正高级专业技术人员研究成果汇编.1

联大的足迹 2014
（上册）

付晨光 主编

知识产权出版社
Intellectual Property Publishing House

图书在版编目（CIP）数据

联大的足迹：正高级专业技术人员研究成果汇编．1，2014／付晨光主编．—北京：知识产权出版社，2015.7
ISBN 978 - 7 - 5130 - 3440 - 1

Ⅰ.①联… Ⅱ.①付… Ⅲ.①北京联合大学—专业技术人员—研究成果—汇编 Ⅳ.①G644

中国版本图书馆 CIP 数据核字（2015）第 070822 号

内容提要

本书以北京联合大学部分校领导任编委会主任、校人事处负责组织编辑的本校正高级专业技术人员研究成果汇编。主要包括研究论文、学术专著和发明专利等栏目。成果汇编包括对当前的学术理论、学术热点的探讨；教育教学改革的探索；教学管理工作经验探讨；等等。

责任编辑：兰　涛	**责任校对**：董志英
封面设计：乔鸿雁　王竹宝	**责任出版**：孙婷婷

联大的足迹：正高级专业技术人员研究成果汇编．1，2014
付晨光　主编

出版发行：知识产权出版社有限责任公司	网　　址：http://www.ipph.cn
社　　址：北京市海淀区马甸南村 1 号	邮　　编：100088
责编电话：010 - 82000860 转 8325	责编邮箱：lantao@cnipr.com
发行电话：010 - 82000860 转 8101/8102	发行传真：010 - 82000893/82005070/82000270
印　　刷：北京中献拓方科技发展有限公司	经　　销：各大网上书店、新华书店及相关专业书店
开　　本：787mm×1092mm　1/16	印　　张：63
版　　次：2015 年 7 月第 1 版	印　　次：2015 年 7 月第 1 次印刷
字　　数：2041 千字	定　　价：200.00 元
ISBN 978 -7 -5130 -3440 -1	

出版权专有　侵权必究
如有印装质量问题，本社负责调换。

编委会

主　任　徐永利　卢振洋

副主任　付晨光　黄先开　鲍　泓

成　员（以姓名笔画排序）

　　　　　王　静　卢振洋　叶　晓

　　　　　付晨光　曲学利　杨　鹏

　　　　　徐永利　黄先开　鲍　泓

前　言

　　北京联合大学是1985年经教育部批准成立的北京市属综合性大学，其前身是1978年北京市依靠清华大学、北京大学等大学创办的36所大学分校。北京联合大学以培养适应国家特别是首都经济社会发展需要的高素质应用型人才为己任，经过30多年的建设与发展，学校的综合实力显著增强，逐步形成了以本科教育为主，研究生教育、高职教育和继续教育协调发展的人才培养体系，是北京市重点建设的应用型人才培养基地，也是北京地区规模最大的高校之一。学校多年来坚持以突出应用研究、推动学科发展、坚持科技创新、服务首都建设为宗旨开展科学研究。

　　为贯彻落实学校第四次党代会提出的"学术立校、人才强校、开放兴校"三大战略目标，加强和促进全校正高级专业技术人员的学术研究和学术交流，提高学术水平，学校将正高级专业技术人员2012年1月1日至2014年2月28日期间的研究与实践成果汇集成册，以学术论文、学术著作和发明专利的形式展现出来，编印成《联大的足迹——正高级专业技术职务人员研究成果汇编.1，2014年》。本汇编分为三大板块，按照成果所属学科进行了分类，涉及论文成果157篇、著作成果概要29个以及发明专利概要两项。

　　高级专业技术人员是学校事业发展的领军人群，是学校核心竞争力的关键所在。他们的研究成果真实记录了我校建设应用型大学的成长足迹，体现了学校学科、专业建设的水平，也关系到学校今后可持续发展的潜力。成果有很多已公开发表或获得不同级别的奖励，不仅是他们对实践的总结、反思过程，也是教育教学智慧的结晶，是学校的宝贵财富。希望此次成果的交流与推广，让更多人得益受惠，营造更加浓厚的学术科研氛围，鼓励更多教师积极、深入地开展教育教学及学术研究，更好地督促教师严谨治学，提升专业化水平，推动学校内涵发展。

编委会

目 录

研究论文

球形磷酸铁锂正极材料制备方法的研究进展 …………………………………… 于春洋（3）
苯胍胺改性三聚氰胺甲醛树脂的合成研究 ………………………… 权 靖 马榴强（7）
Genetic Algorithm for the Single Machine Earliness and Tardiness
　　Scheduling Problem with Fuzzy Processing Times ……………… Wang Chengyao（11）
混合数据模型在建筑物三维建模中的应用 ………………… 王育坚 许承福 刘立平（19）
一种新型管口整形机的结构设计 ……………………………… 毛智勇 刘 建 胡西南（25）
基于小波分析和概率 Hough 变换的书脊视觉识别 ………… 方建军 杜明芳 庞 睿（30）
DP780 熔化极气体保护焊工艺参数优化 ……………… 卢振洋 汤 超 熊 威 黄鹏飞（37）
聚合物膜材料在油水分离过程中的应用 …… 叶 晓 谢 飞 罗孝曦 全升武 刘 巍 叶志伟（41）
Intelligent Control of Welding Gun Pose for Pipeline
　　Welding Robot Based on Improved Radial Basis Function
　　Network and Expert System Regular Paper …………… Tian Jingwen　Gao Meijuan　He Yonggang（45）
Discussion of Building a Tourist Information Service Platform
　　Based on Cloud Computing ……………………………… Sun Lianying　Peng Tao
　　　　　　　　　　　　　　　　　　　　　　　　　　　Liu Chang　Zhang Qixiu（55）
多校区环境下分布式资源共享平台 ……………………… 孙建华 林德强 刘元红 李 媛（61）
云计算技术在大学生计算机应用大赛中的应用 …………… 杜 煜 许菁菁 刘振恒（65）
Model Reference Adaptive Control Based on GANN for
　　Vertical Electric Furnace ………………………… Li Hongxing　Kong Xiangling　Zhang Yinong（69）
基于路由功能的 BACnet/Modbus 协议转换器设计 …………… 李春旺 孙育英 吴义民 施 方（78）
基于现场总线的双容液位模糊控制系统设计 ……………………… 李 微 邵志勇 李 媛（83）
Research on Characteristics of Plastic Materials and
　　Plastic Optical Fiber ………………… Zhang Ning　Han Zeyuan　Song Luqin　Lu Yueming（88）
我国焊接设备的技术水平及发展趋势 …………………………………………… 张明贤（92）
某病房行政楼采暖空调系统节能潜力分析与效果评估 ……………………… 张恩祥（107）
真实世界中的虚拟与虚拟世界中的真实 ………………………………………… 张 楠（112）
Integration of Tree Models into a Real-time
　　Pollution Dispersion Simulation ……………………… Chen Shihong　Shangguan Dayan（116）
毛细管电泳电致化学发光法同时测定氯丙嗪、
　　异丙嗪及其主要代谢物 ……………………………… 李旭菲 杨燕英 周考文（119）
流域水质改善的公共偏好问题研究 ……………………………… 郑海霞 张陆彪（125）
The Design and Simulation of Electric Vehicle Cruise
　　Control System Based on MATLAB ……………………… Zhang Wenjuan　Wang Xue &
　　　　　　　　　　　　　　　　　　　　　　　　　　　Jin Tong　Niu Wenliang（132）
The Design and Implementation of GR-MV Image Inpainting …………… Yuan Jiazheng
　　　　　　　　　　　　　　　　　　　　　　　　　　Liu Hongzhe　Zheng Yongrong（138）

Analysis on Flow Field of the Valveless Piezoelectric Pump with Two Inlets and One Outlet and a Rotating Unsymmetrical Slopes Element ……………………… Xia Qixiao　Zhang Jianhui　Lei Hong　Cheng Wei（145）

基于流固耦合有限元法的汽车发动机液力悬置动力学分析 …………… 徐志军　刘福水　于增信（157）

Comprehensive Risk Evaluation in the Phase of Setting Information System Project ……………………………………………… Gao Yinmin（161）

A Sludge Compost Quality Evaluation Method Based on Chaos Genetic Support Vector Machine ……………… Gao Meijuan　Tian Jingwen　Zhang Zhenbin（167）

基于 CDIO 教育理念的数据库课程实验设计 ………………………………… 逯燕玲　戴红　侯爽（175）

HPLC Fingerprint of Solid–State Fermentation of Fugui Gutong Compound Prescription ……………… Su Jianshu　Tian Pingfang　Lin Qiang　Liu Baining　Zheng Laili　Ge Xizhen（178）

四色套印偏差视觉检测系统软件设计与实现 ………………………… 董南萍　于丽杰　高宗余（185）

Crowd Density Estimation Based on Texture Feature Extraction … Bobo Wang　Hong Bao　Shan Yang（190）

The Application of Permanent Magnet Electric Machine on Electrical Wheelchair ……………………………………… Dou Xiaoxia　Tong Qiming（199）

Study on Active Ingredient of Ailanthus Leaves ………………………… Gu Tiaohao　Liu Wanying　Huo Qing　Yu Xiao（204）

"衣可衣，非常衣"
　　——三宅一生设计思想解析 ……………………………………………………………… 李红梅（209）

从内画艺术的发展历程看民间美术的当代传承之路 ………………………………………… 张旗（213）

媒介的权力
　　——一种全景透视方法 ……………………………………………………………… 郝家林（220）

探索色彩力量在商品色彩营销中的应用 …………………………………………………… 鲁彦娟（226）

近代北京基督教史研究现状及史料利用综述 ……………………………………………… 左芙蓉（229）

湖北郧县刘湾旧石器时代遗址发掘简报 ……………… 冯小波　王昊　王正华　黄旭初　周兴明　张俊（236）

门头沟区宗教文化遗产的保护与利用 ……………………………………………… 杨靖筠　于洪（246）

兵家与儒、道、法等诸家思想的交融与区别 ……………………………………………… 张连城（251）

对北京历史文化遗产空间重构的思考 ……………………………………………………… 张宝秀（256）

清代三山五园兴衰及其启示 ………………………………………………………………… 赵连稳（260）

民俗类非物质文化遗产保护三议 …………………………………………………… 顾军　苑利（264）

庙底沟时代与"早期中国" …………………………………………………………………… 韩建业（269）

从后现代主义到浪漫主义
　　——一种史学观念的回归 …………………………………………………………… 王利红（278）

莫言与幻觉现实主义 ………………………………………………………………………… 王德领（286）

《喜福会》的叙事艺术 ………………………………………………………………………… 王毅（292）

海明威小说《雨中的猫》主题思想探究 …………………………………………………… 牛洁珍（297）

日本社会的右倾化与相对化意识 …………………………………………………………… 纪廷许（300）

金末遗民词联章双线章法结构研究 …………………………………………………………… 李艺（305）

新媒体语境下对科技期刊编辑的新要求 …………………………………………… 李亚青　柴智（309）

音系学理论教学与实证研究 ………………………………………………………………… 宋长来（311）

跨文化交际课程中多元识读教学模型的建构与实践 ……………………………………… 张义君（316）

从乞巧节到中国情人节——七夕节的当代重构及意义 …………………………………… 张勃（323）

媒体融合条件下的学术期刊新媒体转型 …………………………………………………… 周小华（330）

| 留学生汉语需求分析的理论与方法 | 郭素红 吴中平 (339) |

留学生汉语需求分析的理论与方法 …………………………………………… 郭素红 吴中平 (339)

赵萝蕤先生汉译《荒原》艺术管窥 …………………………………… 黄宗英 邓中杰 姜君 (344)

调查性报道"事实建构"的机制与特征 …………………………………………… 惠东坡 (351)

论西欧中世纪后期基于文字媒介的知识传播 …………………………………… 程德林 (355)

房地产的财税法调控研究 …………………………………………………… 王平 刘慧勇 (360)

共同富裕的历史选择和实现条件考察
　　——以中国农村为例 ……………………………………………………………… 王维国 (365)

两岸法律适用问题研究
　　——一个政治与法律互动的视角 ………………………………………………… 刘文忠 (369)

中国台湾与日本钓鱼岛纠纷与马英九当局的应对策略 ………………………… 李振广 (376)

民间资本运行的危机透视与法制思考 …………………………………………… 杨积堂 (382)

城镇化过程中失地农民权益的整体性保障 ……………………………………… 郑广永 (388)

人大常委会监督途径的确立与运行 ……………………………………… 徐永利 王维国 (395)

关于财产公开的可实施性 ………………………………………………………… 崔英楠 (403)

经济增加值模型在商业银行价值评估中的应用 ……………… 朱传华 詹细明 黄金英 (406)

后危机时代中国金融创新模式选择 ……………………………………………… 刘迎春 (411)

中国向低碳经济转型的制约因素及发展模式 …………………………………… 李慧凤 (414)

亚洲著名科技园区金融支持体系比较研究 …………………… 杨宜 徐鲲 王俊文 (420)

大宗商品国际市场价格变化趋势分析
　　——国家发展与改革委员会"十三五"规划前期研究重大课题子课题 ……… 吴勤学 等 (425)

基于相对熵的证券市场参与者对监管的态度偏好研究 ……………… 张士玉 郝旭光 (430)

基于资本增值的知识协同效益评价研究 ……………………… 陈建斌 郭彦丽 徐凯波 (439)

"碳关税"对我国出口贸易的影响及对策 ……………………………… 郑春芳 赵亚平 (449)

论我国特定非金融机构反洗钱监管 ……………………………………………… 赵永林 (454)

低碳经济背景下零售企业"绿色商业"发展策略
　　——基于本土与跨国企业比较的研究 ……………………………………………… 崔玮 (461)

产业链的传导机制与通货膨胀机理研究 ………………………………………… 符亚明 (468)

我国《小企业会计准则》与《中小主体国际财务报告准则》差异的原因分析 …… 傅宏宇 (473)

基于变量聚类和COX比例风险模型的企业财务预警研究 ……… 鲍新中 陶秋燕 傅宏宇 (480)

Research on Network Marketing Performance Evaluation
　　Based on GIOWA Operator ……………………………… Xue Wanxin　Pei Yilei　Li dandan (489)

环境资源定价及其实现途径
　　——基于边际机会成本定价理论 ………………………………………………… 穆红莉 (495)

中国共产党加强先进性建设的当代创新
　　——有关马克思主义执政党跳出"历史周期率"的思考 ………………………… 马小芳 (499)

"中国梦"的时代价值 ……………………………………………………………… 许晓平 (503)

海外中国学研究的发展前瞻
　　——北京联合大学海外中国学研究中心成立大会暨学术研讨会述要 …………… 许峰 (506)

提升高校学生党建科学化水平的思考 ……………………………………… 李九丽 马俊红 (510)

关于北京高校大学生马克思主义大众化水平调查研究 …………………………… 李俊卿 (513)

"以人民为本":马克思"跨越论"的主体价值观 ……………………………… 孟宪东 (518)

新媒体视角下大学生思想政治教育的新探索 …………………………… 郭堃 孙瑞婷 (522)

中国特色的社会主义道路及其核心价值体系
　　——坚持共产党员的精神追求 …………………………………………………… 唐小恒 (525)

利益关系多样化与保持党的纯洁性 ……………………………………………… 韩强 (529)

Global Solutions for Second Order Impulsive Integro – differential
  Equations in Banach Spaces ·················· Wang Xinfeng Liu Dalian Li Chong（533）
联想记忆系统学习算法的改进 ·· 邢春峰（550）
Crystal Structure of $(Bu_4N)_2$ $[Mo_6O_{18}N(o-CH_3C_6$
  $H_3OOCCH_2CH_3)]$, $C_{42}H_{83}Mo_6N_3O_{20}$ ················ Zhu Li Zhong Yanfang Cao Xiyan（554）
白藜芦醇诱导 Raji 细胞死亡的自噬途径研究 ··· 劳凤学（559）
超临界 CO_2 密度对全反式番茄红素吸光系数的影响 ··················· 何强强 惠柏棣 宫 平（566）
植物甾醇的安全性研究进展 ····················· 张 波 刘河汝 安秀峰 代晓曼（573）
学生宿舍设计方案的模糊综合评价与集对分析 ············· 张晓晞 邓 岩 董 巍 骆 腾（578）
北京建设国际活动聚集之都的现状及推进对策 ·· 张景秋 甄茂成（582）
太行山区传统民居建筑空间研究 ·· 张路光 李 苹（588）
Quantum Spectra and Classical Orbits in Artificial Atom ··· Lu Jun（591）
The Effect of Taurine on Cholesterol Metabolism ················ Chen Wen Guo Junxia Chang Ping（597）
壳聚糖/β - 环糊精交联聚合物的制备及其对葛根素的吸附性能 ········· 苏 苗 王丽丽 林 强（609）
小蓟中氧化蒲公英赛酮和醇的分离鉴定和细胞毒活性测试 ············· 院珍珍 吴春彦 王阿利
                            李金杰 李 斌 尚小雅（616）
基于社会属性的北京市居民通勤满意度空间差异分析 ············· 孟 斌 湛东升 郝丽荣（624）
北京早园竹叶不同提取组分对 CHO
  细胞 Akt 信号通路的影响 ················ 梅 晶 祖桂芳 赵晓红 何 颖 孙 健（632）
Comparisons of Walnut Quality Stability of Yunnan – Santai
  Walnut in Different Packing Conditions ················ Li Dapeng Wang Wenqian Luan Na
                           Rong Ruifen Xu Huilian（637）
Curcumin Attenuates Amyloid – β – Induced Tau Hyperphosphorylation in Human Neuroblastoma
  SH – SY5Y Cells Involving PTEN/Akt/GSK – 3β Signaling Pathway ······ Huang Hanchang Tang Di
                           Xu Ke Jiang Zhaofeng（645）
The Effects of Vitamin C on DDP – induced Anemia in Rats ·················· Gao Liping Li Zen
                         Guo Zhuoyu Zhao Yanmeng（659）
加权线性支持向量分类机的数据扰动分析 ·· 蔡 春（667）
不同地类春小麦拔节期冠层光谱与叶绿素差异研究 ············ 靳彦华 熊黑钢 张 芳 王莉峰（673）
Regulatory Effects of Xylooligosaccharides on Intestinal Microbial
  Flora Proliferation and Defecation of BALB/c Mice ······ Wei Tao Shang Hongtao Gao Zhaolan
                       Wang Li Li Siyu Huang Xue Zeng Mengrui（678）
Effects of preparation conditions on characters of hydrophobic
  silica granular aerogel and its Applications ······ Wei Wei Zhang Jingyi Wu Liping Qin Guotong（683）
校企联动构建餐旅类人才培养体系 ·· 王美萍 张丽娟 朱 莉（687）
随班就读孤独症儿童对不同句子类型理解的个案研究 ·· 王 梅 周梦佳（691）
地方普通高校学生学习动力的制度影响分析及对策研究 ··················· 尹庆民 马丽仪 牟 书（695）
中青年教师专业化发展的院校培训支持体系构建 ······ 付晨光 曲学利 周华丽 张军辉 韩忠强（699）
以开放式教育推进大学内涵式发展 ·· 乔东亮（702）
高校学生成绩管理的问题与对策研究 ·· 刘在云（705）
基于互联网培训管理方案的研究与设计 ·· 刘 莹（708）
科学构建一体化人才培养体系提升高职教育教学品质 ··················· 齐再前 孙晓鲲 黄先开（723）
地方院校高等教育国际化的影响要素析评 ·· 杨亚军（726）
网络环境下的英语听力学习策略培训 ····························· 何 芳 王 玮 郁 震（731）

研究论文

一种高精度电子微距测量装置简介 ……………………………………………………………………（950）

学术著作

汽车发动机构造、原理与维修	于增信	（953）
建筑智能化系统工程实训 ………………………… 苏 玮 阴振勇 杜明芳 杨晓玲		（954）
高寒地区矿山深部通风防尘技术研究 ………………………………………… 杨 鹏 吕文生		（955）
建筑供配电与照明 ………………………………………………………… 范同顺 苏 玮		（957）
工业工程现场改善与应用 …………………………………………………………… 程 光		（958）
服饰品设计 …………………………………………………………………………… 张嘉秋		（959）
《中国民族电影审美鉴赏》 …………………………………………………… 茹秀华 赵 华		（960）
英语口语比喻词语词典 ……………………………………………………………… 张东昌		（962）
汉英衔接文化性研究 ………………………………………………………………… 张殿恩		（964）
现代流通企业知识资产评价研究简介 …………………………………… 王 卓 王晓文		（965）
金融创新与北京国际金融中心发展		
——基于环境金融理论的研究 …………………………………………………… 张 蓉		（966）
投资项目金融价值评估 …………………………… 庞昊勇 秦 江 吕 强 王立军		（968）
北京零售业绿色经营发展研究		
——基于理论与跨国零售实践 …………………………………………………… 赵亚平		（970）
稀土催化材料在环境保护中的应用 …………………………… 赵 卓 彭 鹏 傅平丰		（971）
《实用特殊教育研究方法概论》 ……………………………… 刘全礼 邓 猛 熊 琪		（972）
教育基本问题专论 …………………………………………………………………… 刘彦文		（974）
学校食堂从业人员培训教材 ……………………………… 闫喜霜 许荣华 姜 慧 张 琦		（975）
残疾儿童随班就读支持体系的研究与实践 ……………………………… 王 洙 许家成		（976）
职业教育分级制研究		
——职业教育分级框架与分级标准建构研究 …………………………………… 李宇红		（977）
《职业教育教师教育研究》 ……………………………………………………… 李娟华		（978）
汉语盲文简写方案 …………………………………………………………………… 钟经华		（979）
《新时期职业院校创业教育理论与实践》 ……………………………………… 段素菊		（982）
"思想道德修养与法律基础"课教学设计 …………………… 陈 勇 王 易 贾少英 王滨有		（983）
大学生职业发展教育实证研究 ……………………………………………………… 葛海燕		（984）
心理学实验与生活 ……………………………………… 曾美英 晏 宁 毛荣建 李 伟		（985）
高校英语教师专业发展研究 ………………………………………………………… 谢职安		（986）
喀斯特洞穴旅游开发与景观保护研究 ……………………………………………… 王 静		（988）
《旅游标准化导论》 ………………………………………………………… 张凌云 朱莉蓉		（989）
旅游公共服务：理论与实践 ………………………………………………………… 徐菊凤		（991）

北京高等院校校内创新实践基地建设探索
　　——以北京联合大学普通与特殊教育相结合校内创新实践基地为例 ………… 汪艳丽　等（735）
社会资本视角下民办高校教师专业发展影响机制研究 ………………… 秦立栓　宋　哲（739）
以职业需求为导向的高职旅游财务管理专业培养模式研究 …………………… 张玉凤（744）
青教赛为服务青年教师全面发展提供正能量 ……………… 张俊玲　罗　丹　邹佳霖（747）
治理理念下高校创新人才战略的实施 ………………………………………… 张祖明（750）
基于网络学堂的高职数学精品课程建设 …………………… 陈玉花　张　耘　王新苹（755）
师范教育应走在教育改革发展的前列 ………………………………………… 陈志刚（757）
基于协同理论的应用型大学学科、专业一体化建设研究 ………… 陈　琳　龚秀敏（761）
构建以"创新"为核心控制点的财会本科毕业论文质量控制体系 ……………… 邵　军（767）
规则导向下竞技健美操成套动作艺术性的研究 ………………………………… 范清惠（770）
专业化发展视域下的职教教师职业核心能力培养路径 ………………………… 徐英俊（776）
传承、借鉴和发展
　　——基于学生工作管理的中外比较分析 ……………………………………… 唐少清（780）
信息化背景下旅游高等教育改革与发展的思考 …………… 黄先开　范　蓓　冯爱秋（789）
多校区高校实验教学集中管理体系构建研究 ………………………………… 董　焱（793）
我国残疾人高等教育宏观结构研究 ……………… 滕祥东　郝传萍　吕淑慧　朱　琳（798）
基于云计算的电子商务安全问题研究 ………………………………… 于　平　马桂真（802）
大数据技术背景下的服务外包人才培养 …………………………………… 于丽娟（806）
档案部门参与非遗保护工作的优势与劣势分析 …………… 王巧玲　孙爱萍　陈文杰（809）
Investigation and Study on the Present Situation of Enterprise
　　Website Construction of Intellectual Property Agencies …… Wang Xiaohong　Wu Jianping（813）
广州会展企业空间集聚特征与影响因素 ……………………………………… 方忠权（825）
旅游权内涵解析及其保险保障机制探讨 ……………………………………… 孔令学（836）
会展旅游带动效应的统计研究
　　——以北京为例 ……………………………………………………… 石美玉　王春才（843）
旅游吸引力与城市休闲气质的探讨 …………………………………………… 宁泽群（853）
开展人力资源开发研究　促进中青年教师队伍建设 ……… 曲学利　孔　军　方祖成（860）
农村老年人休闲生活方式研究
　　——以北京郊区农村调查为例 ………………………………………………… 李　享（863）
刍议我国中小企业发展面临的困境与突破 …………………………………… 张永敬（868）
网络时代听力有障碍年轻群体娱乐休闲研究 ………………………………… 陈文力（871）
旅游服务外包的理论建构研究 ………………………………………… 范　蓓　田彩云（880）
Studies on the Issue of Trust in Tourism Group - buying ………………………… Li Zheng（888）
云数字档案馆安全运营管理机制研究
　　——以区域性档案局（馆）为承建方为例 ……………… 徐　华　薛四新　刘宗渊（894）
"金蝉"不再"脱壳"
　　——论营业转让中债权人的利益保护 ……………………………………… 郭娅丽（899）
中小企业社会网络与其成长绩效的关系研究
　　——基于北京地区 200 家企业的调研 …………… 陶秋燕　汪昕宇　陈雄鹰（907）
保险合同可争议制度研究 ……………………………………………………… 常　敏（916）
建筑师事务所绩效考核管理体系设计 ………………………………… 蔡　红　李树贤（928）

发明专利

关于"助眠卧室系统"的说明 ………………………………………………………（945）

{工学类}

球形磷酸铁锂正极材料制备方法的研究进展

于春洋

橄榄石结构的磷酸铁锂（$LiFePO_4$）自1997年[1]被报道具有可逆脱嵌锂特性以来，因其安全性能好、循环性能优异、环境友好、原料来源丰富等优点，而成为当前锂离子电池正极材料的研究热点之一。该材料导电性差的缺点可借助表面包覆导电碳材料[2]、体相掺杂高价金属离子[3]或者细化颗粒[4]等予以改善，然而，振实密度低[5]的缺点尚未得到有效解决。目前商业生产的$LiFePO_4$振实密度普遍较低，一般只能达到$1.0g/cm^3$左右，远远低于钴酸锂约$2.2g/cm^3$的振实密度。这就意味着要得到相同的放电容量，基于$LiFePO_4$的电池体积将远远大于基于钴酸锂的电池。所以，如何在保证$LiFePO_4$材料的电性能基础上，提高材料的振实密度，进而提高材料的体积比容量，成为该材料大规模商业化应用亟待解决的问题。

球形$LiFePO_4$纳米颗粒由于相互间的接触面小，不易出现团聚和架桥现象，具有界面自由能较低、体积能量密度较高、流动性能较好、振实密度高等优点，合成球形纳米材料可以满足高比能量锂电池对正极材料的要求[6-10]。因此，提高$LiFePO_4$材料振实密度重要思路之一为制备球形颗粒。目前，主要有以下几种常用的球形$LiFePO_4$颗粒制备方法。

1 球形$LiFePO_4$纳米粒子的制备

1.1 控制结晶法制备球形$LiFePO_4$颗粒

Ying等[11]采用控制结晶的方法制备振实密度高达$1.8g/cm^3$ Cr掺杂的球形$Li_{0.97}Cr_{0.01}FePO_4/C$，该材料在0.05C和1.0C下放电容量分别为$151mA·h/g$和$110mA·h/g$。该方法制备的材料虽然振实密度高但是颗粒粒径太大，容易在充放电过程中形成"死角"。Kim等[12-14]用机械活化法合成了近球形的纳米级$LiFePO_4$与$LiFePO_4/C$正极材料。采用喷雾干燥-碳热还原法有利于制备多级结构的球形$LiFePO_4/C$正极材料，碳热还原的还原气氛有利于还原Fe^{3+}，多余的碳作为导电极包覆在$LiFePO_4$周围，有利于提高材料的电导率和阻止颗粒的长大。

1.2 用高密度球形$FePO_4$前驱体合成球形$LiFePO_4$颗粒

制得高密度球形前驱体是得到高密度球形产物的有效途径之一[15]。先合成高密度球形$FePO_4$前驱物，再与其他原料混合均匀，通过高温反应，使锂通过球形前驱体颗粒表面的微孔向各方向均匀、同步地渗入前驱体的中心，保持球形形貌[16]。此法中，球形前驱体可以消除反应过程中由于扩散途径不同而引起的微观组分差异，生成组成均匀的$LiFePO_4$，从而提高材料的性能。

雷敏等[17]通过控制结晶法制备出球形前驱体$FePO_4·xH_2O$，经过520℃预烧得到高密度的无水$FePO_4$晶体，将$FePO_4$与Li_2CO_3和葡萄糖均匀混合，采用碳热还原法合成了球形$LiFePO_4/C$，振实密度高达$1.8g/cm^3$，在$0.1mA/cm^2$电流密度条件下，首次放电比容量为$129.7mA·h/g$，首次放电体积比容量达$233.5mA·h/cm^3$。Xie等[18]合成出$FePO_4·2H_2O$球形前驱物，将其与Li_2CO_3和苯酚甲醛树脂球磨

[作者简介] 于春洋，北京联合大学生物化学工程学院。

混合后,在还原性气氛中得到球形 $LiFePO_4$-PAS(聚并苯)复合物,振实密度为 $1.6g/cm^3$,比起不规则形貌颗粒,振实密度有了 33% 的提高。Sung 等[19]用共沉淀法合成了球形 $FePO_4$ 前驱体,然后与 Li_2CO_3 还有作为碳源的 PVP(聚乙烯吡咯烷酮)一起在惰性气氛中煅烧得到了直径为 $6\mu m$ 球形的 $LiFePO_4/C$,振实密度为 $1.6g/cm^3$,在 0.1C 下的放电比容量为 $150mA·h/g$。常照荣等[20]用控制结晶法制备了振实密度分别为 $1.08g/cm^3$ 和 $1.56g/cm^3$ 的 $FePO_4$,这两种 $FePO_4$ 再与 Li_2CO_3 和葡萄糖制得的 $LiFePO_4/C$ 的振实密度分别为 $1.43g/cm^3$ 和 $2.14g/cm^3$。后者在 0.1C 下的首次放电比容量为 $121.5mA·h/g$,体积比容量达到 $260.0mA·h/cm^3$,并表现出较好的高倍率性能。

1.3 喷雾干燥法制备球形 $LiFePO_4$ 颗粒

喷雾干燥/热解法利用载气将前驱体溶液、溶胶或悬浊液带入高温的干燥器中,由于液体的表面张力自动收缩形成球形液滴,在瞬间实现溶剂蒸发、溶质沉淀、颗粒干燥、颗粒预分解和烧结程序等一系列过程。若改变溶剂体系或添加辅助模板剂还可以制备出具有特殊的二级结构的球形 $LiFePO_4$,该方法还极容易实现工业化。

孙学磊等[21]以碳酸锂、草酸亚铁、乙酸镁和磷酸二氢铵为原料,以蔗糖为碳源,按含碳量 5%(质量分数)添加。用湿法球磨—喷雾干燥法制备 $LiFe_{0.98}Mg_{0.02}PO_4/C$ 复合正极材料,振实密度可达 $1.67g/cm^3$,在 0.1C、0.5C 和 1.0C 倍率下的首次放电比容量分别为 $151mA·h/cm^3$,$143mA·h/cm^3$ 和 $132mA·h/cm^3$。Gao 等[22]将 $CH_3COOLi·2H_2O$、$FeC_2O_4·2H_2O$ 和 $(NH_4)_2HPO_4$ 为原料,采用喷雾干燥法所得类球形的 $LiFePO_4$ 的振实密度为 $1.4g/cm^3$,在 0.2C 下的首次放电比容量为 $139.4mA·h/g$,且循环性能良好。

Gómez 等[10]采用氩气作为载气将前驱体溶液带到高温石英管式炉中热解得到均匀球形材料。在高倍透射电镜下显示该球形颗粒是由 15~30nm 左右的一次颗粒团聚成的。虽然该方法制备的材料形貌漂亮但是不纯,可能是由于作者使用悬浊液作前驱体,载气将前驱体载入的过程中成分发生了偏析。

Yu 等[23-25]以溶液或溶胶作为前驱体,采用喷雾干燥技术制备了多孔球形 $LiFePO_4/C$。通过聚焦离子束(FIB)测试表明该球形颗粒是由 30nm 小颗粒组成的,该材料不仅具有比表面积大,流动性和分散性优异,易于涂片等物理性能,而且充放电测试表明该材料具有优异的电化学性能。Konarova 等[26]联合采用喷雾干燥法和湿球磨法合成了几何平均直径为 58nm 的 $LiFePO_4$ 纳米颗粒,样品在 0.1C 和 10C 充放电速率下的首次放电容量分别为 $164mA·h/g$ 和 $100mA·h/g$。

1.4 熔盐法制备球形 $LiFePO_4$ 颗粒

熔盐法通常采用一种或数种低熔点的盐类作为反应介质,合成过程会出现液相,反应物在其中有一定的溶解度,这大大加快了反应物离子的扩散速率,使反应物在液相中实现原子尺度混合,反应就由固固反应转化为固液反应。反应结束后,采用合适的溶剂将盐类溶解,经过滤洗涤后即可得到合成产物。近年来,熔盐法广泛用于正极材料制备的研究当中。Ni 等[27]采用 KCl 熔盐法合成了球形 $LiFePO_4/C$。方法是以 Li_2CO_3、$FeC_2O_4·2H_2O$ 和 $NH_4H_2PO_4$ 为原料,蔗糖为碳源,先球磨后在 450℃ 下煅烧 5h,然后与适量的 KCl 混合再次球磨后,在 755℃ 下煅烧 3h,再将 KCl 洗去,得到了球形的 $LiFePO_4/C$ 材料,振实密度达到了 $1.55g/cm^3$。KCl 的熔融状态不仅加快了 $LiFePO_4$ 的结晶过程,而且有利于球形颗粒的形成。在 0.1C 下,材料的首次放电比容量为 $130.3mA·h/g$,循环 40 周后放电比容量可达 $137.2mA·h/g$,具有比较优良的循环性能。

1.5 共沉淀法制备球形 $LiFePO_4$ 颗粒

共沉淀法具有易于控制形貌,原材料成本低,易于大规模生产和工业化等优点。不足之处为不同组分的沉淀速度不同,因而会使材料组成发生偏离,出现不均匀现象[28]。Wang 等[29]通过共沉淀与原位聚合 2 种方法联用合成了碳包覆的纳米尺寸的 $LiFePO_4$ 正极材料。所得到的 $LiFePO_4$ 由 40~50nm 的主要颗粒与 100~110nm 的次要颗粒构成。每个颗粒都呈球形,且均匀地包覆有厚度为 3~5nm 的无定形碳层。在共沉淀过程中,苯胺单体发生聚合,覆盖到每一个新形成的 $FePO_4$ 颗粒表面,从而阻碍了核的进一步生长。即使 $LiFePO_4$ 在 650℃ 下煅烧 15h,主要的颗粒尺寸也在 40~50nm 范围之内,并有连续的碳包覆层。合成的 $LiFePO_4$ 在 1C 下初始放电容量为 $150mA·h/g$,且有优良的容量保持能力与循环稳定性能。

2 粒径分布对振实密度及电化学性能的影响

LiFePO$_4$ 的振实密度与颗粒的粒径之间存在着密切的联系，研究表明[30]，纳米级别的 LiFePO$_4$ 振实密度一般较低，而微米级别的 LiFePO$_4$ 具有较高的振实密度。曹寅等[31]利用控制结晶法制备了粒径约为 1μm、5μm、10μm 的球形 LiFePO$_4$，以此为前驱体通过碳热还原法合成了小、中、大三种不同粒径的球形 LiFePO$_4$ 正极材料，它们的振实密度分别为 1.09g/cm^3、1.65g/cm^3 和 2.03g/cm^3。合成的材料较好地保持了球形形貌。小粒径的样品的振实密度不高，但不同倍率下质量比容量最优，0.1C、0.5C 和 1.0C 充放电电流下分别为 160.6mA·h/g、149.4mA·h/g 和 141.8mA·h/g。而中粒径的样品具有最高的体积比容量，0.1C、0.5C 和 1.0C 倍率下分别对应为 230.4mA·h/g、192.0mA·h/g 和 176.5mA·h/cm^3。大粒径的样品振实密度虽然最高，但其电化学性能不佳。

3 结束语

从上述各种文献中可以发现，要想制得高密度的 LiFePO$_4$ 材料，使产物粒子球形化是一种很普遍且效果也很好的方法；如果球形颗粒组成的粉体具有理想的粒度分布，使得小球尽可能填补大球之间的空隙，则可以进一步提高振实密度。由于多孔 LiFePO$_4$ 粉体材料特殊的三维孔状结构，能在提高材料振实密度的同时兼顾材料的电性能。

参考文献

[1] PADHI A K, NANJUNDASWAMY K S, GOODENOUGH J B. Phospho - olivines as positive - electrode materials for rechargeable lithium batteries [J]. J Electrochem Soc, 1997, 144 (4): 1188 - 1194.

[2] ELVIRA M B, CARLO B, MAURO P, et al. Versatile synthesis of carbon - rich LiFePO$_4$ enhancing its electrochemical properties [J]. Electrochem Solid - State Lett, 2004, 7 (4): A85 - A87.

[3] WANG D Y, LI H, SHI S Q, et al. Improving the rate performance of LiFePO$_4$ by Fe - site doping [J]. Electrochim Acta, 2005, 50 (14): 2955 - 2958.

[4] ARNOLD G, GARCHE J, HEMMER R, et al. Fine - particle lithium iron phosphate LiFePO$_4$ synthesized by a new low - cost aqueous precipitation technique [J]. J Power Sources, 2003, 121: 247 - 251.

[5] YUAN L X, WANG Z H, HUANG Y H, et al. Development and challenges of LiFePO$_4$ cathode material for lithium - ion batteries [J]. Energy Environ Sci, 2011 (4): 269 - 284.

[6] Yu F, Zhang J, Yang Y, et al. Porous micro - spherical aggregates of LiFePO$_4$/C nanocomposites: A novel and simple template - free con - cept and synthesis via sol - gel - spray drying method [J]. J Power Sources, 2010, 195: 6873 - 6878.

[7] 于锋, 张敬杰, 杨岩峰, 等. 正极材料球形 LiFePO$_4$ 的制备方法综述 [J]. 电池, 2009, 39 (3): 170 - 172.

[8] Xie H M, Wang R S, Ying J R, et al. Optimized LiFePO$_4$ - polyacene cathode material for Lithium - Ion batteries [J]. Advanced Materials, 2006, 18: 2609 - 2613.

[9] 应皆荣, 高剑, 姜长印, 等. 控制结晶法制备球形锂离子电池正极材料的研究进展 [J]. 无机材料学报, 2006, 21: 291 - 297.

[10] Gómez L S, Meatza I D, Martin M I, et al. Morphological, structural and electrochemical properties of lithium iron phosphates synthe - sized by Spray Pyrolysis [J]. Electrochim Acta, 2010, 55: 2805 - 2809.

[11] Ying J R, Lei M, Jiang C Y, et al. Preparation and characterization of high - density spherical Li$_{0.97}$Cr$_{0.01}$FePO$_4$/C cathode material for lithium ion batteries [J]. J Power Sources, 2006, 158: 543 - 549.

[12] Kim J K, Cheruvally G, Choi J W, et al. Effect of mechanical activation process parameters on the properties of LiFePO$_4$ cathode mate - rial [J]. Journal of Power Sources, 2007, 166: 211 - 218.

[13] Kim J K, Choi J W, Cheruvally G, et al. A modified mechanical activation synthesis for carbon - coated LiFePO$_4$ cathode in lithium batteries [J]. Mater Lett, 2007, 61: 3822 - 3825.

[14] Kim J K, Cheruvally G, Ahn J H. Electrochemical properties of LiFePO$_4$/C synthesized by mechanical activation using sucrose as carbon source [J]. J Solid State Electr, 2008, 12: 799 - 805.

[15] [9] LOU X M, ZHANG Y X. Synthesis of LiFePO$_4$/C cathode materials with both high - rate capability and high tap density for lithium - ion batteries [J]. J Mater Chem, 2011, 21: 4156 - 4160.

[16] 时喜喜,郭春雨,易炜,等.关于提高 LiFePO$_4$ 振实密度的研究进展 [J].电源技术,2010,48 (3):848-851.

[17] 雷敏,应皆荣,姜长印,等.高密度球形 LiFePO$_4$ 的合成及其性能 [J].电源技术,2006,30 (1):11-13.

[18] SUNG W O, SEUNG - TAEK M, SEUNG - MIN O, et al. Polyvinylpyrrolidone - assisted synthesis of microscale C - LiFePO$_4$ with high tap density as positive electrode materials for lithium batteries [J]. Electrochim Acta, 2010, 55: 1193-1199.

[19] 常照荣,吕豪杰,汤宏伟,等.高密度 LiFePO$_4$/C 正极材料的合成及其电化学性能研究 [J].功能材料,2009,40 (4):618-620.

[20] 孙学磊,戴永年,姚耀春.球形 LiFePO$_4$ 正极材料制备中试研究 [J].中国有色金属学报,2011,21 (1):125-130.

[21] GAO F, TANG Z Y, XUE H J. Preparation and characterization of nano - particle LiFePO$_4$ and LiFePO$_4$/C by spray - drying and post - annealing method [J]. Electrochem Acta, 2007, 53 (4): 1939-1944.

[22] Yu F, Zhang J, Yang Y F, et al. Porous micro - spherical aggregates of LiFePO$_4$/ C nanocomposites: A novel and simple template - free concept and synthesis via sol - gel - spray drying method [J]. J Power Sources, 2010, 195: 6873-6878.

[23] Yu F, Zhang J J, Yang Y F, et al. Preparation and characterization of mesoporous LiFePO$_4$/C microsphere by spray drying assisted template method [J]. J Power Sources, 2009, 189: 794-797.

[24] Yu F, Zhang J J, Yang Y F, et al. Up - scalable synthesis, structure and charge storage properties of porous microspheres of LiFePO$_4$@ C nanocomposites [J]. J Mater Chem, 2009, 19: 9121-9125.

[25] Konarova M, Taniguchi I. Physical and electrochemical properties of LiFePO$_4$ nanoparticles synthesized by a combination of spray pyrolysis with wet ball - milling [J]. J Power Sources, 2009, 194: 1029-1035.

[26] NI J F, ZHOU H H, CHEN J T, et al. Molten salt synthesis and electrochemical properties of spherical LiFePO$_4$ particles [J]. Mater Lett, 2007, 61: 1260-1264.

[27] 倪聪,莫祥银,俞琛捷,等.纳米磷酸铁锂的研究进展 [J].化工新型材料,2010,38 (5):1-4.

[28] Wang Y, Sun B, Park J, et al. Morphology control and electrochemi - cal properties of nanosize LiFePO$_4$ cathode material synthesized by co - precipitation combined with in situ polymerization [J]. Journal of Alloys and Compounds, 2011, 509: 1040-1044.

[29] WANG M, YANG R, ZHANG Y X. Synthesis of micro - nano hierarchical structured LiFePO$_4$/C composite with both superior high - rate performance and high tap density [J]. Nanoscale, 2011, 3: 4434-4439.

[30] 曹寅,王子港,杨晖.不同粒径球形 LiFePO$_4$ 的制备及其性能研究 [J].功能材料,2011,42 (3):448-451.

苯胍胺改性三聚氰胺甲醛树脂的合成研究

权 靖 马榴强

目前普遍采用的有机外墙外保温材料主要是聚苯乙烯泡沫塑料和聚氨酯泡沫塑料等。他们具有保温效果好的特点，属于高效保温材料。但此两种材料热熔温度不超过100℃，且极易燃烧，许多事例表明，一旦发生火灾，会造成火势沿建筑外立面迅速蔓延，同时伴随着大量有毒气体的释放，不但会造成财产损失，人员伤亡，也会对环境造成极大的污染[1]。

按照许多欧洲国家建筑设计标准的最新要求，在高层建筑或防火等级较高的工程中，将采用难燃材料代替易燃材料作保温层。国内工程设计也开始向这个方向发展。因此，研制一类既具有良好保温特性，易于施工操作及满足节能设计标准，又具有阻燃性能，以弥补目前品种有限的建筑外墙保温隔热材料，这是当前我国建材市场中的一个迫切需要解决的课题[2]。

三聚氰胺加热分解时会释放出大量氮气，其与甲醛反应所生成的三聚氰胺甲醛树脂具有阻燃性能，属于耐燃材料[3]。但高固含量的三聚氰胺甲醛树脂的反应活性很高，贮存稳定性较差，不利于制备发泡材料。因此，研究一种适合于制备泡沫材料的三聚氰胺甲醛树脂成为了一种迫切的需求。

1 实验部分

1.1 仪器与药品

实验所采用的仪器设备包括三口烧瓶、温度计、冷凝器、精密pH试纸、电热套和搅拌器等常规实验设备。

实验用药品均选用分析纯试剂，包括三聚氰胺、多聚甲醛、苯胍胺、尿素和NaOH等。

1.2 实验方法

将三聚氰胺、甲醛、改性剂按一定比例加入三口瓶中反应，调节pH值，升温反应。反应一定时间，测试合格后出料，进行相关性能测试。

1.3 检测方法

黏度的测定：将所合成的树脂倒入烧杯中，恒温至25℃，使用NDJ-4旋转黏度计，使待测溶液没过转子刻度，打开黏度计，待转盘刻度转3圈读数稳定后读数。

贮存期的测定：取部分树脂，观察树脂在常温下的流动性、颜色等现象，直至其失去流动性为止所需要的时间。

2 结果与讨论

2.1 树脂制备的预实验

根据相关文献[1]，我们采用表1中所列药品及数量。首先向三口瓶内依次加入三聚氰胺、多聚甲醛、尿素，再倒入37%甲醛溶液和聚乙二醇200，开始搅拌，同时用30% NaOH溶液调pH至8.5，并匀速升温至80℃，保温反应1h后，降温出料。从反应结果看，上述方法能够制备出三聚氰胺甲醛树脂，但树脂黏度与固含量均较低，并且树脂的贮存稳定性较差，仅为1d。

[基金项目] 本课题获北京市教委科技项目及北京市政府转化项目资助。
[作者简介] 权靖，北京联合大学生物化学工程学院，主要研究合成树脂发泡材料。

表1 制备实验用三聚氰胺甲醛树脂的基本配方

药品	用量/g
三聚氰胺	75
多聚甲醛	35
37%甲醛溶液	50
聚乙二醇200	25
尿素	25
30% NaOH	适量

2.2 三聚氰胺与苯胍胺的不同配比对树脂稳定性的影响

分析上述树脂储存期过短的原因,我们认为与树脂的反应活性较高有直接关系。为有效降低树脂的活性,我们加入活性相对较低,比三聚氰胺的官能团少的苯胍胺为改性剂对树脂进行改性。实验结果见表2。

表2 三聚氰胺与苯胍胺的不同质量比对树脂稳定性的影响

质量比(三聚氰:苯胍胺)	储存期/d	黏度/cp
75:0	0.8	850
65:10	3.0	1000
55:20	0.8	1000
45:30	3.5	800
35:40	3.4	700
25:50	6.0	720
15:60	6.0	620

通过表2以及图1可以看出,随着苯胍胺含量的增加,树脂的储存期有增长的趋势,树脂的黏度有下降趋势。但与实际要求仍然有较大的差距。虽然如此,由于本实验产品的最终目的是制备一种稳定的、可用于发泡的树脂,所以配合发泡实验一起进行。通过发泡实验发现,苯胍胺含量过低时不能用于发泡。当苯胍胺含量在20~60g时,树脂可以发泡,且随着苯胍胺含量的增加,发泡质量略有提高。

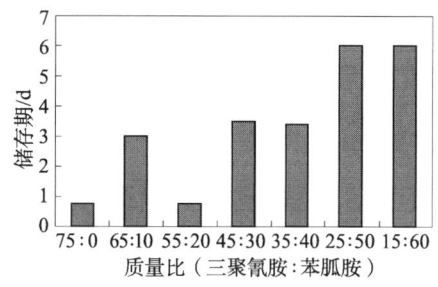 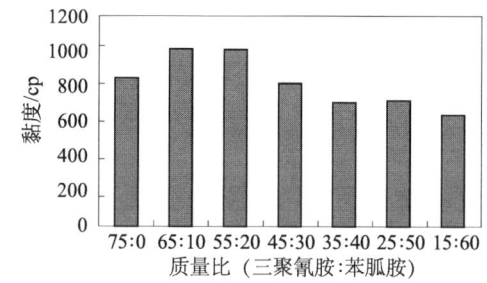

图1 三聚氰胺与苯胍胺的不同　　图2 三聚氰胺与苯胍胺的不同
质量比对树脂稳定性的影响　　配比对树脂黏度的影响

2.3 固含量对树脂稳定性的影响

为解决树脂固含量过低的问题,我们采用在反应初期即逐步脱水以逐步提高树脂固含量的的方法。根据基础配方,控制树脂的含水量不同,实验结果见表3。通过表3可以看出,树脂的固含量与树脂的稳定性间没有明显的规律。

表3 固含量对树脂稳定性及黏度的影响

固含量/(%)	储存期/d	黏度/cp	发泡效果
92.86	3.2	1000	可发，泡沫细腻
89.66	9.2	6200	可发，泡沫细腻，内部有少量气孔
86.67	1.3	2450	可发，泡沫细腻，有轻微缩泡现象
83.87	1.0	1200	可发，泡沫细腻，内部有少量气孔
81.25	6.0	620	可发，泡沫细腻
78.79	1.8	540	可发，泡沫细腻，内部有少量气孔

通过发泡实验发现，当固含量达到80%以上时，树脂可以发泡，且随着固含量的提高，发泡效果、泡沫质量越来越好。尤其是固含量为90%左右时，泡沫质量最好。

通过图3可以看出，树脂的黏度随固含量的增加而增大。其主要原因是因为三聚氰胺经羟甲基化后，分子间极不稳定，羟甲基间能进一步交联，使聚合度增高，使树脂黏度变大，溶解程度降低，直至絮凝、凝胶和固化。

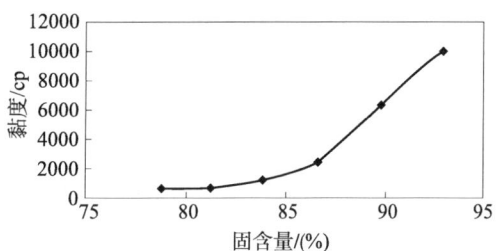

图3 固含量对树脂黏度的影响

2.4 乙二醇对树脂质量的影响

改性树脂的黏度随固含量的增加而增加，为解决树脂黏度过大的问题，我们采取用黏度相对较低的乙二醇逐步替代基础配方中的聚乙二醇200。实验结果见表4及图4。

表4 乙二醇含量对树脂稳定性及黏度的影响

乙二醇/g	储存期/d	黏度/cp
0	9.2	6200
5	10.0	6000
10	2.8	4500
15	4.8	3200
20	6.9	2800
25	0.8	2000

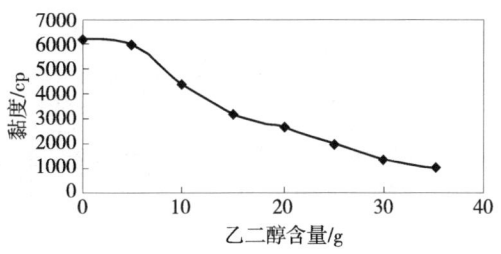

图4 乙二醇含量对树脂黏度的影响

通过表4和图4可以看出，树脂的黏度随乙二醇含量的增加而降低。

通过发泡实验发现，当用乙二醇替代聚乙二醇 200 时，树脂可以发泡，但其含量若大于 25 g 时，则发泡效果不佳，会出现塌泡、缩泡等。同时，随着乙二醇含量的增加，发泡效果越来越差。

通过表 4 可以看出，乙二醇的加入对树脂体系的稳定性的影响没有规律可循。

3 结　　论

苯胍胺的加入对三聚氰胺甲醛树脂体系的稳定性有所提高。乙二醇的加入能够有效地降低树脂的黏度。树脂的固含量、黏度等指标与树脂的储存稳定性没有明显的规律可循。作为发泡用树脂，树脂的固含量在 80% 以上时才能发泡，且固含量为 90% 左右时，发泡效果最好。

参考文献

[1] 刘春生. 浅谈建筑保温材料的分类和应用 [J]. 广东建材 - 建筑与装饰, 2005, (8): 113 - 114.
[2] 张泽平, 李珠, 董彦莉. 建筑保温节能墙体的发展现状与展望 [J]. 工程力学, 2007, 24: 121 - 128.
[3] 张宇, 王桐雨, 马榴强, 等. 可发性三聚氰胺甲醛树脂的合成研究 [J]. 广州化工, 2010, 38 (3): 109 - 111.
[4] 曹莲莲. 三聚氰胺甲醛树脂发泡保温材料的研究 [D]. 北京联合大学生物化学工程学院, 2011.

Genetic Algorithm for the Single Machine Earliness and Tardiness Scheduling Problem with Fuzzy Processing Times

Wang Chengyao

1 Introduction

In today's rapidly changing global markets, companies are under increasing pressure to short lead times and to maintain high on time delivery performance. Just – In – Time (JIT) philosophy has been the current interest corresponding to this changing. In a JIT scheduling environment, jobs that complete early must be hold in the inventory until their due date, it increase the cost of the inventory so will be discourage. On the contrast, jobs that complete late may be penalty by the customer or loss the credit of the customer. An ideal scheduling is that every job completed exactly on its due date. Unfortunately, in practice, the scheduling that every job completed exactly on its due date not always exists. The scheduling problems which objective minimizes the distant of job completion times between these due dates are earliness and tardiness scheduling problems.

In the past several years, many researchers have considered various earliness and tardiness (E/T) scheduling problems. Many of the E/T scheduling problems are NP – complete (Garey et al., 1978). This reinforces the need for effective heuristics and search techniques to solve larger problems. The class of the E/T scheduling problems is a vast class and can be divided by different criterions. Classed by the due dates – common due dates, distinct due dates and deadline due dates, Baker and Scudder (1990) indicated that the common due dates problems have been well researched than has been made with other classes. Classed by the number of machines – single machine scheduling problems and parallel machine scheduling problems, many research papers are interested in single machine scheduling (Liaw, 1999; James, 1998 and Lee, 1995) and less in the parallel (Funda, 1999 and Adamopoulos, 1998). In the real manufacturing systems, only a machine constructed the system is rarely existed, but when a machine act as a bottleneck for the whole system, the scheduling problems can be regarded as the single machine scheduling problems (French, 1990). The parameters of the E/T scheduling problems are usually regarded as deterministic value, Only a few papers regarded the some parameters as stochastic values. Sorouth (1999) studied an E/T scheduling problems on a single machine where processing times are random variables and job earliness and tardiness cost are distinct, the objective is to determine the optimal sequence and the optimal due – date which jointly minimize the expected total earliness and tardiness cost. In the open papers, there is not a paper to research the E/T scheduling problems with fuzzy parameters.

This paper is studies E/T scheduling problem that with difference penalties of earliness and tardiness on a single machine where processing times are fuzzy variables and job due dates are distinct. The objective is search the optimal sequence and minimize the possibility total earliness and tardiness cost. A method is presented to rank two fuzzy scheduling schemes. Genetic algorithms are used to solve the problem.

The paper is organized as follows. In Section 2, we introduce the fuzzy scheduling problems and give the definition of the fuzzy processing times in this paper. In Section 3, the E/T scheduling problems with fuzzy processing times is formulated, also a rule to rank different schemes is presented. In Section 4, genetic algorithms are proposed to generate near optimal schemes. In Section 5, the computational results of the proposed algorithms are discussed. In Section 6, Conclusions are presented.

2　Fuzzy scheduling problems

Fuzzy set theory has been studied extensively over the past 30 years. Since Tanka (1974) and Zimmermann (1976) formulated fuzzy mathematical programming problems, many approaches have been proposed in the field of fuzzy optimizations. Over the years, there have been several successful applications and implementations of fuzzy set theory in production planning and management.

Dubios (1983) formulated a fuzzy constraint satisfaction problem. In their model the release and due dates are fuzzy variables. Based on three basic procedures: consistency enforcing, tree search, and look – ahead analysis, a solving scheme is presented.

Ishii (1992) introduced the concept of fuzzy due dates to scheduling problems. In these fuzzy scheduling problems, the membership function of a fuzzy due date assigned to each job represents the grade of satisfaction of a decision – maker for the completion time of that job. Furthermore, Hisao (1994) and Sansu (1994) also studied different models of scheduling problems with fuzzy due dates.

McCahon and Lee (1990) study the job sequencing problems with fuzzy processing times. The fuzzy processing times are represented by the triangular or trapezoidal fuzzy numbers. McCahon and Lee (1992) studied a job shop problem that processing times are represented as the triangular numbers. The article provides a framework for interpreting and utilizing fuzzy makespan and mean flow time performance measures. The objective is the minimizing makespan and mean flow time.

Tzung – Pei Honghas (1998) studied the LPT scheduling for fuzzy tasks. Each task has a fuzzy processing time. The processing time is supposed as a fuzzy number. The membership function of the job processing times is not continuous, but discrete, and assumes that the number of possible execution time for each task is finite. In the article, two methods are assigned to ranking fuzzy numbers, which called the maximizing method and the averaging method.

Sakawa and Ryo (2000) study job shop scheduling problems with fuzzy due dates and fuzzy processing times. The fuzzy due date is a trapezoidal fuzzy number and the processing time is triangular fuzzy number. Three objectives that maximize the minimum agreement index, maximize the average index and minimize the maximum fuzzy completion time are studied. The article is also provided a method to rank and add the different fuzzy numbers. A genetic algorithm is applied to solve the problem.

In these articles, the fuzzy variable of processing times are regard as fuzzy number, the membership function represents the grade that the processing time equal to a value. For example, in the article of Sakawa and Ryo (2000), the fuzzy processing time is represented by a triangular fuzzy number and denoted by a triplet as shown in Fig. 1.

Where the horizontal axiom of the Fig. 1. represents the processing time, the vertical axiom represents the possible grade that a job processing time equals to a value. From this definition, it concerns about what the crisp processing time is.

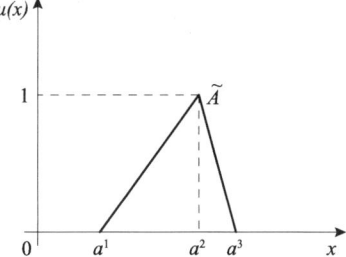

Fig. 1　Fuzzy processing time of other articles

Sometimes the manager may be concern about a job that processed under a constant processing time whether or not be completed. Especially, scheduling deals with determining the time – sequencing of jobs or orders, and with the allocation of required resources (personnel, machines, tools, etc.) to accomplished the related set of operations. Scheduling is the process of deciding what to do in the future. In the planning time, the manager may be more attention to concern about how much processing time allocated to a job that the possibility of the job completed than to concern about what the grade that the job processing time equal to a crisp value.

In real world, when a job is first to process or the new techniques are first implement a job, the job processing time must be forecasted during the scheduling period. Skilled workers and dispatchers estimate the job processing time by their accumulated experience. The processing time is estimated by human subjective views, we consider that is a fuzzy variable. Usually they set a lower bound and the upper bound of the job j. When the processing time is given to job j less than lower bound, the job will be not completed. When the processing time large than upper bound, the job j will be certainly completed. The job processing time is varying in the interval. The membership of the fuzzy processing time scheduling problems is established as follow.

Definition 1. Completed Job Set is a set that the job belonging to it is completed.

If $j \in T$ then j is a completed job

Definition 2. The membership function is the grade that job j belonging to the Completed Job Set under a constant processing time. Denoted as $\mu_j(x)$.

Properties 1. The membership function is a non-decrease function.

Proof: from the definition 2, the membership function is the grade of the job belonging to the Completed Job Set under a constant processing time. In a practice, when the processing time increasing, the job belonging to the set will not decreasing. So the membership function is a non-decrease function.

There are some assumptions are applied in the article.

Assumption 1. The membership function is a strictly increasing and continuous in the interval.

The membership function of a job processing times can be a linear function or non-linear function. The linear function can be described as follow.

$$\mu(x) = \begin{cases} 0 & x \leq a_j \\ \dfrac{x - a_j}{b_j - a_j} & a_j < x \leq b_j \\ 1 & b_j < x \end{cases}$$

Fig. 2 is a graph of the linear membership function. The horizontal axiom represents the processing time; the vertical axiom represents the grade of a job j belonging to Completed Job Set.

By the assumption 1, the membership function of job j in the interval (a_j, b_j) has an inverse function. The inverse function is also strictly increasing and continuous in the interval, denotes as.

Assumption 2: In the planning, for any job, the processing time allocated must maintain that the job grade belonging to Completed Job Set large than or equal to a predetermine value α_0 $(0 < \alpha_0 \leq 1)$.

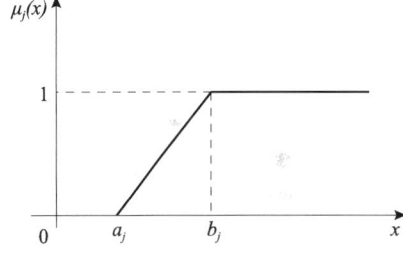

Fig. 2 the membership function of the fuzzy proessing time in this paper

Given a value α_0, there is a criterion to guarantee the planing available that avoid the grade equal to zero meaning job not completed.

Now the E/T scheduling problem with fuzzy processing time on the single machine is formulated as follow.

3 E/T scheduling problem with fuzzy processing time

The single machine earliness and tardiness scheduling problem with a fuzzy processing time addressed in this paper may be described as follows. Let $N = \{1, 2, \cdots, n\}$ be a set of n jobs to be processed in a single machine. Each job j $(j \in N)$ is available at time zero, has a fixed due date d_j, and a fuzzy processing time varying in the interval $(a_j, b_j]$. The membership function of job j is a linear function. Each job cannot be interrupted during processed time and must be completed. The machine can only process one job at a time and shall not be idle. If $c_{s,k}$ denotes the completion time of job that at position k of a scheme s, it is a fuzzy number. It also can be describe by a function of variable α. $c_{s,j} = \mu_{s,[k]}^{-1}(\alpha) = \sum_{t=1}^{k} \mu_{s,j}^{-1}(\alpha)$ Where, $\mu_{s,i}^{-1}(x)$ denotes the inverse membership function of the job that at position k of a scheme s, $\mu_{s,[k]}^{-1}(x)$ denotes the inverse union membership

$$t_{s,j} = (c_{s,j} - d_{s,j}) = (\mu_{s,[k]}^{-1}(\alpha) = d_{s,j}) = \left(\sum_{i=1}^{k} \mu_{s,i}^{-1}(\alpha) - d_{s,j} \right)$$ function of a job that at position k of a scheme

s. It is dependent on the inverse membership function of jobs that before position k. For the job j then is its earliness and is its tardiness. If a nonnegative penalty β_j is defined for each unit of time job j ($j \in N$) is early and a nonnegative penalty γ_j is defined for each unit of time job j ($j \in N$) is late. Then the total cost function of a scheme s may be described as follow.

$$f_s = \sum_{k=1}^{n} (\beta_{s,j} e_{s,j} + \gamma_{s,j} t_{s,j})$$

In the planning period, the of the scheme s is a fuzzy number, we do not know the exact total cost value of the scheme until the all jobs are processed completed. It is very important to select the optimal or best scheduling scheme that how to compare and rank two different schemes during the planning period. To rank fuzzy numbers, is a difficult thing, because that every fuzzy number represents a set. Between the two sets can not always yield a totally ordered set as real numbers do. To resolve this problem, many authors have proposed different fuzzy ranking methods that yield a totally ordered set or ranking. For more about fuzzy members ranking can be found in (Yoon, 1996; Tseng, 1988; and Lee, 1988).

In this paper, we give a method to rank two schemes. Firstly, assumption that in a scheme all jobs belonging to Completed Job Set's grade is equal. So the changes into a function of the grade α ($\alpha \in [\alpha_0, 1]$).

Secondly, because for any inverse function $\mu_j^{-1}(\alpha)$ is a strictly increasing and continuous function in the interval $[\alpha_0, 1]$, and the function by the countable continuous functions summed is also a continuous function, so the f_s is a continuous function in the interval $[\alpha_0, 1]$. By the Extreme Value Theorem (Wade, 1995), the function is bounded on $[\alpha_0, 1]$. There exist points $\alpha_{max}, \alpha_{min} \in [\alpha_0, 1]$ such that $f_s(\alpha_{max}) = \sup_{\alpha \in [\alpha_0, 1]} f_s(\alpha)$ and $f_s(\alpha_{min}) = \inf_{\alpha \in [\alpha_0, 1]} f_s(\alpha)$.

Finally, we calculate by the equation as follow.

$$f_s = \frac{f_s(\alpha_{min}) \, f_s(\alpha_{pro}) + f_s(\alpha_{max})}{6}$$

Where the α_{pro} means the maximum possibility that α equal to. In this paper, the $\alpha_{pro} = 0.5$ is assumptive.

So the objective can be describe as follow crisp equations.

min $\quad \{f_s \mid s = 1, 2, \cdots, n!\}$

st. $\quad f_s(\alpha_{min}) = \inf_{\alpha \in [\alpha_0, 1]} \sum_{k=1}^{n} \{\beta_{s,j}[d_{s,j} - \sum_{i=1}^{k} \mu_{s,i}^{-1}(\alpha)]^+ + \gamma_{s,j}[\sum_{i=1}^{k} \mu_{s,i}^{-1}(\alpha) - d_{s,j}]^+\}$

$\quad f_s(\alpha_{min}) = \sum_{k=1}^{n} \{\beta_{s,j}[d_{s,j} - \sum_{i=1}^{k} \mu_{s,i}^{-1}(0.5)]^+ + \gamma_{s,j}[\sum_{i=1}^{k} \mu_{s,i}^{-1}(0.5) - d_{s,j}]^+\}$

$\quad f_s(\alpha_{min}) = \sup_{\alpha \in [\alpha, 1]} \sum_{k=1}^{n} \{\beta_{s,j}[d_{s,j} - \sum_{i=1}^{k} \mu_{s,i}^{-1}(\alpha)]^+ + \gamma_{s,j}[\sum_{i=1}^{k} \mu_{s,i}^{-1}(\alpha) - d_{s,j}]^+\}$

This problem is a NP – hard problem. It is not likely that an algorithm can be developed which can solve the problem in 'reasonable' time. Optimization approaches (branch – and – bound algorithm) can only resolve the small – scale problems, for large – scale problems must be using heuristic rules or intelligent algorithms. The genetic algorithms are applied in this paper.

4 Genetic algorithms

Genetic Algorithms were developed by Holland (1975) as artificial systems to simulate natural evolution. Motivated by the biological adaptation, they generate a new set of offspring from parent chromosomes via stochastic operation. The chromosomes with high fitness value have more opportunity to survive and those with low fitness values have little opportunity. The chromosomes are improved from generation to generation, it is regard that the chromosomes will search the optimal solution or near optimal solution. By the more points to search and the improving of random, the GAs effectiveness and efficiency used to resolve NP – hard problems. In this section, the details of the GAs used for this paper are discussed.

4.1 Representation

A feasible solution called a chromosome is represented as a sequence of jobs. The chromosome is encoding by the natural number. The number of gene represents the job number and the position of gene represents the job position in the sequence. For example, the chromosome {3, 4, 1, 2} represents a solution that process the job by the sequence {3, 4, 1, 2}.

4.2 Reproduction

The fitness value of a chromosome is equal to the objective function value. Using roulette wheel as the basic selection mechanism to reproduce next generation based on parent population, in which a fitter chromosome has a large chance to be reproduced into next generation. In the generation M, chromosome k's probability of being reproduced is

$$P_M(k) = \frac{f_M - f(k)}{\sum_{j=1}^{pop\_size} [f_M - f(j)]}$$

where, $f_M = \max_j \{f(j)\}$, is the maximum fitness value in population.

4.3 Crossover and Mutation

Crossover plays the important role of exchanging information among chromosomes. In this algorithm, five crossover different operators are separately used to get five different Genetic Algorithms. Four typical crossover operators: Partially Matched Crossover (PMX), Order Crossover (OX), Circle Crossover (CX) (Goldberg, 1989), and Uniform Crossover (UN) (Syswerda, 1989).

The last crossover operator is a new crossover—Hybrid Crossover (HX) which combination of the other four crossover operators. It selects one of the four operators as its crossover method randomly, with the probability of 40% for UN, 40% for PMX, 10% for OX and 10% for CX. Thus it is expected to improve the performance of the algorithm by enhancing the variety of crossover method.

Mutation operator is used the inversion operator to do the mutation.

4.4 Elitist selection

Randomly remove one chromosome and add the best one of parent population into the offspring population.

5 Computation results

In this section, the computational results of the GAs are discussed. The GAs developed in this paper is coded in VC++ on the PC586. The termination criterion of the algorithms is iteration generations. The maximum generation is 500 (iter_num = 500). The crossover rate is 1 ($p_c = 1$) and the mutation rate is 50% ($p_m = 0.5$). The population size at each generation of the genetic algorithms is kept at 20 (pop_size = 20).

5.1 Algorithm of the test problems

Two type sets of job numbers are produced. Type set I contain 10 jobs and Type set II contain 50 jobs. Each set has 50 problems. The job processing time is estimated by the linear membership function. For example the job j membership function is

$$\mu(x) = \begin{cases} 0 & x \leq a_j \\ \frac{x - a_j}{b_j - a_j} & a_j < x \leq b_j \\ 1 & b_j < x \end{cases}$$

The given grade $\alpha_0 = 0.2$.

The follow algorithms produce the job parameters.

Step1. Randomly generate the low bound of job processing time of the integers 10, 11, ⋯, 19.

Step 2. The upper bound of job processing time is adds a number that randomly generate of the integers 1, 2, ⋯, 5.

Step 3. The earliness penalty of each job j, is randomly selected from 0, 0.1, 0.2, ⋯, 0.9, and the tardiness penalty of job j, is randomly selected from 0, 0.05, 0.1, ⋯, 0.95.

Step 4. The due date of each job j, is an integer that is randomly selected from the interval $[5, Max]$. where $Max = \sum_{j=1}^{n} b_j$.

5.2 Calculate the function value

In the genetic algorithms, it contains many chromosomes that via different job sequence. The important thing is to calculate the fitness value of each chromosome. In this paper, the fitness values are equal to the objective function value. So effectively calculated the objective function value is important to improve the algorithm characters.

Generally, a function is continuously in the closed interval, can get the maximum and the minimum value by the differentiable method that the maximum and the minimum value is obtained at the point x where the $f'(x) = 0$ or the bound of the closed interval. But it is difficult to get the differentiable function of the objective values, because the objective function is difficult to be clearly to describe in the closed interval.

In this paper, the job membership function is a linear function, and the inverse function is also a linear function. For a scheme s, the function $f_s(\alpha)$ is a sum of the countable linear functions. It is a linear function during several closed interval of the interval $[0, 1]$. The slope of the function $f_s(\alpha)$ will not be change until at some points that there is a job at this grade the job is on time (the completion time equal to due date). So any shift point will via no less than a job that on time. During two shift points, the function $f_s(\alpha)$ is a non – increasing or non – decreasing function. By the assumption 2, we only exchange the shift points that make a job of the scheme s change from earliness to tardiness in the closed interval $[0.2, 1]$. The maximum and the minimum value is can be obtained from these shift points, the upper bound 1, or the lower bound 0.2.

5.3 Results

The results is listed in table 1 and table 2, where the comparison is made in terms of mean objective value of 50 problems through evolution of 100 generations, 200 generations, 300 generations, 400 generations and 500 generations. And in the table, GA_ PMX, GA_ OX, GA_ CX, GA_ UN and GA_ HX means the genetic algorithms using PMX, OX, CX, UN and HX crossover operator. The value in the tables is average of the 50 problems search result at the same crossover operator.

Table 1 Results of 10 job with different crossovers

Crossover operator	100	200	300	400	500
GA_ PMX	1.65	1.51	1.41	1.38	1.38
GA_ OX	1.74	1.50	1.42	1.40	1.38
GA_ CX	1.87	1.65	1.49	1.38	1.38
GA_ UN	1.63	1.53	1.44	1.38	1.38
GA_ HX	1.57	1.41	1.41	1.38	1.38

Table 2 Results of 50 job with different crossovers

Crossover operator	100	200	300	400	500
GA_ PMX	12.34	11.18	11.18	10.54	9.06
GA_ OX	12.44	11.40	10.86	10.41	9.59
GA_ CX	12.57	11.54	10.96	10.68	9.40
GA_ UN	12.68	12.54	11.46	9.89	8.97
GA_ HX	12.58	12.45	10.44	9.73	8.92

Furthermore, in order to making comparison between results gained by genetic algorithm and optimal solution, we developed a branch and bound algorithm. For the same 50 problems of the 10 job, we brought out that the mean of objective functions is 1.38. In the small-scale problems, the genetic algorithms can search the optimal solution. There is a little difference of different crossover operator. But in the large-scale problems, there is a difference of GAs with different crossover operator. For 50 jobs problem, is difficulty to get the optimal solution by the branch and bound algorithm. Thus we regard the optimal solution is the smallest value of different GAs searched after 500 generations. Compare the GA with 5 crossover operators in terms of relative deviation and frequency of reaching the optimal objective through evolution of 500 generations, which is listed in table 3. Where the $f*$ means the average of the regard optimal solutions, the Δf is the difference between the average value of the same crossover operator and the f^*.

Table 3 Comparison of genetic algorithms using different crossovers

Crossover operator	$\Delta f / f^*$	Frequency
GA_PMX	1.68%	78%
GA_OX	7.63%	56%
GA_CX	5.49%	58%
GA_UN	0.67%	86%
GA_HX	0.11%	90%

The results show that: for the 50-job problem, the genetic algorithm using any crossover operator is little deviation to the regard optimal solutions, it means that genetic algorithms search the near optimal solution effectively. The results of GA_PMX and GA_UN are better than that of GA_OX and GA_CX, while GA_HX is more effective than GA_PMX and GA_UN. The hybrid crossover algorithm can gain quite near optimal solution, and its frequency of reaching the optimal objective is 4% higher than that of GA_UX.

6 Conclusion

A new kind of membership function of the fuzzy processing time is presented. The model, that earliness and tardiness scheduling problem with fuzzy processing time, is formulated. The criterion of ranking different fuzzy schemes is also discussed. To resolve problem, genetic algorithms are used. Five different crossover operators are used and compared. By the computational results, it shows that the genetic algorithms can get the optimal solution of 10-job size problems. For the 50-job size problem, the search result of the different genetic algorithm has little deviations, it shows that genetic algorithm can obtained the near optimal solution of the large-scale problems. The computation results also shows that the new HX crossover operator is better than other four typical ones.

References

[1] Adamopoulos, G. L. and Pappis, C. P. Theory and methodology scheduling under a common due-date on parallel unrelated machines [J]. European Journal Operation Research, 1998 (105): 494-501.

[2] Baker, K. R. and Scudder, G. D. Sequencing with earliness and tardiness penalties: A review [J]. Operation Research, 1990 (38): 22-36.

[3] French, S. Sequencing and scheduling, an introduction to the mathematics of the job-shop [J]. Ellis Horwood, 1990.

[4] Funda, S. S. and Ulusoy, G. Parallel machine scheduling with earliness and tardiness penalties [J]. Computer & Operation Research, 1999 (26): 773-787.

[5] Dubios, D., et al. Fuzzy constraints in job-shop scheduling [J]. J. of Intelligent Manufacturing, 1995 (6): 215-234.

[6] Garey, M. R. Gramham, R. L. and Blackstone, J. H. Performance guarantees for scheduling algorithms [J]. Operation Research, 1978 (26): 3-21.

[7] Goldberg, D. E. Genetic algorithms in search, optimization & machine learning. Addison Wsley, Reading, Mass.

[8] Hisao Ishibuchi, et al. Genetic algorithms and neighborhood search algorithms for fuzzy flow shop scheduling problems [J]. Fuzzy Sets and Systems, 1994 (67): 81 – 100.

[9] Holland, J. Adaptation in natural and artificial systems. Ann Arbor, The University of Michigan Press.

[10] Ishii, H., Tada, M. and Masuda, T. Two scheduling problem with fuzzy due dates [J]. Fuzzy Sets and Fuzzy Systems, 1992 (46): 339 – 347.

[11] Lee, E. S. and Li, R. J. Comparison of fuzzy number based on the probability measure of fuzzy events [J]. Computer Mathematics Application, 1998 (15): 887 – 896.

[12] Liaw Ching – fang. A branch – and – bound algorithm for the single machine earliness and tardiness scheduling problem [J]. Computer & Operation Research, 1999 (26): 679 – 693.

[13] James, R. J. W. and Buchanan, J. T. Performance enhancements to tabu search for the early/tardy scheduling problem [J]. European Journal of Operation Research, 1998 (106): 254 – 265.

[14] Lee, C. Y. and Choi, J. Y. A genetic algorithm for job sequencing problems with distinct due dates and general early – tardy penalty weights [J]. Computer & Operation Research, 1995 (22): 857 – 869.

[15] McCahon, C. S. and Lee, E. S. Job sequencing with fuzzy processing times." Computers & Mathematics with Applications [J]., 1990 (19): 31 – 41.

[16] McCahon, C. S. and Lee, E. S. Fuzzy job sequencing for a flow shop [J]. European Journal of Operation Research, 1992 (62): 293 – 301.

[17] Sakawa, M. and Ryo, K. Theory and methodology fuzzy programming for multiobjective job shop scheduling with fuzzy processing time and fuzzy duedate through genetic algorithms [J]. European Journal of Operation Research, 2000 (120): 393 – 407.

[18] Sansu Han, et al. One machine scheduling problem with fuzzy due dates", European Journal Operational Research, 1994 (79): 1 – 12.

[19] Soroush, H. M. Theory and methodology sequencing and due – date determination in the stochastic single machine problems with earliness and tardiness costs [J]. European journal Operation Research, 1999 (113): 450 – 468.

[20] Syswerda, G. Uniform crossover in genetic algorithms", Proc. 3^{d} International. Conf. On Genetic Algorithms. George Mason University, 1989.

[21] Tseng, T. Y., Klein, C. M. and Leonard, M. S. A formalism for comparing ranking procedures. Proc. 7th Ann. Meeting of the North American Fuzzy Information Processing Society, 1989: 231 – 235.

[22] Tanaka, H., Okuda, T. and Asai, K. On fuzzy mathematical programming [J]. J. Cybernetics, 1974 (3): 37 – 45.

[23] Tzung – Pei, Hong, Cheng – Ming, Huang and Kun – Ming, Yu. LPT Scheduling for Fuzzy Tasks [J]. Fuzzy Sets and Systems, 1998 (97): 226 – 286.

[24] Wade, W. R. An introduction to analysis. Prentice – Hall, Inc.

[25] Yoon, K. P. and Hwang, C. L. A probabilistic approach to rank complex fuzzy numbers [J]. Fuzzy Sets and Systems, 1996 (80): 167 – 176.

[26] Zimmermann, H. J. Description and optimization of fuzzy systems [J]. Inter. J, General Systems, 1976 (2): 209 – 215.

混合数据模型在建筑物三维建模中的应用

王育坚　许承福　刘立平

建筑物是城市中的主要地物，建筑物三维建模是计算机图形学、地理信息系统、摄影测量学及相关学科研究的热点，并在虚拟现实、复杂场景设计、计算机视觉和三维 GIS 等领域得到了广泛应用[1-2]。建筑物三维建模方法直接影响到城市三维可视化的速度和效果，如何快捷、逼真地构建建筑物三维模型是很多研究人员重点研究的课题。笔者在分析了多种三维空间数据模型的基础上，针对建筑物的结构特点，提出了一种基于八叉树和 NURBS 的混合三维数据模型。

1 三维空间数据模型

空间数据模型是在实体概念的基础上发展起来的。近年来，国内外很多学者对三维空间数据模型理论和应用进行了深入的研究，提出了多种三维空间数据模型建模方法[3-4]。按照模型的存储元素类型分类，三维空间数据模型可分为栅格数据模型、矢量数据模型、栅格和矢量混合模型 3 类。按照模型的构成元素分类，三维空间数据模型可分为基于面元的模型、基于体元的模型和面元体元混合模型 3 类。

基于面元的模型是利用微小的面元素来描述空间实体的几何形态，通过表面表示形成实体的三维空间轮廓。基于面元的模型包括格网（Grid）、不规则三角形格网（TIN）、线框（Wire Frame）、边界表示（Boundary Representation）、断面（Section）和参数函数表示（Parameter Function）等。其中，基于三角形格网的模型已成为三维空间数据建模的通用方法。

基于体元的模型是以基本体元分割空间实体，将三维空间实体抽象为一系列邻接但不交叉的三维体元的集合，通过对体元的描述实现三维实体的空间表示。基于体元的模型包括四面体格网（TEN）、八叉树（Octree）、结构实体几何法（CSG）、三维栅格（Array）、块段（Block）、六面体（Hexahedral）、多面体（Polyhedral）和棱柱体（Prism）等。

基于面元模型的优点为数据存储量小，建模快捷，实体显示和更新的速度快，不足之处为不能描述实体的内部属性，难以进行实体的三维空间分析和查询。基于体元模型的优点为适于空间操作和分析，不足之处为数据结构复杂，存储空间大，建模速度慢。

面元模型和体元模型有不同的特点和适用对象，而混合模型综合了面元模型和体元模型的优点[5]，实际应用中可以根据实体的不同特性采用不同的混合模型。构造混合模型需要考虑以下 3 个维：模型的构成元素维，包括面元、体元和混合 3 种；存储类型维，包括栅格、矢量和混合 3 种；构成元素的形状维，包括规则、不规则和混合 3 种。研究者根据不同需要将这些维组合起来构造了多种混合模型[6-7]，有同一维上的混合模型，如 TIN – CSG 面和体混合模型、Octree – TEN 矢量和栅格混合模型、混合面片的规则和不规则体素混合模型；还有不同维之间的混合模型，如 TIN – Oc – tree 面和栅格的混合模型。

2 三维混合数据模型

2.1 八叉树结构

八叉树结构是一种规则的数据结构，通过树结构对模型进行递归，按 X、Y、Z 3 个不同方向，将所要表示的三维空间实体 V 分割为 8 个大小相等的子立方体。然后根据每个子立方体中所含的目标来决定是否对子立方体继续进行 8 等分的划分。一直划分到每个子立方体被一个目标所充满，或没有目标，或

[基金项目] 北京市属高等学校人才强教计划基金资助项目（PHR200907120）；北京市教育委员会科技计划基金资助项目（KM201111417014）。

[作者简介] 王育坚（1963—），男，北京联合大学信息学院教授。

其大小已成为预先定义的不可再分的体素为止。如图 1 所示，八叉树每个节点有 8 个子节点或者没有子节点。图 1（c）中，小圆圈表示该立方体未被某个目标填满，需要继续划分。灰度小矩形表示该立方体被某个目标填满，空白小矩形表示该立方体中没有目标，这两种情况都不需继续划分。八叉树每个维度每划分一次，其分辨率都将增大到原来的两倍。

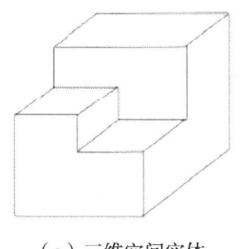 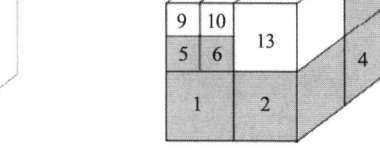 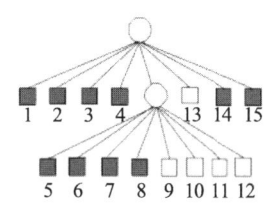

（a）三维空间实体　　　　　（b）八叉树分割　　　　　（c）树结构表示

图 1　八叉树结构

八叉树体素分解是将空间三维物体逐级分解，最终形成八叉树体素表示的结构。八叉树的主要优点为可以方便地实现物体的并、交、差等集合运算，适用于较规则实体的建模，但对于不规则实体的建模则不太适用[8]。

2.2　NURBS 参数函数表示

参数函数表示的指导思想是利用有限的空间数据，构造一个函数的解析式，用这个解析式来生成新的空间点，用以逼近原有物体。参数函数表示包括解析函数模型和非解析函数模型。解析函数模型的优点为数学运算简便、数据存储量小，但复杂的空间对象很难用统一的函数参数方程来表达。为了克服解析函数的局限性，人们提出了非解析函数。B 样条函数是比较实用的参数函数，具有存储量小、分析运算速度快、空间几何不变性等特点，是构建三维空间实体边界曲面的有效方法。

非均匀有理 B 样条（non-uniform rational B-splinc，NURBS）函数是在 B 样条函数基础上发展起来的，已被广泛应用于工程设计中。计算机图像处理技术的发展，推动了 NURBS 技术在三维建模领域中的应用[9]。

如图 2 所示，一条 NURBS 曲线 $s(u)=(x(u),y(u),z(u))$ 可通过式（1）表示：

$$s(u) = \sum_{i=0}^{n} w_i P_i N_i^k(u) \Big/ \sum_{i=0}^{n} w_i N_i^k(u)$$
$$u \in [u_{k-1}, u_{n+1}] \tag{1}$$

式中：$P_i=(x_i,y_i,z_i)$ $(i=0,1,\cdots,n)$ 为控制点；w_i $(i=0,1,\cdots,n)$ 为权因子；k 为阶数；N_i^k $(i=0,1,\cdots,n)$ 为 B 样条基函数，其递推定义如下：

$$N_i^1(u) = \begin{cases} 1 & u_i \leq u \leq u_{i+1} \\ 0 & 其他 \end{cases}$$

$$N_i^k(u) = \frac{(u-u_i)N_i^{k-1}(u)}{u_{i+k-1}-u_i} + \frac{(u_{i+k}-u)N_{i+1}^{k-1}(u)}{u_{i+k}-u_{i+1}} \tag{2}$$

图 2　NURBS 拟合曲线

u 向节点矢量为 $\{u_0,u_1,\cdots,u_{n+k} | u_i \leq u_{i+1}, i=0,1,\cdots,n+k-1 |\}$。

$s_i(u)$ $(i=0,1,\cdots,n)$ 为由控制点分段拟合的曲线段，$u \in [u_i, u_{i+1}]$，$i=k-1, k, \cdots, n$。

如图 3 所示，设一个 NURBS 曲面给定了 $(n+1)(m+1)$ 个网格控制点 P_{ij} $(0 \leq i < n, 0 \leq j < m)$，则该 NURBS 曲面可定义为：

$$S(u,v) = \frac{\sum_{i=0}^{n}\sum_{j=0}^{m} w_{ij} P_{ij} N_i^k(u) N_j^l(v)}{\sum_{i=0}^{n}\sum_{j=0}^{m} w_{ij} N_i^k(u) N_j^l(v)}$$

式中：w_{ij} $(0 \leq i < n, 0 \leq j < m)$ 为相应于控制点 P_{ij} 的权因子；k、l 为阶数；$N_i^k(u)$ $(0 \leq i \leq n)$ 和

$N_j^l(v)$ $(0 \leq j \leq m)$ 分别是定义在 u、v 向节点向量：$U = \{u_0, u_1, \cdots, u_{n+k} | u_i \leq u_{i+1}, i = 0, 1, \cdots, n+k-1\}$，$V = \{v_0, v_1, \cdots, v_{m+l} | v_j \leq v_{j+1}, i = 0, 1, \cdots, m+l-1\}$

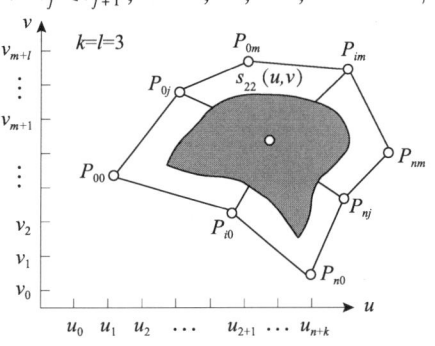

图 3　NURBS 拟合曲面

k、l 阶 B 样条基函数递推定义同式（2）；$S_{ij}(u, v)$ 表示拟合的曲面段，$u \in [u_i, u_{i+1}]$，$i = k-1$，$k, \cdots, n$；$v \in [v_j, v_{j+1}]$，$j = l-1, l, \cdots, m$。

2.3　建筑物三维混合数据模型

建筑物在几何和拓扑上有较大差异，传统的八叉树模型表示不规则的实体不够精确，很难用于各种类型建筑物的建模。针对城市建筑物种类繁多、结构复杂、信息量大的特点，笔者采用八叉树与 NURBS 曲面相结合的混合数据模型。

在混合数据模型中，利用八叉树对建筑物实体进行三维空间分割，利用 NURBS 拟合建筑物不规则的表面。当分割后的建筑物子体位于实体边界且外形不是规则立方体时，采用 NURBS 曲面描述该体元的表面，如图 4 所示。将实体转换为八叉树结构时，在边界灰度节点中加入子体的面、边、顶点信息，从而形成扩展的八叉树结构[10]。

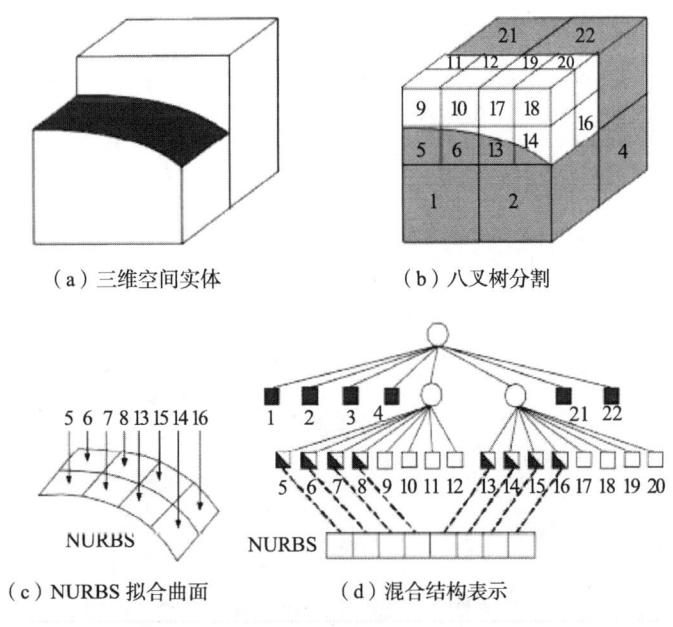

（a）三维空间实体　　　（b）八叉树分割

（c）NURBS 拟合曲面　　（d）混合结构表示

图 4　八叉树 – NURBS 混合结构

空间分割首先采用八叉树空间分解法生成曲面离散点集，选取一个立方体包围盒圈定空间曲面，将包围盒作为八叉树的根节点来初始化八叉树数据结构。然后将该包围盒分解成 8 个子区域，作为大立方体的 8 个子节点，生成子体曲面上的空间离散点集。空间分割时注意采集实体不规则部分的外围散点，将不规则体元剖分成参数函数曲面，生成子体的 NURBS 曲面。

混合结构用一个特殊的属性值实现八叉树与 NURBS 曲面的链接，若八叉树某节点编码的属性值为 N，表示该节点关联一个局部的 NURBS 曲面。通过节点与对应的 8 个子节点体内的特征点相结合，形成局部 NURBS 曲面。实现时采用网格细化和求交切割的方法[11]，用不规则体元填充八叉树与表面模型之间的空隙，完成模型的自适应分割。

曲面模型的数学表示是一个带符号的代数距离函数，为了简化曲面建模，也可以采用一个均匀的双三次 B 样条函数[12]。假设在二维平面上有 n 个点 (x_i, y_i) $(i = 1, 2, \cdots, n)$，并有 $h_i = F(x_i, y_i)$，这样在三维空间中可以构成一个点的集合 $P = \{(x_i, y_i, z_i)\}$。构造一个均匀的双三次 B 样条曲面来逼近集合 P，该双三次曲面片由覆盖在子节点的控制点网格 φ 来定义。设 φ_{ij} 是网格 φ 中序号为 ij 控制点的值，则由这些控制点定义的双三次 B 样条函数为：

$$f(x,y) = \sum_{k=0}^{3} \sum_{l=0}^{3} B_k(s) B_l(t) \varphi_{(i+k)(j+l)} \tag{3}$$

式中：B_k、B_l 为均匀双三次 B 样条基函数。

控制点阵列 $\varphi_{kl}(k,l = 0,1,2,3)$ 决定了点 (x_c, y_c) 的函数值 $f(x_c, y_c)$，即有：

$$h = \sum_{k=0}^{3} \sum_{l=0}^{3} B_k(s) B_l(t) \varphi_{kl} \tag{4}$$

式中：$s = x_c - 1$；$t = y_c - 1$。

有许多组的值可以满足式 (4)，根据最小二乘法原理，用伪逆矩阵可以求出一组解为：

$$\varphi_{kl} = \frac{B_k(s) B_l(l) z_c}{\sum_{a=0}^{3} \sum_{b=0}^{3} \omega_{ab}^2}$$

2.4 建筑物数据结构

随着城市化进程的加快，城市建筑物的结构和形状不断发生变化。数据结构是三维建模的基础，必须设计出合理的数据结构，以便高效地存储建筑物的属性和几何数据。根据八叉树 – NURBS 混合三维数据模型，采用面向对象的程序设计语言 C ++ 为建筑物设计相应的数据结构，其形式化表示如下：

```
class BuildingObject {                      // 建筑物对象
private：
    int buildingID；                        // 建筑物编号
    float length；                          // 建筑物主体长
    float width；                           // 建筑物主体宽
    float height；                          // 建筑物主体高
    float roofheight；                      // 建筑物屋顶高
    float ridgelength；                     // 建筑物屋脊长
    TreeNode octree[8]；                    // 定义 8 个子八叉树
public：
    void initialize（）；
    Octree *   CreatOctree（）             // 八叉树生成函数
    Nurbs *  pNurbs  CreatNURBS
    （NurbsPoint ** point）                // NURBS 曲面生成函数
}；//树节点的数据结构：
struct TreeNode {                          // 八叉树节点
    long code；                            // 节点编码
    int size；                             // 节点大小
    int type；                             // 属性
    int layer；                            // 节点所在层
    int index；                            // 节点在兄弟节点中的序号
    struct TreeNode *    pParent；         // 父节点指针
    struct TreeNode *    pChd [8]；        // 子节点指针
```

```
    bool leaf;                          // 是否为叶子节点
    bool Polygon;                       // 节点是否关联 NURBS 曲面对象
    NurbsPoint **   point;              // NURBS 曲面控制点,用指针定义二维动态数组
    int nNurebsCtrl;                    // NURBS 曲面控制点数
    Nurbs *   pNurbs;                   // 关联 NURBS 曲面指针
    int NurbsObjectID;}                 // 曲面对象的 ID 码
```

在存储结构上,采用扩展节点(面、边、顶点)和混合式的八叉树结构,在八叉树较高的层次上使用指针式结构建立节点的索引,而在较低的层次上按节点编码的大小排序,建立该局部空间内包含的所有非空叶节点的线性表。这样既减少了存储空间,又提高了显示的精度和搜索效率。

通过八叉树节点编码可以得到其对应的 8 个子节点,编码方案直接影响节点的存取效率。这里采用八进制前缀编码方案,即对同一父节点的 8 个兄弟节点,其具有最小 (x, y, z) 值的节点编号为 0,相邻兄弟节点的编号沿 x 方向增加 1,沿 y 方向增加 2,沿 z 方向增加 4,并将父节点的编码作为其 8 个子节点编码的前缀。为保证八叉树中每一节点编码的长度相同,在编码后增加一串区别于 0~7 八进制数的特殊字符"T",使每个节点编码的长度均为树的最大深度 H。这样,节点编码可表示为 $q_1q_2\cdots q_iTT\cdots T$,其中 q_1, q_2, $\cdots$, $q_i \in \{0, 1, \cdots, 7\}$,$0 \leq i \leq H$。显然,$q_1q_2\cdots q_n$ 表示了空间最低层次(第 n 层)立方体网格单元,$q_1q_2\cdots q_iTT\cdots T$ 表示了空间分割至第 i 层时的立方体网格。

实体模型的多个子体相互关联,多个子体结合成为模型总体。每个子体由一组节点和一个 NURBS 曲面重构形成,CreatNURBS( ) 函数用于建立建筑物的 NURBS 曲面对象。一些八叉树叶节点可能被同一个 NURBS 曲面对象包含,即一个 NURBS 曲面对象可能同时与多个八叉树节点相关联。通过对八叉树按层次遍历逐步细分作用区域,在求交层中对区域内的每个节点进行精确的 NURBS 关联运算。实际应用中,有些建筑物的墙体或屋顶为曲面,需要采集或内插一些特征点,然后按一定的规则对建筑物的子体建立 NURBS 曲面模型。

3 基于 OpenGL 的建筑物三维可视化

模型系统以 Visual C ++6.0 为开发平台,采用面向对象的建模方法,利用 OpenGL 技术实现实体的三维建模和可视化。在建立 NURBS 曲面模型时,以 OpenGL 的 NURBS 接口函数为基础,通过编写程序对节点相关联的 NURBS 曲面建模。NURBS 对实体表面的拟合,主要通过计算控制点实现。先求出控制多边形的顶点,根据已知的数据拟合 NURBS 曲面,通过插值法最终实现所有子体表面的 NURBS 曲面构造。该模型系统不仅可以表达规则实体,也可以表达不规则实体,使用该模型系统生成的三维模型如图 5 所示。

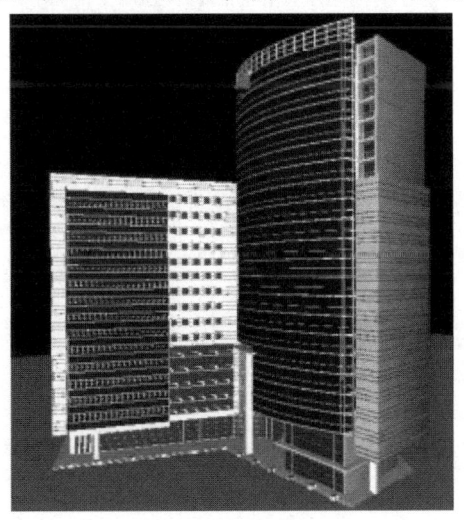

图 5 建筑物三维模型

对于简单结构建筑物的建模,混合模型并没有表现出比传统的八叉树模型更优越。但在处理不规则的建筑物时,在相同分辨率要求的前提下,混合模型对三维空间实体的分割次数要远远小于八叉树模

型。如对弧面形状的建筑物，前者的分割次数为后者的 1/8 左右。因此，即使考虑 NURBS 曲面对象的建模，混合模型的数据存储量比八叉树模型少 50% 以上，相应的模型显示速度提高了 20%，模型的精度也更高。

4 结论

笔者在对城市建筑物三维建模理论和方法进行深入研究的基础上，设计了一个基于八叉树和 NURBS 的混合数据模型系统。实践证明，该模型具有一定的实用性和可行性，可视化效果较好，具有较精确表示复杂空间实体的特点。由于数据结构的复杂性，该模型在判断何时需要构造 NURBS 曲面时，条件不够精确，理论和算法还需深入研究。

参考文献

[1] Thiele A, Cadario E, Schulz K, et al. Building Reconstruction from InSAR Data by Detail Analysis of Phase Profiles [C] // The International Archives of the Photogrammetry, Remote Sensing and Spatial Information Sciences. 2008: 191-196.

[2] 杨淼. 基于图像的城市建筑物三维自动重建参数化建模方法研究 [D]. 青岛：中国海洋大学图书馆，2009.

[3] 王彦兵，吴立新，李小娟. 3 维 GIS 空间建模方法评述 [J]. 中国图象图形学报，2007，12（8）：1430-1434.

[4] KATSIANIS M, TSIPIDIS S, KOTSAKIS K, et al. A 3D digital workflow for archaeological intra-site re-search using GIS [J]. Journal of Archaeological Science, 2008, 35 (3): 655-667.

[5] 张传明，潘懋，徐绘宏. 基于分块混合八叉树编码的海量体视化研究 [J]. 计算机工程，2007，33（14）：33-78.

[6] 吴慧欣，薛惠锋. 基于块段模型的三维 GIS 混合数据结构模型研究 [J]. 计算机应用研究，2007，24（10）：273-275.

[7] 荆永滨，王李管，毕林，等. 复杂矿体的块段模型建模算法 [J]. 华中科技大学学报：自然科学版，2010，38（2）：97-100.

[8] FREY P J. Generation and adaptation of computational surface meshes from discrete anatomical data [J]. International Journal for Numerical Methods in Engineering, 2004, 60 (2): 1049-1074.

[9] HU S M, LI Y F, JU T, et al. Modifying the shape of NURBS surfaces with geometric constraints [J]. Computer Aided Design, 2001, 33 (12): 903-912.

[10] 郭锐锋，刘春辉，丁万夫. 改进的八叉树模型在 3D 刀轨显示系统中的应用 [J]. 小型微型计算机系统，2010，31（2）：373-376.

[11] 任铭，李振平. 基于八叉树与 RBF 神经网络的曲面三角网格生成 [J]. 中原工学院学报，2011，22（1）：32-34.

[12] 李鹏，刘永鸿. 一种运用 OpenGL 快速构建三维模拟地形的方法 [J]. 计算机仿真，2005，22（12）：174-177.

一种新型管口整形机的结构设计

毛智勇　刘　建　胡西南

引　言

管口整形机是一种主要用于管道施工现场对焊接管组端口部位整形的焊接辅助设备,它能够代替人工实现焊接管口组对的定位、自动定心及整形。

在管口组对焊接过程中,若管口组对圆度一致性精度不够,则焊缝增大,将造成烧穿、漏焊和未焊透等焊接缺陷。管道在运输和装卸过程中,管口处经常出现磕碰变形,当两段管道管口组对实施焊接时,由于管口变形,使得焊口很难整圈对齐,加之管道铺设一般是在预先设置的管道沟中进行,施工空间狭窄,管口整形很难实施。

本文设计的管口整形机已获国家发明专利[3],笔者应用管道弹性变形的力学理论,进行了管组端口在整形过程中的受力分析,并通过计算和实验确定了该规格管道设备整形力的大小及液压系统的工作压力,为该类不同规格设备的液压系统工作压力的确定提供了一种计算方法。

1　结构设计及工作原理

管口整形机主要由液压控制阀2（超高压液压系统）、定位盘3、整形盘4和行走滚轮（前后）1四部分组成,管口整形机如图1所示。

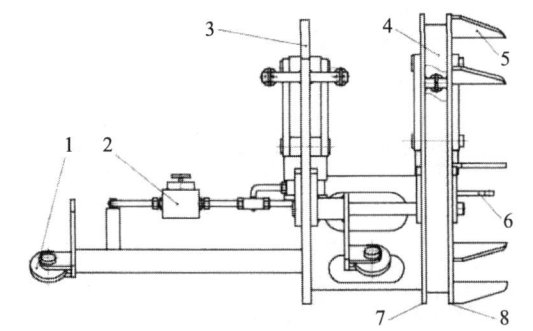

1—行走滚轮（后）　2—液压控制阀　3—定位盘　4—整形盘
5—导板　6—牵引板　7—内侧盘　8—外侧盘

图1　管口整形机

定位盘的作用是使整形机定位并使整形盘与焊接管口组对定心,定位盘如图2所示。定位盘主要由上动盘7和下盘1组成,上动盘7分左/右两部分,分别通过推杆5与高压油缸4连接,上动盘7上还固定有滚轮支架3并通过销轴8与下盘1连接。当高压油缸4通入高压油、活塞杆伸出时,推动推杆5上行并迫使左/右上动盘7绕销轴8旋转,左/右上动盘7张开,使上动盘7和下盘1与管道内壁沿周圈卡紧,整形盘完成中心定位。同时,上动盘7带动滚轮支架3一同绕销轴8旋转,使前滚轮2脱离管壁缩回。复位弹簧6的作用是在高压油缸4回油时,使油缸活塞杆退回、左/右上动盘7回位、松卡,前滚轮2伸出,支撑起整形机,使下盘1脱离管道内壁,为设备移动做好准备。

［基金项目］北京联合大学人才强校计划资助项目。
［作者简介］毛智勇,北京联合大学机电学院;刘建,北京联合大学机电学院;胡西南,北京市电子科技情报研究所。

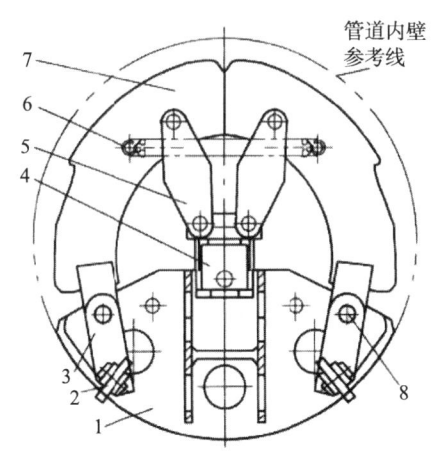

1—下盘　2—前滚轮　3—滚轮支架　4—高压油缸
5—推杆　6—复位弹簧　7—上动盘　8—销轴

图 2　定位盘

整形盘为双盘结构。靠近定位盘一侧的称为内侧盘，另一侧为外侧盘，两盘刚性连接（见图1）。整形盘也分为上动盘和下盘两部分，整形盘如图3所示。整形盘是在定位盘完成与管口组对卡紧定心后，由液压系统自动控制开始工作的。工作时，内侧盘与外侧盘分别卡位在管口组对管口处。其工作原理与定位盘原理相同，通过高压油缸的作用力使上动盘、下盘沿管道内壁产生径向推力，迫使管口组对在同一轴心同一外径尺寸上变形，达到焊口整形的目的。在整形盘的外侧盘沿周圈焊有九块导板2，在整形盘进入待连接管道时起导向作用。

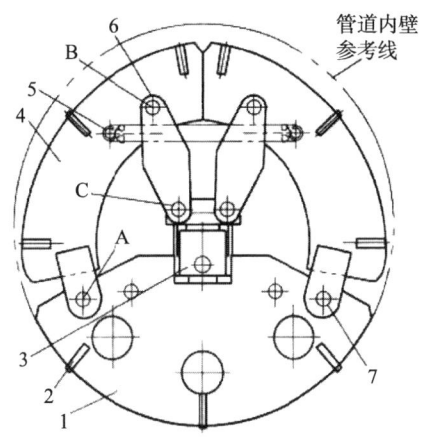

1—下盘　2—导板　3—高压油缸　4—上动盘
5—复位弹簧　6—推杆　7—销轴

图 3　整形盘

2　整形盘受力分析

2.1　管道弹性变形区内径向压力 p_i 的计算

整形机工作时，整形盘首先接触管口的变形部位，纠正变形。之后，随着整形盘进一步扩张，整形力进一步增大，管口整个横截面将依贴整形盘外边缘发生材料的弹性变形。因此，可以利用厚壁圆筒弹性力学理论进行研究。

在材料的弹性变形区内，管口内壁所受径向压力 p_i 与管口内壁各点的径向变形量 u 的关系为：

$$p_i = \frac{uE(K^2-1)}{R_i\left[(1-v)k+(1+v)\dfrac{K^2}{k}\right]} \tag{1}$$

式中：E 为材料的弹性模量；$K = R_0/R_i$，R_0 为管道外半径，R_i 为管道内半径；v 为材料的泊松比；$k = r_i/R_i$，r_i 为所求管道内壁径向压力 p_i 处的半径，按其焊接处管道外半径计算，即 $r_i = R_0$。

受内压厚壁圆筒的弹性极限压力 p_e 是指使筒体内壁开始屈服的压力，当管道内壁径向压力达到 p_e 值时，管道开始发生塑性变形。按密赛斯屈服条件，p_e 为：

$$p_e = \frac{K^2 - 1}{\sqrt{3}K^2} \sigma_s \tag{2}$$

式中：σ_s 为管材的屈服强度。

式（1）为管道内壁均匀受压且在弹性变形区范围内，压强与径向变形量之间的线性关系。根据整形机的工作原理，当管道在弹性变形区范围内直径开始发生微小弹性变化（u 值很小）时，管口即已达到整形目的。因此，可以将此时管道内壁径向压力 p'_i 作为整形机整形力的设计依据。此时管道内壁的径向压力 p'_i 应远远小于弹性极限压力 p_e。

2.2 整形盘受力 F_1 的分析

由整形机工作原理可知，管口组对所需的整形力 F_1（一侧的）均匀分布在整形盘的外圆弧轮廓面上，方向指向圆弧的圆心。由于结构对称，对一侧上动盘进行受力分析，整形盘受力分析如图4所示。

取微圆弧 $ds = rd\theta$，r 为上动盘外圆弧半径；微面积 $dA = lds = lrd\theta$，l 为上动盘宽度；则管道内壁的回弹压力 p'_i 作用在 dA 上的力 $dF1 = p'_i dA$，该力沿 $-X$ 轴方向的分力为：

$$dF_x = dF_1\cos\theta = p'_i dA\cos\theta = p'_i lr\cos\theta d\theta \tag{3}$$

对式（3）积分，可得一侧上动盘在 $-X$ 方向所受的作用力 F_1 为：

$$F_1 = \int_{-\frac{\pi}{4}}^{\frac{\pi}{4}} dF_x = \int_{-\frac{\pi}{4}}^{\frac{\pi}{4}} p'_i lr\cos\theta d\theta = \sqrt{2}p'_i lr = p'_i A_x \tag{4}$$

式中：A_x 为上动盘在 X 方向的投影面积，$A_x = \sqrt{2}lr$。

由于管道内壁的回弹力是均匀分布在上动盘上的，所以可以将上动盘简化成长度为 $\sqrt{2}r$ 的直杆，其中间位置作用有合力 F_1，如图4（b）所示。

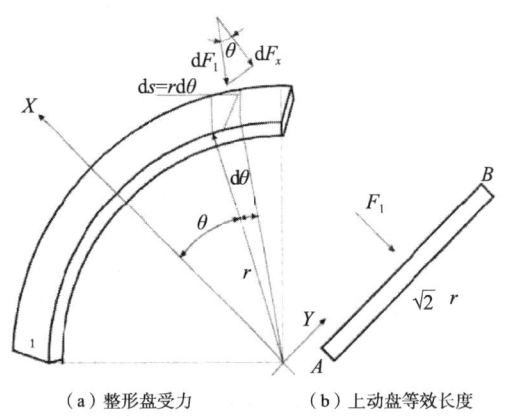

（a）整形盘受力　　（b）上动盘等效长度

图4　整形盘受力分析

2.3 推杆受力 F_2 的计算

如图3所示，上动盘外侧为一段圆弧，接近1/4圆，下端经销轴7与下盘1在点 A 铰接，上端与推杆在点 B 铰接。由于整形机工作时整形力是均匀分布在整形盘上，可以将其简化为集中力 F_1，作用在上动盘简化杆 AB 的中点位置，如图4b所示。图3所示中推杆6的上端与上动盘点 B 铰接、下端与油缸推块在点 C 铰接。推杆6可以简化为二力杆 BC。上动盘受力简图如图5所示。

参考图3所示，当整形盘开始工作时，由简化杆 AB、BC 组成的三角形 ABC 近似于直角三角形（见图5）。由于一般整形量很小，所以三角形 ABC 在设备整形过程中基本维持直角三角形形状。因此，可按直角三角形受力进行分析。高压油缸经推块将推力作用于二力杆 BC，其大小为 F_2，F_2 在杆 AB 垂直方向的分力 $F_3 = F_2\cos\beta$。

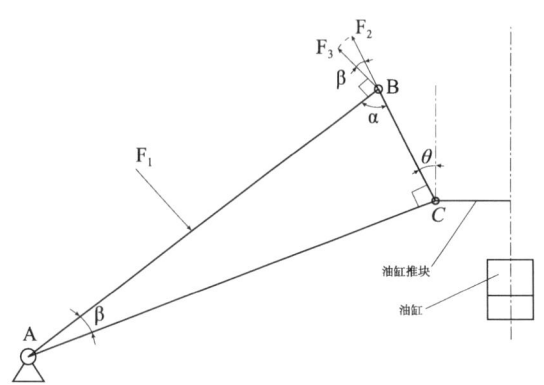

图 5　上动盘受力

由杆 AB 对点 A 的力矩平衡可得：

$$F_1 \frac{L}{2} = F_3 L = F_2 L \cos\beta$$

得：

$$F_2 = \frac{F_1}{2\cos\beta} \tag{5}$$

式中：L 为杆 AB 长度，$L = \sqrt{2}r$。

2.4　高压油缸推力 $F_缸$ 的计算

如前所述，高压油缸是通过油缸推块将力传递给整形盘的。所以，整形力通过油缸推块反作用在油缸活塞杆上，该力为 F_2，其垂直分力 F_{2y} 与 F_2 的夹角为 θ，高压油缸与推杆受力如图 6 所示。

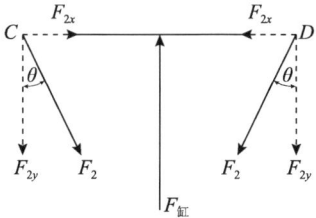

图 6　高压油缸与推杆受力

根据高压油缸输出力平衡可得：

$$F_缸 = 2F_{2y} = 2F_2\cos\theta \tag{6}$$

将式（5）代入式（6）可得：

$$F_缸 = 2F_2\cos\theta = F_1\frac{\cos\theta}{\cos\beta} \tag{7}$$

θ、β 角由结构尺寸而定。液压系统的工作压力和高压油缸活塞直径根据高压油缸推力 $F_缸$ 确定。

3　结　语

该设备结构紧凑，采用超高压液压系统可在有效缩小体积前提下获得较大的整形力，具有体积小、重量轻、输出力大、定位整形一次完成等优点。在管道施工中，可有效减轻工人劳动强度，缩短焊接准备时间，提高焊接质量和工作效率，适合在中等直径管道施工现场使用。在实际应用中，整形开始阶段，整形盘是局部接触管道内壁的变形位置。此时，较小的液压系统压力增加即可获得较大的变形量恢复；随着压力增高，当管口处凸凹变形量为零后，整形盘整体接触工件，随后进入材料的弹性变形区，变形量与系统工作压力成线性关系。实际上，在刚刚进入弹性变形区时，管口组对圆度已达到一致性，满足焊接要求。考虑到施工中可能出现的焊接管道材质不同、管道壁厚不同、凸凹变形程度不同等因素，在选择液压系统压力时其最高工作压力应留有充分余地。

参考文献

[1] 雷天觉. 液压工程手册 [M]. 北京：机械工业出版社，1990.
[2] 徐灏，邱宣怀，蔡春源，等. 机械设计手册 [M]. 北京：机械工业出版社，1992.
[3] 管口整形机：中国，ZL 2009 1 0242225.7 [P]. 2012-03-14.

基于小波分析和概率 Hough 变换的书脊视觉识别

方建军　杜明芳　庞　睿

1　引　言

目前，世界上成功应用图书馆机器人的有德国洪堡大学、美国犹他州大学、日本早稻田大学等，这些图书馆机器人的应用大大节省了图书管理成本，同时使读者借还图书更加便捷。2002年，美国约翰·霍普金斯大学的 Suthakom J. 等人[1]研制了一种完整意义上的图书馆机器人实验装置，它由移动机器人、机械手及其升降装置、摄像头等几部分组成，可以实现图书的自动存取。同年，新加坡国立大学 Yuan K. H. 等人[2]研究了基于 RFID 定位技术的无人化图书馆系统，可利用机器人完成图书存取工作。以往有关图书馆机器人的研究已经很好地解决了机器人进行图书搬运、装卸及辅助图书管理员完成图书管理等工作，但在图书上下架时，机械手如何利用机器视觉进行书脊正确快速识别问题并未得到很好的解决[1~4]。书脊视觉识别的难点在于书脊图像本身比较复杂，每本书的轮廓与图像细节部分不易区分，且在实际应用中，机械手与书脊之间存在相对运动，这也给视觉识别增加了难度。美国的 LeeD. J. 等人[5]对自动化图书馆中书脊的视觉识别问题曾进行过深入的探讨。本文结合实际项目，针对书脊视觉识别的特点，将小波分析、Hough 变换等多种算法相结合，提出一种新的书脊视觉识别方法，该方法的有效性已在实验中得到较好的验证。

2　机器人视觉识别系统框架

机械手移动到确定的位置区间后，便可利用视觉系统通过图像处理算法精确识别出每本书的厚度，进而完成机械手的抓取操作。

通过反复实验，确定出如图1所示的图书视觉识别流程。

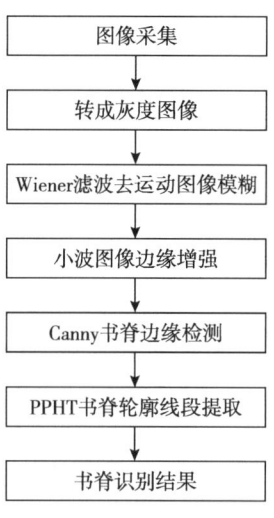

图1　书脊视觉识别流程

本系统选择 MDC – D80 2 自由度云台摄像机用于图像采集，该摄像机具有470线高分辨率，SONY

［基金项目］北京市属高等学校人才强教计划资助项目（PHR201107149）；北京市教委科技计划面上项目（SQKM201311417010）。
［作者简介］方建军（1970—）男，博士，北京联合大学自动化学院教授，研究方向为智能机器人；杜明芳（1976—）女，博士生，北京联合大学自动化学院副教授，研究方向为智能机器人；庞睿（1990—）男，北京理工大学自动化学院教师，研究方向为电气工程与自动化。

HAD CCD，10 倍光学变焦，旋转 120°/s，俯仰 60°/s。

3 运动图像去模糊处理

由于机械手靠近书架时与图书之间存在相对运动，因此会造成获取的图像模糊。本系统中机械手的运动速度并不要求很快且可以通过控制使其保持匀速，因此模糊后图像 $f(x,y)$ 上任意点的值为：

$$g(x,y) = \int_0^{T_r} f[x - x_0(t), y] dt$$

其中，T_r 是运动终止时间，$x_0(t)$ 是起始时刻 x 方向上的像素坐标。

将模糊图像近似认为是由摄像机在 x 方向上做水平匀速直线运动引起的，上式可简化为：

$$g(x,0) = \int_0^{T_r} f[x - x_0(t), y] dt$$

将机械手摄像机拍摄到的书脊图像信号近似看作平稳随机过程。Wiener 滤波器的基本原理是将原始图像 f 和对原始图像的估计 $\hat{f}$ 看作随机变量，按照使 f 和估计值 $\hat{f}$ 之间的均方误差达到最小的准则进行图像复原。运用 Wiener 滤波去书脊图像模糊，结果如图 2 所示。

（a）运动造成的模糊图像　　（b）Wiener 滤波去图像模糊

图 2　Wiener 滤波去书脊图像模糊实验效果图

实验表明，运用 Wiener 滤波时，运动位移和运动角度两个参数需根据机械手的实际运动情况合理设置，才可得到好的滤波结果。

4 小波分析法增强书脊轮廓

4.1 小波图像分解原理

设 $\{V_k\}$ 为多分辨率分析，W_k 为 V_k 关于 V_{k+1} 的补空间。图像为 $f(x,y)$，$f(x,y) \in L^2(R^2)$，$f_N(x,y)$ 是 $f(x,y)$ 在空间 V_N 中的投影。对 $f_k(x,y) \in V_k$ 与 $g_k(x,y) \in W_k$，有[6]：

$$f_{k+1}(x,y) = f_k(x,y) + g_k(x,y)$$

而 $g_k(x,y) \in W_k$ 还可进一步分解为：

$$g_k = g_k^{(1)} + g_k^{(2)} + g_k^{(3)}$$

其中，$g_k^{(i)} \in W_k^{(i)}$，$i = 1, 2, 3$。

设 $\{a_{l,j}\}$，$\{b_{l,j}^i\}$ ($i = 1, 2, 3$) 是由两个一元分解序列生成的二元分解序列：

$$a_{l,j} = a_l^1 a_j^2$$
$$b_{l,j}^1 = a_l^1 b_j^2$$
$$b_{l,j}^2 = b_l^1 a_j^2$$
$$b_{l,j}^3 = b_l^1 b_j^2$$

记：

$$f_k(x,y) = \sum_{n,m} c_{k,n,m} \phi(2^k x - n, 2^k y - m)$$

$$g_k^{(i)}(x,y) = \sum_{n,m} d_{k,n,m}^i \varphi^i(2^k x - n, 2^k y - m), i = 1, 2, 3$$

其中，$C_{k;n,m}$，$d_{k;n,m}^i$ 是小波系数，ϕ 是 V_k 的基底，φ^i 是 W_k 的基底。

则图像分解算法为：

$$C_{k,n,m} = \sum_{l,j} a_{l-2n,j-2m} c_{k+1,l,j}$$

图像分解示意图如图 3 所示，其中，L 表示低频，H 表示高频。图像做小波变换后，可得到不同分辨率的子图像序列。

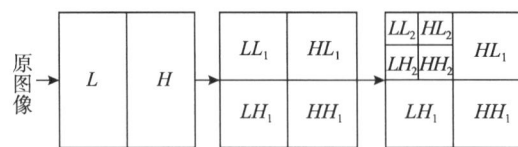

图 3　图像小波两层分解

设 $\{p_{l,j}\}$，$\{q_{l,j}^i\}$（$i=1$，2，3）是由两个一元两尺度序列得到的二元两尺度序列，即：

$$p_{l,j} = p_l^1 p_j^2$$
$$q_{l,j}^1 = p_l^1 q_j^2$$
$$q_{l,j}^2 = q_l^1 p_j^2$$
$$q_{l,j}^3 = q_l^1 q_j^2$$

可得重构算法为：

$$c_{k+1;n,m} = \sum_{i,j} \left(p_{n-2l,m-2j} c_{k,l,j} + \sum_{i=1} q_{n-2l,m-2j}^i d_{k,l,j}^i \right)$$

图像做小波变换后，可得到一系列不同分辨率的子图像，不同子图像对应的频率不同。

4.2　设计与实验

小波变换将一幅图像分解为大小、位置、方向均不相同的分量，图像经二维小波分解后，轮廓主要体现在低频部分，细节主要体现在高频部分[7]。由于机械手抓取图书时需要知道的是每本书的厚度，因此在做图像识别时应更多关注书脊的外部轮廓而非书脊上的文字细节信息。这可以通过对图像做小波增强处理来实现。本系统的做法是：对书脊图像进行两层分解，对分解系数进行处理，即使低频分解系数增强以突出轮廓，高频分解系数衰减以弱化细节，再对处理后的系数进行小波重构，最终得到轮廓增强的图像。为得到理想的图像，小波分解系数的阈值选取是关键，即如何界定高低频分解系数问题。设系数阈值为 T，对大于 T 的系数进行加权处理，设权值为 α；对小于 T 的系数也进行加权处理，设权值为 β。书脊轮廓增强实验效果如图 4 所示。

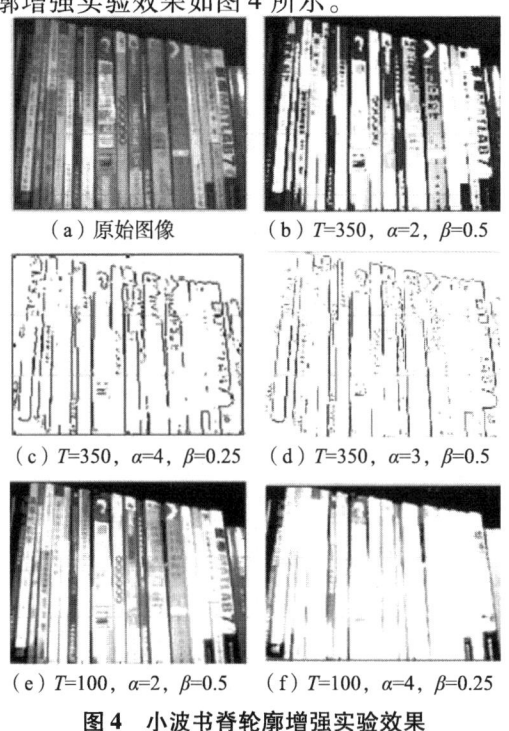

图 4　小波书脊轮廓增强实验效果

比较处理后的图像效果可知，系数阈值的大小对图像的灰度有直接影响，权值的选择对轮廓与细节的保留程度有影响，只有在适中的情况下，才可获得理想的结果。选择图4（e）作为进一步检测和识别的对象。

5 视觉检测与识别实验

5.1 书脊边缘检测实验

机器人图书视觉检测系统对边缘检测的要求是：（1）能检测出预抓取的目标书籍的完整外部轮廓；（2）尽可能少检测出书脊上文字的轮廓；（3）对当前机器视野中所有书脊的轮廓能够很好地区分开。

图5为调整到最佳阈值后对同一幅图像分别用Sobel算子和Canny算子所做的书脊边缘检测效果。

（a）原始图像　　（b）Sobel算子

（c）Canny算子

图5　书脊边缘检测实验效果图

比较后发现，运用Canny算子对书脊边缘进行检测的效果更好，可以更加完整地检测出书脊轮廓，有利于后续的Hough变换提取书脊线段。除边缘检测算法外，检测效果与摄像机拍摄图像时的位置及拍摄到的图像角度、范围都有关。

Canny算子采用双阈值法从候选边缘点中检测和连接出最终的边缘。OpenCV中通过函数 $cvCanny$ 访问Canny算子边缘检测算法，其函数原型为 $cvCanny$（$constCvArr * image$，$CvArr * edges$，$double\ threshold1$，$double\ threshold2$，$int\ aperture\_size$），参数 $threshold1$ 为第一个阈值，参数 $threshold2$ 为第二个阈值。运用Canny算子对书脊进行边缘检测时应恰当设置阈值参数，阈值设置的目的是尽量使图像的细节部分边缘减少，尽可能多地保留每本书的外部轮廓边缘，以利于外部轮廓的直线查找。图6是选用不同阈值时的边缘检测效果，显然图6（b）的阈值设定更符合图像分割需求。

 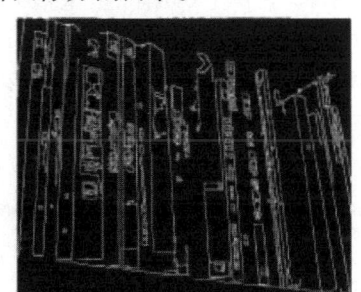

（a）threshold1=100，threshold2=150　　（b）threshold1=30，threshold2=350

图6　Canny算子阈值设定结果比较

通过实验"试凑法"得到合理的Canny算子阈值是一种有效方法，但对于动态的移动机器人视觉系统来讲并不实用。移动机器人视觉系统应能在每次采集图像并进行预处理时自适应地调整边缘检测算法的阈值。常用的自适应阈值选取方法有：双峰法、迭代法、大津法（OTSU法）及其改进算法。在以上实验的基础上，本文采用迭代法选取最佳阈值，解决不同书脊图像分割时的阈值自动切换与识别问题。迭代法的公式是：

$$T_{i+1} = \frac{1}{2}\left[\frac{\sum_{k=0}^{T_i} h_k \cdot k}{\sum_{k=0}^{T_i} h_k} + \frac{\sum_{k=T_i+1}^{n-1} h_k \cdot k}{\sum_{k=T_i+1}^{n-1} h_k}\right]$$

其中，n 为灰度级的个数，h_k 是灰度为 k 的像素点的个数，T_i 是迭代 i 次后的阈值。

迭代法的实现步骤是：

（1）根据实验结果求出图像的最大灰度值和最小灰度值，分别记为 Z_{MAX} 和 Z_{MIN}，令初始阈值 $T_0 = (Z_{MAX} + Z_{MIN})/2$；

（2）根据阈值 T_i（$i = 0, 1, 2, \cdots$）将图像分割为前景和背景，分别求出两者的平均灰度值 Z_0 和 Z_B；

（3）求出新阈值 $T_i + 1 = (Z_0 + Z_B)/2$；

（4）若 $T_i = T_i + 1$，则所得即为阈值；否则转（2），迭代计算直至迭代收敛于某个稳定的阈值时，此阈值即为最终结果。

5.2 书脊线段查找实验

本系统采用累计概率霍夫变换 PPHT（Pro-gressiveProbability HoughTransform）算法实现书脊线段的查找。

采用霍夫变换检测直线，其基本思想是利用点—线的对偶性，点—线在两个坐标系中的对偶关系如图 7 所示。

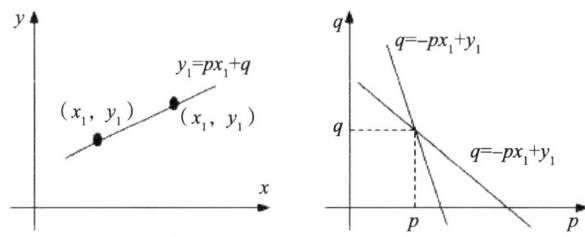

图 7　霍夫变换检测直线原理

Hough 变换采用一种"投票机制"，输入空间（$x-y$ 空间）中的每一个点，对对应的输出空间（$p-q$ 空间）的某些参数组合（由 q、p 组成的数组）进行投票，获得票数最多的参数组合（如某对（p, q）值）胜出。

在 OpenCV 中通过函数 *cvHoughLines*2 访问 PPHT 算法。*cvHoughLines*2 的函数原型是：

CvSeq * *cvHough Lines*2（CvArr * *image*, void * *line_ storage*, int *method*, double *rho*, double *theta*, int *threshold*, double *param*1, double *param*2）[8]。将参数 *method* 设置成 CV_HOUGH_PROBABILISTIC 表示选择 PPHT 算法。实验表明，参数 *threshold*、*param*1、*param*2 的设置对检测结果有直接影响，恰当地配置这些参数才能得到使机械手臂准确定位的目标图像。*Threshold* 是阈值参数，如果相应的累计值大于 *threshold*，则认定为一条直线。*param*1 设置将要返回的线段的最小长度，*param*2 表示在同一条直线上进行碎线段连接的最大间隔值（gap），即当同一条直线上的两条碎线段之间的间隔小于 *param*2 时，将其合二为一。

图 8 为修改各参数值时得到的不同检测结果（为简便，用 f1 表示原始图像，用 f2 表示小波轮廓增强后的图像，*th* 表示 *threshold*，*p*1 表示 *param*1，*p*2 表示 *param*2）。

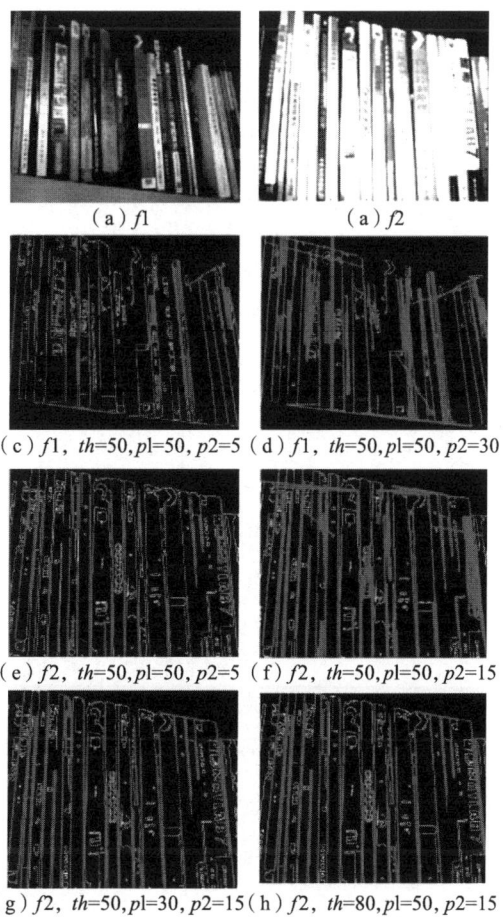

(a) *f1*   (a) *f2*

(c) *f1*, *th*=50, *p1*=50, *p2*=5   (d) *f1*, *th*=50, *p1*=50, *p2*=30

(e) *f2*, *th*=50, *p1*=50, *p2*=5   (f) *f2*, *th*=50, *p1*=50, *p2*=15

(g) *f2*, *th*=50, *p1*=30, *p2*=15 (h) *f2*, *th*=80, *p1*=50, *p2*=15

图 8 PPHT 算法参数选择实验

实验结果表明，在 *threshold* 固定时，当 *param2* 偏大时，Hough 变换连成的直线太多，很多直线是不想要的，这些直线的干扰使书脊边界无法提取；当 *param2* 偏小时，连成的直线又太少，检测不出相对较长的书脊直线，也不好提取书脊边界。*Threshold* 的设置对书脊的判定影响较大。由于该图书馆机器人工作在自主作业模式，因此需根据作业对象自适应地调整 *threshold* 的设定值，以达到环境适应性强的目的。为加快系统计算速度，这里仍采用迭代法自适应地设定阈值参数。

5.3 识别结果优化处理

摄像头拍摄角度、距离以及图书本身的高度不等客观事实会带来所拍摄图像的某些区域检测结果有较大失真，此时应放弃对此部分区域的处理结果，圈定出检测效果相对完善的区域，即能够有效分离出每一本书并确定出每一本书厚度的区域，将此区域定义为有效检测区域，如图 9 中矩形 *R* 所包围的区域。在有效检测区域内再做下一步的计算与处理。

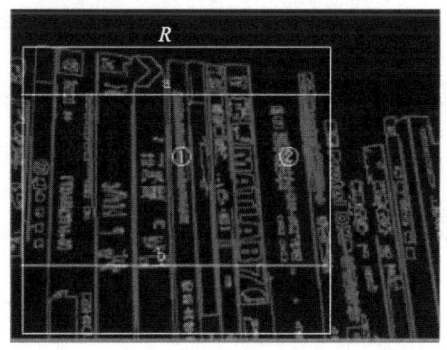

图 9 识别结果优化处理

进一步的计算与处理包括两个方面：(1) 在有效检测区域中划出虚拟的两条线段 a 和 b，使 a、b 之间为最有利于提取出书脊直线特征的区域。(2) 消除多余线段带来的检测误差，如图中书脊上的文字可能被误检测成书之间的分割线段（图中的线段①、②），这会给机械手控制器发出抓取指令时带来强干扰。解决此问题的方法是：对同一幅图像进行多次采集，对每次的处理结果进行比较，采用表决融合准则，降低误判率。为减少计算量，最多采集 3 次。

为验证方法的有效性和普遍适用性，借鉴模糊智能计算思想，对书脊厚度类别做出如下模糊划分：{厚，较厚，中等厚度，较薄，薄，混合}，其中"混合"是指厚、薄书脊随机混放情况。在以上 2 种情况下分别采集 100 幅不同书脊图像，用文中提出的方法进行书脊识别实验，得到书脊位置有效检出率分类统计结果，如表 1 所示。

表 1 书脊位置有效检出率分类统计表

厚度类别	霍夫变换的阈值	有效检出率/(%)	耗时/s
厚（每本书厚度 >1000 页）	50	100	1.0
较厚（500≤每本书厚度≤1000 页）	50	99	1.2
中等厚度（300≤每本书厚度<500 页）	60	95	1.8
较薄（100≤每本书厚度<300 页）	60	90	1.9
薄（每本书厚度<100 页）	80	85	2.0
混合（厚、薄随机混放）	80	70	2.5

从表 1 中可看出，当书脊厚度较大且均匀时，有效检出率较高，且算法耗时较少，基本可满足鲁棒实时识别的需求；当书脊厚度较小且均匀时，有效检出率相对低一些，但仍能满足实时识别的需求；当书脊厚度不一，即随机混合时，检出率最低，耗时也最大，这种情况为最难识别的极端情况。

6 结束语

图书馆机器人机械手的图书识别问题实际上属于摄像机运动、目标静止的移动机器人视觉系统问题，这也是目前运动视觉研究的一个重要方向。常用的处理方法是通过分析运动过程中获得的图像序列，可能是对某一感兴趣区域的各个角度的观察图像序列来建立目标的 3D 结构信息[9]。考虑到此种方法在程序处理时的复杂性，本文采取了一种新型综合处理方法，实验结果已充分表明，该方法可通过编程实现，且计算量较小、识别率较高、实时性较强，已成功应用到我们研制的图书馆机器人装置中。

参考文献

[1] Suthakom J A. robotic library system for an off – site shelving facility [C] //Proc of 2002 IEEE International Conference on Robotics & Automation, 2002：1010 – 1012.

[2] Yuan K H., Hong A. C., Ang M, etal. Unmanned library：An intelligent robotic books retrieval & return system utili – zing RFID tags [C] //Proc of 2002 IEEE International Confer – enceon Systems, Man and Cybernetics, 2002：50 – 55.

[3] Miller C. An investigation of an automated shelf reading and inventory system for the clemson university cooper library [EB/OL]. [2006 – 01 – 07]. http：//www.ces.clemson.edu/ie/academics/isaris.pdf.

[4] Anderson D R. Method without madness：Shelf – reading meth – ods and project management [J]. College and Undergraduate Libraries, 1998, 5 (1)：1069 – 1072.

[5] Lee D J. Matching book – spine images for library shelf – read – ing process automation [C] //Proc of the 4th IEEE Confer – ence on Automation Science and Engineering Key Bridge Marriott, 2008：1004 – 1008.

[6] 程正兴. 小波分析与应用实例 [M]. 西安：西安交通大学出版社, 2006.

[7] 胡昌华, 李国华. 基于 MATLAB7.X 的系统分析与设计：小波分析 [M]. 3 版. 西安：西安电子科技大学出版社, 2008.

[8] BradskiG., KaehlerA. Learning OpenCV：ComputerVision withtheOpenCV Library [M]. 北京：清华大学出版社, 2009.

[9] 张毅, 罗元, 郑太雄. 移动机器人技术及其应用 [M]. 北京：电子工业出版社, 2007.

DP780 熔化极气体保护焊工艺参数优化

卢振洋　汤　超　熊　威　黄鹏飞

序　言

能源危机和环境问题的加剧，使得汽车用钢日趋高强化，以期降低车重，减少油耗[1]。先进高强钢以其高强度和良好的延展性成为车身的理想材料[2]，其中双相钢是目前使用最普遍的先进高强钢钢种之一。

先进高强钢具有较高的碳当量，焊接过程中在焊接热循环的作用下母材微观组织的变化极大地改变了接头的力学性能，同时不同钢材供应商生产的钢材的化学成分和冶金工艺大不相同，这些给先进高强钢的焊接带来了许多挑战。先进高强钢电弧焊搭接接头在汽车制造中具有广泛应用，其工艺参数的优化[3-5]及接头性能的研究对先进高强钢弧焊技术的应用具有重要的工程应用价值，也是国际上研究的前沿课题，对此国内还没有深入系统的研究。文中以2.0mm板厚DP780钢为研究对象，通过正交试验研究了熔化极气体保护焊的主要工艺参数对接头强度的影响规律，为先进高强钢焊接参数的优选提供了理论和试验依据。

1　试验方法

本研究采用的DP780钢材由宝山钢铁公司提供。DP780的化学成分和力学性能如表1和表2所示。

表1　DP780化学成分（质量分数,%）

C	Si	Mn	P	S	Al	Fe
0.094	0.14	1.99	0.0056	0.0023	0.036	余量

表2　DP780力学性能

屈服强度 $R_{eL0.2}$/MPa	抗拉强度 R_m/MPa	断后伸长率 A_{80mm}/(%)
500~650	≥780	≥10

焊接试验两板重叠部分为25mm，焊接方法为熔化极气体保护焊，保护气体为Ar（80%）+ CO_2（20%），填充金属为ER70S-6。文中选取了对焊接热输入有直接影响的参数：送丝速度、焊接速度、电弧电压，以及对焊缝成形有直接关系的参数，包括焊枪倾角和焊丝伸出长度，其余参数恒定不变，每个参数选取5个水平以便在较大范围内优化工艺参数。通过预备性试验确定因素水平表，如表3所示。

表3　试验因素及水平

	送丝速度 v_s/(m/min)	焊接速度 v/(m/min)	电弧电压 U/V	焊丝伸出长度 D/mm	倾角 E/(°)
1	3.0	1.0	17.0	10	65
2	3.6	1.1	17.5	12	75
3	4.2	1.2	18.0	14	90
4	4.8	1.3	18.5	16	105
5	5.4	1.4	19.0	18	115

[基金项目] 国家科技重大专项资助项目（2009ZX04014-072）；国家自然科学基金资助项目（51075011）。
[作者简介] 卢振洋，男，1957年出生，博士，北京工业大学焊接研究所教授。主要从事材料加工工程领域的研究工作。发表论文50多篇。Email：xwlxkf@163.com.

2 试验结果及分析

2.1 直观分析

表4给出了根据正交试验设计得到的不同因素及水平搭配下对应的接头抗拉强度的结果。其中,k_n($n=1\sim5$)分别为因素A、B、C、D、E的第n水平所在的试验中对应的抗拉强度的均值。极差R代表k_n($n=1\sim5$)中的最大值与最小值之差。

比较表4中各列的k值,送丝速度在3.0~5.4m/min变化时,随着送丝速度的提高,接头的抗拉强度增大;焊接速度在1.0~1.4m/min变化时,随着焊接速度的提高,接头抗拉强度减小;焊丝伸出长度和焊接倾角分别在k_2和k_3水平下接头抗拉强度达最大值。

表4 正交试验表(部分)

试验编号	因素A	因素B	A×B	A×B	A×B	A×B	因素C	因素D	因素E	误差列	误差列	抗拉强度R_m/MPa
1	1	1	1	1	1	1	1	1	1	1	1	576.4
2	1	2	2	2	2	2	2	2	2	2	2	568.9
3	1	3	3	3	3	3	3	3	3	3	3	493.9
4	1	4	4	4	4	4	4	4	4	4	4	519.4
5	1	5	5	5	5	5	5	5	5	5	5	518.6
…	…	…	…	…	…	…	…	…	…	…	…	…
45	4	5	3	4	3	5	1	4	1	2	2	594.3
46	5	1	5	2	5	2	3	4	4	3	1	600.5
47	5	2	1	3	1	3	4	5	5	4	2	612.6
48	5	3	2	4	2	4	5	1	1	5	3	620.9
49	5	4	3	5	3	5	1	2	2	1	4	616.0
50	5	5	4	1	4	1	2	3	3	2	5	602.6
k_1	537.0	599.57	576.04	580.54	576.42	591.13	585.96	577.03	579.33			
k_2	565.7	584.66	585.95	572.56	582.41	572.18	572.67	586.52	574.17			
k_3	576.0	572.13	570.19	572.28	574.49	570.49	573.54	567.82	581.31			
k_4	579.1	571.17	582.80	581.37	570.10	576.08	569.28	580.41	577.19			
k_5	606.9	561.81	568.36	576.59	579.60	567.46	581.89	571.56	579.34			
R	69.9	37.76	17.59	9.09	12.31	23.67	16.68	18.70	10.98			

注:A×B代表送丝速度和焊接速度交互作用。

极差R的大小代表因素对指标影响的主次。由表4中的数据结果可以看出,该试验中对接头抗拉强度影响的主次顺序依次为送丝速度、焊接速度、送丝速度和焊接速度的交互作用、焊丝伸出长度、电弧电压、焊接倾角。

接下来是确定优化方案。由表4的计算结果可知,当送丝速度为5.4m/min,焊接速度为1.0m/min,电弧电压为17V,焊丝伸出长度为1.2mm,焊接倾角为90°时,接头的抗拉强度均为最大值,故为优化方案。由于该方案正交试验中并未出现,故通过补充试验得到该方案在相同工艺下的抗拉强度为640MPa,高于正交试验中数据,证明该优化方案合理。

2.2 方差分析

表5给出了方差分析结果。其中,F'为各因素的平均离差的平方和与误差的平均离差平方和的比值,反映了各因素对结果影响程度的大小。显著性水平取0.1。F代表各效应项与误差项均方差的比值。从结果来看,送丝速度和焊接速度的F'均大于临界值,因此对抗拉强度影响显著,而其他因素F'小于临界值,因此影响不显著。

表5 抗拉强度方差分析结果

因素	偏差平方和 ε	自由度 σ	比值 F'	临界值 F	显著性
A	29960.05	4	14.192	2.81	显著
B	6339.31	4	3.003	2.81	显著
A×B	9031.33	16	1.29	2.39	不显著
C	1939.61	4	0.919	2.81	不显著
D	2155.74	4	1.021	2.81	不显著
E	713.74	4	0.338	2.81	不显著
误差	4223.23	8			

2.3 回归分析

试验建立的多元线性回归模型为
$$y = \beta_0 + \beta_1 x_1 + \beta_2 x_2 + \beta_3 x_3 + \beta_4 x_4 + \beta_5 x_5 + \varepsilon,$$
$$\varepsilon \sim N(0, \sigma^2)$$

式中：$\beta_0 \sim \beta_5$ 都是未知的参数；$x_1 \sim x_5$ 分别代表因素A、B、C、D、E的独立试验。利用最小二乘法估计这些参数，在最小二乘法估计运算中运用矩阵的运算方法解正规方程组，引入矩阵如下。

$$X = \begin{bmatrix} 1 & x_{11} & x_{12} & x_{13} & x_{14} & x_{15} \\ 1 & x_{21} & x_{22} & x_{23} & x_{24} & x_{25} \\ \cdots & \cdots & \cdots & \cdots & \cdots & \cdots \\ 1 & x_{n1} & x_{n2} & x_{n3} & x_{n4} & x_{n5} \end{bmatrix}$$

$$Y = \begin{bmatrix} y_1 \\ y_2 \\ \cdots \\ y_n \end{bmatrix}, \beta = \begin{bmatrix} \beta_1 \\ \beta_2 \\ \cdots \\ \beta_n \end{bmatrix}$$

由此，正规方程组可表示为 $X^T X \hat{\beta} = X^T Y$。$\hat{\beta}$ 为 β 的估计。假定 X 为列满秩的，即 $R(X) = 6$，则 $R(X^T X) = R(X) = 6$，故 $(X^T X)^{-1}$ 存在，解正规方程组得 $\hat{\beta} = (X^T X)^{-1} X^T Y$，则经验回归方程为 $y = \beta_0 + \beta_1 x_1 + \beta_2 x_2 + \beta_3 x_3 + \beta_4 x_4 + \beta_5 x_5$。利用Minitab软件对文中进行多元回归计算得到回归方程为 $y = 578 + 28.4x_1 - 67.0x_2 - 2.31x_3 - 0.85x_4 + 0.150x_5$，这里用 P 值表征方程与因子的置信水平，P 值越小，效果越显著。方程的 P 值为0，该回归方程高度显著。5个因素的 P 值分别为 $P_1 = 0$，$P_2 = 0.003$，$P_3 = 0.584$，$P_4 = 0.419$，$P_5 = 0.354$。在置信水平为0.05下，仅因素A、B的回归系数是高度显著的。把因素C、D、E去掉后，再进行两元一次回归分析计算，其回归方程为 $y = 538 + 28.4x_1 - 67.0x_2$，回归方程的 P 值为0，所以回归方程为高度显著。因素A、B的回归系数的 P 值分别为0和0.002。所以因素A、B的回归均为高度显著。R^2 代表方程与试验数据的拟合程度。方差分析中输出结果中 $R^2 = 62.6\%$，R^2（调整）$= 61.0\%$，R^2（预测）$= 57.29\%$，Durbin – Watson统计量为2.18542。R^2 值表明这些预测变量可以解释抗拉强度中62.6%的方差。调整后的 R^2 为61.0%，这说明了模型中预测变量的个数。这两个值都表明模型与数据拟合较好。预测的 R^2 为57.29%，由于预测的 R^2 值与 R^2 及调整的 R^2 值都很接近，因此模型并没有过度拟合而且具有足够的预测能力。Durbin – Watson统计量为2.18542，表明残差不存在相关性。

根据回归方程可知，在较大的送丝速度和较小的焊接速度下能得到最大的抗拉强度。图1和图2给出了在不同送丝速度和焊接速度下的曲面和等值线。

从图1和图2可以看出，送丝速度和焊接速度是该试验中影响接头抗拉强度最大的因素。无论是用直观分析法、方差分析法，还是多元线性回归法，都能够充分说明这一点。

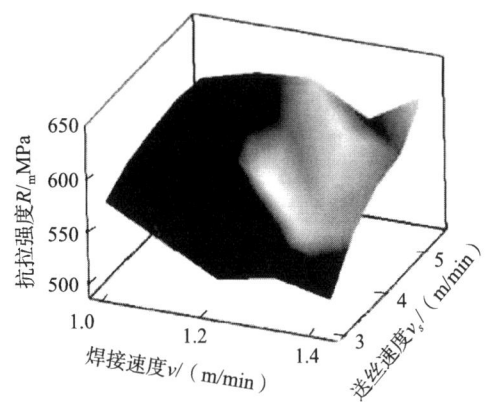

图1 在各种送丝速度和焊接速度下抗拉强度的曲面

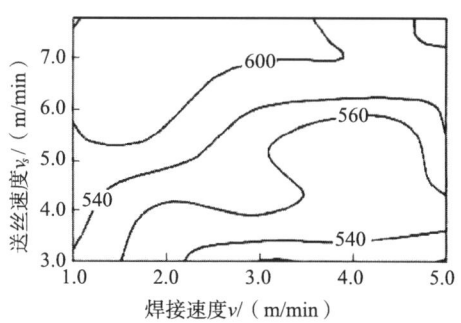

图2 在各种送丝速度和焊接速度下抗拉强度的等值线（MPa）

3 结 论

（1）通过正交试验的直观分析得到了控制接头抗拉强度的优化方案，即送丝速度为5.4m/min，电弧速度为1.0m/min，电弧电压为17V，焊丝伸出长度为1.2mm，焊接倾角为90°。

（2）方差分析结果表明，送丝速度、焊接速度对接头抗拉强度影响为高度显著，送丝速度与焊接速度的交互作用、电弧电压、焊丝伸出长度、焊接倾角的影响不显著。

（3）利用多元线性回归分析得到了控制接头抗拉强度的近似数学模型，由此可以进行接头抗拉强度的预测，为工程实际中焊接结构设计提供参考。

（4）较大的送丝速度和较小的焊接速度下能得到更大的抗拉强度。大的送丝速度和小的焊接速度会熔敷更多的填充金属，同时有更大的熔深，这些将导致更大的抗拉强度。

参考文献

[1] 康永林. 汽车轻量化先进高强钢与节能减排[J]. 钢铁, 2008, 43 (6): 1-8.

[2] Koganti R, Angotti S, Joaquin A, et al. Static tensile strength of gas metal arc welded (GMAW) joints of uncoated dual phase 600 (DP600) steels [C] // 2008 American Society of Mechanical Engineers International Mechanical Engineering Congress and Exposition, Evanstion, Illinois, 2008: 1-9.

[3] 张本生, 周红, 于永利. 电弧喷涂粉末管状丝材的工艺参数优化[J]. 焊接学报, 2000, 21 (4): 58-60.

[4] 徐文立, 刘雪松, 方洪渊, 等. 薄板高强铝合金LY12CZ焊接工艺参数的优化[J]. 焊接学报, 2004, 25 (2): 39-42. Xu Wenli, Liu Xuesong, Fang Hongyuan, et al. Parameters optimization for welding aluminum alloy 2024 sheet with high strength [J]. Transactions of the China Welding Institution, 2004, 25 (2): 39-42.

[5] 刘双宇, 张宏, 刘凤德, 等. CO_2激光-MAG电弧复合焊接工艺参数优化[J]. 焊接学报, 2011, 32 (10): 61-64.

聚合物膜材料在油水分离过程中的应用

叶 晓 谢 飞 罗孝曦 全升武 刘 巍 叶志伟

在物料分离过程中，油水混合物是常见的分离对象。含油水体的来源很广，从工业生产诸如石油开采、石油化工、机械制造、毛纺、皮革等领域，到食品、屠宰、医药以至家居生活无所不有，无论从环境治理还是各类油的回收、水的再利用等各方面都要求进行良好的油水分离。按油在水中的形态通常把油分为四类：油的粒径大于 $150\mu m$，称之为浮油；油的粒径在 $20\sim150\mu m$ 之间，称之为分散油；油的粒径小于 $20\mu m$，称之为乳化油；油的粒径小于几微米时则为溶解油。油和水都是很特殊的物质，水有强极性；油本是单纯的碳氢化合物，是非极性疏水的物质，但由于种种原因它们常和表面活性剂等化学物质混合，成为难以处理的、被乳化的甚至溶解的油。要去除水体中的乳化油和溶解油，需经过破乳—分离过程。其主要技术方法有聚结（粗粒化）、重力分离、离心分离、气浮、过滤、膜分离等。传统的分离方法对乳化油和溶解油分离较为困难。而利用膜分离技术，可根据膜本身结构的特点，选择适宜的膜过程和膜组件，就能一次性去除水体中 $100\mu m$ 以下的油珠，对分散油和乳化油乃至溶解油的适应性也很强，去除率大于 90%；分离过程在常温下进行，过程无相变，设备能耗低，膜组件结构简单，流程缩短，分离过程可高度自动化；适用领域广泛，油的回收相对容易，且分离过程中只需添加极少或不需添加化学试剂，无二次污染，易于保护环境[1,2]。

1 用于油水分离的聚合物膜材料

常见的油水分离膜过程有超滤和微滤过程，这两种膜分离过程均能截留乳化及溶解态油。乳化油基于油滴大小而截留，溶解油则基于它与膜表面的分子作用而截留。用于油水分离的膜材料可分为无机陶瓷膜和有机聚合物膜两大类，无机膜具有耐高温、强酸、强碱、有机溶剂和耐微生物侵蚀、机械强度高、孔径分布窄等优点，但也存在着制膜工艺复杂（锻烧）、膜的重现性差、制备小孔径膜困难、质脆柔韧性差、成本高、制成的组件装配困难等缺点；有机膜制备工艺简单，膜材料品种多，容易改性，柔韧性好，价格便宜，可制成各种形式的膜组件，但有机膜具有孔径分布宽、机械强度低、渗透率低、容易水解、耐温差、pH 值适用范围窄等缺点。然而，随着聚合物科学的不断发展，通过聚合物材料的改性、共混或复合等方法，可以使性能不同的聚合物材料，或是聚合物与无机材料复合制备成可以满足油水分离需要的膜材料。

1.1 单一聚合物分离膜的应用

目前已经报道的用于油水分离的有机膜材料有：聚砜（PS）、聚醚砜（PES）、聚丙烯腈（PAN）、聚偏氟乙烯（PVDF）、纤维素类、聚四氟乙烯（PTFE）和聚丙烯（PP）等[3]。对于不同材质的膜，由于聚合物材料自身结构和所带基团的不同，因为膜材料具有亲水或疏水性，其油水分离效果不同。一般情况下，膜的亲水性越好，油的截留率及水的渗透通量越高。

李发永等[4]用有效膜面积为 $0.4m^2$ 外压管式聚砜超滤膜装置现场处理石油类含量为 $20\sim100ppm$ 的采油污水，在适宜的操作条件下，膜通量为 $80\sim490L/m^2\cdot h$，石油类物质的截留率为 97.7%，所处理过的污水达到了低渗透油田注水标准。李红剑等[5]以 α 纤维素为原料，聚乙二醇（PEG400）为添加剂，采用浸入相转化法制备用于油水分离的中空纤维非对称超滤膜，油水乳液的截留率可达到 99% 以上，渗

[基金项目] 北京联合大学本科生科学研究计划项目资助。

[作者简介] 叶晓（1965—），北京（汉），博士，北京联合大学教授。主要从事高分子材料改性及膜分离应用技术研究。E-mail: shtyexiao@buu.edu.cn；谢飞（1972—），北京（汉），硕士，北京联合大学生物化学工程学院讲师。主要从事高分子材料和生物材料方面研究。E-mail: xf0124@126.com。

透液含油量小于10mg/L达到国家环境保护排放要求。同时，在20℃下，纤维素膜与PS、PVDF、PES和陶瓷（ZrO_2）膜的油水通量衰减率进行了对比，纤维素中空纤维超滤膜的油水通量衰减仅为9.5%，远低于其他膜材料，但膜的通量较小，尚需改进。魏风玉等[6]用0.45μm亲水性混合纤维素酯微孔膜对O/W型乳液进行了破乳研究，在0.3MPa、水相体积与油相体积之比为4:1时，破乳率可达67%。Kong等[7]利用PVDF平板膜对去除水包油体系中的油进行了研究，油的去除率为77%。Gryta等[8]将PVDF超滤膜和液膜集成来处理含油废水，超滤膜处理后含油量低于5mg/L，进一步经液膜处理后TOC去除率达到99.5%，TDS去除率达到99.9%。新加坡的Xu等[9]利用不同分子量聚乙烯吡咯烷酮（PVP）作为聚醚酰亚胺（PEI）膜的制孔剂，所得超滤膜用于分离油水乳化体系，其中油的节流率高于99%。

无论亲水膜还是疏水膜材料，在分离油水体系中，单一聚合物膜还不能满足分离性能的要求。因而，在此基础上通过聚合物与聚合物复合，聚合物与无机物的复合，聚合物间的共混以及聚合物的填充改性成为研究的重点内容。

1.2 复合聚合物分离膜的应用

复合分离膜主要是在聚合物支撑层或无机陶瓷膜上通过化学接枝或物理涂复的方法，将具有油水分离性能的材料附着在其表面，一方面提高油水分离性能，另一方面保持膜材料的力学强度及制作要求。

王枢等[10]采用界面聚合法对具有陶瓷基膜的聚偏氟乙烯（PVDF）超滤膜进行表面改性，制备出具有聚酰胺/聚乙烯醇（PVA）复合功能表层的抗污染有机/无机复合膜。所制备的复合膜对平均油滴粒径为2.365μm的油水乳化液，在0.4MPa操作压力下进行分离，结果表明复合膜的油截留率随界面聚合反应物浓度增加而增大，滤液油含量小于1.6mg/L，油截留率大于98.5%，优于未经复合的PVDF超滤膜。Faihish等[11]在ZrO_2陶瓷膜上担载CSP及PVP所制备的超滤膜用于处理O/W乳化液，膜污染、通量和截留率均有改善。关福伟[12]在机械强度好、孔隙率高、阻力小的涤纶滤布上涂覆强亲水性的聚乙烯醇材料，制备了滤布-PVA亲水膜。该膜在操作压力为0.05MPa下处理质量浓度为1000mg/L的O/W型乳化液，可获得140L/$m^2 \cdot h$的膜通量，除油率达到82.3%。

1.3 共混或填充聚合物分离膜的应用

在制膜工艺上，共混和填充是比较容易实现的方法。因而在此方面得到的成果也较多。涂郑禹等[13]采用非化学计量掺杂Ce纳米SiO_2聚砜复合膜对油田回注水进行处理。纳米SiO_2复合粒子添加量为PS质量的10%时，复合膜的机械强度最大，接触角为最小值41.7°，渗透通量最大。在操作压力为0.1MPa，处理含油量为98mg/L的油田回注水，经过6h的过滤，得到的滤液达到国家水质排放标准（含油量1.01 mg/L，截留率为98.97%）。王静荣等[14]采用氯甲基化聚砜和聚砜共混中空纤维膜（CMPS/PS）处理乳化油水，经过8h实验，该膜的透水通量衰减较其他PAN、PS膜都小，抗油污染性能最佳，透液中的含油量60mg/L，符合生产回用标准。Ochoa等[15]对PVDF/PMMA共混膜进行了系统的研究，当PMMA为50%时，共混膜的接触角由84°下降到64°，亲水性增加，处理油水混合物的COD值由935ppm下降到89ppm。姜云鹏等[16]在PVA超滤膜中添加纳米SiO_2粉末制备SiO_2-PVA复合超滤膜，纳米SiO_2的适宜加入量为2%，该复合膜在对油田废水的过滤实验中，其水通量及截留率随时间的变化基本保持恒定，说明纳米SiO_2-PVA复合膜具有较强的抗污染能力及稳定性。此外还有聚砜/聚醚砜（PSF/PES）、聚酰亚胺/聚醚酰亚胺（PI/PEI）等聚合物共混膜。

2 膜材料的改性研究

对于油水分离膜材料，按其分离机理，膜的亲水或疏水性对分离效果有显著的影响。此外，有效缓解膜在油水分离过程中的膜污染情况的途径之一是提高膜表面的亲水性[17,18]。因此针对膜材料的改性研究主要集中在疏水膜表面亲水化改性这一研究热点上。

2.1 亲水改性的研究

膜材料的亲水性改性分为永久性改性和非永久性改性。一般非永久性改性采用含表面活性剂的溶液处理膜，使膜表面吸附一层表面活性剂[19]，以提高膜的亲水性，但在分离过程中，表面活性剂极易损失，不能长期保持膜的亲水性。永久性改性是通过膜材料共混复合改性，有机物接枝改性，等离子聚合，辐射聚合，有机物嵌段共聚改性和界面聚合等方法，改变膜表面聚合物分子的化学结构，形成亲水性功能层。此方法可确保膜在分离过程中长期保持膜的亲水性。

丁健等[20]用聚醚砜和聚丙烯腈通过共混方法制备油水分离膜，其制得的共混膜性能良好，亲水性大大改善，水的接触角由改性前得107°减少到37°，从而有效降低了膜的污染。聚砜膜亲水性差，但其压密性和抗氧化性良好，用1，2－二氯乙烷及氯磺酸磺化后，在保持了其原有物化性质的同时极大地改善了透水性。另外，膜材料亲水性的强弱还可通过适当选择添加亲水基团来控制。张裕卿[21]按10:5的质量比在PS中添加Al_2O_3微粒制成的PS－Al_2O_3膜，不仅改善了膜的亲水性，还提高了膜的机械强度，用此膜处理华北油田油浓度64.0 mg/L，油滴粒度25.4 μm的原水，可获得出水浓度0.47mg/L、油滴粒度0.084 μm的良好效果。王枢等[22]以PES为支撑层的聚哌嗪酰胺/聚乙烯醇复合膜，其截留率大于99.1%，水通量保持在280 L/$m^2 \cdot h$，滤液油含量小于0.1 mg/L，复合膜过滤性能在水通量和油相截留率两方面都大大优于PES超滤膜，这表明复合膜一方面提高了膜表面亲水性，另一方面有效减小了膜孔径，从而同时增大了水通量和截留率。Hamza等[23]对聚醚砜超滤膜表面改性后用于处理乳化油废水比未改性的超滤膜取得了更好的效果。

2.2 疏水改性的研究

通常过滤技术是使大量流体通过过滤介质，将相对量少的物质截留在介质面上。对于体系中油的含量相对较少的油水体系，疏水膜易于使油滴聚结粗化，从而有利于油水分离。

首先提出将超疏水表面应用在油水分离领域的是中科院江雷研究组[24]，2004年报道了一种由疏水材料制备的具有纳米结构的兼有超疏水与超亲油性质的网膜，并提出可应用于油水分离的设想。他们用含有低表面能的聚四氟乙烯（PTFE）均相乳液，通过比较简单的喷枪雾化喷涂—烘干的方法，在孔径115 μm的不锈钢网上，制得超疏水—超亲油网膜，该网膜对水的接触角

约156.2°±2.8°。Wang等[25]将经过预处理的不锈钢网浸泡在含有1H，1H，2H，2H－六氟化三乙氧基硅烷（PFAS）的涂覆溶液中，随后烘干后得到具有超疏水和超亲油的网膜，并设计成油水分离装置对油和水进行有效地分离，对柴油和水的分离结果为最后混合液中水含量为95.1wt%，滤液（油）中水含量为0.028wt%。Neena等[26]考察了一系列聚丙烯疏水膜（0.02～0.2 μm）对油水乳液的破乳情况，研究表明，油通过膜的速率在0.14～5.79 cm/s范围内，透过液中水浓度小于49 ppm。且油滴可在透过膜后生长100倍以上，破乳效果甚佳。

Mark Hiavacek[27]利用膜作为聚结介质进行了破乳研究。实验选用了亲油的0.2 μm聚丙烯膜来处理制铝工业中产生的O/W乳液，可使平均粒度为（1.7±0.5）μm的乳滴全部透过膜，且生长到100 μm左右，能够自动聚结，达到分离效果。

2.3 其他改性研究

在实际工业应用中，分离膜除要满足分离要求外，还要考虑其力学性能、成型性能、以及价格等因素。因此在研究提高分离膜油水分离性能的同时，利用物理或化学方法对膜材料其他性能进行必要的改善也是研究者的目标之一。只是这点无异于膜材料在其他领域上的研究工作，在此不再赘述。

3 结 论

在油水分离领域，大多数膜材料都得到了研究者的关注，其中以膜的亲水性改性研究最为活跃。

用于油水分离的膜材料主要为价格较高的工程材料，少量通用型材料还存在使用上的缺陷。寻找性价比更为合适的膜材料，利用通用聚合物材料改性，以满足油水分离的要求应成为研究的目标。

通过共混或复合改性的方法可预期得到通量大、截留效果好的油水分离材料。

参考文献

[1] 刘国强，王铎，王立国，等. 膜技术处理含油废水的研究 [J]. 膜科学与技术, 2007, 27 (1): 68－72.

[2] Lin S H, Lan W J. Waste oil/water emulsion treatment by membrane processes [J]. Journal of Hazardous Materials, 1998, 59: 189－199.

[3] 左文蕊,张国亮,孟琴,等. 用集成膜过程对含油废水进行资源化回收利用处理 [J]. 膜科学与技术, 2007, 27 (6): 63-67.

[4] 李发永,李阳初,孙亮,等. 含油污水的超滤法处理 [J]. 水处理技, 1995, 21 (3): 145-148.

[5] 李红剑,曹义鸣,杨林松,等. 抗油污染 α 纤维素中空纤维超滤膜油 – 水分离性能的研究 [J]. 高等学校化学学报, 2005, 26 (10): 1890-1895.

[6] 魏风玉,肖翔. 亲水性混合纤维素酯微孔膜对 o/w 乳液的破乳 [J]. 应用化学, 2006, 23 (8): 881-885.

[7] Kong J, Li K. Oil Removal from Oil – in – water Emulsions Using PVDF membranes [J]. Sep. Purif. Technol., 1999, 16: 83-93.

[8] Gryty M, Karakulski K, Morawski A W. Purification of oily wastewater by hybrid UF/MD [J]. Wat Res, 2001, 35 (15): 3665-3669.

[9] Xu Z L, Chung T S, Huang Y. Effect of polyvinylpyrrolidone molecular weights on morphology, oil/water separation, mechanical and thermal properties of polyetherimide/ polyvinylpyrrolidone hollow fiber membranes [J]. J Appl Polym Sci., 1999, 74: 2220-2233.

[10] 王枢,褚良银,陈文梅,等. 有机/无机复合型抗污染油水分离膜研究 [J]. 高校化学工程学报, 2005, 19 (1): 11-16.

[11] Faibish R S, Cohen Y. Fouling – resistant Ceramic – supported Polymer Membranes for Ultrafiltration of Oil – in – water Microemulsions [J]. J. Membr. Sci., 2001, 185: 129-143.

[12] 关福伟. 滤布 – PVA 亲水膜的制备及处理油水乳化液的研究. 中国利技信息 [J].

[13] 2009, 16: 116-117.

[14] 涂郑禹,李栋,柳琦,等. 用于油水分离的非化学计量掺杂 Ce 纳米 SiO_2 聚砜复合膜的研究 [J]. 化学工程师, 2009, 4: 37-40.

[15] 王静荣,吴光夏,王正军,等. 超滤法处理乳化油废水的研究 [J]. 环境科学, 1997, 18 (4): 53-55.

[16] Ochoa N A, Masuelli M, Marchese J. Effect of hydrophilicity on fouling of an emulsified oil wastewater with PVDF/PMMA membranes [J]. J. Membr. Sci., 2003, 226: 203-211.

[17] 姜云鹏,王榕树. 纳米 SiO_2 – 聚乙烯醇复合超滤膜的制备及应用 [J]. 工业水处理, 2002, 22 (5): 12-14.

[18] Faibish R S, Cohen Y. Fouling and rejection behavior of ceramic and polymer – modified ceramic membranes for ultrafiltration of oil – in – water emulsions and microemulsions [J]. Colloids and Surfaces A: Physicochemical and Engineering Aspects, 2001, 191: 27-40.

[19] Tansel B, Regula J, Shalewitz R. Treatment of fuel oil and crude oil contaminated waters by ultrafiltration membranes [J]. Desalination, 1995, 102: 301-311.

[20] Anderson G K, Saw C B, Le M S. Oil/Water separation with surface modified membranes [J]. Environmental Technology, 1987, 8 (1): 121-132.

[22] 丁健,谭欣,张裕卿,等. 用于油水分离的具有 IPN 结构的耐污染复合超滤膜的研究 [J]. 天津理工学院学报. 1999, 15 (4): 85-88.

[23] 张裕卿. 聚砜 – Al_2O_3 复合膜处理油田含油污水 [J]. 工业水处理, 2000, 20 (2): 24-34.

[24] 王枢,褚良银,陈文梅,等. 界面聚合表面改性法制备高效抗污染油水分离复合膜 [J]. 化工学报. 2004, 55 (4): 664-667.

[25] Hamza A, Pham V A, Matsuura T, et al. Development of membranes with low surface energy to reduce the fouling in ultrafiltration applications [J]. J Membr. Sci, 1997, 131: 217-227.

[27] Feng L, Zhang Z Y, Mai Z H, et al. A Super – Hydrophobic and Super – Oleophilic Coating Mesh Film for the Separation of Oil and Water [J]. Angew. Them. Int. Ed., 2004, 43: 2012-2014.

[28] Wang Q J, Cui Z, Xiao Y, et al. Stable highly hydrophobic and oleophilic meshes for oil – water separation [J]. Appl led Surface Science, 2007, 253: 9054-9060.

[30] Tirrnizi N P. Demulsification of Water/Oil/ Solid Emulsions by Hollow – Fiber Membranes [J]. AIChE Journal, 1996, 42 (5): 1263-1276.

[32] Hiavacek M. Break – up of oil – in – water emulsions induced by permeation through a microfiltration membrane [J]. J Membr. Sci, 1995, 102: 1-7.

Intelligent Control of Welding Gun Pose for Pipeline Welding Robot Based on Improved Radial Basis Function Network and Expert System Regular Paper

Tian Jingwen   Gao Meijuan   He Yonggang

1 Introduction

At present, welding robots are used in shipping, chemistry, the automobile industry and the mechanism producing industry. Most of these industries need only flat welding or spot welding, which can be easily finished by a robot[1]. In the petrochemical, boiler and other industries, pipe insertion is generally used in pipeline connection. The welding seam for pipe insertion is a typical and complicated space welding seam. For the welding of a rotundity pipe in a level position, the gravity endured by the welding drop will form a different angle with the pipe in a different position and so will affect the contiguity degree of the weld slot which directly influences production efficiency and quality. Production practice shows that when the welding seam is in a flat or boat – shaped welding position, excellent welding quality can be guaranteed. The more deviation of weld seam from the flat position, the more difficult it is to guarantee the quality of the welding. The welding gun pose relative to the weld also affects the quality of welding. Many scholars have studied weld models and obtained certain achievements[2-5].

Many scholars have studied intelligent control methods for seam tracking applications. D. Lakov proposed using the fuzzy model to describe the uncertainty of the arc welding process according to the teaching content for weld seam tracking[5]. S. Murakami developed the weld seam tracking system based on fuzzy control and the control effect is good[5]. Y. Suga studied neural networks applied to seam tracking and the experimental results show that the system can be effectively used in seam tracking[6]. At present, a domestic study of the programming of the welding gun pose is far less required, thus, the study of intelligent control of the welding gun pose contains a lot of academic worth and much application value[5,7,8].

The artificial neural network is a new technique in recent years. Its ability to approach nonlinear functions and its strong self – adaptation has been proved in theory and has also been validated in actual applications[9]. Artificial neural network solves some problems that expert systems possess, such as knowledge representation, knowledge acquisition, paralleled inference etc[10]. The RBFNN adopted a local approaching network. It has a superior fast learning speed and is capable of a strong functional approach. It can effectively overcome the weakness of the BP network, such as slow convergence and its frequently being trapped in local minima[9, 11]. With the aim of shortening the traditional genetic algorithm, an improved genetic algorithm which is adaptive is used to optimize the RBFNN structure which can enhance the accuracy and global search efficiency. At the same time, the development of neural network theory which features in the nonlinear parallel distribution process provides an effective method to solve the problems of the traditional expert system.

As we all know, classic control theories are very effective in solving control problems in a linear constant system, however, the control of the welding gun pose is a complex nonlinear controlling target that cannot be captured in a mathematical model[7]. With the aim of solving the control problem of the welding gun pose in the case

---

[Author Introduction] Tian Jingwen, Beijing Key Laboratory of Information Service Engineering, Beijing Union University.

of whole – position welding, an intelligent control system based on the IRBFNN and expert system is presented in this paper. ADXRS300 micro – mechanicalgyro is used as the welding gun pose sensor in this system. When the welding gun position is obtained, an appropriate pitch angle can be obtained through expert knowledge and the numeric reasoning capacity of the IRBFNN. ARM is used as the controller to drive the welding gun pitch angle step motor in order to adjust the pitch angle of the welding gun in real – time.

2 Improved radial basis function network (IRBFNN)

2.1 Radial basis function neural network (RBFNN)

The radial basis function neural network is composed of three layers. Those are the input layer, hidden layer and output layer. The input layer nodes transmit input signals to reach hidden layers, hidden layer nodes are described by the gauss kernel function and output layer nodes are described by the linear function. The structure of the radial basis function neural network is shown in Fig. 1.

In this paper, the basic function is defined as follows:

$$\alpha_i(x) = epx\left[\frac{-\|X - C_i\|^2}{2\sigma_i^2}\right], \quad i = 1, 2, \cdots, m \tag{1}$$

where $\alpha_i(x)$ is the output of number i node of the hidden layer; $X = (x_1, x_2, \cdots, x_n)^T$ is the input samples; C_i is the centre of the Gauss kernel function, and it has the same dimensions as X; σ_i is the variable of the number i of hidden layers, it is called the standardized constant; m is the total number of hidden layer nodes.

The output of the radial basis function neural network is given by the following formula:

$$y_k = \sum_{i=1}^{m} \omega_{ik} \alpha_i(x) \quad k = 1, 2, \cdots, p \tag{2}$$

where ω_{ik} is the weight value of the network; p is the number of the output layer nodes.

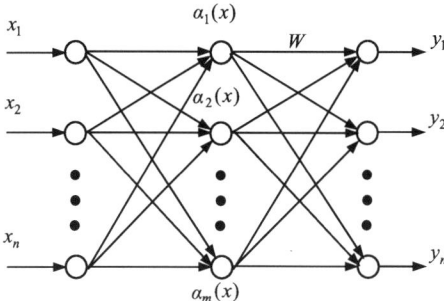

Fig. 1 Structure of the radial basis function neural network

2.2 Improved genetic algorithm[12-16]

The genetic algorithm (GA) is a kind of self – adapting heuristic global search algorithm which is derived from an imitation of how natural biological evolution is thought to occur. In nature, it is a cyclical process made up of reproduction – crossover – mutation operators. An adaptive genetic algorithm is a kind of GA that has to – scale reproduction and self – adaptive crossover and mutation operations.

$$P_c = \begin{cases} k_1 (f_{max} - f) / (f_{max} - f_{avg}) & \text{if } f' > f_{avg} \\ k_3 & \text{if } f' < f_{avg} \end{cases} \tag{3}$$

$$P_m = \begin{cases} k_2 (f_{max} - f) / (f_{max} - f_{avg}) & \text{if } f > f_{avg} \\ k_4 & \text{if } f < f_{avg} \end{cases} \tag{4}$$

where P_c is the exchanging probability, P_m is mutation probability, f_{max} is the biggest fitness of the colony, f_{avg} is the average fitness of the colony, f' is the bigger fitness of two strings used for an exchange, f is the fitness of the individual to mutate.

2.2.1 Code

A key problem is completing the mapping from the solution space of the optimization problem to the coding space. There are two main encoding modes of the genetic algorithm: binary – coding and decimal – coding. The improved genetic algorithm denotes the parameters directly with binary – coding.

Concerning hidden random nodes of RBFNN, the control vector (individual) L = (l_1, l_2, $\cdots$, l_i, $\cdots$, l_M) of hidden nodes is expressed in the binary coded form, where the l_i value is 1 or 0, which separately correspond to the existence or not of the i hidden node. The selection of hidden nodes and the gene of the chromosome is one to one correspondence.

2.2.2 Initial solution and adaptation function

A large number of individuals will be generated in the initialization phase, which is called the colony. The adaptation function is given as follows:

$$f = \begin{cases} C_{max} - E & E < C_{max} \\ 0 & E \geqslant C_{max} \end{cases} \quad (5)$$

$$E = \frac{1}{2p} \sum_P \sum_k (t_{pk} = o_{pk})^2 \quad (6)$$

where the C_{max} can be the maximum value E of the evolutionary process, E is the object function. p is the number of training samples, k is the node number of the network output layer, t_{pk} is the RBF network output and o_{pk} is the real output.

2.2.3 Operation operator

The operation operator of the genetic algorithm is composed of three operators, namely the reproduction operator, crossover operator and mutation operator.

The reproduction operator reproduces the individuals in the new colony according to the probability of their success in proportion to their adaptive value. After reproduction, preponderant individuals are preserved and the inferior individuals are weeded out, and the average fitness degree of the colony is increased, but the variety of the colony is lost at the same time. The role of the reproducing operator is to realize the principle of winner priority for preserving the predominance and natural selection, and making the colony converge on the optimum solution.

The crossover operator first selects two individuals stochastically according to a certain adaptive exchanging probability P_c, then it can produce two new individuals by exchanging parts of the chromogene stochastically. The two – point crossover is adopted in this paper, which randomly generates two crossover points; this is shown in Fig. 2. The genetic algorithm can generate a filial generation colony which has a higher average fitness and better individuals due to the reproduction and crossover operators, and makes the evolutionary process proceed to the optimum solution.

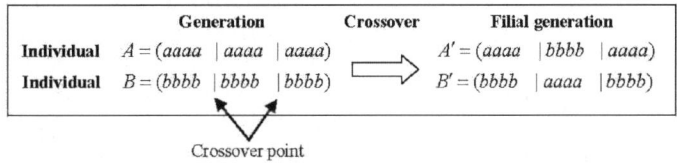

Fig. 2 Two – point crossover

The mutation operator changes several bits of the chromosome string stochastically with a small probability P_m, namely turn 0 to 1 and 1 to 0. The mutation operator is very important in recouping the loss of colony diversity.

2.3 RBFNN structure optimization with an improved genetic algorithm

Network optimization and parameter learning are divided into two phases, which are training and evolution. Firstly, N individuals are randomly generated and are regarded as the initial colony. Then the centre parameter c_i is trained as is the width parameter σ_i of the basis function and network weights w_i using the gradient descent method (GDM) and the least squares method (LSM). Secondly, the number of hidden layer nodes is optimised as are the other parameters using an improved genetic algorithm. We can obtain the least number of hidden layer nodes that satisfy the accuracy requirement through alternate training and evolution.

Introduce Boolean vector $U^T = (u_1, u_2, \cdots, u_M)$, of which $u_i = \{0, 1\}$, $u_i = 1$ represents the existence of the hidden, $u_i = 0$ represents the non-existence of the hidden node.

Every Boolean vector U^T can generate two chromosomes with binary-coding, one is the central parameter chromosome U_c^T, another is the width parameter chromosome U_σ^T.

The algorithm flow is shown in Fig. 3.

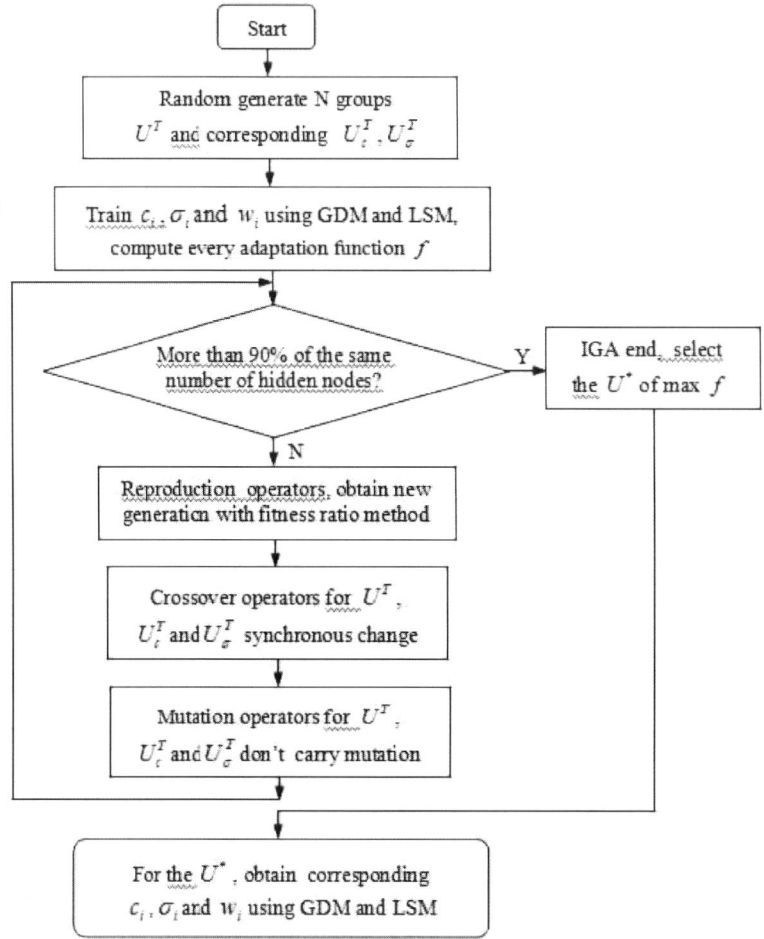

Fig. 3 Flow chart of RBFNN structure optimization with improved genetic algorithm

3 System structure

3.1 Total framework of the control system based on the IRBFNN and the expert system

The intelligent control system of the welding gun pose for a pipeline welding robot based on an IRBFNN and expert system is shown in Fig. 4. This system is mainly composed of an expert controller, an IRBFNN controller, a position sensor and a controlling target. The expert controller and the IRBFNN controller compose a knowledge sharing and parallel control compound controller.

The operating principle of the expert controller and the IRBFNN controller is described as follows: establish a knowledge base and the expert experience is formed with learning samples and stored in every node of the neural network in nonlinear mapping form. Start the expert controller to control the system, the inference mechanism implements the inference according to the knowledge of the knowledge base and the control information that the user provided, at the same time the IRBFNN controller is trained using the learning samples. When the IRBFNN controller is stable, the IRBFNN controller is used to control the system instead of the expert controller. Using the forward computation of the IRBFNN, we can obtain the output quantity of the control signal. When the performance of the IRBFNN controller does not meet the system requirements, the expert controller is restarted and the IRBFNN controller is trained again.

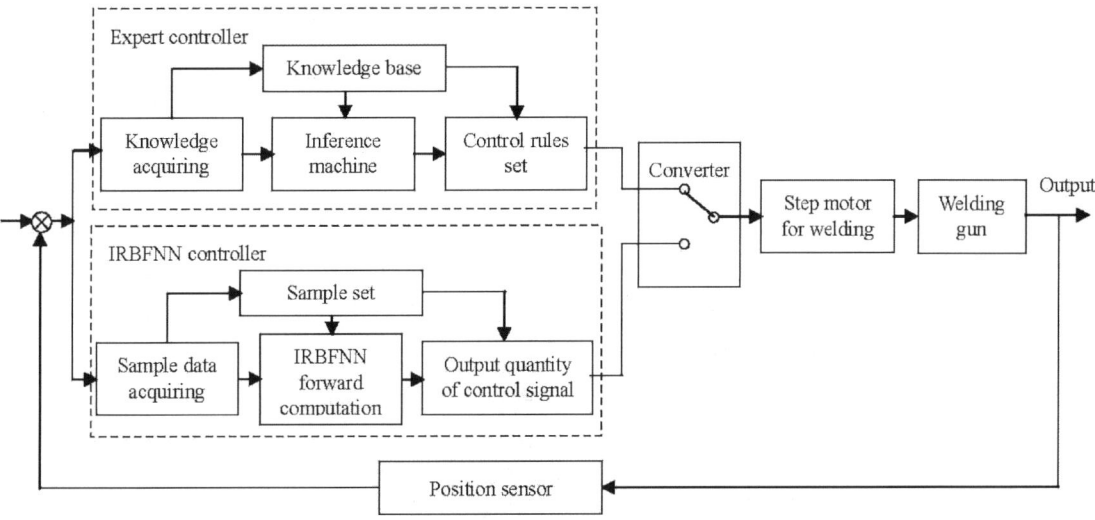

Fig. 4 **Control system of the welding gun pose structure**

When the system runs, the position sensor will detect the space position of the welding gun of the welding robot, and the IRBFNN controller will educe an appropriate pitch angle control signal for each sampling time, based on the measured real space position and the forward computation of IRBFNN. ARM is used as the controller to drive the welding gun pitch angle step motor in order to adjust the pitch angle of the welding gun in real – time, which realizes the real - time conditioning of the pitch angle of the welding gun. The compound controller composed of the expert controller and the IRBFNN controller and the welding gun on the pipe – welding robot composes a closed loop which completes a real – time control.

3.2 Knowledge acquisition

Based on the experience of an expert, in the control system, the circle of the pipeline is divided into 360 entries, for each space position, the welding gun has a corresponding experience value of the pitch angle. The information is formed using learning samples in a certain code form. This system adopted the semi – automatic method to obtain knowledge. For the IRBFNN controller, the knowledge is gained automatically through continuous learning from samples in the IRBFNN. The expert experience is stored in every node of the neural network in a nonlinear mapping form. By this means, the expert knowledge database is formed and the bottleneck problem of knowledge acquisition of the traditional expert system is overcome.

3.3 Inference mechanism

The inference mechanism of the expert system based on the neural network and the traditional inference mechanism has essential differences. The traditional inference mechanism is an inference based on the logic symbol and the inference mechanism of the expert system based on the neural network is a numerical calculation process. This system adopts a forward reasoning strategy driven by data. For the IRBFNN controller, firstly, the space position of the welding gun and the width and depth of the welding seam are inputted to every input node of the IRBFNN. Then the hidden layer output is computed through the formula (1) and acts as the input to the output layer, the output of the output layer neuron is computed by the formula (2). The output of the output layer neuron is the final inference result. Compared with the forward inference of the traditional expert system, theneural network forward inference is a paralleled inference and is implemented through numericalcalculation, so the inference speed based on the neural network is enhanced greatly.

4 Welding gun pitch angle control

4.1 Position sensor

The effect of the position sensor in the intelligent control system of welding gun pose is to detect the space position of the welding gun. ADXRS300 micro machine gyro is used as the welding gun position sensor. In reality, to use the micro machine gyro it has to be fixed to the welding gun and, along with the welding robot. s circle turning around the pipe, the micro machine gyro will run at the same time.

The type ADXRS300 micro machine gyro is a kind of micro gyro on – chip [17]. Its important indexes are as follows: Measuring range is ± 300°/s. Supplied output current is 6mA. Supplied voltage is 4.75V to 5.25V. The marked factor is 5mV/°/s. Bandwidth is 0.04kHz, nonlinearity is 0.1% of FS. Examining the micro machine gyro, we find that its circumvolution is around the centre axis and its positive going voltage related to the circumvolution angle speed will be outputted, the two have a linear relationship, as shown in Fig. 5. By carrying out the integral operation for voltage, we can get the real space position of the welding gun.

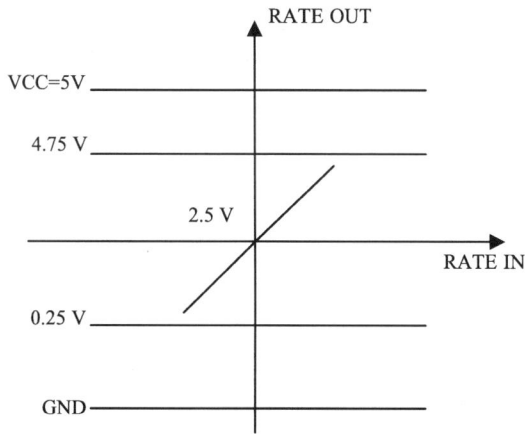

Fig. 5 Relationship of output and circumgyrate angle speed

4.2 Control for step motor of welding gun pitch angle

After the space position of the welding gun is ascertained, we take the normal plane of the welding seam tangent vector through the welding spot as the default plane. In real welding, the welding technique usually needs a certain forward pitching angle between the welding gun and the default plane. So the real plane of the welding gun is ascertained after the default plan is pitched at a certain angle. Based on the forward inference of the expert system and the IRBFNN controller, we can get an appropriate pitching angle. Meanwhile, the step motor will adjust the pitching angle of the welding gun.

This design scheme is adopted by the ARM processor as the control kernel. ARM technology is the mainstream of the embedded system [18]. At present, ARM chips available in the market can even reach a speed of several trillion and systems which use these chips as their main controller can build up a system of data collection, data process and communication with a high speed and highprecision. The system in this paper adopted the Samsung Company's S3C2410 processor, combined with the μC Linux operating system to realize the control of the welding gun pose of the welding robot. S3C2410 is a type of low price, low power loss and high performance microprocessor of 16/32 bits, which performs quite well in the application field of the embedded system.

The aim of the control system is to realize the control of the welding gun pose of the welding robot. The kernel question consists in the start, stop and control of the speed and direction. Aimed at the working principle of the step motor, we adopted the frequency conversion timing control method, let the electricity level signal control the inside convert circuit of the driver to change the pulse list. In this way, the direction exchange of the motor is realized. The control pulse is supplied by the outside V/F circuit. After power magnification, the welding gun pitch angle step motor transforms the signal outputted by ARM into angular displacement. This project adopted the step motor SANYO 103H7123 and adopted the Parker Company OEM750 as the driver, which accomplishes the digital fractionalization of the motor. The fractionized steps of the motor can be as many as 4000~20000 steps/circle and this fractionized motor is used as the motor to control the pitch of the welding gun.

4.3 Working flow of pose control system

The work of the control system can be divided into two sections: the manual part and the auto part. The working flow of this system is shown in Fig. 6.

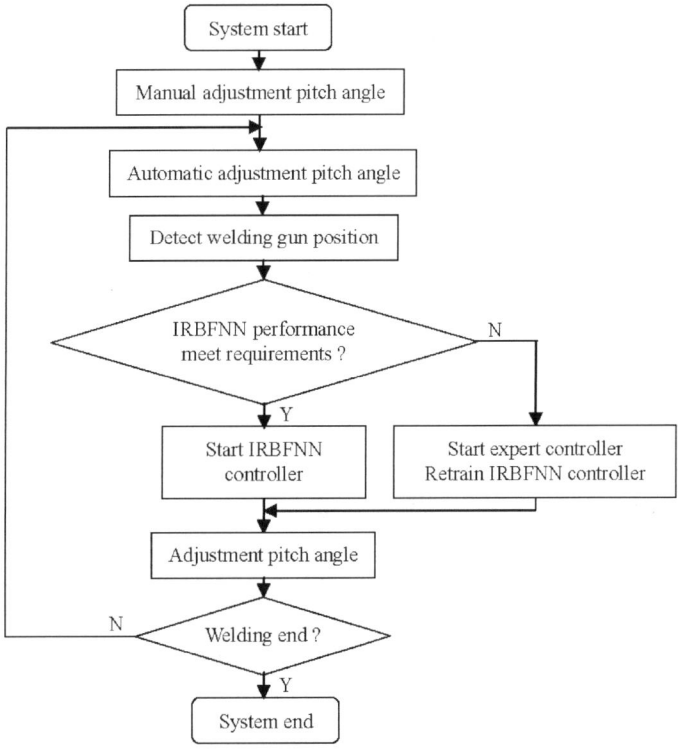

Fig. 6 Work flow of the welding gun pose control system

When the system operates, first the manual state is entered. The pitch angle of the welding gun can be adjusted by the operator through the adjustment mechanism. When the control system enters auto state, the welding gun position is detected by the ADXRS300 micro machine gyro and the welding gun position is inputted to the compound controller which is a combination of the expert controller and the IRBFNN controller. Once the IRBFNN controller performance meets requirements, the IRBFNN controller is used to control the system instead of the expert controller. With the IRBFNN forward computation, the output quantity of the control signal can be obtained and the pitch angleof the welding gun is adjusted. Otherwise, the expert controller is restarted to control the system, the inference mechanism implements its inference based on the knowledge of the knowledge base and the control information that the user provided, and the pitch angle of the welding gun is adjusted, at the same time the IRBFNN controller is trained using the learning samples.

5 Application study

Through correlative analysis between the characteristic parameters and the welding gun pose angle, we find the characteristic parameters which have the maximum correlativity with the welding gun pose angle. Combining expert experience, finally, we select 3 kinds of characteristic parameters to input as neurons of IRBFNN, these parameters are space position of the welding gun (expressed by angle), the width of the welding seam and the depth of the welding seam. The output layer ofIRBFNN contains one node, which stands for the value of the pitch angle.

We wrote some programs for the corresponding algorithm using C + +. In order to show the advantage and feasibility of IRBFNN, we adopted the expert system based on IRBFNN, RBFNN and BP network to complement the forward inference. The structure of RBFNN and the BP network is the same as the IRBFNN. According to the actual sample data and the RBFNN structural optimization with the improved genetic algorithm, the number of hidden layer nodes in IRBFNN is 12. The effect of different numbers of hidden nodes on the properties of RBFNN is shown in Fig. 7.

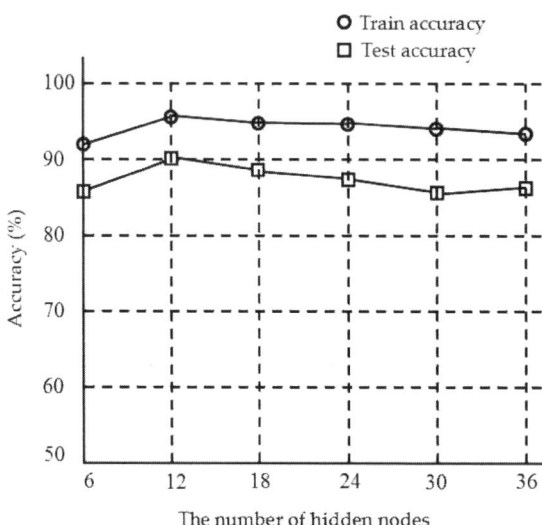

Fig. 7 **The effect of different numbers of hidden nodes on the properties of RBFNN**

From Fig. 7, we can see that when the number of hidden nodes is 12, the average train accuracy and test accuracy are higher than that of the number accuracy of the other hidden nodes number accuracy. So the topology structure of the IRBFNN network is 3 – 12 – 1.

After all the samples are normalized, we randomly separate 500 samples into 5 groups and take out 80 pieces of sample data as training samples each time, while the other 20 samples are testing samples. The IRBFNN, RBFNN and BP network are trained 5 times respectively using 5 groups with different training samples; thenceforth we used the corresponding testing samples to test. The results of the training and testing by the IRBFNN, RBFNN and BP network are shown in Table 1. Tables 2 and 3 are the results of training and testing by IRBFNN, RBFNN and BP networks in different training samples and test samples.

Table 1 **Training and testing results by IRBFNN, RBFNN and BP network (80 training samples and 20 testing samples)**

Method	Training error	Testing error	Average iteration times
IRBFNN	0.047	0.093	219
RBFNN	0.062	0.105	282
BP network	0.088	0.197	916

Table 2 **Training and testing results by IRBFNN, RBFNN and BP network (70 training samples and 30 testing samples)**

Method	Training error	Testing error	Average iteration times
IRBFNN	0.042	0.107	246
RBFNN	0.065	0.126	312
BP network	0.091	0.215	1055

Table 3 Training and testing results by IRBFNN, RBFNN and BP network (60 training samples and 40 testing samples)

Method	Training error	Testing error	Average iteration times
IRBFNN	0.045	0.113	265
RBFNN	0.069	0.139	387
BP network	0.098	0.296	1279

From Table 1, we can see that the mean squared error of training samples of IRBFNN is smaller than that of the RBFNN and BP network. Moreover the mean squared error of testing samples of IRBFNN is also smaller than that of the RBFNN and the BP network. Furthermore, the iteration times of the IRBFNN are obviously smaller than those of the RBFNN and BP network with the same system error. From the Table 2 and Table 3, we can obtain the same result. It shows that the IRBFNN is superior to the RBFNN and BP network with regards to estimation accuracy and convergence rate. So the control system based on an improved radial basis function network and expert system has higher stability and faster real-time controlled speed.

6 Conclusion

This paper presented an intelligent control system of welding gun pose based on an improved genetic algorithm radial basis function network and an expert system. This system integrated AI, robotics and other technologies, and combined computer science and mechanism science. It supplied a new way and method for the whole position auto-programming of pipeline welding gun pose of the welding robot, it has some use for reference with regards to the intelligent control of robots. Experiments proved that using the expert system based on an improved radial basis function network to control the welding gun pose is feasible. It can enhance the welding quality. This system will have a wide prospect for application.

7 Acknowledgments

This work is supported in part by the National Natural Science Foundation of China under grant no. 40674028 and the Funding Project for Academic Human Resources Development in Beijing Union University no. 11101501105.

References

[1] Ke Zhang, Xueqin Lu, Yixiong Wu and Changjian Wang. Research Status and Development Trend about Mobile Welding Robots [J]. Welding & Joining, 2004 (8): 5-9.

[2] Zhixiang Chen, Zhenyang Lu, Shuyan Yin and Yonglun Song. Models of Weld Pose and Welding Gun Pose [J]. Chinese Journal of Mechanical Engineering, 2003 (39): 59-62.

[3] Kehong Wang and Yong Liu. Study of geometric model and attitude of typical workpiece welded in robot [J]. Electric Welding Machine, 2003 (33): 29-32.

[4] Xiaofeng Wang, Huanming Chen and Shuyuan Jiang. Discussion on welding pose parameters and model of typical workpieces [J]. Journal of Nanchang Institute of Aeronautical Technology (Natural Science), 2006 (20): 24-28.

[5] Jiaping Liao, Chenshu Zhang and Yi Yin. Conditions and trend about the development of the tracking technology of welds of welding robots [J]. Modern Welding Technology, 2010 (11): 1-3.

[6] Y. Suga, M. Naruse and T. Tokiwa. Application of neural network to visual sensing of weld line and automatic tracking in robot welding [J]. Welding in the world, 1994 (34): 275-282.

[7] Liting Cao, Jingwen Tian and Wei Jiang. Intelligent Control System of Welding Torch's Gesture Based on Expert System [J]. Control & Automation, 2006 (22): 91-93.

[8] Su Wang, Xingang Miao and Xiaohui Li. Torch pose fitting for intersection line welding robot based on fuzzy control [J]. Journal of Beijing University of Aeronautics and Astronautics, 2010 (36): 771-775.

[9] Licheng Jiao. Neural network system theory [M]. Xian: Xian electronic science and technology university press, 1995.

[10] Zhaoqing Yin. Artificial Intelligence and Expert System [M]. Beijing: China Waterpower Press, 2009.

[11] Jingwen Tian and Meijuan Gao. Artificial Neural Network Algorithm Study and Application [M]. Beijing Institute of Technology Press, 2006.

[12] J. W. Tian and M. J. Gao. Thin interbedded reservoir parameters predicting based on high speed and precise genetic algorithm neural network [J]. Control and Decision, 2002 (17): 599 – 603.

[13] Y. Sun and J. W. Tian. WSN Path Optimization Based on Fusion of Improved Ant Colony Algorithm and Genetic Algorithm [J]. Journal of Computational Information Systems, 2010 (6): 1591 – 1599.

[14] J. W. Tian, M. J. Gao and Z. B. Zhang. Web Text Mining Based on Improved Genetic Algorithm and Radial Basis Function Neural Network [J]. Journal of Computational Information Systems, 2012 (8): 1195 – 1202.

[15] R. Geetha Ramani, R. Subramanian and P. Viswanath. Genetic Programming Method of Evolving the Robotic Soccer Player Strategies with Ant Intelligence [J]. International Journal of Advanced Robotic Systems, 2009 (6): 79 – 90.

[16] Za'er S. Abo – Hammour, Othman MK. Alsmadi, Sofian I. Bataineh, Muhannad A. Al – Omari and Nafee'Affach. Continuous Genetic Algorithms for Collision – Free Cartesian Path Planning of Robot Manipulators [J]. International Journal of Advanced Robotic Systems, 2011 (8): 14 – 36.

[17] Zhanyou Sha. The Principle and Application of Single Chip Yaw Rate Gyroscope [J]. Sensor World, 2004 (9): 31 – 34.

[18] Xuewen Ma, Mingri Zhu and Xiaohui Cheng. The Design and Realization of Network Communication Based on uCLinux and S3C4510B [J]. Control & Automation, 2004 (20): 53 – 55.

Discussion of Building a Tourist Information Service Platform Based on Cloud Computing

Sun Lianying　Peng Tao　Liu Chang　Zhang Qixiu

I Introduction

With the development of the tourism industry continuously and the emerging of a variety of smart phones constantly, computers and other mobile terminals supported by the technology of cloud computing and networking, it become a possibility to get the information you need by fingertips. Tourist information is complicated extensively, including direct description of tourist activity information (including tourist information, tourist destination information, travel service agency information, etc.) and travel activities are closely linked to indirect information (such as political, economic, cultural, legal, technological environment, etc.), and has comprehensive, sensitive, timeliness, development and non – definitive characteristics that have a significant impact on tourism activities [1]. With the development of computer networks, all people have changed the way of access to information, most of the tourists search the tourist information from the traditional media organizations turned to the channels of communication through the network to collect information, such as the forum, blog, micro – blog, so performance of machine and ability of software must be provided, some customs have difficult to obtain the service freely. Cloud computing technology joined a huge systems and resources together, changed the service mode, with the advantages of a very large scale, visualization, high reliability, versatility, highly scalable, on – demand service, easy use, etc., which can be used to build public platform travel services.

The cloud travel services technology model, system design and implementation method for the construction of diversified, three – dimensional, networked public travel service platform are discussed in the paper, which will provide technical support to share information resources, improve the level of modern service.

II Analysis of services

As we known, different groups have different target in the trip. Some concern landscape, anther concern geography and religious. How to make them obtain the information that they are eager for become a problem eager to be solved. Cloud travel service platform need to provide information services with the characteristics of popular, comprehensive, behavioral, feature and so on, so classified information of serviceis discussed firstly.

A. Service object analysis

Service platformservice for four categories of users mainly, the first category are a registered user, with the features of long – term service; The second is the casual user, that need to get topical information, with the features of temporary, targeted strong; The third category user are mobility customers which visit in a tourist area, with temporal and spatial characteristics, they are need to provide emergency services. The fourth category is travel suppliers, travel suppliers, travel agencies or travel companies such as hotels, scenic spots. Cloud services platform service user objects and key service requirements shown in Fig. 1.

[Author Introduction] Sun Lianying, College of information technology, Beijing Union University. E – mail: sunlychina@ buu. edu. cn; Peng Tao, College of information technology of Beijing Union University. E – mail: pengtao@ buu. edu. cn; Liu Chang, College of information technology Beijing Union University. E – mail: xxtliuchang@ buu. edu. cn; Zhang Qixiu, College of information technology, Beijing Union University. E – mail: hack_ ok_ 25@ qq. com.

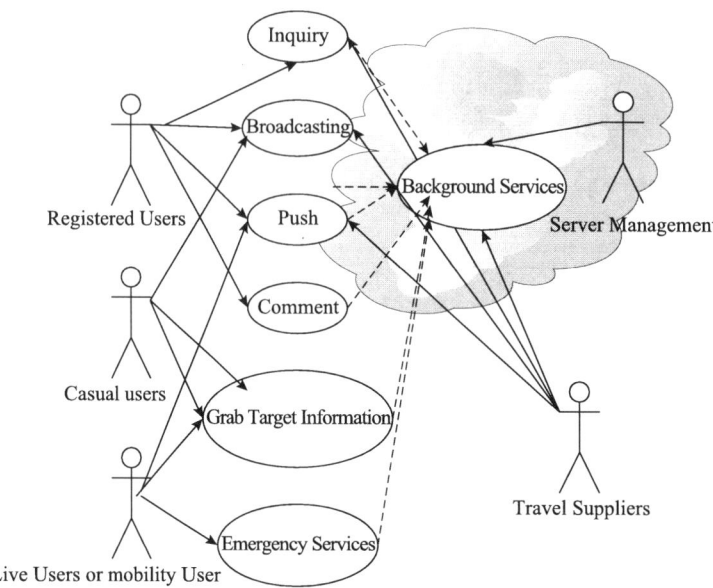

Fig. 1　User objects and key service requirements of cloud services platform service

B. Introduction of main services

1) Information inquiry

Information inquiry is shown by two forms in this system, one type information is classified according to attractions characteristics, another is searched by location map, classified information inquiry is shown in details as fig. 2.

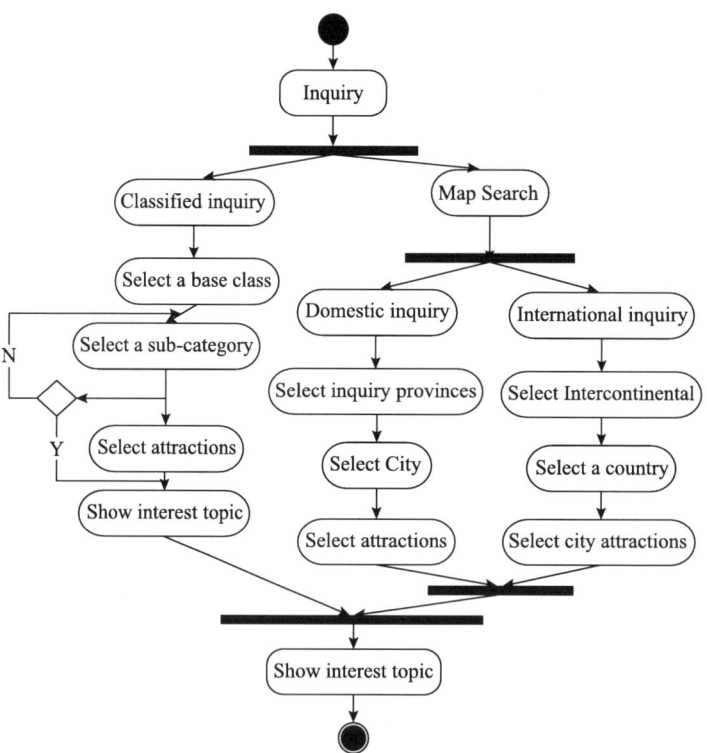

Fig. 2　Classified information inquiry

Attractions Classified inquiry first select the basic classification: natural, cultural, religious, urban civilization。 when the user determines that the base class, the system will be a detailed list of categories attractions. If you select a detailed list of categories of natural, mountains, valleys, forests, grasslands, deserts, caves, lakes, rivers, streams, springs lake, hot springs, waterfalls, etc. Vill be shown, Similarly, a detailed list of categories humanities include: site, residence, folklore, ancient, ancient architecture, towns, houses, arches, castles, ruins ruins, ancestral halls, palaces, tombs, monument towers, pavilions, etc. ; religious detailed list of categories, including: Islam, Buddhism, Indian Buddhism, thirteen, Tibetan Buddhist / Lamaism, Taoism, Confucianism, Christianity, the Roman Catholic / Catholicism, Orthodoxy / Orthodox, Protestant / Christian / Protestant; Choose from the detailed list of categories , you can enter information interface that you're interested in.

Map search display information in the form of maps. The information classed by region, the user first selects the domestic information query or abroad information inquiries by clicking on the map. If you choose the international information query, the interface will appear with a world map , then the user clicks to query Intercontinental (including Asia, North America, South America, Africa, Europe, Oceania, Antarctica), and then select the country you want to query, system interface will display the country's famous attractions, click on these attractions can view the attractions in details.

2) Broadcast and push

Currently many tourist products message spread by more use of paper flyers, newspaper or SMS with higher costs, greater consumption. Our products are designed based on mobile Internet network, travel suppliers to provide customers with information by mobile push service, and includes:

■ Living broadcasts. The brief text description of promotional activities are send to all APP users.

■ Delay regional push. When users enter a attractions nearby area, will receive more latest promotional information by technology of location – based push driven.

The system design is C/S mode based on the idea of mobile Internet. Server – side includes data server and push server, data server is responsible for data registration and data storage, push server is responsible for pushing the message. Android platform mobile client side is chosen to be in charge of receiving and displaying messages. Registered on the server data, tourism services providers input the information which will be pushed, and then the push server push information to the customer phone. Push process: Travel Service Provider→Data Servers→push server→client→data server (for push details).

3) Topic information searching

As the development of mobile Internet and Web technology continually, mobile Internet (for example micro – blog, etc.) gradually become an basic tools of communication and entertainment everyday. To the end of December 2012, Sina micro – blog had more than 500 million registered users, 46. 29 million daily active users, 75 percent of daily active users from the mobile client. It is very large amount of data and information (such as news, forums, blog, micro – blog, social networking sites) collected from the mobile Internet. But how to effectively solve the "pieces of information" and "information overload", "spam content" and other issues has become a challenge. People are creating data on the internet while also browsing data, Therefore, the ultimate goal of tourism services is to provide users with location – based and user interest – based personalized recommendation by mining the user's interest and needs, clustering behavior characteristics. Meanwhile, the government, enterprise information can be pushed to users in the most efficient way to make users receive the hot topic information with timeliness, authenticity and higher propagation. It has higher political significance and social and cultural significance to provide users with faster, more efficient service.

A multi – level, multi – dimensional search model is designed by way of analyses the open API and traditional way of web crawlers comparatively in the process of system design.

4) Emergency Services

Emergency services includes three cases:

The first is the traveler eager to learn how to reach the destination or achieve a particular purpose, such as how to ride, how to go to the hospital, how to find the ideal hotel, etc. , at this moment his most needed services is to obtain objective information by use of handy tools such as mobile phones and other mobile devices, with the characters of specific needs and rapid response.

The second is how toacquire and release the warning information. Timely warning information is published in accordance with authority, which includes: early warning level, the incident area or place, time of the incident, impact assessment and response measures. The information is released or adjusted through radio, communications, information networks or other means, for special people, special places the targeted push inform ways should be taken individually.

The third isinformation release and comments the tourist can release accident information and comments by the public travel service platform. The accident information includes: event information sources, time of the incident, the site of the incident, the scope of the nature of the incident, the incident momentum, tourists casualties and missing people and so on. Comments containing the user's understanding of attractions, real-life experience, user information collected archive by topic searching.

III Model of Travel servicesbased on cloud computing

"Cloud tourism" isa travel service mode based on cloud computing technology, with non-download, non-installation, non-upgrade hardware. You not only through the cloud server obtain the instant travel service, but also read the same tourist information by multi-terminal, which get rid of the hardware device control. With the living standards and quality of life improved, the capabilities of modern tourism services is growing up, how to improve the quality of service and emergency service capabilities has become a hot research many experts and scholars. It is become a necessity to integrate multi-level, multi-faceted tourism resources. The cloud computing technology has changed the service mode, improved the level of tourism services, which achieved the sharing of information resources. A huge systems and resources are connected together by cloud computing technology. Through Internet technology the extended elastic IT-related capabilities is provided customers as a service.

Users only need to make use of relevant cloud services, no longer need to purchase expensive hardware investments, to overburden the frequent maintenance and upgrades. They can enjoy a variety of cloud services provide travel services, just to use a terminal to access the network. The infrastructure of public cloud tourism service model shown in Fig. 3.

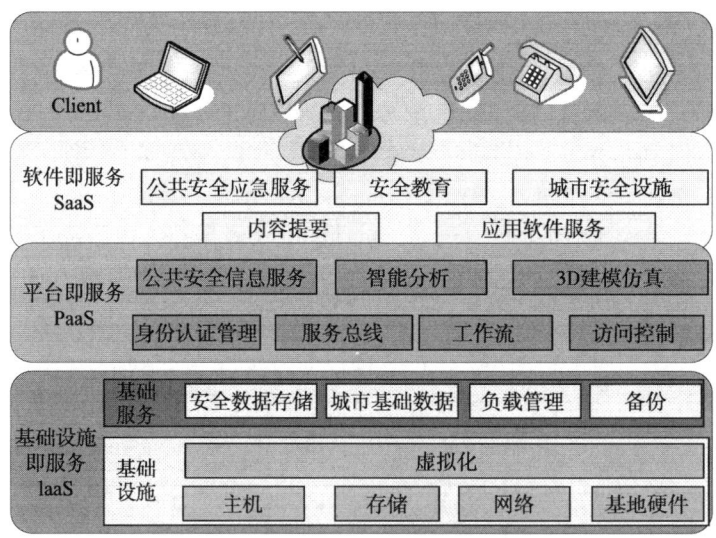

Fig. 3 Theinfrastructure of public cloud tourism service model

According to the characteristics of tourism services, the cloud travel services model is designed corresponding to the classic architecture of cloud computing. SaaS layer does not require users to install software on their computers or servers, get its own needed, with the corresponding software-enabled services through a service level agreement (SLA) directly. Customers do not need to purchase hardware and software, can create, test, and deploy applications and services only by use of the PaaS platform. The IaaS layer provides users with computing resources remotely, including computers, storage, and related functions provided by the network. But they do not need to support the computing power of the IT hardware and software to pay the corresponding original investment cost.

Ⅳ Design and Practice

In order to cloud travel platform used by different customer groups anywhere, this system take the combined mode of B/S and C/S.

A. User information acquisition

The userinformation is recorded through complete user registration, select individual registration, groups registered or travel provider to enter the registration interface, fill in the information submitted to complete the registration.

As an example, group information registration interface include group name, basic information of the group head, group size. User must fill out the information and submit it, and then the registration is completed.

B. Developing thesearching functions

Users input the name of the interesting attractions interested in the search box, the system will find attractions according to user input information and find matches returned to the user, the user clicks to search for points of interest, they can enter into the attraction Attractions Introduction interface to view the corresponding information on attractions, it is shown as Fig. 4.

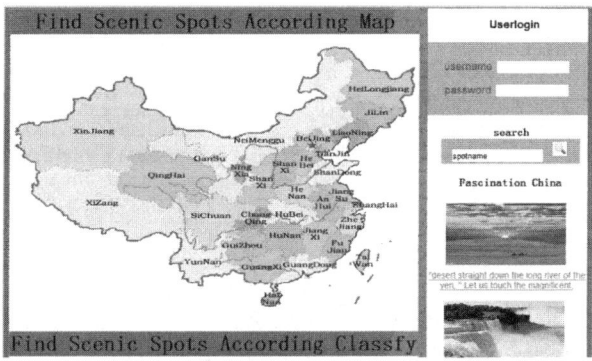

Fig. 4　Attractionsinformation inquiry

After selected the topic attractions information, the system will appear the interface corresponding attractions. Including traffic information, accommodation information, gourmet specialty information, customs information, weather information, attractions profile, price information, user's evaluating information.

C. Comments and emergency service

Evaluation function includes your friends to check all the attractions evaluation.

If you are a backpacker, then click on the interface looking for backpackers, input arrival date of the attractions, you can see all the attractions the date of backpackers and contact information, so that you canhave companions easily.

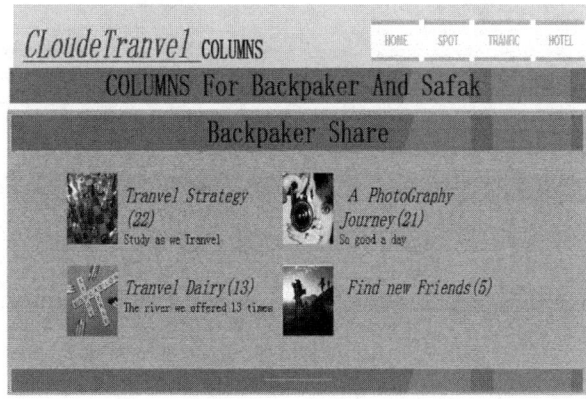

Fig. 5　Comments and emergency service

V Conclusion

Studied in thekey technologies to construct the tourist cloud public services platform is a hot problem, which can solve how to share information resources, construct information classification push model, Software development techniques and other issues. Practice shows that the cloud service mode of travel services such as user behavior analysis, themes grab and push, emergency services and other functions has a practical value for the urban public travel service platform, and provide technical support for the tourism cloud.

Acknowledgment

We thank all program and local committee members, and volunteers for their hard work and contributions to the ICSECS conference. This work is partially supported by Funding Project of National Science Foundation of China (NSFC, 40672104), Talents Support Project of Talents Enhancing University Development Plan in Beijing Union University (BPHR2011A04, BPHR2012F01). And thank all of experts and scholars referenced in my paper, and all of devoting to this study.

References

[1] Wei Yu, Docking of Slow Travel and Tourism cloud – a new semi – portability travel packages, and Model Construction, Chinese foreign investment, 2011, 16

[2] Chen Kang, Zheng Weimin, cloud computing: system instances and Research, Journal of Software, 2009, Vol. 20 (5), pp. 1337 – 1348

[3] CHENQuan, DENG Qianni, cloud computing and its key technologies, Computer Applications, 2009, Vol. 29 (9), pp. 2562 – 2567

[4] Qinliang Juan. Tourism Tourism cloud era public information services. Tourism Tribune, 2012, Vol. 27 (2) pp. 9 – 10

[5] ZhouXiangbing, MAHongjiang (etc.) AnArchitectureApproachofTourismCloudBasedonCloudComputing, JournalofChongqingNormalUniversity (NaturalScience, 2013, Vol. 30 No. 2, pp. 79 – 86

[6] SunLianying Liu Chang. Investigate of Urban Safety Service Model based on Cloud Computing, Computer Science, 2011, vol. 38 (10), pp. 89 – 91

多校区环境下分布式资源共享平台

孙建华　林德强　刘元红　李　媛

引　言

如何存储、调度、管理海量信息，以及如何从海量信息中查找和提取所需要的信息是迫切需要解决的问题，也是最为棘手的问题。同样，在办公信息化建设日益深入的进程中，国内高校几乎无一例外的从单一的管理系统开始建设，如：教学管理系统、人事管理系统、资产管理系统、科研管理系统、网络学堂，以及专用的教学资源管理和实验教学模拟系统等。各个专业信息系统的建立使得终端用户的使用非常烦琐，即使建设了统一的一次性登录的网络管理平台，但是信息的检索，特别是教学资源的全文检索尚没有一个方便的访问平台。

实现对业务应用系统、业务网站以及办公系统进行统一全文检索、查询和共享成为网络资源使用者的共同需求。特别是在多校区环境下，实现业务系统、业务网站、OA办公系统、邮件系统、多媒体等资源统一平台的全文检索、查询、共享和应用的需求尤为迫切。现在也有一些应用云平台的解决方案。云平台的应用对于新系统的建设是个不错的方案，但是对于原系统整合、已有数据的迁移，还存在一些有待解决的问题。

1　建设思路

我校设有14个学院，分布在13个校区，校区分布在北京的6个城区，形成了以校本部为中心，集中与分散相结合的办学布局。学校已经建成各种办公业务系统、邮件系统、国家级特色专业建设点、服务外包基地、应用文科综合实验教学示范中心建设单位网站，以及教学资源系统等。作为国家级示范实验中心建设单位，应用文科综合实验教学中心面向北京联合大学分布在13个校区的14个学院的全体师生提供服务。因此，实现统一的资源检索、共享和管理平台势在必行。

除了上述教学、科研系统的各类信息的全文检索外，还有大量的办公多媒体信息的管理。目前，国家正在大力推进办公信息化和电子政务，政府机关和企事业单位越来越多地利用和依赖互联网与计算机，绝大多数纸质公文和文件都来自于电子文件，许多文件则直接采用电子文件形式。任何一个机构的各种办公业务、邮件、网站以及教学资源系统等资源大致分为几类：各种多媒体信息，如：doc、docx、jpg、pdf、xls、xlsx等；网页；邮件，如：outlook, foxmail等。

大量的电子文件存储在各个部门相关工作人员所使用的电脑中。有些电子文件包括重要数据信息，其中既有可公开使用公用的信息，也有需要严格或局部保密的非公开信息。现阶段对于办公、工程建设、教学相关的纸质文件都是每年整理存放于学校档案室，这类文件的检索非常麻烦，检索效率低。对现有电子资源的整合优化是非常必要的，也是今后的发展趋势。

通常，当领导需要查找具体信息和数据时，一般的做法是：领导→主管部门→办事人员→在电脑中查找或翻阅档案→找出相关的多个文件→逐个文件阅读→可能查到、也可能查不到→找到后，上报给领导→领导拿到相关文件后，可能是需要的，也可能是不需要的→如果是需要的，当感觉内容不符合需求时，还需要再查找→新的循环开始。

然而，对于校区多、办学分散的环境，上述问题就更加突出。现已广泛使用的关系数据库难以实现海量信息的高速全文检索。

目前在全球广泛使用的非结构化数据库有很多，目前欧美在新闻出版行业和情报研究机构广泛使

[基金项目] 北京市属高等学校人才强教计划资助项目（PHR201107302）。

[作者简介] 孙建华（1960—），女，硕士，研究员，北京联合大学应用文理学院实践教学中心主任，主要研究计算机网络技术。

用，具备高效检索效果的 TRIP 数据库具有很好的应用前景[1]。TRIP 是最早、最成熟的全文检索系统之一。TRIP 最初是瑞典 Paralog AB 的产品，它源于瑞典皇家工学院图书馆 1972 年开发的、面向非结构化数据处理的图书情报检索专用软件 3RIP，这可谓是世界上最早、最成熟的全文检索系统。自 1985 年在 3RIP 的基础上开发成为 TRIP 后，已在图书情报界外，尤其是在企业、公共机关中找到了更多的用户。应用最多的领域是化学、化工公司、医药公司、政法部门、议会、海关、警厅、报业、交通、电信、广播、保险等[2-3]。系统需求的应用模型见图 1 所示。

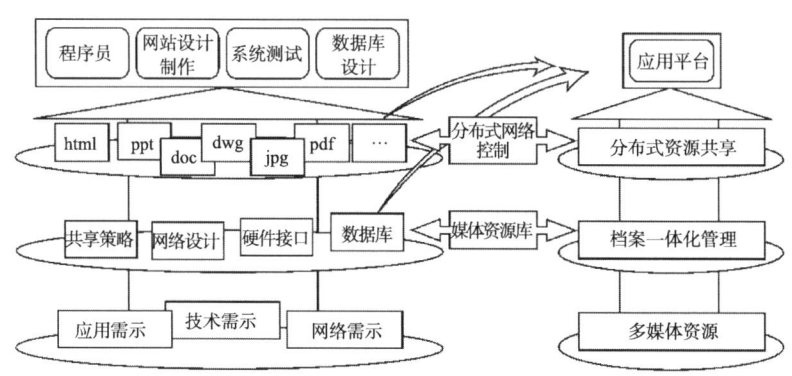

图 1　资源共享系统的应用模型

2　系统实现

TRIP 是一种面向对象的全文数据库系统，更准确地说，TRIP 是一种具有非常快速查找功能的信息档案管理系统，最适用于在公共网 Internet 上或局域网 Intranet 上管理、检索、出版像法律法规、合同文本、技术文件、来往书信、报刊杂志、备忘录、报告、图书馆系统等任意规格的文本数据，以及照片、图像、图表等二进制数据。

TRIP 系统也同样擅长处理像日期、时间、数值（实数、虚数）、人名、地名等一般关系型数据库所擅长处理的规格化数据[4-5]。

2.1　系统需求

本系统通过对现有电子资源进行分类、整合，采用 TRIP 全文数据库技术，存储文本、OFFICE 文档、工程制图文件及各种多媒体文件，提供对各类资源的多样化全文检索；为用户备份、共享、管理各类资源提供支持。通过摘要算法对资源的存储和检索进行优化，不存在随着数据记录的增大而降低检索效率的问题，从而改变了传统信息的查找方法。

系统实现了关系数据库不易实现的数据库和系统程序的分离，可以对建立的 TRIP 数据库进行拆分、合并和移动。TRIP 数据库的跨平台数据存储机制，可以实现在各种系统平台下建立的数据库，如：Windows、Linux、Unix 等，可以按需拆分、合并、迁移和复原。

系统的最大特点是：跨平台的数据库任意拆分组合；对各类文档全文检索，又能够实现文档备份与管理，有利于对于历史文件的查询；高效全文检索；各种媒体资源统一检索平台，如：在图 2 中所示的各种文件，包括图片、邮件和网页等；分布式的资源访问策略。

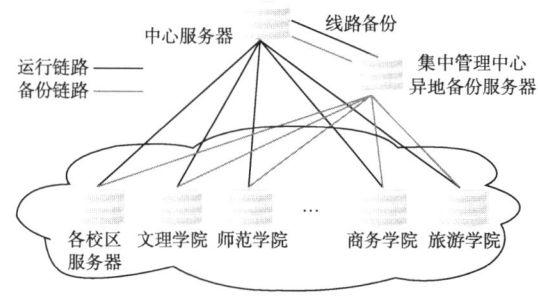

图 2　系统总体架构

2.2 系统的总体架构

针对学校校区的特点，系统采用集中控制、分层分布式应用管理的模式。中心控制部分采用双机热备以保障系统提供不间断服务，分层分布式是指在各个校区设二级管理功能对分布在各个校区的分服务器进行本校区的资源管理和总校区资源共享的授权。

2.3 系统功能

整个系统由多媒体资源管理、网站信息资源管理、电子邮件资源管理和身份管理4个模块构成。

（1）多媒体资源管理。针对200多种电子文档进行管理。用户通过B/S或C/S模式访问服务器。包括数据库管理、权限或属性管理、资源全文检索和日志管理。资源进入数据库有两种方式：①批量入库，只需设定文件夹或盘符即可将路径内的所有资源批量入库。②逐一入库，通过浏览器页面逐条编辑入库[6-8]。属性管理：所有资源都有自身的属性，属性类别包括：公共、私有和群组。任何人不得越权查看没有权限查看的资源。资源全文检索：所有多媒体资源的检索结果均可在浏览器中播放显示[9]。

（2）网站资源管理。模块提供Web资源检索，包括：读取网站对象信息、抓取进程管理、抓取网页信息、解析网站内容、日志文件信息记录、信息入库等模块。还提供自定义数据库结构的功能，包括定义数据库模板和创建数据库。用户在创建数据库之前都需要对数据库的字段类型、名称和备注等信息进行设计[10]。最终数据库会根据用户所设计的数据库结构进行创建。为减少应用的复杂性，引入数据库模板。

（3）电子邮件资源检索。实现动态读取用户邮箱，并进行资源的抓取。从而实现对邮件的本地备份和对邮件内容全文检索功能。电子邮箱资源检索的全文检索与网站资源检索类似。模块启用之前首先要设定邮箱，理论上可以设定任意多个邮箱，系统定时在邮件服务器抓取信件内容以备检索之用。邮箱的安全也是系统安全的重要内容之一，使用者只能依据权限访问相关内容，否则不能查看任何内容。

（4）一体化的检索平台。系统不仅提供了上述三个模块的检索功能，还可在授权的前提下在上述三个资源数据库中进行一次性一体化检索。方便使用。用户权限的核心功能分为两个方面：用户管理和权限管理。用户管理可以通过添加、删除、修改和查询实现；权限管理从两个方面进行控制：功能模块的使用和资源的访问。优先级为功能模块、资源。权限类别有公共、群组和私有[11-13]。

2.4 系统资源分布式策略

系统考虑到多校区，分布式校园网络的拓扑结构和应用需求，设计实现资源的分布式访问和控制策略。通常的分布式策略：划分式（partitioned）、全重复方式（fully replicated）和部分重复方式（partiallyreplicated）。划分式，将数据分布于不同结点，彼此间没有任何重复。划分式在共享部分较多时，事务的分布式执行也就越多，会使性能下降。全重复方式，每一个节点拥有全部数据的一个复本。全重复方式对只读事务，可做到完全本地访问，但对更新操作，则需要访问每一个节点。部分重复方式，根据应用的需要，将有些数据只分布在一个节点上，有些数据分布在多个节点上，这种分布方式应用比较广泛。3种分布式策略的复杂性、灵活性和引发问题的比较见表1。本系统采用部分重复式资源分布部署策略，将面向特定校区或面向局部人群的资源置于一个节点，而面向多个校区或共享范围较大的资源置于多个特定节点。

表1 3种分布式策略比较

分布方式	复杂性	灵活性	由分布引出的问题
划分式	低	小	少
全重复	中	中	中
部分重复	高	大	多

3 系统安全设计

系统安全性要求是指对整个系统（包括系统硬件、软件、使用、保障及有关人员）和系统全寿命期的各阶段（包括论证、设计、研制、使用、维护及报废）的所有活动，都要贯彻安全方面的需求，逐项、全面地识别系统中存在的危害，采取保证安全的工程和管理措施，达到消除风险或者将风险控制到可以接受的水平，以防止灾难的发生[14]。系统安全主要包括：

（1）物理安全。物理安全主要包括环境安全、设备安全、媒体安全等方面。处理秘密信息的系统中心机房应采用有效的技术防范措施。

（2）运行安全。运行安全主要包括备份与恢复、病毒的检测与消除、电磁兼容等。涉密系统的主要设备、软件、数据、电源等应有备份，并具有在较短时间内恢复系统运行的能力。应采用国家有关主管部门批准的查毒杀毒软件适时查毒杀毒，包括服务器和客户端的查毒杀毒。

（3）信息安全。确保信息的保密性、完整性、可用性和抗抵赖性是信息安全保密的中心任务。对于涉及个人知识产权的资源设置密级，只有得到授权才可以访问。

（4）安全保密管理。涉密计算机信息系统的安全保密管理包括各级管理组织机构、管理制度和管理技术三个方面。要通过组建完整的安全管理组织机构，设置安全保密管理人员，制定严格的安全保密管理制度，利用先进的安全保密管理技术对整个涉密计算机信息系统进行管理。在设计时，要尽最大努力将安全方面的需求与其他方面的需求作整体考虑，从而达到设计上的优化[15]。

4 结　　语

总之，由于网络和资源的特殊性质，决定了信息共享和信息安全问题的客观存在。因此，真正解决这一矛盾，仅靠技术手段是不够的。还应从法制上提高公民的法律意识，从管理上提高管理者的法律意识和执政能力。

参考文献

[1] 杨小莉. 国内常见全文检索系统比较［J］. 图书与情报，2006（2）：94-96.
[2] 徐飞. 基于TRIP数据库的公文电子化管理系统的设计与实现［J］. 中原工学院学报，2012（5）：14-16.
[3] 战小漪. TRIP中英文全文数据库管理系统新华社综合数据库的应用与开发［J］. 中国新闻科技，1998（5）：21-22.
[4] 杨恒宇. 基于TRIP的全文检索系统的应用及研究［J］. 电脑知识与技术，2012（25）：25-26.
[5] 程传鹏. 基于Trip数据库的档案管理系统的设计与实现［J］. 中原工学院学报，2012（1）：44-45.
[6] 陈金水. 非结构化数据存储管理的实用化方法［J］. 计算机与现代化，2006（8）：25-26.
[7] 张德政. 非结构化信息管理［J］. 微计算机信息，2006（9）：218-220.
[8] 韦琳. E-learning非结构化数据管理系统的构建与实现［J］. 中国科学技术大学学报，2010（6）：14-16.
[9] 冯宇. 非结构化数据管理平台研究与建设［J］. 电力信息化，2012（2）：69-71.
[10] 文永革. 基于Web的非结构化数据管理方法的研究与实践［J］. 计算机系统应用，2008（5）：101-104.
[11] 张志军. 分布式数据库在信息化管理系统中的应用［J］. 无线互联科技，2012（2）：26-28.
[12] 王春晓. 分布式数据库数据复制技术的研究［J］. 中山大学学报，2009（S1）：366-368.
[13] 孙碧燕. 非结构化档案信息管理对策分析［J］. 企业研究，2010（6）：72-74.
[14] 何淑娟. 非结构化数据库及其应用分析［J］. 信息系统工程，2009（7）：49-51.
[15] 吴广印. 非结构化网络数据库在图书情报服务中的应用［J］. 图书情报工作，2000（9）：52-56.

云计算技术在大学生计算机应用大赛中的应用

杜　煜　许菁菁　刘振恒

1　简　介

云计算将大量价格低廉的服务器通过虚拟化技术进行松散耦合，构成大规模的可扩展计算中心和海量存储系统，通过互联网交付服务。用户对计算资源的使用可以像水、电等公共基础服务设施一样，随用随到、按需扩展，而不需要了解、控制支持这些服务的技术基础构架。

计算机应用大赛对作品要求相对特殊，用户提交的是作品代码。传统的软件设计竞赛通常是通过邮箱提交作品，由竞赛组织者进行作品部署供专家评审。由于移动互联网开发技术的应用须进行较复杂的环境部署，因此结合云计算的服务交付模式，提供给用户多开发平台的、在线部署作品、在线评审的云计算平台。

2　面向计算机应用大赛的云计算应用架构

云计算技术可使用户用较少的资本支出，获得计算功能、扩展能力、服务和更多商业价值。云计算的核心特征包括：以服务为基础、具备可扩展性、支持共享、按使用计量、基于互联网技术。云计算的关键技术包括网格计算、网络存储、虚拟化技术等。

云计算在建制架构上可以分为3个层次，即应用程序、平台和基础设施，这决定了云计算能够提供如下3种类型的服务，即IaaS/PaaS/SaaS。IaaS（Infra-structure as a Service，基础设施即服务）为用户提供虚拟的计算资源、互联网资源和存储资源；PaaS（Platform as a Service，平台即服务）为用户提供应用程序开发的服务环境、中间件和数据库；SaaS（Software as a Service，软件即服务）为终端用户按需提供完整的应用程序。IaaS/PaaS/SaaS服务提供的云计算可以满足不同用户的业务需求。云计算为用户带来了新的计算模式和新的客户体验。

云平台基于E2Cloud的系统框架如图1所示。

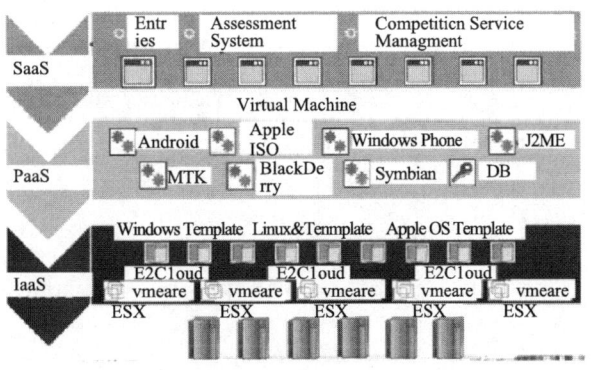

图1　计算机应用竞赛的云计算服务平台架构

2.1　基础设施

云平台在IaaS层采用硬件服务器集群并行计算，基础设施采用服务器耦合成内存资源池和存储资源池，依据不同等级提供动态、虚拟、可管理的计算能力、存储空间和平台服务。竞赛的相关原始数据经过处理进行存储、分享、分析和服务。

2.2　服务平台

云平台在PaaS层提供操作系统和围绕特定应用的必需服务。通过VMware虚拟化技术提供Windows

［作者简介］杜煜，北京联合大学信息学院教师。

操作系统、Linux 操作系统和 IOS 操作系统等模板；提供竞赛规定的全部 7 个移动开发平台（Android、Apple IOS、Windows Phone、J2ME、MTK、BlackBerry、Symbian）。

2.3 应用程序

在 SaaS 层由参赛团队部署作品和远程调试，并为大赛评审系统、大赛服务系统等提供技术支撑服务。

3 面向计算机应用竞赛的云计算应用实现

本届大赛，首次应用云计算虚拟化技术为各参赛团队提供按需使用的计算资源，为竞赛评委提供跨区域评审环境。通过大赛云计算平台，参赛团队可以通过 Web 随时随地访问云端开发环境，云平台分为教育网（http://ecloud.bjcac.buu.edu.cn）和公网（http://cloud.bjcac.buu.edu.cn）两个登录通道。

云计算平台采用负载均衡技术、网络安全技术等，提高云平台的硬件支撑能力、数据的访问速度，确保应用系统的可用性和可靠性，如图 2 所示。

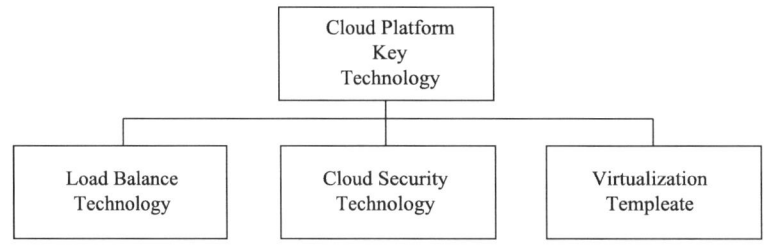

图 2　云平台关键技术

云平台在解决云计算下的负载失衡的过程中，首先通过建立云计算环境下的负载均衡模型，再运用马尔可夫过程理论建立起负载失衡时的转移概率矩阵。云平台应交付安全的服务，本系统平台从数据安全、互联网安全、虚拟化安全和用户鉴权的角度考虑云安全解决技术。无论使用哪种云计算的服务模式（SaaS/PaaS/IaaS），数据安全都很重要，将数据备份，若受到损坏，可在 1h 内恢复，这样能够保证竞赛评审。在云端部署的 Web 应用程序应当充分考虑来自互联网的威胁。由于引入虚拟化技术，因此还需考虑虚拟机安全和虚拟服务器的安全。另外，需要给用户提供安全的用户鉴权接口。

参赛团队根据参赛需求向云平台申请资源，资源使用时长可以由团队根据开发需求选择（30min 到 12 个月）；可选择 7 大移动开发平台，仅需 2min，所申请资源即可交付用户使用。开发版本根据大赛需求定制，资源信息（虚拟资源与开发环境）如图 3 所示。云端资源可以轻松维护、建立快照、备份多个开发测试环境和版本，方便团队成员进行协同开发工作，在云平台上实现作品远程调试与运行，从而提高团队效率。

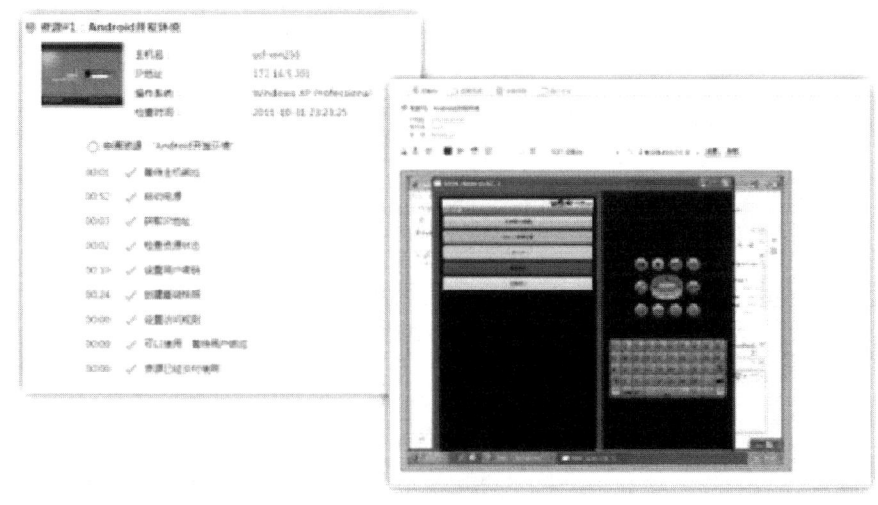

图 3　云计算平台虚拟计算资源使用界面

根据竞赛的需要，定制相应的管理，如表 1 所列，定制模板管理分为基础模板和应用模板。将不同的所需操作系统设置为基础模板，将所需开发环境定制为应用模板，包括 Android、AppleIOS、Windows Phone、J2ME、MTK、BlackBerry、Symbian。基于模板的资源申请仅需 2min，所申请资源即可交付用户使用。

表 1　模板管理

基础模板	Windows Template、Linux & Unix Template、Apple OS Template
应用模型	Android、Apple IOS、Windows Phone、J2ME、MTK、BlackBerry、Symbian

本届大赛覆盖"京、港、澳、台"地区，评审专家也来自这四个地区，采用集中式现场评审方式比较困难。大赛依托云计算平台，为评议环节提供跨区域网络评审服务，提高了效率，节约了成本。专家网络评审可以通过云计算平台查看每个参赛队在虚拟资源上部署的作品的运行情况及源代码，界面如图 4 所示。专家评审意见通过网页向组委会提交。

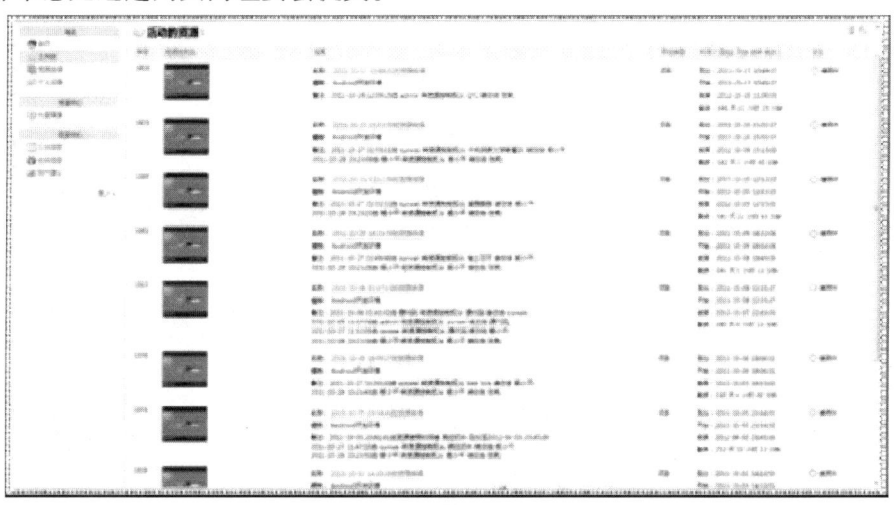

图 4　评审云平台界面

4　结束语

该平台是云计算技术在教育服务应用领域的成功落地，竞赛期间 99 个参赛作品部署在云端，参赛学生按需自主申请虚拟资源超过 400 次。统计数据及图表如下。

大赛期间（2011 年 6 月—2011 年 10 月）大赛平台虚拟资源共 439 次服务访问，如图 5 所示。

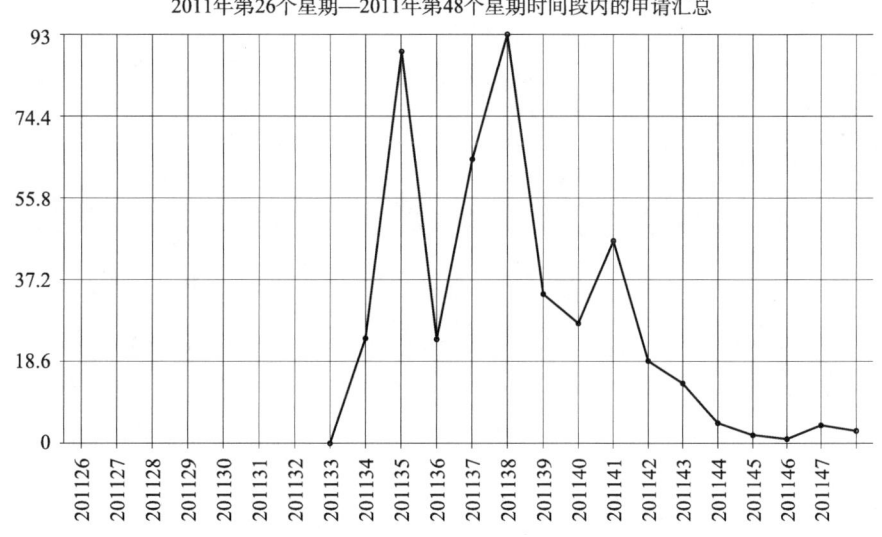

图 5　2011 年计算机应用大赛期间资源申请统计

该项目支撑平台从投入使用至今，接受超过712次用户自主资源申请，如图6所示。

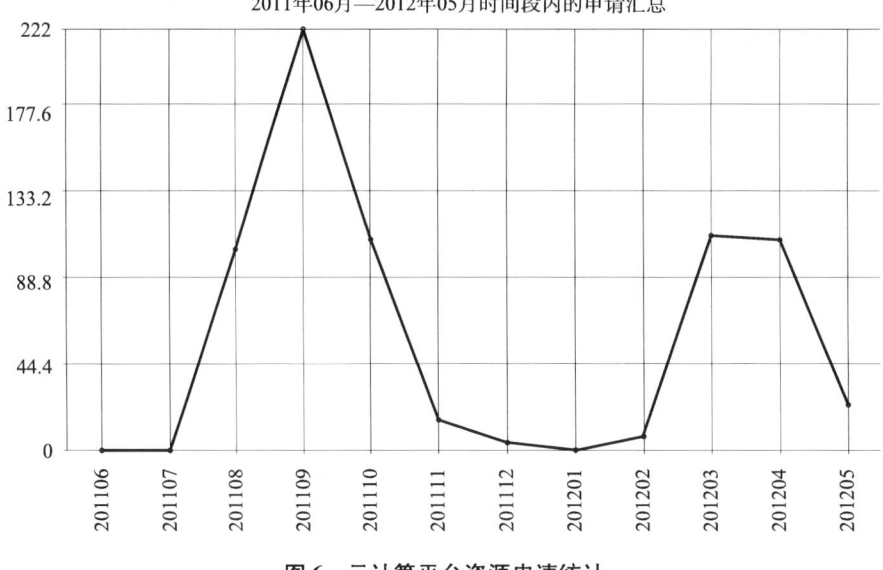

图 6 云计算平台资源申请统计

面向计算机应用竞赛的云平台通过负载均衡、模板定制等技术，通过互联网交付服务，为用户提供作品部署和评审接口。今后还将对平台应用进行进一步研究，以推进云计算在学科竞赛领域的服务应用。

参考文献

[1] Lei W Y, Zhu J Z. Cloud computing platform and case [M]. Beijing: Tsinghua University Publishing House, 2011: 7 - 13.

[2] Liu P. Cloud Computing [M]. 2nd ed. Beijing: Publishing House of Electronics Industry, 2011: 5 - 15.

[3] He Chen – liang, Shi Liang. The . ew Usage Model of PXE for Enterprise Based on Cloud and Virtualization [J]. Microcomputer Applications, 2011, 27 (12).

[4] Shi Yong – ge, Bian Fu – ling. The Study of Public Service for Remote Sensing Information Based on Cloud Platform [Z]. Geomatics World, 2011.

[5] Liu Yu. Research on Technology of Building Enterprise Private Cloud Platform [J]. Computer Era, 2011 (6).

[6] Liu Zhi – jia. A Research into Cloud – computing – based Load Balance Technology [J]. Journal of Guangxi Teachers Education University (Natural Science Edition), 2011 (2).

[7] Zhang Yun – yong, Chen Qing – jin, Pan Song – bai, et al. Key Security Technologies on Cloud Computing [J]. Telecommunications Science, 2011 (9).

Model Reference Adaptive Control Based on GANN for Vertical Electric Furnace

Li Hongxing   Kong Xiangling   Zhang Yinong

INTRODUCTION

The vertical electric furnace is a multi – variable control system. It is used to test the mechanical properties of the high temperature alloys with the aviation in the steel. The internal structure of the vertical electric furnace is shown as Fig. 1. According to the technical requirements, the test temperatures of different materials are not the same. Generally, the test temperature is in 100 to 980°C range. We demand that the test temperature stably rise from room temperature to the setting point and long – term stability in the settings and the errors are ±2°C.

The outside wall of the ceramic bushing in the vertical electric furnace is heated by the upper and the lower resistance wires. Then, the steel specimen and clamp in the centre of the ceramic bushing are heated by multi – thermodynamic process. Two outcrop sheathed thermocouples of K (EU – 2) type are installed two points that is away from 25 mm in the steel specimen surface. According to the technical requirements, the temperature error of the two points on the steel specimen surface must be less than ±4°C in 400 to 900°C range. This means the steel specimen has a small temperature gradient in the length of 25 mm, or there is a symmetrical temperature field.

The temperature of the vertical electric furnace is heated and kept by the resistance wires, but the drop in temperature depend on natural cooling. When the temperature of the vertical electric furnace has overshoots, it will not be able to use control method to cool. Thus, the vertical electric furnace only has a heating input control phase and large time delay yet. It is more difficult to control than two phase plant to obtain good control performance. Besides, the upper and the lower temperature regions of the vertical electric furnace exist in the characteristic of mutual coupling. In addition, the temperature control is non – linear, so it is very difficult to obtain satisfactory control effect by using the conventional control methods and estimate an appropriate dynamic model for model – based controller design. Especially, the temperature control problem with heating input only has time – delay and asymmetric control behavior. How to design a practical temperature controller with good response speed, smaller steady – state error and without overshoot for industrial implementation is still a challenge in the control research field.

Hornik *et al.* (1989) reported that Artificial Neural Networks (ANNs) have shown an excellent ability to model any nonlinear function to a desired degree of accuracy. Because of this property, they are suitable for the identification and control of nonlinear plants.

Genetic Algorithms (GAs) are a parallel global search technique that emulates natural genetic mechanics and biological evolution theory. Because they exploit strategies of genetic information and survival of the fittest to guide their search, it needs not calculate the gradient and assume that the search space is differentiable or continuous. Besides, they simultaneously evaluate many points in the parameter space, so it is more likely to converge toward the global solution. Genetic algorithms are very suitable for searching discrete, noisy, multimodal and complex space (Goldberg, 1989). They have been successfully applied to engineering in search and optimization problems because it has many remarkable features, which are reported by Goldberg (1989), Li *et al.*

[Author Introduction] Li Hongxin, Automation College of Beijing Union University; Kong Xiangling, Information College of Beijing Union University; Zhang Yinong, Information College of Beijing Union University.

(2005), Teng *et al.* (2003) and Sharma *et al.* (2005).

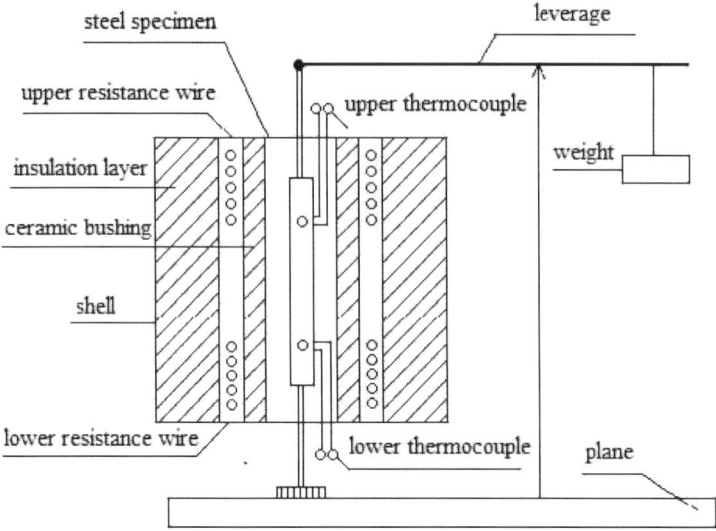

Fig. 1 The internal structure diagram of the vertical electric furnace

The hybrid control methods of the genetic algorithm and neural network are used for the complex system. In this study, the Model Reference Adaptive Control (MRAC) strategy is considered, due to its excellent robustness and stability (Wang *et al.*, 2003; Araz and Salum, 2010). The MRAC strategy based on ANN consists in training a network to learn the process dynamics of the vertical electric furnace. Another ANN is trained to learn the inverse dynamics so that it can be used as a nonlinear controller.

In general the inversion of nonlinear models is not an easy task and analytical solutions may not exist, so solutions have to be found numerically. One important point is that the inversion of the process model may lead to unstable controllers when the plant has unstable zeros.

In this study, the Back – Propagation (BP) neural network is used to identify the model and inverse model of the vertical electric furnace. The power of the BP network has been demonstrated by a number of workers and research has indicated that a BP neural network has the potential to approximate any continuous nonlinear function with arbitrary accuracy, provided that there are enough hidden neurons. In order to overcome the disadvantage of BP algorithm, the improved genetic algorithm is used to train the neural network and present an interesting alternative to optimize the weight and threshold of BP structure. It is very efficient that the genetic algorithms are used to train the NN (Sharma et al., 2005). Based on the model and inverse model of the neural network, an effective MRAC method is proposed for the temperature control of the vertical electric furnace.

NEURAL NETWORK MODELLING

The NN modeling for the vertical electric furnace: Artificial neural networks have been increasingly used in many aspects of controlling and modelling in the industry (Hsu et *al.*, 2005). The traditional use of neural network modelling is a black – box approach; i.e., a neural network is trained on the available process data. However, in the real world, quite often the available process data are not sufficient to develop a good neural network model. The main difficulties arise from lack of excitation in the training data, uneven distribution of the data samples, significant noise in the modeling data, etc. They will result in the inaccurate neural network model and the not converged process of learning algorithm.

A normal network contents input layer, hidden layer, output layer, the hidden layer may not be only one. In BP network the output of every nodes in one layer only affect the output of the next layer. The nodes of different layers are connected by the weights.

The BP NN is trained to learn the dynamics of the temperature of the vertical electric furnace using the genetic algorithm, as shown in Fig. 2.

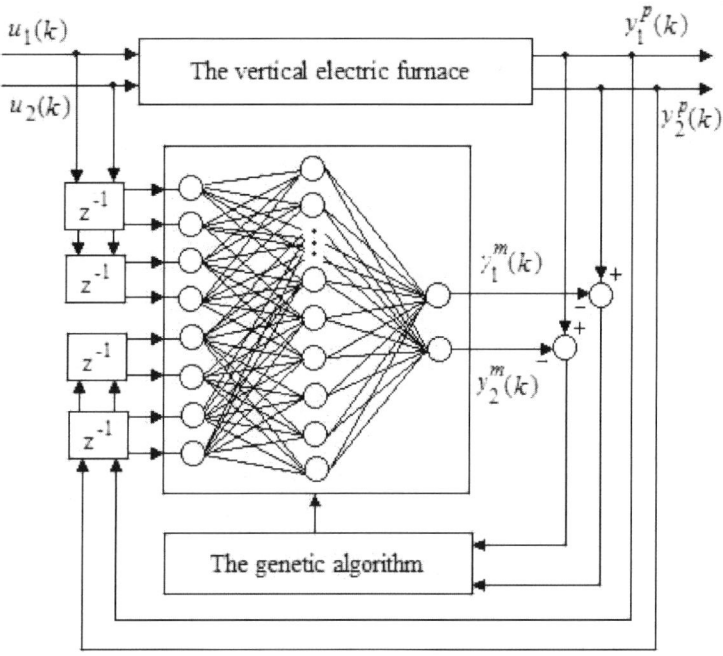

Fig. 2 BP NN is trained to learn the dynamics of the vertical electric furnace

The output of the neural network is denoted by:

$$y_k^m(x) = \sum_{j=0}^{m} f(\sum_{i=0}^{n} x_i w_{ji}) v_{kj} \qquad (1)$$
$$= \sum_{j=1}^{m} f(\sum_{j=1}^{n} x_i w_{ji} + w_{j0}) v_{kj} + v_{k0}, k = 1, \cdots, l$$

where, w_{ji} and vkj are the input – hidden weight and hidden – output weight respectively and f is activation function that it is used in the hidden layer and the output layer, as follows:

$$f_{ij}(x) = \frac{e^x - e^{-x}}{e^x + e^{-x}} \qquad (2)$$

In the training scheme of the neural network, the determination of parameters usually involves the minimization of an error function that, typically, is the Mean Squared Error (MSE) between the actual outputs and the targets for the whole training set. For a multi – output system, MSE is calculated using all the training examples over each network output, denoted by:

$$MSE = \frac{1}{nl}\sum_{i=1}^{n}\sum_{1}^{l}(y_{ij}^p - y_{ij}^m) \qquad (3)$$

where,

l, n = The number of NN outputs and the number of training data respectively

y_{ij}^p = The actual output of the vertical electric furnace

y_{ij}^m = The output of NN model

Since GA is usually applied to maximize a fitness function, a transformation is required to convert the error function into a suitable fitness function. A common method for this purpose is given by:

$$f = \frac{1}{MSE + a} \qquad (4)$$

where, a is a small positive constant ($0 < a < 1$) that is used to avoid dividing by zero. Thus, f can now be treated as the absolute fitness function of the genetic algorithm.

The parameter vector θ of the genetic algorithm is described as:

$$\theta[W, V] \qquad (5)$$

where,

$W = (W_{ij})^T$ ($i=1, \cdots, 8, j=1, \cdots, 16$) is the weights between input layer and hidden layer

$V = (v_{ij})^T$ ($i=1, \cdots, 16, j=1, 2$) is the weights between hidden layer and output layer

Each real parameter of the vector θ needs to be given a specified interval $[\theta_{jmin}, \theta_{jmax}]$ so that the L_j-bit substring of the binary code is interpreted as the binary integer on the interval $[0, 2^{L_j}]$ and this integer can be mapped to this interval according to the following:

$$\theta_j = \theta_{jmin} + \frac{binrep}{2^{L_j}-1}(\theta_{jmax} - \theta_{jmin}) \qquad (6)$$

where,

$binrep$ = The integer value represented by an L_j-bit string, θ_j = j^{th} real parameter of the vector θ

In this study, the reproduction is implemented using stochastic remainder without replacement. Expected string count values are calculated as $NF_i / \sum_{i=1}^{N} F_i$ and integer parts are assigned the reproduction numbers of the strings and the fractional parts of the expected number values are treated as probabilities. One by one, whether the fractional parts will be able to reproduce one string is decided by the stochastic probability. This process continues until the population is full.

An effective method of adaptive probabilities of crossover and mutation is used in the study. In this method, the crossover probability P_c and the mutation probability P_m are varied with the fitness values of the solution. Therefore, low values of P_c and P_m are assigned to high fitness solutions, while low fitness solutions have very high values of P_c and P_m. The method can maintain diversity in the population and sustain the convergence capacity of the GA. The expressions for P_c and P_m are given as:

$$P_c \begin{cases} k_1 (f_{max} - f') / (f_{max} - \bar{f}), & f' \geq \bar{f} \\ k_2, & f' < \bar{f} \end{cases} \qquad (7)$$

and

$$P_m = \begin{cases} k_3 (f_{max} - f) / (f_{max} - \bar{f}), & f \geq \bar{f} \\ k_4, & f < \bar{f} \end{cases} \qquad (8)$$

where, $k_1, k_2, k_3, k_4 \leq 1.0$, f_{max} is the maximum fitness value, $\bar{f}$ is the average fitness value, f' is the largest of the fitness values in the two stings to be crossed and f is the fitness value of the string to be mutated.

The procedure of the NN model training by the GA is described as Fig. 3.

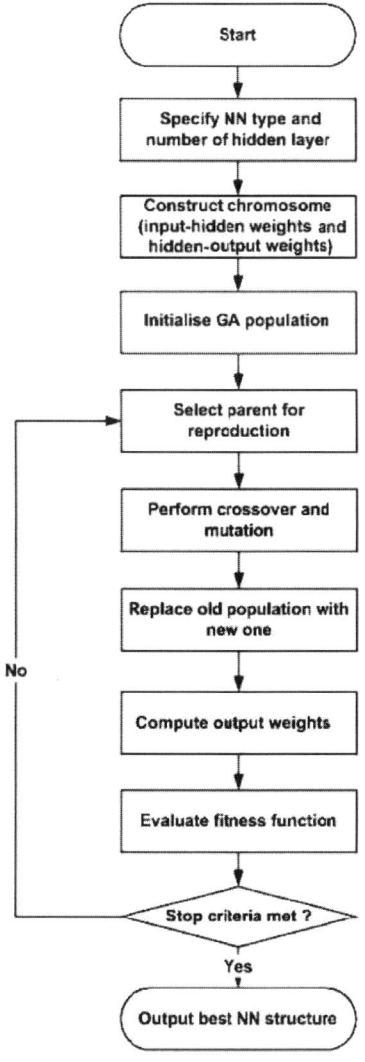

Fig. 3 Flowchart of neural network training by the GA

SIMULATION RESULTS

Once the model structure has been defined, the next step is to train this particular NN by the proposed method. In experiment, the data of inputs and outputs are acquired from the actual temperature of the vertical electric furnace, i.e., gather once data from the two inputs and outputs every 10 sec, collected a total of 5 sets of data, each consisting of 720 data. After they are pretreated, the two sets of data are selected, which one set of data is used to train the NN, another is employed to enhance its generalization capabilities. Our method can automatically choose the best weights and thresholds for each generation. We set the initial weights between -1 and 1. The goal of error is 0.001, learning rate is 0.005 and the largest training time is 3000.

The genetic parameters for the NN model training are chosen as follows:

Population size N = 80

Coefficients of crossover probability $k_1 = 0.9$ and $k_2 = 1.0$

Coefficients of mutation probability $k_3 = 0.02$ and $k_4 = 0.1$

After the NN model training algorithm is implemented, the error curve is obtained in the Fig. 4, the dotted line is shown as the error – goal and the solid line is shown as error – trained. From the Fig. 4, we can see that about 1024 epochs the sum – squared error reached error – goal.

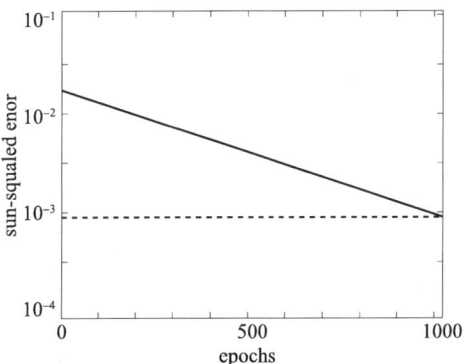

Fig. 4 Error curve of the NN model

In the Fig. 5 and 6, ' – o – ' stands for the actual temperature of the vertical electric furnace, ' – * – ' stands for the model output. It is clearly seen that the NN model obtained by the proposed method produces a good approximation to temperature of the vertical electric furnace, the MES is 0.00019.

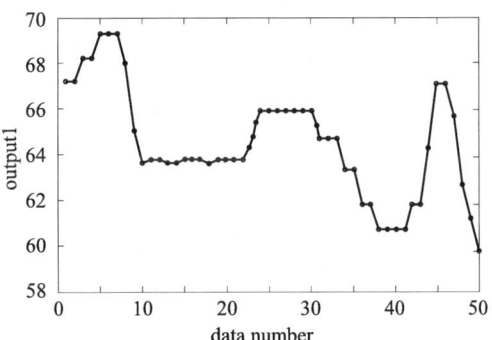

Fig. 5 Actual output 1 versus model output 1

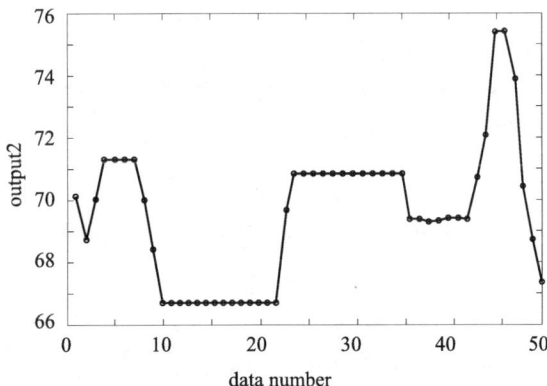

Fig. 6 Actual output 2 versus model output 2

The inverse NN modelling for the vertical electric furnace: In the model reference adaptive control strategy, another ANN needs to be trained to learn the inverse dynamics of the vertical electric furnace so that it can be used as a nonlinear controller.

The BP NN is trained to learn the inverse dynamics of the vertical electric furnace using the genetic algorithm, as shown in Fig. 7.

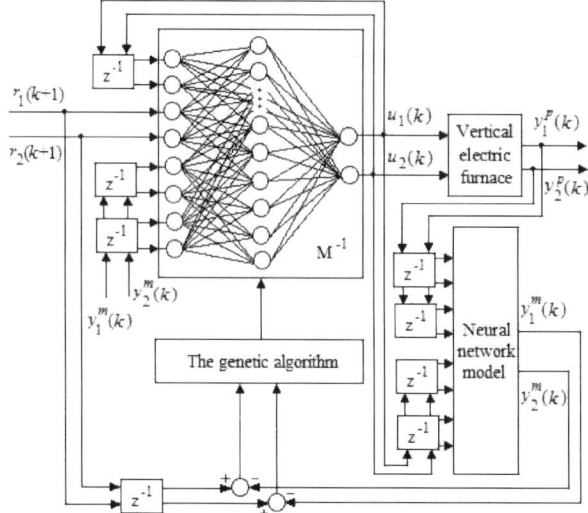

Fig. 7 BP NN is trained to learn the inverse dynamics of the vertical electric furnace

The output of the neural network for the inverse model is denoted by:

$$u_k(x) = \sum_{j=0}^{m} f\left(\sum_{i=0}^{n} x_i w_{ji}\right) v_{kj}$$
$$= \sum_{j=0}^{m} f\left(\sum_{i=1}^{n} x_i w_{ji} + w_{j0}\right) v_{kj} + v_{k0}, k = 1, \cdots, l \quad (9)$$

The input vector of the neural network is denoted by:

$$\begin{aligned} X(k) & \; y_1^m(k), \cdots, y_1^m(k-n), r_1(k+1)] \\ & u_1(k-1), \cdots, u_1(k-m), \\ & y_2^m(k), \cdots, y_2^m(k), r_2(k+1), \\ & u_2(k-1), \cdots u_2(k-m)]^T \end{aligned} \quad (10)$$

where $r_t(k+1)$ ($t=1, 2$) is the input of the controller, replace with $y_t^m(k+1)$ because it can be not measured in the actual plant.

The other parameters are the same with the aforementioned those. The NN inverse model is trained by using the proposed genetic algorithm.

After the NN model training algorithm is implemented, the error curve of the inverse model is obtained in the Fig. 8, the dotted line is shown as the error – goal and the solid line is shown as error – trained. From the Fig. 8, we can see that about 5160 epochs the sum – squared error reached error – goal. It is clearly seen that training time of the NN inverse model needs longer by the proposed method.

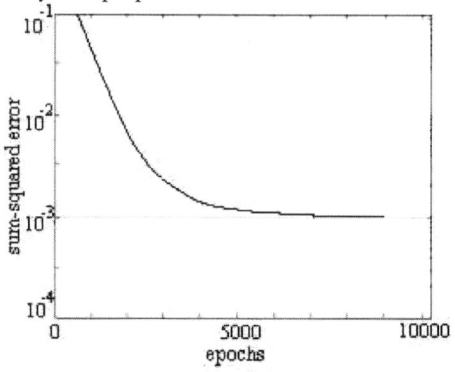

Fig. 8 Error curve of the NN inverse model

THE MODEL REFERENCE ADAPTIVE CONTROL

The model and the inverse model using the neural network have been identified by above section. A model reference adaptive control based on the GA – NN is presented in this study.

MRAC for temperature of vertical electric furnace: In the MRAC strategy, the model of the neural network is used as the estimator of the vertical electric furnace and the inverse model is employed as the controller. The configuration of MRAC for the temperature control the vertical electric furnace is shown as Fig. 9. The d is disturbance of the system. The reference model is selected as:

$$y_m(k+1) = ay_m(k) + r(k) \tag{11}$$

where, a is constant.

In Fig. 9, $y_1(k)$, $y_2(k)$, $u_1(k)$ and $u_2(k)$ are the two output and input of the vertical electric furnace respectively. $r_1(k)$ and $r_2(k)$ are the input of the control system.

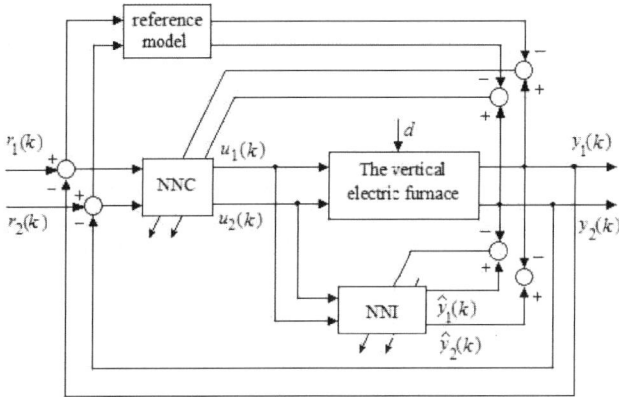

Fig. 9 The configuration of MRAC for the vertical electric furnace

Simulation result: The traditional PID control is employed in order to compare with the proposed method MRAC in the study. In all disturbances d = 0, the parameter of the reference model is selected as a = 0.56. The input of the temperature is 500℃, a plot of the response of the system appears in Fig. 10. The green line and purple line are the output of the MRAC, which they denote the upper and the lower temperature regions of the vertical electric furnace respectively. The red line and blue line are the output of the PID control. It is clearly seen that the transient and steady – state response of the system has the advantage of the MRAC method over the traditional PID control. Thus, the response parameters of the system, as the overshoot, the settling time and the steady – state value is very satisfied. We now consider that the system has disturbance. Assume that the disturbance signal d is 10% of the system input, i.e., d = 60, the plot of the response of the system is shown in Fig. 11. It is clearly seen that the MRAC system proposed has a good capability of resisting disturbance.

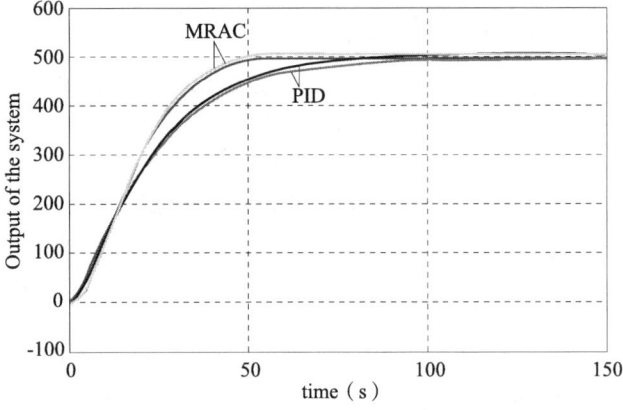

Fig. 10 The response of the temperature control system

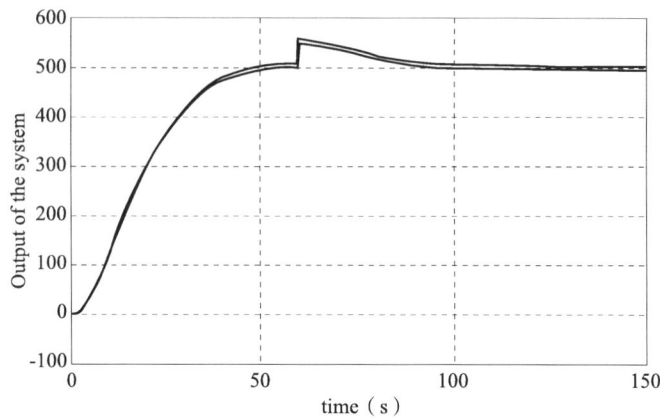

Fig. 11　The response of the MRAC under the disturbance signal d = 60

When the parameters of the temperature model of the vertical electric furnace is increased by 25%, the response of the system of the two control methods is shown in Fig. 12. After the parameters of the temperature model of the vertical electric furnace is decreased by 25%, the response of the system of the two control methods is shown in Fig. 13. It is clearly seen that the MRAC is robust.

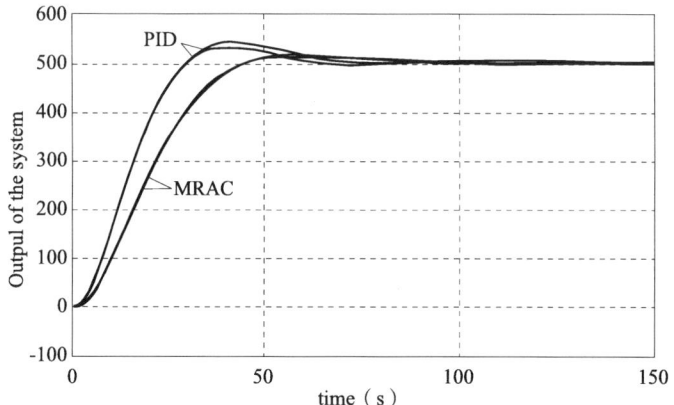

Fig. 12　The response of the system in parameters of the vertical electric furnace is increased by 25%

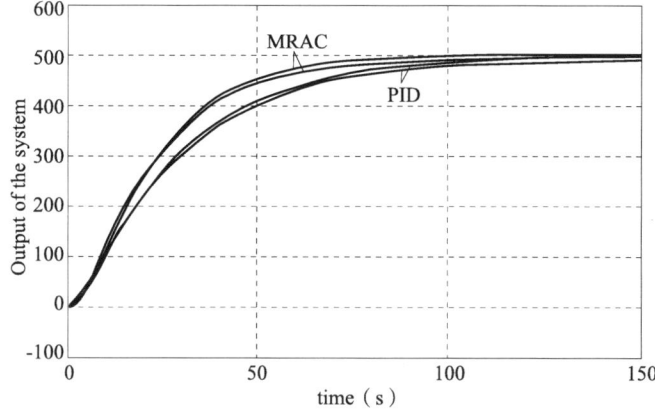

Fig. 13　The response of the system in parameters of the vertical electric furnace is decreased by 25%

CONCLUSION

The temperature of the vertical electric furnace is strongly coupled and disturbed, nonlinear and slow time – variant. It is difficult to control the temperature of the vertical electric furnace with conventional methods. The model reference adaptive control strategy based on the GA and NN is considered to control the temperature of the vertical electric furnace in this study. The model of the neural network of the system is identified. Another NN is trained to learn the inverse dynamics of the system. In order to overcome the disadvantage of BP learning algorithm, the genetic algorithm is used to train the neural networks to learn the dynamics and inverse dynamics of the system. The simulation results show that the method proposed for controlling the temperature of the vertical electric furnace is effective.

ACKNOWLEDGMENT

This study was supported by the project of science and technology development plan of Beijing Municipal Commission of Education under Grant KM201111417011, Beijing, China.

REFERENCES

[1] Araz, O. U. and L. Salum. A multi-criteria adaptive control scheme based on neural networks and fuzzy inference for DRC manufacturing systems [J]. Int. J. Prod. Res., 2010, 48 (1): 251-270.

[2] Goldberg, D. E. Genetic Algorithms in Search, Optimization and Machine Learning. Addison-Wesley, Reading, Massachusetts, 1989.

[3] Hornik, K., M. Stincheombe and H. White. Multilayer feed forward networks are universal approximators [J]. Neural Networks, 1989 (2): 359-366.

[4] Hsu, C. F., C. M. Lin and T. Y. Chen. Neural network identification based adaptive control of wing rock motions [J]. IEE P-Contr. Theor. Ap., 2005, 152 (1): 65-71.

[5] Li, H. X., J. S. Lu and H. S. Yan. Model reduction using the genetic algorithm and Routh approximations [J]. J. Syst. Eng. Electr., 2005, 16 (3): 632-639.

[6] Sharma, S. K., S. F. McLoone and G. W. Irwin Genetic algorithms for local controller network construction [J]. IEE P-Contr. Theor. Ap., 2005, 152 (5): 587-597.

[7] Teng, T. K., J. S. Shieh and C. S. Chen. Genetic algorithm applied in online autotuning PID parameters of a liquid-level control system [J]. T. I. Meas. Control, 2003, 25 (5): 433-450.

[8] Wang, X. S., H. Hong and C. Y. Su. Model reference adaptive control of continuous-time systems with an unknown input dead-zone [J]. IEE P-Contr. Theor. Ap., 2003, 150 (3): 261-266.

基于路由功能的 BACnet/Modbus 协议转换器设计

李春旺　孙育英　吴义民　施　方

引　言

BACnet 协议是楼宇自控网络协议领域的唯一 ISO 标准（ISO 16484-5），几十家著名公司开发了相关产品，在工程中得到广泛应用[1]。Modbus 通信协议作为规范工业自动化网络协议的国家标准之一，成为楼宇机电设备控制器和测控仪表串行通信接口的常规配置。传统 BACnet/Modbus 网关的设计思路是在 BACnet 和 Modbus 两种通信协议之间通过数据共享来实现数据交换，即 Modbus 通过轮询方式获取数据后暂存在数据共享区，当 BACnet 发出请求时，直接从数据共享区读取数据并进行相应的解析和封装处理，保证 BACnet 和 Modbus 协议的正确映射[2]。但这种方式存在两个问题：①软、硬件资源占用大，真正需求数据的实时转换效率不高；②从 BACnet 软件或硬件环境中，无法直接识别 Modbus 侧设备，导致 Modbus 设备管理产生盲区。针对以上问题，笔者研制了一种具有路由定向功能的 BACnet/Modbus 协议转换器，可以实现 Modbus 设备与 BACnet 软件或硬件之间的数据透明传输，并将 Modbus 设备封装成 BACnet 设备，可直接支持各种 BACnet 软件或硬件对 Modbus 设备进行的管理和操作功能，实现了真正意义的无缝集成。

1　BACnet Ethernet 与 Modbus 报文

1.1　BACnet Ethernet 报文结构[3]

BACnet 协议具有应用层、网络层、数据链路层和物理层 4 层架构。在数据链路层和物理层提供 5 种选择，其中以太网选择之一是由 ISO 8802 Type1 定义的逻辑连接控制协议、媒体访问控制 MAC 和物理层协议组合在一起。ISO 8802 Ethernet 协议的报文比 IP 通信协议报文短，通信效率较高，可以避开使用 IP 地址技术的一些弊端，是路由器、网关以太网端口的通信协议首选。图 1 所示的 BACnet Ethernet 通信协议报文由 6 个部分构成：应用层协议数据单元（APDU），网络层协议控制信息（NPDU），数据链路层数据单元（LPDU），逻辑链路控制（LLC），X82X82X03 是服务访问点信息，物理层报文负责具体硬件收发字节内容。

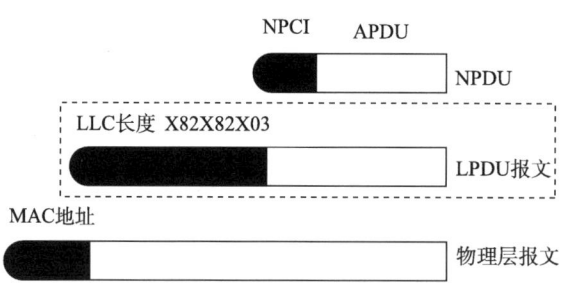

图 1　BACnet Ethernet 通信协议的报文结构

1.2　Modbus 报文结构

标准的 Modbus 网络通信可以设置成 ASCII 或 RTU 两种传输模式。Modbus 报文结构包括设备地址、功能代码、所要发送的数据和错误检测域。Modbus 通信使用主从方式，即主设备能发送查询报文帧进行

［基金项目］北京市科技发展计划资助项目（KM201011417014）。

［作者简介］李春旺（1972—），男，北京联合大学副教授，硕士，主要研究方向为建筑设备自动化；孙育英，北京工业大学；吴义民，北京联合大学；施方，北京施能通智能科技开发有限公司。

查询，从设备根据主设备查询提供的数据发送回应报文帧作出反应。查询报文帧中的功能代码告之被选中的从设备要执行何种功能，数据段包含了从设备要执行功能的任何附加信息，错误检测域为从设备提供了一种验证消息内容是否正确的方法[4]。如果从设备产生正常的回应，在回应报文帧中的功能代码是在查询消息中的功能代码的回应，数据段包括了从设备收集的数据，如寄存器值或状态，如果有错误发生，功能代码将被修改以用于指出回应报文是错误的，同时数据段包含了描述此错误信息的代码。错误检测域允许主设备确认消息内容是否可用。

2 基于 BACnet 路由功能的报文转换方法

2.1 BACnet Ethernet 报文转化为 Modbus 报文的解析和封装

图 2 为 BACnet Ethernet 报文转化为 Modbus 报文的过程。如图 2 所示，BACnet NPDU 报文中的 NPCI 存放的是 Modbus 设备地址，当 BACnet 软件或 BACnet 以太网设备发出 BACnet NPDU 报文时，直接将 Modbus 设备地址解析出来，传递给处理 Modbus 设备通信协议的任务中，Modbus 设备通信处理任务的下一次指令则直接针对这个地址的 Modbus 设备进行主从查询，即发出对这个地址的 Modbus 设备的查询指令字节。

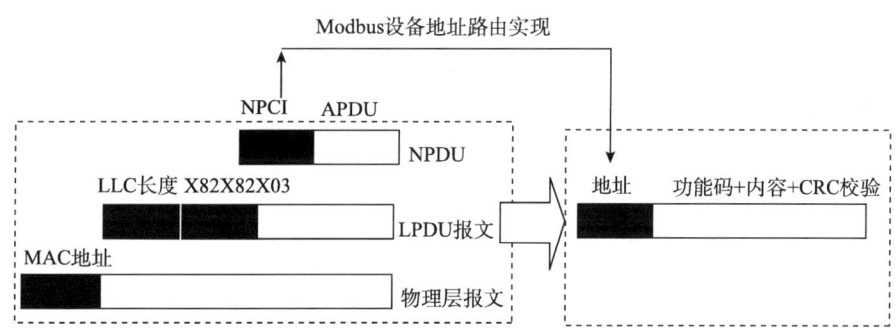

图 2　BACnet Ethernet 报文转化为 Modbus 报文的过程

2.2 Modbus 报文转化为 BACnet Ethernet 报文的解析和封装

如图 3 所示，将 Modbus 设备回复的应答数据报文中的 Modbus 设备地址直接解析出来，传递给处理 BACnet 设备通信协议的任务中，其下一次任务执行则回复给查询软件或其他以太网设备所查询的Modbus 设备的地址及数据内容。

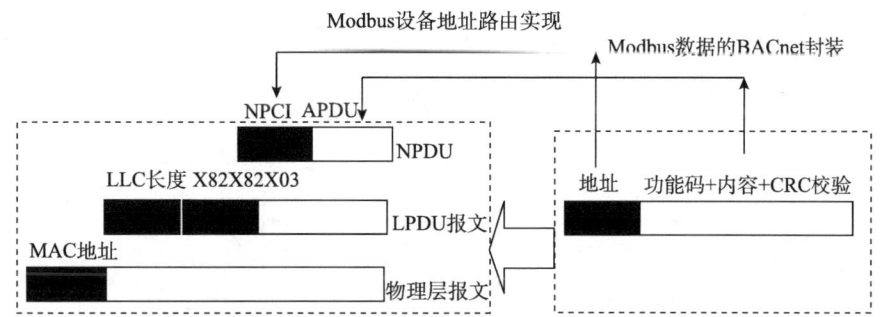

图 3　Modbus 报文转化为 BACnet Ethernet 报文的转化过程

2.3 BACnet 路由功能的实现

2.3.1 BACnet "I am" 响应功能

当转换器收到 BACnet 软件或其他 BACnet 以太网设备发出的 BACnet 对象 "Who is" 查询指令时，转换器根据已经在线 Modbus 设备的地址，为每个 Modbus 设备自动分配生成 BACnet 通信协议必需的器件编号。例如，假设 Modbus 设备所在的 RS485 通信网络被定义为 BACnet 通信网络，网络编号为 61，则硬件地址为 1 的 Modbus 设备的 BACnet 器件编号为 6101，硬件地址为 2 的 Modbus 设备的 BACnet 器件编号为 6102，……，以此类推，将每个在线的 Modbus 设备均分配一个独立的 BACnet 通信时惟一辨识的编号，完成了 Modbus 设备的 BACnet 封装的基本条件准备。然后，就在 Modbus 设备地址的前后封装网络编号和其器件编号，组成标准的 BACnet 报文，并向 BACnet 软件或其他 BACnet 以太网设备发回“I am”回应报文。如图 4 所示。

"1, 0x28, 0xff, 0xff, 0, 0, 0x3d, 1, 1, 0xfe, 0x10, 0, 0xc4, 2, 0, 0x2, 0x17, 0xd5, 1, 0x0, 0x91, 3, 0x21, 0xff"
网络编号 61
Modbus 地址
器件编号6101

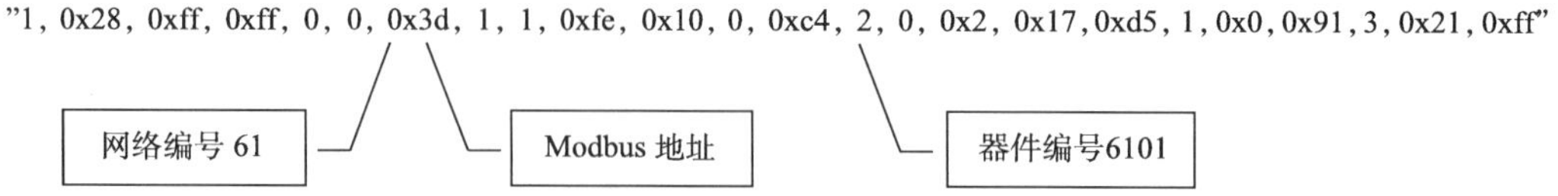

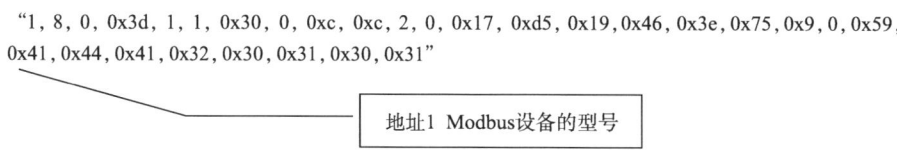

图 4 “I am”响应报文结构举例

2.3.2 BACnet“Read”响应功能

当 BACnet 软件或其他 BACnet 以太网设备收到转换器发出的“I am”回应报文后，发出查询该 Modbus设备型号、数据等信息的 BACnet 报文。当转换器收到该报文时，将报文中的 NPCI 网络报文头部中的 Modbus 设备地址信息解析出来，立即启动 Modbus 侧的查询任务，将查询该地址设备相关信息的 Modbus 报文发送出去。当收到查询结果时，封装为 BACnet 报文进行回复，实现对 BACnet 的“Read”响应功能。当转换器收到查询地址 1 Modbus 设备型号的报文时，回复的响应报文，如图 5 所示。

"1, 8, 0, 0x3d, 1, 1, 0x30, 0, 0xc, 0xc, 2, 0, 0x17, 0xd5, 0x19, 0x46, 0x3e, 0x75, 0x9, 0, 0x59, 0x41, 0x44, 0x41, 0x32, 0x30, 0x31, 0x30, 0x31"
地址1 Modbus设备的型号

图 5 “Read”响应报文结构举例

3 协议转换器的设计与实现

3.1 协议转换器的硬件设计

图 6 所示电路包括控制单元、以太网接口、串行接口和系统电源。控制单元采用 TI 的微控制器 Lm3s6911 + 实现，用于路由定向、Modbus 与 BAC - netEthernet 报文的双向解析和封装。在通信方面，Lm3s6911 + 有 3 个可编程的 UART，2 个同步串行接口 SSI 和可编程 MAC 地址的 10/100MHz 以太网控制器。其中 2 个同步串口作为 Modbus 的通信端口，MAX485CPA 芯片分别与 Lm3s6911 + 的 PA2 和 PA3 引脚连接，用于接收和发送封装好的 Modbus 网络数据。100MHz 以太网接口作为 BACnetEthernet 通信端口。本设计中，系统电源提供标准 5V 和 3.3V 两种电压，5V 用于给接口电路供电，3.3V 用于给控制单元供电，再通过 Lm3s6911 + 中可编程片内低压差稳压器调整到 2.75V 以满足芯片的要求。

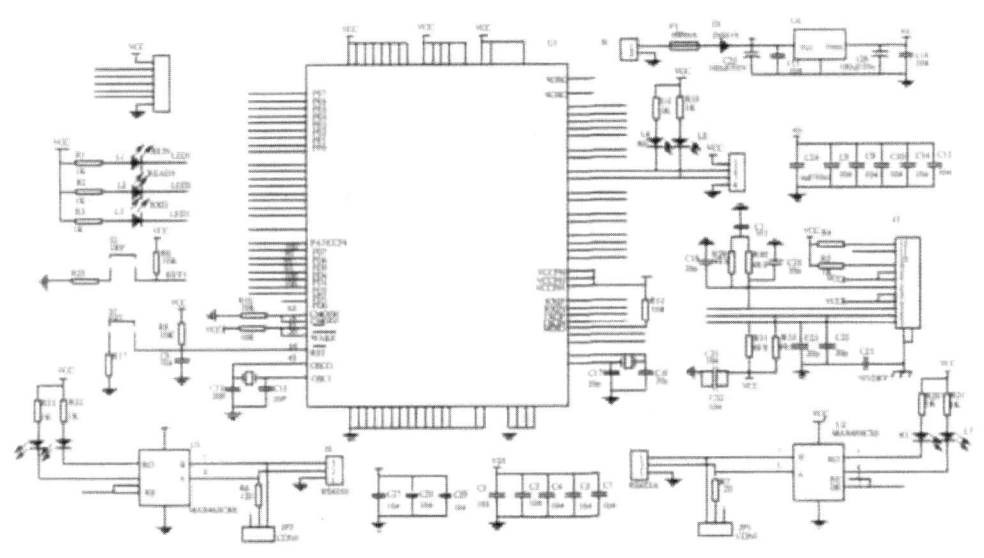

图 6 硬件电路原理图

3.2 协议转换器软件设计

转换器软件为 BACnet 和 Modbus 通信协议的实现各分配一个独立任务，在两个任务之间建立路由关系，传递 Modbus 设备的通信协议地址和数据内容。为实现多任务功能，软件系统架构采用免费开源的嵌入式操作系统 ucOSII，具有小巧、可裁减、实时的特点[5-6]。将 ucOSII 移植到 Lm3s6911 + 微控制器上，并根据转换器的需要对其内核进行配置，连同用 ANSIC 编写的应用程序一同编译下载到控制单元，实现了可同时侦听和处理 BACnet Ethernet 通信协议帧和 Modbus 通信协议帧的功能。

转换器 Modbus 侧的任务要同步跟随 BACnet 侧的需求，当 BACnet 侧查询某个地址的 Modbus 设备信息时，转换器的路由功能则惟一定向在这个地址上，启动 Modbus 侧的查询任务，并将查询结果 BACnet 封装后返回 BACnet 侧。为了实现上述任务的协同工作，转换器在软件设计上采用了"消息"机制，即在 BACnet 和 Modbus 通信协议处理任务中分别建立了"消息"标记，用来同步 BACnet 报文中的 NPCI 段和 Modbus 报文地址段，及 BACnet 报文的 APDU 段和 Modbus 报文数据段的相关信息。

需要注意的是，为了提高通信效率，转换器需要每次 Modbus 查询能回复该 Modbus 设备的全部寄存器表数据，因此 Modbus 设备必须支持批读查询指令，而且能够提供寄存器表内的全部数据值的固定格式，以便于解析封装为对应的 BACnet 点位 AV 或 BV 值。

4 实验测试

4.1 Modbus 设备封装为 BACnet 设备测试

传统的 BACnet/Modbus 网关，在 BACnet 软件环境下只能显示该网关及其全部已经完成数据共享的 Modbus 数据，而无法看到每个 Modbus 设备的状态。笔者采用带 Modbus 通信接口的 YD2010 数字电表作为 Modbus 设备，典型的 Navigator 楼宇自动化组态软件作为 BACnet 设备。如图 7 所示，新型协议转换器直接将 Modbus 设备封装为具有 BACnet 对象属性的 BACnet 设备，Navigator 软件将 YD2010 数字电表等同于 BACnet DDC 设备进行管理，并正常显示了读取的全部数据。

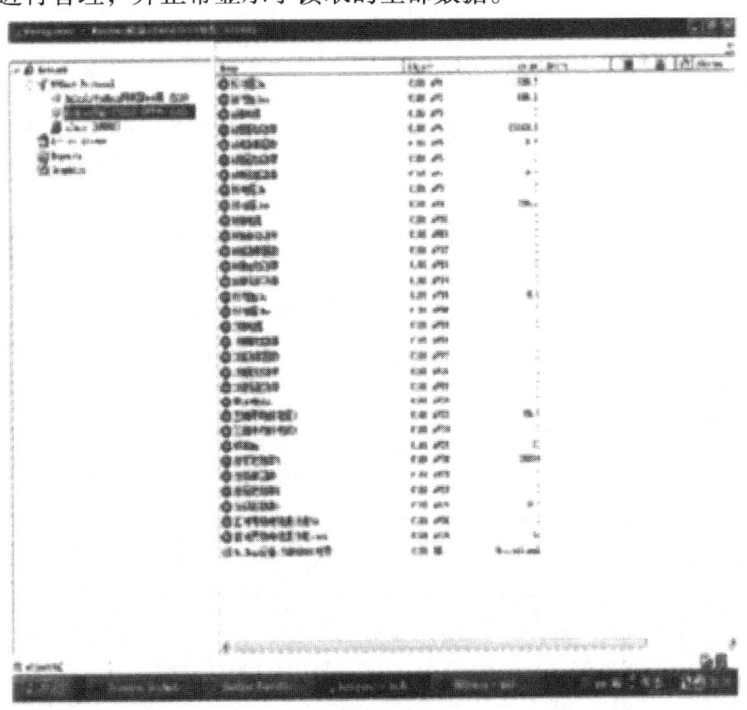

图 7 Modbus 设备封装为 BACnet 设备测试

4.2 实时性测试分析

基于路由功能的 BACnet/Modbus 转换器，通过路由功能直接根据 Modbus 设备地址进行地址定向查询，无须将资源浪费在没有查询需求的 Modbus 设备数据上，保证了 BACnet 设备读取的均为实时值。图 8 为采用逻辑分析仪对查询 - 响应速度测试的结果，白色数据块为电表回复字节信息，可以看出回复内容本身需要 100ms 左右的发送时间。白色数据块之间的黑色间隔时间长度加上白色数据块的时间长度则为软件发送查询命令的间隔时间，约为 200ms 左右，达到了每秒钟查询 5 块 Modbus 电表内的所有电量值的速度。若采用传统的 BACnet/Modbus 网关，则无法保证实时性和效率。以集成 30 个联网的 Modbus 数字电表为例，每秒钟顺序查询 5 个 Modbus 电表内所有数据，则需要 6s 完成网关内数据共享区的所有数据更新，从而导致 BACnet 设备通过网关读取的 Modbus 电表数据已经滞后实时值 6s，还未必都是 BACnet 侧所需查询数据。

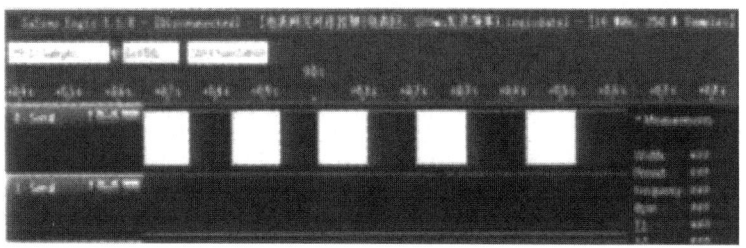

图 8　逻辑分析仪显示的 Modbus 设备回复字节信息

5　结　论

采用嵌入式技术实现基于路由功能的 BAC – net/Modbus 转换器，直接将 Modbus 设备封装为具有 BACnet 对象属性的 BACnet 设备，可以利用现有的各种 BACnet 软件进行管理和操作，弥补了传统 Modbus 网关管理不透明的缺陷，提高了实时性，方便了在 BACnet 环境中 Modbus 设备的调试和维护，提高了系统集成的价值。

参考文献

[1] 董春桥，刘贤德，惠晓实．楼宇自动控制网络通信协议 BACnet 实现模型的研究 [J]．计算机工程与应用 2003，39 (5)：172 – 174．
[2] 廖方诚，周祖德．基于 BACnet 和 Modbus 协议转换器的设计 [J]．武汉理工大学学报．2009，31 (23)：89 – 91．
[3] ANSI/ASHARE Standard, BACnet – A Da – ta Communication Protocol for Building Automation and Control Networks, USA, 2001.
[4] 线岩团，许江淳，鄢大鹏．基于单片机的 MODBUS 的协议实现 [J]．云南大学学报：自然科学版．2009，31 (S2)：120 – 124．
[5] 张桂，金国强，李辉．基于 ARM 平台 Modbus RTU 协议的研究与实现 [J]．电力科学与工程，2011，27 (1)：23 – 27．
[6] 邵贝贝．嵌入式实时操作系统 ucOSII [M]．北京：北京航空航天大学出版社，2006．

基于现场总线的双容液位模糊控制系统设计

李 微 邵志勇 李 媛

1 系统概述

现场总线是用于现场仪表与控制主机系统之间的一种开放的、全数字化的、双向和多站的通信系统。它由三层组成，即现场级、控制级和监控级。本系统控制级与监控级之间由工业以太网进行通信，控制级与现场级采用 Profibus – DP 进行通信。在 PC 上通过 STEP7 软件组态、编程下载到 S7 – 300 PLC 中，PLC 根据编写的指令进行相应的控制；同时通过 WINCC 软件的监控界面监视现场状态，并将现场级的信号进行显示、保存。现场总线系统以其强大的功能及可靠性高等特点在过程控制、楼宇自动化、飞机制造、车辆制造等行业都有广泛的应用。

系统以 QXLTT 三容液位控制实验装置为被控对象，它具有多输入和多输出的非线性耦合物理模型。实验装置的主体是由用透明的有机玻璃制成的三个圆形容器罐和一个蓄水池，并配以相应的执行机构和传感器组成，即由 2 个水泵 P1 和 P2，6 个手动阀 V1～V6，2 个 PWM（脉宽调制）型线性比例调节阀 V7 和 V8，3 个反压式液位传感器 LT1、LT2 和 LT3，以及两个旁路阀 V9、V10 组成。本实验装置可以实现单容、双容和三容水箱液位控制，与现场的实际控制装置具有相同的工作原理，可以为实际装置的控制提供仿真实验和验证。

本系统是双容液位控制系统，以 2#容器即 T2 的液位为被控参数，调节阀 V7 是执行机构，采用现场总线控制器形成单回路控制系统，系统结构如图 1 所示。

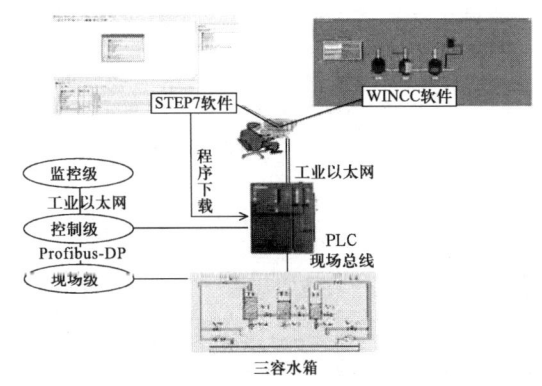

图 1 现场总线系统

2 控制算法

2.1 PID 控制算法

对于温度、压力、流量和液位的控制是属于慢变过程的控制，在工业生产中经常采用 PID 控制，即通过调试 PID 的比例、积分和微分 3 个参数来改变被控量的变化速度、消除误差和减小振荡。PID 控制器进行控制是将给定值与实际值进行比较，将误差最终减小为零，并且要求调节的速度要快、准、稳。但这三个条件之间是相互矛盾的，要使系统调节得快，就要降低稳定的性能，会产生一些振荡；反之，要使系统稳定的调节，在速度上就不可能有很高的要求，调节时间也要加长。在实际工程中，许多系统

[基金项目] 北京联合大学校级科研项目资助（zk200920x）；北京联合大学 2011 年学生科技立项项目（北京市级项目）资助（12222993101）。

[作者简介] 李微（1988—），女，研究方向为智能控制网络技术；邵志勇，李媛，北京联合大学自动化学院。

和过程都十分复杂，难以建立精确的数学模型和设计出通常意义下的控制程序，K_p、K_i 和 K_d 参数往往整定困难。此时，采用模糊控制就有可能获得满意的控制效果。

2.2 模糊控制算法

模糊控制的核心部分为模糊控制器。模糊控制器的控制规律由计算机的程序实现，模糊控制的基本思想是：将偏差信号和偏差变化率信号作为模糊控制器的输入量，经模糊化后，用相应的模糊语言表示，得到模糊语言集合的一个子集。再由模糊子集和模糊控制规则（模糊关系）根据模糊推理合成规则进行模糊决策，得到模糊控制量；经解模糊（也称清晰化），得到了精确地数字控制量输出给执行机构。

因此，模糊控制过程可概括为以下 4 个步骤。

1) 根据本次采样得到的系统输出值，计算所选择系统的输入变量；
2) 将输入变量的精确值变为模糊量；
3) 根据输入变量（模糊量）及模糊控制规则，按照模糊推理合成规则推理计算输出控制量（模糊量）；
4) 由上述得到的控制量（模糊量）计算精确的输出控制量，并作用于执行机构。

3 系统组态

本设计的硬件和网络结构均采用西门子 S7 控制系统，利用 STEP7 软件实现系统硬件组态、通信组态和控制算法组态；采用 WINCC 软件实现系统监控层设计。

3.1 硬件组态

STEP7 软件是用于 SIMATIC S7 – 300/400 站创建可编程逻辑控制程序的标准软件，应用 STEP7 软件可以方便地构造和组态 Profibus – DP 网络。本系统采用 S7 – 300 控制器，硬件包括电源模块、CPU 模块、信号模块、功能模块、接口模块和通信处理器 CP。机架的 1~3 槽位分别放置电源模块、CPU 模块。CPU 模块型号为 314 – 2DP，带有集成的数字量和模拟量的输入、输出；以太网通信模块采用 CP343 – 1，由于带有以太网通信接口，因此会自动弹出 Ethernet（以太网）接口属性对话框，创建一个新的以太网子网，并输入一个唯一的 MAC 地址与之相对应。

3.2 算法编程

从系统建模的角度看，双容液位系统是一个二阶惯性环节，也可以等效为一个惯性环节加滞后环节，由于双容系统存在容积滞后，给系统控制增加了难度。

3.2.1 PID 控制设计

STEP7 软件中提供了多个功能块，用于实现多个控制算法。本文首先采用 STEP7 软件提供的 PID 控制模块对双容水箱液位进行控制。PID 控制中有三个重要的参数。

（1）比例系数 K_p 的作用是加快系统的响应速度，提高系统的调节精度。K_p 越大系统的响应速度越快，系统的调节精度越高，但易产生超调，甚至会导致系统不稳定。

（2）积分作用系数 K_i 的作用是消除系统的稳态误差。K_i 越大，系统的静态误差消除越快。但 K_i 过大，在响应过程的初期会产生积分饱和现象，从而引起较大的超调。

（3）微分作用系数 K_d 的作用是改善系统的动态特性，其作用主要是在响应过程中抑制偏差的变化，对偏差变化进行提前预报。但 K_d 过大，会使响应过程提前制动，从而延长调节时间，降低系统的抗干扰性能。微分作用可以消除时间滞后，但对容积滞后无能为力。

根据 3 个参数的特点，通过先期的仿真研究和参数整定，确定了 3 个参数值。

3.2.2 模糊控制器设计

模糊控制器最基本的形式被称为"查询表"式的模糊控制器，它将模糊控制规则最终转化为一个查询表，又称为控制表，存储在计算机中供在线查询使用。这种形式的模糊控制器具有结构简单、使用方便的特点，因此又称为简单模糊控制器。这种设计思想是其他形式模糊控制器的基础。本文采用模糊控制算法，结合液位控制系统特点设计一个合理的二维模糊控制器。

液位模糊控制器设计为 2 个输入、1 个输出，1 个输入为液位设定值与液位实际值偏差 E，另一个输入为偏差的变化率 EC，模糊控制器的输出是 U，用来控制进水调节阀开度。

描述输入变量及输出变量的语言值的模糊子集为 {负，零，正}，通常采用如下简记形式 N=负，Z=零，P=正。其中，设偏差 E、偏差变化率 EC 和控制量 U 的论域相同为 X，量化为五个等级，即 $X = \{-2, -1, 0, 1, 2\}$。采用三角形隶属函数曲线，如图 2 所示。根据经验和被控对象的先验知识，经过反复实验建立了模糊控制规则，如表 1 所示。

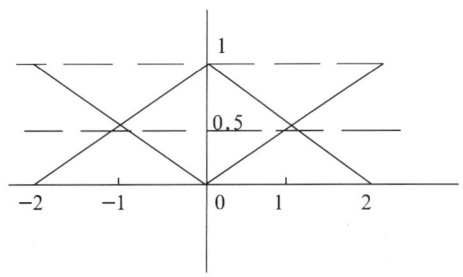

图 2　隶属函数曲线

表 1　模糊控制规则表

U	EC		
	N	Z	P
E	N	N	N	Z
	Z	N	Z	Z
	P	Z	P	P

应用 STEP7 软件中 SCL 语言编写模糊控制程序。

```
FUNCTION_ BLOCK FB5
VAR_ INPUT // 定义输入参数
    pv: REAL: =0.0;
    sp: REAL: =0.0;
    e_ H: REAL: =500.00;
    e_ L: REAL: =0.0;
    ts: TIME: =TIME#1.00S;
    deadb_ w: REAL: =0.0;
    ec_ H: REAL: =0.00;
    ec_ L: REAL: = -5.0;
    BIPOLAR: BOOL: = false;
    END_ VAR
VAR_ IN_ OUT
    // I/O Parameters
        END_ VAR
            ……
```

源程序编译完成后生成模糊控制功能块 FB5，就可以直接用于功能块编程。

3.3　监控程序设计

通过 WINCC 软件可以实现对现场设备的实时监控，WINCC 与 PLC 的通信是通过"SIMATIC S7 Protocol Suite"驱动程序，通道单元为工业以太网"Industrial Ethernet"。因此在 WINCC 中建立项目后，添加"SIMATIC S7 Protocol Suite"协议组，在"Industrial Ethernet"下建立与 S7 – 300 PLC 站连接的逻辑通道，添加监控所需的与 PLC 地址变量 相对应的 WINCC 外部变量。该组态在监控层 PC 中进行，与 PLC 通过工业以太网连接即可监控现 场运行状态。本项目在 WINCC 中建立了实时监控界面和趋势控制曲线。

4 系统运行分析

图 3 是系统的监控运行界面,被控量是 2#水箱液位,其设定液位值是 250,当前实际液位值是 252,出现超调量,因此阀门的开度是零,系统还处于动态的调节过程中。1#和 3#水箱可以实时监控,随着现场的实际液位值实时变化、动态显示。

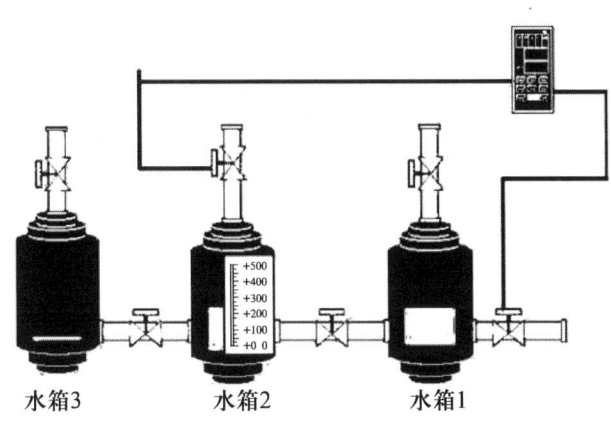

图 3 系统运行界面

图 4 和图 5 分别是 2#水箱液位值在 PID 控制和模糊控制作用下的动态响应曲线,描述了液位参数值从动态到稳态的变化过程,以及执行器的变化情况。其性能指标分析如表 2 所示。

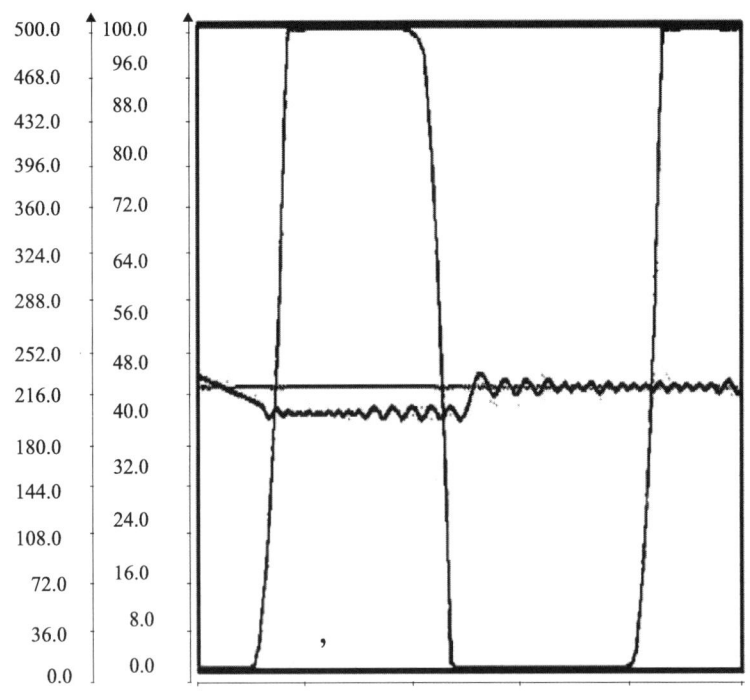

图 4 PID 控制曲线

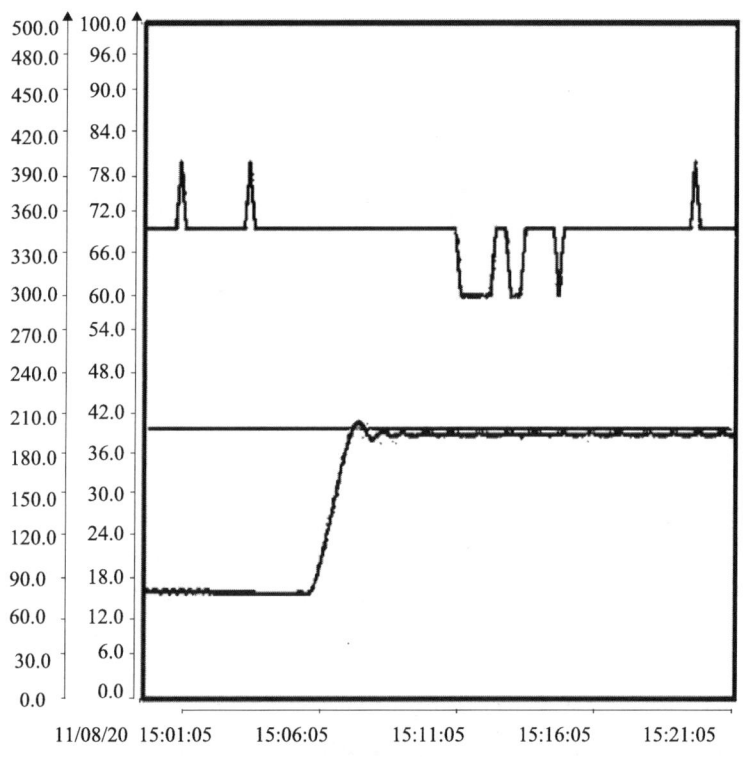

图 5　模糊化控制曲线

表 2　性能指标比较

性能指标	PID 控制结果	模糊化控制结果
超调量	4.5%	2.5%
调节时间	2min	3min
上升时间	0.8min	1.2min
峰值时间	1min	1.5min
延迟时间	0.6min	0.8min

由表 2 可见，PID 控制调节时间较短，有相对较大的超调量，而且执行器（阀门）处于全开/全关状态，执行器（阀门）磨损较大；模糊控制虽然时间稍长，但超调量小，且阀门小幅运动，保持固定状态的时间较长，执行器（阀门）磨损小。从过程控制角度看，更强调系统的稳定性和装置的状态，因此模糊控制具有更好的控制效果。

参考文献

[1] 高志宏. 过程控制与自动化仪表［M］. 杭州：浙江大学出版社，2006.
[2] 丁肇红，舒光伟，孙国琴. 基于 PLC 的液位模糊控制系统设计［J］. 微计算机信息，2008：74 - 75.
[3] 罗启平. 基于西门子 WinCC 和 S7 - 400 的过程控制研究［J］. Equipment Manufaetring Technology，2007.
[4] 刘泽祥，李媛. 现场总线技术［M］. 北京：机械工业出版社，2011.

Research on Characteristics of Plastic Materials and Plastic Optical Fiber

Zhang Ning   Han Zeyuan   Song Luqin   Lu Yueming

Introduction

The plastic materials are plasticity of synthetic polymeric organic compound (resin). In modern society, fiber - optic communications is indispensable primary means of communication for optical network[1]. With the continuous development of communication, people's lives more and more dependent on these high - tech technologies. In the past two decades, due to the information society, a lot of information quickly produced in the form of an explosion around the exchange to the communications equipment and communications cable transmission[2]. It is well known that silica fiber with its attenuation small, frequency bandwidth, etc. is used as a long - distance, high - speed, large capacity, and the optical transmission medium of the public communication network[3]. But because of the required starting material purity, the manufacturing process is complex and expensive, and the splice difficulties for a large number of short distance optical access network transmission medium is uneconomical[4]. It is in order to reduce the cost of short distance for access network fiber client, the birth of the plastic optical fiber (POF) is emerged. The biggest advantage of the optical fiber communication is that a great deal of transmission capacity, low transmission loss and dispersion characteristics. Optical fiber access networks can provide sufficient bandwidth to meet the changing requirements telecom services to multimedia broadband services for voice, data, image combining, and is really suitable for the development of an access technology[5]. With the advancement of technology, the FTTH era has arrived, the "last mile" problem will soon be solved, and this has become an irreversible trend. The plastic optical fiber will play an important role in this process.

Characteristics of Plastic Materials

Plastic is an organic synthetic resin as a main component, adding or not adding other compounding ingredients (additives) of constituting the artificial material, and it is usually in the heating, the plastic made with a certain shape of the device under pressurized conditions. The plastic optical fiber is made from a lower cladding layer of the core and the refractive index of refraction higher. Plastic optical fibers compared to the optical glass fibers, despite poor translucent, light loss large, the transmitted light with a narrow, and it is difficult to adapt to the needs of the multimedia communication network and other shortcomings, but it has a soft texture, high impact strength, low production price, anti flexural properties, radiation resistance, ease of processing. It can be made into a series of advantages of large diameter. Production of plastic optical fiber, usually require the selection of plastic optical fiber material. It should have good transparency, uniform optical properties suitable refractive index, and is easy to adjust, easy to process, stable performance of the chemical, physical, and cheap. The structure of POF

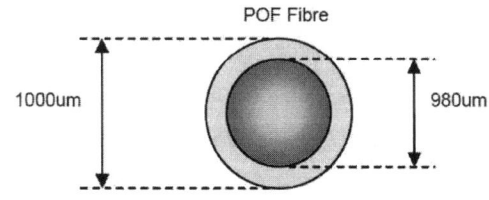

Fig. 1 Structure of POF

[Author Introduction] Zhang Ning, Han Zeyuan, Song Luqin, Beijing Key Laboratory of Information Service Engineering of Beijing Union University Beijing; Lu Yueming, Key Laboratory of Trustworthy Distributed Computing and Service, Ministry of Education Beijing University of Posts and Telecommunications.

is shown in Fig. 1. The coupling efficiency of light is higher, the terminal device of the connection with a personal computer, etc. connected between the fibers are very easy. This makes the plastic optical fiber installation costs are very low, installation very simple and align the connector plug easily.

POF is a transmission medium with low cost, good transparency, light weight, softness, and the core diameter is easy to install, as shown in Fig. 2. Plastic optical fiber has some advantages.

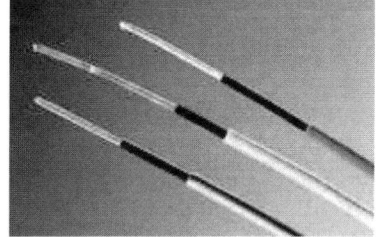

Fig. 2 POF

(1) Resistance to electromagnetic interference: the POF is not sensitive to electromagnetic interference, nor occurs radiation. In different data rates, it keeps the attenuation constant, the error rate can be forecast, it can be used in an electrically noisy environment.

(2) The price is low: POF cost is quite symmetrical cable, and POF and its accessories cost continues to decline, largely being affected by the price of copper and copper lower cost constraints, limited decline in space.

(3) Fast install: POF can be easily installed through a narrow conduit.

(4) Easy connection: POF without polishing solution can achieve a good connection effect without dedicated equipment in order to connect.

(5) Rugged: POF cable is softer than quartz fiber optic cable durability, small bending.

Application of POF

With the rapid development of network technology, the Internet, video telephony, distance education, high - definition television, video on demand and TV shopping has put forward higher requirements for the development of the communications business. The access network is the direct user - oriented, is an important part of the telecommunications network as a whole, and its quality of service and content directly affects the development of the communication network. Network cost reduction, performance improvement, the introduction of digital communication technologies, the reduction of electromagnetic interference and plastic optical fiber standard formulation and improvement make plastic optical fiber to have been widely used in industry, agriculture, national defense construction, and gradually promote plastic optical fiber industry become the mainstream of the optical communication industry. The plastic optical fiber is mainly used in low - speed, short - range communication transmission. The biggest advantage of the optical fiber communication is that a great deal of transmission capacity, low transmission loss and dispersion properties of optical fiber access network can provide enough bandwidth to meet the ordinary telecommunication services to voice, data, image combining multimedia broadband services changing needs, and it is really suitable for the development of an access technology. POF optical switch. The switch is composed of the core of the network system equipment, and it is a simplified, low - cost, high - performance and high port - intensive features of switching products. It can provide greater bandwidth for each operating point, and the transparency of the agreement makes the switch software simple configuration directly installed in a multi - protocol network. The POF optical switch as shown in Fig. 3.

Fig. 3 POF Optical Switch

For TV, coaxial cable has to meet the needs of users, but from the trend of the development of future large – screen high – definition TV, and TV shopping will require a great deal of bandwidth and the amount of data, connect to a TV with a plastic optical fiber that is the development trend. The network with POF optical switch is shown in Fig. 4.

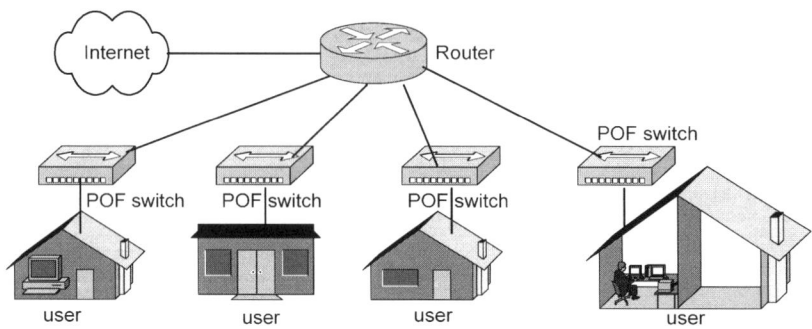

Fig. 4 Access network with POF optical switch

Networking using the IEEE 1394 bus, plastic optical fiber, smart appliances (home PC, HDTV, telephone, digital imaging devices, home security equipment, air – conditioning, refrigerator, sound system, kitchen appliances, etc.), to reach home automation and remote control and management, can improve the quality of life. Making Internet phone calls through the Internet, you can greatly reduce the costs of international calls; watch HD network television (IPTV); to upgrade plastic optical fiber access can provide a bandwidth of 100 megabytes, so do not worry quite a long period of time; printable coping, faxing and scanning, suitable for the needs of the home office, and at the same time network monitoring, no matter where you are, as long as the network can see the home at any time. Modern home network is connected by a single or multiple computers, IP telephony, IPTV, printer, network set – top boxes, digital home appliances and other equipment, to implement the Internet, communications, television, telephone, monitoring, print, and other purposes. The implementation of the POF home network will promote the popularity of "fiber to the home", so that at the same time promote IPTV and HDTV services. POF has a high degree of flexibility, and security, and stability.

Summary

In this paper, the characteristics of plastic materials and the plastic optical fiber are studied, and a novel application for access network is proposed. Plastic optical fiber has a soft, pliable, large core diameter, easy coupling, immunity to electromagnetic interference and electromagnetic radiation manufacturing process. With the continuous advancement of POF manufacturing technology and raw materials preparation technology, POF production costs will continue to decrease. From the view of the laser, optoelectronic integrated device, connector development situation, domestic and international technology made rapid progress. With forward to the continuous expansion of production scale, it is believed that the cost of sending and receiving devices have decreased significantly, and POF is more advantage in access communications.

Acknowledgment

This work was supported by Qimingxing Program (2012 – 2013), scientific and technological innovation projects.

References

[1] S. Yan, C. Okonkwo, D. Visani, E. Tangdiongga, T. Koonen, Distribution of broadband service over 1 – mm core diameter plastic optical fiber for point – to – multipoint in – home networks [J]. Journal of Lightwave Technology, 2013, 31

(6): 874.
[2] D. Dinakar, P. Rao, P. Kishore, K. Srimannarayana, M. Shankar, S. Rao, A simple plastic optical fiber force sensor [J]. Optical Engineering (ICOE), 2012: 1.
[3] K. T. Kim, B. J. Han, High-performance plastic optical fiber coupler based on heating and pressing [J]. Photonics Technology Letters, 2011, 23 (24): 1848.
[4] Atef, R. Swoboda, H. Zimmermann, 1.25 Gbit/s over 50 m step-index plastic optical fiber using a fully integrated optical receiver with an integrated equalizer [J]. Journal of Lightwave Technology, 2012, 30 (1): 118.
[5] N. Schlepple, M. Nishigaki, H. Uemura, K. Obara, H. Furuyama, Y. Sugizaki, H. Shibata, Y. Koike, 10 Gb/s High-speed link over thin GI 50/125 plastic optical fibers and compact optical sub-assembly [J]. Photonics Technology Letter, 2012, 24 (19): 1670.

我国焊接设备的技术水平及发展趋势

张明贤

近 20 年来，我国焊接装备制造行业取得了长足的进步，国产焊接装备的成套性、自动化程度、制造精度和整体质量都有明显的提高，其应用范围正逐步扩大。进入 21 世纪以来，我国焊接结构制造业的发展令世人注目。其主要特点是趋向规模化、大型化、高参数化和精密化。例如火力、水力和核能发电设备的单机容量已达 1000MW，化工炼油装置的年产量提高到 100 万吨，煤液化装置设计年产量为 1000 万吨。远洋货轮和大型油轮的载重吨位已超过 20 万吨。各类冶金和重型机械、航天、航空工程、大型和高层建筑结构、大跨度桥梁、省际/国际输油输气管线、海洋建筑、汽车、大型客车、轨道交通车辆和高速铁路车辆都已进入世界顶级水平。2008 年，我国焊接结构的钢耗量已突破 2 亿吨，跃居世界首位，使我国成为名副其实的焊接大国。在上述发展形势下，各类焊接结构生产企业都迫切需要各种高性能、高精度、高度自动化和集成化的先进焊接装备，并对其技术特性和质量提出了愈来愈高的要求。

1 我国焊接装备制造行业现状的评价

1.1 焊接装备类型的发展

近 10 年来，国产焊接装备的类型和品种有了很大的发展，已从传统的焊接操作机、滚轮架、座式变位机和头尾架翻转机扩展到各种成套自动化焊接专机、焊接生产线和焊接机器人工作站。

焊接操作机的种类已从通用的立柱横梁式操作机发展成多种结构形式的焊接操作机，如龙门式、悬臂式、门框式、侧梁式和台式焊接操作机。焊接操作机的规格渐趋大型化，目前已能生产最大规格为 10m×10m 重型载人立柱横梁式焊接操作机。

焊接操作机的成套性已能满足国内大多数用户的需求，不仅可配备传统的埋弧焊系统，而且也可配备精度要求较高的 TIG 焊、MIG/MAG 焊和等离子弧焊系统，以及技术难度较大的窄间隙埋弧焊系统。焊接操作机与滚轮架或变位机（回转平台、翻转机）在电气上可实现联动或程序控制，使其真正成为一台功能齐全的焊接中心。

在焊接操作机的自动控制方面已广泛采用 PLC 可编程控制器和人机界面、微处理机和工控机，实现了焊接过程的全自动程序控制。焊接操作机的传动系统，可按焊接工艺的要求分别采用普通导轨、交流变速电机和齿轮齿条传动，以及精密直线导轨和交流伺服电机驱动系统。

与焊接操作机配套使用的焊接滚轮架，除了传统的可调式滚轮架和自调式滚轮架外，已能生产不同类型的自动防窜滚轮架，防窜精度达 ±1.0mm，以满足特殊焊接工艺的需要，如厚壁容器筒身环缝的窄间隙埋弧焊和筒体内壁的螺旋线连续自动堆焊等。

为适应 TIG、MIG/MAG 等离子弧焊等精密焊接的需求，也生产了精密型焊接滚轮架，其传动系统采用交流伺服电机驱动和相应的控制装置。此外，为满足重型容器焊接的需要，目前已生产了最大吨位达 1000t 的焊接滚轮架。

焊接变位机、头尾架翻转机和回转平台既可单独用于焊接件的装配和手工焊接，也可与各类焊接操作机配套使用。焊接变位机的品种已发展成多种结构形式，包括通用的座式变位机、双座式变位机、L 形双回转变位机和提升式变位机等。国产座式焊接变位机的最大吨位已达 70t，双座式焊接变位机的最大吨位已达 160t。

目前，我国已能自行设计和制造与焊接机器人配套的精密焊接变位机，其由交流伺服电机和 RV 减

[作者简介] 张明贤，北京联合大学生化学院。

速箱驱动。机器人控制系统协调控制，重复定位精度可达±0.1mm。最大载重达10t，最大工作平台直径为3m。这为焊接机器人系统的国产化奠定了坚实的基础。

我国焊接装备制造行业已能自行设计制造各类自动焊接生产线，其中包括轻型/重型 H 型钢焊接生产线、箱形梁焊接生产线、管道焊接生产线、矩形管焊接生产线、螺旋管焊接生产线和钢板拼焊生产线等。生产线的基本组成包括自动切割机、组装机、自动焊接装置、矫正机和各种输送辊道和翻转机等，基本满足了我国建筑钢结构和管材制造行业的需要。

我国自行开发、设计和制造焊接机器人配套装备已取得可喜的进步。近10年来，已生产焊接机器人配套设备300多套，基本掌握焊接机器人系统的核心技术和高精度配套外围设备的设计和制造技术，具备了为用户提供完整技术解决方案的能力，技术水平已接近国际先进水平。

1.2 焊接装备制造行业的生产规模

近几年来，我国焊接装备制造行业的生产规模以较快的速度逐年扩大。据2008年统计，全行业的年总产值已达到20亿元，相当于我国通用焊机年总产值的1/5。

我国现有从事焊接装备生产企业20多家，都具有相当规模，且年产值超亿元的生产企业共有8家。如昆山市华恒焊接股份有限公司、成都焊研威达自动焊接设备有限公司、无锡阳通机械设备有限公司、无锡华联科技集团公司、唐山开元自动焊接装备有限公司、伊萨罗马重工自动设备（无锡）有限公司、无锡洲翔焊接设备有限公司和无锡肯克焊割科技有限公司等。

我国生产的各类焊接装备的技术性能和质量水平基本上已达到国际水准，已有部分企业的产品出口至北美、欧洲、东南亚、中东和韩国等地。

2 与国际同行业先进水平的差距

我国焊接装备制造行业与国际同行业的先进水平相比，在下列各方面尚存在相当大的差距。

2.1 科研与开发力量方面的差距

世界工业发达国家，如美国、英国、法国、德国、意大利、日本和瑞典等国对焊接装备的研究和开发颇为重视，大部分焊接装备生产企业都建有规模较大的焊接技术研究所和研发中心，装备有现代最先进的焊接设备和试验手段，其规模大大超过了我国国家级的焊接研究所，为企业自行开发新型焊接装备提供了坚实的、强有力的科技基础资源，其中包括全面掌握世界最先进技术，综合开发能力较强的人力资源，使所生产的焊接装备的技术性能始终处于世界领先地位。

目前，我国焊接装备生产企业已开始重视科技投入，并相继成立了科技开发中心、研究所和试验基地，但在规模、开发研究手段和科研人员的配备方面仍大大落后于工业发达国家，尚存在相当大的差距。

2.2 焊接装备技术特性方面的差距

国外工业发达国家生产的现代化自动焊接装备的技术特性，包括规格大型化、传动机构的精密化、自动化程度、系统集成化、智能化、数字信息化方面都已达到了相当高的水平，采用了当代最先进的计算机控制技术、传感技术、网络信息化技术、系统集成技术和遥测技术等。除了已能稳定商品化生产数字控制的焊接操作机、滚轮架和焊接变位器外，还能够提供运行可靠的计算机集成控制的各类焊接生产线。在各种自动焊接装备中，焊接机头行走定位的最高精度可达±0.05mm，速度控制的最高精度可达±0.1%。各种自动焊接生产线大多已采用计算机直接数字控制（DNC），部分焊接生产线已采用计算机集成控制和网络化控制。

在焊接装备大型化方面，英国 Keyplant 公司已生产出迄今世界上最大规格的重型立柱横梁操作机，其工作行程为12.5m×10m，外形结构见图1；意大利 Ansaldo 公司曾生产出高度×宽度为11.7m×13.0m 的大型龙门式焊接操作机，可焊容器的最大外径达到7200mm，垂直升降行程5200mm，总体结构如图2所示，所配焊接机头为双丝串列电弧埋弧焊和窄间隙埋弧焊，可焊最大壁厚为400mm。

德国 DEUMA 公司座式变位机产品样本中已列出承重250t标准座式变位机，图3示出该公司生产的承重为100t的座式变位机外形。重型双座变位机的最大负载可达1000t，其结构外形如图4所示。

图1　12.5m×10m 重型立柱横梁操作机外形

图2　大型龙门式焊接操作机总体结构

图3　承重100t的标准座式变位机

图4　最大负载1000t的双座式变位机

为满足重型厚壁压力容器、熔量汽轮机和发电机转轴装配焊接的需要，法国 Lambert – jouty 公司最近推出了载重 2500t 的重型滚轮架，如图5所示。

在焊接装备的系统集成技术方面，国外的发展速度也相当快，例如，为满足集装箱需求量的快速增长，德国 OXYTECHNIK 公司曾开发出集装箱外壳整体组装焊接中心，如图6所示。该公司还为机车车辆壳体组装与焊接设计制造了以机器人为主要执行元件的生产线，其布置图见图7。

图5　2500t 重型焊接滚轮架外形

图6　集装箱外壳整体组装焊接中心

图7 机车车辆壳体组装与焊接生产线

对于加工精度要求较高的焊件，例如涡轮机导流盘，意大利 Ansaldo 公司曾为这类部件设计和制造了柔性制造系统，其流程布置图见图8，组装与焊接装置外形如图9所示。

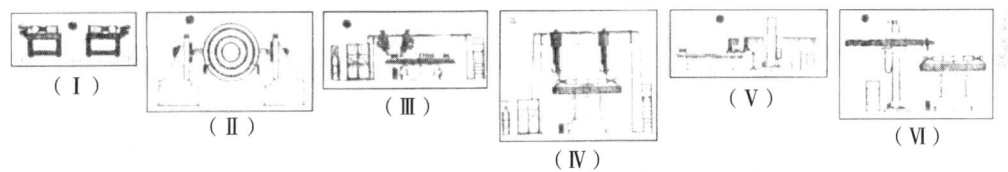

Ⅰ—导流盘组装工作站；Ⅱ—导流盘预热工作站；Ⅲ—喷管机器人焊接中心；
Ⅳ—导流盘机器人焊接中心；Ⅴ—磨光操作机

图8 涡轮机导流盘制造流程布置图

（a）组装机　　　　　　　　　　　（b）焊接装置

图9 涡轮机导流盘组装与焊接装置外形

2.3 焊接装备采用高新技术方面的差距

国外工业发达国家焊接装备制造行业采用各种高新技术的速度十分惊人，而且从科研成果转变为实用工业商品的周期相当短，通常1～2年。国外各大焊接装备生产企业几乎每年都有新型焊接装备推向市场。在焊接装备上采用高新技术主要集中在两方面，即采用先进高效的焊接工艺方法及最先进的计算机控制技术和传感技术。

2.3.1 采用新的焊接工艺方法

近10年来，世界先进国家在自动焊接装备上采用新的高效焊接工艺方法主要有以下6项。

(1) 双丝串列电弧 MIG/MAG 焊。其效率比普通 MIG/MAG 焊提高了 3 倍以上。目前已有大量的自动化焊接专机和机器人工作站配备这种新的高效焊接工艺方法。图 10 和图 11 分别示出其典型的应用实例。

图 10　双丝串列电弧 MIG/MAG 焊自动化焊接专机

图 11　双丝串列电弧 MIG/MAG 焊机器人工作站

(2) 激光/MIG 复合焊接法。激光/MIG 复合焊是 21 世纪初焊接技术领域内的一项重大创新，实现了两种焊接工艺方法的优势互补，进一步提高了焊接效率，增强了工艺适应性，扩大了应用范围。图 12 示出激光/MIG 复合焊焊接 Audi A8 轿车顶盖连接缝的实况。

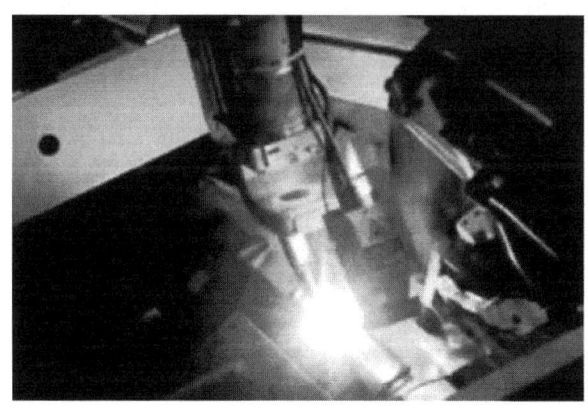

图 12　激光/MIG 复合焊焊接 Audi A8 轿车顶盖连接缝实况（机器人工作站）

(3) 激光切割和焊接技术。激光和焊接技术在工业发达国家已得到大规模的推广应用，特别是在薄板加工工业中应用广泛。有关的统计数据表明，自 2003 年以来，日本激光切割和焊接设备的年产值相当于所有通用焊机的年总产值。可见，激光切割和焊接工艺方法在许多应用领域具有压倒性的优势。图 13 示出瑞士 Bystronic 公司近期生产的大型门架式激光切割机的外貌。

图 13　大型门架式激光切割机外貌

(4) 多丝高效埋弧焊接法。多丝高效埋弧焊接法包括双丝串列电弧埋弧焊、3 丝埋弧焊和 4 丝以上至 9 丝的埋弧焊，主要用于大型船舶、厚壁压力容器和管道、海洋建筑和风力发电装备的风塔主柱等大型焊件的焊接，为此必须研制相应的焊接装备。图 14 示出正在厚壁管生产中使用的 3 丝和 6 丝埋弧焊装备。

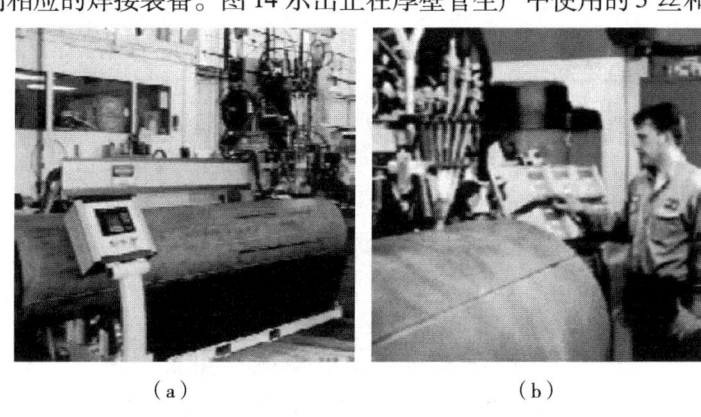

(a)　　　　　　　　(b)

图 14　用于厚壁管生产的 3 丝和 6 丝埋弧焊装置

(5) 搅拌摩擦焊技术。搅拌摩擦焊发明于 1991 年，被焊接界公认为 20 世纪最重要的焊接技术创新之一。其突出的优点是焊接效率高、焊缝质量优、焊接变形小、不需要添加填充金属、对工作环境不产生污染，主要用于焊接塑性较好的金属材料，如铝及其合金和铜及其合金，已在飞机、航天飞行器、火箭壳体、铝制船舶、高速列车车箱中成功应用。其先决条件是必须配备相应的焊接装备，图 15 示出大型铝板拼接搅拌摩擦焊装备外形。

图 15　大型铝板拼接搅拌摩擦焊装备外形现代焊接

(6) 窄间隙电弧焊技术。窄间隙电弧焊是在间隙为 10～20mm 范围内完成全厚度接缝的一种工艺方法。按焊接方法可分窄间隙 TIG 焊、窄间隙热丝 TIG 焊、窄间隙 MIG/MAG 焊和窄间隙埋弧焊。其共同的特点是，与传统的宽坡口焊接相比，焊接效率至少可提高 1 倍，焊接材料节约 50% 以上，并可改善焊缝金属的金相组织，提高接头的力学性能。因此窄间隙电弧焊的应用范围不断扩大，同时研制出了满足窄间隙焊要求的技术性能先进的各种窄间隙焊接装备。图 16 示出法国 Polysoude 公司研制的厚壁管环缝热丝

TIG焊装置，图17示出瑞典ESAB公司最近推出的双丝窄间隙埋弧焊装置，并采用了三维激光跟踪系统。

图16　厚壁管环缝热丝TIG焊装置

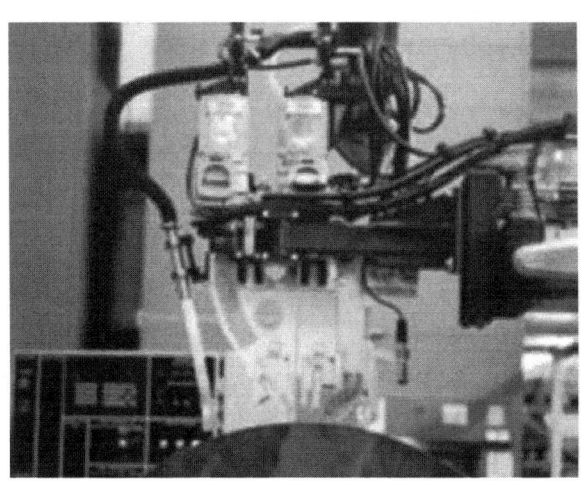

图17　厚壁容器环缝双丝窄间隙埋弧焊装置

2.3.2　广泛应用工业计算机控制技术

根据自动化程度的要求，国外现代自动化焊接装备和焊接生产线广泛应用了以下不同等级的计算机控制技术。

（1）采用微处理机、PLC与人机界面工业计算机及DSP等数字控制技术，实现焊接过程的自动程序控制，并同时提高焊接装备的定位精度和行走精度以及焊接参数的控制精度。

（2）应用计算机集成控制技术，结合先进的传感检测技术，实现焊接装备和焊接生产线全过程的自动控制。

（3）利用网络信息技术。利用现代的网络信息技术可对数字控制的自动焊接装备和焊接生产线实行脱机编程、远程监控、远程诊断和远程检修等功能，可大大缩短焊接生产准备和检修周期，明显提高焊接装备和生产线的利用率。

（4）充分利用计算机软件技术。利用CAD/CAM/CAE/CAPP/PDM等通用计算机软件和焊接装备控制系统的专用软件，可将设计、制造、工艺编制、生产计划与管理和生产过程的监控实行全面集成，并可通过脱机编程实现生产线或生产车间无人操作的全自动化生产。

图18示出美国Jetline公司最新开发的9900型工业计算机控制器，装有15英寸全彩触摸屏，采用Windows XP操作系统和直观性的焊接软件，通过局域网通信接口和光纤电缆，可与刚性自动化焊接装备及数字控制焊接电源实行无缝连接，可以控制15个焊接工艺参数，适用于TIG焊、等离子弧焊和双弧焊，对高频电流具有很强的抗干扰性，保证了焊接装备的可靠性和焊接质量的一致性。图19示出配备9900型控制器的自动TIG焊装备的焊接实况。

图20示出了计算机集成控制板材切割中心的总体布置图，其由板材存放架、板材起吊输送设备、输

送辊道、预钻孔设备、数控切割机、切割零件分选装箱系统、余料切割机、余料回送系统和中央控制台等组成。该切割中心采用 ops 专用切割软件，按图 21 所示的系统结构框图由计算机群集成控制。该系统可通过通信接口与计算机辅助设计系统连接，可直接读取 CAD 图样数据，大大简化了操作程序。这种计算机集成控制板材切割中心可以最高的效率、均衡而合理地安排生产流程，可取得最好的经济效益。

图 18　9900 型工业计算机控制器界面图形

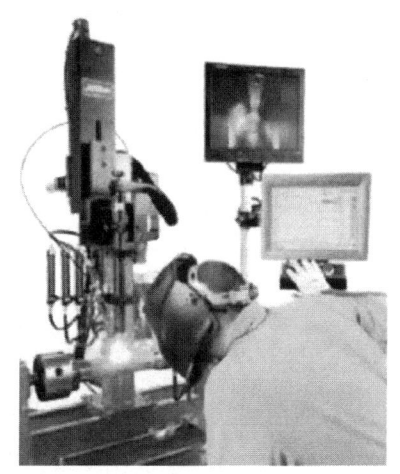

图 19　配备 9900 型工业计算机控制器的自动 TIG 焊装备全貌

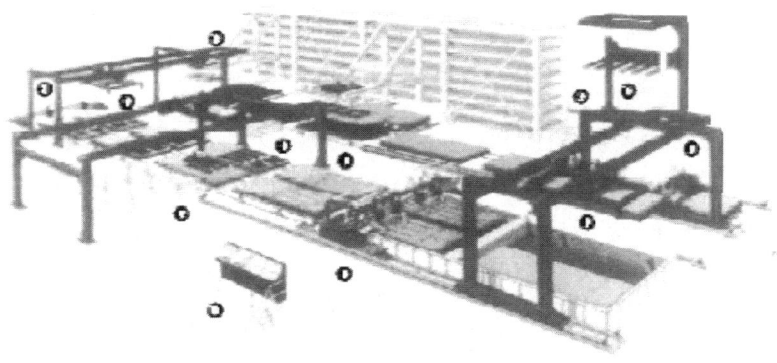

A—板材存放架；B—板材起吊输送设备；C—输送辊道；
D—预钻孔设备；E—板材移位装置；F—数控切割机；
G—切割零件分选装箱系统；H—余料切割机

图 20　计算机集成控制板材切割中心

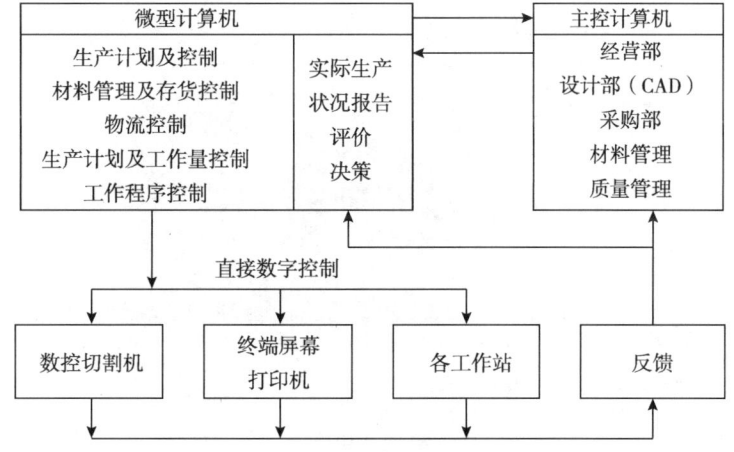

图 21　板材切割中心计算机集成控制系统结构框图

2.3.3 利用高级传感技术

为实现焊接装备的自适应控制，包括焊缝轨迹的自动导向和跟踪，以及焊接工艺参数的闭环反馈控制，并对自动焊接装备赋予智能化的功能，国外一些先进的自动焊接装备充分利用了各种高级传感元件，如视觉传感器、触觉传感器、光敏传感器、听觉传感器和激光扫描器等，并借助计算机软件、数据库和专家系统而使其具有识别、判断、实时检测、运算、自动编程、参数优化、自动编排焊道顺序、焊接参数存储和调用等功能。

国外在自动化焊接装备上利用各种传感器技术已经达到成熟的发展阶段。图 22 示出英国 Meta 公司生产的激光视觉传感器在厚壁容器环缝埋弧焊中应用的实例。所焊厚壁接头横剖面宏观金相检验表明，焊道排列整齐，无论是根部焊道、填充焊道，还是盖面焊道，焊接机头的跟踪精度均令人满意，解决了盖面层焊道不能准确跟踪的难题。

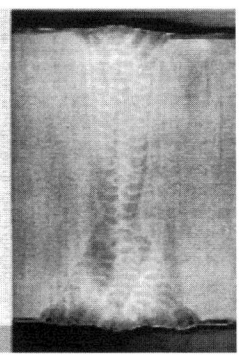

图 22 激光视觉传感器在厚壁容器环缝埋弧焊自动跟踪系统中的应用实例

图 23 示出激光图像传感器在大型埋弧焊装备中的应用实例。该装备配置了串列电弧双丝埋弧焊机头和 ABW 自适应控制系统。在厚壁环缝的连续焊接过程中，激光图像传感器连续测量接头坡口的外形尺寸，并将测量数据通过计算机由智能软件快速处理，从而确定所要求的焊接工艺参数（焊接电流和焊接速度）和焊枪的位置，即每道焊缝的尺寸和焊道的排列由系统软件自适应控制，图 24 示出该装备主控计算机和监视器的外貌。

图 23 大型埋弧焊装备的串列电弧双丝焊头及其激光传感系统

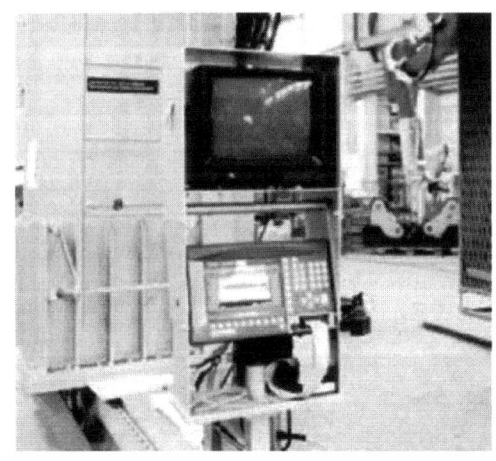

图 24 自适应控制埋弧焊装备的主控计算机和监视器外貌

图 25 示出日本三菱重工公司最近研制成功的大直径管全位置自动焊管机的基本结构和系统原理框图。它是一种模拟高级熟练焊工的智能和操作技能的全自动焊管机。这在世界上尚属首次。

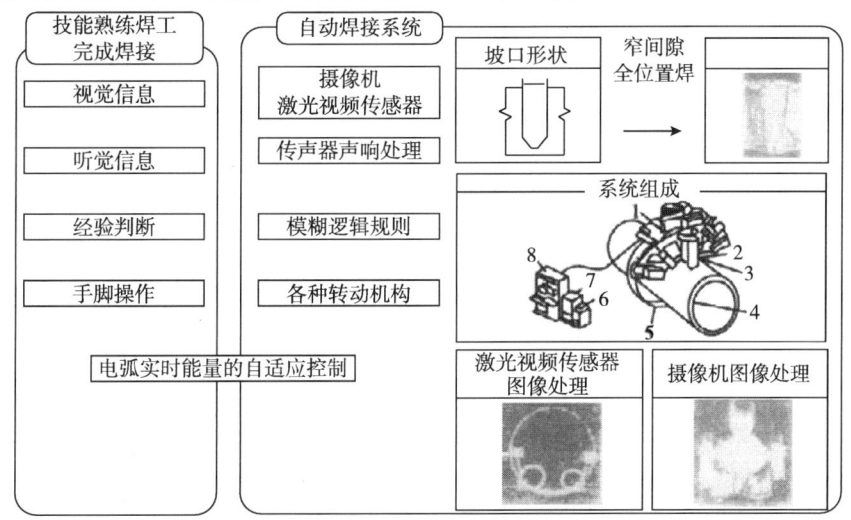

1—焊接机头；2—摄像机；3—激光视频传感器；4—感件；5—导轨；
6—冷却水箱；7—焊接电源；8—控制系统

图 25　自适应控制的全位置焊管机的基本结构和系统原理框图

这种自适应控制系统主要是通过高分辨率的视觉传感器实时检测焊接区的信息，并经计算机图像处理，按模糊逻辑的规则实时控制钨极相对于坡口边缘的位置，填充焊丝相对于钨极的位置以及决定焊接熔池尺寸的焊接工艺参数。焊缝质量监控系统则按照激光视频传感器、听觉传感器和电流传感器的信息实时修正焊接熔池的尺寸，焊道形状、钨极尖端的形状、电弧燃烧的稳定性和焊接电流，以保证焊缝质量的一致性。

从中可见，国外在自动焊接装备中利用现代高灵敏传感器提高自动化程度方面已达到相当高的水平。

2.4　焊接装备标准化和质量认证方面的差距

我国目前已对焊接操作机、焊接滚轮架和焊接变位机制订了相应的行业标准，即 JB/T 6965—1993《焊接操作机》、JB/T 9187—1999《焊接滚轮架》和 JB/T 8833—2001《焊接变位机》。这些标准的内容基本上沿用了原苏联 20 世纪 60 年代相应的标准，且未作重大改动，未能体现这三种焊接装备的当代技术水平，使我国焊接装备制造行业执行的标准大大落后于国际先进的标准。更值得注意的是，除上述三种焊接装备外，其他类型焊接装备的设计与制造尚处于无标准可循的状态，致使国产焊接装备的技术特性和质量水平的提升相对滞后。

在一些工业发达国家，不仅相关的国家标准齐全，而且大多数焊接装备生产企业都制订了内容完整、技术指标先进的产品企业标准，促使这些企业的产品技术性能始终处于国际领先地位。

我国大多数焊接装备生产企业，虽然已取得 ISO 9000 质量体系认证，但因上述相关技术标准落后，仍然改变不了国产焊接装备的总体质量达不到国际先进标准的落后局面。

鉴于我国已加入 WTO 组织，焊接装备制造行业也必将面向世界市场。虽然部分企业已开始出口各类焊接装备，但必须注意的是，我国大多数焊接装备生产企业都未取得国际市场准入证，即国际质量认证，如欧洲的 CE 认证、美国的 UL 认证。在这种情况下，只能通过国内外中介组织的渠道出口，不仅售价低廉，而且不能打出自己的品牌，也难以促进出口产品技术水平的提升。

为彻底改变这种被动局面，焊接装备生产企业应积极准备取得国际质量认证，直接自主经营出口业务，树立自己的品牌，全面推进企业的技术进步。

3　焊接装备的发展趋势

焊接技术的发展有两个方向：一是高效化焊接，提高焊接速度和熔敷率；二是优秀的焊接工艺性能，减少飞溅，美化成形。任何一种应用中的焊接技术都是两者的结合体。自 20 世纪 80 年代开始，出现了很多优秀的焊接技术，对焊接工业的发展有不可替代的作用。

3.1 数字化弧焊电源

3.1.1 软开关逆变技术

焊接技术发展的基础是焊机的发展，焊机的发展又依赖于电力电子器件的成熟。几种电力电子器件和相应焊机的发明时间如表 1 所示。

表 1 几种电力电子器件和相应焊机发明时间

器件	实际应用时间	焊机	制造时间
大功率晶体管	1950 年	晶体管整流弧焊机	1970 年
晶闸管	1958 年	晶闸管整流弧焊机	1972 年
功率场效应晶体管	1977 年	大功率场效应管逆变焊机	20 世纪 80 年代末
绝缘栅双极型晶体管（IGBT）	1986 年	IGBT 逆变焊机	1990 年

从表 1 可以看出，随着电力电子器件特别是新型焊机的出现，焊接技术的发展越来越快。其中，IGBT 逆变焊机的出现为优秀焊接技术的出现提供了先决条件。

世界上首台投放市场的逆变焊机应当是 1977 年在埃森焊接展览会上推出的 KEMPPI 公司的 Hilarc250。逆变焊机一经产生，其体积小、重量轻、控制灵活的特点就使其成为研究的热点和发展方向。到了 2000 年，各种 IGBT 焊机成为市场的主流。IGBT 逆变焊机工作频率为 20kHz，输出等级为 200~2000A；从工作频率、焊机容量、焊机可靠性方面综合考虑，200A 以上的 IGBT 逆变焊机已成为逆变焊机的主流。

软开关技术则使逆变焊机可靠性提高、减小开关损耗和谐波的影响，使用户更加青睐逆变焊机。软开关技术在逆变焊机中的真正应用是在全负载范围软开关技术的出现后。国外逆变焊机中的软开关电源技术并不十分普遍，特别是 20kHz 的逆变焊机多数仍以硬开关为主，但其所用开关器件的容量余度比国内焊机大很多，从而保证了逆变电源的高可靠性。这是由于不同的人力成本所决定的，因为软开关电路所需附加的电磁元件的制造和组装成本，在人力成本较高的地方会超过增加开关器件容量的材料成本。国外的软开关电源技术主要用于工作在 60~120kHz 的高频大功率的焊机，主要是为了提高电源的响应速度，便于更精密的波形控制过程。

3.1.2 数字化技术

焊机的数字化技术可以分为 3 个方面：数字化的控制核心、先进的控制算法和焊机网络化。

（1）数字化的控制核心

现代焊机很多都应用 MCU、DSP、CPLD/FPGA 等大规模集成电路作为控制核心，ARM 芯片的应用还比较少，只在一些高端焊机上见到。应用数字化的控制核心解决了模拟控制不灵活、器件不一致造成的问题，使焊接电源具有更稳定的控制精度、更灵活的控制性能。典型应用数字化控制的焊机是 Fronius 公司的 TPS 系列焊机。MCU 作为事件管理器并处理参数的输入输出，DSP 负责控制算法的实现，CPLD/FPGA 形成 PWM。

（2）先进的控制算法

传统的 PI 控制用比例环节调节速度，积分环节调节误差，稳态精度较高，但是需要建立精确的数学模型，这在焊接过程中比较困难，一般通过不断的调试来确定参数。随着数字化技术、控制理论的发展，一些现代的控制方法，如重复控制、模糊控制、滑模变结构控制、神经网络控制等非线性控制方法也被尝试应用于弧焊电源的控制电路中，这些控制方法应用前景广阔。

（3）焊机网络化

焊机间的网络通讯也是数字化的重要特点。一方面，在多丝焊接系统中不同焊机的电弧需单独控制且互相协调，此情况一般使用设备网；另一方面，焊机群控的实现及焊接规范的接收和焊接状态的监控，此情况一般使用 CAN 总线。

逆变电源的高响应速度为焊接控制技术提供了一个理想的功率平台，数字化技术在焊接电源中的应用进一步提高了电源控制技术的水平和可操作性。逆变焊机的数字化控制无疑会有强势的发展，因为它在控制方面极大地简化了电路结构，提高了焊机控制系统的稳定性，且应用方便。目前，国内与国外数字化焊机的最大差距在于焊接工艺性能。可以说，数字化焊机的最大卖点不是数字化技术本身，而是先进的焊接工艺技术。同时，数字化的最大优势还在于与逆变焊机相结合后可以承载先进的焊接工艺技术。

3.1.3 数字化焊接新工艺

逆变技术和数字化技术为焊接技术的发展创造了基础条件。世界各大焊接研究所（英国TWI、美国EWI、乌克兰PWI等）和焊接设备生产公司（Fronius、EWM、Lincoln等）以及许多高等院校在此基础上提出了很多优秀的焊接方法。

逆变焊机对于电焊机行业的影响无疑是一场电源技术的革命，但是对于整个焊接领域来说，与其说是电源技术的革命，不如说是焊接工艺技术的革命。可以说，逆变焊机促进了焊接工艺技术的深化。

数字化技术搭载在逆变焊机的技术平台上进一步改变了电焊机行业的技术状态。

数字化控制的逆变焊机的最大优势体现在MIG/MAG焊接工程中，因此除了电源问题之外，送丝机的控制也非常重要。如果没有稳定的送丝速度，很多先进的控制方法都无法实现，如脉冲MIG焊的核心问题就是电流波形与送丝速度之间的合理搭配。目前，国内外脉冲MIG焊机的主要差距不是在电源方面，而是在送丝机方面。国外同类产品都是采用具有速度反馈控制的送丝机，而国内大多还在使用电压反馈控制的送丝机。

随着焊接工艺要求的提高，对于送丝机要求不仅仅是速度稳定，对于响应速度的要求也将越来越高。例如CMT技术的核心就是焊丝的反抽控制，这点同样在引弧技术中起到关键作用。数字化控制的交流伺服电机已经替代传统的直流电机在高档焊机中使用，由此可见逆变焊机的数字化控制从电源部分扩展到送丝机也是一种发展趋势。

众所周知，数字化技术可以提高控制系统的干扰性、控制精度，从而提高焊机的焊接精度、可靠性和稳定性等整机性能。同时，还可通过变换外特性曲线、输出电流波形、动态特性参数等，实现多种焊接方法、多种焊材、多功能、多焊接参数的调节及其最佳匹配的控制，在把焊机做成"精品"的同时，把焊接工艺、焊件也做成"精品"。福尼斯公司的CMT（冷金属过渡）焊接系统在此方面做了很好的诠释。CMT熔滴过渡的方式新颖，与传统焊接工艺比较，过渡熔滴温度相对较低，可以实现异种金属连接，可以把焊丝的熔化和过渡分别作为两个相对独立的过程，对于焊接线能量的控制更加灵活。通过精确的弧长控制，CMT过程结合脉冲电弧，实现了无飞溅焊接，大大降低了焊接的热输入量。通过控制脉冲电弧影响热输入量，实现无电流状态下的熔滴过渡；母材熔化时间极短，起弧速度提高了两倍，热输入低、焊接变形小，搭桥能力显著提高，焊接性能优异；焊缝成形美观。

3.2 实现高速高效的MIG/MAG

除焊接机器人自动化、高效化以外，随处可见的就是熔化极焊接的大量展出和广泛应用。熔化极焊接除个别特殊情况外，几乎全是MIG/MAG焊机，适应集装箱等行业需要的薄板高速高效焊接的需求。珠海金宝热融公司代理的德国克鲁斯公司展示的TANDEM焊接系统，焊接2~3mm薄板的焊接速度可达6m/min，焊接8mm以上厚板的熔敷效率可达24kg/h。在焊接一些要求控制线能量的低合金高强度钢等材料时，气体保护焊是替代埋弧焊工艺的最新选择。

当使用脉冲电流焊接时形成脉冲过渡，可在较小的平均电流时得到相当稳定的焊接过程，适宜于全位置焊接和薄板焊接。在厚板焊接时脉冲过渡可使用3mm以上的焊丝和500A以上的电流焊接，适宜于MAG焊或CO焊各类钢材，还适用于MIG焊不锈钢、高合金钢、铝及铝合金和铜及铜合金。0.5~2.0mm小直径焊丝小电流焊接一般用于半自动焊，大直径焊丝大电流焊接用于自动焊。目前使用最多的是实芯焊丝CO焊、MAG焊，其次是药芯焊丝CO焊。药芯焊丝的构成比例很低，发展速度也较慢。日本在1981年药芯焊丝只占焊材总量的1%，1990年就达16.5%，2004年已达27%，手工焊条生产已由1981年的63%降到2004年的14%。我国焊材生产总量2005年为270~280万吨，其中手工焊条要占63%，气体保护焊丝占22%，埋弧焊丝占12.4%，但药芯焊丝只占2.6%。看来要将目前大量的手工焊发展成为气体保护半自动焊和自动焊，特别药芯焊丝气体保护半自动焊和自动焊是必然趋势，但还有很长的路要走。

3.3 多丝焊接技术

单面多丝焊焊接速度快、熔敷率高，在大型生产场合应用较多。一般采用多个电源分别控制多条焊丝，焊丝采用并联或者串联结构。由于电弧距离较近，需要考虑电弧之间的相互作用力，因此多个电源要协调控制以得到最佳焊接效果。在整个焊接系统中，数字化网络极为重要。例如在 Lincoln 公司由 Power Wave AC/DC 1000 组成的多丝埋弧焊中，用 ArcLink 技术和 DeviceNet 技术组成焊机网络，利用 ETHERNET 技术组成局域网并与上位机相连监控多个焊机的焊接状态及进行控制。

在 MIG/MAG 焊中最常用的是双丝焊接，例如 Fronius 公司的 Time Twin 技术。它由两台数字化 TPS4000/5000 焊接电源组成，在焊接过程中，作为电极的 2 根焊丝处在同一保护气环境下，需要保护气流量比较大（40~50L/min）。焊丝由 2 个独立、相互绝缘导电嘴送出后熔化并形成同一熔池，2 个电弧相位相差 180°，同时提高焊接速度和熔敷效率。焊接速度是普通 MIG/MAG 焊的 3~4 倍，可达 4m/min；具有高熔敷效率，焊接碳钢时熔敷率超过 30kg/h。

在双丝焊接中，应用最多的还是 Tandem 技术。Tandem 的意思就是一前一后。Tandem 技术以奥地利 Fronius 和德国 Cloos 公司为代表，美国的 Lincoln 公司在 20 世纪 90 年代早期也引进 TandemMIG 技术。该技术中，可将 2 个电弧分为前导弧和跟踪弧。前导弧控制熔深，跟踪弧控制焊缝外观。也可以只用 1 个电弧进行单丝焊以增加持续焊接时间，减小焊接周期；2 根焊丝也可分别为实芯或药芯焊丝。Fronius 的 Tandem 系统通过选择"标准电弧"或者"脉冲电弧"产生 4 种不同的结果。表述如下。

A：脉冲/脉冲模式。这是最常用的工作状态。前导弧和跟踪弧为同步脉冲模式且每个电弧的峰值产生在另一个电弧的基值上。

B：脉冲/标准模式。前导弧为脉冲，跟踪弧为持续电压。这样可以达到最快焊接速度和最宽焊缝。

C：标准/脉冲模式。前导弧为持续电压模式可以使熔深增加并提高焊接速度，跟踪弧为脉冲模式减小热输入量控制焊缝成形。

D：标准/标准模式。前导弧和跟踪弧都为持续电压模式。此时一般只用单丝焊接，当更换焊接方向时，同时更换工作电极以减小工作周期。

通过运用 Tandem 技术，可以极大提高焊接效率，相对单丝焊提高 40%~80%；焊接速度翻倍甚至更高；熔深加大；通过离线编程可以用任一焊丝按任意方向焊接，适应性强、生产成本降低，可提高生产率。

3.4 高能束焊接与复合热源焊接技术

高能束流（High Energy Density Beam）加工技术包含了以激光束、电子束和等离子弧为热源对材料或构件进行特种加工的各类工艺方法。高能束流焊接技术是现代高科技与先进制造技术相结合的产物，国内在高能束流焊接设备水平上与国外有一定差距，但在工艺研究上水平较为接近，在某些方面甚至还有自己的特色。当前高能束流焊接被关注的主要领域是高能束流设备的大型化，如功率大型化及可加工零件的大型化、设备的智能化以及加工的柔性化、束流品质的提高、束流的复合及相互作用、新材料焊接及应用领域的扩展。

高能束流焊接设备向大型化发展有两层含义，一是设备的功率增大，二是采用该设备焊接的零件大型化。由于高能束流焊接设备一次性投资大，特别是激光焊和电子束焊设备。因此增大功率、提高焊接深度和焊接过程的稳定性，相对降低焊接成本，才能为工业界所接受。大型焊接配套设备建立之后，高能束流焊接成本可以进一步降低，有利于在军用工业、民用工业等各个领域中扩大应用。

3.4.1 电子束焊接

电子束焊在工业上的应用已有 50 多年的历史，随着电子技术、高压和真空技术的发展，电子束焊接技术的研究及推广应用极为迅速，在大批量、大厚度件生产、大型零件制造以及复杂零件的焊接加工方面都显示出独特的优越性。目前，在工业中实际应用的电子束焊接设备的功率一般小于 150kW，加速电压在 200kV 以内。一次可焊最大厚度钢板约为 300mm，铝合金约 50mm。

随着国内外对电子束焊接设备及控制、同种及异种材料焊接工艺、电子束焊接理论等方面研究的深入，电子束焊接技术在航空燃油测量系统、飞机发动机上得到了广泛应用。焊接产品涉及航空装备、卫星导航、雷达通讯、舰载机箱，尤其是变截面电子束焊接技术的出现，为航空工业的发展起到了促进作用。正是由于这项技术使得许多复杂的飞机和发动机零部件的一次性焊接成为可能，避免了多次焊接出现的局部焊接缺陷和重复加热所造成的组织性能下降，提高了飞机的整体性能。

进入21世纪，随着人类活动空间向太空的进一步扩展，电子束焊接技术的应用也逐步拓展到太空领域。高低温度交替冲击、失重、真空及宇宙线辐射等特殊的太空环境，对宇航零部件的结构设计、材料选择及加工工艺提出了极为苛刻的要求。实践证明，为了满足上述特点，电子束焊接技术是必不可少的强有力的工具之一。为适应特殊的焊接环境，空间所用电子束焊机应具有以下特点：一是重量轻、体积小，以方便火箭运载及宇航员操作；二是要对宇宙辐射线进行防护；三是需要考虑失重、超高真空、空间温度交变的影响。

由于电子束焊接过程中电子束与金属之间的深穿透和快速物理化学冶金作用，以及当前研究分析手段上的局限性，使得电子束焊机理的本质研究有待进一步深入。同时，借助于计算机系统更新、软件升级，有望在脉冲电子束焊、电子束焊缝自动跟踪系统上寻求突破，从而实现超薄零件、不规则焊缝的自动化和半自动化焊接。

3.4.2 激光焊接

激光焊是以聚焦的激光束作为能源轰击焊件所产生的热量进行焊接的方法。激光焊接技术经历了由脉冲波向连续波的发展、有效功率薄板焊接向大功率厚件焊接的发展、由单工作台、单工件向多工作台、多工件同时焊接的发展，以及由简单焊缝形状向可控的复杂焊缝形状的发展。目前激光焊接技术几乎已涉及各个工业领域，尤其在航空航天、汽车制造业，激光焊技术能够显著降低成本、提高生产效率、减轻飞机、航天武器和飞行器的重量，成为传统焊接技术的有效补充，显示出某些独特的优势。

激光焊接技术是飞机制造业的一次技术革命。例如空客A380是欧洲空中客车公司设计生产的运输力最大的民用飞机，空客A380之所以能大大减轻飞机重量（机身重量减轻18%），减少油耗排放，降低营运成本的主要原因就是将激光焊接技术应用于飞机机身、机翼的内隔板与加强筋的全部连接，取代了原有的铆接工艺，被称为航空制造业中的一大技术革命。

激光技术已成功用于焊接航空发动机主要结构件，如叶片、燃烧室、机匣等。普惠公司在美国空军项目计划资助下，建立了涡轮叶片激光焊接中心，可以完成涡轮叶片所需部件的自动激光焊接，如JT9D和FLO的二级涡轮转子叶片以及V2500、F100-PW-220等发动机的涡轮叶片、导向叶片、机匣、燃烧室等均采用激光焊接技术。V2500发动机的风扇机匣前后段是采用6kW的CO_2激光束将其焊成一整体。美国GE公司也成功完成了发动机导向叶片组件的激光焊接，解决了镍基合金零件激光焊接变形与裂纹等问题，并用CO_2激光设备焊接喷气发动机燃烧室衬套。钛合金飞行舵翼外型面为空间曲线型面，要求连接强度高，焊接过程采用计算机编程，实现了焊接轨迹和激光焊枪的精密调整，保证焊接过程与局部保护等技术的协调运动控制，提高了焊接质量。

激光焊接技术用于航空航天工业仍面临新型激光器研发、先进工艺研究、焊接性能预测及质量控制等方面的问题。目前，激光焊接所用的激光器主要为大功率CO_2激光器、脉冲YAG激光器和光纤激光器，激光器的发展应集中于高性能激光设备的研发，如提高电源的稳定性和寿命，对于CO_2气体激光器要解决大功率激光器的放电稳定性，对于YAG固体激光器要研制大容量、长寿命的光泵激励光源。

在激光焊接过程控制和质量预测研究中，关键问题是建立熔池形状参数与焊接工艺之间的关系。一些研究者根据激光深熔焊中的小孔机制，对激光焊接的温度场、液体流动及小孔形状、尺寸等用计算机进行模拟计算并取得了一定效果。随着图像传感方法的改进，人们可以从熔池图像获得熔池形状更多的特征信息，如熔池宽度、长度和面积，这对激光焊焊缝质量控制有着重要的作用，这也是激光焊接研究的一个重要方向。

3.4.3 高能束流的复合技术

近年来，国内外关于束流复合—焊接新工艺、新技术的研究报道推动了束流复合焊接技术的发展。其中最主要的是采用激光—电弧复合热源的高效焊接技术。高能束流焊接的优势很明显，但目前高能束流焊接的成本仍较高，因此以激光为核心的复合技术受到人们的关注。事实上，激光—电弧复合在20世纪70年代就已提出，然而稳定的加工应用直至近几年才出现，这得益于激光技术以及电弧焊设备的发展,尤其是激光功率和电弧控制技术的提高。

束流复合加工时,激光产生的等离子体有利于电弧的稳定;复合加工可提高加工效率,提高焊接性差的材料(如铝合金、双相钢等)的焊接性,增加焊接稳定性和可靠性;激光加丝焊对参数变化是很敏感的,通过与激光—电弧的复合,则变得容易而可靠。

激光—电弧复合主要是激光与钨极氩弧、等离子弧以及活性电弧的复合。通过激光与电弧的相互影响,克服每一种焊接方法自身的不足,产生良好的复合效应。

熔化极活性电弧成本低,使用填丝,适用性强;缺点是熔深浅、焊接速率低、工件承受热载荷大。激光焊可形成深而窄的焊缝,焊接速率快、热输入低,但设备成本高,对工件制备精度要求高,对铝等材料的适应性差。激光—MIG/MAG 的复合效应表现在:电弧增加了对间隙的桥接性,其原因一是填充焊丝,二是电弧加热范围较宽;但复合电弧的功率决定了焊缝顶部宽度;激光产生的等离子体减小了电弧引燃和维持的阻力,使电弧更稳定;激光功率决定了焊缝的深度。也就是说,复合电弧导致了焊接效率增加,增强了焊接适应性。

激光—电弧复合对焊接效率的提高十分显著,这主要基于 2 种效应:一是较高的能量密度导致了较高的焊接速度,工件热流损失减小;二是两热源相互作用的叠加效应。焊接钢时,激光等离子体使电弧更稳定;同时电弧也进入熔池小孔,减小了能量的损失。

激光—MIG/MAG 的复合可增加焊接速度,约为钨极氩弧焊的 2 倍。钨极烧损也大大减小,坡口夹角也可显著减小,焊缝截面积与激光焊时相近。与激光单弧焊相比,激光双弧复合焊接的焊接热输入可减小 25%,而焊接速度可增加约 30%。

激光—电弧(或等离子弧)复合焊接的优点主要是提高了焊接速度和熔深。由于电弧加热,金属温度升高,降低了金属对激光的反射率,增加了对光能的吸收。这种方法在小功率 CO_2 激光器试验基础上,还在 12kW 的 CO_2 激光器以及光纤传输的 2kW 的 YAG 激光器上进行试验,并为应用机器人进行激光—电弧(或等离子弧)复合焊接打下了基础。

激光焊接复合技术还有激光—高频焊、激光—压焊、激光—搅拌摩擦焊等。激光—高频焊是在高频焊管的同时,采用激光对熔焊处叠加热量,使待焊件在整个焊缝厚度上的加热更均匀,有利于提高焊管的接头质量和生产率。激光—压焊是将聚焦的激光束照射到被连接工件的接合面上,利用材料表面对垂直偏振光的高反射将激光导向焊接区。由于接头特定的几何形状,激光能量在焊接区被完全吸收,使工件表层的金属加热或熔化,然后在压力作用下实现材料的连接。这样不仅焊缝强度高,焊接速度也得到大幅度提高。

搅拌摩擦焊是近年来发展起来的先进焊接技术。激光—搅拌摩擦焊是采用激光束在 FSW 搅拌头前方进行预热的复合搅拌摩擦焊,可以大幅度加快焊接速度。这种方法采用 YAG 激光发生器,自左而右和自上而下采用氩气保护。

近年来,通过激光—电弧复合而诞生的高能束流复合焊接技术获得了长足的发展,在航空航天、军工等部门复杂构件上的应用受到重视。目前,高能束流与不同电弧的复合焊接技术已成为高能束流焊接领域发展的热点之一。

某病房行政楼采暖空调系统节能潜力分析与效果评估

张恩祥

根据统计,发达国家的建筑物能耗已占全国总能耗的30%~45%左右,在民用建筑中暖通空调能耗达到65%。为保证建筑的舒适性要求,暖通空调设计通常考虑较大的负荷余量,造成冷热源能量的供给与末端负荷需求之间能量匹配矛盾越来越明显,导致冷水机组、输送系统和末端设备长期在低效率下运行,运行成本居高不下。因此,有针对性的研究既有建筑物暖通空调系统形式和运行情况,从负荷需求与合理运行的角度,研究分析其节能潜力与措施显得尤为重要,对建筑设备节能具有重要意义。

1 某病房行政楼采暖空调系统概况

该建筑物总建筑面积约15000m^2,空调系统为无新风的风机盘管系统,风机盘管数量为509台,制冷机为10台模块化冷水机组RC130,最大输出冷量为1300kW,最大名义使用电功率为407kW。冷冻水泵KQW200—315和冷却水泵KQW200—250均为一用一备,冷却塔LRCM—LN—350一台。中央空调每年的使用时间为5月下旬到10月1日前,使用天数约130d。在使用期空调系统的每天开机时间随室外温度的增减而变化,每年中央空调系统运行约2800h。热源采用燃气锅炉,末端设备为暖气片。

2 冷负荷需求分析与节能措施

2.1 冷机运行冷负荷次数与时间频数分析

中央空调系统的工作一般分为两个阶段,第一阶段将空调房间的室温降低到设定温度,第二阶段维持空调房间的室温。在各阶段空调系统投入的负荷比例不同。表1是根据2008年5月至2008年8月20日间该楼空调系统的不同负荷率下运行次数,统计分析的平均时间频数情况。

表1 空调运行冷负荷时间频数表

负荷(%) 次数	5	10	15	20	25	30	35	40	45	50	55	60	65	70	75	80	85	90	95	100
5月	2	0	0	24	0	0	9	1	0	4	0	0	0	0	0	0	5	0	0	
6月	5	2	0	120	5	5	64	2	31	11	1	27	0	3	3	8	0	5	0	1
7月	0	0	0	39	2	5	71	4	89	2	2	60	5	5	58	3	25	2	0	0
8月	0	0	0	27	6	1	51	5	50	0	1	53	1	2	25	2	14	0	0	2
次数累计	7	2	0	210	13	11	186	12	170	17	4	140	6	10	86	13	39	15	0	3
平均时间频数(%)	0.7	0.4	0	22.3	1.3	1.17	19.8	1.28	18.1	1.8	0.4	14.9	0.6	1.1	9.1	1.3	4.1	1.6	0	0.3
平均负荷(%)	46.87								36.88						16.26					

由表1可见,在2008年供冷季运行的85天内,有47%的开机时间空调的负荷低于名义装机容量的40%,高于75%的空调负荷时间仅占开机时间的17%。

2.2 空调循环水温差变化趋势分析

空调水系统普遍存在着大流量小温差的问题,特别是在供冷季初期,由于室外的温度较低,导致空调负荷的需求较少。根据运行记录表2所示,在20%负荷的时候,冷冻水的温差仅为0.5℃,冷却水温

[作者简介] 张恩祥,北京联合大学生物化学工程学院。

差仅为 1.5℃。RC130 冷水机组为恒水量型，标准工况为冷冻水出水温度 7℃，进水/出水温差 5.6℃，冷却水出水温度 35℃，进水/出水温差 5.6℃。

表2 空调系统循环水温差随空调负荷变化趋势表

运行负荷率（%）	冷冻水/℃			冷却水/℃		
	进水	出水	温差	进水	出水	温差
20	12	11.5	0.5	23	24.5	1.5
35	12.5	11	1.5	23.5	26	2.5
45	13	11.5	1.5	24	27	3
60	13.5	11.5	2	25.5	29.5	4
70	13	11	2	29	33	4
80	13.5	11	2.5	26.5	30.5	4
90	14	10.5	3.5	27	32.5	5.5
95	15	12.5	2.5	28.5	34	5.5

2.3 冷源系统节能措施

针对上述冷负荷需求和空调循环水温差变化趋势的分析，若将配备的冷水机组按照空调系统的实际需求进行分组运行，并采用变频调速装置实现恒温差控制，可有效减低水泵功耗，保持冷机和水泵运行在高效区间。如图1所示，将冷机按照 4:2:4 的形式进行拆分，模块之间的管道用电动蝶阀连接。采用专用的控制系统一方面根据冷水机组的负荷需求，确定电动蝶阀的开闭数量，实现 4:2:4 分组控制；另一方面又要实时跟踪和调整冷冻泵、冷却泵的运行流量，满足冷水机组 4:2:4 分组运行的流量需要，在此基础下，把供回水温度差恒定在 5℃左右的一个狭窄的区间内，使冷冻水，冷却水温差不随空调的热负荷变化而变化。

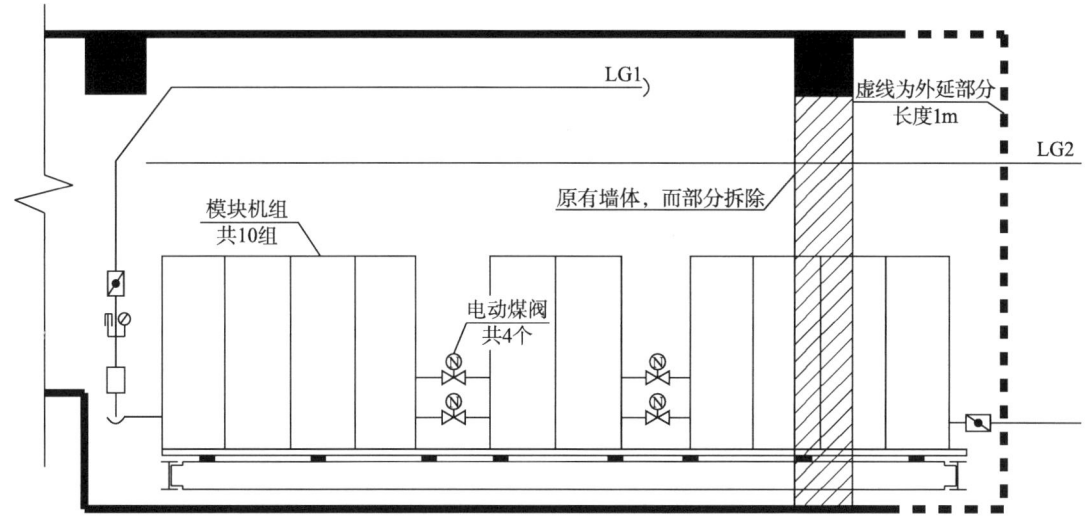

图1 模块化冷水机组分组安装示意

3 中央空调末端运行工况测试与节能措施

2007 年 7 月 29 日下午 2：00～3：00，对病房楼中央空调末端工况进行测试，测试结果见表3。空调系统在全天热负荷最大时间内均能满足室温 26℃的需求。在 50 个测试点，一个小时的测试时间内有 22 个测试点的室温低于 26℃ 的设定温度，占全部测试点的 44%。因此，通过改进风机盘管控制器，当空调房间的温度达到设定值时，停止风机盘管继续向空调房间供冷，使这一部分冷量回流，可有效的减低冷水机组的负荷，达到节省能源的目的。

表3 中央空调末端工况测试表

层号	测试时间	房间号	室温/℃	出风温度/℃	层号	测试时间	房间号	室温/℃	出风温度/℃
10区	2:00	大厅	26.1	17.8			护士站	25.3	16.5
		5310	25.9	17.5	3区	2:30	大厅	26.3	17.3
		5306	26.0	17.2			2110	27.0	未开
		护士站	25.4	16.9			2108	26.1	16.9
9区	2:05	大厅	25.9	17.2			护士站	25.4	16.6
		5110	27.0	未开	11区	2:35	大厅	25.8	17.8
		5108	26.1	17.1			6病室	26.2	18.2
		护士站	25.3	16.8			3病室	27.3	没开
7区	2:10	大厅	25.9	17.5			护士站	27.0	18.0
		4114	26.3	15.1	4区	2:40	大厅	26.0	16.8
		4113	27.1	未开			2308	27.4	未开
		护士站	25.3	17.0			2306	25.9	17.1
8区	2:15	大厅	26.2	17.7			护士站	25.5	16.4
		4310	25.8	17.2	2区	2:45	大厅	26.1	17.2
		4308	26.0	16.8			1313	26.1	16.9
		护士站	25.2	16.4			1308	27.0	未开
6区	2:20	大厅	26.2	17.7			护士站	25.3	16.9
		3309	25.5	17.3	1区	2:50	大厅	26.0	17.1
		3305	26.0	16.7			1108	26.9	未开
		护士站	25.5	16.3			1106	25.9	17.0
5区	2:25	大厅	26.1	17.8			护士站	25.9	16.7
		3108	26.0	17.1	特需门诊	2:55	大厅		
		3106	25.9	17.8	门诊	3:00	大厅	25.5	17.0
12区	3:05	大厅	26.2	17.4					
		321	25.7	未开					
		343	26.0	17.2					
		护士站	25.4	17.0					

4 办公区域采暖方式的节能潜力分析与措施

4.1 采用中央空调供暖方式的节能潜力分析

病房行政楼冬季采暖采用传统的暖气片，热源由燃气锅炉提供，冬季最高供水温度为65℃，全年供暖时间为150d，采暖面积为15520m^2，其中病区（包括区内的病房、公共区、护士站等）采暖要求24h，室温达到18~22℃，占总采暖面积的48%；办公室区（包括实验室、会议室等）除值班室和少数加班的办公室外，采暖仅要求在上班时间，供暖房间的室温达到18~22℃，其余时间可低温保持，占总采暖面积的52%。由于采暖系统没有能量输出的调节功能，即使办公区在非工作时间内采暖房间的室温也只能保持和病区采暖房间的室温相一致，造成较大的能耗浪费。若采用中央空调供暖，当管道中通入50℃热水时，风机盘管（以风机盘管型号为803为例）可输出热量8770W，达到平均219 W/m^2的供暖要求。当风机盘管的风机停止工作后，风机盘管的输出热量低于额定输出热量的5%，这就意味着末端将节约90%以上的热量。

4.2 供暖系统节能改造措施

在锅炉房负一层泵房内新增引管DN125，将锅炉热水通过锅炉房外公共管沟，接入行政楼的中央空调主干输送水管进入中央空调系统,重新调整病房行政楼的暖气系统的工作参数。在走廊、卫生间、浴室、地下室无风机盘管的地方,保留原暖气供暖功能,其余部分关闭。为解决在低负荷末端热水过流量问题,在供水端增加了一个电动三通阀实现分流控制,以达到负荷与流量的匹配,见图2和图3。

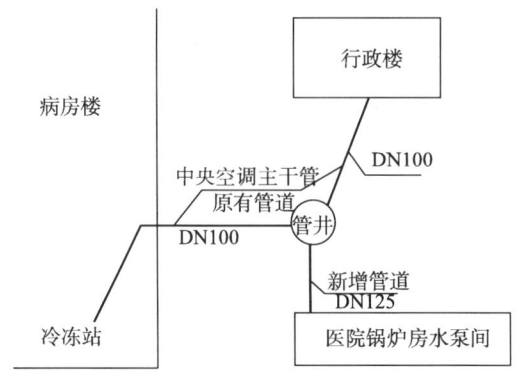

图2 空调供暖管道改造方案示意图

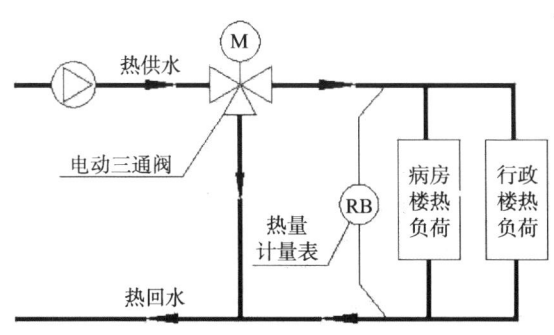

图3 采暖流量控制示意图

5 节能效果评估

5.1 冷源系统节能效果

模块化冷水机组根据动态负荷需求按照4:2:4模式分组运行后,使中央空调冷冻水泵和冷却水泵的实际电功率相应减少,节能效果分析计算,见表4。考虑到水系统恒温差变频控制是在冷水机组4:2:4分组运行模式对水量需求的基础上进行的频率精细调节,运行工况复杂,具体节能效果很难准确计算,若根据经验按节约5%统计,则节电6118kW·h。

表4 冷水机组4:2:4分组运行冷冻水泵与冷却水泵节能效果

组别	流量/(m³/h)		水泵功率变化/kW			运行时间		节约度
	设计值	改造后	当前	改造后	节约	(%)	/h	(kW·h)
10组	223 (330)		27.45 (16.02)			100	2816	0
4组	/	89.2 (132)	/	10.98 (6.41)	16.47 (9.61)	46.9	1320	21740 (12692)
4+2组	/	133.8 (198)	/	16.47 (9.61)	10.98 (6.41)	35.2	991	10881 (6353)
4+2+4组	/	223 (330)	/	27.45 (16.02)	0	17.9	505	0
总计								16310 (9522)

注:( )中数据为冷却水泵数据。

5.2 中央空调末端节能效果

由于空调房间的温度的控制受使用者人为喜好的因素的影响较大,所以风机盘管控制器改造的节能潜力一般为冷水机组负荷的5%~15%之间。根据统计,在平均负荷45%的情况下,冷水机组的平均耗电

149.4kW，按节能率低限5%计算，节约功率7.47kW，取运行时间2816h，可节约电20106kW·h。

5.3 采暖系统节能效果

按照办公区在工作时间（周一～周五）内每天工作10h，其余时间内有15%区域在加班，非工作时间内风机盘管输出热量只有5%的输出，办公区在供暖季其供暖的能量最大的节省空间可达50%。

6 结 论

针对某病房行政楼暖通空调系统的形式、运行方式和运行数据，分析其动态空调负荷需求，研究其节能潜力和节能措施。冷源系统采用模块冷水机组分组优化控制和水系统恒温差变频控制，按供冷季运行2816h计算，共节电31950 kW·h，节能率可达26.1%；中央空调末端通过改进控制器，节能率达到5%；改变办公区域供暖方式，由中央空调替代传统的暖气片，节能率可达到50%，大大提高了既有建筑物暖通空调系统的运行效率，具有很好的经济性。

参考文献

［1］Thomas B. Hartman，P. E，Design issues of variable chilled – water flow through chillers ［J］，ASHRAE Transactions：Symposia，v102. n2. 1996，679 – 683.
［2］高养田. 空调变流量水系统设计技术发展［J］. 暖通空调，1996（3）.
［3］汪训昌，林海燕，杨书渊，等. 办公楼空调冷热负荷的计算分析——关于北京地区办公楼外区冬季冷负荷的几点看法［J］. 暖通空调，2004，34（7）：33 – 39.
［4］孙志高，马荣生. 空调系统的节能研究［J］. 节能技术，2004（4）.

真实世界中的虚拟与虚拟世界中的真实

张 楠

信息技术的迅猛发展，使网络世界与现实世界的深度融合加剧，网络世界依附现实世界的初始形态发生突变，网络世界与现实世界的交融日益深化，传统意义的现实世界的内涵更加丰富。虚拟的网络世界已成为人类实践活动的崭新空间，人在真实与虚拟之间穿梭，在真实与虚拟中转换角色。真实世界中的虚拟与虚拟世界中的真实、虚拟世界中的真实与虚拟的本质、真实与虚拟与人的存在样态的关系等问题，成为颇具研究价值的理论与现实问题。

一、真实世界中的虚拟与虚拟世界中的真实之现象

所谓真实世界，有广义和狭义之分。广义的真实世界是指包括网络世界在内的整个现实世界；狭义的真实世界是指传统意义上的现实世界，即不包括网络世界的现实世界。本文在狭义上使用"真实世界"这一概念。虚拟世界专指利用信息技术发展建造起的网络世界。

1. 真实世界中的虚拟表象

网络技术应用以前，人们生活在一个现实的世界之中。真实，是那种可以确证的存在：真实的生产活动、真实的生活空间、真实的岁月流逝、真实的性别和职业、真实的交往对象和情感交流，等等。世界的真实性存在触手可及。虚拟作为一种不真实的存在，在真实的现实世界中，多存在于科学研究、文学艺术创作之中。譬如，科学研究中的假设、假定、假想、假说，文学艺术中的想象、幻想、虚构、虚拟、模拟，等等。虚拟既是科学研究、文学创作的方法，也是科学研究不可或缺的重要环节和文学艺术创作的构成要素，是人类特有的文化现象和精神活动。不仅如此，随着信息技术的快速发展，虚拟作为一种技术手段也已广泛应用于国防、工业设计、医学等领域。真实世界中的虚拟伴随着科学研究、文学艺术创作以及技术应用的发展而发展。在此意义上可以说，"虚拟贯穿人类文明发展的始终，渗透于生活的方方面面，是我们生活的一部分，是人类独有的文化实践"。[1]

真实世界中的虚假不属于虚拟范畴，它与真实相对，是与实际不符的不真实，却是一种真实的存在。

如经济增长中的泡沫成分、商业活动中的弄虚作假、商品交换中的以次充好，以及假话、假唱、假球、假钞、假案等，都是为达到某种目的而采取的欺诈手段和行为。另一种情形，如信仰危机、价值迷茫、诚信缺失、道德失范等社会现象，亦不属于真实世界中的虚拟范畴，它们一般发生在社会转型或社会动荡时期，是社会存在的真实反映。但在真实的现实社会中，它们的表象有些是显性的，有些是隐性的。这些显性的社会现象通过新型价值体系的重建或构建寻求解决路径；其隐性的社会现象一般通过个体或群体的深度迷茫、焦虑、痛苦等精神活动和心理症状表现出来。

2. 虚拟世界中的真实表征

对于传统的现实世界而言，网络世界的虚拟性毋庸置疑——虚拟的国籍、地域、民族、种族、职业、性别、年龄、交往；虚拟的时空变换；虚拟的生产、经营、交换；虚拟的战争、自然灾害，等等。在虚拟的网络世界中，现实世界中的真实几乎都可以虚拟的样态存在，虚拟世界不仅可以模拟现实世界的存在，还可以创造现实世界中的非存在。然而，透过网络世界中的虚拟，可以发现虚拟世界中的真实表征和真实存在。

依据真实性特点，网络世界中的真实可分为真真实、虚真实、合真实。（1）真真实，是指网络世界与现实世界具有同一性的活动或事物，包括作为现代信息技术的载体——物质的网络世界——的真实存

[作者简介] 张楠（1963—），女，吉林榆树人，北京联合大学副教授，从事马克思主义理论研究。

在；网络活动主体——人的真实存在；网络活动主体人的网络活动时空的真实存在；网络世界中的网络活动本身的真实存在，如真实的信息传递、知识传播、商业活动、情感交流等。（2）虚真实，是网络世界中剥去虚拟形式后的活动主体及其活动过程、活动内容、活动结果的真实，包括网络世界中虚拟的活动主体的真实存在，虚拟活动本身的真实存在，如以虚拟身份进行的交往、交流等精神活动。（3）合真实，是指虚拟的网络世界对真实的现实世界的整体性影响，包括网络世界对现实世界影响本身的真实存在，网络技术引发人类的生产方式、生活方式和思维方式的深刻变革，引发整个世界的经济、政治、文化、军事等方面的深刻变化，引发人们交往方式和社会组织结构的深刻变化等。可见，网络技术已全面渗透于社会生活的各个方面，从根本上改变了人类的生产方式、生活方式和思想观念。因此，虚拟世界中的真实表征，本质上是网络技术进步带来的人类实践活动的拓展，"不管哪一种虚拟，都是人类文化所必需的。科学、历史、艺术等都会由于虚拟而显示出自身的深度和真实性。"[2]

二、虚拟世界中的真实与虚拟之本质

1. 虚拟世界中的真实

如前文所述，虚拟世界中的真实可归结为真真实、虚真实、合真实三类，三者的共同特点是都具有真实性，都是真实存在。不同于以往的技术进步只是延伸人的大脑、五官、四肢，信息技术延展的是包括人在内的整个世界，这个世界无边无际、无所不包。

真真实是人作为主体性存在，在一定的时空条件下，在信息技术创造的网络世界中从事的真实的社会实践活动。真真实本质上是依赖技术进步实现的现实世界和人类实践活动的延展。

虚真实主要是指虚拟主体（隐去真实身份的真实主体）以信息、思想、情感、心理为主要内容的网络交往、交流等精神活动，包括网上信息传递、交友、恋爱、交流以及网络论坛、网络答疑、网络游戏等，这是网络世界独有的文化现象，在真实的世界中是不存在的。信息技术把真实世界模拟成一个地球村。地球村的环境污染、能源危机、战争不断、恐怖威胁、自然灾害，以及技术进步带来的诸多道德问题、心理问题等，无时无刻不在困扰着人们；不论从农业社会向工业社会、工业社会向现代社会、现代社会向后现代社会的发展，世界范围内的科技进步，在给人类带来巨大的物质财富和精神财富的同时，人类精神却不能在这个世界上找到安稳的栖息之地；经济的全球化使资本、生产、经营、消费、人才在世界范围内加速流动，世界政治经济形势的多变性、复杂性、不可预见性，给人们带来诸多的生存压力和焦虑，"社会的隔离感和孤独感使人们强烈意识到自身的存在成为一种被压抑的存在，一种放弃了自我意识的存在。"[1]在虚真实中，人们可以一定程度地认识自我、释放自我、把握自我和确认自我。因此，虚真实是技术进步的结果，本质上是人类在网络世界中的精神活动，是人的精神需求在网络世界中的真实投射。

合真实涉及虚拟世界与真实世界的关系问题，主要是指网络世界对现实世界的整体性影响，这种影响是全方位的、立体式的、快捷的、无形的。网络技术从根本上引发了人类生产方式、生活方式和思维方式的变革，对人类生存与进步带来巨大影响，为人的全面发展创建了前所未有的环境与空间。然而，网络世界会在多大程度上影响人类社会的发展方向和历史进程？人类的主宰是谁？是人类自身还是科技进步？网络技术引发整个世界的经济、政治、文化、军事等方面的深刻变化，给人类带来无限遐想与无数梦魇，网络技术对世界经济、政治秩序的影响是偶然的还是必然的？合真实启示人类要洞悉和把握科技进步与技术异化的关系，探索如何驾驭人类自身创造的科技成果，最大限度地降低技术异化带来的负效应。人类面对技术异化表现出无奈后，还会有什么样的表情和办法？还有没有普遍的人类正义、人类良知？人类需不需要终极关怀？人类个体要不要关注如此巨大而久远的人类困惑？合真实从本质上而言，是虚拟的网络世界对真实的现实世界的整体性的强烈的影响，真实的现实世界与虚拟的网络世界之间的深度交融加剧。因此，虚拟的网络世界中的真实，不管是哪一种真实，都是人类实践活动的现实拓展。正如技术进步的两面性一样，网络世界在最大限度地延展现实世界、为人类提供更为便捷的技术手段的同时，也给人类带来了无形的威胁。

2. 虚拟世界中的虚拟

作为一种纯粹的非存在，虚拟世界中的虚拟活动的主体仍然是真实存在的，只不过是一种虚拟存在。如虚拟生产和虚拟经营，除虚拟主体是真实的存在外，其生产或经营的全过程都是虚拟的，包括生产产品和经营收益，这些产品和收益既不是真实的存在，也不能进入现实世界之中，确切地说，这种虚拟活动是一种生存训练或生命体验。在此意义上，诸如网络农庄、网络婚姻等亦属于虚拟世界中的虚拟。除了生存训练或生命体验，虚拟世界中的虚拟还有更深层的意蕴。试拿网络"偷菜"现象为例，"偷菜"现象何以能风靡一时，何以能影响现实生活中的夫妻关系，值得反思。远离色情和战争游戏的网络"偷菜"，是老少咸宜的网络消遣活动，在种菜、收获的整个过程中，"偷菜"成为一个焦点环节，"偷"成为游戏中的游戏。没有法律制约，没有道德约束，也不需要承担责任，在他人不在场的情况下完成偷菜，便赢得游戏，产生"成就感"和"愉悦感"。虚拟与游戏"与现实性相对，他们体现出一种超越性与非日常性……有很大的自主性"。[1]因此，虚拟世界中的虚拟，实质上是人的一种本质需求，是人的思想、道德、情感、心理、意志、欲望等方面的需求，它反映的是人作为真实存在的真实生存愿望和存在样态。

三、真实世界与虚拟世界中人的存在样态

1. 人的存在样态的本质关联

人的存在样态与人的本质密切相关。"人来源于动物界这一事实已经决定人永远不能完全摆脱兽性，所以问题永远只能在于摆脱得多些或少些，在于兽性或人性的程度上的差异。"[3]人作为社会存在物，是自然属性与社会属性的统一体，马克思把人的本质界定为"不是单个人所具有的抽象物，在其现实性上，它是一切社会关系的总和"。人的本质是多方面的、多层次的、动态的复杂系统，因此，人的存在样态也是多样的、多层次的、动态的。人的存在样态又与人的需要直接相关。马斯洛把人的需要分为生理需要、安全需要、归属和爱的需要、自尊需要、自我实现需要五个层次。这五个层次的需要又可归结为物质需要和精神需要。物质需要作为基础性、保障性需要，精神需要作为发展性、价值性需要，两者既相对独立，又相互影响、相互制约，在现实生活中以极其复杂的状态表现出来。

2. 人的存在样态的基本形式

从历史上看，人的存在样态可归结为三种基本形式，即"对人的依赖"、"对物的依赖"和"对物与灵的依赖"。（1）在对人的依赖性社会和时期中，人们的活动受血缘和地域关系的限制，物质生产活动是人们主要的生产活动，人们的生产活动深深陷于对一定群体的依赖之中，无自由可言。（2）在对物的依赖性社会和时期中，由于商品经济的发展，在世界范围内形成了普遍的社会物质交往，人虽然从对人的依赖中解脱出来，却落入了对金钱关系和商品关系的依赖之中，人成为异化的个人，成为自由仍旧受限制的个人，这种对物的依赖历史地存在于现实社会之中。（3）在对物与灵的依赖性社会和时期中，不同程度依附金钱关系和商品关系的人们，在追逐物质需要的同时，必然会寻求精神需要，追求生存价值和自我实现，因此，人们往往在醉心于物质追求与享受的同时，又总是试图冲出物欲的羁绊，摆脱物欲带来的身心疲乏、精神空虚和生存价值的否定，试图获得情感慰藉和精神自由。人对物与灵的依赖体现人的双重属性，即趋乐避苦与道德情感。然而，人之社会性的理性更能标志人的存在。因此，对物与灵的依赖是人类的永恒依赖。

3. 人的存在样态的网络变化

网络世界的出现，深刻影响着现实世界人的存在方式，人的存在样态也表现出鲜明的网络特征。网络世界出现后，人的存在样态发生诸多变化：人对物的依赖从对现实的、真实的物的依赖向对现实世界中真实的物的依赖与虚拟世界中真实的物的依赖相结合转变；对灵的依赖从对一元的或一定的价值追求和道德生活的依赖向多样的、多层次的价值追求和道德生活的依赖转变；对灵的依赖从现实世界中显性与隐性并存向虚拟世界中全部显性的呈现并外溢于现实世界转变，在现实世界中以隐性形式存在的精神生活和心理、情感诉求，在虚拟的网络世界中以毫无遮掩的显性的形式存在。因此，虚拟的网络世界已全面渗入真实的现实世界之中，成为广义的真实的现实世界的组成部分。

四、真实世界中的虚拟与虚拟世界中的真实的共同诉求

世界范围内科技进步带来的物质财富的剧增，并没有降低人对物的依赖程度，人更加深陷物欲之

海，人不仅被异化，还流连忘返于拜金主义的狂潮之中，人之自由精神、价值追求被排斥在物欲之外。网络世界为人的全面而自由的发展创造了一个崭新空间，在一定程度上改变了现实世界人与人之间"咫尺天涯"的无奈与困境，最大限度地拉近了人与人之间的距离，增加了人与人之间交流的频度，不同地域、种族、身份、年龄的人都可以在一定时空实现思想交流、情感倾诉、心理释放；现实世界中隐性存在的精神困惑、心理焦虑等问题，亦可在网络世界中自由安全地得到适度消解；人在虚拟的网络世界中不断尝试变换角色，试图实现自我认识、自我释放、自我确认和自我提升，确认自我的真实存在。人作为社会性的主体存在，"天生就处于一个公共的社会关系网络中"，"只有当他进入了张开双臂拥抱他的社会公共空间之中，他才成为一个人"[4]。网络世界不仅全面而深刻地拓展了现实世界，还因其平民化、平等性、开放性、自由性、隐蔽性等特征独具神秘和魅力，使人们乐于穿梭于现实世界与网络世界之间，穿梭于真实与虚拟之间。

真实世界中的虚拟，无论是科学研究、艺术创造，还是虚拟现实的实际应用，都是人类理性的本质反映，是人类超越有限和暂时的生命冲动。虚拟世界中的真实，一方面确证科学技术进步和人类社会的发展，确证人类理性的光芒；另一方面也反映出人在科学技术迅猛发展中表现出的无奈、无助、孤独、困惑，以及永不停歇的精神的、道德的、情感的和心理的追求与探索，这亦是人的本质属性的表征，是人的存在样态的真实投射。因此，真实世界中的虚拟与虚拟世界中的真实的共同诉求，是人的存在样态的真实流露，是人对物与灵的本质依赖，是人对物质与精神的历史的、现实的和永恒的需求。

参考文献

[1] 朱珊. 作为人类一种存在方式的虚拟[J]. 哲学研究，2009（12）.
[2] 张世英. 现实·真实·虚拟[J]. 江海学刊，2003（1）：12.
[3] 马克思恩格斯选集：第3卷[M]. 北京：人民出版社，1995：442.
[4] 哈贝马斯. 公共空间与政治公共领域——我的两个思想主题的生活历史根源[J]. 哲学动态，2009（6）：5-10.

Integration of Tree Models into a Real – time Pollution Dispersion Simulation

Chen Shihong   Shangguan Dayan

Introduction

Along with the enhancement of human environment protection consciousness, the harm of air pollution to the environment, to human health and social development, is more and more universal concerned by the whole society. Protecting humanity's living environment has become the common aspiration of the people.

Researchers are working to understand the process of pollution dispersion and the influence of air pollution within the urban environment. This paper discusses the virtual interaction system about particle dispersion and wind simulation in an urban surrounding. The system can be used to get some information to help about emergency response training and preparedness, urban planning, and education about environmental concerns. [1]

During the simulation process, this system can promptly and with real – time interaction display a live simulation of pollution particles in a virtual city, showing the interactions between pollution particles and buildings. The current system does not support the interactions between pollution particles and trees. Trees and other woodlands add important structure to urban environments, and as such, the air pollution will have different effects to the environment of the city.

This paper refers to the real – time animation of 3D trees as a result of wind force and direction. Our work is being developed as part of an atmospheric, wind display project for real – time virtual environments. This paper discusses the techniques used in our creating tree models in real – time. The animation trees described in this paper will eventually be integrated into the TPAWT's system. Trees will be animated along with the wind speed and direction and the system will express the process of the air pollution in real – time interaction environment.

Related Work

The focus of this paper is on the implementation of tree animation along with wind. It uses two techniques, which can be applied in tree modeling of virtual environment and in constructing the combination of skinned mesh and tree modeling to simulate the movement of trees in the wind.

There is a lot of works have been done about creating tree model[2][3]. According to mathematic methodology of parameter, such as particle system, L system and IFS, etc, programming languages or modeling tools of generating tree and plants in developing languages of 3D design software are used to make tree models. Particle system is a stochastic modeling approach, which is consists of a large number of particles, the particles are independent of each other, change and make dynamic movement, over time. Reeves proposed a structurized particle system to simulate meadows, forests as a background environment[4]. L – systems in particular have being used extensively for modeling trees[5,6,7,8]. An L – system is a recursively defined algorithm, by increasing the recursion level the form slowly grows and becomes more complex, then the tree model will be generated. However the form created by L – system is similar, it is hard to generate trees with distinct shapes. Some people take the way which extract the information of three – dimensional skeleton trees from acquired one or more images. Tree models can be generated

---

[Author] Chen Shihong, College of Arts & Science, Beijing Union University, E – mail: csh398@126.com; Shangguan Dayan, School of Information & Technology, Beijing Forestry University, E – mail: 604567322@qq.com.

based on three-dimensional control points coordinates of framework and the width obtained from the segmentation of each control point[9].

It is important to use models with smaller numbers of polygons for real-time virtual environment simulation. However, the models generated by L-system based methods do not readily apply themselves for use in virtual environments due to the geometric complexity found in these models. The way of tree modeling is studied plenty, but not so much with regard to animating it.

Create Tree Model

There are many kinds of ways for plant modeling, which can be mainly categorized to the following two, one is 2D image-based modeling, and the other is 3D graphics-based. The modeling method based on 2D image replaces the 3D solid modeling by the images, which greatly reduces the number of the geometrical object's faces to increase the real time rendering rate, but the simulation effect is not lifelike in other words, the tree model is not physically representative of the actual tree model. The modeling graphics-based method imitates the character and details of the object themselves according to structure and characteristics of object, which can truly reflect the real shape characteristics. The modeling method based on graphics can be achieved to construct the objectives use 3D design software or the programming language according to the parameterized mathematics means. [10]

The effects of the detailed constructed trees such as the trunks, branches and leaves, using 3D solid modeling, are distinctly portrayed, but it requires large number of polygons, and thus, more rendering time for the system hampering cannot real time display.

Considering the problem of balancing the real scene and real time rendering, linking up with the characteristics of the system, in this paper, the software of 3D max has been adopted and the modeling method based on image and graphics blended has been adopted to construct the tree models. During the construction, the following key steps should be paid attention.

Trunk Construction. The tree truck is constructed with the adoption of the real 3D solid modeling, by the operation of moving, rotating, and scaling, the Figure 1 was achieved. After constantly using the EXTRUDE command, the branches were extruded from the trunks, as is shown in Fig. 2.

Leaves Construction. The leaves are represented by two cross patches, each of which has been texture mapped with images depicting sets of leaves, as shown in Fig. 3. Through the commands of the copy, moving, rotating, scaling, they were placed around the branches. During the process of placing, pay attention to the distribution of the leaves from the different view, especially from the top view, and try to achieve the effects of three dimensional and artistic effects. By doing this, we not only achieve the effect of a plausible, physically-based tree model, but also save the rendering time.

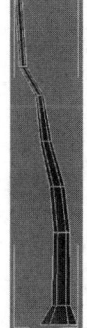  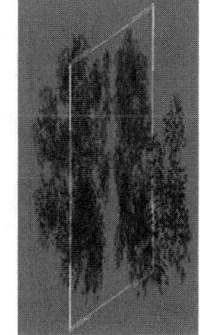

Fig. 1 Tree's trunks   Fig. 2 Tree's Branches   Fig. 3 Tree's Leaves

Summary

In this paper, we discuss the techniques used in our creating tree models in real-time. The model of the tree is created in 3D max platform. The approach which combines the way of based – on graphics and based – on image is effective for decrease the numbers of polygon. It is handled by the CPU into the GPU, and which is integrated into a real – time pollution dispersion simulation system. The experimental results show that this method is proper and efficient for simulating tree animation. Giving related parameters, the movements of the tree will be altered just like the whole tree under the wind force in the current. We will continue to develop this system to be more comprehensive. We believe that real – time pollution dispersion simulation system will help for recognizing the significance of environment protecting and city planning, and educating people about the relation between urban form, wind, trees and pollution.

AKNOWLEDGEMENT

Project supported by the key projects of the State Forestry Administration: The key technology research of wireless sensor gateway for forest monitoring (2011 – 04).

Finally, thank Peter Willemsen (University of Minnesota Duluth) for his advising and help during completing the paper.

Reference

[1] P. Willemsen, A. Norgren., B. Singh, and E. R. Pardyja. Integrating Particle Dispersion Models into Real – time Virtual Environments [J]. EGVE Symposium, 2008.

[2] P. Prezemyslaw, A. Lindenmayer. The Algorithmic Beauty of Plants [J]. Springer – Verlag, New York, NY, USA, 1996 (4).

[3] M. Fuhrer, H. W. Jensen, and P. Prusinkiewicz. Modeling Hairy Plants, In Proceedings of Pacific Graphics [J]. Seoul, Korea, 2004 (10): 217 – 226.

[4] Reeves, W. T. and Blau, R. Approximate and probabilistic algorithms for shading and rendering structured particle systems [J]. In SIGGRAPH '85. 1985.

[5] P. Prusinkiewicz, A. Lindenmayer and J. Hanan, Developmental. Models of Herbaceous Plants for Computer Imagery Purposes [J]. Computer Graphics, 1988, 22, (4): 114 – 150.

[6] P. Prusinkiewicz and A. Lindenmayer. The Algorithmic Beauty of Plants, Springer – Verlag. New York, 1990.

[7] Ilya Shlyakhter, Max Rozenoer, Julie Dorsey, Seth Teller, Reconstructing 3D Tree Models from Instrumented Photographs [J]. IEEE Computer Graphics and Applications, 2001 (5): 53 – 61.

[8] Wang kelun, Wang deqiang, Liu Ying. 3D Trees Simulation based on L – System. Proceedings of System Simulation Technology and Applications Conference, 2007: 509 – 511.

[9] YanTao, Wu enhua. Multiple – image – based Modeling of Trees [J]. ACTA SIMULATA SYSTEMATICA SINICA, 2000 (5): 565 – 571.

[10] Chen Shihong, Zhai Haijuan. Modelling Virtual Forest Park and its Implementation [J]. Computer Applications and Software, 2010 (27): 58 – 61.

毛细管电泳电致化学发光法同时测定氯丙嗪、异丙嗪及其主要代谢物

李旭菲　杨燕英　周考文

氯丙嗪（CPZ）和异丙嗪（PMZ）为重要的吩噻嗪类临床药物。CPZ 具有特殊的中枢抑制作用，主要用于治疗精神分裂症、躁狂症等；PMZ 具有较强的抗过敏及显著的中枢安定作用，能提高止痛、麻醉、镇静的效果，主要用于治疗过敏性疾病。在配药学上把二者混合制成安定类药物能降低中枢神经系统多巴胺的活性。这两种药物的代谢产物有很多种，其中亚砜类是其主要代谢物。因此建立 CPZ、PMZ、氯丙嗪亚砜（CPZSO）和异丙嗪亚砜（PMZSO）的快速测定方法对研究该类药物的剂量、利用率以及代谢途径都有十分重要的意义。

CPZ、PMZ、CPZSO 和 PMZSO 的分子结构相似，文献中对 CPZ 或（和）PMZ 测定方法的研究有很多报道，包括液相色谱法[1,2]、化学发光法[3,4]、光谱法[5,6]、电化学分析法[7-10]和色谱-质谱联用法[11-14]等，而对其代谢物的测定报道较少[12-14]。

毛细管电泳（CE）具有分离速度快、效率高、样品用量小等特点，它的出现使分析科学进入了纳升级水平，为小体积样品的分析提供了可能；而电致化学发光技术（ECL）可为微体积环境提供高灵敏检测；因此，CE 与 ECL 结合可以成为一种简便快速的分离分析技术。近年利用 CE-ECL 技术进行单组分或双组分药物分析的研究有很多报道[15-30]，而对 3 个或 3 个以上组分的连续测定则报道很少。

李云辉等[29]在检测电位 1.15V、钌联吡啶（$Ru(bpy)_3^{2+}$）浓度 5.0mmol/L、检测池磷酸缓冲溶液（pH 7.5）浓度 50mmol/L 和分离磷酸缓冲溶液（pH 4.0）浓度 30mmol/L 的条件下建立了 CPZ 和 PMZ 的 CE-ECL 分离检测方法。本文通过实验发现，在适当的电解电位下，$Ru(bpy)_3^{2+}$ 在铂电极上的弱电化学发光信号也可以被 CPZSO 和 PMZSO 不同程度的增敏。通过对分离条件和检测条件的优化，建立了同时测定 CPZ、PMZ、CPZSO 和 PMZSO 的 CE-ECL 方法，可在无需预分离的情况下用于较复杂混合溶液中 CPZ、PMZ、CPZSO 和 PMZSO 的同时连续测定。

1　实验部分

1.1　仪器、试剂与材料

MPI-B 型多参数化学发光分析测试系统（西安瑞迈分析仪器有限公司）；未涂层毛细管（50cm×25μm，河北永年光导纤维厂）。钌联吡啶纯品（Alfa Aesar）；磷酸氢二钠（分析纯，北京化工厂）；磷酸二氢钾（分析纯，北京化工厂）；CPZ、PMZ、CPZSO 和 PMZSO 标准品（中国药品生物制品检定所）；所用水为二次蒸馏水。

1.2　溶液制备

磷酸盐缓冲溶液：用磷酸氢二钠、磷酸二氢钾和二次蒸馏水配制；1g/L CPZ、PMZ、CPZSO 和 PMZSO 标准溶液：准确称取标准品 10.0mg，用 5mL 0.05mol/L HCl 溶解，转移至 10mL 容量瓶中并用水定容，避光于 4℃储存备用。

1.3　实验条件

检测池采用三电极系统：直径 500μm 的铂盘工作电极，直径 300μm 的 Ag/AgCl 参比电极，直径 1mm 的铂丝辅助电极。采用循环伏安法和恒电位法测定。毛细管在使用前分别用 0.1mol/L NaOH 溶液冲

[作者简介] 周考文，北京联合大学生物化学工程学院教授，研究方向为化学发光分析。

洗 20min，二次蒸馏水冲洗 10min，运行缓冲液冲洗 10min。检测池中的钌联吡啶 - 磷酸盐缓冲液每 3h 更新一次。实验中所用溶液需用 0.22μm 的醋酸纤维素膜过滤。

2 结果与讨论

2.1 检测条件的优化

2.1.1 检测电位

图 1 显示了在 5.0mmol/L Ru(bpy)$_3^{2+}$ 和 40mmol/L 磷酸盐缓冲溶液（pH 6.5）的检测溶液中检测电位对 CPZ、PMZ、CPZSO 和 PMZSO 增敏钌联吡啶电化学发光信号的影响。

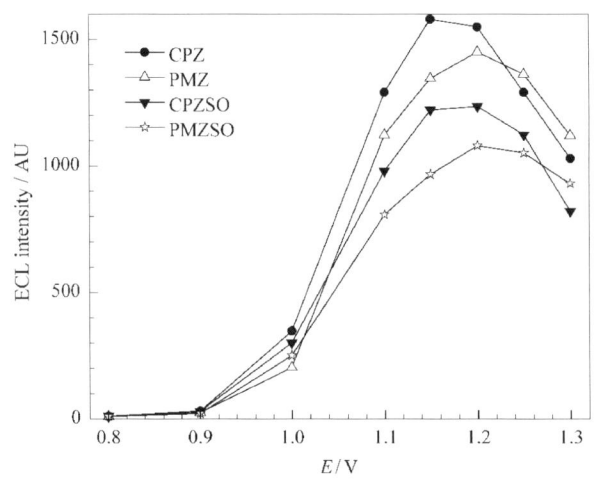

图 1 检测电位对电化学发光强度的影响

在检测电位低于 1.0V 时，没有达到 Ru(bpy)$_3^{2+}$ 的氧化电位，电化学发光强度很弱。随着检测电位的增加，电化学发光强度迅速增加，CPZ 在 1.15V 附近达到最大，CPZSO 的最大发光强度在 1.15～1.20V 范围内，而 PMZ 和 PMZSO 都在 1.20V 附近达到最大，此后，发光强度都开始不同程度的下降。综合考虑，选择 1.20V 为检测电位。

2.1.2 Ru(bpy)$_3^{2+}$ 浓度

实验采用毛细管电泳柱后电化学发光检测模式。当体系中存在叔胺类还原性共存物时，Ru(bpy)$_3^{2+}$ 的电化学发光机理是"氧化 - 还原型"的，即 Ru(bpy)$_3^{2+}$ 在工作电极上被氧化成 Ru(bpy)$_3^{3+}$，然后与还原性共存物作用产生激发态产物 [Ru(bpy)$_3^{2+}$]*，该产物返回基态时放出光子[31]。可见，Ru(bpy)$_3^{2+}$ 的初始浓度对电化学发光强度是有影响的。

实验发现，随着 Ru(bpy)$_3^{2+}$ 的初始浓度增大，发光强度也不断增大；但是，当其浓度大于 15.0mmol/L 时，发光信号基线变得不稳定，检测重现性也变差。实验中选用 5mmol/L Ru(bpy)$_3^{2+}$ 进行检测，可以获得较好的信噪比和较大的发光强度。

2.1.3 检测池缓冲液的 pH

实验发现，发光反应受溶液 pH 影响很大。磷酸盐缓冲溶液稳定性好，容易配制，pH 范围宽，故选用磷酸盐缓冲溶液来调节溶液酸度。图 2 为发光强度随检测池中磷酸盐缓冲溶液 pH 的变化曲线，从图 2 可见，CPZ、PMZ、CPZSO 和 PMZSO 的最佳发光酸度环境不完全相同，CPZ 在 pH 值为 6.0~6.5 时发光信号较大，PMZ 则为 6.5~7.0，CPZSO 为 5.5～6.5，而 PMZSO 为 5.5~7.5。综合考虑，选择 pH 值 6.5 的缓冲溶液基本能兼顾 4 种药物。

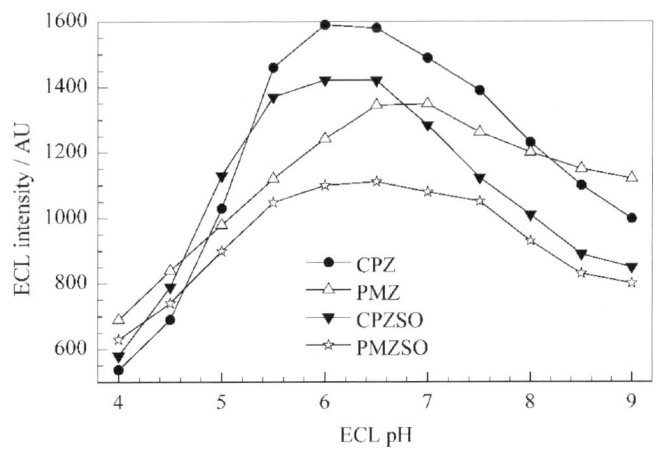

图2 检测池中磷酸盐冲溶液 pH 对电化学发光强度的影响

2.1.4 检测池中缓冲液的浓度

进一步的研究发现，磷酸盐缓冲溶液的浓度对发光强度也有影响，这可能是由于溶液离子强度对 Ru(bpy)$_3^{3+}$ 氧化能力有一定的影响所致。图3为发光强度随检测池中磷酸盐缓冲溶液浓度变化的曲线，从图3中可见，CPZ 在 40~45mmol/L、PMZ 在 35~45mmol/L、CPZSO 在 35~45mmol/L 和 PMZSO 在 35~50mmol/L 的磷酸盐缓冲溶液中发光强度较大。因此，选择磷酸盐缓冲溶液浓度为 40mmol/L 时，可以使4种药物均获得较高的灵敏度。

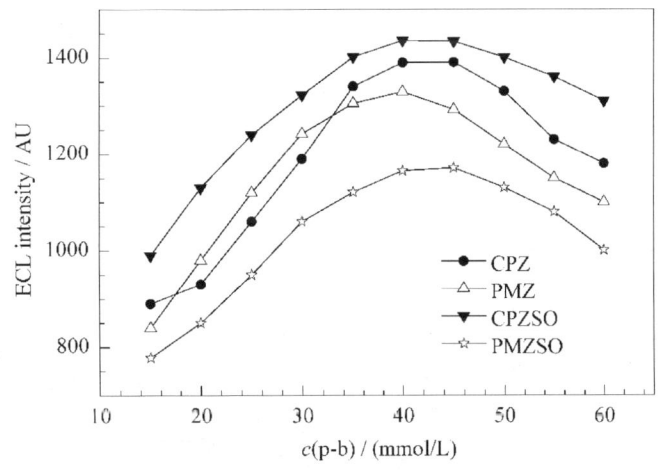

图3 检测池中磷酸盐缓冲溶液浓度对电化学发光强度的影响

2.2 分离条件的优化

2.2.1 进样时间和进样电压

毛细管电动进样量与进样电压和进样时间成正比，而进样量又直接影响电化学发光强度。把进样时间固定为 10s，在 4~20kV 内研究了 CPZ、PMZ、CPZSO 和 PMZSO 受进样电压的影响，实验发现4种药物受进样电压的影响趋势基本相同，即在 4~11kV 范围内，电化学发光强度随进样电压增加而迅速增大，11kV 以后趋势减缓，16 kV 以后重现性变差。将进样电在 12 kV，在 2~20 s 内研究了 CPZ、PMZ、CPZSO 和 PMZSO 的发光强度受进样时间的影响，实验发现4种药物受进样时间的影响不尽相同。其中，CPZ 和 PMZ 的发光强度在 10s 前随着进样时间的增长而迅速增大，10s 以后缓慢增大；而 CPZSO 和 PMZSO 在 8s 前随着进样时间的增长而迅速增大，8~13s 缓慢增大，13s 以后基本不变。

实验中还发现，高的进样电压会使峰形变宽，从而导致柱效降低。综合考虑，最佳进样电压可以在 11~16 kV 之间选择，最佳进样时间应该在 8~10s 间确定。

2.2.2 分离电压

随着分离电压的升高，目标组分的迁移时间逐渐变短，其流出毛细管的瞬间浓度逐渐增加，因此发光强度也逐渐增大。实验发现，在分离电压从 2kV 升高到 15kV 时，CPZ、PMZ、CPZSO 和 PMZSO 的发光强度都在不断增强，但是当分离电压大于 15 kV 时，基线噪声变大且发光强度开始有不同程度的下降。这可能是由以下原因造成的：其一，高电压使毛细管焦耳热变大，导致噪声变大；其二，高电压下，流入检测池的缓冲溶液增多，从而显著降低了电极表面的 $Ru(bpy)_3^{2+}$ 浓度。此外，4 种药物的迁移时间都随分离电压的增加有一定缩短，可见，分离电压对多组分物质的分离十分重要。

2.2.3 分离缓冲溶液浓度和 pH

实验表明，分离缓冲溶液的浓度变化时发光强度变化不大，但是当其浓度超过 24mmol/L 时，发光信号的基线变得不稳定。这可能是由于随着分离缓冲溶液浓度的增大，离子强度增加，从而导致了焦耳热的增加。

分离缓冲溶液的 pH 值影响电渗流，在较高 pH 下电渗流增大，迁移时间缩短，重现性变差。实验发现，当分离缓冲溶液的 pH 大于 6.0 时，发光信号下降明显，当 pH 大于 7.4 时重现性变差，pH 值大于 9.2 时甚至有少量沉淀物。

综上所述，分离缓冲溶液浓度应小于 24mmol/L，pH 应不超过 6.0。

2.2.4 分离条件

多种组分同时测定时，分离条件的总体优化尤为关键。实验发现，样品迁移时间和组分峰形是影响各组分分离的主要因素。迁移时间主要由电泳离子强度和分离电压控制，而电泳离子强度又可以通过调节缓冲溶液的浓度和 pH 值来适当改变；组分峰形则与样品量和迁移时间有关，样品量可以通过进样时间和进样电压来调节，迁移时间长虽然有利于组分分离，但峰形变宽、柱效下降。为此，通过大量的综合优化实验，获得了 4 种目标组分混合溶液的电泳分离图（见图 4），确定的最佳分离条件为：电泳磷酸缓冲溶液 18 mmol/L（pH 4.8），进样高压 11kV，进样时间 8s，运行高压 13.5kV。

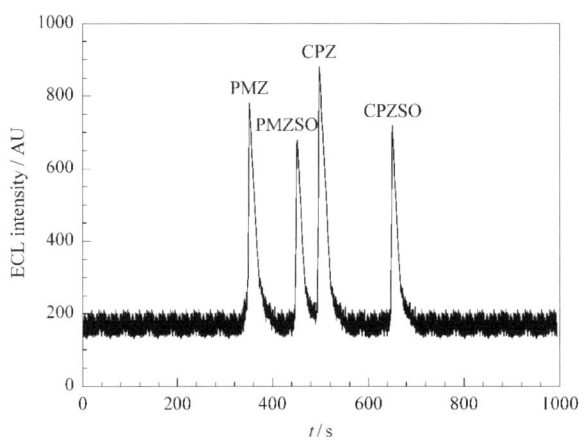

图 4 氯丙嗪、异丙嗪、氯丙嗪亚砜和异丙嗪亚砜混合溶液的电泳分离图

2.3 工作曲线、检出限和重现性

在最佳实验条件下，即检测电位 1.20V、钌联吡啶浓度 5mmol/L、检测池磷酸缓冲溶液 40mmol/（pH 6.5）、分离磷酸缓冲溶液 18mmol/L（pH 4.8）、进样高压 11kV、进样时间 8s、运行高压 13.5kV 时，测定不同 CPZ、PMZ、CPZSO 和 PMZSO 质量浓度 C（mg/L）下各自的电化学发光强度（I）以考察其相关性；分别用 0.50mg/L 的各组分标准溶液连续进样 12 次以考察其重现性。各组分的工作曲线、线性范围、电化学发光强度的相对标准偏差、迁移时间的相对标准偏差，以及依据 3σ 方法计算的检出限见表 1。

表1 4种药物的回归方程、重现性和检出限

Drug	Regression equation*	Linear range/(g/L)	RSDI/(%)	RSDt/(%)	Detection limit/(g/L)
CPZ	$I = 624.1C + 211.3$	$7.1 \times 10^{-6} - 6.3 \times 10^{-3}$	2.2	0.77	8.3×10^{-7}
PMZ	$I = 260.7C + 92.1$	$7.5 \times 10^{-5} - 4.6 \times 10^{-3}$	2.7	0.61	7.2×10^{-6}
CPZSO	$I = 844.8C - 33.5$	$9.7 \times 10^{-5} - 3.6 \times 10^{-3}$	1.9	0.85	1.9×10^{-5}
PMZSO	$I = 472.0C + 501.6$	$8.1 \times 10^{-5} - 7.7 \times 10^{-3}$	1.7	0.91	3.7×10^{-6}

* I：ECL intensity (AU)；C：mass concentration，g/L．RSDI：RSD of ECL intensity；RSDt：RSD of migration time．

2.4 家犬尿样的测定

选18~20kg的健康家犬，将氯丙嗪和异丙嗪各25mg研细后拌食给药，收集1~2h的尿液，过滤后直接测定，结果见图5a。向上述尿样中适量加入4种标准物质的混合溶液，混合均匀后再进行CE-ECL测定，结果见图5b。与图5a相比，图5b有4个峰的发光强度明显提高了，据此可以准确确定CPZ、PMZ、CPZSO和PMZSO的位置。张思敏等[13,14]利用色谱分离和质谱分析的方法测定了氯丙嗪和异丙嗪在大鼠体内的代谢情况，并发现其代谢物中还包括2-氯吩噻嗪、丙嗪、2-羟基吩噻嗪、去甲基氯丙嗪、3-羟基丙嗪、7-羟基氯丙嗪、去甲基氯丙嗪亚砜、去甲基异丙嗪、2-羟基去甲基丙嗪、吩噻嗪亚砜、去甲基异丙嗪亚砜等多种代谢物，这些代谢物多数都具有叔胺结构，因此，可以推测出现的杂质峰应为其他代谢物的电化学发光信号。

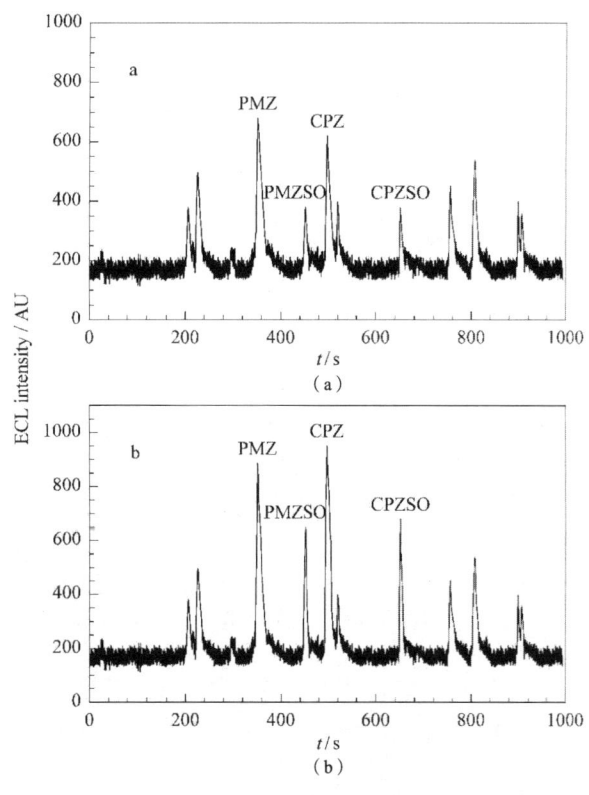

图5 (a)尿样及(b)加标尿样的CE-ECL图

3 结 论

本文通过对分离条件和检测条件的优化，建立了同时测定CPZ、PMZ、CPZSO和PMZSO的CE-ECL分析方法，可在无需预分离的情况下用于复杂混合溶液中CPZ、PMZ、CPZSO和PMZSO的同时测定。本方法具有速度快、线性范围宽、重现性好、样品及缓冲液用量少、自动化程度高等优点，具有广泛的应用前景。

参考文献

[1] Broeders J J W, Blaauboer B J, Hermens J L M. J Chromatogr A, 2011, 1218 (47): 8529.
[2] Bazhdanzadeh S, Talebpour Z, Adib N, et al. J Sep Sci, 2011, 34 (1): 90.
[3] Mokhtari A. Rezaei B. Anal Methods [J]. 2011, 3 (4): 996.
[4] Zhang Y X, Zhang Z J. Chinese Journal of Analysis Laboratory（张迎雪，章竹君. 分析试验室），2010, 29 (12): 16.
[5] He L L, Wang X, Liu B, et al. J Lumin, 2011, 131 (2): 285.
[6] Chen P L, Hu X L, Liu S P, et al. Spectrochim Acta, Part A, 2010, 77 (1): 207.
[7] De Jesus C G, Sampaio Forte C M, Wohnrath K, et al. Electroanalysis, 2011, 23 (8): 1814.
[8] Karimi M A, Hatefi-Mehrjardi A, Ardakani M M, et al. Russ J Electrochem, 2011, 47 (1): 34.
[9] Parvin M H. Electrochem Commun, 2011, 13 (4): 366.
[10] Alizadeh T, Akhoundian M. Electrochim Acta, 2010, 55 (20): 5867.
[11] Borges N C, Rezende V M, Santana J M, et al. J Chromatogr B, 2011, 879 (31): 3728.
[12] Qi S L, Wu M, Yan L J, et al. Journal of Instrumental Analysis（齐士林，吴敏，严丽娟，等. 分析测试学报），2009, 28 (6): 677.
[13] Zhang S M, Huang K J, Li H S, et al. Journal of Instrumental Analysis（张思敏，黄克建，李宏森，等. 分析测试学报），2011, 30 (10): 1088.
[14] Huang K J, Zhu D J, Li H S, et al. Journal of Instrumental Analysis（黄克建，朱定姬，李宏森，等. 分析测试学报），2010, 29 (3): 220.
[15] Zhou K W, Gu X M, Cui X C, et al. Acta Chimica Sinica（周考文，顾雪梅，崔晓超，等. 化学学报），2011, 69 (2): 221.
[16] Li X, Xu X Y, Albano D R, et al. Analyst, 2011, 136 (24): 5294.
[17] Wang Y C, Xiao L, Cheng M R. J Chromatogr A, 2011, 1218 (50): 9115.
[18] Deng B, Shi A, Kang Y, et al. Luminescence, 2011, 26 (6): 592.
[19] Yang H, Li X C, Yang F, et al. Microchim Acta, 2011, 175 (1/2): 193.
[20] Yang R, Zeng H J, Li J J, et al. Luminescence, 2011, 26 (5): 374.
[21] Zhou M, Li Y J, Ma Y J, et al. Luminescence, 2011, 26 (5): 319.
[22] Huang Y S, Chen S N, Whang C W. Electrophoresis, 2011, 32 (16): 2155.
[23] Sun J, Du H, You T. Electrophoresis, 2011, 32 (16): 2148.
[24] Liu H J, Yuan R, Chai Y Q, et al. Talanta, 2011, 84 (2): 387.
[25] Deng B Y, Ye L, Yin H H, et al. J Chromatogr B, 2011, 879 (13): 927.
[26] Xiang Q, Wang H, Xu Y, et al. Asian J Chem, 2011, 23 (4): 1553.
[27] Yu C X, Du H W, You T Y. Talanta, 2011, 83 (5): 1376.
[28] Liu Y M, Peng L F, Mei L, et al. Chinese Chem Lett, 2011, 22 (2): 197.
[29] Li Y H, Wang C Y, Tian J, et al. Asian J Chem, 2008, 20 (5): 3833.
[30] 任小娜，马永钧，周敏，等. 色谱），2008, 26 (2): 223.
[31] 李云辉，王春燕. 电化学发光 [M]. 北京：化学工业出版社，2008.

流域水质改善的公共偏好问题研究

郑海霞 张陆彪

1 引言

流域水质改善的最大支付意愿存在着公共偏好。不同收入阶层、年龄、性别和职业等对流域水质改善的认知和需求不同，最大支付意愿也存在很大差异。定量模拟 WTP 的公共偏好，可以为不同的政策目标的制定提供参考。由于不同的模型结构不同，模拟的结果也有差异。研究发现，利用分位数模型可以为不同的水资源管理政策提供更全面、综合的不同分位的影响因素，尤其发现 WTP 的高分位和低分位 WTP 影响因素系数的大小和统计显著性存在明显不同[1]。本研究利用分位数模型对不同分位 WTP 及其被调查者个人信息的模拟，考察是否影响高分位数的因素也同样影响低分位数。如果不是，政策制定者也许想知道谁从某项特殊的政策中受益最大。同时，是否这种定向目标的政策精确地使这些目标人群而不是其他人群受益，从而减少公共环境政策执行中的搭便车现象。分位数模型可以通过界定 WTP 在高分位上的决定因素确定政策目标的主要受益人群。本研究通过 QR 模型与 Tobit 模型、最小二乘模型的对比，分析密云水库流域水质改善 WTP 的决定因素，通过实证研究，了解什么指标驱动更高的 WTP（也就是对于执行水质改善付费更高受益者）。由于驱动高 WTP 的指标比驱动低的 WTP 的指标更有效，研究结果可以为设计流域水质改善环境服务付费政策和宣传方案的制订提供重要参考。

2 模型方法

利用支付卡引导的 WTP 数据可以用多种方法进行分析。标准最小二乘法（OLS）能处理 WTP 的值，以支付者直接选择的支付卡的点数据进行分析。断点回归是利用支付者选择的值和下一个值的中点数据（midpoint）进行回归分析。另外，支付卡引导的 WTP 数据是最小值为 0（零支付时）的普查数据，支付者仅仅给出正的支付值。考虑到具有普查数据的特征，Tobit 模型可以很好地应用[2]。分位数回归模型（Quantile regression，QR）可以更详细地描述变量的统计分布，分析不同支付层次、支付能力和收入水平人群的最大支付意愿的影响因素的不同，从而为政策制定者提供更为精准的定量参考[3]。本研究利用这 3 种方法进行对比，分析 WTP 的决定因素及其在不同分位上的差别。

2.1 Tobit 分析模型

Tobit 模型是用来解决耐用消费品支出 y_i 和解释变量 x_i 之间关系的模式，而最大支付意愿 WTP 是对环境服务商品（Environmental goods）的消费。本研究通过对最小二乘法（Ordinary Least Squares，OLS）模型、Logistic 回归模拟和 Tobit 模型模拟结果的对比，选择模拟结果最优的 Tobit 模型对最大支付意愿及其影响因素进行模拟和分析。Tobit 模型通常在利用支付卡方法调查的 WTP 数据分析中，因为这类数据具有明显的检索数据特征。

Tobit 模型是经济学家、1981 年诺贝尔经济学奖获得者 J. 托宾（James Tobin）于 1958 年在研究耐用消费品需求时首先提出来的一个经济计量学模型。

Tobit 模型假设被观察的独立变量 $y_i(i = 1,2,\cdots,n)$ 满足如下条件：

[基金项目] 国家自然科学基金项目（41271527，70703001，70973013）；教育部人文社科发展项目（11YJC790300）；北京市属高等学校高层次人才引进与培养计划项目（IDHT201304078），北京市教委人文社科规划项目（SM2008 11417009），北京学研究项目（BJXJD-KT2011-A03）。

[作者简介] 郑海霞（1975—），中国科学院地理科学与资源研究所博士，北京联合大学教授，北京市青年拔尖创新人才，北京联合大学首都经济与企业管理研究所所长，北京大学经济与人类发展研究中心客座研究员。研究方向：资源与环境经济、环境价值评估、环境服务补偿。E-mail：haixiazheng@126.com。

$$y_i = \max(0, y_i *) \tag{1}$$

而潜变量 y^* 满足经典线性假设，可以用如下回归模型表示：

$$y^* = \beta_0 + \beta x_i + u_i, \quad u \mid x \sim N(0, \sigma^2) \tag{2}$$

式中：y 为被解释变量；β_0 为截距项；x 为回归系数向量；β 为解释变量向量；u 为误差项；$N(0, \sigma^2)$ 表示以 0 为均值、σ^2 为方差的正态分布。Tobit 模型的基本原理如下：

设某一耐用消费品为 y_i（被解释变量），解释变量为 x_i，则耐用消费品支出 y_i 要么大于 y_0（y_0 表示该耐用消费品的最低支出水平），要么等于零。因此，在线性模型假设下，耐用消费品支出 y_i 和解释变量 x_i 之间的关系为

$$y_i = \begin{cases} y_i^* & \text{若 } y_i^* \geq y_0 \\ 0 & \text{若 } y_i^* < y_0 \end{cases}$$

Tobit 模型的一个重要特征是，解释变量 x_i 是可观测的（x_i 取实际观测值），而被解释变量 y_i 只能以受限制的方式被观测到：当 $y_i^* > 0$ 时，取 $y_i = y_i^* > 0$，称 y_i 为"无限制"观测值；当 $y_i^* \leq 0$ 时，取 $y_i = 0$，称 y_i 为"受限"观测值。也就是说，"无限制"观测值均取实际的观测值，"受限"观测值均截取为 0。

更为一般意义的的模型为

$$y_i^* = \beta_0 + \beta x_i + u_i, \quad (i=1, 2, \cdots, N) \quad u \mid x \sim N(0, \sigma^2) \tag{3}$$

式中：

$$y_i^* = \begin{cases} a & \text{若 } y_i \leq a \\ y_i & \text{若 } b > y_i > a \quad y_i \sim N(\mu, \sigma^2) \\ b & \text{若 } y_i \geq b \end{cases} \tag{4}$$

2.2 断点回归模型

我们利用断点回归模型考虑数据的断点特征。断点数据模型指的是被调查者真实 WTP 的可能性，用字符 Y 表示，Y 可以用断点 [BIDL, BIDH] 表示，假设断点 [BIDL, BIDH] 可以由 $\Phi(BID_H \mid Y) - \Phi(BID_L \mid Y)$ 估算，在此 WTP 属于标准正态累积分布函数 (Φ)。具体 [BIDL, BIDH] 可以用调查的断点数据推出。例如，CVM 调查的中点（midpoint）（5, 10, 15, 20, 25, 30, 35, 40, …），如果被调查者选择的 WTP 是 5，断点 [BIDL, BIDH] 分别是 [5, 10]；如果被调查者选择的 WTP 是 17，断点 [BIDL, BIDH] 分别是 [20, 25]。与 OLS、Tobit、Logit 相似，模型被用最大似然方程评估[4]。

2.3 分位数回归模型

分位数回归（Quantile regression, QR）可以在整个分布维度上评估变量之间的关系，能够提供更完整的自变量和因变量之间关系的统计图。分位数回归（Quantile regression, QR）是 Koenker 和 Bassett (1978) 发展的多元分位回归模型，该模型为研究者提供了一个日益重要的工具，用于评估因变量 Y 在整个分布区域与解释变量之间的关系。对比传统的 OLS 和最大似然评估的归回模型，如 Tobit、Logit、断点回归（Interval regression）等，QR 方法通过分析不同分位（例如：0.1, 0.25, 0.5, 0.75, 0.9）因变量及其对应的自变量的关系，能提供更完整和综合的统计关系，解释高分位和低分位因变量的主要影响因素。同时，QR 回归是离群极值（Outliers）和偏态双尾（skewed tails）的一种稳健的展示[5]，这种特征也可能特殊地应用到 CVM 中，因为在 CVM 研究中经常出现少量很高的 WTP 投标值（离群值, Outliers）和大量很小的投标值。QR 方法可以通过分别明确它们的主要决定或影响因素，更详细地评估 WTP 分布高支付和低支付值的有效性。本研究用 QR 模拟了 WTP 在不同分位的主要影响因素。同时，为了验证分位数回归方法的有效性，本研究利用该方法与断点回归（Interval regression）、Tobit、OLS 的模拟结果进行了对比分析。

利用 QR 方法进行 CVM 数据的分析可以更好地揭示相关政策影响因素。例如，分析影响高分位 WTP 支付的影响因素是否也同样影响低分位 WTP 支付群体。如果影响不同，政策制定者也需要知道谁对特定政策的受益最大，是否臆想的政策接受者实际从政策中受益。QR 可以通过分析高分位最大 WTP 的决定因素分析，明确知道政策影响的主要群体。QR 分析的相关结果可以用于政策制定时的参考。本研究中，

通过 QR 分析收入、教育、年龄、认知等不同因素对水质改善的最大支付意愿在整个 WTP 分布点影响的不同，为流域保护和生态补偿政策制定提供参考。

另外，分析和掌握什么指标驱动更高的 WTP（因此也是更高的政策受益者），并据此制订项目的执行方案、宣传教育材料可以获得更多的支持（更高的 WTP）。如果执行方案和宣传材料是依据 WTP 低驱动指标，则项目的执行效果没有高 WTP 驱动指标更有效。

Belluzzo（2004）利用 QR 分析了 CVM 双边界调查的水资源改善 WTP 数据，发现对于不同水管理政策的多层次影响，QR 比标准的 Logit 模型提供了更综合的结果。他指出在双尾分布中系数的统计显著性和大小的不同，表明水管理政策的受益者（在右尾）和损失者（在左尾）也许被非常不同的因素驱动。

OLS、Tobit、Logit 和断点回归（Interval Regression）方法模型都假设解释变量沿着因变量整个分布的影响是同质的，这也许不足以证明因变量真正的影响而不是平均影响，OLS 等方法给出的是平均影响（Koenker & Bassett，1978；Koenker，2003）。在 WTP 研究案例中，QR 模型为

$$WTP_i = X_i\beta_\theta + \mu_{i,\theta} \tag{5}$$

$$Quant_\theta(WTP_i \mid X_i) = X_i\beta_\theta \tag{6}$$

式中 X_i 是外生变量的向量，β_θ 是被评估的向量参数。$\mu_{i,\theta}$ 误差项。$Quant_\theta(WTP_i \mid X_i)$ 指对应 X_i 的 WTP_i 的分位数。为了评估分位数，当 $0 < \theta < 1$ 时，可以利用线性回归方程解决，如下：

$$\min b_\theta [\sum_{i:WTP_i \geq X_i\beta} \theta \mid WTP_i - X_i\beta_\theta \mid + \sum_{i:WTP(X_i\beta)} (1-\theta) \mid WTP_i - X_i\beta_0 \mid] \tag{7}$$

式中 β_θ 是评估系数，QR 方程是最小化绝对残差值的权重之和。通过 θ 的变化，在 WTP 分布的任何分量的系数都能够被评估。QR 回归中的系数可以解释为与 OLS 系数评估相似的方法。例如，WTP 收入回归中，第 25 分位收入的系数（$\theta = 0.25$）给出当收入边际变化被给定时 WTP 的边际变化。

QR 模型被用于经济、教育等方面的分析[6]，工资收入的决定因素和工资的不公平性[7]和收入收敛性增长等方面[8]，在环境经济价值评估方面的研究主要是 Belluzzo（2004）利用 QR 模型，并结合 OLS 和最大似然评估方法对比分析 CVM 支付卡数据，揭示影响水资源管理 WTP 的主要决定因素。O'GARRA 和 MOURATO（2007）利用 QR 模型研究了伦敦引入氢气清洁公交系统增加的 WTP 及其决定因素。

3 结果分析

本研究是利用 CVM 方法的支付卡法调查获得密云水库最大支付意愿 WTP，调查地点在密云水库用水区，包括北京市海淀、朝阳、丰台、石景山、西城、东城、宣武、崇文、昌平等 9 个主要分区。密云等郊区县也有少量调查，调查显示水源区也有支付意愿，这说明了环境服务的价值被广泛认可，也显示了环境服务在水源区和用水区都共享的事实。

问卷调查时间是 2009 年 12 月至 2010 年 2 月，总计发放问卷 370 份，除去填写不完整、抗议性回答等问卷，回收有效问卷 329 份，其中密云水库有支付意愿（非零支付）的受访者 256 份，但是其中 14 份支付意愿仍然为 0，尽管他们选择了愿意支付。他们不支付的原因是：由于收入低没有支付能力，或者认为污染者或政府应该支付。因此，我们认为这些被调查者实际上也不具有支付意愿。具有正支付意愿的有 242 份，拒绝支付或无能力支付（零支付）的有 87 份，分别占 73.56% 和 26.44%。

3.1 WTP 影响因素的描述性统计

通过多次初步拟合，我们从许多可能影响 WTP 的指标中选择 9 个拟合度较好的指标分析 WTP。指标的定义和描述性统计见表 1。

表 1 解释变量描述性统计

指标	指标描述	观察值 N	Mean	Std. Dev.	Min	Max
WTP_MIYUN	最大支付意愿（Max WTP）	329	18.89	35.667	0	500
PERWAT（x_1）	假设：1 表示被调查者知道密云水库是北京市水源区；2 表示不知道	326	1.29	0.457	1	2

续表

指标	指标描述	观察值 N	Mean	Std. Dev.	Min	Max
ENVIMPT (x_2)	环境的相对重要性,1 表示非常重要;5 表示非常不重要	325	1.59	0.787	1	5
BUYBOTWAT (x_3)	假设:1 表示被调查者购买瓶装水以改善水质;2 表示被调查者不购买瓶装水以改善水质	326	1.33	0.472	1	2
DEMWATQ (x_4)	假设:1 表示被调查者有改善水质的需求;2 表示被调查者没有改善水质的需求	328	1.18	0.383	1	2
Gender (x_5)	1 表示男性;0 表示女性	329	0.41	0.493	0	1
Age (x_6)	被调查者的年龄(≥18)	326	35.56	11.959	18	73
Edu (x_7)	被调查者受教育的年限	324	14.66871	3.433868	2	23
HOUSHOLDINCOM (x_8)	被调查者户均收入(Yuan/户/月)	329	7267.173	4776.358	1000	40000
Ocupation (x_9)	被调查者的职业 1. 政府工作人员 2. NGO 和私有公司工作人员 3. 商人、医生或者律师等个人营业者 4. 工人、农户和服务人员 5. 其他人:非雇用、学生、全职在家和退休等人员	329	4.7	3.947	0	5

可以看出,密云水库支付意愿的中位值是 10 元/户/年,最小值是 0,最大值是 500 元/月/户。被调查者的年龄处于 18~73 岁,平均年龄 35.56 岁,平均受教育年限 14.7 年,最高 23 年(博士学位),最低 2 年,被调查者户均家庭收入最低 1000 元/户,最高 40000 元/户。

3.2 结果分析

本研究选择以上 9 个变量作为自变量,以密云水库最大支付意愿 WTP 为因变量,利用 STATA 11.2 软件对 3 种模型进行模拟。利用双边审查(double censored)的 Tobit 模型对 WTP 进行模拟。由于根据原始数据统计,只有一个人选择大于 100 元/月/户。故 Tobit 回归的截断点分别选取 0 和 100。实际调查 WTP 是被调查者支付意愿的中点数据,结合支付卡推导出断点的 BID_L 和 BID_H,进行断点回归模拟。为了进行分位数分析,我们计算了不同分位数上 WTP 的值。分位数回归仅选取正 WTP,观察值为 242(见表 2)。

表 2 在不同分位数中 WTP 的分布

	分位值	最小值	分布指标	指标对应值
1%	5	5		
5%	5	5		
10%	5	5	观察值	242
25%	10	5	权重和	242
50%	10	5	均值	25.68
		最大值	标准差	39.45
75%	30	100		
90%	50	100	方差	1556.28
95%	100	100	偏度	7.62
99%	100	500	峰度	87.88

表2给出了分位数以及每一个分位数所对应的WTP的值,这个值是用支付卡断点数据的中点(mid-points)计算得到的,不同分位数上的分位值分别是5、10、30、50、100,同时给出了最大值、最小值。我们利用STATA 11.2软件模拟Tobit、断点回归和分位数回归模型,分析WTP的主要决定因素,分析不同模型的显著性差异。同时,分析QR模型在不同分位上影响因子的显著性差异。

整体上,Tobit模型与指标拟合的结果比断点模型更优,模拟的结果有更多指标具有显著性,与QR模拟结果有一定的相似性。正如预料,断点模型、Tobit与QR模型结果都显示:平均WTP与家庭收入在1%上具有显著性,系数为正值,呈正相关关系,说明收入是WTP的重要影响因素,与多个研究结果结论一致[9-12]。同时,断点模型和Tobit模型均显示,性别也与WTP在10%的显著性上呈正相关关系,说明男性的支付意愿强于女性。

在断点模型中,WTP还与教育年限(x_7)呈正相关。在Tobit回归模型中,WTP与环境相对经济的重要性(x_2)环境重要性呈正相关关系,与年龄(x_6)、是否知道密云水库是北京市水源(x_1)、购买瓶装水以改善水质(x_3)等因素呈负相关关系。令人奇怪的是,知道密云水库是北京市水源的被调查者反而支付的更少,这可能是因为密云水库近10年水量减少和水质恶化。

分位数回归分析的结果揭示了更有趣的发现,在Tobit和断点回归分析中许多不显著的指标,在WTP分布的某些分位上也变得显著了。例如,被调查者有水质改善需求(x_4)在Tobit分析和断点回归分析中均不显著,在高分位99%上却变得非常显著(1%)。同时,环境相对重要性(x_2)、购买瓶装水以改善水质(x_3)、具有水质改善的需求(x_4)、年龄(x_6)在断点回归中均不显著影响WTP,但是在高分位99分位上却是存在1%的显著——这表明这些指标不是平均WTP(mean WTP)的决定性因素,但是却在高分位投标值上具有显著影响。因此,高分位上具有显著影响的指标及回归系数决定的影响程度,可以为政策的制定提供参考。

同时,从QR模型在不同分位数上,具有显著性指标的对比分析,可以看出:

(1)仅仅有1个指标在所有分位上都显著——家庭收入。家庭收入对WTP具有正向的、显著的影响。

(2)影响低分位的指标和高分位的指标不同:除了家庭收入以外,在低分位上仅仅环境相对重要性(x_2)在25分位上、具有水质改善的需求(x_4)在10分位上具有显著性,在中位数之后,具有显著性的指标增加。这主要是由于低分位上的支付仅仅是家庭月均收入中很少的一部分,这也与国际上相关研究结果相似[13]。

(3)在不同分位上指标的正负影响发生转变。例如,是否知道密云水库是北京市水源(x_1)、购买瓶装水以改善水质(x_3)在Tobit分析中呈负相关,在最后的高分位99分位上是正相关,这与基本的常理判断相符,这也表明分位数回归模型比Tobit回归以及其他利用似然法开展的回归更符合实际情况。

(4)结果也表明,反映收入和环境态度的9个指标在右尾高分位上对WTP均具有重要影响,在1%上显著性。除了年龄显示负相关以外,其他因素都具有正相关关系,这与WTP及其影响因素的经济学理论预期相符,反映了调查结果的有效性和可靠性。这也从另一个角度说明,通过大量陈述性方法的调查获取的WTP确实具有多种不同的驱动,也反过来暗示在CVM调查中解释变量的同质性(homogeneity)影响并不总是存在,本研究所选择的9个指标不具有同质性。

4 结 论

本研究通过对比分析断点模型、Tobit模型和分位数回归模型方法,模拟流域水质改善WTP的公共偏好,研究发现如下。

(1)断点模型、Tobit与QR模型结果都显示:平均WTP与家庭收入在1%上具有显著正相关,进一步印证了收入是WTP的重要影响因素。

(2)Tobit模型拟合的结果比断点模型更优,有更多指标具有显著性,与QR模拟结果有一定的相似性。

(3)QR模型在高分位和低分位上受影响的解释变量不同,除了家庭收入以外,在低分位上仅仅环境相对重要性(x_2)、具有水质改善的需求(x_4)具有显著性,在中位数之后,具有显著性的指标增加,这主要是由于低分位上的支付仅仅是家庭月均收入中很少的一部分。

(4) 所选择的9个指标均在右尾高分位上对WTP具有重要显著性影响。除了年龄显示负相关以外，其他因素都具有正相关关系，这与WTP及其影响因素的经济学理论预期相符，也表明调查结果具有有效性和可靠性。

研究结果正如所料，QR模型在支付卡数据的价值评估中具有明显的优势。三种模型分析参数对比见表3。

表3 密云水库水质水量改善的断点回归、Tobit和分位数回归分析（$n=307$，242 for QR）

Variable		Intreg	Tobit	QR_10	QR_20	QR_25	QR_50	QR_75	QR_90	QR_99	BSQR_50
PERWAT (x_1)	Coef	-8.142	-6.312	0.145	-1.200	-1.546	-1.891	-5.184	-19.337	17.186	-1.891
	S.E.	4.452	3.024	0.288	1.295	1.097	2.024	5.311	10.586	0.582	2.277
	t	-1.83*	-2.09**	0.5	-0.93	-1.41	-0.93	-0.98	-1.83*	29.53***	-0.83
ENVIMPT (x_2)	Coef	2.533	4.505	0.195	0.941	1.941	5.268	10.740	13.655	-11.824	5.268
	S.E.	2.516	1.713	0.195	0.857	0.673	1.184	3.421	5.490	0.329	3.333
	t	1.01	2.63***	1	1.1	2.88***	4.45***	3.14***	2.49*	35.89***	1.58
BUYBOTWAT (x_3)	Coef	-0.639	-6.415	-0.301	-1.577	-1.090	-0.199	-3.655	-10.130	70.904	-0.199
	S.E.	4.296	2.920	0.346	1.357	1.090	1.977	5.380	9.130	0.566	2.267
	t	-0.15	-2.2**	-0.87	-1.16	-1	-0.1	-0.68	-1.11	125.37***	-0.09
DEMWATQ (x_4)	Coef	-7.185	-5.554	0.876	2.812	2.056	1.814	-1.270	-7.764	33.466	1.814
	S.E.	5.434	3.690	0.510	1.789	1.496	2.755	7.328	10.082	0.797	3.632
	t	-1.32	-1.51	1.72*	1.57	1.37	0.66	-0.17	-0.77	42.01***	0.5
Gender (x_5)	Coef	7.741	4.589	0.477	0.437	1.094	1.947	4.908	3.961	78.567	1.947
	S.E.	4.016	2.731	0.312	1.225	1.005	1.805	4.900	9.498	0.513	2.333
	t	1.93*	1.68*	1.53	0.36	1.09	1.08	1	0.42	153.3***	0.83
Age (x_6)	Coef	-0.136	-0.210	-0.008	-0.041	-0.048	-0.136	-0.392	-0.640	-0.745	-0.136
	S.E.	0.181	0.123	0.012	0.051	0.044	0.080	0.222	0.321	0.023	0.093
	t	-0.75	-1.71*	-0.65	-0.79	-1.09	-1.69*	-1.76*	-1.99**	-32.64***	-1.460
Edu (x_7)	Coef	1.280	0.501	0.027	0.219	0.270	0.207	0.556	1.022	5.469	0.207
	S.E.	0.723	0.492	0.059	0.225	0.172	0.304	0.810	1.731	0.087	0.355
	t	1.77*	1.02	0.46	0.97	1.57	0.68	0.69	0.59	63.02***	0.580
Househdincom (x_8)	Coef	0.002	0.001	0.0002	0.0004	0.001	0.001	0.003	0.004	0.019	0.001
	S.E.	0.000	0.000	0.000	0.000	0.000	0.000	0.001	0.001	0.000	0.0004
	t	4.55***	4.59***	8.07***	2.67***	5.79***	7.12***	7.16***	5.6***	361.9***	3.18***
Occupation (x_9)	Coef	0.436	-1.022	-0.047	-0.389	-0.137	-0.406	-0.233	-0.670	4.810	-0.406
	S.E.	1.483	1.008	0.105	0.476	0.368	0.662	1.914	3.828	0.187	0.827
	t	0.29	-1.01	-0.45	-0.82	-0.37	-0.61	-0.12	-0.17	25.74***	-0.490
_cons	Coef	4.921	25.797	2.901	3.356	0.203	0.542	9.228	59.909	-237.255	0.542
	S.E.	19.225	13.071	1.308	6.081	4.523	8.120	20.796	43.767	2.342	8.999
	t	0.26	1.97**	2.22**	0.55	0.04	0.07	0.44	1.37	-101.3***	0.060
/lnsigma		87.10***									
sigma		23.77***									
Log likelihood		-1016.904	-1361.011								
LR chi2 (9)		45.35	62.39								
Pseudo R^2			0.0224								

* 在10%水平上显著；** 在5% 水平上显著；level；*** 在1%水平上显著

参考文献

[1] Belluzzo, W. J. Semiparametric Approaches to Welfare Evaluations in Binary Response Models [J]. Journal of Business and Economics Statistics, 2004, 22 (3), 322 – 330.

[2] Halstead, J. M., B. E. Lindsay and C. M. Brown. Use of the Tobit Model in Contingent Valuation: Experimental Evidence from the Pemigewaset Wilderness Area [J]. Journal of Environmental Management, 1991 (33): 79 – 89.

[3] Tanya O'Garra & Susana Mourato. Public Preferences for Hydrogen Buses: Comparing Interval Data, OLS and Quantile Regression Approaches'Environmental & Resource Economics, European Association of Environmental and Resource Economists, 2007, 36 (4): 389 – 411.

[4] Cameron, T. A. and D. D. Huppert. OLS versus ML Estimation of Non – market Resource Values with Payment Card Interval Data [J]. Journal of Environmental Economics and Management, 1987 (17): 230 – 246.

[5] Koenker, R. and K. Hallock. Quantile Regression [J]. Journal of Economic Perspectives, 2001 (15): 143 – 156.

[6] Bauer, T. K. and J. P. Haisken – DeNew. Employer Learning and the Returns to Schooling [J]. Labour Economics, 2001, 8 (2): 161 – 180.

[7] Martins, P. S. and P. T. Pereira. Does Education Reduce Wage Inequality? Quantile Regression Evidence from 16 Countries [J]. Labour Economics, 2004, 11 (3): 355 – 371.

[8] Mello, Marcelo & Perrelli, Roberto. Growth equations: a quantile regression exploration [J]. The Quarterly Review of Economics and Finance, Elsevier, 2003, 43 (4): 643 – 667.

[9] Bateman, I., R. T. Carson, B. Day, M. Hanemann, N. Hanley, T. Hett, M. Jones – Lee, G. Loomes, S. Mourato, E. Ozdemiroglu, D. W. Pearce, R. Sugden and J. Swanson. Economic Valuation with Stated Preference Techniques: A Manual. Cheltenham: Edward Elgar, 2002.

[10] 郑海霞, 张陆彪. 流域生态服务补偿市场的形成机制及其政策建议——基于金华江的实证研究 [J]. 资源科学, 2006 (3): 192 – 204.

[11] 张志强, 徐中民, 王建, 等. 黑河流域生态系统服务的价值 [J]. 冰川冻土, 2001, 23 (4): 360 – 366.

[12] 杨凯, 赵军. 城市河流生态系统服务的 CVM 估值及其偏差分析 [J]. 生态学报, 2005 (6): 1391 – 1396.

[13] G. D. Garrod and K. G. Willis. Economic Valuation of the Environment [M]. Edward Elgar, Cheltenham, 1999.

The Design and Simulation of Electric Vehicle Cruise Control System Based on MATLAB

Zhang Wenjuan Wang Xue & Jin Tong Niu Wenliang

1 Introduction of PID

PID control algorithm a classical control algorithm in industry has a wide application in process control system because of the advantages of simple principle and convenient operation. As a controller, it only needs a simple calculation of proportion, integral and differential of system error and its rate of change in order to achieve the object of fast, stable and accurate control. The equation of PID controller is,

$$u(t) = k_p \left[e(t) + \frac{1}{T_i} \int_0^t e(t) \, dt + T_d \frac{de(t)}{dt} \right] \quad (1)$$

k_p is coefficient of proportionality, T_i is integral time constant, T_d is differential time constant.

The characteristics of three kinds of control of PID controller which are proportional control, integ – ral control and differential control will be discussed in the following three chapters (Kefei. 2012).

1.1 Characteristic of proportional control

The proportional controller will immediately have an effect on the controlled object and make it to be controlled to the direction of reducing the error when the control system runs. And the strong or weak degree of control effect depends on the big or small size of the proportional coefficient k_p. It can reduce the error with increasing the size of the proportional coefficient k_p. But if the k_p is set too large, it will lead to increase the system overshoot and destroy a dynamics balance of the system.

1.2 Characteristic of integral control

The integral controller is capable of storing and integrating the system error and is propitious to eliminate the static error of the system. But it has a strong delay characteristic and if the integral effect is too strong, it will lead to lower control precision of the controlled object and make the system become unstable under closed loop control.

1.3 Characteristic of differential control

The differential controller differentiates the system error. The differential controller could increase differential effect to accelerate the system reaction speed and make the overshoot reduce gradually with predicting the system error trend.

At present, the conventional PID controller is widely used in industrial process control, and achieves a good control effect. But the conventional PID regulator don't have the online tuning parame – ters function, therefore it can't meet the require – ments of system parameter self – tuning in different working conditions, leading to affect the further enhancement of the control effect.

Fuzzy controller has the advantages of no requirement of accurate mathematical model, the weaker dependence on the object model and good robust performance. It is very suitable for control systems of nonlinear, large delay and time vary – ing. Given that the characteristics of PID control algorithm and fuzzy control algorithm, electric automobile cruise control system in the paper is composed of a parameter self – turning fuzzy PID controller

[Author Introduction] Zhang Wenjuan, Institute of Information, Beijing Union University; Wang Xue, Jin Tong, Niu Wenliang, College of Applied Science and Technology, Beijing Union University.

based on MATLAB.

2 Fuzzy PID Controller

2.1 Fuzzy PID control algorithm

Fuzzy PID controller is based on traditional PID controller, and its control process is complicated. First, it uses fuzzy sets to represent control rules' conditions and operation, then it stores the know – ledge of fuzzy control rules and related information (such as the initial PID parameters) in computer knowledge base. Finally the computer automatically adjusts optimal PID parameters using fuzzy inference according to the actual response of the control system.

In the automobile cruise control system, cruise control system consists of a classic PID and a two – dimensional controller. The frame of vehicle cruise control system with a fuzzy PID controller (Min et al. 2005) is shown in Fig. 1.

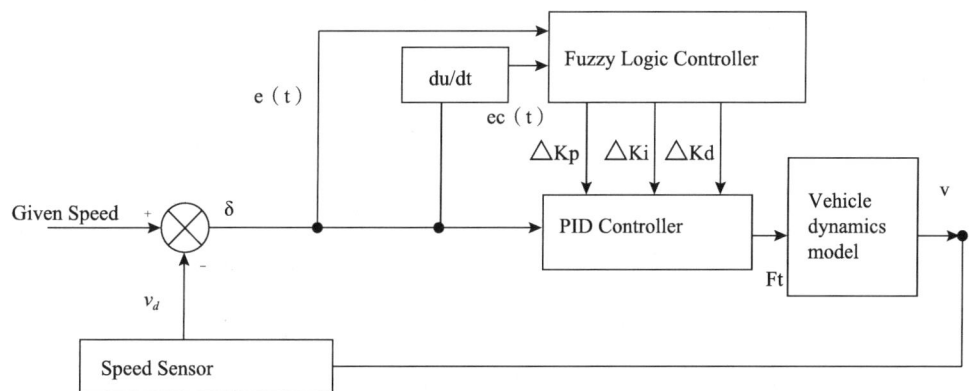

Fig. 1 the frame of Vehicle cruise control system

The two – dimensional fuzzy controller considers the error e (t) and the error rate ec (t) as input signals and k_p, k_i, k_d as output signals. We can get the fuzzy PID final adjustment parameters by correcting the PID parameters online, here is the calculation formula.

$$kp = k'p + \Delta kp;$$
$$ki = k'i + \Delta ki;$$
$$kd = k'd + \Delta kd \qquad (2)$$

In order to implement PID parameters tuning, it has to figure out the fuzzy relation among three PID parameters, the error e (t) and the error rate ec (t). Then we could carry out online correction of three PID parameters according to the fuzzy control principle with continuously monitoring the error e (t) and the error rate ec (t). This kind of tuning PID parameters online can meet requirements of different error e (t) and different error rate ec (t), so that the controlled object will have a good dynamic and static performance. And it is easy to tune PID parameters online because of a small amount of calculation.

2.2 Fuzzy logic controller

Seven linguistic variables which are NB, NM, NS, Z, PS, PM and PB are considered as input and output parameters. The quantization domain of input and output parameters could be (– A, A), and the size of A affects accuracy of the system. Here, the quanti – zation domain of the error e (t), the error rate ec (t) and three output parameters of fuzzy controller could be [– 5, 5]. The membership function of input and output parameters (Hougwei. 2010) are shown in Fig. 2 – 4.

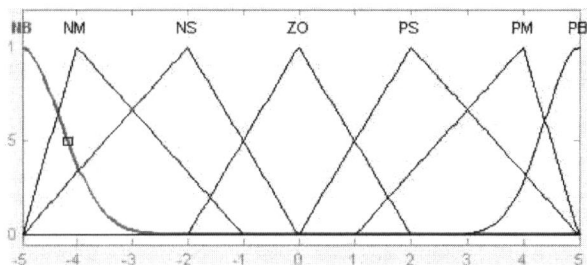

Fig. 2 the membership function of e (t)

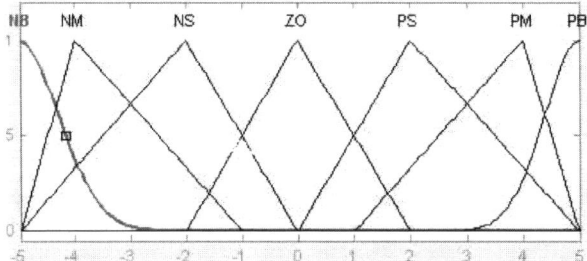

Fig. 3 the membership function of ec (t)

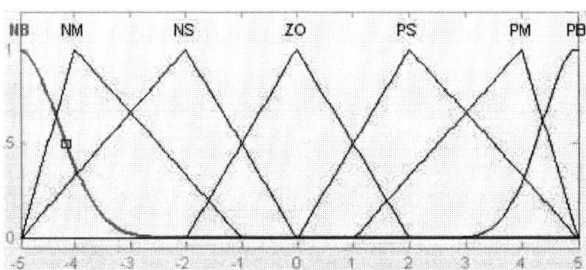

Fig. 4 the membership function of output parameters

The effect of k_p, k_i and k_d on system has been discussed in the chapter 1. The proportional k_p coefficient can not only accelerate response speed of system, but also improve regulation accuracy of system. The integral coefficient k_i can eliminate steady error of system. The differential coefficient k_d can improve dynamic characteristics of system and predict the variation trend of the error signal, namely while predicting a big variation trend of the error signal, system will generate an effective correction signal to accelerate the movement speed and reduce the adjusting time.

The fuzzy control rules that engineering staff gains through technical knowledge and practical experience is shown in Table 1. And the control rules of fuzzy controller should be described like this: If (e (t) is NB) and (ec (t) is NB) then (k_p is PB) (k_i is NB) (k_d is PS). Here, fuzzy controller totally has 49 rules which are edited in the rule editor of GUI.

The internal structure of PID controller is shown in Fig. 5.

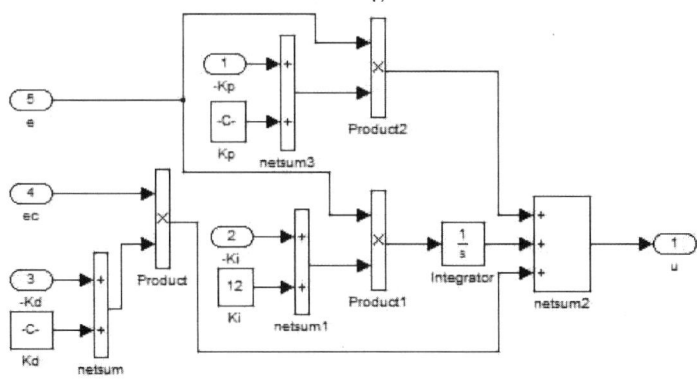

Fig. 5 internal structure of PID controller

Table 1 fuzzy control rules

$k_p/k_i/k_d$		ec(t)						
		NB	NM	NS	Z	PS	PM	PB
e(t)	NB	PB/NB/PS	PB/NB/NS	PM/NM/NB	PM/NM/NB	PS/NS/NB	Z/Z/NM	Z/Z/PS
	NM	PB/NB/PS	PB/NB/NS	PM/NM/NB	PS/NS/NM	PS/NS/NM	Z/Z/NS	NS/Z/Z
	NS	PM/NB/Z	PM/NM/NS	PM/NS/NM	PS/NS/NM	Z/Z/NS	NS/PS/NS	NS/PS/Z
	Z	PM/NM/Z	PM/NM/NS	PS/NS/NS	Z/Z/NS	NS/PS/NS	NM/PM/NS	NM/PM/Z
	PS	PS/NM/Z	PS/NS/Z	Z/Z/Z	NS/PS/Z	NS/PS/Z	NM/PM/Z	NM/PB/Z
	PM	PS/Z/PB	Z/Z/NS	NS/PS/PS	NM/PS/PS	NM/PM/PS	NM/PB/PS	NB/PB/PB
	PB	Z/Z/PB	Z/Z/PM	PM/PS/PM	NM/PS/PM	NM/PM/PS	NB/PB/PS	NB/PB/PB

3 Vehicle Dynamics Model

Vehicle longitudinal dynamic model is based on the transmission system, driving system and vehicle motion system. This model takes into account only the vehicle longitudinal motion (Xiaoju. 2014).

There are some assumptions during establishing vehicle longitudinal dynamics model.

(1) The transmission shaft and transmitting gear of power transmission system are rigid;

(2) The nonlinear factors such as tire slip could not be considered when the road is good and the ground adhesion is big enough.

The force analysis in the running process of vehicle is shown in Fig. 6 and the force balance relation is shown in the following equation.

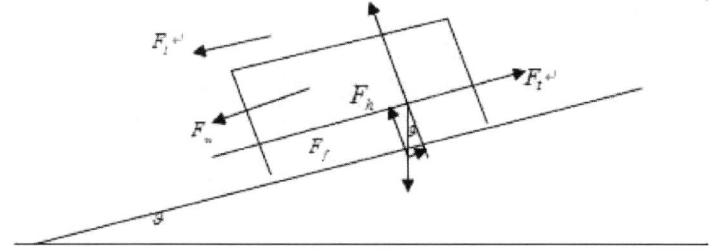

Fig. 6 force analysis in the running process of vehicle

$$F_t = F_f + F_w + F_l + F_h \tag{3}$$

F_t is driving force, F_h is gradient resistance, F_l is accelerating resistance, F_w is air resistance and F_f is rolling resistance. Here are their definitions.

$$F_t = \frac{T_d}{r} = \frac{T_0 i_o \eta_t}{r} \tag{4}$$

$$F_h = mg\sin\theta \tag{5}$$

$$F_l = \delta m v \tag{6}$$

$$F_w = \frac{1}{2} C_d A \rho u^2 \tag{7}$$

$$F_f = mgf\cos\vartheta \tag{8}$$

We can get formula (9) after combining formula (3) with formula (4) ~ (8).

$$\delta m v = \frac{T_0 i_o \eta_t}{r} - mg\sin\vartheta - mgf\cos\vartheta - \frac{1}{2} C_d A \rho u^2 \tag{9}$$

In the formula (3) ~ (8): δ is vehicle rotating mass transfer coefficient, m is gross vehicle weight, v is absolute velocity, i_0 is the main reducer transmission ratio, θ is slop, f is rolling resistance coefficient, C_d is air resistance coefficient, A is front face area, ρ is air density, and u is relative velocity.

According to Newton's Law, we can get formu – la (10) and formula (11) (Fan. 2010).

$$mv = F_t - (F_f + F_w + F_l + F_h) \tag{10}$$

$$mv = F_t - mg\sin\vartheta - mgf\cos\vartheta - \frac{1}{21.15}C_d A (v - v_\alpha)^2 - \delta mv \tag{11}$$

Finally we have

$$mv + \delta mv = F_t - \frac{1}{21.15}C_d A (v - v_\alpha)^2 - mg\sin\vartheta - mgf\cos\vartheta \tag{12}$$

The vehicle dynamics model of BAIC electric vehicle C30 that considers driving force F_t as input signal and absolute velocity v as output signal can be established in SIMULINK of MATLAB according to formula (12) and it is shown in Fig. 7.

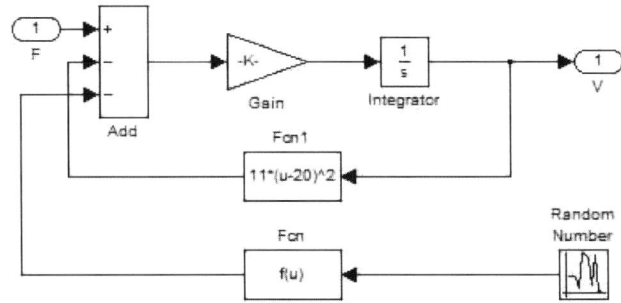

Fig. 7 vehicle's dynamics model

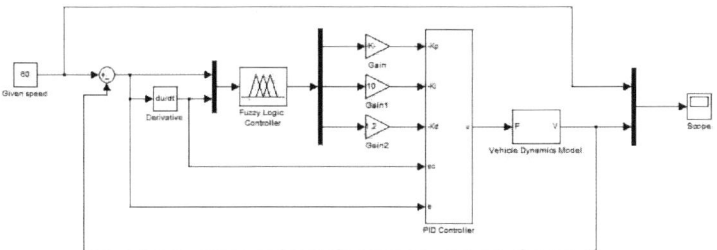

Fig. 8 vehicle cruise control system on MATLAB

Random signal will be used to simulate the road slope in order to truly reflect influence that road have on vehicle when the vehicle is running.

4 Simulation of Parameters Self – tuning Fuzzy PID Controller

Vehicle cruise control system which is shown in Fig. 8 on MATLAB will be gained combined with fuzzy PID controller and vehicle dynamics object. First, the error e (t) and the error rate ec (t) are processed by fuzzy logic controller, then fuzzy logic controller outputs k_p, k_i and k_d parameters. These output parameters will be considered as the input parameters of PID controller after amplifying these three parameters.

The simulation results of fuzzy PID controller are shown in Fig. 9.

It can be seen from simulation results that output parameters' response time that self – tuning fuzzy PID controller outputs is very fast. It can be seen that the output signal has a small overshoot and reach a stable state in short time. It turns out that parameters self – tuning fuzzy PID controller could control the object well.

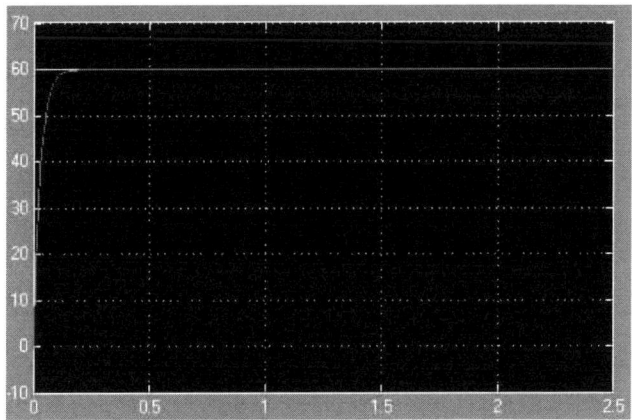

Fig. 9 simulation results of fuzzy PID controller

5 Conclusion

The conventional PID controller can't adapt to systems that have complex conditions and whose object's parameters often change. Sometimes it even exacerbates the instability of system. But fuzzy PID controller could adapt to these systems according to different input conditions, so that parameters of system can adapt to change of the error and error rate of system in real – time. Moreover, fuzzy PID controller has a weak dependence of the controlled object model and can timely adjust its parameters according to information of input signal. With the increasing industrial demand, fuzzy control algorithm will be widely used in industry based on PID control algorithm and the control rules also will be more perfect with industrial experience.

6 Acknowledges

This work was financially supported by "The Project of Construction of Innovative Teams and Teacher vehicleeer Development for Universities and Colleges Under Beijing Municipality" and "The Importation and Development of High – Caliber Talents Project of Beijing Municipal Institutions" (CIT&TCD201304074 and IDHT20130513). And this paper's corresp – onding author is Wenliang Niu whose email is xxtwenliang@buu.edu.cn. His telephone number is +139 1086 4617 and his address is No. 97 Beisihuan East Road, Chao Yang District, Beijing, P. R. China, 100101.

REFERENCES

[1] Yueming, Hou. Research on Constant Speed Cruise Control of Electric Vehicle. Harbin: Harbin Institute of Technology, 2001.

[2] Zhenjun, Zhang. Research on Control Strategy of Adaptive Cruise Control System for Battery Electric Vehicle. Changchun: Jinlin University, 2013.

[3] Kefei, Hu. The Design of Cruise Control System. Wuhan: Wuhan University of Technology, 2012.

[4] Min, Zhang & Chun, Yu. MATLAB – based Design of a Fuzzy – tuning PID controller. Techniques of Automation and Application, 2005, 24 (7).

[5] Hougwei, Liu. Research on Automobile Adaptive Cruise control system. Shanghai: Donghua University, 2010.

[6] Xiaoju, Lu. The Research and Realization of Automated Cruise Control System. Beijing: Beijing Union University, 2014.

[7] Fan, Yu. Vehicle Dynamics and Control. Machinery Industry Press, 2010.

The Design and Implementation of GR - MV Image Inpainting

Yuan Jiazheng   Liu Hongzhe   Zheng Yongrong

1 Introduction

Image inpainting is an important research topic in the area of image restoration[1]. Inpainting is the process of reconstructing lost or deteriorated parts of images. Image restoration is one of the current hot research field which computer graphics, computer vision and image processing. Image inpainting is great importance in a variety of applications, such as protection of cultural relic and paintings, restoration of damaged images caused by network transmission, removal of caption, scratches and target objects in images and videos etc.

At present, the image inpainting algorithm basically has two kinds: one is image inpainting based on the geometric image models[2,3,4,5]. The other is image completion based on texture synthesis[1,6]. The former is suitable to inpaint the small scale scratches in images[1], but larger regions and rich texture information damaged image restoration poor effect, at present this kind of method includes the based on partial differential equations (PDE)[7,8] repair methods and based on the total variational (TV)[3,9] model of the repair methods. The latter is very good at completing the large objects[1], but the results are not good for contain structure information and these algorithms have high time complexity[10]. The representative algorithms like references [6,8,11,12,13,14,15,16,17,18].

According to the merits and demerits about the image inpainting based on the geometric image models and image completion based on texture synthesis, we try to propose a novel image inpainting algorithm between the two kinds of important and traditional algorithms.

In order to synthesize the merits of the image inpainting algorithm based on the geometric image models and based on texture synthesis. This article puts forward the idea that golden ratio[19] and mean variance image inpainting algorithm. The algorithm will apply the technology of golden ratio[20,21] in image processing.

The problem of image segmentation basing on color and texture region differences is considered[11]. We can use the golden ratio as segmentation line. And use the high correlation between adjacent pixels, according to the golden section to choose the local image area, and analysis the gradient information. Through calculating the pixels, and synthesized the relevant gradient damaged pixel information, makes the area around the neighborhood and the information fusion image in order to get the purpose of repair. The algorithm has better performance validated by experiments. It has two kinds traditional repair algorithm's advantages, not only be suitable to inpaint the small scale scratches in images, but also be suitable for large continuous area damaged images.

This paper is organized as the following. We discussed the essential principle in section 2. The detailed description and the implementation steps of our proposed algorithm will be described in section 3. The evaluation method in section 4, with results and conclusion in sections 5 and 6, respectively.

2 Basic Principle of GR - MV Algorithm

According to the research in the field of perception theory, GR - MV algorithm's mechanism of repair is the

[Foundation Item] Project supported by the Natural Science Foundation (No. 61271369, No. 41101111), Natural Science Foundation of Beijing (No. 4102060, 1122016), the science - technology development plan of Education Committee of Beijing (No. KM201111417014), and Funding Project for Academic Human Resources Development in Institutions of Higher Learning Under the Jurisdiction of Beijing Municipality (PHR201107302).

[Author Introduction] Yuan Jiazheng, Liu Hongzhe, Zheng Yongrong, Beijing Key Laboratory of Information Service Engineering, Beijing Union University. Yuan Jiazheng Email address: xxtjiazheng@ buu. edu. cn.

image pixels are highly relevant in most of the images, and the farther the distance, the correlation of pixel weaker. By studying correlated relation of neighborhood pixel[22], so we can choose a local area form the damaged images, and to study the pixel related gradient[23], this is

$$\nabla \partial = \sqrt{\frac{\sum_{i=1}^{n}(x_i - x_0)^2}{n-1}} \quad (1)$$

The x_i is a pixel, and the x_0 is the average pixel of the image area, this is

$$x_0 = \frac{1}{n}\sum_{i=1}^{n} x_i \quad (2)$$

About the choice of the object regions φ, we introduce the Golden Ratio, we set the size of φ is γ times than the image θ, namely

$$\frac{\varphi}{\theta} = \gamma \text{ or } \varphi = \theta \cdot r \quad (3)$$

We suppose that the image's length is α pixel, and the width is β, so we can express the image by the matrix θ [α] [β]. Every pixel point can be expressed by $x(i, j)$ and $i < \alpha$, $j < \beta$ namely

$$\theta = \begin{bmatrix} x(1,1) & \cdots & x(1,\alpha) \\ . & \cdots & . \\ . & \cdots & . \\ . & \cdots & . \\ x(\beta,1) & \cdots & x(\beta,\alpha) \end{bmatrix} \quad (4)$$

We can get the local area ϕ by golden section, and the local area's length and width is a and b respectively. It has

$$a = \alpha \cdot \gamma, \quad b = \beta \cdot \gamma \quad (5)$$

We can get four local area were ϕ_1, ϕ_2, ϕ_3, ϕ_4 by gold ratio and the four corners $x(1,1)$, $x(1,\beta)$, $x(\alpha,1)$, $x(\alpha,\beta)$. There are

$$\varphi = \begin{bmatrix} x(1,1) & \cdots & x(1,a) \\ . & \cdots & . \\ . & \cdots & . \\ . & \cdots & . \\ x(b,1) & \cdots & x(b,a) \end{bmatrix} \quad \varphi_2 = \begin{bmatrix} x(1,\alpha-a) & \cdots & x(1,\alpha) \\ . & \cdots & . \\ . & \cdots & . \\ . & \cdots & . \\ x(b,\alpha-a) & \cdots & x(b,\alpha) \end{bmatrix} \quad (6)$$

$$\varphi_3 = \begin{bmatrix} x(\beta-b,1) & \cdots & x(\beta-b,a) \\ . & \cdots & . \\ . & \cdots & . \\ . & \cdots & . \\ x(\beta,1) & \cdots & x(\beta,a) \end{bmatrix} \quad \varphi_4 = \begin{bmatrix} x(\beta-b,\alpha-a) & \cdots & x(\beta-b,\alpha) \\ . & \cdots & . \\ . & \cdots & . \\ . & \cdots & . \\ x(\beta,\alpha-a) & \cdots & x(\beta,\alpha) \end{bmatrix} \quad (7)$$

And there will be a public area ϕ^*, as follows

$$\varphi^* = \begin{bmatrix} x(\beta-b,\alpha-a) & \cdots & x(\beta-b,a) \\ . & \cdots & . \\ . & \cdots & . \\ . & \cdots & . \\ x(b,\alpha-a) & \cdots & x(b,\alpha-a) \end{bmatrix} \quad (8)$$

We can express a damaged pixel by $x(p, q)$, and we can know which region in the damaged pixel in by the nearby principle and the region in ϕ_1, ϕ_2, ϕ_3, ϕ_4 4. If the pixel $x(p, q)$ in the public area φ^*, the pixel

x (p, q) belong to the area which the pixel x (p, q) closer to the center. Then compute the related gradient $\nabla \partial$ of the area which the pixel x (p, q) in.

According to the damaged pixel x (p, q), we can get the surrounding pixels average $\bar{x}$, we define the surrounding area as δ, and the δ is a ring area near the center point with 3 by 3, they are x ($p-1$, $q-1$), x ($p-1$, q), x ($p-1$, $q+1$), x (p, $q-1$), x (p, q), x (p, $q+1$), x ($p+1$, $q-1$), x ($p+1$, q), x ($p+1$, $q+1$). And there is

$$\bar{x} = \frac{1}{8}\sum_{p \in \delta} x_p = \frac{1}{8}\left(\sum_{i=-1}^{1}\sum_{j=-1}^{1} x(p+i, q+j) - x(p,q)\right) \tag{9}$$

According to the adjacent related principle, we can give the sum of $\bar{x}$ and $\nabla \partial$ to the damaged pixel x (p, q), namely

$$x(p, q) = \bar{x} + \nabla \partial \tag{10}$$

3 GR – MV Image Restoration Algorithm Implemented

3.1 Recognition gezer choice

Recognition gezer[24] which a color for distinguishing the damaged image. We know that a picture has a lot of pixels, and each pixel have RGB three color information, so the picture have a lot of pixel information, however, damaged image's part pixels information is blank, it is not good for intelligent identification, therefore, we select a color as the recognition gezer to distinguish the damaged pixels in the process of image inpainting. Research showed that the general image is hardly containing pure white; therefore, the pure white is the best choice. So we define the recognition gezer as pure white, its RGB ratio is 255∶255∶255. In other words, if the pixel's information data is 255, it is a damaged pixel.

3.2 Algorithm idea of GR – MV

To restore a broken image, we must repair damaged color information, and how to get that information? Because a pair of damaged the image may be small range of damaged also may be big range, we can to repair the whole image according to the distribution and peripheral environment and the color information simulate the damaged information. So the missing information in the texture layer can be generated with a texture synthesis method[25].

We can design it like this, to chose a block, and get the mean square deviation as related gradient, as the whole image of processing information; According to the information data around the damaged pixel, we can get their average information data, we will get mean value add relevant gradient then give the sum to damaged pixel spot, to achieve the purpose of repair. This thought comprehensive considers repairing the whole and the parts of the image, the relationship between the structure and texture, cleverly combining both the different characteristics of the repair of the image, more applicable.

3.3 Algorithm steps

We judge whether a pixel is a damaged pixel or not. If it is a damaged pixel, replace it by the average of non – damaged pixels. If it is a non – damaged pixel, simply skip the process and preserve that pixel[6]. The following are the details about the five steps:

Step 1 The first step. Segment the image need to repair by the gold ratio, the image will be segmented into four areas ϕ_1, ϕ_2, ϕ_3, ϕ_4, and compute respectively the pixel related gradient $\nabla \partial_1$, $\nabla \partial_2$, $\nabla \partial_3$, $\nabla \partial_4$ by the formula (1), (2).

Step 2 To find the damaged pixel x (p, q), and determine its area φ' by the nearby principle.

Step 3 To compute the average pixels $\bar{x}$ (p, q) of the damaged pixel x (p, q) neighbourhood surrounding by the formula (9).

Step 4 To give the ($\nabla \partial + \bar{x}$) to the damaged pixel x (p, q) by the formula (10).

Step 5 It is turn next damaged pixel, and executes the algorithm circularly until image restora – tion is intact.

4 Valuation Method of GR – MV

4.1 Standard related gradient

The purpose of the image inpainting is to repair the damaged image, make the repaired damaged image as near the original image, we need to have an objective evaluation to check the quality of the image restoration[24,26,27,28,29,30,31,32].

As we known, if two images are same, their data and information are same and the same index's ratio is 1. So their data and information are more and more similar, the ratio closer to 1. We can adopt standard related gradient image quality as the image inpainting evaluation index. Standard related gradient ∇l is

$$\nabla l = \frac{\nabla \partial'}{\nabla \partial} \tag{11}$$

the $\nabla \partial'$ is the related gradient after the inpainting, the $\nabla \partial$ is the original image's related gradient. The standard related gradient closer to 1 the quality higher.

4.2 Standard contrast test

The GR – MV image inpainting algorithm is combined with the geometric image models and texture synthesis, is synthesized the whole and part. In order to compare their performance, we use the same data term as the comparison. To keep the contrast test terse, we only compare the GR – MV algorithm to the traditional algorithm based on the total variational (TV) model method.

5 Analysis of Experimental Results

5.1 The experiment results of GR – MV

Now we will show the application effect of the GR – MV image inpainting algorithm. The image (b) is the damaged image, and the image (c) is the results restored by the GR – MV algorithm. The experimental effect is as follows:

(a) Master map

(b) Damaged image

(c) The results

Fig. 1 Experimental results show

5.2 Standard contrast test

We compared the GR – MV image inpainting algorithm to the TV model image inpainting algorithm, image (a) is the master map, image (b) is the damaged image need to be repaired, image (c) is the results of the the GR – MV image inpainting algorithm, image (d) is the results of the TV model image inpainting algorithm. Experiment results are as follows: Through the contrast test we knew that the repair results of the GR – MV image inpainting algorithm keep highly consistent with the original image, and the repairing effect is obvious better than the TV model image inpainting algorithm.

(a) Master map (b) Damaged image (c) GR-MV algorithm (d) TV model algorithm

Fig. 2 The results of the standard contrast test

5.3 Standard related gradient analysis

Through the formula (4.1) we can get the GR – MV image inpainting algorithm's standard related gradient and the TV model algorithm's standard related gradient, the results are as follows: Through the comparison of the related standard gradient, we found that the algorithm of standard related gradient ∇l closer to 1, the algorithm is obviously higher than the TV model image inpainting algorithm in the aspect of quality. But the GR – MV image inpainting algorithm needed time is more than TV model image inpainting algorithm.

Table 1 Standard related gradient analysis

	∇l	$T(s)$
GR – MV algorithm	1.092 074	4.506 337
TV model algorithm	1.220 392	2.697 052

6 Conclusion and Future Work

The results of the experiment showed that GR – MV image inpainting algorithm is simple and easily understand and high repair ability. The algorithm has high intelligence and accuracy. Use of combining the whole and the parts processing, to avoid the ladder effect, and retained the characteristic of image, avoided feature points dim in the repair process. Applicability is wider than traditional algorithms, and the repaired quality is better. GR – MV image inpainting algorithm had great research value and practical value in the current image restoration field.

We will try to overcome the shortcoming of slow speed, to reduce the image inpainting time, to improve the GR – MV image inpainting algorithm.

Acknowledgement

This work is supported by a grant from Nation Natural Science Foundation (No. 61271369, No. 41101111), Natural Science Foundation of Beijing (No. 4102060, 1122016), the science – technology development plan of Education Committee of Beijing (No. KM201111417014), and Funding Project for Academic Human Resources Development in Institutions of Higher Learning Under the Ju – risdiction of Beijing Municipality (PHR201107302).

References

[1] Zhang Hong ying, Peng Qi cong. A Survey on Digital Image Inpainting [J]. Journal of Image and Graphics, 2007 (1): 6 – 15.

[2] Wei Xin, Jiang Hua wei. Study on Inpainting Algorithm Based on Image Structure and Texture [J]. Computer Technology and Development, 2010, 20 (9): 90 – 93.

[3] Hou Zheng xin, He Yu – qing, Xu Wei. A Fast Algorithm of Image Inpainting [J]. Journal of Image and Graphics, 2007, 12 (10): 1909 – 1912.

[4] Bai Zong wen, Zhang Wei hu, Zhou Mei li. Algorithm designed for image inpainting adopt f + v decomposition and fractal [J]. Electronic Design Engineering, 2011, 19 (12): 160 – 171.

[5] Sun Yu gang, Li Kai yu, CHeng Wei ping, Xu Gui li. Exemplar based inpainting algorithm con – strained by continuity [J]. Application Research of Computers, 2011, 28 (5): 1951 – 1953.

[6] Hung Jason C, Hwang Chun – Hong, Liao Yi – Chun, Tang Nick C, Chen, Ta – Jen. Exemplar – based Image Inpainting base on Structure Construction [J]. Journal of Software, 2008 (8): 57 – 64.

[7] Gao Xin, Liu Fu lai. Image Processing Methods Based on PDE [J]. Mathematics in Practice and Theory, 2001, 31 (2): 206 – 210.

[8] Lian Xiao li, Xu Zhong yu, Feng Li li, Chao Yu zhong. Novel Image Inpainting Based on Partial Differential Equation [J]. Computer Engineering, 2009 (6).

[9] Zhao Yan wei, Li Xiang lin. A Rapid Image Inpainting Algorithm Based on TV Model [J]. Micro – electronics & Computer, 2009, 26 (6): 253 – 260.

[10] Peng Kun yang, Dong Lan fang. A Fast Image Inpainting Algorithm Based on Average Gray Value [J]. Journal of Image and Graphics, 2010 (1): 55 – 60.

[11] P. A. Chochia. A pyramidal image segmentation algorithm [J]. Journal of Communications Technology and Electronics, 2011 (12): 1550 – 1560.

[12] Jisheng Zhou, Zhenkuan Pan, Weibo Wei, Guohao Liang. Variational Models for Color Image Inpainting and Their Split Bregman Algorithms [J]. Science & Technology Information, 2011 (6): 159 – 162.

[13] Mengxin Li. A New Image Inpainting Method Based on TV Model [J]. CCCM: 2010 (3): 390 – 392.

[14] Folkmar Bornemann. Fast Image Inpainting Based on Coherence Transport [J]. Journal of Mathe – matical Imaging and Vision, 2007 (3) 259 – 278.

[15] Ubirat A. Igncio, Cludio R. Jung. Block – based image inpainting in the wavelet domain [J]. The Visual Computer, 2007 (9): 733 – 741.

[16] Chen Fang, Ye Zheng lin, Wang Ji hong. Image inpainting based on statistical features [J]. Computer Engineering and Applications, 2007 (22): 60 – 62.

[17] Wang Zhipeng, Zhang Guixu. Digital Image Inpainting Based on Group Marching Method [J]. Journal of Image and Graphics, 2007 (5): 52 – 57.

[18] Tan Jieqing, Wang Zhongqing. A novel image inpainting algorithm based on adjacent pixels [J]. Journal of Hefei University of Technology (Natural Science), 2006 (9): 22 – 26.

[19] J. N. Kapur. Some generalizations of the golden ratio [J]. International Journal of Mathematical Education in Science and Technology, 1988, 19 (4): 1464 – 5211.

[20] Li Yanbin, Du Juanlong. Golden ratio – haar wavelet in image encryption. Journal of Xian Poly – technic University, 2008, 22 (3): 309 – 314.

[21] Cai Xiumei, Fan Jiu – lun. Directional filter mask for fingerprint image based on golden segmen – tation ratio [J]. Computer Engineering, 2011, 37 (10): 14 – 15.

[22] He Wenxi, Ding Xinghao. Image inpainting based on 1 Norm. Computer Engineering and Ap – plications. 2010 (19): 168 – 169.

[23] Zhou Chunxia, Wu Xisheng. Adjacent pixels image inpainting based on deviation and edge interpolation [J]. Computer Engineering and Applications, 2008 (14): 188 – 190.

[24] Tony F. Chan, Sung Ha Kang, Error Analysis for Image Inpainting. Journal of Mathematical Imaging and Vision, 2006 (1): 85 – 103.

[25] Hrestha Kedar, Chuan Qin, Shuo – zhong Wang. Layered image inpainting based on image decom – position [J]. Journal of Shanghai University (English Edition), 2006 (6) 580 – 584.

[26] Chen Ke, Fan Yingle, Li Yi. Bistable stochastic resonance mechanism and its application to the image restoration. Journal of Image and Graphics, 2011, 16 (7): 1170 – 1177.

[27] Shih Timothy K., CHANG Rong – chi, Super – resolution inpainting [J]. Journal of Zhejiang University Science A (Sci-

ence in Engineering), 2005 (6): 6-10.

[28] Yang Yong, Wang Ji-wen. Research on Image Completion by Solving Poisson Equation and Gradient [J]. Computer Technology and Development, 2008 (2): 104-109.

[29] Derina R. Holtzhausen, Glen F. Roberts. An Investigation into the Role of Image Repair Theory in Strategic Conflict Management [J]. Journal of Public Relations Research, 2009, 21 (2): 165-186.

[30] William L. Benoit, Shirley Drew. Appropriateness and effectiveness of image repair strategies [J]. Communication Reports, 1997, 10 (2): 153-163.

[31] Karen L. Legg. Religious Celebrity: An Analysis of Image Repair Discourse [J]. Journal of Public Relations Research, 2009, 21 (2): 240-250.

[32] Susan L. Brinson, William L. Benoit. Dow corning's image repair strategies in the breast implant crisis [J]. Communication Quarterly, 1996, 44 (1): 29-41.

Analysis on Flow Field of the Valveless Piezoelectric Pump with Two Inlets and One Outlet and a Rotating Unsymmetrical Slopes Element

Xia Qixiao Zhang Jianhui Lei Hong Cheng Wei

1 Introduction

Valveless piezoelectric pump has no mechanical transmission chain involved. So there are no lubricant leak pollution and abrasion caused by sliding friction or rolling friction in the machine. With the advantages of simple structure, easy manufacturing and convenient microminiaturization, it has been applied widely in the areas of medical treatment and health care[1].

Until now, the researches on the valveless piezoelectric pump were concentrated on the cause of net flow[1-3], flow field in the chamber[4-5], hydrodynamies feature[6], and the relationship between the flow and the drinving voltage and frequency[7-9]. On the other hand, some specific functions of the pump were explored and applied extensively. For instance, the piezoelectric pump with Y – shape elements was designed for transfusing cells or macromolecules[10-12]. And the pump with unsymmetrical slopes element (USE) in another instance, can mix solute fluid and solvent fluid during pumping[13-15].

The working principle of the piezoelectric pump with USE is built on the difference of flow resistances due to the unsymmetrical slope feature of the USE. And the mixing function of the pump comes from the strong turbulent flow and vortices in the chamber generated by USE. Till now, researches has been concerned with the theory on the valvelessness of the USE pump, and the causation of the flow field and the vortices in the chamber. However, there was little attention on the mixing applications.

This paper presents a valveless piezoelectric pump to realize the integration of mixing and pumping functions based on the theory of the USE pump. It contains two inlets and one outlet, and a rotational USE (RUSE). The RUSE means a USE can be rotated around its axis. This pump was developed based on the principle of valveless piezoelectric pump with USE and combined mixing function with it. The developed pump has three channels, two of them connecting inlets and one connecting outlet, with a RUSE equipped in its chamber. Two fluids are sucked into the chamber from the two inlets, respectively, when the pump works. The RUSE in the chamber can be rotated at a desired angle to tune the flow resistances of fluids flowing through all the channels at the same time, by which the adjusting of the flow ratio of the two inlets comes true. Meanwhile, the RUSE also serves as USE to produce net flow and pumps the solution, mixed by the turbulence field, out of the outlet. Therein, the mixing function and pumping function are integrated into a mixing pump.

This paper will describe the principle of this proposed pump, firstly. And then, numerical analysis on the flowing field in the chamber will be processed. Finally, comparison between the results from experiment and the simulation will be carried out to verify the theoretical analysis.

[Foundation Item] This project is supported by National Natural Science Foundation of China (Grant No. 50735002, Grant No. 50775109, and Grant No. 51075201) Chinese Mechanical Engineering Society and Springer – Verlag Berlin Heidelberg 2012.

[Author Introduction] Xia Qixiao, Lei Hong, College of Mechanical and Electronic Engineering, Beijing Union University; Zhang Jianhui, Cheng Wei, Precision Driving Laboratory, Nanjing University of Aeronautics and Astronautics.

2 Piezoelectric Mixing Pump

RIFE, et al.[16], reported a piezoelectric mixing pump in 2000. It actually is only a mixing pool, with piezoelectric vibrators mounted on the wall to drive the solute and solvent flowing when the pump is working. The blocks in the pool are used to generate vortices in order to form a homogeneous solution. This device can only blend fluids, but cannot transport them.

SHEEN, et al[17], presented another piezoelectric mixing pump from China Taiwan in 2007, which integrates functions of mixing and transporting of fluids. The pump has two inlets connected with two channels which converge to a mixing channel. However, this mixing pump cannot be controlled to adjust the ratio of the two fluids through inlets. Besides, the volum of the pump is larger than the regular piezoelectric pump with diffuser/nozzle elements owing to the mixing channel. Otherwise, regular diffuser/nozzle elements fixed outside the chamber, equivalent to the trapezoid obstacle in the channel, are always a bar for further minimization of regular valveless piezoelectric pump.

Fig. 1 shows the valveless piezoelectric pump with USE, proposed by ZHANG, et al[13] and XIA, et al[14-15] from China in 2006. This pump contributes a new idea to minimize the size of the valveless piezoelectric pump by elimination of the diffuser/nozzle elements outside the chamber. In this pump, the bottom of the chamber is developed into an innovative structure, named USE, which is composed of a set of slope pairs. Each slope pair is in triangle shape, made up of two slopes with different angles of α_1 and α_2, illustrated in Fig. 2. The USE in the chamber can work to produce net flow. Another function of USE is to drive fluids to form a complex flow field in the chamber, comprising large vortices with different measures, different directions and complex shapes. This function can be used to develop a new minimized valveless piezoelectric pump integrating mixer and pump to mixing and transporting fluids.

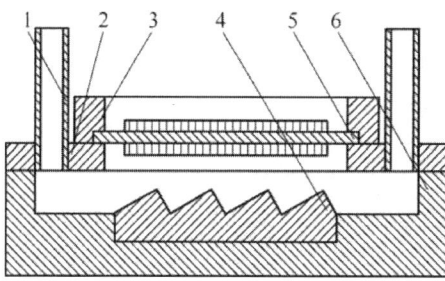

Fig. 1 Assembled pump with USE

1. Lucite conduit (vertical conduit) 2. Cover
3. Upper fixing plate 4. USE 5. Piezoelectric vibrator 6. Pump body

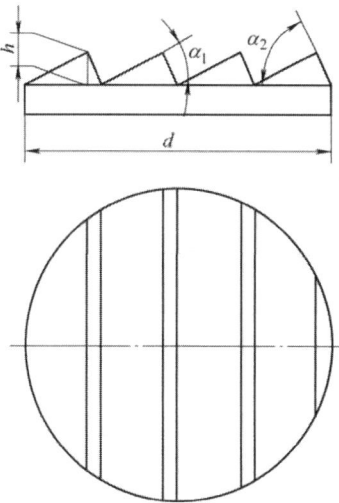

Fig. 2 Unsymmetrical slopes element

Fig. 3 shows the sketch of the proposed valveless piezoelectric pump comprised of two inlets and one outlet with RUSE.

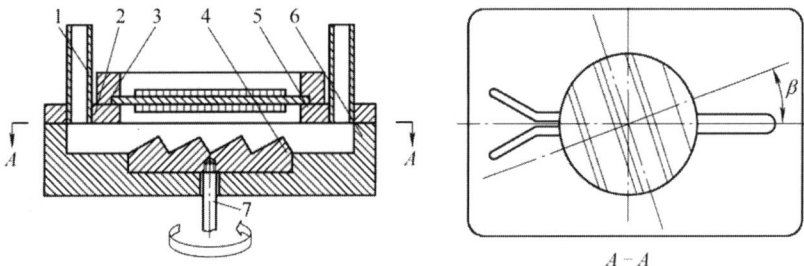

Fig. 3 Sketch of the proposed valveless piezoelectric pump
1. Lucite conduit (vertical conduit)　　2. Cover　　3. Upper fixing plate
4. USE　　5. Piezoelectric vibrator　　6. Pump body　　7. Adjusting handle

By rotating the adjusting handle, the relative position of the RUSE can be changed. And the flow field and vortices in the chamber will vary as the rotation angle changes. Therefore, the fluids sucked from the two inlets can be controlled to a desired flow ratio by rotating the RUSE at a corresponding angle when the pump works, and then the fluids are mixed under the effect of turbulent flow field in the chamber. It has also been proved that the mixing capability of the pump will be enhanced under the effect of intense and complex vortices occurring in the flow field[18].

3 Working Principle

The RUSE explored in this paper is modified based on the USE shown in Fig. 2. As can be seen in Fig. 3, the RUSE works when it turns round its axis under the control of an adjusting handle. The working part of the RUSE has the same structure as the USE, composed of two groups of slopes with different angles, $\alpha_1 \neq \alpha_2$. In addition to that, the RUSE has an adjusting handle fixed to it. It is mounted on the bottom of the chamber.

The RUSE employed in this research is designated with α_1 as 20° and α_2 a right angle. The attack angle of the slopes facing the inlets α_1 will vary to γ when the RUSE is rotated through a β degree on the basis of its axis, but there is no change of α_2, as indicated in Fig. 4. The relationship among α_1, α_2, γ, and β is

$$\tan \gamma = \tan \alpha_1 \cdot \cos \beta, \tag{1}$$

and followed by

$$\gamma < \alpha_1 < \alpha_2. \tag{2}$$

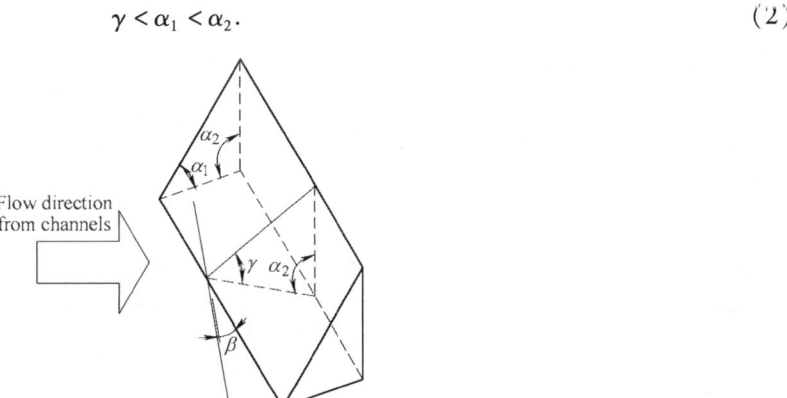

Fig. 4 Diagram of the relationship of the flow and the rotation angle of the RUSE

The direction of net flow in the pump will not be changed because the slopes with a smaller attack angle are always involved in inlet and those with a larger attack angle involved in outlet[14-15].

It can be deduced that the flowing direction will not change when the RUSE is rotated at an acute angle of β according to its axis. So, in this structure, the two inlets of this pump are arranged facing α_1 slopes of the RUSE and α_2 slopes face the outlet. Channel 1 is equivalent to Channel 2 on the condition that the symmetric axis of the RUSE coincides with that of the pump. This is set as the initial position of the RUSE.

In Fig. 5, the dash – double – dot lines denote the initial position of the RUSE, when β is equal to zero. With β degree of rotation, the distance from Inlet 1 to the slope is shortened from L to L_1, and the distance between Inlet 2 and the slope increases from L to L_2. The RUSE in the chamber impedes the fluids in both flowing – in and flowing – out directions. And the coefficients of flow resistance difference will lead to the diversion effect on the net flows through Inlet 1 and Inlet 2. Because of $L_1 \neq L_2$, the net flows through Inlet 1 and Inlet 2 are different. The variations of L_1 and L_2 can be expressed as

$$\begin{cases} L_1 = L - l\cos\beta, \\ L_2 = L + l\cos\beta. \end{cases} \quad (3)$$

It can be seen from Eq. (3) that L_1 and L_2 are all the functions of β. And the flow ratio of channel 1 to Channel 2 can be controlled by adjusting the rotation angle of β.

The chamber of the pump is composed of the pump body and the piezoelectric vibrator. The chamber volume will vary along with the deflection of the piezoelectric vibrator driven by AC voltage periodically. The chamber volume increases when the vibrator deflects up and the chamber pressure decreases. In this condition, fluid flows into chamber from the three channels simultaneouly, and the pump works in suction mode. However, the flows through the three channels into the chamber are different because of the different coefficients of flow resistance as illustrated in Fig. 6.

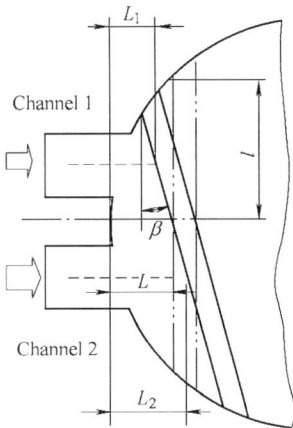

Fig. 5 Top sketch of the part of the chamber corresponding to the inlets

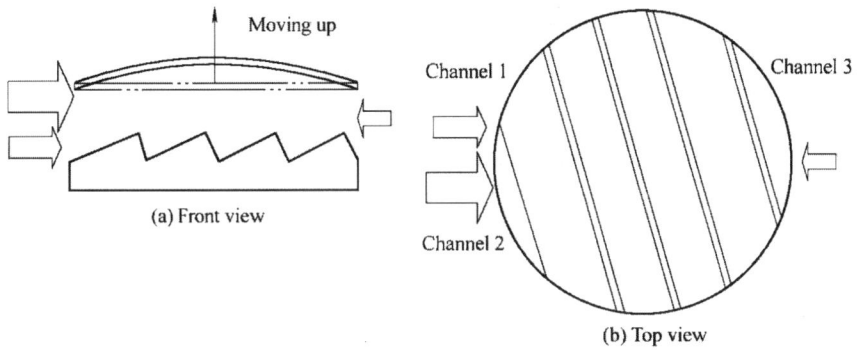

Fig. 6 Suction mode of the piezoelectric pump with RUSE

When the vibrator deflects down and the pressure in the chamber rises, the fluid is expelled out of the chamber through the three channels, shown in Fig. 7. The pump works in the discharge mode in this condition. Similar to the suction mode, the flows are different because the three channels face to the different places of the RUSE. The attack angle γ of the left slopes is always smaller than α_2 of the right slopes. Therefore, the direction of the net flow is always from left to right[14]. The value of the net flow can be obtained according to the continuous principle[15]:

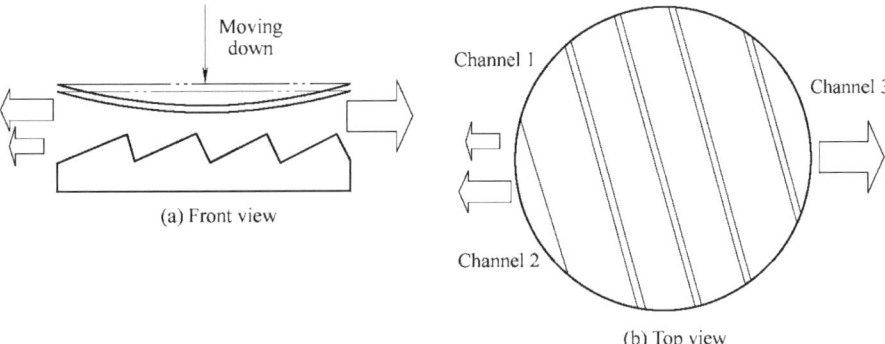

Fig. 7 Discharge mode of the piezoelectric pump with RUSE

$$Q = (Q_{1s} + Q_{2s}) - (Q_{1e} + Q_{2e}) = Q_{3e} - Q_{3s}, \tag{4}$$

Q—Net flow,
Q_{1s}—Flow in Channel 1 in suction mode, $i = 1, 2, 3$,
Q_{1e}—Flow in Channel 1 in discharge mode, $i = 1, 2, 3$.

4 Numerical Analysis on RUSE Pump

In this research, the cross sectional areas of Channels 1 and 2 are different from that of Channel 3. The former two channels on the left side of the chamber have the same values of width and height, which are 3 mm and 2 mm, respectively. The other channel on the right of the chamber is 3 mm in width and 4 mm in height. Thus the outlet channel has double sectional area of the inlet.

The chamber is 30 mm in diameter and 4 mm in height. α_1 and α_2 are designed as 20° and 90°, respectively. Fig. 8 shows the 3D model of the chamber filled with fluid. For the convenience of explanation, the part of the chamber higher than the upper edge of channels is colored in blue, named Upper–region, while the lower part of the chamber is dyed in crystal brown, named Lower–region. Water is adopted in this research as working substance, which is assumed to be viscous, incompressible Newton fluid. The governing equations of fluid motion are the continuity equation and the Navier–Stokes momentum equation.

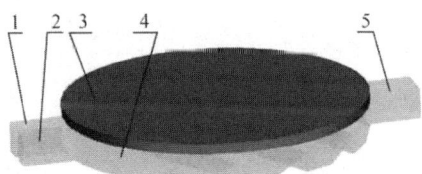

Fig. 8 Model of the RUSE pump while the liquid is filled
1. Channel 1 2. Channel 2 3. Upper–region
4. Lower–region 5. Channel 3

Continuity equation is
$$\nabla v = 0. \tag{5}$$

Navier–Stokes equation is
$$\rho\left(\frac{\partial v}{\partial t} + v \cdot \nabla v\right) = -p + \mu \nabla^2 v; \tag{6}$$

v—Velocity of flow,
p—Pressure,
t—Time,
ρ—Density of fluid,

μ—Dynamic viscosity of fluid,

∇—Hamilton operator.

The RNG $k-\varepsilon$ model was used in this research. The governing equations for incompressible flow can be expressed as follows:

$$\rho \frac{\partial k}{\partial t} + \rho \frac{\partial (ku_i)}{\partial x_i} = \frac{\partial}{\partial x_i}\left(a_k \mu_{\text{eff}} \frac{\partial k}{\partial x_i}\right) + G_k + \rho \varepsilon, \tag{7}$$

$$\rho \frac{\partial \varepsilon}{\partial t} + \rho \frac{\partial (\varepsilon u_i)}{\partial x_i} = \frac{\partial}{\partial x_i}\left(\alpha_\varepsilon \mu_{\text{eff}} \frac{\partial \varepsilon}{\partial x_j}\right) + C_{1s}^* \frac{\varepsilon}{k} G_k - C_{2\varepsilon} \rho \frac{\varepsilon^2}{k}; \tag{8}$$

k—Kinetic energy of turbulence flow,

ε—Dissipation rate,

μ_{eff}—Efficient viscosity, $\mu_{\text{eff}} = \mu + \mu_t$,

μ—Dynamic viscosity,

$\mu_t = \rho C_\mu \dfrac{k^2}{\varepsilon}$, $C_\mu = 0.045$, $\alpha_k = \alpha_\varepsilon = 1.39$,

G_k—Stress term generated by Velocity gradients,

$G_{1\varepsilon} = C_{1s}^* = C_{1s} - \dfrac{\eta(1 - \eta/\eta_0)}{1 + \beta\eta^3}$, 1.42, $C_{2\varepsilon} = 1.68$,

$\eta = \sqrt{2E_{ij} \cdot E_{ij}} \dfrac{k}{\varepsilon}$, $E_{ij} = \dfrac{1}{2}\left(\dfrac{\partial u_i}{\partial x_j} + \dfrac{\partial u_j}{\partial x_i}\right)$,

$\eta_0 = 4.377$, $\beta = 0.012$.

The density of the water $\rho = 998.2$ kg/m^3, and dynamic viscosity $\mu = 0.001\,003$ kg/(m·s) under the condition of standard atmosphere.

The Lower – region is described firstly. Fig. 9 shows the streamlines of the fluid flowing into the chamber from Channel 1 on condition that $\alpha_1 = 20°$ and $\beta = 0°$ in suction mode. It can be seen that the complex flow field is generated in the ways of counterclockwise vortices in horizontal planes and complex vortices in vertical planes, while part of the fluid flows spirally to the region facing Channel 2 in the chamber. Due to symmetry when $\beta = 0°$, the fluid from Channel 2 is generated to produce clockwise vortices in horizontal planes and some of it flows spirally to the region facing Channel 1 as shown in Fig. 10.

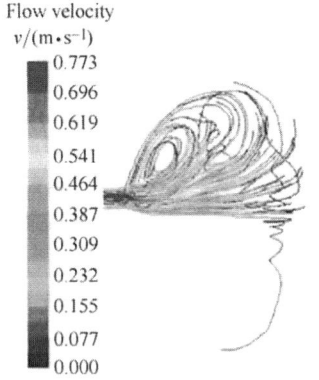
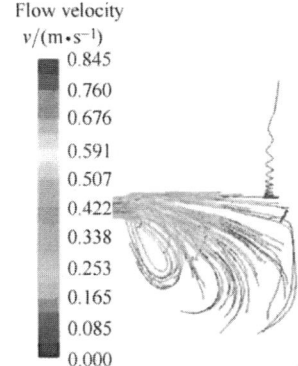

Fig. 9 Streams from Channel 1 in the Lower – region in suction mode when $\beta = 0°$ (top view)

Fig. 10 Streams from Channel 2 in the Lower – region in suction mode when $\beta = 0°$ (top view)

Fig. 11 illustrates the circumstance that the chamber works in suction mode. Under the resistance of the streams from Channel 1 and Channel 2, the stream coming from Channel 3 is split into two parts in the chamber. The two streams flow around into the chamber by both sides, respectively with vortices in the horizontal direction and stronger vortices in the vertical direction under the effect of the RUSE. And the two streams meet in the center of the chamber accompanied with strong spiral flow finally.

Fig. 12 shows the distribution of the flow field in the Upper-region in suction mode, which is mainly comprisedof vortices with different measures. It can be seen from Fig. 9 to Fig. 12 that the fluids flowing into the chamberfrom the three channels form complex vortices in different directions and in various measures. According to mixing theory, complex and strong vortices produce strong shear flows and intense turbulence field, which are sufficient conditions for mixing. Therefore, under the effect of the vortices and turbulent flows, these fluids will mix with each other. It is very suitable to mix two kinds of fluid into a mixture when pumping them.

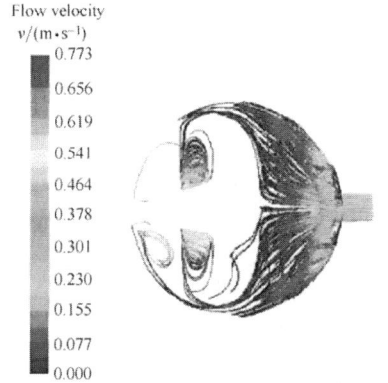

Fig. 11 Streams from Channel 3 in the Lower-region in suction model when $\beta = 0°$ (top view)

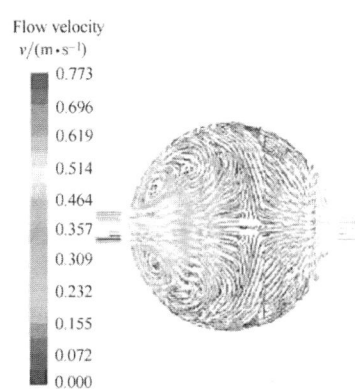

Fig. 12 Flow field in the Upper-region in suction mode when $\beta = 0°$ (top view)

Fig. 13 shows the streamline in discharge mode. Almost no vortices occur in horizontal planes, although some do in vertical planes. Thereby, there is not so much effecton mixing fluids in discharge mode as in suction mode.

What will happen if the RUSE is rotated at an acute angle of β? The net flows of Channel 1 and Channel 2 vary, and the flow field in the chamber is also transformed. This paper gives illustrations with only instance about thetransformed flow fields on Condition that β varies to 16°, while α_1 and α_2 remain. The Lower-region in suction mode is described firstly. Fig. 14 shows the streamlines formed by fluid flowing into chamber from Channel 1. It is very different from the case of $\beta = 0°$ mentioned above. It can be seen that the vortices occurring in horizontal planes are more various and complex in spite of flow direction sill counterclockwise. And the vortices in vertical planes are much stronger. Also, more fluid flows into the region Channel 2 faces.

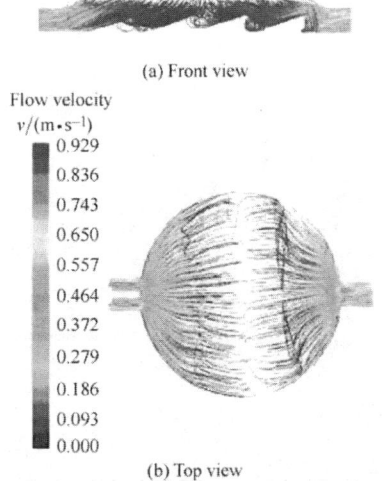

Fig. 13 Flow field in the chamber in discharge mode when $\beta = 0°$

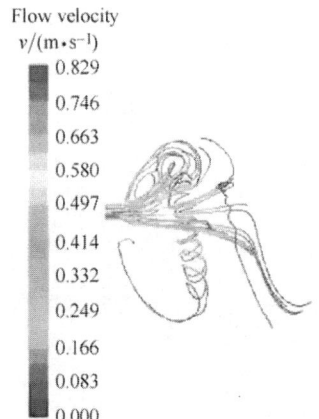

Fig. 14 Streams from Channel 1 in the Lower-region in suction mode when $\beta = 16°$ (top view)

The streamlines of the fluid coming from Channel 2 are transformed below, shown in Fig. 15. There are still clockwise vortices occurring, but their region is compressed. The flow field varies to some simple. There is less fluid flowing to the region Channel 1 faces. The fluid from Channel 3 into the chamber is illustrated in Fig. 16. It is also split into two parts. But most of it flows by upside into the upper part of the chamber and then runs through the entire chamber, producing some clockwise vortices in horizontal planes and very strong vortices in vertical planes. Another small fluid flows in by downside, generating counterclockwise vortices in horizontal planes, shown in Fig. 16. Fig. 17 is the flow field occurring in the Upper – region, in which the flow field is more turbulent than that when $\beta = 0°$. Compared to the case of $\beta = 0°$, the flow field features violent turbulence and the vortices behave with a variety of measures and shapes.

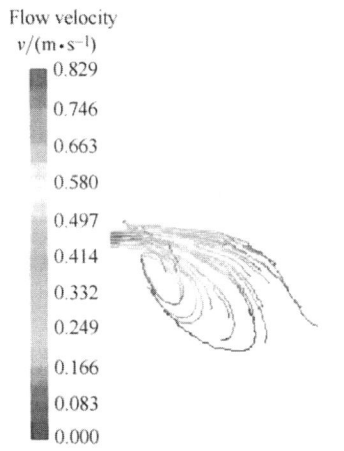

Fig. 15　Streams from Channel 2 in the Lower – region in suction mode when $\beta = 16°$ (top view)

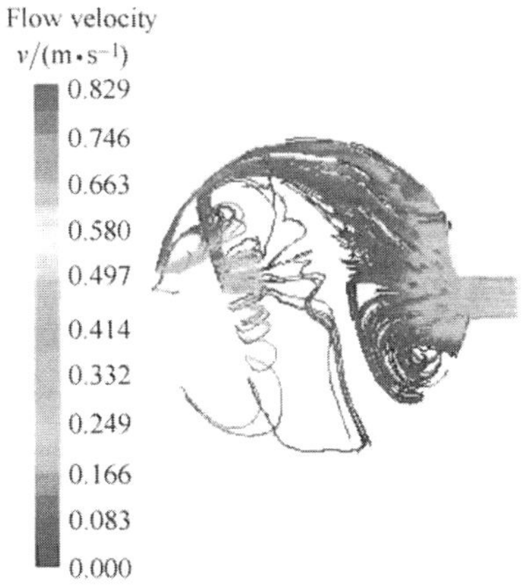

Fig. 16　Streams from Channel 3 in the Lower – region in suction model when $\beta = 16°$ (top view)

Fig. 18 shows the flow field occurring in discharge mode. It is mainly constructed by vortices generated in vertical planes. All patterns of the flow fields shown above indicate that strong turbulence field and intense shear flows also occur in the chamber when the RUSE is rotated. According to the analysis above, if $\beta \neq 0°$, this pump has the function to distribute the flows from Channel 1 and Channel 2 in proportion. Also, the complex vortex field can mix and blend the fluids from the three channels sufficiently. These features provide prospect for integration of mixer and pump, by which two fluids can be mixed together into a homogeneous mixture while they are being transported.

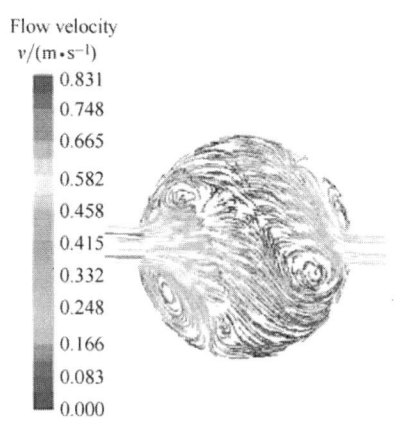
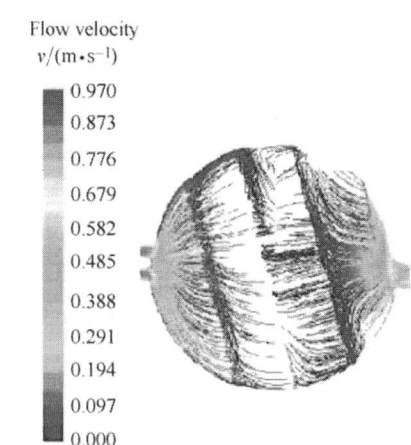

Fig. 17　Flow field in the Upper – region in suction mode when $\beta = 16°$ (top view)

Fig. 18　Flow field in the chamber in discharge mode when $\beta = 16°$ (top view)

The direction of the net flow of the RUSE pump is from left to right if the pump is arranged as Fig. 3. Fig. 19 shows the flow changes of the three channels at the RUSE rotation angle of β. With the increase of β, the configuration of the RUSE about the two inlets varies, and the flows also vary.

The total flowing trend increases when β is increasing. But their rates of increasing are different. The net flow from Channel 2 increases more quickly than that from Channel 1. Fig. 20 shows the ratio of the flows from the two channels. Accompanying with the increase of β, the ratio of the flow from Channel 1 to Channel 2 varies from 1 to 0.61 accompanied by β from 0° to 16°. Also, the net flows in all channels increase with β rising, which means that the flow of the pump increases. When $\beta > 16°$, the RUSE will block Channel 1, beyond the research of this paper. Therefore, this paper only pays attention to the study in range of β from 0° to 16°. It is obvious that the RUSE makes the flow field complex, and generates much more vortices, which feature diverse measures and various shapes in all directions.

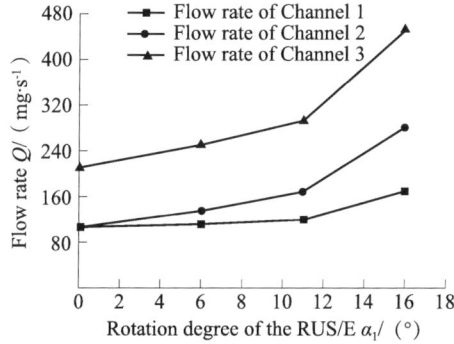

Fig. 19 Relationship between flows and the rotation angle of the RUSE

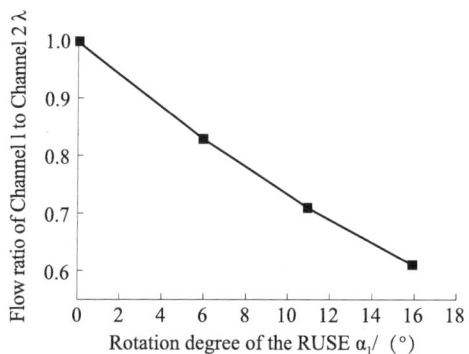

Fig. 20 Relationship between the flow ratio of the two channels with the rotation angle of the RUSE

Compared to the flow fields shown in Ref. 17, the flow field in the RUSE pump is far more turbulent, and more suitable to mixing and blending two fluids while transporting them. The rotation angle has more effect on the flows of the two inlets and their ratio. It features that both flows in the inlets increase with the rotation angle of RUSE increasing, while the flow ratio of the inlets varies. These features can be used to assign the flows from the inlets and adjust the mixing ratio of the two kinds of fluid within a certain range. Therefore, it is superior to the pumps presented in Ref. 16 and Ref. 17.

5 Experiment on a Physical RUSE Pump

In this research, a physical RUSE pump is developed for the sake of verification of the theoretical analysis. All the technical parameters involving the chamber, the channels and the RUSE are the same as the numerical model. Fig. 21 shows the pictures of the experimental pump.

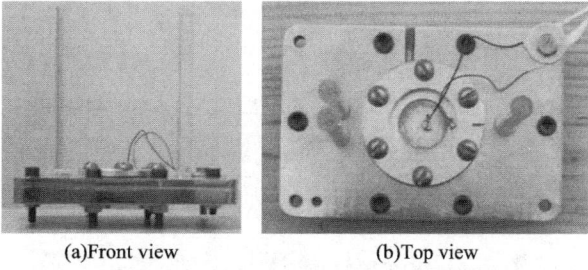

Fig. 21 Pump with RUSE for experiment

Fig. 22 shows the 20° RUSE employed in the experiment, which has the exactly same working sizes to the numerical model. Fig. 23 shows the working part of the RUSE. Four undulating salient parts are distributed at a constant distance on the RUSE, having the same height h of 2 mm. The diameterd of the RUSE is 30 mm, and the distance L is 1.5 mm.

Fig. 24 shows the interior structure of the RUSE pump. The two inlet channels on the left side are filled with water, and their flows vary with the different rotation angles of the RUSE in the chamber.

The pressure differences of the three channels produced by the different configurations of the RUSE are calculated and verified. The geometric parameters and driving parameters of the experimental pump are given in Table1.

(a) Front view

(b) Top view

Fig. 22 RUSE used in the experiment pump

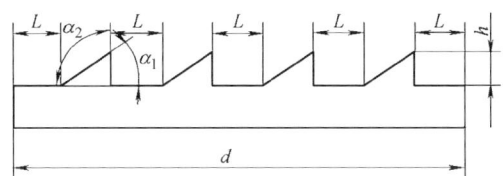

Fig. 23 Sketch of the USE used in the experiments

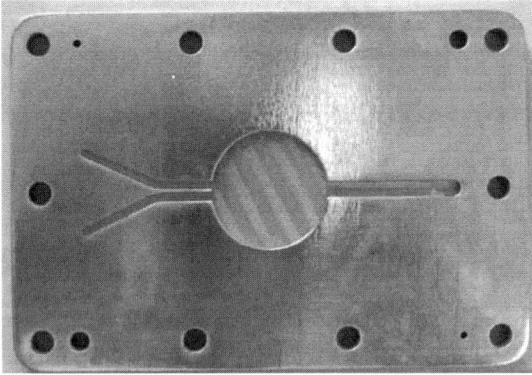

Fig. 24 Interior structure of the experiment pump

Table 1 Geometric parameters and driving parameters of the experimental pump

Working voltage U/V	Working frequency F/Hz	Diameter of the chamber D/mm	Height of the chamber h/mm
220	50	30	4

Figs. 25 – 27 show the comparison of the theoretical analysis and the experimental conclusion. The result shows that the theoretical data and the experimental data share the same tendency. But the errors increase with the increasing of the RUSE rotation angle. It is mainly due to the rough faces in the chamber and the channels, which is hard to be expressed in numerical model. The flow speeds in channels rise accompanying with the RUSE rotation angle increasing. It results to pressure losses rise due to rough faces. Fig. 28 shows the flow ratio of Channel 1 to Channel 2 according to the RUSE rotation angle rising, from which it is concluded that the theoretical ratio and the experimental ratio agree with each other very well, though the net flows from experiment are somehow lower than those from theoretical calculation. The experiment result is a further verification of the theoretical analysis.

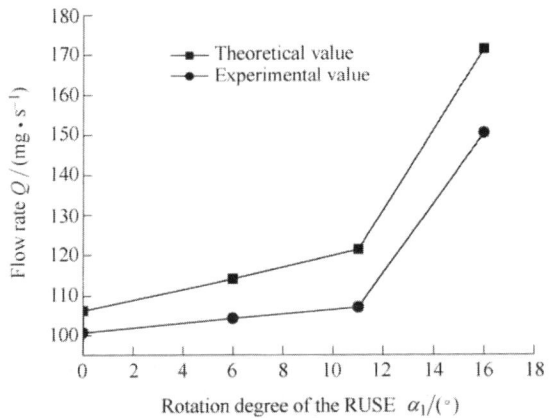

Fig. 25　Net flow of Channel 1

Fig. 26　Net flow of Channel 2

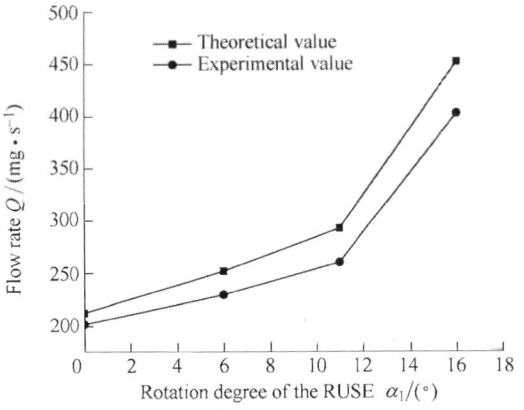

Fig. 27　Net flow of the pump

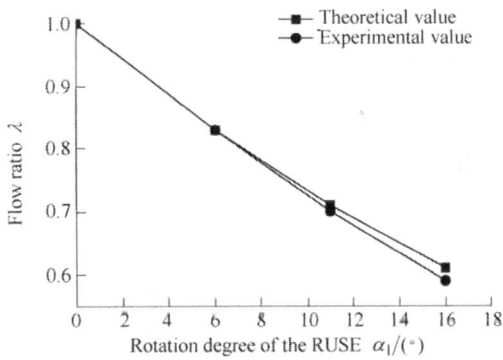

Fig. 28　Flow ratio of Channel 1 to Channel 2

6　Conclusions

(1) A piezoelectric pump with two inlets and one outlet and a RUSE is proposed. It can be used in mixing two fluids while transporting them. This paper analyzes the mixing and pumping principle of this pump. It is shown that the RUSE makes the pressure in the chamber uneven, resulting in strong turbulence and large complex vortices occurring. The rotation of the RUSE can affect the flow resistances of the two inlets, and varies their flows, and, accordingly, can achieve fluids mixing in a desired ratio.

(2) This research analyzes and simulates the flow field in the chamber when the proposed pump is working. Its flow field is composed of the vortices that have different sizes, various directions and strong intension. This feature performs particularly in the suction stage. According to mixing theory, the flow field is suitable to mix fluids to produce homogeneous mixture. Therefore, it has broad prospects in mixing field.

(3) This research assigns $\alpha_1 = 20°$ because the largest flow can be obtained according to Ref. 15. And an ex-

perimental pump is designed for the sake of verification of the theoretical analysis and numerical calculation. The rotation range of β is from 0° to 16° on condition that each of the inlets is blocked. Thereby, the theoretical analysis and experimental verification are all carried out in this range. The conclusion shows that the errors between the theoretical flow and the experimental flow are no more than 11.14%. The errors of flow ratio of the two inlets are no more than 2.5%. It verifies the theoretical analysis.

(4) The proposed RUSE pump features that the lowest flow is achieved when the flow ratio of the two inlets is 1, corresponding to $\beta = 0°$. The flow of the pump will increase with the rotation angle of β rising. And the flow will reach its top when the flow ratio of the two inlets drops to 0.61, corresponding to the maximum rotation angle of the RUSE, $\beta = 16°$. The ways to keep a constant pump flow with any mixing ratio in its range, and to keep a constant mixing ratio with any pump flow remain to be issues to future research.

References

[1] ERIK S, GORAN S. A valve-less diffuser/nozzle-based fluid pump [J]. Sensors and Actuators A, 1993, 39 (12): 159-167.

[2] GERLACH T. Microdiffusers as dynamic passive valves for micropump applications [J]. Sensors and Actuators A, 1998, 69 (2): 181-191.

[3] IVANO I, DINO A, ARIANNA M, et al. Modeling and experimental validation of a piezoelectric micropump with novel no-moving-part valves [J]. Sensors and Actuators A, 2007, 133 (1): 128-140.

[4] KAN Junwu, YANG Zhigang. Research on piezoelectric pump and its development [J]. Optics and Precision Engineering, 2002, 10 (6): 619-625.

[5] Cheng Guangming, Li Peng, Zeng Ping, et al. Piezoelectric pump used in bionic underwater propulsion unit [J]. Journal of Bionic Engineering, 2007, 4 (3): 159-164.

[6] Li Yili, Zhang Jianhui, XIA Qixiao, et al. Research on the dynamic characteristics of the actuator for the piezoelectric pump [J]. China Mechanical Engineering, 2007, 18 (17): 2,088-2,093 (in Chinese).

[7] MARTA F T Ribeiro, JOAO L M Santos, JOSE L F C Lima. Piezoelectric pumping in flow analysis: Application to the spectrophotometric determination of gabapentin [J]. Analytica Chimica ACTA 600, 2007, 4 (20): 14-19.

[8] Morris C J, FORSTER F K. Low-order modeling of resonance for fixed-valve micropumps based on first principles [J]. Journal of Microelectromechanical Systems, 2003, 12 (3): 325-334.

[9] Nguyen N T, HUANG Xiaoyang. Numerical simulation of pulse-width-modulated micropumps with diffuser/nozzle elements [C] //Technical Proceedings of the 2000 International Conference on Modeling and Simulation of Microsystems, March 27-29, 2000, San Diego, California, USA, 2000: 636-639.

[10] Zhang Jianhui, LI Yili, XIA Qixiao. Analysis of the pump volumeflow rate and tube property of the piezoelectric valveless pump with Y-shape tubes [J]. Chinese Journal of Mechanical Engineering, 2007, 43 (11): 136-141 (in Chinese).

[11] Zhang Jianhui. Valveless piezoelectric pump with Y-shape elements: China, ZL99110248.7 [P]. 2001-01-17.

[12] Zhang Jianhui, LU Jizhuang, XIA Qixiao, et al. Working principle and flux characteristics of valve-less piezoelectric pump with Y-shape tubes for transporting cells and macromolecule [J]. Chinese Journal of Mechanical Engineering, 2008, 44 (8): 92-99 (in Chinese).

[13] Zhang Jianhui. Valveless piezoelectric pump: China, ZL200510090255.2 [P]. 2007-09-19.

[14] Xia Qixiao, Zhang Jianhui, LI Hong. Valve-less piezoelectric pump with unsymmetrical slope chamber bottom [J]. Optics and Precision Engineering, 2006, 14 (4): 641-647.

[15] Xia Qixiao, Zhang Jianhui, LEI Hong, et al. Theoretical analysis and experimental verification on flow field of piezoelectric pump with unsymmetrical slopes element [J]. Chinese Journal of Mechanical Engineering, 2009, 22 (5): 735-744.

[16] RIFE J C, BELL M I, HORWITZ J S. Miniature valveless ultrasonic pumps and mixers [J]. Sensors and Actuators A, 2000, 132: 135-140.

[17] Sheen H J, HSU C J, HORWITZ J S, et al. Experimental study of flow characteristics and mixing performance in a PZT self-pumping micromixer [J]. Sensors and Actuators A, 2007, 139: 237-244.

[18] Hessek V, LOWE H, SCHONFELD F. Micromixers - a review on passive and active mixing principles [J]. Chemical Engineering Science, 2005, 60: 2,479-2,501.

基于流固耦合有限元法的汽车发动机液力悬置动力学分析

徐志军　刘福水　于增信

合适的发动机悬置是减小发动机振动和噪声向车身传递的关键，理想的发动机悬置应在不同的频率和振幅下有不同的隔振性能。在发动机低频大振幅的振动范围内，悬置应有足够大的动刚度和较大的阻尼；在中高频范围内，悬置应具有较大的动刚度以降低振动振幅，同时具有较小的阻尼以降低振动和噪声向车内传递。

液力悬置是目前较为流行的发动机支承型式。发动机液力悬置是在传统橡胶悬置中设有上下液腔，中间由带惯性通道或节流孔的隔板隔开。液体在上下液腔之间流动，振动能量被消耗，从而实现衰减振动的目的[1]。设计液压悬置时，一般首先进行仿真计算来确定液力悬置的结构参数和液力参数，如惯性通道长度、横截面积、液体黏度等[2]。

本研究的主要目的是为开发高性能的发动机悬置进行仿真计算。一般对液力悬置的仿真研究都是采用集总质量法，即在计算时引入了各种假设：橡胶主簧无质量、液体在惯性通道内形成振动液柱、上下液室的体积柔度是常数等，需要大量的试验和经验才能确定液体流动阻尼和橡胶主簧体积刚度。

随着计算机技术的发展，数值方法已成为求解工程问题的主要工具。有限元法在求解三维立体结构振动问题上有很大优势。

液力悬置充入液体后，在外界激励的作用下，橡胶的位移和变形对上液室内的液体施加载荷，引起上液室内液体压力的变化，同时橡胶的底面受到反作用力，对这时的液力悬置进行动力学分析就要研究流固耦合力学。

本研究采用基于流固耦合的 ALE 方法。使用 Ansystm 程序，利用流固耦合有限元方法模拟液力悬置动态响应特性。计算时考虑了橡胶主簧的非线性和液体流动的紊流，仿真计算的精度较集总质量法有较大提高。

1 流固耦合有限元理论和 ALE 算法

流固耦合力学是流体力学与固体力学交叉而生成的一门力学分支，它是研究变形固体在流场作用下的各种行为以及固体位形对流场影响这二者交互作用的一门科学。流固耦合力学的重要特征是两相介质之间的交互作用；变形固体在流体载荷作用下会产生变形或运动，而变形或运动又反过来影响流场，从而改变流体载荷的分布和大小[3]。

发动机振动给液力悬置施加激励。液力悬置橡胶主簧的变形使液体的压力变化并使液体在上下液室之间流动。同时，液体流动和压力变化又影响橡胶主簧，改变了橡胶主簧初始约束条件。为准确分析液压悬置动态特性，这种相互作用必须耦合计算。

有两种方法可以计算耦合问题：一类是液体作为模拟固体，采用直接耦合法；另一种是固体和液体动力学方程分别计算，统一处理。前者具有较高的计算效率，较小的费用，但要符合"流体不流动，小扰动"的假设。后者的计算较复杂和烦琐，但可以计算大流量、大变形的流固耦合问题[3]。液体在惯性通道内流动的流量较大，橡胶主簧变形较大，因此，用第二种耦合方法模拟液力悬置的动态特性。

[基金项目] 北京市教委科技发展项目（KM2010114V7008）。
[作者简介] 徐志军（1966—），男，博士，主要研究方向汽车振动与噪声控制，jdtzhijun@buu.edu.cn；刘福永，北京理工大学；于增信，北京联合大学机电学院。

使用第二种耦合方法，遇到的最大困难是两相界面的协调问题。为了解决不同坐标系的困难，文献[4]中提出的用于流场计算的 ALE 方法被用于流固耦合分析[5-6]，以处理界面协调及自由面的问题：ALE 坐标系可以任意速度在空间运动，若其速度为 0，它即为 Euler 系，若其速度等于质点速度，它即为拉氏（Lagrange）系，因而 ALE 坐标系提供了两种坐标系的统一描述。

ALE 方法具有可按规定速度运动的灵活性，它将某一时间步的计算分为 3 个阶段：第一阶段为显式拉格朗日计算，网格保持不动；第二阶段是隐式的压力迭代求解过程，运用放大压力梯度法，求出速度的新值；第三阶段把各网格节点按预先规定的速度移到新的位置重新划分网格。

ALE 的坐标系：

$$\frac{\partial \Phi}{\partial t}\bigg|_{\text{fixedframe}} = \frac{\partial \Phi}{\partial t}\bigg|_{\text{movingframe}} - \vec{w} \cdot \nabla \Phi 。$$

式中：Φ 为任意自由度；$\vec{w}$ 为运动坐标系的速度。

2 流固耦合有限元计算模型和流体计算模式选择

液力悬置一般由橡胶主簧（承载发动机）、金属外壳（安装在车架上）、橡胶底膜（软橡胶，容纳流体）、惯性通道体、液体组成。惯性通道体内有细长的惯性通道，上下液室内的液体在惯性通道内流动。图 1 示出了所使用的发动机惯性通道式液力悬置示意。

为了减少计算量，提高计算效率，液力悬置的钢壳（液力悬置借此安装在车体或基础上）和惯性通道体用零位移约束来代替。图 2 示出了流固耦合的有限元网格模型。该模型由 115218 个节点组成，包括 9672 个固体单元（橡胶）和 101831 个流动单元（fluid142）。流固耦合表面有耦合标记。

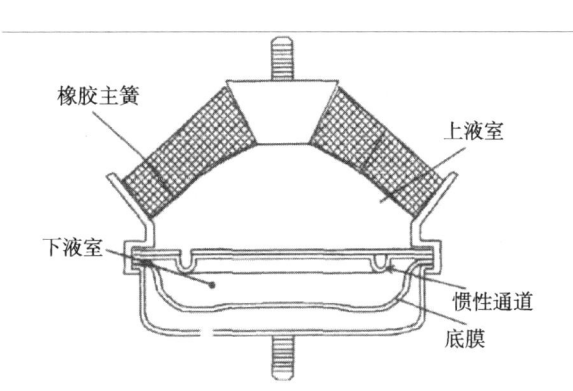

图 1 惯性通道式液力悬置示意

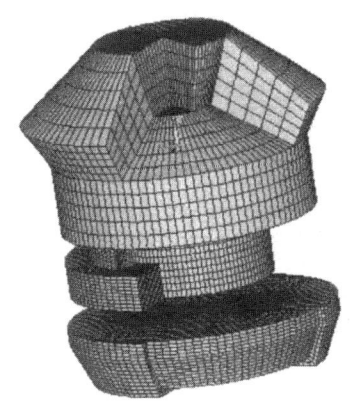

图 2 液力悬置的流固耦合有限元网格模型

计算过程中的计算模式及假设如下：
1) 液力悬置充满了液体，液体满足斯托克斯关于牛顿流体的 3 个假设，属于牛顿流体；
2) 液体是不可压缩流体；
3) 采用瞬态计算模式；
4) 液力悬置中，液体受到橡胶主簧交变载荷的激励，在惯性通道内的流动速度随时间变化，而且 Re 较大，流动属于紊流；
5) 用等效阻尼系数来模拟流体摩擦阻力和局部阻力；对于惯性通道内壁不够光滑、液体进出惯性通道时流通面积的突然缩小或扩大使液体受到的附加阻力，采用一个等效阻力系数施加给液体来模拟。

3 液力悬置的流固耦合动态特性

给液力悬置上表面中心节点施加简谐激振位移（见图 3），对橡胶主簧、橡胶底膜与液体进行耦合分析，运算方式选为"瞬态"，流体力学计算模式选为"紊流模式"，固体计算模式选为"非线性"。

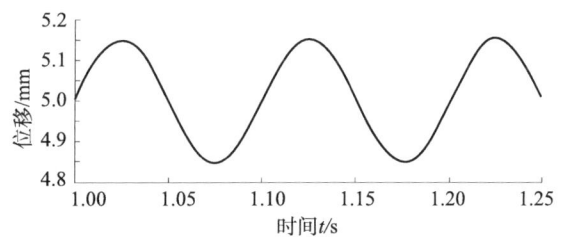

图 3　橡胶主簧上表面中心节点的输入激励

计算首先从固体的动力响应分析开始，第一次计算结果传给流体，进行坐标系变换（ALE 方法）后计算流体的运动，得到流体在与固体耦合面上节点的速度和压力，计算固体节点对此速度和压力的响应，这样完成了一次流固耦合的迭代[4]。反复进行迭代，直到收敛，得到第 1 个时刻的耦合结果。将此结果作为下一次耦合计算的初始条件，进入上一级迭代循环，计算结束后得到上表面中心节点处的节点支反力。利用动刚度和滞后角的定义，求出液力悬置在该频率下的动刚度和滞后角。

图 4 示出了输入图 3 所示的激励时第 1.075s 的液力悬置内流场。液体从下液室经过惯性通道流进上液室（为表示清楚，图中只绘出了惯性通道上开口附近的速度矢量），惯性通道的进出口附近液体的压力梯度很大，说明两处的液体流动阻尼很大；上液室橡胶主簧底面处的压力为 1.088×10^5 Pa，对主簧的向上运动起促进作用，上液室内液体压力大于大气压。

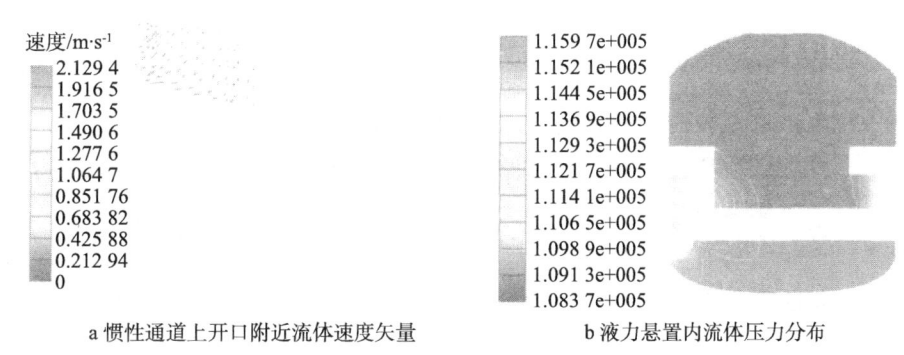

a 惯性通道上开口附近流体速度矢量　　b 液力悬置内流体压力分布

图 4　1.075s 液力悬置内的流场

图 5 示出液力悬置上表面中心节点的支反力响应。响应也是正弦曲线，与输入之间有一个 30°的相位差。将支反力除以输入位移得到液力悬置的复刚度，复刚度的实部是动刚度，虚部为滞后角。

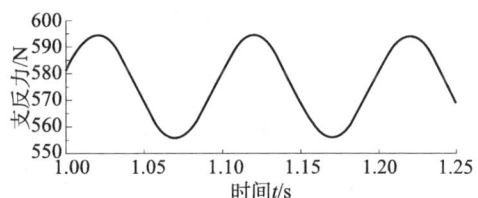

图 5　主簧上表面的支反力响应

改变激励的频率，得到其他频率激励下的节点支反力，求出液力悬置在其他频率下的动刚度和滞后角，得到液力悬置在这个频率范围内的动态特性。图 6 示出液力悬置（橡胶主簧硬度为邵氏 55）在图 3 所示激励下的动态特性。有限元仿真结果说明，液力悬置充入液体后，动刚度在 11Hz 处有一最小值，滞后角在 12Hz 附近最大。

在振动试验台上对惯性通道式液力悬置进行了试验研究。液力减振器台架试验系统由液力激振器及控制系统、力传感器、数据采集分析仪组成，在台架试验系统中，液力减振器样件按照其工作状态安装，即激振器在上，对试件施加向下的正弦激振力，激振频率为 0~80Hz，激振器对液力减振器样件施加预载荷[7]。

将有限元仿真、集总质量法仿真与试验的动态特性曲线绘在一起（见图 6），可以看出，高于液柱共振频率时,有限元仿真的动刚度曲线较平,与试验结果相比,误差只有10%。这是因为有限元计算过程中较好地模拟了橡胶的刚度和阻尼的非线性性质。而集总质量法对这些参数都是线性化处理的,与试验结果相比,误差为22%;两种仿真曲线的滞后角峰值都小于实测值,这是因为有限元流固耦合仿真时将通道壁面的粗糙度和惯性通道拐弯处的局部阻力用一个平均分布在流体各质点上的阻力系数来代替,这种简化的处理方式使得液体的仿真流动与实际流动之间存在一定的差距。

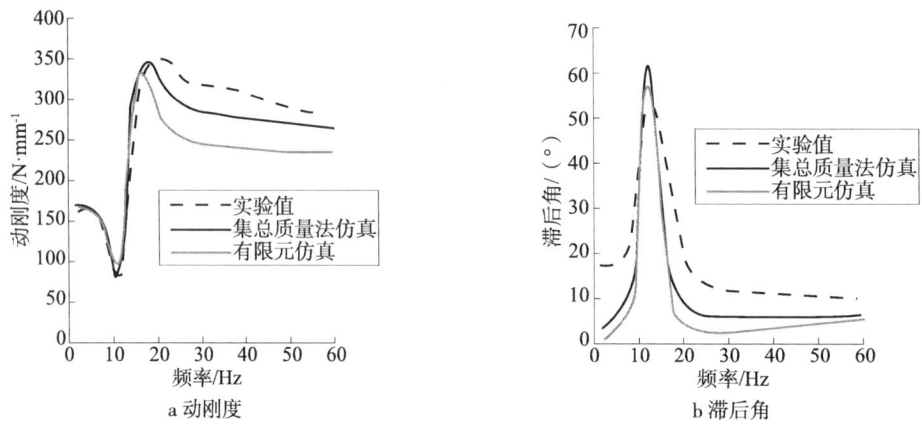

图6 液力悬置动态特性

4 结束语

流固耦合的有限元方法较好地模拟了液体在上下液室和惯性通道内的运动及对橡胶主簧的反作用,计算时考虑了橡胶的非线性特性。与集总质量的液力悬置线性仿真方法相比,基于流固耦合的有限元仿真和实际情形更为接近,精度更高。

参考文献

[1] 谭达明. 内燃机振动控制 [M]. 成都:西南交通大学出版社,1993.
[2] 严济宽. 机械振动隔离技术 [M]. 上海:上海科学技术文献出版社,1985.
[3] 邢景裳,周盛,崔尔杰. 流固耦合力学概述 [J]. 力学进展,1997,27 (1):19 - 38.
[4] Hirt C W, Amsden A A, Cook J L. Anarbitrary Lagrangian - Eulerian Computing Method for all Flowspeeds [J]. J. of Comp. Phys.,1974 (14):227 - 253.
[5] Nomura T. ALEFE Computations of Flu id - structure Interaction Problems [J]. Comput Methods Appl. Mech. Eng.,1994,112 (1/2/3/4):291 - 308.
[6] 钱勤. 分析撞水和动接触问题的计算方法和数值模拟 [D]. 武汉:华中理工大学,1994.
[7] 徐志军,汪建华,刘福水. 液力减振器结构参数和液力参数的优化试验研究 [J]. 内燃机工程,2002 (3):39 - 42.

Comprehensive Risk Evaluation in the Phase of Setting Information System Project

Gao Yinmin

1 Introduction

Failing to understand and manage Information System Project risk can lead to a variety of problems, including cost and schedule overruns, unmet user requirements, and the production of systems that are not used or do not deliver business value. A simple definition of "risk" is aproblem that hasn't happened yet but could cause some loss or threaten the success of your project if it did (Wiegers, 1998). A number of research studies have investigated the issue of the relative importance of various risks in software development projects and have attempted to classify them in various ways. Much has been written about the causes of information systemsproject failures. Poor technical methods is onlyone of the causes, and this cause is relatively minor in comparison to larger issues, such as failures in communications and ineffective leadership. Managing the risk associated with them becomes a critical area of concern[1,2]. Advocates of IS risk management argue that identifying and analyzing threats tosuccess allows actions to be taken to reduce the chance of failure. Articles have stressed the importance of empirically categorizing. the sources and types of risks associated with software development projects[3] Unfortunately, despite these recommendations there are relatively few tools available to help project managers identify and categorize risk factors in order to develop effective strategies. While various risk checklists (e. g., the "top – 10" list of risk factors described by and frameworks[4] have been proposed, the underlying dimensions of the software project risk construct and their influence on a project remain largely unexplored.

With systems that involve the use of new client – server technology, it is often critical to acquire external expertise, including vendor support, to facilitate successful implementation. Also, the costs of training and support are often under – estimated, and these costs may be many times greater than originally anticipated. Client – server implementations often bring "surprises" with respect to cost, because of the costs of decentralized servers, systems integration software, technical support, and software updates and version control. In actuality, the total cost of a client server implementation can be three to six times greater than for a comparable mainframe – based system. Even thoughthere are great cost reductions possible through moving off the mainframe, the costs of learning the new technology and of acquiring technical support are substantial.

By applying the principle and method off uzzy comprehensive evaluation, the article establishes evaluation system for comprehensive risk evaluation design of the setting IS project (shortened form SISP) risk which is suitable for the present status of setting IS project decision in our country. I intend to provide a relatively scientific method for SISP in our country through my preliminary exploration. I also expect there can be more experts to concern about Information System Project risk evaluation, so as to make contribution for enhancing manage Information System Project risk.

2 Index System Design of the Evaluation of the SISP Risk.

The first step of the evaluation is to construct the evaluating index system scientifically, which is the key to

---

[Author Introduction] Gao Yin min, Department of e – business Business College of Beijing Union University (phone: 8601065086749; fax: 86 – 010 – 65940655; e – mail: Cgaoyinmin@ 126. com.).

success of evaluation. The evaluation of the IS project – setting risk is a complex system with a large number of functional parameters. The overall risk level is determined by the parameters, that is, by

$$TRL = f(RMI, RTL, RUL, \cdots) \quad (1)$$

Where in TRL = total SISP risk level; RMD = risk level with respect to management risk; RTL = risk level with respect to technology risk, RUL = safety level with respect to user involvement and training risk, and so on.

On the basis of the code for the "top – 10" list of risk factors described by and frameworks study, experts' investigation and also referring other papers[4,5], an index system has been established for The evaluation of the IS project – setting risk The first hierarchy indexes consist of four parts: inherent management risk, technology risk, user involvement and training risk and Implementing risk each of which has its own sub – indexes. Index system is shown in Fig. 1.

3 The Weighting of the Attribute for Evaluation

Not all risk criteria have equal importance. Parameter weights serve to express the importance of each criteria compared with the others. Hence the assignment of weights is a key component of multi – attribute evaluation. The accuracy of the evaluation depends on the accuracy of the weighting assigned to each criterion, which can be determined by setting up an expert panel and synthesizing—for example, by approximate reasoning – the average ranking of the criteria for evaluation purposes. Since a large number of criteria are needed and it is difficult to obtain a consistent result from each of the experts, a systematic method is required to rank the criteria.

The Analytical Hierarchy Process (AHP), developed by Saaty[7], is one of the methods used in multi – criteria decision – making and may be employed to assist individuals and groups in ranking the fire safety attributes. By incorporating both subjective and objective data into a logical hierarchical framework, AHP provides decision – makers with an intuitive approach to evaluating the importance of every element of a decision through pairwise comparison. The AHP is best suited for multi – criteria problems for which it is not possible to accurately quantify the impact of each of the alternatives. For this reason, the AHP is effective for ranking each fire safety attribute in The evaluation of the IS project – setting risk because the attributes that involve people interacting are difficult to quantify the paper uses AHP to calculate the weight of each index. The results are shown as followings:

$$W = (W_1, W_2, W_3, W_4) = (0.28, 0.33, 0.19, 0.20)$$
$$W_1 = (W_{11}, W_{12}, W_{13}, W_{13}, W_{14}, W_{15})$$
$$= (0.23, 0.12, 0.29, 0.21, 0.15)$$
$$W_2 = (W_{21}, W_{22}, W_{23}, W_{24}, W_{25}, W_{26}, W_{27})$$
$$= (0.11, 0.25, 0.15, 0.16, 0.12, 0.11, 0.10)$$
$$W_3 = (W_{31}, W_{32}, W_{33}, W_{34}, W_{35})$$
$$= (0.28, 0.21, 0.20, 0.17, 0.14)$$
$$W_4 = (W_{41}, W_{42}, W_{43}, W_{44}, W_{45})$$
$$= (0.24, 0.24, 0.21, 0.20, 0.11)$$

4 Fuzzy Comprehensive Evaluation Model for the comprehensive evaluation Risk Degree of ISSP

The comprehensive evaluation risk degree of ISSP involves many factors. What is more, there are abounding uncertainty factors and dynamic variable withhigh fuzziness. An assessment model for the comprehensive evaluation risk degree of ISSP is established by applying fuzzy mathematics theory in this paper.

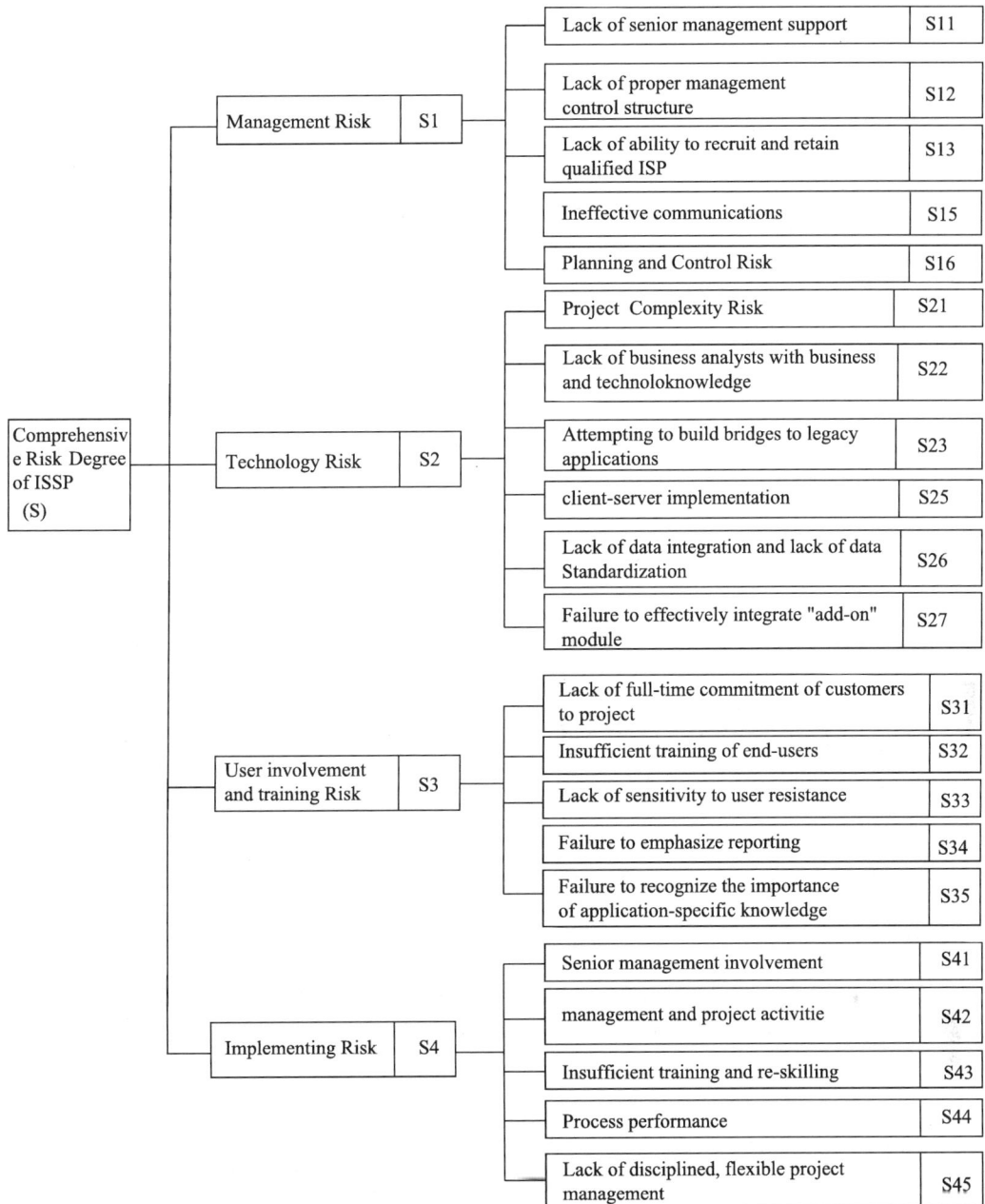

Fig. 1 Index system of Comprehensive evaluation for ISSP

4.1 SimpleFuzzy Comprehensive Evaluation

Index set is $X = \{x_1, x_2, \cdots, x_n\}$. Evaluation set is $Y = \{y_1, y_2, \cdots, y_m\}$ (in the paper, m = 4, y_1 = very risk, y_2 = risk, y_3 = basicallyrisk, y_4 = low risk). Fuzzy relation R between index and evaluation represents the possibility of making all kinds of evaluation on various indexes. x_i For example, r_{ij} represents the possibility of making evaluationon. y_j on x_i. w is a weight distribution. $w = (w_1, w_2, \cdots, w_n)$ represents the significance of each index in evaluation. For example, w_i represents the significant value of factor x_i in evaluation. The result of evaluation is fuzzy sets, $B = (b_1, b_2, \cdots, b_m)$, which represents the degree of subordination of making all kinds of evaluation. For example, b_j represent the degree of subordination of comprehensive evaluation for y_j.

4.2 Multi-hierarchy Fuzzy Comprehensive Evaluation

There are many factors affecting the comprehensive evaluation Risk Degree of ISSP, and their structure is very complex. In the above research, we have already set up theindex system of evaluation according to the internal relations of each factor. Therefore, we set up the multi-hierarchy fuzzy comprehensive evaluation model.

$$B = (b_1, b_2, \cdots b_m) = (w_1, w_2, \cdots, w_n) \circ \begin{bmatrix} r_{11} & \cdots & r_{1m} \\ \vdots & \vdots & \vdots \\ r_{n1} & \cdots & r_{nm} \end{bmatrix} \quad (2)$$

Multi-hierarchy fuzzy comprehensive evaluation is implemented in the following steps:
$X = \{X_1, X_2, \cdots, X_n\}$ into s subsets

$$X_i = \{x_{i_1}, x_{i_2}, \cdots, x_{i_{ni}}\}, i = 1, 2, \cdots, s \quad (3)$$

Which meets the conditions of

$$\sum_{i=1}^{s} n_i = n; \bigcup_{i=1}^{i=1} X_i = X; X_i \cap X_j = \Phi, i \neq J$$

(1) Implement comprehensive evaluation on each X_i with above-mentioned simple fuzzy comprehensive evaluation model, respectively.

Set up remark set. $Y = \{y_1, y_2, \cdots, y_m\}$. The weight distribution of each factor in x_i is:

$$w_i = (w_{i_1}, w_{i_2}, \cdots, w_{i_{ni}}),$$

$$\sum_{j=1}^{n_i} w_{ij} = 1 \, w_{ij} \geq 0, j = 1, 2, \cdots, n_i \quad (4)$$

If the single-factor assessment matrix of x_i is R_i, then the first order comprehensive evaluation of the index is:

$$B_i = w_i \cdot R_i = (b_{i1}, b_{i2}, \cdots, b_{im}), i = 1, 2, \cdots, s \quad (5)$$

(2) If each x_i is considered as one index and the single-factor evaluation result is b_i, then the single index evaluation matrix of $X = \{x_1, x_2, \cdots, x_s\}$ will be R

$$R = \begin{bmatrix} B_1 \\ B_2 \\ \vdots \\ B_s \end{bmatrix} = \begin{bmatrix} b_{11} & b_{12} & \cdots & b_{1m} \\ b_{21} & b_{22} & \cdots & b_{2m} \\ \vdots & \vdots & \vdots & \vdots \\ b_{s1} & b_{s2} & \cdots & b_{sm} \end{bmatrix} \quad (6)$$

As a part of X, each X_i reflects a kind of attribution of X. In this way, the weight distribution $W = (w_1^*, w_2^*, \cdots, w_s^*)$ can be presented in terms of their importance.

So, the second order comprehensive evaluation vector is:

$$B = W \cdot R = (b_1, b_2, \cdots, b_m) \quad (7)$$

If the first order index set, $X_i, i = 1, 2, \cdots s$, still contain more factors, X_i can be separated into lesser sets. So the three-stage model or four-stage model can be obtained in the same way.

4.3 The Determination of Logical Operation Method

The logical operator of the above-mentioned fuzzy comprehensive evaluation model $B = w \cdot R$ is " $\circ$ ".
This paper adapts the weighted average model:

$$b_j = \sum_{k=1}^{n} w_k \cdot y_{kj} \quad (8)$$

Compared with other common models, such as ($\vee$, $\wedge$) Model and ($\vee$, $\bullet$) Model, the model can furthest reserve the evaluation opinions of all those specialist with least information distortion.

4.4 The Criteria for Evaluation

In this paper, the result is obtained on the principle of greatest membership. That is to say, if $b_j = \max\{b_1, b_2, \cdots, b_m\}$, and then the comprehensive evaluation result will be y_j.

5 An Example of Application

Provided that 10 experts are invited to participate in the comprehensive evaluation Risk Degree of ISSP, the single-factor evaluation matrix of inherent management risk, technology risk, user involvement and training risk and Implementing risk is represented respectively as follows:

$$R_1 = \begin{bmatrix} 0.00 & 0.70 & 0.30 & 0.00 \\ 0.10 & 0.60 & 0.30 & 0.00 \\ 0.00 & 0.90 & 0.10 & 0.00 \\ 0.90 & 0.10 & 0.00 & 0.00 \\ 0.50 & 0.50 & 0.00 & 0.00 \end{bmatrix}$$

$$R_3 = \begin{bmatrix} 0.00 & 0.70 & 0.20 & 0.10 \\ 0.10 & 0.60 & 0.10 & 0.20 \\ 0.00 & 0.70 & 0.20 & 0.10 \\ 0.10 & 0.30 & 0.30 & 0.30 \\ 0.10 & 0.60 & 0.20 & 0.10 \end{bmatrix}$$

$$R_2 = \begin{bmatrix} 0.10 & 0.40 & 0.50 & 0.00 \\ 0.00 & 0.20 & 0.70 & 0.10 \\ 0.80 & 0.20 & 0.00 & 0.00 \\ 0.00 & 0.60 & 0.30 & 0.10 \\ 0.10 & 0.80 & 0.10 & 0.00 \\ 0.00 & 0.50 & 0.50 & 0.00 \\ 0.40 & 0.60 & 0.00 & 0.00 \end{bmatrix}$$

$$R_4 = \begin{bmatrix} 0.00 & 0.70 & 0.30 & 0.00 \\ 0.80 & 0.20 & 0.00 & 0.00 \\ 0.00 & 0.70 & 0.20 & 0.10 \\ 0.40 & 0.20 & 0.40 & 0.00 \\ 0.10 & 0.70 & 0.20 & 0.00 \end{bmatrix}$$

So the result of simple fuzzy comprehensive assessment can be obtained as following:

$$B_1 = W_1 \cdot R_1 = (0.276, 0.590, 0.134, 0.000)$$
$$B_2 = W_2 \cdot R_2 = (0.184, 0.431, 0.345, 0.040)$$
$$B_3 = W_3 \cdot R_3 = (0.052, 0.597, 0.196, 0.155)$$
$$B_4 = W_4 \cdot R_4 = (0.283, 0.480, 0.216, 0.021)$$

The fuzzy matrix of multi-factors assessment can be obtained as following:

$$R = \begin{bmatrix} B_1 \\ B_2 \\ B_3 \\ B_4 \end{bmatrix} = \begin{bmatrix} 0.276 & 0.590 & 0.134 & 0.000 \\ 0.184 & 0.431 & 0.345 & 0.040 \\ 0.052 & 0.597 & 0.196 & 0.155 \\ 0.283 & 0.480 & 0.216 & 0.021 \end{bmatrix}$$

Then the obtained result of fuzzy comprehensive assessment is:

$$B = W \cdot R = (0.204 \quad 0.517 \quad 0.232 \quad 0.047)$$

According to the principle of greatest membership (the greatest value is 0.517), we can draw a conclusion that the setting IS decision is the characteristic of high risk.

Conclusions

With the help of the evaluation model established in the paper, the comprehensive risk evaluation design of the IS project – setting risk a can be evaluated with higher accuracy. The result of evaluation can be used as the scientific basis for setting IS decision, carrying out IS management in a reasonable way.

This paper outlines the framework of fuzzy comprehensive evaluation for setting IS decision. Further studies are needed to clarify the details of setting up the system, including forming expert panels to formulate the numerical values of the attributes' weights, carrying out sensitivity analysis, determining the most suitable method for evaluation, and verifying the accuracy of the method. The rationality of each index and its weight should undergo continuous examination through practical application. We shall adjust index and its weight flexibly to make it more reasonable to meet the requirements of practical application. The precise definition and quantification of each index is not stated in the paper. We will do it in the next research work.

References

[1] R. Kumar, Managing risks in IT projects: an optionsperspective [J]. Information and Management, 2002 (40): 63 – 74.

[2] J. S. Osmundson, J. B. Michael, M. J. Machniak, M. A. Grossman, Quality management metrics for software development [J]. Information and Management, 2003 (40): 799 – 812.

[3] P. P. Tallon, et al. Using Real Options Analysis for Evaluating Uncertain Investments inInformation Technology [A]: Insights From The ICIS 2001 Debate, Communications of the Association for Information Systems, 2002, 9: 136 – 167.

[4] M. Keil, P. Cule, K. Lyytinen, R. Schmidt, A framework foridentifying software project risks [J]. Communications of the ACM41 (11), 1998: 76 – 83.

[5] Walsh, K. R. & Schneider, H. The role of motivation and risk behaviors in software development success [J]. Information Research, 2002, 7 (3).

[6] Keil, Mark; Cule, Paul E.; Lyytinen, Kalle; andSchmidt, RoyC. A Framework for identifying software project risks [J]. Communications of the ACM, V. 41, No. ll, Nov. 1998, 76 – 83.

[7] Thomas L. Saaty and Luis G. Vargas. Models, Methods, Concepts & Applications of the Analytic Hierarchy Process [M]. Boston: Kluwer Academic Publishers. 2001: 1 – 13.

A Sludge Compost Quality Evaluation Method Based on Chaos Genetic Support Vector Machine

Gao Meijuan　Tian Jingwen　Zhang Zhenbin

1　Introduction

The compost technology is a new biologic treatment method. It can decompose the multiphase organic matter by means of the mixed microbial community in special condition, and change the organic solid wastes into the stabile humus which used for fertilizing the field or improving soil. Because the compost technology can realize the effects of the harmless, resourceful realization and reduce quantification in the practice application, hurtles decrement and callback resource effect. So it obtains wide attention and has become the research hotspot in the field of environmental protection.

The compost quality is the key factor of affecting the resourceful realization of sludge compost. The quality evaluation parameters of sludge compost include five kinds indexes that are innocuity, reduce quantization, resourceful realization, microbial activity and maturity degree. Because the relationship between the evaluation grade of compost quality and evaluation parameters is a complicated and nonlinear, the traditional comprehensive analysis methods cannot avoid the index weight problem, the determination of weight needs expert knowledge and experience which with the inevitable subjective factors, so the traditional comprehensive analysis methods such as the exponential method[1] and the fuzzy mathematics method[2,3] are limited[4].

Genetic algorithm is a new optimum algorithm developed fast recently[5]. Chaos is a universal phenomenon in nature. Chaos has randomization, ergodicity and regularity etc characters. In a certain range, it can travel all the unrepeated states according to itself regulation. The chaos operation is added to the genetic algorithm, the convergence rate of genetic algorithm is improved. Support Vector Machine proposed by Vapnik is a newly developed technique which based on statistical learning theory[6,7], it adopts Structure Risk Minimization principle which avoids local minimum and effectively solves the over learning and assures good generalization ability and better classify accuracy. The special predominance of SVM in resolving limited samples, non - linear function and multidimensional pattern recognition makes it become a kind of excellent machine learning method[8]. However, the selection of parameters of SVM affects the SVM classification capacity significantly. In view of the parallel search and powerful global convergence capability of chaos genetic algorithm, the chaos genetic algorithm is used to optimize SVM parameters which can enhance the convergence rate and the classification accuracy of SVM classification model. Considering the special predominance of chaos genetic algorithm and SVM possess, a sludge compost quality evaluation method based on chaos genetic support vector machine is proposed in this paper.

2　Chaos genetic support vector machine

2.1　Classify support vector machine

SVM is proposed which is based on the idea of optimal classify hyperplane of linearly separable. The sketch map of optimal classification hyperplane is shown in Fig. 1. There are two classes samples of linearly separable, H

is the class line which divides the two classes without mistake, H_1 and H_2 are the line that pass through the points which are the nearest to the class line in each classes samples and parallel to the class line. The distance between H_1 and H_2 is called the separating margin of the two classes. We want the optimal class line not only can separate the two classes correctly which ensure the experience risk minimization, but also can have the maximum separating margin of the two classes which ensure the real risk minimization. For the high dimension, the optimal class line is the optimal classify hyperplane.

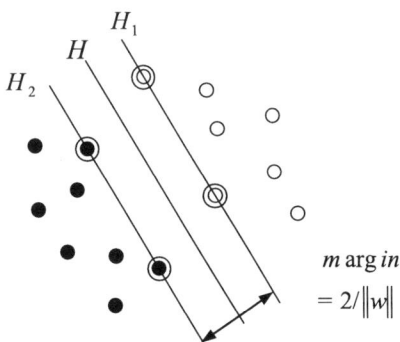

Fig. 1 The sketch map of optimal classification hyperplane

Suppose the linearly separability sample set (x_i, y_i), $i = 1, \cdots n$, $x \in R^d$, $y \in \{+1, -1\}$ is the classes number. The problem that SVM should solve can be formulated as follows:

$$\min \phi(w) = \frac{1}{2} \| w \|^2 = \frac{1}{2} (w \cdot w) \tag{1}$$

Suibject to $y_i [(w \cdot x_i) 4b] - 1 \geqslant 0 \quad i = 1, 2, \cdots, n$

Where w is the normal of the hyperplane, b decides the place which relative the origin point.

Lagrange function is used to translate the original problem to its dual problem:

$$\max Q(\alpha) = \sum_{i=1}^{n} a_i - \frac{1}{2} \sum_{i,j=1}^{n} a_i a_j y_i y_j (x_i \cdot x_j) \tag{2}$$

$$subject\ to \begin{cases} \sum_{i=1}^{n} y_i \alpha_i = 0 \\ \alpha_i \geqslant 0 \end{cases} \quad i = 1, 2, \cdots, n$$

The classify function be described as follows:

$$f(x) = \text{sgn}\{(w^* \cdot x) + b^*\} = \text{sgn}\left\{\sum_{i=1}^{n} a_i^* y_i (x_i \cdot x) + b^*\right\} \tag{3}$$

For the non-linear classification, the optimal solution problem can be described as follows:

$$\min \phi(w) = \frac{1}{2} \| w \|^2 + C \sum_{i=1}^{n} \xi_i \tag{4}$$

subject to $y_i; (w \cdot x_i) + b] \geqslant 1 - \xi_i \ i = 1, 2, \cdots, n$

Where C is the penalty factor, ξ is relaxatiton term r*.

The optimal solution problem is translated by quadratic programming as follows:

$$\max Q(\alpha) = \sum_{i=1}^{n} \alpha_i - \frac{1}{2} \sum_{i,j=1}^{n} \alpha_i \alpha_j y_j y_i (x_i \cdot y_j) \tag{5}$$

$$subject\ to \begin{cases} \sum_{i=1}^{n} y_i \alpha_i = 0 \\ 0 \leqslant \alpha_i \leqslant C \end{cases} \quad i = 1, 2, \cdots, n$$

If the dot product $(x \cdot x_i)$ is replaced by the kernel function $K(x, x')$, equal that transforms the original characteristic space to a new characteristic space, the optimal classify function as follows:

$$f(x) = \text{sgn}\left(\sum_{i=1}^{n} \alpha_i^* y_i K(x_i, x) + b^*\right) \tag{6}$$

Other conditions of the algorithmic keep changelessness, this is Support Vector Machine.

The classify function obtained by the support vector machine is analogous to a neural network in formally. The sketch map of the support vector machine is shown in Fig. 2.

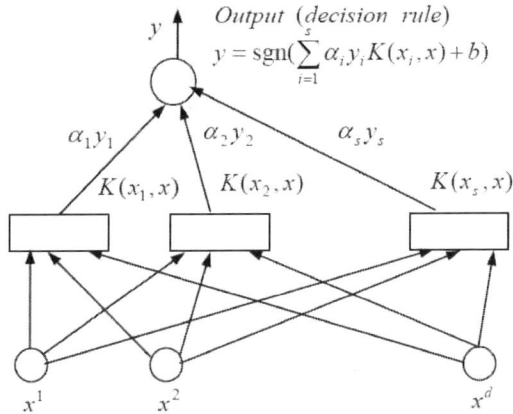

Fig. 2 The sketch map of support vector machine

In above classify problem, only consider two classify problem. In this paper, the compost quality evaluation can be regarded as a problem of pattern recognition. The compost quality can be classified into "good", "preferable", "common" and "bad", this is a multi-classify problem, so the system needs a combination multi-SVM to classify. In this paper, we adopt "one to one" method of multi-SVM.

In this method, we will construct all the possible two classes classifier for the multi-kinds training samples, every classifier only executes training on two kinds training samples of those other kinds, in this way, if the compost quality can be divided m kinds, then the classification system will need $m \times (m-1)/2$ SVM two classes classifier, we use the "ballot" fashion to decide the finally classify result.

Suppose we need to classify the data of the i classes and the j classes, then we need to solve the two classes classify problem, this is as follows:

$$\min_{w^{ij}, b^{ij}, \xi^{ij}} \frac{1}{2} (w^{ij})^T w^{ij} + C \sum_{i=1}^{n} \xi_i^{ij} \quad (7)$$

$$subject\ to \begin{cases} (w^{ij})^T \phi(x_i) + b^{ij} \geq 1 - \xi_i^{ij}, & y_i = i \\ (w^{ij})^T \phi(x_i) + b^{ij} \leq -1 + \xi_i^{ij}, & y_i \neq i \\ \xi_i^{ij} \geq 0 \end{cases}$$

Where, ϕ is the kernel function, C is the penalty factor.

These two classes classifier are combine using the "ballot" fashion in this paper, if the result that obtained by the sgn $((w^{ij})^T \phi(x) + b^{ij})$ shows that the x belongs to the i classes, then the side that belongs the i classes is added a ballot, else if the result that obtained by the sgn $((w^{ij})^T \phi(x) + b^{ij})$ shows that the x belongs to the j classes, then the side that belongs the j classes is added a ballot, the class that obtain the most ballot is the class that test sample x belongs to. If the two classes possess the same ballot to a turn, then we can simply select that the small indexed class is the class that the test sample x belongs to.

2.2 Chaos genetic algorithm[9-15]

The genetic algorithm (GA) is a kind of self-adapting heuristic global search algorithm which derived from imitating the thought of natural biological evolution. In nature, it is a cyclical process made up of reproduction-crossover-mutation operators. Adaptive genetic algorithm is a kind of GA that has scale reproduction and self-adaptive crossover and mutation operations.

$$P_c = \begin{cases} k_1 (f_{max} - f') / (f_{max} - f_{avg}) & if\ f' > f_{avg} \\ k_3 & if\ f' < f_{avg} \end{cases} \quad (8)$$

$$P_m = \begin{cases} k_2 (f_{max} - f) / (f_{max} - f_{avg}) & if f > f_{avg} \\ k_4 & if f < f_{avg} \end{cases} \quad (9)$$

Where P_c is exchanging probability, P_m is mutation probability, f_{max} is the biggest fitness of colony, f_{avg} is the average fitness of colony, f' is the bigger fitness of two strings used for exchange, f is the fitness of the individual to mutate.

The basic principle of chaos genetic algorithm is that optimize variables with chaos states, and extend the ergodic range of chaos movements to the numeric area of optimization variables. Then the chaos variables were coded and expressed "chromosome". According to the rule of "survival of the fittest", the operating of reproduction, crossover, mutation is executed and gets new chaos variable, then adds little chaos disturbance to every new chaos variable. Through the uninterrupted evolution, we can obtain the optimal solution of the problem.

The random disturbance is ascertained as follows:

$$\delta'_k = (1 - \alpha) \delta^* + \alpha \delta_k \quad (10)$$

Where δ^* is a vector formed by mapped the current optimal solution to $^{[0,1]}$ interval, which is called optimal chaos vector, δ_k is a chaos vector of iterated k times, δ_k is a chaos vector corresponding current solution after added random disturbance, $0 < \alpha < 1$, it can be chosen self-adaptive. The α is decided as follows:

$$\alpha = 1 - \frac{(k-1)^m}{k} \quad (11)$$

Where m is an integer, which ascertained by the optimal object function; k is an iterative times.

The process of chaos genetic algorithm is described as follows:

(1) Supposed the numeric area of variable is $[a_\mu, b_\mu]$, colony scale is m, the attractor of chaos operator is μ_i.

(2) Generate the initial colony $y_1^0, y_2^0, \cdots, y_i^0 \in [a, b]$ randomly, $i = 1, 2, \cdots, N$.

(3) Generate the initial value of chaos sequences, and put the y_i^0 mapping into interval $^{[0,1]}$ by mapping formula (12).

$$\beta_i^0 = (y_i^0 - a_\mu) / (b_\mu - a_\mu) \quad (12)$$

Where, u is the order number of colony, i is the order number of chaos variables, $i = 0, 1, \cdots, n$;

(4) The chaos variable β_i can be produced as follows:

$$\beta_i^{(u+1)} = \mu_i \cdot \beta_i^{(u)} (1 - \beta_i^{(u)}) \quad (13)$$

Where i is the sequence number of chaos variable, $i = 1, \cdots, n$; u is the sequence number of colonial $u = 0, 1, \cdots, m$, β_i, is chaos variable, $0 \leq \beta_i \leq 1$, μ_i is attractor.

(5) Select n chaos variables $\delta_i^{\mu+1}$ and change them to the corresponding optimized variables respectively through the formula (14).

$$Y_i^\mu = a_\mu + \delta_i^\mu (b_\mu - a_\mu) \quad (14)$$

(6) Selection: Calculate fitness function f, the individual whose fitness is good will be the parent.

(7) Crossover: Execute the crossover operation, the exchange probability between parentgenerations is p_c.

(8) Mutation: Mutation is that adding a random disturbance to the individuals. Both crossover and mutation are insurance strategy to avoid postmaturity.

(9) The individuals which are more feasible will be done chaos operation by step (3) to step (6), the old individual will be replaced if the new one is more feasible, else, the old one hold constant and execute the follow step (7) to (8), repeat the above steps until the termination conditions are met and optimal solution is obtained.

There are two main encoding mode of the genetic algorithm: binary-coding and decimal-coding. The chaos genetic algorithm denotes the parameters directly with decimal-coding instead of binarycoding, thus, it can avoid the encode difficulty and enhance the learning speed of the algorithm.

For the crossover operation: Execute crossover operation for two stochastic individuals according exchanging probability P_c, and two new individuals are generated by the following formula:

$$a_1 = ra_1 + (1-r)\ a_2 \qquad (15)$$
$$a_2 = ra_2 + (1-r)\ a_1 \qquad (16)$$

Where $r \in (0, 1)$ is a random number.

For the mutation operation: Execute mutation operation for someone individual according mutation probability P_m, and a new individual is generated by the following formula:

$$a_i = v + (u - v) \times r \qquad (17)$$

Where u and v are the boundary values of the parameters to optimize, $r \in (0, 1)$ is a random number.

For adaptation function: The adaptation function is given as follows:

$$f = \begin{cases} C_{max} - E & E < C_{max} \\ 0 & E \geq C_{max} \end{cases} \qquad (18)$$

$$E = \frac{1}{2p} \sum_p \sum_k (t_{pk} - o_{pk})^2 \qquad (19)$$

Where the C_{max} can be the maximum value E of evolutionary process, E is the object function. p is the number of training samples, k is the node number of the network output layer, t_{pk} is the RBF network output, o_{pk} is the real output.

2.3 SVM parameters optimize by chaos genetic algorithm

The parameters of SVM have important influence for the classification capability, if the parameters do not enactment appropriate, we can't get the good classification result. In this paper, the radial basis function $K(x, x_i) = \exp\left\{\frac{-|x - x_i|^2}{\sigma^2}\right\}$ was used as the kernel function of SVM.

The chaos genetic algorithm is used to optimize SVM parameters in order to obtain the optimum parameter combination of the penalty factor C and the width coefficient σ^2 of the radial basis function. The parameter combination which needs to optimize can be expressed $P = \{C, \sigma\}$, C and σ are positive number with decimal – coding.

The classification ability of SVM classifier is regarded object function in order to optimization the capability of SVM. We adopt the classification SVM method based on the radial basis function. The steps of optimizing the parameters as follows:

Step1: First, construct the samples for pattern classification and get the training sample set.

Step2: Decide colony numbers of the chaos genetic algorithm, and decide the initial value and scope of the penalty factor C and the width coefficient σ^2 of the radial basis function.

Step3: Use SVM to establish different classifier model for every class, and estimate the forecast classification error of every classifier. If forecast classification ability of classifier satisfier the request, then turn step5, if the forecast classification ability of classifier does not satisfy the request, then turn Step4.

Step4: Get the next generation parameters of SVM classifier using chaos genetic algorithm, namely, execute reproduction, crossover and mutation adaptive genetic operation on the current colony parameters; then turn Step3.

Step5: Get optimal SVM parameters and put out the result, then stop.

3 Application study

3.1 Compost quality affect factors

The treatment of high temperature compost meets the demand of innocuity, resourceful realization and reduces quantity of sludge. So the three indicators, as well as the microbial activity and compost maturity degree in the composting process can be chosen as the index of compost quality.

Innocuousness is eliminating the virus, bacteria, protozoan and heavy metal. In high – temperature composting fermentation stage, the insect nit, pathogens, helminthes, sporule and so on would be killed as the compost temperature keeps at 50~55 degrees for 5~7 days. So we can select the duration which is higher than 55 degrees to as the parameter of the innocuous estimation.

The reduction quantity means two. One is to use the biological or chemical method to reduce the production of the sludge in the sewage treatment, the other is to increase the rate of solid sludge as reducing the volume of the sludge of before the final processing. The degradation rate is the ratio of the degradation weight to the original material weight at the end of the compost, whose size indicates the degradation effect of the compost macroscopically. So we can take it as a parameter of the reduction estimation. The degradation rate at the end of the compost would be about 30%~50%. The bigger the degradation rate is, the better the reduction effect is.

Resourceful realization is to recycle the organic fertilizer using the N, P, K element in the sludge. As taking the compost as farm using, the higher of the N' content, the better the fertilizer efficiency of composting is. So the N's content at the end of composting can be taken as the estimating parameter of the resourceful realization. Generally, N' content is required higher than 0.5%. The higher of the N's content, the better of the resourceful realization.

Oxygen concentration is the macroscopic index of the microbial activity. Its size characterizes the intensity of the microbial activity, which can be taken as the parameter to estimate the microbial activity. We can get the result that the most fitted rate of the oxygen should be bigger than 18% and could not be smaller than 8% by analytical study. The ratio of the carbon and nitrogen is a traditional and effective method to evaluate the maturity degree of compost, so we take the ratio of carbon and nitrogen (C/N) as the estimating parameter of the maturity of compost. The city sludge compost, when the ratio of carbon and nitrogen (C/N) is smaller than 12, then the compost is mature.

In this paper, the compost quality index referred to the provision and several correlative research findings about agricultural utilization of sewage sludge, dejection and organic matter at home and abroad[16]. The compost quality can be classified into 4 categories: good, preferable, common and bad. The evaluation criterion is shown in Table 1.

Table 1 Evaluation criterion of compost quality

Compost quality level	High temperature duration (Day)	Degradation rate (%)	N content (%)	Oxygen concentration (%)	C/N (%)
Good	>7	>50	>0.5	>18	<12
Preferable	5-7	45-50	0.4-0.5	15-18	12-14
Common	4-5	40-45	0.3-0.4	12-15	14-16
Bad	<3	<3	<0.2	<8	>20

3.2 Application study

Through correlative analysis between the characteristic parameters and the sludge compost quality, we find the characteristic parameters which have the maximum correlativity with the sludge compost quality. Combining expert experience, finally, we select 5 kinds of characteristic parameters to as input vectors of chaos genetic algorithm support vector machine, these parameters are the high temperature duration, degradation rate, N content, oxygen concentration and the C/N.

Collecting training samples which be requested to have categoricalness, namely the training samples should include which the output mode is "good", "preferable", "common" and "bad". We can get many group training samples and testing samples and every training sample is composed of 5 - input and 4 - output. We construct all the possible two classes classifier for the four kinds training samples. Every classifier only executes training on two kinds training samples of those four kinds, in this way we need $4 \times (4-1)/2 = 6$ SVM two classes classifier.

We write the corresponding algorithm program using C++. In order to show the advantage andfeasibility of chaos genetic algorithm support vector machine (CGA - SVM), we adopt CGA - SVM and radial basis function neural network (RBFNN) to identify the sludge compost quality of sewage treatment, CGA - SVM uses radial basis function, the best parameters of SVM through the chaos genetic algorithm optimize is $C = 300$, $\sigma^2 = 10$. For the RBFNN, the width of kernel function σ^2 is 10, equal to the width of kernel function of SVM. The input layer of CGA – SVM and RBFNN has the same number of input neurons, and that is 5, and the output layer has the same 4 output neurons.

After all samples are normalized, we select different training sample numbers and different test samples numbers every time and input training samples into the CGA – SVM and RBFNN to learn, and then use the test samples to test the result. We randomly separate 1000 samples into 5 groups, and take out 150 sample data as training samples each time, while the other 50 samples as testing sample. The CGA – SVM and RBFNN were trained 5 times respectively using 5 groups different training samples, thenceforth we used the corresponding testing samples to test. The training error and testing error were respectively the average value of 5 times training error and 5 times testing error. The results of training and test by CGA – SVM and RBFNN are shown in Table 2. Concrete evaluation results by CGA – SVM and RBFNN are shown in Table 3.

Table 2　Train and test results by CGA – SVM and RBFNN

Method	Training error	Testing error
CGA – SVM	0.036	0.108
RBFNN	0.055	0.178

Table 3　Concrete evaluation results by CGA – SVM and RBFNN

Compost quality level	CGA – SVM		RBFNN	
	Train accuracy	Test accuracy	Train accuracy	Test accuracy
Good	97.3%	92.3%	96.3%	84.8%
Preferable	93.9%	86.3%	92.2%	78.2%
Common	95.8%	85.7%	92.8%	78.5%
Bad	98.6%	92.5%	96.7%	87.3%

From the Table 2, we can see that the mean squared error of training samples of CGA – SVM is smaller than that of RBFNN. Moreover the mean squared error of testing samples of CGA – SVM is also smaller than that of RBFNN. From the Table 3, for the training sample set, we can see that the average classification accuracy by CGA – SVM is about 96.4%, and the RBFNN is about 94.5%, for the testing sample set, the average classification accuracy by CGA – SVM is about 89.2%, and the RBFNN is about 82.2%, the fluctuating range of the generalize error of CGA – SVM is smaller than the RBFNN. These show that the CGA – SVM is all superior to the RBFNN at the classification accuracy, convergence rate and the degree of depending on the sample data aspects. So the compost quality evaluation method based on CGA – SVM has higher stability, and can obtain higher classification accuracy.

4　Conclusion

Owing to the SVM is a convex quadratic optimization problem, it can assure the extremum result is the global optimum result, and it can effectively solve the overfitting problem of ANN. It has good generalization ability and better classification accuracy. In view of the parallel search and powerful global convergence capability of chaos genetic algorithm, therefore, the compost quality evaluation method based on the chaos genetic algorithm support vector machine can enhance the converging speed and the classification accuracy to a great extent. The real classification result shows that the method presented in this paper can truly evaluate the level of sludge compost quality. Along with the sewage quantity of the city is increasing, the sludge compost quality evaluation method has extensive application foreground in the sewage treatment.

5　Acknowledgement

This work is supported in part by the National Natural Science Foundation of Chin under Grant No. 40674028 and Funding Project for Academic Human Resources Development in Beijing Union University No. 11101501105.

References

[1] California Compost Quality Council Compost Maturity Index [EB/OL]. 2001.
[2] Huashuai Cai, Xuya Peng, Ming Li. Applacation of fuzzy Mathematics in the Evaluation of MSW Compost quality [J]. Journal of Chongqing Jianzhu University, 2006, 11 (4): 87 - 89.
[3] X. L. QIAN, Y. SUN, D. T. Li. Study on Degree of Maturity of Compost Using Fuzzy Comprehensive Assessment [J]. Shanghai Environmental Sciences, 2001, 20 (2): 85 - 87.
[4] W. H. Zeng, R. C. Chen, Y. Shi. A model for evaluating ability of professional innocent production based on artificial neural network [J]. Environmental Engineering, 2003, 21 (6): 70 - 72.
[5] J. W. Tian and M. J. Gao. Artificial Neural Network Algorithm Study and Application [M]. Beijing: Beijing Institute of Technology Press, 2006.
[6] V. Vapnik. Statistical Learning Theory. Wiley, 1998.
[7] Nello Cristianini, John Shawe - Taylor. An Introduction to Support Vector Machines and Other Kernel - Based Learning Methods [M]. Beijing: Electronic Industry Publishing House, 2005.
[8] J. Weston and C. Watkins. Support vector machines for multi - class pattern recognition [M] //In Proceeding of the 6th European symposium on Artificial Neural Network (ESANN), 1999.
[9] Y. Sun, J. W. Tian. WSN Path Optimization Based on Fusion of Improved Ant Colony Algorithm and Genetic Algorithm [J]. Journal of Computational Information Systems, 2010, 6 (5): 1591 - 1599.
[10] J. W. Tian, M. J. Gao and Z. B. Zhang. Web Text Mining Based on Improved Genetic Algorithm and Radial Basis Function Neural Network [J]. Journal of Computational Information Systems, 2012, 8 (3): 1195 - 1202.
[11] Z. X. Wang, R. H. Tian, Y. Li. Improved Chaos GA and Structural Optimum Design [J]. Coal Mine Machinery, 2006, 27 (2): 213 - 215.
[12] M. J. Gao, J. Xu, J. W. Tian, H. Wu. Path Planning for Mobile Robot Based on Chaos Genetic Algorithm [M] //In Proceeding of The 4th International Conference on Natural Computation, 2008: 409 - 413, 2008.
[13] Hongying Huo, Shaobin Zhan. Improved Grey Model GM (1, 1) and Its Application based on Genetic Algorithm [J]. JDCTA: International Journal of Digital Content Technology and its Applications, 2012, 6 (9): 361 - 368.
[14] Xiangmei Li, "Tuning the Structure and Parameters of a Neural Network by a New Network Model Based on Genetic Algorithms [J]. JDCTA: International Journal of Digital Content Technology and its Applications, vol. 6, no. 11, pp. 29 - 36, 2012.
[15] Hongyu Jia. A Novel Classification Algorithm based on Rough Sets and RVM Classifier [J]. JDCTA: International Journal of Digital Content Technology and its Applications, vol. 6, no. 11, pp. 116 - 123, 2012.
[16] DOMINIC H, JOSEF B, ENZO F, Review of compost standards in New Zealand, The Waste and Resources Action Programme, 2002.

基于 CDIO 教育理念的数据库课程实验设计

逯燕玲　戴　红　侯　爽

数据库技术应用日益广泛深入，与社会生活的各个领域息息相关，为适应国家"以信息化带动工业化，发挥后发优势，实现社会生产力的跨越式发展"的需要，高等学校普遍面向非计算机专业开设数据库课程，以满足国家信息化建设人才需求。但社会对高校不同学科专业的人才培养在知识结构、信息技术应用能力与素养上的需求是有差异的，因此，数据库课程在不同学科专业的教学目标和应用能力培养既有共性，又存在很大差异。而数据库技术不仅内容广泛，而且技术发展迅速，在涵盖理论、技术和应用的同时，数据库新思想、新概念和新技术不断涌现，高等学校数据库课程的教学内容在一定程度上落后于数据库技术发展，尤其对人文社科类专业学生的数据库工程实践能力和数据库系统应用能力培养不够，学生普遍缺乏实践动手能力、分析问题和解决问题的能力，不能满足企事业单位信息化建设的用人需求。如何使人文社科类专业的学生掌握数据库应用能力，是数据库课程教学改革亟待解决的关键问题。

1 基于 CDIO 教育理念设计数据库应用能力结构

地方本科高等学校的办学定位是培养应用型人才，在地方高校中的人文社科类专业中，数据库课程承担着培养具有较强的数据库技术应用能力、具有与专业结合的实践创新精神的应用型人才的任务。数据库技术本身属于一种工程技术，课程内容本身具有较强的理论性和抽象性特点，讲解和学习难度较大，对学生工程实践要求高。实验教学不仅可以补充、深化和拓展理论教学，还可以加深学生对数据库理论知识的理解，从而培养学生数据库工程实践能力、团队合作精神和数据库系统应用能力。

CDIO 代表构思（Conceive）、设计（Design）、实施（Im – plement）、运行（Operate），作为国际上普遍认可的工程教育理念，它以产品从研发到运行的生命周期全过程为载体，以主动的、实践的、课程之间有机联系的方式学习工程的理论、技术与经验，让学生掌握从构思、设计、实现到运行的全过程所必须拥有的工程实践能力、个人专业基本能力、人际交流能力和系统综合应用能力[1-2]。引入 CDIO 教育理念强化数据库技术应用能力培养，以企事业单位信息化建设实际岗位为着眼点，以培养数据库技术的应用能力为主线，面向人文社科类专业设计培养学生的 CDIO 能力结构，如图 1 所示。在此基础上进行理论和实验教学方面的改革与创新，在数据库课程的教学过程中强调工程项目实践全生命周期的教育，着眼于能力培养与知识的教、学、做过程的关联，而不是只专注于数据库技术的理论知识[3-4]。

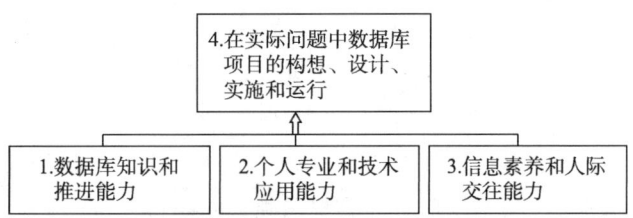

图 1　数据库课程 CDIO 能力结构框图

［基金项目］全国教育科学规划教育部重点课题"地方本科高校文科专业群综合实验教学研究"（DIA 110276）阶段性成果。
［作者简介］逯燕玲（1963—），女，工学硕士，教授，北京联合大学应用文理学院教务处处长，主要从事离散数学、算法分析和软件工程研究。

2 构建基于 CDIO 的数据库课程体系

2.1 理论与实践相融合的课程体系

为使 CDIO 工程教育理念在数据库课程教学中得以体现，坚持理论联系实际地构建基于 CDIO 的数据库课程体系，注重由单纯的传授理论知识转向能力培养，尤其强调培养学生数据库技术应用能力。以数据库理论知识、技术应用能力、信息素养和人际交往能力培养为核心，构建理论教学、实验教学、素质拓展三位一体的课程体系，如图 2 所示。

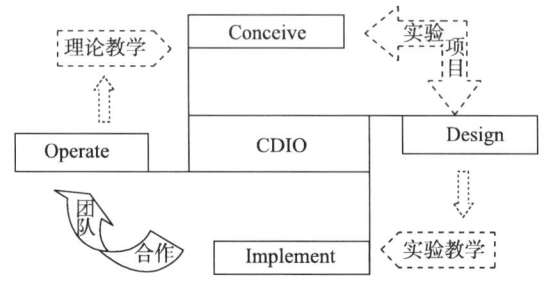

图 2 基于 CDIO 的数据库课程体系

将 CDIO 教育理念的各项标准引入和渗透到课程教学过程中，以全面提升学生的 CDIO 能力为目标，倡导"做中学""学中做"，让知识技能的讲授服务于数据库技术应用能力和学生个人综合素质的培养[5-6]。在理论课堂教学中采用边讲、边实验、边讨论的灵活方式，强调"精讲多练"，引导学生对实验项目展开构思，以多练、多实践使学生成为课堂上的"主动者"；在实验教学过程中坚持以实际项目为导向，提倡学生体验式自主学习教学模式，以解决各专业实际问题为背景，将数据库项目的构思、设计、实施和运用贯穿于整体训练，让学生从解决问题出发，强调分析问题、探索实践和解决问题的能力培养，激发和训练学生主动学习的兴趣、动手实践探索的精神和掌握解决问题的途径。

基于 CDIO 的数据库课程体系对于学生来说，重点是以共同完成小组项目等形式强化学生个人综合素质和数据库技术应用能力培养，将不同专业的教育与数据库系统的整体认识统一起来，通过"团队合作性学习"，锻炼学生的个人能力、团体交流能力以及数据库系统的运用和调控能力，特别是跨专业组建团队，更有利于实践"工作情境模拟教学法"，可以使学生将不同学科的基本原理和数据库技术放到具体的环境制约之中，从而达到拓展学生个人综合素质的目标[7]。

2.2 "多层次递进式"实验项目设计

在理论知识、实验教学和素质拓展三位一体的课程体系中，实验项目设计是关键。基于 CDIO 的数据库实验教学，从构思阶段的数据库概念设计开始，经历数据库设计和实施阶段，以实际数据处理工作以及信息化建设项目全生命周期的实验项目为载体整合数据库知识，重在培养分析问题、解决问题的能力和数据库系统的运用与调控能力[8-9]。

CDIO 实验项目划分为三级，一级项目以学生所在专业实际问题为背景，引导学生自主研究，通过需求分析构思、逻辑结构和物理设计、数据库实施和运行，全面培养学生的综合应用能力，同时促进实践创新精神的发展；二级项目以数据库综合设计"任务"为驱动，引导学生理清问题实质，确定结构和解决问题的方法，注重数据库理论知识和技术的综合运用，培养学生对关联知识的理解与应用、团体交流合作能力以及实践探索精神；三级项目以基础或验证型实验项目使学生验证、理解、巩固并掌握基本教学内容[10]。

以基础验证型、综合设计型、实践创新型三层次实验方案组成的递进式实验教学体系如图 3 所示[11]。在课程教学过程中，以基础验证型实验项目为载体引导学生自主地、循序渐进地学习；以综合设计型实验为突破口，将"工作情境模拟教学法"引入实验课程，引导学生结合本专业实际问题完成数据库应用系统"大项目"，激发学生学习兴趣和实践探索精神，引导学生团体交流合作，从选题开始，经构建框架、设计到制作调试完成，使学生将所学知识贯穿起来，提高学生的实战能力和综合运用知识的能力。

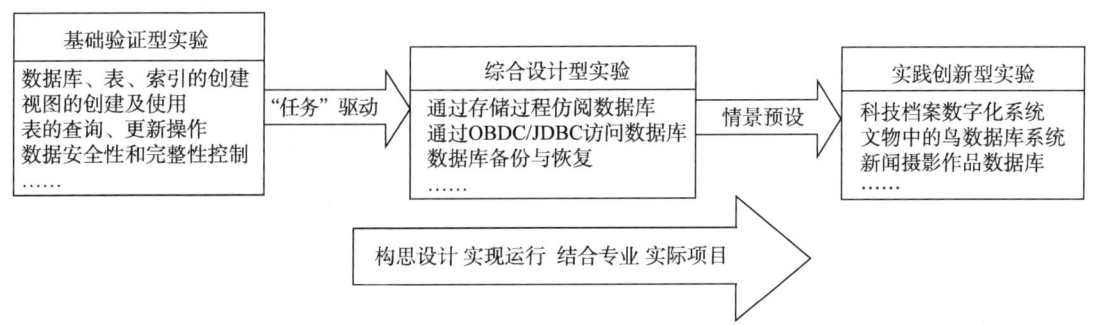

图3 "多层次递进式"实验教学体系框图

3 结束语

建立在CDIO教育理念基础之上、包含"三层次递进式"实验教学的数据库课程体系，有效地体现了应用型人才培养宗旨，三级实验项目的开展让学生充分体验"构思—设计—实现—运行"的全过程，有效地解决了理论教学与实践教学脱节和人文社科类专业学生数据库工程实践能力薄弱的问题，提升了学生系统思维和独立解决问题的能力[12]。在课程教学过程中，通过建立教学资源库和网络交流平台，为培养应用数据库技术解决实际问题的人才发挥了重要作用。

参考文献

[1] Accreditation Board of Engineeringand Technology. Criteriafor Accrediting Engineering Programs [Z]. Effectivefor Evaluations During the 2000—2001 Accreditation Cycle, 2000.
[2] 张红霞. 高等教育课程国际化的文化思考：兼谈通识教育课程改革 [J]. 清华大学教育研究, 2007 (1): 91-96, 104.
[3] 温涛. 基于TOPCARES—CDIO的一体化人才培养模式探索与实践 [J]. 计算机教育, 2011 (11): 23-29.
[4] 单家凌. 基于CDIO理念的网络工程专业教学改革 [J]. 计算机教育, 2012 (7): 45-49.
[5] 查建中. 论"做中学"战略下的CDIO模式 [J]. 高等工程教育研究, 2008 (3): 1-6.
[6] 赵娅, 薛继伟. CDIO教育理念在"数据库原理与应用"课程中的应用 [J]. 中国电力教育, 2011 (1): 97-98.
[7] 袁旦, 苏志强, 钱慧娜. CDIO模型的理念对工程类大学生学业评价的启示 [J]. 中国高等教育评估, 2008 (4): 67-69.
[8] 郭皎, 鄢沛, 应宏, 等. 基于CDIO的计算机专业实验教学改革 [J]. 实验技术与管理, 2011, 28 (2): 155-157.
[9] 董晨, 戴敏, 张桦. 基于CDIO模式的数据库系统课程实践教学 [J]. 计算机教育, 2012 (9): 81-85.
[10] 林泽铭, 李姗姗, 蔡伟鸿. 基于CDIO的计算机网络课程项目设计与实践 [J]. 计算机教育, 2012 (7): 73-77.
[11] 杨毅, 唐西西. 基于CDIO的开放实践教学模式 [J]. 中国高校科技, 2011 (7): 72-74.
[12] 李春英, 汤志康. CDIO模式下的软件工程课程设计实践 [J]. 实验技术与管理, 2011, 28 (6): 173-174.

HPLC Fingerprint of Solid – State Fermentation of Fugui Gutong Compound Prescription

Su Jianshu　Tian Pingfang　Lin Qiang　Liu Baining
Zheng Laili　Ge Xizhen

INTRODUCTION

Fu – Gui – Gu – Tong, a Chinese compound prescription used for curing arthritis and related disorders such as rheumatoid arthritis, hyperosteogeny and lumbago, is composed of eight traditional Chinese herbs (Table – 1) and has been approved by the Ministry of Health of the People's Republic of China. Two kinds of herbs Radix aconiti and Radix aconiti Lateralis preparata in the formula were rich in alkaloids, such as aconitine, mesaconitine, hypaconitine and jesaconitine1, all are active and toxic ingredients2. Of them, aconitine belongs to diester – diterpenoid aconitum alkaloid, which is also highly toxic. Our previous studies showed that when the fungus Aspergillus niger (E6.22) was fermented with Radix aconiti or Radix aconiti Lateralis preparata, some diester – diterpenoidaconitum alkaloids were changed into hydrolysis monoesterditerpenoid alkaloids, which have less toxicity3, 4. Paeoniflorin from Radix paeoniae alba is another major active component showing anti – inflammatory and analgesic activity. In order to obtain better activity and less toxicity, myriads of methods were adopted to ensure the safety and curative effects, such as processing, compatibility of different herbs, decoction, et al. 5. In recent years, solid – state fermentation has attracted great interest to produce fermented foods, enzymes, organic acids and to decrease the toxicity l6, 7. Therefore, in the present study, A. niger (E6.22) was used to ferment the prescription, the fermentation parameters were optimized and the fermentation stability was estimated by HPLC fingerprint, the half lethal dose (LD_{50}) was applied to evaluate the potential safety of Fu – Gui – Gu – Tong.

EXPERIMENTAL

Eight traditional Chinese herbs were purchased from TongRenTang Co. Ltd., (Beijing, China) and authenticated by Prof. Ge Xizhen in Biochemical Engineering College, Beijing Union University. A voucher was deposited at the College. Paeoniflorin and aconitine were purchased from Sigma, USA. A. niger (E6.22) was stored in this lab. All chemicals were of analytical or chromatography grade.

Solid state fermentation

Medium of solid – state fermentation Fu – Gui – Gu – Tong compound prescription (Table. 1) containing eight traditional Chinese herbs were used as natural substrate for solid state fermentation according to the prescription ratio and no other constituent was added. The herbs were milled, sieved (10 – 20 mesh), mingled and heat – sterilized at 122℃ for 30 min prior to inoculation.

Spore suspension: A. niger (E6.22) was propagated on beef extract peptone medium (beef extracts 10 g, peptone 10 g, dextrose 20 g, sodium chloride 5 g), 30° for 5 – 8 d, stored on slants at 4℃. The spores were suspended with sterile water. The density of spore suspension was adjusted to $1.8 \times 10^2 - 1.8 \times 10^5$ spore/mL.

[Author Introduction] Su Jianshu, Lin Qiang, Liu Baining, Zheng Laili and Ge Xizhen, Biochemical Engineering College, Beijing Union University; Tian Pingfang, College of Life Science and Technology, Beijing University of Chemical Technology.

TABLE. 1 HERBS USED FOR PREPARING FU – GUI – GU – TONG DECOCTION OR MEDIUM

Family names	Botanical names	Chinese names	Ratio
Radix Aconiti Lateralis Preparata	Aconitum carmichaeli Debx.	Fuzi	4
Radix Aconiti	Aconitum carmichaeli Debx.	Chuanwu	2
Radix Paeoniae Alba	Paeonia lactiflora Pall.	Baishao	3
Radix Codonopsis Pilosulae	Codonopsis pilosula (Franch.) Nannf.	Dangshen	3
Radix Angelicae Sinensis	Angelica sinensis (Oliv.) Diels.	Danggui	3
Herba Epimedii	Epimedium brevicornum Maxim.	Yingyanghuo	3
Olibanum	Boswellia carterii Birdw.	Ruxiang	2
Cortex Cinnamomi	Cinnamomum cassia Presl.	Rougui	1

Fermentation procedure: Fermentations were carried out in a tray, 250 mL of spore suspension were added to 500 g of sterilized natural substrate and a exact amount of water to fit a moisture content of 60 % at last. The trays were incubated under static, constant temperature at a specific condition. Fermentation parameters selected: Different fermentation conditions were studied in the present work, including fermentation temperature, fermentation time, pH and spore density.

Experiment temperatures were 25, 30, 35 and 38℃. Fermentation time was 5, 7, 9 and 11 d. Spore density was 1.8×10^2, 1.8×10^3, 1.8×10^4 and 1.8×10^5/mL. The pH was 5.5, 6.5, 7.5. All experiments were conducted in triplicate.

Preparation of crude extract of solid state fermentation Fu – Gui – Gu – Tong: At the end of fermentation, the substrates in each experiment were extracted with water for 2 h, 90℃, 3 times, the suspension collected from every extractionwas centrifuged (4000 rpm, 15 min) and the supernatant wasfiltered and concentrated to become a sticky glue – like substancein a rotary shaker under vacuum. After concentration, the residue was dissolved in a small volume of analytical pure methanol and this methanol solution was used as crude extract, stored at -20℃ until needed for the later experiments. The fermentation method was compared with the traditional water extracting method.

Determination of the dry weight of extract: According to appendix X. A. the first section of Chinese Pharmacopoeia (2005), 10 mL of extract solution was transferred into a evaporating dish, dried by a water bath, then dried in oven at 105℃ for 3 h, cooled for 30 min, weighted accurately, t he weight of dry extract was calculated.

Detection of total alkaloids: The total alkaloids in the prescription was determined by previous method[8] based on acid dye colourimetry, in brief, the spectrometric features of the ion – pair compounds produced in the reaction between the aconitine – type alkaloids and bromcresol green.

Construction of HPLC of solid state fermentation Fu – Gui – Gu – Tong: A mixture solution of reference substances containing paeoniflorin and aconitine were diluted to be the appropriate concentration for establishing calibration curves (Fig. 1). The appropriate HPLC conditions were as follows: waters analytical HPLC:

LC – 10AT vp HPLC pump, CTO – 10AS vp thermostated column compartment, SPD – 10A vp detector and controller. Diamonsil C_{18} (250 × 4.6 mm, 5 μm) (DIKMA, American) chromatogram column, the flow rate was 1.0 mL/min, the column temperature was maintained at room temperature (25 – 30℃), detection at 230 nm was to analyze the product of solid state fermentation Fu – Gui – Gu – Tong, the mobile phase consisted of A (water) and B (acetonitrile), gradient elution was as follows: 0.01min, A:B = 96:4; 20min, A:B = 90:10; 30min, A:B = 85:15; 60min, A:B = 60:40; 70min, A:B = 10:90; 80min, A:B = 4:96; 85min, A:B = 96:4. The linearity of the peak area versus concentration curve for paeoniflorin and aconitine was used to calculate the contents of the biomarker substances in Fu – Gui – Gu – Tong.

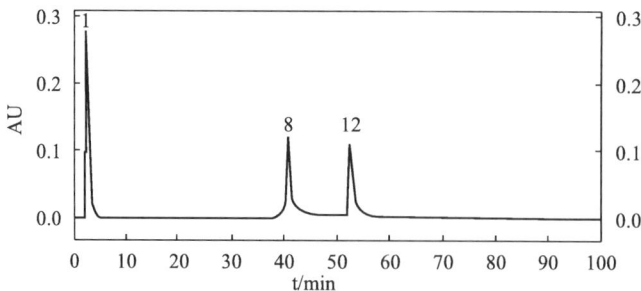

Fig. 1 HPLC analysis of standard solution. The peaks were identified as: 8 = Paeoniflorin; 12 = Aconitine.

Establishment of fingerprint for solid state fermentation Fu – Gui – Gu – Tong: Through optimization of solid state fermentation condition, the process was repeated for 10 batches, 100 minutes of chromatogram was recorded, meanwhile, the superposition chart (Fig. 6) was obtained using similarity evaluation system of traditional Chinese medicine chromatographic fingerprints provided by state pharmacopoeia committee (Version 2004A). The software was employed to calculate the correlative coefficient and evaluate the similarities of different chromatograms[9].

Study on acute toxicity (oral): According to the method of Bliss[10] and our reported toxicity through preliminary study, the lethal dose (100) of Fu – Gui – Gu – Tong was 190.0 g/kg and the survival dose (0) was 57.8 g/kg. Fifty mice were divided into five groups according to a random number table. The mice were orally administered with graded doses of solid state fermentation Fu – Gui – Gu – Tong 176.0, 140.9, 112.8, 90.2 and 72.2 g/kg (the ratio is 1: 0.8) to five different groups of mice, all groups were orally administered twice a day and then closely observed for any abnormal or toxic manifestation and mortality up to 14 d. The half lethal dose (LD_{50}) was calculated. Meanwhile, another fifty mice with Fu – Gui – Gu – Tong was designed and operated as the control group.

RESULTS AND DISCUSSION

Optimization of fermentation process parameters:

Solid state fermentation was used for production of Fu – Gui – Gu – Tong, according to preliminary experiments, four important parameters (incubation temperature, time, pH and spore density) were considered as the independent variables and their effects on active ingredients were given in Figs 2 – 5.

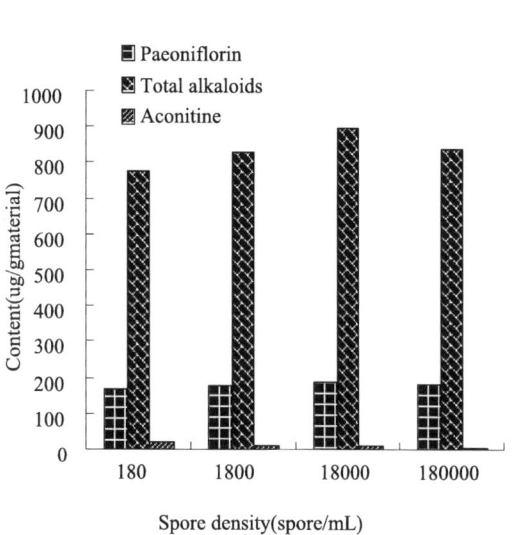

Fig. 2 Effect of spore density on the contents of paeoniflorin, total alkaloids and aconitine in fermentation extracts

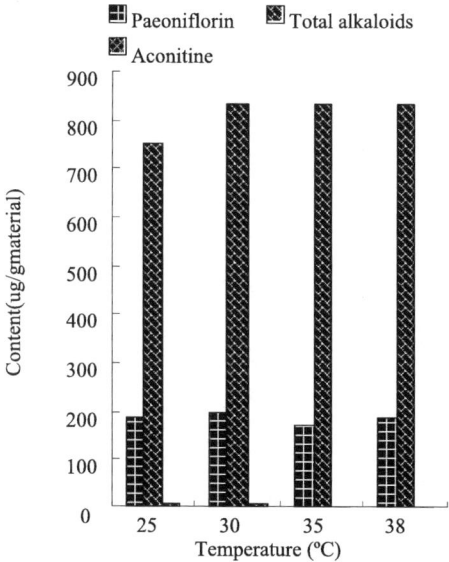

Fig. 3 Effect of temperature on the contents of paeoniflorin, total alkaloids and aconitine in fermentation extracts

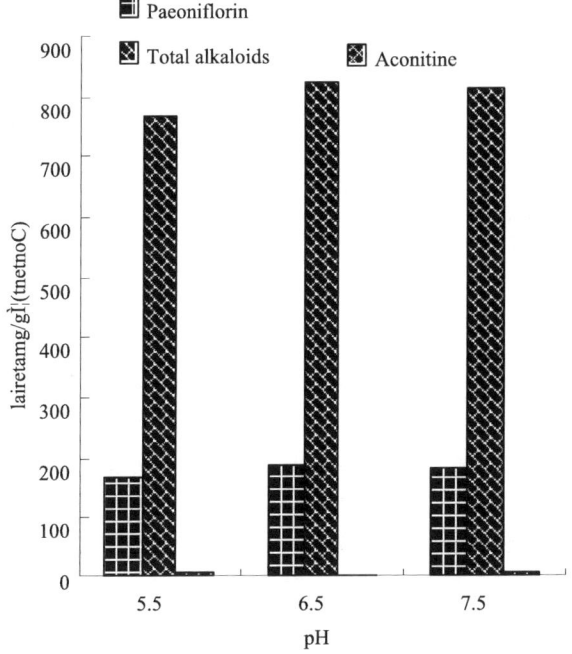

Fig. 4 Effect of pH on the contents of paeoniflorin, total alkaloids and aconitine in fermentation extracts

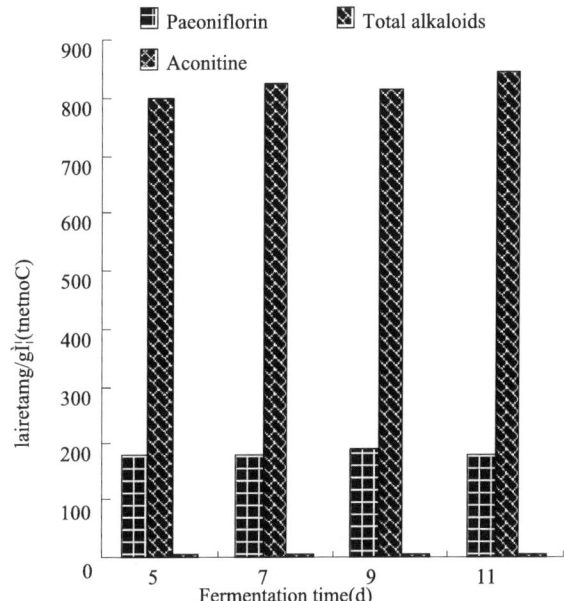

Fig. 5 Effect of fermentation time on the contents of paeoniflorin, total alkaloids and aconitine in fermentation extracts.

The content of paeoniflorin at 30℃ was higher. In contrast, aconitine became lower when the temperature rose.

The contents of paeoniflorin and total alkaloids at 1.8×10^4 spores/mL were higher, but the aconitine was lower.

The contents of paeoniflorin and total alkaloids at 9 or 11 d were higher. In contrast, aconitine became lower with the increase of fermentation time.

The total alkaloids varied in different fermentation process, in general, the total alkaloids rose up with the increase of the spore number, incubation time, or the incubation temperature. Conversely, the aconitine decreased, which is one of the major aconitum alkaloid typically symbolizing the prescription's toxicity2. Considering the labor cost, material, time cost and the growth status, the optimal setting of experimental parameters for solid state fermentation Fu – Gui – Gu – Tong were as follows: spore density, 1.8×104 spore/mL; incubation time, 7d; pH, 6.5; incubation temperature, 30℃.

Comparison of this fermentation with conventional methods: Solid state fermentation (Table – 2) was showed to bebetter for optimum production of paeoniflorin (245.2 μg/g) and total alkaloids (853.7 μg/g), both of them were higher than traditional method (181.4, 421.9 μg/g), though the dry extract (30.56 g/g) in solid state fermentation was lower, the extraction liquid was clear with low viscosity, it was thus deduced that the microbes most possibly the A. niger (E6.22) decomposed the polysaccharide in the extract[11]. The data revealed that the amount of aconitine in solid state fermentation FGG extract was very low (4.01 μg/g), because the oral lethal dose 50 % (LD_{50}) of aconitine for mice is 1.8 mg/kg[12] and the lethal dose of these alkaloids for humans is 1 – 2 mg[13]. It could be deduced that the solid state fermentation FGG extract was safe.

TABLE – 2 COMPARISON OF FERMENTATION WITH TRADITIONAL METHOD

Methods	Paeoniflorin μg/g material	Total alkaloids μg/g material	Aconitine μg/g material	Weight of dry extract (g) /100 g herbal material
Tradition	181.4	421.9	33.14	32.31
Fermentation	245.2	853.7	4.01	30.56

The contents of paeoniflorin and total alkaloids at pH 6.5 were higher, while the aconitine was lower. The A. niger grow well, suggesting that pH 6.5 is appropriate.

Fingerprinting and similarity index of solid state fermentation Fu – Gui – Gu – Tong: Fu – Gui – Gu – Tong was a compoundprescription containing diverse active compounds, while the paeoniflorin in Radix paeoniae alba was the main constituent with high concentration, the peak height is moderate with good separation from the adjacent peaks (Fig. 6). Hence, the chromatography of paeoniflorin was regarded as reference peak. The retention times of this biomarker substance and aconitine were 41.242, 52.275 min, respectively. Among all peaks observed, 18 peaks of them (denoted from 1 to 18) were defined as common peaks because they showed up in all samples. The relative retention time and relative retention area of these 18 peaks were not shown. The similarity index of 10 samples was higher than 0.978 (Table – 3), indicated that the samples from different batches in the same solid state fermentation condition shared the similar chromatographic pattern, thereby suggesting the stability of the constituents of solid state fermentation Fu – Gui – Gu – Tong in different batches, as well as the reliability and applicability of this fermentation procedure.

TABLE – 3 SIMILARITY FOR 10 BATCHES OF SOLID STATE FERMENTATION FU – GUI – GU – TONG

Sample No.	1	2	3	4	5	6	7	8	9	10	Control
Similarity	0.978	0.982	0.995	1.000	0.978	0.992	0.998	0.978	0.984	0.994	1.0

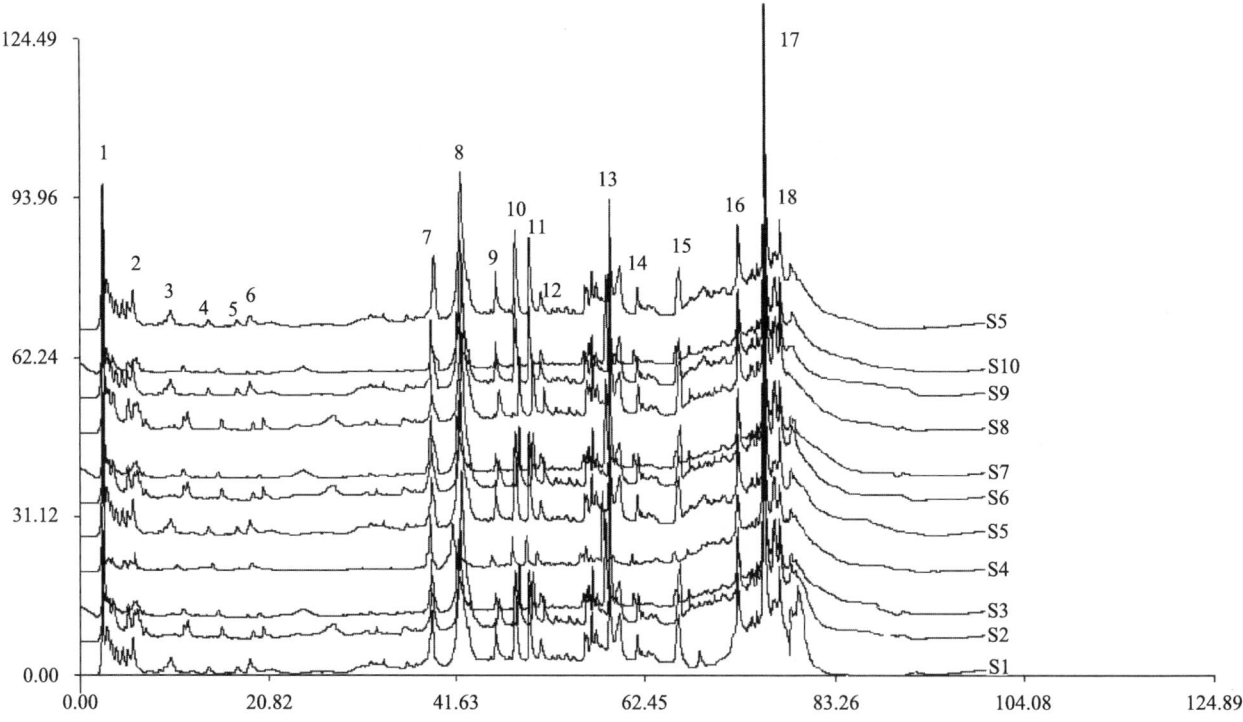

Fig. 6 Matched chromatographys of 10 patches of solid state fermentation Fu – Gui – Gu – Tong

Acute toxicity results: The mice became dispirited, some moved slowly or died after being orally administered with Fu – Gui – Gu – Tong or solid state fermentation Fu – Gui – Gu – Tong[14] days later. Before dying, the mice manifested toxic symptoms with a low respiratory rate, gasping for breath and flapping of nose wing. The death numbers could be clearly seen from Table – 4, in control group, the LD_{50} was 118.16 g/kg, its 95 confident limit was 101.77 – 139.53 g/kg. For the solid state fermentation Fu – Gui – Gu – Tong group, the LD50 was 133.70 g/kg, which was higher (118.16 g/kg), its 95 confident limit was 114.73 – 166.67g/kg. The above results indicated that when Fu – Gui – Gu – Tong treated by solid state fermentation, its toxicity became less and safer than the original prescription Fu – Gui – Gu – Tong. Therefore the solid state fermentation Fu – Gui – Gu –

Tong is helpful for the goals: low toxicity and safety[10,14].

TABLE-4 RESULTS OF DIFFERENT DOSES OF SOLID STATE FERMENTATION (SSF) FU-GUI-GU-TONG (FGGT) ORALLY GIVEN TO MICE

Dose (g/kg)	Dose (g/kg)	n	Death number	Percentage mortality	LD_{50} (g/kg)
SSF FGGT	176.0	10	8	80.0	133.70*
	140.9	10	6	60.0	
	112.8	10	3	30.0	
	90.2	10	1	10.0	
	72.2	10	1	10.0	
FGGT	176.0	10	9	90.0	118.16**
	140.9	10	7	70.0	
	112.8	10	4	40.0	
	90.2	10	2	20.0	
	72.2	10	1	10.0	

* LD_{50} 95 % was 133.70g/kg, 95 confident limit was 114.73 – 166.67g/kg;

** LD_{50} 95 % was 118.16 g/kg, 95 confident limit was 101.77 – 139.53g/kg

Conclusion

Three conclusions have been drawn from this study. (i) the optimal parameters for fermenting Fu – Gui – Gu – Tong were as follows: A. niger (E6.22) spore density, 1.8×10^4 spores/mL; incubation time, 7d; pH, 6.5; incubation temperature, 30℃. In this condition, paeoniflorin and total alkaloids could be increased, whereas, the composition of aconitine was decreased. (ii) the appropriate HPLC conditions for solid state fermentation Fu – Gui – Gu – Tong were as follows: diamonsil C_{18} (250×4.6 mm, 5 μm) chromatogram column, the flow rate was 1.0 mL/min, the column temperature was 25 – 30℃, detection was at 230 nm, the mobile phase was gradient elution consisting of A (water) and B (acetonitrile). The similarity index of samples was 0.978. HPLC fingerprinting was stable and feasibility to test the fermentation procedure of Fu – Gui – Gu – Tong. (iii) when Fu – Gui – Gu – Tong was treated by solid state fermentation, its toxicity became less and was safer than the original prescription Fu – Gui – Gu – Tong. It is concluded that the procedure of solid state fermentation was stable and reliable and the fermented Fu – Gui – Gu – Tong was safe.

ACKNOWLEDGEMENTS

This study was supported by a grant from the Beijing Municipal Education Commission of the People's Republicof China (KM200911417011).

REFERENCES

[1] K. Wada, M. Nihira and Y. Ohno [J]. J. Ethnopharmacol, 2006, 105, 89.

[2] K. Wada, M. Nihira, H. Hayakawa, Y. Tomita, M. Hayashida and Y. Ohno. Forensic. Sci. Int., 2005, 148, 21.

[3] W. L. Liu, Z. Q. Liu, F. R. Song and S. Y. Liu. Chem. J. Chineses U., 2011, 32, 717.

[4] J. S. Su, B. N. Liu, P. F. Tian, Q. Lin, Y. X. Zhao and X. Z. Ge. J. Beijing U. Chem. Technol., 2010, 37, 97.

[5] L. P. Zhu and Z. P. Xu, Chin. Traditional Pat. Med., 2005, 27, 8202.

[6] A. Sharma, V. Vivekanand and R. P. Singh, Bioresour. Technol., 99, 3444 (2008).

[7] R. R. Singhaniaa, A. K. Patel, C. R. Soccolc and A. Pandeya, Biochem. Eng. J., 44, 13 (2009).

[8] L. L. Zheng, P. F. Tian, Y. S. Li, X. Y. Qiao, R. Wang and X. Z. Ge, J. Beijing U. Chem. Technol., 36, 80 (2009).

[9] B. H. Cai and X. H. Liu, Determination technology of HPLC fingerprint for common Chinese Herbal Medicines, Chemical Industry Press, Beijing (2005).

[10] Q. Chen. Method Study of Traditional Chinese Medicine Pharmacology [M]. Beijing People's Health Press, 1993.

[11] A. B. Diaz, I. Caro, Ory. I. De and A. Blandino, Enzym. Microb. Technol., 2007, 41, 302.

[12] Y. Ohno, J. Tox. Rev., 1998, 17, 1.

[13] T. Y. K. Chan, Hum. Exp. Toxicol., 10.1177/0960327111407224 (2011).

[14] M. W. Carey, N. V. Rao, B. R. Kumar and G. K. Mohan, J. Ethnopharmacol., 130, 179 (2010).

四色套印偏差视觉检测系统软件设计与实现

董南萍 于丽杰 高宗余

套印偏差是印刷过程中的一个重要参数,其准确性直接影响印刷质量。为了检测套印偏差,通常在每一底色旁边设计专用的估计套印偏差的测量标记(如带十字线的圆)[1]。目前,国内常用的四色胶印机一般采用叠印式套印标记,套印偏差的检测主要采用离线人工方式,通过放大镜对印刷品边缘的套印标记进行观察,来估计套印偏差大小,然后根据经验调整套准机构,检测精度和速度取决于工人的经验[2-3]。随着印刷技术水平的提高,现代印刷机正在向高质量、高精度、高速度和高自动化方向发展,以往人工检测套印偏差的方法已不能满足需要,因此,研究套印偏差的快速、准确自动检测及实时调整控制,是保证印品质量、提高印刷机的自动化水平的重要措施。图案模式的快速辨识和颜色的快速辨识等视觉检测问题,肉眼根本无法连续稳定地做到,其他物理量传感器也难有用武之地。相比较而言,机器视觉检测技术成为套印偏差检测的必然发展趋势,例如文献[4-5]研究了基于图像处理的套印误差检测方法,文献[6-7]中研究了叠印式套印标记的套印偏差检测方法及检测系统的设计。在已有的工作基础上,以四原色CMYK为例,研究适用于重叠标记的胶印机套印偏差自动检测方法,并给出配套的系统软件的设计方法,拓宽视觉检测技术的应用范围。

1 视觉检测系统组成及工作过程

为了实现彩色胶印机套印偏差自动检测,自行设计了基于视觉检测技术的套印偏差离线检测系统的样机。系统主要由3部分组成:工作台和图像采集系统(包括CCD摄像机、镜头、光源、计算机)以及视觉检测软件系统。系统选用大恒 DH-HV2000 数字摄像机、环形光源以及日本 Computar 公司 MLM-3XMP 可调焦镜头组成图像采集部分,摄像机通过 USB 总线与计算机通信。

检测时,将印刷页面置于工作台上,通过手动调整摄像机位置,获取页面不同位置上的套印标志图像。系统可以通过 LED 光源的电源调整,实现照明光源光照强度的调整,并进行 Z 轴调焦,CCD 摄像机将被测物体(彩色套印标志)在光的照射下所反映的信息记录下来,同时合成完整的数字图像信号,输入计算机,进行数字图像分析和处理,计算出4种彩色套印偏差的实际偏离值。之后,把检测得到的套印偏差数据统计分析,进行印刷机工况结果判定,并把数据结果记录到数据库中,显示输出套印偏差检测数据和判定结果。

2 系统软件工作流程及功能模块

软件通过图像采集系统来采集待检测印刷品的图像,进行图像分析处理,处理过程包括图像分色、图像分割和边缘提取。对于单张的印刷品,本软件的工作流程见图1。

[基金项目] 北京市属高等学校人才强教计划资助项目(PHR201008320,PHR201106149);北京联合大学校级科研项目(zk200923x)。

[作者简介] 董南萍(1964—),女,北京联合大学教授。主要研究领域为计算机网络、软件设计;于丽杰(1970—),女,博士,北京联合大学副教授。主要研究领域为计算机视觉、人工智能。

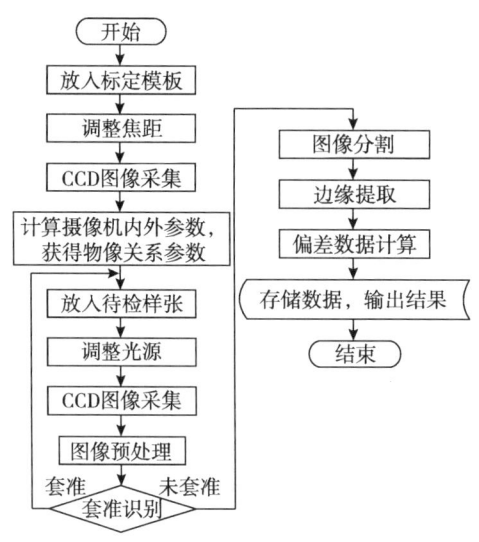

图 1　套印偏差检测工作流程

根据软件的需求，将软件分为 8 个功能模块，包括：图像采集及显示模块、摄像机参数标定模块、光源调整模块、套准识别模块、图像处理模块、数据存储模块、打印报表模块以及用户管理模块等。

3　色标分割及边缘提取

软件用到的图像处理方法主要有：彩色图像分割、直线边缘提取等。

3.1　色标分割

从图像采集系统采集的彩色图像为 24 位真彩色图像，由红（R）、绿（G）、蓝（B）三基色组成，R，G，B 三基色间存在很强的相关性，改变任一分量都会导致颜色的失真与偏离[8]，因此图像处理时通常从相关性强的 RGB 色彩空间转换到相关性不强的色彩空间。选择 HSI 色彩空间作为彩色图像处理的模型。在 HSI 色彩空间，H、S、I 3 个分量是相互独立的，I 分量与图像彩色信息无关，H 和 S 分量通常通称为色度，表示颜色的类别与深浅程度。HSI 模型各分量可以根据下面公式[8]计算得到：

$$H = \begin{cases} \theta, & B \leq G \\ 360 - \theta, & B > G \end{cases} \tag{1}$$

$$S = 1 - \frac{3}{R+G+B}\left[\min(R, G, B)\right] \tag{2}$$

$$I = \frac{1}{3}(R+G+B) \tag{3}$$

其中：

$$\theta = \arccos \frac{\left[(R-G)+(R-B)\right]/2}{\left[(R-G)^2 + (R-B)(G-B)\right]^{1/2}}$$

CMYK 四原色是印刷色彩模式，四原色相互叠加能够产生其他颜色，如青色和黄色叠加产生绿色，青色和品红叠加产生蓝色等。由图 2 可知，叠印式套色标志可分为以下几种情况：（1）完全未重叠的部分，包括 Y（黄色），C（青色），M（品红）；（2）两两交错的部分，包括 G（绿色，由 Y 与 C 交叠而成），B（蓝色，由 C 与 M 交叠而成），R（红色，由 M 与 Y 交叠而成）；（3）3 个套色标记交叠的部分，这部分理论上是黑色。从以上分析看，套印标志图像的颜色种类包括：黑色、青色、黄色、品红、红色、绿色以及蓝色共 7 种颜色。与其他丰富颜色信息的彩色相比，套印标志图像的场景简单，图像中的目标和背景有各自的颜色，容易区分，因此本系统软件根据套印标志的颜色特征进行图像分割。在 HSI 颜色空间，像素的颜色由 H、S、I 3 个分量组成，它们的值构成描述像素颜色的向量 C_k，k 为像素编号，$C_k[C_{kH}, C_{kS}, C_{kI}]^T$，$C_{kH}$，$C_{kS}$，$C_{kI}$ 表示图像的第 k 个像素

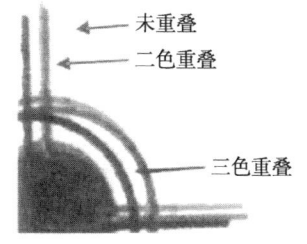

图 2　样本重叠类型

点的 H, S, I 分量的值。理想状况下常见颜色的 HIS 的分量值见表1。

表1　常见颜色的描述方法（归一化数值）
Tab 1　Common colors description method（Normalized value）

	H	S	I
R（红）(1, 0, 0)	0	1	0.333
Y（黄）(1, 1, 0)	0.167	1	0.667
G（绿）(0, 1, 0)	0.334	1	0.333
Cy（青）(0, 1, 1)	0.5	1	0.666
B（蓝）(0, 0, 1)	0.667	1	0.333
Mg（品红）(1, 0, 1)	0.833	1	0.667
黑 (0, 0, 0)	—	0	0
白 (1, 1, 1)	—	0	1

实际采集的套印标志图像由于受光照、摄像机和印刷油墨的影响，各像素的值会有变化，以理想数值为中心波动，通过实验观察，设定 H, S, I 三个分量的阈值：$T_{kS} = 0.2$, $T_{kH} = 0.085$, $T_{kI} = 0.2$。

白色像素属于背景像素，满足：$C_{kI} = 1$, $C_{KS} = 0$；黑色像素理论上应该满足条件 $C_{kI} = 0$, $C_{KS} = 0$，但是黑色的效果与印刷的着墨效果有关，着墨效果好，其黑色比较纯正，其灰度分量 I 很小，有时着墨较少，或者拍摄时光线较强等因素，导致灰度分量 I 较大，在满足 $C_{kI} < T_{kI}$ 时就作为黑色像素处理。

青色像素满足条件：$C_{kH} - 0.5 \leqslant T_{kH}$, $C_{kS} > 1 - T_{kS}$, $C_{kI} = 0.667 \pm T_{kI}$。

品红像素满足条件：$C_{kH} - 0.833 \leqslant T_{kH}$, $C_{kS} > 1 - T_{kS}$, $C_{kI} = 0.667 \pm T_{kI}$。

黄色像素满足条件：$C_{kH} - 0.167 \leqslant T_{kH}$, $C_{KS} > 1 - T_{kS}$, $C_{kI} = 0.667 \pm T_{kI}$。

红色是品红和黄色叠加的结果，红色像素归入红色像素群和黄色像素群，满足条件：$C_{kH} \leqslant T_{kH}$, $C_{kS} > 1 - T_{kS}$, $C_{kI} = 0.333 \pm T_{kI}$。

绿色是青色和黄色叠加的结果，绿色像素归入青色像素群和黄色像素群，满足条件：$C_{kH} - 0.334 \leqslant T_{kH}$, $C_{KS} > 1 - T_{kS}$, $C_{kI} = 0.333 \pm T_{kI}$。

若像素颜色值不满足以上任何条件，作为特殊颜色处理。以上分割使用的阈值可根据实验系统的情况进行微调。因此，系统的基于目标特征的彩色阈值分割详细算法流程见图3。套印标志图像的分割结果见图4。

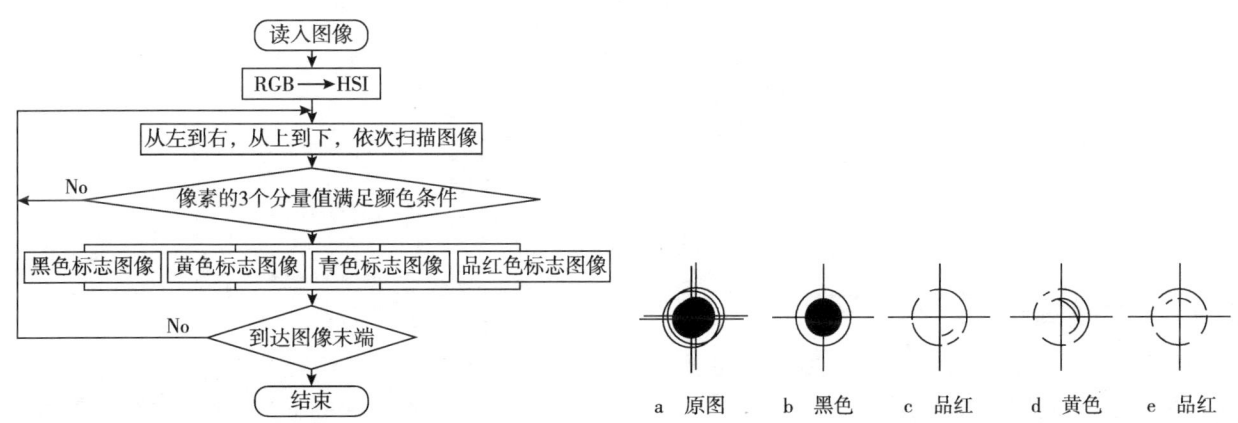

图3　基于目标特征的阈值分割算法流程　　　　　　图4　真实标记分割结果

3.2　直线边缘拟合

经过彩色图像分割后，套印标记的图像分割成只有单一色标的图像，图像中目标和背景都只有单一的颜色，可以直接转换为灰度图像进行处理。在此基础上，采用 Canny 算法进行边缘提取。

图像中的套印标志是圆和具有一定宽度的直线相交形成的,直线型边缘点具有如此的特征:(1)垂直边缘方向的像素梯度值变化迅速;(2)沿着边缘方向的像素梯度值变化缓慢;(3)同一条直线上像素点的梯度方向基本相同;(4)标识两侧边缘的梯度方向相反。

经过了 Canny 算法提取边缘后,图像中的每个像素点都具有了相应的梯度矢量方向,根据梯度方向设定阈值,将像素点划分为左侧、右侧、上侧和下侧边缘像素点集合,并可剔出圆形标记边缘像素点,形成直线边缘像素点的集合。在每个边缘像素点集合内,采用最小二乘法拟合方法,将相关离散点拟合成为直线。原色标志的多条边缘直线确定后,可以计算图像中轴向和周向的套印偏差,通过视觉标定转化为物空间中的套印偏差。

4 软件实现结果

4.1 软件工作主界面

系统软件是在 VC ++ 6.0 开发平台上开发设计的,系统软件的工作主界面见图5,右侧为控制面板,包括检测方式选择、检测内容、检测样本选择,以及手动检测时检测标志线位置调整按钮等检测控制内容。左侧为图像显示区域,可以实时显示检测图像,在标定和测量时显示图像的处理结果。窗口左下角的状态栏可以实时显示图像测量数据,右下角的状态栏在光照强度调整优化时可实时显示光照强度标定数值,便于在检测过程中观察测量数据。工具栏的图形化命令按钮可以方便地控制摄像机工作。

4.2 软件的工作方式

根据需要,软件系统设计了手动检测和自动检测 2 种工作方式。手动检测为人工交互形式,在套印标记图像中通过鼠标移动"十字线"检测线图标选择特征点,也可以通过右侧控制面板的微调按钮微调"十字线"图标的位置,并可以调整控制"十字线"旋转角度。窗口的上面和左边可显示水平标尺和垂直标尺作为参照,在标尺上会有对应到当前鼠标位置的 2 条线来显示鼠标的当前位置坐标,通过肉眼观察标尺可直接观察到检测结果。手工检测方式适用于多种不同类型的套印标志的测量,测量精度取决于 CCD 图像传感器的分辨率,以及人员操作的定位精度。自动检测是本系统的主要检测方式,图像采集后,一键测量,结果显示在测量环境中,不受操作人员的影响,测量精度取决于摄像机标定精度、特征点提取精度、CCD 图像传感器的分辨率等因素,计算速度与计算机性能直接相关。

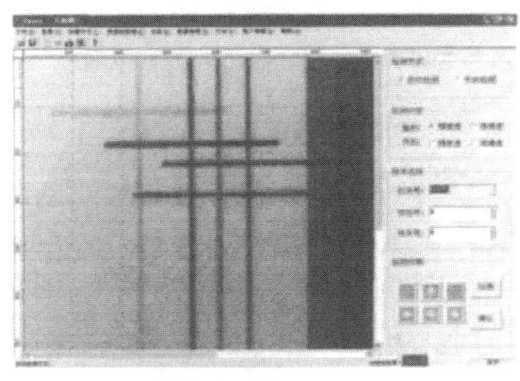

图5 系统软件的工作主界面

4.3 报表显示输出

胶印机性能的评价参数主要包括输纸套准准确度、输纸套准精密度、传纸套准准确度、传纸套准精密度 4 个参数,是在连续印刷的 500 张印样中随机抽取 100 张印刷样张作为样本,分别测量每个样张上 8 个位置的套印标记作为样本点,取样本点同侧边宽度值,采用式(1),计算各颜色的套印精度,胶印机的输纸精密度为相应样本套印精密度的最大值,即取 8 个位置点计算结果中的最大值,作为胶印机的输纸精密度。

$$\delta_{kn} = \sqrt{\frac{1}{m-1}\sum_{i=1}^{m}(d_{kni} - \bar{d}_{kni})^2} \quad (4)$$

式中：$\bar{d}_{kni} = \frac{1}{m}\sum_{i=1}^{m} d_{kni}$，$d_{kni}$ 为十字线同侧边距离；i 为样张顺序（$i = 1,2,\cdots,m$）；m 为样张总数；k 为叠印（套印）十字线位置序号（$k = 1,2,3,4,5,6,7,8$）；n 为色数。

系统检测采用离线方式，将印刷机的印刷样品置于检测平台，通过人工操作依次检测样本，检测系统工作见图6，检测系统软件运行在普通P4，2.8 G 台式计算机上，完成一个标记的检测计算时间是1.6ms。在检测过程中，软件将各样本点检测的套印偏差数据存储于数据库表中，待所有样本检测完成后统计生成打印报表，可用于印刷机出厂性能评价，也可以单独输出每个样本点检测的详细数据。

图6 检测系统工作示意图

5 结　　论

研究了四色叠印套印标记图像的分割方法及系统软件的设计方法，软件的所有功能均在 VC ++ 环境下实现并调试完成，解决了常见的 CMYK 四色叠印标记胶印机的套印偏差自动检测问题，拓宽了视觉检测技术的应用范围。实践应用表明：配合相应的硬件系统，该检测误差较小，满足彩色印刷机出厂时套印精度检测的需求。系统软件使用简单，操作方便，已经应用于北人集团印刷机套印偏差的检测。

参考文献

[1] hiwen G, Wenhe L, Yu G, et al. Manufacturing Resource Planning Technology Based on Genetic Programming Simulation [J]. Chinese Journal of Mechanical Engineering, 2009, 22（2）：177 - 183.
[2] 孙园园, 陈长缨. 彩色印刷套印误差检测系统的设计与实现[J]. 陕西科技大学学报, 2010, 28（2）：100 - 103.
[3] 谢志萍. 基于 PLC 与图像联合控制的印刷套准系统关键技术研究[J]. 包装工程, 2011, 32（9）：71 - 73.
[4] 王梅, 李克天, 赵荣丽. 印刷自动套准偏差检测软件的主要技术问题分析[J]. 包装工程, 2008, 29（12）：122 - 124.
[5] 赵明炎, 徐艳芳, 王瑜. 基于数字图像处理的套印误差检测方法[J]. 北京印刷学院学报, 2009, 17（2）：1 - 4.
[6] 于丽杰, 李德胜. 彩色套印偏差检测中的图像处理技术研究[J]. 计算机工程与应用, 2010, 46（11）：190 - 195.
[7] 于丽杰, 李德胜. 彩色印刷套准识别方法研究[J]. 计算机工程与应用, 2011, 47（5）：163 - 165.
[8] 冈萨雷斯. 数字图像处理[M]. 2 版. 北京：电子工业出版社, 2005.

Crowd Density Estimation Based on Texture Feature Extraction

Bobo Wang   Hong Bao   Shan Yang

1 INTRODUCTION

With the rapid economic development and increasing people's social activities, the flow density of large malls, supermarkets and places such as subway station is growing more and more serious and brings security risks by the crowd congestion. According to news agency reports: On February 27, 2013, LaoHeKou of Hubei province occurred a stampede caused by crowd of local elementary school, 11 students were injured, 4 students died. Therefore, if we can analyze the events in advance and predict the likelihood of the risk, then timely and effective measures can be took to ease the crow. It can effectively avoid the social security problem that caused by the high crowd density. According to the different feature extraction methods, crowd density estimation techniques can be divided into three categories: ①estimation based on pixels statistical categories; ②estimation based on texture analysis technique; ③estimation based on individual characteristics. For the first category, Davies, Chow et al proposed a approach of using foreground – pixels, which is based on the relationship between number of people and crowd density using a linear methods for estimating the density. The Hong Kong Chow et al proposed a neural network method by using a mix of global learning algorithm for the crowd density. The method is mainly based on the extraction of the three characteristics of the crowd: population object edge length, a proportion of object pixels in the image and the background of the object pixels in the image. Paragios[1] proposed a method based on Markov Random Field (MRF) real – time crowd density estimation. The method is divided into two steps: The first step is to distinguish the image's foreground and background by Markov Random Field; The second step is to get the image by changing detection combined with a geometric module to perspective correction, and then estimate the population density of the monitored area. Chow et al. joined the body template matching module and match for human body for the people who are clearer individual characteristics and near camera. The performance of the system has been obviously improved and is applied in the subway system in Hong Kong. In the method of crowd density estimation based on texture analysis technology: it was proposed by Brazilian Marana as early as in 1998. Marana think that images of crowds with different densities tend to present distinct texture patterns. High density crowded areas are often made up of fine patterns (which correspond to high frequencies in the frequency domain), while images of low density crowded areas are mostly made up of coarse patterns (which corresponds to low frequencies in the frequency domain), especially when their backgrounds are also made up of coarse patterns. H. Rahmalan[2] take the crowd image as texture image, and extract gray level co – occurrence matrix and the min Khodorkovsky fractal dimension, scale invariant orthogonal Chebyshev torque characteristics. Finally, crowd density is classified by using self – organizing mapping learning and classification algorithms. Wu[3] segments image into different sizes by adopting the method of projection transformation in accordance with the different distances from the camera. Then extract texture feature vectors from each input image grid and use support vector machine (SVM) method to get the population density in each grid. Finally, the support vector machine (SVM) method id used again to detect abnormal density distribution based on the estimated density vector. CHAN[4] established the regression equation by comprehensive utilization the groups of pixels and texture feature information, and get the function relation the number of sce-

---

[Foundation Item] This work was supported by the National Nature Science Foundation of China (Grant No. 61271370).

[Author Introduction] Bobo Wang, Beijing Key Laboratory of Information Service Engineering, Beijing Union University; Hong Bao, Professor of Beijing Union University; Shan Yang, Beijing Union University.

narios and the characteristics of the crowd. The Qing WEN et al[5] proposed the mathematical method by the texture characteristics of the crowd and the number of the scene to statistics the number. The method of using the 2 - d Gabor filter to extract the crowd global texture characteristics can effectively avoid the overlap between the crowd and perspective distortion. In paper[6], the authors put forward a new kind of approach which through the accumulation of Mosaic image difference feature to represent these complex random motion models for accurate detection. Then, through the perspective distortion correction model, the observed field achieved considerable population density measurements obtained on the basis of the foreground image. Chow methods cannot solve the problem of high density crowd to distinguish, but crowd density estimation method based on texture analysis technology can solve it. This method is currently under further development. In crowd density estimation based on individual characteristics, Shengfim Lin etc. put forward a kind of through the crossing transform to extract the head contour feature to locate each one, to determine the number of a crowded environment. D. B. Yang[7] obtained images of the same scene by multiple sensors from different angles computes scenario 2d projection and used background difference method to detect prospect. Then, prospects are detected from various angles for fusion. Finally, geometric algorithms are used to calculate the projection area of the body contour, and count. Antonio etc. [8] proposed a new feature which is used for people counting and statistical method, which made use of feature points to count the number. They assumed that the number of feature points and the crowd density and the quantity have some corresponding relation. The method achieved ideal effect, and some gesture recognition is studied by using characteristic points at the same time. Conte[9] classified the feature point of prospects for detecting movement in the scene. Then the feature points in each category, the number of parameters such as the distribution of feature points were trained in SVM for ultimately determining the number of pedestrians.

Currently, many researchers who are devoting the crowd behavior analysis usually use the PETS data sets[14]. The PETS (Performance Evaluation of Tracking Systems) meeting is AVSS BBS annual meeting on crowd behavior analysis. In recent years, the meeting has been held in the United States, Britain, Australia, Italy and many other countries. The meeting is mainly on crowd behavior analysis, including population statistics, crowd density estimation, individual staff and tracking individuals in the group, special groups and special events detection, etc. The PETS data set includes the background and normal flow for the training data, and the density estimation data, the data used for pedestrian tracking and behavior analysis and event detection.

This paper is a new kind of texture feature of crowd density estimation. Tamura feature is a kind of common texture feature in image retrieval. Through the feature extraction and PCA dimension reduction[10], the obtained feature vector has high correlation with crowd density, which can improve the accuracy of crowd density estimation.

The rest of this paper is organized as follows. In Section II, the details of our proposed method are elaborated. Section III demonstrates the experiment results. Finally, some concluding remarks are presented in Section IV.

2 PROPOSED METHOD

The flowchart of our proposed method is illustrated in Figure. 1. We can see that, the images are firstly preprocessed, which mainly includes: get gray image, deal with the noise, and extract the interested area. Secondly, the 13 image texture features are extracted in the area of interest by gray level co - occurrence matrix. Then dimension reduction is implemented by principal component analysis (PCA) to get the high correlation of 4 - D feature vector. Four Tamura image texture features are extracted by Tamura. Through feature fusion, an 8 - dimensional feature vector is got. Finally, classification and prediction are obtained by using the SVM[11] to get the estimation of crowd density.

A. The image preprocessing and interest region extraction

Usually, there are laws in the pedestrian route of movement in the scene, namely, they walk along a certain route. For this experiment, the road that the pedestrians are walking on is the area of interest[12]. After picking up the area of interest, we can remove the influence caused by the background in the image, which can improve the estimated accuracy and efficiency. Fig. 2 are the area of interest extracted by graying image and Wiener filter denoising for each set of source images.

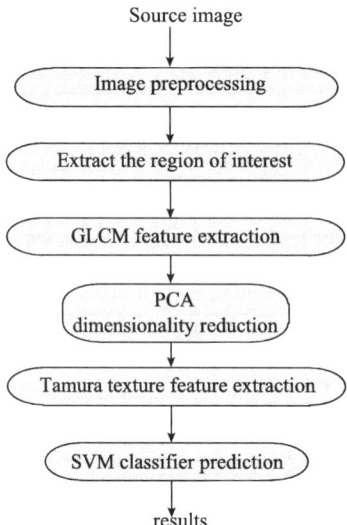

Fig. 1 Flowchart

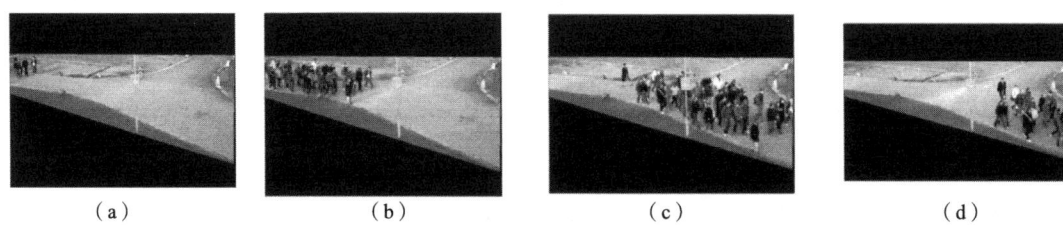

Fig. 2 (a), (b), (c), (d) are the area of interest extracted by graying image and Wiener filter denoising for each set of source images.

B. GLCM texture feature extraction and dimension reduction

In texture feature extraction[13], Marana used GLCM texture analysis methods. The method calculates GLCM of the crowd image and extracts the texture feature. Then the feature vectors into neural network classification. Because the different density of the population images corresponds to a different texture pattern, in the high density of population, the texture is a fine and coarse mode in the low – density populations' image.

Texture is alternately repeated by the gray scale distribution on space position change. So there must be some gray relation between two pixels separated by a distance in the image space. This is called the image gray – scale spatial correlation properties[14]. Through the study of spatial gray level correlation to describe texture, this is the thinking foundation of gray level co – occurrence matrix. Gray level co – occurrence matrix is the probability of i point to the gray j point and the distance is $d = (Dx, Dy)$. Gray level co – occurrence matrix express with P_d (i, j) $(i, j = 0, 1, 2, \cdots L-1)$, which L is the gray scale of the image, i, j, respectively pixel gray level and d is the space position relation between two pixels. Different d determines the distance and direction between two pixels. Θ is the generating direction of gray level co – occurrence matrix. Usually the four directions are 0°, 45°, 90° and 135°. As shown in Fig. 3.

When d is selected, it generates gray level co – occurrence matrix. One element of the co – occurrence matrix represents the number of occurrences of combinations of a gray scale. In general, the gray scale of a image is 25. When calculating the texture feature which are from the the gray level co – occurrence matrix, it request the gray scale image is far less than 256. That is mainly because of matrix dimension is larger and the size of the window is smaller. If the texture is very good

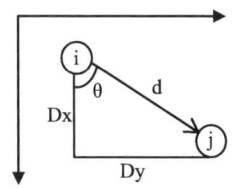

Fig. 3 Pixel gray level co – occurrence matrix

to describe, window size is larger, and it can greatly increase the amount of calculation. Furthermore, each type of boundary areas of the error rate is bigger when the window size is big. So we need do image histogram specification before calculation of gray level co-occurrence matrix to reduce the image gray scale. General the gray scale of a image is 8 or 16 after image histogram specification.

In this paper, we extract texture features from GLCM. Haralick[15] export some of the statistical parameters that describe the texture characteristics, Then 13 features (step d = 1, the angle of 0 degree direction) are extracted: Energy, Correlation, Inertia, Entropy, Inverse Difference Moment, Sum Average, Sum Variance, Sum Entropy, Difference Average, Difference Variance, Difference Entropy, Information measure of correlation, Information measure of correlation. The common used definitions are shown as follows:

Energy:

$$ASM = \sum_{i=1}^{l} \sum_{j=1}^{l} P(i, j)^2 \tag{1}$$

Energy mainly reflects texture thickness. The targer the value, the more coarse texture. The maximum of 1, p (i, j) is sonly one element in the value of 1, other is 0. The minimum is 1/L. uniform distribution of p (i, j), image gray difference.

Entropy:

$$Ent = -\sum_{i=1}^{l} \sum_{j=1}^{l} P(i, j) \, lb \{P(i, j)\} \tag{2}$$

Entropy reflects texture complexity. The greater the entropy value, texture is more complex; The maximum is lb (L^2), p (i, j) is evenly distributed. Smaller entropy value, texture, more simple, the minimum is 0, p (i, j) only one element value is 1, the other is 0.

Inverse Difference Moment:

$$IDM = \sum_{i=1}^{l} \sum_{j=1}^{l} P(i, j) / (1 + (i-j)^2) \tag{3}$$

Inverse Difference Moment local image gray balance metric, A maximum of 1, p (i, j) are located in the main diagonal, the local image gray unchanged, A minimum of 1/ (1 + (L-1)²), p (i, j) only distributed in the (L1) or (1, L) point, the whole image and gray-scate difference.

$$Con = \sum_{i=1}^{l} \sum_{j=1}^{l} (i-j)^2 P(i, j) \tag{4}$$

It reflects the image intensity and texture. The larger the value, texture groove deeper, the visual effect was clear. The maximum (L-1), p (i, j) are only distributed in the (L1) or (1, L) point. Minimum of 0 and P (i, j) are located on the main diagonal, the local image completely uniform, no gray-scale difference, no contrast.

In order to find feature vector with the crowd density high correlation, we use PCA in the 13 feature vector for data dimension reduction, and strong correlations of four dimensional feature vector is obtained. Figures (4-7) are the contribution rate of the 4-dimensional feature vector dimensionality reduction for each group of experimental images respectively; they are accounted for more than 99%.

C. Tamura texture feature extraction

In the psychological research Based on human visual perception, Tamura et al. [16] proposed the expression of texture feature. Tamura texture characteristics of six components corresponding to the psychology Angle on the texture characteristics of six kinds of properties. They are coarseness contrast directionality line likeness regularity and roughness. When the crowd density is high, coarseness, contrast, direction, roughness of Tamura texture features is smaller. On the other hand, the population density is small, the value of Tamura texture features is high. The data of some experiment images as follows:

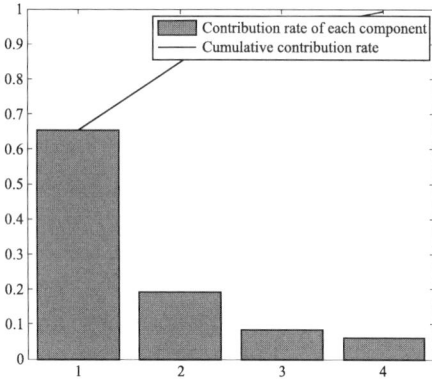
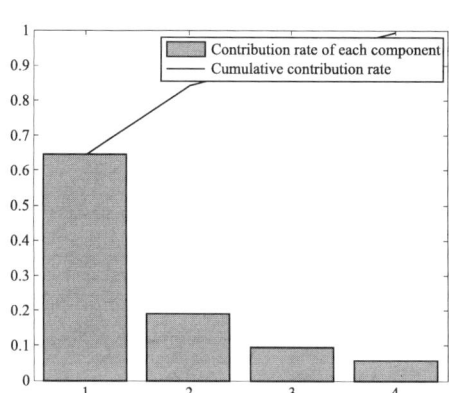

Fig. 4 The contribution rate of the first group of experiments

Fig. 5 The contribution rate of the second group of experiments

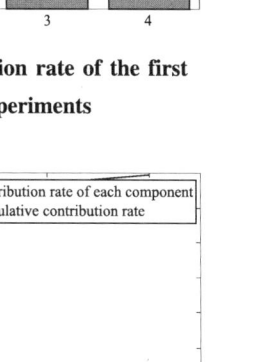
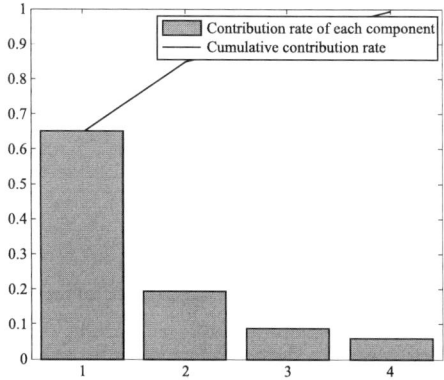

Fig. 6 The contribution rate of the second group of experiments

Fig. 7 The contribution rate of the forth group of experiments

The experiment images are from a video of the crowd. The crowd flow is from little to much and then gradually reduce after the monitoring scope. So, the density of crowd is small at beginning, and then it becomes high gradually. From table I, we can know that the value of Tamura texture feature become small when the density is high. (there is a little exception when calculate the value of direction for some reasons.)

The formula of Coarseness, contrast, direction, roughness is as follows:

Coarseness:

1) calculating moving averages, for the window $2k*2k$, the moving average are:

$$a_k(i,j) = \sum_{i=i-2^{k-1}}^{i+2^{k-1}-1}\sum_{j=j-2^{k-1}}^{j+2^{k-1}-1} \frac{p(i,j)}{2^{2k}} \tag{5}$$

2) Calculate the horizontal and vertical deviation:

$$c_k(i,j) = \max(|a_k(i-2^{k-1},j) - a_k(i+2^{k-1},j)|, |a_k(i,j-2^{k-1}) - a_k(i,j+2^{k-1})|) \tag{6}$$

3) To determine the size of the window:

$$\hat{k}(i,j) = argmax\, c_k(i,j) \tag{7}$$

4) Calculate the average size of the window and get the

$$Fcrs = \frac{1}{wh}\sum_{(i,j)} 2^{k(i,j)} \tag{8}$$

Contrast:

$$Fcon = \frac{\sigma}{\sqrt[4]{\alpha^4}} \tag{9}$$

Direction:

$$\text{Fdir} = \sum_{p}^{n_p} \sum_{\theta\mathit{l}w_n} (\theta - \theta_p)^2 H_D(\theta) \tag{10}$$

Roughness is the synthesis of the Coarseness and contrast two properties.

D. SVM classifier prediction

LIBSVM is a library for Support Vector Machines (SVMS). The LIBSVM is developed and designed by Lin Chih – Jen Taiwan University. It is a simple and easy – to – use support vector machines tool for classification (C – SVC, nu – SVC), regression (epsilon – SVR, nu – SVR), and distribution estimation. The package can be obtained on the Internet for free[17]. The goal is to help users to easily apply SVM to their applications. LIBSVM has gained wide popularity in machine learning and many other areas.

In this part, we fused four texture features extracted by Tamura and GLCM. Crowd density leveled by manual calibration. Qualitative description the crowd density monitoring area, it is classified according to crowd density. Crowd density is usually divided into five types. They are very low, low, medium, high, and very high. The scope of each type is related to the service level. Table II shows the Polus about the definition of service level in 1983. Table III shows the relationship between density of classification and the service level (monitoring area is 15 m^2). Due to the camera is stationary in this the experimental data. Population flow is from little to much and then gradually reduce after the monitoring scope. According to the number of features in the data sets, this paper will divide into the crowd density four parts: low, low, medium and high, which are labeled 1, 2, 3, 4 respectively.

TABLE 1　THE EXTRACTION RESULTS OF EXPERIMENTAL IMAGE TAMURA TEXTURE FEATURES

Tamura texture feature	Coarseness	contrast	direction	Roug – hness
Image1	56.9190	46.7000	1.0884	101.889
Image2	56.8888	46.0192	1.0753	101.179
Image3	56.8801	45.3414	1.0207	100.562
Image4	56.8708	45.0668	1.0169	100.345
Image5	56.8671	44.6839	1.0069	101.003
Image6	56.8580	44.3157	0.9727	99.8334
Image7	56.8198	43.6214	0.9870	99.6587
Image8	56.8187	43.3374	0.9959	99.4735
Image9	56.7711	42.9091	0.9509	94.3515
Image10	56.7367	42.7787	0.9397	94.2932

TABLE 2　THE SERVICE LEVEL DEFINITION

The service level	Crowd density (person/m^2)
A: Normal people	≤0.6
B: Dense stream of people	0.6 ~ 0.75
C1: Dense stream of people	0.75 ~ 1.25
C2: Very dense stream of people	1.25 ~ 2.0
D: Congestion crowd	>2.0

TABLE 3　RELATIONSHIP BETWEEN DENSITY CLASSIFITON AND THE SERVICE LEVEL

Density classification	The number range	Density level	service level
Very low	0 ~ 10	1	A, B
low	11 ~ 20	2	C1
medium	21 ~ 35	3	C2, D
high	36 ~ 50	4	D

TABLE 4   BENCHMARK DATA Data set (PETS2009)

Data set (PETS2009)	Total images	training set	test set
S1_ L2.14 - 06 (1)	200	160	40
PETS2009 S1_ L2.14 - 31 (1)	130	90	40
PETS2009 S1_ L1.13 - 57 (1)	220	—	40
PETS2009 S1_ L1.13 - 59 (1)	240	200	40

3   EXPERIMENTAL RESULTS

All the images used in this paper are derived from PETS2009 benchmark data[18]. Table IV shows that the training set and test set of every experiment group. The total number of images is 790 in our experiment.

The four groups of images were adopted from the same camera in the same scene but at different times and under different lighting conditions. Images are JPG format of the size 768 * 576. Final experiments classification prediction results as shown in Figure (8, 9, 10, 11).

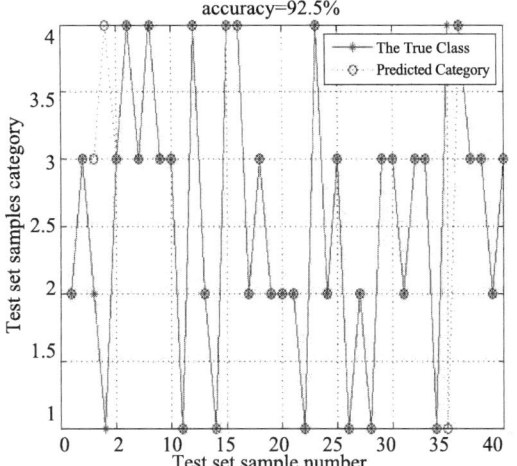

Fig. 8   The predicted results of the first set of data

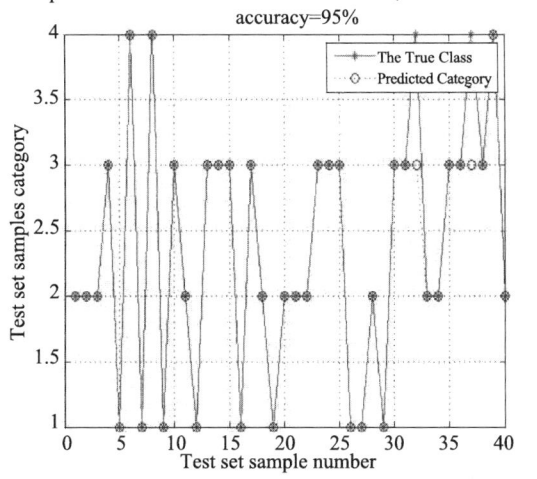

Fig. 9   The predicted results of the second set of data

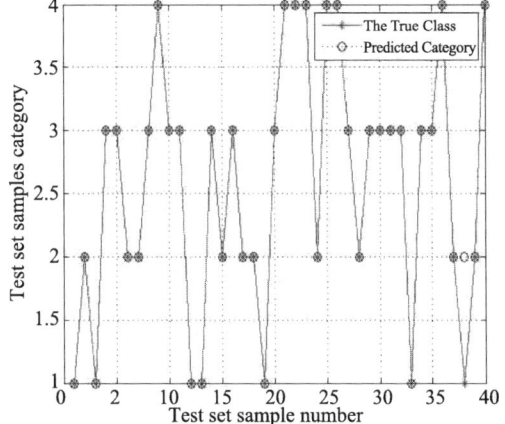

Fig. 10   The predicted results of the third set of data

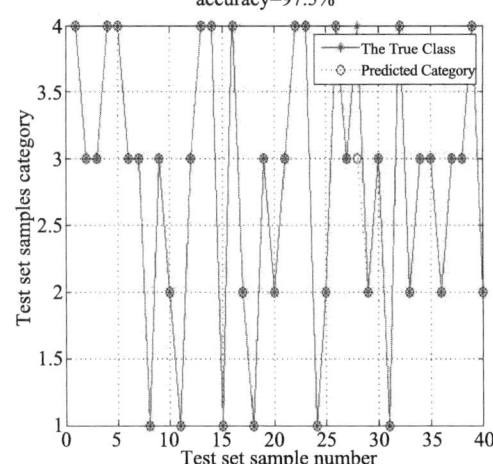

Fig. 11   The predicted results of the fourth set of data

The experimental groups are shown in table IV and V. The numbers of first group are 200 images. we selected 160 images randomly for training and the remaining 40 to test. The numbers of second group are 130 images and then selected 90 images randomly for training and the remaining 40 to test. The numbers of third group are 220 images and we selected 180 images randomly for training and the remaining 40 to test. The numbers of forth group are 240 images. we selected 200 images randomly for training and the remaining 40 to the test. If we extract the texture feature only with GLCM to estimate the density of crowd, the average accuracy rate is 90%. Table VI is the result compared with the method which just use gray level co-occurrence matrix (GLCM) to extract the texture features. At the same time, the comparison with other methods by the similar way is shown in table VII[19]. From table VII We can know that Marana and Wu extracted the same texture feature but the feature pretreatment are different. Chan used Pixel and texture feature to estimate the crowd density. Our method extracted texture feature by GLCM and Tamura and the feature pretreatment was PCA. Finally, we can see that the accuracy rate of our method is more exact than others.

TABLE 5 PREDICTION ACCURACY STATICS TRAINING SAMPLE AND TEST SAMPLE

Experimental group	Accuracy of training samples	Accuracy of test samples
The first group (S1_ L2.14-06)	99.375% (159/160)	92.5% (37/40)
The second group (S1_ L2.14-31)	97.778% (88/90)	95% (38/40)
The third group (S1_ L1.13-57)	99.444% (179/180)	97.5% (39/40)
The fourth group (S1_ L1.13-59)	99.5% (199/200)	97.5% (39/40)
average accuracy rate	99.024%	95.5%

TABLE 6 COMPARED WITH THE METHOD ONLY USE GLCM TO EXTRACT TESTURE FEATURE

Experimental group	Accuracy of training samples	Accuracy of test samples
(S1_ L2.14-06)	90% (36/40)	92.5% (37/40)
(S1_ L2.14-31)	87.5% (35/40)	95% (38/40)
(S1_ L1.13-57)	90% (36/40)	97.5% (39/40)
(S1_ L1.13-59)	92.5% (37/40)	97.5% (39/40)
average accuracy rate	90%	95.5%

TABLE 7 COMPARED WITH OTHER EXPERMIMENTAL RESULTS

Author	People feature	Feature pretreatment	crowd analysis	Accuracy
Marana[3]	GLCM	...	neural net	High-density: 93.0%
Wu[8]	GLCM	Projection deformity correction	SVM	91.3%
Chan[9]	Pixel and Texture	Projection deformity correction	Statistical-regression	more than 90%
Our	GLCM and T-amura	PCA	SVM	95.5%

4 CONCULSION

Considering the real-time and accuracy of the estimation the crowd density, extracting feature vector which has high correlation with the crowd density is worth studying. This paper introduces a new image texture feature called Tamura for crowd density estimation. The features GLCM are reduced dimension by PCA method, which can obtain the features with high correlation to the crowd scenes. The experimental results show that the method can improve the classification accuracy of prediction. However, the calculation of support vector machine (SVM) method is large, and how to obtain the optimal parameters which will be further studied in the future.

ACKNOWLEDGEMENT

This work was supported by the National Nature Science Foundation of China (Grant No. 61271370). We thank PETS for sharing its source images, and the reviewers for insightful comments. We also would like to thank teachers Jinhua Wang and Haitao Lou's guidance and help in the process of writing my paper.

REFERENCES

[1] Nikos Paragios, Visvanathan Ramesh. A MRF – based Approach for Real – time Subway Monitoring. IEEE Trans, 2001 (1): 1034 – 1040.

[2] H. Rahmalan, M. S. Nixon, J. N. Carter. On Crowd density estimation for surveillance [M] //IEEE Int Conf. Crime Detection and Precention, 2006: 540 – 545.

[3] Wu Xinyu, Liang Guoyuan, Lee Ka Keung, Xu Yangsheng. Crowd Density Estimation Using Texture Analysis and Learning. [M] //IEEE International Conference on Robotics and Biomimetics. 2006: 214 – 219.

[4] CHAN A B, LIANG Z S J, VASCONCELOS N. Privacy preserving crowd monitoring: Counting people without people models or tracking [EB/OL]. 2008.

[5] Qing WEN, Chengcheng JIA et al. People Number Estimation in the Crowded Scenes Using Texture Analysis Based on Gabor Filter [J]. Journal of Computational Information Systems, 2011, 7 (11): 3754 – 3763.

[6] Zhaoxiang Zhang, Min Li. Crowd density estimation based on statistical analysis of local intra – crowd motions for public area surveillance [J]. Optical Engineering, 2012, 5 (14).

[7] D. B. Yang, H. H. Gonzalez – Banos, L, J, Guibas. Counting people in crowds with a real – time network of simple image sensors. Proceedings [M] //Ninth IEEE International Conference on Computer Vision, 2003, 1: 122 – 129.

[8] Antonio Albiol, Maria Julia Silla, Alberto Albiol and Jos'e Manuel Mossi: Video Analysis using Corner Motion Statistics [M] //Proceedings 11th IEEE International Workshop on PETS, Miami, 2009 (16).

[9] Donatello Conte, Pasquale Foggia, Gennaro Percannella et al. A Method for Counting Moving People in Video Surveillance Videos, Eurasip Journal on Advances in Signal Processing Volume, 2010.

[10] Shafin Rahman, Sheikh Motahar Naim et. al. Performance of PCA Based Semi – supervised Learning in Face Recognition Using MPEG – 7 Edge Histogram Descriptor [J]. Journal of Multimedia. 2011 (10).

[11] Shaobo Zhong, Dongsheng Zou. Web Page Classification using an Ensemble of Support Vector Machine Classifiers [J]. Journal of Network. 2011 (11).

[12] [Haiyu Song, Xiongfei Li et al. Adaptive Feature Selection and Extraction Approaches for Image Retrieval based on Region [J]. JOURNAL OF MULTIMEDIA. 2010 (2).

[13] Gang Xie, Tianrui Cao, Chengdong Yan. Texture Features Extraction of Chest HRCT Images Based on Granular Computing [J]. Journal of Multimedia. 2010 (12).

[14] Chengcheng Gao, Xiaowei Hui. GLCM – Based Texture Feature Extraction [J]. Journal of Computer Applications. 2010.

[15] Haralick R M. Statistical and Structural Approaches to Texture [J]. Proc. of the IEEE, 1979 (5): 786 – 804.

[16] Ideyuki Tamura, et al. Texture Features Corresponding to Visual Perception [J]. IEEE Trans. on Systems, Man and Cybernetics, 1978, 8 (6): 460 – 473.

[17] http: //www. csie. ntu. edu. tw/ ~ cjlin/.

[18] http: //www. cvg. rdg. ac. uk/PETS2009/.

[19] Su Hang, Zheng Shibao et al. Survey of Crowd Flow and Density Estimation in Video Surveillance [J]. Video Engineering. 2009, 33 (11).

The Application of Permanent Magnet Electric Machine on Electrical Wheelchair

Dou Xiaoxia　Tong Qiming

I INTRODUCTION

China is the earliest country in finding the characters of permanent magnet materials and applying into production. Permanent magnet DC motor not only keeps its advantage of its good performance of separately excited DC motor but also omit the exciting windings. It has simple structure, reliability operation, and small in size, light in weight, and even more with high efficiency. It is widely applied in many areas in modern society. With the worse trend of aging of population and increased living standard, both aged people and disabled have eager desires to electrical wheelchairs. Electrical wheelchair is used for disabled and people in walking difficulties as small walking tools for indoor and outdoor use. Advanced countries (Japan, Germany, etc) have developed such equipment into the market in 1970s while at that time China had not realized it. Driving motor, as the core part in electrical wheelchair will directly influence its function. ZD281 type permanent magnet DC motor is applied in the DLY-1 type electrical wheelchair which is the first prototype in China. This may be an inspiration to increase the performance and cost ratio and to improve the quality of wheelchair and its driving motor.

II COMPOSITION OF ELECTRICAL WHEELCHAIR SYSTEM AND THE CHARACTER OF DRIVING MOTOR

A. Basic Function and Composition of Electrical Wheelchair

Electrical wheelchair uses its sole control handle to adjust the speed. It can easily move forth and back and turn left and right so to ensure safety. These rely on the coordination among electrical control part, mechanical transfer part and structure part. It is a typical mechanical and electrical integrated comprehensive product.

The wheelchair system is composed of: main frame, left and right handrail and supporting foot. The executive mechanism includes motor and driving system. The control system is located on top of the right handrail. Operation handle and indications of normal and under voltage are equipped on the control box. Direction and speed can be freely adjusted within the range which the handle can move. Junction box and power are also could be found. The electrical wheelchair uses battery as the power, with two motors driving. The signal which produced by the control part control the terminal voltage of the motor after amplified. Step less speed regulating in wide range and synchrony control of two motors can be realized. The circuit is controlled by photoelectric to change the two motors' direction which has different logic order to reach movement on each direction.

B. Technical Data and Specification

The motor should transfer sufficient torque to be driven safely and reliable within the speed limit under load as it is the core executive part in the electrical wheelchair. Meanwhile its voltage and current should match the power. Technical target should be determined during design stage. That is under rated voltage, with rated load deflecting torque, the motor should meet designed speed and current. After this, the data of quantity of electricity and mechanics of driving motors can be decided. This is the guarantee to ensure the motor moving reliability and with good performance.

[Author Introduction] Dou XIaoxia, Tong Qiming, Beijing Union University.

Main technical parameters are: rated voltage U_N, rated speed n_N, rated power P_N, rated working current I_N, etc. Current and speed with no load and brake data sometimes also regulated when considering production control and commissioning. The motor can rotate clock and counter clock and in continuously operation with good mechanical feature.

The specific design point of permanent magnet DC motor when compared with general purpose DC motor is that the motor used for wheelchair should strictly meet the special operational requirements. Condition should also be considered.

- Voltage should match power. Because the reasonable fluctuation of battery (see relevant standard), above mentioned rated voltage means nominal voltage. Tolerance should be considered to ensure the wheelchair will be driven normally when actually voltage higher or lower than the rated voltage.

- The motor drives the wheelchair moving by transmission mechanism. The actual torque, force, flywheel moment and mass should be reduced on motor shaft according to speed ratio. Improvement of loading capacity and transmission system will influence the requirement of motor performance.

- Temperature rising, noise and life period which are common design data should also be considered. Normally there is only general limitation for motor current. Efficiency will be decided according to economical regulations. Under some circumstances, being the limitation of the whole wheelchair volume and battery capacity, and long time operational life period, more strictly requirements on current and efficiency will be raised.

Generally speaking, strictly requirements on electrical wheelchair motors are necessary. That is based on meeting the sufficient output torque or power; the input current should be as low as possible with the efficient as high as possible. Meanwhile, the volume of the motor should be as small as possible with the weight as low as possible.

III STRUCTURE AND ELECTROMAGNETISM DESIGN

A. Structure of Permanent Magnet DC Motor used in Electrical Wheelchair.

ZD281 prototype structure is shown in Fig. 1. The sketch is a small power permanent magnet DC motor applied in the fist electrical wheelchair in China.

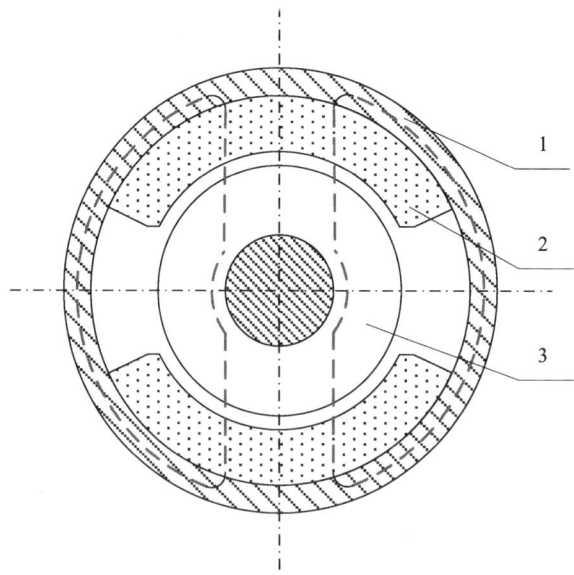

Fig. 1 Prototype structure of driving motor

1 – Housing case; 2 – tile shape magnet pole; 3 – armature

There are all kinds of permanent magnet materials with different performance data. When designing the motor, big enough magneto motive force and magnetic flux which produced in the magnetic circuit by the permanent magnetic material should be guaranteed. Different permanent magnet material has different shape of magnetic steel. For the design of small power permanent magnet DC motor, ferrite permanent magnet materials with low cost should be considered first. Only when the ferrite permanent magnet materials could not meet the requirements, can rare earth permanent magnet materials be considered. The customers in driving the electrical wheelchairs are normally aged and disabled people, reduce cost is more important.

Considering ferrite permanent magnet materials which have higher coercivity and economic factor, the magnet pole of the permanent magnet motor applied in electric wheelchair use single structure that is tile shape ferrite material is chosen as the pole. Its outstanding features are higher residual magnetism and coercivity, lower relative permeability response, strong anti-magnetic capability. Try to design the working point above the turning point in the demagnetize curve, thus the return line will overlap the demagnetize curve. [1]

B. Electromagnetism Design Method and Key Data

The ideal magnet design method of permanent magnet DC motor is based on setting up a system of equations between performance data and the data to be confirmed then derivation. [2] As it is know the interior structure of the motor is complicated, it is not easy to set up equation and derive the evaluation. Thus makes the procedure uncertainty. In order to get the best solution, a lot of programs have been carried and compared. That is under similar conditions like volume, weight and materials, different results can be reached to meet the design data. This is the uncertainty. Theoretically, there exists the most perfect solution, but each solutions have its advantages and disadvantages, how to decide which is the most perfect one? When viewing at different point or under specific conditions, different the most perfect solutions will be made.

People are looking for a bright new method on motor design and analysis for many years. Up to now, MATLAB is the most popular interaction software. [3] It is used for calculation, design and analysis in the motor design process.

In the wheelchair motor design, theory analysis with computer aided design has been carried on. During design stage, first, think of the rated data and technical requirements, main dimension relationship equations and experienced formula to determine the main dimension of the motor and relevant data. Then calculate the magnet circuit, electrical circuit and performance. After this, analysis the results to judge if it is meet the given technical target. If not, adjust structure and winding, etc data, recalculation. And so on to get the best result.

According to the performance requirements of the wheelchair, its equipped driving motor should reach the following data.

Nominal voltage: 24V, speed: 2800r/min, current: 4.5A, power: 80W, current with no load: ≤2A

Some parameters have decision function to the results in the design stage. Traditional design is based on experienced data to determine the parameters then after many times adjustment to reach a satisfied result. Now this time the design is based on analyzing manual calculation program then testing and adjusting by self developed permanent magnet motor computer aided design software. This can avoid the mistakes by manual calculation so to increase the accuracy. Moreover, this reduced the design period rapidly and increased the efficiency. A better result can be reached. Results of the key structural parameters of the design are shown in Table 1.

TABLE 1 KEY DATA OF THE WHEELCHAIR MOTOR

outside diameter of the base	$D_j = 9$ cm	thickens of the case	$\Delta j = 0.2$ cm
inside diameter of magnetic steel	$D_{mi} = 6.7$ cm	outside diameter of magnetic steel	$D_{me} = 8.6$ cm
outside diameter of armature	$D_{c2} = 6.5$ cm	length of steel core in armature	$l_{Fe} = 3.1$ cm

IV MOTOR CHARACTERS AND OPERATIONAL TEST

Under laboratory conditions, the wheelchair motor starts with no load, and then gradually increases load torque. Record the motor testing voltage, armature current, speed and other physical data. The curve by testing and calculation is shown in Fig. 2. These are speed and efficiency characters of wheelchair motor. From the curve, it is found that under rated voltage and specified load condition, both the armature current and the motor speed can satisfy the design requirements.

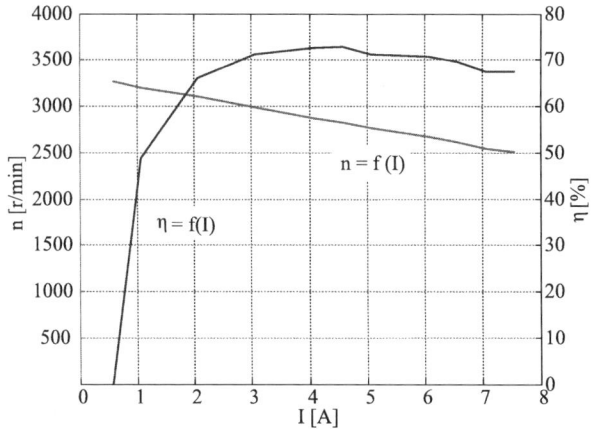

Fig. 2　Character of the wheelchair motor

The ZD281 type permanent magnet DC motor is equipped on the DLY－1 type electrical wheelchair prototype and put into use. At 24V voltage, the prototype carried the items per the listing on table 2 for moving, driven on slope, speed adjusting and brake performance test. The results show that the wheelchair and its equipped motors reached the technical requirements using the Japanese JIS9203 as a reference. And it passed the technical authentication by relevant department in HeBei province.

TABLE 2　PERFORMANCE TEST OF THE WHEELCHAIR MOTOR

items	contents and results
moving test	Five motions can be finished: move forward and backward with two motors synchrony, one forward and the other backward, the left turns and the right stops, the right turns and the left stops. Whiling driving on even road, no aberration.
speed adjusting	the speed adjusting range of driving wheel meets the requirement: 0 ~ 100r/min
driven on slope	No abnormal happened when driving over stairs of 25mm in height, ditch with 25mm in width and slope and with 5° driving along S shape. Good performances when motor start on slope top and bottom.
current test	Current without load is 1.9A, working current is 4.5A, start current is 7A, and stall current is 30A.
brake performance	Stall test is for 30s when meet obstacles. Temperature rise is within permission range.

V　CONCLUSIONS

Electrical wheelchair is a typical mechanical and electrical integrated device. The driving motor as the core executive part has a direct influence in realizing the function of the wheelchair. After understanding the features of the motor, use theory analysis combined with computer aided method to adjust reduced the design period and increased the efficiency. The motor is now equipped in DLY－1 type electrical wheelchair which is the first produce in China. It also passed the authentication by HeBei province. With the science and technology developed, modern direct current driven technique combined with digital design method will provide brighter space to optimize the motor. Device for aged and disabled people has a huge potential market.

ACKNOWLEDGMENT

The authors acknowledge the assistance of Beijing Jing Wei Electrical Motor and Appliance limited company, Department of Civil Affairs of Hebei Province, etc. during the product design and development period. Also research team of DLY－1 electrical wheelchair and volunteers in driving the model made very valuable suggestions.

REFERENCES

[1] Renyuan TANG. Theory and Design of Modern Permanent Magnet Electric Machine [M]. Beijing: Machinery Industry Press, 1997. 12.

[2] Xiaoxia DOU. Computer Aid Design System for Electric Windshield Wiper Assembly—The Design of Windshield Wiper Motor [J], Journal of Beijing Union University [J]. 1997, 29 (3): 19 – 25.

[3] Jimmie J. Cathey. Wenjin DAI. Electric Machines: Analysis and Design Applying MATLAB [M]. Beijing: Electronic Industry Press, 2006. 7.

[4] Edwards. J. D. Electrical Machines [M]. British: 1986.

Study on Active Ingredient of Ailanthus Leaves

Gu Tiaohao Liu Wanying Huo Qing and Yu Xiao

INTRODUCTION

Ailanthus altissima commonly known as tree of heaven, in Standard Chinese as chouchun is a deciduous tree in theSimaroubaceae family. It is native to both northeast and centralChina and Taiwan. A. altissima is a medium – sized tree thatreaches heights between 17 and 27 metres with a diameter atbreast height of about 1 metre. The leaves are large. They rangein size from 30 to 90 cm in length and contain 10 – 41 leafletsorganised in pairs. The leaflets are ovate – lanceolate with entiremargins, somewhat asymmetric and occasionally not directlyopposite to each other. Each leaflet is 5 to 18 cm long and 2.5to 5 cm wide. They have a long tapering end while the baseshave two to four teeth, each containing one or more glands atthe tip. The leaflets' upper sides are dark green in colour withlight green veins, while the undersides are more whitish green. The flowers are small and appear in large panicles up to 50cm in length at the end of new shoots.

Recent research determined that the extract could applyin amebicide1 and insecticide2 as well. Other than those, a newtest shows that the extract had prominence control effect ontobacco mosaic virus3. They found that the extract not onlyinhibits the spread of infection, but also controls the speeds ofthe virus to reproduce.

Lv[4], determined that components of the bark of A. altissima which was extracted by Soxhlet extraction and withdiethyl ether as solvent, played a repellent effect on Linposcelispaeta (Pearman). A bioactivity experiment on tobacco pestsfurther shows the status of the research5. In brief the methodology is as: diposed of samples 1, 2 and 3 day, respectively, the repellent rate accounted for 93.71, 87.75 and 76.14%. Even the contact toxicity of extract is feeble to against tobacco beetle, there is a significant suffocating effect to the tobacco beetle. There is a high adjust mortality ratio, about 100%, when the concentration of extract upper than 1.50×10^{-4} and processing under suffocation for 48 h.

In test of toxicology, Cao et al. 6 determined that the active ingredients in water, ethanol, diethyl ether and acetone extract of tree bark and leaf had evident toxic effect against the longicron pest6. In comparison, we found that the acetone extract had the best toxic effect and the diethyl ether could be the best solvents that extract active ingredients from plant and its ability of extracting active ingredients is superior to others.

EXPERIMENTAL

A. altissima leaves were collected from Beijing Union University College of chemical engineering, biological Baicao garden collection. Ethanol, chloroform, ethyl acetate, acetone, petroleum ether, methanol, formic acid and silica gel G were procured from silica gel G Beijing chemical reagent company.

Rotate evaporator RE – 52 A, Dual wavelength UV lamp, (Shanghai biochemical instrument factory), Electric heatingsleeve: model number ZDHW (Beijing zhongxingweiye Instrument Co. Ltd), chromatography column $\Phi 2$ cm × 70 cm, chromatography cylinder: size 150 × 100 × 200 mm; gas chromatography – mass spectrometry: GCMS – QP2010 Shimadzu, glass capillary (hard neutral glass): bore size 0.9 – 1.1mm, wall thickness 0.10 – 0.15mm, length 100 mm (Instrument factory of West China University of Medical Sciences), thin layer plate: the self – made; U – 1810 PC double beam UV – Vis spectrophotometer, Japan Shimadzu; constant temperature water bath oscillator: model number THZ – 82; Shimadzu LC – 10 ATVP high performance liquid chromatograph,

---

[Author Introduction] Gu Tianhao, Liu Wanying, Huo Qing, Yu Xiao, Biochemical Engineering College of Beijing Union University.

Shimadzu Shimadzu – CLASS – VP. V6. 12. SP4 workstation; electronic balance: BS210S, (Beijing Saiduolisi balance limited production); three ultraviolet analyzer (Shanghai Kang Huasheng instrument factory); sprayer (Zhejiang Huangyan City, sprayer Co. Ltd.); circulating water type multipurpose vacuum pump: SHB – 95 (Henan Yuhua Instrument Co. ltd.)

VARIAN Prosta 210 Preparative chromatography workstation, C18 VARIAN Dyamax 250 * 21.4 mm (L * ID).

Extraction of major components of the leaf: Clean off the dirt with water and stored it in a cool dry place. Once theleaf starts to dry, chopping it in patches. The leaf is extracted by ethanol through heating reflux about 2 h then purified by rotary evaporator Separated by TLC: Using the silica gel G as the adsorbent mix with the water (1:3). When it turns out to be mushy, spread it on the layer about 2 mm thickness. Using the capillary absorbs the sample and drops it on the layer. Putting the ethyl acetate, methanol, petroleum ether together as the developing solvent and then pouring the developing solvent in chromatography cylinder. After about 20 min that the developing solvent was saturated, putting the complete layer in and waiting for 20 min approximately. Observe the location and the color of spot under the UV.

GC – MS analysis: Shimadzu Corporation GC – MS QP2010 gas chromatography mass spectrometry; gas chromatography conditions: column type: DB – 5 ms 30m, 0.25mm; column temperature programmed conditions: initial temperature 80℃, keep the time 2 min, 20℃/dL to 250℃, keep the time: 30 min; split ratio: 10:1; inlet temperature: 250℃. Mass spectrometric conditions: ion source temperature: 250℃; electron energy: 0ev; scanning range: 20 – 650m/z.

RESULTS AND DISCUSSION

Chromatographic separation of active ingredients: The separation of TLC is choosing appropriate developing solvent, which depending on the activity of adsorbent and the polarity of separated samples. Because of different action of various components in a developing solvent, in the layer, the larger polar solvent could moves compounds further, the small polar solvent that could drops off the elusive power and the Rf value of the larger polar solvent, in the medium polar solvent, two solvents which had vast polar difference were mixed uniformly. According to the theories of chromatography, the polarity of the developing solvent must close to the separated components in order to get a superior effect of separation.

The result of using ethyl acetate, petroleum ether, methanol as mobile phase are proved by mass of preliminary experiment results and the separating effect was evident by means of changing the proportion of them. The chromatography result of A. altissima leaf extracts in different solvent systems is shown in the Table – 1.

TABLE – 1 ACTIVE INGREDIENT OF A. altissima LEAF ISOLATED BY TLC

Expand system (v/v/v)	Expand the case	Expand results
Ethyl acetate: petroleum ether: methanol = 6:16:1.5	Spots huddled together	
Ethyl acetate: petroleum ether = 8:16	Spots huddled together	
Ethyl acetate: petroleum ether: methanol = 5:16:1	Spots huddled together	

续表

Expand system (v/v/v)	Expand the case	Expand results
Ethyl acetate: petroleum ether: methanol = 6:17:1	Four spots clear separation	
Ethyl acetate: petroleum ether: methanol = 8:17:1.5	Spots huddled together	
Ethyl acetate: petroleum ether = 5:17	Spots huddled together	
Ethyl acetate: petroleum ether = 6:15	Spots huddled together	
Ethyl acetate: petroleum ether: methanol = 8:15:1	Unexpanded	
Ethyl acetate: petroleum ether: methanol = 5:15:1.5	Severe tailing	

This graph shows that the effective components of A. altissima leaf could be separated sufficiently by using ethylacetate (6mL), petroleum ether (17mL) and methanol (1mL) as the developing solvent. Sorted spots which appeared on the layer in ascending order from 1 to 8. When the developing solvent evaporated, scooping the silica gel which corresponding to every spot and then dissolved it in ethyl acetate. After filtration and precipitation, preserving the solution in penicillin bottle. Those above samples would be analyzed by GC – MS.

Analysis of active ingredient of A. altissima leaf by GCMS: We used GC – MS by standard material to identical allkinds of chromatograph peaks of compounds. Calculate the percentage composition of all kinds of compounds, according to peak area normalization method. According to the performance of the test, the DB – 5 capillary has the advantage of both non – polar column and polar column and indicated a better separating effect. Direct sample injection method are adopted in accordance with the condition of analysis as above and then established a chromatographic fingerprint of GC – MS (Fig. 1).

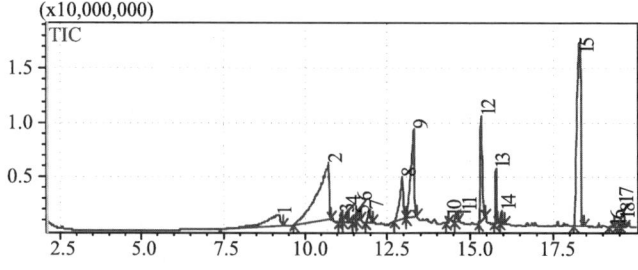

Fig. 1 Ingredient of A. altissima leaf of total ion current (TIC) chromatogra

Through analyzing by GC – MS technology, 45 chromatographic peaks were separated and 18 compounds wereidentified. The main constituents are long – chain higher fatty acids and their esters and a mass of alkylates. The data was processed by a chemical workstation and the identified components are shown in Table – 2.

TABLE-2 ANALYTICAL RESULTS OF SAMPLE BY GC-MS

No.	Chemical composition	m. f.	m. w.
1	Decane $C_{10}H_{22}$	142	
2	Tetradecane	$C_{14}H_{30}$	198
3	2,6-bis(1,1-Dimethyl-ethyl)-4-methyl-phenol	$C_{15}H_{24}O$	220
4	Nonadecane	$C_{19}H_{40}$	268
5	Octadecane	$C_{18}H_{38}$	254
6	Heneicosanoic	$C_{21}H_{44}$	296
7	Phthalic acid-2-Methyl alcohol-two ester	$C_{16}H_{22}O_4$	278
8	Sixteen alkyl acid	$C_{16}H_{32}O_2$	256
9	9,12-Diene-eighteen alkanoic acid	$C_{18}H_{32}O_2$	280
10	Hexacosane	$C_{26}H_{54}$	366
11	Hexatriacontane	$C_{36}H_{74}$	506
12	Tetracosane	$C_{24}H_{50}$	338
13	Tetratriacontane	$C_{34}H_{70}$	478
14	Heptadecanoyl	$C_{17}H_{36}$	240
15	Phthalic acid isobutyl alcohol two ester	$C_{16}H_{22}O_4$	278
16	Seventeen acid methyl ester	$C_{17}H_{34}O_2$	270
17	8,11-Diene-eighteen acid methyl ester	$C_{19}H_{34}O_2$	294
18	Methyl stearate	$C_{19}H_{38}O_2$	294

Making analysis and study on components of A. altissima leaves and we realized that 9,12-diene-eighteen alkanoic acid could treat arteriosclerosis and high blood lipid. The allelopathy of the phthalic acid isobutyl alcohol two ester on verticillium wilt of eggplant and seedling growth. The antibacterial, anti-viral effect of 3-chloro-octane is superior to berberine, mequindox and ofloxacin obviously and same as the florfenicol, otherwise, has antitumor effects[3]. Sixteen alkyl acid could inhibited the effects on inflammation and pain[7].

Isolation of components by preparative chromatography: On the base of research in TLC, the Ailanthus leaves extracts could be concentrated the extracts to 10 mL by the rotary evaporation in 75℃. Using Varian prosta 210 preparative chromatograph with C_{18} column and mobile phase of ethyl acetate, petroleum ether, methanol (25:71:4), flow rate of 2 mL/min, detection wavelength of 220 nm and 30℃ as column temperature. Collected the separated chemical components by means of interceptor technique, preparative chromatography (Fig. 2) There are seven components were separated and purified.

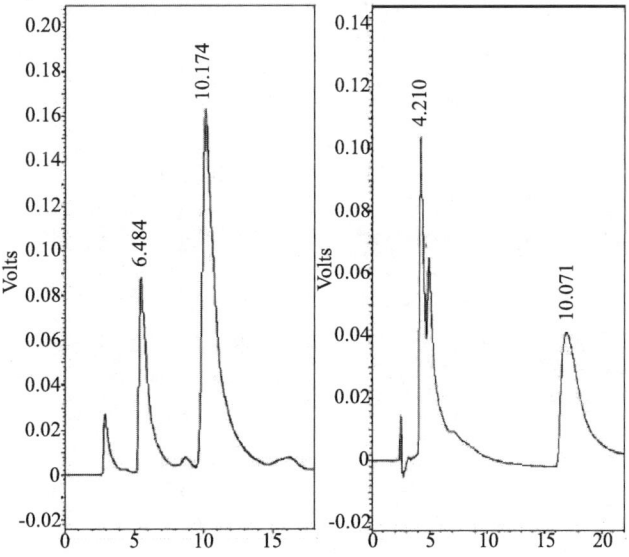

Fig. 2 Ingredient of A. altissima leaf isolated by preparative chromatography

Conclusion

According to the analysis by GC – MS, it is observed that the major active ingredients of A. altissima leaf are long – chain alkane, long chain fatty acids and their esters. The content of 9, 12 – diene – octadecane acid is highest.

REFERENCES

[1] W. J. Sun and J. F. Sheng, The Brief Book of Natural Active Constituents [M]. Peking, Press of Traditional Chinese Medicine, 1988: 16 – 17.
[2] M. J. Pascual – Villalobos and A. Robledo, Ind. Crops prod. , 8, 183 (1998).
[3] J. G. Sheng, Z. K. Zhang and Z. J. Wu, China J. Chinese Materia Medica, 32, 27 (2007).
[4] J. H. Lu, Grain Storage Pests, 36, 17 (2007).
[5] J. H. Lu, L. Li, L. Cheng, L. Jia and S. – H. Wu, Tobacco Sci. Technol. , 6, 59 (2007).
[6] B. Cao, Z. Z. Li, X. L. Ji and X. Z. Xu, J. Nanjing Forestry Univ. (Nat. Sci. Ed.), 28, 47 (2004).
[7] Y. Xiang and G. J. Zhang, The Research on the Extraction and Isolation of Liposoluble Compounds, The Pharmacological Action of Angelica sinensis, University of Chinese Medicine Institute of Traditional Chinese Medicine (TCM), Peking, 2007: 159 – 166.

艺术学类

"衣可衣,非常衣"
——三宅一生设计思想解析

李红梅

　　三宅一生(Issey Miyake)是一位伟大的时装艺术大师,他的作品集质朴、功能、现代于一体,极具创造力和视觉冲击力,被誉为"我们这个时代中最伟大的服装创造家"。自20世纪70年代以来,他不断地以全新的服装造型、独特的设计思想、不羁的陈列方式傲然独立于欧美的高级时装之外。他的设计思想似乎超越了所谓的东方文化或者西方文化的羁绊,将东方传统的含蓄之美与西方现代的设计理念不着痕迹地糅合起来,出于其中又超乎其外,极富创造性和哲理性。正如美国著名画家劳生伯格所言:"三宅是一位国际艺术家,是影响最大的日本艺术家。"

1　形式之美

　　三宅一生的服装充满了美轮美奂的形式之美,服装的外轮廓线丰富夸张,尽管设计师偏爱黑灰色系,但凡用到彩色,他的色彩就极度鲜艳饱和,具有强烈的视觉冲击力。看似不经意的折叠、印染、缠绕,其实经历了他的独具匠心。1977年,他开始设想仅用一块布就能制成一件衣服,"一块布"(APOC)的概念就此诞生。他仅仅用一个简单的几何形状,却有数种披挂缠绕的方法,服装依附于人体,呈现出不同的形式和观感。在他的手下,衣服被简化成最精华的朴素、最奢侈的简单。1990年,三宅一生对创立品牌以来独特的"一生褶"进行了改造,推出了新的"我要褶皱(Pleats Please)"系列。在这个系列中,三宅一生将永久性皱褶的面料与简单的几何图形融合在一起,一维的面料变成了立体形状的服装。更令人惊叹的是,在这些设计理念的基础上,立体主义大师三宅一生从日本折纸中吸取灵感,又推出了1325.系列(1代表简单的一块面料,3代表三维立体的廓形,2表示折叠后的二维形状,5则代表全新的多样的穿衣体验)。他把三维立体的时装折成了一个个规则的平面几何图形,将这些几何图形轻轻提拉就变出一套时装,这让整个时装界瞠目结舌,人们都不由得感叹大师的创造力。

2　材质之美

　　三宅一生被称为"面料的魔术师"。在材料的设计和运用上,三宅一生偏爱有肌理感觉的材质,日本传统的宣纸、亚麻布、白棉布、针织棉布等,都在他的创意下展现出独特的时代美感。那具有独特肌理感觉的"褶皱",就成了三宅一生招牌式的符号。每当在设计与制作之前,三宅一生总是与布料寸步

[作者简介]李红梅,北京联合大学师范学院。

不离,他会把它裹在、披挂在自己身上,感觉它、理解它,他说:"我总是闭上眼,等织物告诉我应去做什么。"三宅一生希望自己设计的褶皱能够像人体的皮肤一样,既舒适服贴而又随心所欲;同时,三宅一生又充分考虑到人体造型和运动的特点,在机器压褶的时候直接依照人体曲线或造型需要来调整裁片与褶痕。这样的材质,造就了他的服装不止是装饰性的艺术——平放的时候像一件雕塑品,更是人体着装的极致状态——穿在身上呈现出符合身体曲线和运动规律的立体几何图案,这种与西方美学及成衣传统截然相反的东方神秘主义,让全世界的人为之疯狂。

在服装材料的运用上,三宅一生也突破了时装及成衣平整光洁的材料定式,以各种各样的材料,如日本宣纸、白棉布、针织棉布、亚麻等,创造出各种肌理效果。三宅一生的"我要褶皱"系列(Pleats Please)获第八届东京原创大奖,获奖理由是"单纯而富有功能性,美丽而让人感到快乐,称之为21世纪的时尚是颇为恰当的。不仅是设计,从面料的处理开始坚持艺术性和实用性的融合,这样的创造不愧为'服装革命'"。

  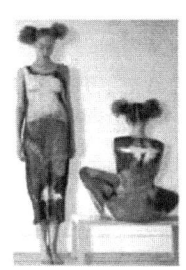

3　结构之美

三宅一生的作品,看似随心所欲,其实都是经过了严谨科学的计算,赋予"一块布"看似无结构的结构,也正是这种独特的"结构",构成了三宅一生服装艺术的核心,充分体现了他对东方服装内外空间尺度的把控能力。

三宅一生擅长立体主义设计,"服装是覆盖在运动着的身体上的一块布",他希望自己设计的服装能够和人体互动,共同来创作各种形态和表情。多年来,三宅一生秉承着这一设计理念,既借鉴东方传统的宽衣平面制衣技术,又融合了西方传统的窄衣立体裁剪技术,将传统的合体造型的结构掰开、揉碎、再组合,包裹缠绕形成惊人奇妙的构造,看似无形,却疏而不散。这种基于东方制衣技术、超越西方设计理念的创新模式,开创了服装设计上的解构主义风格,释放出无拘无束创造力激情的同时,又赋予作品宽泛、雍容的内涵,服装设计具有了哲学的意味。

 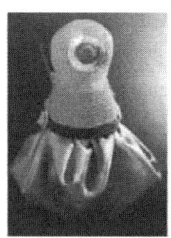 

4　工艺之美

三宅一生在制作工艺上打破了东西方的界限,将平面裁剪与立体裁剪融会贯通。他吸取日本和服的结构和裁剪特点,将披挂、包裹、缠绕、褶皱等民族工艺运用到现代服装设计中,东方的结构、西方的精神,使得他的成衣工艺超然脱俗。

三宅一生认为日本的传统纺织技术是非常出色的,但是却没有得到重视,甚至面临消亡的命运。于是,他坚持不懈地四处游走,去寻访那些各地的小染织工厂和老匠人,对那些古老的材质和面料重新改造开发,使它们焕发出新的生命力。同时,三宅一生对新技术也非常敏感,他认为技术或新材料的发明对社会而言往往是革命性的,会对设计产生重大影响。他总是及时利用新材料和新技术,对服装与身体的空间表达作出积极有效的尝试。把古典画家安格尔的名作《泉》绘制在褶皱的长裙子上或者将裙子设计成折叠的纸灯笼……衣服随着模特的肢体动作呈现出动态的褶皱，令衣者和观者如入无人之境，安然忘我。这种美，是艺术、技术和科学的和谐统一，是设计的最高境界。

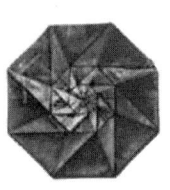

5　文化之美

三宅一生在服装界被誉为"哲人""思辨家""创造家""魔术师"等，集哲学家的智慧与设计师的灵性于一身。从"一块布"（APOC）到"我要褶皱"（Pleats Please），再到1325.系列，他的作品无不充盈着视觉上的独特性和内涵的深刻性，表达着三宅一生深邃的哲学思想，而这种思想的根源，就是植根于广博而深厚的东方文化基础之上的日本民族文化。

"东方遭遇西方"，三宅一生成功的最直接原因就是找到了东方文化和西方文化的契合点。他从东方服饰文化与哲学思想中探求全新的服装功能、装饰与形式之美，设计出了前所未有的新观念服装，即蔑视传统、舒畅飘逸、尊重个性、使身体得到最大自由的服装。"我要褶皱"就是东方服装注重空间感和西方服装注重结构严谨的有机融合。褶皱面料的设计是根源于东方宽衣文化中顺应自然，以及日本民族"折叠小宇宙"的时空观，直线裁剪更是东方服饰文化理念的精髓，而这些理念，又承借着新材料、新技术的运用以及西方服饰文化中的立体裁剪技术，赋予了服装以全新的观感和哲学的意味。

文化的核心内容是其价值和意义体系。三宅一生的设计充满着人道、人本主义的思考。他认为人们需要的是随时都可以穿的、便于旅行的、好保管的、轻松舒适的服装，而不是整天要保养、常送干洗店的"难伺候的"服装。因此，三宅一生设计的褶皱面料可以随意一卷，捆绑成一团，不用干洗熨烫，要穿的时候打开，依然是平整如新。同时，"一块布"的理念，其实是最大程度地节约资源，最优化地呈现着衣状态，最完美地表现人体与服装的空间关系。"艺术大师"关注的是生活中的每一个人，是每一个人艺术的生活方式，这是设计的本质所在，但这并不是每一位设计师都能够做到的。

6　结束语

总之，三宅一生品牌是优秀的世界女装品牌。它根植于日本的民族观念、习俗和价值观，他的产品是一些流行于全世界的，但却张扬着鲜明的日本民族风格的东西。它不仅确立了三宅一生自身的国际地位，同时也确立了东京为国际时装之都的地位。

中国先秦的《周礼·冬官·考工记》是中国早期记载传统设计工艺的一部论著，其中对于优良的设计有这样的论述："天有时，地有气，材有美，工有巧，合此四者，可以为良。"三宅一生的服装设计既遵循了这样的设计原则，又超然物外，跳出了对具体服装元素一招一式的模仿，继承了具有精神性的东方审美文化。在他的设计中，材质本身和服装与人体的关系成为被关注的中心，结构的设计往往游离于人体曲线之外，体态被完全隐蔽在服装造型当中，再加上设计师对黑、灰等晦涩色彩的偏爱，使这种极端隐藏的神秘诡异的气息与东方特有的对服装空间的演绎方式完美的结合，形成了独具日本风格的现代服装艺术。形式、材质、结构、工艺，这些都不过是外在的物质手段，是用来传达其设计思想的载体，而其真正的设计思想是站在时代高度对日本传统服装审美文化的全新演绎。

参考文献

[1] 卫臻. "一生褶"的设计特色与文化底蕴 [J]. 郑州轻工业学院学报（社科版），2007（6）.

[2] 焦宝娥. 国际服装设计大师——三宅一生 [J]. 装饰，1994（3）.

从内画艺术的发展历程看民间美术的当代传承之路

张 旗

在我国种类众多的民间美术中,中国内画壶艺术(以下简称"内画艺术")是个很有意思的民间美术类别,它的发展史就是一部流动的历史,内画艺术不仅在流动中生存下来,而且在我国民间美术保护面临极大困难的情况下,在流动中实现了发展和繁荣,它的代表流派"冀派"还在2003年被列入了我国的第一批国家级非物质文化遗产名录。

一、内画的起源和四大流派

内画艺术的产生源于内画鼻烟壶,随着400多年前鼻烟传入中国后,在清嘉庆道光(1790—1850年)年间,出现了内画艺术这一新的民间美术类别。在此后的发展中,由于种种原因,内画技艺自北京先后流动到河北、山东、广东等地发展,并在这四个地方开花结果,最终形成了中国内画艺术的"京""鲁""冀""粤"四大流派。可以说中国内画艺术的四大流派是在流动中产生和发展起来的。

当今内画鼻烟壶四派均起源于北京,其中京派的历史最为久远。北京是中国明清两代王朝的京都,内画鼻烟壶为当时皇宫贵族、达官贵人所喜爱。内画画工们汲取了京都深厚的文化底蕴和文人士大夫的审美情调,使诗书画印并茂成为京派艺术风格的主流,内画鼻烟壶的创作在清光绪年间达到鼎盛,当时名家辈出,有名有姓的内画大师就有30多位,代表人物有周乐元、马少宣、叶仲三等人(见图1、图2)。

图1 周乐元作品　　　　图2 叶仲三作品

鲁派内画主要集中在山东博山,是因山东博山籍的内画艺人毕九荣在清光绪十六年(1890)从北京回到博山后发展起来的。北京的内画鼻烟壶艺术因此传到了琉璃之乡——山东博山。画师毕九荣利用本地生产的高级琉璃水晶料做壶坯,开始创作琉璃内画鼻烟壶。自此,自成一派,即鲁派。

新中国成立后,为保护内画等民间艺术,北京市政府成立了北京工艺美术研究所(可惜早已经取消了),聘请京派内画传人叶仲三之子叶晓峰、叶菶祺任教。1958年,王习三考入北京工艺美术研究所,成为叶派内画的第一个外姓传人。"文化大革命"期间,由于内画鼻烟壶被贴上政治标签,王习三也因此被遣回老家——衡水阜城县杨庄。王习三在乡下继续创作,在阜城县杨庄村以副业形式搞起内画。内

[作者简介] 张旗,北京联合大学广告学院。

画艺术由此在河北衡水生根，由此逐渐形成了冀派内画。

20世纪六七十年代内画艺术从北京流入广东，逐渐形成了粤派内画艺术，主要在广东汕头地区，代表人物为吴松龄。

二、流动中丰富的内画技艺

内画的艺术风格受传统文人绘画风格的影响最为显著，如清末内画画工们就把"以形写神""气韵生动"等传统绘画精神作为内画画工的一个内在追求。画工们将不同的绘画题材结合自身的情感创作出具有艺术个性魅力的内画作品，从而使内画艺术呈现出多元丰富的艺术格局，如周乐元、叶仲三等人的作品是此种风格的代表。另外，清末画坛中西结合的倾向也体现在内画创作中，内画画工将西画的明暗、透光等技法及表现等造型观念，融入内画创作中，并与传统绘画的"线性"造型相结合，体现出中国审美趣味的写实性特征，体现在内画人物刻画上尤为明显，如清末著名京派内画艺人马少宣的内画人物便是中西结合的典型（见图3）。

图3　马少宣作品

内画艺术流动到不同的地域后，在当地的人文环境、地域特点的影响下，不断在继承中创新，逐渐形成了富有中华民族审美特征以及地域文化特点的内画技艺风格。因此，中国内画艺术从宫廷风格的京派，发展出了气势恢弘又细致入微的鲁派画风，中西合璧、形神兼备的冀派画风，以及线条纤秀、色彩鲜艳的粤派画风。四派在内画工具、技巧、材料等方面都有很大的创新和发展。

（1）京派内画艺术风格突出了上层文人士大夫的审美习惯，题材多取自历史故事、神话传说和文学戏剧题材，如叶仲三先生的红楼梦人物作品、其他戏剧人物作品是典型代表；在艺术元素的运用上大量选取传统山水画中的常见内容，如山水楼阁、花鸟虫鱼、人物场景等；艺术风格上追求符合当时中国画的写意特点，形成了既有精工的写实描写、又有写意表现的内画艺术特征。当今京派传承人为刘守本先生（见图4）。

（2）山东博山是琉璃之乡，盛产鼻烟壶，为鲁派内画发展提供了得天独厚的条件。鲁派最有特色的技法是能够利用瓷器上用的釉彩在鼻烟壶的内壁上作画，然后，烘烧形成内画鼻烟壶的瓷釉画，即使盛水画面也毫不受损；再一个革新是以毛笔代替竹笔作画，使博山琉璃内画成为鲁派独有的技艺。艺术风格上则融入到了源远流长的齐鲁文化中，表现题材以历史故事和神话传说见长，如以李克昌（见图5）等为代表的鲁派内画大师们创作的《水浒108将》《清明上河图》《红楼梦》《阿房宫赋》《泰山雄姿》等一大批内画艺术珍品。这些作品场面宏大、构图饱满、层次分明、刻画细微；形成了独特的鲁派内画艺术风格。

（3）冀派内画表现是在继承叶派厚朴古雅之风的基础上，糅进了鲁派细腻流畅的画法，把国画的皴、擦、染、点、勾、丝等技法引入内画，将国画技法发挥得淋漓尽致。1981年，冀派创始人王习三又成功掌握了油彩内画技法，改变了传统单一水彩作画的方式，使内画艺术呈现了形神兼备、中西结合的表现技法。王习三还发明了金属杆钩毛笔——习三弯钩笔，这种笔的笔杆可随创作需要任意改变，比以往的竹钩毛笔更灵活、牢固、耐用，成为冀派的代表工具。在内画创作题材上，冀派代表人物王习三突破了京派内画人物画只画古代人物的传统，他除创作了《清朝历代帝王帝后像》《美国历届总统肖像》《当代英国皇室成员肖像》等作品外，使内画表现题材和现实社会生活结合起来，其作品还涵盖了山水、花卉、草虫、鸟兽等众多题材。

（4）由吴松龄创始的汕头瓶内画虽是"后起之秀"，但从作画工具、绘画技法、构图形式，到瓶体造型、瓶外装饰，汕头瓶内画都具有强烈的粤派特征。其一，由于瓶内画是从鼻烟壶发展而来的，多用扁瓶。唯独汕头瓶内画受潮汕陶瓷造型影响，多用圆形玻璃瓶，这给瓶内作画增加了难度。其二、汕头瓶内画常描以金线和珐琅，突破了瓶内画无外饰的局限，更显华贵绚丽。其三、汕头瓶内画艺术风格受岭南派画风影响，线条纤秀，色彩鲜艳。在吴松龄先生之后，粤派内画的传承人为赖乙宁先生（见图6）。

图 4　刘守本作品　　　　　　图 5　李克昌作品　　　　　　图 6　赖乙宁作品

三、在流动中发展的冀派内画

  冀派的当代发展过程中，经历过两次流动。第一次流动是在"文化大革命期间"，王习三被"流动"到家乡阜城县杨庄村后，开始把内画作为一项农村副业发展起来。和在北京不同的是，内画在河北获得了空前的发展空间；在北京很少有年轻人愿意学习内画艺术，在河北却吸引了大量的年轻人加入。例如，王习三第二次招徒弟，在众多的应试者中进行挑选，最后录取了 12 名各方面素质都很优秀的年轻人。在王习三悉心培养下，这批弟子很快在全国乃至海外崭露头角，王习三创立的"冀派"由此在海内外声名远扬。另外、政府、社会、企业等各个层面的倾力支持也是在北京难以实现的，自此冀派内画在短时期内形成了广泛影响力，逐渐成为年产值 10 亿元，从业人员上万人的大型文化产业。2006 年 6 月，以原产地命名，衡水内画成功申报成为第一批国家级非物质文化遗产，2007 年 6 月 5 日，经国家文化部确定，河北省衡水的王习三成为该文化遗产项目代表性传承人，并被列入第一批国家级非物质文化遗产项目 226 名代表性传承人名单。

  第二次流动是冀派内画从河北流向北京，流向海外。2003 年，王习三先生（见图 7）和长子王自勇筹资创建了"中国内画艺术之乡展览馆"，还在石家庄市、北京市也建起了中国内画艺术博物馆。一批批冀派内画传人从河北来到北京发展，内画艺术从河北又流回了北京。从河北流向世界则标志着冀派内画发展到了走出国门、走向世界的一个新阶段，冀派传人们频繁在海外进行展览和艺术交流活动，开发新产品和新市场；还成立了冀派内画协会进行市场管理，组织扩大对外贸易，积极开拓海外市场，扩大内画艺术的文化影响力。冀派的流动发展对京派乃至整个中国内画事业发展都起到了极大的推动作用。简言之说，第一次流动属于王习三先生的被动返乡；第二次流动则是冀派内画的为赢得市场、扩大文化影响力的主动出击。在主动出击的背后，有一个关键因素起到决定性的作用和许多民间美术的家族相传、作坊相传方式不同。从 1990 年开始，王习三和儿子王自勇在衡水创建了全国唯一一所国家承认学历的内画中等专业学校——习三工艺美术中等专业学校。学校以系统、科学的教育方式，在素描、书法、美术理论和内画专业等方面给学生打下了坚实的基础，使学生毕业后既掌握了一定的理论，又能独立进行创作，为冀派内画艺术队伍的发展壮大源源不断地输送着人才。涌现出了王百川、雨农等众多内画高手（见图 8、图 9），这正是冀派能主动出击、发展繁荣的关键所在，体现了冀派内画传人面向未来、全面开放的传承观念。

图7 王习三作品　　　图8 雨农作品　　　图9 王百川作品

与冀派在流动中发展不同的是，其他三大流派固守一隅造成了发展的停滞甚至消失。作为内画艺术起源地的北京，和历史上的辉煌时期已不可同日而语，全盛期的北京知名内画师有30多人，而今天北京内画从业者也就10人左右，从技法、题材等方面来看，也是创新少，啃老本的多。鲁派历史上一度和京派同领风骚，在内画艺术技法创新、艺术表现上做出了很大的贡献，但如今随着博山的琉璃资源开发殆尽，内画传承人的减少，博山内画也处在一个发展的停滞期。作为四大流派之一的粤派就更惨了，已经处于了消失的边缘。

四、流动的实质

从内画艺术的发展历程来看，流动起到了决定性的作用；但流动只是一个表面现象，流动的实质是什么呢？对于民间美术来说，流动是一种共性的还是个性的特征？对今天的民间美术传承又有什么启示呢？下面从非物质文化遗产的流变性和活态性特征来分析流动的实质。

（1）流变性。"通常而言，物质文化遗产的传播通过复制就可以获得，依据图纸和建造方案进行复制就可以了，但非物质文化遗产的传播是一种活态流变，是继承与变异、一致与差异的辩证结合。在它的传播过程中，常常与当地的历史、文化和民族特色相互融合，从而呈现出继承和发展并存的状况"。[1]从这个论述能看到内画的流动体现了非物质文化遗产的流变性特征，既是包含民间美术在内的非物质文化遗产的共性特征，也是促使民间美术生存、发展的重要因素。从内画艺术的历史发展来看，没有流动就没有今天的四大流派，没有今天中国内画技艺丰富多样的面貌，也没有今天的冀派内画事业蓬勃发展的局面。因此，中国内画的流动发展是非物质文化遗产的流变性特征的一个典型案例。在今天的民间美术传承中，这种流变性的特征应该为民间美术的传承者们所认知，民间美术只有走出去、迎进来，和不同时间和空间的地域文化、时代文化相结合，才能不断地传承和发展下去。

（2）活态性。流动使水成为活水，流动使内画艺术成为活态的内画艺术，流动实际上是非物质文化遗产活态传承特征的一种体现。民间美术的活态性特征可以理解为两个方面，一个是传承主体的能动参与，内画流动中吸引了更多更广泛的传承主体的积极参与；另一个是指该内画艺术在当代社会、自然、生活的互动中不断生发、变异和创新[2]。例如，《非物质文化遗产概论》中写道："非物质文化遗产重视人的价值，重视活的、动态的、精神的因素，重视技术、技能的高超、精湛和独创性，重视人的创造力，以及通过非物质文化遗产体现出来的该民族的情感及表达方式、传统文化的根源、智慧、思维方式和世界观、价值观、审美观等这些意义和价值的因素"。[3]因此，我们理解流动是内画艺术乃至民间美术生命力的一个本质特点，流动在内画艺术的传承中起到了不可或缺的作用，内画艺术跨时间和空间的流动，使内画艺术成为"活"的艺术，不断焕发出创新创造的生命活力。

从以上论述可以看出，流动背后的实质是非物质文化遗产所具有的流变性和活态性特征。体现了创新和发展的思维，使内画艺术的传承和时代发展结合起来，和不同的地域文化结合起来，在新时代、新地域开出时代之花。因此，对整体处于"保护"状态的我国民间美术来说，内画艺术流动历程给出了一个有价值的传承思路和途径。

五、流动背后的原因

除了特殊的原因外，出现流动的根本原因是生存和发展的需要，和其他类别的非物质文化遗产比较而言，大部分民间美术生存和发展主要依赖市场。可以说，没有市场，就没有中国内画的四大流派；没有市场需要，冀派内画就不会向北京、向海外流动。因此，民间美术的传承，离开市场是不可能实现的。对于今天我们的大多数民间美术而言，面向市场、开发市场才是实现当代传承的根本出路。王松华等在《产业化视角下的非物质文化遗产保护》一文中写道："市场是非物质文化遗产传承的载体与传播的空间，市场是推广某种东西的最有力的载体，非物质文化遗产要保护与发展，市场化是最好的手段。当前社会的各种强势文化正是通过市场的途径得以全球化的。例如，足球运动的全球普及，市场发挥了推波助澜的作用，并形成了数额巨大的全球足球消费市场"[4]。还有刘云升在《非物质文化遗产保护的理性回归》一文中写道："既然引起文化变迁的因素是外因，文化变迁的内因是什么？不管是信仰、习俗、手工技艺都是人们在同大自然、外来入侵进行抗争，以此维护和扩展生存环境的过程中产生和发展的。"[5]刘先生写的与大自然、外来入侵进行抗争，应该还包括各种政治、经济、社会等原因，都是民间美术在流动中传承的可能动因。

从创新的角度来看，市场上不同需求的驱动也是民间美术的创新的重要原因，如鲁派内画结合博山特产的琉璃进行的技法变革，把京派技法和山东地域文化结合形成鲁派风格，这些创新活动就适应了新的市场需求；冀派代表人物王习三的代表作品系列内画鼻烟壶《美国历届总统肖像》，能看到他对内画技法的创新；其形神兼备、中西结合的内画油彩新艺术风格，也体现了内画艺术对于新市场的适应和开发。从市场角度来看，市场促使冀派内画艺术在时代语境中不断创新发展。所以说，在民间美术的当代传承中，我们应该认识到市场在民间美术历史发展中的特殊意义。要正面认识市场在民间美术传承中的载体作用。例如，刘魁立先生在《论全球化背景下的中国非物质文化遗产保护》一文中写道："在市场经济体制下，社会生活发生极大变化，生活的诸多因素大都打上了市场经济的烙印，保护一种文化传承，不让它受到市场经济的干扰是不大可能的。"[6]从冀派名家付国顺、卢俊为、苏凤羽、郑世魁、王东瑞、王自勇等人的创作中能充分体现这种适应和创新。（见图10～图16）

冀派的繁荣体现了产业化发展的巨大威力，产业化使冀派迅速发展壮大，从河北走向全国，从国内走向国外，对于中国内画艺术的传承和发展起到了重要作用。王松华等在《产业化视角下的非物质文化遗产保护》一文中写道："而产业化追求规模经济的动机与非物质文化遗产得以存续和发展的规模前提是可以有机契合的，走产业化道路，将零散学习、私相授受的传承方式转变为按照市场运作的经济形式，并统一规范、整合资源、形成规模、产生利润。只有这样，非物质文化遗产才能顺应新的历史潮流，并找到自我图强、自我发展的道路。"[7]另外，民间美术和旅游产业的结合也是产业化发展的有效途径，早就为政府、界者所看好；山东大学王德刚教授认为："旅游模式，是将'非遗'作为一种旅游资源进行有效利用，开发成可供游客游览、体验、学习和购买的旅游产品，使'非遗'在现代社会中以一种新的方式进行生存和发展的模式。"[8]

图10 付国顺作品

图11 卢俊为作品

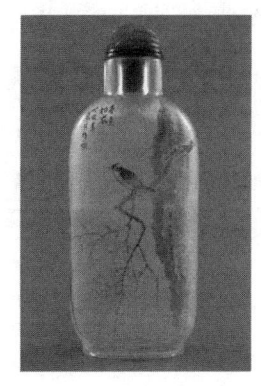

图12 苏凤羽作品

图 13　郑世魁作品　　图 14　郑世魁作品　　图 15　王东瑞作品　　图 16　王自勇作品

总之，民间美术作为我国优秀的传统文化艺术资源，完全可以在产业发展的道路上大胆尝试，内画艺术的发展证明产业化是民间美术发展和走向世界的一条重要路径。

六、对民间美术当代传承的启示

当代中国民间美术的传承问题一直在探索中前行，经历了从20世纪八九十年代的全面开发利用，到21世纪的"活态保护"和"生产性保护"阶段。从各种论述中可以看到"静态保护还是动态保护"是民间美术研究中的一个焦点问题。例如，刘志军在《非物质文化遗产保护的人类学透视》一文中写道："静态保护还是动态保护非物质文化遗产的问题，涉及的是非物质文化遗产的旧有形式应当保持不变，还是应当被允许作与时俱进的改进，而这种改进又能做到什么样的程度的争论。虽然大多数论者都主张动态保护，但由于缺乏深入探讨，因而在实际工作中往往堕入静态保护的窠臼"。[9] 从民间美术传承的实际情况来看，20世纪八九十年代过度市场化带来的恶果至今还在学者们的头脑中发酵，以致"保护"几乎成为唯一的共识。"保护"概念的强化，除了学界对于过度市场化的反思，以及对于我国民间美术不断消失的现实担忧之外；还有一个原因是我国政府和主流学术圈对联合国教科文组织有关非物质文化遗产保护思想的引进。

从内画艺术流动的历程来看，实现传承的关键是对我国民间美术要有正确的认识。要多从田野考察中，从实践中研究并了解我国民间美术的传承特点，尊重民间美术自身的传承规律，我们所要做的就是激发出民间美术自身的生命活力，而不是人为要让它怎么样或不该怎么样。例如，刘魁立先生在《论全球化背景下的中国非物质文化遗产保护》一文中写道："我们往往看到有些文化事象随着历史时代的发展和前进不断地变异，有的由于不再与新的社会生活环境相适应而被淘汰，但同样还有相当多的事像在继续展示自己强大的生命力，或者在变异中获得新的发展。"[10] 因此，仅从我们的主观臆想出发，让某个民间美术种类在今天再保持原汁原味是不现实的；我国在贵州等地建立的生态保护区的失败已经说明了这条路是走不通的，事实证明建立民间美术生态特区的想法是一种脱离时代、脱离现实的幻想。对于已经或正在失去原有生存土壤的民间美术类别而言，守是守不住的，该进博物馆的就进博物馆，该流动的就应该流动，该改变的就应该改变，去寻找时代赋予的土壤；当代的民间美术应该在与时代语境的互动中生发、创新和发展，形成属于当代的民间美术内容和形式。因此，在保护方式、生产方式、创作方式等方面给民间美术的传承设置底线是保守的，不利于民间美术的活态传承。刘魁立先生认为："非物质文化遗产是流动的、发展的，它不可能脱离生产者和享用者而独立存在，它是存在于特定群体生活之中的活的内容，是发展着的传承方式，它很难被强制地凝固保存。"[11] 方李莉在《探索非物质文化遗产保护的新高度》一文中写道："非物质文化遗产跟物质文化遗产不是一个形而下的、具体的文物，它首先是一种观念，是一种认识，是形而上的，是一种意识形态。观念和意识形态是流动的、变化的和活态的，严格来讲它不是遗产，也不是过去了的产物，而是还存在于我们生活中的活生生的传统文化。如果我们能认识到这一点并有意识地传承它、发展它、记录它、认识她，让它成为当今文化的一部分，成为当今文化发展的基础和文化创新的资源，成为中国实现"文化自觉"中的一种教育方式，那么，有关它的保护工作才有可能成为中国文化复兴的起点，同时可能成为中国创意产业的一个新的增长点。"[12]

联合国教科文组织《非物质文化遗产保护公约》中强调创新和可持续发展是传承的主要目的。从内画艺术在流动中发展的历程来看，内画的流动过程实际上也是一个不断创新创造的过程。对于今天的民间美术而言，走出去显得尤其重要，会给民间美术带来创新创造的活力，会使民间美术在当代文化语境中体现出新的面貌。刘云升在《非物质文化遗产保护的理性回归》一文中写道："族群的传统文化在自愿或是非自愿的交流中，在继承与创新中不断演变，有些文化形式就改变了原有发展轨迹而走向衰落直至消失，这就是文化发展的规律"。[13]在苏州举行的"非物质文化遗产保护、研究与工艺美术的可持续发展"学术研讨会暨2006年中国工艺美术学会理论委员会年会上。诸葛铠先生在题为《适者生存：工艺美术的蜕变和再生》的发言中指出：传统手工艺的市场日渐缩小、对手工艺品价值认识的偏移、手工艺的创作观念难以与时代同步是手工在近代潜在的蜕变因素；与市场经济不相适应的生产方式、与生活方式脱离的产品、"推陈出新"中的误区必然导致现代工艺美术的蜕变；而再生之路则可通过形式与思想内涵的分离和移植、形式与技艺的分离和移植、形式与实用性的分离与移植等途径实现脱胎换骨。[14]

笔者认为：对于民间美术的可持续发展而言，要实现创新发展，就应该把保护与发展这两个概念统一起来，只有保护和发展都做好了才能有活态的民间美术，才能实现创新和可持续发展。从内画的流动现象可以看到流动的根本原因是市场强大的引导力和向心力，大多数民间美术自诞生之日起，就生活在市场里，没有市场就不能生存、不能发展。因此，民间美术传承中要充分运用市场的作用。对市场和资本的介入的担忧和排斥，实质上是脱离了大部分民间美术的历史和现实，也是对民间美术和市场的关系认识不足所造成的。在经济高度市场化的今天，市场生存、产业开发将可能是解决民间美术当代传承的根本途径之一。

近年的民间美术研究界普遍对民间美术的传承人青黄不接、后继乏人感到忧虑。的确，缺少传承人以及传承人素质不高都将使民间美术传承走到死胡同。但冀派内画却很好地解决了这个问题，通过学校教育的传承方式彻底打破了过去民间美术行业蔽塞的老师傅带小徒弟的小作坊生产状态，打破了父传子、子传孙的传统传承观念，把现代学校教育模式正式写入了民间美术的当代传承事业，值得我们借鉴和反思。

结　语

综上所述，从对内画艺术的流动历程的描述中，可以看到流动所带来的巨大创新和发展活力。流动使民间美术的文化传承得以实现，使人们重新思考民间美术的流动原因、根本出路等问题。从内画艺术的案例来看，做好民间美术的研究工作和传承工作，需要我们俯下身去，到田野考察中去，在现象中考察，认真观察民间美术的本质属性，研究这种传统文化传承的内在规律和特征，了解我们究竟要保护什么，传承什么？如果对这个问题没有清醒的认识，讨论保护或是传承都是有问题的。再者，对于民间美术的研究和传承要有一个全面开放、面向未来的观念。不要人为地给民间美术的传承设置过多障碍，要辩证地理解保护和发展的概念，保护是为了发展，发展也是为了保护，保护和发展做到了也就实现了传承。例如，2002年的《伊斯坦布尔宣言》在强调非物质文化遗产的重要性时指出：非物质文化遗产是人类文明"文化多样性的熔炉"和"可持续发展的保证"。

参考文献

[1] 王文章. 非物质文化遗产概论 [M]. 北京：教育科学出版社，2008.
[2] 王松华，廖嵘. 产业化视角下的非物质文化遗产保护 [J]. 同济大学学报：社会科学版，2008（1）：108–109.
[3] 王德刚. 再论旅游权利 [J]. 北京第二外国语学院学报，2010（1）：17.
[4] 刘志军. 非物质文化遗产保护的人类学透视 [J]. 浙江大学学报：人文社会科学版，2009（7）：28.
[5] 刘魁立. 论全球化背景下的中国非物质文化遗产保护 [J]. 河南社会科学，2007（1）：30–31.
[6] 方李莉. 探索非物质文化遗产保护的新高度 [J]. 徐州工程学院学报：社会科学版，2011（4）：1.
[7] 刘云升. 非物质文化遗产保护的理性回归 [J]. 河北师范大学学报：哲学社会科学版，2009（5）：162–163.
[8] 李明. 非物质文化遗产保护、研究与工艺美术的可持续发展 [J]. 装饰，2007（2）：6.

媒介的权力
——一种全景透视方法

郝家林

媒介权力（media power）意指现代传播媒介对个人和社会进行影响、操纵及支配的力量。随着人类传播技术的发展，媒介的力量已深入社会生活的各个领域，并"构成了社会权力结构中一种具有强大影响力的部分"。西方国家尤其美国对媒介权力的研究已有近百年的历史。相比之下，我国在这一领域的研究才刚刚起步。鉴于此，在我们有能力提出自己的理论假说前，对媒介社会影响力问题进行一番全景透视，把握西方媒介理论的方法论意义，就是一件有价值的工作。我们的分析是基于传媒曾经或正在发生的作用这一客观经验。依据历史客观经验是阐释媒介系统与社会其他系统之间相互关系的准则。任意贬低或夸大媒介影响力的做法都是不恰当的。

一、政 治

（一）安排议程

安排议程源于对特定政治活动（大选）的观察，后被人们引入对媒介社会影响力的研究之中。

奥斯坎普于1977年提出："也许大众媒介最重要的效力即在于其形成议题的功能"。[1]赛弗林则解释："大众媒介形成议题的功能即大众媒介选择并突出报道某些问题，从而使这些问题引起公众重视的能力"。[1]自20世纪50年代后期，人们开始对于媒介"安排议程"的功能有了较明确的认识。此后20年间，政治学家、传播学家对此寄予了极大期望。例如，诺顿[1]、朗伯·科恩[4]、西奥多·怀特（白修德）[5]、希尔斯曼[6]等人，均在不同时期和不同研究课题中触及这一问题。而真正为它提供可统计的数据支持的及经验基础的人，公认的是麦库姆斯和肖。他们在20世纪60年代末70年代初所进行的调研显示：媒介议题与公众议题之间存在着惊人的相应关系。不过这一结论有一个弱点，即它并未指出两者孰因孰果。有观点认为，媒介是从公众那里获得议程的，媒介的注意力反应并非替代公众的注意力。进入80年代，随着研究工作深入展开。施拉姆提出"安排议程"的理论基础基于两个观点：其一，媒介是新闻报道的把关人，它们要对大量消息进行选择；其二，公众经常感到需要对复杂的政治世界为他们指出方向。这就是说，把关人帮助人们决定哪些超出他们有限感受的那些事件和那些问题，是值得关心和加以注意的。而注重制度分析的阿特休尔则认为，并非媒介单独安排议程，是他们与社会的政治（经济）权力共同传播新闻或共同确定议事日程。无论怎样，媒介若要成功引导公众的注意力，需要有一个基本条件：它们得采取联合一致的行动。媒介即使不能改变公众的观点，至少能够做到"使人们把某一议题看得比其他议题更重要"。

（二）统一规范

"规范是一个群体的所有成员均理解和遵循的普遍规则"。传媒凭借大量信息向社会成员传输规范化的意义，促使其养成与规范相适应的行为习惯，从而维护现实的社会秩序。在这方面传媒潜移默化的宣传效力往往胜过政府的强制力量。阿特休尔在分析西方新闻传播制度时就直言不讳地道出："广播电视也许是迄今为止所能设想出的社会控制的最有效的工具。"因为"广播电视主宰人类生活超过了以往任何一种传播媒介，这一事实是无可置疑的"。[7]

统一规范的方法有两种：一是通过宣传报道赋予个人或组织高出一般性的地位和荣誉，奖励那些遵

[作者简介] 郝家林，北京联合大学应用文理学院。

守规范并协助群体达到目标,表现突出的成员,从正面肯定规范的普遍性意义,即所谓"肯定性制约";二是通过公开揭露违反规范的行为,惩戒犯规者并威慑那些尚未造成事实的潜在犯规者,从反面校正人们的行为偏差,即所谓"否定性制约"。传媒之所以能够承担这一政治性功能,与其自身特点是分不开的。研究表明,由于传媒在其社会属性方面所具有的某种意义上的权威性色彩及其巨大的技术能量,使其对事物的态度可以迅速转化为社会的普遍认可。

(三)监视环境

政治学家哈·拉斯韦尔在1948年发表的《社会传播的结构与功能》一文中,明确把"对环境进行监视"列为社会传播的功能之一。此后,人们便将大众传媒比喻为社会监视器。传媒广泛报道消息、意见和指导性评价,向公众报告他们的生存条件和质量,帮助公众认识并理解生活于这个世界的历史、现实及面临的问题。传媒的报告经常成为公众对现实作出反应和抉择的主要依据。

对社会消极现象的报告是环境监视的重要内容。它公开了原本隐蔽的问题,突出了问题性质的严重性,唤醒公众的政治意识,从而推进社会变革。在美国新闻史上,20世纪初的"掏粪者"时代(揭发丑闻的时代)最初确立了监视环境的道德性准则,即腐败行为与"要求社会正义的革新运动"是不相容的。这一传统后来被美国及西方的负有社会责任感的新闻工作者继承了下来。对政治环境的监视除对社会心理的宏观估价或对其取样测评之外,主要是媒介针对权力行为的合法性与合理性的监视。当然,媒介监视既非行政法意义上的监督法律关系,也非政治学所讲的权力制衡机制。它属于社会监督范畴,体现或代表公民的宪法权利。

二、经　　济

(一)广告

在19世纪大众报纸诞生的最初的日子里,它的创办人的商业动机便将它与广告结成了天然盟友。进入20世纪,随着电子媒介的普及,人类社会的经济生活便步入了广告时代。施拉姆曾假定:如果排除广告作用,电台、电视台将不复存在。这一假定并不具理论性质,仅道出了一个常识:媒介靠广告收入而生存。可口可乐公司自创办一百多年来,广告费投入年均达1.84亿美元,就证明了这一点。但是,施拉姆的假定完全可以颠倒过来:如果失去媒介,广告也将不复存焉。而广告一旦消失,我们将无法想象现代经济活动包括企业经营计划的制订、公众消费行为的选择、跨国公司的海外市场开拓等,将会是怎样的一种局面。

(二)产业结构

传播行业作为现代产业之一,在国民经济中所占比重不断增大,日益改变着传统产业结构。1988年,美国视听收入达80亿美元,占出口总额中的第二位,仅次于航天工业。1993年,世界CD-ROM(只读光盘)的销售额超过百亿美元。据预测,世界电子出版物的市场销售将以每年30%~40%的速度增长。中国自改革开放以来,传播业的兴起构成了经济繁荣的一道醒目风景线。家庭对媒介更新换代的追求为市场带来了巨大的潜力。例如,1995年,大屏幕彩电是拉动消费品零售总额较快增长的主要商品之一。

(三)科技与劳动力

现代传播业的发展带动了印刷技术、电子技术、摄影摄像技术,以及光学、电学、声学、材料科学的进步,为科学技术研究迅速转化为生产力开拓出广阔前景。同时,大众传媒的普及还为从根本上改变劳动者的知识结构提供了社会化手段。在未来学家眼中,最优秀的工人是善于处理问题的。他们善于追踪新思想、新风尚,关注经济和政治领域的变化。他们能够意识到竞争的压力、文化的变迁以及许多从前只是管理人员才考虑的问题。未来学家在思考人类历史发展进程时,敏锐地观察到信息时代发生在工人身上的这种深刻变化,并充分肯定了大众传媒为促成这种变化而发挥的作用。阿·托夫勒指出:"这些广博的知识并非来自教室,也不来自技术手册,而是来自我们经常收看或收听的报纸、杂志、电视和广播刊登或播发的大量新闻。它也间接地来自娱乐。因为许多娱乐节目都在无形中传递着关于新的生活方式、人际关系和社会问题,甚至是外国顾客和市场的信息。"[6]

许多人也许并不在意生活中所发生的种种细小变化，但恰恰是这些变化很可能会改变人的一生。细小的变化可能就是历史变迁的征兆。我们在分析大众传媒的社会影响力问题时，不应忽视在各个方面诸如企业管理者、公司职员、家庭、社会团体等所发生的"小事情"，因为我们往往会在"细小变化"中寻找到所需要的有力论据。

（四）消费时尚

媒介促成"流行"，对此竹内郁郎作出了完整的论证。他从三个层面来阐述媒介对流行的作用。其一，促进流行的产生。大众媒介将以新方式构筑成人共同认知的环境世界，迫使人们与之相适应，于是媒介奠定了流行产生的基础。其二，促进流行的普及。媒介通过报道新方式被采用的实际情况及新方式得到怎样的社会支持，鼓励那些虽关心流行但还未采用新方式的人加入流行行列，结果扩大了流行规模。其三，促退流行。媒介不断制造新环境，诱使人们喜新厌旧，从而支配流行的周期。[7]

上述论证无疑具有价值，它至少为信息发布者制订宣传计划展示出一种带定理意味的程序模式。但是，论证忽略了一个重要的消费心理现象，即消费者在行为选择上所表现出的主动性。而且，作为理论研究，竹内郁郎也未进一步探讨出媒介在促成流行时是如何创造出某种来自心理方面的消费文化氛围，这一点恰恰是媒介影响力在本质意义上的表现。

需要说明的是，在注意日常"细小变化"的同时，还应强调那些制度性因素对传媒影响力的制约，否则我们的观察将失去客观的标准。西方国家的传播体制已作为一个不可分割的部分深入其政治、经济结构中，并成为制度的一个象征性解释。西方传播学的批判学派正是站在制度分析的高度，来给大众传播活动定性的。这种"定性分析"方法值得我们借鉴。例如，我们分析传媒的政治影响力，一方面要指出传媒为政治行为构建了社会舞台，另一方面也必须看到，传媒又是政治舞台上的一个社会角色，自然要受到这个舞台的规则的制约。传媒绝非在政治之外影响政治，它就身在其中，因为"新闻媒介就是一个政治机构。"我们分析传媒对社会经济生活的影响，当然也就不能排除以下因素的作用：一国经济发展的战略目标和策略手段，政府干预经济的能力，企业现代化程度，政府关于精神产品生产的政策性限制，等等。中国是社会主义国家，新闻机构是党和人民的喉舌，这是我国新闻传播制度的本质特征。只有结合中国实际来研究大众传媒对我国社会生活所发生的种种影响，才能得出合乎逻辑的结论。

三、文　　化

（一）融合与侵略

法国社会学家卡森奈在1969年出版的《广播电视社会学》一书中写道：大众媒介"使各个国家间、各种风俗和文化间存在的障碍正在减少"。[8]卡森奈的话无须再加以证明。今天当人们正在热烈讨论"跨文化交流"这一严肃的学术话题时，我们的大众传媒早已在最通俗的层面上为实现这一话题的实践性目标铺陈道路。但是，"障碍的减少"一方面为各民族间文化的顺畅交流创造了条件，同时这些条件也为一民族文化向他民族的扩张提供了便利。伴随着世界政治、经济一体化的进程，世界文化格局也发生着深刻变化。20世纪80年代末，美国的视听节目在拉美国家占77%，在欧洲占到44%，在阿拉伯地区占32%，在非洲占47%，在加拿大占到70%，而美国进口节目仅占2%。国际视听贸易的这种不均衡状态引起各国普遍不安。欧洲人担心如果自己的娱乐活动、节日活动和幻想中充满了欧洲以外的形象、符号、声音和象征，那么被征服、被占领的将是他们自身的形象、自身本质的特征。一位法国总统向同胞们发出警告："对欧洲来说，这将是一次文化上的惨败，政治上的失败，欧洲将不能向自己的公民乃至向全世界公民显示自身文化的统一性，或者说完整性。在经济上也将是一次严重的失败，因为文化财富的生产——它已经衍生出若干地道道的产业——将被窒息，从而革新、创造性和活力的基本支柱之一也就被拆除了。"[9]

军事征服、经济掠夺、文化渗透似乎可以构成近现代国际关系史上一条显性线索，它勾画出了人类社会近百年来风云变幻的历史轨迹。在世界文化大融合的今天，异质文化的介入会导致某些社会在历史传统、生活方式、价值观念等方面发生重大变化。这些变化可能会平缓地进行，也可能会采取对立因素之间的对抗形式。异质文化对本土文化的强烈冲击，必然使后者提出维护自身具有象征性价值的（甚至激进的）要求，这一要求显而易见地超出了民间性质。自20世纪80年代末以来，法国、加拿大、澳大利亚、英国、德国等国政府,纷纷制定措施以限制外国节目的进口,保护和扶植本国视听产业。一些发展中国家也联合呼吁,要求建立符合各国情况的信息和传播政策,以保证文化和政治的多元性,维护民族主权。上述国家的反映当然不会导致文化壁垒的形成,但它向世界表明,要解决由于大众传播所引发的那些深刻影响一个国家赖以存在的价值基础的问题,将是各国政府所面临的一个艰难而长期的任务。

(二) 普及与庸俗化

大众传播时代的到来,结束了文化作为上流阶层的特权进而垄断人类精神生活的历史。文化在今天已被大多数人列入他们的日常性消费。人类精神产品的世俗化对于提高社会整体文明水准,增强较低阶层的公共生活意识具有划时代意义。但人们同时需注意到大众文化(有人定义为工业化生产、商业化运作、快餐式消费的文化)所带来的功能性负效应,即文化的庸俗化。文化制造商们为了迎合"大众对庸俗、色情以致野蛮行为的渴求心理",每天都在向社会大批量生产粗俗低劣的传播品,在社会上营造出了一种功利的、浮躁的、乃至浅薄滑稽的文化氛围。人们受这种氛围熏染会逐渐消磨掉——至少会疏远——他们原本具有的那些高品格鉴赏趣味。这正是哥伦比亚社会学派首领人物、被人视为传播学奠基人之一的拉扎斯菲尔德曾经感叹的,人们在宝贵的自由时间内不是同大学而是同大众媒介打交道的原因。然而问题的严重性不仅于此,庸俗文化还在撼动着一个社会赖以世代维系的传统根基。布热津斯基认为,电视对观众施加的文化和哲学影响无与伦比,它正在取代家庭、教会和学校而成为社会教育的最重要工具。但这位前国家安全顾问指责电视所展现的关于幸福生活的定义更多的是自我享乐和贪婪,所以它完全有理由被指为道德败坏和文化堕落的罪魁祸首。"电视在破坏代代继承的传统和价值观念方面起了特别大的作用"。[10]中国在大众文化勃兴的现阶段,人们也已经注意到现代传媒更多地传达出平庸和低劣,构成对一个民族道貌岸然的公开化的文化戕害,同时认为,电视虽体现了时代较敏感的那部分特征,它却不能(也无力)代表时代的发展方向。[11]

(三) 语言

梅·德弗勒和他的合作者在为他们的意义构成论寻找理论依据时,提出大众媒介影响语言和意识的方式是:它们建立具有新的关联意义的单词;引申现有词汇的意思;用新意义代替旧意义;最重要的是,它们稳定我们语言词汇中现有的意义常规。他们还指出:"虽然媒介的说话风格绝没有取代各个地区、不同种族群体或经济水准较低的人们的口音、语法或句法,但它们也许会最终消除这些区别。"[12]媒介潜移默化地模糊着人们的语言差异,有可能形成不同民族之间相同的语言习惯,而同一种语言习惯的形成则意味着民族语言个性的消失。

四、意识与行为

(一) 转述现实

传播学界普遍承认关于媒介转述现实的论点最早出自美国著名政治专栏作家沃尔特·李普曼于1922年发表的经典著作《舆论》。李普曼论点的理论基础可表述如下:现代人的生存环境实在太大、太复杂,它稍纵即逝,太难以直接经历了。人要认识环境并在此环境中作出行为抉择,在我们能够直接与它发生关系之前,我们必须把它改造成一个比较简单的模式。于是新闻媒介承担起"改造"任务。媒介将人们无法直接经历的现实裁剪成某种概念化的东西,再将这个可以被称之为现实的"副本"的东西提供给人们,人们便依据媒介的提供去认识客观世界。所以,"我们目前过渡到大众传播时代的一个主要特点是我们越来越多地接触复杂的物质世界和社会世界的媒介表述,而不只是我们狭小个人环境的客观特征。"[13]

但问题是,媒介的表述是否可靠。李普曼的主要结论之一就是媒介表述常常具有"欺骗性",使人产生误解。媒介利用可选择的符号并经过精心加工在人与客观现实之间制造了一幅被歪曲的甚至完全虚假的图象。人们曾找出许多实例来验证这一结论的正确性,因此也就有了对媒介更为激进的批评。法国人沙菲尔在1970年出版的《传播机器》一书中指出,所有传播工具所提供的,都不是现实的社会,不是现实的事件,而只是现实的幻影。关于非洲的例子就更生动些,"在以往的电视节目里,非洲成了'动物世界',这是成功的西方电视人的特别奉献。"[14]阿·托夫勒则较为温和,他承认在一部内容经过刻意安排的电视节目中，它的情节和主要人物的行为举止经常为人们描绘出一幅虚假的社会现实的图画，但他同时认为，在所有电视节目、广告和电影中，总是存在着所谓的"无意性内容"，它给日常生活中的现实描绘了一幅相当准确的图画。它是通过背景中的细节如街景、汽车、录音电话等自然流露出来的，表现流行的时尚和风气，表现人们对性、宗教、金钱和政治生活的一般态度。人们把这些印象储进大脑，成为一个人对世界看法的知识总库里的一部分。

如李普曼所言，人们不是根据真实发生的情况采取行动，而是根据媒介所提供的人们信以为真的描述采取行动。"我们把世界设想成的哪个模样，决定我们做什么，决定我们的努力、感受和希冀，却不能决定我们一定获得成就和结果"。[15]这是因为，媒介的描述作为人们行为的依据，它导致了人们与客观世界真正性质不大相干的不适当行动。那么谁应对此承担责任？阿特休尔认为在新闻媒介从事工作的男男女女，包括新闻商人，具有至关重要的作用。德弗勒则认为，消息的选择性和曲解是记者、编辑、制片人或发行人所控制不了的因素的产物，是某种"先决条件"的后果。这一观点为人们认识媒介权力的性质及其构成拓展出更多的思路。

（二）心理压力

如果说大众媒介是人们宣泄紧张情绪的渠道，倒不如说它们是造成这种情况的原因。在信息时代，信息的快速增值迫使人们以一种远远超过缓慢演变的社会所必需的快速来处理信息，迫使人们在快速增值的选择中作出抉择，结果抉择本身构成了心理负担。对于传播者（我们指的是世界上大大小小的新闻传播机构及其记者、编辑们）来说，向大众尽可能多地倾泻信息是他们的社会职责和职业骄傲，或许他们希望所有人和他们一样对人类日新月异的科技力量感到同样鼓舞和振奋人心。但是对于那些不受表面现象迷惑的并对自身及社会具有强烈责任感的人来说，他们却越来越深切地感到，要真正认识并应付周围环境所需要关心和思考的问题实在太多、太复杂，而这些问题大都没有答案。他们从意识深处生出一种关于人类前途和命运的焦虑感。较多的选择机会，较多的行为参数，伴随着多元价值观和多重判断标准；相互矛盾的信息还会把人引入进退两难的迷宫。所有这一切又使得他们的焦虑呈现出一种极度无所适从的状态。这正是体现于现代人身上的那种难以排遣的、躲藏于人类灵魂深处的无奈。人们把大部分自由时间花费在媒介消费上，习惯于坐在电视机前欣赏世界、评价世界，满足于间接地认识生活，而不是主动直接地干预生活。所谓新闻就是只需人去读、去听、去观看，问题被提出了，结论有了，社会共鸣产生了，于是一切便完美无缺了。大众传媒用信息编织成一张巨大的网，人便是这网中永难逃离的生物。

（三）行为

有学者认为，媒介的使用使人们独处的时间更多，有组织行动的时间更少。人们喜欢谈论甚于行动，患上了因"情报太多造成的无所作为的冷漠症"。对此在尚未见到通过定量统计得出的经验数据之前，我们无法证实信息超载在多大程度上导致人的行为冷漠。

至于媒介的"示范"作用则可靠得多。媒介塑造出各类典型人物，他们身处其中的境遇，通过这些人物解决问题的方式所展现的人类多样化的品格特征，向人们提供认知和模仿的材料。尤其对青少年而言，媒介人物已成为他（她）们行为经验的主要源泉。德弗勒和他的合作者在讨论心理模仿理论时，观察了大众传播如何通过媒介的表述而成为人们学习行为方式的源泉。人们可以采用媒介展现的行为方式作为应付各自环境的手段。他们还排列出模仿过程的六个阶段。据说，模仿论对大众传播学是很有发展前景的理论，尽管这一理论在实践上主要是针对个人而言。

媒介的权力是如何形成的，构成媒介权力的资源有哪些？要回答这个问题需要我们对近些年来西方以结构主义为代表的新马克思主义观点的批判文化研究成果投以更多的热情。[16]同时，我们需要开拓我们的理论思维空间，除政治学、社会学、心理学外，寄希望于语言学、符号学、现象学、解释学、文学、精神分析学等学科的介入，那时，针对中国大众传播实践提出我们自己的理论假说和解释的时机、条件也许就成熟了。

参考文献

[1] [美] 沃纳丁·赛弗林，等. 传播学的起源、研究与应用 [M]. 福州：福建人民出版社，1985.

［2］［美］J·赫伯特·阿特休尔. 权力的媒介［M］. 北京：华夏出版社，1989.
［3］［美］威尔伯·施拉姆，等. 传播学概论［M］. 北京：新华出版社，1984.
［4］［美］希尔斯曼. 美国是如何治理的［M］. 北京：商务印书馆，1988.
［5］［美］J·赫伯特·阿特休尔. 权力的媒介［M］. 北京：华夏出版社，1989.
［6］［美］阿尔温·托夫勒. 权力的转移［M］. 北京：中共中央党校出版社，1991.
［7］［日］竹内郁郎. 大众传播社会学［M］. 上海：复旦大学出版社，1989.
［8］中国社会科学院新闻研究所. 传播学［M］. 北京：人民日报出版社，1983.
［9］［墨西哥］阿·瓦·阿雅拉. 拉美的视听贸易和文化完整性［J］. 编译参考，1991（1）.
［10］［美］兹·布热津斯基. 大失控与大混乱［M］. 北京：中国社会科学出版社，1995.
［11］张宏森. 中国电视剧给我们带来了什么［N］//张炜. 怀疑与信赖，新华文摘，1995（10）.
［12］［美］梅尔文·德弗勒，等. 大众传播学诸论［M］. 北京：新华出版社，1990.
［13］尹吉男. 决非野生动物的文化眼光［M］. 读书，1996（2）.
［14］［美］沃纳丁·赛弗林，等. 传播学的起源、研究与应用［M］. 福州：福建人民出版社，1985.
［15］王怡红. 认识西方"媒介权力"研究的历史与方法［J］. 新闻与传播研究，1997（2）.

探索色彩力量在商品色彩营销中的应用

鲁彦娟

色彩营销（Color Marketing），就是在了解消费者心理的基础上，给商品一个恰当定位，然后在产品本身、产品包装、产品展示环境装饰等环节配以适当的色彩，利用色彩架起商品与消费者之间沟通的桥梁，实现"人—色彩—商品"的统一，将商品的所有信息第一时间通过色彩传递给消费者，从而提高商品营销的效率，同时减少营销成本。国外色彩研究的权威人士法伯·比兰曾指出：在商品广告中往往不在于其使用了多少色彩，而关键在于色彩运用的是否恰当，因此在广告中选择色彩时就既要根据目标市场的色彩需求、偏好特征，并结合企业的文化、产品的特色与环境相协调，形成企业独特的广告宣传效应。

随着色彩营销理论的发展与传播，色彩策略在企业营销活动中的运用越来越频繁，并逐渐成为企业在激烈的市场竞争获得优势的一个重要手段。色彩是世界通用的语言，它超越国界，让世界上的人们得以相互交流。21世纪，色彩战略将在商品企划和推广中越来越占有重要的地位。

1 色彩的力量

色彩是人与人沟通交流的重要武器，色彩具有触动心灵的力量。在古希腊时期，人们就已经开始探索和利用色彩，发展到近现代，歌德和弗洛伊德都从心理学的角度开始追寻色彩与心理之间的关系，开启了利用色彩的能量治疗心理疾病的阶段。色彩无论在什么时代，都会带来不同的使用价值。

从20世纪60年代的CIS（企业形象识别系统）创建以来，在商业空间中有计划地使用色彩开始盛行，特别是在设计领域，如果不能合理地运用色彩，就不是一个合格的设计人员。由于受到来自西方和日本色彩研究的影响，色彩作为一门独立的专业在中国也得到认可。

2 商品滞销与商品色彩

目前市场上的某些大企业的企划部负责人经常陷入到这样的困惑："我们的产品质量非常好，与竞争对手相比毫不逊色，而且价格上面更具有优势，但是为什么就是卖不出去，是因为宣传方式不对，还是经营方式不行？"一般我们都会认为，物美价廉的产品自然会受到消费者的喜欢，所以不明白自己的企业为什么市场占有量和销售量无法超越竞争对手。"明明我们的质量更好一点，商业推广广告也大受好评，为什么卖不出去？"其实，有些商品别说广告就连宣传都没有做过，但市场上却非常畅销的实例也有不少。可见，影响商品销售的原因并非单纯在于是否宣传或者宣传力度的状况。

资生堂的"SINOADORA"系列，虽然没有做过商业广告宣传，但是一上市就非常畅销。良好的品牌形象、一贯优良产品品质自然是该系列产品成功的首要原因，除此之外，"SINOADORA"系列的成功营销还要归功于其准确传导了产品理念的包装设计。2004年8月，资生堂公司提出了一个化妆品业界从未有过的新方案：将东西方文化融合的一个新品牌"SINOADORA"诞生了。品牌创意来自中医美容理论，原理是平衡全身的"气、血、水"的流通。而包装设计方案采用中国的"方圆"象征，色彩战略五行五色加上表示阴阳的金银两色的组合，图形采用中国画和西方插画结合的手法，通过伦敦和上海两个公司的合作绘制而成。只要你看到这个包装，心就会被它所俘获，因为该系列商品的优秀品质通过包装上的视觉信息传达给消费者，所以"SINOADORA"系列产品一上市就大受消费者的欢迎。

［基金项目］本项目获得北京市属高等学校人才强教计划（项目号：1221093103）和北京联合大学校级科研项目（项目号：1107HB1003）资助。

［作者简介］鲁彦娟，北京联合大学特殊教育学院教授。

3　色彩营销

色彩营销理论是由美国的卡洛尔·杰克逊女士在 20 世纪 80 年代创办的 Color Me Beautiful（简称 CMB）公司在企业营销实践中总结和提炼出来的。该理论的实质是根据消费者对色彩的心理需求，运用色彩营销组合来促进商品的销售。色彩营销理论是把上百种颜色按四季分为四大色彩系列，每个系列的色彩形成和谐的搭配群，根据不同人的肤色、发色和眼睛的颜色等自然生理特征，以及个人的体貌特征、性格和职业等外表特征选取最合理的色彩系列，从而最大限度地发现美。

在美国色彩研究领域，有一种理论叫"7 秒钟色彩"，就是对一个人乃至对一种商品或事物的认识，可以在 7 秒钟之内以色彩的形状留在人们的印象里。因为根据国外相关机构的研究表明：能被消费者瞬间进入视野并留下印象的产品，其时间是 0.67 秒。第一印象是影响购买决定因素的 60%，而这 60% 是由色彩带来的。由于商品和色彩的密切关系，色彩营销理论一开始就受到美容美发、化妆品、服饰等行业的重视，并在企业商品的营销活动中加以运用。

商品企划中最重要的就是色彩。随着技术改革的发展，产品生产厂家的技术水平和设计水平的差别并不大，商品的宣传广告语经常充斥着"高品质""高性能""最尖端"等词语，但是市场销售还是会产生一定的差别，最后决定销售量的主要因素就是色彩。

销售不好的企业早 10 年最关注商品自身的原因，当这个原因不那么凸显时，企业就会陷入困惑，发现不了问题又如何解决问题呢。对于色彩在包装、宣传等环节上的重要性，大家现在都越来越重视。但是一般情况下人们不会认为销售不好的原因是配色不好，当企业寻找影响销售原因的时候，我们不妨观察一下竞争对手或其他大受欢迎的商品成功的原因，把商品自身的相似之处抛弃后，我们就可以得到这样一个结论：受欢迎的商品都是成功利用了色彩的案例。

色彩不能凭感觉去选定，虽然我们称它为色感，而实际上它也是有科学依据的。因此决定色彩不能根据设计师的喜好，而是要从针对商品的消费层得到的信息，相应决定适合的色彩。色彩具有让人心动的力量，将这种力量作为战略使用的话，就能使销售量得到提升。色彩在拥有力量的同时，也有它的价值，色彩不是商品的附属品，它的价值包含在物品当中，你在花钱买下某件商品时，也等于花钱买下了这种颜色。

4　色彩与设计的关系

使用色彩传达内心的东西，这是色彩战略的根本。某种商品能直接传达出商品精髓的就是色彩，也就是商品的内容、本质，甚至是价值，这些东西可以通过外包装一目了然，就像中医通过观察人的脸色来进行病情的初步判断一样。

如果我们把商品和消费者两者之间的关系比喻成单相思的恋情，商品包装的内容（MIND）时刻准备好是想引起对方（TARGET）的关注很相似。大多数情况下"对方"对这种爱慕是不知情或者不很关心，因此，为了让"对方"注意到自己，就要向对方送出可以表达自己心情的信息，想方设法让"对方"关注自己，即使表达露骨也在所不惜。如果"对方"没有接受这份关怀和好感，这段恋情就无始而终，也就是所谓的失恋，而在商品营销中就是产品没有得到消费者的认可。

色彩战略的价值在于：在将你的心情传达给"对方"的同时，还要抓住"对方"的心，要想抓住"对方"的心，就必须要了解"对方"喜欢什么颜色。这时候色彩市场学就派上了用场，采用时下流行风还是追求个性色彩，在了解清楚之后才能采取行动，考虑使用什么方式来传达自己心中的色彩。为了让"对方"了解自己的优点，要让自己更具有吸引力是很重要的。色彩战略中，广告的活用是不可或缺的，而重点就是颜色的正确选择。

色彩包含在设计之内，是重要的设计要素之一。设计战略和色彩战略的目的是一致的，设计是通过活用色彩的力量，来达到抓住人心的效果，因此使用什么色彩绝不是设计师一个人可以决定的。以前的理论认为，颜色给人以心理暗示，例如：蓝色主要代表"清澈""青春""沉着"和"寒冷"等，这种时候"要从色彩心理学角度出发"进行说明。那么，色彩心理学的根据是什么呢？这是无法体验的心理。当然人们看到冰冷的水时，就会存储下蓝色是冰冷的这种体验信息，所以在看到蓝色时会觉得冷，不过这种感受有疑点，水真的是蓝色的吗？答案当然是否定的。在心理学上，红色和火焰重叠，被称为暖色，但是温度最高的不是蓝色的火焰吗？人们看到红色就感到热，是不是有其他的原因？但是，却从来没有人怀疑过"红色是热情"这种说法。近年来，针对这种疑问，大脑生物学有了相当的进展，特别是对视觉细胞和视觉神经，以及大脑之间的关系的研究还在继续，这将很大程度影响到色彩革命。

5 结 论

色彩营销改变了人们对色彩的理解方式，使我们关注并了解色彩的本质。色彩的定义正在从感观向科学领域转变。从"色表"到现在，色彩心理疗法一路走来长盛不衰，色彩以惊人的势头融入了现代人们的生活，这也让我们意识到色彩离我们越来越近的发展历程，这个历程让我们也看到色彩的力量是如何深入人心的，色彩的机能就是让我们每天的生活变得快乐。

{历史学类}

近代北京基督教史研究现状及史料利用综述

左芙蓉

基督教与近代北京的关系约始于19世纪中期英国伦敦布道会传教士进京,传入北京的基督教亲历了历史变迁并且在其中异常活跃。近代北京基督教史既反映了基督教在近代北京发展历程的曲折,又展现了基督教与近代北京社会变迁的互动关系,还揭示出近代北京基督教广泛而深远的影响,因此引起教内外人士的关注和学者的兴趣。

1 中外人士对近代北京基督教史的研究状况

1.1 国外主要相关研究

从笔者掌握的信息看,国外有关近代北京基督教史的专门研究主要集中在美国。20世纪50年代出版的《燕京大学》(Yenching University)一书是早期代表作之一。该书由艾德敷(Dwight W. Edwards)[1]编著,有许多人参与了该书的写作,书中详细论述了燕京大学从筹建、成立到发展,以及抗战后期一度停办、战后复校再到最终停办的历程。参与该书编写的人多有近代来华传教的经历,有的人甚至亲历了燕京大学的创办和发展。因此,书中提供的资料比较直接,所述事件具有较大的真实性,此为该书的特点之一。将燕京大学的历史置于中国社会变迁的大背景之中加以考察,比较全面地再现了该教会大学在一个动荡环境中的发展及其与中国社会变迁的互动,此为该书的特点之二。但作者很强调中国基督教教会大学的正面影响,绝少提及其负面的社会效应,艾德敷甚至称燕京大学不只是一所高等学校,而且是一种精神力量[2],充分体现了作者的传教士立场。尽管如此,该书仍不失为研究近代北京基督教史,以及近代中国基督教高等教育活动的一部重要参考文献。关注燕京大学的还有美国学者韦斯特(Philip West),1976年出版的《燕京大学与中西关系》(Yenching University and Sino-Western Relations 1916-1952)是其力作。该书深入分析了基督教在民国北京开办高等教育及其对中西关系的影响,指出燕京大学既成功又失败,成功之处在于它是植根于新教传教事业和中国土壤里的世界主义埋想的实现,曾经具有很高的学术地位。作者指出,"如果说20世纪曾有过超越东西文化差异的事情,那应该就是燕京大学";失败之处既反映在它的易受攻击又反映在它后来的完全停办,"首先是来自西方宗教的原教旨主义的攻击,更为严重的是来自中国的民族主义的抨击,最后是来自韩战时期国际政治的影响"。韦斯特认为,"1949年以后俄国在中国政治中的影响与燕京大学的关闭是有关系的。美国与中国的联系在与日本的战争中得到加强。但是在战后,学生开始憎恨美国支持蒋介石,司徒雷登个人对蒋的忠诚以及他作为支持国民政府的美国大使,都影响了燕京大学所谓的事业。"尽管韦斯特认为中国的民族主义和共产主义革命,以及"韩战"都成为燕大继续存在的不可克服的障碍,但他更强调"外交是燕京大学结束的决

[基金项目] 本文是笔者承担的北京联合大学中青年骨干教师资助计划项目(人文社会科学类)《中国基督教女青年会史》的部分成果。本文所述的基督教主要指新教。

[作者简介] 左芙蓉,北京联合大学应用文理学院历史系。

[1] 艾德敷,美国人,1905年硕士毕业于普林斯顿大学,1906年来到北京,是北京基督教青年会创建人之一,20世纪上半期长期居留中国,曾先后担任北京基督教青年会副总干事和总干事、中国基督教青年会华北区总干事、中国华洋义赈救灾总会代理总干事、燕京大学校董会董事和司库等职,1945年离华返美,1949年被普林斯顿大学授予荣誉哲学博士学位。

[2] DwightW. Edwards, Yenching University, NewYork: United Board for Christian Higher Education in Asia, 1959, Preface.

定性因素",所以,"使燕大结束的政治力量可以说是既有中国的又有西方的"❶。不可否认,韦斯特对燕京大学的兴亡及其原因的分析有其独到之处,与艾德敷将燕京大学历史的终结主要归因于共产主义在华的胜利相比,韦斯特的视角更宽广、更开阔一些。不过笔者以为,外交因素对燕京大学失败的影响不宜过分强调,毕竟它还是属于外在的因素。1995年,美国学者哈里斯(Marjorie Jean Har-ris)对近代北京的基督教女子高等教育产生了浓厚兴趣,以《美国的传教与中国的现实——对华北协和女子大学/燕京大学女部发展的跨文化影响的历史分析》(American Missions, Chinese Realities – An Historical Analysis of the Cross – Cultural Influence Upon the Development of North China Union Women's College/Yenching Women's College 1905—1943)为题完成了其博士论文。该文以近代北京也是近代中国最早的女子大学——华北协和女子大学为中心,从跨文化的视角深入探究美国传教活动与近代中国女子教育的关系,主要侧重对该校几任女校长的分析。该文的选题富有新意,正如作者本人所说,之前"尽管有一些学者研究传教史,但是无人深刻地考察过中国妇女的基督教教育",这也是该文的特色之一。特色之二在于作者对文化传播的双向影响有着深刻的理解,比较清楚地认识到"美国女传教士教育家在帮助中国妇女接受高等教育以适应妇女生活不断变化的特征和中国政治环境的转变时,也使她们自己的生活、信仰和认知发生了改变"❷。但作者对美国女传教士教育家的作用和影响也很高估。20世纪末,留美中国学生邢文军以《社会福音、社会经济和基督教青年会——甘博和普林斯顿—北京中心》(Social Gospel, Social Economics and the YMCA: Sidney Gamble and Princeton – in – Peking)为题撰写博士论文,详细考察了北京基督教青年会研究干事美国人甘博和普林斯顿-北京中心在20世纪上半期的中国开展社会调查、社会服务和社会改革等活动及其影响。在作者看来,甘博和普林斯顿—北京中心的作用就在于"以一种非常重要的方式,展现了西方和中国之间丰富的知识和文化的普遍互动——美国和中国之间特殊的互动"❸。以 一个与基督教青年会相关的人物和机构为切入点,深入探究美国青年参与基督教海外传教运动、将社会福音的改革精神带入中国,并通过基督教青年会使社会福音影响北京,进而证明基督教与中国文化是可以和谐共存的,这是该文最大的特色。但作者对普林斯顿—北京中心在后期的活动介绍较少。

不难看出,在美国的学者对近代北京基督教史研究开始得较早,其研究对象也比较集中,在教会大学和基督教青年会等方面着力较多,而且多从近代中美关系、中西文化交流的角度入手,研究重点为与美国关系密切的人物和事件及其影响,其视角独特,分析深刻,但多为专题性研究,而有关近代北京基督教史的综合性研究很少。

1.2 中国大陆的主要相关研究

改革开放以来,近代北京基督教史的研究在中国大陆逐渐受到重视,较早开始这项工作的当推北京基督教女青年会理事王毓华,她于1996年完成编写的《北京基督教史简编》一书可以说是奠基之作。该书收编了自19世纪中期至新中国成立初期基督教(新教)在北京的很多史实和相关资料,其史料来源于各教会档案、出版物和《北京基督教史料选辑》,北京市政府的《专门登记》档案,个人口述或书面材料,以及外国传教士的一些书籍❹。该书所收史料多与教会宗教活动相关,作者对史料也做了一些梳理,但其史料多来自中文文献,英文档案较少收录,反映教会社会活动的内容也很少。但是,该书所提供的文献信息十分珍贵,是学者们从事北京基督教会史研究不可或缺的参考书籍。大陆学者对近代北京基督教史的专门研究始自20世纪90年代,以陈月清和刘明翰两人合著的《北京基督教发展述略》为代表,该书于1998年由首都师范大学出版社出版,对基督教三大宗派——天主教、东正教和新教——在北京的传播与发展进行了综合考察。基督教(新教)只是其中的一部分,内容以20世纪30年代以前的

---

❶ Philip West, Yenching University and Sino – Western Relations, 1916 – 1952, Harvard University Press, 1976, Intro – duction and Conclusion.

❷ Marjorie Jean Harris, American Missions, Chinese Realities – An Historical Analysis of the Cross – Cultural Influence Upon the Development of North China Union Women's College/Yenching Women's College 1905—1943, A Ph. D dissertation University of North Carolina, 1995, Abstract.

❸ Xin Wenjun, Social Gospel, Social Economics and the YMCA: Sidney Gamble and Princeton – in – Peking, A Ph. D ThesisofUniversityof-Massachusetts, 1992, Abstract.

❹ 王毓华,北京基督教史简编. 北京市基督教三自爱国运动委员会、北京市基督教教务委员会办公室印制,1996:2-3.

基督教研究为主，其篇幅有限，对一些重要事件和人物的论述不够深入，对档案资料的利用不足，但该书的研究思路和研究方法为后人提供了一定的参考和借鉴。

进入21世纪以后，有关近代北京基督教史的研究逐步深入，相关研究成果不断涌现，包括《社会福音、社会服务与社会改造——北京基督教青年会历史研究1906—1949》《基督教与近现代北京社会》《北京地区基督教史迹研究》等专著，以及《历史·性别·社会：北京市基督教女子中学初考——以贝满女中为中心》等文章，研究不断向纵深拓展。《社会福音、社会服务与社会改造——北京基督教青年会历史研究1906—1949》一书主要以北京基督教青年会为个案，深入描述和详细分析基督教青年会是如何进入中国和北京、如何将提倡社会服务与传播社会福音相结合、探索改造近代中国社会之路的。该书是国内第一部深入研究城市基督教青年会历史的学术专著，利用了大量的英文档案文献，对基督教青年会的源流、发展，以及在近代北京的活动和影响进行了深入探究，再现了20世纪上半期北京基督教青年会的历史，分析了基督教青年会与近代北京社会的互动❶，对中国大陆的城市基督教青年会历史研究有一定带动作用。但由于史料所限，该书对抗战时期北京基督教青年会在北平的活动介绍略显不足。《基督教与近现代北京社会》一书主要探究基督教（新教）从19世纪中期传入北京直到21世纪初的历史。该书的时间跨度约150年，其间又以1949年为界，分出近代和现代两大阶段，前者主要考察基督教在近代北京的传播及其相关活动和多方面的影响，后者重点探讨基督教与社会主义社会相适应，以及为构建社会主义和谐社会所做出的种种努力。该书的特别之处在于采用了较多的中文档案文献和期刊杂志上的文献资料，深入考察了一些名人与近代北京基督教的关系，对北京基督教从传统向现代的转变及相关问题进行了一些分析❷。但有关新中国成立初期特别是"文革"时期北京基督教会的历史论述显得比较简略。《北京地区基督教史迹研究》一书运用考古学和历史学的方法，以北京现存的基督教史迹和文物为对象考察其现状及历史。作者指出，历史上的北京发生过许多重大历史事件，至今在地面和地下还保存着许多年代久远、种类丰富、价值很高的遗迹遗物，而基督教文物遗存是其中的重要内容之一，本书的目的就是为了唤起人们对它们的抢救保护，使其有用于现代北京的社会文化发展❸，其现实意义显而易见。该书所述的基督教包括了天主教、东正教、新教甚至景教，时间从唐代到明清时期，近代基督教（新教）只是其中很小的部分，所占篇幅仅几页，对相关遗迹的介绍不足不详。《历史·性别·社会：北京市基督教女子中学初考——以贝满女中为中心》一文以近代北京的一所基督教会中学——贝满女中——为例，探究基督教中等教育的兴起、发展和影响，以及其针对挑战的回应和面对机遇的努力。该文的特点在于从多角度入手和分析，如笔者所说"从历史语境、性别问题和社会参与这三个角度，来探讨基督教女子教育在北京地区的思想转型和社会变迁中的发展形态和历史意义"❹，深化了近代中国基督教教育史的研究，但在相关档案资料的利用上还可以再挖掘。

综观上述成果，笔者对大陆学界有关近代北京基督教史的研究概括出如下一些特点。

一是起步较早。基督教在近代北京的历史是基督教在近代中国的历史的一个缩影，近代北京基督教史是近代中国基督教区域史的组成部分，近代北京基督教史研究开始于改革开放初期，与同一时期其他区域的基督教史研究一起带动了中国基督教区域史研究。20世纪90年代以来，中国基督教区域史方兴未艾，研究成果陆续问世，较早的一批当属20世纪最后10年间出版的一批专著，包括陈友平、李少平的《基督教与福建民间社会》（厦门大学出版社，1992年）、张坦的《"窄门"前的石门坎——基督教文化与川滇黔边苗族社会》（云南教育出版社，1992年）、姚民权的《上海基督教史》（上海市基督教三自爱国运动委员会和上海市基督教教务委员会，1994年）、陶飞亚、刘天路的《基督教与近代山东社会》（山东大学出版社，1995年）、莫法有的《温州基督教史》（香港建道神学院基督教与中国文化研究中心，1998年）、钱宁的《基督教与少数民族社会文化变迁》（云南大学出版社，1998年）等。前面述及的《北京基督教史简编》和《北京基督教发展述略》也是这一时期的研究成果。

二是研究范围逐步扩大、不断深入。进入21世纪以后，中国基督教区域史的研究不断向纵深推进，

---

❶ 左芙蓉. 社会福音、社会服务与社会改造——北京基督教青年会历史研究1906—1949 [M]. 宗教文化出版社，2005：绪论.
❷ 左芙蓉. 基督教与近现代北京社会 [M]. 巴蜀书社，2009：绪论与结语.
❸ 吴梦麟，熊鹰. 北京地区基督教史迹研究 [M]. 文物出版社，2010.
❹ 尹文涓. 基督教与中国近代中等教育 [M]. 上海人民出版社，2007：346.

不仅总的研究成果增多,而且反映同一区域基督教研究成果的数量也多起来。例如,反映华南地区基督教的研究成果就有吴义雄的《宗教与世俗之间——基督教新教传教士在华南沿海的早期活动研究》(广东教育出版社,2000年)和《开端与进展:华南近代基督教史论集》(台北宇宙光出版社,2007年)、林金水的《福建基督教史初探》(台北宇宙光出版社,2006年)、郭德焱的《基督教新教传教士与广州口岸》(广东人民出版社,2002年)、赵春晨等的《基督教与近代岭南文化》(上海人民出版社,2002年)等。而有关西南地区基督教研究的成果则有韩军学的《基督教与云南少数民族》(云南人民出版社,2000年)、昆明市宗教事务局编写的《昆明基督教史》(云南大学出版社,2005年)、肖耀辉、刘鼎演的《云南基督教史》(云南大学出版社,2007年)、秦和平的《基督教在四川传播史稿》(四川人民出版社,2006年)等。此外,还有反映基督教在东部沿海城市的历史研究成果,如龚缨晏的《浙江早期基督教史》(杭州出版社,2010年)、孙顺华的《基督教传播与近代青岛社会文化研究》(中国社会科学出版社,2010年)等。而关于北京地区基督教史的研究也出现同样的趋势,从前面述及的《社会福音、社会服务与社会改造——北京基督教青年会历史研究1906—1949》《基督教与近现代北京社会》《北京地区基督教史迹研究》等著述不难看出,有关近代北京基督教史研究既有总体性论述,也有专题讨论;既有对北京基督教历史的综合考察,以及对基督教在近现代北京的传播、发展及影响的纵向研究,也有针对基督教青年会和教会中学等方面的个案考察,从而大大丰富了中国基督教区域史的研究。

三是研究方法逐渐多元化。比较明显的是,学者们在改革开放初期对于近代北京基督教史的研究主要采用的是历史学的研究方法,以梳理史料和论述史实为主,后来逐步向跨学科研究方向发展,尝试运用历史学、宗教社会学以及性别学、考古学等方法,既注重史料的广泛收集和梳理,也重视基督教与近代北京社会互动的分析,还将视角转向基督教青年会以及女性与教会中等教育,反映了学者们的研究视野不断开阔、研究思路逐渐扩大以及研究方法日益多元。

四是研究范式的非单一性。改革开放以来,近代北京基督教史的研究范式总的来看具有非单一性,或者说是混合型的。学者们对不同阶段的史实、对不同的历史事件和人物及其影响所采用的范式是有差别的,即具体事件和人物具体分析,既指出基督教传入近代北京的强权政治背景及其影响,也从世界文化交流复杂的大背景来分析判断基督教入华所带来的中西文化相遇、碰撞、互渗、沟通,及其与北京近代化的关系❶。因此,在同一著述中采用两种以上范式的情况并不少见。

需要指出的是,从总体来看大陆学者对近代北京基督教史的研究也还存有一些遗憾。例如,由于史料挖掘不够,致使很多问题难以得到深入细致的剖析,现有研究成果也不能取得尽如人意的效果,还有不少相关领域因此被学者们忽视。此外,学者们多关注基督教与北京社会的关系,但对基督教会自身发展演变的历程少有专门深入的考察。另外,现有研究多侧重于史料梳理和史实分析,但对相关理论的深度阐释较少,更缺乏理论上的突破或创新。因此,该研究领域的中外学者加强交流、相互学习、彼此借鉴是很有必要的。

2 近代北京基督教史的相关资料及利用

详细占有史料是历史研究的最基本条件,同样,近代北京基督教史研究也离不开相关史料的利用。从保存来看,现有的相关资料主要在北京的各大图书馆(如国家图书馆和首都图书馆等)、各综合性大学图书馆(如北京大学图书馆、中国人民大学图书馆、北京师范大学图书馆等)、北京市档案馆、北京基督教会以及中国社会科学院等单位保存,港台和美国也存有一些。从内容来看,有关近代北京基督教史的资料很多,包括各类基督教报刊杂志、基督教会会议文件、基督教年鉴、教会会务活动记录、男女青年会的会刊和报告及纪念刊、教会学校刊物、相关人士回忆录、基督徒知识分子的论著以及普通报刊的相关报道等,非常丰富。其中基督教报刊杂志有《救世报》《生命月刊》《真理与生命》《暗中之光》《北平青年》《华北公理联合月刊》《中华基督教公理会联合月刊》《灵食季刊》《燕大团契声》《燕京神学丛刊》《恩友》《团契》《田家》《紫晶》❷等多种。基督教会会议文件、会务活动记录及年鉴等也有

---

❶ 卓新平. 中国宗教学30年(1978—2008)[M]. 中国社会科学出版社,2008:297.

❷ 该刊创办于1931年,会址在燕京大学燕南园内,刘廷芳任编辑,从第4卷第2期起,该刊的印刷及发行事务委托位于上海博物院路19号的广学会代办。

不少，如《基督教全国大会报告书》《中华基督教青年会全国干事大会报告书》《华北基督教宗教工作研究会会刊》《北京公理会会议记录》《北京基督教女青年会会务纪闻》《中华基督教会年鉴》《华北宗教年鉴》等。相关报告和纪念刊有：《北平基督教女青年会社会服务工作报告书》、青年会年度报告（英文）、《北平基督教女青年会三十周年纪念刊》《中华基督教青年会五十周年纪念册1885—1935》等。教会学校刊物则包括了各校校刊、一些名校如崇实中学、汇文中学、慕贞女校，以及燕京大学等印制的年刊、纪念刊和报告书等。相关人士回忆录有：《在华五十年——司徒雷登回忆录》《亲历晚清四十五年——李提摩太在华回忆录》《燕京大学—1945—1951级校友纪念刊》《北京基督教青年会会史片断》丁韪良的《花甲忆记》和《北京被围目击记》、刘廷芳和谢景升的"司徒雷登年谱"、陆志伟的"司徒雷登与燕京大学"等。此外，一批与近代北京基督教有关的基督徒知识分子的论著，如吴雷川的《基督教与中国》《基督教研究课程》，张钦士的《国内近十年来之宗教思潮》，徐宝谦的《基督教与中国文化》，吴耀宗的《社会福音》《大时代的宗教信仰》，赵紫宸的《从中国文化说到基督教》《中国基督教教会改革的途径》等也是重要的参考资料。值得一提的是，民国时期的一些报刊如《大公报》《晨报》等也经常刊登近代北京基督教的一些活动，不失为学者相关研究的辅助文献。从利用来看，目前利用率较高的近代北京基督教史文献有：《生命月刊》《真理与生命》《华北公理联合月刊》，以及北京基督教青年会英文档案等。其中，《生命月刊》是研究20世纪20年代基督徒知识分子与新文化运动的关系的重要依据之一，其内容广泛，涉及宗教教育讨论、《圣经》研究、神学研究、社会问题研究、教会问题研究，以及基督教革新运动的提倡等，而且该刊各卷保存完整❶，为中国大陆和港台学者较多地参考和引用。《真理与生命》以讨论中国教会问题、阐发基督教真理以促进中国基督教运动为宗旨，其发行时间自1926至新中国成立初期，抗战期间一度停办。该刊为民国后期基督教史和基督教思想史研究的重要参考资料，广受学者关注和利用。《华北公理联合月刊》（从第4期起更名为《华北公理会月刊》）为传入中国的基督教宗派之一——公理会所办刊物，刊址在北平，以报道华北地区公理会的活动为主，该刊近来也受到研究近代北京公理会史学者的重视。基督教青年会在民国时期的北京非常活跃，影响较大，但相关的史料在中国大陆保存得很少，大陆学者对它的研究较多地依靠在美国保存的英文档案，但这些英文档案也多限于1937年以前，1937年以后至1949年期间的档案文献存留至今的仍不多。

总之，改革开放以来大陆学者对近代北京基督教史料的利用经历了由稀少到逐渐增多的过程。由于"文革"等原因造成的相关史料散落或流失，加之改革开放初期很多相关档案不予开放，学者早期所做的相关研究可利用的史料很有限。随着改革开放的持续和深入、大陆与海外交流活动的增多，以及一些历史档案的解封等，越来越多的历史文献向社会开放，地方志、教会档案、教会报刊，以及其他相关文献和外文资料等为学者的研究提供了重要的史料支撑。但是由于不少宗教期刊卷数不全、档案文献片面等原因，成为制约学术研究的不利因素。还有一些档案在大陆已经消失殆尽，而在海外保存较好，尽管获取它们存在交通方面的某些不便，但毕竟有希望获取，而且随着图文信息技术的不断进步和广泛应用，一些在海外的档案文献也逐渐可以通过互联网在国内查阅，这对大陆学者来说无疑是福音。因此，从前述大陆学者的研究成果中可以清楚地看到这样的变化：早期研究所参阅的一手资料不多，外文资料也较少，而近期研究所利用的史料较为丰富，其中包括大量的中英文档案资料以及其他外文文献。但总的来看，由于多种因素的影响，已经面世的研究成果对史料尤其是档案资料的利用仍不够充分。

3 对未来研究的展望与建议

由于近代北京基督教史在近代北京史、近代中国基督教史、近代中外关系史中占有重要地位，还由于近代北京基督教与当代北京基督教的承继关系，重视对它的研究很有必要，不仅有助于北京史研究领域的拓宽和中国基督教史研究的深入以及中外关系史研究的丰富，而且对基督教的中国化与本土化、中国基督教的历史影响与现实作用等理论问题的探索也具有重要意义。

从现有研究成果来看，近代北京基督教史的综合性研究虽然比较广泛但仍然不够全面，有些问题虽然涉及但没有得到充分论述，而专题研究仅局限于个别议题，很多领域有待开拓。以笔者之见，今后还

---

❶ 1920—1926年，《生命月刊》共出版6卷56期。

需要重视以下五个方面的专门研究。

一是近代北京基督教会的历史，包括各宗派、教派或教会的演变、组织结构、成员构成及宗教活动等。近代北京基督教宗派林立，门户众多，既有外来的宗派，如伦敦布道会、长老会、圣公会、卫理公会、公理会、神召会、救世军、基督复临安息日会、圣洁教会、圣经会等，也有自办的教派或教会，如真耶稣教会、圣城新教会、基督徒会堂、基督徒聚会处及一些福音堂等，而有关它们的专门深入研究至今几乎是空白。

二是近代北京基督教神学教育，包括各类神学院校的开办及宗旨、课程设置、师生来源、毕业生流向及影响等方面。基督教神学院校在近代北京有很多，包括华北协和道学院、汇文大学校神科、燕京大学宗教学院、联合女子圣道学院、北京神学院、真理学院、北平圣书学院、基督教灵修院、香山灵修学院等，这些神学院校不仅培养了一批中国传道人，而且涌现出一批中国基督教教育家和神学思想家，他们曾对中国基督教神学思想体系的构建作出过重要贡献，赵紫宸、刘廷芳、吴雷川等是其代表人物。总的来看，有关近代北京基督教神学教育的现有研究成果主要集中在与燕京大学宗教学院相关的人和事方面，对其他神学院校及相关人物的深入研究极少。

三是教会附属机构，如学校、医院、出版社、图书馆、慈善组织等。一般而言，学界对近代北京的教会大学关注较多，但对教会中学和小学较少专门研究。事实上，教会初级和中级教育是教会高等教育的基础。以1865年裨治文夫人开办的贝满女子小学为例，后来的贝满女中和华北协和女子大学（中国第一所女子大学，后并入燕京大学）都要寻根到这里。此外，近代北京的一些教会中学在今天仍然存在，如育英中学（现为北京市立25中）、汇文中学和潞河中学等校的地址没有改变，有的甚至校名依旧，如汇文中学（一度改名为市立26中）和潞河中学（一度改名为通县1中）等，其历史影响由此可见，加强对它们的研究有助于理解近代北京的教育近代化。此外，有关近代北京教会医院的历史至今仍缺少有份量的专门研究成果。近代北京最早的西医院和西医学校是由伦敦布道会开办的，今天的协和医院和协和医科大学的历史都要从此开始。北京同仁医院也曾是教会医院，初名叫做美以美会医院，1886年由美以美会在崇文门内孝顺胡同创办，1903年扩建后取名同仁医院，以眼科见长。上述医院在今天仍然闻名全国，这与其传统因素的影响是分不开的。有关近代北京基督教的出版机构、图书馆、慈善组织等专门研究也基本上处于边缘地位。

四是相关方面。例如，近代北京基督教与其他宗教的关系、与全国各地基督教的关系、与中外名人的关系等。近代北京有很多宗教并存，主要有佛教、道教、回教、天主教，还有民间宗教，基督教与它们的关系如何？有无对话？等等，这些问题至今没有受到学者的重视，少有深入专门的研究成果。近代北京长期作为政治和文化中心，吸引并聚集过很多名人，他们与近代北京基督教关系密切。例如，有着"基督将军"称号的冯玉祥就曾与近代北京基督教会来往频繁，他接受洗礼成为基督徒是在北京的亚斯立教堂[1]，他曾在北京发起成立"基督徒祈祷会"，其夫人李德全曾是北京基督教女青年会干事。又例如，当代北京著名作家老舍早年曾在北京西城缸瓦市教堂接受基督教洗礼，并且参与缸瓦市教堂的自立自养，起草《北京缸瓦市中华基督教会现行规约》。名人与近代北京基督教会的关系从一个方面反映了基督教的广泛影响，这一研究还有待深入。

五是1937—1949年期间北京基督教的历史，特别是抗战时期的北京基督教史。1937年日本帝国主义者发动全面侵华战争，北平较早沦陷。在日伪统治下，基督教会面临严峻考验，虽然在抗战前期，基督教因为与英、美的密切关系，属英、美差会的各教会仍然在英、美传教士和外国经济的支持下照常活动，但是大环境的改变还是令其发展严重受挫，尤其是"珍珠港事件"爆发后英、美对日宣战，一些传教士包括燕京大学校务长司徒雷登等人被日本人拘留。为监视、利用和控制基督教会，日本在北平组织华北基督教团，迫使教会参加，否则予以解散；燕京大学被迫关闭，一部分师生逃往中国西南地区复校……当时基督教会及其相关组织面临着非常艰难的境地。另一方面，广大基督徒坚决反对日本对中国的侵略，尽其所能、竭尽全力以不同形式参与抗日救亡，例如，服务抗日将士和伤兵、救济贫民和难

---

[1] 该教堂现名崇文门教堂，它是北京现存历史悠久的新教教堂，也是一所涉外教堂，接待过不少外宾。每个主日都有外国使馆的官员、国外信徒来此做礼拜。美国前总统乔治·布什和克林顿曾专门到该教堂做礼拜，英国坎特伯雷大主教乔治·凯瑞博士、著名布道家葛培理牧师曾经多次到访。

民、多方募集钱物为抗战出力等。抗战胜利后，基督教会进入重建和奋进阶段，战后提出的"三年计划"希望教会在1946—1949年中不但可以重建而且有所发展。实现这一计划的运动名为"三年奋进运动"，其目标是增加信徒的人数、加强教会力量以使教会富有生命力、促使教会合一与合作、提高社区和国家的精神生活。这一运动取得了较明显的成效，反映在信徒人数增加，堂会数量增多，一些外国传教士再度进入北平，福音传播、文字宣教等活动急速发展，燕京大学回迁北平，各神学院校复校开学等方面。另一方面，战后时局动荡，内战再起，信徒的社会责任感增强，教会领袖对时局的主张及对国民党政府的认识分歧加大，一部分教会人士在中华人民共和国成立后成为"三自"爱国运动的发起者和领导者。大陆学界目前对这段历史的深入研究极少，相关史料缺失较多、存在一些敏感问题等是其中重要原因。

从现有研究方法来看，专家学者对近代北京基督教史的研究多采用历史学、兼用宗教社会学、考古学和性别学的一些方法，但从神学、历史文献学、文化遗产学等角度深化研究的不多。事实上，基督教在近代北京的传播过程中，基督教神学思想也得到丰富发展，系统深入的研究有助于理解基督教的中国化与本土化以及一些相关问题。此外，有关近代北京基督教史的文献资料十分丰富但又比较分散，包括中文和外文的资料，对它们加以系统地收集整理和编译出版，不仅有利于学者的研究而且有助于历史文献的保护。从文化遗产学的角度看，近代北京基督教文化及相关遗址、遗迹和遗存也是北京文化遗产的一部分，重视对它们的利用、保护和深入细致的研究对于推动北京文化的建设和发展具有重要意义。

4 结　语

把近代北京基督教史放到中国基督教史的发展历程中看，说它太短暂绝不为过，然而，这并没有成为中外学人忽视它的理由，相反，它却成为吸引学者的因素之一，因为它的影响度与它的时间段并不成正比。从20世纪50年代开始的美国学者对教会大学及青年会的专门研究，到改革开放以来大陆学者对基督教的综合性研究及某些专题的研究都不难看出，它对学者们研究的吸引力不但没有因为时间的推移而减弱，反倒还有增加的趋势。近代北京基督教史的研究现状一方面反映了中外学人的不懈努力及所取得的成绩，另一方面也反映出了某些不足和遗憾，足资日后研究借鉴。正是从这个角度来看，回顾和分析中外学人对近代北京基督教史的研究现状，介绍和梳理相关历史文献，不仅有利于学术界的沟通与交流，也有助于相关研究水平的不断提升，对深刻理解北京基督教从传统向现代的转变及其原因也有一定的启发性。

湖北郧县刘湾旧石器时代遗址发掘简报

冯小波 王 昊 王正华 黄旭初 周兴明 张 俊

刘湾旧石器时代遗址位于湖北省十堰市郧县杨溪铺镇刘湾村4组（图1），埋藏于汉水左岸第Ⅲ级阶地上（丹江口水库未淹没时之地貌），距郧县县城约20千米。在南水北调中线工程湖北省地下文物保护工作中，遗址于1994年调查发现，2010年4~7月，中国科学院古脊椎动物与古人类研究所、郧县博物馆组成的联合考古队对该遗址进行了正式发掘，同时在遗址周边区域进行了详细调查。本文即是这次发掘和调查的收获。

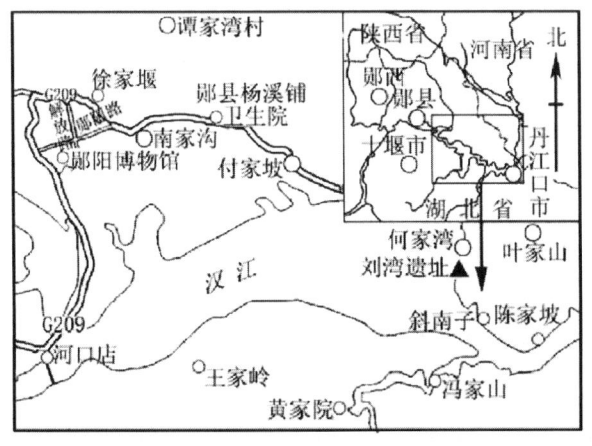

图1 刘湾旧石器时代遗址地理位置示意图

1 地质背景与地层堆积

刘湾旧石器时代遗址所在的汉水第Ⅲ级阶地（现为第Ⅱ级阶地，丹江口水库已将原来的第Ⅰ级阶地淹没）形成于新生代的新构造运动时期。这个区域在第四纪是河流发育的主要时期，由于构造运动和河流侵蚀作用使得河流两岸发育有多级河流阶地，在丹江口地区形成了5级层状地貌，同时也反映出该区有五次构造运动上升和稳定。新近纪是一个新构造运动相对稳定的时期，形成高度在380米左右的分布较广的夷平面。新近纪末受喜马拉雅造山运动的影响，有一次较剧烈的新构造运动上升期，上升幅度达200米。在早更新世新构造运动又处于一个相对稳定时期，形成了Ⅳ级基座阶地，早更新世末又有一次新构造运动上升，上升幅度为30米左右。在中更新世也有一次较长时期新构造运动稳定和下降时期，形成了分布较广的Ⅲ级冲积阶地。

刘湾旧石器时代遗址紧邻汉水，在遗址的东边是一处面积约10000平方米的新石器时代遗址，已经由湖北省文物考古研究所发掘，其海拔高度在160米左右。为了寻找最佳的发掘区域，我们在这个新石器时代遗址周围进行了详细的踏勘，布设了7条探沟，然后选择了石制品分布较为丰富、地层堆积较厚的两个地点进行了正式发掘，编号分别为刘湾旧石器时代遗址Ⅰ、Ⅱ号地点，Ⅰ号地点在Ⅱ号地点的南

[基金项目] 本次发掘得到国家社科基金（课题编号：12BKG002）；国家文物局文化遗产保护科学和技术研究课题（课题编号：20090105）；南水北调文物保护科研课题（课题编号：NK04）；北京联合大学人才强校计划人才资助项目；北京市哲学社会科学规划项目（项目编号：11LSB004）；国家重点基础研究发展计划项目（2006CB806400）的资助。
[作者简介] 冯小波，北京联合大学应用文理学院教授，历史文博系副主任。
[绘图] 陈曦，冯小波。
[照相] 郝勤建。

边，两个地点直线距离约为200米。根据湖北省文物局南水北调中线工程文物保护领导小组办公室规划，确定Ⅰ、Ⅱ号地点发掘面积分别为500平方米、200平方米。我们共布5×5米的探方28个。

刘湾旧石器时代遗址Ⅰ、Ⅱ号地点的海拔高度均为150~155米，地理坐标分别为N32°49′05″，E110°53′15″；N32°48′41.6″，E110°53′31。

Ⅰ号地点的地层堆积如下（图2a）。

第1层为灰黑、灰褐色耕土层，粉砂质黏土，局部夹杂零星小砾石和现代残留物，结构疏松。厚0~0.2米。

第2层为红褐色黏土，钙质结核发育。结构致密，胶结坚硬，柱状节理发育。钙质结核呈结核状和透镜状发育于节理中，垂直状展布。含石制品。厚1.3米。

第3层为棕红色、褐红色黏土，土质坚硬，局部发育柱状节理，节理空隙内局部充填黑色粉砂，呈垂直状展布。红色黏土下部夹有土黄色细粉砂。与下伏地层呈过渡接触。含石制品。厚1.8米。

Ⅱ号地点的地层堆积如下（图2b）。

第1层为灰黑、灰褐色耕土层，粉砂质黏土，结构疏松。厚0~0.3米。

第2层为红褐色黏土，钙质结核发育。结构致密，胶结坚硬没，柱状节理发育。钙质结核呈结核状和透镜状发育于节理中，垂直状展布。含石制品。厚1.2米。

第3层为棕红色、褐红色黏土，局部发育柱状节理。与下伏地层呈过渡接触。含石制品。厚1.7米。

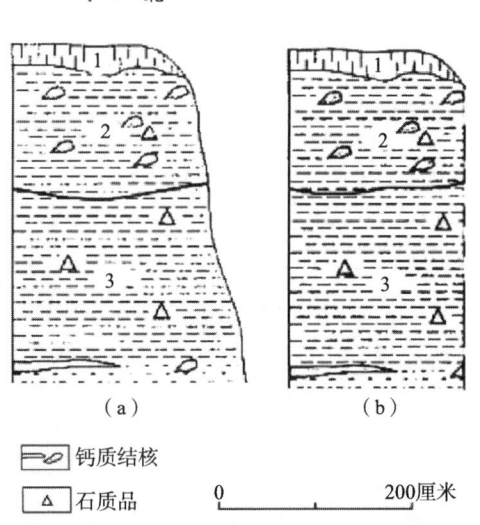

图2 刘湾旧石器时代遗址Ⅰ、Ⅱ号地点地层剖面图
1—Ⅰ号地点地层剖面图；2—Ⅱ号地点地层剖面图

2 遗 物

我们在刘湾旧石器时代遗址Ⅰ、Ⅱ号地点没有发现遗迹现象，所发现的均为遗物，依照田野考古发掘规程，我们将这两个地点出土及采集的石制品分别统计。但由于这两个地点的地层堆积相同，出土及采集的石制品的埋藏环境也相同，因此两个地点的文化内涵也应相同。据此我们将它们出土及采集的石制品统一在一个文化面貌内来描述。

刘湾旧石器时代遗址Ⅰ、Ⅱ号地点出土及采集所得遗物共计320件，其中除了1件为鹿科的牙齿化石外，其余319件都是石制品。

2.1 动物化石

此次发现的动物化石只有1件，为1颗鹿科动物的上白齿化石。

2.2 石制品

共319件，其中采集品25件，出土石制品Ⅰ号地点177件，Ⅱ号地点117件。

2.2.1 采集石制品

25件,分别为石核2件、石片1件、碎片4件、砍砸器10件、手镐2件、手斧6件。没有发现砾石、石锤和刮削器。

石核 2件。10YLC:18,单台面石核。长9.6厘米、宽10.2厘米、厚7.2厘米,重866克。岩性为脉石英,台面在底面,有两个剥片面,分别在近端的左、右两侧面,有5块石片疤阴痕,台面角分别为49°、78°、78°、82°、89°(图3a)。

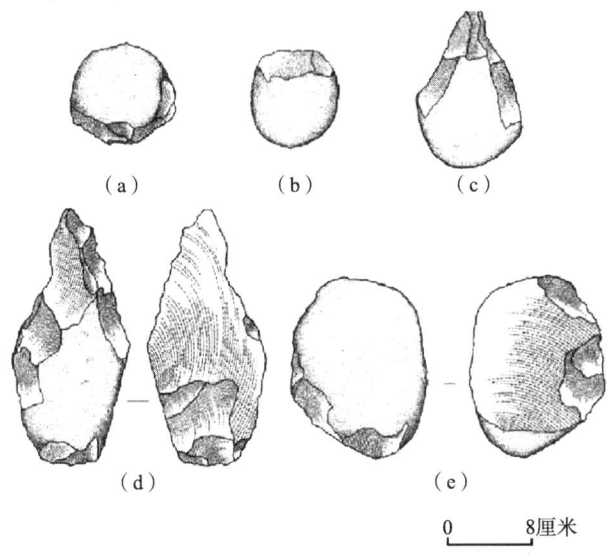

图3 刘湾旧石器时代遗址Ⅰ、Ⅱ号地点采集石制品
(a) 单台面石核(10YLC:18);(b)(e) 单刃砍砸器(10YLC:10、10YLC:17);
(c)、(d) 手镐(10YLC:25、10YLC:5)

砍砸器 10件。10YLC:10,单刃砍砸器。长8.9厘米、宽8.4厘米、厚4.6厘米,重488克。岩性为脉石英,素材为砾石,刃缘在远端边,由2块疤单向加工而成,刃角分别为51°、57°(图3b)。10YLC:17,单刃砍砸器。长17.2厘米、宽13.1厘米、厚5.3厘米,重1135克。岩性为硅质岩,呈黑色,素材为完整石片。刃缘在左端边,为凸刃,由5块疤加工而成,其中2个是正向加工,其余3个为反向加工,刃角分别为45°、52°、46°、61°、67°(图3e)。

手镐 2件。10YLC:25,长15厘米、宽10.2厘米、厚4.8厘米,重506克。岩性为娃质岩,素材为砾石,刃缘在左、右两侧边,由6块疤加工而成,其中5块为正向加工,1块为反向加工,刃角分别为41°、65°、49°、58°、73°、82°(图3c;彩版一,1)。10YLC:5,长23.9厘米、宽11.5厘米、厚4.3厘米,重1133克。岩性为闪长岩,素材为砾石,刃缘在左、右两侧边,由7块疤加工而成,其中6块为正向加工,1块为反向加工,刃角分别为48°、63°、56°、37°、53°、54°、45°(图3d;彩版一,2)。

手斧 6件。10YLC:4,长16厘米、宽10.2厘米、厚4.1厘米,重725克。岩性为娃质岩,素材为石乐石,刃缘在左、右两侧边,由6块疤加工而成,其中4块为正向加工,2块为反向加工,刃角除一个难以测量外,其余分别为67°、67°、51°、50°、50°(彩版一,3、4)。10YLC:6,长15.2厘米、宽10.7厘米、厚6.2厘米,重949克。岩性为含砾砂岩,素材为砾石,刃缘在左、右两侧边,在近端也有加工,有11块加工小疤,有7块为正向加工,4块为反向加工,刃角除一个难以测量外,其余分别为63°、75°、75°、57°、65°、73°、81°、73°、62°、87°(彩版一,5、6)。10YLC:16,长14.9厘米、宽8.3厘米、厚6.1厘米,重1010克。岩性为硅质岩,素材为砾石,刃缘在左远、右远两侧边,有5块加工小疤,3块为正向加工,2块为反向加工,刃角分别为73°、78°、65°、73°、77°(彩版一,7、8)。10YLC:1,长20.1厘米、宽10.7厘米、厚5.2厘米,重1064克。岩性为娃质岩,其素材为5乐石,刃缘在左、右两侧边,在近端也有加工,有16块加工小疤,其中2块为修理把手的疤,1块为去薄的疤,其余13块疤有8块为正向加工,5块为反向加工,刃角除两个难以测量外,其余分别为60°、95°、64°、59°、59°、29°、39°、60°、82°、62°、51°(彩版二,1、2)。

湖北郧县刘湾旧石器时代遗址采集石制品

2.2.2 出土石制品

（1）Ⅰ号地点出土石制品

177件，分别为砾石17件、碎片82件、石锤1件、石核17件、石片20件、砍砸器31件、手镐2件、手斧3件、刮削器4件。

石锤 1件（10YLⅠT10②:7），长17.2厘米、宽9.9厘米、厚5.2厘米，重1215克。岩性为斑岩，在近端有1块反向的疤。

石核 17件。10YLⅠT1②:11，单台面石核。长9.4厘米、宽9.4厘米、厚3.7厘米，重685克。岩性为脉石英，台面在左侧面，有一个剥片面，在远端，有2块石片疤阴痕，台面角分别为87°、88°。

石片 20件。10YLⅠT15②:2，完整石片。长10.6厘米、宽9.2厘米、厚4.7厘米，重495克。岩性为石英砂岩，天然台面，背面全部为砾石石皮，石片角为119°（图四,1）。10YLⅠT5②:4，完整石片。长4.3厘米、宽3.8厘米、厚1厘米，重15克。岩性为砂岩，人工台面（一个平疤），背面全部为片疤阴痕，可测量的台面角分别为82°、83°、86°，石片角为104°（图四,2）。10YLⅠT12②:4，完整石片。长5.3厘米、宽4.7厘米、厚1.1厘米，重28克。岩性为硅质岩，天然台面，背面砾石石皮比率约为30%，台面角为60°，石片角115°（图四,3）。10YLⅠT10②:4，完整石片。长6.5厘米、宽6.2厘米、厚1.7厘米，重56克。岩性为硅质岩，天然台面，背面砾石石皮比率约为25%，台面角难测量，石片角124°（图四,4）。10YLⅠT14②:6，完整石片。长4.7厘米、宽3.5厘米、厚1.3厘米，重22克。岩性为脉石英，天然台面，背面均为片疤阴痕，台面角为63°、68°，石片角111°（图四,5）。10YLⅠT3②:6，完整石片。长4.8厘米、宽5.5厘米、厚1.8厘米，重54克。岩性为脉石英，天然台

— 239 —

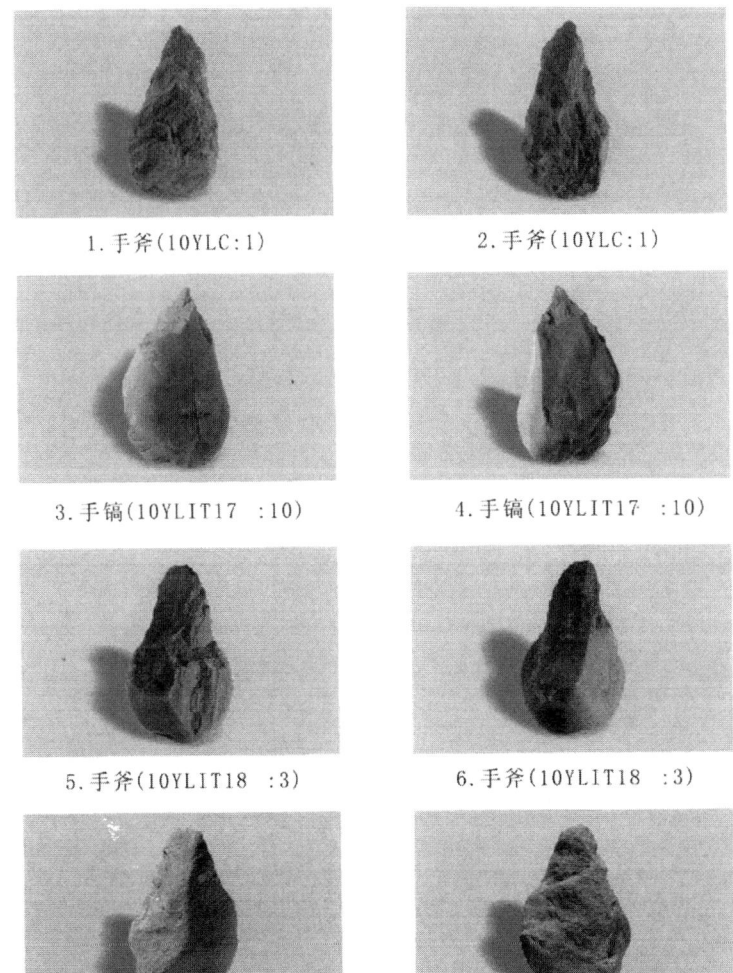

湖北郧县刘湾旧石器时代遗址采集及出土石制品

面,背面全部为砾石石皮,石片角97°(图四,6)。

砍砸器 31件。

单刃砍砸器 23件。10YLⅠT17②:5,长8.5厘米、宽7.2厘米、厚4.2厘米,重360克。岩性为脉石英,素材为砾石,刃缘在右侧边,由1块疤单向加工而成,刃角为65°(图五,1)。

10YLⅠT2②:10,长8.2厘米、宽8.2厘米、厚5厘米,重414克。岩性为脉石英,素材为砾石,刃缘在近端边——右侧边,由3块疤单向加工而成,刃角分别为83°、93°、80°(图五,2)。10YLⅠT2②:1,长11.8厘米、宽11.5厘米、厚3.5厘米,重548克。岩性为硅质岩,素材为砾石,刃缘在近端边,由3块疤双向加工而成,刃角分别为45°、47°、53°(图五,3)。10YLⅠT12②:3,长12.1厘米、宽7.8厘米、厚3.7厘米,重442克。岩性为砂岩,素材为砾石,刃缘在远端边,由4块疤单向加工而成,有两个刃角难以测量,其余两个刃角分别为48°、54°(图五,4)。

双刃砍砸器 4件。10YLⅠT17①:1,长13.5厘米、宽11.6厘米、厚4.4厘米,重821克。岩性为闪长岩,素材为砾石断块,刃缘在近端边和左侧边,由4块疤单向加工而成,刃角分别为68°、65°、62°、78°。

多刃砍砸器 4件。10YLⅠT2①:6,长12厘米、宽12厘米、厚4.8厘米,重1152克。岩性为砂岩,素材为砾石,刃缘在近端边、左侧边和右侧边,由10块疤双向加工而成,刃角分别为72°、73°、78°、72°、81°、67°、73°、61°、70°、58°。

手镐 2件。10YLⅠT17①:10,长16.4厘米、宽9.1厘米、厚6.4厘米,重1054克。岩性为砂岩,其素材为砾石,刃缘在左、右两侧的远端边,由3块疤单向加工而成,刃角分别为55°、69°、75°

（图五，5；彩版二，3、4）。

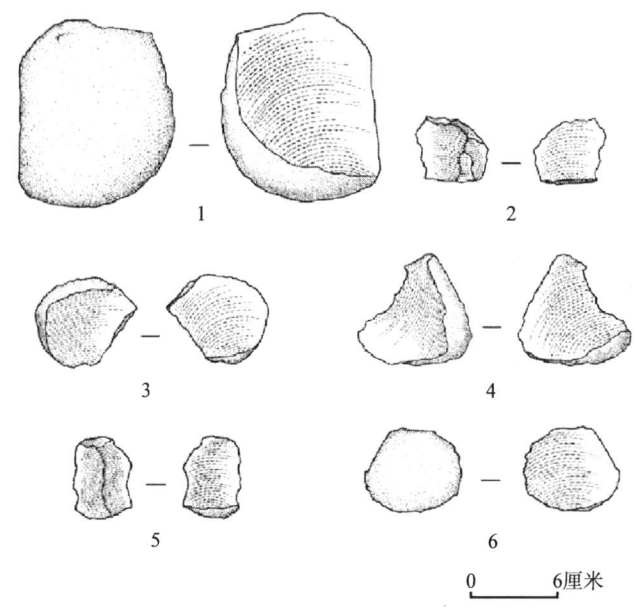

图4　刘湾旧石器时代遗址 I 号地点出土石片
1. 10YL I T15②：2　2. 10YL I T5②：4　3. 10YL I T12②：4
4. 10YL I T10②：4　5. 10YL I T14②：6　6. 10YL I T3②：6

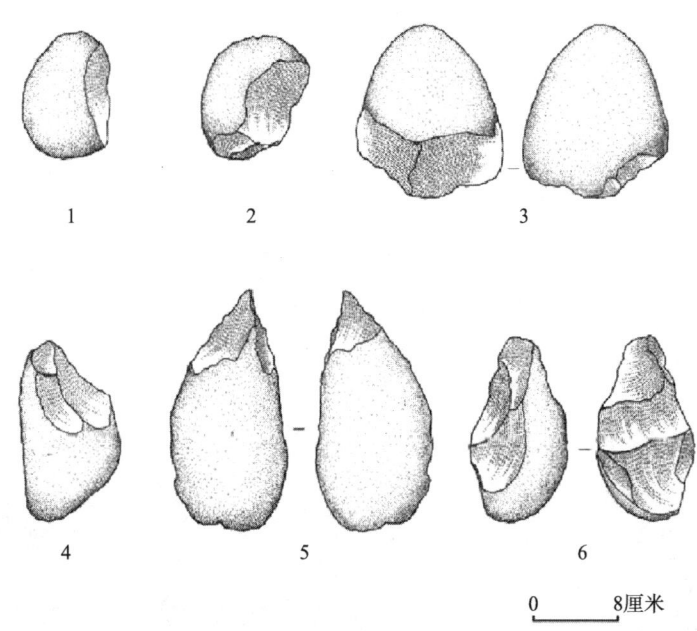

图5　刘湾旧石器时代遗址 I 号地点出土石器
1~4. 砍砸器（10YL I T17②：5、10YL I T2②：10、10YL I T2②：1、10YL I T12②：3）
5. 手镐（10YL I T17①：10）　6. 手斧（10YL I T8②：5）

手斧　3件。10YL I T18①：3，长15.7厘米、宽9.5厘米、厚6.2厘米，重742克。岩性为硅质岩，素材为砾石，刃缘在左、右两侧边，有6块加工小疤，有4块为正向加工，2块为反向加工，刃角除三个难以测量外，其余分别为70°、75°、83°（彩版二，5、6）。10YL I T8②：5，长12.4厘米、宽7.7厘米、厚4.8厘米，重433克。岩性为闪长岩，素材为砾石，刃缘在左、右两侧边，由8块疤加工而成，其中3块为正向加工，5块为反向加工，刃角分别为73°、96°、78°、71°、77°、67°、88°、85°（图五，6；彩版二，7、8）。

刮削器　4件。10YL I T14②：1，长11.8、宽8.2、厚3.2厘米，重244克。岩性为砂岩，素材为砾石断块，刃缘在近端边，由2块疤加工而成，刃角分别为41°、45°。

(2) Ⅱ号地点出土石制品

117件，分别为砾石15件、碎片79件、石核7件、石片8件、砍砸器7件、手镐1件。没有发现手斧和刮削器。

石核 7件。10YLⅡT2②：8，单台面石核。长7厘米、宽8.5厘米、厚3.1厘米，重401克。岩性为脉石英，台面在底面，有一个剥片面，在近端面，有3块石片疤阴痕，台面角分别为60°、78°、73°。T1②：5，双台面石核。长7.8厘米、宽5.7厘米、厚4.9厘米，重273克。岩性为脉石英，台面在底面和右侧面，有两个剥片面，在近端面和远端面，有3块石片疤阴痕，台面角分别为68°、74°、80°。

石片 8件。10YLⅡT3②：1，完整石片。长5.9厘米、宽3.3厘米、厚1.3厘米，重21克。岩性为脉石英，天然台面，背面没有保留砾石石皮，台面角分别为83°、64°，石片角为114°（图六，2）。

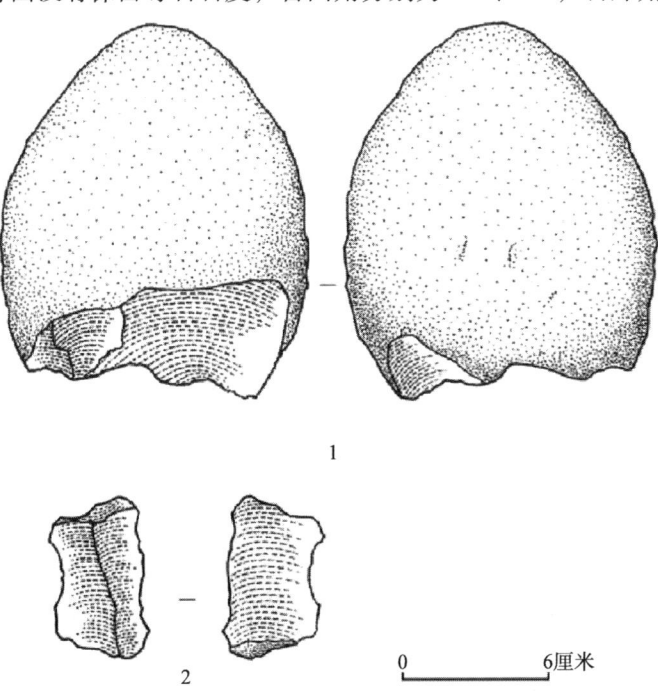

图6 刘湾旧石器时代遗址Ⅱ号地点出土石制品
1. 砍砸器10YLⅡT3②：10) 2. 石片（10YLⅡT3②：1）

砍砸器 7件。

单刃砍砸器 6件。10YLⅡT3②：10，长12.6厘米、宽10.5厘米、厚6.5厘米，重1125克。岩性为脉石英，素材为砾石，刃缘在近端边，由4块疤加工而成，刃角分别为75°、88°、75°、88°（图六，1）。10YLⅡT3②：7，长9.8厘米、宽10厘米、厚8厘米，重861克。岩性为脉石英，素材为砾石，刃缘在近端边，由2块疤双向加工而成，刃角分别为83°、79°。

多刃砍砸器 1件（10YLⅡT6②：9），长9.4厘米、宽8.8厘米、厚3.5厘米，重579克。岩性为脉石英，其素材为砾石，刃缘在远端边、左侧边和右侧边，由6块疤双向加工而成，刃角分别为85°、85°、78°、73°、85°、75°。

手镐 1件（10YLⅡT3②：11），长12厘米、宽9.6厘米、厚4.4厘米，重952克。岩性为砂岩，素材为石乐石，刃缘在左、右两侧的远乡而边，由7块症加工而成，刃角除一个难以测量外，其余分别为56°、62°、68°、83°、73°、83°。

3 文化特征及时代

刘湾旧石器时代遗址Ⅰ、Ⅱ号地点出土及采集的石制品因为埋藏环境相同，可视为同一文化遗存的石制品。

表1 刘湾旧石器时代遗址Ⅰ、Ⅱ号地点出土及采集石制品岩性统计表

岩性	沉积岩						火成岩			变质岩	小计
	砂岩	硅质岩	含砾砂岩	泥质岩	石英砂岩	细砂岩	脉石英	闪长岩	斑岩	石英岩	
采集	2	9	1	0	0	0	12	1	1	0	25
Ⅰ号地点	34	18	0	3	1	1	112	5	1	2	177
Ⅱ号地点	1	0	0	0	0	0	116	0	0	0	177
小计	37	27	1	3	1	1	240	6	1	2	319
百分比（%）	11.6	8.4	0.32	0.94	0.32	0.32	75.2	1.94	0.32	0.64	100

从表1中可看出，刘湾旧石器时代遗址石制品中岩性以火成岩标本最多，有247件，占石制品总数的77.5%；其次为沉积岩标本，有70件，占21.9%；变质岩标本最少，只有2件，占0.6%。从岩性大类上看，沉积岩最多，有6种，火成岩有3种，变质岩只有1种。再细分，总共10种岩性中，以脉石英标本为大宗，有240件，占75.2%；其次为砂岩标本，有37件，占11.6%；第三为硅质岩标本，有27件，占8.4%；第四为闪长岩标本，有6件，占1.94%；其他如泥质岩、石英岩、含砾砂岩、石英砂岩、细砂岩、斑岩等标本，均不到1%。可见刘湾旧石器时代的远古居民制作石器最喜好的岩石种类是脉石英、砂岩和硅质岩，其他的较少选用，以沉积岩种类最多。

我们将刘湾旧石器时代遗址石制品分为三大类：加工工具、素材（或称原料）和石器。加工工具主要是指石锤、石砧及其他用来加工石器的工具；素材主要指被加工的对象，如砾石、石核、石片、碎片、碎块、断块等；石器指各种素材经过加工后得到的石制品，主要分为两个大类，砾石（石核）石器和石片石器，每大类又分为若干小的类型，如砍砸器、刮削器、手镐、手斧等。

经统计，素材中完整砾石、断裂砾石、碎片（碎块）数量不少，石核和石片的数量稍少。石核中，单台面、双台面、多台面和石核剩块分别有15件、9件、1件、1件。石片中，完整石片有26件，半边石片3件。全部319件石制品中，石核、砾石石器等有89件，石片、碎片、石片石器有198件，大致从每件砾石（石核）上可产生的石片（碎片）数量为2.2块。不到3块，可知当时对石核的利用率不太高，可能和当时的古人类获取原料非常方便有关。

表2 刘湾旧石器时代遗址石制品类型统计表

类型	加工工具	素材	石器		小计
	石锤		砾石石器	石片石器	
数量	1	252	62	4	319
百分比（%）	0.3	79	19.4	1.3	100

表3 刘湾旧石器时代遗址石器类型统计表

类型	砍砸器	手镐	手斧	刮削器	小计
数量	48	5	9	4	66
百分比（%）	73	8	13	6	100

从表2、表3中我们可以看到，石器在全部石制品中只有66件，占总数的20.7%，约1/5，即成品率只有20%，成品率并不低。石器大类中，砾石石器占绝大多数，有62件，占石器总数的94%；石片石器有4件，占6%。砾石石器的种类较多，有砍砸器、手镐、手斧等；石片石器的种类只有刮削器一种。石器小类中，砍砸器有48件，占石器总数的73%，其次为手斧，有9件，占13%；再其次为手镐，有5件，占8%；最少的是刮削器，有4件，占6%。

砍砸器中，以单刃砍砸器为主，有37件，占石器总数的56%；其次为多刃砍砸器，有6件，占9%；最少的是双刃砍砸器，只有5件，占8%。

手斧中真正意义上完全加工的只有2件，另外7件均为加工不完全的部分手斧。手镐的加工往往比较简单，其尖端通常只由几块简单加工的片疤构成。

刮削器均为单刃，没有双刃和多刃的刮削器，也没有发现其他类型的石片石器，说明在石器组合中，刮削器处于非常次要的地位，甚至是到了可以忽略不计的地位。

刘湾旧石器时代遗址石制品的剥片和加工方法均为硬锤锤击法，加工石器的方式以向一面（单向）加工为主，有39件，占59%；双面（双向）加工的也不少，有27件，占41%。

刘湾旧石器时代遗址Ⅰ、Ⅱ号地点没有做过年代测定工作，也没有发现更多的可以断定其相对年代的动物化石。上述我们提到在其东边有一个面积巨大的新石器时代遗址（年代距今6000年左右），我们曾试图在那个新石器时代遗址发掘完后继续向下发掘，以期找到旧、新石器时代地层叠压的证据，遗憾的是由于种种原因，效果并不理想。但是刘湾旧石器时代遗址Ⅰ、Ⅱ号地点与该新石器时代遗址紧紧相连，海拔高度一致，埋藏环境基本一致，两者时代相距应不会太遥远。同时我们根据汉水河流阶地的发育情况，以及与丹江口水库库区已经发掘的其他类似遗址相对比，推测刘湾旧石器时代地点的年代在距今10~5万年之间。

4 讨 论

刘湾旧石器时代遗址的文化面貌有以下一些特点：石制品的岩性大类中以火成岩为多，种类以沉积岩为多，变质岩标本最少；岩性多样，有10种，以脉石英为主，其次为砂岩、硅质岩，其他种类较少；素材以河床中磨圆度较高的河卵石为主，石器的素材以砾石（石核）为主，且占绝对优势，以石片为素材的石器处于可忽略的地位；石制品的剥片和加工方式均为硬锤锤击法，没有发现砸击法等其他方法的产品；剥片时对石核的台面不进行预先修理，石核利用率不低；石器类型以砍砸器为主，其次为手斧、手镐，刮削器最少；石器的加工方式以单向加工的为多，但双向加工的石器也有相当的比例。

刘湾旧石器时代遗址所处的丹江口地区是中国南方旧石器时代早、中期文化分布的重要区域，以前没有发现旧石器时代遗址时代中、晚期的遗址，近些年来，随着南水北调中线工程湖北库区文物保护工作的开展，发掘了大量和刘湾旧石器时代遗址埋藏环境相似、海拔高度相近的遗址，如双树、彭家河、北泰山庙、尖滩坪、红石坎、刘湾等10余处旧石器时代遗址[1~13]。这些遗址的文化面貌都有一定的相似性，如均以大型工具为主，以砍砸器、手镐、手斧等大型石器为多，小型工具较少，以刮削器为主；所有遗址中都出土有手斧；均以硬锤锤击法为主加工石器，有时也用砸击法等。

刘湾旧石器时代遗址Ⅰ、Ⅱ号地点的发掘，为研究中国南方旧石器时代文化提供了非常重要的实物资料，从该遗址的石制品面貌看，和这个区域旧石器时代早、中期的一些遗址有着惊人的一致性，证明中国南方旧石器时代文化发展的连续性，南方砾石文化传统有着自己的发生、发展的演化谱系[14~17]。刘湾旧石器时代遗址Ⅰ、Ⅱ号地点的发掘证明在汉水流域不仅有距今100万年的旧石器时代早期的"郧县人"文化，也有距今10~5万年的文化。汉水流域的远古文化是土生土长的文化，在其发展过程中，不断地吸收其他外来的文化因素，从而形成了具有自己特色的远古文明。

附记：刘湾旧石器时代地点的发掘是在中国科学院古脊椎动物与古人类研究所高星研究员的指导下完成的，领队冯小波，参加发掘的有中国科学院古脊椎动物与古人类研究所硕士研究生王昊、湖北省十堰市博物馆的黄旭初、湖北省郧县博物馆的王正华、周兴明、张俊等。

参考文献

[1] 陈铁梅,杨全,胡艳秋等. 湖北"郧县人"化石地层的ESR测年研究[J]. 人类学学报,1996(2):114-118.

[2] 黄培华,李文森. 湖北郧县曲远河口地貌、第四纪地层和埋藏环境[J]. 江汉考古,1995(4):83-86.

[3] 李天元,王正华. 湖北郧县人颅骨化石初步观察[J]. 史前研究,1990~1991年合刊:1-12.

[4] 李天元,王正华,李文森. 湖北省郧县曲远河口化石地点调查与试掘[J]. 江汉考古,1991(2):1-14.

[5] 李天元,王正华,李文森等. 湖北郧县曲远河口人类颅骨的形态特征及其在人类演化中的位置[J]. 人类学学报,1994(2):104-116.

[6] 李天元,武仙竹,李文森. 湖北郧县曲远河口发现的猴类化石[J]. 江汉考古,1995(3):4-7.

[7] 李天元,艾丹,冯小波. 郧县人头骨形态特征再讨论[J]. 江汉考古,1996(1):40-44.

[8] 李炎贤. 中国最早旧石器时代文化的发现与研究[J]. 中国文物报,1999年1月20日三版;1999年1月,27日三版。

[9] 阎桂林. 湖北"郧县人"化石地层的磁性地层学初步研究[J]. 地球科学—中国地质大学学报,1993(4):221-226.

[10] 阎桂林. 考古磁学-磁学在考古中的应用[J]. 考古,1997(1):85-91.

[11] 张银运. 郧县人类头骨化石与周口店直立人头骨的形态比较[J]. 人类学学报,1995(1):1-7.

[12] Li Tianyuan, Etler DA:《New Middle Pleistocene Hominid crania from Yunxian in China》),《Nature》,1992(357):404-407.

[13] 李炎贤,计宏祥,李天元等. 郧县人遗址发现的石制品[J]. 人类学学报,1998(2):94-120.

[14] 李莉. 碰砧法与锤击法的打片实验研究[J]. 华南方民族考古,1992(5):180-197.

[15] 裴文中,贾兰坡. 丁村旧石器[M]. 裴文中主编:山西襄汾县丁村旧石器时代遗址发掘报告[M]. 北京:科学出版社,1958:97-111.

门头沟区宗教文化遗产的保护与利用

杨靖筠　于　洪

1　门头沟区宗教文化遗产概述

北京门头沟区自古就是京西古道，是京城连接河北、山西、内蒙古地区的重要通道，更是守护北京城的京西天然屏障，有"神京右臂"之美誉，不仅自然环境优美，而且历史悠久，人杰地灵，民风淳朴，文化资源丰厚。其中，宗教文化资源尤为突出。

门头沟区的宗教文化遗产具有极为深厚的底蕴、完整的类型和丰满的层次，是北京地区宗教文化集中展现之地。门头沟区主要的宗教有佛教、道教、基督教（新教）、天主教、伊斯兰教五大宗教，以及多种民间信仰，宗教文化遗址遗存众多。经过调查研究，大体将区内宗教文化资源划分为四大类，即佛教文化资源、其他宗教文化资源、民间信仰文化资源和与宗教文化相关的文化资源。

门头沟区信教总人数约为1万余人，占全区总人数的3.7%。其中，佛教信徒近9000余人、基督教信徒5000余人、天主教信徒约1200人、伊斯兰教信徒1000余人，还有若干道教信众。[1]

1.1　佛教文化遗存

佛教是门头沟区也是北京地区流行最早的宗教，历朝僧众纷纷在名山上建寺设坛。据统计，门头沟区旧有229个自然行政村，元、明以来遗留下的各类佛道庙宇达300座。其中得到了比较好的传承、保护和发掘，具有历史价值至今开放，或具有开发利用前景的仍有近百处之多。就佛教宗派传承而言，历史上的门头沟地区各大流派异彩纷呈，禅律交辉，演变至今。

最具有代表性的当属潭柘寺与戒台寺。潭柘寺始建于西晋，历史悠久，堪称北京地区佛教寺院之源始。发展到金代，潭柘寺成为禅宗曹洞宗中心，号称"京都第一寺"。元明清几代皇帝与此寺颇有渊源。民国时期，潭柘寺与政界联系密切，形成了举足轻重的宗教、政治势力，展示出潭柘寺典型的皇家文化风格和浓厚的"庙系天下"的政治色彩。戒台寺始建于隋朝，曾是中国北方佛教律宗中心，号称"神州第一坛"。从辽代开始，律宗发展很快，律宗高僧法均和尚在此建造戒坛，并开坛演戒。辽代道宗帝召见法均，封以"崇禄大夫、守司空"[2]，并将自己抄写的《大乘三聚戒本》授予法均。此后这件戒本被公认为佛教律宗正统代表的信物，戒台寺也因此成为中国佛教北方律宗的中心。戒台寺拥有全国规模最大、等级最高的戒台。戒台，是佛为学有所成的僧侣颁发戒牒的地方，只有修行很高的僧人才有资格在戒台寺受戒。除此之外，现在每年5月举行的"戒台梵音"音乐会也非常有特点。古曲唱诵、丹青古琴、唢呐独奏，内涵丰富、历史悠久的佛学歌曲，使人心境自然、平和。潭柘寺、戒台寺均为国家级的文物保护单位。寺院的规模庞大，文物资源珍贵，自然景观优美，对于北京佛教文化，乃至世界佛教文化具有潜在的深厚影响力。

其他诸如西峰寺、灵严寺、灵岳寺及下院宝峰寺、栖隐寺、崇化寺也都保存相对完整，历史悠久，文化底蕴较深，有一定的开发价值。

1.2　道教、天主教、基督教（新教）、伊斯兰教等宗教文化遗存

门头沟区的道教宫观遗迹也很丰富，但多数规模不大，保存的也不够完好，遗存至今相对完整的不多。其中，燕家台的通仙观是门头沟区的第一座道观。金正大七年（1230年），尹志平到燕家台隐居修行，传播全真教，在当地驻军元帅刘津的资助下，开始修造道观。道观建成后，全真教主长春宫（白云观）住持李志常题名为"通仙观"，作为长春宫的下院。石门营玄贞观以"老公庙"闻名。这座庙系清廷太监所建，观内道士全是出宫的太监，因此，当地人称其为"老公庙"。同治十年（1871年），清后

[作者简介] 杨靖筠（1963—），女，北京联合大学应用文理学院教授；于洪（1973—），女，北京联合大学应用文理学院副教授。

宫二总管刘多生拜白云观方丈耕云道长张宗璇为师，后创立全真教龙门派的分支霍山派，作为太监信奉的道教宗派。光绪年间，刘多生修整玄真观，作为出宫年老太监们终老之所，并在旁边购置一块土地，作为太监们的墓地。

天主教从元代开始传入门头沟，在后桑峪村建立教堂，目前有后桑峪和曹各庄两座天主教堂。后桑峪天主教堂历史悠久，为教友村，更是北京市惟一有天然圣母山的天主教活动场所。基督教（新教）于1942年传入门头沟区，目前全区有聚会点87个，一座教堂。伊斯兰教从光绪年间进入门头沟，1951年将回民煤窑及煤场改做清真寺。目前有一座清真寺，即城子清真寺。

1.3 民间信仰文化遗存

门头沟区还流传多种民间信仰文化，极具区域文化特色。首先是金顶妙峰山娘娘信仰。这一信仰源于当地民众到金顶妙峰山娘娘庙中朝圣，祈求生活美满、婚姻幸福、一世平安。这一习俗不仅使得娘娘信仰广为流传，还推动了庙会文化在清代达到鼎盛。庙会文化传承的是金、元、明、清以来北京历史上最为独特而精深的民间传统文化遗产，是北京民间传统文化中最直观、最生动的部分，是北京历史文化遗产的精华所在，最集中地代表着非物质文化遗产的主流。这类民间艺术声情并茂、技艺精湛，内涵之丰富、艺术水准之高超、传承之久远、摄人魂魄之强烈，是传统文化中的精品。其次是窑神信仰。门头沟蕴藏着丰富的煤炭，上千年的开采史形成了门头沟煤窑颇具特色的生产、生活和信仰民俗，具体表现在采煤、运煤、用煤、语言、生活、祭神等各个方面。通过窑神，所有的窑工几乎成为一个整体，人们要经过相同的祭奠仪式之后才会开窑、采煤，这也形成了窑工对窑神的虔诚膜拜。因此门头沟具有惟一供奉窑神的圈门窑神庙，保佑煤业的安全生产的九龙山娘娘庙等民间信仰。

1.4 与宗教相关的非物质文化遗产

宗教文化信仰往往伴随着非物质文化遗产的展示。如祭拜窑神中的节日祭祀后，人们通常举办京西幡会习俗。幡旗队列，乐曲演奏，最为繁盛。一是幡，二是乐，盛况空前。还有灵水村的转灯会习俗。转灯之前，有请神活动，即把村民所信仰的诸路神灵请到灯场的神棚供奉，让神灵与民同乐。其中即有煤窑之神，在神棚中放上煤窑神牌位，接受人们的崇祀。另一事例是妙峰山庙会的民俗活动，如五虎少林会、中幡会、高跷会、秧歌会、小车会、旱船会等活动。这些都能够构成独特的"京西门头沟民间民俗文化体系"。

2 门头沟区宗教文化遗产的定位

2.1 北京宗教文化的缩影

北京宗教文化的特征主要表现在历史传承性、吸纳包容性、多元共存性、中心引领性、民众民俗性五个方面。门头沟宗教文化既构成北京宗教文化中不可或缺的重要组成部分，又反映出这五大特征。门头沟的佛教文化是北京佛教文化的源头，在历史上曾经是北京佛教的中心，起到了引领性的作用。门头沟佛教的法脉从未中断，潭柘寺、戒台寺的历史发展折射出北京佛教历史与文化，体现了历史传承性。门头沟区宗教文化总特点是典型的"金字塔"结构，高踞顶端的皇家寺院文化和广大区域、数量众多的村落宗教文化遗存共存互生，表现出独特的多元共生性；门头沟宗教分布地域广，可以说村落文化发达，村村有村庙，反映出民众民俗性。后桑峪天主教堂是北京西部乡村历史悠久、文化厚重的山村教堂，是展示我国宗教信仰自由政策的窗口。城子清真寺是门头沟区惟一的清真寺，是展示民族团结的窗口。这些都表现出了门头沟宗教文化的吸纳包容性。

2.2 门头沟宗教文化遗产的特殊地位

门头沟区宗教文化遗产带有强烈的区域文化特色，是北京历史文化中平原、丘陵、山地三种类型中的山地文化的典型代表，具有鼎足之势，必须高度重视和挖掘。这种文化特色的形成、发展与其独特的地理环境，以及北京地区政治和经济的发展脉络息息相关、紧密相连。门头沟作为北京的京西古道，军旅、商旅、香客及车马等川流不息，在此留下了积淀深厚、种类繁多的民间信仰文化资源。从经济上讲，门头沟以采煤业为经济的支柱产业，在千百年的采煤历史中，自发地形成了京西煤业的专用术语和某些风俗。在门头沟的煤矿业，窑主希望产业兴旺，窑工祈求平安，各窑台都贴有神码（即窑神纸像）

和吉祥辞语，并在窑口摆上供桌。清代在圈门修建的"窑神庙"，就是专祭窑神的地方。此外，在门头沟保存下来的有关煤业的一些碑刻、契约都极具史料价值。上述内容都是京西煤业文化的重要部分。

3 门头沟区宗教文化遗产保护中存在的问题

3.1 缺乏突出宗教文化遗产保护与开发的总体规划

一个地区总体规划的制定对于其社会经济可持续发展、对土地的开发、利用、治理、保护等所做的总体安排和布局，起着至关重要的作用。门头沟地区发展的总体规划中对于自身具有丰厚底蕴的宗教文化资源，规划、整合、开发、利用不够具体和全面。在考察了门头沟区十余座古寺院并进行分析后，总体感觉，除了戒台寺、潭柘寺、妙峰山之外，其余众多的宗教文化遗产仍处于断壁残垣、整修无序的境况，规划整合余地大。

3.2 宗教文化遗产的管理体制尚未理顺

与全国一些寺院相似，门头沟的宗教文化遗产管理体制尚未理顺。目前，区内重要的宗教文化资源存在着国家明文制止和纠正的佛教寺庙、道教宫观"被承包""被上市"等现象，突出反映在潭柘、戒台两寺。除此之外，仰山栖隐禅寺、白瀑寺由于管理体制未理顺，有些古建不合规制，体量超标过大。尤其是目前部分宗教活动场所多头管理现象严重，甚至为争夺经济利益不断发生矛盾，使得宗教文化资源很难加以合理使用，发挥其原有的社会功用与效能。

3.3 保护的力度不够，破坏现象严重

门头沟区对宗教文化遗址进行了一些有效的保护，但由于遗址很多，一些宗教遗址保护的力度不够。如，下苇甸村龙王庙、三家店村古刹龙王庙、三家店村关帝庙铁锚寺、崇化寺遗址。更有一些以旅游开发为目的修复的寺院，虽然是经过文物部门批准的文物恢复项目工程，而且建筑规模和投资数额巨大，但由于缺乏专业人员的指导，恢复重建的寺院建筑违背了文物修复的基本原则，体量过大、超标、违规现象严重，而且保护性的破坏较为严重。

3.4 文化内涵提炼宣传力度不够

应该说，对于旅游资源后起开发的区域，发展文化旅游是提高竞争力的重要突破口，文化旅游不仅可以拓展外延，更能提升品牌辨识度，是整体带动区域产业发展的根基所在。但总的看来，门头沟区宗教文化资源没有充分挖掘，"文化兴区"的意识还不够强，直接显现为宗教文化资源整体宣传力度不大，深度不够，产品不多。实际上，无论是潭柘寺的由来、潭柘寺中的帝王树还是配王树都是有典故的。妙峰山是佛、道、儒、俗四者于一身的集合体，不同的庙会传说内涵丰富多样有所不同，它不仅仅记载着神灵的故事、庙会的演绎，也暗含了庙会所在的村落曾经发生的事件与行为，而现在许多这种文化资源被忽略，"门头沟之源"文化也如此。

4 门头沟区宗教文化遗产保护与利用的建议

4.1 强化对宗教文化遗产的保护意识

将门头沟区的宗教文化遗产列入全区宣传的重要内容，在全国和北京市及各区进行形象推介，对潭柘寺、戒台寺、妙峰山等进行重点宣传报道。做好宣传策划，借助平面媒体、网络媒体、广播电视媒体等进行立体宣传，提高社会各界对门头沟区宗教文化遗产的保护意识。

将门头沟区宗教文化遗产变为国内外专家、学者深入研究的热点内容。如潭、戒两寺组织门头沟区宗教文化遗产保护与利用的高层论坛，召开学术会议，提高高层的关注度。还可以整合一批民间民俗活动和创意文化节庆活动等，成为非物质文化遗产的调查点和展演点。

4.2 研究制定保护与利用整体规划

应在对门头沟区的宗教文化遗存进行价值评估的基础上，制定相关政策，依照政策法规对于纳入规划的寺庙观堂进行保护、修缮，提升原住民文物保护知识与文化素养。

总体规划门头沟宗教文化资源，包括"门头沟之源"的规划、潭柘寺、戒台寺以及金顶妙峰山的深

度开发与利用，适度恢复历史上典型的宗教遗存，把门头沟宗教文化资源开发融合于休闲旅游产业之中，形成一系列的旅游线路，推动"城区资源进山区、山区资源进城区"的双向流动与要素互补，实现合作共赢。推出以宗教文化旅游为主线，生态旅游、商务会展、修学旅游、农业观光采摘和民俗旅游等相互结合的多样化旅游产品链条，并以此为基础进行综合开发。结合民俗文化、红色文化、古村落文化、边城文化等，对众多的民间宗教文化资源进行有规划的综合开发，实现门头沟区文化的融合发展。重点开发知名度高的潭柘、戒台两寺及妙峰山，将资金集中在这几个点上，其他的宗教寺庙可有选择性地进行开发。

总体规划要细分为初期规划、中期规划和远期规划。初期规划主要是做好规划区域内的基础设施建设，中期规划主要是做精、做细宗教文化内涵，远期规划是在现有基础上增加软性服务，打造独具区域文化特色的文化旅游产业系列产品。只有打好文化牌，才能真正提升旅游业品质，提高品牌知名度。要努力探索将宗教文化元素全方位植入旅游经典和线路，改变过去游客简单看山看水欣赏自然风景的模式。

4.3 理顺宗教文化遗产管理体制

目前，门头沟区宗教场所多头管理现象较为严重，甚至为了争夺经济利益不断发生矛盾。应明确宗教、文化、文物、建设部门的责任，共同参与重要宗教文化场所的建设、改造。2012年10月22日，国家宗教局等10部门联合下发文件，就涉及佛教寺庙、道教宫观管理有关问题提出意见，制止和纠正佛教寺庙、道教宫观"被承包""被上市"等现象。寺观应在政府宗教事务部门的行政管理下，在当地政府有关部门指导、监督下，由佛、道教按照民主的原则负责管理，任何单位和个人不得插手其内部宗教事务。严禁党政部门参与或纵容、支持企业和个人投资经营或承包经营寺观，不得以任何方式将寺观搞成"股份制""中外合资""租赁承包""分红提成"等。寺庙保护后应加以合理使用，由具备资质的佛教、道教人士进驻，发挥其原有的社会功用与效能。

4.4 门头沟区宗教文化遗产利用的建议

4.4.1 潭柘寺、戒台寺宗教文化遗产的利用

历史上潭柘寺曾多次易名，最终还是以龙潭、柘树而得名，但龙潭已干涸近20年，柘树也是屈指可数；开发龙潭、保护柘树必须加大投入力度，应让它名至实归。可以依据龙潭泉水、帝王树、石鱼等传说故事，开展有关宣传活动，提高人们对潭柘寺的认知程度。潭柘寺还可以着力打造成为高端的养心、休闲度假的场所。戒台寺历来是古人受戒之所，更是我国三戒坛之首，虽已历经沧桑，但还可以沿袭传统，作为现代都市人受戒、反省、祈愿之地，也可以让它成为全国律宗教中心。佛教需要培养高素质人才，可以引进北京佛教学院。北京佛教学院原来在广化寺，后来迁到通教寺，由于地方狭小，常年未招生，不利于培养佛教人才，也不利于展示宗教信仰自由政策。潭柘寺、戒台寺空间大，环境清幽，适合读书、修身。戒台寺在历史上就是中国佛教的最高学府之一，具有良好的办学条件，若将北京佛教学院建在这里，可进一步提升其文化地位。

4.4.2 进一步打造金顶妙峰山民俗文化景区

妙峰山是一座历史名山、文化名山，其内涵十分丰富，范围非常广泛，尤其是碧霞元君在民间信仰中有着深厚的尊奉基础。应利用妙峰山得天独厚的历史、地理、文化优势，重点规划、策划、运作，使之成为著名的民间宗教信仰的旅游和朝圣之地。

妙峰山庙会文化中博大精深的民族品格，民间传统道德文化的撼人感召力，是具有珍罕价值的首都品牌的优秀文化遗产。妙峰山庙会文化中优秀的传统文化技艺表演，不仅是北京的，完全可以走向全国，走向世界，展示中华传统文化艺术的无穷魅力。这些流传近千年的民间文艺、技艺表演形式，是北京民间传统文化遗产连续的传承与发展，体现了妙峰山庙会文化恒久的、真正的历史价值。妙峰山庙会已列入国家级非物质文化遗产名录，应予以挖掘、整理、保护和利用。需进一步提高妙峰山的知名度，加大宣传力度，加强报纸、广播、电视及网络等媒体的宣传力度，出版妙峰山导游、妙峰山志之类的明信片和画册。将妙峰山一年四季的美景，拍成风光片，并制作光盘。进一步提高妙峰山的文化品位，定期举办有关妙峰山的学术研讨会、展览等活动。可以通过博物馆的建设，赋予景区历史文化以载体。当年顾颉刚等人到妙峰山考察的成果，香客进香之路图，五条香道图，香客文化、庙会

习俗，都有其独特的文化价值，形成感知度极高的博物馆，依此带动和提升认知度，用科技的手段将文化展现出来。重点实施金顶妙峰山风景区、妙峰山古香道、龙凤岭水土保持科技示范基地等"妙峰八景"建设；提高沟域内民俗旅游业发展水平，使沟域内5个民俗村全部达到市级民俗村标准，发展市级民俗旅游户100户，区级民俗旅游户300户。可以在妙峰山大力发展运动健身产业。开发建设杨岭山场自行车俱乐部、妙峰山沟露营地及环妙峰山50公里自行车赛道、涧沟村环山纵走路线、妙峰山顶登山线路。还可以在妙峰山建设旅游集散中心、咨询中心、宾馆、会议中心、旅游保障和报警等旅游服务设施。经过几年的努力，使妙峰山成为全国知名的5A级综合文化景区。

4.4.3 重点打造以"门头沟之源"为代表的沟域民间信仰文化

门头沟之名，随时代发展，有广义和狭义的多种解释。广义之门头沟是指今日之门头沟区区界之内。狭义之门头沟，是指从峰口庵往东至圈门的山沟。基本上是今龙泉镇的门城地区。门头沟之门，即指圈门。圈门为一横跨狭义之门头沟上的过街楼。门头口村名得于圈门，门头口即为圈门之旁，进入门头沟的沟口。门头口村在明、清之际曾是北京地区最重要的产煤基地，分布有煤窑上百家。此地又是西山大路中路古道的必经之地，商旅往来，昼夜不断。清末至民国初年，一度成为门头沟最为繁华的地区。民国以后，圈门外煤炭开采增多。1920年，中英门头沟煤矿在圈门外开凿立井，井深矿大。1925年，治水公司在圈门外开凿立井。门头沟的工商中心随煤业发展从圈门里逐步移入圈门外。

门头沟采煤业发达，与之相适应的是窑神信仰。京西惟一供奉窑神的庙宇——窑神庙的繁盛，以颂神、祭神为主要内容的京西古幡会发达，二者均具有惟一性。还有九龙山上娘娘庙，是京西煤炭行业的保护神，是财富的象征，备受窑主、窑工、煤商们的尊崇。每到农历五月初一和九月初一，以圈门"十三会"为主的数十档民间花会一起出动，转遍圈门一带各村，载歌载舞，走十几里山路上山朝奉。附近数十里各村的窑工和农民也分走四条香道上山，在娘娘庙举行盛大的祭神仪式，规模之大，享誉京城。除了九龙山庙会，每年腊月十七祭窑神是门头沟煤业的共同节日，众多大小煤窑各自予以祭祀，上层人士在窑神庙举办祭祀窑神的隆重仪礼。除了祭祀，还要在圈门的大戏楼唱三天大戏，酬谢煤窑神。据九龙山顶的残碑记载，京城内不少的行业亦到此参加庙会活动。门头沟煤业地区的本地香会计有：东辛房开路会，西辛房狮子会、中幡，门头口村大鼓会，宽街娘娘驾，西辛房杠箱会，东店村大旗会、铙子会，西店音乐会，官厅村中幡，岳家坡中幡，孟家胡同中幡，韩家沟、匣石窑村拜驾烧香会（号佛会），西店村持单会（会谱），13个村合编吉祥会（吹打音乐班）。

应深层次、宽角度地挖掘窑神文化的历史文化内涵，形成整体风貌格局，使之成为北京著名的古乡村风貌旅游区。重点打造以数字模拟再现的方式，向人们展示"门头沟"地名的由来，圈门过街楼的形成及演变过程；门头沟区采煤的煤窑历史演变过程，京西古道的用途、古道上的文化遗迹、独特的九龙山庙会、煤窑神的崇拜等内容，以突出沟域文化的特色。同时，要结合城市改造，使庙宇形成新型社区的文化景观。如圈门过街楼、大戏楼、窑神庙修复后与圈门里村落形成古风貌景观。在三家店村的改造中，把庙宇、古村落以及沿街古宅院的保护结合起来，整合资源，形成新的文化亮点。要合理规划、整合，形成整体优势。

参考文献

[1] 北京市门头沟地方志编纂委员会. 北京门头沟区志[M]. 北京：北京出版社，2006：668.
[2] 张云涛. 北京戒台寺石刻[M]. 北京：北京燕山出版社，2007：97.

兵家与儒、道、法等诸家思想的交融与区别

张连城

我国兵家的渊源，可追溯到原始社会末期的战争实践，兵家学说中的一些基本概念在甲骨文中便已开始形成，如"兵""武""征""伐""戍""卫""御""败"等。西周时期出现了吕尚论兵法的兵书，如《军政》《军志》等。春秋战国时期，兵家正式形成一个独立的学派，和诸子百家并驾齐驱，交相辉映。《韩非子》曰："境内皆言兵，藏孙吴之书者家有之。"[1]虽言过其实，但反映了战国后期兵家学说的影响之巨。吕思勉也说："（汉志）诸子略外，又有兵书、术数、方技三略。兵书与诸子，实堪并列。"[2]班固在《汉书·艺文志》中记载的兵家著作有53家、790篇，流传下来的只有《孙子兵法》《孙膑兵法》《吴子》《六韬》《尉缭子》《司马法》6家。值得注意的是，兵家作为先秦诸子百家之一，在保持自身特征的同时，十分注意吸收借鉴诸子百家中的合理内核，借以丰富和发展自己的学说。本文将对先秦兵家和诸子百家的思想联系与区别等问题作一论述。

一、先秦兵家与儒、道、法等诸家思想的交融

兵家产生于我国春秋战国时期，由于诸雄争霸，战乱频仍，兵家思想格外引人注目，因此，兵家成为先秦诸子百家中一个很有影响的学派。在先秦典籍中，兵家思想不但与诸子及其他各家相互渗透、交融，而且相互扬弃。纵观中国古代兵家思想，尤其是在先秦时期，始终不是孤立的、封闭的流派体系，如孙武虽然属于兵家，但他兼通儒法；又如商鞅，他不仅是战国时期法家学派的代表人物，同时也是一位杰出的军事家和战略家，他的著作《商君书》中部分篇章，诸如《农战》《更法》《开塞》等，也讨论了兵学内容。还有吴起，他兼法家与兵家于一身，其著作《吴子》以阐发兵学内容为主。诸子百家思想相互滋润，相互激荡，吸取其他学派的合理内核，丰富着自己的学说，发展着自己的学派。

（一）兵家与儒家思想的融合

兵家和儒家两者之间的关系十分密切，在先秦有代表性的兵家著作中，对于儒家最为核心的概念"仁义"，不仅被广泛地引用和强调，而且形成了一种基本的认知。例如，《孙子》主张军队将领应该具备"智、信、仁、勇、严"5个方面的品德，也就是后人所概括的"五德"，其中"仁爱"思想占据重要地位，其要义在于要"视卒如婴儿""视卒如爱子"，对士兵要仁爱，即使是降卒，也要"善而养之"，而不是坑而杀之。这种对于将帅仁义的要求，基本成为先秦兵家的共识。又如孙膑所倡导的"义、仁、德、信、智"，《六韬》的"勇、智、仁、信、忠"，都无一例外地将"仁义"视作将帅品德的核心。《尉缭子》把战争区分为"挟义而战"和"争私结怨"两大类，提出"义战"论，强调战争的目的是为了"诛暴乱、禁不义"，而并非为了私怨从事"不义"的战争，诚如《孙子》所说："不可以怒而兴师""不可以愠而致战"。与《司马法》一样，《尉缭子》也强调战争本于"仁义"，"不攻无过之城，不杀无罪之人"。《吴子》将儒家的"德""义"观念借鉴过来，多处谈到"仁"和"义"，在兵家中首先提出"义兵"的思想，主张"内修文德，外治武备"[3]。可见，兵家思想中也讲求仁义，其与孔子所强调的仁德，虽然使用的范畴和界定的领域有所区别，但本质上是相通的。

尉缭子曾从辩证分析的角度谈到文和武两者之间的关系，"兵者，以武为栋，以文为植；以武为表，以文为里；以武为外，以文为内。能审此三者，则知所以胜矣"[4]可见，尉缭子主张文和武两者是武栋文植、武表文里、武外文内的关系，这也可看作是兵家与儒家关系的绝妙注脚。

《司马法》是西周时期军事礼仪、军队编制、军事操练、军事典章等的汇编，是西周礼乐内容在军

[作者简介] 张连城（1965—），男，辽宁锦州人，北京联合大学副校长，副教授。

事领域中的反映，故又称《军礼司马法》。班固在修撰《汉书》时，注重考虑的是《司马法》一书中的军礼内容，把其列入礼经类。司马迁则根据《司马法》的军事内容，把其看作兵书。在此姑且不谈《司马法》的产生是否早于诸子百家，但是，从司马迁和班固如此看重《司马法》，就从另一角度验证了兵家与儒家兼通的论断。可以看出，若真正地理解先秦兵家思想，应该说兵家的主张不是专攻杀伐、不尚文德，而应是内修文德、外事攻略的辩证统一。同样，儒家也并非从根本上排斥战争，而是主张对战争的性质和类型进行区别，如儒家提出的"慎战""义战"思想，成为对兵家思想的杰出贡献，兵家吸收了这些思想，提倡以战止战，以杀去杀。《孙子》说："非危不战。"其意是指在受到战争威胁的情况下才进行战争，即使在万不得已的情况下，也要尽量利用其他手段，通过各种非军事途径达到战争的目的，即所谓"不战而屈人之兵""不战而胜"。《六韬》则更加直接地说："兵为凶器，不得已而用之。"[5]《尉缭子》也说："富治者，车不发轫，甲不出橐，而威制天下。"[6]

可见，不能简单地、片面地认定兵家是杀伐废德，儒家是修德弃兵。从某种意义上讲，兵家与儒家是相辅相成、水火相济的，有互补相长的妙用，总体而言，儒家思想制约着兵家的精神境界，形成其"中庸"的合理内核。

（二）兵家对道家思想的借鉴

对于兵家和道家两者之间的关系，首先应该肯定的是：道家尤其是其中所包括的丰富的思辨哲学，极大地充实丰富了中国的兵家思想，成为兵家诡道思想的渊源所在，使其逻辑思辨体系逐渐完善。

道家主张去兵无为，老子对战争是持反对态度的，这是客观事实。但是战争是不以人的意志为转移的，从人类进入阶级社会，战争就难以避免。因此，老子对于战争也并非简单地反对了事，而是进行了深入的思考，提出了许多重要的兵学论断，诸如"以正治国，以奇用兵，以无事取天下"[7]。而"用兵以奇"的论断在《孙膑兵法》和《六韬》等兵家著作里也作过多方面详尽的发挥。《六韬》则大量吸收了"道法自然"等道家治国理念，具有浓重的黄老道家特征，但却实实在在的是一部集先秦兵家思想之大成的著作。

"道"是道家思想的主要概念，道家强调人道、天道并重，主张遵循天地自然之法则，求得人与天地的和谐。孙膑则把"道"的概念运用到兵法之中。《孙膑兵法·八阵》提出上知天之道，下知地之理，内得其民之心，外知敌之情，阵则知八阵之经。"孙膑认为，要取得战争的胜利，必须讲"天时、地利、人和"，如果天人不合，即使取得胜利也是暂时的，最终也会遭受失败，所谓"三者不得，虽胜有殃"[8]。《司马法》也主张"取法天地"[9]"顺天奉时"[10]。

"以静制动""后发制人"是老子思想中的精髓。诸如《老子·四十章》曰："反者，道之动。"《老子·六十八章》曰："善为士者，不武；善战者，不怒；善胜敌者，不与；善用人者，为之下"等，充分体现了老子哲学思想中辩证思维的特性，隐含着互为转化的辩证法命题。在先秦兵家论述中也有着与之一脉相承的思想，如《六韬·文韬·大礼》记载："安徐而静，柔节先定；善与而不争，虚心平志，待物以正"等。而《尉缭子·勒卒令》"正兵贵先，奇兵贵后，或先或后，制敌者也"，更是对老子后发制人哲学思想的绝妙发挥，提出先后的取舍完全出自于战争的需要，而非僵硬教条。《战国策》曰："骐骥之衰也，驽马先之；孟贲之倦也，女子胜之。夫驽马女子筋骨力劲，非贤于骐骥孟贲也，何则？后起之借也。"[11]后发制人的命题在中国战略思想史上产生了广泛的影响。道家与先秦兵家之间的密切关系由此可见一斑。

（三）兵家与法家思想的交融

兵家和法家两者有着密切的关系，可谓二位一体，相伴产生[12]。譬如，管仲、子产既为法家鼻祖，但其著作中同时又有兵家的言论，其论述之精辟，有些甚至为兵家所不及。进一步讲，有的兵家同时又是法家，如吴起、商鞅；有些法家如荀子和韩非子，虽不是兵家，但在其著作中有论述军事的篇章。可见，法家与兵家之间相互交融的东西是比较多的。

众所周知，法家对于"法治"是十分重视的，堪称法家立身之本。法家强调"法"的威严，主张"法不私亲"，"法不阿亲"，崇尚"重刑"理论，讲求赏信罚明，如《韩非子·饰邪》"赏刑明则民尽死，民尽死则兵强主尊"。而先秦兵家也同样十分重视"法治"，这在先秦兵家著作中有十分详尽的阐述。

先秦兵家主张法治,也重视刑罚。如《尉缭子·兵令》中"赏如日月,信如四时,令如斧钺,制如干将,士卒不用命者,未之有也"。力主治军"重赏重罚"。《司马法》更进一步提出了要及时行罚,令行禁止,以维护法治的威严。如《司马法·天子之义》讲"赏不逾时,欲民速得为善之利也;罚不迁列,欲民速睹为不善之害也"。《吴子》更是把严明军纪、厉行执法作为治兵的重要法宝,指出若"法令不明,赏罚不信,金之不止,鼓之不进,虽有百万,何益于用。"[13]应该说,兵家和法家一样,都是重视和强调以法的意志和行为来约束或发挥人的主观能动性。兵家在吸收法家思想后,在强调法律的威严前提下,一方面从人的"趋利避害"的本性出发,重视赏罚的严明;另一方面,又突出了重视"权变"的兵法精神,主张"将在外,君命有所不受",维护了将帅在外独立作战、见机行事的决策权威。可以说,兵家对于法家思想是在吸收继承的基础上,结合兵家的特殊性进行发挥,从而形成兵家的法治思想体系。

此处着重提出儒家、道家和法家对于兵家的影响,并不意味着先秦其他诸子对于兵家没有影响。实际上,有的流派对兵家的影响还非同凡响,需要特别指出的就是墨家。

墨家虽然主张"非攻"等非暴力的论述,主张尽量采用非战手段和途径来击败敌人,以减少战争给社会和人民生活所带来的破坏性,却十分注重军械技术和战术方式。如果兵家思想没有墨家思想的渗入,那么,兵家在兵器器械上的长足发展是难以想象的。《卫公兵法·守城篇》称:"禽滑厘问墨翟守城之具,墨翟答以六十六事。"应该说,先秦兵家的兵械技巧的渊源就在于墨家。

二、讲求用兵操作功能和构建用兵思想境界是兵家和其他诸子百家的根本区别

兵家和诸子百家之间最大的区别在于执着功利原则和崇尚人本精神的对立,从而决定了在军事思想方面的差异,即讲求用兵操作功能和追求用兵思想境界的分歧。

儒家、墨家和法家等诸子崇尚人本精神,按照自己的主观愿望,对战争的性质和宗旨加以理想化地阐述,把原本是残酷、恐怖的战争改造成为合乎自己政治理念的事物,进而批判、否定现实中的战争活动,但现实中残酷的军事斗争又迫使他们不得不在具体论述中注意、肯定兵事的迫切性和必要性。这是其追求理想境界与现实矛盾的必然现象。这突出地表现在"义战"理论上。

"义战"理论的提出是儒家在构筑战争的理想境界方面的主要标志。同时,在实践中,儒家也积极推行"义战"在军事斗争中的运用,并且认为"义战"是顺应天道而合乎民心,因此,凡是推行"义战"的军事家一定所向披靡,天下无敌,并据此加以演绎,得出逻辑性的结论。从事"义战",就是用兵的最高理想境界,是任何战斗指挥员都应该执着追求的军事理念。至于应该通过何种手段才能达到这种境界,儒家人物是不曾也不屑于从军事操作层面去考虑的。墨家则主张以"兼爱""德义"服天下,提倡"非攻",与儒家的"义战"理论有着异曲同工之妙。

然而,不论是儒家,还是墨家,他们所倡导的"义战""非攻"纯粹是自己虚构与假设的理念,只是理论上的概念表述而已,在现实生活中是无法实现的。值得注意的是,墨家在构筑用兵理想境界的同时,也讲求战争实施方面的可操作性问题,这反映在其具体的"救守"理论中。《墨子》中有《城守》诸篇,讲的就是如何运用有效的工具与手段达到"救守"的目的,在以守城为中心的防御作战理论方面,提出了重要的见解。由此可见,墨家构筑用兵理想境界与讲求实战操作功能是并行不悖的,在这一点上,墨家的军事思想要比儒家全面和辩证。

道家主张"不以兵强于天下",提倡以"无为""不争"的方式来实现战争上的全胜,做到"虽有甲兵,无所陈之"。但是,这只是道家的一厢情愿的设计,是无法实现的主观意念,非但不能达到消灭战争的目的,反而助长军事冒险家的战争行为。

法家学派强调军事理论在实践中的有效使用,主张运用各种行之有效的手段去争取战争的胜利。从这一点上讲,法家与兵家是一致的,更注重掌握驾驭战争的实际要领,把主要的精力投入到讲求具体的操作方法之中。法家学说的特点是注重实事,讲究效益。它关心的是战争准备与实施上的可操作性,而不是去追求什么虚无缥缈的理想用兵境界。这既是法家政治立场在军事理论上的反映,也是其学说特点的逻辑必然。与儒家和道家相比,法家关于作战指导的见解是丰富和深刻的,尤其是《管子》一书,在这方面的言论更是精到,值得重视。但是法家毕竟不是专门论述军事理论的学说,对具体作战理论的论

述仍然显得比较单薄，比较简单。

由于兵家和诸子百家之间存在着构筑理想境界与讲求操作功能两种不同的差异，这就形成了点的深化与宏观的把握、面的兼顾与微观的操作之间的区别。

儒家、道家等学派虽然不去专门讨论具体的军事学术问题，但总体而论，其军事思想的基本特点之一，乃是点的深化，即关于战争理论的高度成熟，并对后世产生深远的影响，尤其是高度重视军事与政治的关系，深刻认识到民心向背与战争胜负的关联，提出了"取信于民""得道者多助，失道者寡助""天时不如地利，地利不如人和""夫慈，以战则胜，以守则固"等一系列著名命题，从总揽全局的高度，为古代兵学解决了政治原则问题，使古代战争理论在哲理上得到了升华。

兵家以讲究可操作性为特征，努力包容兼顾军事理论的各个侧面、各个层次，构成比较系统完整的军事理论体系，以便于在实践中加以操作。从这个意义上说，在面的兼顾与微观的操作方面明显高出其他诸子学派。

三、结　　论

第一，兵家作为一个开放的思想体系，以海纳百川的胸怀，对于其他诸子百家的思想，凡是有利于丰富或发展自身思想体系的，大都加以借鉴或吸收。先秦兵家的思想学说体系从一个侧面反映了中国的传统文化蕴涵。先秦兵家汲取众家之所长，同时，反过来又影响和丰富了其他学派的思想内涵。从某种意义上讲，起源于我国先秦时代的几大思想流派，无一例外都影响了先秦兵家的思想，为其形成发展提供了丰厚给养。同时，先秦的各大思想流派又互相彼此影响，相互补充和贯通，"你中有我，我中有你"，兼容并包和交叉发展，包括兵家在内的先秦诸子均讲求天、地、人三者的和谐与统一，既肯定天、地的作用，又重视人的价值。这种兼容并蓄的文化品格正是中国古代文化的真谛之所在，否则就难以领悟先秦兵学的文化底蕴。

第二，诸子百家各个学派之间相互包含和相互渗透的前提是各个学派仍然坚韧地保留着自己学派的特点，乃至于学派体系的特质与精华，如果抹杀和取消每一学派自身的特点，各自流派的成立与存在便无从谈起。拿兵家来说，虽说它在不同程度上吸收、借鉴和融会了儒家、法家、道家和阴阳五行家等的思想，但却是以兵法、兵谋的形式表现出来的，保留有自己鲜明的特色。甚至于兵家和诸子百家的有些论述在字句上几乎都是相同的，但仔细推究其内涵，实际上存在着很大差异。例如，道家和兵家都讲"无为"，但道家所讲的"无为"的含义是以弱者的身份静观事物本身的变化，忽视人的主观努力；兵家的看法却与之截然相反，其更多的是发现在无为背后的更深层次的东西，即"无为"绝不是坐以待变，而是积极积蓄力量，运用人的各方面主观努力，争取局势朝着对己方有利的方向发展和转变，"无为"实际上蕴含的是积极的"有为"。这种似是而非的相类似字句还有许多，其主要区别在于兵家不仅吸纳诸子学说的理论学说，更从操作层面更进一步地思考、衍生、发挥和升华。

第三，任何一种思想学说，要想发展，都必须吸收其他学说的合理内核，并且保持自己的特征，缺一不可。兵家这种重视思想体系内容和诸子百家的协调与交融，同时又十分重视保持自身体系的完整与独立，正是先秦兵家在诸子百家中卓然独立的根本原因。

参考文献

[1] 韩非子，著. 王先慎，集解. 韩非子集解（卷19）·五蠹（第四十九）[M]//诸子集成本（第5册）. 上海：上海书店影印出版，1986：346.
[2] 吕思勉. 先秦学术概论 [M]. 北京：中国大百科全书出版社，1985：15.
[3] 晁罡. 儒家和兵家治道思想的整合及其历史影响——从"儒兵家"看《十一家注孙子》[J]. 现代哲学，2003（4）：85–91.
[4]《中国军事史》编写组. 银雀山简本《尉缭子·兵令》（附录）[M]//武经七书注译·尉缭子. 北京：解放军出版社，1986：252.
[5]《中国军事史》编写组. 武经七书注译·六韬·兵道第十二 [M]. 北京：解放军出版社，1986：294.
[6]《中国军事史》编写组. 武经七书注译·尉缭子·兵谈第二 [M]. 北京：解放军出版社，1986：148.

[7] 王弼,注. 老子道德经下篇(第五十七章)[M]//诸子集成本(第3册). 上海:上海书店影印出版,1986:34.
[8] 银雀山汉墓竹简整理小组. 临沂银雀山汉墓出土《孙膑兵法》释文[J]. 文物,1975(1):2-5.
[9] 《中国军事史》编写组. 武经七书注译·司马法·天子之义第二[M]. 北京:解放军出版社,1986:89.
[10] 《中国军事史》编写组. 武经七书注译·司马法·定爵第三[M]. 北京:解放军出版社,1986:103.
[11] 刘向,集录. 范祥雍,笺证. 齐五·苏秦说齐闵王[M]//战国策笺证(卷12). 上海:上海古籍出版社,2011:578.
[12] 杨用成,龚留柱. 论先秦兵家的性质及其产生[J]. 河南大学学报:社会科学版,2005(4):103-110.
[13] 吴起. 吴子·治兵第三[M]//诸子集成本(第6册). 上海:上海书店影印出版,1986:5.

对北京历史文化遗产空间重构的思考

张宝秀

1 相关概念梳理

1.1 空间与文化空间

《现代汉语词典》界定：空间（Space），是物质存在的一种客观形式，由长度、宽度、高度表现出来，是物质存在的广延性和伸张性的表现。❶ 空间与时间相对。时间（time）是物质运动中的一种存在方式，由过去、现在、将来构成的连绵不断的系统，是物质运动、变化的持续性、顺序性的表现。❷ 空间有物理空间、宇宙空间、数字空间、网络空间、思想空间、数学上的空间等。在地理学中，空间是指地球表层的一部分。

文化空间（cultural space），有广义和狭义之分。狭义的文化空间，也称为"文化场所"（culture place），是联合国教科文组织在保护非物质文化遗产时使用的一个专有名词，主要用来指人类口头和非物质遗产代表作的形态和样式。1998年联合国教科文组织发布《人类口头和非物质遗产代表作条例》，明确将"文化空间"作为非物质文化遗产的重要形态，界定文化空间（文化场所）的人类学概念被确定为一个集中了民间和传统文化活动的地点，但也被确定为一般以某一周期（周期、季节、日程表等）或是以一事件为特点的一段时间。这段时间和这一地点的存在取决于按传统方式进行的文化活动本身的存在。在我国，《国务院办公厅关于加强我国非物质文化遗产保护工作的意见》（国办发〔2005〕18号）界定"非物质文化遗产是各族人民世代相承、与群众生活密切相关的各种传统文化表现形式和文化空间"。文件的附件1《国家级非物质文化遗产代表作申报评定暂行办法》第三条明确说明："非物质文化遗产可分为两类：一是传统的文化表现形式，如民俗活动、表演艺术、传统知识和技能等；二是文化空间，即定期举行传统文化活动或集中展现传统文化表现形式的场所，兼具空间性和时间性。"

广义的文化空间，可以理解为人类在社会历史发展过程中所创造的物质财富和精神财富的承载空间，应该包括各种物质文化空间、制度文化空间和精神文化空间，当然也包括作为非物质文化遗产类型的文化空间。

1.2 结构与空间结构

结构（structure），原意为屋宇构建的式样，引申为各个部分的配合、组织。《现代汉语词典》界定：结构是各个组成部分的搭配和排列。❸ 哲学上将结构定义为不同类别或相同类别的不同层次按程度多少的顺序进行有机排列。结构既是一种观念形态，又是物质的一种运动状态，具有主观世界与物质世界的结合构造之意。

空间结构（spatial structure），是空间系统内各组成要素的搭配和排列，是各组成要素之间的相互联系、相互作用方式，是空间系统组织化、有序化的标志。空间结构将空间视为一种网络，强调空间内部各要素之间的关系。

1.3 空间解构与重构

解构（deconstruction），或译为"结构分解"，就是打破现有单元化的秩序，把原结构解体分解还原

［基金项目］本文是北京市属高等学校高层次人才引进与培养计划项目（The Importation and Development of High – Caliber Talents Project of Beijing Municipal Institutions）"——"北京历史文化遗产空间重构与城市文化建设研究"（项目编号 CIT&TCD20140313）成果之一。

［作者简介］张宝秀，北京联合大学应用文理学院院长、北京学研究基地主任、北京学研究所所长、教授、博士。研究方向：历史地理、人文地理。

❶ 中国社会科学院语言研究所词典编辑室. 现代汉语词典［M］. 商务印书馆，2007（5）：778.
❷ 中国社会科学院语言研究所词典编辑室. 现代汉语词典［M］. 商务印书馆，2007（5）：1235.
❸ 中国社会科学院语言研究所词典编辑室. 现代汉语词典［M］. 商务印书馆，2007（5）：697.

成每个局部的基本原始单位，是法国后结构主义哲学家德里达提出的一个术语，一种研究态度和思想方法，以其创立的批评学派为代表。重构（reconstruction）就是重新组合，构成一个全新的、不同于以前新的结构。解构与重构的思想方法，目前在很多领域都有应用，其中在艺术设计、建筑学、文学、城市规划等领域应用较多。

空间解构（spatial deconstruction），可以理解为将某类空间的结构分解还原成每个局部的基本原始单位。空间重构（spatial reconstruction），是空间各要素在特定条件下重新建构其相互关系的过程，由于空间不能独立于时间而存在，空间重构强调一种持续的状态，而非固定的结局。❶ 空间重构的目的在于激发空间的活力与韧力，使空间释放出新的能量和意义。

对文化空间的研究，也常使用建构和构建这两个关键词。建构（construction）是一个借用自建筑学的词语，原指建筑起一种构造，主要应用在文化研究、社会科学和文学批评的分析上，是指在已有的文本上，建筑起一个分析、阅读系统，使人们可以运用一个解析的脉络，去拆解那些文本背后的因由和意识形态，强调建造的过程。构建（structure），是指全方位、多角度、深层次地建立，多用于抽象事物。

1.4 文化空间重构

文化空间重构，是对文化空间的体系结构进行重新构建。文化遗产空间重构，是对文化遗产（包括物质文化遗产和非物质文化遗产）的文化空间进行重构，即在现代城市、区域文化建设的背景下重新整理和思考文化遗产现存要素及其空间构建方向和思路，利用现存文化遗产重构城市、区域的文化空间，改变零散的、不成体系的、内在关系表现不强烈的格局现状，推动构建面向未来的、前瞻性的、既有继承又有发展的实体和非实体相结合的城市、区域文化空间新格局。

对于文化遗产的空间结构与重构，我们可以从解构与重构方法在艺术设计中的应用得到启发。"解构"和"重构"在设计中是共同存在的，后者是前者的提炼升华过程，也是一个创新的过程。一个特定的设计主题，可以经过对设计本源合理、规范、科学的解构后，分解为数个甚至更多的个体元素；然后，同样通过合理、规范、科学以及设计本身的基础技巧对解构后的个体元素进行重构，求得与特定的设计主题的谋和，并使特定的设计主题得以充分表现。解构过程也是针对特定的设计主题表现元素的应用和重构的思维成熟过程，也是继承的过程；而重构则是对设计主题最终表现设计本身的视觉效果的综合升华过程，是创新的过程。设计本源的解构是单一的，可是对设计的重构却又不是局限于对设计本源解构后所产生的设计元素。设计本源在解构后通过重构可以表现出多个设计主题。重构过程中思维空间的扩展、思维模式的变幻，以及逻辑的强化和技巧手法的发挥运用使设计获得成功。❷

2 有关研究概述

长期以来，空间一直主要是地理学的研究对象。1974年，法国马克思主义哲学家、城市社会学家亨利·列斐伏尔（Henri Lefebvre，1901-1991）在巴黎出版了一部集其哲学和社会学思想于一体的城市研究力作《空间的生产》（The Production of Space），此后哲学、社会学、经济学、城市规划等学科领域关注和研究社会空间的学者越来越多，地理学者也参与其中。亨利·列斐伏尔在《空间的生产》一书中对空间概念及空间历史进行了系统研究和全新阐释，导致了空间一词的使用及其内涵发生了巨大的改变，这至今对法国的社会学、地理学、政治学、文学批评以及建筑学和城市科学都有着深刻的影响。❸ 如今这种影响已经波及到世界上其他国家，对于空间的意义，各个学科都给予了更多的关注。

为了弥补精神空间与物质空间传统二元论之间的分歧，亨利·列斐伏尔引入了社会空间（social space）、生活空间（the space of social life）以及社会实践（social and spatial practice）、空间实践（spatial practice）的概念，并形成了集物质空间（real space）、精神空间（mental space）、形式抽象以及人对社会空间的感知为一体的一元化的空间理论。他认为空间是一种社会产品，每一个社会和每一种生产模式都会"生产"出自己的空间，不能再把社会的空间与社会的时间当作"自然的"事实来看待，而必须按照

---

❶ 郁枫. 空间重构与社会转型 [D]. 博士学位论文，清华大学，2006：20.
❷ 陈强. 学会怎样与"千手观音"握手——浅析设计中的"解构"与"重构" [J]. 中国包装工业，2013（4）：59.
❸ 汪原. 关于《空间的生产》和空间认识范式转换 [J]. 新建筑，2002（2）：59.

某些层次等级加以规范化，作为第二自然的基本特征，作为社会多种活动作用于"第一自然"（如感性的资料、物质与能量等）之上的结果。空间是一种具有特殊意义的全方位的产物，空间并不是某种特定的产品，而是一束关系。在对社会空间的引入中，亨利·列斐伏尔认为必须考察三个重要的环节：即空间实践（spatial practice）、空间表征（representations of space）和表征空间（representational space）。[1]

空间实践涉及空间组织和使用的方式，在新的资本主义环境中，空间实践使日常生活和城市现实之间体现了一种紧密的联系。空间表征涉及概念化的空间，是一种科学家、规划师和专家治国论者所从事的空间，这种空间在任何社会中都占有统治地位，它趋向一种文字的和符号的系统。表征空间是通过相关的意向和符号而被直接使用的空间，是一种被占领和体验的空间，是居住者和使用者的空间，它与物质空间重叠并且对物质空间中的物体做象征（符号）式的使用。从意大利"文艺复兴"到19世纪，西方城市大都经历了这三个环节，但19世纪之后，尤其是现代主义盛行之后，城市空间的历史性被抽象性所打断和代替；城市空间与自然、历史、宗教、政治等因素之间的因果关系也因此被忽略了。[2]

近些年，西方人文社会科学各领域都出现了"文化转向"和"空间转向"趋势，从文化和空间的角度对相关问题进行深入分析和研究已成为各学科共同关注的焦点和方法论基础。[3] 西方人文地理学强调文化和制度转向，侧重从文化和制度层面诠释人文现象的空间规律。关于社会空间、文化空间、地理空间解读、重构的研究成果不断问世，而且已注意从空间角度研究物质文化遗产。英国Routledge公司出版社出版发行的学术期刊International Journal of Heritage Studies集中发表了很多关于文化遗产研究的高水平论文，其中包括文化遗产空间研究的成果，如Susan Pearce的The Construction and Analysis of the Cultural Heritage：Some Thoughts。国内文化遗产保护与利用方面的研究成果非常丰富，对于非物质文化遗产文化空间的研究日益增多，从地理学、社会学、文学等学科视角研究城市化空间的成果也在不断涌现。但是，对城市或区域物质和非物质文化遗产整体文化空间重构的关注还不多，研究还不够深入，特别是关于北京历史文化遗产空间重构的研究成果还很缺乏。截止到2013年5月底，在中国知网文献总库中对公开发表的相关中文文献进行检索，检索出的文献多数是发表于期刊的论文，少量是硕士、博士学位论文和发表于会议论文集和报纸上的文章。

以"文化空间"为主题词进行精确高级检索，共检索出3763条结果。以"文化空间"为篇名进行精确检索，共检索出498条结果，其中最早的文章发表于1988年，2003年以前每年发表文章数量只有数篇，2004年以后增长到每年10篇以上，2007年以来每年发表文章数量在50篇以上，增长速度较快。

以"空间重构"为篇名进行精确检索，排除数学和物理学意义的"相空间重构"文献以外，有193篇文献是有关城市、区域空间重构的，最早的文章发表于2001年，是赵云伟发表在《国外城市规划》2001年第5期的《当代全球城市的城市空间重构》。

同时以"文化空间"和"重构"为篇名进行精确检索，只检索出3篇文献，最早的文章发表于2007年，时间较晚。3篇文章分别是刘勇、杨志的《"乡下人进城"与京城文化空间的重构》（《文艺报》2007年6月12日）、谢纳的《现代空间重构与文化空间想象》（《文学评论》2010年第1期）和马琳的《灾后汶川羌文化生态旅游区文化空间的重构》（《云南民族大学学报（哲学社会科学版）》2010年第6期）。

同时以"文化"和"空间重构"为篇名进行精确检索，共检索出9篇文献，最早的文章发表于2006年，是陈蕴茜、刘炜发表于《史林》2006年第6期的《秦淮空间重构中的国家权力与大众文化——以民国时期南京废娼运动为中心的考察》。关于文化空间重构的研究成果较少，具有代表性的是矫伶、孙萍发表于《上海城市规划》2008年第1期的文章《上海城市空间重构的文化初探》，该文通过理论上对城市空间的文化解读，结合上海的实际情况，探索上海城市空间重构中文化因素的作用，探寻文化对城市空间布局的影响，从而对今后上海城市空间的发展方向做出展望。

此外，以"空间解构"为篇名进行精确检索，有6篇文献是有关城市、区域空间解构的，最早的文章发表于2004年，是聂承锋发表于《南方建筑》2004第5期的《城市空间解构分析》。同时以"文化

---

[1] Henri Lefebvre. The Productionof Space. Translated by Donald. icholson - Smith. Oxford：BlackwellLtd, 1991：33.
[2] 汪原. 关于《空间的生产》和空间认识范式转换 [J]. 新建筑, 2002（2）：60.
[3] 姜楠. 空间研究的"文化转向"与文化研究的"空间转向" [J]. 社会科学家, 2008（8）：138 - 139.

空间"和"建构"为篇名进行精确检索,共检索出 18 条结果,同时以"文化空间"和"构建"为篇名进行精确检索,共检索出 17 篇文献,这些文献主要都发表于近五年。

3 北京文化遗产空间重构的意义

北京是世界著名的历史文化名城,历史悠久,文化底蕴深厚,文化遗产项目数量最多,物质文化遗产和非物质文化遗产都非常丰富。目前,仅不可移动文物就多达 3840 处,已确定为各级文物保护单位的 1012 处,其中全国重点文物保护单位 125 处(含世界文化遗产 6 处),市级文物保护单位 255 处。非物质文化遗产,列入国家级非物质文化遗产名录项目 108 个,列入北京市级名录项目 235 个。这些文化遗产承载着丰富的历史文化内涵,是弘扬民族优秀传统文化、建设中华民族共有精神家园的重要载体,是实现"人文北京"和"世界城市"战略目标的重要资源,合理重构文化遗产的文化空间是充分发掘和展示文化遗产的内涵和影响力,推动城市社区文化发展和新农村文化建设的重要切入点,是展示首都形象、提升北京文化软实力和国际影响力、建设全国文化中心的重要抓手和途径。

在已取得的丰富的历史文化遗产研究成果基础上,选择从文化空间重构角度研究北京历史文化遗产保护、利用与首都城市文化建设是十分必要和有意义的,是建设现代城市文化空间和发展城市文化的有效途径和手段。"对城市空间的解析与认知,除了要考察物质空间要素相互交织、组合构成的空间形式所具有的形态和格局特征外,还要考察这种空间形式背后的深层文化内涵和社会动因。"❶

从理论方面看,基于丰富的文化遗产调查研究成果,运用文化地理学的空间研究视角和方法,研究北京文化遗产的空间重构,有利于丰富文化遗产研究和保护、利用实践的理论认识,扩展研究视角和研究方法;运用历史地理学的研究方法和视角,不仅关注文化遗产的静态空间,还有利于加强文化遗产空间变迁的动态过程研究;北京历史文化遗产空间重构研究亦有利于推动历史地理学研究向现代城市文化空间建设延伸,更好地发挥学科服务现代城市文化发展与建设的作用。

从实践方面看,北京市的经济社会发展已进入新的阶段,经济实力大大增强,在继续加强文化遗产保护的基础上,进一步深入地充分地挖掘文化遗产的内涵,对各类文化遗产项目进行宏观整体和微观局部文化空间重构,有利于明确北京文化遗产系统的网络化整体架构和文化遗产保护与合理利用的丰富路径,对提升遗产的文化影响力、推进北京城市文化建设具有重要意义;利用 GIS 技术建立一套北京文化遗产空间关系系统,可以丰富正在建设中的北京历史文化地理信息系统的内容,提升系统的层次和水平,为其他相关工作奠定基础,也有利于文物、旅游、规划等政府部门、单位和公众查询使用。

4 北京历史文化遗产空间重构的路径设想

第一,在国内外已有城市空间重构和文化空间理论研究的基础上,借鉴国际经验,搭建文化遗产空间重构研究的理论框架与方法体系。

第二,分析北京城市空间结构的演变过程及其文化内涵和底蕴,明确各种文化要素在北京城市的空间位置和文化地位,作为解读并重构现存遗产文化空间的本底和基础。

第三,收集、分析北京市现存各类文化遗产信息和资料,以翔实的资料、数据为基础,在 GIS 技术支持下,分析北京现存文化遗产系统各组成要素之间的空间关系、文化联系、相互作用方式和影响程度,及其与城市文化内涵建设、文化空间建设的关系,可以利用 GIS 技术建立一套北京文化遗产空间关系系统。

第四,明确北京文化遗产的文化空间保护与重构路径,构建城市宏观整体和微观局部及专题性、专项性遗产空间网络和系统,并将其嵌入北京现代城市文化空间体系中。对北京文化遗产系统进行组织化、有序化整体设计,连点成线,组线成网,挖掘遗产项目的文化联系和地方响应,加强文化遗产的综合性、联动性开发利用,扩展文化遗产的文化影响力,推进北京城市文化建设,彰显首都的文化特色和文化魅力,提升文化软实力。

---

❶ 田宝江. 城市空间解析与设计 [D]. 同济大学建筑与城市规划学院,博士学位论文,1998:83.

清代三山五园兴衰及其启示

赵连稳

三山五园作为北京西郊的皇家园林，位于京西海淀，这里山清水秀、环境优美。论及三山五园的兴衰史，笔者认为从三山五园的整体上来说，其从兴到衰经历了自清圣祖玄烨至清末几代帝王的时间。清圣祖玄烨时期是三山五园建造的初始阶段，如三山五园中的畅春园和圆明园都是在这一时期建造的。清世宗胤禛时期，主要是对三山五园中的建筑进行了进一步的扩建，如圆明园中的二十八景就是在这一时期建造而成的。到了清高宗弘历年间，随着国力的强盛，大事兴建，三山五园中的大多数建筑都是在这一时期建造完成的，三山五园达到了其建筑的鼎盛时期。三山五园的衰落是从清文宗奕詝时期开始的。清宣宗旻宁以后，清朝政局经常处于动荡之中，国库的空虚使得清政府再也无力经营皇家园林，三山五园中的多数园林在这一时期开始荒废。清文宗奕詝及清德宗载湉年间是三山五园急剧衰落的时期。咸丰十年（1860年）八月，英法联军攻入北京西郊，对以圆明园为首的三山五园进行了大规模的抢夺和焚烧，使得三山五园中的建筑所剩无几。光绪二十六年（1900年），八国联军的入侵，三山五园再遭劫难，其辉煌历史成为人们的记忆。

一、三山五园的兴起

（一）京西的地理环境和园林的兴起

北京西郊作为皇家园林的所在地，其地理环境十分优越。这里不仅有众多的河流，还有许多山丘为依托，使得其成为依山傍水的绝佳之地。（康熙）《大兴县志》对北京西郊的地理环境有清晰的记载："西山秀色甲天下，寺则香山、碧云，水则玉泉、海淀，而卢沟桥关门巘立，即古之桑乾河，京邑之瀍、涧也。"[1]从这段史料中可以看出，京西不仅有优越的自然环境，还有众多的庙宇衬托其中，如著名的香山寺和碧云寺。不仅如此，"从西山峡谷中流出的永定河，如同流经洛阳城的瀍水、涧水一样，"[2]绵延不绝。

三山五园作为整体的皇家园林建筑群兴起于清代，但是其中的多数园林都是在之前朝代园林的基础上修建的。其中最早的园林可以追溯到辽代，如在作为三山五园之一的"香山静宜园"的基址上就有辽代中丞耶律阿勒弥的别业。到了金代，金世宗又在原耶律阿勒弥的别业的基址上修建了香山寺。金章宗完颜璟对于香山的景色十分喜爱，并多次前往香山游览。《金史·章宗纪》记载了这一过程："明昌四年三月，幸香山永安寺及玉泉山；承安三年七月，幸香山，六年九月，幸香山。"[3]P228 元代对于香山寺的经营范围进一步扩大，据《元史》记载："皇庆元年四月，仁宗给钞万锭修香山永安寺。"[4] "沈榜的《宛署杂记》中记载了元代曾有'香山八景'：护驾长松、饮仙寒井、香莲金界、松顶明珠、佛阁云梯、祭台星影、乳峰古寺、妙高云堂"。[5]P37 明代对于香山进行了更大规模的建设，不仅增加了多处建筑，还兴修了许多新的庙宇，成为许多文人墨客作诗的绝佳之地。三山五园中另一皇家园林"玉泉山静明园"的历史最早可以追溯到金章宗完颜璟时期。金章宗完颜璟为了便于其在玉泉山游玩，命人修建了自己的行宫——芙蓉殿，据《金史·章宗记》记载，金章宗于"明昌元年八月，幸玉泉山；六年四月，幸玉泉山。承安元年八月，幸玉泉山。泰和元年五月，幸玉泉山。三年三月，幸玉泉山；七年五月，幸玉泉山。"[3]P228 从这则史料中金章宗去往玉泉山的次数上可以看出其对于玉泉山的喜爱程度。到了金章宗明昌年间，玉泉山的"玉泉垂虹"被誉为了"燕山八景"之一，这使得玉泉山的名气也随之加大。到了元明时期，玉泉山的规模更加扩大，众多的庙宇和独特的建筑兴建起来，例如"昭化寺、上下华严寺、金山

[作者简介] 赵连稳（1962—），男，北京联合大学三山五园研究院研究员。

寺、崇真观、观音寺、补陀寺等。"[5]P127而作为三山五园中修建最早的畅春园则是在明武清侯"清华园"基址上修建而成的。《帝京景物略》对清华园内的景观有精细的介绍："（丹棱）沜而西，广可舟矣，武清侯李皇亲园之。方十里，正中，挹海棠。堂北亭，置'清雅'二字，明肃太后手书也。亭一望牡丹，石间之，芍药间之，濒于水则已……园中水程数十里，舟莫或不达，屿石百座，槛莫或不周。灵璧、太湖、锦川百计，乔木千计，竹万计，花亿万计，阴莫或不接。"[6]后随着明王朝的衰败，清军的入关，清华园也就成为了清人的园林。

（二）静宜园、静明园和畅春园的修建

到了清代，为了皇帝休憩的需要，更为了皇帝们避喧理政的需要，上文中提到的三个园林（香山静宜园、玉泉山静明园、畅春园）得到了大规模的修建。香山静宜园在清代最早是作为清圣祖玄烨的香山行宫而修建的，其正式修建的年代是在康熙十六年（1677年）。根据张宝章先生在《京西名园》一书中的介绍可知，清圣祖玄烨在游览香山时留下了一些诗词，如《来青轩临眺二首》，"来青高敞眺神京，斜倚名山涧水清。此日君臣同览赏，村村鸡犬静无声。"[5]P38玉泉山静明园正式命名的年代是在康熙三十一年（1692年）。虽然是在此时期命名的，但玄烨自康熙十四年（1675年）起便经常游览玉泉山，并于康熙十九年（1670年）修建了玉泉山行宫。康熙二十一年（1672年）将其命名为"澄心园"，而"静明园"的名称就是在原"澄心园"旧名上更改的。自静明园建成后，玄烨便经常在这里游览，有时还会处理一些朝廷政事。畅春园正式修建的年代在康熙二十六年（1687年）。对于畅春园修建的原因，笔者认为有两个：第一个原因就是清圣祖玄烨首次南巡时，由于对江南园林非常青睐，归来后立即命人在原武清侯的别墅"清华园"废址上修建了这座大型的皇家园林，这只是一个表面的原因，清圣祖玄烨修建畅春园更深层次的原因还是在于它的地理位置极为适宜，与静宜园、静明园相比，这里距京城较近，既可以避免喧嚣，又可以免除臣僚觐见的奔波之苦，以实现最初的建园目的——游园不废政务。清圣祖玄烨在畅春园的活动及其丰富，不仅处理朝政，还经常与一些名儒谈诗作画，并十分关注皇子们的学习情况。自畅春园建成之后，玄烨便经常在此活动，最终也是病逝于畅春园清溪书屋。

（三）雍正时期对京西皇家园林的扩建

清世宗胤禛时期对京西一带的皇家园林进行了大规模的扩建，而最值得一提的要数三山五园中以"万园之园"著称的圆明园。圆明园最早是在康熙四十六年（1707年）作为皇四子胤禛的赐园而建造的。清世宗胤禛时期对圆明园进行了大规模的扩建，圆明园四十景中的二十八景就是在这一时期建造完成的。这二十八景主要包括勤政亲贤、正大光明、九州清晏、镂月开云、天然图画、碧桐书院、慈云普护、上下天光、杏花春馆、洞天深处、坦坦荡荡、长春仙馆、茹古涵今、四宜书屋、平湖秋月、蓬岛瑶台、廓然大公、夹镜鸣琴、西峰秀色等精美的建筑。

二、三山五园的鼎盛

三山五园在清高宗弘历年间达到其强盛时期，而这一时期园林的强盛在很大程度上源于国力的强盛。上文中提到的圆明园四十景中的其余十二景在乾隆时期建造完成。在圆明园四十景建造完成后，清高宗弘历仍觉得不能体现皇家园林的整体气势，为此继续大兴土木，陆续建成了长春园和绮春园两座园林作为圆明园的附园，也就是通常所谓的"圆明三园"。玉泉山静明园虽然是在清圣祖玄烨时期建造的，但是其真正达到鼎盛的时期也是从乾隆十五年（1750年），也就是清高宗弘历加大对静明园建设这一年开始的，直至乾隆十八年（1753年）静明园内的主体建筑群基本建造完成。而作为三山五园中最后建造的一座皇家园林——"万寿山清漪园"也是在乾隆时期建造的。清漪园在乾隆十五年（1750年）开始兴建，到乾隆十九年（1754年），园内的大部分建筑基本完工，"包括万寿山前山、昆明湖和东宫门一带的工程，共一百零一处建筑。"[7]

直至乾隆十九年（1750年），"三山五园中"最后一座皇家园林——"万寿山清漪园"的建成，标志着整个三山五园建筑群的整体完工，也标志着京西皇家园林进入了它最鼎盛的时期。从三山五园整体布局上来看，它所呈现出的是一种众星捧月的建筑格局，这也是体现了"皇权至上"的皇家园林建造理念。三山五园全盛时期，自海淀镇至香山，散布着静宜园、静明园、清漪园、圆明园、长春园、绮春

园、畅春园、西花园、熙春园、镜春园、淑春园、鸣鹤园、朗润园、弘雅园、澄怀园、自得园、含芳园、墨尔根园、诚亲王园、康亲王园、寿恩公主园、礼王园、泉宗庙和圣化寺等几十多处皇家离宫御苑与赐园，连绵二十余里。

三、三山五园的衰落

（一）乾隆中期以后三山五园步入衰落

三山五园自修建到鼎盛，历经了清圣祖玄烨、清世宗胤禛、清高宗弘历三代帝王，直至乾隆前期，达到了其最鼎盛的时期。但到了乾隆中期以后，随着清政府的财政危机，三山五园随之失修，也随之走向衰落。而其中以"畅春园"表现的最为明显。"畅春园"的衰落是从乾隆四十二年（1777 年）开始的。据史料记载，乾隆四十二年（1777 年），孝圣皇太后去世，弘历下旨畅春园今后将作为奉养皇太后的所在地。但是，乾隆年间以至嘉庆年间，都不再有皇太后，畅春园只好闲置下来。对于闲置的园林，其管理人员自然也不会很多。据《（光绪）顺天府志》记载："（乾隆）四十二年裁撤畅春园汛十五处，仍留门班五处，日以副参领、署参领一人，护军校、护军五十八人守卫。嘉庆七年裁撤畅春园守卫护军营官兵，交巡捕营官兵看守。"[8] 到了清宣宗旻宁时期，畅春园已被荒废多年，此时期的畅春园又遭到了人为的大规模拆毁。道光二十二年（1842 年）第一次鸦片战争的失败，《南京条约》的签订，使得清政府陷入严重的财政危机中。此时的大清王朝已无力经营除了"圆明园"以外的其他园林。畅春园几乎与废园相差无几，到了清文宗奕詝时期，畅春园已经完全变成了废园。

（二）咸丰十年（1860）英法联军焚烧三山五园

咸丰六年（1856）10 月，英法联军为了攫取更多的在华利益，利用"亚罗号事件"和"马神甫事件"挑起了第二次鸦片战争。三山五园也正是在第二次鸦片战争中进入了它的焚毁阶段。咸丰十年（1860），英法联军攻入北京，但是他们并没有直接进入北京城，而是在北京西郊一带大肆掠夺，其中处于西郊的圆明园成为他们进攻的主要目标。据史料记载，法军于咸丰十年（1860）10 月 6 日晚，首先闯入圆明园，英军于次日紧随其后。进入圆明园后，英法联军开始了疯狂的掠夺，园内珍贵的宝物几乎荡然无存。不仅如此，为了掩盖他们的罪行，避免留下犯罪证据，英军决定于 10 月 18 日清晨纵火焚烧圆明园，大火连烧三天三夜，使得圆明园葬身于火海之中。圆明园的焚烧并没有满足英法联军的侵略欲望，他们接着又将畅春园、玉泉山静明园、香山静宜园、万寿山静宜园等其他园林一并焚烧。焚烧之后的三山五园，除了"圆明园"和"清漪园"内的一些建筑因未被侵略者发现而幸存下来以外，其他园林几乎荡然无存。

（三）光绪二十六年（1900）八国联军再次焚毁三山五园

第二次鸦片战争使得三山五园遭到了大规模的毁坏，也使得清政府的财政危机进一步加深，为了满足慈禧太后晚年享乐的需要，三山五园中的"万寿山清漪园"在光绪十二年（1886 年）得到了重新的建造，截至光绪十四年（1888 年），被焚毁的大部分建筑得到了修复，并将其原有的名称"清漪园"正式更名为"颐和园"。到光绪二十一年（1895 年），园内的全部建筑修建完成。颐和园的修建虽耗资巨大，但终究使这座"虽由人作，宛自天成"的皇家园林散发出它往日的光辉，但这样的辉煌却如昙花一现，光绪二十六（1900 年）八国联军的再次入侵，使得以"颐和园"为中心的三山五园再遭劫难，三山五园也是在这次浩劫中彻底失去了它昔日的辉煌。

四、三山五园兴衰的启示

三山五园伴随着清王朝的兴盛而兴衰，伴随着清王朝的衰落而衰落，三山五园的兴衰史就是一部浓缩的清朝国家兴衰史，从中我们可以得出以下几点启示。

（一）随着政治地位变化而兴衰

作为理政和休憩合二为一、而首先是理政场所的皇家苑囿，其兴衰必然与理政地点的变化密切相关。畅春园的全盛时期是在康熙年间，其原因就是因为清圣祖玄烨把畅春园作为处理朝政的重要场所。清圣祖玄烨二十六年（1687）二月二十二日，清圣祖玄烨首次驻跸畅春园，以后经常在畅春园理政，至六十一年（1722）十一月十三日病逝于清溪书屋，36年间，计居住畅春园257次3800余天，年均驻园7次107天，最短者为29天，最长者为202天。雍正时期，圆明园政治地位上升，成为御园，清帝理政地点改在圆明园。清高宗弘历时期，将畅春园定为皇太后的居所。清高宗弘历经常赴畅春园内向皇太后问安，并在园中随时处理一些政事，清高宗弘历的母亲活到乾隆四十二年（1777）。应该说，雍正和乾隆时期的畅春园还是处于盛期。可是自乾隆四十二年后，至嘉庆朝的40多年内，清朝没有皇太后，畅春园便始终处于关闭状态，一直未得到修缮，到了道光年间已经是破败不堪。清宣宗旻宁即位后，以畅春园年久失修、不堪使用为由，便将其母亲奉养在圆明园绮春园。此后，没有了政治地位的畅春园加速败落下去，甚至把畅春园九经三事殿拆毁。颐和园在乾隆时期达到鼎盛，虽然由于英法联军和八国联军的焚烧掠夺，一度衰落，但由于慈禧太后要在此园理政避暑，因此还能够维持着皇家园林的气派。

（二）与国家民族命运紧密相连

三山五园在乾隆时期达到鼎盛，以后随着国力的衰退而步入衰落之境地。清朝在嘉庆以后对三山五园没有再进行大规模的修缮。鸦片战争后，清朝国力逐步衰落下去，咸丰十年（1860），英法联军入侵北京，在疯狂掠夺之后，一把大火将三山五园焚烧，英法联军的暴行受到世界爱好和平的人们的谴责，法国大作家雨果在《致巴特雷上尉的信》中怒斥英法侵略者是"两个强盗"。清政府在和西方列强签订了一系列屈辱的条约后，又苟延残喘了几十年，虽然其间有洋务运动，但仍然没有挽救其颓势，甲午中日战争，天朝帝国被蕞尔小国打败，举国震惊，戊戌变法遂起，可惜的是仅仅维持了一百零三天便失败了。光绪二十六年（1900），八国联军侵入北京，三山五园再次惨遭洗劫。此后，除去颐和园以外的西郊皇家园林，加速衰败下去。

（三）随着国家经济实力的消弱而衰落

清圣祖玄烨至清高宗弘历前期，清王朝正值康乾盛世，政局稳定，国库充足，为此这一时期的三山五园也达到了其发展的鼎盛时期，但随着乾隆中期国家财政日渐吃紧，三山五园也随之走向衰落，道光时期已经只能够对园林进行一些维修而已，特别是第一次鸦片战争的惨败，每次和西方列强的冲突基本上都以失败告终，随之而来的是巨额赔款，使得清政府再也无力经营皇家园林，例如同治年间，清廷很想重修圆明园，但因财力不足，不但拆了清漪园、静明园和静宜园所存枋木2800余件，而且还向大臣借款，还是仍然无法重修下去，被迫停止下来。

三山五园与清代国家的盛衰是相辅相成的，其兴衰史就是一部浓缩的清朝国家兴衰史，如何从三山五园的兴衰过程中汲取教训，实现中华民族伟大复兴的中国梦，是摆在每个中国人面前的重大问题，中国从来没有像今天这样接近实现民族复兴的中国梦，我们再也不能失去这次难得的机会！

参考文献

[1] 张茂节. 大兴县志（卷1）形胜考. 康熙二十四年刊本.
[2] 赵连稳. 京西文化初探 [M] //三山五园和京西文化研究与保护利用，北京：研究出版社，2014：72.
[3] 脱脱. 金史（卷10）章宗本纪. 北京：中华书局，2005.
[4] 宋濂，王祎. 元史（卷24）[M] //仁宗本纪，北京：中华书局，1976：194.
[5] 张宝章. 京西名园 [M]. 北京：开明出版社，2000.
[6] 刘侗，于奕正. 帝京景物略（卷5）西城外·海淀 [M]. 上海：上海古籍出版社，2001：320.
[7] 张宝章. 京西名园记盛 [M]. 北京：开明出版社，2009：338.
[8] 周家楣，缪荃孙. （光绪）顺天府志（卷8）京师志·兵制 [M]. 北京：北京古籍出版社，1987：258.

民俗类非物质文化遗产保护三议

顾 军 苑 利

所谓"民俗类非物质文化遗产",泛指传统仪式与传统节日,有些分类亦将食品制作技术与服饰制作技术一并纳入此范畴。

那么,什么是传统仪式类遗产?所谓"传统仪式",是指那些专门为确认、强化某种关系而举行的认证或纪念活动。如为解决人与人之关系而产生的仪式(包括祖先神祭祀仪式、英雄神祭祀仪式、行业祖先神祭祀仪式以及各种各样的人生礼仪等),以及为解决人与自然之关系而产生的仪式(如祭山仪式,祭水仪式、祭祀五谷神仪式等)等。而所谓传统节日类遗产,主要是指人类在历史上创造并以活态形式原汁原味传承至今的、具有重要历史价值、艺术价值、文化价值、社会价值以及科学价值的传统节庆活动。由于中国90%以上的传统节日都是从远古祭祀仪式的基础上发展起来的,因此,两者在传承模式以及保护模式上均不存在太大差异。

1 民俗类非物质文化遗产:一种重要的遗产类型

如果进行民意测验,让大家说出自己喜欢的非物质文化遗产,得票最高的恐怕就是民俗类非物质文化遗产。在众人心目中,传统节日与传统仪式无论如何都是十分重要的。

其实,细想起来这个结论也不难理解:一年有365天,但并非每一天都同等重要。一年中总有那么几天,在传承一国物质文明与精神文明的过程中发挥着重要作用,而这几天就是传统节日。同样,在个人的成长过程中,也有数不胜数的节点,其中总有那么几个节点,标志着个人社会属性的质的变化,这几个节点,就是由诞生礼、成年礼、婚礼、葬礼等种种仪式组成的人生礼仪。

民俗类遗产虽然从表面上说只是非物质文化遗产总类中的一种,但由于绝大多数传统表演艺术、传统工艺技术都依附于传统节日与仪式,因而这类遗产也就成了民间文学、表演艺术、传统工艺技术等非物质文化遗产表现形式的重要载体。从文化生态学的角度来说,保护好这类遗产,其意义已经不仅仅局限于民俗类非物质文化遗产的本身,而且还直接关系到其他非物质文化遗产事项的生死存亡。

那么,作为一个民族非物质文化遗产重要载体的传统节日、仪式,在传承一国文明的过程中究竟发挥着怎样的作用呢?

[作者简介] 顾军,北京联合大学历史文博系主任、教授,文化遗产研究所所长;苑利,中国艺术研究院研究员、博士生导师、国家非物质文化遗产保护工作委员会委员。

1.1 民俗节日仪式类遗产是传统节日食品及其制作技术的重要载体

传统节日食品大体上可以分为娱神食品与娱人食品两大类。中国传统节日90%以上都是从古老仪式的基础上发展起来的。出于对神灵的敬畏，每当节日来临之时，人们都会根据神灵们的"口味"与"嗜好"，为他们准备好各种各样的美味佳肴。这类食品（更确切地说应该叫"祭品"）的最大特点是，它不是根据当代人的口味而是根据所祭神灵的口味烹制而成的。它的存在可以为我们了解远古人类的饮食，提供一个绝佳的窗口。当然，传统节日也是娱人的重要时段。在传统节日中，除需要准备各种娱神祭品外，人们还会想方设法为自己准备一份不小的节日大餐。且每个节日的节日大餐，都会根据节日功能或祭祀对象的不同而有所区别。如正月初一吃饺子，正月十五吃元宵，五月端午吃粽子，八月十五吃月饼，腊月初八喝腊八粥等。这些美食在今天可以说是想吃就吃，但在缺吃少穿的年代，只有当过节时人们才会享用到这些美食。因此，在传统社会中，传统节日也就成了传承一个民族最优秀饮食文化的重要时段。没有传统节日仪式，中华民族的饮食文明就不可能得到如此顺畅的传承，中国也不可能成为世界上少有的美食大国。

贵州黎平黄岗侗族

1.2 民俗节日仪式类遗产是传承节日服饰及其制作技术的重要载体

中华民族在漫长的历史岁月中，创造出了丰富多彩的服饰文化。这些服饰文化的诸多元素有些是通过壁画、国画、石刻、木雕等实物传承下来的，有些则是通过家庭妇女，特别是那些民间巧女之手，以活态形式传承下来的。这些独具特色的传统服饰，既是研究传统服饰史的重要佐证，也是当代服饰创新的重要参考。

传统服饰有盛装、便装之分。所谓盛装，是指在传统节日仪式中穿戴的节日正装；而所谓便装，则是指在日常劳作中穿戴的常服。从功能上讲，简洁、明快、利落、素朴的常服便于劳作，而雍容、华贵、繁复、讲究的节日盛装更注重文化内涵的表达与展示，凝聚有更多的历史信息、文化信息、审美信息与科技信息，应该成为我们的保护重点。

作为一种传统文化，节日盛装的传承同样需要特定的人文环境作支撑。而这个人文环境便是一个民族的传统节日或是传统仪式。如果没有了传统节日与仪式，这些传统节日盛装便会因为载体的缺失与功能的丧失而逐渐消亡。因此，要保护好传统服饰文化，就必须从保护传统节日仪式做起。

1.3 民俗节日仪式类遗产是传统工艺美术技艺赖以存活的重要载体

每当节日到来之前或仪式举行之前，人们都会张灯结彩以营造节日气氛。而繁简不一的节日装潢，又为民间社会彩扎业、彩塑业、搭棚业、油漆业、描金业、鞭炮业、香烛业、印染业等行业的技艺传承，提供了一个非常广阔的施展空间，而面人、泥人、糖人、空竹、风车等各种民间手工艺品也借助节日平台得以展示与传播。因此，传统节日与仪式是中国传统工艺美术行业借以发展壮大的重要载体，更为以假日经济为主轴的民间传统工艺美术的传承提供了无限可能。传统节日和传统仪式一旦消失，那些与之息息相关、唇齿相依的手工技艺，就会因功能和市场的丧失而彻底消亡。

1.4 民俗节日仪式类遗产是传统表演艺术的重要载体

节日源于祭仪，今天我们所看到的传统节日庆典，实际上都是在古老祭仪的基础上发展起来的。既然是祭祀，就必然会祭神、娱神，使神在高兴之余满足祭祀者的请求。而愉悦神灵的通常做法，除供品、香火外，便是歌舞大戏。人们通过载歌载舞，使神灵大饱眼福，并在获得快乐之后，满足祭祀者的请求。大量史料告诉我们，今天在我们看来完全是出于娱人需要而出现在祭坛上的戏剧、歌舞，在古代几乎都是娱神的手段。如当下中原地区祈雨仪式中的唱雨戏习俗、祭祀关老爷仪式中的唱神戏习俗，都是这些古老祭神仪式的残留。而这些具有特定功能的戏曲表演艺术是否还在，也应成为评估一个传统节日或传统仪式是否仍原汁原味保存至今的一个重要标准。

1.5 民俗节日仪式类遗产是传承一个民族传统道德的重要载体

传统节日与传统仪式在协调人与人之关系以及人与自然之关系方面，在构建人类社会伦理观与自然伦理观方面发挥着重要作用。而我们在推选民俗节日仪式类遗产时，最看重的一点，也是这些传统节日与仪式在协调人与人之关系以及在协调人与自然之关系的过程中，到底发挥了怎样的作用。如果我们忽略了这份遗产，忽略了传统节日或传统仪式这样一种周期性强化的集体记忆，我们优美的自然环境与和谐的人文环境，就很可能会因为人类社会伦理观与自然伦理观的缺失而遭到彻底破坏。

2 民俗类非物质文化遗产：需要宽容对待

民俗类非物质文化遗产是包含民间信仰成分最多的遗产类型之一。由于这类遗产一直被视为"封建迷信"，因此，很少有官方问津。

打钢花

但随着思想解放运动的不断深入，特别是联合国教科文组织《非物质文化遗产保护公约》的颁布和中国非物质文化遗产保护工程的启动，民俗类非物质文化遗产又一次被推到风口浪尖。那么，对待这类传统文化现象，我们究竟应该欣然继承还是应该彻底摒弃？这是每位遗产保护工作者都应直面的问题。而中国非物质文化遗产保护领域的思想解放运动，也正是从这个领域开始的。从第一批《国家级非物质文化遗产名录》看，民俗类遗产的申报与审批首先是从"保险系数"最高的民族祖先神祭典开始的。除黄帝陵祭典、炎帝陵祭典、女娲祭典外，少数民族祖先神的祭典如成吉思汗祭典、苗族鼓藏节（苗族祖先祭典），甚至包括规模较大并已获得中国社会普遍认可的大型民俗活动（如白族绕三灵、厂甸庙会）也开始走进非物质文化遗产大视野。到第二批《国家级非物质文化遗产名录》评审时，原来一直被斥为"封建迷信活动"的保生大帝信俗、妙峰山庙会、武当山庙会等一大批被禁锢了几十年的传统庙会活动，也走进了中国《国家级非物质文化遗产名录》。

其实，对这类传统文化事项究竟应该采取何种态度，主要还是看它们到底具有怎样的价值，在一国文明的传承过程中究竟发挥着怎样的作用。传统祖先神祭祀仪式、行业神祭祀仪式，在增进民族团结、家族团结以及行业团结等方面显然发挥过重要作用，我们没有理由对这类充满"正能量"的传统仪式横加指责甚至随意抛弃。同样，我们也没有任何理由将在调整人与自然关系方面发挥过重要作用的传统祭山仪式、祭水仪式拒之门外。但是，在现实生活中，有些遗产所呈现给我们的价值有时确实很难判断，这就需要我们通过深入考察，认真研究，做出审慎的价值判断。

通常，凡事有"利"必有"弊"，关键看是"利"大，还是"弊"大。凡"弊"大于"利"者，就要坚决摒弃；凡"利"大于"弊"者，就要继承。从目前我们所掌握的资料看，我国民间社会所保留下来的绝大多数民俗类遗产都很难说得上是"根红苗正"，有些甚至还带有相当程度上的"俗信"甚至"迷信"色彩。如今天我们所看到的端午节、重阳节、奠基仪式、祭祖仪式等，哪个不包含这方面内容？但考虑到它们在创建和谐社会以及在调整人与自然之关系方面所发挥的巨大作用，我们仍应对这类遗产报以更多的宽容。如果我们连这样一点儿瑕疵都不能忍受，我们就很难将这笔遗产真正地继承下来。

3 民俗类非物质文化遗产：保护工作将面临的几个问题

民俗类非物质文化遗产保护面临着很多问题，但目前需要重点解决的是以下三个方面的问题：一是申报问题；二是保护问题；三是商业化经营与产业化开发问题。

3.1 申报问题

民俗类遗产数量多，范围广，又是许多非物质文化遗产项目的重要载体，因此，应该成为我们申报工作的重点。但在现实生活中，这类遗产也是在审批过程中最容易出现的一种问题。问题主要表现在以下三个方面。

（1）以规模大小作为评审民俗类遗产的重要尺度。在有些人看来，能否成为一国或一地遗产，首先要看其规模如何，政府投入力度如何。政府投入越多，规模越大，也就越容易入选非物质文化遗产名录。而这种观念一旦获得社会的认可，许多从遗产角度看并不优秀，甚至不是非物质文化遗产的"遗产项目"，特别是一些地方政府刻意打造出来的所谓"遗产项目"——如某某祭祀大典一类的文化创意活动，就会因为规模足够宏大而被堂而皇之地列入非物质文化遗产名录。其实，历史上由官方传承的大型仪式并非不能进入非物质文化遗产名录，韩国李氏王朝宫廷祭祀列入联合国教科文组织《人类非物质文化遗产名录》，就是最典型的一例。但关键要看你是否真传承有序，是否真的原汁原味。如果整个仪式所用的音乐都是当代乐人所创，所用舞蹈都是当代舞人所编，所用服装都是当代服装大师所设计，祭坛上所用祭品都是布景师精心制作的仿品，这样的官办仪式还有什么历史认识价值可言？

（2）以当代审美标准作为评审民俗类非物质文化遗产的重要尺度

是否具有审美价值，确实是遴选非物质文化遗产的一个重要尺度。但这里所说的"审美价值"，不是指当代审美价值——当代人的审美喜好，而是指传承了千百年之久的传统审美价值。它不但是我们了解历史上不同时代审美特性的重要参考，同时也是我们了解不同地域审美特性的重要参考。如果我们偷换了评审尺度，用当代审美取代传统审美，那些根本就不属于非物质文化遗产的当代创作，就会因为非常符合当代审美主流而顺势混入非物质文化遗产名录。如果真是这样，我们的非物质文化遗产名录，就会变成非物质文化遗产转基因项目名录，我们的保护就会因保护对象的误判而失去其应有的作用。目前，一些已经被艺术家改编过的，已经不再具有原生性质的"遗产项目"，之所以能堂而皇之地进入非物质文化遗产保护名录，显然与我们错把当代审美价值当成非物质文化遗产评审尺度有关。其实，这种误判不仅会影响到非物质文化遗产的申报，同时也会影响到非物质文化遗产的保护与传承。一些地方之所以将苗族舞蹈改成霹雳舞，将侗族大歌改成美声唱法，将传统剪纸改成剪纸画，将五音山歌改成七音山歌，实际上都与这种错误理念的泛滥有关。

（3）以经济价值即盈利多少作为评审民俗类非物质文化遗产的重要尺度

非物质文化遗产具有经济价值，但与其他价值相比，其经济价值并非必不可少。因此，经济价值永远不会、也不应该成为遴选民俗类遗产的基本尺度。但在GDP至上的现实生活中，经济利益常常会成为各地政府申报非物质文化遗产项目的关键尺度。在这种错误理念的引导下，那些可以获得较高经济回报的传统节日仪式项目，很容易成为地方政府的申报重点，而那些远离市场、但确确实实又需要保护的濒危型遗产项目反倒因为无利可图而被冷落。

3.2 保护问题

纵观我国传统节日仪式类遗产的流变过程，我们不难发现，除少数官祭外，绝大多数节日仪式类遗产无论是除夕、端午，还是中秋、重阳，都是在民间自主传承的。"民间事儿民间办"，是这类遗产有序传承的一般规律。只要我们认真遵循这一规律，最大限度地调动民间社会的积极性，这类遗产的传承当不存在大的问题。但由于这类遗产规模宏大，影响广泛，比较容易成为地方政府打造"地方名片"的重要手段，所以，这类遗产的归属权正在被迅速蚕食。许多地方政府如果想利用非物质文化遗产做文章，他们瞄准的第一目标，往往就是当地的传统节日。而通常的情况是，这节日一旦经了政府的手，虽然称得上又"大"又"强"，但同时也一定变成了一个毫无滋味的"官俗"。目前，凭借行政力量，将本属民间社会的传统节日改造成毫无特色之某某艺术节的做法非常普遍。这样做不但破坏了这些传统节日的原有风貌，同时对这类遗产的有序传承也造成了不小的负面影响，成为这类遗产保护工作中纠偏的重点。纠偏方法很简单：将节日还给民间，让节日在民间自主传承。在这个过程中，政府的工作不要凭借自己的行政优势去取代民间，而是应该利用自己的行政优势为传统节日的自主传承创造更多更好的机会和条件。

民俗类遗产保护方面还有一项重要工作，便是尽快为那些"无主"项目找到"婆家"。在2006年颁布的《国家级非物质文化遗产名录》中，春节、清明、端午、中秋、重阳以及二十四节气等传统文化事项，基本上都是在尚未找到合适传承人的情况下暂以中央政府的名义申报的。这无疑反映出中国政府对于这类正在迅速消失的传统节日类遗产的强烈关注。作为一种权宜之计，未尝不可。但这类遗产项目一旦进入名录而又无法落实到人，一方面会影响到这类项目的有效传承，另一方面也很容易被人们误读为各级政府亦有权取代民间社会，并成为非物质文化遗产传承人。而这样做的一个必然结果，便是在政策层面为非物质文化遗产的"官俗化"打开了方便之门。所以，作为各级政府有责任为这些在特定历史条件下匆忙上马的"空壳"项目，找到真正的传承群体，让它们名正言顺地承担非物质文化遗产的传承重任，并使那些已经进入"官俗化"程序的非物质文化遗产项目尽快"还俗"民间。

3.3 商业化经营与产业化开发问题

传统节日仪式的本身自有其庄严性，这就决定了这类遗产很难通过仪式自身实现这类遗产项目的商业化经营。试图通过仪式来获得经济效益，既不现实，也不明智。但这并不意味着传统仪式所带来的庙会没有商机可寻。庙会通常是一个客流量非常集中的时空，有人气必然有商机。因此，我们完全可以通过仪式之外的"市场"，完成商业化经营。只要政府不对传统庙会进行过多干预，不将庙会办成一个显示政绩的"群众大会"，传统庙会很容易成为当地社会的一个重要的经济增长点。

我们在发掘这些传统节日资源时，一要注重挖掘的深度，二要注重挖掘的广度。所谓"深度"，就是对传统节日仪式所具有的文化内涵——传统节日服饰、饮食、表演等各种文化因子进行全方位发掘，并尽量将它们转化为可以被游客购买的文化商品。所谓"广度"，就是指不要仅局限于对一两个民俗节日进行单体发掘。实践证明，由于传统节日周期短，一年中仅凭一两个传统节日是很难获得很大的经济回报的。相反，如果我们对当地所有传统节日都进行发掘，我们就会开发出更多的文化产品。这种情况在相对封闭的少数民族地区表现得尤为明显。如贵州省一年之中，光是各民族的传统民俗节日就有2000多个（因支系不同，文化传统不同，每个村落的节期都会有所差异，叠加起来数目相当可观）。如果我们肯下大气力将这些独具魅力的传统节日资源统统发掘出来，年年有节，月月有节，天天有节；我们的民俗旅游天天有看点，日日有活动，其市场前景岂不变得非常可观！

但目前我们民俗节日仪式类遗产的商业化经营问题较多。其中最主要的问题有二：一是政府介入过多，二是太急功近利。目前，各个地方对这部分遗产所进行的商业化经营基本上都是由政府操作的。譬如各地举办的各种"民间艺术节"，就是这类遗产项目开发过程中的初级产品。由于人们并没有真正把握住这些传统节日仪式的灵魂，也没有很好地利用这类遗产的传承规律，所以，开发出的产品个个雷同，了无新意，不但在经济上所得回报不多，而且还破坏了这些传统节日的原有生态，真可谓"赔了夫人又折兵"。第二类情况是开发过程中人们太过急功近利，而忽略了对这类遗产的保护与传承。原生态是传统节日仪式的最大卖点，也是招揽游客的重要前提。原有生态一旦遭到破坏，传统节日仪式就会因为客流量的减少而不再具有经济价值。

庙底沟时代与"早期中国"

韩建业

仰韶文化东庄—庙底沟类型时期，中国大部地区的考古学文化首次交融联系形成以中原为核心的文化共同体，这个文化共同体所处的新时代即为本文所谓"庙底沟时代"[1]。仰韶文化庙底沟类型实力强盛且对外产生了很大影响，这已基本成为学术界的共识。早在 1965 年，苏秉琦就注意到庙底沟类型"对远方邻境地区发生很大影响"[2]。此后，严文明指出"庙底沟期是一个相当繁盛的时期，这一方面表现在它内部各地方类型融合和一体化的趋势加强，另一方面则表现在对外部文化影响的加强"[3]。张忠培认为此时是"相对统一的时期"[4]，庙底沟类型（或西阴文化）对周围同期考古学文化产生了积极作用[5]。王仁湘称庙底沟期的彩陶扩展是"史前中国的艺术浪潮"[6]。在前人研究的基础上，本文试图论证，庙底沟时代是在东庄—庙底沟类型的强力扩张影响下形成，该时代的到来标志着"早期中国文化圈"或文化上"早期中国"的形成。

一

仰韶文化东庄类型和庙底沟类型主要分布在晋西南和豫西地区，时当新石器时代晚期，其绝对年代大约在公元前 4200 ~ 公元前 3500 年[7]。

东庄类型以山西芮城东庄村仰韶文化遗存[8]和翼城北橄一、二期[9]为代表，时代介于半坡类型和庙底沟类型之间[10]，绝对年代约在公元前 4200 ~ 公元前 4000 年。东庄类型是在当地仰韶文化枣园类型的基础上，接受东进的半坡类型的强烈影响而形成[11]。具体来说，其钵、盆、罐、瓮等主要陶器兼具枣园类型和半坡类型的特点，尖底瓶的雏形双唇口为仰韶文化枣园类型内折唇口和半坡类型杯形口的结合（图一，1 ~ 3）；杯形口尖底瓶和雏形双唇口尖底瓶的尖底特征，绳纹和宽带纹（图二，1、2）、三角纹、菱形纹、鱼纹等黑彩，以及头骨和肢骨成堆摆放的二次葬等特征[12]，都来自半坡类型；素面壶、鼎，尖底瓶的瘦长特征，墓葬基本不见随葬品的质朴习俗等，基于枣园类型；葫芦形瓶、火种炉以及豆荚纹、花瓣纹等彩陶纹饰（图三，1、2）则为新创。总体看，来自半坡类型的影响巨大，甚至从某种程度上可视其为半坡类型的关东变体[13]。其大口勾鋬罐的勾鋬呈鸟首状，暗示该类型或许有崇拜鸟的习俗。东庄类型大致可以细分为两期，早期以北橄一期为代表，尖底瓶无颈且雏形双唇口的下唇不突出；晚期以北橄二期为代表，尖底瓶出颈且雏形双唇口的下唇较突出。同属东庄类型的豫西陕县三里桥仰韶遗存[14]、三门峡南交口仰韶文化一期[15]等，仅见杯形口尖底瓶而不见雏形双唇口尖底瓶，也不见火种炉，推测东庄类型的核心当不在豫西而在晋西南地区。

庙底沟类型以河南陕县庙底沟一期[16]为代表，绝对年代约在公元前 4000 ~ 公元前 3500 年（下限或许更晚），总体是在东庄类型基础上的继续发展，新出的直领釜和灶等陶器则体现出来自郑洛地区的影响。该类型流行鸟纹彩陶，见有鸟形鼎、灶、器盖等。庙底沟类型大致可以分为三期，北橄三、四期和南交口仰韶文化二期早段代表早期，庙底沟遗址一期和西阴村庙底沟类型主体遗存[17]代表中期，西坡墓葬和 H110[18]代表晚期。小口尖底瓶先是上唇圆翘、下唇突出下垂而成为真正的双唇口，然后双唇逐渐尖平，最后上唇几乎消失而变为近于喇叭口，器底则由尖向钝变化（图一，4 ~ 6）。葫芦形瓶上部由斜弧向斜直转变，最后变为颈部出棱近似喇叭口。钵和宽沿盆由浅弧腹向深曲腹发展，罐、瓮的腹部由矮弧向深直演变，弦纹和附加堆纹越来越常见。彩陶中花瓣纹逐渐繁复，最后又趋于简化（图三，3 ~ 5）；钵口沿先是由宽带纹变为窄带纹，最后彩带基本消失（图二，3 ~ 5）。就级别甚高的西坡墓地来看，至

［基金项目］本文为国家社会科学基金项目、北京市属高等学校人才强教计划资助项目。
［作者简介］韩建业，北京联合大学应用文理学院历史文博系。

少晚期时庙底沟类型的核心已转移至豫西。

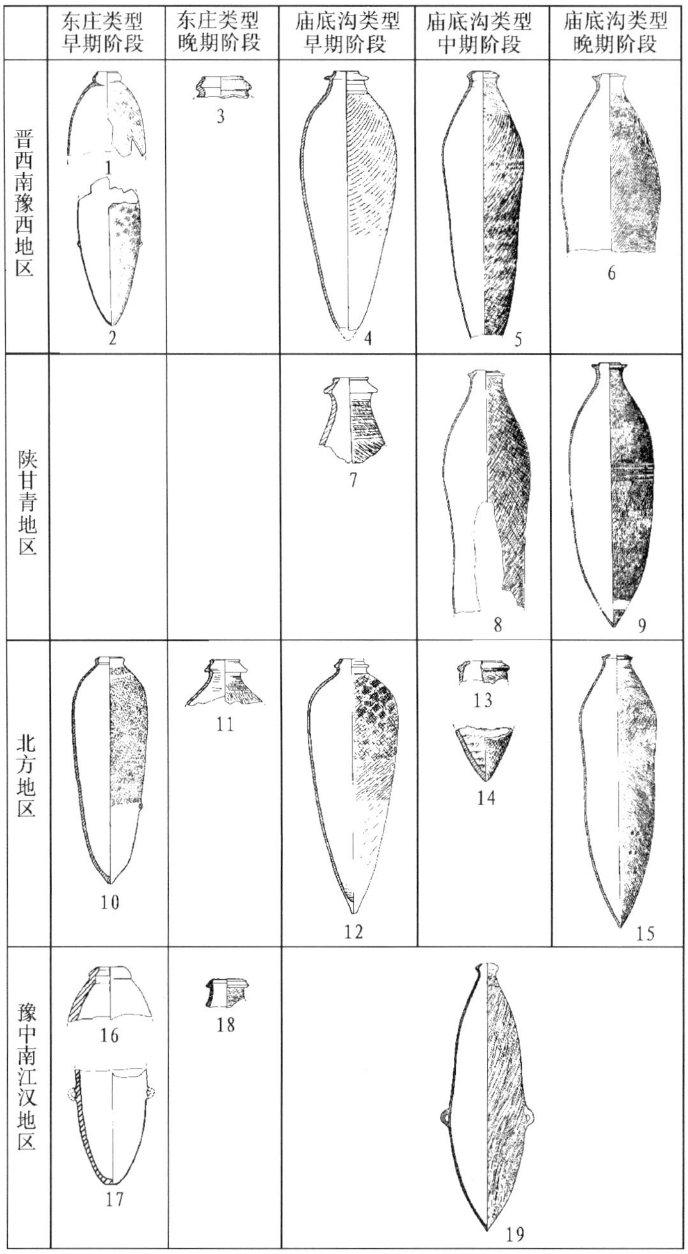

	东庄类型早期阶段	东庄类型晚期阶段	庙底沟类型早期阶段	庙底沟类型中期阶段	庙底沟类型晚期阶段
晋西南豫西地区	1、2	3	4	5	6
陕甘青地区			7	8	9
北方地区	10	11	12	13、14	15
豫中南江汉地区	16、17	18			19

图1 庙底沟时代各地区的陶双唇口小口尖底瓶

1~3. 仰韶文化东庄类型（北橄 H34：27、H34：5、Ⅱ T1302④：6）4~6. 仰韶文化庙底沟类型（南交口 H90：1、西阴 G1：28、西坡 H110：5）7~9. 仰韶文化泉护类型（大地湾 T704③：P50、案板 GNDH24：7、福临堡 H37：8）10~15. 仰韶文化白泥窑子类型（白泥窑子 F1：1、王墓山坡下ⅠF1：21、王墓山坡下ⅠF11：13、段家庄 H3：15、段家庄 H3：27、杨家坪 F1：3）16、17. 仰韶文化大河村类型（大河村 T56⑯：27、28）18. 大溪文化（关庙山 T63⑤A：27）19. 仰韶文化阎村类型（水地河 W1：2）

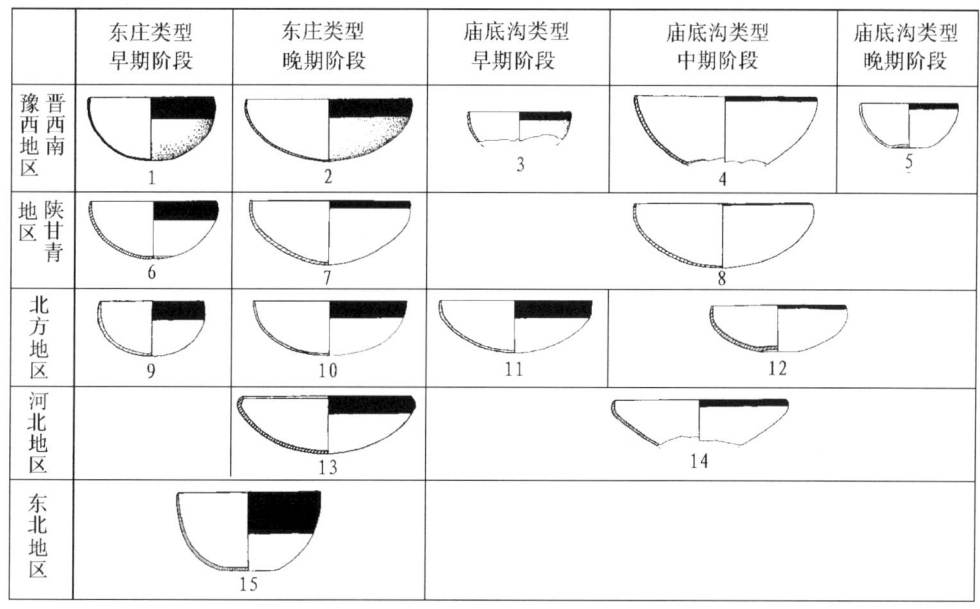

图 2　庙底沟时代各地区的黑彩陶钵

1、2. 仰韶文化东庄类型（北橄 H34：20、H32：2）3～5. 仰韶文化庙底沟类型（北橄Ⅱ T402③：2、西阴 H33：54、西阴 H30：9）6、7. 仰韶文化史家类型（原子头 H126：1、大地湾 T302③：21）8. 仰韶文化泉护类型（大地湾 F709：1）9～12. 仰韶文化白泥窑子类型（白泥窑子 F1：11、王墓山坡下Ⅰ H1：4、Ⅰ F6：13、段家庄 H3：5）13. 仰韶文化后岗类型（南杨庄 T40④：1）14. 仰韶文化钓鱼台类型（钓鱼台 H1）15. 红山文化（西水泉 T7②：20）

东庄类型形成以后，就以其极具活力的姿态迅速拓展；庙底沟类型青出于蓝而胜于蓝，进一步扩张影响。

二

东庄类型和庙底沟类型向周围邻近地区的扩张影响，造成仰韶文化的"庙底沟化"和空前统一的局势。

东庄类型一经形成，就迅速反馈影响关中地区，使半坡类型进入晚期亦即史家类型阶段[19]。陕西渭南史家墓葬[20]、临潼姜寨二期[21]等史家类型遗存，总体上继承半坡类型早期而有所发展，如钵、盆类器向尖圆底、折腹方向转变，小口尖底瓶、细颈壶变小退化等；但不少则为东庄类型因素，如葫芦形瓶以及彩陶中的花瓣纹、豆荚纹等。考虑到半坡类型尚鱼，而东庄类型崇鸟，则此时新出的鸟鱼合体纹不啻为半坡类型和东庄类型融合的象征[22]。这次文化浪潮还一直延伸到关中西部乃至于甘肃中东部，形成陕西陇县原子头仰韶一、二期遗存[23]、甘肃秦安大地湾第二期遗存[24]等（图二，6、7；图三，6），西北可能已延伸至河西走廊东缘[25]。只是这些西部遗存流行仰身直肢葬而基本不见东部的多人二次合葬，双腹耳罐、双腹耳钵、葫芦口小口尖底瓶、人头形口平底瓶等也具有一定地方特点。庙底沟类型向西影响更加强烈，使得关中和甘肃东部由史家类型发展为泉护类型，如陕西华县泉护一期[26]、白水下河一期[27]、扶风案板一期[28]、宝鸡福临堡一、二期[29]、甘肃秦安大地湾第三期等；花瓣纹、鸟纹彩陶和双唇口小口尖底瓶（图一，7～9；图二，8；图三，7～9）等典型因素和庙底沟类型大同小异，区别只在鼎较少等细节方面。类似遗存还向西北扩展至青海东部[30]和宁夏南部[31]，西南达陇南至川西北[32]，偏晚阶段彩陶明显繁缛化（图三，10），与关中东部逐渐简化的趋势正好相反，反映出核心区和"边远地区"逐渐分道扬镳。至于汉中地区的陕西汉阴阮家坝、紫阳马家营等遗存[33]，流行釜形鼎而与泉护类型有所不同，当受到过晋南豫西核心区文化的直接影响。

东庄类型同时北向深刻影响晋中北、内蒙古中南部、陕北北部和冀西北——狭义的北方地区，形成仰韶文化白泥窑子类型和马家小村类型[34]。内蒙古中南部至陕北北部此前分布着仰韶文化鲁家坡类型和石虎山类型，一定程度上可视为后岗类型和半坡类型的融合体，此时却变为白泥窑子类型，早、晚期分别以内蒙古清水河白泥窑子C点F1[35]和凉城王墓山坡下第1段遗存[36]为代表,新出锥形双唇口小口尖底瓶(图一,10、11)和火种炉,钵、盆流行宽带纹(图二,9、10)和花瓣纹黑彩装饰,显然与东庄类型因素的大量涌入有关;甚至早、晚期的尖底瓶口特征正好与北橄一、二期对应,充分显示其与晋西南亦步亦趋的关系。但白泥窑子类型缺乏鼎、釜、灶等,花瓣纹彩陶也较简单,仍体现出一定的地方特色。晋北和冀西北此前属后岗类型,此时则演变为地方特征浓厚的以山西大同马家小村遗存为代表的马家小村类型[37],宽带纹和花瓣纹彩陶少而简单,小口尖底瓶个别卷沿外附加一圈泥条似双唇口,多数为单圆唇直口。至庙底沟类型早、中期,晋中北和冀西北文化面貌已与庙底沟类型基本相同[38],而内蒙古中南部仍更多延续此前的风格(图一,12~15;图二,11、12;图三,11~13)。庙底沟类型晚期,由于红山文化的南下影响,冀西北孕育出最早的雪山一期文化[39],岱海地区形成装饰较多红彩的王墓山坡下第3段遗存,北方地区文化与晋西南的关系日渐疏远。

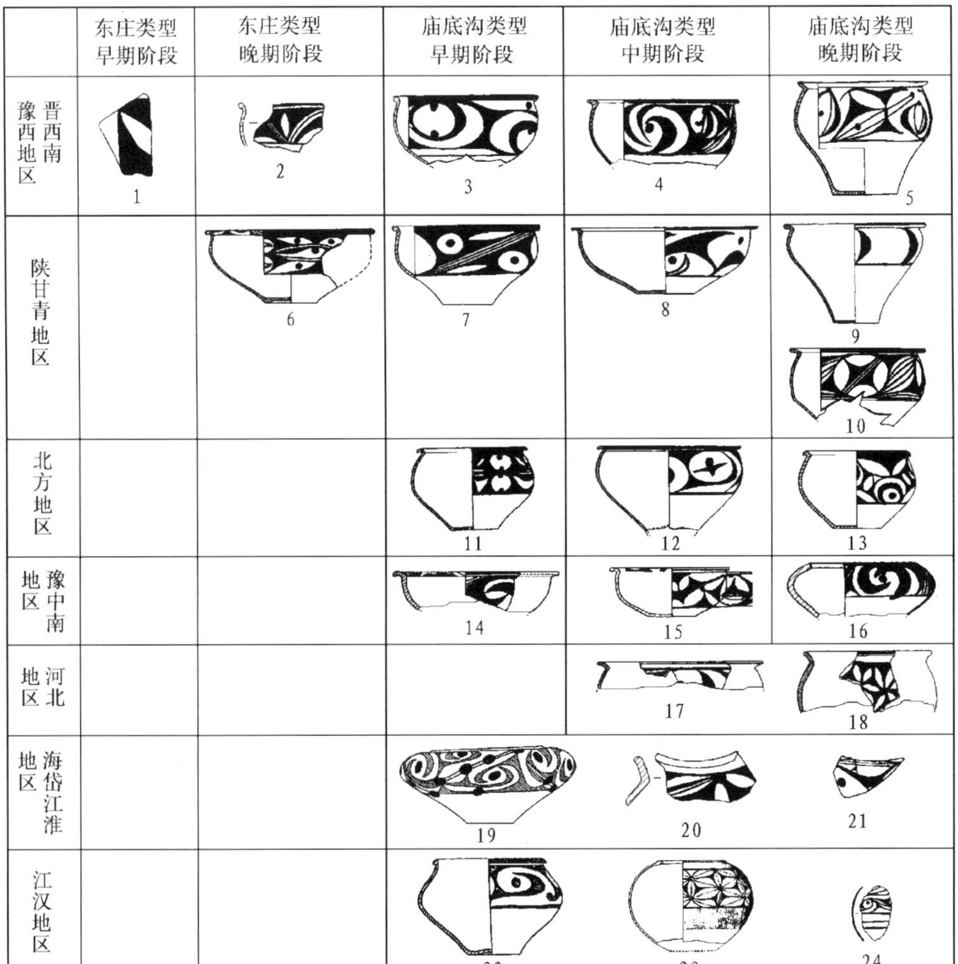

	东庄类型早期阶段	东庄类型晚期阶段	庙底沟类型早期阶段	庙底沟类型中期阶段	庙底沟类型晚期阶段
豫西南晋西地区	1	2	3	4	5
陕甘青地区		6	7	8	9 / 10
北方地区			11	12	13
豫中南地区			14	15	16
河北地区				17	18
海岱江淮地区			19	20	21
江汉地区			22	23	24

图3　庙底沟时代各地区的花瓣纹彩陶盆

1、2. 仰韶文化东庄类型(北橄H38:11、东庄H104:1:01) 3~5. 仰韶文化庙底沟类型(北橄T8①:1、西阴H33:7、西阴H30:63) 6. 仰韶文化史家类型(原子头H42:1) 7~10. 仰韶文化泉护类型(大地湾T700④:19、泉护H5:192、泉护H1127:871、胡李家H14:2) 11~13. 仰韶文化白泥窑子类型(章毛勿素F1:4、段家庄H3:07、白泥窑子A点F2:2) 14~16. 仰韶文化阎村类型(大河村T1¾D:113、点军台F3:7、大河村T11½A:83) 17、18. 仰韶文化钓鱼台类型(南杨庄H108:1、钓鱼台T4④) 19. 大汶口文化(刘林M72:1) 20、21. 崧泽文化(青墩下文化层、草鞋山T304:6) 22~24. 大溪文化(螺蛳山1号墓、关庙山T37¼B:9、T4④:9)

东庄类型同样东南和南向对河南中南部及鄂北产生很大影响。郑洛及以南地区,此前为大河村前二期类遗存[40],此时则转变为大河村类型遗存,新出现锥形口小口尖底瓶[41](图一,16、17)和花瓣纹、豆荚纹黑彩等东庄类型因素,但流行釜形鼎、崇尚素面和红彩带等仍为当地传统的延续,小口折腹釜形鼎的出现当为北辛文化影响的结果,豆、杯等则体现出与江淮地区的文化联系。豫西南和鄂西北地区,此前为仰韶文化大张庄类型[42],此时则发展为以河南淅川下王岗二期下层[43]、邓州八里岗M53[44]为代表的下王岗类型,新出现宽带纹、豆荚纹、花瓣纹黑彩和多人二次葬等东庄类型因素,小口尖底瓶则多为杯形口。庙底沟类型的影响更加深入,花瓣纹彩陶成为这些地区的典型因素(图三,14~16),双唇口小口尖底瓶(图一,19)和葫芦形瓶也见于各地,只是距离豫西越远越少。但地方性特征仍然浓厚,郑洛地区的河南汝州阎村、郑州大河村一、二期、荥阳点军台一期[45]、巩义水地河三、四期[46]之类遗存,小口尖底瓶更多为矮杯形口,浅腹釜形鼎发达,常见在白衣上兼施黑、红彩,流行成人瓮棺葬,被称为仰韶文化阎村类型[47]。豫西南和鄂西北地区仍为下王岗类型的延续,以下王岗二期中、上层为代表,扩展至鄂西北的郧县、枣阳、随州一带[48],流行圆腹釜形鼎,小口尖底瓶多为杯形口,彩陶黑、红、白搭配。偏晚阶段接受大汶口文化、大溪文化和崧泽文化影响,出现太阳纹、"互"字纹等彩陶图案,豆、杯、圈足碗、附杯圈足盘等陶器增多,与晋西南和豫西核心区的差异逐渐增大。

东庄类型向太行山以东的影响最小,仅在河北正定南杨庄三期[49]、永年石北口中期四段和晚期的H52[50]等遗存中,见有少量黑彩宽带钵(图二,13)、凹折沿绳纹罐和弦纹罐等东庄类型因素,这当与后岗类型的顽强抵制有关。公元前4000年左右庙底沟类型正式形成之后,其与后岗类型的对峙局面终于宣告结束。这时除磁县钓鱼台、正定南杨庄四期为代表的少量与庙底沟类型近似的钓鱼台类型遗存[51](图二,14;图三,17、18)外,河北平原大部呈现出文化萧条景象,或许与庙底沟类型进入太行山以东引起的激烈战争有关。这也从另外一个侧面见证了庙底沟类型强势扩张的剧烈程度。

三

东庄类型和庙底沟类型对仰韶文化区以外的东北、东部沿海和长江中游地区都产生了较为深远的影响。

(一) 东北地区

东庄类型和庙底沟类型东北向的影响渗透,导致了西辽河流域红山文化的兴起。约在公元前4200年以前,东北西辽河流域分布着以内蒙古敖汉旗小山遗存为代表的晚期赵宝沟文化[52],其中已经渗透进仰韶文化下潘汪类型和后岗类型的泥质红陶钵、盆类因素。东庄类型形成后向北方强烈影响,形成仰韶文化白泥窑子类型和马家小村类型,其中前者已扩展至内蒙古锡林郭勒盟境,后者到达冀西北[53]。这两个类型继续东北向强力渗透的结果,就是使西辽河流域的赵宝沟文化转变为以内蒙古赤峰蜘蛛山T1③[54]、西水泉H2[55]为代表的早期红山文化,面貌焕然一新,出现大量装饰黑彩的泥质红陶钵、盆、壶类,尤其宽带纹黑彩钵(图二,15)明确为东庄类型因素。庙底沟类型继续东北向施加影响,不但在冀西北地区留下蔚县三关F3那样与其很类似的遗存,而且使得以敖汉旗三道湾子H1[56]、赤峰西水泉F13为代表的中期红山文化开始流行涡纹彩陶,那实际上是花瓣纹彩的变体。

苏秉琦先生曾以"华山玫瑰燕山龙"的诗句,对中原和东北这种文化联系进行了高度概括。他指出花瓣纹等仰韶文化因素正是从华山脚下开始,经由晋南、北方地区而至于东北地区,并说红山文化"是北方与中原两大文化区系在大凌河上游互相碰撞、聚变的产物"[57]。但到以辽宁凌源牛河梁主体遗存为代表的红山文化晚期[58],红山文化已经开始反向对仰韶文化产生较大影响[59]。

(二) 东部沿海地区

东庄类型和庙底沟类型向东部沿海地区的扩张影响,使海岱地区刚诞生的大汶口文化的面貌发生一定程度的改观,刺激了江淮和江浙地区文化的"崧泽化"进程,并促进了中国东部区"鼎豆壶杯鬶(盉)文化系统"的形成。

大约公元前4100年,在江淮地区龙虬庄文化北向渗透的背景之下,海岱地区增加了杯、豆、盉等崭新因素,从而由北辛文化发展为以山东泰安大汶口H2003为代表的最早期的大汶口文化[60],东庄类型因素仅表现在兖州王因M2558那样的多人二次合葬方面[61]。约公元前4000年以后,庙底沟类型的影响显著增强,在大汶口、王因等早期大汶口文化遗存中,除多人二次合葬外,突然新增较多花瓣纹彩陶以及敛口鼓肩深腹彩陶钵、宽折沿彩陶盆等庙底沟类型因素(图三,19),这使得大汶口文化的面貌发生了一定程度的改观。不过从其彩陶的黑、红、白彩组合,以及钵敛口较甚等情况来看,与阎村类型更为接近,说明庙底沟类型间接通过阎村类型对大汶口文化产生影响。

约公元前4100年以前，江淮地区为龙虬庄文化一期[62]或类似遗存[63]，江浙地区为马家浜文化；之后在马家浜文化向崧泽文化转变的同时，还出现北阴阳营文化、薛家岗文化、龙虬庄文化二期等与崧泽文化大同小异的遗存，本文暂称这些类似遗存的形成为"崧泽化"过程。这些遗存普遍新出现小口鼓腹鼎，有的肩部还饰多周弦纹，当是受到庙底沟类型和阎村类型小口折腹釜形鼎的影响所致。安徽肥西古埂早期H2[64]、江苏海安青墩下文化层[65]、吴县草鞋山T304[66]等所见的花瓣纹彩陶（图三，20、21），以及龙虬庄二期M141的葫芦形瓶等，都更明确为庙底沟类型因素。由此推测，东庄—庙底沟类型尤其是后者的影响在这次"崧泽化"进程中起到重要刺激作用。

（三）长江中游地区

东庄类型和庙底沟类型还向长江中游地区顽强渗透，不但为其增添了新的文化内容，而且使其文化活力大为增强。

约在公元前4200年以前，长江中游地区文化可分为两个系统。汉江以东的湖北钟祥边畈类遗存[67]，流行高锥足釜形鼎、红顶钵、盆等，实际上与豫西南和鄂北地区的下王岗一期遗存近似，大致属于仰韶文化系统。而在汉江以西，则是以湖北枝江关庙山大溪文化一期[68]、湖南澧县城头山一期[69]为代表的早期大溪文化，流行釜、折腹钵、圈足碗等陶器。稍后至约公元前4100年，大溪文化向东渗透，为汉江东部地区增加了大量圈足盘、圈足碗等器类，使其形成大溪文化油子岭类型[70]；与此同时，东庄类型的花瓣纹彩陶、锥形口小口尖底瓶（图一，18）、小口鼓腹弦纹鼎等因素也进入汉江两岸，见于关庙山二期、城头山二期等遗存。此时大溪文化中新出现的薄胎彩陶杯，也不排除是受到仰韶文化彩陶影响而产生。

庙底沟类型对长江中游大溪文化的影响更加深入，其典型因素如花瓣纹、鸟纹彩陶装饰和多人二次葬，均发现于湖北宜昌中堡岛新石器时代Ⅰ期[71]、关庙山大溪文化三期（图三，23、24）、四川巫山大溪遗存[72]等当中，在湖北黄冈螺蛳山M1甚至还随葬庙底沟类型风格的彩陶鼓腹盆[73]（图三，22）。通过这种交流影响，大溪文化进入蓬勃发展时期。

四

总体来看，由于公元前4000年前后仰韶文化东庄—庙底沟类型从晋南和豫西核心区向外强力扩张影响，使得中国大部地区的考古学文化交融联系形成相对的文化共同体[74]。其空间结构自内而外至少可以分为三个层次。核心区在晋西南、豫西及关中东部，即仰韶文化东庄类型和庙底沟类型分布区及泉护类型东部，最具代表性的花瓣纹彩陶线条流畅，设色典雅；双唇口小口尖底瓶、折腹釜形鼎等典型器造型规整大气。向外是主体区即黄河中游地区（南侧还包括汉水上中游、淮河上游等），也就是除核心区之外的整个仰韶文化分布区，花瓣纹彩陶的造型因地略异，线条迟滞，其中偏东部彩陶多色搭配；西北部多双唇口小口尖底瓶而少鼎，东南部少双唇口小口尖底瓶而多鼎，也体现出区域性差异。再向外是边缘区即黄河下游、长江中下游和东北等仰韶文化的邻境地区，时见正宗或变体花瓣纹彩陶，以及黑彩带钵、折腹釜形鼎、双唇口小口尖底瓶、葫芦形瓶等。这个三层次结构共同体初定于东庄类型，成熟于庙底沟类型，是一个延续达六七百年的相对稳定的文化共同体，其所处的时代构成庙底沟时代。这一文化共同体与东北亚地区的筒形罐文化系统、华南地区的釜文化系统在边缘地带略有交叉，但总体上自成系统（图四）。

庙底沟时代是社会开始走向分化的时代，稍后铜石并用时代的社会变革和复杂化趋势都于此开端。具体来说，东庄类型和庙底沟类型早、中期，核心区和主体区农业生产工具爪镰和石铲大增，表明农业有长足发展；作为专门武器的穿孔石钺已经少量出现，或许已经具有军权象征意义[75]，暗示战争在社会中的作用越来越重要。聚落中房屋大小有别，成排分布[76]，社会秩序井然，显示当时已有较为强有力的社会组织管理能力。至于墓葬基本不见随葬品，一方面说明贫富分化和社会地位分化还很有限，一方面也是当时社会平实质朴的表现。我们曾将之后铜石并用时代的此类社会发展模式称为"中原模式"[77]，则此时这一模式已见雏形。边缘区的大汶口文化、崧泽文化、北阴阳营文化的同时期墓葬分化显著，尤其玉石器制作水平远高于仰韶文化，似乎在社会发展方面走在前面，这也是其社会发展的"东方模式"初步显露的反映。但归根结底，这些文化的迅猛发展还是离不开仰韶文化庙底沟类型的启发。到庙底沟类型晚期，核心区附近的河南灵宝西坡、陕西白水下河、陕西华县泉护等遗址已经出现二三百平方米的大型"宫殿式"房屋和大型墓葬，表明社会已经复杂到相当程度，已经站在了文明社会的门槛，但西坡大墓阔大特殊而珍贵随葬品不多,仍体现"中原模式"的质朴习俗。而东部诸文化——大汶口文化、崧泽文化、北阴阳营文化、薛家岗文化、红山文化等,贫富分化、社会地位分化和手工业分化则愈加显著,"东方模式"的特点越来越明显。

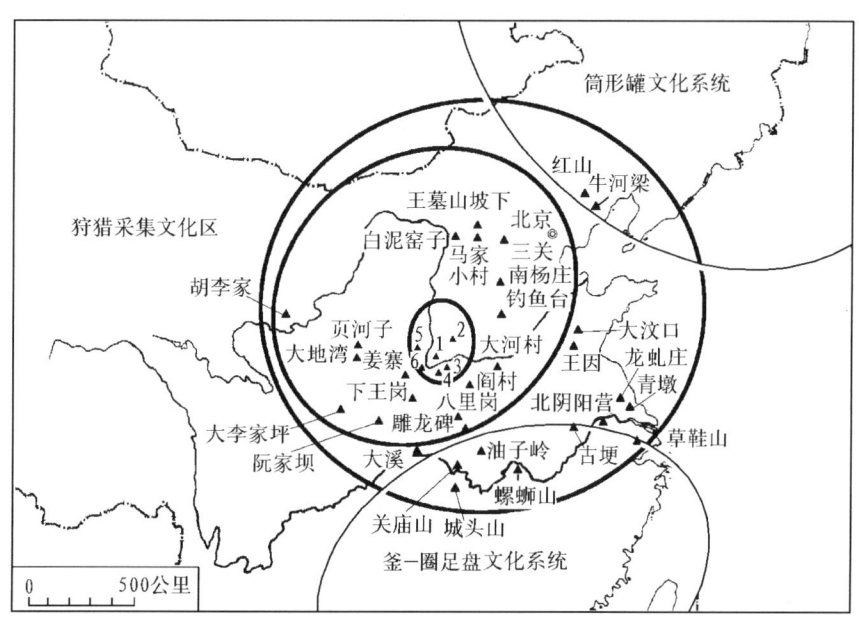

图 4　庙底沟时代《早期中国》三层次文化结构图
1. 东庄　2. 北橄　3. 庙底沟　4. 西坡　5. 下河　6. 泉护

庙底沟时代这个三层次的文化共同体,与商代政治地理的三层次结构竟有惊人的相似之处[78]。这一共同体无论是在地理还是文化上,都为夏商乃至于秦汉以后的中国奠定了基础,因此可以称为"早期中国文化圈",或者文化上的"早期中国",简称"早期中国"[79]。究其原因,中原东庄类型和庙底沟类型的崛起,大约与距今6000年前后全新世适宜期最佳的水热条件有关。而其强力扩张影响乃至于形成庙底沟时代,则得益于中原所处"天下之中"的特殊地理位置。

参考文献

[1] "庙底沟时代"是与"龙山时代"相对应的概念。参见严文明:《龙山文化和龙山时代》,《文物》1981年第6期。
[2] 苏秉琦:《关于仰韶文化的若干问题》,《考古学报》1965年第1期。
[3] 严文明:《略论仰韶文化的起源和发展阶段》,见《仰韶文化研究》,文物出版社,1989年。
[4] 张忠培:《关于内蒙古东部地区考古的几个问题》,见《内蒙古东部区考古学文化研究文集》,海洋出版社,1991年。
[5] 张忠培:《仰韶时代——史前社会的繁荣与向文明社会的转变》,《文物季刊》1997年第1期。
[6] 王仁湘:《史前中国的艺术浪潮——庙底沟文化彩陶研究》,文物出版社,2011年。
[7] 同[3]。
[8] 中国科学院考古研究所山西工作队:《山西芮城东庄村和西王村遗址的发掘》,《考古学报》1973年第1期。
[9] 山西省考古研究所:《山西翼城北橄遗址发掘报告》,《文物季刊》1993年第4期。
[10] 张忠培、严文明:《三里桥仰韶遗存的文化性质与年代》,《考古》1964年第6期。
[11] a. 田建文、薛新民、杨林中:《晋南地区新石器时期考古学文化的新认识》,《文物季刊》1992年第2期。
　　b. 同[9]。
[12] 陕西华县元君庙墓地一期就流行摆放成仰身直肢葬式的二次葬,二期以后流行头骨和肢骨成堆摆放的二次葬(北京大学历史系考古教研室:《元君庙仰韶墓地》,文物出版社,1983年),这两种二次葬之间当存在演化关系。元君庙一、二期属于半坡类型早期,相对年代略早于北橄一期。
[13] a. 严文明:《论半坡类型和庙底沟类型》,《考古与文物》1980年第1期。
　　b. 戴向明:《试论庙底沟文化的起源》,见《青果集——吉林大学考古系建系十周年纪念文集》,知识出版社,1998年。
[14] 中国科学院考古研究所:《庙底沟与三里桥》,科学出版社,1959年。

[15] 河南省文物考古研究所：《三门峡南交口》，科学出版社，2009年。
[16] 同［14］。
[17] a. 李济：《西阴村史前的遗存》，清华学校研究院丛书第三种，1927年。
　　 b. 山西省考古研究所：《西阴村史前遗存第二次发掘》，见《三晋考古》第二辑，山西人民出版社，1996年。
[18] a. 河南省文物考古研究所、中国社会科学院考古研究所河南一队等：《河南灵宝市西坡遗址2001年春发掘简报》，《华夏考古》2002年第2期。
　　 b. 中国社会科学院考古研究所、河南省文物考古研究所：《灵宝西坡墓地》，文物出版社，2010年。
[19] 王小庆：《论仰韶文化史家类型》，《考古学报》1993年第4期。
[20] 西安半坡博物馆、渭南县文化馆：《陕西渭南史家新石器时代遗址》，《考古》1978年第1期。
[21] 半坡博物馆、陕西省考古研究所、临潼县博物馆：《姜寨——新石器时代遗址发掘报告》，文物出版社，1988年。
[22] 赵春青：《从鱼鸟相战到鱼鸟相融——仰韶文化鱼鸟彩陶图试析》，《中原文物》2000年第2期。
[23] 宝鸡市考古工作队、陕西省考古研究所：《陇县原子头》，文物出版社，2005年。
[24] 甘肃省文物考古研究所：《秦安大地湾——新石器时代遗址发掘报告》，文物出版社，2006年。
[25] 在甘肃古浪三角城遗址曾采集到1件史家类型阶段的细黑彩带圜底钵。参见甘肃省文物考古研究所、北京大学考古文博学院：《河西走廊史前考古调查报告》第65页图三五，1，文物出版社，2011年。
[26] 北京大学考古学系：《华县泉护村》，科学出版社，2003年。
[27] 王炜林、张鹏程：《陕西白水下河新石器时代遗址》，见《2010中国重要考古发现》，文物出版社，2011年。
[28] 西北大学文博学院考古专业：《扶风案板遗址发掘报告》，科学出版社，2002年。
[29] 宝鸡市考古工作队、陕西省考古研究所宝鸡工作队：《宝鸡福临堡——新石器时代遗址发掘报告》，文物出版社，1993年。
[30] a. 青海省文物考古队：《青海民和阳洼坡遗址试掘简报》，《考古》1984年第1期。
　　 b. 中国社会科学院考古研究所甘青工作队、青海省文物考古研究所：《青海民和县胡李家遗址的发掘》，《考古》2001年第1期。
[31] 北京大学考古实习队等：《隆德页河子新石器时代遗址发掘报告》，见《考古学研究》（三），科学出版社，1997年。
[32] a. 北京大学考古学系、甘肃省文物考古研究所：《甘肃武都县大李家坪新石器时代遗址发掘报告》，见《考古学集刊》第13集，中国大百科全书出版社，2000年。
　　 b. 成都文物考古研究所等：《四川茂县波西遗址2002年的试掘》，见《成都考古发现》（2004），科学出版社，2006年。
[33] 陕西省考古研究所等：《陕南考古报告集》，三秦出版社，1994年。
[34] 韩建业：《中国北方地区新石器时代文化研究》，文物出版社，2003年。
[35] 崔璇、斯琴：《内蒙古清水河白泥窑子C、J点发掘简报》，《考古》1988年第2期。
[36] 内蒙古文物考古研究所等：《岱海考古（三）——仰韶文化遗址发掘报告集》，科学出版社，2003年。
[37] 山西省考古研究所、大同市博物馆：《山西大同马家小村新石器时代遗址》，《文物季刊》1992年第3期。
[38] 如山西汾阳段家庄H3、柳林杨家坪F1（国家文物局、山西省考古研究所、吉林大学考古学系：《晋中考古》，文物出版社，1999年）、河北蔚县三关F3（张家口考古队：《一九七九年蔚县新石器时代考古的主要收获》，《考古》1981年第2期）等，只是仍少见鼎。
[39] 以河北平山中贾壁遗存为代表。参见滹沱河考古队：《河北滹沱河流域考古调查与试掘》，《考古》1993年第4期；韩建业：《论雪山一期文化》，《华夏考古》2003年第4期。
[40] 郑州市文物考古研究所：《郑州大河村》，科学出版社，2001年。
[41] 《郑州大河村》将其划分为M型罐。
[42] 南阳地区文物队、方城县文化馆：《河南方城县大张庄新石器时代遗址》，《考古》1983年第5期。
[43] 河南省文物研究所等：《淅川下王岗》，文物出版社，1989年。
[44] 北京大学考古实习队、河南省南阳市文物研究所：《河南邓州八里岗遗址发掘简报》，《文物》1998年第9期。
[45] 郑州市博物馆：《荥阳点军台遗址1980年发掘报告》，《中原文物》1982年第4期。
[46] 张松林、刘彦锋、刘洪淼：《河南巩义水地河遗址发掘简报》，见《郑州文物考古与研究》（一），科学出版社，2003年。
[47] a. 同［3］。
　　 b. 袁广阔：《阎村类型研究》，《考古学报》1996年第3期。
[48] 以郧县大寺H98、枣阳雕龙碑第一期为代表。参见湖北省文物考古研究所、湖北省文物局南水北调办公室：《湖北

郧县大寺遗址 2006 年发掘简报》，《考古》2008 年第 4 期；中国社会科学院考古研究所：《枣阳雕龙碑》，科学出版社，2006 年。

[49] 河北省文物研究所：《正定南杨庄——新石器时代遗址发掘报告》，科学出版社，2003 年。

[50] 河北省文物研究所、邯郸地区文物管理所：《永年县石北口遗址发掘报告》，见《河北省考古文集》，东方出版社，1998 年。

[51] 同［3］。

[52] 中国社会科学院考古研究所内蒙古工作队：《内蒙古敖汉旗小山遗址》，《考古》1987 年第 6 期。

[53] 以河北蔚县三关 F4 为代表。参见张家口考古队：《一九七九年蔚县新石器时代考古的主要收获》，《考古》1981 年第 2 期。

[54] 中国社会科学院考古研究所内蒙古工作队：《赤峰蜘蛛山遗址的发掘》，《考古学报》1979 年第 2 期。

[55] 中国社会科学院考古研究所内蒙古工作队：《赤峰西水泉红山文化遗址》，《考古学报》1982 年第 2 期。

[56] 辽宁省博物馆、昭乌达盟文物工作站、敖汉旗文化馆：《辽宁敖汉旗小河沿三种原始文化的发现》，《文物》1977 年第 12 期。

[57] 苏秉琦：《中华文明的新曙光》，《东南文化》1988 年第 5 期。

[58] 辽宁省文物考古研究所：《辽宁凌源市牛河梁遗址第五地点 1998～1999 年度的发掘》，《文物》2001 年第 8 期。

[59] 韩建业：《晚期红山文化南向影响的三个层次》，见《文物研究》第 16 辑，黄山书社，2009 年。

[60] a. 山东省文物考古研究所：《大汶口续集——大汶口遗址第二、三次发掘报告》，科学出版社，1997 年。
b. 韩建业：《龙虬庄文化的北上与大汶口文化的形成》，《江汉考古》2011 年第 1 期。

[61] 中国社会科学院考古研究所：《山东王因——新石器时代遗址发掘报告》，科学出版社，2000 年。

[62] 龙虬庄遗址考古队：《龙虬庄——江淮东部新石器时代遗址发掘报告》，科学出版社，1999 年。

[63] 例如江苏高淳薛城遗址早期、金坛三星村一期遗存等。参见南京市文物局、南京市博物馆、高淳县文管所：《江苏高淳县薛城新石器时代遗址发掘简报》，《考古》2000 年第 5 期；江苏省三星村联合考古队：《江苏金坛三星村新石器时代遗址》，《文物》2004 年第 2 期。

[64] 安徽省文物考古研究所：《安徽肥西县古埂新石器时代遗址》，《考古》1985 年第 7 期。

[65] 南京博物院：《江苏海安青墩遗址》，《考古学报》1983 年第 2 期。

[66] 南京博物院：《吴县草鞋山遗址》，见文物资料丛刊（3），文物出版社，1980 年。

[67] 张绪球：《汉江东部地区新石器时代文化初论》，《考古与文物》1987 年第 4 期。

[68] 中国社会科学院考古研究所湖北工作队：《湖北枝江县关庙山新石器时代遗址发掘简报》，《考古》1981 年第 4 期；湖北枝江关庙山遗址第二次发掘》，《考古》1983 年第 1 期。

[69] 湖南省文物考古研究所：《澧县城头山——新石器时代遗址发掘报告》，文物出版社，2007 年。

[70] 张绪球：《长江中游新石器时代文化概论》，湖北科学技术出版社，1992 年。

[71] 国家文物局三峡考古队：《朝天嘴与中堡岛》，文物出版社，2001 年。

[72] 四川省博物馆：《巫山大溪遗址第三次发掘》，《考古学报》1981 年第 4 期。

[73] 中国科学院考古研究所湖北发掘队：《湖北黄冈螺蛳山遗址的探掘》，《考古》1962 年第 7 期。

[74] 张光直：《中国相互作用圈与文明的形成》，见《庆祝苏秉琦考古五十五年论文集》，文物出版社，1989 年。此文早已提出公元前 4000 年前开始形成"中国相互作用圈"。

[75] 河南汝州阎村遗址发现的"鹳鱼石斧图"，其"斧"身似有穿孔，当为石钺，此图或可称为"鹳鱼石钺图"。严文明认为此斧（或钺）当为军权的象征（《〈鹳鱼石斧图跋〉》，《文物》1981 年第 12 期）。

[76] 以内蒙古凉城王墓山坡下Ⅰ聚落为代表，最大的 F7 居于最高处，其余房屋成排分布。参见内蒙古文物考古研究所等：《岱海考古（三）——仰韶文化遗址发掘报告集》，科学出版社，2003 年。

[77] 韩建业：《略论中国铜石并用时代社会发展的一般趋势和不同模式》，见《古代文明》第 2 卷，2003 年。

[78] 宋新潮：《殷商文化区域研究》，陕西人民出版社，1991 年。

[79] 其实质与严文明所说"重瓣花朵式的格局"（《中国史前文化的统一性与多样性》，《文物》1987 年第 3 期）含义近同，与张光直提出的"中国相互作用圈"（《中国相互作用圈与文明的形成》，见《庆祝苏秉琦考古五十五年论文集》，文物出版社，1989 年）和苏秉琦所说"共识的中国"（《中国文明起源新探》第 161 页，生活·读书·新知三联书店，1999 年）也相近。

从后现代主义到浪漫主义

——一种史学观念的回归

王利红

关于后现代主义史学,学者们已从不同的角度进行了解读,但对于它与浪漫主义史学的关联,所论不多。本文拟从新的视角,对此展开论述,以期对浪漫主义史学与后现代主义史学有新的认识,对史学的未来发展有所展望。

一

伴随着浪漫主义❶运动和后现代主义的发生,被称为浪漫主义史学和后现代主义史学的历史观念和历史写作方式随之出现。稍加比较,就会发现,这两种出现在不同时代的历史写作存在着诸多相似之处。浪漫主义与后现代主义都带有强烈的时代特征,都表现和沾染了一种相似的时代情绪。这种情绪从文学、建筑、政治、哲学和审美领域生发,最终弥漫整个社会,影响到历史学的书写。学者黄进兴认为:"整体而言,后现代主义乃反启蒙运动,特别是后者所象征的理性与进步。它侧重变异性、个体性与在地性,仿若浪漫主义浴火重生,而与启蒙的普世性格有所违碍。但后现代主义与浪漫主义仅止于貌似,因为它首重当下意识,而绝不会发思古之幽情。"❷

这段话既道出两者的相似之处,又指出它们的不同。就后现代主义是浪漫主义的浴火重生而言,的确所言非虚。浪漫主义和后现代主义都与现代性紧密相关,分别反映了资本主义工业化初期和后期人们面对科技进步、社会发展、自然生态变迁和人类自身存在时所遭遇的巨大困境和失落。如果说浪漫主义对现代性表现出最初的不满和忧伤,那么后现代主义则是对现代性最激烈的反叛与抨击。

基思·特斯特在《后现代性下的生命与多重时间》中认为:"要想使后现代性这种境况具备意义,就得结合现代来思考它。如此一来,'那些选择栖居于后现代境况中的人,也同时生活在现代人和前现代人当中。这是因为,后现代性的根基本身就在于认为,世界是由多重异质性空间和时间性构成的'。"❸伊·哈桑认为,现代主义和后现代主义之间并没有一层铁幕隔开,我们都同时带着些许维多利亚、现代和后现代的气质,"在叙述抽象的层次上,现代主义完全可能被纳入浪漫主义,浪漫主义与启蒙运动有关,后者又与文艺复兴相联"。❹如此一来,浪漫主义史学与后现代主义史学就共享了同一片领域,同一种时代精神和情绪,即都与启蒙运动和现代性相关,只不过一个处于开端,一个处于终点。

斯蒂芬·巴恩在谈到后现代主义时曾说,他更喜欢使用维柯所用的词 ricorso(回归)来指后现代主义,"因为它径直就意味着返回。它指的是回到并重新采取原先就潜藏在那里的立场,然而,这当然也意味着第二度时某些东西已有所不同。它所预设的,是一种循环式的运动而非线型的运动。现代主义建

[作者简介] 王利红,北京联合大学人文社科部教授。

❶ 本文所讲的浪漫主义和后现代主义都不是泛指而是特指。浪漫主义特指 18 世纪末 19 世纪初影响和波及整个欧洲的浪漫主义运动,是对欧洲乃至整个世界产生重要影响、充满哲理思辨、文学和美学色彩的浪漫主义运动,它是对启蒙运动理性主义的反动,即历史的浪漫主义。这里所说的后现代主义也不是一般理解的一种非常激进的立场,而是指在历史研究中可以采取的一种更好的态度和方法意义上的后现代主义。它指的是对于传统的、"现代的"历史思维概念所进行的富有成效而让人信服的批判。参见埃娃·多曼斯卡编:《邂逅:后现代主义之后的历史哲学》,彭刚译,北京大学出版社 2007 年版,第 186—187 页,对耶尔恩·吕森的访谈。

❷ 黄进兴. 后现代主义与史学研究 [M]. 三联书店,2008,203.

❸ 基思·特斯特. 后现代性下的生命与多重时间 [M]. 李康,译. 北京大学出版社,2010:30.

❹ 让-弗·利奥塔,等. 后现代主义 [M]. 赵一凡,等,译. 社会科学文献出版社,1999:118.

基于线型的观念、进步的观念和启蒙的观念,等等。"斯蒂芬·巴恩认为,后现代主义的"这种回归——对于原先被占主导地位的现代主义意识形态排斥了的元素的回归——不仅是一种非常重要的史学现象,因为我们突然以新的方式来看待事物了,而且也是对于我们关于这个世界的当代经验的指南。"❶ 让—弗·利奥塔在谈到后现代主义时说,后现代主义的"后"字不仅意味着纯粹的接替,意味着一连串历时性的阶段,而且意味着一种类似转换的东西;从以前的方向转到一个新方向。❷ 在这种转换中,出现了类似斯蒂芬·巴恩所说的那种回归,即向浪漫主义的回归。

我们可以从时空关系来考察浪漫主义与后现代主义的相似性。浪漫主义史学和后现代主义史学最大的相似之处在于它们都反对启蒙运动理性主义的线性历史观,这种历史观强调理性的进步、人类历史的单向和直线发展。与之相反,浪漫主义和后现代主义都认为历史发展是多重的、复线的,不存在单一的、整体的历史这样的东西,主张历史的复杂性、多元性、偶然性、地域性、异域性、开放性、变动性及其差异性。浪漫主义和后现代主义在史学观念上的相似,与它们的时空观紧密相关。它们在处理和面对时空关系时,采取了近似的立场。时空观是阐释两者相似性的重要媒介和参照。

二

安克施密特认为,后现代主义的历史意识即在于把时间"空间化"了:时间上的差异转变成为空间的弥散。这也解释了为什么后现代主义历史编纂与人类学紧密关联。因为人类学在全球不同的部分相继向我们展开的正是同时存在的人类进化的不同历史阶段。❸ 这种展示体现了后现代主义史学对空间性的寻求,这正是两者契合之处。同样,浪漫主义史学与人类学也有亲缘性。柯林武德称浪漫主义史学家赫德尔为"人类学之父","赫德尔把人类生命看作是与其在自然世界中的背景密切相联系着的"。❹ 他对人类本身以及人类生存的自然界和社会环境的考察,充满人类学意味。

需要强调的是,浪漫主义史学和后现代主义史学从未放弃对时间的关切,因为时间始终是形成变化和差异、发展和连续的另一个重要维度。不过相比于现代主义的单向和线性,浪漫主义史学和后现代主义史学更重视空间的维度。后现代主义对空间的着迷不是要取消时间,而是在时间的轴上同时展现人物和事件发展的多样性和多层次性。这一点和浪漫主义史学一致。浪漫主义史学的理论来源之一是莱布尼茨的单子论。单子不是别的,只是组成复合物的单纯实体,莱布尼茨认为,整个宇宙就是由单子组成的有机总体。但他在强调单子组成宇宙万物有机整体的同时,也突出了单子本身具有的特异性和繁多性,完满性和自足性。他认为每个单子自身形成一个独立的自成一体的空间。赫德尔据此在其历史哲学中论述每个民族都有自己的幸福中心。莱布尼茨说:"物质的每个部分都可以设想成一座充满植物的花园,一个充满着鱼的池塘。可是植物的每个枝桠,动物的每个肢体,它们的每一滴体液,也是一个这样的花园或这样的池塘。"❺ 这里的花园和池塘呈现的正是空间的概念。可以说单子论开启了浪漫主义史学对人类历史发展多样性、多层次性、差异性、特殊性、异域性的重视和书写。

G. W. 斯多京在描绘 18 世纪末历史意识的转变时认为,虽然 18 世纪后期的进步主义者们往往认识到在孟德斯鸠那里获益良多,但是在他与他们之间,文化比较的首要轴心已经发生 90°转变,即从水平的(或空间的)变成垂直的(或时间的)。安克施密特指出,如果 G. W. 斯多京是正确的,在后现代主义的历史编纂中,人们或许发现回返到前历史主义的历史意识的愿望。❻ 而这里所谓的前历史主义,无疑与浪漫主义及其史学相关。

安东尼·吉登斯在分析现代性与时间—空间转换之间的关系时,曾拿它与前现代的时间关系作比较。他认为,在机械钟发明之前(最早出现在 18 世纪后半期的计时方式),对农业社会里的大多数人来说,构成日常生活基础的时间计算,总是把时间与地点联系在一起,而且通常是不精确和变化不定的,

---

❶ 埃娃·多曼斯卡. 邂逅:后现代主义之后的历史哲学 [M]. 第 294-295 页.
❷ 包亚明. 利奥塔访谈、书信录:后现代性与公正游戏 [M]. 谈瀛洲,译. 上海人民出版社,1997:143.
❸ F. R. 安克施密特. 历史与转义:隐喻的兴衰 [M]. 韩震,译. 北京出版社,2005:288.
❹ 柯林武德. 历史的观念 [M]. 何兆武,张文杰,译. 商务印书馆,2003:141.
❺ 北京大学哲学系. 西方哲学原著选读 [M]. 商务印书馆,1999:489.
❻ F. R. 安克施密特. 历史与转义:隐喻的兴衰 [M]. 288.

如果不参照其他的社会—空间标记,没有人能够分清每天的时间。"什么时候"一般总是与"什么地方"相联系,或者是由有规律的自然现象来加以区别。这表明前现代社会人们对空间、地理及其环境的重视往往大于时间,时间需参照空间来确立。然而,机械钟的发明和在所有社会成员中的实际运用和推广,打破了时间和空间的紧密联系,对时间从空间中分离出来具有决定性意义。时钟体现了一种"虚化"时间的统一尺度。时间的虚化导致了空间的虚化,并使它具有了超越空间的因果关系上的优先性。❶ 这种优先性被现代性无限扩大。现代性的线性时间观正建立在这种时空的转换之上。随着时间从空间中分离出来,空间在历史研究中具有的重要意义被极大地忽略,表现在历史观念上,启蒙、进步、理性、单向、线性成为历史研究的主体。

浪漫主义史学的主要观点在于"主张历史的复杂性、偶然性及其变动的各种可能性。"❷ 浪漫主义历史哲学不赞同启蒙派所说的"进步论"。他们认为:"历史的前一阶段和后一阶段之间,没有必然的联系,不存在因果性,更没有由'低级'向'高级'发展的规律;有的只是跳跃性、片段性、裂变性和多维度性。在哈曼、荷尔德林和施莱尔马赫等人的历史描述中,看不到有规律的'发展'和'进步',只有充满斗争、矛盾和悖论的复杂可能性的表演过程。"❸ 而正是无限的空间为这种表演提供了各种场景。因此,早在后现代之前,浪漫主义就看到了启蒙运动进步理性的局限。在资本主义尚未充分发展、后现代尚未到来之际,他们敏锐地发现了前现代的时空观念在历史研究中的重要意义,并用它来克服启蒙运动线性历史观的缺陷。

因此,不妨说后现代主义重新开启和延续了浪漫主义对空间的关注。丹尼尔·贝尔论证说:"把现代主义带向极点的各种运动必须按空间和运动的概念设计出一种新的逻辑。空间的结构已经'随着时间问题(在柏格森、普鲁斯特和乔伊斯那里)成为这个世纪头几十年里主要的美学问题而成为了 20 世纪中叶文化中主要的美学问题。'弗里德里克·杰姆逊(1984 年)把后现代的转移归因于我们对空间和时间之体验中的危机,在这种危机中,各种空间范畴终于支配了时间范畴。"❹ 福柯认为:"我们处于同时的时代,处于并列的时代,邻近的和遥远的时代,并肩的时代,被传播的时代。我们处于这样一个时刻,在这个时刻,我相信,世界更多地是能感觉到自己像一个连接一些点和使它的线束交织在一起的网,而非像一个经过时间成长起来的伟大生命。也许我们可以这样说,一些激起今天论战的意识形态上的冲突发生于时间和空间之中。结构主义,或者至少是我们集中于这个有些笼统的名词下的东西,是为了在那些能够通过时间来分配的元素中间建立一个关系的集合而做的努力,这一关系的集合使那些元素似乎是并列的、相对的、彼此相互包含的,总之,使那些元素作为一种结构出现;坦率地说,在这里不涉及否认时间;这是探讨我们称作时间和历史的某个方法。但是,必须指出今天出现在我们的忧虑、我们的理论、我们的体系的前景下的空间不是一次革新。在西方的经验中,空间本身是一段历史,无可否认时间与它的必然联系。"❺ 在这段话中,福柯突出强调了空间在认识历史和诸多社会意识形态问题上的重要性以及空间自身的历史,并明确我们现在所处的时代是一个空间性占据主导地位的时代。福柯的作品充满对空间和场景的描述,不管是精神病院、监狱还是学校。正是通过这些特定空间,福柯向我们讲述了充满变异、断裂、偶然性、不连续性和差异的历史。

我们也可以从后现代主义与建筑的关系来探讨这种空间性的转换。众所周知,后现代主义最初发生在建筑学领域,建筑本身寓意的正是空间。从 20 世纪 70 年代开始,美国那些激进的都市规划者们把都市发展看成是差别极大的空间与各种混合物的一种"拼贴",他们找到了"多元论的"与"有机论的"战略来反对此前的建筑形式。与"现代主义的"城镇规划者们通过有意设计一种"封闭的形式"追求"控制"作为一个"总体"的大都市不同,后现代主义者们把都市进程看成是不可控制的和"混乱无序的"。在其中,"混乱无序"和"变化"可以在一种完全"开放"的情景中"起作用","拼贴城市"成

---

❶ 安东尼·吉登斯. 现代性的后果 [M]. 田禾译,黄平校,译林出版社,2000:15-16.
❷ 高宣扬. 德国哲学通史 [M]. 第 1 卷,同济大学出版社,2007:247.
❸ 高宣扬. 德国哲学通史(第 1 卷),247.
❹ 戴维·哈维. 后现代的状况:对文化变迁之缘起的探究 [M]. 阎嘉译,商务印书馆,2003:251.
❺ 福柯. 另类空间 [M]. 王喆译,《世界哲学》2006,6:52.

为主题。❶

这种从建筑学领域蔓延开来的后现代主义观念，表现在史学领域就形成了安克施密特所说的"水平性取代了垂直性"的史学研究模式。因为空间意味着水平和转移，同时也意味着无深度性和形式主义。安克施密特在分析现代主义历史学家和后现代主义历史学家对证据的不同看法时打了一个比喻。他认为："对现代主义者来说，证据是他拣起瓦片以便看下面是什么；相反，对后现代主义者来说，证据是他踩着脚下的瓦片以便转移到另外的瓦片上。"❷ 对后现代主义史学，安克施密特还有另一个隐喻。他认为，如果把历史与一棵树相比，西方历史编纂中的本质主义传统，其中包括启蒙运动和现代主义传统，使历史学家们把注意力集中到树干和树枝上。而后现代主义的历史编纂学，由于与本质主义传统的首次断裂，把关注的重点集中到历史的片段上，也就是历史之树的树叶上；或者用本质主义者的话来说，后现代主义认为本质并不处于树枝上，也不是树干上，而是在历史之树的叶子上。因为叶子与树相对松弛的关系以及秋冬的来临，树叶被风吹落。安克施密特认为可以假定，西方历史编纂学的秋天已来临，这使得西方历史编纂学研究的重点转为收集被吹落的树叶，并独立于它们的起源来研究它们，这也意味着我们的历史意识已经从内部转向了外部。❸ 由于打破了关于过去的本质主义模式，后现代主义历史研究走向多样化的同时趋于碎片化。这种碎片展开的正是无数细小的空间和细节，因此我们看到后现代主义突出"微小"（micro -）、"差异"（hetero -）和"多元"（poly -）主义。后现代主义的微观故事、日常生活史和心态史的大部分历史编纂学，正是后现代主义历史学家着迷于细节、差异、偶然性和空间性的表现。❹

通过上述分析，可以发现，后现代主义发展了在浪漫主义时期就已萌发的对空间性、地域性、特殊性、奇异性、差异和他者的关注，并使其得到了更大的发展。我们可以从后现代主义与结构主义、后结构主义和人类学的密切联系看到这一点，因为结构二字呈现的正是空间与集合。正如斯蒂芬·巴恩指出的那样，后现代主义径直就意味着返回。它回到并重新采取了原先就潜藏在浪漫主义那里的立场，这当然也意味着第二度时某些东西已有所不同。

三

从时空关系出发，我们可以发现浪漫主义史学与后现代主义史学的另一个相似之处，即"怀乡"。怀乡呈现的既是时间的意向，更是空间的意向，或者可以说是在空间中呈现的时间意向或在时间中呈现的空间意向。这多重的视角使它别具审美和诗性。如果说"怀"代表的是记忆与追忆的话，那么"乡"无疑是"怀"所指向的空间，是更重要的所在。当我们关注浪漫主义史学与后现代主义史学所"怀"之"乡"时，会发现二者如此相似，不仅在空间性上，而且在表达和呈现的时代情绪上。

让—弗朗索瓦·利奥塔说："后现代的并不意味着是最新的。后现代指的是，就广义的思想和行动而言，书写在遭受现代性沾染并试图自愈之后如何确定自己的位置和时间。"❺ 耶尔恩·吕森认为："历史中的后现代性的确是一种新的定位，是一种非常特殊的定位：它是一种与梦幻相参照的对人类生活的一种定位方式。精神分析教导我们为了与现实妥协，我们需要梦幻。而对于我来说，这似乎是后现代主义的历史著述与历史理论的定位功能。它是对现代化的否定性结果的补偿；它是与进步观念的危机和大毁灭——现代化进程的简单延续将把全世界带入大毁灭——的威胁相关联的那种历史记忆的一种美学的安慰。"❻ 戴维·哈维认为，"后现代"这个词语实际上指的是人们感受性方面的一种变化，是人们"情感结构"的深刻转变。这种转变，早在浪漫主义时期人们就已经感知和经历，到后现代主义时期则进一步加剧。

如前所述，浪漫主义和后现代主义都与现代性相关，只不过一个处于起点，一个处于终点，但两者

---

❶ 戴维·哈维. 后现代的状况：对文化变迁之缘起的探究 [M]. 58 - 63.
❷ F. R. 安克施密特. 历史与转义：隐喻的兴衰 [M]. 216.
❸ F. R. 安克施密特. 历史与转义：隐喻的兴衰 [M]. 221 - 224.
❹ F. R. 安克施密特. 历史与转义：隐喻的兴衰 [M]. 244.
❺ 让—弗朗索瓦·利奥塔. 后现代道德 [M]. 莫伟民, 译, 学林出版社, 2005：63.
❻ 汤因比等. 历史的话语——现代西方历史哲学译文集 [M]. 张文杰编, 广西师范大学出版社, 2002：80.

感受到的变化和时代情绪是相似的，只不过程度不同。埃娃·多曼斯卡说："后现代主义在某种意义上就仿佛是19世纪悲观主义的延续以及与现代主义的对立。现代文化无法以令人满意的方式来应对存在性的人类需要。这一'受挫'的过程开始于19世纪中期。一方面，那是一个进步的时代、工业化的时代。但是，另一方面，那又是一个绝望、忧郁、对于人类生存中神圣的维度充满渴求的时代。那种挫折感表现在浪漫主义、德国唯心主义和先锋派之中。……如今，这种悲观主义以其对于人和'生活'的特别肯定，带着后现代主义的面罩又回来了"，"它诉诸情感和潜意识。它提供了一种全新的观察世界的方式，透过直觉和情感来看世界，那个失去已久的世界，神圣的世界"。❶

对浪漫主义和后现代主义来说，那个失去已久的世界应该是充满审美和诗性的世界，即前现代的世界，中世纪的世界，前苏格拉底的世界，人类的直觉和情感尚未受到理性、科技和进步沾染的世界。浪漫主义和后现代主义选择这样的世界其实并非偶然。以中世纪为例，按照传统的看法，中世纪相对于近代和现代社会，具有更大的稳定性。在那漫长的一千年里时光似乎停滞了，但在同一时期的不同地方（主要是欧洲），人们的生活却仍在继续，并呈现出截然不同的状态与场景。这些场景因其遥远、陌生、神秘、多彩、奇特、另类，可以引发人们许多奇异的想像与发现，因其所谓迷信、野蛮、愚昧、落后、黑暗，可以和所谓光明、理性、进步、文明进行比对，从而展现人类自身和历史发展的多样性、多层次性、差异性、神秘性、精神性、异域性和独特性。历史的发展不再是单向、单线和唯理性的。不论就审美还是诗性来说，中世纪都是一个理想的选择。所以，不管是浪漫主义史学家赫德尔、米什莱、诺瓦利斯、卡莱尔，还是后现代主义史学家勒华拉杜里、金兹堡和戴维斯，都选择了中世纪来展开他们的历史叙述。

维柯认为，各异教民族所有的历史全部从神话故事开始，而神话故事就是各异教民族的一些最古的历史。❷ 诺瓦利斯用诗句吟唱："如果人们从童话和诗句，认识真实的世界历史，于是整个颠倒的存在，随一句密语飞逝。"❸ 安克施密特认为，后现代主义的历史编纂对前苏格拉底的早期历史有天然的留恋。因为希腊最早的历史编纂是史诗；希腊人以叙述史诗传递他们祖先的事迹。他们讲给别人的故事首先由伦理和审美的沉思所激发。❹ 诚如耶尔恩·吕森所言，浪漫主义和后现代主义需要梦幻来达成与现实的妥协。前苏格拉底的早期历史和中世纪很好地满足了浪漫主义史学家和后现代主义史学家对审美和诗性的需求。

基思·特斯特曾对怀旧/恋乡产生的缘由，以及它与现代性的关系进行了论述。他说："未来性与怀旧/恋乡之间的关联值得深入探讨。不妨认为，这种关联证明，怀旧/恋乡感可能并非一种非历史性的常项，任何人在任何时刻都有可能产生这样的情感。相反，只有在特定的地点，特定的时刻，才有可能产生怀旧/恋乡感。""怀旧/恋乡是现代性的一项特征。它既为确定性奠定了丰厚的根基，也为解构提供了肥沃的土壤。它是针对现代性中的文化冲突所作出的一种反应。"他进一步指出："怀旧/恋乡感意味着一种双重的渴求，而其核心便是对于某种缺失的东西的欲望。首先，怀旧/恋乡意味着某种思乡。它预设从某种角度上说，产生渴念的主体要么无家，要么去国……其次，怀旧/恋乡意味着渴求某种属于远方或往昔的东西。"❺

基思·特斯特的分析对于理解浪漫主义和后现代主义的怀乡提供了很好的维度。无疑，浪漫主义和后现代主义的怀乡，正是特定地点、特定时刻的怀乡，是对现代性给人类生活与处境带来的缺失表达不满。安克施密特认为："怀乡病必定是有关我们置于时间和空间之中的最'基本的'情感。""我们在怀乡病中历史地经验到的东西并不是'过去本身'，而是现在和过去之间的差异和距离。"❻ 这种差异和距离穿越时间通过空间展现出来。于是，浪漫主义和后现代主义不约而同选择了前现代作为所怀之"乡"，这一空间所表达和呈现的情绪如此相似，而那个失去的世界和他们实际所处的世界是如此不同。

---

❶ 埃娃·多曼斯卡编. 邂逅：后现代主义之后的历史哲学 [M]. 242-315.
❷ 维柯. 新科学（上册）[M]. 朱光潜，译，商务印书馆，1997：55.
❸ 刘小枫. 夜颂中的革命和宗教——诺瓦利斯选集 [M]. 第1卷，林克，等，译，华夏出版社，2008：22.
❹ F.R. 安克施密特. 历史与转义：隐喻的兴衰 [M]. 228.
❺ 基思·特斯特. 后现代性下的生命与多重时间 [M]. 70、71、72.
❻ F.R. 安克施密特. 历史与转义：隐喻的兴衰 [M]. 252、254.

加斯东·巴什拉在其著作《空间的诗学》中说，人们总认为能在时间中认识自己，然而人们认识的只是在安稳的存在所处的空间中的一系列定格。这个存在不愿意流逝，我们的回忆所指其实是空间在千万个小洞里保存压缩的时间。在此空间是一切，这也是空间的作用，因为时间不再激活记忆。回忆是我们关于给人安慰的空间的经验，这种经验特别需要被占有，我们无法重新体验那些已经消失的绵延，我们只能思考它们，在抽象的、被剥夺了一切厚度的单线条时间中思考它们，正是凭借空间，是在空间之中，我们才找到了经过很长的时间而凝结下来的绵延所形成的美丽化石。❶

不管是浪漫主义还是后现代主义，其所走向的怀乡之旅，都预示着在现实世界中遭受的不如意和创伤，这才使得它们需要另一个时空来宣泄和表达内在的诉求。安克施密特分析了浪漫主义史学家米什莱的怀乡病，认为他感受到的其实是腐朽的现在和光荣的大革命岁月之间的差异。这种持续的差异意识，既带给他痛苦也带给他甜蜜，而这正是他所需要的全部。耶尔恩·吕森在谈到著名的后现代史学家勒华拉杜里和金兹堡的作品时，分析了为什么它们让我们感觉亲切入迷的原因。他说："我觉得勒华拉杜里的《蒙塔尤》或者金兹堡的《奶酪与虫》等这类著作的引人入胜之处，在于它们给我们当前的生活经验提供了一个反面的图景。《蒙塔尤》以及磨坊主梅诺丘的世界，乃是现代化社会的反面图景。《蒙塔尤》描绘了人类生活中一个卢梭主义的时代（在其偏离现代性的意义上乃是接近于'自然'的），这种历史编纂中充满了投影，它有着非常特殊的文化功能，它给那些被现代世界的'进步'挫伤的人们提供了某种补偿。它以一种全然不同的、前现代的生活风格以及似乎永恒不变的特质，补偿了我们对于社会生活的经验。甚至于，它在使人们了解早期现代历史中某种别样的生存方式的同时，还有助于人们承受现代化生活方式的经验。卡罗·金兹堡的磨坊主梅诺丘也是如此。倘若你观察这个让人同情的磨坊主的品质，就会发现，他身上累积了1968时代知识分子们希望通过革命而在他们的社会中成其为文化价值的诸多品质。……它提供了一幅历史肖像，将1968年一代的理想付诸现实。他们将自己的将来丢失在了过去。这就是补偿：让过去承载着对于将来的已经破灭了的希望。"❷ 透过时光之河，我们感受到作品呈现的多重异质性空间带给我们的冲击。

戴维斯的《马丁·盖尔归来》同样如此。戴维斯通过马丁·盖尔的故事，向我们传达了一种讯息，即在像中世纪那样相对平静的时代，也会有像马丁·盖尔那样不安于现状的人。他所有的故事都源于他的一次出走，而他的出走对当时的人们来说本身就是一次传奇。对于在现代社会每天都疲于奔命追赶新目标、缺乏稳定感的人们来说，马丁·盖尔的时代是如此令人向往。而处在马丁·盖尔的地位，他全部希冀所系其实只是一次远行。历史的发展就是这样经历着二律背反，在一个动荡不安的时代人们所需要的和在一个过于安稳的时代人们所期冀的，也许正好相反，而这就构成了传奇。人类的历史也许就是在这样的二律背反中寻求着综合，时而化身为理性，时而化身为浪漫，总是欠缺着。

诺瓦利斯曾经给浪漫派下过一个定义："世界必须浪漫化。这样人们会重新发现本真的意义。浪漫化无非是一种质的强化。当我给卑贱物一种崇高的意义，给寻常物一幅神秘的模样，给已知物以未知物的庄重，给有限物一种无限的表象，我就将它们浪漫化了。"❸ 对后现代主义，埃娃·多曼斯卡说："抛开后现代主义，并不会有助于我们解决当今文化种种让人烦忧的问题。……历史学本质上乃是一种生活故事；它提醒历史哲学家们，历史学同时也是文学，而真理乃是一个道德概念。……如今我们应该思考，如何将平庸之物转化为艺术，如何使世俗之物再度神圣化，如何将日常生活的活动转换为一种仪式，如何将深藏在文化层累中的稳定不变的模式揭示出来。一句话：我们这一次如何能够让世界生魅。"❹

以上两段引文传达的信息是，不管是浪漫主义还是后现代主义，都从事着相同的工作，即让世界生魅。如果说启蒙运动进步理性和现代性从事的主要工作是让世界祛魅的话，那么浪漫主义和后现代主义则把让世界生魅作为追求的目标。这一过程无疑是一个审美和诗意的过程，特别是在现代性让一切诗意尽失的时候。而在这一过程中，浪漫主义和后现代主义让我们重新认识到，世界和历史是如此广大，如

---

❶ 加斯东·巴什拉. 空间的诗学 [M]. 张逸婧，译，上海译文出版社，2009：7-9.
❷ 埃娃·多曼斯卡编. 邂逅：后现代主义之后的历史哲学 [M]. 174.
❸ 刘小枫. 夜颂中的革命和宗教——诺瓦利斯选集 [M]. 第1卷，134.
❹ 埃娃·多曼斯卡编. 邂逅：后现代主义之后的历史哲学 [M]. 322.

此生机盎然,如此多姿多彩,如此层层叠叠。"过去的奇异性一直是我们自我知识的条件。……我们越是使外部世界(例如,过去)让我们感到奇异、异化,我们就变得越充分地洞悉我们自己。"❶

这样,"在主导性的历史经验的概念化中,后现代历史著述从人类学和民俗学中获得灵感。关于历史记忆的定位功能,后现代历史研究呈现一种对历史经验的美感性质的兴趣。历史学必须产生一种图像,一种具有美感的关于过去的形象。"❷

安克施密特说,两个世纪以前,只有在穿越理性主义后,人们才能接近浪漫主义,而现在,他希望实现从理性主义到浪漫主义的转向,在思考历史和历史写作时,重温灵魂深处的回声,复兴浪漫主义的心情和感受的世界。❸ 而后现代主义向浪漫主义的转向,将使它们一同踏上返乡的历史之途。

四

浪漫主义史学和后现代主义史学从空间性展开的对历史发展多样性、多层次性、差异性、神秘性、精神性、内在性、具体性、异域性和独特性的研究,最终需要落实到具体的历史写作层面。其表现就是对普通大众历史、微观历史、日常生活史、心态史、女性史以及各种文化史和人类史的书写。所谓历史的碎片化,其实就是从现代主义的宏大叙事转为后现代主义的微观叙事。

最早把关注的目光投向普通大众和民间的是浪漫主义史学家赫德尔。他认为人民的心灵是最自然、最质朴、最纯真的。通过研究民歌和民俗,他给德国和当时的欧洲带来了新的民族观念。他认为民歌是无名的集体表白,与人民的语言浑然一体,是一个民族内心深处的独特声音,即人民之声。❹ 赫德尔开启了对普通民众及其文化、语言、风俗和历史的研究。在他之后,米什莱把写作普通大众的历史当作自己的神圣使命。他自称历史领域的普罗米修斯和祭司。他说:"即使在庸俗的事物当中,每个灵魂也有一个特殊的、个别的侧面,它们终归是各个不同的。"❺ 他把关注的目光投向每一个普通人。他认为每个人的存在都是独一无二的,都是值得历史学家书写的。他说:"每一个人都是人类,一部世界史……不过,尽管体内有着无限的普遍性,这个存在同时也是一个特殊的个体,一个人,一个唯一的、无法弥补的、任何东西都不能替代的存在。身前与身后都没有一样的人。上帝绝不会重新来过。另外一些人无疑还会出现;不知疲倦的世界将会把另外一些人引入生命,也许是更优秀的人,但永远不会相同,永远不会。"❻

后现代主义的微观史和日常生活史,延续了浪漫主义史学对普通民众和个体的关注。这种关注本身突破了传统史学的藩篱,拓展和深入开掘了史学研究的领域。"后现代主义是关于未被述说、重新述说、不可述说的诸种历史。历史学再也不像往昔一般,它拒绝把历史视为直线的、且可用某种可认知的模式直接带向今日。"❼

伊格尔斯说:"假如我们希望把无名的人从备受漠视之下解救出来,就得号召有一种新的概念上的和方法论上的历史学研究途径,它不再把历史看作吞没了许许多多个人的一个统一过程、一篇宏伟的叙述,而看作有着许多个别中心的一股多面体的洪流。这时候作数的就不是一份历史而是许多份历史了,或者更好是说许多份故事了。"❽ 缪尔认为:"微观历史学的一项基本承诺就是要向'被其他方法所遗漏了的人们打开历史的大门',并且要'在绝大部分的生活所发生于其中的那些小圈子的层次上阐明历史的因果关系'。"❾ 伊格尔斯和缪尔对微观史的论述,抓住了问题的实质,只是他们并没有使用空间一词。空间所展开的从来不是一个巨大无朋或无限狭小的封闭领域。空间恰似福柯所认为的,是能感觉到自己像一个连接一些点和使它的线束交织在一起的网,每一个网格里都生活着许多人,发生着许多故事。当

---

❶ F. R. 安克施密特. 历史与转义:隐喻的兴衰 [M]. 117.
❷ 汤因比等. 历史的话语——现代西方历史哲学译文集 [M]. 83.
❸ F. R. 安克施密特. 崇高的历史经验 [M]. 杨军,译,东方出版中心,2011:5-8.
❹ 卡洛·安东尼. 历史主义 [M]. 黄艳红,译,上海人民出版社,2010:63.
❺ 转引自罗兰·巴尔特. 米什莱 [M]. 张祖建,译,中国人民大学出版社,2008:98.
❻ 转引自罗兰·巴尔特. 米什莱 [M]. 100-101.
❼ 基思·詹金斯. 论"历史是什么?"——从卡尔和艾尔顿到罗蒂和怀特 [M]. 江政宽,译,商务印书馆,2007:31.
❽ 伊格尔斯. 二十世纪的历史学——从科学的客观性到后现代的挑战 [M]. 何兆武,译,辽宁教育出版社,2003:118.
❾ 伊格尔斯. 二十世纪的历史学——从科学的客观性到后现代的挑战 [M]. 126.

我们像打开一扇由无数层叠的扇面组成的历史之门的时候，我们就能走近那些曾被我们忽略的人们和他们生活的场景。

勒华拉杜里正是在一次偶然的发现中，通过宗教裁判所的文件和1500年前两个普通人写下的回忆录"深入观察了'我们失去的世界'，以及在这个'旧日美好年代'中生活的庄稼汉们。"❶ 卡罗·金兹堡"在《奶酪与虫》中写道，要紧的是要表明，籍籍无名的人们的历史是可以（而且应该）写出来的。"❷ 我们不知道，还有多少这样的领域等待我们去发现。

浪漫主义史学和后现代主义史学所展开的历史写作空间，使我们感到过去距离我们并不遥远。我们不仅通过历史之门，而且透过历史之窗，看到了与我们如此相似又如此不同的别样的生活场景。"当我们阅读这些故事时，我们就能将自己认同于生活于过去的人们。我们几乎能够'触摸'过去。"❸ 通过"变陌生为熟悉"，"变熟悉为陌生"，我们再次感受到历史本身的丰富性、生动性，"我们的确应该承认：历史是多种多样的，而决不只存在着作为事实实体的此等历史。"❹

卡罗·金兹堡在谈到历史的碎片化时曾说过一段意味深长的话。他说："我知道有许多历史学家抱怨历史的碎片化；我不这样。观点的碎片化的出现在我看来很有好处。毕竟，历史学是一门前于范式的学科……换句话说，历史学就像是波义耳之前的化学或者欧几里得之前的数学；也就是说历史学中还从来没有出现过创造了强有力的统一性范式的一位伽利略或者一位牛顿。而且，也许也不会有这样的人了，而这就意味着历史学也许永远就维持在一个前伽利略或者前牛顿的阶段。……在历史学中人们可以说很多很多不同的东西、甚至是相互冲突的东西，然而依旧是在这个专业之内。"❺

我们的确需要说很多很多不同的东西。在这个后现代的时代、全球化的时代，当元叙事被宣布不复存在，展开的也许就是普通人的语言游戏。"对过去的后现代'私化'。"❻

浪漫主义和后现代主义其实在很多意象上具有相通之处。当谈到后现代主义把过去实在的整体解体成为大量自给自足的碎片（安克施密特语）时，总是令我想起莱布尼茨的"单子"。洛夫乔伊在给浪漫主义下定义时曾说过，没有单数的浪漫主义，只有复数的浪漫主义。他在这样说时也许没有料到，在后现代主义时期，当历史整体碎裂成为独立的存在或要素时，科塞莱科也说过类似的话，没有唯一的整体历史，只有各种历史，"历史（History）让位于各种历史（histories）"。❼

---

❶ 埃马纽埃尔·勒华拉杜里. 蒙塔尤 [M]. 许明龙、马胜利，译，商务印书馆，2011：1.
❷ 玛丽亚·露西娅·帕拉蕾丝—伯克. 新史学：自白与对话 [M]. 彭刚，译，北京大学出版社，2006：245.
❸ 埃娃·多曼斯卡. 邂逅：后现代主义之后的历史哲学 [M]. 174.
❹ 汤因比等. 历史的话语——现代西方历史哲学译文集 [M]. 85.
❺ 玛丽亚·露西娅·帕拉蕾丝—伯克编. 新史学：自白与对话 [M]. 250.
❻ F. R. 安克施密特. 历史表现 [M]. 周建漳，译，北京大学出版社，2011：154.
❼ F. R. 安克施密特. 历史与转义：隐喻的兴衰 [M]. 234.

莫言与幻觉现实主义

王德领

我一直认为，很难将莫言的创作归类，他本身就是一个极为独特的存在。想象力是鉴别一个作家是否伟大的试金石。在中国，最富有想象力的作家，非莫言莫属。他的天马行空的想象力，汪洋恣肆的文笔，一泻汪洋的情感，文字呈现的是飞翔的姿态，仿佛不是在纸上而是在空中游走。一般作家只能望其项背。而中国文学，自五四新文学以来，不乏优雅和崇高，不乏精致与绝伦，不乏深刻和奇谲，惟独缺乏的是天马行空的想象力。我们虽然有鲁迅的奇谲与高蹈、沈从文物我相融的淡然、张爱玲的凄艳华美、穆旦的丰富与矛盾、曹禺的博大与激情，但这些中国经典作家身上，似乎缺少一种狂放的东西，缺少骨子里的放浪形骸。100年来的汉语写作，所谓的现实主义、现代主义、浪漫主义，都让人意犹未尽。一句话，我们都是在杜甫的影响下写作，而严重缺乏李白的"白发三千丈"的豪迈与超拔。所幸，我们有了莫言。莫言的出现，颠覆了我们对中国新文学的想象。

一、超越魔幻与发现自我

瑞典文学院在颁给莫言诺奖的理由中，hallucinatory realism 在中国被译为"魔幻现实主义"，随即有人指出，应译为"幻觉现实主义"，或者是"谵妄现实主义"[1]，"和莫言获奖原因相关的'幻觉'（hallucination）属于精神分析学的病理范畴，这种幻觉包括幻听、幻视、幻触等"❶。目前通行的译法是"幻觉现实主义"。

瑞典文学院对莫言写作的这个命名，我认为具有特别的意义，不仅意味着对莫言小说的概括是准确的，更重要的意义在于对当代中国文学的独特性和创造力的承认。20世纪80年代以来，我们一直是在西方的影响下写作，外国文学的影响，一直是我们挥之不去的一个话题。一些优秀的中国作家总有自己追摹的外国作家。正如残雪之于卡夫卡，扎西达娃、莫言之于马尔克斯，余华之于法国新小说，马原、孙甘露之于博尔赫斯，等等。自然，中国作家出众的才华使得他们在比照西方作家进行写作时，进行了富有中国特色的创造，但是，不可否认的是，80年代他们创作出的文本，"外国文学特征"更为容易指认。从80年代到今天，中国文学取得了辉煌的成就，莫言的获奖，充分证明了这一点，表明中国文学已经走出了外国文学影响的阴影，崛起在世界文学的版图上。

幻觉现实主义区别了拉美的魔幻现实主义，清晰地勾勒出了莫言小说的主要特征。拉美魔幻现实主义一直在影响着中国作家的创作。不可否认的是，莫言的小说深深地打上了《百年孤独》的烙印。他曾说："在中国人的经验里，在我这样作家的乡村经验记忆里，类似于《百年孤独》里很多的细节描写比比皆是，可惜我们知道得太晚。我最早听说这本书是1984年底，读这本书第一个感觉就是震撼：原来小说可以这样写；紧接着是遗憾：自己为什么早不知道小说可以这样写呢？"[2]可以说是马尔克斯开启了莫言的想象力。莫言小说里的神异情节，灵感无疑是来自于马尔克斯的。在《生死疲劳》里，"文革"中"大喇叭发出震天动地的声响，使一个年轻的农妇受惊流产，使一头猪受惊头撞土墙而昏厥，还使许多只正在草窝里产卵的母鸡惊飞起来，还使许多狗狂吠不止，累哑了喉咙"，"一群正在高空中飞翔的大雁，像石头一样噼里啪啦地掉下来"[3]。这些富有魔幻色彩的情节，给莫言的小说蒙上了一层诡异的气氛。这使他的写作，超越了日常生活的平庸景象。

马尔克斯在《百年孤独》的开头写道："许多年以后，面对行刑队，奥雷良诺·布恩地亚上校将会

[作者简介] 王德领，男，北京联合大学师范学院教授，文学博士。

❶ 而美国加州州立大学的童明教授则认为，"Hallucinatory realism 可直译为'幻觉现实主义'。如果按关键词的内涵，译为'谵妄幻觉现实主义'或'谵妄现实主义'则更准确传神。文学中的'谵妄'现象虽然存在已久，'谵妄现实主义'却是一个新词，暗示诺贝尔委员会在莫言作品中看到一种特殊的文学乃至文化现象。"见《莫言的谵妄现实主义》，2012年10月19日《南方周末》。

回想起,他父亲带他去见识冰块的那个遥远的下午。"这个经典的开头,包含了过去、现在和未来三种时态。莫言在《生死疲劳》中多处运用了这种叙述方式:

这时,从远处那条土路上,一个草绿色的方形怪物,颠颠簸簸、但是速度极快地驶来,屁股后面还拖着一溜黄尘。现在我当然知道那是一辆苏制吉普车……但那时我是一头驴,一头1958年的驴。这个下边有四个胶皮轮子的怪物,奔跑的速度,在平坦的道路上显然比我快,但到了崎岖的路上它就不是我的对手了。莫言早就说过:山羊能上树,驴子善爬山。[3]

这是站在现在的立场上向未来、向过去叙述。莫言在这种三维时态的交叉叙述中,还屡屡引用"莫言说",融进了元小说的叙述技巧。

莫言的丰富性在于,他从许多现代外国作家身上吸取了营养,他是转益多师的。在中国作家中,莫言的文体意识大概是最强的了。他尤其对西方现代主义文学情有独钟。除了马尔克斯,还有福克纳、卡尔维诺、卡夫卡等。与古典小说不同,现代小说注重叙述,带有很大的炫技成分,以期创造出一个高度陌生化的新现实。莫言显然对西方现代主义深深迷恋。他大量吸纳了外国现代小说技巧,如意识流、魔幻、荒诞、黑色幽默等,行文带有鲜明的炫技色彩,他新世纪以来创作的小说尤其如此。很少有中国作家这么密集地使用现代小说技巧。他的中篇小说《欢乐》,通篇用意识流手法写成,书写了一个高考屡试不中的农村青年在自杀前的意识活动。莫言酣畅淋漓的文笔,使得整个小说元气淋漓,如行云流水,气韵生动,这是我所读到的用意识流手法写成的最为成功的中国小说。他的《生死疲劳》,叙述了人死后变为动物来到人间的经历,荒诞而又真实。在这里,魔幻、荒诞变形、乃至黑色幽默统统交织在一起了。这是一次众声喧哗,人类的声音、地狱里的声音、动物界的声音混杂在一起,而高踞在这些声音之上的,是人的尊严、人的价值的庄严与神圣。

莫言的伟大之处在于,他有摆脱外国作家影响的超强能力。比如最近的《蛙》,他基本放弃了令人眼花缭乱的叙述方式,回归朴素。哈罗德·布鲁姆说:"诗的影响并非一定会影响诗人的独创力;相反,诗的影响往往使诗人更加富有独创精神。"[4]"对于尼采而言,'影响'意味着活力的增补。"[4]50超越魔幻,是莫言从一开始就定下的清晰目标。早在1986年,莫言在一篇文章里,将马尔克斯和福克纳比作两座灼热的高炉,充分意识到他们对自己的巨大影响。他对这种影响保持了足够的警惕,不敢离他们太近,担心被融化掉,表现了强烈的逃离意识。他说:"我如果不能去创造一个、开辟一个属于我自己的地区,我就永远不能具有自己的特色。我如果无法深入进我的只能供我生长的土壤,我的根就无法发达、蓬松。我如果继续迷恋长翅膀老头、坐床单升天之类诡奇细节,我就死了。我想:一、树立一个属于自己的对人生的看法;二、开辟一个属于自己领域的阵地;三、建立一个属于自己的人物体系;四、形成一套属于自己的叙述风格。这些是我不死的保障。"[5]莫言在20多年后,以自己的创作实绩,发现了自我,实现了自己的艺术雄心。

莫言在《檀香刑》后记中说:"1996年秋天,我开始写《檀香刑》。围绕着有关火车和铁路的神奇传说,写了大概有五万字,放了一段时间回头看,明显地带着魔幻现实主义的味道,于是推倒重来,许多精彩的细节,因为很容易有魔幻气,也就舍弃不用。最后决定把铁路和火车的声音减弱,突出了猫腔的声音,尽管这样会使作品的丰富性减弱,但为了保持比较多的民间气息,为了比较纯粹的中国风格,我毫不犹疑地做出了牺牲。"[6]莫言有意识地摆脱魔幻现实主义的影响,从而形成了自己的叙述风格,即在大力张扬想象力的基础上,将人的感觉无限放大,从而描绘了一个基于感觉之上的幻觉现实主义世界。

在《檀香刑》里,孙丙从曹州学会了义和拳,领着两个打扮成猪八戒和孙悟空模样的徒弟回到高密,在高密设坛,在百姓面前表演义和拳的举动,活脱脱是一场梦幻般的场景:

孙丙一个鲤鱼打挺,从地上跃起。他那魁梧沉重的身体,竟然如一片羽毛轻飘飘地腾空而起,飞了足有三尺高,然后稳稳地落在地上……[6]

……孙悟空运了一口气,指指脑袋。猪八戒抡起捣粪耙,对准孙悟空的头,擂了一家伙。孙悟空脖子一挺,脑袋安然无恙。

猪八戒把一口气运到肚子上。孙悟空抡起如意棒,对准猪八戒的肚子,打了一棒。巨大的力量把孙悟空反弹回来。八戒揉揉肚皮,呵呵地笑起来。[6]

这个荒诞不经的故事,在莫言的笔下,叙述得极为可信。这是一种莫言式的"幻觉现实主义",深深地打上了中国的烙印,已经不再是那个翻译过来的拉美"魔幻现实主义"。莫言终于创造了幻觉现实主义这个属于自己的言说方式。

二、狂放与夸张:幻觉现实主义

莫言曾经把余华称为"清醒的说梦者",对余华的《十八岁出门远行》等作品的梦幻色彩做了精彩的描述,并认为梦幻叙述并非余华首创,而是来自外国文学:"如奥人卡夫卡的作品,可以说篇篇都有梦中境界,最典型的如《乡村医生》等,简直是一个梦的实录,也许是他确实记录了一个梦,也许他编织了一个梦,这都无关紧要。余华曾坦率地述说过卡夫卡对他的启示,在他之前,加西亚·马尔克斯在巴黎的阁楼上读《变形记》后,也曾如梦初醒地骂道:'他妈的!小说原来可以这样写。'"[7]在我看来,莫言对余华的评述也可以用在他自己的创作上。莫言的作品,也是充满了梦幻色彩,更确切地说,是一种幻觉现实主义。

"幻觉现实主义"这个命名,如一道闪电,照彻了莫言的小说世界。自五四新文学运动以来,从来没有一个作家,能像莫言一样调动各种感官,在幻化的场景中,描绘出一个听觉、味觉、视觉、触觉等各种感觉浑融、爆炸的世界。在40年代的上海,受日本文学的影响,曾经崛起了一个新感觉派小说。穆时英的《夜总会里的五个人》等小说,调动了各种感觉,将上海光怪陆离的生活描绘得有声有色。但是,描绘人在都市的感觉,想象力很难飞腾起来,总是带着一股颓废气和放浪感,那是人的灵魂被都市过分压抑之后的变态释放,带着扭曲的人性的印痕,与莫言小说里的感觉描写有着巨大差别,有着质的不同。莫言从乡野走来,他生于1955年,1976年才离开农村去当兵,在农村待了21年。乡野已化为他的血肉,他的写作,无疑是沾地气的。在他的小说里,回荡着大自然的万千繁响,游走着民间最自由舒放的生命。他的感官,向着大自然敞开,向着动物、植物、大地、天空敞开,尽情地舒展着自己的触觉。在这个辽阔的乡村背景上,在高密东北乡的红高粱地里,蓬勃着的,是无尽的生命的波涛。

在莫言早期的作品里,这种感觉的狂放姿态就已呈现了出来。1985年创作的《秋水》是传奇性的,在大洪水面前,各种生命都以一种狂放与夸张的姿态罂粟花一般绽放,读完以后仿佛做了一个绚丽奇谲的长梦。尤其是小说里的那个盲女,天真无邪,仿佛是人类大美的象征。"盲姑娘穿一身白绸衣,怀抱着一个三弦琴,动作迟缓,悠悠飘飘,似梦幻中人。"盲女对色彩是没有感知的,但是却拨着三弦琴,唱着一个色彩绚丽的动物世界:

绿蚂蚱,紫蟋蟀,红蜻蜓。

白老鸹,蓝燕子,黄鹈鸪。

绿蚂蚱吃绿草梗。红蜻蜓吃红虫虫。紫蟋蟀吃紫荞麦。

白老鸹吃紫蟋蟀。蓝燕子吃绿蚂蚱。黄鹈鸪吃红蜻蜓。

绿蚂蚱吃白老鸹。紫蟋蟀吃蓝燕子。红蜻蜓吃黄鹈鸪。

来了一只黑毛大公鸡,伸着脖子叫:"哽哽哽——哦——"[8]

这是一个相互"吃"的世界,盲女寻找的色彩世界,却是这样的无情!这看似无心唱出的歌谣,有着弱肉强食的人世的投影和命定的悲凉。

在90年代创作的《拇指铐》中,莫言讲述了一个看似不可思议的荒诞故事。整个小说给人以恍兮惚兮的感觉。少年阿义在为生命垂危的母亲抓药回来的途中,被人莫名地拷上了拇指铐,结果谁也无法把它打开。阿义为了挣脱拇指铐咬断了两根拇指。阿义不时陷入幻觉之中,整个小说宛如一场离奇的梦幻。小说的结尾,阿义的幻觉又一次出现了:

后来,他看到有一个小小的赭红色的孩子,从自己的身体里钻出来,就像小鸡从蛋壳里钻出来一样。那小孩身体光滑,动作灵活,宛如一条在月光中游泳的小黑鱼。他站在松树下,挥舞着双手,那些散乱在泥土中的中药——根根片片颗颗粒粒——飞快地集合在一起。他撕一片月光——如绸如缎,声若裂帛——把中药包裹起来。他挥舞双臂,如同飞鸟展翅,飞向铺满鲜花月光的大道。从他的两根断指处,洒出一串串晶莹圆润的血珍珠,叮叮咚咚地落在仿佛玛瑙白玉雕成的花瓣上。他呼唤着母亲,歌唱着麦子,在瑰丽皎洁的路上飞跑。他越跑越快,纷纷扬扬的月光像滑石粉一样从他身上流过去,馨香的风灌满了他的肺叶。一间草屋横在月光大道上。母亲推开房门,张开双臂。他扑进母亲的怀抱,感觉到从未体验过的温暖与安全。[9]

莫言的许多作品，都有这种感觉的飞升状态，在写这些灵光频现的片段时，莫言一定是陷入了柏拉图所说的灵感的"迷狂"状态，不然，怎么能解释这些神来之笔的由来。

莫言在一篇短篇小说《学习蒲松龄》中，写到了一个梦境：我梦见自己拜蒲松龄为师，蒲松龄从怀里摸出一只大笔扔给我："回去胡抢吧。"一句胡抢，道出了莫言对打破常规、自由自在的写作状态的向往。正是这种写作的自由状态，才产生了许多在现实中匪夷所思的情节。在山东民间有许多鬼狐故事，莫言有一些小说，如《奇遇》《夜渔》，就写出了人的世界和鬼魅世界的交融状态，此岸与彼岸、生者与死者在这里是合一的。《奇遇》中死去的赵三大爷与"我"的交谈，《夜渔》中巧遇的仙女，与其说是根据民间传说写成，又何尝不是我们人类的幻觉造成？可能在某个瞬间，我们的感觉逸出了常规，于是就产生了一个非理性的世界。《嗅味族》中的长鼻人，鼻子很长，只有一个鼻孔眼，长在鼻尖上。他们吃饭只嗅嗅肉味儿就饱了。在那个饥饿的年代，长鼻人嗅过的肥肉就成了"我"和于进宝的美食。这个故事，何尝不是饥荒年代人们产生的幻觉？

《生死疲劳》整部小说在奇幻氛围里展开。主人公西门闹死后灵魂幻化成动物来到人间，和家人一起生活，经历了50年代以来中国农村的坎坷、磨难与变革。灵魂是人，肉体却是动物，作为人的痛苦和欲念，与动物的身份所造成的局限之间，形成了巨大的张力，使得整部小说的叙述，蒙上了幻觉色彩。笔墨在亦真亦假、荒诞夸张、幽默辛辣之间游移，以狂欢化叙事的方式颠覆了主流意识形态对历史的叙述。这是何等大手笔的叙事！

《檀香刑》也呈现出很强的幻觉特征。小说的第一章，是以孙眉娘的口吻来叙述情节的。她的爹爹赵甲因率民众抗击德国人要被处以残忍的檀香刑，在行刑的前一天，孙眉娘精神亢奋而又恍惚，决意前去设法搭救爹爹，于是整个故事就在孙眉娘的这种高度紧张、亢奋而又恍惚的心态下展开，故事的行进如同梦魇般恍然。在她的叙述中，刽子手公爹赵甲身上凉气逼人："刚住了半年的那间朝阳的屋子，让他冰成一个坟墓；阴森森的，连猫都不敢进去抓耗子"，夏天"为了防止当天卖不完的肉臭了，小甲竟然把肉挂在他爹的梁头上"。[6]在孙眉娘的眼里，赵甲的手在杀人之前都会突然发红滚烫，需要用凉水降温。当赵甲把手伸进凉水里，"俺恍惚觉得他的手是烧红了的钢铁，铜盆里的水支支啦啦地响着，翻着泡沫，冒着蒸汽"。[6]孙丙学成义和拳归来、扮演成岳武穆转世的情形，小甲拿着"虎须"透视人的动物原形的举动，都好似发生在梦幻中，呈现出鲜明的超现实色彩。

《丰乳肥臀》被认为是莫言的代表作，同样在现实的场景中融进了奇幻色彩。对此孙郁先生曾做过精彩的评述："这部作品弥漫着奇幻的历史图景。比如写送葬的场景，天地之色大变，魔鬼般的乌鸦的合唱，有诸多巫气。在庄重里增加一种玄奥的因素，就把死亡的痛感与命运的无常以怪诞之笔完成了。母亲对故乡的叙述里，传奇与志怪式的笔意笼罩在作品的上空，故土的人与事，都以非理性的方式衍生着苦意。大姐的私奔，相亲的哑巴的受辱，都有邪气的流转，我们在这种梦幻的叙述里，看到了有形与无形的存在。而那些无形的存在在现实人体里的跳动，就把空寂的乡村世界历史化与精神化了。"[10]

莫言的幻觉现实主义，是以人的各种感觉为根基的，带有强烈的狂放与夸张色彩。莫言最擅长描述头脑里产生的幻觉，迄今为止，他的最美的文字，都是写幻觉的，飞升的文字仿佛一个个精灵在舞蹈。在别的作家静止的地方，他能够把视觉、味觉、听觉、触觉充分调动起来，描绘出一个喧哗的活色生香的感官世界，这个世界与中国的现实紧密相关，对中国"猪圈生活"的反映和揭露前所未有的深刻。

三、幻象的狂欢：动物意象

动物意象，是莫言对中国当代文学的独特贡献。在他之前，从来没有一个中国当代作家，这么集中、大量、富有创造性地描述一个动物世界，一个和人相厮守、物我不分的高密东北乡动物世界。正如诺贝尔文学奖颁奖词所说："高密东北乡体现了中国的民间故事和历史"，"驴与猪的吵闹淹没了人的声音，爱与邪恶被赋予了超自然的能量"。在这样一个莫言所营造的乡村世界中，动物的狂欢几乎压倒了人类世界的喧闹声。在这个人日益成为世界的主宰、日益为欲望所驱使、愈来愈成为整个大自然命运的裁决者的今天，莫言将物的声音凸显了出来，颠覆了现代人对物的宰制关系人与物的关系。

如果说，伟大的蒲松龄在山东这块土地上借狐仙创造了一个动物性的世界，那个世界和人的世界有着高度的一致性,反衬了人间的肮脏、阴暗、污浊。不过,人最终还是鬼狐世界的主宰者和评判者,在《聊斋志异》400多个故事中,异史氏在故事的结尾,总是扮演了一个高明的评判者角色。在那里,人是上帝,是立法者,人的优越性还是无所不在的。

莫言的独特性在于,与蒲松龄不同,他对这个动物世界赋予了更为丰富的意义。正如孙郁先生所说:"传统的读书人描述乡村是单线条的,莫言却贡献了一个翻腾摇动的神幻的世界。那里没有道学气,没有静穆的泥土,所有的空间都是精灵的舞动之所。这里有乡下泥土气的哲学和萨满教式的巫歌。……莫言知道这种表述符合自己的本意,乃一种放逐与逍遥,人只有和非人的存在体相处的时候,才知道自己的世界在什么地方。"[10]

在莫言的笔下,动物意象的内涵大体在以下几个层次上展开:

首先是人性的动物性。动物是人的镜像,人在动物身上找到了自己的归属,人的动物化是人的退化,是人性消泯。莫言在《檀香刑》中,将视角放得很低。那个屠夫小甲,是个傻子。他小时候听母亲讲过一个虎须的故事。人透过虎须,可以看出人的原形。于是小甲就着魔一般地寻找虎须。吊诡的是,他只得到了妻子孙眉娘的一根阴毛,透过这根毛发,他看到了人间纯然是一个动物世界。这是他看到的妻子孙眉娘的形象:

一条水桶般粗细的白色大蛇,站在炕前,脑袋探过来,吐着紫色的信子,两片嘴唇一开一合,竟然从那里发出了老婆的声音:"小甲,你想干什么?"[6]

这是小甲看到的父亲赵甲的形象:

俺看到,紫檀木太师椅子上坐着的还是那头黑豹子,而不是俺的爹……它的毛茸茸的大头上,扣着一顶红缨子瓜皮小帽,两只长满了长毛的耳朵在帽子边上直竖着,显得十分地警惕。几十根铁针一样的胡须,在它的宽阔的嘴边往外参煞着。它伸出带刺的大舌头,灵活地舔着腮帮子和鼻子,吧哒,吧哒,然后它张开大口,打了一个鲜红的哈欠。它身上穿着长袍子,袍子外边套着一件香色马褂。两只生着厚厚肉垫子的大爪子,从肥大的袍袖里伸出来,显得那么古怪、好玩,俺既想哭又想笑。那两只爪子,还十分灵活地捻着一串檀香木珠呢。[6]

孙眉娘是一条大白蛇、刽子手赵甲是一条豹子、县官钱丁是一只老虎,袁世凯是一只大鳖,那些清军、德国兵则是一些豺狼。小甲也看到了自己的原形:山羊。这是一次意味深长的还原。他所看到的那个晚清末年的高密东北乡,是一个动物的世界。作为万物的灵长,人的堕落达到了一个惊心动魄的程度。在福克纳的《喧哗与骚动》中,傻子班吉的视角只是一种平视的视角,目的是减弱对生活的意识干预和评判,有助于呈现生活的原生态。与福克纳不同的是,莫言在《檀香刑》中赋予傻子小甲更加形而上的意义,让他扮演人的命运的审视者和裁决者。一个傻子充当了裁判的角色,历史的荒诞感由此产生。小说对现代人的卑琐、污浊的揭露,对人类进化所带来的文明退化,对人的动物性的揭露和批判,其讽刺的力度前所未有。小说里面有一句经典的话:"到处都是畜生,你还怎么活下去?"[5]87面对"猪圈生活",莫言提出了作为人,在这个冷漠、荒诞的世界上,应该如何生存这样的大问题。

其次是动物性的人性。在2005年问世的《生死疲劳》中,动物的意象从另外一个角度展开,通过人与动物的轮回,人性通过动物这个载体来展开。中国一直有生死轮回的观念,在这个轮回的观念里,人的生死和动物紧密相关。人在生前是否行善,作为死后或下地狱、或托生为动物、或托生为人的依据。地主西门闹被镇压之后,在阎罗殿大喊冤枉,阎王让他依次托生为驴、牛、猪、狗,重新返回自己的家中,但是政治运动早已使他的家支离破碎。西门闹转世为动物后,灵魂犹存,有着人的喜怒哀乐。在这里动物性和人性得到了高度的统一,或者说是二者原本就是寄生在一起的。从本源上说,人原本就属于动物世界,而由人所豢养的动物,诸如驴、马、猪、狗、羊之类,在人类长期的驯化史中也沾染了人性,而人由于和这些动物相厮守,也在它们身上确证了自己的动物性。人性和动物性,在波澜壮阔的历史场景上展开,莫言写出了人和动物的相互交融状态。

再次是人和动物的合一。如上所述,如果说人与动物之间的转换有逻辑可循,在《小说九段·狼》中,莫言干脆省略了人与动物之间的区别,二者已经完全合一,作家直接将变形记的结果呈献出来。小说的开篇写道:

那匹狼偷拍了我家那头肥猪的照片。我知道它会拿到桥头的照相馆去冲洗,就提前到了那里,躲在门后等待着。我家的狗也跟着我,蹲在我的身旁,脖子上的毛耸立着,喉咙里发出呜呜的声音。

……

上午十点钟,狼来了。它变成了一个白脸的中年男子,穿着一套洗得发了白的蓝色咔叽布中山服,衣袖上还黏着一些粉笔末子,看上去很像一个中学里的数学老师。我知道他是狼。它无论怎么变化也瞒不了我的眼睛。它俯身在柜台前,从怀里摸出胶卷,刚要递给营业员。我的狗冲上去,对准它的屁股咬了一口。它大叫一声,声音很凄厉。它的尾巴在裤子里边膨胀开来,但随即就平复了。我于是知道它已经道行很深,能够在瞬间稳住心神。[11]

动物幻化成人,出神入化,恍兮惚兮,标准的蒲松龄笔法。动物不再是人的世界的附庸,不再是旁观者,而是直接介入了人的生活。莫言写得臻入化境,神来之笔不时涌现。

而在《屠户的女儿》中,人是兼具动物的外形的。这仿佛回到了中国古代传说。伏羲与女娲不就是人首蛇身吗?女孩香妞生下来没有双脚,生着像鱼一样的尾巴。人和鱼,奇特地结合在一起。可是,人一旦与动物结合在一起,也就注定了悲剧的命运。人类世界对她是排斥的,她受到了孩子们的围攻。天真烂漫的香妞对大自然的好奇心超过了任何人,她和万物之间是一种对话的关系,这是他看到小牛犊时的感觉:

我看到它站在那儿,瞪着水汪汪的大眼睛看着我,仿佛要对我说什么话,但是它没有说话——我知道它不好意思和我说话,它故意不跟我说话,它总有一天会对我说话。[12]

这个叫香妞的小人鱼不再以人类超功利的俯视的目光看待万物,而是放低姿态,将自己放到与万物平等的地位,与万物对话。人,还原成自然的一个分子,还原成最为原始、朴拙的状态。莫言小说中的大多数动物意象还是有着明确的意蕴内涵,是对人的世界的隐喻,但是在《屠户的女儿》中,人鱼形象则包含了更加深刻的文化内涵。这里反思的是在这个技术主义的工业时代,人类的终极命运这类大命题。现代的人是异化的人,人与人、人与自然万物的关系出现了全面的异化。莫言更加向往的是一个人与万物平等交往、和谐共处的世界。在这里,所隐含的追问是:人凌驾于万物之上的姿态是否应该改变?人如何才能与万物达成和谐的关系?文明的进化是否意味着人类的进步?在人类的贪婪和骄横面前,诗意地栖居如何成为可能?

参考文献

[1] 童明. 莫言的谵妄现实主义 [N]. 南方周末, 2012-10-19.
[2] 莫言. 我始终在跟马尔克斯搏斗 [N]. 光明日报, 2011-07-31.
[3] 莫言. 生死疲劳 [Z]. 北京:作家出版社, 2006.
[4] 哈罗德·布鲁姆. 影响的焦虑 [M]. 南京:江苏教育出版社, 2006.
[5] 莫言. 两座灼热的高炉——加西亚·马尔克斯和福克纳 [J]. 世界文学, 1986 (3).
[6] 莫言. 檀香刑 [Z]. 北京:作家出版社, 2001.
[7] 莫言. 清醒的说梦者 [A]. 莫言. 会唱歌的墙 [Z]. 北京:人民日报出版社, 1998.
[8] 莫言. 秋水 [A]. 莫言. 白狗秋千架 [Z]. 上海:上海文艺出版社, 2005.
[9] 莫言. 拇指铐 [A]. 莫言. 与大师约会 [Z]. 上海:上海文艺出版社, 2005.
[10] 孙郁.《丰乳肥臀》印象. 中国图书评论 [J]. 2012 (11).
[11] 莫言. 小说九段 [A]. 莫言. 与大师约会 [Z]. 上海:上海文艺出版社, 2005.
[12] 莫言. 屠户的女儿 [A]. 莫言. 与大师约会 [Z]. 上海:上海文艺出版社, 2005.

《喜福会》的叙事艺术

王 毅

《喜福会》是一部反映第一代中国人移民美国的生活纪实，或者说是一部被西方人称之为关于"他者"的传记文学作品。作者以真实的生活素材为基础，增添了一定的虚构情节，创新性地运用第一人称，虚实结合，撰写了"母女"的传记，主题突出、完整。在《喜福会》中，作者借别人之口，说自己的事，再现了其亲人们的过去，并使过去与现在相结合，母女同心同德，完成了共同的心愿，使一个家庭从分离破碎到团圆重逢，完整了其传记主线，谱写了传记文学作品的新篇章，成为传记文学作品家族中的新成员。按照传记文学作品的特点，如果把《喜福会》翻译成《喜福会记》就更有传记文学作品的意味了。

1 《喜福会》叙事的历史性和真实性

传记文学作品的历史性在于作品或相关作者或事件的真实性和纪实性。《喜福会》的叙事是在尊重、记录历史的基础上进行的，是根据作者的母亲、外婆和一些她自己的经历撰写的。《喜福会》记录了20世纪40年代的中国女性在中国和移民到美国后的生活经历，只是作品中没有启用她们的真名实姓，她们不具有为其立传的因素，但其真实性和纪实性是有一定依据的。

首先，从《喜福会》的题献就可以看出此书写的就是对她母亲的的尊敬、爱戴和记忆。《喜福会》的卷首语这样写道："给我的母亲，且谨以此纪念她的母亲，有一次您问过我，我将留下怎样的记忆，喏，就是这本书，还有这意外的很多很多……"[1]卷首语这无疑说明《喜福会》记录了很多关于作者母亲的真实经历。

2006年9月15日，谭恩美在接受上海《第一财经日报》记者专访时坦率地说，希望了解母亲更多，是她创作《喜福会》的最初动因。对于她来说，母亲是她灵感和创造的源泉："我的母亲总是想感知更多，但同时她又感觉自己承受太多痛苦。我故事中的叙述者和她的情况一样，她的母亲死了，她从没感觉到什么是爱，她总是想更深地感知。"[2]而在现实中，谭恩美的外婆年轻守寡，遭强暴后被迫为妾，最后吞生鸦片而亡。谭恩美的母亲当年9岁，在一旁目睹母亲自杀的经过。这段经历被移植在《喜福会》中许安梅的故事里。对此，谭恩美在她的散文集《我的缪斯》中写道："在写'姨太太的悲哀——许安梅的故事'一章时，我对听来的这些细节做了些修改，小说中是这样的：年轻的寡妇被富翁强奸，不得不做了地位谦卑的四姨太，还给这个富翁生了他的第一个儿子，这是那次奸污的结果。孩子从小就被地位比她高的三姨太抱走，愤怒之余，她越发感觉自己的生命毫无意义。四姨太并非意外死亡，她是出于报复才结束了自己的生命。"[3]23谭恩美从小就听她母亲极其生动地讲述自己的故事，对鬼魂、龙骨、妾等诸多事物有耳闻，一点都不觉得神秘、奇怪。每当听时，她就把一切记录下来，再辅以阅读，以了解当时当地发生的故事，保证细节真实准确。在小说中，作者采用了很多移花接木的写作手法，来记录历史的真实。在小说中"割肉救母"时，谭恩美解释道："读者可能认为，书中某些细节是我编造的，但它们确是事实。母亲要死了，做女儿的会从手上割一小块肉下来烧成汤喂给母亲喝，我外婆就曾这样做。有人说'妾'很过时，我的外祖母被逼成为人家的四姨太，她住在巨鹿路（上海），后来在崇明岛自杀，这是我认为重要的事情。"[2]4这一情节写在《喜福会》的第二个故事，"伤疤——许安梅的故事"里。故事的讲述人是其母亲的化身许安梅。

此外，在现实生活中，谭恩美在上海有三位同父异母的姐姐；她幼年学弹钢琴，和母亲时常发生争

[基金项目] 北京联合大学英语语言文学研究项目《谭恩美和她的作品研究》（11WL016）。
[作者简介] 王毅（1956—），男，北京联合大学新闻与传播系教授，主要研究方向：英美文学。

执;谭恩美的母亲临终前,她为她母亲"放了一张肖邦钢琴曲的CD,并伏在她耳边小声说:这是我弹得曲子,我已经开始刻苦练琴"[1]6。这些经历都再现在《喜福会》中女儿吴精美弹琴风波、母亲去世后再次在喜福会弹奏钢琴、代替妈妈去中国见她的姐姐们等事件中。另外,在拍摄《喜福会》电影中一幕关于映映与她男友在舞会后做爱的镜头时,谭恩美也曾与导演王颖发生争执,也反映了《喜福会》中一些情节的真实性。

还有,谭恩美在她母亲生前给她读到《喜福会》中,"……孩子从小就被地位比她高的三姨太抱走,她越发感到自己的生命毫无意义。四姨太并非意外死亡……"时,她母亲问道:"你怎么知道你外婆事实上是四姨太?你怎么知道真相的?你怎么能写出这些你根本不知道的事情?"[3]130这真实母女的对话也道出谭恩美对实情的了解。

上述林林总总都说明《喜福会》具有相当的真实性、纪实性和历史性。用谭恩美的话概括,《喜福会》记录了:"……从六岁至今陆续发生的事情,全部都是我的想象,至于现在我是个作家,这也只是我的想象罢了。为了让我自己确信这些并不是真的,为了证明我确实仍然活在现实世界,我像所有作家所做的一样,赋予小说真实感。我开始动笔记下种种往事,往事与回忆交错,如此充斥着复杂与平庸的一生,怎么可能是一种虚构呢?"[3]23据此,我们可以完全相信《喜福会》具有真实性、纪实性和历史性,是一部关于作者亲人的传记文学作品,而不是一部虚构的小说。

2 《喜福会》叙事的完整性

《喜福会》不是仅仅记录一个人的传记文学作品,而是记录了母女三代人,这也是其有别于其他一般传记作品的地方。《喜福会》由两部分组成:第一部分记录了作者母亲和她外婆在旧中国的心酸、血泪史。这里的母亲们代表了她们那个时代部分中国女性,她们是小说中的吴素云,映映·圣克莱尔、许安梅和她的母亲,她们都是作者母亲和外婆的化身。这些母亲们用她们的亲身经历讲述了一些20世纪40年代中国女性纪实生活,展示了中国传统文化在她们身上的影响和作用,让世人较全面地了解当时中国女性和她们的地位与处境,认识当时中国女性的历史;第二部分讲述了这些中国母亲和她们移民到美国后出生的美国女儿们相处的真实生活写照,记录了中美文化差异、冲突与融合。这两部分有机的结合,勾画了第一代和第二代中国移民在美国生活画卷的一角。

《喜福会》中的母亲们把关于她们自己的故事讲给女儿们听,教她们做人、做事、懂中国文化、用中国人的智慧、做中国人,使母亲的文化、思想和精神在女儿身上得以延续,是母亲的中国传统思想和文化行为帮助她们的女儿长大、成熟,接受和继承中国人的思维方式和传统文化。《喜福会》的结尾就是母亲吴素云的女儿吴精美代替和作为"母亲"去中国,见她在那里女儿们,而她、吴精美则同时已成为"一个中国人",一个妹妹去见她同母异父的姐姐们。在中国,当吴精美和她的姐姐们相见的瞬间,她想到的是:"现在我又见到妈妈了,两个妈妈……"见到她们,吴精美感到有"一种无法描绘的亲切和骨肉之情。我终于看到属于我的那一部分中国血液了。啊,这就是我的家,那融化在我血液中的基因,中国的基因,经过这么多年,终于开始沸腾昂起"[1]216。此时此刻,母女完全融为一人,女儿成为母亲的化身,"母女"彼此拥抱着,实现了母亲的愿望和梦想,"母女"重逢,团圆。至此,母女的传记得以完成,《喜福会》叙事之完整性和其魅力可以说是不言而喻的。在这里,我们看到的不仅是母亲的精神、文化和思想在女儿身上得以传承,在一定程度上,更是中国人、中国女人的精神、文化和思想在美籍华人身上得以传承,其传记人生又可以连绵不断、持续永远地在异国他乡续写下去,其完整性已远远高于一般传记文学作品应有的完整性。

3 《喜福会》叙事的独特性

3.1 《喜福会》与一般传记文学作品的差异

传记文学作品通常都是讲述伟人、名人、历史人物、有一定历史影响和地位的人或有相当成就的成功人士的故事。但是《喜福会》不然,虽然读者看到的是在讲述四位中国母亲和她们与她们四位美国女儿的故事,但实际讲述的是有关作者一家母女三代人的故事。作者创造性地把其家人:外婆、母亲和作者本人(女儿)化身为《喜福会》中的人物,把她们的故事移植在其中的两个家庭吴素云家和许安梅家中进行演绎，同时还虚构了另外两个家庭《喜福会》中的龚琳达家和映映·圣克莱尔家，借用这两位母亲的经历，补充和完整了20世纪40年代中国女性相似的生活经历，以使读者较全面了解当时中国部分女性的生活状态和处境。此外，《喜福会》还清晰地记录了这些中国母亲和她们的美国女儿们的纪实生活。母亲们的过去和她们与女儿的现在的结合，有机地构成"中国移民母女"的"他者"传记文学作品。

《喜福会》首次使普通百姓登上传记文坛，成为传记文学描写的对象，并使其传记内容多样化，注重对传记人物多视角、多侧面、多层次的描写，立体地展现了传记人物的生存状态与精神世界，此举在传记文学作品创作中，可谓开创了先河。《喜福会》是在尝试着一种全新创作理念，是在用一种平常的语言讲述母女的故事，写她们的情感，写她们的苦恼，写她们的过去和现在，写她们的文化，写她们的新生活。从这个意义上来说，《喜福会》呈现给读者的是普普通通而有个性的中国女人。

中国人在西方人眼里是神秘的，中国女人和母亲就更加神秘。《喜福会》揭开了这层神秘的面纱，让世界看到了一些真实的中国女人、中国母亲和中国传统文化对她们的影响和作用。旧社会、封建社会和解放前的中国女人是极为让人感兴趣的群体，这是《喜福会》的定位，作者写出了真实的、活灵活现的、朴实而又智慧的中国女人。与此同时，作者还写出了她们移居美国后和她们美国女儿的生活，作者通过记录母女的人生，让世人看到中美文化的差异和融合，使她们的传记人生得以发展和延续。《喜福会》以人物的过去寻觅自身的价值所在，着重表现其真实性、客观性和中国性，突出传主的个性和其延伸性，使其具有传记的文学性和完整性，成为"他者"的传记，与众不同，深得欧美读者的喜爱。

3.2 《喜福会》叙事中不同的"我"

传记文学作品多用第三人称写作，传者采用传主的名字或根据其性别用其代词"他"或"她"来讲述其人生，也有用第一人称"我"来叙述或自述传主人生的。《喜福会》则不然，这部传记文学作品打破了传统叙事模式，虽也采用了第一人称叙事，但是"我"讲的不是一个人的故事，而是三个人的故事，讲的是关于"母女"们的故事。故事中的"我"既是叙述者，也是被叙述者，在整部作品中，是变化的，"我"一会儿是"叙述者，讲自己的故事，一会儿是被叙述者，成为故事中的主人公或主人公的叙述者，如吴精美在讲她妈妈初建"喜福会"的故事时，她是叙述者，她妈妈则是故事中的主人公"我"，一个被叙述的人："喜福会这一名字，起缘于我母亲的第一次婚姻，那还是在日军占领桂林前。所以一提到喜福会，就会使我想到她的桂林故事。每当她把碗碟擦干净，塑料台面也已擦拭了两个来回，而父亲已开始将脸躲在报纸后面，一支接一支地抽他的黑猫牌香烟——这往往是一种"不要打搅"的警告，这便是她觉得无所事事之时，于是，她便会对我讲起她的往事。这个时候她总会拉出一箱旧毛衣，那是我们在温哥华的一个从未见过面的亲戚送给我们的。"[1]256

但当吴精美讲她妈妈去世后"喜福会"的故事时，她则是叙述者的"我"："我母亲总是用中国话开始她的叙述："我在还未去桂林前，就梦见它好几回了。群山环绕中，一条小河蜿蜒而过，河上漂着青色的浮萍。天幕上衬着锯齿般的山峦，层层叠叠的，白云缭绕其间。如果你在河面上漂浮，仅以浮萍果腹，也能毫无难色地爬上山峰。如果你不慎滑跌下来，也只是坠入一张柔软的浮萍织成的大床上。一旦你爬至顶峰，你会因眼前祖露的一切而欣喜若狂，它会涤净你的一切烦恼不快，扫尽一切腌臜之气"[1]15。

但纵观整部作品，"我"的角色不是母亲，就是女儿；而"我"的女儿身份随着故事的展开可以是女儿吴精美、许露丝、丽娜·圣克莱尔或龚琳达；做为母亲的"我"，在故事中也在不停地变换着角色，"我"一会儿是吴素云，一会儿是许安梅、映映·圣克莱尔或龚琳达；但故事的主线从头到尾都是围绕着"我"在讲述母亲吴素云和女儿吴精美的故事；而其他母亲和女儿关于的"我"的故事则是具有史实性的虚构故事，是谭恩美的文学创作，是在补充、丰富和完善吴素云和吴精美母女相似和相同的经历，以增加其全景效果和可信度，更真实地展示"母女"的人生经历，如龚琳达的童养媳的故事、映映·圣克莱尔婚后受丈夫虐待、杀死自己孩子的故事、薇弗莱·龚下棋的故事和许露丝离婚的故事等。

传记文学作品采用第一人称叙事，多是由于叙述人是当事人，所叙述的人与事，只能是"我"所能接触的活动范围内的人物和事，但其活动范围以外的人物和事情就不能成为作品中的叙事内容。这也是第一人称写作最大的局限性和不足。但事物都是一分为二的，就是其不足和局限性使得其叙事更显得自然天成，更具有强烈的逼真感,同时还有利于深入开掘"我"的内在世界,完整展示"我"的心路历程。谭恩美选择第一人称"我"的运用也从另一面说明和证实了其故事的真实性和其"亲力亲为"的纪实性。

传记文学常常是一种逆时写作。谭恩美采用第一人称"我"讲述她外婆和母亲的过去和她与母亲相处的现在独具匠心。因为谭恩美深知她在写什么,她所写的多与她的家人有关,但毕竟又不尽详细,因此,她特别选用第一人称来写,这样,她就可以驾轻就熟,只写她知道的,或是说知道的就提,不知道的就避开,这样写起来,就方便了许多,实为明智之举。如此这样,谭恩美才得以在作品中自由地穿梭于历史与现实、过去与当今之间,将深受不同文化影响下的中国母亲和她们的美国女儿两辈人的思想意识活动和行为展示在世人面前,对比东西方文化,唤起世人对民族传统文化进行自醒、反思和传承。

《喜福会》中不同的叙述者"我"和被叙述者的"我"的故事使史实、现实和虚构的情节有机统一,使现实世界与文本世界高度融合,真实地反映了在美国的中国第一代和第二代移民生活。这实乃第一人称"我"所特有的属性所为。在谭恩美的《命运的另一面》一书中,她对其创作有这样的观点:"记忆孕育想象""我的想象和现实几乎无异""我对现实和想象生活记忆的把玩犹如女孩们对于芭比娃娃、男孩们对于他们的阳物那样痴迷。"[4]因此,我们可以说,谭恩美在其作品中充分运用记忆、想象和现实材料,对中国传统文化中的诸多元素进行利用并以服务作品的中心——纪实和再现历史为其创作目的。

3.3 《喜福会》叙事的"他者"情结

在西方后殖民理论中,中国移民已成为当今美国社会的"他者"之一,《喜福会》也因之极具"他者性"。因此,美国人、西方人可以通过阅读《喜福会》或看《喜福会》电影可以了解和认识关于一些中国人移民美国的历史、文化、阶级背景,以及他们在美国的生存和发展状况,和其中国传统文化与美国文化的冲突与融和的过程。客观上,小说《喜福会》本身已具有一定的功效,但更主要的是谭恩美在《喜福会》叙事中的"他者"情结使然。谭恩美的"他者"情结表现为:在母女的叙事中,她们相对彼此,都是互为"他者"被叙述着,因为在家或在"喜福会",母亲是主人,"本地人或当地人"(native),女儿是美国人,是"他者"(the other),女儿的一切言行举止都不符合中国人的要求和标准,她们都太美国化了;而对女儿来说,在美国,她们是美国人,是"本地人或当地人"(native),她们的母亲则是"他者",她们来自中国,有着与她们不同的文化理念,做事方法和不同的信仰,她们相差太远,彼此做事太不习惯,甚至产生反感和厌恶。

在《喜福会》中,我们随处可以看到女儿对她们的"他者"母亲的叙述和描写,她们以美国人自居,看待和评价她们的"他者"妈妈。母亲们主要被叙述为:按照中国古老的"五行"理解世事、做人做事;打麻将,谈天说地;聚会时,"她们用她们自己特殊的语言谈天:一半是洋不洋腔不腔的英文,一半是她们自己的中国方言"[1]20。她们都喜爱"都穿着有趣的硬邦邦的立领中国式衣衫,前胸绣着花卉,这样的衣服对真正的中国人来说,是太时髦了,而在美国的聚会上穿,又显得太古怪"。"我想象中的喜福会,是一个有着特殊仪式的社团,好比三K党的集会及电视片中印第安人出征前的典礼,反正有着一套神秘古怪的仪式。"[1]15"这些人的吃相,可真是不大雅观!好像人人都处在饥饿状态,一个个狼吞虎咽。"[1]18

这些都使女儿们苦不堪言。此外,她们认为美国是个让人自由、独立的国度,怎么做人做事是自己的事,其表现的方式又有个人的好恶,别人不能横加干预。可是在《喜福会》的家里,情况就大不相同了:母亲非常中国,总是强加于她们许多她们不喜欢的东西,母亲时刻进入了她们的生活,支配或左右着她们的生活,这让她们难以理解。然而,在母亲们的眼里,她们的美国"他者"女儿们又是怎样的呢?"她们,只会大口大口往肚里灌可口可乐!"[1]4母亲认为女儿总是:"与我隔着一条河,我永远只能站在对岸看着她,不得不接受她的那套生活方式——美国的生活方式。"[1]224"……教不会她有关中国的气质;如何服从父母,听妈妈的话,凡事不露声色……她才不听这一套,在苦口婆心给她讲这些时,她只顾嚼口香糖,吧嗒吧嗒的,然后吹起一个比她脸还大的泡泡。"[1]227母亲们为此感叹着:"除了她的头发和皮肤是中国式的外,她的内部,全是美国制造的。"[1]227

谭恩美通过以上种种叙述和描写,把《喜福会》中母女彼此看待为"他者"的言行和思考展示于世,清晰地表明了中国移民两代人不同的思想意识和价值取向,并揭示了其缘由所在。正是由于谭恩美采用这种母女互为"他者"的叙事方式,她才能游离在中国与美国,在东方与西方、过去与现实之间来回穿梭、跳跃,精心构筑美国文化和中国传统文化两种完全不同的世界,把中美文化的差异、冲突和融合表现得淋漓尽致，让世人看到"他者"的过去、现在与未来。

谭恩美有这种叙事的"他者"情结，是因为她是美国人，她是美国作家，她写的是美国小说。"我是一个美国作家，我了解的中国文化是"二手信息"。我写作是从美国人的角度，着笔以中国文化为基础的家庭。我不可能有中国人的视角，我并非在中国成长。"[5] "如果我不得不给自己某种身份，我会说我是一位美国作家……我相信我创作的是美国小说，因为我生长在这个国家，我的情感、想象和兴趣都是美国人才有的。我的特征可能是华裔美国人，但我认为华裔美国人也是美国人。"[2]

《喜福会》的叙事手法具有"他者性"，也是谭恩美独到的叙事艺术。在欧美人的眼里，中国第一代移民、第二代移民、第三代移民等对美国社会而言，都是"他者"，他们的生活写照、生存状况自然都是欧美人所关注和感兴趣的。谭恩美的《喜福会》刚好满足了他们的好奇和猎奇。因为《喜福会》不仅展示了中国移民、中国女人、中国母亲过去的历史经历和她们具有美国公民身份的女儿们的生活和处境，还让世界看到了中美文化的差异、冲突和融合，以及今后世界的发展趋势——多元文化的融合与和谐共处。因此，《喜福会》之"他者性"叙述可谓妙不可言。

《喜福会》是一部与众不同的传记文学作品，其情节构建虚实相间、写实演绎交织成辉，相得益彰，传主刻画得更加具体、鲜活、生动，其中一个个故事深深地印刻在每一个读者的脑海中——其实，就是中国传统文化那点事让人回味无穷。此外，从文学和社会角度上看，《喜福会》第一人称的运用、"他者"的叙事方式和传主的非单一性也给传记文学作品的创作留下了浓重的一笔。《喜福会》不仅有对于"他者"生活的探求和反思，还掀开了世界多元文化融合画卷的一角，为构建和谐大同的世界开辟了一条新路，展示了光明的前景。

参考文献

[1] 谭恩美. 喜福会 [M]. 程乃珊, 译. 上海：上海译文出版社, 2010.
[2] 罗敏, 段武宁. 谭恩美访谈录 [N]. 第一财经日报, 2006-10-01.
[3] 谭恩美. 我的缪斯 [M]. 上海：上海远东出版社, 2007.
[4] 余军. 记忆、想象、现实——谭恩美小说的创作策略 [J]. 译林, 2006 (6).
[5] 张璐诗. 华裔作家谭恩美专访：我是一个美国作家 [N]. 新京报, 2006-04-14.

海明威小说《雨中的猫》主题思想探究

牛洁珍

《雨中的猫》（Cat in the Rain）是海明威于1923年创作的一篇以女性为主体的短篇小说佳作，后收录于他的短篇小说集《在我们的时代里》（In Our Time）。故事讲述的是一对美国年轻夫妇到意大利旅游，因外面下雨而呆在旅馆里。太太感到百无聊赖，站到窗口向外望时，发现有只猫蜷缩在一张桌子底下躲雨，于是心生恻隐，想把它抱上楼来。当她下去寻猫之时，猫却消失不见，于是只得回到房间开始向丈夫一番絮叨。正在这时，旅馆老板差遣女侍把一只大玳瑁猫送到她面前，故事至此戛然而止。

故事情节简单，语言简练、睿达。小说通篇以猫为主线，通过描写女主人公见猫、寻猫、得猫过程中内心的情绪起伏与变化，揭示了美国20世纪20年代初新女性充满矛盾、彷徨、苦闷与挣扎的现实状况这一主题思想。尽管叙述者对故事中人物之间的深层关系没有做任何交待和评论，然而作者通过场景描写及人物关系塑造，让读者能够从多个角度深切体会并理解一个被孤独惆怅、失落空虚的心绪所笼罩的美国新女性，描述了她渴望回归传统性别角色，但又迷惘彷徨、患得患失、充满矛盾与挣扎的内心世界。

1 小说创作的时代背景

小说表现的背景是第一次世界大战之后的20世纪20年代。一方面，美国和欧洲的青年思想中弥漫着一股迷惘的情绪，人们都处于一种冷漠之中；而另一方面，新女性的出现让女性角色有了翻天覆地的变化。她们追求自由和平等，无拘无束地参加各种活动，颇具男性特征。她们剪掉了传统女性的飘飘长发，代之以活泼简洁的短发，以青春健康的形象吸引了美国人的视线。新女性还一反女性温柔、顺从、谦卑的传统，追求时尚，讲求享乐。这些快乐、摩登的年轻女性很快成了20世纪20年代最亮丽的一道风景线。随意和开放的社会风气使老一辈女权主义者感到震惊和失望。新女性不仅在外表和行为上有明显变化，她们还追求经济独立和自由的生活方式，其精神上的独立意识也不断提高，她们积极融入到时代潮流中，从一个没有自己思想、习惯于依赖丈夫和家庭的人转变为有自己想法和追求的人，向男女平等迈出了重要的一步。

然而随着经济大萧条的到来，一切犹如幻梦一场。一方面，新女性发现自己依然走着前辈妇女相同的道路，因为当时的美国社会对妇女的性别定义仍然是作妻子和母亲，大众文化的新手段也在不断强化那些传统价值观，新女性迫于社会和舆论压力，回归传统价值观，把婚姻和家庭作为她们生活的中心；而另一方面，新女性们对自由的渴望并没有停止，她们仍然向往外边精彩的世界，仍然期待拥有自由和平等的生活[1]。

2 小说场景描写与主题体现

众所周知，海明威对小说场景的选择是非常挑剔甚至达到了吝啬的程度。在海明威的世界里，某一个故事只能发生在它的那一种场合而且没有任何可替换性[2]。因为舞台和场景本身就可以节省大量的语言而直截了当地代替描述[3]。

Bradbury指出："海明威的写作并不是我们所熟悉的心理描写，他不直接描写内心感受，而是写外在表现，所以故事发生的地点就非常重要，而且还得选对场景。角色是生活在一定的外部条件下的，所以外部世界也就是心理的反映。"[4]《雨中的猫》一文也不例外，其场景的选择并非偶然。一对美国夫妇投宿一家意大利旅馆，这家旅馆朝着海，也朝着公共花园和战争纪念碑。空荡荡的广场象征着人们精神生活的空虚。在诗人眼里，大海往往是大自然永恒魅力的象征，它充满了神秘和力量。作者这样描写：

[作者简介] 牛洁珍，北京联合大学。

"海水在雨中冲上沙滩，留下一条长长的线，然后退回去又冲上来，再冲出一条长长的线。"在这里作者暗示女主人公在阻力中不屈不挠反复抗争，奋力追求着自己的自由和幸福。公共花园留给人们的是祥和幸福的生活印象，而战争纪念碑连同来瞻仰它的人们不由地让人联想到刚过去不久的战争场面，这种矛盾与对立的场景恰恰映衬出当时虽是战后的和平时期，但战争带来的负面影响依然存在。同时这幅场景画面也象征着女主人公心中向往的情感生活和精神生活与现实的差距，就像是"花园"和"战争纪念碑"一样，是对立和冲突的。可见，海明威在开篇第一段的场景描写看似写景，实为传情，为故事的发展奠定了基调，埋下了伏笔。

另外，这篇故事是在下雨的背景中进行的。"战争纪念碑在雨中闪闪发光"等处多次提到雨，雨始终伴随着故事的发生和发展。海明威喜欢写雨，也擅长写雨。在短短的叙事中，除标题外，雨被重复多达10次。此外，与雨相关的或类似于雨的意象如水、海等词语则贯穿全文。不断重复的意象看似是对自然现象的素描，实则渲染了情境气氛，烘托了人物心境。如故事开始的描写："公园里有大棕榈树，天气好的时候，常常可以看到一个带着画架的艺术家。艺术家们都喜欢面对着公园和海的旅馆的那种鲜艳的色彩。"其景致静谧而和谐，宛如一幅优美的风景画，让游客陶乐其中，给读者一种祥和安宁的印象。接着作家写道："天正在下雨。雨水打着棕榈树滴下来，海水夹着雨，空荡荡的广场。"明快、亮丽的景致经作者笔锋一顿转为阴郁而灰色的雨景。不断冲刷的海水和空无一人的广场，徒添几分凄凉和孤独。雨的不断重复与战争纪念碑相呼应，压抑气氛跃然纸上。后面"雨下得更大了"，看似写景，实则叙情。它体现了美国妻子激烈斗争的内心情感。最后一句场景描写："这会儿，天很黑了，雨仍在打着棕榈树。"表明她雨中寻猫未果之后内心不断增长的焦虑与不安。

可见，海明威之所以能做到对心理描写抑而不露但又让读者能真切感受到人物情绪，其法宝就是寓情于景，借景抒情的高超技巧。

3 小说的角色关系塑造与主题展示

海明威在该小说中刻画了四个人物。其中一个主角即妻子，三个配角，即丈夫、旅店老板及女侍。除此四个人物之外，文中的猫也是一个重要的角色，虽然它不是人，但却是某种人物角色的象征，每个角色在小说中象征着不同的群体，小说的主题意义正是通过女主人公与猫、女主人公与丈夫、女主人公与旅店老板，女主人公与女侍这四层关系得以展示的。

3.1 女主人公与猫

"雨中的猫"固然是文章出现的一个真实角色，但它更是故事发展的一条重要线索和对女主人公命运的映射。同病相怜的情绪促使她展开了拯救行动，要把那只"雨中的猫"从凄风苦雨的困境中解救出来，拯救这只猫也就是拯救自我，能使她获得自我安慰。当丈夫说："让我去吧"，她说："不，我去"，她不顾外面下着雨，拒绝丈夫的帮助，执意要亲自去抱回雨中的猫，甚至忘了打伞，女主人公"救猫"这个举动表明了她企图扮演强者角色，这是典型的"新女性"的行为。

然而，女主人公在店老板面前产生了渺小感。在伞送来之前，女主人公曾被大雨挡住了去路，屋外披着雨披冒雨行走的陌生男人衬托出了她的无助感和对保护的渴望。因此，伞在给她提供安全保护的同时，让她意识到了男性的强大以及自己的弱小。她觉得自己渺小或许还因为她未能寻回那只雨中的猫所产生的挫败感。从女主人公对店老板的喜欢程度看出，她内心非但不排斥这种渺小感，还生出"自己无比重要"的幸福感，显示出了她对传统柔弱女性形象的认同。于是回到房间之后，这位新女性不再满足扮演与男人平等的强者角色，而是渴望回归传统女性的形象，想"把头发留起来，梳到脑后，扎得又紧又光滑，在后脑勺扎个大结儿"，"希望现在是春天"，"希望自己能有一只小猫"。但这种愿望遭到了丈夫的否定，他的态度表现了其对新女性回归传统角色的否定。虽然后来旅馆老板派人送回一只大玳瑁猫，但这个行为从某种程度上粉碎了女主人公扮演新女性"拯救者"角色的企图。海明威正是通过描写女主人公在寻猫过程中经历的心绪起伏和情感变化，揭示出当时新女性的艰难而尴尬的处境。

3.2 女主人公与丈夫

海明威把小说中的丈夫乔治塑造成了一个20世纪初新兴的妇女解放运动的支持者形象。他年轻而有知识、有修养，能够较快地接受新鲜事物。他欣赏独立、自信的新女性；喜欢妻子那头突破了传统形象的短发，给妻子以充分的信任。当妻子"想下去救那只猫时"，乔治说："我去捉"，这说明他是对妻子疼爱的；当妻子仍然坚持下楼去捉猫，他说："别淋湿了"，说明他对妻子是关心体贴的；他让妻子在雨天独自去捉小猫显示了他对妻子行动能力的尊重与信任，相信她完全有能力独自解决捉猫的任务；当妻子没有捉住猫空手而归时，乔治马上放下了手中的书，问她："猫捉到了吗？"这表示了他给予妻子的及时关注；当妻子坐在床上就开始唠叨她是多想要那只猫时，乔治"又在看书了"则说明他认为妻子的想法不切实际。后来妻子又坐在梳妆镜前说道："你不认为我把头发留起来是个好主意吗？"乔治说："我喜欢你现在的样子。"后来乔治还"在床上移动了一下位置。他的眼神一直注视着她，并且说'你看起来很漂亮'。"这体现了他对新女性的欣赏与肯定。妻子继续唠叨："我想把头发拉到后面打一个舒服的结。我想要一只猫，想让它坐在我的大腿上。"而丈夫反应了一句"是吗？"这个简短的回答表示了丈夫对妻子回归传统心愿的明确否定。妻子继续喋喋不休："我想用自己的银器用餐，而且要用蜡烛。我还想现在就是春天，我可以在镜子前梳我的头发，我也想要猫和新衣服。"说到这时，丈夫忍无可忍了，说了一句："住口，找点东西来看吧。"可以看出他不希望妻子退回依附型的性别角色，而是希望妻子成长为独立、有思想的个体，所以建议她去"读点书"充实和提升自我，避免空虚、无聊与不切实际的遐想。然后，妻子继续说："不管怎么样，我要一只猫。如果我不能留长发或有其他的乐趣，那么我总可以有只猫吧。"她哀求丈夫给自己一些关爱。可是丈夫仍然"在读自己的书"。这说明丈夫虽然是新女性的支持者，但他忽略了女性的性别特征和情感需求，以至于本身也忽略了自身性别差异的妻子倍感受到冷落，希望回归传统女性角色以获得一种平衡。丈夫的反对令她陷入苦闷与彷徨。

3.3 女主人公与旅馆老板

意大利旅馆老板是一个传统男性性别建制的传承者和维护者。店老板的年纪和一丝不苟的工作作风显示出他对男权传统的笃信和执著。他还通过他掌控的另一个女性——女侍，实现了对女主人公的控制。然而，女主人公对店老板的倾心又为我们揭示了女人的真实心理诉求：在她"寻猫"时，店老板派出了侍女帮她打伞；当她回到旅店时，这个老板让她觉得自己极其了不起，这种了不起来源于自己被店老板尊重和关怀，这让妻子感受到自我存在的价值，让她有了一种被人重视的感觉，而这种感觉是她与丈夫相处时感受不到的。于是她向往贵族阶层女性享受型的生活方式，想找个百般呵护她的男人做依靠，她宁愿做个小女人享受男人的恭维和宠爱。

3.4 女主人公与旅馆女侍

小说中的意大利女侍象征着传统女性群体。她不理解受到美国妇女解放运动影响的美国女性的所作所为，也不能感受到新女性在争取解放时所受到的排斥、压抑和苦闷。所以，女侍对女主人公的"寻猫"行为先是感到好笑，后是完全不解。她忠实地履行着男性上级指派给她的任务，不折不扣地服从男性店老板的指挥。

4 结 语

《雨中的猫》寥寥千字，然意蕴深厚，全方位解读着实不易。本文仅从时代背景、场景设计和人物关系塑造三个方面入手进行了研究，较清晰地展示了场景设计及角色关系塑造等与美国新女性的孤独惆怅、苦闷失落和彷徨困惑这一主题的深层次关联性，从分析角度和切入点进行了一定的创新。同时，也期望能对以后的海明威小说研究者有所启示。

参考文献

[1] 周莉萍. 20世纪20年代美国新女性初探 [J]. 2003 (6).
[2] 苗木兰. 海明威其人、作品及其写作风格 [M]. 南京：南京师范大学出版社，2002.
[3] 贝茨. 海明威的短篇小说 [M]. 上海：上海译文出版社，1981.
[4] MalcolmBradbur, David Palmer. The American Novel and the Nineteen Twenties [M]. London：1971：24，25.
　　注：文中未标记的《雨中的猫》引文均来自陈良廷所译《海明威短篇小说全集》，上海：上海译文出版社，2004：189-193.

日本社会的右倾化与相对化意识

纪廷许

一、日本社会右倾化的社会思想成因及其危险性和局限性

追根溯源,日本社会的右倾化有着远近两大成因。其远因首先体现在四面环海而又与中国大陆一水之隔的地理位置下,相对封闭却又易于吸收外来文化的岛国环境,以及表现为日本人根深蒂固的精神气质的所谓岛国根性,即轻理论而重实践;薄历史而厚现实;寡言而敏行为主体特征的思维行为模式。这种以内向封闭为基质的日本民族性格,既渊源于约一万年前狩猎采集型的原始部落形态(所谓"大和魂"的原点),又真正形成于公元前3世纪至公元3世纪自中国大陆经朝鲜半岛东渐日本九州及全列岛的(弥生时期)稻作文化。一言以蔽之,自古以来的村落社会形态,以及被称为"国、藩"的实质上的长期地方自治割据状态,是形成其内向封闭民族性格的主要因素。在这种长期军事封建社会文化及其制度体制下,形成了异常沉稳的保守排他的社会政治氛围和纵式的人际关系结构。基于二战战败的历史教训,以及昙花一现式的反战反核反安保的大众运动,日本在保守政党执政下发展成为世界第二位的经济大国后,以政治及军事大国为目标的右倾化趋势可谓水到渠成,对内表现为近乎天然地抵触激烈的社会变革,特别是厌共及蔑视高度集权主义的政治制度和国家;对外崇拜遵从国际经济政治军事上的绝对霸权国家,并将根本国策定位于与世界最强国结盟。其近因则是在国家及民族史上唯一一次被军事占领,即二战被美军占领并被施以外科手术式的"民主化改革",但却在美国的远东反共战略下既保留了天皇制又仿效构建了欧美的政体,特别是未在政治上及思想意识上清算军国主义、皇国史观,更欠缺源于普世价值的民族道德和国家道义的反省,甚至于日本民族本应具有的对自甲午战争开始的反人类的侵略者加害者的悔罪意识,大大弱于因遭受美军空袭特别是原子弹轰炸而产生的受害者意识。再加上近代以来,在所谓日本近代思想之父福泽渝吉的摈弃中朝等东方恶友,加入西方列强的"食人者行列",即"脱亚入欧"的思想及战略的引导熏陶,导致厌恶中朝的"下流思想情绪"自130余年前延续至今。同时,日本自古而然的功利主义、现实主义的思想行为模式,由于二战后依赖美国、脱亚入美带来的巨大现实利益和经济奇迹而更加根深蒂固,对美一边倒的背后是美国的绝对强权和"意识形态的正确"。上述综合因素奠定了日本社会易于向右倾化转变的思想和制度上的基础。

从20世纪90年代以来日本社会右倾化的演变轨迹而论,新民族主义的泛起是其主流。这股政治思潮虽然与战后日本的右翼思想与行为一样欠缺基于人类理性思维的理论体系,但却不乏战略设想及策略手段。其核心内容是将在日本拥有巨大精神感召力的"国民性作家"司马辽太郎所说的"国家应有的形态"加以发挥,提出日本近代以来继明治维新、战后改革之后的"第三形态",或称"第三次开国"、"第三次维新"。其主要目标是始自20世纪80年代中曾根执政时期的大国战略,并于20世纪90年代以后,特别是21世纪初形成日本的综合国策,即以体制改革为手段,用立法和解释改宪为突破口,最终达到明文修改现行《日本国宪法》,特别是第九条,最终摆脱战后国际秩序格局对日本的约束,达到从属于美国,而与英法等相当的政治军事大国目标。阶段性策略方面,以改宪并获得集体自卫权为基本前提,在此基础上重新修订教育基本法,新建财政、国家安全保障基本法等,从而摆脱战后日本持续了半个多世纪的"不依靠军事力量的和平"国策,构筑以政治、经济、军事大国为依托的美国式霸权体系,或至少获得从属于美国的东亚区域霸权地位。2012年以来,以石原与桥下为代表的攻击性的右翼民族主义政治势力,借持续20余年的经济低迷下民粹主义社会思潮的泛起,特别是所谓来自北朝鲜的"军事威胁"及中日钓鱼岛及海洋资源之争,公然提出修改和平宪法甚至制造和拥有核武器的极端纲领。这一直接越过战后愈来愈脆弱的和平民主主义底线的右翼民族主义的跳梁,可以说在2012年12月16日的众

[作者简介] 纪廷许,北京联合大学旅游学院教授、博士。

院选举和 2013 年 7 月的参院选举中得到了不少日本选民的投票支持，而最终使这个第三极政治势力坐大甚至成为了影响日本政局的一只重要力量，这也使始自小泉政府时期的闹剧型政治出现了向极端国家主义倒退的危险苗头。换言之，缺乏对侵略战争的思想意识清算和国家道义反省的现实日本，其可能的政治走向之一是，从"二战"时期的松散的德意日法西斯同盟改变为紧密的美日军事同盟，且直接威胁东亚地区的区域平衡与和平安全。虽然这种可能尚面临日本民众根深蒂固的和平民主主义心理的屏障，距成为现实尚有诸多不确定因素。但其趋势值得关注与深入客观地把握。

根据丸山真男对战前日本的总体把握，"有国家无民族"的状态导致极端国家主义思潮的统治地位。从这个定义上说，战后日本右翼民族主义总是执着地以国家主义的形态出现也就不足为怪了。旧思想的惯性作用及对恢复战前一个主义、一种思想的社会政治状况的冲动，既有 20 世纪 70 年代初三岛由纪夫剖腹自杀的行为展示，也有 20 世纪 80 年代"新国家主义"名称的思想标明。如果在丸山的上述定义下予以延长，可以说战后至今 68 年以来日本的社会思想状况，本来已经有了深刻的变化，即岛国型的不成熟的民主主义与和平主义已然化为了比较沉稳的社会心理。许多日本学者从不同角度揭示的现在的日本人"有个人无国家"、"有自我无民族"的特殊性精神结构。只不过右翼将其称为"民主主义过了头"、"民主主义的自我摧毁"，[1]左翼将其归纳为"市民"及"市民社会"的成熟。

无论其视角如何，右翼民族主义在战后日本的不同阶段，总是挑起事端且力图将水搅浑的缘由，正是在于日本大众的"自我"意识及"个人生活中心主义"价值取向强烈，缺乏国家意识及民族认同感的总体性精神结构。右翼文人政客骂得愈狠，煽情炒作得愈烈，愈说明日本社会在泡沫经济崩溃前的主要思想潮流与国家主义，右翼民族主义的距离与隔膜之大。然而，值得引起充分警惕的是 90 年代中期以后日本右翼宣扬的历史观及编写教科书等新的活动方式，迷惑了不少青年人甚至教育机构的中青年教员。加上保守政治势力的大力呼应，使右翼民族主义形成了一股浪潮。如同《美国展望》主编罗伯特·莱克所说："民族主义不是危险，真正的危险在于允许消极民族主义者为了自己的某种目的而披上爱国主义的外衣。"[3]日本右翼民族主义的嚣张一时，主要是借助于 20 世纪 90 年代以后持续 20 余年的日本经济低迷下形成的闭塞感，以及日本人意识的内向化（更关注国内经济形势对个人生活的影响）趋向。但是，如同"新历史教科书编纂会"的历史教科书被采用率不足 1%（公立学校中只有东京、爱媛地区的聋哑等残疾人学校，以及私立等五县六校）。现代日本人已不是六十余年前麦克阿瑟所说的"12 岁的少年"，日本知识界主流所指出的加速日本社会从国民向"市民"的过渡进程，同时更加关注公共性、世界性，而非私人性，民族性的观念，在日本社会逐步深入人心。丸山真男指出过战前日本的极端国家主义源自"有国家无民族"的特殊性。从这个定义上说，战后的日本右翼民族主义总是以国家主义面目出现，乃至执着地以战后"有个人无国家"的日本人的精神结构为靶子，原因皆在于此。

新民族主义的政治目标，与日本政界主流的一些战略设想既有相通之处，亦有不同。前者专以粉饰日本的过去和妖魔他国为业，后者触及的却是严肃的现实课题。以政策研究机构"世界和平研究所"为舞台继续发挥"余热"的原日本首相中曾根康弘，在 2001 年 4 月 7 日的《朝日新闻》上撰文谈"日本如何摆脱国家危机"，指出"当前日本进入了政治、经济和社会三种泡沫都已破灭的时代。这是战后英国极端的功利主义、法国的个人主义、以及美国的利己主义在日本泛滥，进而冲击日本固有的道德和社会规范的结果。现在的改革在于医治这种'文明病'。最近的调查表明，赞成修改宪法的国民已经达到约 60%，反对者只占 30%。今后十年内可以完成对宪法的修改。同时，还需制定作为今后国家支柱的三项基本法。第一项是修改教育基本法；第二项是制定财政结构改革基本法，第三项是制定国家安全保障基本法，以使日本在政府和国会监督下行使集体自卫权。"同时，中曾根还强调"日本历史上一直缺乏国家战略，应建立政府战略机构。"值得密切关注的，倒是这类被日本知识界视为理性民族主义派的观点，正被愈来愈多的日本民众所接受。同时，又极易被右翼民族主义所利用，特别是在日本内政外交的叠加困境刺激之下，近年内对和平宪法放弃战争的第九条的明文修改，可能在安倍的右翼内阁执政期内形成水到渠成的结果。

在此文中，年逾 83 岁的中曾根一方面将战后日本社会的思想状况归纳为功利主义、个人主义和利己主义的泛滥，另一方面也抨击了日本政治决策层缺乏国家战略，治标不治本，迟迟不将修改宪法提上政治日程，堪称保守政治主流派对日本社会的政治及思想状态的焦虑心理的真实写照。这也从一个侧面说明了战后日本社会思潮形成、发展及演变的背景，以及对日本政治走向的巨大影响力。同时，又使新民族主义的局限性暴露无遗。也就是说，日本社会的思想意识主流仍是"个人主义、功利主义、利己主义"，日本大众患上的这种现代"文明病"与极端民族主义、国家主义有着天然的抵触。毕竟战后日本民主化改革带来的不仅仅是和平宪法和议会民主制及地方自治等制度法律约束，更深刻的实质性变化是日本人的价值观体系、社会意识乃至国家观念都发生了革命性的变化。在可预见的时期内，无论石原、桥下的"日本维新会"等右翼民族主义势力如何跳梁，具有坚定反战反核意识的多数日本民众最终将不会投票将危及他们现实富足生活的右翼扶上执政地位，即便默认修改宪法第九条，也不会送自己或亲人上战场。日本社会的和平民主主义即便已不成潮，但作为历久弥新的沉稳社会心理，仍足以对以改宪和拥有核武器为目的的攻击型民族主义喊"不"或用公投踩刹车。

如此，右翼民族主义既囿于自身的排他性、狭溢性、煽情性的窠臼不能自拔，否则将无立身之地。同时，又突破不了日本社会自我中心主义的基本价值结构及绝对和平主义的心理屏障。21世纪初经济低迷下的社会闭塞状况虽然为右翼民族主义的滋生提供了一定的条件，但其主客观的局限性又使其无法扭转大局。对于只能在经济持续低迷导致的大众不安心理下逞一时之勇的右翼民族主义来说，上述两难之境几乎是不可克服的。其最终的结局，恐怕不外乎或持续对社会民主主义进行思想外围战式的吞噬，或被相对化到经济及政治大国主义的潜在意识范围之内。总之，在极端主义与激进主义仍被日本社会及大众思想视为大忌的现实下，右翼民族主义要么自生自灭，亦或随波逐流，在"爱国主义"的躯壳上再披上一件"社会变革、平成维新"的外衣。总之，在战后68年日本社会之沧桑巨变前，在和平富足和现实生活第一的社会氛围中，日本快速倒退回战前的军国主义既缺乏必需的社会土壤，亦不具备国际环境。因此，可以说现实条件下桥下彻连北一辉也做不成，石原慎太郎也扮演不了石原莞尔的历史角色。

二、积极的民族主义与相对化意识的合理性及局限性

20世纪90年代中期以来，日本市民阶层要求撤除美军基地，反对日美新防卫合作指针的运动，实际上是战后使日本从对美国的追随下"独立"出来，以推进民主主义革新力量政治目标的继续。从实质上说，也是1960年反安保运动为顶峰的战后民主主义的延续。

一般而言，战后日本社会思潮演变过程的背后，存在着战后日本书化形成上三个主要因素的影响。即（一）高速经济增长及其大众社会化；（二）日本社会各个领域的美国化；（三）大众传播媒介的作用与影响。特别明显的一个现象是：战后日本的市民运动及其思想观点，亦围绕美国的文化与政治展开。美国式的价值观、政治文化模式及市民运动方式，例如多元文化主义、环境及生态保护、女权主义运动，以及网络化、非政府民间组织（NGO）、非营利团体（NPO）等等，都很快地被移植到当代日本社会之中，并潜移默化地影响着日本大众意识的潮变。美国针对日本的政治支配、军事同盟、经济压力及文化渗透，在战后长期对日本社会的精神渗透和同化的同时，也孕育出了抗美、反美的思想和社会运动。其中，右翼民族主义利用反对美国的政治军事及文化霸权的意识刺激，试图重建日本人的民族认同和确立军事大国化的国家战略。而积极的民族主义警惕和竭力试图防止的是美国霸权政治下日本陷入战争的危险，以及对自身和平生活的现实威胁。最具典型意义的是集中了美国在日基地总数75%的冲绳地区。自1945年起长期处于美国的直接施政权下，既使1972年回归日本后仍是美国在亚洲的最大军事基地的冲绳地区，形成了日本各地区中对美国文化，乃至美国化最具抵抗力的区域文化和地方的独特民族性格。20世纪90年代以后日本社会规模在万人以上的大众政治运动的绝大部分都发生在冲绳。其他较大规模的签名、示威、集会等也多是针对日美新防卫合作指针，或是抗议驻日美军的暴行，并要求撤除驻日美军基地等。这种积极的民族主义的内在动因，在于不使日本民族成为美国对其他国家及民族发动战争的帮凶；同时维护自身的基本人权不受美国霸权的践踏，并进一步从根本上解决冲绳及遍布日本各地区的美军基地对日本发展空间的占据和破坏。反战、基本人权、和平发展的正义性自不待言，对冷战结束后一强多极的世界格局中日本的政治走向，亦具有大众意识的强大制约作用。

针对日本政治长期在美国卵翼下偏安于岛国环境，而缺乏明确思想理念支撑的现实，以及20世纪90年代后，战后长期积聚的矛盾表面化，而使日本社会不得不进入大的变革阶段，亦有人大声疾呼"没有思想"的日本国民及政治家们要"先行选择思想"。"现实的日本面临三种思想的选择，保守主义、自

由主义、还是社会民主主义。在当今冷战结束,资本主义对社会主义的明确的意识形态对立关系已经消失的现实下,对每个日本国民来说,都面临着在上述三种思想中选择其一的课题。在新的历史已拉开序幕,经济业已成熟化的今天,没有思想支撑的政治早已过时,现时期的政治、经济蓝图脱离思想是无法描绘的。长期以来一直有意识地规避思想理念的日本政治与政治家们,在进行政策及对策抉择前,必须先行选择思想。"[4]

上述论述的语境虽然表述的十分明确,但改变现实又谈何容易。让原本没有,或疏于理性与战略性思维的民族和政治"精英"们选择一种思想并一以贯之,恐怕首先要先行改变这个民族的思想惰性及其妥协型、应变型的政治因习。因此,相对化思维不但有其现实性和合理性,还拓留出一个民族的思想意识结构逐步转变所必需的时间过渡的余地。在这个过渡期中,似乎保守主义、自由主义、社会民主主义中的任何一个都不可能占据日本大众思想及政治决策的绝对优势地位,而只能根据不同历史阶段的时代课题,在相对化中偏重于其中的某一个。具体到20世纪末21世纪初的日本社会,可以说政治改革上的保守主义、经济体系变革中的自由主义处于相对强势的地位。而面对这个改革的阵痛及对自身利益的波及,日本大众思想中社会民主主义的意识及情绪比较强烈。这几种因素和倾向反映在主流思潮的流向及日本政策的形成上,自然地表现为协调变通与调整改革的过程。

与针对美国化及美国霸权政治的日本特有的民族主义相比较,相对化意识是从思维方式和行为模式上对美国强权政治仍坚持不放的绝对化倾向的反应。在日本大众意识疏离政治,摒弃左右两个极端,走中间妥协道路的总体倾向下,相对化意识体现的是不以强权为中心,中和及协调不同观点的现实合理主义。虽然相对化意识本身的模糊性和妥协性,使其容易被误解为缺少民族主义、保守主义、自由主义、社会民主主义等思潮的明确性和指向性。但正如坂本义和从1960年反对安保运动以后就主张的日本和平共存与中立主义的道路,以及近年来大力倡导相对化思维那样,相对化的时代与"市民"及"市民主义"的成熟,将超越以国界、民族、文化制度及体制形成的障碍。近年来围绕揭露和惩处政治腐败,日本社会的政治透明度及市民知情权意识迅速提高,社会改革与转型时期大众靠近并运用民主主义的思想倾向日益明显。1989年11月起步的亚太经合(APEC)及近年来中日韩三国与东盟(ASEAN)关系的加深(10+3),进一步使和平与发展、民主与共生成为当今东亚各国时代的主旋律。即便在领土纠纷愈演愈烈的2012年临近岁末之时,中日韩互贸区谈判仍获重启,无疑是一个积极的信号。溯及2001年,由伊朗哈塔米总统倡导并被联合国规定为"世界不同文明间对话的一年。"它所反映的,正是在全球化趋势下思想融合与协调共生这一相对化思潮的核心理念。

相对化意识的主流虽然具有合理性和积极意义,并且在当今世界意识形态的对立日渐消失,文明间的对话与融合已打破坚冰的大趋势下显示出合乎潮流的思想活力,但亦内含丧失传统社会思想体系中明确的指向性和方向感的另一种倾向。这虽然是"主义"消失后伴随文化与思想多元化而出现的必然结果,但却给刚刚亲历过剧烈思想与政治动荡的20世纪的东西方大多数国家的人们以沉重的不适应感和思想的又一次"虚脱感"。仿佛对失去重心的不安一样,习惯于非左即右,无对立面即意味着失去"原则"而无立身之本的传统社会思维模式而言,相对化意识可能无异于历史相对主义的主观随意性。在人与人之间只有利益之争,而无道德纽带,国与国之间只有利害关系,绝无道义可言的价值判断面前,相对化意识顿显苍白和疲软,就像把"小而闪光的日本"视为鲁迅笔下阿Q的现代版,或将中立与共生斥为"和平痴呆"一般。尤其是在美国重返亚太的战略下,日本极端功利主义的政治传统势将在石原、桥下等攻击性民族主义的裹挟下,挟持民意去删改和平宪法第九条甚至开拥核之禁。战后持续67年之久的日本和平民主主义可能很快面临危急的关头。实际上右倾化绝非始自今日,而是在内政外交、政治经济的综合困境的叠加效应下加速向攻击型的右翼民族主义转化。[5]

在日本社会闭塞和思想混沌的今天,右翼民族主义借日本大众意识的保守化和内向化倾向,希图以本国历史的无罪主义,与日本发展的大国主义重构民族认同及时代意识,并以美国的强权政治为蓝本,竭力将日本向绝对化的方向导引。在树欲静而风不止的复杂现实中,相对化意识难免"中看不中用"之嫌,但与"退一步进两步"的道理一样,思想与现实性既有表现为日本战败至20世纪60年代和平民主主义思潮的激流澎湃,亦有冷战结束后全球化时代背景下日本社会相对化意识以柔克刚的水滴石穿。现实问题是,日本民众的和平民主主义思想底蕴虽然是友好相处、和平共生的普世价值,但欠缺对侵略战争的道德道义的深刻反省的日本政界自不必说,日本民众的防御型民族主义能否长期抵御右翼攻击型民族主义亦不乐观。以中国人的大局观审视日本社会的政治文化特点,东京都民与大阪市民只认能力魅力,不讲政治大德地长期选举石原、桥下之流的现象,如果在经济低迷和领土纠纷下漫及日本全国,当代日本社会主流意识的正能量氛围恐将急速减退。

从日本社会的思想资源的生产性而言,相对化意识与和平主义与民主主义的"永久革命"式的不断再生产,凸现出过渡性和手段性的特征。它的思想强势表现在基于和平主义理念的兼容性和调和性之中,但思想资源的生产性不应是一个固定概念,它似乎应该含括给 21 世纪的思想空间提供了更富选择性和可能性的相对化意识。因为在 21 世纪初本没有路的荆棘丛生的日本思想荒原中,积极的民族主义思潮与相对化意识,毕竟是在曲折中开辟着一条将日本的生产性思想资源与东亚乃至世界的和平多元的国际关系原则相融通,相合流的道路。最重要的是,这个思想潮流是取向于和谐共生这一现代国家基本道义原则的。这才是日本的政界及文化知识界精英们应该不懈追求和坚定维护的真正的"政治的正确"。

本文试提出当代日本社会思想动态研究的前沿课题,即 2012 年以来日本社会的加速右倾化,特别是 2012 年 12 月中旬的众院选举、2013 年 7 月的参院选举的结果及其后日本政治的走向,应视作对日本知识界长期标榜的"市民社会"的真伪,以及"和平民主主义"社会理念是否仍是民意主流的试金石。其对战后日本社会思想史,特别是当代日本政治思潮与社会思想的流变之间的关系,似值得深入探究。因为这一课题兼具重要的现实意义及理论意义。偏颇之处,企盼指教。

注 释

[1] 佐伯启思. 现代民主主义的病理 [M]. NHK 出版协会,1997.
[2] 坂本义和. 相对化的时代 [M]. 岩波书店,1997.
[3] [美] 罗伯特·莱克. 民族主义应突出积极方面 [N]. 洛杉矶时报,2000-11-24.
[4] 佐和隆光. 平成衰退的政治经济学 [M]. 中央公论社,1994:208、209.
[5] 关于右倾化的定义,参见《岩波小辞典·政治》及自由国民社编《现代用语的基础知识》1983 年版内田健三撰写的辞条。右翼的基本定义及内容为:日本右翼团体及其运动,具有与天皇制结合起来形成并发展的特殊性,以欠缺政治理论的精神至上主义与英雄性行为主义为其特色。它从针对日本的近代化及自由主义的反动起步,主要表现为强烈反对民主主义、社会主义、共产主义。战后这类右翼运动曾一度偃旗息鼓,随着反对战后民主主义的政治保守化及其舆论的抬头,20 世纪 80 年代以后又呈现复活的势头。战后右翼标榜反共、重整军备及修改宪法。右翼中分为亲美派、反美派、亚洲派等。

关于日本 20 世纪 80 年代以后社会思想意识上的右倾化,主要指的是 70 年代末 80 年代初开始形成的以政治潮流为核心的右倾现象的社会基础。它表现为由日本内外形势变化所触发的范围广泛、影响深刻的一系列思想现象。这种思想状况不仅存在于改宪运动、外交政策、防卫问题、靖国神社问题、教科书审定及内容、领土纠纷等政治层面,还涉及到日本的经济运行、财政改革以及福利政策等经济层面的多个领域。在意识形态方面,流行一时的 20 世纪 80 年代的"苏联威胁论"和 20 世纪 90 年代以后的"中国威胁论"以及对战后民主主义的批判抨击和鼓吹自主防卫论等,十分突出。进入 21 世纪后,围绕日本与韩国之间的独岛、中日之间的钓鱼岛等领土争端,以及持续 20 余年的经济低迷特别是东日本地震造成的核泄漏事故,紧张的社会氛围使日本政治思潮的右倾化向极端化发展。其典型表现是 2012 年攻击型的右翼民族主义形成了坐三望二的政治势力,原东京都知事石原慎太郎与大阪市长桥下彻合并组建的"日本维新会"公然提出修改宪法放弃战争的第九条,甚至主张日本拥有核武器。日本右倾化的主要社会背景是经济低迷和政局混乱,以及目标方向的丧失。

思想言论界中,战后右倾化思潮的主要代表人物有清水几太郎、江藤淳、舛添要一、高坂正尧、佐藤诚三郎、伊藤宪一、西部迈、长谷川庆太郎等人。政界中,长期执政的保守政党自民党的中曾根康弘、民主党的小泽一郎虽被视为"理性的民族主义",但亦是右倾化的思想理论支撑"新保守主义"的代表人物,在国家发展战略及基本政策等方面具有体系性和代表性。自民党的小泉纯一郎及现任首相安倍晋三是近年来日本政界右翼主流派的代表。极端右翼、攻击性民族主义的典型人物是已解散的"日本维新会"的石原慎太郎和桥下彻。

金末遗民词联章双线章法结构研究

李 艺

1234年，金朝在经历了120年的历史之后终于衰亡了。汴京失守以后，元好问等人被羁管于聊城（今山东聊城），两年后元好问移居冠氏县（今山东冠县）。一直到蒙古太宗十年（1238年）元好问才离开冠氏县回到自己的家乡。太宗十二年（1240年），元好问回到了自己的家乡忻州。另外像李俊民、二段等文人也都避居山林之间。

元好问虽然不仕蒙元，但他能舍弃传统的忠君忠国的观念，审时度势，以救民于涂炭之目的，在金亡后的几十年间他或者周旋于地方上的汉人世侯间，劝导其施行仁政；或者力促蒙古统治者实行汉法。值得一提的是，元好问力劝自己的门生等仕于蒙元，只有这样才能影响蒙元统治者加快汉化的进程。事实也正是如此，例如元好问的学生郝经在入仕于元后深得忽必烈的信任，后来在忽必烈继承皇位时曾发挥了相当的作用。而忽必烈正是元好问等人认为最适合于做中原最高统治者的人选，元好问曾私下同张德辉一齐觐见当时还"在潜邸，思大有为于天下"[1]的贤王忽必烈，并奉之为"儒教大宗师"。这对于促进蒙元由对汉人的大肆血腥杀戮转为以儒治国，加快蒙元政权的汉化都起到了一定的作用。

从这种政治态度出发，元好问等人在创作中所表露出的思想、情趣便有其不同于前人的特征。他们的创作与金亡之前的金词有着不同的创作倾向，我们称之为金遗民词人群体。金末"遗民词人群体"活动的时间大致限定在金末元初，主要有元好问、段克己、段成己、李俊民，此外还有李天翼、李节等人。

金元易代，蒙古国的统治集团入主中原，取代了原来的统治者金，这对于金末元初的金遗民词人们来说，无论是外在的生存状况，还是内心的深层意识，都是无比残痛和哀伤的。对故国的怀想，使得他们在作品中抒发着自己的感慨，表露着自己的心曲。在作品中一往情深抒写的同时，他们的思想意识也无意识地得到了某种升华。因其所写的每一个物、每一件事都无意识地或多或少地折射出华夏的影子。这也许是金遗民词人群体在创作上的一个独特现象。

我们来看一下元好问37首《鹧鸪天》中的《宫体八首》。（在《遗山乐府》中有集《鹧鸪天》词37首为一组的。另还有散见词籍中各处的《鹧鸪天》十余首。）这里以"宫体八首"名之，至少表明这八首词是作于同一时期内的，或者是同一种心理状态的展示。从词中所写可以看出是写于金亡之后的。

如《鹧鸪天·宫体八首》第一首：
候馆灯昏雨送凉。小楼人静月侵床。多情却被无情恼，今夜还如昨夜长。
金屋暖，玉炉香。春风都属富家郎。西园何限相思树，辛苦梅花候海棠。

从第一句的"候馆灯昏雨送凉"可知是写于聊城羁管结束后在华北一带漂泊之时。"多情却被无情恼"句表面看是艳句，但实际上可能是元好问复杂、矛盾心理的显露。他觐见忽必烈等的行为，曾遭人误解，面对"多情却被无情恼"，词人坦然处之，丝毫没有后悔的想法。

《鹧鸪天·宫体八首》第二首：
憔悴鸳鸯不自由。镜中鸾舞只堪愁。庭前花是同心树，山下泉分两玉流。
金络马，木兰舟。谁家红袖水西楼。春风殢杀官桥柳，吹尽香绵不放休。

那故国的一草一木、一人一物，就像那春风吹散的无休无止的柳絮一样，一朵接着一朵回旋于词人心头，抹之不掉，挥之不去。词以宫体的外在形态，实际是抒写山河易主的哀伤。

《鹧鸪天·宫体八首》第三首至第六首，词人从各个不同的角度表达抒写了对中华数千年历史与传

[作者简介] 李艺，北京联合大学师范学院语言文化系。

[1] 〔明〕宋濂：《元史》卷四，《世祖一》。北京：中华书局，1987年点校本，第57页。

统的一往深情。第七首："花烂锦，柳烘烟。韶华满意与欢缘。不应寂寞求凰意，长对秋风泣断弦。"作者认为江山虽易代，而山河仍在，词人主张应向前看。还有第八首：

好梦初惊百感新。谁家歌管隔墙闻。残灯收罢空明月，腊雪消融更暮云。

鸾有伴，雁离群。西窗寂寞酒微醺。春寒留得梅花在，剩为何郎瘦几分。

关于这"宫体八首"的创作过程：从第一首"候馆灯荤雨送凉，小楼人静月侵床"以及第八首上片"好梦初惊百感新，谁家歌管隔墙闻。残灯收罢空明月，腊雪消融更暮云。"可以看出这一组词是词人在某地客居时所作。一天晚上，月光初上，那绵绵不尽的秋雨带来阵阵寒意。在这孤馆寒秋，飘忽难安的凄苦境况中，词人铺开纸笔，一口气将前七首挥洒而出，词人心中的无限忧愤暂时解脱开了。这时大约已是晚上九十点钟，不知是谁家的歌管之声从墙外边传进来，他竟然感觉是那样动听。尽管现在我像离群之雁，常常寂寞地呆在西窗前以酒解愁（作者的一些作为不被当时一些人所赞同。），但是，只要"梅花"还在，即使"衣带渐宽"，又有何妨呢？这里既是明志之语，又是对整个一组词的总结之语。明乎此，对元好问当时那种复杂矛盾、深隐婉曲的由眷恋故国进而升华为眷恋华夏文明的心路历程就能够理解了。

恋旧情结是一般人所共有的，尤其当国破家亡之时，这种情结往往会成为当时文人学者的创作主题，不仅元好问是这样，李俊民、二段等也都是这样。但是如果能够把这种恋旧情结有所升华，和眷恋整个华夏文明连结起来的话，这样的恋旧就不是一般意义上的恋旧了。元好问做到了这一点，李俊民、二段等人也做到了这一点。这不能不说是一个让人深思的现象。

《蕙风词话》卷三中在谈到元遗山这一阶段所写之词作时深刻地指出："元遗山以丝竹中年，遭遇国变，崔立采望勒授要职，非其意指。卒以抗节不仕，憔悴南冠二十余稔。神州陆沉之痛，铜驼荆棘之作，往往寄托于词。《鹧鸪天》三十七阕，泰半晚年手笔。其《赋隆德故宫》《宫体八首》《薄命妾辞》诸作，蕃艳其外，醇至其内，极往复低徊，掩抑零乱之致。而其苦衷之万不得已，大都流露于不自知。此等词宋名家如辛稼轩固尝有之，而犹不能若是其多也。遗山之词，亦浑雅，亦博大，有骨干，有气象。以比坡公，得其厚矣，而雄不逮焉者。豪而后能雄，遗山所处，不能豪，尤不忍豪。牟瑞明《金缕曲》云："'扑面胡尘浑未扫，强吹讴、还肯轩昂否？'知此可与论遗山矣。"其词"各句有指，知者可意会而得。其词缠绵而婉曲，若有难言之隐，而又不得已于言，可以悲其志而原其心矣。"

同时我们还应看到，社会的巨变所影响的并不仅仅是元好问一个人，而是影响了整个一代的文人创作。比如与元好问同被羁管聊城的李天翼。李天翼（生卒年不详）字辅之，固安（今河北省固安县）人。贞祐二年（1214年）进士。历荥阳、长社、开封三县令，迁右警巡使。李天翼在汴京失陷后与元好问一样，同被羁管于聊城。两个人真可谓患难之交。俩人自聊城分别，元好问去了冠氏，李天翼去了济南，从此人各一方，但二人的友谊却丝毫未减。元好问客济源，曾写一首《临江仙》寄赠李辅之，词曰：

荷叶荷花何处好，大明湖上新秋。红妆翠盖木兰舟。江山如画里，人物更风流。

千里故人千里月，三年孤负欢游。一尊白酒寄离愁。殷勤桥下水，几日到东州。

词前小序曰："李辅之在齐州，予客济源，辅之有和。"可知此小序及李辅之所和之词均是后来编辑词集时所后加的。我们来看一下李辅之所和之词，《临江仙·和元遗山》：

南去北来人自老，落花飞絮悠悠。思君一度一登楼。无穷烟水里，何处认并州。

忽见姓名双泪落，新诗聊浣离愁。若为重醉绣江秋。芙蓉明月下，来往一扁舟。

词的上片抒写对友人的思念之情，天荒地老，劫后余生。下片写接到友人寄赠的词后的激动心情。最后两句写的是自己的情怀，表明自己并不想随波逐流。那种同为天涯沦落人的遗民心态跃然纸上。

在金国灭亡后的相当一段时间内，那些沉痛的悲恋"旧时情愫"的心态在当时遗民词人群体中的许多词人身上都有表露。再如李俊民的词作，也强烈地体现出了这一点。不过在总体心态的大体相似的情况下，由于各人身世经历的不同，其创作又都有各人不同的风貌。

李俊民，字用章，号鹤鸣老人，家泽州（今山西省晋城），唐韩王元嘉之后。生于大定十六年（1176年）。承安五年（1200年）举经义进士第一，应奉翰林文字。中统元年卒，时年85岁。从李俊民《李氏家谱》得知："俊民男扬，伊阙商酒监。扬一子道儿。甲戌兵火，值甲午，二十年间，皆物故矣。"

在李俊民60岁以后，时局逐渐稳定下来，蒙元的泽州长官段直把李俊民由河南迎回到泽州家乡，李俊民一直活到85岁。李俊民在家乡兴办教育，为泽州培养了大量人才。这段时期他的生活虽然终于安定了，但是对家国亲人的怀念之情，却深深地隐藏于他的内心深处。其十二首连章体《谒金门》词可以说是给了词人一个释放这一深埋于心中情感的合适场所。整个十二首连章体《谒金门》从起始、过渡、发展到高潮有始有终，意脉贯通。由于词人在"梅"与"人"（甚至还有故国）之间结合转换得不露一丝痕迹，竟使得况蕙风也发出疑问："抑何缠绵郑重乃尔？"从章法结构上看，这十二首连章体词内，一条明线"梅"与一条暗线"人"，两个线索相得益彰，使整个作品更有韵味，更有深意，愈回味愈觉有余意。

从元好问《鹧鸪天·宫体八首》到李俊民十二章《谒金门》，我们似乎看到了词体文学在金末词坛所形成的一种新的趋尚，即在词中讲究那种具有深美闳约、醇厚沈着的风尚。（也就是后来清代的"常州词派"所提出的"寄托"说。）正如陈廷焯所言："黍离麦秀之悲，暗说则深，明说则浅。"❶ 沈约斋（祥龙）所言："词贵意藏于内，而迷离其言以出之，令读者郁伊怆怏，于言外有所感触。"❷

元好问、李俊民等人的一些词是达到了上述要求的，并且他们的词有一个比较突出的特点，就是用联章体的形式来写作，而这又形成了当时词体文学创作上章法的一种形式，这里称之为"联章双线"章法结构形态。所谓联章，就是同一词调的多次重复使用，使同一词调的多首词作在整体上有着章法结构上的统一安排；所谓双线，就是字面上有一条线索（明线）而字面后还隐含着的另一条线索（暗线）。

这里的"联章双线"章法与南宋赵令畤的《商调蝶恋花》等作品还有所不同，赵的词作虽也是联章体，但似乎所表现出的"双线"意识还不太明显，而元好问等人的这些联章体词已明显在使用"双线"手法以达到其抒写情意的目的。那么这种联章双线章法结构形态具体有哪些新的特征呢？下面作一简单阐释。

第一，由于联章体的数量可根据需要任意增大或缩小，在容量上就突破了单篇的限制，可以尽情地多方面反复抒情写意而没有任何篇幅上的局限。这就把散文的这方面优势转化到了词的手上。这里有着宋词的影响，（比如赵令畤《商调蝶恋花》）同时也会受到当时在金代盛行的诸宫调的影响。这种联章体词在词体文学发展史上可以说是小令的一种变通形式，由此小令便又可与长调慢曲相抗衡，并且抒情、叙事效果可以说比单篇长调更佳。如元好问的《鹧鸪天·宫体八首》、李俊民的十二章《谒金门》等，读之感觉既雅致、又华美，令人浮想连翩。

第二，在这种联章形式之内，更容易敷设明、暗两条线索来进行创作。明线是字面上的一条线索，暗线则是字面以外隐含着的另一条线索，在写作时，一般通过对明线的字面上的描写叙述而达到暗线所寄托的含义的释放。这是一种虚实相生的章法技巧。当然在单篇之内，通过字面上含义的抒写而显露其所深含的寄托之情的也有，像辛弃疾的《摸鱼儿》等，但是在仅仅一章之内，因篇幅有限，两方面的抒写均受一定限制。而联章体则大大扩展了容量，可以完全根据内容需要设定创作层序。在连章体内，回旋的余地大为增加，其明暗两条线索均可获得充分体现，甚至于还可以根据内容的需要，在某一章内突出某一线索，而仅在总体气氛，含蕴上对另一线索有所顾及照应即可。这样作者所受到的体裁上的限制就进一步减少，其灵活多变的特点给了作者以更大的创作自由。

这种章法结构形态可以说在元好问《鹧鸪天·宫体八首》，李俊民十二章《谒金门》等词作中已经得到了成熟的体现，其风格可用深美闳约、醇厚沈着来概括。与南宋同时期词体文学创作相比较，吴文英与元好问从生卒年来看是同时代人，而吴文英的"以绵丽为尚，运意深远，用笔幽邃……"（清戈载《宋七家词选》）的风格与金遗民词人的"联章双线"章法结构形态的风格，虽地处一南一北，却声息相通，异曲同工。

正是通过这样巧妙的艺术形式的杰出运用，遗民词人群的作者们使得其词作在强烈的恋旧情结的凸显之后，进一步使其恋旧情结又得到了升华！在其深婉的情感波澜的背后，我们似乎能感觉得出一种升华了的情感抒发！

元好问同时代人王中立曾有一首诗《题裕之乐府后》曰：

---

❶ 陈廷焯. 白雨斋词话 [M] //自詹安泰. 论寄托, 词学季刊, 三卷三期.
❷ 沈约斋（祥龙）. 论词随笔 [M] //载唐圭璋. 词话丛编. 北京：中华书局，1986：4043.

常恨小山无后身，元郎乐府更清新。
红裙婢子那能晓，送于凌烟阁上人。

虽然其所指为元好问中年所作之词，但用来阐释金亡之后的遗民词人群的词作似更显得恰如其分。

遗民词的这种创作风尚在二段的词作中也有体现。段克己（1196—1254年），段成己（1199—1279年），成己乃克己之弟，绛州稷山（今山西稷山）人。从总的创作倾向来看，成己的二段词与元好问、李俊民词一样，都体现出了以承续华夏传统为自己精神寄托的一种历史使命感。

段氏兄弟的词，读之能给人一种自树其骨的感觉。一般来说，越是在民族生死存亡的危难关头，一些守节之士便越是对民族的、传统的东西倍加珍视，往往将其精华部分加以整理、进行传扬。元李二段等人正是这样。比如段克己的连章体《渔家傲·送春六曲》一组词。这种连章体的形式，在宋人作品中虽也偶有所见，但并不太多。而在金末遗民词人中，由于独特的时代风会的影响，词人的审美趋向有了变化，不约而同地用连章体这种回旋余地较大，易于表达深沉、浩渺情怀的形式进行创作。他们往往是将时代的巨变所产生的深刻体验、非凡经历等浓缩在一组词中，用连章体的形式反复进行咏叹。

我们看段克己的《渔家傲·送春六曲》第一首：

龙尾沟边飞柳絮。虎头山下花无数。花底醉眠留杖屦。花上露。随风散漫飘香雾。

老去逢春能几度。不妨且作风光主。明日不知风共雨。回首处。夕阳又下西山去。

作者正面描写烂漫春光、柳絮、山花，是那么迷人，词人醉眠其间，不愿离去，一直到"夕阳又下西山去"，仍徜徉其间。这第一首是起兴，是写迎春的欢快心情。起始得有力。因《渔家傲》词调本身就比较带有旷达、辽阔的味道。不过词人的重心是在"送春"，就是说其所寓之感是在"送"上面。显然这第一首词作并没有这条隐含的第二条线索。

《渔家傲·送春六曲》第二首这样写道：

不是花开常酹酒。只愁花尽春将暮。把酒酬春无好句。春且住。尊前听我歌金缕。

醉眼看花如隔雾。明朝酒醒那堪觑。早是闲愁无着处。云不去。黄昏更下廉纤雨。

从第二首开始，明（春）、暗（故国）两条线索逐渐露出端倪。作者之所以常醉眠花丛之中，不是为了别的，而是怕花落春尽，无处寻春。那么一种失落、怅惘的情感，不正和故国沦亡相同吗？就此便可知作者为什么是那么地恋春、留春了。"春且住"，是作者发自内心的深情呼唤，"尊前听我歌金缕"，是要一泄自己久藏于内心深处的对故国的婉惜之情，是对故国所唱的高亢的挽歌！这里的感情不能说不浓烈。但是，和元好问的《鹧鸪天》与李俊民的《谒金门》相比，格调又有所不同。这里的自我意识更强烈，"春"（故国）虽然会有尽时，但来年必然还会再来，作者对此深信不疑，因此，才能吟出高亢的金缕曲。吴澄在《二妙集序》中说："中州遗老值元兴金亡之会，或身没而名存，或身隐而名显，其诗文传于今者，窃闻一二矣。有如河东二段先生者，则未之见也。心广而识超，气盛而才雄，其蕴诸中者参众德之妙，其发诸外者综群言之美，夫岂徒从事于枝叶以为诗文者之所能及哉？"洵为的论。况蕙风言："金词清劲能树骨。""二段"词确如况氏所言，自树其骨，气盛而才雄。由于他们弟兄二人入元后皆不仕，又被时人目为儒林标榜，成为一代名士。从其词作中可以看出自金中期以来所形成的刚方亢爽词风丝毫未曾减弱。

金末遭亡国之痛比南宋早，以词来反映这一巨变及词人的生活和感怀确是词人们的不幸，但他们在词作中所表露出的强烈的承续华夏传统情怀却在金词史中具有不平常的意义，在词史上是应有其相当的地位的。金比南宋早四十多年而亡，在文学史上用词体文学的形态，以金词特有的刚方亢爽之气，抒写神州陆沉之痛，这形成了一种新的风格，比之南宋末的遗民词人，时间早了几十年。尤其是金末遗民词人群体使用的"联章双线"章法结构形态，用明、暗两条线索来进行创作，使其作品更具有独特的风格和魅力，800年来传唱不衰。

新媒体语境下对科技期刊编辑的新要求

李亚青 柴 智

一、新媒体语境下科技期刊面临的困境

新媒体语境下,作为主要承担科技成果传播的科技期刊不再垄断科技成果发布的话语权。以往只有经过专家审核、编辑修改、主编批准的科技成果,且以科技论文的形式,才能通过科技期刊发表,进而传播。而在新媒体语境下,这种相对权威的话语权被分解了,现实中的每个人都可随时发布自己的新成果,传播自己的新思想。网络民主以不可阻挡的力量冲击权威和独断,各种声音得以顺畅地表达,新媒体改变了传统科技成果的传播状态,由一点对多点变成了多点对多点。[1]

新媒体的即时性、快捷性、海量性的特征,对传统的科技期刊以月甚至以季为周期的出版模式造成巨大的冲击。以网络、手机为代表的新媒体使即时传播成为可能,打破一切时间、空间、所有权的限制,实现任何人、任何时间、任何地点的自由传播。相比新媒体海量信息的特征,科技期刊传播的信息少之又少。科技期刊有限的发行量,也使其传播效果只能在有限的范围之内。

互动传播是新媒体的另一个重要特点。互动传播使作者与读者站在同等的位置上。传统科技期刊在传播时是单向与封闭的,一般是自上而下地传递,选题也常常从编辑自己的兴趣出发,很难顾及读者的感受,仅有的反馈就是读者来信,因而显出很大的封闭性,以至于有论者称其为"孤芳自赏""自说自话"。

在新媒体语境下,传统的科技期刊仍有自己的生存空间,并且结合新媒体的某些特征,运用其有益的技术,科技期刊正在焕发新的生机与活力。

二、新媒体语境下科技期刊发展的趋向[2]

1. 借助新媒体,强调内容为王。内容的准确性与权威性一直是科技期刊的优势。新媒体信息发布的自主性,使网络等新媒体刊发的信息呈现随意性与碎片化,信息接受者需自己去甄别;新媒体传递的海量信息还容易造成信息冗余,读者需在海量的信息中发掘自己所需要的、正确的信息。据此,科技期刊应抓住内容这一核心优势,"借力"新媒体,打造核心竞争力。首先,借助新媒体优选选题,运用新媒体信息传播的即时性与舆论聚集作用,挖掘出公众关注的热点与焦点问题,结合科技期刊的办刊方向,对相关信息去粗取精、去伪存真,选定主题。其次,充分发挥科技期刊积聚着一批高水平的专家、学者的优势,依托专家等社会知识生产系统,围绕选定的主题,约请相关专家、学者进行特定问题的研究,再经过同行专家匿名审核,编辑人员编辑校对,组建起有深度、有创意的内容。最后,经过印刷、出版,发布可靠的、权威的、前沿的知识和思想。

2. 开拓新的阅读方式。在互联网发展带来的网络阅读的基础上,移动互联终端的广泛应用,催生了移动阅读这种新型阅读方式的诞生。据调查,现在大部分的手机上网用户已开始使用手机阅读。鉴于此,科技期刊应在传统的纸质媒体的基础上,延伸发展网络媒体和移动媒体,使数字化的科技期刊不仅可以在电脑上阅读,还可随时随地在各种移动终端,如 iPad、手机等上阅读,这已成为科技期刊传播的新趋向。

3. 创新科技期刊数字化盈利新模式。科技期刊往往不以经济效益为唯一目标,而更多注重社会效益,但科技期刊的发展壮大需要经济基础的支撑。新媒体语境下,要求科技期刊创新盈利模式,在继续维持好纸质期刊读者群和广告客户的基础上,开展数字化盈利。一是付费阅读,与数字杂志阅读服务商

[基金项目] 中国高校科技期刊研究会科技期刊学研究计划项目资助(GBJXB1108);北京联合大学校级科研资助(sk201028x)。
[作者简介] 李亚青,柴智,北京联合大学学报编辑部。

或移动终端提供商合作,读者可根据自己的需要按期或按栏目或按篇付费订阅、下载阅读。二是广告盈利,传统的纸质期刊发展到网络期刊时,已对纸质的平面广告带来革命,音频、视频的运用丰富了原来静止的文字图像,移动网络终端的发展,结合数字媒体具有多元素、互动性的特质,再借助合理的移动互联网广告的支付渠道,移动互联网广告将实现大的发展,这是科技期刊的价值新趋向。

三、对科技期刊编辑的新要求

新媒体时代,对科技期刊编辑提出了新的要求,编辑不仅需要运用业务知识对稿件初审把关、编辑加工、设计版面、审改校样等,还需要熟练运用新媒体技术,跟上数字化技术发展的步伐,以及培养、挖掘与新媒体时代科技期刊发展相关的能力。

1. 努力提高科技期刊编辑的个人素养。新媒体语境下,科技期刊编辑在具备编辑的基本素质——政治思想素质、编辑出版业务知识、掌握必要的专业知识与广博的各科知识、文字水平与逻辑思维能力、策划与创新能力等[3]的基础上,还须具有较强的技术能力。其中,主要包括熟练掌握一门外语、熟练应用计算机、具备一定的网络应用技术能力。

2. 强化培养科技期刊编辑的学习能力。在新媒体语境下,新生事物不断涌现,新知识、新技能日新月异地发展,更要求科技期刊编辑具有搜集和阅读科技文献、熟练使用学习工具的能力,通过不断学习,把新知识融入已有知识,从而改变其知识结构,适应新媒体时代科技期刊发展的要求。科技期刊编辑还要注重在实践中学习,在与作者、读者的互动中学习,借助新媒体多向传播、即时传递、图文并茂等优势,建立起新媒体语境下科技期刊的新型的、互动的充满创造性的编辑、作者、读者、专家等相互学习、优势互补的新局面。

3. 注重养成科技期刊编辑的沉潜能力。沉潜力是一个人成长的定力,也就是我们在生活中所说的:做事要能沉下去。只有沉下心来,不急不躁,努力学习,稳步提高,才能站稳脚跟、厚积薄发,承担起科技期刊编辑的职责。

4. 鼓励发展科技期刊编辑的国际视野。新媒体时代,出版界的国际化、全球化趋势日趋明显,国际学术文化交流日益增多,要求科技期刊编辑视野开阔,了解、借鉴国外的经验教训,主动地选择,巧妙地运用。国际视野是指在能力和素质方面的国际化,也就是国际眼光或者国际视角,能够站在全球或更广阔的角度上观察期刊运行、市场营销,从而为科技期刊的发展服务。国际视野并不是一定要去海外留过学,精通几门外语,语言只是用于交流的工具,会几门外语并不一定就是具有国际视野。当然,没有任何外语知识也是不行的。应培养鼓励科技期刊编辑多掌握几门外语知识,以此作为"敲门砖",走向国际。[4]

参考文献

[1] 王珑玲. 新媒体语境下传统媒体的核心竞争力培育[J]. 当代青年研究,2010(12):18-22.
[2] 路艳艳. 新媒体时代:期刊的创新之道. 圣才学习网[EB/OL]. (2011-06-26)[2011-09-01] http://bjcb.100xuexi.com/HP/20110626/OTD303448.shtml.
[3] 郑一奇. 编辑的悟性[M]. 北京:首都师范大学出版社,2009.
[4] 杨牧之. 编辑要有国际视野[J]. 编辑之友,2009(2):6-10.

音系学理论教学与实证研究

宋长来

一、引　言

由于国际交流日益频繁，全球化趋势逐渐加深，加之英语专业就业形势更加严峻，更多大陆的英语本科毕业生远赴欧美读研深造。令人欣喜的是，更多学生选择音系学或句法学为主攻方向，而以前更多深造者却选择文化交流，跨文化交际等偏重应用性研究的方向。

二、音系学理论基础

人们一般都认为，语言学习主要包括语音、句法与语义，而其首要任务则是学习目标语言的语音系统。

1. 语言学基础

语言学的基础是掌握语音知识，包括语音学和音系学知识。国内以前的外语教学主要以语音学为主，音系学则常被忽视。其后果是学习者只好以模仿操练为主，这造成他们只知"所以然"，而不知"之所以然"。由于学习者千差万别，没有理论指导，以致外语教学效果较差，因而语音教师只好为示范者，而不是解释者，更不是母语与外语之间有效的系统对比研究者。学习效率低下，更有甚者，导致昙花一现的"双向式英语""疯狂英语"等劳民伤财的教学实践与市场操作，这些都是我国外语教育的经验教训，值得主管部门与社会的借鉴与警惕。

2. 音系学与语音学之异同

语音学与音系学都以语音为研究对象，语音学为音系学之基础，但是两者却存在差异。其研究范围目的与任务各不相同。语音学的界定为：

Phonetics studies speech sounds, including the production of speech, that is, how speech sounds are actually made, transmitted and received, the description and classification of speech sounds, words and connected speech, etc. （胡壮麟，姜望琪，钱军，2011：15）

语音学是描写性的，而非规定性的（应该与传统的规定性外语教学区分开来）。而音系学界定为：

Phonology studies the rules governing the structure, distribution and sequencing of speech sounds and the shapes of syllables. It deals with the sound system of a language by treating phoneme as the point of departure. （胡壮麟，姜望琪，钱军，2011：16）

音系学主要研究语言的语言规则与系统，属于索绪尔所说的 langue 范畴，而语音学则研究具体发音方法，因而属于索绪尔所谓的 parole 范围。

因此语音学研究人类能发出的语音，而音系学则研究这些语音子集，它们构成语言与意义。前者研究整体语音，而后者则主要研究其规则。（胡壮麟，姜望琪，钱军，2011：16）

换言之，语音学、音系学研究角度不同。前者提供描写单个语音及其语音属性，而后者研究的是这些语音组合方法与模式（陈林华，1999：63 - 4）。

总之，语音学为音系学的基础，音系学对外语教学与学习则更具指导意义。

3. 音系学基本概念

为更好地了解一门外语，外语教师需掌握一定音系学知识，特别是关于 phone, phoneme, allophone 的区分。对于 minimal pair, complementary distribution, distinctive features 等音系学理论都要有深刻理解与掌握。语音学与音系学的区分是布拉格学派的主要贡献之一。下文以案例为导向，具体介绍这些理论。

［作者简介］宋长来，男，山东安丘人，北京联合大学旅游学院国际旅游系教授，英语博士，研究方向为英语语言学及英汉互译。

三、音系学理论的案例研究

音系学的案例研究可以考查外语学习者对外语语音知识的实际了解以及分析能力。

1. 音系学理论的具体案例分析

在对学生进行课后答疑和出国留学考试的咨询中，我们发现，学生对研究生入学试题的理解有一定困惑和困难，本文以香港中文大学的入学试题为例，提供解题思路和指导策略，以供参考。

首先，我们来看 Part One (2008-9 CUHK MA (LIN/CLLA) Recruitment Test)

B. Examine the following words from Malayalam, a Dravidian language spoken in India, and answer the questions that follow.

(1) [koṭːa]	'basket'	(2) [kiṭːi]	'got'
(3) [apːam]	'bread'	(4) [aṭːam]	'end'
(5) [keṭːu]	'burnt out'	(6) [kati]	'biting'
(7) [palam]	'a weight'	(8) [keṭːi]	'tied'
(9) [keːṭːu]	'heard'	(10) [kaːti]	'sour gruel'
(11) [paːta]	'a tree'	(12) [ciri]	'smile'
(13) [koṭːi]	'drummed'	(14) [kuti]	'drinking'
(15) [ciːri]	'shrieked'	(16) [wiːṭə]	'house'
(17) [kuːti]	'increased'	(18) [koːṭːa]	'castle'
(19) [katːi]	'thickness'	(20) [aːnə]	'man'
(21) [wenːa]	'butter'	(22) [kuṭːi]	'child'

Question：

(1) How are long and short vowels distributed?

(2) Is vowel length phonemic (音位) or allophonic (音位变体)?

首先阅读试题，语料来源于 Malayalam, a Dravidian language spoken in India。第一问考查该语言的长元音和短元音的分布；第二问则考查元音长短是音位变化，还是音位变体。

对于第一问，根据语料 6、7、12、14，该语言短元音分布在开音节里或词尾音节（音节划分根据 Maximal Onset Principle（Radford, et al, 1999：91-92））；长元音分布在首个闭音节里。对于第二问，根据 5 和 9、6、10 和 19、12 与 15、14 和 17，就是因为长元音与短元音之差异而导致了语义不同，构成不同词项，因此元音长度是音位单位，而不是音位变体。类似情况出现在我们比较熟悉的日语里。例如ぃえ［家］（房屋；家；家庭）和ぃぃぇ（不，不是）（感叹词），正是因为ぃ的长短不同，而导致两个词语，因此在日语和达罗毗荼诸语（Dravidian languages）中，元音长度是个音位。据说，已故的季羡林老先生留德十年主攻语言学研究，有人称他为东方文化大师，他自己曾公开否认，因为他首先是语言学家。他留德读博的主系为"梵文，巴利文等所谓印度学"，副系为"英语语言学和斯拉夫语言学（学习俄文和南斯拉夫文）"（季羡林，2005：184-185）有人批评，现在的博士根本不像博士，攻读一种语言文学或文学或翻译，"深而不博"，主攻翻译不懂语言学，主攻文学却不会翻译，语言功底差得要命。但也有人辩驳道"隔行如隔山"！实际上，随着社会的发展，要想成为真正的博士，要求越来越高，因此困难越来越大。

英语回答是：①The long vowels are distributed in the initial closed syllables and the short vowels are distributed in the open syllables and word-ending syllables。②Vowel length is phonemic because it is contributed with the minimal pair contrast.（以下英语答案略）

另一案例是：

Phonology (Turkish) (2011-12 CUHK Recruitment Test)

en	*width*	em	*suck*	in	*cave*
im	*sign*	dʒam	*glass*	dʒan	*life*
tym	*all*	tyn	*afternoon*	son	*end*

som	*solid*	un	*flour*	um	*hope*	
baŋk	*sand bank*	zamk	*glue*	kent	*city*	
semt	*neigbborhood*	kamp	*camp*	reŋk	*color*	

1) Are [n] and [m] contrastive in Turkish? Please explain your answer with examples.

2) In which environment does [ŋ] occur? Does [ŋ] contrast with [n] or [m]? Explain your answer with examples.

3) What phonological process affects the distribution of [ŋ]?

首先阅读试题，有些学生反映，他们参加留学笔试时，读不懂试题。这反映两个问题：一是英语基础薄弱，二是专业知识有所欠缺。试题给出的语料来自于土耳其语。第一题问 [n] 和 [m] 是否为两个不同音位，根据音位定义 "the word PHONEME simply refers to a 'unit of explicit sound contrast'" （胡壮麟，姜望琪，钱军，2011: 39）。又根据 the existence of a minimal pair automatically grants phonemic status to the sounds responsible for the contrast (Roca & Jonson, 1999: 53); One word can be distinguished from another by selecting one type of sound instead of another (Spenser, 1996: 3) 便可以得出判断。第二题第一问是 [ŋ] 分布情况，即 [ŋ] 在什么条件下出现？第二问是 [ŋ] 和 [n] 或 [m] 是否是不同音位？第三题求问 [ŋ] 的音系过程分布规律。

认真理解试题后，考生必须首先审查语料。对于第一题，必须找到跟 [n] 和 [m] 有关语料，例如，em/en; in/im; dʒam/dʒan; tym/tyn; som/son; un/um。在每一组中，两者唯一差异就是 [n] 和 [m]，而这种差异导致每组词的意义差异，根据 "phonological analysis relies on the principle that certain sounds causes changes in the meaning of a word or phrase, whereas other sounds do not" (Crystal, 1997: 162)，所以我们可以得出结论: [n] 和 [m] 是两个不同音位，例如 em (suck) 和 en (width), in (cave) 和 im (sign) 都是因为 [n][m] 的差异而导致意义变化，如 width/suck, cave/sign。另外四组词以此类推。

对于第二题第一问，[ŋ] 在什么条件下才出现？根据语料，[ŋ] 出现在 k 之前。k 的语音描写是 [-voiced, stop, velar]。对于第二问，[ŋ] 和 [n]/[m] 是否形成对比，根据 minimal pair 定义: "two words in a language which differ from each other by only one distinctive sound (one phoneme) and which also differ in meaning (Richards, Jack C. et al, 2005: 429)，在以上语料 baŋk, reŋk 中我们找不到最小对比对，所以 [ŋ] 与 [n]/[m] 在给出的语料中不形成对比。对于第三题，考查 [ŋ] 音系过程分布情况，[ŋ] 出现在 [voiced plosive velar] ([k]) 之前。

另一案例是:

(2011 - 2 CUHK MA (LIN/CLLA) Recruitment Test)

Part One Answer all the questions in this section

Olsk

The sounds [ç h s] are in complementary distribution in native words in the Olsk dialect of Even, a Tungusic language spoken in Yakutia, Siberia. By examining the following Even words, decide what governs this distribution ([ie] and [iæ] are diphthongs consisting of [i] + [e] / [æ])

bead	nɪsa	*blows*	huːn	*bottom*	hɛr	*cave*	hor
foundation	hat	*his skill*	hɔːn	*hot*	hoːksi	*knife*	çɪrqan
knows	haːn	*pocket*	ciep	*poplar*	hol	*rotted*	ciævʊs
sad	bʊlʊs	*sole*	hɛssə	*soup*	çilj	*soviet*	havjɛːt
spectacles	bʊsqjɪ	*star*	ɔsɪqam	*vein*	hula	*weapon*	us

首先阅读试题，语料来自雅库特的通古斯满语。其语音 [ç h s] 为互补分布，这说明它们是音位变体，其条件是互补分布和语音类似性（胡壮麟，姜望琪，2002: 96）。根据 complementary distribution 定义 (Bussmann, 2000: 87) 和胡壮麟，姜望琪 (2002: 95) 可以得出这样结论，那么它们的分布到底是什么样的？第一，根据 hat, hot, hor 等语料，[h] 位于词首: #__且在后元音或 ɛ 之前）。另外根据，çiep, çiljj, çɪrqn, çiævʊs 可以得出 [ç] 位于 ie, i, ɪ 或 iæ 之前: 出现在高前元音 (i/ɪ) 之前。最后

［s］出现在后元音之后或之后 ε。

最后的案例：

(2012-13CUHK MA (LIN/CLLA) Recruitment Test)

Question 1 Analyze the following data and decide if ［s］ and ［z］ are allophones of the same phoneme or belong to different phonemes.

1. ［esféʃa］ 'sphere'
2. ［kása］ 'houses'
3. ［asustáʃ］ 'frighten'
4. ［péska］ 's/he fishes'
5. ［rúsos］ 'Russians'
6. ［lósas］ 'tiles'
7. ［sʊéňo］ 'dream'
8. ［asʊéto］ 'vacation'
9. ［izla］ 'island'
10. ［ezβélto］ 'slender'
11. ［dézðe］ 'since'
12. ［sésos］ 'brains'
13. ［eleksjón］ 'election'
14. ［píso］ 'apartment'
15. ［kási］ 'almost'
16. ［késo］ 'cheese'
17. ［desjérto］ 'desert'
18. ［sjérto］ 'certain'
19. ［mizmo］ 'same'
20. ［áznos］ 'asses'
21. ［rázro］ 'feature'

根据音位变体特征：如果［s］和［z］有互补分布和语音相似性，那么它们就是同一个音位的音位变体，否则就不是。［s］是［-voiced fricative alveolar］，［z］是［+voiced fricative alveolar］因此可以说［s］和［z］有语音相似性。因而如果［s］和［z］形成互补分布，那么它们就是一个音位的音位变体。［z］分布在闭音节里（非词尾），为韵尾（coda）参见语料 9，10，11，19，20，21。［s］出现在其他情况：词尾或节首（oneset），因此［s］和［z］是同一音位的不同音位变体。

2. 促进对普通语言学理论研究

通过以上分析研究，我们理解音系学研究与学习的重要性，无论传统语文研究也好，盛行的 TG 语法也罢，音系学都占有重要一席，因为音系学研究是语言研究的起始点与基础。对于具体语言的研究都有一定指导意义。

四、音系学理论对外语教学的思考

音系学研究对于中国外语教育尤其具有指导意义。

1. 对外语教学与学习的指导意义

对于中国外语教学与学习，音系学有现实指导意义。作为教师，如果听力和口语薄弱，那么他们就很难胜任教学与科研任务。对于学生而言，口语与听力较差，那么他们是很难通过面试这一关，也谈不上有效就业，更无法出国进修。至于与国际接轨，促进国际交流，实现全球化双赢，更是无从谈起。

2. 对于翻译的指导

对于翻译，国内翻译研究与实践又掀起了新一轮热潮，莫言获得诺贝尔文学奖更为此创造了新的契机。文学翻译，尤其是诗歌翻译注重韵律和意象传递，而音系学研究就是培养外语学习者逻辑思维能力和想象力。如果翻译的诗歌既没有意象的再创造,也没有语言韵律的传递,那绝对谈不上好的译文,甚至谈不上是诗歌。具体问题,由于篇幅所限,此处不在赘述。

3. 对认知语言学的指导

有人说,21 世纪是认知科学世纪。在跨进入 21 世纪之后,中国外语界开始关注认知语言学,外语教学研究同人开始研究认知语义学及认知句法学。我们建议有条件的院校应关注认知音系学,因为一般院校开设音系学的还凤毛麟角。

五、结 语

基于以上分析与讨论,我们呼吁加强音系学教学与学习,投入更多精力,提高外语学习效率,尽早摆脱哑巴外语的困境。为积极参与国际交流,做出我们更大的努力与贡献。

参考文献

[1] Bussmann, H (Translated and Edited by Trauth Gregory. P & Kerstin Kazzazi). Routledge Dictionary of Language and Linguistics [M]. Beijing: Foreign Language Teaching and Research Press, 2000.
[2] Crystal, David. Cambridge Encyclopedia of Language [M]. Cambridge: Cambridge University Press, 1992/1997.
[3] Radford, Andrew, et al. Linguistics: An Introduction [M]. Cambridge: Cambridge University Press, 1999.
[4] Richards. Jack I. et al. Longman Dictionary of Language Teaching and Applied Linguistics [M]. Beijing: Foreign Language Teaching and Research Press, 2005.
[5] Roca, I. & W. Johnson. A Course of Phonology [M]. Oxford: Blackwell, 1999.
[6] Spencer, Andrew. Phonology: Theory and Description [M]. Oxford: Blackwell, 1996/1999.
[7] 陈林华. 语言学导论 [M]. 长春:吉林大学出版社,1999.
[8] 胡壮麟,姜望琪. 语言学高级教程 [M]. 北京:北京大学出版社,2002.
[9] 胡壮麟,姜望琪,钱军. 语言学教程 [M]. 4 版. 北京:北京大学出版社,2011.
[10] 林洁. 季羡林名篇佳作 [M]. 北京:东方出版社,2005.

跨文化交际课程中多元识读教学模型的建构与实践

张义君

引 言

在国内跨文化交际课程研究领域,至今未见从培养学生批评识读能力方面开展的探讨,而且让学生带着问题到实践中去验证,通过与不同文化背景的人在异文化语境下进行人际交流以消除"文化定式"的研究也较为欠缺。我们认为,在跨文化交际课程中建构多元识读教学模型有助于培养和提高学生的批评识读能力。批评识读能力是在社会实践中通过解决跨文化交际问题培养和发展起来的,使得学生对各种文化持有理解、尊重、宽容和批评的态度。在多元化的信息社会中,跨文化交际教学不再是简单地了解和比较文化,而是通过批评性识读和人际交流实现思想提升和知识创新的过程。

1 批评识读能力的概念

批评识读能力(critical literacy)是多元识读能力的一种。正如 Thwaites(1999)所言,多元识读能力内容丰富,包括科技识读能力、媒体识读能力、文化识读能力、政治识读能力和批评识读能力(Lotherington 2007)。批评识读能力具有多元识读能力的特征,即学习者具备有效使用现代技术和多媒体的能力,具有理解全球性多元化文化差异的能力(Kalantzis&Cope2000)。批评识读能力强调社会环境中的交流和实践,强调意义构建、学习和与他人互动,强调参与者不仅能识读语篇信息,也能解释符号和图像,并能利用多媒体和互联网等技术工具。批评识读特别关注批评性思辨能力。具有批评性思辨能力的人会更多地包容和移情,更关注社会的权利分配和不公,从而改变社会(Gee 2000)。批评识读能力就是批评、质疑和改变因传统偏见所造成的不公平社会现象和利益关系的能力。这就涉及要鼓励学生将他们的生活经验与书本相联系,注重对知识和文化多样性的理解(Comber 2002;McLaughlin & DeVoogd 2004)。批评性识读强调在教学方面,要从知识传授向知识产出转变,也就是说,学生要积极参与知识的构建和产出,同时教师的作用在于设计和构建学习的环境(Kapitzke 2000:227)。

2 多元识读教学模型的理论基础

本研究构建的多元识读教学模型主要基于新伦敦小组(New London Group 1996)提出的教学设计方法,Unsworth(2001)归纳的识别识读(recognition literacy)、生成识读(reproductionliteracy)、反思识读(reflection literacy)3种识读表现形式以及 Luke 和 Freebody(2005)的"识读者的4种身份"(Four Roles of the Literacy Learner)理论。

研究在梳理相关成果的基础上,从不同时期教学的关注点出发,将识读教学分为指导性识读教学、社会建构主义教学和多元识读教学,并对它们进行比较分析。

2.1 指导性识读教学

指导性识读教学是指在认知层面强调人脑对文字进行解码和重新组码的过程,肯定了识字、写字以及分析文章和句法在读写学习中的重要作用。联合国教科文组织指出,识读是一种区别、理解、阐释、创新、交流、计算和在不同语境下使用印刷与书写资料的能力,它包含了学习的连续性,但随着时代和社会的演变,信息传播使识读教学的内涵发生了相应变化,它已摆脱传统单一的文字形式而借助各式各

[基金项目] 本文是北京市教育科学"十二五规划"重点课题"当前我国大学生多元识读能力现状、问题及对策研究"(项目编号:ADA11086)的阶段性成果和北京市高等教育学会"十二五"高等教育科学研究规划课题"多媒介语境下外语教学新视野:多元识读实践教学研究"(项目编号:BG125YB010)的部分成果。

[作者简介] 张义君,北京联合大学旅游学院国际旅游系。

样的媒体呈现出多样化表达方式（UNESCO Education Sector2004）。

指导性识读教学通常采用传统的语言学习模式，即从学习语音、阅读、语法、词汇到学习写作。教学大纲内容按简单到复杂顺序安排，呈现一种静态的知识输出过程。教学模式常常是以教师为中心，教授的内容基本上是正式、标准和书面的知识。在这种教学过程中，很少运用文化知识和学生已有的经验。如果说有涉及社会的文化识读方面，这种文化识读也是与社会的权利关系相关，其结果是没有鼓励学生成为批判性思维者，没有鼓励学生质疑社会秩序。指导性识读教学所关注的只是语言本身，强调的是一种国家语言的标准形式，并设定语言的正确用法是能够识别和描写的。这种语言教学观点和与之相匹配的教学法被称为"教学权威主义型"教学（Cope & Kalantzis 2000：5）。虽然基于语言的识读教学法有许多值得保留的成分，但其显然不能满足当今信息时代的识读发展需求，因为21世纪的识读概念应该是多样性的识读。

2.2 社会建构主义教学

社会建构主义教学领域很多关于知识建构方法的理论都是基于维果茨基的社会学习理论，特别是他的"最近发展区（ZPD）"理论发展而成的（Kourtis – Kazoullis & Skourtou 2007）。该理论认为人的高级心理机能只能通过人们的协同活动、人与人的交往产生。学习也不例外，它只有在同伴或师生的互动中才能协同建构。教学活动应保证学习者能在真实的情境下通过解决复杂的真实问题建构新知识。不同于"从简单到复杂"的传统原则和教学论的还原思想，建构主义强调学生的咨询、合作学习、已有经验运用以及社会交往以促进认知能力发展（Cummins & Sayers 1995）。社会建构主义教学认同文化差异，但基于建构主义的教学仍然不能关注社会的权利关系，其结果是尽管学生的思想有可能是自由和包容的，但他们还是不能反思自己的经验和社会现实（Cummins 2000）。Gee（2000：62）认为认知主义教学培养的学生能进行"高层次思考（higher order thinking）"，但批评性思考能力欠缺。换句话说，学生不能充分理解和批评所处世界的权利与不公平的体系，而只是简单地将其看成经济上的必然结果。因此，社会建构主义教学同样不能解决社会权利关系的问题，也不能处理与之相关的学习问题。

2.3 多元识读教学

多元识读教学的核心概念是"设计"（New London Group 1996：73 – 77）。设计包括意义的主动设计和社会未来的积极设计，它将学习与知识的创新、改变紧密结合起来。多元识读教学的目标是实现多元识读倡导者提出的双重识读目的：一是理解并掌握不断演变的语言；二是培养学生的批评识读能力，使他们能够设计自己的社会未来并通过完成工作获得成功。通过反思，学习者能够在他们的学习过程中获得必要的空间、构建性地判断、创造性地拓展和应用，最终创新出自己的东西。多元识读教学强调对文本的分析和改变，因为文本的意识形态不是中立的，而是代表某种特殊的观点，并能影响其他人的观点（张义君 2011）。因此，文本始终处在批评性的环境中，可以用新的方法对其重新设计（New London Group 1996：60）。Lankshear 等（2000）认为，从根本上说，所有的识读实践都包含"批评性特征"。Cummins（2001）将批评性识读的内涵与社会环境、权利分配相结合，表明其与知识的构建、学习密不可分，从而鼓励学生探讨如何通过社会行为和社会参与来改变社会现实。Kalantzis 和 Cope（2000：9）认为，识读教学的内容不仅仅是学习语言的标准形式、唯一语言和唯一文化，识读教学应该被看成是能营造引导学生参与社会活动的学习环境的教和学的关系。多元识读教学强调反省型语言学习，关注语言与权力的关系，鼓励学习者对所学的知识和书本的权威性进行反思，而不是一味接受、内化来自教材、教师或同伴的观念。同时，多元识读教学要求教师向学习者提供不同于传统语言学习的实践活动，让学习者通过多种信息传递方式和信息网络理解各种模态的语篇，帮助学习者反思学习，发展批评性思维能力。总之，多元识读教学就是使"识读"过程转变成"设计"过程，并在这些"设计"过程中实现学生批评识读能力的培养。

对识读教学理论的分类是为了突显不同阶段识读教学的导向和目的，并非是机械式和分离式的教学区分。因为有效的教学不可能只涉及一种方法，而是有机运用多种方法的结果。由此，在构建多元识读教学模型的过程中，我们综合了指导性识读教学强调的学习基础性和连续性，融入了社会建构主义教学在合作学习方面的观点，应用了多元识读教学鼓励学生通过反思社会行为、社会参与来改变社会现实的创新理念。在跨文化交际课程中研究和构建多元识读教学模型不仅符合跨文化交际的特点，能够培养学生的批评识读能力,反思跨文化交际中的"文化定式"问题,而且能够将学生带入真正的跨文化交际语境,缩短书本知识和真实交际之间的距离。

3 多元识读教学模型的实践研究

3.1 研究问题和方法

本研究以多元识读理论的"设计"三要素,即可用的设计(available design)、设计(designing)和重新设计(the redesigned)为指导思想,构建跨文化交际课程的多元识读教学模型(见图1),从项目任务的建立、参与、分析与重构4个阶段阐述多元识读教学对学生批评性识读能力的影响和作用。研究采用质性研究方法。质的研究不是用现有的学术模式来评析某一社会现象或事例,而是基于调查主体的经验,从科研对象的经验视角出发来了解研究客体,客观地阐释某一群体的经验,并达到普遍化的目的。

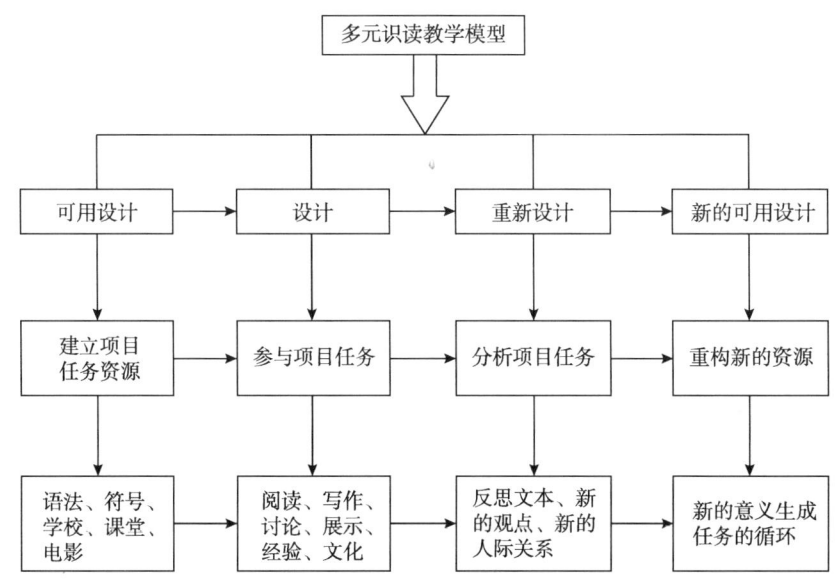

图1 跨文化交际课程的多元识读教学模型

本研究在北京市某高校英语专业的跨文化交际课程中开展,参与研究的学生共85人。跨文化交际课程的课时为16周,前8周主要是教师授课,后8周是实践项目任务。实践项目任务的具体课时和内容安排见表1。

表1 实践项目任务的课时和内容安排

课时安排	阶段任务	任务主要内容
第9周	建立项目任务资源	(1)自主学习 (2)小组讨论
第10至11周	参与项目任务	(1)写计划纲要 (2)以小组形式选择交流方式
第12至14周	分析项目任务	(1)观察和体验 (2)理解文化定式 (3)反馈
第15周	重构新的(项目)资源	(1)完成项目报告 (2)构建新的可用资源
第16周	问卷调查	反馈任务目的和意义

本研究围绕基于设计的项目任务内容,分4个阶段对项目进行观察和分析,主要探讨以下问题:(1)基于设计的多元识读教学模型能否培养学生的批评识读能力?(2)学生对"文化定式"的理解是否会随着跨文化人际交流发生改变?

本研究的内容包括以下3个部分:第一部分,确定项目任务实施步骤;第二部分,参考Walsh和

Grant（2002）的批评识读框架（critical literacy framework）对项目任务中的选项进行分析；第三部分，教师了解学生对项目任务的看法。因受时间和条件的限制，学生选择3种交流方式开展项目活动，即与来华留学生交流；与海外中国留学生交流（通过视频和邮件）；与回国留学生交流。

3.2 任务实施步骤

1）建立项目任务资源。学生以小组为单位进行整合性学习，结合教师授课和同伴的话语，借助文本、案例、电影和网络等媒介，归纳总结跨文化交际课程中的理论观点、文化现象等内容。这些可用设计资源能使学生充分理解信息传递行为所表达的各种符号意义和对意义的不同选择，并使学生理解在特定的社会空间与符号行为相联系的结构设置，如话语形式、风格和语态等元素。

2）参与项目任务。（1）学生阅读教师推荐的参考书，结合自己的经验和知识确定项目计划和调查内容，就相关问题咨询教师后进行相应修改；（2）根据兴趣和条件，以小组为单位选择以下交流方式中的一种：与来华留学生交流、与海外中国留学生交流和与回国留学生交流。参与项目任务是跨文化交际课程中设计概念的具体表现形式，包括学生可接触的所读、所看和所听等，是一种创造性活动，时时体现对可用资源的改变，并生成新的意义。

3）分析项目任务。（1）在与他文化人的交际中检测和反思所学知识、理论与观点；（2）形成新的观点，建立跨文化人际关系；（3）理解和消除文化定式，产生新的文化认同。分析项目任务不仅承载了历史和文化的意义，完成重新设计的过程，更具备改变意义的特征，证实积极介入现实世界的设计也能改变设计者（学习者）自身。通过这种设计，学生不仅改造了自己已有的知识，同时在与他人合作的过程中改善了人际关系，进而对自己的文化身份有了新的认识。分析项目任务是一种原创性活动，也被看成是日常经验积累的核心部分，因而需在教育过程中加以强调。

4）重构新的资源。（1）整理、完成项目报告；（2）实践中的问题和方法生成新的可用资源。重构新的资源指由设计过程产生的资源或意义又可成为一种新的可资利用的设计，形成具有意义潜势的新的资源。

上述任务实施步骤体现了"设计"的概念，即学习和生成，包括复杂的人际体系、环境、技术、信念和文本，这些都是设计的结果（New London Group 1996）。设计这一概念与创新、改变密切相关，使"识读"过程转变成"设计"过程，并使学生的批评识读能力在"设计"过程中得到发展。

3.3 学生问题调查

参考 Walsh 和 Grant（2002）的批评识读框架，本研究首先把学生项目任务中的问题分为以下两种：权利关系和文化定式，然后让学生对海外留学生、回国留学生和来华留学生展开调查。

4 结果与讨论

4.1 学生对权利关系的认识

本研究中的权利关系指学校的师生关系、教与学的关系以及学习与活动的关系。

目前国内的高等教育仍具有以下特点：教师过于看重自己身份的权威性，没有意识到与学生地位平等的重要性；教育强调的是教师的认真教学，忽视学生的自主学习，注重书本知识的传授和记忆，忽视社会现实的经验和活动。多元识读教学则强调培养学生的批评识读能力，使他们能够设计自己的社会未来，反思、改善人际关系，并通过实践工作获得成功。在探讨"学生未来"的各种问题及其答案方面，我们认为多元识读教学是十分有效的途径，其目的就是如何让学生具备批评识读能力，加强他们对不同语言和文化的认同，使他们通过与其他人的交流在"全球化世界"中占有一席之地。有同学在项目总结中写道：

"在项目开始前，我想我们与西方的教育只是在教学方法和学校制度方面有所不同，但在我与他们（法国、加拿大留学生）交谈后，才知道还有很多的不同，远远超过我在书本上看到的内容。这种经历让我明白，实际的调查研究才是知道事实的有效途径。给我印象最深的是，他们几乎一致认为教师和学生是平等的，学生更喜欢把老师当作朋友。他们表示学生去上课是对老师的尊敬，这一点给了我很大启示，意识到上课不仅是学知识，也是尊重老师。但我们和老师还是经常有距离感，希望以后会有所改变。"

接受调查的一位回国留学生说道:

"在国内读书时,有大量的公共必修课,觉得听的课太多,几乎没有时间自己读书,一学期下来没有读多少书。在国外(德国)就不一样了,如果要完成老师的作业,必须要查阅很多资料,要看很多东西。特别是和老师做项目时,虽然很忙碌,但感到很充实,很快乐。"

接受调查的一位海外留学生说道:

"我感觉美国的课程都贯穿'学以致用'的观点。比如,宏观经济学的老师在第一节课就说'希望你们学完后能读懂财经类报纸杂志'。课程的目的性和实践性很强,关注点放在以后的应用上,学生就容易产生学习的激情。"

上述调查结果表明学生开始关注师生关系、教与学的关系以及学习与活动的关系。他们摆脱了传统教学模式的束缚,认真思考,理性判断,"更关注社会的权利关系"(Gee 2000)。然而,在教学中,很多教师还没有认真思考与学生建立平等关系的重要性,忽视了将课堂内容与学生将来的社会活动紧密联系,也没有意识到学生的批评识读能力其实就是通过每一个设计的社会活动培养起来的。

4.2 学生对文化定式的认识

文化定式简而言之就是预先设定性的判断和由此形成的观念与意见。在跨文化课程教学中,用定式(stereotype)来区别群体间的文化差异比较普遍。这种方法在很大程度上方便了教学,但如果应用不当,则容易使人以静止不变的眼光看待世界。在全球化背景下,信息的更新和渗透都达到了前所未有的速度和深度。世界现实在不断变化,而人们头脑中的定式如果未及时调整和改变,必然会造成跨文化交际障碍,引发误解。美国社会心理学家 Raiper 通过实验揭示了实际交往具有消除偏见的积极作用(李媛,范捷平 2007)。这一理论在跨文化交际实践中的表现就是:对异文化的"文化定式"可以通过亲身接触、体验该文化而得以匡正和消解。下面以进行调查学生(Investigating Students,IS)与来华留学生(Foreign Students,FS)的对话(由笔者翻译成中文)为例进行分析:

IS:一般认为,西方人喜欢低语境交流方式,即说话直白,不拐弯抹角,而不喜欢高语境交流方式,即不直接的、含蓄的交流方式。我想问,你喜欢用哪种方式交流呢?

FS:我想用什么方式交流要看不同的场景,看不同的交流对象。我会交替使用不同的方式。在这里(北京)我认为高语境更合适,因为我知道中国人说话大多比较含蓄。当然,我会看书或上网查资料了解我要打交道的人的文化背景。

IS:你在这里学习时是否觉得与人交流有什么困难?

FS:没有,也许因为我妈妈是德国人,我爸爸是法国人,我想我与拥有其他文化的人相处得很好。

上述对话有利于我们理解文化定式观点会随着交通的日益便捷、互联网的普及、世界经济的全球化以及人们的全球化意识和多元文化意识的增强而发生改变。正如一位学生在报告中所写的:

"通过与外国留学生的交往,我认为不能从定式的窗口观察某文化个体及其行为,不能忽视交际者的个性。比如,以前我以为国外的大学生都要参加很多学校活动,当他们(法国、德国留学生)告诉我其实没有很多学校活动时,我真的很吃惊。还有关于是否要读博士学位的问题,他们认为如果不是为了进高校或做研究,读博士学位意义不大,找工作硕士学位就够了,是否找到好工作、是否晋升与是否有博士学位没有直接联系。他们通常把读博士学位看成一种荣誉。这些观点与我们想的很不一样。"

如果说"因为定式使我们对人类的活动或跨文化交际活动的认识局限在一两个层面上,并把这种简单的认识当作人类的活动或跨文化交际活动的全部"(Scollon & Scollon 2000),那么让学生与不同文化的人交流不仅可以在一定程度上消除"文化定式",体现多元文化环境下跨文化交际的真实需求,而且能真正促进跨文化实践走向人际交往。

胡文仲(1989)从应用语言学角度提出,要提高学生的跨文化交际意识,培养跨文化交际能力,最好的方法应该是让他们沉浸于目标语文化的氛围中,同英语本族语者亲身接触。这种亲身接触是十分有意义的,正如一位学生所总结的:

"我很感谢老师安排我们做这个调查项目,让我们有机会与同龄的外国学生交流,不仅了解了很多书本上没有的文化知识,还和他们成了朋友,常常共同探讨问题,相互学习。"

4.3 学生对实践项目的认识

在跨文化交际课程教学中，教什么以及怎么教才能使学生真正成为应对全球化机遇与挑战、成功开展跨文化交际的人？解决这些问题是广大教师面临的新的挑战。当前，人们获取的信息大部分由媒体提供，这就决定了人们的感知与认识在很大程度上受媒体的支配和制约。媒体对个体与群体心理的影响是人类迄今为止所创造的任何事物都无法比拟的。由于不了解也没有机会亲身接触世界其他国家的民族和文化群体，网络、报刊、图书、电影、广播、电视等媒介所提供的标签式概括和归类便成为人们了解其他群体文化的主要途径，这就难以避免出现描述过时、片面甚至是错误的情况。只有面对面的接触才真正有助于人们了解某一群体的真实面貌。这也是我们开展基于设计的实践项目研究的目的之一。由于首次进行这样的项目活动，有必要了解学生对项目任务的态度及对完成项目任务意义的看法（见表2），以便改进项目任务，更有效地实施项目任务。

表2 学生对项目任务的反馈（N = 85）

	选项	人数	百分比（%）
态度	喜欢做这个项目	82	96.5
意义	了解异国真实文化	71	83.5
	促进人际交往能力	80	94.1
	能够选择恰当话题	60	70.6
	理解异文化幽默	33	38.8

表2说明学生对项目任务的认同度很高，很喜欢这样的实践机会，这一点也体现在学生的总结报告中。关于项目任务促进人际交往能力的作用方面，学生的认同度也很高，这一结果与本研究项目设计的初衷是一致的。至于是否理解异文化幽默，学生表示只能听懂比较简单的、字面的幽默，而涉及历史、地理，特别是政治、经济方面的幽默故事就不容易理解，还常常感到很尴尬，可见学生在这一点上没有什么自信心。此外，学生表示在交流中，特别是初次交流时，选择双方感兴趣的话题不是件容易的事，特别担心由于了解不够深入会涉及异文化中的某些禁忌话题而引起误解。这些都是需要我们在跨文化交际课程中关注和解决的问题。

5 结束语

本研究首次尝试在跨文化交际课程教学实践中应用多元识读教学模型。根据本次调查结果，本研究提出的两个问题得到了初步解答：（1）基于设计的多元识读教学模型能够培养学生的批评识读能力；（2）学生对"文化定式"的理解会随着跨文化人际交流而发生改变。

通过本研究，我们可以得到以下启示：（1）多元识读教学模型不仅能够培养学生的责任意识和自主学习能力，而且创造了开展社会活动的学习环境，有利于构建新的知识体系，这样的学习观和学习方式有助于培养学生的批评识读能力。（2）跨文化交际学科的知识是动态的，会随着环境和时代的不断发展而变化。教师和学生都要有发展的意识和创造性，要学会甄别文化现象的真假，避免形成"文化定式"。（3）跨文化交际的目的是真正走向有效的人际交往。为实现有效的人际交往，必须关注交际者参与交际时的心理变化过程以及交际者的交际行为背后两种或多种文化之间的相互作用，关注交际中文化结构的解构和重构问题。

本研究运用多元识读理论来诊断当前跨文化交际教学中存在的问题，同时也论证了该理论在跨文化交际课程教学中的可操作性和应用价值。

参考文献

[1] Comber B. (Critical Literacy)：(Maximising Children's) (Investments in School Learning) [R]. Christchurch, New Zealand：The Resource Teachers' Literacy Training Programme, 2002.
[2] Cope B & Kalantzis M (eds.). Multiliteracies：(Literacy Learning and the Design of Social Futures) [C]. London：Rout-

ledge, 2000.

[3] Cummins J. 《Language, Power and Pedagogy: Bilingual Children in the Crossfire》[M]. Clevedon: Multilingual Matters, 2000.

[4] Cummins J. 《Negotiating Identities: Education for Empowerment in a Diverse Society》(2nd Ed.) [M]. Los Angeles: California Association for Bilingual Education, 2001.

[5] Cummins J & Sayers D. 《Brave New Schools: Challenging Cultural Illiteracy through Global Learning Networks》[M]. New York: St. Martin's Press, 1995.

[6] Gee J P. New people in new worlds: Networks, the new capitalism and schools [A]. In Cope B & Kalantzis M (eds.). 《Multiliteracies: Literacy Learning and the Design of Social Futures》[C]. London: Routledge, 2000. 43 – 68.

[7] Lankshear C, Snyder I & Green B. 《Teachers and Technoliteracy: Managing Literacy, Technology and Learning in Schools》[C]. Sydney: Allen & Unwin, 2000.

[8] Lotherington H. From literacy to multiliteracies in ELT [A]. In Cummins J & Davison C (eds.). 《International Handbook of English Language Teaching》[C]. New York: Springer, 2007. 897 – 898.

[9] Luke A & Freebody P. 《Further Notes on the Four Resources Model》[EB/OL]. http://readingonline.org/research/lukefreebody.html, 2005.

[10] Kalantzis M & Cope B. A pedagogy of multiliteracies: Designing social futures [A]. In Cope B & Kalantzis M (eds.). 《Multiliteracies: Literacy Learning and the Design of Social Futures》[C]. London: Routledge, 2000. 9 – 37. (4): 36 – 40.

[11] Kapitzke C. Cyber pedagogy as critical social practice in a teacher education program [J]. 《Teaching Education》, 2000, 11 (2): 211 – 229.

[12] Kourtis – Kazoullis V & Skourtou E. The Internet and English language learning [A]. In Cummins J & DavisonC (eds.). 《International Handbook of English Language Teaching》[C]. New York: Springer, 2007.

[13] McLaughlin M & DeVoogd G L. 《Critical Literacy: Enhancing Students' Comprehension of Text》[M]. New York: Teaching Resources, 2004.

[14] New London Group. A pedagogy of multiliteracies: Designing social futures [J]. 《Harvard Educational Review》1996, 66 (1): 60 – 89.

[15] Scollon R & Scollon S W. 《Intercultural Communication: A Discourse Approach》[M]. Beijing: Foreign Language Teaching and Research Press, 2000.

[16] Thwaites T. 《Multiliteracies: A New Direction for Arts Education》[EB/OL]. http://www.swin.edu.au/aare/99pap/thw99528/htm, 1999.

[17] UNESCO Education Sector. 《The Plurality of Literacy and Its Implications for Policies and Programmes》[EB/OL]. http://unesdoc.unesco.org/images/0013/001362/136246e.pdf, 2004.

[18] Unsworth L. 《Teaching Multiliteracies Across the Curriculum: Changing Contexts of Text and Image in Classroom Practice》[M]. Buckingham: Open University Press, 2001.

[19] Walsh C & Grant H. 《Investigating Identity and Power Relations》[EB/OL]. http://www.decs.sa.gov.au/thenetwork/files/pages/identity_web/introduction.html, 2002.

[20] 胡文仲. 英语的教与学 [M]. 北京: 外语教学与研究出版社, 1989.

[21] 李媛, 范捷平. 跨文化交际中模式固见发展变化动态分析 [J]. 外语教学与研究, 2007 (3): 123 – 124.

[22] 彭世勇. 中国跨文化交际研究的现状与困境 [J]. 汕头大学学报, 2010 (4): 14 – 18.

[23] 张义君. 英语专业学生多元识读能力实证研究 [J]. 外语界, 2011 (1): 45 – 51.

从乞巧节到中国情人节——
七夕节的当代重构及意义

张 勃

当前,七夕节——这个历史悠久的传统节日正发生从乞巧节到中国情人节的重要变化。本文旨在确认这种变化不是文化想象而是文化事实,并探讨其性质和意义。

1 从乞巧节到中国情人节:七夕节的当代蜕变是一种文化事实

笔者曾将节日的构成要素概括为如下五点:(1)节日名称的特殊性;(2)在历法中位置的特殊性;(3)活动内容的特殊性;(4)活动空间的特殊性;(5)参与主体体验和情感的特殊性。[1] 节日名称、节日时间、节日活动以及活动空间共同构成一整套节日规范,社会成员通过对这一套规范的实践形成自己的节日生活,产生特殊的体验和情感。这五种构成要素是节日与常日区别开来的标志,也可以用来作为区别不同节日,以及同一节日不同历史形态的分析性工具。从这五个方面入手,能够发现,七夕节——这个历史悠久的传统节日在当代正发生重要的变化。

首先,从节日名称上说,传统社会的七夕节有许多专名,其中有根据节日所在历法中的位置命名的,如七月七、七夕;有根据节日活动主体命名的,如女儿节、小人节;有根据节日的活动内容命名的,如乞巧节、穿针节、巧夕。但这些名称如今已在很大程度上让位于中国情人节、七夕情人节或中国爱情节。这不仅表现在商家的广告中,也表现在许多人的日常生活中。用这种专名称呼农历七月七日已是普遍现象。

其次,从活动内容方面说,传统七夕节习俗活动主要有乞巧(包括拜祷乞巧、穿针乞巧、观影占巧、用蜘蛛乞巧,看巧云、吃巧等)、乞美(包括用凤仙花染红指甲、采树叶洗头发、接露水洗浴等)、乞子、准备享用专门的饮食以及祭祀占卜等信仰活动,而当下,尽管乞巧等习俗仍在一定范围内存在,但发送手机短信,享受烛光晚宴,饮用香槟红酒,开始爱情之旅,赠送玫瑰、巧克力和珠宝首饰等成为七夕节的主要活动内容。

其三,从活动空间方面说,传统七夕节的活动主要是在庭院中进行。庭院本是私人空间,由于七夕节习俗活动往往由来自不同家庭的多人共同参与,私人空间便公共化了。又由于多有祭祀织女等信仰活动,本来的世俗活动空间便神圣化了。如今,七夕节的活动空间较少公共化,不仅如此,像酒店、咖啡馆等公共空间也因为活动主体主要是恋人而变得私人化了。由于信仰活动的缺失,活动空间也缺少了神圣的意味。

其四,从活动主体及其体验和情感而言,过去七夕节尽管也有男性参与活动,但主要是一个以女性为主体的民俗节日,是女子们表达美好愿望的关键时刻,反映了女子们对心灵手巧的热盼、对生儿育女的祈愿和对美丽容貌的渴望。[2] 如今,七夕节的活动主体主要是具有婚姻恋爱关系的男女双方,七夕节主要成为他们表达爱情的重要节日,反映了人们对美好爱情的向往和追求。对此,当下流行的众多七夕节短信可以为证。比如"送祝福"网站的"七夕节短信"中,有"最新彩信""热门彩信""最新短信"

[基金项目] 本文为北京市哲学社会科学规划项目"北京文化日历构建研究"(项目编号:12ZHB013)、北京联合大学人才强校计划人才资助项目"国际比较视野下的北京文化日历构建研究"的系列成果之一。

[作者简介] 张勃(1972—),女,历史学博士,北京联合大学北京学研究所研究员。

[1] 张勃. 当前语境下传统节日的困境与出路——兼及建构新兴节庆活动的一点思考[J]. 山东社会科学,2011(3).
[2] 张勃. 压力下的憧憬——七夕节俗中的女性心理和情感分析. 袁学骏等编. 七夕文化论文集[M]. 北京:中国文联出版社,2002:71-83.

"搞笑短信""爱情短信""朋友短信""经典短信"栏目的设置，几乎全与爱情有关。❶ 节日所带来的体验和情感也多与男女爱情有关。比如朗姆-可乐在2013年7月25日16点左右发布的微博中这样说："刚刚同事在讨论快七夕了，我突然觉得很失落，这些节日那些感情已经不再是我所能参与的话题，原本以为自己大大咧咧什么都可以不在乎，原来我也是个可以让伤心跟随这么久的人……越是刻意想去忘记一个人，那些发生过的事情越是清晰的回放……"❷

在以上五个构成要素中，惟一没有改变的是节日的标志性时间。正是这个没有改变，提示我们上述的种种改变只是七夕节内部的变化。

七夕节的当下变化是人们可以看到、感知的文化事实，考虑到乞巧主题的退隐、爱情主题的突显，这个文化事实可以概括为从乞巧节到中国情人节的变化，这个变化显著且具有质变意义，因而是一种"蜕变"。

从乞巧节到中国情人节的蜕变是进入21世纪以来发生的事情。这个蜕变的过程大致可以概括为：在文化交流频繁的情况下，圣瓦伦丁节以"情人节"的名称与玫瑰花、巧克力、烛光晚宴等文化符号进入中国社会（主要是城市社会），并为一些人所喜欢和践行。一种外来文化大行其道令国内一些具有较强民族主义情结、文化自觉意识和文化安全意识的人倍受刺激，他们开始在本土文化中寻找可以与之相抗衡的"中国情人节"，于是一些中华民族的传统节日如元宵节、清明节、三月三、七夕节的情爱要素被发现和被发掘。尽管在谁应该成为"中国情人节"方面存在着一些讨论，但七夕节还是更受认可而成为"中国情人节"，圣瓦伦丁节也相应成为"西方情人节"。与此同时，已从西方情人节中获益的商家从中国情人节中看到巨大商机，他们采借西方情人节的过节方式和文化符号，在农历七月七日来临前，推出针对"有情人"的商品和服务。各种媒体也推波助澜，不断引发公众围绕七夕节进行辩论和思考，并组织以爱情为主题的大型活动，越来越多的人在观念上认可了七夕节作为中国情人节的正当性，并在行动上参与到和爱情有关的活动中。七夕节不仅拥有了情人节之名，而且拥有了情人节之实。

2 重新命名、发现爱情、活动内容的采借与发明：七夕节的蜕变是典型的文化重构

在七夕节从乞巧节向中国情人节的蜕变过程中，2002年由河北省文联、河北省民间文艺家协会、石家庄市文联等单位联合发起的"七月七爱情节"起了十分重要的作用。一方面，它率先以七夕节为爱情节，组织开展了多项丰富多彩的文化活动，从而使"数十万人参与其中，沐浴了爱情的幸福与快乐"。❸ 另一方面，它举办了七夕节文化研讨会，引发了学者对七夕节作为爱情节合理性和正当性的系统思考，思考的部分成果呈现于由袁学骏等人编辑的《七夕文化论文集》中。❹ 时任河北省文联主席的冯思德在"河北省会首届七月七爱情节开幕式"上的讲话中，回顾了倡办首届七月七爱情节的过程并阐述了将七月七定位为爱情节的合理性与重要意义。他说：

"没想到牛郎织女的美丽传说竟可以打破国界，在异国异族（这里指在日本，笔者注）中扎根，但我转而又有些黯然，七夕节（乞巧节）在我国早已被人们淡忘了，事实上它已经让位给了西方传过来的'情人节'。

去年12月，在中国文联第七次代表大会上，江泽民总书记在报告中再三强调了弘扬和振奋民族精神的问题。在讨论中，我重提了日本七夕节的话题。石家庄市文联主席袁学骏同志便找到我，说他想与省文联联手张罗一个节，与西方情人节相抗衡。想来想去，最好还是把我国的七月七乞巧节捡起来，重新定义一下，然后大张旗鼓搞一个中国的爱情节。我非常赞成学骏同志的意见，一拍即合，我们还征求了省会党、政、文各界一些人士的意见，大家普遍对这一想法予以肯定和支持。

---

❶ 网址 http://m.szhufu.com/qixi/.

❷ 网址 http://weibo.com/z/bdkzym/index.html? search =%E6%88%91%E7%9A%84%E4%B8%83%E5%A4%95&uid=3298053125&refer=baidu.

❸ 杨守勇. 河北：七月七爱情节演绎中国"情人节"[OL]. http://news.sohu.com/20040719/n221073466.shtml.

❹ 袁学骏，等，七夕文化论文集[M]. 北京：中国文联出版社，2002。这次"七月七爱情节"还包括"七夕文化研讨会"，该论文集收录了研讨会的数十篇会议论文，以及"首届省会七月七爱情节资料"。

过去，仅仅把七月七说成是乞巧节，定位是不准确、不全面的。我认为应当把七月七定位于爱情节。关于牛郎、织女的爱情故事，在我国可以说是家喻户晓，有着深厚的传统渊源和群众基础。

把七月七定位于爱情节，不单单是为了与西方情人节抗衡，更重要的是，可以倡导忠贞爱情、稳定家庭，符合我国《公民道德建设实施纲要》要求。大家知道，家庭是社会组成的细胞，家庭稳定是社会稳定的基础。改革开放以来，随着世界优秀文化的传入，一些腐朽没落文化也乘机侵入。诸如'包二奶''找情人''泡妞'之类丑恶行为严重妨害了我国家庭稳定。所以，搞'七月七爱情节'将是绝对适时的，十分有意义的。"❶

上述讲话表明中国本来没有情人节，为了与"西方情人节相抗衡"，他们就要"张罗一个节"，而"张罗"的策略和路径是对七夕节进行重新命名，并从中发现爱情。

2.1 重新命名

正如前面已经说明的，农历七月七日作为节日，本来有自己的多个专名，但在抗衡西方情人节的诉求中，被进行了重新命名。2002年河北省文联的命名是"七月七爱情节"，2006年时，"根据中央有关领导的提议"这个名字被更改为"情侣节"。目前社会上比较流行的名称则是"中国情人节""七夕情人节"。不过已有专家明确指出这一名称并不合适，因为："七夕节表达的是已婚男女之间恪守双方对爱的承诺，不离不弃、白头偕老的情感，不是表达婚前情人或恋人的情感，这是在不同人生阶段的两种感情，因此将七夕节作为'中国情人节'并不妥当，'七夕节'应称作'中国爱情节'。"❷ 尽管围绕着七夕节的重新命名至今仍有争议，情侣节、情人节、爱情节的所指也有一些不同，但不可否认的是，新名称中都含有一个"情"字。新名字让七夕节更多与"男女之情"联系了起来。

中国人历来重视"名实"之辨，根据"取实予名"和"循名责实"的逻辑，对七夕节的重新命名既需要人们在七夕节传统中发现爱情，又需要人们在实际生活中运用表达爱情的文化符号、从事与爱情相关的节日活动，从而表明七夕节果然是一个"名副其实"的爱情节（情人节、情侣节）。

2.2 发现爱情

从七夕节中发现爱情是一个多人参与的持续过程，早在1999年，汪玢玲就发表长文论证七夕本就是"中国的情人节"。❸ 冯思德更多从牛郎织女传说中发现了七夕节蕴含着的爱情元素。因为广为流传的牛郎织女传说讲述了两人被迫隔开但依然不离不弃、最终得以一年一度鹊桥相会的浪漫爱情故事。2002年未能参加七夕文化研讨会但积极支持"七月七爱情节"的乌丙安、冯骥才同样肯定这则附着于七夕节的传说与爱情相关。乌丙安说："流传百世的牛郎织女鹊桥会的故事，始终颂扬着中华民族历代民众为爱情坚贞、婚姻自由而奋斗牺牲的壮丽精神。"冯骥才说："若向爱情求真谛，且问牛郎织女星。""牛郎织女身上寄托了中国人的爱情理想"❹。在这次会议上，"还有大量的文章，是阐发弘扬七夕文化的社会意义和时代意义，呼吁要让古老的文化传统与时俱进，这与冯、乌二人的论述形成了本次会议的最强音"❺。之后，不少学者继续从传说、诗词、习俗、典籍中寻找、发掘，以发现七夕节与爱情的固有关联性，许多民众也纷纷参与其中。

在这个过程中，秦观的《鹊桥仙》、白居易的《长恨歌》得到反复吟咏，"两情若是久长时，又岂在朝朝暮暮""在天愿为比翼鸟，在地愿为连理枝，天长地久有时尽，此恨绵绵无绝期"成为七夕节富含爱情因子的表征；在这个过程中，含有二人被迫分开却不离不弃的牛郎织女传说版本得到反复讲述，他们成为忠贞爱情的代表；牛郎织女传说的其他异文则被忽略，在这些异文中，或者织女与牛郎的生活并不怎么和谐，或者织女总是想方设法主动离开牛郎而终于成功。从七夕中发现爱情的过程，是将七夕

---

❶ 冯思德. 弘扬民族节庆文化的一次尝试——在河北省会首届七月七爱情节开幕式上的讲话［M］//袁学骏，等. 七夕文化论文集. 北京：中国文联出版社，2002：199-200.

❷ 今天不是"情人节". 参见网址：http://news.sina.com.cn/o/2006-07-31/09559614675s.shtml。

❸ 汪玢玲. "七夕"——中国的情人节——牛郎织女传说考释［M］//袁学骏，等. 七夕文化论文集. 北京：中国文联出版社，2002：6-17.

❹ 黄玉. 守望民间咏赞七夕——访中国民间文艺家协会主席冯骥才、乌丙安. 中华"七夕"爱情节的祝愿［M］//袁学骏，等. 七夕文化论文集. 北京：中国文联出版社，2002：1-5.

❺ 冯思德. 序［M］//袁学骏，等. 七夕文化论文集. 北京：中国文联出版社，2002：2.

节中原本零散的、潜在的爱情因子发掘出来、加以筛选、整合、阐释并集中呈现的过程。

2.3 活动内容的采借与发明

"人类的姓名是建立在实践和认知基础上的分类系统，既是社会、文化和历史的产物，也直接或间接地参与了社会、文化和历史的生产和再生产。"[1] 七夕节的重新命名让七夕节在社会上有了新的定位、内涵和指称。按照循名责实的逻辑，重新命名必然引导和激发人们在节日期间从事与爱情有关的活动。由于中国节日体系中原本没有一个情人节，中国情人节的设置原本深受外来文化的影响，所以如何过中国情人节，人们很自然地从西方情人节那里寻找合适的资源，采借西方情人节的文化符号，运用西方情人节的活动模式，将玫瑰、蛋糕、巧克力、烛光晚餐纳入自己的节日实践。与此同时，又发明出诸多具有中国元素的文化符号与节日活动，如彩虹鹊桥、相亲大会、情歌对唱、抛绣球、放飞许愿灯等。

七夕情人节因对抗西方情人节而生，本身却打上西方情人节的深深印痕，并以一种崭新的样态出现，不仅改变了活动主体，而且改变了活动内容、活动空间和活动情感，甚至改变了节日名称。如果我们将文化重构理解为一个社会群体对既有文化现象的再加工、再创造，那么七夕节从乞巧节到情人节的蜕变就是典型的文化重构。它是人们在外来文化的刺激下重新发现、发掘传统，并将其与外来文化结合在一起的结果。它融合本土资源与外来资源、传统资源与现代资源，并具有主动谋求的鲜明特征。

3 节日复兴与文化反思：七夕节当代重构的重要意义

七夕节的当代重构具有重要意义，大致可以概括为如下三点。

3.1 有效地帮助七夕节摆脱生存困境，促进了节日的重振复兴

中国传统节日植根于农业社会，源远流长，是传统社会生活的有机组成部分。近代以来，在全球化、现代化的过程中，在多种因素的共同作用下，传统节日地位明显下降，七夕节也面临生存的危机。如果说节日的活态存在，乃在于特定时代、特定区域处于不同社会地位、承担不同社会角色的社会成员在特定情境下对节日习俗活动的全部或部分实践，或者简言之，在于社会中有一定数量的人把这段时间当作"节日"来度过，那么在20世纪末期，除了个别地方，七夕这个曾经广为流行的传统节日因没有多少过节主体已名存实亡。但十几年后的今天，我们可以从花店售卖鲜花的庞大数据中、从节日尚未到来关于七夕活动的预告宣传就纷至沓来的现象中，看到这个节日的蓬勃生机。七夕节复兴态势明显，其生存状态已今非昔比。尽管七夕节复兴背后有多种因素的共同作用，也并非只有七夕这一个传统节日经历着复兴的过程，但毫无疑问，文化重构对七夕节的命运逆转起了至关重要的作用。因为正是这一重构，使爱情成为七夕节的主题，它契合了当代人的价值观念和社会需求，并因此迅速吸引了众多商家和都市男女的注意力，迅速发展壮大了过节的群体。不仅如此，这一重构还使七夕节重新回到公众的视野，不仅勾起许多中老年人对七夕节的早年记忆而使其首先在记忆中复活，而且使个别地方如甘肃西和、温州石塘、广州珠河等地仍然活跃的传统七夕节俗得到更多关注，这也促进了七夕节的当代复兴。

传统节日是一套与生活密切相关的文化，包括一系列何人在何时应做何事或不应做何事以及应如何做的规则，处于时间长河中的传统节日犹如一个生命体，有其自身生长发展演变的历史。它可以生，也可以死。由生而死通常被视为一个传统节日正常的生命历程。七夕节的蜕变表明，传统节日的命运其实更为复杂：不仅可以生，可以由生而死，而且还可以死而复生。在一定条件下，能够在传承中断后以一种崭新的样态重新回归社会成员的日常生活，为其所遵循、操演和践行。七夕节的蜕变同时表明，在多元文化背景下，对于本土传统文化的传承而言，外来文化不仅是冲突的来源、竞争的对手，它还有可能成为激活本土传统的一把钥匙，并成为传统复兴过程中可以取用的重要资源。文化重构具有起死回生、化腐朽为神奇的巨大力量。

3.2 在中国节日体系中增加爱情节的设置，丰富了社会成员的生活内容

"中国人有爱情，但中国神话中没有爱神。中国有情人，但中国节日中没有情人节。"[2] 七夕节的文

---

[1] 纳日碧力戈. 姓名 [M]. 北京：中央民族大学出版社，2000：1.
[2] 王善民，凡雨. 一个被权力扭曲的节日——"七夕"演变中民间叙事与主流话语的对抗 [M] //. 袁学骏，等. 七夕文化论文集. 北京：中国文联出版社，2002：55.

化重构填补了这一空白，凸显了爱情的意义和价值，为当代人坦率地表达爱情、寻求浪漫提供了时机。而围绕爱情主题采借和发明的多种节日活动，也极大地丰富了社会成员的生活内容。从最新的一些新闻报道中，我们已能够感知2013年七夕节（阳历8月13日）生活内容的丰富性。比如《七夕"浪漫经济"提前来袭玫瑰花预定异常火爆》一文中提到："尽管距离七夕还有段时间，但各路商家却已提前备战七夕商机……除了传统的花店、蛋糕店、电影院，各大商场、超市的七夕节气氛也日渐浓厚，一股'浪漫经济'悄然来袭。"除巧克力、蛋糕、毛绒玩具等常规礼物外，萤火虫、玫瑰香皂花、竹筒情书等许多创意类礼物也非常受年轻情侣们的欢迎。❶ 又比如，北京市通州区将于8月9～13日举办首届北京七夕节，共包括"七夕歌会"、"相爱运河"婚礼文化展、"大美运河"七夕传统文化展等17项活动；❷ 而七夕节当晚7点零7分，首都体育馆也上演了一场盛大的"七夕中国2013情歌演唱会"，主办方向社会公开征选的77对情侣参与互动，现场万余名观众与众多明星共同见证爱的表达。❸

3.3 多种社会力量共同参与了七夕节的文化重构，客观上起到了促进全社会进行文化反思的巨大作用

七夕节的文化重构归功于多种社会力量的共同参与。其中专家主要发挥了启动引领作用，并从学术角度承担了正当性的论证工作。商家也扮演了重要角色。由于传统节日往往是消费时间，以赢利为目的的商家总是会介入传统节日当中，繁荣的市场往往成为节日期间的动人景致。通常认为，商家主要是为人们按约定俗成的方式过节而提供各种物品。但在七夕节的蜕变过程中，商家不仅提供了节日主体在节日中需要的物品和服务，而且提供了节日活动的空间，尤其重要的是，他们还在引导节日主体如何过节，如何消费。通过引导如何消费，他们生产了人们对特定物品和服务的认可、偏好和需求，也生产出了节日的活动内容和文化符号，因而也就形塑了节日本身。当前七夕节在事实上成为了情人节，鲜花、巧克力、红酒、香槟、烛光晚宴、浪漫之旅等成为七夕节的文化符号，很大程度上要归因于鲜花店、巧克力经营商、红酒经营商、餐饮店和旅行社等商家，他们比其他行业的商家更加积极地以节日所需的名义推销自己的商品和服务。民众是七夕节蜕变的决定性力量，他们基于生活需要和文化自觉参与了七夕节的文化重构，不仅包括参与对正当性的讨论，更重要的是用自己的选择确证了七夕节的爱情主题，并基于追求个性、博取爱人欢心的目的而不断推陈出新并不断要求推陈出新，由此促进了七夕节节日活动的采借和发明。大众媒体则关注舆论、传递信息、发表意见、引发思考，并为各种力量的作用发挥提供了交流碰撞的平台。总之，具有不同利益诉求和目标追求的学者、民众、商家、媒体等多种社会力量通过共处在同一个中华文化空间里而互相影响，彼此激发，一起营造了七夕乞巧节向情人节蜕变所必需的文化氛围和文化空间，推动了这一蜕变所必需的正当性论证和主体性选择，为七夕节的文化重构发挥了各自独到的作用。

值得一提的是，七夕节的文化重构过程并非一团和气，在应该如何给七夕节重新命名、是否应该承认七夕节是中国情人节等方面，均存在不同意见。这些争议影响深远，颇具意义。

在中国人的观念中，"名不正则言不顺，言不顺则事不成"。关于七夕命名的争议，前文已有叙述。命名争议明显地延续了"必也正名"的思维逻辑，其背后，则是公众尤其是知识分子对一度式微的传统节日能够复兴并长期传承下去的殷切希望，是对这个节日以何种状态复兴的设计与理想，是企盼复兴的节日能够经世致用、传递文化价值、解决社会问题、维护社会秩序的良苦用心。

在是否应该承认七夕节是中国情人节方面，争议更多。比如2006年有一位学者提出"把七夕当作情人节来过不合乎传统"的观点，❹ 就引起了许多民众的强烈反对，演化成一个文化事件，掀起了一场轩然大波。又比如2009年8月14日腾讯QQ论坛上开设了一个帖子，让七夕节PK情人节。辩论设置了正反双方，正方的代表观点是："我觉得无所谓，与时俱进嘛！牛郎织女也是爱情的象征，只要有需求、有市场，人们又喜欢这种氛围，就不要这么较真，毕竟传统也是人造出来的！"反方的代表观点是："我觉得应该抵制这种崇洋的情节，原本七夕的内涵就不是情人节，因为商业利益而改变传统文化，那老祖

---

❶ http：//news.163.com/13/0725/11/94KIRG5I00014Q4P.html.
❷ 通州七夕节上演"皇室嫁女". http：//news.163.com/13/0725/03/94JLF9HD00014AED.html.
❸ 七夕对抗情人节2013情歌演唱会做爱情见证. http：//news.xinhuanet.com/ent/2013-07/22/c_125046735.htm.
❹ 刘宗迪. 七夕故事考［J］. 民间文化论坛. 2006 (5).

宗留下的东西都要慢慢变味了！"❶ 无论是正方观点还是反方观点，都有不少跟帖。比如正方 11 辩的辩词如下：

"自从新中国建立以来，新中国不断地与外国建立外交关系，在加入 WTO 后，与世界交流更加密切。随着社会发展，非主流和西方的思想也不断涌入进来，既然七夕节能够带动市场消费，我们又和乐而不为呢。而对于情人，特别是对于我国的情人而言，不是又增加了一次创造温馨、甜蜜的机会么。我们不能拒绝西方的文化，我们需要做的是发扬自己的文化传统。我们不能闭门造车，要勇于交流，把我们的文化发扬光大，让七夕节成为一个世界性的传统爱情节日。"❷

反方 3 辩则说：

"我们应该好好保护现有的传统文化，进一步弘扬'牛郎织女的爱情文化'，这是祖先遗留下来的文化遗产。我们应该好好地接续历史，把传统文化一代一代传承下去，这是中华民族世世代代都要做的事。我们要不断增强中华民族凝聚力，增强我国在世界竞争中的软实力，不要让外国人看笑话。"❸

这些围绕着七夕节是否应该向情人节靠拢的跟帖，表达出普通中国人关于如何对待本土文化与外来文化、传统文化与现代文化的认知和理解。这是公众参与七夕节文化重构的过程，也是参与文化讨论进行文化反省和文化批判的过程，同时也是公众文化自觉性、文化自信力、文化鉴赏力、文化反思力、生活自主性的培养过程。从不同观点的碰撞交锋中，我们看到这个时代的多元价值取向，纳异包容的与坚守民族本位的共同在场。我们也看到，碰撞交锋激发、推动着不同观点的持有者对多元文化及其相互关系进行着更加深入的思考。而这些思考，无论对于七夕节的未来发展，还是对于所有传统节日的传承，乃至对于当代中国文化的建设，无疑都大有助益。可以说，七夕节的文化重构客观上起到了促进全社会进行文化反思的作用，它所产生的实际影响已远远超出七夕节本身。

4 结　语

民众有权利过自己想要的节日生活，并有权利选择自己喜欢的方式。在当前中国人的生活方式、爱情观念已经发生重大变化、民族意识高涨、传统复兴已成大势的情况下，中国人要过情人节而且要过自己的情人节的诉求理应得到充分表达，也理应受到充分尊重，七夕节向中国情人节的蜕变是这种诉求的现实化，是民众凭借一定的民族文化自觉意识和纳异包容的文化开放态度进行文化选择的自然结果，不仅无可厚非，而且值得珍视。不过，在笔者看来，这并非七夕节文化重构的终点，而只是一个阶段性成果，并且也应该只是一个阶段性成果。因为尽管七夕节由乞巧节向中国情人节蜕变的文化重构具有重要意义，但也有缺陷，即一定程度形成了对传统七夕活动的遮蔽。

有着两千年历史的七夕节在其不断发展演进的过程中，早已形成了丰富多彩的习俗活动，而且具有多样的地方性表现。比如甘肃西和仍然活跃的"乞巧节"是典型的女儿节，参加者主要是未婚的少女，节日历时七天八夜，包括迎巧、祭巧、唱巧、跳麻姐姐、拜巧、迎水、巧饭会餐、照瓣卜巧和送巧等一系列仪式，且有相应的仪式歌舞相伴。❹ 浙江温岭石塘箬山村的七夕节则是"小人节"，它的主要参加者是小于 16 岁的孩童及其家人，主要活动是祭祀七女神，祈愿小孩健康发展。❺ 七夕节的众多习俗活动及其地方性表现，以及"七夕"这个具有诗意、浪漫气质的名字，具有重要的生活价值、历史价值、艺术价值和认同价值，应该有比当下更好的生存空间。换句话说，未来的七夕节应该是既吸纳外来文化的优长又有更多中国元素（不只是节日时间，还有节日活动及其所具有的文化内涵）的有机融合，能够同时作为情人节、乞巧节乃至小人节等在更大空间里共生共荣。

目前来看，突破情人节遮蔽、实现共生共荣的重要路径，是七夕节历史记忆的日常生活化和目前仍然活跃的地方七夕节俗活动一定程度的普遍化。前者是指有意识采取一些措施使曾经活态存在、目前仅

---

❶ http://bbs.vip.qq.com/t-30161-1.htm.
❷ 同上注.
❸ 同上注.
❹ 杨克栋.仇池乞巧民俗录.西和县文学艺术界合会印制.李凤鸣,韩宗坡,王亚红.西和乞巧民俗研究[M].兰州：甘肃人民出版社,2013：348-428.
❺ 陈勤建.当代七月七"小人节"的祭拜特色和源流——浙江温岭石塘箬山与台南、高雄七夕祭的比较[J].广西师范学院学报（哲学社会科学版）,2005（2）.

仅保存于文献和头脑中关于传统七夕节的历史记忆重回日常生活，得到实践。后者是指有意识采取一些措施使当下为个别地方民众所传承享用的七夕习俗在更大的空间内被更多的人所共享和传承。这两种路径无疑都存在一定的障碍。前者需要克服的主要是时间变换所带来的挑战：毕竟历史记忆中的七夕节是传统社会的七夕节，更多体现了农耕社会的理想和追求，而我们目前所面临的是工业文明、现代社会。后者需要克服的主要是空间位移所带来的挑战：地方七夕节俗活动毕竟是特定空间内生长发育出来并适合其水土的节日文化，普遍化则意味着将其置于非本土的环境之中。而这也决定了无论选择哪一种路径，都不可能是传统七夕节俗和特定地方七夕节俗的全面照搬，而只能是以其为资源从中汲取若干元素、结合其他元素重新加以组织并应用实践的文化重构过程。

未来的七夕节重构仍然需要包括学者在内的多种力量共同参与。需要说明的是，学者既没有权利也没有能力要求民众选择专家学者偏爱的节日生活和过节方式，但专家学者可以通过研究提出自己的观点，从而为人们如何过节提供更多的选择项。这是学者的社会责任，也是学者的社会贡献所在。

媒体融合条件下的学术期刊新媒体转型

周小华

在媒介融合的新形势下，如何运用新媒体技术，有效利用网络集聚、集合和集成效应，发挥学术研究与学术期刊的内容资源优势，在学术研究体系内，将传统媒体与新媒体相融合，将学术研究成果与成果的终端需求用户直接联系，在思维观念、运作模式、产品呈现上实现真正意义上的转型，形成以新媒体技术为平台，内容相互转化，终端共享，传播体系健全，受众广泛的学术研究与学术期刊共生平台，打造学术期刊和学术研究共同体多方共赢的生态圈，是学术期刊在新媒体转型进程中重点关注的问题。这种平台模式，目前在世界范围内还找不到成功的模板，需要我们在理论和实践中加以探索。

1 新媒体平台上学术期刊与学术研究的融合现状

1.1 传统媒体时代的学术期刊与学术研究关系分析

学术研究是学术期刊的源头活水，学术期刊是学术研究成果的传播渠道之一。无论在传统或新媒体中，学术研究的提升在某种程度上促进了学术期刊的发展，学术期刊影响力的大小也反映了国家学术研究的发展程度，在中国学术研究的发展进程中，学术期刊发挥着举足轻重的作用。在学术研究的生态圈中，学术期刊是其中的一个重要组成部分。

在传统媒体时代，研究者没有更多的渠道与方式进行彼此间的学术交流及成果转换，但学者的学术观点和学术成果，又有交流、展示和传播的需要，于是，作为学术信息传递中介的学术期刊（学术著作）产生了，就这样，学术研究以知识产品（专著、论文、报告等）的形式呈现其最终成果。随着学者及研究机构研究成果的逐渐丰富，学术期刊和学术出版也不断发展着，学术期刊和学术出版是学术研究的重要传播媒体之一，"刊号"和"书号"则成为学术研究成果是否属于"正式出版"的身份证。

1.2 新媒体的出现结束了学术期刊对学术成果传播的绝对垄断地位

在学术期刊上发表论文，绝对不是学术研究的终点，学术研究的目的应该是发现问题和解决问题，在学术期刊上发表论文只是学术研究成果的传播途径之一。

随着互联网的发展，基于学术传播的工具、手段及渠道的更新，学术期刊与学术出版对学术成果的交流、展示和传播，将不会永远是"唯一"，因为现在几乎所有的研究者都能够比较容易地获得从前只有学术期刊和学术出版编辑者才能拥有的工具、技能与手段。在这里，我们借用纽约大学新闻学教授杰·罗森对新闻传播所提出的"不在场"理论，在新媒体平台上的学术传播，完全可以让学术期刊的编辑和刊物"不在场"。由此，我们不可忽视的是，学术成果的传播方式正在发生重构，只要国家放开"刊号"和"书号"的限制，或者放开"刊号"和"书号"对学术研究成果的惟一社会认可价值，改变现有的学术研究评价体系，突破现有的学术研究管理模式，国家根据新媒体的传播规律和要求，重新建立和健全一套适合新媒体传播的学术成果传播体系，形成一套行之有效的学术成果评价体系，那么，谁是学术成果的出版者以及学术成果发表在什么期刊上，就不再重要了，重要的是所传播的学术观点或学术成果的意义。只要人们就学术传播的基本功能和目标达成共识，那么传播学术成果的手段、渠道、媒介都只是技术问题而已。由此，传统体制下自娱自乐的学术期刊，将不能完全担当起互联网时代真正意义上的学术传播的重任，长期以来学术期刊或学术出版对学术成果传播的垄断发布权面临瓦解。

当然，我们所说的学术期刊对学术成果传播的垄断发布权的瓦解，是指传统体制下作坊式运作的学

[基金项目] 2013年北京市哲学社会科学规划项目"信息网络化条件下政府形象传播研究"（项目编号：13KDB012）。
[作者简介] 周小华，《北京联合大学学报》编辑部主编、编审。

术期刊组织形式和经营方式。在这里我们必须明确的是，即使在"人人都是麦克风"的新媒体平台上，社交网站也不能替代学术期刊的发布平台，学术成果的正式发表，不同于新闻传播，不是任何个人和机构都可以做的，它必须有专业门槛和标准，其中编辑和同行专家评审的角色不能缺位。编辑通过他们深厚的学术背景、长期养成的学术判断力、严谨的科研态度及开阔的视野，用严格的同行评审制度及录用标准，去判断学术成果的品质，对作者所撰写的研究成果，负有把关的责任；具备专业特长的同行专家的评审可以保证所发表成果的学术性和公正性。学术出版是需要门槛的，门槛实质上也就是准入机制。在发达国家，学术成果的发表也几乎是由专业学术期刊所"垄断"，那些不适合做学术成果发表的期刊社会逐步被淘汰。如果学术成果的发表门槛缺失或过低，就会造成"学术垃圾""学术不端"和"假学术"的泛滥。

1.3 学术研究的规律性，要求学术研究和成果传播的内容和功能在新媒体平台上实现交叉呈现

学术研究具有其自身的复杂体系，它包括三个主要环节，一是科学发现和知识创新；二是将创新的知识孵化为新技术；三是对新技术的采用。而这三个环节，涉及产学研不同主体间的合作与互动：大学和专业科研机构提供研究成果；各种类型的孵化器（科技园、创意园区）将成果孵化为技术；企业将学术研究转化为现实。而学术期刊，在学术研究的各个环节中，都是他们之间信息的交流与传递者。由此，这个传递者没有理由长期游离于学术圈而独立存在，更不只是简单地将各专业的学术期刊嵌入到相关学术研究的网站中，而是要建立学术期刊与学术共同体双方共同的平台和机制，研究者与编辑者在同一平台上密切协作，两方面主体在学术研究的各领域、层次和进度上协同作用，借用互联网的链接，借力整合学术期刊与学术研究的平台资源，用检索让内容信息的碎片互联互通，让学术研究各自分属的内容相互连通，实现对学术期刊所涉及的学术研究整体内容的有效把握，让学术领域和学术研究成果传播的内容和功能实现交叉呈现。

1.4 互联网时代学术研究范式的改变和学科间的交叉融合，要求新媒体平台的学术期刊必须通过链接服务实现信息的有效利用

在互联网时代，"与学术期刊处于同一环境体系的学术创新模式、学术研究范式、知识形态、知识获取、知识交流及处理机制的改变，都直接影响着学术期刊的生存和发展环境。""特别是学术研究的方法，正从过去的单一领域向全领域的方向发展，各学科间的研究视角和研究方法的相互借鉴，学科间的深入交叉融合，使研究得以不断深入。"[ii]同时，由于互联网传播的双向性，过去单向度被动的"受众"概念也受到挑战。这样，大众对信息的需求就呈现出多角度、全方位、双向度和智能化。如果说在以"内容为王"的传统媒体时代以及互联网初级时期，学术期刊最大的优势就是内容，但在大数据时代，互联网的海量信息，已经远远超出了受众的注意力所能关注的能力，"内容"在互联网中的价值比例已经下降，取而代之的是如何通过信息服务，实现有效信息的链接。而传统学术期刊，包括目前以数字化形式出现的学术期刊，它们只是独立的期刊网站或期刊群，最多也就是个期刊数据库，还没有真正融入学术共同体中，还不能反映学术研究的全貌，提供更完整、更方便的信息链接服务，更不能实现学术研究所需要的有效的信息提供、畅通的传播渠道，以及有效的媒体经营和学术成果转化经营。

新媒体正在改变学术研究和学术成果传播间的关系、结构和方式，也在改变研究者对成果传播的需求，在新媒体的推动下，"世界各国传统媒体纷纷进军新媒体领域，在媒体融合战略中不断推进媒体的组织架构调整、体制机制改革和传播体系创新。"[iii]这种局势在给我们带来新的发展机遇的同时，也让我们面临着严峻的挑战。2014年8月18日，中央全面深化改革领导小组第四次会议审议通过了《关于推动传统媒体和新兴媒体融合发展的指导意见》。该指导意见对媒体的融合发展提出了五项要求，即立足于整合资源、研究设计传播渠道、注重个性化服务、强化互动功能、要有商业模式。从理念上、机制上、技术上、流程上、体制上融合，实现信息内容、技术应用、平台终端、人才队伍的共享融通，加速传统媒体和新兴媒体融合，优势互补、一体发展。

2 新媒体时代的学术成果传播方式面临重构

学术期刊在新媒体的转型方面还存在不少问题，需要我们在实践中加以解决。

2.1 从体系上看，学术期刊平台与学术共同体，在新媒体平台上缺乏关联性和协调性，还处于"疏离"的状态，没有形成一个协同共生的系统

由"三网融合"带来的"媒信通"产业已经形成，新媒体的发展给整个学术研究生态圈带来了巨大的影响，"平台"和"跨界"成为互联网思维的特征之一。在互联网思维引导下学术期刊的协同创新，是学术期刊和学术共同体在新媒体平台上各要素的组合，它包括内容创新、技术创新、市场创新和组织制度创新。但目前，在新媒体平台上，学术期刊平台与学术研究平台，还始终处于"疏离"的状态，还没有成融合成一个协同共生的系统。

2.2 从平台模式上看，数字化学术期刊还没有实现真正意义上的新媒体转型

我国学术期刊主要分布在高校、科研机构、出版社和行业协会，如大学多为综合类学术期刊；研究机构和行业协会多为专业期刊；出版社多为系列期刊等。国际上较有影响的学术期刊则主要分布在各著名的大型出版集团及相关研究机构，如施普林格（Springer）出版公司、牛津大学出版社（OUP）、爱思唯尔（Elsevier）出版社、泰勒—弗朗西斯（Taylor & Francis）出版集团、自然出版集团（NPG）、威立—布莱克唯尔（Wiley Blackwell）出版集团、英国物理学会出版社（IOPP）等。国内外在学术期刊的网络出版方面，已经开始了探索，其发展的路径基本是：由传统的"期刊"到"网站"，再到"数据库"，上升为综合网站，这是一个学术期刊的传统媒体与新媒体融合的逐级向上发展过程，后者在包括前者的同时，又是前者的升级版和高级版，同时，后者又在不断地颠覆或替代前者。即使这样，在学术共同体与学术期刊公共平台的建设方面，还没有成功的模式。国际上，最接近这个模式的如 Sharon Rogers 和 Charlene Hurt 在 1990 年提出建立一个跨学科的学术交流网络出版系统，用于网络电子期刊的出版，[iv]但这个系统也只是一个学术期刊的工作系统，没有扩大到研究领域。美国物理学会在《2020 年电子出版展望》报告中，提出由物理学科的期刊社将其出版物以超媒体文稿的形式提交到国家物理数据库中，[v]这种模式只是对专业学术期刊进行了横向整合。与这种整合模式类似的有施普林格（Springer），它把在线期刊、电子书和参考书全部放在一个平台上实现互联和增值，同时通过"在线优先出版"，实现了将研究成果快速推向市场的出版理念。[vi]1999 年，John W. T. Smith 提出了论文作者将自己所撰写的文章提交至一个服务器，由一个独立的文章质量评估组织来实施和完成论文的发表。[vii]2010 年，爱思唯尔（Elsevier）也提出了"按文章出版"，即在一篇文章的最终版编排完成之后就直接将之放至网络平台上正式出版，这种"在线优先出版"能使文章得到更早的引用。这种期刊的分解出版模式也仅仅是提供了一个学术期刊整合编辑出版流程的大平台。美国科学公共图书馆（PLoS）则提出了开放存取出版模式，即开放共享、开放访问、开放阅览，这也是学术期刊的单向信息，没有形成学术研究的互动。在我国，目前学术期刊的网络出版主要有五种模式：一是加入大型的数据库。这个模式只是简单地将纸质内容数字化；二是编辑部自建网站。这个模式沿袭着作坊式编辑部的体制，所起的作用大多只能算是一个编辑部的审稿、编辑、出版和发行流程工作平台而已；三是创建同行专业学术期刊权威数据库。这种窄众化的横向联合，相对于综合性大型权威数据库来说，大部分内容属于重复建设。四是"中国高校系列专业期刊"的做法。它虽然突破了传统学术期刊一校一刊、各自为政的局面，但也还是纸质版学术期刊的集合体，同时学术共同体的内容在这里也没有得以呈现。五是由中国社会科学杂志社牵头建立的"中国社会科学期刊网络群"。这个网络群同样没有脱离纸质内容简单转化为网络内容的窠臼，同样不属于真正意义上的网络出版。

2.3 数字出版从观念、技术手段到体制机制上，都没有实现真正意义上的新媒体转型

我国的学术期刊的新媒体转型，还处于利用数字技术，实现刊物采编印发的全流程信息化，将纸质媒体的内容简单数字化的阶段，学术期刊的纸质版和电子版的内容大多一致，只是介质不同，即将纸质换成了智能电脑和显示屏，而没有在流程上实现"再造"。作为专业的学术成果发表平台，数字化的学术期刊与纸质化的相一致，还属于主流平台，它包括学术成果的传播需要按照学术出版的固定格式要求，规范摘要、关键词、图表、参考文献，经过编委会、同行评议，以保证学术成果出版的专业性和严谨性外，还包括国家政策规定的在有正式刊号的学术期刊发表论文与研究人员的各项评价指标相挂钩。到目前为止，在我国的学术研究评价体系中，是以刊定文，即论文发表的数量和所发表学术期刊级别，

已经成为衡量学者学术水平的标准,是学者获得职称评定、项目评审、职务晋升、争取更多的研究资源、赢得学术荣誉的重要途径。也正是以这种评价方式,将学术研究与学术期刊紧密联系起来,也使得大多数规模小、无法投入足够的资金进行数字化建设的学术期刊只能够在自己的一亩三分地上自娱自乐。

2.4 缺乏科学的顶层设计,重复建设、学术信息不平等循环现在严重

在我国,如果说新华网、人民网等大型新媒体平台,是由国家财政扶持起来的主流媒体,那么,在学术研究平台上,国家还没有扶持和建立统一的新媒体平台。为了适应互联网时代的发展,国内多个期刊社、出版社、数字出版基地,都分别建设起学术期刊的数字平台或公共服务平台,所耗费的财力和人力也不少,但由于资金、技术和人员有限,国内期刊社大多都将"千刊一面"的纸质期刊变成了"千网一面"的网刊,而一些学术期刊的数据库或公共服务平台则是功能相似重复,标准不一,如中国知网、维普、万方数据等,即使这样,他们目前也是我国学术期刊数字出版收益的主要来源,全国各教育、科研单位的图书馆,基本都订购了一个以上的学术期刊数据库。对中文学术期刊数据库来说,全国各大图书馆购买最多的是中国知网、维普和万方三大数据库,在外文数据库中,购买最多的是Springer、EBSCO、Elsevier等数据库平台商旗下的期刊数据库。国内学术期刊社也大都加入了中国知网、维普和万方数据库,并且在数字化建设方面,国内学术期刊几乎完全依赖于大型数据库。部分国外数据库,也同我国的部分期刊社建立了合作关系。数据库平台商与学术期刊社的合作,在客观上提高了学术期刊的数字化程度,但他们的根本目的还在于自身的商业利益。由于中国知网、维普和万方等数据库平台商分别与部分期刊社签订了"独家协议",由此,他们各自所收入的学术期刊,虽然绝大多数是重复的,但各自也都有部分的缺失。各大型图书馆为了保障文献的完整率,不得不将三个数据库全部购买,无形中降低了数据库资源的利用率,增加了数据的使用成本。这样,在学术期刊的数字化进程中,形成了一个生产与收益的信息不平等循环现象:由国家支付科研人员的工资、资助产出学术研究成果,同时还资助学术出版,期刊社(或出版社)用国家的经费编辑、出版和支付稿酬,最后国家(图书馆等)再出钱从中外数据商手中购买本属于国家的东西,利益链的终端落在了数据平台商一方,业内将这种学术信息恶性循环的现象,借用经济学的名词称为"斯蒂格利茨怪圈"。

2.5 缺乏统一布局和标准,缺乏完善的学术研究和学术期刊评价体系

学术研究网站之于学术期刊,是个天然的大数据库,每一个研究机构的网站都是一个数据中心,但长期以来,都零散地分布在各个教学机构和科研机构,无论国际还是国内,大多都是以学术期刊为主体的数据库网站。之中链接有学术机构的网站;或者是在学术机构的网站中链接着与其专业相关联的期刊网站。由于所投入数字化平台建设的财力分散,都还没有成功的学术期刊与学术研究融合的平台模式,没有一个完整的学术研究与产出的主体展现平台,更没有形成真正意义上的学术研究与研究成果传播的网络生态环境。

同时,各个网站之间、各大型数据库之间,缺乏整体性的统一标准,缺乏统一的布局和长远目标,不仅浪费了大量的建设资金,也不便于具体、深层次、整合性地利用数据,对实现内容的共享交互操作带来了一定的困难,无法充分挖掘出学术传播的内容价值。

在公共平台上,缺乏完善的学术研究和学术期刊评价体系。对学术成果的评价与对期刊的评价,本属于相互联系的不同范畴,学术研究与办学术期刊,有各自不同的规律。但是在目前,国内的7大核心期刊(或来源期刊)遴选体系和国际公认的六大检索系统所属的评选机构,将学术期刊评价、学术研究评价以及学术国际化相连接。即,评价学术成果的标准就是在"核心期刊"上发表文章,学术研究国际化的标志和评价标准就是在国际公认的六大检索系统的期刊上发表文章。这个标准同时又作为大学和专业排行的依据以及获得政府学术资源的重要依据,所以成为各高校及研究机构争相追逐的目标。期刊的"等级"决定了论文的"等级",这种将理科、工科、医科、社会科学和人文学科都一刀切、量化、外在的学术评价体制,不符合学术研究中各学科的内在逻辑。由此,必须在学术共同体与学术期刊公共平台上,建立学术共同体内的学术评价和学术期刊评价体制和价值标准。

总之,新媒体不是单纯地为学术成果的传播提供一个简单的数字"版面",学术期刊不能只是消极被动地成为"展示"现有学术成果的窗口,而应当成为学术研究的参与者、学术前沿信息的及时发布

者、服务者和提供者，这样，学术期刊与学术研究在新媒体平台上才能走向融合。

3 学术期刊公共平台模式探讨

数字出版公共平台的建构是对技术、内容、体制问题的综合解决，在内容寻找平台和渠道的同时，平台也在探讨如何增加新的表现形式与传播手段。目前，各个学科间互相渗透，在学术共同体与学术期刊公共平台上进行解构、构造和构架，虽然它不能代替学科本身的专门研究，但是，作为各学科平台的构架，它能够站在传播的高度，提供研究的框架、规则和逻辑，将学术研究的各个领域、学科、单位、圈子等之间打通，让彼此之间有沟通和对话的渠道，让学术成果得以更有效地传播。正如喻国明认为的："传媒的概念就是，以传播为介质的这样的一种配置社会资源、商业资源及一切社会生活的整合架构，这就是传媒。"[viii]

3.1 公共平台的基本定位和目标

学术共同体与学术期刊公共平台的基本定位是用互联网思维探讨融入学术共同体的学术期刊公共平台的新格局，整合国内外学术期刊与学术研究的资源，创造方便快捷的连接服务，强化用户参与和分享，打造以学术期刊为纽带的产学研合作、人才对接、协同创新的互动平台。在该平台上，参与单位既要维护好自己的"一亩三分地"，又要走出去与各种资源进行对接整合，去搜索与自己相匹配的相关资源，发挥自己所长，在融合中发展。将传统媒体与新媒体相融合，将学术研究成果与成果的终端需求相连接，实现学术研究"全过程、全媒体、全媒介"的传播。这种连接将创造学术共同体与学术期刊公共平台的新格局，产生出超越现有学术期刊平台的传播价值和商业价值，造就学术期刊在为学术研究服务中的巨大可能性。这个融入学术共同体的学术期刊公共平台，不仅能深刻揭示学术研究对人类科学和社会进步以及人类精神世界的影响，还能提出有价值的问题，引导未来的学术研究方向，是一个反映学术研究的科学思想及人文内涵相结合的平台，也是一个集学术性、思想性和新闻性于一体的平台。

3.2 公共平台的特点分析

学术共同体与学术期刊公共平台的特点，概括说来就是连接、整合、开放、共享。互联网的价值体现在连接当中，连接就是互联网本身的逻辑，在关联当中形成服务、形成价值。在学术共同体与学术期刊公共平台上，通过对编辑机构的整合、阅读形式的整合及效益链条的整合，统和学术研究内容，并渗透到其他终端平台，达到学术成果传播与学术研究过程的资源共享、现代技术手段与编辑手段的共享，打造学术研究的"全过程、全媒体、全媒介"产业链，实现该平台的连接价值。

3.3 公共平台的构成要素

在这个平台上，将不同系统、不同专业和学科集群和集约化，同时与国外学术共同体（如学术机构和学术期刊数据库等）相链接，使资源优势最大化，产生叠加效应。平台的建构要素，一是在技术层面的基础网络平台、编辑出版发行的二级工作平台、终端平台、全媒介平台，以及版权代理、广告运营、电子支付、技术支持等相关辅助平台。二是汇集全球学术期刊和学术研究成果内容资源，建立庞大的内容数据库，如中外期刊数据库、研究人员数据库、研究机构数据库、研究项目数据库、各类相关数字发布等。三是聚集与学术研究相关的机构层面的二级平台，包括国家和政府的相关体系、教育体系、研究机构体系、相关学会等民间团体、社会化产学研协同合作体系的相关机构等。四是在成果呈现上实现方便检索、在一定权限下实现开放获取、定制服务、按需印刷、线上线下互动、一次编辑多渠道出版的全媒体、全媒介呈现等功能。五是保护知识产权，实现信息收费。六是构造平台的价值链和商业模式。七是国际化问题。这是一个多语种、国际化的开放平台。

3.4 公共平台的优势

一是有利于实现学术研究与学术传播的跨界、跨学科融合发展。融入学术共同体的学术期刊公共平台提供了产学研协同发展的基础，在该公共平台的大数据基础上，打通研究领域之间、研究领域与研究机构之间、研究机构与研究机构之间、研究机构与媒体之间、研究机构与产业之间、媒体与产业之间、产业与产业之间的界线，各个研究专业由于聚合，使得内容更丰富、细化和深化，为产学研的线上资源和线下资源提供"OTO"的结合和互动，不仅建立了研究与传播的共同体，同时也建立了产学研与传播相结合的互利共赢的利益共同体，以实现跨界、跨学科融合发展。

二是有利于学术期刊与学术研究的相互借力发展。在这个系统中，学术期刊在论文质量、学术视野、理论深度、作者层次、审稿流程、国际化程度等方面，在学术出版的"流程再造"方面，甚至包括学术期刊编辑部体制机制的改革等诸方面，将有极大的提升空间。学术期刊不再是简单地呈现给读者一本杂志、一篇文章或一次阅读，而是将专业的、精细的、不同形式的服务延伸到从学术研究到成果运用的各方面和各层面。同时，这个平台上的期刊编辑部，再也不是单打独斗的小团队了，它实现了专家群共享、作者群共享、翻译群共享、读者群共享等，作者与编辑部实现了投稿与发稿的双向选择。平台所设置的专题研讨、话题领袖等在这个平台上可以与国内外学术机构和研究者进行充分的互动。尽管如此，学术期刊在这个平台上，也仅仅是该系统的一个标配，虽然也起着关键性的作用，但是已经不是目前的学术成果传播的终点和主体。

三是有利于提升我国学术研究成果的国际显示度和影响力。一直以来，学术期刊都在努力通过国际合作，融入国际学术共同体；而国际学术机构和知名出版商同样也在积极寻求与中国学术期刊及学术研究的合作机会。[ix] 在这个融合平台上，我国的学术期刊，将有更多的渠道和机会开展国际合作，学者和学术期刊的从业人员，能与国际学者、学术期刊编辑和出版商建立更有效的沟通、联系与对话。更重要的是，在这个平台上，能让大家开阔视野，立足全球学术研究的制高点，利用世界先进的理论、技术和方法，在吸收的同时进行有效地传播，提升中国学术研究成果的国际影响力。

学术研究与学术期刊在新媒体平台上的融合，使产学研及其传播的主体在这里交汇和互动。学术研究与学术期刊在新媒体平台上的互动。在这个平台上，传统的学术研究与成果发表的边界被改变，形成"内容—平台—用户"的最短渠道。

4 推进学术期刊在学术共同体中的新媒体转型

在深化文化体制改革的背景下，中国进入了一个信息传播技术持续演进、国家信息传播战略不断升级的发展时期。媒介产品形态的更替、学术成果传播模式的变化以及受众的变化，使得媒介环境发生了根本性的变化，人们对媒介的依赖程度也随之加强，在学术共同体中实现学术期刊的新媒体转型，是一项系统工程，涉及流程再造、体制机制改革、价值重塑、品牌创新、边界拓展、战略设计等方方面面，必须加快思想观念的转变，以国家的力量，推动它的生成和发展。

中共中央《关于推动传统媒体和新兴媒体融合发展的指导意见》，给我们提出了新的紧迫的任务，在大数据和媒体融合的背景下，进一步探索中国学术期刊的新媒体发展规律，为推动中国学术期刊在学术共同体中建设新媒体传播体系，很有必要。

4.1 加快从"传统媒体思维"向"互联网思维"的转变

其一，链接和服务思维。过去我们通常把学术传播理解为学术成果的内容传播，在学术共同体与学术期刊公共平台上，应该是以内容为中心，同时"加入越来越多非内容的服务、非内容的价值创造的传播与服务，而且它的非内容的价值创造远比内容带来的市场价值大得多。"[x]

其二，平台思维。要打破现有学术期刊编辑部单位的小而全机制，同时打破学术期刊平台与学术共同体平台"两张皮"的状态，树立学术期刊与学术共同体一体化发展思维，在内容、渠道、终端、技术、手段、资金及人才队伍上，实现共享融通，形成一体化的组织结构、传播体系和管理体制，这是中国学术期刊新媒体转型的内在要求和基本方向。[xi]

其三，跨界和流量思维。我国目前的学术期刊平台，还停留在数字化阶段，而"数字化"并不是数据化。真正意义上的新媒体，不是简单地将纸质版的内容，通过电子版在互联网上简单呈现。这种呈现虽然也能通过搜索引擎找到信息，但这种由搜索引擎所带来的信息，带有明显的纯技术和平面化的局限。学术共同体与学术期刊公共平台，其不同数据之间的内在联系，能建立起用户和信息之间的有效联系，并通过对数据的挖掘和分析，找出不同事物之间的相关关系，实现跨媒体、跨行业、跨所有制、跨地域的跨界多元化以及全过程、全媒体、全媒介、立体、互动传播，进而实现学术研究的最大价值。

其四，社会化、公众体系思维。在传播体系的构建上，用"互联网思维"改革传统媒体的组织结构、传播体系和管理体系，突破现有行政体系的限制，从行政体系转变到公众体系，以公众需求为出发点,打破传统媒体的"分立化"行政体系,在新媒体中,将不同学科之间、不同部门之间、不同期刊社之间、不同管理层级之间打通,塑造"一体化"的传播体系。

其五,大数据和迭代思维。在资源的整合及边界的延伸方面,从单一媒介到媒介与学术共同体的融合,首先应做好整合工作,在发挥骨干科研机构和期刊的作用的同时,应尽可能加大规模;其次,在平台建设的原则上,要遵循学术成果的传播规律和新媒体发展规律,按照新媒体的规律来融合平台,要先研究新媒体的优势,再将学术研究与学术期刊的资源优势相匹配。

其六,极致和简约思维。学术共同体与学术期刊公共平台的建设,由于涉及的面多且广,更要注重每个步骤、每个环节、每个节点以及每个页面设计的极致,达到阅读的权威、方便及简约。这就需要处理好五个关系:整体性与单一性的统一、顶层设计与分层设计的衔接、统一性与差异性的结合、长期性与阶段性的有序推进以及关联性、协调性和法律的刚性协调。

4.2 政府的推动是实现学术期刊新媒体转型的关键

政府对科学研究的指导及投入的合理性和科学性程度,体现了政府治理体系和治理能力水平。当前,国家鼓励媒体融合,在学术期刊层面,国家肩负着引领、规划和助推学术期刊数字化、国际化发展的重要使命。在学术共同体中实现学术期刊的新媒体转型进程中,由于牵涉的参与行业、单位和个人不仅数多而且面广、启动建设阶段的资金需求大,在开始阶段,需要政府的大力扶持,通过积极的鼓励政策加以引导,通过资金的投入搭建公共平台,推动平台的形成和发展。

政府对在学术共同体中实现学术期刊的新媒体转型的介入和推动,可以从如下方面着手。

第一,做好顶层设计。在国家层面的目标确定方面:中央《关于推动传统媒体和新兴媒体融合发展的指导意见》强调:"要着力打造一批形态多样、手段先进、具有竞争力的新型主流媒体,建成几家拥有强大实力和传播力、公信力、影响力的新型媒体集团。"融合的基本路径是"以中央主要媒体为龙头,以重点项目为抓手,坚持传统媒体和新兴媒体优势互补、一体发展,坚持先进技术为支撑、内容建设为根本,推动传统媒体和新兴媒体在内容、渠道、平台、经营、管理等方面深度融合。"融合的主要方法是"重组媒体内部组织结构,构建现代化的立体传播体系,建立科学有效的媒体管理体制。"[xii]明确了媒体融合的方向和路径。

第二,在国家的政策支持方面:2014年4月,国家新闻出版广电总局、财政部颁布的《关于推动新闻出版业数字化转型升级的指导意见》中提出的政府重点支持如下方面的工作:开展数字化转型升级标准化工作、提升数字化转型升级技术装备水平、加强数字出版人才队伍建设、探索数字化转型升级新模式。该"指导意见"在财政扶持方面提出:"加大财政对新闻出版业数字化转型升级的支持力度,将新闻出版业数字化转型升级项目作为重大项目纳入中央文化产业发展专项资金扶持范围,分步实施、逐年推进。发挥财政资金杠杆作用,推动重点企业的转型升级工作,引导企业实施转型升级项目。"[xiii]

第三,在学术共同体与学术期刊公共平台建设的初始阶段,需要政府的扶持性投入。一是政府数据的开放,在政府的数据开放和政府采购:政府的相关政策信息、学术信息和有关数据在学术共同体与学术期刊公共平台中有着重要的价值。二是政府采购,政府采购学术共同体与学术期刊公共平台的数字资源,能解决目前学术期刊数据库功能重复、建设重复、购买重复、资金投入重复、建设力量分散等问题,优化资源配置,走出"斯蒂格利茨怪圈"。三是政府的财政扶持,学术共同体与学术期刊公共平台在起始的平台建设阶段,必须得到政府财政的扶持性支持,用以进行内容资源建设、软件配备和硬件购置,为建设数字内容资源投送与运营服务平台奠定基础,待这个平台形成了成熟的运营模式,再依靠自身的力量发展壮大。

4.3 在学术期刊的新媒体转型中必须进行"流程再造"

"流程再造"是指在媒体融合中,通过对新媒体传播流程的再设计,以期取得在成本、质量、服务、速度等关键绩效上的重大突破。建立学术共同体与学术期刊公共平台,将为学术研究、学术成果传播以及学术成果的转换应用,提供专业的、全方位的、有影响力的学术研究全过程信息平台。陆小华认为:"互联网的两个核心要素,就是便利性匹配和超细分匹配",[xiv]只有在同一个协同创新系统中,才能在流程再造中实现学术研究与成果运用的高匹配度。学术研究的目的不是发表论文,而是成果的有效运用,研究与运用的匹配,才是新媒体的关键所在。

其一，通过搭建精细化的管理平台，重构组织机制和管理结构。"学术共同体"的概念不同于"产业价值链"，学术共同体与学术期刊在新媒体平台上的融合是一个系统工程，只有平台是不够的，还必须有良好的组织机制和管理结构。在网站构建中，要设计精细的、统一的多媒体编辑出版工作平台，对加入平台的单位、作者、出版者、内容资源、渠道资源、版权资源、品牌资源等方面，通过先进的电子技术，设计有效可行的程序，实现精细化管理。建立标准统一的学术期刊编辑库、审稿专家库、作者库、技术研发库等，在新媒体流程中共享资源，实现学术研究的传播信息一次编辑、一次同行专家评审，多种生成、多元传播。在平台上要加强国际合作，在合作中借鉴国外经验，瞄准和利用世界最新技术推动融合发展，通过多种形式，充分利用别人成熟的技术、平台、渠道、手段等借力推进，实现更好更快发展。

其二，要建立扁平化管理机制，激发新的发展活力。目前，传统学术期刊大都还属于分立单干的小、散、弱的现状，与之相联系的体制机制问题，还不能适应学术期刊与学术共同体在新媒体平台上融合发展的要求。我们必须重构包括学术期刊在内的学术共同体传播生产流程，各研究机构和期刊单位要从实际出发，积极探索适合自己的融合发展模式，将个体的发展，融合到平台的发展中去。同时，通过整合并升级包括编辑出版工作系统在内的学术研究网站，解决长期以来形成的学术期刊同质化现象。在此基础上，通过流程的再造，重构学术研究与学术期刊的评价标准。

4.4 建立健全机关法律法规，严格保护知识产权

作为一个统一开放的新媒体服务平台，在资源共享的过程，必然同时会产生大量的版权资源在不同角色中流转，而由于新媒体出版尚属新兴领域，现行的法律法规对新媒体，有些已不具备现实的可操作性。虽然2012年全国人大常委会已通过了《关于加强网络信息保护的决定》，工信部也有保护个人信息的新规等，但作为法律法规体系，还没有健全和完善。比如，如何在确保知识产权的前提下，加入国际开放获取的行列等问题，还缺乏新的比较完善的法规条文。由此，在学术共同体与学术期刊公共平台上，很容易导致各种不同类型的版权保护问题。由此，必须强化法律意识，明确合作主体，制定相应健全完善的相关的法律法规，建立新的著作权管理保障体系，做好网络授权，规避版权纠纷，促进版权产品的使用，强化网络监管，提升消费者合法使用版权产品的意识，科学严密地保护知识产权，使著作权人的利益最大化。

4.5 探索可持续发展的商业模式

一是发挥财政资金的扶持作用，比如，申请国家关于科研和出版方面的基金、关于支持文化创意产业发展的资金等。二是争取该平台上参与单位的资金、民间资本、社会资本等的支持。三是各类数据库的收入。四是探索平台资源与成果转换对接、平台资源与资本对接的新机制。在研究成果与成果转换以及与金融的对接过程中，探索平台新的盈利增长模式与途径，比如，政府采购、各研究机构订阅、成果孵化、成果转化、专利、国际版权贸易等。通过以上资本的扶持，壮大学术期刊新媒体平台的产业链，形成"政府引导、市场主导、企业主体"的发展模式，实现学术期刊平台的实体与金融资本、社会资本、高等学校资源、研究机构资源及民间资本的战略合作与对接，形成多种所有制共同发展的格局。[xv]

参考文献

[1] 洪银兴. 科技创新路线图与创新型经济各个阶段的主体［J］. 南京大学学报（哲学·人文科学·社会科学版），2010（2）.

[2] 周小华. "大数据"时代中国学术期刊的转型与发展机遇［J］. 科技与出版，2014（4）.

[3] 刘笑盈，康秋洁. 转型迎战数字化大潮，没有完成时［N］. 人民日报，2014-07-17.

[4] 王华生. 数字网络环境下学术期刊传播方式的变革及因应策略［J］. 河南大学学报（社会科学版），2011（6）.

[5] 王华生. 数字网络环境下学术期刊传播方式的变革及因应策略［J］. 河南大学学报（社会科学版），2011（6）.

[6] 苗晨霞. 以客户为中心：国际出版社的重要理念［N］. 中国社会科学报，2011-03-29.

[7] 臧国全. 网络电子期刊出版模式研究［J］. 中国图书馆学报，2003（1）.

[8] 高海珍. 喻国明：未来的世界离不开传播学［J］. 新闻与写作，2014（8）.

[9] 朱剑. 学术评价、学术期刊与学术国际化——对人文社会科国际化热潮的冷思考［J］. 清华大学学报：哲学社会科学版（京），2009（5）：126~137.

[10] 高海珍. 喻国明：未来的世界离不开传播学［J］. 新闻与写作，2014（8）.

[11] 刘奇葆. 加快推动传统媒体和新兴媒体融合发展［N］. 人民日报，2014-04-23.

[12] 刘奇葆. 加快推动传统媒体和新兴媒体融合发展［N］. 人民日报，2014-04-23.

[13] 中央政府门户网站. http://www.gov.cn/xinwen/2014-04/30/content_2669106.htm.

[14] 陆小华. 媒体未来将出现颠覆性的创新. 搜狐传媒：http://media.sohu.com/20140421/n398570891.shtml.

[15] 周小华，乔东亮，孙俊青. 共建中国高等学校学术期刊航母——关于组建"全国高等学校学术期刊出版传媒集团"的设想［J］. 科技与出版，2014（1）.

留学生汉语需求分析的理论与方法

郭素红　吴中平

引　言

需求分析（Needs Analysis）最早用于外语教学中的"专门用途英语/语言"（ESP/LSP = English/Language for Specific or Special Purposes）中，目的是为成人学习专门用途英语的课程设置提供依据，即通过分析语言学习者所处的目标环境及语言特征，最后制定专门用于英语教学理论大纲的方法。

国外教育界对需求和需求分析的含义有不同的解释。Brindley（1989）和Robinson（1991）提出了客观需求（Objective Needs）与主观需求（Subjective Needs）这一组概念，把所有关于学习者的客观情况（如学习者目前的外语水平、语言学习中的难点等）笼统地称为客观需求，而把学习者在语言学习中的认知和情感需求（信心、态度等）概括为主观需求。Hutchinson T. & A. Waters（1993）则提出了目标需求（Target Needs）和学习需求（Learning Needs）两个概念，认为目标需求是指学习者为在将来的目标情景中顺利完成工作所必须掌握的知识，而学习需求则是指学习者为了学会而需要做的一切。

Waters, A. & C. Vilches（2001）区分了两种不同层次的需求，即"打基础"和"开发潜能"，认为采用这种模式开展需求分析必须实行自下而上的方式，即从了解和分析"打基础"方面的需求开始逐步过渡到"开发潜能"方面的需求。而用来了解、分析学习者学习需求的过程则被称作"需求分析"。从内容上看，需求分析主要包括目标需求分析和学习需求分析两个方面。目标需求分析是对课程结束时学生应达到的目标进行分析，主要是针对学生的个人学习情况、学习目的和目前的外语水平开展的分析。学习需求分析主要是了解在课程开始讲授前学生的语言现状，调查学生当前的目的语水平、学习态度、学习偏爱、个人愿望、需求与期望等。

对外语学习者各种需求的数据和资料进行需求分析的方法在不断完善。Richterich（1972）首次提出了外语教学中需求分析的模式，指出如何满足外语学习者在未来的语言使用环境中交际需求的系列范畴。Munby（1978）提出了在一门外语教学课程结束后对学生的需求开展分析的模式，并称其为目标情况分析，认为可以利用一些工具对学生开展需求分析，并将其提出的交际需求转换成具体的语言技能和编写目标大纲的系列语言微功能。Munby提出的模式尽管考虑了语言学习者个人的语言需求，却忽视了学习者的认知和情感变量，如学习者的学习态度、学习动机和学习风格等，这种需求分析模式就与语言教学中的交际模式分离开来。尽管该需求分析模式可以作为编写目标语言课程大纲的依据，但是这种模式却不能为根据真实交际环境开展外语教学活动提供帮助。Richterich & Chancerel（1980）提出了建立PSA模式的系列方案，成为对TSA的一种补充。PSA即当前情况分析（Present Situation Analysis），主要是在外语课程开始讲授前了解学生的语言现状，调查学生的语言优势和欠缺。

新近出现的需求分析各种模式拓宽了收集数据的重点范围，不仅含有各种客观数据，而且包含了有关外语学习者偏爱的学习方式、学习者对于所学课程的需求与期望、以及课堂所处的环境等方面的内容。国内学者通过归纳需求分析文献，将外语需求分析涉及的主要内容划分为核心需求和外围需求。外语需求的核心内容即目标需求和学习需求，外围外语需求是外语需求的外围内容，包括学习动机、学习风格、语言态度等，由此外语需求分析也可分为"强式"和"弱式"需求分析两种（倪传斌2006）。

需求分析涉及有关教学活动客观信息和主观信息等数据的收集，属于评估研究的范畴，其关键是要找出学习者现有的语言运用能力和专业知识水平与他们所期望达到的程度之间的距离。需求分析属于实

［基金项目］本文得到北京市教委2012年度社科计划资助项目"来华留学生学历教育中的全英文授课问题研究"（项目编号：SM201211417011）的资助，谨致谢忱。

［作者简介］郭素红，吴中平，北京联合大学国际交流学院。

证调查与研究,通过收集课程开始前和课程结束时的有关需求,为教学大纲的设计与实施、教学的组织、教材的使用以及教学效果的评估等方面提供依据,最终目的是为了使教师能更多地关注最需要重视的需求方面。外语需求分析的研究理论是为所有以目的语作为外语教学所通用的,也为对外汉语教学中留学生的汉语需求分析提供了理论上的借鉴和支持。

1 留学生汉语需求分析的方法

针对留学生的汉语需求分析一般按照以下步骤进行:确定调查对象、设计问卷、收集资料、分析信息。以下依次展开讨论。

1.1 确定调查对象

在进行需求分析之前,首先确定好调查对象,明确所需要的信息,根据不同的研究需要,可以侧重不同的研究方面,设计不同的调查问题。分析外国留学生的汉语需求,调查对象为来华学习汉语的留学生,而选取生源相对稳定集中的来华长期进修的留学生作为调查对象,是因为汉语长期进修的留学生是对外汉语教学的核心和重点,因而这部分调查对象具有较强的代表性。

进行需求分析,需要设计研究方法。外语需求分析可用的方法多达10余种,如预先文件分析法、专家语言测试法、入学语言测试法、自我评估法、观察法、班级进步测试法、问卷法、访谈法、日记法、个案研究法、终结测试法、评估法、跟踪调查法和前瞻性研究法等(Braine G. 2001)。外语需求分析常用的方法是问卷法和访谈法。问卷法在外语需求分析中应用最广,适用于外语需求分析的大面积调查,但设计问卷的信度和效度控制需要有丰富的经验。访谈法分个别访谈法和小组访谈法两类。访谈法的优点是信息量大、灵活性高,但访谈标准不一,其结果难以进行定量研究,因而访谈法经常与其他方法结合使用,以获取更加丰富的信息。

1.2 设计问卷

一般而言,留学生汉语需求分析经常采取问卷调查和访谈的形式。依据需求分析模式,在文献分析的基础上先尽可能详细地收集与留学生汉语需求相关的调查条目,再参照如倪传斌(2006)调查问卷的设计,将留学生汉语需求分析的相关内容,如目标场景、目标水平、汉语学习和应用困难、学习动机、学习偏好、语言态度、学习目的等,放在一个共同的框架内进行分析,以确定所做研究需要分析的主要内容。

问卷调查具体包括如下六个方面:(1)留学生个人基本情况;(2)留学生的汉语语言态度;(3)留学生的汉语学习目的;(4)留学生使用汉语的目标场景;(5)留学生的汉语学习需求;(6)留学生汉语学习的目标水平等。研究者可以根据以上内容自行设计调查问卷,留学生作为被调查对象按照要求对问卷内容进行单选或多选。所用调查问卷均以留学生问卷为蓝本,其他如针对教师的调查均在此基础上改换描述角度和适当增减调查条目。

为了尽可能全面地囊括所有相关情景和内容,需要对预试卷的信度和效度进行评估。调查问卷的信度即调查的一致性,是指重复调查时产生同样结果的程度。效度指调查问卷反映所需要调查内容的程度。研究者可以先组织部分留学生参加座谈会,并对部分教师进行访谈,对他们所提供的信息进行归纳、认真分析、修改问卷中的每一个问题和选项。随后,用复测信度(Test-Retest Reliability)的方法对问卷进行信度评估。用初步设计出来的问卷,由同一位调查者对若干名留学生(不参加本调查)前后间隔两周时间重复施测,用 Kappa 一致性系数来评估重测信度,对 $K < 0.75$ 的某些问卷的选项进行修改或删除,最终确定调查问卷的设计。

1.3 收集材料

收集资料采用按自然班随机抽样、当场收回的办法发放和收回问卷。问卷调查结束后,研究者针对问卷反映出的情况,对参加问卷调查的部分学生进行访谈。对访谈数据运用"主题一致"分析法进行归纳。数据分析采用 Spss13.0 统计软件。问卷数据由研究者手工录入,多选题数据采用多重二分法输入(把多选题的每一个选项都定义为一个单选变量,被选中的选项定义为数值1,未被选中的选项定义为数值0),用频次分析的方法计算出每个选项的频数和该选项占全部有效问卷的百分比。

1.4 分析信息

资料收集完整以后要对所收集到的资料进行分析。分析应是需求分析中非常重要的环节，问卷调查、访谈等仅仅是获取所需资料的手段，而非目的。只有详细分析所获取的信息，才能成为教学决策者安排教学、设置课程和组织教学活动的依据。需求分析可以采用定量分析和定性分析相结合的方法。定量分析一般用于确定需求的广度与范围，从被调查对象的语言调查中获取数据，如问卷调查、测试、成绩评定和考试中获取数据。定性分析一般用于确定需求的本质，包括课堂观摩、案例调查、正式讨论会等形式。开展需求分析最理想的方式应该是尽量把定性分析和定量分析结合起来，从多种渠道，用多种工具了解和获取多方面的相关信息与观点。

尽管收集和分析留学生汉语需求的数据和资料存在困难，但却具有重要意义。需求分析可以在留学生学习的不同阶段进行。如开设课程之前对留学生目标情景进行需求分析，其结果可应用于设置课程；课程中途的留学生需求分析对目前情境进行分析，目的是调整教学内容和教学方式；课程结束以后的留学生需求信息，就成为评估学习目标是否实现、课程设置是否合理的依据。

2 留学生汉语需求分析的意义

外语需求分析的应用价值在外语教学领域已逐渐显现出来。对外汉语教学属于外语教学的一个重要分支。陆俭明（1999）曾指出，对外汉语教学学科体系建设的核心目标是"怎样在尽可能短的时间里让外国学生尽快学好汉语"。对外汉语的学科体系由四个层面构成，即本体论、认识论、教育学方法论和现代教育技术工具论。离开了汉语需求分析的指导和调节，对外汉语学科体系中的"教什么""如何学""怎样教""使用什么教育技术和手段"等都将是盲目的，完善对外汉语教学学科建设也将无从谈起。孙德金（1997）认为，需求分析是影响对外汉语教学学科发展的重要因素："应当明确对外汉语教学的本体研究不同于一般意义上的本体研究，它的基点和归宿点都是对外汉语教学的实际需要，只有这样才能构筑对外汉语教学中汉语本体的理论框架。"

汉语需求分析在对外汉语教学过程中具有核心性的地位，教学过程的各个环节都离不开需求分析成果的具体指导。需求分析从多方面决定和影响着对外汉语课程设置、教材选用、课堂教学开展和教学评估。

首先，汉语需求分析能使汉语教师更有效地设置课程、制定和执行教学大纲。而设置一门外语课程的前提就是做好需求分析，只有充分了解学生在学习过程中各方面的需求，才能科学地设置课程，制定出符合实际的教学目标和授课方案。而要使教学大纲具体落实到课堂教学中，就需要对学生的自身情况、学习的各种环境因素和所有目标因素进行深入细致的调查研究，从中找出满足这些需求的途径。Nunan（1988）把对学习者的需求分析和学习目的看成是课程计划的首要环节，在具体施教过程中，教师讲授的内容与学习者需求保持一致非常关键（Brindley G. 1989）。通过需求分析，可了解学习者希望通过这门课程学到的内容、掌握的外语技能，从而为课程设置的必要性论证提供可靠信息。针对学习者需求开设的外语课程更能激励他们学好外语，开发他们自主学习和使用外语的能力（Crookes G. 1991）。在设计课程和选定教材之前，非常有必要进行一次深入全面的需求分析。能否做好深入细致的需求分析，对于设置课程大纲，选用合适的教材，都起着至关重要的作用。

其次，汉语需求分析强调学习的步骤和过程，注重留学生个人的实际情况（包括学习动机、学习方法、个体差异等），对于汉语教师改进教学方法、提高教学效果也有重要意义。王钟华（1995）曾指出留学生在对外汉语教学中的地位，学习首先是学生自己的事，学习过程需要学生自己来完成，教师教学效果也由学生来体现。学生想学就能学好，不想学，由再好的教师来教也无济于事。学生的学习意图、目的、年龄、文化程度和文化教养等因素决定了学习过程是一个选择的过程。外部条件能否起作用关键在于能否与这种选择协调一致。心理语言学研究证明：只有当学生意识到他们正在获取他们所需要和感兴趣的东西时，他们才能产生自觉学习的动力，并取得丰硕的成果。从这个意义上讲，学生是主体。课程规范必须树立主体意识，规范的各项内容要从学生的需求和特点出发。

刘珣（1997）认为，"以学生为中心，教师为主导"的教学原则应该强调从学生的特点和需求出发，制订教学计划、教学大纲并确定教学内容、教材和教学方法，学习的内容应是真实而实用的，为学生迫切需要的。"学以致用"才能提高学生的学习兴趣。在对外汉语教学课堂上有不少问题是由于汉语教师对留学生的兴趣和需求关注不够,通过需求分析即可利用需求分析成果,有的放矢地制定教学目标、教学大纲和适时安排教学。对于教学目标的清晰把握可以使教师消除教学中的盲目性,提高教学效率。总之,需求分析属于实证调查与研究,有助于教师认识学习者的需求以及未来的工作情景对学习者语言技能的要求,并有效地实现教学目标。

3 留学生汉语需求分析的现状与问题

3.1 汉语需求分析的现状

目前,需求分析已广泛应用于教育、经贸、制造和服务等行业。其中,外语需求分析已广泛应用于外语教学的各个领域,并在课程设置、教材编写、教学大纲设计、课程评估、试题编制和教育政策制定等方面取得了丰硕的成果。在对外汉语教学领域,对需求分析特有的应用价值,国内学者早在20世纪90年代初就已论述了开展需求分析的必要性。

程棠(1997)曾指出,实际交际需要在对外汉语教学中具有重要作用:实际交际需要是一个大的原则。到底需要什么?这是一个十分复杂的问题。需要我们以语言学理论为指导,对日常交际中最需要最常用的话语进行调查。需要编制一个语言功能大纲,以便有计划地安排功能项目。国家汉办曾组织力量编制功能大纲,但至今尚无成果。功能大纲的难产,原因是多种多样的,而对功能本身的研究却不成熟,对外国人在交际中对汉语的需求不够清楚是主要的原因之一。

竟成(1999)谈及语法教学大纲的设计时认为:"第一批教学大纲的出现是对外汉语教学从经验型向科学型转变的标志,有着十分重要的意义,大纲的修订需要有一个'务实'的阶段。……经过'务实'阶段后,可以尝试性地'调查不同学生需要什么不同的语法知识'"。《高等学校外国留学生汉语教学大纲(长期进修)》也明确指出了对外汉语的教学原则:"从学习者的实际需要出发,注重教学内容的实用性。"但目前外国留学生汉语需求分析的实证研究还处于起步阶段。外国留学生虽然来自不同的文化背景,使用不同的母语,来华求学的目标也不尽相同,但他们都有共同的汉语学习需求。已经有研究者意识到,要了解学生的实际需求,需要使用问卷调查方法,收集数据进行分析,以真正有效地了解学生及教师对教学活动的看法。也有学者采用问卷调查的方法分析了外国留学生的学习需求,从入学、课堂学习和测评几个方面进行调查和讨论。这些研究为了解一定范围内的留学生需求和改进对外汉语教学产生了积极作用。

3.2 汉语需求分析存在的问题

对外汉语领域中的需求分析也在逐渐显示出不足之处。迄今为止,有文献记载的汉语需求分析均属于"强式"或"弱式"中的一种,需求分析的具体内容还不够完整,所得结论仅局限于目标场景、目标水平、学习动机、学习偏好、语言态度、学习目的等单方面的研究成果。需求分析的方法尚未进行可靠性监控和评估,大多数需求分析为单维统计。另外,由于需求分析统计软件和分析方法复杂,其应用范围仅限于大纲设计、课程设置和教育政策制定等宏观领域,普通汉语教师无法应用这些技术开展简单可行的汉语需求调查,这些因素都影响了留学生汉语需求分析的实际应用。

对于留学生的汉语教学,需要结合语言学、教育心理学等相关学科的研究方法和成果,从理论上指导教学,从课程设置、教学方法、编写教材等方面满足留学生的实际需求,以提高对外汉语教学质量。对外汉语教学中存在的一系列值得深入研究的课题,汉语需求分析正是这些课题研究的基础,因而有必要针对外国留学生汉语需求分析进行理论与方法上的梳理和研究。只有从留学生汉语需求的视角出发,用自下而上的方式,分析留学生汉语学习中的主客观需求,才能系统地探索提高对外汉语教学质量的途径与方法,为留学生汉语教学中的实际问题,如课程设置、教材选择、教师角色、课堂形式等,从留学生汉语需求的角度提供实证支持。

参考文献

[1] 竟成. 我们究竟需要什么样的语法大纲[J]. 世界汉语教学, 1999(3).

[2] 李绍林. 对外汉语教学中语言要素和言语技能的关系［J］. 汉语学习, 2011（1）.
[3] 刘珣. 对外汉语教学概论［M］. 北京：北京语言大学出版社. 1997.
[4] 刘珣. 试论汉语作为第二语言教学的原则［J］. 世界汉语教学, 1997（1）.
[5] 陆俭明. 关于开展对外汉语基础研究之管见［J］. 语言文字应用, 1999（4）.
[6] 倪传斌. 汉语作为外语的需求分析［M］. 南京：河海大学出版社, 2006.
[7] 孙德金. 对外汉语教学研究的回顾与前瞻性研讨会纪要［J］. 语言教学与研究, 1997（1）.
[8] 王钟华. 学习主体与外部条件［J］. 汉语学习, 1995（5）.
[9] Braine, G. Twenty years of needs analysis：Reflections on a personal journey. In J. Flowerdew, & M. Peacock (Eds.), Research perspectives *on English for Academic Purposes*［M］. Cambridge University Press, 2001.
[10] Brindley, G.. The role of needs analysis in adult ESL program design［A］. In R. K. Johnson, ed. The Second Language Curriculum［C］. Cambridge：Cambridge University Press, 1989.
[11] Child, D. Psychology and the Teacher［M］. London：Butler & Tanner Ltd., 1981.
[12] Crookes, G. &R. W. Shmidt. Motivation：Reopening the research agenda［J］. Language Learning, 1991（4）.
[13] Flowerdew, J. Research Perspectives on English for Academic Purposes［M］. Cambridge：Cambridge University Press, 2001.
[14] Hutchinson, T. &. A. Waters. English for Specific Purposes［M］. Cambridge University Press, 1987.
[15] Munby, J. Communicative Syllabus Design［M］. Cambridge：Cambridge University Press, 1978.
[16] Nunan, D. Syllabus Design［M］. Oxford：Oxford University Press, 1988.
[17] Richard, J. C. Curriculum Development in Language Teaching［M］. Cambridge University Press, 2001.
[18] Richterich, L. & Chancerel, J. Identifying the Needs of Adults Learning a Foreign Language［M］. Oxford：Pergamon, 1980.
[19] Richterich, R. Model for the Definition of Language Needs of Adults Learning a Modern Language［M］. Strasbourg：Council of Europe, 1972.
[20] Robinson, P. ESP Today：A Practitioner's Guide［M］. New York：Prentice Hall International (UK) Ltd, 1991.
[21] Weir, C. J., H. Zh. Yang & Y. Jin. Studies in Language Testing［M］. Cambridge University Press, 2000.
[22] Waters, A. & Vilches, C. Implementing ELT Innovations：A Needs Analysis Framework［J］. *ELT Journal*, 2001（2）.

赵萝蕤先生汉译《荒原》艺术管窥

黄宗英 邓中杰 姜 君

引 言

根据赵萝蕤（1912—1998 年）先生的回忆，她是在 1935 年 5 月间，无意中试译了《荒原》的第一节。当时，赵萝蕤先生年仅 23 岁，在清华大学外国文学研究所攻读硕士学位；她喜欢写诗并在戴望舒先生主编的上海《新诗》刊物上发表过诗作。1936 年底，上海"新诗社"戴望舒先生约赵萝蕤先生翻译艾略特的《荒原》全诗。她于 1936 年年底一个月内译完全诗，并将诗人原注和译者注释整理编译在一起。1937 年夏天，这本译著由叶公超先生作序，伴随着"七·七卢沟桥事变"的枪炮声，悄然问世。1939 年，邢光祖先生在《西洋文学》杂志上发表评论说："艾略特的《荒原》是近代诗的'荒原'中的灵芝，而赵［萝蕤］女士的译本是我国翻译界的'荒原'上的奇葩。"[1]3 赵萝蕤先生在如此短的时间内能将这首艰深晦涩的现代派"怪诗"译成我国文学翻译史上的一朵"奇葩"。关于文学翻译工作，赵萝蕤先生曾提出三个基本条件："对作家作品理解越深越好""两种语言的较高水平"和"谦虚谨慎的工作态度"[2]607-08。笔者希望通过对赵萝蕤先生汉译《荒原》手稿与几位国内外国文学研究专家和翻译家的不同译本之间的比较分析，来重新审视赵萝蕤先生所提出的从事文学翻译工作的三个条件，进而讨论她在翻译严肃的文学作品时始终坚持的直译法的艺术造诣。

1 "对作家作品理解越深越好"

赵萝蕤先生对从事文学翻译工作提出的第一个条件是"对作家作品理解越深越好"。她认为对作家作品的研究大致有三种情况：①有些作家作品只需要译者有一个大致的理解就可以进行翻译，比如朗弗罗的《哈依瓦撒之歌》；②有些作品要求译者必须对作者的思想认识、感情力度、创作意图和特点等都有深刻全面的研究，比如惠特曼的《草叶集》；③还有些作家本身不难理解，但其作品却需要译者做一番比较艰苦的研究工作，比如艾略特的《荒原》。[2]607-08 艾略特认为，当代社会变得复杂多样，因此表现这个复杂多样的时代与社会的诗歌艺术形式就必然变得艰涩。[3]289 赵萝蕤先生认为，《荒原》之所以难懂，主要是因为作者引经据典太多，而且诗中的典故盘根错节，在结构上有许多交叉点，让人感到"剪不断理还乱"[4]20。因此翻译这类作品，译者首先必须认真研究作者和研读作品。

众所周知，第一次世界大战后，整个西方世界呈现出一派大地苦旱、人心枯竭的现代"荒原"景象[5]83-89；那是一段掺杂着个人思想感情和社会悲剧的"历史"[6]55-56，人们的精神生活经常表现为空虚、失望、迷惘、浮华、烦乱和焦躁，而艾略特《荒原》一诗"确实表现了一代青年对一切的'幻灭'"[4]19。在《荒原》第一章《死者葬礼》的第 22 行中，出现了这么一个画龙点睛的短语："A heap of broken images"，尤其是其中的英文单词"image"比较耐人寻味。首先，请看赵萝蕤先生 1936 年的译文手稿：

原文：

What are the roots that clutch, what branches grow

Out of this stony rubbish? Son of man,

You cannot say, or guess, for you know only

A heap of broken images, where the sun beats,

And the dead tree gives no shelter, the cricket no relief,

［作者简介］黄宗英（1961—），男，文学博士，北京联合大学应用文理学院教授；邓中杰（1972—），男，高等教育出版社首席编辑；姜君（1980—），男，北京联合大学应用文理学院讲师。

And the dry stone no sound of water. [7]38

译文：

什么树根在捉住，什么树枝在从

这堆石头的零碎中长出？人子啊，

你说不出，也猜不到，因为你只知道

一堆破碎的偶像，承受着太阳的鞭打，

枯死的树没有遮阴，蟋蟀不使人放心，

焦石间没有流水的声音。[8]31

再看国内其他译者对第22行中这个短语的译法：

查良铮译（1985）："一堆破碎的形象"[9]47

赵毅衡译（1985）："一大堆破碎的形象"[10]198

裘小龙译（1985）："一堆支离破碎的意象"[11]70

叶维廉译（2009）："一堆破碎的象"[12]80

汤永宽译（2012）："一大堆破碎的形象"[13]80

不论是译成"形象""意象""象"甚至是"图像"[14]818，不同译者都会有各自不同的解释和道理。但是，不同的译法给读者传递的信息（量）是不同的。赵萝蕤先生也曾经对自己1936年的译本做过几次修改，但是始终没有改动第22行的译法。那么，赵萝蕤先生为什么把这个短语中的"image"一词翻译成"偶像"呢？

首先，赵萝蕤先生研究了诗人为第20、23行分别提供的两个原注："对照《旧约·以西结书》第二章第一节"和"对照《旧约·传道书》第十二章第五节"[7]50。《旧约·以西结书》第二章第一节上说："他对我说：'人子啊，你站起来，我要和你说话'。"《旧约·以西结书》讲述的是上帝与先知以西结之间的谈话。上帝选择以西结作为他的代言人，去警告以色列人并让他们悔过自新。然而，上帝告诫以西结说，以色列人是一个叛逆的民族。他们对他的警告将听而不从[15]568。因此，从某种意义上说，以西结可以被看成是来拯救荒原的使者。由于上帝已不再是以色列人所崇拜的偶像，所以他们的灵魂就无法得到拯救，他们也就只能像荒原上的人那样，饱受无端的磨难："在你们一切的住处，城邑要变为荒场，邱坛必然凄凉，使你们的祭坛荒废，将你们的偶像打碎，你们的日像被砍倒，你们的工作被毁灭。"[15]568不仅如此，《旧约·传道书》第十二章第五节上说："人怕高处，路上有惊慌，杏树开花，蚱蜢成为重担，人所愿的也都废掉，因为人归他永远的家，吊丧的在街上往来。"[15]568艾略特在这里想提醒读者的是"那些背叛上帝的人是注定要生活在一块事与愿违、寸草不长的荒地上"[15]568。赵萝蕤先生在此将"image"一词翻译成"偶像"可谓达到了画龙点睛的艺术效果，点明诗中的主题：偶像已破碎，"焦石间没有流水的声音"。

其次，《荒原》一诗发表于1922年。艾略特虽然不同意许多评论家对这首诗歌的评论，不愿意承认《荒原》的主题是表现西方"一代人的精神幻灭"（"disillusionment of a generation"）[16]368。他认为，《荒原》只不过是他"个人对生活的满腹牢骚"（"a personal and wholly insignificant grouse against life"）[17]1。然而，"牢骚"是有思想内容的语言。当语言受情感所控制却未被情感所征服的时候，这种语言综合了情感和理智的元素，或许也就是艾略特所谓"有节奏的牢骚"（rhythmical grumbling）。这种"牢骚"一旦发出，它便成为西方人情感与精神枯竭的直接宣泄和对西方现代文明"荒原"的极写。美国小说家弗·斯科特·菲茨杰拉德（F. Scott Fitzgerald，1896—1940年）将第一次世界大战后的整个西方世界描写成一个"所有的上帝都死光了，所有的战争都打完了，所有人的信仰都动摇了的"所谓的"人间天堂"[18]255。上帝已不再是人们心灵中崇拜的偶像，人们惧怕贫穷，崇拜金钱和成功。同样，在艾略特笔下的这个现代"荒原"中，我们窥见了西方病态的文明、反常的内心世界和畸形的社会。在这么一个"迷惘"的时代背景之下，赵萝蕤先生译笔下的这"一堆破碎的偶像"真可谓画龙点睛的互文之笔了！它不仅让读者联想起《圣经·旧约》中典型的荒原意象，而且让我们联想到西方许多现代作家笔下人们没有信仰、虽生犹死的"人间天堂"。可见，《荒原》不同汉译文本的比较研究可以打开一个新的文本释读视角，而赵萝蕤先生强调在对作家作品深刻理解的基础上传神地译出原作与译作之间所蕴涵的这种简单深邃的互文关系，又为推进我国文学翻译批评理论建构提供了一个崭新的启示。

2 "两种语言的较高水平"

赵萝蕤先生提出文学翻译的第二个基本条件是："两种语言的较高水平"[2]808。赵萝蕤先生认为有不少作品是可以采用直译法（即保持语言的一个单位接着一个单位的次序，用准确的同义词一个单位一个单位地顺序译下去），但要绝对服从每一种语言自身的特点和规律。如果要避免直译法沦为僵硬的对照译法，那么关键在于译者驾驭句法的能力是否灵活，是否传神[1]185。而"两种语言的较高水平"对一位从事文学翻译工作的人，特别是主张直译法的译者非常重要。

对照《荒原》英文原诗开篇的 7 行，赵萝蕤先生 1936 年的译文如下：

原文：

April is the cruellest month, breeding
Lilacs out of the dead land, mixing
Memory and desire, stirring
Dull roots with spring rain.
Winter kept us warm, covering
Earth in forgetful snow, feeding
A little life with dried tubers. [7]37

赵萝蕤原译：

四月天最是残忍，它在
荒地上生丁香，掺和着
回忆和欲望，让春雨
挑拨呆钝的树根。
冬天保我们温暖，大地
给健忘的雪覆盖着，又叫
干了的老根得一点生命。[8]27

这段开篇诗行是诗人对极度空虚、贫乏、枯涩、迷惘的西方社会现代荒原的形象描写。中世纪乔叟《坎特伯雷故事》开篇诗行中"春之歌"所描写的"甘霖""花蕾"和"新芽"在艾略特笔下都已消失得无影无踪。现代人已经听不见春天树上鸟儿的歌声，也看不到那"通宵睁开睡眼"的小鸟[19]1。往日的"丝丝茎络"变成了如今"呆钝"的"老根"，没有春的气息，只剩下"一点生命"。现代荒原上的人们似乎经历了一个懒洋洋的、不情愿的、甚至是愤懑不平的苏醒过程。赵萝蕤先生早在 1940 年 5 月 14 日的《时事新报》上发表过一篇题为《艾略特与〈荒原〉》的文章，讨论了她是如何努力做到让译文传达原诗的"情致""境界"和"节奏"：

这一节自第一到第四行都是很慢的，和残忍的四月天同一情致。一、二、三行都在一句初开之时断句，更使这四句的节奏迟缓起来，在原诗亦然。可是第五行"冬天保我们温暖"是一口气说的，有些受歌的陶醉太深的人也许爱在"天"字之下略顿一下，但是按照说话的口气，却是七个字接连而下的，和原文相似：(Winter kept us warm) 是一气呵成的句子，在一至七行中是一点生命力，有了这一点急促琐屑，六与七行才不至疲弱而嘶哑。[1]10-11

赵萝蕤先生的评论至少说明了三个问题。首先，她注意到了诗人在前四行中用"断句"来达到"节奏迟缓"的艺术效果，其译诗的句法与原诗完全对称；其次，赵萝蕤先生注意到了原诗前三行的弱韵结尾（feminine ending），而且是一连三次连续使用动词分词形式的弱韵结尾。虽然弱韵结尾不容易汉译，但是赵萝蕤先生选用了"生""掺和"和"挑拨"三个及物动词来翻译原诗中"breeding""mixing"和"stirring"三个及物动词，而且做到了前四行的重音节数与原诗基本吻合，锁定了原诗的情致和节奏；第三，赵萝蕤先生在文章中说："在译文中我尽力依照着原作的语调与节奏的断续徐疾。"[1]10 "断续徐疾"恐怕是表现孤独无序、焦躁不安的现代荒原人生命光景最逼真的节奏，而赵萝蕤先生却用一句貌似简单的口语，改变了前面迟缓的语速："冬天保我们温暖。"这句话口气"急促琐屑"，却又耐人寻味：

冬天何以保人们温暖呢？原来诗人是在抨击现代荒原上无所事事、无可奈何的人群。可见，译者当时将原诗中的"kept"一词译成"保"字也是基于对原文的透彻理解和对汉语运用的游刃有余。赵萝蕤先生在此既直译了原诗的句法结构，又传神地译出了原诗的讽刺口吻，足见赵萝蕤先生掌握两种语言的深厚基础。

3 "谦虚谨慎的工作态度"

赵萝蕤先生提出文学翻译的第三个基本条件是："谦虚谨慎的工作态度。"[2]608 在半个世纪的翻译生涯中，赵萝蕤先生始终坚持用直译法从事文学翻译。她认为"直译法能够比较忠实地反映原作"[2]613，因为直译法的基本原则是追求形式与内容的相互统一。此外，赵萝蕤先生认为："译者没有权利改造一个严肃作家的严肃作品，只能十分谦虚地、忘我地向原作学习。"[2]607 尤其是在翻译严肃作家的严肃作品时，译者应当"处处把原著的作家置于自己之上，而不是反之"[2]608。那么，赵萝蕤先生是如何在《荒原》原译中实践她的这种"忘我"精神的呢？

原文：

"My nerves are bad to–night. Yes，bad. Stay with me.

"Speak to me. Why do you never speak. Speak.

"What are you thinking of? What thinking? What?

"I never know what you are thinking. Think."[7]40

赵萝蕤原译：

"今晚上我精神很坏。对了，坏。陪着我。

"跟我说话。为什么总不说话。说啊。

"你在想些什么？想什么？什么？

"我从来不知道你在想什么。想。"[8]51

《荒原》原著中诗体繁多、句法复杂、语气微妙。赵萝蕤先生始终是"尽力使每一节译文接近原文而不是自创一体"[2]610。从以上这一节译文看，赵萝蕤先生可谓不折不扣地在实践她的"忘我"精神。对照原文，我们发现赵萝蕤先生连一个标点符号都舍不得改动！然而，这种"直译"并非一种简单的对译，而是一种深思熟虑的艺术创造。如果我们把原文中的"Stay with me"译成"留下陪我"[10]202，不仅比原文多出一个音节，而且可能会让读者对诗中的"你"和"我"之间的关系多了几分揣测。假如我们把第 113 行译成"你在想什么？想什么？想什么？"[10]202，可能就把这行诗简单地理解为一个问句了。读者就难以感觉到原诗中所掺杂着的孤独、焦躁、疑虑、疑惑的"精神"状态。假如我们把第 114 行翻译成"我老是不明白你在想什么。想吧"[10]202，这种译法就比赵萝蕤先生的原译似乎多了几分宽容。实际上，这最后一个字"想"恰恰是艾略特笔下现代荒原人自我封闭、自我捆绑的典型行为："你，/你什么都不知道？不看见？不记得/什么？"（第 121–123 行）、"你是活的还是死的？你脑子里竟没有什么？"（第 125 行）、"我现在该做什么？我该做什么？/我就这样跑出去，走在街上/散着头发，这样。我们明天做些什么？/我们都还做什么？"（第 131–134 行）[8]57。可见，艾略特笔下的现代荒原人根本就没有希望过梭罗笔下的那种"深思熟虑的生活"[20]444，也无法想象弗罗斯特笔下那个"事实是劳动才能知晓的美梦"[21]73–74。

赵萝蕤先生谦虚谨慎的工作态度还体现在她为读者提供的详细注释上。赵萝蕤先生在其"译后记"中说，翻译这首诗的难处之一就是"需要注释：若是好发挥的话，几乎每一行皆可按上一种解释（interpretation），但这不是译者的事，译者仅努力搜求每一典故的来源与事实，须让读者自己去比较而会意，方可保原作的完整的体统"[8]243。艾略特为《荒原》提供了 52 个原注[7]50–55，多数只指出用典的出处，而不提供典故文本，说明性文字很少，对不熟悉这些典故的读者帮助不大。因此，在翻译原著时，赵萝蕤先生首先给原注增加了必要的"译者按"，为读者提供典故文本或者故事概要；其次，赵萝蕤先生另外增补了 26 条"译者按"，弥补了原注的不足。难能可贵的是赵萝蕤先生旁征博引，钩隐抉微，提供了大量权威可靠的注释，大大减少了阅读难度，同时拓展了读者的想象空间。比如，《荒原》第三章《火的教训》12 开篇的前 15 行诗：

河上的帐篷倒了,树叶留下最后的手指
握紧拳,又沉到潮湿的岸边上去了。那风
经过了棕黄色的大地听不见。仙女们已经走了。　　175
可爱的泰晤士,轻轻地流,等我唱完我的歌。
河上不再有空瓶子,夹肉面包的薄纸,
绸手绢,硬皮匣子,和香烟头儿
或其他夏夜的证据。仙女们已经走了。
还有她们的朋友,城里那些总督的子孙;　　180
走了,也不曾留下地址。
在莱茵河畔我坐下来饮泣……
可爱的泰晤士,轻轻地流,等我唱完我的歌。
可爱的泰晤士,轻轻地流,我不会大声,也不多说。[8]65-67

关于这一节诗文,艾略特给第176行加了一个注释:"见斯宾瑟的《祝婚曲》(Spenser: Prothalamion)。"赵萝蕤先生另外为第176行增补了"译者按:斯氏曲中形容泰晤士河上的愉快,并有这样一句作为全诗的副歌"。此外,赵萝蕤先生又给第179行增补了一个"译者按:这是指现代的河上仙女"。赵萝蕤先生的两个注释帮助我们更好地理解诗人在此借古讽今的手法。首先,"可爱的泰晤士,轻轻地流,等我唱完我的歌"这一行来自斯宾塞《祝婚曲》:"……银波荡漾的泰晤士河岸/河岸上繁枝密布,为河水镶边,/绘出了姹紫嫣红,百花齐放,/所有的草坪有玉石珠翠镶嵌,/适合于装饰闺房,/戴在情人们头上,/迎接她们的佳期,它就在不久/可爱的泰晤士河轻轻流,流到歌尽头"[15]575。它带给读者的联想是"文艺复兴"时期祝婚曲中那神秘浪漫的"仙女"。其次,相形之下,那些现代泰晤士河上的仙女们"只是城里老板们后代的女伴,曾在这里度过几个夏夜,也不知除野餐一通外还干了什么荒唐事,没有明说,但可以猜测"[4]23。那些少爷们仅仅是寻欢作乐,"也不曾留下地址"。赵萝蕤先生在此的注释虽然简约,但并不简单。它们还是让读者联想到了现代泰晤士河畔那一幕幕令人触目惊心、至深至痛的肮脏的两性关系。

然而,每当涉及诗歌主题、核心人物、意象、情景的时候,赵萝蕤先生总是努力提供细微具体的注释,帮助读者把握正确的意思。比如,虽然赵萝蕤先生没有对第三章《火的教训》的题目补充注释,但是由于火的形象是这一章的核心意象,因此在这一章结尾处的第308行,赵萝蕤先生还是做了一个全诗最长的注释,长达800余字,将西方佛学研究鼻祖亨利·柯拉克·华伦(Henry Clarke Warren)的《翻译中的佛教》(Buddhism in Translation)一书中关于佛陀的火诫全文译出,暗示读者:"尽管人们受情欲之火的百般奴役,但是炼狱之火却能净化一切赖于感官的感觉印象,使现代生活返璞归真"[15]575。那么,艾略特在这首诗中所做的最长的注释当推第218行中"Tiresias"(帖瑞西士)这一角色的注释:

帖瑞西士(Tiresias)虽然只是一个旁观者,而并非一个真正的"人物",却是诗中极重要的一个角色,联络全篇。正如那个独眼的商人和那个卖小葡萄干的,一齐化入那个非尼夏水手这个人物中,而后者也与奈波士(Naples)的福迪能(Ferdinand)王子没有明显的区别,所以所有的女人只是一个女人,而两性在帖瑞西士身上融合在一起。帖瑞西士所见的,实在就是这首诗的本体。欧维德的一段,在人类学上看来,很有价值。[7]183-185

帖瑞西士之所以是诗中"极重要的一个角色",又能够"联络全篇",是因为他具有两性人的属性。根据法兰克·吉士德斯·弥勒氏的英译《变形记》第三卷,帖瑞西士有一次因为手杖打了一下,触怒了正在树林里交媾的两条大蟒。突然,他由男子一变而为女人,而且一过就是七年光景。到了第八年,他又看见这两条蟒蛇,就说:"我打了你们之后,竟有魔力改变了我的本性,那么我再打你们一下。"说着,他又打了大蟒,自己又变回出生时的原形。因此,帖瑞西士既经历过男人的生活又有女人的经历,在《荒原》中变得十分重要。那么,究竟该怎么翻译这一行诗呢?原文:

"I Tiresias, though blind, throbbing between two lives,"[7]43

译文:

赵萝蕤译:"我,帖瑞西士,虽然瞎眼,在两种生命中颤动"[8]73

赵毅衡译:"我,梯雷西亚斯,虽然眼瞎,心却跳在两个生命中之间"[10]206-07
查良铮译:"我,提瑞西士,悸动在雌雄两种生命之间,"[9]55
裘小龙译:"我,铁瑞西斯,虽然失眠,在两条生命之间颤动,"[11]83
汤永宽译:"我,泰瑞西士,虽然双目失明,跳动在两个性别之间,"[13]91

对照几种译文,笔者认为赵萝蕤先生的直译法比较自然传神,遣词精当,句法合理,语气含蓄。赵毅衡先生试图用增词法译出动词"throbbing"的逻辑主语,使译文表述更加明白:"虽然眼瞎,心却……",但是诗人似乎没有意思要具体描写诗中人"我"的心态,而是更多地暗示诗中人"我"所代表的那种无法掌握自己命运的现代人的生命光景。查良铮先生此处出现了漏译现象,没有译出"though blind",而且"悸动在雌雄两种生命之间"同样存在增词法带来的麻烦,因为假如读者没有搞清楚"Tiresias"两性人的特征,那么"雌雄两种生命"的出现也只能起到提醒读者的作用,也无法译出典故的内涵,况且"悸动"一词显得比较温文,文体特征过于正式。裘小龙先生的译法虽然改动不多,但"失眠"应该是一个误译,而且"两条生命"似乎比"两种生命"更加明确,但实际上所传达的信息反而不够准确。汤永宽先生的译文流畅上口,但是将原文中的"two lives"译成"两个性别"似乎阐释的成分多了点。从这个例子可以看出,赵萝蕤先生的直译法是可取的,其译文比较接近原作的风格。

4 "直译法是我从事文学翻译的惟一方法"

赵萝蕤先生对从事文学翻译提出了三个基本条件——深入研究作家作品、两种语言的较高水平和谦虚谨慎的"忘我"精神。这三个基本条件虽然语言朴素,但哲理深刻,不容易做到。假如我们对作家作品缺乏正确的理解和深入的研究,我们就无法译出原作的风格和特点,更不用说把握严肃的文学作品的"思想认识和感情力度",去挖掘像《荒原》这样艰涩复杂的现代文本之间的互文关系;假如我们缺乏两种语言的较高水平,我们就无法保证对原作内容的正确理解和正确反映;假如我们缺乏谦虚谨慎的工作态度,我们在翻译过程中就很容易"玩世不恭,开作家的玩笑,自我表现一番"[2]608。就《荒原》而言,赵萝蕤先生认为"这首诗很适合于用直译法来翻译"[2]613,因为"直译法是能够比较忠实反映原作……使读者能尝到较多的原作风格"[2]613。如果说"诗就是翻译中所丧失掉的东西"[22]159,那么译诗难就难在如何保留原诗的诗味。译诗常常是形式移植完美无缺,但诗味荡然无存。然而,赵萝蕤先生的译笔每每体现出形式与内容相互契合的艺术境界。从以上我们对《荒原》第111-114行和第218行的讨论可以看出,形式与内容的契合不仅是文学创作的原则,同样是文学翻译的基本原则。因此,赵萝蕤先生说:"我用直译法是根据内容与形式统一这个原则。"[2]607

就文学翻译的标准而言,赵萝蕤先生强调"信"与"达",但说:"独立在原作以外的'雅'似乎就没有必要了。"[2]610她认为译者应该自觉"遵循[两种语言]各自的特点与规律","竭力忠实于原作的思想内容与艺术风格"[2]608。赵萝蕤先生的直译法所强调的"形式与内容统一的原则"既尊重两种语言的特点与规律,又强调译出原作的思想内容与艺术风格。她抓住了译诗最核心的要素。赵萝蕤先生的文学翻译理论,简洁朴素,但意韵深邃。她说:"直译法是我从事文学翻译的惟一方法。""直译法,即保持语言的一个单位接着一个单位的次序,用准确的同义词一个单位一个单位地顺序译下去"[2]608,但是要传神地译出《荒原》中"各种情致、境界和内容不同所产生出来的不同的节奏"[23]10,译者需要选择相应的语言单位,使译作的形式与内容相互契合。可见,赵萝蕤先生既强调"形似",也追求"神似",属于形神并蓄的二维模式,她的直译法文学翻译理论有着深厚的文艺学和美学基础。

"艾略特汉译研究几乎可以说仍是个盲点。"[24]119虽然《荒原》汉译文本比较丰富,但是对这些译作的评论却是凤毛麟角。1996年10月,第一次全国T. S. 艾略特专题研讨会在辽宁师范大学召开。在会上,王誉公教授在论文《〈荒原〉的理解与翻译》中说:"赵萝蕤先生的《荒原》是我国当前最优秀的翻译作品。她以直译法,用现代汉语将原作的思想内容、诗歌形式和语言风格表达得清清楚楚,惟妙惟肖。"[25]19同时,傅浩先生通过比较《荒原》的六种汉译本,得出结论:"赵萝蕤先生的译本虽然完成于30年代,但今天看来,仍流利畅达,不失为佳译。"[26]43

既然赵萝蕤先生的《荒原》译本至今仍是"最优秀的翻译作品",那么笔者认为我们有必要认真梳理和研究赵萝蕤先生的《荒原》汉译文本及其翻译思想,更深刻地理解、体会和揭示她所主张的用"直译法"翻译严肃的文学作品的学术价值。从文学翻译批评视角比较和研究《荒原》的不同汉译文本，可以更深刻地揭示赵萝蕤先生的《荒原》译本在表现"原作的思想内容、诗歌形式和语言风格"等三个译诗要素的独到之处，进而推进我国英诗汉译批评理论的建构和发展，同时为诗歌翻译实践提供一个不可多得的案例参照与理论指导。

参考文献

[1] 赵萝蕤. 我的读书生涯［M］. 北京：北京大学出版社，1996.
[2] 赵萝蕤. 我是怎么翻译文学作品的［M］. 王寿兰，编. 当代文学翻译百家谈. 北京：北京大学出版社，1989.
[3] T. S. Eliot. The Metaphysical Poets［M］. Selected Essays by T. S. Eliot. London：Faber and Faber Limited，1951.
[4] 赵萝蕤.《荒原》浅说［M］. 赵萝蕤. 我的读书生涯. 北京：北京大学出版社，1996.
[5] 黄宗英."我个人的满腹牢骚"：艾略特的《荒原》［M］//抒情史诗论. 北京：北京大学出版社，2003.
[6] 张剑. T. S. 艾略特：诗歌和戏剧的解读［M］. 北京：外语教学与研究出版社，2006.
[7] Eliot T S. The Complete Poems and Plays：1909—1950［M］. New York：Harcourt，Brace & World，INC，1971.
[8] 黄宗英，赵萝蕤. 译.《荒原》手稿［M］. 北京：高等教育出版社，2013.
[9] 查良铮译. 英国现代诗选［M］. 长沙：湖南人民出版社，1985.
[10] 赵毅衡编译. 美国现代诗选（上）［M］. 北京：外国文学出版社，1985.
[11] 裘小龙译. 荒原［M］//裘小龙译. 获诺贝尔文学奖作家丛书——四个四重奏. 桂林：漓江出版社，1985.
[12] 叶维廉. 众树歌唱：欧美现代诗100首［M］. 增订版. 北京：人民文学出版社，2009.
[13] 汤永宽译. 荒原［M］//陆建德，主编. 荒原·艾略特文集·诗歌. 上海：上海译文出版社，2012.
[14] 周明译. 荒原［M］//苏欲晓等译. 基督教文学经典选读（下）. 北京：北京大学出版社，2004.
[15] 黄宗英注释. 荒原［M］. 英国名诗详注. 胡家峦编. 北京：外语教学与研究出版社，2003：565-585.
[16] Eliot, T. S. Selected Essays［M］. London：Faber and Faber Limited，1951.
[17] Eliot, Valerie. Ed. The Waste Land：A Facsimile and Transcript of the Original Drafts［M］. New York & London：HBJ，1971.
[18] Fitzerald, F. Scott. This Side of Paradise［M］. New York：Charles Scribner's Sons，1920.
[19] 杰弗雷·乔叟. 坎特伯雷故事［M］. 方重，译. 上海：上海译文出版社，1993.
[20] 梭罗著. 瓦尔登湖或林中生活［M］. 梭罗集（上）. 许崇庆、林本椿译. 北京：三联书店，1996.
[21] 黄宗英."离经叛道"还是"创新意识"？［J］. 北京联合大学学报（人文社科版）. 2009（4）：69-74.
[22] Frost, Robert. Conversations on the Craft of Poetry［M］. Robert Frost on Writing. Elaine Barry. New Brunswick（New Jersey）：Rutgers University Press，1973：155-162.
[23] 赵萝蕤. 艾略特与《荒原》［M］赵萝蕤. 我的读书生涯. 北京：北京大学出版社，1996.
[24] 董洪川."荒原"之风：T. S. 艾略特在中国. 北京：北京大学出版社，2004.
[25] 王誉公、张华英.《荒原》的理解与翻译［M］. 外国文学研究. 1996（2）：19-26.
[26] 傅浩.《荒原》六种中译本比较［M］. 外国文学研究. 1996（2）：36-43.

调查性报道"事实建构"的机制与特征

惠东坡

新闻报道事实是记者在特定话语系统的约束下对客观事实进行符号或话语建构的产物。调查性报道也是一种话语建构的结果,其事实建构的过程实际上就是信息的采集、转化、表达、整合的过程。作为深度报道的一种类型,"调查报道"一直是媒体实现舆论监督和提升影响力的重要手段。调查话语事实建构的机制和特征主要体现在信息来源、信息转化、信息呈现、信息整合四个方面。

1 信息来源:新媒体推动了事实建构的社会化

未知或被遮蔽的客观事实信息总是以零星或碎片化的形态呈现,这种不规则的信息放射源就是信息来源。接触信息来源是调查报道生产的第一步,记者通过对信息源的调查研究来建构报道事实。"消息来源是记者生命的血液。没有通过消息来源得来的情况,记者就无法活动。"[1]作为"一出生就风华正茂"的主流都市报,《新京报》十分重视通过"新闻报料"来拓展信息来源。创刊伊始,就万元重奖新闻线索。新媒体给调查报道带来的不只是冲击,更多的是契机。擅长调查报道的《财经》《南方都市报》《21世纪经济报道》充分利用新媒体的丰富信息来源,拓宽调查报道的深度和广度。从目前的发展实践来看,深挖信息来源已经成为调查报道生产的重要运作机制。调查报道的信息来源,除传统的渠道和24小时报料热线电话、读者来信之外,更多的是建立在新媒体技术平台上的短信报料、QQ新闻线索、互联网报料、电子邮件和微博等。

目前,以移动终端和互联网技术为平台的微博正成为一支不容忽视的传播力量,其便捷、全民、及时、精炼、互动的特点极大地影响着新闻生产的方式。《新京报》非常重视利用这一途径拓展信息来源,要求记者注册微博,甚至把在微博上抢先发布新闻纳入绩效考核。《新京报》还在新浪和腾讯网这两大微博平台上开放爆料功能,欢迎知情人士向他们提供信息线索。2012年5月5日,《新京报》新浪微博已经有139万多粉丝。其微博还开设了"在线报料"功能,可以在线填报"事发时间""事发地点""爆料主题""爆料内容""添加图片""联系电话"等。《南方都市报》新浪微博粉丝为248万多人,其深度的粉丝为12万人,《财经》新浪微博粉丝为19.8万人,《21世纪经济报道》新浪微博粉丝为111万多人。调查记者在微博上获取的事实信息是碎片化、零散的和无效的,这在一定程度上为新闻生产指明了方向、提供了内容,但是它还需要记者谨慎求证、深入采访才可能建构报道事情的真相。新媒体信息来源途径,为调查报道的生产提供了更多、更快、更广泛的新闻线索,也改变了其生产方式。传统的调查报道生产模式是从中心到边缘,也就是事实信息是经过严格的个人认证和组织集体认证后才可以传播到受众那里。这是一种以"媒介组织"为中心的组织化生产模式。但是,随着新媒体技术的飞速发展,信息来源不再局限于媒体记者、专门机构和其他媒体,处于事实中心的个人以及由个人临时组成的松散群体(飞信群、BBS、QQ群、微博群等)却成了信息的重要来源。这时,新闻信息传播形态呈现"面-点-面"的模式,调查话语的生产也就转化为从边缘到中心的机制。因此,调查报道的事实建构越来越依赖于媒介外部的多元信息来源,从而呈现出社会化、开放性、多元联动的特点。

2 信息转化:突破性采访保证了建构事实真相的可能

事实建构的基础是首先获取有关事实的信息。信息体系包括自在信息和认知信息。自在信息是未进入记者认知视野的信息,是不可知的事实或被遮蔽的事实信息。只有把自在信息转化为认知信息,媒介才可以按照新闻生产逻辑进行事实建构。而这种信息转化的过程,就是在事实被极度隐瞒或掩饰的情况

[作者简介] 惠东坡,北京联合大学应用文理学院副教授。

下,调查记者通过采取非凡的战略、步骤和手段努力把"自在信息"转化为"认知信息",无限逼近事实真相的过程,这就是采访突破。突破能力是调查媒体制胜的法宝,它越来越成为考察调查记者业务能力的一个重要标准。

采访突破是一个艰难的过程,《财经》杂志记者"为获知一个信源,拨打上百个电话,将每一个细微的收获,拼接成完整的图景;记者甚至主编在知情人家外守候,希冀打动受访者,获得关键信息,即便只是一个态度的回应"。[2]《庄家吕梁》《银广夏陷阱》《基金黑幕》等一系列产生重大影响的报道都是由于记者缜密、严谨的调查采访才把被权力或利益遮蔽的事实信息转换为认知信息的。记者的采访突破有时是打动和争取了一位深知内情的"深喉",有时是在层层迷雾中发现了一些关键信息。例如,《庄家吕梁》第一次系统曝光了中国股票市场的黑暗内幕,就是由于采访到了"内部人"吕梁。《银广夏陷阱》作为完整意义上的调查报道,记者凌华薇持续一年的采访,历经波折。银广夏造假的弥天骗局,最终在天津海关得到确切证实后才被揭露。从 2007—2010 年《新京报》年度调查报道金奖及入围奖作品来看,每一篇报道都是建立在"采访突破"的基础上的。记者绕过重重障碍,通过抽丝剥茧式的调查取证,更多的"自在信息"得以呈现,由此,调查得以延伸,深度因此获得。2010 年获得金奖的《石家庄原团市委书记王亚丽造假骗官》这篇报道,就是两名记者历时半年调查,一点点地把这个骗局的未知谜团独家揭开,用转化的自在信息建立了完整的证据链,最终直指事实真相。

通过采访突破把更多被遮蔽的自在信息转化为认知信息,这是调查性报道生产的第一步,也是至关重要的一步。调查记者要善于从已经展现出来的"浅表事实"开始,由"认知信息"去探知"自在信息"。突破性采访是记者证伪的调查过程,是接近深层事实、转化更多"未知信息"的过程,它使得调查报道建构事实真相成为一种可能。

3 信息呈现:零度修辞成就了事实建构的客观、理性

调查性报道杜绝任何形式的主观臆测和评价,只让新闻事实本身说话,这是零度修辞手法。零度修辞是指用本真的事实记录方式获得一种意义上相对"中立"的文本。它强调以相对隐蔽的方式叙述有关事实的片段、场景、细节和语言,尽量以客观公正的姿态最大限度地呈现事件原貌,避免或隐没其评价意义。零度修辞并不是不讲究修辞,它是一种不着痕迹、最为深刻的修辞。对调查报道来说,它是一种最佳的修辞策略。《财经》调查报道重分析、重事实,克制主观意见的流露。《"如烟"真相》这篇报道就是通过呈现官方、医学专家、烟草管理方、企业方等多因素调查,把事实建构成了一个零度修辞文本。《新京报》零度修辞的叙事原则使其调查报道呈现出理性、客观、冷峻的特点。这主要归因于其生产团队修正了传统的新闻叙事模式,基本不用全知视角叙事,坚持"从外部呈现"的客观视角。《新京报》2007—2010 年的 18 篇金奖和入围奖调查报道都采用的是以内焦点叙事和有限的外焦点叙事相结合的客观视角。客观视角强调如实记录事情的表象,不描摹人物的内心活动。因而,这种叙事视角受到调查性报道的青睐。《新京报》2007 获得金奖的调查报道《贫病夫妻相缚投江》是外聚焦叙事视角的典范。记者像一台摄像机那样客观记录贫病夫妻相缚投江的场景。"夫妻俩被打捞上岸时相互揽拥,拽也拽不开……一条麻绳捆在两人腰间,腰带也相互绞缠在一起。"[3]对于这样一个使人欲哭无泪的事件,如果用内聚焦视角来写,不管是采用记者视角还是第一人称视角,都不太好控制情绪,很容易走入情感失控的误区。用外聚焦的叙事方式,就可以达到客观的报道要求。

零度修辞叙事并不排斥叙述的生动性,相反,它往往通过巧妙的布局谋篇和展现细节、场景来体现其行文的优美。调查性报道写作中的蒙太奇手法突破了传统的强调完整故事情节的写作模式,突出了有效的事实信息,提升了报道的感染力和影响力。在《新京报》《贫病夫妻相缚投江》这篇报道中,记者大量使用镜头叙事,白描的、工笔的、浓墨渲染的"画面"铺展开一个个最打动人的鲜活细节,勾勒出一个普通农村家庭,在疾病折磨下挣扎生存的残酷样本。在《山西运城十余少年连遭跨国绑架》这篇调查报道中,村落、熊牢、宾馆、赌场等闪现出跨国绑架案的震撼人心,筹款、捐资、解救又活现出打击罪犯的难度和无奈。记者亲赴迈扎央采访调查,他看到的是:"野象皮、老虎牙当街叫卖,背着长枪的克钦士兵在人流中穿梭。街道两边,赌场林立。赌场门口,妓女、赌客大声地讨价还价。"在探寻跨国绑架的深层原因时,记者向我们展示了迈扎央博彩业萎缩的景象:"大理石铺就的弧形停车场上,车辆

稀疏而停，保安们蹲在地上，懒散地吸着烟。迈达赌城对面，一座钢结构四周环绕玻璃幕墙的建筑已经停工。"[4]这种蒙太奇式的叙事把杂乱的情节有机连缀成事件发展的有机逻辑，从而启发我们探寻少年落难背后复杂的社会原因。总之，在不违背新闻真实性的前提下，调查报道用场景和细节建构事实，用跳跃的文字，超越常规的时间与空间顺序展示事件的发生和发展，可以体现零度修辞建构事实的客观与理性。

4 信息整合：稿件配置平衡了事实建构的时效性和深刻性

信息整合是谋求新闻报道事实建构资源配置最优化和最大化挖掘新闻事实价值的过程。它是在初级事实的基础上，建构出新闻报道事实的更立体化图景。新媒体时代，报纸一方面要发挥深度报道的优势，另一方面还要体现新闻的及时性。《新京报》刚创刊那两年，原创的深度报道或者独家报道能占到大概五成以上，近两年最多也就占两成或三成。现在的媒体环境要求快速地去操作深度报道，要把操作深度当作操作消息一样。[5]《新京报》调查报道通过稿件配置对新闻事实进行了"二次建构"，在报道动态的时候，进行了深度拓展，真正做到了时效性与深刻性并存。这主要是通过以下手段来实现的。

4.1 为每篇调查报道配置"核心提示"或"关注焦点"

《新京报》为调查报道配置的"核心提示"或"关注焦点"相当于导读，它提炼出调查报道的核心，让读者在极短的时间内迅速获得整篇报道的精华。在2007—2010年的18篇金奖和入围奖调查报道中，17篇有提示配置。"吉林通钢事件"和"邳州非法占地致死调查"这两个系列调查，共有两篇调查报道是放在"中国新闻·关注"版并配置了"关注焦点"。其他调查报道都刊发在"核心报道"版并配置了"核心提示"。核心提示采用纯客观叙事手法，不做任何主观的猜测和评价。"核心提示"好像是把几千字的调查报道改写成了100字、200字左右的消息。除了揭示调查核心外，"核心提示"还通过使用设问等修辞手法设置悬念，引导读者阅读。例如，《"造假书记"王亚丽的官场现形记》的核心提示为"被称作'一身是假'的王亚丽，是如何一路过关斩将，从一名普通的农村女子，一步步升迁至团市委副书记？当地相关部门在王亚丽升迁中是如何审核把关的，为何没有及时发现其身份及档案造假？近日，记者再次赴当地对此进行深入调查。"[6]再如，《神医张悟本的幕后推手》《神医张悟本的身份》也使用了这种手法，以便迅速吸引读者阅读。

4.2 在头版为每篇调查报道设置"导读"

头版是报纸的"橱窗"，是最具有强势的区域。在新媒体的优势越来越明显的时代环境下，头版的导读具有很强的索引和导读功能，是对新闻及时性的强调和对新闻影响力的渲染，也是新媒体时代报纸的"救赎"策略。在《新京报》18个调查报道中，除沧州多名农民被指敲诈政府后获刑、民警高作喜奇遇记、寻找"消失"的辽东"5·11"海难这三篇报道外，其他调查报道都在头版设置了导读。这对没有时间阅读较长篇幅调查报道的读者来说，只通过导读简练的概述也可以马上知晓这一新闻事件。

4.3 在调查报道所在的同一版面配置消息

《新京报》的调查报道一般刊登在"核心报道"版，在"核心报道"版为调查报道同时配发消息的情况比较少，18个调查报道中，只有"甲氨喋呤"这篇调查报道。2007年12月13日在"核心报道"版刊发了调查报道"几种药品挤在一条生产线上生产"，同时配发了消息"药厂有组织隐瞒事实"。假如新闻事件没有进一步调查的可能和必要，《新京报》一般会在"核心报道"版之外的版面同时刊发消息和一次性调查。2007年11月15日在"各地新闻"版刊发事件调查"拿走警察证倒车掉头，枪声响起"的同时，配发消息"公安部派员了解枪击副教授事件"。有些新闻事件，在没有掌握足够多的信息时或者在没有深入调查前，《新京报》通常的做法是：先在其他版发消息或小调查，随着调查的深入，再在"核心报道"版跟进。这种配置既兼顾了新闻的时效性和深刻性，又为读者提供了阅读的多种选择。

4.4 在其他版面为调查报道配置消息

同一天的报道中，在不同的版面进行不同报道形式的整合。2010年6月7日"核心报道"版刊发调查报道"养生市场乱象六问"，在同一天的"北京新闻"版配发消息"悟本堂贴通知，预交费者可退款"。2007年12月13日"核心报道"A20版刊发核心报道"上海市政府责成药厂赔付患者"，同一版组的 A19 版刊发了 1 条相关信息和另一篇核心报道。2010 年 9 月 9 日在"核心报道"版刊发调查报道"蜱虫怪病揭秘",同一天的"中国新闻·时事"版配发消息"河南卫生厅:蜱虫中毒三年 18 人亡"和"北京无蜱虫伤人报告"。通过这样配置,就使调查的事件处在不同的时间维度上,调查报道和消息也各自发挥了报道体裁的优势,相互补充,达到了立体传播的效果。

4.5 为跟进性调查报道配置连续报道

调查报道所关注的新闻事件背后一般都具有深厚的历史、体制背景,由于受到采访对象和记者采写状态的制约,报道不可能一次性完成,整个调查一般会呈现一条纵深的过程。所以,报纸通过系列报道、连续报道等报道形式实现报道配置,实际上是对新闻事实的连续建构,以呈现其发展脉络和深广的社会背景。这是一种特殊的稿件配置形式。《21 世纪经济报道》2006 年震动海内外的"上海社保案"持续了一个多月。通过连续报道配置,一组组调查扎实、反思有力的报道以每期数篇的规模形成了一次规模和级别都空前的连续性调查报道。《新京报》蜱虫夺命调查共进行了四次连续报道。分别从小虫夺命、怪病揭秘、锁定元凶、防治空白等四个层次进行了动态跟踪。整个报道既体现了认知逐渐深入的特点,也展现了调查推进的过程。该报"通钢事件调查"更是动态跟进,深度拓展的典型。前后 6 次报道,先是 2009 年 7 月 27、28 日在"中国新闻"版刊发了 3 篇消息。第三天在"中国新闻·关注"版刊发"吉林通钢事件始末"。这是一般社会新闻的报道思路。有了深入的调查采访后,7 月 31 日在"中国新闻·社会"版刊发消息的同时,配发了 1 篇调查报道。随后继续跟踪事件进展,8 月 2 日在"中国新闻"版刊发了 2 篇消息。最终,在掌握大量调查资料的基础上于 8 月 14 日在"核心报道"版刊推出了 2 篇核心报道"建龙吉林并购折翼路线图"和"建龙十年钢铁征战"。《新京报》的阜阳白宫、邳州征地、李庄案等报道也都采用了连续报道这一配置形式。调查报道通过连续报道这一稿件配置形式,连续跟进和深入解读了新闻事件,发挥了议程设置的作用,也体现了其监测环境、主导舆论走向的策略。

总之,作为调查话语建构基础的事实建构,其运作机制遵循信息的采集、转化、表达、整合的规律和逻辑。调查报道事实建构的特征表现为:新媒体信息来源推动了事实建构的社会化,信息转化过程中的突破性采访保证了建构事实真相的可能,信息的零度修辞呈现保持了事实建构的客观与理性,稿件配置作为一种信息整合手段平衡了事实建构的时效性和深刻性。

参考文献

[1] 麦尔文·曼切尔. 新闻报道与写作 [M]. 北京:中国广播电视出版社,1981:151.
[2] 张志安. 潜入深海 [M]. 广州:南方日报出版社,2010:207.
[3] 杨万国. 贫病夫妻相缚投江 [N]. 新京报,A25,2007-04-05.
[4] 崔木杨. 山西运城十余少年连遭跨国绑架 [N]. 新京报,A13-15,2009-01-19.
[5] 刘炳路. 新闻如果离开了现场就没有真相 [OL]. 凤凰网,2010-12-11.
[6] 黄玉浩. "造假书记"王亚丽的官场现形记 [N]. 新京报,A24,2010-03-03.

论西欧中世纪后期基于文字媒介的知识传播

程德林

在知识传播过程中，媒介是知识从传播的主体（传播知识者）到传播的客体（接受知识者）之间一个不可或缺的要素，它不仅是用以完成知识传播的手段或工具，而且直接影响到知识传播的效果。

媒介之于人类文明的作用可谓大矣！正如传播学家欧阳康教授所说："无论人们的学识有多么渊博，当他们在人类两千多年有文字记载的历史和六千多年文明史的浩瀚大海中漫游之时，无论是地理的、经济的、政治的、智力的、伦理道德的和精神的，他们的记忆或多或少都是朦胧的。然而，就是媒介使朦胧变成了清晰。"[1]正是由于有各种不同的媒介为人类保存了大量的信息，古人的业绩、创造发明、知识成果等才跨越时空传播给今人。

知识传播产生于人类生存与发展的需要，而人类社会的递进发展又对知识传播不断提出新的要求。传播媒介发展到今天，人们完全可以根据不同的需要和可能选择一种或多种媒介传播知识，知识传播有了越来越多的可能性，同时也有了越来越广阔的空间，这充分体现了人类文明的进步。然而，处于中世纪后期的西欧人用于传播知识的媒介只有两种：一是口语，二是文字（严格说来是非印刷文字）。本文只讨论西欧中世纪后期基于文字媒介的知识传播，基于口语媒介的知识传播将另文讨论。

1 西欧印刷书籍出现之前的书

书籍是人类记录和传播知识的工具。在印刷书籍出现之前，西欧人用来传播知识的书籍有两种：一是纸草书，二是羊皮卷。

纸草书是欧洲人最早使用过的书。纸草（Papyrus）是古埃及人发明的书写材料，后来传入希腊、罗马。纸草对西欧文明的影响至今犹在，这不仅因为西欧文明中含有通过纸草传播的古希腊、古罗马文明，而且从"纸"的英文单词 Paper、法文单词 Papier 以及德文单词 Papier 与"纸草"Papyrus 一词的渊源关系也可见一斑。

羊皮卷是继纸草书之后欧洲人使用过的书，由于是把字写在用羊皮做成的纸上，可以卷起来收藏，故称"羊皮卷"。最早的羊皮纸出自罗马帝国时期小亚细亚的贝尔格姆城（Pergame）。当时的埃及皇帝为了保持亚历山大里亚图书馆藏书量世界第一的地位，下令禁止芦叶纸输出到小亚细亚。这样一来，贝尔格姆城图书馆便失去了书的来源。于是，贝尔格姆的国王只好命令国内的能工巧匠用羊皮造纸，以替代纸草。后来，贝尔格姆城就成了制造羊皮纸的中心。现在英文"羊皮纸"一词 Parchment 就源于 Pergame。

西欧曾经经历了一段纸草书与羊皮卷同时使用的时期，后来羊皮卷就取代了纸草书。据英国学者沃尔夫的研究，"早期从埃及输入的易损坏的纸莎草手稿，由于地中海航运的衰落逐渐变得越来越稀少和昂贵，到 8 世纪中叶已或多或少地被文稿誊抄者所淘汰，而代之以一种更结实的羊皮纸"[2]。作为书写材料，羊皮纸比芦叶纸有着更多的优点：它很容易切开，而且可以随意折叠，还可以用线把它装订成册。实际上，羊皮卷才是真正意义上的书。在 8 世纪中叶以后，羊皮卷已基本取代纸草书而成为主要的文字传播媒介。虽然羊皮卷是有史以来真正意义上的书，但这种书还是很特别的。羊皮做成的书又大、又厚、又重，"装订很坚牢，封面是两块布做成的板，里外包上一层皮，四角镶上铜或别的金属，这样角头不会碰坏，而且样子也好看，另外再加上一副铜制的锁，以使里面的羊皮书页不会移动。这样的一册书，看上去实在有些像保险箱的模样"[3]。

[作者简介] 程德林，(1958—)，男，江西万年人，历史学博士，北京联合大学应用文理学院副教授。研究方向：西欧中世纪的知识传播、世界中世纪史。

如果说纸草文书代表了古典文明，那么羊皮卷之类的书则代表了西欧的中世纪文明，后人正是通过保存下来的羊皮卷了解和研究西欧中世纪文明的。

2 修士抄书

西欧中世纪后期除原始手稿外的书籍都是以手抄本的形式出现的。抄书是中世纪人们复制知识信息的惟一办法，抄写好的书被称为"手写文书"（Scriptoria）。当时有不少人从事抄书的工作，其中一部分就是修道院的修士。

修道院（Monastery）是基督教会的一个基本组织，是那些发誓要绝财、绝色、绝意的基督徒潜心修行的场所。不过，中世纪西欧的修道院不单单是一个宗教组织，它集宗教活动、生产劳动、学术研究、教育活动于一身，具有多种功能。美国知识史专家戴勒斯说："修道院成了一个主要的知识中心，它利用自己积累的手稿，办成一个很好的图书馆，以一个较高水平的教育训练和学术研究的场所提供服务。"王亚平教授也认为："西欧的修道院从建立之初起就是基督教文化教育的学校，许多著名的修道院：莱兰、蒙特卡西诺、吕克索耶、富尔达等都是基督教神学的研究中心。"而那些有一定文化的修士们，则是"文化的传播者"。[4]应该说，在中世纪后期，修道院既是西欧一个知识活动的中心，也是一条传播知识的重要途径。

抄书是需要一定条件的，一是要有书可抄，二是要有人能抄，三是要有兴趣也有精力去抄。当时，修道院的修士便具备这三个条件：其一，在那个时代，书是宝贵之物，轻易不能见到，惟修道院存有一些图书资料（包括宗教经典和古典文化典籍）；其二，当时整个社会处于文化落后状态，真正具有读写能力的人不多，而修道院的修士既能读又会写；其三，那时候，即使有的人既有书、又有文化，也不一定有兴趣和精力去抄书，而修士们却有。于是，具备抄书3条件的修士们便扮演了"抄书手"这样一个历史赋予的角色。

修士抄书源于公元6世纪，而最早把抄写经典著作作为修道内容之一的是威维尔斯（Viviers）修道院。当时，这座修道院的院长是意大利人卡西奥多鲁斯（Cassiodorus，约480—575年），他将自己多年收集的古典著作置于威维尔斯修道院，责令修士们进行抄写，他本人也亲自抄，不管是基督教的经典著作、还是异教徒或世俗人士的作品都抄。这以后，修士抄书便形成了一个传统。

在漫长的中世纪，许多修道院的修士夜以继日、认真勤勉地伏案抄书。更有一些修士把抄书视作毕生的事业。美国史学家汤普逊在他的《中世纪图书馆》一书中这样写道："加斯藤（Garsten）修道院的修士用毕生精力抄书。"[5]专门研究宗教与文化之关系的道森先生也说：修士们"坐在阴森的隐修院里艰难地抄写、再抄写他们保存下来的手稿"。[6]

修士们的抄书工作是在十分艰难的条件下进行的："修道院将其回廊分隔成一个个小卧室，有些宽度不足2英尺9英寸，提供给专门抄书的修士居住。……每个修士要自己准备好抄写用的兽皮（羊皮或牛皮）。先用刮刀把皮上的毛刮掉，用浮石把皮磨光，再打上四次蜡，使皮子变得既软又亮，然后展平铺在桌子上，使用那种用小刀削尖的羽毛笔醮着黑墨水进行抄写。……修士们极少有人能在一年里抄完一本书，进展总是十分缓慢而令人疲劳的。"[7]72-73修女也参与抄书，德国韦索布鲁恩修道院的修女蒂姆迪斯就以抄书闻名，"此修女誊写技巧极其娴熟。尽管她不曾因编写任何著作而为人所知，但是她亲手以十分漂亮而清晰的字体誊写出许多卷书，既有为神学祈祷的，也有为修道院公共图书馆誊写的"。[8]

修士抄写的内容并不像人们经常以为的那样只限于神学教义、信条、圣徒的神奇故事、修道院编年史等，而是包含了世俗作品。许多古代著作和手稿正是经修士之手才保存下来的。尤其是在12世纪，有不少希腊文和阿拉伯文的著作被译成拉丁文，而修道院的修士们是较早读到这些译本的人，这些拉丁文著作也因他们的抄写而得以保存，并且流传至今。因此可以说，修道院修士从事抄书工作并不只是完成"上帝"所交给的一部分工作，而且也是在从事知识传播工作。

3 非教会人士的抄书活动

西欧中世纪后期，从事抄书活动的不仅有修道院的修士，也有专门以抄书为业的抄书匠。

意大利著名私人藏书家柯西莫·美第奇曾问佛罗伦萨的书籍收集者维斯帕西诺，怎样才能使图书馆的书多起来？维斯帕西诺回答说：只有抄书。于是，柯西莫·美第奇就委托他从事这项工作。维斯帕西诺只用了很短的时间就请来了45名抄书匠，这些抄书匠在22个月之内抄完了200卷图书。[8]91因为抄书可以使图书馆的书多起来，所以当时的图书馆都设有抄写室，供人专门从事书籍的抄写与装订工作。此外，也有一些书商自行开设抄写室，雇用很多的抄书人进行抄书，大量复制书籍。据《历史上的传播——技术、文化、社会》一书的作者考证，中世纪后期西欧"最有名的抄写室在佛罗伦萨。它是一个名叫韦斯帕西阿诺·达·比斯梯希（Vespasiano da Bisticci）的书商开设的。……有一段时间，比斯梯希雇了50个抄书人在抄写室工作，他按每人抄书的多少付给他们工资"。[7]76抄写室同时拥有50个抄书人在从事抄书工作，可见抄写室的规模之大。

勒戈夫研究过中世纪后期大学里的抄书活动，他在《中世纪的知识分子》一书中说："准备传播的著作的第一个正式副本抄在四开页的分册上，这些分册各自独立。每本由折成四页的熟羊皮制成的分册叫'卷'（Pecia）。抄写者们依次使用它们，它们合在一起称为'样本'（Ex－Emplar）。假如有一本60卷的著作，在一个抄写者单独完成一个独立副本所需要的时间内，依靠这些卷册，就足以让40个抄写者同时完成40份在大学监督下经过润色和在一定程度上成为正式文本的抄本。"[9]当时，在博洛尼亚、萨勒诺和巴黎等地的大学附近出现了一批依附于大学的一种集抄书、售书并兼营书写材料为一体的手工作坊，即"定点书坊"（Stationarii）。

布克哈特也研究过中世纪后期的抄书问题，他在其名著《意大利文艺复兴时期的文化》中说："随着15世纪的到来，开始有了很多新发现，有了用抄写方法系统地制作出的许多丛书。"[10]

总之，在中世纪后期的西欧，抄书活动是比较频繁的。抄书者既有教会人士，也有非教会人士，社会上有抄书活动，大学里也有抄书活动，所抄之书既有单册书，也有丛书。据沃尔夫研究，"阿得拉德（Adelard）所著的《自然问题》一书有20多个抄本流传下来"。[2]有资料表明：英国"通过伦敦进口了大量抄本，仅在1480至1481年间就超过1300本"。[11]中世纪传播史专家詹姆斯·博克先生对中世纪后期大规模频繁抄书之原因进行过研究，他认为13世纪乃至其后人们大量抄书的原因，一是由于不断有新的知识出现，二是当时人们的经济与文化水平都有所提高，对手抄本的需求量越来越大了。[7]71

4　抄本与知识传播

不管是印刷的书还是手抄的书，都是知识的载体。在印刷书籍出现之前，手抄本是以文字为载体传播知识的重要媒介，也是后人研究古典及中世纪文化遗产的重要途径。

从负载的知识内容看，西欧中世纪后期的抄本里不仅有古代学者的知识成就，也有中世纪学者总结的知识成果。据《人类文明编年纪事》记载：1390年，巴黎出现了一本附有插图的介绍风车知识的手抄本，其中提到一种方向固定的风车。1405年，德国学者康拉德·凯泽尔·冯·艾希施泰特用拉丁文著《勇士》一书，并附有插图，这是德国最早的一本有关武器的羊皮卷手抄本。手工业技术知识通过书籍这一媒介的传播，大大促进了德国手工业技术的提高和城市文化的发展。[12]另外，一些手抄的《祈祷书》之类的宗教书籍也在一定程度上向人们传播了知识。而在中世纪后期的西欧，《祈祷书》的拥有量是比较大的。据近年出版的《中世纪后期的日常生活》一书记载，当时英国约克郡的"一些城市家庭拥有祈祷书，人们可以在家里作祷告"。应该说，中世纪后期的手抄书籍在传承和传播人类文明方面发挥了重要的作用。

手抄书籍是中世纪后期人们获取知识的重要渠道。当时，西欧各类学校所使用的教材，绝大部分是手抄本（Codex），西欧各种图书馆的藏书，除了一小部分是古代学者或中世纪学者的手稿外，绝大部分也是手抄书籍。中世纪后期意大利有一位名叫尼科洛·德·尼科里的著名私人藏书家，他在有钱的朋友帮助下雇了不少人从事收集珍本（包括原著和抄本）的工作，"到1437年他去世时已经收集了800卷珍本。此外，他也收集地图。他那藏书丰富的家成为一批学者们聚集的中心。这些学者中有商人、教士和官吏。比如有詹诺佐·马内蒂，他既是商人又是哲学家、神学家和语言学家。还有1431年成为卡马尔多里教派会长的安布罗焦·特拉韦尔萨里。……官吏中我们可以举出前后相继任职的三位共和国秘书官，他们是萨卢塔蒂、莱奥纳尔多·布鲁尼和波焦。这些都仅是很多名人中的少数几个。……其他一些著名学者也在那里停留过，如奥里斯帕（1424年），菲莱尔福（1429—1434年），乔瓦尼·阿尔吉罗普罗

（1456年）"。

5 中世纪后期以文字为媒介传播知识的障碍

在中世纪后期，以文字为媒介传播知识远不像现在这样方便，而是存在着一些障碍，其中最大的障碍就是书少价贵，人们想通过书籍获取知识比较困难。

尽管中世纪西欧的修道院、大学、图书馆、书商家里都设有抄写室，也有不少抄书人专门从事抄书的工作。但是，由于抄书是一项艰苦劳动，一本书从买进羊皮纸到抄写到制作成书更是一个非常复杂的过程，因而书的成本很高，书的数量也很有限。以大学为例，巴黎大学最有名的索邦学院图书馆，1289年只有1000多本藏书，1338年的藏书量也只有1700种。牛津大学著名的奥里尔学院图书馆，1375年只有100多本藏书，著名的新学院图书馆，1380年也只有374本藏书。剑桥大学皇后学院图书馆，1472年时才有199卷书。海德堡大学图书馆，1461年时也才有840卷藏书。堂堂著名学府尚且只有如此之少的图书，其他诸如修道院学校、城市学校等就更少藏书了。据美国的图书馆史专家哈里斯考证，在印刷术传入之前，西欧很少有图书馆能收藏到上千卷的图书。由此可见，中世纪后期的西欧是多么缺乏书籍。

物以稀为贵。因为当时书籍稀少，而在这些稀少的书籍中不是原著孤本就是手抄的珍本，所以书的价格特别昂贵。有材料说："里纳尔多·德格尼·阿尔比兹在其回忆录中记载，他1406年在阿雷佐花了11枚金弗罗林才买到一部《圣经》。"有位名叫博索·德依斯特的人，"1469年，他花了40杜克特买了一本论优素福和克温图斯·库尔提乌斯的书。据说他的两卷本大《圣经》曾价值1375古意大利金币"[8]210。

当然，中世纪后期西欧书价之昂贵还有一个原因，那就是当时手抄的书籍中有些制作得很精美，从而增加了书籍的成本，抬高了书籍的价格。有材料说：一些手抄的书"扉页由优质羊皮纸制成，上面配有插图，大写字母编排醒目，字体花饰，使图案精致增彩。抄写员费心地完美复制字体，用深红色、金色和兰色装饰页边。然后，将烤干的纸张予以装帧，并装进丝绒或牙雕和木雕的富丽嵌座，配上金子和宝石。边缘烫金并贴上花案。银制书夹上面镶嵌乌银。这般杰作，价格自然高昂。1464年，买一本彩饰的书，要支付8枚杜克特（Ducat）金币"[8]94。这样的书籍简直就是一件珍贵的艺术品！正因为当时"法国的书籍具有艺术性的设计风格，所以在上流社会受到格外的珍视"。还有材料说："15世纪初欧洲经济增长以后，对那些关于时间、诗歌和《圣经》等书的需求也开始稳定地增加。当然，一些著名的书，比如坎特伯雷的伊德蕴（Eadwine）诗集、爱尔兰人克尔斯（Kells）的作品等都是价值极高的。它们用皮革装订，包上精致的饰以珠宝的外壳，使之光辉灿烂。……这些名著同金银餐具和圣洁的容器一起放在国库里"[7]74。为什么要把图书做得如同艺术品一样精致呢？这是因为："在中世纪，教士、皇帝、以及诸侯们都想拥有豪华型图书，这样就可以提高他们的显赫地位。"

正因为当时的书籍非常缺乏，所以人们对书籍倍加珍惜，并采取一些措施保护书籍。当时不论是修道院、世俗学校，还是图书馆、藏书楼，都要用重杠和链条将珍贵的书籍栓在专门的读书台的脚上，或者固定在书架上，不让读者搬动书籍。这样的书被称为 Chained Book，意为"加锁的书"。当时还有一种保护书籍的习惯做法，那就是在书卷里写上警告语或咒语，进一步防止书籍被人盗走或被损坏等。

据《发现者》一书记载："一本圣奥古斯丁和安布罗西著作的12世纪手抄本上有这样的警告：'此书属于罗伯特桥的圣玛丽修道院，凡盗窃或出卖此书、或以任何方式将此书带出屋外、或损坏此书者，当永受诅咒。阿门！'"这一手抄本现收藏在牛津大学博德利学院图书馆。"

还有些书里留着这样的咒语："无论何人以何种诡计或何种手段于此地窃取本书，他的灵魂将受到惩罚的报应而遭难，他的名字就会从生命簿上抹掉，不再记入升天之列。""但愿毁坏此书的人，但愿以赠送、出售、借贷、交换、偷盗和其它任何手段……故意转让本书的人，在其一生中招致耶稣基督、其母最光荣的玛利亚、神圣的殉教者托马斯的诅咒。"

以上事实说明，中世纪后期的人们把书籍视如宝贝。面对昂贵的书价，穷人是买不起书的，经济比较宽裕的人买书时也要考虑再三。那些馆藏书籍不是用链条将书栓在读书台的脚上，就是固定在书架上，这样做大大降低了藏书的使用效率。至于那些豪华型图书也只是一种满足某些人虚荣心的装饰品而已，基本失去了其作为书籍传播知识的使用价值。而那些同金、银餐具和圣洁的容器一起放在国库里的珍本书，却更像是专门摆放在一个固定的地方仅仅用于供神，而不是作为每天都要接触的东西给普通人看的。诸如此类都成了障碍，直接影响了书籍的流通和知识的传播。

后来，用亚麻纤维制成的纸逐渐代替昂贵的羊皮纸，这样一来便促进了知识的普及。以前从来还没有产生过这么好的手抄本书籍，也从未进行过如此大量的抄写工作。由于对书籍的需求的增长，致使抄写和装璜书籍的工作从宗教团体的手稿誊写者转移到商业行会的手中，如在布鲁几的圣约翰基尔特，或在布鲁塞尔的宾氏兄弟基尔特。事实上，正是这种对书籍、小册子、传单的需求的增加，其中特别是15世纪中叶关于文法和宗教法的书籍需求的增加，导致了印刷术的采用。而印刷术的采用就使得知识传播的媒介从抄写文字发展到印刷文字，实现了人类知识传播的革命性进步。这一进步的标志，在中国是在868年首次采用雕版印刷技术印出了第一本印刷书籍《金刚经》，在西欧是1445年德国人谷登堡首次用金属活字印刷了有关末日审判的诗歌。以印刷文字为媒介的知识传播，既加大了知识传播的深度与广度，也加快了人类文明的发展进程。

参考文献

[1] 欧阳康. 大众媒介通论 [M]. 广州：中山大学出版社. 1991：28.
[2] Philippe Wolff. The Awakening of Europe [M]. Penguin Books, 1985：60, 280.
[3] (俄) 伊林. 书的故事 [M]. 胡愈之译. 沈阳：辽宁教育出版社, 1993.
[4] 王亚平. 修道院的变迁 [M]. 上海：东方出版社, 1998：33 - 34.
[5] James Westfall Thompson. The Medieval Library [M]. The University of Chicago, 1936.
[6] (美) 克里斯托弗·道森. 宗教与西方文化的兴起 [M]. 成都：四川人民出版社, 1989.
[7] David Crowley&Paul Heyer, Communication in History—Technology, Culture, Society [M]. Longman, 1991.
[8] (美) E. P. 克伯雷. 外国教育史料 [M]. 武汉：华中师范大学出版社, 1990.
[9] (法) 雅克·勒戈夫. 中世纪的知识分子 [M]. 张弘译. 北京：商务印书馆. 1999：77 - 78.
[10] (瑞士) 雅各布·布克哈特. 意大利文艺复兴时期的文化 [M]. 何新译. 北京：商务印书馆, 1991.
[11] Kenneth O. Morgan edited. The Oxford Illustrated History of Britain [M]. Oxford University Press, 1984：215.
[12] (德) 维尔纳·施泰因. 人类文明编年纪事·科学技术分册 [M]. 北京：中国对外翻译出版公司, 1992：59 - 60, 68.

房地产的财税法调控研究

王 平 刘慧勇

1 涉税房地产调控措施及评价

1.1 培育阶段的基本税收制度

从1988年开始，我国启动了城镇住房制度改革，直到1994年，这个阶段主要以调整低租金、出售公有住房、集资建房、加快经济适用房建设等措施为主，逐渐实现住宅商品化、社会化，同时，拉开了房地产业发展的序幕，房地产业还算新生事物，还需要多方政策扶持，才能逐步培育起来，以便推动住房制度改革。这个阶段除了涉及房地产的基本税收制度之外，并无额外的涉税调控措施。

1.2 支持阶段的优惠税收政策

1997年亚洲金融危机以来，为了应对危机、扩大内需，继续将房地产业作为新的经济增长点，直到2000年前后，主要以促进房地产业发展为主要政策取向，相关的税收制度也主要以"优惠"为主题。在营业税方面，表现为对"二手房"交易的优惠以及住房公积金收入免税，体现对产业优惠的同时，支持和促进了住房制度的改革；对个人转让"二手房"、出租房屋实行减免税；在契税方面，对个人购买普通住房减半征税，职工购买单位"房改房"免税；在土地增值税方面，还主要表现为税收宣传、解释和一般的征管，同时确定了房地产开发企业堂而皇之"欠税"的预征制度，为日后清算难埋下了伏笔。❶

1.3 发展阶段的适度调控政策

2000年至2004年前后，房地产业慢慢进入了发展的"春天"，房地产开发一片繁荣，房地产交易日益活跃，但房价一路高升，露出了局部地区房地产投资增幅过大、土地供应过量、房地产市场结构不合理、价格增长过快等不健康的苗头，国家和金融主管部门曾出台了相应的调控措施，❷ 但具体涉税的不多，主要体现为对土地增值税的依法征管。

1.4 "繁荣"阶段的严厉调控政策

2005—2007年，房地产业达到空前的繁荣，房地产交易日新月异，居住性购房、投资性购房、投机性购房并存，尤其是投机性购房占到了房地产交易量的半壁江山，出现了诸如"温州炒房团""山西炒房团"等团体型投机购房，提高了商品房价格，也提高了住房租赁市场价格，扰乱了房地产市场秩序，加重了普通居民购房压力，偏离了国家城镇住房制度改革的既定轨道，使老百姓在满足住房需求方面享受不到"改革开放的成果"。这个阶段，国家陆续出台了相应的调控政策。在税收政策方面，以调整住房供应结构、抑制投机性购房为主。在营业税方面，"二手房"交易的免税条件由购买2年后调整为5年后，严格了免税流程；在土地增值税方面，对个人"二手房"交易实行暂免征税，但对房地产开发企

[基金项目] 本文受2011年度北京市属高等学校人才强教深化计划人才项目（项目编号：PHR201108386）、北京联合大学2011年度校级科研项目——基于财税、金融法的房地产价格控制研究（项目编号：sk201005x）资助，也是北京市法学会2011年度专项课题——经济法视角下房地产市场调控长效机制研究的研究成果。

[作者简介] 王平（1970—），女，汉族，四川安岳人，北京联合大学应用文理学院副教授；刘慧勇（1976—），男，汉族，山西阳泉人，北京联合大学生物化学工程学院讲师。

❶ 这其实也是悖论，如果不实行预征而实行每次转让后都申报纳税的征管制度，征纳成本则太高，也不现实。

❷ 2002年建设部、国家计委、财政部、国土资源部、人民银行、国家税务总局联合发布的《关于加强房地产市场宏观调控促进房地产市场健康发展的若干意见》，即住建房（2002）217号文件；2003年人民银行发布的《中国人民银行关于进一步加强房地产信贷业务的通知》，即银发（2003）121号文件；2003年国务院《国务院关于促进房地产市场持续健康发展的通知》，即国发（2003）18号文件。

业则强化了税额清算，增加了企业的开发营运成本，一定程度上抑制了投资过热，挤压了房地产市场的泡沫；修订了《城镇土地使用税暂行条例》《耕地占用税暂行条例》，调高土地使用税、耕地占用税税额标准；明确了居民住宅区经营用房房产税的征管。尽管采取了较为严厉的税收调控措施，❶ 但实际作用却不够理想，"投机性购房依然不减"❷ 土地增值税的清算"在执行中被地方政府打了折扣"，❸ "没能很好地起到预期的税收杠杆调节作用"。❹

1.5 经济危机阶段的保障性住房税收优惠政策

2008年，受美国金融危机引发的国际经济危机的影响，全球经济处于低迷状态，房价呈现了增长放缓的趋势，国家一方面为了刺激实体经济包括房地产业及其产业链的各行业发展，另一方面也力争完善保障性住房体系，回归住房制度改革的初衷，出台相应的政策措施，这一阶段的政策主要偏向于对保障性住房的优惠。

1.6 新时期的综合严厉调控政策

2009年后，房价又"反弹性"高涨，许多一线城市的平均房价达每平方米20000元以上，投资性、投机性购房更加活跃，房地产市场泡沫明显，住房供应结构不合理，普通居民购房更加困难，在一定程度上导致了较为严重的民生问题，与住房制度改革的初衷渐行渐远。这一时期，国家陆续出台了涉及土地、金融、财税、保障性住房建设，甚至购买资格限制（"限购"）等方面的措施，力图使住房供应结构、消费结构合理，房价合理回落，租售并举，达到"居有定所"的基本要求。在税收制度方面，基本上也是配合国家的调控政策进行调整的，从严调控的包括：营业税方面，将应对2008年经济危机修订的"二手房"交易减免税条件变回了5年标准，使之更加严厉，更能凸显其调控作用；在土地增值税方面，发布了《土地增值税清算管理规程》，更加严格地执行土地增值税清算制度，合理调节房地产开发收益，充分发挥土地增值税制度对房地产市场的调控作用；在个人所得税方面，为了堵塞税收漏洞，明确了无偿受赠房屋免征个人所得税的范围；规定了对单独建造的地下建筑用土地使用税，此外还包括在重庆、上海两地试行对居民个人非营业用房征收房产税。优惠制度包括对居民家庭首次购买普通住房实行契税减税优惠，以及经营公租房的免征房产税。在各项调控措施的综合作用下，从2011年下半年到2012年初，各地房价确实出现了涨幅减小或者价格略有回落的局面，房产、地产交易量明显减少。❺ 而这其中，税收（包括与房地产开发、经营相关的营业税、土地增值税、房产税、契税、土地使用税、耕地占用税、个人所得税）起的作用，很难说有多大的分量，甚至是在重庆、上海试点实行的对个人拥有非营业性住房征税的房产税也没能起到很好的调控作用。❻

一般认为，起主要作用的还是"限贷""限购"这样的行政措施，但行政措施对市场的调控是"非常规"的、也不长久，要真正使房地产业、房地产市场持续健康发展，房价回归合理水平，除了遵循一般的市场规律之外，还应发挥行政手段之外的金融的、财税的杠杆作用。前述分析表明，税收的调节作用是有限的，相关的税收不外乎是两大类，一是交易环节的税收，多属流转税，纳税人可以通过交易转嫁出去，除了有资金占用负担之外，纳税人无实际负担，因此，调控功能不会太强；二是房地产保有阶段的税收，对于投资性、投机性房地产交易主体来说，本来交易就有很大的获利空间，即使不能转嫁，也是能够消化得了的，也不能构成真正的负担，就很难影响其交易意愿。❼

要对房地产市场进行有效调控，促使房价回落，还应该从房地产本身寻找突破口，房地产发展的基本要素涉及土地、资金（自有、融资）、原材料等，以下就土地这个要素从财政角度进行分析。

---

❶ 这个阶段，陆续还出台了相关税收政策，对房地产市场进行综合调控，例如强化涉及房地产转让征收个人所得税的政策、修订城镇土地使用税暂行条例提高土地使用税税额、强化耕地占用税和房产税的依法征管等。
❷ 王平. 住房制度改革与政府职能 [J]. 法学杂志, 2007 (4)：134、135.
❸ 王平. 住房制度改革与政府职能 [J]. 法学杂志, 2007 (4)：134、135.
❹ 王平. 住房制度改革与政府职能 [J]. 法学杂志, 2007 (4)：134、135.
❺ 这种情况，应该一分为二来看：一方面力争房价回落的调控目的达到了，但另一方面，房地产市场发展却受到了一定程度的影响，短期内会出现一些负面的问题，例如企业发展受阻、政府国有土地使用权转让收入减少等。
❻ 两地的具体做法虽然不同，但共同点都是涉及面不广、税额小，对纳税人影响不大，据统计披露，重庆市一年试点征收房产税2亿元左右，上海21亿元左右。
❼ 即使实行房产税试点的沪、渝两地，普通居民购房大多也符合减免税条件，并无多大负担。

2 "土地财政"对房地产调控的影响

2.1 土地财政的缘起和发展

2.1.1 分税制改革后地方财政收入减少，在实践中增强了对卖地收入的依赖

1993年底进行的分税制改革，明确了中央和地方的财力分配关系，实现了二者在税种、税权、税管的划分，解决了当时中央政府财力小、宏观调控能力偏弱的问题，扭转了在财力上"中央弱、地方强而不平衡"的局面，为经济发展特别是强化中央政府的宏观调控能力发挥了巨大作用。但随着形势的发展，问题日益暴露：此次改革只是触及财权的分配，但与之相应的事权却没有作相应调整，中央的财力日益雄厚，中央政府的预算内财政收入占整个财政收入的比例逐年提高，相反，地方政府的则逐年下降，但是，当时改革并未将事权界定清楚，没有做到事权与财权的科学统一，导致地方政府的财政支出日益吃紧。据统计，中央政府的预算内财政收入占整个财政收入的比例从1993年的22%提升到了2011年的49%（其中，2007年占54.1%，2009年占52%，2010年占46%），地方政府则由1993年的78%下降到2011年的51%。而与此相对应的是，地方预算内财政支出占整个财政支出的比例在2011年则为近85%。❶ 即地方政府以51%的财政收入来承担85%的支出责任，❷ 事权与财权极度不匹配。随着社会的进步发展，地方政府的事权范围也在不断扩大，财政支出压力也不断增加。鉴于此，为了保证满足支出需要，地方政府不断挖掘各种制度外资金、土地收入和负债，导致财政混乱、政府信誉受损。在土地管理领域，政府扮演双重角色，混淆了价值判断和职能发挥，大量无序供应土地以换取大量资金充实政府财力，刺激了房地产投资，也推高了房价。

2.1.2 "城市经营"的理念，从理论上支撑了土地财政的发展

1998年，汪道涵提出城市现代化建设要走经营城市的新路，继而有学者提出城市土地经营、城市基础设施经营、城市无形资产经营三项城市经营内容❸。在此理念指引下，各城市广泛展开了相关"经营活动"，尤其以土地经营的收效最为可观，尤其是在一些经济发达城市，如北京、上海、广州、杭州、深圳等城市短期内就聚集了数百亿元的收入，❹ 马上就使"捉襟见肘"的财政状况有了明显的改观。随着"招拍挂"的土地出让制度的实施，各地政府大量出让土地，大幅度提高土地价格，使得土地转让收入越来越多，在政府财政收入中所占比重也日益提高，例如北京市2011年全市公共财政收入3006.3亿元，政府性基金收入1352.8亿元（其中土地出让金收入1233.68亿元，还因为房地产市场不景气没有完成全部预算）。❺

2.2 "土地财政"在房地产调控中的利弊分析

2.2.1 "土地财政"的积极方面

（1）能够有效补充地方政府财力

分税制改革以后，地方税中有些税种进行了改革或被取消，从2000年起，先后停征或者废止了固定资产投资方向调节税、筵席税、农牧业税、屠宰税、农业特产税（其中烟叶税目改为烟叶税保留下来），将车辆购置附加费改为车辆购置税、并作为中央税，将车船使用税和车船使用牌照税合并改为车船税，地方政府的财政收入来源渠道日益减少。但地方事权支出却并没有减少，地方政府通过经营土地取得收益，可以有效补充政府财力，个别城市"土地出让金收入已占所在城市地方财政的半壁江山"，以解决实际困难。❻

（2）有利于保障性住房建设

各地各类保障性住房建设，均属地方事权范畴，需要由地方政府解决❼，国务院、财政部明确规定，

---

❶ 根据财政部相关数据统计计算，财政部网站：http://news.mof.gov.cn. 访问日期：2011年8月20日。
❷ 当然，支出来源中也包括中央政府的税收返还及转移支付。
❸ 王明浩，肖翊. 对城市住宅若干问题的剖析［J］. 城市发展研究，2010（9）：8-9.
❹ http://news.mlr.gov.cn. 访问日期：2011年10月10日。
❺ 北京市财政局. 关于北京市2011年预算执行情况和2012年预算草案的报告. 2012年1月12日北京第十三届人民代表大会第五次会议。
❻ 仇保兴. 对地方政府"土地财政"的理性分析及兴利除弊之策［J］. 城市发展研究，2010（4）：8.
❼ 中央政府每年也划拨保障性安居工程补助资金2011年累计达1709亿元。

各地土地出让金收入主要应该用于保障房建设、耕地整理与必要的城市基础设施建设。尤其是自2008年起，国家重申强调要求各地完善住房供应结构，大力发展"两限房"、经济适用房、公共廉租住房等保障性安居工程，需要投入大量资金，包括保障房专项资金、土地出让收益、住房公积金增值收益，以及试点地区的房产税等财政资金和各种渠道的融资资金。

2.2.2 "土地财政"的缺陷

（1）城市土地无序供应，房地产投资过热，出现野蛮拆迁等问题

为了获取更多土地收益，许多地方不断增加土地供应量，有的地方甚至不惜更改土地用途，把本属于教育用地、公共绿化用地等变更为商业开发用地。由于大量土地入市，使得部分地方房地产投资过热，房地产市场出现供需两旺的"繁荣"景象，投资性、投机性购房严重扰乱市场秩序，导致房产价格不合理上涨。为增加土地供应，各地方进行大规模拆迁、征用农地，为此，甚至出现野蛮拆迁❶、毁坏文物❷，农业用地日益被蚕食，引发许多社会矛盾。

（2）"炒地""屯地"现象严重，推高房地产价格

政府大量供应土地的同时，催热了房地产业，由于城市土地资源的稀缺性，为了获取更高的利润，房地产开发企业通过各种渠道大量购入土地资源，要么自己开发，要么转手倒卖"炒地"，甚至还有"屯地"等待时机，赚取更加高额的利润。无论怎样，这种"炒地""屯地"行为，无疑是炒高了土地资源的价格，从而在源头上推高了房产价格。

（3）过分依赖"土地财政"，寅吃卯粮，不利于城市可持续发展

"土地财政"的实质是政府一次性收取土地资源的交换价格，而房地产权是70年，对于某房地产而言，购买人一次性支付的交换价格从法理上将拥有70年的权益年限，政府在这70年内将不会再获得土地收益。❸ 基于不理性的政绩观，对于每届政府而言，当然是能够最大限度地获取土地收益，这对土地资源有限的城市来说，这种收入渠道是有限的、不可持续的，从长远来看，这种局面也不利于房地产业的健康持续发展。

3 改革财税制度，促进房地产市场良性发展

3.1 改革财政体制，增强地方财力，改变"土地财政"局面，降低房地产价格

从首次交易的房产（简称房产）价格构成成本来看，一般包括：土地出让金、税费、建安成本、财务管理等费用，其中，土地出让金部分，在北京、上海等城市，能够占到四至五成，二三线城市占到二至三成。因此，如果能够降低土地出让金，那房产价格自然就会降下来，政府"使房地产价格回落"的调控目标就能达成。如前所述，房地产业发展的十几年来，地方政府对"土地财政"的依赖程度越来越高，因为调控政策的缘故，2011年各地土地交易均呈下滑态势，地方财政对这部分短收有很强烈的感受。❹

为此，需要下决心改革我国目前这种中央强、地方弱的财力配置格局，在保证中央政府宏观调控需要的前提下，适当提高地方财政在整个财政收入中的比重，使地方财权与事权的匹配度更趋合理。由于分税制施行以来，我国陆续停征、废止、改革了部分地方税种，还将一些税种调整为中央收入，同时还将进一步扩大增值税征税范围、缩小作为地方主要税种的营业税的征税范围，有必要在科学测算的基础上重新划分中央、地方管理的税种，或者以其他科学方式来确定中央和地方的收入划分。同时，加强城市土地资源管理，科学合理进行建设用地长期、中期、短期规划，合理控制土地资源的使用，从源头上掌控房地产业的发展。惟有如此，才能从体制上解决地方财政"入不敷出"的问题，进而自觉遏制通过增加卖地来增加财政收入的"土地财政"欲望，使房地产价格回归应有的正常水平，使房地产市场健康

---

❶ 这样的事件比比皆是，"钉子户"也是野蛮拆迁的结果。
❷ 近期发生了北京华润置地拆毁梁思成、林徽因故居，重庆"保护性"拆除抗战遗迹——国民政府军事委员会重庆行营（蒋介石行营）的事件。
❸ 当然，如因再交易而产生的相关税收则依法成为政府财政收入。
❹ 北京市2011年全市土地出让收入1233.68亿元，完成不到逾期的80%，2012年调低至900亿元。参见《北京日报》2012年2月6日网络版。

稳定发展，使得住房制度改革与房地产业发展并行不悖。

3.2 改革完善房地产税收制度，充分发挥税收制度对房地产的调控作用

3.2.1 修订《中华人民共和国房产税暂行条例》，对个人所有非营业用的房产恢复征税❶

配合改变地方政府"土地财政"局面，在土地交易阶段，降低土地出让金、降低房产交易价格，促进房价合理回落，保证有需求、有购买能力的居民能够买到房。但是在房屋保有阶段，应该负担房产税，将房产中所含的土地出让金转化为房产税，依然归地方政府管理。这样一方面可以在资金方面降低居民的购房门槛，将一次性高投入变更为拥有住房后的持续性投入，另一方面可以抑制投资性、投机性购房，以及不合理的住房高消费，有利于恢复房地产交易的正常秩序，引导居民进行理性的住房消费。同时，解决了地方政府土地收益不可持续的问题。

3.2.2 严格土地增值税清算

由于我国在1995年就确立了对房地产开发企业实行按比例预征税额的土地增值税征管制度，房地产开发企业对于"拖欠"、占用这部分税款已经习惯了，一定程度上助长了房地产热。同时，由于房地产开发、转让周期较长导致征管难度大，一些地区对此产生了畏难情绪，一些地区放松了征管工作，不利于国家税款及时入库，甚至造成应收税款的流失，即使是从2006年开始国家就一直强调要按规定对符合条件的要实行清算，"在执行开始就被地方政府打了折扣"❷，弱化了土地增值税对房地产市场的调控作用。2009年，国家税务总局发布了《土地增值税清算管理规程》，严格了土地增值税清算的条件、程序、具体要求，2010年又连续颁布两个重要文件，重申严格清算制度，促进房地产行业健康发展，合理调节房地产开发收益，充分发挥土地增值税调控作用。为此，需要地方税务部门严肃认真对待，与土地、建设等部门密切配合，共享信息，不折不扣执行中央文件精神，以达到预期调控目标。

3.2.3 强化"二手房"交易相关税收征管

"二手房"交易中，有很大一部分是属于投机性购房后的转手交易，这类投机性购房在很大程度上不合理地抬高了房产价格、催生了房地产泡沫，扰乱了房地产市场，挤占了刚性购房需求空间，使房地产业的发展严重背离了住房制度改革对其互相补充、互相配合的关系定位。因此，调整"二手房"交易相关税收政策、强化征管，是发挥税收调节功能的良好举措。在营业税制度方面，几经反复，确立了目前较为严厉的减免税条件，即不足5年"二手房"，全额征税；超过5年（含5年）的非普通"二手房"，差额征税；超过5年（含5年）的普通"二手房"，免税❸；个人所得税方面，明确销售"二手房"收入为"财产转让"税目，应依法纳税，2010年规定，销售"二手房"并在1年内重新购房的，不再减免个人所得税❹。到目前，相关实体税收制度已经基本完善，能够从制度层面起到对"二手房"交易的调控作用，需要在具体的税收征管过程中强化实施、严格征管。

---

❶ 2011年沪、渝两地已经开始试点征税。
❷ 王平. 住房制度改革与政府职能［J］. 法学杂志，2007（4）：135.
❸ 财政部、国家税务总局关于调整个人住房转让营业税政策的通知. 财税〔2011〕12号.
❹ 财政部、国家税务总局住房和城乡建设部关于调整房地产交易环节契税、个人所得税优惠政策的通知. 财税〔2010〕94号.

共同富裕的历史选择和实现条件考察
——以中国农村为例

王维国

改革开放以来，中国国内经济总量日益增大，社会财富快速增加，贫富差距却日益拉大。面对日益扩大的贫富差距，越来越多的人开始关注政府对共同富裕的"价值承诺"和兑现能力。共同富裕不仅成为我国当前经济社会矛盾的焦点，而且也是理论界高度重视的一个"中心课题"。目前，中国不仅城乡发展不平衡，而且农村内部的贫富差距也日益增大，根据华中师范大学中国农村研究院研究报告，中国农村居民基尼系数在 2011 年已达 0.3949。维护社会公平，实现共同富裕最繁重、最艰巨的任务在农村。实现农村共同富裕寄托了中国共产党的几代领导人和几亿中国农民太多的希望和憧憬。因此，以中国农村为例，对共同富裕的历史选择和实现条件进行考察具有重要的理论意义和实践意义。

一、人类对合作方式的选择及其限度

由于人体生理结构和自然界所能提供的食物的状况方面均存在局限，因而每个人既是独立的个体，又是类存在物，只有在与他人的合作中才能获得生存和发展。就人类已经实现及可能选择的合作方式看，有主要依靠生存法则的自发合作；主要依靠管理者的棍棒、皮鞭的强迫或半强迫性合作；主要依靠国家行政权力，或通过控制住房、医疗、教育、养老等生存必需品的半自愿性合作；主要依靠市场和法律的自觉的合作；主要依靠道德规范的自愿自觉的合作。合作方式不同，合作成果就不同，当然合作者分配成果的方式也就不同。在原始社会，主要依生存法则，自发合作，合作成果较小，只能按人平均分配合作成果。在奴隶社会和封建社会，主要为强迫性或半强迫性合作，这时由于生产力水平有所提高，因而合作成果的数量和质量有了一定提高，但合作成果的分配只能是按照拥有强迫权力的管理者的意愿进行。在计划经济条件或集体经济条件下的社会，主要靠国家行政权力实行半自愿合作，合作成果按国家政策规定分配，即通过控制住房、养老、医疗、教育等生存必需品的半自愿性合作，合作成果在基本生存必需品平均分配的基础上，根据贡献实行适度差别性分配。在市场经济条件下的社会，主要靠市场和法律，自觉合作，合作成果快速增加，按投入的要素分配。在未来的共产主义社会，主要为依靠道德规范的自愿自觉的合作，合作成果极大丰富，可以实行按需分配。我们这里所讲的分配指的是初次分配，在国家条件下，国家可以进行再分配。显然，共同富裕不仅与合作成果的大小有关，而且与合作成果（收入）的分配方式直接关联。

人类对合作方式的选择是由人类自身的特性和人类劳动能力水平所决定的。在我们看来，所谓人类自身的特性其实就是人类在生存中的共同取向，那就是：每个人总希望比以往比其他人生活得好一些，只不过有的人希望在物质方面好一些，有的人希望在精神方面好一些，当然也有人希望两方面都比别人好一些。正是人类的这一特性影响了人们对合作的态度。如果合作能够使个人的生活比以往、比他人更好一些，其合作的积极性就高，合作的成效就明显。对此马克思有过形象的描述："一座小房子不管怎样小，在周围的房屋都是这样小的时候，它是能满足社会对住房的一切要求的。一旦在这座小房子近旁耸立起一座宫殿，这座小房子就缩成可怜的茅舍模样了。这时狭小的房子证明它的居住者毫不讲究或者要求很低；并且，不管小房子的规模怎样随着文明的进步而扩大起来，只要近旁的宫殿以同样的或更大的程度扩大起来，那么较小房子的居住者就会在那四壁之内越发觉得不舒适，越发不满意，越发被人轻视。"[1]

[作者简介] 王维国（1967—），男，陕西子洲人，北京联合大学人民代表大会制度研究所研究员。

人类对合作方式的选择，除了受人类自身特性的影响外，还要受人类的劳动能力水平的制约，即我们经常讲的生产力水平。也就是说，在人类社会，和谁合作，如何合作是有限度的。改革开放后，江苏的华西村、北京的韩村河等在中国崛起的强村富村之所以得到了村民们的认同，愿意继续走集体主义的合作方式，就是因为村民一方面劳动能力不断提高，另一方面通过集体主义的合作方式，无论是村民们的生活水平，还是生活条件都比以往、比周边村庄好，甚至在全国农村中，都处于最前列。

当然，这些强村富村的崛起，得益于改革开放后中国社会生产力水平的快速提高和外部市场经济条件的确立。

二、新中国对农村共同富裕的探索

旧中国不仅积贫积弱，而且贫富差距悬殊。基于此，尽快消灭贫穷并且实现共同富裕就成为共和国第一代领导人的理想和追求。尤其是如何使广大农民脱贫致富、实现共同富裕，就成为毛泽东考虑新中国建设的出发点和着眼点之一。1953年中共中央通过了《关于发展农业生产合作社的决议》，从此中国开始了通过走集体合作化的道路使全体农村人民共同富裕起来的试验。随后，党和国家在救济、医疗、教育等方面采取了一些具体措施，帮助农民摆脱贫困，走向共同富裕。然而，为了防止两极分化，一味片面追求均富，结果导致在农业科学技术方面的支撑缺乏和不足，在劳动者的合作方式简单而机械且愿望不足的情况下，农村不仅没有富裕起来，而且人们的消费欲望在受到限制的同时，创造的热情也受到了打击，共同富裕变成了共同贫穷。当然，国家通过工农业的"剪刀差"，将一部分农业收入用来支持工业和城市发展也是导致农村贫困的一个不可忽视的因素。这就表明当人们的劳动能力没有很大提高的条件下，大规模地实行集体主义政策有其历史和时代的功能局限，当它在完成它的历史使命时，带来的只能是消极作用。

三、改革开放以来合作方式的转变及其影响

共同的贫穷不仅使社会失去了活力，而且使人民失去了幸福，更使人们对社会主义的价值产生了怀疑。对此，改革开放的总设计师邓小平决定改革原来的那种简单合作的农业集体化生产方式，实行包产到户的农业生产责任制，城市工商业也进行了承包制等调动生产经营者积极性的新的生产经营方式，并逐步推行市场经济。随着行政性权力在人们分工合作中作用的减弱，市场机制的作用日益增强，这不仅使全社会的物质财富迅速增加，而且也使得人们的生活条件得到了改善，生活水平得到了较大的提高，中国共产党的改革开放政策得到人民的普遍拥护。但随着农村集体经济的不断弱化，国有和集体工商企业普遍转轨改制，社会贫富差距日趋拉大，社会弱势群体不断遭到排斥。

对于集体主义的未来前景，邓小平同志曾多次说明。1980年5月31日，他在同中央负责同志的一次谈话中明确指出："我们总的方向是发展集体经济。实行包产到户的地方，经济的主体现在也还是生产队。这些地方将来会怎么样呢？可以肯定，只要生产发展了，农村的社会分工和商品经济发展了，低水平的集体化就会发展到高水平的集体化，集体经济不巩固的也会巩固起来。关键是发展生产力，要在这方面为集体化的进一步发展创造条件。"[2]此时，邓小平同志就已经深刻地认识到，在生产力发展的基础上，低水平的集体合作只有发展到高水平的集体合作，才能真正有助于实现共同富裕。1985年，邓小平更加明确地指出："社会主义的目的就是要全国人民共同富裕，而不是两极分化。如果我们的政策导致两极分化，我们就失败了。如果产生了什么新的资产阶级，那么我们就真是走了邪路了。"[3]1990年3月，邓小平在谈到农业问题时再次强调："中国社会主义农业的改革和发展，从长远的观点看，要有两个飞跃。第一个飞跃，是废除人民公社，实行家庭联产承包为主的责任制。这是一个很大的前进，要长期坚持不变。第二个飞跃，是适应科学种田和生产社会化的需要，发展适度规模经营，发展集体经济。这是又一个很大的前进，当然这是很长的过程。"[3]1992年南方讲话中，邓小平更是将共同富裕提升到社会主要本质的重要组成部分的高度。这就表明，在邓小平同志看来，社会主义与共同富裕是同一的，只要我们坚持走社会主义道路，就必然最终实现共同富裕。

面对我国经济发展新阶段出现的新情况、新问题，新的中央领导集体在进行了深入细致调查研究的基础上，为我国农民脱贫致富采取了一系列重要的政策措施。中共中央从2004年起将"三农"工作摆

在"重中之重"的地位上，2005年制订"十一五"规划时将建设新农村放在各项任务之首，并作出"工业反哺农业，城市支持农村"的决策，努力提高农民收入。胡锦涛同志曾明确指出："在促进发展的同时，把维护社会公平放到更加突出的位置，综合运用多种手段，依法逐步建立以权利公平、机会公平、规则公平、分配公平为主要内容的社会公平保障体系，使全体人民共享改革发展的成果，使全体人民朝着共同富裕的方向稳步前进。"[4]

这些制度政策创新，一定程度上改善了弱势群体的生活水平和条件，但由于未能触动强势群体在生产要素方面的垄断控制优势，因而未能遏制两极分化的势头。这就表明，实现共同富裕的合作方式及其所依赖的条件还有待于我们进一步明确，并在实践中不断去探索和改进。

四、共同富裕的实现条件

唯物史观否定之否定规律决定了人类合作方式必然是一个由自发合作到非自愿合作再到自觉自愿合作的过程。自觉自愿合作是超越市场机制的完全依赖道德规范的合作，也是人类真正意义上的合作。人类要超越市场机制，一方面要求人类个体的能力要有超越性的进步；另一方面，与此相联系，人类财富增加的关键因素或主要因素是劳动力，而非其他生产要素。人类个体能力的普遍提高，消除了其成为弱者的可能性。劳动力成为财富增加的关键因素或主要因素，一方面使得个体占有生产资料的意义减弱，另一方面，人类个体合作由谋生的需要变成了自我确证的需要。人类不断超越市场机制的过程，也就是逐步建设共同富裕社会的过程。

以上仅仅是对人类的合作方式的演变的逻辑分析。人类历史发展到今天已进入后现代社会。在西方发达国家，生产资料私有制已由资本家独有发展为股份制（企业、公司的员工和社会也有份额），财富的增加由主要靠科技含量转变为科技含量和设计者管理者的创意并重。劳动力所获得的收入占公司、企业总利润中的份额越来越大。与此同时，对那些因先天疾病、天灾人祸等原因造成的能力缺陷者或能力不足者，政府给予了基本的生活保障。只要有工作岗位（处于就业状态），人们的生活就不会有问题。就中国目前来说，推行市场经济后，之所以会再次出现两极分化，其中一个重要的原因就是劳动者的收入同其他生产要素所获得的收益相比，所占份额不断下降。我国的企业、公司虽然大部分实行了股份制改造，但缺陷明显；同时，我国的就业不足一直伴随着改革开放的进程，而且就业形势日益严峻。政府对劳动能力不强者或缺陷者的基本生活保障也是低水平且有欠缺的。就那些改革开放后崛起的共富村来说，一方面，所有有劳动能力的村民实现了充分就业，使每一位劳动者获得了一定的劳动收入；另一方面，实行集体所有制后，劳动力以外生产要素的收益以福利的形式平均地返还给了每位村民，老弱病残者得到了特殊的照顾。虽然这些共富村村民的个人能力从整体上讲，并未超出全国的平均水平，但由于其作为劳动者被平等对待，生活无忧，这时带领者又通过唤起毛泽东时代的集体记忆，使人们再次燃起了集体主义的激情。共产主义作为人们对毛泽东时代的集体记忆，常常用来对社会上日益滋生蔓延的自私自利、消极腐败现象进行道德的批判。而人们对共产主义最直接的感受和体验就是集体主义，尽管集体主义一度曾使人们经受了共同贫困的生活。然而，物质上的贫困，生活的单一，个性齐一，却使人们通过斗私批修，在理想道德上站上了高地。许多观察者就是因为看到了这些村的集体主义激情，因而对其持久性和思想道德至上性产生了质疑。其实，对这些村民来说，虽然其个性化需要受到了一定程度的抑制，但其劳动人权得到了最公平的对待，因而即使个人生活自由权受到一定程度的抑制，也还是可以包容的。都是村民，其能力差异本来就不是很大，对收入分配上的平均主义意见自然就不会太多。即使是那些能力较强的带领者，也并未领受超出普遍村民太多的报酬，作为普遍村民还能对平均分配说些什么呢？个人自由同好生活、道德比起来，似乎成为叛逆，得不到彰显也就自然而然了。

综上所述，共同富裕的实现条件就是：大力提高全民的劳动能力水平，实现劳动者的充分就业，提高劳动者收入在生产要素收益中的份额，扩大和提高劳动能力不强者和缺陷者的基本生活保障覆盖面和水平，让劳动者对劳动力以外的生产要素收益的分享不断增加。

参考文献

[1] 马克思，恩格斯. 马克思恩格斯选集（第1卷）[M]. 北京：人民出版社，1997：367-368.

[2] 中共中央文献研究室. 邓小平年谱1975—1997（上）[M]. 北京：中央文献出版社，2004：641.
[3] 邓小平. 邓小平文选（第3卷）[M]. 北京：人民出版社，1993.
[4] 中共中央文献研究室. 十六大以来重要文献选编（中）[M]. 北京：中央文献出版社，2008：712.

两岸法律适用问题研究

——一个政治与法律互动的视角

刘文忠

历史上许多重大的社会变革或伟大的改革家,都是以一些微小甚至不重要的问题作为切入点,从而展开深刻的社会转型与变革的。两岸法律适用在两岸关系的框架下显然属于比较微观与中观的层次,但法律适用的方法、技术、规则等可以能动地牵引两岸统一的进程,展现出法律与政治关系更为多元的互动关系。

两岸四地经贸往来日益频繁,产生越来越多的民商事纠纷,而这种跨越不同法域的纠纷涉及法律适用问题。法律适用[1],在一般意义上是指行政主体(公权力的代表者:司法机关和行政机关)依照法定职权和程序实施法律(行使公权力)的一种专门活动;在冲突法学中,法律适用就是准据法的确定。在法律体系统一的国家,不存在国家冲突法意义上的法律适用问题。在国家未统一之前且我国实行"一国两制"的特定的历史时期内,都存在着区际"准涉外法律适用"问题。台湾由于内战遗留问题作为独立法域而存在,香港和澳门分属于西方法系传统中的普通法系和大陆法系,有独立的法源,大陆、台湾、澳门、香港构成一国范围内的四个相对独立的"法域"。

1 两岸法律适用问题的意义

台湾与大陆都是重视法律的社会,将两岸和平发展的成果法律化更容易获得台湾的认同。两岸的法律问题从宏观上是两岸的宪政安排与宪政结构问题,立法权与主权者如何统一问题;从中观上是两岸公权力如何对接,是区际法律冲突和选择问题;微观上是两岸经贸交往中法律适用问题。无论两岸的哪一个法律层次的安排,都可以形塑两岸的政治过程,将微观的法律问题发展为宏观的政治性议题,或者将宏观的宪政结构展示为对两岸交往中的民生关怀,例如涉台的民商法律关系。适时解决两岸法律适用问题,实质上是从两岸关系框架的一个微观与中观视角介入两岸未来的一个实践性问题,是探讨法律行为与政治现象一个个案分析框架。一旦两岸法律适用的框架被能动地创造出来,成为一种制度,就会成为外在于人们的强大力量,有助于理解行为与事件对于两岸的意义,从而对两岸冲突起着疏导与调节的作用,确保两岸关系沿着健康的轨道前进。

1.1 前瞻性探索法律体系与主权如何实现统一的需要

法律不仅仅要提供正确的司法判决,还要为社会提供思想,发挥积极的建构社会的功能;法律在现代社会里不可或缺,并与政治、历史、哲学、社会等共生,在树立基本人类秩序上意义非凡。我国是单一制国家,但却是典型的复合法域国家。[2]在我国相互独立和平行的四个法域(拥有独立的审判权),立法者与主权者并未实现统一。研究两岸法律适用的意义在于通过制度建设,使四法域内在协调有序运行,形成政治与法律双向良性互动的格局。在规则体系没统一之前,可以借助法律原则与两岸共有的法律文化实现规范内涵的统一。

两岸民间交往衍生大量的法律问题,仅仅以默契和政策灵活是解决不了的,必须求助于公权力和制度化的机制才能确保有序发展。[3]两岸公权力的对接和进行事务性的合作与磋商是早晚的事情,实际上两岸的法律事务合作已经开始。随着两岸全面直接双向"三通"的实现,海峡两岸经贸交流、人员往来日益频繁,涉台婚姻、继承、经贸投资等民商事纠纷越来越多,无疑增加了审判难度,而障碍主要集中

[作者简介] 刘文忠,北京联合大学台湾研究院,教授,法学博士。

在两点：规范援引和判决的执行。最高人民法院一贯重视依法保护海峡两岸当事人的正当权益，自1988年至2010年12月以来，共发布了7个司法解释，对于两岸法院及时、公正审理互涉民事案件发挥了积极作用。其中2010年《最高人民法院关于审理涉台民商事案件法律适用问题的规定》明确了涉台民商事案件的法律适用规则，该最新司法解释规定："根据法律和司法解释中选择适用法律的规则，确定适用台湾地区民事法律的，人民法院予以适用。"而且尤其值得重视的是，台湾方面也于2010年4月三读通过"涉外民事法律适用法修正案"，一定程度衔接了国际私法发展的基本规律，但"新法"继续延续"小"国际私法观，仍停留在冲突规范的层面。在两岸复杂的政治环境下，务实解决两岸的经济与法律事务，更多地通过仲裁、ADR纠纷解决机制不可避免，而台湾民事诉讼法律适用修正条文远没有表现出对两岸经济与法律事务高度的预见性和适应性。

1.2 解决两岸经贸交流常态化与法律冲突并存的需要

有独立的法律制度和管辖权是"法域"的本质特性。"法域"就是拥有独立法律体系的区域，该区域内实行独立于其他区域的法律制度，并拥有独立的司法管辖权[4]。如果仅从司法管辖权的角度分析，法域与主权国家有共同之处但并不重叠，但它特指一个主权国家内部实行不同的法律制度和享有相互独立的司法管辖权的地理区域。中国各法域之间，存在着不同的法律传统，有些法律只能在本法域内行使，各法域间互不隶属，彼此之间是相互平等的关系。

独立与具有平行地位的法域引发法律适用中的冲突，实质上是主权统一行使过程中障碍性与阶段性的问题。法域间需要协商与合作，共同促进，共享发展。当今世界经济全球化趋势明显，在区域层面上表现为区域经济一体化。随着香港、澳门的回归和台湾问题的最终解决，不同法域之间建立一种比现在更紧密的经贸关系，乃至最终在中国境内形成一个统一的市场体系是一种不可阻挡的趋势。作为具有统一主权的中国境内四法域之间有必要加强司法领域的协调与合作，以推进这一历史进程；而且两岸四地共有的人文传统，是谋求民商法律适用的统一模式的基础；现代市场经济使经济与社会生活变得越来越不具本地化色彩，是四地共有的制度基础。当然世界经济的一体化及两岸四地经济的区域化，使得确认四地法律传统所使用的标准变得越来越复杂，成为政治性和法律性、国际性与区域性相互交织的问题。

1.3 建立两岸纠纷解决机制的需要

两岸交往中一系列影响两岸民生的问题，都需要以务实和理性的态度多角度来构建两岸争端解决的法律机制。一个有效的争端解决机制，对于两岸经贸往来是必要的，它可以提高两岸争端解决的预见性和法律安全，减少经贸纠纷，维系两岸人民的感情，有利于区域经济一体化的实现。争端解决机制就是ECFA其中重要部分，是逐步破解政治难题的一部分。

2 目前两岸法律适用存在的主要问题

随着两岸关系和平发展，两岸法律适用的研究成果与两岸法律事务不断推向前进。目前两岸法律适用研究与法律事务重点集中在两岸司法互助层面，主要包括民商事司法互助、刑事司法互助。加强两岸司法实务领域的交流合作，针对案件管辖、罪犯移管、文书送达、协查取证、证据采信、判决认可等方面互助事宜，设定更为具体的操作制度和标准，构建顺畅、高效、平稳的协作机制，是顺应两岸民心、惩治互涉犯罪、提高司法效率的必然要求。

两岸法律适用包括规则适用、法律冲突、判决的承认与执行等多层次问题，这些层次既有体制性问题，也有技术性与程序性问题，既有政治无关乎法律问题，也有法律无涉政治问题，因此应区别对待，分层次推进。

2.1 法律适用规则的完善

首先，完善两岸四地的双边规则。大陆先后与港澳签订了《更紧密经贸关系的安排》（CEPA），2010年6月与台湾签订了《海峡两岸经济合作框架协议》（ECFA）；台湾为解决四地间民商法律适用制定了"两岸关系条例""港澳关系条例"；香港立法会也审议了《香港特别行政区与内地相互执行商事判决》的安排；四地都有涉外民事诉讼规则但区别很大。最高法院对港澳台的民事判决与仲裁的执行、诉讼文书的送达做了司法解释，先后出台了涉台的7个司法解释，并于2010年12月颁布了《关于审理涉台民商事案件法律适用问题的规定》。

其次，为了更好地促进两岸四地经济发展与错综复杂的法律关系，除了要完善双边规则外，还要科学架构两岸四地的多边规则。在经济高度一体化的区际之间，为了减少歧视，降低跨法域交易成本和风险，必须有相适应的区际法律适用制度与规范。

最后，科学协调国际组织规则和区际间规则的关系。CEPA、ECFA 是在 WTO "一国四席"的背景下签订的，四方是一个主权国家下单独关税区，又是 WTO 体制下的独立成员，增加了法律适用的难度。签订 CEPA、ECFA 后，这种制度缺陷导致的问题更加突出。两岸四地涉外民事诉讼法虽分别对民商法律适用问题做了单方约定，但司法实践中难以统一，加之两岸四地之间的政治、法律关系纵横交错，法律文化与法治水平发展极其不平衡，且涉及国际条约适用上的冲突，两岸四地民商法律适用规则协调是一个亟待解决的问题，应当适时而前瞻地推出区际法律冲突的"示范法"或者协商制定统一的区际冲突规范。

2.2 单边立法的冲突

两岸四地现有民商立法体系"同"的因素与"异"的因素并存，法律规则难以统一，而指导司法实践的法律原则又常态性地受到政局的影响，一些法律原则诸如"公共秩序"和"善良风俗"是不能通过明确列举得以阐释的概念（很大程度上是解释性的），带有不可预见性。

两岸四地的法律冲突客观存在，它具有合法性但是不具有合理性。例如，两岸四地管辖权的确立，我国虽然没有对区际民商事管辖权进行直接协调，适用于中国数个法域的有关国际公约对个别的民商事纠纷的司法管辖权问题进行了间接的协调，导致了大量涌现的平行管辖和平行诉讼的存在。目前在中国各法域，国际和区际民商事诉讼管辖权的规定是一致的，各法域均将区际民商事管辖权问题与国际民商事管辖权问题同样对待，这与统一主权的要求是不相符合的，也反映了我国各法域尤其是内地和港、澳地区在区际民商事管辖权立法问题上的滞后。

2.3 判决承认与执行的障碍

相互认可与执行民商事裁判是两岸民事司法协助的重要内容，目前两岸主要通过各自立法的方式对此加以规范。自 1988 年至 2010 年 12 月以来，最高人民法院先后出台了 7 个司法解释，就申请认可台湾地区有关法院的民商事裁判的范围、法律效力以及程序等问题做出了明确的规定。[5]

台湾地区认可与执行大陆地区民商事裁判的主要依据是 1992 年 7 月颁布的"台湾地区与大陆地区人民关系条例"第 74 条。该条规定，"在大陆地区做成之民事确定裁判、民事仲裁判断，不违背台湾地区公共秩序或善良风俗者，得申请法院裁定认可"。此原则是台湾方面在判决的承认与执行的主要原则，即"不违背台湾地区公共秩序或善良风俗"。由于该条规定过于原则，因此缺乏可操作性。

两岸民商法律适用如能够取得更好的发展，必须在管辖权问题、扩大法院相互认可与执行民商事裁判的范围、完善对仲裁裁决认可和执行的规定等方面取得突破，特别应当对公共秩序的内容、公共秩序保留的适用范围与标准做最低限度的原则性限制，并通过权威判例明确公共秩序的具体判断标准，逐步对公共秩序的内涵加以界定。[6]

3 两岸法律适用的制度构建

两岸法律适用主要解决两岸案件的管辖权、裁判案件的程序与规范选择、既判力等法律问题，作为阶段性目标目前在于立体性完善三个层面的问题：争端解决机制，明确争端解决的主体、方式和程序，确立案件的管辖权；法律冲突与冲突规范的选择，明确在法律适用中哪些规范可以选择，排除哪些规范，法律原则在司法判决的效力；司法互助，主要解决既判力问题，以及发生在判决中的证据和文书交换与互助。三个层面又立体性地辐射诸多两岸法律事务性问题，共同构成两岸法律适用的制度。

3.1 争端解决机制的完善

两岸关系经历一个发展过程，随着政治局势的不断变化，从战争状态、结束战争状态、累积互信、共同化解分歧与解决争端、形成局部的利益共同体、形成某种政治协议、进行政治宣誓，形成政治共同体，最后成为国家共同体，争端解决机制显然处于两岸关系发展过程的中观结构。争端解决机制的建立能够对两岸稳定发展做出最独特的贡献，保证 ECFA 后期协议与前期收获能够如期执行。两岸应遵守共同拥有的社会责任以及幸福、和谐的争端解决理念，才能共享两岸发展成果，增强两岸经贸往来，以及和平发展时期的可靠性与可预见性。两岸人应该做出承诺并且信守，不应采取单边行动以对抗其发现的违反和平发展规则的事件，而应在争端解决制度下寻求救济，并遵守其规则与裁决而不是斥逐报复措施。

争端解决机制要解决两个核心问题，即争端解决的规则与程序，它们是保障双边与多边贸易体制的可靠性和可预见性的核心因素。两岸通过 ECFA 的签署建立起制度化的经贸合作框架，通过"两会"建立起协商性谈判机制。但必须看到"两会"机制受台湾政局变化的影响很大，ECFA 签订后尚需一系列后期协商，两岸交流的日益频繁和立体化需要完善许多制度，存在两岸协商后制度供给的严重不足，因此进一步完善 ECFA 后的争端解决机制意义重大。

3.1.1 完善法律适用规则

规则包括双边规则和单边规则。从 1990 年"海峡两岸红十字会组织有关海上遣返协议"到 2010 年 6 月签订 ECFA，海峡两岸共签订 22 个协议[7]，这是两岸的双边规则，主要包括两岸签订的双边协议；单边规则是两岸法域的各自立法，现在两岸的单边立法逐渐增多，涵盖实体与程序法。

3.1.2 程序正当

就程序而言，涉及几个核心要件：争端解决机制的主体、争端解决的时间表和争端解决的方式。如何设置科学的争端解决程序，可以借鉴 WTO 争端解决的相关原则，科学地设定 ECFA 框架下的争端解决机制的正当程序原则。WTO 争端解决机制具有中立性原则、听审原则、参与原则和证明原则等一系列原则为 ECFA 提供了一个典范。

3.1.3 完善争端解决方式，完善公力救济机制和私力救济机制

两岸争端解决机制涉及公力救济与私力救济，仅仅通过大陆、台湾彼此单向的公力救济是远远不够的。公力救济受两岸政治生态的影响，而私力救济机制尚不完善。

首先，要完善公力救济机制，ECFA 签订后，两岸共同约定"两岸经济合作委员会"负责处理与本协议相关的事宜，包括但不限于任何关于本协议解释、实施和适用的争端，采用了与 CEPA 一样的传统的政治争端的解决方法，且规定得很原则，并没有赋予任何司法解决争端的方式，是一种临时性、过渡性的安排。

其次，要扩展私力救济机制。ADR（Alternative Dispute Resolution）以妥协而不是对抗的方式解决争端，有利于维护两岸的商业关系和人员往来；ADR 更快捷，更简易和直接，避免了送达、执行和取证难的诸多不便；在两岸规则对接相对滞后的情况下，ADR 不必局限于规则的条条框框，允许当事人自主选择适用的实体规范，如地方惯例、行业习惯和标准或者 WTO 条款等，做出的结果更符合商业惯例和道德标准。在目前可在香港建立 ADR 机构，由台湾律师、香港律师、大陆律师或法律工作者联合组成一个 ADR 机构。

3.1.4 政治与法律方法相结合的原则

WTO 争端解决机制将政治说理方法与法律方法结合起来，形成了独特的和平解决争端制度。国际及其区域经济组织一般采用的争端解决方式包括磋商、专家组和上诉机构审理，以及在当事方自愿基础上的仲裁、斡旋、调解或调停，结合了争端解决的政治方法与法律方法，体现了综合性争端解决机制，采用了多种争端解决方式。由于两岸关系受岛内政局影响大，在争端解决时应特别强调政治方法与法律方法相结合，充分借鉴 WTO 争端解决机制。

总之，应在两岸共同利益的前提下，采用非强制的争端解决方式平衡两岸的共同利益，求同存异，才是 ECFA 的实质。

3.2 法律冲突与冲突规范的选择

两岸法律冲突在性质上是区际法律冲突（Interregional Conflict of Laws），区际法律冲突是指一个主权国家内不同法域的法律相互之间适用效力上的冲突。[8]多法域并存是区际法律冲突产生的前提条件和根本原因。区际法律冲突是一个主权国家内不同法域的法律之间的冲突，区际法律冲突是不同法律在空间上的冲突，是不同法律在效力上的冲突，或不同法律在同一平面上的冲突。一般认为，区际法律冲突是

指一个国家内部不同地区的法律制度之间的法律冲突，或者说是在一个国家内部不同属地性法域之间的法律冲突。区际法律冲突是解决统一国家内部因不同地区的民法不一致所造成的法律冲突的法律，这种法律冲突多见于复合法域的国家，又称多元法域。在一个中国的前提下，存在四个相对独立的"法域"（大陆、香港、台湾和澳门）。"区"是法律概念，四个"法域"的法律体系相对独立，但在国际法上中华人民共和国是唯一且必须的国际法主体；在国内法上则是如何有效处理四者关系，实践性解决一国内具有中国特色的法律冲突。中国区际冲突是指中国范围内大陆、香港、澳门、台湾四个法域之间的利益冲突及法律冲突；不仅是大陆与香港、澳门、台湾之间的冲突，也包括香港、澳门、台湾三个地区相互之间的冲突。区际法律冲突包括三方面的内容，即区际管辖权、区际法律适用和区际司法协助。

3.2.1 国际复合法域国家解决区际法律冲突的经验

国际上没有关于解决区际法律冲突的统一模式，按照目前有关国家的理论与实践，采用区际冲突法的解决方式主要有以下几种形式："分别立法"模式、"统一立法"模式、"示范法"模式、类推适用国际私法解决等方法。

A. 制定统一的区际冲突法。有的国家专门制定了区际冲突法法典或法规，如1926年的《波兰区际私法典》；有的国家将区际冲突法与国际私法合并起来规定，如1891年瑞士颁布的《关于定居的或者暂住的公民的民法关系的联邦法》；有的国家是颁布解决某些方面的区际法律冲突的区际冲突法，如南斯拉夫于1979年颁布的《解决关于民事地位、家庭关系及继承的法律冲突与管辖权冲突的条例》。

B. 制定各自的区际冲突法。各个法域分别制定各自的区际冲突法来解决本法域与其他法域之间的区际法律冲突，许多国家都是先产生各个法域自己的区际冲突法，再逐渐发展成全国统一的区际冲突法的，例如美国、加拿大和澳大利亚等国。

C. 类推适用国际私法解决。采用这种方式解决区际法律冲突的国家，既认为区际冲突法与国际私法有不同之处，又强调二者之间的相似之处，因此并不单独制定区际冲突法，只是通过本国的国际私法的相关规定来类推适用国际私法规范解决区际法律冲突。在英美法系国家，一法域的法院把本国的其他法域视为同其他主权国家一样的外法域，因此，在解决区际法律冲突的时候，适用的区际冲突法与国际私法的基本规则是一致的。但是由于国际法律冲突与区际法律冲突之间的区别，这些国家一般是指适用国际私法的基本规则和原则，在具体的适用上并不完全一致。

D. "示范法"模式。在美国，为了解决区际法律冲突问题，各州于1892年共同成立了一个半官方机构，即"统一州法委员会全国会议"。该组织在比较研究各州的法律法规以后，负责制定一个统一立法的最低标准。草案经全体会议通过后，建议各州采用。这种模式对于建立和统一区际民商事司法协助制度无疑是有积极意义的，它不仅可免除各法域之间进行谈判、协商、签约等复杂的环节，能够充分发挥专家学者的作用，自由、简便，易于被各方所采用和接受。[9]

3.2.2 我国复合法域解决区际法律冲突的路径选择

灵活、多样不拘泥于法律体系的区际私法应成为两岸构造两岸民商交往统一运动的基本原则，适用区际法律冲突模式处理两岸法律问题，可渐进的分为三个步骤：两岸各自以域内冲突法调整法律冲突；统一区际冲突法调整，两岸相互谅让，共同制定统一区际冲突法；统一实体规范调整。两岸出于同一文化母体，具有极强的民族亲合力，法律差异逐渐消除并渐趋一致，最终过渡到统一实体法阶段，也将是两岸法律冲突解决的最终走向。解决区际法律冲突可以采取灵活多样的区际私法统一模式，不必囿于法典化的模式。目前的复合法域国家解决区际法律冲突既有通过区际冲突法模式，也通过统一实体法模式解决。虽然区际冲突法只是间接解决法律冲突，但是通过统一实体法解决的法律障碍较多，仍然需要区际冲突法调整区际法律关系。随着实践的发展，区际冲突法的统一和各个法域实体法的统一已经成为我国区际法律冲突解决的趋势。

要充分发挥宪法在解决区际法律冲突的作用。在复合法域的美国很少支持各州使用公共秩序保留作为对抗诉权的理由，反观两岸法律体系中都主张公序良俗与公共秩序保留原则[10]，成为对抗彼此判决与裁定执行的主要理由。在美国复合法域较少发生这种情况的原因是在相当大的程度上得益于美国联邦宪法对"联邦主义"的确立和"充分诚意和信任"条款的存在。美国各州法院在法律适用和区际司法协助中均不排除适用公共秩序保留制度，只是在实践中较为少用。各州在区际司法协助中所要考虑的公共秩序的内容，主要还是美国联邦法律和联邦宪法关于美国社会的一系列重大利益的规定，如正当法律程序[11]、平等保护条款[12]、商业条款[13]、联邦制度[14]等。美国宪法的"充分诚意和信任条款"不仅是一项宪法原则，也是一项具有可操作性的规则，这一义务性条款的规定最大限度地推动了区际法律冲突的开展。中国可以在宪法层面尝试使用这一法律方法，将"充分诚意和信任条款"发展成为适用四个法域的法律（宪法）原则。

3.3 司法互助与既判力问题

开展区际司法协助是解决区际法律冲突问题的具体举措，而解决两岸法律冲突的核心应该是两岸判决的既判力问题。两岸的司法互助的核心特征是它不是来自法律义务，而是来自两岸的意愿。在 ECFA 签订之后，两岸双方将陆续对相关的补充协定进行协商和签订，以进一步促进两岸的经贸领域有序高效的向前发展，在这种良好的政策环境之下，提升双方的法律环境既是一种必然要求也是一种可期待的结果。大量的经贸合作涌现必然需要完善的法律规定作为保障和救济的依据，两岸司法协助领域的很多不完善制度亟待解决。同时目前双方有着良好的合作氛围，非常适合对两岸的区际司法协助制度进行整合，借鉴 ECFA 协议民间形式进行司法协助协定的设计和鉴定，在此基础上逐步地完成两岸正式司法协助制度的构建。

本文据此认为，两岸的法律适用实际上密切关联了三个核心问题：（1）争端解决机制，它所确立的规则制定者、参与者、规则、行使规则的程序本身成为法律适用最直接的依据；（2）法律适用和规范冲突，它直接明确哪些行政主体通过何种方式（协商、调节、仲裁、判决）行使哪些国家公权力，排除哪些法律以及援引哪些法律，通过何种方法消除法域的冲突；（3）司法互助和既判力，它是法律适用的实际行为和最终结果，包括文书送达、证据调取和判决的承认和执行，而其中的核心是判决的承认和执行。

在现代社会，法律更加被理解为政治行为设立边界的活动，使之成为政治理性和原则框架下的任务，一种立足于基本权利保护要求的法律框架无疑会重塑政治的实践方式，产生广泛的民族认同、社会认同与国家认同。两岸法律适用产生的问题，是单一制国家里多法域并存引发的区际法律冲突，它虽区别于国家间冲突法，但具有很大的关联性，因而它必然是走向法律体系统一的过渡性与工具性问题之一。

参考文献

[1] "法律适用"概念有广狭二义。广义的法律适用概念通常指司法机关和行政机关实施法律的活动，即司法和行政两方面。狭义的法律适用是指司法机关或行政机关适用法律活动中的一个重要环节，即这些国家机关选择、解释、推理并运用法律规范的活动。汪金胜. 法律适用概念再商榷［J］. 黑龙江省政法管理干部学院学报，2000（2）：100-101.

[2] 英国、美国、欧盟和中国代表了当今世界上复合法域的几种典型情况。英国是单一制国家结构下传统复合法域国家，形成了两个法域：英格兰（威尔士）法域、苏格兰法域和北爱尔兰法域，各法域都拥有独立的立法权和司法权，其法律传统也各具特色；美国是联邦制复合法域国家，按照美国宪法的规定联邦政府的权力由宪法赋予，其余权力由各州保留，从而导致了在同一主权国家下复合法域的形成；中国则代表了内战形成国家尚在分裂中形成的复合法域国家；欧盟则是在经济全球化和文化、法律趋同化的国际大趋势下，新的国家联合体形成的多法域地区。

[3] 黄嘉树. 关于两岸政治谈判的思考［M］//北京联合大学台湾研究院. 北京台研论坛，九州出版社，2010：177.

[4] 黄进. 中国的区际法律问题研究［M］. 法律出版社，2001：16.

[5] 大陆地区认可与执行台湾地区民商事裁判的法律依据，主要体现在最高人民法院制定的相关司法解释之中。自1988年至2010年12月以来，最高人民法院先后出台了7个司法解释，就申请认可台湾地区有关法院的民商事裁判的范围、法律效力以及程序等问题做出了明确的规定。它们是：《关于人民法院处理涉台民事案件的几个问题》《关于当事人持台湾地区有关法院民事调解书或者有关机构出具或确认的调解协议书向人民法院申请认可人民法院应否受理的批复》《关于当事人持台湾地区有关法院支付命令向人民法院申请认可人民法院应否受理的批复》《关于人民法院认可台湾地区有关法院民事判决的规定》《关于人民法院认可台湾地区有关法院民事判决的补充规定》《关于涉台民事诉讼文书送达的若干规定》和《最高人民法院关于审理涉台民商事案件法律适用问题的规定》7个司法解释。

[6] 王传丽，张薇. 论两岸四地经贸争议解决［J］. 法学杂志，2006（3）.

[7] 包括海峡两岸经济合作框架协议（2010.06.29）、海峡两岸知识产权保护合作协议（2010.06.29）等22个。资料来源：中国台湾网 http://www.chinataiwan.org/flfg/ygxy/。
[8] 丁伟.冲突法论（第二版）[M].法律出版社，2005：304.
[9] 黄进，黄风.区际司法协助研究[M].中国政法大学出版社，1993：5-6.
[10] 台湾：修正"涉外民事法律适用法"第1条涉外民事，本法未规定者，适用其他法律之规定，其他法律无规定者，依法理；第8条也同时规定，违反公共秩序或善良风俗者，不得适用。
[11] 美国联邦宪法第14条修正案规定，无论何州，不得制定和实行剥夺合众国公民之特权或豁免的法律，亦不得在未经正当程序前，使任何人丧失其生命、自由或财产。正当程序要求"基本公平"，如果在法院地与当事人或诉讼之间不存在合理联系，适用法院地法律将不是基本公平的，因为这种结果不是当事人所能预见和期望。如果一州法院拒绝适用与案件有合理连接关系的外州法，而适用本州法或其他州法律，由此导致不利的一方当事人可以以违背适当程序为由，依联邦宪法请求救济。
[12] 美国联邦宪法还规定，各州不得对其管辖区域内的任何人拒绝给其法律上的平等保护，此即平等保护条款。
[13] 美国联邦宪法第1条第8款规定，国会对美国与外国间、各州间及与印第安部落间的商业关系有规范的权利，此即商业条款。
[14] 美国联邦政府的权力源自宪法的规定，各州有其固有的主权，但受联邦宪法的限制。根据联邦宪法第10条修正案，联邦宪法未授予联邦政府或未禁止各州行使的权力，均由各州保留。

中国台湾与日本钓鱼岛纠纷与马英九当局的应对策略

李振广

多年来，中国台湾与日本之间频频发生的钓鱼岛纠纷对中国台湾与日本关系构成一定的冲击和影响。在处理中国台湾与日本钓鱼岛纠纷中，马英九当局逐渐形成了一套应对钓鱼岛危机的政策与策略。2013年4月10日，中国台湾与日本签订渔业协议，扩大了中国台湾渔民在钓鱼岛周边海域的作业范围，这是被中国台湾有关方面视为多年来中国台湾在钓鱼岛问题上获得的一项重大利益突破。这一结果显然与当前的中日钓鱼岛争端有关，同时也与马英九当局的钓鱼岛政策与策略有密切关系。本文考察梳理了马英九担任中国台湾地区领导人以来台日钓鱼岛之争的主要类型，并对马英九当局处理钓鱼岛问题的政策目标与策略进行了分析。

1 马英九上台以来日本与中国台湾钓鱼岛纠纷的主要类型

从2008年6月迄今，中国台湾与日本之间几乎年年都会围绕钓鱼岛问题发生冲突与纠纷。其中，2008年6月台湾联合号渔船被撞沉事件，2010~2011年的保钓护渔运动，2012年日本所谓钓鱼岛"国有化"等都对中国台湾与日本关系产生了很大的冲击和影响。在这些事件中，既有日本方面故意侵害中国台湾渔民利益而造成的事件，也有中国台湾民众主动进行的保钓维权活动。日本作为窃取钓鱼岛的一方，运用实力并依仗美国的支持控制着钓鱼岛及其周边海域，因此，近几年来日本与中国台湾围绕钓鱼岛发生的一系列冲突大多是因日本的挑衅或非法侵害中国台湾权益而造成的。

总体而言，中国台湾与日本钓鱼岛冲突可分三大类型，第一种是侵害——反击型，即日本在钓鱼岛海域直接侵害台湾渔民、保钓人士权益，中国台湾被迫回应；第二种为挑衅——宣示型，是日本在钓鱼岛问题上进行政治挑衅，中国台湾当局为保钓护航，借机宣示权益；第三种是主动出击型，即中国台湾保钓人士勇闯钓鱼岛海域，开展保钓活动。

第一种类型：侵害——反击型。典型案例是2008年6月中国台湾"联合号"渔船被日本巡逻舰撞沉事件。这是马英九刚刚上台执政才20天就面临的一次中国台湾与日本关系风波，更是对素有"保钓健将"之称的马英九的一次政治考验。

2008年6月10日凌晨，中国台湾"联合号"海钓船在钓鱼岛南方6海里处遭日本巡逻舰撞击沉没。这就是"联合号事件"。虽然中国台湾渔船在钓鱼岛海域被日本巡逻舰驱离、扣押，船员被逮捕的事件屡见不鲜，[1]但是中国台湾渔船被日舰故意撞沉却是第一次，也是日本在钓鱼岛问题上开了一个危险的先例。因此，这一事件在中国台湾引起了轩然大波和对日本野蛮行径的强烈愤慨。为反击日本的野蛮行径，中国台湾保钓人士于6月16日早晨乘"全家福号"在中国台湾"海巡署"舰船的护航下，冲破日本舰船的阻挠，进入距钓鱼岛0.4海里处宣示主权并成功绕行钓鱼岛一周后返航。这是自日本窃取钓鱼岛管辖权37年来中国台湾渔船与"海巡署"舰艇第一次在钓鱼岛海域绕行钓鱼岛一周，具有突破性意义。

由于"联合号"是被日本舰艇故意撞沉，"联合号"钓鱼船自身没有过错，在中国台湾群情激奋和强烈要求日本放人、道歉、赔偿的压力下，2008年6月20日下午，日本驻中国台湾代表机构——"日本交流协会台北事务所副所长"舟町仁志带着道歉函，到被撞的船长何鸿义家鞠躬道歉。这是日方因为钓鱼岛问题对中国台湾方面的第一次正式道歉。[2]

[基金项目] 本文为北京市属高等学校高层次人才引进与培养计划项目之"长城学者培养计划"——"美国重返亚太战略对台湾问题的影响"课题（项目编号：IDHT 20130319）的阶段性研究成果。

[作者简介] 李振广，北京联合大学台湾研究院政类所所长、教授。

第二种类型：挑衅——宣示型。近几年来，在美国"重返亚太"战略的鼓舞下，日本在钓鱼岛问题上进行政治挑衅的频度与力度越来越大，最终引发中日钓鱼岛危机。与此同时，中国台湾地区的保钓人士也对日本在钓鱼岛问题上的政治挑衅展开一系列反击，马英九当局借着为保钓船只护航之机进行政治宣示。

2010年8月25日，日本众议院安全保障委员会成员搭乘自卫队飞机赴"东海油气田"及钓鱼岛海域进行空中视察，主动进行挑衅；另外，当时的台湾媒体报道，日本政府已经决定在2011年3月把25个离岛"国有化"，以作为"划定大陆架面积和确保海底资源的据点"。这些岛屿中，也包括钓鱼岛。[3] 为反击日本这一系列的政治挑衅行为，2011年9月13日，来自中国台湾、香港、澳门等地的10位保钓人士，聚集台北县野柳渔港，准备赴钓鱼岛海域宣示主权。由于中国台湾当局不允许香港、澳门的保钓人士登船出海，最终只有中国台湾籍的中华保钓协会执行长黄锡麟及理事殷必雄获准出海前往钓鱼岛海域。9月14日凌晨，搭载2名保钓人士的中国台湾渔船"感恩99号"在距离钓鱼岛约41公里处，遭到10艘日本巡逻船围阻，台湾"海巡署"则派出6艘大型舰和5艘中型艇围绕"感恩99号"进行保护。保钓船最终到达距钓鱼岛18.5海里处后被8艘日本舰艇团团包围而无法继续前进，保钓宣示活动宣告结束。

2012年日本实施"钓鱼岛国有化"等挑衅行为再次引发中国台湾渔民和保钓人士赴钓鱼岛海域宣誓主权。2012年初，日本政府片面决定为钓鱼岛群岛周边4个小岛命名，并将其记载入所谓日本的"国有财产地籍册"。[4] 随后，在日本东京都知事石原慎太郎不断鼓噪要购买钓鱼岛等因素的刺激下，钓鱼岛争端愈演愈烈。6月26日，日本东京都议员乘船闯入钓鱼岛周边海域进行挑衅。中国台湾保钓团体为反击日本的挑衅，于7月4日再次发起保钓宣示活动。中华保钓协会会长黄锡麟等9人搭乘"全家福号"渔船前往钓鱼岛海域进行保钓活动，中国台湾"海巡署"派出5艘舰艇全程戒护。在前往钓鱼岛海域途中，日本派出3艘舰船企图登上"全家福号"进行检查，但在中国台湾"海巡署"舰艇的阻拦下，没有成功，"全家福号"得以顺利返航。

2012年9月11日，日本政府与所谓"钓鱼岛地主"完成签约手续，将钓鱼岛收归"国有"。日本政府的这一挑衅行为直接威胁到中国台湾渔民的渔权与生存权。9月24日，中国台湾宜兰渔民发起"为生存、护渔权"活动，组织大批渔船赴钓鱼岛海域，捍卫中国台湾渔民在钓鱼岛海域的传统渔权。中国台湾民间这次自发性的保钓护渔行动得到了马英九当局的大力支持。中国台湾"海巡署"出动12艘舰艇全程护航，保钓护渔船队一度深入钓鱼岛海域。期间，数度遭日本海上保安厅舰艇阻挠及喷水，中国台湾"海巡署"舰艇坚定保护保钓渔船，也以水柱还击日舰，保护中国台湾渔船平安宣示并顺利返航。这次护渔保钓活动是台湾历年最大规模的民间保钓行动，共有58艘渔船，292位渔民参与。与此同时，中国台湾"海巡署"的舰艇也驶抵与钓鱼岛只有2.1海里的地方。总之，这次保钓护渔行动成功宣示了中国台湾的立场和态度，对于防止日本借"钓鱼岛国有化"把窃取钓鱼岛的行为合法化发挥了重要作用。

第三种类型：中国台湾主动出击保钓型。自20世纪70年代初开始，中国台湾的保钓运动一直就是反对日本窃占钓鱼岛、捍卫中国对钓鱼岛主权的重要力量。中国台湾保钓力量的重要活动形式之一就是主动赴钓鱼岛海域展开保钓示威活动。

2011年4月是中国台湾保钓运动兴起40周年之际，中国台、港、澳等地的保钓人士原本计划以保钓运动40周年为契机，举行大规模海上保钓示威活动。由于这一年日本发生"3·11大地震"，保钓人士不愿"趁人之危"，因此，延至6月底举行了一场小规模的海上保钓活动。6月29日上午，保钓人士黄锡麟等人搭乘"大发268号"渔船进入距钓鱼岛23.7海里处，遭日方公务船阻挡，只好掉头返航。在此期间，台湾"海巡署"5艘舰艇全程护卫"大发268号"。

2013年初，在中日因钓鱼岛问题处于紧张博弈之际，中国台湾保钓人士于1月24日又组织了一次赴钓鱼岛海域宣示保钓的活动。"全家福号"保钓船在中国台湾"海巡署"4艘舰艇的戒护下赴钓鱼岛海域宣示主权，在距钓鱼岛16海里处遭到日本8艘舰船的阻挡，"全家福号"保钓船在日本舰船强大水柱的冲击下设备受损，不得不结束行动返航。

中国台湾保钓人士主动发起的保钓行动得到了马英九当局的支持和保护，对于反击日本窃占钓鱼岛，展示台湾民众保卫钓鱼岛的决心，有着积极的意义。

2 马英九当局在钓鱼岛问题上的政策目标

钓鱼岛问题是马英九自2008年上台以来一再面临的一个棘手问题。这一问题涉及中国台湾渔民的渔权、中国台湾与日本的关系、亚太地区局势、两岸关系等，是一个长期而复杂的问题。在应对这一问题的过程中，马英九当局逐渐确立了处理钓鱼岛问题的政策目标。纵观马英九执政以来在处理钓鱼岛问题的方式与原则，马英九在钓鱼岛问题上的政策目标体现在两个方面。

2.1 坚决维护中国台湾自身的权益及中华民族的主权与领土权益

在争取和维护中国台湾渔民利益的同时，从中华民族的整体利益出发，坚持捍卫钓鱼岛主权，明确反对日本把窃取钓鱼岛合法化。马英九当年作为第一代保钓青年和多年研究钓鱼岛问题的法律专家，其政治情怀、学术认知和民族感情都促使他在钓鱼岛问题上把捍卫钓鱼岛主权作为首要原则，担任中国台湾地区领导人使马英九有机会在钓鱼岛问题上执行这一原则。马英九上任之初，"联合号"被撞事件发生后，马英九办公室立即发表声明，对日本表达强烈抗议，召回"驻日代表"，要求日本立即释放被扣船长并予以赔偿。有中国台湾媒体评论指出，马英九对这一问题的处理上，"姿态上已经较李登辉、陈水扁20年任期间要强硬许多。"[5] 几年来，无论是在言论上、政策上还是行动上，马英九努力把维护中国台湾自身的权益和中华民族的主权与领土权益作为处理钓鱼岛问题的首要目标是明确的，是不容置疑的。

2.2 不使钓鱼岛问题冲击"友日政策"的大格局

"亲美、友日、和中"战略是马英九上台后为营造稳定、良好的周边环境而精心打造的政策框架。"友日政策"是这一战略的重要组成部分。鉴于马英九的保钓背景及其上台后两岸关系获得突飞猛进发展的现实，日本对马英九的"友日政策"有疑虑是不言而喻的。钓鱼岛问题长期以来就是中国台湾与日本关系中所面临的一个敏感问题。除了钓鱼岛问题，能够导致中国台湾与日本之间对抗与冲突的问题并不多。处理钓鱼岛问题是马英九对日政策的试金石，对其"友日政策"的成败有直接的影响。从2008年以来马英九处理钓鱼岛问题的方式与原则来看，马英九所确立的一个重要政策目标就是掌握分寸、理性应对，不使钓鱼岛问题冲击"友日政策"这一大格局。

钓鱼岛问题之所以复杂，不仅在于这个问题是一个历史问题，而且这个问题中还夹杂着民族感情、地缘政治、海洋权益、渔民利益等因素。对于马英九而言，对钓鱼岛问题的处理不仅关系到中国台湾渔民的权益、自己的民族感情与历史责任，也涉及中国台湾民意的压力、美国的态度、日台关系发展等因素，而且中国台湾在钓鱼岛问题上不占主导地位，基本属于弱势应对的一方。尽管如此，马英九当局在几年来处理钓鱼岛问题的过程中探索出了一套应对策略，基本达到了上述两大政策目标。

3 马英九当局处理中国台湾与日本钓鱼岛问题上的基本策略

马英九当局应对钓鱼岛问题处理也是一个逐渐发展的过程，其在努力为中国台湾渔民争取最大利益的同时，也通过策略性地支持保钓活动等方式回击日本在钓鱼岛问题上的挑衅，尽力防止中国台湾与日本钓鱼岛纠纷过分冲击中国台湾与日本的关系。马英九当局在处理台日钓鱼岛纠纷问题的应对策略主要有以下4个方面。

（1）及时作出反应，伸张权益，争取中国台湾民意支持

积极捍卫钓鱼岛权益既是马英九作为第一代保钓青年的个人政治理想，同时也是马英九当局的集体政治职责与赢得中国台湾民意支持的需要。无论是在日本侵害中国台湾渔民权益或野蛮对待保钓人士之时，还是在日本议员巡视钓鱼岛、日本政府为钓鱼岛列岛命名或购买钓鱼岛之时，马英九当局总是第一时间作出强烈的反应。在行动上，马英九当局敢于作出反击，宣示权益。例如，2008年6月"联合号"海钓船被撞沉后，马英九当局派出数艘舰艇为保钓船护航、保驾，成功环绕钓鱼岛巡航一周。在陈水扁执政的8年时间里，中国台湾"海巡署"只进行了5次护渔行动，而马英九当政后的4年多时间里先后派出舰船10余次赴钓鱼岛海域保钓护渔。在舆论宣传上，对于日本议员乘船或乘飞机赴钓鱼岛海域巡视，日本给钓鱼岛列岛命名及钓鱼岛"国有化"等行为，马英九当局都及时对日本提出抗议。马英九也一再指出："不管日本进行钓鱼岛国有化、还是私有化，当年窃占我领土的本质不变"，基于民族大义，

钓鱼岛主权一寸都不能让步。[6]尽管马英九当局的这些努力暂时不能改变日本窃占钓鱼岛的事实，但是，敢于对日本的非法行为进行抗争，用实际行动捍卫中华民族在钓鱼岛的权益，有助于保持钓鱼岛问题的争议性，使日本侵吞钓鱼岛计划无法得逞，也赢得了中国台湾民众和舆论的支持。

（2）把中国台湾与日本钓鱼岛冲突当做实现中国台湾权益突破的契机

自20世纪70年代以来，钓鱼岛一直处于日本的控制之下，日本对于中国台湾在钓鱼岛问题上的各种要求根本不予理睬，而中国台湾与日本钓鱼岛纠纷则是中国台湾冲击日本对钓鱼岛的实际控制权，实现权益突破的重要契机，更是中国台湾提高与日本谈判渔权等问题要价的机会。钓鱼岛冲突越是扩大，争议性就越大，越对中国台湾有利。2008年中国台湾"联合号"渔船被撞沉事件后，马英九当局把"和平解决争端""尽速重启渔权谈判"确立为应对这一事件的两大主轴。[7]从1996年起中国台湾与日本多次进行渔业谈判，而2005年7月第15次渔业谈判之后便中断了。2008年6月的"联合号"被撞后，中国台湾方面便把这次撞船事件作为重启中国台湾与日本渔业谈判的契机，要求与日本尽快开展渔权谈判。也正是在这一事件的影响下，2009年2月，在中断3年半之后，中国台湾与日本在台北举行了第16次渔业谈判并达成建立渔业争端紧急通联机制等成果。2012年9月，当日本计划对钓鱼岛进行所谓"国有化"，引爆中国台海两岸民众的反日情绪之际，日本为分化两岸保钓力量，拉拢台湾，牵制中国大陆，随即主动向中国台湾提出"尽早举行"第17次渔业谈判的建议。尽管有很多日本、中国香港、中国台湾的媒体都指出，日本此时提议重启日本与中国台湾渔业谈判是离间计，意在"诱使中国台湾在钓鱼岛冲突上不要与日方激烈对抗"，避免两岸联手对付日本。[8]但马英九当局依然要借此难得的机会争取扩大中国台湾地区在钓鱼岛海域的权益。中国台湾与日本在2013年4月10日达成"渔业协议"，日本同意扩大中国台湾渔民在钓鱼岛海域的作业范围。这是马英九当局借机争取钓鱼岛海域权益的典型例证。

除了渔业谈判外，马英九当局也借中国台湾与日本钓鱼岛纠纷之机，努力冲破已有的限制，扩展台湾的权益。例如，2008年6月16日，中国台湾保钓人士驾船赴钓鱼岛海域宣示，中国台湾"海巡署"派出舰艇护航并绕行钓鱼岛一周，离钓鱼岛最近时只有0.4海里。在这一过程中，中国台湾舰艇还与日本舰艇对峙，互射水炮。台湾这一大胆举动是自日本窃占钓鱼岛以来的第一次。与此同时，中国台湾海巡部门提出，未来若有必要将不排除再次派遣舰艇进入钓鱼岛12海里海域护渔。[9]2012年9月14日，马英九提出，只要有中国台湾渔民到钓鱼岛海域作业，"海巡署"就一定会派出舰艇保护渔民作业，透露出中国台湾方面进入钓鱼岛海域护渔的决心。[10]自2008年以来，中国台湾保钓船、"海巡署"舰艇也数次大胆进入钓鱼岛海域。应该说，中国台湾方面充分利用中国台湾与日本钓鱼岛纠纷的机会不仅扩大了自身的权益，而且也对日本控制钓鱼岛的局面构成一定的冲击。

（3）把握分寸，避免钓鱼岛纠纷激化升级

尽管在每一次中国台湾与日本钓鱼岛纠纷发生后马英九当局都会在态度和言论上表现出强硬，以疏导民意，发泄对日本霸道行为的不满，并会寻机进行一些政策和行动上的突破，但总体而言，马英九当局把"和平解决"钓鱼岛争端作为首要原则，控制事态的发展，避免过度冲击中国台湾与日本关系。2008年6月"联合号"事件发生后，中国台湾一些民意代表情绪激动，提出要在6月18日搭乘军舰赴钓鱼岛海域宣示权益，但经过马英九当局的协调最终放弃了这种激化问题的行动。[11]马英九当局派遣"海巡署"舰艇为保钓船进入钓鱼岛海域护航，事先也与日本方面有过多次沟通。马英九当局这样做的目的就是既要从中国台湾利益出发又要照顾到美国、日本的感受，以尽快促使"此事件顺利落幕，避免台日双输"。[12]由此可见，马英九当局处理钓鱼岛问题还是有相当的克制和理性。

（4）顾及美国和日本的态度，不与大陆联合保钓

钓鱼岛是台海两岸中国人的共同"祖产"，钓鱼岛海域也是台海两岸渔民的传统渔场。反对日本窃据钓鱼岛，捍卫中国的钓鱼岛主权是台海两岸中国人的共同责任。在历次中国台湾与日本之间的钓鱼岛纠纷中，中国台湾是受害一方，也是弱势一方，日本在应对来自中国台湾方面的抗争时往往游刃有余，但是，如果台海两岸联合起来反对日本窃占钓鱼岛，将足以打乱日本对钓鱼岛的主控权，使日本左支右绌，捉襟见肘，难以应付。因此，在钓鱼岛问题上，日本最担心的就是中国台湾与中国大陆联合起来对付日本，争夺钓鱼岛主权。不仅日本最不希望看到两岸联手捍卫钓鱼岛主权，而且美国也不愿看到中国台湾在钓鱼岛问题上与大陆联手，共同对付日本。从地缘政治的角度看，中国台湾与日本都是美国在亚

太地区的安全伙伴，中国台湾与日本之间的钓鱼岛纠纷属于美国控制下的"安全同盟内部小伙伴"之间的问题。一旦中国台湾在钓鱼岛问题上与大陆联手对付日本，不仅使日本倍感压力，同时也是对美国领导下的西太平洋安全秩序的冲击。这是美国最不希望看到的。对于美国而言，在钓鱼岛问题上"中国台湾应该低调，不要反日，不要让美国担心，不要让人以为中国台湾与大陆合作"，中国台湾不能成为"北京的盟友"。[13] 正是由于这一问题的复杂性、敏感性，特别是美国的压力，马英九当局从一开始就明确表态在钓鱼岛问题上不与大陆联手，以使美国放心。与此同时，避免过度刺激日本也是一项重要的考虑因素。不与大陆联手，可以使日本对马英九当局更为放心，为中国台湾在渔权谈判、加强中国台湾与日本经贸联系等方面争取更多利益创造条件。2008年6月17日，中国台湾"联合号"渔船被撞后，针对民进党质疑马英九"联中反日"，马英九第一次公开发表讲话时明确表示："此次联合号渔船事件，从头到尾都未与北京政府接触。"[14] 自此以后，每每遇到钓鱼岛问题，马英九当局就一再申明不会与大陆联手解决钓鱼岛主权问题，与此同时，拒绝两岸民间要求两岸联合保钓的呼声，在行动上刻意与大陆捍卫钓鱼岛主权的行动保持距离，以便消除美国和日本的疑虑。

（5）提出"东海和平倡议"，避免在钓鱼岛问题上被边缘化

钓鱼岛问题总体而言是台海两岸与日本之间的领土权益争端。长期以来，由于日本对钓鱼岛及其周边海域实施实际控制，在历次中国台湾与日本钓鱼岛纠纷中日本占据了主导地位。在日本的压制下，中国台湾当局只能借助渔民和保钓人士的保钓行动来表达对日本控制钓鱼岛的不满和反对，同时展示台湾在这一问题上的存在与影响，但在总体趋势上，中国台湾处于弱势和被边缘化的一方。2012年之前钓鱼岛问题基本以中国台湾渔民与日本之间的冲突为主。进入2012年后，日本抛弃了中日两国老一代领导人在钓鱼岛问题上达成的"搁置争议"的默契，企图通过钓鱼岛"国有化"，将日本对钓鱼岛的"行政管辖"转变为"主权归属"日本。日本这一引发钓鱼岛争议质变的举动引起中国大陆的强烈反应。大陆派遣海监、渔政船赴钓鱼岛海域巡航执法，维护中国在钓鱼岛的主权，凸显了中国大陆和日本是钓鱼岛问题争端的两大主角的地位。中国台湾虽然与大陆在钓鱼岛问题上有共同利益和义务，但是由于整体实力有限，加之不愿与大陆联手保钓，中国台湾在钓鱼岛问题上逐渐成为配角，被边缘化的趋势越来越明显。为了避免边缘化趋势的发展，马英九于2012年8月5日就钓鱼岛问题提出"东海和平倡议"，呼吁各方搁置争议，和平解决争端，制定东海行为准则。马英九的这一倡议意在强化中国台湾在钓鱼岛问题上的话语权和影响力。9月7日，马英九进一步提出了"东海和平倡议推动纲领"，希望在钓鱼岛问题上从中国台湾与日本、两岸、大陆与日本"三组双边"对话开始，逐步走向中国台湾、日本与中国大陆"一组三边"共同协商。其战略意图就是在处理钓鱼岛问题上"让中国台湾与大陆、日本成为对等实体"。[15] 这也是马英九为中国台湾在钓鱼岛问题上扩大参与、避免被边缘化所进行的一次努力。

4 结　　语

钓鱼岛是中国的固有领土，在反对日本窃占钓鱼岛、维护中国主权领土完整的斗争中，中国台湾地区也是一个重要的参与者。中国台湾与日本之间经常围绕钓鱼岛问题发生纠纷，且大多是因日本的挑衅或非法侵害中国台湾权益而造成的。近几年来，马英九当局在钓鱼岛问题既坚持固有的立场，支持保钓运动，试图以此争取中国台湾权益的最大化，其积极参与保钓活动对日本窃占钓鱼岛构成较大冲击；但与此同时，面对美日对两岸联手保钓的疑虑，马英九当局也公开表示两岸不会联合保钓。此外，马英九当局还力求通过提出"东海和平倡议"等措施，避免中国台湾在钓鱼岛问题上"被边缘化"。尽管马英九当局应对中国台湾与日本钓鱼岛纠纷的政策措施扩大了中国台湾在钓鱼岛问题上的权益，其策略取得了初步的成功。但是我们也必须指出的是，由于大陆加强了在钓鱼岛海域捍卫主权领土完整的力度，更加有利于中国台湾渔民争取在钓鱼岛海域的权益。因此，从两岸中华民族整体利益考虑，只有两岸联合起来，才能取得保钓斗争的胜利。

参考文献

[1] 从2003年11月到2008年6月10日中国台湾"联合号"渔船被撞沉之前，共计有132艘中国台湾渔船在钓鱼岛海域

被日本公务船驱离、19艘被日本扣押。"海巡署"平时联合护渔及战时纳入"国防"体系［N］. 中国台湾：中国时报，2008－06－18.

［2］黄筱筠. 钓鱼岛事件日方将到船长家鞠躬道歉［N］. 中国台湾：中国时报，2008－06－20.

［3］日相候选人小泽：钓鱼岛没一天隶属中国［N］. 中国台湾：联合报，2010－09－08.

［4］钓鱼岛北小岛日列"国有财产"我严正抗议［N］. 中国台湾：中国时报，2012－03－28.

［5］高凌云. 人召回有姿态　没影响［N］. 中国台湾：联合晚报，2008－06－16.

［6］马英九：已召回"驻日代表"［N］. 中国台湾：联合报，2012－09－12.

［7］李明贤."国安"高层会议：和平解决争端重启渔权谈判［N］. 中国台湾：联合报，2008－06－17.

［8］张凯胜. 日促重启渔业谈判恐是离间计［N］. 中国台湾：旺报，2012－10－08.

［9］唐孝民. 护渔：我舰不排除再入钓鱼岛12浬海域［N］. 中国台湾：联合报，2008－06－18.

［10］黄国梁. 钓鱼岛之争　我方会进水域护渔［N］. 中国台湾：联合晚报，2012－09－15.

［11］林新辉."府"党高层出手"立委"护渔喊卡［N］. 中国台湾：联合报，2008－06－18.

［12］萧旭岑. 马设停损点　避免情势失控［N］. 中国台湾：中国时报，2008－06－17.

［13］美专家：钓岛争议台湾应低调［N］. 中国台湾：中国时报，2012－11－22.

［14］马重申钓岛主权驳"联中反日"［N］. 中国台湾：中国时报，2008－06－18.

［15］王光慈. 马将台湾拉到与陆、日对等［N］. 中国台湾：联合报，2012－09－08.

民间资本运行的危机透视与法制思考

杨积堂

几乎所有的疯狂都逃脱不了毁灭的魅影，任何无序的运行都无法真正走得长远。在资本的狂欢中，当资本在严格法律规制的状态下运行时，它是创造财富的天使，一旦资本冲出法律规制的藩篱，它会成为毁灭财富的魔鬼。当前，民间资本运行的乱象频现，危机已现端倪。本文拟透过民间资本运行的乱象，揭示民间资本运行中法律机制的缺失和监督机制的失灵，从而探索如何为民间资本运行构建良性的法律保障机制。

一、民间资本运行的危机透视

所谓民间资本，一般是指非政府拥有的资本，即民营企业的流动资产和公民个人及家庭所拥有的金融资产的统称。在党和国家有关重要的政策文件和法规中，一般以"非公有资本"或"民间资本"的称谓表述。改革开放以来，随着生产力的解放，民间资本大幅聚积，据报道，全国民间资本总量约为30多万亿元。[1]这些民间资本，对我国的经济和社会发展起到了重要的促进作用。近年来，由于民间资本所面临的行业壁垒和身份歧视，使民间资本的流动渠道不畅；随着民间资本的不断聚积和资本逐利本能的刺激，民间资本暗流涌动，使得民间资本运行中爆发各种乱象，给民间资本的健康发展带来危机。

（一）民间资本运行乱象之状

近段时间以来，从民间资本发达的温州，到异军突起的鄂尔多斯，再到江苏泗洪的"宝马乡"等地，出现了一系列非法集资、资金链断裂、老板出逃等各种民间资本运行的典型案件，这些案件投射出民间资本运行的各种混乱迹象，根据其运行特征，略举如下。

1. 非法集资猖獗。近年来，非法集资大案频发，涉及资金巨大，人数众多，危害严重。湖南湘西荣昌建设集团责任公司（简称"荣昌集团"）涉嫌非法集资、诈骗一案，涉及集资群众23778人共62615人次，涉案金额高达37.7亿余元人民币，至案发时止，仍有集资本金18.7亿余元无法归还。包头金利斌案，从2004年6月至2011年4月13日，陆续非法吸收公众存款22.25亿元，因无力偿还巨额欠款，金利斌自焚身亡。内蒙古鄂尔多斯市石小红非法集资案，涉及金额高达7.4亿元，由于资金链断裂，4亿元财富瞬间蒸发，被骗的大都是妇女、老人、学生，甚至还有拾荒者。浙江"亿万富姐"吴英非法集资案，非法集资人民币77339.5万元。这些众多非法集资案例，成为民间资本的乱象的典型。

2. 高利贷疯狂。众多非法集资能够得逞并聚集数十亿元民间资本，与民间资本暗流中的另一机制"高利贷"密不可分。"高利贷"指的是索取特别高额利息的贷款，盛行于中国旧社会，最为常见的有所谓"驴打滚"利滚利，它被作为一种残酷剥夺借贷者私人财产的手段。传统的高利贷的借高利贷者都是迫于生活急需资金的穷苦人，因而绝大多数都是消费借贷，很少是为了扩大再生产或投资。随着市场经济的发展，大量个体工商户、中小企业的涌现，加之中小企业面临融资困难，在此情况下，高利贷成为众多中小企业解决资金困难的渠道。中小企业用户的生产性需求，催生了高利贷链条化、产业化。金字塔式分级分层的传销模式，使民间资本运行的链条失去了理性，众多民众以暴富的心理参与其中，在利率链上层层加码，使得雪球越滚越大，风险越集越重，最终资金链断裂。根据2010年4月中旬人民银行温州市中心支行关于温州民间借贷的一项调查显示，有89%的家庭个人和59.67%的企业参与了民间借贷，其中中小企业有60%左右参与其中。目前，温州人亲友间的借贷利息达到月息0.2元，而民间借贷

[基金项目] 本文系北京联合大学北京市级重点建设学科"经济法学"建设科研项目"民间资本运行的法律问题研究"（项目编号：LD11JIF01）的阶段性成果。

[作者简介] 杨积堂（1971—），男，汉族，宁夏彭阳人，北京联合大学应用文理学院法律系主任，首都法治研究中心主任、教授。

的极端利率甚至已达月息 0.3~0.6 元。内蒙古鄂尔多斯市石小红非法集资案显示，参与高利贷的房贷者包括大多妇女、老人、学生，甚至还有拾荒者。据当地金融监管部门估计，在东胜区 60 万人口中，民间放贷规模达 300 多亿元。甚至出现了"在鄂尔多斯不放高利贷，会被人笑话"的疯狂局面。

3. 传销模式介入民间资本运行。无论是江苏泗洪县的"宝马乡"，还是鄂尔多斯、宁夏、新疆等地发生的非法集资案件中，出现了传销模式介入民间资本运行的新动向。这种模式往往是由放贷人员利用网络建立网站发展下线吸引投资，再根据发展下线的人数，按比例提取酬劳。主要策化者常居于幕后，或者在外地逍遥。一些先期投入者本来是受害者，但在利益诱惑下又去发展其他人加入，从中获利。而被发展加入的人往往是他们的亲朋好友，使得民间资本传销犯罪更具有智能性、隐蔽性和快速的传导性。在泗洪非法集资案件中，也是以分级分层，高息向村民集资，并逐渐形成了庞大的网络。[3]

4. 披理财外衣，以高科技手段障眼。在民间资本运行的各种乱象中，高科技手段被违法分子利用，并以理财为诱饵，设计了各种骗局和陷阱，使得很多受害人被蒙蔽，利益受损。在新疆发生的集资诈骗案，就是犯罪嫌疑人在江苏虚构制作了"美国天使基金"的网页，而后伙同他人来到新疆实施集资诈骗。"他们打开'美国天使基金'的网页让受害人浏览，承诺投资 1000 元每天可返利 15 元，投资 3000 元每天返利 60 元……诱骗投资人发展下线按比例给予推荐奖"[4]。在内蒙古发现的"电子币"集资诈骗案，也是骗子使用了网络、电子币、资金流等多种新型手段，通过编造所谓的美国 MDIC 投资策略集团公司等方式，以专门为个人和企业的共同基金、股票、私募基金投资者选择专业的理财项目为名，附以高额回报为诱饵实施的诈骗行为[5]。

（二）民间资本运行乱象之源

民间资本运行中的各种案件频发，据公安部的一份数据显示，自 2008 年以来全国公安机关共破获各种类型的非法集资（含非法吸收公众存款和集资诈骗）案件 5000 余起，其中非法集资类案件每年约以 2000 起、集资金额以 200 亿元的规模快速增加。[6] 就其根源，笔者认为原因如下。

1. 民间资本运行的渠道不畅。近年来，由于世界性金融危机的影响，加之国内通货膨胀加剧，为了应对金融危机和抑制通胀，国家实施了较为紧缩的货币与财政政策，从而给传统的制造业造成了冲击，抑制了民间资本对传统实业的投资热情，转而加入了房地产、矿山、股票、贵金属、农产品等各种暴利炒作的浪潮，进而使实业产业的资金需求更加紧张和饥渴。在此情况下，国家现有民间资本的运行机制又缺乏良性的桥梁和疏通机制，就导致地下钱庄、民间高利贷、资本传销等灰色资金渠道暗流涌动。这些灰色渠道由于无法监控，因此，每每都是基于资金链断裂而引发重大案件，才引起政府及司法部门的重视，但是为时已晚，往往造成巨额损失，无法弥补。

另外，对于民间资本的出路，国务院曾在 2005 年 2 月 19 日颁布了《国务院关于鼓励支持和引导个体私营等非公有制经济发展的若干意见》（国发〔2005〕3 号），俗称"旧 36 条"。在 2009 年 9 月 19 日颁布了《国务院关于进一步促进中小企业发展的若干意见》（国发〔2009〕36 号），俗称"国 29 条"。2010 年 5 月 7 日再次颁布了《国务院关于鼓励和引导民间投资健康发展的若干意见》（国发〔2010〕13 号），俗称"新 36 条"。以上三个重要文件对民间资本的出路规定了较为明确的去向和政策鼓励。但是，由于长期以来的行业壁垒和身份歧视难以改变，垄断机制难以打破，上述政策的落实不尽如人意，民间资本汹涌的波涛并未得到真正疏浚，"堰塞湖"之剑依然高悬。

2. 狂热逐利让理性丧失。任何事物的运行，都有其应当遵循的基本规律，如果想用狂热的冲动打破规律去创造奇迹，其结果就只有承受规律的惩罚。"人，作为一个'物理的存在物'来说，是和一切物体一样，受不变的规律的支配。"[7] 同样，民间资本的运行，也必须遵循资本的规律。但是，逐利之心却常常让人们的理性迷失，错把泡沫当希望，让眼前晃动的诱饵蒙蔽了脚下的陷阱。于是，国家级贫困县江苏泗洪县石集乡村民狂热地相信了眼前飞驰而过的宝马、奔驰也会成为明天现实，鄂尔多斯的妇女、老人、学生，甚至拾荒者也相信财富梦想的实现就在那个"高利贷"的馅饼里。同样浙江"亿万富姐"吴英非法集资案、丽水市"小姑娘"杜益敏集资诈骗 7 亿余元、温州乐清高秋荷非法集资诈骗 1.16 亿元案、台州王菊凤非法集资 4.7 亿元案等案件也暴露了民间资本逐利的集体狂热。

钱本身是不能生钱的。当有些地方的高利贷的年利息回报率高达 50% 以上，部分达 100%，甚至最高达到三个月利息 100%，年息在 400% 以上的暴利借贷时，如果参与其中的放贷者略有理性，就不至于集体抱团在薄冰上狂欢。一个人的狂热并不可怕，可怕的是出现区域性的群体性狂热。当前民间资本的运行生态，在某些区域，便被高额逐利的诱惑激发了群体性狂热，这是需要高度警惕的。

3. 法律观念和安全意识淡薄。民间资本的运行中所发生的各种案件，在我国现行法律中均有相关规定。我国《刑法》明确规定了高利转贷罪、非法吸收公众存款罪、用账外客户资金非法拆借、发放贷款罪、集资诈骗罪、贷款诈骗罪等罪名，对上述行为均规定了相应的刑事责任。在禁止高利贷方面，1991年8月13日，最高人民法院印发《关于人民法院审理借贷案件的若干意见》的通知，明确规定民间借贷的利率不得超过银行同类贷款利率的四倍（包含利率本数）。超出此限度部分的利息不予保护。并规定"出借人不得将利息计入本金谋取高利"，从而禁止了高利贷的利滚利行为。这一系列的法律及司法解释的有关规定，在民间资本的运行中被忽略了，由此可见民间资本运行的各个环节法律观念的淡薄。很多民间资本借贷案件也反映了资金持有人安全意识的淡薄，很多地方的放贷人与借款人之间只是口头承诺，连一纸合同都没有，当资金链断裂，需要追债时，最基本的借款依据都没有。如此淡薄的法律观念和安全意识，也是导致当前民间资本运行乱象的根源之一。

（三）民间资本运行乱象之灾

民间资本的狂热运行中酿造的各种案件，其结局几乎都是一个模式，就是资金链断裂，肇事者要么自杀，要么出逃，要么被绳之于法。但是所引发的连锁反应影响深远。其一，民众财富蒸发，利益严重受损，给家庭带来灾难，殃及社会稳定。其二，资本成本畸高，企业负担增加，资金链条断裂，毁及企业倒闭破产，伤及社会经济。其三，民间资本信用受损，非公经济活力受挫，市场经济的互补缺失，损及整体经济的平稳较快发展。

二、民间资本运行中法律机制的失范

（一）民间资本运行缺乏疏通的法律机制

当前法律机制中，以刑事之责禁非法集资、禁高利转贷、禁非法吸收公众存款、禁集资诈骗。如此之禁，恰如铁板封门。澎湃的民间资本，就被收束在庞大的资本池中。

在民间借贷方面，虽然《民法通则》第90条规定"合法的借贷关系受法律保护"，《合同法》第196条也规定"借款合同是借款人向贷款人借款，到期返还借款并支付利息的合同"，但是，在民间借贷出路方面，中国人民银行制定的《贷款通则》第61条规定："企业之间不得违反国家规定办理借贷或者变相借贷融资业务。"《贷款通则》第73条规定："企业之间擅自办理借贷或者变相借贷的，由中国人民银行对出借方按违规收入处以1倍以上至5倍以下罚款，并由中国人民银行予以取缔。"根据上述规定，民间资本储量丰富的民营企业之间以借贷方式进行资本流动，就被依法禁止了。民间资本如潮，堵而不疏，则如堰塞之势，堵之愈久，则决堤之害愈凶。

剩下的民间资本的流动通道，就是按照1991年7月2日最高人民法院审判委员会第502次会议讨论通过的《关于人民法院审理借贷案件的若干意见》的精神，准许公民之间、公民与法人之间以及公民与其他组织之间的借贷关系，似乎我国在法律意义上的民间借贷就只能是这三者之间的借贷往来。该意见同时规定民间借贷的利率可以适当高于银行的利率，但最高不得超过银行同类贷款利率的四倍（包含利率本数）。这一司法解释就算是我国民间资本借贷在法律层面的唯一出口和保障了。这一出口，只是给了民间资本这个庞大的资本池开了一道小小的缝隙。

正是上述以堵漏为主的法律机制，才使得民间资本发达的各地都存在着尽人皆知的地下钱庄和地下资金链。这些地下钱庄和地下资金链，非法承载着民营资本流动的桥梁作用。由于是非法的地下交易，监管部门就无法监控，这便形成了民间资本池下的众多"管涌"。这些"管涌"如不及时整治，民间资本池的基土将被淘空，决堤、垮坝之险在所难免。因此，民间资本运行最缺失的就是可靠的疏浚机制，需要在民间资本的出路方面有明确的法律机制予以疏通，否则民间资本乱象就无法根除。

（二）民间资本运行缺失阳光法案

关于民间资本运行的"堵"与"疏"，国家并不是没有相关的政令和决策，但是，相关政令和决策没有上升到基本法律或者行政法规等立法的高度，却始终停留在国务院的《若干意见》《通知》的层面，有些重大规定甚至停留在部门规章或者司法解释的层面。这就给民间资本治理的效率打了折扣。

对于民间资本的出路，《国务院关于鼓励支持和引导个体私营等非公有制经济发展的若干意见》《国务院关于鼓励和引导民间投资健康发展的若干意见》这"新旧36条"之规定堪称完美。但是，这些看上去很美的《意见》，到底能否落到实处呢？以"旧36条"为例，该《意见》自2005年实施以来，效果并不是十分理想，并没有如"旧36条"所鼓励的那样，将民间资本顺利地引入电力、电信、铁路、民航、石油等垄断行业和领域，也没有使民间资本在公用事业和基础设施领域、社会事业领域、金融服务业、国防科技工业建设领域、参与国有经济结构调整和国有企业重组等领域顺利地施展拳脚，反而一度在某些领域有"国进民退"之势。2010年实施的"新36条"，正在经历着实践的考验。

反观上述"新旧36条"的完美规定，诚如"新旧36条"《意见》标题名称及正文中的诸多的"鼓励""引导"等核心字眼，在实施中缺乏"刚性"规定，在落实中缺乏"责任"追究机制，从而使党和国家的重大决策及对民间资本的重大政策没有得到如其规定的那样"完美实现。"笔者认为，将国务院在"新旧36条"中的重要规定，以立法的形式，明确制度，细化流程，规范责任，从而赋予民间资本以真正阳光法案，民间资本运行才会真正归于平稳健康。

（三）民间资本运行缺乏系统的法律保障机制

民间资本的健康运行是一个系统工程，从法律保障机制来看，并不是一两部单行的法律或者法规就能得以实现的。笔者认为，加强民间资本管理，疏导民间资本运行渠道，保障民间资本良性发展需要系统性的法律保障机制，这是当前所缺失的。具体而言，民间资本运行的法律保障中，至少在下列方面需要有明确的法律保障机制。

1. 民间资本主体的权利义务的法律规制。在目前的各种规范性文件中，均没有对民间资本主体加以清晰界定，更没有对民间资本主体的权利和义务进行规范。在"旧36条"中使用的是"非公有资本"之称谓，在"新36条"中又变为"民间资本"之称谓，此"民间资本"与彼"非公有资本"之间是何关联，并无交代。一般而言，学界将民营企业的流动资产和公民个人及家庭所拥有的金融资产统称为民营资本，但是民营企业和公民个人这两种不同主体在民间资本的运行方面有何差异，均需要法律给予明确的规定。

2. 民间资本市场准入机制的法律规制。民间资本的市场准入，关乎民间资本的流动与出路，因此，除了在国务院的鼓励和引导意见中予以体现外，更需要将民间资本的市场准入范围和准入标准用法律的形式加以规定。

3. 民间资本运行的程序的法律保障机制。目前民营资本运行缺乏有效的程序机制，处于较为无序的状态。民间资本的真正有效运行，还有赖于完善的程序机制加以保障。

4. 民间资本运行的法律责任机制。无责任则无制约，在民间资本运行的各种法律保障机制的建设和健全过程中，法律责任机制不能缺失。也就是说，需要明确民间资本运行各个环节的职能与职责，并明确运行各有关方面的法律责任，从而保障有法可依，违法可究。

三、民间资本运行中监督机制的失灵

构建公平竞争的市场环境，充分发挥市场配置资源的基础性作用，是社会主义市场经济发展的根本要求。但是，当市场机制失灵时，政府的干预和监督职能就显得尤为重要。近年来在民间资本领域，由于很多民间资本在地下钱庄等灰色体系中运行，从而导致了大量性质严重的案件爆发，给经济平稳发展、社会稳定、群众生活及民间资本的自身安全造成了较大的影响，暴露了在民间资本运行中有效的监督机制的失灵。

（一）民间资本运行的监督意识不强

从鄂尔多斯、温州、泗洪等地爆发的民间资本运行的恶性案件来看，其显著的特点就是参与非法资本流转的人数众多，当地包括公务员在内的各种人群均有参与，尤其是高利贷、非法集资在有些地方成为普遍现象。即使如此，在资金链断裂导致重大案件爆发前，各级政府有关部门的监督意识淡薄，没有实施及时的管控和警示，从而使民间资本运行中监督缺位。

（二）民间资本运行的监督主体不清

由于民间资本运行关系复杂，既有民间资本投资，又有资本的民间借贷，既有合法的市场行为，也有非法的地下操作，因此，在各地民间资本运行监督不力的背后，凸显了民间资本运行的监督主体不清的尴尬。所以，有关政府部门必须协调机制，分工合作，从金融监管、工商管理、治安监管等多部门多渠道配合监督，才能真正遏制民间资本的非法运行。

（三）民间资本运行的监督依据不足

民间资本运行的法律机制不健全，所以民间资本的不同运行情况和不同的运行阶段，应该符合怎样的运行规范本身缺乏法律依据。另外，有关部门就民间资本运行的监督职权也缺乏法律支持，从而导致了职能部门在实施监督时依据不足，这也是导致民间资本案件频发而监督缺位的原因。

四、思考与建议

（一）加强立法，健全民间资本运行的法律保障机制

市场经济就是法制经济，市场经济发展的每一个链环，都需要有法律规范的定位和保障，否则将会导致角色缺位，规范缺失，秩序受损。"法律规范作为秩序的组成部分，行使着社会控制的职责。"[8]改革开放三十多年来，民间资本得到了极大的扩充，但是民间资本的法律保障却极不健全。因此，加强民间资本立法，健全民间资本运行的法律保障机制势在必行。

首先，在立法层次上，应该由全国人大制定"民间资本保护与促进"的基本法律规范。在基本法律规范之下，再分层次构建一个系统的民间资本法律保障体系。"政府作为市场监管的主体，既要全面、有效、合理地执行市场监管法律所赋予的职责，行使相应的权力，也要根据执行法律的需要制定层级低一些的规范性文件，如法规、规章。"[9]改革开放以来，我国非公有制经济不断发展壮大，已经成为社会主义市场经济的重要组成部分。民间资本的不断聚积，也成为促进社会生产力发展的重要力量。只有健全的法律保障体系，才能促进民间资本在市场经济建设中更好地发挥作用。

其次，在立法内容上应该全面系统，既要有民间资本运行的主体立法，规范民间资本主体的市场地位；也要有民间资本的市场准入立法，明确民间资本的市场准入范围和条件；还要有民间资本运行的程序立法，规范民间资本的运行秩序。民间资本运行的监督与责任机制立法，明确监督主体及监督职能，规范法律责任的追究机制。

（二）加强监督，规范民间资本运行的市场行为

"国家对市场的规制，是指国家不仅为参与市场活动各方制定规则，而且予以直接管束和制约（有时还包括对市场的培育和组织）。"[10]我国民间资本分散，主体众多，影响面广，管理难度大。因此，在国家加强民间资本立法的基础上，更应当加强对民间资本的监督和制约。在监督机制方面，相应的监督主体需要强化监督意识，明确监督职责，规范监督行为，以监督促进民间资本的合法运行，健康发展。将民间资本市场中的非法行为消灭在萌芽状态，而不是任其疯狂壮大，贻害群众，损坏民间资本自身的良性发展。

（三）加强宣传，增强群众的法律意识和安全意识

民间资本的畸形狂欢中，那些受损的群众，除了正常的逐利之心的驱使外，淡薄的法律意识和资金安全意识也是他们裹入高利贷和非法集资链条的重要原因。因此，加大普法宣传力度，将国家现行的法律、法规及政策宣讲给群众，增强群众的法律意识，使群众在参与民间资本运行时知法守法。同时，需要把各地发生的各种各样新型的资本骗局和陷阱及时地宣传给群众，使群众增强安全意识和鉴别能力，避免被不法分子利用欺骗手段引入资本陷阱，以维护民间资本安全。

参考文献

[1] 莫开伟. 三十万亿民间资本该向何处流. http://www.banyuetan.org/rtdj/hot/110925/54363.shtml.

[2] 李玉波. 非法集资案受害人：在鄂尔多斯不放高利贷会被人笑话. http://finance.ifeng.com/news/20110613/

4140086. shtml.
[3] 江苏泗洪县民间借贷疯狂贫困县里惊现"宝马乡". http：//www. chinanews. com/cj/2011/09 – 11/3320454. shtml.
[4] 吴亚东. 借网络虚拟基金币传销骗财 57 万　3 人集资诈骗新疆获刑. http：//www. legalinfo. gov. cn/index/content/2010 – 06/03/content_ 2162337. htm？node = 7880.
[5] 史万森. 画个馅饼也有人信　内蒙古现"电子币"集资诈骗案. http：//news. sohu. com/20100819/n274315964. shtml.
[6] 李玉波. 非法集资事件频发　暴利让民间借贷者铤而走险. http：//news. xinhuanet. com/society/2011 – 06/13/c_ 121527215. htm.
[7] （法）孟德斯鸠. 论法的精神. 北京：商务印书馆，1961.
[8] （德）阿图尔·考夫曼，温弗里德·哈斯默尔. 当代法哲学和法律理论导论. 北京：法律出版社，2002.
[9] 杨紫烜. 经济法［M］. 3 版. 北京：北京大学出版社，2008.
[10] 漆多俊. 经济法基础理论［M］. 3 版. 武汉：武汉大学出版社，2006.

城镇化过程中失地农民权益的整体性保障

郑广永

中国共产党第十八次全国代表大会的政治报告指出:"坚持走中国特色新型工业化、信息化、城镇化、农业现代化道路,推动信息化和工业化深度融合、工业化和城镇化良性互动、城镇化和农业现代化相互协调,促进工业化、信息化、城镇化、农业现代化同步发展。"同时提出要显著提高城镇化质量。显然,高质量的城镇化是我国下一步发展的目标之一。根据以人为本的科学发展观的要求,城镇化的高质量不仅要体现在城镇外表上,更应该体现在民生上。民生与民权是紧密相联的。我们要更加清楚地认识到,在城镇化过程中必须以充分的民权来保障民生,这一点对于参与城镇化的农民而言尤其重要。尽管早在中共十七届三中全会的报告中就提出了要保护农民的政治、经济、文化、社会权益,但在具体的实施中却不够全面。也就是说,过去我们许多同志对于农民权益的认识不够全面,往往只重视农民当下的经济权益,致使城镇化过程中农民长远的经济权益,以及其他权益受到了损害。如果城镇化损害了农民权益,那就违背了科学发展观,同时也违背了中国共产党为人民服务的宗旨。这样的城镇化显然不能实现与工业化、农业现代化的良性互动。所以,在今后的城镇化过程中,探索如何整体性保护农民权益就是十分必要的了。本文集中探索城镇化过程中失地农民权益的整体性保障。

一、保障失地农民权益就是尊重公正原则

公平正义是维系社会正常运转的核心原则,类似于康德所说的令人敬畏的道德律令。然而,这个道德律令不仅仅是道德要求,在现代社会则具有极其深刻的经济根源,那就是市场经济的等价交换原则。其实,马克思早就明确说过,商品经济是天生的平等派[1]。当前城镇化过程中,失地农民权益受损的原因之一就是违背等价交换的公平原则。具体来说,就是农民出让自己的承包地,改变自己的身份,换来的应该是能够保障其生存和发展的各种权益。如果失地农民获得的权益不足以保障其生存和发展,那就说明这种交易是不公平的。以不公平交易推进的城镇化必然遭受挫折。

城镇化是一个自然历史过程,是市场经济发展的产物。要在城镇化过程中对农民权益进行整体性保障,就首先需要搞清楚,城镇化是市场经济发展的必然产物。在一定意义上说,农民市民化、农村城镇化本身是一个市场交易过程。市场交易就要遵循等价交换的原则。农民放弃原本作为农民的权益而成为市民,应该获得市民所应该享有的全部权益,这是一个公平的交易过程。在这个意义上,农民的权益是天然的,而不是什么人恩赐的。我们今天之所以要谈保障农民的权益,其原因就在于在当今城镇化过程中,公平交易的市场原则没有得到充分的尊重,强势的资本和权力剥夺了农民应得的部分权益。

关于城市的起源有各种说法,特别是在古代政治和军事的原因也促使城市产生和发展。但是根据马克思主义的常识,在根本的意义上来看,生产力的发展特别是社会分工的发展是城市产生和发展的最根本原因,尤其是现代城市是工业化的直接产物。马克思、恩格斯在《共产党宣言》中就说过:资产阶级"创立了巨大的城市,使城市人口比农村人口大大增加起来"。而"现代资产阶级本身是一个长期发展过程的产物,是生产方式和交换方式的一系列变革的产物。"[2]马克思、恩格斯在这里所指的生产方式和交换方式就是指资本主义市场经济。所以,从逻辑上顺理成章地就可以得出现代城市是市场经济产物的结论。

有了现代意义的城市,人类开始了城市化的步伐。当然,由于最初的现代意义的大工业只是集中在西欧和南欧,所以,城市化也只是在这些地区展开。后来,伴随着现代工商业文明遍及世界,城市化才在世界范围内逐渐展开。

[作者简介] 郑广永(1965—),男,山东费县人,北京联合大学社会建设研究院研究员,哲学博士。

中国古代也曾经出现过许多繁华的大都市，诸如马可·波罗笔下的大都、苏州、扬州等。这些城市诚然也是生产力高度发展的产物，但是与现代工商业城市相比，它们没有现代工业基础，更为根本的是这些城市并没有从根本上改变封建的生产方式，从而也就不可能引导国家走向城市化。鸦片战争以后，随着帝国主义的入侵和本国民族资本主义的发展，现代资本主义工商业开始在中国发展起来，由此中国逐渐发展起了现代工商业城市。尽管现代工商业在近代中国整个国民经济中所占比例很低，城市人口占总人口的比例同样也很低，但是毕竟开始改变自给自足的封建生产方式，开始引领中国缓慢步入城市化轨道。

新中国成立后，我国大力推进工业化，在工业化基础上，城市化取得了巨大进步。但是，由于建国后很长一段时间，我国实行计划经济，市场原则受到了极大限制，特别是采取了实行工农业产品剪刀差等方式从农业积累资本推动工业化的方针，并且严格限制农村人口流入城市的城乡二元户籍制度，因此，我国的城市化进程十分缓慢，而且城市发展水平也很低。可以说，我国的城市化并没有进入良性发展的轨道。与此相对应，农民的权益也未得到充分的保障。具体来说，就是在强调为国家工业化做贡献的号召下，农民不但没有享受到工业化、城市化的成果，反而做出了巨大的牺牲。尽管这些都是在特殊历史条件下造成的，但是无论如何都必须承认，我们没有遵循等价交换、公平交易的市场规则来推进城市化，所以这种以损害一方权益来推进的城市化是不可持续的。20 世纪 90 年代，党的十四大确立了建设社会主义市场经济的目标，等价交换、公平交易的原则逐渐主导了国家的经济生活，城镇化的步伐大大加快了。但是，由于计划经济的影响还没有完全消除，社会主义市场经济体制还在完善过程中，我们对于城镇化过程中的市场规则还没有充分的认识，所以在急于推进城镇化时没有完整地考虑到农民的权益，在一定程度上以牺牲农民的权益为代价展开了城镇化。这种牺牲最直接的表现是为了降低工业化的成本，在征收农民土地时，压低给农民的补偿，而且没有充分考虑被征地农民的就业、社会保障等，实质就是一种要地不要人（农民）的工业化和城镇化方式。与这种明显的直接经济侵权相并存的，还有隐含的对农民政治、文化、社会、生态权益的损害。马克思说过，商品经济是天生的平等派。从理想的角度看，如果我们真正尊重市场规律，实行公平交易，农民的权益是不会受到损害的。所以，从本质上说，当前的城镇化在一定意义上受非市场化因素的干扰，即依靠资本和权力强势推进的城镇化，从根本上违背了公平正义的原则，这也是导致农村群体性事件的原因之一。

二、农民整体性的权益状况

中国共产党第十八次全国代表大会提出"要坚持以经济建设为中心，以科学发展为主题，全面推进经济建设、政治建设、文化建设、社会建设、生态文明建设，实现以人为本、全面协调可持续的科学发展"。这个总目标体现在城镇化过程中农民的权益上，就是要保障失地农民的经济权益、政治权益、文化权益、社会权益、生态权益。其中经济权益是核心，是基础，政治权益是保障。

（一）经济权益

城镇化过程中农民的经济权益包括两种类型。一种是因为人多地少，农业收益低，而使得一部分农民在没有失去土地的情况下，从事非农业生产而获得的工资性收入。确保这种工资性收入不受侵害主要是农民在付出与城镇职工同等劳动时应该获得与城镇职工相同的劳动报酬，即同工同酬。农民的这种经济权益基本得到了实现。这不是本文所要讨论的问题。另外一种，也是最主要的一种，就是城镇化过程中，农地转化为城镇用地，农民失去了原有的土地而得不到公平的补偿，这是最突出的，也是本文所探讨的。

按照公平交易的市场规则，农民转让自己的土地，国家获得工业化、城镇化所需要的土地，这应该是一个双赢的过程。作为农民而言，出让土地后要享受工业化、城镇化的成果。从直观看，至少要保证农民生活水平不下降，而且要提高到与城镇居民同样的水平，同时必须保证失去土地的农民各种长期的潜在的权益，诸如就业、教育培训等发展权益。而要实现农民的这些经济权益，一个直接有效的办法就是按照公平交易的规则，给农民适合的征地补偿，而不是故意压低征地补偿。至于这种补偿到底是多少，应该按照市场价格来确定。

土地作为一种特殊的商品，其收益因用途不同而不同。作为农业用地的收益远远小于作为工商业用地的收益，这本身也是社会发展的结果。在我国，当农业用地转化为城镇建设用地后，土地立即升值几十倍，甚至上百倍。当前农民出让土地后的补偿标准主要是基于原先作为农业用地的产值来计算的，而没有考虑到出让后的增值部分。根据现行的《中华人民共和国土地管理法》第二十二条规定，国家建设征用土地，建设单位应支付土地补偿费、青苗和附着物补偿费、安置补助费。但是补偿的标准还是偏低，而且还特别规定"土地补偿费和安置补助费的总和最高不得超过土地被征用前三年平均年产值的二十倍"。即使按照最高二十倍的标准给予补偿，也不能满足失地农民作为城市市民长期的正常生活。究其原因在于这个规定没有考虑土地转变使用用途后的增值收益。很显然，这种规定并没有依据马克思的级差地租理论。正因为如此，一些农民失去土地后生活水平下降了。根据有的学者研究，"在有的县市，征地后家庭收入减少的农户接近四成。根据国务院发展研究中心课题组对全国 2749 个村的调查，约 40% 的村民上访反映的是土地征用问题。中国社会科学院 2004—2005 年'社会形势分析与预测'课题报告中明确指出，在当前困扰中国的七大社会问题中'农民失地引起的社会矛盾加剧'排在首位。"[3] 一些被征地农民成为"三无"人口：种田无地，就业无岗，社保无份。现实来看，增值收益主要由地方政府和土地使用者来分配，而农民只得到了其中的 5%～10%。这也就是说，农民只是在为城镇化做贡献，实际上却被排除在城镇化之外了。难怪农村 65% 以上的群体性事件都与征地有关。在这种情况下，这些地区建设和谐的社会主义新农村，实现科学发展就是一句空话。

（二）政治权益

城镇化过程中失地农民的政治权益不是通常宪法和法律所规定的当家做主的权利，而是指这种权利在城镇化过程中的具体表现。还没有开始城镇化的农民，以及已经转变为城镇居民的公民权益都不属于本文讨论的城镇化过程中的失地农民权益。党的十七大政治报告中提出要保障公民的知情权、参与权、表达权和监督权。参与城镇化的农民的这四种权利要通过具体的法律体现出来。目前我国实行农村基层自治制度，确保这个制度实施的是《中华人民共和国村民委员会组织法》（以下简称《村民委员会组织法》）。本文所要探讨的保障城镇化过程中农民的政治权益，就是保障该法律在城镇化过程中的实施。实际上，当前城镇化过程中农民政治权益受到损害，就是《中华人民共和国村民委员会组织法》还不能得到完整的贯彻实施。

无论是主动还是被动，卷入城镇化过程中的农民都有权全面了解涉及自身权益的各种政策、措施以及结果，并对全过程进行监督和表达自己的意见。《村民委员会组织法》第二十四条规定涉及村民利益的事项，经村民会议讨论决定方可办理。比如其中第七款列出的"征地补偿费的使用、分配方案"就属于必须经村民会议讨论决定方可办理的事项，第三十条规定本款也属于村务公开和村民监督的内容。

如果真正按照这些规定执行，就不会出现或者是少出现侵害农民权益的情况。而实际上，在一些地区，当涉及被征地的村民的住房安置、征地补偿等具体问题时，村民就没有了知情权、参与权、表达权和监督权。往往是上级政府决定以后以通知、公告的方式告知村民，村民只能遵照执行。有的地方即使召开村民会议，也往往因为村民代表不能真正代表村民而只是形式地走过场，村民的意见得不到尊重。

需要进一步说明的是，《村民委员会组织法》的宗旨是民主选举、民主决策、民主管理、民主监督。住房安置、征地补偿等具体问题当然需要民主决策。民主决策包括协商民主和票决民主。当讨论协商达不成共识时，就需要票决。遗憾的是《村民委员会组织法》并没有明确规定票决民主的形式。当协商不成，就强征强拆。在这种情况下，《村民委员会组织法》的规定往往形同虚设。所以，当村民由于权益受损而缺乏正常的表达渠道时，最终导致群体性事件的爆发。这需要我们做进一步的思考。

导致一些地区不能依法推进城镇化，不能依靠《村民委员会组织法》来保障城镇化过程中农民的权益有许多原因，但是我国村民自治过程中存在着一些内在的矛盾，于建嵘教授曾经进行过分析。[4] 涉及城镇化农民权益的矛盾主要有以下几点。

"两委"矛盾凸显。在当今农村，同时存在着两个进行村务管理的组织，即村党支部和村委会。根据《中国共产党农村基层组织工作条例》规定，村党支部是农村各种组织的领导核心，讨论决定本村经济建设和社会发展中的重要问题。但同时村委会作为村民自治组织，也是以国家法律的授权为依据、以全体村民的民主选举为基础的，在法律上并不具有服从村党组织的义务。两者的权力来源和职权的不同必然影响到农村政治的统一性。目前，党支部和村委会之间的关系和矛盾越来越成为村民自治进程中一个不容忽视的焦点。

村务公开存在盲点。主要是公开不及时；假公开；难监督。

更为深刻的是自治权与行政权冲突。国家行政权与村民的自治权是两种不同来源的权力。在农村，以乡镇政府为代表的国家基层政权组织，其权力来源于国家。乡镇政府代表国家所行使的权力是社会公共权力的组成部分，是政权意志的体现。而以村民委员会为代表的自治组织，其权力来源于村民的选举和授权，是一种社区自治权。这样就出现了"乡镇管理权与村民自治权二元并存"的局面。一方面乡镇政府要行使国家行政权，另一方面，村民要行使自治权，二者冲突难免。实际上，乡镇管理权往往要比村民自治权强势，经常性地侵蚀村民自治权。在城镇化过程中，由于土地财政和急功近利观念的驱使，国家行政权严重侵害村民自治权的情况已经常态化了。这种常态化的侵害就是对失地农民政治权益侵害的具体表现。

以上这些问题虽然不仅仅出现在城镇化过程中，但是的确影响了城镇化过程中农民的政治权益。因此，同我国其他方面的改革和发展情况一样，失地农民政治权益的保障也有赖于政治体制改革的推进。

（三）社会权益

城镇化过程中农民的社会权益是指农民所应该获得的与城镇居民相同的社会保障。具体来说，包括养老保障、医疗保障、最低生活保障、失业保障、工伤和生育保障。在城镇化中，被征用土地后农民获得的经济补偿不属于社会保障的范围。在我国，城镇化过程中，农民分为两个部分。一部分是那些虽然进城务工，但还有承包地的农民，另一部分则是指因工业化、城镇化承包地被征用后的农民。相应地，农民的社会权益也分为两个部分，即仍然拥有承包地的农民工的社会权益和失去土地后的农民的社会权益。在我国，农民的承包地不仅是生产资料，而且是生活资料，承担了农民社会保障的功能。许多农民不愿放弃承包地，不是因为这些承包地可以为他们带来多大的物质财富，实现他们的富裕梦想，而是因为当他们失业后，这些承包地可以提供生活的保障。根据国际通行的标准，人均耕地0.8亩时，这些土地仅有最低社会保障的功能。现在我国许多省份人均耕地已经不足一亩，仅仅依靠人均不足一亩的耕地根本不可能实现农村、农业、农民的发展，耕地的社会保障功能日益突出。

当前，我国还没有统一的关于失地农民社会保障的法律规定，只有国务院以及各地行政部门的一些行政法规和条例。各地都是结合本地的情况对失地农民进行社会保障。缺乏法律保障的失地农民权益很难得到充分的尊重。当然，总体来说，改革开放之初，那种不管被征地农民社会保障权益的状况已基本上改变了，各地都在探索如何保障失地农民的社会权益。但是，实际上失地农民的社会权益还没有得到充分的保障，在一些地区仍然存在侵害失地农民社会权益的现象。在我国目前的农村社会保障体系中，保险项目以养老保险和医疗保险为主，以救济救灾和社会福利的对象为最广，失地农民由于不符合救济条件而无法享受到救济。此外，2009年推行的新型农村社会养老保险规定，年满60周岁的农民才可按月领取养老金，排除了失地的青壮年。因此，失地农民社会保障覆盖面窄，保障水平比较低，不具有长期可持续性等特点，远不符合社会经济发展和失地农民的合理需要。

当前各地失地农民的保障模式都存在一些缺陷，农民出让土地后所获得的是不可持续、低水平、一元、不稳定的社会保障[5]。一是保障的不可持续性。从保障对象来看，失地农民中真正得到实惠的是那些即期领取养老金的老年人，而青壮年失地农民需要靠自己的能力买社会保险，这对于既失地又需要缴纳保险费用的年轻劳动力来说，没有吸引力，很难长久坚持下去。从保障资金来看，政府从土地收益中只拿出10%~30%用于保障，这种过度依赖失地农民征地补偿费来建立社会保障制度的情况是很难持续的。从保障运行机制来看，保障资金的运行机制和监督机制不健全，不利于失地农民社会保障安置的长远发展。二是保障的低水平性。主要体现在对失地农民的保障限于生存型保障，缺乏发展型保障。三是保障内容的一元性。一般仅包括养老保险，而医疗保险、失业保险、工伤保险等仅在沿海一些经济比较发达地区出现。四是保障的不稳定性。一些失地农民尤其是那些在经济发展水平较低地区、文化层次不高的失地农民对养老保险、医疗保险等存在着许多认识误区。这导致了一些地区的失地农民不愿意参保、害怕参保，或者参保后又退保，加大了社会保障的不稳定性。这种社会保障与工业化、城镇化中国家、地方政府、开发商等获得的巨大利益相比，对这些农民而言，显然是不公平的。

(四) 文化权益

文化作为人们在社会实践和意识活动中长期絪蕴化育出来的价值观念、审美情趣、思维方式以及丰富的表现形态，除了能够直接增强当代农民对党和国家政策的认同感，提升农民道德修养，和谐农民人际关系，缓解农民心理危机外，更重要的是提高农民的社会主义公民意识。胡锦涛同志在党的十七大报告中明确提出要积极培育社会主义公民意识。社会主义公民意识作为一种意识形式，最深刻的基础是社会主义市场经济。无论愿意与否、认识到与否，城镇化过程中的失地农民都不可避免地被卷入社会主义市场经济的大潮中。在这个大潮中，传统自然经济条件下的人身依附关系被独立的商品关系取代，独立人格得以健全，以独立人格为核心的公民意识日益发育成熟。马克思在《路易·波拿巴的雾月十八日》中对法国小农的批判反衬了这个道理。所以在这个意义上，文化在城镇化中的作用自不待言。

但是，在当下的中国社会，除了高层和知识精英，部分地方政府、普通民众包括农民自身并没有真正重视农民的文化权益，特别是与经济权益、政治权益、社会权益、生态权益相比，人们对于农民文化权益的关注度本来就不高。在城镇化过程中，人们的注意力集中在了经济补偿、社会保障等方面，很少有人关注农民的文化权益。这也反映了我国当前社会发展的阶段特征，即先生存，后发展的现实。但是这并不意味着农民的文化权益不重要。恰恰相反，要提高城镇化的水平，提高社会的文明程度，必须保障城镇化过程中农民的文化权益，提高转化为城镇居民的人口的文化素质，核心内容在于培育失地农民的社会主义公民意识。在一定意义上说，没有人的现代化，就没有现代工业化和城镇化。

党中央历来重视农民的文化权益。十六大以来，中央多次强调并出台相应的措施来推进农村文化建设，保障农民的文化权益。目前主要的政策性文件有《中共中央关于深化文化体制改革推动社会主义文化大发展大繁荣若干重大问题的决定》《国家"十二五"时期文化改革发展规划纲要》。实事求是地讲，这些规定缺乏明确的社会主义公民意识这个根本的价值导向。在许多人看来，保障农民的文化权益就是让农民看上书、看上戏，于是不外乎建图书馆、电影院等硬件建设。其实这只是问题的表面，根本目的是通过看书、看戏提高公民素养。失地农民转化为城镇居民后还不能，或者是还没有能力自觉享受城镇居民所享受的文化权益。尤其是那些就地城镇化的农民，他们的生活环境并没有太大改变，更主要的是他们的思维方式、心理状态、风俗习惯、价值观念等文化气质并没有因为身份的转变而立刻转变。这对于提高市民素质，提高城镇化水平，提高社会的文明程度是不利的。因此，从根本上说，现在对失地农民的文化权益需要有一个清醒的认识。总的来看，现在还没有关于城镇化过程中，农民文化权益保障的认识，没有认识当然也就没有相关规定，这需要我们进一步研究。

(五) 生态权益

公民的生态权是指公民享有在适宜的生态环境中生活的权利，是公民在生态系统中对生态安全、生态选择、生态保护、生态发展等所拥有的各项权利的总和。"农民生存在农村生态系统中，是农村生态系统的拥有者、使用者、经营者和维护者。农民的衣、食、住、行都依赖于农村的生态系统，生态权是农民最基本的权利，农民没有生态权就不可能进行农业生产，农民的生态权遭到破坏，其利益就会受到损害。只有实现农民对生态环境参与的制度化、法律化，才能切实保证农民生态权益的稳定化、持续化，确保农民平等享受环境权。"[6]实际上，在城镇化过程中，失地农民的生态权益受到了损害，没有得到公正的补偿。

我国城镇化过程中农民生态权益遭受侵害包括两种情况。一种是随着全国性的工业化、城镇化的快速推进、产业升级换代，大批污染严重的企业陆续迁往农村。工业三废超标排放已成为影响农村环境质量的主要因素。农村环境日趋恶化对农民的身心健康和生命安全构成了极大的威胁，并且严重影响了农业生产。这种对农民生态权益的损害是全国性的。另一种是直接卷入城镇化中的农民所遭受的生态权益的损害。本文强调的是后者。因为前一种损害，还无法得到直接补偿，后者则有可能。

在我国当前城镇化过程中，农民在出让自己的承包地，转换身份后，已经没有权利干预土地的用途。在利益驱动下，许多给环境带来严重污染的工业项目上马了。农民转换身份后，直接遭受环境污染的侵害。但是，在确定给农民补偿内容时，政府包括农民自己大都没有考虑到生态权益的补偿，只是把经济补偿看作补偿的全部。实事求是地说，对于一些农民而言，由于生态权益遭受侵害，他们的身心遭受严重伤害，做一个城镇居民反倒不如做一个农民。这样的城镇化对于农民乃至城镇居民和国家都是弊大于利。

尽管工业化、城镇化所造成的环境污染损害了全体社会成员的生态权益，但是，相对而言，农民所遭受的损害更大，农民是环境不公正的最大受害者。有学者对此进行了如下分析。[6]

由于我国长期实行城乡二元体制，走的是一条从农业积累资本支持工业化的道路，因此，从根本上造成了城乡环境不公正的制度背景。

首先，城市的快速发展很大程度上以侵害农村环境为代价，在城乡居民生产生活中，城市的环境服务和农村的环境污染存在着明显的不公正。农村的环境支出大于其所得到的环境收益，而城市的环境支出远小于其得到的环境收益。农村的环境支出是指农村向城市的资源供给而引起农村环境质量的下降和生态的破坏所导致的经济损失，农村的环境收益主要是指农村从城市获得的经济收益。从公正的逻辑上讲，农村的环境收益应等于城市的环境支出。但是，我国长期实行以农村积累支持城市的政策，其中包括牺牲农村生态环境以满足城市经济社会发展的需求。农村为城市付出了环境污染的代价，却并没有得到合理的补偿，城市的环境支出并没有转移到农村，而是用于城市自身的治理。农村承受着巨大的环境负担，农民的环境生态权受到了不公正的对待。

其次，城乡环境不公导致农民生态享有权缺失。根据环境权理论，环境权主体应平等地享有环境资源权、环境使用权和环境处理权。在各类能源和资源的消费量以及各类生活消费品的结构和数量上，城市人均消费量远远高于农村，因此，城市人均排放的污染物就比农村多。农村居民相对于城市居民来说较少使用资源，相应较少产生污染，这样实际上是农民对自己应享有的环境使用权向城市居民的让渡的生态享有权的缺失。

当然除了上述两点外，还有其他因素。但是，无论哪种因素，在城镇化过程中都没有考虑到农民生态权益的保护。所以，应该本着环境公正的原则，在城镇化过程中对失地农民的生态权益给以补偿。

三、整体性保障农民权益的对策

实事求是地说，本文不可能给出一个完整而详细的保障农民整体性权益的对策。其实，单就某一权益的保障对策的制定，就十分困难。因为这不仅是一个技术问题，更是一个法律和政治问题。但是，我们至少可以进行一些有益的探索。

首先，提高人们对于保障农民权益重要性的认识，特别是高层对这个问题的认识。人们已经认识到，城镇化过程中需要保障农民的权益。工业化、城镇化是社会发展的必然趋势，是提升人们生活水平，提高社会文明程度的必然之路。城镇化是一个城镇与乡村、城镇居民与农村居民互利共赢的过程。这个过程不可能长期通过侵害一方权益来满足另外一方权益的方式完成，只有互利共赢才能实现和谐发展。为此，最重要的是对城镇化有一个正确的认识。党的十八大提出了要走新型城镇化的道路。2012年4月，李克强发表在《求是》杂志上的文章指出，推进城镇化，要努力在改革攻坚中破解深层次矛盾。围绕城镇化发展中面临的发展方式转变和结构调整、土地节约集约利用、户籍和社会管理、资源支撑和生态环保等问题。2013年1月15日，李克强在国家粮食局科学研究院考察调研时指出，推进城镇化，核心是人的城镇化，关键是提高城镇化质量，目的是造福百姓和富裕农民。要走集约、节能、生态的新路子，着力提高内在承载力，不能人为"造城"，要实现产业发展和城镇建设融合，让农民工逐步融入城镇。要为农业现代化创造条件、提供市场，实现新型城镇化和农业现代化相辅相成。

其次，坚持以人为本的科学发展观。党的十八大提出，必须更加自觉地把以人为本作为深入贯彻落实科学发展观的核心立场，始终把实现好、维护好、发展好最广大人民群众的根本利益作为党和国家一切工作的出发点和落脚点，尊重人民首创精神，保障人民各项权益，不断在实现发展成果由人民共享、促进人的全面发展上取得新成效。在城镇化过程中，贯彻这个要求的具体体现就是充分保障农民的各项权益。城镇化中的人民群众绝不是抽象的，而是每一个实实在在的农民。保障了他们的权益就是贯彻了科学发展观，否则就是一句空话。

再次，坚持社会主义市场经济的原则。公平交易是市场经济的灵魂。在城镇化过程中，农民出让自己的承包地，转换身份，必须取得相应的市民权益。对农民权益的保障不能仅仅停留在道义的层面。所以，在这个意义上，应该把城镇化定义为一个市场交易的过程，一个自然历史过程。那种强权与资本合力推进的城镇化，往往会侵害农民的权益，造成社会的冲突，导致社会的不和谐。同时，市场经济是法制经济，所以城镇化还必须依法进行。当然，我们也需要清楚地认识到，目前的一些法律对于保障农民的权益是不力的，有的甚至成为剥夺农民的依据，这是必须改变的。

最后，积极推进政治体制改革。政治体制改革似乎与城镇化没有直接关系，其实不然。政治体制改革的本质是推进社会主义民主政治建设。社会主义民主政治不是抽象的，它具体体现在人民当家做主上。在城镇化过程中，农民是城镇化的主体，而不应"被城镇化"。农民对于自己的权益必须有知情权、参与权、表达权和监督权。失去了这些权利，农民权益必然受到侵害，事实也证明了这一点。没有民权，民生自然不保。

总之，改革开放前，农民为国家的工业化、城镇化做出了巨大牺牲，改革开放后，国家不能再让农民为城镇化做出牺牲。因为，牺牲农民权益实现的城镇化不仅违背道义原则，而且，随着农民权利意识的清醒，也很难再推行下去。所以，保障农民权益，实现和谐发展的城镇化是必由之路。

参考文献

[1] 马克思. 资本论（第1卷）[M]. 北京：人民出版社，1975.
[2] 马克思，恩格斯. 马克思恩格斯选集（第1卷）[M]. 北京：人民出版社，1995.
[3] 王朝华. 城市化过程中失地农民利益受侵害的制度根源分析[J]. 农业经济，2012（8）.
[4] 于建嵘. 村民自治的价值和困境[J]. 学习与探索，2010（4）.
[5] 钟水映，李魁. 失地农民社会保障安置：制度、模式与方向[J]. 中州学刊，2009（1）.
[6] 贾凤姿，杨驭越. 城乡环境公正缺失与农民生态权益[J]. 大连海事大学学报（社会科学版），2010（4）.

人大常委会监督途径的确立与运行

徐永利 王维国

虽然《中华人民共和国各级人民代表大会常务委员会监督法》（以下简称《监督法》）已颁布施行有几年了，但人大常委会行使监督权的实效一直与宪法法律规定，与党的要求和人民的期待有一定的差距。也就是说，人大常委会行使监督权的实效问题仍然突出。对此，有人认为是监督途径不足所致；有人认为是监督途径闲置所致；也有人认为是监督途径运行不畅所致。三种解读看起来大相径庭，实际上都与"监督的目的、监督途径的确立与运行"密切相关。监督途径的确立与运行状况会影响到监督目的的实现及其程度，而监督目的的实现程度直接影响监督实效。因此，探索和研究人大常委会监督途径的确立与运行，以进一步增强其监督实效具有重要的理论意义和现实意义。

一、监督的目的

人类发展史，在某种意义上讲，也是一部监督制度与实践发展史。一般意义上的监督广泛存在于各个共同体之间、个人之间及共同体与个人之间，但这样的监督是基于共同体关系或契约关系的一种监督，主要依靠的是一种信誉，监督关系随着共同关系或契约关系的解除而丧失，不以国家的强制力为保证，是一种非刚性监督。虽然中西方关于"监督"一词的含义相近；但总的来看，不同时代不同国家的监督制度与实践类型多样，形态各异，关于监督的本质属性及其目的仍有很大差异，从而影响了不同时代不同国家的监督实效。

从中国国家层面的监督制度与实践看，首先源于对军队将领的管理。《后汉书·荀彧传》："古之遣将，上设监之重，下建副贰之任，所以尊严国命，谋而鲜过也。"其意思是说，古时候派兵打仗，一般在最高统帅之侧设立几名官员，负责监督督促元帅按皇帝的命令用兵。[1]作为一种国家活动，秦朝就已经开始通过上级对下级官员的考绩来予以监督（以下所讲的监督都指作为一种国家活动意义上的监督）。汉代设立了较为健全的监察机关，制定了专门的监察法典，加强了对各级官吏的监督。在整个封建君主专制时期，通过建立和完善御史制度，监督普遍实行于吏治之中。中国最后一个封建王朝被推翻后，由于封建残余势力仍然很强势，尤其是在社会的民主法治意识普遍不强和西方列强不断入侵的条件下，民主革命党人所推崇的以议（国）会为主导的国家监督制度未能真正建立起来，更谈不上有效运行。新中国成立后，中国共产党领导人民建立了人民代表大会制度，不仅实现了民主监督制度的突破，而且在实践中不断丰富和完善了该制度。

就新中国成立前的监督制度和实践看，官吏在政治、法律上出了问题往往被认为是由其道德缺失所致，对官吏进行道德教化和惩戒，是为了让本人及其他官员避免在政治、法律上再出问题。最高统治阶层普遍认为，官吏的道德主要应是忠、孝、廉、耻等。在他们看来，官吏最大的优点是对道德的自觉，最大的错误就是道德的缺失。因此，监督的重点在于发现哪些官吏的道德是有缺失的，监督的关键在于对那些道德缺失的官吏进行道德教化，乃至惩戒，以使其道德得以尽快复归。即使在北洋政府及民国政府时期，虽然对官吏的教化、惩戒方面，多了一些政治法律手段，但监督的理念未能有重大转变。在中国整个封建专制社会，最高统治阶层主要是通过道德来解决官吏的违规（法）问题，即不仅把道德功利化、工具化，而且将监督问题转化为一个道德问题。对此，我们从"正心、修身、齐家、治国、平天

［基金项目］国家社科基金项目《加强人大常委会依法行使监督权的途径研究》（12BZZ010）阶段性研究成果。
［作者简介］徐永利（1955—），男，北京人，北京联合大学党委书记，研究员，博士生导师，人民代表大会制度研究所所长，主要从事教育管理和人大制度理论与实践研究；王维国（1967—），男，陕西子洲人，北京联合大学人民代表大会制度研究所研究员，博士，硕士生导师，主要从事人大制度与工作研究。

下"这一直被奉为有政治抱负的人必须遵循的原则中，也可以明确地看出这一点。

在西方，"监督"（Supervision）是一个复合词，由 super 和 vision 两部分组成，前者指位居上方，后者指观察、察视，二者连用，即位居上方，加以察看，也就是上级对下级进行督察、督导的意思[1]。从古希腊看，政治被功利化，而道德却成为目的本身。在古希腊的思想家看来，对官吏的监督是一个政治、法律问题，因而解决途径也只能通过政治、法律活动，而不是道德。反而，个人的道德（德性），只有通过政治、法律活动才能得以提升。对此，亚里士多德明确指出："人是天生的政治动物。"在现实中，古希腊人也是如此践行的，对苏格拉底的处置就是一个典型的事例。由于苏格拉底向青年人传播了与主流信仰不一致的新神思想，因而城邦通过政治投票的方式决定将其处死。他本人在完全能够逃亡的情况下，却放弃了逃亡，而是选择按照法律程序饮毒酒而亡，以此来彰显他的德性修养。苏格拉底用自己的亲历而为诠释了政治法律活动何以提升一个公民的德性。

中世纪的欧洲社会，是一个上帝的时代，因而监督问题被认为是违背和遵循上帝旨意的问题，监督问题变成了信仰问题。

西方近现代社会，随着议会制度的建立及其日益完善，监督成为在议会主导下的政治法律活动。在这种条件下，监督过程就变成了发现违规（法）事实及纠正和问责的过程。在近现代西方的政治法律学家看来，监督作为一个政治法律问题，只能通过政治法律手段解决，并就如何通过政治法律手段解决监督问题提出丰富而深刻的思想观念。

综合中外监督制度与实践，在民主法治国家，监督本质上是政治法律问题，这样的监督是以国家的强制力为保证的，监督关系是不可以解除的，是一种刚性监督。对监督问题的解决，从针对性上讲，政治法律方式是有效的选择；从人的社会价值看，道德方式具有终极意义，但这需要每一位官吏对自身的道德价值要有完全的自觉和深厚的修养，从目前看，这只能作为一种期待和追求。在民主法治国家，解决监督问题就是发现监督对象的违规（法）事实，并予以纠正和问责，纠正和问责就是刚性的约束和惩戒。发现监督对象的违规（法）事实，并予以纠正和问责，就是监督的目的。当然，对于中国人大常委会来说，基于中国的政治法律制度和政治司法体制，无论是违规（法）事实的判断标准，还是纠正和问责的方式与其他国家相比都有自己鲜明的特色。对于人大常委会监督的目的及其性质，吴邦国同志在十届全国人大常委会第二十三次会议闭幕式上的讲话中明确指出："人大监督的目的在于确保宪法和法律得到正确实施，确保行政权、审判权、检察权得到正确行使，确保公民、法人和其他组织的合法权益得到尊重和维护。人大监督工作涉及我国政治制度和国家体制，政治性很强。"吴邦国同志的讲话，重点强调了公权力的正确行使和社会权益的不受侵犯；相反，就是违规（法），人大及其常委会应该予以纠正和问责。这一论述对于我们理解人大常委会监督途径的确立与运行具有重要的指导意义。

二、人大常委会监督途径的确立

我国《宪法》第 2 条规定："人民依照法律规定，通过各种途径和形式，管理国家事务。"这就表明，途径和形式既有不同之处，又密切关联，只有搭配使用，才能真正发挥作用。途径，狭义上讲，就是起点和终点之间的通道，甚至可以将其看成由此岸通往彼岸的"船"或"桥"。途径作为通道、"船"或"桥"，有承载物时，才能发挥作用，因而其在运行中有饱和状态和非饱和状态之分，饱和状态意味着作用发挥充分，非饱和状态意味着作用发挥不足。一般来说，形式是相对于内容而言的，是针对具体内容的一种特定规范；同时，形式也是使某事物或活动同其他事物或活动区别开来的结构特点。监督途径，狭义上讲，就是监督主体用于发现监督对象违规（法）事实的渠道。监督途径本身不具有肯定意义或否定意义，其直接作用是查清监督对象是否存在违规（法）事实。也就是说，监督途径的主要作用在于发现问题，而不是解决问题。解决问题是监督对象自己的事，监督者只负责纠正和问责，以强制监督对象把问题解决好。作为发现违规（法）事实的渠道，监督途径还要明确判断违规（法）的标准、确定违规（法）事实的主体以及流程。由于违规（法）行为的危害性有大有小，导致违规（法）行为的原因有简单有复杂，涉及的人员、机构有多有少，因而要求采用不同类型的方式方法去查清监督对象的违规（法）事实。查处监督对象的违规（法）事实的方式方法不同，其启动条件、人员力量安排、程序环节设置、时间节点限制、资源配置、规模力度大小等也就不同。这些因素的不同配置、组合，就形成了不同的监督途径。由于监督的本质属性是政治法律活动，因而这些因素的配置、组合不能超出政治制度和法律领域；否则，不仅难以从根本上解决问题，而且本身也可能违反政治法律。因此，要让监督的目的得以完全实现，不仅要采取一定的监督形式，而且必须借助监督途径。尤其在民主法治国家，由于监督形式是法定的，因而在增强监督实效方面，监督途径所能发挥作用的空间更大。这就表明：提高监督实效的关键在于监督形式，但重点在于充分发挥监督途径的作用。只有最大限度地利用监督途径，使其处于饱和状态，彻底弄清楚监督对象的违规（法）事实及其原因，才能合法合理地适用监督形式，从而最大程度地实现监督的目的，真正体现出监督实效。

就中国当前来说，监督对象的违规（法）事实主要是指监督对象为了谋取本区域、本部门和本单位甚至个人利益，擅自突破国家及部门的有关规定，甚至触犯法律，给国家、社会和民众造成损失。可见，违规（法）事实，不外乎人、财、事这三项。具体来说，要么是负责人有违法问题；要么是部门或单位财政资金使用不当、不合理、绩效不高，甚至违法；要么公共项目、公共事务没办好，成效低，甚至违法，损失大。要弄清楚这些问题，只能通过调（视）查、调研、审议（询问）、审查等途径。依此来看，我国一些地方政府及其部门、法院、检察院，甚至个别国家部委，均不同程度存在上述违规（法）事实。因此，中国人大常委会监督途径的确立，只有着眼于弄清楚上述违规（法）事实，才能具有较强的合理性、现实性；才能有助于监督形式的合法合理地适用，最大程度地实现监督目的。不过，就目前的监督途径看，监督启动条件、人员力量安排、程序环节设置、时间节点限制、资源配置、规模力度大小等方面在制度规定方面有明显不足，影响了运行状态和作用发挥。

监督主体通过监督途径，有可能查出监督对象存在违规（法）事实，也有可能不存在违规（法）事实。而监督形式（狭义）作为一种惩戒和问责措施和规范具有否定意义，根据监督对象的违规（法）事实的性质对其予以纠正和问责。人大常委会监督正是根据所查情况，提出审议意见，作出决议、决定，责令监督对象限期改正违规（法）行为，并予以问责。审议意见、决议和决定就是我们所说的狭义的监督形式。如果监督形式都是肯定性和支持性的，那就丧失了监督的本质，不是真正意义上的监督，监督实效也就自然而然无从谈起。

总之，从狭义上讲，监督途径和监督形式是监督工作中两个密切关联的环节，离开监督途径，监督形式难以合法合理适用；离开监督形式，监督途径作用难以真正发挥，甚至会失去存在的意义。监督途径和监督形式相互搭配、衔接，才能实现监督目的，体现监督实效。也就是说，要说清楚监督途径，离不开对监督形式的说明。对于中国人大常委会的监督途径与形式及其关系问题，虽然多年前就受到人大专家学者的关注，但真正成为一个热点问题，是在监督法的颁布实施之后。人大专家学者关于监督途径和监督形式的说明，对于我们理解监督途径及其运行具有重要的启发意义。事实上，人们之所以对人大常委会的监督实效存疑，就是因为不仅在监督形式适用方面过于柔性，而且监督途径的运行缺乏强度。

早在1996年，有人大专家就撰文指出："国家权力机关监督同级其他国家机关的方式应当有监督途径和监督形式之分。所谓监督途径是指实施监督所通过的渠道；监督形式是指实施监督所运用的手段。"[2]关于监督途径与监督形式的关系，"监督途径是实施监督的一条必由之路，但是，它本身不具有监督的性质（最多只具有准监督的性质）。如果没有发现违法问题，也就没有监督的必要。只有发现违法问题，才可以根据不同的违法问题运用不同的监督形式进行纠正。"[2]也就是说，"并不是所有的监督途径都能够通向监督的殿堂。有的人大常委会通过监督途径，发现了应当进行监督纠正的违法问题。但是，由于各种原因，会议未能进入监督程序，进行监督纠正。它说明产生监督疲软问题，不是因为监督途径太少，不了解执法情况，而是因为应当运用监督形式的，不敢运用、没有运用，或在运用时不力。"[2]因此，"引入监督途径的概念，根本目的是为了正确认识和运用监督形式，增强监督的力度和实效。如果把监督途径当作监督形式加以运用，就会使监督流于形式，陷入疲软无力的境地，失去应有的权威。因此，把监督形式同监督途径加以区分，有着极其重要的现实意义。"[2]显然，在上述阐述中的监督途径与监督形式，都是在狭义上所使用，对于我们正确区分监督途径与监督形式具有重要的启发意义。

大部分人大专家与学者往往是在广义的意义上使用监督形式或监督途径。广义上的监督形式或监督途径，实际上指的就是监督工作。如果在监督工作的意义上使用监督途径这一概念，实际上不仅涵盖了狭义的监督形式，而且包括监督主体、监督对象、监督内容、监督方法、监督程序等。如果在监督工作的意义上使用监督形式这一概念，实际上不仅涵盖了狭义的监督途径，而且同样包括监督主体、监督对象、监督内容、监督方法、监督程序等。《监督法》通过后，吴邦国同志在十届全国人大常委会第二十三次会议闭幕式上的讲话指出："本届全国人大常委会高度重视监督工作，从一开始就确定了围绕中心、突出重点、增强实效的工作思路，综合运用听取和审议专项工作报告、开展执法检查等形式，不断加强监督工作，取得了明显成效。"显然，吴邦国同志把听取和审议专项工作报告、执法检查等既作为不同方面的监督工作，又看作具体的监督形式。此后，不少人大专家、学者围绕监督法的实施，进行了权威解读和分析研究。2007年，全国人大法工委国家法室主任许安标在其所撰写的《监督法的特点与创新》一文中指出："《监督法》规定了人大常委会开展监督的七种形式。这七种形式按照使用的频率，大体可分为三类：一是日常性的监督，即常年都要开展的监督，如听取和审议专项工作报告、执法检查、规范性文件的备案审查等；二是例行监督，即在特定时间内必须进行的监督，如审查和批准决算、年中听取和审议计划和预算执行情况的报告、审计工作报告等；三是在特定情况和条件下启动的监督，如质询、特定问题调查和审议决定撤职案等。前两种是人大常委会经常性的监督形式，也是监督法的重点内容。"[3] 显然，许安标是在广义上使用监督形式概念的。2008年，十一届全国人大常委会副秘书长乔晓阳在全国人大常委会专题讲座第三讲中作了题为"监督法和全国人大常委会的监督工作"的报告。乔晓阳的报告把监督法的第二章至第五章概括为经常性的监督工作，把监督法的第六章至第八章概括为非经常性监督工作。由此可以看出，乔晓阳把"听取和审议人民政府、人民法院和人民检察院的专项工作报告；审查和批准决算，听取和审议国民经济和社会发展计划、预算的执行情况报告，听取和审议审计工作报告；法律法规实施情况的检查；规范性文件的备案审查；询问和质询（实际上，近年来询问也变成了一项经常性的工作）；特定问题调查；撤职案的审议和决定"看成是人大常委会的七项监督工作。就监督法中所规定的每一项监督工作的具体内容来说，包括监督主体、对象、内容、途径（狭义）、形式（狭义）、方法等。不过，由于工作要具有全面性、全程性，而监督法目前的规定又未能完全达到这一要求，因而乔晓阳在报告中讲全国人大常委会的监督工作时，把上述七项监督工作又称为人大常委会开展监督的具体形式。显然，把七项监督工作又称为监督形式时，是在广义上使用了监督形式一词。也有人大学者从广义上使用监督途径。如有学者指出："对权力的监督一般可以分为两条途径，一是内部监督，二是外部监督。"[4] "听取和审议'一府两院'的专项工作报告，是监督法规定的各级人大常委会行使监督权基本的、也是主要的形式，是人大常委会加强监督、实施经常性监督的有效途径。"[5] 尤其是后一种观点，把监督形式与监督途径甚至在同一意义上交替使用。

现在我们就监督法中的第二章"听取和审议人民政府、人民法院和人民检察院的专项工作报告"作一个简要分析，以对我们的上述观点作进一步的说明。就"关于听取和审议人民政府、人民法院和人民检察院的专项工作报告"这项监督工作来说，《监督法》第9条规定：常务委员会听取和审议本级人民政府、人民法院和人民检察院的专项工作报告的议题，根据下列途径反映和发现的问题确定：（1）本级人民代表大会常务委员会在执法检查中发现的突出问题；（2）本级人民代表大会代表对人民政府、人民法院和人民检察院工作提出的建议、批评和意见集中反映的问题；（3）本级人民代表大会常务委员会组成人员提出的比较集中的问题；（4）本级人民代表大会专门委员会、常务委员会工作机构在调查研究中发现的突出问题；（5）人民来信来访集中反映的问题；（6）社会普遍关注的其他问题。

也就是说，监督议题可以是人大常委会、人大代表、常委会组成人员、人大专门委员会、常委会工作机构、公民在工作中或调查研究中所发现或反映的问题。当然这些问题，有的事实清楚，有的不很清楚，需要进一步调查核实。对此，《监督法》第10条规定：常务委员会听取和审议专项工作报告前，委员长会议或者主任会议可以组织本级人民代表大会常务委员会组成人员和本级人民代表大会代表，对有关工作进行视察或者专题调查研究。视察或专题调查研究其目的仍是为了进一步查清事实。第14条规定：常务委员会组成人员对专项工作报告的审议意见交由本级人民政府、人民法院或者人民检察院研究处理。人民政府、人民法院或者人民检察院应当将研究处理情况由其办事机构送交本级人民代表大会有关专门委员会或者常务委员会有关工作机构征求意见后，向常务委员会提出书面报告。常务委员会认为必要时，可以对专项工作报告作出决议；本级人民政府、人民法院或者人民检察院应当在决议规定的期限内,将执行决议的情况向常务委员会报告。常务委员会听取的专项工作报告及审议意见,人民政府、人民法院或者人民检察院对审议意见研究处理情况或者执行决议情况的报告,向本级人民代表大会代表通报并向社会公布。显然,这一条就是最重要的也是最后的环节,亮出人大常委会根据事实和相关法律所作出的纠正和问责措施。这一条也是同其他监督工作区别开来的关键所在,也就是我们所说的狭义的监督形式。

这一项监督工作,共有7条,其中1条是规定监督内容的,5条是规定监督途径的,1条是纠正或问责措施。也就是说,作为一项或一个方面的监督工作,既有对监督途径的规定,又有对监督内容的规定,也有作为监督标志的监督(纠正或问责)形式。对不同监督工作用不同监督形式或监督途径称谓都是一种借代表达,当然从突出特征上讲,用监督形式称谓监督工作更具有代表性。

三、人大常委会监督途径的运行

监督途径处于饱和运行状态时,才能真正发挥作用,才能有助于使监督目的得以实现,从而体现出监督实效。对于人大常委会的监督途径,宪法、监督法都有规定,在各级人大常委会监督工作中,监督途径也在不同程度上发挥作用。只不过,人们感觉到行政腐败、司法腐败往往都是纪检部门、检察院、审计部门及网络媒体所发现,而人大常委会通过自身监督途径所发现的监督对象的违规(法)问题不仅少,而且轻,因而刚性的监督形式很少使用,就是经常使用的监督形式,也没有多少实质性的纠正和问责措施,因而所发挥的作用并不理想,监督实效还有很大的提升空间。就人大常委会的监督途径的运行状况来说,目前存在的主要问题是未能以饱和的状态运行,主要原因在于中国特色的社会主义民主政治的优势彰显不够。由于人民代表大会制度是根本政治制度,因而中国特色的社会主义民主政治的优势也就是人民代表大会制度的优势。就人大常委会自身来说,至少存在两方面的问题,一是人大常委会自主作为不够,二是人大常委会自身能力有限。从近几年人大常委会组成人员看,有许多都是同级党委、政府部门领导转岗过来的,还有的是律师、业界名人等,应该说素质越来越高。不过,人大专门机构和人大常委会工作机构建设有待加强。概括来说,就是外部压力、内部动力都不足。

既然监督的本质是政治法律活动,其目的在于发现监督对象的违规(法)事实;那么,人大常委会监督途径的运行就必须遵循中国特色政治法律制度,体现中国特色社会主义民主政治优势。从党的最权威的文献看,中国特色社会主义民主政治最根本最显著的特色和最大的优势就是党的领导、人民当家做主和依法治国的有机统一(以下简称"三者有机统一")。

从人大监督工作的发展进程看,什么时候立足于三者有机统一,人大监督工作就能取得重大成就和重要进步,什么时候脱离了三者有机统一,人大监督工作就要受到挫折。监督法本身集中体现了三者有机统一。对此,吴邦国同志在十届全国人大常委会第二十三次会议闭幕式上的讲话中明确指出:"监督法坚持以邓小平理论和三个代表重要思想为指导,以宪法为依据,充分体现了坚持党的领导、人民当家做主和依法治国的有机统一,正确处理了加强人大监督工作和坚持党的领导的关系,正确处理了加强人大监督工作和支持'一府两院'依法开展工作的关系,充分体现了民主集中制、集体监督、有序监督的原则,是一部符合我国国情和人大工作实际的重要法律。"目前,三者有机统一的理念已成熟了,认识明确了,也以一定的方式在实践中运行。因此,对于增强人大常委的监督实效来说,重点在于立足于三者有机统一,通过完善人大常委会监督途径制度建设和改进其运行状态,使人大常委会监督途径的运行处于一种饱和状态。

(一)立足于三者有机统一,进一步完善人大常委会监督途径制度建设

三者有机统一涉及了党委、人大、政府及其他国家机关的关系问题,因而牵一发而动全身。"有机统一的'有机',是指每一者都离不开另外两者,每一者离开了另外两者都不再是它自身,而变成了别的什么东西或不复存在。党的领导如果离开人民当家做主和依法治国,就成为改革开放前的那种高度集中的一元化的党的领导,像邓小平在《党和国家领导制度的改革》中激烈批评过的那样;人民当家做主如果离开了党的领导和依法治国,要么就不复存在,要么就成为无序的大民主或者个人专制,像'文化大革命'中发生的那样;依法治国如果离开了党的领导和人民当家做主,要么法治国家根本无从建立,要么走向以党治国的老路,而不是按照人民的意志来依法治国。"[6]从党和国家的领导制度文本看,党委

行使谋划决策权,人大及其常委会行使立法权、重大事项决定权和监督权,政府行使执行权。如果完全按照制度文本逻辑推演,就会出现决定和执行重大事的不谋划事,或很少参与谋划。如果事情做不好,每一方都有充足的理由,为自己辩护。党委可以说,人大及其常委会作决定的时候由于情况发生了变化但未能把好关,政府也有可能在执行中有偏差。人大及其常委会可以说,事情既不是我谋划的,也不是我执行的,因而事情做不好,有可能是谋划方和执行方有失误的地方。政府可以说,事情是你们谋划好的,也是你们决定的,我只是按照你们的决定执行而已,有问题说明你们的谋划和决定本身可能是有失误的。不过,从三者有机统一现实的运行方式看,在我国现行的政治体制中,领导干部往往实行交叉任职,如党委常委、委员兼政府首长;党委常委、委员,政府首长也都兼任人大代表。每一方都不同程度地参与了谋划,也参与了决定和执行,取得成效是三方共同的,有了失误也应由三方共同承担。这就叫集中智慧谋大事,集体行使决定权,集中人力办大事。现在的问题是对于每一方组成人员来说,由于具有多重身份,因而有时难免会出现角色冲突问题,从而影响对问题的判断和行动方向的把握,集中表现在一些党政领导干部常常不以人大代表的身份思考问题、处理问题(人大是集体有权,个人无权),习惯于个人说了算,或小范围讨论决定。你中有我,我中有你,相互交织,相互支撑,在避免了互相推诿的缺陷的同时,往往留下人大及其常委会对监督对象予以纠正和问责时感到为难顾虑的遗憾。要解决这一遗憾,首先要在具体的实施制度建设上下功夫;这是因为人大常委会监督实施制度的完善对于增强人大常务委员会的监督实效具有突破口的作用。由于党的领导是政治领导、思想领导和组织领导,党必须在宪法法律范围内活动;因此,人大常委会判断违规的标准只能是四项基本原则和党的路线、方针和政策。人大常委会判断监督对象违法的标准就是宪法法律,以及具有法律效力的其他规范。对此,《监督法》的第2条明确规定:各级人民代表大会常务委员会依据宪法和有关法律的规定,行使监督职权。第3条明确规定:各级人民代表大会常务委员会行使监督职权,应当围绕国家工作大局,以经济建设为中心,坚持中国共产党的领导,坚持马克思列宁主义、毛泽东思想、邓小平理论和"三个代表"重要思想,坚持人民民主专政,坚持社会主义道路,坚持改革开放。监督途径制度,作为人大常委会监督实施制度之一,其建设的重点就在于解决好如何发现监督对象的违规(法)事实,如何弄清楚其违规(法)事实的性质、危害程度大小、涉及组织和人员身份的特点等。这就要求监督途径要有调查(视察)、检查与审议等形式;而且调查(视察)要深入、检查与审议要求真务实;否则,监督途径将难以达到饱和状态或应有的强度。这就要求监督权应该是一种综合性权力,由许多具体权力所构成。其中,知情权、检查权和审议权,不仅是人大常委会监督职权的重要组成部分,而且是增强其监督实效性的重要保证。众所周知,没有约束的权力,不仅会导致权力滥用,而且难以常态化有效运行。这就要求对任何权力都要用制度加以约束规范。制度规范越完善越具体,权力自由度越小,运行越规范、有序、顺畅和有效。因此,要使人大常委会监督途径的运行到达饱和状态,就需围绕知情权、检查权和审议权,立足于三者有机统一,抓好调查研究、检查和审议制度建设。

一是围绕人大常委会知情权的行使,完善调查研究制度建设。没有调查就没有发言权。人大常委会的调查研究就是通过深入实际调查,发现问题,找出导致问题的原因,形成调研报告。调研成果转化成为人大常委会的审议意见、决议决定,便有了法律效力,才能发挥实际作用。对人大常委会来说,组织调查研究工作是其经常性的基础工作,不仅为人大常委会提供充分履行职责的基础,也是增强其工作实效性的重要保证。人大常委会作出的审议意见、决议、决定要符合其实际情况,维护人民群众的根本利益,都离不开深入的调查研究。目前,有的人大工作者对调研工作还存在着一些片面的看法,有的地方人大调研主体力量薄弱、调研时对象不清、具体调研过程中调研方式方法不够完善和科学,调研后形成的调研成果转化力度不够等[7]。《监督法》也只在第10条规定:常务委员会听取和审议专项工作报告前,委员长会议或者主任会议可以组织本级人民代表大会常务委员会组成人员和本级人民代表大会代表,对有关工作进行视察或者专题调查研究。第七章、第八章就特定问题的调查作了一些原则性的规定。为了使人大常委会审议意见及决定决议具有针对性、合法性、合理性和权威性,还须从调查(视察)、调研活动的启动、遵循原则、调研内容、参与人员、被调研对象职责义务、时间安排、程序流程、调查调研成果使用等作出更加明确的规定,这样才有利于形成高质量的调查调研报告。各级党委也要制定相应的联动工作制度,充分发挥其与人民群众联系密切的优势,对于哪些阻挠、消极抵制人大常委会调研调查的组织和个人予以党纪政纪的处分，以支持和保障人大常委会充分行使知情权，进一步做好调查调研工作。

二是围绕人大常委会检查权的行使，完善检查制度建设。检查权是监督权的基本条件与关键要素。要建立有效的监督制度，就要建立完善的检查制度。目前，监督法只是对执法检查作了较为细致的规定。人大常委会需要对于一些重要的违法行为检查时，既没有专职的检查人员，也没有明确的检查程序和流程。这就须对除执法检查之外其他检查年度计划公布时间、检查的时间节点、检查的人员、专门委员会、常务委员会工作机构职责、被检查视察对象的职责义务等作出更加明确的规定。各级党委也要制定相应的联动工作制度，对于那些阻挠、消极对待人大常委会检查的组织和个人予以党纪政纪的处分，以支持和保障人大常委会充分行使检查权，进一步做好检查工作[8]。

三是围绕人大常委会审议权的行使，完善审议审查制度建设。有了调查、调研、视察、检查报告，只是为听取审议、审查"一府两院"的工作报告和其他规范性文件提供了准备材料，听取审议、审查本身才是真正意义上的监督活动。目前，监督法只是对听取审议、审查在内容、时间节点方面作了一些原则性规定。因此，还须就听取审议、审查"一府两院"的工作报告和其他报告及规范性文件的年度计划公布时间，听取审议、审查的时间节点、听取审议审查人员、报告人员、报告内容，专门委员会、常务委员会工作机构职责、被听取审议、审查对象的职责义务等作出更加明确的规定。各级党委也要制定相应的工作制度，对于那些阻挠、消极对待人大常委会听取审议审查的组织和个人予以党纪政纪的处分，以支持和保障人大常委会充分行使审议权，进一步做好听取审议审查工作。

（二）立足于三者有机统一，改进人大常委会监督途径的运行状况

在中国国家监督体系中，人大及其常委会的监督是具有最高法律效力的监督；在人大及其常委会的监督之下，才使各国家机关之间按照权力分工形成纵横交错、层级制的监督体系。人大及其常委会代表人民行使国家权力。中国共产党代表最广大人民群众的根本利益，作为执政党掌握有实际权力。这就表明二者的目标一致、任务一致，只不过工作的方式不同。如果双方在工作方式上能相互协调一致，就会取得事半功倍的效果。根据前述，人大自身的监督力量和监督资源明显不足，而党内纪检、行政监查审计、司法检察、媒体网络从上到下都有系统完整的监督力量和监督资源配置。《监督法》第19条规定，人大常委会每年审查和批准决算的同时，听取和审议本级人民政府提出的审计机关关于上一年度预算执行和其他财政收支的审计工作报告。尤其是国家审计署近年的审计报告，常常就国务院各部委财政资金违规使用情况进行曝光，被媒体称为"审计风暴"，为全国人大常委会行使监督权提供了重要支撑。因此，立足于三者有机统一，改进人大常委监督途径运行状况要抓好以下几个方面的工作。

一是充分发挥人大民意机关职能与党内民主相结合。人大常委会的重要意见，通过党内民主的途径进入党的纪检程序，然后根据党委的正确意见，人大常委会科学、合理、合法、公平、公正地作出审议意见和决定决议。然后，人大常委会党组再将审议意见、决定和决议向同级党委报告，同级党委从党纪的角度监督一府两院认真执行人大常委会的审议意见、决定和决议。

二是人大常委会开展监督工作与人民群众直接行使民主权利相结合。结合人大信访工作、网络民意等途径，人大常委会综合运用明察暗访、调查、约见"一府两院"领导等方式，以及接待选民、走访选民、召集小型选民座谈会，把人民群众强烈反映的有关"一府两院"的工作作风问题、消极腐败问题纳入人大常委会的监督议题，然后再经过人大常委会专门组织的专题视察、调研、调查、检查等获得更加深入全面准确的事实情况，科学合理、合法、公平、公正地作出审议意见和决定决议。

三是人大常委会开展监督工作与检察机关、监察审计部门履行职责相结合。司法监督解决法纪问题，行政监督解决政纪问题。借助司法行政的专业监督，通过人大的宏观监督和司法、行政的微观监督有效衔接和良性联动，使得人大常委会监督途径处于饱和状态。

四是人大常委会开展监督工作与充分发挥人大常委会机关协调、支持体系作用相结合。常委会监督工作涉及经济建设、政治建设、文化建设、社会建设等各个领域，每一项工作都关系到党和国家工作大局，关系到人民群众的根本利益。所以，人大常委会监督工作，涉及面广、难度大、要求高。开展好人大常委会监督工作，要注重各工作机构、专家、顾问组的统筹协调和资源整合，除了要发挥每一位组成人员的主体作用，发挥各工作机构的参谋助手作用之外，还应该积极借助外力，发挥"外脑"作用。

当工作需要的时候，各专门委员会要加强沟通协商，相互支持，相互帮助，加快工作节奏，提高办

事效率，保证各项任务的圆满完成。专门委员会在常委会集体领导下，各负其责，各尽其能，形成强大的工作合力。各专委会和工作机构要积极主动地采取多种方式，从各方面收集信息，并经过分析、综合后，归纳出要点，及时提供给常委会组成人员，为组成人员更好履职提供更多信息资料。

五是人大常委会开展监督工作要自觉接受人民代表大会和人民的监督。为了使人大常委会开展监督工作内有动力外有压力，就要使其自身接受监督。人大常委会要接受两方面的监督："一是受本级人大的监督。各级人民代表大会是国家权力机关，常委会是本级人大的常设机关。常委会是由本级人大选举产生的，向本级人大负责并报告工作，接受本级人大的监督。正是这样一层监督一层，从而保证国家权力始终掌握在人民手里，真正用于为人民服务。"[3]

对此，监督法第6条规定：各级人民代表大会常务委员会行使监督职权的情况，应当向本级人民代表大会报告，接受监督。同时，监督法还相应规定，人大常委会听取和审议的专项工作报告、计划执行情况报告、预算执行情况报告、审计工作报告以及执法检查报告，常委会组成人员对这些报告的审议意见，政府、法院或检察院对审议意见的处理情况或者执行决议的情况报告，要向本级人大代表通报。"二是受人民监督。对人民负责，受人民监督，是我国一切国家机关的活动原则。将国家机关的活动公开，是将其置于人民监督之下的重要保证。"[3]

对此，监督法第7条规定：各级人大常委会行使监督职权的情况，向社会公开。"为了保证公开原则落到实处，监督法作了一系列具体的、可操作的规定。人大常委会行使监督职权的情况，凡是向本级人大代表通报的内容，同时要向社会公布。同时，常委会会议原则上要公开举行，允许新闻媒体采访、报道，这也是公开的重要方式。"[3]

参考文献

[1] 吴超. 中华苏维埃共和国监督制度研究 [D]. 湖南师范大学，2006.
[2] 刘今定. 应当把监督形式同监督途径加以区分 [J]. 人民政坛，1996，(9).
[3] 许安标. 监督法的特点与创新 [J]. 国家行政学院学报，2007，(11).
[4] 董敏志. 制度化权力监督与政治体制改革 [J]. 江苏行政学院学报，2013，(1).
[5] 公艳萍. 对监督法的再认识、再思考 [J]. 时代主人，2007，(8).
[6] 席文启. 关于"三者有机统一"问题的几点思考 [J]. 新视野，2012，(2).
[7] 陈旷. 地方人大常委会组织的调研工作存在的问题及对策研究 [D]. 中南大学，2011.
[8] 刘文忠. "实体正义"和"程序正义"的一种后现代主义视角 [J]. 河北法学，2005，(5).

关于财产公开的可实施性

崔英楠

财产公开的可行性与可实施性

多年来，对财产公开（申报）制度的研究一直为学界所关注。[1]其核心就在于论证我国建立财产申报制度的合法性、必要性和可行性，但是讨论该制度的可实施性并不多。

在讨论可实施性之前，需要厘清可行性与可实施性两个概念。可行性的英文是"feasibility"，可实施性的英文是"enforceability"，前者意味着在现有的环境和条件下能够实行，而后者还包含着"可强制性"。这样，财产公开的可行性，意味着在当前条件下，通过立法建立财产公开制度是可行的，并且可以顺利推行；而财产公开的可实施性，意味着在当前条件下，财产公开制度可以依法实施，当有违法情形时，可追究其违法责任。因此，严格来说，财产公开的可实施性与可行性相比，有两个差异。其一，可实施性强调财产公开制度的贯彻与落实，即强调制度实施的结果和实效；而可行性强调财产公开推行的环境和条件。其二，可实施性强调实施的国家强制性和违法的责任追究，而可行性则没对此着重强调。此外，目前，我们讨论财产公开制度可行性的时候，往往包括立法与实施两个阶段，并不加以区别。[2]

上述差异导致了另一个差异，一项法律制度建立和实施，所依赖的条件并不完全相同。也许人们会认为，如果当前建立财产公开制度是可行的话，那么其实施是不言而喻、水到渠成的事情。但是事实上，制度建立了，也许难以顺利实施或者实施效果不理想。因此，财产公开制度的可行性和可实施性两个概念存在着差异。

一般而言，人们讨论财产公开制度建立的可行性时，往往考虑如下几个因素：其一，在理论上，隐私权不得援引来保障官员财产不予公开；其二，配套制度的不完善并不影响财产公开制度的建立；其三，公开财产制度的建立（和实施）并不会导致社会动荡；其四，公民的民主素质得到了很大的提高。[3]财产公开制度的可实施性，考量的核心问题是：一旦制度建立，其实施存在哪些阻碍，以及如何排除这些阻碍。因此，虽然可实施性考量的问题与可行性考量的问题有着重合，但是毕竟有着差异，其考虑的问题有着独特性。归纳起来，考量的问题主要包括三个方面：其一，民众是否形成权力监督共识？其二，有效的责任追究机制是否建立？其三，在我国，实施关键是否是在党的领导下进行？

财产公开可实施性的前提：权力监督的共识

财产公开的可实施性的前提，不是存在一个"财产公开法律制度"，而是民众的"权力监督共识"。固然，财产公开立法对于财产公开可实施性具有重要作用，但是事实上，一项法律制度是否实施以及实施状况，却依赖于各种条件，其中最为重要的是，社会各个阶层对该法律制度的认可度和接受度。

财产公开可实施性的认可和接受，其核心在于"权力监督的共识"。这是因为，官员的财产公开，其本质就是在于对于官员监督、对权力监督。对权力的监督，可以有多种方式，但是最为有效而且最基本的方式，就是让权力公开运行，所谓"阳光是最好的消毒剂"，就是反映这一监督方式的法谚。财产公开，又是所有公开方式中最为基本、最为重要的方式，是反腐最为有效的利器之一，因此，全世界许多国家都制定了有关财产公开的法律。那么，目前我国对"通过财产公开监督权力"这一共识是否形成呢？

从执政党的角度来看，通过财产公开实现对权力的约束已经成为党重点考虑的问题。1987年，全国人大常委会提出要研究是否建立领导干部财产申报制度。1994年，《财产申报法》被正式列入全国人大立法规划，虽然最后未能进入实际立法程序。1995年4月20日，中办与国办联合印发的《关于党政机

[基金项目] 国家社科基金项目"财产申报与公示制度的中外比较研究（14BFX029）"。
[作者简介] 崔英楠，北京联合大学人民代表大会制度研究所教授。

关县（处）级以上领导干部收入申报的规定》，第一次明确提出对中国官员的收入实行申报。2010年6月，两办再次印发《关于领导干部报告个人有关事项的规定》。尤其是近年来，中央领导人多次就财产公开问题发表谈话。[4]

从理论界来看，财产公开作为反腐倡廉、权力监督的重要方式早已经达成了共识。在一个民主法治的社会，作为国家权力的授权者，公民"有权知悉国家所颁布的法律、法规、政策以及国家机关及其工作人员的活动和背景资料，有权知道自己所选举或由政府任命的公职人员是否服务于社会，并在此基础上参与公共决策和政府监督"。因此，为了公共利益的需要，完全可以对掌握国家权力的官员的隐私权加以限制。[5]

综前所述，我们可以认为，目前，我国社会整体来说，都认可财产公开是实现权力监督、反腐倡廉的有效手段。固然，还有一部分人认为，当前财产公开的条件还不具备，必须等待条件成熟再予以实施。但是，我们必须认识到，财产公开条件的完全成熟一定需要经过实践的摸索才能形成，因此，财产公开先行实施才是前提；另外，财产公开的实施，并不依赖于完美的条件，而是依赖于核心条件的成熟。而核心条件之一，就在于社会公众对"财产公开"形成共识，这一共识，是保障财产公开有效实施的前提和基础。

财产公开可实施性的保障：有效的责任追究机制

财产公开实施的有效性，还必须有赖于有效的责任追究机制的建立。如果没有责任追究机制的刚性约束，就无法保障每一个公务员凭借党性和道德遵守法律，将自身的财产诚实地依法公之于众。

责任追究制的建立，在理论上主要有如下两个来源。第一，委托—代理理论。该理论认为，代理人同样是具有自利和有限理性特征的经济人，同时，由于委托人和代理人之间存在的信息不对称，因此委托人有必要通过建立有效的约束机制克服代理人的滥用权力和错误选择的可能性。公务员受人民的委托来行使公共权力，其基本职责就是实现公共利益、保障公民权益。当公务员未能依法履行财产公开的义务时，委托人——人民就有权要求追究其违法责任。第二，责任政府理论。责任政府是"指政府所担负的全部责任的范围、政府在承担各种责任过程中所分别具有的行政权限以及履行对应义务的法治运作状态"。它意味着公民可以依法监督政府及其官员的权力行使，可以通过各种法定方式参与权力运行，并且可以依法对政府及其官员的违法行为追究其法律责任。[6]因此，如果财产公开制度建立，那么，建立有效的责任追究机制则是其当然内容和必然要求。

如何建立财产公开的有效责任追究机制呢？归纳起来，主要有三个方面。

其一，明确和细化违反财产公开制度的法律责任。拒报、瞒报、虚报等行为，根据其情节轻重，承担相应的违法责任。总体来说，违法责任的构建，应该坚持两项原则：第一，过错推定为归责依据，即只要存在违反财产公开制度的行为即承担责任，除非有足够的理由证明非出于本人的故意或过失；第二，加重责任为责任理念，即，违反财产公开制度导致的法律责任，应该让违法者或潜在的违法者感受到违法成本明显超过违法收益，这可足以阻止本人或其他人试图违法。之所以如此，是因为从公共权力行使者的角度来说，他们早知道财产公开是其一项重要的法定义务，明知而违法，则彰显其主观恶意；从惩戒和预防腐败的角度来说，只有通过重典才能收到成效，如果腐败的收益大于腐败的成本，就无法有效惩戒和预防腐败了。

其二，建立独立的责任追究主体。要有效地追究违法者的责任，必须有独立的责任追究主体，否则，责任追究也成为形式。当前，责任追究主体似乎由纪委承担比较适宜。但是，纪委是党的组织，而非国家机关，而追究违法责任，必须由国家机关实施。检察机关，从职能来说，适宜担任责任追究主体。因为宪法明确规定，检察机关专门从事法律监督工作，由人大产生对人大负责，独立于政府行使检察权。就人事部门、监察部门来说，独立性不够，很难胜任监督工作。至于预防腐败局，由于目前主要从事政策研究，也难担当此任。不过，如果从中央到地方建立预防腐败局垂直管理体制，并且法律赋予其财产公开的监督职能，那么，预防腐败局作为责任追究主体是非常适宜的。不管最终由哪一国家机关担任责任追究主体，必须坚持独立性这一根本原则。

其三，更为重要的是，要促进责任追究机构积极履行职责，要确保违法者实实在在承担应有的法律责任,就必须建立相应的新闻舆论监督制度。这一制度,意味着公民和新闻媒体,对有关人士的财产公开存在合理怀疑时,有权通过法定渠道了解其财产状况。比如,建立房产信息联网制度,公民有权对官员的房产信息查询;再比如,制定新闻保护法,保护新闻记者的合法采访权利,保护媒体的合法报道权利。需要注意的是,这并不意味着这些监督制度的建立是财产公开制度建立的前提。实际上,这些监督制度往往是财产公开制度的必然要求和逻辑结果。

财产公开可实施性的关键:党的领导

财产公开制度的建设,是依法治国的一项重要内容。依法治国、建设社会主义法治国家,其目的之一,就是防止官员违法乱纪、腐败堕落,从而导致损害公共利益和公民权利。如前文所述,限制权力滥用、预防官员腐败是财产公开制度的主要目的和根本保障。但是,财产公开制度,又必须在党的领导下进行,才能取得成效,也就是说,党的领导,是财产公开制度具有可实施性的关键。具体而言,有如下几个理由。

第一,党对财产公开的意志是全国人民意志的集中体现。人民对于财产公开制度的意见和认识,是分散的、片面的、感性的。要将这些意见上升为国家意志,必须是理性的、较为全面和系统的,而这一工作,需要由真正代表人民利益的中国共产党通过一系列艰辛的工作和复杂的程序来完成。

第二,将全国人民财产公开的意志转变为法律,即立法工作,也是在中国共产党的领导下进行的。我国宪法规定,最高权力机关——全国人民代表大会也是由中国共产党来领导的。这种领导,虽然不是上下级的行政领导,而是政治领导、思想领导和组织领导,即把握政治原则、政治方向、重大决策和向各级人大及其常委会推荐重要干部,但是这种领导关系,确保党的主张要通过人大及其常务委员会依照法定程序上升为国家意志。

第三,财产公开制度要顺利得以实施,就必须坚持党的领导。顺利实施,包括三个方面:一是官员自觉遵守;二是对财产公开制度的违法行为进行制裁;三是社会对官员的财产公开行为进行监督。就第一个方面来说,官员大多是共产党员,因此共产党员带头遵守法纪,是中国共产党领导的本质所决定的;就第二个方面来说,实施制裁的机关和组织,无论是纪委、行政机关还是司法机关,都是在党的领导之下,要保障制裁的合法、及时和公平,都有赖于党的领导;就第三方面来说,公民对监督权的有效行使,又不得不依赖于一系列制度的建设,而这些制度的建设又必须在党的领导下进行。

综上所述,我们有理由认定,财产公开可实施性的关键在于党的领导。

结　语

近年来,财产公开不但成为理论界研究的焦点,也成为公众讨论的热点。这意味着我国法治建设进入了新的领域,也标志着我国依法治国达到了一个新的高度。财产公开立法工作,将会在党的领导下顺利完成。

习近平总书记近日指出:"宪法的生命在于实施。"财产公开法律制度也应作如是观。财产公开法律制度,要真正建立权威性,不仅仅是来自于制定机关——作为最高权力机关的全国人民代表大会,更重要的是,来自于实实在在的实施。财产公开制度只有实施,民众才能真正感受到其生命与活力,才能对其油然而生出尊崇感,而这才是财产公开制度权威性的生动而具体的体现。

参考文献

[1] 孙龙桦. 近二十年国内外财产申报制度研究综述 [J]. 理论月刊, 2012 (4).
[2] 解薇薇. 我国建立公务员财产申报制度的必要性和可行性 [J]. 劳动保障世界, 2011 (1).
[3] 陈小斌. 我国建立官员财产申报制度的可行性与路径分析 [J]. 云南行政学院学报, 2011 (3).
[4] 27 市县试点财产公开 [EB/OL]. http://news.fznews.com.cn/guonei/2012-12-26/20121226upbzodtGll101815.shtml, 2013-03-11.
[5] 屠振宇. 财产申报制度中的隐私权保护 [J]. 法商研究, 2011 (1).
[6] 杨鸿台. 论法治政府、责任政府、服务政府及政府职能转变 [J]. 毛泽东邓小平理论研究, 2004 (7).

{经济学类}

经济增加值模型在商业银行价值评估中的应用

朱传华　詹细明　黄金英

在经济全球化及在资本市场环境中,企业价值最大化是上市银行企业财务管理的最大目标,也是提高企业核心竞争力的必要策略,本文应用经济增加值(Economic Val-ue Added,简称 EVA)模型评价企业经营业绩,评估企业价值,并以民生银行为例进行实证分析,剖析了导致商业银行整体价值低估的因素,旨在激励商业银行利润增长,注重企业投入资本的经济增加值,提高商业银行创造价值能力和水平。

1 构建适应于商业企业的经济增加值(EVA)估价模型

1.1 会计科目的调整

会计科目的调整方法如表1所示。

表1　会计科目的调整方法

会计科目	调整方法
提取的各项准备金	税后净利润中计入本期各项准备的变化额,把会计准备冲回,在投资资本计算时,将各项准备金计入作为资本成本
营业外支出	税后净利润+营业外支出—营业外收入
递延税项	用当期递延税项的变化调整税后净利润,投资资本+递延税项的贷方余额-递延税项的借方余额
商誉	不对商誉进行摊销。资本总额中将过去累计摊销金额加回,税后净营业利润当中将本期的摊销额加回
研发费用	净利润中将冲销后的研发费用加回

1.2 经济增加值(EVA)的指标调整

按照经济增加值(EVA)的定义,可用公式表示为:

$$EVA = NOPAT_1 TC \times WACC$$

上式中,NOPAT 为调整后的税后净营业利润,TC 为累计投入资本总额,$WACC$ 为加权平均资本成本。

考虑到商业银行业务的特殊性,其业务与工业企业存在显著区别,如存款业务是银行的主要负债,若按传统的经济增加值(EVA)计算将会导致高估资本成本,而且投资于银行资本的机会成本和投资于不同行业或金融机构时的机会成本可能产生不一样的收益,导致机会成本不同,因此,经济增加值(EVA)模型在商业银行价值评估中应用时,必须调整商业银行经济增加值(EVA)计算方法,调整如下:

$NOPAT$ = 税后净利润

加:本年商誉摊销

各种准备金变化额的增加(包括:拆出资金减值准备、固定资产减值准备、在建工程减值贮备变化额、存货跌价准备变化额、坏账准备变化额、长期应收款减值准备变化额、持有至到期投资减值准备变

[作者简介] 朱传华(1963—),女,教授,研究方向:财务管理;詹细明(1977—),男,硕士,讲师,研究方向:商业银行;黄金英(1959—),女,会计师,研究方向:财务会计。

化额、可供出售金融资产减值准备、贷款损失减值准备）

营业外支出

减：营业外收入

加：递延税款贷方余额的增加

减：递延税款借方余额的增加

加：研发和市场开拓费用

减：本年的摊销的研发费用

TC = 权益资本

加：融资性债务成本

累计商誉摊销

各种准备金变化额的增加（同上）

营业外支出

减：营业外收入

加：递延税款贷方余额的增加

减：递延税款借方余额的增加

加：研发费用余额

WACC =（债务资本成本率×债务资本＋权益资本成本率×权益资本）／总资本

债务资本包括短期借款、一年内到期长期借款、长期借款、应付债券和交易性金融资产，权益资本包括归属于母公司股东的权益和少数股东权益，根据资本资产定价模型（CAPM），权益资本成本率计算公式为：

$$K_B = R_f + \beta \times (R_m - R_f)$$

其中，K_B 为权益资本成本率，R_f 是无风险收益率，β 为证券收益率与市场组合收益率之间的系数，R_m 是市场组合收益率。

1.3 建立经济增加值（EVA）估价模型

1.3.1 经济增加值（EVA）估价模型的假设条件

经济增加值（EVA）估价模型的假设条件有三，其一，持续经营假设，在管理、技术水平等内部因素不发生明显变化的情况下，银行会保持稳定增长。其二，外部环境不变。通货膨胀率、利率、汇率等外部因素稳定，以使资本成本率和贴现率不变。其三，资本结构趋于稳定，股本和债务规模不发生大的变化。

1.3.2 稳定增长的经济增加值（EVA）估价模型

未来经济增加值（EVA）现值 $= \sum_{i=1}^{\infty} \frac{EVA_i}{(1+WACC)^i}$ 则，企业的价值 $= I_0 + \sum_{i=1}^{\infty} \frac{EVA_i}{(1+WACC)^i}$

其中，企业初始投入资本为 I_0，EVA_i 表示第 i 年度的 EVA 值，加权平均资本成本表示为 $WACC$。

1.3.3 阶段性经济增加值（EVA）估价模型

未来经济增加值（EVA）现值 $= \sum_{i=1}^{\infty} \frac{EVA_i}{(1+WACC)^i} + \frac{EVA_{n+1}}{(WACC+-g)} \times \frac{1}{(1+WACC)^n}$

企业价值 $= I_0 + \sum_{i=1}^{\infty} \frac{EVA_i}{(1+WACC)^i} + \frac{EVA_{n+1}}{(WACC-g)} \times \frac{1}{(1+WACC)^n}$

其中，EVA_i 为高速增长期第 i 年的 EVA 值，EVA_{n+1} 为稳定增长期第一年的 EVA 值，g 为稳定增长期的增长率，I_0 为初始投入资本，$WACC$ 代表加权平均资本成本率。

2 应用经济增加值（EVA）模型对商业银行价值的评估

民生银行是在资本市场上具有代表性的商业银行。近年来，民生银行成长速度惊人，特别是2007年事业部制改革进行以来，各个领域都取得了较大的突破，在上市银行中比较具有代表性。因此，在模型构建的基础上，对该银行2007—2011年经济增加值（EVA）价值进行分析评估。

2.1 经济增加值（EVA）模型中主要指标确定

2.1.1 税后净营业利润

近几年，民生银行的税后净营业利润体现了较快的增长，计算过程如表2所示。

表2　2007—2011年税后净营业利润的计算　　　　　　　　　　　　　　　　（单位：百万元）

项目＼年份	2007	2008	2009	2010	2011
净利润	6 335	7 893	12 108	17 688	28 443
加：本年商誉摊销	28	46	42	68	274
拆出资金减值准备变化额	-2	2	92	0	0
固定资产减值准备	—	—	—	—	—
在建工程减值准备	—	—	—	—	—
存货跌价准备变化额	—	—	—	—	—
坏账准备	0	122	34	-61	8
持有至到期投资减值准备	0	54	-54	0	0
可供出售金融资产减值准备	0	599	-243	523	-15
贷款损失减值准备变化额	1 246	4 222	3 356	4 607	7 088
递延所得税贷方增加额	8	200	0	0	0
营业外支出	20	34	65	23	155
研发费用本年投入	8	39	11	1 310	3 250
减：递延所得税借项增加额	274	1 015	1 047	1 140	2 587
营业外收入	41	97	40	-63	80
研发费用本年摊销	27	0	0	0	568
NOPAT	7 301	12 099	14 324	23 081	35 968

2.1.2 资本总额

由于民生银行企业债务资本占比例很低，因此将权益资本当作资本总额。计算过程如表3所示。

表3　2007—2011年资本总额的计算　　　　　　　　　　　　　　　　（单位：百万元）

项目＼年份	2007	2008	2009	2010	2011
权益资本	50 187	54 672	88 894	105 257	134 110
加：累计商誉摊销	80	80	80	80	568
拆出资金减值准备余额	94	92	0	0	0
固定资产减值准备余额	—	—	—	—	—
在建工程减值准备余额	—	—	—	—	—
存货跌价准备余额	—	—	—	—	—
坏账准备余额	86	208	242	181	189
持有至到期投资减值准备	0	54	0	0	0
可供出售金融资产减值准备	0	599	-243	523	-15
贷款损失减值准备余额	7 663	11 885	15 241	19 848	26 936
递延所得税贷方余额	2 914	1 451	0	0	0
营业外支出	47	81	146	169	324
研发费用余额	159	198	209	1519	4770
减：递延所得税借项余额	1 608	2 530	3 181	4 455	6 982
营业外收入	60	157	197	134	214
TC	59 562	66 633	101 191	122 988	159 686

2.1.3 资本成本

对于权益资本成本率，国内外主流学者分析经济增加值（EVA）时一般都以一年期活期存款利率为无风险收益率；选取了以GDP增长率作为市场风险收益率，β系数取自WIND资讯数据库，计算过程如表4所示。

表4 2007~2011年资本成本的计算 （单位：百万元）

年份 项目	2007	2008	2009	2010	2011
无风险收益率	3.39%	5.74%	3.69%	3.73%	5.43%
BETA系数	0.94	1.00	0.86	1.07	0.93
市场风险溢价	9.20%	9.60%	9.20%	10.30%	9.20%
权益资本成本率	12.04%	15.34%	11.60%	14.75%	13.99%
权益资本比率	84.26%	82.05%	87.85%	85.58%	83.98%
WACC	10.14%	12.59%	10.19%	12.62%	11.75%

2.2 经济增加值（EVA）估值确定

在计算出了税后营业利润、资本总额和资本成本后，需要计算出民生银行5年的经济增加值（EVA）值，计算结果如表5所示。

表5 2007~2011年经济增加值（EVA） （单位：百万元）

年份 项目	2007	2008	2009	2010	2011
NOPAT	7301	12 099	14 324	23 081	35 968
TC	59 562	66 633	101 191	122 988	159 686
WACC	10.14%	12.59%	10.19%	12.62%	11.75%
EVA	1261	3 710	4 013	7 560	17 205

从表5可知，民生银行的经济增加值（EVA）在近几年呈大幅度上升态势，2007年仅为12.61亿元，而到2011年已经增加到172.05亿元，年均增长率为104.56%。从历史EVA值我们可以看出事业部制改革的成果渐渐显现，体现股东价值快速增长的过程。因此，民生银行具有的潜力和发展能力是不容置疑的，这也是该银行吸引产业资本在二级市场持续增持股票的重要原因。

运用经济增加值（EVA）模型对民生银行估值分析，从净利润价值、权益资本价值以及特许权价值等方面的评估，剖析了民生银行企业价值提升的根源，说明了在资本市场上民生银行不愧于在上市银行中具有其代表性。

（1）净利润价值评估。

净利润从2007年的63.35亿元增长到2011年的284.43亿元，5年间民生银行的净利润平均增长率为50.69%，这5年是民生银行高速发展的时期，受益于我国经济的稳定增长和民生银行自身的良好的盈利能力和公司的战略。同时，民生银行的各项准备金一直保持着高速的增长，2011年年末，各项准备金年末余额总额近270亿元，体现出民生银行较高的资产质量和安全性。

（2）权益资本价值评估。

民生银行权益资本从2007年的501.87亿元增长到2011年的1341.10亿元，年均增长率为55.46%，由于2007年实施了资本公积金转增资本方案，权益资本增长率达到159.97%。营业外收入和递延税款虽然波动比较大，但是从总体上看比例较小，因此对经济增加值（EVA）的影响也就较小。

（3）特许权价值评估。

民生银行的每年商誉的摊销额及累计商誉摊销额增长速度越来越快，2011年摊销的商誉为2.74亿元，比起2007年的0.28亿元增长了近10倍；累计摊销额2007年的0.80亿元增长到2011年5.68亿元，民生银行的特许权价值得到了进一步的提升。

3 结　　论

本文应用经济增加值（EVA）模型对商业银行价值评估，以资本市场上有代表性的民生银行为例进行实证分析，针对商业银行业务特殊性，构建经济增加值（EVA）适应于商业银行价值评估，论证经济增加值（EVA）模型在商业银行价值评估中的应用，剖析了导致商业银行整体价值低估的因素，有利于商业银行创造价值能力和水平的提高。

参考文献

[1] 刘建德．经济资本——风险和价值管理的核心［J］．国际金融研究，2004（8）．
[2] 刘素梅，安琳．EVA具体项目会计处理的调整与应用［J］．财会通讯，2006（5）．
[3] 曹萍，靳长巍．EVA模型与企业价值评估研究［J］．商业经济，2010（3）．
[4] 谈际佳．我国上市股份制商业银行风险系数测算［J］．经济论坛，2007（3）．
[5] 谭三艳．企业价值评估方法研究［J］．财会通讯，2009（8）．
[6] Peter C Brewer，Cyan Chandra，Clayton A Hock．Economic Value Ass？es：its Uses and limitation［Z］．1999．

后危机时代中国金融创新模式选择

刘迎春

对于一个经济体而言，金融创新模式的演进与其经济发展阶段和金融市场发展水平密切相关，在不同的历史时期影响金融创新模式的各种要素居于不同的支配地位，也决定了金融创新模式的发展与变化。在金融全球化的背景下，经济体外部的经济金融环境变化对其金融创新模式的演变也具有越来越重要的影响。

1 金融创新模式分类

金融创新模式是金融市场参与主体为实现各种金融创新活动而采取的一系列方法。金融创新的过程涉及很多因素，这些因素组合与配置的方式及其结构上的差异，构成了金融创新的不同模式。本文主要从金融创新的宏观和微观两个层次对金融创新模式进行分类。

1.1 市场主导模式和政府主导模式

从宏观层面看，金融创新模式问题主要体现在金融制度创新领域。从创新的主体来看，金融制度创新模式可以分为市场主导型创新模式（需求诱导型创新模式）和政府主导型创新模式（供给主导型创新模式）。市场主导型创新模式是指金融创新主体（如金融企业）在给定的约束条件下，为实现自身利益最大化而自发组织和实施的"自下而上"的制度创新，它以清晰产权界定和自主决策为前提条件。在市场主导型制度创新模式中，金融机构是创新的主要推动者，它们在充满不确定性的经营环境中，为获得利润而进行制度创新，并独自承担风险，因而它们只有在制度创新的潜在收益大于消除各种潜在风险的成本时，才可能开展制度创新行为。政府主导型创新模式是指政府的金融管理部门通过直接和间接的手段"自上而下"组织实施的创新，它是以大量的公共产权和集权型决策体制为前提条件。在政府主导型制度创新模式中，政府金融管理部门则直接成为创新活动的组织者和推动者，由于法律赋予其相应的权力，一旦它发现局部或整体性制度创新方案的预期收益大于零，就可以借助行政力量进行强制性局部试点，这种试点由于权力部门减少了外部性及不确定因素，因而风险较小。

在市场主导型创新模式中，最先推动创新的金融机构不可能持久地独占制度创新的潜在利润，这是由于以利润为目标的其他金融机构为分享这一利润会模仿其创新行为，实际上这也是创新的模仿与扩散过程，也正是因为模仿、扩散、创新才引起金融制度结构的变化；而在政府主导型制度创新模式下，金融管理部门对制度创新往往采用试点先行的方式，这也就意味着试点范围外的金融企业不得模仿先行试点单位的创新做法，这样创新的潜在收益就无法被扩散。可见，这两种制度创新模式各有利弊，因而只有联系金融制度目标及相关约束条件，并对之进行成本—收益的分析，才能判断二者各自适应的对象及范围。

1.2 自主创新模式和合作创新模式

在微观层面上，金融创新主要是指金融产品和服务的创新，包括股票、债券等金融基础工具的创新，以及期权、期货等复杂的金融产品的创新。从区分创新主体的角度可将微观层面的金融创新模式区分为自主金融创新和合作金融创新两种模式。自主金融创新模式具有率先性，通常率先创新者只是个别金融企业，其他后来者只能跟随和模仿；而合作金融创新模式则是金融机构之间或金融机构与科研机构、高等院校、政府部门之间联合开展金融创新的做法。合作金融创新能综合发挥产、学、研各方在各

［作者简介］刘迎春，（1965—）男，北京联合大学商务学院副教授，哈尔滨工程大学经济管理学院博士研究生，主要从事金融投资研究。

领域的优势，联合推动金融创新发展。这两种金融创新模式既相互联系又相互影响，金融创新主体根据自身的资源能力和战略需求将两种模式组合运用以实现内外部协调。

2　金融创新模式在西方发达国家的实践

从发达国家的金融市场演进历程来看，20世纪30年代以前，金融创新主要通过市场主导型创新模式实现，金融创新行为主要由商业银行在利润驱动下完成。而政府的行为则主要是适应金融市场发展，对金融企业的金融创新活动并不直接参与，对新创立的金融机构、新开发的金融产品以及新形态的金融交易并不进行过多的约束，而仅仅以法律或制度规定等方法加以确认。"大萧条"成为这种金融创新模式变革的转折点。20世纪30年代以后，由于市场自发性和盲目性导致的"市场失灵"经常对金融市场造成恶性冲击，从而影响到经济安全。"大萧条"之后，西方国家普遍对金融创新模式进行反思并进行政策调整，加强对金融市场的监管并开始逐渐成为金融制度创新的推动者。此后，政府主导型金融创新模式日益发挥显著作用。

西方国家金融产品创新经历了四个阶段：20世纪60年代，为了逃避国家及地区间严格的金融管制，提高利润率，西方国家纷纷掀起金融产品创新浪潮，新推出了大量资产型金融产品，如出口信用、平行贷款、可转换债券、可赎回债券等；70年代，为了防范和转嫁通货膨胀、利率、汇率等风险，西方国家又推出了外汇远期、物价指数相关的公债、利率期货、联邦住宅抵押贷款、自动转账服务等金融创新产品；80年代，为了扩大融资渠道，货币互换、零息债券、期权交易、动产抵押债券等新的金融产品相继问世；90年代，金融产品创新朝多样化、衍生化进一步发展，成熟、统一的金融市场逐渐形成。[1]

总之，从发达国家的金融创新历程看，金融产品创新多数是采取自下而上的以市场为主导的创新模式，而金融制度创新则相对比较稳定，往往是在原有金融制度的弊端累计到一定程度甚至引发金融危机之后才会发生大的制度变革，"大萧条"之后西方国家普遍加强金融监管就是一个典型的案例。而在金融市场平稳发展的过程中，金融制度创新更多地是对金融产品创新的成果加以规范化和合法化，并使其最终保存下来，两者在实践中相互推动，共同促进金融发展。[2]

3　后危机时代中国金融创新模式选择

源于2007年美国次贷危机所引发全球金融危机，向全世界各国金融创新活动提出警告，并促使人们反思：金融创新对金融市场发展和经济发展的作用是毋庸置疑的，但也会创造一些新的风险，甚至带来灾难性危机，只有风险可控的金融创新活动才能创造真正的经济效益和社会效益。基于此，西方国家在经历此次危机的洗礼后，开始重新审视自己的金融创新活动，纷纷进行一系列创新模式的调整，这也必然对融入全球经济体系的中国产生深远影响，促使我们进行后危机时代的金融创新的模式选择。

与西方国家相比，我国的金融创新历史很短，开始于20世纪80年代，且长期以来，我国金融制度创新是由政府主导推动的。这样的创新模式客观上对我国金融市场的发展起到积极作用，但政府干预在一定程度上替代了金融市场的资源配置功能，致使广大金融机构缺乏主动开展金融创新活动的积极性，造成金融产品创新严重滞后。为了在最大程度上发挥金融创新的积极作用，我们在进行金融创新的制度取向及金融创新模式的选择时，既要考虑我国金融市场发展的实际，也要考虑本次金融危机对金融市场带来的深远影响。

3.1　金融创新模式的制度取向

随着我国金融市场的迅速发展，金融市场参与主体进行金融创新活动的自觉性得以发挥，在局部出现了"自下而上"的金融制度创新，市场主导型模式有所发展。但是，我们必须清醒地认识到，在我国当前经济发展水平下，政府控制着金融市场的定价权，同时规模庞大的国有金融机构在金融市场处于近乎垄断者的市场优势地位，因此，在相当长的一个时期内我国在金融模式创新上仍将由政府主导。

金融危机之后各国政府的一个普遍共识是，政府在金融发展中应当发挥更加重要的作用，诸如加强金融监管、积极开展金融救助、维护市场信心等。对我国而言，政府在金融创新中本就居于主导地位，金融的影响无疑会进一步强化这种态势。但是，同样的政府主导模式可以通过结构调整实现更高的创新效率。后危机时代我国金融管理部门应更加注重风险管理，提高市场监管水平，减少对微观主体创新活动的行政干预，营造科学、审慎的金融监管环境，维护公平的金融交易，这样才能为各种金融创新活动提供稳健的制度基础，降低金融创新活动的市场风险，防范金融危机的发生。但是，从长期来看，我国的金融模式创新应以市场化为导向。其原因有二：一是中国的市场经济体系发展急需有充分市场化的金融体系的配套；二是中国不断追求的、融入的当代全球经济体系，是一个以商品、资本自由跨境流动、汇率自由浮动为特征的自由化市场体系。这决定了不管政治、社会、经济的矛盾如何复杂，国情如何特殊，中国想通过继续参与经济全球化获得高速的经济增长，金融的市场化是必须遵循的首要原则。[3] 而在一个充分市场化的金融体系中金融创新主体必然由微观的金融机构担当，因此，我们对中国金融创新模式在制度上演进的判断是，随着金融市场的发展和金融体制改革的不断深入，我国当前政府主导型的金融创新模式必将被市场主导型的创新模式所取代。

3.2 金融产品创新模式选择

金融产品创新是金融创新的核心内容，在金融创新活动中居于基础性地位。国际金融危机给我们的启示是，脱离有效金融监管的过度泛滥的金融创新会给金融市场乃至整个实体经济带来灾难性后果。因此，在后危机时代我国金融产品创新中必须遵循的两条基本原则是：一是金融产品创新必须立足于服务实体经济，避免金融市场的过度虚拟化；是金融产品创新必须与金融当局的监管能力同步协调发展，对于发展中国家来说不宜盲目发展高风险的金融衍生品市场。

我国金融监管体制要求金融机构"分业经营"，但随着市场竞争的加剧，如大型国有商业银行和一些股份制银行成立海外机构，通过这些机构再回到国内经营证券、保险等业务；另外一些银行则通过控股国内信托公司，利用信托公司的全牌照优势参与资本市场业务；而一些中小银行则通过与非银行金融机构进行战略伙伴合作的方式经营投行业务，突破分业经营界限。由此可见，在商业银行开展投行业务的金融创新中，实力雄厚的大银行通过自主创新的模式整合自身资源优势突破分业经营限制，而一些区域性中小银行则采取合作创新的模式实现业务综合化。所以，在进行金融产品创新模式的选择时，不应一味强调采用自主创新模式抑或合作创新模式，而应因地制宜，综合金融机构的资源条件和市场需求情况选择成本低、效率高的创新模式。

受金融危机影响，发达国家的金融市场业务萎缩，而新兴市场国家的金融市场会成为主要利润增长点，中国庞大的金融市场需求更会成为各类跨国金融机构的必争之地。国外金融机构的加入无疑会加剧本已激烈的国内金融市场竞争，也给国内金融机构带来更大的竞争压力。在金融创新方面，跨国金融机构更加富有经验，而国内金融机构则相对较弱，但其扎根本土，更加了解国内市场，具有成熟的渠道网络和大量客户。因此，在竞争中寻求合作，以合作创新实现共赢，将成为未来中国金融产品创新的主要模式。

参考文献

[1] 孙诗. 中国金融改革创新研究 [J]. 现代商业，2012 (5).
[2] 葛颖培. 论我国金融创新模式的转变 [J]. 金融理论与实践，2003 (9).
[3] 夏斌，陈道富. 中国金融战略 2020 [M]. 北京：人民出版社，2011：381.

中国向低碳经济转型的制约因素及发展模式

李慧凤

1 引 言

工业化、城市化大量消耗化石能源而引发的全球气候变暖正威胁着全球的生态平衡,给社会经济的发展带来严重损失,触及能源安全、生态安全、水资源安全和粮食安全,甚至威胁到人类的生存。因此,全球气候变暖引起了国际社会的极度关注和对现有经济发展模式的反思,从《京都议定书》到"巴厘岛路线图",世界各国都在为解决气候变暖问题而努力,在经济发展的同时,降低经济增长所带来的二氧化碳排放量,减缓气候变化的速率,避免给人类和自然生态系统带来不可逆转的负面影响。由此,以低碳经济为基本内涵的发展模式在世界范围内得到普遍的认同,并成为新时期人类发展的目标。

低碳经济是以低能耗、低污染、低排放为基础的新经济发展模式,是人类社会继农业文明、工业文明之后的又一次重大进步。低碳经济的宗旨是降低经济发展对生态系统中碳循环的影响,实质是能源利用效率和清洁能源结构问题。中国一方面能源紧张、人均资源占有量低、环境污染严重,发展低碳经济有利于提高能源效率、改善能源结构和加强能源安全;另一方面,全球气候变暖,发展低碳经济是《中国应对气候变化国家方案》所必然要求采取的经济发展模式。因此,作为发展中的温室气体排放大国,中国如何从自己的国情出发实施节能减排,转变经济增长方式,构建环境友好型的低碳经济模式,是化解中国刻不容缓的现实压力和承担国际责任的迫切需要。

2 低碳经济国内外研究进展

低碳经济作为低能耗、低污染、低排放为基础的新经济发展模式,得到了国内外学者的普遍关注,本文将目前国内外关于低碳经济的相关研究成果进行梳理、归纳、总结如下。

2.1 低碳经济国外研究进展

国外学者关于低碳经济的研究主要集中在以下 3 个方面。

(1) 低碳经济的内涵研究

"低碳经济"首先由英国在《我们未来的能源—创建低碳经济》白皮书中提出。该白皮书认为,低碳经济是通过更少的自然资源消耗和更少的环境污染,获得更多的经济产出。但英国并没有界定低碳经济的概念,也没有给出低碳经济的评价指标体系。气候集团在发布的报告《赢余:低碳经济的成长》中介绍了低碳经济的概念,回顾了市场的发展并分析了低碳经济道路带来的收益,表明低碳经济具有更高的投资回报率,能够显著地增加产量、缩短生产周期、提高生产可靠性、改善产品质量、改善工作环境并鼓舞员工士气,在新增就业方面具有出色的潜力,其增长速度也大于其他经济形态。

(2) 低碳经济的必要性、实现的可能性研究

约翰斯顿(Johnston)等学者[1]探讨了英国大量减少住房二氧化碳排放的技术可行性,认为利用现有技术到 21 世纪中叶实现在 1990 年基础上减排 80% 是可能的。特莱佛斯(Trefers)等学者[2]探讨了德国 2050 年实现在 1990 年基础上减少温室气体排放 80% 的可能性,认为通过采用相关政策措施,经济强劲增长和温室气体排放减少的共同实现是可能的。川濑(Kawase)等学者[3]回顾和描绘了长期气候稳定的情景,指出为实现 60%~80% 的减排目标,总的能源强度改进速度和二氧化碳强度减少速度必须比以

[基金项目] 本文系北京市教委人文社会科学面上项目"北京低碳城市发展路径研究"(项目编号:SM201111417003)的阶段性成果。

[作者简介] 李慧凤(1965—),女,湖北省武汉市人,北京联合大学应用科技学院教授,博士生,主要研究方向为环境污染的经济分析。

前40年的历史变化速度快2~3倍。岛田（Shimada）等学者[4]构建了一种描述城市低碳经济长期发展情景的方法，并将此方法应用到日本滋贺地区。

（3）城市碳排放构成研究

美国哈佛大学经济学教授格来赛（Glaeser）等[5]从家庭生活和能源消费结构的角度系统地研究了城市二氧化碳的排量计算方法及应用分析，对美国10个典型大城市中心与郊区单位家庭采暖、空调、交通及生活能耗进行了实证分析，从碳排放的经济学角度，按照每吨二氧化碳排放折合43美元的经济成本，提出了实现城市低碳化发展的政策建议。格来赛还对碳排放量与城市规模、土地开发密度的关系进行了实证研究，发现城市规模与碳排放存在一定的正相关关系，随着城市规模的扩大，新增人口的人均碳排放量要高于存量人口；而土地开发密度与碳排放量存在较为明显的负相关关系，城市规划对土地利用的限制和约束越严格，居民生活的碳排放量水平越低。英国学者克里斯·古多尔（Chris Goodall）[6]通过对英国国民家庭生活中电能、石油、天然气等能源的统计，把国民的生活支出及各种物质消耗定量转化为二氧化碳排放，并通过英国家庭调查取样进行实证分析，以具有说服力的数据表达了英国家庭生活碳排放的未来情景及低碳化生活方式的迫切需求，提出在不改变目前生活水平及福利标准的情况下，如何把英国家庭生活的人均碳排放从每年6吨的标准降到人均年碳排放3吨的水平。

通过对国外低碳经济相关研究成果的梳理、总结，发现在低碳经济的研究领域，国外低碳经济研究是以发达国家，尤其是以经济合作与发展组织（OECD）国家的情况为背景进行的，对于发展中国家的情况考虑较少，但其研究方法及思路对于中国低碳经济的研究是有借鉴意义的。

2.2 低碳经济国内研究进展

国内学者关于低碳经济的相关研究起步较晚，随着《联合国气候变化框架公约》和《京都议定书》的签订而全面展开，取得了一些研究成果，主要集中在以下3个方面。

（1）低碳经济特征研究

中国较早研究低碳经济的学者庄贵阳[7]认为，低碳经济的实质是能源效率和清洁能源结构问题，核心是能源技术创新和制度创新，目标是减缓气候变化和促进人类可持续发展。鲍健强等[8]指出，碳排放量成为衡量人类经济发展方式的新标识，将全方位地改造建立在化石能源基础之上的现代工业文明，并促使其转向生态经济和生态文明。胡鞍钢[9]认为，在中国从高碳经济向低碳经济转变过程中，低碳城市是一个重要的方面，包括低碳能源、提高燃气普及率、提高城市绿化率、提高废弃物处理率等方面的工作。刘细良[10]强调现代意义上的低碳经济是对人与自然、人与社会、人与人和谐关系的一种理性认知。陈飞等[11]认为城市作为地区经济和社会发展的核心单元，不可避免地成为中国低碳发展关注的重点，低碳城市内涵包括从宏观层面上经济增长与能源消耗增长及二氧化碳排放相脱钩；在微观物质流过程，即经济过程进口环节、转化环节、出口环节中全面实现低碳化。

（2）低碳城市的空间规划、社区规划研究

近年来，国内学术界对低碳经济的研究包括了低碳城市的空间结构规划和城市能源结构等内容，均涉及城市社区层面。潘海啸等[12]研究了低碳城市的空间结构，在区域规划、城市总体规划和居住区规划3个层面，从城市交通与土地使用、密度控制和功能混合方面提出了改进规划编制的建议。顾朝林等[13]提出为实现低碳城市和社区发展，规划应该在不同的方面有所作为。在城市社区空间层面，应强调混合使用和适度高密度社区开发的策略，打破传统方式上的功能分区，不同的社区组团作为城市最小功能体，依靠公共交通联系，减少小汽车使用，发挥城市地缘性作用。肖荣波[14]等提出开展以低碳社区为基础的城市节能应用，将社区能源规划纳入城市社区规划的内容体系和设计过程中。

（3）中国发展低碳经济的建议及策略研究

对于中国如何发展低碳经济，中国学者进行了积极的探索。金起文等[15]提出，从中国建设资源节约型、环境友好型社会和节能减排的工作需求出发，结合国家的"发展规划""循环经济规划"和"节能减排规划"，加快制定低碳经济"国家方案"和行动路线图，并将发展低碳经济纳入"十二五"规划，形成一个具有国家意志的可操作的发展低碳经济的总体思路与实施方案。潘家华[16]指出，应从国际经济角度分析碳税、碳交易、国际技术经济合作框架、碳转让、经济激励的控制途径及全球合作模式来降低总的碳排放量。通过对碳产生的驱动因子、控制因子及约束因子的划分，探索低碳路径的社会经济及技术选择，提出适应中国国情及GDP指标的适应性排放量。宋德勇等学者[17]强调有效的政策工具是发展低碳经济政策目标得以实现的根本保障，中国的低碳经济政策体系必须跟上市场化改革的进程，政策工具设计应从主要依靠行政手段向以主要依靠市场机制转变。

综观中国国内有关低碳经济的相关研究，可以概括为以下两个方面的特征。

其一，对低碳经济的内涵、特征等方面进行了较深入研究。尽管他们研究的角度不同，所提出的概念也有所差异，但都是为了表达同样的内涵，即通过技术创新和制度创新，尽可能最大限度地减少温室气体排放，实现经济和社会的可持续发展。

其二，关于中国发展低碳经济必要性方面的研究较多，但对中国向低碳经济转型的制约因素、发展模式及改革方向缺乏深入分析。因此，深入分析中国低碳经济发展的现状及制约因素，构建中国低碳经济模式的总体框架及实现策略是中国低碳经济发展面临的迫切问题。

3 中国低碳经济发展现状及制约因素

3.1 中国低碳经济发展现状

中国作为世界第二大能源生产国和消费国，第二大二氧化碳排放国，高度重视全球气候变化问题，先后发布了《国家中长期科学和技术发展规划纲要》《气候变化国家评估报告》以及《国家环境保护"十一五"规划》3个大的纲领性文件，明确提出把解决能源、水资源和环境保护技术放在科学技术发展的优先位置，并加强节能技术、可再生能源技术以及煤炭清洁高效利用技术等减缓温室气体排放技术的研发。2003年以来，国务院还先后发布了《节能中长期专项规划》《关于做好建设节约型社会近期重点工作的通知》《关于加快发展循环经济的若干意见》以及《关于加强节能工作的决定》等政策性文件，并根据《联合国气候变化框架公约》和《京都议定书》的规定，制定了《中国应对气候变化国家方案》，并于2007年正式颁布实施，表明中国推进节能减排和发展低碳经济的决心与勇气。近两年，中国依法淘汰了一大批落后生产能力，如关停小火电2 157万千瓦、小煤矿1.12万处，淘汰落后炼铁产能4 659万吨、炼钢产能3 747万吨、水泥产能8 700万吨；全国环保投入达到5 500多亿元，占同期GDP的1.24%；启动10大重点节能工程；燃煤电厂脱硫工程取得突破性进展；中央政府投资支持重点流域水污染防治项目691个。2007年单位国内生产总值能耗比2006年下降3.27%，化学需氧量、二氧化硫排放总量近年来首次出现双下降，比2006年分别下降3.14%和4.66%。但与世界其他国家相比，中国单位GDP的碳排放强度依然很高，单位GDP的碳排放强度为印度的1.86倍，日本的1.69倍，西欧发达国家的1.6倍。据美国能源署预测，由于中国经济规模的逐年增加以及煤炭主导的能源结构，中国二氧化碳排放总量呈快速增长趋势（年均增长2.6%），2020年将达到81.45亿吨，届时将超过美国，成为世界第一大二氧化碳排放国。可见，中国面临巨大的温室气体减排压力，发展低碳经济具有紧迫性。

3.2 中国向低碳经济转型的制约因素

结合中国现阶段发展的实际情况，可以发现中国向低碳经济模式转型面临着一系列制约因素。

（1）以煤为主的能源结构

中国的一次能源消费结构中，煤炭的比重超过2/3，这与世界能源消费结构中以石油、天然气为主的格局大不相同。2007年在全球一次性能源消费构成中煤炭仅占27.8%，发达国家煤炭消费比例大多不到20%，而在中国能源消费中，煤炭所占比重高达69.5%。根据中国的能源资源条件，到2020年中国的能源结构中煤炭比重仍将维持在60%以上。由于石油的二氧化碳排放系数平均仅相当于煤炭的80%，天然气仅相当于煤炭的60%，煤炭消费比重大，二氧化碳排放强度高，导致经济发展过程中"高碳"特征非常明显。

（2）加速增长的能源消费

目前中国正处于工业化、城市化、现代化快速发展时期，随着经济社会不断发展，人口数量不断增加，城市和农村基础设施建设以及居民消费结构升级，对能源需求不断增加，呈现快速增长的态势。我国能源消费总量从2000年的13.86亿吨煤当量上升至2007年的26.56亿吨煤当量，年均增长9.7%。能源消费在短期内将延续加速增长的趋势，到2020年中国能源需求量将达到50亿吨标准煤以上。"高碳"特征突出的"发展排放"成为中国可持续发展的一大制约。

(3) 高耗能的产业结构

中国经济的主体是第二产业，决定了能源消费的主要部门是工业，特别是重化工业比重偏高，低能耗的第三产业和服务业比重偏低，发展滞后。统计资料显示，2005年、2006年、2007年，日本每万美元能耗分别是1.34、1.31、1.07吨油当量，德国是1.31、1.28、1.21吨油当量，中国是3.15、3.06、2.83吨油当量。

(4) 全球产业分工体系所处的低端位置

现阶段全球产业分工体系中，发达国家已进入服务经济时期，在全球产业分工体系中处于领先地位，而中国产业仍处于低端位置，在产业技术含量、附加值和竞争力等方面均与发达国家有较大落差。中国在成为"世界制造业基地"的同时，付出了巨大的环境代价。有关资料显示，中国2004年净出口产品排放的二氧化碳约为11亿吨，约占总排放量的23%。

4 中国低碳经济模式及实现策略

4.1 中国低碳经济模式

作为发展中的温室气体排放大国，中国向低碳经济模式转型刻不容缓。根据中国低碳经济发展现状及制约因素，中国的低碳经济模式设计如图1所示，这种模式不同于自由市场经济模式，也不同于政府高度掌控的环境治理模式，而是一种政府、市场、微观经济主体（企业、居民）三方共同参与、相互作用、相互影响的发展模式。

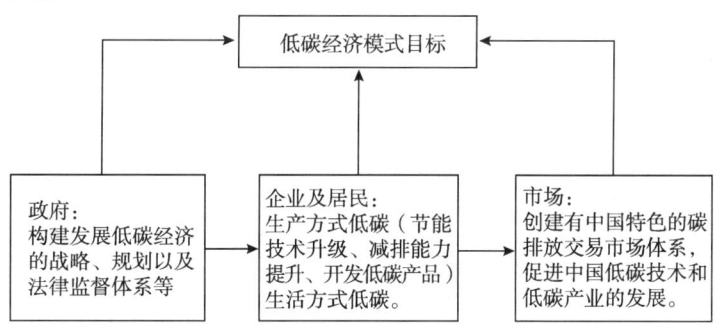

图 1　中国低碳经济模式

首先，政府在低碳经济模式中起指导、引导和监督的作用。中国政府应尽早制定中国低碳经济发展战略及规划，并进行法律监督体系建设，发挥看得见的手的作用；其次，创建有中国特色的碳排放交易市场体系，将现有的市场体系引导到低碳方向，发挥看不见手的作用；最后，通过"看得见的手"和"看不见的手"的双重作用，引导企业生产方式及居民生活方式的低碳化，完成产业节能技术的升级和减排能力的提升，形成低碳技术开发的大环境，并积极开发低碳产品，进行低碳消费引导、低碳理念教育和低碳生活宣传。

这种发展模式摒弃了政府作为解决经济发展模式问题的单一主体的认识，强调的是政府、市场、企业及居民之间形成的合力，通过有效的激励约束机制，促进微观经济主体的生产、消费方式由"高碳"向"低碳"转变。

4.2 实现中国低碳经济模式的策略

根据中国发展低碳经济面临的制约因素以及中国低碳经济模式中政府、微观经济主体、市场的关系，实现中国低碳经济模式的策略主要包括以下3个方面的内容。

(1) 加快构建和形成发展低碳经济的国家战略框架及法制保障体系

中国的长期发展战略要积极地借鉴、吸收、消化低碳经济的发展理念，要在中国已有的应对全球气候变化的国家方案、行动规划、方针措施的基础上，加快实施低碳经济发展的国家战略部署，将发展低碳经济纳入"十二五"规划，形成一个具有国家意志的、可操作的发展低碳经济的总体思路与实施方案。

在促进低碳经济发展方面，还应建立发展低碳经济的法制保障体系，为有效推动低碳经济提供法律依据。中国现有立法工作包括：①《清洁生产促进法》（2003年1月1日实施）、《促进循环经济法》（2009年1月1日实施），是中国节能减排，发展低碳经济的基本法制保障；②《能源法》正在起草，是促进中国能源发展战略实施的重要法律基础；③《可再生能源法》与《节约能源法》的配套规范性文件正在抓紧制定等。此外，中国还将在下一步适时开展一些环境和资源领域法律的修改工作，如《环境保护法》《环境影响评价法》《大气污染防治法》《矿产资源法》等。总的来说，到目前为止，中国正在逐步形成有关环境保护和低碳发展的法律体系框架，但与环境保护和低碳发展的要求相比，还应在以下两个方面改进：一是环境保护的法制建设应尽快与国际接轨，积极开展环境保护的国际合作，借鉴吸收国外环境法制的经验教训；二是环境法制建设要有全局观，防止与地方环境保护法规的不一致甚至冲突。

（2）优化能源结构，大力发展替代能源和可再生能源

低碳经济的实现形式是合理调整能源结构，优化能源利用方式，提高能源利用效率，积极开发替代能源和可再生能源。在近期，中国应把节能和煤炭的清洁利用作为重点，不断提高能源的利用效率，加快新能源、可再生能源、低碳和固碳技术的研发；在中期，要大幅提高可再生能源的比重，推进氢燃料等新能源技术以及碳收集与埋存技术的应用；在长期，建立以可再生能源、洁净煤、先进核能等为主体的可持续能源体系，并加快开发清洁的替代能源，尤其是战略性地提高可再生能源的消费比重，向"低碳富氢"的方向发展。[18]

（3）探索利用市场化机制，建立中国的碳交易市场

随着全球二氧化碳排放权交易的蓬勃发展，各国纷纷建立碳交易市场，为其国内的清洁发展机制（Clean Development Mechanism，CDM）项目产生的核证碳减排量及相关衍生品搭建交易平台，这是运用市场机制遏制温室气体排放的有效手段。中国应积极借鉴发达国家的有效经验，思考和建立比较合理的中国碳交易市场。目前，北京、天津和上海已建立环境交易所，但国内市场仍处于起步和探索阶段，业务仅限于项目信息介绍服务，还未成为真正意义上的金融交易平台。当前，中国节能减排工作的最大难点在于企业节能减排技改能力不足和技改成本高昂。建立碳交易市场，为国际买家与中国企业交易搭建平台，一是可以吸引更多的国际力量参与中国清洁发展机制项目合作，有利于对国外先进技术的吸收和利用；二是企业可通过出售碳排放权获利，直接提高节能减排的主动性。

5 结 论

低碳经济作为一种新的经济发展模式，是实现可持续发展的具体路径和必由之路。但由于中国以煤为主的能源结构、以第二产业为主体的产业布局、全球产业分工体系所处的低端位置，以及工业化、城市化、现代化快速发展带来的能源消费加速增长等因素，使目前中国经济的"高碳"特征非常明显，中国向低碳经济模式转型刻不容缓。中国的低碳经济模式设计强调的是政府、市场、企业及居民之间形成的合力，促进微观经济主体的生产、消费方式由"高碳"向"低碳"转变。而实现中国低碳经济模式的策略是在加快构建和形成发展低碳经济国家战略框架及法制保障体系的基础上优化能源结构，构建中国碳交易市场，实现发展与低碳的双赢。

参考文献

[1] Johnston D, Lowe R, Bell M. An Exploration of the Technical Feasibility of Achieving CO_2 Emission Reduction in Excess of 60% Within the UK Housing Stock by the Year 2050 [J]. Energy Policy, 2005 (33): 1643-1659.

[2] Trefers T, Faaij APC, Sparkman J, Seebregts A. Explor-ing the Possibilities for Setting up Sustainable Energy Systerm for the Long Term: Two Visions for the Dutch Energy System in 2050 [J]. Energy Policy, 2005 (33): 1723-1743.

[3] Kawase R, Matsuoka Y, Fujino J. Decomposition Analy-sis of CO_2 Emission in Long-term Climate Stabilization Sce-narios [J]. Energy Policy, 2006 (15): 2113-2122.

[4] Koji Shimada, Yoshitaka Tanaka, Kei Gomi, Yuzuru Matsuoka. Developing a Long-term Local Society Design Methodology towards a Low-carbon Economy: An Application to Shiga Prefecture in Japan [J]. Energy Policy, 2007 (35): 4688-4703.

[5] Edward L Glaeser, Matthew E Kahn. The Greenness of City, Rappaport Institute Taubman Center Policy Briefs [D]. 2008: 1-11.
[6] Chris Goodall. How to Live a Low-Carbon Live: the In-dividul's Guide to Stopping Climate Change [M]. London: Earthscan, 2007: 201-231.
[7] 庄贵阳. 中国经济低碳发展的途径与潜力分析 [J]. 国际技术经济研究, 2005 (3): 79-87.
[8] 鲍健强. 用循环经济理念重构传统经济流程 [J]. 自然辩证法研究, 2007 (4): 91-94.
[9] 胡鞍钢. "绿猫"模式的新内涵—低碳经济 [J]. 世界环境, 2008 (2): 26-28.
[10] 刘细良. 低碳经济与人类社会发展 [N]. 光明日报 2009-06-02 (10).
[11] 陈飞, 等. 低碳城市研究的理论方法与上海实证分析 [J]. 城市发展研究, 2009 (10): 71-79.
[12] 潘海啸, 等. 中国"低碳城市"的空间规划策略 [J]. 城市规划学刊, 2008 (6): 57-64.
[13] 顾朝林, 等. 气候变化、碳排放与低碳城市规划研究进展 [J]. 城市规划学刊, 2009 (3): 38-45.
[14] 肖荣波. 欧洲低碳城市发展的节能规划与启示 [J]. 现代城市研究, 2009 (11): 27-31.
[15] 金起文, 等. 中国发展低碳经济的策略选择 [J]. 中国国情国力, 2009 (10): 13-15.
[16] 潘家华. 怎样发展中国的低碳经济 [J]. 中国市场, 2009 (11): 61-65.
[17] 宋德勇, 等. 我国发展低碳经济的政策工具创新 [J]. 华中科技大学学报（社科版）, 2009 (3): 85-91.
[18] 谢军安, 等. 我国发展低碳经济的思路与对策 [J]. 当代经济管理, 2008 (12): 1-7.

亚洲著名科技园区金融支持体系比较研究

杨 宜 徐 鲲 王俊文

1 引 言

科技园区作为新技术革命和知识经济时代出现的一种高层次"经济特区",在国家与地区的技术革新和产业升级过程中发挥了先导作用。亚洲作为全球科技发展的新高地,近年来其科技园区发展成效显著,不仅对区域性科技创新方面做出巨大贡献,而且在科技与金融的协同发展下结合自身定位和区域特色形成了具有一定差异化的科技金融模式。

2 研究综述

科技园区运动已经成为一个世界性现象,它在促进地方经济增长、推动技术创新、加速知识转移等方面发挥着不可替代的作用。针对金融对科技创新的影响方面的论述,首见于经济学家 Schumpeter 的信用创造论。他在 1912 年出版的《经济发展理论》一书中,论证了货币、信贷和利率等金融变量对经济创新与经济发展的重要影响。随后众多学者从不同视角分别研究了科技创新与金融系统的发展问题(Gurley,1967;King、Levine,1993;Moon、Schwartz,2000;Auken,2001;Carlota Perez,2002;王松奇,2000;王海,2003;廖添土,2007);科技金融国际比较研究(丁涛,2009;顾峰,2011;李俊霞,2013;孙长学,2009;李兴伟,2011)等。

然而国内外众多学者的研究主要着眼于科技与金融的互促机制、国家或地区层面的科技金融系统的比较分析等,然而着眼于亚洲范围,基于科技园区分析金融支持体系的研究却相对较少,同时随着科技园区的不断升级,也对优化科技金融体系提出了新的要求,因此本文基于科技园区发展的视角,针对亚洲情况对各典型科技园区科技金融体系的优化和发展问题展开研究。

3 亚洲典型科技园区金融支持体系的比较

3.1 日本筑波科技园区

日本筑波科技园区成立于 1963 年 9 月,位于筑波市中心。筑波是日本政府第一个尝试建立的科学城,完全由中央政府资助,以基础科研为主,采用集中式布局,属于国家级研究中心。其科技金融支持体系以政策性金融为主,并注重金融服务的多样化。

3.1.1 强有力的政策性金融体系

日本设立了一系列政府机构和政策性金融机构,如中小企业厅(局),通过建立中小企业的信息网络,为中小企业提供技术和资金信息,促进科技与金融紧密结合。并专门设立了中小企业金融公库、日本开发银行等各类政策性融资机构,为企业提供中长期优惠贷款。同时政府不仅相继颁布了《国民金融公库法》《中小企业金融公库法》和《日本开发银行法》等法律,为政策性金融的发展提供法律保障,而且针对以筑波科学城为代表的高新技术园区制定"筑波研究学园都市建设法""筑波研究学园都市建设计划大纲""高技术工业积集地区开发促进法""技术城促进税则""增加试验研究费税额扣除制度"等法规和政策[1]。此外还有一些其他优惠措施,如减免税、发补助金、低息长期贷款等,有力地保障和

[基金项目] 北京市委组织部优秀人才资助项目(2012D005022000018);北京市哲学社会科学北京学研究基地项目(BJXJD - KT 2013 - B05)。

[作者简介] 杨宜(1966—),女,北京联合大学商务学院院长,教授,博士生导师。研究方向:科技金融;徐鲲(1981—),女,北京联合大学管理学院讲师,在读博士研究生。研究方向:公司金融;王俊文(1967—),男,内蒙古自治区乌海市政府金融办公室主任。研究方向:科技金融。

促进了科学城区的发展。

3.1.2 多样化的金融服务

日本的科技金融体系主要以科技信贷、科技保险和信用担保的形式存在。在日本的银行导向型金融体系的影响下，银行系统的间接融资是科技型企业融资的主要渠道，同时结合科技园区的特点还有科技保险与信用担保等多重保障。日本中小企业贷款保险公司（JCIC）由通产省和大藏省共同管理，为中小科技企业的科技创新提供覆盖率高、总量较大的贷款保险。此外，中小科技企业为其贷款进行保险甚至再保险，比信用担保成本更低。

3.1.3 发展中的风险投资金融体系

日本是亚洲地区风险投资发展最早的国家，但由于风险投资公司大部分为金融机构所有，风险投资几乎成为债权融资的变种，投资对象也以大中型企业为主，很少涉足高风险的技术创新领域，发展较为缓慢。日本筑波科技园区政府的资金投入占主导地位，同时充分调动企业和社会的财力，发挥民间企业的积极性，风险投资系统正在积极探索与发展过程中，目前资金来源主要靠地方公开团体、财团和企业、财团与政府合建，投资渠道的多元化为筑波的发展注入了长久的发展动力。

3.2 印度班加罗尔科技园区

班加罗尔软件产业科技园成立于 1991 年，是印度第一个计算机软件技术园区，被誉为印度的"硅谷"，是全球第五大信息科技中心。其强有力的政策性支持和独特的风险投资系统给园区的科技金融发展提供了重要支持。

3.2.1 强有力的政策性支持

印度政府大力支持科技金融发展，科技研发经费的 85% 由中央及各邦政府提供，设立技术开发和应用基金推动园区发展。同时采取一些具体有效的保障措施。一方面，对软件出口实行零关税、零流通税和零服务税，并提供劳动合同税、个人所得税等多税种的优惠；另一方面，制定和修改了《信息技术法》和《版权法》等法律法规，保护软件知识产权，促进软件业发展，并创造合适的法律环境[2]。

3.2.2 独特的风险投资

印度风险投资基金的初步构想可以追溯到 1973 年，随后政府颁布长期财政政策、进行试点、颁布减免税收条例、建立不同层次的风险基金等。目前印度最大的风险投资公司印度技术发展与信息有限公司以及另外两个著名的个人风险投资公司均将总部或办事处设在班加罗尔。班加罗尔软件科技园的风险投资公司主要具有两方面特点：①主要由金融机构发起设立，包括由中央联邦政府控制的金融发展机构、由州政府控制的金融发展机构、由公共商业银行、外资银行及私人银行发起设立；②风险投资主要投资于风险企业的成长期、后期及已上市风险企业。

3.2.3 商业性金融

针对班加罗尔科技园区的特点，商业性银行为其发展也提供了大力支持。其中印度工业发展银行提供优惠的贷款给软件企业，而且商业银行的分支行设立一个专门的 IT 金融部门来为软件企业服务。另外，类似于硅谷银行，印度的不少商业银行也采取债权投资与股权投资相结合的方式，经常以股本模式参与企业投资，为企业提供增值服务。

3.3 中国台湾新竹科技园区

台湾新竹科学工业园成立于 1980 年，经过"技术引领、人才培训、科技生根、市场开拓、科技创新、产品创新"等多个历史阶段的发展，目前已成为台湾经济的重要支柱，并形成了具有特色的科技金融支持体系。

3.3.1 政策性金融体系

新竹科技园区的特色化政策性金融系统主要体现在政策性信贷支持、创业投资基金、颁布的法规等。①中国台湾当局积极发放低于一般银行放款 2% 的低息贷款，如由"行政院"从开发基金中拨出专款，配合银行信贷发放低息贷款。

②中国台湾当局通过设置各种基金（如中小企业信用保证基金、创业投资基金），参与科技产业的投融资，推动高科技产业的发展。另外，在新竹科学工业园，投资人可以申请政府参与投资，出资额最高可达总资本额的 49%；园区管理局提供创新技术研发奖助金，最高可获得新台币 500 万元；中国台湾

地区政府每年补贴工业技术研究院及其相关研究机构的经费高达 4.2 亿美元[3]。③在法规保障方面，早在 1983 年，台湾就颁布了《创业投资事业管理规则》《奖励（创业）投资条例》和《产业升级条例》等有关创业投资的管理法规和奖励。

3.3.2 商业性金融体系

交通银行、中国台湾中小企业银行等商业银行是台湾高科技企业的重要资金供给者。根据台湾《银行法》规定，中小企业银行以供给中小企业中长期信用，协助其改善生产设备、财务机构及健全经营管理为主要任务。而交通银行在改制为开发银行后，加大了高科技企业的长期股权投资。

3.3.3 风险投资体系

中国台湾地区的风险投资业是以外资介入为主的运营模式。1986 年，由"行政院发展基金"、交通银行、中国发展公司共同设立"种子基金"，以后陆续开放保险公司及民营银行等，通过政策引导，吸引了数百亿元的国际资本投入，包括日本的和通、信友、大和及美国的 H&Q 等。

3.4 中关村科技园区

北京中关村科技园区成立于 1980 年 10 月，从当初的"中关村电子一条街"逐步发展为"一区十园"的跨行政区域的高端产业功能区，随着园区的不断发展，园区企业的融资渠道不断拓展，并形成了多元化的融资体系。

3.4.1 政策引导与政策性金融

政策不仅积极推进产学研合作，而且为开展科技贷款、科技保险、股权激励、多层次资本市场、科技银行等"科技金融套餐式"服务，初步建立科技金融服务体系提供了有力的保障[4]，真正实现了将政府之力与市场机制有机结合。同时政策性银行也不断探索新机制、新模式支持科技型企业的发展。国家开发银行北京市分行专门成立科技金融处，面向中关村示范区开展业务，截至 2012 年 10 月，国家开发银行累计发放中关村基础设施建设贷款突破 325 亿元，为中关村重点项目提供贷款近 216 亿元，累计支持中关村高新技术企业 97 家，"十百千"工程企业 25 家，形成了富有特色的中关村金融合作模式[5]，并对园区及企业的发展给予了有力的金融支持。

3.4.2 商业性金融

商业性金融是中关村园区企业采用的仅次于内源融资的第二大融资途径，截至 2009 年底，中关村科技园区企业银行贷款为 1 909.5 亿元，同比增长 24.1%。在"科技北京"战略的引领下，各大金融机构尤其是商业银行以此为契机，纷纷开展金融创新，不断推出针对科技型企业、中小企业融资的金融服务和产品，甚至设立了专门服务科技型企业的特色支行，拓展新领域，发掘新的利润增长点。

3.4.3 股票融资

随着我国资本市场的日趋完善，特别是由主板、中小板、创业板构成了多层次的股票融资市场，IPO 融资越来越受到科技型企业的青睐。截至 2012 年底，园区内符合境内创业板财务指标的企业近千家，上市公司总数 224 家，其中境内 145 家，境外 79 家，创业板 62 家，占全国的 1/7，在创业板形成了创业板中的"中关村板块"。[6]在创业板上市企业数、IPO 融资额和总市值三方面都高于深圳、江苏、浙江、上海等地。

3.4.4 债券融资

与较为活跃的股票市场相比，我国的债券市场发展相当滞后，但是近年来推出的中小企业集合债券融资还是成为了中关村科技型企业的重要融资方式之一。中关村园区内企业相继成功发行了"07 中关村债"和"10 中关村债"，发债规模分别为 3.05 亿元和 3.83 亿元，参与发债企业额数量也从 4 家增加到了 13 家，两只债券的信用级别分别为 AAA 和 AA +。集合债券融资模式不仅高效地发挥了群内企业的协同效应，而且也为科技型中小企业提供了崭新的融资平台[7]。北京市还推出了"区县信托集合计划"，组成北京市海淀、昌平、石景山、顺义等 9 个区县信托项目包，集合信托规模为 39 家企业，资金规模达 3.98 亿元，同期中关村示范区企业新增债券融资额 93.9 亿元，同比增长 34.6%。

3.5 各典型科技园区金融支持体系比较分析

上述介绍的 4 个著名的亚洲科技园区，虽然属于不同的国家和地区、处于不同的经济背景之下、植根于不同的经济与金融土壤，但是由于地域相近性，它们的成功仍然存在一些共同特征：①都依托于国家和地区原有的金融系统建立了适合自身发展的资金筹措体系；②基本上均以政策性金融体系、商业性金融体系、风险投资体系作为三大金融支撑体系；③政府及政策性的支持与保障作用显著。此外，各园区基本都依托于高校和科研机构形成密集的科技人力资源；在高校、研究机构、企业、政府多元主体共同参与作用下形成完备的创新网络。

总体而言，上述国家和地区的金融基础设施较好，科技创新资金来源多样，金融市场层次丰富，银行体系健全，配套体系完善，各园区在其发展历程和金融支持体系的特色构建方面也各具特色，各园区比较分析详见表1。

表1 亚洲科技园区发展情况比较分析表

类型	要素	筑波	班加罗尔	新竹	中关村
基本情况	管理体制	政府主导型	政府主导型	政府主导逐步过渡到市场主导	市场自发+政府引导
基本情况	园区企业主体	大、中、小企业群体结构	以中小企业为主体	以中小企业为主体	大、中、小企业群体结构
基本情况	高校支持	筑波大学	—	交通大学、清华大学等	清华大学等
金融支持体系	代表性融资方式	政府财政拨款为主	特殊的风险投资与多种融资方式相结合	风险投资、政策性金融、商业性金融	内源融资、商业性金融
金融支持体系	金融支持特点	政府引导下的主银行模式为主导	政府引导下的风险投资与政策性金融	政府设立创投基金，参与投资，资金来源多元化	政府给予大力支持和高度重视，但内源融资所占比例过高

资料来源：根据参考文献及本文研究内容整理。

3.5.1 科技园区所处金融系统不同

基于国别层面的金融系统的状况体现了科技园区所处的宏观环境分析，是园区金融支持体系构建的基础，正是由于金融系统特征各异，才产生不同模式的金融支持体系。亚洲国家（地区）的金融系统与美洲和欧洲的相比主要在于资本市场成熟度不同，因此上述四国（地区）科技金融系统中政策性金融发挥了主导作用。最典型的是以"关系型"银行融资为主的日本[8]，政策性金融支持力度大，资本市场融资则处于次要地位，因此其风险投资体系还处于不断发展和完善之中。园区的管理体制也在一定程度体现了金融系统的特点，中、日、印度则以政府为主导，较为特殊的是中国台湾新竹在前期是政府开展计划性建设并承担主导地位，到中后期随着中介机构的介入，政府渐渐退出，并进入到市场主导阶段。

3.5.2 科技园区金融支持体系的构成和主导融资方式不同

不同的金融系统决定了园区不同的科技金融支持体系。日本筑波强有力的政策性金融、强大的商业银行体系和科技信贷、科技保险和信用担保等多样化的金融支持对园区的发展助力不少；印度班加罗尔除了政策性金融支持以外就是印度政府主导的特色化的风险投资成效显著；中国台湾新竹的三大支柱性金融支持系统发展较为均衡；我国中关村已初步形成了多层次、多元化的金融支持体系，但内源性融资所占比例过高也成为制约融资高效化的主要"瓶颈"。

3.5.3 政府对科技金融的推动作用不同

政府发挥的作用主要体现在政策性金融的引导和科技金融的立法支持方面。我国、日本和印度政府在科技金融的推动力度方面较为显著，如我国政府高度重视中关村的发展建设，国务院先后6次作出重要决定，逐步规范和推进园区的发展，并成立中关村国家自主创新示范区，并针对园区特点大力推进科技银行、股票市场、债券市场、产权交易市场的建设。日本筑波科技园区得益于以政策性金融为主的银行导向型金融体系，形成了以政府资金投入为主导，鼓励银行体系为企业的科技创新提供融资服务，园区内企业贷款既可得到信用担保的支持，又可以得到贷款保险公司的保障。印度班加罗尔的成功也离不开政府的支持，印度增加国家对科研经费的财政开支，设立技术开发和应用基金，出台征收研究与开发税的条例，同时鼓励科研机构与企业联合创新开发，促进科研成果的商业化和产业化。

4 结 论

科技金融体系的不断完善成为科技园区迅猛发展的重要推动力，亚洲各著名科技园区成功具有一定的共性：①都依托于国家和地区原有的金融系统建立了适宜的资金筹措体系；②基本上均以风险投资体系、政策性金融体系和商业性金融体系作为三大金融支撑体系；③政府和政策性的支持与保障都起到了相对重要的促进作用。然而由于园区植根于不同的经济与制度土壤，发展的重点与进程也不尽相同，因此不同园区的发展历程和金融支持体系各具特色：①各科技园区所处的金融系统不同；②各科技园区金融支持体系的构成和主导融资方式不同；③政府对各科技金融的推动作用不同。

参考文献

[1] 刘芹，张永庆，樊重俊．中日韩高科技园区发展的比较研究［J］．科技管理研究，2008（8）：122－125．
[2] 陈平．印度班加罗尔信息产业集群研究［J］．商业研究，2007（11）：125－128．
[3] 丁涛，胡汉辉．金融支持科技创新国际比较及路径设计［J］．软科学，2009（3）：50－54．
[4] 刘璇，马秋君．北京市科技型企业融资瓶颈及对策探析——基于中关村"一区十园"的分析［J］．科学管理研究，2011（5）：111－115．
[5] 国家开发银行积极探索融资模式创新支持示范区建设［EB/OL］．http：//www.zgc.gov.cn/zxdt2010/84377.htm，2012－10－08．
[6] 汪川，武岩，桂青．中关村科技园区融资现状分析及对我国资本市场支持科技型企业发展的启示［J］．科学管理研究，2013（5）：102－105．
[7] 徐鲲．高科技中小企业集合债融资问题研究［J］．科技管理研究，2012（8）：231－235．
[8] 杨宜，徐鲲．中小企业关系型融资的国际比较研究［J］．改革与战略，2009（8）：179－183．

大宗商品国际市场价格变化趋势分析

——国家发展与改革委员会"十三五"规划前期研究重大课题子课题

吴勤学 等

一、近年大宗商品国际市场价格的变化特征

纵观最近 10 余年来的全球经济发展形势,自从 2000 年泡沫经济崩溃之后,全球经济始终处于调整与低速增长的状态之中。伴随着 2003 年伊拉克战争的结束,在美国经济连续采取扩张性经济政策的带动下,自 2003 年第二季度开始,全球经济迎来了久违的复苏。此后,虽然有石油价格上涨、全球经济失衡与发达国家房地产泡沫经济隐患的担心,但全球经济在 2004—2007 年间仍保持了较高的增长速度。但到了 2008 年,世界经济剧烈动荡,美国次贷危机升级演变为全球金融危机,严重影响到各个实体经济部门,导致世界经济又一次出现衰退。世界银行和联合国的数据表明,2008 年的世界经济增长率为 2.5%,是自 2002 年以来的最低增长水平。而 2009 年受到美国次贷危机及金融危机的影响,全球经济更是经历了"二战"以来的首次经济负增长。

与世界经济发展的趋势类似,大宗商品国际市场的价格也表现出与世界经济相同的走势:从图 1 可以看出,国际货币基金组织 IMF 发布的大宗商品价格指数走势几乎同步于经济增长走势;而从 CRB 指数反映的大宗商品国际市场价格来看,自 2004 年以来,大宗商品国际市场价格开始大幅上涨,且波动加剧。2004—2008 年,CRB 指数持续走高,在此以后的年份也在高位维持振荡状态,具体如图 2 所示。

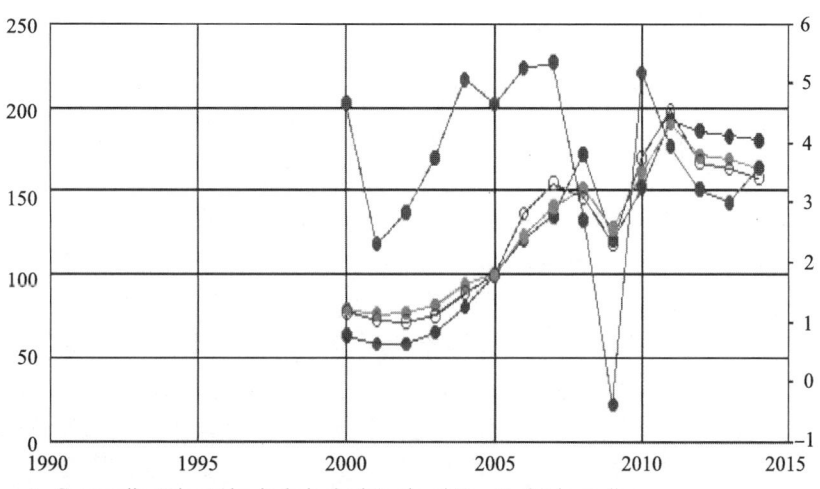

图 1 世界经济与大宗商品价格趋势

注:商品价格指数以 2005 年为 100 点,GDP 以 2000 年不变价格为准

数据来源:国际货币基金组织 IMF 网站 www.imf.org

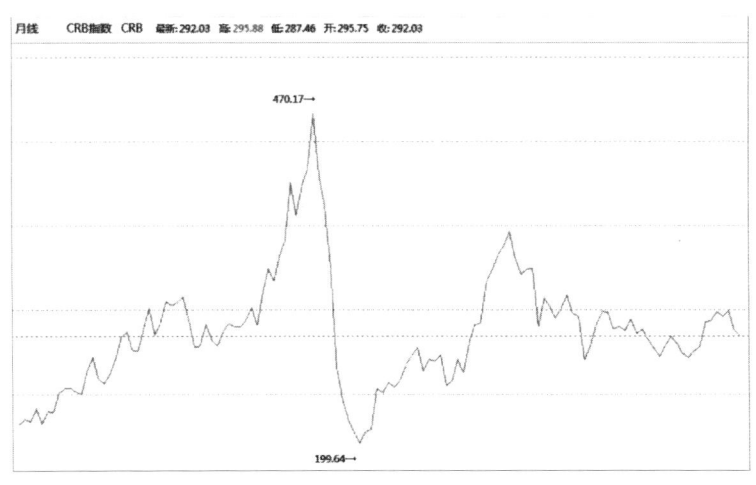

图 2　CRB 指数走势（2004 年 3 月—2014 年 8 月 CRB 月线）

二、影响大宗商品国际市场价格的主要因素

引起大宗商品国际市场价格波动的因素有很多，包括基本供求因素、市场资金或流动性因素、作为商品标价基准的美元走势、全球经济增长以及大宗商品定价机制等因素。其中，供求关系因素是影响大宗商品价格波动的根本因素。

（一）大宗商品供求因素

按照现代经济学理论，供给和需求是同一个问题的两个方面，商品的价格是由供求关系决定的。供大于求，价格下降；供不应求，则价格上涨。纵观大宗商品近 40 年的价格变动情况可以发现，供求关系是影响大宗商品价格波动的根本性因素，供求关系发生变动则引起大宗商品价格的波动。20 世纪 70 年代初期，两次石油危机使得石油供不应求，从而石油价格大涨，直接导致 CRB 指数从 70 年代以前的 100 左右上涨到 1972 年的 200 以上，此后一直在 250 左右波动。

进入 21 世纪以来，由于中国、印度等新兴经济体的经济快速增长，引起对大宗商品需求的增加，从而导致大宗商品价格持续上涨。21 世纪初，世界经济持续快速增长，特别是中、印、俄、巴金砖四国经济增长加速，工业化、城镇化进程加快，这极大地刺激了大宗原材料商品的需求。

而在 2008 年金融危机中，全球经济遭受重挫，这使得大宗商品价格急剧下挫。不过，金融危机之后，由于世界各国为恢复经济而采取了一系列刺激性政策，自 2009 年下半年开始，世界经济开始复苏，特别是中国等国家经济强劲复苏，又使得大宗商品价格再次走上上涨快车。

此外，石油、铁矿石等矿产类大宗商品越来越趋于集中，被一些大的集团控制，形成寡头垄断格局，也是推动大宗商品国际市场价格的重要因素。不同于一般商品，大部分大宗商品的需求价格弹性小，而其生产具有专用性、高风险性的特征，这样，大宗商品的供给方长期处于优势地位，使得价格容易被少数集团控制。例如，必和必拓等三大巨头控制了铁矿石 70% 的产量、欧佩克石油组织控制了 65% 的世界石油产量。而大宗商品一旦被少数巨头控制之后，这些巨头容易形成价格联盟，进而推高大宗商品市场价格。

最后，由于大宗商品具有一定的保值性和增值性，使得大宗商品市场成为机构和个人投资者的重要投资和投机渠道，机构和个人投资者的加入进一步引起了大宗商品国际市场的供求不平衡。

在机构和个人投资者加入之前，大宗商品主要的投资主体包括现货市场上的生产商、经销商、中间加工商及部分规模参差不齐的投机者。而随着机构和个人投资者进入后，大宗商品市场格局发生变化。商品基金在做多时，期货的投机性增强，在市场利多的情况下，大量投资和投机性资金看多买进，导致大宗商品价格大幅上涨，而在市场利空时，这些资金也会迅速撤离，从而导致大宗商品价格的暴跌。2004 年以来，机构投资者开始大量涉足商品期货市场，而受到游资和对冲基金的追捧，大宗商品价格的波动甚至出现了对基本供求关系的偏离。有学者（Masters，2008）甚至提出游资炒作是大宗商品价格剧烈波动的主要根源。

（二）市场资金因素

一方面，世界各国为了应对经济周期的波动而采取的各种财政政策和货币政策组合，使得市场流动性不断变化，而市场流动性的变化必然导致大宗商品市场资金的变动，从而引起大宗商品市场价格的变动。

以美国为例，为了应对2008年的全球性金融危机，美联储除了采用降息等常规措施外，还采用了直接向金融市场注入流动性和国有化银行等应急措施。美联储的资产额在金融危机后的两年时间里扩张了近2倍。在这些措施之后仍未看到经济的持续复苏，美联储又启动了通过增加其资产负债表规模的量化宽松货币政策，进一步影响金融市场上的利率水平、资产价格和经济产出。在美国增加流动性的同时，大宗商品国际市场的价格也持续上涨。

另一方面，如前所述，由于大宗商品具有一定的保值性和增值性，特别是自2004年商品期货指数投资兴起以来，大量的个人和机构投机者纷纷加入这个市场，大宗商品的价格波动不再仅仅归因于大宗商品本身的供求关系。

（三）美元走势

美元是大部分商品和服务贸易的定价和结算货币，大宗商品也不例外。在其他条件不变时，美元币值变动必然会影响大宗商品的标价变动：美元走弱，则以美元标价和计算的大宗商品价格就会上涨；反之若美元走强，则以美元标价和计算的大宗商品价格就会下降。

2008年金融危机之后，全球主要经济体都推出了各种恢复本国经济的扩张经济政策。美国作为金融危机的发源地，不仅采用降息等常规措施，还采用直接向金融市场注入流动性和国有化银行等紧急措施以恢复本国经济。在实行近乎"零利率"的货币政策，仍未看到经济复苏迹象后，美国启动了量化宽松货币政策，即央行通过增加其资产负债表的规模或结构，影响金融市场上的利率水平、资产价格和经济产出。美国一系列政策的结果导致美元指数持续走低，而相应地大宗商品的价格则不断创出新高。同时，美国宽松的货币政策形成美元贬值的预期之外又形成了资金的避险情绪，而作为保值增值重要选择的大宗商品作为主要投资对象，进一步推动了大宗商品价格上涨。

（四）大宗商品定价机制

在国际市场中，大宗商品贸易的定价方式主要有两种：一种是期货价格主导模式，即以国际期货市场的期货合约价格为基准价格，供需双方在确定基准价后，根据一定的升贴水幅度来确定最终的贸易价格，绝大多数大宗商品都以这种方式进行定价；另一种是商业谈判模式，即由供需双方以商业谈判的方式来确定贸易定价，如我国的铁矿石进口就主要采用这种方式。

在期货价格主导模式中，作为形成大宗商品基准价格的期货市场，是一个集中、统一、公开的市场，且是近似完全竞争的市场，能最大限度地反映社会对大宗商品价格的预期，真实地反映市场供求关系和真正的市场价格。而在商业谈判模式中，可能由于贸易双方力量不对等，弱势一方的权益容易被侵害。以我国铁矿石进口贸易为例：一方面，我国的钢铁企业数量众多，而拥有铁矿石进口资质的企业过少。在中国与境外矿山的铁矿石价格谈判中，几乎大多数的中方机构和企业都希望铁矿石价格上涨，与外国矿山的利益一致，而不是与国内钢铁企业的利益一致。与此同时，大宗商品的供给方由于地理优势等容易形成联盟，形成谈判优势。另一方面，我国的铁矿石进口采用长协合同，境外铁矿石供给方定死了供货的数量，期限长达5~10年甚至20~30年，但贸易价格却是一年一谈。这种定价方式对我国的铁矿石进口极为不利。

三、大宗商品国际市场价格走势展望

展望大宗商品国际市场价格的未来走势，由世界经济走势主导的大宗商品的供求关系仍然是影响大宗商品价格走势的最主要因素。

（一）世界经济筑底回升决定大宗商品价格走势稳定或下行

世界经济筑底缓慢回升。2014年应是全球经济"筑底企稳"回升年，多数经济体将好于前两年。据国际货币基金组织（IMF）估计，2014年世界经济将增长3.6%，好于2013年。这与经济合作与发展组织（OECD）和联合国的预测值一致。其中，新兴市场与发展中国家和发达国家经济将分别增长5.1%和

2%，分别高于 2013 年的 4.5% 和 1.2%。

发达经济体增势明显上升：欧元区经济止跌回升，2014 年可望增长 1%；美国经济增速将由 2013 年的 1.6% 上升到 2.6%；日本受消费税提高影响及"安倍经济学"边际效应下降影响，2014 年经济增速将由 2013 年的 2% 回落到 1.2%。

新兴市场与发展中国家经济发展依然温和。中国经济增速换挡到中速，据联合国预测，2014—2015 年中国经济将分别增长 7.5% 和 7.3%。IMF 则认为，2015—2018 年间中国经济年均增速将放缓到 7%。

当然，世界经济总体看好，但是仍有众多不稳定和不确定因素：美国量化宽松政策逐步退出和国债上限问题将对美国乃至全球经济产生负面影响；"安倍经济学"的政策效果呈现下降趋势；新兴经济体面临结构性改革压力。

第一，美国联邦储备银行的货币政策走向对全球经济的不确定性。自 2014 年 1 月起，美联储将量化宽松额度逐渐减少，最近的 7 月 31 日，美联储在为期两天的货币政策会议后，宣布维持利率 0~0.25% 不变，进一步缩减每月购债（QE）规模至 250 亿美元，并从 8 月开始，每月购买 100 亿美元抵押贷款支持证券（MBS）和 150 亿美元美国国债。

第二，欧洲的经济形势仍具有挑战性。欧债危机似乎过去了，但欧洲仍然面临区域性的政治危机，这是债权国和债务国之间的危机。华尔街金融大鳄索罗斯表示，除非欧洲政治家们进一步整合欧元区，改变政策使欧洲银行愿意发放贷款，否则欧洲可能面临长达 25 年的日本式经济增长的停滞状态。根据欧盟统计局的数据显示，随着俄罗斯和乌克兰危机，以及中国经济增速放缓，欧元区经济不可能快速增长，预测 2014 年经济增长为 1.2%，2015 年为 1.8%；工业信心指数从 3 月份的 -3.3，降至 4 月份的 -3.6，服务行业信心指数从 4.5 下降到 3.5。

欧洲在一个统一的金融监管体系方面取得了重大进步，但是，其结构改革还没能成功。失业率水平仍然是一些国家的社会承受能力面临的新的挑战，欧洲在经济全面复苏的进程中任重而道远。

欧债危机的不利影响逐渐在消除，但欧洲货币联盟体制的弊端已经暴露，且仍未解决，欧元区内部竞争力和增长前景将继续分化。日本经济在安倍货币财政政策短期刺激后，面临更加实质而艰难的结构改革，难以持续复苏。

第三，新兴经济发展的不确定性，面临着美联储缩减 QE 和中国对大宗商品需求减弱的双重压力。自 2013 年 5 月美联储宣布推出量化宽松货币政策的进程开始，新兴市场国家经济出现了震动，但一些国家加大了结构调整，印度、巴西等情况有明显改善，但土耳其、俄罗斯等国家还是出现了较大的困难。于此同时，中国正在进行经济结构调整和增长方式调整，逐步减少对能源及原材料等大宗商品的依赖程度。

第四，新的地缘政治的挑战。目前，乌克兰与俄罗斯之间的政治矛盾不仅对乌俄两国经济产生了不利影响，而且对欧洲乃至全球经济都产生了影响。国际货币基金组织正在研究对乌克兰的救助。

综合来看，虽然全球经济面临众多不确定性因素，但总体筑底回升的趋势不会改变，受此影响，大宗商品国际市场价格也将稳步上升。

（二）美元指数随着美国经济逐渐恢复而企稳向上

资金和大宗商品市场是关联的——资金成本上升会影响美元币值。从历史数据看，资金成本上涨、债券收益率上升和美元升值三者之间存在一定时滞，趋势上是依次牵引关系。资金成本上升是市场最关键的逻辑起点，正是它导致全球资金流动发生变化，从而影响币值波动。

从一个中性角度讲，美元很可能结束底部震荡，走入上升周期。尽管 2013 年没有表现出这一点，但是未来美元结束震荡的概率不能排除。目前美元还在底部，进入上行通道的概率较大。根据前述的资金成本上涨——债券收益率上升——美元升值的逻辑，美元可能结束底部盘整，从而逐步走上振荡上升之路，美元指数走势与 CRB 指数走势如图 3 所示。

从历史经验来看，美元指数的走高将促使大宗商品价格的下跌。但这一变化的同步相关性不会很强，中间会有时滞。因为影响大宗商品市场的各种因素逐渐累积，在某一时点由事件性因素作为催化剂，集中释放此前累积的影响力。

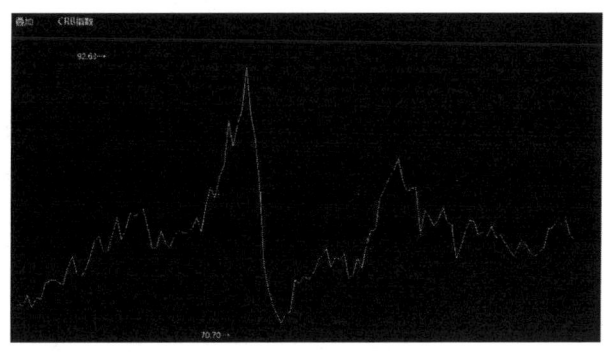

图 3 美元指数走势与 CRB 指数走势

（注：红线代表美元指数，白线代表 CRB 指数；均为月线。）

数据来源：智通智能软件。

（三）受地缘政治的影响，大宗商品价格难以持续走高

历史上，原油价格非常容易受到中东地区地缘政治紧张局势的影响。在中东和东欧地区，伊朗核危机出现缓解迹象，但是叙利亚、伊拉克问题和乌克兰危机导致地区形势恶化。同时，是否有新的地区政治危机还不能确定。从地缘政治角度来看，大宗商品国际市场价格仍有上涨的趋势，但长期看难以持续。

参考文献

[1] N. 格利高利·曼昆. 宏观经济学 [M]. 5 版，北京：中国人民大学出版社，2005.

[2] （美）多恩布什，费希尔，斯塔兹. 宏观经济学 [M]. 1 版. 王志伟，译. 北京：中国财政经济出版社，2003.

[3] 杨浩，林丽红. 中国与国际大宗商品价格关联性研究 [J]. 经济问题探索，2011（9）.

[4] 唐衍伟，王逢宝，张晨宏. 中国大宗商品国际定价权的缺失及相关对策研究 [J]. 中国物价，2006（1）.

[5] 余军. 量化宽松货币政策对大宗商品价格的影响 [J]. 金融经济，2012（2）.

[6] 李敬辉，范志勇. 利率调整和通货膨胀预期对大宗商品价格波动的影响 [J]. 经济研究，2005（6）.

[7] 吴开尧，李榕. 美元指数与大宗商品价格相关性分析 [J]. 价格理论与实践，2013（6）.

[8] 韩立岩，尹力博. 投机行为还是实际需求——国际大宗商品价格影响因素的广义视角分析 [J]. 经济研究，2012（12）.

[9] Frankel. J. A. The Effect of Monetary Policy on Real Commodity Prices. Asset Prices and Monetary Policy, Inc. Campbell (Ed.), University of Chicago Press, 2008.

[10] Akram, Q. F.. Commodity Prices, Interest Rates and the Dollar. Energy Economics, 2009, 31 (6): 838–851.

基于相对熵的证券市场参与者
对监管的态度偏好研究

张士玉 郝旭光

一、引　言

在社会科学研究中，经常通过问卷量表研究社会群体的某种态度[1]。大量观察和研究表明，由于人的心理、性格和情绪等特点的综合作用，在评价某事物的各项指标时，常常表现出某种非理性信息。例如，构成某事物的评价指标有A、B、C三个。要求被调查者对这三个方面给以分数评价，从1分至5分，1分为最差，5分为最好。这三个指标具有明显的各自特殊内容，基本没有重叠，同时也很难同时达到很好或很不好。但是被调查者在进行分数评价时，会出现两种情况：一种是对各个指标评价的差距很小，表现为都给高分，或者都给低分，又或者都给中等分数；另一种就是对各个不同指标所给分数差距较大。

仔细观察人们对社会问题的反映，通过问卷调查反映出的态度往往与通过访谈和人们诉说、行动表现等现象不尽一致。举个例子，在研究人们对某社区管理的态度和意见时，常常将社区管理分为若干指标，包括清洁程度、绿化程度、治安状况、维修服务、购物环境，等等。每一项按照1~5个等级评分，1分为最差，5分为最高。可能社区中有一部分人总是对清洁问题不满，向管理人员提出意见，反映地面不及时清扫、垃圾没有及时运走。但是这些人在问卷中对清洁程度的评分不一定是最低的，例如这些人在该项给出的平均分数为2分或3分，而那些给予该项平均1~2分的群体可能默不做声，并不去社区管理中心诉说意见。这是什么原因呢？如果仅从对"清洁程度"这个指标的评价来看，确实无法解释这一现象，但是如果从两个类型人群对各个指标的评分的总体上看，就很容易解释。对社区的清洁问题付出行动去诉说和反映问题的这个群体，尽管与其他人相比对"清洁程度"的评分不是最低，但是相比他们对其他指标的评价是最低的，这个群体对治安状况的评价可能是5分，对绿化程度的评价可能是4分，而对清洁程度的评价相对最低，也许是2分，也就是说这个群体对各个指标的评价差距较大，可以理解为这个群体目光敏锐、爱憎分明。对清洁程度评价最低而并不付诸行动诉说意见的群体，可能对所有的指标评价都很低，各项之间的差距不大。如果这个社区在事实上仅是清洁问题不太好，而其他方面都不错的话，那么对各个指标评价都较低而差距不大的群体，其原因可能并不全是他们理性的评价，而是具有一些非理性的因素，如性格悲观等。那些对各个指标评价差距较大的人，表现出了他们的真实意见偏好的情况很多。

几乎所有调查研究的本质目的都是为了真正了解被调查者的态度和意见偏好，突出这些明显的偏好，了解反映比较强烈的诉求，而根据常规的统计方法则有悖这种研究目的，在一定程度上掩盖了本质。因为其前提是对每个被调查者的数据都同等对待，不论这个人是对各个指标同时给以5分、或者同时给以1分，或者经过思考对不同指标给以不同分数。本文的基本观念就是，为了达到研究目的，即有效地突出被调查者的态度和意见偏好，在数据分析中，应该对那些对不同指标的评价差距较大的人给以更高重视，在计算过程中使其对结果的影响更大，而对那些对各个指标评价的差距较小甚至相同的人，给以较小的重视，在计算过程中使其对结果的影响相对较小一些，但不是零。重要的是，要寻求一种合理的计算方法，而不是人为地进行加权。

本文的来源是一项对中国证券监管效果评价的研究。自从1990年中国内地建立证券市场以来，在20多年的发展历程中，股市经常暴涨暴跌、熊市时间远长于牛市时间，导致各方市场参与者对监管层抱

[基金项目] 国家社科基金重点项目"我国资本市场系统稳定性评估和监测研究"（11AZD010）。
[作者简介] 张士玉，男，北京人，北京联合大学管理学院教授；郝旭光，男，山东烟台人，对外经济贸易大学国际商学院教授。

怨很多,对监管效果不满意。所以有必要通过对市场参与者的调查研究对监管效果进行评价[2-3]。调查问卷将证券监管分为若干方面,将市场参与者分为五类群体[4]:监管者、上市公司管理者、个人投资者、基金公司管理者、证券公司管理者。要求被调查者对各个方面进行分数评价。项目在采用传统方法完成了第一轮分析后,经过对研究结论的思考,认为没有突出主要本质与核心要素,掩盖了某些本质因素。究其原因,就是在数据分析中没有充分重视不同人员的偏好,对每个被调查者的数据都给以同等重视,使其对结果的影响同等重要,而那些诉求最强烈的愿望,正是通过那些对不同方面所给的评价差距较大的人群所反映出来的。

本文基于相对熵的方法构造了计算方法,较好地解决了这一问题,并且具有一定的普遍性。

二、文献综述

偏好性(preferences)是一个被广泛应用的概念。诺贝尔经济奖获得者 Kenneth Joseph Arrow(1963)在其著作[9]中对偏好性作了阐述。当人面对一个由若干选择项目构成的备选对象(alternative)时,这些选项可以用 x, y, z, …表示,由此构成了集合 S,选择者的偏好性表现在不是同等看待 S 中的各个选项,而是在经过比较之后进行排序,或优先选择某项。Arrow 首先定义了偏好或无差异关系,这种关系是一个公理,其表述为:

对于任意两个备选对象 x 和 y,必有 xRy,或者 yRx。

xRy 意为"x 不次于 y",yRx 意为"y 不次于 x",这种关系被称为"弱排序"关系。弱排序关系包含了偏好或无差异,而如果将无差异关系排除,仅仅针对偏好关系作出定义,Arrow 的定义是:

如果 yRx 不成立,就称 xPy。

"xPy"就是指"x 优于 y",Arrow 将其称为严格偏好关系。

由此可见,比较是偏好的前提,偏好性是人在比较和选择不同事物时所产生的现象。由于每个人在面对选择时具有偏好性,要得到社会大众对某问题的态度,正如 Arrow 指出的那样,这个问题就变成了集结个体偏好类型以致产生由这些个体组成的社会唯一的偏好类型。

通过对大量数据的汇总来反映人的偏好,可以有多种方法。最经典的方法就是传统的统计学方法,即计算每个人对每个变量评价的平均分或对各个选项选择的比率,以及对不同群体数据的平均数或比率的差异显著性检验,这也是最基本的方法,但是其局限性也很明显。在采用平均数和比率汇总数据时,数据表中的每行数据,也就是每个被调查者对一系列变量的选择数据,不论其差异大小,都给以同等重视,使其对结果的影响都一致。这也就在一定程度上削弱了偏好性对结果的影响。对于平均数和标准差在数据分析中的局限,以及熵理论及其方法可以弥补这些局限的问题,早已有学者指出[5](何大义,2005)。

数据挖掘中的关联规则(Association Rules)方法[8,10],其产生就是为了对超市客户的购货偏好进行分析,称为货篮分析,即分析"大部分顾客会在一次购物中同时购买什么商品"。关联规则的基本算法是 Rekesh Agrawal 等人(1993)提出的 Apriori 算法。但是这种分析的结果是发现一系列有关联的项目组,而不是将大量数据集结为一个参数。而这正是许多研究所需要解决的问题,即用一个参数来表述偏好性,而不是将数据的分布展示出来。

统计学中的方差只是反映了数据的离散情况,却难以反映不同群体数据的偏好型。用熵理论和相对熵的方法来集结大量被调查者的数据,可以有效地反映被调查者的偏好。业界一般公认 Shannon(Claude E. Shannon)于1948年发表的文献[11]是信息论诞生的重要标志。信息论把熵理解为一个信息源发出的信号的状态的不确定性程度,所获得的信息就是消除了不确定性,所以信息量就是负值的熵。使熵理论获得飞跃性发展的另外两个重要里程碑,一是 Jaynes 于1957年提出最大熵原理[12],即在满足所有给定约束的概率分布中,应选择最接近一致的概率分布,即熵最大的概率分布;二是相对熵(Relative Entropy)理论,是在早期由 Kullback(1959)提出的直接散度(Directed Divgenceer)基础上发展而来[13]。利用相对熵可以度量两个概率分布的接近程度。

信息熵的发展历程、主要理论及其应用在邱菀华、钟义信和罗伯特的著作中都有比较详细的论述[6-7,13]。自从将熵与信息联系起来之后,开拓了信息熵在经济学、管理学和社会科学等领域广泛的应用。按照信息熵理论[6-7],如果某事物具有 m 种状态,每种状态的概率为 P_i($i=1, 2, …, m$),则该

系统的信息熵定义为

$$H = -\sum_{i=1}^{m} p_i \ln p_i, \quad (1)$$

其中：$0 \leq p_i \leq 1, \sum p_i = 1$

系统的熵值高，则说明系统的混乱程度高，数据分布均匀，变异程度小，所包含的信息量小，极端情况是每种状态的概率相等，即 $p_i = 1/m$，熵取得最大值。系统的熵值小，则数据的变异程度大，所包含的信息量大。

根据最大熵原理，在事物自然状态或没有外力干涉的情况下，系统倾向熵增加；如果使得熵降低，必须对系统施加外力。对于反映某事物状态的数据系统，随机状态下应该是数据分布均匀，如果数据分布不均匀，变异程度大，往往是受某种系统因素决定，具有值得研究的原因存在。如本文的问题，当被调查者面对若干指标进行选择时，如果没有偏好性的影响，其数据分布是均匀的，各个选项之间没有差别，如果数据分布不均匀，以及各个选项之间具有差异，不同选项被选择的比率不同，则必然受到偏好性的影响。由此可见，熵理论的基本定义公式反映了人的偏好性，而要度量不同人或不同群体的偏好型，还要利用相对熵的概念。相对熵（Relative Entropy）的定义是基于两个概率分布的比值。如果有两个概率分布 P 和 Q，则将 P 对于 Q 的相对熵 $D(P:Q)$ 定义为

$$D(P:Q) = \sum_i P_i \ln \frac{P_i}{Q_i} \quad (2)$$

相对熵 $D(P:Q)$ 定义了概率分布 P 与概率分布 Q 之间的接近程度，相对熵的绝对值越小，二者越接近，极端情况是，如果 $P_i = Q_i$，则 $D(P:Q) = 0$。根据相对熵原理，如果要取得优化结果，在满足给定约束的所有概率分布中，集结的结果应该最接近各类人员的选择概率（先验概率）分布。

同时满足上述最大熵原理和相对熵原理的条件，显然解决了本研究数据分析中的两个问题，即最终的集结参数要反映整体性要求和人的偏好特点。符合最大熵原理，较好地反映了整体性要求，而符合相对熵原理，则反映了人的偏好特点。

三、问题与解决路径

（一）问题

上述对社会群体偏好型研究的要求可以转化为三方面具体目标：第一，分别度量不同群体的态度倾向程度；第二，按照不同群体的态度对变量进行排序；第三，度量不同态度群体的区别大小。

（二）问题的模型与解决目标

将某一现实问题转化为 j 个衡量指标，$j=1, 2, \cdots, k$，假设所有指标都具有共同数量的取值，最为常用的是5级或7级取值，典型的5级取值为[5]：（1）很不好；（2）不好；（3）一般；（4）较好；（5）很好。用数字1、2、3、4、5表示测量变量取值级别。每个被调查者记为 i，$i=1, 2, 3, \cdots n$，每个被调查者都对构成该问题的各个指标进行评价，所有被调查者的评价数据就构成了一个 $n \times m$ 阶矩阵 x。

$$x = (x_{ij})_{n \times k} = \begin{bmatrix} x_{11} & x_{12} & \cdots & x_{1k} \\ x_{21} & x_{22} & \cdots & x_{2k} \\ \cdots & \cdots & \cdots & \cdots \\ x_{n1} & x_{m2} & \cdots & x_{nk} \end{bmatrix} \quad (3)$$

同时被调查者又分为 g 类群体，$g = 1, 2, 3, \cdots m$。解决目标就是将所有原始数据 X 集结为一个能够代表这些数据的参数，前已述及，平均数和简单的比率统计就是这种经典参数，尽管具有其天然的优势，但是在反映人的偏好性方面具有局限性，而本方法希望在数据集结过程中，对于偏好明显的数据行给以比较大的权重，使其对最终结果具有较大的影响。

（三）模型构造

1. 基于相对熵方法的数据集结

针对不同群体对某事物若干指标计分评价后的数据分析，同决策的问题一样，本质上是一个数据集

结问题，即将以数字表示的许多人和群体的评价数据集结为一个参数，这个参数应该能够反映个人偏好，即每个人的偏好与该参数的距离最小，使得参与者的意见被最大程度地反映。由于每个人的偏好不同，要使得最终的集结参数与每个人的偏好平均最小，即极小化集结参数（决策结果）与个人偏好的不一致，最大化群体偏好的一致性，也就是最大化群体选择的一致性。这种优化问题在数学上被归为对模型求最优解。模型的建立依据两个原理，一是极大熵原理，二是相对熵原理。

根据极大熵原理，如果要取得优化结果，在满足给定约束的所有概率分布中，应该选择最接近一致分布的概率分布，即选择使熵最大的概率分布。

邱菀华[8]在解决群决策问题中提出了相对熵模型并给出了解。对于决策方案集合 $A = \{a_j, j = 1, 2, \cdots, n\}$；决策者群体集合 $E = \{e_i, i = 1, 2, \cdots, m\}$，$x_{ij}$为决策者$e_i$对方案$a_j$的评价值，假设评价值越大则越肯定该方案，集合 $W = \{w_i, i = 1, 2, \cdots, m\}$ 是决策者的权重集合，合计为1，规划模型 (p) 形式如式（4）。

$$(p)\begin{cases} \min Q(X_g) = \sum_{i=1}^{m} w_i \sum_{j=1}^{n} \left[\log x_{gj} - \log \frac{x_{ij}}{\sum_{j=1}^{n} x_{ij}}\right] x_{gj} \\ s.t. \sum_{j=1}^{n} x_{gj} = 1, \ x_{gj} > 0 \end{cases} \quad (4)$$

通过解此数学规划模型，得到规划问题 P 的最优解 $X_g^* = (X_{g1}^*, X_{g2}^*, \cdots, X_{gN}^*)^T$，称之为偏好量，如式（5）。

$$x_{gj}^* = \frac{\prod_{i=1}^{m} (b_{ij})^{w_i}}{\sum_{j=i}^{n} \prod_{i=1}^{m} (b_{ij})^{w_i}}, \ b_{ij} = \frac{x_{ij}}{\sum_{j=1}^{n} x_{ij}} \quad (5)$$

在群决策中，这个模型被成功地用于解决多个专家对某问题若干方案的评价数据集结问题，由于原理相同，完全可以将这一成果用于不同群体对某一社会问题的若干指标评价的数据分析，即求出上述 $n \times m$ 阶矩阵 x 的集结参数。

2. 基于相对熵方法的数据之间距离测量

偏好量是某群体数据的最终集结，尽管其中包含了群体的偏好因素，但仍是一种集中趋势，需要一个与之相应的参数度量其离散趋势，这种思路与平均数和标准差的构造思路类同。

（1）对诉求程度的度量。由于偏好量是一个相对指标，在数据表中任意i行的偏好量合计值为1，符合式（1）中的信息熵条件，所以可以用信息熵反映各行数据对于该行各个指标偏好量的离散程度。定义任意i行的偏好熵为H_g，根据式（1）得

$$H_g = -\sum_{j=1}^{n} x_{gj} \ln x_{gj}, \ s.t. \sum_{j=1}^{n} x_{gj} = 1, \ x_{gj} > 0 \quad (6)$$

偏好熵反映了某个体或群体对各个指标数据评价的离散程度，H_g越小，说明数据离散，所包含信息量大。反映到现实中，说明被调查者对不同指标的偏好区别程度大，其"爱憎分明"程度大，所要诉求的信息较多。反之，如果H_g越大，说明数据分布均匀，反映在现实中，就是被调查者对不同指标的偏好区别程度小，对各个指标的评价大体相同，可能所要诉求的信息较少。由此可见，偏好熵H_g的倒数，即$1/H_g$可以用于衡量"爱憎分明"程度，即诉求的强烈程度。

（2）分量对总量距离的度量。与平均数不同，偏好量是一个相对数，所以其单独的数据意义不大，有意义的偏好量数组，该数组合计值为1。比较不同偏好量数组的接近程度，实际是比较两组数据分布的距离。数据总体的偏好量数组为$X_g^* = (X_{g1}^*, X_{g2}^*, \cdots, X_{gj}^*)^T$，设某分量偏好量数组为$X_i^* = (X_{i1}^*, X_{i2}^*, \cdots, X_{ij}^*)^T$，可以依据式（2）度量二者的距离，这属于数学上的$K-L$测度。但是利用$K-L$测度要求符合一个条件，即：对任意$i$，有$P_i \geq Q_i$，以保证结论非负。为了解决这一问题，当然可以采用取绝对值的方法，不过数学上常不采用此方法，而是采用平方后再开方的方法。基于相对熵理论和数学惯例，定义两个分布，即分量X_i^*对总量X_g^*的距离D_i为

$$D_i = \sqrt{\sum_{j=1}^{m}(x_{ij}^* \ln \frac{x_{ij}^*}{x_{gj}^*})^2} \tag{7}$$

四、对证券监管效果的评价研究

中国大陆自1990年开始建立的证券市场，已经运行了20多年。在市场获得飞速发展的同时，社会对于监管效果问题存在广泛争议，所以必须经过对市场参与者的调查，明确回答三个问题：

第一，从总体上度量市场各方对证券监管效果的满意程度；

第二，按照市场参与者的评价结果，对衡量中国特色证券市场监管效果的主要指标进行排序；

第三，不同市场参与者的主要意见区别。

（一）测量变量的形成

将证券市场参与者分为5类群体进行调查，即监管者、一般投资者、上市公司、基金公司和券商，要求他们对如下5个指标进行评价。

（1）您认为监管部门以往对股市的监管政策是否见效？

（2）您认为以往股市暴跌时出台的一系列政策措施效果如何？

（3）您认为股权分置改革是否成功？

（4）2008年4月20日证监会发布的《上市公司解除限售存量股份转让指导意见》，实践证明如何？

（5）您认为证监会对市场操纵和内幕交易的监管政策及其实施是否成功？

答案是A、B、C、D四个选项之一，并赋以分值（括弧中数字），即

A. 非常成功（7）；B. 失败（1）；C. 没有完全成功（5）；D. 不清楚（3）。

这5个问题，其中前两个问题是从整体的角度调查监管效果，后三个问题是从具体政策执行的角度调查监管效果，本研究分析其中五类人共139份有效问卷数据。

（二）平均数与偏好量排序对比

将常用的平均数和本研究提出的偏好量汇集同一表中，以便对照，如表1所示。从表1中可以看出，不论是平均数排序还是偏好量排序，在本项目的合计上都是一致的，即题2＞题3＞题5＞题4＞题1，说明不论从绝对值的评价上还是相对偏好上，这个排序都是一致的，因为平均数强调的是各个指标单独评价的绝对值，而偏好量是从各个指标的联系上表现出的相对偏好程度，两个视角达成一致，进一步印证这个排序的可靠性。

表1　五类市场参与者针对证券监管问题的评价指标

		题1	题2	题3	题4	题5
监管者 （19人）	偏好量	0.130	0.259	0.219	0.203	0.188
	均值	3.32	5.42	4.68	4.37	4.05
一般投资者 （40人）	偏好量	0.145	0.242	0.236	0.191	0.186
	均值	3.25	4.50	4.15	3.55	3.65
上市公司 （32人）	偏好量	0.140	0.275	0.217	0.190	0.177
	均值	3.06	4.88	3.88	3.44	3.44
基金公司 （26人）	偏好量	0.125	0.280	0.198	0.196	0.200
	均值	3.23	5.69	4.15	4.15	4.15
券商 （22人）	偏好量	0.152	0.275	0.216	0.151	0.207
	均值	3.64	5.73	4.36	3.18	4.36
合计 （139人）	偏好量	0.139	0.264	0.219	0.187	0.190
	均值	3.27	5.13	4.19	3.69	3.86

题2是"您认为以往股市暴跌时出台的一系列政策措施效果如何？"，题1是"您认为监管部门以往对股市的监管政策是否见效？"，题3、题4和题5分别是关于三项具体政策的提问。调查结果说明被调

查者尽管对证券市场监管效果从总体上的评价程度和偏好程度都较低，但是对于在暴跌时的所谓"救市政策"的评价和偏好都明显最高。

从各个群体对各个指标的评价上看，多数情况下均值的排序与偏好量排序一致，但也有部分不一致的情况。一般投资者，即散户群体，其题5的平均数（3.65）大于题4的平均数（3.55），但是对题4的偏好值（0.191）大于对题5的偏好值（0.186），说明一般投资者对制止内幕交易措施的效果不满倾向实际更高。基金公司对题1的平均分（3.64）明显高于对题4的平均分（3.18），但是对题1的评价偏好（0.152）只是略高于对题4的评价偏好（0.151），说明基金公司在绝对值的评价方面对二者评价的差距较大，但是其相对偏好相差并不大。

（三）通过显著性检验发现主要矛盾

方差分析表明，各个不同群体分别对5个问题评价的平均分都没有显著性差异。再利用独立样本比率之差检验的方法，分别对5类群体对各问题的偏好量进行两两之间差异显著性检验，取显著性系数为0.05，同样未发现显著性差异。这样就得到了一个结论，从平均数的绝对值评价和偏好量的相对评价这两个角度来看，市场参与者的5类群体对各个问题的评价都没有显著差别，说明这5类群体态度基本一致。

再从平均数和偏好量这两个角度考查5个问题之间的差异性。用t检验方法检验各个问题配对的平均值差异，偏好量是一种比率，同样可以用比率之差的显著性检验，为了便于比较，将检验结果合并在表2之中。

表2　各个问题之间平均数的差异检验和偏好量差异检验

问题组合	平均值			偏好值		
	二者之差	Sig.（双侧）	差异性	二者之差	Sig.（双侧）	差异性
题1～题2	-1.856	.000	显著	-0.125	.000	显著
题1～题3	-.921	.000	显著	-0.08	.005	显著
题1～题4	-.417	.078	不显著	-0.048	.095	不显著
题1～题5	-.590	.018	显著	-0.051	.075	不显著
题2～题3	.935	.000	显著	0.045	.245	不显著
题2～题4	1.439	.000	显著	0.077	.052	显著
题2～题5	1.266	.000	显著	0.074	.061	不显著
题3～题4	.504	.003	显著	0.032	.373	不显著
题3～题5	.331	.075	不显著	0.029	.418	不显著
题4～题5	-.173	.312	不显著	-0.003	.928	不显著

从表2中可以看出，5个问题共有10对组合，对于平均数来说，只有三对问题组合，即题1～题4、题3～题5和题4～题5之间的差异不显著，其他7对组合的差异都显著。而对于偏好量，只有三对问题组合之间的差异显著，而且这三对之间的平均数差异也显著，也就是说，只有三对问题组合，即题1～题2、题1～题3和题2～题4，从分数的绝对值高低和相对偏好这两个角度考查，其差异都显著。可以认为，这三对问题之间的差距即整个问题系统的主要矛盾，而定性解释和分析的重点应以这三对问题为主。前已述及，平均数比较和偏好量比较，都是题1＞题2，说明调查者尽管对证券市场监管效果从总体上的评价程度和偏好程度都最低，但是对于在暴跌时的所谓"救市政策"的评价和偏好都明显最高。而此处两方面的检验都表示这种差距的显著性，说明这个差距具有必然因素。定性分析和现实经验也完全可以证实这点，当股市发生暴跌时，管理层的救市政策是最受欢迎的政策，同时也是短期内最有作用的政策，但总体上对监管效果的评价不高。当然本文只是定量地描述和客观分析被调查者的态度，至于这种态度是否理性和有利则不在本文讨论范围内。

再看题1～题3的差异，题1是"您认为监管部门以往对股市的监管政策是否见效？"，题3是考查被调查者对"《上市公司解除限售存量股份转让指导意见》实践效果"的态度。从两方面看，题3的分数都大于题1的分数，而且显著性检验证明差异显著，同样说明市场参与者对待二者的态度本质不同。

实际上,《上市公司解除限售存量股份转让指导意见》,俗称"大小非限售政策",也是一种减轻股市压力、缓解下跌的政策,被许多市场人士认为也是一种救市政策,所以问题3类同问题2,其被评价的分值仅次于问题2,但是如果仅依靠对平均数的显著性检验,对于二者差异显著的结论解释起来似乎理由欠缺,现实依据不充分,而依据偏好量的差异显著性检验,二者偏好差异不显著的结论正好对于现实经验形成互相印证。

题4是"您认为证监会对市场操纵和内幕交易的监管政策及其实施是否成功",就两方面的评价分数排序,题2大于题4,而且其差异显著。尽管题4被评价较低,但只与被评价位居第一位的题2具有显著区别,而与其他问题的区别都不显著。

在5个问题共10对关系之间,解释了上述3对问题之间关系即抓住了主要矛盾。如果没有偏好量及其显著性检验的引入,面对平均数差异显著的7对问题,如果都进行解释,则过于烦琐,不但没有抓住主要矛盾,而且也与实际不尽相符,如果不进行解释而只是展示数据结果,则显然分析得不够深入。同时又不能凭主观意愿挑选出几种关系人为地认定其为主要矛盾进行解释。由此看出,不但偏好量的引入解决了在数据分析中反映人类思维的整体性和偏好性特点,而且对偏好量的显著性检验和对平均数的显著性检验共同使用,为掌握问题的主要矛盾提供了科学依据。

(四)对不同群体的特征分析

如果仅依据平均数体系进行分析,那么就只能是局限在对某个问题的平均数是否具有差异,或局限在对总体平均数是否具有差异,而没有反映不同群体分别对各个问题评价分数的分布差异,这种分数的分布差异是由于人类思维的整体性和偏好性所决定的。通过本文构造的指标,即偏好熵和中心距,可以解决本问题。

由表3可以看出,中心距最大的群体是券商,为0.041,仔细观察券商和基金公司对各个问题偏好量的排序并与总体和其他群体比较,会发现一个有趣的现象。在题4和题5的偏好量排序上,监管者、一般投资人和上市公司这三类群体的评价,都是题4>题5,基金公司的评价是二者很接近,只是题5微大于题4,只有券商的评价是比较明显的题5大于题4,基金和券商的人数比率合计仅占被调查者的35%,就导致了总体结果是题5大于题4,足见券商对总体结果的影响。

表3 五类群体数据分布的离散性

群体	比率(w_i)	偏好熵(H_g)	中心距
监管者	0.137	1.59	0.020
一般投资人	0.288	1.59	0.029
上市公司	0.23	1.58	0.017
基金公司	0.187	1.58	0.032
券商	0.158	1.58	0.041
合计	1	1.59	0.000

五、结束语

(一)主要结论

在比较分析不同群体的社会态度和倾向的研究中,采用常规统计方法具有一定局限性,而熵理论和相对熵方法提供了较好的解决问题的途径。通过引入基于相对熵理论的偏好量,弥补了以往基于平均数、方差和比率统计的分析方法的不足,反映了人类思维中整体性和偏好性这两个特点。平均数和偏好量这两个参数共同使用,可以从评价的绝对值和相对偏好这两个方面、两个角度反映被调查者的态度。

采用基于相对熵方法研究不同群体的偏好,可以发现以传统统计学方法难以发现的微妙规律,以证券监管效果的数据分析证明了这点。在分析监管者、一般投资人、上市公司、基金公司和券商这5类对象的基本特点时,在通过方差分析没有发现显著差异后,本文基于相对熵理论构造了中心距这一参数,从整体上度量不同群体对各个问题评价的数据分布的差异,由此发现了不同群体的差异。其中,监管者和上市公司的数据分布最接近,也最接近总体数据分布;券商的数据分布与总体数据分布的差距最大,可以认为在这5类群体中,券商是最"离群"的群体,与券商最接近的群体是基金公司。此结论对进一步的研究起到了重要指导作用。

在通过对各个问题之间偏好量的显著性检验中,可以发现被调查者在某方面意愿诉求的主要矛盾,而这一矛盾常常被数据的整体特征掩盖。对证券监管效果的研究表明:尽管对证券市场监管效果从总体上的评价程度和偏好程度都较低,但是对于缓解股市暴跌的政策效果评价和偏好却都明显较高。

(二)政策建议

1. 依据科学的模型调节市场供求关系

尽管各个参与群体的诉求有所差异,但是达成共识的愿望就是不希望市场长期下跌,并希望在长期非理性下跌后采取"救市措施"。尽管以往的"救市措施"临时性强,缺乏系统性,但是都受到市场各方的好评。鉴于参与者达成共识的呼声和以往的经验教训,建议制定长期维护市场的措施,既要保护市场的上涨与国民经济的发展相适应,同时又要具有一定的规范性,给市场以一定的预期。本文建议研究制定IPO的发行量与股票价格指数相配合的数学模型,并公开发布。在市场低迷时,依据模型计算的IPO发行量较小甚至停止,而当市场涨幅较大时IPO发行量较大。依据模型控制IPO发行量是一个连续的调节过程,可以有效地控制暴涨暴跌,同时又避免了以往临时性的、人治性的"救市措施"的不足,将调整供求关系以科学的方法纳入法制化的轨道。

2. 建立监管者听取和采纳多类群体意见的制度

通过中心距分析表明,监管者与上市公司的距离最接近,而与其他群体的距离明显较远。由于基于熵理论的计算方法是从整体上考虑各个指标要素,所以此处可以理解为,我国的证券监管者在价值观、思想意识、政策意见和情感方面与上市公司最接近,与券商的差距最大。这种定量分析的结论与定性经验和我国证券市场的发展历史基本吻合。改革开发后所建立的证券市场初衷就是"为国企解困服务",时至今日没有根本改变,又包括了为民营企业创业融资服务。这种指导思想在当今明显过于片面,不但违背"三公原则",而且明显违背中共中央的群众思想路线。正是在这种过分重视融资而轻视投资的思想指导下,导致我国证券市场长期"熊冠全球"。因此,必须从制度上保证监管者重视并定期听取其他群体,包括券商、基金公司、投资者等群体的意见。

参考文献

[1] (美)弗洛德·J. 福勒. 调查问卷的设计与评估 [M]. 蒋逸民,等,译. 重庆:重庆大学出版社,2010.
[2] 郝旭光. 中国证券市场监管有效性研究 [J]. 中国工业经济,2011,(06):16-25.
[3] 宋云玲,李志文,纪新伟. 从业绩预告违规看中国证券监管的处罚效果 [J]. 金融研究,2011,(06):136-149.
[4] 郝旭光,朱冰,张士玉. 中国证券市场监管政策效果研究——基于问卷调查的分析 [J]. 管理世界,2012,(07):44-53.
[5] 何大义. 熵在数据分析中的应用研究 [J]. 统计与决策,2005,(8):27-29.
[6] 邱菀华. 管理决策与应用熵学 [M]. 北京:机械工业出版社,2002.
[7] 钟义信. 信息科学原理(第三版)[M]. 北京:北京邮电大学出版社,2002.
[8] 张士玉,郝旭光. 基于关联规则的调查问卷多项选择题分析 [J]. 图书情报工作,2011,55(10):41-45.
[9] Arrow K J. Social Choice and Decision Individual Values [M]. Yale University Press, New Haven, 1963.
[10] Han Jia Wei, Kamber Micheline. Data Mining Concepts and Techniques [M]. New York: Academic Press, 2001.
[11] Shannon C E. A mathematical theory of communication [J]. Bell System Technical Journal, 1948, 27: 623-656.
[12] Jaynes E T. Information theory and statistical mechanics [J]. The Physical Review, 1957, 106 (2): 620-630.
[13] Robert M. Gray. Entropy and Information Theory (Second Edition) [M]. Springer Berlin Heidelberg, 2011.
[14] Agrawal R, Imielinski T, Swami A. Mining association rules between sets of items in large databases [M] //In: Proceeding of 1993 ACM SIGMOD International Conference on Management of Data. Washington DC, 1993. 207-216.
[15] Hwarg C L, Lin M L. Group Decision Making Under Multiple Criteria [J]. Spring-Verlag, 1987.
[16] Toque, Carole Terraza, Virginie. Time Series Factorial Models with Uncertainty Measures: Applications to ARMA Processes

and Financial Data [J]. Communications in Statistics: Theory & Methods, 2011, 40 (9): 1533 – 1544.

[17] Zhao K, Karsai M, Bianconi G. Entropy of dynamical social networks [J]. Plos One, 2011, 6 (12): 28116.

[18] Hu M, Liang H. Adaptive multiscale entropy analysis of multivariate neural data [J]. IEEE Transactions On Bio – Medical Engineering. 2012, 59 (1): 12 – 15.

[19] Hollisaaz MT, Khedmat H, Effatmanesh – Nik M, Yousefvand M, Mansouri S, Saadat SH, Rafati – Shaldehi H, Ebrahiminia M. Data – entropy analysis of renal transplantation data [J]. Transplantation Proceedings. 2007, 39 (4): pp. 930 – 931.

[20] van Wieringen WN, van der Vaart AW. Statistical analysis of the cancer cell's molecular entropy using high – throughput data [J]. Bioinformatics. 2011, 27 (4): 556 – 563.

[21] Richman, Joshua S. Sample Entropy Statistics and Testing for Order in Complex Physiological Signals [J]. Communications in Statistics: Theory & Methods. 2007, 36 (5): 1005 – 1019.

[22] Razmkhah M., Morabbi H., Ahmadi J. Comparing two sampling schemes based on entropy of record statistics [J]. Statistical Papers. 2012, 53 (1): 95 – 106.

基于资本增值的知识协同效益评价研究

陈建斌　郭彦丽　徐凯波

引　言

我国服务外包一直面临着领域专注、产业升级、价值链"微笑曲线"攀升的发展"瓶颈"[1]，究其深层原因主要有两个：一是发包企业向接包企业知识转移存在着认知差异、信息不对称、合作关系不稳定、机会主义等天然障碍[2]；二是接包企业内部由于项目团队之间的隔离、团队成员跨国分布（客户现场和后方技术）、隐性知识默会性等所形成的知识共享和知识转移的高阻滞[3-5]。

知识协同是近年来知识管理研究的热点[6]。知识协同微观上强调知识转移的时效性和准确性，强调高效知识协作[7]；宏观上强调"1+1>2"效应，强调知识资产增值[8]。知识协同为服务外包企业提升竞争力提供了新思路：强调知识资本增值评估，引导业务领域知识的快速积累，部分解决客户知识依赖问题，并有利于垂直行业优势的培养；强调社会资本增值评估，增强知识在员工、客户、团队之间的流转与协作，部分解决隐性知识转移困境，并有利于员工/客户信任的培养，提高协同效应。

本文基于接包企业视角，首先对服务外包虚拟团队及其知识协作特点进行分析，探讨知识协同的需求背景；其次，梳理知识协同内涵，结合虚拟团队知识活动特点，以知识资本与社会资本理论为支撑，探讨虚拟团队知识协同效率和效果评价，进而构建知识协同评价指标体系。

1 研究综述

1.1 服务外包知识转移与绩效评价的研究

服务外包是一种包含发包商和接包商不断互动的、复杂的跨组织合作关系网络，表现出明显的关系导向特征，项目完成期间伴随着双方不断的正式和非正式的知识传递行为，是一种知识密集的协同工作模式[3]。在知识传递过程中，接包商处于从属地位，需要不断努力从发包商获取业务知识，并进行内外知识整合以交付符合客户需求的知识产品。但是，接包商一直存在着较大的知识整合困境[2]，由于知识复杂性、契约不完备性、组织差异性及客户知识保护行为等因素，知识传递并不顺利。

此前研究多集中于揭示接发包商之间知识传递的影响因素，并对知识转移与外包绩效（或外包成功）之间关系进行探讨，如Lee、Karhu等、Liu等、田野等[9-12]，试图解决接发包商之间、项目团队之间的知识转移问题，尤其是隐性知识转移难题。研究表明，接发包企业之间的知识共享、接包商的知识获取能力均对外包绩效或外包成功有着重要作用。

对于接包商的外包绩效，一致认为项目质量、项目成本、客户满意是衡量其成功的关键指标[3,13]。社会资本经常被当作前置条件，考察其与知识共享/转移、知识管理能力、外包绩效之间的关系[14]。但是，知识转移/共享对知识资本和社会资本的影响，外包项目成功后的知识资本和社会资本的增值，一直未能纳入绩效评价的研究范畴。

1.2 知识协同研究概述

最早提出"知识协同"概念的Karienzig认为，知识协同是一种组织战略方法[15]，可以动态集结内外部系统、商业过程、技术和关系，以最大化商业绩效。其后，在企业层面分别把知识协同定义为一种知识活动、组织能力或管理模式和战略手段[7,16-17]；在产业或供应链层面，则界定为一种特殊的关系模

［基金项目］北京市哲学社会科学规划项目（11JGB039）；组织部优秀人才资助项目（2012D005022000004）；北京市教委人才强教深化计划项目（PHR201108389）。

［作者简介］陈建斌（1970—），男，博士，教授，北京联合大学商务学院科研处处长。研究方向：知识管理等。

式[18]。目前研究多集中于知识协同过程的分析，如表1所示。

表1　国内知识协同过程研究文献综述

作者	知识协同过程	备注
曾德明、文小科等（2010）[19]	知识获取、转移、创造实现新知识的生成和创新	供应链
王聪颖、管晓东等（2009）[20]	发现、创新、传播、观察再到发现的闭环过程	集群环境
佟泽华（2012）[6]	包含知识协同需求、确定知识协同主题、知识协同活动、知识协同成果等几个过程	
施慧斌（2008）[21]	知识协同过程模型表示为4元组：知识协同环境、知识协同活动、知识流、知识协同的目标	
吴绍波等（2008）[22]	知识协同过程包括知识共享、知识转移、组织学习、知识创造	
王悦（2009）[23]	知识协同的核心过程为知识获取、知识发现、知识处理、知识传播与共享、知识使用和创新	

综上，可以得出以下结论：

（1）知识创造是知识协同的目标。

（2）知识转化（包括知识共享、转移、内外、外化等）是知识协同的有效构成。这也意味着现有关于知识转化影响因素的研究成果是知识协同研究的基础。

（3）知识协同过程中有知识搜寻、知识转移、知识创新等多种微观过程。

1.3　知识协同的测度

施慧斌从系统角度分析了知识协同效应的内涵[21]，指出知识协同效应是"预期目标与预期目标增量效应之和，反映了知识协同活动过程中各个阶段相变的积累"：

$$E = f(k_1, k_2, \cdots, k_n) + \varphi(r_1, r_2, \cdots, r_m) \tag{1}$$

式中：E 为知识协同总效应；$f(k_1, k_2, \cdots, k_n)$ 表示预期目标效应函数；k_i（$i=1, 2, \cdots, n$）是依附于行为主体的知识单元；$\varphi(r_1, r_2, \cdots, r_m)$ 表示预期目标增量函数，是协同效应增值；r_i（$i=1, 2, \cdots, m$）是协同过程中的知识活动。

王慧认为[24]，企业集团内部知识协同效应与主体（A）；客体（O）；媒介（M）以及情境（C）四个因素有关。因此，企业集团知识协同效应可表示为一个数学模型：

$$P = F(A, O, M, C) \tag{2}$$

上述研究初步探讨了协同效应的组成要素，但仍处于概念层面，缺乏深入地探讨。比如，增量的性质是什么？增量部分如何测度？如何促进增量的实现？因此，还需要对知识协同机理的进一步分析和创造性的研究设计。

2　知识协同与资本增值

服务外包商业模式导致虚拟团队知识协同的困境[25]。其跨时空分布造成了语境缺乏和隐性知识转移障碍；跨组织形态造成了管理与协调障碍；跨文化造成了知识情境障碍。知识协同是一种克服诸多障碍、多主体协调一致、知识转移高度有效的协作状态。

2.1　知识协同的本质

知识协同是团队知识协作过程和结果的综合反映。在微观层面，Leijen 和 Baets 指出[26]，知识协同是一个知识请求者首先认识到自己没有能力解决某个问题，而另一知识提供者恰好有这方面的能力，如能达成共识，则可以整合双方知识，达到解决问题的目的。在宏观层面，陈昆玉和陈昆琼认为[8]，企业通过整合组织的内外部知识资源，使组织学习、利用和创造知识的整体效益大于各独立组成部分总和的效应，它的目的在于获得"1+1＞2"的知识协同效应。知识协同在微观上强调协作的"恰当性"，在宏观上强调效果的"增值性"。

综合上述宏微观理解，知识协同四个特点明显与知识转移、知识共享存在不同[27]。

（1）要素综合性：知识主体、知识客体、时间、环境综合一体。

（2）要素准确性：知识传递的时间、对象、空间的恰当准确。

（3）要素动态性：协同过程与时间密切相关。

（4）知识增值性：目标是创造更具价值的新知识，同时实现企业社会资本和知识资本的增值。

2.2 知识协同与社会资本

社会资本最初被定义为个体利用社会关系网络获取外部资源的一种能力[28]。此后，其概念和范围延伸至团体、企业、区域、国家等层面，强调它是内部成员通过社会机制获得的一种联合行动能力[29]。柯江林等指出[30]，社会资本无论宏观微观，都具有资源动用能力和社会关系网络嵌入性两个关键的特征。据此，本文认为，虚拟团队社会资本是指嵌入团队成员的关系网络中、通过关系网络可获得的、来自于关系网络的资源集合体，代表了团队成员获取和交换资源的能力。

知识协同的目的是创造新知识，知识创造本质上是一个社会化过程。在 SECI 模型中，知识创造四阶段中的三个阶段，即社会化、外在化、组合化，都包含着个体间的社会互动[31]。个体间的社会互动必然导致社会网络的形成，知识创造便在知识网络中产生。知识个体通过协同问题求解触发了相互之间的连接，新的连接导致新知识。进一步，社会资本是由社会连接和社会互动所产生的利益、价值或资产等，当分析知识创造时，研究者都将社会资本作为主要研究要素之一[32]。现有不少针对知识创造所进行的实证研究，往往都是从社会资本对知识创造的影响入手的[33-35]。

服务外包虚拟团队成员间只有不断通过所属社会网络获取社会资本，才能克服由于团队结构特点带来的诸多障碍创造新知识。可见，虚拟团队的社会资本对知识创新有促进作用，有利于知识协同；知识协同意味着知识网络中连接的增强和新连接的增加，促进了社会资本的增值。

2.3 知识协同与知识资本

2.3.1 知识资本及其构成

知识资本的本质是企业拥有或者控制的知识和能力，是组织中隐性知识以及能被组织明文化或结构化的显性知识的总和。目前知识资本的研究重点集中在其构成、各部分与企业绩效关系等方面[36]。研究表明，知识资本对企业绩效有正向影响，但各部分贡献不一；人力资本只有与结构资本相结合，才能产生应有效益。张丹等研究了 IT 业上市公司知识资本与企业绩效之间的关系[37]，发现影响程度由高到低依次为关系资本、人力资本、结构资本。

与上述方法不同，王大勇根据知识的显性和隐性分类[38]，把企业的知识资本划分为显性和隐性两种。服务外包中，接包企业从发包企业获得的行业知识既对当前项目有益，也对长期专注领域发展有利；每个外包项目的完成，总是伴随着一定过程成果增补进入规则库、模块库、知识库等。因此，为便于研究知识的协同效益，本文采纳显性知识和隐性知识资本的二分法。

2.3.2 知识协同与知识资本的关系

知识资本包括所有经过知识的获取、创新以及有价值关系的建立等智力活动所创造的资产。而知识协同中知识工人的能力得到提升，知识得以更新和扩展，企业的组织环境和业务流程得到改善，交付知识产品提升了客户关系，这些都属于企业知识资本的增值范畴。

从现有文献看，知识协同与知识资本之间的关系还未引起业界研究的重视，知识协同如何促进知识资本的增值，在知识资本各个组份之间的作用大小及其作用机理等，需进一步展开。另外，由于服务外包企业知识密集的特点，知识协同的绩效对企业知识资本、尤其是隐性知识资本的积累与增值影响比较明显，如何进一步通过企业知识资本来判断企业知识协同绩效，需进一步研究。

2.4 知识协作效率与知识协同

2.4.1 知识协作效率

由于服务外包虚拟团队的特殊性，团队成员需要通过频繁的社会互动与沟通、共享语言与目标等，对团队内部知识进行有效认知，形成基于"谁知道什么""谁知道谁"的协作状态[39]。知识协同所实现的"恰当性""有效协同"与上述状态有基本相同的内涵，并且由社会资本和知识资本共同决定了这种状态的有效性。

根据系统论，知识协同是众多微观知识传输、转化的有序表现，知识协作的时效性和准确性决定了这种状态的有序化程度。在知识流量相对稳定的企业系统中,知识协作的时效性和准确性是两个难以同时满足的量。知识传递过程中,一个量的增加总是以牺牲另一个量为代价。增加知识流通的路径和层次可以有效提高知识传输的准确性,却延缓了知识流通;反之,又会使知识流通的时效性增加而准确性降低。因此,当评价和研究企业知识系统有序度时,必须综合考察时效性和准确性。

2.4.2 知识资本、社会资本与知识协作效率

研究表明,企业社会资本对知识获取或知识共享具有显著的正向影响[40]。反过来,知识活动在人与人之间加强了联系,增进了信任,推动了共享认知,因此也可以推论:知识资本对社会资本也有显著正向影响。

知识协作效率由知识流通时效性与准确性共同决定。知识资本提供了知识客体的数量和质量,社会资本提供了知识流通的路径和层次,影响着人们有限时间内搜寻到正确知识的能力,因此影响着知识传输的准确性和时效性。根据学习曲线理论,随着知识资本和社会资本的增加,知识传输的准确性和时效性将随之提高;当知识资本与社会资本增加到一定程度时,知识搜寻、鉴别成本将递增,知识协作效率边际递减。

2.5 知识协同的效果与效率

综合知识协同与知识资本、社会资本、知识协作效率关系的讨论,知识协同既表现为协同效果的获取(知识资本、社会资本增值),也表现为协作效率的提高(准确性与时效性的提高),存在着一定的相关关系。基于此,本文构建知识协同效益的概念分析如图1所示。

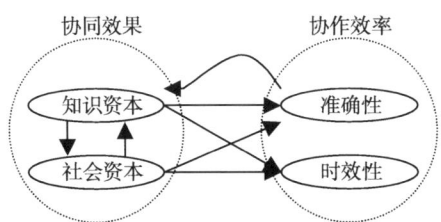

图 1 知识协同概念分析图

3 知识协同效益评价

3.1 知识协同效益评价指标

3.1.1 知识协同效果的度量

知识协同的效果从知识资本和社会资本的增值两个方面进行测度。

(1) 知识资本增值的度量。由于知识资本的共享性、非损耗性,知识协同效果除了交付给客户的最终知识产品外,内含的知识成果同时成为企业知识资本的增值部分,表现为个人、团队能力的提高、经验的积累、流程的改善,也表现为显性知识的增加(经验总结、过程文档、知识库等的增加)。根据野中郁次郎的分类模型(见表2)[41],显性知识资本的增值,主要测量的是知识协同最终形成的、被组织或团队共同拥有的知识成果,如专利、工艺、章程等,程序库、规则库、知识库、案例库等可复用知识单元的增加;隐性知识资本的增值,主要测量个体经验和技巧的增加、团队能力的提升、组织文化和惯例的改善等。

表 2 野中郁次郎关于知识的分类模型

分类	个人层次	群体层次	组织层次	跨组织层次
显性知识	知识积累	绩效分析文件	组织章程	供应商的专利和工艺文件
隐性知识	跨文化沟通技巧	团队协调	企业文化	顾客对产品的态度和期望

(2) 社会资本增值的度量。Nahapiet 和 Ghoshal 将企业社会资本分为三个维度[32],即结构、关系和认知。知识协同过程中,结构维度表现为知识主体之间的联系趋强、连接增加;关系维度表现为信任、互惠、尊重认可增强,语言、立场、观点趋于一致;认知维度表现为规则、规范更为明确。这些增量,就形成了社会资本总量的增加。因此,本文关于社会资本增值的测量,主要从社会互动、信任、共享认知三个变量的变化进行测度[40]。

3.1.2 知识协作效率的度量

曹勇等在研究隐性知识转化效果测度时[42],提出了包含五个方面的影响因素层次结构图(见图2)。在不考虑知识转移主体能力和客体载体的情况下,隐性知识转移的效率主要受技术转移平台(知识距离、准则距离、空间距离、关系距离)的影响。

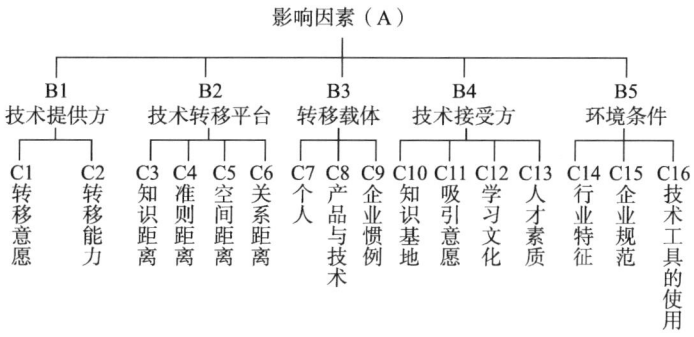

图 2　隐性知识转移效果影响因素的层次结构图

研究表明,影响知识获取的关键因素有知识源转移意愿、知识可达性和知识吸收能力。其中知识可达性,除了受知识属性约束外,更受知识网络连通性的约束;知识吸收能力则很大程度上取决于知识关联度[42]。要高效获取所需要的知识,准确性方面需要考虑可获取资源的丰富度和关联度、解决问题协作的次数;及时性方面需要考虑搜寻知识的时间、知识转移的时间以及技术的可靠性。

综合以上论述,本文提出知识协同效益的评价指标体系及其含义如表3所示。

表 3　知识协同效益评价指标体系

构念	变量	维度及其表征	参考文献
知识协同效果	社会资本增值	社会互动增强:连接强度增强、新连接增加	刘佳佳(2013)[40]
		信任增强:信任、互惠、认可、归属	
		共享认知增强:共同的语言、目标、观点	
	知识资本增值	显性知识资本增值:专利/工艺/流程/模块/知识/案例库等增加量	HedlundG.,Nonaka I.(1993)[41]
知识协作效率	准确性	隐性知识资本增值:个体经验和技巧的增加、团队能力的提升、组织文化和惯例的改善	
		知识资源可获性、丰富性与关联性	曹勇,等(2010)[42]
	时效性	解决问题所需协作的次数	张晓棠,等(2012)[43]
		知识搜寻时间、知识转移时间、技术可靠性	

3.2　因子分析

为了验证表3中的综合测量指标,本文有针对性地选取北京市IT服务外包公司进行了问卷调研,共回收有效问卷158份。回收数据的描述性统计结果见表4,其中97.5%的被调查者年龄在40岁以下,87.3%的被调查者学历在本科以上,这符合IT行业从业者的年龄特征和学历结构。而被调查者所在团队属于研发团队的占到了38%,属于服务团队的占到了44.9%;且91.3%的团队规模小于50人。

表 4　描述性统计

变量	题项	占比/%
性别	男	55.4
	女	44.6
年龄	≤30岁	46.2
	31—40岁	51.3
	41—50岁	1.9
	>50岁	0.6

续表

变量	题项	占比/%
学历	专科及以下	12.7
	本科	68.4
	硕士及以上	18.9
团队类型	研发团队	38
	服务团队	44.9
	科研团队	7.0
	非任务型合作团队	7.6
	其他	2.5
团队规模	≤10 人	36.7
	11—30 人	41.8
	31—50 人	14.6
	51—100 人	5.7
	>100 人	1.2

被调查者的职位分布比较广泛，其中 CEO、高层经理、主管层次的管理约占 20%；研发工程师约占 30%；测试人员约占 10%；运营、培训、数据管理、市场推广等人员约占 30%，科研人员及其他一般员工约占 10%。

为了检验数据的可靠性进行了信度检验，经检验 α 值等于 0.907，大于 0.9，数据可靠，可以用于后续分析。且 KMO 检验结果显示，KMO 值等于 0.806，大于 0.8，小于 0.9，适合进行因子分析，因此采用 SPSS 进行了探索性因子分析（EFA），共提取出 7 个因子，其解释的总方差及旋转成分矩阵见表 5 和表 6。

表 5 解释的总方差

成分	初始特征值			提取平方和载入			旋转平方和载入成分		
	合计	方差比/%	累积/%	合计	方差比/%	累积/%	合计	方差比/%	累积/%
1	8.411	33.643	33.643	8.411	33.643	33.643	3.416	13.663	13.663
2	2.222	8.887	42.531	2.222	8.887	42.531	3.022	12.088	25.751
3	1.840	7.359	49.890	1.840	7.359	49.890	2.608	10.432	36.184
4	1.459	5.838	55.728	1.459	5.838	55.728	2.540	10.162	46.346
5	1.302	5.207	60.935	1.302	5.207	60.935	2.207	8.830	55.176
6	1.174	4.694	65.629	1.174	4.694	65.629	2.010	8.039	63.214
7	1.149	4.596	70.225	1.149	4.596	70.225	1.753	7.011	70.225

注：提取方法：主成分分析，下同。

表 6 旋转成分矩阵

项目名称	成分						
	1	2	3	4	5	6	7
互相帮助	0.765	0.110	−0.040	0.023	0.028	0.115	0.042
相互尊重/信任	0.726	0.137	0.309	−0.016	0.131	−0.070	0.269
容易谅解	0.707	0.138	0.268	0.153	−0.094	−0.097	0.256
自由分享	0.673	0.164	−0.030	0.199	0.225	0.166	0.154

续表

项目名称	成分						
	1	2	3	4	5	6	7
任务目标一致	0.669	-0.046	0.141	0.109	0.254	0.272	0.048
合作默契	0.588	0.252	0.203	0.037	0.264	0.346	-0.033
知识交换途径便捷	0.132	0.832	0.065	0.142	0.182	0.030	0.061
交流和沟通及时	0.212	0.788	0.094	0.208	0.076	0.110	0.059
交流平台/工具统一	-0.009	0.787	0.194	0.117	0.182	0.082	0.055
资源获取快速	0.265	0.620	0.124	0.244	-0.108	0.212	0.257
协同文化增强	0.154	0.111	0.829	0.175	0.185	0.107	0.136
流程/制度完善	0.170	0.031	0.804	0.188	0.026	0.300	0.069
分享知识的氛围	0.131	0.327	0.652	0.044	0.223	0.100	0.048
能得到需要的资源	0.049	0.170	0.019	0.863	0.026	0.015	0.090
准确的知识技术支持	0.185	0.130	0.064	0.806	-0.011	0.019	0.246
成员提供恰当的支持	0.014	0.140	0.261	0.622	0.161	0.128	0.025
统一的共享知识库	0.158	0.388	0.221	0.556	0.143	0.098	-0.240
积累管理经验	0.112	0.090	0.116	0.016	0.846	0.148	0.023
任务完成高效	0.299	0.209	0.123	0.286	0.662	0.097	0.076
相互讨论的习惯	0.059	0.292	0.491	0.150	0.530	-0.107	0.217
积累了新知识	0.164	0.073	0.210	-0.044	0.505	0.394	0.145
积累了文档资料	0.187	0.151	0.284	0.148	0.073	0.820	-0.030
积累了案例资料	0.130	0.138	0.057	0.053	0.204	0.788	0.254
增加了新成员	0.258	0.067	0.159	0.081	0.050	0.042	0.805
与其他团队建立合作	0.202	0.194	0.090	0.174	0.203	0.255	0.755

注：旋转法：具有Kaiser标准化的正交旋转法；旋转在7次迭代后收敛。

从表6可以看出，25个题项与7个因子之间的关系。其中25个题项为测量变量，7个因子为潜变量。结合本文在表3中提到的测量指标，以上7个因子分别是：因子1为隐性社会资本增值，包括信任和共享认知增强；因子7为显性社会资本增值，指社会互动增强；因子3和因子5为隐性知识资本增值，其中因子3表示组织层次的隐性知识资本增值，而因子5则表示个体层次的知识资本增值；因子6为显性知识资本增值；因子2为知识协同的时效性，因子4表示知识协作的准确性。修正后的知识协同效益评价体系如表7所示。

表7 修正后的知识协同效益综合评价体系

构念	变量	意义
知识协同效果	隐性社会资本增值	信任和共享认知增强：信任、互惠、认可、一致性、归属
	显性社会资本增值	社会互动增强
	隐性知识资本增值（个体）	个体经验和技巧的增加、团队能力的提升
	隐性知识资本增值（组织）	组织文化和惯例的改善
	显性知识资本增值	显性知识资本增值：专利/工艺/流程、模块/知识/案例库等增加量
知识协作效率	准确性	知识资源可获得性、丰富性与关联性
		解决问题所需协作的次数
	时效性	知识搜寻时间、知识转移时间、技术可靠性

3.3 知识协同度量方法的应用

由于知识本身的精确度量存在较大的困难，与知识相关的度量方法均存在较多的缺陷，既难以定量把握知识活动的客观成果，也难以进行企业、团队之间的纵横向比较。本文关于知识协同概念的讨论及其效益评价方法的研究虽无法根本突破这种困境，但主要应用意义在于：

（1）全方位理解知识协同本质，指导企业实践。拓宽和深化了"知识协同"的内涵，有利于企业管理者综合运用技术和管理手段优化知识资源的配置，提升知识活动的效率和水平。

（2）为知识协同研究提供理论借鉴。为具象化研究提供了理论借鉴。以此为基础，可以进行知识协同影响因素的研究、演化路径的研究等，并能够实现一定技术支持下定性讨论与定量测度相结合的综合研究。

知识存在的形式多样，难以进行定量测度。但在 Web2.0 环境下，尤其是企业 2.0 在各类组织内部的推广应用，为知识协同的定量研究提供了可能。企业 2.0 下，员工之间的知识交流过程、知识创造成果都有数字化存储和记录，基于这个平台进行员工之间连接强度、连接数量、问题解决效率、知识文档存量与增量等的测度，能够部分解决知识资本与社会资本增值、知识协作时效性和准确性的定量计算问题，有利于开展知识协同可计量性研究。

4 结 论

本文探讨了 IT 服务外包知识协同的本质，建立了以虚拟团队为组织单元的知识协同分析模型，试图建立知识协同效果与知识协作效率相结合的效益综合评价方法。在知识协同效果方面，强调度量社会资本和知识资本的增值，在知识协作效率方面强调准确性和及时性的综合平衡。通过分析，建立了"知识协同"效益评价的构念体系及其测度指标，为知识协同的深度研究奠定了基础。

5 研究局限性

EFA 和 CFA 是研究过程的两个阶段。本文仅做了 EFA，并没有进行 CFA 检验。根据 Anderson 等学者观点[44]，在发展理论的过程中，可以先通过探索性因子分析建立模型，再做验证性因子分析去检验和验证模型，这被称为交叉验证。本文完成了第一阶段建立模型阶段的因子分析，尚未进行对该模型的验证研究。原因在于：交叉验证的过程应该是首先在一个样本中通过 EFA 分析找到变量的因素结构，其次在另一个样本中用 CFA 对因素结构进行验证和修改。因此，进行交叉验证必须采用不同的样本。本文由于时间限制，先完成了利用第一批样本数据的 EFA 研究，构建了理论模型；尚未开展第二阶段的验证性研究。尽管现在也有不少学者利用"一个样本"进行交叉验证，即在同一样本中先用 EFA 找出因子、再用 CFA 来验证。但很显然，这样的 CFA 起不到证伪的作用，完全没有验证的意义和价值。因此，本研究拟采取两阶段研究的思路进行不同样本下的交叉验证。本文完成了第一阶段的 EFA 研究，在后续研究中，将重点进行第二批数据采集，在不同样本中开展针对因素结构模型的 CFA 验证研究。

参考文献

[1] 黄烨菁. 跨国服务外包中的知识转移：以软件外包为对象[J]. 科研管理, 2012, 33（6）：40-47.

[2] 赵大丽, 左美云. IT 服务接包企业知识整合的困境及其治理策略[J]. 兰州学刊, 2011（1）：58-62.

[3] 周海炜, 姜骞. IT 外包接包企业知识管理对外包成功的影响研究：知识黏滞性的调节作用[J]. 科学学与科学技术管理, 2012, 33（11）：71-78.

[4] ChristopherD, Tanwar A. Knowledge management in outsourcing environment：People empowering people[J]. The IUP Journal of Knowledge Management, 2012, 10（2）：61-87.

[5] 李红玲. 知识转移阻隔解析：从知识本体的视角出发[J]. 科技管理研究, 2009（3）：216-219.

[6] 佟泽华. 知识协同及其与相关概念的关系探讨[J]. 图书情报工作, 2012, 56（8）：107-112.

[7] Glogel L, Howell P, Hugh H, et al. Knowledge collabo - ration for IT support [EB/OL]. http：//www.thinkhdi.com/hdi2006/files /strategicAdvisoryboardpaperknowledgecol - laboration. Pdf.

［8］陈昆玉，陈昆琼．论企业知识协同［J］．情报科学，2002（9）：986－989．

［9］Lee J. The impact of knowledge sharing, organizational capability and partnership quality on IS outsourcing suc－cess［J］. Information & Management，2001（38）：323－335．

［10］Karhu K, Taipale O, Smolander K. Outsourcing and knowledge management in software testing［C］. Evalua－tion and Assessment in Software Engineering Proceed－ings，2007．

［11］Liu C, Ghauri P N, Sinkovics R R. Understanding the impact of relational capital and organizational learning on alliance outcomes［J］. Journal of World Business，2010（45）：237－249．

［12］田野，杜荣．离岸IT服务外包中的跨文化知识共享研究［J］．情报杂志，2011（4）：95－101．

［13］邓春平，毛基业．关系契约治理与外包合作绩效：对日离岸软件外包项目的实证研究［J］．南开管理评论，2008，11（4）：25－33．

［14］田雯．通过激活社会资本在虚拟社区中实现知识共享：来自中国在线社交网络的发现［D］．合肥：中国科学技术大学，2011．

［15］Karlenzig W. Tap into the Power of Knowledge collab－oration［EB/OL］. Dimension Data, http://www.tmcnet.com/.

［16］Mckelvey M, Almb H, RiccaboniI M. Does co－loca－tion matter for formal knowledge collaboration in the Swedish biotechnology－pharmaceutical sector［J］. Re－search Policy，2003（32）：483－501．

［17］樊治平，冯博，俞竹超．知识协同的发展及研究展望［J］．科学学与科学技术管理，2007（11）：85－91．

［18］杨利军．供应链知识协同对企业竞争力提升的作用分析［J］．科技管理研究，2011（5）：173－175．

［19］曾德明，文小科，陈强．基于知识协同的供应链企业知识存量增长机理研究［J］．中国科技论坛，2010（2）：77－81．

［20］王聪颖，管晓东．基于市场导向的产业集群知识协同模式研究［J］．科技进步与对策，2009，26（10）：69－71．

［21］施慧斌．知识协同概念分析及其心理契约研究［D］．沈阳：东北大学，2008．

［22］吴绍波，顾新．知识链组织之间合作的知识协同研究［J］．科学学与科学技术管理，2008（8）：83－87．

［23］王悦．基于知识链的供应链协同知识创新模式研究［J］．工业技术经济，2009，28（1）：125－128．

［24］王慧．企业集团内部知识协同研究［D］．济南：山东大学，2009．

［25］方德英，陈建斌，徐凯波．IT服务外包中复杂知识网络协同演化概念模型研究［C］．重庆：第六届（2011）中国管理学年会论文集，2011．

［26］Leijen H V, Baets W J. A cognitive frame work for reengineering knowledge intensive Proeesses［C］. Ha－waii：Proeeedings of the 36th Hawaii international Conference on System Seiences（HICSS'03），2002．

［27］陈建斌，徐凯波，薛云．企业2.0视角下的知识协同自组织分析模型研究［J］．经济问题，2013（4）：55－58．

［28］郑晓涛，郑兴山，石金涛．员工社会资本对其组织承诺的影响［J］．管理评论，2008，20（5）：15－20．

［29］王凤彬，江鸿，吴隆增．社会资本与核心能力关系研究：以知识创造为中介变量［J］．科学学研究，2008，26（3）：612－618．

［30］柯江林，孙健敏，石金涛，等．企业R&D团队之社会资本与团队效能关系的实证研究：以知识分享与知识整合为中介变量［J］．管理世界，2007（3）：89－101．

［31］Chua A. The Influence of Social Interaction on Knowl－edge Creation［J］. Journal of Intellectual Capital，2002，3（4）：375－392．

［32］Nahapiet J, Ghoshal S. Social capital, intellectual capi－tal, and the organizational advantage［J］. Academy of Management Review，1998，23（2）：242－266．

［33］Chun W, Hung W. A Social Network Analysis of the Multidisciplinary Knowledge Creation Process［D］. Can－ada：University of Waterloo，2006．

［34］Gonzalez－Brambila. Social Capital and the Creation of Knowledge［EB/OL］. http://isapapers.pitt.edu/101/1/2008－18_Gonzalez－Brambila.pdf.

［35］Artigues C. Predictors of Knowledge Creation Perfor－mance：A Quantitative Qualitative Comparative Study of European Doctorandi［D］. Girona：University of Gi－rona，2009．

［36］李东琴．知识资本与企业绩效的关系研究［M］．杭州：浙江大学出版社，2004．

［37］张丹，吕程．知识资本与企业绩效的关系研究：基于信息技术业上证A股上市公司的实证分析［J］．会计之友，2013（3）：81－84．

［38］王大勇，陈方正．论知识资本价值增值性质［J］．南京理工大学学报（社会科学版），2007，20（6）：1－7．

［39］曲刚，李伯森．团队社会资本与知识转移关系的实证研究：交互记忆系统的中介作用［J］．管理评论，2011，23（9）：109－118．

[40] 刘佳佳,陈涛,朱智洺. 企业社会资本与知识共享关系研究:以知识获取为中介变量[J]. 科技进步与对策,2013(4):86-90.
[41] Hedlund G, Nonaka I. Models of knowledge manage – ment in the West and Japan //Lorange B. Implement – ing Strategic Processes, Change, and Cooperation [M]. London:Macmillian, 1993.
[42] 曹勇,黎仁惠,王晓东. 技术转移中隐性知识转化效果测度模型及其应用[J]. 科研管理,2010,31(1):1-8.
[43] 张晓棠,荆心. 关系型社会资本与企业知识获取绩效研究[J]. 商业时代,2012(18):90-91.
[44] Anderson R E. Multivariate Data Analysis [M]. New York:Prentice Hall International, 1998.

"碳关税"对我国出口贸易的影响及对策

郑春芳　赵亚平

自英国政府2003年发表《我们能源的未来——创建一个低碳经济体》白皮书首次明确提出"低碳经济"概念后，低碳经济发展模式成为全球关注的热点。特别是2008年末国际金融危机发生后，一些国家相继采取"绿色新政"措施。可以说，低碳经济是人类从工业文明向生态文明转变的一种新的经济模式与生活方式。在当前国际金融危机余波未退、世界经济增长乏力的国际环境下，发达国家出于全球气候变暖和对碳排放的担忧拟开征"碳关税"。"碳关税"的制定将对发展中国家特别是我国的外贸出口产生一定影响，本文对此进行深入分析，找出我国应对之策。

1 发达国家拟征收"碳关税"的现状

"碳关税"也称边境调节税（BTAs：Border Tax Adjustments），指对在国内没有征收碳税或能源税、存在实质性能源补贴国家的出口商品征收特别的二氧化碳排放关税，是发达国家对从发展中国家进口的碳排放密集型产品，如铝、钢铁、水泥和一些化工产品征收的进口关税。目前，发达国家"碳关税"正处于策划或制定阶段，美国拟于2020年开始对从发展中国家进口的商品征收"碳关税"，法国宣布从2010年初开始对环保立法不及欧盟严格的发展中国家的进口商品征收"碳关税"。目前，虽然各发达国家还没有实施"碳关税"，但其一系列的前期工作证明"碳关税"的征收已经确定，其实质是一种新型的影响较大的贸易保护措施。

在未来的10年内，发达国家将通过协商最终确定各国的碳减排量、碳交易规则及"碳关税"征收的对象、范围和标准。"碳关税"的征收是以发达国家与发展中国家同时减排为前提，还是以工业化国家单独减排为前提？是采取排放权不可交换为征收方法，还是以排放权可交换但要扣除私人转移支付，或排放权可交换但通过公共转移支付，或是排放交易抵消减排的成本等4种不同排放情形之一征收"碳关税"？"碳关税"是以进口商品的碳含量为标准对所有进口商品征收，还是按照本国生产碳含量为标准对所有进口商品扣除出口商品征收，或是按进口商品碳含量为标准对能源密集型进口商品征收？在这个过程中，各国都将尽力争取对本国有利的规定，因为不同的规定产生的各国应征"碳关税"额度有很大不同。

2010—2020年的10年间，不仅将在世界范围内塑造"碳关税"征收新规则，也必将打破现有的世界贸易和经济格局，并建立低碳经济模式下的世界经济新格局。而我国进入21世纪以来，能源密集型产品出口增长迅速。仅2004—2008年，我国钢铁、化工产品和纺织品出口占世界总量的份额分别从5.12%、2.68%和16.98%上升到12.09%、4.65%和26.08%。[1]而且我国能源利用效率不高，隐含碳排放量❶情况不容乐观。钢、火电、水泥、玻璃、石化和碱等高耗能产品单产能耗分别是世界平均水平的1.15倍、1.17倍、1.53倍、1.47倍、1.45倍和1.34倍。可见，针对所有工业品征收的"碳关税"，对我国的影响可能要比特别保障措施、反补贴或反倾销的影响更严重。因此，"碳关税"对我国未来外贸出口和经济发展等将产生重要影响。

[基金项目] 本文为2010年北京市人才强教深化计划"中青年骨干人才培养项目"："'碳关税'对我国外贸和产业安全的影响及应对策略"的成果。

[作者简介] 郑春芳（1974—），女，北京联合大学商务学院副教授。研究方向：国际贸易理论与政策。

❶ 隐含碳排放量（Embodied Carbon）指产品生产全过程（包括原材料开采、产品加工制造甚至把最终运输至终端用户的整个过程）中的二氧化碳排放总量。

2 "碳关税"对我国外贸出口的影响

"碳关税"对我国外贸出口最直接的影响是增加我国高碳行业产品出口的成本和国际市场价格,削弱我国产品的国际竞争力。同时,"碳关税"还有可能引起我国外贸出口额不同程度的下降,改变出口结构并恶化出口环境。

2.1 增加我国高碳企业产品出口的成本

如果开征"碳关税",我国高碳企业产品出口成本必然上升。如果对我国黑色金属冶炼及压延加工业、非金属矿物制品业、造纸及纸制品业和有色金属冶炼及压延加工业四大能源密集型产品生产部门征收较高水平"碳关税",即按丹麦和瑞典国内281.9—369.0欧元/千升轻质燃料油税和241.8—300.6欧元/千立方米的天然气税,我国非金属制品业的碳税总额最高可达出口总额的32.8%,行业总碳税成本占总主营业务成本的13.4%,这样我国出口企业无利可图。如果征收中等水平"碳关税",即按德国国内61.4欧元/千升轻质燃料油税和59.6欧元/千立方米的天然气税,碳税总额占出口总额的比重最高可达10%;按照较低"碳关税"水平,即按美国或英国国内的碳税和能源税征收,"碳关税"可能达到出口总额的比重为3%—7%。[2]以2008年为例,我国上述4个行业的成本费用利润率仅为3.61%、7.95%、6.17%和4.34%,[3]这就意味着我国现有高碳企业无法承受中等和较高水平的"碳关税"。

2.2 引起我国制造业出口额不同程度的下降

世界银行一份研究报告显示,以工业化国家单独减排17%为前提,如果按进口商品的碳含量为标准对所有进口商品征收"碳关税",2020年我国所有制造业出口降幅将达20.8%,其中能源密集型制造业和其他制造业出口降幅分别为16.6%和21.6%,而服务业和农业的出口增幅将达46.3%和31.0%。[4]如果以发达国家与发展中国家同时减排、发达国家到2020年减排为2005年基准的30%、发展中国家在正常交易水平基础上减排30%为前提,与正常交易水平相比较而言,2020年在排放权可交换且通过公共转移支付和排放交易抵消减排的成本情形下,减排将导致我国工业出口下降幅度高达11.7%,远高于世界工业出口的平均降幅1.9%,而预计同时期美国和欧盟的工业出口却分别有5.0%和6.5%的增幅。[5]

以我国工业品出口的隐含碳排放量为基础,如果征收30美元/吨和60美元/吨的"碳关税",可使我国工业品出口量分别减少3.53%和6.95%。而且,机械制造业的出口和就业可能会受到"碳关税"的较大冲击。[6]如,以能源密集型制造业为代表的石油加工业的出口降幅将达12.39%和23.70%,即使是不属于能源密集型或碳排放密集型行业的电气机械器材制造业,其出口降幅也可能达到3.97%和7.79%。[7]在30美元征收标准下,我国制造业需要经过7年以上的时间才能逐步消除对制造业产品出口造成的冲击。[8]不仅如此,不同"碳关税"征收标准和碳排放交易规则确定的我国应征"碳关税"的数额不同,引起我国外贸出口的降幅也不同。按照进口商品的碳含量对所有进口商品征收"碳关税"(BTAFU)、本国生产碳含量对所有进口商品征收(BTADU)、本国生产碳含量对所有进口商品扣除出口商品征收"碳关税"(BTADE)、进口商品碳含量对能源密集型进口商品征收"碳关税"(BTAFR)和本国生产碳含量对能源密集型进口商品征收"碳关税"(BTADR)5种不同征收标准,将导致2020年我国制造业产出和出口分别下降3.6%和20.8%、0.5%和3.4%、0.5%和1.8%、0.3%和3.2%、0.2%和1.5%。[9]

在发达国家与发展中国家同时减排、发达国家到2020年减排2005年基准的30%、发展中国家在正常交易水平基础上减排30%的前提下,按照排放权不可交换(NTER)、排放权可交换但要扣除私人转移支付(TER1)、排放权可交换且通过公共转移支付(TER)和排放交易抵消减排的成本(TERWMT)4种碳排放交易规则,将导致我国工业产出和出口不同程度地下降。其中,在TERWMT情形下,降幅分别为7%和11.7%;在TER1情形下降幅均为5.8%;在TER情形下分别下降6.5%和9.4%;在NTER情况下降幅最小,分别为2.9%和4.5%。[10]

2.3 改变我国商品的出口结构和贸易方式

"碳关税"对我国出口结构的影响主要体现在出口商品结构和贸易方式方面。首先,"碳关税"将引起我国工业制成品出口比重下降。在30美元/吨的碳税征收标准下,我国制造业需要较长时间才能逐渐消化开征碳税对产量造成的负面影响,由此可能会引起工业制成品出口比重下降。其次,"碳关税"将引起高耗能产品出口下降。进入21世纪以来,我国出口的能源密集型产品增长迅速,工业发达国家通过征收"碳关税",将提高我国能源消费成本,改变我国企业投入要素组合,导致我国传统出口产品的劳动力成本比较优势难以为继,使我国高碳行业产品出口比重下降。再次,"碳关税"将引起加工贸易出口比重下降。2007年,我国加工贸易出口占比为50.71%,2008年为47.19%,[11]而企业从加工贸易中获得的利润却远低于研发、销售等环节。如,中国为苹果公司组装的iPod音乐播放器每出口一件到美国,意味着中国出口增加150美元,实际上中国组装每一件仅获得增加值4美元,其余146美元则归美国为主的科研和实验设计部门及工业设计、营销和复杂零部件生产部门所有。[12]因此,征收"碳关税"将会迫使我国从战略制定和企业实践层面促进出口产品升级,以赚取较高的利润,加速改变上述现状。预计到2015年左右,加工贸易出口占我国全部出口的比重将下降到40%以下。[13]

2.4 在一定程度上恶化出口环境

2009年初以来,我国出口频频遭受贸易救济调查,并始终是被调查的头号目标。2010年第一季度,在世界贸易组织13个成员发起的新的贸易救济调查中,我国的出口商成为贸易救济调查案的头号目标,共有约47%的新增调查针对我国。尽管我国遭受的贸易救济措施频繁,但只是针对个别行业、个别企业或个别商品征收,且最多有5年的时间限制。而美欧各国积极筹划的"碳关税"实际上是对未承担约束性减排目标的主要发展中国家实行的惩罚性关税,是针对所有出口产品征收的,覆盖面大且长期征收。因此,"碳关税"是贸易制裁的一种形式,无疑将抬高我国产品出口的门槛。

近两年,在部分发达国家和地区提出征收"碳关税"的提案或决定中(见表1),欧盟的决定遭到国际航空运输协会理事会的反对,美国法案尚未最终通过,法国的提议也在哥本哈根联合国气候变化大会上遭到其他欧盟国家的反对。[14]但"碳关税"的实质是美欧各国积极筹划、对未承担约束性减排目标的主要发展中国家实行的惩罚性关税,是贸易制裁的一种形式,尤其在国际金融危机爆发之后,这不仅意味着将抬高发展中国家产品出口的门槛,更意味着气候谈判可能在未来引发较严重的国际贸易争端。

表1 近两年部分发达国家和地区提出拟征收碳关税情况

时间	提出方	约束性规定
2008.7	欧盟	从2012年开始,所有在欧盟机场起降的飞机都要缴纳温室气体排放费
2009.6	美国	《清洁能源与安全法案》提出将从2020年开始征收"碳关税"
2009.11	法国	从2010年1月1日开始对环保立法不及欧盟严格的发展中国家的进口品征收碳关税

资料来源:International Air Transport Association. Annual Report 2009。

3 碳关税对我国工业化进程的影响

我国政府有两个节能减排目标:近期目标是"十一五"规划建议提出的到2010年单位GDP能耗比"十五"期末降低20%左右;远期目标是在2009年哥本哈根国际气候变化框架公约缔约国会议上承诺的,到2020年单位GDP二氧化碳排放量比2005年下降40%—45%。两个指标的实现难度都很大。我国应对碳关税和国际气候变换而提出的节能减排目标将对我国工业化进程产生一定影响。

一方面,节能减排限制传统产业上升的空间。我国是后起工业化国家,工业化发展的"两高一低"模式还将在一定时间内存在。尽管中国社科院《中国工业化进程报告——1995～2005年,中国省域工业化水平评价与研究》指出,中国工业化进程整体进入工业化中期的后半阶段,但其在衡量地区工业化进程的五个指标中,并没有考虑单位GDP的能源消费水平。而我国工业生产的隐含碳排放情况不容乐观。2005年,中国单位GDP能耗是英国的2.8倍、美国的1.69倍;2009年全国单位GDP能耗为1.077吨标准煤/万元;2006—2009年单位GDP能耗降幅分别为2.74%、5.04%、5.20%和3.61%;2010年7月,国家统计局将2009年GDP增速从8.7%修正为9.1%,2009年GDP现价总量增加了5154亿元,为340507亿元。即使在增加了GDP基数的情况下,距离实现"十一五"规划建议提出到2010年单位GDP能耗比"十五"期末降低20%左右的目标还有一定距离。

另一方面,从工业化规律来看,战略性新兴产业目前还处于布局阶段。未来国际减排规则的最终确定和欧美出于对碳泄漏的担忧而积极筹划征收的碳关税,都意味着当今世界将不再具备沿袭以往发达国家高能源和高消费为支撑的现代化道路的国际环境,我国只能探索低碳发展的新型工业化和现代化道路。

4 我国应对"碳关税"问题的对策

在当前国际金融危机余波未退、各国经济增长乏力的国际环境下,我国作为出口大国的敏感身份极易激发他国抵制和报复情绪。因此,对"碳关税",我国应积极应对,以减少其可能对外贸出口造成的影响。

4.1 积极利用WTO现有法律机制

WTO一般例外条款(GATT)的第20条允许WTO成员国在某些情况下采取基于环境理由的贸易限制。这给欧盟和美国等发达国家征收"碳关税"提供了可能。因此,应对进口国将实施的"碳关税",我国面临的首要问题就是判断其实质,是可获得WTO第20条款"保护用尽的自然资源"的豁免,还是强行推行发达国家高标准以保护进口国本国产品竞争优势,被争端机构定性为推行贸易保护主义的隐形"绿色壁垒"。同时,我国要根据WTO的"国民待遇"原则,要求进口国产品承担与进口产品相同的碳减排责任;根据最惠国待遇原则,要求我国与其他国家出口产品适用同样的"碳关税"征收原则和标准;并尽力争取WTO体系内其他针对发展中国家的"特殊及优惠待遇",例如一定期限的过渡期,为我国实现产业升级、工业化和现代化争取时间和更大的发展空间。

4.2 积极参与国际气候变化规则和"碳关税"征收规则的制定

在国际气候变化规则制定过程中,应重视我国作为发展中国家应承担"共同但有区别的责任",争取确立对我国有利的碳排放额度、减排额度、碳排放交易规则和"碳关税"征收标准。因此,在"碳关税"征收标准的制定中,尽量争取对我国外贸出口影响最小的标准。在碳交易规则的制定中,尽量避免实行使我国工业出口降幅最大的"排放权可交换且通过公共转移支付和排放交易抵消减排的成本(TER‐WMT)"规则,争取对我国外贸出口影响最小的"排放权不可交换(NTER)"规则。

4.3 从产业转型升级入手改善我国出口结构

为更好地抓住低碳经济发展机遇,我国需大力改善出口产品结构:一方面从产业结构调整入手,推进我国传统的能源消费结构优化,加快制定"新能源产业发展规划",大力发展非化石可再生能源的转化利用,如水电、核电、风能、太阳能和生物质能等,以此降低制成品生产过程中耗费的能源和碳排放;改善我国出口结构,还应大力发展碳排放较低的服务产业,提高出口服务的附加值和竞争力,不断优化我国的出口商品和服务结构。

4.4 整合供应链以降低企业成本

制造业出口企业应从整合供应链入手,改变只占制造业低利润环节的现状,不断提升企业的技术水平,抢占产品设计、原料采购、批发经销等环节的控制权,优化产品研发设计及生产决策,不断提高企业运行效率,摆脱征收"碳关税"造成的成本上升约束。认真做好市场调研,提高产品质量,努力成为跨国公司的供应商。在此过程中,不断提高本企业的设计能力和营销能力。

参考文献

[1][2] 吴立波,汤维祺. 碳关税的理论机制与经济影响初探 [J]. 科学对社会的影响,2010 (3).

[3][11] 中华人民共和国国家统计局编. 中国统计年鉴 (2009) [M]. 北京:中国统计出版社,2009.

[4][9] Mattoo, A. et al. Reconciling Climate Change and Trade Policy. Policy Research Working Paper, No. 5123. The World Bank Devel‐opment Research Group, Trade and Integration Team, Nov. 2009.

[5][10] Mattoo, A. et al. Can Global De‐Carbonization Inhabit Developing Country Industrialization? Policy Research Working Paper, No. 5121. The World Bank Development Research Group, Trade and Integration Team, Nov. 2009.

[6] 沈可挺,李钢. 碳关税对中国工业品出口的影响——基于可计算一般均衡模型的评估 [J]. 财贸经济,2010,(1).

[7] 沈可挺. 碳关税争端及其对中国制造业的影响 [J]. 中国工业经济,2010 (1).

［8］李进. 碳关税或冲击中国工业品出口［EB/OL］. 商务部网站，2010 – 06 – 23.

［12］"中国制造"含多少"中国成分"［N］. 参考消息，2008 – 08 – 04.

［13］陈长缨. 后危机时期中国对外贸易变化的六大趋势［N］. 上海证券报，2010 – 03 – 29.

［14］张昕宁. "碳关税"的性质界定研究［J］. 求索，2010（9）.

论我国特定非金融机构反洗钱监管

赵永林

近些年来，随着全球经济的不断发展，洗钱犯罪活动日渐猖獗，对于国际经济秩序的稳定与安全的威胁日益凸显。在当前的洗钱犯罪活动中，一个突出的特点是随着金融经济全球化态势的发展，国家对金融机构安全监管力度的不断加强，洗钱犯罪分子利用银行业、证券业、保险业等传统的社会资金流通主渠道实施洗钱犯罪活动的成本，以及所可能引发的风险正在逐渐加大，因而将洗钱的视角向安全监管措施相对薄弱的一些特定的非金融机构转移、以拓展更加安全便捷的洗钱渠道成为趋势，使得洗钱犯罪活动的隐秘性更强，犯罪形式与犯罪手段日趋多样化、复杂化，由此也加大了对洗钱犯罪活动查处的难度。

为了防范犯罪分子利用特定非金融机构实施洗钱犯罪活动，强化对我国境内特定非金融机构的反洗钱监管力度，于2007年1月1日开始施行的《中华人民共和国反洗钱法》中规定了在中国境内设立的特定非金融机构应当与金融机构一样依法采取预防、监控措施，建立反洗钱相关制度，依照有关规定履行反洗钱义务。我国反洗钱法的这一规定，将金融机构与特定非金融机构同时纳入反洗钱的主体范围，明确金融机构与特定非金融机构均应承担反洗钱使命、履行反洗钱义务。然而，由于该法中对特定非金融机构在反洗钱行动中的地位、责任、制度，以及如何履行反洗钱义务等方面的规定并不具体清晰，并且至今我国基本没有相应的配套法律、法规出台，致使反洗钱法中关于特定非金融机构履行反洗钱义务的规定事实上成为一纸空文，客观上造成了特定非金融机构反洗钱监管的缺失，以及犯罪分子利用特定非金融机构实施洗钱犯罪活动而不能予以及时、有效应对与查处的局面。因此，强化非金融机构反洗钱监管，明确特定非金融机构反洗钱义务与责任，已经成为我国当前反洗钱所面临的一个极为紧迫的问题。

1 当前犯罪分子利用特定非金融机构洗钱的特点

1.1 洗钱渠道不断拓宽，涉及行业领域众多

特定非金融机构日常经营活动的一个明显特征就是其经营活动内容范围甚为广泛，基本上涵盖了社会经济生活的各个方面，其经营活动在极大程度上为社会经济发展和人们的物质文化生活提供广泛空间与需求的同时，客观上也极大地便利了犯罪分子的洗钱活动，使洗钱犯罪分子的洗钱空间大为拓展。近些年我国国内大量的洗钱犯罪活动事实证明，犯罪分子早就已经将其视野转向了一切可以用作洗钱的渠道和途径，涉猎房地产、贵金属现货、金银饰品、翡翠珠宝、古玩字画、娱乐场所、洗浴中心、甚至影视制作等诸多行业领域，利用这样一些安全监管相对薄弱的新兴产业或特定非金融行业、机构的经营活动进行洗钱，不仅可以实现犯罪分子掩饰、隐瞒犯罪所得及其收益性质与来源的目的，更由于通过资本孳息使犯罪分子获取更加可观的经济效益，为其犯罪后利用犯罪所得及其收益追求腐败奢靡的生活方式提供了物质基础和保障。如原内蒙古自治区党委政法委副书记杨汉中在2000—2012年，利用担任满洲里市人民政府市长、满洲里市委书记、兴安盟盟委书记、内蒙古自治区党委政法委副书记等职务上的便利，为多名请托人在土地征用、工程项目落实税款返还、道路工程、光缆下线工程、机场设备安装工程土地出让金补交等多个事项上提供帮助，谋取非法利益，伙同其妻子、弟弟、情妇、司机等人先后49次非法收受和索取19人给予的财物共计人民币4037余万元、美元35万元、澳元4万元，其中索贿共计人民币1320余万元、美元15万元，其使用犯罪所得在国内6个大、中城市置办了20多处房产，以掩饰隐瞒犯罪所得的性质及来源；❶ 因犯贪污罪于2005年11月被人民法院一审判处无期徒刑的广西桂林贪官

[基金项目] 北京市哲学社会科学规划项目《反洗钱机制与法律问题研究》（编号：09BaFX049）阶段研究成果。
[作者简介] 赵永林（1955—），男，北京联合大学应用文理学院法律系教授。研究方向：刑法学，金融法学。
❶ 资料来源：北京晨报，2013-09-04。

李和平，被捕前用违法所得 3000 多万元人民币购买了 55 套房产进行洗钱；而在若干年前案发的中国银行广东开平支行前行长许超凡，以及其之后的两位继任者余振东、许国俊等人利用职权监守自盗贪污犯罪案，其中余振东携 3 亿美元贪污款逃往境外后，在加拿大购买了 3 幢豪宅洗钱。[1] 近些年在全国各地先后屡屡被举报揭露、并经有关部门查处的所谓"房叔""房嫂""房哥""房姐"等涉嫌职务犯罪的刑事案件，几乎无不显现出洗钱犯罪的这一特点。犯罪分子在实施犯罪、获取大量赃款之后，或者由其家属、亲戚、朋友出面，或者使用虚假的身份证明，尽可能地通过一切可以利用的渠道，大量购买动产或不动产，或者自己居住使用，或者对外出租、转让，从而达到掩饰、隐瞒犯罪所得及其产生收益的性质、实现将所获赃款表面合法化的目的，是当下国内许多贪污受贿腐败分子犯罪后清洗赃款普遍采用的方式。

1.2 利用特定非金融行业、机构间信息壁垒跨行业洗钱操作

行业间信息壁垒严重，在我国现阶段经济活动中表现得较为普遍，其原因皆由于保护主义作祟，行业壁垒森严，其不仅表现在同一行业不同的经营者之间没有建立起信息资源共享机制，信息共享程度低下，更突出地表现在不同行业之间信息沟通渠道闭塞，缺乏信息资源互通互补机制，相互之间的信息沟通与情报交流不畅。尽管这一问题近些年已经开始受到国家有关主管部门的关注，并在一些金融机构间得到某种程度的纠正与改善。如在商业银行之间建立起的企业与公民个人信用平台，以求达到信息资源共享、互通有无的目标，但信息壁垒的问题在特定非金融行业、机构中仍然反映得尤为突出。由于各种类型的特定非金融机构分属于不同的行业领域范围，涉及的行业领域范围极其广泛，而特定非金融行业、机构日常经营活动的内容又涵盖社会经济生活的方方面面，这就导致不同行业之间、即使是同一行业中的不同经营者之间的经济往来活动并不普遍，甚至更由于行业之间、不同经营者之间不可避免的相互竞争关系而导致相互间壁垒森严，基本谈不上信息交流与资源共享，这就恰恰为犯罪分子跨行业、跨机构进行洗钱操作提供了可乘之机。因为他们根本不用担心自己利用某个行业、某一经营机构的日常交易活动实施洗钱致使其在另一行业、另一经营机构中为相类似的行为受到经营者的怀疑。因此，犯罪分子不再单纯地仅仅依托于某一个行业或者某一个机构实施洗钱犯罪活动，而是在多个行业、机构之间将犯罪所得的资金循环往复地流动、周转，进行复杂的跨行业操作，最终实现洗钱的目的。

1.3 法律服务职业机构成为洗钱的理想途径

寻求法律专业人员的协助，通过法律服务职业机构洗钱，不仅可以利用法律的公信力掩饰洗钱行为的真实意图，实现洗钱交易形式上的"合法性"，而且由于法律服务职业机构及其从业人员具有相关的专业知识和专门的技能，可以通过他们的"服务"有效地为洗钱犯罪分子化解风险，寻求洗钱操作安全程度的最大化，因而愈加受到犯罪而是在多个行业、机构之间将犯罪所得的资金循环往复地流动、周转，进行复杂的跨行业操作，最终实现洗钱的目的。而某些法律职业机构以及少数该类机构的从业人员受非法利益的驱使，为了谋取不正当收入，主动帮助犯罪分子洗钱，亦使犯罪分子的洗钱欲望较为顺利地得以实现。有证据表明，通过法律服务职业机构及其从业人员的行为洗钱，正在逐渐成为犯罪分子洗钱的理想途径。

犯罪分子利用法律服务职业机构洗钱，大致上有几种形式：一是通过双方"协商"更改付费方式、数额或"服务"的项目内容，将原付给法律服务职业机构的费用（实际上是犯罪所得赃款）退回或转付其他投资账户，以循环流通的方式完成洗钱；二是与个别法律服务职业机构从业人员相互勾结，以向法律服务职业机构"付费"的方式利用该机构或从业人员个人账户洗钱；三是由法律服务职业机构从业人员利用法律规则直接为犯罪分子策划洗钱方案，设计洗钱流程，协助其清洗犯罪所得，为逃避打击设置法律障碍。

1.4 以现金交易以及各种非金融支付方式洗钱

利用现金交易或者其他各种非金融支付方式，如网络支付交易等方式洗钱，不仅更为简单、快速、便捷，还可以即时清结，便于及时转移资金，有效消除可疑交易痕迹，而且尽管有的时候交易涉及的资

---

[1] 唐韵. 央行反洗钱中心主任怒斥：房地产行业的洗钱明目张胆[J]. 中国经济周报, 2006 (10).

金量可能额度巨大，但由于避开了金融流通环节，能够规避金融机构的交易监管和反洗钱监控，因而操作起来隐秘性、安全性更强。目前我国的特定非金融机构多处在现金密集型经营行业中，而现金密集型行业日常经营活动的主要特征之一就是大多以现金支付作为主要交易方式，特别是在一些大城市以及经济较为发达的地区，经营活动中的大额现金交易现象更加普遍，如在房屋、贵金属现货、金银饰品、钻石珠宝、古玩字画、典当拍卖、洗浴娱乐等特定非金融行业、机构的经营活动中，直接以现金支付方式完成交易的比比皆是。由于现金支付本身并无实名登记要求，而就我国目前的立法现状而言，特定非金融行业、机构也没有法律上确定的需要承担查清交易客户资金来源的责任，同时囿于特定非金融行业、机构自身的能力和所处的经营环境，要想查清客户资金来源绝非易事，这就自然便于巨额资产持有方式的交换与转移，使犯罪分子利用特定非金融行业、机构的经营活动实施洗钱犯罪活动有了可乘之机。我们在以上所列举的几例犯罪分子洗钱犯罪案件，基本上就是以现金交易的方式完成洗钱的。

1.5 非实名制交易掩饰洗钱

非实名制交易，在特定非金融行业、机构的日常经营活动中屡见不鲜。尽管在特定非金融行业、机构的一些日常交易活动中也会有比较严格的实名制要求，比如房地产买卖、典当拍卖等经营活动中的实名登记制度，但更多的交易活动则是以非实名制的方式完成的，而且目前无论是在法律上或者是在行业制度管理中，对于是否需要实名登记，或者无明确的规范性要求，或者虽然有一定的要求，但因缺乏强制约束与有效的监管而流于形式，如金银饰品、贵金属现货、钻石珠宝、古玩字画、洗浴娱乐等的零售交易活动。非实名制交易行为事实上既迎合了一些非金融行业、机构的营销理念，同时也满足了某些参与交易活动的客户讳忌交易隐私泄露的愿望和要求，使得这些特定非金融行业、机构的经营活动少了些许法律上或者制度上的硬性约束，客观上有利于融洽经营者与客户之间的关系，使双方在彼此信任的前提下完成交易行为，甚至由此可能会给这些非金融行业、机构的经营者们带来可观的经济效益，但同时由于客户身份、交易内容等基本信息的缺失，可以极为便利地掩饰客户交易资金的性质、来源及其参与交易活动的真实意图，而且即使事后可能受到怀疑，也会因为缺少实时登记的资料而难以查实，客观上为犯罪分子利用与特定非金融行业、机构之间的交易行为实施洗钱犯罪活动提供了便利条件。

2 当前特定非金融机构反洗钱难点分析

虽然在我国反洗钱法上将特定非金融机构列入国家反洗钱义务的主体范围，但目前诸多不利因素的存在，造成了特定非金融机构反洗钱的难点，直接影响了特定非金融机构反洗钱行动的开展。

2.1 特定非金融机构反洗钱相关法律、法规几近空白

审视我国反洗钱立法体系的现状，不难看出，与反洗钱法有关特定非金融机构履行反洗钱义务规定相配套的相关法律、法规几乎处于一种空白的境地，导致特定非金融机构实施反洗钱基本上无法可依。这突出反映在以下三个方面。

2.1.1 履行反洗钱义务的特定非金融机构具体范围不明

我国反洗钱法在反洗钱主体范围的规定中使用了"特定非金融机构"这样一个概念，并且在反洗钱法的"附则"中规定"应当履行反洗钱义务的特定非金融机构的范围、其履行反洗钱义务和对其监督管理的具体办法，由国务院反洗钱行政主管部门会同国务院有关部门制定"，但时至今日，除了 2012 年 3 月 5 日中国人民银行颁布的《支付机构反洗钱和反恐怖融资管理办法》将包括网络支付、预付卡发行与受理以及银行卡收单在内的非金融支付行业纳入反洗钱监管体系的非金融行业外，对于其他的"特定非金融机构"具体范围的法律界定仍为空白，这就导致应当履行反洗钱义务的"特定非金融机构"的具体范围并不明确。

据了解，我国反洗钱法在立法过程中曾就履行反洗钱义务的特定非金融机构的范围在提请审议的草案中作出规定，明确包括从事房地产销售企业、贵金属和珠宝交易机构、拍卖企业、典当行、律师事务所、会计师事务所等企业与中介机构，但在最终审议通过的反洗钱法中却取消了对特定非金融机构的范围的规定，只在该法"总则"一章中保留了对特定非金融机构反洗钱义务的原则性规定，而如此一来，特定非金融机构具体范围不明这一状况至今延续多年而得不到法律上的界定。

2.1.2 特定非金融机构应当履行的反洗钱具体义务不明

依据反洗钱法的规定，特定非金融机构应当与金融机构履行相同的反洗钱义务，即"依法采取预防、监控措施，建立健全客户身份识别制度、客户身份资料和交易记录保存制度、大额交易和可疑交易报告制度"等，但由于各具体的特定非金融机构自身所处的行业性质的不同，决定了各自工作内容的差异，凸显出特定非金融机构业务范围复杂性、宽泛性的特点，由此也必然决定了特定非金融机构事实上所应当履行的反洗钱义务也会有所差异，而且不可能与金融机构所履行的反洗钱义务完全一致，这就要求在相关法律、法规中根据各特定非金融机构的业务范围在设定其应当履行的具体的反洗钱义务时做出差别化的规定，以与其业务特点相适应，从而提高反洗钱工作的有效性。而我国目前的状况是除了在上述《支付机构反洗钱和反恐怖融资管理办法》中明确了非金融支付行业应当履行的反洗钱具体义务、其中包括差别化的客户身份识别措施、与金融机构不同的以"合理怀疑"为基础的可疑交易报告制度外，在反洗钱法中对一般特定非金融机构的反洗钱义务仅仅做了一般的原则性规定，而并未将特定非金融机构应当履行的反洗钱义务具体化，导致特定非金融机构的反洗钱具体义务不明，面临认知与操作上的困难。

2.1.3 特定非金融机构反洗钱组织架构缺失，职责不清

特定非金融机构反洗钱是一个相当复杂的系统性工程，这是因为洗钱犯罪活动涉及的特定非金融机构数量多、范围广，跨行业特点突出，由此也带来一个复杂而又艰难的问题，就是如何有效协调各不同行业间的反洗钱行动，确保特定非金融机构反洗钱组织架构完整、职责清晰、监管得力。依照有关反洗钱犯罪国际公约的规定，各缔约国应当为反洗钱犯罪努力寻求建立国内的协作机制以及与国际社会间的合作机制。为此，我国早在几年前建立了反洗钱部际联席会议机制，❶ 但这样一个机制事实上非常松散，其绝对的权威性并未在法律层面得到确认，致使该机制对于国内反洗钱行动的协调、制约作用十分有限，加之现实中我国长期存在着的复杂而难以调和的部门之间的协调、权力平衡问题的影响，导致部门之间的掣肘、不协调现象极为普遍，最终在反洗钱问题上难以形成合力。尤为突出的是，由于该机制对特定非金融机构反洗钱行动的指导与制约关系无法可依，而现实中我国特定非金融机构的反洗钱行动似乎又总是游离于这个机制之外，不受这个机制的约束，也就使得履行反洗钱义务的特定非金融机构反洗钱组织架构一直处于不明晰的状态，包括主管部门是谁、履行何种职责等，在法律上都没有比较明确的规定，因此根本谈不上机构之间的协调与合作。

2.2 特定非金融机构反洗钱认识存在盲点

如前所述，当前洗钱犯罪的突出特点之一是犯罪分子将犯罪的目光开始投向经济利益更高、隐秘性更强的行业，以追逐犯罪所得的迅速"合法化"以及经济利益的最大化，使洗钱犯罪活动的重点正在逐步向特定非金融机构转移。于是，在金融机构以外的其他特定非金融机构，诸如房地产经营与代理机构、博彩、贵金属、珠宝、拍卖行业、娱乐场所、洗浴中心、夜总会、乃至影视制作行业，无不留下洗钱犯罪分子驻足的痕迹。这种普遍的现象足以证明一个不争的事实：洗钱犯罪分子正在利用我国特定非金融机构反洗钱法律规定与执行标准的缺失以致于造成反洗钱监管不力的空子大行其道。10多年前有学者在评论我国内地洗钱状况时就曾指出："在建立社会主义市场经济的过程中，（内地的）金融基础设施如此脆弱，根本无法阻止洗钱活动。中国特有的多种因素又进一步促使了洗钱的恶化。"❷ 然而对于这样一个早已呈现出的复杂而又严峻的洗钱局面，某些特定非金融机构及其从业人员却不能保持足够的警觉，对于特定非金融机构参与反洗钱行动的必要性以及重要性缺乏清醒的认识，他们或者认为对洗钱犯罪的防控主要是政府职能部门的职责以及金融机构应当履行的义务，与本行业、本部门无关，因而置身于反洗钱行动之外，或者明知在其业务活动中出现洗钱可疑交易，但为了一己私利而熟视无睹，听之任之，客观上纵容了犯罪分子的洗钱犯罪活动。这种较为普遍存在着的对反洗钱的模糊认知以及反洗钱意识的淡漠导致特定非金融机构反洗钱行动的开展缺乏广泛的群众基础和支持力度，在一定程度上加大了

---

❶ 2002年经国务院批准成立反洗钱部际联席会议；2003年5月经国务院决定，该联席会议由中国人民银行牵头，成员单位有公安部等20几个部、委、局。

❷ 郭建安：《中国的洗钱状况及对策》，2002年6月21日至22日香港大学第三届"大中华的犯罪及其控制"年度讨论会会议论文。

特定非金融机构反洗钱工作的难度。

2.3 特定非金融机构履行反洗钱义务与其执业操守规范冲突

限于我国目前法律、政策的规定或职业行规与特点，某些特定非金融机构履行反洗钱义务事实上与其职业操守规范之间存在着明显的利害冲突，客观上不仅造成具体操作上的难度，而且加大了这些特定非金融机构及其从业人员的从业风险。例如律师事务所、公证机构等法律职业机构一般被认为属于履行反洗钱义务的特定非金融机构范围，而反洗钱金融行动特别工作组（FATF）❶ 的有关洗钱研究报告中也指出，随着许多国家反洗钱制度的健全，洗钱犯罪分子依赖律师、会计师、财务顾问、公证人等专业人员洗钱的案件数量大幅上升，因此在其2003年修订的《40 + 9 条建议》❷ 第12条第4款中明确规定：律师、公证人等法律专业人员在为客户提供列举的服务内容时，应当履行反洗钱义务。可以肯定的是，由于律师、公证人等法律专业人员具有法律专业知识，在反洗钱问题上确实具有独特的优势，可以通过对客户身份、合同及相关文件等资料来审查交易以及客户的真实情况，发现可疑交易线索，但其举报客户交易的行为却与自身职业操守中要求履行的执业秘密义务相冲突，在一定程度上会影响执业人员与客户之间基于保密义务而建立的信任关系，甚至有可能损害到客户的权益；另一方面，由于律师、公证人等未能履行客户身份识别、可疑交易报告等反洗钱义务，其基于与客户之间的委托关系所收取的费用则因有可能是客户犯罪所得的赃款而受到协助洗钱的指控，从而加大了自身执业的风险。这种规范上的冲突使得特定非金融机构及其从业人员在是否以及如何履行反洗钱义务问题上处于两难的尴尬境地，势必影响反洗钱行动的开展。

2.4 特定非金融机构反洗钱信息获取与交流渠道不畅

反洗钱行动的开展必须借助于高速、有效的反洗钱情报网络的沟通和相关信息的交流，以及对各种可疑交易与资金往来的跟踪监察和国际协查，其中信息渠道的畅通尤为重要。

2004年4月经中央机构编制委员会办公室批准，由中国人民银行组建了我国国内反洗钱情报机构，对外称中国反洗钱检测分析中心，承担根据国内有关部门及其他国家反洗钱机构提供的金融情报分析可疑支付交易或寻找洗钱犯罪痕迹、为打击洗钱犯罪提供技术性条件的职责，但由于该机构的性质只是一个事业单位，行使行政权力于法无据，因而导致其职责、信息渠道过窄，要从其他政府职能部门获取反洗钱所需的信息资料和情报具有相当大的难度，对特定非金融机构反洗钱行动提供相关情报信息的作用十分有限。而特定非金融机构囿于自身条件，反洗钱情报信息收集专业性不强，加之洗钱犯罪活动本身就极具隐秘性，经有关部门披露的具有参考价值的特定非金融机构可疑交易的案例数量又十分有限，因而期望于特定非金融机构凭借自身的能力获取比较全面、完整的判断交易是否可疑的足够情报信息，可能性不大。获取反洗钱信息的渠道不畅，相关情报信息不能快速、准确传递和交流的客观现实，决定了特定非金融机构难以依赖于自身的能力准确判定客户交易行为的性质，给其履行反洗钱义务增加了难度。

3 强化特定非金融机构反洗钱监管措施建议

针对我国现阶段犯罪分子利用特定非金融机构实施洗钱犯罪活动的现状和特点，为强化我国特定非金融机构反洗钱监管，以适应我国反洗钱法中有关特定非金融机构应当履行反洗钱义务的要求，我们认为有必要积极采取相应的反洗钱监管措施。

---

❶ FATF 是 Financial Action Task Force on Money Laundering 的简称，即反洗钱金融行动特别工作组，反洗钱和反恐融资领域最著名的国际组织。1989年，根据西方七国首脑会议提出的7月16日经济宣言，以经济合作发展组织（即OECO）加盟各国为中心成立了以推进洗钱犯罪的对策为目标的政府间合作组织机构，即FATF。FATF事务局设置在经济合作发展组织机构内。中国于2005年1月被接纳为该组织观察员，2007年6月28日成为该组织正式成员。

❷ 1990年2月，反洗钱金融行动特别工作组提出了关于全球洗钱问题的专题报告——《关于洗钱问题的建议》，即《40条建议》。该建议就政府间合作、有关可疑资料的交流、其他合作形式确立了反洗钱行动的国际标准。《40条建议》一经提出，首先被各成员国所接受并实施；之后，《40条建议》逐渐被越来越多的国家和地区所接受，成为反洗钱行动的国际标准。此后，《40条建议》经多次修订补充，最终形成现在的以反洗钱和恐怖融资为目标的《40 + 9 条建议》。

3.1 尽快制定特定非金融机构反洗钱配套法律、法规

由于我国现行反洗钱法中对于特定非金融机构履行反洗钱义务的规定存在诸多不明确之处，客观上不利于规范特定非金融机构的反洗钱行动，因此，当务之急是需要尽快以立法形式制定颁布与特定非金融机构反洗钱行动相配套的有关法律、法规，完善我国反洗钱法律体系框架内的各项具体规范，以使特定非金融机构参与国家统一的反洗钱行动有法可依。

制定与特定非金融机构反洗钱配套的法律、法规，要从立法上解决三个基本问题：一是我国履行反洗钱义务的特定非金融机构的主体范围。事实上，鉴于目前世界各国反洗钱形势的实际，各个国家反洗钱立法以及有关反洗钱国际公约、国际组织反洗钱规范对于履行反洗钱义务的主体范围的规定并不完全一致，但一般还是有比较明确的范围界定，如FATF在其《40+9条建议》中明确了承担反洗钱义务的特定非金融机构的范围包括赌场（包括网络赌场）、房地产代理商、贵金属和宝石交易商、律师、公证人、其他独立法律专业人员、会计师、信托和公司服务提供者等；德国反洗钱法中亦对履行反洗钱义务的机构、人员的范围以及不履行反洗钱义务应当承担的法律责任作出比较详尽的规定。❶ 这些规定值得我国进行相关立法时参考借鉴；二是对我国特定非金融机构在反洗钱行动中应当履行的具体义务加以明确。在反洗钱法规定我国特定非金融机构履行的反洗钱普遍义务的基础上，应当根据特定非金融机构的行业性质，以及经营活动的范围、特点，依据权利与义务对等的原则，有针对性地规范特定非金融机构反洗钱的具体义务，并要求承担义务的特定非金融机构必须履行，以体现义务普遍性与特殊性的相统一，以及不同性质主体之间义务的差别化；三是严格设定特定非金融机构不履行反洗钱义务的法律责任。目前我国反洗钱立法中存在着一个比较明显的缺陷，就是针对特定非金融机构不履行反洗钱义务的法律责任的规定事实上还是个空白，对特定非金融机构不依法履行反洗钱义务的行为没有相应的追究责任的法律依据。在我国现行反洗钱法中，虽然专章设定了法律责任，但其所针对的对象只是违反反洗钱法律规定的反洗钱行政主管部门和其他依法负有反洗钱监督管理职责的部门、机构中从事反洗钱的人员，以及金融机构、包括对金融机构直接负责的董事、高级管理人员和其他直接责任人员，而没有任何法律责任的条款约束到特定非金融机构及其主管人员或直接责任人员。当然，这一缺陷的存在，与我国目前反洗钱法中对特定非金融机构所应当履行的反洗钱义务规范不够明确有着直接的关联。由于对特定非金融机构履行反洗钱义务的行为缺少法律上的约束，自然会使一些特定非金融机构及其经营者对其不依法履行义务的行为所可能带来的不利后果没有任何忌惮，这种立法现状自然会在无形中助长某些特定非金融机构及其从业人员的侥幸心理，也使对特定非金融机构履行反洗钱义务的要求及反洗钱监管难以落到实处。因此，有必要通过立法把不履行反洗钱义务而需要承担的法律责任的对象范围扩大到特定非金融机构及其从业人员，将其履行反洗钱义务的行为纳入法律的监督与制约之下，使追究特定非金融机构及其从业人员不履行或者不正确履行反洗钱义务的法律责任规范化、明确化。

3.2 提高对特定非金融机构反洗钱监管的重视程度

就我国现状而言，一方面是由于特定非金融机构经营活动中存在着现金交易为主、实名制交易弱化、跨行业操作频率高等诸多的特点，因而受到洗钱犯罪分子的极大关注，致使洗钱犯罪活动的重点逐渐向特定非金融机构转移，另一方面则由于反洗钱法律规定的不明确性，以及特定非金融机构及其从业人员主观重视程度不够，特定非金融机构基本上是游离于反洗钱行动之外的，这显然不利于国家反洗钱行动的统一实施。因此，必须以强化特定非金融机构及其从业人员的反洗钱意识与反洗钱责任为目标，采取各种积极的措施加大对特定非金融机构参与反洗钱的宣传力度，提高对特定非金融机构反洗钱监管的重视程度，进而积极研究、探索、建立健全特定非金融机构反洗钱监管的有效模式和监管机制，营造出一个统一组织、职责明确、机制健全、从业人员积极参与的特定非金融机构反洗钱防控体系，为特定非金融机构反洗钱工作的开展创造客观上的有利条件。

---

❶ 德国《反洗钱法》第3条规定：从事为客户设计运作房地产买卖，管理现金、证券和其他财产，开设及管理银行、储蓄和证券账户，买卖、管理基金、信托公司等业务的律师或法律顾问，注册会计师、审计师、税务师，房地产经纪人，赌场负责人，以及其他管理他人财产的人需要识别客户。该法第17条规定：有关义务人不遵守法定义务的，处以5万至10万欧元罚款。

3.3 建立、完善特定非金融机构反洗钱组织机构与协调机制

特定非金融机构反洗钱工作能否取得成效，很大程度上取决于组织工作是否有力、协调机制是否完善。我国反洗钱法虽然在立法层面上明确了国家反洗钱行动的组织结构与协调机制，但更多是规范国家反洗钱行政主管部门与其他政府部门、金融机构之间的组织架构，而并未明确特定非金融机构的反洗钱行动组织形式、特别是行业自律组织在反洗钱监管中的地位与职责，这就影响了特定非金融机构反洗钱行动的开展。因此，建立、完善特定非金融机构反洗钱组织机构与协调机制的基点应当包括：一是鉴于国家反洗钱行动的一致性，确立国家反洗钱主管部门在特定非金融机构反洗钱行动的绝对权威性，将特定非金融机构的反洗钱统一纳入国家反洗钱行动中，明确国家反洗钱主管部门对特定非金融机构反洗钱行动的指导、监督职能；二是针对特定非金融机构涉及行业面广、信息交流不对称、跨行业监管成本高等诸多客观因素，为提高反洗钱监管的有效性，明确行业主管部门、自律组织在反洗钱监管中的职责，充分发挥行业主管部门、自律组织在反洗钱监管方面的作用，加强行业主管部门、自律组织与国家反洗钱主管部门之间的沟通联系和信息交流，形成监管合力，真正建立起优势互补、资源共享、协调一致的特定非金融机构反洗钱组织机构与协调机制。

3.4 建立特定非金融机构反洗钱激励机制

为了调动特定非金融机构及其从业人员参与反洗钱行动的自觉性、积极性，发挥其履行反洗钱义务的主观能动性，在以法律的形式规范特定非金融机构必须履行的反洗钱特定义务、强化义务约束机制的同时，可以考虑建立起特定非金融机构反洗钱激励机制，以提高反洗钱监管的有效性。

特定非金融机构反洗钱激励机制的构成体系可以设计两方面的重点内容：一是对特定非金融机构日常反洗钱工作开展及其成果的评价体系。即设定对特定非金融机构反洗钱义务履行状况的科学评价量化指标，根据特定非金融机构性质以及经营活动的特点，结合其日常经营活动中履行反洗钱义务的实际情况，对其所开展的反洗钱工作进行定期的绩效评估，包括内部反洗钱防控制度的建立与完善、反洗钱措施的落实与执行、反洗钱专业队伍的构建与技能、反洗钱义务履行的实际与效果等方面的内容进行综合检查评定，了解和掌握特定非金融机构反洗钱工作开展的基本状况及动态变化，确保特定非金融机构履行反洗钱义务的合规性和有效性；二是对特定非金融机构日常反洗钱工作开展取得成效的奖励体系。即设定对特定非金融机构反洗钱义务履行贡献成就的奖励手段，可以考虑由国家反洗钱主管部门或相关部门从破获洗钱犯罪案件所收缴的犯罪所得及其产生的收益中提取一定比例的资金作为奖励基金的来源，对于在日常经营活动中注意发现洗钱活动线索、可疑交易线索、并主动向主管部门和有关机关报告的，以及积极协助有关机关对洗钱案件调查取证、认真并卓有成效地履行反洗钱义务的特定非金融机构及其从业人员给予适当的物质奖励，充分体现出义务约束与物质激励并举、权利与义务统一，促使特定非金融机构能够依照法律的规定在其日常经营活动中切实承担起反洗钱的责任。

特定非金融机构反洗钱，是国家反洗钱行动整体中的重要组成部分，并且直接关系到我国反洗钱行动及监管的效果。只有通过相关法律的立法、制度的建立及措施的完善，使特定非金融机构及其从业人员明确自身在国家反洗钱行动中的职责和义务，自觉将自己的行动与国家反洗钱行动保持一致，才能确保我国反洗钱法的真正贯彻施行，实现对反洗钱行动的有效监管。

参考文献

[1] 于光远. 反洗钱的理论与实践 [M]. 北京：中国金融出版社，2006.
[2] 张军. 反洗钱立法与实务 [M]. 北京：人民法院出版社，2007.
[3] 黄子文. 国际视角：洗钱渠道研究 [M]. 北京：中国金融出版社，2011.
[4] 于光远. 中华人民共和国反洗钱法实用手册 [M]. 北京：中国财政经济出版社，2006.
[5] 刘泽华. 建立健全我国反洗钱法律制度体系的思考 [J]. 河北法学，2004（1）.
[6] 吴忆萍. 我国反洗钱措施的完善势在必行 [J]. 河北法学，2003（6）.
[7] 千宏武，魏旭明. 特定非金融机构洗钱风险及防范 [N]. 金融时报，2012-02-06.

低碳经济背景下零售企业"绿色商业"发展策略
——基于本土与跨国企业比较的研究

崔 玮

1 问题的提出

由于资源与环境对社会发展的制约日益严重,绿色、环保、健康、公益等理念日益贯穿社会各领域,商业领域也不例外。通过实施"绿色商业"战略,商业企业已经成为推动低碳经济发展的重要一员。绿色商业是指有利于促进人类、自然及社会协调发展,创造良好生态环境,节约并合理利用自然与社会资源,促进社会可持续发展的商业行为的总称。跨国零售企业通常在全球范围内实施可持续发展战略并积极采取相应的绿色经营措施,包括降低能源消耗、减少碳排放、提倡绿色消费、销售环保健康产品、承担更多社会责任等。其绿色商业经营行为涵盖了广泛的环境与社会领域。本土零售企业也日益注重自身商业行为的绿色化,逐渐改变单纯追求商业利润的传统商业行为,力争实现企业利润与社会可持续发展的协调,但与跨国零售企业相比仍存在较大的差距。

商业界与理论界已日益重视对绿色商业培育与发展的研究。Bibi Van Der Zee 研究了传统商业进行"绿色革新"的必要性,并对企业如何制定绿色商业战略进行了分析[1]。周殿昆等利用外部性理论定义了"绿色商业",提出绿色商业涉及生产企业、商业企业、消费者和政府,它们之间健全的良性互动机制是绿色商业发育的动力源[2]。胥树凡分析了绿色商业的含义,提出了推动绿色商业体系的建立和发展的对策[3]。此外,一些学者也对主要零售企业开展绿色经营的具体实践包括绿色供应链构建、低碳环保示范店建设等措施与成效进行了研究。如 Edward Humes 系统研究了沃尔玛的绿色经营战略与策略[4]。总体而言,目前针对绿色商业所进行的理论与实践研究仍较少,相关研究主要集中在绿色消费与绿色供应链上。研究并借鉴国外零售企业绿色经营的先进经验,对于推动我国绿色商业的发展,构建低碳经济具有重要的意义。

2 本土与跨国零售企业绿色经营的比较

2.1 "绿色商业"理念的比较

跨国零售企业通常将"绿色经营""节能环保"纳入可持续发展的范畴,作为其商业战略的核心,并制定相应的目标。如沃尔玛将可持续发展作为其全球至关紧要的使命,并为此制定了"可持续发展 360"战略,把环保理念融入供应链和业务发展的各个环节,提出了三大发展目标:百分之百使用可再生能源;"零"浪费;出售利于资源和环境的商品。❶而澳大利亚的 Coles 自 1995 年起就加入了可持续能源发展项目,并由于有效节约能源和进行废弃物管理而获得零售和服务领域能源节约奖。❷家乐福则提出企业的目标是:在与消费者日益变化的生活方式相一致,与文明社会的期望以及主要的经济、社会、环境挑战相一致的同时实现企业业务的增长。Tesco 则设定了长远发展目标:到 2020 年成为低碳排放企业,到 2050 年成为零碳排放企业。

同时,跨国零售商在对内、对外宣传中也十分注重强调"节能环保",努力在政府及公众面前树立"绿色企业"的形象。2010 年世界零售百强排名前 15 的企业中,有 13 家企业的网站主页上设立了与企业可持续发展目标和节能环保实践相关的板块,主要进行门店节能环保建设、推广节能环保产品、倡导低碳生活方式等内容的宣传。❸如 TESCO 在英国专门开设了"Greener Living"网站,为顾客提供节能环

[作者简介] 崔玮(1970—),女,经济学博士,教授。研究方向为国际服务贸易、国际贸易理论与政策。

保建议，倡导低碳生活方式。此外，许多跨国零售企业每年还会公开发布企业的《可持续发展报告》，公布该年度企业在世界各地的分店在"节能环保""承担社会责任"等方面所采取的措施与取得的成绩。

在我国全面构筑资源节约型和环境友好型社会的背景下，本土零售企业也逐渐认识到发展"绿色商业"的重要性与紧迫性，但在对"绿色商业"概念的认识、重视程度以及"绿色商业"在企业发展中的地位等方面仍与跨国企业有较大差距。近80%的企业，节能环保仍停留在低成本投入的基础层。❹企业管理决策层能够在一定程度上重视节能环保工作，并设立企业年度节能目标，但普通员工的节能意识相对薄弱，节能环保还没有成为企业文化的组成部分，制度保障仍不完善；绝大多数本土企业能够做到定期对员工就节能降耗开展各种形式的培训和宣传，但仍有部分企业缺乏对员工节能意识和技能培训的持续宣传和实施。在对企业"绿色形象"的宣传方面方法较为肤浅、单一，如只是通过在社区推广环保购物袋的使用等类似活动进行企业宣传。此外，本土零售商很少利用网络宣传企业的"绿色经营"实践及成果，网上宣传更多集中在参与公益慈善活动的介绍上。

2.2 "绿色产品"销售策略的比较

绿色产品是指从生产、运输、购买到消费及回收处置的整个过程都符合特定的环保标准，对生态环境无害或危害极小、有助于人类健康并有利于资源保护与再生回收的产品。发达国家消费者环保意识较强，绿色产品认同率相对高于我国，消费者更关注商品在生产、购买、使用，甚至回收过程是否有利于环境保护，愿意为无污染、有利于健康的商品支付更高的价格。为更好地满足消费者的绿色消费需求，国外零售商非常注重销售"绿色商品"，包括有利于环境与资源保护的商品，有助于身体健康的商品以及循环再生的产品等。

中国消费者的绿色消费观念较为淡薄，购物时仍主要考虑商品的质量、价格等因素，较少考虑商品的生产、消费等是否会对环境造成不利影响。由于绿色产品成本较高，通常售价会远远高于普通产品，这成为阻碍消费者购买的主要障碍。同时，由于我国绿色产业刚刚兴起，绿色产品的生产尚未形成规模，且产品单一、技术含量低，未形成品牌效应，难以得到消费者的认可；而且，绿色市场管理较为混乱，真假绿色产品鱼龙混杂，甚至有一些零售商滥用绿色产品概念，使消费者失去对绿色产品的信任，这也为零售商的销售带来了较大的困难。

2.2.1 环保商品相关措施

跨国零售商已开始关注所销售的商品是否会对环境造成破坏，并逐渐引入环保产品。2010年，美国沃尔玛商场中销售的100%的复印纸及80%以上的纸质笔记本所使用的原材料都产自经认证、有专人管理的森林，所有自有品牌木制产品均获得森林管理委员会（FSC）的认证。TESCO在英国推出了200种"GreenLiving"系列自有品牌商品，包括节能灯泡、环保型纸制品和厨房用品，为顾客提供更环保的购买选择。同时，还通过降价、促销及产品推广等营销措施宣传商品的环保特征，引导顾客选择低碳生活方式。❺

此外，许多跨国零售商已开始在所销售商品上使用"碳标识"，即在商品外包装上贴上一种特殊的标签，标注出该商品从原材料到制成品的过程中所消耗二氧化碳的数量，使消费者对该种商品的生产过程对环境所造成的破坏形成量化认识，从而对于是否购买该商品做出选择。目前，TESCO已对包括灯泡、牛奶、洗衣粉等在内的114种产品标注了碳标识，这一做法既对供应商提出了更高的环保要求，也改变了消费者的消费观念。另外，一些国外零售企业还实行绿色会员卡制度，会员购买环保商品能够有相应的积分或其他优惠，从而鼓励消费者更多的购买环保产品。

与跨国零售商相比，我国零售企业所经营的绿色环保产品种类仍较少。目前主要销售节能家电、节能灯泡、无磷洗衣粉及可降解塑料包装制品等环保型产品；家电产品都有明显的能效标识；对于耗电量低的节能家电，通常会通过价格及促销措施促进其销售。虽然环保商品销售比重有所提高，但数量仍较少，涵盖的范围也较小，很少有零售商能够设置长期的环保商品专柜。而且，企业针对消费者所做的绿色环保产品的宣传、推广较少，方式单一，未能更好地发挥对绿色消费的引导作用。

2.2.2 绿色食品相关措施

所谓绿色食品是指生产地环境质量、生产过程中生产资料使用、产品质量等方面符合国家相关技术标准，无污染、无公害的优质食品。国内外零售企业都较为重视对绿色食品的销售。一些企业通过设置完整的产品追溯系统、供货商管理措施、内部警示系统及检测机制等，达到对食品安全的控制，同时承诺"逐步禁止农药使用"与"拒绝转基因食品"。

(1) 商品可追溯系统与供货商管理制度的建立。

零售企业的供货商包括农民、生产基地、制造商、代理商等，范围广泛。因此，大多数零售企业都在逐步建立供货商的管理制度，对供货商的商品质量安全情况、价格水平、供货及时性、整体服务水平、商品销售实绩等进行统计、评价，并采取相应的奖惩措施，甚至关注供货商内部组织是否完善，质量管理体系是否健全，财务状况是否稳定等。此外，跨国零售企业通过建立可追溯系统实现产品质量保障，即在产品供应的整个过程中对产品的各种相关信息进行记录存储，当产品出现质量问题时，零售企业就能够快速、有效地查询到是哪种原料或哪一加工环节出现了问题，从而有针对性地实施惩罚措施甚至进行产品召回。通过建立这种可追溯系统实现对产品质量水平的控制。家乐福、乐购、沃尔玛、永旺、欧尚等跨国零售商都承诺设置完整的产品追溯系统、供货商管理措施、内部警示系统及检测机制，并对公众公开供货商管理措施、内部警示系统及检测机制等相关信息，达到全程无污染的目的。本土零售企业中做出相同承诺的只有华普超市和农工联超市。此外，华润万家、百佳超市已对所销售生鲜蔬果建立一定程度的追溯系统，以及针对农药的检测系统。但其他企业还没做出相关的承诺和行动，虽然像永辉超市等也开展了农超对接项目，但对于产品源头的监管力度仍不够。

(2) 农药禁用与拒绝转基因食品的承诺。

对于生鲜食品，国内外都已有许多大型超市承诺逐步禁用世界卫生组织列为剧毒和高毒的农药、有机磷农药，对自有品牌生鲜食品还承诺禁用造成环境严重污染的农药，以及毒性可能对蜜蜂产生影响的农药等；对于生鲜食品设有拒绝转基因食品政策；承诺公开与消费者直接相关的拒绝转基因食品政策及逐步禁止农药使用政策。

根据国际环保组织"绿色和平"的调查，绝大多数跨国零售企业在国外市场上都做出了"逐步禁止农药使用"与"拒绝转基因食品"的承诺，但沃尔玛、乐购及伊藤洋华堂等部分企业对于中国市场实行了"双重标准"；而国内仍有很多大型超市还未做出任何承诺，或未采取有关的措施，这是造成京客隆、华润万家等超市被检测出所售蔬果中有农药残留或销售转基因食品的原因之一。

(3) 健康食品销售。

跨国零售商也在采取措施，努力使自己所销售的食品更加有利于消费者健康，如沃尔玛承诺到2015年之前将美国店内自有品牌数千种食品中的钠含量降低25%，糖含量降低10%，同时不再使用工业用反式脂肪。

本土企业为了满足消费者日益增强的对健康生活方式的追求，也越来越重视对健康食品的销售，具体体现在以下几个方面：(1) 绝大多数超市中都设有有机蔬菜专柜，为追求健康、环保并愿意为此支付更高价格的消费者提供更多的选择；(2) 许多大型超市中都设有杂粮专柜，为消费者提供更健康的主食产品；(3) 乳制品、豆制品专柜也是超市近年来重点经营的商品专区，低脂乳品、黑豆豆浆等健康食品成为主要的销售品种；(4) 日用必需品中，含铁、锌食盐、果糖等新型健康产品也逐渐摆在了超市货柜的显著位置。总体而言，本土超市中绿色食品涵盖的范围仍不够广泛，企业的宣传也仍不够充分。

表1 主要跨国零售商所采取的农产品供货商管理措施

跨国零售企业	供货商管理措施	具体做法与成效
沃尔玛	食品安全监督体系	通过与农户和农民组织对接，为农民提供食品安全管理、种植技术培训等，提高食品安全水平
	农超对接基地	基地必须取得无公害、绿色或者是有机产品基地认证，空气、水质、土壤都需符合检验标准；种植菜品的种类、种子、播种、技术、检测、采收、冷藏、包装、配送等各个环节必须在第三方机构指导下进行
乐购	传统的农超对接方式	企业与农户和农民组织直接对接
	自有品牌农场模式	对自有品牌供应商设置较高的食品安全准入门槛，并对供应商进行培训，签订责任合同，实现全程监控
家乐福	直采模式	挑选产品符合采购标准的合作社签订长期订货合同，通过合作社来控制生产流程

2.2.3 循环再生产品相关措施

跨国零售企业大多已经建立了物品回收利用的相关管理制度，并能够对废弃产品进行回收再利用。如 2010 年，沃尔玛回收利用了 1400 万磅的废弃汽车和卡车的轮胎，并利用这些轮胎橡胶制成了户外地垫进行销售。此外，沃尔玛用包装用废料再生了 325000 磅的聚苯乙烯，并用这些材料制成了海报和图片相框。❻北京沃尔玛与生物科技公司合作，将废弃的熟食、海鲜、肉类、面包、饼干等进行处理，作为饲料、肥料、土壤的改良剂，应用于农业、畜牧业等产业，实现了有机循环。西尔斯在商店内回收塑料衣架，仅 2008 年就回收了 2250 吨衣架，其中 75% 的衣架会被循环再用，损坏或过时的衣架则被用于生产新产品；此外，西尔斯公司还通过闭环回收系统对 97% 的铅酸电池进行了回收。

许多本土零售企业也面向消费者提供了废弃物的回收服务。调查显示：50% 的企业对淘汰的家电进行回收，48% 的企业对废旧瓶罐进行回收，44% 的企业会回收废旧电池，而只有 35% 的企业会面向消费者进行纸张的回收。❼但是，本土企业对于废弃物仅仅是停留在回收的初级阶段，大部分回收品只是作为废品销售，对于如何对废弃物进行再利用或循环再生，转变为可供企业销售的环保产品，为企业创造利润，则有待于企业进行深层次的探索。

2.3 "绿色包装"措施的比较

绿色包装（green package）又可以称为无公害包装和环境友好包装，指对生态环境和人类健康无害，能重复使用和再生，符合可持续发展的包装。首先，包装减量化是国内外零售商发展绿色包装的首选措施。通过与供货商的合作，减少包装用料，既达到了环保的目的，又能够节省包装成本与物流成本。沃尔玛对商品包装制定了严格规定，如有冠菠萝包装纸箱尺寸为 60×40×14.5 厘米，无冠时包装缩小为 50×40×15.5 厘米，从而减少 4% 的纸浆使用量。沃尔玛的目标是在 2013 年前实现总体包装用料减少 5%，并要求与之联系的中国 2 万家供应商行动起来减少包装。这一行动能够为其自身供应链节省近 34 亿美元。[5] 欧尚中国将关注减量包装作为其可持续发展实践的一部分，2009 年对 80 个品项进行减量包装，节约了近 19.4 吨包装材料。其次，利用可循环材料或绿色材料替代原有高污染材料进行包装，利用纸质包装或是可回收的复合式材料包装，既有利于回收利用，又不会对环境造成大量污染。

本土零售企业也逐渐重视包装的减量，调查显示：超过 34% 的企业关注包装环节的减量化，2010 年实现多个品项的减量包装，每家门店年平均节约包装材料 6.8 吨。❽此外，2008 年，中国商务部下发了《商品零售场所塑料购物袋有偿使用管理办法》，超市"限塑"效果最明显，塑料购物袋减少量平均在 75% 以上，相当于减少塑料消耗约 27 万吨。一些超市还推出了"无塑料袋快速通道"、购物篮租用、换购环保袋等各种配套服务。此外，一些企业对内部包装废弃物进行回收利用，但目前纸箱等包装物返回配送中心和返回供应商再循环再利用的比例仅为 13% 和 15%。

2.4 节能降耗措施的比较

由于各国环保节能的政策和侧重点不同，如欧洲的环境标准日益严格、环境税已经普及，所以英国零售业比较侧重低碳或零碳排放；而美国则相对比较注重绿色供应链和可持续发展。但无论怎样，都是秉承着节能环保的宗旨。

跨国零售商通常凭借其资本与技术优势对其门店投资进行节能改造，建设智能化能源管理控制中心或能源管理数据平台。通过在连锁分店中安装能源管理系统，将能耗情况随时上传至总部能源管理中心，通过远程控制实现对门店的能耗即时管理，降低碳排放。此外，跨国零售商在世界各地建设节能示范店，通过在用水管理、冷冻冷藏、照明、循环再利用、清洁能源等方面采取综合措施，推行低碳营销。TESCO 从 2005 年开始将建设低碳超市纳入战略规划，并在全球几十个国家陆续开设低碳超市。2008 年 10 月在韩国开办的低碳超市运用了 69 项节能措施，实现减排 50%。2010 年 2 月正式运行的朗姆锡超市更是实现了零碳排放目标，成为全球首家零碳超市。这家超市在建筑中不仅仅应用了大量可持续资源的材料、在供热发电方面采用了可再生资源，而且在停车场和加油站均使用了 LED 灯照明，在制冷、加热、通风及空调系统方面几乎没有对环境产生影响。沃尔玛则在其全球 7400 多家分店中全面采取提高能效、减少浪费的措施。

目前，我国零售业节能减排与发达国家相比还有较大差距。国内大型零售企业的能源消耗占费用总支出的 10%—30%，比发达国家同类商场高出 2~3 倍。即使在能耗较低的北京，本土商场单位面积能耗仍然高出气候相近的日本同类商场40%左右。在节能环保方面，本土企业仍处于起步阶段，虽然大型零售商已对门店的节能设施加大了投入，但一般只是节电节水等若干分散的单项措施，缺乏系统性和综合性的节能意识与措施。在节能示范店的建设方面，由于大部分店铺是租赁经营，且店面系统改造成本高，风险大，短期内很难收回成本，而且本土企业资金有限，因此绝大多数仍处于观望状态。

2.5 绿色供应链构建的比较

绿色供应链管理是一种在整个供应链内综合考虑环境影响和资源效率的现代管理模式。零售企业作为消费者与供应商之间的桥梁，在绿色供应链的构建中发挥着越来越重要的作用。"与供应商共同构建可持续发展的绿色供应链，打造一个彼此共赢的公益模式"已成为跨国零售商可持续发展战略的核心。一方面，通过逆向整合供应商，与其建立绿色供应链战略联盟，与供应商在产品开发、包装、运输等方面通力协作，引导供应商提高技术创新和可持续发展能力，减少不必要的包装，增加包装循环再利用次数，提高物流配送能力和运输效率，降低物流成本；另一方面，零售商通过回收包装及旧产品供制造商再次使用等行为，既加强了绿色供应链管理，又向消费者传递低碳生活理念。2008年，沃尔玛提出建立对环境和社会发展负责任的全球供应链，到2015年底，沃尔玛将从全球供应链中减少2000万吨的温室气体排放量。沃尔玛已与200余家中国顶级供应商工厂合作，提高能效达20%。同时，沃尔玛已在部分供应商中实行"碳揭露计划"，公布这些供货商的温室气体排放量，并最终实现碳足迹标识。此外，沃尔玛还在全球设立了10家"返品中心"，从客户手中回收用过、退还或者损坏的产品和包装，通过构建绿色逆向物流，实现节约资源、保护环境，提升企业竞争力的目标。

跨国企业虽然在物流配送方面根据实际情况采取了不同的模式，但都能够通过采取绿色措施，降低物流成本，减少配送过程中的能耗和环境影响。

本土企业也已经认识到将环保节能向供应链延伸的重要性。根据中国连锁经营协会的调查，超过半数的企业设定了物流环节的节能目标；46%的企业关注本地产品的销售，以减少商品运输过程的碳排放；超过半数的企业对供应商提出了节能环保要求和限制，并开展针对供应商能效提升的培训等。但是，在"绿色供应链"构建方面，本土企业仍处于起步阶段：大多数零售商和供应商之间没有建立长期合作的战略伙伴关系；在物流配送方面，零售企业虽拥有自己的配送车辆以及仓库，但自有车辆实载率只有25%，信息化程度低，物流效率低下，能耗及成本较高，物品的损耗率也相对较高。

2.6 承担企业社会责任的比较

跨国零售企业之所以能够成功进入国际市场，一个重要的因素就是将社会责任纳入企业的战略环节，积极与东道国政府及非政府组织合作，在食品安全、节能降耗、环境保护、雇员权益等方面积极开展"绿色行动"，树立符合低碳社会流通价值观的绿色企业形象，从而赢得消费者的高度认可。沃尔玛正是通过与政府部门、学术机构、NGO及行业协会在可持续发展的各个领域开展形式多样的合作，积极承担社会责任。

本土企业也积极尝试采取丰富多样的形式向社区、顾客、商场员工推广环保节能理念：如通过开展"地球月"、回收月饼盒、开设节能环保产品专区、设置环保宣传栏、举办"环保低碳"社区公益教育等活动，向公众宣传低碳环保生活方式。但本土企业在承担社会责任方面更为注重开展慈善捐助、爱心奉献等活动，低碳环保行动较少，对社会责任的认识仍较浮浅和单一，与跨国企业相比，本土企业所采取的绿色行动仍处于较低的层面。

表2 主要跨国零售企业的绿色物流模式比较

跨国零售企业	绿色物流模式	具体措施与成效
乐购	建立绿色物流乐购	整体采用节能设计，应用太阳能面板、可再生能源等大量绿色节能技术及设备，使物流中心本身成为一个绿色有机整体，并通过物流中心节省运输成本，降低运输途中产生的不必要浪费
沃尔玛	集权化物流管理模式	通过所拥有的世界上最大的民用卫星和数据库系统管理绿色物流环节，将分布在世界各地的分店和供应商有机连接，能够在1小时内完成全球几千家分店的库存盘点。各门店没有自主进货权，由配送中心统一进货再配送到各门店
家乐福	分散配送模式	在中国没有采取常规的集中采购管理体制，没有配送中心，各门店拥有自己的供应商体系，利用先进信息技术提高物流效率、减少库存成本

表3 沃尔玛在中国承担企业社会责任的具体措施

时间	采取的"绿色行动"
2008年10月	与科技部直属事业单位中国21世纪议程管理中心签署《环境可持续发展备忘录》，在供应商企业中推广"企业创新与可持续发展能力建设项目"；与中国林业产业协会签署《环境可持续发展合作谅解备忘录》，分享森林认证的专业意见
2009年10月	与科技部直属事业单位中国21世纪议程管理中心签署《关于可持续发展竞赛的谅解备忘录》
2009年10月	与商务部和农业部签署《共促"农超对接"合作备忘录》
2010年4月	中国饮料工业协会签订《饮料产品绿色生产和绿色运营推进计划》
2010年10月	同国家林业局中林天合（北京）森林认证中心签署《环境可持续发展合作谅解备忘录》
2010年12月	同北京大学签署《沃尔玛中国超市废弃物处理的合作协议》
2012年2月	同重庆市对外贸易经济委员会签订《经贸合作战略框架备忘录》

3 借鉴跨国零售发展我国"绿色商业"的对策

3.1 政府层面

首先，完善"绿色商业"发展配套政策。包括完善绿色补贴和税收政策，通过经济手段鼓励企业的节能环保行为；降低对零售商节能改造补贴和奖励的门槛，扩大辐射面；制定政府绿色采购政策推动绿色低碳产品的销售；加大对绿色产品研发与生产的支持力度等。如建立"流通业节能环保扶持基金"，通过政府专项基金形式带动企业增加对节能设备及管理技术的投入。

其次，建立健全零售业绿色环保法律与标准体系。制定、完善"绿色产品"的相关标准，包括农产品农药禁用及残留、转基因食品管理、食品可追溯性等方面的法律法规，如建立图1所示的产品可追溯系统；促进产品环保性的评估与申报制度的建立；建立节能减排能耗统计指标体系，形成零售业监测平台；制定绿色超市的环保标准及绿色超市的认证体系等。

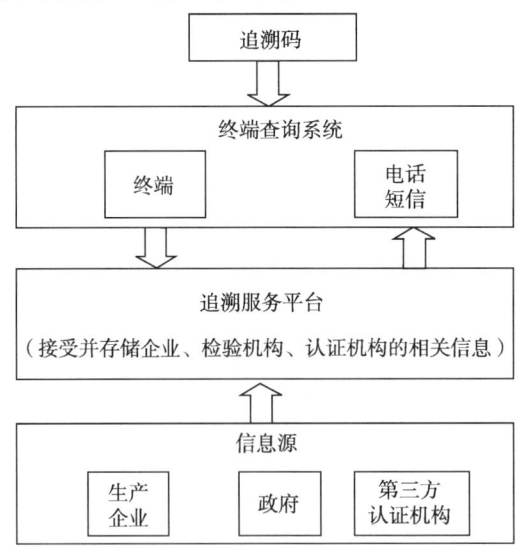

图1 产品可追溯系统

再次，制定绿色消费的相关法律法规。借鉴发达国家经验，制定《废弃物管理法》《可再生能源优先法》《绿色消费法》等，为实现绿色消费创造良好的法律环境。

最后，加强针对消费者与零售商的"绿色宣传"。一方面，向消费者宣传绿色低碳消费理念，传播绿色消费知识，引导消费者自觉自愿接受绿色消费模式和低碳生活方式；另一方面，引导零售企业提高环保意识与责任感，并加强政府的监督与管理。

3.2 企业层面

首先,树立绿色经营理念,宣传企业绿色形象。零售企业应将绿色经营作为企业的可持续发展战略和系统运营模式,而不仅仅是简单地在某些经营环节实施节能环保措施。积极学习跨国企业的绿色商业理念、制度、行为与方法,制定本企业可持续发展的战略与目标,并开展多途径、多角度的宣传。通过与政府机构、非政府组织、科研机构、高校等的合作,开展节能环保项目,积极承担企业社会责任,树立企业绿色形象;同时,利用自身直接接触消费者的优势,加强针对消费者的宣传与引导。

其次,实施"绿色商品"销售及"绿色包装"策略。零售企业应进一步加大健康产品、环保产品、循环再生产品等绿色商品的销售比例,设置绿色产品销售专柜或专区;通过建立农超对接基地或自有品牌基地,加强对农户的培训、监督与管理,建立完善的产品追溯制度,从源头上保证产品的安全;通过使用环境标示、实行绿色会员卡制度、合理制定绿色产品价格等方式引导消费者更多地购买绿色商品;与供应商合作,研究包装减量及回收再利用的有效方式等。

再次,对店面进行系统的节能改造。本土企业应创造条件进行节能示范店的建设,采用先进的节能设备和技术,构建智能能源管理系统,全面实现空调通风系统、食品冷冻冷藏系统,以及照明系统的安全运行和低能耗。在资金不足的情况下,则可因地制宜,利用各种节能措施对店面进行系统化改造,减少能源消耗。

最后,构建绿色供应链。第一,实现绿色采购。与供应商建立战略伙伴关系,不仅对于产品本身还包括整个生产过程是否符合环保标准进行监控,与供应商合作提高能效,减少对资源的消耗;第二,实现绿色配送。零售企业应根据自身条件及店面分布选择适宜的物流配送方式,包括:自建绿色物流中心或是利用供应商和使用第三方物流公司。通过科学管理减少配送中的能耗及货损;第三,实现绿色逆向物流。自建或以合伙形式建立"返品中心",通过对废品的回收和循环再生,达到节能环保及树立企业绿色形象的目的。

参考文献

[1] van der Zee B. 绿色商业[M]. 广州:世界图书出版公司,2010.
[2] 周殿昆,李荣庆,郭红兵. 构建促进绿色商业发展的良性互动机制[J]. 财贸经济,2007(11):103-107,129.
[3] 胥树凡. 绿色商业的发展与思考[J]. 环境经济,2010(6):44-46.
[4] Humes E. Force of nature:How Wal-Mart started a green busi-ness revolution-and why it might save the world[M]. New York,NY:HarperBusiness,2011.
[5] 莫姬. 沃尔玛"绿色战略"大变革[J]. 中国商贸,2008(8):82-83.

注　释

❶❻ 资料来源:Walmart 2012 Global Responsibility Report。
❷ 资料来源:中国连锁经营协会,《超市行业节能情况调查报告2006》。
❸❹❺❼❽ 资料来源:《2011年中国零售业节能环保绿皮书》。

产业链的传导机制与通货膨胀机理研究

符亚明

产业是指国民经济的各种生产或服务部门，"三次产业"理论出现后，就泛指各种提供商品生产和流通、技术服务的企业或经济组织，它既指具有某种相同或相近属性的企业或组织的集合，又可指某一类别产品生产的总称。国民经济就是由这些相互联系、相互影响、相互作用的产业组成，所以，产业经济的的发展状况直接决定国民经济的发展速度和质量。同时，在国民经济发展过程中，各产业间都存在着直接或间接的联系，与其它产业脱离的产业是难以生存和发展的。某个产业增长或衰退，对上、下游产业都产生直接影响，并通过产业链一层一层地向其它相关产业传导，进而影响该产业及相关产业的生产过程，最终影响整个国民经济。所以，研究产业链的构成、特点及内在规律，对理解产业经济运行规律、调整产业结构和国民经济结构，保持国民经济稳定健康的发展，具有重要的理论意义和现实意义。

产业链理论是我国理论界和学者在 20 世纪末提出的[1]。近几年来，经过专家和学者的研究和推广，形成了丰富的研究成果和理论基础，并在实践中得到了应用，也逐渐为世界理论界所接受，并得到了进一步完善[2]。综合研究成果，产业链理论研究大致可划分为三个层次：一是对产业链基础理论的研究，如产业链的概念、类型的研究，对产业链的定义、内涵、特点的等基础理论[3]；二是产业链内在规律的研究[4]，研究产业链的内在规律[5]；三是应用研究[6]，运用产业链理论解决实际问题[7]，特别是分行业研究产业链的应用[8]。但整体而言，产业链的研究目前还处于理论系统的完善阶段，基础研究需要进一步加强，应用研究需要进一步充实，特别是要将新的研究方法和工具运用到应用研究中，使应用研究得到更科学，更具有实际意义。综合来说，产业链要形成一整套系统理论还有待进一步于完善，需要在实践中不断丰富和发展，使之成为研究产业结构和国民经济结构的理论工具和政策依据。

一、产业链的形态与结构

产业链在理论界还没有一个较为明确且公认的定义，通常是指在一种产品生产过程中的上下游产业间的关联关系[3]。在综合产业链的定义基础上，本文将产业链定义为：在最终产品的生产过程中，从最初的自然资源到最终产品所包含的各个生产环节由供应关系所形成的链条。一个产品的产业链就是一个由多个相互链接的生产链条所构成的。

任何能持续生产的产品或服务，要么是满足居民生活、政府机构、社会团体消费需要的，将之称为最终品；要么是用来满足企业生产需要，作为生产要素，作为产品生产经营过程中的原材料，经过生产加工，最后形成最终品的构成部分。将这类产品称之为投入品；要么兼而有之。既可以是消费品，也作为投入品。

(1) 产业链形态

如果把最终品作为分析的起点，分解其产品的生产过程。每个最终品都是通过对材料进行加工而成的。将直接构成最终品的材料即投入品，定义为一级投入品。构成一级投入品的材料定义为二级投入品，依次类推，直到从自然界中直接获得的原材料，称之为原始材料，这样就形成了一个产品生产过程中上下产业层次关系。将最终品、各级投入品和原始材料用链条联接起来，就形成了这个产品的产业链。如图 1。最终消费品处于一个产业链的顶端，投入品位于产业链的中间环节，原始材料处于产业链的末端。

[作者简介] 符亚明，北京联合大学。

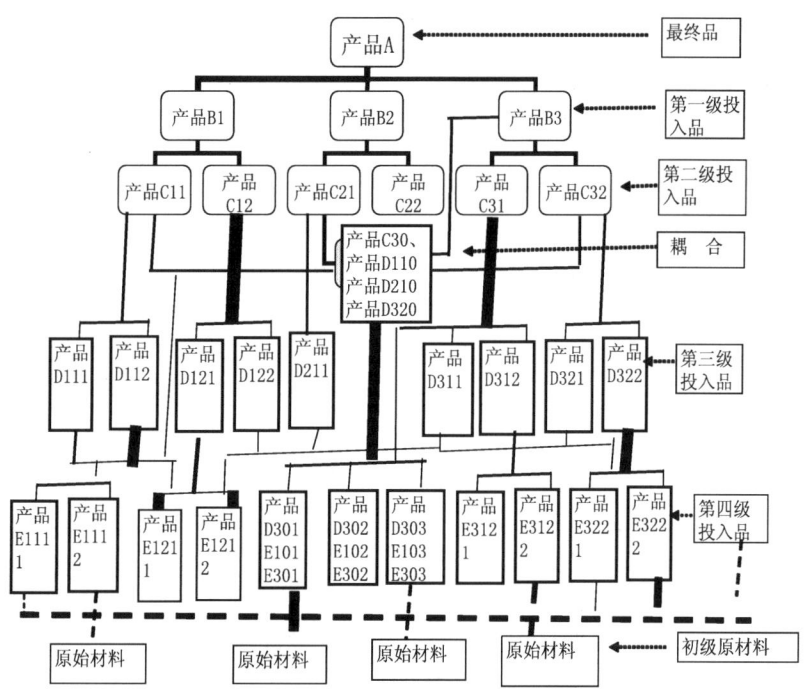

图1 产业链形态

在一个产品的产业链中，从最终品经过投入品至每个原始材料都形成一条贯穿某个生产环节的链条，把这种从最终品、某个投入品和某一个原始材料构成的链条称之为子链，它覆盖着从原始材料到最终品的某一个生产环节，每个产品产业链都由数量不同的子链构成。在图1中，每个从最上端的最终品到最末端的原始材料构成一个产品A产业链的子链，如产品A——产品B_1——产品C_{11}——产品D_{111}——产品E_{1111}——原始材料，就是产品A这个产业链的一个子链。一个产业链有很多条长度不同的子链构成，这些子链相辅相成，相互影响，缺一不可。这些子链的数量和比例就决定了这个产品的产业链的结构，而产业链结构一旦形成，在一定时期内就会相对稳定，只要产品的生产技术和产品结构不发生变化，产业链结构也不会发生变化。所以，一个产品的产业链结构是由产品结构和生产技术决定的。一旦产品的结构和生产技术发生变化，比如某些成份增加，而另一些成份减少甚至消失，那么成份增加的材料对应的产业链的子链比例就会增加，而成份减少的材料所对应的产业链中的子链比例就会下降。同样，产品中消失的成份对应的子链就会消失，增加成份就会出现新的子链。

产业链是由社会分工和专业化生产过程中形成的，产品生产过程越复杂，子链越多，产业链越长，产业链覆盖的范围也越广，对国民经济影响也就越大。在图1中，每个从最上端的最终品到最末端的初级原材料都构成一个产业链的子链，如产品A——产品B_1——产品C_{11}——产品D_{111}——产品E_{1111}——初级原材料，就是产品A这个产业链的一个子链。一个产业链有很多条这样长度不同的子链构成。同时，除原始材料外，每个产品及投入品都有其作为生产要素的下一级投入品。不同的产品及投入品有不尽相同的下一级投入品，但也可能不同级别的投入品可能具有相同的下一级投入品，这种现象称之为产业链耦合。如图1中的同一个产品C_{30}、产品D_{110}、产品D_{210}、产品D_{320}就是同时是产品B_3、产品C_{11}、产品C_{21}和产品C_{32}的投入品。产业链耦合对整个产业链正常运行至关重要，它是产业链的交汇点，它的增长或衰退，影响整个产业链的扩张或萎缩。

（2）产业链的长度和广度

每个产业链都由数量不同、长短不一、错综复杂子链组成，多个产业链子链相交于产业链耦合点。某个产业链的子链越多，其产业链覆盖范围越广。产业链子链数量能表明该产业在国民经济中涉及的范围，称之为产业链广度。同时，在同一个产业链中，其子链在生产过程中的重要性也不同，有的支链在整个产业链中占主导的生产地位，其增长或衰退直接导致整个产业链的扩张或收缩。将这种子链称之为产业链的主链。产业链主链主要特点是在最终品和各级投入品的生产过程中，下一级投入品都是上一级产品的主要构成。对应主链的其他子链称之为支链，如图1中的粗线条都表示主链。一个产业链中可能有一个或多个主链，同时也有一个或多个支链。在产业链中，其主链对整个产业链的生产和发展比支链影响更大。虽然主链和支链在生产过程的重要性不同，但主链和支链同样都是产业链不可或缺的组成部分，缺少任何一个支链，产业链都不能正常的运行。

同时，不同产业链子链以及同一个产业链的不同子链的长短也不相同，产业链生产过程中经过的环节越多，产业链层次越多，其产业链越长。由于主链在产业链占有主导地位，在产品生产起着重要影响，而支链对产业链影响相对较小。所以，决定产业链延伸范围的应该是主链，产业链主链的延伸长度作为产业链的长度，是产业链中从最终品经投入品到原始材料的纵向长度，也表示产业链层次的数量。

产业链的广度和长度是产业链两个重要的特征，从横向和纵向两个方面描述产业链在国民经济中的地位和影响。产业链广度是指产业链主链和支链的数量特别是指主链数量的多少。某个产业链的主链及支链越多，其广度越宽。从层次上来看，产业链链条数量是呈几何级数增长的，产业链越延伸，其主链和支链数量越多，广度也就越宽。但产业链延伸到一定程度后，最终都会归结到最基本的原始材料上。所以，产业链延伸到一定程度后，就出现链条逐渐减少的现象，产业链广度也就逐渐减小。

产业链的长度和广度描述的是产业链经过的生产环节数量，生产环节越多，涉及的中间品生产过程越多，产业链长度和广度值越大，产业链的广度和长度是由产品的特性和生产过程的特点决定的。长度和广度越大的产业链，在国民经济中所覆盖的范围越大，对国民经济和经济增长影响也就越大。所有最终品所组成的产业链就完全覆盖了国民经济，这些产业链结构也就形成了国民经济结构，产业链结构的变化也必然会引起国民经济结构的调整和生产方式的转变。

二、产业链中的物质流及传导机制

产业链从最终品、投入品到原始材料间的链接主要是通过物质流和资金流链接的。即投入品为最终品提供生产要素的供给，最终品形成对投入品的需求，形成了物质和资金的双向流动。所以，产业链是个双向链条，如图2。产业链中某个产品价格发生变动时，都会通过信息流和物质流的传导给产业链中的其他产品价格产生影响，这就是产业链的价格传导机制。

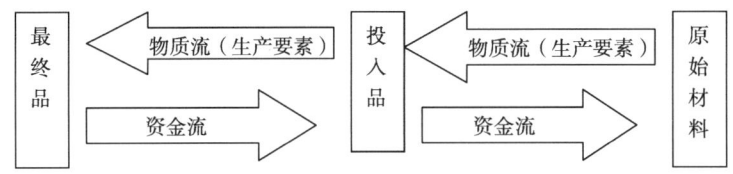

图 2　产业链双向结构链条

物质流和资金流构成了产业链中的上、下产品链接的链条。物质流和资金相向流动，且价值对等，即货币计量的物质流的流通量应该与资金流的流通量相等（如果不考虑支付延迟）。用 W 表示资金流通量，P 表示物质流的价格，Q 表示物质流数量，是产业链上一级投入品或最终品对下一级投入品或原始材料的需求量。则有 $W = P * Q$。显然，W 代表用货币表示的产业链的上一级投入品或最终品对下一级投入品或原始材料的总需求，Q 也表示产业链下一级投入品或原始材料对产业链总供给，$P * Q$ 是用货币表示的产业链下一级投入品或原始材料的总供给。W 或 $P * Q$ 称为产业链的流量。

要保持产业链正常、稳定的运行，用货币计量的物质流量和资金流量应该相等，即总需求等于总供给。一旦物质流和资金流均衡打破，产业链链条就会削弱，甚至会断裂。在产业链中，产业链的主链对应的流量大，产业链中的支链地流量相应比较小。

影响产业链中的流量的因素是价格 P 和需求量 Q。在正常情况下，价格 P 和需求量 Q 成反向变动关系，即价格上涨时，需求量减少，价格下跌时，需求量增加。而决定价格变动的主要因素是商品的供求关系。

当最终品供求关系产生变化时，最终品价格也会发生变化，进而影响下一级投入品的需求量，从而影响该投入品的价格，并通过产业链向下传导，最终影响整个产业链的价格。同样，产业链中某一投入品价格发生变化时，也会影响该产品的供给量与需求量，并同时向上、下游产业传导，影响上一级投入品和下一级投入品的供给量与需求量，进而影响其产品价格。这就是产业链中的价格传导。

由于投入品都作为生产要素，当作为原始材料或某一投入品价格发生变化时，必然会影响上一级投入品或最终品的成本，成本作为价格的组成部分，通过价格传导机制，传导到整个产业链，使总成本发生变化。这就是产业链中的成本传导。

首先研究最终品价格传导。如果整个产业链中的生产技术都没有发生变化，那么，产业链中每个产品其构成成份也不会发生变化，也就是说每个产品的材料构成比例不发生变化。所以，最终品、投入品和原始材料的需求量变化率都相同。比如，最终品产量增长了10%，由于产品生产技术没有发生变化，产品的每个构成材料比例也不会发生变化，对每个材料需求量都会增长10%，这样最终品对其产业链中每个一级投入品需求也将增加10%。依此类推，整个产业链中在这个生产过程中的每个投入品和原始材料的需求量都将增加10%。

如果最终品的产品需求价格弹性系数 E_0，当最终品价格变化量为 $\triangle P_0/P_0$ 时，根据需求价格弹性定义[9]

$$E = \frac{\frac{\Delta Q}{Q}}{\frac{\Delta P}{P}}, 即 \frac{\Delta Q}{Q} = E \times \frac{\Delta P}{P}$$

那么最终品的需求量变化量为 $E_0 * \triangle P_0/P_0$。若投入品需求价格弹性系数为 E_{1i}，第一级各投入品的产品作为生产要素，在生产技术不变的情况下，最终品的构成成份也不会发生变化，所以，一级投入品的需求量同样变化 $E_0 * \triangle P_0/P_0$。得到产业链一级投入品价格变化为

$\frac{\Delta P_{1i}}{P_{1i}} = \frac{E_0}{E_{1i}} \times \frac{\Delta P_0}{P_0}$，其中 E_{1i} 为某一级投入品的需求价格弹性系数

依此类推，产业链中的各级投入品和原始材料的价格变化率为

$$\frac{\Delta P_{ij}}{P_{ij}} = \frac{E_0}{E_{ij}} \times \frac{\Delta P_0}{P_0},$$ 公式1

其中 E_{ij} 为第 i 级投入品中第 j 个投入品的需求价格弹性系数

显然，最终品价格变化，对产业链各级投入品都会产生影响，影响大小与需求价格弹性系数的比值有关。如果某个投入品的需求价格弹性系数大于最终品的需求价格弹性系数，这种投入品的价格变化幅度会更大，相反就会较小。

再研究原始材料的价格传导。当某一个原始材料的价格变动时，会引起产业链中与之链接的子链中上一级投入品的需求量发生变化。原始材料价格上涨会使上一级投入品成本上升，引起投入品的价格上涨。如果投入品生产企业转嫁成本能力强，就会完全将成本转嫁给上一级投入品，价格相应提高。

若原始材料在上一级投入品构成所占的比例是 α，该投入品的成本转嫁能力系数为 β[10]（即价格与成本上涨幅度的比值）。如果原始材料价格变化 $\triangle P_m/P_m$，由这种原材料价格变化这一种因素导致其所在产业链子链的上一级投入品的价格变化率为。

$$\frac{\Delta P_{i,m-1}}{P_{i,m}} = \alpha \times \beta \times \frac{\Delta P_m}{P_m},$$ 公式2

其中 $P_{i,m-1}$ 为某一个原始材料某一产业链子链的上一级每时 j 个投入品的价格。

这样，可以计算出该产业链中某个投入品因原始材料价格变动，所引起的产业链其它投入品的价格变化。

$$\frac{\Delta P_{m,n}}{P_{m,n}} = \prod_{j=m-1,m-2,\cdots,1}^{i=m-1,m-2\cdots,1} \alpha_i \times \beta_j \times \frac{\Delta P_0}{P_0},$$ 公式3

$P_{m,n}$ 为产业链中距原始档 m 级第 n 子链的投入品的价格。

将原始材料价格变化引起的各个投入品的价格变化，称之为成本传导。

最后分析产业链中投入品价格变化对产业链的影响。产业链某个子链中某个投入品的价格发生变化时，可以将它作为最终品，用公式1分析对产业链所有下级投入品进行价格传导，又可将它视为原始材料，用成本传导分析它对所有上级投入品进行成本传导。

三、结论与建议

从公式1可以得出这样的结论：在消费品价格上涨时，其投入品价格上涨幅度取决于其需求价格弹性系数与最终品的需求价格弹性系数的比例，当比值大1时，投入品的价格会上涨，比值越大，上涨幅度越大。当比值小于1时，投入品的价格会下降，比值越小，其价格下降的幅度越大，由于最终品一般都是消费品，其需求价格弹性系数一般较小，所以，最终品与投入品的需求价格弹性系数的比值一般会大于1。也就是说，由消费品价格指数上涨决定的通货膨胀发生时，大部分投入品价格会上涨更大，从而导致社会整体物价水平的上涨。消费品价格的上涨，常常是由需求拉动的通货膨胀，这类通货膨胀会引起会从消费品传导到投入品，引起社会物价的普遍上涨。

从公式2可以看出，由于 α 小于1，成本传导过程中对产业链其他产品的价格影响，主要取决于这种产品的成本转嫁能力 β 的大小，β 越大，其价格上涨幅度越大。如果产品的成本转嫁能力小，产品价格反而可能下降。所以，在成本传导过程中，其价格上涨大小不一，并且会呈现出这样一个规律：随着产业链中延伸，价格上涨效应逐渐减弱。所以产业链中离原始材料越远的投入品，价格变化越小，成本传导具有递减规律。

治理需求拉动的通货膨胀时，应该采取抑制消费品物价上涨的措施，比如收紧流动性、减少货币发行量等措施来降低通货率。治理成本推动的通货膨胀，应该用提高利率抑制投资等手段来控制通货膨胀。

参考文献

[1] 刘志迎，赵倩. 产业链概念、分类及形成机理研究述评 [J]. 工业技术经济，2009（10）：51-55。
[2] 魏然. 产业链的理论渊源与研究现状综述 [J]. 技术经济与管理研究. 2010（6）：140-143。
[3] 刘贵富. 产业链的基本内涵研究 [J]. 工业技术经济. 2007（8）：92-96。
[4] 郁义鸿. 产业链类与产业链效率基准 [J]. 经济与管理研究. 2005（11）：35-40。
[5] 邵昶，李健. 产业链"波粒二象性"研究——论产业链的特性、结构及其整合 [J]. 中国工业经济. 2007（9）：8-11。
[6] 刘志迎，赵倩. 产业链概念、分类及形成机理研究述评 [J]. 工业技术经济，2009（10）：51-55。
[7] 张利庠，张喜才. 我国农业产业链中价格波动的传导与调控机制研究经济理论与经济管理 [j]. 2011（1）：104-110。
[8] 高阔，甘筱青. 基于FDL模型的猪肉供应链价格传导机制研究 [J]. 统计与决策 2012（24）：132-135。
[9] 高鸿业. 微观经济学. 人民邮电出版 [M]. 2012年：50-100。
[10] 董理，史小龙垄断产业规制中的风险和成本转嫁研究 [J]. 价格月刊，2008（9）：63-66。

我国《小企业会计准则》与《中小主体国际财务报告准则》差异的原因分析

傅宏宇

一、引　言

2011年11月18日，我国财政部正式发布了《小企业会计准则》。比较IASB 2009年7月发布的《中小主体国际财务报告准则2009》（以下简称IFRS for SMEs），两者存在很大的差异。在适用范围上，IFRS for SMEs适用于中小主体，即不具有公共受托责任的主体；而我国《小企业会计准则》适用于小企业，即除了不承担社会公众责任外，还需符合国务院发布的中小企业划型标准所规定的小企业或微型企业标准。采用的文本体例上，IFRS for SMEs基本沿用了《国际财务报告准则》（以下简称IFRS）的体例，除了准则正文还有"结论基础"和"解释性财务报表以及列报与披露一览表"；而我国的《小企业会计准则》增加了附录部分，包括"会计科目、主要账务处理和财务报表""主要会计事项分录举例"等内容。在涉及的交易事项范围上，IFRS for SMEs涉及了许多《小企业会计准则》没有涉及的内容，如权益变动表和收益与留存收益表、合并财务报表和单独财务报表、其他金融工具问题、合营中的投资、投资性房地产、企业合并和商誉、租赁、准备和或有事项、政府补助、借款费用、以股份为基础的支付、资产减值、雇员福利、所得税、外币折算、恶性通货膨胀、报告期后事项、关联方披露、特殊活动等。在采用的计量属性上，IFRS for SMEs中"常用的计量属性是历史成本和公允价值"（2.34），但在存货的计量中仍采用了可变现净值；而《小企业会计准则》则只采用历史成本计量。在资产减值方面，IFRS for SMEs中保留了大量资产减值的内容；而《小企业会计准则》完全没有资产减值的内容。在确认计量的方法上，IFRS for SMEs也远比《小企业会计准则》复杂。例如，对长期股权投资IFRS for SMEs的适用方法有成本法和权益法，而《小企业会计准则》只采用成本法。在披露要求方面，《小企业会计准则》较之IFRS for SMEs不要求披露综合收益表、权益变动表，选编现金流量表，且附注披露的内容也大幅度减少。整体来看，我国《小企业会计准则》的简化力度大大超过IFRS for SMEs。在我国会计准则已经与国际财务报告准则全面趋同的背景下，我国《企业会计准则》与完整版《国际财务报告准则》只存在极少数的个别差异。因此，我国《小企业会计准则》与IFRS for SMEs存在很大差异的原因非常值得探讨和分析。

IASB制定准则的方法与发达国家和地区（以美国为代表）制定准则的方法基本是一致的，即先由准则制定机构根据其秉持的理念目标、结合了解的情况制定准则的初步文稿（讨论稿和征求意见稿），再根据反馈意见进行认真修改，其间还可能包括实地测试，最终形成发布的准则文件。我国准则制定机构在国际趋同的大背景下，其制定准则的方法也在逐步接近国际通用的方法。这样，准则制定机构在制定准则时秉持的理念和后续修订的依据对于准则最终文件的形成起到关键的作用。

二、IASB制定《中小主体国际财务报告准则2009》的基本理念

通过阅读《中小主体国际财务报告准则2009》中的"基础结论"（Basic Conclusion）可以看出，IASB在2001—2009年长达8年的IFRS for SMEs制定过程中一直秉持着如下几个基本理念。

（一）提高财务报告信息的可比性

提高全世界财务报告信息的可比性是IASB及其前身IASC自1973年以来一直秉持的理念。IASB在

[作者简介] 傅宏宇（1959—），男，福建人，北京联合大学副教授，研究方向：财务会计概念框架。

制定 IFRS for SMEs 过程中自然坚持这一理念。"一致应用的全球财务报告准则，能够提高财务信息的可比性。"（BC36）"全球财务报告准则带来的益处不只限于其证券在公开资本市场上交易的主体。根据理事会的判断，中小主体及其财务报表使用者都能从一套通用的会计准则中获益。基于下列原因，人们需要在不同国家可比的中小主体财务报表之间进行抉择：（1）金融机构跨境发放贷款并进行跨境经营。……（2）供应商希望在他们赊销商品或服务之前评估位于其他国家的买主的财务状况。（3）信用评级机构尝试跨境制定统一的评定等级。……（4）许多中小主体有海外供应商，……（5）风险投资公司跨境为中小主体提供资金。（6）许多中小主体有外部投资者，他们不参与主体的日常经营。"（BC37）

（二）制定《中小主体国际财务报告准则》只是 IASB 工作的次要目标

"国际会计准则委员会基金会的目标是：（1）本着公众利益，制定一套高质量、可理解的且可实施的全球性会计准则，这套准则要求在财务报表和其他财务报告中提供高质量的、透明的且可比的信息，以帮助世界资本市场的参与者和其他使用者进行经济决策；（2）促使这些准则得到使用和严格的应用；（3）在履行与（1）和（2）相关的目标时，适当考虑中小主体和新兴经济体的特殊需要；以及（4）促使国家会计准则与国际会计准则和国际财务报告准则达成高质量解决方法的趋同。"（BC79）显然，国际会计准则委员会基金会的主要目标在（1）（2）（4），即制定针对全球资本市场的高质量、统一的会计准则，而对中小主体包括新兴经济体的特殊需要只是"适当考虑"，是其次要工作目标。这也使我们理解为什么 IASB 只要求具有公共受托责任的主体执行完整版 IFRS，除此之外的其他主体一律执行 IFRS for SMEs。

（三）以 IFRS 为起点且不远离 IFRS

IFRS for SMEs 是对完整版《国际财务报告准则》的简化，即是以 IFRS 为起点。而且，IASB 在简化过程中还持有不远离 IFRS 的理念。

首先，IASB 坚持 IFRS for SMEs 与 IFRS 一样秉持通用财务报告目标。"国际财务报告准则的目的是适用于所有以营利为目的的主体的通用财务报表和其他财务报告。通用财务报表旨在满足广泛使用者的信息需求，如股东、债权人、雇员和广大公众。通用财务报表旨在满足那些无权要求主体按其特定信息需求编制报告的使用者需求。"（BC49）确定应税收益和可分配收益以及向直接经营企业的所有者提供信息以帮助其作出决策都不是 IFRS for SMEs 的目标。（BC49~54）"《中小主体国际财务报告准则》为那些应外部使用者要求或自行选择来发布通用财务报表的主体设计的，而不考虑其规模。……对微型和规模稍大的中小主体都是如此。"（BC71）

其次，IASB 坚持认为 IFRS 完整版同样适用于中小主体包括微型企业。"《中小主体国际财务报告准则》的采用并不意味着完整版国际财务报告准则不适合中小主体。"理事会注意到研究表明，目前超过 80% 的国家或地区要求或允许中小主体采用完整版国际财务报告准则。"（BC48）

第三，IASB 制定 IFRS for SMEs 的方法使其无法获得对 IFRS 大幅度简化的依据（详见下文"三"）。

（四）实质上更多地考虑发达国家和地区的情况

第一，国际会计准则委员会基金会的目标，只是"适当考虑新兴经济体的特殊需要"（BC79）。

第二，IASB 认为执行复杂的会计准则或是执行相对简化的会计准则在执行成本上没有显著差异。这一判断实际上是基于发达国家和地区企业会计岗位设置和会计人员素质情况作出的。在分析制定 IFRS for SMEs 必要性时 IASB 指出："中小主体的情况和那些更大规模的公众受托责任的主体在一些方面是不同的，包括：（1）主体财务报表的使用者和他们的信息需求；（2）这些使用者如何使用财务报表；（3）主体可利用的会计专业知识的深度和广度；以及（4）中小主体遵循与更大规模的公众受托责任的主体相同的准则的成本承受能力。"（BC42）对于这4点的后续分析，"结论基础"只分析了（1）（2）（BC45）和（4），至于（3）则未作分析。对于（4）的分析如下："按照理事会的判断，完整版国际财务报告准则与《中小主体国际财务报告准则》之间差异的性质和程度，必须基于使用者的需要和成本效益分析来确定。实务中，报告主体应用会计准则的效益各不相同，主要取决于其财务报表使用者的性质、数量和信息需求。相关成本可能没有显著差异。"（BC46）类似忽视不同准则执行成本的表述在"结论基础"中多次出现（BC71~75，81~88）。

由于 IASB 制定 IFRS for SMEs 的方法使其无法获得不同复杂程度准则执行成本差异的实务依据（详见下文"二"），则上述"相关成本可能没有显著差异"只是一种推断。这种推断更多地是基于发达国家和地区企业会计岗位设置较为健全和会计人员素质较高的情况作出的。在这种情况下，企业执行更为复杂的会计准则一方面需要较少的培训或者不需要培训，另一方面增加的工作量也较为有限（如更多地测算公允价值）。但如果会计人员的专业素质较差且企业会计工作岗位设置缺陷较为严重，则执行较为复杂会计准则的成本会有很大增加。一方面，培训的时间长、任务重。例如，公允价值计量（包括现值计量）的大量应用需要会计人员有一定的专业素质水平和职业判断能力，在短期内迅速提升专业素质水平和职业判断能力是不容易的；另一方面，企业相应岗位不健全会使执行复杂准则的人力成本投入有较多增加。根据卢新国 2008 年对我国 891 家小企业的调研，每家企业平均拥有会计人员不足 2 人，会计人员中本科及以上学历占比不足 8%。以这样的岗位设置和人员专业素质要有效地执行完整版国际财务报告准则的培训成本和人力投入成本可想而知。显然，这一现实是 IASB 作出判断时没有考虑的。

（五）对重新构建概念框架的实用主义态度

由于中小主体财务报表使用者及其对信息的需求有别于完整版国际财务报告的信息需求，从而可能导致财务报表目标甚至后续整个概念框架的重构。但 IASB 没有重新构建概念框架，只是"（1）从国际财务报告准则（包括解释公告）的《框架》、原则以及相关强制性指南中摘录的基本概念，以及（2）考虑了基于使用者需求和成本效益的适当修改"。（BC95）实际上，IFRS for SMEs 第二章"概念和一般原则"是对完整版国际财务报告准则的相关内容的简化和修订。简化包括篇幅和考虑了后面具体准则需要的内容的简化（如计量属性主要只包括历史成本和公允价值两种）；修订则根据近年具体准则内容的发展，如增加了有关金融资产和金融负债后续计量等。

其之所以采用上述方案，IASB 围绕使用者需求和成本效益原则给出了如下两点解释。

第一，"理事会认为这种方案是适当的，因为中小主体财务报表使用者的需求在许多方面与公众受托责任的主体财务报表使用者的需求是相似的。因此，完整版国际财务报告准则是制定《中小主体国际财务报告准则》的逻辑出发点"。（BC96）"在理事会看来，具有和不具有公众受托责任的主体的通用财务报表使用者的需求，存在大量趋同。"（BC97）这一理由基本上是成立的。大致看来，具有或不具有公众受托责任主体的通用财务报表使用者需求确实存在大量的"相似"或"趋同"，如都注重获利能力、偿债能力、营运能力、现金流量情况，等等。但需要指出的是，大量的"相似"或"趋同"并非完全一致。具有或不具有公众受托责任主体的通用财务报表使用者需求存在差异是不可否认的，起码对不同信息类别需求的侧重上存在差异。而且不同国家和地区中小主体财务报告信息使用者的情况及其需求差异会比具有公众受托责任主体的更大，因为不同国家和地区对资本市场和大金融机构的规范和监管较之对中小主体的相关监管更为接近。至于这些差异是否有充分的理由导致有明显区别的概念框架尚待大量深入细致的研究。

第二，"理事会拒绝了可供选择的'新起点'方案，因为该方案可能导致不同的财务报告目标、不同的财务信息质量特征、不同的财务报表要素定义以及不同的确认和计量概念。理事会认为'新起点'方案将花费大量成本和时间而最终徒劳无功"。（BC97）这一点是基于成本效益原则。其一，重新制定中小主体的概念框架实在是工程浩大，令人望而生畏。财务会计概念框架涉及的理论问题本身存在很多争议。当然，概念框架不是一般争鸣性的会计理论。它的基本目的是作为规范性的理论框架，用以兼顾各方利益，指导具体会计准则和实务。即便如此，其每一个命题都必须基于对现实的深入研究和理论分析，见仁见智，争议在所难免。以财务报告目标为例，目标包含的三个问题（谁是信息的使用者？他们需要怎样的信息？如何提供相关信息？）即使是在成熟的资本市场也很不容易得到确定没有非议的答案。1971 年，美国的特鲁博罗特委员会（Trueblood Committee）认为信息使用者主要关注企业现金流的金额、时间安排以及不确定性（以便评估企业未来产生现金流入的能力），这一结论在 30 余年前即被 FASB 的概念框架接受，且在 2010 年 9 月 IASB—FASB 联合发布的新概念框架文件（FASB 第 8 号概念公告第一章）中仍然被采用。但至今尚有争议。更何况情况更为复杂的中小主体财务报告目标，不经过非常大量的充分调研和深入细致地分析研究，是不可能得出令人信服的结论的。而且，就算是做了这样的研究，结论也未必能出新，未必没有争议。至于概念框架中的信息质量标准、要素定义、确认计量的概念和标准等则更为复杂。可以说，IASB 面对这样浩繁的工程既无意也无力完成，只好知难而退了。其二，若真的形成了较大差异的另一套概念框架，则其对后续实务规范的影响也必须考虑。而沿用现有的概念框架中小主体的实务规范并非无法完成。长期以来，会计规范的制定始终遵循或契合着实用主义哲学，由此可见一斑。

三、IASB 制定《中小主体国际财务报告准则2009》的路径和现实依据

（一）制定路径和现实依据的基本情况

"基础结论"的"背景"（BC1~35）部分介绍了 IASB 制定 IFRS for SMEs 的整个过程。从 IASB 2001 年刚刚成立即着手展开中小主体会计准则的相关工作，到 2009 年 7 月 IFRS for SMEs 正式发布，历时 8 年。2004 年 6 月发布了讨论稿，并就一系列基本问题（需求、目标、服务主体、与完整版 IFRS 的关系、与原来的概念框架的关系、公布形式等）征求意见，收到反馈意见 120 份，反馈需求强烈。2005 年 4 月，就确认计量问题进行问卷调查，收到反馈意见 101 份。2005 年 10 月公开举行为期 2 天的圆桌会议，有 43 个团体派代表出席。2007 年 2 月，基于讨论稿及收到的反馈意见修订后发布了征求意见稿，对 IFRS 作了 5 种简化：减少涉及的主题、会计政策选择、简化确认计量原则、披露减少、简化了重新起草的程序。征求意见稿收到 162 份反馈意见。同时，在 20 个国家的 116 个小规模主体（其中 35% 为只有 10 位或更少雇员，35% 有 11~50 位雇员，30% 有 50 位以上雇员，超过半数有银行贷款或相当数量的透支，有 1/3 有国外经营）进行实地测试，目的针对如下问题：征求意见稿的可理解性、主题范围、企业应用的负担、对现执行规范的变动程度性质、会计政策选择、评估微型主体及发展中经济体应用的特殊问题、指南在何种情况下有助于测试者。最终正式发布的 IFRS for SMEs 对征求意见稿做了 34 项变化（BC34）。客观地讲，8 年间 IASB 在力所能及的范围内认真地做了大量工作。

（二）对制定路径和现实依据的分析

1. 现实依据有限。一般来讲，影响一国或地区会计规范繁简程度以及规范执行情况的因素主要包括如下方面：第一，经济发达程度。大致来看，通常情况下，经济越发达，社会就拥有越多的财富和规范的管理，作为财富创造主体的企业也就拥有越多的资源和对资源更为有效的管理，其中包括更规范的会计实务和信息披露。第二，政治制度及政治的稳定程度。就政治制度看，对权力的制约越有力，社会的公平程度就越高。财务会计规范究其本质是为了解决信息不对称导致的不公平。所以，若有制约和监督的政治体制，则会给财务会计规范及其实施创造更好的氛围。而政治的稳定是经济乃至整个社会稳定规范运行的前提，更是财务会计规范良好运行的前提。第三，法律体系及其执行效力。普通法和成文法法律体系会影响会计规范的制定程序。公司法、证券法、税法等法律法规的完善会对会计规范的制定实施起到协同配套的作用。法律的执行效力会给会计规范的实施提供氛围。第四，资本市场的发达程度。资本市场的发展会极大地影响会计信息的披露规范，尽管中小主体不具有公共受托责任也会深受影响。第五，会计人员的专业能力、职业操守等多方面的综合素质。第六，企业会计岗位设置的完善程度和会计人员的数量。第七，税收征管与会计信息的相关性。第八，企业的融资方式，即企业通过金融机构融资的程度以及金融机构在融资过程中对企业会计信息的依赖程度。IASB 的中小主体会计准则面向 100 余个国家或地区，它们在上述诸方面有很大差异。显然，IASB 无意为了"次要目标"兴师动众，针对所有面向的国家或地区就上述各方面展开全面的调研；即使是选择有代表性的国家或地区展开全面调研，其工作量也非常巨大。而且，真正进行了这样的调研，不同国家或地区巨大的差异也会使 IASB 不易抉择。所以，IASB 采取了被动的通过收集反馈意见获得现实依据的方法。这使其获得现实依据在数量、覆盖的国家或地区的范围和深度方面有限（根据"基础结论"提供的信息，IASB 制定 IFRS for SMEs 整个过程共收到反馈意见 383 份，估计多数来自发达国家）。这样的依据很难全面完整地反映各个国家或地区中小企业会计实务的实际情况，进而使得 IASB 无法获得对 IFRS 有针对性的大幅度简化的现实依据，也使得 IFRS for SMEs 无法有依据地远离完整版 IFRS。

2. 客观上有利于发达国家和地区的企业。

IASB 采用的方法也是 IASB 和 FASB 制定会计准则过程中采用的方法，它源于英美普通法系国家。这些国家或地区的企业熟悉这一程序，懂得积极利用反馈意见在会计准则制定的利益博弈中为自己争取

利益最大化。新兴市场国家和欠发达国家相对表现较弱。例如，以往 IASB 发布修订某些会计准则的征求意见稿，在收到的上百份反馈意见中，中国作为世界上最大的新兴市场国家往往只有财政部会计司的 1 份反馈意见。

四、我国制定《小企业会计准则》遵循的原则

（一）促进小企业发展的重要制度安排

财政部会计司在 2010 年 11 月 8 日发布的《〈小企业会计准则（征求意见稿）〉起草说明》（下简称《起草说明》）中指出："小企业是我国国民经济和社会发展的重要力量。……小企业会计准则是加强小企业管理、促进小企业发展的重要制度安排。"

（二）国际趋同背景下完善我国的会计准则体系

2006 年 2 月 15 日，我国发布了与国际会计准则趋同的《企业会计准则》，并自 2007 年 1 月 1 日起在上市公司、金融企业、大中型企业陆续实施。

《起草说明》指出："按照我国企业会计改革的总体框架，基本准则是纲，适用于在中华人民共和国境内设立的所有企业；企业会计准则和小企业会计准则是基本准则框架下的两个子系统，分别适用于大中型企业和小企业。"在我国《小企业会计准则》的制定过程中，"……我国制定小企业会计准则的基本设想得到了国际有关方面的认同"。因此，《小企业会计准则》的正式发布，在国际趋同的背景下完善了我国的会计准则体系。

（三）符合我国国情，有助于切实提高小企业会计信息质量

《起草说明》指出，制定小企业会计准则应当立足国情、借鉴《中小主体国际财务报告准则》简化要求，同时与我国税法保持协调，并有助于银行等债权人提供信贷。

"小企业会计准则应当按照基本准则，规范小企业会计确认计量报告要求。但考虑到我国小企业规模小、业务简单、会计基础工作较为薄弱、会计信息使用者的信息需求相对单一等实际，小企业会计准则应当简化要求。本稿注意了这两个方面的结合。例如，在会计计量方面，要求小企业采用历史成本计量；在财务报告方面，要求小企业编制资产负债表和利润表，自行选择编制现金流量表。"（《起草说明》）

"小企业外部会计信息使用者主要为税务部门和银行。税务部门主要利用小企业会计信息作出税收决策，包括是否给予税收优惠政策、采取何种征税方式、应征税额等，他们更多希望减少小企业会计与税法的差异；银行主要利用小企业会计信息作出信贷决策，他们更多希望小企业按照国家统一的会计准则制度提供财务报表。为满足这些主要会计信息使用者的需求，本稿减少了职业判断的内容，基本消除了小企业会计与税法的差异。"（《起草说明》）

五、我国制定《小企业会计准则》的依据

（一）我国准则制定机构获取制定依据的情况

《起草说明》中定性地阐述了《征求意见稿》制定过程中征求意见和调研的情况：2010 年 4 月份印发《关于征求〈小企业会计准则〉意见的通知》（财会便〔2010〕15 号），就小企业会计信息需求、小企业会计准则的适用范围、与税法的协调、与企业会计准则的协调等问题，征求社会各方面意见。深入开展调查研究：多部门进行沟通交流，先后赴国家税务总局、银监会、工信部等部门调研，了解相关部门信息需求，取得相关部门理解支持配合；多地区开展实地调研，先后赴江苏、河北、上海、北京等地调研，收集大量一手资料；多层面召开座谈会，认真听取税务部门、银监部门、工信部门、银行、小企业的政策建议；多角度着手政策研究，完成了多份国内、国际比较研究报告。

（二）一份我国小企业会计工作相关情况调研报告的佐证

2009 年 12 月，《会计研究》发表了卢新国的文章《〈小企业会计制度〉执行情况分析及对策》。文章结合《小企业会计制度》的执行情况调研了我国小企业会计工作相关情况。2008 年 5~8 月调研共发放调查问卷 2000 份，回收有效问卷 891 份，涉及 6 个省。

文章反映的我国小企业会计准则制定工作的相关情况如下。（1）执行会计规范的选择情况：

50.60%选择《小企业会计制度》，19.75%选择行业会计制度，13.69%选择《企业会计制度》，9.76%选择行业会计制度与《小企业会计制度》交叉，4.60%选择《企业会计准则》，1.58%选择自定规范。(2) 会计人员数量：1~2人占65.32%，3~4人占25.25%，5~6人占5.06%，6人以上占4.37%，平均1.9732人，即平均不足2人，这使得会计基本不相容的岗位无法分离，如出纳不得兼任稽核、会计档案管理、收入费用、债权债务账目的登记工作等。(3) 会计机构设置情况：独立设置并配备专职会计人员的占39.39%，其余则为兼职会计或代理记账等。(4) 会计人员的学历和职称：研究生占0.28%，本科生占7.62%，专科生占47.61%，中专生及高中生占28.38%，初中及以下占16.11%；高级会计占2.22%，中级会计占19.51%，初级会计占61.04%，无专业技术资格占17.24%。(5) 税收征管方式简化：不以会计资料为征收标准，简化为核率或定额征收。这使得小企业管理者更坚定地认为会计人员的素质高低以及实施什么样的会计制度对企业的影响不大，甚至建账不建账都一样。(6) 小企业的筹资状况：债权人是业主的亲友、金融机构。金融机构贷款大部分基于房屋等不动产抵押或信誉好的企业担保，对企业会计信息需求较少。(7) 小企业管理者认识不到位：一是认为企业规模小，情况管理者都了解，无须会计信息辅助管理，且其对纳税又没有影响，所以会计信息不重要；二是怕实施《小企业会计制度》科学管理，按章办事，削弱自己的权力；三是怕实施《小企业会计制度》财富公开、"露富"。

文章结合调研的情况认为，我国2004年发布的《小企业会计制度》在实施过程中存在如下问题：(1) 纳税调整任务较重，影响制度执行者的积极性。虽然我国《小企业会计制度》对所得税核算采用应付税款法，不确认暂时性差异对所得税的影响金额，但是在坏账准备、存货跌价准备、短期投资跌价准备的计提等方面，仍与税法不一致。这就使得期末纳税调整任务较重，导致一部分会计人员因担心增加工作量而不愿意实施《小企业会计制度》。(2) 会计职业判断要求太高。例如，对有形资产的减值测试和谨慎性原则的具体运用中，应收款项可收回金额、可变现净值、资产减值额的估计以及计提和确认预计负债等问题，要求会计人员有较高的职业判断能力，而绝大部分小企业的会计人员无法胜任。(3) 部分业务处理没有纳入制度中。例如，对职工薪酬福利的核算过于简单，没有将养老金核算、辞退福利等内容纳入其中。有鉴于此，文章对修订《小企业会计制度》提出如下建议：(1) 制度的有关规定尽量与税法一致，减少会计与税收之间的差异。(2) 针对我国小企业会计人员素质整体不高的实际情况，会计制度中资产的计量应以历史成本原则为准，减少公允价值、市场价值、未来现金流量现值的应用，尽可能减少会计选择与职业判断。

上述卢新国的调研文章是对我国《小企业会计准则》的一个非常好的佐证。它使我们理解为什么在会计准则国际趋同的背景下我国没有采用或基本采用IFRS for SMEs，而是自己制定差别很大的《小企业会计准则》，即我国小企业会计工作的情况与大中型企业有很大的差异，有必要单独为其制定简化的会计准则；它也使我们理解了我国的《小企业会计准则》不仅对《企业会计准则》作了大幅度的简化，而且对2004年发布的《小企业会计制度》也作了进一步的简化的原因。这种大幅度的简化是有针对性的、有现实依据的。

六、结　论

IASB在制定IFRS for SMEs和我国准则制定机构制定《小企业会计准则》时在准则的应用范围、秉持的基本理念、制定依据等方面存在的差异，导致了两个准则的很大差异。

第一，在准则面向的国家和地区方面，IFRS for SMEs是面向全球100多个国家和地区的中小企业，而《小企业会计准则》只是面向我国的小企业。

第二，秉持的基本理念方面，双方的差异为：IASB更关注全球中小企业会计信息的可比性，更多地考虑发达国家和地区的情况，坚持不远离IFRS。我国准则制定机构则更注重切实有助于提高我国小企业会计信息质量，只是考虑我国作为新兴市场国家的实际情况，结合国情对已与IFRS趋同的《企业会计准则》大幅简化。双方的相同点在于相对于完整版会计准则制定中小主体或小企业会计准则只是次要目标；对于重新制定概念框架的实用主义态度。

第三，获取的现实依据的充分性方面，IASB面对复杂且差异巨大的现实，无力也无意开展全方位的大幅度的主动调研，采取了传统的被动征求意见和少量主动企业测试的方法，获取的简化依据有限。我国准则制定机构只面对我国小企业的现实，不仅进行征求意见且主动开展调研，积极总结我国 2004 年《小企业会计制度》实施的经验，借助学者的研究成果，比较全面深入地了解了我国小企业会计工作的相关情况，为我国《小企业会计准则》的制定获取了较为充分的现实依据。

总的来看，我国准则制定机构在制定《小企业会计准则》过程中，在准则国际趋同的大背景下，充分争取和利用了 IASB 给予的空间，依据我国的具体国情制定了与 IFRS for SMEs 差别很大的《小企业会计准则》。相信《小企业会计准则》的实施将在实质上有利于提高我国小企业会计信息的质量。

参考文献

[1] 国际会计准则理事会. 中小主体国际财务报告准则 2009 [Z]. 北京：中国财政经济出版社，2010. 1 - 226.
[2] IASB. International Financial Reporting Standard for Small and Medium - sized Entities (IFRS for SMEs) Basis for Conclusions (2009) [Z]. 1 - 52.
[3] 中华人民共和国财政部. 小企业会计准则 (2011) [Z]. 准则：1 - 33；附录：1 - 85.
[4] 中华人民共和国财政部.《小企业会计准则（征求意见稿）》起草说明 (2010) [Z]：1 - 5.
[5] 国际会计准则理事会. 国际财务报告准则 (2008) [Z]. 北京：中国财政经济出版社，2008. 70 - 92.
[6] 中华人民共和国财政部. 企业会计准则 (2006) [Z]. 北京：经济科学出版社，2006. 1 - 189.
[7] 中华人民共和国财政部. 企业会计准则——应用指南 (2006) [Z]. 北京：中国财政经济出版社，2006. 1 - 263.
[8] 财政部会计司. 企业会计准则讲解 (2010) [Z]. 北京：人民出版社，2010. 1 - 18.
[9] 卢新国.《小企业会计制度》执行情况分析及对策 [J]. 会计研究，2009 (12)：47 - 54.
[10] 赵小克，任静梅. 对我国会计准则变迁的思考 [J]. 兰州商学院学报，2006 (4)：49 - 52.
[11] 葛家澍，林志军. 现代西方会计理论（第三版）[M]. 厦门：厦门大学出版社，2011. 43 - 134.
[12] 胡成. 论会计准则弹性影响的优化 [J]. 兰州商学院学报，2011 (1)：107 - 126.

基于变量聚类和 COX 比例风险模型的企业财务预警研究

鲍新中　陶秋燕　傅宏宇

1　引　言

建立适合我国上市公司特点的财务预警系统，及早识别和实时监控上市公司是否会发生财务风险，对不同利害关系人均有着非常重要的意义。对企业财务预警的研究经历了趋势分析、判别分析、人工智能技术三个阶段。

20 世纪 30—60 年代，学者们主要采用对财务指标的特征和趋势进行分析的趋势分析方法。20 世纪 60 年代到 20 世纪末，学者们采用的主要方法是单变量判别分析、多变量判别分析方法和条件概率模型。20 世纪末至今，人工智能技术越来越多地被学者们采用，包括数据挖掘技术[1-3]、案例推理分析[4-5]、生存分析[6]、人工神经网络[7-10]、支持向量机[11-12]、系统动力学[13]、指数加权移动平均控制图模型[14]等。

生存分析方法最早被应用在医学方面，由于该方法有预测生存时间的能力，因此有些学者将生存分析方法运用到业财务状况评价中。马超群、何文[15]将生存分析方法应用到上市公司财务困境的预测，研究表明，模型不受样本观测期选择不同的影响，具有较稳定的预测能力。卢永艳[16]的研究表明，行业差别是影响财务困境风险的一个重要因素，在研究财务困境时应该尽可能地考虑到行业的影响。倪中新、张杨[17]采用 COX 比例风险模型对影响财务困境企业恢复的因素进行了系统的分析。研究发现：主营业务利润率、每股净资产与财务困境恢复呈正相关，销售期间费用率、销售现金比率、净资产增长率与财务困境恢复呈负相关，而偿债能力及营运能力与财务困境恢复不显著相关，流通股比例对困境恢复有负的影响，管理层更换对困境恢复有正的影响，而在发生困境后进行资产重组及关联交易的困境企业更容易从困境中恢复。

生存分析方法具有从动态的角度考虑问题，不要求样本数据符合某种分布，允许样本数据有缺失等优势，因此本文将采用生存分析方法中的 COX 比例风险模型进行上市公司财务预警分析。将企业从上市开始到第一次因财务状况原因被特别处理即 ST 看作企业的一个生存过程，将这期间经历的时间段看作企业的生存时间，进而可以建立生存分析模型来预测企业发生财务困境的概率。目前学者们运用生存分析方法中的 COX 比例风险模型进行财务预警的研究很少，而 COX 还能够通过基准生存率描绘出上市公司陷入财务困境的变化趋势，即时点预测功能，而其他模型却很难实现这样的动态预测功能。

在建立财务预警模型时，选择指标的选取尤为重要，指标选取不当，就会使模型准确率大大降低。事实上，非财务指标在财务预警中越来越多地受到学者们重视[18-20]。而在运用生存分析建立财务预警模型时，目前学者们的研究仍然选用财务指标作为分析对象。并且，在财务指标的筛选中，有的是基于指标的重要性进行筛选，而有些是基于指标间的相关性程度进行筛选，很少能兼顾指标的重要性和相关性两个方面进行财务指标的筛选。本文在进行指标的筛选时，在传统财务指标的基础上，考虑了现金流量、公司治理结构特征等因素，从 8 个方面初选了 32 个指标，并运用变量聚类方法进行指标约减，最后选取 11 个指标来建立 COX 比例风险模型，使得指标的选择更加全面，也更加合理。将聚类分析与 COX 比例风险模型有机地结合，选取了 T-3 年的样本数据进行建模，以便于企业提早发现财务困境，并有充足的时间进行改善。

[作者简介] 鲍新中，陶秋燕，傅宏宇，北京联合大学管理学院。

2 相关理论方法

2.1 变量聚类分析

根据分类对象不同,聚类分析分为样品聚类和变量聚类。样品聚类是根据被观测的对象的各种特征,即反映被观测对象的特征的各变量值进行分类。变量聚类是根据所研究的问题选择部分变量对事物的某一方面进行研究。在实际工作中,变量聚类法十分重要。一方面,在系统分析或评估过程中,为避免遗漏某些重要因素,人们往往在一开始选取指标时,会尽可能多地考虑相关因素。而这样做的结果,则是变量过多,变量间的相关度高,给系统分析与建模带来很大的不便。因此,人们常常期望研究变量间的相似关系,按照变量的相关关系把它们聚合成若干类,从而观察和解释影响系统的主要特征。另一方面,通过变量间相似关系的研究,可以确定这些变量间相互关联的情况。

变量聚类是一种降维的方法,用于在变量众多时寻找有代表性的变量,以便在用少量、有代表性的变量代替大变量集时,损失信息很少。它将变量进行分类,使得同一类中的变量之间相似性比其他类的变量相似性更强,达到了类内同质性最大化和类间异质性最大化的目的。因此可以从每一类中选择一个典型指标来达到降维的目的。典型指标的选择主要根据专业知识,同时根据下列原则综合确定代表变量。考察在一类指标中:①最有代表性的变量;②最容易测得的变量;③如果从专业角度不好确定,还可以通过进一步计算每个指标的相关指数来确定,公式为

$$\overline{R_J^2} = \frac{\sum r^2}{m_j - 1}$$

选择最大一个相关指数对应的变量作为该类的典型指标。

2.2 生存分析与 COX 比例风险模型

生存分析(Survival analysis)方法常用来探讨特定危险因子与生存时间的关联性,现已广泛地应用于生物医学统计、药学统计及各类临床试验上,后来逐渐渗透到保险和社会经济问题等各个行业。本文中将企业因财务状况被特别处理即被 ST 看作企业发生财务困境。

生存分析方法常见的模型有非参数模型、参数模型和半参数模型三类。本文选用的是属于半参数模型的 COX 比例风险模型。COX 比例风险模型不要求生存函数的分布类型,更重要的是它是处理带有删失数据样本的经典方法。COX 模型的基本形式为

$$h(t,X) = h_0(t)\exp(\beta X)$$

其中 $h(t,X)$ 表示具有协变量 X 的个体在 t 时刻的风险概率函数,也称作顺势死亡率,即具有预警指标 X 的企业在 t 时刻发生财务困境的概率;$h_0(t)$ 表示基线风险率,是指所有危险因素为 0 时的基础风险率;$exp(\beta X)$ 中,X 是协变量,也就是本文中的各个预警指标,可以通过回归分析找到系数 β,β_i 表示当其他变量不变时,X_i 没变化一个单位,风险率的自然对数变化 β_i 个单位,若 $\beta_i > 0$,该因素为危险因素,若 $\beta_i < 0$,该因素为保护因素,若 $\beta_i = 0$,该因素为无关因素。又因为

$$RH(t) = \exp(\beta X) = \frac{h(t,X)}{h_0(t)}$$

因此可以将 $RH(t)$ 看作企业在 t 时刻发生死亡事件即发生财务困境或者被 ST 的相对风险度。

3 研究样本与预警指标的选择

3.1 生存时间的界定

由于企业财务困境是一个动态持续的过程和状态,因此本文主要对上市公司从正常状态到发生财务困境的过程进行预警。在财务困境预警研究中,由于在观察期内,一部分公司已陷入财务困境,而另一部分公司仍保持正常经营状态,无法继续观测保持正常经营状态的公司将来是否会陷入困境,以及何时陷入困境,因而用生存时间数据类型分别表示为非截尾数据和截尾数据(又称删失数据),即本文中将已陷入"财务困境"的上市公司样本称为非截尾样本,将仍保持正常经营状态的"非财务困境"上市公司样本称为截尾样本。根据前文所述,本文沿用大多数学者的研究,采用因财务状况被特别处理(ST)

作为财务困境的界定标准,即"财务困境"样本为在观测期内被实施 ST 的上市公司,"非财务困境"样本为在观测期内从未被实施 ST 的上市公司。

对于生存时间的界定,由于公司在核准上市前需要符合证监会企业上市的规定要求,公司在初次上市时是同质的。因此本文界定公司首发上市交易时间作为生存时间的起点,这样所有上市公司生存时间数据的起点信息均可以获取,从而有效避免删失数据对模型分析的干扰。观测期终点以样本构成的不同来区别设定。对于财务困境样本,将上市公司被首次实施 ST 时间设为观测终点;对于非财务困境样本,将观测期的终点设定为 2011 年 12 月 31 日。此外,将上市公司以"财务状况异常"而被证监会施以"特别处理"作为生存分析中的"死亡"事件,以此作为生存时间的终点,所采用的时间尺度统一为月。

3.2 样本选择

本文在选取研究样本时是基于以下方面的考虑。

(1)行业原则。目前,国内外学者在选取样本时都注意到了行业差别对模型预测结果造成的影响,不同行业具有明显不同的行业特征,且财务比率相差巨大,因此分行业构建模型能有效避免因行业特性不同对模型的预测效果和适用性的影响。制造业行业不仅占据了所有行业财务困境上市公司的半壁江山,而且再次陷入财务困境的概率也较大,这也与中国经济发展长期以制造业为主的实际情况相符,因此本文选取具有代表性的制造业作为研究对象以避免行业因素带来的偏差。

(2)时间原则。根据我国上市公司年报披露制度,上市公司公布其年报的截至日期为下一年的 4 月 30 日,上市公司在 T 年度是否被特别处理与 T-1 年的年报是发生在不同时间却具有相同性质,因此用 T-1 年的数据预测 T 年度是否会被特别处理是没有实际意义的。再者,从实际经营情况来看,公司陷入财务困境不是一朝一夕发生的,而是一个连续动态的过程。证监会是根据上市公司前两年的年报判断其是否出现财务状况异常的,公司首次出现亏损的前一年应是 T-3 年,此时公司仍然保持着账面上的盈利,在以后年度才连续发生亏损,若采用上市公司前两年的年报预测显然会高估了模型的预测能力。因此本文选择采用公司提前三年,即 T-3 年的财务数据,试图为有关部门提供及时的财务困境的信号,使其能预先采取有效措施以避免第二年发生亏损或有效防止财务困境的发生。

本文的样本数据主要来自 CCER 中国经济金融数据库和 RESSET 金融研究数据库。国内外研究学者在选取样本时都注意到了不同行业具有不同的特征,财务比率相差较大,如果用不同行业的数据进行综合建模的话,预测效果不是很好。因此本文以 2002—2011 年期间制造业的公司为样本基础,将在这 10 年间被 ST 的公司视为完全数据样本,剔除了数据不完整的公司,最终选取了 60 家此类公司作为完全数据样本;另外选取了 120 家截至 2011 年 12 月 31 日未被 ST 的公司作为删失数据样本,这 120 个公司按照股票代码随机抽取,以保证样本公司的代表性。通常研究学者采用 1:1 配对方式建立模型,而为了增大样本容量,确保模型的较高准确性,本文采用的是 1:2 的配对方式建立模型。并且将 ST 企业和非 ST 企业按照 1:2 的比例分成两组,120 家企业作为训练样本建立模型,60 家企业作为测试样本检验模型准确性。综上,本文将所选取的企业样本简单地用表 1 进行描述。

表 1 训练样本和测试样本统计表

类别	训练样本数量	训练样本百分比/%	测试样本数量	训练样本百分比/%
ST 企业	40	33.33	20	33.33
非 ST 企业	80	66.67	40	66.67
合计	120	100.00	60	100.00

此外,由于证监会是根据上市公司前两年的年报判断其是否出现财务状况异常,因此采用上市公司前两年的年报预测显然会高估了模型的预测能力。故本研究选择在上市公司被 ST 的前三年数据进行预测,故需剔除样本中生存时间小于 36 个月的公司。同时提前三年预测,还可以给企业一段比较充裕的时间来进行改善,以摆脱发生财务困境的命运。因此,假设公司 T 年发生财务困境,本文针对财务 T-3 年的数据进行预测。

3.3 财务预警指标筛选

1. 预警指标初步选取

本文构建的财务预警备择指标体系,主要考虑反映公司经营状况的偿债能力、盈利能力、营运能力、成长能力和现金流量能力、资本结构、股本结构和董事会结构八个方面的预警指标。具体指标如表2所示。32个初选指标中,$X_1 \sim X_6$是反映企业偿债能力的预警指标,$X_7 \sim X_{14}$是反映企业盈利能力的预警指标,$X_{15} \sim X_{19}$是反映企业成长能力的预警指标,$X_{20} \sim X_{24}$是反映企业营运能力的预警指标,$X_{25} \sim X_{26}$是现金流量指标,$X_{27} \sim X_{28}$是资本结构指标,$X_{29} \sim X_{30}$是股本结构指标,$X_{31} \sim X_{32}$是董事会结构指标。

表2 初选财务预警指标

序号	名称	计算公式
X_1	产权比率	(负债/所有者权益)×100%
X_2	流动比率	(流动资产/流动负债)×100%
X_3	速动比率	(速动资产/流动负债)×100%
X_4	现金流动负债比率	(现金/流动负债)×100%
X_5	经营净现金流量/带息债务	(经营净现金流量/带息债务)×100%
X_6	利息保障倍数	[(利润总额+利息费用)/利息费用]×100%
X_7	销售净利率	(净利润/营业收入)×100%
X_8	销售期间费用率	[(财务费用+销售费用+管理费用)/营业收入]×100%
X_9	资产报酬率	[2×净利润/(期初资产总额+期末资产总额)]×100%
X_{10}	净资产收益率	[2×净利/(期初股东权益余额+期末股东权益余额)]×100%
X_{11}	销售费用率	(销售费用/营业收入)×100%
X_{12}	财务费用率	(财务费用/营业收入)×100%
X_{13}	管理费用率	(管理费用/营业收入)×100%
X_{14}	营业利润率	(营业利润/营业收入)×100%
X_{15}	每股收益增长率	[每股收益(t)-每股收益(t-1)]/每股收益(t-1)
X_{16}	营业收入增长率	[营业收入(t)-营业收入(t-1)]/营业收入(t-1)
X_{17}	营业利润增长率	[营业利润(t)-营业利润(t-1)]/营业利润(t-1)
X_{18}	股东权益相对年初增长率	[股东权益(t)-股东权益(t-1)]/股东权益(t-1)
X_{19}	经营活动现金流量净额增长率	(本期经营活动现金流量净额-上期经营活动现金流量净额)/上期经营活动现金流量净额
X_{20}	应收账款周转率	[2×营业务收入/(期初应收账款+期末应收账款)]×100%
X_{21}	存货周转率	[2×营业务成本/(期初存货+期末存货)]×100%
X_{22}	流动资产周转率	[2×营业务收入/(期初流动资产+期末流动资产)]×100%
X_{23}	固定资产周转率	[2×营业务收入/(期初固定资产+期末固定资产)]×100%
X_{24}	总资产周转率	[2×营业务收入/(期初总资产+期末总资产)]×100%
X_{25}	销售商品劳务收入现金/收入	(销售商品劳务收入现金/营业收入)×100%
X_{26}	销售现金比率	(经营现金流量净额/营业收入)×100%
X_{27}	资产负债率	(负债总额/资产总额)×100%
X_{28}	长期负债/股东权益	(长期负债/股东权益)×100%
X_{29}	第一大股东持股比例	(第一大股东持股股份/股份总额)×100%
X_{30}	股权制衡度	第二至第五大股东持股比例和/第一大股东持股比例
X_{31}	董事会规模	董事会人数总额
X_{32}	独立董事比例	(独立董事人数/董事会人数总额)×100%

2. 利用变量聚类进行指标筛选

32个预警指标数量太多,因此在建模之前需要对该财务指标体系进行进一步处理和筛选,以获得信息含量最大的预警指标。这里采用变量聚类分析的方法来起到降维的作用。

通过 SPSS 对本文的变量进行聚类,结合得到的聚类树形图以及学者们的经验变量个数,本文将变量分为 11 类。这 11 类的变量组成分别为:(X_6、X_7、X_9、X_{10}、X_{14}、X_{15}、X_{16}、X_{17});(X_2、X_3、X_5);(X_4、X_{25}、X_{26});(X_{19});(X_{30});(X_{21}、X_{22}、X_{23}、X_{24});(X_{29}、X_{20});(X_1、X_{12}、X_{27}、X_{28});(X_{18});(X_8、X_{11}、X_{13});(X_{31}、X_{32})。再从每一类中选择一个典型指标来达到降维的目的。这里通过计算每个指标的相关指数 $\overline{R_J^2} = \dfrac{\sum r^2}{m_j - 1}$ 来确定每一类中所选择的指标,这里以第一类 8 个指标为例来选择指标。首先计算第一类中 8 个变量 X_6、X_7、X_9、X_{10}、X_{14}、X_{15}、X_{16}、X_{17} 的相关矩阵从表 3 中读取相关系数,根据相关指数公式计算各相关指数,得到如下结果:$X_9 > X_{14} > X_{10} > X_7 > X_6 > X_{15} > X_{16} > X_{17}$,因此第一类中选取 X_9 也就是资产报酬率作为典型指标。同理,其余各类中分别选取 X_3 速动比率、X_5 经营净现金流量/带息债务、X_{19} 经营活动现金流量净额增长率、X_{30} 股权制衡度、X_{24} 总资产周转率、X_{20} 应收账款周转率、X_{27} 资产负债率、X_{18} 股东权益相对年初增长率、X_8 销售期间费用率、X_{32} 独立董事比例作为典型指标。经过变量聚类分析筛选后的预警指标体系见表 2。

表 3 通过变量聚类分析筛选后的预警指标体系

指标内涵	序号	名称	指标内涵	序号	名称
偿债能力指标	X_3	速动比率	营运能力指标	X_{20}	应收账款周转率
	X_5	经营净现金流量/带息债务		X_{24}	总资产周转率
盈利能力指标	X_8	销售期间费用率	资本结构指标	X_{27}	资产负债率
	X_9	资产报酬率	股本结构指标	X_{30}	股权制衡度
成长能力指标	X_{18}	股东权益相对年初增长率	董事会结构指标	X_{32}	独立董事比例
	X_{19}	经营活动现金流量净额增长率			

因此,通过变量聚类之后,从 32 个预警指标中筛选了 11 个预警指标,为之后进行财务预警分析减少了工作量。

4 基于 COX 比例风险模型的财务预警实证分析

根据前面的研究方法介绍,可以将 $RH(t)$ 看作企业在 t 时刻发生死亡事件即发生财务困境或者被 ST 的相对风险度。通过利用 $t-3$ 的指标数据建立生存分析模型,计算企业在 t 时刻的被 ST 的相对风险度来预测企业是否会发生财务困境。在本文中,将截至 2011 年 12 月 31 日被 ST 的企业的生存状态记作 1,将截至 2011 年 12 月 31 日未发生过被 ST 状况企业的生存状态记作 0;完全数据样本的生存时间 t 为从企业上市到第一次因财务状况被 ST 的时间段,删失数据样本的生存时间为从企业上市到 2011 年 12 月 31 日的时间段。

4.1 COX 回归

通过 SPSS 建立训练样本关于 $T-3$ 期数据的 COX 回归模型,得到如下一系列结果。

表 4 案例处理摘要

Case Processing Summary		N	Percent
Cases available in analysis	Event[a]	40	33.3%
	Censored	80	66.7%
	Total	120	100.0%
Total		120	100.0%

a. Dependent Variable:生存时间(月)

表 4 显示了建立生存分析模型的总样本数、财务健康和财务困境各自的比例,本模型的生存时间是以月为单位。由该表可以看出,120 个训练样本中有 40 个企业样本发生了财务困境被 ST,另外 80 个企

业样本未发生财务困境即未被 ST，成为了删失数据样本。

表 5　模型外变量的统计量

(Variables not in the Equation)

		Score	df	Sig.
Step 7	X_5	.351	1	.553
	X_8	2.220	1	.136
	X_9	.132	1	.716
	X_{19}	.040	1	.841
	X_{20}	1.037	1	.308
	X_{30}	2.197	1	.138

表 5 为拟合结束时，未进入模型变量的统计量。检验结果 Sig 都大于 0.05，表明对模型无统计意义的变量 X_5 经营净现金流量/带息债务、X_8 销售期间费用率、X_9 资产报酬率、X_{19} 经营活动现金流量净额增长率、X_{20} 应收账款周转率、X_{30} 股权制衡度都没有进入模型。

表 6　进入方程的统计量

(Variables in the Equation)

		B	SE	Wald	df	Sig.	Exp (B)
Step 7	X_3	1.251	.294	18.103	1	.000	3.493
	X_{18}	.011	.004	8.892	1	.003	1.011
	X_{24}	-.994	.535	3.449	1	.043	.370
	X_{27}	4.174	1.421	8.628	1	.003	64.970
	X_{32}	-5.755	1.235	21.720	1	.000	.003

如表 6 所示，经过一步步剔除对模型没有统计意义的协变量，最后剩下 X_3 速动比率、X_{18} 股东权益相对年初增长率、X_{24} 总资产周转率、X_{27} 资产负债率、X_{32} 独立董事比例 5 个对模型具有显著意义的变量。

表 7　回归系数相关矩阵

(Correlation Matrix of Regression Coefficients)

	X_3	X_{18}	X_{24}	X_{27}
X_{18}	.183			
X_{24}	.085	-.215		
X_{27}	.305	.262	-.017	
X_{32}	-.212	-.115	-.346	-.155

表 7 为回归系数的相关矩阵，相关系数均不大，说明进入模型的变量之间相互是独立的，共线性问题不明显。由此建立的 COX 模型为

$$RH(t) = \frac{h(t,X)}{h_0(t)} = \exp(\beta X)$$
$$= \exp(1.251 \times X_3 + 0.011 \times X_{18} - 0.994 \times X_{24} + 4.174 \times X_{27} - 5.755 \times X_{32})$$

通过上述 COX 回归模型可以得出如下结论。

（1）X_3 速动比率相对风险度为 3.493，回归系数为 1.251 > 0，速动比率为危险因素，增加了发生财务困境的危险性，每增加一个单位，相对风险度增加 3.493 倍。从经济含义来讲，速动比率的高低能直接反映企业的短期偿债能力强弱，它是对流动比率的补充，并且比流动比率反映得更加直观可信，一般比率为 1 最好，过小的话容易发生偿债危机，而过大则容易影响企业的正常经营。

（2）X_{18} 股东权益相对年初增长率相对风险度为 1.011，回归系数为 0.011 > 0，速动比率为危险因素，增加了发生财务困境的危险性，每增加一个单位，相对风险度增加 1.011 倍。

（3）X_{24} 总资产周转率相对风险度为 0.370，回归系数为 -0.994 < 0，总资产周转率为保护因素，降低了发生财务困境的危险性，每增加一个单位，相对风险度降低 1 - 0.370 = 0.630 倍。从经济含义来讲，

总资产周转率综合反映了企业整体资产的营运能力,一般来说,资产的周转次数越多或周转天数越少,表明其周转速度越快,营运能力也就越强。因此,总资产周转率越高,企业发生财务困境的危险性概率越小,生存时间越长,模型得出的结论与实际经济意义相一致。

(4) X_{27} 资产负债率相对风险度为 64.970,回归系数为 4.174 > 0,资产负债率为危险因素,增加了发生财务困境的危险性,每增加一个单位,相对风险度增加 64.970 倍,由此可见,资产负债率显著性最强。从经济含义来讲,资产负债率是指公司年末的负债总额同资产总额的比率,该指标是评价公司负债水平的综合指标。如果资产负债比率达到 100% 或超过 100% 说明公司已经没有净资产或资不抵债,对于企业来说非常危险。

(5) X_{32} 独立董事比率相对风险度为 0.003,回归系数为 -5.755 < 0,独立董事比率为保护因素,降低了发生财务困境的危险性,每增加一个单位,相对风险度降低 1 - 0.003 = 0.997 倍。从经济含义来讲,独立董事是指独立于公司股东且不在公司内部任职,与公司或公司经营管理者没有重要的业务联系或专业联系,并对公司事务作出独立判断的董事,独立董事比率越大,企业发生财务困境的危险性越小,生存时间越长。

由图 1 可以看出,制造企业一般在 100 个月(约 9 年)之后,生存率开始下降,之后进入一个稳定期,250 个月(约 20 年)之后,生存率就急剧下降,变得很低。

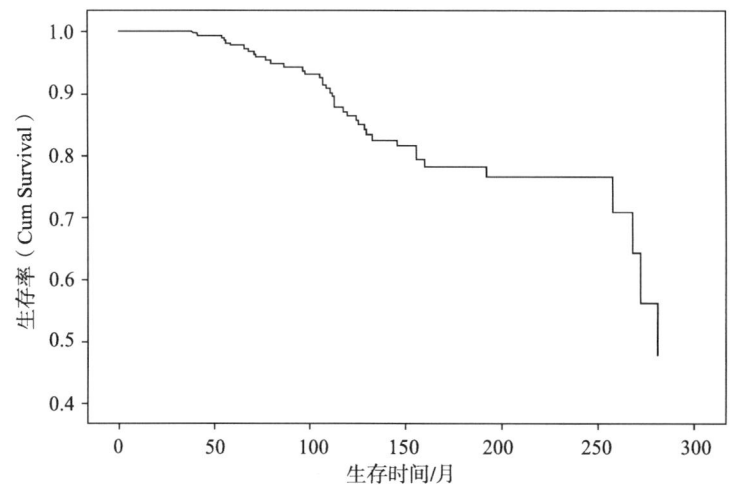

图 1 生存函数的图形

4.2 COX 模型判别能力检验

在利用 COX 模型进行预测时,还必须先确定某一分界值,若估计的生存概率小于这一特定分界值 C,则其被判定为财务困境公司,反之,若估计生存概率大于 C,则其被判定为财务健康公司。因此检验模型判别能力前,还涉及分界点选取的问题,它的选取会造成不同的分类结果,并直接影响到模型的判定效果。

一般而言,分界点 C 主要有两种,一种是指定分界点 C = 0.5,其想法是基于公司发生财务困境或财务健康的概率均各占一半,即如果通过模型计算出来的某事件的概率 ≥ 0.5 就判定该事件会发生,否则该事件不会发生。另一种为 Lane 等人对 COX 模型研究的建议,采用样本中正常样本占总样本的比例为分界点(C)。

由于 COX 模型在理论上不存在最优的临界点,故其选取取决于模型使用者具体的目标。实际上,对于任意一个临界点,所有模型都会犯两类错误:将财务困境公司误判为财务健康公司,或者将财务健康公司误判为财务困境的公司。前者错误的增加意味着后者错误的减少,但犯前者错误的成本要远远大于后者错误。由于不同的分界点的指定和不同的样本比例均会影响前者错误和后者错误的概率,为避免因选取不同分界点而影响模型的判别能力,本文沿用上述方法将 ST 与非 ST 公司又按 1:2、1:1 的比例对样本进行组合,并采用不同的分界点对比分析模型的判别能力。

通过众多医学学者研究,生存概率 = 活过时间 t 的观察例数/观察总例数,同理采用样本中正常样本占总样本的比例作为分界点更为精确,所以本文的分界点 C = 80/120 = 0.667。当生存概率 < 0.667 时,认为企业发生财务困境;当生存概率 > 0.667 时,认为企业财务状况健康。

由表 8 可以看出,COX 模型针对训练样本和测试样本的综合识别准确率均达到了 80% 以上,测试样本中财务困境样本的识别准确率未达到 80%,主要是因为该类样本量太小,因此,COX 比例风险模型具有较好的财务预警判别能力。

表 8 训练样本的识别准确率

观测	训练样本预测			测试样本预测		
	0	1	准确率/%	0	1	准确率%
0	71	9	88.75	35	5	87.50
1	7	33	82.50	5	15	75.00
合计			86.67			83.33

综上,通过 COX 比例风险模型进行建模回归,发现速动比率、股东权益相对年初增长率、资产负债率为危险因素,增加了发生财务困境的危险性;总资产周转率、独立董事比例为保护因素,降低了发生财务困境的危险性。同时 COX 比例风险模型具有较好的财务预警判别能力。

5 结 论

本文以沪深两市 A 股上市公司的 180 家制造企业为样本进行实证研究,按照 1∶2 的比例将 180 个样本分为样本量为 120 家的训练样本和 60 家的测试样本。通过从企业盈利能力、企业偿债能力、企业成长能力、企业运营能力、反映企业资本结构、股本结构和董事会指标以及现金流量指标等 8 大方面初步选取 32 个财务预警指标,随后运用变量聚类方法进行指标约减,选取了 11 个指标作为典型指标,最后建立 COX 比例风险模型,通过这一系列的实证研究得出如下几点结论。

(1) 变量聚类分析方法能够有效地筛选指标,降低工作量,使得同一类中的变量之间相似性比其他类的变量相似性更强,达到了类内同质性最大化和类间异质性最大化的目的。本文通过变量聚类之后,从 32 个预警指标中筛选了 11 个预警指标,为之后进行财务预警分析减少了工作量。

(2) 通过 COX 比例风险模型进行建模回归,发现速动比率、股东权益相对年初增长率、资产负债率为危险因素,增加了发生财务困境的危险性;总资产周转率、独立董事比例为保护因素,降低了发生财务困境的危险性。COX 比例风险模型得出的结论与现实的经济含义是相一致的。

(3) 通过 COX 比例风险模型的判别能力检验,COX 模型针对训练样本和测试样本的综合识别准确率均达到了 80% 以上,因此,COX 比例风险模型具有较好的财务预警判别能力。

参考文献

[1] Jie Sun, Hui Li. Data mining method for listed companies' financial distress prediction [J]. Knowledge – Based Systems, 2008, 21: 1 – 5.
[2] De Andrés J, Lorca P, De Cos – Juez F J, et al. Bankruptcy forecasting: a hybrid approach using Fuzzy c – means clustering and Multivariate Adaptive Regression Splines (MARS) [J]. Expert Systems with Applications. 2011, 38: 1866 – 1875.
[3] 鲍新中. 基于粒子群的 K 均值算法和粗糙集理论的财务预警研究 [J]. 系统管理学报. 2012, 21 (04): 461 – 469.
[4] Yip A Y N. Predicting business failure with a case – based reasoning approach [J]. Lecture Notes in Computer Science, 2004, 3215: 665 – 671.
[5] 李清, 刘金全. 基于案例推理的财务危机预测模型研究 [J]. 管理科学与工程, 2009, 462: 123 – 131.
[6] Ayse Y. Evrensel. Banking crisis and financial structure: A survival – time analysis [J]. International Review of Economics and Finance, 2008, 17: 589 – 602.
[7] 张玲, 陈收, 张昕. 基于多元判别分析和神经网络技术的公司财务困境预警 [J]. 系统工程, 2005 (11): 49 – 56.
[8] 吴应宇, 蔡秋萍, 吴芃. 基于神经网络技术的企业财务危机预警研究 [J]. 东南大学学报, 2008, 10 (1): 22 – 26.
[9] Cho S, Kim J, Bae J K. An integrative model with subject weight based on neural network learning for bankruptcy prediction

[J]. Expert Systems with Applications, 2009, 36: 403-410.

[10] Boyacioglu M A, Kara Y, Baykan O K. Predicting bank financial failures using neural networks, support vector machines and multivariate statistical methods: a comparative analysis in the sample of savings deposit insurance fund (SDIF) transferred banks in Turkey [J]. Expert Systems with Applications, 2009, 36: 3355-3366.

[11] Yang Zijiang, You Wenjie, Ji Guoli. Using partial least squares and support vector machines for bankruptcy prediction [J]. Expert Systems with Applications, 2011, 38: 8336-8342.

[12] Min Sung-Hwan, Lee Jumin, Han Ingoo. Hybrid genetic algorithms and support vector machines for bankruptcy prediction [J]. Expert Systems with Applications, 2006, 31: 652-660.

[13] 蔡岩松, 杨茁, 王聪. 基于系统动力学的企业财务危机预警模型研究 [J]. 管理世界, 2008, 5: 176-177.

[14] 陈磊, 任若恩. 公司多阶段财务危机动态预警研究 [J]. 系统工程理论与实践, 2008 (11): 29-35.

[15] 马超群, 何文. 基于COX的财务困境时点预测模型研究 [J]. 统计与决策, 2010, 21: 38-42.

[16] 卢永艳. 上市公司财务困境风险的行业差异性研究 [J]. 宏观经济研究, 2012, 3: 80-84.

[17] 倪中新, 张杨. 基于COX比例风险模型的制造业财务困境恢复研究 [J]. 统计与信息论坛, 2012, 27 (1): 15-20.

[18] 郭斌, 戴小敏, 曾勇, 方洪全. 我国企业危机预警模型研究——以财务与非财务因素构建 [J]. 金融研究, 2006, 308: 78-87.

[19] 王克敏, 姬美光. 基于财务与非财务指标的亏损公司财务预警研究——以公司ST为例 [J]. 财经研究, 2006, 32 (7): 63-71.

[20] 邓晓岚, 王宗军, 李红侠, 杨忠诚. 非财务视角下的财务困境预警——对中国上市公司的实证研究 [J]. 管理科学, 2006, 19 (3): 71-80.

Research on Network Marketing Performance Evaluation Based on GIOWA Operator

Xue Wanxin   Pei Yilei   Li dandan

Introduction

Network marketing is a new marketing mode, which brings broader and broader space for development to modern enterprise marketing, increasingly showing its value. Evaluation of Network marketing performance is a necessary task that enterprises must carry out. How to evaluate the effect of network marketing is an important top in the development of network marketing. Enterprises can use the performance evaluation system to conduct the cost – effectiveness evaluation regularly, understand the status quo of network marketing, and take effective measures to improve network marketing performance continually. Enterprises attach great importance to the evaluation of network marketing performance. There is a certain difficulty in research and practice of performance evaluation of network marketing.

Zhao Tingwei put forward evaluation index system of network marketing performance consisted of social benefits, network effects, and economic benefits three dimensions based on the analytic hierarchy process method[1]. Dai Wenfeng used website design, website promotion, website traffic and network marketing effectiveness to establish evaluation system of network marketing performance[2]. Gao Wenhai proposed a comprehensive evaluation model of network marketing performance based on multi – level fuzzy method, and built evaluation index system from the perspectives of website effectiveness, network marketing efficiency and network marketing effectiveness[3]. The research method is based on the analytic hierarchy process method and multi – level fuzzy method, in which uncertain factors influencing evaluation are not well avoid. The evaluation of network marketing performance is a multi – attribute decision – making problem, of which consists of both numeric value and fuzzy language. Zhang Aimin, Zhang Chunrun conducted the effective evaluation of the performance of vehicle maintenance readiness based on GIOWA operator method[4]. Ding Fei used GIOWA operator method to effectively evaluate optimal allocation of water resources and selected the optimal solution[5]. Li Hua combined GIOWA operator method with gravity method to conducted the effective research on the issue of logistics center location[6]. GIOWA operator can be directly applied language to describe the problem that is difficult to quantify, and weights of GIOWA operator play the role of balancing factors or adjusting the evaluation to make it more reasonable[4].

This paper establishes evaluation system of network marketing performance based on GIOWA operator method and fuzzy linguistic assessments, and uses the AHP method to determine the weights, finally applies the example to verify the validity of the evaluation system.

Evaluation method and model of multi – attribute group[7,8,9,10,11,12]

Triangular fuzzy numbers. Set $\hat{a} = [a^L, a^M, a^U]$, in which $0 < a^L \leq a^M \leq a^U$, so $\hat{a}$ is a triangular fuzzy number. Its characteristic function (membership function) can be expressed as follows:

[Author Introduction] Xue Wanxin, Management College of Beijing Union University, E – mail: xuewanxin@126.com; Pei Yilei, Management College of Beijing Union University, E – mail: peiyilei@126.com; Li Dandan, Management College of Beijing Union University, E – mail: Lidandan@126.com.

$$U_{\hat{a}} = \begin{cases} \dfrac{(x - a^L)}{(a^M - a^L)} & a^L \leqslant x \leqslant a^M \\ \dfrac{(x - a^U)}{(a^M - a^U)} & a^M \leqslant x \leqslant a^U \\ 0 & else \end{cases} \quad . \tag{1}$$

Algorithms of triangular fuzzy numbers. Set $\hat{a}$ and $\hat{b}$ are two triangular fuzzy numbers, then:

$$\hat{a} + \hat{b} = [a^L, a^M, a^U] + [b^L, b^M, b^U] = [a^L + b^L, a^M + b^M, a^U + b^U] . \tag{2}$$

$$\lambda \hat{a} = [\lambda a^L, \lambda a^M, \lambda a^U], \text{ in which } \lambda > 0 . \tag{3}$$

This paper uses the method for multiple attribute decision making based on generalized induced ordered weighted averaging (GIOWA) operator to conduct the evaluation of network marketing performance, and then determine the optimal solution of network marketing.

Generalized Induced Ordered Weighted Averaging (GIOWA) operator. If $GIOWA_W(< \xi_1, \pi_1, a_1 >, \cdots < \xi_n, \pi_n, a_n >) = \sum_{j=1}^{n} w_j b_j$, in which $w = (w_1, w_2, \cdots, w_n)$ is a weighted vector associated with GIOWA, $w_j \in [0, 1] (j \in N)$, $\sum_{j=1}^{n} w_j = 1$, $< \xi_i, \pi_i, a_i >$ is a ternary datum, its first component ξ_i represents the second component π_i is the main body of the third component a_i, and b_i is the third component of a ternary datum corresponding to the jth biggest element among $\xi_i (i \in N)$. (That is b_i can be obtained by the following way: First, sort all ternary data in the set according to the size of the first component $\xi_i (i \in N)$ of each ternary datum, then put b_i in the third component of the third datum in the ternary data at the jth position), then the function GIOWA can be called generalized GIOWA operator.

GIOWA operator is characterized by: Data $< \xi_i, \pi_i, a_i >$ is not related to w_i, w_i is only related to the ith position in the order of the assembly process. Element $a_i (i \in N)$ is weighted and assembled not by the size of its own value, but based on the value of $\xi_i (i \in N)$ corresponding to a_i from $< \xi_i, \pi_i, a_i >$, π_i is generally the attribute of the case, and represented by language or numeric values; ξ_i is generally the importance degree and feature of π_i (such as weight, serial number and achievements), and is represented by language or numeric values; a_i is generally an attribute or a value of other a_i, and represented by numeric values (such as real number, interval number, triangular fuzzy number, etc.).

Methods and procedures of the multi-attribute group decision making based on GIOWA operator.

For a multi-attribute group decision making problem, assume solution set $X = \{x_1, x_2, \cdots x_m\}$, attribute set $G = \{g_1, g_2, \cdots g_n\}$, decision maker set $D = \{d_1, d_2, \cdots d_j\}$.

Decision maker $d_j \in D$ conducts the fuzzy linguistic evaluation $r_{ij}^{(k)}$ of solution $x_m \in X$ under attribute $g_n \in G$, and gets evaluation matrix $R_k = (r_{ij})_{n*m}$, and $r_{ij}^{(k)} \in S$, in which $S = \{$extremely bad (EB), very bad (VB), bad, (B) relatively bad (RB), common (C), relatively good (RG), good (G), extremely good (EG)$\}$ is language scale, its corresponding triangular fuzzy numbers are: EB = [0, 0.1, 0.2]; VB = [0.1, 0.2, 0.3]; B = [0.2, 0.3, 04]; RB = [0.3, 0.4, 0.5]; C = [0.4, 0.5, 0.6]; RG = [0.5, 0.6, 0.7]; G = [0.6, 0.7, 0.8]; VG = [0.7, 0.8, 0.9]; EG = [0.8, 0.9, 1]. In which, EB < VB < B < RB < C < RG < G < VG < EG.

Use GIOWA operator to assemble the language evaluation information of line i of evaluation matrix R_k, and then get the comprehensive attribute evaluation $r_i^{(k)} (i \in N, k = 1, 2, \cdots t)$ of solution x_i.

$$r_i^{(k)} = GIOWA_w(< r_{i1}^{(k)}, U_1, \hat{a}_{i1}^{(k)} >, \cdots, < r_{im}^{(k)}, U_m, \hat{a}_{im}^{(k)} >) = \sum_{j=1}^{m} w_j b_{ij}^{(k)} . \tag{4}$$

In which, $r_{ij}^{(k)} \in S, U_j \in U, \hat{a}_{ij}^{(k)}$ is the triangular fuzzy number corresponding to $r_{ij}^{(k)}$, $w = (w_1, w_2, \cdots, w_n)$ is the weighted vector associated with GIOWA operator, $w_j \in [0,1] (j \in M)$, $\sum_{j=1}^{m} w_j = 1$ and $\hat{b}_{ij}^{(k)}$ is the third component of the ternary data corresponding to the jth biggest element of $r_{ij}^{(k)} (i \in M)$.

Use GIOWA operator to assemble the comprehensive attribute evaluation $r_i^k (k = 1, 2, \cdots t)$ of solution x_i of t decision makers, and then get the group comprehensive attribute evaluation $z_i(w) (i \in N)$ of solution x_i:

$$z_i(w) = GIOWA'_w(<r_i^1, \pi_1, \hat{a}_i^1>, \cdots, <r_i^t, \pi m, \hat{a}_{im}^t>) = \sum_{j=1}^{t} w'_j b_i^{(k)}. \quad (5)$$

In which, $z_i^{(k)}(w) \in S, d_k \in D, \hat{a}_i^{(k)}$ is the triangle fuzzy number corresponding to $z_i^{(k)}(w)$, $w' = (w'_1, w'_2, \cdots w'_t)$ is the weighted vector of GIOWA operator, $w'_t \in [0,1]$, $\sum_{k=1}^{t} w'_k = 1$ and $\hat{b}_{ij}^{(k)}$ is the third component of the ternary data corresponding to the kth biggest element of $z_i^{(k)}$.

Use $z_i (i \in N)$ to determine and optimize all the solutions.

Case study

Performance evaluation of network marketing is a multi-attribute decision-making problem. According to the meaning and characteristics of the network marketing, learn from domestic and international research results of network marketing performance evaluation and multi-attribute decision-making problems, through a wide range of social research and network marketing experts' advice, this paper selects five evaluation indicators (attributes), which are as follows: website ranking (G_1), website traffic (G_2), user visits (G_3), security situation (G_4) and customer satisfaction (G_5). The evaluation system is established as shown in Fig. 1:

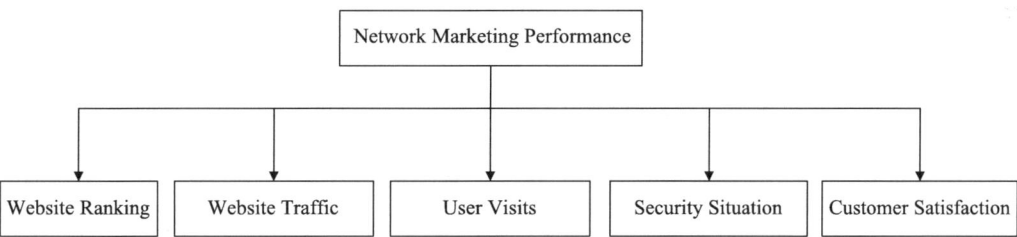

Fig. 1 Evaluation Indicators of Network Marketing Performance

The contents of evaluation indicators are as follows:

Website ranking reflects the status and popularity of the website and also affects customer's consumption tendency. The higher the website popularity is which indicates that the enterprise has the greater influence, the more forward the website ranking usually is. This paper gives not only the comprehensive ranking of the website, but also the Chinese ranking of the website.

Website traffic is the amount of data generated by the user in the process of accessing the website. Some websites limit the traffic, when more than this amount, the website can not be accessed.

User visits refers to the number of people accessing the website during a given period, here it refers to the number of people accessing the website per million people. The number of users is an important manifestation of the website value, and reflects the results of network marketing.

Security situation refers to the situation that in the process of online transactions, information on transaction goods and parties can not be stolen or intercepted illegally. Safety is very important for a website, and it is the key indicator affecting website marketing.

Customer satisfaction is a comprehensive indicator which reflects the user's evaluation of the overall operation of the enterprise. The low customer satisfaction can directly or indirectly lead to the loss of a large number of users. Without users, there can be no good network marketing performance.

According to the network marketing performance results in actual operation of six related enterprises x_i (i = 1, 2, 3, 4, 5, 6), attribute sets can be determined as shown in Table 1:

Table 1 Attribute Sets of Enterprises' Network Marketing

G \ X	Website Ranking comprehensive/Chinese	Website Traffic (MS/minute)	User Visits (per million people)	Security Situation	Customer Satisfaction
1	14/3	1731	41500	relatively safe	relatively satisfied
2	73/25	1641	9600	safe	very satisfied
3	89/18	1201	7700	relatively safe	relatively satisfied
4	57/11	2243	1283	relatively safe	relatively satisfied
5	461/85	1578	1590	relatively safe	satisfied
6	283/40	11238	3100	Safe	satisfied

Note: All the data are from Alexa 2013-11-25 statistics

The three decision-makers $d_k(k=1,2,3)$ evaluate the various indicators of enterprises, and the following evaluation matrix is got as shown in Table 2. Evaluation results are: very good (VG), good (G), relatively good (RG), common (C), relatively bad (RB), bad (B), very bad (VB).

Table 2 Evaluation Matrix

	d_1					d_2					d_3				
	G1	G2	G3	G4	G5	G1	G2	G3	G4	G5	G1	G2	G3	G4	G5
x_1	VG	G	VG	C	RG	VG	VG	G	RG	C	VG	VG	VG	G	RG
x_2	VG	G	VG	G	VG	RG	RG	G	G	G	RG	G	G	VG	VG
x_3	VG	RG	RG	C	RG	VG	C	C	RG	C	G	RG	G	G	RG
x_4	VG	VG	RG	C	RG	VG	G	C	RG	C	G	VG	C	G	RG
x_5	B	B	RB	C	G	C	RB	B	RG	G	B	RB	C	G	RG
x_6	C	C	B	RG	G	RG	B	G	G	G	C	C	RG	VG	VG

In this paper, the Analytic Hierarchy Process (AHP) is used to determine weights. According to the literature, weights can be obtained as shown in Table 3:

Table 3 Weights

Website Ranking	Website Traffic	User Visits	Security Situation	Customer Satisfaction
0.037	0.072	0.13	0.38	0.38

Use GIOWA operator to assemble the language evaluation information at Line I of evaluation matrix R_k, and then get comprehensive attribute evaluation $r_i^k (i=1,2,3,4,5,6; k=1,2,3)$ of network marketing x_i given by d_k. According to the corresponding relations between scale and triangle fuzzy function of Table 2, based on the comprehensive evaluation information of network marketing from decision-maker d_1 and by language scale, get the triangle fuzzy number corresponding to $\hat{a}_{1j}^{(1)} (j=1,2,3,4,5)$, and then get the triangle fuzzy number corresponding to $\hat{b}_{1j}^{(1)} (j=1,2,3,4,5)$ as follows:

$\hat{b}_{11}^{(1)} = \hat{a}_{11}^{(1)} = [0.7\ 0.8\ 0.9]$; $\hat{b}_{12}^{(1)} = \hat{a}_{13}^{(1)} = [0.7\ 0.8\ 0.9]$; $\hat{b}_{13}^{(1)} = \hat{a}_{12}^{(1)} = [0.6\ 0.7\ 0.8]$; $\hat{b}_{14}^{(1)} = \hat{a}_{15}^{(1)} = [0.5\ 0.6\ 0.7]$; $\hat{b}_{15}^{(1)} = \hat{a}_{14}^{(1)} = [0.4\ 0.5\ 0.6]$.

By the weight vector $W = (0.037\ 0.072\ 0.13\ 0.38\ 0.38)$, use GIOWA operator and the algorithm of triangle fuzzy number to get:

$$z_1^{(1)}(w) = GIOWA_w(<r_{11}^{(1)}, g_1, \hat{a}_{11}^{(1)}>, \cdots <r_{16}^{(1)}, g_6, \hat{a}_{16}^{(1)}>) = \sum_{j=1}^{6} w_j b_{1j}^{(1)} = [0.5\ 0.6\ 0.7] = RG;$$

Similarly, get:

$z_2^{(1)} = [0.6\ 0.7\ 0.8] = G$; $z_3^{(1)} = [0.5\ 0.6\ 0.7] = RG$; $z_4^{(1)} = [0.2\ 0.3\ 0.4] = B$; $z_5^{(1)} = [0.4\ 0.5\ 0.6] = C$; $z_6^{(1)} = [0.2\ 0.3\ 0.4] = B$;

For decision-maker d_2:
$z_1^{(2)} = [0.5\ 0.6\ 0.7] = RG; z_2^{(2)} = [0.5\ 0.6\ 0.7] = RG; z_3^{(2)} = [0.4\ 0.5\ 0.6] = C;$
$z_4^{(2)} = [0.4\ 0.5\ 0.6] = C; z_5^{(2)} = [0.4\ 0.5\ 0.6] = C; z_6^{(2)} = [0.4\ 0.5\ 0.6] = C;$

For decision-maker d_3:
$z_1^{(3)} = [0.5\ 0.6\ 0.7] = RG; z_2^{(3)} = [0.6\ 0.7\ 0.8] = G; z_3^{(3)} = [0.5\ 0.6\ 0.7] = RG;$
$z_4^{(3)} = [0.5\ 0.6\ 0.7] = RG; z_5^{(3)} = [0.3\ 0.4\ 0.5] = RB; z_6^{(3)} = [0.4\ 0.5\ 0.6] = C;$

Set $W' = (0.3\ 0.4\ 0.3)$, use GIOWA operator to assemble the comprehensive evaluation $z_k^i(w)$ ($k = 1, 2, 3, 4, 5, 6$) of website network marketing x_i from three decision-makers, and then get the group comprehensive attribute $z_k(w')$ ($k = 1, 2, 3, 4, 5, 6$) of website network marketing x_i, finally get the comprehensive attribute evaluation of each enterprise network marketing as follows:

$z_1(w') = GIOWA_{w'}(<z_1^1(w), d_1, \hat{a}_1^1>, <z_1^2(w), d_2, \hat{a}_1^2>, <z_1^3(w), d_3, \hat{a}_1^3>) = [0.5\ 0.6\ 0.7] = RG;$
$z_2(w') = GIOWA_{w'}(<z_2^1(w), d_1, \hat{a}_2^1>, <z_2^2(w), d_2, \hat{a}_2^2>, <z_2^3(w), d_3, \hat{a}_2^3>) = [0.6\ 0.7\ 0.8] = G;$
$z_3(w') = GIOWA_{w'}(<z_3^1(w), d_1, \hat{a}_3^1>, <z_3^2(w), d_2, \hat{a}_3^2>, <z_3^3(w), d_3, \hat{a}_3^3>) = [0.5\ 0.6\ 0.7] = RG;$
$z_4(w') = GIOWA_{w'}(<z_4^1(w), d_1, \hat{a}_4^1>, <z_4^2(w), d_2, \hat{a}_4^2>, <z_4^3(w), d_3, \hat{a}_4^3>) = [0.3\ 0.4\ 0.5] = RB;$
$z_5(w') = GIOWA_{w'}(<z_5^1(w), d_1, \hat{a}_5^1>, <z_5^2(w), d_2, \hat{a}_5^2>, <z_5^3(w), d_3, \hat{a}_5^3>) = [0.4\ 0.5\ 0.6] = C;$
$z_6(w') = GIOWA_{w'}(<z_6^1(w), d_1, \hat{a}_6^1>, <z_6^2(w), d_2, \hat{a}_6^2>, <z_6^3(w), d_3, \hat{a}_6^3>) = [0.3\ 0.4\ 0.5] = RB;$

The order of the six enterprises' network marketing performance is $x_2 > x_1 \approx x_3 > x_5 > x_4 \approx x_6$. The evaluation value of comprehensive attribute shows: the second enterprise has the optimal network marketing performance.

Conclusion

The multi-attribute decision making method of GIOWA operator has features of practicability, systematization and simplicity, and it can be applied in more fields. Using GIOWA operator and AHP method to conduct a comprehensive evaluation on network marketing performance and doing comparison analysis of advantages is a research focus in the future. When evaluating network marketing performance, evaluation purposes are different, so the selected indicators are different; and economic benefits, social benefits, and service need to be considered. This paper selects five evaluation indicators, in which there are no economic benefits. The reasons are that on the one hand, economic data is more difficult to obtain; on the other hand, the economic benefits of website marketing have time delay characteristics and are poorly defined. Usually online and offline entities are linked, it is difficult to define clearly how many economic benefits are from the website marketing. In the future, other indicators are applied to conduct a comprehensive evaluation on network marketing performance, according to different evaluation goals.

References

[1] D. W. Zhao, W. Lian. Network Marketing Performance Evaluation Based on Analytic Hierarchy Process [J]. Science Technology and Management, 2010 (1): 137-140.

[2] W. F. Dai. Research on Network Marketing Performance Evaluation Method [J]. New Marketing, 2009 (5): 42-43.

[3] W. H. Gao, N. Su. Network Marketing Performance Comprehensive Evaluation Model Based on Multi-level Fuzzy Method [J]. Market Modernization, 2006.

[4] A. M. Zhang, C. R. Zhang. Readiness Performance Evaluation of Vehicle Maintenance [J]. Ordnance Industry Automation, 2009: 26-28.

[5] F. Ding, T. Yamashita. Scheme Choice for Optimal Allocation of Water Resources Based on Fuzzy Language Evaluation and the Generalized Induced Ordered Weighted Averaging Operator [J]. Original Article Fuzzy Inf. Eng, 2011 (2): 169-182.

[6] H. Li, X. S. Cha, B. D. Wang. Research of Logistics Center Location Based on GIOWA Operator Logistics Technology, 2009 (6): 82-84.

[7] Z. S. Xu. Uncertain Multiple Attribute Decision Making Methods and Application [M]. Beijing: Tsinghua University Press, 2004.

[8] Z. S. Xu. Method Based on Fuzzy Linguistic assessments and Linguistic Ordered Weighted Averaging (OWA) Operator for Multi-attribute Group Decision-making Problems. Systems Engineering. 2002: 79-82.

[9] X. C. Bai, L. Kang, C. Z. Guo. The Fuzzy Synthesizing Evaluation of City's Environmental Quality Based on GIOWA Operator, A Case of 13Cities of Jiangsu province. Journal of Population, Resources and Environment (In Chinese) 2005 (3): 51-58.

[10] Zhou shan, the performance evaluation of real estate enterprises network marketing research [D] the chongqing university, 2013 (5).

[11] ZhuYan, Internet marketing performance evaluation based on analytic hierarchy process [J] modern business. 2014.

[12] Rajshekhar (Raj) G. Javalgi, patricia R. Todd, Wesley Johnston, Elad Granot, Entrepreneurship, muddling through, and Indian Internet-enabbled SMEs [J]. Journal of Business Research, 2012, 6 (65): 740-744.

环境资源定价及其实现途径

——基于边际机会成本定价理论

穆红莉

环境资源是人类赖以生存和发展的物质基础。然而，近年来，由于企业过度使用环境资源而引发的问题日益突出。2011 年，国家环境保护部发布的《中国环境状况公报》显示：在监测的 26 个湖泊中，呈富营养化状态的湖泊占 53.8%；在监测的 200 个城市 4727 个地下水监测点中，较差－极差水质的监测点比例为 55.0%；多数城市的空气颗粒物指标超过了 PM2.5 二级标准。环境污染问题已成为制约我国经济健康发展、影响社会和谐安定的关键因素。

在市场经济条件下，企业作为追求利润最大化的经济主体，缺乏治理污染的内在动力。如果环境资源可以无偿或低价使用时，企业就会选择将污染不经治理直接排放，由社会承担其治理成本。长期以来，我国环境资源价格水平长期偏低，导致企业选择高污染排放的生产方式。2005 年，中国环境与发展合作委员会《环境和自然资源定价与税收》课题组进行了历时两年的研究后，在研究报告中指出："在大多数情况下，环境定价还没有做到完全真实地反映长期环境治理和环境损害成本。这样的价格机制无法激励环境治理和改变生产者、消费者破坏环境的行为。"全国人大环境与资源保护委员会在 2012 年进行的调查中也发现，我国现行排污收费标准偏低，排污收费数额远远低于企业治理污染的成本。"企业宁可交费，也不愿投资治理污染"在一些高污染企业中变成普遍现象。我国目前迫切需要推进环境资源价格改革。同时，也迫切需要学术界进行环境资源价格改革的理论研究。本文将基于边际机会成本定价理论对环境资源的定价问题进行探讨。

1 环境资源的价格构成

1.1 边际机会成本定价墙理论

随着人类经济活动范围的不断扩大，稀缺性成为各种资源被广泛使用的"瓶颈"。许多过去可以自由取用的免费资源逐渐变为必须付费才能使用的经济资源。如河水、森林、草场和具有纳污能力的环境资源等。我们应该为这些资源确定一个合理价格，以避免出现资源滥用。在为这些资源确定价格时，要充分考虑其稀缺性。任何稀缺资源的使用，无论实际上是否为之支付代价，都能形成机会成本，即为了这种使用所放弃的其他使用能够带来的益处。边际机会成本（MOC）包括使用一单位资源时全社会（包括生产者）所付出的全部成本。就环境资源来说，使用一单位环境资源的边际机会成本等于其边际生产成本（MPC）、边际使用者成本（MUC）与边际外部成本（MEC）三者之和。

1.2 环境资源价格构成

企业排放污染物，消耗了周边环境的纳污能力，并且企业的排污行为使得周边环境资源在未来无法使用。边际使用者成本（MUC）是指自然资源数量的单位变动所引起的使用者成本总额的相应变动。使用者成本就是当代人使用环境资源而牺牲的后代人使用该资源所产生的成本。在环境资源价格中计入边际使用者成本体现了资源使用的代际公平性原则。

工厂排放废气污染空气，导致周围居民呼吸污浊的空气，但工厂没有进行治理。工厂排污造成的损失不是由工厂承担，而是由居民负担，那么这种成本就是外部成本。边际外部成本（MEC）是利用一单

［基金项目］本文系教育部人文社会科学研究项目基金项目（项目批准号：08JA790008）；国家自然科学基金项目：（项目批准号：70703001）。

［作者简介］穆红莉，北京联合大学生物化学工程学院。

位环境资源给他人造成的没有得到相应补偿的损失。

分析环境资源价格构成的三个组成部分，可以发现边际生产成本（MPC）实际上是环境资源的生产、维护和开发成本。这部分成本是由环境资源生产或管理部门付出的。在制定环境资源价格时，边际生产成本作为资源使用者需要补偿的私人成本计入价格。边际使用者成本（MUC）和边际外部成本（MEC）二者反映了资源的社会价值，应作为资源使用者需要补偿的社会成本计入环境资源价格。

对于日益稀缺的环境资源，如果低估其价格，必然会出现企业随意排放污染物，大量消耗环境资源的情况。而按照使用资源的边际机会成本（MOC）=边际生产成本（MPC）+边际使用者成本（MUC）+边际外部成本（MEC）为环境资源定价，企业除付出私人成本 MPC 之外，还必须付出反映资源社会价值的 MUC 和 MEC。以边际机会成本为其定价可以准确反映将有限的环境资源用于某项经济活动时社会所付出的全部成本，从而促使人们合理地分配和使用环境资源。

2　环境资源价格的实现机制

除确定环境资源价格构成之外，在经济活动中，还必须解决环境资源价格的实现机制问题。具体来说，就是谁是索取主体，以何方式索取的问题。这是目前学术界讨论的薄弱环节。本文将从主体与方式两个方面深入探讨环境资源价格的实现机制。

2.1　环境资源价格的索取主体

边际生产成本是生产、维护环境资源过程中产生的直接成本。边际使用者成本和边际外部成本是使用环境资源所造成的社会成本，这两部分成本需要政府向排污企业索取。

2.1.1　边际使用者成本是排污企业对环境资源的未来使用者的补偿

可持续发展原则要求后代人具有和当代人同等的
享用资源的权利。由于后代人无法亲自向排污企业索取这部分成本，政府应该代为行使该权利。目前，一些国家的政府已经开始为后代人索取资源使用补偿。如在 2011 年颁布的加纳《石油收入管理法案》中，明确规定一定比例的石油收入要划入政府管理的遗产基金，遗产基金用于确保后代人也能享有不可再生资源的收入。

2.1.2　边际外部成本是企业对污染排放受害者的补偿

一般情况下，企业排污会造成空气污染、水污染、土壤污染等。污染受害者通常是区域中的全体居民。当存在众多污染受害者时，出于"搭便车"心理，往往没有人愿意出面索取补偿。因此，理当由政府作为公众利益的代表可排污企业要求经济补偿。

2.2　环境资源价格的索取方式

为了使环境资源的价格体现其稀缺性，政府要代表整个社会对资源使用者进行索取。市场经济条件下，政府一般不使用行政命令手段，而是以经济手段为主的环境管理制度对企业进行生产成本追加，使企业使用环境资源所付出的成本既包括资源的私人成本，也包括资源的社会成本。使用经济手段有利于企业自主选择，企业可以在购买资源用于排污和治理不排污两者之间进行选择。一般情况下，企业会对治理污染成本与环境资源价格进行比较。治理污染成本低的企业将选择自己治理污染。另一些企业会选择购买环境资源排污，然后政府用出售资源的收入治理污染。最终的结果将达到对环境资源的最优配置。

3　环境资源价格的实现途径

环境管理制度是解决环境问题的社会规则。环境管理制度中的经济手段（简称环境经济手段）的特点，是从影响企业成本收益因素入手，引导企业进行选择，最终达到保护环境的目的。环境资源价格的实现途径，是使用环境经济手段对排污企业进行成本追加。目前，政府经常使用的环境经济手段包括排污费、排污权交易、环境补贴和环境押金等。在使用不同的环境经济手段时，环境资源价格有不同的体现。

3.1　排污费——排污收费标准是环境资源价格的体现

1972 年，经合组织（OECD）环境委员会提出"污染者付费原则"即"污染者必须承担削减污染措施的费用"。在该原则的指导下，OECD 成员国在环境管理中采用了排污费（税）制度。我国在 1979 年 9 月颁布的《环境保护法》从法律上确立了排污收费制度。1982 年 7 月，我国国务院发布《征收排污费暂行办法》，排污收费制度在全国范围内得以实施。排污收费制度要求排污企业必须以所排放污染物的种类、数量和浓度按照收费标准缴纳排污费。排污收费标准是环境资源价格的体现。科学制定排污收费标准，使收费标准高于污染治理成本，是排污收费制度发挥作用的前提。

3.2 排污权交易——排污权交易价格是环境资源价格的体现

实施排污权交易要经过以下步骤：首先，根据本地区环境质量目标确定一定时间内可容纳的污染物总量；其次，将可容纳的污染物总量划分为若干排污权；再次，通过拍卖手段进行排污权初始分配，分配给排污企业；最后，准许各个持有排污权的厂商进行交易。在这种情况下，排污权就成为厂商在一定条件下对环境资源的占有、使用、处置和收益的权利。环境资源的价格通过排污权交易的价格得以实现。企业如果要排放污染物，就必须购买排污权。由于一个地区允许排放的污染物总量有一定限额，随着新企业加入和原有企业生产规模扩大，排污权的需求量上升，排污权的价格就会提高。这就意味着企业需要支付更高的价格才能购买到用于排污的环境资源，企业为降低成本会主动选择清洁生产工艺。

3.3 环境补贴——环境补贴率是环境资源价格的体现

为了保护环境和自然资源，政府对企业在治理环境污染、提高清洁生产技术和设备的投入进行补贴。环境补贴的主要方式包括赠款、软贷款、税收补贴等。通过环境补贴可以使企业加大对清洁生产的投入，从而减少污染排放。环境补贴率是环境资源价格的体现。如果环境补贴足够补偿企业的清洁生产改造投入，就可以激励企业持续地选择清洁生产，节约对环境资源的使用。环境补贴的实质是政府激励企业进行污染削减活动的财政转移支付。德国政府于 2000 年制定了《可再生能源法》，根据不同的太阳能发电形式，政府给予为期 20 年、每千瓦时 0.45 – 0.62 欧元的补贴。

3.4 环境押金——押金标准是环境资源价格的体现

某些产品的残留物对环境具有潜在的威胁，如电池、电子产品、瓶装饮料等。对于这些产品可以使用环境押金制度达到保护环境的目的。具体操作步骤是：政府强制企业在销售这些产品时向购买者收取一定数量的押金，购买者如果将产品残留物送到指定的收集系统，就把押金退还给购买者。收取押金后，消费者随意丢弃产品残留物就要承担一定数额的成本。这个成本实际上就是消费者对使用环境资源的支付。在环境押金制度下，押金标准是环境资源价格的体现。押金标准的确定应参考残留物对环境的损害程度。考虑到旧电池、塑料瓶对环境损害的长期性和严重性，这类产品的押金标准应高到足以激励人们送还残留物。目前，环境押金制度在我国实施的情况不容乐观。工信部 2011 年进行的一项抽样调查显示，平均每人一年使用 11 节干电池，目前 90% 的市民对废旧电池的处理是随意丢弃。在这种情况下，迫切需要政府扩大环境押金制度覆盖的产品范围，提高押金标准。通过利益驱动，引导公众改变不利于环境的消费习惯。

4 结论与建议

党的十八大报告中指出，我国要"深化资源性产品价格和税费改革，建立反映市场供求和资源稀缺程度、体现生态价值和代际补偿的资源有偿使用制度和生态补偿制度"。这为我国今后的环境资源价格改革指明了方向。合理的环境资源价格应补偿使用资源所带来的全部成本。

4.1 我国环境资源价格的确定应基于边际机会成本定价理论

其价格中既应包括体现环境资源私人成本的边际生产成本，也应包括体现环境资源社会成本的边际使用者成本和边际外部成本。这就为从根本上解决我国的环境污染问题奠定了基础。

4.2 环境资源的价格应由政府代表当代和未来的公众向排污企业索取

具体途径是政府采用经济手段对排污企业的生产成本进行追加。企业在进行了成本收益分析后，可以在购买环境资源排污或投入成本进行清洁生产二者之间进行选择。企业自由选择的结果能够使环境资源配置达到帕累托最优状态。

4.3 为了使环境资源的价格反映其真实的稀缺程度，环境保护部门应不断优化环境经济手段的使用

目前用于实现环境资源价格的环境经济手段主要包括排污权交易、排污收费、环境补贴、环境押金等。针对我国目前存在的排污收费标准偏低、议价收费、环境押金标准偏低且覆盖面较小的问题，环境保护部门应根据具体情况调高排污收费标准和环境押金标准，扩大环境押金制度覆盖面，使环境资源的价格对生产和消费起到正确导向作用。

参考文献

[1] 马中，杰米拉，渥福德. 环境和自然资源定价与税收研究报告 [R]. 北京：中国环境与发展合作委员会，2005.
[2] 张亚连，邓德胜. 构建反映生态成本的企业产品定价机制 [J]. 价格理论与实践，2012（4）.
[3] 孙乾. 我国排污费偏低致企业宁交费认罪也不愿投资治污 [N]. 京华时报，2012-08-28.

正高级专业技术人员研究成果汇编.1

联大的足迹 2014

（下册）

付晨光 主编

知识产权出版社
Intellectual Property Publishing House

图书在版编目（CIP）数据

联大的足迹：正高级专业技术人员研究成果汇编.1，2014/付晨光主编.—北京：知识产权出版社，2015.7
ISBN 978-7-5130-3440-1

Ⅰ.①联… Ⅱ.①付… Ⅲ.①北京联合大学—专业技术人员—研究成果—汇编 Ⅳ.①G644

中国版本图书馆 CIP 数据核字（2015）第 070822 号

内容提要

本书以北京联合大学部分校领导任编委会主任、校人事处负责组织编辑的本校正高级专业技术人员研究成果汇编。主要包括研究论文、学术专著和发明专利等栏目。成果汇编包括对当前的学术理论、学术热点的探讨；教育教学改革的探索；教学管理工作经验探讨；等等。

责任编辑：兰 涛　　　　　　　　　　　　　　责任校对：董志英
封面设计：乔鸿雁　王竹宝　　　　　　　　　　责任出版：孙婷婷

联大的足迹：正高级专业技术人员研究成果汇编.1，2014
付晨光　主编

出版发行：知识产权出版社有限责任公司	网　　址：http://www.ipph.cn
社　　址：北京市海淀区马甸南村1号	邮　　编：100088
责编电话：010-82000860 转 8325	责编邮箱：lantao@cnipr.com
发行电话：010-82000860 转 8101/8102	发行传真：010-82000893/82005070/82000270
印　　刷：北京中献拓方科技发展有限公司	经　　销：各大网上书店、新华书店及相关专业书店
开　　本：787mm×1092mm　1/16	印　　张：63
版　　次：2015年7月第1版	印　　次：2015年7月第1次印刷
字　　数：2041千字	定　　价：200.00元
ISBN 978-7-5130-3440-1	

出版权专有　侵权必究
如有印装质量问题，本社负责调换。

哲学类

中国共产党加强先进性建设的当代创新
——有关马克思主义执政党跳出"历史周期率"的思考

马小芳

1945年7月,我国著名教育家和爱国民主人士黄炎培先生访问延安。他向中共领导人毛泽东提出,中国存在着"历史周期率",即许多团体、地方和王朝呈现出兴亡更替的现象。黄炎培说:我生60多年,耳闻的不说,所亲眼看到的,真所谓"其兴也勃焉","其亡也忽焉"。一部历史,有'政怠宦成'的,有"人亡政息"的,也有"求荣取辱"的。总之,一人、一家、一团体、一地方,乃至一国,不少单位没有跳出由盛及衰的历史周期率。从过去到现在,中共诸君希望找出新路,跳出这个周期率的支配。[1]

力争跳出这个"历史周期率",中国共产党几代中央领导集体带领全党坚持根本宗旨,全面加强党的建设,永葆中国无产阶级先锋队和中华民族先锋队的政治本色。党的十六大以来,以胡锦涛为核心的党中央领导集体引领执政的中国共产党继续探索、不断实践,防止陷入这个"历史周期率"的怪圈和出现红色江山变质、易帜的悲剧。

1 加强先进性建设,为跳出"历史周期率"提供根本保证

纵观中国历代封建王朝的"兴盛亡忽",横看当今世界一些大党、老党,尤其是曾经在苏联和东欧地区执政的共产党相继失去执政地位,其源盖出于不能够最大限度地满足民众的利益诉求,即丧失了先进性而跳不出"历史周期率"。

"一个政党的执政地位不是与生俱来的、也不是一劳永逸的,过去拥有不等于现在拥有,现在拥有不等于永远拥有;一个政党的先进性不是一蹴而就的、也不是一成不变的,过去先进不等于现在先进,现在先进不等于永远先进。"[2]先进性是马克思主义政党的本质属性,是马克思主义政党的生命所系、力量所在。共产党提高执政能力的根本和巩固执政地位的关键,就在于牢牢抓住先进性建设毫不动摇。中国共产党始终保持先进性也必在于此。

2005年1月,在新时期保持共产党员先进性专题报告会上,胡锦涛首次提出加强中国共产党先进性建设的重大命题。其核心是代表中国先进生产力的发展要求、代表中国先进文化的前进方向、代表中国最广大人民的根本利益;决定因素是正确的理论、纲领、路线、方针、政策;组织基础是党员的先进性;重要任务是以党的执政能力建设为重点,全面加强和改进党的思想、组织、作风方面的制度建设和反腐倡廉建设;根本标准是实现好、维护好、发展好最广大人民的最大利益。

马克思主义的政党和执政党的先进性是具体的、历史的,既一以贯之又与时俱进。在新的历史条件之下,中国共产党面临着执政考验、改革开放考验、市场经济考验、国际风云变幻考验。经受住这些长期的、复杂的、严峻的考验,中国共产党必须切实加强先进性建设,不断提高执政能力和拒腐防变能力,做到科学执政、民主执政、依法执政,成为中国特色社会主义事业的坚强领导核心,从而实现先进性。先进性保证它的全部理论和全部工作体现时代性、把握规律性、富于创造性,推动它始终走在时代前列,永不脱离群众和永具蓬勃活力,能够承担起人民和历史赋予的使命。

[作者简介] 马小芳(1968—),女,法学博士,北京联合大学人文社会科学教研部副教授。

2 建设社会主义核心价值体系，为跳出"历史周期率"提供价值认同

社会主义核心价值体系适应当代中国经济体制的深刻变革、社会结构的深刻变动、利益格局的深刻调整、思想观念的深刻变化。它表述社会主义初级阶段的价值观念，回答中国共产党人用什么样的精神品格带领全国人民开拓前进，回答中华民族以什么样的精神状态屹立于世界民族之林。它揭示我国社会主义制度的内在精神、生命之魂和价值规定，以及经济、政治、文化、社会的发展动力。它提出富强、民主、文明、和谐的社会主义现代化国家的发展要求，反映全国各族人民的核心利益和共同愿望，奠定中国特色社会主义的思想根基。

2006年10月，党的十六届六中全会首次提出社会主义核心价值体系。它包括4个方面的基本内容，即马克思主义指导思想，是社会主义核心价值体系的灵魂；中国特色社会主义共同理想，是社会主义核心价值体系的主题；以爱国主义为核心的民族精神和以改革创新为核心的时代精神，是社会主义核心价值体系的精髓；社会主义荣辱观，是社会主义核心价值体系的基础。它们相互联系、相互贯通、相互促进，构成有机统一的整体。

我国建立社会主义市场经济体制和深入进行改革开放，带来人们的价值取向、道德观念、文化生活的日趋多样化。在思想大活跃、观念大碰撞、文化大交融的时代背景下，只有用社会主义核心价值体系引领观念更新和引导社会思潮，促进社会全方位和谐发展，才能避免"历史周期率"。首先，坚持用马克思主义统领社会意识形态，用共同的理想信念和价值追求团结各个阶级、阶层的人们，从而持久地凝聚人心，向着共同的目标奋进。其次，坚持兼容并存的方针，在尊重差异中扩大认同，在包容多样中增进共识，从而借鉴和吸纳其中的优秀成果和有益内容，调动一切可以调动的积极因素。

3 树立科学发展观，为跳出"历史周期率"提供理论支撑

科学发展观是现阶段中国特色社会主义社会发展道路、发展模式的理念和理论。有关科学发展观，在2003年，由党的十六届三中全会首次提出；在2005年，由党的十六届五中全会通过的《中共中央关于制定国民经济和社会发展第十一个五年规划的建议》全面阐发；在2007年，由党的十七大进一步系统而深刻地论述，并且被写入《中国共产党章程》。

科学发展观立足社会主义初级阶段的基本国情，总结我国的发展实践，借鉴外国的发展经验，适应新的发展要求。作为马克思主义与当代中国实际和时代特征相结合的产物，作为中国共产党首次提出的、系统的社会主义社会发展理论，科学发展观实现了发展问题的认识飞跃，丰富了马克思主义理论宝库，是马克思主义中国化的最新成果，是发展中国特色社会主义必须坚持的重大战略思想。

科学发展观的第一要义是发展，核心是以人为本，以最广大人民群众的根本利益为出发点和落脚点，强调发展为了人民、发展依靠人民、发展成果由人民共享。基本要求是全面协调可持续。全面发展，就是以经济建设为中心，全面推进经济、政治、文化和社会的建设，实现经济发展和社会进步。协调发展，就是推进生产力与生产关系、经济基础与上层建筑相协调，推进经济、政治、文化、社会建设的各个环节、各个方面相协调。可持续发展就是坚持走生产发展、生活富裕、生态良好的文明发展之路，实现经济社会永续发展。根本方法是统筹兼顾。统筹城乡发展、区域发展、经济社会发展、人与自然和谐发展、国内发展与对外开放，统筹中央与地方、个人利益与集体利益、局部利益与整体利益、当前利益与长远利益的关系，统筹国际和国内两个大局。

马克思主义执政党要实现长期执政、执好政，就必须解决发展问题。科学发展观为我们正确处理经济发展与政治、文化、社会发展的关系和经济与人口、资源、环境的关系，提供了理论指导。深入贯彻落实科学发展观，实现全面协调可持续的发展，就能够为跳出"历史周期率"奠定坚实的基础。

4 科学执政、民主执政、依法执政，为跳出"历史周期率"提供执政方式

面对新世纪以来世情国情党情社情的深刻变化，党的十六届四中全会总结历史经验，首次提出"科学执政、民主执政、依法执政"。这是中国共产党人新近求解"黄炎培难题"、落实长期执政问题、实现政治现代化获得的新飞跃。

科学执政，强调用科学的思想、理论、制度和方法治国理政。在领导中国特色社会主义事业的过程中，中国共产党不断探索共产党执政规律、社会主义建设规律和人类社会发展规律，把加强党的执政能力建设建立在自觉地运用客观规律的基础之上。提出"科学执政"，并且放在执政基本要求的首位，成为新的时代条件下马克思主义执政党跳出"历史周期率"的基本前提。

民主执政，突出为谁执政、靠谁执政。中国共产党坚持为人民执政、靠人民执政，支持和保证人民当家做主人，强调运用民主的制度和科学的程序行使公共权力、管理国家，因此体现了马克思主义政党执政的本质。

依法执政，主张执政要符合法治精神、法治原则和法律规范。中国共产党运用宪法、法律治理国家和社会，坚持依法治国和领导立法、带头守法、保证执法，不断推进国家的经济、政治、文化和社会生活的法制化、规范化，使制度和法律不因领导人的改变而改变，不因领导人的看法和注意力的改变而改变。依法执政是马克思主义政党执政的保障。

把科学执政、民主执政、依法执政当作执政的整体目标，表明中国共产党认识执政规律达到了新高度，标志其执政方式不断深化。科学执政是前提和基础，民主执政是核心和实质，依法执政是途径和保障。三者相辅相成、有机统一，构成中国共产党执政方式的基本框架。

中国共产党执政60多年，不断完善执政方式并且积累丰富的执政经验，扎实地推进科学执政、民主执政、依法执政，中国共产党一定能够彻底破解"黄炎培难题"，带领全国各族人民实现社会主义现代化和中华民族的伟大复兴。

5 开展执政能力建设和反腐倡廉建设，为跳出"历史周期率"提供内在动力

开展执政能力建设和反腐倡廉建设，是当代中国共产党人践行马克思主义的重大贡献。历史和现实都证明，办好中国的事情，关键在于共产党搞好包括执政能力建设和反腐倡廉建设在内的党的建设，以赢得人民群众的信任和拥护，承担起历史、时代赋予的重任，真正跳出"历史周期率"。

加强党的执政能力建设是执政的马克思主义政党的一项根本性建设。进入新世纪新阶段，中国共产党加强执政能力建设的问题更加突出。而执政能力强不强，事关中国特色社会主义事业的兴衰成败、中华民族的前途命运。苏联共产党丢掉国家政权、丧失执政地位的一个重要原因，就是其执政能力不强，不能正确应对国际国内的形势变化，没能在执政舞台上及时解决经济、政治、社会、意识形态、自身建设等一系列重大问题，没能长期赢得老百姓的拥护和支持。中国共产党必须汲取这个教训，居安思危，增强忧患意识，自觉加强执政能力建设。

《中共中央关于加强党的执政能力建设的决定》（2004年）深刻总结中国共产党的执政经验，完整提出执政能力建设的指导思想、总体目标和主要任务，要求提高5个方面的执政能力。党的十七大报告把党的执政能力建设和先进性建设，作为全面推进党的建设新的伟大工程的主线、总体要求和根本思路。党的十七届四中全会把坚持执政能力建设和先进性建设，作为中国共产党始终走在时代前列的6条基本经验之一。

加强党的执政能力建设包括不断提高驾驭社会主义市场经济的能力、发展社会主义民主政治的能力、建设社会主义先进文化的能力、构建社会主义和谐社会的能力、应对国际局势和处理国际事务的能力。这5个能力涉及经济、政治、文化、社会的各个方面。真正具备这些能力，有助于中国共产党保持执政地位，实现长期执政。

反腐倡廉建设关系人心向背和执政党的生死存亡。中国共产党越是长期执政，反腐倡廉的任务就越艰巨，就越要提高拒腐防变的能力。它是一项根本的执政要求，必须抓紧抓实。中国共产党执政60多年的实践证明，反腐倡廉建设抓得好，社会就稳定，老百姓就能够安居乐业，中国共产党就会建立最广泛、最可靠的群众基础，真正赢得人民群众的支持和拥护，切实稳固执政地位。

2007年6月，胡锦涛在中央党校发表重要讲话，提出反腐倡廉建设的新概念。党的十七大报告则把反腐倡廉建设升华为党风廉政建设和反腐败斗争，与思想建设、组织建设、作风建设、制度建设处于同等重要地位，强调以改革创新精神全面推进党的建设新的伟大工程。党的十七届四中全会则提出推进反腐倡廉的制度创新。

反腐倡廉建设包括廉政文化建设、廉政思想建设、廉政制度建设和惩治腐败行为。其中，最根本的是廉政制度建设。它是反腐败斗争最终取得成功的必由之路。搞好廉政制度建设，需要不断完善权力运行机制，使官员不必腐败；需要不断完善权力监控机制，使官员不能腐败；需要不断加强惩治腐败力度，使官员不敢腐败。

6 构建社会主义和谐社会，为跳出"历史周期率"提供良好社会环境

马克思主义执政党跳出"历史周期率"，实现长期执政，必须具备相应的执政观念、执政理论、执政方式、执政能力和执政基础（阶级的、群众的、经济的、政治的、文化的、社会的）和执政环境（国际的和国内的）等。构建社会主义和谐社会为中国共产党提供了良好的社会基础和社会环境。

社会和谐是中国特色社会主义的本质属性，是国家富强、民族振兴、人民幸福的重要保证。构建社会主义和谐社会，是建设中国特色社会主义的必然选择，是中国共产党带领全国各族人民全面建设小康社会、实现执政使命的必然要求。中国共产党的执政实践证明，只有社会和谐了，实现长期执政才有牢固的社会基础和安定有序的社会环境。

党的十六届四中全会首次提出构建社会主义和谐社会的战略任务，并且明确其主要内容。党的十六届六中全会通过的《中共中央关于构建社会主义和谐社会若干重大问题的决定》，全面、深刻地阐明社会主义和谐社会的性质和定位，指明其指导思想、目标任务、工作原则和重大部署。这是中国共产党认识和实践中国特色社会主义的又一重大成果。党的十七大深化社会主义和谐社会的认识和实践，全面部署以改善民生为重点的社会建设。

我们要建设的社会主义和谐社会，应该是民主法治、公平正义、诚信友爱、充满活力、安定有序、人与自然和谐相处的社会。这6个方面相互联系、相互作用，包括社会关系的和谐、人与自然关系的和谐。它体现民主与法治的统一、公平与效率的统一、活力与秩序的统一、科学与人文的统一、人与自然的统一。这6个方面共同揭示社会主义和谐社会的本质内涵，也是构建社会主义和谐社会的总要求。

社会主义和谐社会，是中国共产党实现长期执政的基本要求。能否建设全体人民各尽所能、各得其所而又和谐相处的社会，是对中国共产党执政能力的重大考验。构建社会主义和谐社会，是艰巨复杂的系统工程，需要经过经济、政治、文化可持续的长期协调发展，需要全党全社会坚持不懈地共同努力。有中国特色社会主义理论体系的指引，有中国共产党的领导和社会主义制度，有新中国成立以来、特别是改革开放以来不断发展而奠定起来的坚实物质基础，有各民族、各阶层、各党派、各团体利益的根本一致，我们一定能够扎实地推进中国特色社会主义的伟大事业。

参考文献

[1] 薄一波. 若干重大决策与事件的回顾：上卷 [M]. 北京：中共中央党校出版社，1991：156-157.
[2] 习近平. 加强和改进新形势下党的建设的纲领性文献 [N]. 北京：人民日报，2009-10-09，(1).

"中国梦"的时代价值

许晓平

"中国梦"是当下党报聚焦的主题和百姓热议的话题。那么，什么是"中国梦"？它的提出有什么历史意义？它的实现过程蕴含着怎样的价值？这些是我们畅谈"中国梦"首先要思考的问题。习近平总书记在参观复兴之路大型展览时这样定义"中国梦"："实现中华民族伟大复兴，就是中华民族近代以来最伟大的梦想"，而且满怀信心地表示这个梦想"一定能实现"[1]。习近平提出的"中国梦"的宏伟奋斗目标，凝聚了新中国几代中央领导集体的智慧，在坚持和发展中国特色社会主义的实践中打开了新视域，体现了中国人民的共同夙愿和中华民族的整体利益，也是每一个中华儿女的共同期盼，它触动并点燃了每个中国人内心深处实现民族复兴的渴望。

1 "中国梦"的提出，表明中国共产党为凝聚全党全国各族人民团结奋斗的精神力量树起了新旗帜

真正把中国人民和中华民族带上实现"中国梦"人间正道的，是中国共产党。在党的领导下，我们已经站在了近现代史中从未有过的新平台上，我们所遇到的阻力和挑战前所未有，我们所面临的机遇前所未有，我们离民族复兴从没有如此之近。从旧中国的无数中华儿女为实现民族复兴的前赴后继、上下求索，到新中国的共产党从"中国式的现代化"的改革初梦、到小康梦、再到党的十八大的两个"百年梦想"的重申以及"中国梦"的提出，是中国共产党领导中国人民边行走边梳理我们到底想要什么、走向哪里的过程，给我们的奋斗赋予了现实意义。习近平总书记同时强调："中国共产党历代领导人都把'中国梦'作为社会主义社会的精神支柱，都把人民群众效用最大化作为评价资源配置的价值取向和实践标准。"[2]这也使得当代中国人民更有了前进的方向和动力、更富有责任感和使命感，"天下兴亡、匹夫有责"，这种责任意识在中国共产党人和中国人民心中进一步强化。

习近平总书记强调，实现"中国梦"，必须走中国道路，必须弘扬中国精神、凝聚中国力量，彰显了"中国梦"是拓展中国道路、弘扬中国精神、凝聚中国力量的目标导向，指明了发展中国特色社会主义的前进方向。"中国梦"是中国人民利益的汇合点，是中国力量的着力点、聚焦点、落脚点，全国各族人民在"中国梦"的感召下，正在形成各族人民大团结的磅礴力量。中国共产党在开辟中国特色社会主义道路的过程中形成了道路自信；在创立毛泽东思想和中国特色社会主义理论过程中形成理论自信；在坚定理想、百折不挠中，无论遭受多少困难和挫折都不动摇、不退缩、不屈服，创造出中国特色社会主义制度，形成了制度自信；在坚持立党为公、执政为民，以人民对美好生活的向往为奋斗目标，坚持同一切腐败行为作斗争，保持党同人民群众血肉联系的过程中，形成了政党自信。在如今中华民族伟大复兴展现出光明前景的历史时刻，我们不但应该进一步增强道路自信、理论自信、制度自信和政党自信，同时要进一步赋予"中国梦"以更加丰富的价值内涵，那就是"富强、民主、文明、和谐、平等、公正、法治、爱国、敬业、诚信、友善"，只有这样，通向圆梦的道路才会有坚实的路基。

中国人民在党的强有力的领导下，也迸发出前所未有的活力。"梦在前方，路在脚下"，所有中国人的梦想都可以归结为一个最简单而平实的希望：国家富强，人民幸福。现实的"中国梦"，是所有中国人理想信念的汇集。它首先是一份责任担当，是全体国民为了实现国富民强的不懈努力，也是几千年生生不息文明古国在新世纪对于人类发展的殷切期盼；它也是一股精神能量，是在凝聚民族复兴共识的基础上获取的源源不断的意志动力；它还是一种文化气质，彰显了传统文化的色彩，谱写了天下大同的基调，绘就了和谐发展的前景。

[作者简介] 许晓平（1964—），女，北京联合大学生化学院公共基础课教学部教授、哲学硕士。主要研究方向为马克思主义基本原理。

2 "中国梦"的提出,表明以爱国主义为核心的价值观得以彰显,民族共识重新汇聚

"中国梦"是对近代以来中国人民争取民族独立、人民解放和实现国家富强、人民富裕伟大事业的继承和发展,是"振兴中华""民族复兴""中国崛起""四个现代化"以及"富强、民主、文明、和谐"与"自由、平等、公正、法治"等国家社会层面核心价值的高度概括和精炼浓缩,蕴含着凝聚共识和汇聚力量的价值。

中华民族的伟大复兴是鸦片战争以来中华儿女以爱国主义为核心的伟大民族精神共同构造的热切期盼,也是"中国梦"作为国家梦想和民族梦想不同于其他国度梦想的独特历史文化渊源。这个道理是全民族用血泪换来的共识,它已经深深地融入每一个中国人最深层的认知当中。这使得中国人民无论面对多少挑战、多大困难,都能够始终以伟大的民族智慧为底蕴,给人以希望、给人以信心、给人以力量。"中国梦"是中华民族自强不息的不竭动力,牵引着中国砥砺前行的脚步。在此过程中,爱国主义始终是把中华民族坚强团结在一起的精神力量,改革创新始终是鞭策我们在改革开放中与时俱进的精神力量。全国各族人民在"中国梦"的感召下,不断弘扬伟大的民族精神和时代精神,不断增强团结一心的精神纽带、自强不息的精神动力。

开放变革的中国也是社会转型分化的中国,在社会转型分化的背景下,每个人都有自己的梦想,每个阶层、群体也都有自己的梦想,这些梦想往往各有诉求甚至大相径庭。如今,通过"中国梦"把不同阶层、不同群体、不同个人的梦想汇聚为一个共同的追求,共同的愿景,在不同中寻找和呵护共同,在共同中尊重和保护差异,这样就可以把13亿人的力量汇集于一处,使其心往一处想、劲往一处使,这种汇集起来的力量,就是中国各族人民大团结的力量。因此,"中国梦"能够促进多元时代中国社会对政治和思想共识的构建,为表层逐渐松散的社会扎牢精神内核,促进我们团结一切可以团结的力量,发掘一切可以发掘的"正能量",调动社会各方面的积极性、主动性和创造性,齐心协力,共同推动中国特色社会主义取得新胜利。

3 "中国梦"的提出,表明应在强调国家、集体和个人三者统一中成就个人梦想

由于受传统文化的浸润,中国人特别看重家庭和宗族,在走上社会主义道路后,又尤其注重集体主义所发挥的作用,众人拾柴火焰高的观念深入人心,现实的"中国梦"在我国的基本国情下是国家富强与个人命运的高度统一。社会主义核心价值体系作为与西方国家个人主义价值观相异的精神支柱,在中国国家梦想的实现中扮演着举足轻重的作用。社会主义核心价值体系认为,人的全面发展和利益实现是社会主义的价值目标,也是社会全面进步的条件和标志。同时,坚持集体利益高于个人利益,要求在为国家前途奋斗的过程中实现个人发展和个体利益。在科学认识国家、集体与个人关系的基础上,构建新的伦理观、价值观,汇聚精神能量,增强"中国梦"的吸引力。

"中国梦"也不排斥个人积极性及其价值和创造性的发挥。在国家梦的塑造和实现过程中,每一个普通公民都应该是梦想的主角,每一个中国人的"中国梦"都是"中国梦"的具体展开。也就是说,"中国梦"的最终实现,是以一个又一个"我"的"中国梦"的实现为基础的。尊重个人创造,成就个人价值,并不意味着否认集体的作用。"中国梦"在中华文化滋润下萌生,推崇"国家好,民族好,大家才会好"。"'中国梦'的价值维度就是要实现人的自由全面发展,这也在价值层面上极大提升了'中国梦'的吸引力、凝聚力和感召力"[3]。

"中国梦"的动力之源全面激活,极大地激发了中国人实现民族复兴的内心渴望和高涨热情。无论多元化走多远,中国人都有共同的理想,只要我们紧密团结,万众一心,为实现共同梦想而奋斗,实现梦想的力量就无比强大,我们每个人为实现自己梦想的努力就拥有广阔的空间。"生活在我们伟大祖国和伟大时代的中国人民,共同享有人生出彩的机会,共同享有梦想成真的机会,共同享有同祖国和时代一起成长与进步的机会。有梦想,有机会,有奋斗,一切美好的东西都能够创造出来。"[4]

4 "中国梦"的提出,为世界和谐发展和丰富多样注入了新活力

世界各国交往的不断扩大与深入,全球化的进一步发展,都向我们证明着这样一个事实:"中国梦"的最终实现不太可能仅仅在一个相对封闭的范围内由中国人自行完成。"中国梦"应该是"中国梦"和"世界梦"的统一,中华文明与世界文明的统一,中国与世界共享战略机遇和共同应对挑战的统一。当今时代,任何国家都是与世界紧密相联、密不可分的。自身的发展往往与世界的发展具有联动性。如果以自我为中心,只考虑本国利益,甚至牺牲别国利益谋求自身发展,人类就会陷于纷争与冲突之中,最终也会危及自身发展。所以任何国家在抢抓战略机遇的过程中,都应该摒弃"独占""独有""独霸"思维,树立"共有""共享""共赢"理念,与其他国家一起共享战略机遇,共担国际风险和责任。"处于伟大复兴进程中的中国,在谋求本国发展中促进各国共同发展;处于伟大复兴进程中的中国,坚持把本国人民利益同各国人民共同利益结合起来,以更加积极的姿态参与国际事务,共同应对全球性挑战,共同破解人类发展难题。"[5]

首先,从中华民族伟大复兴的角度来说,中国的和平发展有利于世界的和谐稳定。由于中国奉行"互信、互利、平等、协作"的新安全观,中国要走的是和平崛起的道路,即通过争取和平的国际环境来发展自己,又以自己的发展来维护世界的和平。从这个意界,这个伟大梦想不仅属于中国,也属于世界。中国坚决走和平发展道路,中国利用和平的形势,快速地发展自己;中国快速地发展又加强了世界和平、发展、合作的潮流。

其次,从个人自我实现的角度来说,只有增强"中国梦"的吸引力才能在世界公民中汇聚圆梦的能量。中国人可以走出去圆"中国梦",外国人也可以来到中国圆"中国梦",中国与世界共享"中国梦",目的是为了使世界更美好。中国13亿人共圆"中国梦",发展自己,同时又与世界分享自己的发展。所以说实现"中国梦"是世界的重大"利好",是全世界人民的福祉。

最后,从促进世界和平与发展的角度来说,"中国梦"的大力倡导和实践,能够促进世界各国取长补短、互惠互利。由于中国秉持"和而不同"的文化传统,"中国梦"不是政治强制,它所容纳的社会千姿百态,不仅刷新了中国历史,也必将展现全球意义上的丰富多样性。"中国梦"为探索人类文明多样化发展道路开辟了更加美好、光明的前景。"在我们实现'中国梦'的过程中,已经开始了与国际社会互利共赢和平发展的崭新实践,它必将给全球带来巨大的机会,为人类社会向更高级的文明形式演进提供新范式。"[3]

参考文献

[1] 王逸吟,龚亮. 新一届中央领导集体参观《复兴之路》展览引发社会各界热烈反响 [N]. 光明日报,2012 - 11 - 30.
[2] 习近平. 毫不动摇坚持和发展中国特色社会主义 [EB/OL]. 新华网,2013 - 01 - 05.
[3] 赵周贤,刘光明. 沿着中国特色社会主义道路奋力实现"中国梦" [N]. 经济日报,2013 - 01 - 04.
[4] 习近平. 在第十二届全国人民代表大会第一次会议上的重要讲话 [EB/OL]. 新华网,2013 - 03 - 17.
[5] 中央党校中国特色社会主义理论体系研究中心 ". 中义上讲中国梦"就是和谐世界的梦想,以自己的意国梦":内涵·路径·保障 [N]. 人民日报,2013 - 01 - 04.

海外中国学研究的发展前瞻

——北京联合大学海外中国学研究中心成立大会暨学术研讨会述要

许 峰

为了贯彻落实教育部关于《高等学校哲学社会科学"走出去"计划》，积极推动海外中国学研究工作，北京联合大学成立了海外中国学研究中心。中心成立大会暨学术研讨会于2012年9月28日在北京会议中心隆重举行，这是北京市属高校成立的第一个以海外中国学为研究对象的专门研究机构。

在研讨会上，与会者围绕"海外中国学研究的发展前瞻"这一中心主题展开了热烈而富有成效的讨论。全国人大常委会法制委员会委员、中共中央党史研究室原副主任章百家，教育部社科司副司长徐维凡，中央编译局副局长魏海生研究员，中国社会科学院当代中国研究所副所长武力研究员、王爱云副研究员，北京大学张注洪教授，北京师范大学张静如教授，中共中央党史研究室李向前研究员、马贵凡研究员，中共中央党校柳建辉教授，中国社会科学院国外中国学研究中心何培忠研究员，华东师范大学萧延中教授，北京外国语大学李雪涛教授，以及北京联合大学徐永利、韩强、梁怡等领导和专家教授共70多人参加了会议。

与会专家普遍认为，当下的海外中国学研究应以追踪和评析国外对现实中国问题的研究成果为重点，不断增强中国学术界在这个问题上的话语权；在做好学术研究的同时，发挥好海外中国学研究的资政作用，为政府及时提供具有较高学术价值和富有可操作性的建议；要注意借鉴国外研究新的技术手段，特别是利用好互联网带来的快捷信息检索和学术交流平台，扩大国内海外中国学研究的视野和渠道；要充分发挥多学科优势，深化对学科领域内热点和难点问题的研究和评析；在海外中国学不断发展的今天，还要注意加强和扩大国内研究机构的多种形式的协作和交流。现综合本次研讨会的主要内容如下。

1 关于海外中国学发展的历史进程

关于海外中国学的研究可溯源于汉学。就中国学发展的历史进程，有学者认为，海外中国学的鼻祖是美国著名的中国问题专家费正清先生。费正清从对以中国传统文化为研究重点的汉学中开辟出了一个新的园地，把对中国历史的研究与对中国现实问题的研究真正结合在一起。这一举措被事实证明是一种很有战略眼光的举措。相比之下，欧洲人对中国的研究长期停滞在汉学范围内，直到20世纪80年代末，才开始认识到开展中国学研究的重要性。从发展历程可以看出，海外中国学的发展主要受两个因素的推动，一个是中美关系正常化进程的开启。自此，国外有一批历史学家和政治学家开始研究中国问题。当代中国的政治、外交、中共党史是这个时候研究的热点。另一个最根本的因素就是中国的崛起。随着中国经济的持续发展和影响力的不断提升，20世纪90年代以后，中国学已经成为显学。许多国家和地区都加强了对中国的研究，无论政界、学界和商界都有大批人士对中国产生浓厚兴趣，研究队伍的规模在不断扩大，大批学术成果不断涌现，各国的智库纷纷设立了研究中国问题的部门，大批有才华的学者开始专注于中国问题研究。

有学者以译介和评析国外中国近现代史研究为例进行了阶段性的划分，认为大致可分为四个阶段：(1) 1949~1966年，为初始阶段。此时仅有对个别国外中国近现代史研究者如裨治文、柔克义、马士、丹涅特、赖德烈、费正清等人部分著作的翻译和对国外研究近现代史状况的零星介绍和评价。(2) 1967~1976年，为沉寂阶段。因为"文革"十年期间中国对外联系骤然减少，个别大型图书馆的

[作者简介] 许峰，北京联合大学海外中国学研究中心教授。

外文书刊仍可见到，但很少有学者能对海外中国学的研究进行评析。(3) 1977～1999年，为勃兴阶段。改革开放后，始有国外中国学著作大量出版。在专著方面，有侯且岸的《当代美国的"显学"——美国现代中国学研究》（人民出版社，1995年）、张注洪、王晓秋的《国外中国近现代史研究述评》（中国文史出版社，1999年）、梁怡的《英、法、德、澳、加对中国近现代史的研究》（《北京联合大学学报》多期连载刊登）等；在工具书方面，则有冯燕的《近三十年国外"中国学"工具书简介》（中华书局，1981年）、杨诗浩的《国外出版中国近现代史书目（1949—1978）》（上海人民出版社，1980年）、《美国中国学手册》（中国社会科学出版社，1993年）、《俄苏中国学手册》（中国社会科学出版社，1986年）等陆续面世。(4) 2000年至今，为发展阶段。此时，对国外研究的关注范围更加扩大，研究内容更加全面，提供的信息更加新颖，分析渐趋深入。研究成果主要有何培忠的《当代国外中国研究》（商务印书馆，2006年）、何寅的《国外汉学史》（上海外语教育出版社，2006年）、黄长著等的《欧洲中国学》（社会科学文献出版社，2005年）、张海惠的《北美中国学》（中华书局，2010年）、陈君静的《太平洋彼岸的回声——美国中国史研究考察》（中国社会科学出版社，2003年）、朱政惠的《美国中国学史研究》（上海古籍出版社，2004年）等。

2 关于海外中国学研究的意义与旨归

与会专家结合十七届六中全会精神、教育部2011年11月提出的哲学社会科学"走出去"和"推动海外中国学研究"的有关论述，从各自的角度阐发了进一步开展海外中国学研究的重要意义。

有学者谈到，从30多年的总体发展结果来看，海外中国学领域已形成一个颇具影响的学者群，有了代表性的学术刊物、学会组织以及年报的出版。在海外的中国学成为国际学术界"显学"的同时，"海外中国学研究"也成为我国实施改革开放政策以来，自主创建的、成长最为迅速的学科之一。用北京大学严绍璗教授的话来说，海外中国学的创立，"意味着我国学术界对中国文化所具有的世界历史性意义的认识愈来愈深化；学术界愈来愈多的人士意识到，中国文化作为世界人类的共同的精神财富，作为世界文明的重大存在，在世界文明互动的历史进程中，对它的认知和研究，事实上具有世界性。或许可以说，这是自20世纪70年代中期以来的30余年间，中国人文科学的学术观念最重要的转变，也是最重大的提升的标志之一"。❶

有党史专家回顾了胡乔木生前对海外中共党史问题研究的指示，进而提出研究海外中国学的两个意义：一是对我们自己正在研究的问题可以深入，可以借鉴外国人有益的方面；再者，可以有针对性地在国际学术界上发出我们的声音。在这方面，中国和俄罗斯学术界通过接触和学术交流，增强了双方的相互理解，取得了比较明显的成效。有学者认为，加强海外中国学研究的意义和作用不仅在于学术方面，还表现为可以借助于海外的视野和研究方法进行比较研究，让世界了解中国，让中国融入世界，可以在一定程度上解决话语权不对称的问题。也有学者认为，开展海外中国学研究，一个重要目的是为借助外界帮助我们深入认知当今全球化体系下中国自身的问题，增加多向度的观察视角和广阔开放的参照系。这是我们不断升华自我认知、认清自身方位、探索现实主动性的内在基点。这种参照和反省越自觉，眼光与声音越真切，越有利于我们的判断与辨析，这无疑是对我们"只缘身在此山中"的时代和历史局限性的有效超越。

大家还讨论了海外中国学研究对外传播的意义。有学者认为，改革开放30多年以来，我们强调加强海外中国学研究，其意义不是一般地开展中外学术交流，重要的是要说明：一个改革开放的中国需要世界的了解，中国也需要了解世界，包括外部世界对我们的看法，而且这种了解必须是实时的，是与中国和世界的变化同步的。作为沟通中外相互理解的一个重要而特殊的学术渠道，海外中国学可以缩短我们的自我认知和外部认知之间的差距，可以使我们更客观地了解中国的外部形象，进而发挥引导作用，多方位地树立中国在国际上的积极形象。至于中国的价值理念怎么传出去、怎么有效传播的问题，有学者提出：通过海外中国学的研究，第一，要充分了解其他国家和民族现代化道路的特点，民族文化、价值的特点，这样才能够求得大同。第二，他山之石可以攻玉。我们要充分了解外国人是怎么认识中国的。

---

❶ 严绍璗. 对国际中国学研究的再思考 [J]. 国家图书馆学刊, 2010 (1).

他们的价值理念在中国问题上是怎么反映出来的。第三，应该通过我们的研究和了解，能够逐渐形成中国在全球的话语体系中的主导地位，这一点日益显得重要。

3 关于海外中国学的学科特性及研究定位

大家讨论认为，海外中国学其实是一个综合性的学科。有学者认为，它涉及面广，边缘比较模糊。国外要强调的就是对中国进行综合性、全方位的研究，这是中国学不同于历史学、政治学的地方。有学者认为，从广义上看，海外把中国研究作为一门学问，在西方有200年的历史，在东方则更为悠久，至少也有600年或800年的历史。但作为一门学科，海外中国学研究在我国起始于20世纪70年代中期，是由中国社会科学院有远见卓识的学者发动、联合学术界的众多学人创建的。一个新的学科的出现、成长和壮大，不仅有时代需求的背景，也需要时间的付出、学人的努力和行政管理部门的支持。就目前来说，这一学科的发展还面临许多需要讨论和研究的问题，例如对其学科意义的认识如何提高、学理的阐述如何加强、学科的称谓是否需要统一等，尤其是在我国的学术体系列表中如何体现这一学科的存在，已成为制约这一学科进一步发展的关键。

大家一致认为，海外中国学研究的主要对象和关注重心应该是海外对当代中国问题的研究。中国学的研究重心已转向当代中国问题，特别是与中国发展战略和政府决策相关的研究。近年来，在海外中国问题的研究中涉及中国党和政府的执政理念、制度模式、发展道路、发展经验和发展成就方面的关注度显著上升，如何认知中国、解读中国已经成为一个世界性的舆论话题。"当代中国研究"正牵动着世界相关领域专家的问题意识。因此，我们的海外中国学研究应该有清晰的划界和定位，应把更多的关注点放在海外当代中国问题研究上，更好地服务于当前中国的改革与发展。

有学者从国外党史研究资料译介的角度发现，近年来随着国内学术界对加强国史、党史资政育人功能及加强现实性研究的认识不断加深，对国外相关研究的译介和评析范围也拓宽了，不仅将国外的党建研究纳入了党史研究范围，还把国外对中国当代社会问题、环境问题的研究纳入了国内学者的译介范围。

4 关于海外中国学研究面临的问题

梳理好当前海外中国学研究面临的问题，对于研究的深入和拓展有着特别的意义。有学者系统地归纳了5个方面的问题：第一，对理论的探讨还较滞后。这主要是对于渗透于各种成果中的理论基础往往未作或缺乏全面、深入的评价。第二，对海外研究的状况反映不够全面。在内容上多集中于政治类研究情况的了解，在国别和地区上对东南亚地区、拉丁美洲和非洲地区的中国研究很少介绍。第三，对海外研究的历史考察未尽系统，对各个国家间的中国学研究追踪也不平衡。第四，对研究的个案分析还欠普遍。第五，对研究方法的借鉴仍有偏颇。

关于意识形态与价值观层面的问题。有学者提出，在当前海外中国学研究中，有一个常见的问题，就是在讨论国外的东西时会意识形态化，而不是从辩证唯物主义和历史唯物主义的角度来看待问题。对于与我们相左的观点，容易在脑子里先入为主，然后嗤之以鼻。其实，这些观点有学术探讨，也有恶意攻击，应多注意深层面的分析，全面了解外国学者的立场和观点。也有学者认为，美国学是由美国人自己主导的，美国人借此来引导和吸引外国学者来关注美国问题，同时也通过这个途径输出美国的文化观和价值观，这一点值得我们注意。虽然中国学的成果也在不断增加，但总体上说，它在世界范围内发挥的影响还是比较有限的。这就需要我们有一套自己的中国学研究的体系。我们对应该向外部世界展示哪些东西、怎样引导外国人对中国的看法并不清晰。

5 关于加强海外中国学研究的建议

与会学者从方法论原则、发展方向、队伍建设以及基础工作等多个方面，对加强海外中国学研究提出了十分中肯的建议。

有学者强调，海外中国学的健康发展有赖于以下4个方面的努力：第一，必须以马克思主义唯物史观为指导，全面、真实、准确地进行调查研究，才可以科学地理解这一学科的性质、特点、范围和方向。第二，应具有较好的国内中国学的基础和学术素养，具有严肃的反思精神，才能更好地审视海外中国学研究的历史和现状，取长补短，促进学科发展。第三，需要把对海外研究成果的历史考察上升到学术、理论高度，既坚持中国学术的优秀传统，又重视吸收海外中国学研究中的新思潮和新方法。第四，对海外中国学的研究，国内各高校和科研单位均有创新或建树，宜加强联系、增进交流，这对于避免重复劳动，丰富和发展对海外中国学的研究都是十分必要的。

有学者认为，海外中国学研究中需要坚守一定的原则和态度。第一，研究中国问题，应该以中国为主，包括研究资料的来源和话语权问题。第二，在国际学术交流中，要旗帜鲜明地表明中国学者的态度，明确我们的立场，在是非面前不含糊。第三，对国外的研究成果取客观、平等和商榷的学术态度。在坚持公平和客观的交流原则下，就某一具体的学术观点和研究结论进行商榷乃至争鸣是非常必要的，这有助于提升研究结论的科学性，更有助于扩大中国学术的正面影响。

就进一步拓展和深化国外中共党史研究问题而言，有学者提出，由于国外学者选择研究对象的多元化、多样性，国外的中共党史研究作为一个整体的概念，与当代中国研究有同质化的趋势。在新的历史条件下，我们需要继续开展人物研究、专著论文的译介和对"问题"的综合研究；需要不断开阔眼界，从"以我为主"的解读模式到开启国际比较视野；需要直面现实，注意从"现实诉求"中找到研究的点和题。

有学者认为，在加强对海外当代中国的研究的评、译、介的过程中，准确地对外使用学术词汇和政治语汇很重要。应重视学术话语的对称性问题，尤其应注意坚持中国的学术话语权，特别是应注意选择外国人听得懂的话语体系和表述方式，这对于更好地宣传党和政府的执政理念、树立中国的国际形象有着重要的意义。也有学者认为，海外中国学研究不能照搬照抄海外的专门术语，唯"洋"是尊，而应该用马克思主义的立场、观点和方法进行辨析和运用。

有学者分析了汉学和中国学研究的不同任务和彼此关联，开展海外中国学与汉学研究所不同的侧重点和效果，并提出海外中国学研究数据库建设的重要性和迫切性问题。不少学者还提出解决研究队伍建设的重要性问题。海外中国学涉及的研究领域比较宽泛，对多语种人才的需求比较大，对使用外语开展评析的学术能力要求比较高。因此，尤其应重视对那些有专业研究背景、外语条件好的青年学者进行培养，重视从硕士、博士研究生中进行选拔和培养。

提升高校学生党建科学化水平的思考

李九丽　马俊红

随着社会的发展和高校体制的改革，大学生的价值取向日趋多元，大学生党建工作出现了一些新问题，遇到了新挑战。如何在党的十八大精神指导下，积极创新高校学生党建工作，探索新思路、新模式和新途径，努力提升学生党建的科学化水平，是摆在高校学生党建工作者面前的一项紧迫任务。

1 提高学生党建的科学化水平必须有科学的理论指导

党的十八大把科学发展观同马克思列宁主义、毛泽东思想、邓小平理论、"三个代表"重要思想一道，确立为党必须长期坚持的指导思想并写入党章，实现了党的指导思想的又一次与时俱进。科学发展观是指导党和国家全部工作的强大思想武器。实现全面建成小康社会的宏伟目标、全面提高党的建设的科学化水平，必须深入贯彻落实科学发展观。首先，要把加强学生党组织的思想理论建设放在更加突出的位置，抓好思想理论建设这个根本，引导广大学生党员学习马克思列宁主义、毛泽东思想、中国特色社会主义理论体系，深入学习实践科学发展观，推进学习型学生党支部的创建，引导广大学生党员为中国特色社会主义共同理想而刻苦学习，掌握为人民服务的本领。其次，要加强对广大学生党员的党性教育。党员是党的细胞，党的先进性要通过每一个党员的先进性来体现。因此，要引导学生党员不断加强党性修养，树立崇高的共产主义理想和中国特色社会主义信念，帮助他们明确奋斗目标和方向。最后，要教育广大学生党员模范遵守社会主义荣辱观，讲党性、重品行、做表率，做社会主义道德的示范者、诚信风尚的引领者、公平正义的维护者。

2 提升学生党建的科学化水平必须有科学的目标

2.1 要把高校学生党组织建设成学习型党组织

学习型政党，是指在坚持重视学习、善于学习优良传统的基础上，通过更新学习理念，创新学习制度，形成一套科学的学习机制，推动党内学习不断走向科学化、制度化、规范化，提高全党的马克思主义理论水平，增强全党的理论思维能力、认识规律能力和创新发展能力。把各级党组织建设成为学习型党组织是建设马克思主义学习型政党的基础工程；学习型学生党支部建设是在学习型政党理论指导下的具体实践。高校党支部是党的最基层组织，在建设学习型政党和学习型党组织的过程中，高校建设学习型党支部具有重要的现实意义，是学习型政党建设的基础工程。

2.2 要把高校学生党组织建设成服务型的党组织

建设马克思主义服务型的学生基层党组织，是党的先进性、纯洁性和根本宗旨的本质要求。建设马克思主义服务型学生党组织必须坚持以科学理论为指导，必须体现保持和发展党的先进性和纯洁性的特质，必须将社会主义核心价值体系建设融入党组织和党员服务工作全过程，必须体现党服务于普通学生的根本要求，必须努力探索新形势下执政党服务群众、服务社会、服务发展的规律等。

2.3 要把高校学生党组织建设成创新型的学生党组织

建设创新型的学生基层党组织，就是要不断增强基层党组织的生机与活力，不断创新学习方法和服务方式。创新是我们党的鲜明特征，也是党和人民事业不断取得胜利的重要保证。在新的历史起点上，以改革创新精神全面推进党的建设新的伟大工程，提升学生党建的科学化水平，关键在于建设一个马克思主义创新型政党。改革创新型的中国特色社会主义事业必然要求建设创新型政党实现科学领导；中国

[作者简介] 李九丽，北京联合大学自动化学院党委副书记，教授；马俊红，北京联合大学管理学院学生办公室主任，助理研究员。

社会发展的转型必然要求党在治国理政方式上实现变革；党自身建设的发展必然要求党在管党治党方式上实现创新。

3 提高学生党建科学化水平必须有科学的方法

3.1 进一步加强学生党组织思想建设

在建设和改革时期，我们党把马克思主义的普遍原理同中国的具体实际相结合，探索形成了中国特色的社会主义。只要我们八千多万共产党员进一步坚定对中国特色社会主义的理论自信、道路自信、制度自信，就可以形成排山倒海、无坚不摧的力量，领导人民取得中国特色社会主义事业的新胜利。要以社会主义核心价值体系为引领，在全体党员中开展坚定理想信念教育。高校学生党组织是党在高校的战斗堡垒，是高校党建工作的重要组成部分，肩负着培养有中国特色的社会主义事业建设者和接班人的重任，讲政治始终是最根本的原则，提高各级党组织和党员干部的思想政治素养始终是第一位的要求。特别是广大大学生党员正处在心智即将成熟的特殊时期，处在即将进入社会，成为社会建设新生力量的过渡时期，如果思想政治素养不过关、不合格，就会在错综复杂的发展形势中迷失方向，就难以抵御各种错误思潮和腐朽思想的影响。加强学生党支部的思想建设，一个很重要的任务就是要坚持以马克思主义为指导，以理想信念教育为核心，以爱国主义教育为重点，以思想道德教育为基础，以大学生全面发展为目标，帮助大学生树立正确的世界观、人生观和价值观。要提高他们的认知水平，防止和减少认识偏差，从而能正确地认识人类社会的各种现象，正确处理人与社会的各种关系和矛盾。确立正确的人生态度和人生信仰，树立正确的价值取向和崇高的人生理想。

3.2 进一步加强学生党组织的组织建设

结合学生党员特点，探索多维、立体的党支部设置方式。基层党支部是党的全部工作和战斗力的基础，是贯彻落实党的路线方针政策和各项工作任务的战斗堡垒。党的十七届四中全会明确要求，要"做好抓基层打基础工作，夯实党执政的组织基础"。而党支部设置方式对开展基层党支部工作有着直接的影响，因此，优化党支部设置，不仅可以扩大党组织的覆盖面和影响力，还可以直接推动党支部开展工作。一般高校党支部大多依据年级、专业来设置，党支部建在年级上、党支部建在专业上。《中共中央国务院关于进一步加强和改进大学生思想政治教育的意见》中明确指出，要努力实现本科生班级"低年级有党员、高年级有党支部"的目标。《中国共产党普通高等学校基层组织工作条例》第十三条也明确要求："大学生党的支部委员会要成为引领大学生刻苦学习、团结进步、健康成长的班级核心。"首先，党支部建在班上，可以强化党组织在基层的领导。其次，还要积极探索支部建在宿舍的方法与途径。在坚持以年级和专业等学习行政单位为区划支部的同时，尝试以学生的生活区划为中心设置党支部，建立党员宿舍，从学生的生活区进行覆盖和攻略，可以把工作真正做到学生的心坎上，使学生党员参加双重组织生活。最后，还要积极探索支部建设的"网络化"。网络已经成为思想政治教育的重要阵地，支部建设的网络化，是新媒体时代的一种必要的尝试。利用QQ群、飞信群、BBS、社区等网络形式进行党组织建设，有利于党支部建设的网络化，可以有效整合资源，提高工作效率。高校学生基层党支部设置要避免扁平化的单线设置，要探索多维、立体的设置方式，这样可以加强学生党建工作的影响力和覆盖面，有利于丰富高校党建工作的内涵。

3.3 进一步加强学生党组织的作风建设

加强学生党组织的作风建设，就是要坚持以人为本，执政为民，始终保持党同人民的血肉联系。我们要永远牢记，密切联系群众是我们党最大的政治优势，脱离群众是我们党执政以后的最大危险。要始终把人民的利益放在第一位，把实现好、维护好、发展好最广大人民的根本利益作为我们一切工作的出发点和落脚点，这样才能更好地依靠人民，推进中国特色社会主义的伟大事业。

建立党支部的实践锻炼平台是非常重要的。实践是最生动的课堂。支部应引导学生党员在校园内外积极参与各种类型、层次的实践锻炼活动，加深学生党员与现实社会生活的接触，在真实真切的感官接受和身心体会中潜移默化地受到启发教育，从而把党的基本理论和基本知识与对学生党员进行全面素质培养结合起来。比如，组织支部成员积极参加各级各类学科竞赛和课外科技作品比赛活动，在竞赛的平台上夯实专业基础，提升专业技能，以学参赛、以赛促学；通过党员担任新生导师、党员宿舍挂牌、党员校内流动服务站等形式，发挥学生党员在校园内的带动与示范作用；通过党员社区服务岗、党员百时奉献、党员校外志愿服务、校外党日活动等，增强学生党员的主人翁意识和解决实际问题的能力。在参与这些实践活动中，学生党员既可以培养自己的竞争意识和团队合作精神，也可以提高自己的实际动手能力，还可以锻炼自己的创新意识和创新能力。

3.4 进一步加强学生党组织的制度建设

制度建设是党的建设的重要方面，不断加强高校基层党组织制度建设对于提高基层党建的科学化水平起着重要的保障作用。制度是基础，有了合适的制度，党的建设才有了基本的规范，党组织和党员就有了行为准则。要不断固化已有的制度，积极探索符合高校学生党员特点的新制度。坚持政治理论例会学习制度、组织生活制度、党员佩戴党徽制度、群众教师测评制度、入党承诺书制度、学生党员行为规范等。

参考文献

[1] 黄乌密．关于科学开展高校学生党建工作的思考［J］．佳木斯教育学院学报，2010，(10)．
[2] 徐泽胜，周述波．新时期高校学生党建工作的理性思考［J］．改革与开放，2009，(10)．

关于北京高校大学生马克思主义大众化水平调查研究

李俊卿

高校大学生马克思主义大众化水平指高校在大学生中推进和实施马克思主义大众化所达到的程度及效果。大学生作为社会大众中的高知群体，是未来对马克思主义进行进一步阐释和大众化传播的核心人群，其掌握、认同马克思主义理论的程度将直接影响马克思主义大众化的社会推广效果，因此研究这一群体的马克思主义大众化水平，有着极其重要的意义。事实上，积极探讨大学生马克思主义大众化实现的有效路径，既是大学生健康成长的根本保障，也是马克思主义大众化的内在要求。笔者立足实证研究，通过设计问卷，对北京部分高校大学生进行马克思主义大众化现状的调查，以反映当前北京高校大学生马克思主义大众化的程度，为高校进一步提升马克思主义大众化水平提供一些可行性建议。

1 调查的方法与对象

高校大学生马克思主义大众化水平具体表现为大学生对马克思主义的理论认知、情感认同、信仰坚定的程度，以及指导自己实践的广度和深度四个渐进的层次。据此，问卷以大学生为基点，对高校推行马克思主义大众化过程中的重要因素进行梳理，问题涉及三个方面：一是北京高校大学生接受马克思主义教育的水平现状；二是北京高校思想政治理论课发挥主渠道作用的效果现状；三是北京高校实施马克思主义大众化各种途径的效果及校园环境的影响。

本研究以上述三个方面为基础展开，笔者自编《北京高校大学生马克思主义大众化水平调查问卷》，测评的维度包括大学生马克思主义的理论认知、情感认同与信仰的目的性、意志的坚韧性及对马克思主义的践行意识等方面，并收集大学生的人口统计学变量（性别、专业、年级等）信息，进行各因素影响的差异检验。课题调查组采用分层整群抽样的方法，于 2011 年 6~8 月向北京市 18 所高校 2750 名本科生发放了调查问卷，有效问卷 2590 份，有效回收率为 94.18%，之后应用 SPSS16.0 统计软件对结果进行处理，对北京高校在大学生中推行马克思主义大众化的水平现状进行描述性的分析。

2 调查数据的呈现与分析

2.1 北京高校大学生马克思主义大众化的总体水平

本部分是调查数据的主体，主要围绕受众自身对马克思主义理论认知状况的评价，对马克思主义的情感接受情况、信仰信念水平、行为意志的坚定性、对确立的信仰能否践行等方面进行考察。调查呈现的总体情况是，学生对马克思主义理论认知的程度较高，大部分同学认同马克思主义，并升华为信仰，但由于受社会风气的影响，信仰虚空或无信仰的现象也在一定范围内存在。在践行层面，多数同学会自觉运用或想到用马克思主义的观点、方法去解决现实问题，但若使全体学生形成一种完全自觉的思维习惯，还需进一步引导。

具体而言，就理论认知部分来看，调查数据显示学生对自身掌握马克思主义理论的程度评价有别，其中 71.80% 的学生认为系统掌握或了解了马克思主义理论的基本内容；21.31% 的学生仅了解少部分理论观点；而基本不清楚马克思主义理论的仅为 6.87%，表明学生对马克思主义理论认知的程度较高。

[基金项目] 本文系中共北京市委教育工作委员会首都大学生思想政治教育重点课题"北京高校马克思主义大众化水平调查研究"（项目批准号：BJSZ2011ZD17）的阶段性成果。

[作者简介] 李俊卿，北京联合大学社科部。

为了更准确地考察学生对马克思主义基本观点的掌握情况，课题组设计了3道具体的问卷题目，主要涉及马克思主义最根本的世界观和方法论、当代中国马克思主义所指的对象、中国特色社会主义理论体系与马列主义、毛泽东思想的关系，对学生进行实测，学生正确答案率分别为27.22%、59.15%、84.98%，考虑一年级学生未学习有关思想政治理论课的课程，这样的结果可以令人满意。尽管这样的基础问答不足以准确反映学生实际掌握马克思主义理论知识的全貌，但也可以略见一斑，反映出大学生学习马克思主义理论的基本素养。由于知识信息层面接受度的高低，并不能反映学生对马克思主义情感层面的认同度的大小，因此，问卷接着又对大学生学习马克思主义基本理论的主要原因进行了调查。结果显示，48.61%的大学生认为学习马克思主义理论有助于自身的提高和未来发展；7.64%的大学生是出于个人兴趣的目的；35.44%的学生则认为学习的原因主要出于完成学分考虑。可见，大学生在接受马克思主义传播时，多半同学能主动接受马克思主义理论知识，但也存在少量学生的被动参与。

大学生的信仰心态是其认知、情感和意志的统一，它关涉人的内心世界，触及的是精神理念和价值追求。本调查显示，大部分学生明确表示信仰马克思主义。从信仰动机看，59.23%的学生对马克思主义的性质和作用有较为理性的认识而选择主动接受；49.65%的学生信仰的原因是缘于马克思主义是执政党的指导思想，并出于对主流意识形态的认同而信仰；也有29.5%的学生表示对马克思主义理论认同部分观点，少量学生信仰中抱有功利主义的想法。这表明大部分大学生对马克思主义是持理性思考后的接受态度。但是由于我国社会不断发展，受各种社会思潮的影响，信仰虚空作为一种文化现象，在高校大学生中也有一定的存在。调查中部分学生表示目前没有最终的选择，处于无明确信仰的状态，还有极少数学生选择信仰宗教。

调查显示，大部分大学生对信仰马克思主义是坚定执著的，但小部分学生思想处于一种摇摆的状态。这种情况的出现表明，在认知层面部分学生还未达到真知真懂的理想状态，由此导致了思想的困惑和价值选择取向的相对模糊化。

践行方面主要考察学生是否用马克思主义的理论指导自己的实践，是否已将马克思主义的理论、观点、方法变为个人言行的精神指南，成为生活秩序运行的内在规则，成为学生建立意义系统之内在的根据。数据显示，当学生在生活、学习中遇到问题时，多数学生（26.18%）会自觉运用或会想到（41.16%）用马克思主义的观点、方法去解决现实问题，即大部分学生已经意识到用马克思主义的观点或方法指导自己的学习生活，并在日常领域发挥主导作用。只是若使化理论为方法的过程在全体大学生中形成一种完全自觉的思维习惯，还需进一步引导。

2.2 高校思想政治理论课发挥主渠道作用的效果现状

高校思想政治理论课教学作为高校马克思主义大众化的主渠道，不仅进行马克思理论知识方面的教育而且包括意识形态的价值教育，不仅要教会学生事实判断，还要引导学生进行价值选择。从调查数据来看，高校思想政治理论课是学生获取马克思主义相关理论知识的主要渠道，教师的理论水平、教学效果得到大多数同学的认可，但教师在实践环节、教学方法等方面还有改进的空间。

具体数据显示，74.56%的学生认为获取马克思主义相关知识的渠道是思想政治理论课，其他方式（如学术讲座、理论社团、网络等）所占的比重则相对较少。从对信仰部分调查的数据看，影响学生信仰马克思主义的因素有多种，但是除马克思主义理论本身的魅力位列比例最高（44.17%）外，其他依次为思想政治理论课教师的影响为41.81%；那些真正信仰马克思主义的人所发表的言论为34.67%；社会实践的亲身感受占33.75%；主流媒体宣传为29.77%；专业课教师的言论占22.93%。此外，学生感觉在信仰马克思主义方面，思想政治理论课教师信仰的程度与其他群体相比得分最高，其他依次为学校领导、专业课教师、学生工作人员。由此可知，教师的信仰对学生有很强的正面引导作用，思想政治理论课与思想政治理论课教师在高校大学生马克思主义大众化的推行过程中作用不容忽视。另外，从学生对授课教师的评价来看，82.63%的学生承认老师理论水平较高，在此前提下，37.80%的同学认为教师具有学识魅力，授课有吸引力；44.83%认为教师授课的吸引力方面可以进一步改善；7.95%的同学认为尽管教师的理论水平不太高，但授课的方法灵活、有吸引力；只有7.30%的同学认为有些教师理论水平不高，授课也缺少吸引力，此外还有2.12%的同学有其他的选择。由此可见，高校学生对思想政治理论课教师的基本政治素养和理论水平持肯定的态度，同时抱有希望改革教学方式，增加授课吸引力的想法。最后，在思想政治理论课存在问题需要改进的方面，一些同学选择了增大实践环节等，表明思想政治理论课教学有进一步的提升空间。

2.3. 马克思主义大众化其他载体的效用

理论社团和网络媒介是马克思主义大众化载体的重要形式，校园文化、整体氛围对大学生马克思主义大众化也会有一定的影响。调查数据显示：红色社团的作用已得到学生的充分认可，但高校的红色网站影响的范围尚有拓展的空间，校园文化的隐性浸染作用需进一步加强。调查的题目如下。

第一是学生参加政治理论类社团的态度情况。在愿意参加的学生中，所持理由为加入理论社团可以学习很多理论知识，提高理论水平的占34.32%；认为参加理论社团可以展示才华，锻炼自我，增加见识的所占比例最大为41.58%；强调加入社团可以扩大朋友圈，消除寂寞，有归属感的为33.28%；认为对仕途有利，进行功利性参与的占19.46%；受周围同学影响而被动参与的占16.41%；而20.19%的学生表示虽感兴趣，但因学习紧张，无时间参加；21.35%的学生感觉理论社团活动缺少吸引力，不感兴趣，而未参加。

第二是对学生平日浏览红色网站情况的了解。大学生并不是处在一个与世隔绝的真空地带，信息化时代的学生随处可接触大众传媒，网络、广播电视、报刊杂志，尤其是网络已成为大学生日常生活不可缺少的重要内容。然而就目前来看，有些高校并未建立红色网站或校园理论学习网络，或建立起来的相应网站缺少足够的吸引力，以致马克思主义理论宣传的平台作用未得到充分发挥。调查数据显示，15.52%的学生会经常浏览相关网页，以了解关心的信息，并学到知识；46.49%的学生会间歇浏览，平日更多关注的是与自己生活关联密切的网站；表示不会浏览，对红色网站不感兴趣的学生占19.85%；因不了解这些方面网站的信息，因而不浏览的学生占15.95%。

第三是校园文化浸染对学生的影响。校园文化作为环境因素对大学生的马克思主义理论修养的提高具有隐性感染力，通过大学校园文化影响、提升学生对马克思主义的认识水平，具有润物细无声的作用。调查显示，32.28%的学生认为学校开展的与马克思主义大众化相关的大型活动多，身在其中很受感染；31.54%的学生认为学校的整体氛围积极向上；但也有29.46%的学生认为在学校感受不到什么。这表明学校在推行马克思主义大众化过程中采取的态度和支持的力度不一，学生感受的影响效果也差异较大。

3 提升北京高校大学生马克思主义大众化水平的对策建议

3.1 提高学生对马克思主义理论的认知水平，培养学生对理论的正向情感

理论知识的系统普及过程是马克思主义大众化的基础和前提，其目的是为了形成正确的理性认知，并引发进一步学习、了解理论的兴趣和热情。在马克思主义大众化的过程中，知、信、行三个层面，知是基础，其能直接影响信和行。从调查数据反映的情况看，尽管大学生对马克思主义基础层面的认知程度较高，但也不能过分乐观，需要反思。笔者认为：

第一，提高学生认知层级的路径。如何让学生跨越认知的门槛，除了教授马克思主义的基本观点外，还要引导学生精读原著。通过坚持不懈地开展阅读原著的活动，使大学生更完整、更准确、更科学地掌握马克思主义的思想精髓和理论实质。

第二，保持、巩固大学生对马克思主义理论的正向情感的方法。在实际学习中，要找准突破点，找到兴趣提升的一个门槛或切入点，由知到有吸引力再达到有热情和渴望，寻得马克思主义的信仰生长点，以此达到信的程度，真正触及心灵，在学习、解读和领悟之后，达到高度共鸣和自觉认同，并将其作为一种精神支柱、价值内核、理想信念、科学方法等在大学生的心灵中占有特殊的地位，发挥积极的作用。要达到以上目标，需要用马克思主义理论给予学生日常生活、学习以关照和指导，以满足其内心的需要，将马克思主义从高深的科学殿堂引到学生的视野中。正如恩格斯所说："马克思的整个世界观不是教义，而是方法。它提供的不是现成的教条，而是进一步研究的出发点和供这种研究使用的方法。"[1](P742-743)

第三，建立分层目标，使工作更具操作性。"马克思主义大众化所面对的'大众'，是个在文化程度、知识结构、职业特点、生活状况、年龄、兴趣等方面有着多样差异的群体，因此，大众化必须有重

点、必须分层次。"[2] 在高校，由于大学生中不同的群体对马克思主义理论认知、情感认同和信仰的程度有别，因此，应建立符合大学生特点和大众化要求的分层目标，区别于学生党员、积极分子和普通同学；不同的年级采取不同的教育内容及教育目标，以满足不同人群对理论的期待、理解和需求，提高工作的针对性和可操作性。

3.2 活化思想政治理论课的教学内容，强化社会实践

马克思主义大众化的成效最终要由受众是否以及多大程度上理解、认同和接受马克思主义理论来检验和衡量，从这个意义上说，受众才是马克思主义大众化的最终决定因素。从调查结果判断，高校马克思主义大众化重点在课堂教学。思想政治理论课教师不仅要传授学生知识，还要教会方法，授课不仅要有理论魅力，还需具备逻辑力量。

作为高校马克思主义大众化主渠道的思想政治理论课教学效果可以进一步提高。在教学内容上，除了教授理论之外，还可以告诉学生创造这些理论的伟人有什么样的信念，并通过讲解让学生感受这些伟人的人格魅力、语言魅力等。作为具有视野开阔、思维活跃、勇于创新等思想特点的高校学生，往往偏爱质疑先于接受，简单地否定或者肯定，很可能引起他们的叛逆想法，这就要求教师在教材体系向教学体系转换过程中要增加理论的论证，在授课中把思想政治理论课中的"思想"性特别突出出来，使学生真正在思辨、反思的层面接触、接受马克思主义理论。这首先需要教师提高自己的理论水准，通过转变单一教学方式，并尽量使用易于为青年学生接受的语言风格，采用专题讨论、案例教学等多种讲课方法，形成师生互动的学习机制，使教师授课中传达的理念进入到学生心灵，起到内化认同的效果。

此外，马克思主义大众化要求实现知、信、行的有机统一，而实现此目标的一个重要途径就是加强实践教学环节。马克思主义大众化不只是让学生掌握马克思主义理论的基本知识，最重要的是教会学生如何运用马克思主义的立场、观点、方法去思考、分析和解决实际问题，将马克思主义的基本要求内化为品德，外化为行动，使学生达到知与行的统一。社会实践作为课堂教学的延伸，学生学以致用，其现场的感受胜过千言万语，学生通过多经历，多体验，可以开阔视野。但是社会实践是一个非常复杂的体系，教师要精心设计，将内容具体化，切合学生的实际，与学生心理结合，制定实施方案，并对学生提出具体要求。

3.3 加强学生理论社团的管理，创新传播平台，实现传播渠道的多样化，强化校园文化的隐性作用

首先，加强理论社团管理。大学生"红色社团"是大学生理论社团的形象称谓，一般是指由高校在校学生组成的研究马列主义、毛泽东思想和中国特色社会主义理论体系的理论宣传和学术研究社团，是大学生自发形成的以共同志趣、爱好为出发点的非正式群体组织，是联系大学生与社会的桥梁和纽带。大学生社团在推动马克思主义大众化进程中，具有重要的载体功能，能够将深奥的马克思主义理论与丰富多彩的实践活动结合起来，并将马克思主义大众化的主体传播者与受众群体连接起来，真正达到理论与实践、主体与客体的有机统一。大学生"红色社团"所具有的桥梁和纽带作用，一方面使其成为马克思主义大众化传统实现路径不可或缺的补充；另一方面它也不失为马克思主义大众化实现路径的全新探索。调查表明，红色社团是学生喜闻乐见的载体，高校有关部门应增大培育的力度。

其次，开发高校红色网络系统。在信息化时代，学生们随处可接触大众传媒，如网络、广播电视、报刊杂志等。由于传播渠道的多样和受众个体的差异性，只有富有个性的、有吸引力的传播内容才能对受众产生好的传播效果，才能提升传播力、影响力。目前，高校红色网络的影响力相对有限。高校应将网络作为育人的重要载体，采取多种手段，如：建立相关论坛、网站、学者、专家主页等多种方式，积极引导学生学习和研究马克思主义的理论，并"努力提升传播方式的亲和力和感召力，其是马克思主义大众化获得最佳传播效果的重要因素"。[3]

最后，加强校园文化的塑造。在校园氛围中，应加强渗透马克思主义的价值观和社会规范，让大学生在无意识的心态下自然地接受与内化马克思主义的理论、观点和方法，使马克思主义大众化中包含的价值性、规范性的内容通过隐性教育得到很好的实现。高校在推进马克思主义大众化的过程中，应充分利用隐性教育的影响，通过校园文化的建设和多种活动形式，如知识竞赛、人文讲座、社科图片展、征文活动等，营造高校浓厚的理论学习氛围，增强马克思主义大众化的渗透性，达到润物细无声的作用。

参考文献

[1] 马克思恩格斯选集，第 4 卷［M］．北京：人民出版社，1995．
[2] 秦宣．问题与对策：提高马克思主义大众化的实效［J］．思想理论教育导刊，2011（5）．
[3] 冯培．实现马克思主义大众化的有效传播［J］．高校理论战线，2011（3）．

"以人民为本：马克思"跨越论"的主体价值观

孟宪东

晚年的卡尔·马克思深入研究当时的世界历史环境和以沙皇俄国为代表的落后国家，提出经济文化落后的国家"可以不通过资本主义制度的卡夫丁峡谷"而走上社会主义道路、实现跨越式发展。这一著名论断所形成的"跨越论"构想，以独特的视角审视落后国家的革命和发展问题。其中蕴含的社会主义主体价值观，为我们更好更快地推进中国特色社会主义事业提供了坚实的理论支撑。

1 "跨越论"奠定落后国家的社会主义发展基础

20世纪世界社会主义事业跌宕起伏的变迁证明，马克思提出的"跨越论"构想与落后国家的社会主义发展具有内在的逻辑关系。

1.1 落后国家创新社会主义理论的逻辑起点

众所周知，早年的马克思重点关注发达资本主义国家的无产阶级革命和社会主义前景。由于世界形势的发展和人类学研究成果的涌现，1870年以后，马克思重点研究以俄国为代表的落后国家的革命和发展问题，投入相当大精力思考俄国、中国、印度等东方落后大国的革命形势与世界革命的前途。他坚持唯物史观，提出在整个世界社会主义革命的大背景中，在旧的社会形态向新的社会形态转变的过程中，东方大国凭借特殊条件可以走出不同于西方发达国家的全新革命道路——经济文化落后的俄国"不通过资本主义制度的卡夫丁峡谷，而吸取资本主义制度所取得的一切肯定成果"[1-1]，走社会主义道路，实现跨越式发展，最终使那里的无产阶级和广大劳动人民获得新生。

在马克思看来，这是关乎经济文化相对落后的所有国家寻找社会发展新路，以及在特定条件下实现民族独立和国家富强的重大探索，是科学社会主义的崭新命题。尽管马克思针对俄国问题提出的这一设想并没有得出肯定的结论，其理论表述也欠完整，但散见于手稿、信件中的那些文字，让我们领悟到关于落后国家可以实现跨越式发展的深刻思想内涵。它给我们留下许多值得思索的问题，为我们深入探究社会主义的历史命运提供了宝贵的指南。

马克思逝世以后，弗里德里希·恩格斯和领导20世纪落后国家社会主义事业的列宁、斯大林、毛泽东、邓小平等领袖们，都在新的历史时期和特殊的国情环境中，为成功地实现社会主义的"跨越式"发展进行了实践探索和理论创新。也许，他们不完全了解晚年的马克思提出的"跨越资本主义卡夫丁峡谷"的构想，但通过各自的实践，在逻辑上延伸和丰富了这一"跨越论"中蕴含的科学思想。诸如，列宁的帝国主义论、毛泽东的新民主主义论、邓小平的中国特色社会主义论等一系列关于落后国家开展社会主义革命、建设、改革的科学理论。它们都是在特定意义上继承和发展了这一"跨越论"。如果我们把现实的社会主义与马克思的"跨越论"构想及其后世的发展联系起来，就会从中感受到这一"跨越论"所蕴含的理论力量，以及对科学社会主义的进步所发挥的理论作用。马克思主义本身所具有的"与时俱进"的理论品质，在这个问题上得到淋漓尽致的表现。马克思提出的"跨越资本主义卡夫丁峡谷"的构想，为落后国家寻求社会主义道路提供了独特的思维指向，也成为落后国家创新社会主义理论的逻辑起点。

1.2 落后国家寻求社会主义实践的历史之门

马克思的"跨越论"具有科学社会主义的实践意义。20世纪社会主义的理论与实践同马克思的

[作者简介] 孟宪东（1954—），男，北京联合大学人文社会科学教研部教授，研究领域为马克思主义基本原理。

"跨越论"构想存在诸多不同。但有一个基本事实,就是社会主义的成功实践和有效制度均出现在经济文化相对落后的国家,其主题都是解决历史跨越问题。这些国家曾有和现有的社会主义发展,实实在在地证明马克思"跨越论"构想的正确性。

马克思不可能脱离当时的历史条件实际地预见后世的社会主义。但是,他觉察到时代的进程和即将出现的变化,意识到西方发达国家与东方落后国家之间的矛盾已经前沿化、尖锐化,以及资本主义时代的这种矛盾将导致社会主义的实践及其结果,可能不同于他和恩格斯的早期预见。历史的发展给予了证实。在垄断资本主义时代,社会主义革命的确出现新的特点。经济文化相对落后的东方国家,率先发生社会主义革命,比西方资本主义国家更早地进入社会主义社会,从而打破资本主义的一统天下。而俄国"十月革命"胜利后近百年来的社会主义历程,无论是凯歌行进还是失误倒退,中心都是围绕着如何通过社会主义道路去实现和展开跨越式发展。以俄国和中国为代表的世界社会主义运动,循着马克思指出的"跨越论"路径,去探索社会主义"幼驹"用最小代价跨越式赶超发达资本主义"老马"。年迈的马克思以他最后的气力叩响和开启落后国家走上社会主义道路的历史大门。在人类进步的大潮中,马克思提出的"跨越论"构想中的若干具体观点,已经转化为马克思之后的科学社会主义理论成果及其指导下的现实社会主义生动实践。

2 "跨越论"彰显"以人民为本"的主体价值观

马克思提出的"跨越论"构想,凸现了以无产阶级和全人类的解放为己任,以实现劳动人民的利益幸福为准则的政治立场与价值追求。而贯穿始终的是"以人民为本"的主体价值理念,即高举"为人民而发展"的旗帜。

2.1 坚持真理尺度与价值尺度并举、社会历史观与主体价值观统一

马克思以真理尺度与价值尺度并举和社会历史观与主体价值观统一为基本原则,研究人类社会的发展问题。所谓社会历史观,就是探讨人类社会发展的客观规律,强调的是社会发展的必然性和现实性;所谓主体价值观,就是探求人类社会发展对于人的生存和进步所具有的价值目标、评价尺度,并以此衡量社会的文明程度、进步幅度,强调的是社会发展中的人的主体性和能动性。

实事求是地认识资本主义创造丰厚财富和取得丰硕成就,承认其确实推动社会生产力实现巨大发展,同时不能否认这是以牺牲无产阶级和广大劳动者的利益为代价的。马克思从生产力与生产关系矛盾运动的角度,本质地揭示资本主义的弊端,用人的生存与进步的价值尺度深刻地批判资本主义的罪恶。在马克思看来,研究落后国家的发展问题,目的是给生存在那里的劳动人民寻求发展条件和光明出路。他尊重客观规律,运用客观规律把握社会发展脉络,也非常重视广大劳动者的生存状态和发展结果,运用实际状况评说社会现实,引导他们通过历史发展和现实可能进行价值判断、目标选择,进而探索如何改造现实社会,使他们摆脱苦难获得幸福,最终实现人的解放和全面发展。

马克思提出的"落后国家的人民走社会主义道路可以实现跨越式发展"的思想,既是反映客观规律的真理性判断,又是涉及实践主体的价值性判断。因为,社会形态的存续和更替,离不开主体人的需要与努力。这是社会主体进行有目的的价值选择和价值实现的过程。

2.2 思考落后国家的发展问题是"为了人民"

马克思研究落后国家的发展问题,一贯坚持"以人民为本"的价值理念。其出发点和落脚点凸显一切"为了人民"的政治立场。

早在19世纪中期,马克思就站在劳动人民的立场上关注东方。他考察中国、印度等东方落后大国的社会状况,分析那里发生的一切社会变化,把"为了人民"当作评价东方国家专制制度的根本尺度。马克思认为,东方社会的专制制度压抑人民的创造精神,"使人的头脑局限在极小的范围内,成为迷信的驯服工具,成为传统规则的奴隶,表现不出任何伟大的和任何历史的首创精神"[2-1],因而迟滞了社会进步。同时,他抨击英国资产阶级统治印度的罪恶,也以"是否带给人民自由和幸福"作为衡量社会合理性的价值尺度。马克思认为,英国殖民者在印度的统治表明,"他们既不会给人民群众带来自由,也不会根本改善他们的社会状况。因为,这两者都不仅仅决定于生产力的发展,而且还决定于生产力是否归人民所有。"[2-2]就是说,马克思评价社会是否进步,并不是简单地看是否推进了生产力的发展。马克

思认为，生产力不是衡量社会进步的惟一尺度。问题的关键，要看是否做到"生产力归人民所有"。在他看来，生产力发展的结果只有惠及劳动人民，社会才真正实现了进步。他提醒人们，在东方落后的国家发展资本主义，将严重压抑人民的创造性。社会生产力即使有所发展，也不能归人民所有。就一般情况而言，即使生产力暂时有所发展，经济暂时有所繁荣，只要这一成果只被少数剥削者占有而与广大劳动者无关，那么，这个社会也毫无进步价值可言。因为，人民才是社会历史发展的主体和动力，他们理应是自己劳动成果的享用者。只有人民成为社会发展的主体，才能高度体现合规律性与合目的性的统一。社会才是进步的社会。

马克思创立并始终坚持的唯物史观，是唯物主义与辩证法在历史领域的有机统一。人类社会发展的实际过程表明，生产力从来都不是抽象的存在。孤立地看待生产力的发展，单纯地认识财富的增值，只能离开生产力的主体——劳动者的生存价值，割裂财富的创造与财富的享用。这样的发展，不可能带来社会的进步。而抓住"生产力归人民所有"，便掌握创造财富与享用财富的辩证统一，即生产力发展，财富增加，不是用多数人的创造仅供少数人去享用，不是要劳动人民遭受苦难和付出沉重代价。它最终必定是满足全体人，首先是全体人中的多数人——劳动者自身的需求。有人认为，西方殖民主义者的侵略推动东方殖民地国家的生产力发展。这种观点是极其错误的。

2.3 贯穿着"人民为本"的价值取向

马克思提出"生产力归人民所有"的论断，为后来研究沙皇俄国摆脱资本主义、转向社会主义提供了思想基础。他明确指出，为了那里的无产阶级和劳动人民免于"背负牛轭"行走在资本主义道路，免除资本主义制度带来的无尽痛苦，俄国有可能利用国际和国内的特殊条件，"跨越资本主义的卡夫丁峡谷"，完成由资本主义到社会主义的革命转变。这一立场贯穿着以人民为本、实现无产阶级和劳动人民的根本利益的最高价值取向。

其实，马克思早年提出的追求人民的幸福和自由、"不仅决定于生产力的发展，还决定于生产力是否归人民所有"的科学论断，已经为其晚年提出落后国家"不通过资本主义卡夫丁峡谷"的科学构想，作出了理论铺垫。马克思指出："只有在伟大的社会革命支配了资产阶级时代的成果，支配了世界市场和现代生产力，并且使这一切都服从于最先进的民族的共同监督的时候，人类的进步才会不再像可怕的异教徒那样，只有用人头才能喝下甜美的酒浆。"[2-3] 1877年，马克思写的《给〈祖国纪事〉杂志编辑部的信》中，深沉地表达了他对俄国人民的同情和告诫："如果俄国继续走它在1861年所开始走的道路，那它将会失去当时历史所能提供给一个民族的最好的机会，而遭受资本主义制度所带来的一切极端不幸的灾难。"[1-2]

马克思的"跨越论"构想所蕴含的"人民为本"的主体价值理念，表象是人民渴望主宰自己的命运，追求自由、自尊的幸福生活，本质是落后国家的劳动者不通过资本主义的"卡夫丁峡谷"去推动本国的社会发展。因此，可以说，马克思提出"跨越论"构想的理论价值之一，就是突出人民是社会发展的主体。

3 社会主义必须始终坚持马克思的主体价值观

研究马克思提出的"跨越论"构想，目的是坚持"以人民为本"的主体价值理念，指导我们解决当今社会主义发展过程中遇到的问题。

3.1 坚持"以人为本"，像马克思那样"关注人民"

"跨越论"的基本价值理念是"人民主体"和"以人民为本"。中国共产党人的政治立场、价值取向和根本宗旨是一切为了人民，把最广大人民群众的根本利益当作思考问题、解决问题的出发点与落脚点。马克思和恩格斯指出：过去的一切运动都是少数人的或者为少数人谋利益的运动。无产阶级的运动是绝大多数人的，为绝大多数人谋利益的独立的运动。在新世纪新时期，我们党反复强调：要把人民高兴不高兴，人民答应不答应，人民拥护不拥护，人民赞成不赞成，作为各项工作的出发点和归宿。此后，我们党又提出科学发展观的指导思想，强调核心是以人为本，目标是实现人的全面发展，从人民群众的根本利益出发来谋发展、促发展，不断满足人民群众日益增长的物质文化需要，切实保障人民群众的经济权益、政治权益、文化权益。党的十七大报告报告提出，要做到发展为了人民、发展依靠人民、发展成果由人民共享，早日建成人民共同富裕的社会主义和谐社会，尽快实现人的全面发展。这不仅是马克思"跨越论"构想的政治理念和社会理想，也是中国共产党人推进中国特色社会主义实现跨越式发展、在2020年全面建成小康社会的根本目标。

3.2 坚持"科学发展"，努力构建"和谐的小康社会"

用科学发展观指导中国特色社会主义的跨越式发展，必须把全面性、协调性、可持续性结合起来。这是对跨越式发展的基础性要求，是顺利推进跨越式发展的必要条件。经过30多年的改革开放和现代化建设，我国各个方面的发展均取得惊人成就。但是，不能不看到，人民群众生活水平普遍提高，同时也积聚了不少矛盾。随着贫富差距、城乡差距、地区差距的扩大，中国特色社会主义的跨越式发展面临着巨大挑战，极易导致发展的失衡乃至社会动荡。解决这些问题，必须坚持社会主义的、以人为本的主体价值观，落实符合最广大人民根本利益的举措，努力构建公正的社会主义和谐社会，真正做到人与人、人与社会、人与自然的全面的和谐发展，尽快走出落后国家的发展"瓶颈"，让马克思的美好意愿在东方社会主义大国——中国的土地上成为现实。

参考文献

[1] 中共中央编译局. 马克思恩格斯全集：第19卷 [G]. 北京：人民出版社，1963：451[-1]，128[-2].
[2] 中共中央编译局. 马克思恩格斯全集：第9卷 [G]. 北京：人民出版社，1961：148[-1]，250[-2]，252[-3].

新媒体视角下大学生思想政治教育的新探索

郭 堃 孙瑞婷

当前，社交网站、博客、微博、微信等新媒体极大地改变了大学生原有的生活方式、思维方式和价值观念，已经成为大学生的第二生存空间，对于当代大学生来说，"刷微博""发微信"等已不再是一种兴趣爱好，而是一种生活习惯。作为思想政治教育工作者应充分关注新媒体的影响，积极利用微信、微博等新媒体为思想政治教育工作服务，不断丰富工作手段，努力创新工作思路，有效提高大学生思想政治教育工作的针对性和实效性。

1 微信、微博等新媒体给大学生思想政治教育带来的新挑战

随着数字通信技术的飞速发展，微信、微博等新媒体的应用日益普及。由于新媒体具有超媒体性、超时空性、开放性、交互性和虚拟性等特点，因此，相对于传统媒体而言具有不可比拟的传播优势。大学生思维活跃、接受新生事物快的心理特点决定了他们是使用新媒体最频繁、最主要的群体，也是受其影响最深刻的群体。新媒体对当代大学生的交往方式、学习思维方式和性格塑造等产生了深刻影响，既给大学生思想政治教育开辟了新领域、提供了新手段，也带来了新挑战。

1.1 微信、微博等新媒体的开放性影响思想引导的统一性

新媒体的开放性冲击了思想政治教育的主旋律。微信、微博等新媒体给大学生创造了自由交流的平台，它的开放性使大学生可以接触多元化的价值观念、生活方式和社会思潮，这些自由平等交流的方式和观念，一方面，容易使大学生对自由平等的方式产生盲目崇拜，滋长极端个人主义和自由主义，如不加以正确的引导，势必造成大学生习惯于我行我素，张扬个人的观点和主张，难以保持一致，形成统一。另一方面，西方意识形态和价值观念以前所未有的速度和力度在大学校园内蔓延，大学生作为容易接受新思想、新事物的特殊群体，其辨别是非的能力还不是很强，他们在新媒体中频繁接触的西方国家的宣传论调、文化思想等必然会扰乱他们对中国特色社会主义核心价值观的认识，冲击社会主流价值观，进而冲击高校思想政治教育的主旋律。

1.2 微信、微博等新媒体的草根性弱化思想政治教育的权威性

新媒体的草根性使每个大学生都拥有一份自己的"廉价报纸"（微博）"免费电话"（微信），这使得他们可以轻而易举地获取信息、自由互动、发表言论、获得自己的追随者（"粉丝"）。在学习新知识时，从习惯性"问老师"，转变成习惯性"搜百度"；从习惯性"听老师，学知识"，转变成习惯性"晒微博，听我说"，弱化了学生对教师的依赖；从学生对老师学术权威的"深信不疑""敬畏仰视"，转变成"半信半疑""不屑一顾"。在这种背景下，思想政治教育工作者依靠自己的光辉形象、专业知识、社会阅历等优势的主导性话语权正在逐渐被削弱。

1.3 微信、微博等新媒体的虚拟性阻碍思想政治教育的约束性

新媒体的虚拟性使得使用者具有较强的隐匿性，容易诱发大学生的诚信危机。大多数大学生使用微信、微博等新媒体不以真实身份与他人进行交流，言行内容无法规范，其真实性得不到保证。这种交流的虚拟性容易造成大学生道德意识的弱化、责任感的降低和言行的失范，也使交流的可信度降低。从而大大弱化了思想政治教育工作对大学生的道德约束功能，使大学生极易沦为传播不良信息的主体，这无疑给大学生思想政治教育工作增添了极大的阻力。此外，长期使用甚至沉迷于新媒体交流，导致部分大

[作者简介] 郭堃（1955—），男，北京联合大学师范学院教授。研究方向：党建和大学生思想政治教育；孙瑞婷（1981—），女，北京联合大学师范学院讲师。研究方向：大学生思想政治教育工作。

学生对现实生活中的人际交往感到无所适从，长此以往，不少大学生会产生人际交往障碍，在现实中进行人际交往时会陷入"失语"等心理困境。比如，有些大学生在网络上可以恰到好处地与很多人交往，但是在生活中却沉默寡言，害怕与人交流。

2 微信、微博等新媒体下大学生思想政治教育的新优势

2.1 微信、微博等新媒体增强了思想政治教育的辐射力

微信、微博等新媒体具有信息容量大、资源丰富，传输快捷、交互性强、覆盖面广等优势，极大地吸引着大学生，随时随地地"发微信""晒微博"，使得大学生几乎每天都离不开微信、微博等沟通交流的新媒体。大学生思想政治教育可以充分利用新媒体信息量大、速度快、覆盖面广的特点，通过微博、微信、论坛、网络课程、数字化校园平台等新媒体和数字化教学形式，主动地、大规模地对大学生进行思想理论、价值观念教育，这就改变了传统的学生必须在规定的时间到规定的地方接受一定的教育内容和模式，学生可以在任何时间和任何地点获取知识和教育，极大地增强了思想政治教育的辐射力。

2.2 微信、微博等新媒体丰富了思想政治教育的形式

长期以来，传统的大学生思想政治教育多以课堂教学为主，形式单一陈旧，缺乏吸引力，新媒体的灵活性和快捷性丰富了大学生思想政治教育的形式。"新媒体能够更便捷地发布个性化的信息，并且在较短的时间内，通过文字、语言、图片、影像等多种方式把教育内容迅速传递给受教育者，使得思想教育更直接、更便捷、更深入。通过新媒体，大学生不必受时空等条件的制约，通过网络、手机等新媒体可以在任何地点、任何时间获取任何他们所需的任何知识和信息，这样就大大提高了思想教育信息传播的速度和效率。"思想政治教育工作者可以将大学生感兴趣的丰富的网络资源进行加工整理，采取声音、文字、图像等生动的多元化表达形式，把教育内容迅速传递给受教育者，使思想教育更直接、更深入、更形象。

2.3 微信、微博等新媒体增强了大学生思想政治教育的感染力

师生之间的平等互信是提升大学生思想政治教育质量的关键。现实中"师道尊严"的传统心理作用往往使师生处于一种非平等状态，加之人的思想隐蔽性的客观存在，导致很多大学生不愿意向老师讲真话、说实情，甚至对老师居高临下的教育方式产生抵触情绪。在微信、微博等新媒体环境下，思想政治教育工作者可与大学生随时随地平等地进行网络聊天、发布信息和接受信息，平等地与大学生交流感情，有助于消除大学生的心理戒备和隔阂，增强师生之间的信任度，传统意义上的单向"灌输""说教"模式，逐渐转化为"积极引导""帮助选择"的思想政治教育模式，进一步增强了思想政治教育的吸引力和感染力。

3 借助新媒体创新大学生思想政治教育的新思路

新媒体是一把"双刃剑"。一方面，它能够在第一时间内为大学生提供及时和丰富的信息，可以适当地帮助大学生解决心理疑惑，是大学生发泄负面情绪的出口和媒介。在一定意义上缩短了大学生和世界的距离，能够开拓他们的视野和思路，使得大学生在思考问题时具有世界眼光。另一方面，新媒体也会导致大学生过分追求个人的绝对自由，出现价值观念自我化，人生理想庸俗化，行为取向呈现无政府化。如此种种，最终导致大学生的价值取向出现重个人轻群体、重功利轻道德、重时尚轻传统、重索取轻贡献的不良倾向。因此，借助新媒体的力量，创新手段，做好大学生的思想政治教育，是新媒体环境下的"必修课"。

3.1 净化新媒体信息内容，优化思想政治教育环境

一是，国家要高度重视新媒体网络建设，以更加前瞻的眼光、更加创新的思维建设新媒体。立足本国，放眼世界，以科学统筹的意识和理念，构建布局合理、结构优化的新媒体传播网络，以社会主义核心价值观引领大学生价值取向的选择。二是，要积极适应互联网的特点及传播规律，改变以往对传统媒体的管理模式，变封、堵、压为普遍的交流、沟通和疏导。通过立法规范，建立完善的监控体系，大力消除不良信息流通，警示和引导公众自觉遵守网络道德，共同营造文明健康的精神家园。三是，要利用

新媒体技术，特别是网络的力量广泛开展中国特色社会主义理论体系宣传普及活动，推进马克思主义大众化和通俗化。要加快培养网评队伍，建设一支有影响力、有说服力、贴近网民、令人信服的网络评论员队伍，培养造就一批拥有娴熟的写作技巧和言论权威的"网络意见领袖"。大力宣传社会主义核心价值观，有效利用新媒体主导社会舆论。

3.2 打造校园新媒体平台，创新思想政治教育方式

校园新媒体是影响大学生生活学习和思想价值观最为直接的信息传播平台，高校应积极强化新媒体对大学生价值取向的积极影响。一是，完善思想政治教育体系，整合教育资源。大学生思想政治教育应整合各种教育资源和教育力量，坚持学校教育、社会疏导、家庭辅导、自我提高多种方式构建立体教育网络，形成大学生思想政治教育的整体模式，将新媒体作为新形势下有效的思想政治教育载体。针对大学生开展思想教育是一项全新的社会工作，信息行业主管部门要加强网络、手机等的信息监管，履行社会责任。高校思想政治工作者和教育科研机构，要注重对新媒体的研究和思考，积极探索新媒体环境下大学生思想政治教育工作的规律和特点，开发适合大学生身心发展特点的高质量的新媒体教学软件和数据库，加快大学生思想政治教育的数字化教材体系建设，构筑大学生思想政治教育的新媒体阵地，逐步建立起适应新媒体时代发展需要的立体化的大学生思想政治教育的理论体系。二是，打造校园新媒体平台，构建和谐校园文化。新媒体时代的高校文化建设需要将新媒体文化建设与校园文化建设紧密结合，把以微博、微信、QQ等校园网络文化、手机文化等在内的文化建设纳入和谐校园文化建设的总体格局，丰富校园文化内容，拓展校园文化内涵，延伸校园文化功能。

3.3 加强新媒体信息监控，健全思想政治教育信息监管机制

高校思想政治教育工作者要完善自身的信息素质，了解新媒体特征和新媒体文化特点，有效掌握新媒体传播技术，探究新观念、新途径和新方法，及时发现大学生中存在的思想问题并进行针对性的教育，提前防范，从而切实建立和健全大学生思想政治教育中的新媒体信息监管机制，对新媒体的价值影响实施有效的监控和合理的引导，在校园形成健康的新媒体教育环境。此外，还应加强大学生的媒介素养教育，提升他们的信息辨别能力，引导他们树立正确的价值观。媒介素养是人们面对媒介的各种讯息的选择能力、理解能力、质疑能力、评估能力、思辨性应变能力以及创造和制作媒介讯息的能力。提高大学生的媒介素养水平不仅仅只是学校的责任，媒介素养教育的实施主体应该是一个"教育共同体"，即以从事新闻传播学理论研究与教育工作者为核心，包括各类教育工作者、社会学者、传播技术工作者、政府主管部门、家长以及大众传媒机构广泛参与的共同体。提高大学生的媒介素养就是为了引导大学生学会区分良莠，获得有用、健康、有效的知识，树立积极健康的人生观、价值观和思想道德观念。

参考文献

[1] 蒋宏，徐剑. 新媒体导论 [M]. 上海：上海交通大学出版社，2006.
[2] 付长海，陈占安. 传播学在思想政治教育中的应用研究综述 [J]. 现代传播，2003（2）.
[3] 钱文彬. 浅析新媒体与大学生思想政治教育 [J]. 当代教育论坛，2008（6）.
[4] 姜恩来. 新媒体环境下的大学生思想政治教育 [J]. 高校理论战线，2009（6）.

中国特色的社会主义道路及其核心价值体系
——坚持共产党员的精神追求

唐小恒

一、中国特色社会主义道路

中国特色社会主义道路之所以是中国发展进步之路，关键在于既坚持了科学社会主义基本原则，又根据时代条件赋予其鲜明的中国特色，这就是党的十八大报告中所说的实践特色、理论特色、民族特色、时代特色。丰富中国特色社会主义的时代特色，就是要紧贴时代脉搏、顺应时代潮流、吸纳时代精华，从而具有远大美好前景。

党的十八大中国特色社会主义道路是中国共产党对现阶段纲领的概括。要求把马克思主义的普遍真理同本国的具体实际结合起来，一方面要坚持马克思主义的基本原理，走社会主义道路；另一方面必须从中国的实际出发，不照抄、照搬别国经验、模式，走适合中国特点的道路，逐步实现工业、农业、国防和科学技术现代化，把中国建设成为富强、民主、文明、和谐的社会主义国家。

从理论层面来看，就是邓小平理论、"三个代表"重要思想和科学发展观；从实践层面上来看，就是党的十一届三中全会以来我国进行的卓有成效的探索；从制度层面来看，就是改革开放以来我国在政治、经济、文化和社会等领域已经形成并且不断完善着的一系列制度、体制和机制。

从发展经验上来说，我国处于并将长期处于社会主义初级阶段，社会的主要矛盾是人民群众日益增长的物质文化需要同落后的社会生产之间的矛盾；坚持解放思想，实事求是，与时俱进；坚持以经济建设为中心，贯彻全面、协调、可持续的科学发展观；坚持以人为本和"三个代表"重要思想；坚持改革开放，建立健全社会主义市场经济体制；坚持以公有制为主体、多种所有制经济共同发展，实行按劳分配和按生产要素分配等多种分配方式；坚持共产党的领导、人民当家作主和依法治国相统一，建设社会主义民主政治；建设社会主义核心价值体系；追求公平与正义，构建社会主义和谐社会；坚持"一国两制"、和平统一，以高超的民族智慧坚决维护中华民族的根本利益、国家统一和主权完整；坚持独立自主的和平外交方针，走和平发展道路，推动和谐世界的构建等。

中国特色社会主义道路，就是在中国共产党领导下，立足基本国情，以经济建设为中心，坚持四项基本原则，坚持改革开放，解放和发展社会生产力，建设社会主义市场经济、社会主义民主政治、社会主义先进文化、社会主义和谐社会、社会主义生态文明，促进人的全面发展，逐步实现全体人民共同富裕，建设富强、民主、文明、和谐的社会主义现代化国家。

中国特色社会主义制度，就是人民代表大会制度的根本政治制度，中国共产党领导的多党合作和政治协商制度、民族区域自治制度以及基层群众自治制度等基本政治制度，中国特色社会主义法律体系，公有制为主体、多种所有制经济共同发展的基本经济制度。中国特色社会主义道路是实现途径，中国特色社会主义理论体系是行动指南，中国特色社会主义制度是根本保障，三者统一于中国特色社会主义伟大实践——最鲜明特色。

建设中国特色社会主义，总依据是社会主义初级阶段，总布局是五位一体，总任务是实现社会主义现代化和中华民族伟大复兴。中国特色社会主义，既坚持了科学社会主义基本原则，又根据时代条件赋予其鲜明的中国特色，以全新的视野深化了对共产党执政规律、社会主义建设规律、人类社会发展规律的认识，从理论和实践结合上系统回答了在中国这样一个人口多、底子薄的东方大国建设什么样的社会主义、怎样建设社会主义这个根本问题，使我们国家快速发展起来，使我国人民生活水平快速提高起

[作者简介] 唐小恒，北京联合大学应用文理学院。

来。实践充分证明,中国特色社会主义是当代中国发展进步的根本方向,只有中国特色社会主义才能发展中国。

中国特色社会主义道路有着丰富的科学内涵和强大的生命力。这条道路是自鸦片战争以来先进的中国人、先进的中国知识分子,尤其是先进的中国共产党人以民族独立自由和国家繁荣富强为己任,在几个世纪的探索中,历尽曲折,在中华民族伟大复兴和社会主义现代化建设的征途中找到的惟一正确的道路。习近平同志指出:中国特色社会主义道路是实现我国社会主义现代化的必由之路,是创造人民美好生活的必由之路。中国特色社会主义理论体系是马克思主义中国化最新成果。在当代中国,坚持中国特色社会主义理论体系,就是真正坚持马克思主义。中国特色社会主义制度符合我国国情,集中体现了中国特色社会主义的特点和优势,是中国发展进步的根本制度保障。中国特色社会主义事业不断发展,中国特色社会主义制度也需要不断完善,从而为夺取中国特色社会主义新胜利提供更加有效的制度保障。

二、改革开放是中国特色社会主义道路的重大创新

中国特色社会主义是当代中国发展进步的根本方向,改革开放是坚持和发展中国特色社会主义的必由之路。改革开放是发展中国特色社会主义的强大动力,是解放和发展社会生产力、创新体制机制的必然要求。

党的十一届三中全会以来党中央提出的理论路线和制定的一系列方针政策,集中体现了改革,并形成了对外开放的全新格局,开辟了中国特色社会主义的伟大道路。通过改革开放,我们实现了党的工作重点的转移,从以阶级斗争为转变到以经济建设为中心。改革开放所带来的历史性突破,从高度集中的计划经济转变到社会主义市场经济。改革开放极大地解放和发展了社会生产力,冲破了束缚生产力发展的体制障碍,推动了社会主义市场经济体制的初步建立,从而开创了我国经济、政治、文化、社会全面发展的崭新局面。

中国的历史大转折和事业大发展,变成了有强大市场活力的世界第二大经济体,国民经济持续快速健康发展,综合国力显著提升,国际影响力和民族凝聚力大大增强,社会政治稳定,人民生活总体上实现了由温饱到小康的历史性跨越。在改革开放中,国有企业走出了困境,国有资产大幅度增值,劳动、知识、技术、管理和资本的活力竞相迸发,创造社会财富的源泉充分涌流;在改革开放中,亿万人民群众以极大的热情投身并推动着波澜壮阔的社会变革,创造了许多新事物、新经验,精神面貌焕然一新。

事实证明,改革开放顺应时代潮流,符合人民意愿;没有改革开放,就没有今日中国的繁荣富强,就没有人民生活的显著改善,就没有中国特色社会主义在现代化进程中的起步与发展。社会主义中国能够在国际风云变幻中站稳脚跟,能够战胜各种困难和风险,原因就在于改革开放以来,我们党带领人民开辟了中国特色社会主义道路,这条道路之所以正确、之所以能够引领中国发展进步,关键在于我们既坚持了科学社会主义的基本原则,又根据我国实际赋予其鲜明的中国特色。全党全国各族人民在这条道路上万众一心,团结奋进,为中国特色社会主义伟大事业奠定了坚实的物质基础,凝聚起了强大的精神力量。历史雄辩地证明,改革开放是决定当代中国命运的重大抉择,是强国之路、富民之路,是发展中国特色社会主义、实现中华民族伟大复兴的必由之路。

历史表明,不改革开放只能是死路一条;中国今天只有深化改革、扩大开放,才能巩固成果、再创辉煌。只有坚定不移地推进改革开放,才能为中国未来经济社会发展提供强大的动力,使中国特色社会主义始终充满生机和活力;才能使关系经济社会发展全局的重大体制改革取得突破性进展,推动经济社会又好又快发展;才能更好地解决人民群众最关心、最直接、最现实的利益问题,做到发展为了人民、发展依靠人民、发展成果由人民共享。

三、社会主义核心价值体系是我们团结奋斗的共同思想基础

中国特色社会主义道路,是历史的选择、人民的选择,是中国全面建成小康社会、加快推进社会主义现代化、实现中华民族伟大复兴的惟一正确道路。文化建设要加强社会主义核心价值体系建设,提高公民道德素质,丰富人民精神文化生活。社会主义核心价值体系深入人心,公民文明素质和社会文明程度明显提高。从构建社会主义和谐社会到推动建设和谐世界,从建设社会主义核心价值体系到建设社会

主义文化强国。

必须把社会主义核心价值体系建设融入国民教育、精神文明建设的全过程。要坚持用社会主义荣辱观引领社会风尚，深入推进社会公德、职业道德、家庭美德、个人品德建设，加强对青少年的德育培养，在全社会形成积极向上的精神追求和健康文明的生活方式。

中国共产党领导人民发展社会主义先进文化。加强社会主义核心价值体系建设，坚持马克思主义指导思想，树立中国特色社会主义共同理想，弘扬以爱国主义为核心的民族精神和以改革创新为核心的时代精神，倡导社会主义荣辱观，增强民族自尊、自信和自强精神，抵御资本主义和封建主义腐朽思想的侵蚀，扫除各种社会丑恶现象，努力使我国人民成为有理想、有道德、有文化、有纪律的人民。

新党章总纲充实了发展社会主义先进文化的内容，强调加强社会主义核心价值体系建设。党的十八大对建设社会主义文化强国作出部署。总纲增写了"建设社会主义文化强国、加强社会主义核心价值体系建设"的内容。这样有利于全党牢牢把握发展社会主义先进文化的前进方向，树立文化自觉和文化自信。

中国共产党领导人民发展社会主义先进文化。加强社会主义核心价值体系建设，坚持马克思主义指导思想，树立中国特色社会主义共同理想，弘扬以爱国主义为核心的民族精神和以改革创新为核心的时代精神，倡导社会主义荣辱观，增强民族自尊、自信和自强精神，抵御资本主义和封建主义腐朽思想的侵蚀，扫除各种社会丑恶现象，努力使我国人民成为有理想、有道德、有文化、有纪律的人民。

党的十八大提出：加强社会主义核心价值体系建设。社会主义核心价值体系是兴国之魂，决定着中国特色社会主义发展方向。要深入开展社会主义核心价值体系学习教育，用社会主义核心价值体系引领社会思潮、凝聚社会共识。推进马克思主义中国化、时代化和大众化，坚持不懈用中国特色社会主义理论体系武装全党、教育人民，深入实施马克思主义理论研究和建设工程，建设哲学社会科学创新体系，推动中国特色社会主义理论体系教材进课堂、进头脑。广泛开展理想信念教育，把广大人民团结凝聚在中国特色社会主义伟大旗帜之下。大力弘扬民族精神和时代精神，深入开展爱国主义、集体主义、社会主义教育，丰富人民精神世界，增强人民精神力量。倡导富强、民主、文明、和谐，倡导自由、平等、公正、法治，倡导爱国、敬业、诚信、友善，积极培育社会主义核心价值观。牢牢掌握意识形态工作领导权和主导权，坚持正确导向，提高引导能力，壮大主流思想舆论。

四、坚守共产党人精神追求

对马克思主义的信仰，对社会主义和共产主义的信念，是共产党人的政治灵魂。要教育引导党员牢固树立正确的世界观、权力观、事业观，坚定政治立场，明辨大是大非。要教育引导党员模范践行社会主义荣辱观，讲党性、重品行、作表率，做社会主义道德的示范者、诚信风尚的引领者、公平正义的维护者，以实际行动彰显共产党人的人格力量。

中华文明史几千年，中国特色社会主义道路方向性探索上百年（从被动到能动），起势30多年（从十一届三中全会——十二大提出中国特色社会主义；十三大初级阶段；十四大市场经济；十五大邓小平理论；十六大三个代表；十七大科学发展观；十八大道路自信）。中国特色社会主义理论：邓小平理论——什么是中国特色社会主义；三个代表——建什么样的党；科学发展观——怎么实现发展。十八大解决了举旗、走路、目标、任务四大问题。不走封闭僵化的老路，也不走改旗易帜的邪路；民族复兴，全面实现小康。

当前的世情、国情、党情：面临的发展机遇和风险挑战前所未有。高举中国特色社会主义伟大旗帜，坚定不移沿着中国特色社会主义道路前进，为全面建成小康社会而奋斗。回首近代中国史，展望中华民族充满希望的未来，我们的结论是：全面建成小康社会，加快现代化，实现中华民族的伟大复兴，必须坚定不移走中国特色社会主义道路。

道路关乎党的命脉，关乎国家前途、民族命运、人民幸福。在中国这样一个经济文化十分落后的国家探索民族复兴道路，是极为艰巨的任务。九十多年来，我们党紧紧依靠人民，把马克思主义基本原理同中国实际和时代特征结合起来，独立自主走自己的路，历经千辛万苦，付出各种代价，取得革命建设和改革的伟大胜利，开创和发展了中国特色社会主义，从根本上改变了中国人民和中华民族的前途命运。

以毛泽东同志为核心的第一代中央带领全党全国各族人民完成了新民主主义革命、社会主义改造，确立了社会主义基本制度，奠定了根本政治前提和制度基础。为新的历史时期开创中国特色社会主义提供了宝贵经验、理论准备和物质基础。以邓小平为核心第二代中央集体，以经济建设为中心、实行改革开放，明确提出走自己的路、建设中国特色社会主义，科学回答了建设中国特色社会主义的一系列基本问题，成功开创了中国特色社会主义。

江泽民、胡锦涛十多年一以贯之。如今习近平领导我们的接力探索发展，坚定不移高举中国特色社会主义伟大旗帜，既不走封闭僵化的老路、也不走改旗易帜的邪路。中国特色社会主义道路，中国特色社会主义理论体系，中国特色社会主义制度，是党和人民九十多年奋斗、创造、积累的根本成就。

发展中国特色社会主义是一项长期的艰巨的历史任务，必须准备进行具有许多新的历史特点的伟大斗争。我们一定要毫不动摇地坚持、与时俱进地发展中国特色社会主义，不断丰富中国特色社会主义的实践特色、理论特色、民族特色、时代特色。在任何情况下都要牢牢把握社会主义初级阶段这个最大国情、最大实际。党的基本路线是党和国家的生命线，必须坚持把以经济建设为中心同四项基本原则、改革开放这两个基本点统一于中国特色社会主义伟大实践（一个中心两个基本点）。

只要我们胸怀理想、坚定信念，不动摇、不懈怠、不折腾，顽强奋斗、艰苦奋斗、不懈奋斗，就一定能在中国共产党成立一百年时全面建成小康社会，就一定能在新中国成立一百年时建成富强、民主、文明、和谐的社会主义现代化国家。全党要坚定这样的道路自信、理论自信、制度自信！

利益关系多样化与保持党的纯洁性

韩 强

利益关系多样化是我国经济社会发展出现的明显变化之一，正在日益广泛深入地从经济领域渗透到政治、文化和社会领域，从党外影响到党内。目前，我国利益关系多样化表现出利益主体多元、贫富差距扩大、利益表达愿望强烈、利益矛盾复杂、利益观念更加普及、利益来源方式更加多样、财产权公平更受关注等突出特点，这些新特点和新变化对保持党的纯洁性带来了极大的挑战。为此，只有正确应对这些挑战，我们党才能永葆纯洁性，不断巩固执政地位，完成执政使命。

1 利益关系多样化对保持党的纯洁性的挑战

利益关系多样化作为一种广泛的社会存在，必然反映到党内，反映到党员干部的思想、言行上，从而在思想纯洁、组织纯洁、作风纯洁、清正廉洁等方面对党的建设构成冲击。

1.1 思想纯洁面临冲击

在利益关系多样化背景下，保持思想纯洁面临的挑战主要表现在以下几个方面：

第一，对马克思主义的科学性产生怀疑和动摇。马克思主义是科学的世界观和方法论，是指导无产阶级解放的强大理论武器，其中无产阶级没有自己的特殊利益，以解放全人类最终实现共产主义为己任，是马克思主义理论的一个基本论断。但是，一些党员看到传统产业工人生活、发展面临的困难，看到工人阶级队伍中贫富差距的扩大，看到一批包括民营企业家在内的其他社会阶层人士陆续进入党的队伍，他们不是从理论上正确分析这些现象，而是简单地认为马克思主义的一些理论或论断过时了，因而滋长了怀疑和动摇的情绪。

第二，对党的先进性和为人民服务的宗旨产生怀疑。党的先进性从根本上在于党全心全意为人民服务的本质，过去战争和计划经济年代，党员、干部吃苦在前、享受在后已经成为人们对党的先进性的普遍认知，但是在社会主义市场经济条件下，一方面越来越多的党员凭着辛勤劳动和诚实经营率先走上了致富之路，另一方面也确有一些党员、干部靠着投机取巧、权力寻租甚至权钱交易积累了大量财富，对于部分党员、干部比普通群众富裕的现象，有的党员既不能正确理解，心态也极不平衡，从而怀疑党的先进性和党的宗旨，甚至怀疑党的性质。

第三，奉献奋斗精神减弱，革命意志严重衰退。由于一些党员、干部对自己的个人利益过于关心，因此为了维护自己的既得利益，或者为了争取更大的利益，往往不惜说假话、套话、空话，把实事求是原则抛到脑后。也有的人对改革开放以来党的理论创新、党的政策不是去积极学习、科学理解，而是人云亦云、道听途说，致使思想偏激，牢骚满腹，不思进取，得过且过，萎靡不振，精神懈怠。

1.2 组织纯洁形势严峻

在利益多元化的条件下，党的组织纯洁面临着突出的考验。

第一，党员、干部多元化的阶层背景、多样化的利益诉求影响党的队伍纯洁。在计划经济年代，党员、干部主要来自工人、农民、知识分子、军人几个阶层，其利益诉求也相对统一，便于实现利益一致基础上的高度团结。但是，随着来自不同阶层的党员人数的增长，导致党员干部的利益诉求日益多样，来自新兴阶层和传统阶层的党员之间利益诉求差距在不断扩大，而且阶层利益群体性特征的外显也增加

[基金项目] 国家社科基金重点项目"保持党的纯洁性研究"（12AZD024）、中组部 2012 年委托课题，负责人韩强。
[作者简介] 韩强（1965—），男，北京联合大学人文社科部主任，教授、法学博士，海外中国学研究中心主任，北京市高教学会中国近现代史纲要研究会副会长。主要研究方向为中共党史党建、党的制度建设、干部制度改革。

了利益协调的难度,加剧了党内因利益问题而引发的各种矛盾,并在干部选拔、党内决策、政策制定等方面表现出来,从而影响党的团结统一。

第二,一些党组织协调解决利益矛盾的能力不强致使党组织公信力下降。面对利益关系的复杂和利益矛盾的加剧,各级党组织理应不断提高协调能力,及时化解党内外各种利益矛盾和冲突,但是仍有一些党组织协调重大利益关系的能力不强,有的党组织的领导干部还介入了一些利益冲突,从而引发了党内外的利益矛盾和危机,有的甚至酿成了一些影响极坏的群体事件。可以说,许多群体事件的爆发,不仅与党组织内部在处理利益矛盾问题时的失误、失当有直接的关系,而且其中不少事件更是党内利益矛盾积累外显化的结果。

1.3 作风纯洁受到考验

党的优良作风源于党的全心全意为人民服务的根本宗旨,源于党在长期的革命建设实践中形成的光荣传统,党员、干部只有忠实践行这一基本观点、根本宗旨和光荣传统,才能确保党的作风纯洁先进,得到人民群众的支持拥护。但是,在利益关系多样化的背景下,这一观点、宗旨和传统正在受到越来越严重的冲击。具体表现在:

第一,群众是历史的创造者的基本观点受到削蚀。群众是历史的创造者,群众的力量是无穷的,只有真正坚持这一历史唯物主义的基本观点,才能真正甘当人民的小学生,虚心向人民群众学习,才会真心尊重群众、理解群众、支持群众、带领群众,而不是以群众的主人自居,把自己的个人意志凌驾于群众的意愿之上。但是,有不少领导干部只是看到资本、能人、大款的作用,看到对 GDP 的拉动,看到对其个人政绩的支撑,而忘记了广大人民群众才是财富的创造者,才是历史和社会的主人。错误的认识必然导致错误的行动,这些领导干部看不到群众的作用,必然会看不起群众,必然会脱离群众,其结果必然是形式主义、命令主义、官僚主义的盛行,必然是首长工程、形象工程、面子工程的愈演愈烈,对党的作风纯洁的危害不可小视。

第二,领导干部对个人升迁的过分追求严重地侵蚀党的优良作风。有为才能有位,有位更要有为。领导干部为了实现政治抱负,更好地发挥作用,注重通过追求人民群众满意的政绩而实现个人升迁本无可厚非。但是,如果不是为了广大人民群众的利益而是为了个人的私利去争取权力和地位,不仅会不可避免地使权力的行使走形变味,而且会使公权力的公信力受到难以挽回的伤害,进而对党的形象、对领导干部的权威造成极大的损害。虽然绝大多数干部在权力面前能够做到权为民所用,交出了一份合格的答卷,但是,也有不少干部在利益诱惑面前打了败仗,成了利益的奴仆,说到底,这正是把个人利益置于公共利益之上所造成的恶果。

1.4 清正廉洁任重道远

清正廉洁是共产党人的政治本色,反腐倡廉是党一贯的政治立场,在党发展的各个阶段我们都旗帜鲜明地反对腐败,严厉打击腐败分子,保证了党的清正廉洁。改革开放以来,反腐倡廉的形势趋于严峻,消极腐败的危险成为我们党面临的四大危险之一,清正廉洁面临严峻考验。

首先,腐败现象的高发频发考验党的清正廉洁。虽然我们建立了惩治和预防腐败体系,完善了工作格局,查处了一批大案要案,但是,腐败现象仍然比较严重。在 2012 年 1 月 6 日召开的中纪委监察机关查办案件工作情况新闻通气会上,中纪委公布的数据表明,2011 年全国纪检监察机关立案 137859 件,结案 136679 件,处分 142893 人,呈现出腐败人数增加、腐败类型增多、腐败情节增重的趋势。[2]腐败现象的增多,一方面直接影响党员干部队伍的纯洁性,另一方面也具有很强的腐蚀作用。如果一个单位主要领导人搞腐败,那么整个领导班子往往会被拉下水,许多窝案串案的被查处,表明这种情况绝非个别。

其次,党员干部对党能够真正解决腐败问题的信心受到影响。广大党员干部对腐败现象深恶痛绝,对中央严厉打击腐败分子的决心和政策积极支持,对近年来反腐败工作取得的成绩也感到满意。但是,许多党员干部也目睹了日常工作和生活中存在的大量消极腐败现象,加之一些大案要案的频繁曝光,以及一些谣言的广泛传播,使一部分党员干部对党能否真正解决腐败问题产生疑问,有的甚至因此失去信心,进而对党的政策产生怀疑。

最后,反腐败的最有力武器——领导干部财产公示制仍未出台,制约着反腐败斗争的推进。领导干部财产公示制是国际通用的反腐败的有力武器,我们只对领导干部的收入申报有一个规定,但非指财产申报,虽然各地屡有探索,但终究难以推广实施。目前党内外对出台这一制度热心期盼,如果迟迟不能推出,对腐败现象的遏制力度势必受到影响,也会损害党的清正廉洁形象。

2 利益关系多样化条件下保持党的纯洁性的对策

利益关系多样化对党的纯洁性的影响是直接的、全面的,我们应对这一挑战也要从党内外共同着眼,全方位地化解这一风险。

2.1 把科学发展作为解决党的纯洁性问题的根本出路

发展是硬道理,发展是解决一切问题的出路所在。保持党的纯洁性遇到的挑战,也要用发展的眼光、发展的思路来解决。从目前看,利益矛盾是影响党的纯洁性的主要问题,这一问题的本质在于我国经济发展水平还不够高,满足人民群众日益增长的物质文化需求的能力还不够强。要解决这一问题,只能通过进一步发展生产力,转变经济发展方式,提高生产效率,同时注重分配公平来实现。党的十八大报告对实现收入分配公平高度重视,并作出了安排,提出:"初次分配和再分配都要兼顾效率和公平,再分配更加注重公平。多渠道增加居民财产性收入。"无疑,通过发展提高效率,通过改革分配制度实现社会公平是我们解决分配公平的可行出路。分配公平得到保证,低收入民众的收入水平明显提高,反映到党内,因收入问题而产生的党员干部在党内关系上的差异性就会降低,党员干部也会更关注于党的事业而非个人利益,对党的忠诚度也会增强。

2.2 切实处理好党内外各种利益矛盾

从党内外利益矛盾对党的纯洁性的影响来看,首要的任务是各级党组织要解决好本地区、本单位发展中面临的突出利益问题,避免问题日积月累、久拖不绝。尤其是对于那些有可能或者已经酿成群体事件的重大利益矛盾,必须站在最广大人民群众的立场上,依照法律和程序妥善解决,绝不能动辄用强行压制的手段,压制人民的利益诉求。社会重大利益矛盾如果能得到及时解决,作为社会矛盾反映的党内矛盾也会易于化解。当然,有些矛盾先从党内解决也可以对全面解决起到促进作用,这就需要分清矛盾的性质、范围、程度,抓住主要方面有重点地加以解决,以收到事半功倍的效果。

2.3 在党员管理中把好入口、畅通出口

保持党的纯洁性,关键在队伍纯洁,关键在保证党员干部的质量。历史经验告诉我们,把好入口关和出口关是可行的思路。把好党员的入口关,这是保证党的纯洁性的基础。一方面要严格按照党员标准吸收党员,做到"徒有其名的党员,就是白给,我们也不要"。[3]

另一方面,也要创新发展党员的模式,比如,加强对入党积极分子的筛选和培养,变上级单位每年下派发展党员指标为基层单位根据需要申报,变在优秀单位发展党员为注重在落后单位发展等,这些都是提高党员发展质量的好方法,而且一些地方在探索中也已收到较好的效果。畅通不合格党员的出口也非常重要,只有及时淘汰不合格党员,留下的党员才能增强党员意识,强化党员责任,发挥模范作用。保持干部队伍的纯洁也是如此,要在干部选拔环节严格标准和程序,扩大民主,使干部能够选得准。同时要把经过实践检验证明能力、政绩平庸的干部坚决地拿下来,用任期制等方式使他们离开干部岗位,对于存在严重问题的干部则要及时严肃处理,保证干部队伍的素质能力经得起各种考验。

2.4 继续坚定不移地反对腐败,构建自我净化机制

党的十八大提出要增强党的自我净化、自我完善、自我革新、自我提高能力,这是保持纯洁性的重要任务,尤其是自我净化能力,更需要全党在全面推进反腐倡廉建设中切实提高。当前反腐倡廉建设的预防功能有待进一步加强,要规范领导干部的权力行使,明确其权力边界,加强对干部的考核监督,尤其是干部德的考核要进一步加强,努力构建起一个干部不想贪、不能贪、不敢贪的工作环境,这才是真正对干部负责的表现,以免有些干部致身陷囹圄而悔之晚矣。要积极稳妥地加快领导干部财产公示制度出台的步伐,争取尽早施行。

参考文献

［1］范平．新时期党的建设教程［M］．北京：中共中央党校出版社，2003．

［2］林立权，甄成明．中央纪委监察部召开纪检监察机关2011年查办案件工作情况新闻通气会［J］．时代中国之声，2012（1）．

［3］列宁全集：第37卷［M］．北京：人民出版社，1986．

Global Solutions for Second Order Impulsive Integro-differential Equations in Banach Spaces

Wang Xinfeng Liu Dalian Li Chong

1 Introduction

Around the last fifteen years, a lot of works[1-10,13,14] have been done for the following initial value problem for nonlinear second order impulsive integro-differential equations of mixed type in a real Banach space E

$$\begin{cases} u'' = f(t, u, u', Tu, Su), \quad \forall t \in J[0, a], \ t \neq t_k \\ \Delta u|_{t=t_k} = I(u(t_k), u'(t_k)), \\ \Delta u'|_{t=t_k} = \bar{I}_k(u(t_k), u'(t_k)), \ k = 1, 2, \cdots, m \\ u(0) = x_0, \ u'(0) = x_1 \end{cases} \quad (1)$$

where $Tu = \int_0^t q(t,s) u(s) ds$, $Su = \int_0^a h(t,s) u(s) ds$, $h(t,s) \in C(J \times J, R)$, $q(t,s) \in C(D, R)$, $D = \{(t, s) \in J \times J : t \geq s\}$. $\Delta u|_{t=t_k} = u(t_k^+) - u(t_k^-)$, $(k=1, 2, \cdots, m)$ denote the jump of $u(t)$ at $t=t_k$, $u(t_k^-)$ and $u(t_k^+)$ represent the left and right limits of $u(t)$ at $t=t_k$ respectively, and $\Delta u'|_{t=t_k}$ has a similar meaning for $u'(t)$.

In many investigations, for examples[1-4,9,10,15], non-compactness type conditions, combined with fixed point theorem, play an important role in the proof of those results. In 1996, Guo[4] studied the unique solution of system IVP (1) employing Banach's fixed point theorem. Zhang[15] studied IVP (1) for the case in which f does not include derivative x' and obtained a golbal solution by Schauder's fixed point theorem. Zhang et al.[10] improved the results of Zhang[15] by Mönch's fixed point theorem with a new established comparison result. Rechntly, Liu et al.[9] and Zhang et al.[2] generalized the results of Guo[4] by using Banach's fixed point theorem. Almost at the same time, Guo et al.[3] established the existence of global solutions of IVP (1) by Schauder's fixed point theorem. And then Zhang et al.[1], based on the generalization of Darbo's fixed point theorem, extended the the results of Guo et al.[3] step by step through extending integro-differential equation without impulses on subinterval $\bar{J}_k$ to one with impulses on global interval J. Zhang et al. used the following compactness-type condition:

(H0). For any $r > 0$, f is bounded and uniformly continuous on $J \times B_r \times B_r \times B_r \times B_r$, and there exist non-negative Lebesgue integrable functions $L_k \in L(J, R^+)(k=1, 2, 3)$ such that for any bounded sets $B_i \in E$ ($i = 1, 2, 3, 4$) and $t \in J$,

$$\alpha(f(t, B_1, B_2, B_3, B_4)) \leq L_1(t) \alpha(B_1) + L_2(t) \alpha(B_2) + L_3(t) \alpha(B_3) \quad (2)$$

Apparently, the effect of operator Su in f of IVP (1) is overlooked.

Compactness type condition with both u' and Su is very difficult to deal with in proof. By introducing an operator and transforming IVP(1) into first order IVP without u', Wang et al.[8] obtained some results by using the monotone iterative technique. In this paper, the novelty of our approach is to introduce a vector with components

---

[Author Introduction] Wang Xinfeng, Basic Course Department of Beijing Union University, E-mail: wangxf728@263.net; Liu Dalian, Basic Course Department of Beijing Union University, E-mail: ldtdalian@buu.edu.cn; Li Chong, Basic Course Department of Beijing Union University, E-mail: lichong@buu.edu.cn.

being $u(t)$ defined on each subinterval $[t_k, t_{k+1}]$ (where $t_0 = 0$, $t_{m+1} = a$, $u(t_k) = u(t_k^+)$) at the left point of subinterval and $k = 0, 1, \cdots, m$), then a corresponding integro differential equation is derived for such an unknown vector system. Further, by means of the Mönch fixed point theorem, we establish the existence of solution – s of IVP(1). Under more general form with the item $L_4(t)\ \alpha(B_4)$ than the condition(2), we obtain some new results.

2 Some Lemmas

Let $PC[J, E] = \{u | u: J \to E$ is comtinuous at $t \neq t_i$, left continuous at $t = t_i$, and its right limit $u(t_i^+)$ at t_i exists, $i = 1, 2 \cdots, m\}$. Evidently, $PC[J, E]$ is a Banach space with the norm $\|u\|_{PC} = \sup_{t \in J} \|u(t)\|$.

Let $PC^1[J, E] = \{u \in PC[J, E]\ u'(t)$ is continuous at $t \neq t_i$, and $u'(t_i^-), u'(t_i^+)$ exist, $i = 1, 2, \cdots, m\}$. We can obtain that $u'(t)$ is continuous at the left of t_i by the mean value theorem, and then $PC^1[J, E]$ is a Banach space with the norm

$$\|u\|_{PC^1} = \max\{\|u\|_{PC}, \|u'\|_{PC}\}$$

Let $J' = J \setminus \{t_1, t_2, \cdots, t_m\}$, $J_0 = [0, t_1]$, $J_1 = (t_1, t_2]$, $\cdots$, $J_{m-1} = (t_{m-1}, t_m)$, $J_m = (t_m, a]$, $t_0 = 0$, $t_{m+1} = a$, $d_i = t_{i+1} - t_i$, $\bar{J}_i$ is the closure of J_i and $B_r = \{x \in E: \|x\| \leq r\}$ for any $r > 0$. For $H \subset PC^1[J, E]$, let $H' = \{x': x \in H\} \subset PC[J, E]$ and

$$H_i = \{x|_{\bar{J}_i}: x \in H\} \subset C^1[\bar{J}_i, E],$$
$$H'_i = \{x'|_{\bar{J}_i}: x \in H\} \subset C[\bar{J}_i, E],$$
$$A_i H = \{(Ax)|_{\bar{J}_i}: x \in H\} \subset C^1[\bar{J}_i, E],$$
$$(A_i H)' = \{(Ax)'|_{\bar{J}_i}: x \in H\} \subset C[\bar{J}_i, E],$$

Where $x(t_i) = x(t_i^+)$, $x'(t_i) = x'(t_i^+)$, $(A_i x)(t_i) = (Ax)(t_i^+)$, $(Ax)'(t_i) = (Ax)'(t_i^+)$, $(i = 1, 2, \cdots, m)$. For any $t \in J$, set

$$H(t) = \{x(t): x \in H\} \subset E,$$
$$H'(t) = \{x'(t): x \in H\} \subset E,$$
$$(TH)(t) = \{(Tx)(t): x \in H\} \subset E,$$
$$(SH)(t) = \{(Sx)(t): x \in H\} \subset E.$$

For any $t \in J_i$ ($i = 0, 1, \cdots, m$), set

$$H_i(t) = \{x(t): x \in H, t \in J_i\} \subset E,$$
$$H'_i(t) = \{x'(t): x \in H, t \in J_i\} \subset E,$$
$$(A_i H)(t) = \{(Ax)(t): x \in H, t \in J_i\} \subset E,$$
$$(A_i H)'(t) = \{(Ax)'(t): x \in H, t \in J_i\} \subset E.$$

Let $\alpha(\cdot)$, $\alpha_1(\cdot)$ and $\alpha_2(\cdot)$ denote the Kuratowski measure of non – compactness in E, $C^1(I, E)$ and $PC^1(J, E)$ respectively. For the details please to refer the references[11][12].

Lemma 1:[3]. *If $H \subset PC^1(J, E)$ is bounded and the elements of H are equicontinuous on each J_k ($k = 0, 1, \cdots, m$), then $\overline{co}(H) \subset PC^1(J, E)$ is bounded and equicontinuous an each J_k ($k = 0, 1, \cdots, m$). (Here $\overline{co}(H)$ denotes the closed convex hull of H.*

Lemma 2:[3]. *If for any $r > 0$, f is bounded and uniformly continuous on $J \times B_r \times B_r \times B_r \times B_r$ and $H \subset PC^1(J, E)$ is bounded and equicontinuous on each J_k ($k = 0, 1, \cdots, m$), then*

$$\{f(t, x(t), x'(t), (Tx)(t), (Sx)(t): x \in H\} \subset PC(J, E)$$

is bounded and equicontinuous on each J_k ($k = 0, 1, \cdots, m$).

Lemma 3:[11] *If $H \subset PC^1[J, E]$ is bounded and the elements of H' are equicontinuous on each J_k ($k = 0, 1, \cdots, m$), then*

$$\alpha_2(H) = \max\{\sup_{t \in J}\alpha(H(t)), \sup_{t \in J}\alpha(H'(t))\}$$

Lemma 4:[15] *If $H \subset PC^1[J, E]$ is bounded and equicontinuous on each J_k ($k = 0, 1, 2, \cdots, m$),*

then $\alpha(\{u(t) \mid u \in H\})$ is continuous on $t \in J_k$ ($k = 0, 1, 2, \cdots, m$) and
$$\alpha\left(\left\{\int_0^a u(t)dt \mid u \in H\right\}\right) \leq \int_0^a \alpha(\{u(t) \mid u \in H\})dt.$$

Lemma 5:[12] *Let E be a Banach space, $\Omega \subset E$ be a bounded open set, and $\theta \in \Omega$, $A: E \to E$ be continuous such that, (i) $x \neq \lambda Ax$ for $\forall \lambda \in [0, 1]$ and $x \in \partial\Omega$; (ii) than $H \subset \overline{\Omega}$ is conutable and $H \subset \overline{co}(\{\theta\} \cup (AH))$ imply that H is relative compact. Then A has at least one fixed point in Ω.*

Lemma 6:[15] *The problem IVP (1) is equivalent to the first-order nonlinear impulstive integro-differential equation*
$$u(t) = (Au)(t) \tag{3}$$
where
$$\begin{aligned}(Au)(t) &= x_0 + tx_1 + \\ &\int_0^t (t-s)f(s, u(s), u'(s), Tu(s), (Su)(s))ds \\ &+ \sum_{0 < t_k < t} I_k(u(t_k), u'(t_k)) \\ &+ \sum_{0 < t_k < t} (t - t_k)\bar{I}_k(u(t_k), u'(t_k)).\end{aligned} \tag{4}$$

Lemma 7: *Let $V_1, V_2 \subset PC^1[J, E]$ be two countable subset satisfying $V_1 \subset \overline{co}(u_0 \cup V_2)$ for some $u_0 \in PC^1[J, E]$. Then*
$$V_{1i} \subset \overline{co}(\{u_{0i}\} \cup V_{2i}), \quad i = 0, 1, 2, \cdots, m$$
$$V'_{1i} \subset \overline{co}(\{u'_{0i}\} \cup V'_{2i}), \quad i = 0, 1, 2, \cdots, m$$
and for any $t \in J_i$ ($i = 0, 1, 2, \cdots, m$).
$$V_{1i}(t) \subset \overline{co}(\{u_{0i}(t)\} \cup V_{2i}(t)),$$
$$V'_{1i}(t) \subset \overline{co}(\{u'_{0i}(t)\} \cup V'_{2i}(t)).$$

Proof: $V_1, V_2 \subset PC^1[J, E]$ are countable imply that $V'_1, V'_2 \subset PC[J, E]$ are countable and $u_0 \in PC^1[J, E]$ imply that $u'_0 \in PC[J, E]$.

For any $x \in V'_{1i}$, there exists $u \in V_1$ such that $u'|_{J_i} = x$. From $u \in V_1 \subset \overline{co}(u_0 \cup V_2)$, there exist
$$u_n = \lambda_0^{(n)} u_0 + \sum_{k=1}^{m_n} \lambda_k^{(n)} v_k^{(n)} \in \overline{co}(\{u_0\} \cup V_2),$$
$$n = 1, 2, \cdots,$$
such that $\|u_n - u\|PC^1 \to 0$ ($n \to \infty$), where
$$v_k^{(n)} \in V_2, K = 1, 2, \cdots, m_n,$$
$$\lambda_k^{(n)} \geq 0, k = 0, 1, \cdots, m_n,$$
$$\sum_{k=0}^{m_n} \lambda_k^{(n)} = 1.$$

Hence $\|u'_n|_{\bar{J}_k} - u'|_{\bar{J}_k}\|C \to 0$ ($n \to \infty$) and
$$u'_n | \bar{J}_k = \lambda_0^{(n)} u'_0|_{\bar{J}_k} + \sum_{k=1}^{m_n} \lambda_k^{(n)} (v_k^{(n)})'|_{\bar{J}_k}$$
$$\in \overline{co}(\{u'_{0i}\} \cup V'_{2i}), n = 1, 2, \cdots,$$

so $x = u'|_{J_k} \in \overline{co}(\{u'_{0i}\} \cup V'_{2i})$, which imply $V'_{1i} \subset \overline{co}(\{u'_{0i}\} \cup V'_{2i})$ and $V'_{1i}(t) \subset \overline{co}(\{u'_{0i}(t)\} \cup V'_{2i}(t))$ for any $t \in J_i$ ($i = 0, 1, 2, \cdots, m$).

For the same reasons, we have $V_{1i} \subset \overline{co}(\{u_{0i}\} \cup V_{2i})$ and $V_{1i}(t) \subset \overline{co}(\{u_{0i}(t)\} \cup V_{2i}(t))$ for any $t \in J_i$ ($i = 0, 1, 2, \cdots, m$).

Lemma 8: *Let $X \in R^{n \times n}$ be a matrix with following form*

$$X = \begin{pmatrix} t_{11} & 0 & \cdots & 0 \\ t_{12} & t_{22} & \cdots & 0 \\ \cdots & \cdots & \cdots & \cdots \\ t_{1n} & t_{2n} & \cdots & t_{nn} \end{pmatrix}.$$

Then for any $\varepsilon > 0$ there exists a norm $\|.\|_{mon}$ on $R^{n \times n}$, which is reduced by monotone vector norm, such that
$$\|X\|_{mon} \leq p(X) + \varepsilon.$$

Proof: It is from the proof of theorem 3.7 of[16].

For any $\delta > 0$, let
$$D_\delta = \text{diag}(1, \delta, \delta^2, \cdots, \delta^{n-1}),$$
then
$$D_\delta^{-1} X D_\delta = \begin{pmatrix} t_{11} & 0 & \cdots & 0 & 0 \\ \delta t_{12} & t_{22} & \cdots & 0 & 0 \\ \cdots & \cdots & \cdots & \cdots & \cdots \\ \delta^{n-1} t_{1n} & \delta^{n-2} t_{2n} & \cdots & \delta t_{n-1\,n} & t_{nn} \end{pmatrix}$$

For any $\varepsilon > 0$, let $\delta > 0$ such that
$$\sum_{i=1}^{j-1} |\delta^{j-i} t_{ij}| < \varepsilon, \quad j = 2, 3, \cdots, n,$$
and define
$$\|G\|_{mon} = \|D_\delta^{-1} G D_\delta\|_\infty, \quad \forall G \in C^{n \times n}$$
then we can prove the function $\|.\|_{mon}$ is an operator norm reduced by following vector norm
$$\|x\|_{D_\delta} = \|D_\delta^{-1} x\|_\infty, \quad x \in C^n \tag{5}$$
and
$$\|X\|_{mon} = \|D_\delta^{-1} X D_\delta\|_\infty \leq \rho(X) + \varepsilon.$$

It is easily to see that $\|.\|_{D_\delta}$ is a monotone vector norm. Lemma 8 holds.

In what follows, set $u_k(t) = u(t)$ as $t \in \bar{J}_k$ for $u \in PC[J, E]$, i.e. $u_k = u|_{\bar{J}_k}$ (where $u_k(t_k) = u(t_k^+)$ at the left point of interval $\bar{J}_k$ and $u|_{\bar{J}_k}$ denote the section of u restricted on $\bar{J}_k$), then (3) can be recast into the following form
$$u_k(t) = (A_k u)(t), \quad t \in \bar{J}_k, \quad k = 1, 2, \cdots, m \tag{6}$$

where
$$(A_k u)(t) \triangleq x_0 + t x_1 + \sum_{i=0}^{k-1} \int_{t_i}^{t_{i+1}} (t-s) \Gamma(i, s, u(s)) ds$$
$$+ \int_{t_k}^{t} (t-s) \Gamma(k, s, u(s)) ds$$
$$+ \sum_{i=1}^{k} I_i(u_{i-1}(t_i), u'_{i-1}(t_i))$$
$$+ \sum_{i=1}^{k} (t - t_i) \bar{I}_i(u_{i-1}(t_i), u'_{i-1}(t_i))$$
$$+ \sum_{i=1}^{k} (t - t_i) \bar{I}_i(u_{i-1}(t_i), u'_{i-1}(t_i))$$

and
$$\Gamma(i, s, u(s)) =$$
$$f(s, u_i(s), u'_i(s), (T_i u)(s), (Su)(s)),$$
$$(T_k u)(t) = \sum_{i=0}^{k-1} \int_{t_i}^{t_{i+1}} K(t, r) u_i(r) dr +$$

$$\int_{t_k}^{t} q(t,r) u_k(r) dr, t \in \bar{J}_k,$$

$$(Su)(s) = \sum_{i=0}^{m} \int_{t_i}^{t_{i+1}} h(s,r) u_i(r) dr.$$

3 Main Results

For convenience, we give the assumptions as follows.

(H1) For any $r > 0$, f is bounded and uniformly continuous on $J \times B_r \times B_r \times B_r \times B_r$, I_k and $\bar{I}_k$ are bounded on $B_r \times B_r$.

(H2) For any $r > 0$, there exist non-negative Lebesgue integrable functions $L_k \in L(J, R^+)$ ($k = 1, 2, 3$) such that for any bounded sets $B_i \subset E$ ($i = 1, 2, 3, 4$) and $t \in J$,

$$\begin{aligned}
\alpha(f(t,B_1,B_2,B_3,B_4)) &\le \sum_{i=1}^{4} L_i(t) \alpha(B_i), \\
\alpha(I_k(B_1,B_2)) &\le a_k(t) \alpha(B_1) + b_k \alpha(B_2), \\
\alpha(\bar{I}_k(B_1,B_2)) &\le a_{\bar{k}}(t) \alpha(B_1) + \bar{b}_k \alpha(B_2), \\
k &= 1, 2, \cdots, m.
\end{aligned} \tag{7}$$

(H3) $\beta = \limsup\limits_{\|x\| + \|y\| \to +\infty} \left(\sup\limits_{t \in J} \dfrac{f(t, x, y, Tx, Sx)}{\|x\| + \|y\|} \right)$ is finite.

Let $q_0 = \max\{|q(t,s)| : (t,s) \in D\}$, $h_0 = \max\{|h(t,s)| : (t,s) \in J \times b\}$.

Theorem 9: *If the assumptions (H1)-(H3) are satisfied and the spectral radius $\rho(M_0^T M_0)$ of matrix $M_0^T M_0$ satisfies*

$$\rho(M_0^T M_0) < 1, \tag{8}$$

where

$$M_0 = \begin{pmatrix} \Delta_0 & d_1 \mu_0 & \cdots & d_m \mu_0 \\ \Delta_{012} & \Delta_1 & \cdots & d_m \mu_1 \\ \cdots & \cdots & \cdots & \cdots \\ \Delta_{01m} & \Delta_{02m} & \cdots & \Delta_m \end{pmatrix} \tag{9}$$

and

$$\begin{aligned}
\Delta_{ijk} &= \delta_i + d_i \sigma_{ik} + \lambda_{jk}, \\
\Delta_k &= \delta_k + d_k \sigma_{kk}, \\
\delta_i &= \max\{t_{i+1}, 1\} \int_{t_i}^{t_{i+1}} [L_1(s) + L_2(s)] ds, \\
\mu_k &= h_0 \max\{t_{k+1}, 1\} \int_0^{t_{k+1}} L_4(s) ds, \\
\sigma_{ik} &= \mu_k + q_0 \max\{t_{k+1}, 1\} \int_{t_i}^{t_{k+1}} L_3(s) ds, \\
\lambda_{ik} &= \max\{(a_i + b_i) + (t_k - t_i)(a_{\bar{i}} + b_{\bar{i}}), \bar{a}_i + \bar{b}_i\}, \\
d_i &= t_{i+1} - t_i, i = 0, 1, \cdots, k, \\
j &= i+1, i+2, \cdots, m, k = i+1, i+2, \cdots, m.
\end{aligned} \tag{10}$$

Then IVP (1) has at least one solution $u \in PC^1(J, E) \cap C^2(J', E)$.

Proof: We divide the proof into two steps.

(i) Firstly, let

$$\Omega_0 = \left\{ \begin{array}{l} x \in PC^1(J, E): \\ \exists\, 0 \le \lambda \le 1 \text{ such that} \\ x = \lambda A x \end{array} \right\} \tag{11}$$

We will prove that Ω_0 is bounded set in $PC^1(J, E)$.

From the hypothesis (H3), there exists the constant $\beta' > \beta$ and $d > 0$ such that
$$\|f(t, u, v, Tu, (Su))\| \leq \beta'(\|u\| + \|v\|), t \in J, \|u\| + \|v\| > d.$$

Since f is bounded and continuous, we get
$$\|f(t, u, v, Tu, (Su))\| \leq \beta'(\|u\| + \|v\|) + G, t \in J, u, v \in E, \quad (12)$$

where $G = \sup\{\|f(t, v, v, Tu, Su)\| : t \in J, \|u\| + \|v\| \leq d\} < \infty$.

On the other hand, $\forall u \in \Omega_0$, from (11) there exists $0 \leq \lambda \leq 1$ such that
$$u(t) = \lambda Au(t), t \in J. \quad (13)$$

If $t \in J_0$, from (4), (12) and (13), we have
$$\|u(t)\| \leq \|x_0\| + t_1\|x_1\| + \beta' t_1 \int_0^t (\|u(s)\| + \|u'(s)\| + G) ds$$

$$\|u'(t)\| \leq \|x_1\| + \beta' \int_0^t (\|u(s)\| + \|u'(s)\| + G) ds.$$

Let $m_0(t) = \max_{t \in \bar{J}_0}\{\|u(t)\|, \|u'(t)\|\}$, then we have
$$m_0(t) \leq C_0 + \gamma_0 \int_0^t m_0(s) ds$$

where $C_0 = \max\{\|x_0\| + t_1\|x_1\| + \beta' t_1^2 G, \|x_1\| + \beta' t_1 G\}$ and $r_0 = 2\beta' t_1 G\}$ and $\gamma_0 = 2\beta' \max\{t_1, 1\}$.

From the Gronwall lemma, we get
$$\max_{t \in \bar{J}_0}\{\|u(t)\|, \|u'(t)\|\} = m_0(t) \leq C_0 e^{r_0 t_1} = K_0, t \in J_0.$$

And then $\|u\|_{C^1} \leq K_0$ for any $t \in J_0$. From the hypothesis (H1) there exists the constant $\beta_0 > 0$
$$\|f(t, u, u', Tu, (Su))\| \leq \beta_0,$$
$$\|I_1(u, u')\| \leq \beta_0, \|\bar{I}_0(u, u')\| \leq \beta_0\|. \quad (14)$$

If $t \in J_1 = (t_1, t_2]$, then (13) change into
$$u(t) = \lambda(x_0 + tx_1) + \lambda \int_0^t (t-s)f(s, u(s), u'(s), Tu(s), (Su)(s)) ds + \lambda[I_1(u(t_1), u'(t_1)) + (t-t_1)\bar{I}_0(u(t_1), u'(t_1))]. \quad (15)$$

(12)(14)(15) imply that
$$\|u(t)\| \leq \|x_0\| + t_2\|x_1\| + t_1^2 \beta_0 + \frac{(t_2-t_1)^2}{2}\beta' G + \beta_0 + (t_2-t_1)\beta_0 + \beta' t \int_{t_1}^t (\|u(s)\| + \|u'(s)\|) ds$$

$$\|u'(t)\| \leq \|x_1\| + t_1 \beta_0 + (t_2-t_1)\beta' G + \beta_0 + \beta' \int_{t_1}^t (\|u(s)\| + \|u'(s)\|) ds.$$

Let $C_1 = \max\{\|x_0\| + t_2\|x_1\| + (t_2 - t_1 + t_1^2 + 1)\beta_0 + \frac{(t_2-t_1)^2}{2}\beta' G, \|x_1\| + t_1\beta_0 + (t_2-t_1)\beta' G + \beta_0\}$, $\gamma_1 = 2\beta' \max\{t_2, 1\}$, and therefore
$$m_1(t) \leq C_1 + \gamma_1 \int_{t_1}^t m_1(s) ds$$

where $m_1(t) = \max_{t \in \bar{J}_1}\{\|u(t)\|, \|u'(t)\|\}$. And then
$$m_1(t) \leq C_1 e^{r_1(t_2 - t_1)} = K_1, t \in J_1.$$

Analogously, there exist $K_i > 0$ such that
$$m_i(t) \leq k_i, t \in J_i, (i = 2, 3, \cdots, m)$$

where $m_i(t) = \max\limits_{t\in \bar{J}_1}\{\|u(t)\|, \|u'(t)\|\}$. Let $m(t) = \max\limits_{t\in J}\{\|u(t)\|, \|u'(t)\|\}$ and $K = \max\limits_{0\leq i\leq m} K_i$, then $m(t) \leq \max\limits_{0\leq i\leq m} m_i(t) \leq K, t\in J$, i.e. $\|u\|_{PC^1} \leq K$

So Ω_0 is a bounded set on $PC^1[J, E]$.

ii) Let $R_0 > K$ and $\Omega = \{u \in PC^1(J, E)\}$:
$\|u\| < R_0$, then Ω is open bounded set which satisfy that $x \neq \lambda Ax$ for $\forall \lambda \in [0, 1]$ and $x \in \partial\Omega$. As follows, we prove that $H \subset \overline{\Omega}$ is relative compact for any countable set $H \subset \overline{co}\{\theta\} \cup (AH)$.

From (4) and (H1), we have that the operator

$A: PC^1[J, E] \to PC^1[J, E]$ is bounded and continuous. And the $(AH) \subset PC^1[J, E]$ is bounded and $(AH), (AH)'$ are equicontinuous on J_k $(k = 0, 1, m.)$

Since $H \subset \overline{\Omega}$ is countable, $H \subset \overline{co}\{\theta\} \cup (AH)$ and $(AH), (AH)'$ are bounded and equicontinuous on J_k, then H, H' are bounded and equicontinuous. Thus all of H_i, H'_i, A_iH and $(A_iH)'$ $(i = 0, 1, \cdots, m)$ are countable, bounded and equicontinuous on $\bar{J}_i$ and $H_i \subset \overline{co}(\{\theta_i\} \cup (A_iH))$ from lemma 7. From lemma 1, lemma 2 and (H1), we have $f(t, H, H', (TH), (SH)) \subset PC[J, E]$ is bounded and equicontinuous on each J_k $(k = 0, 1, \cdots, m)$. Hence from Lemma 7, Lemma 4 and (H2), we have

$$\alpha(H_0(t)) \leq \alpha(A_0H)(t))$$
$$\leq t\int_0^t [L_1(s)\alpha(T_0H(s)) + L_2(s)\alpha(H'_0(s))]ds +$$
$$t\int_0^t [L_3(s)\alpha(T_0H(s)) + L_4(s)\alpha(SH(s))]ds$$
$$\leq t\int_0^t ([L_1(s) + L_2(s) + t_1L_3(s)q_0]\alpha_1(H_0)]ds +$$
$$t\int_0^t [L_4(s)h_0\int_0^\alpha \alpha(H(r))dr]ds$$
$$\leq t\int_0^t \{[L_1(s) + L_2(s) + t_1L_3(s)q_0]\alpha_1(H_0)\}ds +$$
$$t\int_0^t [h_0L_4(s)\sum_{i=0}^m (t_{i+1} - t_i)\alpha_1(H_i)\}ds,$$

and

$$\alpha(H'_0(t)) \leq \alpha(A_0H)'(t))$$
$$\leq \int_0^t [L_1(s)\alpha(H_0(s)) + L_2(s)\alpha(H'_0(s))]ds +$$
$$\int_0^t [L_3(s)\alpha(T_0H(s)) + L_4(s)\alpha(SH(s))]ds$$
$$\leq \int_0^t \{[L_1(s) + L_2(s) + t_1L_3(s)q_0]\alpha_1(H_0)\}ds +$$
$$\int_0^t [h_0L_4(s)\sum_{i=0}^m (t_{i+1} + t_i)\alpha_1(H_i)\}ds.$$

So from lemma 3 and (10),

$$\alpha_1(H_0) = \max\{\sup_{t\in J_0}\alpha(H(t)), \sup_{t\in J_0}\alpha(H'(t))\}$$
$$\leq (\delta_0 + d_0\sigma_{00})\alpha_1(H_0) + \sum_{i=1}^m d_i\mu_0\alpha_1(H_i). \tag{16}$$

For $t \in \bar{J}_1$, we have

$$\alpha(H_1(t)) \leq \alpha(A_1H)(t))$$
$$\leq t\int_0^t [L_1(s)\alpha(H(s)) + L_2(s)\alpha(H'(s))]ds +$$

$$t\int_0^t [L_3(s)\alpha(T_1 H(s)) + L_4(s)\alpha(SH(s))]ds$$
$$+ a_1\alpha(H_0(t_1)) + b_1\alpha(H'_0(t_1)) +$$
$$(a - t_1)[\bar{a}\alpha(H_0(t_1)) + \bar{b}_1 a(H'_0)(t_1))]$$
$$\leq t\int_0^{t_1}[L_1(s) + L_2(s) + t_1 L_3(s)q_0]\alpha_1(H_0)ds +$$
$$t\int_0^{t_1}[h_0 L_4(s)\sum_{i=0}^m (t_{i+1} - t_i)\alpha_1(H_i)]ds +$$
$$+ t\int_{t_1}^t [L_1(s) + L_2(s)]\alpha_1(H_1)ds +$$
$$t\int_{t_1}^t [t_2 - t_1]L_3(s)q_0\alpha_1(H_1)ds +$$
$$t\int_{t_1}^t [t_1 q_0 L_3(s)\alpha_1(H_0)]ds +$$
$$t\int_{t_1}^t h_0 L_4(s)\sum_{i=0}^m (t_{i+1} - t_i)\alpha_1(H_i)ds +$$
$$((a_1 + b_1) + (t - t_1)(\bar{a}_1 + \bar{b}_1)\alpha_1(H_0)$$

and
$$\alpha(H'_1(t)) \leq \alpha((A_1 H)'(t))$$
$$\leq \int_0^{t_1}[L_1(s) + L_2(s) + t_1 L_3(s)q_0]\alpha_1(H_0)ds +$$
$$\int_0^{t_1}[h_0 L_4(s)\sum_{i=0}^m (t_{i+1} - t_i)\alpha_1(H_i)]ds +$$
$$\int_{t_1}^t [L_1(s) + L_2(s) + (t_2 - t_1)L_3(s)q_0]\alpha_1(H_1)]ds +$$
$$\int_{t_1}^t [t_1 q_0 L_3(s)\alpha_1(H_0)]ds +$$
$$\int_{t_1}^t h_0 L_4(s)\sum_{i=0}^m (t_{i+1} - t_i)\alpha_1(H_i)ds + (\bar{a}_1 + \bar{b}_1)\alpha_1(H_0)$$

then from lemma 3 and (10), we get
$$\alpha_1(H_1) = \max\{\sup_{t\in J_1}\alpha(H)(t), \sup_{t\in J_1}\alpha(H'(t))\}$$
$$\leq \sum_{i=0}^1 (\delta_i + d_i\sigma_{i1})\alpha_1(H_i) + \lambda_{12}\alpha_1(H_0) + \sum_{i=2}^m d_i\mu_1\alpha_1(H_i). \tag{17}$$

In general, for $t\in \bar{J}_k$ ($k = 2, 3, \cdots, m$), we have
$$\alpha(H_k(t)) \leq \alpha((A_k H)(t))$$
$$\leq t\int_0^t [L_1(s)\alpha(H(s)) + L_2(s)\alpha(H'(s))]ds +$$
$$t\int_0^t [L_3(s)\alpha(T_k H(s)) + L_4(s)\alpha(SH(s))]ds +$$
$$\sum_{i=1}^k [(a_i + b_i) + (t - t_i)(\bar{a}_i + \bar{b}_i)]\alpha_1(H_i)$$
$$\leq t\sum_{i=0}^k \int_{t_i}^{t_{i+1}} [(L_1(s) + L_2(s))\alpha_1(H_i)]ds +$$
$$t\sum_{i=0}^k \int_{t_i}^{t_{i+1}} [k_0 \sum_{j=0}^i (t_{j+1} - t_j)L_3(s)\alpha_1(H_j)]ds$$
$$+ h_0 t\int_0^{t_{k+1}} L_4(s)\sum_{j=0}^m (t_{j+1} - t_j)\alpha_1(H_j)ds$$
$$+ \sum_{i=1}^k [(a_i + b_i) + (t_k - t_i)(\bar{a}_i + \bar{b}_i)]\alpha_1(H_{i-1}),$$

and
$$\alpha(H'_k(t)) \leqslant \alpha((A_k H)'(t))$$
$$\leqslant \sum_{i=0}^{k} \int_{t_i}^{t_{i+1}} [L_1(s) + L_2(s)] ds \alpha_1(H_i) +$$
$$\sum_{i=0}^{k} \int_{t_i}^{t_{i+1}} [k_0 \sum_{i=0}^{k} \int_{t_i}^{t_{k+1}} (t_{i+1} - t_i) L_3(s) \alpha_1(H_i) ds +$$
$$h_0 \int_0^{t_{k+1}} L_4(s) \sum_{j=0}^{m} (t_{j+1} - t_j) \alpha_1(H_j) ds +$$
$$\sum_{i=1}^{k} (\bar{a}_i + \bar{b}_i) \alpha_1(H_{i-1}).$$

Thus for $k = 2, 3, \cdots, m$,
$$\alpha_1(H_k) = \max\{\sup_{t \in J_k} \alpha(H(t)), \sup_{t \in J_k} \alpha(H'(t))\}$$
$$\leqslant \sum_{i=0}^{k} (\delta_i + d_i \sigma_{ik}) \alpha_1(H_i) +$$
$$\sum_{i=k+1}^{m} d_i \mu_k \alpha_1(H_i) + \sum_{i=1}^{k} \lambda_i \alpha_1(H_{i-1}), \tag{18}$$

where δ_i, σ_{ik}, μ_i, λ_i and d_i are defined by (10). Hence from (16)(17)(18), we obtain

$$\begin{pmatrix} \alpha_1(H_0) \\ \alpha_1(H_1) \\ \cdots \\ \alpha_1(H_m) \end{pmatrix} \leqslant M_0 \begin{pmatrix} \alpha_1(H_0) \\ \alpha_1(H_1) \\ \cdots \\ \alpha_1(H_m) \end{pmatrix} \tag{19}$$

where M_0 is defined by (9). Let

$$\begin{pmatrix} y_0 \\ y_1 \\ \cdots \\ y_m \end{pmatrix} = M_0 \begin{pmatrix} \alpha_1(H_0) \\ \alpha_1(H_1) \\ \cdots \\ \alpha_1(H_m) \end{pmatrix} \tag{20}$$

From (19) and (20), we have
$$[\alpha_1(H_0)]^2 + [\alpha_1(H_1)]^2 + \cdots + [\alpha_1(H_m)]^2$$
$$\leqslant y_0^2 + y_1^2 + \cdots + y_m^2. \tag{21}$$

From the definition and the properties of the 2-norm $\|\cdot\|_2$, we have
$$\left\| \begin{pmatrix} \alpha_1(H_0) \\ \alpha_1(H_1) \\ \cdots \\ \alpha_1(H_m) \end{pmatrix} \right\|_2 \leqslant \left\| \begin{pmatrix} y_0 \\ y_1 \\ \cdots \\ y_m \end{pmatrix} \right\|_2 \leqslant \|M_0\|_2 \left\| \begin{pmatrix} \alpha_1(H_0) \\ \alpha_1(H_1) \\ \cdots \\ \alpha_1(H_m) \end{pmatrix} \right\|_2$$
$$= \sqrt{\rho(M_0^T M_0)} \left\| \begin{pmatrix} \alpha_1(H_0) \\ \alpha_1(H_1) \\ \cdots \\ \alpha_1(H_m) \end{pmatrix} \right\|_2 \tag{22}$$

where $\|M_0\|_2$ denote 2-norm of the matrix M_0. (8) and (22) imply $\alpha_1(H_k) = 0$ ($k = 0, 1, 2, \cdots, m$), and then from lemma 3,
$$\alpha_2(H) = \max\{\sup_{t \in J} \alpha(H(t)), \sup_{t \in J} \alpha(H'(t))\}$$
$$\leqslant \max\{\max_{0 \leqslant k \leqslant m} \sup_{t \in J_k} \alpha(H_i(t)), \max_{0 \leqslant k \leqslant m} \sup_{t \in J_k} \alpha(H'_i(t))\} = 0,$$

i.e. H is relative compact. So the operator A defind by (3) has at least one fixed point in Ω from lemma 5. Thus IVP (1) has at least one solution $u(t) \in PC^1(J, E) \cap C^2(J', E)$ from lemma 6.

If we replace the norm in (22) into anyone of the others, which is reduced by monotone vector norm, we obtain the following conclusions.

Theorem 10: *Let the matrix M_0 be defined by (9) and the matrix norm $\|\cdot\|_{mon}$ be an operator norm reduced by some monotone vector norm. If the assumptions (H1) – (H3) hold and*
$$\|M_0\|_{mon} < 1, \tag{23}$$
then IVP (1) has at least one solution $u \in PC^1(J, E) \cap C^2(J', E)$.

Proof: For the proof of theorem 9, we replace the (21) into that
$$0 \leq \begin{pmatrix} \alpha(H_0) \\ \alpha(H_1) \\ \cdots \\ \alpha(H_m) \end{pmatrix} \leq \begin{pmatrix} y_0 \\ y_1 \\ \cdots \\ y_m \end{pmatrix}$$
imply
$$\|(\alpha(H_0), \alpha(H_1), \cdots, \alpha(H_m))^T\|_{mon}$$
$$\leq \|(y_0, y_1, \cdots, y_m)^T\|_{mon},$$
then we get the conclusion of theorem 10.

Remark 1. Since δ_k, μ_k, σ_{ik}, λ_{ik}, d_i ($i = 0, 1, \cdots, k$, $k = 0, 1, \cdots, m$) are nonnegative and $t_k \leq a$, $\sigma_{ik} \leq \sigma_{im}$, λ_{im} ($i < k$, $k = 1, 2, \cdots, m$), then
$$\delta_0 + \delta_1 + \cdots + \delta_m \leq \max\{a, 1\} \int_0^a (L_1(s) + L_2(s)) ds,$$
$$d_0 \sigma_{0m} + d_1 \sigma_{1m} + \cdots + d_1 \sigma_{mm}$$
$$\leq a \max\{a, 1\} \int_0^a [q_0 L_3(s) + h_0 L_4(s)] ds.$$
Thus
$$\|A\|_\infty \leq \max\{a, 1\} \int_0^a L(s) ds + \sum_{i=0}^m \lambda_{im},$$
where $L(s) = L_1(s) + L_2(s) + a q_0 L_3(s) + a h_0 L_4(s)$.

We can see that our conclusions imply those of[4] since the vector norm $\|\cdot\|_\infty$ reducing the matrix norm $\|\cdot\|_\infty$ is monotone.

Remark 2. Most of those conclusions in theorem 10 are new, since the compactness – type conditions (H2) involve both the derivative x' and the linear integral operator Su. Usually, it will be convenient that we verify (23) by using the operator norms $\|\cdot\|_1$, $\|\cdot\|_2$ and $\|\cdot\|_\infty$. Only if one of the three norms satisfy (23), we can obtain the conclusion of theorem 10.

Specially, let $L_4(t) = 0$, then we get the following conclusion.

Theorem 11: *Let $L_4(t) = 0$, If the assumptions (H1) – (H3) are satisfied and*
$$\max_{0 \leq k \leq m} \{\delta_k + d_k \sigma_{kk}\} < 1. \tag{24}$$
Then IVP (1) has at least one solution $u \in PC^1(J, E) \cap C^2(J', E)$.

Proof: $L_4(t) = 0$, then we get $\mu_k = 0$ ($k = 0, 1, 2, \cdots, m$). then the matrix M_0 defined by (9) changes into
$$M_0 = \begin{pmatrix} \Delta_0 & 0 & \cdots & 0 \\ \Delta_{012} & \Delta_1 & \cdots & 0 \\ \cdots & \cdots & \cdots & \cdots \\ \Delta_{01m} & \Delta_{12m} & \cdots & \Delta_m \end{pmatrix} \tag{25}$$
where Δ_{ijk} and Δ_k are defined by (10) and σ_{ik} ($i = 0, 1, 2, \cdots, m$, $k > i$) change into
$$\sigma_{ik} = q_0 \max\{t_{k+1}, 1\} \int_{t_i}^{t_{k+1}} L_3(s) ds. \tag{26}$$

Apparently, the eigenvalues of M_0 are $\delta_k + d_k \sigma_{kk}$ ($k=0, 1, 2, \cdots, m$), and then

$$\rho(M_0) = \max_{0 \leq k \leq m} \{\delta_k + d_k \sigma_{kk}\} < 1. \tag{27}$$

Let $\varepsilon < 1 - \rho(M_0)$, then from Lemma 8, there exist a operator norm $\|\cdot\|$, which is reduced by monotone vector norm, such that

$$\|M_0\| \leq \rho(M_0) + \varepsilon < 1. \tag{28}$$

Thus theorem 11 is valid from the theorem 10.

Remark 3. In some sense, theorem 11 indicate that the result with impulses t_i is equivalent to one without impulse defined in every subinterval $[t_i, t_{i+1}]$ ($i=0, 1, \cdots, m$) only if we ignore the influence of the operator S. This is fair and reasonable. Thus our results improve and generalize ones of the paper[1].

4 An Example

Consider the IVP of infinity systems for nonlinear impulsive integro-differential equation

$$\begin{cases} u''_n = \dfrac{t}{2}(t + u_n) + \dfrac{3t}{5}u'_n + t^2 \int_0^t e^{-ts} u_n(s) ds + \\ \dfrac{t^3}{18} \sin^3 \int_0^1 \dfrac{u_n(s)}{1+t+s} ds, t \in [0,1], t \neq \dfrac{1}{2} \\ \Delta u_n \big|_{t=\frac{1}{2}} = \dfrac{1}{10} \cos^2 u_n\left(\dfrac{1}{2}\right) + \dfrac{1}{5} u'_n\left(\dfrac{1}{2}\right), \\ \Delta u'_n \big|_{t=\frac{1}{2}} = \dfrac{1}{4} u_n\left(\dfrac{1}{2}\right) + \dfrac{1}{4} u'_n\left(\dfrac{1}{2}\right) \\ u_n(0) = 0, u'_n(0) = \dfrac{1}{n}, n = 1,2,3,\cdots. \end{cases} \tag{29}$$

Then IVP (29) has at least one solution $u^*(t) = (u_1^*(t), u_2^*(t), \cdots, u_n^*(t), \cdots)$ which is continuously differentiable twice on $\left[0, \dfrac{1}{2}\right] \cup \left(\dfrac{1}{2}, 1\right]$ and $u_n^*(t) \to 0 (0 \to \infty)$ for any $t \in [0, 1]$.

Proof. By all appearances, $u_n(t) \equiv 0$ is not a solution of IVP (29) Let $\|u\| = \sup_n |u_n|$ is a norm of $E = \{u = (u_1, u_2, \cdots, u_n, \cdots) \mid u_n \to 0\}$, then we know that IVP (29) can be regard as a form of IVP (1) in E. In this situation, $k(t, s) = e^{-ts}$, $h(t, s) = (1+t+s)^{-1}$, $x = (x_1, x_2, \cdots, x_n, \cdots)$, $y = (y_1, y_2, \cdots, y_n, \cdots)$, $z = (z_1, z_2, \cdots, z_n, \cdots)$, $w = (w_1, w_2, \cdots, w_n, \cdots)$, $f = (f_1, f_2, f \cdots, f_n, \cdots)$, $I_1 = (I_{11}, I_{12}, \cdots, I_{1n}, \cdots)$, $\bar{I}_1 = (\bar{I}_{11}, \bar{I}_{12}, \cdots, \bar{I}_{1n}, \cdots)$ and

$$f_n(t, x, y, z, w) = \dfrac{t}{2}(t + x_n) + \dfrac{3t}{5} y_n + t^2 z_n + \dfrac{t^3}{18} \sin^3 w_n$$

$$I_{1n}(x, y) = \dfrac{1}{10} \cos^2 x_n + \dfrac{1}{5} y_n, \quad I_{\bar{1}n}(x, y) = \dfrac{1}{4} x_n + \dfrac{1}{4} y_n$$

where $m = 1$, $t_1 = \dfrac{1}{2}$, the assumption (H1) holds and

$$\|f_n(t, x, y, Tx, Sx)\| \leq \dfrac{1}{2} \|x\| + \dfrac{3}{5} \|y\| + \|Tx\| + \dfrac{5}{9}$$

$$\leq \dfrac{3}{2} \|x\| + \dfrac{3}{5} \|y\| + \dfrac{5}{9}.$$

i. e. the assumption (H3) holds too. On the other hand, for any bounded set B_i ($i=1, 2, 3, 4$), since

$$\alpha(f(t, B_1, B_2, B_3, B_4))$$

$$\leq \dfrac{t}{2} \alpha(B_1) + \dfrac{3t}{5} \alpha(B_2) + t^2 \alpha(B_3) + \dfrac{t^3}{6} \alpha(B_4)$$

$$\alpha(I_1(B_1, B_2)) = \dfrac{1}{5} \alpha(B_1) + \dfrac{1}{5} \alpha(B_2),$$

$$\alpha(\bar{I}_1(B_1, B_2)) = \frac{1}{4}\alpha(B_1) + \frac{1}{4}\alpha(B_2)$$

the assumption (H2) hold and $L_1(t) = \frac{t}{2}$, $L_2(t) = \frac{3t}{5}$, $L_3(t) = t^2$, $L_4(t) = \frac{t^3}{6}$, $\alpha_1 = b_1 = \frac{1}{5}$, $\bar{a}_1 = \bar{b}_1 = \frac{1}{4}$. So $\delta_0 = \frac{11}{80}$, $\delta_1 = \frac{33}{80}$, $\mu_0 = \frac{1}{384}$, $\mu_1 = \frac{1}{24}$, $\sigma_{00} = \frac{17}{384}$, $\sigma_{01} = \frac{1}{12}$, $\sigma_{11} = \frac{1}{3}$, $\lambda_1 = \frac{13}{20}$. Thus

$$M_0 = \frac{1}{3840}\begin{pmatrix} 613 & 5 \\ 3184 & 2224 \end{pmatrix} = \begin{pmatrix} \frac{613}{3840} & \frac{1}{768} \\ \frac{199}{240} & \frac{139}{240} \end{pmatrix}$$

Calculating the row norm of the matrix M, we have

$$\|M_0\|_1 = \max\left\{\frac{3797}{3840}, \frac{743}{1280}\right\} < 1.$$

So the formula (23) holds. Thus the conclusions of our example hold from theorem 10.

Remark 4. Farther calculating two rest common norms in the example, we have

$$\rho(M_0^T M_0) > 1.04 > 1 \text{ and } \|M_0\|_\infty = \frac{169}{120} > 1.$$

In addition, set

$$f_n(t, x, y, z, w) = \frac{t}{2}(t + x_n + y_n) + \frac{t^2}{8}z_n + \frac{t^3}{24}\sin^3 w_n$$

$$I_{1n}(x, y) = \frac{1}{8}\cos^2 x_n + \frac{1}{4}y_n, \quad \bar{I}_{1n}(x, y) = \frac{1}{4}x_n + \frac{1}{4}y_n,$$

we have

$$\rho(M_0^T M_0) < 0.98 < 1, \quad \|M_0\|_1 = \frac{3139}{3072} > 1$$

and

$$\|M_0\|_\infty = \frac{125}{96} > 1$$

As well as we set

$$f_n(t, x, y, z, w) = \frac{t}{8}(t + x_n) + \frac{t}{4}y_n + \frac{4t^2}{3}z_n + \frac{t^3}{3}\sin^3 w_n$$

$$I_{1n}(x, y) = \frac{1}{16}\cos^2 x_n + \frac{1}{8}y_n, \quad \bar{I}_{1n}(x, y) = \frac{1}{8}x_n + \frac{1}{8}y_n$$

and $t_1 = \frac{7}{8}$, then

$$\rho(M_0^T M_0) > 1.1 > 1, \quad \|M_0\|_1 = \frac{1694431}{1179648} > 1$$

and

$$\|M_0\|_\infty = \frac{4597}{4608} < 1$$

So each norm of the matrix M_0 in theorem 10 is corresponding to one of the conclusions. Thus theorem 10 include many different results.

5 An Annotation

This idea, that differential equations with impulses are transferred into differential system and are studied, can be used to the following boundary value problem (BVP) for second order impulsive integro-differential equations of mixed type in a real Banach space E

$$\begin{cases} u'' = f(t, u, u', Tu, Su) & \forall t \in J = [0, 1], t \neq t_k \\ \Delta u \mid_{t=t_k} = I_k(u(t_k), u'(t_k)) \\ \Delta u' \mid_{t=t_k} = \bar{I}_k(u(t_k), u'(t_k)) \\ u(0) = \hat{x}_0, u(1) = \hat{x}_1 & (k = 1, 2, \cdots, m), \end{cases} \quad (30)$$

where the symbols is identical with that of IVP (1). In this section, we use the following assumption:

(**H4**). There exist non-negative Lebesgue integrable functions $L_i \in L[J, R^+]$ $(i = 1, 2, 3, 4)$ such that

$$\|f(t, x, y, u, v) - f(t, \bar{x}, \bar{y}, \bar{u}, \bar{v})\|_E$$
$$\leq L_1(t) \|x - \bar{x}\|_E + L_2(t) \|y - \bar{y}\|_E +$$
$$L_3(t) \|u - \bar{u}\|_E + L_4(t) \|v - \bar{v}\|_E,$$
$$t \in J, x, \bar{x}, y, \bar{y}, u, \bar{u}, v, \bar{v} \in E,$$
$$\|I_k(x, y) - I_k(\bar{x}, \bar{y})\|_E \leq a_k \|x - \bar{x}\|_E + b_k \|y - \bar{y}\|_E,$$
$$x, \bar{x}, y, \bar{y} \in E \quad (k = 1, 2, \cdots, m)$$

and

$$\|\bar{I}_k(x, y) - \bar{I}_k(\bar{x}, \bar{y})\|_E \leq \bar{a}_k \|x - \bar{x}\|_E + \bar{b}_k \|y - \bar{y}\|_E,$$
$$x, \bar{x}, y, \bar{y} \in E \quad (k = 1, 2, \cdots, m).$$

Theorem 12: *If the assumption (H4) holds and the spectral radius of matrix $M_1^T M_1$ satisfy*

$$\rho(M_1^T M_1) < 1, \quad (31)$$

where

$$M_1 = \begin{pmatrix} \delta_0 + \mu_1 & \delta_1 + \mu_2 & \cdots & \delta_m \\ \delta_0 + \mu_1 + \lambda_1 & \delta_1 + \mu_2 & \cdots & \delta_m \\ \cdots & \cdots & \cdots & \cdots \\ \delta_0 + \mu_1 + \lambda_1 & \delta_1 + \mu_2 + \lambda_2 & \cdots & \delta_m \end{pmatrix} \quad (32)$$

and

$$\mu_k = (a_k + b_k) + (1 - t_k)(\bar{a}_k + \bar{b}_k),$$
$$\lambda_k = \max\{\mu_k, (\bar{a}_k + \bar{b}_k)\},$$
$$k = 1, 2, \cdots, m,$$
$$\delta_i = (t_{i+1} - t_i) \int_{t_i}^1 (L_3(s) K_i + L_4(s) H_i) ds +$$
$$(t_{i+1} - t_i) \int_0^{t_i} L_4(s) H_i ds +$$
$$\int_{t_i}^{t_{i+1}} [L_1(s) + L_2(s)] ds,$$
$$i = 0, 1, 2, \cdots, m, \quad (33)$$

then BVP (30) has an unique solution $u \in PC^1[J, E] \cap C^2[J', E]$. Moreover, for any $z_0 \in PC^1[J, E]$, the iterative sequence defined by

$$z_n(t) = \varphi(t) + \int_0^1 G(t, s) F(s, z_{n-1}(s)) ds +$$
$$t \sum_{k=1}^m [Q_k(z_{n-1}(t_k)) + (1 - t_k) \bar{Q}_k(z_{n-1}(t_k))] +$$
$$\sum_{0 < t_k < t} [Q_k(z_{n-1}(t_k)) + (t - t_k) \bar{Q}_k(z_{n-1}(t_k))],$$
$$n = 1, 2, 3, \cdots \quad (34)$$

converges to $u(t)$ uniformly on $t \in J$, and the sequence

$$z'_n(t) = \varphi'(t) + \int_0^1 G'_t(t,s)F(s,z_{n-1}(s))ds +$$

$$\sum_{k=1}^m [Q_k(z_{n-1}(t_k)) + (1-t_k)\overline{Q}_k(z_{n-1}(t_k))] +$$

$$\sum_{0<t_k<t} \overline{Q}_k(z_{n-1}(t_k)), n=1,2,3,\cdots \tag{35}$$

converges to $u'(t)$ uniformly on $t \in J$, Here

$$F(s, u(s)) = f(s, u(s), u'(s), Tu(s), Su(s)),$$
$$Q_k(u(t_k)) = I_k(u(t_k), u'(t_k)),$$
$$\overline{Q}_k(u(t_k)) = \overline{I}_k(u(t_k), u'(t_k)).$$

Proof: At first, (30) is equivalent to the following first-order nonlinear impulsive integro-differential equation

$$u(t) = \varphi(t) + \int_0^1 G(t,s)F(s,u(s))ds -$$

$$t\sum_{k=1}^m [Q_k(u(t_k)) + (1-t_k)\overline{Q}_k(u(t_k))] +$$

$$\sum_{0<t_k<t} [Q_k(u(t_k)) + (t-t_k)\overline{Q}_k(u(t_k))] \tag{36}$$

where

$$G(t,s) = \begin{cases} s(t-1) & 0 \leq s \leq t \\ (s-1)t & t \leq s < 1 \end{cases},$$

and

$$\varphi(t) = \hat{x}_0 + t(\hat{x}_1 - \hat{x}_0).$$

For any $x, y \in PC^1[J, E]$, let $x_k(t) = x(t)$, $y_k(t) = y(t)$ as $t \in \overline{J}_k$ ($K=0, 1, \cdots, m$), where $x_k(t_k) = x(t_k^+)$, $y_k(t_k) = y(t_k^+)$ at the left point of each subinterval $\overline{J}_k$ ($k=1, 2, \cdots, m$). Since $\max_{t,s\in J}\{|G(t,s)|, |G'(t,s)|\} \leq 1$, from (H1) and (36), we have

$$\|(A_0x)(t) - (A_0y)(t)\|_E$$

$$\leq \sum_{i=0}^m \int_{t_i}^{t_{i+1}} |G_0(t,s)|[L_1(s)\|x_i(s) - y_i(s)\|_E$$

$$+ L_2(s)\|x'_i(s) - y'_i(s)\|_E$$

$$+ L_3(s)\sum_{j=0}^i \int_{t_j}^{t_{j+1}} K_j(s,r)\|x_j(r) - y_j(r)\|_E dr$$

$$+ L_4(s)\sum_{j=0}^i \int_{t_j}^{t_{j+1}} H_j(s,r)\|x_j(r) - y_j(r)\|_E dr]ds$$

$$+ t\sum_{i=0}^m [a_i\|x_{i-1}(t_i) - y_{i-1}(t_i)\|_E$$

$$+ b_i\|x'_{i-1}(t_i) - y'_{i-1}(t_i)\|_E$$

$$+ (1-t_i)(\overline{a}_i)\|x_{i-1}(t_i)\|_E$$

$$+ \overline{b}_i\|x'_{i-1}(t_i) - y'_{i-1}(t_i)\|_E)]$$

$$\leq \sum_{i=0}^m \int_{t_i}^{t_{i+1}} [L_1(s) + L_2(s)]\|x_i - y_i\|_{C^1 J_i}$$

$$+ \sum_{j=0}^i (t_{j+1} - t_j)L_3(s)K_j\|x_j - y_j\|_{C^1 J_j}$$

$$+ \sum_{j=0}^m (t_{j+1} - t_j)L_4(s)H_j\|x_j - y_j\|_{C^1 J_j}\}ds$$

$$+ \sum_{i=1}^m [a_i + b_i + (1-t_i)(\overline{a}_i + \overline{b}_i)]\|x_{i-1} - y_{i-1}\|_{C^1 J_{i-1}}$$

and
$$\| (A_0x)'(t) - (A_0y)'(t) \|_E$$
$$\leq \sum_{i=0}^{m} \int_{t_i}^{t_{i+1}} \{ [L_1(s) + L_2(s)] \| x_i - y_i \|_{C^1_{J_i}} +$$
$$\sum_{j=0}^{i} (t_{j+1} - t_j) L_3(s) K_j \| x_j - y_j \|_{C^1_{J_j}} +$$
$$\sum_{j=0}^{i} (t_{j+1} - t_j) L_4(s) H_j \| x_j - y_j \|_{C^1_{J_j}} \} ds +$$
$$\sum_{i=1}^{m} [a_i + b_i + (1 - t_i)(\bar{a}_i + \bar{b}_i)] \| x_{i-1} - y_{i-1} \|_{C^1_{J_{i-1}}}.$$

So we have
$$\| (A_0x) - (A_0y) \|_{C^1_{J_0}} \leq \sum_{i=0}^{m} \delta_i \| x_i - y_i \|_{C^1_{J_i}} + \sum_{i=0}^{m} \mu_i \| x_{i-1} - y_{i-1} \|_{C^1_{J_{i-1}}}. \tag{37}$$

Let $Q(x,y) = \sum_{i=0}^{m} \big[\int_{t_i}^{t_{i+1}} (L_1(s) + L_2(s)) \| x_i - y_i \|_{C^1_{J_i}} + \sum_{j=0}^{i} (t_{j+1} - t_j) L_3(s) K_J \| x_j - y_j \|_{C^1_{J_j}} + \sum_{j=0}^{m} (t_{j+1} - t_j) L_4(s) H_j \| x_j - y_j \|_{C^1_{J_j}} \big] ds + \sum_{i=1}^{m} [a_i + b_i + (1 - t_i)(\bar{a}_i + \bar{b}_i)] \| x_{i-1} - y_{i-1} \|_{C^1_{J_{i-1}}}$. We obtain
$$\| (A_1x)(t) - (A_1y)(t) \|_E \leq Q(x,y) + [(a_1 + b_1) + (1 - t_1)(\bar{a}_1 + \bar{b}_1)] \| x_0 - y_0 \|_{C^1_{J_0}},$$
$$\| (A_1x)'(t) - (A_1y)'(t) \| \leq Q(x,y) + (\bar{a}_1 + \bar{b}_1) \| x_0 - y_0 \|_{C^1_{J_0}}.$$

and then
$$\| (A_1x) - (A_1y) \|_{C^1_{J_1}} \leq Q(x,y) + \lambda_1 \| x_0 - y_0 \|_{C^1_{J_0}} \tag{38}$$

In general, we obtain that
$$\| (A_kx_k) - (A_ky_k) \|_{C^1_{J_k}} \leq Q(x,y) + \sum_{i=1}^{k} \lambda_i \| x_{i-1} - y_{i-1} \|_{C^1_{J_{i-1}}},$$
$$k = 2,3,\cdots,m. \tag{39}$$

So from (37), (38) and (39), we get
$$\begin{pmatrix} \| A_0x_0 - A_0y_0 \|_{C^1_{J_0}} \\ \| A_1x_1 - A_1y_1 \|_{C^1_{J_1}} \\ \| A_mx_m - A_my_m \|_{C^1_{J_m}} \end{pmatrix} \leq M_1 \begin{pmatrix} \| x_0 - y_0 \|_{C^1_{J_0}} \\ \| x_1 - y_1 \|_{C^1_{J_1}} \\ \cdots \\ \| x_m - y_m \|_{C^1_{J_m}} \end{pmatrix}, \tag{40}$$

where M_1 is defined by (32) (Here and in what follows the vector inequality $x \leq y$ denotes that all of the corresponding components of vectors satisfy $x_i \leq y_i$ ($i = 0, 1, \cdots, m$)). Then we have
$$\left\| \begin{matrix} \| A_0x_0 - A_0y_0 \|_{C^1_{J_0}} \\ \| A_1x_1 - A_1y_1 \|_{C^1_{J_1}} \\ \| A_mx_m - A_my_m \|_{C^1_{J_m}} \end{matrix} \right\|_2 \tag{41}$$

$$\leqslant \sqrt{\rho(M_1^T M_1)} \left\| \begin{array}{c} \|x_0 - y_0\|_{C_{J_0}^1} \\ \|x_1 - y_1\|_{C_{J_1}^1} \\ \cdots \\ \|x_m - y_m\|_{C_{J_m}^1} \end{array} \right\|_2$$

From (31), (41) and the Banach fixed point theorem, the operator $A = (A_0, A_1, \cdots, A_m)$ has an unique fixed point. Thus BVP (30) has an unique solution $u(t) \in PC^1[J, E] \cap C^2[J', E]$.

Moreover, if $u(t)$ is the unique solution of BVP (30) and $z_n(t)$ is defined by (34), let $u_k(t) = u(t)$, $t \in J_k$ and $z_{n,k}(t) = z_n(t)$, $t \in J_k$ ($k = 0, 1, \cdots, m$). Similar to the reduction process of (40), we can get

$$\begin{pmatrix} \|A_0 z_{0,0} - A_0 u_0\|_{C_{J_0}^1} \\ \|A_1 z_{0,1} - A_1 u_1\|_{C_{J_1}^1} \\ \cdots \\ \|A_m z_{0,m} - A_m u_m\|_{C_{J_m}^1} \end{pmatrix} \leqslant M_1 \begin{pmatrix} \|z_{0,0} - u_0\|_{C_{J_0}^1} \\ \|z_{0,1} - u_1\|_{C_{J_1}^1} \\ \cdots \\ \|z_{0,m} - u_m\|_{C_{J_m}^1} \end{pmatrix}.$$

Considering that the components of A are nonnegative, from mathematical induction, it is easy to obtain that

$$\begin{pmatrix} \|A_0 z_{n,0} - A_0 u_0\|_{C_{J_0}^1} \\ \|A_1 z_{n,1} - A_1 u_1\|_{C_{J_1}^1} \\ \cdots \\ \|A_m z_{n,m} - A_m u_m\|_{C_{J_m}^1} \end{pmatrix} \leqslant M_1^{n+1} \begin{pmatrix} \|z_{0,0} - u_0\|_{C_{J_0}^1} \\ \|z_{0,1} - u_1\|_{C_{J_1}^1} \\ \cdots \\ \|z_{0,m} - u_m\|_{C_{J_m}^1} \end{pmatrix}.$$

So $z_n(t)$, $z'_n(t)$ uniformly converge to $u(t)$, $u'(t)$ respectively for any $t \in J$. In other words, the conclusion of Theorem 12 holds.

If we replace the norm in (40) by p-norm of matrix, we can obtain following conclusion esaily.

Theorem 13: *If the assumption (H4) holds and the matrix M_1 defined by (32) satisfies*

$$\|M_1\|_p < 1, \tag{42}$$

where $1 \leqslant p \leqslant +\infty$, then we have the conclusions of theorem 12.

Remark 5. Let $M = \max\limits_{(t,s) \in J \times J} |K(t,s)|$ and $N = \max\limits_{(t,s) \in J \times J} |H(t,s)|$, Since

$$\sum_{i=0}^{m} \delta_i \leqslant \int_0^1 [L_1(s) + L_2(s)] ds + N \int_0^1 L_4(s) ds + M \sum_{i=0}^{m} (t_{i+1} - t_i) \int_{t_i+1}^1 L_3(s) ds$$

$$\leqslant \int_0^1 [L_1(s) + L_2(s)] + ML_3(s) + NL_4(s)] ds,$$

then we have

$$\|M\|_\infty = \sum_{i=0}^{m} \delta_i + \sum_{i=1}^{m} (\mu_i + \lambda_i)$$

$$\leqslant \int_0^1 L_0(s) ds + \sum_{i=1}^{m} (\mu_i + \lambda_i),$$

where $L_0(s) = L_1(s) + L_2(s) + ML_3(s) + NL_4(s)$. The condition (42) is more general than one obtained directly by (36). So the conclusion of Theorem 13 is an extension of those in[4] for initial value problems.

Remark 6. Most of those conclusions of theorem 12 and 13 are new, since the conditions (H4) involve both the derivative x' and the linear integral operator Su. Usually, for convenience, we can use $\|\cdot\|_1$, $\|\cdot\|_2$ or $\|\cdot\|_\infty$ as the operator norm in (42).

References

[1] X. G. Zhang, L. S. Liu, Y. H. Wu, Globalsolutions of nonlinear second – order impulsive integro – differential equations of mixed type in Banach spaces, *Nonlinear Anal.* 67 (2007), pp. 2335 – 2349.

[2] X. G. Zhang, L. S. Liu, Initial value problems for nonlinear second order impulsive integrodifferential equations of mixed type in Banach spaces, *Nonlinear Anal.* 64 (2006), pp. 2562 – 2574.

[3] F. Guo, L. S. Liu, Y. H. Wu, P. F. Siew, Global solutions of initial value problems for nonlinear second – order impulsive integro – differential equations of mixed type in Banach spaces, *NonlinearAnal.* 61 (2005), pp. 1363 – 1382.

[4] D. J. Guo, Initial value problems for nonlinear second – order impulsive integro – differential equations in Banach spaces, *J. Math. Anal. Appl.* 200 (1996), pp. 1 – 13.

[5] D. J. Guo, Initial value problems for second orderintegro – differnetial equations in Banach spaces, *Nonlinear Appl.* 37 (1999), pp. 289 – 300.

[6] J. L. Sun, Y. H. Ma, Initial value problems for thesecond order mixed monotone type of impulsive differential equations in Banach spaces, *J. Math. Anal. Appl.* 247 (2000), pp. 506 – 516.

[7] L. S. Liu, Y. H. Wu, X. G. Zhang, On wellposednessof an initial value problem for nonlinear second – order impulsive integro – differential equations of Volterra type in Banach spaces, *J. Math. Anal. Appl.* 317 (2006), pp. 634 – 649.

[8] W. X. Wang, L. L. Zhang, Z. D. Liang, Initial value problems for nonlinear integro – differential equations in Banach space, *J. Math. Anal. Appl.* 320 (2006), pp. 510 – 527.

[9] L. S. Liu, C. X. Wu, F. Guo, Existence theoremsof global solutions of initial value problems fornonlinear integro – differential equations of mixedtype in Banach spaces and applications, *Comput. Math. Appl.* 47 (2004), pp. 13 – 22.

[10] X. Y. Zhang, J. X. Sun, Solutions of nonolinear second order impulsive integro – differential equations of mixed type in Banach spaces, *J. Systems Sci. Math. Sci.* 22 (2002), pp. 428 – 438 (inchinese).

[11] D. J. Guo, V. Lakshmikantham, X. Z. Liu, *Nonlinear Integral Equations in Abstract Spaces*, Kluwer Academic Publishers, Dordrecht, 1996.

[12] K. Deiming, *Nonlinear Functional Analysis*, Springer – Verlag, Berlin, 1985.

[13] L. S. Liu, Iterative method for solutions and coupled quasi – solutions of nonlinear Fredholm integral equations in ordered Banach spaces, *Indian J. Pure Appl. Math.* 27 (1996), pp. 959 – 972.

[14] L. S. Liu, F. Guo, C. X. Wu, Y. H. Wu, Existence theorems of global solutions for nonlinear Voterratype integral equations in Banach spaces, *J. math. Anal. Appl.* 309 (2005), pp. 638 – 649.

[15] J. Q. Zhang, The solutions of second order impulsive integro – differential equations in Banachspaces, *Acta. Math. Scientia*, 19A (5)(1999), pp. 565 – 572 (in Chinese).

[16] S. F. Xu, *Theory and method of matrix computation*, Peking University Press, Beijing, 2001 (in Chinese).

联想记忆系统学习算法的改进

邢春峰

在文 [1] 中借助于牛顿向前插公式给出了一种新的联想记忆系统 (NFI – AMS) 的学习算法。其学习算法如下：

$$\begin{cases} \delta_i^{(n)} = p_i - \tilde{p}_i^{(n)} \\ \omega^{(n+1)}(a_{i_1+l_1,i_2+l_2,\cdots,i_N+l_N}) = \omega^{(n)}(a_{i_1+l_1,i_2+l_2,\cdots,i_N+l_N}) + d_{l_1l_2\cdots l_N}^{(i)}\delta_i^{(n)} \\ \tilde{p}_i^{(n+1)} = \sum_{l_1=0}^{\mu}\sum_{l_2=0}^{\mu-l_1}\cdots\sum_{l_N=0}^{\mu-l_{N-1}} \omega^{(n+1)}(a_{i_1+l_1,i_2+l_2,\cdots,i_N+l_N}) \cdot d_{l_1l_2\cdots l_N}^{(i)} \end{cases}$$

该学习算法虽然具有所需存储单元数量较少（恰好是 $C_{N+\mu}^{\mu}$，根据多项式插值理论 $C_{N+\mu}^{\mu}$ 是最小记忆单元数）、收敛速度快、学习精度高等优点，但是在实际应用时发现，这种新的联想记忆系统的学习算法和 J. S. Albus 在 1975 年基于 CMAC (Cerebellar Model Articulation Controller) 提出的联想记忆系统 (CMAC – AMS) 相比，虽然内存备用量大大减少，但 CMAC – AMS 本身具有的局部泛化 (generalaization 亦称推广) 能力降低；虽然学习算法收敛速度快，但对周围信息的收集能力相对减弱。等等。

基于上述原因，有必要对 NFI – AMS 的学习算法进一步改进。

1 牛顿插值公式

在文 [1] 中已经基于牛顿向前插公式给出了插值算法的一种显示格式：

$$f(S_1,S_2,\cdots S_N) \approx \sum_{l_1+l_2+\cdots+l_N=\mu} f_{i_1+l_1,i_2+l_2,\cdots i_N+l_N} \cdot d_{l_1l_2\cdots l_N} \tag{1}$$

其中
$$d_{l_1l_2\cdots l_N} = \sum_{j_1=l_1}^{\mu}\sum_{j_2=l_2}^{\mu-l_1}\cdots\sum_{j_N=l_N}^{\mu-l_{N-1}} \left[\prod_{i=1}^{N} \frac{(-1)^{j_i-l_i}C_{j_i}^{l_i}}{j_i!}t_i(j) \right]$$

$$t_i(j) = \begin{cases} t_i(t_i-1)(t_i-2)\cdots[t_i-(j-1)] & j>0 \\ 1 & j=0 \end{cases} \quad i=1,2,3,\cdots,N$$

这里利用文 [1] 中类似的推导方法基于牛顿向后插公式给出插值算法的另外一种显示格式：

$$f(S_1,S_2,\cdots S_N) \approx \sum_{l_1+l_2+\cdots+l_N=\mu} f_{i_1+1-\mu+l_1,i_2+1-\mu+l_2,\cdots i_N+1-\mu+l_N} \cdot d'_{l_1l_2\cdots l_N} \tag{2}$$

其中 $d'_{l_1l_2\cdots l_N} = \sum_{j_1=l_1}^{\mu}\sum_{j_2=l_2}^{\mu-l_1}\cdots\sum_{j_N=l_N}^{\mu-l_{N-1}} \left[\prod_{i=1}^{N} \frac{(-1)^{j_i-2l_i}C_{j_i}^{l_i}}{j_i!}t'_i(j) \right]$

$$t'_i(j) = \begin{cases} -t_i(-t_i-1)(-t_i-2)\cdots[-t_i-(j-1)] & j>0 \\ 1 & j=0 \end{cases} \quad i=1,2,3,\cdots,N$$

2 改进的学习算法的设计

将（1）、（2）两式相加除以 2 并整理得

[作者简介] 邢春峰，北京联合大学基础部。

$$f(S_1, S_2, \cdots S_N)$$

$$\approx \frac{1}{2}\left(\sum_{l_1+l_2+\cdots+l_N=\mu} f_{i_1+l_1, i_2+l_2, \cdots i_N+l_N} \cdot d_{l_1 l_2 \cdots l_N} + \sum_{l_1+l_2+\cdots+l_N=\mu} f_{i_1+1-\mu+l_1, i_2+1-\mu+l_2, \cdots i_N+1-\mu+l_N} \cdot d'_{l_1 l_2 \cdots l_N}\right)$$

$$= \sum_{l_1+l_2+\cdots+l_N=\mu} f_{i_1+l_1, i_2+l_2, \cdots i_N+l_N} \cdot \frac{1}{2} d_{l_1 l_2 \cdots l_N} + \sum_{l_1+l_2+\cdots+l_N=\mu} f_{i_1+1-\mu+l_1, i_2+1-\mu+l_2, \cdots i_N+1-\mu+l_N} \cdot \frac{1}{2} d'_{l_1 l_2 \cdots l_N}$$

简记为 $\sum_{l_1+l_2+\cdots+l_N=\mu} f(p) \cdot d$ \hfill (3)

这里还是使用 AMS 学习下列形式的映射：

$$S^{(i)} = \{s_j^{(i)}\}_{N\times 1} \Rightarrow f(S^{(i)}) = f(s_1^i, s_2^i, \cdots s_N^i) = p_i$$

AMS 的学习过程采用了两种学习方式：有规则学习和无规则学习，一般地，在实际中用的最多的还是无规则学习，所以下面给出无规则的学习过程。

在无规则的学习过程中，样本点是任意给定的。这时学习采用一种循环方式来完成，在每次循环过程中，基于输入信号 $S^{(i)} = (s_1^i, s_2^i, \cdots s_N^i)^T$，在相应的区域内，AMS 就根据相应的地址 $a_{i_1+l_1, i_2+l_2, \cdots i_N+l_N}$ 与 $a_{i_1+1-\mu+l_1, i_2+1-\mu+l_2, \cdots i_N+1-\mu+l_N}$ 内的存储单元的权值 $\omega(a_{i_1+l_1, i_2+l_2, \cdots i_N+l_N})$ 和 $\omega(a_{i_1+1-\mu+l_1, i_2+1-\mu+l_2, \cdots i_N+1-\mu+l_N})$ 得到实际输出值

$$\tilde{p}_i^{(n)} = \sum_{l_1=0}^{\mu} \sum_{l_2=0}^{\mu-l_1} \cdots \sum_{l_N=0}^{\mu-l_{N-1}} \omega^{(n)}(a) \cdot d^{(i)} \tag{4}$$

其中 $\omega^n(a)$ 是在第 n 次循环时地址 $a_{i_1+l_1, i_2+l_2, \cdots i_N+l_N}$ 与 $a_{i_1+1-\mu+l_1, i_2+1-\mu+l_2, \cdots i_N+1-\mu+l_N}$ 内的权值，$d^{(i)}$ 是（1）（2）两式中相应的 $d_{l_1 l_2 \cdots l_N}$ 和 $d'_{l_1 l_2 \cdots l_N}$。然后使用增补式学习，即用希望的输出 p_i 与网络回代的结果 $\tilde{p}_i^{(n)}$ 之间的误差

$$\delta_i^{(n)} = p_i - \tilde{p}_i^{(n)} \tag{5}$$

以一定的比例增补到相应的存储单元内

$$\omega^{n+1}(a) = \omega^n(a) + d^{(i)} \cdot \delta_i^{(n)} \tag{6}$$

改进的 NFI – AMS 的学习仍采用 δ 学习（所谓 δ 学习就是用已知的样本点对网络的权进行学习）进行。用 $P = (p_1, p_2, \cdots, p_m)^T$ 表示希望的输出值；$\tilde{p} = (\tilde{p}_1, \tilde{p}_2, \cdots, \tilde{p}_m)^T$ 表示实际输出值，它可通过调节与输出有关的地址中权 $\omega(a_{i_1+l_1, i_2+l_2, \cdots, i_N+l_N})$ 而得到。

设定一个误差要求 ε(ε>0)，如果 ||$P - \tilde{p}$|| < ε，则停止学习；否则按下面的改进的学习算法公式进行修改，

$$\begin{cases} \delta_i^{(n)} = p_i - \tilde{p}_i^{(n)} \\ \omega^{(n+1)}(a) = \omega^{(n)}(a) + d^{(i)} \delta_i^{(n)} \\ \tilde{p}_i^{(n+1)} = \sum_{l_1=0}^{\mu} \sum_{l_2=0}^{\mu-l_1} \cdots \sum_{l_N=0}^{\mu-l_{N-1}} \omega^{(n+1)}(a) \cdot d^{(i)} \end{cases} \tag{8}$$

直到满足设定的精度为止。

下面就改进前的 NFI – AMS 的学习算法和改进后的 NFI – AMS 的学习算法在一维和二维的情况下，对每个区域 D_i 内的存储单元的分布图进行了比较（如图 1 和图 2 所示）。

通过对图 1 和图 2 进行比较可以看出，改进的联想记忆系统的学习算法对周围信息的收集能力大大增强。

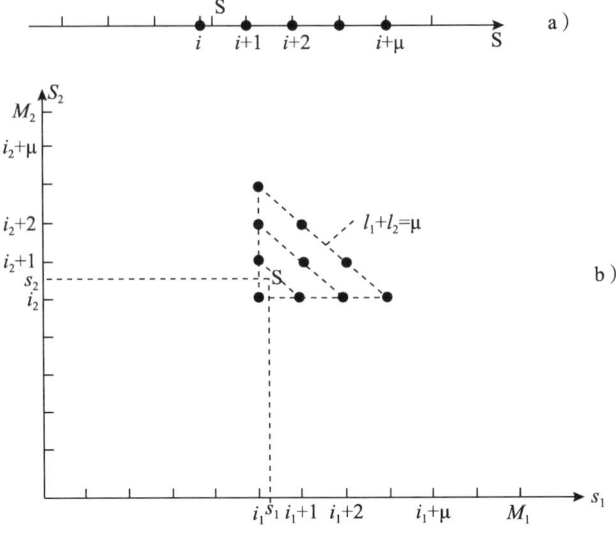

图 1　NFI-AMS 在区域内存储单元的分布

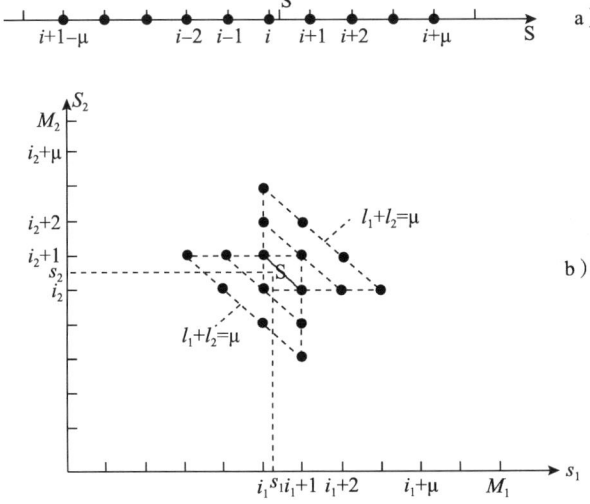

图 2　改进的 NFI-AMS 在区域内存储单元的分布

3　数值模拟

由公式（8）可以得到一维的学习算法公式

$$\begin{cases} \delta_i^{(n)} = p_i - \tilde{p}_i^{(n)} \\ \omega^{(n+1)}(a) = \omega^{(n)}(a) + d^{(i)}\delta_i^{(n)} \\ \tilde{p}_i^{(n+1)} = \sum_{l=0}^{\mu} \omega^{(n+1)}(a) \cdot d^{(i)} \end{cases}$$

同样可以得到二维的学习算法公式

$$\begin{cases} \delta_i^{(n)} = p_i - \tilde{p}_i^{(n)} \\ \omega^{(n+1)}(a) = \omega^{(n)}(a) + d^{(i)}\delta_i^{(n)} \\ \tilde{p}_i^{(n+1)} = \sum_{l_1=0}^{\mu} \sum_{l_2=0}^{\mu-l_1} \omega^{(n+1)}(a) \cdot d^{(i)} \end{cases}$$

例　映射函数 $f(S_1, S_2) = \sin(S_1)\cos(S_2)$，$(S_1, S_2)^T \in [0, \pi] \times [0, \pi]$

解　参数：输入维数 $N = 2$；

输出维数 $N_p = 1$；

步长 $h = 0.314$，即分段数 $M_1 = 10, M_2 = 10$

无规则学习：$(S_1, S_2) \Rightarrow f(S_1, S_2) = P$

结果如表 1 所示。

表1 二维正余弦函数的逼近结果

AMS 类型	迭代次数	误差	
		均方差	最大值
CMAC – AMS（2次）	20	0.01346	0.11390
NFI – AMS（2次）	20	0.00055	0.00475
改进的 NFI – AMS（2次）	10	0.00008	0.00300

表1 说明：改进的 NFI – AMS 的学习算法在无规则学习情况下与一般的 AMS 相比，具有较高的逼近精度和快速的收敛速度。

4 结　　论

本文是在牛顿插值公式的基础上，对 NFI – AMS 的学习算法进行了改进，改进的 NFI – AMS 学习算法对非多项式函数可以做到高精度逼近，从理论上讲，这可由著名的 Weierstrass 多项式逼近定理所保证。改进后的联想记忆系统的学习算法不但具有原来学习算法的收敛速度快、学习精度高等优点，而且还具备了 CMAC – AMS 本身具有的局部泛化（generalaization 亦称推广）能力以及对周围信息的收集能力大大增强等等。数值模拟表明，这种改进的 NFI – AMS 在信号处理、模式识别及高精度的实时智能控制等领域具有很大的应用潜力。

参考文献

[1] 邢春峰, 柳重堪：联想记忆系统的学习算法设计（Ⅰ）[J]. 北京联合大学学报, 1998, 12 (3)：38 – 45。

[2] 邢春峰, 柳重堪：一种新的联想记忆系统的学习收敛性（Ⅱ）[J]. 北京联合大学学报, 2000, 14 (4)：48 – 49。

[3] Albus J S. A new approach to manipulator control：the cerebella model articulation controller（CMAC）[J]. Trans ASME Series G J Dynamics System, Measurement &Control, 1975, 97：220 – 227

[4] 颜庆津. 数值分析 [M]. 北京：北京航空航天大学出版社, 1994.

[5] 焦李成. 神经网络理论的应用 [M]. 西安：西安电子科技大学出版社, 1995.

[6] 张立明. 人工神经网络的模型及其应用 [M]. 上海：复旦大学出版社, 1994.

Crystal Structure of $(Bu_4N)_2$ $[Mo_6O_{18}N(o-CH_3C_6H_3OOCCH_2CH_3)]$, $C_{42}H_{83}Mo_6N_3O_{20}$

Zhu Li Zhong Yanfang Cao Xiyan

Source of material

Reference to literature[1], a mixture containing organoimido derivative (1.0mmol), a carboxylic acid (1.5mmol) in anhydrous acetonitrile (15mL) was heated ahead for 15 min, then 1,3-dicyclohexylcarbodiimide (DCC, 2.0mmol in 5mL anhydrous acetonitrile) was added. The reaction mixture was refluxed at a temperature of 85℃ for 7h. After being cooled to room temperature, the tesulting redbrown solution was filtered to remove some yellow-green precipitates. The red-brown filtrate was poured into 40 mL ice-water mixture with stirring continuously. Then the resulting brown solid product was collected by filtration. After being dried, the crude product was dissolved in 15mL acetonitrile for recrystallization, and the product was obtained by slow diffusion of the layered on Et_2O into an acetonitrile solution of the crude product.

Discussion

The title compound $(Bu_4N)_2[Mo_6O_{18}N(o-CH_3C_6H_3OOCCH_2-CH_3)]$ is an esterified product of Lindqvist organoimido derivative $(Bu_4N)_2[Mo_6O_{18}N(o-CH_3C_6H_3OH)]$. There are some typical features of the reported organoimido derivatives in the crystal structure of the title compound[2,3]. For example, the bond length of Mo-N is 1.734(8) Å showing special triple bond character, and the bond angle of Mo-N-C = 173.3(9)° is almost in a straight line. While the bondC(4)-O(19) = 1.41(2) Å is much longer than phemolic hydroxyl of raw material C(4)-O(19) = 1.353(5) Å[3], as the result of acylation.

Table 2 Atomic coordinates and displacement parameters (in Å²)

Atom	Site	x	y	z	U_{iso}
H(11A)	2i	0.9428	0.4347	-0.2285	0.093
H(11B)	2i	1.0645	0.4537	-0.2376	0.093
H(12A)	2i	1.0259	0.2751	-0.2801	0.141
H(12B)	2i	1.1415	0.3176	-0.3012	0.141
H(13A)	2i	1.0199	0.3924	-0.4012	0.298
H(13B)	2i	0.9616	0.4800	-0.3522	0.298
H(14A)	2i	1.1099	0.5281	-0.4343	0.417
H(14B)	2i	1.1793	0.4198	-0.4010	0.417
H(14C)	2i	1.1211	0.5073	-0.3534	0.417
H(15A)	2i	0.9932	0.3569	-0.0499	0.076
H(15B)	2i	1.0345	0.4533	-0.1148	0.076

[Author Introduction] Zhu Li, Beijing Union University; Zhong Yanfang, Hunan University of Science and Technology, School of Chemistry and Chemical Engineering; Cao Xiyan, Hunan University of Science and Technology, School of Chemistry and Chemical Engineering.

续表

Atom	Site	x	y	z	U_{iso}
H(16A)	2i	0.8157	0.4089	−0.0657	0.086
H(16B)	2i	0.8569	0.5051	−0.1316	0.086
H(17A)	2i	0.8594	0.4869	0.0171	0.090
H(17B)	2i	0.9061	0.5811	−0.0484	0.090
H(18A)	2i	0.7254	0.6434	0.0158	0.156
H(18B)	2i	0.6791	0.5514	−0.0001	0.156
H(18C)	2i	0.7258	0.6457	−0.0653	0.156
H(19A)	2i	0.8608	0.2902	−0.1404	0.083
H(19B)	2i	0.9569	0.2005	−0.1686	0.083
H(20A)	2i	0.8959	0.2200	−0.0213	0.117
H(20B)	2i	0.9747	0.1219	−0.0526	0.117
H(21A)	2i	0.8087	0.0987	−0.0856	0.140
H(21B)	2i	0.8155	0.0527	−0.0034	0.140
H(22A)	2i	0.6461	0.1463	−0.0079	0.310
H(22B)	2i	0.6999	0.2506	−0.0544	0.310
H(22C)	2i	0.7062	0.2039	0.0278	0.310
H(23A)	2i	1.1475	0.2064	−0.1792	0.084
H(23B)	2i	1.1242	0.2163	−0.0973	0.084
H(24A)	2i	1.2422	0.3574	−0.2227	0.110
H(24B)	2i	1.2096	0.3797	−0.1426	0.110
H(25A)	2i	1.3463	0.1882	−0.1814	0.136
H(25B)	2i	1.3157	0.2133	−0.1023	0.136
H(26A)	2i	1.4942	0.2556	−0.1675	0.234
H(26B)	2i	1.4143	0.3631	−0.1521	0.234
H(26C)	2i	1.4458	0.3368	−0.2307	0.234
H(27A)	2i	1.3147	0.0061	0.2701	0.134
H(27B)	2i	1.3059	0.1268	0.2245	0.134
H(28A)	2i	1.4994	−0.0265	0.2021	0.211
H(28B)	2i	1.4871	0.0936	0.1550	0.211
H(29A)	2i	1.4539	−0.0583	0.1098	0.249
H(29B)	2i	1.3317	−0.0321	0.1597	0.249
H(30A)	2i	1.3510	0.0738	0.0458	0.357
H(30B)	2i	1.4507	0.1180	0.0547	0.357
H(30C)	2i	1.3296	0.1443	0.1044	0.357
H(31A)	2i	1.2529	0.0640	0.3800	0.140
H(31B)	2i	1.2441	0.1873	0.3396	0.140
H(32A)	2i	1.3605	0.2139	0.4066	0.155
H(32B)	2i	1.3609	0.0917	0.4496	0.155
H(33A)	2i	1.1477	0.1407	0.4954	0.296
H(33B)	2i	1.2176	0.1837	0.5333	0.296
H(35A)	2i	1.5036	0.0414	0.3645	0.132
H(35B)	2i	1.5435	0.0003	0.2908	0.132

续表

Atom	Site	x	y	z	U_{iso}
H (36A)	2i	1.4203	−0.1259	0.3392	0.169
H (36B)	2i	1.3739	−0.0822	0.4123	0.169
H (37A)	2i	1.5834	−0.1293	0.4068	0.280
H (37B)	2i	1.4950	−0.2008	0.4578	0.280
H (38A)	2i	1.6336	−0.2812	0.4310	0.709
H (38B)	2i	1.6454	−0.2335	0.3462	0.709
H (38C)	2i	1.5520	−0.3055	0.3927	0.709
H (39A)	2i	1.5202	0.1815	0.2267	0.150
H (39B)	2i	1.4817	0.2157	0.3027	0.150
H (40A)	2i	1.3583	0.2946	0.1934	0.172
H (40B)	2i	1.3228	0.3308	0.2691	0.172
H (41A)	2i	1.5194	0.3735	0.1588	0.299
H (41B)	2i	1.4848	0.4089	0.2348	0.299
H (42A)	2i	1.4348	0.5547	0.1441	0.354
H (42B)	2i	1.3265	0.5203	0.2040	0.354
H (42C)	2i	1.3615	0.4852	0.1280	0.354
H (34A)	2i	1.0872	0.3210	0.4989	0.680
H (34B)	2i	1.1288	0.3050	0.4173	0.680
H (34C)	2i	1.2052	0.3485	0.4499	0.680
H (7A)	2i	−0.8957	1.8487	0.5179	0.208
H (7B)	2i	−0.9830	1.8704	0.4713	0.208
H (7C)	2i	−0.8854	1.9403	0.4452	0.208
H (3)	2i	−0.7661	1.6902	0.5039	0.157
H (5)	2i	−0.6448	1.5957	0.3153	0.220
H (6)	2i	−0.7596	1.7432	0.2599	0.143
H (9A)	2i	−0.4701	1.3528	0.4586	0.281
H (9B)	2i	−0.4566	1.3488	0.3766	0.281
H (10A)	2i	−0.3077	1.4029	0.3955	0.351
H (10B)	2i	−0.3864	1.5102	0.4124	0.351
H (10C)	2i	−0.3583	1.4851	0.3337	0.351

Table 3 Atomic coordinates and displacement parameters (in Å).

Atom	Site	x	y	z	U_{11}	U_{22}	U_{33}	U_{12}	U_{13}	U_{23}
Mo (1)	2i	−0.98855 (8)	2.00106 (7)	0.28207 (5)	0.0640 (6)	0.0482 (5)	0.0692 (6)	−0.0024 (4)	−0.0231 (5)	−0.0040 (4)
Mo (2)	2i	−0.96592 (8)	2.16642 (8)	0.12076 (5)	0.0560 (6)	0.0662 (6)	0.0571 (5)	−0.0056 (5)	−0.0111 (4)	−0.0107 (4)
Mo (3)	2i	−1.19366 (8)	2.05253 (8)	0.20519 (6)	0.0598 (6)	0.0510 (5)	0.1034 (8)	−0.0115 (5)	−0.0278 (6)	−0.0240 (5)
Mo (4)	2i	−0.99275 (8)	2.25961 (7)	0.26759 (5)	0.0644 (6)	0.0535 (6)	0.0795 (7)	−0.0102 (5)	−0.0312 (5)	−0.0160 (5)
Mo (5)	2i	−1.20131 (8)	2.31512 (7)	0.18878 (5)	0.0538 (6)	0.0454 (5)	0.0736 (6)	−0.0052 (5)	−0.0231 (5)	−0.0078 (4)
Mo (6)	2i	−1.22068 (9)	2.14557 (8)	0.35215 (5)	0.0658 (7)	0.0678 (7)	0.0626 (6)	−0.0084 (5)	−0.0036 (5)	−0.0086 (5)
O (1)	2i	−1.0915 (5)	2.1533 (5)	0.2372 (3)	0.045 (3)	0.044 (3)	0.054 (4)	−0.009 (3)	−0.013 (3)	−0.009 (3)
O (2)	2i	−0.8786 (7)	2.1770 (7)	0.0368 (4)	0.073 (5)	0.101 (6)	0.067 (5)	−0.004 (5)	0.000 (4)	−0.025 (4)
O (3)	2i	−1.2715 (7)	1.9801 (6)	0.1850 (5)	0.076 (5)	0.060 (5)	0.173 (8)	−0.010 (4)	−0.051 (6)	−0.048 (5)

续表

Atom	Site	x	y	z	U_{11}	U_{22}	U_{33}	U_{12}	U_{13}	U_{23}
O (4)	2i	−0.9188 (7)	2.3390 (6)	0.2861 (5)	0.089 (6)	0.069 (5)	0.131 (7)	−0.010 (5)	−0.056 (5)	−0.036 (5)
O (5)	2i	−1.2795 (6)	2.4305 (6)	0.1533 (4)	0.073 (5)	0.053 (4)	0.098 (6)	0.004 (4)	−0.038 (4)	−0.009 (4)
O (6)	2i	−1.3131 (8)	2.1414 (8)	0.4345 (5)	0.098 (7)	0.109 (7)	0.081 (6)	−0.008 (6)	0.011 (5)	−0.018 (5)
O (7)	2i	−1.1108 (6)	2.0249 (6)	0.3699 (4)	0.074 (5)	0.068 (5)	0.067 (4)	−0.011 (4)	−0.009 (4)	−0.003 (4)
O (8)	2i	−0.9241 (6)	2.1152 (6)	0.2989 (4)	0.069 (5)	0.062 (5)	0.079 (5)	−0.007 (4)	−0.033 (4)	−0.013 (4)
O (9)	2i	−1.0903 (6)	1.9422 (5)	0.2511 (4)	0.071 (5)	0.042 (4)	0.106 (6)	−0.011 (4)	−0.024 (4)	−0.018 (4)
O (10)	2i	−0.9033 (6)	2.0355 (6)	0.1807 (4)	0.055 (4)	0.060 (4)	0.074 (5)	0.009 (3)	−0.017 (4)	−0.021 (3)
O (11)	2i	−0.9096 (6)	2.2484 (6)	0.1673 (4)	0.059 (4)	0.062 (4)	0.080 (5)	−0.022 (4)	−0.019 (4)	0.002 (4)
O (12)	2i	−1.2773 (6)	2.0648 (6)	0.3056 (4)	0.052 (4)	0.057 (5)	0.102 (6)	−0.017 (4)	−0.009 (4)	0.003 (4)
O (13)	2i	−1.0736 (7)	2.0782 (6)	0.1195 (4)	0.079 (5)	0.069 (5)	0.082 (5)	0.006 (4)	−0.031 (4)	−0.040 (4)
O (14)	2i	−1.2615 (6)	2.2018 (6)	0.1738 (4)	0.057 (4)	0.061 (4)	0.094 (5)	−0.004 (4)	−0.034 (4)	−0.022 (4)
O (15)	2i	−1.0979 (6)	2.3691 (5)	0.2196 (4)	0.063 (4)	0.047 (4)	0.088 (5)	−0.008 (3)	−0.033 (4)	−0.014 (3)
O (16)	2i	−1.1147 (7)	2.2373 (6)	0.3523 (4)	0.082 (5)	0.069 (5)	0.072 (5)	−0.004 (4)	−0.022 (4)	−0.025 (4)
O (17)	2i	−1.0794 (6)	2.2893 (6)	0.1049 (4)	0.066 (5)	0.059 (4)	0.071 (4)	−0.010 (4)	−0.026 (4)	−0.002 (3)
O (18)	2i	−1.2822 (6)	2.2785 (6)	0.2903 (4)	0.057 (4)	0.061 (4)	0.083 (5)	0.004 (4)	−0.013 (4)	−0.022 (4)
N (1)	2i	−0.9043 (8)	1.8865 (7)	0.3178 (5)	0.067 (6)	0.043 (5)	0.086 (6)	0.003 (4)	−0.025 (5)	−0.001 (4)
N (2)	2i	1.0166 (8)	0.3252 (6)	−0.1516 (4)	0.085 (7)	0.046 (5)	0.065 (5)	−0.017 (5)	−0.024 (5)	−0.013 (4)
N (3)	2i	1.396 (1)	0.100 (1)	0.3004 (7)	0.070 (7)	0.14 (1)	0.120 (9)	−0.039 (8)	−0.034 (7)	−0.018 (8)
C (11)	2i	1.018 (1)	0.3980 (9)	−0.2285 (6)	0.11 (1)	0.065 (7)	0.062 (7)	−0.015 (7)	−0.027 (7)	−0.012 (6)
C (12)	2i	1.061 (2)	0.340 (1)	−0.2918 (7)	0.19 (2)	0.08 (1)	0.075 (9)	−0.02 (1)	−0.02 (1)	−0.028 (8)
C (13)	2i	1.029 (3)	0.429 (2)	−0.366 (1)	0.49 (6)	0.17 (2)	0.08 (1)	−0.18 (3)	0.05 (2)	−0.05 (1)
C (14)	2i	1.115 (4)	0.474 (3)	−0.390 (2)	0.41 (6)	0.24 (4)	0.15 (3)	−0.03 (4)	−0.01 (3)	−0.08 (3)
C (15)	2i	0.9829 (9)	0.4004 (8)	−0.0974 (6)	0.075 (8)	0.050 (6)	0.075 (7)	−0.013 (6)	−0.026 (6)	−0.020 (5)
C (16)	2i	0.869 (1)	0.4602 (9)	−0.0850 (6)	0.070 (8)	0.068 (7)	0.082 (8)	−0.001 (6)	−0.025 (6)	−0.027 (6)
C (17)	2i	0.850 (1)	0.5325 (9)	−0.0301 (6)	0.087 (9)	0.066 (7)	0.071 (7)	−0.011 (7)	−0.010 (6)	−0.023 (6)
C (18)	2i	0.735 (1)	0.599 (1)	−0.0189 (7)	0.10 (1)	0.11 (1)	0.10 (1)	0.007 (9)	−0.024 (9)	−0.049 (9)
C (19)	2i	0.931 (1)	0.2470 (8)	−0.1332 (6)	0.081 (8)	0.049 (6)	0.085 (8)	−0.012 (6)	−0.021 (7)	−0.027 (6)
C (20)	2i	0.909 (1)	0.176 (1)	−0.0573 (7)	0.10 (1)	0.085 (9)	0.11 (1)	−0.053 (9)	−0.016 (8)	−0.005 (8)
C (21)	2i	0.809 (2)	0.119 (1)	−0.0412 (9)	0.13 (2)	0.11 (1)	0.12 (1)	−0.05 (1)	−0.02 (1)	−0.03 (1)
C (22)	2i	0.707 (2)	0.185 (2)	−0.017 (1)	0.13 (2)	0.27 (3)	0.24 (3)	−0.07 (2)	0.04 (2)	−0.16 (2)
C (23)	2i	1.130 (1)	0.2581 (8)	−0.1477 (6)	0.075 (8)	0.047 (6)	0.094 (8)	−0.013 (6)	−0.017 (6)	−0.025 (6)
C (24)	2i	1.228 (1)	0.323 (1)	−0.1704 (8)	0.09 (1)	0.076 (9)	0.10 (1)	−0.017 (8)	0.002 (8)	−0.032 (7)
C (25)	2i	1.330 (1)	0.246 (1)	−0.155 (1)	0.068 (9)	0.09 (1)	0.18 (2)	−0.008 (8)	−0.02 (1)	−0.06 (1)
C (26)	2i	1.430 (1)	0.306 (2)	−0.179 (1)	0.09 (1)	0.15 (2)	0.25 (2)	−0.03 (1)	−0.03 (1)	−0.10 (2)
C (27)	2i	1.357 (1)	0.066 (1)	0.2446 (9)	0.08 (1)	0.13 (1)	0.13 (1)	−0.02 (1)	−0.02 (1)	−0.03 (1)
C (28)	2i	1.447 (2)	0.033 (2)	0.183 (1)	0.11 (2)	0.30 (3)	0.16 (2)	−0.02 (2)	−0.04 (1)	−0.12 (2)
C (29)	2i	1.401 (2)	−0.003 (3)	0.133 (2)	0.15 (2)	0.28 (4)	0.17 (2)	0.02 (2)	−0.05 (2)	−0.01 (2)
C (30)	2i	1.382 (2)	0.090 (3)	0.081 (2)	0.16 (2)	0.31 (4)	0.29 (4)	−0.05 (3)	−0.11 (3)	−0.07 (3)
C (31)	2i	1.293 (1)	0.126 (1)	0.3611 (8)	0.070 (9)	0.18 (2)	0.11 (1)	−0.03 (1)	−0.015 (8)	−0.04 (1)
C (32)	2i	1.317 (2)	0.154 (2)	0.425 (1)	0.11 (1)	0.14 (2)	0.13 (1)	−0.01 (1)	−0.03 (1)	−0.04 (1)
C (33)	2i	1.201 (3)	0.190 (2)	0.487 (1)	0.21 (3)	0.16 (2)	0.30 (4)	−0.06 (2)	−0.02 (3)	0.05 (3)
C (35)	2i	1.479 (1)	0.014 (1)	0.3313 (9)	0.068 (9)	0.13 (1)	0.14 (1)	−0.014 (9)	−0.035 (9)	−0.03 (1)

续表

Atom	Site	x	y	z	U_{11}	U_{22}	U_{33}	U_{12}	U_{13}	U_{23}
C(36)	2i	1.440(2)	−0.094(2)	0.373(1)	0.10(1)	0.16(2)	0.16(2)	−0.04(1)	−0.03(1)	−0.01(1)
C(37)	2i	1.534(3)	−0.177(2)	0.406(2)	0.22(3)	0.10(2)	0.34(4)	−0.00(2)	−0.11(3)	0.05(2)
C(38)	2i	1.593(5)	−0.252(4)	0.394(3)	0.49(9)	0.39(7)	0.6(1)	0.22(7)	−0.26(8)	−0.35(8)
C(39)	2i	1.455(1)	0.200(2)	0.265(1)	0.08(1)	0.16(2)	0.15(1)	−0.03(1)	−0.03(1)	−0.03(1)
C(40)	2i	1.387(2)	0.308(2)	0.231(1)	0.09(1)	0.14(2)	0.17(2)	−0.01(1)	−0.03(1)	0.00(1)
C(41)	2i	1.456(2)	0.396(2)	0.198(2)	0.12(2)	0.15(2)	0.43(4)	−0.06(2)	−0.13(2)	0.11(3)
C(42)	2i	1.389(2)	0.498(2)	0.166(2)	0.20(3)	0.17(2)	0.40(4)	−0.05(2)	−0.16(3)	−0.07(3)
C(34)	2i	1.151(5)	0.300(5)	0.461(2)	0.8(1)	0.47(7)	0.25(4)	−0.41(9)	−0.23(6)	0.08(5)
C(1)	2i	−0.835(1)	1.802(1)	0.3517(8)	0.074(8)	0.066(8)	0.10(1)	0.003(7)	−0.041(7)	−0.013(7)
C(2)	2i	−0.834(1)	1.789(1)	0.4251(8)	0.078(9)	0.066(8)	0.11(1)	0.002(7)	−0.038(8)	−0.010(8)
C(7)	2i	−0.906(2)	1.869(2)	0.4688(8)	0.12(1)	0.19(2)	0.09(1)	0.02(1)	−0.03(1)	−0.03(1)
C(3)	2i	−0.764(2)	1.701(2)	0.454(1)	0.14(2)	0.10(1)	0.16(2)	0.01(1)	−0.10(1)	0.00(1)
C(4)	2i	−0.697(2)	1.634(2)	0.418(2)	0.16(2)	0.09(1)	0.36(4)	0.06(1)	−0.17(3)	−0.07(2)
C(5)	2i	−0.693(2)	1.645(2)	0.342(2)	0.10(2)	0.10(2)	0.39(4)	0.04(1)	−0.10(2)	−0.11(2)
C(6)	2i	−0.762(1)	1.732(1)	0.310(1)	0.09(1)	0.09(1)	0.17(2)	0.028(9)	−0.02(1)	−0.07(1)
O(19)	2i	−0.625(2)	1.551(1)	0.453(1)	0.24(2)	0.102(9)	0.46(3)	0.08(1)	−0.24(2)	−0.12(1)
O(20)	2i	−0.6256	1.431	0.3831	0.31	0.095	0.452	−0.017	−0.229	−0.019
C(8)	2i	−0.5792	1.4699	0.4107	0.364	0.087	0.266	−0.009	−0.247	−0.016
C(9)	2i	−0.4673	1.3975	0.4093	0.191	0.108	0.345	0.025	−0.119	0.065
C(10)	2i	−0.372(2)	1.454(2)	0.386(2)	0.30(4)	0.10(2)	0.37(4)	0.01(2)	−0.17(3)	−0.08(2)

Acknowledgments. The Project was supported by the Natural Science Foundationof Hunan Province of China (grant no: 07JJY5005) and the DoctorFoundation of Hunan University of Science and Technology (E50901).

References

[1] Zhu, L.; Zhu, Y.; Meng, X.; Hao, J.; Li, Q.; Wei, Y.; Lin, Y.: DCC - Assisted Esterification of a Polyoxometalate - Functionalized Phenol with Carboxylic Acids (DCC: Dicyclohexylcarbodiimide). Chem. Eur. J. 14 (2008) 10923 - 10927.

[2] Wei, Y.; Xu, B.; Barnes, C. L.; Peng, Z.: An Efficient and Convenient Reaction Protocol to Organoimido Derivatives of Polyoxometalates. J. Am. Chem. Soc. 123 (2001) 4083 - 4084.

[3] Roesner, R. A.; McGrath, S. C.; Brockman, J. T.; Moll, J. D.; West, D. X.; Swearingen, J. K.; Castineiras, A.: Mono - and di - functional aromatic amines with p - alkoxysubstituents as novel arylimido ligands for the hexamolybdate ion. Inorganica Chimica Acta 342 (2003) 37 - 47.

[4] Sheldrick, G. M.: A short history of SHELX. Acta Crystallogr. A64 (2008) 112 - 122.

白藜芦醇诱导 Raji 细胞死亡的自噬途径研究

劳凤学

肿瘤细胞死亡可通过多种途径，近年针对肿瘤治疗方案的设计多集中在克服肿瘤细胞的抵抗力和触发肿瘤细胞凋亡方面。然而，许多肿瘤细胞经历的是非凋亡（non-apoptosis）死亡，例如自噬（autophagy）死亡等。自噬是一种特殊的细胞死亡方式，近年吸引了越来越多细胞生物学家的注意。白血病在我国人口中的发病率为 2-4/10 万人，是导致恶性肿瘤死亡的主要疾病之一。其中急性白血病占 35 岁以下人类肿瘤死亡病因中的首位。但目前治疗白血病所用的药物多为重金属制剂，药物副作用大，一些患者经过几个疗程后难以持续使用。因此寻找低毒高效的死亡诱导剂尤显迫切。

白藜芦醇是从多种葡萄属植物中提取的多酚类化合物。它具有引起细胞周期阻滞和诱导细胞凋亡等多种生物学功能。近几年也有白藜芦醇诱导肿瘤细胞自噬的报导。但它对 Burkitt B 淋巴瘤 Raji 细胞作用未见明确报导。本研究主要通过白藜芦醇对 Burkitt B 淋巴瘤 Raji 细胞的增殖抑制、死亡诱导，探讨其诱导肿瘤细胞死亡途径，分析白藜芦醇治疗白血病的可能作用。

1 材料与方法

1.1 材料

Burkitt B 淋巴瘤 Raji 细胞株、Jurkat 细胞株购自北京协和医科大学细胞库；白藜芦醇、MDC（Monodansylcadaverine）、MTT、小牛血清购自 Sigma 公司；RPMI-1640 培养基购自 Invitrogen 公司；兔抗 Caspase-3 多克隆抗体、兔抗细胞色素 c 多克隆抗体、兔抗 β-actin 多克隆抗体购自 Cell Signaling 公司；z-VAD-fmk、z-DEVD-fmk、z-LETD-fmk、z-LEHD-fmk 购自 BD Biosciences Pharmingen 公司。BX51 型 Olympus 倒置荧光显微镜，日本 Olympus 公司；JEM-100CXII 型透射电子显微镜，日本电子光学公司（JEOL）；LSR 流式细胞仪，美国 BD 公司。

1.2 细胞培养

Raji 细胞株、Jurkat 细胞株在含 10% 新生牛血清的 RPMI 1640 培养基中，5% CO_2、37℃ 培养。细胞生长至对数生长期用于实验。

1.3 Raji 细胞增殖测定

取对数期生长的 Raji 细胞分组加药，加药的细胞初始浓度 $2×10^5$ 个/ml。处理组分别加入含 0.1、0.15、0.2、0.25、0.3mmol/L 终浓度的白藜芦醇，另设阴性对照、空白对照，每组设 3 复孔，培养 48h 后，常规 MTT 法检测，全自动酶标仪读取波长 570nm 的 OD 值，计算细胞生长抑制率，求出半数抑制浓度 IC50。测生长曲线则设空白孔和加药孔（半数抑制浓度 0.23mmol/L），分别在 12h、24h、36h、48h 检测 570nm 的波长，计算细胞生长抑制率，绘制生长曲线。

抑制率 =（1-实验组平均 OD 值/对照组平均 OD 值）×100%

1.4 Raji 细胞 DNA 片段化检测

用白藜芦醇（终浓度 0.23mmol/L）处理 Raji 细胞，孵育 8h、16h、24h、36h、48h，处理 Jurkat（0.18mmol/L，48h）作对照，分别收获细胞，冷 PBS 洗 2 次；加裂解液［20mmol/L EDTA，100mmol/L Tris-HCI，pH8.0，0.8%（w/v）SDS］，RNaseA，37℃ 孵育 2h，蛋白酶 K 37℃ 过夜，1.8% 琼脂糖凝胶电泳，EB 染色并照相。

［作者简介］劳凤学，北京市生物活性物质和功能食品重点实验室；北京联合大学应用文理学院。

1.5 Raji 细胞的 caspase 活性的检测

用白藜芦醇处理 Raji 细胞（终浓度 0.23mmol/L），孵育 12h、24h，分别收获细胞（同时设对照组），1×10^7 的细胞用 PBS 洗两次，裂解液（MOPS 20mmol/L，NaCl 0.15mol/L，NP-40 1%，去氧胆酸盐 1%，EDTA 1mmol/L，1mmol/L PMSF，1.5μg/ml Pepstatin A）裂解（冰浴）30min，离心，上清贮存在 -80℃。调整样品至相同的蛋白浓度，12% 的聚丙烯酰胺凝胶电泳，半干转印法转印至 PVDF 膜上。PVDF 膜用 BSA 封闭液室温封闭 1.5h，TBST 洗膜 3 次，然后将 PVDF 膜孵育于含兔抗 Caspase-3 多克隆抗体缓冲液中，4℃过夜。TBST 洗膜三次后，在含有辣根过氧化物酶标记的二抗缓冲液中孵育 1h，洗膜后 DAB 显色，照相。

用 z-VAD-fmk（75μmol/L）、z-LETD-fmk（50μmol/L）、z-LEHD-fmk（50μmol/L）分别处理 Raji 细胞 1h，再分别加入 0.23mmol/L 终浓度的白藜芦醇，孵育 24h、收获细胞（同时设对照组），PBS 洗两次，PI 染色，流式细胞仪检测。

1.6 Raji 细胞透射电镜观察

用白藜芦醇（终浓度 0.23mmol/L）处理 Raji 细胞 48h，冷 PBS 洗 2 次，4% 戊二醛固定，2 000r/min 离心 10 min，加入 2% 琼脂糖搅匀，冷却后切块，1% 四氧化锇固定，醋酸双氧铀——柠檬酸铅双重染色，透射电镜观察。

1.7 Raji 细胞荧光显微镜检测

参照 Daniela 等人的方法，用白藜芦醇（终浓度 0.23mmol/L）处理 Raji 细胞，孵育 48h 收获细胞，PBS 洗 1 次；细胞在 37℃ 含 0.05 mmol/L MDC 的 PBS 缓冲液中孵育 10min。收集细胞，用 PBS 洗 4 次，立即用倒置荧光显微镜观察，激发波长 380-420nm，照相。记数在 200 个细胞中，MDC 阳性细胞数，重复三次实验，计算 MDC 阳性细胞的百分率。

1.8 亚细胞结构分级分离及细胞色素 c 的免疫印记检测

用白藜芦醇分别处理 Raji 细胞（终浓度 0.23mmol/L）和 Jurkat 细胞（终浓度 0.18mmol/L），孵育 24h 分别收集细胞（同时设对照组），冷 PBS 洗两次，用缓冲液 A（20 mmol/L HEPES-KOH（pH 7.5），10 mmol/L KCl，1.5 mmol/L MgCl2，1 mmol/L EDTA，1 mmol/L EGTA，1 mmol/L DTT，and 0.1 mmol/L phenylmethylsulfonyl fluoride）悬浮细胞，用玻璃匀浆器研磨（抽拉）15 次，4℃ 1000g 离心 10min。收集含线粒体的上清液，4℃ 12,000g 离心 30min。收集上清液，作为细胞质成分，线粒体富集成分（沉淀）用缓冲液 A 洗一次，溶解在含有蛋白酶抑制剂的裂解缓冲液，贮存于 -80℃。

调整样品至相同的蛋白浓度，分别取含等量的蛋白质（30μg）的样品，β-actin 作为细胞质成分的内参照，用 12% 的聚丙烯酰胺凝胶电泳，半干转印法转印至 PVDF 膜上。将 PVDF 膜孵育于含抗细胞色素 c 兔多克隆抗体缓冲液中，在含有辣根过氧化物酶标记的二抗缓冲液中孵育 1h，洗膜后 DAB 显色，照相。

1.9 Cathepsin D 免疫印记检测

用白藜芦醇分别处理 Raji 细胞（终浓度 0.23mmol/L）和 Jurkat 细胞（终浓度 0.18mmol/L），孵育 12h、24h、36h、48h 分别收获细胞（同时设对照组），1×10^7 的细胞用 PBS 洗两次，裂解液（MOPS 20mmol/L，NaCl 0.15mol/L，NP-40 1%，去氧胆酸盐 1%，EDTA 1mmol/L，1mmol/L PMSF，1.5g/ml Pepstatin A）裂解（冰浴）30min，离心，上清贮存在 -80℃。调整样品至相同的蛋白浓度，12% 的聚丙烯酰胺凝胶电泳，将 PVDF 膜孵育于含抗 cathepsin D 兔多克隆抗体缓冲液中，在含有辣根过氧化物酶标记的二抗缓冲液中孵育 1h，洗膜后 DAB 显色，照相。

2 结 果

2.1 Raji 细胞的增殖抑制

不同剂量白藜芦醇的处理组，对 Raji 细胞均有抑制作用，0.1、0.15、0.2、0.25、0.3mmol/L 处理组的抑制率分别为 21.7%、28.6%、37.2%、49.2%、64.4%，与对照组比较有显著性差异（$P<0.02$），且随白藜芦醇浓度增加，抑制作用逐渐增强。0.23mmol/L 白藜芦醇处理组，随培养时间的延长，抑制作用亦逐渐增强（图1）。

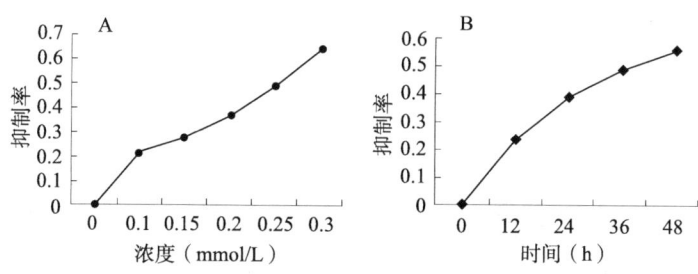

图 1　Raji 细胞生长曲线

A. 不同浓度白藜芦醇处理组　B. 0.23mmol/L 白藜芦醇处理组

2.2　Raji 细胞的 DNA 片段化检测

白藜芦醇处理 Raji 细胞 8h、16h、24h、36h、48h 均未见 DNA "梯形" 图谱，而对照组 Jurkat 细胞，处理 48h 可见见 DNA "梯形" 图谱（图2）。

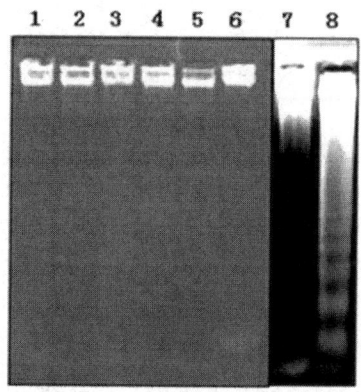

图 2　琼脂糖凝胶检测白藜芦醇诱导 Raji 细胞中染色体 DNA 断裂的电泳图谱

Raji 细胞（1. 正常细胞；2. 处理 8h；3. 处理 16h；4. 处理 24h；5. 处理 36h；
6. 处理 48h）；Jurkat 细胞（7. 正常细胞；8. 处理 48h）

2.3　Raji 细胞的 caspase-3 活化检测结果

用 0.23mmol/L 的白藜芦醇处理 Raji 细胞 12h、24h 后，未检测到 caspase 3 活化的片段。

用 z-VAD-fmk、z-LETD-fmk、z-LEHD-fmk 处理 Raji 细胞后，再分别加入 0.23mmol/L 终浓度的白藜芦醇处理 24h，经检测几种 caspase 抑制剂均不能明显减少黎芦醇诱导的 Raji 细胞死亡，单独白黎芦醇诱导细胞死亡比率为 48.92%，而 z-VAD-fmk、z-LETD-fmk 和 z-LEHD-fmk 处理后的白黎芦醇诱导的死细胞比率分别为 31.5%、41.22% 和 36.6%（图3）。

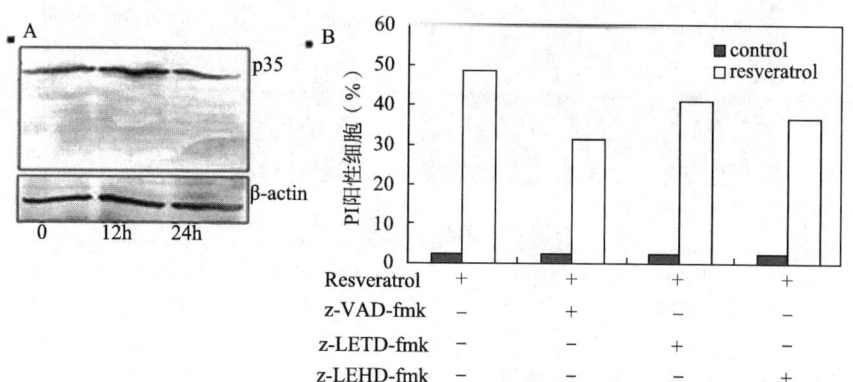

图 3　白黎芦醇诱导 Raji 细胞死亡的 caspase 活性分析

Casapase-3 活化的免疫印记分析；B. Caspase 抑制剂对白黎芦醇诱导 Raji 细胞死亡的影响

2.4 Raji 细胞的透射电镜观察

白黎芦醇处理组可见 Raji 细胞出现双层膜结构包围的细胞质或细胞器的结构，形成自噬小泡和空泡（图4）。

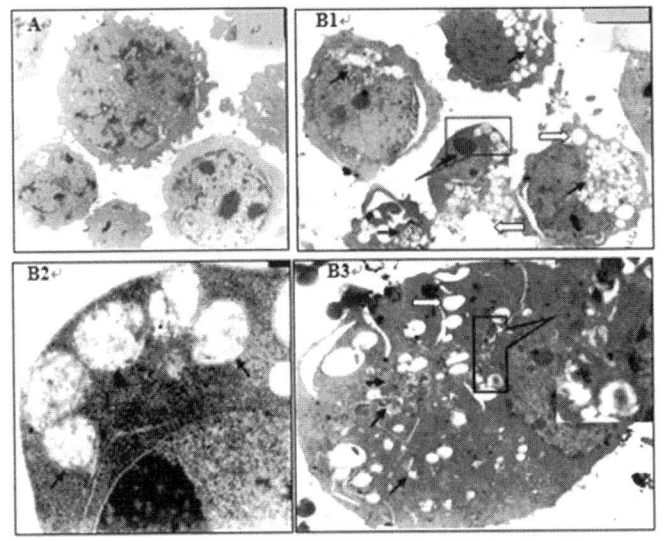

图4 白黎芦醇诱导 Raji 细胞株自吞噬死亡的透射电镜形态

A. 正常细胞；B. 白黎芦醇处理48h 的细胞；
B1（×2700）；B2（×14000）；B3（×4000）. （自吞噬小泡或自吞噬体→，空泡⇨）

2.5 Raji 细胞的荧光显微镜检测

白黎芦醇处理组的 Raji 细胞荧光显微镜观察，MDC 标记的阳性的细胞（即小囊泡的数量和分布面积都明显增加细胞）数量明显增加，未处理的 Raji 细胞只有很少的细胞呈 MDC 阳性（图5）。

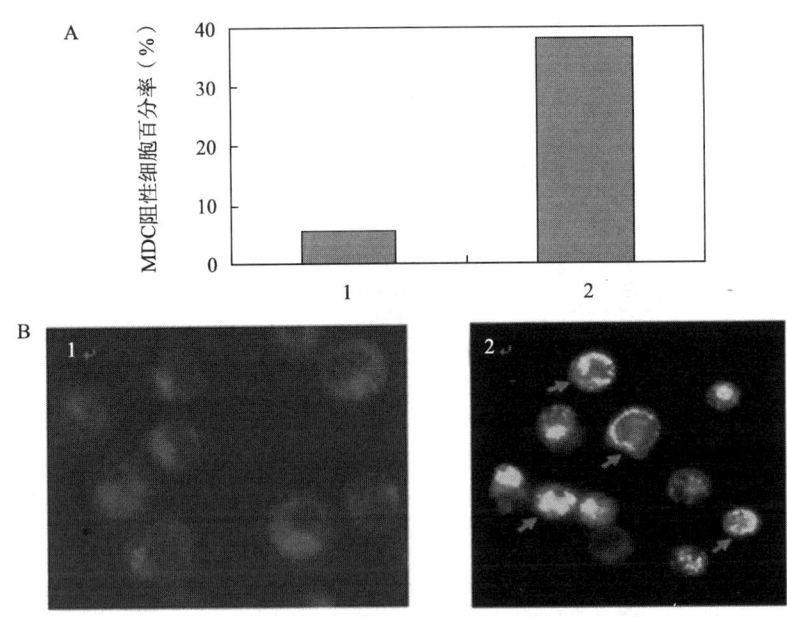

图5 白黎芦醇诱导 Raji 细胞株的自吞噬

A. Raji 细胞自吞噬的定量1 未处理组；2. 白黎芦醇处理48h 组；
B. MDC 染色的光镜照片1 未处理组；2. 白黎芦醇处理48h 组；MDC 阳性细胞（▲）

2.6 Raji 细胞线粒体释放细胞色素 c 的检测

分别取细胞质和线粒体片段成分的等量蛋白质（30μg）进行 Western blot 分析，β-actin 作为细胞质的内参照，结果显示如图6，在 Raji 和 Jurkat 细胞中，线粒体均释放细胞色素 c，但 Raji 细胞质中细胞色素 c 的含量明显减少。提示白黎芦醇作用于线粒体只活化少量的线粒体。

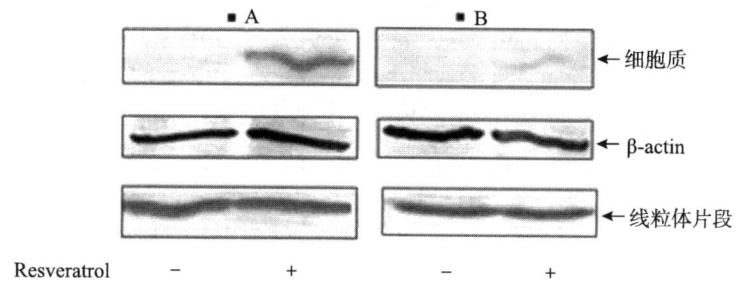

图6　白黎芦醇诱导 Raj、Jurkati 细胞死亡引起线粒体细胞色素 c 的释放
A. Jurkat 细胞；B. Raji 细胞

2.7　Raji 细胞 Cathepsin D 的 Western blot 检测结果

用 0.23mmol/L 的白黎芦醇处理 Raji 细胞后，可检测到 32kDa 的 Cathepsin D 的形成，随白黎芦醇处理时间的延长，含量逐渐减少。白黎芦醇处理 Jurkat 细胞细胞后，随白黎芦醇处理时间的延长，cathepsin D 的含量变化不大。β-actin 作为内参照（见图7）。

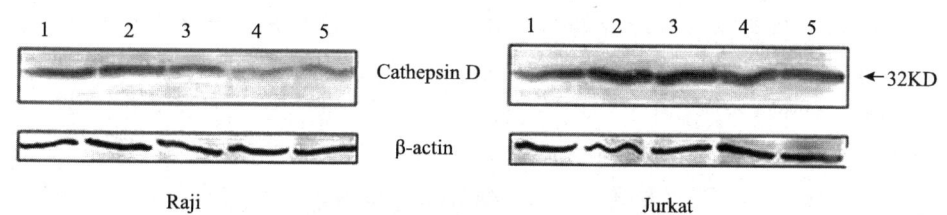

图7　Western blot 分析 Cathepsin D 在 Raji 细胞表达水平
1. 未处理组，2. 处理12h；3. 处理24h；4. 处理36h；5. 处理48h

讨　论

肿瘤细胞自噬与凋亡的死亡形式、机制不同。自噬表现为自噬体和自噬溶酶体的形成，高电子密度的膜状自噬小泡形成，鞘磷脂螺旋状，多泡体和细胞器被吞噬等现象。白黎芦醇是一种植物抗毒素，在植物体中具有抗病原体感染的功能[1]；白黎芦醇在动物体内、体外具有抗肿瘤作用[2-4]，白黎芦醇抑制 Jurkat 细胞增殖和诱导细胞凋亡的功能已经得到证实[5]，国内外许多学者开始致力于此化合物及类似结构物质的研究工作，希望通过阐明白黎芦醇的作用机理，使其有效的用于疾病治疗，尤其是对肿瘤的治疗。

本研究为了探索白黎芦醇诱导肿瘤细胞死亡的作用机制，选择了白血病细胞株，即 Burkitt 淋巴瘤 Raji 细胞株作为实验材料。实验首先观察了白黎芦醇对 Raji 细胞株的作用。数据显示，白黎芦醇可以抑制白血病细胞 Raji 细胞株的增殖，具有明显的时间、剂量依赖关系。但 Raji 细胞经白黎芦醇处理后，细胞染色体未见明显的凝集和边缘化，细胞核变化不明显，在细胞死亡的后期之前，多数核是完整的。且通过 DNA 片段化分析，未见梯状 DNA 产生，这些数据提示白黎芦醇可能通过活化非凋亡细胞死亡程序诱导 Raji 细胞株死亡。

自噬是一种生理机制，通过吞噬体包围细胞内多余细胞质和细胞器，使其酶解而自我保护或细胞自杀式死亡的一种特殊形式[6]。自噬细胞形态学上最主要的特征是细胞内出现大量的双层或多层膜的细胞质囊泡结构。本研究通过透射电镜检测发现，白黎芦醇处理 Raji 细胞后，细胞出现双层膜结构包围的细胞质或细胞器的结构，形成大量的自噬小泡和空泡，这些超微形态表现与自噬特征一致，说明白黎芦醇可以通过诱导自噬途径诱导 Raji 细胞死亡。

为进一步证实白黎芦醇通过自噬途径引起 Raji 细胞死亡，采用 MDC 染色法[7]，显示 Raji 细胞株的吞噬小泡（AVs）的形成。实验通过分析 MDC 阳性细胞，即小囊泡的数量和分布面积都明显增加细胞的百分率，来检测白黎芦醇诱导 Raji 细胞自噬死亡的作用。MDC 阳性细胞的数量在白黎芦醇处理48h 后显著增加，可达到40%。用三苯氧胺处理 MCF-7 细胞、塞来考昔衍生物 OSU-03012 处理 Huh7 细胞，均显示了诱导自噬现象[8,9]。以上数据进一步证明白黎芦醇通过自噬途径诱导 Raji 细胞死亡。

细胞凋亡和自噬死亡是细胞死亡的两种不同途径，在胚胎发育，机体的生长发育及非增殖组织的线粒体再循环等正常生理过程均可发生。以往的报导显示，两种途径细胞死亡的发生是由不同的死亡信号如营养因子的剥夺，药物或激素处理所触发，而本研究数据显示，同一种物质——白黎芦醇可诱导 Jurkat 细胞和 Raji 细胞通过凋亡[5]和自噬不同途径死亡，显示细胞凋亡和自吞噬死亡的机制在某些环节上是相互联系的。

Lemasters[10]等认为自噬可以阻断凋亡，通过清除损伤的线粒体而阻止促凋亡线粒体因子释放到细胞质。这个信号从线粒体损伤到刺激自噬的传导，可能与 mTor 有关，其蛋白片段伴随线粒体外膜存在，当渗透性应激时，能诱导线粒体异常。线粒体损伤诱导自噬细胞死亡，可能发生在线粒体为基础的凋亡不明显或被 caspase 抑制剂阻滞的条件下。Raji 细胞具有抗化学药物诱导凋亡特征，白黎芦醇处理 Raji 细胞，能引起细胞线粒体细胞色素 c 的释放，但与 Jurkat 细胞比较，释放到细胞质的细胞色素 c 量明显减少，可能白黎芦醇引起的线粒体损伤较小，不能引起下游物质包括 caspase-3 的有效活化，而通过旁路途径，即自噬途径诱导死亡。这个结果与 Lemasters 等提出的假设一致。

Cathepsin D（Cath D）是凋亡上游的细胞色素 c 释放的调节者，在调节细胞死亡方面有重要作用[11,12]。为进一步探讨组织蛋白酶 D 在凋亡和自噬两种途径中的作用，本研究检测了在两种死亡模型中组织蛋白酶 D 的变化情况。数据显示，在白黎芦醇诱导 Raji 自噬死亡过程中，Cath D 表达水平下调。而白黎芦醇诱导 Jurkat 细胞凋亡过程中，Cath D 表达水平变化不明显。这种表达的不同，与细胞种类有关。可能由于白黎芦醇处理 Raji 细胞，Cath D 表达水平下调，对线粒体损伤较小而引起的自噬死亡途径。可见，Cath D 表达水平在白黎芦醇诱导 Jurkat 细胞凋亡和诱导 Raji 细胞自噬死亡的分子机制方面存在差异。这也进一步说明白黎芦醇诱导两种白血病细胞死亡的作用机制存在差异。同时提示 Cath D 基因与自噬死亡途径有关

总之，该研究证实了白黎芦醇对白血病治疗新的活性，即能够诱导自噬，为白黎芦醇临床治疗肿瘤提供理论参考，也为进一步从事细胞自噬工作提供可靠的实验素材。

参考文献

[1] Fremont L. Biological effects of resveratrol. Life Sci, 2000 (66)：663-673.

[2] Banerjee S, Bueso-Ramos C, Aggarwal B. Suppression of 7, 12-dimethylbenz (a) anthracene-induced mammary carcinogenesis in rats by resveratrol: role of nuclear factor-B, cyclooxygenase 2, and matrix metalloprotease 9. Cancer Res, 2002 (62)：4945-4954.

[3] Li ZG, Hong T, Shimada Y, et al. Suppression of N-nitrosomethylbenzylamine (NMBA)-induced esophageal tumorigenesis in F344 rats by resveratrol. Carcinogenesis (Lond.), 2002 (23)：1531-1536.

[4] Schneider Y, Duranton B, Gosse F, et al. Resveratrol inhibits intestinal tumorigenesis and modulates host-defense-related gene expression in an animal model of human familial adenomatous polyposis. Nutr. Cancer, 2001 (39)：102-107.

[5] 劳凤学，冯骥良，柳忠辉，等。白黎芦醇抑制急性 T 淋巴母细胞白血病 Jurkat 细胞增殖、引起 S 期阻滞和诱导凋亡的研究。吉林大学学报（医学版），2006, 32 (2)：289-292

[6] Reggiori F & Klionsky DJ. Autophagy in the eukaryotic cell. Eukaryot. Cell, 2002 (1)：11-21.

[7] Biederbick A, Kern HF, Elsasser HP. Monodansylcadaverine (MDC) is a specific in vivo marker for autophagic vacuoles. Eur. J. Cell Biol, 1995 (66)：3-14.

[8] Bursch W, Ellinger A, Gerner C, et al. Programmed cell death (PCD). Apoptosis, autophagic PCD, or others? . Ann. NY Acad. Sci, 2000 (926)：1-12.

[9] Ming Gao, Pei Yen Yeh, Yen-Shen Lu, et al. OSU-03012, a Novel Celecoxib Derivative, Induces Reactive Oxygen Species-Related Autophagy in Hepatocellular Carcinoma. Cancer Res, 2008 (68)：9348-57

[10] Jia L, Dourmashkin RR, Allen PD. et al. Inhibition of autophagy abrogates tumour necrosis factor induced apoptosis in human T-lymphoblastic leukaemic cells. Brit. J. Haematol, 1997 (98): 673-685.

[11] Jaattela M, Cande C, and Kroemer G. Lysosomes and mitochondria in the commitment to apoptosis: a potential role for cathepsin D and AIF. Cell Death Differ, 2004 (11): 135-136.

[12] Yin L, Stearns R, and Gonzalez-Flecha B. Lysosomal and. mitochondrial pathways in H_2O_2. -induced. apoptosis of alveolar type II cells. J. Cell. Biochem, 2005 (94): 433-445.

超临界 CO_2 密度对全反式番茄红素吸光系数的影响

何强强　惠伯棣　宫　平

番茄红素（lycopene）是一种胡萝卜素（carotene），系统命名为 ψ,ψ - 胡萝卜素（ψ,ψ - carotene），分子式为 $C_{40}H_{56}$，相对分子质量为 536.85。番茄红素的分子由多聚烯链构成，含 11 个共轭双键和 2 个非共轭双键，末端无芳香环，为开环结构。由于分子中存在多个双键，番茄红素普遍存在几何异构现象。天然来源的番茄红素主要以全反式（allE - isomer）的形式存在（图 1），是最稳定的一种构型。在目前的研究工作中，反式异构体的性质是关注的重点[1-4]。

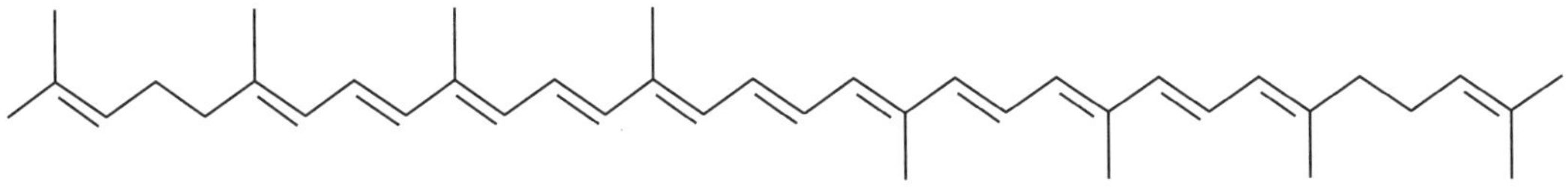

图1　全反式番茄红素的分子结构

超临界流体是物质处于临界压力和临界温度之上的一种状态。超临界流体技术（包括超临界流体萃取和色谱）已被大量应用于类胡萝卜素的制备和分析上[5-6]。由我国新疆红帆生物科技有限公司研发的世界上第一条应用超临界 CO_2 为第一萃取溶媒从番茄果皮中萃取天然番茄红素的生产线在我国新疆维吾尔自治区巴音郭楞蒙古自治州已经运行了 6 年[7]。以番茄红素为功能因子的保健食品和食品添加剂产品在我国市场上呈畅销趋势。在这些应用中，类胡萝卜素的检测主要依靠其在紫外—可见区的吸收光谱（电子吸收光谱）。因此，研究超临界流体溶媒对类胡萝卜素（尤其是番茄红素）电子吸收光谱的影响具有十分现实的意义。

这一领域的研究始于 20 世纪 90 年代初期，由惠伯棣等[8]报道。到目前为止，惠伯棣等[1,2,6,8]所报道的结果包括：1）在超临界 CO_2 中，番茄红素和 β - 胡萝卜素的最大吸收波长较其在有机溶剂中的小；2）二者的最大吸收波长与 CO_2 密度呈正相关；3）二者的跃迁能与 CO_2 的极化率呈负线性相关[9]。在方法上，由惠伯棣等进行的番茄红素在超临界 CO_2 流体中电子吸收光谱的研究工作均使用的是流动检测设备。与使用静态电子吸收光谱收集设备的方法相比，这种方法所需的设备较为普及，一般耐高压的液相色谱检测器即可。所得数据重复性较好，经统计学分析后具有较好的置信度。

本项研究的目的为：根据在超临界 CO_2 色谱上测定的 CO_2 流动相密度与全反式番茄红素组分峰面积的相关性，推算 CO_2 密度变化对全反式番茄红素的吸光系数（$A_{1cm}^{1\%}$）的影响。

1　材料与方法

1.1　材料与试剂

DSM redivivo™ 全反式番茄红素样品（番茄红素含量≥10%）瑞典帝斯曼公司。该产品为人工合成全反式番茄红素的微结晶油悬浮物，含有少量的 α - 生育酚。使用前应用 UV - Vis 法对其中总番茄红素含量进行标定[10]，标定含量为质量分数 10.03%。随后应用 C_{30} - HPLC - PDA 对其几何异构体组成进行了

[基金项目]"十一五"国家科技支撑计划项目（2008BAI58B06）；2010 年北京联合大学"创新人才建设计划"项目（2010 - 05 - 20）。
[作者简介] 何强强（1986—），男，硕士研究生，研究方向：生物活性物质制备及天然产物化学；惠伯棣（1959—），男，教授，博士，研究方向：类胡萝卜素化学及生物化学。

分析[4,11]。分析结果表明：该样品中全反式异构体的含量超过97%。

CO_2（纯度为99.9%）北京气体公司；乙腈、甲醇（色谱纯）美国迪马公司；二氯甲烷、正己烷、N, N-二异丙基乙胺（分析纯）美国JK化学品公司。

1.2 仪器与设备

超临界流体色谱设备（该系统由CO_2源、CO_2泵、夹带剂泵、进样器、紫外—可见光检测器（具扫描功能）、尾压阀及控制器和数据采集设备组成，详见图2）、HPLC设备（PU-2080 Plus智能输送泵、CO_2输送泵PU-1580-CO_2、尾压控制器BP-1580-81、检温箱CO-2065Plus）日本分光（Jasco）公司；N2000色谱数据工作站浙大智达公司；DiamonsilC8色谱柱（250mm×4.6mm，5μm）美国迪马公司。Multi Spec-1501紫外—可见光分光光度计 日本岛津公司；Waters PDA-2996二极管阵列检测器 美国Waters公司。

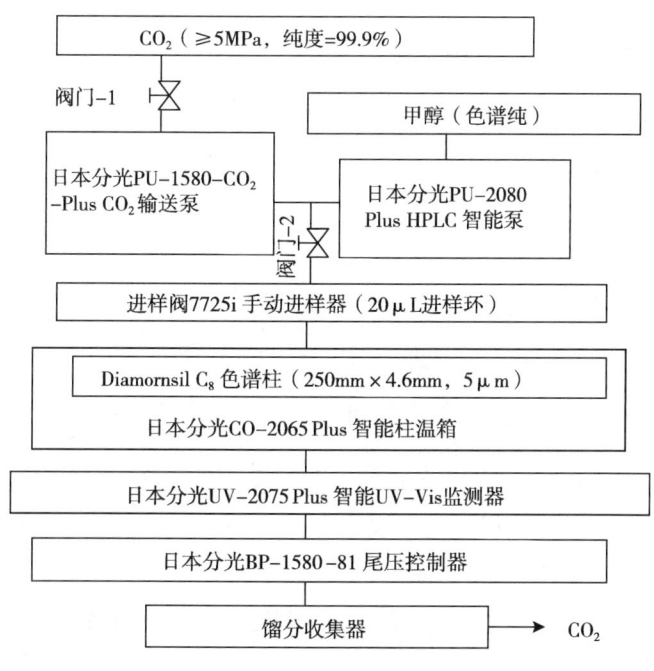

图2 超临界CO_2流体色谱仪

1.3 方法

1.3.1 样品溶液的配制

将样品在开启前置于40℃水浴中15min，并不时摇动，使样品具有一定流动性。开封后迅速称取0.1775g样品于10mL棕色容量瓶中，用二氯甲烷溶解并定容，制成0.01775g/mL的样品储备液。储备液贮存于-80℃冰箱中，于48h内使用完毕。根据各实验的需要用贮备液配制成不同质量浓度的工作液。

1.3.2 色谱操作

1.3.2.1 超临界流体色谱

由于样品中番茄红素的含量仅为10%，因此，在采集组分的电子吸收光谱前，需经过色谱的分离和纯化过程，以确保组分在被收集光谱时处于纯度较高的状态。同时，在采集样品组分的光谱时，组分的溶媒也必须单一，为超临界态的CO_2；否则，组分的吸光强度会受到干扰。因此，在采集光谱前，使用了C_8固定相对组分进行了超临界流体色谱纯化。组分的色谱纯化及光谱采集过程操作如下：关闭阀门-2，打开阀门-1，打开气瓶阀门。打开CO_2泵的制冷机电源，等待约30min，待绿色指示灯亮后，打开所有设备的电源。设定柱温箱温度为45℃，开启反压阀。约10min后，系统中空气排尽。随后，设定CO_2泵的流速为2mL/min，反压阀调控方式为恒流模式。在所有的实验中，样品导入体积均为20mL。在色谱柱载量测定中，设定压力为13MPa，柱温箱温度为45℃。根据之前研究[8-9]，检测波长设定为453nm。

在压力变化研究中，设定压力分别为11.5、13、14.5、16、17.5MPa，柱温箱温度为45℃。检测波长设定为453nm。样品导入量为1.2μg。

在温度变化研究中,设定压力为13MPa,柱温箱温度分别为35℃、40℃、45℃、50℃、52℃。检测波长设定为453nm。样品导入量为1.2μg。

1.3.2.2 高压液相色谱

色谱条件:流速:0.7mL/min;温度:室温25℃;流动相:乙腈-甲醇-二氯甲烷-正己烷-N-乙基-迪索丙胺(850:100:25:25:0.5,V/V);检测波长:470nm;样品导入量:1.2μg。

1.4 数据处理

色谱系统在使用前用番茄红素样品进行重复性测试,6次进样中番茄红素组分峰面积的RSD≤3%。在实验中,每个样品重复进样3次以上,直到采集到RSD小于3%的平行数据。

2 结果与分析

2.1 全反式番茄红素的超临界CO_2色谱行为

Jasco UV 2705 Plus Intelligent UV-Vis型检测器具有进行实时光谱扫描的功能。因此,全反式番茄红素组分的超临界CO_2色谱行为如图3所示。

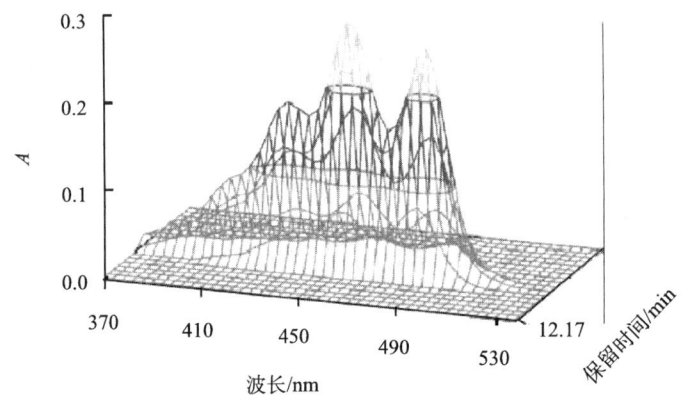

图3 全反式番茄红素组分的超临界二氧化碳色谱行为

2.2 压力变化对保留时间的影响

由图4可知,当CO_2流动相的压力自11.5MPa升至17.5MPa时,全反式番茄红素组分在453nm波长处的保留时间呈缩短趋势。

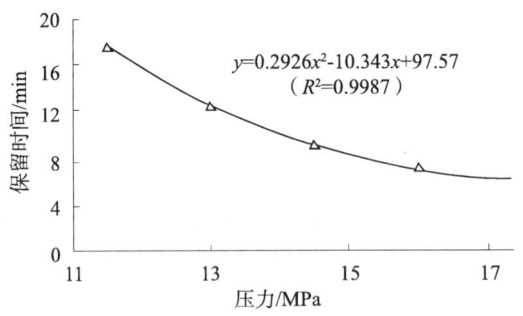

图4 压力变化对全反式番茄红素组分保留时间的影响

2.3 温度变化对保留时间的影响

由图5可知,当CO_2流动相的温度自32℃升至52℃时,全反式番茄红素组分在13MPa压力和453nm波长处的保留时间呈延长趋势。

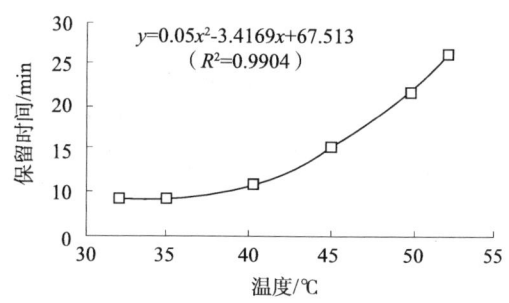

图5 温度变化对全反式番茄红素组分保留时间的影响

2.4 密度变化对保留时间的影响

由于超临界CO_2流体的压力和温度变化会引起其密度的变化,可根据全反式番茄红素组分在453nm波长处的保留时间与CO_2压力和温度变化的相关性(图4、5),得到组分保留时间与CO_2密度变化的相关性(图6)。

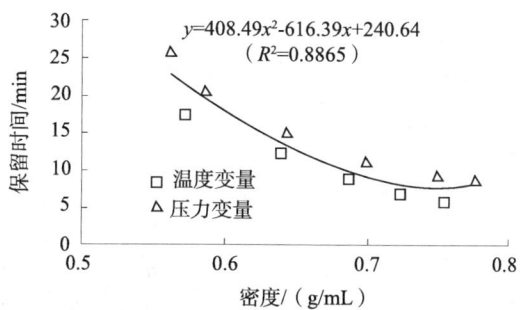

图6 CO_2密度变化对全反式番茄红素组分保留时间的影响

2.5 色谱柱的最小检测限、载量与线性测定

在压力为13MPa、温度为45℃、流速为2mL/min、检测波长为453nm、进样体积为20μL时,本色谱系统的全反式番茄红素最小检出量为60ng。

本项研究的目的是在色谱系统上根据组分的峰面积推算全反式番茄红素的吸光系数,并观察色谱流动相条件的变化对吸光系数的影响。因此,样品进样量与组分峰面积的线性相关是保证实验结果准确性的必要条件。由图7可知,当样品量在0~11.836μg时,样品进样量与组分峰面积可以被认为呈线性相关($R^2=0.9967$)。色谱柱的载量值>15μg。

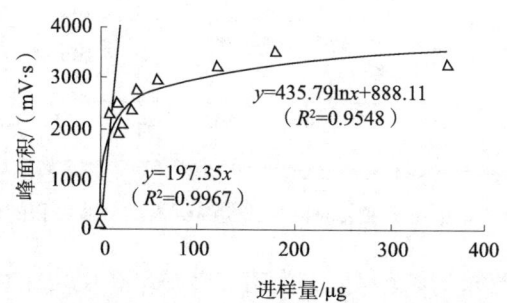

图7 样品进样量对全反式番茄红素组分峰面积的影响

2.6 压力变化对峰面积的影响

在以下的实验中,进样量均为1.2μg,小于色谱柱的载量,以保证样品量与组分峰面积的线性关系。由图8可知,当CO_2流动相的压力自11.5MPa升至17.5MPa时,全反式番茄红素组分在453nm波长的

峰面积呈增加趋势。

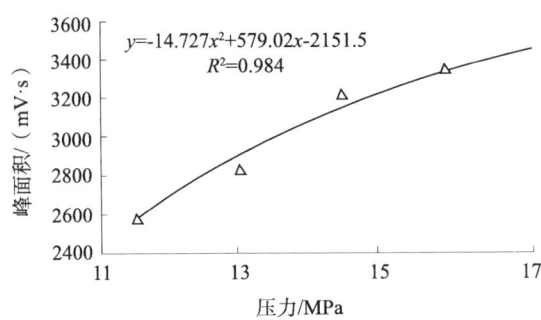

图8　压力变化对全反式番茄红素组分峰面积的影响

2.7　温度变化对峰面积的影响

由图9可知，当CO_2流动相的温度自32℃升至55℃时，全反式番茄红素组分在453nm波长的峰面积呈减少趋势。

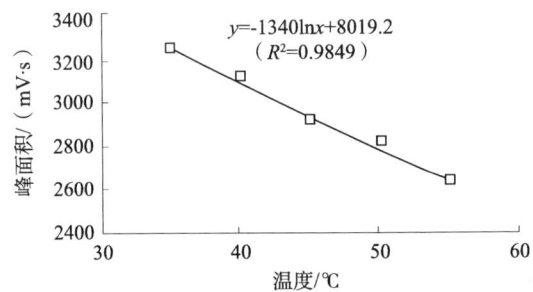

图9　温度变化对全反式番茄红素组分峰面积的影响

2.8　CO_2密度变化对峰面积的影响

如上所述，超临界CO_2流体的压力和温度变化可引起其密度的变化。根据全反式番茄红素组分在453nm波长处的峰面积与CO_2流动相压力和温度变化的相关性（图8、图9），其峰面积与CO_2密度变化的相关性见图10。

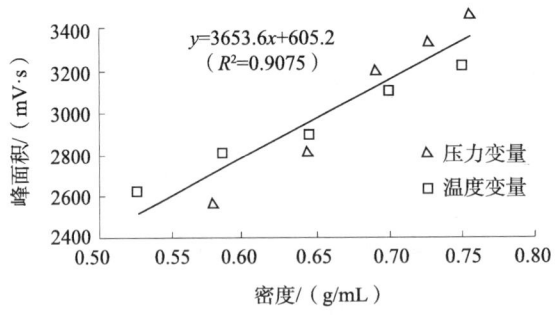

图10　CO_2密度变化对全反式番茄红素组分峰面积的影响

由图10可知，在0.53～0.75g/mL范围内，当超临界CO_2密度增加时，其中全反式番茄红素组分的峰面积呈增加趋势。本项研究所得数据表明：关于超临界CO_2密度与组分峰面积的数量相关性尚不能确定。但在这个密度范围内，其$R_2=0.9075$。如要确定二者的关系，需扩大检测密度的范围。即使如此，在本项研究中，亦可根据所得二者的线性关系推算了在不同CO_2密度条件下的全反式番茄红素组分吸光系数。

2.9 全反式番茄红素组分在HPLC流动相中的吸光系数测定与计算

在本项研究中，也对1.2μg全反式番茄红素组分在乙腈为主的流动相（乙腈体积分数85%）中的峰面积进行了测定。随后，在UV-Vis上，根据惠伯棣等[8]报道的方法，测定了该组分在流动相中的$A_{1cm}^{1\%}$值为3430。

根据全反式番茄红素组分在HPLC流动相中的峰面积和$A_{1cm}^{1\%}$值（3430），以及全反式番茄红素组分在SFC流动相中的峰面积，计算出该组分在SFC流动相中不同密度条件下的$A_{1cm}^{1\%}$值。

虽然根据本项实验的结果，超临界CO_2密度与组分峰面积的数量相关性尚不能确定。但在这个密度范围内，线性回归方程为：

$$y = 3653.6x + 605.2 \tag{1}$$

式中：x为超临界CO_2密度/（g/mL）；y为全反式番茄红素组分峰面积/（mV·s）。

其中：$R^2 = 0.9075$。在本项研究中，根据所回归的线性关系按式（2）推算全反式番茄红素组分在密度为0.53~0.75g/mL范围内超临界CO_2流体中的吸光系数（$A_{1cm}^{1\%}$，结果见表1。

$$A_{SF} = \frac{A_{HPLC} \times S_{SF}}{S_{HPLC}} \tag{2}$$

式中：A_{SF}为全反式番茄红素组分在超临界CO_2流体中的吸光系数（$A_{1cm}^{1\%}$）；A_{HPLC}为全反式番茄红素组分在HPLC流动相中的吸光系数（A）；S_{SF}为全反式番茄红素组分在超临界CO_2流体中的峰面积/（mV·s）；SHPLC为全反式番茄红素组分在HPLC流动相中的峰面积/（mV·s）。

表1 溶媒密度变化对全反式番茄红素吸光系数（$A_{1cm}^{1\%}$）变化的影响

溶媒名称	密度/（g/mL）	吸光系数（$A_{1cm}^{1\%}$）	状态
HPLC流动相	0.790	3430	液态
超临界CO_2	0.757	2238	超临界态
	0.750	2221	超临界态
	0.727	2165	超临界态
	0.699	2098	超临界态
	0.691	2078	超临界态
	0.644	1964	超临界态
	0.586	1823	超临界态
	0.578	1804	超临界态

3 结 论

本项研究的结果表明：全反式番茄红素组分在超临界CO_2色谱中最大吸收波长下的峰面积是可变的，与CO_2密度呈线性正相关。由此，可以得出结论：全反式番茄红素的吸光系数与超临界CO_2流体密度变化呈线形正相关。

参考文献

[1] 惠伯棣. 类胡萝卜素化学与生物化学[M]. 北京：中国轻工出版社，2005：261-266.
[2] 惠伯棣，朱蕾，欧阳清波，等. 类胡萝卜素的命名[J]. 中国食品添加剂，2003（4）：48-54.
[3] 李京，惠伯棣，裴凌鹏. 番茄红素：被关注的功能因子[J]. 食品科学，2005，26（8）：461-464.
[4] 李京，惠伯棣. 番茄红素在体内代谢中的几何异构体组成变化[J]. 食品科学，2008，29（9）：591-594.
[5] FAVATIP, KING J W, FRIEDRICH J P, et al. Supercritical CO_2 extraction of carotene and lutein from leaf protein concentrate [J]. Food Science, 1988, 53（5）：1532-1536.
[6] 惠伯棣. 胡萝卜素、叶黄素和叶绿素在反相超临界色谱中的分离初探[J]. 食品科学，2005，26（8）：162-166.
[7] 庞善春，惠伯棣，刘沐霖. 天然番茄红素软胶囊的生产工艺和质量控制点分析[J]. 食品科学，2007，28（8）：

619-624.

[8] HUI Bodi, YOUNG A J, BOOTH L A, et al. Detection of carotenoids on supercritical fluid chromatography (SFC). A preliminary investigation on the spectral shifts of carotenoids in supercritical carbon dioxide [J]. Chromatographic, 1994, 39 (9/10): 549-556.

[9] 惠伯棣. 超临界 CO_2 中全反式 β, β - 和 ψ, ψ - 胡萝卜素的电子吸收光谱位移研究 [J]. 食品科学, 2008, 29 (10): 125-128.

[10] 白鸿. 保健食品功能因子检测 [M]. 北京: 中国中医药出版社, 2011: 270-273.

[11] 李京, 惠伯棣. 秋橄榄果实中番茄红素含量与几何异构体组成分析 [J]. 食品工业科技, 2006, 27 (10): 64-65.

植物甾醇的安全性研究进展

张 波 刘河汝 安秀峰 代晓曼

植物甾醇（phytosterols）主要存在于植物细胞膜中，在各种植物油、坚果及植物种子中含量丰富，尤其是在米糠油、菜籽油以及玉米油中含量较高，植物甾醇的含量平均为总油量的 0.3%~0.4%。植物甾醇主要成分为 β-谷甾醇（β-sitostero）、豆甾醇（stigmastero）和菜油甾醇（campesterol），其中以 β-sitostero 为主，占总植物甾醇的 60%~90%。近十余年的研究表明[1]，每天摄入一定量的植物甾醇可降低血清胆固醇浓度。美国食品药物管理局（FDA）、欧盟食品科学委员会（SCF）等发布相关健康声称：适量摄入植物甾醇和植物甾烷醇可降低血液中的胆固醇并确证了植物甾醇类食品的功效性和安全性[1]。美国 FDA 指出，每天总服用量不少于 1.3g 植物甾醇酯，可降低心血管疾病的发病率[2]。1999 年，美国 FDA 允许在食品涂抹用料中加入 20% 的植物甾醇酯，世界其他国家的食品公司也相继推出含植物甾醇的功能食品投放市场。近年来，植物甾醇作为功能性食品和添加剂受到了国外食品行业的高度重视，美国、加拿大、澳大利亚、新西兰和许多欧洲国家均允许销售添加植物甾醇的功能食品，用于降低人群血液胆固醇的含量[2-3]。在我国，随着人们对植物甾醇保健功能认识的不断深化，功能性植物甾醇食品的开发速度也逐步加快。2010 年 3 月我国卫生部正式批准植物甾醇和植物甾醇酯为新资源食品，由此引起了我国食品行业对开发富含植物甾醇的食用油以及添加植物甾醇食品的重视。目前，我国卫生部、美国 FDA 以及欧盟推荐的植物甾醇摄入量为 1.3~3.0g/d。植物甾醇及植物甾醇酯在多种食品中的应用呈现不断增加的趋势。

1 植物甾醇的化学结构

植物甾醇的结构与动物甾醇（主要是胆甾醇，也称为胆固醇）相似，都属于 4-无甲基甾醇。结构上惟一不同之处是环戊烷全氢菲骨架带有侧链，正是这些侧链上的微小差异导致了植物甾醇与胆固醇生理功能的极大不同。主要的植物甾醇以及胆固醇的结构式如图 1 所示。

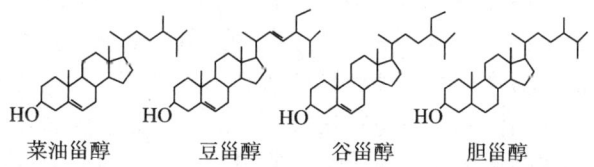

图 1 主要的植物甾醇以及胆甾醇（胆固醇）的结构

2 植物甾醇的吸收与作用

植物甾醇的结构与胆甾醇（胆固醇）相似，其在人体的吸收途径和胆固醇一样，通过胆固醇吸收蛋白（Niemann Pick C1 like 1，NPC1L1）进行吸收[3]，故食用植物甾醇可竞争性地抑制人体肠道对胆固醇的吸收，从而起到降低血液中胆固醇的作用。目前普遍认为，植物甾醇通过抑制小肠对外源性胆固醇（从食物中摄取）以及内源性胆固醇（来源于胆汁）的吸收从而起到降低血清中胆固醇的作用[4-5]。前期的研究表明，每天服用 2.2g 左右的植物甾醇或植物甾醇酯即可使血浆中胆固醇降低 60% 左右，低密度脂蛋白胆固醇降低 12% 左右[6-9]。而血清中高水平的总胆固醇或低密度脂蛋白胆固醇是冠心病和缺血性脑卒中等心脑血管疾病的独立危险因素之一。因此近年来，植物甾醇以及植物甾醇酯常作为辅助降低

[作者简介] 张波，女，北京联合大学应用文理学院生物活性物质与功能食品北京市重点实验室教授。研究方向：生物活性物质的功能与毒理。

胆固醇的膳食补充剂或功能性食品用于预防动脉粥样硬化和心血管疾病。Demonty等人[10-11]的研究表明，低密度脂蛋白胆固醇5年中保持较低水平可使冠心病的发病风险降低27%。我国学者陈茂彬等人[12]将3种植物甾醇酯（植物甾醇乙酸酯、油酸酯和硬脂酸酯）对小鼠高脂血症的作用进行比较研究，结果表明，3种植物甾醇酯可不同程度地降低高脂血症小鼠的血清总胆固醇、低密度脂蛋白胆固醇以及动脉硬化指数（AI），同时还降低了高血脂小鼠的肝重、肝脏总胆固醇和低密度脂蛋白胆固醇。付佳等[13]运用系统评价方法对植物甾醇/甾烷醇的降血脂作用进行了系统评价，Meta分析结果显示，当饮料以及人造黄油等食品中添加植物甾醇/甾烷醇（每人1.5~3.0g/d）时，与对照组比较，可以明显降低血浆总胆固醇、低密度脂蛋白胆固醇、甘油三酯的水平。武韬等[14]对100名血脂异常的患者进行了植物甾醇酯的干预试验。干预组每人每天服用含1.35g植物甾醇酯的奶粉，对照组服用安慰剂，试食期为48d。结果表明，植物甾醇酯对血脂异常患者具有辅助降总胆固醇和低密度胆固醇的作用。

3 植物甾醇的安全性研究

3.1 动物试验研究

近年来，有关大量摄入植物甾醇以及植物甾醇酯会引起机体的毒副作用的研究引起学者的广泛关注[15-16]。Naito等人[17-19]在膳食中添加10%的菜籽油（总植物甾醇含量为0.71g/kg饲料）给予自发性高血压脑卒中大鼠（SHRSP）、自发性高血压大鼠（SHR）和正常血压的Wistar-Kyoto（WKY）大鼠，共13周，与添加10%的大豆油对照组（总植物甾醇含量为0.29g/kg饲料）比较，收缩压显著升高，故认为菜籽油中较高的植物甾醇含量可引起大鼠的血压升高。后来的研究也得出了类似的结果，如Chen等人[20]用SHRSP大鼠和WKY大鼠进行植物甾醇酯的干预试验，食物中添加2.0g/kg的植物甾醇酯，共5周。试验结果表明，食物中添加2.0g/kg植物甾醇酯可引起SHRSP大鼠心脏舒张压明显升高2~3倍，血管紧张素原（angiotensinogen，Agt）、血管紧张素转换酶1（angiotensin I - converting enzyme 1，Ace1）、一氧化碳氧合酶1和3（nitric oxide synthase，Nos1，Nos3）、环氧合酶2（cyclooxygenase 2，Cox2）等的表达量明显升高。因此，作者认为植物甾醇酯引起SHRSP大鼠血压明显升高有可能与肾脏的血压调节基因表达的改变有关，尤其与Ace1、Nos1、Nos3、Cox2和Spon1基因表达的上调有关。进一步，CHEN等人[21]采用雄性WKY大鼠进行试验，每天分别给予WKY大鼠0.2g/kg的植物甾醇和植物甾烷醇，共5周。结果表明，植物甾醇组其肝脏、主动脉以及肾脏中植物甾醇含量增加了3~4倍，而胆固醇分别降低了40%、31%和19%。植物甾烷醇组其肝脏、主动脉以及肾脏中植物甾醇含量增加了9倍而胆固醇分别降低了16%、20%和14%。植物甾醇和植物甾烷醇组大鼠其胆固醇/植物甾醇或植物甾烷醇比值也均明显降低。另外，植物甾醇和植物甾烷醇还使大鼠的收缩压和舒张压明显升高，肾脏血管紧张素肽原的表达水平明显提高，即大量摄入植物甾醇和植物甾烷醇会引起WKY大鼠在低盐膳食条件下血压仍明显升高，故该作者提出在临床上使用植物甾醇和植物甾烷醇是否对心血管患者有利还有待研究，尤其对一些敏感个体。摄入这类物质可能会增加其与其他物质的相互作用。因此，尽管植物甾醇和植物甾烷醇可显著降低血液中胆固醇的含量，但是对心血管健康的综合效应急需进一步研究。Weingärtner等人[21]通过膳食给予小鼠0.2g/kg的植物甾醇酯，共4周。结果表明，小鼠的血管舒张能力受损并增加了大脑缺血性损伤程度。为了研究植物甾醇酯对胆固醇的降低作用，该研究将载脂蛋白E基因敲除小鼠（apolipoprotein E gene knockout mice，ApoE-/-）随机分成高脂饲料加植物甾醇组和高脂饲料加降脂药组。结果表明，高脂饲料加植物甾醇酯组血小板含量明显高于高脂饲料加降脂药组，血浆中植物甾醇浓度与动脉粥样硬化程度呈正相关。该研究表明，食品中添加植物甾醇酯会损伤血管内皮细胞功能，加重缺血性脑损伤，加重小鼠动脉粥样硬化的程度。同时，Weingärtner等人[22]还分别给予ApoE-/-小鼠0.34g/kg的植物甾醇和植物甾烷醇，共6周。结果表明，在食物中添加植物甾醇和植物甾烷醇使血浆中胆固醇浓度明显降低，但也使植物甾醇和植物甾烷醇在血浆中的浓度明显升高，而且在肝脏和脑组织中的含量也明显增加，另外还增加了血液中单核细胞的数量以及超氧化和脂质过氧化产物的含量。基于这些结果，该作者强调指出，有必要深入研究食物中添加植物甾醇和植物甾烷醇的安全性和临床有效性。Vanmierlo等人[23]的研究也表明，每天从食物中给予C57BL/6NCrl小鼠0.2g/kg体重的植物甾醇，共6周，可使血液中低密度胆固醇降低10%左右，但同时也使血液中植物甾醇含量增加2倍以上，并对动脉血管产生不利影响，使血压升高，有促动脉粥样化作用以及促炎症作用。植物甾醇还大量积累在脑和肝脏等组织中高达2～3倍。同时还发现，不同的植物甾醇穿过血-脑屏障的能力不同，体外培养脑内皮细胞试验也表明，菜油甾醇透过血-脑屏障的能力远大于谷甾醇。该项试验结果表明，植物甾醇可透过血-脑屏障，不可逆地积累在脑组织中，其对机体及各个器官的影响还需进一步深入研究。Marttinena等人[24]在最新的一项研究中指出，用含植物甾烷醇0.8%的饲料饲喂Apc^{Min}小鼠9周，测定盲肠内容物以及肠黏膜的植物甾醇和植物甾烷醇的含量，采用Western blotting测定β-catenin（β-联蛋白）、细胞周期蛋白cyclinD1以及表皮生长因子受体EGFR（epidermal growth factor receptor，EGFR）、细胞外信号调节激酶1或2（extracellular signal-regulated kinase1/2，ERK1/2）的含量。试验结果表明，植物甾烷醇可诱导小肠腺瘤数量的增加但没有影响腺瘤的大小。另外，植物甾烷醇也使磷酸化β-catenin、核细胞周期蛋白cyclin D1、总EGFR以及磷酸化EGFR的含量增加，即植物甾烷醇可能通过激活EGFR等，EGFR通过促使β-catenin磷酸化并转移到核内，刺激细胞周期蛋白cyclin D1的高表达，从而诱导小肠肿瘤的形成。

3.2 人类流行病学研究

人类流行病学研究结果也表明，大量补充植物甾醇可使血液中低密度脂蛋白胆固醇降低，但也可能对心血管系统产生不利影响。如Weingärtner[22]的研究表明，受试者食用含植物甾醇酯的人造黄油后，血浆和总动脉瓣膜中植物甾醇酯含量明显增加，尤其是总动脉瓣膜中植物甾醇酯含量增加了5倍。Assmann等人[25]的研究结果表明，血浆中高植物甾醇含量会增加患动脉粥样硬化的风险，尤其对于植物甾醇血症患者，目前认为其血浆中高浓度的植物甾醇是患冠心病的高风险因子。Rajaratnam等人[26]的研究表明，绝经期后的妇女谷甾醇/胆固醇、菜油甾醇/胆固醇比值较高者其患冠状动脉粥样硬化的风险也较高。Sudhop等人[27]的研究表明，冠心病家族史受试者的患病风险与性别、年龄以及血浆中甘油三酯以及低密度脂蛋白胆固醇和高密度脂蛋白胆固醇没有明显的相关性而与植物甾醇含量相关，受试者血浆中菜油甾醇和谷甾醇的含量较高且菜油甾醇/胆固醇以及谷甾醇/胆固醇的比例也明显高于正常人。这些结果均支持植物甾醇可能是冠心病的致病因子。但也有一些相反的研究报道，如Pinedo等人[28]对373名冠心病患者以及758名正常人群的研究表明，血浆中较高的但仍然在生理允许范围内的植物甾醇含量与冠状动脉粥样硬化性心脏病（CAD）没有明显的相关性，在身体健康状况正常的个体也没有观察到冠状动脉粥样损害。因此该作者指出，在生理范围内，膳食中添加植物甾醇还是比较安全的。Windler等人[29]对绝经期前后的妇女进行的人群研究数据也并未显示血清中植物甾醇含量与冠心病之间有明显的相关性。Fassbender等人[30]在一项研究人类老龄化问题的研究项目中，对1242名平均年龄65岁的人群研究表明，冠心病患者血浆中植物甾醇含量以及植物甾醇/胆固醇比值明显低于正常人，但是高β-sitostero浓度可明显降低冠心病的风险（$OR=0.78$，CI：$0.62\sim0.98$，$P<0.05$）。相反，研究组中各个体间植物甾烷醇、胆固醇合成标志物（烯胆固烷醇、羊毛甾醇和链甾醇）以及植物甾烷醇、胆固醇合成标志物与胆固醇的比值差异无统计学意义。因此该项研究认为，植物甾醇对于冠心病的作用是中立的或许还有保护作用。Richelle等人[31]的临床研究还表明，每人每天以饮料的形式补充2.2g植物甾醇，与对照组比较，胆固醇的吸收降低60%，但同时人体对β-胡萝卜素的吸收也降低了50%、α-生育酚的吸收降了20%，而维生素A、D、K在血浆中的浓度变化差异无统计学意义。Hendriks等人[32]通过在面包中添加植物甾醇，研究植物甾醇对胆固醇的降低作用以及对脂溶性维生素的影响作用。结果表明，与普通面包组比较，食用添加了较低剂量的植物甾醇面包（每人0.83、1.61、3.24g/d）的受试者，其血清中总胆固醇以及低密度脂蛋白胆固醇含量降低，低密度脂蛋白胆固醇和高密度脂蛋白胆固醇的比值也降低，差异均有统计学意义。食用添加了不同剂量植物甾醇面包的受试者血清中维生素K1、25-羟基-维生素D、番茄红素以及α-生育酚含量变化差异无统计学意义，但是中、高剂量植物甾醇面包组（植物甾醇含量分别为1.61和3.24g）受试者，其血清中胡萝卜素（包括α-胡萝卜素和β-胡萝卜素）含量分别降低了11%和19%。该研究的结论是，大量摄入植物甾醇会影响脂溶性维生素的吸收。造成这种作用的原因可能是，植物甾醇在小肠中不仅仅抑制胆固醇的吸收也可抑制其他亲脂分子的吸收以及影响在乳糜颗粒中的相互作用。因此学者们认为，膳食补充植物甾醇可降低血浆中胆固醇的含量但也降低了人体对脂溶性维生素以及脂溶性抗氧化物质如β-胡萝卜素、叶黄素、番茄红素等的吸收。降低这些物质的生

物利用度，需要另外补充这些物质以维持体内的平衡。但植物甾醇以低于1.6g的剂量添加到食品中就可明显降低胆固醇以及低密度脂蛋白胆固醇的含量而不至于引起脂溶性维生素吸收的改变。

4 总 结

综上所述，目前的动物研究以及临床和流行病学资料还无法确定长期膳食补充植物甾醇和植物甾烷醇对人类心血管疾病以及其他器官的利弊。目前惟一能肯定的是，膳食补充植物甾醇和植物甾烷醇能够降低血浆中胆固醇的含量。因此，进一步全面深入地研究植物甾醇和植物甾烷醇的作用机理，明确其对人类心血管疾病以及其他器官的影响是目前急需进行的研究内容。

参考文献

[1] Food and Drug Administration, Health and Human Services. // Food labeling: health claims; plant sterol/stanol esters and coronary heart disease; interim final rule [J]. Fed. Regist, 2000, 65 (8): 54685 – 54739.
[2] Wester I. Cholesterol – lowering effect of plant sterols [J]. Eur J Lipid Sci Tech. 2000, 102 (1): 37 – 44.
[3] L'abbé M R, Dumais L, Chao E. et al. Health claims on foods in Canada [J]. J Nutr, 2008, 138 (6): 1221S – 1227S.
[4] Ostlund RE Jr. Phytosterols in human nutrition [J]. Annu Rev Nutr, 2002, 22: 533 – 549.
[5] Weststrate J A, Meijer G W. Plant sterol enriched margarines and reduction of plasma total and LDL cholesterol concentrations in normocholesterolemic and mildly hypercholesterolaemic subjects [J]. Eur J Clin Nutr 1998, 52: 334 – 343.
[6] Lees A M, Mok H Y I, Lees R S, et al. Plant sterols as cholesterol – lowering agents: clinical trials in patients with hypercholesterolemia and studiessterol balance [J]. Arteriosclerosis, 1977, 28 (3): 325 – 328.
[7] Harry R D, ZHU L J, Lizbeth M H, et al. Niemann – Pick C1 Like 1 (NPC1L1) is the intestinal phytosterol and cholesterol transporter and a key modulator of whole – body cholesterol homeostasis [J]. The Journalof Biological Chemistry, 2004, 279 (32): 33586 – 33592.
[8] Lichtenstein A H, Appel L J, Brands M, et al. Summary of American Heart Association Diet and Lifestyle Recommendations revision [J]. Arterioscler ThrombVascBiol, 2006, 26: 2186 – 2191.
[9] Law M. Plant sterol and stanol margarines and health [J]. BMJ, 2000, 320 (7238): 861 – 864.
[10] Von Bergmann K, Sudhop T, Lütjohann D. Cholesterol and plant sterol absorption: recent insights [J]. Am J Cardiol 2005, 96 (1):10 – 14.
[11] Demonty I, Ras R T, Knaap van der Knaap HC, et al. Continuous dose – response relationship of the LDL – cholesterol – lowering effect of phytosterolintake [J]. J Nutr, 2009, 139 (2): 271 – 284.
[12] 陈茂彬，黄琴，吴谋成. 三种植物甾醇酯预防小鼠高脂血症作用的比较 [J]. 中国粮油学报，2005，20（2）：80 – 82.
[13] 付佳，杨月欣，张立实，等. 植物甾醇/甾烷醇对血脂作用的系统评价研究 [J]. 营养学报，2008，30（2）：181 – 189.
[14] 武韬，卢长林，马小丽，等. 植物甾醇酯对血脂异常患者血脂调节作用的临床观察研究 [J]. 首都公共卫生，2012，6（3）：105 – 109.
[15] Weingärtner O, Lütjohann D, Shengbo Ji, et al. Vascular effects of diet supplementation with plant sterols [J]. J Am CollCardiol 2008, 51 (16): 1553 – 1561.
[16] Calpe – BerdielL, Méndez – GonzálezJ, Blanco – VacaF, et al. Increased plasma levels of plant sterols and atherosclerosis: a controversial issue [J]. Curr Atheroscler Rep, 2009, 11 (5): 391 – 398.
[17] Naito Y, Kasama K, Yoshida H, et al. Thirteen – week dietary intake of rapeseed oil or soybean oil as the only dietary fat in Wistar Kyoto ratschange in blood pressure [J]. Food Chem Toxicol, 2000, 38 (9): 811 – 816.
[18] Naito Y, Konishi C, Katsumura H, et al. Increase in blood pressure with enhanced Na +, K + – ATPase activity in stroke – prone spontaneously hypertensive rats after 4 – weeks intake of rapeseed oil as the sole dietary fat [J]. Pharmacol Toxicol, 2000, 87 (3):144 – 148.
[19] Naito Y, Yoshida H, Nagata T, et al. Dietary intake of rapeseed oil or soybean oil as the only fat nutrient in spontaneously hypertensive rats and Wistar Kyoto rats – blood pressure and pathophysiology [J]. Toxicology, 2000, 146 (2 – 3): 197 – 208.
[20] CHEN Q, Gruber H, Swist E, et al. Influence of dietary phytosterols and phytostanols on diastolic bloodpressure and the ex-

pression of blood pressure regulatory genes in SHRSP and WKY inbred rats [J]. Br J Nutr, 2009, 102 (1): 93-101.

[21] CHEN Q, Gruber H, Swist E, et al. Dietaryphytosterols and phytostanols decrease cholesterol levels but increase bloodpressure in WKY inbred rats in the absence of salt-loading [J]. Nutr Metab (Lond), 2010, 7 (1): 2-11.

[22] Weingärtner O, Ulrich C, Lütjohann D, et al. Differential effects on inhibition of cholesterol absorption by plant stanol and plant sterol esters in apoE-/- mice [J]. Cardiovasc Res, 2011, 90 (3): 484-492.

[23] Vanmierlo T, Weingärtnerc O, Pol Svd, et al. Dietary intake of plant sterols stably increases plant sterol levels in the murine brain [J]. The Journal of Lipid Research, 2012, 53 (4): 726-735.

[24] Marttinena M, Päivärintaa E, Storvikb M, et al. Plant stanols induce intestinal tumor formation by up-regulating Wnt and EGFR signaling in Apc Min mice [J]. J Nutr Biochem, 2013, 24 (1): 343-352.

[25] Assmann G, Cullen P, Erbey J, et al. Plasma sitosterole levations are associated with an increased incidence of coronary events in men: results of a nested case-control analysis of the Prospective Cardiovascular Muönster (PROCAM) study [J]. Nutr Metab Cardiovasc Dis, 2006, 16 (1): 13-21.

[26] Rajaratnam R A, Gylling H, Miettinen T A. Independent association of serum squalene and noncholesterol sterols with coronary artery disease in postmenopausal women [J]. J Am. Coll Cardiol, 2000, 35 (5): 1185-1191.

[27] Sudhop T, Gottwald B M, von Bergmann K. Serum plant sterols as a potential risk factor for coronary heart disease [J]. Metabolism, 2002, 51 (12): 1519-1521.

[28] Pinedo S, Vissers M N, von Bergmann K, et al. Plasma levels of plant sterols and the risk of coronary artery disease: the prospective EPIC-Norfolk Population Study [J]. J Lipid Res, 2007, 48 (1): 139-144.

[29] Windler E, Zyriax B C, Kuipers F, et al. Association of plasma phytosterol concentrations with incident coronary heart disease. Data from the CORA study, a case control study of coronary artery disease in women [J]. Atherosclerosis, 2009, 203 (1): 284-290.

[30] Fassbender K, Lutjohann D, Dik M G, et al. Moderately elevated plant sterol levels are associated with reduced cardiovascular risk - The LASA study [J]. Atherosclerosis, 2008, 196 (1): 283-288.

[31] Richelle M, Enslen M, Hager C, et al. Both free and esterifiedplant sterols reduce cholesterol absorption and the bioavailability of ß-caroteneandα-tocopherol innormocholesterolemichumans [J]. Am J Clin Nutr, 2004, 80: 171-177.

[32] Hendriks H F J, Weststrate J A, Van Vliet T, et al. Spreads enriched with three different concentrations of vegetable oil sterols and the degree of cholesterol lowering in normocholesterolemic and mildly hypercholesterolemic subjects [J]. Eur J Clin Nutr, 1999, 53 (4): 319-327.

学生宿舍设计方案的模糊综合评价与集对分析

张晓晞 邓 岩 董 巍 骆 腾

0 引 言

学生宿舍事关学生在校期间的生活品质,直接或间接地影响学生的生活、学习和健康成长,本文对 2010 高教社杯全国大学生数学建模竞赛 D 题中学生宿舍设计方案中 4 种比较典型的设计方案[1]中存在的问题进行讨论,学生宿舍的使用面积、布局和设施配置等的设计既要保证学生生活舒适,也要方便管理,同时还要考虑成本和收费的平衡,这些与所在城市的地域、区位、文化习俗和经济发展水平有关。因此,学生宿舍的设计必须考虑经济性、舒适性和安全性等问题。经济性:建设成本、运行成本和收费标准等;舒适性:人均面积、使用方便、互不干扰、采光和通风等;安全性:人员疏散和防盗等。

1 模型的建立

设给定两个有限论域[2-3]:$U = \{u_1, u_2, \cdots, u_n\}$,$V = \{v_1, v_2, \cdots, v_n\}$,其中 U 代表综合评判因素所组成的集合,V 代表评语所组成的集合,模糊变换:

$$B = A \cdot R。 \tag{1}$$

其中 A 是 U 上的模糊子集,而评判的结果 B 是 V 上的模糊子集,V 标准如表 1 所示。

表 1 模糊隶属度评价标准

评语	评分值
很好	0.6 ~ 1
好	0.3 ~ 0.6
较好	0.2 ~ 0.3
一般	0.1 ~ 0.2
差	0 ~ 0.1

现在用模糊综合评价法对某大学宿舍方案进行评价。在 2010 年 9 月 10 日通过人人网 Blog 投票,共计 108 名学生进行了投票,取得了如下数据:经济性所占百分比为 26%,舒适性所占百分比为 30%,安全性所占百分比为 44%。

我们给出指标因素集合:

$$A = \{a_1(经济性), a_2(舒适性), a_3(安全性)\},$$

所以得到权重:

$$A = (0.26, 0.30, 0.44)。 \tag{2}$$

2 因素分析

2.1 经济性分析

1) 建设成本[4]:$G_1(x_i) = D_i \cdot S_i \ (i = 1, 2, 3, 4)$; \(3\)

2) 运行成本:$G_2(x_i) = D_i \cdot S_i \cdot 30\% \ (i = 1, 2, 3, 4)$; \(4\)

[基金项目] 北京市高等教育学会"十二五"高等教育科学研究规划课题(BG125YB025);高等学校大学数学教学研究与发展中心项目(20110901)。

[作者简介] 张晓晞(1957—),男,北京联合大学师范学院教授。研究方向为运筹学与数学建模。

3) 收费价格：$G_3(x_i) = \dfrac{D_i \cdot S_i \cdot 50\%}{M_i}$ $(i=1, 2, 3, 4)$。 (5)

其中 x_i 为第 i 种方案；D_i 为第 i 种方案建设单价；S_i 为第 i 种方案建筑面积；M_i 为第 i 种方案能居住学生总人数。

由公式（5）可得：

$$G_3(x_1) = \dfrac{592 \times 877.35 \times 50\%}{184} = 1411.39,$$

$$G_3(x_2) = \dfrac{592 \times 2660 \times 50\%}{220} = 3578.91,$$

$$G_3(x_3) = \dfrac{592 \times 2229 \times 50\%}{228} = 2893.79,$$

$$G_3(x_4) = \dfrac{592 \times 1886.64 \times 50\%}{132} = 4230.65。$$

归一化处理得：

$G_3(x_1) = 0.11$，$G_3(x_2) = 0.30$，$G_3(x_3) = 0.24$，$G_3(x_4) = 0.35$。

考虑到价格越低越好，故经济性定义为：

$$G(x_i) = 1 - G_3(x_i)。 \tag{6}$$

由公式（6）可得：

$G(x_1) = 0.89$，$G(x_2) = 0.70$，$G(x_3) = 0.76$，$G(x_4) = 0.65$。

归一化处理：

$G(x_1) = 0.30$，$G(x_2) = 0.23$，$G(x_3) = 0.25$，$G(x_4) = 0.22$。

2.2 舒适性分析

1) 人均使用面积系数[5]（使用面积总和 Q_i 与能居住学生总人数 M_i 的比值）：

$$H_1(x_i) = \dfrac{Q_i}{M_i} (i=1, 2, 3, 4)。 \tag{7}$$

2) 采光系数（南北朝向的寝室数量总和 C_i 与寝室、盥洗室、卫生间、沐浴室等数量总和 N_i 的比值）：

$$H_2(x_i) = \dfrac{C_i}{N_i} (i=1, 2, 3, 4)。 \tag{8}$$

3) 通风系数（寝室的通风口即外门窗总数 E_i 与寝室总数 R_i 的比值）：

$$H_3(x_i) = \dfrac{E_i}{R_i} (i=1, 2, 3, 4)。 \tag{9}$$

舒适性定义为：

$$H(x_i) = H_1(x_i) + H_2(x_i) + H_3(x_i)。 \tag{10}$$

由公式（10）可得：

$H(x_1) = 6.10$，$H(x_2) = 11.28$，$H(x_3) = 9.34$，$H(x_4) = 15.30$。

归一化处理：

$H(x_1) = 0.15$，$H(x_2) = 0.27$，$H(x_3) = 0.22$，$H(x_4) = 0.36$。

2.3 安全性分析

1) 人员疏散系数[6]（人均所占楼梯与楼道的面积 L_i）：

$$A_1(x_i) = \dfrac{L_i}{M_i} \tag{11}$$

2) 防盗系数（宿舍进出口安全门个数 F_i 与宿舍进出口个数 T_i 的比值）：

$$A_2(x_i) = \dfrac{A_i}{T_i} \tag{12}$$

安全性定义为：
$$A(x_i) = A_1(x_i) + A_2(x_i)。 \tag{13}$$

由公式（13）可得：
$$A(x_1) = 2.13, A(x_2) = 6.39, A(x_3) = 5.08, A(x_4) = 7.34。$$

归一化处理：
$$A(x_1) = 0.10, A(x_2) = 0.31, A(x_3) = 0.24, A(x_4) = 0.35。$$

3 模糊综合评价

由上述分析结果得到模糊综合评价矩阵：

$$\mathbf{R} = \begin{pmatrix} 0.30 & 0.23 & 0.25 & 0.22 \\ 0.15 & 0.27 & 0.22 & 0.36 \\ 0.10 & 0.31 & 0.24 & 0.35 \end{pmatrix}。$$

由公式（1）可得：

$$B = A \cdot \mathbf{R} = (0.26, 0.30, 0.44) \cdot \begin{pmatrix} 0.30 & 0.23 & 0.25 & 0.22 \\ 0.15 & 0.27 & 0.22 & 0.36 \\ 0.10 & 0.31 & 0.24 & 0.35 \end{pmatrix}$$

$$= (0.17, 0.28, 0.23, 0.32)。$$

由此可得：$Design_4 > Design_2 > Design_3 > Design_1$。

故 $Design_4$ 的设计综合量化评价和比较最高，由表 1 可知 $Design_4$ 的评价最好，$Design_2$、$Design_3$ 较好，$Design_1$ 一般。

4 SPA 发展趋势分析

4.1 SPA 模型

我们应用集对分析的方法[7]进行研究，集对分析（Set Pair Analysis）是一种新的系统分析理论，其基本思路为：在一定的问题背景下对所论的两个集合所具有的特性作同、异、反分析并加以度量刻画，得出这两个集合在所论问题背景下的同、异、反联系度表达式。

集对分析（SPA）的基本思路是把所研究的问题看做一个既确定又不确定的系统，并可用一个能充分体现其思路的联系度式子 $\mu = a + bi + cj$ 来描述各种不确定性。a 表示同一度，b 表示差异度，c 表示对立度。其中 a, b, c 满足归一化条件 $a + b + c = 1$，可以考察 $j = -1$，$i \in [-1, 1]$ 时的计算结果，分析设计方案的主要因素的发展态势。

4.2 舒适性、经济性的 SPA 分析

由公式（2）中的权重可得：$a = 0.30$ 为舒适性的隶属度，$c = 0.26$ 为经济性的隶属度，$b = 1 - a - c = 0.44$ 为差异度。

由此可得：

$$\mu（舒适性、经济性） = 0.30 + 0.44i + 0.26j。$$

当 $j = -1$，$i = 0$ 时，μ（舒适性、经济性）$= 0.30 + 0.44 \times 0 + 0.26 \times (-1) = 0.74 > 0$，说明学生宿舍的设计发展趋势将更多地着重于舒适性。

4.3 安全性的 SPA 分析

由公式（2）中的权重可得：$a = 0.44$ 为安全性的隶属度，由《中国青年报》社会调查中心通过新浪教育频道，对千名大学生进行的在线调查结果，非安全性学生宿舍占 15%，故取 $c = 0.15$ 为非安全性的隶属度，$b = 1 - a - c = 0.41$ 为差异度。

由此可得：

$$\mu（安全性） = 0.44 + 0.41i + 0.15j。$$

当 $j = -1$, $i = 0$ 时：

μ（安全性）$= 0.44 + 0.41 \times 0 + 0.15 \times (-1) = 0.29 > 0$，说明学生宿舍的设计发展趋势将更多地着重于安全性。

5 结束语

综上所述，用模糊综合评价法就它们的经济性、舒适性和安全性做出综合量化评价和比较，在计算过程中所用的方法层次分明、思路清晰，可以推广到其他领域应用。随着人们对住宿条件量化的重视，运用集对分析法分析了学生宿舍设计方案的主要因素的发展态势，可以为学生宿舍的评价提供更为科学的依据。

参考文献

[1] 全国大学生数学建模竞赛组委会. 2010 年竞赛题 [EB/OL]. [2010-09-14]. http://www.mcm.edu.cn.
[2] 张晓晞. 数学控制理论与应用 [M]. 赤峰：内蒙古科学技术出版社，1999.
[3] 贺仲雄. 模糊数学及其应用 [M]. 天津：天津科学技术出版社，1983.
[4] 金敏求. 建筑经济学 [M]. 2 版. 北京：中国建筑工业出版社，2003.
[5] 周越. 室内设计专业毕业设计指南 [M]. 北京：中国水利水电出版社、知识产权出版社，2007.
[6] 北京中建建筑科学技术研究院. 建筑施工安全技术统一规范 [M]. 北京：北京中建建筑科学技术研究院，2001.
[7] 赵克勤. 集对分析及其初步应用 [M]. 杭州：浙江科学技术出版社，2000.

北京建设国际活动聚集之都的现状及推进对策

张景秋　甄茂成

1 国际活动的特征和分类

城市自产生起就具备了集会场所的特性,是人类进行交易和交流活动的重要载体。交易和交流活动的等级越高、范围越大,其所依附的城市影响力也就越显著,而国与国之间或多国之间的国际活动则是最高等级的交易与交流活动。

1.1 国际活动的词义界定与特征

作为交易与交流活动的一种,国际活动本身就是个动态的、复杂的过程,它涉及政治、经济、文化、生活、环境等众多领域,很难给国际活动以精准定义。本文以"国际活动"的词义解析为着眼点,诠释国际活动。

"国际"一词,依据边沁的界定,其直接含义是指"国家之间的",它主要有两层含义:指涉及到多个国家或者其公民的事务,比如国际条约;作为形容词,"国际"也常用来表示超出一个国家国界的事物[1]。而"活动"一词,按照《牛津高阶英汉双解词典》的注解,它强调的是正在发生某种事情的环境状况或者正在做的诸多事务,或者为了兴趣、娱乐及为了达到一定目的而做的事情[2]。结合两词的词义,可以这样界定"国际活动",即它是一项至少有两个国家以上的代表、企业组织或政府机构就相互关心的事务,所做的定期或不定期的有目的、有主题、有计划且具有一定影响力的会议、会展及节庆活动。

对"国际活动"的理解还应把握以下几个特征。

第一,多国性。国际活动可以由一国发起,也可由几个国家联合发起;也有一国倡议或数国发起的情况,但不论发起的形式如何,它是有多个国家参与的活动。

第二,目的性。国际活动通常要消耗大量的人力、物力和财力,其结果是为了扩大影响,达成共识。因此,无论国际活动的规模如何,均具有鲜明的目的性,如奥运会除了弘扬"更快、更高、更强"的体育竞赛精神外,增进交流、扩大影响、塑造地方和国家的形象、拉动经济发展,也是其所要实现的目的。

第三,主题性。国际活动因其鲜明的目的性要求而附带有突出的主题性特征,如2008年北京奥运的主题——"同一个世界同一个梦想",表达了全世界在奥林匹克精神的感召下,追求人类美好未来的共同愿望;2010年上海世博会的主题——"城市,让生活更美好",第17届北京国际图书博览会活动(2010)的主题——"低碳阅读",均提倡一种新的城市生活方式。由此可以看出,国际活动通过其主题性特征,来表明参与国的共同愿望,突出活动的特色,引导活动主张的理念。

第四,规划性。国际活动的举办周期通常较长,要经历发起阶段、准备阶段和实施阶段。如此,规划性对于国际活动具有至关重要的意义。国际活动的流程具有复杂化、多样化的特点,每一项国际活动的背后都有一个甚至多个"智囊团",来组织、推动和保障国际活动的顺利进行。

1.2 国际活动的分类

基于国际活动的词义界定,可以看出国际活动的种类繁多,涉及领域广泛。本文对国际活动的分类将按照活动内容、组织性质、地理区域等将其划分为不同的类型,见表1。

[基金项目] 北京市哲学社会科学规划项目(11CSB005)——北京五个之都建设功能区布局优化及实施对策研究。
[作者简介] 张景秋(1967—),女,北京联合大学应用文理学院城市科学系主任,教授,博士,研究方向为城市地理学、城市与区域规划;甄茂成(1987—),男,首都师范大学资源环境与旅游学院硕士研究生,研究方向为城市与区域规划。

表1 国际活动分类

分类标准	类型	典型案例
按内容划分	政治性会议	亚太经合组织领导人会议（APEC）、中日韩首脑会议等
	经济活动	国际经济发展会议、国际货币基金组织会议等
	文体活动	奥运会、国际音乐节、国际电影节等
	科技会展	世博会、国际交通展览会、北京国际旅游文化节等
	学术交流	国际水会议、中欧知识产权保护高级论坛、国际科技园区北京论坛等
按组织性质划分	政府组织	各国首脑会议等
	非政府组织	奥运会、世界杯等
按地理区域划分	世界或洲际	奥运会、世界杯、世博会、世界大学生运动会等
	地区级	东亚国家首脑会议、欧盟会议、石油输出国会议等

从表1可以看出，国际活动的类别之间的界限并不十分严格，分类不具有惟一性和排他性，不同类别的国际活动之间存在着交叉，如亚太经合组织会议即是政治性会议，也具有经济活动的性质；上海世博会既是国际会展活动，也具有文化交流的性质；一些学术交流会议也带有经济商贸洽谈的目的。至于国际活动的规模很难作为划分依据，规模大小与影响力并不成正比关系。国际活动的规模可以依照参加国家和地区的数量而定，也可以根据参加的人数而定，还可以依照其重要程度而定。

通过对国际活动的词义界定、特征及分类的辨析可以看出，规模类型多样、高投资性、高关注度是国际活动的一个鲜明特点，其不容忽视的影响力和带动作用，对提高举办城市的国际地位和国际形象具有积极的作用，由此产生的经济效益更是难以估量。

此外，从卡斯特（M. Castells）基于网络社会理论的世界城市概念出发，世界城市不仅限于地方的空间等级体系，还包括一种新的流的空间体系，即全球的流的空间（global spaces of flows）。卡斯特认为，流的空间的节点和枢纽就是世界城市，这为世界城市提供了一种更直接的分析理论和方法[3]。而类型规模多样的国际活动即是一种流的空间形态，世界城市则是其重要的空间组织形式和载体。对国际政治、经济和文化生活具有广泛影响力、控制力的节点城市，其主要指标和突出特点之一，是必须具备汇聚国际活动的能力，即其必定是国际活动聚集之都。

2 北京举办国际活动现状

2.1 举办国际会议的次数低于纽约、伦敦和东京等世界城市

根据国际协会联盟（UIA）对国际会议和体育赛事的界定标准，可看出北京与纽约、伦敦、东京三大世界城市在举办大型国际活动数量方面的差异，见表2。

表2 北京、纽约、伦敦、东京承办大型国际活动数量比较

项目	纽约（2008）	伦敦（2008）	东京（2008）	北京（2009）
大型国际体育赛事（次）	37	22	—	12
国际会议（次）	128	103	126	88

数据来源：参见参考文献4：《北京世界城市指标体系的构建与测评》。

表2显示，与纽约、伦敦、东京这世界三大城市相比，北京在承办大型国际体育赛事和国际会议方面尚存在着比较明显的差距。这表明北京吸引国际活动的能力相对较低。

2.2 国际会议会展比例低，大型展览不多

会议会展是国际活动的重要组成。2010年北京会展业的数据显示，2010年在北京举办的会议会展总量不少，但国际会议会展所占比例较低，国际会议只占会议总数的2.3%，出席国际会议的人数不及出席会议总人数的5%；国际展览比例接近展览总数的四分之一；北京具有较强的国际展览吸引力，尽管能举办大型展览的场地设施较少，5万平方米以上的只有21个，但国际展览的累积面积约占展览场馆总

面积的 49%，国际展览观众数达到 165 万人次，约占观众总数的 20%；国际会议和展览带来的收入却甚少，两者加起来仅占会展总收入的 9.58%，见表 3。

表 3 2010 年北京会展业活动情况

项目	数值	所占百分比（%）
会议情况		
会议总数（个）	256771.0	
国际会议（个）	5912.0	2.30
接待会议人数（万人）	1731.3	
与会国外人数（万人）	78.0	4.50
展览情况		
展览总数（个）	1196.0	
国际展览（个）	291.0	24.33
展览面积 5 万平方米及以上的展览（个）	21.0	
展览累计使用面积（含室外展览面积）（万平方米）	899.5	
国际展览累计使用面积（万平方米）	436.8	48.56
展览观众数（万人次）	839.4	
国际展览观众数（万人次）	165.0	19.66
收入情况		
会展收入（万元）	1724839.5	
国际会议收入（万元）	101217.5	5.89
国际展览收入（万元）	63655.0	3.69

数据来源：《北京统计年鉴》（2011）。

2.3 国际活动场馆建设不足

国际活动能在北京聚集，必须要有足够的场馆设施。从北京市 2006—2010 年主要场馆情况可以看出，公共图书馆的数量在这 5 年内没有增加，群众艺术馆及文化馆数量有所下降，博物馆变化不大，见表 4。另外，据相关研究，北京城区市级以上的展览馆只有 16 座，且分布不均匀，主要集中在朝阳区（4 座）和海淀区（6 座）[5]。以上数据表明，北京能承载国际活动的场馆设施建设还很不充足，需要进一步加强。

表 4 2006—2010 年北京图书馆、文化馆、博物馆数量（个）

年份	公共图书馆	群众艺术馆、文化馆	博物馆
2006	25	21	33
2007	25	21	34
2008	25	20	37
2009	25	20	40
2010	25	20	41

数据来源：《北京统计年鉴》（2011）。

2.4 组织形式单一，缺少具有北京特色的国际活动

自 2008 年北京奥运会之后，在北京举办的国际活动数量逐年增加，但是受关注程度并不高。北京每年举办的国际会展，以商务会展居多，规模大多局限于两三个国家，特别是缺乏以"北京"为主题的定期举行的具有国际影响力和美誉度的世界性国际活动。此外，国际活动组织形式单一，大多数都是由政府主导举办的，缺少在国际上具有重大影响的企业机构在京举办的大型活动。

3 北京建设国际活动聚集之都的可行性

3.1 首都优势与后奥运契机

北京是我国的首都，是全国的政治、文化中心，随着中国在世界政治和经济格局中地位的提升，北京的影响力和吸引力也日益增长，这对于北京吸引国际活动聚集是十分有利的。而奥运会的成功举办，进一步塑造了北京的国际形象，知名度和影响力更是显著提升，比较奥运会前后北京新批境外投资数和投资总额（见表5）可以看出，2007年北京外商投资企业为3900个，到2009年增加至4733个，增加了833个；实际利用外资2009年比2007年增长了20.7%。同时各种以奥运为主题的政治、经济、文化活动频繁在京举办，由此可以看出，后奥运阶段给北京的发展带来了更大的机遇。

表5　2006—2009北京市外商投资企业数和实际利用外资额

年份	新批境外投资企业数量（家）	境外企业投资总额（亿美元）
2006	76	3.81
2007	87	4.22
2008	103	4.93
2009	140	6.35

数据来源：《北京统计年鉴》（2006—2010）。

3.2 产业结构不断优化，服务业发展较成熟，发展环境稳定

从2005—2010年北京市第三产业占GDP的比重变化可以看出，北京市产业结构正处于不断优化的进程中，第三产业增长迅速，已经成为城市经济的主导产业（见图1）。

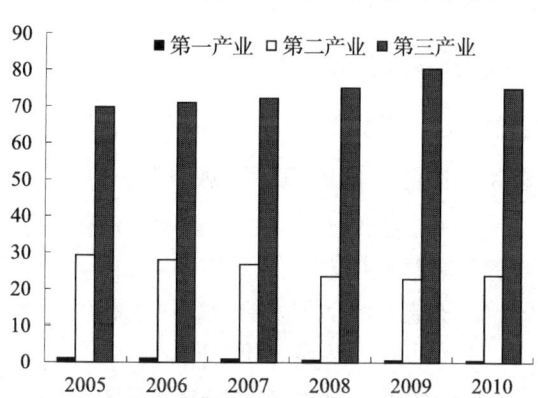

图1　2005—2010年北京市三次产业占GDP比重变化
数据来源：《北京统计年鉴》（2011）

国际活动对主办城市的服务业要求较高。近年来，北京在交通运输、金融保险、信息通信、住宿和餐饮等与承办国际活动相关的服务业数量和质量均有不同程度的提升（见表6），这是举办国际活动的必备条件。服务业的快速发展，为北京举办国际活动奠定了坚实的基础。

表6　2005—2010年北京市主要服务业年生产总值　　　　　　　　　　　　　　　　（单位：亿元）

服务业类型	2005年	2006年	2007年	2008年	2009年	2010年
交通运输、仓储和邮政业	404.7	455.2	502.6	498.9	556.6	712.0
信息传输、计算机服务和软件业	583.2	696.4	855.9	999.1	1066.5	1214.1
金融业	836.6	1302.8	1286.3	1519.2	1603.6	1863.6
房地产业	455.3	821.5	644.2	844.6	1062.5	1006.5

续表

服务业类型	2005 年	2006 年	2007 年	2008 年	2009 年	2010 年
批发和零售业	654.1	872.5	879.4	1426.7	1525.0	1888.5
住宿和餐饮业	182.8	218.4	247.0	274.4	262.5	317.3
租赁和商务服务业	346.8	447.1	554.5	765.3	809.6	953.2
科技研究、技术服务和地质勘探	341.8	438.6	539.3	706.7	816.9	941.1
教育	315.2	320.6	441.5	402.1	444.1	516.2
文化体育娱乐业	171.3	189.0	227.4	247.4	259.0	294.6

数据来源：《北京统计年鉴》(2011)。

2008年发生的金融危机使全球经济重心开始转移。相对而言，北京政治、经济环境稳定，经济发展平稳。这些因素对举办和吸引国际活动来说是非常有利的。

3.3 独特的文化优势和包容性

纵观纽约、伦敦、巴黎、东京这些国际活动聚集的重要城市，巴黎因其在文化上的独特性，成为以文化立市的典范[6]。一说到"浪漫之都""艺术之都"，人们首先想到的就是巴黎，它独特的历史文化，众多的名胜古迹，多姿多彩的文化，吸引了大量的国际活动在巴黎聚集，使之成为当之无愧的国际活动聚集之都。在文化软环境方面，北京也同样具有突出的优势。北京是一座具有3000多年建城史、850多年建都史的历史文化名城，有着深厚的文化底蕴、独特的故都风貌和丰富的现代文化资源[7]；北京作为历史上多元文化交融的都城，其文化包容性已经成为北京的一种品质。这种独特的城市魅力吸引着世界各地的人们，是北京建设国际活动聚集之都的重要优势。

4 关于北京建设国际活动聚集之都的建议

北京要打造国际活动聚集之都，建设世界城市，需要做好以下几个方面的工作。

4.1 学习先进经验，制定促进举办国际活动的政策法规

首先，要加强国际间的交流，积极借鉴世界城市建设国际活动聚集之都的理念、方法和经验，结合北京城市建设的实际和发展规律，不断总结和创新，找寻出适合北京建设国际活动聚集之都的路径。其次，要制定促进举办国际活动的政策法规和活动准入标准，规范和引导多元组织机构在北京举办国际活动，让国际活动的举办有法可依，有章可循，逐步趋于规范化。

4.2 以国际会展为"龙头"，加强国际会议和节庆活动的定期化和长效化建设

国际活动聚集之都的建设可以在极大程度上缩小北京与世界城市的差距，提升北京的影响力和竞争力，促进城市的快速发展。因为一项世界级国际活动将吸引众多的知名企业、跨国公司和游客涌向举办城市，将会有力地推动当地乃至整个区域的政治、经济、文化的发展，特别是某一城市定期举办的国际活动将会成为该城市极富影响力的"名片"。

目前，北京已经取得了一定的国际会展办展经验，应以此为"龙头"，引导国际会议和节庆活动比例的提升，策划定期化、长效化、有影响力的国际会议和节庆活动，并以经营企业的方式经营国际会展、会议和节庆活动。同时，北京还应在提高国际活动的收入上多下功夫，如多吸引境外游客参加国际会展，与有影响力的国际会议组织者协商将北京纳入主办城市，以促进北京国际活动聚集之都建设的进程。

4.3 进一步完善城市基础设施建设，优化布局国际活动场所

便捷的交通网络、发达的通信网络、设备齐全的场馆、完善的接待服务设施等，是举办国际活动必备的硬性条件。目前，北京在这些方面还存在着一定的差距。因此，北京仍要继续加大城市基础设施的建设，要进一步优化布局和建设一批符合举办国际活动要求的场所。目前来看，北京四星级及以上的宾

馆、酒店及接待大型国际会议的场地仍然不足，且一些大型活动场所还多集中在主城区。今后，一方面要结合城市功能区的优化调整，从全市角度有重点地在石景山、顺义、通州和大兴布建几个大型会展中心；另一方面要在高等级星级宾馆集中的区域，整合会议场所资源，形成高级别的国际会议聚集区。

4.4 培养国际活动组织策划和实施管理人才

北京建设国际活动聚集之都的关键在于人才建设。对于种类繁多的国际活动而言，要求具备国际视野、通晓举办国际活动的惯例和规则，以及具备专业知识和技能的活动组织策划和管理人才队伍，尤其是举办大型国际活动，更需要专业化的国际团队。北京作为全国的文化中心，虽然高校云集、科研机构众多，但符合要求的国际活动策划和管理人才却呈紧缺状态。因此，应将国际活动策划和管理作为一门学科，在高校设置相关专业与课程，培养适应国际活动策划和管理要求的专业团队，以此奠定北京建设国际活动之都的人才基础。

4.5 深入挖掘文化资源，以文化优势吸引国际活动

北京建设国际活动聚集之都的绝对优势在于其多元文化的兼容并蓄，应充分利用和深入挖掘北京的文化资源，结合国家文化中心的建设，以城市历史文化街区的保护和更新为载体，形成特色鲜明的文化功能区，以此吸引国际活动落户北京。

5 结　语

中共北京市委十届八次全会通过的"十二五"规划《建议》提出，要以更高的标准推动"人文北京、科技北京、绿色北京"建设，努力打造"国际活动聚集之都、世界高端企业总部聚集之都、世界高端人才聚集之都、中国特色社会主义先进文化之都、和谐宜居之都"，推动北京向中国特色世界城市迈进。在"五个之都"的建设目标中，国际活动聚集之都是树立城市形象、提升城市影响力的关键。本文立足北京的城市特性，解析了国际活动的特点和分类，分析了北京国际活动聚集之都建设的现状。本文认为，国际活动聚集之都是世界城市的重要标志，北京应在立足自身优势的基础上，积极借鉴国际先进经验，不断总结创新，以争取国际活动落户北京，以此推进北京建设国际活动聚集之都的进程，提升北京的影响力和竞争力。

参考文献

[1] 杰里米·边沁. 道德与立法原理导论（英文珍藏版）[M]. 西安：陕西人民出版社，2006：296-297.
[2] 霍恩比著，石孝殊等译. 牛津高阶英汉双解词典 [M]. 北京：商务印书馆，2004：17-18.
[3] Castells M. The Rise of Network Society [M]. Oxford: Blackwell. 1996: 378-469.
[4] 齐心，张佰瑞，赵继敏. 北京世界城市指标体系的构建与测评 [J]. 城市发展研究，2011（4）：1-7.
[5] 陈卓，张景秋. 北京城区展览馆空间布局演变及特征 [J]. 城市问题，2008（12）：34-38.
[6] 张景秋. 论北京的文化包容性与世界城市的建设 [J]. 北京规划建设，2010（5）：39-41.
[7] 田丽凤. 北京迈向世界城市的发展要点 [J]. 城市问题，2010（9）：36-39.

太行山区传统民居建筑空间研究

张路光　李莘

国外对传统民居建筑的研究由来已久，对乡土建筑的保护和传承也是我国学界关注的焦点。以河北太行山区井径县和邢台县英谈村为例，井怪县 2006 年就被联合国地名专家组评定为"千年古县"，河北邢台县的英谈村，被誉为"江北第一古石寨"，两地都因至今保存完好的明清以来传统民居建筑而著称，它们是体现太行山地区传统民居建筑特色的典型案例。其不同的村落形态、建筑形制、布局、材料、技术不但反映出个性的建筑文化，同时解读着太行山区的民居文化和地域人文精神。

1 太行山区传统民居建筑空间的形成和形制特征

"太行山像一只虎，诗沱河额水，黄河岸摆尾[1]。"这只猛虎，不仅蕴含了原始纯朴的自然环境，雄奇独特的自然景观，也形成了太行山区传统的农耕文化。这就表现为讲究与自然和谐，以人为本，天人合一的深厚文化内涵和丰富的人文景观。

1.1 建筑空间的形成

太行山山势东陡西缓，西翼连接山西高原，东翼过渡到华北平原，太行山区传统民居建筑就处于这相对闭塞、地形复杂的山脊山墙环境中。这种山地自然生态环境和特殊的地理地势，在客观上决定了太行山区传统民居建筑风格和形态特征，主要村落的选址和整体布局也取决于村落所依存的山势，背山面水或四面环山。太行山石材遍布，建筑材料就地取材，石材多为喀斯特地貌延展基岩层石灰岩，坚固结实、冬暖夏凉。在古村落中，石材不但被用作建造房屋的主要材料，也被用于铺设道路、垒砌水井，甚至许多生活必需品和一些艺术装饰品也都用石头制作而成。

1.2 民居建筑空间的形制特征

由于山区地理地势的影响和当时的经济条件、生产技术、运输方式的落后，使得居民改造自然环境的能力有限，因此在建筑取材上因地制直、建筑空间上存在延展变化，而这种错落的空间布局并没有完全遵循传统北方民居的直线形制，而是依据不同的地理环境以及生活需要在轴线对称的基础上进行了延伸，从村落形态、建筑形制到院落空间都沿山体走向依形营造，呈现出更为自由有序的形态，形成了独属于太行山区民居建筑的形制特征。如具有典型古太行建筑风格的河北井径县和邢台县英谈村。

地处太行山东麓的井径县，地貌复杂，峰谷交错，崖台叠置，地势险峻。《太平寰宇记》说"四方高，中央下，如井之深，如灶之怪，故谓之井径。"更为典型的就是井径县太行深山的于家石头村，整个街道全部取材于太行山青石造筑，由低洼之地始建朝高地势发展，依山坡蜿蜒起伏、千姿百态、层层叠叠、步步高升，就像从太行山脉生长出的有机建筑体，与大山完美呼应，成为太行山区古村落独树一帜最具代表性的特征。

而位于太行山东麓深山腹地、被太行山崎峰雾子墙、和尚墙紧紧包围的邢台县英谈村，则是由当地盛产的红石材靠山而建、顺势构筑的古寨。其城墙围绕古村大多以两三层建筑垒就，高低俯仰、阁楼错落、石板铺路、错落有序，这些没有经过人工精细加工的红石墙体，其色彩、肌理形成了与大山的视觉延续，呈现出粗矿但同一，简单且丰富的地域建筑特色。

[作者简介] 张路光，北京联合大学师范学院；李莘，中国戏曲学院新媒体艺术系。

2 太行山区传统民居建筑空间类型和构成要素

2.1 建筑空间类型

太行山区民居建筑多以窑洞以及合院为主要建筑形式。传统村落无论是南北纵向,还是东西横向,村落中的合院民居正房多为坐北朝南,两侧厢房成对称布置,纵向或者横向递进院落。与陕北窑洞直掏式方法施工不同,太行山民居主要依赖山墙崖壁建筑,多采用填充发券结构建造,以一米左右厚度的墙体抵御侧推力,平的屋顶用作粮食晾晒,房檐设置排水槽储存降雨。

建筑形式上有石头房和瓦房。石头房屋不仅在建材上有着便直性和坚固性的特点,同时还具有优于砖块的隔热性。厚重石块为基础墙体,用白石灰黏合,屋顶则采用薄而宽的石板。瓦房民居与传统形式的瓦房建筑形制大致相同,屋顶采用起脊铺瓦、四梁八柱的建筑格式,外部墙体采用青石砖,内部墙体则用灰泥饰面。

2.2 建筑平面布局

太行山传统民居建筑的平面布局因山地环境的地势变化而变化,多数以单进院落纵向进深为主要布局,并由此发展出更为多变和自由的空间布局,同时承袭了河北传统民居的建筑形制,正房坐北朝南成主轴起点,两侧厢房以南北轴线为中心左右堆成,院落在南北纵向上成矩形空间布局。正房开间面积大于两侧厢房。前院和后院由中间的厅房连接,无论是正房或者是厢房,都在房屋的中心开门洞,左右两侧开窗洞,两侧窗户也是以门为中心呈左右对称的布局。

2.3 建筑院落空间

太行山区的院落在建筑空间中并不是一个绝对私密的空间,它是半开放的,并因其敞开性成为居民生活中最易接触外部自然环境的场所。最常见的有三或五开间坐北朝南的正房,且多中心轴线,正房中间是厅堂,左右两侧为卧室以及灶房,正房前为廊檐统一贯通的"一明两暗三开间"的独院式院落形式;基于独院院落形式的以正房轴线为中心对称,左右两侧布置厢房,正房和左右厢房围以及院落墙体围合成的空间的三合院式院落;还有因为山地地势变化发展出更多灵活的矩形四合院院落;以及在四合院的基础上以正房庭院为中心东西横向由两个或两个以上独立小合院组合形成进深不同的组合院院落。

2.4 建筑构成要素

太行山传统民居建筑以合院形式为主要建筑形制。合院是以院落为中心成向内聚集的建筑组合体,建筑形制主要由以下要素组成在合院中线的端头,是建筑体量最高大、建筑装饰最精致,象征家庭中最高等级的正房,也是合院建筑中最为重要的中心部分;与正房围合成院落空间的是左右两侧厢房,正房和厢房由檐廊连接;街道进入合院院落内部的过渡空间称为倒座,两层形制的倒座是太行山区传统民居建筑的一个特色;内部空间与外部空间的交界点是大门,在建筑形态上反映了院落主人的地位和贫富程度,一般位于建筑中心轴线上,有与倒座相连接的规格比较高的屋宇式大门和结构简单的墙垣式大门的区别;在两进合院院落中还有次门,在体量、装饰上都次于大门;影壁在太行山区民居建筑空间中有着重要含义,为阻挡院落外部的冲煞之气进入院内,也防止院内才气散去,它与大门共同塑造了一个过渡空间,也为建筑增加了视觉层次。

3 太行山区传统民居建筑空间面临的问题与保护措施

当今我国城镇化发展势头迅猛,新农村建设日趋深入,人类征服自然的能力不断增强,大量传统民居建筑遭到损毁甚至被废弃,太行山区传统民居建筑也正在面临着前所未有的危机。

3.1 太行山区传统民居建筑面临的问题

随着经济建设的快速发展,社会变迁以及人民的生活方式、居民的居住意识都发生着改变,新民居建设及公共基础设施不断完善和提高。但由于对传统民居建筑空间的内涵认识不够,缺乏专业规划和科学管理,使其内部的文化内涵必然无法得到延续;农村人口流动的日趋频繁,外部文化的渗透和影响,改变了相对稳定、封闭的生活环境和几百年延续下来的社会生活方式;传统民居建筑聚集的古村落内基础设施不健全,生活、卫生条件简陋,使之逐渐失去了往日生活的气息;传统民居建筑的建造与改造一般属于居住者的个人行为，他们在投入新居建设中，因无力对传统民居建筑进行维护，从而加剧了对于传统民居建筑的破坏。上述种种原因导致了传统民居建筑空间的物质形态的变化。

因此，在新时代的环境下，保持太行山人传统的社会生活方式和社会观念，是传承和发展传统民居建筑空间形式与内涵文化的当务之急。

3.2 太行山区传统民居建筑空间保护可行性方法

首先，要尊重环境，树立保护原生态环境的意识。随着新材料和新技术的不断开发，在现代社会建筑建造的过程中，应建立起保持民居建筑空间和自然生态环境之间的平衡观念，树立对传统民居建筑空间进行保护的意识，这是传统民居建筑空间在新时期延续的物质基础。

其次，科学管理和规划，保护古村落原始风貌。规划保护区，在保护区内，由建筑群和街道所形成的空间结构要严格控制；规划新建区，处理好新建区与保护区之间的过渡关系；规划新建建筑规模和形制，使其与传统民居建筑形成和谐统一的整体[2]；规划村落，控制保护区内的人口密度，保证原生态的生活氛围，避免环境承载超负荷而遭到破坏；规划交通，在保护区外围设置过境交通，严格控制古村落内的机动车通行。

第三，改善保护区内的基础设施，提高居民的生活质量。在保护其建筑格局的同时，还要清理村落中的私搭乱建，治理外部环境污染、疏通水系，重点对建筑内部加以调整改造，使用当地的材料、当地的工艺改造给水、排水、燃气、供热、道路等，修旧如故，体现当地的文化特色，满足居民对现代生活的追求。

第四，政策上建立全面的保护机制。保护、传承和发展，须借助政府力量，加大宣传力度，推行保护的社会化和市场化，因地制宜建立相关保护体系，下放部分市场的经营开发权，以调动经济力量为村落发展增添力量。

本文基于太行山区传统民居建筑空间的形成和形制特征，分析其形制类型和构成要素，总结其现状、面临的问题与保护措施，希望借此能为乡土建筑的保护、传承及传统民居建筑空间形制在现代居住建筑设计的研究提供理论依据。

参考文献

[1] 王佳. 太行山东麓旅游资源的 RMP 分析及其创新开发策略 [J]. 生态经济, 2008 (8).
[2] HudsonF. S. B. A. Geography of Settlements. 2nd. Edition [M]. London: Macdonald & Evans, 1976.

Quantum Spectra and Classical Orbits in Artificial Atom

Lu Jun

I INTRODUCTION

It is characteristic of the classical theory that within it exist objects, phenomena, and events that are distinct and well - defined and events that exhibit reliable and reproducible properties with the aid of which they can be identified and compared. However, when we come to describe quantum concepts, we find that the precision of our customary scientific language leads to difficult and unwieldy modes of expression. As is well known, the quantum properties of matter are to be associated with incompletely defined potentialities, which can be more definitely realized only in interaction with a classically describable system.

In fact, instead of having well - defined variables that are in a one - to - one correspondence with the actual behavior of matter, we have at the quantum level a wave function that is only in statistical correspondence with this behavior. Nevertheless, it is only at the classical level that definite results for an experiment can be obtained, in the form of distinct events which are associated in a one - to - one correspondence with the various possible values of the physical quantity that is being measured. This means that quantum theory presupposes the classical level and the general correctness of classical concepts in describing this level. It does not deduce classical concepts as limiting cases of quantum concept. Thus, the correspondence principle is simply a consistency condition which requires that when the quantum theory plus its classical interpretation is carried to the limit of high quantum numbers, the simple classical theory will be obtained. Hence, classical definiteness and quantum potentialities complement each other in providing a complete description of the system as a whole.

Since the periodic - orbit theory of states density was introduced by Gutzwiller[1,2], the researches about the relationship between classical and quantum mechanics of dynamical behavior are continual for the integrable and chaos systems[2,3]. These researches have extended our comprehension to the chaos dynamics extremely. The results of research have become indispensable tools for understanding some new physical phenomenon. For example, Du and Delos[4-6] have recognized that the periodic - orbit theory is the right theoretical tool for atomic spectra. They found that it was not periodic orbits, but close orbits that produce the visible signal in the absorption spectrum, and the "quasi - Landau resonance" phenomenon can be explained successfully in this theory. Thus the form of periodic - orbit theory that gives a description of atomic spectra is known as closed - orbit theory.

The closed - orbit theory has been extended and refined in a number of ways, and used to study a variety of phenomena[7-9]. We can determine the periods and the classical actions of orbits of the electron, and see the creation and bifurcation of these orbits as the dynamics of the system changes from orderly to chaotic. The interpretation of atomic spectra in terms of classical orbits has been called "Recurrence Spectroscopy". Recently the theory has been reformulated to consider the effects of time - dependent fields acting on the electron[10]. There have also been interesting recent proposals for retrieving long - time quantum information from short - time classical orbits[11].

In this paper, we will propose a kind of new classical - quantum correspondence principle. We will define a new quantum spectrum function using the eigenvalues and the eigenfunctions of a system in section II. As an instance, in section III we will calculate the quantum spectrum function in the system of two - dimensional artificial

---

[Author Introduction] Lu Jun, Department of Foundational Science, Beijing Union University, E - mail: lujun@ buu. edu. cn.

atom. In section IV, we will show the correspondence relationship between the quantum spectrum function and the classical orbits. These orbits are neither Gulzwiller's periodic orbits nor Du and Delos's closed orbits.

II QUANTUM SPECTRUM FUNCTION

We consider a multi-dimensional system with the Hamiltonian

$$H = \frac{p^2}{2} + V(q). \tag{1}$$

If $A(x_1, y_1)$ and $B(x_2, y_2)$ are two arbitrary fixed point in the system, we define the new quantum spectrum function as

$$\rho_{AB}(E) = \sum_n \psi_n^*(A)\psi_n(B)\delta(E - E_n), \tag{2}$$

where n is the quantum number, E_n is the energy eigenvalue, and ψ_n is the corresponding eigenfunction.

In analogy with the reckon of closed-orbit theory, $\rho_{AB}(E)$ can always be written by

$$\rho_{AB}(E) = \rho_{AB}^0(E) + \sum_i C_i \sin(S_i + \varphi_i) \tag{3}$$

It is apparent that there are a background term and a summation of many sine resonance terms in Eq. (3). The summation includes all the classical reasonable orbits from point A to point B. Here the amplitude C_i is related to the stability of orbits, the action variable $S_i = \int_A^B p dq$ is the integrals along the orbits, and φ_i is the phases, including the Maslov phase corrections. It should be pointed that Eq. (3) shows the relationship between the quantum spectrum function [Eq. (2)] and the classical orbits. We will describe the uses of Eq. (3) by means of an instance in next sections.

III QUANTUM SPECTRA IN ARTIFICIAL ATOM

As a simple explicit example of the calculation of quantum spectrum function, we consider the two-dimensional motion of an electron with unit mass in the artificial atom, which length a and width b. The electron is restrained by reflecting walls that terminate a region of constant potential energy. The potential function for the system can be expressed as

$$V(x, y) = \begin{cases} 0, & 0 < x < a, \ 0 < y < b. \\ \infty, & \text{otherwise} \end{cases} \tag{4}$$

The corresponding stationary state Schrödinger equation is

$$-\frac{1}{2}\left(\frac{\partial^2}{\partial x^2} + \frac{\partial^2}{\partial y^2}\right)\varphi(x, y) = E\varphi(x, y) \tag{5}$$

This equation can be solved by separation of variables. The energy eigenvalues of Eq. (5) can be given by

$$E_{mn} = \frac{\pi^2}{2}\left(\frac{m^2}{a^2} + \frac{n^2}{b^2}\right), \quad m, n = 1, 2, 3, \cdots, \tag{6}$$

and the corresponding eigenfunctions are

$$\varphi_{mn}(x, y) = \sqrt{\frac{2}{ab}}\sin\left(\frac{m\pi}{a}x\right)\sin\left(\frac{n\pi}{b}y\right). \tag{7}$$

If we set that $A(x_1, y_1)$ and $B(x_2, y_2)$ are two arbitrary points in the two-dimensional artificial atom (not on the boundary), we can write the new quantum spectrum function as

$$\rho_{AB}(E) = \sum_{mn} \varphi_{mn}^*(x_1, y_1)\varphi_{mn}(x_2, y_2)\delta(E - E_{mn}) \tag{8}$$

Now we will prove that the new quantum spectrum function Eq. (8) has contained the information of classical orbits from point A to point B, by means of the Fourier transformation. Considering the characteristic of the motion for an electron in the two-dimensional artificial atom, we can write the action variable as $S = kL$, where k is the absolute value of momentum, and L is the length of orbit. We then define the Fourier transformation as

$$\tilde{\rho}_{AB}(L) = \int_{E_{min}}^{E_{max}} \rho_{AB}(E)\exp(ikL)\,dE, \qquad (9)$$

here it should be noticed that

$$E = \frac{k^2}{2} \qquad (10)$$

Substitution of Eq. (8) into Eq. (9) and integral give

$$\tilde{\rho}_{AB}(L) = \sum_{mn} \varphi_{mn}^*(x_1,y_1)\varphi_{mn}(x_2,y_2)\exp(ik_{mn}L), \qquad (11)$$

where $k_{mn} = \sqrt{2E_{mn}}$. The summation in Eq. (11) includes all the energy levels between E_{min} and E_{max}.

For Eq. (3), considering that kCi changes slowly in the integral regions and can be regarded as constants approximately, through the same Fourier transformation we obtain

$$\tilde{\rho}_{AB}(L) \approx \tilde{\rho}_{AB}^0(L) + \sum_i \bar{k}_i C_i \Big[-\frac{\exp(-i\varphi_i)}{2i}\Big]\Delta(L-L_i), \qquad (12)$$

where

$$\Delta(x) = \int_{k_{min}}^{k_{max}} \exp(ixk)\,dk \qquad (13)$$

is a function which peak is at the point of $x = 0$, $\bar{k}_i$ is a kind of average value of k in the region $[k_{min}, k_{max}]$, and

$$\tilde{\rho}_{AB}^0(L) = \int_{E_{min}}^{E_{max}} \rho_{AB}^0(E)\exp(i\sqrt{2E}L)\,dE. \qquad (14)$$

Here the revolving wave approximation is used. From Eq. (12) it can be found that the positions of peaks of function $|\tilde{\rho}_{AB}(L)|^2$ will correspond with the length of the classical orbits from point A to point B.

IV QUANTUM SPECTRA AND CLASSICAL ORBITS

Losing no generality, as an illustration we choose the following parameters

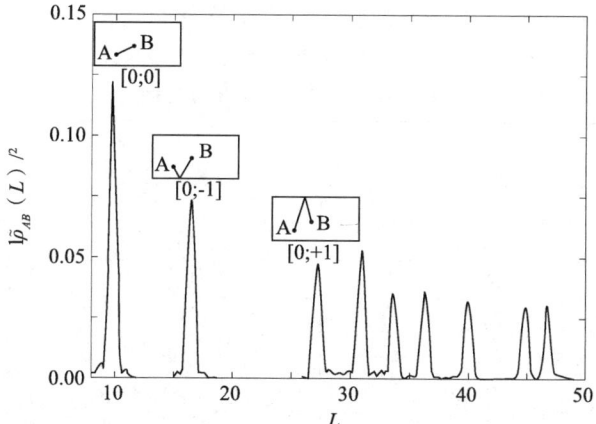

Fig. 1 Norm of Fourier transformation of quantum spectra $|\tilde{\rho}_{AB}(L)^2|$ changes with the self-variable L. The forms of corresponding classical orbits are drawn on the first three peaks.

$$a = 25\sqrt{3}, \quad b = 14\sqrt{2},$$
$$x_1 = 10.92, \quad y_1 = 4.76$$
$$x_2 = 19.73, \quad y_2 = 9.15,$$

to calculate the function. All the states that energy eigenvalue is less than $E_{max} = 40$ are calculated in the summation. Fig. 1 describes the situation that the norm of Fourier transformation of quantum spectra $|\tilde{\rho}_{AB}(L)|^2$ changes with the self-variable L.

The electron does the rectilinear motion in the system, until coming into collision with the walls of artificial atom and reflected. We have found all the classical orbits from point A to point B, which length is less than 50 (see Fig. 2). We will depict the forms of every orbit with the following method.

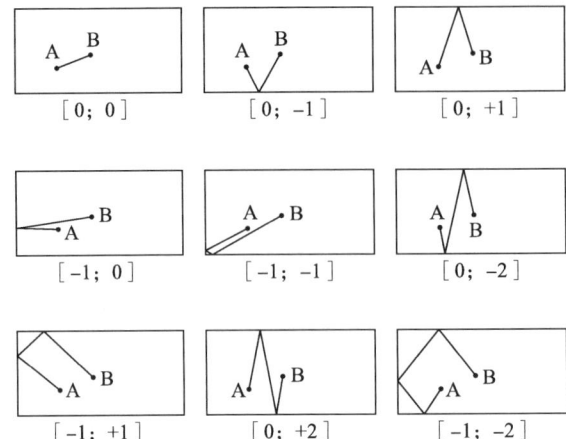

Fig. 2 Classical orbits from point A to point B in the two – dimensional artificial atom, which length is less than 50. The classical orbits correspond with the peaks in Figure1 one by one.

- All of the orbits are expressed with two integers in square brackets. A semicolon separates the two integers.
- The absolute value of the first integer means the number of times that the orbit collides with the two walls vertical to x – axis, and the absolute value of the second integer means the number of times that the orbit collides with the two walls vertical to y – axis.
- The sign of the first integer means the direction of x – axis when the electron leaves from point A. The " + " means in the same direction as x – axis, and the " – " means in the reverse direction as x – axis. The sign of the second integer means the direction of y – axis when the electron leaves from point A. The " + " means in the same direction as y – axis, and the " – " means in the reverse direction as y – axis.

TABLE I CONTRAST ABOUT POSITIONS OF QUANTUM PEAKS AND NATURE OF CLASSICAL ORBITS

Number	Positions of quantum peaks	Forms of classical orbits	Length of classical orbits
1	9.83	[0; 0]	9.84
2	16.47	[0; -1]	16.46
3	27.21	[0; +1]	27.16
4	30.96	[-1; 0]	30.96
5	33.57	[-1; -1]	33.66
6	36.29	[0; -2]	36.29
7	39.97	[-1; +1]	39.99
8	44.86	[0; +2]	44.86
9	46.72	[-1; -2]	46.68

The last two lists in Table I give the nature of classical orbits. It is easy to find that, all the classical orbits of the electron correspond one by one with the positions of the quantum peaks in Fig. 1 (the norm of Fourier transformation of quantum spectra). From Table I, we can also find that, the length of each classical orbit is just consistent with the position of each quantum peak in the range of allowable error.

On the other hand, If we let point B coincide with point A, i. e. ,
$$x_1 = x_2 = 10.92,$$
$$y_1 = y_2 = 4.76,$$
we can also obtain the closed orbits. Fig. 3 describes the situation that the norm of Fourier transformation of quantum spectra $|\hat{\rho}_{AA}(L)|^2$ changes with the self – variable L. Table II gives the positions of quantum peaks and the

nature of classical orbits from point A coming back to point A. It is interesting that the 6th and 7th quantum peaks in Fig. 3 are degenerate. They correspond with two classical closed orbits respectively.

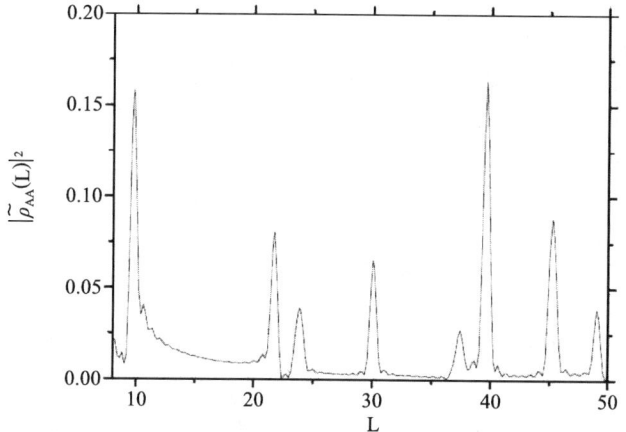

Fig. 3 Norm of Fourier transformation of quantum spectra $|\tilde{\rho}_{AB}(L)|^2$ changes with the self-variable L. It is interesting that the 6th and 7th quantum peaks are degenerate.

TABLE II CONTRAST ABOUT POSITIONS OF QUANTUM PEAKS OBTAINED BY CALCULATION AND NATURE OF CLASSICAL ORBITS IN ARTIFICIAL ATOM (FROM POINT A COMING BACK TO POINT A)

Number	Positions of quantum peaks	Forms of classical orbits	Length of classical orbits
1	9.74	[0; -1]	9.52
2	21.74	[-1; 0]	21.84
3	23.90	[-1; -1]	23.82
4	30.09	[0; +1]	30.08
5	37.36	[-1; +1]	37.17
6	39.59	[0; +2], [0; -2]	39.60
7	45.23	[-1; +2], [-1; -2]	45.22
8	49.06	[0; -3]	49.12

V CONCLUSIONS

This research has showed that, in the system of two-dimensional artificial atom, there is the quantitative correspondence relation between the classical orbits and the quantum spectra defined in this paper. We find that, these orbits are the opened orbits from point A to point B, and points A and B can be chosen arbitrarily. It should be noticed that, though the discussion about classical-quantum correspondence is only in the system of two-dimensional artificial atom, we believe that all the methods and results can be used in a lot of other systems, including some one-dimensional and three-dimensional systems.

On the other hand, the dynamics of all kind of artificial atom is closely related to the transport nature of nano-device, hence, the research about these systems is very important in the field of applied science.

VI ACKNOWLEDGMENT

This work was supported by the Innovative Talent Foundation of Beijing Union University, PHR (IHLB) (Grant No. PHR200907120), and the Science and Technology Research Program of Beijing Municipal Education Commission.

REFERENCES

［1］ M. C. Gutzwiller, "Periodic orbits and classical quantization conditions," J. Math. Phys. , vol. 12, pp. 343 – 358, 1971.

［2］ M. C. Gutzwiller, Chaos in Classical and Quantum Mechanics. New York: Springer – Verlag, 1990.

［3］ D. Kleppner and J. B. Delos, "Beyond quantum mechanics: insights from the work of Martin Gutzwiller," Found. Phys. vol. 31, pp. 593 –612, 2001.

［4］ M. L. Du and J. B. Delos, "Effect of closed classical orbits on quantum spectra: ionization of atoms in a magnetic field," Phys. Rev. Lett. vol. 58, pp. 1731 – 1733, 1987.

［5］ M. L. Du and J. B. Delos, "The effect of closed classical orbits on quantum spectra: ionization of atoms in a magnetic field I. Physical picture and calculations," Phys. Rev. A, vol. 38, pp. 1896 – 1912, 1988.

［6］ M. L. Du and J. B. Delos, "The effect of closed classical orbits on quantum spectra: ionization of atoms in a magnetic field II. Derivation of formulas," Phys. Rev. A, vol. 38, pp. 1913 – 1930, 1988.

［7］ D. A. Sadovskii, J. A. Shaw, and J. B. Delos, "Organization of sequences of bifurcations of periodic orbits," Phys. Rev. Lett. , vol. 75, pp. 2120 –2123, 1995.

［8］ P. A. Dando, T. S. Monteiro, and S. M. Owen, "Periodic orbit theory for Rydberg atoms in external fields," Phys. Rev. Lett. , vol. 75, pp. 2797 –2800, 1998.

［9］ A. Matzkin, P. A. Dando, and T. S. Monteiro, "Closed – orbit theory for molecules in fields," Phys. Rev. A, vol. 66, pp. 013410, 2002.

［10］ M. R. Haggerty and J. B. Delos, "Recurrence spectroscopy in time-dependent fields," Phys. Rev. A, vol. 61, pp. 053406, 2000.

［11］ J. Main and V. A. Mandelshtam, and H. S. Taylor, "Periodic orbit quantization by harmonic inversion of Gutzwiller's recurrence function," Phys. Rev. Lett. , vol. 79, pp. 825 – 828, 1997.

The Effect of Taurine on Cholesterol Metabolism

Chen Wen Guo Junxia Chang Ping

1 Introduction

Taurine (2 - aminoethanesulfonic acid), rich in sea food, is a conditionally essential amino acid which is not incorporated

Correspondence: Dr. Wen Chen, Beijing Key Laboratory of Bioactive Substances and Functional Foods, Beijing Union University, Beituchengxi Road 197, Haidian District, Beijing 100191, P. R. China

E - mail: chenwen@ygi.edu.cn

Fax: +86 - 10 - 6238 - 8927

Abbreviations: ABCG5, ATP - binding cassette G5; ABCG8, ATPbinding cassette G8; ACAT, acyl - coenzyme A: cholesterol acyltransferase; ApoB - 100, Apolipoprotein B - 100; ApoE, Apolipoprotein E; BSEP, bile salt export pump; BARE, bile acid response element; BHT, 2,6 - di - tert - 2,2 - butyl - p - cresol; CYP7A1, cholesterol 7a - hydroxylase; FGF19/FGFR4, fibroblast growth factor 19/fibroblast growth factor receptor 4; FXR, farnesoid X receptor; HDL, high density lipoprotein; HMG - CoA, 3 - hydroxy - 3 - methyl - glutaryl coenzyme; HNF4α, hepatocyte nuclear factor 4α; I - BABP, ileal bile acids binding protein; I - BAT, ileal bile acids transporter; IDL, intermediate density lipoprotein; LDL, low density lipoprotein; LDLR, low density lipoprotein receptor; LRH - 1, liver receptor homolog - 1; LXR - , liver X receptor α; MAPK/JNK, mitogen - activated protein kinase/Jun N - terminal kinase; OST - α/OST - β, organic solute transporter α and β heterdimer; PAN, puromycin aminonucleoside; PB, phenobarbital; PCB, polychlorinated biphenyl; RXR, retinoid X receptor; SHP - 1, small heterodimer partner; STZ, streptozotocin; TAG, triacylglycerol; TC, total cholesterol; TNF, tumor necrosis factor; VLDL, very low density lipoprotein into proteins, but rather is found free in most mammalian tissues, such as heart, retina, liver, brain, and platelets, leukocytes[1]. It was considered as a nonessential nutrient in human beings until 1975 when it was found that formula - fed, pre - term infants were not able to sustain normal plasma or urinary taurine levels[2]. Signs of taurine deficiency have also been detected in children on long - term, total parenteral nutrition[3] and in the patients with "blind - loop" syndrome[4]. Furthermore, in vivo studies have demonstrated that low levels of taurine are associated with various pathological lesions, including cardiomyopathy, retinal degeneration, and growth retardation, etc.[5]. Now it is well known that taurine has many biological and physiological properties, such as antioxidation, osmoregulation, membrane stabilization, modulation of cellular calcium levels and serving as a neurotransmitter and neuromodulator, etc.[1,6-9]. In lipids metabolism, the effect of taurine is considered only because of its conjugation with bile acids, which is perhaps its best - known function although that just accounts for a small proportion of total available taurine in the body[10].

A great number of studies with guinea pigs, rats, mice, and hamsters revealed that taurine affected cholesterol metabolism since Tsuji et al. published their research results in 1979[11-21]. In the early feeding studies dealing with taurine, different types of hypercholesterolemia model were used, and taurine showed cholesterol lowering effect in exogenous hypercholesterolemia induced by high cholesterol diet[12,14,18,19], and on the contrary, it

[Author Introduction] Chen Wen, Guo Junxia, Chang Ping, Beijing Key Laboratory of Bioactive Substances and Functional Foods, Beijing Union University.

showed cholesterol improving effect in endogenous hypercholesterolemia caused by diabetes and some xenobiotics, etc.[13, 15-18]. These observations suggest that cholesterol lowering effect of taurine is due to the increased biotransformation of cholesterol to bile acids and the excretion of bile acids[12, 14, 15, 18], and cholesterol improving effect is due to the increased De Novo synthesis of cholesterol[16]. As the elevated plasma cholesterol level is one of the high risk factors for the development of atherosclerosis, the cholesterol lowering effect of taurine has been studied intensively, and the possible metabolic and molecular mechanisms have also been discussed in the last two decades.

This review, first, summarizes the change of cholesterol concentration in metabolism observed in feeding studies of hypercholesterolemia animal dealing with taurine, and, second, addresses the possible metabolic and molecular mechanisms of cholesterol lowering effect by taurine.

2 The effect of taurine on serum and liver cholesterol levels in different types of hypercholesterolemia

Table 1 summarizes an overview about some published studies reporting taurine's effects on serum (or plasma) and liver total cholesterol (TC) levels in rat, mouse, hamster, and rabbit with exogenous or endogenous hypercholesterolemia.

It is evident that taurine shows cholesterol lowering effect in exogenous hypercholesterolemia rat and mouse by high cholesterol/sodium cholate diet, with the range between -22% and -67% in serum (or plasma) TC, and with the range between -26% and -42% in liver TC. In particular, high density lipoprotein (HDL) - cholesterol level changed from +11% to +43%, and very low density lipoprotein (VLDL) + low density lipoprotein (LDL) - cholesterol concentration varied from -48% to -66%. It is also observed that taurine reduces TC concentrations in serum and liver and decreases non HDLcholesterol level in hamster[21]. These indicate that the decrease in serum (or plasma) TC level by taurine supplementation is mainly due to the decrease in VLDL and LDL cholesterol, and the effect is already clear in the condition of 1% taurine supplemented in diet with 7 days feeding. In the case of exogenous hypercholesterolemia induced by high cholesterol diet (without sodium cholate), the results are different. Serum and liver TC were decreased by taurine onlymarginally by approximately 3% and 5%, respectively, in rat, and decreased by 20% and 15%, respectively, in mouse; however, serum TC concentration was raised by 10% and liver TC level declined by 5% in rabbit.

In the presence of sodium cholate, high dietary cholesterol is easy to be assimilated because cholate is well known for its activity on cholesterol uptake. Therefore, most of dietary hypercholesterolemia model is induced by high cholesterol diet with sodium cholate, especially rat. It has been reported that rat is a poor model for development of experimental atherosclerosis as it is capable of facilitating disposal of excess cholesterol[22, 23]. Chen et al.[19] also reported that mouse and rat showed different responses to dietary cholesterol and sodium cholate, cholesterol degradation in rat was more susceptible and to be improved by dietary cholesterol to keep the relative stability of serum and liver TC concentrations, whereas it was more sensitive and to be repressed by cholate in mouse. Thus, cholesterol lowering effect of taurine has been consistently observed in hypercholesterolemia mouse induced by high cholesterol diet without sodium cholate, but not hypercholesterolemia rat. In 2009, Zulli et al.[24] reported that taurine has no action to reduce plasma TC concentration in rabbit fed with the diet containing 0.5% cholesterol/0.5% methionine/5% peanut oil for 4-weeks. In this study, a multiple model was made with hyperhomocysteinemia, hypermethioninemia, and hyperlipidemia to determine whether taurine could specially protect against coronary artery disease during an atherogenic diet, and taurine showed its antiatherogenic property bymarkedly inhibiting the increase in plasma methionine and completely inhibiting the increase in total homocysteine level, but no decline of TC or LDL concentration was observed. Balcan et al.[25] also indicated that taurine has no effect to reduce plasma and liver TC levels in atherosclerotic rabbit during regression period. The above results suggest that different species respond differently to increased cholesterol intake with elevations in blood cholesterol, and taurine may show its antiatherogenic property without having any effect on plasma lipid levels in rabbit.

Table 1 Effect of taurine on TC concentrations of blood and liver as observed in studies with different hypercholesterolemia types

Species	Rat	Rat	Rat	Rat	Mouse	Mouse	Rat	Rat	Rat	Rat	Rat	Rat	Hamster	Rabbit
Hypercholesterolemia type	High cholesterol/fat/sodium cholate diet induced	High cholesterol/sodium cholate diet induced	High cholesterol/sodium cholate diet induced	High cholesterol diet induced	High cholesterol/sodium cholate diet induced	High cholesterol diet induced	Genetic diabetes induced	Genetic diabetes induced	PAN induced	Thiouracil induced	PB induced	PCB induced	High fat/cholesterol diet induced	High cholesterol/peanut oil/methionine diet induced
Taurine feeding	5% in diet	5% in diet	1% in diet	1% in diet	1% in diet	1% in diet	3% in high cholesterol diet	3% in cholesterol free diet	500 mg/kg body weight i.p.	3% in diet	3% in diet	3% in diet	0.7% in drinking water	2.5% in diet
Feeding period (days)	21	14	7	7	7	7	14	21	10	14	10	15	28	28
Percental change of serum or plasma TC concentration (compared with control)	−67%	−42%	−42%	−3%	−22%	−20%	−30%	+14%	−13%	−2%	+5%	+36%	−14%	+10%
Percental change of serum or plasma HDL−C concentration (compared with control)	+43%	+14%	+11%	+8%	+35%	−12%	+25%	+17%	+34%	−6%	n. d. a)	+50%	0%	0%
Percental change of serum or plasma (VLDL + LDL)−C concentration (compared with control)	n. d. a)	n. d. a)	−66%	−15%	−48%	−26%	−54%	+9%	−20%	−16%	n. d. a)	+25%	−24%	n. d. a)
Percental change of liver TC concentration (compared with control)	−42%	−26%	−28%	−5%	−26%	−15%	−27%	−5%	−26%	−8%	+25%	+59%	−15%	n. d. a)
Reference	[12]	[14]	[19]	[19]	[19]	[19]	[18]	[18]	[13]	[15]	[16]	[17]	[20]	[24]

a) Not determined.

Endogenous hypercholesterolemia is often caused by nephritis, hypothyroidism, diabetes, and some xenobiotics. Intraperitoneal or subcutaneous administration of puromycin aminonucleoside (PAN) to rats results in nephrosis associated hypercholesterolemia, and the reduction of plasma and liver TC levels and the increase of HDLcholesterol by daily taurine injection were observed[13], mainly due to its therapeutic effects in attenuating PAN induced nephrotic syndrome. In the case of endogenous hypercholesterolemia induced by hypothyroidism, which is characterized by an increase of LDL - and intermediate density lipoprotein (IDL) - cholesterol caused by an enhancement of the defective receptor - mediated catabolism of lipoproteins[26], cholesterol lowering effect of taurine was not observed[15]. One of the complications in diabetes is atherosclerosis, thus it is also be concerned for the effect of taurine on cholesterol metabolism in diabetes rat. The result was observed that taurine did not decrease serum TC concentration in genetic diabetes rat fed with cholesterol - free diet, but marginally increased by 14%, whereas taurine significantly reduced serum and liver TC concentrations in genetic diabetes rat fed with high cholesterol/sodium cholate diet by 30% and 27%, respectively[18]. It has been reported that the administration of polychlorinated biphenyl (PCB), 2, 6 - di - tert - 2, 2 - butyl - p - cresol (BHT), and barbital derivatives to rat caused hypercholesterolemia[16, 27, 28]. PCBs are synthetic organic compounds and harmful contaminants which are widely distributed in the environment, and PB is one of the well used sleeping drugs. Interestingly, in the case of endogenous hypercholesterolemia induced by phenobarbital (PB) and PCB, taurine did not reduce serum and liver TC concentrations but caused a significant enhancement. These were mainly attributed to the stimulation of liver cholesterol synthesis, as taurine increased the conversion of $[C^{14}]$ acetate to nonsaponifiable compounds which close related to the activity of 3 - hydroxy - 3 - methyl - glutaryl coenzyme A (HMG - CoA) reductase[16, 17].

Although the effect of taurine on cholesterol metabolism is very different from different types of endogenous hypercholesterolemia, cholesterol lowering effect has been consistently observed in many independent experiments performed by rat and mouse with exogenous hypercholesterolemia caused by high cholesterol/sodium cholate loading diet.

3 The effect of taurine on cholesterol clearance pathway from blood circulation in hypercholesterolemia

Although cholesterol is an essential element of biological membranes, hypercholesterolemia increases the risk of developing cardiovascular diseases. In particular, LDL cholesterol is a well - established risk factor for susceptibility to atherosclerosis and coronary artery disease[29,30]. VLDL is synthesized in the liver and secreted to the circulation to forming IDL and LDL. VLDL and LDL are removed from circulation by LDL receptor (LDLR), which binds to Apolipoprotein B - 100 (ApoB - 100) and Apolipoprotein E (ApoE) moieties on them. LDLR plays an important role in the regulation of plasma LDL cholesterol by mediating about two - thirds of LDL clearance from circulation[31]. Thus, VLDL secretion, plasma VLDL + LDL cholesterol, and LDLR protein level or activity are closely related, and are thought to be keeping in a dynamic equilibrium.

It has been reported by Murakami et al.[32] that taurine increased ^{125}I - labeled LDL binding to LDL receptor by 52% and 58% in hamsters fed either a normal chow or high - fat diet respectively for 14 days, and LDL kinetic analysis showed that taurine intake resulted in significant faster plasma LDL fractional catabolic rates. Their results suggest that taurine elevates hepatic LDLR activity and thereby decreases serum cholesterol level. Furthermore, in 2011, Chang et al.[21] demonstrated taurine significantly upregulated LDLR gene expressions in hamster for 4 - weeks feeding with high - fat/cholesterol dietary. With taurine deficient model generated by giving mouse 0.5% guanidinoethyl sulfonate (GES) GES solution, the inhibitor of taurine transport[33], Chen et al.[34] reported that LDLR protein level was not affected by either taurine deficient or taurine supplemented, whereas triacylglycerol (TAG) secretion rate was significantly repressed by taurine supplementation. Since dietary TAG is transported in chylomicrons and endogenous TAG is transported as VLDL, and VLDL catabolism can be blocked by injection of tyloxapol, finally results in TAG accumulation in the circulation[35]. Therefore, VLDL release rate can be expressed by TAG secretion rate at a certain extent when tyloxapol is injected to animal. The above results observed in different groups indicate that taurine lowers cholesterol concentration by repressing VLDL (TAG) secretion from the liver and improves cholesterol clearance from blood circulation by upregulating LDLR binding capacity.

The liver is the organ to synthesize and secrete the apolipoproteins containing apoB – 100, which is recognized by LDLR. ApoB – 100 is an essential structural component of VLDL and LDL and is required for the intracellular assembly and the secretion of these lipoproteins[36]. As the elevation of the concentration of apoB – 100 as well as of LDL cholesterol is also regarded as a risk factor for coronary artery disease[29, 30, 36], it is important to investigate the factors controlling the secretion rate of apoB by the liver. The study was designed by Yanagita et al.[37] to test taurine's effect on apoB – 100 secretion and lipid metabolism by using the human hepatoblastoma cells HepG2, which have been found to retain many typical functions of the normal human hepatocytes including lipoprotein and apolipoprotein synthesis. Their results demonstrated taurine at the concentrations of 10^{-4} and 10^{-3} M reduced apoB – 100 secretion from HepG2 cells preincubated with oleatemedium in DMEMby 42% and 45%, respectively[37]. In addition, their data also indicated taurine (10^{-3} M) significantly reduced the cellular cholesterolmass by 19% and decreased the synthesis of cholesterol ester from [^{14}C] oleic acid by 58% in the cells and reduced its secretion into medium by up to 43%[37]. It is well known that cholesterol ester formation is catalyzed by acyl – coenzyme A: cholesterol acyltransferase (ACAT) from free cholesterol and acyl – CoA. Reduction of the synthesis of cholesterol ester may suggest that relatively high amount taurine exerts for ACAT inhibitor.

The above findings reveal that taurine lowers cholesterol concentration by reducing apoB and VLDL secretion from the liver, and improving cholesterol clearance from the circulation by upregulating LDLR binding capacity led to increase of LDL uptake, and suggest indirectly that taurine accelerates the degradation of cholesterol in the liver, thus results in reduction of VLDL release to the circulation.

4 The effect of taurine on cholesterol catabolism or bile acid synthesis pathway in hypercholesterolemia

Cholesterol is an extremely important biological substance that has roles in membrane structure as well as being a precursor for the synthesis of steroid hormone and bile acid. About half of the cholesterol in the body derives from de novo biosynthesis. Except utilized in the formation of membranes and in the synthesis of steroid hormone, the greatest proportion of cholesterol from both diet and synthesis is used in conversion to bile acid in the liver. Thus, cholesterol conversion to bile acids plays a vital role for elimination of cholesterol, which is one of the main factors regulating cholesterol homeostasis in the body[38].

Table 2 summarizes taurine's effects on bile acid synthesis in rat, mouse and hamster with hypercholesterolemia reported by several research groups. Apparently, taurine improves fecal bile acid excretion in hypercholesterolemia rat regardless of being caused by high cholesterol diet or endogenous factors such as diabetes and hypothyroidism, with the range between +24% and +75%, but not significantly affects fecal cholesterol excretion except that +16% increasing is observed in lard supplemented high cholesterol diet induced hypercholesterolemia rat. In the case of hypercholesterolemia mouse led by cholesterol or cholesterol/sodium cholate loading diet, +16% enhancement of fecal bile acid excretion is observed, and the change of fecal cholesterol is not observed. In hypercholesterolemia hamster induced by high fat/cholesterol diet, fecal bile acid and cholesterol level increased +35% and +19% respectively by taurine.

There are two pathways in bile acid biosynthesis, one is the classic (also known as neutral) pathway which is the main pathway in the conversion of cholesterol to bile acid, and the other is alternative (also known as acidic or mitochondrial) pathway. Cholesterol 7a – hydroxylase (CYP7A1) is the rate – limiting enzyme in the classic pathway[39, 40]. In Table 2, it is evident that taurine remarkably increases CYP7A1 activity with the range between

+82% and +151%, and improves CYP7A1 mRNA level with the range between +95% and +119% in hypercholesterolemia rat and mouse caused by high cholesterol/sodium cholate diet. About +30% elevation of CYP7A1 activity and +63% enhancement of CYP7A1 mRNA expression are observed in hypercholesterolemia rat and hamster, respectively, which induced by high cholesterol/ fat diet, and no improvements of activity and mRNA level of CYP7A1 are observed in hypercholesterolemia mouse led by high cholesterol diet without sodium cholate.

The above studies reveal that cholesterol – lowering effect of taurine is carried out by enhancing CYP7A1 activity or mRNA expression and fecal bile acid excretion in hypercholesterolemia hamster and rat with high cholesterol/fat diet and in hypercholesterolemia rat andmouse with high cholesterol/ sodium cholate diet. Interestingly taurine does not improve CYP7A1 activity /or mRNA expression in hypercholesterolemia mouse by cholesterol diet without sodium cholate.

Chen et al.[19] reported there was an apparent difference in the regulation of cholesterol degradation or bile acid biosynthesis between mice and rats, the diet rich in cholesterol induced CYP7A1mRNA expression in rats (but not inmice), and CYP7A1 mRNA level was significantly repressed by diet high in combination of cholesterol and sodium cholate, but still notably higher than that of the rats with normal chows. In mice, CYP7A1 mRNA level was marginally increased by the diet rich in cholesterol, and markedly decreased by adding sodium cholate to cholesterol diet, even far less than that of the mice with normal chows[19]. Boone et al.[41] also reported that western blotting analysis showed dietary cholesterol significantly increases CYP7A1 protein levels in rats but not inmice. Other reports[42,43] showed that dietary cholesterol may act to increase or decrease CYP7A1 mRNA levels in C57BL/6J mice depending on the type of fat added to the diet, and olive oil supplement caused increased expression of CYP7A1. These studies suggest there is considerable variation among animals in terms of their responses to consumption of excess dietary cholesterol. Hamsters and mice are not resistant to dietary cholesterol and exhibit marked elevations in serum cholesterol level when given diets supplemented with cholesterol, whereas rats show very little increase in serum cholesterol level when given a similar cholesterol challenge[44,45]. According to Chen's paper, taurine induced CYP7A1 expression only in the present of sodium cholate in high cholesterol diet, subsequently showed its more efficient cholesterol lowering effect in rat and mouse[19], although they displayed different response to dietary cholesterol. In addition, in vitro study reported by Lam et al.[46] demonstrated taurine remarkably induced CYP7A1 expression in HepG2 cells with time – and dose – dependent in the presence of cholesterol in medium. This paper also suggests Hep G2 cell line may be an appropriate model to study the effects of taurine on human cholesterol metabolism[46].

Cholesterol degradation or bile acid biosynthesis is critically regulated in order to maintain cholesterol or bile acid homeostasis in the body. CYP7A1, the rate – limiting enzyme in the classic pathway of bile acid biosynthesis[39], has been widely reported to being regulated by several nuclear receptors at the level of gene transcription to balance the elimination of cholesterol responsive to the physiological status in the body[47,48]. Two regions for transcription factor binding (bile acid response element – I (BARE – I) and BARE – II) have been identified in the CYP7A1 promoter[49]. BARE – I in mouse binds liver X receptor α (LXRα), a nuclear receptor identified as a positive regulator of CYP7A1 transcription[50,51], whereas LXR binding site is not present in the CYP7A1 gene in human[52]. The ligands that activate LXR are oxysterols[53], which increaseed after cholesterol feeding. BARE – II contains binding regions for hepatocyte nuclear factor 4α (HNF – 4α) and liver receptor homolog – 1 (LRH – 1), which were reported to be essential for basal level expression of CYP7A1[54,55]. Farnesoid X receptor (FXR), a bile acid receptor, plays a critical role in the regulation of bile acid synthesis and homeostasis. FXR represses CYP7A1 transcription by promoting the transcription of the atypical nuclear receptor small heterodimer partner (SHP – 1), which interacts withHNF4α and LRH – 1 and then suppresses CYP7A1 gene transcription[56,57]. Bile acids such as lithocholic acid, chenodeoxycholic acid, and deoxycholic acid are ligands that activate FXR. Although studies in CV – 1 cells did not show cholic acid had strong affinity to activate FXR[48], it has been demonstrated in mice that cholic acid was a powerful activating ligand for FXR in vivo[58]. These findings support the idea that bile acid pool size and components proportion are responsible for inhibition of CYP7A1 by providing additional activating ligands to activate FXR, the negative regulator of CYP7A1.

Table 2 Effect of taurine on fecal excretion of bile acid and steroid, and CYP7A1 activity and mRNA level as observed in studies with hypercholesterolemia animal model

Species	Hypercholesterolemia type	Taurine feeding	Feeding period (days)	Percental change of fecal bile acid concentration (compared with control)	Percental change of fecal neutral steroid or fecal cholesterol concentration (compared with control)	Percental change of CYP7A1 activity (compared with control)	Percental change of CYP7A1 mRNA (compared with control)	Reference
Hamster	High fat/cholesterol diet induced	0.7% in drinking water	28	+35%	+19%	n.d. [a]	+63%	[20]
Rat	High cholesterol/lard/sodium cholate diet induced	5% in diet	21	+75%	−6%	+151%	n.d. [a]	[12]
Rat	High cholesterol/sodium cholate diet induced	5% in diet	14	+60%	5%	n.d. [a]	+95%	[14]
Rat	High cholesterol/lard diet induced	1% in diet	7	+46%	+16%	+30%	n.d. [a]	[68]
Rat	High cholesterol/sodium cholate diet induced	5% in diet	14	+59%	+5%	n.d. [a]	+95%	[68]
Mouse	High cholesterol diet induced	1% in diet	7	+16%	+4%	−4%	−4%	[19, 59]
Mouse	High cholesterol/sodium cholate diet induced	1% in diet	7	+16%	−2%	+82%	+119%	[19, 59]
Rat	High cholesterol/sodium cholate diet induced (STZ-induced Diabetic rats)	5% in diet	14	n.d. [a]	n.d. [a]	n.d. [a]	+98%	[69]
Rat	High cholesterol/sodium cholate diet induced (Genetic Diabetic rats)	3% in diet	14	+42%	n.d. [a]	n.d. [a]	n.d. [a]	[18]
Rat	Cholesterol-free diet (Genetic Diabetic rats)	3% in diet	21	+49%	n.d. [a]	n.d. [a]	n.d. [a]	[18]
Rat	Thiouracil induced	3% in diet	14	+24%	+12%	n.d. [a]	n.d. [a]	[15]

a) Not determined.

Molecular mechanism of CYP7A1 induction by taurine is rarely discussed although its regulation pathway and relative nuclear receptors and factors have been studied extensively. In 2006, Lam et al.[59] reported that C57BL/6 mice were fed with cholesterol or cholesterol/sodium cholate diet supplemented taurine for 1 week in their experiment, and mRNA levels of CYP7A1, LXR α, HNF - 4α, LRH - 1, FXR, and SHP were determined. Their results showed no alternation in the mRNA levels of nuclear receptors were observed by diet treatment, although the mRNA level of CYP7A1 was significantly decreased by cholesterol/sodium cholate diet (but not by cholesterol diet) and then two - fold increased by taurine supplementation[59]. Their results suggest (1) although there are no changes on mRNA level, FXR is indeed activated by sodium cholate diet and then functions as a down - regulator to CYP7A1; (2) taurine may interrupt the activation of FXR via any unknown pathway, in spite of enhancement synthesis of bile acid, which is the activating ligand for FXR; and (3) taurine also may activate LXR, HNF4 α or LRH - 1 by any indirect route because it is not a probable ligand for LXRα[59]. The exact mechanism of upregulating effect of CYP7A1 by taurine remains unclear at present.

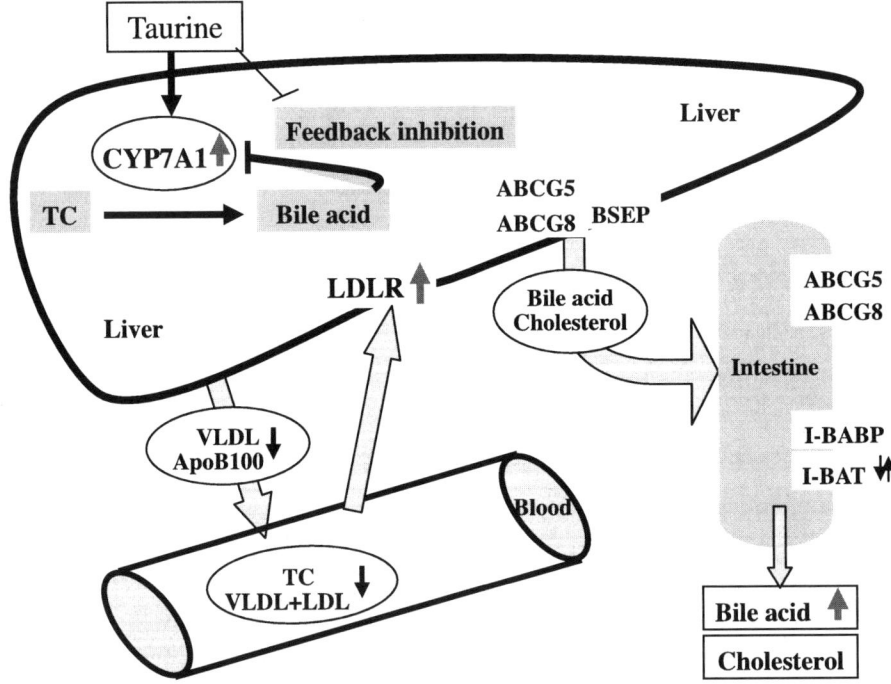

Fig. 1 Proposed model explaining cholesterol lowering effect of taurine. Reduction of serum (or plasma) TC concentration by taurine is mainly due to the decrease in VLDL and LDL cholesterol. First, taurine reduces apoB and VLDL secretion from the liver, and improves cholesterol clearance from blood circulation by upregulating LDLR binding capacity led to increase of LDL uptake; second, taurine activates bioconversion of cholesterol to bile acid via enhancing CYP7A1 activity or mRNA expression, and may also interrupt the feedback inhibition of bile acid to CYP7A1 by repressing the activation of FXR, a negative regulator of CYP7A1; third, taurine increases excretion of fecal bile acid, and possibly improves and represses I - BAT expression in different feeding situations, to affect re - absorption of bile acid from enterohepatic circulation; and fourth, taurine do not affect fecal cholesterol excretion mediated by ABCG5 and ABCG8. ABCG5/8, ATP - binding cassette G5/8; BSEP, bile salt export pump; CYP7A1, cholesterol 7a - hydroxylase; FXR, farnesoid X receptor; I - BABP, ileal bile acids binding protein; I - BAT, ileal bile acids transporter; LDL, low density lipoprotein; LDLR, low density lipoprotein receptor; TC, total cholesterol; VLDL, very low density lipoprotein.

5 The effect of taurine on cholesterol excretion and bile acid re - absorption in hypercholesterolemia

Decrease of De Novo synthesis, increase of degradation and large excretion of cholesterol are three auto - regulation mechanisms to maintain cholesterol homeostasis when high cholesterol is present in the diet. Except the excretion, degradation of cholesterol by taurine has been discussed, and de novo synthesis is not under consideration as being interrupted by high cholesterol diet. ATP - binding cassette G5 (ABCG5) ABCG5 and ATP - binding cassette G8 (ABCG8) ABCG8, exist in the hepatocytes and enterocytes, are induced by LXR to enhance cholesterol efflux into biliary ducts and intestinal lumen[60]. Significant evidence indicates that deletion of ABCG5 and ABCG8 in mice leads to a marked decrease (90%) in biliary cholesterol[61], and furthermore, cholesterol secretion is linearly correlated with the gene copy number of Abcg5/Abcg8 in mice[62].

The three important sides in bile acid homeostasis in the body are biosynthesis, excretion to feces, and re – absorption from the ileum. Besides re – absorption, the other two points have been demonstrated to be increased by taurine. Conjugated bile acids are secreted into bile by canalicular bile salt export pump (BSEP) and stored in the gallbladder and then emptied into the intestinal tract after meal. When passing through the intestinal tract, most bile acids (95%) are reabsorbed in the ileum by apical sodium – dependent bile acid transporter (also known as ileal bile acids transporter (I – BAT)) located in the brush border membrane, and transdiffused across the enterocyte to the basolateral membrane where organic solute transporter and heterodimer (OSTα/OSTβ) discharges bile acids into portal blood circulation, and finally taken up into hepatocytes to complete enterohepatic circulation[63]. BSEP is FXR target gene, which is the driving force for bile formation[64]. FXR induces I – BAT expression in mouse and inhibits I – BAT expression in rabbit but does not affect I – BAT in human[65]. FXR also induces the expression of ileal bile acids binding protein (I – BABP), which is the first target gene of FXR identified in the gastrointestine system and may bind bile acids and reduce intracellular bile acid concentrations in the ileum[66].

Few studies revealed taurine's effects on cholesterol excretion and bile acid re – absorption in hypercholesterolemia. Lam et al.[59] reported the effect of taurine on some factors involved in cholesterol and bile acid homeostasis in mice. In their experiments, mRNA levels of liver ABCG5 and ABCG8 were increased by high cholesterol diet, and further improved by high cholesterol/sodium cholate diet, but not mediated by taurine. Expression of liver BSEP and jejunum ABCG5 and ABCG8 were induced by both of high cholesterol and high cholesterol/sodium cholate diets, and also not regulated by taurine. These data suggest that taurine supplementation do not affect not only the excretion of cholesterol and bile acids from the liver to bile, but also cholesterol excretion from the intestine. These are well consistent with their results of unchanged fecal neutral sterol excretion by taurine. In enterohepatic circulation of bile acid, mRNAlevel of I – BABPwas not affected by the diets, whereas I – BAT was notably reduced by both of high cholesterol and high cholesterol/sodium cholate diets. The interesting is a reduced and an induced I – BAT expression was observed by taurine supplemented high cholesterol diet and high cholesterol/sodium diet, respectively. According to the results of fecal bile acid excretion and I – BAT mRNA level, it is conceivable that taurine lowers serum and liver cholesterol concentrations through improving excretion and suppressing re – absorption of bile acids when taking high cholesterol diet without exogenous sodium cholate, because both of expression and activity of CYP7A1 were not improved in this case. On the contrary, taurine has no effect on repressing bile acid re – absorption but notably improved CYP7A1 mRNA level in the case of sodium cholate added cholesterol feeding. These suggest that taurine may deregulate the feedback inhibition of bile acids to CYP7A1 gene expression under this special physiological condition although the mechanism is unknown at present.

6 Conclusions and future perspectives

The obvious reduction of serum (or plasma) and liver TC concentrations by taurine are the most striking observation from a number of feeding experiments with cholesterol/cholate loading diets. The decrease in serum (or plasma) TC level by taurine supplementation was mainly due to the decrease in VLDL and LDL cholesterol. Mechanistic studies dealing with this topic indicate that these effects of taurine are mediated by improved LDLR binding capacity, reduction of VLDL and apoB – 100 secretion from the liver, and activated bioconversion of cholesterol to bile acid via upregulating CYP7A1, and consequently, increased excretion of fecal bile acid, and a possible improved and repressed I – BAT expression in different feeding situations that related to re – absorption of bile acid from enterohepatic circulation. The comprehensive mode of action of taurine is shown in Fig. 1.

Regulation of bile acid synthesis has been extensively studied, and CYP7A1 mRNA expression is a biomarker for studying cholesterolmetabolism in animalmodels of hypercholesterolemia. Mouse and rat models are widely used; however, some differences exist in bile acid synthesis and regulation when they were given by cholesterol challenge with or without sodium cholate. CYP7A1 expression is markedly induced by taurine in both of rat and mouse fed with cholatecontaining cholesterol diet. The action mechanism of taurine to relieve the feedback inhibition of CYP7A1 transcription by bile acid remains to be further elucidated, such as FXR – dependent pathway including FXR/SHP and FXR/ fibroblast growth factor 19/fibroblast growth factor receptor 4 (FXR/FGF19/FGFR4) pathway, and FXR – independent pathway including tumor necrosis factor (TNF) receptor and mitogen – activated protein kinase/Jun N – terminal kinase (MAPK/JNK) pathway, etc. Moreover, a study provided evidence that FXR – mediated repression of bile acid synthesis requires the complementary actions of FXR in both liver and intestine[67].

Somehow, cholesterol lowering action of taurine indicates that taurine may be important during states with high dietary cholesterol habits or where cholesterol metabolism is disturbed.

The authors have declared that they have no conflict of interest.

References

[1] Huxtable, R. J., Physiological actions of taurine. *Physiol. Rev.* 1992, *72*, 101 – 163.

[2] Raiha, N., Rassin, D., Heinonen, K., Gaull, G. E., Milk protein quality and quantity: biochemical and growth effects in low birth weight infants (LBWI). *Pediatr. Res.* 1975, *9*, 370.

[3] Geggel, H. S., Ament, M. E., Heckenlively, J. R., Nutritional requirement for taurine in patients receiving long – term parenteral nutrition. *N. Engl. J. Med.* 1985, *312*, 142 – 146.

[4] Sheik, K., Toskes, P., Dawson, W., Taurine deficiency and retinal defects associated with small intestinal bacterial overgrowth. *Gastroenterology* 1981, *80*, 1363.

[5] Sturman, J. A., Taurine in development. *Physiol. Rev.* 1993, *73*, 119 – 147.

[6] Kuriyama, K., Taurine as a neuromodulator. *Fed. Proc.* 1980, *39*, 2680 – 2684.

[7] Wright, C. E., Tallan, H. H., Lin, Y. Y., Taurine: biological update. *Annu. Rev. Biochem.* 1986, *55*, 427 – 453.

[8] Thurston, J. H., Hauhart, R. E., Dirgo, J. A., Taurine: a role in osmotic regulation ofmammalian brain and possible clinical significances. *Life Sci.* 1980, *26*, 1561 – 1568.

[9] Pasantes, M. H., Wright, C. E., Gaull, G. E., Taurine protection of lymphoblastoid cells from iron – ascorbate – induced damage. *Biochem. Pharmacol.* 1985, *34*, 2205 – 2207.

[10] Danielsson, H., Present states of research on catabolism and excretion of cholesterol. *Adv. Lipid Res.* 1963, *1*, 335 – 385.

[11] Tsuji, K., Seki, T., Iwao, H., Cholesterol – lowering effects of taurine and sulfur – containing amino acids in serum and liver of rats. *Sulfur – Containing Amino Acids* 1979, *2*, 143 – 145.

[12] Sugiyama, K., Ohishi, A., Ohnuma, Y., Muramatsu, K., Comparison between the plasma cholesterol – lowering effects of glycine and taurine in fats fed on high cholesterol diets. *Agric. Biol. Chem.* 1989, *53*, 1647 – 1652.

[13] Venkatesan, N., Rao, P. V., Arumugam, V., Inhibitory effect of taurine on puromycin aminonucleoside – induced hyperlipidemia in rats. *J. Clin. Biochem. Nutr.* 1993, *15*, 203 – 210.

[14] Yokogoshi, H., Mochizuki, H., Nanami, K., Hida, Y. et al., Dietary taurine enhances cholesterol degradation and reduces serum and liver cholesterol concentrations in rats fed a highcholesterol diet. *J. Nutr.* 1999, *129*, 1705 – 1712.

[15] Mochizuki, H., Takido, J., Yokogoshi, H., Improved suppression by dietary taurine of the fecal excretion of bile acids from hypothyroid rats. *Biosci. Biotechnol. Biochem.* 1999, *63*, 753 – 755.

[16] Mochizuki, H., Takido, J., Yokogoshi, H., Effect of dietary taurine on endogenous hypercholesterolemia in rats fed on phenobarbital – containing diets. *Biosci. Biotechnol. Biochem.* 1999, *63*, 1298 – 1300.

[17] Mochizuki, H., Oda, H., Yokogoshi, H., Dietary taurine potentiates polychlorinated biphenyl – induced hypercholesterolemia in rats. *J. Nutr. Biochem.* 2001, *12*, 109 – 115.

[18] Nishimura, N., Umeda, C., Oda, H., Yokogoshi, H., The effect of taurine on plasma cholesterol concentration in genetic type 2 diabetic GK rats. *J. Nutr. Sci. Vitaminol.* 2002, *48*, 483 – 490.

[19] Chen, W., Suruga, K., Nishimura, N., Gouda, T. et al., Comparative regulation of major enzymes in bile acids biosynthesis pathways by cholesterol, cholic acid and taurine in mice and rats. *Life Sci.* 2005, *77*, 746 – 757.

[20] Kibe, A., Wake, C., Kuramoto, T., Hoshita, T., Effect of dietary taurine on bile acid metabolism in guinea pigs. *Lipids* 1980, *15*, 224–229.

[21] Chang, Y. Y., Chou, C. H., Chiu, C. H., Yang, K. T. et al., Preventive effects of taurine on development of hepatic steatosis induced by a high–fat/cholesterol dietary habit. *J. Agric. Food. Chem.* 2011, *59*, 450–457.

[22] Jones, M. P., Pandak, W. M., Hylemon, P. B., Chiang, J. Y. L. et al., Cholesterol 7α–hydroxylase: evidence for transcriptional regulation by cholesterol and/or metabolic products of cholesterol in the rat. *J. Lipid Res.* 1993, *34*, 885–892.

[23] Doerner, K. C., Gurley, E. C., Vlahcevic, Z. R., Hylemon, P. B., Regulation of cholesterol 7α–hydroxylase expression by sterols in primary hepatocyte cultures. *J. Lipid Res.* 1995, *36*, 168–177.

[24] Zulli, A., Lau, E., Wijaya, B. P. P., Jin, X. et al., High dietary taurine reduces apoptosis and atherosclerosis in the left main coronary artery: association with reduced CCAAT/enhancer binding protein homologous protein and total plasma homocysteine but not lipidemia. *Hypertension* 2009, *53*, 1017–1022.

[25] Balkan, J., Oztezcan, S., Hatipoglu, A., Cevikbas, U. et al., Effect of a taurine treatment on the regression of existing atherosclerotic lesions in rabbits fed on a high–cholesterol diet. *Biosci. Biotechnol. Biochem.* 2004, *68*, 1035–1039.

[26] Scarabottolo, L., Trezzi, E., Roma, P., Catapano, A. L., Experimental hypothyroidism modulates the expression of the low density lipoprotein receptor by the liver. *Atherosclerosis* 1986, *59*, 329–333.

[27] Oda, H., Yoshida, A., Effect of feeding xenobiotics on serum high density lipoprotein and apolipoprotein A–I. *Biosci. Biotechnol. Biochem.* 1994, *58*, 1646–1651.

[28] Nagaoka, S., Masaki, H., Aoyama, Y., Yoshida, A., Effects of excess dietary tyrosine or certain xenobiotics on cholesterogenesis in rats. *J. Nutr.* 1986, *116*, 726–732.

[29] Campos, H., Granest, J. J. Jr., Bilijievents, E., McNamara, J. R. et al., Low density lipoprotein particle size and coronary artery disease. *Arterioscler. Thromb.* 1992, *12*, 187–195.

[30] Coresh, J., Kwiteroviwich, P. O. Jr., Smith, H. H., Bachorik, P. S., Association of plasma triglyceride concentration and LDL particle diameter, density and chemical composition with premature coronary artery disease in men and women. *J. Lipid Res.* 1993, *34*, 1887–1897.

[31] Brown, M. S., Goldstein, J. L., A receptor mediated pathway for cholesterol homeostasis. *Science* 1986, *232*, 34–47.

[32] Murakami, S., Kondo, Y., Toda, Y., Kitajima, H. et al., Effect of taurine on cholesterol metabolism in hamsters: upregulation of low density lipoprotein (LDL) receptor by taurine. *Life Sci.* 2002, *70*, 2355–2366.

[33] Huxtable, R. J., Laird, H. E., Lippincott, S. E., The transport of taurine in the heart and rapid depletion of tissue taurine content by guanidinoethyl sulfonate. *J Pharmacol. Exp. Ther.* 1979, *211*, 465–471.

[34] Chen, W., Matuda, K., Nishimura, N., Yokogoshi, H., The effect of taurine on cholesterol degradation in mice fed a high-cholesterol diet. *Life Sci.* 2004, *74*, 1889–1898.

[35] Li, X., Catalina, F., Grundy, S. M., Patel, S., Method to measure apolipoprotein B–48 and B–100 secretion rates in an individual mouse: evidence for a very rapid turnover of VLDL and preferential removal of B–48–relative to B–100–containing lipoproteins. *J. Lipid Res.* 1996, *37*, 210–220.

[36] Olofsson, SO., Boren, J., Apolipoprotein B: a clinically important apolipoprotein which assembles atherogenic lipoproteins and promotes the development of atherosclerosis. *J. Intern Med.* 2005, *258*, 395–410.

[37] Yanagita, T., Han, S. Y., Hu, Y., Nagao, K. et al., Taurine reduces the secretion of apolipoprotein B100 and lipids in HepG2 cells. *Lipids Health Dis.* 2008, *7*, 38–43.

[38] Sjovall, J., Fifty years with bile acids and steroids in health and disease. *Lipids* 2004, *39*, 703–722.

[39] Chiang, J. Y. L., Regulation of bile acid synthesis. *Front. Biosci.* 1998, *3*, 176–193.

[40] Vlahcevic, Z. R., Pandak, W. M., Stravit, R. T., Regulation of bile acid biosynthesis. Gastroenterol. *Clin. North Am.* 1999, *28*, 1–25.

[41] Boone, L. R., Brooks, P. A., Niesen, M. I., Ness, G. C., Mechanism of resistance to dietary cholesterol. *J. Lipids* 2011, *10*, 1242–1251.

[42] Cheema, S. K., Cikaluk, D., Agellon, L. B., Dietary fats modulate the regulatory potential of dietary cholesterol on cholesterol α–hydroxylase gene expression. *J. Lipid Res.* 1997, *38*, 315–323.

[43] Dueland, S., Drisko, J., Graf, L., Machleder, D. et al., Effect of dietary cholesterol and taurocholate on cholesterol 7α–hydroxylase and hepatic LDL receptors in inbred mice. *J Lipid Res.* 1993, *34*, 923–931.

[44] Biddinger, S. B., Almind, K., Miyazaki, M., Kokkotou, E. et al., Effects of diet and genetic background on sterol regulatory element–binding protein–1c, linebreak stearoyl–CoA desaturase 1, and the development of the metabolic syndrome. *Diabetes* 2005,

54, 1314-1323.

[45] Ness, G. C., Gertz, K. R., Hepatic HMG-CoA reductase expression and resistance to dietary cholesterol. *Exp. Biol. Med.* 2004, *229*, 412-416.

[46] Lam, N. V., Chen, W., Suruga, K., Nishimura, N. et al., Enhancing effect of taurine on CYP7A1 mRNA expression in HepG2 cells. *Amino Acids* 2006, *30*, 43-48.

[47] Janowski, B. A., Willy, P. J., Devi, T. R., Falck, J. R., Mangelsdorf, D. J., An oxysterol signalling pathway mediated by nuclear receptor LXR alpha. *Nature* 1996, *383*, 728-731.

[48] Wang, H., Chen, J., Hollister, K., Sowers, L. C., Forman, B. M., Endogenous bile acids are ligands for the nuclear receptor FXR/BAR. Mol. *Cell* 1999, *3*, 543-553.

[49] Stroup, D., Crestani, M., Chiang, J. Y. L., Identification of a bile acid response element in the cholesterol 7 alphahydroxylase gene CYP7A. Am. *J. Physiol.* 1997, *273*, G508-517.

[50] Chiang, J. Y. L., Kimmel, R., Stroup, D., Regulation of cholesterol 7-hydroxylase gene (CYP7A1) transcription by the liver orphan receptor (LXRα). *Gene* 2001, *262*, 257-265.

[51] Peet, D. J., Truly, S. D., Ma, W., Janowski, B. A. et al., Cholesterol and bile acid metabolism are impaired in mice lacking the nuclear oxysterol receptor LXR-α. *Cell* 1998, *93*, 693-704.

[52] Agellon, L. B., Drover, V. A., Cheema, S. K., Gbaguidi, G. F., Walsh, A., Dietary cholesterol fails to stimulate the human cholesterol 7alpha-hydroxylase gene (CYP7A1) in transgenic mice. *J. Biol. Chem.* 2002, *277*, 20131-20134.

[53] Lehmann, J. M., Kliewer, S. A., Moore, L. B., Smith-Oliver, T. A. et al., Activation of the nuclear receptor LXR by oxysterols defines a new hormone response pathway. *J. Biol. Chem.* 1997, *272*, 3137-3140.

[54] Crestani, M., Sadeghpour, A., Stroup, D., Gali, G., Chiang, J. Y. L., Transcriptional activation of the cholesterol 7α-hydroxylase gene (CYP7A1) by nuclear hormone receptors. *J. Lipid Res.* 1998, *39*, 2192-2200.

[55] Nitta, M., Ku, S., Brown, C., Okamoto, A. Y., Shan, B., CPF: an orphan nuclear receptor that regulates liver-specific expression of the human cholesterol 7α-hydroxylase gene. *Proc. Natl. Acad. Sci. USA* 1999, *96*, 6660-6665.

[56] Sinal, C. J., Tohkin, M., Miyata, M., Ward, J. M. et al., Targeted disruption of the nuclear receptor FXR/BAR impairs bile acid and lipid homeostasis. *Cell* 2000, *102*, 731-744.

[57] Goodwin, B., Jones, S. A., Price, R. R., Watson, M. A. et al., A regulatory cascade of the nuclear receptors FXR, SHP-1 and LRH-1 represses bile acid biosynthesis. *Mol. Cell* 2000, *6*, 517-526.

[58] Li-Hawkins, J., Gåfvels, M., Olin, M., Lund, E. et al., Cholic acid mediates negative feedback regulation of bile acid synthesis in mice. *J. Clin. Invest.* 2002, *110*, 1191-1200.

[59] Lam, N. V., Chen, W., Suruga, K., Nishimura, N. et al., Effects of taurine on mRNA levels of nuclear receptors and factors involved in cholesterol and bile acid homeostasis in mice. *Adv. Exp. Med. Biol.* 2006, *583*, 193-202.

[60] Yu, L., Li-Hawkins, J., Hammer, R. E., Berge, K. E. et al., Overexpression of ABCG5 and ABCG8 promotes biliary cholesterol secretion and reduces fractional absorption of dietary cholesterol. *J. Clin. Invest.* 2002, 110, 671-680.

[61] Yu, L., Hammer, R. E., Li-Hawkins, J., Von Bergmann, K. et al., Disruption of Abcg5 and Abcg8 in mice reveals their crucial role in biliary cholesterol secretion. *Proc. Natl. Acad. Sci. U. S. A.* 2002, *99*, 16237-16242.

[62] Yu, L., Gupta, S., Xu, F., Liverman, A. D. B. et al., Expression of ABCG5 and ABCG8 is required for regulation of biliary cholesterol secretion. *J. Biol. Chem.* 2005, *280*, 8742-8747.

[63] Chiang, J. Y. L., Bile acid: regulation of synthesis. *J. Lipid Res.* 2009, *50*, 1955-1966.

[64] Ananthanarayanan, M., Balasubramanian, N., Makishima, M., Mangelsdorf, D. J., Suchy, F. J., Human bile salt export pump promoter is transactivated by the farnesoid X receptor/bile acid receptor. *J. Biol. Chem.* 2001, *276*, 28857-28865.

[65] Li, H., Chen, F., Shang, Q., Pan, L. et al., FXR-activating ligands inhibit rabbit ASBT expression via FXR-SHP-FTF cascade. Am. J. Physiol. Gastrointest. *Liver Physiol.* 2005, *288*, G60-66.

[66] Tu, H., Okamoto, A. Y., Shan, B., FXR: a bile acid receptor and biological sensor. *Trends Cardiovasc. Med.* 2000, *10*, 30-35.

[67] Kim, I., Ahn, S. H., Inagaki, T., Choi, M. et al., Differential regulation of bile acid homeostasis by the farnesoid X receptor in liver and intestine. *J. Lipid Res.* 2007, *48*, 2664-2672.

[68] Chen, W., Nishimura, N., Oda, H., Yokogoshi, H. et al., The effect of taurine on cholesterol degradation and bile acids pool. *Adv. Exp. Med. Biol.* 2003, *526*, 261-268.

[69] Mochizuki, H., Takido, J., Oda, H., Yokogoshi, H., Improving effect of dietary taurine on marked hypercholesterolemia induced by a high cholesterol diet in streptozotocin induced diabetic rats. *Biosci. Biotechnol. Biochem.* 1999, *63*, 1984-1987.

壳聚糖/β-环糊精交联聚合物的制备及其对葛根素的吸附性能

苏 苗 王丽丽 林 强

1 前 言

壳聚糖（Chitosan）是一种从甲壳类动物外壳中提取的天然高分子化合物，具有无毒、价廉、可生物降解及良好的吸附性能。壳聚糖分子含游离氨基，属碱性多糖，其分子链上含氨基和羟基，可进行衍生化反应[1-4]。β-环糊精是由7个葡萄糖单元以α-1,4-糖苷键连结而成的环状低聚糖，具有独特的内疏水、外亲水结构，能通过范德华力、疏水作用和主客体分子间的匹配等与许多有机和无机分子形成包合化合物[5,6]。壳聚糖和环糊精的交联聚合物具有环糊精的包络识别性能和壳聚糖的生物降解性、无毒性、吸附功能等双重特性，有更好的吸附能力[7-10]。

近年来，壳聚糖/环糊精的合成方法多是壳聚糖先合成微球，然后再接枝环糊精，或是活化后的壳聚糖与环糊精接枝，或活化后的环糊精与壳聚糖接枝等。本工作用活化的环糊精与壳聚糖接枝，然后再对接枝产物进一步交联，制备出聚合物，可避免环糊精只是在外部固载，也可对接枝物进一步交联，改善其形态、机械强度和重复使用性。壳聚糖/环糊精聚合物作为吸附材料可吸附金属离子、苯酚类物质、胆固醇等，对葛根素的吸附还未见报道。本工作研究了壳聚糖/环糊精聚合物新的合成方法及其对葛根素的吸附性能。葛根素是从中药葛根中提取分离出来的一种异黄酮类化合物，它在葛根总黄酮中所占比例最大，具有降低心肌耗氧量、改善局部微循环障碍及降低血糖等多种药理作用[11]，近年来葛根素需求迫切，其吸附材料的研究具有应用价值。

2 实 验

2.1 试剂与仪器

壳聚糖（北京惠康源生物科技有限公司），β-环糊精（天津市赢达稀贵化学试剂厂），硼氢化钠（天津市福晨化学试剂厂），高碘酸钠（天津市福晨化学试剂厂），环氧氯丙烷（天津市福晨化学试剂厂），葛根素（中国食品药品检定研究所），液体石蜡（西陇化工股份有限公司），Tween-80及Span-80（天津市光复精细化工研究所），乙酸乙酯（广东汕头市西陇化工厂）。

UV-1700紫外分光光度计（日本岛津公司），数显水浴恒温振荡器（金坛市精达精密仪器制造厂），SB-1000水浴锅（上海爱郎仪器有限公司），SHB-B循环水式多用真空泵（郑州长城科工贸有限公司），电子分析天平[梅特勒.托利多仪器（上海）有限公司]；冻干机（德国MarinChrist公司），扫描电镜（荷兰FEI公司），JJ-1A精密定时电动搅拌器（江苏省金坛市荣华仪器制造有限公司），NEXUS-470傅里叶变换红外光谱仪（美国Nicolet公司）。

2.2 壳聚糖/环糊精的制备

2.2.1 环糊精的活化

参照文献[12]中β-环糊精氧化产物的合成方法。称取适量β-环糊精溶解于100mL蒸馏水中，在10℃温度下逐滴加入25mL 12%高碘酸钠溶液，避光条件下继续搅拌20min，放置暗处5℃保存过夜。次日用5%亚硫酸氢钠溶液滴定未反应的高碘酸钠，然后用处理好的717树脂搅拌吸附30min，再用732树脂吸附30min分别除去溶液中的杂质阴离子和阳离子。溶液冷冻干燥得到环糊精氧化产物。

[作者简介] 苏苗（1986—），女，北京联合大学生物化学工程学院硕士研究生。

2.2.2 壳聚糖/环糊精交联反应

将90mL液体石蜡倒入三颈瓶中,加入一定量Span-80和Tween-80,乳化30min后,加入5%(w)壳聚糖乙酸溶液和1mL乙酸乙酯,油水体积比为1:3,搅拌30min。在40℃下加入环糊精醛基衍生物搅拌2h,用硼氢化钠还原得到稳定的中间物。在60℃下用环氧氯丙烷在碱性条件下交联反应2h,用石油醚、甲醇、蒸馏水分别洗涤,抽滤得到壳聚糖/环糊精聚合物。

2.3 葛根素的标准曲线

用蒸馏水配制60g/mL葛根素储备液,用移液管分别精密量取储备液1,2,3,4,5mL,然后用蒸馏水稀释至10mL,制得不同浓度的系列溶液,采用分光光度法在波长250nm处测其吸光度。

2.4 醛基含量分析测试

参照文献[13]的方法,采用半微量盐酸羟胺法,盐酸羟胺甲醇溶液与醛基定量反应,生成希夫碱,释放出的盐酸用NaOH甲醇溶液滴定,精确称取0.1g干燥样品,用移液管吸取20mL浓度0.3mol/L的盐酸羟胺甲醇溶液与之混合,加入15滴0.04%百里酚蓝甲醇溶液,70℃水浴下回流2h,冷却至室温,用已标定好的0.03mol/L NaOH甲醇溶液进行滴定,至溶液颜色由粉红变为黄色,同时做空白实验。

醛基含量 H (mol/g) 计算公式为:

$$H = 30X/(1000G),$$

式中,X 为消耗的NaOH体积(mL),G 为试样质量(g)。

2.5 壳聚糖/环糊精聚合物对葛根素的吸附性能测定

取一定壳聚糖/环糊精聚合物于三角烧瓶中,加入一定量葛根素溶液,振荡一段时间后抽滤,在250nm处测定滤液的吸光值,计算吸附容量 Q (mg/g):

$$Q = V(C_0 - C_e)/m,$$

式中,V 为溶液体积(mL),C_0 为葛根素的初始浓度(mg/mL),C_e 为吸附后葛根素的浓度(mg/mL),m 为所用壳聚糖/环糊精聚合物的质量(g)。

3 结果与分析

3.1 壳聚糖/环糊精的制备

壳聚糖/环糊精的制备反应见图1。

图1 反应示意图

环糊精在高碘酸钠的氧化作用下，C2，C3 选择性氧化成醛基，环糊精醛基衍生物在适当条件下与壳聚糖的氨基发生 Schiff 结合反应，产物经 $NaBH_4$ 还原得到稳定的中间产物，在碱性条件下，用双官能团交联剂环氧氯丙烷对其进行交联反应，交联主要发生在 C6 伯羟基上，得到壳聚糖/环糊精交联物。

3.2 红外分析

采用 KBr 压片法，环糊精、环糊精醛基衍生物、壳聚糖/环糊精及壳聚糖的 FT－IR 光谱见图2。比较曲线 a，b 可知，由于 $NaIO_4$ 开环氧化破坏了环糊精的结构，曲线 a 的指纹区不同于曲线 b；此外，它在羰基吸收区域 $1650cm^{-1}$ 有新的吸收带，为新醛基产生。比较曲线 c，d 可知，随壳聚糖氨基取代为 N－环糊精衍生物，$1157cm^{-1}$ 处的峰增强，C—N 峰增强，曲线 c 在 $1560cm^{-1}$ 附近的—NH_2 吸收峰明显减弱，而 $1652cm^{-1}$ 附近的 C＝O 吸收峰有所增强，表明部分—NH_2 与醛基的 C＝O 发生了反应。其他吸收峰变化不大，而原属壳聚糖 C—H 伸缩振动的 $2879cm^{-1}$ 和原属 β－环糊精 C—H 伸缩振动的 $2925cm^{-1}$ 的振动峰在曲线 c 中明显增强[14]。

3.3 扫描电镜图像

图3 是不同放大倍数的扫描电镜照片，可看出，壳聚糖/环糊精聚合物呈不规则球状结构，且其表面凹凸不平呈蜂窝状，也有一些空腔结构，从而可增加起接触表面积，所以该聚合物会对被吸附物有一定的吸附和包埋作用。

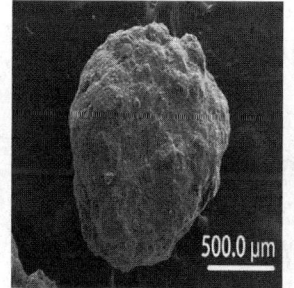
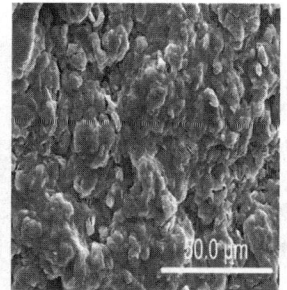
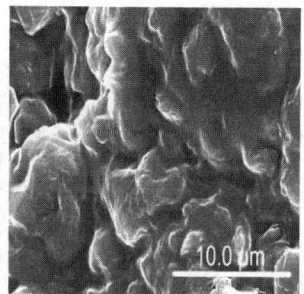

图3 壳聚糖/环糊精的 SEM 照片

3.4 醛基分析

滴定法测定环糊精衍生物的醛基。滴定结果显示 $NaIO_4$ 氧化环糊精的醛基量为 5.1mol/g，高碘酸钠是邻位二醇经典的氧化剂。它以开链方式将环糊精 C2，C3 位的仲羟基选择性氧化成醛基（如图1反应式）。

3.5 葛根素的标准曲线

以葛根素浓度为横坐标，吸光度为纵坐标，绘制标准曲线见图4，经回归得到葛根素浓度与吸光度的线性回归方程为 $y = 75.5x + 0.0036$（$R^2 = 0.9998$），该方程在溶液浓度范围为 2～14μg/mL 时线性关系良好。

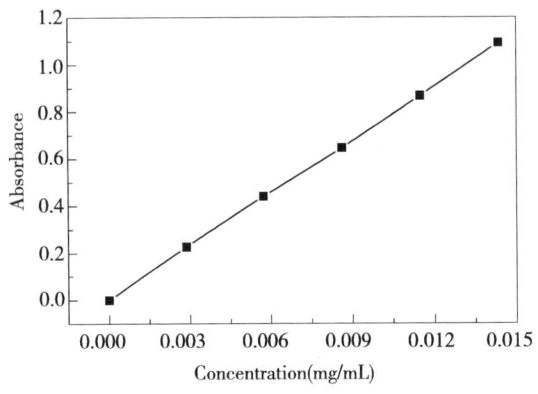

图 4　葛根素水溶液的标准曲线

3.6　壳聚糖/环糊精聚合物的溶胀性

将 0.10g 干树脂置于不同 pH 值的缓冲溶液中浸泡 3h，过滤，称重，按 $S_w = (m_t - m_d)/m_d$ 计算溶胀率（m_t 和 m_d 分别为湿树脂和干树脂的质量）。由图 5 可见，pH = 3.0～7.0 时溶胀率下降，pH = 7.0～9.0，溶胀率稳定。pH = 7.0 时溶胀率达最小，且壳聚糖/环糊精的耐酸性优于壳聚糖。

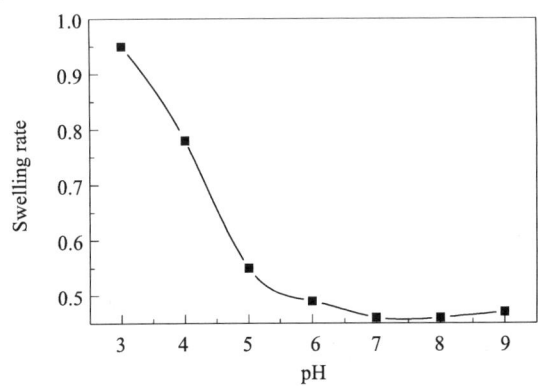

图 5　壳聚糖/环糊精聚合物的溶胀率曲线

3.7　不同条件下对葛根素吸附的影响

3.7.1　时间对吸附的影响

在吸附温度 30℃、吸附剂用量 0.05g、葛根素浓度 6mg/100mL、振荡速率 150 次/min 条件下研究振荡时间对壳聚糖/环糊精聚合物吸附性能的影响，结果如图 6 所示。随时间增加，吸附量增加，2h 内吸附速度较快，4h 时壳聚糖/环糊精聚合物对葛根素的吸附量达最大，4h 后基本平衡。吸附的最佳时间是 4h。

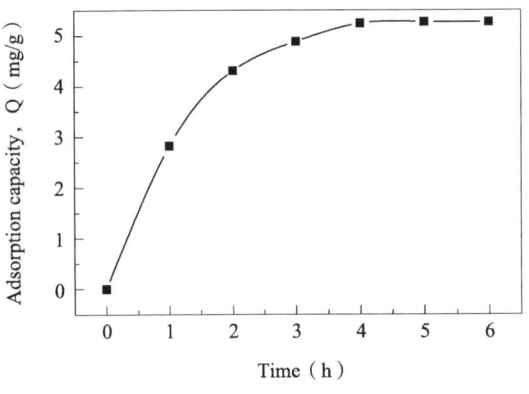

图 6　时间对吸附的影响

在固液吸附过程中，存在着吸附剂对溶质的吸附和对溶剂的吸附，在吸附的初始阶段，由于吸附剂对溶质的吸附占主导，导致吸附量上升快，当吸附剂对溶质的吸附趋于饱和，其对溶剂的吸附速度相对加快，从而导致吸附量趋于平稳，当两种吸附速度相同时，溶液的浓度不再变化。

3.7.2　温度对吸附的影响

取 0.05g 样品加入 10mL 一定浓度的葛根素溶液中，振荡 4h 后取出过滤，测定吸光值，计算其吸附量。由图 7 可知，35℃时吸附量最大。吸附和解吸过程均需活化能，且吸附活化能小于解吸活化能，故在低温范围内，吸附量随温度升高而增大；在一定范围内随温度升高而变小，35℃时吸附效果最好。

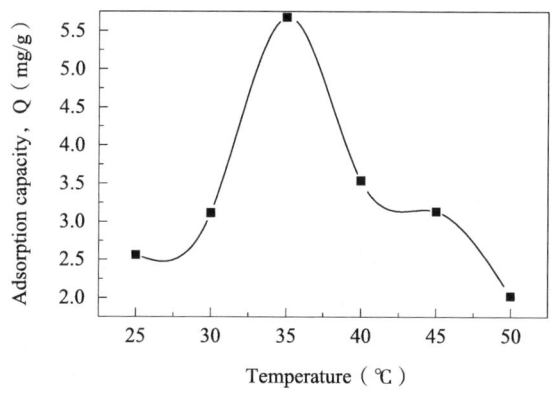

图 7　温度对吸附的影响

3.7.3　pH 值对吸附的影响

取 0.05g 样品，加入 10mL 一定浓度的葛根素溶液中，振荡 4h 后取出抽滤测定吸光值，图 8 显示 pH =7 时吸附量最好。pH 值较小时，溶液中有大量的 H^+，抑制溶液中葛根素的电离，不利于葛根素的吸附。pH 值增大时，OH^- 浓度增大，不利于葛根素与壳聚糖/环糊精的氢键作用及环糊精的疏水包合作用，从而使吸附减少[15]。吸附剂与葛根素之间的作用力可能主要是氢键和疏水交互作用，溶液酸性太强或碱性太强都会减弱这种作用力。

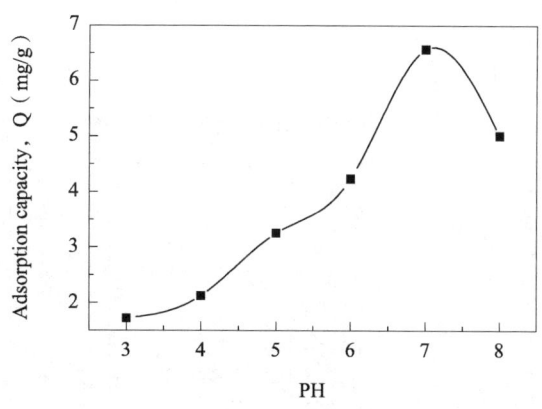

图 8　pH 值对吸附的影响

3.7.4　初始浓度对吸附的影响

取 0.05g 样品，在 pH =7 及 35℃条件下放入不同浓度的葛根素溶液中振荡 4h 后，抽滤测定其吸光值，计算吸附量。由图 9 可见，随着葛根素初始浓度增加，壳聚糖/环糊精聚合物对葛根素的吸附容量逐渐增加，当葛根素初始浓度至 0.5mg/mL 时，吸附容量达 52.43mg/g，吸附达到饱和。因此葛根素最佳初始浓度为0.5mg/mL。

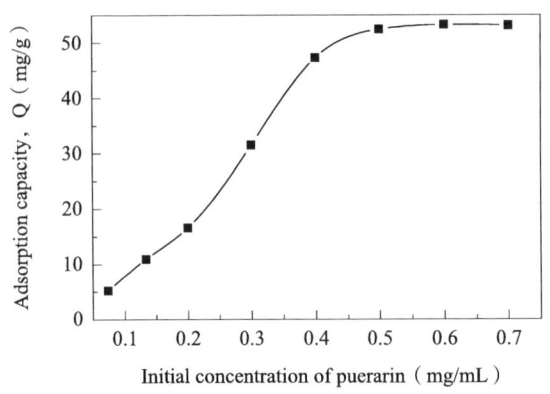

图 9　葛根素初始浓度对吸附的影响

3.8　壳聚糖/环糊精聚合物的脱附

壳聚糖/环糊精聚合物对葛根素的最大吸附量为 52.43mg/g，饱和吸附后过滤，取相同质量聚合物分别加 40%，50%，60%，70% 和 80% 乙醇溶液 20 mL，振荡 12h，测溶液的吸光度，计算洗脱液中葛根素的量，计算洗脱率，结果见表 1。从表 1 可看出，当乙醇浓度为 70% 时洗脱效果较好，且其洗脱率达 89.69%。

表 1　壳聚糖/环糊精聚合物对葛根素的洗脱率

Alcohol concentration（%）	Elution rate（%）
40	74.30
50	77.73
60	82.22
70	89.69
80	82.79

3.9　壳聚糖/环糊精的重复使用性

葛根素脱附后，壳聚糖/环糊精可实现重复利用。用 70% 乙醇洗脱，其重复使用性能见图 10。经 5 次循环吸附后，吸附性能变化不大，实验结果表明其重复使用性能较好。

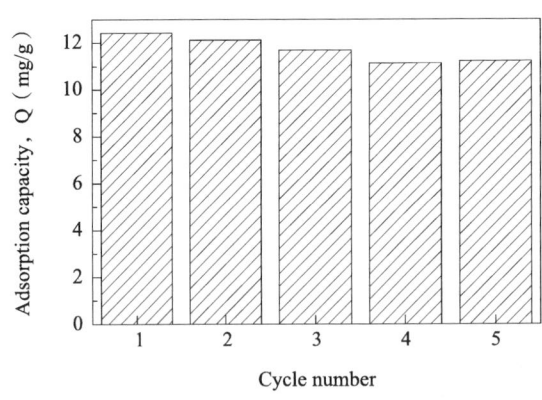

图 10　壳聚糖/环糊精聚合物的重复使用性

3.10　吸附机理探讨

葛根素分子的结构中有 1 个葡萄糖基，还有 1 个黄酮母核，又有酚羟基结构、酚羟基和糖苷链，有一定的极性和亲水性，生成氢键的能力较强。由于壳聚糖氨基上的氢原子与电负性大得多的氮原子结合，共用电子对强烈地偏向氮一方，使氢原子成为带正电几乎暴露的质子，当带负电荷氧原子的葛根素靠近时，便与其上的氧原子形成氢键，这就是壳聚糖氨基与葛根素的氢键作用力，是第一个吸附作用力；

空间结构上,壳聚糖/环糊精的蜂窝状结构使其具有较高的比表面积,对吸附将较有利,这是第二个吸附作用力;另外,环糊精具有疏水腔体结构,能与葛根素形成主客体超分子化合物,这是第三个吸附作用力。

4 结　　论

（1）用高碘酸钠氧化环糊精修饰壳聚糖,用环氧氯丙烷交联制备的壳聚糖/环糊精表面凹凸不平呈蜂窝状且有空腔结构,对葛根素有较好的吸附性能。

（2）温度、时间、pH值及葛根素初始浓度对吸附效果均有影响。

（3）本实验条件下的壳聚糖/环糊精对葛根素吸附量为52.43mg/g,且有较好的洗脱性,洗脱率可达89.69%,重复使用性较好。

参考文献

[1] Zha F, Li S G, Chang Y. Preparation and Adsorption Property of Chitosan Beads Bearing β – Cyclodextrin Cross – linked by1, 6 – Hexamethylene Diisocyanate [J]. Carbohydr. Polym., 2007, 72 (3): 456 – 461.

[2] Liu K H, Liu T Y, Chen S Y, et al. Effect of Clay Content on Electrostimulus Deformation and Volume Recovery Behavior of a Clay – Chitosan Hybrid Composite [J]. Acta Biomater., 2007, 3 (6): 919 – 926.

[3] Chen C Y, Chen C C, Chung Y C. Removal of Phthalate Esters by α – Cyclodextrin – linked Chitosan Bead [J]. Bioresour. Technol., 2007, 98 (13): 2578 – 2583.

[4] Xia Y Q, Guo T Y, Song M D, et al. Selective Separation of Quercetin by Molecular Imprinting Using Chitosan Beads as Functional Matrix [J]. React. Funct. Polym., 2006, 66 (12): 1734 – 1740.

[5] Khaled E T, Mohamed A G, Safaa E R. Novel Method for Preparation of β – Cyclodextrin/Grafted Chitosan and Its Application [J]. Carbohydr. Polym., 2006, 63 (3): 385 – 392.

[6] Wang H D, Chu L Y, Song H, et al. Preparation and Enantiomer Separation Characteristics of Chitosan/β – Cyclodextrin Composite Membranes [J]. J. Membr. Sci., 2007, 297 (1/2): 262 – 270.

[7] Krauland A H, Alonso M J. Chitosan/Cyclodextrin Nanoparticles as Macromolecular Drug Delivery System [J]. Int. J. Pharm., 2007, 340 (1/2): 134 – 142.

[8] Zha F, Li S G, Chang Y, et al. Preparation and Adsorption Kinetics of Porous Glycidoxypropyltrimethoxysilane Crosslinked Chitosan β – Cyclodextrin Membranes [J]. J. Membr. Sci., 2008, 321 (2): 316 – 323.

[9] Prabaharan M, Jayakumar R. Chitosan – graft – β – cyclodextrin Scaffolds with Controlled Drug Release Capability for Tissue Engineering Applications [J]. Int. J. Biol. Macromol., 2009, 44 (4): 320 – 325.

[10] 葛亚芳,李明春,辛梅华. 壳聚糖固载环糊精微球的制备及吸附硝基酚 [J]. 化工进展,2010,29 (2): 233 – 237.

[11] 桂本,郭嘉,池汝安,等. 大孔吸附树脂对葛根总黄酮吸附性能的研究 [J]. 应用化工,2007,36 (5): 451 – 453.

[12] 韩薇妍,龚平,田平. 超氧化物歧化酶修饰产物结构和性能研究 [J]. 北京化工大学学报,2010,37 (2): 117 – 120.

[13] 钱军民,李旭祥. 高碘酸钠氧化纤维素的研究 [J]. 现代化工,2001,21 (7): 27 – 30.

[14] 吴坚,柴灵芝,李俊,等. 乙二醛或戊二醛交联. – 环糊精与壳聚糖交联物的制备 [J]. 科技通报,2008,24 (1): 1 – 4.

[15] 刘廷岳,聂素双,彭露婷. 离子交换纤维对葛根素静态吸附和解吸作用的考察 [J]. 沈阳药科大学学报,2008,25 (2): 148 – 152.

小蓟中氧化蒲公英赛酮和醇的分离鉴定和细胞毒活性测试

院珍珍　吴春彦　王阿利　李金杰　李　斌　尚小雅

小蓟〔*Cirsium setosum* (Willd.) MB.〕为菊科蓟属植物刺儿菜的干燥地上部分或全草，味微苦、甘，性凉，具有凉血止血、祛瘀消肿、利尿之功效，适用于血热性出血，痈肿疮毒等症，尤长于治尿血、血淋[1]。小蓟俗称"刺儿菜"，其嫩茎和叶可以食用，为人们喜爱的民间野菜[2]。

小蓟由于药源广泛、廉价、无毒副作用，在民间用其单方或作为药饮和其他药物联用治疗甲状腺癌[3]、肺癌[4]、脑干肿瘤[5]和膀胱癌，具有较好的效果[6]。在药理学方面，小蓟水提液对人白血病细胞K562、肝癌细胞HepG2、宫颈癌细胞Hela和胃癌细胞BGC823均具较强的抑制作用[7]。本课题组前期根据体外MTT药理活性筛选结果，发现小蓟粗提取物的石油醚萃取部位具有较强的细胞毒活性，申请了专利并已被授权[8]。继续对具细胞毒活性的石油醚部位的化学成分进行系统研究，分离得到3个氧化蒲公英赛酮和醇类化合物，其在人结肠癌细胞、肝癌细胞、胃癌细胞、肺癌细胞和卵巢癌细胞的体外细胞毒活性测试中，均显示一定程度的细胞毒活性。

1　材料与方法

1.1　材料与试剂

小蓟药材采自安徽九华山，经安徽省池州市九华山黄精研究所柯云武工程师鉴定为菊科植物小蓟〔*Cirsium setosum* (Willd.) MB〕，标本（20081028）保存于北京联合大学生物活性物质与功能食品北京市重点实验室。

试验中所用各种分析纯溶剂，北京化学试剂厂生产；HPLC用色谱纯溶剂，美国Fisher公司产品；试验用水，超纯水；Sephadex LH-20，美国Pharmacia公司产品；柱色谱和薄层色谱硅胶，青岛海洋化工厂生产；四甲基偶氮唑盐（MTT），德国Serva公司产品；1640培养液用时临时配制。

1.2　仪器与设备

Inova 500核磁共振仪；Micromass Autospec-Ultima ETOF型质谱仪（EI离子源）和Agilent1100 SL离子阱质谱仪（配有APPI和ESI离子源）；Waters 600高效液相色谱仪（Alltima C_{18} 制备柱，250mm×22mm×5μm，Waters 2996型检测器），Alltech公司；Waters 2545二元高压液相色谱仪（SunFire C_{18} 制备柱，250mm×19mm×5μm，Waters 2998型检测器，2767型自动纯化进样器兼馏分收集器），Waters公司；CombiFlash快速分离仪〔正反相硅胶（43~60m）制备柱〕，ISCO公司产品；Pall纯水机，美国Pall公司；5840R冷冻离心机，德国Eppendorf公司；MR700型酶标仪，美国Dynex公司。

1.3　单体的制备方法

小蓟干燥地上部分20kg，用不同浓度的乙醇超声提取后，合并3次提取液，减压浓缩得到浸膏；将浸膏分散于水中，用石油醚、醋酸乙酯依次萃取，减压浓缩得到石油醚、醋酸乙酯和水萃取部位3个部分。经体外细胞毒活性筛选发现石油醚部分显示了较好的细胞毒活性。

将石油醚部分（468.5g）进行硅胶柱色谱，石油醚-丙酮〔（100∶1）~（0∶100）〕梯度洗脱，薄层色谱检识，合并相似流分，得到Sh1-Sh11共计11个组分。Sh4亚组分经正相硅胶和氰基flash柱色谱，

［基金项目］北京市自然科学基金面上项目资助（7142028）。
［作者简介］院珍珍（1988—），女，北京联合大学生物活性物质与功能食品北京市重点实验室硕士研究生。

石油醚 - 丙酮〔(200∶1) ~ (50∶1)〕梯度洗脱,再经制备液相97%甲醇洗脱,得到化合物11α,12α - oxido - taraxerone (20mg)。Sh7亚组分先经正相硅胶色谱,石油醚 - 丙酮〔(100∶1) ~ (2∶1)〕梯度洗脱,再经 SephadexLH - 20 柱色谱石油醚 - 氯仿 - 甲醇(5∶5∶1)反复洗脱,最后经过制备液相97%甲醇洗脱,得到化合物11α,12α - 氧化蒲公英赛醇(35mg)。Sh2亚组分先经正相硅胶色谱,石油醚 - 丙酮〔(100∶1) ~ (50∶1)〕梯度洗脱,再经快速分离仪反相 flash 柱甲醇 - 水〔(90∶10) ~ (100∶0)〕反复梯度洗脱,得到化合物11α,12α - 氧化蒲公英赛醇棕榈酸酯(18mg)。

2 结果与分析

2.1 化合物的结构鉴定

2.1.1 11α,12α - 氧化蒲公英赛酮的结构鉴定

白色粉末,ESI - MS 给出分子离子峰 m/z 439 [M + H]$^+$。13C - NMR 谱显示有30个碳,低场有1个双键碳信号 δ_C156.9 和 119.4,1个酮羰基碳信号 δ_C216.9。1H - NMR 谱高场显示8个甲基单峰质子信号:δ_H1.24,1.13,1.10,1.08,1.01,0.98,0.87 和 0.83;低场有1个三取代的烯键质子信号 δ_H5.58 (1H, dd, J = 3.3, 8.3Hz);1个与羰基碳相连的亚甲基质子信号 δ_H2.66 (1H, ddd, J = 16.3, 12.0, 7.0Hz),2.43 (1H, ddd, J = 16.3, 6.5, 3.0Hz);氢谱结合碳谱推断结构中还存在1个环氧乙烷基团 [δ_C51.8 和 58.4,δ_H3.17 (1H, t, J = 5.3Hz) 和 2.83 (1H, d, J = 4.5Hz)]。根据上述碳氢谱的特征数据,推断此结构为含有羰基、环氧乙烷基和三取代烯键官能团的五环三萜类结构,再根据低场烯键质子的 dd 峰信号 δ_H5.58 (1H, dd, J = 3.3, 8.3Hz),判断此化合物为蒲公英赛烯型三萜。查阅文献,其碳氢数据与文献[9-10]报道的11α,12α - 氧化蒲公英赛酮 (11α,12α - oxidotaraxerone) 的数据一致,故确定化合物为11α,12α - 氧化蒲公英赛酮 (11α,12α - oxido - taraxerone)。

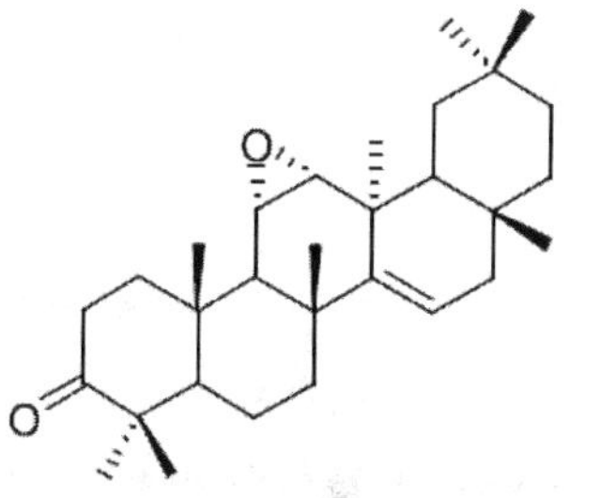

图1 11α,12α - 氧化蒲公英赛酮的结构

2.1.2 11α,12α - 氧化蒲公英赛醇的结构鉴定

白色粉末,EI - MS 给出分子离子峰 m/z 440 (M$^+$)。此化合物的氢谱和碳谱与上述11α,12α - 氧化蒲公英赛酮十分相似:^{1}H - NMR 谱高场显示8个甲基单峰质子信号:δ_H1.08 (6H, s),1.00 (3H, s),0.99 (3H, s),0.96 (3H, s),0.86 (3H, s) 和 0.82 (^{6}H, s),低场有1个三取代的烯键质子信号 δ_H5.55 (1H, dd, J = 8.0, 3.0Hz),较低场有1个环氧乙烷基团 [δ_C52.1 和 58.4,δ_H3.12 (^{1}H, t, J = 5.0Hz) 和 2.80 (^{1}H, d, J = 4.5Hz)],1个连氧的次甲基质子信号 δ_H3.24 (^{1}H, dd, J = 11.0, 5.5Hz);^{13}C - NMR 谱显示有30个碳,低场 δ_C157.3 和 119.0 显示了双键的存在,较低场 δ_C79.1 显示了有结构中羟基的存在。与化合物11α,12α - 氧化蒲公英赛酮的氢谱和碳谱图仔细对照后,推测该化合物为11α,12α - 氧化蒲公英赛醇。查阅文献,与文献[10,11]报道的化合物11α,12α - 氧化蒲公英赛醇 (11α,12α - oxidotaraxerol) 数据一致。

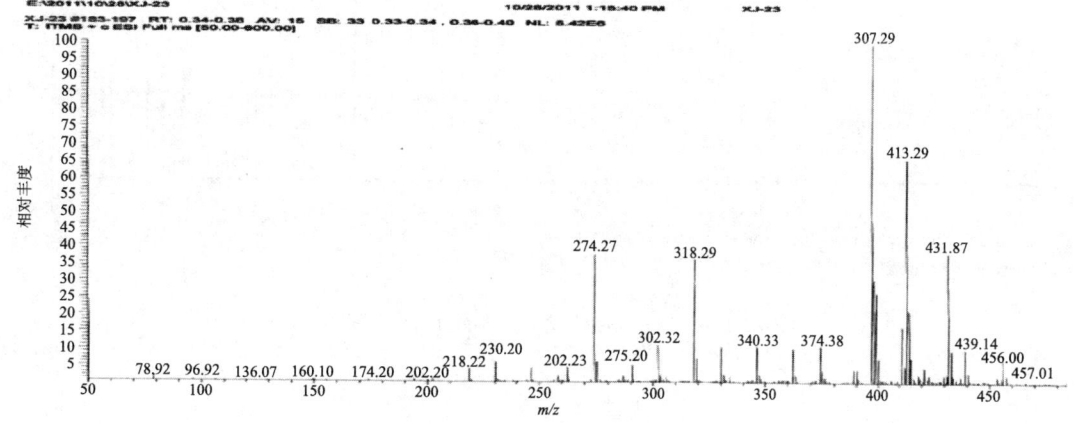

图2 11α,12α - 氧化蒲公英赛酮的 ESI - MS 谱

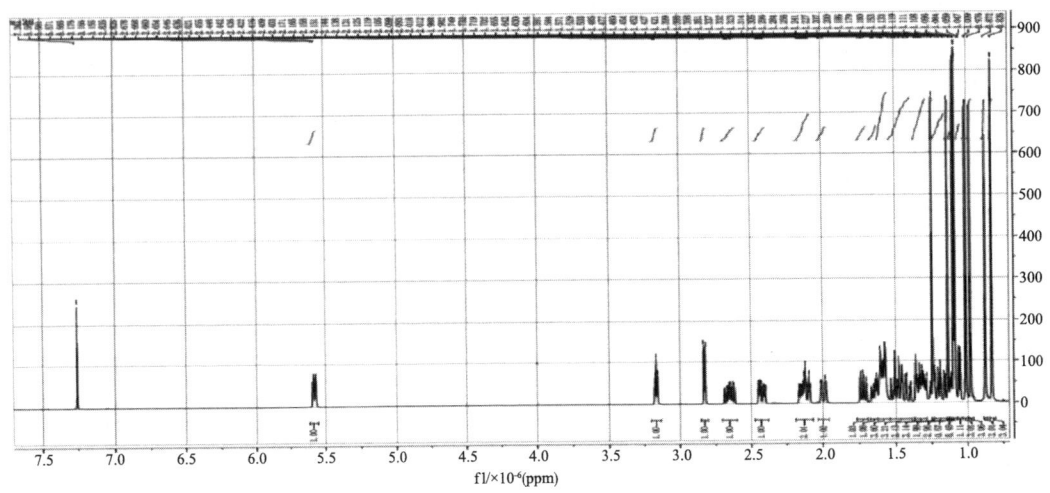

图3 11α,12α-氧化蒲公英赛酮的 ^{1}H-NMR 谱

2.1.3 11α,12α-氧化蒲公英赛醇棕榈酸酯的结构鉴定

白色粉末,EI-MS 给出分子离子峰 m/z 678（M$^{+\cdot}$）。此化合物的氢谱和碳谱与上述 11α,12α-氧化蒲公英赛醇十分相似,差别是结构中多了个长链脂肪烃。^{1}H-NMR 谱高场显示 9 个甲基的质子信号,其中 8 个是单峰甲基质子信号:δ_H1.11,1.08,1.00,0.97,0.90,0.87（^{6}H,s）和 0.82,1 个三重峰甲基质子信号 0.88（^{3}H,t,J=5.5Hz）,同时,高场区 δ_H1.26 处显示 10 个以上亚甲基的质子信号存在,低场有 1 个三取代的烯键质子信号 δ_H5.55（^{1}H,dd,J=3.0,8.0Hz）,较低场有 1 个环氧乙烷基团[δ_C52.0 和 58.3,δ_H3.10（^{1}H,t,J=5.5Hz）和 2.79（^{1}H,d,J=5.0Hz）],1 个连氧的次甲基质子信号 δ_H4.52（^{1}H,dd,J=5.0,10.5Hz）。^{13}C-NMR 谱显示 30 个以上的碳信号,低场有 1 个双键碳信号 δ_C157.3 和 119.0,1 个酯羰基碳信号 δ_C173.6,较低场 δ_C80.5 显示了结构中还存在连氧的碳,高场区 δ_C29.6 处显示有多个亚甲基的重叠信号。以上碳氢特征数据表明此结构为 11α,12α-氧化蒲公英赛醇的 3 位羟基与 1 个长链脂肪酸成酯了,再根据质谱 ED-DMS 给出的分子离子峰 m/z 678（M$^{+\cdot}$）,推断结构为 11α,12α-氧化蒲公英赛醇棕榈酸酯。与已知文献[10,12]中报道的数据对比完全吻合,故确定出化合物结构为 11α,12α-氧化蒲公英赛醇棕榈酸酯（11α,12α-oxido-taraxerol palmitate）。

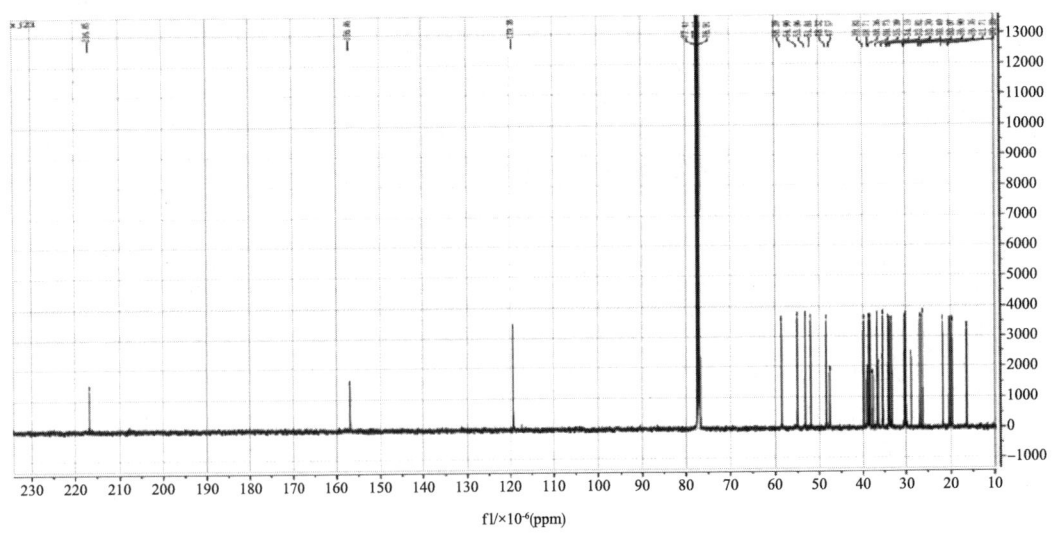

图4 11α,12α-氧化蒲公英赛酮的 ^{13}C-NMR 谱

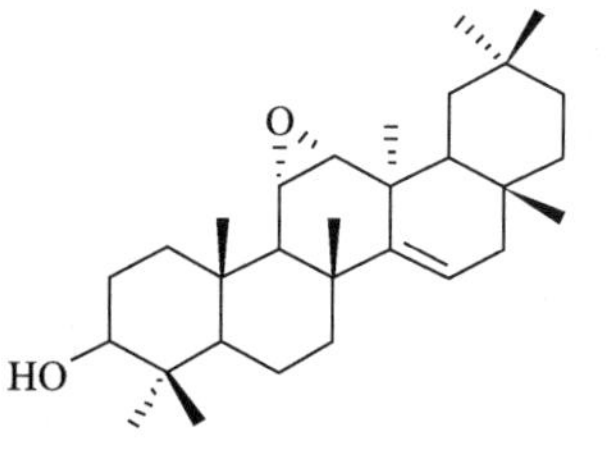

11α,12α-氧化蒲公英赛醇

图 5　11α,12α-氧化蒲公英赛醇的结构

2.2　化合物的波谱数据

2.2.1　11α,12α-氧化蒲公英赛酮的波谱数据

白色粉末，ESI-MS m/z 439 [M+H]$^+$。^{1}H-NMR（CDCl$_3$，500 MHz）δ：5.58（^{1}H，dd，J=8.3，3.3Hz，H-15），3.17（^{1}H，t，J=5.3Hz，H-11），2.83（^{1}H，d，J=4.5Hz，H-12），2.66（^{1}H，ddd，J=16.3，12.0，7.0Hz，H-2b），2.43（^{1}H，ddd，J=16.3，6.5，3.0Hz，H-2a），2.15（^{1}H，ddd，J=13.3，6.8，3.0Hz，H-1b），2.11（^{1}H，dt，J=13.3，3.0Hz，H-1a），2.00（^{1}H，dd，J=15.0，3.0Hz，H-16b），1.73（^{1}H，dd，J=15.0，8.5Hz，H-16a），1.65（^{1}H，dd，J=7.8，6.3Hz，H-6），1.24（^{3}H，s，H-25），1.13（^{3}H，s，H-26），1.10（^{3}H，s，H-23），1.08（^{3}H，s，H-24），1.01（^{3}H，s，H-29），0.98（^{3}H，s，H-30），0.87（^{3}H，s，H-28），0.83（^{3}H，s，H-27）；^{13}C-NMR（CDCl$_3$，125MHz）δ：39.8（C-1），34.1（C-2），216.9（C-3），47.6（C-4），54.9（C-5），20.2（C-6），39.0（C-7），38.7（C-8），53.1（C-9），36.5（C-10），51.8（C-11），58.4（C-12），37.7（C-13），156.9（C-14），119.4（C-15），38.4（C-16），35.5（C-17），48.3（C-18），36.7（C-19），28.9（C-20），33.3（C-21），35.4（C-22），21.7（C-23），26.4（C-24），16.3（C-25），26.9（C-26），19.7（C-27），30.4（C-28），33.8（C-29），30.1（C-30）。

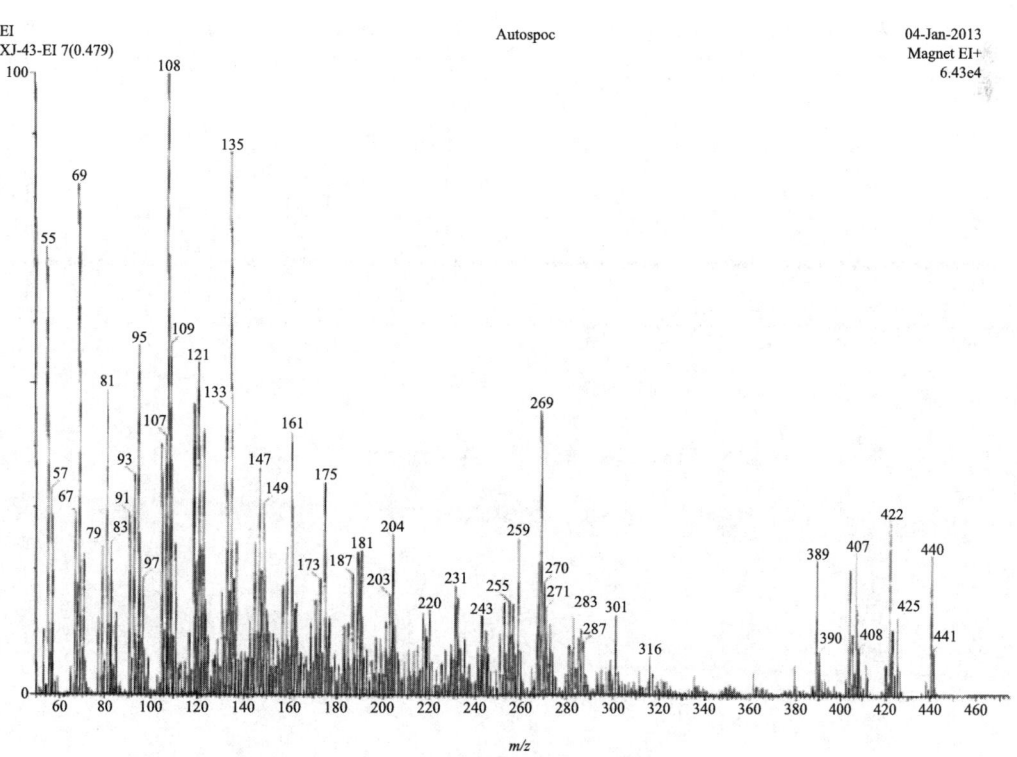

图 6　11α,12α-氧化蒲公英赛醇的 EI-MS 谱

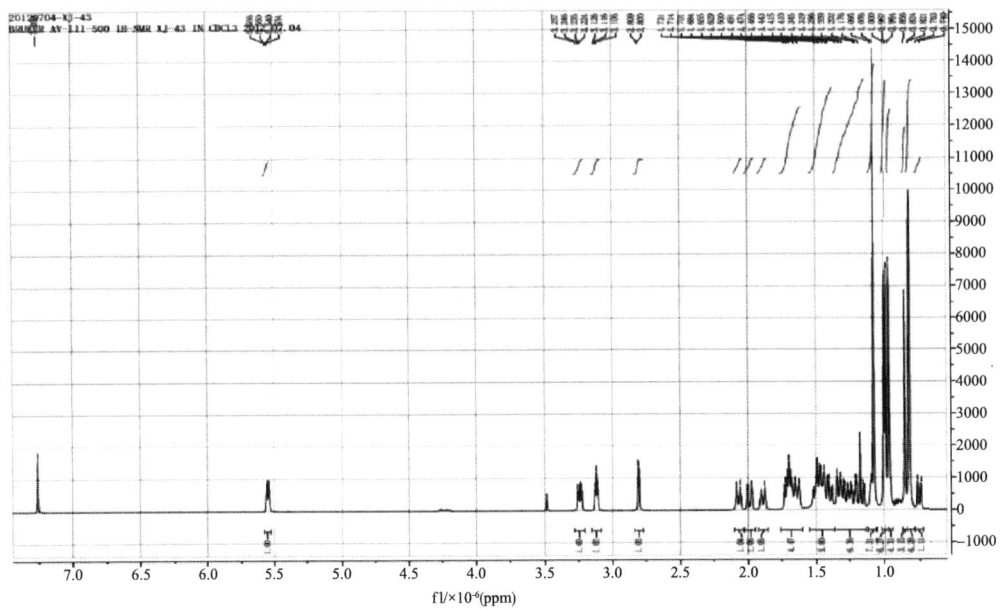

图7 11α,12α-氧化蒲公英赛醇的 1H-NMR 谱

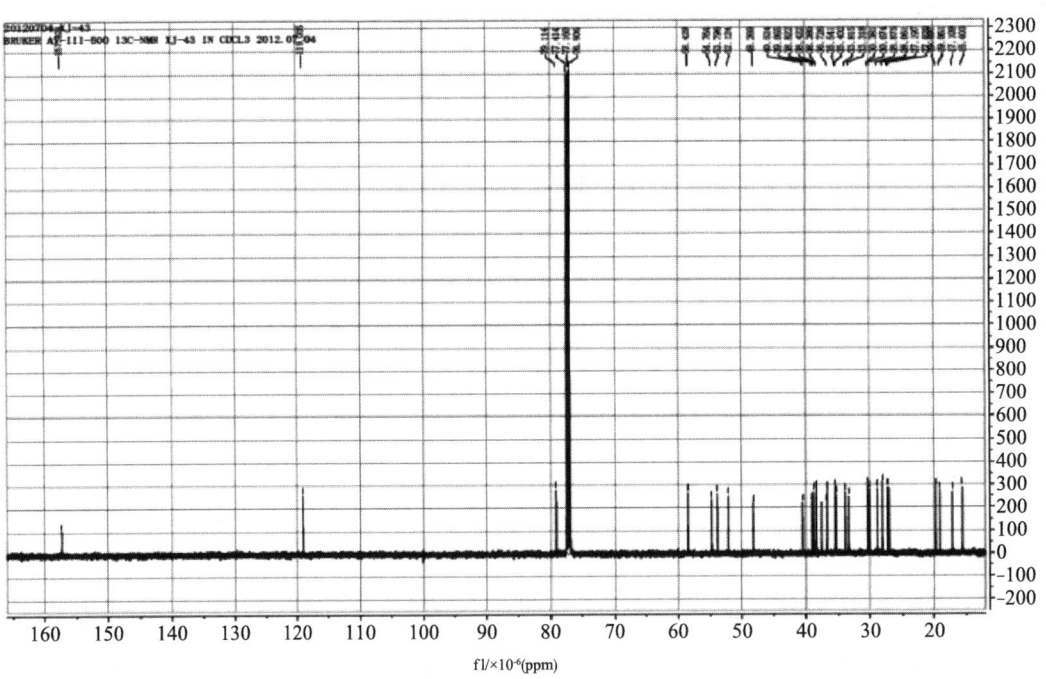

图8 11α,12α-氧化蒲公英赛醇的 ^{13}C-NMR 谱

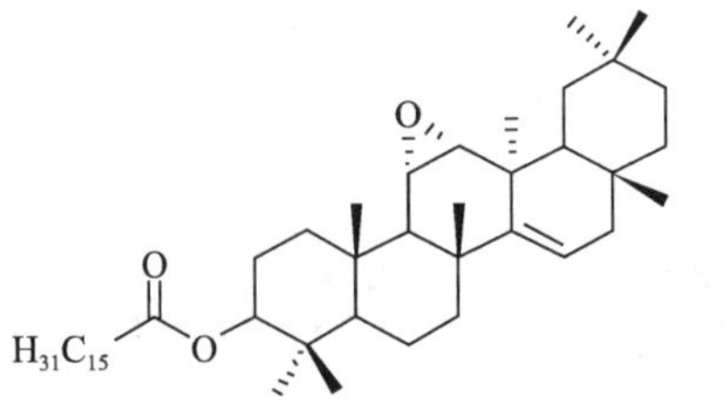

11α,12α-氧化蒲公英赛醇棕榈酸酯

图9 11α,12α-氧化蒲公英赛醇棕榈酸酯的结构

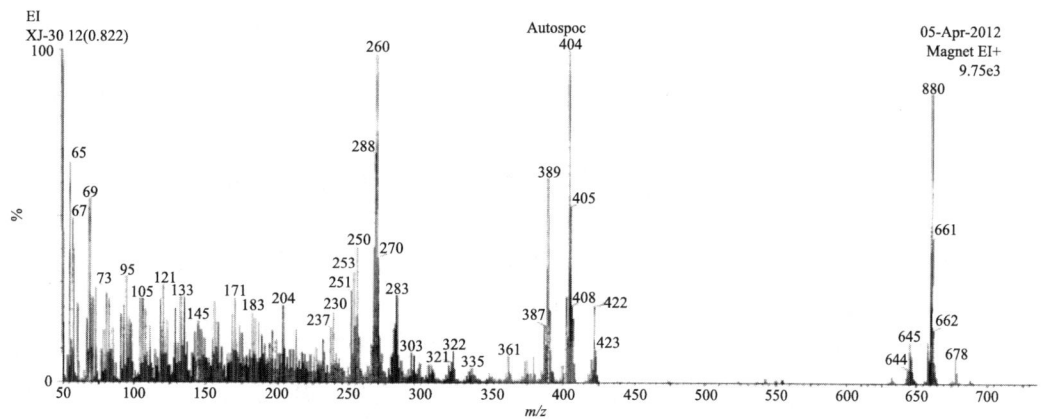

图10　11α,12α-氧化蒲公英赛醇棕榈酸酯的 EI-MS 谱

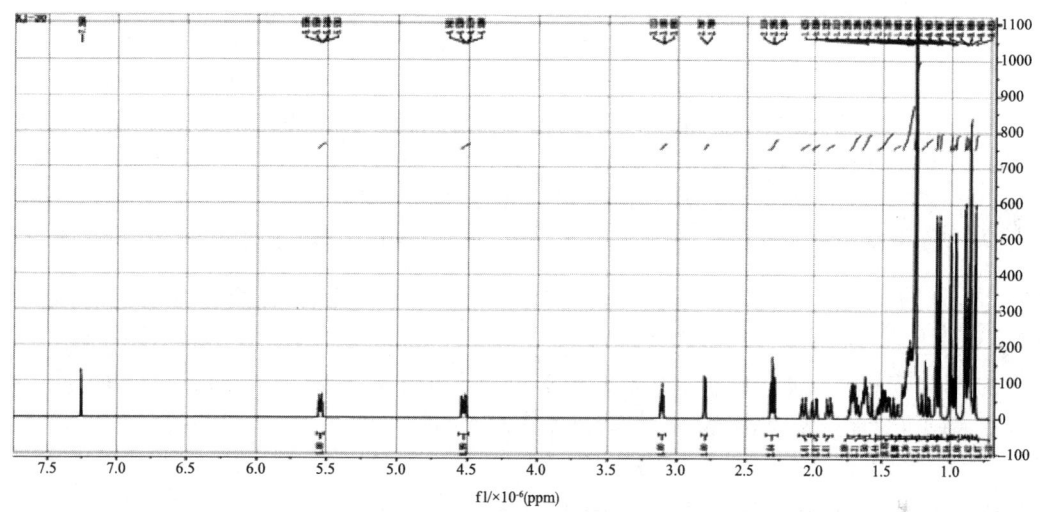

图11　11α,12α-氧化蒲公英赛醇棕榈酸酯的 ^{1}H-NMR 谱

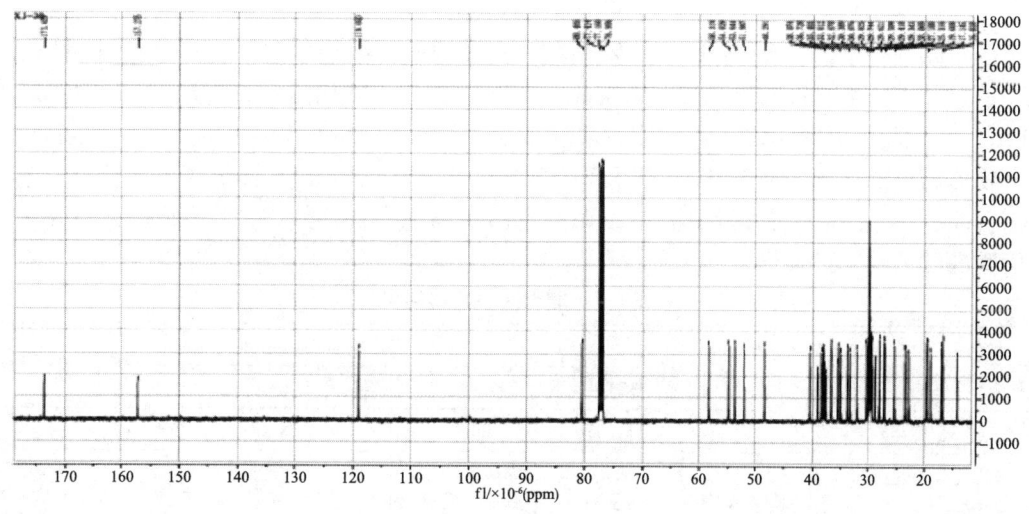

图12　11α,12α-氧化蒲公英赛醇棕榈酸酯的 ^{13}C-NMR 谱

2.2.2　11α,12α-氧化蒲公英赛醇波谱数据

白色粉末，EI-MS m/z 440（M$^+$）。^{1}H-NMR（CDCl$_3$，500 MHz）δ：5.55（^{1}H，dd，J = 3.0，8.0Hz，H-15），3.24（^{1}H，dd，J = 5.5，11.0Hz，H-3），3.12（^{1}H，t，J = 5.0Hz，H-11），2.80

(^{1}H, d, J = 4.5Hz, H - 12), 1.08 (^{6}H, s, H - 25, 26), 1.00 (^{3}H, s, H - 29), 0.99 (^{3}H, s, H - 30), 0.96 (^{3}H, s, H - 24), 0.86 (^{3}H, s, H - 28), 0.82 (^{6}H, s, H - 23, 27); ^{13}C - NMR (CDCl$_3$, 125MHz) δ: 38.4 (C - 1), 27.0 (C - 2), 79.1 (C - 3), 38.8 (C - 4), 54.8 (C - 5), 19.1 (C - 6), 40.5 (C - 7), 39.1 (C - 8), 53.8 (C - 9), 36.7 (C - 10), 52.1 (C - 11), 58.4 (C - 12), 37.7 (C - 13), 157.3 (C - 14), 119.0 (C - 15), 38.4 (C - 16), 35.5 (C - 17), 48.3 (C - 18), 36.8 (C - 19), 28.9 (C - 20), 33.3 (C - 21), 35.4 (C - 22), 28.1 (C - 23), 15.6 (C - 24), 17.1 (C - 25), 27.2 (C - 26), 19.7 (C - 27), 30.4 (C - 28), 33.8 (C - 29), 30.1 (C - 30)。

2.2.3 11α,12α-氧化蒲公英赛醇棕榈酸酯的波谱数据

白色粉末，EI - MS m/z 678 (M$^+$)。^{1}H - NMR (CDCl$_3$, 500 MHz) δ: 5.55 (^{1}H, dd, J = 3.0, 8.0Hz, H - 15), 4.52 (^{1}H, dd, J = 5.5, 11.0Hz, H - 3), 3.10 (^{1}H, t, J = 5.0Hz, H - 11), 2.79 (^{1}H, d, J = 4.5Hz, H - 12), 1.11 (^{3}H, s, H - 25), 1.08 (^{3}H, s, H - 26), 1.00 (^{3}H, s, H - 29), 0.97 (^{3}H, s, H - 30), 0.90 (^{3}H, s, H - 24), 0.88 (^{3}H, t, J = 5.5Hz, H - 16? - CH$_3$), 0.87 (^{6}H, sH - 23, 28), 0.82 (^{3}H, s, H - 27); ^{13}C - NMR (CDCl$_3$, 125MHz) δ: 38.1 (C - 1), 23.4 (C - 2), 80.5 (C - 3), 37.8 (C - 4), 54.8 (C - 5), 19.0 (C - 6), 40.4 (C - 7), 39.1 (C - 8), 53.6 (C - 9), 36.7 (C - 10), 52.0 (C - 11), 58.3 (C - 12), 37.7 (C - 13), 157.3 (C - 14), 119.1 (C - 15), 38.4 (C - 16), 35.5 (C - 17), 48.3 (C - 18), 36.9 (C - 19), 28.9 (C - 20), 33.3 (C - 21), 35.4 (C - 22), 28.1 (C - 23), 16.8 (C - 24), 17.1 (C - 25), 27.2 (C - 26), 19.7 (C - 27), 30.4 (C - 28), 33.8 (C - 29), 30.1 (C - 30), 173.6 (C - 1′), 35.0 (C - 2′), 32.1 (C - 3′), 29.8 ~ 29.3 (C - 4′ ~ C - 13′), 25.3 (C - 14′), 22.8 (C - 15′), 14.3 (C - 16′ - CH$_3$)。

2.3 细胞毒活性筛选结果

用MTT法对筛选出具有体外细胞毒活性的石油醚部位进行系统分离，并对分离得到的化合物在5种人肿瘤细胞中继续进行体外细胞毒活性的测试，计算公式和结果如下：

肿瘤细胞生长抑制率（%）=（1 - 实际孔测定值/对照孔测定值）×100%

由表中数据可知，在测试浓度条件下，3个化合物对5种人肿瘤细胞均有一定的抑制作用，其中对人结肠癌细胞显示了较强的细胞毒活性。

3 结 论

利用常压正相硅胶色谱、SephadexLH-20、闪式正反相低压液相色谱和反相高压液相色谱，从小蓟乙醇提取物的显示细胞毒活性的石油醚萃取部位分离鉴定了3个氧化蒲公英赛烷型三萜类化合物，分别为11α,12α-氧化蒲公英赛酮，11α,12α-氧化蒲公英赛醇和11α,12α-氧化蒲公英赛醇棕榈酸酯，这3个化合物均为首次从蓟属植物中分离得到。文献报道，11α,12α-氧化蒲公英赛酮具有细胞毒活性[11]，11α,12α-氧化蒲公英赛醇具有抗细菌、真菌和细胞毒的活性[13-15]，而11α,12α-氧化蒲公英赛醇棕榈酸酯的活性未见报道。

表1 细胞毒活性筛选结果

化合物	IC_{50}/μmol·L^{-1}				
	HCT - 8	Be - 7402	BGC - 823	A549	A2780
11α,12α-氧化蒲公英赛酮	11.57	28.05	26.24	21.98	30.12
11α,12α-氧化蒲公英赛醇	9.84	27.83	24.35	18.55	27.45
11α,12α-氧化蒲公英赛醇棕榈酸酯	15.12	28.67	24.74	18.67	27.72
紫杉醇（阳性对照）	0.18	0.15	0.46	0.35	0.10

本文对分离得到的3个化合物，利用MTT法进行了体外抗人结肠癌细胞（HCT-8）、人肝癌细胞（Bel-7402）、人胃腺癌细胞（BGC-823）、人肺癌细胞（A549）和人卵巢癌细胞（A2780）的筛选，3个化合物对人结肠癌细胞均显示了较强的细胞毒活性，对其余肿瘤细胞显示了中等程度的细胞毒活性。

此结果提示11α,12α-氧化蒲公英赛醇体外抗细胞毒的活性比11α,12α-氧化蒲公英赛酮稍强,然而当11α,12α-氧化蒲公英赛醇的3位羟基被酯化后活性就变弱了。尽管分离得到的3个化合物显示了一定的细胞毒活性,还是从石油醚部位显示的体外细胞毒活性,和分离得到的3个化合物的细胞毒活性并综合其在石油醚部位的含量比较,推测这3个化合物对石油醚部位显示较强细胞毒活性具有一定的贡献,而不应该是石油醚部位具细胞毒活性的主要成分。今后需要对石油醚部位的化学成分进行系统深入研究,以期找到具有强细胞毒活性的化合物单体。

参考文献

[1] 魏彦,邱乃英,欧阳青. 大蓟、小蓟的鉴别与临床应用[J]. 北京中医杂志, 2002, 21 (5): 296-297.

[2] 李桂凤,董淑敏,李兴福,等. 野生刺儿菜营养成分分析[J]. 营养学报, 1999, 21 (4): 478-479.

[3] 许新琳. 甲状腺癌瘤淋巴结胶囊:中国, 03148840.4 [P]. 2004-03-31.

[4] 郝来勤,赵明,郝玉成. 1种治疗肺癌及其他各种癌症的强效中药:中国, 200710106868.X [P]. 2007-10-10.

[5] 王峰. 一种治疗脑干肿瘤的外用中药组合物及其制备方法:中国, 201010300434.5 [P]. 2010-06-09.

[6] 李虹. 小蓟饮子加减治疗膀胱癌的体会[J]. 中国中医药信息杂志, 2001, 8 (9): 80-80.

[7] 李煜,王振飞,贾瑞贞. 小蓟水提液对4种癌细胞生长抑制作用的研究[J]. 中华中医药学刊, 2008, 26 (2): 274-275.

[8] 尚小雅,李金杰,李泠鸰. 从小蓟中提取抗肿瘤活性物质的方法以及小蓟抗肿瘤药物:中国, ZL 2009 1 0085297.5 [P]. 2009-10-28.

[9] Kuo YH, Way ST, Wu CH. A new triterpene and a new lignan from *Saussurea japonica* [J]. J. Nat. Prod., 1996, 59 (6): 622-624.

[10] 李泠鸰,孙珍,尚小雅,等. 小蓟三萜类化合物成分的研究[J]. 中国中药杂志, 2012, 37 (7): 951-955.

[11] Hu J, Shi XD, ChenJG, et al. Cytotoxic taraxerane triterpenoids from *Saussurea graminea* [J]. Fitoerapia, 2012, 83: 55-59.

[12] Barreiros ML, David JM, Pereira PA de P, et al. Fatty acid esters of triterpenes from *Erythroxylum passerinum* [J]. J. Braz. Chem. Soc., 2012, 13 (5): 669-673.

[13] Abu-Sayeed M, Abbas AM, Bhattacharjee PK, et al. Biological evaluation of extracts and triterpenoids of *Euphor-bia hirta. Pak* [J]. J. Sci. Ind. Res., 2005, 48 (2): 122-125.

[14] Kheyrodin H, Ghazvinian K. Assessment of plant extract toxicity in *Euphobial Spease* [J]. J. Rec. Adv. Agri., 2012, 1 (3): 77-83.

[15] Ekpo OE, Pretorius E. Asthma, Euphorbia hirta and its anti-inflammatory properties [J]. S. Afr. J. Sci., 2007, 103 (5/6): 201-203.

[16] Vallisuta O, Olimat SM. Drug discovery research in pharmcognosy [M]. Croatia: InTech, 2012: 165-180.

基于社会属性的北京市居民通勤满意度空间差异分析

孟 斌 湛东升 郝丽荣

近年来，北京城市化处于快速发展时期，城市人口规模和用地规模都进一步扩大，居住空间不断向郊区迁移。交通发展进一步促进了住宅郊区化进程，但郊区居住功能相对单一，就业岗位缺乏[1]。人口郊区化快速发展与就业发展相对滞后导致居住-就业空间错位、交通拥挤等一系列问题[2]，职住分离引起的城市通勤问题逐渐受到社会关注。

城市通勤是由于居住-就业的空间分离而产生的交通行为[3]，城市的居住和就业空间结构一定程度上决定了通勤的空间格局，反过来，通勤行为也可以反映城市空间结构特征[4]。目前，城市地理和城市规划领域的学者对通勤的关注也越来越多，通勤和交通问题成为城市地理学和城市规划研究的重要课题之一。国外学者对通勤问题的相关研究主要集中在城市形态和通勤[5~7]、居住-就业平衡和通勤[8,9]、空间不匹配与通勤[10,11]、过度通勤[12~14]等方面，这些研究在实证和理论层面都对国内相关研究产生巨大影响。

国内学者大多围绕职住分离背景下居民通勤行为变化开展实证研究，如孟斌[15]、孟庆艳[16]、周素红[17]分别对北京、上海和广州居民的通勤特征进行研究，认为职住分离对大城市居民的通勤行为影响较大；一些学者则从居民通勤特征和居民迁居前后的通勤时间变化反映北京等大城市职住分离现象普遍存在[2,18]。也有学者更加关注城市空间结构因素对通勤的影响，如李峥嵘和柴彦威[19]通过对大连居民通勤特征的研究，得出通勤现象的距离衰减规律及其空间结构模式；孟斌[20]、周素红等[21]则关注到通勤和城市空间组织的关系。一些研究则试图解释通勤行为差异的产生原因，如张艳等[22]比较了不同居住区居民的通勤行为差异；刘志林等[23]则研究了居民属性和居住特征对通勤距离的影响。

上述文献大多基于对案例城市或某种属性居民的通勤特征研究，但鲜有学者基于居民主观评价的角度来研究北京城市居民的通勤问题。通勤满意度是居民在特定城市发展背景下对通勤状况的一种主观评价和心理感受，也是居民对职住分离程度及其影响的直接反映。国内一些学者已经在宜居城市研究中关注到通勤满意度[24]，但从居民对通勤满意度评价的角度来考察城市居民的通勤现状和职住分离程度的研究还较为缺乏[25]，能从不同时间断面进行对比研究则更少。从人群的社会属性角度，研究通勤满意度差异和空间分布，对理解城市物质空间结构与社会空间结构的互动具有重要意义。因此，本文基于不同时间问卷调查数据，采用多元统计分析和空间分析技术比较北京不同居民群体的通勤满意度差异和空间分布格局，试图揭示居民社会属性对通勤满意度的影响及其在城市空间中的映射，对深化职住关系研究和城市空间结构研究具有重要意义，也对城市建设中改善居民通勤出行环境、提高居民的通勤满意度具有一定的借鉴作用。

1 数据来源和研究方法

1.1 数据来源

本文采用2010年"北京职住关系调查"的问卷数据，结合2005年的"北京宜居满意度"问卷调查

[基金项目] 国家自然科学基金项目（41171136，40871079），北京市属高校人才强校计划资助项目（PHR201007146，PHR201108374），北京联合大学人才强校计划人才资助项目（BPHR2012E01）资助。

[作者简介] 孟斌（1971—），男，北京联合大学应用文理学院教授。主要研究方向为地理信息科学、城市地理等；湛东升，北京联合大学北京学研究所；郝丽荣，首都师范大学资源环境与旅游学院。

数据开展研究。两次问卷调查均以北京城区为主要研究区域，另外包括回龙观、天通苑、亦庄开发区以及通州等典型地区，按照各个街道人口所占比例采用分层抽样和街头拦访的调查方法。2005 年共发放问卷 11000 份，回收有效问卷 7647 份，有效率达到 69.5%。2010 年共发放并回收问卷 4269 份，剔除回收问卷中有遗漏信息的部分调查对象，最终用于本研究的有效问卷共计 4060 份，有效率达到 95.1%。调查对象为常年居住（半年以上）在北京居住的全职工作者，调查样本属性构成见表 1。

表 1 样本属性构成

属性		样本数（个）	比例（%）	属性		样本数（个）	比例（%）
年龄	30 岁以下	2695	63.2	家庭构成	单身独住	1658	39.0
	30~39 岁	1048	24.6		单身和父母同住	736	17.3
	40~49 岁	383	9.0		夫妻独住	817	19.2
	50~59 岁	124	2.9		夫妻和父母同住	135	3.2
	60 岁以上	15	0.4		夫妻携子女	621	14.6
学历	初中及以下	270	6.3		三代以上同住	144	3.4
	高中	712	16.7		其他	142	3.3
	大专	1219	28.6	交通方式	步行	454	10.7
	本科	1661	39.0		自行车	301	7.1
	研究生	393	9.2		电动车/摩托车	105	2.5
家庭月收入	3000 元以下	909	22.0		公交车	1606	37.7
	3000~4999 元	1180	28.6		地铁/轻轨	1003	23.6
	5000~9999 元	1183	28.7		单位班车	135	3.2
	1~1.5 万元	444	10.8		出租车	88	2.1
	1.5~2 万元	218	5.3		私家车	566	13.3
	2 万元以上	191	4.6				

1.2 研究方法

1.2.1 主成分分析

主成分分析是利用降维处理技术把原来多个变量划为少数几个综合指标的多元统计方法，利用较少的新变量去解释原始变量的大部分信息[26]。首先对居民的属性即年龄、学历、家庭月收入、家庭规模、交通方式 5 种属性按照一定规律进行数值化处理，再进行主成分分析，通过降维处理得到新的综合指标来反映居民原有社会属性特征。

1.2.2 聚类分析

聚类分析是研究多要素事物分类问题的数量方法，其基本原理是根据样本自身的属性，用数学方法按照某种相似性或差异性指标，定量地确定样本之间的亲疏关系，再对样本进行分类[26]，当样本量比较大时，适宜采用 K-均值法，实现快速聚类。基于主成分分析结果，再对居民综合属性进行 K-均值聚类分析，把社会属性相似的居民聚成一类，有助于更好地把握不同居民群体的通勤满意度特征和空间分布格局。

1.2.3 空间集聚分析

全局空间自相关可以反映空间对象在整个区域内的空间分布状态和模式。空间全局自相关的测度指标很多，如 Moran's I，Geary's C 和 Getis' G。其中，最常用的是 Moran's I，常采用 Z 统计量检验全局空间自相关的显著性[27]。Moran'I 的取值范围在 $[-1,1]$ 之间，当 $I<0$，表示存在空间负相关；$I>0$，表示空间正相关；$I=0$，表示不存在空间相关性。正相关表明某单元的属性值变化与其相邻空间单元具有相同的变化趋势，负相关则正好相反。

全局空间自相关假定空间是同质的，即只存在一种充满整个区域的趋势。局域空间自相关主要反映空间对象与其临近区域的空间关联程度，主要用来探寻空间对象在局部空间上的集聚性，反映要素的空间异质性。常用 Local Moran's I（LISA）表示，一般常将经过统计检验之后的 LISA 分为四类，其中"HH（高高）"表示某一点（区域）和其周围点（区域）的属性值都较高，"HL（高低）"表示某一点

（区域）的属性值较高，但其周围点（区域）的属性值较低。"LH（低高）"与"LL（低低）"的意义正好相反。"高高"和"低低"表明具有较高的空间正相关，提示区域的集聚和相似性。"高低"和"低高"则表示存在较强的空间负相关，区域具有异质性[27]。

首先，基于每个街道各类人群所占的比例，分别做全局空间自相关和局域空间自相关分析，用来探寻不同居民群体的空间分布格局和集聚特征。

其次，将居民通勤满意度为很满意、基本满意、不太满意、很不满意、不清楚或不关注分别赋值为4、3、2、1、0分，计算出每个街道居民通勤满意度的平均得分再对其进行空间自相关分析，主要分析不同人群空间分布对街道通勤满意度的影响和街道通勤满意度的空间分异特征。

2 不同居民群体空间分布格局

2.1 居民属性的聚类分析

单一的属性划分往往无法全面地反映出居民的社会属性特征，因此，利用SPSS17.0软件对数值化处理后的居民5个属性值进行主成分分析，并用最大方差旋转法最终得出反映居民综合社会属性的两个主成分因子（表2）。两个主成分因子共解释了原有属性变量信息的59.896%，其中，第一主成分因子和第二主成分因子分别解释了变量信息的34.095%、25.081%。从旋转后的因子载荷可以看出，第一主成分因子在"学历、家庭月总收入、交通方式"这3个指标上的因子载荷较高，主要反映居民的"经济知识水平"；第二主成分因子在"年龄、家庭规模"这两个指标上的因子载荷较高，主要反映居民的"家庭负担压力"。

表2 居民社会属性特征的主成分分析

		F1 经济知识水平	F2 家庭负担压力
主成分	特征值	1.705	1.290
	贡献率	34.095	25.801
	累计贡献率	34.095	59.896
旋转后因子载荷	X1 年龄	−0.003	0.800
	X2 学历	0.763	−0.246
	X3 家庭月总收入	0.715	0.344
	X4 家庭规模	0.082	0.755
	X5 交通方式	0.705	0.091

基于上述分析结果再进行聚类分析，得出4分类的最优分组结果。在2010年的4060份有效问卷中，聚类得到的1、2、3、4类居民所占的比例分别为17.3%、23.1%、24.6%、34.9%。为了更清楚的反映每类居民的属性特征，再对每一类结果和居民属性进行交叉分析后，可以概括出以下4类人群：一般平民、年轻打工族、高收入阶层、年轻白领。每类人群的社会属性特征见表3。

表3 不同人群的社会属性特征

	年龄	学历	家庭规模	家庭月总收入	交通方式
一般平民	30~49岁	高中、大专	3人为主、包括一些5人	3000~9999元	公交车为主，其次步行、自行车
年轻打工族	30岁以下	高中、大专	1人为主	3000元以下	公交车为主，其次步行、自行车
高收入阶层	30~40岁	本科	3人为主	5000~15000元	私家车为主，其次地铁
年轻白领	30岁以下	本科	1人为主	3000~9999元	公交车、地铁

2.2 不同居民群体分布的全局空间自相关

检测每类人群在整个区域的空间相关性（表4）可以看出，一般平民和年轻白领在全市空间存在显著的集聚性（$P<0.05$），Moran's I 值都为0.11，说明一般平民和年轻白领在全市空间分布具有明显的集

聚特点，即某类人群比例高的街道趋向于和该类人群高比例的街道接近，或某类人群比例低的街道趋向于和该类人群低比例的街道接近。年轻打工族和高收入阶层在全市空间上呈随机分布格局，并不存在显著地全局空间依赖性。

表4　不同人群的全局自相关检验

	Moran's I	Z 值	P 值
一般平民	0.11	2.28	0.02
年轻打工族	0.06	1.30	0.19
高收入阶层	−0.07	−1.19	0.23
年轻白领	0.11	2.36	0.02

目前，北京城市的就业中心主要集中在城市中心地区，内城的住宅存量相对较少，住宅不断向郊区迁移，而郊区住宅的配套设施和交通条件均不完善，居住区位优势无法和城市中心地区相比，城市中心仍是人们较为理想的居住地。不同居民群体的社会经济属性差异和个人住房偏好不同导致一定规模的居住空间分异格局，表现为不同社会属性的居民群体在城市空间上集聚分布与随机分布并存的格局，居民的社会空间结构更加复杂，这和冯健等[28]的研究结论相吻合。

2.3　不同居民群体分布的局域空间自相关

对不同人群进行局域空间自相关分析（图1），可以看出不同居民全体分布特征。一般平民的热点地区主要聚集在北京城市西部，如苹果园、广宁、香山等，这个区域是传统工业集中地区，随着产业升级和转型，下岗工人增多，并且由于年龄、教育等因素限制，就业活动空间受限。

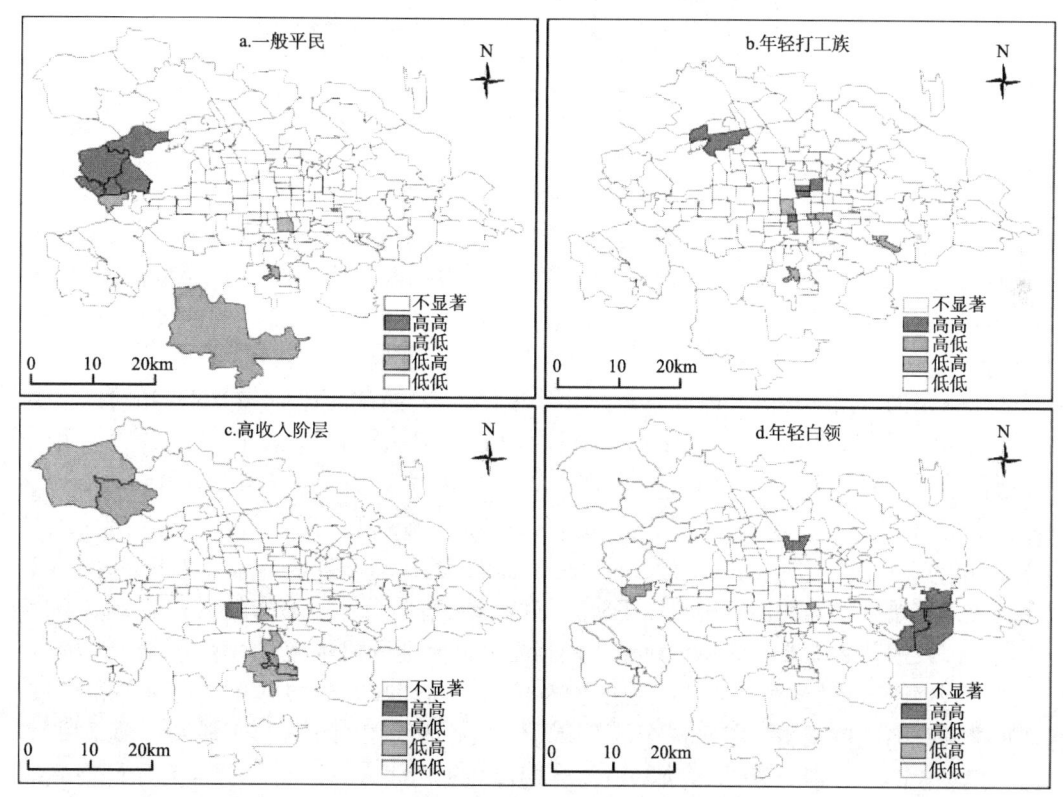

图1　不同人群分布的局域空间自相关格局

年轻打工族的热点区域主要集中在中关村附近的北新桥、青龙桥，以及内城的大栅栏、景山等地。中关村是北京的重要就业中心之一，而内城区的消费性服务业比较发达，这一群体就业引导居住特征显著造成这样的居住空间格局。

高收入阶层的热点区主要集中在广外，主要由于该地靠近城市中心，居住区位优越；而温泉镇却是高收入阶层分布的异质热点区，这里的居住环境质量较高，成为高收入阶层的理想别墅区之一。

年轻白领的热点区域主要聚集于亚运村和东五环外的官庄、豆各庄等地；亚运村附近公司和科研院所相对较多，许多年轻白领事业在此聚集，利于他们就近上班；而东五环外地区房价相对便宜并且靠近CBD，成为年轻白领购房的理想区域。

3 通勤满意度的社会属性特征和空间分布格局

3.1 不同居民群体的通勤满意度特征

在2010年问卷调查过程中要求被访者对通勤满意度总体感受进行了回答，选项包括很满意、基本满意、不太满意、很不满意、不清楚或不关注5类。通过对不同群体居民的通勤满意度比较分析（图2），可以得出以下结论。

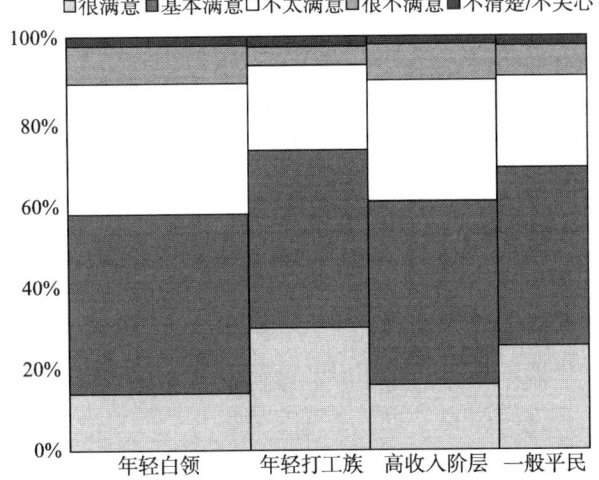

图2 不同人群及其通勤满意度构成特点

1）北京市6成以上居民对通勤持满意态度，但与2005年相比，居民满意度明显降低。如果把居民通勤满意度调查中的"很满意""基本满意"归为一类，"基本不满意""很不满意"的归为一类。在2005年样本中，居民对通勤持满意态度比例为82.2%，不满意人群比例仅为17.8%，而2010年居民对通勤持满意态度降低到63.4%，有36.6%的居民对目前通勤时间持不满意态度，通勤不满意度较2005年增加了18.8%。

居住郊区化带来的居民平均通勤时间延长是导致这种结果的直接原因。在2005年的样本中，居民的平均通勤时间为38min，而2010年居民的平均通勤时间增至43.6min，增加了14.7%[15]。另一方面主要与北京市交通拥堵程度恶化有关。2010年北京市人口已达到1961万人，比2005年增加27.5%，此外，2010年北京市机动车保有量达到480.9万辆，是2005年的1.86倍，其中私人小微型客车数量有356.6万辆，是2005年的2.66倍。庞大的城市人口规模和高增长的机动车数量给北京城市交通带来巨大压力，交通拥堵现象普遍直接导致居民通勤满意度下降。影响居民通勤满意度下降的因素还有很多，土地利用结构、交通规划以及居住和就业空间错位所带来的通勤时间和通勤成本增加可能是更深层原因。

2）一般平民和年轻打工族对通勤满意程度相对较高，而高收入阶层和年轻白领却相对较低。四类人群对通勤基本满意的比例相当，集中在43%～45%。低收入阶层的年轻打工族和一般平民对目前通勤很满意的比例相对较高，分别为29.3%和25.1%，远远高于高收入阶层的15.6%和年轻白领的13.9%；反之，这也说明了高收入阶层和年轻白领的通勤不满意程度相对较高。

年轻打工族受学历和技能限制往往从事一些低端的服务性行业，用人单位大多提供住宿或倾向于选择就业地附近的廉价住宿，通勤时间相对较短。一般平民中大多是城市近远郊地区自由职业的居民或下岗职工，职住相对接近。而高收入阶层大多是商品房住户，交通方式以出租车、私家车较多，通勤距离相对较长而导致其通勤满意度不高。年轻白领的学历较高并且事业刚刚起步，面临的家庭住房压力相对较大，择居地点一般选择房价相对便宜的近远郊，较长的通勤时间使其通勤满意度大大降低。

3）年轻打工族对通勤不清楚或不关注的比例相对略高。可以看出年轻打工族对北京市通勤不清楚或不关注的比例为2.7%，较其他3类人群略高，这说明年轻打工族对北京城市的了解和关注程度并不多，社会融入程度还相对较低，在通勤满意度上的比较优势并不能代表他们的社会优势，背后可能隐含着这一群体在交通方式、住房条件和家庭月收入等更多弱势地位。

3.2 街道通勤满意度分布格局

对街道通勤满意度得分进行全局自相关分析，得到Moran's I值为0.25（$Z=5.16$，$P=0.00$），这表明北京城市各个街道的通勤满意度得分在空间上存在显著的正相关，说明通勤满意度存在空间集聚的特点，即通勤满意度得分相近的区域趋于集中，这反映出城市总体空间结构对通勤满意度影响。

进一步进行局域空间自相关分析来看，通勤满意度的热点区（HH）主要集中在大栅栏、前门、和义、东高地，异质热点区（HL）分布在香山街道，城市西北区域和大兴是通勤满意度的冷点区（LL），异质冷点区主要分布在天桥街道（LH）（图3）。

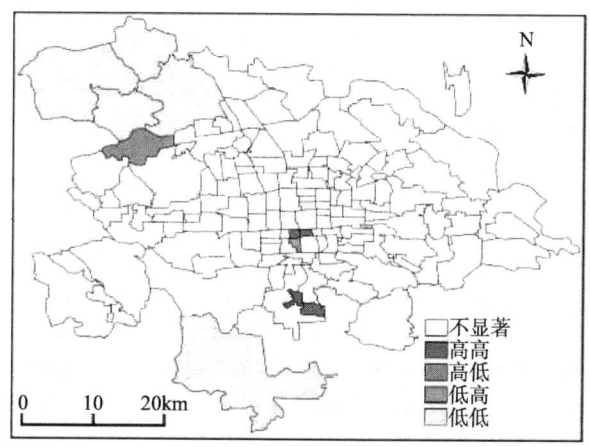

图3 街道通勤满意度的局域空间自相关格局

街道通勤满意度空间分异明显，其空间差异与人群分布格局密切相关：一般平民和年轻打工族分布比例较高的街道，其通勤满意度得分往往也相对较高，更可能成为通勤满意度的热点区。相反，以高收入阶层和年轻白领人群为主的街道则更可能成为通勤满意度的冷点区。如大栅栏、前门、东高地街道的年轻打工族和一般平民分布较多，两类人群占街道总人数比例均达66%以上，群体通勤特征使这些街道成为通勤满意度的热点区。在调查样本中，和义街道的居民分布数量很少并且以高收入阶层为主，个体随机性导致这一街道也成为通勤满意度的热点区。香山街道的一般平民和年轻打工族两类人群的比例超过85%，成为通勤满意度的异质热点区。分布在苏家坨、上庄乡附近等地和大兴的居民数量很少或者空白，并且这些区域离城市中心较远，成为居民通勤满意度的冷点区。天桥街道的高收入阶层和年轻白领的比例超过半数以上表现为异质冷点区。

4 结论与讨论

本文通过问卷调查获得北京城市居民的社会属性和通勤满意度数据，采用多元统计方法对居民进行分类，探讨了通勤满意度的社会属性差异，并通过空间分析技术对不同人群的空间分布格局和通勤满意度的空间分异特征进行了分析，研究结果表明：

1）2010年北京城市居民的通勤满意度总体较好，但和2005年相比，通勤满意度明显降低。"十一五"期间，北京城市居民的通勤满意度降幅明显，这主要是由于城市人口、机动车数量快速增长带来的交通拥堵现象；但北京城市土地利用结构、交通规划以及居住和就业空间错位导致的通勤时间延长也是造成居民通勤满意度下降的主要原因。

2）不同人群的通勤满意度特征差别明显。一般平民和年轻打工族的通勤满意度相对较高，而高收入阶层和年轻白领的通勤满意度却相对较低。不同社会属性居民群体之间的就业机会、择居能力差异造成居民通勤时间的不同，居民通勤满意度也因此分化。此外，年轻打工族对通勤满意状况不清楚或不关注的比例略高，从而折射出这一群体存在的通勤优势和社会融入劣势。

3）在整体城市空间上，居民群体呈现集聚分布和随机分布并存，在局部空间上，不同居民群体空间集聚明显，反映出城市社会阶层的空间分异值得关注。从全局空间自相关可以看出，一般平民和年轻白领在全市空间上呈集聚分布，而年轻打工族和高收入阶层在全市范围内却呈随机分布。从局域空间自相关来看，一般平民主要聚集在城市西部老工业区附近的街道；年轻白领却主要集中在亚运村和东五环以外区域；年轻打工族聚集在北新桥、大栅栏等街道，而广外的高收入阶层比重相对较大。

4）通勤满意度空间分异现象显著。通勤满意度热点区集中在大栅栏、前门、和义、东高地这4个街道，冷点区主要分布在城市郊区的街道；香山街道成为通勤满意度的异质热点区，异质冷点区域分布在内城的天桥街道。其中，街道人群构成状况对通勤满意度空间差异具有显著影响，一般平民和年轻打工族构成为主街道的通勤满意度更可能成为热点区域，高收入阶层和年轻白领构成为主街道的通勤满意度更可能成为冷点区域。

本文基于居民社会属性分类的基础上，结合居民对通勤满意度评价，可以有效地反映居民通勤满意度的社会差异和空间差异，针对北京城市居民的通勤满意度格局和人群属性特征，可以制定出更有效的交通规划方案和公共政策以提高居民通勤满意度。本研究仅仅揭示了北京城市居民整体的通勤满意度格局和人群分布特点，但对其背后的成因分析还有待进一步深入研究。

参考文献

[1] 马清裕，张文尝. 北京市居住郊区化分布特征及其影响因素 [J]. 地理研究，2006，25（1）：121-130.

[2] 徐涛，宋金平，方琳娜，等. 北京居住与就业的空间错位研究 [J]. 地理科学，2009，29（2）：174-180.

[3] 刘望保，闫小培，陈忠暖. 西方国家关于城市通勤的研究回顾与展望 [J]. 经济地理，2009，29（3）：402-430.

[4] Sohn J. Are commuting patterns a good indicator of urban spa-tial structure? [J]. Journal of Transport Geography, 2005, 13 (4): 306-317.

[5] Handy S L. Methodologies for Exploring the Link between ur-ban form and travel behavior [J]. Transportation Research Part D, 1996, 1 (2): 151-165.

[6] Giuliano G, Narayan D. Another Look at travel patterns and ur-ban form: the US and Great Britain [J]. Urban Studies, 2003, 40 (11): 2295-2312.

[7] Horner M. A multi-scale analysis of urban form and commuting change in a small metropolitan area (1990-2000) [J]. The An-nals of Regional Science, 2007, 41 (2): 315-332.

[8] Cevero R. Jobs-housing Balance and Regional Mobility [J]. Jour-nal of the American Planning Association, 1989, 55 (2): 136-150.

[9] Giuliano G. Is jobs-housing balance a transportation issues [J]. Transportation Research Record, 1991, 13 (5): 305-312.

[10] Mc Lafferty S, Preston V. Spatial mismatch and employment in a decade of restructuring [J]. Professional Geographer, 1996, 48 (4): 420-431.

[11] DeRango K. Can commutes be used to test the spatial mismatch hypothesis? [J]. Urban Studies, 2001, 38 (9): 1521-1529.

[12] White MJ. Urban Commuting Journeys are not "Wasteful" [J]. Journal of Political Economy, 1988, 96 (5): 1097-1110.

[13] Small K A, Song S. Wasteful Commuting: a Resolution [J]. Jour-nal of Political Economy, 1992, 100 (4): 888-898.

[14] Horner M W. Extensions to the Concept of Excess Commuting [J]. Environment and Planning Part A, 2002, 34 (3): 543-566.

[15] 孟斌，郑丽敏，于慧丽. 北京城市居民通勤时间变化及影响因素 [J]. 地理科学进展，2011，30（10）：1218-1224.

[16] 孟庆艳，陈静. 城市居民通勤活动行为的时空特征研究-以上海浦东新区为例 [J]. 交通规划，2006（1）：6-9.

[17] 周素红，杨利军. 广州城市居民通勤空间特征研究 [J]. 城市交通，2005（1）：62-67.

[18] 冯健，周一星. 郊区化进程中北京城市内部迁居及相关空间行为——基于千份问卷调查的分析 [J]. 地理研究，2004，23（2）：227-241.

[19] 李峥嵘，柴彦威. 大连市民通勤特征研究 [J]. 人文地理，2000，15（6）：67-72.

[20] 孟斌. 北京城市居民职住分离的空间组织特征 [J]. 地理学报, 2009, 64 (12): 1457-1466.
[21] 周素红, 闫小培. 城市居住-就业空间特征及组织模式——以广州市为例 [J]. 地理科学, 2005, 25 (6): 664-670.
[22] 张艳, 柴彦威. 基于居住区比较的北京城市通勤研究 [J]. 地理研究, 2009, 28 (5): 1327-1340.
[23] 刘志林, 张艳, 柴彦威. 中国大城市职住分离现象及其特征——以北京市为例 [J]. 城市发展研究, 2009, 16 (9): 110-117.
[24] 余建辉, 张文忠. 基于社会属性的北京城市居民居住环境安全性评价 [J]. 地理科学, 2009, 29 (2): 167-173.
[25] 高晓路, 季钰, 张文忠. 北京市交通出行环境的空间评价 [J]. 地理科学, 2009, 29 (6): 817-824.
[26] 徐建华. 现代地理学中的数学方法 [M]. 北京: 高等教育出版社, 2002: 69-84.
[27] 孟斌, 王劲峰, 张文忠, 等. 基于空间分析方法的中国区域差异研究 [J]. 地理科学, 2005, 25 (4): 393-400.
[28] 冯健, 周一星. 转型期北京社会空间分异重构 [J]. 地理学报, 2008, 63 (8): 829-844.

北京早园竹叶不同提取组分对 CHO 细胞 Akt 信号通路的影响

梅 晶　祖桂芳　赵晓红　何 颖　孙 健

我国竹子资源丰富，但绝大部分尚未得到充分的开发利用。早园竹作为主要的观赏竹类，在北京各处均有分布，具有一定的开发应用价值。竹叶黄酮是从竹叶中提取出来的具有生理活性的生物黄酮，包括黄酮类、内酯类和酚酸类化合物，是一组复杂而又具有相互协同增效作用的混合物[1]。许多研究已证明，竹叶提取物具有较强的抗自由基、抗氧化、抗衰老、抗菌、抗病毒及保护心脑血管、防治老年退行性疾病等生物学功效[2-4]。植物提取物对健康具有有益和有害的双重作用，目前的研究更多关注的是其有益的生理作用，而对植物提取物可能的不良作用研究资料比较少见。我们的前期工作以北京早园竹为材料，初步提取和分离出竹叶中的主要活性组分为黄酮类和酚酸类化合物，并观察总提取物和这两个组分对细胞增殖的影响和抗 H_2O_2 诱导的 DNA 损伤作用，研究发现不同组分在低剂量范围内都具有促进细胞增殖作用并具有抗 H_2O_2 诱导的 DNA 损伤作用，也发现不同组分在较低剂量下呈现一定的 DNA 损伤作用，以黄酮类的作用效果最为明显[5]。竹叶提取物中是哪些组分发挥主要的生物活性作用、其作用机制如何，有待于深入研究。

磷脂酰肌醇3激酶（phosphatidylinositol 3 kinase，PI-3K）/蛋白激酶 B（protein kinase B，PKB），简称 PI3K/Akt。PI3K/Akt 信号通路是参与细胞生长、增殖、分化调节的信号转导通路。其中 Akt 是 PI3K 信号转导途径中一个重要的下游靶激酶。把 Akt 作为分子靶点筛选活性物质，可直接揭示化合物与靶点之间的作用机制[6]。研究表明，PI3K/Akt 通路的异常激活是多种人类癌症的突出特征。Akt 在大多数肿瘤中表现为过度活化，因此被认为是一个极有意义的癌症治疗靶点[7]。研究证明生物活性物质，如白藜芦醇可通过抑制 Akt 信号通路和下游靶分子抑制人类肿瘤细胞的增殖[8]，而活性物质对正常细胞的 Akt 信号通路是否也有影响尚未见报道。因此本课题选择竹叶提取物的3种不同组分分别作用于 CHO 细胞，观察其对细胞增殖、凋亡及 Akt 信号通路的影响并比较其作用差别，为进一步开展活性物质有益及有害作用的研究提供科学依据。

1　材料与方法

1.1　材料与试剂

CHO-Akt-EGFP 细胞株，由美国 GE 公司提供。竹叶提取物制备[9]：采集新鲜竹叶（北京鹰山国家森林公园）经晾干、粉碎、过80目筛后，称取400g 竹粉，用80%乙醇，温度70℃，料液比为1:15，提取时间为120min，提取两次，合并提取液，旋转蒸发仪蒸至无乙醇味，冻干，得竹叶粗提取物54.5g，作为总提取物组。将总提取物重新溶水、SP825大孔树脂过柱，依次用10%、30%、60%的乙醇水溶液洗脱，干燥，用高效液相色谱（HPLC）分析并获得黄酮苷类组分和酚酸类组分样品。在10%乙醇洗脱液中主要为酚酸类，含量约0.31%，作为酚酸类组；30%乙醇洗脱液中主要为 C-黄酮苷类，含量约5%，作为黄酮苷类组；60%乙醇洗脱液中未检测到明显活性成分，不再进一步使用。所得到的竹叶总提取物和不同组分分别用去离子水配成质量浓度为5000mg/L 的母液（加样前稀释）。

F-12培养基、新生小牛血清（NBS）美国 Gibco 公司；青链霉素（PS）、胰蛋白酶（0.25% Tryp-

[基金项目] 北京市自然科学基金项目（70922015）；北京联合大学学生课外科技学术作品项目。

[作者简介] 梅晶（1984—），女，北京联合大学应用文理学院硕士研究生，主要从事生物活性物质的功能与毒理学研究；赵晓红（1961—），女，北京联合大学应用文理学院研究员，博士，主要从事生物活性物质的功能与毒理学研究。

sin）美国 Invitrogen 公司；四甲基偶氮锉蓝（MTT）美国 Amresco 公司；细胞凋亡检测试剂盒北京宝赛公司；胰岛素样生长因子 -1（IGF-1）、渥曼青霉素（Wortmannin）美国 Sigma 公司。

1.2 仪器与设备

超净工作台 北京百剑空气净化设备厂；Forma3110 系列 CO_2 培养箱 美国 ThermoElectron 公司；TE2000-M 倒置显微镜 日本 Nikon 公司；MLS-3750 型高温蒸汽灭菌器 日本 Sanyo 公司；5840R 冷冻离心机德国 Eppendorf 公司；MQX200 微板分光光度计 美国 Bio-Tek 公司；FACSCalibur 流式细胞仪 美国 BD 公司；INCellAnalyzer1000 活细胞成像系统 美国 GE 公司。

1.3 方法

1.3.1 MTT 法检测细胞增殖

将 CHO 细胞以 5×10^4 个/mL 接种于 24 孔培养板，培养 24h 后用 D-Hanks 液洗 3 次，加入 0、50、100、200、400、800、1600μg/mL 竹叶提取物组分，每个质量浓度设 3 个平行样，培养 20h，弃上清，每孔加入 0.9mL 无血清培养液和 0.1mL MTT（5mg/mL），继续培养 4h，离心 10min，弃上清，每孔加入 DMSO1mL，振荡待其充分溶解后，于 96 孔培养板中每孔加入 100μL，每孔设 3 个平行，测 OD_{570nm} 值，按公式（1）计算细胞增殖率，其中零加药组为溶剂对照组，空白组为不加细胞的溶剂对照组。

$$细胞增殖率/\% = \frac{OD_{加药} - OD_{空白}}{OD_{零加药} - OD_{空白}}$$

1.3.2 流式细胞仪检测细胞凋亡

将 CHO 细胞以 5×10^4 个/mL 接种于 6 孔培养板，培养 24h 后加入 0、200、400、800、1600μg/mL 的竹叶提取物的总提取物、酚酸类及黄酮苷类组分，继续培养 18h，胰酶消化收集细胞，4℃ 预冷 PBS 洗两次，重悬于 300μL Binding Buffer 中，参照宝赛公司试剂盒操作方法进行 Annexin V-Cy5 与碘化丙啶（PI）双染，用 FACS Calibur 流式细胞仪对进行凋亡检测，计算细胞凋亡率。

1.3.3 IN Cell Analyzer1000 检测 Akt 通路

将处于对数生长期的稳定转染了 GFP-Akt 的 CHO 细胞接种到 96 孔板上，每孔 200μL，细胞浓度为 5×10^4 个/mL，先室温培养 1h，再置 37℃、5% CO_2 培养箱 24h，弃去上清，用检测培养基洗涤，于 150μL 检测培养基室温培养 1h，每孔加入 50μL 的待测样品，同时设空白对照组（加不含血清培养基）对绿色荧光细胞进行实时拍照，拍照间隔为 30min，连续取像 24h。选用 Plasma Membrane Spot Analysis Module 分析模板对图像进行分析，以荧光细胞占所有细胞的百分比值，即激活率（%）来反映 Akt 通路激活的情况。

1.4 统计学分析

数据均以 $\bar{x}\pm s$ 表示。应用 SPSS12.0 进行数据统计分析，不同处理与对照组比较采用单因素方差分析（ANOVA）中的 Dunnet 检验，多组均数比较采用单因素方差分析及多重比较 LDS 方法。

2 结果与分析

2.1 竹叶提取物不同组分对 CHO 细胞增殖的影响

由图 1 可知，作用时间为 24h 时低质量浓度的总提取物组分的细胞增殖率略高于黄酮苷类和酚酸类，而在较高质量浓度时，黄酮苷类组分的细胞增殖率均高于总提取物组分和酚酸类组分。在各质量浓度下，均以酚酸类组分的细胞增殖率最低，说明不同竹叶提取物组分对细胞增殖的影响作用不同，以酚酸类组分的细胞毒性作用最强。观察受试物不同剂量对细胞增殖的影响，结果可见在 50～400μg/mL 范围内对细胞存活的影响不明显，当质量浓度 ≥800μg/mL 时细胞增殖率明显下降（$P<0.05$），显示明显的细胞毒性作用，说明竹叶提取物的细胞毒性作用较低。

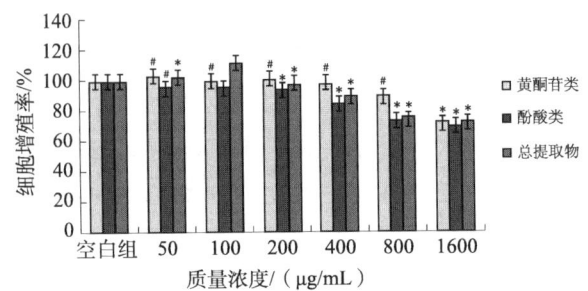

#. 与相同质量浓度总提取物比较，有显著性差异（$P<0.05$）；
*. 与空白组比较，有显著性差异（$P<0.05$）。下同。

图1 不同竹叶提取物作用24h对CHO 细胞增殖的影响（$\bar{x}\pm s$, $n=3$）

2.2 不同提取物对细胞凋亡的影响

由表1可见，不同组分的竹叶提取物在200~800μg/mL 范围内与空白组比较均可降低细胞凋亡率（$P<0.05$），总提取物和黄酮苷类在质量浓度为1600μg/mL 时可诱导CHO 细胞的凋亡明显增加，与空白组比较有显著差异（$P<0.05$）。3种不同组分诱导细胞凋亡的作用不同，高剂量组以黄酮苷类诱导的细胞凋亡率最高，达14.21%。由此可见，竹叶提取物不同组分在低质量浓度下能抑制CHO 细胞凋亡，但在毒性剂量下可诱导细胞凋亡率增加。

表1 竹叶提取物不同成分对CHO 细胞凋亡的影响（$\bar{x}\pm s$, $n=3$）

质量浓度/（μg/mL）	凋亡率/%		
	总提取物	黄酮苷类	酚酸类
空白组	6.59±0.12	6.59±0.06	6.59±0.05
200	1.72±0.15*	2.30±0.10*#	1.46±0.10*
400	1.67±0.02*	3.64±0.04*#	3.63±0.13*#
800	5.55±0.1*	3.48±0.21*#	4.98±0.69**
1600	9.73±0.02*	14.21±0.25*#	5.29±0.07**

2.3 竹叶提取物对CHO 细胞 Akt 激活影响

CHO 细胞以5×10^4个/mL 铺板，培养24h后加入不同质量浓度的提取物，培养24h，同时设Akt 激活剂IGF-1（2μg/mL）、抑制剂Wortmannin（500ng/mL）作为对照，Akt 激活的细胞图像见图2。分析不同质量浓度竹叶提取物组分荧光细胞占所有细胞的百分比值。所得激活率见图3。

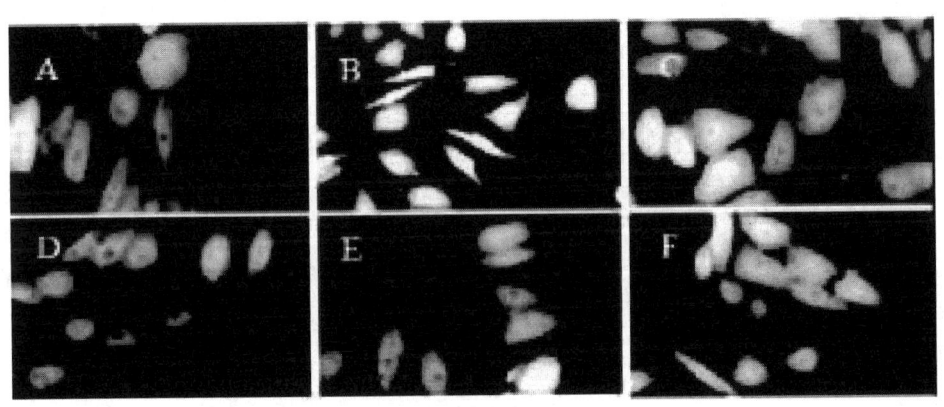

A. 空白组；B. IGF-1（对照组）；C. Wortmannin（对照组）；D. 总提取物（200μg/mL）；
E. 黄酮苷类（200μg/mL）；F. 酚酸类（200μg/mL）。

图2 不同竹叶提取物组分对CHO 细胞 Akt 的激活作用

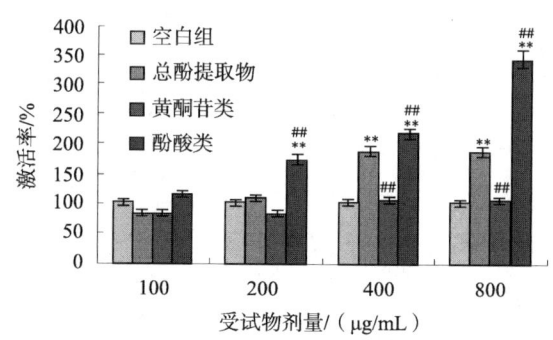

**. 与空白组比较,差异极显著($P<0.01$);
\#\#. 与总提取物比较,差异极显著($P<0.01$)。
图3　不同竹叶提取物组分对 CHO 细胞 Akt 激活的影响

由图2可见,当加入激活剂 IGF-1 后,细胞形态没有变化,但边缘明显变亮,Akt 蛋白被激活,从胞质聚集到细胞膜上,而抑制剂 Wortmannin 作用后细胞没有明显变化,说明实验方法可行。与空白组比较,加入不同提取物组分后 CHO 细胞边缘略有变亮,以酚酸类最明显,但对细胞形态无明显影响。通过统计荧光颗粒的数量及面积用激活率表征 Akt 的活化水平。

由图3可见,与空白组比较,在受试剂量下,黄酮苷类对 Akt 的活性无明显影响,总提取物在 400、800μg/mL 时 Akt 的激活率明显增加($P<0.01$),而酚酸类在 100~800μg/mL 范围内,随剂量增加,激活率增高,呈明显的剂量-反应关系($r=0.996$,$P<0.01$)。比较3种不同提取物组分对加 Akt 激活的影响,可见酚酸类的作用最明显,总提取物的增高与其含酚酸类物质相关,由此说明,不同竹叶提取物组分对 CHO 细胞 Akt 活性的影响不同。

3　讨　论

细胞凋亡是机体生长、分化、发育和病理过程中由基因编码调控的细胞主动自杀过程,正常的细胞凋亡在维持生物机体细胞增殖与死亡的平衡过程中起重要作用,但异常的细胞凋亡是某些重要疾病发病的重要原因,因此细胞凋亡是当前生命科学研究中最热门的领域之一[10]。本研究结果表明,竹叶提取物的3种组分对正常细胞的凋亡没有明显影响。

高通量筛选评价系统是目前新兴的细胞组学研究的一个重要技术手段,可应用于细胞内目标分子核转移、靶蛋白表达、报告基因表达、受体激活等方面的研究[11,12]。IN Cell Analyzer 1000 活细胞图像分析系统将荧光共聚焦细胞成像系统和全自动图像分析系统整合,实时检测受试物对细胞的作用,且可得到整个细胞群和单个细胞的具体数据。由于绿色荧光蛋白(GFP)容易被荧光显微镜跟踪检测的特性,在信号转导通路研究和细胞筛选中适合作为报告标记因子。当筛选化合物作用于不同的稳定表达 GFP 融合蛋白的细胞时,不同的 GFP 融合蛋白呈现出与活性反应相关的转运,因此可用于评价与确认活性物质对细胞内相应信号通路的影响与作用[13]。

PI3K/Akt 是一条重要的维持细胞生存的信号通路,能刺激细胞增殖并抑制细胞凋亡。生理状态下,Akt 蛋白以低活性(失活状态)存在于细胞浆。当其暴露于各种刺激因素如生长因子缺乏、紫外线照射或 DNA 损伤等时,Akt 蛋白从细胞质转移至细胞膜而获得催化活性。CHO-AKT-EGFP 中的 Akt-EGFP 在未受到刺激时,绿色荧光呈弥散分布,受刺激后 Akt 蛋白活化,Akt-EGFP 迅速转移到细胞膜上形成高亮度的荧光颗粒,通过统计这种荧光颗粒的数量及面积就可以表征 Akt 的活化水平[6-14]。本实验采用 INCell Analyzer 1000 系统中的稳定细胞株 CHO-Akt-EGFP 作为细胞模型,以竹叶总提取物,经过分离的黄酮苷类以及酚酸类为实验材料研究了竹叶提取物对 CHO 细胞的细胞毒性作用、凋亡诱导作用和刺激 Akt 蛋白活化的作用,结果显示,3种不同组分对细胞的影响不同,由于酚酸类组分的细胞毒性作用比较强,因此导致其激活 Akt 蛋白的作用也最强。而对细胞增殖的影响在<1600μg/mL 质量浓度下没有明显差异。

植物化学物质毒性作用评价及其机制研究是保健食品风险评估与安全性保障的基础,而目前更多关注的是其有益的生物活性作用，大多数研究报道主要是针对植物总提取物和不同组分的研究，但单体物质毒性作用特点与提取物间可能存在较大差异，因此需要对这些组分中的主要单体物质进行进一步的研究，用活细胞成像系统进行动态观察，以明确其作用时间及特点，为竹叶活性物质的开发与应用提供基础数据。

参考文献

[1] 张英. 天然功能性竹叶提取物：竹叶黄酮 [J]. 中国食品添加剂, 2002 (3)：54-58.

[2] 郭雪峰, 岳永德, 孟志芬, 等. 用清除羟自由基法评价竹叶提取物抗氧化能力 [J]. 光谱学与光谱分析, 2010, 30 (2)：508-511.

[3] 刘璇, 米生权, 张宇轩, 等. 北京早园竹叶提取物的抗氧化活性研究 [J]. 环境与健康杂志, 2009, 26 (3)：239-241.

[4] 付晓春, 李少鹏, 王希, 等. 竹叶提取物对缺氧/复氧心肌细胞的保护作用 [J]. 现代食品与药品杂志, 2006, 16 (1)：18-21.

[5] 单梁, 肖乐乐, 赵晓红, 等. 北京早园竹叶有机提取物对细胞DNA断裂损伤的保护与修复作用 [J]. 环境与健康杂志, 2011, 28 (2)：118-121.

[6] 王维, 张琍. PI3K/Akt信号转导通路的研究进展 [J]. 现代医药卫生, 2010, 26 (7)：1051-1052.

[7] LINDSLEY C W. The Akt/PKB family of protein kinases：a review of small molecule inhibitors and progress towards target validation：a 2009 update [J]. Curr Top Med Chem, 2010, 10 (4)：458-477.

[8] SHAKIBAEI M, HARIKUMAR K B, AGGARWAL B B. Resveratrol addiction：to die or not to die [J]. Mol Nutr Food Res, 2009, 53 (1)：115-28.

[9] 祖桂芳, 彭辉, 赵晓红. 北京早园竹叶活性成分的分离与鉴定 [J]. 食品工业科技, 2009, 30 (12)：123-125, 129.

[10] DAGHER Z, GARÇONÇ BILLET S, et al. Role of nuclear factor-kappa B activation in the adverse effects induced by air pollution particulate matter (PM2.5) in human epithelial lung cells (L132) in culture [J]. Appl Toxicol, 2007, 27 (3)：284-290.

[11] WOLFF M, WIEDENMANN J, NIENHAUS G U, et al. Novel fluores-cent protein for highcontent screening [J]. Drug Discov Today, 2006, 11 (23/24)：1054-1060.

[12] GOUGH A H, JOHNSTON P A. Requirements, features, and performance of high contentscreening platforms [J]. Methods Mol Biol, 2007, 356：41-61.

[13] 李韶菁, 杜冠华. 细胞水平的高通量药物筛选技术研究进展 [J]. 中国药学杂志, 2008, 43 (2)：84-87.

[14] HENSHALL D C, ARAKI T, SCHINDLER C K, et al. Activation of bcl-2 associated death protein and counter-response of Akt within cell populations during seizure-induced neuronal death [J]. Neurosci, 2002, 22 (19)：8458-8465.

Comparisons of Walnut Quality Stability of Yunnan – Santai Walnut in Different Packing Conditions

Li Dapeng   Wang Wenqian   Luan Na
Rong Ruifen   Xu Huilian

Introduction

Walnuts contain high – quality proteins and fatty acids, and receive affections of consumer because of its unique taste and high nutritional value. Walnuts contain approximately 65 ~ 75% of fat, over 90% of which belongs to unsaturated fatty acids, especially with the polyunsaturated fatty acids as the main components[1,2]. Walnuts have good equilibrium ratio of polyunsaturated fats, with ω – 6/ω – 3 as 4/1 approximately, which play important roles in reduction of risk of cardiovascular and cerebrovascular diseases[3,4]. In addition, walnuts contain massive antioxidative functional ingredients such as polyphenols, flavones, vitamin E and so on, which are effective in health improvements by lowering blood fat and cholesterol, preventing the atherosclerosis and postponing aging[5,6]. High content of unsaturated fat makes the walnuts extremely easy to oxidize and turn rancid, producing materials harmful to human body. O_2 content in storage environment imposes the serious impact on the rancidity of the walnuts and loss of nutritional components. However, researchers have only studied the stability to oxidation[7-10], with the research on functional nutrition ingredients focused only on composition and content[11,12]. There are very few research reports on stability of the functional nutrition quality. Therefore, there is an urgent need to carry out the research on the quality stability of the functional fatty acids and anti – oxidant compounds in walnuts as affected by different packing conditions, clarify the importance in health improvement of walnut shelf – life nutrition, and provide a guidance to quality maintenance during storage, full uses of walnuts for health improvement and walnut crop production practices.

Materials and Methods

Plant materials and experimental equipment: Used as experimental materials, walnut (*Juglans sigillata* Dode) was obtained Qiaosheng Walnut Processing Factory, Yangbi County, Yunnan Province, China. The following reagents at analytically pure levels were used in the experiment: chloroform, glacial acetic acid, potassium iodide, sodium thiosulfate, starch, trichloroacetic acids, 2, 4 – dinitro naphthol phenylhydrazine, caustic potash, ethanol, methanol, caustic potash, absolute ethyl alcohol, ascorbic acid, petroleum ether, anhydrous sodium sulfate, sodium bisulphate, gallic acid and grass cutter. The assay standards of γ – tocopherol, methyl oleate, methyl linoleate, and linolenic acid methyl ester were obtained from Sigma. The following equipment were used: vacuum packing machine (DZQ400 Youtian, Hangzhou, China), electric heating blast drying oven at constant temperature (HG – 940A Yiheng Instrument, Shanghai, China), spectrophotometer (UV – 9200 Ruili Analytical Instrument, Beijing, China), rotatory evaporator (RE – 52 Yarong Biological Instrument, Shanghai, China), digital water – bath at constant temperature (HH6 Guohua Appliances, Changzhou, China), HPLC (1525 Waters, Mas-

---

[Author Introduction] Li Dapeng, Wang Wenqian, Luan Na, Rong Ruifen, College of Applied Art and Science of Beijing Union University; Xu Huilian, International Nature Farming Research Center.

sachusetts, USA) and gas chromatography (6820 Agilent, California, USA).

Treatments: The walnuts were packed in PE bags, vacuum bags and silicon window gas adjustment bags and stored from December 2010 to June 2011 under room temperature. The relative vacuum degree of vacuum packing is −0.1 MPa. The walnuts packed in a silicon window gas adjustment bag was 5 kg, repeated 3 times and the samples were taken only one time in June 2011. In other treatments, one bag contained 10 kg walnuts and repeated 3 times with 40 walnut samples taken monthly. Five walnuts were used for sense evaluation and other 35 walnuts were stored under 25oC for use in analyses.

Analyses of various evaluations

Sensory quality evaluation: The sensory quality evaluation was made from smell (odor), shell color, pellicle color, seed color, taste and mildew or worms, as shown in Table 1.

Table 1 The sensory quality evaluation criteria.

Grade	Odor	Shell color	Pellicle color	Seed color	Taste	Mildew
Excellent	No rancid	Shallow yellow	Yellowish white	Yellowish white	Slightly astringent	No mildew and worms
Good	Slight rancid brown	Yellowish brown	Yellowish	Yellowish with worms	Astringent	Slight mildew brown
Bad	Strong rancid	Brown	Deep brown	Deep brown	Severe astringent	Severe mildew with worms

Assays: The peroxide value (POV) was estimated according to GB/T 5009.37 − 2003 (CHINA). The carbonyl value was estimated according to GB/T 5009.37 − 2003 (CHINA). Measurement of the total phenolics (TP) was made using the Forint Phenol method according to GB/T 8313 − 2008 (CHINA). Content of the total flavonoids (TF) was measured according to Rong et al. 13. The content of g − vitamin E (g − VE) was measured according to GB/T 5009.82 − 2003 (CHINA). Fatty acids were measured according to GB/T 17376 − 2008 (CHINA) and GB/T 17377 − 2008 (CHINA) with modifications as described below. Samples of 10 walnuts were unhulled, grinded into powder and mixed into petroleum ether (boiling range 30 − 60℃) with a ratio of 10∶1. The mixture was transferred into flask, covered and placed in dark overnight. The mixture was vacuum evaporated, spin stilled and the oil was obtained. The saponification of fatty acid was made using 0.15 − 2.0 g of oil sample. The oil sample was filled into a tube with 4 ml normal heptane added, dissolved by vibrating the tube. Then the mixture was added with 1 ml 2 M KOH − methanol solution, well vibrated for 30 s, and silenced for 10 min. Then, 1 g NaHSO4 was added and vibrated for 30 s, silenced for 5 min and then the supernatant was taken for use of measurement.

Statistic analysis: The data were analyzed using SPSS 12.0 and the graphs were plotted using Origin 8.0.

Results

As the storage duration prolonged, the color of walnut hull, pellicle and seed all darkened steadily, tasted more astringent with rancid smell, indicating that the walnuts got oxidized with sensory quality lowered down (Table 2). When stored in vacuum packing for 6 months, the color of pellicle and seed got darkened and tasted more astringent but the nutritional quality maintained good. Storage in silicon window gas adjusting bags showed the same effective as the vacuum packing although slight rancid odor appeared. When stored at room temperature for 5 months, the walnuts showed slight rancid odor and the sensory quality still maintained between excellent and good at the 6th month with good nutritional quality. The worms appeared in the walnuts at room temperature and this might be attributed to the mal − sealed bags.

Table 2 Changes in sensory quality of the Yunnan – Santai walnuts stored in different packaging.

Duration (month)	PE bag	Vacuum	Silicon window
3	No rancidity, shallow yellow hull, yellowish white pellicle, yellowish white seed, slightly astringent, no mildew and worms	No rancidity, shallow yellow hull, yellowish white pellicle, yellowish white seed, slightly astringent, no mildew and worms.	No rancidity, shallow yellow hull, yellowish white pellicle, yellowish white seed, slightly astringent, no mildew and worms
4	No rancidity, shallow yellow hull, darkened pellicle color, partly yellow – brown, yellowish white seed, strongly astringent, a few worms.	The same as above.	No data
5	Slight rancidity, shallow yellowish white hull, pellicle color darkened and partly yellow – brown, yellowish white seed.. strongly astringent, a few worms.	The same as above.	No data
6	Strong rancidity, shallow yellowish white hull, pellicle color darkened and partly yellow – brown, yellowish white seed, strongly astringent, a few worms.	No rancidity, shallow yellowish white hull, pellicle color darkened and partly yellow – brown, yellow seed.. strongly astringent, a few worms.	Slight rancidity, shallow yellowish white hull, pellicle color darkened and partly yellow – brown, yellowish white seed.. strongly astringent, no mildew and worms.

Changes in hygienic quality related with oxidation in walnuts as affected by different packing in storage for 6 months:

Changes in peroxidation value (POV) in walnuts: POV value is one of the criteria for the hydroperoxides produced at the beginning of oxidation and increases along with the deepening oxidation degree. When the POV is larger than the authority standard 0.25 g per 100 g, the walnuts do not conform to the hygienic quality standard since the fat oxidation is intensified and the quality is reduced.

As shown in Fig. 1, when stored for 6 months, POV of the walnuts in all the three treatments increased, with an increase of 0.0233 g per 100 g (3.48 times) in PE bag packing from 0.0067 g per 100 g at the beginning to 0.030 g per 100 g, an increase of 0.0127 g per 100 g (1.90 times) in vacuum packing from 0.0067 g per 100 g to 0.0194g per 100g, significantly lower ($P < 0.01$) than in PE, and an increase of 0.0107 g per 100 g (1.60 times) similar to POV in vacuum packing and far lower than in PE packing.

The increasing trend of POV in vacuum packing was more sloping than in PE packing, indicating that the oxidation was slower in vacuum packing than in PE packing. After 6 month storage in PE bags, POV was only of 0.030 g per100 g, far below the upper limit of GB/T2716 – 2005, 0.25 g per 100 g.

Changes in carbonyl group value (CGV): The fat can be oxidized to superoxide as affected by the external environment conditions such as air, temperature, microbes, heat and light, and further degraded into carbonyl compounds. The accumulation quantity of the secondary products (aldehydes and ketones) can be indicated by the carbonyl group value (CGV). CGV is a criterion of secondary oxidation and also related with the sensory quality of the walnuts. As shown in Fig. 2, after 6 month storage, CGV increased in all the three packing treatments, with an increase of 2.48 meq kg^{-1} (1.48 times) in PE packing from 1.68 meq kg^{-1} to 4.16 meq kg^{-1}, an increase of 1.63 meq kg^{-1} (98%) in vacuum packing from 1.68 to 3.31 meq kg^{-1}, and an increase of 1.20 meq kg^{-1} (71%) in silicon window packing from 1.68 to 2.87 meq kg^{-1}, lower than in PE and vacuum packing. As shown in Fig. 2, the increasing trend of CGV was steeper in PE packing than in other two treatments, especially the increase is apparent from the 5th month. This indicated that the oxidation was accelerated from the 5th month and consistent with the appearance of rancid odor at this time.

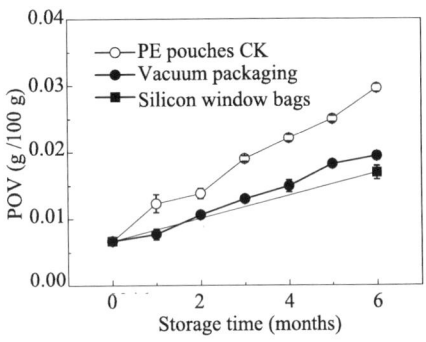

Fig. 1　Changes in POVs of the Yunnan Santai walnuts stored at different packaging.

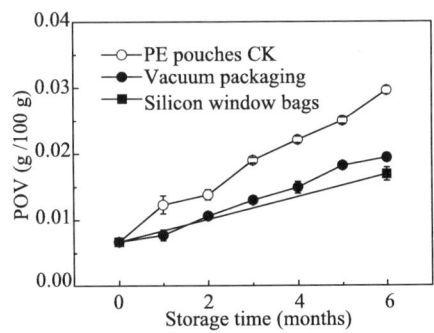

Fig. 2　Changes in carbonyl values of the Yunnan Santai walnuts stored at different packaging.

Changes in functional nutrition quality in walnuts stored in different packing：

Changes in functional fatty acids in walnuts：The oleic acid, a monounsaturated fatty acids, consists of 18 carbons and is effective in adjustment of blood fats and reduction of cholesterol. As shown in Fig. 3, oleic acid content decreased fast in the first 4 months during the storage and the decrease slowed down during the last 2 months, with a decrease of 19.5% from 222.28 to 179.02 g kg^{-1}. The oleic acid content in vacuum packed walnuts decreased fast in the first 2 months, with little change in the middle 2 months and fast decreases in the last two months. The decrease was 15.4% from 222.28 to 188.1 g kg^{-1}, significantly higher ($P<0.05$) than in PE packed walnuts. The oleic acid content in silicon window packed walnuts decreased 11.3% from 222.28 to 197.22 g kg^{-1}, 8.2% less than in PE packed walnuts and 4.1% less than in vacuum packed walnuts. The oleic acid stability is better in silicon window gas adjustment bag packing treatment than in PE plastic bag packing treatment and this was consistent with the above mentioned results of peroxidation value (POV) and the carbonyl group value (CGV).

The linoleic acid belongs to a series of ω−6 fatty acids, one of the two kinds of indispensable fatty acids, and effective in lowering blood cholesterol and preventing the atherosclerosis. As shown in Fig. 4, the linoleic acid content of the PE packing walnuts significantly decreased in the first two months with a large change and then the change lowered down with a total change of 14.0% from 479.47 to 412.49 g kg^{-1}. However, in the vacuum packed walnuts, the linoleic acid content was stable without large changes in the first two months, increased from the 3rd month with the changes slowing down thereafter and the total increase was 9.0% ($P<0.01$) from 479.47 to 522.78 g kg^{-1}.

In the silicon gas adjusting packing treatment, linoleic acid content decreased 2.2% from 479.47 to 468.85 g kg^{-1} and the decrease was 11.8% less than in PE packed walnuts. In all the three treatments, linoleic acid content was unstable in early period and got stable in the later period during the 6 months storage.

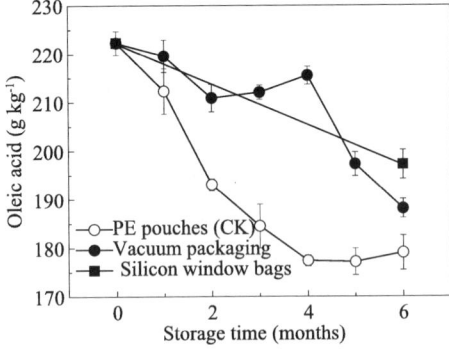

Fig. 3　Changes in oleic acid content of the Yunnan Santai walnuts stored in different packaging.

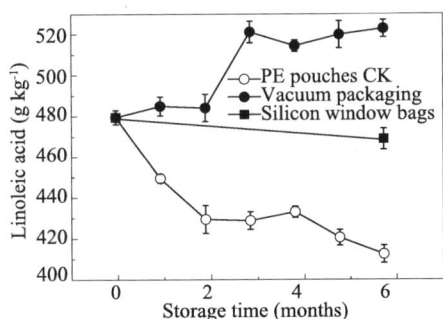

Fig. 4　Changes in linoleic acid content of the Yunnan Santai walnuts stored in different packaging.

The linolenic acid belongs to the series of ω−3 polyene fatty acids and is one of the two kinds of indispensable fatty acids to human body, with a high nutritional value. As shown in Fig. 5, the linolenic acid content in PE packed walnuts decreased significantly in the first month, changed very little from the 2nd to 4th months and decreased to a large extent again from the 5th to 6th months. In PE packed walnuts, the linolenic acid content decreased 12.9% from 78.27 to 68.18 g kg^{-1}. In vacuum packed walnuts, the linolenic acid content showed an increasing trend during the early 3 months with a peak at the 3rd month and showed a decreasing trend from the 4th to 6th month, with a final total increase of 16.7% from 78.27 to 91.38 g kg^{-1}, significantly different from PE packing.

In silicon window gas adjusting packing, the linolenic acid content decreased only 1.1% from 78.27 to 77.40 g kg^{-1}, with 11.8% less decreasing than in PE packed walnuts. In both treatments, the linolenic acid content was unstable during the early storage period but changed little during the later period and this might be related with the property of the linolenic acid being easily oxidized.

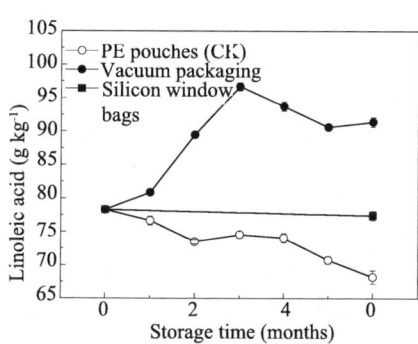

Fig. 5 Changes in linolenic acid content of the Yunnan Santai walnuts stored in different packaging.

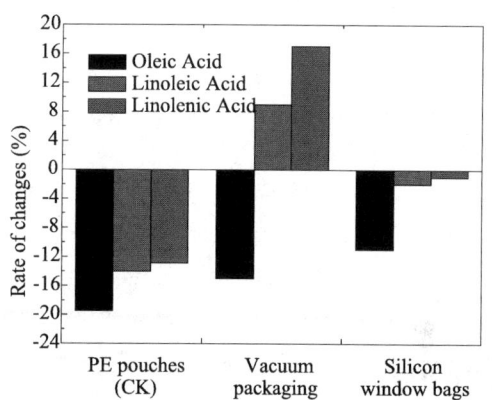

Fig. 6 The reduction of unsaturated fatty acid of the Yunnan Santai walnuts stored in different packaging for 6 months.

Oleic acid, linoleic acid and linolenic acid are all the important nutritional ingredients. As shown in Fig. 6, in PE packing conditions, the decreasing extents of three kinds of fatty acids were oleic acid (19.5%), linoleic acid (14.0%) and linolenic acid (12.9%) in order. In silicon window gas adjusting packing conditions, the decreasing extents in order were oleic acid (11.3%), linoleic acid (2.2%) and linolenic acid (1.1%). In vacuum packing conditions, both linoleic and linolenic acids showed an increasing trend and only the oleic acid showed decreasing trend with total decrease of 15.4%, which was less than in PE packing conditions and more than in gas adjusting packing conditions. In general, the decrement of oleic acid was larger than those of linoleic and linolenic acids, indicating that the stability of oleic acid was lower than those of linoleic and linolenic acids, while the decrements of all fatty acids was lower in vacuum packed and gas adjusting packed walnuts than in PE packed walnuts.

Changes in polyphenolics: Walnuts are rich in polyphenols, which taste bitter and astringent and are the important substances affecting taste and good antioxidants. As reported by Christopoulos[8], the content of total polyphenols decreased 27% after 4 months of storage. As shown in Fig. 7, content of total polyphenols in walnuts stored for 6 months decreased steadily, with a decrease of 34.5% in PE packed walnuts from 17.0686 to 11.1801 g kg^{-1}, a decrease of 20.7% in vacuum from 17.0686 to 13.5415 g kg^{-1}, and a decrease of 10.4% in gas adjusting packing from 17.0686 to 15.2958 g kg^{-1}, which was 24.1% less decrease than in PE and 13.8% less decrease than in vacuum. This suggested that polyphenols are unstable in PE packed conditions but stable in gas adjusting conditions.

Changes in the total flavone content: Compared with the total polyphenols, the total flavones were in low content in Yunnan – Santai walnuts. As shown in Fig. 8, during the storage of 6 months, content of flavones showed a steady decreasing trend, decreased 22.4% from 2.0461 to 1.5881 g kg^{-1} in PE package, decreased 17.3% from 2.0461 to 1.6931 g kg^{-1} in vacuum package with the remaining content significantly higher ($P < 0.01$) than in PE, and decreased 15.0% from 2.0461 to 1.7395 g kg^{-1} in silicon window gas adjusting bags. It was suggested that the silicon window gas adjusting packing was better than PE and vacuum packing although the flavones were unstable in all the three types of package.

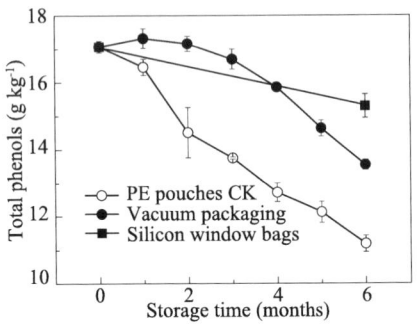

Fig. 7　Changes in TP content of the Yunnan Santai walnuts stored in different packaging.

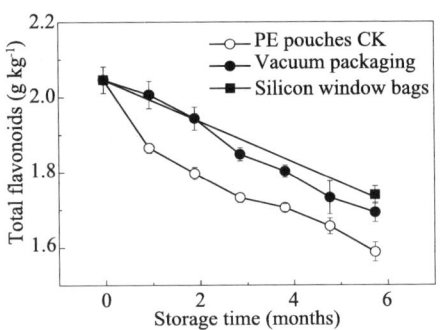

Fig. 8　Changes in TF content of the Yunnan Santai walnuts stored in different packaging.

Changes in γ – vitamin E: V_E is a good antioxidant, improves lipid metabolisms and prevents coronary disease and atherosclerosis. Walnuts are rich in γ – vitamin E, with the content reaching 65% of the total vitamins 14. As shown in Fig. 9, γ – V_E content first increased and then decreased and the decreasing sloped down in PE package with decrement of 40.1% from 47.4 to 28.4 mg kg^{-1}. The γ – V_E content in vacuum package decreased slowly from 47.4 to 39.3 mg kg^{-1}, with a decrement of 17.1%, 23.0% less than in PE package. The γ – V_E content in gas adjusting package decreased 17.3% from 47.4 to 39.2 mg kg^{-1}, similar to that in PE ($P > 0.05$) and significantly lower than in PE ($P < 0.01$). It is suggested that γ – V_E was the same stable in both vacuum and gas adjusting packages compared with PE package.

Changes in the functional ingredients of three antioxidants: Polyphenols, flavones and γ – V_E in walnuts are all function as antioxidants. As shown in Fig. 10, content of γ – V_E decreased 40.1%, total polyphenols decreased 34.5%, and flavones decreased 22.4% under conditions of PE package. Under storage conditions of vacuum, the order of the decrements for the three antioxidants were polyphenols (20.7%) > flavones (17.3%) > γ – V_E (17.1%). Under storage conditions of silicon window gas adjusting package, the order of the decrements for the three antioxidants were γ – V_E (17.3%) > flavones (15.0%) > polyphenols (10.4%).

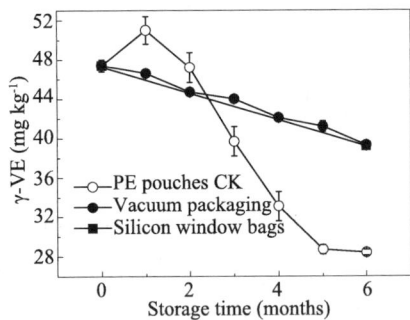

Fig. 9　Changes in γ – VE content of the Yunnan Santai walnuts stored in different packaging.

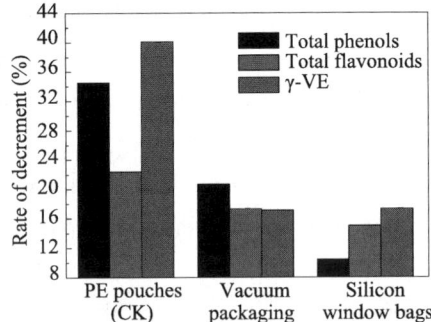

Fig. 10　Reduction of antioxidant functional composition of the Yunnan Santai walnuts stored in different packaging for 6 months.

Discussion

The results of the present study suggested that the Santai walnut of Yunnan variety is a rich source of essential fatty acids. Results showed that stored walnuts' POVs and CGVs in PE packing were much higher than those observed in vacuum packing and silicon window gas adjusting bags. Under simulated shelf life conditions packed in PE bags, antioxidant functional compounds stability was poor, obviously more decreased than in vacuum packing and silicon window gas adjusting bags. In addition, $\gamma - V_E$ and total polyphenolics stability was poorer than that of total flavones.

Stored in PE packing, walnuts' oleic, linoleic and linolenic acids content decreased by less than 20%. UFAs content was more stable in vacuum packing and silicon window gas adjusting bags. UFA was high in the three groups, and walnuts still had a high nutritional value even after six months. During the six months of storage, content of the UFA in walnuts decreased quickly in the earlier period, which was mainly because oxygen content in the PE bags in earlier periods was high and promoted oxidation of the fatty acids. In the later periods of the storage, oxygen content was low and carbon dioxide content increased and thus oxidation of the fatty acids was depressed[8]. Oleic acid is a MUFA, in theory, its stability under oxidation is better than that of linoleic and linolenic acids, but our results showed a discrepancy: the decrements of oleic acid were larger compared with linoleic and linolenic acid, especially, content of linoleic and linolenic acids in vacuum packing increased. The study of walnut powder under shelf conditions showed that the oleic acid content was decreased after 8 - month storage and the PUFA content was first increased and then decreased, represented by an unchanged double bond index[11]. Wang et al.[15] found that the oleic acid content of walnuts stored at room temperature was reduced, while linoleic acid significantly increased. These studies proved that this phenomenon might be attributed the transformation from oleic acids to the two kinds of fatty acids[15,16].

The stability of total polyphenols was significantly larger among the three packages. After six months of storage, the decrement of total polyphenols in the three packages was PE (34.5%) > vacuum (20.7%) > gas adjusting (10.4%), while decrements of $\gamma - V_E$ and flavones were not significantly different among the three types of package. This suggested that polyphenols are more sensitive to oxygen than the other two antioxidants. The decrements of flavones under three kinds of packing conditions were close to each other. This indicated that flavones were not very sensitive to oxygen in the storing environment. Meanwhile, the $\gamma - V_E$ decrements in PE plastic bag package and in the silicon window gas adjustment package were all larger than the decrement of total polyphenols. The $\gamma - V_E$ decrements were also close to those in the vacuum package. This suggested that $\gamma - V_E$ played a more important role in antioxidation and this result was consistent with that reported by Li et al.[17,18].

The functional components of the walnuts stored in vacuum packing and silicon window gas adjusting bags were more stable than in PE packing. The nutritional quality of the walnuts in vacuum packing and silicon window gas adjusting bags after 3 - 4 months were similar to that of walnuts stored in PE packing for 6 months. Oxygen content had great influences on preserving quality.

Conclusions

The present study systematically and comprehensively examined the changes in quality indexes of walnuts in different packing. The changes in antioxidants and their possible impacts on antioxidant properties were analyzed, and comparisons were made between the PE packing, vacuum packing and silicon window gas adjusting bags packing. Studies on this subject have not been comprehensively performed until now. So, this present study provides not only new and useful information for readers, but also a nutritional guide for the production practice and consumption of walnuts.

Acknowledgements

This work was supported by the State Forestry Administration, China (Project No: 201004048 -2).

References

[1] Crews, C., Hough, P., Godward, J., Breton, P., Lees, M., Guiet, S. and Winkelmann, W. 2005. Study of the main constituents of some authentic walnut oils. Journal of Agricultural and Food Chemistry 53 (12): 4853-4860.

[2] Vanhanen, L. P. and Savage, G. P. 2006. The use of peroxide value as a measure of quality for walnut flour stored at five different temperatures using three different types of packaging. Food Chemistry 99 (1): 64–69.

[3] Simopoulos, A. P. 2002. The importance of the ratio of omega–6/omega–3 essential fatty acids. Biomedicine & Pharmacotherapy 56 (8): 365–379.

[4] Sabate, J. 1999. Nut consumption, vegetarian diets, is chemic heart disease risk, and all–cause mortality: Evidence from epidemiologic studies. American Journal of Clinical Nutrition 70 (3): 500–503.

[5] Martinez, M. L., Labuckas, D. O., Lamarque, A. L. and Maestri, D. M. 2008. Walnut (*Juglans regia L.*): Genetic resources, chemistry, by–products. Journal of the Science of Food and Agriculture 90 (12): 1959–1967.

[6] Miraliakbari, H. and Shahidi, F. 2008. Oxidative stability of tree nut oils. Journal of Agricultural and Food Chemistry 56 (12): 4751–4759.

[7] Christopoulos, M. V., Rouskas, D., Tsantili, E. and Bebeli, P. J. 2010. Germplasm diversity and genetic relationships among walnut (*Juglans regia L.*) cultivars and Greek local selections revealed by Inter–Simple Sequence Repeat (ISSR) markers. Sci. Hort. 125 (4): 584–592.

[8] Christopoulos, M. V. and Tsantili, E. 2011. Effects of temperature and packaging atmosphere on total antioxidants and colour of walnut (*Juglans regia L.*) kernels during storage. Scientia Horticulturae 131: 49–57.

[9] Buransompob, A., Tang, J., Mao, R. and Swanson, B. G. 2003. Rancidity of walnuts and almonds affected by short time heat treatments for insect control. Journal of Food Processing Preservation 27 (6): 445–464.

[10] Jensen, P. N., Sorensen, G. B., Brockhoff, P. and Bertelsen, G. 2003. Investigation of packaging systems for systems for shelled walnuts based on oxygen absorbers. Journal of Agricultural and Food Chemistry 51 (17): 4941–4947.

[11] Labuckas, D., Maestri, D. and Lamarque, A. 2011. Lipid and protein stability of partially defatted walnut flour (*Juglans regia L.*) during storage. International Journal of Food Science and Technology 46 (7): 1388–1397.

[12] Isanga, J. and Zhang, G. N. 2007. Biological active components and nutraceuticals in peanuts and related products: Review. Food Reviews International 23 (2): 123–140.

[13] Rong, R.–F., Li, Z.–X., Liu, X. Z., Pei, D., Chen, J. and Wang, Y.–T. 2004. Primary determination study on contents of nutritional and functional components of walnut kernel pellicle. Food Science 29 (11): 541–543.

[14] Lavedrine, F., Ravel, A., Poupard, A. and Alary, J. 1997. Effect of geographic origin, variety and storage on tocopherol concentrations in walnuts by HPLC. Food Chemistry 58 (1/2): 135–140.

[15] Wang, X. Y., Zhang, Z. H., Li, Y. Q., Zhao, H. R. and Zhao, Y. P. 2004. Analysis of fatty acids composition and content in walnut varieties. Acta Nutrimenta Sinica 26 (6): 499–501.

[16] Ma, Y. P., Liu, X. H., Yuan, D. B., Wang, L. M. and Yuan, Y. F. 2010. Changes of respiration intensity and quality of different varieties of fresh walnut during cold storage. Transactions of the Chinese Society of Agricultural Engineering 26 (1): 370–374.

[17] Li, L., Tsao, R., Yang, R., Liu, C. M., Zhu, H. H. and Young, J. C. 2006. Polyphenolic profiles and antioxidant activities of heartnut (*Juglans ailanthifolia var. cordiformis*) and Persian nut (*Juglans regia L.*). J. Agric. Food Chem. 54 (12): 8033–8040.

[18] Li, L., Tsao, R., Yang, R., Kramer, J. K. G., and Hernandez, M. 2007. Fatty acid profiles, tocopherol contents, and antioxidant activities of heartnut (*Juglans ailanthifolia var. cordiformis*) and Persian walnut (*Juglans regia L.*). J. Agric. Food Chem. 55 (4): 1164–1169.

Curcumin Attenuates Amyloid − β − Induced Tau Hyperphosphorylation in Human Neuroblastoma SH − SY5Y Cells Involving PTEN/Akt/GSK − 3β Signaling Pathway

Huang Hanchang Tang Di Xu Ke Jiang Zhaofeng

Introduction

Alzheimer's disease (AD) is one of progressive neurodegenerative diseases. The presence of extracellular senile plaques (SPs) is one of the hallmarks on pathological features (1). Aggregated amyloid − β peptide (Aβ) is a critical member in SPs. Aβ is a proteolytic fragment from amyloid − β precursor protein (APP), which belongs to the type I transmembrane glycoprotein (2). The secreted ectodomain of APP (sAPP) was earliest described as protease nexin 2, a serine protease inhibitor (3). Furthermore, APP was suggested to stimulate and to regulate neurite outgrowth and synaptogenesis (4, 5). Recently, APP is considered to be an intact integral receptor and may play key roles on cell signaling (6, 7); however, the ligands for APP are still unclear. Generally, little is known about the biological function of the APP in organisms. APP is believed to be cleaved by both α − cleavage and β − cleavage pathways. When undergoing β − cleavage pathway, APP is proteolyzed by β − secretase between 671st and 672nd amino acid and by γ − secretase in the transmembrane domain, and Aβ fragment with 39 − 43 residues is generated, dependant on the site cleaved by γ − secretase (1). $A\beta_{1-40}$ is the most abundant fragment among Aβ products. Based on the Aβ deposits in SPs, Aβ is considered to be neurotoxic; however, the pathological mechanisms on Aβ − induced neurotoxicity are little known.

The presence of intracellular neurofibrillary tangles (NFTs) is another feature in the AD pathological process (8, 9). These tangles are bundles of paired helical filaments composed of hyperphosphorylated tau. Tau proteins are microtubule − associated proteins and interact with tubulin to promote tubulin assembly into microtubules and stabilize microtubules, especially in axons. Microtubules are a component of the cytoskeleton. Microtubules are important in a number of cellular processes, such as the movement of secretory vesicles and organelles. The ability of tau to stabilize microtubules is inversely related to the level of tau hyperphosphorylation. Tau hyperphosphorylation leads to depolymerization of microtubule and formation of NFTs. Further, NFTs will eventually lead to the cytoskeleton and cytoplasmic metabolic disorders (10). Besides AD, Some neurodegenerative diseases, such as Parkinson's disease, Pick's disease and Down's disease, are also considered to involve hyperphosphorylated tau protein. So far, more than 30 Thr/Ser residues in tau have been described to be phosphorylated by proline or non − proline directed kinases. Phosphorylations at Thr231 or Ser 396 were most suggested to destabilize microtubules and to contribute to AD pathology. Recently, tau phosphorylation is considered to be required for Aβ − induced impairment of synaptic plasticity in the hippocampus (11), and synaptic hyperphosphorylated tau oligomers were suggested to be an important mediator of the proteotoxicity that disrupts synapses in AD pathology (12). However, the processing mechanism of tau phosphorylation is needed to further investigate.

Although it is over one hundred years since AD was firstly described by Dr Alois Alzheimer and some remark-

---

[Author Introduction] Huang Hanchang, Tang Di, Xu ke, Jiang Zhaofeng, Beijing Key Laboratory of Bioactive Substances and Functional Foods, College of Arts and Scienceof Beijing Union University; Xu Ke, Collegeof Life Science, Capital Normal University.

able progresses have been made on the pathological mechanism and therapy of AD, there are still many questions remained. Based on the fact that Aβ deposits in Senile plaques, hypothesis of Amyloid cascade was first proposed in the 1990s (13, 14). This hypothesis supposes that the accumulated Aβ causes the neuronal damage and death, resulting in the development of AD. Increasing evidence indicated that Aβ induces microtubule – associated protein tau hyperphosporylation and synaptic loss *in vitro* and *in vivo*. However, the mechanisms underlying Aβ – induced neurotoxicity, especially on the links between accumulated Aβ and hyperphosphorylated tau, are still not fully understood. On the treatments for AD, the interventions that inhibit the cellular signals induced by accumulated Aβ may be alternative strategies.

Curcumin, 1, 7 – bis (4 – hydroxy – 3 – methoxyphenyl) – 1, 6 – heptadiene – 3, 5 – dione, is a major ingredient of the yellow pigments (curcuminoids) in spice plant turmeric. For the last few decades, extensive studies have indicated that curcumin shows pharmacological activities, including anti – oxidation, anti – inflammation and anti – cancer. Interestingly, the investigation on epidemiology found that a regular diet of curcumin is one of the responses for reducing the risk of AD among the Indian populations. Therefore, curcumin was regarded as a candidate for AD treatment. On one hand, curcumin binds to oligomeric and fibril Aβ (15, 16) and to inhibit Aβ aggregation, as well as oligomer and fibril formation in AD transgenic mice (17). On the other hand, curcumin decreases Aβ production by the manner of modulating APP processing (18, 19). Recently, curcumin is considered to depress Aβ – induced astrocytes activity and improves rat spatial memory disorders (20). In our previous research, we had indicated that curcumin protects rat cortical neurons against Aβ – induced cell apoptosis (21). Further we found that curcumin inhibits Aβ – induced depolarization of mitochondrial membrane potential and deficiency in energy metabolism (22). However, how curcumin inhibits Aβ – induced cell signaling is still not understood. Therefore, the signaling pathway on tau phosphorylation induced by Aβ was investigated and the protective effects of curcumin on this involved signaling pathway were further studies in this study.

Materials and methods

Preparation of oligomeric Aβ and curcumin stock solutions

$Aβ_{1-40}$ (Sigma – Aldrich, St. Louis, MO, USA) was dissolved in distilled water and then diluted to be 200μM stock solutions in 1.0mM phosphate buffered saline (PBS). The stock solution was incubated in 37℃ for 24 h. The prepared Aβ above is proved to be soluble oligomers with oligomeric number arranged from 2 ~ 8 dominantly (21). The filtered stock solution of 20mM curcumin (>95% HPLC, Chinese National Institute for the Control of Pharmaceutical and Biological Products (NICPBP, Beijing, China) was prepared with DMSO (Sigma – Aldrich, St. Louis, USA).

Cell culture and Treatment

Human neuroblastoma SH – SY5Y cells were cultured in RPMI 1640 culture medium (GIBCO BRL, Life Technologies, Grand Island, NY) supplemented with 10% FBS, 100 unit/mL penicillin and 100μg/mL streptomycin at 37℃ in a humidified atmosphere of 5% CO_2 and 95% air. When treated with drugs, culture medium was changed to serum – free RPMI 1640 supplemented with 100 unit/mL penicillin and 100μg/mL streptomycin. For Aβ – treated group, SH – SY5Y cells were cultured for 24h in culture medium with 1, 5, 10 or 20μM Aβ. For curcumin – protective group, SH – SY5Y cells were cultured with 1, 5 or 10μM curcumin for 4h in culture medium and then were continued incubating with 10μM Aβ for 24 h. The same concentration of DMSO was used as vehicle control.

Western Blotting Analysis

After treatment, cells were digested by 0.25% trypsin and collected by centrifugation at 1000g after washed with phosphate – buffered saline (PBS) three times. The collected cell were lysed in 200μL of lysis buffer (25mM Tris, pH7.5, 1mM EDTA, 1mM DTT, 10mM NaCl, 25mM NaF, protease inhibitors and phosphatase inhibitors) for 30 min on ice. The lysate was centrifuged for 15min at 13,000g in 4℃ and the supernatant was collected, and the concentration of total proteins was determined by bicinchoninic acid (BCA) protein assay kit. Samples (30~40μg protein) were separated by SDS-polyacrylamide gel electrophoresis (PAGE) with a 10% resolving gel and then were electrotransferred to 0.45μm polyvinylidene fluoride (PVDF) membranes (Biotrace™ PVDF, PALL, Gelman Laboratory, Ann Arbor, MI). After transferred, the membrane was washed with PBS to remove guanidine hydrochloride and blocked with 5% skimmed milk in a PBS buffer containing 0.1% Tween-20 for 1h and subsequently incubated overnight at 4℃ with primary antibodies specific for the target proteins. After washed, the membrane was incubated with horse-radish peroxidase (HRP)-linked secondary antibody for 2h. The target protein was visualized using enhanced chemiluminescence (ECL) western blot detection reagents. The optical density was detected with a gel detection system (GE Healthcare, Piscataway, NJ). The densitometry analysis of Western blots was performed using Quantity one 4.62 software. The antibodies used in this study are listed in table 1.

Table 1 antibodies used in this study.

Antibodies	Catalog no and Company	Specific
Tau-5	ab80579, Abcam Inc, Cambridge, UK	monoclonal
pSer396-Tau	ab109390, Abcam Inc, Cambridge, UK	monoclonal
pThr231-Tau	Ab151559, Abcam Inc, Cambridge, UK	monoclonal
GSK-3β	#9832, Cell Signaling Technology, Inc., Beverly, MA	monoclonal
pSer9-GSK-3β	#9336, Cell Signaling Technology, Inc., Beverly, MA	polyclonal
HDAC6	#7558, Cell Signaling Technology, Inc., Beverly, MA	monoclonal
PDPK1	ab31406, Abcam Inc, Cambridge, UK	polyclonal
pS241-PDPK1	ST1073, Abcam Inc., Cambridge, UK	polyclonal
Akt2	ab66129, Abcam Inc, Cambridge, UK	polyclonal
pThr308-pan-Akt	ab38449, Abcam Inc, Cambridge, UK	monoclonal
pSer473-pan-Akt	ab5918, Abcam Inc, Cambridge, UK	polyclonal
IR β-subunit	GR36, Merck-Millipore, Missouri, USA	monoclonal
pTyr972-IR β-subunit	GF1000, Merck-Millipore, Missouri, USA	polyclonal
p85 (Tyr458)/p55 (Try199)-PI3K	4228#, Cell Signaling Technology, Inc., Beverly, MA	polyclonal
p85 subunit of PI3K	4292#, Cell Signaling Technology, Inc., Beverly, MA	polyclonal
PTEN	9559#, Cell Signaling Technology, Inc., Beverly, MA	monoclonal
β-actin	4970#, Cell Signaling Technology, Inc., Beverly. MA	polyclonal

PTEN mRNA RT-PCR analysis

Total RNA was isolated according to the Trizol reagent protocolInvitrogen, Carlsbad, CA) after cells was treated with drugs for 16 h. The quality of isolated RNA was evaluated to be perfect by the absorbance of A260/A280nm (typically 1.6–1.8) and the bands of agarose gel electrophoresis (three rRNA bands and the maximum bright band is about 1.5–2.0 times of secondary bright band). Total RNA was reverse-transcripted into cDNA using the Superscript™ II RNase H Reverse Transcriptase kit (Life Technologies, Carlsbad, CA). PTEN cDNA was amplified by real-time fluorescence quantitative polymerase Chain Reaction (qPCR) using SYBR® green PCR master mix kit (Life Technologies, Carlsbad, CA). The primers for the genes are given in Table 2. PCR was carried out on a Corbett 6000 thermocycler (Corbett Life Science, Sydney, NSW, Australia) with a denaturation step at 94℃ for 15 min followed by 35 reaction cycles composed of 94℃ for 30 s, 55℃ for 30 s and 72℃ for 30s. The final PCR products were carried out melt analysis from 65℃ to 95℃.

To ensure that the correct products were obtained, the products of PCR was analyzed by melting curve and conformed to be only one peak. Further, the molecular weight of RT-PCR products analyzed by 2.5% agarose gel electrophoresis.

Table 2 Primer sequences for quantitative real-time polymerase chain reaction

gene	Primer	sequence (5'→3')	Products (bp)
PTEN	Forward primer	TGTGGTCTGCCAGCTAAAGG	94
	Reverse primer	CGGCTGAGGGAACTCAAAGT	
GAPDH	Forward primer	ACGGATTTGGTCGTATTGGG	210
	Reverse primer	CCTGGAAGATGGTGATGGGATT	

Statistical analysis

Microcal Origin 8.0 software (Microcal Software, Inc.) for windows was used for statistical analysis. Data analysis was performed by one-way analysis of variance (ANOVA) followed by the Tukey test for multiple comparisons. Error bars represent SE of the mean of each group analyzed. The minimum significance level was set at $p < 0.05$.

Results

1. Curcumin attenuates Aβ-induced tau phosphorylation at Thr231 and Ser396

When SH-SY5Y cell was incubated with 10μM Aβ for 24h, there is no significant change in the expression of total tau protein. However, the phosphorylation of tau protein at Ser 396 and Thr231 sites is significantly increased in Aβ-incubated group compared with in control group. The phosphorylation of tau at above sites is significantly decreased in curcumin-protective group (cells was incubated 4h before Aβ was added into cells) compared with Aβ-incubated group (Fig. 1). These experiments indicated that curcumin inhibits Aβ-induced hyperphosphorylation of tau protein. However, the cellular signal pathway is needed to further investigate.

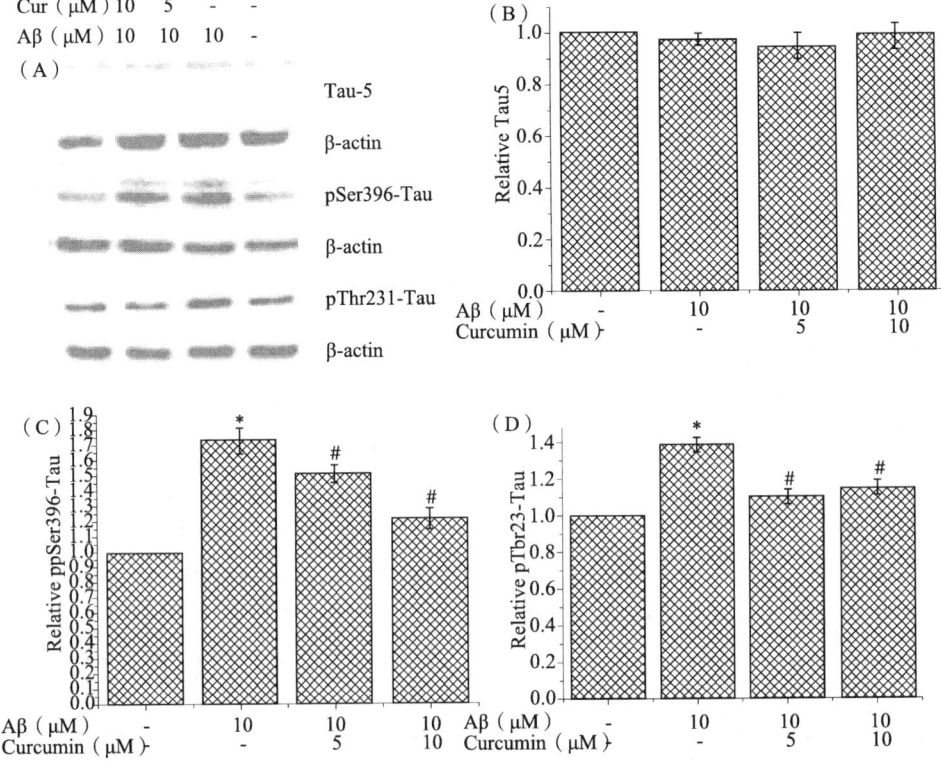

Fig. 1 tau phosphorylation induced by Aβ in the absence or presence of curcumin Tau phosphorylation is increased significantly at Thr231 and Ser396 in the Aβ-treated group compared with control while phosphorylation of tau at both sites is decreased in curcumin-protective group compared with Aβ-treat group. *$p < 0.05$ versus control, #$p < 0.05$ versus Aβ-treated group.

2. Curcumin inhibits Aβ – induced GSK – 3β and HDAC6 activation

Glycogen synthase kinase – 3β (GSK – 3β), a proline – directed serine – threonine kinase, was initially identified as a phosphorylating and an inactivating agent of the enzyme glycogen synthase via catalyzing phosphorylation of this enzyme. Besides energy metabolism, GSK – 3β is considered to be involved in a number of cellular signal transduction pathways, such as insulin, Win/β – catenin and notch signal transduction pathways; cell differentiation, energy metabolism and cell apoptosis process. Recently, GSK – 3β is suggested to participate in Aβ – induced cellular signaling transduction. Previously, we had reported that oligomeric Aβ induces activation of GSK – 3β (amino acid residue at Ser 9 is dephosphorylation when SH – SY5Y cells were treated with Aβ)(22).

The bio – activity of GSK – 3β is dependent on the level of protein phosphorylation. GSK – 3β is activated and induces phosphorylation on downstream protein when it is dephosphorylation at residues Ser9. Increasing evidence indicates that GSK – 3β is also involved in the phosphorylation of tau protein. HDAC6, a member of Class II of histone deacetylases, was suggested to activate by GSK – 3β. Tubacin (a selective inhibitor of HDAC6) was reported to attenuate hyperphosphorylation of tau, suggesting that HDAC6 plays a role in the AD.

As shown in Fig. 2, expression of GSK – 3β protein has no significant change when cells were incubated with Aβ for 24h; however, the level of phosphorylation of GSK – 3β at Ser 9 is significantly reduced. This implies that Aβ results in activation of GSK – 3β. In curcumin – protective group, however, phosphorylation of GSK – 3β at Ser 9 is increased significantly compared with Aβ – incubated group (Fig. 2). This implies that curcumin inhibits Aβ – induced activation of GSK – 3β protein. As shown in Fig. 3, expression of HDAC6 is increased in Aβ – incubated group compared with control group. In SB415286 (a selective inhibitor of GSK – 3β) or curcumin – protective group, the level of HDAC6 is significantly down – regulated compared with Aβ – incubated group, implying that curcumin inhibits Aβ – induced the activation of GSK – 3β and thus attenuates the downstream cellular signal induced by activated GSK – 3β.

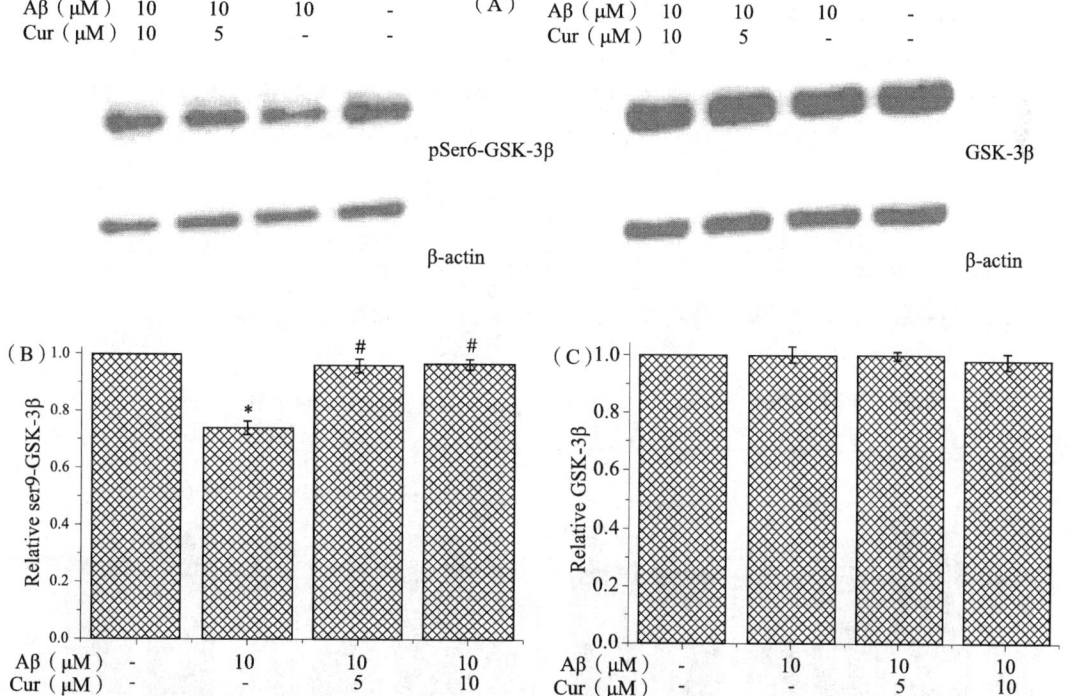

Fig. 2 Aβ induces GSK – 3β phosphorylation in the absence or presence of curcumin GSK – 3β phosphorylation is decreased significantly at Ser 9 in Aβ – treated group compared with control while phosphorylation of GSK – 3β at this site is increased in curcumin – protective group compared with Aβ – treat group.
*$p < 0.05$ versus control, #$p < 0.05$ versus Aβ – treated group.

We had reported previously that Aβ results in oxidative damages in primary rat neurons and SH–SY5Y cells (21, 22). Therefore, it is interesting whether Aβ–induced activation of GSK–3β is directly mediated by cellular oxidative stress. This study further investigated the relationship between cellular oxidative stress and phosphorylation of GSK–3β at Ser9 site. As shown in Fig. 4, neither L–ascorbic acid (V_C), α–tocopherol (an isomer of V_E) nor H_2O_2 has significant impact on phosphorylation of GSK–3β at Ser9 residue, implying that activation of GSK–3β is not directly mediated by cellular oxidative stress.

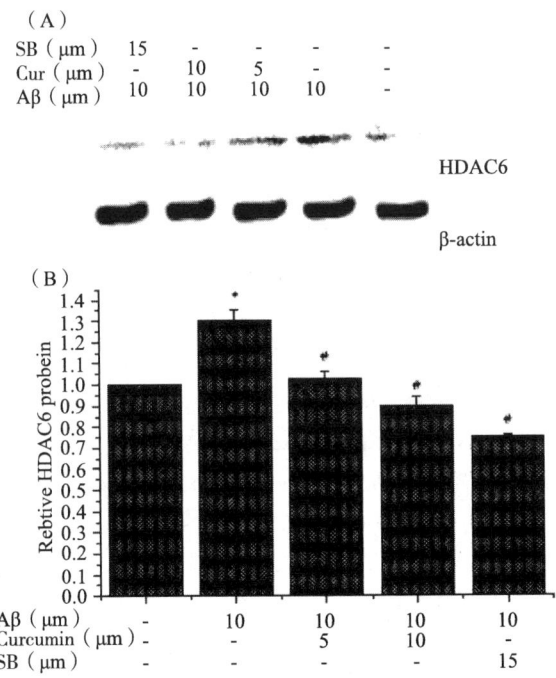

Fig. 3 Aβ's effect on HDAC6 expression in the absence or presence of curcumin expression of HDAC6 is increased significantly in Aβ–treated group compared with control while expression of this protein is decreased in positive control and curcumin–protective group compared with Aβ–treat group.
*$p<0.05$ versus control, #$p<0.05$ versus Aβ–treated group.

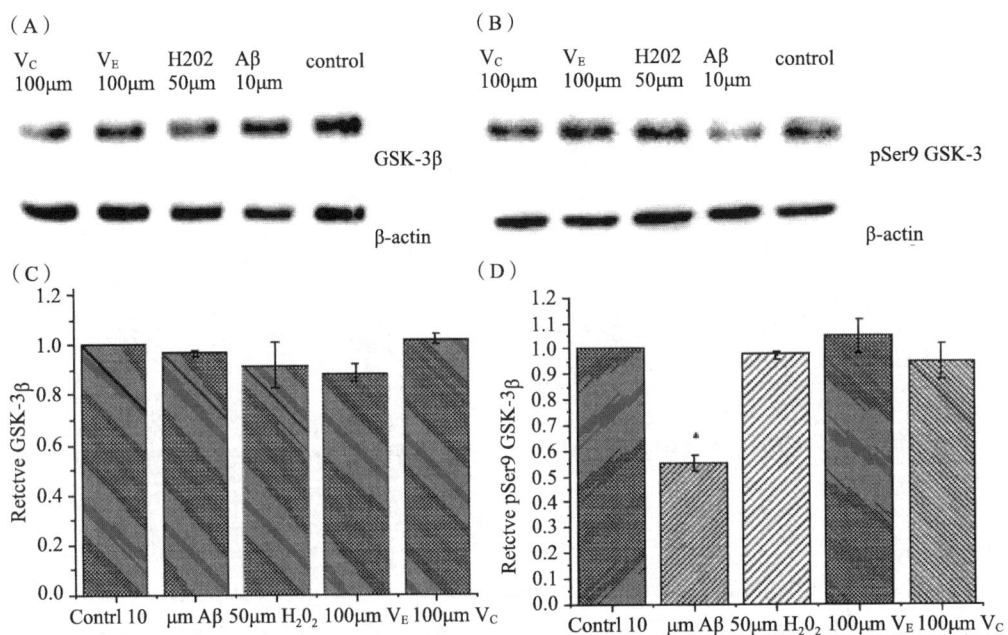

Fig. 4 Effect of oxidative stress on GSK–3β phosphorylation neither H_2O_2 nor V_E/V_C has no effect on GSK–3β phosphorylation at Ser9, implying that direct oxidative stress does not result in activation of GSK–3β. *$p<0.05$ versus control.

These results suggest that Aβ – induced activity of GSK – 3β is not directly achieved by oxidative stress. The cellular signaling is needed to further investigate in order to clarify the mechanism on the Aβ – induced phosphorylation of GSK – β.

Curcumin improves the activity of PDK1/Akt on Aβ – treated cells

As mentioned above, the pathway of Aβ – induced activation of GSK – 3β is needed to further investigate. Akt, also known as protein kinase B (PKB), is a serine/threonine – specific protein kinase. Coupling with 3 – phosphoinositide – dependent protein kinase 1 (PDK1), phosphatidylinositol mediates Akt translocation form cytoplasm to inner side of membrane, resulting in Akt's phosphorylation at Ser473 and Thr308 sites. Phosphorylations at above both sites are required for activation of Akt, and the activated Akt results in phosphorylation of downstream substrate, including GSK – 3β.

This study further studies the activation of PDK1 and Akt under Aβ incubation in the presence or absence of curcumin. As shown in Fig. 5, phosphorylation of PDK1 at Ser241 is decreased in Aβ – treated group compared with control (PDK1 activity is correlated to its phosphorylation levels at this site), and curcumin improves the phosph orylation of PDK1 in curcumin – protective groups compared with Aβ – treated group. Phosphorylations of Akt at Thr308 and Ser473 sites are down – regulated in Aβ – treated group, and they are up – regulated in curcumin – protective groups (Fig. 6). This suggests that Aβ inhibits Akt activity, while curcumin inhibits Aβ – induced inhibition of Akt activity.

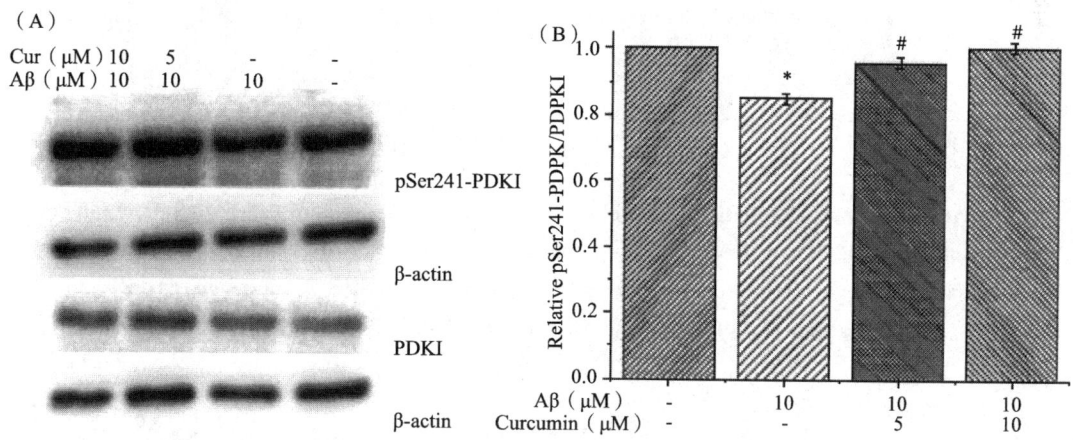

Fig. 5 effect of Aβ on PDK1 phosphorylation in the absence or presence of curcumin PDK1 phosphorylation is decreased significantly at Ser241 in Aβ – treated group compared with control while phosphorylation of this protein is increased in curcumin – protective group compared with Aβ – treat group. *$p < 0.05$ versus control, #$p < 0.05$ versus Aβ – treated group.

Insulin receptor/PI3K does't participate in Aβ – induced transmembrane signaling

The insulin receptor (IR) belongs to the large class of tyrosine kinase receptors and is activated by insulin and IGF. IR is a key upstream regulator of phosphatidyl inositol 3 – kinase (PI3K). IR/PI3K pathway is a very important intracellular signal transduction pathway. PI3K involves intracellular signal transduction, and it is activated by growth factors, cytokines, hormones and other extracellular or intracellular signals stimulated. The activated PI3K results in phosphorylation of membrane phosphoinositides, generating phosphatidylinositol – 3, 4 – biphosphate (PI – 3, 4P2, PIP2) and phosphatidylinositol 3, 4, 5 – trisphosphate (PI – 3, 4, 5P3, PIP3). The generated phosphatidylinositol PIP3, as a second messenger, causes transduction on intracellular signal.

It is attractive whether IR/PI3K pathway involves Aβ – induced transmembrane signal transduction. Activation of PI3K is regulated by the phosphorylation of IR β – subunit at Tyr 972 site. As shown in Fig. 7, the level of p – Tyr of IR β – subunit has no change in Aβ – treated group; as a positive control, insulin results in a significant increase in phosphorylation of IR β – subunit at Tyr 972 site. The phosphorylation of IR β – subunit also has no change in Aβ – treated cells in the presence of curcumin (Fig. 7). Similarly, Aβ has not impact on expression of PI3K – p85/p55 subunit and the protein's phosphorylation (Fig. 8). As a positive control, insulin results in decrease of phosphorylation of PI3K – p85/p55 subunit. These results implied that Aβ – induced deactivation of Akt is not induced by IR/PI3K pathway, and curcumin inhibits Aβ – induced deactivation of Akt also is not mediated by the activation of IR.

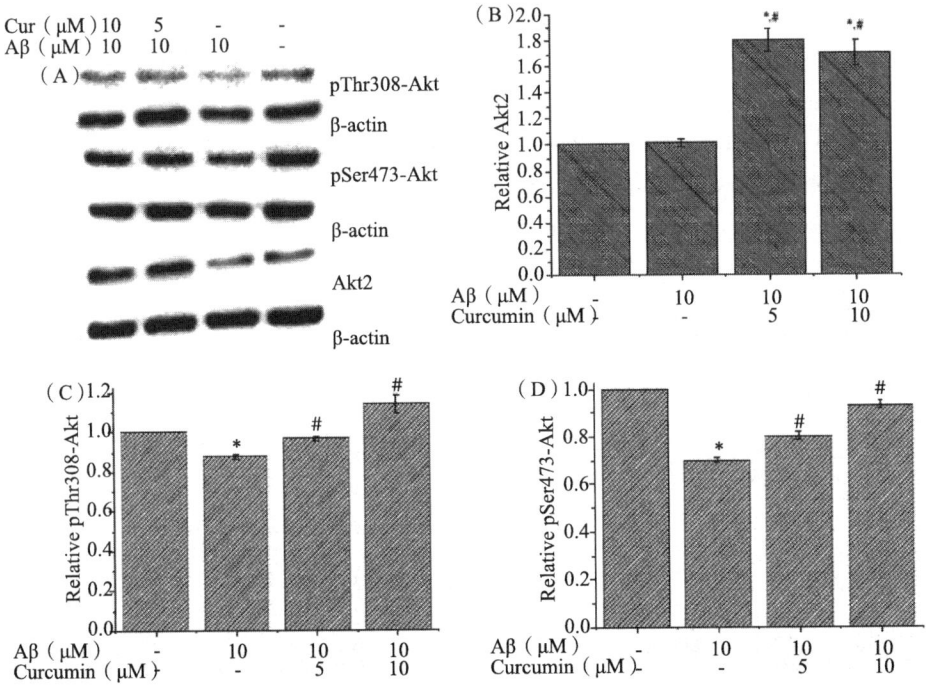

Fig. 6 Effect of Aβ on Akt phosphorylation in the absence or presence of curcumin Akt phosphorylation is decreased significantly at both Thr308 and Ser473 in Aβ – treated group compared with control while phosphorylation of this protein at these sites is increased in curcumin – protective group compared with Aβ – treat group. $*p < 0.05$ versus control, $\#p < 0.05$ versus Aβ – treated group.

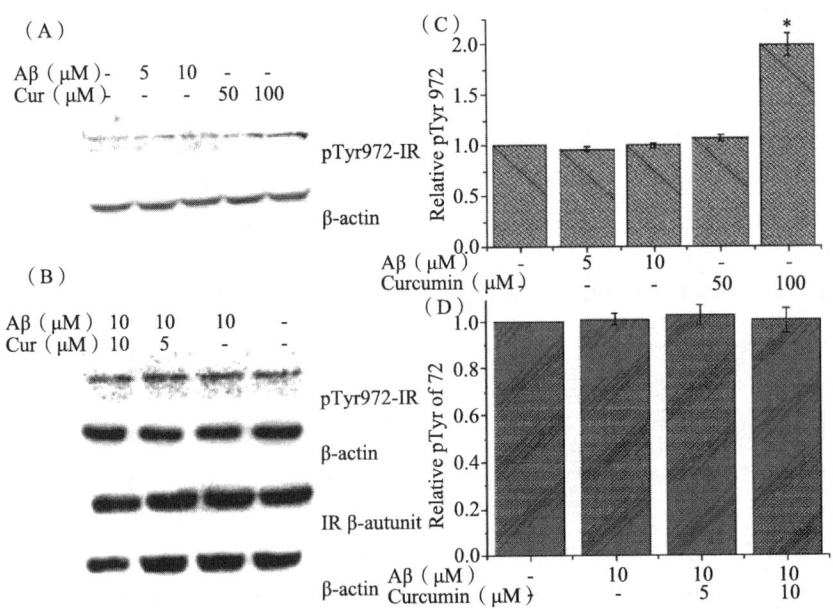

Fig. 7 effect of Aβ on IR phosphorylation in the absence or presence of curcumin phosphorylation of IR at Tyr 972 does not alter in both Aβ – treated and curcumin – protective group while insulin, as a positive control, increases significantly the phosphorylation of this protein. $*p < 0.05$ versus control.

PTEN is involved in Aβ - induced deactivation of Akt

Phosphatase and tensin homolog (PTEN) is a negative regulator of PIP3 signaling and catalyzes phosphoinositide to dephosphorylate. PTEN mRNA expression is sensitive to cellular oxidative stress (Fig. 8); H_2O_2 up - regulates its expression while α - tocopherol decreases this gene mRNA expression. Aβ up - regulates PTEN mRNA expression as the same as H_2O_2. Curcumin's effect on PTEN mRNA expression is differential on concentration, and curcumin at a low dose down - regulates PTEN mRNA expression. Curcumin depresses Aβ - induced PTEN mRNA expression (Fig. 9). On the PTEN protein expression, curcumin also depresses Aβ - induced PTEN protein expression (Fig. 10). These results imply that Aβ results in the hydrolysis of PIP3 and curcumin inhibits Aβ - induced cellular deficiency of PIP3.

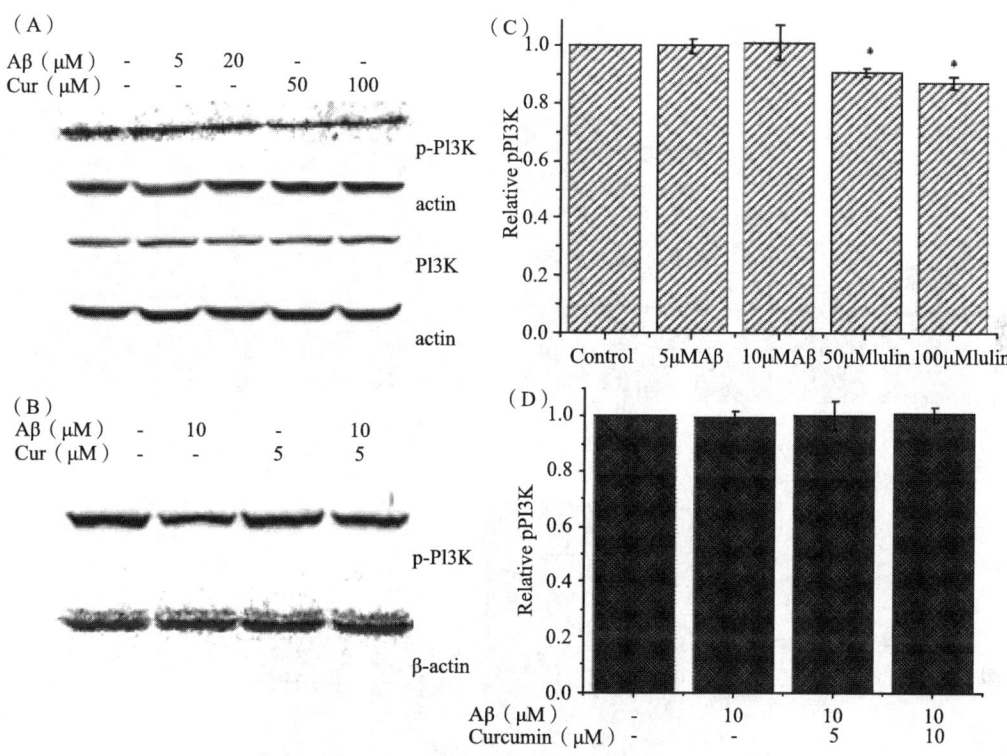

Figure 8 Effects of Aβ and curcumin on phosphorylation of PI3K - p85/p55 subunit phosphorylation of PI3K - p85/p55 subunit has no change in both Aβ - treated and curcumin - protective group while insulin, as a positive control, decreases significantly the phosphorylation of this protein. $*p<0.05$ versus control.

The above results suggested that deactivation of Akt induced by Aβ is achieved by the PTEN - mediated PIP3 deficiency and curcumin inhibits Aβ - induced deactivation of Akt through depression of PIP3 hydrolysis.

Discussion

Besides participates in glycogen synthesis, GSK - 3β is increasingly considered to be involved in a number of cellular signal transduction pathways (23, 24). Recently, GSK - 3β is suggested to links the pathologies between accumulated Aβ and hyperphosphorylated tau (25, 26), and GSK - 3β mediates Aβ - induced tau phosphorylation. Tau is phosphorylated by GSK - 3β at least 15 phospho - sites on Ser46, Thr50 and Thr175; Thr181, Ser199 and Ser202; Thr205, Thr212 and Thr217; Thr231, Ser235 and Ser396; Ser400, Ser404 and Ser413 (1). Substances that can down - regulate Aβinduced activation of GSK - 3β are expected to become a new type of target for the treatment of AD. Tideglusib, a GSK - 3β inhibitor, is currently in phase II clinical trials for the treatment of AD. Tideglusib shows the ability to reduce tau hyperphosphorylation and prevents the loss of neurons in multiple AD animal models (27). However, the manner on Aβ - induced activation of GSK - 3β is still not completely understood.

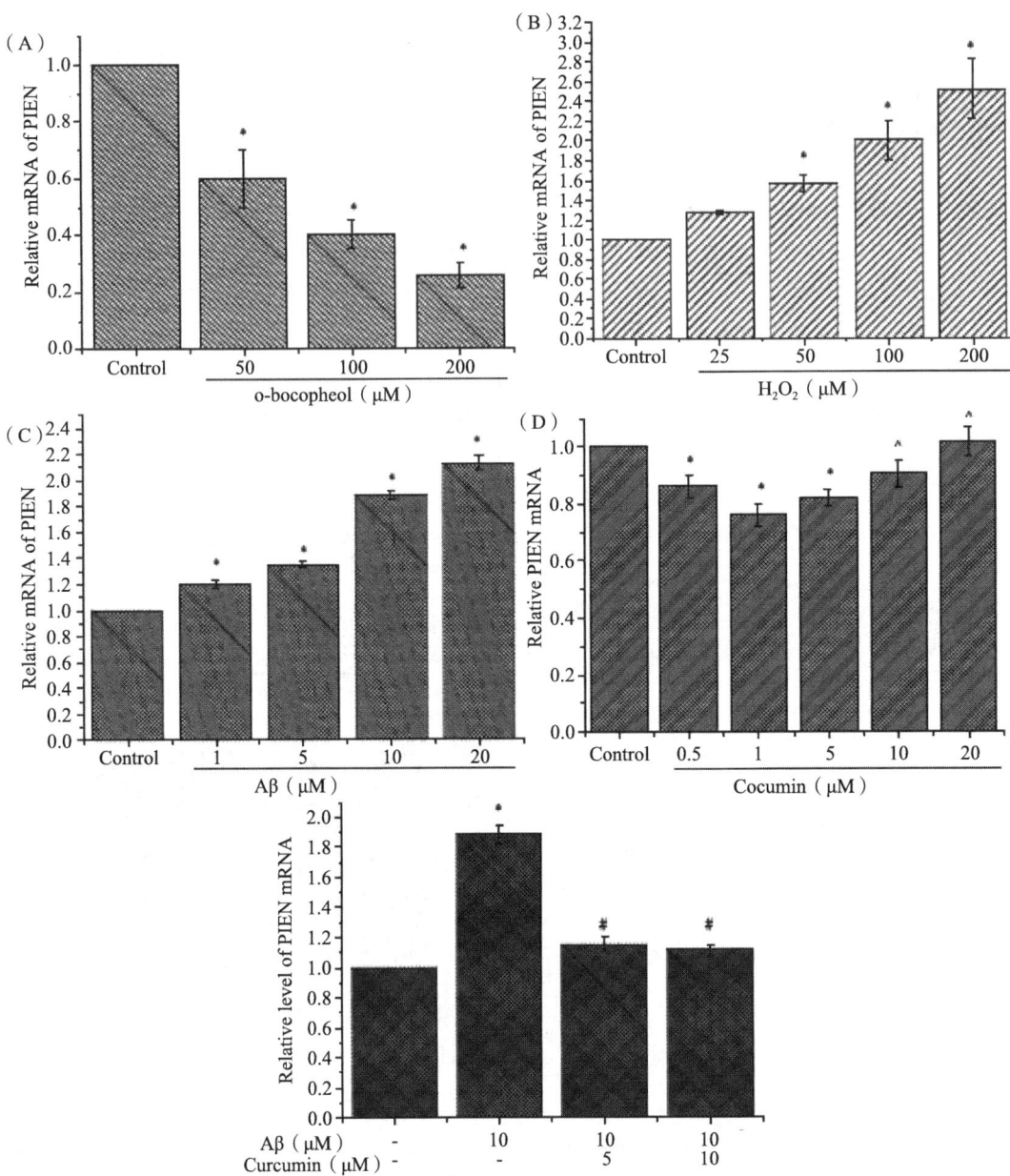

Figure 9 RT-PCR analysis of PTEN mRNA α-tocopherol decreases PTEN mRNA expression while H_2O_2 increases this gene expression. The same as H_2O_2, Aβ increases expression of PTEN mRNA and curcumin normalizes expression of this gene. *$p < 0.05$ versus control, #$p < 0.05$ versus Aβ-treated group and ^$p < 0.05$ versus 1.0μM curcumin.

In this study, phosphorylation of GSK-3β at Ser9 is downregulated when cells were treated with Aβ, and phosphorylation of this protein at Ser9 is increased on cells cultured with Aβ in the presence of curcumin (Fig. 2), implying that curcumin inhibits Aβ-induced activation of GSK-3β. Since the level of cellular oxidative stress is increased when cells were treated with Aβ and curcumin depresses Aβ-induced oxidative damage (21, 22), it is interesting whether activation of GSK-3β induced by Aβ is directly mediated by oxidative stress. As shown in Figure 4, H_2O_2 or Ve has no impact on the phophorylation of GSK-3β at Ser9, implying that Aβ-induced activation of GSK-3β is not directly achieved via cellular oxidative stress.

Akt is a potential upstream regulator of GSK-3β and the activated Akt inhibits phosphorylation of GSK-3β at Ser9. It is interesting whether Akt participates in Aβ-induced phosphorylation of GSK-3β at Ser9. Therefore, Akt/GSK-3β pathway on the effect of tau phosphorylation was investigated in this study. As shown in Fig. 6, Aβ induces dephosphorylation of Akt at both Thr308 and Ser473 sites, and curcumin inhibits both sites' dephosphorylation of Akt induced by Aβ. Furthermore, the phosphorylated PDK1, a direct associate of Akt phosphorylation, is depressed in Aβtreated cells while curcumin inhibits Aβ – induced depression of PDK1 phosphorylation (Fig. 5). This result indicates that Akt mediates the protection of curcumin against Aβ – induced activation of GSK – 3β and tau phosphorylation. However, the upstream regulator of Akt involved in this protection is still needed to investigate.

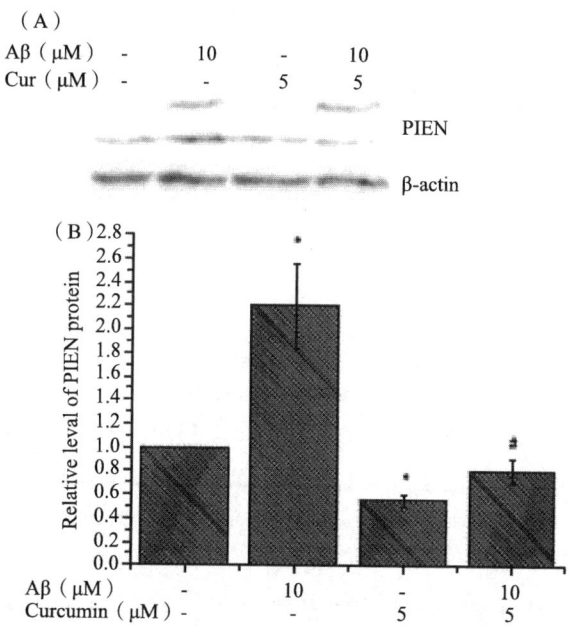

Fig. 10 effect of Aβ on PTEN protein expression in the presence or absence of curcumin PTEN protein is up – regulated in Aβ – treated group compared with control. However, this protein is down – regulated in curcumin – protective group compared with Aβ – treated group.
*$p < 0.05$ versus control, #$p < 0.05$ versus Aβ – treated group.

IR/PI3K signaling pathway plays an important role in prosurvival and pro – growth. About two decades ago, defective insulin signaling was first proposed to contribute to AD pathogenesis (28), and increasing studies have since suggested that type (2) diabetes increases AD risk (29 – 31). IR plays a key role in the regulation of glucose homeostasis, and our previous study indicated that Aβ results in cellular ATP deficiency (22). Therefore, it is appealing whether extracellular Aβ impacts on IR and sequentially induces inactivation of PI3K. In contrast, Aβ has no impact on IR/PI3K signaling pathway and this pathway also does not affected in cells treated with Aβ in the presence of curcumin (Figures 7 & 8). This result indicates that there is another signaling pathway that regulates the activity of Akt in cells treated with Aβ and curcumin may inhibit this pathway up – regulated by Aβ. Notably, PTEN is over – expressed on the levels of transcription and translation when cells were treated with Aβ, and curcumin inhibits Aβ – induced over – expression of PTEN (Figures 9 & 10). Interestingly, although both Aβ and direct oxidative stress (H_2O_2) up – regulate PTEN expression, it seems to be different on the Akt/GSK – 3β signaling. Aβ but no direct oxidative stress induces activation of GSK – 3β.

There is a question remained how extracellular Aβ impacts on intracellular signaling pathway. Actually, this question is like a ghost hovered around the hypothesis of amyloid cascade. There are some potential pathways. Firstly, transmembrane receptors are suspected to directly mediate extracellular Aβ – induced cellular transduction, and it is attractive whether there is the receptor of Aβ. Although recently toll – like receptor 2 (TLR2) is considered to be a primary receptor for Aβ to trigger neuroinflammatory activation (32), until now the receptor of Aβ is still unclear, unfortunately. Some receptors or ion channels are suggested, however, to indirectly mediate Aβ – induced neurotoxicity. On the one hand, Aβ was thought to increase intracellular Ca^{2+} via impact on ion channel and resulted in Ca^{2+} cascade, including tau phosphorylation and loss of synaptic activity

(33 – 35). On the other hand, Aβ is suggested to play a role in activation of extrasynaptic methyl – D – aspartate receptor (NMDAR) and results in selective impairment of synaptic plasticity and microtubule deregulation (36, 37). Selective inhibitors of NMDAR are suggested to be a hope for AD treatment. Memantine, a moderate antagonist of NMDAR, has been used clinically on the treatment of AD (28, 38). Second, extracellular accumulation of Aβ may result in increase of intracellular Aβ. On the one hand, Aβ may be internalized from the extracellular milieu (39); however, more directly evidence is needed. On the other hand, Aβ is secreted intracellularly via the pathway that APP was internalized and proteolyzed in an endosomal/lysosomal pathway (40). Intracellular interaction partner of Aβ has been found and was named Aβ – binding alcohol dehydrogenase (ABAD) (41). Increasing evidence indicates that intracellular Aβ contributes to deficiency of cellular metabolism and mitochondrial dysfunction and impacts on synaptic activity, resulting in deficit in long – term synaptic plasticity (40).

Conclusion

Aβ contributes to tau hyperphosphorylation, and hyperphosphorylated tau protein as well as the formation of NFTs is a significant hallmark of AD. GSK – 3β mediates Aβ – induced tau hyperphosphorylation via Akt signaling pathway but not directly response to cellular oxidative stress. IR/PI3K, as a positive regulator of PIP3, does not involve Akt signaling, but PTEN, as a negative regulator of PIP3, participates in Aβ – induced activation of GSK – 3β via Akt signaling. Curcumin inhibits Aβ – induced tau phosphorylation involving PTEN/Akt/GSK – 3β signaling pathway. The remained questions how Aβ induces over – expression of PTEN and curcumin inhibits over – expression of this protein are needed to further investigate. These results supplement the implication of hypothesisof Amyloid – β cascade and imply the application of curcumin to treatment for AD.

Acknowledgements

This study was supported by the National Natural Science Foundation of China (31071512) and the Scientific Research Common Program of Beijing Municipal Commission of Education (SQKM201411417003).

References

[1] Huang HC, Jiang ZF. Accumulated amyloid – beta peptide and hyperphosphorylated tau protein: relationship and links in Alzheimer's disease. J Alzheimers Dis 2009; 16: 15 – 27.

[2] Huang HC, Jiang ZF. Amyloid – beta protein precursor family members: a review from homology to biological function. J Alzheimers Dis 2011; 26: 607 – 626.

[3] Smith RP, Higuchi DA, Broze GJ, Jr. Platelet coagulation factor XIa – inhibitor, a form of Alzheimer amyloid precursor protein. Science 1990; 248: 1126 – 1128.

[4] Small DH, Clarris HL, Williamson TG, et al. Neurite – outgrowth regulating functions of the amyloid protein precursor of Alzheimer's disease. J Alzheimers Dis 1999; 1: 275 – 285.

[5] Seabrook GR, Smith DW, Bowery BJ, et al. Mechanisms contributing to the deficits in hippocampal synaptic plasticity in mice lacking amyloid precursor protein. Neuropharmacology 1999; 38: 349 – 359.

[6] Gralle M, Ferreira ST. Structure and functions of the human amyloid precursor protein: the whole is more than the sum of its parts. Prog Neurobiol 2007; 82: 11 – 32.

[7] Rama N, Goldschneider D, Corset V, et al. Amyloid precursor protein regulates netrin – 1 – mediated commissural axon outgrowth. J Biol Chem 2012; 287: 30014 – 30023.

[8] García – Sierra F, Jarero – Basulto JJ, Kristofikova K, et al. Ubiquitin is associated with early truncation of tau protein at aspartic acid421 during the maturation of neurofibrillary tangles in Alzheimer's disease. Brain Pathol 2012; 22: 240 – 250.

[9] Goedert M, Spillantini MG, Cairns NJ, Crowther RA. Tau proteins of Alzheimer paired helical filaments: abnormal phosphorylation of all six brain isoforms. Neuron 1992; 8 (1): 159 – 168.

[10] Buee L, Bussiere T, Buee – Scherrer V, et al. Tau protein isoforms, phosphorylation and role in neurodegenerative disor-

ders. Brain Res Brain Res Rev 2000; 33: 95 – 130.

[11] Shipton OA, Leitz JR, Dworzak J, et al. Tau protein is required for amyloid {beta} – induced impairment of hippocampal long – term potentiation. J Neurosci 2011; 31: 1688 – 1692.

[12] Tai HC, Serrano – Pozo A, Hashimoto T, et al. The synaptic accumulation of hyperphosphorylated tau oligomers in Alzheimer disease is associated with dysfunction of the ubiquitin – proteasome system. Am J Pathol 2012; 181: 1426 – 1435.

[13] Hardy JA, Higgins GA. Alzheimer's disease: the amyloid cascade hypothesis. Science 1992; 256: 184 – 185.

[14] Dong S, Duan Y, Hu Y, Zhao Z. Advances in the pathogenesis of Alzheimer's disease: a re – evaluation of amyloid cascade hypothesis. Transl Neurodegener 2012; 1: 18.

[15] Yanagisawa D, Taguchi H, Yamamoto A, et al. Curcuminoid binds to amyloid – beta1 – 42 oligomer and fibril. J Alzheimers Dis 2011; 24: 33 – 42.

[16] Mutsuga M, Chambers JK, Uchida K, et al. Binding of curcumin to senile plaques and cerebral amyloid angiopathy in the aged brain of various animals and to neurofibrillary tangles in Alzheimer's brain. J Vet Med Sci 2012; 74: 51 – 57.

[17] Yang F, Lim GP, Begum AN, et al. Curcumin inhibits formation of amyloid beta oligomers and fibrils, binds plaques, and reduces amyloid in vivo. J Biol Chem 2005; 280: 5892 – 5901.

[18] Zhang C, Browne A, Child D, Tanzi RE. Curcumin decreases amyloid – beta peptide levels by attenuating the maturation of amyloid – beta precursor protein. J Biol Chem 2010; 285: 28472 – 28480.

[19] Liu H, Li Z, Qiu D, et al. The inhibitory effects of different curcuminoids on beta – amyloid protein, beta – amyloid precursor protein and beta – site amyloid precursor protein cleaving enzyme 1 in swAPP HEK293 cells. Neurosci Lett 2010; 485: 83 – 88.

[20] Wang Y, Yin H, Wang L, et al. Curcumin as a potential treatment for Alzheimer's disease: a study of the effects of curcumin on hippocampal expression of glial fibrillary acidic protein. Am J Chin Med 2013; 41: 59 – 70.

[21] Huang HC, Chang P, Dai XL, Jiang ZF. Protective effects of curcumin on amyloid – beta – induced neuronal oxidative damage. Neurochem Res 2012; 37: 1584 – 1597.

[22] Huang HC, Xu K, Jiang ZF. Curcumin – mediated neuroprotection against amyloid – beta – induced mitochondrial dysfunction involves the inhibition of GSK – 3beta. J Alzheimers Dis 2012; 32: 981 – 996.

[23] Flugel D, Gorlach A, Kietzmann T. GSK – 3beta regulates cell growth, migration, and angiogenesis via Fbw7 and USP28 – dependent degradation of HIF – 1alpha. Blood 2012; 119: 1292 – 1301.

[24] Itoh S, Saito T, Hirata M, et al. GSK – 3alpha and GSK – 3beta proteins are involved in early stages of chondrocyte differentiation with functional redundancy through RelA protein phosphorylation. J Biol Chem 2012; 287: 29227 – 29236.

[25] Durairajan SS, Liu LF, Lu JH, et al. Berberine ameliorates betaamyloid pathology, gliosis, and cognitive impairment in an Alzheimer's disease transgenic mouse model. Neurobiol Aging 2012; 33: 2903 – 2919.

[26] Terwel D, Muyllaert D, Dewachter I, et al. Amyloid activates GSK – 3beta to aggravate neuronal tauopathy in bigenic mice. Am J Pathol 2008; 172: 786 – 798.

[27] Dominguez JM, Fuertes A, Orozco L, et al. Evidence for irreversible inhibition of glycogen synthase kinase – 3beta by tideglusib. J Biol Chem 2012; 287: 893 – 904.

[28] Danysz W, Parsons CG. Alzheimer's disease, beta – amyloid, glutamate, NMDA receptors and memantine – searching for the connections. Br J Pharmacol 2012; 167: 324 – 352.

[29] den Heijer T, Vermeer SE, van Dijk EJ, et al. Type 2 diabetes and atrophy of medial temporal lobe structures on brain MRI. Diabetologia 2003; 46: 1604 – 1610.

[30] Haan MN. Therapy insight: type 2 diabetes mellitus and the risk of late – onset Alzheimer disease. Nat Clin Pract Neurol 2006; 2: 159 – 166.

[31] de la Monte SM. Brain insulin resistance and deficiency as therapeutic targets in Alzheimer's disease. Curr Alzheimer Res 2012; 9: 35 – 66.

[32] Liu S, Liu Y, Hao WL, et al. TLR2 is a primary receptor for Alzheimer's amyloid b peptide to trigger neuroinflammatory activation. J. Immunol 2012; 188: 1098 – 1107.

[33] Zempel H, Thies E, Mandelkow E, Mandelkow EM. Abeta oligomers cause localized Ca (2 +) elevation, missorting of endogenous tau into dendrites, tau phosphorylation, and destruction of microtubules and spines. J Neurosci 2010; 30: 11938 – 11950.

[34] Alberdi E, Sanchez – Gomez MV, Cavaliere F, et al. Amyloid beta oligomers induce Ca2 + dysregulation and neuronal death through activation of ionotropic glutamate receptors. Cell Calcium 2010; 47: 264 – 272.

[35] Small DH, Gasperini R, Vincent AJ, et al. The role of Abetainduced calcium dysregulation in the pathogenesis of Alzheimer's disease. J Alzheimers Dis 2009; 16: 225-233.

[36] Mota SI, Ferreira IL, Pereira C, et al. Amyloid-beta peptide 1-42 causes microtubule deregulation through N-methyl-D-aspartate receptors in mature hippocampal cultures. Curr Alzheimer Res 2012; 9: 844-856.

[37] Kervern M, Angeli A, Nicole O, et al. Selective impairment of some forms of synaptic plasticity by oligomeric amyloid-beta peptide in the mouse hippocampus: implication of extrasynaptic NMDA receptors. J Alzheimers Dis 2012; 32 (1): 183-196.

[38] Choi SH, Park KW, Na DL, et al. Tolerability and efficacy of memantine add-on therapy to rivastigmine transdermal patches in mild to moderate Alzheimer's disease: a multicenter, randomized, open-label, parallel-group study. Curr Med Res Opin 2011; 27: 1375-1383.

[39] Mohamed A, Posse de Chaves E. Abeta internalization by neurons and glia. Int J Alzheimers Dis 2011; 2011: 127984.

[40] Gu XM, Huang HC, Jiang ZF. Mitochondrial dysfunction and cellular metabolic deficiency in Alzheimer's disease. Neurosci Bull 2012; 28: 631-640.

[41] Yan SD, Fu J, Soto C, et al. An intracellular protein that binds amyloid-beta peptide and mediates neurotoxicity in Alzheimer's disease. Nature 1997; 389: 689-695.

The Effects of Vitamin C on DDP – induced Anemia in Rats

Gao Liping   Li Zen   Guo Zhuoyu   Zhao Yanmeng

Introduction

Cisplatin (cis – dichlorodiammineplatinum (II), DDP) is one of the most effective anticancer drugs administered to treat a variety of cancers such as ovarian, testicular, bladder, head and neck, and uterine cervix carcinomas (Colpi et al., 2004; Howell & Shalet, 2005). Nevertheless, its full clinical utility is limited due to some adverse side effects including nephrotoxicity and cumulative myelosuppression. Pancytopenia caused by the suppression of bone marrow proliferation and differentiation is a serious risk for chemotherapy. We and some other authors have speculated that DDP nephrotoxicity might lower erythropoietin (Epo) secretion and, by this mechanism, contribute to the anemia that follows therapy with these chemotherapeuticagents (Fjornes et al., 1998; Gao et al., 2006). Although the exact mechanism of DDP – induced nephrotoxicity is not well understood, some investigators have shown that DDP nephrotoxicity is associated with an increase in lipid peroxidation (LPO) in the kidney tissues. This antitumor drug causes generation of reactive oxygen species (ROS), such as superoxideanion and hydroxyl radical, to deplete the glutathione (GSH) levels and to inhibit the activity of antioxidant enzymes in renal tissue. ROS may produce cellular injury and necrosisvia several mechanisms including peroxidation of membrane lipids, protein denaturation and DNA damage (Chirino & Pedraza – Chaverri, 2009; Pérez – Rojas et al., 2011). Our initial experiment also proved this point (Zhang et al., 2012). We hypothesized that ROS may perturb sites of Epo productionin the kidney resulting in anemia and that free radical scavengers may modify this metabolic pathway by scavenging free radical. Vitamin C, as an antioxidant agent, has been shown to be effective in protection from DDP – induced nephrotoxicity (Greggi Antunes et al., 2000; Martinis & Bianchi, 2001). However, the effect of vitamin C on DDP – induced anemia in rats has not been investigated to date. In the present study, we investigated the effects of vitamin C on the level of serum Epo in DDP – induced nephrotoxicity in rats and investigated the effects of vitamin C on DDP – induced anemia in rats.

Materials and methods

Drugs

DDP (Shandong Qilu Pharmaceutical Factory, Shandong, China) was freshly prepared by dissolving in physiologicalsaline solution before use. Vitamin C (Shijiazhuang Siyao Pharmaceutical Co. Ltd, Shijiazhuang, China) was dissolved in distilled water.

Animals

Sprague – awley (SD) rats ($n = 0$, $200 \pm 10g$, Male, Certificate No. SCXK11 – 00 – 0004) were supplied by the Breeding Center of the Institute of Experimental Animals (Peking University Health Science Center, Beijing, China) andhoused in the animal laboratory of our university. The animals were fed with a standard diet and kept on a physiological day – night rhythm.

[Author Introduction] Gao Liping, Li Zen, Guo Zhuoyu, Zhao Yanmeng, Beijing Key Laboratory of Bioactive Substances and Functional Foods, Beijing Union University and College of Arts and Sciences of Beijing Union University

Animal treatments

The rats were divided into six groups; each group containing 10 rats. Anemia was induced with single intravenous (iv) in jection of DDP of 8 mg/kg body weight, which is well documented to induce anemia in rats (Baldwin et al., 1998; Gao et al., 2006; Matsumoto et al., 1990). Vitamin C was administered to animals at the doses of 50 and 100 mg/kg. The dose of vitamin C used in this study was selected on the basis of the previous studies (Greggi Antunes et al., 2000; Martinis & Bianchi, 2001). Group 1 received distilled water by gavage and 10 min after was injected with saline iv. This group served as a negative control. Groups 2 and 3 received a single dose of vitamin C by gavage (50 or 100 mg/kg, respectively) and 10 min later salineiv. Animals of group 4 received distilled water by gavage and were injected with DDP iv. Groups 5 and 6 received the respective doses of vitamin C by gavage and were injected 10 min later with DDP iv. Blood samples were collected by heart puncture under light ether anesthesia 4 and 14 days after saline, DDP injection. Serum was separated in non – heparinizedtubes by centrifugation for 5 min at $1000 \times g$ and stored at $-20℃$ until the analysis. Changes in body weight were also determined during the experiment.

Assays (Epo, Hb, BUN)

Serum Epo was measured by an enzyme – linked immunosorbent assay kit purchased from the Academy of MilitaryMedical Science, EIAAB Inc US, batch number E0028r. The concentration of hemoglobin (Hb) was measured by the cyanmethemoglobin (HiCN) method using an assay kit purchased from the Greatwall Clinical Reagents Corporation (Baoding, China). Blood urea nitrogen (BUN) contents were measured according to the diacetylmonoxime method using an assay kit purchased from the Nanjing Jian cheng Bioengineering Institute (Nanjing, China).

Histopathological examination

Animals were sacrificed on the 14th day after DDP injection. Kidneys were isolated and fixed in 10% formalin forhistopathological studies.

Statistical analysis

Statistical analysis was performed using the analysis of variance (ANOVA) method. Differences between treatments were determined by the Mann – Whitney test. The results were expressed as the meanS. D. in each group, and a statistical probability of $p < 0.05$ was considered to be significant. All the statistical analyses were carried out using SPSS Version12. 0 (SPSS Inc., Chicago, IL).

Results

Effect of DDP – vitamin C combination on body weight

The results of vitamin C on DDP – mediated changes in body weight are shown in Table 1. No differences in body weight were observed among the groups that received only vitamin C compared to the control ($p > 0.05$). A statistically significant weight loss was detected 4 and 14 days after the antitumor injection in the DDP group, when compared to the control group ($p < 0.05$). The decrease in body weight in DDP – treated animals was not changed with the administration of different doses of vitamin C.

Table 1 Effect of vitamin C (VC; 50 or 100 mg/kg) on body weight 4 or 14 days after the administration of cisplatin in travenous (DDP; 8mg/kg).

Groups	Body weight (g)	
	4 days	14 days
Control	170.2 ± 13.91	234.33 ± 20.29
VC50	172.6 ± 10.6	241.5 ± 18.6

Groups	Body weight (g)	
	4 days	14 days
VC100	166.3 ± 12.7	245.3 ± 21.75
DDP	138.1 ± 12.1[a]	196.67 ± 13.63[a]
DDP + VC50	140.66 ± 11.52[a]	203.25 ± 12.98[a]
DDP + VC100	141.6 ± 10.53[a]	190.46 ± 14.75[a]

Each value represents meanSD of six animals.

[a] Statistically significant when compared to control $p < 50.05$.

Effect of DDP – vitamin C combination on serum BUN

Table 2 shows the effects of oral vitamin C on DDP – mediated increases in serum BUN. No differences in serum BUN were observed among the groups that received only vitamin C compared to the control ($p < 0.05$). The antitumor alone led to about 150% and 54% enhancement in the value of serum BUN compared to the control group 4 or 14 days after the i.p. treatment ($p < 0.05$). Administration of vitamin C at doses of 100 mg/kg to rats that received DDP led to a significant reduction in these values.

Table 2 Effect of vitamin C (VC; 50 or 100 mg/kg) on BUN concentrations 4 or 14 days after the administration of cisplatin intravenous (DDP; 8mg/kg).

Groups	BUN (mmol/l)	
	4 days	14 days
Control	5.92 ± 0.78	6.88 ± 1.13
VC50	6.31 ± 0.93	6.57 ± 0.89
VC100	5.39 ± 0.68	5.51 ± 1.32
DDP	14.83 ± 2.65[a]	10.6 ± 2.24[a]
DDP + VC50	12.34 ± 2.33[a]	9.2 ± 2.36[a]
DDP + VC100	9.28 ± 2.71[a,b]	7.56 ± 1.93[a,b]

Each value represents meanSD of six animals.

[a] Statistically significant when compared to control $p < 0.05$.

[b] Statistically significant when compared to DDP alone $p < 0.05$.

Effect of DDP – vitamin C combination on serum Epo

The effect of treatment of adult rats with vitamin C on DDP mediated changes in the levels of serum Epo is shown in Table 3. No differences in serum Epo were observed among the groups that received only vitamin C compared to the control ($p < 0.05$). In the DDP group, the antitumor injection resulted in a decrease in serum Epo 4 and 14 days after the treatment compared to the control group ($p < 0.05$). This decrease was prevented by concurrent administration of vitamin C at doses of 100 mg/kg. ($p < 0.05$).

Effect of DDP – vitamin C combination on Hb

The effects of vitamin C on DDP – mediated changes in Hb content are shown in Table 4. The Hb content was higher in groups treated with only vitamin C than in the control, but this effect was not statistically significant ($p > 0.05$). The DDP treatment resulted in a 35.65% decrease in Hb content 14 days after DDP administration compared to respective controls ($p < 0.05$). This decrease was prevented by concurrent administration of vitamin C at doses of 100 mg/kg ($p < 0.05$).

Effect of DDP – vitamin C combination on pathological changes

Histopathological study of kidney tissue 14 days after DDP administration showed tubular epithelial desquamation, remarkable vaculoation, hyaline casts in some tubules and lymphocytic infiltration in the renal interstitium in comparison with the controls (Fig. 1 and 2). Treatment of vitamin C at doses of 100 mg/kg decreased the nephrotoxic effect of DDP and there were no significant pathological changes apart from an occasional hyaline cast in some tubules (Fig. 3). However, no amelioratipe changes in treatment of vitamin C at doses of 50 mg/kg were observed in DDP-induced pathological changes when compared with the DDP-alone group (Fig. 4).

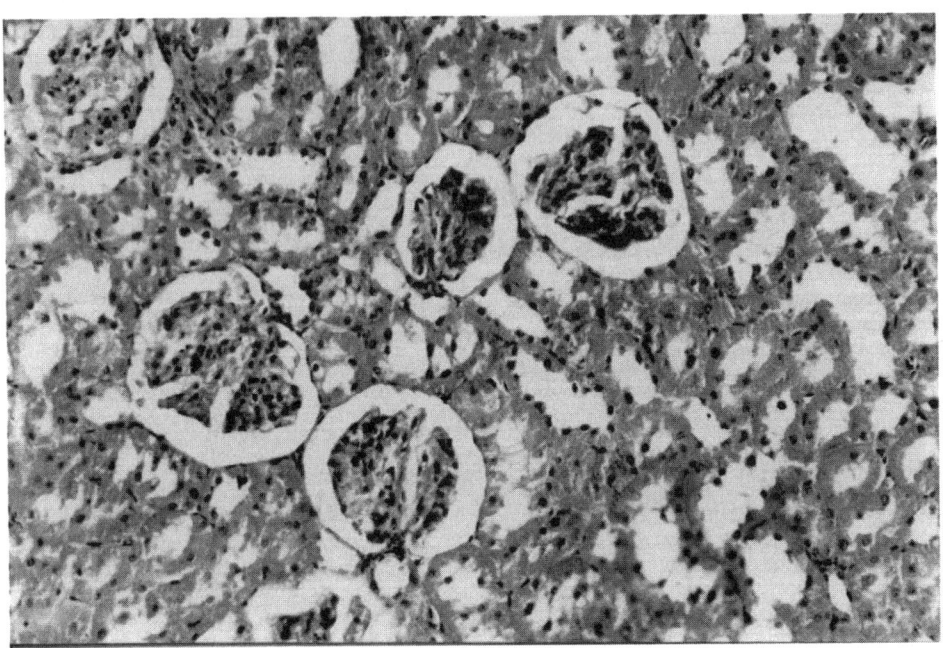

Fig. 1 Light microscopy of renal tissue from rats injecting control. Renal tubules are normal. H&E ×400.

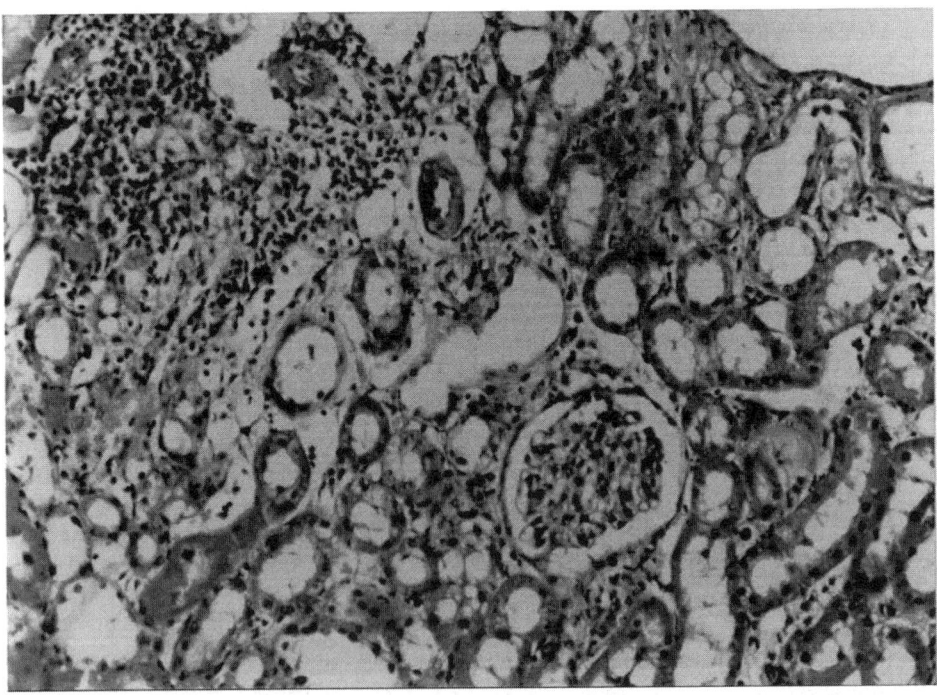

Fig. 2 Light microscopy of renal tissue from rats injecting DDP alone. Significant tubular epithelial desquamation, remarkable vaculoation, hyaline casts in some tubules and lymphocytic infiltration were seen in the renal interstitium. H&E ×400.

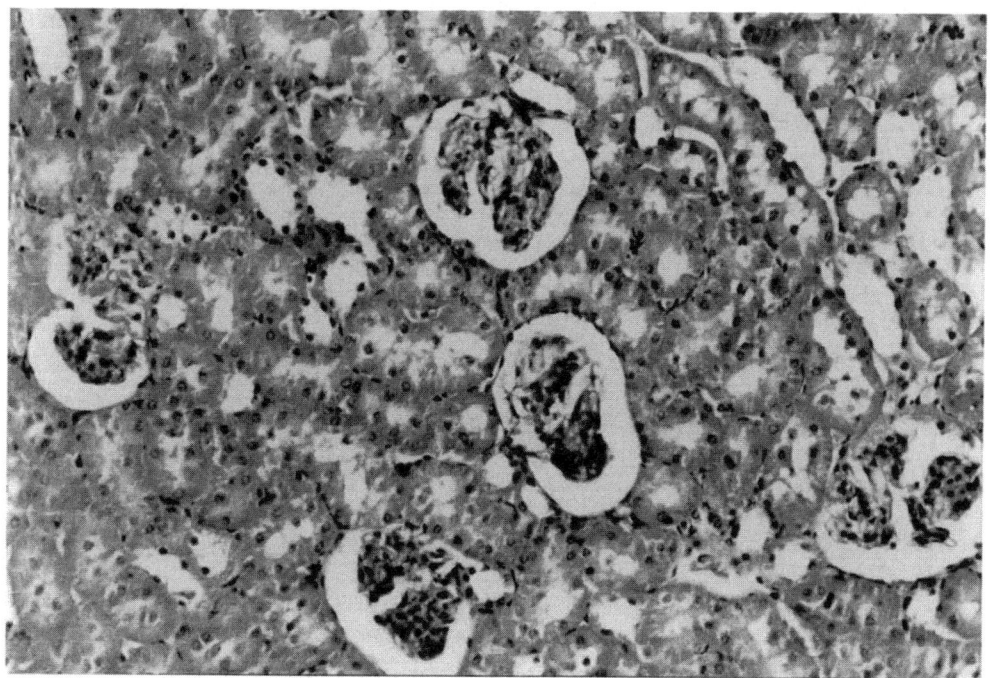

Fig. 3 Light microscopy of renal tissue from rats injecting 100 mg/kg vitamin C plus DDP. There were no significant pathological changes apart from an occasional hyaline cast in some tubules. H&E ×400.

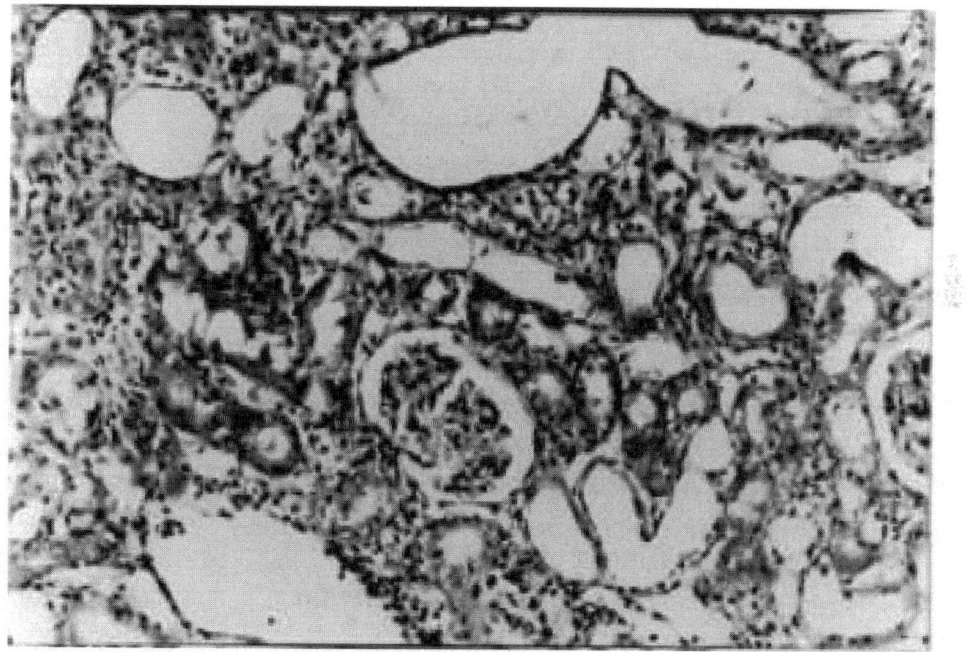

Fig. 4 Light microscopy of renal tissue from rats injecting 50mg/kg vitamin C plus DDP. Significant tubular epithelial desquamation, remarkable vaculoation, hyaline casts in some tubules and lymphocytic infiltration were seen in the renal interstitium H & E ×400.

Discussion

Matsumoto et al. (1990) observed that DDP – suppressed Epo production, with a minimum peak observed 4 days after DDP injection and caused an anemia in rats 14 days after DDP injection. In the present study, blood samples were collected by heart puncture under light ether anesthesia 4 and 14 days after the administration of vitamin C and/or DDP. During the experiment, the rats treated with DDP showed a decrease in body weight. This weight loss was not prevented by the administration of vitamin C. DDP – induced weight loss, already reported by other authors, may be due to the gastrointestinal toxicity or by lessened ingestion of food (Atessahin et al., 2005).

Table 3 Effect of vitamin C (VC; 50 or 100mg/kg) on serum Epo level 4 or 14 days after the administration of cisplatin intravenous (DDP; 8mg/kg).

Groups	Eqo (mU/ml)	
	4 days	14 days
Control	10.8 ± 3.9	11.3 ± 4.8
VC50	11.2 ± 4.1	10.2 ± 3.5
VC100	9.5 ± 3.7	11.6 ± 5.1
DDP	3.6 ± 2.9^a	4.1 ± 5.7^a
DDP + VC50	4.1 ± 3.5^a	4.9 ± 5.3^a
DDP + VC100	6.7 ± 4.3^b	8.3 ± 6.2^b

Each value represents meanSD of six animals.
[a] Statistically significant when compared to control $p < 0.05$.
[b] Statistically significant when compared to DDP alone $p < 0.05$.

Table 4 Effect of vitamin C (VC; 50 or 100 mg/kg) on Hb concentrations 4 or 14 days after the administration of cisplatin intravenous (DDP; 8mg/kg).

Groups	Hb (g/dl)	
	4 days	14 days
Control	129.6 ± 9.3	131.62 ± 13.4
VC50	134.9 ± 12.2	132.8 ± 14
VC100	136.2 ± 11.6	135.3 ± 9.6
DDP	131.47 ± 11.4	84.7 ± 15.6^a
DDP + VC50	133.8 ± 12.4	98.5 ± 11.7^a
DDP + VC100	136.1 ± 11.6	$114.9 \pm 16.3^{a,b}$

Each value represents meanSD of six animals.
[a] Statistically significant when compared to control $p < 50.05$.
[b] Statistically significant when compared to DDP alone $p < 50.05$.

Cancer patients undergoing chemotherapy with DDP containing regiments often develop anemia (Heddens et al., 2002). The exact mechanisms of DDP – induced anemia are still unclear. Recent studies suggested that changes of Epoconcentration plays a significant role. Epo is a cytokine that specifically regulates differentiation and proliferation of erythroid progenitor cells. Studies using *in situ* hybridization show that Epo is synthesized by peritubular interstitium of cortex and out medulla of kidney (Maxwell et al., 1993; Schuster et al., 1992). Epo can also be produced in proximaltubules (Mujais et al., 1999). The DDP nephrotoxicity is predominately in renal proximal tubules (Yildirim et al., 2003). Some studies demonstrated that the decreased serum Epo level in patients treated with DDP is due to its nephrotoxicity (Wood & Hrushesky, 1995). Other studies suggested that during DDP – induced anemia Epo failed to respond to the Hb reduction and Epo was remained at low level (Bokkel Huinink et al., 1998; Cazzola, 2000). It is also reported that anemia induced by DDP is related to iron supply to erythroblasts instead of the lack of Epo (Anat et al., 1993; Baliga et al., 1998). In the present study, it was shown that the administration of DDP to rats caused a reduction in serum Epo on day 4 and 14, which correlated with increased serum BUN. These biochemical parameters were well correlated with the renal histological results. On the other hand, the effect of DDP on Hb was not observed 4 days after the treatment. Hb was decreased by DDP 14 days after the treatment. These data demonstrate that acute renal failure occurs prior to the anemia in DDP – treated rats. Since DDP also decreased serum Epo concentration, this indicated that DDPinduced nephrotoxicity was responsible for the impaired production of Epo and caused anemia.

Although the exact mechanism of DDP – induced nephrotoxicity is not well understood, some investigators have shown that DDP nephrotoxicity is associated with an increase in lipid peroxidation (LPO) in the kidney tissues. This antitumor drug causes the generation of reactive oxygen species (ROS) to deplete the glutathione (GSH) levels and to inhibit the activity of antioxidant enzymes in the renal tissue. ROS may produce cellular injury and necrosis via several mechanisms including peroxidation of membrane lipids, protein denaturation and DNA damage (Chirino & Pedraza – Chaverri, 2009; Pe'rez – Rojas et al., 2011; Zhang et al., 2012). Various free radical scavengers have been shown to be effective in protection from DDP – induced nephrotoxicity and treatment with such agentsprovided significant protection against DDP – induced acute renal failure (Naziroglu et al., 2004; Sueishi et al., 2002; Yildirim et al., 2003). Vitamin C is an antioxidant and strong free radical scavenger (Anderson, 1996). Its antioxidant activity is useful for the protection of cellular macromolecules from oxidative damage induced by different agents. Previous studies have shown that vitamin C treatment resulted in high antioxidant enzymes and also prevented lipid peroxidation induced by Polychlorinated biphenyls (Aroclor, 1254) in hypothalamus of albino rats (Muthuvel et al., 2006). In addition, vitamin C has been shown to significantly attenuate the increase of lipid peroxidation in renal tissue after DDP toxicity (Greggi Antunes et al., 2000; Martinis & Bianchi, 2001). We hypothesized that ROS may perturb sites of Epo production in the kidney resulting in anemia. Vitamin C administration may prevent DDP – induced anemia in rat by its free radical – trapping activity. In the present study, vitamin C at doses of 100 mg/kg result a lower level of serum BUN and a higher level of Hb and serum Epo than only DDP – received group. Vitamin C at doses of 50 mg/kg also provided similar effects on these parameters but at a lower extent. The histological evaluation of the kidney preparations in pre – treatment group also revealed a decrease DDP – induced tubular damage. These observations indicated that vitamin C provided a significant protection against DDPinduced nephrotoxicity and anemia. In conclusion, it was shown that DDP – treatment – induced renal damage and anemia and especially concurrent administration of vitamin C at doses of 100 mg/kg provided protective effect against this DDP – induced nephrotoxicity and anemia.

Declaration of interest

The authors report no conflicts of interest. The authors alone are responsible for the content and writing of this article. This work was supported by grants from the Talents Support Project of Talents Enhancing University Development Plan in Beijing Union University (BPHR2011A01).

References

[1] Anat H, Inanc SE, Dalay N, et al. (1993). Effect of cisplatin on erythropoietin and iron changes. Eur J Cancer 29: 777.

[2] Anderson D. (1996). Antioxidant defenses against reactive oxygen species causing genetic and other damage. Mutat Res 350: 103 – 108.

[3] Atessahin A, Yilmaz S, Karahan I, et al. (2005). Effects of lycopene against cisplatin – induced nephrotoxicity and oxidative stress in rats. Toxicology 212: 116 – 123.

[4] Baldwin MD, Zhou XJ, Ing TS, Vaziri ND. (1998). Erythropoietin ameliorates anemia of cisplatin induced acute renal failure. J ASAIO 44: 44 – 47.

[5] Baliga R, Zhang Z, Baliga M, et al. (1998). In vitro and in vivo evidence suggesting a role for iron in cisplatin – induced nephrotoxicity. Kidney Int 53: 394 – 401.

[6] Bokkel Huinink WW, Swart CA, Van Toorn DW, et al. (1998). Controlled multicentre study of the influence of subcutaneous recombinant human erythropoietin on anaemia and transfusion dependency in patients with ovarian carcinoma treated with platinum – based chemotherapy. Med Oncol 15: 174 – 182.

[7] Cazzola M. (2000). Mechanisms of anaemia in patients with malignancy: implications for the clinical use of recombinant human erythropoietin. Med Oncol 17: S11 – 16.

[8] Chirino YI, Pedraza – Chaverr J. (2009). Role of oxidative and nitrosative stress in cisplatin – induced nephrotoxicity. Exper Toxicol Pathol 61: 223 – 242.

[9] Colpi GM, Contalbi GF, Nerva F, *et al.* (2004). Testicular function following chemo - radiotherapy. Eur J Obstet Gynecol Reprod Biol 113: S2 - 6.

[10] Fjornes T, Wiedemann GJ, Sack K, *et al.* (1998). Serum erythropoietin and creatinine concentrations as predictipe factors for response to recombinant human erythropoietin treatment in anaemic tumor patients on chemotherapy. Oncol Reports 5: 81 - 86.

[11] Gao LP, Ma RY, Cheng SZ. (2006). Changes of serum erythropoietin during cisplatin - or 5 - fluorouracil - induced anemia in rats. Toxicol Mech Methods 16: 501 - 506.

[12] Greggi Antunes LM, Darin JD, Bianchi MdeP. (2000). Protective effects of vitamin C against cisplatin - induced nephrotoxicity and lipid peroxidation in adult rats: a dose - dependent study. Pharmacol Res 41: 405 - 411.

[13] Heddens D, Alberts DS, Hannigan EV, *et al.* (2002). Prediction of the need for red cell transfusion in newly diagnosed ovarian cancer patients undergoing platinum - based treatment. Gynecol Oncol 86: 239 - 243.

[14] Howell SJ, Shalet SM. (2005). Spermatogenesis after cancer treatment: damage and recovery. J Natl Cancer Inst Monogr 34: 12 - 17.

[15] Martinis BS, Bianchi M deP. (2001). Effect of vitamin C supplementation against cisplatin - induced toxicity and oxidative DNA damage in rats. Pharmacol Res 44: 317 - 320.

[16] Matsumoto T, Endoh K, Kamisango K, *et al.* (1990). Effect of recombinant human erythropoietin on cancer drug - induced anaemia. Br J Haem 75: 463 - 468.

[17] Maxwell PH, Osmond MK, Pugh CW, *et al.* (1993). Identification of the renal erythropoietin - producing cells using transgenic mice. Kidney Int 44: 149 - 162.

[18] Mujais SK, Beru N, Pullman TN, Goldwasser E. (1999). Erythropoietin is produced by tubular cells of the rat kidney. Cell Biochem Biophys 30: 153 - 166.

[19] Muthuvel R, Venkataraman P, Krishnamoorthy G, *et al.* (2006). Antioxidant effect of ascorbic acid on PCB (Aroclor 1254) induced oxidative stress in hypothalamus of albino rats. Clin Chim Acta 365: 297 - 303.

[20] Naziroglu M, Karaoglu A, Aksoy AO. (2004). Selenium and high dose vitamin E administration protects cisplatin - induced oxidative damage to renal, liver and lens tissues in rats. Toxicology 195: 221 - 230.

[21] Pe'rez - Rojas JM, Guerrero - Beltra'n CE, Cruz C, *et al.* (2011). Preventive effect of tert - butylhydroquinone on cisplatin - induced nephrotoxicity in rats. Food Chem Toxicol 49: 2631 - 2637.

[22] Schuster SJ, Koury ST, Bohrer M, *et al.* (1992). Cellular sites of extrarenal and renal erythropoietin production in anaemic rats. Br J Haem 81: 153 - 159.

[23] Sueishi K, Mishima K, Makino K, *et al.* (2002). Protection by a radical scavenger edaravone against cisplatin - induced nephrotoxicity in rats. Eur J Pharmacol 451: 203 - 208.

[24] Wood PA, Hrushesky WJ. (1995). Cisplatin - associated anemia: an erythropoietin deficiency syndrome. J Clin Invest 95: 1650 - 1659.

[25] Yildirim Z, Sogut S, Odaci E, et al. (2003). Oral erdosteine administration attenuates cisplatin - induced renal tubular damage in rats. Pharmacol Res 47: 149 - 156.

[26] Zhang HL, Gao LP, Leng HT, Li Z. (2012). Protective effect of *Lycium barbarum* polysaccharide against cisplatin - induced nephrotoxicity in Rats. Food Sci 33: 268 - 271 (in Chinese).

加权线性支持向量分类机的数据扰动分析

蔡 春

1 引 言

设有训练集 $T = \{(x_1, y_1), (x_2, y_2) \cdots, (x_m, y_m)\} \in \{(X \times Y)^m\}$，其中训练输入 $x_i \in X = R^n$，训练输出 $y_i \in Y = \{-1, +1\}$，$i=1, \cdots, m$。数据挖掘问题中的分类问题即根据训练集 T 寻找 R^n 上的实值函数 $f(x)$，以便用决策函数 $\mathrm{sgn} f(x)$ 推断任一输入 x 相对应输出值[1]。支持向量机（Support Vector Machines, SVM）是数据挖掘的新方法。解决分类问题的支持向量机方法称支持向量分类机（Support Vector Classifier, SVC）。支持向量分类机是一种基于训练集的新的分类学习方法[2]它可以寻找出那些对分类有较好区分能力的支持向量[3]。当两类点线性可分时，按照最大化两类样本点的间隔原则找到决策函数[4-8]；当线性不可分时，按照期望风险最小化原则寻找决策函数，因而它有较好的推广性能和较高的分类准确率。支持向量机方法在解决小样本机器学习问题中表现出特有的优势，开始成为克服"维数灾难"和"过学习"等传统困难的有力手段，在应用中表现出令人满意的结果，它已初步表现出很多优于已有方法的性能，成为一种新的通用机器学习方法，并将有力地推动机器学习理论和技术的发展。支持向量机方法在许多领域都获得了成功的应用，如：模式识别[9-11]，回归、函数拟合[12-13]等，现也被国内推广到经济预测[14]、消费信贷信用评估[15]等领域，SVC 正在成为国内外新的研究热点。

考虑较具一般性的加权线性支持向量分类机，其原始问题为

$$\min_{\omega,\xi} \tau(\omega,b,\xi) = \frac{1}{2}\|\omega\|^2 + \sum_{i=1}^m C_i \xi_i$$

$$\text{s.t. } g_i(\omega,b,\xi) = -y_i(x_i \cdot \omega + b) - \xi_i + 1 \leq 0 \quad i=1,2,\cdots,m \quad (1.1)$$

$$g_{m+i}(\omega, b, \xi) = -\xi_i \leq 0, i=1, 2, \cdots, m$$

其中 $(x_i, y_i) \in R^n \times \{-1, +1\}$。

这是一个二次规划问题。Wolfe 对偶理论[1]为问题的求解提供了有效的求解方法。具体说，建立原始问题 (1.1) 的对偶问题

$$\max_{\alpha} W(\alpha) = \sum_{i=1}^m \alpha_i - \frac{1}{2}\sum_{i,j}^m \alpha_i \alpha_j y_i y_j (x_i \cdot x_j)$$

$$\text{s.t } \begin{cases} \sum_{i=1}^m \alpha_i y_i = 0 \\ C_i \geq \alpha_i \geq 0 \quad i=1,\cdots,m \end{cases} \quad (1.2)$$

求得最优解 $\alpha^* = (\alpha_1^*, \alpha_2^*, \cdots, \alpha_m^*)^T$，据此求得原始问题的解 (1.1) 的解：

$$w^* = \sum_{i=1}^m a_i^* y_i x_i \quad b = y_i - w \cdot x_i = y_i - \sum_{j=1}^m a_j(x_j, x_i)(C_i > a_i > 0)$$

同时，对于这一对原始对偶二次规划问题的解的理论，也已有了完整的结果[1]。

对于已有成熟求解理论和方法的支持向量分类机问题，其稳定性和灵敏度分析问题也就自然成为要研究的问题。事实上，问题数据中的训练输入 x_i ($i=1, 2, \cdots, m$) 是某些特征的测定值，它只是真值的近似，使用这些近似值建立起支持向量分类机问题，数据误差必将影响所对应规划问题的解以及决策函数。是不是数据误差很小时，解的误差也很小，从而对决策函数没有本质性的影响？也就是说问题的解稳定性如何？此外，对于能有所限定的数据误差，对它所引起的解的误差大小能否有一个定量的估

[资助项目] 北京骨干教师资助 (PHR201008292); 北京市教委项目 (km201111417004)。
[作者简介] 蔡春, 北京联合大学应用文理学院。

计？甚至计对解随数据变化的依赖关系可否作出一定的推断？我们把这些归于灵敏度分析问题。本文的数据扰动分析方法，一方面是针对支持向量机问题解的稳定性做分析，同时也为支持向量机问题解进行灵敏度分析。

一般非线性规划关于灵敏度分析的定理 1.1 为本文提供了一般的理论基础[16-17]。考虑更一般化的模型：

$$\begin{cases} \min f(x, p) \\ s.t. \ g(x, p) \leq 0 \\ h(x, p) = 0 \end{cases} \tag{1.3}$$

(1.3) 称为非线性参数规划问题，其中 $p = R^t$ 是参数，在某个集合 P 上取值，函数 $f: R^n \times p \to R$，$g: R^n \times p \to R^m$，$h: R^n \times p \to R^l$。Fiacco 针对 (1.3) 建立了定理 1.1。

定理 1.1 考虑问题 (1.3)，设 x^* 是问题 (1.3) 在 $p = p_0 \in P$ 的可行解，假设

在 (x^*, p_0) 的某个邻域中 f、g、h 关于 x 为二次连续可微，g、h 以及它们对于 x 的梯度 $\nabla f(x, p)$，$\nabla_x g_i(x, p)$ 和 $\nabla_x h_i(x, p)$ 对 p 可微，并且所有这些函数和导数关于 (x, p) 为连续。

对于 (1.3) 在 $p = p_0 \in P$ 处对应的最优化问题，x^* 满足二阶充分条件，相应的乘子为 u^*, v^*。

向量组 $\nabla_x g_i(x^*, p_0)$, $i \in I$, $\nabla_x h_i(x^*, p_0)$, $i = 1, 2, \cdots, l$ 线性无关。其中 $I = \{i \mid g_i(x^*, p_0) = 0\}$ 为问题 (1.3) $p = p_0 \in P$ 在 x^* 的起作用集。

严格互补松弛条件成立，即对任意 $i \in I$，u_i^* 和 $g_i(x^*, p_0)$ 不同时为零。那么有下述结论成立：

1) x^* 为问题 (1.3) 在 $p = p_0 \in P$ 的孤立的局部最优解，u^*, v^* 是相应于 x^* 的惟一乘子。

2) 存在 p_0 的邻域 $N(p_0)$，在 $N(p_0)$ 上存在惟一连续可微的函数

$$y(p) = [x(p)^T, u(p)^T, v(p)^T]^T$$

使得

$$y(p_0) = y^* = [x^{*T}, u^{*T}, v^{*T}]^T$$

且对任意的 $p \in N(p_0)$，对于问题 (1.3)，$x(p)$ 为可行解，并且起作用集保持不变；即

$$I(x(p), p) \equiv I(x^*, p_0) \tag{1.4}$$

起作用函数梯度组线性无关性保持成立；$x(p)$ 和 $u(p)$ 使严格互补性质保持成立；$x(p)$ 满足二阶充分条件，相应的乘子为 $u(p)$, $v(p)$。因而 $x(p)$ 为问题 (1.3) 的孤立局部最优解，$u(p)$, $v(p)$ 为相应的惟一乘子。

3) 解的偏导数关系式为：

$$M(p) \begin{pmatrix} \left(\frac{\partial X}{\partial p}\right)^T \\ \left(\frac{\partial u}{\partial p}\right)^T \\ \left(\frac{\partial v}{\partial p}\right)^T \end{pmatrix} = M_1(p) \tag{1.5}$$

其中 $M(p)$ 为 $(n+m+l) \times (n+m+l)$ 矩阵，

$$M(p) = \begin{pmatrix} \nabla^2 L & \nabla_{g_1}(x, p) & \cdots & \nabla_{g_m}(x, p) & \nabla h_1(x, p) & \cdots & \nabla h_l(x, p) \\ u_1 \nabla g_1(x, p) & g_1(x, p) & & & 0 & & 0 \\ \vdots & & \ddots & & \vdots & \cdots & \vdots \\ u_m \nabla g_m(x, p) & & & g_m(x, p) & 0 & & 0 \\ \nabla h_1(x, p)^T & 0 & \cdots & 0 & 0 & & 0 \\ \vdots & \vdots & & \vdots & \vdots & & \vdots \\ \nabla h_1(x, p)^T & 0 & \cdots & 0 & 0 & & 0 \end{pmatrix}$$

(1.6)

$$M_1(p) = -\left[\frac{\partial (\nabla_x L)}{\partial p}, u_1 \nabla_p g_1, \cdots, u_m \nabla_p g_m, \frac{\partial h}{\partial p}\right]^T \tag{1.7}$$

为 $(n+m+l) \times t$ 矩阵；

其中，$L = f(x, p) + u^T g(x, p) + v^T h(x, p)$ 为拉格朗日函数。

本文在第二节针对加权线性支持向量分类机的优化问题建立数据扰动分析基本定理。第三节建立了带有核函数的一般支持向量分类机数据扰动分析定理。第四节小结支持向量分类机数据扰动分析定理。

2 加权线性支持向量分类机数据扰动分析

加权线性支持向量分类机是支持向量分类机的基础，由于模型简单且在实际问题中取得广泛的应用。对于加权线性支持向量分类机优化问题 (1.1)，为表述数据对解的影响，在此假设 p 是数据参数，随数据扰动分析的需要，它可以代表 (1.1) 输入数据的一部分，或全部输入数据，p_0 是参数 p 的一个取值，此处则对应于已知的训练输入数据。这样将输入数据的地位二重化，即一方面是构成问题 (1.1) 的数据，另一方面是可变化的参量，这样我们便有了一个含有参数 p 的线性支持向量分类机问题 (1.1)，从而将我们的数据扰动分析归入定理 1.1 的理论框架。下面给出含参数的支持向量分类机问题 (1.1) 的数据扰动分析基本定理。

为了后面基本定理 2.2 表述方便，设 (w^*, b^*, ξ^*) 是问题 (1.1) 的最优解，相应于 (w^*, b^*, ξ^*)，训练数据 $(x_1, y_1), (x_2, y_2), \cdots, (x_m, y_m)$ 分为如下 A、B、C 三类：

A 类：超平面 $w^* \cdot x + b^* = 1$ 上 $y_i = +1$ 的点和超平面 $w^* \cdot x + b^* = -1$ 上 $y_i = -1$ 的点，为方便，记此类点为 $(x_1, y_1), (x_2, y_2), \cdots, (x_t, y_t)$。

B 类：开半空间 $w^* \cdot x + b^* > 1$ 中 $y_i = +1$ 的点和开半空间 $w^* \cdot x + b^* < -1$ 中 $y_i = -1$ 的点，为方便，记此类点为 $(x_{t+1}, y_{t+1}), (x_{t+2}, y_{t+2}), \cdots, (x_s, y_s)$。

C 类：开半空间 $w^* \cdot x + b^* < 1$ 中 $y_i = +1$ 的点和开半空间 $w^* \cdot x + b^* > -1$ 的点，为方便，记此类点为 $(x_{s+1}, y_{s+1}), (x_{s+2}, y_{s+2}), \cdots, (x_m, y_m)$。

定义了 A、B、C 三类点后，我们同时以符号 A、B、C 记这三类数据点的下标．这样关于起作用约束指标集我们有引理 2.1 和数据扰动分析定理 2.1。

引理 2.1 设 (w^*, b^*, ξ^*) 为 (1.1) 的最优解，则起作用约束指标集为：

$$I(w^*, b^*, \xi^*) = A \cup (m+A) \cup (m+B) \cup C$$
$$= \{1, \cdots, t, m+1, \cdots, m+t, m+t+1, \cdots, m+s, s, \cdots, m\} \quad (2.1)$$

定理 2.1 设 $z^* = (w^* b^*, \xi^*)$ 为 (1.1) 在 $p = p_0$ 的最优解，对应的拉格朗日乘子为 $a^* \Rightarrow (a_1^*, a_2^*, \cdots, a_{2m}^*)^T \geq 0$，假设

1) A 类的输入 $x_1, x_2, \cdots, x_t$ 全为支持向量，且对应的乘子 $\alpha_i < C_i$ ($i=1, \cdots, t$)。

2) 向量组 $\begin{pmatrix} y_1 x_1 \\ y_1 \end{pmatrix}, \begin{pmatrix} y_2 x_2 \\ y_2 \end{pmatrix}, \cdots, \begin{pmatrix} y_t x_t \\ y_t \end{pmatrix}$ 线性无关。

则有下面结论：

1) (w^*, b^*, ξ^*) 为 (1.1) 在 $p = p_0$ 孤立最优解，并且对应的拉格朗日乘子 $\alpha^* = (\alpha_1^*, \alpha_2^*, \cdots, \alpha_{2m}^*)^T \geq 0$ 为惟一的。

2) 存在 P_0 的邻域 $N(p_0)$，在 $N(p_0)$ 上存在惟一连续可微函数 $y(p) = (w(p), b(p), \xi(p), \alpha(p))$．使得①$y(p_0) = (w^*, b^*, \xi^*, \alpha^*) = (z^*, \alpha^*)$，②对任意的 $p \in N(p_0)$，对应于 p 的问题 (1.1)，$z(p) = (w(p), b(p), \xi(p))$ 为可行解，③A、B、C 三类点集合不变，从而起作用集保持不变；即

$$A(z(p), p) \equiv A(z^*, p_0)$$
$$B(z(p), p) \equiv B(z^*, p_0)$$
$$C(z(p), p) \equiv C(z^*, p_0)$$
$$I(z(p), p) \equiv I(z^*, p_0)$$
$$(2.2)$$

④支持向量集不变，即对于 $\xi_i(p) > 0$ 所对应的 $\alpha_i(p) = C_i$ 支持向量以及 $\xi_i(p) = 0$ 的点所对应的 $a_i(p) < C_i$ 保持不变；⑤线性无关性保持成立；⑥$z(p)$ 满足二阶充分条件，相应的乘子为 $\alpha(p)$；⑦因而 $z(p)$ 为问题 (1.1) 的孤立最优解，$\alpha(p)$ 为相应的惟一乘子。⑧$y(p) = (w(p), b(p), \xi$

(p)，$\alpha(p)$）的偏导数满足

$$M(p)\begin{pmatrix}\left(\dfrac{\partial w}{\partial p}\right)^{\mathrm{T}}\\ \left(\dfrac{\partial b}{\partial p}\right)^{\mathrm{T}}\\ \left(\dfrac{\partial \xi}{\partial p}\right)^{\mathrm{T}}\\ \left(\dfrac{\partial \alpha}{\partial p}\right)^{\mathrm{T}}\end{pmatrix}=M_1(p) \tag{2.3}$$

其中

$$M(p)=\begin{pmatrix}\nabla^2 L & \nabla g_1(w,b,\xi,p) & \cdots & \nabla g_{2m}(w,b,\xi,p)\\ \alpha_1 \nabla g_1(w,b,\xi,p)^{\mathrm{T}} & g_1(w,b,\xi,p) & & \\ \vdots & & \ddots & 0\\ \alpha_{2m}\nabla g_{2m}(w,b,\xi,p)^{\mathrm{T}} & & \cdots & g_{2m}(w,b,\xi,p)\end{pmatrix} \tag{2.4}$$

$$M_1(p)=-\left[\dfrac{\partial(\nabla_x L)}{\partial p},\ \alpha_1 \nabla_p g_1,\ \cdots,\ \alpha_{2m}\nabla_p g_{2m}\right]^{\mathrm{T}} \tag{2.5}$$

$$\nabla g_i(w,b,\xi)=(-y_i x_i?\ -y_i?\ -1,\ 0\cdots 0)^{\mathrm{T}}\quad (i=1,2,\cdots,m)$$
$$\uparrow$$
$$\text{第 }(n+1+i)\text{ 个位置}$$

$$\nabla g_{m+i}(w,b,\xi)=(0,0,-1,0\cdots 0)^{\mathrm{T}}\quad (i=1,2,\cdots m)$$
$$\uparrow$$
$$\text{第 }(n+1+i)\text{ 个位置}$$

特别有：

$$M(p_0)\begin{pmatrix}\left(\dfrac{\partial w}{\partial p}\right)^{\mathrm{T}}\\ \left(\dfrac{\partial b}{\partial p}\right)^{\mathrm{T}}\\ \left(\dfrac{\partial \xi}{\partial p}\right)^{\mathrm{T}}\\ \left(\dfrac{\partial \alpha}{\partial p}\right)^{\mathrm{T}}\end{pmatrix}_{p=p_0}=M_1(p_0) \tag{2.6}$$

证明 由 $x_1, x_2, \cdots, x_t$ 为 A 类支持向量，且对应的乘子 $\alpha_i < C_i$（$i=1,\cdots,t$），保证了 (w^*, b^*, ξ^*) 满足二阶充分条件。

现在证明满足严格互补条件。注意
$$I(w^*,b^*,\xi^*)=A\cup(m+A)\cup(m+B)\cup C$$
由假设 $x_1, x_2, \cdots, x_t$ 全为支持向量，则对应的乘子 $\alpha_i^* > 0$（$\forall i \in A$），又 $\alpha_i^* <{}^* C_i$（$i=1,\cdots,t$），则有乘子

$$\alpha_{m+i}^* = C_i - \alpha_i^* > 0 \quad (\forall\, m+i \in m+A)$$

当 $i \in B$，B 类的样本点对应的乘子 $\alpha_i^* = 0$，从而
$$\alpha_{i+m}^* = C_i \quad (\forall\, m+i \in m+B)$$

当 $i \in C$，因为 $\xi_i^* > 0$，$\alpha_{i+m}^* = 0$，所以 C 类的样本点对应的乘子 $\alpha_i^* = C_i$（$\forall i \in C$），严格互补条件成立得证。

现在证明梯度组 $\{\nabla g_i, i \in I(w^*, b^*, \xi^*)\}$ 线性无关。考察所有起作用约束梯度组的线性组合，假设存在系数 $\{c_i \mid i \in I\}$ 使它们的线性组合为 0，即

$$\begin{pmatrix} -y_1x_1 \\ -y_1 \\ -1 \\ 0 \\ 0 \\ 0 \\ \vdots \\ 0 \\ 0 \end{pmatrix} + c_{m+1}\begin{pmatrix} 0 \\ 0 \\ -1 \\ 0 \\ 0 \\ 0 \\ \vdots \\ 0 \\ 0 \end{pmatrix} + \cdots c_t\begin{pmatrix} -y_tx_t \\ -y_t \\ 0 \\ -1 \\ 0 \\ 0 \\ \vdots \\ 0 \\ 0 \end{pmatrix} + c_{m+t}\begin{pmatrix} 0 \\ 0 \\ 0 \\ -1 \\ 0 \\ 0 \\ \vdots \\ 0 \\ 0 \end{pmatrix} + c_{m+t+1}$$

$$\begin{pmatrix} 0 \\ 0 \\ 0 \\ 0 \\ -1 \\ 0 \\ \vdots \\ 0 \\ 0 \end{pmatrix} + \cdots c_{m+s}\begin{pmatrix} 0 \\ 0 \\ 0 \\ 0 \\ 0 \\ -1 \\ \vdots \\ 0 \\ 0 \end{pmatrix} + c_{s+1}\begin{pmatrix} -y_{s+1}x_{s+1} \\ -y_{s+1} \\ 0 \\ 0 \\ 0 \\ 0 \\ \vdots \\ -1 \\ 0 \end{pmatrix} + \cdots c_m\begin{pmatrix} -y_mx_m \\ -y_m \\ 0 \\ 0 \\ 0 \\ 0 \\ \vdots \\ 0 \\ -1 \end{pmatrix} = 0 \tag{2.7}$$

首先可以得到

$$c_{m+t+1} = \cdots = c_{m+s} = c_{s+1} = \cdots = c_m = 0$$

于是（2.7）简约为：

$$c_1\begin{pmatrix} -y_1x_1 \\ -y_1 \\ -1 \\ 0 \\ 0 \\ 0 \\ \vdots \\ 0 \end{pmatrix} + c_{m+1}\begin{pmatrix} 0 \\ 0 \\ -1 \\ 0 \\ 0 \\ 0 \\ \vdots \\ 0 \end{pmatrix} + \cdots c_t\begin{pmatrix} -y_tx_t \\ -y_t \\ 0 \\ -1 \\ 0 \\ 0 \\ \vdots \\ 0 \end{pmatrix} + c_{m+t}\begin{pmatrix} 0 \\ 0 \\ 0 \\ -1 \\ 0 \\ 0 \\ \vdots \\ 0 \end{pmatrix} = 0 \tag{2.8}$$

由 2.8 得到

$$c_1\begin{pmatrix} y_1x_1 \\ y_1 \end{pmatrix} + c_2\begin{pmatrix} y_2x_2 \\ y_2 \end{pmatrix} + \cdots + c_t\begin{pmatrix} y_tx_t \\ y_t \end{pmatrix} = 0$$

$$c_i = -c_{m+i} \ (i = 1, 2, \cdots, t)$$

又由于 $\begin{pmatrix} y_1x_1 \\ y_1 \end{pmatrix}$, $\begin{pmatrix} y_2x_2 \\ y_2 \end{pmatrix}$, $\cdots$, $\begin{pmatrix} y_tx_t \\ y_t \end{pmatrix}$ 线性无关，则得

$$c_1 = c_2 = \cdots = c_t = 0, \ c_{m+1} = c_{m+2} = \cdots = c_{m+t} = 0$$

根据线性无关的定义，可以得到所有起作用约束梯度组线性无关。

综合上述证明，非线性规划数据扰动定理的假设条件全部满足，因而有该结论 1 成立。关于结论 2 中的结论①、②直接得到，由起作用集不变，得到此处的 A, B, C 和 I 均保持不变，此即③，进一步由严格互补保持成立，得到支持向量集保持不变，此即④，至于线性无关性的⑤和二阶充分条件的⑥都直接得到。而⑦则是④、⑤、⑥的直接推论。关于结论⑧，直接为非线性规划数据扰动定理 1.1 结论 3 的转述。

3 结　论

本文针对加权线性支持向量分类机优化问题的各个模型建立了数据扰动分析理论。通过数据扰动分析定理可以回答支持向量分类机问题解的稳定性问题和灵敏度分析问题。该理论完善了支持向量机的优化理论，为其广泛应用奠定坚实基础。

参考文献

[1] 邓乃扬，田英杰. 数据挖掘中的新方法—支持向量分类机 [M]. 北京：科学出版社，2004.
[2] Vapnik V. 统计学习理论的本质 [M]. 张学工，译. 北京：清华大学出版社，2000.
[3] Cristianini N, Shawe–Taylor J. An Introduction to Support Vector Machines [M]. Cambridge University Press, Cambridge, UK, 2000.
[4] Boser B, Guyon L, Vapnik V. A training algorithm for optimal margin classifier [C] //In fifth annual workshop on computational learning theory, Baltimore, MD：ACM Press, 1992：144 – 152.
[5] Cortes C, Vapnik V. The soft margin classifiers, Technical memorandum 11359 – 931209 – 18TM, AT&T Bell Labs, 1993.
[6] Burges C J C. A tutorial on support vector machines for pattern recognition [J]. Data mining and Knowledge Discovery, 1982 (2)：121 – 167.
[7] Bennett K, Bredensteiner E. Duality and geometry in SVM classifiers [C] //In：Proc. of Senventeenth Intl. Conf. on Machine Learning, Morgan Kaufmann, San Francisco：2000：57 – 64.
[8] Scholkopf B, Burges C J C, Smola A J. Advances in Kernel Methods – Support Vector Learning [M]. MIT Press, Cambridge, MA, 1999：327 – 352.
[9] Joachims T. Text Categorization with Support Vector Machines [M]. Technical report, LS VIII Number 23, University of Dormund, 1997.
[10] Scholkopf B, Burges C J C, Vapnik V. Extracting support data for a given task [C] //In：Fayyad UM, Uthurusamy R, eds. Proceedings of First International Conference on Knowledge Discovery and Data Mining, German：AAAI Press, 1995：262 – 267.
[11] Deng Naiyang, Liu Guangli, Zhang Chunhua. A new version of support vector classification and its application to early warning of food security [J]. OR Transactions, 2003, 7 (2)：1 – 8.
[12] Drucker H, Burges C J C, Kaufinan L et al. support vector regression machines [C] //In：Mozer M, Jordan M, Petsche T eds. Neural Information Processing Systems, MIT Press, 1997. 9.
[13] Kwok J T Y. Support Vector Mixture for Classification and Regression Problems, ICPR, 98, 1998.
[14] 刘广利，邓乃扬. 基于SVM分类的预警系统 [J]. 中国农业大学学报，2002, 7 (6)：97 – 100.
[15] 沈翠华. 基于支持向量机的消费信贷个人信用评估方法研究 [D]. 北京：中国农业大学，2004.

不同地类春小麦拔节期冠层光谱与叶绿素差异研究

靳彦华 熊黑钢 张 芳 王莉峰

引 言

叶绿素含量是植物光合作用能力和发育阶段的指示器[1]。在作物生长环境分析和长势监测中，是非常重要的评估内容之一[2]。传统的作物叶绿素含量监测主要以采摘叶片进行化学实验的方法为主，不仅费时费力，而且破坏作物生长，因此迫切需要寻找高效、非破坏性测量作物叶绿因的监测方法。光谱技术能获得并提取作物的长势和健康状况，并能为遥感监测提供大量地面光谱数据。由于植被和叶子的反射光谱在可见光范围主要受植被叶绿素的影响，而在近红外区域则主要受叶子内部结构的影响[3]，因此，可以用植被冠层和叶片的反射光谱来估算其生化参数，特别是叶绿素含量[4]。国内外学者对光谱与叶绿素关系研究的成果有：植被光谱与叶绿素含量关系密切。光谱"红边"位置可在植被叶绿素含量估计中应用[5]。在"红边"特征参数中，"红边"位置与植物的叶绿素有关[6]。玉米生化成分含量与高光谱反射率之间有关[7]。

目前，对不同地类同一种植物光谱与叶绿素差异的研究较少。本工作主要对水浇地与旱地春小麦拔节期冠层光谱与叶绿素含量的差异进行了探讨，通过反射光谱红边捌点位置与叶绿素含量的回归分析，分别建立了适合水浇地和旱地春小麦叶绿素含量的监测模型，为建立干旱、半干旱地区更为精准、普适的农作物遥感监测模型提供依据。

1 实验部分

1.1 研究区概况

研究区位于奇台县，地处新疆维吾尔自治区东北部，天山山脉东段博格达山北麓，准噶尔盆地东南缘。年平均气温5.5℃，7月份最高气温43℃。1月份极端最低气温-42.6℃。年平均降水176mm，蒸发潜力2141mm，无霜期平均156d，年平均风速$2.9 m \cdot s^{-1}$。夏季炎热，冬季寒冷，四季分明，属于典型的中温带大陆性干旱半干旱气候。

1.2 样地选择

2012年5月22~24日分别在平原区和山前丘陵区选择3块土壤质地相同的春小麦地，二者的平均海拔分别为700和1250m。山前丘陵的3块春小麦地又分为南坡（阳坡）地、北坡（阴坡）地和东西坡（双面坡）地。平原区小麦地由机井灌溉（水浇地），山前丘陵区小麦主要依靠天然降水（旱地）。春小麦播种时间3月28日~4月1日，主要种植新春26号。行距约4cm，株距2cm。

1.3 冠层光谱测定与处理

光谱测量采用美国ASD公司的ASD FieldSpecPro3光谱仪，波段范围为350~2500nm。350~1000nm光谱分辨率为3nm，采样间隔1.4nm。光谱的测定选择在晴朗无云无风天气，测量时间为北京时间12:00~16:00，测量时，传感器探头垂直向下，视场角25°，探头距离冠层顶部垂直高度约15cm。每个样地设5个观测点，每个观测点测量5次，将其平均值作为该点的光谱反射值。各样点测定前都进行

[基金项目] 国家自然科学基金项目（41171165，41261049），北京市属高等学校人才强教计划项目（PHR 20 1007 146），北京联合大学人才强校计划项目（BPHR2012E01），新疆大学博士启动基金项目（BSIIOI24）资助。

[作者简介] 靳彦华，（女，1987—），新疆大学资源与环境科学学院硕士研究生，教育部绿洲生态重点实验室；熊黑钢，北京联合大学应用文理学院；张芳，新疆大学资源与环境科学学院，教育部绿洲生态重点实验室；王莉峰，新疆大学资源与环境科学学院，教育部绿洲生态重点实验室。

白板定标,去除暗电流影响。

采用移动平均法对实测光谱进行去噪处理[8],即选取测定样本某一点前后光谱曲线上一定范围测定它的平均值,作为该点的值。公式

$$R'_i = \frac{1}{2k+1}(R_{i+1} + R_{r-k+1} + \cdots + R_i + \cdots + R_{i+k})$$ (1)

式中:R'_i 为样本第 i 点的反射率值(均值),$i = 1, 2, 3, \cdots, n$。

1.4 春小麦叶绿素含量及植株的测定

测量光谱的同时,在测光谱的位置选用对植物无破坏性的 SPAD-502 叶绿素仪测定春小麦叶绿素含量。测量时在叶尖、中部和叶基三个部位各测三次,最后取其均值作为该叶片的叶绿素含量。

用卷尺测定各样地春小麦的行距、苗高和叶宽,每一项选 5 个点,测 5 次取其平均值测量叶宽时每个叶片均测其中部。

1.5 土壤水分的测定

每块样地选择 5 个样点(CGPS 定位),用土钻法采样,取 0~10,10~20,20~30,30~40 和 40~50cm 五层土样,5 次重复,共获得土壤分析样品 75 个。将采集的土样取部分封入铝盒,采用烘干法测定土壤水分。

2 结果与讨论

2.1 不同地类春小麦叶绿素含量的差异

图 1 为不同地类春小麦叶绿素含量的平均值,水浇地春小麦的叶绿素含量明显高于旱地,水浇地之间叶绿素含量差距不大,但旱地小麦叶绿素含量之间差距较大,其中阴坡地的叶绿素含量最高,其次为双面坡地,阳坡地的最低。

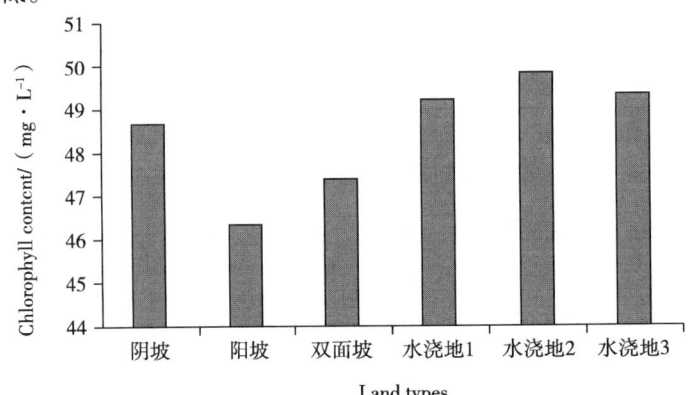

Fig. 1　Choloroghyll content of different types of land

2.2 水浇地与旱地春小麦拔节期冠层光谱的差异

不同地类春小麦冠层光谱存在明显的差异。在可见光区域,水浇地春小麦反射特征表现为"两谷一峰"(蓝紫谷、红谷和绿峰),即小麦反射光谱呈现先降低而后升高再降低的特点,550nm 处反射率达到最大值,形成明显的反射峰 [图 2(a)]。这是因为在蓝光和红光区域叶绿素强烈吸收,反射率较低,而在绿光区域叶绿素吸收较少,形成相对较强的反射峰。

与水浇地相比,旱地小麦的光谱曲线在可见光区域"峰谷"特征没有水浇地春小麦的突出,除阴坡地外,阳坡和双面坡小麦的光谱表现出明显的特殊性 [图 2(b)],主要是因为阴坡地一方面是迎风坡,接受新疆主要的西北向水汽,另一方面避免了阳光直射,土壤水分高,使得春小麦长势(叶宽、苗高)明显优于阳坡和双面坡。而阳坡和双面坡则相反(图 3 和图 4)。因此,造成前者光谱曲线更接近水浇地,而后者因水分不足,长势差,冠层叶面积指数较小,受土壤背景的影响较大,不仅冠层光谱的"峰谷"现象不明显,而且反射率高于水浇地 [图 2(b)]

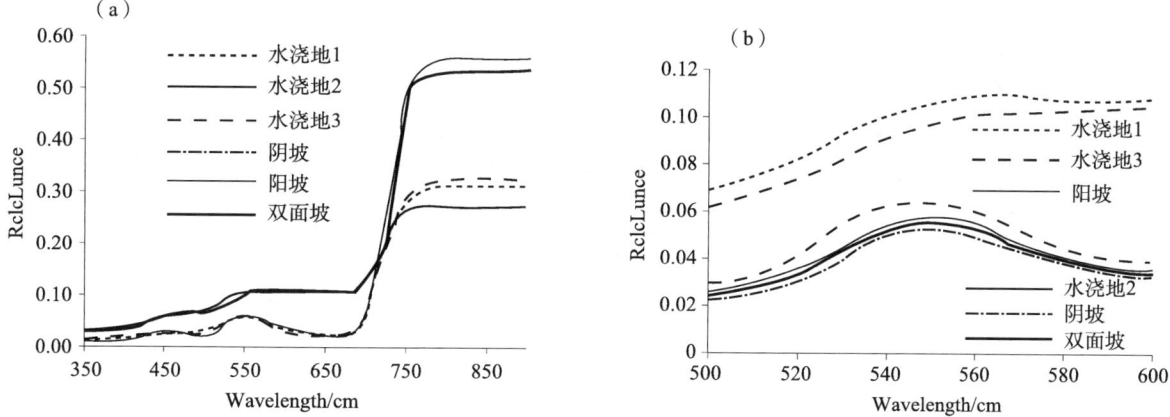

Fig. 2 Spectral variation characteristics of spring wheat at jointing stage in different types hand

(a): Spring wheat spectrum of irrigated and dry land; (b): Trend of visible band

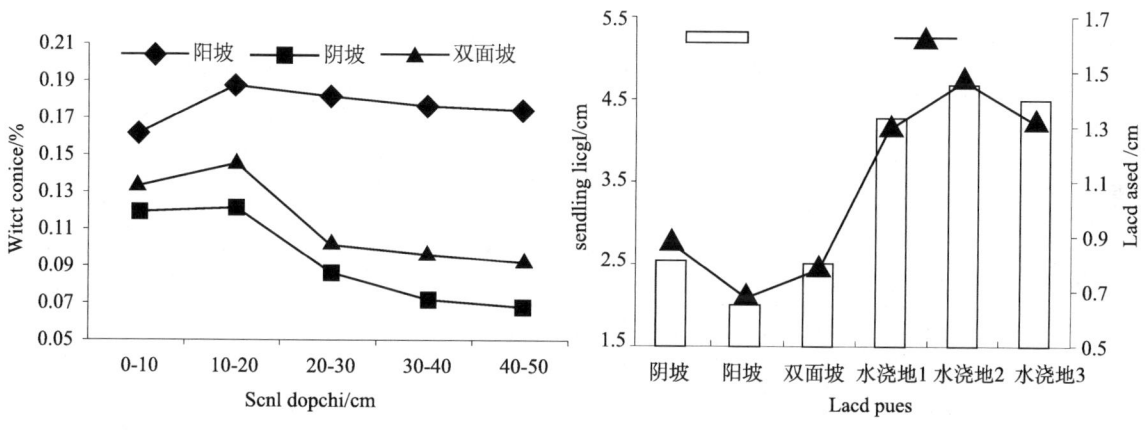

Fig. 3 Water content of dry land wheat

Fig. 4 Correlations between seedling height and leaf width at different kind of land

2.3 不同地类春小麦光谱的反射率与叶绿素含量相关性差异

对水浇地及旱地春小麦冠层光谱反射率与其叶绿素含量进行单相关分析，结果表明：（1）水浇地和旱地春小麦冠层反射率与叶绿素含量均呈正相关关系，且相关系数均大于0.8；（2）在可见光波段，水浇地相关系数明显大于旱地。旱地中，阴坡地的相关系数最大，阳坡地的最小；而进入近红外波段，水浇地的相关系数虽大于旱地，但差值没有可见光区明显；（3）在550 nm附近反射率与叶绿素含量相关关系最大。552 nm处不同地类春小麦冠层反射率达到最大值，水浇地在552 nm处相关系数平均值大于旱地（表1）。

Table 1 Correlations between canopy spectral reflectance and chlorophyll content at different band in irrigated and dry land

	350~900 nm	400~700 nm	700~900 nm	552 nm
水浇地1	0.93*	0.92*	0.93*	0.98**
水浇地2	0.92*	0.94*	0.94*	0.96**
水浇地3	0.89*	0.93*	0.93*	0.91**
阴坡	0.94*	0.87*	0.89*	0.95**
阳坡	0.91*	0.75*	0.87*	0.93**
双面坡	0.93*	0.83*	0.89*	0.90**

旱地与水浇地冠层光谱与叶绿素含量呈上述变化主要由于：（1）春小麦在拔节期只有麦秆和麦叶，冠层反射光谱不受麦芒的影响，故相关性好；（2）反射光谱在可见光范围主要受植被叶绿素的影响，因此，可见光区叶绿素含量能很好的体现春小麦冠层反射光谱与叶绿素含量之间的变化。近红外反射光谱主要由叶片内部结构、外观形态等影响，主要体现光谱与小麦外观形态的变化。（3）由图1可知，可见光区550nm附近是叶绿素的反射峰，水浇地的反射峰比旱地明显，故相关系数也好于旱地。

2.4 不同地类春小麦拔节期叶绿素含量监测模型及差异

在近红外区域，小麦光谱在680～740mm之间有一个斜率较大的陡坡，称为"红边"，"红边的位置、高度和斜率因不同植被及同一植被的不同生长状况而存在差异"[9]，且其位置依据叶绿素含量的变化，沿长波方向移动[10]，计算水浇地和旱地春小麦的一阶导数，得到其红边拐点位置与叶绿素含量值（表2）。

Table 2　Red edge position and chlorophyll content of spring wheat in irrigated and dry land

水浇地		旱地	
红边拐点波长/nm	叶绿素含量/SPAD	红边拐点波长/nm	叶绿素含量/SPAD
728	47.9	727	56.5
727	48.9	722	46.7
732	51.8	723	48.5
735	54.3	720	34.6
733	51.9	725	56.1
731	50.9	721	43.1

选用水浇地和旱地一部分春小麦光谱红边位置与实测叶绿素含量作为试验样本，用于建立回归模型，另一部分作为检验样本，用于模型精度检验。分别以反射光谱红边拐点波长位置为自变量x，叶绿素含量为因变量y，进行线性回归分析，可得两种不同地类春小麦拔节期叶绿素含量监测模型（图5）。

水浇地春小麦线性模型为

$$y = 0.7283x - 481.41 \quad (2)$$

旱地春小麦线性模型为

$$y = 2.9853x - 2110.8 \quad (3)$$

旱地春小麦二项式模型为

$$y = -0.477x^2 + 693.21x - 251.808 \quad (4)$$

水浇地春小麦冠层反射光谱红边拐点位置与叶绿素含量线性模型的R^2达0.93，说明其能很好的体现叶绿素含量。而旱地春小麦二项式模型的R^2达0.93，说明其能很好的体现叶绿素含量。而旱地春小麦二项式模型的R^2达0.97，优于其线性模型（$R^2 = 0.88$）。用以上模型分别对水浇地和旱地春小麦叶绿素含量检验，水浇地的检测模型（$r = 0.96$，$n = 12$）达极显著水平（$p < 0.01$）。RMSE为0.86，预测精度为94.06%；旱地的监测模型（$r = 0.97$，$n = 12$），也达极显著水平，RMSE为0.88，预测精度为97.15%（图5）。表明线性模型适合用于监测水浇地叶绿素含量，而二项式模型则更宜监测旱地小麦叶绿素含量。

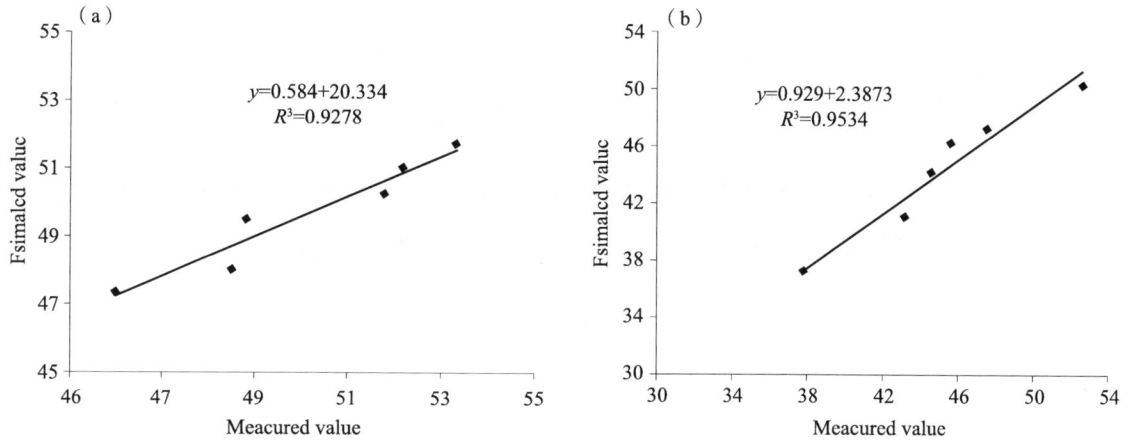

Fig. 5 Examination of the spring wheat model for chlorophyll in irrigated and dry land
(a): Irrigated land; (b): Dry land

3 结 论

（1）不同地类春小麦拔节期叶绿素含量存在较大差异，水浇地春小麦平均叶绿素含量比旱地高 2 SPAO。阴坡因含水量较多，叶绿素含量高于阳坡和双面坡地春小麦。水浇地和旱地春小麦反射光谱与叶绿素含量均呈正相关关系，相关系数较大，但无论是可见风波段，还是近红外波段，水浇地春小麦冠层光谱反射率与叶绿素含量相关性均好于旱地春小麦。

（2）在可见光范围，旱地春小麦叶绿素含量低，冠层光谱反射率大于水浇地春小麦。而在近红外区域，由于水浇地春小麦长势好（叶宽、苗高），冠层光谱反射率比旱地春小麦高。阴坡地的春小麦因长势接近水浇地春小麦，其冠层光谱特点接近水浇地春小麦。

（3）两种地类春小麦反射光谱红边拐点位置与叶绿素含量的线性模型，均能很好地预测春小麦叶绿素含量，但旱地的叶绿素监测二项式模型高于其线性模型。

参考文献

[1] TANG Yan－lin, WANG Ji－hua, HUANG Jing－feng, et al（唐延林，王纪华，黄敬峰，等）[J]. Transactions of the Chinese Society of Agricultural Engineering（农业工程学报），2003，19（6）：167.

[2] CHEN Yan, HUANG Chun－yan, WANG Deng－wei, et al（陈燕，黄春燕，王登伟，等）[J]. Xinjiang Agricultural Sciences（新疆农业科学），2006，43（6）：451.

[3] Gausman H W, Allen W A, Cardenas R. et al. Application of Optics, 1970, 9（3）：545.

[4] Card D H, Peterson D L, Matson P A, et al. Remote Sensing of Environment, 1988, 26（1）：123.

[5] Horler D N H, Dockray M, Barber J. Remote Sensing, 1983, 4（4）：273.

[6] Filella 1. Remote Sensing, 1994, 15（7）：1459.

[7] YI Qiu－xiang, HUANG Jing－feng, WANG Xiu－zhen（易秋香，黄敬峰，王秀珍）[J]. Journal of Infrared Millimeter Waves（红外与毫米波学报），2007，26（5）：393.

[8] HE Ting. WANG Jing, CHENG Ye, et al（何挺，王静，程烨，等）. Geography and Geo－Information Science（地理与地理信息科学），2006，3（2）：30.

[9] TANG Yan－lin, WANG Ren－chao, HUANG Jing－feng, et al（唐延林，王人潮，黄敬峰，等）. Journal of Remote Sensing（遥感学报），2004，8（2）：185.

[10] YANG Min－hua, ZHAO Chun－jiang, ZHAO Yong－chao, et al（杨敏华，赵春江，赵永超，等）. Scientia Agricultura Sinica（中国农业科学），2002，35（6）：626.

Regulatory Effects of Xylooligosaccharides on Intestinal Microbial Flora Proliferation and Defecation of BALB/c Mice

Wei Tao　Shang Hongtao　Gao Zhaolan
Wang Li　Li Siyu　Huang Xue　Zeng Mengrui

Xylooligosaccharides are functional polymeric sugars composed of 2 – 7 xylose molecules by β-1, 4-glycosidic bond. The sweetness of xylooligosaccharides is lower than that of sucrose and glucose, which is about only 40% of the sweetness of sucrose. Xylooligosaccharides have high stability to pH and heat and are basically not decomposed under acidic and heating conditions, which can smoothly pass through the stomach and small intestine without being degraded and utilized due to the lack of xylooligo-saccharide-hydrolysis enzyme system in the gastrointestinal tract; subsequently, xylooligosaccharides directly enter the large intes-tine and are utilized by *Bifidobacterium*, *Lactobacillus* and other beneficial bacteria, while harmful bacteria show very low level or no utilization of xylooligosaccharides, thereby ensuring large-scale growth and reproduction of beneficial bacteria[1-2]. In this study, the effects of xylooligosaccharides on intestinal microbial flora proliferation and defecation of BALB/c mice were investigated, which provided scientific basis for the rational use, supervision and man-agement of xylooligosaccharides.

Materials and Methods

Experiment alanimals

Two-month-old BALB/c secondary female mice weighing 22 – 28g were pur chased from the breeding ground in Animal Center of Chinese Academy of Medical Sciences, which were randomly divided into normal control group, low-dose group and high dose group according to the body weight. Negative control group and model control group were set for defecation regulation experiment.

Experimental samples and administration doses

Xylooligosaccharide powder was produced by Shandong Long-li Biotechnology Co., Ltd. Low-dose [0.5g/(kg·bw)] and high-dose [1.0g/(kg·bw)] xylooligosaccharides were given by intragastric administration for continuous 14d, once a day, 0.02ml/(g·bw) each time. BALB/c mice in control group and model group were administrated with an equal amount of distilled water.

Experimental methods[3]

Counting of intestinal flora

Before intragastric administration and 24h after the final administration, mouse excrements were collected under sterile conditions and placed into sterilized test tubes containing 3ml of dilution liquid, then weighed and mixed evenly with shaking to ensure completely even distribution of excrements in the dilution liquid, which was then diluted to 10^{-8} by 10-fold serial dilution. Appropriate diluent was selected and inoculated to BBL medium, EMB medium, sodium azide-crystal vio-let-esculin agar medium and LBS agar medium. After cultured for 24 or 48h, based on colony morphology, intestinal colonies were counted by Gram staining under the microscope, to calculate the quantities of *Bifidobacterium*, *Escherichia coli* and *Lactobacillus* in each gram of wet excrements, corresponding logarithms were taken for statistical processing.

Intestinal propulsion experiment

After continuous administration of xylooligosaccharides for 14d, BALB/c mice in each group were fasted for24h. In the intestinal propulsion experiment, mice in experimental groups were administrated with xylooligosaccharides and mice in control group and model group were administrated with an equal amount of distilled water. After 30 min, except the normal control group, mice in other groups were intragastrically administrated with 50mg/(kg·bw) of compound diphenoxylate. After 20 min, each mouse in various groups was intragastrically administrated with 0.5ml of 15% carbon black ink. After 20min, BALB/c mice were euthanasized by cervical dislocation, the entire small intestine from the pylorus tocecum was immediately removed and unfolded straightly without traction. The total length of small intestine and the displacement distance of carbon black ink from the pylorus were measured, in order to calculate the rate of intestinal propulsion.

Rate of intestinal propulsion (%) = Displacement distance of carbon black ink (cm) /Total length ofsmall intestine (cm) ×100%

Defecation experiments in mice

After continuous administration of xylooligosaccharides for 14d, BALB/c mice in each group were fasted for 24h. Except the normal control group, BALB/c mice in other groups were intragastrically administrated with 10mg/(kg·bw) of compound diphenoxylate. Mice were placed in the squirrel cage separately with normal drinking and eating. After 1h, each mouse in various groups was intragastrically administrated with 0.5ml of 15% carbon black ink (carbon black ink used in experimental group scontained corresponding dose of xylooligosaccharides). Since the intragastric administration of compound diphenoxylate, the first defecation time of black excrement and the weight of black excrements within 6h of each mouse were observed and recorded.

Results and Analysis

Effect of xylooligosaccharides on body weight ofBALB/c mice

As can be seen from Table1, the intragastric administration of high-dose and low-dose xylooligosaccharides had no effect on body weight of BALB/c mice.

Table 1 Effect of xylooligosaccharides on body weight of BALB/c mice ($\overline{X} \pm SD$, $n=10$, g)

Group	Body weight before intragastric administration	Body weight after intragastric administration
Control group	25.34 ± 1.51	24.63 ± 1.91
Low dose group [0.5/g (kg·bw)]	26.67 ± 1.35	26.23 ± 2.16
High-dose group [1.0g/ (kg·bw)]	26.12 ± 1.30	25.43 ± 1.66

Effect of xylooligosaccharides on intestinal microbial flora of BALB/c mice

As can be seen from Table 2, before intragastric administration, BALB/c mice had no difference in intestinal microbial flora, after continuous administration of high-dose [1.0g/ (kg·bw)] and low-dose [0.5g/ (kg·bw)] xylooligosaccharides for 14 d, quantities of *Enterobacter* and *Enterococcus* had no significant change compared with the control group, while quantities of *Lactobacillus* and *Bifidobacterium* both increased significantly. To be specific, quantities of *Lactobacillus* and *Bifidobacterium* in low dose group were enhanced by 5% ($P < 0.05$) and 9% ($P < 0.05$), respectively quantities of *Lactobacillus* and *Bifidobacterium* in high-dose group were enhanced by 5% ($P < 0.05$) and 9% ($P < 0.05$), respectively. After intragastric administration, quantities of *Enterococcus* and *Lactobacillus* in control group were significantly enhanced by 14% ($P < 0.05$) and 10% ($P < 0.01$), respectively; the quantity of *Enterobacter* in low-dose group was reduced by 5.2% ($P < 0.05$), while quantities of *Lactobacillus* and *Bifidobacterium* were enhanced by 9% ($P < 0.05$) and 14% ($P < 0.01$), respectively; the quantity of *Enterobacter* in highdose group was reduced by 9% ($P < 0.05$), while quantities of *Lactobacillus* and *Bifidobacterium* were enhanced by 8% ($P < 0.05$) and 16% ($P < 0.01$), respectively.

Table 2 Effect of xylooligosaccharides on intestinal microbial flora of BALB/c mice (log CFU/g, $\bar{X} \pm SD$, $n = 10$)

Group	Treatment	Enterobacter	Enterococcus	Lactobacillus	Bifidobncterium
Control group	Before intragastric administration	6.38 ± 0.62	5.43 ± 0.84	7.22 ± 0.68	7.65 ± 0.93
	After intragastric administration	6.31 ± 0.40	6.20 ± 0.43*	7.94 ± 0.31**	8.39 ± 0.52
Low-dose group [0.5g/(kg·bw)]	Before intragastric administration	6.33 ± 0.38	5.60 ± 0.63	7.62 ± 0.74	8.00 ± 0.31
	After intragastric administration	6.00 ± 0.48#	5.84 ± 0.34*	8.34 ± 0.51**	9.11 ± 0.68**
High-dose group [1.0g/(kg·bw)]	Before intragastric administration	6.59 ± 0.76	5.99 ± 0.78	7.75 ± 0.63	7.93 ± 0.43
	After intragastric administration	6.01 ± 0.44#	6.06 ± 0.56*	8.35 ± 0.44**	9.16 ± 0.62**

# indicates significant difference compared with that before intragastric administration ($P < 0.05$); ## indicates extremely signifference compared with that that before intragastric administration ($P < 0.01$); * indicates significant difference compared with that in control group ($P < 0.05$).

Table 3 Effect of xylooligosaccharides on *B/E* value of BALB/c mice ($\bar{X} \pm SD$, $n = 10$)

Group	Before intragastric administration	After intragastric administration
Control group	1.24 ± 0.14	1.34 ± 0.15
Low-dose group [0.5g/(kg·bw)]	1.20 ± 0.08	1.53 ± 0.15##*
High-dose group [1.0g/(kg·bw)]	1.21 ± 0.14	1.52 ± 0.13##*

indicates extremely significant difference compared whth that that before in tragastrie administration ($P < 0.01$); * indicates significant difference compared with that in control group ($P < 0.05$).

Ratio of *Bifidobacterium* to *Enterobacter* (*B/E*) in mouse excrements can be regarded as an indicator of the colonization resistance of intestinal microbial flora and applied in clinical practice, which can evaluate the conditions of the structure of intestinal flora from both positive and negative aspects. *B/E* value ≥ 1 indicates normal colonization resistance of intestinal microbial flora; *B/E* value < 1 indicates reduced colonization resistanc of intestinal microbial flora[4]. As can be seen from Table 3, *B/E* value of BALB/c mice in various groups before and after intragastric administration of xylooligosaccharides were both greater than 1, suggesting normal colonization resistance of intestinal microbial flora in mice. Before administration, *B/E* value of BALB/c mice in various groups had no significant difference. After continuous administration of xylooligosacharides for 14d, *B/E* value of BALB/c mice in control group had no significant difference compared with that before administration, while *B/E* value in low-dose group and high-dose group were respectively enhanced by 28% ($P < 0.01$) and 26% ($P < 0.05$) compared with that before administration, and were respectively enhanced by 14% ($P < 0.05$) and 13% ($P < 0.05$) compared with that in control group, indicating that both low-dose and high-dose xylooligosaccharides can improve the structure of intestinal flora.

Effect of xylooligosaccharides on the rate of intestinal propulsion of BALB/c mice

After continuous administration of high-dose and low-dose xylooligosaccharides for 21d, the rate of intestinal propulsion in negative group and model group were 72.5% and 38.2%, respectively; the rate of intestinal propulsion in negative group was 90% higher than that in model group ($P < 0.01$), suggesting that the model was successfully established. The rate of intestinal propulsion in low-dose group and high-dose group reached

77.4% and 84.0%, which were respectively improved by 102% ($P < 0.01$) and 120% ($P < 0.01$) compared with that in model group, indicating that both low-dose and high-dose xylooligosaccharides can enhance the rate of intestinal propulsion of mice.

Effect of xylooligosaccharides on defecation of BALB/c mice

As can be seen from Table 4, after continuous administration of xylooligosaccharides for 14d, first defecation time of black excrement in model group increased by 186.5% ($P < 0.01$) and total weight of black excrements within 6h was reduced by 55.5% ($P < 0.01$) compared with that in negative group, suggesting that the model was successfully established. In addition, compared with model group, first defecation time of black excrement in low-dose group and high-dose group was reduced by 76.7% ($P < 0.01$) and 85.6% ($P < 0.01$), respectively; total weight of black excrements within 6h was enhanced by 126% ($P < 0.05$) and 183% ($P < 0.01$), indicating that both low-dose and high-dose xylooligosaccharides can effectively improve the defecation of constipation mice.

Table 4 Effect of xylooligosaccharides on frist defecation time of black excrement and total weight of black excrements of BALB/c mice ($\bar{X} \pm SD$)

Group	First defecation time of black excrement/min	Weight of black excrements within 6h/mg
Model group	304.2 ± 72.8	21.8 ± 10.3
Low-dose group [0.5g/(kg·bw)]	70.8 ± 57.8 **	49.3 ± 21.6 *
High-dose group [1.0g/(kg·bw)]	43.8 ± 33.7 **	61.6 ± 38.4 **
Negative group	106.1 ± 96.3 **	91.6 ± 36.5 **

indicates extremely significant difference compared with that that before intragastric administration ($P < 0.01$); * indicates significant difference compared with that in conurol group ($P < 0.05$); ** indicates extremely significant difference compared with that in control group (P < 0.01).

Discussions

With the in-depth study on intestinal microecosystem, it is increasingly recognized that intestinal microorganisms have played important roles in human health. Normal microbial community determine many biological processes of host. Therefore, dysbacteriosis will cause a variety of diseases[5]. In this study, results show that xylooligosaccharides can effectively increase the quantities of *Lactobacillus* and *Bifidobacterium* and significantly reduce the quantity of *Enterobacter* in mouse intestines, which might be due to that *Lactobacillus* and other beneficial bacteria can secrete D-xylosidase and Arab glucosidase to hydrolysize xylooligosaccharides into monosaccharide for use, while harmful bacteria can not secrete these enzymes[6]. Furthermore, results also suggest that xylooligosaccharides have relatively great promotion effects on the intestinal motility and defecation of mice. Digestive tract lacks of xylooligosaccharide-decomposing enzymes, resulting in slow digestion and absorption speed of xylooligosaccharides. Most of the xylooligosaccharides greatly ingested are transported to the intestines and form high concentration the intestines, which causes the increase of osmotic pressure for water entering into the intestine, thereby playing a bowel-relaxing role. In addition, beneficial bacteria absorb xylooligosaccharides as nutrients to achieve large-sacle proliferation, the short chain-fatty acids which are the final products of bacterial metabolism can decrease intestinal pH, which not only inhibits the growth and reproduction of pathogens, but also stimulates the intestinal peristalsis[7]. Results of this study indicate that low-dose and high-dose xylooligosaccharides have similar functions in improving intestinal microbial flora and preventing mice from constipation. Therefore, low-dose xylooligosaccharides can be adopted in practical applications considering the production costs.

References

[1] BHAT MK. Oligosaccharides as functional food ingredients and their role in improving the nutritional quality of human food and health [J]. Recent Res Dev Agric Food Chem, 198, 2: 787-802.

[2] YUAN WANG J, YAO H. Feruloyl oligosaccharides stimulate the growth of Bifidobacterium [J]. Bifidum Anaerobe, 2005, 11: 225-229.

[3] PRC. Technical standards for testing and assessment of health food [M]. 2003: 159-162. (in Chinese).

[4] WU ZW, LI LI, MA WH, *et al*. The new index of intestinal microbial colonization resistance—B/E value [J]. Zhejiang Journal of Preventive Medicine, 2000, 12 (7): 4-5. (in Chinese).

[5] ZHU BL, WANG X, LI LJ. Human gut microbiome: the second genome of human body [J]. Protein Cell, 2010, 1 (8): 718-725.

[6] MICHAEL AC, TERENCE RW. Xylooligosaecharide utilization by the ruminal anaerobic bacterium selenomonas ruminantium [J]. Current Microbiology, 1998 (36): 183-189.

[7] JIANG ZM, YIN JZ, CHEN YX. Xylooligosaccharides and probiotics in the human intestine [J]. China Dairy Industry, 2009, 37 (2): 42-52. (in Chinese).

Effects of preparation conditions on characters of hydrophobic silica granular aerogel and its Applications

Wei Wei   Zhang Jingyi   Wu Liping   Qin Guotong

Introduction

Silica aerogels with pecific surface area, high porosity and low density have attracted more attention due to their potential applications in a variety of technological areas[1-3]. The preparation conditions affect the aerogel characters. Drying of the gel is a critical step. There are three different methods of drying: supercritical drying, freeze drying and ambient pressure drying. A. Parvathy Rao et al[4] prepared hydrophobic silica aerogels by ambient pressure drying method with various silylating agents. The physical properties, including volume shrinkage, density, pore volume, porosity, refractive index, contact angle, thermal conductivity and heat capacity per unit volume were measured. A. Venkateswara Rao et al[5] prepared flexible and superhydrophobic silica aerogels using methyltrimethoxysilane (MTMS) precursor by a two - step sol - gel process followed by the supercritical drying. The effects of various preparation conditions on the flexibility of the aerogels have been investigated. The aerogel can be bent to any shape and acts as a good shock absorber as well. Suzana Štandeker[6] prepared silica monolith aerogels with different degrees of hydrophobicity by incorporating methyltrimethoxysilane (MTMS) or trimethylethoxysilane (TMES) in standard sol - gel synthesis followed by supercritical drying of gels with carbon dioxide (CO_2) at 40℃ and 100 bar. Adsorption capacity measurements show that such modified hydrophobic silica aerogels are excellent adsorbents for different toxic organic compounds (toluene, benzene, ethylbenzene, chloroform, 1, 1 - dichloroethane, xylene, chlorobenzene) from water.

The silica aerogels were used in different applications according to their characters. In this work, we prepared hydrophobic silica aerogels for adsorption using ambient pressure drying. Silica aerogels can either be hydrophilic or hydrophobic, depending on the synthesis conditions. The hydrophobic aerogels can inhibit the liquid water from entering the pores, only allowing the organic compounds to enter the porous materials. Therefore the hydrophobic aerogels are more efficient in adsorption of organics. The various factors that influence the adsorption capacity of aerogel include specific surface area, pore size distribution, pore volume and particle size. We investigated the effects of preparation conditions, including pH and disperse volume on aerogel particle size. The specific surface area, pore size distribution, and pore volume of silica aerogel were tested by nitrogen adsorption. The aerogels were used to absorb phenol from water.

1 Experimental

1.1 Preparation of hydrophobic aerogels

Hydrophobic silica aerogels were prepared by a standard sol - gel procedure, using tetraethyloxylane

(TEOS) as original precursor. Other chemicals include ethanol, 25 wt% solution of NH_3, hydrochloric acid, 1-1-1 trichloroethane, N-hexane, Span 20, isopropanol and distilled water.

First a solution containing NH_4OH and H_2O was prepared. In a separate vessel, TEOS and HCl were mixed and stirred at room temperature. After 1 hour, NH_4OH solution was added to this solution. The mixture was stirred for some time, and then poured into disperse solution which contains 1-1-1 trichloroethane, N-hexane and Span 20 mixed solution. The gel particles were formed within 1 hours. Wet gels were modified in trimethyl chlorosilane solution containing isopropanol and N-hexane for 40 hours. Samples were then dried at 180℃ for 12 hours.

1.2 Analytical methods

The aerogel samples were characterized using N_2 adsorption at 77 K which was carried out on a Micromeritics ASAP 2000. The samples were dried at 100 ℃ before measurement. The BET surface area and pore volume of the sample were evaluated from their N_2 adsorption isotherms. Their pore size distributions were calculated using the BJH (Barrett-Johner-Halendar) theory. Scanning electron microscopy (SEM) was used to characterize the morphology of silica aerogel with a Hitachi S-2400. The average particle size were measured by laser particle size analyzer LS-601.

1.3 Application

About 0.5g of aerogels were introduced into a flask which contained 100 ml of aqueous phenol solution with a initial concentration (C_o) of 1000 mg·L^{-1}. After the adsorption reached equilibrium, the concentration (C_e) of phenol solution was determined. The adsorption amount (Q) was calculated according to:

$$Q = \frac{V(C_o - C_e)}{m}$$

where Q (mg g^{-1}) is the adsorption amount; V (L) is the volume of the phenol solution; m (g) is the weight of the absorbent.

2 Results and discussion

Generally, hydrophilic or hydrophobic silica aerogels were produced by the sol-gel process and supercritical drying which is expensive. In this study we prepared silica aerogels at ambient pressure. We prepared silica aerogels with grain shape for adsorption application.

2.1 Effects of pH and disperse solution volume on aerogel particle size

We investigated the effects of pH and disperse solution volume on aerogel particle size and showed in Table 1. From Table 1, we can conclude that disperse solution volume and pH affect particle size. Particle size increased with disperse solution volume decreasing. The average particle size is 9.7 μm when disperse solution volume is 600 ml while the particle size increased to 25.3 μm when disperse solution volume is 100 ml. Average particle size decreased a little with pH increasing firstly and then increased. When pH increased from 4.5 to 5.5 the average particle size decreased from 9.7 μm to 8.1 μm and increased to 22.7 μm when pH increased to 7.5. Fig.1 is the micrograph of hydrophobic silica aerogels. These aerogels are uniform sphericity.

2.2 Effect of pH on gel time

Gel time (particle formation time) is an important parameter for preparing aerogel because it can affect aerogel characters. Many factors, including raw material concentration, reaction temperature and pH, can affect gel time. In this study, we found that the effect of pH is acutest. Fig.2 showed the relationship between pH and gel time. Gel time decreased with pH increased. Gel time needs 24 minutes when pH is 3.2. When pH exceeds 6, gel time is less than 1 minute.

Table 1 Effects of preparation conditions on aerogel average particle size

Sample	pH	Disperse solution volume (ml)	Average particle size (μm)
1	4.5	600	9.7
2	5.5	600	8.1
3	6.5	600	15.3
4	7.5	600	22.7
5	4.5	300	17.8
6	4.5	100	25.3
7	5.0	300	17.2

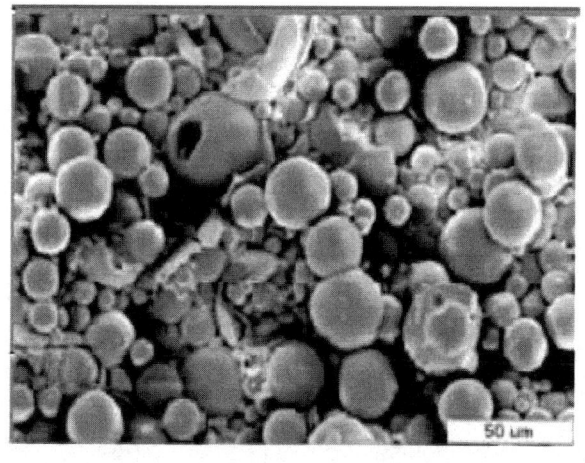

Fig. 1 Micrograph of hydrophobic silica aerogels

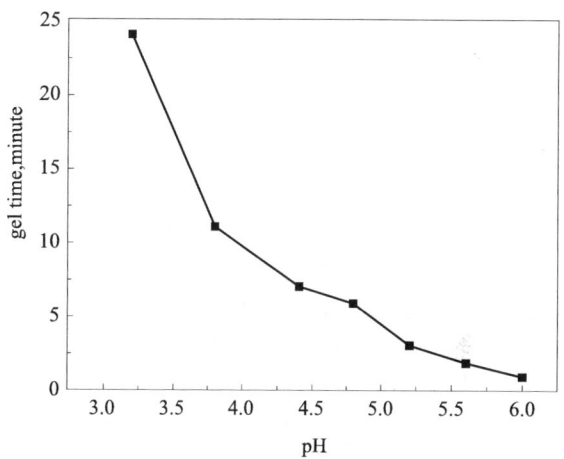

Fig. 2 Effect of pH on gel time

2.3 N$_2$ adsorption experiment

The surface area, pore volume and pore size distribution are important parameters for adsorption application. High BET surface area, high pore volume and appropriate pore size favored adsorption application. N$_2$ adsorption was carried out in order to investigate whether the prepared aerogel is capable of adsorption. The results are shown in Table 2 and Fig. 3. Fig. 3 shows the nitrogen adsorption isotherm of aerogel at 77 K and pore size distribution calculated by the BJH method from isotherms. The isotherm is classified as type II (Langmuir isotherm), which indicates the sample is predominantly mesoporous material. The average pore diameter is 2.81 nm. The S_{BET} and V_{total} are 737 m^2/g and 0.46 cm^{3}g^{-1} respectively. This pore stucture fits adsorption of organic compound from water.

Table 2 Characters of silica aerogel prepared by pH 6.5

pH	S_{BET} (m^2/g)	V_{total} (cm^3 g^{-1})	Average pore diameter (nm)
6.5	737	0.46	2.81

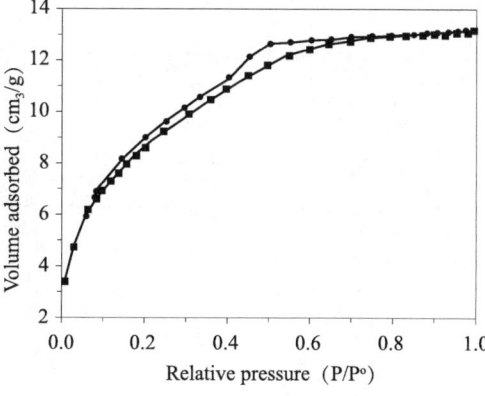
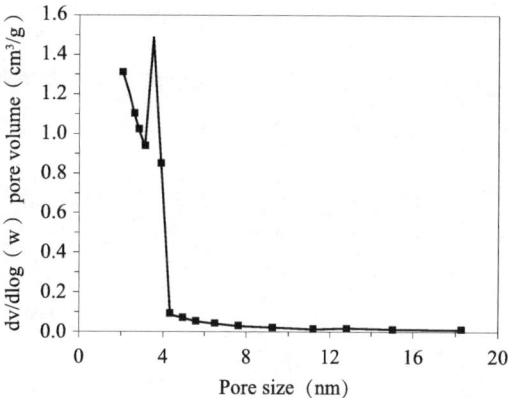

Fig. 3 Adsorption isotherm of nitrogen at 77 K and pore size distribution of aerogel prepared by pH 6

2.4 Application

The flask which contained aerogels and aqueous phenol solution was placed in a shaker at 25 ℃ and was then shaken. After 15 hours, the adsorption reached equilibrium. The concentration (C_e) of phenol solution determined by UV nalysis was 275mg·g^{-1}. The removal of phenol is 72.5% and the saturated adsorption amount is 145mg·g^{-1}.

3 Conclusions

The hydrophobic granular silica aerogels were prepared at ambient pressure. The pH and disperse solution volume can affect aerogel particle size. The prepared silica aerogel is nanostructure materials with high surface area and high pore volume. The aerogels can be used to absorb phenol from water.

Acknowledgements

Project 51172027 supported by NSFC. Project supported by Beijing Municipal Commission of Education (KM200811417013).

References

[1] Soleimani Dorcheh, M. H. Abbasi. Silica aerogel: synthesis, properties and characterization. Journal of materials processing technology 199 (2008) 10 - 26.

[2] L. W. Hrubesh, P. R. Coronado, J. H. Satcher Jr. Solvent removal from water with hydrophobic aerogels. Journal of Non - Crystalline - Crystalline Solids 285 (2001) 328 - 332.

[3] A. Venkateswara Rao, Nagaraja D. Hegde, Hiroshi Hirashima. Absorption and desorption of organic liquids in elastic superhydrophobic silica aerogels. Journal of Colloid and Interface Science 305 (2007) 124 - 132.

[4] A. Parvathy Rao, A. Venkateswara Rao, G. M. Pajonk. Hydrophobic and physical properties of the ambient pressure dried silica aerogels with sodium silicate precursor usingvarious surface modification agents. Applied Surface Science 253 (2007) 6032 - 6040.

[5] A. Venkateswara Rao, Sharad D. Bhagat, Hiroshi Hirashima, G. M. Pajonk. Synthesis of flexible silica aerogels using methyltrimethoxysilane (MTMS) precursor. Journal of Colloid and Interface Science 300 (2006) 279 - 285.

[6] Suzana Štandeker, Zoran Novak, Željko Knez. Adsorption of toxic organic compounds from water with hydrophobic silica aerogels. Journal of Colloid and Interface Science 310 (2007) 362 - 368.

> 教育学类

校企联动构建餐旅类人才培养体系

王美萍　张丽娟　朱　莉

一、引　言

2005年《国务院关于大力发展职业教育的决定》指出"大力推行工学结合、校企合作的培养模式。与企业紧密联系，加强学生的生产实习和社会实践，改革以学校和课堂为中心的传统人才培养模式。" 2006年教育部《关于全面提高高等职业教育教学质量的若干意见》指出"高等职业教育以就业为导向，走产学结合发展道路"。加强"校企合作、工学结合"已成为高等职业教育改革与发展的主要方向。[1]

近十年来，学习借鉴德国的"双元制"、北美的"CBE的合作教育"、英国的"三明治"、日本的"产学结合"等国外职业教育的模式，以及国内推行的"订单式培养""理论实践一体化""工学交替教学"等模式，进行校企联动，协同培养餐旅类应用型人才。我们瞄准酒店、餐饮行业等知名企业，秉持"优势互补、互惠互利、双需双赢"的原则，相继与北京香格里拉饭店、洲际酒店集团、中国全聚德集团股份有限公司（以下简称全聚德集团）等十余家酒店及餐饮集团建立战略合作伙伴关系。

自2005年与全聚德集团合作成立全聚德餐饮管理学院以来，我们根据专业教学和企业生产、经营的实际需要，积极探索产学结合的多种形式。校企协同培养餐旅类应用型人才，共建人才培养模式改革试验区，校企合作、协同培养人才，取得丰硕成果，获得良好的办学效益与社会效益。2006年与全聚德集团合作"订单式"人才培养，2008年《旅游类高职教育实践课程"工作导向同步协作式"教学模式的研究与实践》教学改革项目荣获北京市教育教学成果奖一等奖，2011年作为主要成员校之一参与北京市职业教育分级制改革试验项目，成立企业冠名班。企业参与学校专业教学逐渐变被动为主动，从最初的学生参与企业接待服务工作，到企业工作任务植入专业核心课程教学，企业主动为学校教学提供支持，企业成为促进学校人才培养的平台与载体。2012年《校企联动协同构建餐旅类人才培养体系的创新与实践》荣获北京市教育教学成果奖二等奖。

二、校企联动，协同构建餐旅类人才培养体系实践研究成果

我们依托国家级优秀教学团队建设，以北京市市级校外人才培养基地、全聚德餐饮管理学院、旅游类高技能人才培养创新试验区为平台，校企联动，协同建设餐旅类人才培养新体系（见图1），为首都旅游业的发展培养、输送了大批高素质应用型人才；实现了校企优质资源的"共享"与利益"双赢"，为探索高等职业教育校企合作办学模式和人才培养模式提供有价值的经验总结。

（一）基于"能力本位"教育思想，确立餐旅类高技能人才培养目标

为满足首都旅游业发展对人才的需求，基于"能力本位"教育思想，确立餐旅类高技能人才培养目标，培养具备良好人文素质，熟练掌握旅游行业相关领域技能，能够胜任旅游业、酒店及餐饮企业相关岗位操作和基层管理工作的高技能人才。

（二）基于综合职业能力培养，构建"三层递进、四个模块"课程体系

课程是实现人才培养目标的主要载体。基于综合职业能力培养，校企联动，共同开发专业课程体系

[作者简介] 王美萍（1961—），女，汉族，北京人，北京联合大学旅游学院副院长，教授。研究方向为高等教育管理；张丽娟（1969—），女，汉族，北京人，硕士，北京联合大学旅游学院副教授，研究方向为高等职业教育教学、服务心理。；朱莉（1969—），女，汉族，湖南人，博士，北京联合大学旅游学院教授。研究方向为食品化学、高等教育。

校企联运 协同建设餐旅类人才培养体系的创新与实践

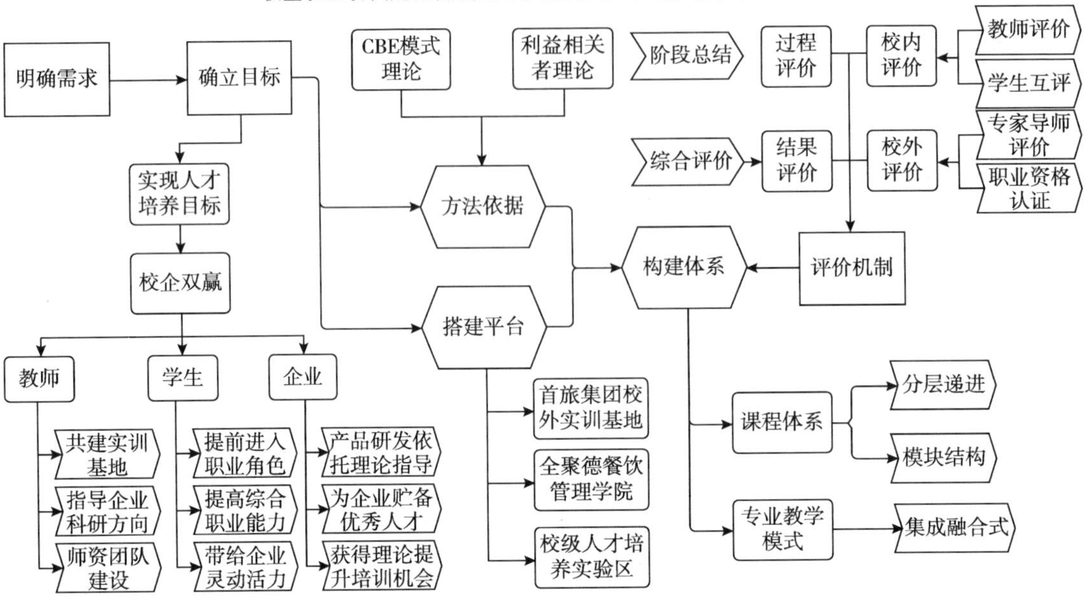

图1　人才培养体系成果图示

（见图2）。形成了以培养高素质应用型人才的目标为出发点和落脚点，创新构建"以职业操作能力、职业综合能力、职业发展能力培养为主线"的"三层递进、四个模块"的课程体系。

课程体系图

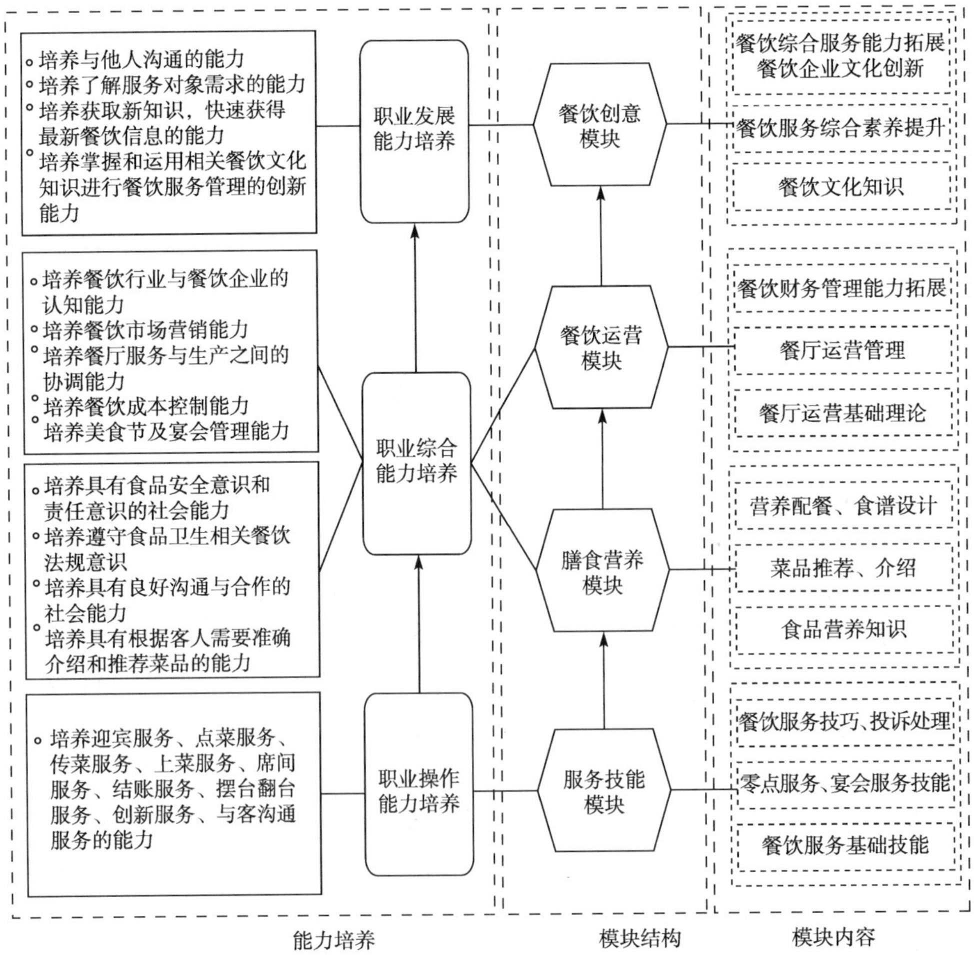

图2　专业课程体系图示

"三层递进、四个模块"的专业课程体系是指以培养学生综合职业能力为目标,通过职业分析及岗位工作分析,以职业岗位工作所需的知识、技能、态度为依据,开发、设计课程模块;模块内容分层逐级递进,培养学生的操作能力、职业综合能力和发展能力,关注学生知识、态度、能力的协调发展。基于此,根据企业岗位工作要求,提取典型的工作任务,分析完成典型工作任务所需要的能力,进行课程内容的开发,构建基于工作任务和工作过程的课程体系。通过新课程体系的实施,实现职业教育与企业需求的对接,满足行业对高技能人才的要求和学生未来可持续发展的需要。

(三)基于工作任务导向,创建"集成融合式"教学模式

"集成融合式"教学模式的核心是通过校企联动、产学合作的形式,将学生带入企业真实的工作环境,以完成职业情境中的实际工作任务为中心,通过服务技能和职业素养类核心课程群的集成,在专业知识与工作任务之间建立关联,引导学生在完成工作任务过程中,建立理论知识和实践技能之间的联系框架,以工作逻辑取代知识逻辑,为学生提供体验完整工作过程的学习机会。

"集成融合式"的教学模式注重学生体验式学习,注重学生实践能力、综合职业素质培养,增强了实践教学与职业活动的融合性。经过"实践—认知—再实践—再认知"的循环往复,学生逐步形成了对服务工作的深度认知,内化了专业知识与技能,培养了学生解决问题能力、合作、沟通的能力。

(四)基于人才需求规格,建立课程考核评价标准

专业课程的考核评估具有评价、反馈和导向功能,科学的考核评价是指导教法、学法和能否实现课程目标的重要检验标准之一。[2]依据企业人才规格标准进行课程教学及课程考核评价,完善校内与校外、教师与学生、过程与结果三结合的考核评价体系,实现人才培养规格与企业人才需求规格的有效"对接"。评价指标涉及职业基本素养(职业修养)、专业基础知识、职业技能等方面。

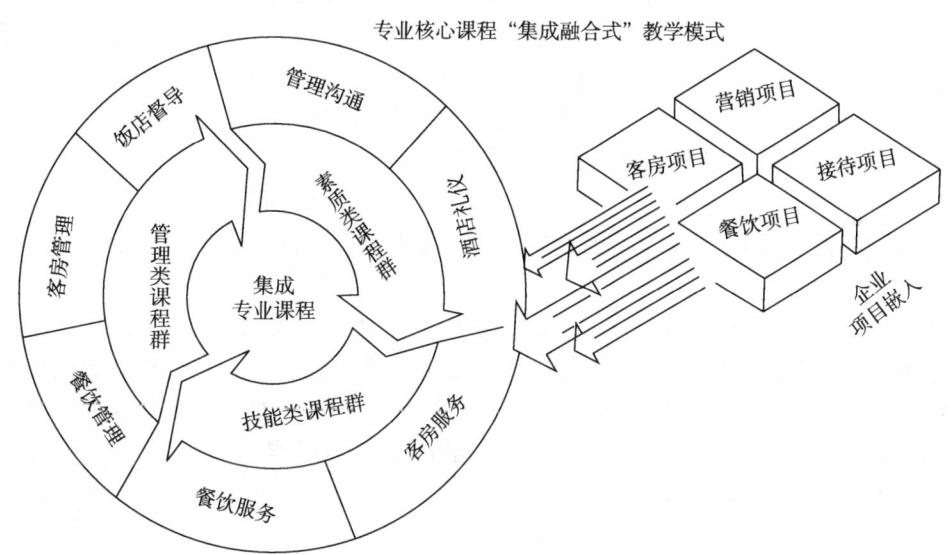

专业核心课程"集成融合式"教学模式

同时,结合企业用人需求标准的变化及时进行课程考核目标的动态调整。建立以工作准备、实时监控与及时纠偏为主线的教学质量监控体系,改变传统的以学业(传统笔试成绩)为导向的考核评价制度。以学生岗位工作实践评价为例,将学生到岗率、现场操作工作绩效、企业导师评价和专业教师评价等作为课程考核的主要指标,采取实际操作、调研报告、方案设计等多种考核形式,专业教师与企业专家协同建构课程考核评价体系,以全面考察学生的专业学习效果及其职业素质的养成效果。

三、校企合作培养人才,双方实现"互利共赢"

借鉴北美CBE(基于能力培养)人才培养模式理论和汲取德国"双元制"职业教育经验,校企联动、协同培养餐旅类应用型人才,共建人才培养体系的实践,有力地促进专业建设和教学改革,利于学生职业能力的培养;在"产学合作、协同培养"人才的过程中,专业教师深入企业挂职锻炼、带领学生进行企业实训(实习)、与企业合作进行产品研发、为企业提供管理咨询服务等;与此同时,聘请行业

专家和企业资深人士作为学生职业导师或学校客座教授（兼职教师）。多年以来已构建了一支稳定的专兼结合的"双师型"师资队伍，形成结构合理的师资团队，更为重要的是，有利地促进了青年教师的专业成长，为不断提高人才培养的质量提供有效保障，解决"双师型"专业师资不足的问题。

基于实现校企双方"合作互惠、互利共赢"的合作目标的校企联动，协同培养餐旅类应用型人才，共建人才培养体系的实践，也同时解决了校企深度、广度合作实施困难、企业方动力不足的问题。

遵循"社会交换"原则，依据"利益相关者理论"，遴选业界影响力大的龙头企业作为校企联动合作伙伴，寻求协同建设的关键点和生长点。明确校企双方的"责权利"，双方优势互补，优质资源共享，使校企双方形成利益"共同体"。充分调动行业企业与学校合作育人的积极性。校企联动、产学结合的内涵之一即学校根据企业需要培养人才、为企业输送符合要求的学生。学校根据行业发展和企业需求，有针对性地设置专业课程体系，实施人才培养方案，共同培养企业和市场需要的人才，实现人才培养与需求的"无缝"对接。通过校企联动，协同构建餐旅类人才培养体系的实践，一方面，有利于专业建设与人才培养；另一方面，追踪行业、企业对人才质量规格的需求动态，学校为企业量身定制培训课程及咨询服务，为企业培养所需后备人才；解决企业用人需求问题，有效降低企业人力资源成本，真正实现校企双方"互利共赢"。

四、结　语

我国职业教育正处于上升发展时期，政府主导、行业指导、企业参与，校企联动、产学结合具有广阔发展空间，校企合作已成为高等职业教育改革发展的主线。在校企联动，协同构建人才培养体系的实证研究中，由兼顾"需求导向"与"就业导向"向同时兼顾"雇主导向"发展，充分体现"二元化"职业教育办学主体，"雇主"（企业）与学校共同成为高等职业教育重要的实施主体。在人才培养模式上，企业深度参与专业人才培养方案制定、专业建设、课程设置、教材开发、师资共建、实训基地建设等工作，将行业企业用人标准融入职业教育人才的全过程。[3]"雇主导向"强调职业教育发展过程中"雇主"积极性和主动性的发挥，"雇主"不应只是学校办学的"合作者"，还应该在"校企关系"中发挥主导作用。[4]北京联合大学旅游学院通过校企合作育人多年的实践，探索构建"人才共育""过程共管""成果共享""责任共担"的紧密型合作办学机制。[5]这一校企合作育人、合作办学的实证研究将有助于总结高等职业教育校企合作培养人才的经验，建立可以推广、复制的相对稳定的校企合作、产学结合的办学模式及人才培养模式。

校企合作作为职业教育办学的重要形式，在推进职业教育可持续发展中扮演着不可替代的作用。[6]校企合作是凝聚资源、凝练特色，实现高等职业教育品牌的重要路径；校企合作教育的实施，使专业教育与人才培养更具"实践性"与"应用性"。今后，我们将探索更深度与更广度的校企合作办学的长效机制，寻求职业教育校企合作制度和机制的不断突破和创新，以推动高等职业教育人才培养质量的提升。

参考文献

[1] 管平. 职业教育国家主导模式的建立—对校企合作、工学结合的再认识 [J]. 中国高教研究, 2013 (6).
[2] 王美萍. 关于"工作过程系统化"教学模式应用的探讨 [J]. 中小企业管理与科技, 2009 (7).
[3][6] 刘占山. 光明网—光明日报：以制度和机制创新推动校企合作 [EB/OL]. http://news.gmw.cn/2013-11/21/content_ 9556674.htm
[4] 王东. 论"雇主导向"职业教育体系的建设 [J]. 中国职业技术教育, 2013 (24).
[5] 唐伯虎. 关于国家骨干高职院校建设校企合作的实践与思考 [J]. 中国职业技术教育, 2013, 25.

随班就读孤独症儿童对不同句子类型理解的个案研究

王 梅 周梦佳

2013年，党的十八大报告中提出，要大力促进教育公平，支持特殊教育。随班就读是发展我国特殊教育事业的重要举措，也是一条符合我国国情的普及残疾儿童少年义务教育的有效途径（朴永馨，2008）。现今，越来越多的家长选择把轻度智力障碍儿童、高功能孤独症儿童等送到普通学校中随班就读，到目前为止，我国随班就读学生超过26万人，占在校特殊学生总数的64%（赵斌，王琳琳，2013）。但他们在学校中能否有质量地学习和生活，摆脱"随班就坐"的局面是个值得深入研究的问题。对教师教学语言和同学交流语言的理解程度影响着他们的学校生活。因此本研究选取一名在普通小学就读的高功能孤独症儿童为被试，分析其在不同情境中对各种句型的理解情况，分析判断原因，以期为随班就读老师和随读生家长提供教育指导的参考。

1 问题的提出

影响随班就读质量的因素很多，学生的语言理解和表达能力是一个十分重要的因素。虽然有的孤独症儿童到普通学校融合，但参与学习的时间往往不尽如人意。分析原因发现，与他们理解语言的能力有紧密关系（李茂2010，孙圣涛，2011），对词义的理解在其听语理解中有重要作用（李伟亚，2009），但孤独症儿童对常用句型理解的具体情况却鲜有研究。本研究选取一名就读于普小二年级的高功能孤独症儿童为研究对象，了解其对教师、陪读人、同学课上、课下常用语言的理解反应情况，分析其句型理解的特点，为其教师、家长、同学更好地与之沟通提供参考，同时也可以为更多的随班就读的教师、随读生家长提供有效沟通的建设性意见。

2 研究对象、方法和过程

研究对象是一位8岁的孤独症女孩，就读于北京市某普通小学，由外婆陪读。她虽主动语言不多，但理解一般用语较好，语言表达比较清晰，情绪比较稳定，能认识书本中多数汉字，语文课基本可以跟上、数学课需要个别辅导。

本研究的方法主要为个案研究法。通过记录教师、同学以及主要监护人日常所说的语言，在一对多情境下和一对一情境下分别观察并记录被试在听到相应语言所做出的反应，被试的反应主要分为两种：有反应和无反应，而有反应又包括正确反应和错误反应。例如教师在上课前和大家说把手背后，被试按照要求完成，记正确反应；被试乱动，记错误反应；被试无动于衷，记无反应并分析这些反应。记录的语句分为陈述句、祈使句和疑问句三类。

3 研究结果与分析

3.1 对三种不同句子类型理解能力的研究结果

本研究共记录了被试教师、同学以及主要监护人所说语言共计843句。通过表1可以看出，陈述句275句，正确反应22句，错误反应48句，无反应205句；祈使句279句，正确反应85句，错误反应48句，无反应146句；疑问句289句，正确反应33句，错误反应55句，无反应201句。在句子的正确反应方面，祈使句的次数最高。在句子的无反应方面，陈述句的次数最高。应用SPSS11.0分别对被试三

[作者简介] 王梅（1968—），女，北京联合大学教授。研究方向：发展性障碍儿童教育、课程与教学设计；周梦佳（1991—），女，北京联合大学学生。

种句型的正确反应、错误反应和无反应的次数进行 F 检验，结果表明：被试对三种不同句型的反应次数的主效应显著（p＜0.001），说明被试对三种不同句型的反应存在显著差异；被试对三种句型的理解能力有差异，祈使句的理解明显好于疑问句句型，对陈述句的理解最差。被试的无反应次数远远多于有反应的次数，且差异显著。

表1 被试对三种不同句型反应数量

		有反应				无反应		合计	
		正确反应	百分比	错误反应	百分比	反应数量	百分比	反应数量	百分比
陈述句	一对一	16	11.35%	23	16.31%	102	72.34%	141	16.73%
	一对多	6	4.48%	25	18.66%	103	76.87%	134	15.90%
祈使句	一对一	42	29.37%	22	15.38%	79	55.24%	143	16.96%
	一对多	43	31.62%	26	19.12%	67	49.26%	136	16.13%
疑问句	一对一	45	29.61%	15	9.87%	92	60.53%	152	11.35%
	一对多	10	7.3%	18	13.14%	109	79.56%	137	11.35%
总数		162	19.22%	129	15.30%	552	65.48%	843	100%
统计检验	被试在有反应和无反应、正确反应和错误反应、正确反应和其他反应中对三种句型的反应次数有显著差异（P＜0.001）								

被试在对大家所说的 843 句话中，无反应和错误反应的语句高达 703 句，且陈述句理解最差，说明她对大多数语句不理解或者注意力分散严重；对包含指令的、多为老师发出的祈使句反应相对较好，可能与她习惯执行指令有关，也可能与祈使句句式短、语气较为强硬、句尾多为降调，同学都在正确反应，易于理解和模仿有关。

通过表 2 的数据可以看出，被试在一对多的情境下，有反应的句子为 125 句，无反应句数为 279 句；在一对一的情境下，有反应的句子为 166 句，无反应的句数为 273 句。检验结果说明了一对一、一对多情境中句子理解没有差别。被试在一对一的情境中对疑问句的正确反应较好；在一对多的情境中对祈使句做出的正确反应较好，但没有显著差异；被试在两种情境中，对陈述句的反应没有显著差异。

表2 被试在不同情境中对三种不同句型反应数量的百分比

	有反应数量	百分比	无反应数量	百分比	合计数量	百分比
一对多	125	30.94%	279	69.06%	404	47.92%
一对一	166	37.81%	273	62.19%	439	52.08%
总数	291	34.52%	552	65.48%	843	100%
检验结果	被试在两种不同情境（一对一、一对多）中对不同句型的反应无显著差异（P＞0.001）					

3.2 不同情境中句子理解能力的研究结果

一对多情境与一对一情景相比更容易分散注意力，但这里的差异并不显著，结合表1结果可以看出，被试反应受理解程度影响较大。进一步分析观察记录可以看出，被试在教师发出"把嘴闭上""我喜欢抓紧时间的孩子"时无反应，但当教师发出"不准说话""快把字抄完"时，被试能做出正确反应。说明被试不能将"把嘴闭上"迁移到"不准说话"，不理解陈述句"我喜欢抓紧时间的孩子"是让儿童抓紧时间，联想能力不足影响了他们的理解；上文提到的语气语调的影响也需要认真考虑。同时，词语理解（思维、想象能力）也影响反应，老师在讲到"柳絮指的是春天的时候柳树长的小白毛"时，同学都表示惊讶，聚精会神地听讲，而被试完全在走神，无任何反应。

3.3 不同沟通对象语言理解能力的研究结果

为了探究不同沟通对象对被试的语言理解有无差异，随机选取被试教师、家长以及同学的语言各 90 句。其中，陈述句 30 句，祈使句 30 句，疑问句 30 句。结果详见表3。

表3 不同对象与三种句型反应数量的百分比

		有反应				无反应		合计	
		正确反应	百分比	错误反应	百分比	反应数量	百分比	反应数量	百分比
陈述句	教师	2	6.67%	5	16.67%	23	76.66%	30	11.11%
	家长	5	16.67%	1	3.33%	24	3.33%	30	11.11%
	同学	0	0	3	10%	27	90%	30	11.11%
祈使句	教师	14	46.67%	3	10%	13	43.33%	30	11.11%
	家长	11	36.67%	4	13.33%	15	50%	30	11.11%
	同学	7	23.33%	1	3.33%	22	73.34%	30	11.11%
疑问句	教师	6	20%	3	10%	21	70%	30	11.11%
	家长	8	26.67%	1	3.33%	21	70%	30	11.11%
	同学	3	10%	1	3.33%	26	86.67%	30	11.11%
总数		56	20.74%	22	8.15%	192	71.11%	270	100%
检验结果	被试在与不同沟通对象（教师、家长和同学）进行沟通时对不同句型的反应有显著差异（P<0.001）								

在随机选取的270句话中，被试有反应的句子为78句。其中，陈述句有反应16，无反应74；祈使句有反应40，无反应50；疑问句有反应22，无反应68。通过表3的检验结果说明被试对三种句型的反应受沟通对象不同的影响。

被试对家长使用的陈述句和疑问句所做出的正确反应优于教师和同学；被试对教师使用的祈使句所做出的正确反应优于家长和同学。

观察记录表明，同样的内容，由教师以及家长用同样的句型与被试进行沟通，被试所做出的反应有所不同。做操时老师说：把手抬起来！被试马上正确执行，而陪读的姥姥说"把手抬起来"，被试不执行。被试有时不是不理解句子，而是受情绪、环境干扰，有意不反应或错误反应。

4 讨论与建议

4.1 多种手段提高理解能力，改变被动参与状态

改变被试对三种常见句型无反应和错误反应高发的情况，提高随班就读的时效性，应多管齐下。首先，结合被试的认知特点，加强图文配合的教学，可以培训陪读人员围绕不易理解和产生新旧经验联系的概念事先准备图画，如讲道柳絮在随机选取的270句话中，被试有反应的句时准备这方面的图片等。其次，加强疑问词语气、语调，陈述句关键词的语气语调或放慢语速。第三，培养表象、联想能力，提高对抽象词汇的理解能力。第四，用观看录像等方式理解隐喻句的实际意思，观察同学的反应，并强化其参照同学反应的能力。

4.2 改善情绪，提高注意力和主动关注

被试情绪不稳定就会影响其注意稳定，更难主动关注老师和同学，如受到老师的直接批评、或看到老师严厉批评同学后，被试会有一段时间无反应或错误反应增多；在一对多的嘈杂情境中也会减弱反应。同时，情绪不佳还容易增加有意不反应或错误反应的可能性。

对祈使句正确反应多，往往说明她被动执行多、主动参与少，这样更容易引起情绪不佳，教师应注意祈使句带来的正、反两方面影响，保护学生的情绪，发展主动配合。

4.3 根据儿童心理甄选沟通用的主要句型

被试在一对一的情境中对疑问句的正确反应最高，主要监护人在与被试的交流过程中，使用疑问句多用来询问被试所熟悉的问题，语气往往和缓，带有商量性质，易于被试理解，把主动选择权交给被试，也有助于集中注意做回应。对家长、同学的疑问句反应较好，对教师疑问句、陈述句反应不佳的现象应引起教师的深思，改变沟通句型、语气，以视觉辅助、语气和蔼并有选择商量性作为辅助沟通手段十分重要。本研究是个案研究，不能全面反应随班就读老师的整体教学语言状态。

总之,通过对孤独症儿童个案不同句型的反应进行调查,反映了该儿童对三种句型的掌握情况依次为:祈使句、疑问句、陈述句。被试对家长使用的陈述句和疑问句反应较好,对教师使用的祈使句反应较好。因本研究是个案研究,数据不具有可推论性,以后应尽可能增加观察者,提高观察有效性。

参考文献

[1] 朴永馨. 改革开放 30 年中国特殊教育的发展与变革 [J]. 现代特殊教育, 2008 (12): 4-13.

[2] 孙圣涛, 姚燕婕. 中重度智力落后学生对不同句类理解的研究 [J]. 中国特殊教育, 2011 (12).

[3] 李茂. 自闭症儿童疑问句个案研究 [D]. 上海外国语大学, 2010.

[4] 李伟亚. 自闭症谱系障碍学生汉语句子理解过程的实验研究 [D]. 华东师范大学, 2009.

[5] 毛倩. 汉语自闭症语障儿童语言的教育基础研究 [D]. 鲁东大学, 2012.

[6] 昝飞, 马红英. 言语语言病理学 [M]. 上海: 华东师范大学出版社, 2005: 1-10.

[7] 赵斌, 王琳琳. 论特殊教育从人文关怀到行动支持走向 [J]. 中国特殊教育, 2013 (1).

[8] 易花萍. 汉语名词陈述句研究 [D]. 复旦大学, 2009.

[9] 李囹. 近 30 年现代汉语祈使及祈使句研究述评 [J]. 重庆工商大学学报, 2010 (6).

[10] 郭婷婷. 现代汉语疑问句的信息结构与功能类型 [D]. 武汉大学, 2005.

[11] 曹漱芹, 方俊明, 顾未青. 高功能自闭症儿童语言交往训练的个案研究——视觉支持性语言教学的探索 [J]. 中国特殊教育, 2009 (7): 60-66.

地方普通高校学生学习动力的制度影响分析及对策研究

尹庆民　马丽仪　年书

1 引　言

随着我国高等教育大众化目标的持续推进，大学生教育质量已成为社会关注的焦点，学生学习动力问题，是当前高等教育研究的重要论题。众多研究成果被应用到教育实践领域，作为教育工作者制定有效的教学行为策略的理论依据（池丽萍，辛自强，2006）。北京联合大学是典型的应用型大学，更加注重学生技术应用能力、理论应用能力、综合应用能力及文化传承和创新能力的培养（徐永利，2012）。探求学生学习动力的影响因素并进行科学测评，制定有效的学习动力制度是实现上述培养目标的有效途径和手段。国内外许多学者对学习动力的影响因素进行了研究，澳大利亚学者毕格斯（1987）的研究将学习动力分为浅层动力、深层动力、成就动力。罗伯特（2001）认为学习动力有目标引力、内部驱力和情境动力三种形式。更多的学者将学习动力划分为内部动力和外部动力。周贤君（2004）、王丹丹（2010）等认为社会、学校、家庭构成了影响大学生学习动力的外部因素。从整体上看，目前国内外的相关研究还存在一定的局限性（范君晖，2012）：一是对于地方普通高校学生学习动力的深入调查研究较少，相关研究还不能适应学校的发展的需要；二是缺乏在一定制度层面通过引导、激励、约束、控制，以增强大学生学习动力等方面系统性的研究。

制度具有指导性、约束性、激励性、规范性等特点。学校制度是指学校为适应社会发展需要，以教育观为指导，依法民主、自主管理，能够促进学生、教职工、学校及其所在地区的协调和可持续发展的一套完整的制度体系。为了探究学生学习动力背后的各种影响因素，本课题参照毕格斯的学习过程问卷和自我效能感问卷，编制了学习动力问卷（包括表层学习动力（以下简称"表层动力"）、深层学习动力（以下简称"深层动力"）和自我效能感三部分，在对北京联合大学 5 个学院、31 个专业、5 个年级（即于 2012 年 7 月对 2008 级、2009 级、2010 级、2011 级和于 2012 年 9 月对 2012 级新生）共 3650 名本科学生深入调研的基础上，使用 SPSS 软件工具，对北京联合大学学生的学习动力进行较为系统的研究。本研究作为系列研究成果之一，旨在研究影响学生学习动力的制度因素，提出学校有关制度改革的建议和具体措施，从而在制度层面正向引导、激励学生的学习动力，促进我校学生的学习效果，并为地方普通高校研究学生学习动力提供借鉴。本次调查共发放问卷 4305 份，回收后剔除缺失数据较多的 655 份问卷，共剩余有效问卷 3650 份，问卷回收有效率为 84.79%。

2 调查结果与分析

学习动力按其作用方式可分为内部动力（内驱力）和外部动力（外驱力）。内部动力是指由于学生内部需要而推动学习的一种力量，属于内因。外部动力是指由客观目标或要求等诱发的一种学习力量，属于外因。表层动力是一种外部动力，学生为应付教师和考试而学习，主要采用机械学习策略，用尽可能少的时间和精力去重复学习可能要考的内容和要点，所学到的只是零散的、孤立的、肤浅而无意义的知识材料。深层动力是一种内在动机，由好奇心产生，为满足兴趣、探究意义而自发、主动学习，主要采用建构主义的编码和有意义学习策略，学到的是结构化的、有意义的知识和内容。自我效能感是指个体对自己是否有能力为完成学习所进行的推测与判断。自我效能感与学生的学习行为密切相关。

［基金项目］北京联合大学教育科学研究课题"地方普通高校学生学习动力研究"资助。
［作者简介］尹庆民（1954—），男，河北人，北京联合大学管理学院党委书记，教授，主要研究方向为经济学、教育管理。

2.1 表层动力与深层动力的关系

对表层动力和深层动力进行配对样本 T 检验的结果显示，$t = 20.2$，$df = 3649$，$P = 0.000$，这表明北京联合大学学生深层动力显著强于表层动力。但学习动力随着年级、性别、家庭背景、生源地的不同而各有差异，从而使调研结果呈现出独特的特点。

2.2 学习动力与学习自我效能感的关系

调查结果显示，学生自我效能感与表层学习动力呈负相关（$r = -0.184$，$P = 0.000$）；自我效能感与深层学习动力呈显著正相关（$r = 0.378$，$p = 0.000$）。这表明，学生的自我效能感越高，表层学习动力越低，而深层学习动力越高。

2.3 学习动力的年级效应

调查结果显示，随着年级的增长，学生的表层学习动力升高，深层学习动力下降。其中，低年级即 2012 级学生的表层动力显著弱于其他年级，深层动力显著强于其他年级。而 2011 级的表层动力也显著弱于 2009 级（$P = 0.016$）和 2008 级（$P = 0.012$），深层动力显著强于 2009 级（$P = 0.04$），其他各年级间没有显著差异。自我效能感也随着年级的增高而减弱，但是在大四出现升高。具体来看，2012 级自我效能感最高，2011 级其次，2009 级和 2010 级显著低于 2011 级（$P = 0.006$，$P = 0.000$），但是 2008 级的自我效能感显著强于 2009 级和 2010 级。

2.4 学习动力的性别差异

男女在自我效能感、表层学习动力和深层学习动力上都有显著差异。男生的自我效能感显著低于女生（$P = 0.01$），表层学习动力显著高于女生（$P = 0.00$），深层学习动力边缘显著高于女生（$P = 0.049 < 0.05$）。

2.5 学习动力的家庭背景差异

自我效能感受家庭因素的影响不显著（$P = 0.156 > 0.05$）；表层学习动力则显著受到家庭因素的影响（$P < 0.001$）。城市学生的表层学习动力最强，农村学生的表层学习动力最弱。深层学习动力受家庭因素的影响不显著（$P = 0.095 > 0.05$）。

2.6 学习动力的生源地差异

京内学生的自我效能感显著低于京外学生（$p = 0.000$），表层学习动力显著高于京外学生（$p = 0.000$），但深层学习动力没有显著差别（$P = 0.169$）。

2.7 学习时间与自我效能感、表层学习动力和深层学习动力的关系

以学习时间为自变量，自我效能感、表层学习动力和深层学习动力为因变量，分别进行方差分析，结果表明，学习时间的效应均为显著，$P < 0.001$。学习时间越多，效能感、表层学习动力和深层学习动力均越高。

2.8 学习成绩自评与学习动力、自我效能感的关系

学生的自我效能感随着成绩的下降而下降，深层学习动力随着学习成绩的下降而下降，表层学习动力随着学习成绩的下降而显著上升。也就是说，相比成绩好的学生，成绩靠后的学生自我效能感和深层动机更低，表层动机更高。

3 讨 论

3.1 联大学生学习特点分析

（1）总体上，主动式学习显著高于被动式学习，且随着年级、性别、家庭背景、生源地的不同呈现不同特点

从总体样本来看，学生的主动式学习显著高于被动式学习。以往的研究认为，作为北京市属的综合性地方普通高校，联大学生书本知识相对薄弱，实用化倾向较为明显，绝大多数学生抱着毕业即马上就业，而不继续深造的目的上学（张妙弟，江小明，2007）。但本次调研结果显示，整体来看，学生的学

习动力更多来自对学习的兴趣，而非为应付考试而学习。这说明随着学校多年改革和生源质量的改变，联大学生的学习动力比以往有了显著变化。但随着年级、性别、家庭背景、生源地的不同，联大学生的学习呈现出如下不同特点。

1) 从年级看，高年级学生主动学习的意愿比低年级时下降，应付考试意愿上升。

2) 从性别看，男生应付考试的意愿显著高于女生，主动学习的意愿也略高于女生，但男生的自我期望与评价显著低于女生。

3) 从家庭背景看，城市学生比农村学生更倾向于为应付考试而学习。

4) 从生源地看，京内学生比京外学生更倾向于为应付考试而学习。

（2）随着年级的增长，学生对自我的期许减弱，但是在大四出现升高

（3）随着学习时间增多，对自我的期许、被动式学习和主动式学习意愿相应增加

（4）学习成绩正面影响对自我的期许和主动式学习意愿，负面影响被动式学习意愿

3.2 原因分析

以上联大学生表现出来的学习特点，其形成原因可以结合本课题同时发放的影响因素问卷进行分析。该影响因素问卷共22道题目，采用4点量表，从1到4代表很强到很弱。对每道题目的得分进行统计，按照得分大小排序，得出学生认为对自己学习影响最大的因素（排名靠前的因素）分别是自身的理想和追求，家长、老师和同学的鼓励和好评，专业的社会认可度，图书馆，奖学金，自习室，同学之间的竞争等。而对学习影响最小的因素则依次是班主任、讲座活动、辅导员、宿舍、食堂。因此，从学生认为对自己影响最大的因素着手，改进或加强现有相关学校制度，将对学生的学习动力起到显著的促进作用。同时，加强和转变学生评价较低的因素的管理，查找不足之处，促使其发挥应有的作用，也可以成为加强学校制度建设的抓手。

4 对　　策

4.1 加强学生思想政治工作，特别是理想信念教育相关制度的建设

（1）理想信念教育应当适应科学发展观的要求，坚持以人为本，促进学生全面发展。学校应有针对性地进行教育和引导，重视学生的应用能力和综合素质的培养。例如，积极组织学生开展志愿服务等社会实践活动；举行校园文化活动，强化提升校园文化建设内涵；设立学生科技活动基金；积极创造条件促进各校区大学生人际活动，包括文艺演出、体育比赛、学术交流等；加强课外社团活动，提高学生参与率；科学设计假期社会实践环节，使学生深入社会、了解社会、参与社会，等等。

（2）要注重教育方法的改革创新，增强思想政治教育的针对性和实效性。深入推进思想政治理论课教学改革和马克思主义理论学科建设。例如，从入学教育、主题军训到毕业教育，纳入人才培养方案，实现德育活动课程化；形成以问题导入式专题教学为主的课堂教学体系、以随堂社会观察和思想政治理论综合实践为主的社会实践体系，以及全校统一的考核体系；加强大学生发展辅导，满足学生学业、职业、情感、身心等多方面发展需要。

4.2 建立家长联系制度，共同帮助学生成长

建立完善家长参与的多方督学机制，以专业、年级、班级为单位建立家长联系制度，通过多种方式，定期通报学生的思想成长、学业发展、奖励处分等情况，对学生异常表现、情绪波动等及时沟通，与家长共同帮助学生成长。

4.3 扩大激励机制的覆盖面，使更多的学生能够脱颖而出

改进优异学生培养机制，在转专业、辅修专业、攻读双学位和考研方面给予一定的支持、指导，并使其享有优先权，激发学生学习热情和积极性，带动学习风气；建立各种激励机制，除评定奖学金、助学金以及优秀生以外，设定单项评优奖和技能型奖学金，解决激励措施单调、激励面窄等多种问题；建立学生自主学习机制，鼓励并支持学生建立学习互助组，激发学习潜能；完善以国家助学贷款为主体、勤工俭学为主导的资助工作体系，解决学生实际困难。

4.4 强化专业建设和办学特色，提升专业社会认知度

（1）打造高水平师资队伍。突出教学业绩考核，改革教师评价办法；完善教师遴选和聘任制度，加大培养和引进力度，优化教师结构。

（2）加快教育教学改革。探索科学基础、实践能力和人文素养融合发展的培养模式，推动交叉培养和联合育人，创新教学方法和学习方式，强化师生交流互动。积极调整完善本科培养方案，大力加强特色专业建设，打造品牌专业。

（3）建立完善导学机制。建立全校学业辅导中心，实施组织机构导学；学院教学系部与学生工作部门配合，试行导师制，从新生入学开始配备导师，由任课教师担任，指导学生学习，开展教师导学；开展专业教育与专业导论，进行专业导学；招生就业处实施全程生涯规划，开展课程导学。

4.5 加强图书馆、自习室的管理和服务，加强宿舍和食堂的服务意识。创造优越环境延长学生学习投入时间

4.6 开展学科竞赛、科技竞赛，鼓励同学们的良性竞争

团委与教务处协作，通过科技立项、设立创新基金等措施，加强对学生的资金与智力支持，鼓励学生广泛参与科研活动。开展学院特色科技竞赛活动，扩大学生参与面，丰富学习生活，提高学习动力。学校教务处与教学部门通过组织学科竞赛、专业比赛与行业竞赛，参加行业认证考试培训，提高学生获取双证书率，促进专业技能与专业兴趣提升。

4.7 加强班主任辅导员队伍建设

认真开展辅导员深度辅导工作，形成辅导员为主体，班主任、党政干部、专业基础课老师及关工委退休老同志"集团化作战"的精细化工作网络，点对点对学生进行深度辅导。积极鼓励辅导员参与思想道德修养与法律基础、大学生职业生涯规划、心理素质教育、形势与政策等课程的教学实践，支持以团队形式进行科研和教学攻关，定期举办各类专题培训班，不断发挥辅导员队伍的团队效应。对辅导员实行导师制，即为辅导员配备一名经验丰富的辅导员导师，对其在工作、学习和职业发展规划上进行全方位指导。加强培训，鼓励其长期从事辅导员工作并向职业化、专业化、专家化方向发展。

参考文献

[1] 池丽萍，辛自强. 大学生学习动机的测量及其与自我效能感的关系 [J]. 心理发展与教育，2006（2）：64-70.

[2] 徐永利. 教学科研并举，提高人才培养质量——在 2012 年学科建设与研究生教育工作会闭幕式上的讲话. 2012，12.

[3] Biggs, J B. Study Process Questionnaire Manual [M]. Melbourne：Australian Council for Educational Research，1987.

[4] 周贤君，张胜利，周笑妮. 独立学院学生教育管理模式探索 [J]. 高等农业教育，2004（8）：71-73.

[5] 王丹丹. 浅析省属高校学生学习动力不足的原因 [J]. 长江大学学报，2010（5）：88-89.

[6] 范君晖. 应用型高校大学生学习动力激励机制 [J]. 高教论坛，2012（9）：77-78，100.

[7] 张妙弟，江小明. 大众化教育背景下应用型大学教学体系的改革与建议 [J]. 中国高教研究，2007（1）.

中青年教师专业化发展的院校培训支持体系构建

付晨光　曲学利　周华丽　张军辉　韩忠强

近年来，我国高等教育快速发展，大学教师特别是中青年教师的专业化发展问题，成为保障和提升高校人才培养质量的关键和瓶颈，日益引起教育主管部门和各高校的重视。教育部"十二五"期间推出"本科教学工程"，正式提出要建设30个左右的国家级大学教师发展示范中心。越来越多的高校逐步建立教师教学发展中心等支持机构，助力教师特别是中青年教师的专业化发展。其中，构建适合中青年教师专业化发展需求的院校培训支持体系成为重中之重。

明确规划目标，重视支持中青年教师专业化发展

北京联合大学的《"十二五"时期改革和发展规划》和2011年"人才强校计划"中特别提出了"实施人才提升计划，完善人才资助和激励措施，构建优秀人才脱颖而出的途径和渠道，有效提升中青年骨干教师队伍的整体素质；实施人才培育计划，分层次、分类别建立青年教师的培育体系，培养青年教师就是培养青年英才，要分学科有计划地培养青年教师。为青年教师搭建快速成长的平台，切实提高青年教师教学和科研能力""培养100名左右具有创新意识、素质精良、发展潜力的中青年骨干人才"。2012年，学校人才工作会进一步通过《关于加强中青年教师培养和资助工作的意见》，加强中青年教师培养和资助的力度，重点加大45岁以下、具有博士学位、副高以下专业技术职务教师的培养与资助；依托学科建设平台，通过向重点学科倾斜，建设团队和协同创新平台，加大对中青年教师的培养资助力度，采取各种措施，进一步加大对中青年教师的培养和资助。

设立教师教学发展中心，有效推进教师专业化发展

学校一直高度重视教师专业化发展。2008年，成立北京联合大学教师培训学校，旨在深化落实学校应用性的办学理念，促进教师和管理人员培训的系统化、规范化，不断提升教师的执教能力和管理人员的履职能力。2012年，成立北京联合大学教师（教学）发展中心（Center for Faculty Development，简称CFD，以下简称"中心"）。中心下设发展中心指导委员会（校领导和学校人事处、教务处、科研处、研究生处、应用型高等教育发展研究中心、工会等有关部门负责人组成）、发展中心专家委员会（聘请兼职校内外教学名师）、发展中心办公室（副处级单位，设立专门职位3人~4人，挂靠校人事处，业务相对独立运行）。2012年3月，教师培训学校纳入教师（教学）发展中心。

中心作为促进全校教师专业化发展的研究与服务机构，致力于搭建教师专业化发展的研究与服务平台。主要职责包括：一是作为学校教师培训主责部门，承担全校教师培训、青年教师指导和培育等工作；以教师教学能力提升为目标，根据不同教师群体特点，聘请教学名师，为教师提供教学理念和技能、研究能力和方法、学术道德和师德等方面的培训。二是进行教师发展研究，探索教师专业化发展规律，开展相关教育科学研究，进行教师评价、教师团队和教学效能方面的研究，并协助有关部门开展相关工作，促进教师专业化发展。三是举办教师发展论坛等学术交流活动，促进教育教学研究。四是提供多样化教师教学咨询指导服务。创建适合学校特点、专业特性、教师个人特质的多样化教学咨询指导机制，开展教师心理咨询等服务。五是促进教师团队建设，鼓励教师组建和参与各种形式的学术共同体，促进不同学科专业教师间交流与经验分享。

［基金项目］本文系北京市委组织部2012年优秀人才培养资助集体项目《北京联合大学中青年教师专业化发展支持体系的研究与实践》（项目编号：2012F-06）的研究成果。

［作者简介］付晨光，北京联合大学党委副书记。

开发教师发展系列活动，构建教师发展院校培训支持体系

经调查发现，不同年龄段教师在教学、科研和职业发展方面希望得到学校帮助的需求重点各不相同，但中青年教师在教师专业化发展各方面的需求都很强，因此，应该成为学校教师教学发展中心工作和服务的主流群体。而在不同的年龄段，中青年教师的专业化发展需求表现出不同特点，如何根据这些不同需求来设计和开发适合中青年教师实际需求的培训支持方案，成为重要研究课题。立足教师实际发展需求调查，教师教学发展中心设计开发了以下比较成熟的品牌活动。

1. 面向新教师，组织开展新教师研习营

教师教学发展中心对每年新入职教师进行职业导入教育，每学年秋季学期组织。内容包括校情介绍、教学理念与方法、教学技能提升、师德修养、职业生涯规划、心理健康辅导、团队拓展训练等。帮助新教师尽快熟悉和适应学校环境，适应学校工作要求，树立信心，为自身职业发展奠定基础。为落实学校人才工作会精神，中心进一步完善了新教师入职教育方案，研习营从新入职教师的特点和需求出发，转变培训为主的活动方式，采用更加丰富多样的系列拓展活动，开设了走进联大、互动拓展、执教能力培养、教学观摩与交流、职业发展导航、在线学习等6个模块的活动，帮助新教师"进校门、进课堂、进团队""近名师、近学生、近管理"，帮助新教师尽快适应学校环境、适应学生、适应教学和科研要求。其中，在执教能力培养阶段，以"让大学课堂更具吸引力"为主线，开展了系列主题活动，聘请教学名师担任小组导师，对新教师进行教学设计的指导和实战演练与公开观摩点评。同时，与学校教务处合作，组织开展了"青年教师执教能力系列培训"活动，截至2012年，已组织1轮，为期2个月，受到新教师好评。

2. 面向新晋升副教授等特定群体组织专题培训班

教师教学发展中心根据学校发展和教师发展的实际需求，面向教师队伍中的关键群体，围绕学校和教师发展中的重点、难点和创新性问题，面向全校不同层面的教师，适时举办各类专题培训班，满足不同教师群体多样化的发展需要，为教师专业化发展提供贴心服务与支持。中心每年面向全校上一年度新晋升的副教授，开设专题培训班，以新晋升副教授的学术能力提升为主线，完善设计了培训方案，开设了教师职业发展、科学研究、学科建设和教学建设改革四个模块的培训，并组织学员结合学校的科研和教育科研课题申报，进行分组申报的实战演练和专家点评。培训班按学科类别分组，由学校相关学科带头人亲自指导，旨在提升新晋升副教授的学术能力。同时采用专题讲座、学术互动、科研项目申报模拟、在线学习等形式，并组织优秀学员赴兄弟院校交流学习。

此外，教师发展中心还根据学校和教师发展需要，组织名师面对面、教师实践计划、中青年教师学术沙龙、教师发展论坛和教师职业发展导航等系列活动，对在教学、科研中遇到问题和困惑的教师提供咨询和帮助。

3. 实施"教师执教能力提升计划"，支持在职教师教学发展

由校教务处牵头，实施"教师执教能力提升计划"。2010年，学校召开教育教学工作会，出台了《北京联合大学教育教学奖励暂行办法》《北京联合大学关于实施教学品质提升计划的意见》和《关于进一步加强教风学风建设的意见》系列文件，明确将"教师执教能力提升计划"列入学校教学品质提升计划，为提升教师执教能力作出了制度规划。学校先后组织了市（校）级名师开放课堂、与北京科技大学"大手拉强手"、举办"中青年教师执教能力提升系列讲座"等活动，要求各教学单位组织中青年教师深入校内外名师课堂系统学习、观摩，学习先进的教学方法；聘请国内外教学督导专家、教学名师、专家学者等来校举办讲座；聘请教学经验丰富、教学效果好的教师担任青年教师导师。截至2012年，约400人次的中青年教师参加为期一学期或两学期的系统观摩学习，累计1000多人次教师参与讲座。2011年，学校启动每学年1次的"中青年教师执教能力比赛"和"教学优秀奖"评选，引导广大教师积极投身教育教学改革研究、教学方法研究和讲课技巧凝练。2012年，学校进一步将"中青年教师执教能力比赛"定位于中青年育苗项目，为"教学优秀奖"提供优秀比赛选手，而"教学优秀奖"则直接为"北京市教学名师"做遴选和人才储备，通过比赛，培育产生一批师德高尚、爱岗敬业、教学效果优秀的教师，成为学校教育教学的中坚力量。

4. 依托学院分中心，开展教师发展特色学术与实践活动

中心积极支持相关特色学院和学科设立教师发展分中心，开展中青年教师专业化发展活动。例如，旅游学院分中心于 2011 年 3 月启动《教师职业生涯规划》，第一期主要以中青年教师为主体，与行业企业合作，提升教师行业企业实践和服务能力。学院实施"教师企业（行业）实践行动计划"，派出 19 人参加企业（行业）实践，选派 6 名青年教师到北京市旅游委进行为期半年的挂职锻炼，坚持每年举办"首都旅游发展论坛""《旅游学刊》中国旅游研究年会"等活动，目前已成为北京乃至全国旅游界的品牌学术活动。商务学院分中心以双语教学为抓手，提升教师国际化能力和素质，制定了相关支持政策，先后选派 65 名教师到国外高校进修学习，帮助青年教师与国外研究机构建立合作关系。通过国内外培训、积极推进网络学堂建设、加强全英语（双语）教学能力培训与交流、基本功大赛等多种形式的活动，从教学理念更新、教学艺术与技巧、教育技术应用等全面提升教师双语教学能力。目前，学院承担全英语教学的教师 33 人，其中专业教师达到 32%，成为学院的鲜明特色。应用科技学院分中心建立青年博士俱乐部，以思想活跃、开放交流、学术自由、交流平等为特点，受到教师欢迎，不仅青年教师踊跃参加，一些教授、副教授、老讲师也参与其中。俱乐部开展的主题活动有：主讲课程的建设思路、青年教师科研方向与方法交流、科研实际问题解决、个人职业生涯规划交流、宣传工作交流、青年教师工作生活和学习的取舍观、电商信管类课程改革方向与思路探讨等。

引入全国精品课程和名师资源，建设校级教师发展在线平台

校级教师发展在线平台是全国高校教师网络培训中心集中全国优质教学资源，整合研发用于解决校级教师培训，提高教师专业发展的整体服务项目。目前，学校借助这个平台建立了自己的校级教师发展在线学习平台，将全国高校教师网络培训中心开发的在线培训课程及相关资源和活动直接接入学校，面向全体教师开放，同时可以在平台上开展校本培训和师资培训管理。现在校级教师发展在线学习平台已经有 1340 门课程，并且计划每年新增 200 门左右，这些在线课程可供本校教师直接选课参训，学校可根据专业设置自由选择课程内容和数量进行组合上线，所选课程及公共辅修资源面向全校教师开放，培训有效期一年，参训教师不限人次。在线学习的方式普及丰富了教师课余学习的方式，教师自己可以自由支配时间，不受空间限制，课程内容丰富，还有名家讲座，从多角度拓宽教师视野，对于教师专业发展尤其是中青年教师有很好的帮助作用。目前，学校已出台政策让所有教师通过本系统进行继续教育学习，并计入继续教育学时。

教师发展是一个古老而崭新的重要领域，对高校教学质量的提升具有基础保障作用，加强教师发展研究和探索实践，任重而道远。因此，建构合理的教师发展院校培训支持体系对于促进高校教师发展能给予很好的保障作用。

以开放式教育推进大学内涵式发展

乔东亮

近年来，伴随教育国际化程度的不断拓展，开放式教育已经成为世界大学教育的潮流。党的十八大报告提出，高等教育要推进内涵式发展，为我们指明了方向。但我国大学教育怎样实现内涵式发展，切实办出一批高水平的世界一流大学，仍是值得国人认真研究和破解的大问题，更是需要大的改革才能做好的大文章。这就需要我们深刻把握当前实际，充分借鉴国外大学办学经验，在办学理念上实现突破，积极探索，大胆实践。

开放式课件计划的启示

1999 年，时任美国麻省理工学院（MIT）校长的布朗先生，向自己学校这个"小社区"提出了一个问题：在当今世界互联网的大环境中，如何给自己学校定位？经过讨论，大家认为，学校在 21 世纪的任务就是面向全世界，推动教育发展。从这个理念出发，MIT 从 2001 年开始启动"MIT Open Course Ware"（OCW）项目，即"开放式课件计划"，逐步把 MIT 的 1800 种课程全部免费推上网络，供全世界有志向学的人免费学习。其中包括授课录音、笔记、作业等一系列内容，并且还在不断增加成本昂贵的免费录影带。为此，MIT 投入大量资金和人力物力，主动承担服务社会的责任，并且是服务超越国境线的国际社会，但并不考虑经济回报，因而被称为"智慧慈善"。后来的 MIT 校长霍克菲尔德女士在谈到"OCW"时说，这是一种"在全世界范围内推进教育的理念。通过 MIT 的开放式课件，世界各地的教育者和学者都能从我们教师的学术活动中受益，同时也加入到了一个世界性的学习型群体中，大家一同公开、自由地分享知识与交流思想，并从中获益"。[1]

由此，我们可以看到一所世界知名大学的前瞻、自信和水平：敏锐洞察社会发展、环境变化对高等教育的影响，把握先机，及时行动，领先世界；理念自信、质量自信、发展自信，以开放突破"小社会"，走向"大社会"，以分享突破"小利"，赢得"大利"；用课程计划这个最能体现大学师资水平、教育水平、办学水平的核心支柱，展示自身的强大与魅力。现在，这项计划已经扩展到全世界包括哥伦比亚大学、杜克大学、约翰霍普金斯大学、卡耐基梅隆大学、塔夫茨大学、犹他州立大学、华盛顿大学、加州大学伯克利分校、耶鲁大学、斯坦福大学等一大批知名大学在内的 200 多个高校，免费向世界提供的开放课程达三四千种。遗憾的是，10 多年过去了，我们尚未看到，我国有哪些高校建立或正在建立 1800 种课程的"OCW"。虽然，我国近 10 多年来，全国评选出了几千门国家级精品课程、10000 多门省级精品课程和若干国家级教学名师，但目前也只有清华大学、北京大学、北京交通大学、北京航空航天大学、中国矿业大学、中央广播电视大学等 6 所大学表示要与 MITOCW 项目合作，且仅局限在继续教育方面。

西方国家的大学在开放式教育方面走在了前面，麻省理工学院引领了开放式教育的方向。美国学者阿特巴赫说，如果教育的边界完全开放，最强势的教育供应商就拥有了无限制的权力，无法与之竞争的国家与机构若想发展真是难于登天。当下，开放式高等教育的最大供应商无疑是美国和欧洲，相比之下，我国高等教育在开放式教育方面差距较大，形势不容乐观。

我国大学教育面临的环境

当前，经济全球化和教育信息化、国际化浪潮汹涌，国外大学人才辈出、硕果累累。我国大学教育面临的发展环境要求我们的办学理念要与时俱进，寻求突破。

[作者简介] 乔东亮，男，北京人，北京联合大学副校长、教授。

（一）教育教学环境正在发生着巨大变化

随着世界经济全球化、贸易自由化的推进，各国都在想方设法利用国内和国际两个教育市场，优化配置本国的教育资源，抢占世界教育的制高点。在科技与信息迅速发展的今天，知识的更新以加速度的方式递增，研究表明，知识更新速度18世纪以前每80至90年翻一番，19世纪60年代每50年翻一番，而20世纪90年代以来，每3~5年翻一番。教育国际化和科技与信息的迅速发展，使传统的教育教学模式发生着巨大变化。

首先，云学习全面拓展。学生手持网络终端，访问各种教学实施平台，获得资料，领取任务，提交作业，在线交流，以学生为主体、教师为主导的新型学习模式正在不断拓展。其次，经典课程网络化加速流行。麻省理工学院、耶鲁、哈佛、剑桥、牛津等世界名校的名师，纷纷借助互联网这种强势的传播手段，把自己的讲课内容在网络上公开传播，供人免费学习。最后，大学之间互认学分，师资力量相互开放。反观我国大学教育，教育模式就显得滞后，已经跟不上形势发展的要求。

（二）传统的教育模式依然强势

第一，封闭的、传统的教学模式，仍然是我国大学教育的基本模式。教师课堂上传授书本上的知识，竭力完成繁重的教学工作量，忙于各种PPT课件设计，而包括借用互联网手段在内的交流、启发、引导和解惑的教学环节却很薄弱。同时，包括教学内容与学习要求等在内的培养方案设计，仍然传统且同质化。

第二，大学与大学之间，大学与社会机构之间的传统"围墙"依然坚固，"象牙塔"依然和大学的概念密切联系在一起。大学之间互选课程、互认学分、优势互补、合作发展的态势还未很好显现，各自依然循着传统的、有科研成果显示度的高水平大学标准而封闭式发展着。大学与其他社会组织之间，围绕人才培养的联系还仅仅停留在一份合作协议、一副基地牌匾、一场启动仪式的前奏曲中，缺乏进一步深入合作的环境和动力，彼此开放、互动、可持续的合作项目却很少。

第三，大学教师队伍管理与学生的培养模式处于封闭的状态。学校强调引进优秀师资为我所用并为我管理，忽视优秀教师资源的社会性。学生的培养模式传统而封闭，如果说国内大学与国外大学之间还有一些互认学分、互派留学生进行"2+2""3+1""3+2"等合作培养人才的尝试，那么国内大学之间的这种机制就极为缺乏。国内大学生大都在封闭的机制下完成学业，各大学只对考入本校的学生有培养责任，不尽"大社会"责任，与大学精神格格不入。

一方面是教育的国际化引起教育模式的巨变，另一方面是我国传统的、封闭的教育模式依然占据主要地位，它表明，我国大学教育已经不能适应教育发展趋势的需要，面对教育国际化和教育模式的新变化，每一所高校领导、每一位教育工作者都有责任对此进行思考，破解难题。

实施开放教育，推动大学发展

开放式教育是伴随着现代教育信息技术的发展而产生的一种新型教育模式，它要求教育对象、教育观念、教育资源和教育过程全部开放。大学教育内涵式发展主要是指通过对内部现有教育资源的优化配置、学科及专业结构的优化调整来提高人才培养质量，是有质量、有特色的发展，当前我国大学面临的环境和问题要求我们通过实施开放式教育，实现大学的内涵式发展。

（一）以开放式教学组织第一课堂，引领课堂教学质量提升

第一课堂教学仍是我国大学教育最主要的教学形式，大学生在校接受教育、获取专业知识的时间70%以上是在第一课堂。提高第一课堂教学质量，对提高教育水平至关重要。目前，大多数高校的第一课堂依然封闭，这与当前社会为人们提供的丰富多彩的获取知识的渠道相比，很不合拍。如果我们设计下面这种第一课堂，就会取得很好的效果。

譬如教师与学生一起分享两个以上国外或国内著名大学的教授，或社会机构的著名专家讲授的网络视频公开课，教师先和学生一起讨论本课程涉及的若干问题，再将学生分成若干小组，开展讨论与实践探索。之后，师生共同分享各小组的交流和辩论，并由教师进行点评。最后由教师和同学间的自评成绩一起加权平均，给出综合成绩。

在这里，课堂是开放、自主、探讨和对话的教学场所，教师的职责主要不是传递知识，而是激励思考，是"一位顾问，一位交换意见的参加者，一位帮助发现矛盾论点而不是拿出现成真理的人"。[2] 如此，即能培养学生的独立思考能力和社会实践能力。一些国际上知名的大学无不采取这种教学方法，如美国的伯克利大学、耶鲁大学，英国的牛津大学和剑桥大学等，鼓励学生质疑和挑战传统权威，鼓励自由探索精神，鼓励学生为自己的观点辩护。

其实，在国内，与开放课堂密切相关，开放课程已不是什么新生事物，教育主管部门在推进质量工程过程中，鼓励教师建设开放课程，评选名师、精品课程都要求有45分钟的"开放课程"，但其数量、质量远不能媲美国外大学。教育主管部门应该在管理机制和办学体制上加强设计，给予政策和专项经费的支持，给教学名师创造开放课程的条件，让社会分享其学术成就，使学生无论在哪所大学就读，都可以通过网络选修这些名师的网络公开课，修满一定学分，经本人申请，通过毕业答辩，均可以取得相应学校的学历和学位。如此就能深度引领我国大学教育内涵式发展。

（二）以开放式平台，组织师资队伍，发挥全社会优秀教育资源的作用

清华大学前校长梅贻琦说："一个大学之所以为大学，全在于有没有好教授。"[3] 可见，一支优秀的教师队伍对一所大学的发展是多么重要。在教育国际化的当下，大学除了从国内招聘部分名师外，更要加大聘用外籍知名教授的力度。面向世界招聘教师，这是现代大学的普遍做法。如世界著名大学新加坡国立大学的教授、副教授，约一半左右是从国外大学聘请的。聘请国际一流的大师来校任教，不仅能为师生学习世界前沿科学知识提供机会，更有利于我们借鉴、吸收国外先进的大学精神、教育理念和教学方法，促进我国大学尽快从半封闭的状态中解放出来，融入到国际教育大乾坤中去。

其次，国内大学之间加大开放优秀师资力度。一方面，大学之间整合教师科研力量，组建学术团队，发挥多种学科优势，实现协同创新；另一方面，教育部门要鼓励大学之间师资力量的对外开放和师资的社会化共享，尽快打破大学师资各自封闭的局面，至少实现优秀教师的地区所有，名师可以同时接受多所高校聘用，而不受现有的教师年度和聘期考核办法的限制。

再次，开放教师国外交流空间。教师的自闭、自高，乃至不学习、不超越，往往源于他们的交流不够、见识不广。新加坡国立大学每年向哈佛大学、约翰霍普金斯大学和麻省理工学院等顶尖大学选派访问学者，使本校教师的教育理念、教学水平得以提升。在这方面，我国大学做得还很不够。

（三）以开放式培养方案，组织教学工作，提升人才培养质量

开放式培养方案，首先要鼓励大学以特色和优势开放式选择生源。鼓励学校公开教学资源、培养方案、招收人数，允许高校在一定分数线之上，不分年龄和原学历，面向国内外选择生源。西方国家的很多大学招生都实现了国际化，芝加哥大学面向世界130多个国家招生，其办学理念是"培养世界公民"。我国大学在国际化招生方面，要尽快打破目前国内外高校联合培养、相互招收留学生的局限，促进国内高校面向所有国家的所有人开放。

其次，改进学习成绩评价方式。大学教育的主要目的是弘扬大学精神，培养完美人格，为经济社会发展服务。因此，对于学生学习成绩评价标准，应采取综合、多元、开放的动态评估系统，以综合素质是否提高、是否具有良好的素养和创新精神以及提出问题、探究问题、解答问题的能力为标准。

最后，结合现实，突出实践环节。开放式培养方案要突出教学实践、科研开发、创新创业于一体的综合性实践基地的建设和应用。美国加州理工大学倡导"少一点演讲，多一次演练"，提倡师生多做社会实践。美国斯坦福大学在学校周围吸引了众多的企业、设立了研发机构，目的也是为了让学生有更好、更便捷的实践去处。我国一些大学虽然建有科技园、创业园，但学生参与的实践太少，今后应当大大加强。

参考文献

[1] 林达. 看麻省理工学院的开放式教育 [DB/OL]. http://www.sina.com.cn 2007-04-16.
[2] 联合国教科文组织国际教育委员会. 学会生存 [M]. 北京：教育科学出版社，1996.
[3] 刘述礼，黄延复. 梅贻琦教育论著选 [M]. 北京：人民教育出版社，1993.

高校学生成绩管理的问题与对策研究

刘在云

成绩管理是高等学校教学管理工作中最核心的部分之一，与教风、学风建设密切相关，更是提高高校社会声誉的重要抓手。在教务管理信息化建设的过程中，与手工管理阶段不同，修改学生课程成绩是客观现实，需要具体问题具体分析。本文针对近几年作者所在高校的教师（或部门）修改学生成绩的现象、原因及解决对策进行了全面的分析。

一、修改学生成绩的现象及原因

1. 修改学生成绩现象

每学期课程考核后，任课教师通过教务管理系统录入、校核、提交学生成绩。教师提交后再申请修改个别学生成绩，主要体现在：（1）对已提交的成绩修改，大多数是提高成绩、将不及格改为及格，理由比较宽泛；（2）对取消考试资格的考生恢复其考试资格并需要录入成绩；（3）将缺考、缓考的信息弄错，特别是只有几个人的学期初补考也往往有弄错的现象发生；（4）申请给未列入系统学生名单的学生成绩，原因很复杂，比较极端的情况如给参军、退学已经离校的、或根本没有报到的新生成绩；（5）未及时给上课的学生成绩，如留级、重修，事后很久再申请补登成绩等。

教学单位或职能部门要求修改学生成绩，主要体现在：（1）给不在政策范围内的个别学生争取政策；（2）争取特殊政策，即没有的政策；（3）因为管理不到位导致的学生成绩缺失的补录入，比如到毕业资审时才发现学生的某科目成绩缺失，往回查找不到过程档案，还有给学生争取到了某个外部政策，并协调好了操作方法，但对下届学生执行不及时，导致需要再次补就学生成绩等。

2011—2013年校教务处处理的教师修改成绩申请，共计813人次、5809条记录，除去符合政策的成绩折算、因为实施某些临时教学改革（如创新试验区等）需要而在系统外运行的课程补录学生成绩数据外，教师（或部门）申请修改成绩的记录为758人次、2034条成绩记录，具体分布为：2011年下半年332人次、1068条成绩记录；2012年275人次、713条成绩记录；2013年151人次、253条成绩记录；而2014年年初到目前为止修改成绩61人次、64条成绩记录。

数据说明，我校修改学生成绩现象呈逐年下降的趋势，这与学校2011年出台《学生成绩管理办法》并严格执行有很大关系；也反映出教师越来越重视、越来越认真对待学生成绩问题；管理部门只要管到位，终会起到良好效果，起到严肃教学、学风的作用。

2. 修改学生成绩原因

从教师提交的书面材料来看，理由是多方面的，大部分是技术性错误，如时间紧、工作忙、教务系统中的学生数据不准确、变化多、系统不友好、系统慢等，的确这些原因一定程度上客观存在；就其深层次的原因而言，可能是个别教师对待教学不太认真，有时连最基本的授课对象是谁都不能准确把握，特别是过程考核执行不过硬，往往经不起学生的质疑，在学生提出疑问后，最简单的处理方式就是修改成绩。教学单位（部门）提交修改成绩申请，涉及政策，影响面更大；深层次的原因可能涉及本部门工作开展的方便程度，这是部门之间的管理协调的永恒问题，最终体现学校的综合管理水平。

二、成绩管理存在的困境

1. 部分教师对学生成绩的责任意识欠缺

教师是学生成绩的唯一责任人，其他管理人员无权修改学生成绩。因此，教师给每位学生成绩更需

[作者简介] 刘在云，北京联合大学教务处。

慎重并做到有据可循，这是最基本的要求；但问题是少部分教师可能存在以下问题。

一是对学生特别是"自我约束能力差的学生"关注度不够。学生学籍变动是常态，往往会导致教师授课对象的变化，这就需要教师至少在学期初、中、后通过教务系统仔细核对所授课的学生名单，另外需要特别关注那些学习吃力、自我管理能力较差的学生。做到给每位学生的成绩心中有数，遇到不清楚的及时与管理部门沟通。这种看似"简单"的要求其实可能是最难达到的，我们需要在教学上将"以生为本"落到实处，教书育人。

二是提交修改成绩的教学档案不全。在成绩管理执行层面，只需教师的修改申请合理就行。学校规定教师在第一次上课须向学生说明本课程考核要求以及成绩构成，课程一般由平时成绩和期末成绩按一定比例构成。期末考核后教师通过教务系统录入、校核并提交成绩；如须更改，需要提供"完整的教学档案即赋分依据"。我们需要教师对修改成绩有绝对的权威依据，但目前，学校在要求教师为修改成绩提供支撑材料方面遇到很大的阻力。

三是不太重视教学过程，最后"一考了之"。教师的权威来源于对整个教学过程的把控，我们在积极推行"3+X"的过程考核，而现实恰恰是不尽如人意，并且发现极个别教师在给学生平时成绩时，存在考核不严、给分标准模糊、给分较随意等现象，不同学生的平时成绩区分度不大，极端情况一律是每人 100 分，或 90 多分、80 多分等少数几种分数水平，导致平时成绩很高，期末闭卷考试成绩偏低。于是教务处不得不设置一个程序，将教师"给全班平时成绩平均分大于 85 分且均差小于 5 分的"暂时不允许提交，需要给出适当的说明后再提交到正式成绩库，结果仅 2012 年下半年就有 321 人次教师被拦截，这对于每学期 4500 人次左右的总录入数不算太多，但这种措施得不到绝大多数教师理解。平时成绩在一定程度上反映一个教师的教学态度和一个班级的学风状况，基于学生、课程等的不同，基准可以不同，但整体要合理，起码有一个科学的分布。不重视教学过程给教师改成绩、学生质疑成绩提供了"土壤"。

2. 职能部门间、部门与教师间沟通不到位

教学管理制度的制定过程不是教务处一个部门的事，需要全校师生、职能部门的积极参与，特别是相关职能部门和教师的"积极介入"，只有这样制度在执行过程中才能得到很好的贯彻。但在实际操作中，由于欠缺共同参与的环境，这导致在政策制定过程中征求意见时，响应者少，但在事后执行时却"意见一大堆"。此外，各项政策应该保持相对的稳定性与延续性，政策出台后要有广泛的宣传。比如成绩管理办法中，规定以等级分制记载的成绩转化为百分制时按就低原则，例如 A 相当于 90 分；但执行时意见就来了，学生和相关部门都要求从学生利益考虑，就高或取中，结果是教师会依据成绩出具单位有无折算说明来执行，而不是严格执行学校自己的文件，其实这样做是不严肃的。

三、解决的对策与建议

1. 进一步理顺校院两级管理模式，提高成绩管理服务水平

尝试基于信息化管理手段的教学管理流程再造，基本思路是向知名大学学习管理经验，建立校院两级成绩管理体系，制定统一的成绩修改规范。统一标准、规范流程后，将批准权限下发到二级教学单位，校教务处以检查为主。校级层面管"总体"，院级层面管"个体"，校教务处依据教务系统管理教师教学、学生学习过程方面的总体数据，并根据数据制定对策，学院依据数据及相关政策面向具体的教师、学生做解释说服工作，在教师登录成绩之前介入，多方协作，有机配合，为教师、学生提供更好的咨询服务，把成绩管理工作做好。

2. 政策导向过程教学，加强对教师过程教学的管理

坚持基础课程全校统一管理、专业课程学院管理。目前针对主要的公共基础课程如外语类、数理类、两课类、计算机基础类，都在试点实施根据该门课程特点的过程教学改革方案，学校一方面从严要求，保障教学质量，实现"统考"、教考分离、"匿名"电子阅卷、严管考试作弊等，另一方面让教师、学生"有努力目标与方向"，根据各门课程的不同特点、教学目标制定并实现有针对性的"3+X"过程教学、考核管理方案，针对不同类型的学生，因材施教，加强教学内容与考核方式的配套改进，提高平时成绩并通过多次多种形式的过程考核强化管理，使得"只要学生学习了、努力了，就有更多的通过机

会",激发学生的学习积极性,并且将不及格率、"成绩进步大小"作为对教师的考核要求,将统考详细数据仅提供给教师作为教学改进的依据。

3. 加强部门间、部门与教师的沟通

教务管理部门与相关教学单位(部门)建立良好的沟通机制,积极搜集特殊政策新要求,为制定(修订)学校成绩管理规定提供政策依据,并将新的成绩管理修订方案或政策及时传达给相关教学单位和教师,确保成绩录入的准确性与严谨性。

4. 强化师生对待学业成绩管理严肃性、严谨性的认识

面向师生积极宣传有关成绩评定政策,广泛树立教师"学生成绩责任第一人"意识,教师与管理部门严谨对待学生的成绩"质疑"。

总之,成绩管理工作是一个涉及制度的刚性与执行的灵活性之间把控平衡的管理问题,是考验教学管理部门管理水平的问题,如何既能较好的地贯彻执行管理制度,又有助于提升我校的办学声誉、服务好师生,促进学生成长成才,需要全校上下共同思考、不断改革完善、探索更合适的方法。

基于互联网培训管理方案的研究与设计

刘 莹

1 需求分析

1.1 内部工作管理平台

协同办公管理系统提供了各种通用的办公管理功能,该系统包括个人事务、协同办公、信息中心、流程审批、知识管理、人事管理、行政管理、个性设置等七大功能平台,可实现任务布置、任务催办、手机短信提醒、邮件收发、公告通知、考勤管理、工作日志、工作计划、绩效考核、会议管理、网络硬盘等内部管理功能,开放的接口设计,满足内部更多协同办公和推进执行力的需求。同时,EIP 统一信息管理平台为管理内部网站提供了完整的内容管理平台,实现了信息的分类组织、编辑、发布、访问控制和全文检索功能。基于 EIP 统一信息管理平台的信息发布功能,可以轻松搭建内部公共信息网,有效地实现信息传递交流、宣传内部制度、文化、提高工作效率,并结合外网全方位展现自身总体概况。

1.2 基础工作服务平台

1.2.1 资讯系统

分为两类:一类是工作新闻通知发布区,另一类是行业业界新闻动态发布区。

主要包括提供工作新闻通知、业界最新信息、市场动态、招标资讯、会议展览信息等。这里包括文字类与数据类两种数据库,后者主要是与采购有关的市场行情数据,如制造业与非制造业采购经理人指数、公路货运价格指数、海运价格指数等。

1.2.2 会员管理服务系统

会员注册(分级别,免费与付费)、登录权限、入会申请、会员信息查询和更新、在线审批、服务项目及优惠、管理办法、表彰奖励、缴费方式。

会员注册及管理系统的作用为:对于网站内的一些重要信息或其他服务,如果网站管理者不希望所有人都能看到,可以将浏览者分为几类人群或几级会员,当他们的个人信息通过了管理员的审核后方可通过自己所设定的用户名与密码登陆网站查看信息。如:普通浏览者可以看到 80% 的网站内容,普通会员可看到 90% 的内容,VIP 会员则可全部浏览网站内容。用户可以在网站上登记注册,选择会员的类别、查看的权限范围并成为预备会员,并提交到用户管理数据库,待网站审核通过后成为不同级别的正式会员,享有网站提供的相应服务或浏览相应信息。

1.2.3 培训认证管理系统

培训、认证管理系统主要内容如下表所示:

类别	内容
教材库	开发与更新
试题库	开发与更新
培训机构管理	培训机构的开发 培训机构的评估 培训机构库的建立与维护

[作者简介] 刘莹,北京联合大学师范学院。

续表

类别	内容
师资管理	师资的审定 师资的评估 师资库建立与管理
考试管理	在线报名 电子准考证发放 考生在线服务与分数查询
认证管理	认证体系的开发建立 证书发放与管理
在线多媒体远程教育与培训	在线培训课程 远程网络视频课程开发

1.2.3.1 C. P. M. 及 CPSM 专区

包括 C. P. M. &CPSM 纵览、C. P. M. &CPSM 培训、C. P. M. &CPSM 考试报名、认证等。考试系统，包括开班报名、考试报名、认证；培训机构管理系统，包括开班信息、在线付款等账务管理系统；师资评审系统。

（1）考试报名需求分析与设计系统原则

网上报名系统的研发必须以方便考生、考试管理为出发点，遵循下列原则：

①对于考生，必须方便他们填写个人信息。

②对于考务工作人员，必须保证信息足够，并能方便地转入常规报名系统。

③对于考试管理人员，提供可以用来进行后续研究的考生背景信息。

④考生报名费的支付方式安全方便。

⑤与常规报名流程顺利地结合。

（2）业务流程

考生自助上网完成报名全过程：

①传统报名开始前若干天，一直开通网上报名服务。

②考生网上选择考点和考试模块，注册个人信息，包括身份证件的名称和号码，获取预定考号。

③考生获得预定考号 3 天之内，通过银行向指定账户划款支付报名费，获得银行交易传票。

④考生在划款 3 天之内，上网输入预定考号和银行交易传票号码。

⑤考试管理人员每日从银行取回交易传票，以此为依据，对于已经上网报名并交费的考生确认其报名有效。

⑥考生在规定的时间内查询报名是否有效（具体时间视银行交易到账承诺等具体情况而定）。如果已经生效，自助打印准考证，与约定的身份证件同时作为参加考试的凭证。如果没有生效（这种情况只发生在银行划款未能到账，因此，数量极少），应与考试管理人员联系。

⑦报名有效后，数据库自动赋予考试准考证号。

其中，第 3 到第 5 步的交费过程，也可通过各商业银行的网上银行系统完成。

（3）应用程序开发

方便考生录入报名信息是应用程序开发的原则。为了遵循这个原则，在应用程序的设计中，应采用如下技术：

①服务有效性的自动判断；

②选择信息、命令按钮和操作提示的动态生成；

③录入信息的二次验证；

④自动处理错误。

应用程序流程如图 1 所示。

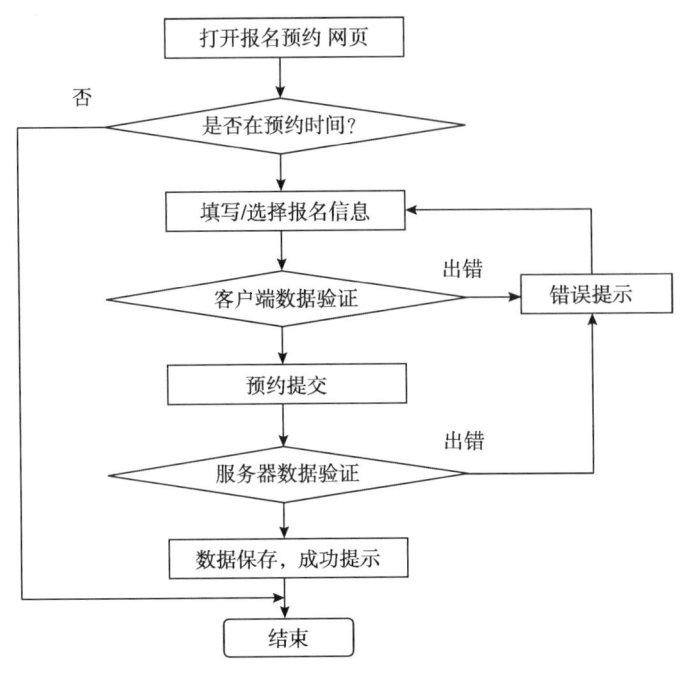

图 1　应用程序流程图

打开报名预约网页时，服务器检查系统时间，如果该时间内没有预约服务，提示考生，将页面设置为不可操作。

考生填写报名信息时，有效的考试模块、考点和考试时间自动生成下拉列表供考生选择。

考生填写结束，客户端进行数据的有效性验证，确保填入必填的项目，以及一些项目在合理的数据区间。

考生提交数据时，服务器端数据验证，对于相同考生多次预约同一次考试给予拒绝。

预约成功时，提示考生记录预约号码，并交费；获得准考证号、打印准考证，以完成整个报名过程。

任何一步操作，以及网络中断或者数据库停止响应时，服务器都给出动态提示，指导考生下一步操作。如此进行应用程序设计，既能保证报名信息录入的方便性，又可以有效地减少网络和数据库访问的数量，提高整个系统的效率。

1.2.3.2　内训专区

包括内训课程体系、师资团队以及成功案例等。

1.2.3.3　在线多媒体培训系统

在线培训系统没有限制用户数，及同时在线用户数，系统实际的在线用户数主要由服务器硬件决定；在线培训系统服务期内提供免费升级；在线培训系统功能齐全，从课程规划，课件制作，到学员学习，学习追踪，在线考核，成绩统计，视频会议等提供全程服务，还可与内部协同办公系统协同使用。在线培训系统支持 SCORM 国际标准，支持课件的在线导入，导出，这样方便进行课件制作和课件交流。

1.2.4　会议会展专区

会议会展分四种形式的会议：中博会跨采会、全球采购与供应链论坛、小型研讨会、采供对接会。每种会议的大致栏目有：往届回顾、会议信息（包括会议背景、会议组织、会议宣传、会议议程、演讲嘉宾介绍）、在线报名、会议在线直播、会议合作条件简介、会后资料的在线观看或阅读、友情支持企业简介。

2 设计与解决方案

2.1 重点技术环节分析

2.1.1 重点技术

（1）门户系统集成的支持能力

本系统采用标准的 WebService 服务接口和 XML 数据接口，能够支持多层次的网站内容浏览权限控制，能够根据门户用户权限不同展现不同的内容。系统能够与符合 J2EE 架构任何应用服务器集成，网站采用 SOA 架构，支持采用 XML 等数据格式的数据交换，因此系统具有良好可扩展性。

（2）多媒体编辑加工

经过多渠道的内容采集到文字、图片、视音频等多种格式丰富的素材资源，这就需要在编辑加工环节具备多媒体内容编辑的能力，实现文字、图片、视音频的混合编辑，制作出整合了各类信息、培训资料等的内容产品。同时，为了满足互联网信息快速报道、传递的特点，需要编辑器具备快速的图文、视音频编辑处理能力。

本系统采用基于 XHTML 的多媒体网站稿件编辑器，能够可视化的进行图片、文字、音频、视频等多媒体内容的混排，通过自动格式化、自动提取关键字、摘要等手段，大大提高文字、音频、视频等编排效率，并且还可通过集成的图片编辑功能如自动缩略图、抽线压缩、添加水印等提高图片处理效率。通过各项编辑功能的整合，使网站内容编辑在集成化的界面中即可完成对多媒体内容的高级编辑加工工作。

（3）先进的技术设计

1）纯浏览器界面基于 JAVA 的三层体系结构的应用

本系统的操作界面完全基于浏览器，系统的体系结构采用了先进的三层结构系统，基于 Java 实现，具有良好的跨平台性，可以运行在 Unix、Linux 和 NT 平台上，系统采用基于 Java 的一系列标准，通过使用第三方厂家提供的中间层产品，从而使本系统可在各种硬件平台、操作系统、WebServer 平台上进行方便的移植。

2）XML 技术

本系统接口数据流采用规范的 XML 数据流，保证了系统的开放性及可扩展性。

XML（eXtensible Markup Language）是从 SGML（Standard Generalized Markup Language）而来的一种新的置标语言，是由 W3C（WWW Consortium）为适应这些新需求而制定的。

2.1.2 系统技术方案的特点

整体方案采用基于 SOA 的松耦合整体应用架构，着重考虑到系统的灵活可扩展，同时，方案还应具有以下特点：

（1）先进性

设计思想先进、起点高，网络结构先进，软件开发工具先进，极大限度地采用市场覆盖率高、符合技术标准的标准化和技术成熟的软硬件产品。

（2）开放性及灵活性

通过采用以下技术，保证系统的开放性及灵活性。

1）数据层访问服务化：同种数据单一数据源，实现数据的数据访问方式服务化，实现数据与应用之间的松耦合；

2）系统模块化、组件化：采用 SOA 的集成方式，使系统模块化，系统接口标准化，渠道系统和客户服务系统，核心计费帐务系统采用松耦合面向服务的集成方式，适合业务流程的快速灵活调整，同时降低对厂商的过分依赖；

3）统一流程调度：使用统一的流程引擎，实现业务流程定义和调整，灵活应对企业业务发展需求。

（3）可靠性

具有容错功能，所有关键软硬件均采用双机方式，提供电信级的可靠性，确保系统的高可靠运行。

（4）安全性

最大满足地提供多层次的安全控制手段，建立完善的安全体系，防止数据受到侵袭和破坏。

（5）经济性

投资合理，优良好的性价比，且综合考虑设备价格的变化、扩展升级等因素。

- 系统的安全需求分析

Web 系统已经渗透到了网络时代的诸多领域，由于各种技术和非技术因素的存在和影响，Web 系统的安全已经成为严重而又深刻的问题。数据库管理系统的安全需求包括以下几个部分：数据库安全、Web 安全、系统安全、硬件安全。

数据库是 Web 系统的核心，是一种可共享的资源。因此，数据库的安全与保密是涉及 Web 系统全局性问题，是保证 Web 系统安全的关键。尤其是对于数据库管理系统中包含的统计数据来说，数据库的安全就显得尤为重要，一旦统计数据被非法访问，将会使本系统无法正常运行，对决策的效率造成严重的影响。

而另一方面，Web 安全包括物理安全、访问控制、传输安全。在平常，网络信息系统的建立遇到了很多问题，Windows 操作系统已经导致了一系列安全漏洞的存在。来自 Internet 上非法黑客的攻击，以及其他途径进入系统的非法用户都能将网络系统置于死地。因此，对于数据库管理系统来讲，要将网络安全风险降低到最小程度，最大程度保证系统中的信息不被非法篡改。

服务器的系统安全更是软件安全的核心。一旦系统被非法访问数据库与统计分析系统都将遭到破坏。所以一旦系统运行出现故障，数据库与分析系统都将瘫痪，造成不可恢复的后果。因此数据库安全为软件安全中的重中之重。

硬件安全包括地震、火灾、水灾等。因此应采用双机热备，可以有效地防止自然灾害以及人为硬件破坏所造成的损失。

2.2 系统设计

这一过程的基本任务是根据系统分析阶段所建立的逻辑模型转化为物理模型，对系统中各个组成部分进行具体的设计。在保证实现逻辑模型的基础上，尽可能地提高系统的各项指标，即系统的运行效率、可靠性、规范性、可修改性、灵活性、移植性、扩展性、通用性和实用性。

- 架构设计

一个系统的架构决定了系统开发的效率与系统运行的质量。因此在系统架构设计上，值得投入大量的时间和精力。既能方便本系统的实现，又可以为以后其他系统的开发，提供一个良好的参考模型。本系统架构的设计主要涉及以下几个方面：类库、卡片 - 列表、菜单 - 导航

类库

本文借鉴了大量的网站信息系统的开发理论，所以可以使用成型的项目类库并进行相应的扩充开发。其中类库中的通用类包括：数据库操纵类（ConnectionPool）、静态变量类（Constant）、通用方法类（Unit）。

数据库操纵类当中，只要通过泛型按表的结构集装数据并给定表名，就可以直接对数据库进行增、删、查、改等操作。本类中的各方法，可以通过泛型及表名，自动生成 SQL 语句，极大地提高了系统的稳定性和开发效率。

卡片 - 列表

卡片—列表模式，是当前最流行的数据输出和输入的方式之一。只要给列表页面传输一个表 ID，就可以方便地显示出表中的数据。而表 ID 则取自与一个管理数据库中所有表的主表。主表中包括替代字段名、连接地址、筛选条件、权限等功能。所以通过列表的形式，无需前台编写 SQL 语句代码，统一的管理模式进一步提高了系统的运行效率。而卡片则根据不同的表，设计了不同的显示界面。但界面的风格要统一，让用户感觉到操作简洁。

菜单 - 导航

此处的菜单，采用的是数据中动态读取的方式，增加了系统的灵活性和控制性。可以提高系统代码的可读性和规范性。将所有的菜单属性保存到数据库中，通过修改数据库中表的形式来完成菜单的开发

和管理。

系统功能模块划分为两个层次，第一个层次主要负责对外网登入用户的管理，包括登入检查、记载、统计、信息上载和查询支持等；第二个层次主要内网信息管理主要处理业务。因此系统的架构层次明确，从内外网开始着手开发。外网通常采用 B/S 模式，而内网通常采用 C/S 模式。B/S 模式有着使用方便的特点。但开发难度大，功能受限，并且受到网速的影响，会影响系统响应的速度。但用户无须安装客户端，只需要一个浏览器即可使用本系统。C/S 模式对网络质量要求高，需要高网速、稳定安全的网络。功能强大丰富、使用简单，但在部署的时候，每个用户都需要安装客户端才可以运行分析系统。因此综合系统的特点分析与设计，本系统对外采用 B/S 模式，对内采用 C/S 模式来整合系统。

系统是由可操作的若干模块构成，每个模块要尽可能的独立、功能明确，要能单独地进行维护、修改和调试，而不影响系统的其他部分。模块设计要遵照面向对象的设计方法，在此基础上，建立相关的业务系统开发平台，以利今后系统的更新和维护。

- 代码设计

代码是代表事物的名称、属性、状态的符号，为了方便计算机的数据处理和存贮，一般用数字、字母或特殊符号混合表示。设计合理的代码体系对提高系统的处理效率及提高信息的使用价值将产生积极影响。在代码设计中，要求代码具有识别性，即唯一性，以区别于其他事物；要求代码具有分类性，即可按照一定的规则进行分类，以便进行存贮和检索。

代码的种类很多，有顺序代码、分类代码、区段代码、关键代码、助忆代码、组合代码等。统计分析系统中要用到的各种代码，都要在分析研究的基础上取得统一，并适当考虑到系统将来可能的扩展。

- 输入输出设计

输入输出设计是整个分析系统与人对话的接口设计。输入设计必须在保证输入数据的准确性和可靠性的同时，做到输入简单、直观、清晰。输入系统要具有各种排错功能。输出设计包括打印报表，输出文件和屏幕显示输出的设计。一般要求报表和屏幕显示格式简明、美观、符合习惯。本系统采用了文件输出、表格输出、图形输出、打印报表 4 种模式。其中文件输出指用户可以将结果保存到计算机上，不受时间的限制。表格输出则通过网格的形式将数据显示在屏幕上。图形输出则通过饼图、折线图、直方图显示到屏幕上。打印报表则需要用户连接打印机来生成物理文件。

- 数据库表设计

数据库表是数据存贮的基本形式，数据库表的设计要本着可靠性、安全性、效率性、扩展性、可维护性、可读性的原则来进行。数据库表设计包括研究数据库文件之间的包容、制约和依赖关系；确定每个数据库表涵盖的项、关键项和辅助关键项；制定各种应用视图；确定用户对各类数据库表的访问权限等。另外，还要确定哪些表是要长期贮存的文件，哪些表是中间过程文件。在表设计中，要遵循数据库结构的规范化原则，减少重复和冗余，节省内存空间，提高系统运行效率。

2.3 系统实现

系统实现的过程主要包括程序开发、系统集成、系统测试、系统发布、人员培训等。

设备方案的选择从局域网设计、广局域网设计和系统支撑软件三个方面予以描述，涉及到了网络中用到的服务器、计算机、交换机及信息安全用到的技术和设备。

2.3.1 设备方案选择

2.3.1.1 网络简述

采购平台系统主要使用两种网络：对外的广域网；对内的局域网。对于本系统，这两种网络的主要差别在于网速和相关的网络设备。在安全上，此处主要通过路由器、防火墙、网管系统来限制外网用户非法访问局域网安全资源。

主要使用设备：负载均衡设备、中高档服务器若干、网线（双绞线、光线）、交换机、网管软件（防火墙、网络管理等相关软件）。见网络结构图。

2.3.1.2 局域网的设计

局域网（Local Area Network），简称 LAN，是指在某一区域内由多台计算机互联成的计算机组。"某一区域"指的是同一办公室、同一建筑物、同一公司和同一学校等，一般是方圆几千米以内。局域网可以实现文件管理、应用软件共享、打印机共享、扫描仪共享、工作组内的日程安排、电子邮件和传真通信服务等功能。局域网是封闭型的，可以由办公室内的两台计算机组成，也可以由一个公司内的上千台计算机组成。

网络的技术规范采用以太网。以太网是当今现有局域网采用的最通用的通信协议标准。该标准定义了在局域网（LAN）中采用的电缆类型和信号处理方法。以太网在互联设备之间以 10-100Mbps 的速率传送信息包，双绞线电缆 10BaseT 以太网由于其低成本、高可靠性以及 10Mbps 的速率而成为应用最为广泛的以太网技术。许多制造供应商提供的产品都能采用通用的软件协议进行通信，开放性最好。成本最低、稳定性高使得此本系统的网络采用以太网规范。如图 2 所示。

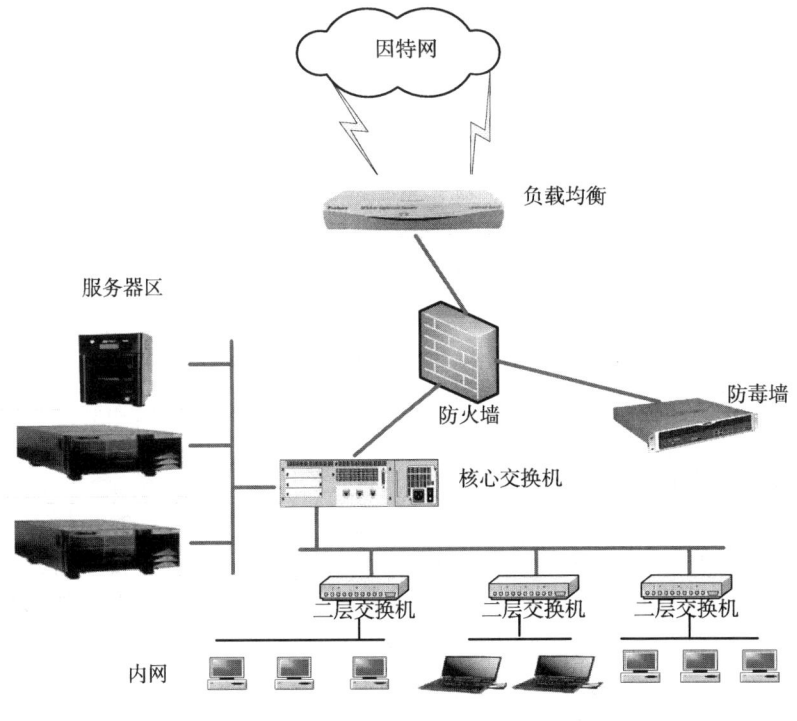

图 2　网络结构示意图

硬件包括电缆、接头、交换机、服务器、光纤等相关设备。光纤成本高，但传输距离远、稳定、速度快，适合远距离使用；双绞线成本低、稳定，适合近距离传输使用。楼与楼之间的远距离连接，应当采用光纤接入，使用其他线路，由于信号的衰减，无法完成通信的任务。而在楼内，则采用普通的双绞线即可。交换机的成本比路由器低，因此本局域网通过交换机来搭建，并且局域网采用统一的网关对外保护局域网安全，对内采用网管软件来控制，因此采用低成本的交换机适宜。本局域网的交换机需求比较大。除了使用必备的交换机外，还应当储备若干台交换机，以防故障时及时更换设备。一般中高档的交换机 24 小时运转的寿命为 1—2 年。因此在网络维护的时候，主要更换部件也应当为交换机与网线。服务器则应当采用中高档的配置。因为网络的用户庞大，一般的小型服务器的承载能力过小，容易使网络瘫痪。鉴于网络的运行效率与稳定，应当采用高档服务器。而网络管理软件也是维护网络必不可少的工具。

2.3.1.3　广域网设计

广域网（Wide Area Network），简称 WAN，是一种跨越大的、地域性的计算机网络的集合。通常跨越省、市，甚至一个国家。广域网包括大大小小不同的子网，子网可以是局域网，也可以是小型的广域网。广域网的设计应当充分考虑网速与安全。在购买网络的时候，应该考虑负载均衡、网络安全、网络管理等。本系统拟定采用 30M/S 光纤接入负载均衡方案。对外购买 3 条或者 3 条以上的网络接口。其中包括电信、网通、铁通、教育网等。将多种网络接在负载均衡设备上，可以提高网络的使用效率，有利于外网用户对统计分析系统的使用。安全机制则主要采用防火墙与网管系统来控制，可防止内外网用户非法访问关键资源，达到合理搭配的效果。负载均衡设备拟采用中心现有的设备。

2.3.2 系统支撑软件
2.3.2.1 操作系统

可以选择的操作系统，主要包括考虑 Windows 与 Unix。其中 Unix 价格低廉，国外盛行，但缺少技术支持，该系统平台下的开发工具及其他相关软件较少，适合上亿的超大项目的深入研究。而 Windows 系统技术支持强大，虽然价格稍微高一些，但开发工具成熟，在国内非常普及。

Windows Server 2008 是微软最新的服务器操作系统，Windows Server 2008 是专为强化下一代网络、应用程序和 Web 服务的功能而设计，可在企业中开发、提供和管理丰富的用户体验及应用程序，提供高度安全的网络基础架构，提高和增加技术效率与价值。

Windows Server 2008 虽是建立在 Windows Server 先前版本的成功与优势上，不过，Windows Server 2008 已针对基本操作系统进行改善，以提供更具价值的新功能及更进一步的改进。新的 Web 工具、虚拟化技术、安全性的强化以及管理公用程序，不仅可节省时间、降低成本，并可为 IT 基础架构提供稳固的基础。

Windows Server 2008 可为所有的服务器工作负载和应用程序需求，提供稳固的基础以及易于部署和管理的特性。全新设计的 Server Manager 提供了一个可使服务器的安装、设定及后续管理工作简化及效率化的整合管理控制台；Windows PowerShell 是全新的命令行接口，可让系统管理员将跨多部服务器的例行系统管理工作自动化；Windows Deployment Services 则可提供简化且高度安全的方法，让您通过网络安装快速部署操作系统。此外，Windows Server 2008 的故障转移群集（Failover Clustering）向导，以及对 Internet 协议第6版（IPv6）的完整支持，加上网络负载平衡（Network Load Balancing）的整合管理，更可使一般 IT 人员也能够轻松地实现高可用性。

Windows Server 2008 全新的服务器核心（Server Core）安装选项，可在安装服务器角色时仅选择必要的组件和子系统，而不包含图形化用户界面。安装较少的角色和功能表示磁盘和服务的占用空间可以减到最少，还可降低攻击表面（attack surface）的影响，并让 IT 人员能更专注于他们所必须支持的服务器角色。

- 内建虚拟化技术

Windows Server Hyper–V 为下一代 hypervisor–based 服务器虚拟化技术，可将多部服务器角色整合成可在单一实体机器上执行的不同虚拟机器，进而让服务器硬件投资的运用达到极致。即使在单一服务器上执行多个操作系统（例如 Windows、Linux 及其他操作系统），仍可拥有同样的效率。只要有了 Hyper–V 技术及简单的授权原则，即可轻易地通过虚拟化节省成本。

利用 Windows Server 2008 的集中化应用程序访问技术，亦可有效地将应用程序虚拟化。因为 Terminal Services Gateway 和 Terminal Services RemoteApp 不需要使用复杂的虚拟私人网络（VPN），即可在终端机服务器上执行标准 Windows 程序，而非直接在用户端电脑上执行，然后更轻松地从任何地方进行远程访问标准 Windows 程序。

- 专为 Web 而打造

Windows Server 2008 整合了 Internet Information Services 7.0（IIS 7.0）。IIS 7.0 是一种 Web 服务器，亦是一个安全性强且易于管理的平台，可用以开发并可靠地存放 Web 应用程序和服务。IIS7.0 更是一种增强型的 Windows Web 平台，具有模块化的架构，可提供更佳的灵活性和控制，并可提供简化的管理，具有可节省时间的强大诊断和故障排除能力，以及完整的可扩展性。

Internet Information Server IIS 7.0 和 .NET Framework 3.0 所提供的全方位平台，可构建让用户彼此连接以及连接到其资源的应用程序，以便用户能够虚拟化、分享和处理信息。此外，IIS 7.0 亦是整合 Microsoft Web 平台技术、ASP.NET、Windows Communication Foundation Web 服务以及 Windows SharePoint Services 的主要角色。

- 高安全性

Windows Server 2008 是迄今为止最安全的 Windows Server，此操作系统在经过强化后，不仅可协助避免运作失常，更可运用诸多新技术协助防范未经授权即连接至您的网络、服务器、资料和用户账户的情形。其拥有网络访问保护（NAP），可确保尝试连接至企业网络的电脑皆能符合企业的安全性原则，而技术整合及部分增强项目则使得 Active Directory 服务成为强而有效的统一整合式身份识别与访问（IDA）解决方案，只读网域控制站（RODC）和 BitLocker 驱动器加密，更可安全地在分支机构部署 AD 数据库。

- 高性能运算

Windows HPC Server 2008 延续了 Windows Server 2008 的优势和节省成本的特性，适合用于高性能运算（HPC）的环境。Windows HPC Server 2008 是建立在 Windows Server 2008 与 x64 位技术上，可有效率地扩充至数以千计的处理核心，并具备立即可用的功能，以改善生产力及降低 HPC 环境的复杂度，而且还提供了丰富且整合的用户体验。由于运用范围涵盖桌面应用程序至群集，而使采用范围更为广泛。此外，还包含一组全方位的部署、管理和监控工具，用户得以轻松地部署、管理及整合既有的基础架构。

2.3.2.2 数据库

在数据库方面，通常可供我们选择的产品有 SQL Server、Oracle、IBM DB2、MySQL 等。

Microsoft SQL Server 是由微软公司所推出的关系数据库解决方案，最新的版本是 SQL Server 2008，已经在 2008 年 8 月 6 日上市。SQL Server 2008 在 Microsoft 的数据平台上发布，它可以将结构化、半结构化和非结构化文档的数据（例如图像和音乐）直接存储到数据库中。SQL Server 2008 提供一系列丰富的集成服务，可以对数据进行查询、搜索、同步、报告和分析之类的操作。数据可以存储在各种设备上，从数据中心最大的服务器一直到桌面计算机和移动设备，用户可以控制数据而不用管数据存储在哪里。

SQL Server 2008 允许用户在使用 Microsoft.NET 和 Visual Studio 开发的自定义应用程序中使用数据，在面向服务的架构（SOA）和通过 Microsoft BizTalk Server 进行的业务流程中使用数据。信息工作人员可以通过他们日常使用的工具（例如 2007 Microsoft Office 系统）直接访问数据。SQL Server 2008 提供一个可信的、高效率智能数据平台，可满足用户的几乎所有数据需求。如图 3 所示。

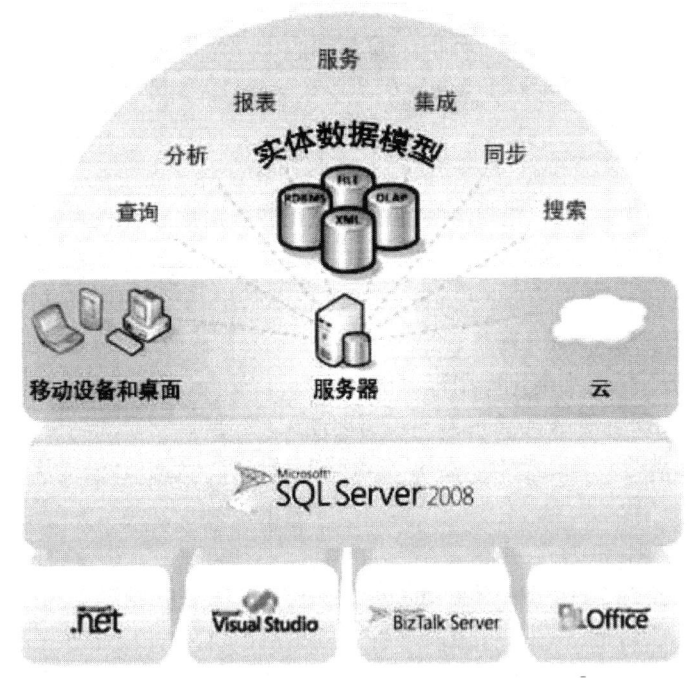

图 3 数据库系统

SQL Server 2008 和 Windows Server 2008 的组合向企业 IT 管理员和专业开发人员提供了一个用于任务关键型应用程序的卓越平台，以及增强的端到端安全性、管理和开发能力。

基于以上考虑我们选用 SQL Server 2008 来搭建数据库系统。它具备以下功能。

- Analysis Services

SQL Server 2008 能帮助组织构建全面、企业级的分析解决方案，并能通过熟悉的工具提供可操作的深入资讯。

- 数据挖掘

SQL Server 2008 具备完整直观的数据挖掘技术，与 Microsoft BI 平台的无缝集成，并且可扩展到任何应用程序，因此能通过预测性分析产生可靠的决策。

- 高可用性 – Always – On

SQL Server 2008 的"Always – On"技术提供完整的选项，可以最小化宕机时间，并将应用程序可用性维持在相应的水平。

- Integration Services

SQL Server 2008 提供可伸缩的企业数据集成平台，并带有杰出的 ETL 和集成能力，使组织能更轻松地管理来自各种数据源的数据。

- 易管理性

Microsoft SQL Server 提供一个基于策略的系统来管理 SQL Server 的一个或多个实例，同时提供用于性能监视、故障诊断和调节的各种工具，使管理员可以更有效地管理他们的数据库和 SQL Server 实例。

- 性能和可伸缩性

SQL Server 2008 提供一个全面的数据平台，包含各种向上扩充单台服务器和向外扩充大型数据库的技术，并提供各种优化性能的工具。

- 可编程性

研究 SQL Server 2008 如何帮助开发人员使用 .NET Framework 和 Visual Studio Team System 构建强大的下一代数据库应用程序。

- Reporting Services

了解 SQL Server 2008 Reporting Services 如何提供一个基于服务器的平台，用于满足各种报表需求，以提供整个企业需要的相关信息。

- 安全性

Microsoft SQL Server 2008 提供安全功能增强，能够有效管理安全功能配置，并可提供强认证和访问控制、强大的加密和密钥管理能力，以及增强的审计功能。

- 空间数据

SQL Server 2008 提供全面的空间支持，使组织能够通过支持空间的应用程序无缝地获取、使用和扩展定位数据，最终帮助终端用户做出更好的决策。

2.3.2.3 数据整合平台

现阶段比较流行的整合平台有 MS BIZTALK、Fiorano、BEA、IBM 的集成平台等。BizTalk Server 是微软企业级 SOA 解决方案的核心组件产品。自 2000 年的 BizTalk Server 2000 之后，历尽 2002、2004 版本，目前是 2006 R2 版本。

微软公司作为国际 SOA 标准的参与、制订者之一，把 SOA 架构的具体实现广泛落实在 BizTalk Server 的内置功能中。BizTalk Server 能够帮助企业搭建高速、互联、健壮的企业服务总线（ESB），担当企业信息枢纽，应用于数据集成（DBI）、企业应用集成（EAI）、企业对企业集成（B2B）和业务流程监控（BAM）等多种业务模式，同时也可以作为企业业务规则的支撑平台。

图 4 是国际著名第三方评测机构 Gartner 公司对"应用系统集成"市场的公平分析报告图（报告时间：2007 年 6 月）。

根据报告图，微软 BizTalk Server 位于"市场领导者"的象限位置，是"功能完整性"和"集成能力"的领导者，并且在"集成能力"方面排名市场第一位。

2.3.3 多媒体信息系统

多媒体信息系统位于底层的是数据采集模块，通过抓取系统完成互联网信息的采集，版面反解完成采编，FIT 文件的信息获取，音视频采集，转码完成多媒体资料的收集。多种信息的采集共同形成网站内容管理系统的数据源，通过统一的采集接口与网站系统进行衔接，将数据汇总入核心采编流程中。

多媒体网站核心的采编流程部分包括：编辑库、发布库、专题库；其间通过工作流引擎加以衔接，使网站新闻内容完全流转起来，通过强大的编辑器，可视化的模板编辑，配以多进程多线程的发布系

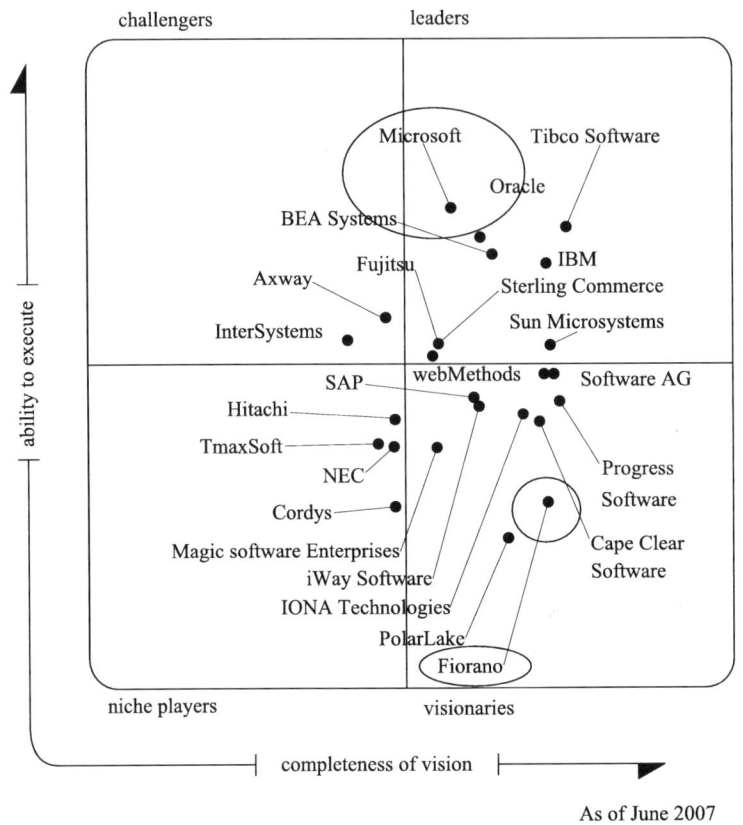

图 4 "应用系统集成"市场分析报告图

统,方便快捷地完成 WEB/WAP 网站的发布。内容管理系统辅助以"系统管理""用户管理""栏目管理"等功能模块,提供完整的内容管理实现。视音频管理系统包括对音视频采集、编辑、转码等全流程的管理,通过与网站系统的无缝集成形成音视频的发布。本系统上端是交互管理平台,实现评论、调查、报料报送、站内检索等多种交互功能形成与网民的互动。本系统最顶层是统一用户管理系统实现整个交互平台各子系统用户的统一注册,统一登录,统一退出,实现网站用户的一站式登录,改善用户体验。访问控制模块能定义网站内容的访问权限,支持正则表达式定义,完成网站内容的分权限访问。多站点管理本网站可以在一套系统中管理多个独立的站点,适应了客户发展的需要,系统可以方便地增加站点,各站点之间有严格的权限管理,具有独立的采、编、发流程,互不干扰,却有可以在多个站点间进行资源的共享,实现了多个站点的统一管理,数据的集中存储。

通过"多媒体信息系统",可以为企业很好地解决信息繁杂和交流不畅的问题。客户可以自主上传市场信息、供求信息,经审核后直接发布到网站;为每家会员企业设置展示页面,并分类管理,更全面的展示产业链条中的企业。通过统一的内容管理生产平台进行内容的采集、加工、整合与发布;通过统一信息平台进行协同交流、题目策划与决策信息的收集分析。可以为不同的群体提供不同的服务,按照分级权限、需求类型的不同,分别提供有针对性的新闻信息服务、远程培训服务、资料检索服务等,为不同类型和不同需求的企业进行差异化的个性服务。目前,"多媒体信息系统"市场上有方正、紫光等技术推广应用提供商,其中方正的"全媒体资源库系统"为该领域应用相对成熟的产品。

2.3.4 系统平台和工具软件

2.3.4.1 开发平台

本系统拟采用 Microsoft. NET Framework 作为开发平台。.NET Framework(.NET 框架)是由微软开发,一个致力于敏捷软件开发(Agile software development)、快速应用开发(Rapid application development)、平台无关性和网络透明化的软件开发平台。.NET 是微软为下一个十年对服务器和桌上型软件工程迈出的第一步。.NET 包含许多有助于 Internet 和 Intranet 应用迅捷开发的技术。

.NET Framework 是微软公司继 Windows DNA 之后的新开发平台。.NET Framework 是以一种采用系

统虚拟机运行的编程平台，以通用语言运行时（Common Language Runtime）为基础，支持多种语言（C#、VB.NET、C++、Python 等）的开发。

.NET 也为编程界面（API）提供了新功能和开发工具。这些革新使得程序设计员可以同时进行 Windows 应用软件和网络应用软件以及元件和服务（web service）的开发。.NET 提供了一个新的反射性的且面向对象程序设计编程界面。.NET 设计得足够通用化从而使许多不同高级语言都得以被汇集。

目前最新的版本为.NET Framework 3.5 SP1，它自动包含.NET Framework 2.0 SP2 以及.NET Framework 3.0 SP2。该版本随 Visual Studio 2008 SP1 发布，此版本提供了以下新的功能。

■ 扩展方法（Extension Method）属性（Attribute），用于为扩展方法提供支持。

■ LINQ 支持，包括 LINQ to Object、LINQ to ADO.NET 以及 LINQ to XML。

■ 表达式目录树（Expression Tree），用于为 Lambda 表达式提供支持。

■ 与语言集成查询（LINQ）和数据感知紧密集成。借助这个新功能，您可以使用相同的语法，在任何支持 LINQ 的语言中编写相关代码，以筛选和枚举多种类型的 SQL 数据、集合、XML 和数据集，以及创建它们的投影。

■ 利用 ASP.NET AJAX 可以创建更有效、更具交互性、高度个性化的 Web 体验，这些体验在所有最流行的浏览器上都能实现。

■ 用于生成 WCF 服务的全新 Web 协议支持，包括 AJAX、JSON、REST、POX、RSS、ATOM 和若干新的 WS-*标准。

■ Visual Studio 2008 中面向 WF、WCF 和 WPF 的完整工具支持，其中包括支持工作流的服务这一新技术。

■.NET Framework 3.5 基类库（BCL）中的新类可满足许多常见的客户请求。

■ 新增的 ASP.NET 功能包括 ASP.NET 动态数据和 ASP.NET AJAX 附加功能，前者提供了无需编写代码就可实现数据驱动的快速开发的丰富支架框架，后者为管理浏览器历史记录提供了支持（后退按钮支持）。

■ ADO.NET Entity Framework。

■ 对 SQL Server 2008 的数据提供程序支持。

■.NET Framework 客户端配置文件是完整版.NET Framework 的子集，面向客户端应用程序。这改善了尚未安装.NET Framework 的计算机上的安装体验。

■ 改进 Windows Presentation Foundation 的性能，其中包括启动速度的位图效果性能的提高。为 Windows Presentation Foundation 增加的功能包括对业务线应用程序的更好支持、本机闪屏支持、DirectX 像素着色器支持以及新的 WebBrowser 控件。

■ ClickOnce 应用程序发布者可以根据具体情况决定是否取消签名和散列，开发人员可以以编程方式安装显示自定义署名的 ClickOnce 应用程序，ClickOnce 错误对话框支持指向网络上特定于应用程序的支持站点的链接。

■ 用于 SQL Server 的.NET Framework 数据提供程序。

（System.Data.SqlClient）完全支持 SQL Server 2008 数据库引擎的所有新功能。有关.NET Framework 对 SQL Server 2008 的支持的更多信息，请参见 SQL Server 中的新功能（ADO.NET）。ADO.NET 数据平台是一种多版本策略，它使开发人员能够针对概念性实体数据模型进行编程，从而减轻他们的编码和维护工作。此平台提供了 ADO.NET Entity Framework、实体数据模型（EDM）、对象服务、LINQ to Entities、Entity SQL、EntityClient、ADO.NET 数据服务及实体数据模型工具。

■ Windows Communication Foundation 现在提供了改进的互操作性支持，增强了部分信任方案中的调试体验，并扩展了集成协议支持以更广泛地应用于 Web 2.0 应用程序，从而使 DataContract 序列化程序更易于使用。

■ Microsoft.VisualBasic.PowerPacks 命名空间引入了新的 DataRepeater 控件，该控件以可自定义的列表格式显示数据。此命名空间还包含新的矢量形状。

2.3.4.2 开发软件

Microsoft Visual Studio Team System 2008 Team Foundation Server——位于系统中心的协作服务器，使每

个团队成员能够更有效率地工作和交付更高质量的软件。它将项目管理、工作项跟踪、版本控制、报告与商业智能、构建管理和流程指南合并到了一个统一的团队服务器中。Team Foundation Server 包括与 Microsoft Office system（Microsoft Excel 和 Microsoft Project）的集成，业务分析师和项目经理可以使用熟悉的应用程序访问它。此外，Team Foundation Server 还允许以 Web 方式访问项目资源和功能。

Microsoft Visual Studio Team System 2008 Team Suite——为体系结构、设计、开发、数据库开发及应用程序测试等多任务的团队成员提供集成的工具集。在应用程序生命周期的每个步骤，团队成员都可以继续协作并利用一个完整的工具集与指南。Team Suite 包含以下软件中的所有功能。

■ Microsoft Visual Studio Team System 2008 Architecture Edition——侧重于改进分布式系统的设计和验证。使用此版本，架构师、运营经理及开发人员能够以可视化方式构造面向服务的解决方案，并在部署之前针对运行环境进行验证。

■ Microsoft Visual Studio Team System 2008 Development Edition——为开发人员提供高级工具集，以找出效率低、不安全或质量差的代码，指定编码的最佳实践，并自动执行软件单元测试。这些工具可帮助团队成员编写质量更高的代码、减少与安全性相关的问题，并避免在开发周期后期出现错误。

■ Microsoft Visual Studio Team System 2008 Database Edition——提供用于数据库更改管理和测试的高级工具与功能，使数据库开发人员和管理员能够提高工作效率和数据库层中应用程序的质量。

■ Microsoft Visual Studio Team System 2008 Test Edition——为 Web 应用程序和服务提供一组集成在 Visual Studio 环境中的综合测试工具。通过这些测试工具，测试人员在 Visual Studio 内即可编写、执行和管理各项测试及相关工作项。此外，Microsoft Visual Studio Team System 2008 Test Load Agent 可生成适用于 Web 应用程序负载测试的其他测试负载。

■ Team System 是一种可扩展的平台，提供自定义并可与第三方工具集成。Visual Studio 行业合作伙伴计划包含 200 多个合作伙伴，提供了 400 多种辅助产品来支持各种软件流程、工具（包括 Java 环境，如 Eclipse）以及平台（如 UNIX 和 Mac OS）。

2.3.4.3 辅助软件

（1）VMware Server 2

VMware Server 是托管虚拟化平台，可像应用程序一样安装在任何现有的服务器硬件上，并且将一个物理服务器分区为多个虚拟机。可以有效地节省运行成本。如图 5 所示。

图 5 VMware 将一个物理服务器划分为多个虚拟机

■ 在几分钟内调配更多服务器，而不用投资购买新硬件。
■ 在同一台物理服务器上运行 Windows、Linux、Solaris 和 Netware 操作系统及应用程序。
■ 提高物理服务器的 CPU 利用率。
■ 将虚拟机从一台物理服务器移动到另一台，而不用重新配置。
■ 捕获虚拟机的完整状态，只需点击按钮即可返回此配置。
■ 通过 服务器整合降低 IT 成本和提高灵活性。
■ 减少计划内和计划外停机以提高业务连续性。

■ 将虚拟化带来的好处扩展到中小型企业。

（2）Microsoft Office SharePoint Server 2007

Microsoft Office SharePoint Server 2007 是一个服务器功能集成套件，它提供全面的内容管理和企业搜索、加速共享业务流程并便利跨界限信息共享以更好地了解业务，从而有助于提高组织的工作效率。Office SharePoint Server 2007 通过一个集成平台而不是依靠分散的系统来支持整个企业内的所有 Intranet、Extranet 和 Web 应用程序。此外，该协作和内容管理服务器还为 IT 专业人员和开发人员提供了实现服务器管理、应用程序可扩展性和互操作性所需的平台和工具。

通过一个集成平台来支持企业范围内的所有 Intranet、Extranet 和 Web 应用程序，从而提高 IT 对业务需求的响应度，同时减少需要维护的平台数。

■ 获得增强的互操作性支持。Office SharePoint Server 2007 构建于可伸缩的体系结构之上，并且支持包括 XML 和简单对象访问协议（SOAP）在内的 Web 服务和互操作性标准。Office SharePoint Server 2007 还具有大量开放的应用程序编程接口（API）以及针对列表和文档的事件处理程序。这样便可与现有系统集成，并可以灵活地合并新的非 Microsoft IT 投资。LDAP 集成支持其他可插入身份验证提供程序，使非 Active Directory 源的使用更容易。直接可用的 WSRP 使用程序 Web 部件支持与其他符合 WSRP 的门户解决方案的集成。

■ 使 IT 部门重点关注更多战略任务。用户现在可以在不需要 IT 部门介入的情况下自行创建网站，启动工作流，自我提供应用程序，访问后端数据，在项目级定义安全性，还原删除的项目以及完成其他任务。用户对 IT 部门的依赖性的下降提高了工作效率，并使 IT 部门可以致力于为组织提供真正的增值服务。通过业务数据目录，您可以定义和部署业务应用程序配置，以访问驻留在后端系统中的数据。企业用户可以重复使用此功能创建业务数据的个性化视图而不必开发任何自定义代码。

■ 简化部署、管理和系统管理。现在管理 Web 服务器场、部署新内容以及管理各网站之间的同步变得更加容易了。部署可以采用"自上而下"或"自下而上"的方式进行。利用公共网站的直接可用的网站启动器模板以及"区域"和"页面版式"模板与预配置导航简化了网站暂存。用于备份和还原内容的增强功能可以帮助 IT 专业人员计划备份，备份多网站集合，然后逐一还原。

■ 可靠的系统监控、使用情况跟踪和监控工具。这些工具有助于更快地确定和解决问题，同时也有助于提高系统基础设施的运行效率。

（3）Microsoft Office Visio 2007

Microsoft Office Visio 2007 有助于 IT 和商务专业人员轻松地可视化、分析和交流复杂信息。它能够将难以理解的复杂文本和表格转换为一目了然的 Visio 图表。该软件通过创建与数据相关的 Visio 图表（而不使用静态图片）来显示数据，这些图表易于刷新，并能够显著提高生产率。使用 Office Visio 2007 中的各种图表可了解、操作和共享企业内组织系统、资源和流程的有关信息。

Office Visio 2007 提供了各种模板：业务流程的流程图、网络图、工作流图、数据库模型图和软件图。这些模板可用于可视化和简化业务流程、跟踪项目和资源、绘制组织结构图、映射网络、绘制建筑地图以及优化系统。

通过用 Office Visio 2007 中的新增功能和改进功能，可以更有效地沟通并以更多方式来影响更广泛的用户。

■ 设计具有专业外观的图表。使用 Office Visio 2007 中新增的主题功能，只需单击一次，即可轻松地设置整个图表中颜色和效果（文本、线条、填充、阴影和连接线格式）的格式。Office Visio 2007 甚至使用了与其他 2007 Microsoft Office system 程序相同的调色板，因此您可以轻松设计与演示文稿和文档匹配的具有专业外观的 Visio 图表。使用新增的三维工作流形状（该形状就是使用新增的主题功能设计的）可以创建更动态的工作流。

■ 影响更多访问群体。将 Visio 图表保存为 PDF 或 XPS 文件格式，可使其更具可移植性，并供更多访问群体使用。1 可在 Microsoft Office Outlook 2007 中查看 Visio 图表附件。

■ 将图表集成到其他 Microsoft Office 应用程序中。将 Visio 图表导入到 Microsoft Office PowerPoint 演示文稿和 Microsoft Office Word 文档中。将业务和流程信息以 Visio 图表和图像文件的形式共享，以便观

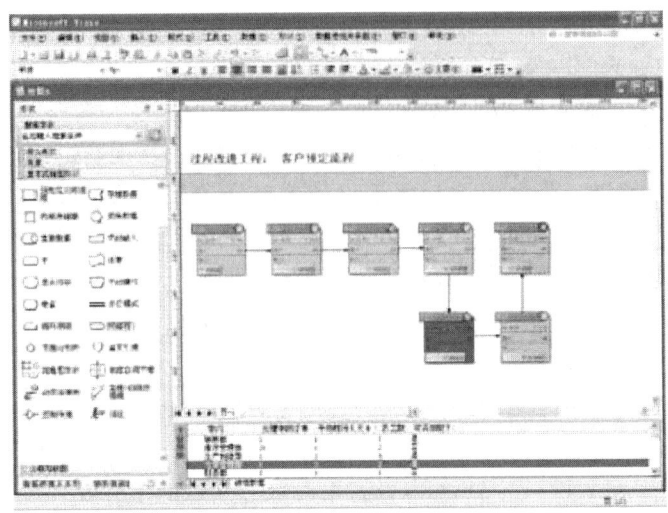

图6 Office Vision 2007 功能

众以一致的方式快速了解复杂的业务流程。

■ 针对同一图表与同事进行协作。借助跟踪标记功能，多个用户可针对同一 Visio 图表进行协作。该功能通常用于审阅图表和合并反馈，跟踪标记有助于其他审阅者和最终将修订并入图表的人员清楚地了解每位审阅者的意见。使用 Microsoft Windows SharePoint Services，可以轻松地在 Office Visio 中直接签入和签出图表。

■ 将图表转换为多种格式并与他人共享。将图表保存为包含导航控件、形状数据查看器、报表、图像格式选择和样式表选项的网页，使组织中的所有人都可使用您的图表。将图表张贴到组织的 Intranet 和 Extranet 上，使任何将 Visio Viewer 与 Windows Internet Explorer 一同使用的用户都可以从 Internet Explorer 中查看该图表。2 将 Visio 图表保存为 PDF 或 XPS 文件格式，可使其更具可移植性，并供更多访问群体使用。

■ 使用 Microsoft Windows SharePoint Services 进行协作。共享的工作区功能支持使用 Microsoft Windows SharePoint Services 进行协作。在 Office Visio 2007 中，可以从网站上直接打开在 Windows SharePoint Services 网站上保存的 Visio 图表，甚至可以在 Office Visio 2007 中签入和签出这些图表。从 Windows SharePoint Services 网站打开图表时，Office Visio 2007 会打开共享工作区任务窗格，其中包含其他文件、成员、任务和链接等工作区中的所有信息。

（4）Office 2007

Microsoft Office 2007 是家庭和小型企业不可或缺的软件套件，使用它可快速轻松地创建外观精美的文档、电子表格和演示文稿，还可以管理电子邮件。最新版本具有 Microsoft Office Fluent 用户界面，它提供了能够创建高质量文档的熟悉的常用命令、增强的图形和格式设置功能，并提供了管理日程的新时间管理工具，以及更为出色的可靠性和安全性（例如，经过改进的用于减少垃圾电子邮件的垃圾邮件筛选功能）。

（5）美工软件

Adobe Photoshop CS 8.0（中文版）与 Dreamweaver 8 是两款专业制作界面的软件开发工具，得到了业界的广泛青睐，它们有着其他工具所不具备的特效制作方案。其代码运行效率高。是美工首选的两款工具。Photoshop 是迄今为止世界上最畅销的图像编辑软件，它已成为许多涉及图像处理的行业的标准，可提供优秀的编码和简单便捷的使用。

科学构建一体化人才培养体系
提升高职教育教学品质

齐再前　孙晓鲲　黄先开

北京联合大学是较早从事高等职业教育的院校之一。学校高等职业教育的建设目标是依托学校整体优势，打造高水平高等职业教育，建立从高职（专科）、专升本（本科）到专业硕士的职业教育人才培养体系，为北京市乃至全国培养高端职业人才。

1　科学构建高职、高职"专升本"相互衔接的人才培养体系

学校将高职、高职"专升本"两个层次的职业教育统筹考虑，探索在学分制管理模式下，高职、高职"专升本"相互衔接的高等职业教育人才培养体系。其目的是解决优秀的高职毕业生进入本科教育阶段的培养目标、课程体系、教学内容、教学方法及管理方式等方面的衔接与深化问题，研究高等职业教育本科与普通本科教育在人才培养模式、培养目标与规格、课程体系与教学模式等方面差异，培养高端职业人才。

1.1　实施一体化培养方案，使高职与高职"专升本"有效衔接

将高职、高职"专升本"两个层次的课程体系均按照基本素质教育平台、专业能力培养平台、实践技能训练平台和职业能力拓展平台进行搭建。通过培养目标以及课程体系的有效衔接，从而达到在教学深度与广度上与本科教育水平的有效衔接，实践技能培养和综合实践水平提升的有效提升。

1.1.1　培养目标的有效衔接

高职人才的培养目标定位在培养生产、建设、管理、服务第一线的高技能专门人才。高职"专升本"的人才培养以此为基础，向高层次延伸和扩展，培养具有扎实的专业知识和较强的实践能力的高级技术应用性专门人才。

1.1.2　课程体系的有效衔接

"专升本"教育课程设置在于适度提升与专业学习和应用相关的理论知识，重点拓展专业知识，安排与专业相关的新科技知识和新技能，注重培养技术应用能力和综合素质。每个课程平台分为必修和选修两部分，给学生一定选择空间。专业任选课程主要是专业拓展和前沿性课程，要求学生必须选取一定学分。考虑到"专升本"学生已经具有一定的基础实践能力和专项训练能力，因此课程设置着重点放在综合应用能力训练上，要求每个专业设置2个以上（含）的综合技术训练项目，每个项目时间2~4周，以强化综合应用能力培养，同时与毕业环节有效衔接。

1.2　以能力培养为主线，综合素质和职业技能培养统筹兼顾

针对目前高等职业教育人才培养过于重视职业技能培养而忽视基本素质教育的现状，着重研究解决高等职业教育人才培养的技能培养与学生可持续发展关系。坚持以能力培养为主线，素质培养和职业技能培养并重。

从培养学生基本素质和职业迁移能力出发，首先加强英语实用能力培养，做到英语教育不断线；其次强化计算机基础及应用能力培养，使学生利用计算机工作的信息化能力、先进软件的应用能力得到全面提高，鼓励学生考取高级别的计算机等级证书。

［基金项目］本文为北京市教育科学规划课题"北京高等职业教育专升本人才培养模式研究"的研究成果。
［作者简介］齐再前，北京联合大学。

对于专业技能课程，从关键技术和最新工艺出发，将专业能力分成若干单项能力贯穿于课程体系中。低年级以单项能力培养为主；高年级以综合能力和综合素质为主，主要以"项目""任务""实务"为载体进行。

2 坚持以学生发展为本，因材施教，创新高等职业教育人才培养模式

学校坚持以学生的发展为本，因材施教，探索个性化的培养途径和方法，解决千人一面、整齐划一的人才培养现状。对学生的来源及需求整体情况进行分析，坚持分类指导，分层培养，因材施教，有效提升教育教学效能。在新生入学之初就进行综合测试，对其职业生涯进行规划，了解其需求然后进行针对性培养。

2.1 通过组建经管类高职创新实验班，探索"3+2"贯通培养的新模式

我校举办本科院校办高等职业教育、高职"专升本"教育已有十几年的办学历史，积累了丰富的办学经验。在不突破国家相关"专升本"政策的前提下，根据学生的意愿，对于整体基础好又目标明确的学生，通过基础课程和心理测试，组建了"经管类高职创新实验班"，采用动态管理机制，学生根据自身发展进行流动。将3年专科和2年本科教育相贯通，探索"3+2"人才培养新模式。

实践证明，实验班有效地调动了学生学习的积极性，改善了学风，在各个方面树立了典范。全国英语三级A测试的一次通过率达到100%，其中1/3学生通过全国英语四级；另外有5人在北京市数学建模竞赛中获奖，且有10余人在各类专业技能大赛中获奖。

2.2 依托北京市职业教育分级制改革试点专业，探索人才培养的新途径

我校市场营销、旅游管理两个专业是北京市职业教育分级制改革试点专业，学校与企业专家共同建立了"学、教、评、做、训"一体的不同级别的人才方案。其课程体系遵循"基础模块+专业模块+职业模块（企业培训课程、职业资格证书课程、顶岗实习）"设置，融合职业培训与专业课程，同时可以根据企业需要灵活调整模块课程，达到不同规格人才培养要求。使职业资格证书、学历教育证书和分级教育证书有机衔接、标准统一。目前两个专业正在进行4级（高职）、5级（专升本）的分级制改革试验工作，为了实现与用人单位的零对接，旅游管理专业与全聚德集团采用订单式培养，市场营销专业与用友集团联合培养。同时还为学生配备了双导师，指导学生学习和实践。

2.3 依托我校国家级服务外包人才培养模式创新实验区，校企联合培养高技能人才

利用学校国家级服务外包人才培养模式创新实验区，运用"外包"的理念，充分发挥企业和学校的核心优势资源，根据专业设置特点，按照"大类培养、行业认知""分流培养、职场体验""实战训练、职业定向"设计人才培养过程。新生入学后参加企业名师讲学计划，增加学生的行业认知；中高年级开始进行企业践学计划，毕业年级进行顶岗实习，达到职业认知培养连续进行的目的。目前学校与多家外包企业合作，培养企业适销对路的技能人才，受到用人单位的普遍欢迎。

3 发挥学校自身优势，实施教学品质提升计划，全面提高人才培养质量

学校根据高等职业教育人才培养目标定位要求，实施了教学品质提升计划。该计划主要围绕实践教学效能、教师执教能力、教学管理效能等教学过程中的关键要素展开，取得了显著成效。

3.1 密切产学研合作，校企互利共赢

依托学校学科优势，主动营造各种机会，建立校企"双赢"的合作机制，探索实践教学最佳模式和有效途径。积极开发校内资源改善实训条件，建立了旅游管理与服务、信息技术服务等9个高水平实训中心；同时与北京首旅集团、全聚德集团、北京同仁堂股份有限公司等100多家行业企业单位建立了长期稳定的产学研合作关系。另外，师资、教材、课程等方面的产学研合作也取得丰硕成果，产学研合作教育已成为北京联合大学高等职业教育的特色和重要平台。

教师参与行业企业技术与职业标准开发、承担或参与行业企业技术研发课题、提供行业企业咨询服务、承接行业企业员工或客户培训等，提供优质社会服务。如：旅游学院拥有北京市劳动局批准的"职业技能培训中心"，承担着为北京市酒店与餐饮业人员提供在职专业培训及考核工作；应用科技学院教

师担任摩托罗拉中国有限公司高级培训师，搭建职业技能证书培训平台，取得了良好的社会声誉。

学生通过参与企业实践、参加教师承担的横向科研项目、毕业实习等方式，贴近行业企业一线需求，提高职业竞争力。学校建立了大学生创新基金，出台并实施了《北京联合大学高等职业教育学生实践能力提升计划》，以立项形式资助学生进行实践项目的训练。目前已经开展3届，共有150个项目结题，有近千名学生参与。建立了国家、北京市、学校和学院四级竞赛体系，出台了各种激励政策，瞄准学生技能提高的兴奋点，积极组织学生参加各级、各类技能竞赛活动，有效地提高了学生实践技能和团队协作能力。

3.2 建立激励机制，打造高水平"双师型"教师队伍

以提高教师整体素质为核心，以培养"双师素质"教师为重点，不断促进教师的教学能力、专业实践能力和学历学位水平的提升。制定优惠政策，聘请一批行业企业专家、技术骨干担任兼职教师，与行业企业在人才培养、技术开发等方面密切合作，促进高水平专兼结合的"双师型"教师队伍建设。出台了《双师素质教师管理办法》《关于提高教师专业实践与应用能力的实施办法》等相关规定，将教师参加企业实践制度化；学校拨专项经费用于在职教师的培训（企业实践技能和业务提升）、高水平师资聘请（企业、相关高校）。通过政策引导和经费支持，我校师资队伍整体水平不断提高。

3.3 根据职业教育特点，不断创新教学管理机制，确保人才培养质量稳步提升

学校根据高职、高职"专升本"学生的具体情况和自身特点，积极推进学分制管理进程，减少必修课程，增加选修课程，给学生自主选择的空间，激发了学生学习的积极性和主动性。制订并实施了学分制管理模式下《北京联合大学高等职业教育学生学籍管理相关规定》、《北京联合大学高等职业教育学生课程重修管理细则》等。

实践教学历来是教学管理的难点和重点，必须强化实践教学中各个环节管理。学校建立了既严格规范又不失灵活的教学管理制度。修订了《北京联合大学校内外实训基地的管理办法》，制订了《北京联合大学高等职业教育学生顶岗实习管理办法》，加强对顶岗实习组织实施的过程管理；发挥校内教学督导和企业专家作用，成立专业指导委员会，共同对教学质量进行监督。

参考文献

[1] 齐再前. 探索高职"专升本"人才培养模式，提高人才培养质量 [J]. 北京教育，2011 (6).
[2] 李论，陈遇春，李彬让. 基于"专升本"制度对完善职业教育体系的思考 [J]. 职教论坛，2007 (7).
[3] 姬慧. 破解高职"专升本"教育困境之研究 [J]. 山西高等学校社会科学学报，2009, 21 (11).
[4] 王叙红. 改进高职"专升本"教育模式的探讨 [J]. 继续教育研究，2009 (1).

地方院校高等教育国际化的影响要素析评

杨亚军

高等教育的国际化是全球化进程中的必然趋势，也是目前高等教育领域发展进程中的显著特征和核心议题。笔者认为：高等教育国际化主要是指在立足本国的基础上，面向世界、把跨国界和跨文化的大学教育理念和办学模式与自身的教育体系和体制、教学工作、科研工作、人才培养模式和社会服务等结合起来的可持续发展的过程。高等院校国际化的程度如何，如何评价，这方面研究也开展了多年，诸多的国内外学者也从不同的角度对高校国际化的评价体系的构建提出了很多不同的指标构件和评价要求。综合分析种种不同国际化指标体系的内容不难看出高等学校的三大主因——教师、学生、课程都是各类国际化指标体系中必不可少的部分[1]。本文拟从教师、学生以及课程相关国际化指标的分析出发，探讨影响地方院校国际化建设中的问题，为地方院校加速国际化进程提供解决问题的对策和思路。

一、研究背景

随着改革开放的日益深入，早在1983年邓小平同志就高瞻远瞩地提出了"教育要面向四个现代化，面向世界，面向未来"的要求，可以说这是中国教育走向世界的先声。1993年中共中央、国务院颁发的《中国教育改革与发展纲要》第14条指出，"进一步扩大教育对外开放，加强国际教育交流与合作，大胆吸收和借鉴世界各国发展与管理教育的成功经验"。1995年公布的《中华人民共和国教育法》明确规定，"国家鼓励开展教育对外合作与交流"，进而从法律意义上明确了教育国际化的发展道路。在教育部《2003—2007年教育振兴计划》中，再次强调将教育国际化作为深化教育改革和制度创新保证的六个重要举措之一："要进一步扩大教育开放"，在这一目标下，教育国际化进程中的诸多具体问题，如加强教育国际合作与交流，搞好出国留学工作，大力推行对外汉语教学和开拓国际教育服务市场等方面的内容都将成为我国高等教育走向国际的工作重心和发展方向[2]。

二、相关研究概述

中国大学教育的国际化是一种必然，也是中国高等教育面向世界、面向未来的内在要求。国内许多专家学者针对大学教育国际化所涉及的诸多问题都展开过有益的研究和论述。如侯俊平、张春河（2003）研究分析了教育国际化对高水平大学建设中的重要作用，认为国际化特色是高水平大学的重要特征，创建高水平大学首先要确立国际化目标，规划国际化发展战略，形成培养具有国际竞争力人才的培养模式[3]。毕家驹（2005）的研究系统地阐述了高等教育国际化的基本概念和内涵，着重分析和论述了中国高等院校国际化建设的特征以及国际化的发展方向和途径[4]。

国内还有很多学者的研究着重于分析我国高等教育在国际化进程中的具体问题、发展思路和应对策略，并提出了许多值得借鉴的建议。例如，乔玉香（2002）探讨了我国大学在全球经济一体化形势下高等教育国际化过程所面临的问题，提出我国的高等教育必须进行多维度的改革才能真正实现国际化，她的研究具体阐述了包括对高等教育的管理体制、培养目标、科研能力等多个方面进行改革的思路和方向[5]。王刚、徐立清（2004）分析认为高等教育的国际化应该涵盖规划国际化的战略目标，并就确立国际化人才培养目标，创建国际化办学体制和机制，设置国际化课程体系，以及营造国际化办学环境等方面的具体内容作了比较全面的分析[6]。

还有一些学者的研究关注高等教育国际化指标体系构建的问题。例如，李盛兵（2005）探讨了大学国际化评价指标体系构建的问题，他的研究基于大学国际化指标体系的观测点和权重，初步构建了一个

[作者简介] 杨亚军，北京联合大学。

包括国际化观念与规划、大学国际化机构的设置、学生结构国际化、教师结构国际化、课程开发和设置的国际化、科研工作的国际化，以及中外合作办学等比较全面的评价指标体系[7]。常永胜（2008）撰文研究了高等教育国际化含义与发展动因，并且重点分析了大学国际化的内涵及发展策略，主张从教师及学生的国际流动、国际学术交流与合作、国际化课程体系的设置和重视外语教学等方面入手，建立大学国际化的评价指标体系[8]。胡亦武（2009）对国内985大学、211大学及一般性大学学生语言与课程设置的国际化程度设计了问卷调查研究并对相关数据进行统计分析，他的研究在分析中国大学对学生外语学习要求以及水平要求的基础上，分析了学生外语水平对大学国际化程度的影响权重，并对大学本科生课程设置的国际化程度的影响状况进行比较研究，探讨了大学课程国际化的改革新思路和创新途径[9]。

综上所述，地方院校高等教育的国际化影响到整个组织的宏观和微观层面，既与大学的发展战略、组织机构、人员交流、教学科研、设施条件及学术成果交流等方面直接相关，也涉及学校、院系、个人发展等诸多层面。从最严格的意义上分析，任何基于科研的评估都难以完整而细致地评估出高校各个层面的国际化进程。因此，基于之前的相关研究成果，笔者认为：高等教育的国际化是在观念、行为、结果等三个层面上的理念和实践发展演变过程，同时也是高等教育体系中相关要素之间交互影响、变化和发展的过程。在高等教育系统国际化建设的相关研究和比较研究方面，一般学者都不可能脱离三个要素去研究高等教育国际化的内容和指标，这三个要素分别是教师流动性、学生流动性、课程设置国际化[10]。

三、地方院校高等教育国际化的三要素：教师、学生和课程

（一）地方院校教师结构的国际化指标

1. 师资队伍国际化的内涵

师资队伍的国际化已成为全球高水平大学的共同特征，是高等教育开展国际合作交流、提高国际影响力的前提，也是大学可持续发展的客观要求。师资队伍的国际化是指培养具有国际视野、国际观念和意识，有国际教育背景和跨文化教育背景的多元化、多民族化的教师队伍。高等教育的国际化归根到底是"人"的国际化，这个观点既包括教育者的国际化，也包括受教育者的国际化。所以师资队伍的国际化在高等教育国际化的建设中处于核心地位，高水平大学非常重视教师的国际合作与学术交流；高水平大学要求教师有不同国家的文化背景和学习经历，吸收世界各国先进的教学、研究方法和教育理念；高水平大学强调师资队伍结构的"远缘交杂"，强调不同专业和学校师资的交叉融合。要了解地方院校教师结构的国际化，我们应该从以下两个方面来分析师资队伍的国际化程度：本土教师的国际化程度和本校聘任外籍教师的比例。

2. 本土教师结构的国际化指标

为了衡量和分析本土教师的国际化程度，本文提出本土教师国际化可从以下16个方面的指标来分析和评估：（1）本校学校领导的国际交流经历；（2）在海外留学获得学位教师的结构比；（3）中外合作境内攻读国外高校学位教师的结构比；（4）本校在境外进修和访学教师的结构比；（5）参与中外合作境内集中培训本土教师的结构比；（6）参与中外科研合作的教师结构比；（7）参与中外合作境内或境外开展的学术交流活动的教师结构比；（8）参与教育代表团互访的教师结构比；（9）合作单位或者相关机构境外工作的教师结构比；（10）中外教师的结构比；（11）担任外国大学客座教授的教师结构比；（12）担任国际协会组织成员的教师结构比；（13）参与合作研究中心或实验室的教师结构比；（14）大学或海外的国际事务办公室的教师结构比；（15）中外机构合作经营的学校教师结构比；（16）在国外期刊发表论文的教师结构比。

通过归纳和分析以上指标，我们可从不同层面了解高等院校教师学习国外先进的教育理念，获取国外先进教育资源，以及将国外教育资源"学以致用"于本土教育环境的程度，换句话说，我们可以通过对以上指标的综合分析来评估地方高校师资队伍构成的国际化程度及其特色。目前地方院校中的教师绝大部分是本土培养的教师，尽管近年来有许多海外归国的高学历人才充实到高校教师队伍中来，但是与庞大的教师群体相比较，具备海外留学或海外工作经历的教师比例还是偏低，仅以笔者所在大学三个学院教师中具备国外学习、工作经历背景的统计数据看，大致不到5%，且因为专业背景的不同，这个指标的比例高低不同。

3. 地方院校外籍教师的结构比

地方院校外籍教师的构成是指院校引进外籍教师数与全体教师数的比例，这个指标能从另一方面了解和说明院校教师结构国际化的程度和目标。这个结构比主要涉及以下方面的指标：(1) 本校长期聘任外籍教师结构比；(2) 短期聘任外籍教师结构比；(3) 授予外国专家职衔的教师结构比；(4) 外籍教师的科研成果；(5) 外国学者的教师结构比。

地方院校外籍教师的结构比也是衡量高校国际化程度的一个重要指标。国际名校的师资队伍中一般外籍教师都超过了50%，有的达到了80%[11]。一流的教育需要一流的大学，一流的大学需要一流的师资，一流的师资才能培养一流的人才。所以地方院校引进外籍教师，有这样四个方面的意义：一是地方院校生存或长远发展的战略考虑，全球国际化的进程给教育最大的影响必将是教育的国际化，而教育国际化的趋势必然促使院校的国际化，教师的国际化，人才培养的国际化，以及本土课程的国际化；二是外籍教师的引进可帮助院校搭建介绍国外先进教育理念，引进国外优秀教育资源的平台；三是形成学术交流和科研合作可持续发展的机制；四是让本土教育体系和教育机制融入新鲜"血液"，共赢发展。

(二) 地方院校人才培养的国际化指标

人才培养是大学的核心功能。在高等教育走向国际化的进程中，人才培养的素质内涵也加入了新的内容：国际化成为大学教育对象的素质要求。关于人才培养国际化的内涵，笔者认为是指所在校学生群体在境内或者境外接触、交流学习国外教育资源的过程，其主要形式有：留学生数量和生源结构、出国留学攻读学位、中外合作培养攻读学位、境外长期或者短期交流学习、由国外高校师资主导的集中培训，以及其他形式的学术或非学术交流活动等。本文主要提出以下指标来分析和评估学生结构的国际化：(1) 全日制境外留学的学生结构比；(2) 中外合作培养攻读学位的学生结构比；(3) 长期学习短期访问留学生数量和生源结构比；(4) 参加境外长短期学习的学生结构比；(5) 中外合作境内集中培训的学生结构比；(6) 海外实习的学生结构比；(7) 在国外期刊发表论文的学生结构比；(8) 参与教育代表团互访的学生结构比；(9) 参与中外合作境内或境外开展的学术活动的学生结构比；(10) 参与中外合作境内或境外开展的竞赛活动的学生结构比；(11) 参加语言类课程学习的学生结构比。

培养学生的全球视野是高等教育国际化的重要目标之一。统计数据表明：2006年之前，中国大学学生国际交流的机会仍然有限。2006年中国除港澳台外的研究型大学平均1.5%的学生出国或出境交流，顶尖大学2006年有3%左右的学生出国交流[12]。近年来中国大学的出国交流学生人数有所增长，但地方院校没有这方面公开的数据来源，估计整体上不会高于2006年研究型大学的比例。

(三) 地方院校课程设置的国际化指标

1. 地方院校课程设置国际化的意义

教育是教师为主导、学生为主体，两者交互影响，以传承道德、文化和知识为主要目的的过程。教学活动是教师和学生相互影响的交集，课程设置是教学活动的核心因素，也是最重要的要素之一。所以教师队伍和学生培养的国际化，必然产生课程设置的国际化。

课程设置的国际化如何理解？课程国际化是高等教育国际化的重要组成部分，是指外语学习课程、国际上通行学术课程的开发和设置，以及"学科知识普及化"的过程。这是从具体一门学科的课程概念出发而言的。如果从广义的课程概念出发，课程国际化还应包含课程目标的国际性与课程体系的国际通行性。这样才能比较完整地理解高校课程国际化的含义[14]。

在具体实施层面，"引进"和"改进"是课程国际化的两个核心观念。所谓"引进"是指借助中外教育合作的平台，将适合本土教育目的的国外优质课程资源课程直接纳入本土课程体系，这包括教材、教学大纲、教学过程以及教学评价手段的全盘吸收和运用，而且可能直接聘用外籍教师担任课程的教学工作；所谓"改进"则是指借鉴国外优质课程资源中的有利因素，同时保留适合本土教学的积极因素，对现有本土课程资源加以改善，形成"洋为中用、中西合璧"的本土课程体系。本文将地方院校课程设置的国际化指标析分为以下几类：(1) 使用外文原版教材的课程比例；(2) 采用外语授课的专业课程比例；(3) 学生的外语水平；(4) 涉外课程的开设比例；(5) 涉外课程的教师培训工作；(6) 课程开发相关的国际合作科研项目与经费。

无论是全盘引进还是改进提升，国际化课程体系的开发和设置是一个长期而又必然的趋势。地方院校课程设置的国际化是衡量和评价院校国际化的一个重要指标，地方院校课程设置的国际化是本土课程体系"吐故纳新"和"改革创新"的必然过程，通过比较研究不同指标对大学课程设置国际化程度的影响状况，探索大学课程设置创新的新思路，期望对正在走向国际化的中国大学从微观的基础层面的课程设置上提供有益的结论和建议，其意义毋庸置疑。

2. 地方院校课程设置国际化须关注的问题

"教师行不行"的问题。地方院校课程设置的国际化，课程的引进和改革是要考虑教师的执教能力能否跟得上的问题。能否将国外优质课程资源吸纳和消化，教师执教能力的同步提升是实现这一目标的关键。课程引进了，教师教不了，或者教不好，都是课程设置国际化过程中可能面临且需要解决的问题。

"学生行不行"的问题。地方院校课程设置的国际化，既要关注教师的执教能力，同时也要考量学生的学习水平。某高校某专业引进了一系列国外优质课程资源，引进了外籍教师，同时也配备了本土教师，本土教师也经过系统的课程教学培训，但开始授课时才发现学生因为语言水平相对较低，听不懂授课，看不懂教材，完不成基本的教学任务。

"多与少"的问题。地方院校课程设置的国际化，一般来说，课程的引进不是问题，最关键的问题是引进多少的问题。比方说，某院校的一个专业要换哪些课程，要留哪些课程？这个多与少的把握，完全在于科学的调研和实地的考证，否则别无他法。

"水土不服"的问题。地方院校课程设置的国际化，课程的引进和改革要考虑其课程设计的科学性和理念的先进性，同时也要考虑其实用性。地方院校的人才培养的基本思路可以理解为"从地方来，回地方去，以服务地方为最终目的"，所以课程的引进既要考虑是否符合学生素质需要，也要考虑学生能力发展的需要，以及未来人才市场的需要。所以国外优秀的课程资源，引进来后能"利于学生学，又便于学生用"，才是课程设置国际化建设的发展方向。

四、地方院校高等教育国际化的对策与思路

（一）重视国际化战略规划，健全人事体制和机制

多数大学重视国际化，有研究表明：81%的研究型大学有明确的国际化战略规划和实施方案。研究型大学59%的校领导有一年或以上的海外经历；在专职外事人员设置方面，近年来研究型大学逐渐将职能比较单一的外事处转变为多职能的国际交流部门，通常为国际交流处（含港澳台办公室）和留学生管理机构（如国际教育学院）。一些研究型大学还设置了对外学术交流中心或海外留学中心这样的机构。研究型大学平均有36名校级专职外事人员，78%的院系设有专职外事人员[12]。地方院校要在学校不同层面，或者说在全校范围内形成"国际化育人"的理念，并在顶层设计时把"培养国际化师资、培养国际化学生，建设国际化课程"作为学校发展战略的要素来考虑。

（二）促进人员国际交流，突出师资队伍的国际化

要解决"教师行不行"的问题，首先是推进师资队伍的国际交流，具体包括外籍教师、外国专家的交流经历以及授予外国专家职衔等方面的工作；其次是教学与科研的国际化工作，包括中外合作办学、校际国际合作协议、国际合作科研项目与经费等方面的内容。从某种程度上说，师资队伍的国际化将极大地影响地方高等院校课程与学术成果交流的国际化程度。有研究表明：在中国进入世界前500名的大学里，师资队伍的国际化程度显著高于非前500名的研究型大学。这些大学吸引的师资不仅有本国培养的优秀人才，而且有来自全球的优秀人才[12]。

关于教师的国际化，笔者认为：一是教师教育观念要国际化。地方院校须借助"外脑"来加快国际化教育理念的更新，使教师能从全球化的视角来认识教育的本质和作用，认识教育改革和发展问题；二是加快海外高层次人才的引进，形成一批高水平国际化师资队伍，并通过改善科研环境和资助条件，充分发挥外籍教师和优秀留学人才的学术能力，完善激励机制；三是加大骨干教师的海外培训，积极选派中青年教师以访学、攻读学位或从事博士后研究的方式到国内外知名大学和研究机构进修学习，推动师资队伍的国际化进程；四是通过与各国政府、国际组织、海外企业以及研究机构建立国际合作实验室，提升科研与人才培养合作的层次，促进海外人才与学校科研骨干的融合；五是鼓励举办系列高水平国际性学术会议，开办教育、文化、语言等相关的系列学术讲座，鼓励本土教师参加国际学术会议；六是创

造条件大力发展留学生教育。近年来,中国教育的潜在市场价值被西方国家频频看好,大量的外国教育机构走进来办学和送留学生出国来华留学,留学生教育事业在近5年内有了突飞猛进的发展,中国逐渐成为全球最大的留学生输出国,21世纪汉语热的出现,又使中国成为留学生的重要接收国之一。所以笔者认为所在院校的来华留学生比例也是地方院校高等教育国际化的重要指标,它体现了一所大学对各国学生的吸引力。大力开办留学生教育,可以充分利用世界高等教育资源,在学习和引进国外高等教育的成熟经验的同时,提高教育质量和效益,提升地方院校的学术地位和国际竞争力。

(三)双语教学和专业课程英语授课入手,实施课程改革

启动双语教学师资培养计划,提高双语教学和专业课程英语授课的比例。加大"双语教学"的力度是提升学生国际化程度的有力举措,能够解决"学生行不行"的问题。笔者认为:双语教学和专业课程英语授课不仅能促进学生的语言能力、思维能力、思考技能,而且有助于提高学生的跨文化交际能力,形成国际视野。开展双语教学和专业课程英语授课对于顺应和促进高校课程改革、增进文化交流和拓展学生未来发展空间等具有重要的意义。

现阶段我国地方院校国际化水平的发展程度不一,发展水平参差不齐,大多数院校的国际化程度还比较低,综合表现为:涉外课程的开发和设置相对比例偏低,专业课程使用外文原版教材的比例偏低,专业课程采用外语教学的比例偏低,学生的外语水平偏低,这些问题都在不同程度上影响一个大学课程国际化的改革进程,因此地方院校须大力推进大学课程的改革和创新,解决课程设置国际化建设中"多与少"的问题,解决"水土不服"的问题。

五、结　论

经济的国际化需求引发了人才的国际化需求,人才的国际化需求引发了教育的国际化需求。教育国际化既是一种客观的必然趋势,也是一种国际性的普遍现象,因此,我们必须对国际化问题进行研究,抓紧建立教育国际化的理念,抓紧考虑如何走好自己的国际化办学之路。随着高等教育国际化实践和理论研究的不断深入,如何衡量和比较大学的国际化程度正走入理论研究者和教育实践者和管理者们的视线,成为教育界关注的热点问题。

本文针对当前高等教育国际化和国家大力开展高水平大学建设的宏观形势,从地方院校教师结构的国际化及学生结构的国际化指标建构出发,提出并分析了影响地方院校课程设置国际化建设中的现状和问题,对地方普通高校通过国际化战略提升自身核心竞争力提出相应的对策思考。为地方院校构建国际化课程,加快国际化进程提出了可供借鉴的视点。

参考文献

[1] 张红. 教育的国际化与未来学校的发展 [J]. 中国基础教育, 2007 (3).
[2] 张妍. 大学国际化水平评价指标体系的构建 [J]. 中国高等教育评估, 2002 (1).
[3] 侯俊平, 张春河. 教育国际化与高水平大学建设 [J]. 国家教育行政学院学报, 2003 (1).
[4] 毕家驹. 大学国际化的实践与展望 [J]. 高教发展与评估, 2005, 21 (2).
[5] 乔玉香. 高等教育国际化与我国大学的发展 [J]. 山西财经大学学报: 高等教育版, 2002, 54 (1).
[6] 王刚, 徐立清. 论大学的国际化: 理念与策略 [J]. 中国高教研究, 2004 (7).
[7] 李盛兵. 大学国际化评价指标体系初探 [J]. 华南师范大学学报, 2005 (6).
[8] 常永胜. 大学国际化: 背景、内容与评价指标体系 [J]. 广东外语外贸大学学报, 2008, 19 (01).
[9] 胡亦武. 基于主成分分析的大学课程国际化程度比较研究 [J]. 系统工程, 2009 (1).
[10] 曾满超, 王美欣, 蔺乐. 美国、英国与澳大利亚高等教育的国际化 [J]. 北京大学教育评论, 2009 (2).
[11] 孙玉中. 比较研究高职师资国际化及重庆高职师资国际化途径 [J]. 重庆电子工程职业技术学院学报, 2011, 20 (4).
[12] 陈昌贵, 曾满超, 文东茅, 等. 中国研究型大学国际化调查及评估指标构建 [J]. 北京大学教育评论, 2009 (4).
[13] 中国教育年鉴编辑部. 中国教育年鉴. 北京: 人民教育出版社, 2006.
[14] 王运来. 论大学课程国际化 [J]. 辽宁教育研究, 2000 (10).

网络环境下的英语听力学习策略培训

何 芳 王 玮 郁 震

语言输入是语言习得的基本条件，没有语言输入就不会有语言习得。英语听力作为主要的语言输入，在英语学习中占有重要的地位。传统的英语听力教学以教师为中心，强调通过为学习者提供大量的可理解性输入来提高他们的英语听力理解水平，即听力教学主要基于语言（language – based instruction）或基于理解（comprehension – based instruction）。但是这种做法忽略了学习者在理解课文、处理信息、学习和保持与学习内容有关的概念时所采取的学习策略。[1]因此，教师应将英语听力学习策略的讲授融入到教学当中。

近年来，随着计算机网络技术的不断发展，通过网络学习英语的方法越来越受到重视，开展基于网络的英语听力自主学习已成为英语教学中的普遍现象，是英语课堂教学的有力补充和拓展。利用网络学习英语听力，一方面，网络上的英语听力学习材料丰富、不受时间和空间限制，学生可以根据自己的兴趣与水平自主选择学习材料等；但另一方面也存在不少问题，比如，学生学习的计划性及自我监管能力不强，面对丰富的网络资源不知该如何取舍，遇到问题得不到教师的及时指导等。如何提高网络环境下的英语听力学习质量成为英语教学研究的新问题。

1 听力学习策略理论概述

在关于学习策略的理论中，O'Malley 和 Chamot[1]的理论受到了广泛的认同。他们提出，学习策略是学习者用于帮助理解、学习和记忆新信息的特殊思想和行为；学习策略既可以是显性的外部行为，也可以是隐性的心理活动；学习策略是可以培训和学习的。他们将学习策略分为三大类：用于监督、调节和自我调整语言行为的元认知策略（计划、自我约束、管理、监察、评估、选择注意等）、认知策略（帮助理解具体语言任务，如记笔记、利用上下文情境预测、整理归类等）和社交/情感策略（学习者主动接触目标语言、合作学习、互动等）。

从 20 世纪 90 年代中期开始，更多研究开始关注学习者外语听力策略的使用。由于自主学习与学习策略有着密不可分的关系，不少研究者试图从策略培训入手促进学习者外语听力自主学习能力的提高。Cohen 认为，听力策略能有效提高学习者的听力水平，建议在外语听力教学中开展听力策略培训。[2] Vandergrift 认为，对学生进行外语听力策略的培训确实可以提高听力教学的效果和学习者的听力水平，元认知策略是成功听力者所必备的。[3] O'Malley 和 Chamot 认为，大量的练习可以促使学习策略的程序化和内化。[1]文秋芳认为，学习策略不但是可以培训的，而且要长期坚持下去，使它成为外语教学课程的一个组成部分。[4]

由上述可知，学习策略研究领域里的重要学者都认为：学习策略是可教的，教师应该对学习者进行学习策略的培训，使学习者更加主动、有效地进行外语听力训练。

2 网络环境下英语听力学习策略的培训方法

为了确保学生网络自主学习英语听力的有效性和可持续性，教师应该有意识地对学生进行系统的英语听力学习策略培训，将学习策略培训融入英语教学中，即通过科学的引导和有针对性的指导，开展一

［基金项目］本文系北京市属高等学校人才强教计划资助项目《多媒体网络环境下大学英语听力学习策略的调查研究》（项目编号：PHR201108428）和北京联合大学新起点计划项目《提升大学英语教师信息素养的对策研究》（项目编号：SK201202）的研究成果。

［作者简介］何芳（1973—），女，北京联合大学外语部副教授、硕士。主要从事英语教育、教师教育研究；王玮（1979—），女，北京联合大学外语部讲师、硕士。主要从事英语教育研究；郁震（1975—），男，北京联合大学外语部讲师、硕士。主要从事英语教育研究。

系列英语听力学习策略的相关培训，教会学生何时使用、如何使用学习策略来帮助他们的英语听力学习。根据 O'Malley 和 Chamot 的分类框架，教师对学生进行网络自主学习英语听力的策略培训也可以从元认知策略、认知策略、社会/情感策略 3 个方面实施。

2.1 元认知策略培训

元认知策略是一个人所具有的关于自己思维活动和学习活动的认知和监控，是自我意识和自我体验，用于评价、管理、监控认知策略的使用，可分为事先计划、指导英语注意力、功能准备、选择注意力、自我管理、自我监控、自我评估。英语听力学习中元认知策略的本质就是有意识地计划、安排听力活动，并对听力行为实施监察，对听力理解进行自我评价。网络环境下教师对学生英语听力学习的元认知策略培训方式有以下 5 种方式。

2.1.1 自我管理

教师要帮助学生树立正确的网络学习态度，对网络环境下的英语听力学习要实事求是、循序渐进，并要引导学生预先计划、确立学习目标、制定具体的网络学习计划；指导学生作出符合自身情况的需求分析，根据自己的学习水平、学习风格、学习习惯、学习困难、已有学习策略等因素，制定有针对性、个性化的学习方案，确定英语听力学习计划和明确学习目标，选择合适的学习策略。

2.1.2 自我监控

由于网络英语听力自主学习缺少教师的直接监督，学生的自我监控能力则在很大程度上决定了网络学习的有效性。教师应要求学生自觉监控学习过程，按时并保质、保量地完成学习任务，以及有计划地巩固与复习等。此外，教师还要逐步指导学生掌握对未完成或未很好完成听力任务的弥补措施等。

2.1.3 自我评价

教师要帮助学生对网络英语听力学习过程和效果作出客观的评价，包括策略的使用效果、计划的实施情况、听力方面取得的进步和存在的不足等，检查自己对某一具体听力材料的理解程度，分析某些内容没听懂的原因，以争取下次能做得更好。同时，教师还可以通过引导学生利用网络互动、在线测试，或下载安装适当的评估软件等，随时监控并检查自己的英语听力学习进度和效果。

2.1.4 集中注意

教师要培养学生集中注意力来完成网上的英语听力学习任务。英语听力学习的特点决定了它比阅读、写作、口语等学习要求学生有更高度的注意力，因为一旦分散注意力就可能错过一个或几个关键信息点。教师要训练学生逐渐延长集中注意力的时间，帮助学生有意识地控制自己集中精力。

2.1.5 选择注意

教师要帮助学生意识到英语听力学习过程中并不需要每个词都全部听懂，对于大部分的听力材料只需抓住一些关键性的主题词或主题句和掌握所听材料的主要信息即可。教师要训练学生把注意力有选择性地放在听力任务的重要信息上，关注关键词句、信息和特定问题；要抓大放小，不需要听懂材料里的每个单词、每个句子，也不能因某个生词或某句话没听懂而影响对后续听力材料的注意力。

总之，网络环境下英语听力学习中的元认知策略培训就是教师指导学生在网络英语听力学习前对学习任务有清晰的认知、制定明确的学习目标和学习方案；要求学生在网络英语听力学习过程中要集中注意力，能够对内容进行有选择的取舍，并学会自觉监控学习过程和调节学习进度等；要求学生对网络英语听力学习的结果进行积极的自我评价、自我校正和自我反思，以提高网络英语听力学习的效能。

2.2 认知策略培训

认知策略用于学习语言的活动之中，可分为使用参考资料、重复、分组/分类、推理、利用图像、听觉再现、利用关键词、联想、转化、推断、做笔记、小结、重新组合、翻译。英语听力学习中的认知策略包括语言学习活动中各种帮助理解语言任务、提高听力水平的具体行动。教师对网络环境下学生的英语听力学习认知策略培训方式有以下 5 种。

2.2.1 利用目标语资源

教师要鼓励学生充分利用网络创设的英语环境，尽可能多地接触网络所提供的真实、生动的英语语料，有意识地选择适合自己听力水平并且感兴趣的学习材料，如英美国家的电影、电视剧、新闻、电台节目、世界名校的公开课视频等。同时，学生要学会利用网络提供的大量国内外英文学习工具书（如在线图书馆、英英词典、金山词霸、有道词典、百科全书、优秀电子教材等），在线学习或下载网络中的各种英语听力学习材料（如学习方法、应试技巧、高分秘籍、历年真题、参考模拟预测题、考试信息等）。

2.2.2 记笔记

在练习听力的过程中，短时记忆只能维持几秒钟的时间，为获得更完整的信息，就要记笔记。教师应教给学生边听边速记的策略，重点记下关键词、人名、地名、数字等（如：年月日、时间、年龄、价格）。为了加快记录速度，教师还可以为学生介绍一些缩写或者简写的符号。如句子"The man bought this $200 camera at a 15% discount"，便可通过记下关键词的首字母和使用特定的符号等方式，迅速记录为"M - B ca $200↓15%"，从而提高记录速度，并加大短时记录的信息量。

2.2.3 整理归类

教师要引导学生学会用电子文档记笔记，通过新建不同的文件夹，对所听过的内容进行归类整理，如针对不同的听力形式（长对话、篇章等）、不同的听力对话场景（校园、餐馆、医院等），分析归纳每一类听力材料的特点，以备日后复习和强化。

2.2.4 利用关键词和上下文情境推断

教师要教会学生尽可能利用听力题目所给出的已知信息（如关键词、图片、标题等），根据上下文情境或背景知识（如预测结果、填补空缺等），结合自身已有知识，对听力材料中的信息进行加工整理，推理预测听力材料的题材结构和大意，同时也将实际获取的听力信息与现存的知识图式相结合，对听力结果进行发挥性运用，并联系各种已知和未知的信息（如新信息与先验知识、个人经历等），对听力材料进行综合归纳和概括，降低听力的盲目性，提高听力的准确性。

2.2.5 听读和听写

根据输出假说，读和写等"输出"活动都会促进听的"输入"活动。因此，教师要让学生意识到，在练习听力这个"输入"环节的同时，也不要忽略对口语和写作两个"输出"环节的学习，因为三者之间是互相促进、相辅相成的。

网络环境下英语听力学习中的认知策略培训就是教师教会学生学会选择并合理调节自己的注意力和知觉，使学生有意识地对所听材料进行积极预测和推理，对所听材料进行高效存储和提取等。在具体的网络英语听力策略培训活动中，教师要侧重于帮助学生提高预测听力材料、接受听力内容、理解听力文章结构、记忆关键信息点、再现听力原文等学习技巧和能力。

2.3 社会/情感策略培训

社会/情感策略为学生提供了更多接触语言的机会，包括提问/澄清，即要求教师或学生对某个语言现象再解释、重复、举例或证实。英语听力学习中的社会/情感策略主要是指学生主动多听英语材料、与同伴协作学习、控制自己的情绪等。教师对网络环境下学生的英语听力学习社会/情感策略培训方式有以下3种。

2.3.1 情感因素

教师应培养学生对英语网络听力学习的积极情感和态度，让他们认识到网络学习对英语听力的良好促进作用。人文主义心理学强调情感与认知的相辅相成，认为如果学习者对学习缺乏积极情感，其认知能力会大打折扣。

2.3.2 降低焦虑感

适度的焦虑感有助于促进学习者的学习，但是过度焦虑会影响学习者的学习成效[5]。焦虑是影响学生学习效率的一个关键因素。教师要引导学生在学习遇到困难时或感到孤单无助时能够调整好自己的情绪，坚持网络学习，而不可半途而废。同时，教师要让学生对网络学习过程中可能会出现的电脑病毒、系统故障、网页打不开或下载教学软件失败等问题，要有心理准备，要尽可能地保持平常心态。

2.3.3 合作学习和寻求解答

教师应鼓励学生在听力活动中积极与他人保持双向或多向交流互动，以促进学生的听力学习。例如，可用博客或微博随时记录并更新自己的网络英语听力学习的心得，与志同道合的学友们互动交流、分享经验；通过各种聊天室、网络BBS论坛等平台，或使用飞信、QQ、微信、skype或Facetime等网络通讯工具与授课教师或朋友交流学习体会、讨论问题或开展合作学习等。

网络环境下英语听力学习中的社会/情感策略培训就是鼓励学生尽可能多地接触语言材料，提高学生对语言学习的兴趣和热情。其中，社会策略培训旨在帮助学生树立良好的心态，从而更好地开展英语学习。情感策略培训旨在帮助学生在网络英语听力学习过程中克服焦虑、控制情绪、分享经验等，从而实现充分利用网络资源，最大程度地达到提高学生英语听力水平的目的。

参考文献

[1] O'Malley & Chamot. Learning Strategies in Second Language Acquisition [M]. Cambridge：Cambridge University Press，1990.

[2] Cohen A. D. Strategies in Learning and Using a Second Lan－guage [M]. Beijing：Beijing Foreign Language Teaching and Research Press，2000.

[3] Vandergrift, L. Orchestrating Strategy Use：Toward a Model of the Skilled Second Language Listener [J]. Language Learning，2003，53（3）：463－496.

[4] 文秋芳. 英语学习的成功之路 [M]. 上海：上海外语教育出版社，2003.

[5] Gass, S. M. & L. Selinker. Second Language Acquisition [M]. Mahwah, N. J.：Lawrence Erlbaum Associates，2001.

北京高等院校校内创新实践基地建设探索

——以北京联合大学普通与特殊教育相结合校内创新实践基地为例

汪艳丽 等

2012年2月,北京联合大学普通与特殊教育相结合的校内创新实践基地(以下简称"普特创新基地")正式投入建设,并于2013年11月成功申报北京高等学校示范性校内创新实践基地。该基地主要依据《北京市教育委员会关于开展北京高等学校校内创新实践基地建设的通知》、结合《北京市中小学三年行动计划》、《北京市学前教育三年行动计划》、《北京市中小学融合教育行动计划》等北京市基础教育和特殊教育发展的迫切需求,立足本校实际,结合学校定位和人才培养目标,充分整合利用各类实验教学中心、工程训练中心、科研实验室、大学生活动中心、校内实习实训基地等现有学生创新实践资源,针对不同学生的特长和兴趣,有计划地组织大学生参与系统性、综合性的创新实践活动。力图建设一个培养适应首都现代教育所需的普通师资与融合教育师资的创新实践教学基地品牌。经过建设现已形成了:"全纳教育"新理念,实现了普通与融合教育师资培养模式的创新;"普特结合"新平台,实现了普通与融合教育师资培养实践教学平台的创新;"协同创新"新举措实现了普通与融合教育师资培养实践教学过程的创新。

一、确立"普特结合、开放共享、自主创新、实践育人"的基地建设理念

普特结合:随着特殊教育的发展,越来越多的残障儿童进入普通学校就读,需要教师不仅要掌握一般的教学技能,还需要掌握适合各类特殊儿童个别差异的特殊教学技能,需要普通教育与特殊教育相结合,培养学生既具备教育普通教育技能又具备特殊教育技能。

开放共享:立足本校实际,结合学校定位和人才培养目标,充分整合利用各类实验教学中心、工程训练中心、科研实验室、大学生活动中心、校内实习实训基地等现有学生创新实践资源,针对不同学生的特长和兴趣,有计划地组织大学生参与系统性、综合性的创新实践活动。

自主创新:依托国家级"应用文科综合实验教学中心""全国残疾人职业教育师资培训基地"、"北京市特殊教育中心"等基地,以及《无障碍理念下残障学生课程建设的研究与实践》《大学生心理素质教育类课程体验式教学的研究与实践》等北京市优秀教学成果奖的基础,围绕创新型融合教育师资培养的需要,校院两级统筹布局,将普通教育的实践基地与特殊教育的实践基地的资源和功能进行整合、拓展,建立了一个培养学生创新意识,充分实践学生创新思想的基地。我校对基地的运行机制进行了规划设计,充分发挥我校学科平台和科研实力的优势,加强科研对本科教学的反哺作用,切实提高大学生实践创新能力。

实践育人:教师是一项操作性极强的职业,需要教师不仅要掌握学科技能,还要掌握教学技能,教师在培养的过程中需要进行大量的实践活动,通过学科实践活动和教师专业技能实践活动,使学生在走出校门之前能够掌握基本职业技能,为将来走上教师岗位奠定职业基础。

二、建设适合基础教育和融合师资培养需要的六个分基地

按功能设置了服务基础教育和融合师资培养的主学科训练分基地,分别为:特殊教育创新实践基地、学前教育创新训练分基地、学科教育训练分基地、心理素质教育分基地、艺术素质教育分基地、工程技术训练分基地。学校整合已有的普通师范教育和特殊教育实验教学场地,根据分基地的功能,从中

[作者简介] 汪艳丽,北京联合大学师范学院。

选择了部分实验室、学生活动中心等纳入本基地建设或主要作为面向大学生创新实验项目开放的实验室。

特殊教育创新实践分基地，针对从事特殊学校教师创新能力不足的问题，参与教师科研项目、手语研究、孤独症儿童的游戏治疗、自闭症儿童的干预研究与实践、特教教师专业技能学科竞赛等活动。

学前教育创新实践分基地，针对普通和融合学前教师创新思维和创新能力不足的问题，参与教师科研项目，组织学前专业学生参加讲故事比赛、教具开发与制作、游戏活动创设等活动。

学科教育创新实践分基地，针对重学科知识、轻教学技能训练，随班就读学校普通教师和融合教师创新意识和创新能力不足的问题，组织全国高师学生教学技能大赛、大学生各类书法类比赛、文学作品创作演讲大赛、全国数学建模竞赛、英语口语大赛等活动。

心理素质教育创新实践分基地，针对普通和融合师资心理素质的提升问题，开展"启明星"科技创新实践活动、朋辈心理辅导活动项目、打工子弟学校校外心理辅导、社区空巢老人团体心理辅导等活动。

艺术素质教育创新实践分基地，针对学生艺术素质、人格培养，普及艺术、设计美化生活的理念，鼓励开展跨学科、跨专业的协同创新类自主实践项目，举办了全国校园音乐舞蹈电视展演、大学生艺术节、服装设计比赛及展演、手工工艺制作、动画片编制、广告设计大赛等活动。

工程技术训练创新实践分基地，针对普通与融合师资理论与实践脱节，动手能力不强的问题，开展开放性项目，如数控直流电流源、波形发生器、自动往返电动小汽车、4人智力竞赛抢答器、交通信号灯设计、简易足球机器人设计等。

依托学校教务管理信息系统，建立基地信息平台，设有九大模块，其功能涉及信息发布、网络办公、安全防控、综合服务等多个层面，已成为基地中心信息化建设的重要阵地。可以提供国内外大学生创新实践活动开展的信息资料；公布基地资源的使用状况；发布基地的项目申报、立项、验收信息；展示基地创新实践成果等。

三、打造一支满足基地建设的"三导师制"队伍

学校实践教学建设指导委员会作为校内创新基地的领导机构，负责总体规划与协调、监督基地实践教育质量。下设创新实践教学指导小组负责确定基地建设发展方向，签署校企战略合作框架，调配各分基地间实践教育资源。为提高创新地实践项目开展的水平，建立了指导教师"三导师制"：即"以校内教师为主体的实践教学指导教师团队、以学校师范教育教师发展中心为主体的学科教学研究教师团队、以北京市优秀中小学学科教师为主体的名师教学团队。"三导师制"师资团队的最大特色是这些教师本身都非常熟悉中小学教育，或来自教学一线，长期从事中小学教育的特级、高级教师，或长期从事师范教育并潜心于基础教育研究的专家学者。

四、建立一个制度完善和规范的保障机制

通过制定发布《关于成立普教与特教相结合的校内创新实践基地管理委员的通知》等指导性文件，补充完善《普教与特教相结合的校内创新·实践基地管理办法》《普教与特教相结合的校内创新实践基地安全管理办法》《普教与特教相结合的校内创新实践基地安全保障管理规定》等管理制度来确定创新实践基地的组织结构、规范创新实践基地的运行流程、建设基地管理信息系统、开发基地运行质量评价标准，使基地始终在制度保障和规范下高效运行。主要的管理制度包括以下四个方面。

①挂牌制度：实行挂牌单位领导下的分基地负责人制。分基地负责人由挂牌单位选任，并报教务处备案。分基地负责人应具有较高的学术水平，热心教学工作，具有较强的组织管理和协调能力。

②项目导师制：实行课题制的人事管理办法和导师制培养模式。指导教师由分基地负责人确定，并报教务处备案。指导教师以副高以上职称为主，同时要求有自己独立的课题。

③课题发布和申报机制：分基地学术委员会根据基地的特点，确定一定数量的符合本科生培养目标的研究课题项目，制订项目指南并报教务处。教务处于每年一度的校大学生科研基金申请时，统一发布各分基地的项目指南，面向全校大学生招标。学生应组成实践创新团队参与投标，每3—5名学生为一个

团队，同时鼓励不同学科背景的学生交叉组合。参加分基地项目申请的学生，应是本校全日制大二或大三的本科生，且主修专业学习成绩优良、学有余力者。分基地学术委员会负责招标，选拔优秀的团队参与基地所立的研究项目，并报教务处备案。

④项目评审和学分认证机制：为了倡导和鼓励大学生个性发展，激发和培养大学生的创新精神、创业意识和实践能力，提高大学生人文素养、科学素质和艺术修养，学校在学生中设立创新实践学分。规定全日制学生在校期间，以我校学生名义参加课外创新实践活动并获得成果者，按规定获得学分。同时为规范创新实践学分的管理，学校将自主创新学习纳入人才培养方案，建立创新实践学分认定标准，将根据学生在创新实践活动中所取得的成绩，给予不同的学分。

其管理模式是：北京联合大学实践教学委员会是校内创新实践基地的最高领导机构，委员会由学校教务处处长、各学院实践教学负责人组成，采用联席会方式，研究确定基地建设发展方向，调配基地创新实践资源，监督基地实践创新活动质量。委员会下设基地学术指导小组和日常运行管理办公室。学术指导小组由校、院专家和校外中小学优秀教师组成，负责创新实践活动的指导。日常运行管理办公室设在学院一级的教学管理部门，负责各分基地日常运行的管理。分基地由各教学单位实验教学负责人担任，具体负责各分基地的建设工作。

专职实验管理和实验技术人员重点负责基地的日常工作，包括基地实验室的建设、实验设备的日常管理与维护、实验教学的准备与安排、实验文档资料的管理等工作；专兼职实践指导教师指导学生自主创新项目的申报、科技小发明、学科竞赛、社会实践；聘请的优秀中小学教师指导学生创新团队建设，引导师范生科技创新方向等。

运行经费保障：充足的经费保障。每学年学校和学院在教学水平提高经费中都单独划拨一定额度的经费，专款专用，以保障基地的日常运行、改善创新实践活动条件及支持学生参加科技活动等。同时学科竞赛、大学生科研训练项目、产学研合作项目、实验室开放项目等都给予了专项经费支持，也纳入了基地的运行经费中。各项经费的投入保证了基地各项活动的正常进行。基地资金来源主要由针对基地的专项投入、教科研项目专项资金、实验室建设经费和校企共建项目投入等组成。近三年，基地特别加强了学生科技活动经费的统筹使用，逐年提高了对学生科技活动的经费支持力度，用于基地实践项目研发、学生科技活动和专业竞赛的投入达416万元。

五、取得丰硕成果并形成特色

以下展示了近三年来基地开展大学生创新实践的内容、项目及主要效果与成果。

1. 开展系统性、综合性的创新实践活动，取得多项国家级、市级奖励

近三年来，校内创新实践基地根据融合教育创新人才培养的规律和我校大学生特点，设计、组织并开展了系统性、综合性的创新实践活动，并将其作为学生"第一课堂"的有益补充与拓展，学生在各级别的比赛、展演、社会实践等活动中，提升了专业技能与综合素养并屡获殊荣。

学生获得"全国高师学生教师技能大赛""全国大学生数学建模竞赛""中国高校大学生戏剧节"等国家级奖项16项，"北京市大学生英语演讲比赛""北京市大学生电子设计竞赛""北京国际合唱节"等市级奖项26项，并成功完成为中央电视台制作《世博中的科学传奇》动画、为北京电视台《红绿灯》《首都经济报道》栏目设计制作节目FLASH等创新实践活动。

2. 通过普特结合的社会实践，树立了适应融合教育需求的全纳教育理念

"有爱才有教育"。基地以融合教育师资的高标准来要求每一名师范生，学生用切身经历践行"全纳教育"的理念。基地充分发挥资源优势和特色优势，积极与社区互动，搭建社会实践平台，成为与学校融合教育师资培养工作协调发展的重要育人环节。持续开展了"走进残疾人温馨家园教授英文""为残障儿童开展游戏活动辅导"，赴牛街敬老院开展"我给奶奶当老师"活动、赴"弘善打工子弟小学支教等活动。通过生动的实践活动，坚定了师范生的正确教育价值观，为培养学教育、爱教育，符合首都教育现代化需求的合格教师提供强有力的保障。

3. 实施跨专业学生自主实践项目，提升了学生自主学习和创新实践的能力

基地针对在校学生学习兴趣不高、学习主动性不强等问题，以项目为驱动、以活动为载体、以鼓励

学生参与实践为手段,以激励学生自主创新为目标开展创新实践活动。学生在与不同院系、专业、年级同伴合作的过程中,通过不断的交流、思想碰撞、协作付出,增强了合作精神与团队意识,人际沟通能力和自主学习能力明显提升。

近三年来,基地开展学生创新活动项目总计 4 类、共 242 项,正是这些有计划的、持续的针对不同学生特长和兴趣开展的创新实践活动,极大地激发了学生的创新意识与创新能力,整个学校逐步形成了积极主动的创新氛围。

4. 创新基地的运行机制,促进了师范教育人才培养模式的改革

基地通过建立挂牌制、项目导师制、课题发布和申报机制、项目评审和学分认证机制等管理制度,改革普通师范教育的人才培养模式,在培养计划中增加创新实践学分,在课内增设融合教育选修课,课外提供适应融合教育需要的实践活动,从而满足了学生的各种不同需求,营造了面向普通生和残障学生共同培养的实践环境氛围。

5. 产生了融合教育师资培养的示范效果,形成了良好的社会声誉

我校师范生近年来就业形势良好,就业率达 100%。近三年,北京联合大学培养的师范毕业生分布在北京各区县的 400 余所教育机构,涉及基础教育、特殊教育等领域,很多毕业生在教师岗位业绩突出,获得市、区级先进教育工作者、青年骨干教师、青年优秀教师等称号。毕业生整体专业水平与综合素养受到用人单位的一致好评。《光明日报》、《中国教育报》等媒体对基地的成果进行了报道。基地具有教育部颁发的全国职业教育师资培训资质,完成了三届国家级中小学骨干教师和学前教育教师培训任务。在承担学生校内实践教学任务的基础上,还面向社会开放,承接基础教育教师的职后培训,以及中小学教师资格证培训等各类社会培训。

参考文献

[1] 王建,杨燕萍. 高等院校校内创新实践基地建设思路探索——以中国人民大学理科公共平台校内创新实践基地为例[J]. 中国大学教学,2013(7).

社会资本视角下民办高校教师专业发展影响机制研究

秦立栓　宋　哲

1　引　言

近年来，国内外学者已将社会资本理论应用于各个领域进行探讨，其中与高校教师相关的研究多集中于社会资本对于教师科研或工作绩效的作用方面。国内对于民办高校教师专业发展的研究成果也日渐丰硕，但多集中于内涵界定、特点分析或对策建议方面，鲜有从社会资本理论出发，专门针对民办高校教师专业发展影响机制的研究，特别是以实证数据为依据的研究更是少之又少。本研究在社会资本理论基础上，深入民办高校，通过问卷调查和数据分析，确定了影响民办高校教师专业发展效果的主要因素，并构建了影响机制模型，提出研究假设，进而采用实证数据对研究假设进行了验证，得到相应结论，并对研究结论带来的启示进行了总结。

2　研究假设及理论模型

2.1　民办高校教师专业发展效果

按照 Guskey（1995）的描述，专业发展是为增进教育者专业知识、技能和态度的过程和活动⋯⋯而且是一个包含多种形式且有意识、有目的、持续的系统过程。为了评价专业发展的具体效果和有效性条件，Guskey 设计了教师专业发展评价模型，该模型分为五个层次，即学员反应、学员学习、组织支持和变化、学员对新知识和新技能的应用、学生的学习结果。[1]一些学者对五层次模型进行了分析，并提出了改进建议，如陈霞（2010）认为应进一步厘清教师专业发展的过程、结果和影响因素，重新划定了评价模型的层次：学习结果、个人绩效、组织成果和学生学习结果。[2]基于有文献的研究，本研究将"民办高校教师专业发展效果"作为因变量，用以考察社会资本视角下专业发展影响因素对于民办高校教师专业发展的正负影响程度，并认为应包括"教师满意度"、"教师新知识收益度"、"高校社会声誉提升程度"、"学生学习结果"等四个层面。

2.2　主要影响因素

社会资本自布迪厄1980年提出后，引起了学术界的大量关注，学者们从不同角度对社会资本进行了研究，至今对于社会资本的概念尚无统一的界定。按照被学术界普遍认可的 Nahapiet 和 Ghoshal（1998）的定义和划分方式，"社会资本是指个体或组织能够从其拥有的关系网络中获取的实际或潜在资源的总量。"，社会资本划分为三个基本维度，即关系维度、结构维度和认知维度。[3]基于对已有文献的分析，本研究就"影响民办高校教师专业发展效果的主要因素"等问题对天津、北京、山东等3所民办高校38名教师进行了访谈，根据所收集的信息进行归纳整理，共得到21项有完整陈述的影响因素，逐步剔除语义模糊以及概念重叠项，挑选出13项影响因素，并以之组成初始测试问卷。经过初测筛选后选取了11个题项对126名教师进行终测，对数据进行因子分析后，最终确定了"跨界机会"、"合作意愿"和"教学能力"等三类主要影响因子，这与 Adler 和 Kwon 在 Nahapiet 和 Ghoshal 所提的社会资本三个维度基础上进一步提出的机会、意愿和能力不谋而合[4]。

［基金项目］1. 天津市高等学校人文社会科学研究一般项目资助：民办高校教师持续性专业发展研究（20102536）；2. 国家软科学研究计划立项项目（2007GXQ4B110）

［作者简介］秦立栓（1965—）男，教授，北京联合大学商务学院。研究方向：人力资源管理、知识管理、战略管理；宋哲，天津天狮学院。

2.2.1 跨界机会

跨界机会是指民办高校教师跨专业、跨学科、跨部门及学校进行专业发展活动的机会,主要包括信息获取难易程度和网络渠道丰富程度两个方面。根据社会资本理论中对于结构维度的解释,对于结构维度可以利用联系的强弱、网络和密度、中心与边缘连接性等特征变量进行分析和描述,而且分析和描述并不受网络所连接的个体差异的影响[5]。因此,本研究认为民办高校社会联系网络密度大小、联系的强度,以及在网络中所处的位置决定了信息获取的效率和网络联系渠道的多寡。并提出以下假设:

H1:跨界机会对民办高校教师专业发展效果有显著的正向影响。

2.2.2 合作意愿

合作意愿是指民办高校教师专业发展活动过程中,参与活动的主体之间进行知识共享和真诚协作的愿望。合作意愿包括合作思维和合作利益两个方面,对于合作意愿的来源可以用社会资本的关系维度来解释。合作思维是产生合作意愿的前提,来源于组织成员之间良好的人际关系和深厚的信任基础,而合作利益是吸引活动主体进行合作的动力,其公平性和吸引力有赖于良好的制度规范。信任、规范与惩罚、义务与期望以及可辨识的身份等正是社会资本关系维度所涵盖的内容,体现了社会联系的人格化层面[5]。基于此,提出假设如下:

H2:合作意愿对民办高校教师专业发展效果有显著的正向影响。

2.2.3 教学能力

教学能力是指民办高校教师的知识吸收、消化、创新和传授能力。为研究方便,本研究将教学能力简要划分为知识吸收能力和知识传授能力两个方面。教师的职责就是"传道、授业、解惑",教师专业发展的根本目的也是为了有效提高教育水平,教学能力是影响民办高校教师专业发展目标实现的重要因素。从社会资本认知维度来看,Nahapiet 和 Ghoshal 认为认知维度的社会资本对于组织智力资本的产生和积累具有非常重要的影响,而后者则是组织竞争优势重要来源[6]。通过提供不同主体间共同理解的表达解释与意义系统的那些资源,如语言、符号和文化习惯,能够有效地改善知识的转移效果,从而提升教学能力。基于此,提出假设如下:

H3:教学能力对民办高校教师专业发展效果有显著的正向影响。

2.3 理论模型

由于跨界机会、合作意愿、教学能力作为变量难以直接进行测量,为了揭示难以观测的变量之间的关系,较为清晰地反映出各影响因素对于民办高校教师专业发展效果的作用大小,本研究采用结构方程模型进行实证分析。基于此,本研究提出如下民办高校教师专业发展影响机制模型路径图(见图1)。

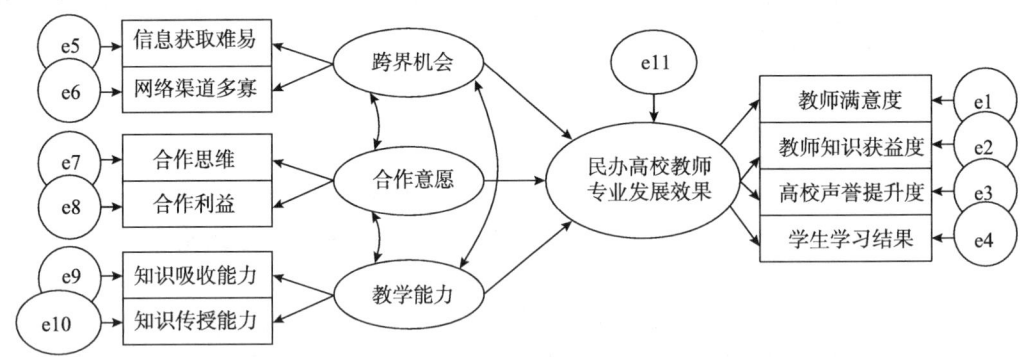

图1 民办高校教师专业发展影响机制路径图

3 实证分析

3.1 问卷设计

问卷共分为三个部分:第一部分:概念说明,向问卷填写者解释问卷中涉及到的重要概念:教师专业发展、合作利益、网络强度、教学能力等,以便被调查者能够更好理解问卷内容。第二部分:基本资料统计,包括问卷填写者的一些个人信息,如性别、年龄、职称、学历等;第三部分:问卷正文。包括两部分内容,一是民办高校教师专业发展效果部分,二是主要影响因素部分。所有测量问项均采用李克特五分量表,1代表"非常不同意",2代表"不同意",3代表"不确定",4代表"同意",5代表"非常同意"。

3.2 数据收集

本研究设计的量表中最大题项数为11,按照Nunnally(1978)的观点,样本量底限应当至少是量表测项数量的10倍,因此有效受测人数不应当少于110位。鉴于此,我们随机调查了天津市、北京市、山东省及河南省8所民办高校的教师及职工,共发放问卷220份,收回169份,有效问卷137份,问卷有效率为81.1%。其中男教师59人,占43.1%,女教师78人,占56.9%;本科84人,占61.3%,硕士44人,占32.1%,博士及以上9人,占6.6%;教授6人,占4.4%,副教授19人,占13.9%,讲师49人,占35.7%,助教63人,占46%。

3.3 信度分析

根据Nunnally(1967,1978)的建议,Alpha系数低于0.35属低信度,应该拒绝使用。介于0.35与0.7之间为可以接受。Alpha系数高于0.7属于高信度。本研究中所涉及到的量表的信度都在可接受的范围之内,具体情况如表1所示:

表1 测量量表的信度

	维度	信度	题项数	量表信度	量表题项数
影响因素	跨界机会	0.816	4	0.951	11
	合作意愿	0.746	4		
	教学能力	0.833	3		
民办高校教师专业发展效果	教师满意度	0.860	3	0.910	10
	教师新知识收益度	0.831	2		
	高校社会声誉提升程度	0.802	3		
	学生学习结果	0.815			

3.4 效度分析

测验或量表所能正确测量的特质程度,一般就是效度。本研究对价值量表的每个维度进行Bartlett和KMO检验,结果显示,Bartlett球形检验统计量的sig<0.01,由此认为各变量之间存在着显著的相关性;而在KMO检验中结果显示各维度的KMO值均大于0.5,说明量表数据的结构效度在可接受的范围之内。(见表2)

表2 测量量表的效度

	维度	KMO	df	Sig.
影响因素	跨界机会	0.716	98	000
	合作意愿	0.819	11	000
	教学能力	0.677	6	000
民办高校教师专业发展效果	教师满意度	0.788	6	000
	教师新知识收益度	0.659	67	000
	高校社会声誉提升程度	0.814	45	000
	学生学习结果	0.703	27	000

3.5 相关分析

本研究主要使用Pearson相关系数分析法,检验跨界机会、合作意愿、教学能力等主要影响因素和民办高校教师专业发展效果等研究变量之间的相关关系。由Pearson相关分析得知,主要影响因素与民办高校教师专业发展效果的线性相关系数为0.538,显著性(双边检验)均小于0.01,从而可以推断二者之间具有显著的正相关关系。各维度之间的相关分析结果见表3。

表 3 相关分析

维度	跨界机会		合作意愿		教学能力	
	Pearson'sr	显著性（0.01）	Pearson'sr	显著性（0.01）	Pearson'sr	显著性（0.01）
教师满意度	0.532	0.000**	0.553	0.000**	0.521	0.000**
教师新知识收益度	0.560	0.000**	0.527	0.000**	0.536	0.000**
高校声誉提升度	0.459	0.000**	0.426	0.000**	0.372	0.000**
学生学习结果	0.452	0.000**	0.448	0.000**	0.415	0.000**

从相关分析结果可以看出，"跨界机会"与"民办高校教师专业发展效果"的相关程度都较高，尤其是"跨界机会"与"教师新知识收益度"的相关程度达到 0.560，可以推论社会资本的结构维度对于民办高校教师获取新知识、提升专业发展水平起着重要作用；主要影响因素的三个维度与"教师满意度"和"教师新知识收益度"的相关程度相对于其他两个维度都比较高，说明民办高校教师专业发展效果更易于从教师的切身感受得以体现；而"高校声誉提升度"与三个影响因素之间的相关程度都偏低，特别是与"教学能力"的相关度只有 0.372，可以推论被调查民办高校教师的知识吸收与传授水平对于高校声誉提升的作用较小；此外，相对来讲，"学生学习结果"与影响因素的三个维度之间的相关程度也比较低。

3.6 路径分析

进行路径分析的目的是验证研究中提出的假设模型，了解各研究变量间的因果关系与关系强度。本研究分别用绝对拟合效果检验 RMR、GFIA、GFI 三项指标和相对拟合效果检验 NFI、IFI、CFI 三项指标来评价结构模型的整体拟和程度。学术界普遍认为，GFI、AGFI、NFI、IFI、CFI 大于 0.90，RMR 小于 0.05，表面模型与数据的拟合程度很好。经测试，模型的拟合度较好，拟合度指标整理见表 4。

表 4 拟合度指标整理

绝对拟合度指标			相对拟合度指标		
RMR	GFI	AGFI	NFI	IFI	CFI
0.028	0.920	0.873	0.909	0.855	0.941

本研究运用结构方程模型进行假设检验，通过 AMOS17.0 软件计算，得出模型潜变量对观测变量的负载拟合结果，限于篇幅，在此仅列出标准化路径系数表（见表 5）。

表 5 标准化路径系数表

	标准化路径系数	P值（0.01）
跨界机会→民办高校教师专业发展效果	0.831	0.000
合作意愿→民办高校教师专业发展效果	0.792	0.000
教学能力→民办高校教师专业发展效果	0.406	0.037
跨界机会→信息获取难易	0.706	0.000
跨界机会→网络渠道多寡	0.842	0.000
合作意愿→合作思维	0.736	0.000
合作意愿→合作利益	0.743	0.000
教学能力→知识吸收能力	0.693	0.000
教学能力→知识传授能力	0.405	0.000
民办高校教师专业发展效果→教师满意度	0.748	0.000
民办高校教师专业发展效果→教师新知识收益度	0.815	0.000
民办高校教师专业发展效果→高校声誉提升度	0.544	0.000
民办高校教师专业发展效果→学生学习结果	0.569	0.000

根据上表，三个研究假设的检验结果为 H1 和 H2 获得支持，H3 被否定。检验结果的具体说明如下：

(1) 跨界机会与民办高校教师专业发展效果之间的路径系数是 0.831，达到显著性水平（P＜0.01），假设 H1 获得验证。这表明，在民办高校中，跨界机会水平越高，其教师专业发展效果越好。

(2) 合作意愿与民办高校教师专业发展效果之间的路径系数为 0.792，达到显著性水平（P＜0.01），假设 H2 成立。这说明一个民办高校教师之间合作意愿越强烈，其专业发展效果就越好。

(3) 教学能力与民办高校教师专业发展效果之间的路径系数为 0.406，（P = 0.037＞0.01），未达到显著水平，假设 H3 不成立。这表示在民办高校中，教师教学能力并不能直接对专业发展效果产生影响。

4 研究结论及启示

综合上述分析结果可知，现阶段民办高校教师专业发展活动相对薄弱，且教师在参与专业发展活动过程中的关注点多集中于为评职称而积累专业知识，而对于如何提升教学效果和学生学习能力，以及高校声誉等方面关注较少。这也从一个侧面反映了我国高等教育管理部门对高校和教师的评价方式和晋升制度对于民办高校教师专业发展的导向作用。本研究认为，为切实提高民办高校教师专业发展水平，应注意以下几个方面：

(1) 加强社会网络建设和现有联系的利用率。民办高校科研资源的有限性决定了必须加强内部教师之间的联系网络建设，同时充分利用与外界的弱联系网络带来的创新灵感，通过广泛联系，提高社会网络密度，逐步确立本校在网络中核心节点位置。

(2) 构建有利于合作的管理制度体系。在民办高校中，教师之间的信任是促进专业发展过程中合作意愿产生的根本，高校管理者应注重建立有利于知识共享的高校管理制度规范和教师评价体系，以利于教师专业发展活动的开展和效果的改善。

(3) 建立育人为先的专业发展导向。民办高校要提高专业发展水平和学校的社会声誉，必须引导教师将工作重点放在教书育人上，要在教师中建立"育人为先"的教育理念，通过相应的激励措施，使教师专注于提高自身的教学能力，使教师专业发展活动效果落到实处。

参考文献

[1] (美) Thomas R. Guskey. 教师专业发展评价 [M]. 北京：中国轻工业出版社，2005：12－13
[2] 陈霞. 教师专业发展效果评价模型评析—以 Guskey 教师专业发展评价模型为例 [J]. 大连教育学院学报，2010（3）
[3] Nahapiet, J. and Ghoshal, S., Social capital, intellectual capital and the creation of value in firms [J]. Academy of Management Proceedings, 1997.
[4] 李志宏，朱桃. 社会资本对个体间非正式知识转移影响的实证研究 [J]. 科学学与科学技术管理，2009（9）
[5] 郭毅，朱熹. 国外社会资本与管理学研究新进展—分析框架与应用述评 [J]. 外国经济与管理，2003（7）
[6] Nahapiet, J. and Ghoshal, S., Social capital, intellectual capital, and the organizational advantage [J]. Academy of Management Review, 1998, 22（2）

以职业需求为导向的高职旅游财务管理专业培养模式研究

张玉凤

随着社会的飞速发展，社会用人需求在不断发生变化，旅游高职财务管理专业学生就业形势面临着愈发严峻的考验。在这种情况下旅游高职教育的培养模式应该以职业需求为导向，培养学生良好的职业道德和素养，系统的专业知识以及持续发展的能力，具备熟练的行业和职业技能，使学生能够很快融入社会，成为有竞争能力的合格"产品"，才能满足社会用人需求。

一、目前高职旅游财务管理专业培养模式存在的主要问题

1. 课程设置与社会需求联系不够紧密。表现在课程体系中，主要偏重知识的系统性，以及知识传授性课程，忽略有利于培养学生文字表达能力、语言表达能力、实务操作能力以及综合分析问题能力的课程。而这些课程对于学生走向工作岗位，尽快适应社会需求有着重要的作用，而且使得学生不知如何处理企业的实务问题，延长了对实际工作的适应期。

2. 教学模式相对滞后。目前一些高职教学还是以传统教科书内容为主，在教学上遵循"基础知识—基本理论—实际案例—毕业实习—毕业论文设计"的模式进行知识的讲授。这样一来，学生的学习知识能力有所提高；在学生考核上也有明确的考核指标。但是，对学生能力培养没有太明确的要求，即没有可量化的考核指标，只能以在校课堂理论教学考试成绩来评价，而且目前考试形式较为单一，对学生的创新能力的培养（包括创新欲望）没有太多的空间。另外社会对人才的需求有一个持续变化的过程，而学校教学要适应这种变化有一个相对滞后的时段。

3. 专业实践课程实施有一定难度。由于旅游财务管理专业实习的对接单位是有关旅游企业的财务部门，而这些部门对实习学生的要求较为严格，学生毕业实习就成为一个较为棘手的问题。另外其他实践课程由于现有一些教师理论知识较为丰富，而实践经验不足，以及专业实习设施、环境不能满足飞速发展的社会需求，因此专业实践课程的实施效果不是很理想。

二、建立以职业需求为导向的高职财务管理专业培养模式

1. 培养模式的理念创新。自主择业引起的激烈竞争，使我们办学有了危机感。如何适应变化的就业环境？通过调研发现旅游高职财务管理专业的毕业生中大多数直接就业，对实际工作技能的要求更迫切，这就要求对传统的培养模式进行理念上的创新。①以人为本的教育理念是时代发展的产物，它主张把人放在第一位，以人作为教育教学的出发点，顺应人的禀赋，提升人的潜能，完整而全面地关照人的发展。那么在具体的高职教育实践中，应该以学生为本，把培养社会需要、具有全面综合素质的学生放在一切教育活动的中心；应用型人才培养的特点是紧贴社会实际，注重知识、能力和素质的协调发展，尤其注重能力和素质的培养；课程结构和教学内容上，以应用性为主，加强理论与实践相结合，注重实践性教学环节的训练。②因材施教，培养高素质人才的理念，高职教育的培养目标在于以职业为导向，以服务为宗旨，培养学生良好的职业道德和素养，使学生具有熟练的职业技能、系统的应用知识以及持续发展的能力。重视学生职业能力的培养，是职业教育区别于普通高等教育的重要特点，也是职业教育的重要特色。因此旅游财务管理专业在人才培养方案中应该以此为依据，制定能够促进学生职业能力的发展，既有一定的专业素养，又有一定的实际工作能力、适应能力、生存能力以及良好的人际协调能力

[作者简介] 张玉凤，北京联合大学旅游学院。

的旅游财务管理专业学生。以"培养具有社会责任感和较强的专业技术能力,具有国际视野的高素质应用型、复合型、创新型人才"为育人目标;以"全员育人,全过程育人,全方位育人",注重学生全面素质提高基础上的个性发展,倡导合格基础上的"扬长教育"。

2. 建立以职业需求为导向的教学模式。①教学方式采用体验式教学,体验式教学模式是指学生通过亲自操作和体验而学得知识和掌握技能的一种教学方式。其精髓在于它是促使学生勤于思考、善于决策,变被动听课为积极思维、主动实践的过程。通过"案例法""角色扮演法""游戏法"等体验式教学法的运用,能较好地培养学生的创新能力和实践能力。例如:引入ERP沙盘的会计实务模拟实训教学模式,既要进行模拟实训,又要进行仿真实训。在模拟实训中让学生充分了解各种凭单的使用条件和填制要求以及账簿报表的登记和编制,初步掌握会计操作的基本技能。在此基础上,将学生置入仿真的企业运营环境中,让他们独立完成并处理在真实企业环境中有可能发生的一切会计核算事务,对已经初步掌握的会计操作基本技能进一步深入和实务化,这对于培养适应社会需要的复合型、应用型人才具有重要的现实意义,是一种切实可行的体验式教学模式。②教学内容采用"任务驱动法"教学,"任务驱动"就是学生在教师的帮助下,紧紧围绕一个共同的任务活动中心,在强烈的问题动机的驱动下,通过对学习资源的积极主动应用,进行自主探索和互动协作的学习,并在完成既定任务的同时,引导学生产生一种学习实践活动。在财务管理专业相关课程教学中使用"任务驱动"教学法,就是让学生在一个个典型的完成"任务"的驱动下展开教学活动,引导学生由简到繁、由易到难、循序渐进地完成一系列"任务",把学习地点进一步推向工作岗位,让学生感性认识所学职业内容和工作环境,完成任务需要经过的工作过程,将"工作过程中的学习"与"课堂上的学习"合为一体,使得理论学习与实践经历得以更好的结合。从而得到清晰的思路、方法和知识脉络,在完成"任务"的过程中,培养分析问题、解决问题以及创新等方面的能力。

3. 开展多种形式的职业能力培养。①企业实地参观考察,一些涉及实训的课程,如:出纳实务、旅游企业会计等课程可以采取"走出去"的办法,让学生到酒店、旅行社等的财会部门实地了解出纳流程和酒店、旅行社财会部门的设置和核算流程。另外还可以组织学生利用课余时间和寒暑假到企业实地考察搜集相关数据资料,从而增加学生的感性认识,培养学生具有理论联系实际的能力。其好处是既减轻了学校集中组织学生实习的压力,又使学生很好地利用了时间,增加了社会实践经验,对学生的发展和成长具有不可小觑的作用。②建立实习基地,由于旅游财务管理专业性质的特殊性,实习安排存在着一定的困难,为了改变这种状况学校应该尽量取得上级主管部门和企事业单位的支持,可以与一些企业建立长期合作关系,把这样的一些企业作为专业实习基地,一方面可以为学生提供更多更有价值的实习机会;另一方面教师接触实务,了解财务、会计方面的信息和动态,又可以为实践单位提供相关专业服务。学校也可以通过与企业联合办学或者是与企业签订合作和研究项目的方式来建立这样的实习基地,这样的好处就是既为企业培养了人才,又为实践教学和学生就业打下了基础。③建立财务管理专业模拟实验,模拟实验是一种亲验性的教学方法,我院财务营销实验室已经成功投入使用,使用后达到了较好的效果。以前学生在学相关专业知识的时候感觉很抽象,现在通过仿真实践,能够将所学理论知识更加生动形象地为学生们展现出来,学生们在学习上能够初步达到由理论到实践的过程,同时能更加深入思考,提出一些问题。另外学生经过实训后,走入社会可以直接上岗,满足了社会对应用型人才的需要。同时专业实验室的建设还可以提高教学效益,常用设备、设施数量的增加,对增加教学知识、技能密度,强化能力训练和合理组织教学具有推动作用。

4. 搞好师资队伍建设。邓小平同志曾经指出:"一个学校能不能为社会主义建设培养合格的人才,培养德智体全面发展、有社会主义觉悟的有文化的劳动者,关键在教师。"教师在教育中始终起着中坚作用。由于一些高职财务管理专业的教师是从"校门"到"校门",有相当一部分教师从来没有接触过会计实务,缺少对具体企事业单位财务、会计实务的全面了解,理论与实践脱节的现象比较严重。因此对如何组织财务管理工作知之甚少。结果一些教师在讲授财务管理、会计实务时往往是"纸上谈兵"。显然,对于一门实践性和操作性很强的学科来说,教师缺乏实务的问题极大地影响了实践教学的正常发展。在条件许可和不影响本职工作的前提下,应该鼓励和支持财务管理专业教师到旅游企事业单位挂职,以增强教师的阅历,锻炼他们的业务能力,提高教师的教学水平和理论研究水平。

参考文献

[1] 覃守云, 袁畅, 熊楚书. 高职教育以职业需求为导向的现实意义 [J]. 黄冈职业技术学院学报, 2003 (12).
[2] 张荣. 体验式教学的创新性与实施条件 [J]. 吉林省教育学院学报, 2007 (11).
[3] 张玉英. 财务管理案例教学法高校运用研究 [J]. 财会通讯学术版. 2007 (4).
[4] 李琳叶. 对高职会计专业教学改革的思考 [J]. 湖南工业职业技术学院学报, 2008 (1).

青教赛为服务青年教师全面发展提供正能量

张俊玲 罗 丹 邹佳霖

青年工作是我党一贯重视的工作。青年教师目前在全国高校占比64%[1]，对青年教师的培养不仅是培养接班人，也是挖掘学校未来发展潜力的一项重要工作，是提高学校未来竞争力的重要基础。为了鼓励和帮助青年教师提高执教能力，激励和引导青年教师有追求有梦想，促进学校协作的向心力，让青年富有永争第一的时代气息，应把青教赛作为社会转型期的强大精神动力，积极培育，稳妥推进。

自2000年起，北京联合大学已成功举办了6届青年教师教学基本功比赛（以下简称"青教赛"），组织选手参加了市青教赛7届。目前获校级以上奖励152人，获市级奖30人，其中获市级一等奖5人，二等奖11人，三等奖14人，获校级奖146人。青教赛培养锻炼了一批青年教师，为使此项活动在学校人才队伍建设、引领、服务青年教师全面成才等方面提供正能量，校工会对获奖选手进行了跟踪调研和培养。其积极意义主要体现在以下几个方面。

一、青教赛搭建了青年教师追求梦想的舞台

青教赛是对青年教师课堂教学的一次较为全面的督促与检查、展示与检阅。旨在考核选手的表达能力、组织教学内容的能力、课堂驾驭和管理的能力（调动气氛、学习的兴趣、学生的主动性和参与度），以及一定的表演能力。对年轻教师而言，每一次精心的课堂准备都是一次教学基本功的磨练与优化，每一次公开课都是一次胆量与才华的展示与提升；同时，这也为青年教师提供了一个向学校领导和同事们展示自我的平台，使得一些教师通过青教赛活动在学校"小有名气"；更为学校考察、选拔和培养青年教师提供了强有力的科学依据。另外，从某种意义上说，每次听课对于一些资历深的"老"教师也是一次吸收新知识，对自己进行充电和向青年教师学习的再教育机会。

二、青教赛提升了选手的自信心和教学技能

青年教师在经历教学基本功比赛的"洗礼"后纷纷表示收获很大。通过比赛，选手们标志性的变化是教学能力有了很大提升，自信心有所加强，自我要求有所提高；在日常教学中表现更加优秀。就参赛的效果而言，主要包括在以下几个方面。

1. 青教赛获奖成果突出

（1）年龄分布。自1998年北京市举办青教赛至今，我校共有152名选手获奖，60%的选手在40岁以下，40%进入中年（超过40岁）。

（2）职称分布。82%的选手仍然是讲师，与参加比赛时进步不大；18%晋升为副教授以上，有的还作为系主任。

（3）其他获奖情况。64%的选手在青教赛获奖后先后获得过校或市级的师德、三育人、教育先锋、先进工作者等荣誉称号，另外还有人获得院级各类先进荣誉称号；45%的选手获得过校级以上的教学、科研的奖励，分别是市中青年骨干教师、北京市精品教材、市教学团队二等奖、校教学成果 一、二等奖、校最佳教案奖。这说明学校派出参加比赛的选手普遍是德艺双馨的。

（4）教学科研能力。73%的被调查选手认为自己目前教学能力更突出，18%认为自己的科研能力更突出。这说明培养获奖选手的科研能力更有助于优秀人才的全面发展。

2. 比赛对青年教师成长赋予正能量

（1）大赛提升了青年教师的自信心。教学基本功更扎实了。通过青教赛，不仅增强了获奖选手教学

[作者简介] 张俊玲，北京联合大学工会。

能力方面的自信心，而且使他们的教学能力也上了一个新台阶，在获奖后的教学生涯中对自己要求更高了，教学更有热情、激情，课堂驾驭能力以及教学内容设计、安排技巧均得到提升，教学设计有想法了，工作干劲更足了，教学效果更好了，增进了对自己教学效果要做得更好的动力和压力，获奖选手近5年的教学评价普遍都在良好以上。

（2）青年教师教学能力有了很大提升。青年教师在教学理念上、教学设计上都有很大的提升，并且认识到讲好课，教师对课程的设计思想、理念很重要，以及在教学方案的设计中要重点考虑面对的群体、如何进行问题的切入，如何引导学生跟着走。

（3）提升了团队协作能力。73%的被调查者认为参加青教赛获奖过程中个人的努力与学校培育相当。27%的选手认为个人的努力大于学校的培育。多数教师认为个人的成长依赖系部，教学团队对自己的获奖有很大帮助，通过自己准备，其他老师帮助，以及在系部反复试讲、团队教师们反复辅导、把关和不断的"洗礼"，选手们增加了胆量，提升了参赛技能。

（4）专家评委帮助大。通过青教赛，青年教师认为能有机会和众多优秀教师近距离学习、请教，对提高教学能力帮助很大。一个选手举例说，通过师范学院教师的指点，对教案的设计能力提升很快。

（5）有利于青年教师脱颖而出。100%的被调查者认为青教赛对学校提高教育教学质量有作用；对学校师资队伍建设有作用；91%的被调查者认为青教赛对青年教师脱颖而出有帮助；73%的被调查者认为青教赛对学校选拔人才有帮助。

3. 青教赛助力选手正确认识自我

（1）树立了明确的近期目标。获奖选手近两年希望在科研方面得到提升，在职称方面得到晋升，实现教学、科研并举，实现做个合格的大学教育工作者的梦想。（获奖选手普遍不希望自己成为只会教课的人）。

（2）明确了影响教学的困难因素。众多青年教师反映，目前工作生活中的困难在于提升职称、科研和学历方面。获奖教师普遍感觉精力不足，在完成教学（自己对自己教学质量和效果要求很高）、科研任务的同时，兼顾照顾孩子和考虑生子等现实生活现状，攻读博士学位压力很大；艺术类等部分专业博士点少，考取很难；职称低，科研项目申报受限制，造成恶性循环；社会服务机会少。

（3）希望获取政策支持。除了对获奖前的帮助，学校还应该有针对性地做好获奖后的帮扶和政策的倾斜，使帮扶政策更实质化；对青教赛获奖在政策上给予更高的认可度，在评聘副教授时给予一定的倾斜；同时加强对教师心理的疏导，改善教学的环境。

4. 明确了助推青年才俊全面成长的方法

一是制定选手优中选优、比赛公平、赛后帮扶并举的政策。在选手遴选工作即要结合教师日常教学考核、评比，以执教能力强的青年教师作为培养和推选对象，让教师们把功夫做在平时，形成了平时工作和比赛活动的有效连接、互动，相得益彰，互相促进。

二是制定了对获奖选手的帮扶计划。对获得校青教赛前10名的教师重点培育，每人配备2名优秀导师，以立项的形式给予每位导师一定的经费支持，导师根据培育对象的实际情况，制订有针对性的指导工作计划，对培育对象的教学和研究工作给予全面的指导，并辅导青年教师制订专业规划。针对培育对象，每位指导教师每学期应至少听课5次，并针对授课情况给予相应的指导意见等指标性的辅导要求。每学期对培育对象的教学工作进行总结，并提出相应的改进措施。同时带领培育对象参加教学研究工作，逐步培养青年教师成为本学科教学、科研的骨干力量。被指导的青年教师在导师的指导下拟订自己的工作和学习计划，并在工作中实施。争取通过两年的培育，在教学上达到北京市教学基本功比赛获奖水平。以上这些举措，均有利地促进了青年教师的全面发展。

青教赛为青年教师搭建平台，在政策、业务上给选手以全方位支持，形成了鼓励优秀青年教师脱颖而出的良好制度环境。

15年来我校六届青教赛的成功举办，在提高教育教学质量，加强教师队伍建设，培养青年教师方面起到了重要作用，得到青年教师的普遍认可。教师们标志性的变化就是教学能力的提高、自信心的增强；通过青教赛，一批批优秀青年教师脱颖而出，很多已经成为教学一线的骨干力量，推进了对课堂教学的研究与探索、促进了教师间的传帮带，在我校制定了对获奖选手的进一步帮扶的政策，为提高教育教学质量、加强师资队伍建设工作中发挥着重要的作用。但是也存在需要进一步完善和加强的方面。

（1）获奖后的培养对青年教师全面成才同样重要

这些获奖教师职称晋升情况并不理想，主要是科研能力需要加强。如何助推这些教师全面成长还需加强赛后的帮扶和政策的支持，使他们全面发展。

青年教师获奖锻炼提升了自己，学校制定帮助政策，切合实际和符合青年教师培养需要，而且是迫在眉睫的，是令青年教师普遍称道的。如何增加政策的实效性，需要导师把重点放在帮助获奖选手制订职业规划和提升科研能力等方面，以帮助这些达到教学基本功要求的青年教师全方位成长、成才。

（2）需进一步提升对青年教师教学基本功的认可度

北京市青教赛在前几届都是以市教育工会为主，市教委相关部门协助组织开展。今年教育主管部门对北京市高校青教赛越来越重视，市委教育工委、市教委、市教育工会联合部署，还出台了对市青教赛获得一等奖的选手优先推荐"五一劳动奖章"政策，这将激励有志青年积极参加。

治理理念下高校创新人才战略的实施

张祖明

当今世界全球化程度逐步加快,科技进步日新月异,知识经济方兴未艾。我国正处在改革发展的关键阶段,工业化、信息化、城镇化、市场化、国际化快速发展,社会经济发展转型势在必行。要在激烈的国际竞争中掌握主动权,就必须提高我国的自主创新能力,在若干重要领域掌握一批核心技术,拥有一批自主知识产权,造就一批具有国际竞争力的企业,全面、大幅度提高我国的国家竞争力。人才在激烈的国际竞争中是最重要的战略资源,是一个国家社会经济发展的重要推动力量。要建设创新型国家,就必要加快创新人才培养步伐,加大创新人才培养力度。

然而,我国现在高层次创新型人才匮乏,人才创新创业能力不强,这严重制约了我国经济的发展。我国经济增长的科技进步贡献率仅为39%,而其他创新型国家则高达70%以上。我国拥有自主知识产权核心技术的企业仅为0.03%,企业对外技术依存度高达50%,而美国、日本仅为5%左右。我国科技成果转化率平均仅为20%,实现产业化的不足5%,专利技术的交易率也只有5%,远远低于发达国家。

一、我国创新人才战略实施的困境

为了彻底改变我国创新人才匮乏的问题,我国从人才、教育、科学技术等制定了一系列相关政策,以培养创新人才。

(一) 我国现在的创新人才培养战略

为了培养国家所需的人才,国家制定了《国家中长期人才发展规划纲要(2010—2020年)》(以下简称《人才规划》)是我国第一个中长期人才发展规划,是当前和今后一个时期全国人才工作的指导性文件。制定并实施《人才规划》,是贯彻落实科学发展观、更好实施人才强国战略的重大举措,是在激烈的国际竞争中赢得主动的战略选择,对于加快我国经济发展方式转变、全面建设小康社会,具有重大意义。

人才是我国经济社会发展的第一资源。当前和今后一个时期,我国人才发展的指导方针是:服务发展、人才优先、以用为本、创新机制、高端引领、整体开发。到2020年,我国人才发展的总体目标是:培养和造就规模宏达、结构优化、布局合理、素质优良的人才队伍,确立国家人才竞争比较优势,进入世界人才强国行列,为在21世纪中叶基本实现社会主义现代化奠定人才基础。

《人才规划》指出人才队伍建设的第一项任务,就是突出培养造就创新型科技人才,建立学校教育和实践锻炼相结合、国内培养和国际交流合作相衔接的开放式培养体系。探索并推行创新型教育方式方法,突出培养学生的科学精神、创造性思维和创新能力。组织实施创新人才推进计划、海外高层次人才引进计划,推进"百人计划"、"长江学者奖励计划"、"国家杰出青年科学基金"等人才项目。加强产学研合作,重视企业工程技术与管理人才培养。为此,《人才纲要》中制定了"实施产学研合作培养创新人才"的政策,要求建立政府指导下以企业为主体、市场为导向、多种形式的产学研战略联盟,通过共建科技创新平台、开展合作教育、共同实施重大项目等方式,培养高层次人才和创新团队。实施研究生教育创新计划,发展专业学位教育,建立高等学校、科研院所,企业高层次人才双向交流制度,推行产学研联合培养研究生的"双导师制"。实行"人才+项目"的培养模式,依托国家重大人才计划以及重大科研、工程、产业攻关、国际科技合作等项目,重视发挥企业作用,在实践中集聚和培养创新人才。对企业等用人单位接纳高等学校、职业学校学生实习等实行财税优惠政策。

[作者简介] 张祖明,北京联合大学继续教育学院。

为了更好地推行这一政策,《人才纲要》中制订了"创新人才推进计划"和"高素质教育人才培养工程"。在创新人才培养上,在我国具有相对优势的科研领域设立 100 个科学家工作室,着眼于培养造就一批世界级水平的科学家;瞄准世界科技前沿和战略性新兴产业,每年重点支持和培养一批具有发展潜力的中青年科技创新领军人才;着眼于推动企业成为技术创新主体,每年重点扶持 1000 名科技创新创业人才;依托一批国家重大科研项目、国家重点工程和重大建设项目,建设若干重点领域创新团队;以高等学校、科研院所和高新技术产业开发区为依托,建设 300 个创新人才培养示范基地。在高素质教育人才培养上,通过研修培训、学术交流、项目资助等方式,每年重点培养和支持 2 万名各类学校教育教学骨干、"双师型"教师、学术带头人和校长,在中小学校、职业院校、高等学校培养造就一批教育家、教学名师和学科领军人才。

人力资源是我国经济社会发展的第一资源,教育是开发人力资源的主要途径。我国制定的《国家中长期教育改革和发展规划纲要》(以下简称《教育规划纲要》)指出,教育要努力培养造就数以亿计的高素质劳动者、数以千万计的专门人才和一大批拔尖创新人才。我国制定的《国家中长期科学技术发展规划纲要》、《中华人民共和国国民经济和社会发展第十二个五年(2011—2015 年)规划纲要》也对创新人才战略培养提出了相应的要求,要求"围绕提高科技创新能力、建设创新型国家,以高层次创新型科技人才为重点,造就一批世界水平的科学家、科技领军人才、工程师和高水平创新团队。创新教育方式,突出培养学生科学精神、创造性思维和创新能力。加强实践培养,依托国家重大科研项目和重大工程、重点学科和重点科研基地、国际学术交流合作项目,建设高层次创新型科技人才培养基地。注重培养一线创新人才和青年科技人才。积极引进和用好海外高层次创新创业人才"。

(二)我国创新人才培养机制不断完善

随着我国教育的发展,我国在创新人才培养方面取得了一定的成效。国家科技部统计资料显示,2007 年度反映原始创新能力的国家自然科学奖和国家技术发明奖项目主要由大学、科研院所完成,而体现科技与经济社会紧密结合、反映集成创新和消化吸收再创新的项目则主要由企业、大学、科研院所分别完成或者合作完成。这表明,我国的国家创新体系正不断趋于完善。

然而,我们也应当清醒地认识到,目前我国创新人才培养的任务十分艰巨。我国目前创新人才培养面临诸多困境,诸如创新人才培养投入不足、企业创新动力与投入不足、创新人才培养方法尚待完善、崇尚创新的社会文化没有形成等等,但其核心问题在于没有建立有效创新人才培养机制。

政策导向需要完成从计划到市场的转变。机制主要包括政府科研激励机制、协调机制和技术创新及人才培养机制。科技人才评价制度和激励机制尚不完善,科研机构、高校对人才的绩效评价和职称评定中,往往忽视具体领域、岗位的不同需求,对不同科技人才的评价指标和职称评定"一刀切",过分依赖论文数量、所获成果奖等量化指标,这种评价体制易导致科研人员较为注重科技成果的技术价值,而忽略其市场价值,导致科研与市场需求的脱节,造成资源的浪费和科研成果难以转化为生产力,不能真正反映科技人才的研究水平和贡献。

培养创新人才主要采用产学研的模式。之所以采用这一模式,实质在于以生产需求为导向,确定学习和科研,所以是"产学研",而不是"学研产"、"研学产"。

但我国现在的产学研培养模式,除了博士、博士后阶段多数是以企业为基地进行产学研的培养外,在本科、硕士这些大面积人才培养阶段,大多仍然是以"学"为主,实质上是"学研产",也就是根据学习内容确定科研内容,根据科研内容寻找企业合作。

高校在创新体系中不能发挥其天然的优势。在和企业进行产学研合作时,往往受制于企业制定的行业或者内容,受到的牵制过多,研发的产品或者技术仅仅针对企业本身,缺乏持续创新的动力。在对学生进行培养时,也是以定向培养为主,向企业输入他们需要的人才,而不是从学生的发展角度而言对学生进行系统的创新教育。高校在产学研体系中的相对弱势,不利于整个创新教育体系的发展。

二、基于治理理念改革高校培养创新人才的措施

当代治理理论(governance theory)是一个纷纭复杂的思想体系。作为一种政治分析和解释途径,它力图说明在激变的社会发展中,世界、国家、地方、社区、组织和秩序发生的变化,阐述当今国家与社

会间关系出现的新结构形态。而作为一种创新性实践行动,它则力图促进传统政治、行政制度的变革,构建分权、参与、多中心的公共政策体系。

从 20 世纪 80 年代开始,伴随着经济全球化浪潮和后现代社会哲学的提出,治理(governance)[1] 的内涵发生了巨大的变化。当代治理概念及其治理理论被作为一种阐释现代社会、政治秩序与结构变化,分析现代政治、行政权力构架,阐述公共政策体系特征的分析框架和思想体系,与传统的"统治"(governing) 和"政府控制"(government) 思想和观念相区别,甚至对立起来。在 1989 年世界银行关于非洲的报告中"治理"一词首次出现,世界银行 1992 年度报告的标题就是"治理与发展"。20 世纪 90 年代以来,西方政治学和经济学家赋予了"治理"一词新的含义,其涵盖的范围已远远超出了传统的经典意义。

治理研究的知名学者格里·斯托克则从五个方面阐述了他对治理特征的理解。第一,治理是出自政府组织但又不限于政府的一套进入公共政策过程的社会公共机构和行为者,即治理主体范围大于政府组织体系;第二,治理是指在为社会和经济问题寻求解答的过程中,存在着行动界限和责任方面的模糊之点,即政策执行的过程更加明显地被分割了,多个行动主体分担着管理职能;第三,治理一定是在涉及集体行动的各个社会公共机构之间存在着权力的相互依赖关系;第四,治理指社会中各类行为者网络组织的自主自治管理;第五,治理观点认定,办好事情的能力既不在于政府的单一的权力和力量,也不在于政府是否下命令或运用其权威,而在于政府与公民社会之间广泛的社会联系,但政府可以动用新的治理工具和技术来控制和引导其发展,政府的能力和责任就在于此。"[2] 这些界定实际上勾勒出当代治理模式运作的基本规则和特点。

从政治学的角度看,治理是指政治管理的过程,它包括政治权威的规范基础、处理政治事务的方式和对公共资源的管理。它特别地关注在一个限度的领域内维持社会秩序所需要的政治权威的作用和对行政权力的运用。治理作为一个政治管理过程,也像政府统治一样需要权威和权力,最终目的也是为了维持正常的社会秩序。尽管治理的主体既可以是公共机构,也可以是私人机构,还可以是公共机构和私人机构的合作,国家治理,也就是国家作为行为对象的治理行为,主要是国家作为公共行政机构的治理行为,也包括市场、社会、公民对国家的治理行为。治理(governance)与统治(ruling)相对应,国家统治是国家的强行政行为,国家治理是国家的软行政行为。治理强调合作、相互作用,是政治国家与公民社会的合作、政府与非政府的合作、公共机构与私人机构的合作、强制与自愿的合作。治理是由多个中心(国家、公民、市场、社会)组成,遵循公正、公平、效率的原则,采用非暴力的方式对公共事务以及一些私人事务中需要公共部门解决的那一部分进行管理的过程[3]。

基于以上治理理念,对于我国的创新人才战略的实施,高校可以进行以下改革:

(一) 建立政府—企业—高校三元互动创新人才培养模式

我国高校迄今的创新人才培养主要是向政府寻求资源,因为我国高校基本上都是在政府管理下的高校,资源由政府进行配置,所以高校习惯于向政府寻求资源。但实际上,社会才是创新、尤其企业是技术创新的需求者,是创新的源泉。但是,企业有着明确的利润导向,企业的创新投入基本上都是技术层面的创新,对于基础性的创新,企业往往缺乏动力,这就需要政府对于基础性创新的支持。

对政府而言,创新型国家建设,中华民族的伟大复兴,需要培养一大批的创新人才。国家的创新能力需要的不仅仅是技术的创新能力,更需要的是基础性学科的创新能力,而基础性创新人才的培养需要很长的时间,而且往往没有眼前的直接的经济效益,这样的人才培养需要国家长期的支持。

对学校而言,培养学生是学校应尽的责任,在当前的经济环境要求之下,学校有义务将学生培养成为有创造力,能够解决实际问题的创新型人才。而学校的教育传达的优势,可以让学校更好的使用思想教育的手段,使学生自觉地接受创新型教育和与之相关的政策。学校应当站在战略高度制订长远的创新

---

[1] Weller, P. (2000). In Search of Governance. In David, A., and M. Keating (Eds.). The Future of Governance. St. Leonards, NSW; Allen Unwin.

[2] [英]格里·斯托克:"作为伦理的治理:五个论点",[J]. 国际社会科学杂志(中文版),1999(2):55;俞可平主编:治理与善治,北京:社会科学文献出版社,2000.

[3] 俞可平. 治理与善治. 北京:社会科学文献出版社,2000;徐勇. 乡村治理与中国政治. 北京:中国社会科学出版社,2003.

人才培养的规划，并形成创新的校园氛围。

对企业来说，企业在培养创新人才的时候更多的是从自身角度考虑培养的人才是否与企业自身的需求相契合。另外由于企业以利润最大化为目标，在执行创新人才培养政策时应当因势利导，更多以经济手段来顺应企业的需求，使企业能够为创新人才的培养提供一定的帮助，达到双方的共赢。

所以，基于治理理念，我们可知，创新人才的培养，不能单纯依靠政府为高校提供资源，而应建构政府、高校、企业之间的三元互动模式，高校从政府、企业争取基于各自的优势的创新人才培养资源。

（二）建立企业主导的双师型导师队伍

"双师型"导师队伍是创新人才培养的基础性工作，反映了国内大学教育自身的发展和人才培养的内在需求。目前对"双师型"导师的理解存在一些误区，有些认为持有"双证"（即教师资格证和职业资格证）的教师就是"双师型"导师，另一种观点认为"双师"就是即具备教师的能力，同时也具备工程师的能力。

从我国高校教师队伍建设的历史可知，我国高校教师都是从高校毕业、获得相应学位后到高校任教。他们往往不具有直接的企业经验，他们对于企业的创新敏感不够直接。我国高校现在也从企业直接调入教师，作为"双师型"教师。但是，这些来自企业的高校教师之所以来到高校任教，则往往是失去了企业工作激情之后的职业转移。他们的创新敏感也不再是他们在企业工作时的状态。

在一些发达国家，在产业界和学术界之间的"双栖"研究人员和教师比比皆是。欧美发达国家研究型大学主要是通过向企业转让专利和鼓励教师到企业兼职，来实现科技成果转化为生产力的。而我国"双师型"导师的资源确是相当稀缺，不仅在以培养学生研究能力的高等学校还是在以培养学生技能为基础的职业学校，"双师型"导师的队伍都有待扩大。我国高校应该大胆从企业直接聘请兼职导师参与创新人才培养，也应该直接派遣学生到企业创新岗位学习、实习。

成立一支兼备专业技能和学术知识的"双师型"导师队伍，需要国家制定和完善有利于人才向企业汇聚的政策，尽快建立机关、事业单位和企业之间基本平衡的人才保障机制，给予在高校、科研院所等事业单位与企业之间流动的人员，在职务聘任、工资福利等方面无障碍地转聘和衔接，从而引导创新型人才向重点行业、关键领域和生产一线流动集聚。这需要建立政府—高校—企业三元互动的人才机制。

（三）建立高校主导的创新人才培养经费使用机制

我国现在的高校培养创新人才的经费都来自政府的财政拨款，高校根据政府计划，向政府申请相关经费，对于经费的使用需要按照财政法律进行定向使用。这一机制中，高校在申请经费项目时具有一定的选择性，可以基于本校优势申请经费，但是项目目录仍然是政府编制的，高校是在政府给出的选择范围内进行选择，而不是高校自主设置项目。国外的创新人才培养的经费则是来自政府的财政拨款和企业捐助，而经费使用则是高校自主确定。美国麻省理工学院的成功得益于20世纪美国政府在自然及工程科学上大量投资，巨大的军工订单使MIT迅速发展，并且带动了128公路高技术产业区的蓬勃发展。斯坦福大学的发展更加得益于美国政府在20世纪40年代后期以来对教育的加大投资。斯坦福大学的迅速发展，推动了硅谷的发展，并最终将二者带入一个良性循环。美国两个科技园（128公路高技术产业区和硅谷）的成功告诉我们，政府在引导大学发展时，必须进行必要的科研经费的投资。

当前我国政府对科研资金的投入虽然力度在加大，但是仍然不能够支持科技发展的需要，科研资金所占比重长期低于世界平均水平，更为严重的是有限的经费往往流向了对设备的添置和更新上，忽视了高层次科研人才、课题负责人、科研助手、博士后等难以量化的智力付出，科研团队的建设和可持续发展受到威胁，这样会导致创新人才的流失，人才缺口将会加大，增加必要的对人力资本的投入显得非常必要。

教育部部长袁贵仁在《国家中长期教育改革和发展规划纲要》征求意见情况发布会上说："我们想建立起一套新的、适合学校特点的管理制度和配套政策，然后逐步取消行政级别和行政化管理的模式。"行政化管理倾向有两个方面：一是政府对学校管理的行政化倾向；二是学校内部管理的行政化倾向。从政府的角度来说，应当明确政府管理的权限和职责，形成不同的办学模式，减少国家对学校自主发展的行政干预，引导学校建立产学研结合的创新体系。[1]

基于治理理念可知，我国现在对于高校的投入应该从大楼大厦的建设转移到基础性学科建设上来，建立高校在法律规定下自主确定经费使用方向与项目的制度，更要地培养创新人才。

综上所述，创新型国家建设是我国改革开放的核心战略之一，创新人才培养是其基础，而承担培养创新人才重任的高校，必须基于治理理念，建立政府—企业—高校三元互动创新人才培养模式，建立企业主导的双师型导师队伍，建立高校主导的创新人才培养经费使用机制，为国家培养一大批创新拔尖人才，实现中华民族的伟大复兴。

---

[1] http://www.gov.cn/jrzg/2010-07/29/content_1667143.htm. 新华社：2010年07月29日.

基于网络学堂的高职数学精品课程建设

陈玉花　张　耘　王新苹

随着现代信息技术的发展，高职数学传统的教学内容、教学方法、教学手段等已不能适应现代高职学生学习的需要，网络学堂已成为高职数学课堂教学以外学生获取数学知识的重要途径之一，是高职数学精品课建设的组成部分。

1 网络学堂概念及主要特征

网络学堂是在现代教育理念、教学理论与学习理论指导下，基于信息网络的教学模式，其学习过程具有交互性、共享性、开放性、协作性和自主性等基本特征。也就是说，现代网络学堂教育突破了时空的限制，将教学活动扩展到每一个地方，学生可以在任何地点、任何时间通过各种智能数字终端连接到网络教学环境中，学习想学的任何课程。

2 网络学堂在高职数学精品课程建设中的地位和作用

随着社会经济的发展，现代课程已走向开放、互动、自主，其特点是开放性、复杂性和变革性。网络学堂所具有的基本特征，满足了现代高职数学精品课程发展的趋势。因此，网络学堂已成为数学高职精品课程建设的重要组成部分。

高职数学精品课程网络学堂是课堂教学的延伸，对课堂教学起到重要的辅助教学作用，即为高职各专业学生学习高等数学提供资源共享及教学辅导。其具体做法是，教师通过在网上发布教学大纲、教学课件、教案、讲义、重点、难点、教学案例、布置作业、在线自主学习辅导、学习讨论、在线测试、探究学习等功能，为学生学习提供教学目的要求、下载教学资料、提交作业、参与课程讨论、进行自我测试和实验演示等自主学习的平台。教师和学生还可以在网上发布BBS、存放文件、开设个人主页、提供链接等。在建设网络学堂时，要结合高职数学课程特点和各专业人才培养要求，把常用的抽象概念、与学生所学专业实际用到的数学知识，以易学、实用、简洁为原则，构建高职数学教学模块；更要考虑到学生学习能力的差异，教学模块中应体现分层教学的设计。

3 高职数学网络学堂的运行形式与构建要素

建设网络学堂，应采用服务器端动态网页技术。在服务器端运行的程序、网页、组件、视频等属于动态网页，动态网页可以直接访问服务器终端资源，可以实现不同用户，在不同时间或地点浏览同一个网页时所提供的内容（数据或功能）有所不同。

高职数学精品课程网络学堂构建要素有：教学大纲、教案、讲义、教学案例、课件、授课视频、实验实训操作系统，以及"教师—学生—学生"交互平台。其技术要求是：教案、课件采用普通网页形式，学生可以下载；授课视频采用"在线播放＋下载播放"，以便于学生随时观看；实验实训操作系统数学实验和参加建模竞赛的帮助系统，包括实验室帮助文档、交互式的辅导系统、实验讨论系统三部分；交互平台包括了学习论坛、答疑系统、作业提交与管理系统、在线考试系统、学生学习成果展示、资料链接等。其中，学习论坛采用Blog、"BBS＋留言板"、E-mail的形式，栏目有学习动态论坛、在线交谈等；在线考试系统包括试卷统计、试卷及试题质量分析、教学质量分析、学生成绩，不受时间、

[作者简介] 陈玉花（1964—），女，北京联合大学应用科技学院，副教授，硕士。研究方向为高等数学教育；张耘（1964—），女，北京联合大学应用科技学院，讲师，研究方向为高等数学教育；王新苹（1978—），女，北京联合大学应用科技学院，讲师，硕士，研究方向为高等数学教育。

地点的限制，学员可以随时随地参加在线考试，并具备考试监控功能；成果展示栏目是学生学习过程中阶段性成果展示平台，体现了学生自主学习的问题和收获；网络学堂要体现学生更多的过程性评价；资料链接包括教师博客主页、有关高职数学资料网站等，通过自主学习，获取课外知识。

4 基于网络学堂的高职数学精品课建设的途径

4.1 改变教学理念，提升教师自身素质

网络学堂改变了传统的课堂教学模式、教学内容、教学方法和教学手段。网络学堂利用网络优势，将信息技术与高职数学资源进行有效的整合，突破了以往班级集中上课的限制，实现了群体教育和个性指导相结合，基础知识学习和能力培养互为补充的人才培养模式。在网络学堂的教学模式下，教师不但为教学和学生服务，而且在教学过程中不断转变自己的教育理念，提升自身专业素质。

4.2 注重能力培养，避免为了"精品"而建设"精品"

教育部 2003 年实施的国家精品课建设工程，对推进课程建设、全面提高教学质量起到了极大的推动作用。精品课程建设的过程是一个集观念、内容、方法、师资、技术、效果、质量等为一体的整体建设的过程。但近 10 年来的精品课建设过程中也出现了一些不正常的情况。建设精品课程不能为了"精品"而建"精品"，不能把精品课程的网络学堂建设停留在知识教育的层面上，无目的地堆砌资源。在课程的教案、课件、授课视频以及案例的呈现形式上应尽量统一；在内容选择上，教案和课件要系统全面，授课视频重视细节，利用现代教育技术将视频、教案、课件与网络学堂的文字稿结合起来，实现互补，切不可有过多重复，给学生造成"教材搬家"的印象，方能有助于学生的自主学习。另外，授课视频要完整，不能是仅有某一章节的代表性视频。

4.3 重视教学内容优化整合

高职数学是高职院校各专业的一门重要的基础课，高职数学的基础理论与方法已成为高职院校学生知识结构中不可或缺的重要组成部分。因此，高职数学精品课程建设的教学内容要从学生现有文化基础出发，在不应过分强调理论体系的完整性和逻辑体系的严谨性下，既要保证不同专业对高等数学知识的实际要求，适度考虑学生的深造发展，又要留给教师和学生更多的选择空间，以适应不同人才培养规格和培养目标的需要。

4.4 建立和完善有效的教学评价体系

教学评价包括两个方面，一是对高职数学精品课程网络学堂的评价，二是对学生的学习评价。前者包括国内外或校内外专家、教师、用人单位、毕业生以及在校生等对该课程的评价，采用的是学生评价与专家、教师评价相结合的评价方式。网络学堂应建有动态的评价体系，为专家、学生等提供网上评价的平台，如针对高职数学课程教学内容和教学效果方面的调查问卷等。在对学生的学习评价方面，应设置教师评价、学生自己评价和同伴的评价，强化过程性评价。学生的考核应由多种内容组成，如调查报告、撰写论文、数学建模、成果制作、使用数学软件求解数学问题的方法等形式，加强学生的数学应用意识，充分调动学生参与的积极性，起到督促学生学习的目的；网络学堂中的作业提交与管理系统，教师通过该系统即时跟踪、了解学生的学习情况和作业完成进展，对学生的学习做出相对客观的评价。同时，教师通过对学生的作业布置和批改情况以及答疑情况，了解学生对学习的关注程度。这些都有助于教师的教学评价和学生的学习评价。

参考文献

[1] 张宁. 现代信息技术条件下的网络学堂教学模式研究 [J]. 梧州学院学报，2007（6）.
[2] （美）小威廉姆·E. 多尔. 后现代课程观 [M]. 王红宇，译. 北京：教育科学出版社，2004.
[3] 薛志俊. 高职应用数学精品课程建设的认识与实践 [J]. 江苏教育学院学报，2010（2）.

师范教育应走在教育改革发展的前列

陈志刚

百年大计，教育为本；教育大计，教师为本。党的十八大报告提出教育是民族振兴和社会进步的基石，要努力办好人民满意的教育。党的十八届三中全会《关于全面深化改革若干重大问题的决定》（以下简称《决定》）明确提出了深化教育领域综合改革的号召，要坚持以立德树人为导向，以促进公平、提高质量为主线，以构建政府、学校、社会新型关系为重要抓手，全面深化教育领域综合改革。实现教育综合改革的目标，关键离不开提升教师队伍的整体素质。师范教育担负着为基础教育培养未来教师的任务，师范教育培养的人才质量将直接关系到基础教育改革目标能否得以实现，因此师范教育必须走在教育改革发展的前列。

1 努力办好人民满意的教育对师范教育提出了更高的要求

教育是国计也是民生，教育涉及千家万户，惠及子孙后代。教育在全面建成小康社会，实现"中国梦"的过程中具有基础性、先导性、全局性的重要作用。我国已进入全面建成小康社会的决定性阶段，社会开始由生存型消费逐渐进入发展型消费阶段，广大人民群众对通过接受良好教育提高自身素质、增强发展能力、改善生活质量，以及更好服务国家社会的愿望愈加迫切，也更为多样化，对教育的需求不仅是数量的增加，更重要的是质量的提高。目前，我国教育的发展水平还不完全适应国家经济社会发展和人民群众接受良好教育的要求。现有的教育状况还是以应试教育为主，教育观念相对落后；学生适应社会和就业创业能力不强，创新型、复合型人才紧缺；教育体制机制不完善，教育发展不平衡，学校办学活力不足。这些与国家对教育和人才的需求是有明显偏差的。因此，党的十八大提出了要努力办好人民满意的教育，党的十八届三中全会提出了要深化教育领域综合改革。

什么是人民满意的教育？这个问题引发了全社会对教育的思考，许多人从不同的角度进行了阐述。本人认为，人民满意的教育首先是要坚持以人为本，立德树人，从学生的实际出发，尊重学生，服务学生，创造适合每一个学生全面发展的教育。其次，人民满意的教育应当是缩小区域、城乡、校际间差距，体现教育公平的教育。教育资源应当向农村、边远、贫困、民族地区倾斜，让适龄的孩子无论走到哪里都能享受到平等的教育。最后，人民满意的教育还应是高质量的教育。要坚持以素质教育为导向，以提高质量为核心，实现由追求学生分数为主的教育向培养德智体美全面发展的高素质人才的教育转变。衡量教育质量高低的根本标准是教育能否促进人的全面发展和适应社会需要。

努力办好人民满意的教育，实现教育的高质量和人才培养的高质量，必须要有一支具有先进的教育理念、师德高尚、教艺精湛的高素质教师队伍。培养教师的任务，特别是培养基础教育教师的任务主要是由师范教育来承担。面向未来的教育首先需要培养面向未来的教师，所以我们说，师范教育责任重大，任务艰巨。师范院校要发挥教育研究的优势，把先进正确的教育理念传授给未来的教师，使师范生能够真正成为一名"学教育、爱教育、懂教育、会教育"的好教师。从这个意义上讲，师范教育的改革与发展水平在很大程度上直接关系到办好人民满意教育的实现。

2 师范教育发展的现状和存在的问题

长期以来，党和政府一直高度重视师范教育，改革开放以来，我国师范教育得到了长足的发展，为教育事业输送了大批优秀教师，做出了重大贡献。2007年教育部直属的6所师范院校，重新实行师范生免费的制度，希望吸引更多的优秀学生报考师范院校，将来成为基础教育的骨干教师。同时我们也看

[作者简介] 陈志刚，北京联合大学师范学院。

到，在教育发展新的历史起点上，按照贯彻落实科学发展观和努力办好人民满意教育的要求，目前教师队伍的整体素质还不能完全适应全面实施素质教育对高水平教师的迫切需要，师范教育的改革发展还不能完全适应建设高素质教师队伍的迫切需要。加强中小学和幼儿园教师队伍建设已经成为一项刻不容缓的战略任务。特别是像北京这样人口急剧增长的特大型城市，中小学、幼儿园师资需求旺盛，但供给严重不足，基础教育和学前教育的师资缺口很大。

据北京市人口统计公报表显示：2006—2012 年北京市常住人口出生呈现显著增长趋势，年平均新增 2.11 万新生婴幼儿，户籍人口出现周期性高峰，北京市适龄儿童呈现显著增长趋势。据预测，北京市 2014 年小学入学适龄儿童将由 2011 年的 13 万人左右增加到 18 万人左右，小学在校生总量将由 68 万人左右增加到 84 万人左右。外来非京籍学龄人口数量同样持续增长，根据北京市相关材料显示，2011 年北京市义务教育阶段随迁子女已达约 47.8 万人，比 2010 年同期增长了 4.4 万人，而这几年这一数字还在持续增长，北京市中小学教师出现严重不足。另据 2012 年《新京报》、《北京晚报》的报道，2010—2012 年这三年北京出生的新生儿约为 56 万人，那么未来三年实际需要的幼儿园班级数为 18666 个，缺额为 7453 个。按照国家教育部发布的《幼儿园教职工配备标准》，每班应配备 3 名教师，那么专任教师的缺口约为 2.2 万人。

除了师范生的培养数量不能满足学前和基础教育迅速发展的需要外，还存在部分师范生毕业后适应工作的时间较长、教学和管理能力有待提高的问题。造成这些问题的原因是多方面的。首先，地方政府对城市人口的急剧增长缺少应有的规划和管控，同时对人口增长所带来的教育问题缺少超前计划性，特别是中师调整后，减少了学前和基础教育教师的培养。其次，部分重点师范院校已经把学校办学目标确定为建设综合性、有特色、研究型高水平大学，对基础教育和学前教育师资的培养不是很重视，招生规模也很有限。最后，由于师范生好就业，有些师范院校存在着"皇帝女儿不愁嫁"的思想，在深化教育改革、提高师范生的培养质量上重视和投入得不够。

3 积极推进师范教育的改革与发展

党的十八届三中全会《决定》明确提出要深化教育领域综合改革，为师范教育改革发展指明了方向。师范教育作为教育事业的"工作母鸡"，是教育发展的基础，必须要有超前意识，只有加快师范教育自身的改革发展才能更好地促进教育事业的发展。

3.1 从招生改革入手，扩大师范生源，提高师范生的招生质量

师范生不同于非师专业的学生，他们一入学就明确了就业方向，毕业后要做教师，所以对师范生的要求就是对未来教师的要求。为保证未来教师的质量，应从招生入手，严把生源质量关，确保报考师范专业的学生热爱教师职业，具有做教师的基本素质。由于教师是一个相对比较稳定的职业，收入水平较好，在目前大学毕业生整体就业形势比较紧张的形势下，师范专业毕业生的就业不成问题，因此，报考师范专业的学生数量比较多，但如何确保师范生的生源质量是需要认真研究和解决的问题。为此，建议进行师范生招生改革，师范院校应当像艺术院校那样提前招生，提前录取，并增加面试环节，这样有利于选拔优秀学生报考师范专业。同时，对于热爱教师职业，符合做教师条件的优秀高中毕业生可以按一定比例免试推荐进入大学师范专业学习。

此外，针对目前北京市基础教育和学前教育师资急需补充的现状，建议在师范院校组织非师范专业的学生自主报名并经过选拔转入师范专业学习，或在非师范专业增加师范专业选修课程，帮助非师范专业的学生考取教师资格证书，使他们能够加入到教师队伍中来，以解目前基础教育和学前教育教师短缺之急。

3.2 坚持立德树人导向，创新师范生培养模式

实施素质教育是我们国家在 20 世纪 90 年代初，针对应试教育和重理轻文、重课堂轻实践、忽视人的全面发展等问题而提出来的教育改革的方向和目标。素质教育提出的真正意义是对教育使命的反思，在于重申人的全面发展，重申知识、能力与社会责任感相互结合的人才标准，在于创造一种激发学生成长成才的培养模式。素质教育是面向全体学生的教育，是促进学生全面发展的教育，是充分开发受教育者潜能、促进学生个性健康发展的教育，也可以说素质教育是以社会文化塑造社会合格成员的教育。素

质教育提出已有 20 多年，但人们对素质教育的理解并不全面，落实得也很不到位。

党的十八届三中全会《决定》为推进素质教育做出了明确部署，《决定》指出："全面贯彻党的教育方针，坚持立德树人，加强社会主义核心价值体系教育，完善中华优秀传统文化教育，形成爱学习、爱劳动、爱祖国活动的有效形式和长效机制，增强学生社会责任感、创新精神和实践能力。强化体育课和课外锻炼，促进青少年身心健康、体魄强健。改进美育教学，提高学生审美和人文素养。"一句话，教育综合改革的目标就是要由"应试教育"真正转到"素质教育"上来。

实施素质教育关键在于教育理念的更新、教育体制的改革、教师素养的提高。实施素质教育要求必须要有符合素质教育的教师，因此，师范教育要率先创新人才培养模式，成为实施素质教育的典范。

首先，要强化立德树人的师德教育。古人云："人可以一生不仕，但不可以一日无德。""才者，德之资也；德者，才之帅也。"才能，是道德的辅助；道德，是才能的统帅。做官要有官德，做教师要有师德。我国现代著名教育家叶圣陶先生曾说过："教育工作者的全部工作，就是为人师表。"如果一个教师没有良好的师德，他就不会有良好的敬业精神，他就难以做到为人师表，他也无法完成教书育人的历史使命。一位中学校长曾说过，教师的思想品德素质对做好一个老师可能要起到 80% 的作用。由此可见，师范教育必须把对师范生的师德培养始终放在首位。师范院校的领导和教师要牢固树立教育的根本任务是立德树人，促进人的全面发展和健康成长这一教育理念，而且要把这一理念落实到师范生培养的全过程，传导到每一个学生。

其次，要把素质教育落实到师范生培养的全过程。对师范生的培养不仅要强调知识，更要强调文化；不仅要强调能力，更要强调素质，要改革原有师范生的培养模式。过去师范生和非师范生的培养区别就是在专业知识学习相同的基础上，加上教育学、教育心理学和学科教学法课程学习，外加短暂的教育实习，这种传统的师范生培养模式已不适应素质教育的要求。我们要积极探索新形势下师范生的培养模式，做到"注重人格塑造、突出综合素养、强化实践训练"，努力培养"人格健全、素养深厚、基础扎实、理念先进、技能突出"的基础教育优秀师资。

为提高师范生的综合素养，师范生的培养方案可以构建成"通识教育、专业教育、教师教育和实践教学"四大模块。在深化教育综合改革，全面推进素质教育，逐渐取消文理分科的形势下，应加强师范生通识教育的课程，特别应加强人文艺术修养类课程如：国学知识、音乐、舞蹈、戏剧、视觉传达艺术等课程，通过这些课程的学习与实践培养师范生认识美、体验美、欣赏美和创造美的能力，形成作为未来教师的审美素养。试想一个不懂艺术、不热爱艺术的老师又怎样去培养学生的美育。此外还可以开设科技与环保、安全与健康等方面的专题学习。教师教育模块除教育学、教育心理学等课程外，应强化师范生教学技能的培养如：板书与口头表达、课程资源开发与教学设计、课外活动组织、教学法研究、现代教育手段的运用和教学评价等。通过这些课程提升教师职业的内涵，增强其专业性，使师范生在从事教师职业时，较之其他未经过教师教育专业学习而从事教师职业的人，具有无可比拟的优势。

在师范生培养过程中，实践教学模块应特别加以重视，一是要强调师范生在校学习过程中的实践锻炼。教师是一个实践性极强的职业，教师不仅要掌握学科技能，还要掌握教学技能。所以，师范生在培养的过程中需要进行大量的实践活动，通过学科创新实践活动和教学技能创新实践活动，使师范生在走出校门之前能够具备教师职业所需的创新实践意识和能力，为将来走上教师岗位奠定职业基础。二是要重视和强化生的教育实习。要改变现有的教育实习安排在高年级，有的甚至安排在最后一学年，且时间短的状况。这样安排实习的效果较差，师范生虽然通过实习发现了不足但是已经快毕业了，来不及改进提高。因此，建议在师范生培养方案中增加教育实习的时间和次数，从低年级开始就安排教育见习，每学期用一周时间让师范生通过入校参观、聆听讲座、课堂观察、远程观摩、视频点播和教学案例分析等活动来初步认识中小学课堂教学，感悟与体验基础教育以及教师职业角色，然后带着问题回到学校来学习，这样会提高他们学习的积极性。高年级以顶岗实习的形式安排一个学期的教育实习，这样有利于他们对一个学期全过程的教学和管理有一个全面的认识和实践，同时由所在实习学校配备经验丰富、工作认真的老师担任实习指导老师，通过实行校内外"双导师"制，提高师范生的培养质量，缩短他们毕业后适应教师岗位的时间。

3.3 校园文化建设一定要突出师范特色

校园文化建设是育人的重要载体，大学不仅通过课堂和实验室教学对学生产生影响，更多地是要通过大学创设的文化环境的熏陶使他们发生潜移默化的变化,并尽快地成熟、成长。大学的文化环境是一种其他因素所无法替代的教育影响和教育力量,大学文化环境的品位极大地影响到大学所造就的人的品位。师范院校更应重视校园文化建设,自觉地把文化营造和文化影响纳入人才培养体系,这也是每一所大学都不能忽视的文化自觉。

校园文化重在建设,重在实践,在以应用为本的师范教育中,更要进一步结合师范生的身心特点,创建文化环境,广泛开展学生参与的校园文化活动,使他们在参与和体验中陶冶情操、提高素养,最大限度地挖掘校园文化的育人功能。苏联著名的教育家苏霍姆林斯基提出了一个理念叫做"让学校的每一面墙壁都会说话"。几年来,我们也在积极地探索带有师范学院特色的校园文化建设。北京联合大学师范学院的前身是北京师范大学分校,建校35年来,如何让面积不大的校园充满教育性、艺术性,体现出师范院校独有的校园文化气息是几代师院人的追求。我们秉承北京师范大学分校的传统,把"学为人师、行为世范"的师大校训雕刻在校园醒目的位置,在校园里修建了体现师范特色的"育师苑""学知亭""桃李廊""莲花池",还有"学院发展历史变迁和名师讲学的浮雕墙"等人文景观,并在校园和楼道空间内开设了学生自主学习交流的场所。通过每年举办校园文化节、艺术展、名师讲学等多种形式的文化活动陶冶师范生的情怀。我院师范生还成立了"师乐社",社团成员通过担任低年级班级助理,强化了师范生的实践能力。多年的实践使我们感受到,带有师范特色的校园文化建设,在师范生的培养过程中,起到了春风化雨、润物细无声的作用。

党的十八届三中全会为深化教育综合改革绘制了蓝图,也提出了时间要求,我们要认真学习深刻领会党的十八届三中全会的改革精神,积极推进师范教育人才培养模式的改革,把"立德树人、全面发展"的教育理念落实到师范教育人才培养的全过程,把"尊师爱生、为人师表"的师德师风作为师范院校校园文化建设的精神力量。

参考文献

[1] 中共中央关于全面深化改革若干重大问题的决定 [M]. 北京:人民出版社,2013.
[2] 袁贵仁. 深化教育领域综合改革 [N]. 中国教育报 2013 – 11 – 20.
[3] 李伦娥. 培养优秀小学教师是学校的根 [N]. 中国教育报 2013 – 12 – 03.

基于协同理论的应用型大学学科、专业一体化建设研究

陈 琳 龚秀敏

协同学（Synergetics）理论是德国著名的物理学家赫尔曼·哈肯于20世纪70年代在研究激光器的自组织现象时提出来的。它是"一门关于协作的科学"，研究那些全然不同学科的极不相同类型的系统之间所普遍存在着的共同特点，即一个由大量子系统所组成的系统，在一定条件下，子系统之间如何通过非线性相互作用产生协同现象和相干效应，使系统形成有一定功能的自组织结构，出现新的有序状态。协同学是关于多组分系统如何通过子系统的协同行为而导致结构有序演化的一门自组织理论。揭示了一个复杂系统从无序到有序，从低级有序到高级有序的演化过程，提出了复杂开放系统有序发展的演化动力是系统内部子系统间协同合作关系。协同学认为，非平衡开放系统在与外界环境进行物质、能量和信息的交换过程中，系统由无序状态逐步演化为有序状态的内在动力是子系统及其内部要素之间的协同作用。没有协同性，子系统的独立性占主导地位，系统整体功能得不到有效发挥。

大学的学科建设和专业建设一体化系统作为一个非平衡开放系统，其学科建设和专业建设子系统常常被人们割裂开，而且由于观念、制度和政策等原因往往导致高校和教师过分重视学科而忽视专业建设，致使两者之间经常出现失衡，难以在实践中产生学科建设和专业建设之间的协同效应。因此，研究高校学科建设与专业建设之间的协同关系，无疑对高校学科建设和专业建设协同发展以更好地实现大学功能具有重要的现实意义。

一、大学的功能及学科、专业建设的协同基础

（一）大学的功能

自1088年意大利的波罗尼亚大学设置法学（随后有医学、神学）学科首开人类高等教育的先河，在长达七百多年的时间里，大学的功能都是单一的，即"人才培养"。1810年，德国的洪堡大学第一次将科学研究与教书育人并列，使大学具有了第二大功能。20世纪30年代，美国的威斯康星大学最早将服务社会作为大学的新功能，至此，形成目前世界范围内对高等教育功能与作用的经典表述，即培养人才、科学研究和服务社会。胡锦涛在庆祝清华大学建校100周年大会的讲话中把文化的传承创新明确为大学的第四大功能，对指导高校建设具有重大的指导意义。我国目前学术界比较公认的观点是，大学要具有培养人才、科学研究、服务社会和文化传承创新四大功能。

（二）学科、专业建设及其与大学的四大功能之间的关系

1. 专业及专业建设

从不同的角度给专业的定义大致可分为以下几种。（1）专业是高等学校或中等学校根据社会分工需要而划分的学业门类。顾远明（1991）将其解释为：中国、前苏联等国高等学校培养学生的各个专门领域，大体相当于《国际教育标准分类》的课程计划或美国学校的主修。根据社会职业分工、学科分类、科学技术和文化发展状况及经济建设与社会需要划分。（2）专业是一种学业门类。《辞海》将其定义为：高等学校或中等专业学校根据社会分工需要而划分的学业门类，各专业都有独立的教学计划，以体现本专业的培养目标和要求。（3）专业是课程的一种组织形式。潘懋元、王伟廉（1995）认为，专业是课程的一种组织形式，因而在谈到课程时，其中也就包含了这种组织形式。（4）从广义、狭义和特指三

［作者简介］陈琳（1966—），河南信阳人，北京联合大学教授，主要研究方向：企业技术创新与核心竞争力。

个层面来界定专业。周川（1992）认为，广义的专业即某种职业不同于其他职业的一些特定的劳动特点；狭义的专业，主要指一些特定的社会职业；特指的专业即高等学校中的专业，它依据确定的培养目标设置于高等学校（及其相应的教育机构）的教育基本单位或教育基本组织形式。薛天祥在2001年版的《高等教育学》中综合了各家的理解后认为，专业有广义与特指之分。狭义的专业是指高等学校的专业，即高等学校培养高级专门人才的基本教育单位，由特定的专业培养目标和课程体系组成。广义的专业是指知识的专门化领域。特指的专业是指一种依据学科分类和社会分工需要进行的培养人才的基本单位，当专业与培养人才的活动相联系时，往往就成为一种培养人才的基本单位，演变为一种实体。

综合以上几种定义，本文认为，专业是指高校根据社会分工的需要而设置的一种课程组织形式。从专业的构成来看，专业主要是由专业培养目标、专业培养方案（课程体系）和专业教学条件构成。专业培养方案即课程体系的设置合理与否、质量高低、实施效果好坏直接影响专业的人才培养质量。

2. 学科及学科建设

学科（discipline）一词最早源于印欧字根——希腊文中的dilako（教）和拉丁语的动词"学习"（discere），以及由它派生出来的名词"学习者"（discipulus）。后来随着人类认识的不断深入，学科概念的含义不断增加，人们从不同的角度赋予了"学科"丰富的含义。我国国家标准GB/T13745-92将学科定义为"相对独立的知识体系"，这一概念为人们所普遍接受。一般认为，一门独立学科的形成需要以下四个要素。一是一定的研究群体负责学科的发展研究。主要包括高等院校、科研院所及其他的科研群体组织。二是研究的对象或研究的领域，即这门学科具有独特的、不可替代的研究对象，具有特殊的规律。三是理论体系，即形成特有的概念、原理、命题、范畴，形成严密的逻辑系统。四是研究方法。要提高一门学科的发展水平，在把握学科发展规律的前提下，需要做到以下三个方面：第一，必须建设一支学术水平较高的研究队伍，形成老、中、青结合，学历与知识结构合理的学术梯队；第二，对学科发展进行设计与规划，确定研究方向，对学科结构进行调整和更新；第三，要提供一定的学术研究条件，包括实验室建设、图书资料建设、学术风气建设、学科管理制度建设与优化等。而这些建设过程就是学科建设。因此，我们可以把学科建设概念界定为：依据社会发展的需求和学科发展的内在规律，结合自身的实际，对学科发展及其结构进行规划和调整、对学术队伍结构进行优化、对学术资源进行维护与完善的过程，其主要内容包括学术梯队建设、学术带头人的培养、实验室和研究基地建设、确定研究方向、争取研究项目、形成科学合理的学科管理制度等。

需要指出的是学科和科研的区别和联系。虽然科研可以形成学科成果，但由于高校的资源、能力及专业设置方面的原因，学校通常会积聚自身的有限科研资源聚焦于有限的学科领域和研究方向。发散型的科学研究难以形成相对稳定的研究团队、获得研究平台的支持，其研究成果又往往很难形成对学校专业发展的较大支持，所以说，只有科研汇聚到学科方向之中才能获得发展的条件，并对专业发展形成很好的支撑。

3. 学科建设、专业建设与大学功能实现之间的关系

学科建设和专业建设是高校实现其培养人才、科学研究、服务社会、文化传承创新四大功能的基本活动。它们之间的关系可用图1表示。

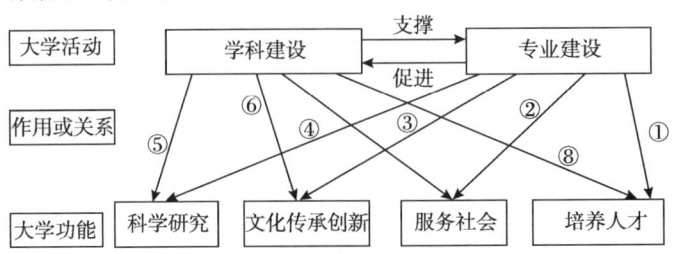

图1　大学功能与学科、专业关系

由图1可以看出，最上一层次是大学活动，大学的基础和核心活动是学科和专业建设活动，总的来说，学科建设是支撑专业建设的，而专业建设又能够促进学科建设水平的提升；最下面的一个层次是大学功能；中间层次是学科建设和专业建设对大学功能的作用或关系，这些关系具体包括：①专业建设从

专业培养目标的确定、培养方案的制订、师资队伍的建设、课程建设、教学环境建设等方面培养人才，这是专业建设的直接和根本的目的；②专业建设通过为社会输送所需人才服务于社会；③专业建设的教学工作本身就是文化知识传播和继承、创新的过程，同时也是社会道德、价值观等形成和传播的活动，是文化传承创新的重要内容；④专业建设为科学研究培养人才，同时拉动科学水平的提升；⑤学科建设通过凝聚科研方向、建设科研团队、搭建科研平台等促进科学研究不断向纵深发展，同时，通过学科建设使科学研究资源和能力聚集到能够支撑学校专业发展的专业或方向上，易于打造优势学科及方向；⑥学科建设在新知识的发现、传播等方面发挥文化传承创新的功能；⑦学科建设主要通过科学研究成果的应用、为社会组织提供咨询服务和课题研究等服务于社会；⑧学科建设一方面通过学位点建设培养研究生等高层次人才，同时通过专业建设间接对人才培养发挥作用，另外，学科建设还通过学生科技活动等培养学生的科研素养和能力。

（三）学科建设与专业建设之间的协同基础

在国外，很少有人把学科建设或专业建设作为一个单独的问题来研究，国外基本上把学科建设与专业建设问题和高校的发展问题综合在一起研究，世界著名大学都是学科建设与专业建设有机融合在一起，通过学科建设促进专业建设，并靠本科教育扬名于世。西方国家认为专业即是不同课程的组合，或者说是不同的课程计划即指一系列、有一定逻辑关系的课程的组织（Program），相当于一个培训计划或课程体系。可见，东西方对专业概念的理解是不大相同的。专业的设置往往取决于社会的需要与可开设课程科目的均衡。从国外学科建设与专业建设的研究与实践来看，国外的学科建设与专业建设始终注重学科与专业对经济社会的适应性；在组织建设和机制设置方面比较灵活，能够从多方面促进学科与专业资源共享、交叉与融合以促进科研与教学水平的提高。

在中国，以学科发展来支持本科专业的研究和实践开始较晚。20世纪末期，建设高水平大学被提上议事日程，国家启动了以学科建设为核心的"211工程""985工程"建设。之后，在学科建设取得成效的基础上，为适应经济与社会发展对创新人才的需求，高校开始注重教学与科研并重，"学科—专业"一体化建设的理念逐渐引入到学校的建设发展之中，并在实践中开始施行。专业建设方面，这些年国家也加大了对本科教育改革的力度，实施高等学校教育教学质量工程，启动了国家级教学名师、学科专业质量评估、国家级精品课程、本科教学工作水平评估等工作。在此背景下，全国高等学校对以学科建设促进专业建设，尤其是科研促进教学方面进行了一系列的理论研究和实践探索，取得了可喜的成绩。谭荣波（2007）对"学科"与"专业"的关系进行了辨析[1]，郭必裕（2004）对"学科"与"专业"建设"两张皮"的问题进行了研究[2]，杜卫等（2010）对新建地方院校学科专业一体化建设进行了初步研究，[3]曾冬梅等人提出高校"学科—专业"一体化建设的学术组织系统建设的设想[4]等，总的来说，国内学者对学科建设和专业建设的研究主要着眼于学科建设或专业建设的管理方面，缺少对学科建设与专业建设协调的动力机制、激励机制、建设环境等的研究；"学科—专业"一体化建设研究还相当初级，缺乏对具体学科与专业一体化建设的实证分析，难以形成能有效指导学科专业一体化建设的理论，从而影响到学科建设与专业建设的融合发展。

事实上，学科建设与专业建设相互作用、相互依赖，共同实现大学的四大功能。中国学者曾冬梅、陈江波对学科建设与专业建设之间的具体协同基础作了比较系统的研究，如见图2所示[5]。

学科建设与专业建设的协同关系可以概括为以下两个方面。

1. 学科建设为专业建设提供支撑。尽管专业建设和人才培养是应用型高校的最核心的功能，但是，专业建设离不开学科建设的支撑。首先，作为专业建设核心的专业课程和专业教学内容来源于学科建设的科学研究成果，专业教学内容是人类长期科学研究的成果。其次，学科建设中的学术队伍建设为培养专业教师和优化师资队伍奠定了基础。另外，学科方向的选定和建设为专业特色的确定奠定了牢固的理论基础，科学研究实验室和研究平台的建设为培养学生的实践能力和科学素养提供了有利条件，而学位点的建设则为本科毕业生的进一步学术深造提供了方向和通道等。

2. 专业建设为学科建设提供动力。作为应用型大学，人才培养和专业建设是其主要和核心的功能，应用型大学的其他活动都将或多或少地围绕专业建设和人才培养进行。首先，专业建设中教学内容、课程、教学方法等方面的建设和改革，需要学科建设进行相关的科学研究，以服务于专业建设。其次，师

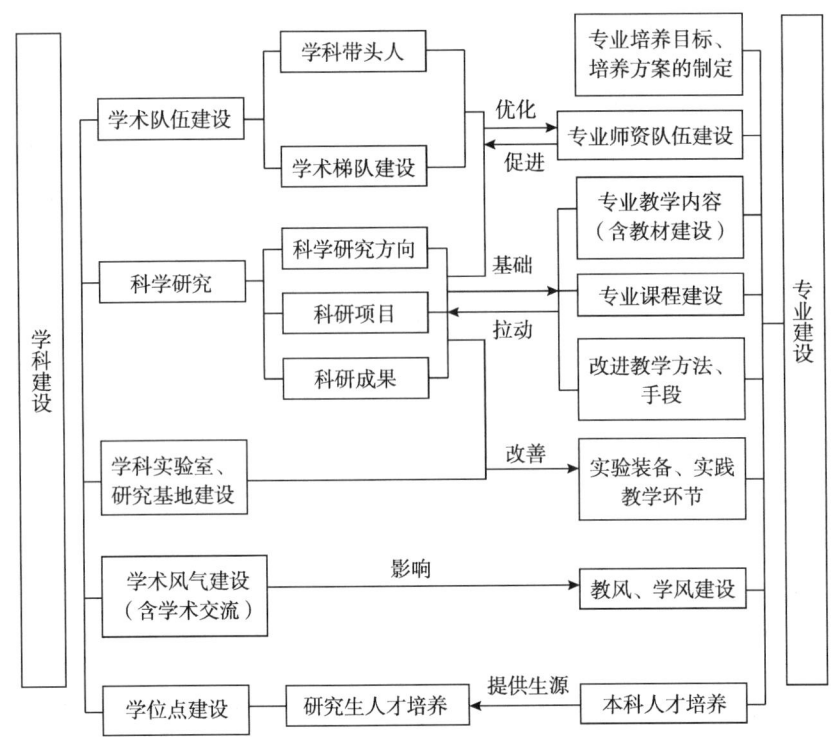

图 2　学科建设子系统与专业建设子系统协同关系

资队伍的建设为学科建设提供了源源不断的学术研究骨干，可以丰富和优化学术研究队伍。最后，专业建设引领应用型大学学科研究的方向和领域。尽管学科建设和科学研究有其自身发展和演进的逻辑，但作为应用型大学的学科建设有其特殊性，应用型大学主要服务于地方经济和社会发展，社会对人才的需求是专业人才培养目标确定的依据，应用型大学学科研究方向和领域应依据由社会需求所确定的专业建设方向和领域，专业建设所培养的本科毕业生也为学位点建设输送源源不断的生源。

另外，学科建设与专业建设的主体和目标的统一性也是两者协同的基础。首先，学科建设和专业建设的主体都是教师，应用型高校的教师首先是专业建设的主体，同时也大多是学科建设的主体，二者合一，使得专业建设和学科建设协同中的知识转化、应用、共享等通过教师本人完成，无须通过其他外部协调机构完成，效率最高、成本最低。其次，学科建设和专业建设的目标是一致的。作为应用型大学的学科建设是要服务于专业建设和人才培养的，而专业建设的目标是培养社会所需要的人才，这也是两者协同的共同的出发点和最终目标。

二、应用型大学"学科—专业"一体化建设思路与对策

尽管目前各高等学校都在强调以科研促教学，但学科建设与专业建设的"两张皮"是普遍现象，除了政策上的原因，主要是缺乏理论指导。由于长期以来国内学者把学科建设和专业建设分开研究，在学科建设与专业建设有机融合方面，理性思考不够，导致在教育改革实践中未将专业建设纳入学科建设的范畴，更没有形成"学科—专业"一体化建设的互动机制，实践中也没有将学科资源真正转化为本科教育资源。

根据协同理论，学科建设与专业建设只有协同发展才能最大程度地发挥大学的功能。鉴于目前应用型大学在学科和专业建设领域存在的各种问题，笔者认为应该从以下几个方面厘清应用型大学"学科—专业"一体化发展的思路，并制定相应的对策，才能提升大学的办学水平和层次。

（一）充分理解应用型大学的学科和专业建设的特殊性

应用型大学的学科和专业建设的协同关系遵从上述论述的规律，与研究型大学相比，应用型大学学科建设和专业建设又呈现出以下不同特征。

1. 学科建设应用性。应用型大学的学科建设不应该模仿研究型大学的做法，一味地追求引进高端科学研究人才、追求高水平的理论研究成果等，这是不现实的，也很难具有竞争力。应用型大学应该找到

自己的定位，找到能够发挥自身优势的领域，那就是在应用性较强的学科领域，这体现在争取各级各类项目上就是要体现出应用性，发表文章也要体现应用性成果，尤其要在研究成果的产业化或商业化方面需要学校大力扶持，充分展现应用型大学在学科建设方面的应用型特色。

2. 专业建设的应用性。应用型大学的专业建设特色主要体现在其培养应用性人才方面，因此在培养目标的定位、培养计划的制订、教学内容的选取、教学方式方法的选择、实践教学环节的设计和安排以及师资队伍的培养等方面都要充分考虑到其应用性，比如师资队伍中企业界人士要占有一定比例，以及双师型教师要保持一定的比例等。

应用型大学的学科建设和专业建设的特殊性使得其"学科—专业"一体化建设中所遇到的问题和解决问题的对策有所不同。

（二）转变观念

造成学科、专业建设矛盾、冲突和"两张皮"这些问题的深层次原因是思想认识上的问题，由于认识上的误区和管理体制等方面的原因，导致人们将学科建设和专业建设分割开来。认识上的不到位，必然导致行动上的偏差。因此，转变观念，牢固确立学科、专业一体化建设理念，以科学的态度和方法实施建设工作，是实现"学科—专业"一体化发展的前提和关键。

（三）完善相关制度

近些年，不少应用型大学把对科研的考核提到前所未有的高度，但由于博士以上人才一般是在进入高校以前就有自己稳定的研究领域和方向，进入高校以后不可能再改变自己的研究方向，从而导致引进人才与学科建设领域"两张皮"现象，这样既不利于学校的学科建设，也不利于人才的发展。所以把好引进人才的关很重要。同时，在绩效考核、职称晋升等关键评价体系中，一般只关注科研成果的质量和数量，在评价时很少考虑学科因素，这也导致"重科研轻学科"的想象。另外，学校的"科研"与"教学"之间"泾渭分明"，其工作任务在基层研究人员身上经常发生冲突，缺乏有效的协调机制，更加重了教师对科研和教学"两者关系不大而且可以分开、经常发生矛盾"的看法，对两者之间的深层次联系缺乏思考，更缺乏将研究成果转化为教学资源的实践。

之所以出现这种情况，根本的原因在于考核和晋升制度以及协调科研与学科建设、科研与教学之间关系的相关制度导向出现偏差，这些制度的导向偏离了应用型大学的轨道，偏离了"学科—专业"协同发展的基本方向。制度为大学的学科专业建设提供必要的机制，这些机制发挥着资源配置作用、评价导向作用等，比如在资源配置方面，学校要统筹安排学科和专业建设资源，建立学科、专业资源共享机制，形成学科、专业之间"共生共赢"机制；在评价导向制度设计上设计一些学科、专业交叉融合性考核指标，有意引导教师在学科、专业融合和一体化发展方面多做贡献等。

（四）以强化课程建设来拉动学科建设

专业是随着社会的发展而变化的，社会需求是专业建设的"风向标"，而专业建设又包括课程的重新组合和课程内容的变化，所以课程建设是专业建设的核心和基础。同时，每一个专业的知识都涉及多个基础学科和应用学科，专业是多个学科知识的固化，应用型大学的学科建设是围绕专业建设所需知识和理论等展开的，所以，加强课程建设必将拉动学科建设，促进科研水平的提高。

（五）以培养学生创新能力来统一学科和专业建设

学科建设的主要任务是探索未知的知识领域，而专业建设的主要任务是培养人才，当今社会所需要的是具有创新素质和创新能力的创新型人才，为培养创新型人才，必须将专业建设的培养学生创新素质和能力的工作与学科建设中的实验室建设、学术队伍建设、学科方向建设、学位点建设等内容紧密结合，只有将学科建设的所有内容充分融入到专业建设之中，才能培养出创新型人才。只有把培养创新型人才作为专业建设的核心，才能充分体现学科建设对学生创新能力培养的功能，才能使学科建设和专业建设日益走向协同和融合发展。

解决当前应用型大学科学处理学科建设、专业建设的关系是一个重大的理论和实践课题。以上运用协同学相关理论对应用型大学学科专业一体化建设的现状及存在的问题进行了分析，并对如何实现应用型大学的"学科—专业"一体化发展提出参考性意见和建议。

参考文献

[1] 谭荣波. 高校"学科专业"的辨析[J]. 湛江师范学院学报（哲学社会科学版），2007（5）：140－142.

[2] 郭必裕. 对"学科"与"专业"建设两张皮问题的对策研究[J]. 高等工程教育研究，2004（3）：23－26.

[3] 杜卫，陈恒. 新建地方院校走学科专业一体化建设之路[J]. 中国高等教育，2010（11）：39－41.

[4] 曾冬梅，唐纪良. 学术组织创新：高校"学科—专业"一体化建设的基础——"学科—专业"一体化建设研究之一[J]. 广西大学学报（哲学社会科学版），2008（4）：150－153.

[5] 曾冬梅，陈江波. 基于协同学视角的"学科—专业"一体化建设初探[J]. 黑龙江教育（高教研究与评估），2007（5）：20－22.

构建以"创新"为核心控制点的财会本科毕业论文质量控制体系

邵 军

1 本科生毕业论文"创新"的必要性与可行性分析

1.1 本科毕业论文创新的必要性分析。

（1）构建创新型国家的人才基础在于具有创新意识和创新能力的本科生。在创新型人才的培养中，本科生的培养处于基础地位和关键环节。本科生毕业论文是培养学生综合运用所学的基本理论知识和实践技能解决实际问题能力的一种基本教学形式。本科生毕业论文的创新能力和深度，不仅是对学生四年的学习成果和综合素质的检验，也是对教师四年教学质量所进行的全面、综合检验。（2）高等教育的培养目标决定了必须将培养本科生的创新意识和创新能力放在首位。培养学生解决问题的能力，发展学生的创新能力，是当代学校教育的重要任务，尤其应该成为高等教育的重要目标。教育部和财政部联合发布的《教育部财政部关于实施高等学校本科教学质量与教学改革工程的意见》明确提出，要以创新教育统领本科教学质量与教学改革。本科生毕业论文作为本科教学的重要环节，在提升本科生的创新意识和创新能力方面有着重要的作用和意义。

1.2 本科毕业论文创新的可行性分析。

（1）大学本科阶段是大学生综合素质飞跃提升时期。大学本科阶段是大学生从青年中晚期向成年期过渡的转折时期，一方面，他们的心理品质全面完整地发展起来，逐步确立了自己的世界观、人生观和价值观；另一方面，大学生头脑中固有的东西少，思想活跃，容易接受新思想、新信息。在毕业论文写作中，学生们被要求针对专业领域的某一问题、某一现象进行解释和分析，并力图找出解决问题的有效途径，这正好具备研究型、实践型学习方式的基本特点，有助于实现学习方式从传统的单纯理论向新型的理论与实践相结合创新模式的转变。（2）大学本科阶段是大学生思维发展最活跃时期。大学时期，刚好是大学生由形式逻辑思维向辩证逻辑思维过渡的阶段，并且在常规性思维继续发展的同时，创新性思维也在发展。大学前三年学习的主要任务是继承前人已经积累起来的知识经验，其思维活动基本上属于常规性思维；大学四年级则是大学生在掌握了系统的专业知识的基础上，通过毕业论文载体实现其早已萌芽了的创新欲望的阶段，他们不再满足于接受已有的知识，更强烈地表现出改造社会、创新社会的愿望，而毕业论文环节就刚好契合了大学生实现自我价值的目标。

2 本科毕业论文"创新"质量控制点的内涵

2.1 思维创新

思维创新，是论文创新的前提，也是创新能力的重要表现。毕业论文的创作过程，也是培养学生独立思考能力的过程，严令禁止抄袭别人的文章。大学生在就业实习中耗费了大量的时间和精力，在撰写论文时常常出现组合改编他人的论文的现象。应鼓励和指导学生探索新方法，打破传统封闭式思维模式，积极提倡新思维。

2.2 科研创新

毕业论文是学生根据自己专业实际，在教师指导下独立进行科学研究的过程。要写作出优秀的毕业

[作者简介] 邵军（1966—），女，北京联合大学商务学院财会教研室主任，教授，硕士。研究方向为财务会计与财务管理。

论文，不仅要有厚实的理论基础，还要具有刻苦钻研的精神，更重要的是要有较强的科研能力。在毕业论文质量管理中，要培养学生刻苦钻研的精神，鼓励和激发学生创新，勇于提出自己的观点，做到层次清晰，结构合理，论证充分。

2.3 技能创新

毕业论文的创作，不仅要求在理论上创新，而且要求在实践上创新。这种实践创新，主要表现在用新方法或数据分析来解决实践中的难题。由于财会专业属于实践性、应用性较强的专业，更需要在技能上创新。仅就论文写作而言，对研究的课题要用财务数据来进行分析，通过数据处理，经验论证，揭示事物的规律或本质。

3 构建以"创新"为核心控制点的本科毕业论文质量控制体系的原则

3.1 以"问题"为导向的原则

科学家爱因斯坦曾说过"：提出一个问题往往比解决一个问题更重要……提出新的问题，新的可能性，从新的角度去看待旧问题，却需要有创造性的想象力，而且标志着科学的真正进步。"本科生限于知识结构和理解能力，解决问题的能力可能会有所欠缺，但是首先要培养他们的"问题"意识，即关注理论和现实社会经济管理中的"问题"。提出有意义和有价值的问题，这是创新的第一步。提出问题之后，在解决问题的过程中，定能培养出解决问题的能力。

3.2 以"结果"为目标的原则

从结果来看，毕业论文是本科四年学生学习和教师教学成果的集中体现，涉及教和学的双方，对毕业论文的质量控制体系的设计，不仅要对学生和学生写作论文过程的控制，还要对老师教学和老师指导论文过程的控制，只有在全程、全方位控制的基础上，才能制造出合格的产品——优质的毕业论文。在整个体系的设计中，要以"创新"为核心，以"毕业论文的创新"带动教学过程的"创新"和"优化"，形成完整的毕业论文质量控制体系。

3.3 以"方法、素材"为保障的原则

毕业论文的创新，不仅表现在选题、观点要新颖，还表现在结论要独特，要想保证两点，其中间环节的论证必然要创新，因此，论证的材料要创新，论证的方法也要创新。所用的材料要新鲜，要把新的事实、新的思想观念作为素材使用；把已经存在，但未被发现、未引起人们普遍重视的事物作为材料使用；从新的角度使用人们已经比较熟悉的材料，把材料所蕴涵的新意揭示出来，做出新的解释，使陈旧的材料成为有新意的材料。所用的论证方法要创新，进行前人尚未做过的实证性研究工作，对某一问题进行首次综合性表述，将某一方法应用于新的研究领域，应用不同的方法论进行交叉学科的研究等。

4 设计以"创新"为核心控制点的本科毕业论文指标评价体系

4.1 体现"创新"质量控制点的指标

根据本科生的创新层次和能力，设计能够体现创新的指标，赋予不同的权重。对于本科生来说，选题的创新相对可行，赋予了18%的权重，而观点的创新对于本科生来说相对较难，赋的权重相对较低，为5%。

（1）论文选题的创新。毕业论文题目的选择是保证毕业论文质量的关键性环节，选题合适，有利于论文写作的顺利完成，可以说，好的论文选题是论文写作成功的一半。一般来说，财经类论文的选题，可以遵循以下三个原则：一是专业为本原则。学生要充分考虑财经专业的特点，将专业和个人兴趣相结合，选择与财经专业密切相关的论题，符合专业培养目标，体现综合训练基本要求。二是小题大做原则。题目的选择要考虑学生自身的实际能力和外部条件的限制，尽量小一点、实一点。三是创新原则。论文应该具有创新性和时代感，即在理论上要有所突破，对实践活动的研究要有新认识，反映时代的要求。根据这三项原则，在"选题"指标下细化三项指标：专业培养目标、工作量与难度、理论结合实践，并分别赋予5%、5%和8%的权重。本科生要通过学术研究，解决理论上、学术上某个重要问题，并有所创新、突破，是比较困难的。而结合实际选题，尤其是财经类专业应用性较强，用已学过的理论

知识分析解决现实社会问题，开展自主创业模拟实验等项目研究，则针对性强，材料丰富，也容易写出水平和特色，因此，在这一指标上赋予了较高的权重。

（2）论文观点的创新。撰写毕业论文，要有自己对题目的独到见解和看法，而不能人云亦云，简单地重复别人的说法。对与选题相关的理论或实际问题要有较深刻的认识，有新的见解，有一定的创新性，但如果在选题时真正做到了真题真做，深入社会、企业，掌握第一手素材，就极有可能找到所研究的实体存在的现实问题，提炼出解决问题的新办法、新措施和新观点。

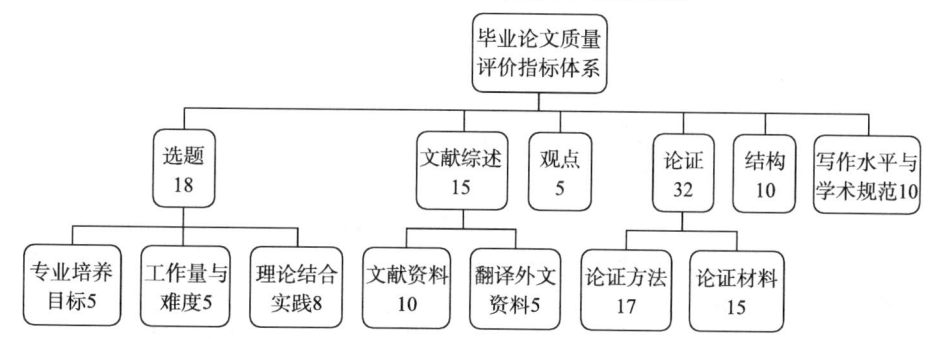

以"创新"为核心控制点的本科毕业论文指标评价体系

4.2. 保证"创新"质量控制点的指标

保证"创新"质量的指标，主要包括文献综述、论证等。

（1）论文论点"创新"保证指标——文献综述15%。文献综述可以保证学生在借鉴学习别人的研究方法和研究成果的基础上，熟悉该题目的研究前沿动态，为选题、论点的创新打下基础。一篇全面客观的文献综述，毕业论文的创新就保证实现了一半，因此这一指标赋予了15%的权重。

（2）论文本身"创新"保证指标——论证。保证学生毕业论文的创新需要严格的论证过程才能够实现，这就要求学生在论证方法及论证材料上要有所创新。论证方法的创新，即选择研究实体的样本数据，运用所掌握的专业基本理论、基本知识和基本技能分析解决相关实际问题；或者，对某一问题进行综合性表述，将某一方法应用于新的研究领域，应用不同的方法论进行交叉学科的研究。论证材料的创新，即毕业论文的创新，不但选题、观点要新颖独特，所用的材料也要能给读者以新鲜感。采取恰当的论证方法，借助新颖的论证材料，是论文论点创新的强有力佐证，应当赋予无法比拟的高权重17%和15%。

（3）论文形式"创新"保证指标——逻辑结构、学术规范与写作水平。论文的形式是指论文的逻辑结构和语言格式。在逻辑结构上，目前普遍存在的问题有：一是没有围绕选题安排论文结构，写作重点不明确或有误；二是思路混乱，结构松散，特别是写作切入点不明确，各个部分联系不紧密，层次不清晰。这样会严重制约论证的有力开展，论点的创新难以显现。在学术规范与写作水平上，保证学生能够形成基本的学术道德，尊重他人的研究成果，正确标注引用的参考文献。行文表述规范，语句通顺，标点、符号、计量单位、图表等的运用和引用均符合各国家标准规定。论文的形式是论文内容的外在表现，笔者给这两项均设计了10%的权重。

参考文献

[1] 赫连，志巍. 经管类本科毕业论文质量控制点选取与对策 [J]. 教学研究，2007 (3).
[2] 杨文超. 本科论文教学质量评价指标体系研究 [J]. 高等教育研究，2009 (1).
[3] 魏东晓，罗梅娟，党传升. 毕业设计（论文）质量监控的研究与实践 [J]. 北京邮电大学学报（社会科学版），2008 (6).

规则导向下竞技健美操成套动作艺术性的研究

范清惠

竞赛规则指导着项目的发展趋向，惟有把握住规则的导向，才能在激烈的比拼中脱颖而出。作为评分类项目，竞技健美操运动员的最后成绩由艺术分、完成分和难度分相加而成，比赛时艺术裁判员对成套动作的复杂性与创新性、空间运用的均衡性、动作连接的流畅性、音乐使用的和谐性，以及运动员的表现力等方面进行综合评判。随着规则的不断修改和完善，竞技健美操的发展愈发趋向艺术性，艺术感染力强的成套动作方能得到裁判员的青睐。本文在详细分析2009版和2013版竞技健美操评分规则的基础上，根据专家访谈，结合项目特点和发展趋势，通过录像观察，对2012年第12届健美操世界锦标赛（简称"世锦赛"）和2013年第9届世界运动会（简称"世运会"）决赛队伍的成套动作编排进行全面剖析，力求细致、深入地探寻出当前世界高水平成套动作艺术性的表现情况，以期为竞技健美操的训练实践和备战竞赛提供参考和借鉴。

1 研究对象与方法

1.1 研究对象

以规则导向下竞技健美操成套动作的艺术性为研究对象。

1.2 研究方法

1.2.1 文献资料法

查阅大量有关竞技健美操动作编排、艺术性、艺术价值的论文，研读2009版、2013版竞技健美操竞赛规则，为论文研究方法的选用及制定总体研究思路框架提供了理论依据。

1.2.2 专家访谈法

根据研究需要设计访谈提纲，采用面谈、电子邮件等方式对我国健美操领域的专家进行访谈，根据访谈结果确立本研究的基本框架。

1.2.3 录像分析法

本研究对2012年第12届健美操世界锦标赛2013年第9届世界运动会健美操比赛中男单、女单、混双、三人、集体项目决赛队伍共60套动作进行录像观察。综合分析各套动作的编排与运动员的表现，为撰写本研究提供数据支撑。

1.2.4 数理统计法

本研究在文献资料、问卷调查和录像观察的基础上，收集并整理得出的数据，最后将统计结果用SPSS软件进行分析。

2 结果与分析

竞技健美操的艺术性既涵盖了艺术家们所创作出来的形象美，还综合了运动过程中所体现出来的律动美。在成套动作中，难度动作的惊险刺激、操化动作的复杂多样、托举配合的新奇巧妙、过渡连接的流畅自然、音乐旋律的优美动听、表现自信且活力四射等，都能对观众和裁判产生视觉上的冲击，因此，美无疑是体现竞技健美操成套动作艺术性的核心。

2.1 竞技健美操竞赛规则艺术评分解析

表1显示，2013年版规则的艺术评分在2009年版规则的基础上，重新进行了拆分、组合与细化。

[作者简介] 范清惠，北京联合大学。

首先2013年版规则将成套动作的艺术评判分为"成套编排"和"表现"两大部分。其中"成套编排"的评判包括"音乐和乐感""操化内容""主体内容"和"空间运用"4项,"表现"则主要针对成套所体现出来的艺术性进行评判,总体分值未有改变,但是评判内容更加具体清晰,分值设定更加准确合理。新加入的"完成质量"和"团队协作"突出了动作规格和团队精神的重要性;操化内容新增加的"强度"以及"空间运用"涵盖的评分点对运动员的身体素质提出了更高的要求,鼓励运动员充分发挥特长优势,拉大与对手的比分;成套音乐所占的分值比重上升,强调了音乐的关键作用。可以看出,规则的变化不仅更加注重项目"难""新""美"的本质特征,同时也使评分观测点更加细化。在竞赛中,只有将以上各部分内容尽善尽美地展现,才能增加成套动作的艺术价值。

表1 2009年、2013年两版规则艺术裁判评分标准

规则版本	评分内容	分值
2009—2012	1. 动作编排（成套动作的动感与流畅性、复杂与创新性、多样性、比赛场地的有效使用和场地内所有成套动作的位置） 2. 操化内容（操化单元的多样性、操化动作的复杂与创新性、连续操化动作的数量与均衡性） 3. 表现与音乐（表现、音乐的结构、音乐的使用）	4.0（每项各1.0） 3.0（每项各1.0） 3.0（每项各1.0）
2013—2016	1. 音乐和乐感（音乐的选择、组成与结构、运用） 2. 操化内容（操化动作的复杂性/多样性、创新性、强度） 3. 主体内容（过渡/连接、托举、身体配合的复杂性/多样性、创新性、流畅性） 4. 空间运用（操化动作数量与移动路线、空间分配与均衡、队形） 5. 艺术性（完成质量、成套表现、团队协作）	2.0分 2.0分 2.0分 2.0分 2.0分

2.2 规则导向下竞技健美操成套动作的艺术展现

2.2.1 音乐的选用

竞技健美操成套动作的完成离不开音乐的伴奏,音乐给了创编者编排动作和运动员表演成套的灵感,使之更具艺术感和生命力。不同的音乐旋律可以表现出不同的风格变化,健美操动作节奏的快慢、幅度的大小变化与音乐风格相得益彰,不仅能够激发人的想象思维,体现出各种各样的情感,同时能对运动员的听觉产生刺激,帮助运动员在完成成套动作过程中表达情感、烘托气氛,与裁判和观众产生心灵上的共鸣。

音乐的选择奠定了成套动作的风格,曲调高亢、旋律激昂、元素丰富、鼓点清晰的音乐能够很好地将运动员的个性特征及整套操的技术风格展现给评委和观众;音乐节奏的变化使整套动作错落有致、高潮迭起;音乐与动作的珠联璧合能够增强成套动作的表演效果和观赏价值。因此,选择时应针对运动员的技术水平、气质特点等择优使用,过于复杂和不必要的多曲混合易产生违和感,降低成套动作的价值。

在第9届世运会上,我国5人操选用音乐《中国龙》,结合舒展大方、精巧绝伦的成套编排,将中华儿女的自信潇洒、豪迈大气展现得淋漓尽致,感染了现场裁判与观众,并以9.0的最高艺术得分夺得比赛冠军。

2.2.2 操化动作的编排

操化动作是在音乐伴奏下,运动员通过多样化的健美操手型、手臂运动形式和基本步伐呈现出优雅、干净、精确、流畅的复杂组合动作。它是竞技健美操项目的特有内容,也是成套动作最基本的组成部分。与一个乐段相配合的一个完整8拍的操化动作称之为操化单元,操化单元编排的复杂性和创新性、分布的均衡性及强度的大小对成套创编的艺术性也起着重要的影响作用。通过对比两次比赛中各单项操化动作的技术指标,可以看出目前世界优秀健美操选手操化动作的编排趋向,见表2。

表2 第12届世锦赛和第9届世运会操化单元的编排

项目	赛事	操化单元	上肢			下肢		
			不对称	对称	不对称/对称	单脚	双脚	单脚/双脚
男单	第12届世锦赛	10.18	24.3	51.10	1/2.10	32.28	47.50	1/1.47
	第9届世运会	10.28	24.32	51.40	1/2.11	35.67	49.15	1/1.38
女单	第12届世锦赛	11.621	38.75	48.90	1/1.26	46.76	55.15	1/1.18
	第9届世运会	11.525	32.25	45.75	1/1.42	42.25	56.25	1/1.33
混双	第12届世锦赛	10.224	32.04	46.50	1/1.45	37.25	44.05	1/1.18
	第9届世运会	10.08	27.25	46.85	1/1.72	37.60	45.25	1/1.20
三人	第12届世锦赛	10.50	27.98	46.10	1/1.65	36.92	46.15	1/1.25
	第9届世运会	10.35	32.25	52.80	1/1.64	37.15	45.28	1/1.22
集体	第12届世锦赛	11.45	27.4	66.68	1/2.43	32.30	58.75	1/1.82
	第9届世运会	10.58	30.27	49.75	1/1.64	29.85	50.65	1/1.70

一定数量的操化单元，能够充分反映成套动作的主题和风格，过多或过少的操化单元都会使成套动作的艺术形象大打折扣，2013年版规则要求单人项目操化单元数量至少9~11个，集体项目至少8~10个。表2数据统计显示，两次比赛中各单项操化单元的数量都达到了规则的规定，以10~11个八拍的数量居多。且操化动作的编排都能呈现多样化的上下肢动作。运动员在动感音乐的伴奏下，通过高强度、复杂化的动作展现充沛体能的同时，还能够发掘潜能、表现个性，使动作的幅度和力度得到提升，进而更好地与观众开展互动与交流。

2.2.3 过渡与连接动作的编排

过渡与连接动作可以将成套动作中的各个元素有机结合，使地面、站立、腾空三个空间之间的关系展现得淋漓尽致。尽管没有难度价值，但新颖多样的过渡与连接动作能够充分点缀成套动作的艺术美感，使内容更加丰富多彩，连接更加流畅紧凑。

如图1所示，随着规则逐渐放宽了对空翻、手翻、滚翻等违例动作的使用，成套中技巧类过渡动作的使用均值大幅提升。例如：在第12届世锦赛上，我国男单运动员黎良发采用后空翻接俯撑的新型过渡方式，将地面—站立—腾空三个空间有效串联，充分发挥了过渡动作的连贯性与流畅性。第9届世运会，中国队三人操以上步转身分腿前滚翻接水平支撑成控腿文森的过渡与连接动作，使站立与地面的过渡、操化与难度的连接显得精彩纷呈，巧妙独特的过渡与连接给成套动作烙上了鲜明的艺术性印记，最终以9.25的艺术分位居榜首。

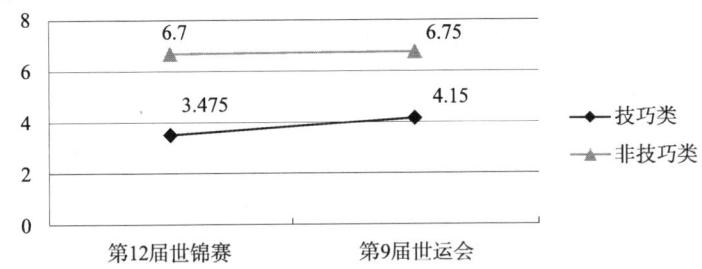

图1 第12届世锦赛和第9届世运会过渡动作类型的使用

通过录像观察还发现，比赛中连接动作的重复次数较多，缺乏一定的创新性，主要表现为起跳准备的上步、并步以及腾空落地后调整重心、填补拍节的步伐，因此连接动作还需要进一步加强编排的创新性。

2.2.4 托举动作的编排

托举动作是多人项目中的特色内容，创意十足的托举往往在成套中起到画龙点睛之效果。托举动作有多种多样的运动形式，要保证托举的完美展示，运动员之间的配合非常重要。托举可分为动力性托举、静力性托举和派生托举三大类，其中动力性托举中包括转体、翻转、劈腿和旋腿动作；静力性托举包括平衡、柔韧、造型动作；派生类托举是指静力性托举和动力性托举组合而成的复杂的托举动作，尖子运动员在完成过程中可以展示以上任何一种或多种动作的结合。

托举动作的新式编排能够展现出成套动作别具一格的风格立意。2013年版规则将成套动作中托举的数量从3次减为2次，数量的减少对托举动作编排的复杂性和创新性有了更高标准的要求。从表3可以看出，两次比赛的托举动作类型主要以翻转和转体居多，特别是第9届世运会，所有的托举中都运用了翻转类动作。托举动作的复杂多样要求尖子运动员不仅要体现出运动轴面和动作形式的变化，还要表现出身体姿态的准确优美。因此，编排时应充分发挥托举动作的装饰与点缀作用，将技巧动作和层次设计相结合，为增加动作艺术性注入能量。

表3 第12届世锦赛与第9届世运会集体项目艺术分第一名队伍托举动作类型

赛事	项目	托举1	托举2	托举3
第12届世锦赛	混双	翻转类+劈腿类	转体类+造型类+平衡类	转体类+翻转类
	三人	翻转类	转体类+造型类	旋腿类+造型类
	六人	转体类	造型类+转体类	翻转类+平衡类
第9届世运会	混双	平衡类+劈腿类+翻转类	旋腿类+翻转类+劈腿类	
	三人	翻转类+劈腿类	翻转类	
	五人	翻转类	旋腿类+翻转类	

2.2.5 场地空间的运用

2.2.5.1 垂直空间的运用

在完成竞技健美操成套动作中，有效利用地面（A）、站立（B）、腾空（C）三个垂直空间的转换，使成套动作的各部分内容流畅衔接并形成跌宕起伏的空间变化。成套中可进行垂直空间转换的动作主要是难度动作和过渡动作，根据录像观察，结合实际应用的可行性，将常用的垂直空间转换类型分为A-B、B-A、B-A-B、B-C-B、B-C-A 5种。

从录像统计结果可以看出，两次比赛中A-B和B-C-B两种类型的应用率相对高于他类型的应用，在个别套路中还出现了A-C-B、B-C-A-B的转换类型，见表4。丰富多变的垂直空间变化，不仅展现了成套动作的多样立体构图，也充分反映出空间过渡的惊险性和复杂性，增强了成套动作的视觉冲击，为提高艺术得分奠定了基础。

表4 第12届世锦赛和第9届世运会垂直空间运用

	A-B	B-A	B-A-B	B-C-B	B-C-A	总计
第12届世锦赛	3.8	2.46	0.78	4.2	1.88	13.12
百分比%	28.96	18.75	5.94	32.01	14.32	100
第9届世运会	3.65	2.82	1.18	4.16	2.06	13.87
百分比	26.32	20.32	8.51	30	14.85	100

2.2.5.2 队形的变化

队形变化是集体项目编排中不可缺少的主要内容，它包括搭档之间的位置，以及改变位置到另一个队形或者保持队形的方式，最能显示出平面空间的构图。

竞技健美操规则规定成套动作必须展现6个以上不同队形，队形移动的路线既要便于动作的连接和展示，还要体现运动员之间的互动关系。通过录像观察发现，两次比赛中集体项目的成套队形运用均值都在15次以上，第9届世运会的队形变化明显高于第12届世锦赛，见表5。队形的变化不仅要跟成套动作的设计巧妙结合，又要在视觉上满足裁判与观众对美的追求，恰到好处地将音乐、动作和时空融为一体，获得完美的艺术效果。

表 5 第 12 届世锦赛和第 9 届世运会集体项目成套队形运用

队形类别	第 12 届世锦赛	第 9 届世运会	总计
竖线形	1.02	1.79	2.81
横线形	1.91	2.16	4.07
斜线形	1.59	1.64	3.23
三角形	3.84	4.04	7.88
四边形	3.17	3.30	6.47
圆形	1.72	1.41	3.13
不规则形	1.84	2.54	4.38
总计	15.12	16.88	32.00

2.2.6 运动员表现力的展示

竞技健美操规则中明确指出，运动员的表现力主要体现在：运动员通过自然和欢乐的面部表情来表现自信，运用准确而娴熟的动作完成展示自己的体能和活力，突出个人气质美和技术风格美，使成套完成更具观赏价值。此外，始终与裁判和观众保持互动，在集体项目中，还要考虑同伴间的眼神交流与身体配合。

世界优秀运动员对成套动作主题的理解、情绪的把握和气氛的营造等越来越趋于"精致和准确"。在第 12 届世锦赛三人操决赛中，韩国队三名男子运动员的表现可谓是独树一帜，巧妙的成套编排和滑稽的成套表现在音乐的伴奏下越发显得亲切自然、逗趣横生，使成套动作更具表演性。最终，韩国队在难度分和完成分相对落后的形势下，凭借极具感染力的表演夺得了 9.10 的最高艺术分，缩小了与对手的总体分差，同中国队一起登上了冠军领奖台。

竞技健美操的艺术美建立在成套动作准确、稳定完成的基础上，是一种综合的表现。在成套动作的完成中，要使运动员达到"美"的最高标准，就必须不断提高运动员的技术规格和完成质量，在此基础上再进行成套动作编排的精雕细琢，才能在视觉、听觉、感觉上让裁判和观众体会到美的全方位享受。

2.3 竞技健美操成套动作艺术性的发展趋势

2.3.1 美中有新，凸显特点

美与新反映着成套动作的魅力和活力，是体现难美性项目竞技性和艺术性的必经之路，也是竞技健美操动作编排的趋势之一。一套动作中若包含了美与新，基本上已经事半功倍，"美"能够体现成套动作的艺术性，"新"能够促进技术技巧的发展。惟有融入美与新的成套动作，才能体现出竞技健美操的特点与价值。

2.3.2 难险结合，完美完成

2013 年版规则放宽了对技巧动作和一些违例动作的使用，丰富了成套编排的元素，大幅提升了这些动作的利用率；难度分值和根命组的调整，促使运动员继续向着高分值难度动作发起挑战；空间运用评分的细化，也更加突出了垂直空间有效运用的重要性。规则的变革和发展使成套动作的编排更加高难化和惊险化。竞技健美操的编排是一个艺术性、灵活性和战术性的创造过程，"美"最终通过运动员的高规格完成来体现，以达到整体的完美统一，更好地展示成套动作的艺术风采。

2.3.3 切合主题，形成风格

音乐的选用与动作的编排决定了竞技健美操成套动作的主题和风格，不同音乐主题能够反映出不同的艺术情境，而切合主题的动作编排可以赋予成套动作更丰富的故事情节，使之更具表演价值和吸引力。根据运动员的性格和气质特点，为其量身打造与之相吻合的成套动作，有利于运动员更完美地抒发情感、诠释内容，使成套动作艺术美的表现无懈可击。

2.3.4 展现优势，发挥特长

一名运动员或一支运动队是否具有突出的特长技术，是衡量其能否跻身高水平运动队行列的标志之一。作为技能主导类表现难美性的项目，竞技健美操不仅要求运动员具备高超的全面技术，还要具有精湛的特长技术。成套的编排应在充分考虑运动员竞技能力的基础上，突出运动员的个性化技术，形成独特的技术风格，将艺术魅力发挥到极致。

3 结论与建议

3.1 结论

（1）2013年版竞技健美操规则艺术评分内容在2009年版规则的基础上，重新进行了拆分、组合与细化，更加注重了项目的本质特征，同时也使评分观测点更加客观和具体。在竞赛中，只有将各部分内容完美地展现，才能使成套动作更具艺术价值。

（2）竞技健美操成套动作的艺术性体现在音乐旋律的动感激昂、操化动作的复杂多样、过渡连接的新颖流畅、托举配合的灵巧美妙、空间运用的自然均衡和表现力的自信热情。成套内容的艺术美建立在各部分内容准确、稳定、高规格完成的基础上，是一种综合的表现。

（3）竞技健美操成套动作艺术性的发展趋势主要包括：美中有新，凸显特点；难险结合，完美完成；切合主题，突出风格；展现优势，发挥特长。

3.2 建议

（1）教练员和运动员应加强自身的艺术修养，注重对各类元素的收集，创编出具有复杂性、新颖性和多样性的成套内容，进一步培养和激发运动员良好的艺术表现力，增加成套动作的艺术效果和观赏价值。

（2）在训练过程中，不仅要巩固和提高运动员的全面技术，还应对运动员的特长技术进一步加以改善和强化，使成套动作通过运动员优势技能的精湛演绎，在赛场上发挥出与众不同的特点和内涵。

参考文献

[1] 2009-2012年竞技健美操竞赛规则[S]. 国际体操联合会.
[2] 2013-2016年竞技健美操竞赛规则[S]. 国际体操联合会.
[3] 李育林,陈敏. 新周期我国竞技健美操成套编排的艺术价值研究[J]. 体育与科学, 2009, 30(6): 53-56.
[4] 查春华,杨建国. 第11届世界健美操锦标赛男子单人项目过渡与连接动作编排分析[J]. 中国体育科技. 2011, 47(5): 25-30.
[5] 周建社,张利芳. 竞技健美操托举与配合动作的创新性[J]. 北京体育大学学报. 2010, 33(2): 129-131.
[6] 张晓莹等. 竞技健美操难度动作制胜因素的研究[J]. 北京体育大学学报. 2013, 36(5): 117-122.

专业化发展视域下的职教教师职业核心能力培养路径

徐英俊

《国家中长期教育改革和发展规划纲要（2010—2020）》进一步明确了未来十年我国教师队伍建设的目标和方向，其核心是"努力造就一支师德高尚、业务精湛、结构合理、充满活力的高素质专业化教师队伍"，[1]这是对我国各级各类学校教师队伍建设提出的目标要求，从国家层面"首次明确提出了建设'高素质专业化教师队伍'的目标要求"。[2]对于职教教师而言，职业核心能力的不断提升则是获得专业发展的必由之路。

1 职教教师专业化与专业发展的内涵

1.1 教师专业化与专业发展

一般认为，教师专业化（teacher professionalization）是职业专业化的一种类型，是指"教师在整个专业生涯中，通过终身专业训练，习得教育专业知识和技能，实施专业自主，表现专业道德，并逐步提高自身从教素质，成为一个良好的教育专业工作者的专业成长过程"。[3]教师专业化包括"五化"：学科专业知识和技能的专业化、专业自主发展的专业化、专业道德的专业化、教育科学素养的专业化和教师专业发展的动态化。教师专业发展（professional development of teachers）是教师专业化发展的核心内容，一般是指"教师的专业成长或教师内在专业结构不断更新、演进和丰富的过程"。[4]有学者指出，教师专业化更多是从社会学角度加以考虑的，主要强调教师群体的、外在的专业性的提升；教师专业发展更多是从教育学维度加以界定的，主要指教师个体的、内在的、专业性的提高。[5]教师专业化在本质上强调了教师群体的成长和发展的历程；教师专业发展在本质上强调了教师个体的成长和发展的历程。

1.2 职教教师专业化与专业发展

我国职教教师专业化除具有教师专业化的一般特征外，还具有自身的特殊性。因此，职教教师专业化一般是指，"以专业标准为依据，通过一定的措施和手段促使职业教育教师从非专业人员或半专业人员转变为专业人员的过程"。[6]有学者从职教教师应具备的特点方面阐述了职教教师专业化的内涵，职教教师"在学科专业方面，具有扎实的专业基础和专业知识。在专业技能运用方面，具有丰富的实践经验，掌握专业领域的研究方法。在教育理论方面，掌握一般的教育理论和职业教育理论，掌握有效教学的技艺，具有较强的教育教学能力。在职业领域，掌握岗位所要求的知识和实践经验，具有专业资格等"。[7]也有学者从职教教师应具备的能力方面阐述了职教教师专业化的内涵，职教教师"能从教育学角度将专业知识融入教学的能力，具有丰富的实践经验和熟练的专业技能，课程开发的能力，职业指导和创业教育的能力，具有教育理论知识，具备科学研究的能力"。[8]职教教师专业发展是职教教师专业化发展的核心内容，一般是指职教教师个体在专业成长过程中，其专业知能、专业经验、职教素养、专业品质和专业自主等方面不断改善、推进和提升的过程。职教教师专业发展包括：专业知识与专业技能的发展、专业实践经验的发展、职业教育科学素养的发展、专业品质的形成与发展和专业自主发展。同样，

[基金项目] 北京市教育科学"十一五"规划2010年度课题"中职师资职业核心能力职前培养策略研究"（编号：DEB10139），主持人：徐英俊。

[作者简介] 徐英俊（1955—），男，北京联合大学师范学院职教研究所所长，北京联合大学教师教育研究所所长，教授。研究方向为职教教师教育。

职教教师专业化也是强调职教教师群体整体的专业性的提升,职教教师专业发展则强调了职教教师个体的专业性的提高。

职教教师在群体的专业化发展过程中,通过自身积极主动的发展,必然会促进和提升其专业发展水平。但仅仅依赖外部群体的发展欲获得自身的专业发展还不够,因群体的发展仅仅为其专业发展提供了良好的外部环境,缺乏专业发展的主动性,必然滞缓其专业发展的速度和进程。由此可见,专业发展的主动性是职教教师专业发展的核心。因此,职教教师必须发挥自身的积极性、主动性,从提升职教教师的职业核心能力入手,以期在专业发展的历程中,提升专业发展的水平和速度,获得良好的专业发展。

2 职教教师职业核心能力的含义与结构

2.1 职教教师职业核心能力的含义

职业核心能力(the professional core competence)是指,在职业院校里,从事专业课教学的教师,经过职前培养和职后培训,在教学实践活动过程中,有效地进行教学活动,顺利地完成专业教学任务所应具备的专业教学能力、实践教学能力及教育教学能力的一种综合教学能力。这一概念包括三层含义,第一,指出了职业核心能力的三个构成要素,即专业教学能力、实践教学能力和教育教学能力;第二,明确了职业核心能力的形成与发展的两条路径,即职前培养和职后培训;第三,强调了职业核心能力的形成与发展所依赖的一项主要活动,即教学实践活动。三种教学能力的不断提升,才能有效地形成职教教师的职业核心能力,而职业核心能力形成,才能使其满足教学需要,胜任教学工作,完成教学任务,提高教育教学质量。

2.2 职教教师职业核心能力的结构

作为职教教师应具备教师的基本素质与能力,这些素质与能力主要包括:专业教学能力,是指专业课教师运用专业教学方法,采取专业教学手段,指导学生学习和掌握专业理论知识,顺利完成专业教学任务的一种基本教学能力。实践教学能力,是指专业课教师能够完成实验、实习实训、毕业综合实习以及社会实践、社会调查、课外科技活动等实践教学环节任务的一种基本教学能力。教育教学能力,是指专业课教师所应具备的教学设计能力(前期分析能力和教学过程设计能力)、课堂教学能力(教学表达能力、教学组织能力、教学管理能力和教学应变能力)、教学评价能力和班级管理能力等基本教学能力。专业教学能力的形成与发展,可以有效地提升实践教学能力;实践教学能力的形成与发展,反过来可以促进专业教学能力的发展,两者相辅相成、相互促进。而教育教学能力则为专业教学能力和实践教学能力的形成与发展提供了有效的支撑。三者之间的关系如图1所示。

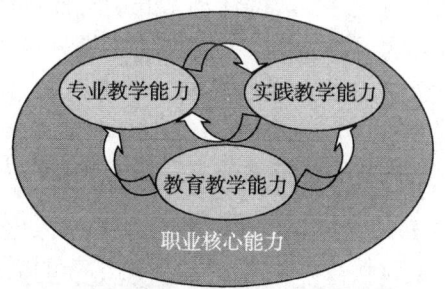

图1 专业、实践、教育教学能力关系图

3 职教教师职业核心能力的培养路径

3.1 专业教学能力培养的路径

从职前培养上看,首先,奠定专业理论教学能力的基础。从七个方面入手:一是对课程内容进行更新和增减,对分量做微调;二是要以掌握基本概念、原理为重点,以应用原理强化专业理论为目标;三是以教学目标分类理论设计教学目标;四是精心设计教学内容,把握教学重点和难点;五是适当适时采用中职学校常用的教学方法；六是精心选用教学媒体；七是采用互动式的教学方式。其次，奠定专业技能教学能力的基础。从三个方面入手：一是通过模拟演示，在观察中巩固理论知识；二是教师进行过程示范，操作应具有示范性、规范性，边操作边讲解或边讲解边操作，做到过程分解，讲清楚每一个操作要领，使其充分看清每一个操作步骤，为模仿操作练习打下基础；三是教师在教学过程中，采取互动式的教学方式与教学组织形式。再次，掌握基本的专业教学法。应在专业教学实践中，根据教学内容的特点，采用案例、模拟、项目、模块、角色扮演和行为导向教学法等，以明确做出运用这些教学方法的示范，以便其深度理解和掌握专业教学常用的教学方法。

从职后培训上看，首先，不断提升专业理论教学能力。通过各级研修培训、学术交流、项目资助、进修学习、自我钻研等方式，不断更新专业理论知识，同时通过企业实践活动获得本专业的新知识。在教学设计过程中更新专业理论知识，充实和完善教学设计方案。在理论教学实践中应用所掌握的新知识，以提升专业理论教学能力。其次，不断提升专业技能教学能力。同样，也应通过上述职后培训和企业实践的方式，学习和掌握本专业新技术，并在教学实践中有效应用。再次，不断提升专业教学法掌握水平。通过开展校本专业教研，在教学设计、听课、说课、讲课、评课、反思等教研活动中，不断提升专业教学法掌握水平。值得一提的是，应在职业院校建立微格实训室，对教师特别是对青年教师进行微格教学实训，可以有效地提升其专业教学能力。

3.2 实践教学能力培养的路径

从职前培养上看，首先，职教师资培养院校应完善职教师资实践教学能力培养体系。各职教师资培养院校不仅有理论教学体系，更有实践教学体系。应根据职业教育发展和中职学校对教师提出的新要求、新标准，不断完善职教师资实践教学能力培养体系。从基本职业能力、专业能力、综合能力等职教教师所需能力层次方面，设计以培养实验教学能力、实习实训教学能力、社会实践教学能力为目标的模块化的实践教学课程体系，以期在职前培养阶段初步形成实践教学能力。其次，采取多种途径实施实践教学能力培养体系。如与中职学校、企业建立共建共管的实践教学基地，搭建学院、中职学校和企业参与的实践教学平台；实施实验课微格教学实训，提升实验课教学能力；实施自主创新实践计划等科技活动，提高实践能力；依托实践教学基地平台，建立职业证书培训基地和学生实验、教师科研、专业技术取证为三位一体的技研中心和培训基地等。

从职后培训上看，首先，应通过校内实践教学环节提高实践教学能力。一是在专业实验室、实训室（中心）进行实验教学和实训之前，熟练使用本专业各种实验仪器设备，特别是熟练使用新仪器、新设备，掌握新工艺、新流程。只有熟练使用各种实验仪器设备，掌握新工艺、新流程，才能在实践教学中有效地应用。二是要利用微格实训室对教师的实验课进行微格教学实训，以提升实验课教学能力和水平。其次，积极参加课外科技活动和组织社会实践活动，开展科技活动和组织社会实践活动也是实践教学的重要组成部分。再次，通过校外实习教学环节和企业实践提高实践教学能力。带领学生在生产、管理和服务第一线进行校外实习，不仅单纯是完成实习教学工作任务，也能使教师获得鲜活的实践经验，这种实践经验有利于提升实践教学能力。特别是要通过本专业企业实践之机，学习岗位知识和专业知识，掌握专业技能和技术。同时尽早取得职业资格证书及技术证书。

3.3 教育教学能力培养的路径

从职前培养上看，首先，应根据职教教师对于职教理论素养的需求，把职教理论课程（职业教育学、职业教育心理学）整合设计成有机联系的、模块化的课程体系。这些模块主要是课程论、教学论、学习论、教学设计、教学评价模块、学生与教师和班级管理模块。模块化的职教理论内容体系反映了职教教师对职业教育理论的实际需求，体现了内容的实用性特点，突出了理论的指导性和技术的可操作性。其次，改善职教理论课程微格教学实训的环节与内容，强化教育教学实习环节。一是加强微格教学实训的设计和组织。教师编写《微格教学实训指导手册》，设计《微格教学实训教案》和《微格教学实训评价表》；受训者编写《微格教学实训教案》。优选微格教学实训内容，抽取其核心的单项教学技能加以训练，设计模拟课堂教学综合技能训练。二是强化教育教学实习环节，在职教教师指导下从事兼职班主任工作、听课、备课、说课、讲课等。形成以职教理论学习为先导，以校内微格实训为基础，以校外教育教学实习为重点的"三位一体"的职教理论素养和教育教学能力提升模式，如图2所示。

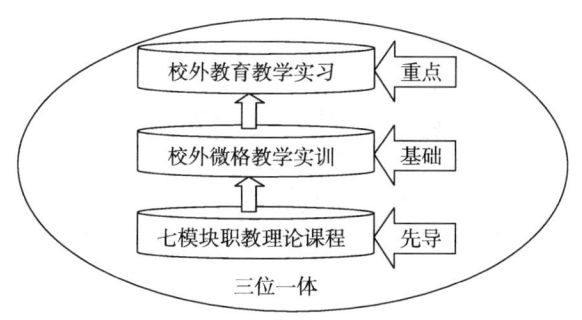

图2 "三位一体"教育教学能力提升模式

从职后培训上看，首先，加强现代教育理论，特别是现代职教理论的学习和应用。应通过各级各类研修培训、学术交流、项目资助、进修学习、自我钻研等方式，不断学习、吸收现代教育理论和现代职教理论，提高掌握程度和应用水平。在现代教育理论中，应重点学习对教师指导性较强的、便于应用于教学实践的理论，如教学设计、教学策略、教学模式、教学艺术等理论。在现代职教理论中，应重点学习"三论"：职业教育课程论、教学论、学习论。其次，在教学实践过程中，应采取教学反思、同行切磋、自我钻研、教学观摩等方式，以提升实际的教育教学能力。并通过教学实践、进修学习、校本培训等途径，特别是要通过教学实践这一主途径，提高自己的教育教学能力。再次，提高教学组织能力。无论是课堂教学，还是实践教学，只有在较好的教学环境中，才能取得良好的教学效果。因此，职教教师应在教学过程中，把所掌握的教育理论有效地运用于教学管理实践中，为有效教学提供良好的教学环境。

参考文献

[1] 中共中央国务院. 国家中长期教育改革和发展规划纲要（2010－2020）[M]. 北京：人民出版社，2010：51.
[2] 《教育规划纲要》工作小组办公室. 教育规划纲要辅导读本[M]. 北京：教育科学出版社，2010：175.
[3][5] 教育部师范司. 教师专业化的理论与实践[M]. 北京：人民教育出版社，2003：11，46.
[4] 叶澜，等. 教师角色与教师发展新探[M]. 北京：教育科学出版社，2001：226.
[6] 邵艾群，刘阳. 对职业教育教师专业化内涵的思考[J]. 成人教育，2008（2）：52.
[7] 朱新生，施步洲，庄西真，等. 职教教师专业化内涵及培养体系构建[J]. 职业技术教育，2011（4）：50.
[8] 史红玲. 关于职业教育教师专业化发展的几点思考[J]. 华章，2011（22）：204.

传承、借鉴和发展

——基于学生工作管理的中外比较分析

唐少清

商务学院经过32年的发展，先后经历了更名转型和国际化跨越式发展的两个重要阶段，提出了培养应用性国际商务人才、建立高水平、有特色的精品学院的目标，面向"十二五"，将面对新的挑战和新的任务，学生工作管理将在传承和借鉴的基础上创新发展。本文在主要借鉴美国、英国、港澳地区学生事务管理的理论与方法的基础上，兼顾日本、韩国[1]、澳大利亚[2][3]的经验与做法，提出商务学院自己的创新发展。

1 商务学院学生工作管理历史沿革与文化传承

2000年，根据学生特点和社会要求，学院提出了以学生为本的"强化管理"教育模式，经过近12年的实际运行，已经逐步形成了惯例。这种理念的提出是基于以下四个方面考虑：第一、适应北京率先实现高等教育普及化的要求；第二、依据学生心理需求。学院学生身上存在的明显特征；第三、顺应新生家长的呼声。学生家长对我们的教育教学管理也寄予了极大的希望，希望学生能够成长为"心性好、灵性高、作用大"的人。从每年新生家长问卷调查和统计分析中发现，家长对学生的综合素质得到提升最为看重（85.7%），并且把始终能够保持积极进取的心（74.3%），与搞好专业学习（74%）放在同等重要的位置。在课业学习方面，77.7%的家长认为掌握英语学习和沟通能力是在校学习的重要部分，在能力培养上，家长认为学生的自立能力、学习能力、交往能力是最需要发展的三个方面。对于学生的在校学习，91.7%的家长对于我院的强化管理的制度比较满意，期望严格记录考勤，加强对早晚自习的管理。第四、来自毕业生的反馈。经过校友会和各种毕业生座谈会的调查反馈，学生们一致认可：强化管理给他们带来的良好后续效果，即：学习习惯养成、遵守纪律、坚持普通而平凡的工作。

大学生养成教育是指以高校为主体，在家庭、社会的配合下，根据大学生的身心形成和发展规律，运用各种途径和手段，对大学生施加系统影响，促使其养成文明的习惯和走向社会后应具备的各种能力。强化管理作为大学生养成教育的有效实施模式，主要在强化班级基本建设、强化学生的基本行为习惯、强化英语等基础课程学习、强化基本实践能力培养等四个方面开展工作，对学生进行规范教育、纠偏教育和陶冶教育，践行养成教育理念，凝炼了"四个强化"体系，即：强化班级建设、强化行为习惯养成、强化基础课程学习、强化实践能力培养。

2 国外学生工作管理比较分析

美国高等教育[5]起步较早、发展较快，与之相对应的是，美国高校学生事务管理在历经200余年发展历史后，已经成为专业化程度很高的职业。科学地教育管理、有效地管理是高校学生管理[6]提高工作效率的关键所在。英国学者帕金说："大学对一切都进行研究，唯独不研究它们自己。"此话提醒了我们，要重视自身问题的研究，积极研究新时期高校学生管理的科学化问题，实现高校学生管理制度化、规范化、科学化，是我国高校学生管理发展的必然趋势。

2.1 美国学生工作管理分析

在美国，学生工作[7]被称为"学生事务"（Student Affairs）或"学生服务"（Students Services）。若以

[作者简介] 唐少清（1965—），男，管理学博士，教授，北京联合大学商务学院党委副书记，中国软科学研究会个人会员，河北大学经济学院硕士生导师。研究方向：企业战略管理、项目评估与管理、教育管理、第三产业、事件管理、学生管理。

高校出现专门负责学生事务的学校领导为标志的话,美国高校学生工作至今已有近120年的历史,可以分成初始期、发展期、成熟期三个阶段。但是景发[8]撰文认为,美国学生事务工作发展可以概括为五个阶段:产生及发展初期(1636—1850年)、多样化时期(1850—1900年)、职业化初期(1900—1945年)、发展期(1945—1985年)、稳定期(1985—)。

美国高校学生工作的育人理念大致可以概括为三句话:一是关注每一个学生,二是挖掘每一个学生的潜力,三是对学生进行"全人教育(主要指促进学生德、智、体、美、群、情、事等7个领域的综合素质的发展)。

2.1.1 美国学生工作的历史进展

(1)初始期(1890's—1920's)。关于学生事务的起源,有人认为学生事务开始于雅典高等教育,也有人认为始于中世纪的大学。然而,学生事务在某种程度上讲是一个美国高等教育的现象,它始于19世纪末,发展于20世纪初期,成熟于20世纪60年代。

在美国高校主管学生工作的男、女院长(Dean)的出现是学生事务领域开始的标志。时至今日,这几个来源发展成颇有影响的三个职业协会组织:全国学生工作者管理协会、美国的大学学生管理协会、全国教育妇女协会。

美国第一位主管学生的院长是哈佛大学的李巴伦·布里格斯(Lebaron Russell Briggs),被任命于1890年;伊利诺依大学的克拉克(Thonias Arkle Clark)是第一位拥有"男院长"(主管男大学生学生工作的)头衔的大学管理者;而"女院长"(主管女大学生工作的)始于1892年的芝加哥大学,首位院长为爱丽丝·帕尔门(Alice Freeman Palmen)。

关注学生需要是导致学生事务领域出现和发展的最主要条件。当时没有人知道应该做什么,如何做,但只是存在为学生服务这种需要。因此,全国学生工作者管理协会(NASPA)的诞生了。

(2)发展期(1920's—1960's),从20世纪20年代到60年代是美国学生事务大发展的时期。在这一时期,全国学生工作者管理协会发表了标志性的文件《学生事务人员的价值观点》(1937),这个报告对于学生事务领域而言是一个奠基式的文件。这一文件中的核心哲学理念认为:高等教育基本目的之一是保留、传授、丰富重要的文化要素;学术,研究,创造性联想,人类经验的产品。实现这一目的和帮助学生发展其潜能,使其更好地为社会做出贡献,正是大学和学院的任务。

这一哲学理念给教育机构赋予了把学生作为一个整体来考虑的义务——他的智力、能力和成就,他的情感构成,他的体育,他的社会关系,他的职业态度和技能,他的道德和宗教价值观,他的经济资源,他的审美能力。简言而之,它把重点放在学生作为一个人的发展之上而不是仅仅放在智力训练上。文件中指出学生事务人员应具备以下信念:

- 相信个人的价值;人的价值最重要,共同利益只有通过帮助每个人按其所能发展到最好才能得到促进。

- 相信平等思想,感觉工作的尊严,这些方面是不可分割的。学生工作人员应致力于学生的整个人而并不仅仅致力于其智力或经济生产力或其他方面。

- 相信世界给每个人都有一个容身之地,社会世界一席之地,家庭生活一席之地,职业世界一席之地。教育的任务并不只是给青年发个邀请,而是根据其需要仔细设计积极的刺激帮助他成长,以适应各种角色。激励和丰富的环境为探索(他是谁,他是什么)提供机会,为将其从青年生活转变成有效的社会生活完成发展任务。

- 相信一个人从其经历的人生所进行的积累会继续;这种积累不是强加的,而是吸收的,将长期存在。学生工作人员应该这样观察人——不是作为一个单位独立于过去和未来时刻,而是一个由婴儿到未来持续不断连续体的一个过渡点;他们坚信每个人都能从依靠逐步走向独立,从兴趣到责任,从自我到社会行为。

《学生事务人员的价值观点》是美国高校学生事务领域的一个重要文件,它正确地预见了"学生事务人员"将会加入商业事务和学术事务,并作为学院和大学主要部门。

学生事务发展的另一个标志是岗位定义清晰。学生事务人员工作是由其所从事的所有活动构成,也即除了课程教学之外的涉及学生个人发展的所有活动是其根本的关注点。院长是学校管理中的办公人员,通过学生工作人员的努力,通过组织动员学校的一切力量,帮助学生到达其个人能发展的最高点。

(3)成熟期(1960's—1990's),随着学生事务的人员、职能不断发展,美国高校学生事务的工作内容也得到有关部门的认可。1966年美国教育、健康、福利部确认了高校学生服务管理的职能是:招生、入学、非学术记录、咨询、纪律、测试、财政资助、外国留学、幼儿园服务、医疗服务、住宿、已结婚学生住宿、就业、学生社团、学生活动、体育、宗教等17项工作。

一个行业是否成熟的重要标志在于其是否职业化。在美国,学生事务成为一个职业已是事实,至少在实践上是如此。从事学生事务的人员必须具备所要求的职业态度、职业实践能力和职业行为。经过120多年的发展演变,学生事务已成为一个大学中的职业——一个承担着涉及学生学术、心理和法律问题等评估的职业。学生事务职业人员不断地增强在与教师建立合作伙伴关系中促进学生成长成才。

一个职业是否成熟,其重要特点或重要标志是标准化。在美国大学,学生工作经历了百年历史,其标准化程度已达到较高水平。GAS(标准提高协会)就学生事务于1988年专门制定了标准,标准分一般标准与部门标准,共有13个部分,它们是:使命、项目、领导与管理、组织与行政、人力资源、资金筹措、设施、法律责任、机会平等、校园与社会关系、多元文化项目与服务、伦理、评价。

美国高校学生工作产生于现实需要,发展于高等教育大众化阶段,成熟于百年积累。经历了一个从无到有,从幼稚到成熟,从定位模糊到职责明确,已成为一个职能多样化,工作标准化,人员职业化,研究学术化,理论综合化,运行高级性的专业领域。经过近130年的风风雨雨,其中学生工作由单一的价值教育发展为价值教育、宗教灌输、心理咨询、就业指导、各种针对性的项目培训、实践活动等综合服务学生的行业。从业人员以此为终身职业。

2.1.2 美国大学生事务管理特点分析

美国在校大学生的全部活动基本分为两类:学术事务和学生事务。学术事务涉及学生学习、课程、课堂及认知发展等,而学生事务则涉及学术指导和后勤服务,如课外活动、食宿、学习资源、各种咨询,并呈现如下特点[9]。

(1)法治化和规范化

美国高校学生管理注重法治化,依照政府法律、法规调整学校与学生之间的关系,在管理规章制度的制定与执行上实现规范化和合法化。美国有完备的高等教育法,如国防教育法(1958)和《2000年目标:美国教育法》(1993),及健全的高校学生管理工作方面的专门性法律、工作规范和规章制度,如《美国高等学校学生事务管理人员行为规范》《美国高等学校学生事务管理人员伦理标准》《学生事务应用手册》《学生服务手册》。各高校遵照联邦政府及州政府法律,依据本校实际情况制定学生事务的规章制度,并以此来规范学生的行为,行使有效的管理。

(2)系统化和专业化

美国学生事务管理系统几乎囊括了学生的非学术性事务,采取垂直化的一级管理体制,由学校一级来设置机构和划分权限,而不在院、系设置学生事务管理机构或组织。根据不同的学生事务,成立校一级的职能部门或中心,以条状管理的工作方式,直接面向学生开展工作。

历经"替代父母制""学生人事工作""学生服务""学生发展",在20世纪末随着学生发展理论的实施,以及职业道德和标准的不断推陈出新,美国大学生事务已步入专业化管理时代,管理人员的角色也随之演变成服务者、教育者、研究者。因此,从事学生事务管理的工作人员需具有领导学、教育学、心理学、医学、法学、咨询学和学生事务等领域的硕士学位,中层管理职位则需拥有相关领域的博士学位。同时,各高校还加大对管理人员的评估力度,从人事处理、领导能力、接触学生、人际传媒、财务管理、专业发展、研究与评估等方面对相关人员进行定期的考评。

(3)人性化和自主化

美国的学生事务管理工作从形成、发展到成熟,始终坚持以学生为本的原则。"一切为了学生,为了学生的一切,为了一切学生"不是口号,而是落实在各项工作中。工作思路为"管理就是服务",工作目标为以服务促发展。关系理顺,学生事务工作的责、权、利更加明确,各部门就齐心协力、全心全意为学生的学习、生活、身心成长与发展着想,竭力提供优质的后勤保障和服务,创设良好的校园环境和和谐氛围来促进学生的学习和全面发展。美国大学生事务管理工作的成功之处正是以其专业化和人性化服务来实现大学生事务管理工作的所有任务和目标。

2.1.3 美国学生管理体制与模式

美国的所有高校都设有一名专管学生事务的副校长，其下设有学生事务处。根据学校的规模、专业设置、学生来源及学生工作智能，在学生事务处下再设立学习中心、宿舍管理办公室、学生活动中心、学生发展中心、国际学生服务部等。

学生事务处统管学校的学生工作，直接向分管副校长负责。学生事务处的职能主要有拟定下属各部门的工作权限、检查监督和协调部门工作、拟定实施学生管理制度，以及向潜在学生介绍学校情况等。学习中心是服务咨询机构，规模可以是一个或由几十人组成的专门机构，其办公地点可以是一栋楼房或者一间办公室。宿舍管理办公室是负责分配和管理学生公寓的机构，主要是给学生提供必要的生活娱乐设施和服务。学生活动中心的主要功能是为学生组织和提供良好的业余文化娱乐活动。学生发展中心主要设有两个部门，一是劳动就业部，主要负责给学生介绍在校内各部门的兼职工作，也为学生假期及在校外谋职牵线搭桥。二是资助部，主要任务是向学生提供各类奖学金、贷款和补助。

2.1.4 美国高校学生工作的挑战和启示

学生结构的多样化、校园文化的多元化以及"每个学生都是一个非常独特的个体"认知，要求学生事务更加多样化、个性化和专业化；美国经济状况恶化，教育开支缩减，高校办学经费减少，对学生事务在资源减少情况下的投入—产出效益提出了新要求；科技的发展、远程化教育模式的兴起，使学生的学习、生活方式发生了变化，对学生事务管理方法手段的更新和学生事务管理的有效性提出了新的要求。

另外，美国国情下的种族问题、同性恋、双性恋、变性人问题、宗教信仰冲突等问题一直以来都是学生工作者必须应对的挑战。

（1）以学生为本，切实提高服务学生的意识和水平

以学生为本，需要我们切实树立服务学生的意识，一切为了学生，将学生的成长放在第一位，对学生有求必应，有忙必帮，尽力为学生排忧解难；需要我们在工作岗位上准确定位，以服务为主，避免以纯粹的教育者、管理者的身份出现，要及时掌握学生的情况、特点、需求，及时提供必要的辅导，有的放矢地开展工作；需要我们不断简化工作程序，拓宽服务渠道，丰富服务内容，提高服务水平，从新生入学教育到毕业生就业各方面的工作上均为学生提供高效的服务。

（2）建立学生工作的专家队伍

未来社会分工愈来愈细，专业化的要求愈来愈高。就像高等教育需要专家、学者一样，学生工作也必须建立自己的专家队伍。目前，我国高校学生工作人员不安心、不专心、不专业的问题没有得到根本地解决，队伍现状未能很好地适应高等教育的发展。为了彻底扭转这一现状，进一步提高学生工作人员的待遇和地位，完善学生工作专业化、终身化的制度，建立学生服务、教育与管理专业学科，培养学生工作的专门人才。只有这样，学生工作队伍才能真正成为大学里不登讲台的教授、专家，学生工作专业化、科学化和规范化才能成为可能，建立具有国际水准的高校学生工作体系的目标才能实现。

（3）建立一套完整、科学、操作性强的学生工作法规

美国高校学生事务工作的一个显著特征就是有一套完善的、可操作的学生事务法，依法管理学生事务。有了这样的法规，学生明白学校要我做什么和怎么做，也十分清楚违纪的后果。同时，工作人员严格依据法规来管理学生事务，并自觉接受法规的制约和被管理人的监督。我国高校学生工作在这方面还存在许多不足，例如：法规不完整、不健全，在教育和管理学生的全过程中常常无法可循；应急性、临时性的"意见、通知、办法"与法规并存，朝令夕改现象严重；部分法规政出多门，口径不同，标准不一，矛盾难以避免。为此，我们需要尽快建立一套完整、科学、操作性强的学生工作法规。第一，学校各级领导要从依法治校、依法育人，建设社会主义的法制国家的高度加强认识，为学生工作的法规建设提供必要的政策、人员和经费支持。第二，要全面、深入研究美国等西方发达国家高校学生工作法规建设的特点，取其精华为我所用，提高法规建设的时效性。第三，要注重自主创新，甘于潜心钻研，逐步建立起一套符合国情和校情的学生工作法规。第四，要真正做到"有法必依、违法必究"，杜绝用临时的意见、通知、办法来取代法规，杜绝人为因素改变执法程序、影响执法结果。第五，要制定相应的配

套措施，使执法者接受法规的制约和被管理人的监督，确保执法的公开、公平和公正。

2.2 中英学生工作管理模式的异同

英国高等教育历经八百多年的岁月洗礼，以其规范的管理，优秀的质量而闻名于世，学生事务作为其中的重要组成部分，形成了理念明确、体系完整、专业化程度高的特点，成为英国高等教育[10]培养优秀人才不可或缺的环节。

2.2.1 工作理念的异同

中英两国高校在学生事务方面都强调"以人为本"的工作理念[11]，以学生为中心的工作态度和服务方针，然而，由于历史渊源、传统习惯的影响，在实践中所体现的效果却是有差异的。

英国高校以学生为中心的观念是"消费者至上"的市场观念在教育领域内的反映。20世纪90年代，英国通过改革建立了统一的高等教育框架，政府将学生人数和财政拨款直接挂钩，使得学生像顾客一样受到重视，1993年颁布的《学生宪章》规定了学生有权享有学校提供的多项服务，这样一来更是赋予了学生顾客的角色。于是学生事务部门通常将自身定义为服务者、支持者而非管理者，体现在名称上多为"学生服务中心""学习支持中心"等，在工作中较多地运用提前契约约定、柔性告知的方法，强调引导为主，慎用强制处罚措施。

英国高校将学生视为独立主体，学校有责任为学生提供合格的学习条件和高质量的服务。许多高校的章程明确规定，在学校的管理机构（如校务委员会、学术评议会等）中设立学生代表席位，以发挥学生的主体作用，使学生参与到学校事务当中，从而保障学生利益。

2.2.2 管理模式的异同

英国高校学生事务管理系统的组织结构呈单一型，通常由学生服务中心一个机构负责全校学生的所有日常事务，学生服务中心在学校占有重要的地位，中心主任是全校最高权力机构大学理事会的秘书。在院系一级，由院长和系主任负责学生事务，每个学生配有一个负责指导学习生活的兼职导师，也有少数兼职人员负责一些具体事务如心理咨询、就业指导等，但没有专职人员负责学生事务，这些兼职人员与学校的学生事务机构保持联系。但院系与校级机构之间只是合作关系，而不存在上下级关系。

我国高校学生事务管理采用民主集中的模式，一般的高校都设有学生工作部，院系一级设有学生工作办公室，从上而下分级管理，下级服从上级并对上级负责。院系一级按学生人数设立学生事务专职人员，有分管学生工作的负责人，还有专职辅导员。一名专职辅导员大约对应200名学生，要全面关心学生的健康成长，以引导为主，帮助学生解决思想、学习、生活方面的各种问题。另外，中国高校还设有各级共青团组织，从思想政治工作的角度对学生事务进行协调管理。

从中、英两国高校不同的学生事务管理模式的比较可以看出，在英国单一型的学生事务管理中，专职的学生事务工作人员相对较少，避免了机构臃肿与人力资源的浪费，而另一方面则对学生的独立和主动性要求较高，学生只有主动提出服务要求，才可以获得相关的服务和支持。相比较而言，我国的学生管理工作能够关注到主动性不足的学生的相关需求，专职辅导员制度从人员上保证了每个学生获得均等的关注，具有主动教育、全面覆盖的优势。同时共青团组织对于学生工作来讲也是一个有力的支撑。

2.2.3 学生事务职能之异同

"学生事务"一词涵盖了学生课堂学习以外的所有活动和事务，中英两国学生事务的范畴大致相同，当然也存在着差异。大体上看，中英两国高校的学生事务部门具有以下相同职能：（1）校园活动管理，包括提供学生活动场所，协助学生团体开展各类文体活动，维持活动秩序等。（2）经济资助，包括奖学金、助学金的评定与发放，学生贷款的办理等。

一般来说，英国大学学生事务部下设招生及学校联络处、扩大招生办公室、学生注册中心、住宿管理中心、考试中心、学部办公室、学生信息系统发展与支持办公室、心理咨询中心、残疾人事务服务办公室、学生事务部办公室、国际学生及留学办公室、就业指导中心、学生资助办公室、音乐中心等，职能涉及招生、学籍管理、宿舍管理、考试、心理辅导、就业指导、学生资助、留学生服务等方面。

相比较而言，英国高校学生事务部门的职能覆盖面更广，更便于将学生事务集中管理。另一方面，我国高校的学生会被纳入学校团委统一管理，而英国高校的学生会是一个独立自治的组织。

2.2.4 英国高校学生事务工作对我们的借鉴[12]和启示

（1）整合力量，优化学工体系，构建与教学工作契合的内外机制

从英国高校"一站式"服务内容来看，其涵盖了学生工作的主要部分，各高校还在进一步进行相关工作的整合及相关部门功能的优化。随着我国社会市场经济的发展和学生成长成才的客观需要，我国高校学生工作需要进一步拓展和整合，不仅包括思想政治教育、日常管理、学风建设、学生资助、心理咨询，还应包括发展指导、素质拓展等工作内容。有些学生工作内容具有相似性和互补性，要重组相关内容和职能，形成新的学工体系。在学生工作中，保证学生良好的学习和生活秩序是最基本的，稍高一层次是围绕学生的发展（或成长、成才）进行指导，最高层次是既完善了学生的知识，也健全了学生的人格，达到又"红"又"专"。此外，高校应加强学生工作与教学工作的沟通与联系，避免学生工作与教学工作"两张皮"现象。从机构的优化到工作内容的安排，我国高校的学生工作和教学工作也应互相渗透，使教学工作真正发挥教书育人的作用，使学生工作在"第二课堂"自觉服务于教学，并最终形成合力，达到育人的目的。

（2）更新理念，改善方式，不断增强学生服务工作的实效性

英国高校的学生"一站式"服务强化了"以学生为中心"的学生事务工作的态度和理念。在此理念指导下，各学生事务部门善于在日常的工作中总结经验教训，发现工作中的不足，不断完善学生服务工作。学生成分和价值观念的多元化、课程类型的多样化，难以实现对学生从教室、图书馆到就餐、住宿的统一管理，学校也难以经常性地开展统一的大规模的课外活动，因此采取灵活多样的工作方法是其最佳选择。为此，学生事务管理部门结合学生个体的心理特点和实际需求，为学生提供个体咨询、小组咨询，定期举办小型研讨会、讲座，学生可以根据自己的需要和兴趣自愿参加，不求规模，但求实效。"一站式"服务中心大楼内的每层楼都备有大量的免费文字资料供学生随时取阅，内容涉及学生事务的方方面面，非常方便。目前，应该说，我国高校在为学生服务方面做得还是不错的，工作重点在学院。而英国学生工作主体在学校，但其工作的特点可能追求更多的是工作整体效应，当然这与我国高校学生事务工作的体制和学生人数有关。因此完善工作方式、方法，结合学生的个体心理和实际需要，加强学生的服务意识，增强学生服务工作的实效性，应是我们努力的方向。

（3）加强队伍建设，提升专业化工作水平

英国学生事务工作者的专业化前提是分工的细化，每个人的工作领域界限清晰。

- 提高学生工作者教育、培养、管理、服务学生的水平基于学生工作面临的政策环境、工作难度、内外影响、发展机遇等各种新形势，只有不断提高学生工作者教育、培养、管理、服务学生的水平，逐步从管理型向教育型、服务型转变，方可保证"服务学生成长成才为本"这个中心，方可有效提高学生综合能力素养。

- 不断强化"三种理念"，即"待生如子""待生如挚友""待生如栋梁"等工作理念，在教育、培养、管理、服务的工作中要像对待自己的孩子（亲人）一样对待学生，充满亲情、关爱和温暖；尽心尽责、周到细致地帮助和服务学生成长成才，应力争和学生结为永久的真挚朋友；要像对待国家栋梁之材一样，以高度负责的态度和精神，尽心尽力地为学生成长成才服务。

- 借鉴英国"个人导师制"，加强育人的合力，加强专业教师（班导师）在学生培养中的作用，形成全员育人、全过程育人、全方位育人的合力。

- 加速学生工作及其队伍的专业化建设借鉴

专职学生工作者要以更多的时间和精力致力于学生日常思想教育、咨询服务和其他学生事务的组织管理，提高学生工作者对学生进行学习指导的能力和水平。

（4）开拓创新，扎实推进，进一步集成学生服务的网上平台

目前，我国学生"一站式"服务的实体部分已经存在，但真正在"一站式"服务的"虚拟"系统的集成上，应该说总体上还处于初级阶段，还存在很多问题。在目前高校信息化建设中重硬件轻软件、重技术轻服务的现象还十分严重的情况下，建设高校"一站式"学生服务信息系统还需要走较长的路。这首先需要学校的各级管理者和建设者能够从整体上、战略上和思想上深入认识"以学生为中心"的理念，解决信息化的整体性和全局性的问题。核心工作是数据接口（共享）、流程优化（边界清晰）和应

用集成（统一），这三项工作说起来容易，但做起来是一个系统工程。

2.3 大陆和港澳学生事务管理的异同

2.3.1 港澳高校学生工作的主要内容

港澳高校的学生事务处下设若干个组（或叫部、中心），各校大同小异，一般包括学生活动辅导、心理辅导、职业规划辅导、学生福利设施管理、学生资助、宿舍管理等内容，几乎涉及除学业以外与学生有关的所有事项。

第一，学生辅导及发展组：是面对全校学生对其心理、思想情绪等各方面身心发展做出指引教育的机构，为学生提供个体和团体辅导，协助学生成长。

第二，独特有效的书院制度。书院的主要职能是管理学生的日常事务，培养学生的德育、体育、美育等综合素质。书院由来自学校不同专业、不同年级的学生构成，为不同专业背景学生的成长提供良好的交流发展平台。书院的管理原则是教授与学生共同管理，管理团队的主体是教授与专职的管理人员。书院和学校层面的学生事务处竞争互补，各显特色，有效地促进了学生的全人发展。

第三，就业策划及发展中心：是以全校学生为对象进行的就业辅导培训和指引的部门，负责就业信息发布、拓宽就业渠道、职前辅导、就业培训、提供就业升学资料等职能。

第四，奖学、助学和经济援助。包括奖学金的评定与发放，助学金和贷款经济援助的策划、评定和发放，勤工助学计划的引导、评定与实施等。香港学费昂贵，为了解决家庭困难的学生的上学问题，各高校都建立了完备的学生经济援助体系。

第五，协助学生会组织课外活动，建设有活力的校园文化。学生会是在香港和澳门政府独立注册的法人，不仅有自己的实体，也有丰富的会费收入。港澳地区高校对学生会不直接干涉，只起到提高、帮助和幕后指导的作用，让学生自己去建设有活力的校园文化氛围。在这种体制下，港澳地区学生会非常活跃，社团活动也开展得有声有色。

2.3.2 港澳高校学生事务管理的特点

港澳高校学生事务管理[14]具有以下五个特点：

（1）服务至上的工作理念。港澳高校学生工作凸显"服务"理念，认为：学生事务处的主要任务是协助学生投入大学生活，并通过不同的活动、援助及辅导，培养学生各方面的才能，为日后升学及就业做好准备。

（2）丰富及时的辅导服务。港澳高校在服务至上理念的指导下，学生服务涉及学生学习和生活的方方面面。

（3）润物无声的潜化德育。港澳高校没有专业的德育工作者队伍，甚至在其整个的工作理念和工作词汇中都很难找到"德育"一词。其独特之处就在于隐性化，把德育化为无形，在润物无声中实现校训目标和教育方针。

（4）学生主体的自我管理。港澳高校学生事务处之所以"不管"学生，并非没有学生事务可管，而是实行学生自我管理。学校除了有很有影响力的学生会外，在大学各有关委员会中均设有学生代表，让学生实质性地参与学校的建设与管理。

（5）全人指向的学生活动。全人教育（holistic education）中的"全人"是指完整的个人，全人教育是指充分发展个人潜能以培养完整个体的教育理念与模式。在此目标指导下，港澳高校学生活动注重课外学习和实践，通过多元化的活动，推动学生的全人发展。这些活动让学生有机会将课本知识学以致用，并补充正规课程未覆盖的范围，旨在启发学生建立发展解难能力、强健体能、培养人际关系、确立工作态度及关心地球发展的生活模式。

3 今后的发展趋势和建议

以美国为代表的欧美高校学生管理模式，经历了"替代父母制""学生人事工作""学生服务"和"学生发展"四个阶段，形成了以"个人本位"作为价值取向，重视学生个体发展，强调"满足和服务于不同天赋、不同需要、不同目的、不同个性的全体同学"的学生工作模式，在教学中实行完全意义的"学分制"，在学生工作中突出"服务"，在管理上实行"开放式"，对我国加强学生管理[15]工作很有借鉴意义。这种学生发展的视角基于 SLI 理论[16]，而 SLI 是英文 student learning imperative 的缩写。它源自美国大学人事协会（ACPA）1994 年提交的一份报告。在这份报告中，美国大学人事协会提出了一个鲜明而新颖的观点：学生的学习是当务之急——学生事务的含义（student learning imperative：implication for Student Affairs，简称 SLI）。其实质是倡导学生事务要以促进学生学习和个人发展为旨趣，体现了"以学生为本"和"以教学为中心"。

SLI 理论进一步发展了对学生事务和学术事务关系的论述，认为把高等教育管理活动分为"学术事务"和"学生事务"的"二分法"不利于学生以后的工作和生活，而是明确地提出：学生的学习是当务之急——学生事务的含义。这就为学生学习和学生发展共同建立了一种有机联系，由此，学生事务人员和学术人员找到了他们服务于学生利益的共同点。学生事务和学术事务有着共同的目标——促进学生学习和发展。学生事务工作者和学术人员要为此目标共同努力，学生事务人员和学术事务人员应该保持"双向"的合作关系，学生事务人员应主动积极地"启动"与学术人员的对话。努力打造一支政治强、业务精、纪律严、作风正、外语好的专业化学生工作团队，建设固化优良学风，着重抓好就业率、出国率、考研率、省部级大赛获奖率和市级以上奖项优秀学生获奖率"5 个率"的提高，提高学生工作绩效的显示度，提升其价值增量，促进学生全面发展，助力培养合格的应用性国际化商务人才。

3.1 有中国特色的高校学生工作事务的传承与发展

我国高等教育学生工作体制的起步较晚，大致可以分为学生工作体制的建立、学生工作体制的恢复与调整，及学生工作步入新的发展时期这样三个阶段。

从建国初期到 1977 年，我国高校的学生工作非常重视对学生的时事教育、党的路线方针政策，及国内外形势、热点问题的学习。1961 年邓小平总结建国以来各领域正反两方面的经验时，确立了"高校辅导员制度"。这个时期学生工作的突出特点是，由校党委组织部、宣传部和学校团委承担起政治功能，没有专门的学生工作机构，在地位上是作为政治工作的附庸而存在。"文革"十年浩劫使高校的学生工作暂时中断。1977 年我国恢复高考制度后，70 年代末 80 年代初各高校都设置了专门机构负责学生思想政治工作。如党委青年部、党委学生部。80 年代后，随着高校招生规模的扩大和向正规化管理方向的发展，部分高校成立了学生处，成为管理学生工作的专门行政机构。从 90 年代到现在，我国又对高校招生制度进行了改革。这一时期学生工作的功能在学生助学体系和就业体系方面得到体现和完善。进入 21 世纪，随着我国社会主义市场经济体制的建立和完善，高校学生工作的内涵也在不断丰富，逐渐形成了具有我国特色的学生工作模式。

3.2 从单一化走向综合化管理

要从单一的只重视政治上的控制，转变为应对与学生有关的各种事务。学生管理的内容综合化发展越来越突出。这就要求学生管理的各职能部门既分工严密，又协作共进，管理服务的内容除了学生活动的日常内容外，学生的政治进步、民族、宗教、学生贫困等问题也成为重要内容，同时还要注重学生对学校各项管理的参与和监督。

如果说我国高校初期的学生管理，是基于处置各种事情而求得学校社会生活的稳定，那么进入 21 世纪以来，随着"学生发展阶段"的提出，学生管理的综合性就凸显出来，而发展到现代的"学生学习"阶段，就需要更高层次的综合化，建立以"学生为中心"的管理与服务综合体系。

3.3 我院学生工作的优势

一是国家重视，从战略高度对大学生思想政治工作进行谋划、布局、设计并逐级领导。学生工作队伍组织严密、体系多层次、规模庞大；二是长期以来坚持"育人为本、德育为先"的工作理念，始终将德育工作长抓不懈、整体推进、主动干预，提倡在学生工作当中将"教育、管理和服务"有机结合；三是在尊重学生个性发展的同时，实施强化管理教育，强调集体主义教育和人在社会化过程中的习惯养成教育，这对于青年人的健康成长至关重要；四是北京经济和谐发展，给高等教育发展包括学生事务工作都带来了跨越式发展；五是学生分散住宿等劣势，不仅有利于建立一个丰富的宿舍文化，而且创造了学生接触社会、相互学习、学会与人相处的良好平台。

3.4 坚持"以学生为本"的管理导向和管理模式

继续坚持"以学生为本"的管理模式，在"敬师敬业、求学求成，爱岗敬业，导学导行"的要求下,坚持强化管理,培养学生的双敬(敬师、敬业)意识、双信(诚信、自信)品质、双能(创新、实践)素质、双求(求学、求成)精神、双责(公民、团队)观念。

(1)以社会主义核心价值体系为基础,抓好大学生党建工作。把好学生培养成学生干部,再由学生干部吸收成为中国共产党党员,使其"政治上信得过,工作上靠得住,学习上站得住"。发挥学生党员的模范和引领作用,成为学生学习的榜样。

(2)大力弘扬"北京精神"和雷锋精神,不断凝炼校园文化,开展形式多样的思想政治教育。通过一年级的志愿服务,二年级的社会实践,三年级的专业实践,四年级的毕业实习,把"第一课堂"和"第二课堂"紧密结合起来,使学生自觉以马克思主义为指导思想,树立有中国特色社会主义的共同理想,确立爱国主义为核心的民族精神和以改革创新为核心的时代精神,建立社会主义荣辱观。

(3)不断提高人才培养质量,提高学生适应社会的能力,做好学生职业生涯规划与就业指导。不断提高学生的就业质量,使学生的社会贡献力和影响力越来越大,关注校友的需求和建议。

(4)关注学生的生理和心理健康,使学生成长成才,逐步使学生能够自我教育、自我管理、自我服务。

(5)加强大学生社团工作,发挥青年团的作用,探索辅导员队伍建设的星型体系。

(6)实现学生事务管理的量化评估。坚持国际化办学特色,把英语四级作为学生的合格标准,英语六级作为优秀标准,把"十个一"作为学工部门管理和考核的标准,持续推动质量增量工程,加强学工干部年轻化、专业化和多样化建设。

基于"90后"大学生的学习特点,在借鉴国内外教学经验的基础上,进行"第一课堂"和"第二课堂"的有效探索,培养学生诚信和服务社会的素质,培养学生的创新能力和实践能力,使他们具有跨文化的沟通能力,努力培养合格的符合北京建设世界城市需要的国际商务人才。[17]

参考文献

[1] 韩秉文、王海燕. 中韩两国高等教育学生管理模式比较分析[J]. 丹东纺专学报,2005,12(1).
[2] 唐晓婷. 澳大利亚大学学生管理模式之借鉴[J]. 东方企业文化,2010(5):211.
[3] 黄海峙,于景华,张向红. 澳中高校学生工作的比较研究[J]. 西安工程大学学报,2011,(25):390-393.
[4] 唐少清,刘春玲,孙鸿飞. 基于学生特点的教学模式探索[J]. 中国大学教学,2010(9):20-22.
[5] 应中正. 美国高校学生事务管理工作的借鉴与启示[J]. 北京教育(德育),2010,(7-8),100-102.
[6] 朱小刚. 国内外高等学校学生工作管理模式的比较及探究[J]. 科技信息,2008(34):218.
[7] 吴志功. 美国高校学生工作的历史和现状[J]. 比较教育研究,2004(9):63-66.
[8] 景发. 美国高校学生工作及启示[J]. 高校辅导员学刊,2011,3(2):89—92.
[9] 裴学梅,胡叶青. 美国大学生事务管理的特点[J]. 高校辅导员学刊,2011,3(2):93-95.
[10] 吴亚玲. 英国高校学生事务概况及启示英国高校学生事务概况及启示[J]. 中国高教研究,2005(5):54-55.
[11] 郭镭. 中英两国高校学生事务之比较[J]. 西南民族大学学报(人文社会科学版),2011(3):222-224.
[12] 孙立军. 英国高校学生事务工作的基本情况及启示[J]. 思想政治教育研究,2009,25(1):115-118.
[13] 王圆圆. 内地与港澳高校学生工作内容的比较研究[J]. 广州广播电视大学学报,2011(4).
[14] 田辉,祝文燕,沈湘平,康震,张天文. 香港高校学生工作的特色及启示[J]. 北京教育(高教),2006(9),63-64.
[15] 辛希贤. 欧美国家高校学生管理模式分析及借鉴[J],理论导刊,2009(2),48-49.
[16] 刘子真,程瑶. SLI理论与美国高校学生事务管理[J]. 航海教育研究,2006(3),37-39.
[17] 唐少清. 国际商务人才培养模式问题的探讨[J]. 中国林业教育,2007(1):13-15.

信息化背景下旅游高等教育改革与发展的思考

黄先开 范 蓓 冯爱秋

20世纪90年代以来，随着信息技术，特别是网络技术的迅猛发展，信息化成为社会普遍关注的焦点。信息化也将对旅游产业带来深刻变革，对旅游高等教育提出新的要求。

一、信息化融入旅游业的发展趋势

旅游信息化是指通过对信息技术的运用来改变传统的旅游生产、分配和消费机制，以信息化的发展来优化旅游经济的运作，实现旅游经济的快速增长。主要包括旅游企业信息化、旅游电子商务、旅游电子政务等。

1. 旅游企业信息化的发展趋势

在旅游企业信息化的发展过程中，旅游管理的信息化和旅游企业网站建设是重要内容。旅游管理的信息化大幅度提高了旅游信息的管理水平和处理速度。20世纪60年代美国航空公司网上订票系统已经出现，随后在酒店中应用了中央预订系统（CRS）、电子门锁系统、自动入住系统，餐饮业中应用了点菜系统、网络订餐系统，旅游景点应用了电子门票等。

旅游企业如酒店、旅行社、餐饮企业、旅游景点、主题公园等网站的纷纷建立，带来吃、住、行、游、购、娱各种服务的网络化，游客可通过网络直接与终端服务提供商联系，跨越中间代理直接完成交易。

2. 旅游电子商务的发展趋势

世界范围的旅游电子商务正在迅猛发展。资料显示，全球旅游电子商务连续5年以350%的速度快速增长，一度占到全球电子商务总额的20%以上。我国目前旅游电子商务收入在整个旅游业收入中所占的比重还不足10%，但目前在线旅游业正在以每年30%的速度迅速成长，2010年在线旅行预订市场规模为61.6亿元，旅游电子商务在我国有着巨大的市场前景。

旅游电子商务的发展带来了旅游消费的升级和转型，旅游消费的个性化成为旅游消费的新特征。网上旅游线路设计与定制服务，满足了旅游消费者个性化出游需求。同时，网络技术为旅游消费者提供了交互平台。

旅游电子商务改变了旅游信息的传递方式，传统旅游营销逐渐向旅游网络营销转变，旅游电子商务成为旅游产品最佳展示台，功能强大的数据库系统，使游客可以很方便地实现吃、住、行、游、购、娱等信息的在线查询和在线交易。

旅游电子商务还可提供虚拟旅游产品。虚拟旅游是网络虚拟技术与现实旅游业的结合，它丰富和拓展了旅游行业经营内容和旅游的内涵，使旅游者足不出户就可感受"旅行"，并有身临其境之感。目前虚拟旅游已应用于酒店体验、旅游体验、景区营销、景区规划等方面。

3. 旅游电子政务的发展趋势

旅游电子政务的发展对政府城市形象宣传、旅游政策信息服务等有积极作用。国家旅游局已推出了网上政务大厅，建立了旅行社管理、酒店管理、导游管理、景区管理和假日旅游预报等系统，提升了旅游政务的信息管理水平。美国几乎每一个州政府旅游管理办公室都建立了网站，提供当地的旅游活动日程表、旅游地图等。旅游主管部门除了建立网站，越来越多的采用交互式触摸电脑，订阅信息传真服务

[作者简介] 黄先开，北京联合大学副校长，教授；范蓓，北京联合大学旅游学院党委副书记，副研究员；冯爱秋，北京联合大学教务处教学科科长，副研究员。

和数据光盘等,为本地旅游业宣传和促销。

新技术在旅游电子政务中也不断得到运用,如物联网技术在智能导游、绿色酒店、智能交通等方面的应用。香港旅游发展局推出名为"香港随身旅游大使"的旅游资讯服务,使游客可以通过手机实时听到一些主要景点的解说。2011年6月,中国电信与武夷山市人民政府签订合作协议,计划完成物联网武夷山示范区的建设,打造"智慧武夷"旅游度假城市;海南省旅游热点地区也已提出开始物联网应用试点。

二、信息化对旅游高等教育的新要求

信息化对旅游高等教育提出了新的要求,主要表现在以下几个方面:

1. 对旅游人才的信息素养提出了更高要求

早在20世纪90年代,美国就把对学生信息素养能力的培养提高到信息社会对人才培养与发展的战略高度来认识。根据美国高等教育图书研究协会提出的"美国高等教育信息素养能力标准",结合旅游信息化发展的要求,旅游人才必须具备的信息素养能力应包括:能决定旅游业务所需要的信息种类和程度;能有效而又高效地获取旅游业务所需要的信息;能准确、系统地评价和遴选旅游信息及来源渠道;能有效地分析、利用旅游信息达到既定目的,解决问题;在获取和使用信息与技术时遵守社会公德和法律[1]。

2. 将信息化素养融入旅游高等教育的人才培养体系

人才培养目标的定位必须适应现代旅游高等教育发展和信息化背景下旅游产业发展的需求。在核心能力中,要体现旅游人才信息素养的要求,培养学生对旅游信息获取、表达和处理的能力,同时加强旅游数据统计处理能力。在课程设置上,要有体现旅游行业信息化的课程,如旅游电子商务、酒店管理信息系统、旅游网络营销,等等。在教学内容中,要融入信息化的要求,通过网络资源建设,扩展课程教学内容。在教学方法上,转变传统教学方式,利用网络教学平台和网络资源,指导学生个性化学习,形成课堂面授教学与网络课程教学混合教学模式。在课程评价方面,将网络作为师生互评与交流的平台。

3. 搭建旅游产学研合作信息平台

搭建集成企业科技需求库、专利和技术成果库、专家信息库、国家政策、科技动态以及技术培训和人才培养等为一体的旅游产学研信息平台。高校等有关研究机构借此根据企业需求有计划开展攻关,将旅游行业企业的需求及问题及时引入课程教学中,开展产学研相结合的实践教学等,同时将高校教学科研方面的成果发布到平台上提供社会服务;旅游企业通过平台了解有关专家的研究背景、技术成果和科技信息,有针对性地开展对接;有关决策部门通过综合信息分析,及时发现下一阶段企业发展的关键难题和共性技术问题,由政府和学校牵头,前瞻性地开展关键问题研究和人才培养。

三、旅游高等教育适应信息化发展的对策建议

1. 充分认识信息化对旅游高等教育的影响

信息化影响着旅游高等教育的人才培养目标和培养模式,影响着旅游高等教育的内容、方法和途径。为适应信息化背景下旅游业对应用型创新人才的需求,要转变观念,明确信息化社会旅游人才培养目标和培养模式,树立"为了旅游""通过旅游""服务旅游"的教育理念。"为了旅游"强调旅游教育的目的,应根据旅游产业信息化发展形势对人才知识结构、职业能力和职业素养的需要,加强旅游人才信息化能力培养,满足旅游业的人才需求。"通过旅游"强调旅游教育的过程,通过在旅游企业的实践,实现旅游教育与旅游实践相融合。"服务旅游"强调旅游教育的落脚点,旅游教育要为旅游产业的发展和旅游信息化发展服务。

2. 构建旅游信息化应用能力与信息素养养成体系

第一,明确对新型旅游人才信息化应用能力要求。在培养目标和核心能力的制定中,强调学生利用信息技术获取、表达、分析和处理旅游信息的能力。主要包括:掌握利用信息技术对旅游管理相关问题进行定性和定量的分析研究方法;掌握信息技术的基础知识、操作技能,掌握旅游专业软件和系统的操

作方法，并具有较好的迁移能力；利用信息技术与他人交流并合作的能力；利用信息技术进行旅游市场调研、发现问题的能力；旅游电子商务的经营能力；旅游企业信息化管理的能力；利用信息化手段，对旅游业市场分析与应用能力；旅游产品的网络营销能力。

第二，应构建支持旅游信息化应用能力和素质培养的课程设置方案。为培养旅游人才的信息技术应用能力和素质，学校应建立支持旅游信息化应用能力和素质培养的课程设置方案。例如，北京联合大学旅游学院构建了"信息技术基础课程群+旅游信息化课程群+旅游专业课程（含信息技术）+旅游信息化讲座"的课程设置方案（见图1）。其中一、二年级为"博识基础、行业认知"阶段，开设信息技术基础课程使学生掌握信息技术基本知识和技能，并通过旅游信息化讲座，让学生了解旅游信息化发展的热点和动向；三年级为"分类培养、职场体验"阶段，通过旅游电子商务、旅游网络营销、旅游调查研究方法等旅游信息化课程群和旅游专业课程的开设，培养学生利用信息技术发现旅游行业问题、掌握旅游企业信息化和旅游电子商务的能力；四年级为"职业定向、实战训练"阶段，学生通过情景仿真实训、旅游企业实习等实践，提高利用信息技术分析和解决问题的能力。

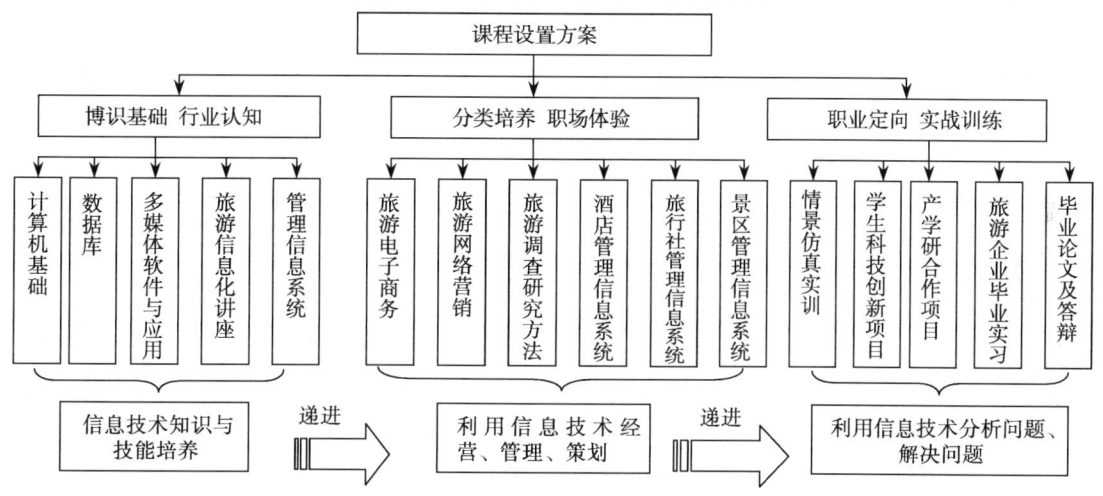

图1　支持旅游信息化应用能力和素质培养的课程设置方案

第三，要构建培养学生信息化应用能力和素质的实践教学体系。旅游信息化应用能力和素质的实践教学体系由演示性实践、感知性实践、虚拟性实践、应用性实践、设计性实践、创新性实践构成。加强实践条件建设，在已有旅游实验室基础上，建设校内虚拟旅游实验室，开展模拟仿真实践教学；搭建学生科技创新平台，为学生参加旅游科技实践提供政策和资金支持；创建校外实践教学基地，开展体验实习、调查实习、毕业实习等实践教学，构建多层次的实践教学体系。

第四，要加强利用信息技术进行教学过程与方法的改革。信息化背景下课程教学信息量远大于传统课程，若仍采用传统授课方式，很难完成既定课程目标，利用信息技术进行教学过程与方法的改革就成为必然选择。要引导学生利用信息技术开展基于问题的学习、自主学习和协作学习等，要加强精品网络课程建设，形成课堂面授教学与网络课程教学的混合教学模式。北京联合大学旅游管理专业的核心课程就采用了基于问题学习（PBL）的教学法，将信息技术的利用和信息素养的培养融入课程教学的全过程，学生被分为若干小组，分别解决一个旅游业中的实际问题，利用网络搜索资料、沟通讨论，利用网络课程自主学习，利用计算机和 SPSS 软件设计、统计分析调查问卷，利用 PPT 汇报问题解决过程和结论，同学和老师通过评分系统评定成绩。

3. 加强师资队伍建设，打造一支掌握信息化技术的教师队伍

通过外引内培，打造一支掌握信息化技术的教师队伍。对外，引进具备信息技术能力和旅游信息化实践能力、教学科研并重的专兼职优秀教师；对内，开展诸如教育信息化发展趋势、基础信息技术、现代统计分析软件及旅游企业专业应用软件等系列培训。此外，制定相关激励政策，提高教师利用信息技术进行教学建设与改革的积极性。

4. 加强信息化教学环境建设，保证旅游高等教育改革的顺利实施

首先要加强教学信息化的软硬件环境建设。硬件环境包括实验室场地、计算机、网络设备、投影仪和大屏幕、课堂自动录播系统等。硬件设施的摆放也要有利于人才培养目标的实现。软件应根据教学实际和教学目标的需要来进行建设。其次要加强学习资源的建设和网络学习工具的提供。

总之，信息化对旅游高等教育提出了新要求，也为旅游高等教育的教学改革提供了难得的机遇。我们要积极探索，勇于实践，把旅游高等教育提高到一个新的、更高的水平。

参考文献

[1] 何高大."美国高等教育信息素养能力标准"及其启示[J]. 现代教育技术, 2002（3）.

多校区高校实验教学集中管理体系构建研究

董 焱

目前,高等学校多校区办学情况日益普遍,一所大学拥有多个校区成为常见的办学格局。多校区发展实现了精英教育向大众化教育的转型,扩大了教育生存空间,提高了高校竞争优势[1]。多校区办学模式在为高校丰富教学资源、拓展生存和发展空间的同时,也带来了诸多管理方面的问题。各高校针对多校区办学给实验教学带来的困境探索解决之道,提供了许多有启发意义的方案。北京联合大学直面多校区办学、实验教学资源难以共享的现实问题,在管理体制方面进行改革,并采用先进的网络信息技术及现代化的管理手段,构建起多校区高校实验教学集中管理体系。本文探讨了多校区实验教学面临的主要困境、实验教学集中管理体系构建的意义、具体的做法、实施过程中存在的问题及解决方案。

1 多校区实验教学集中管理体系构建的意义

1.1 多校区办学造成的实验教学及其管理的困境

多校区办学的主要表现是各校区之间地理位置分散、学生规模大,给学校的教育教学和管理带来相当的困难,特别是在实验教学及其管理方面造成困境,概括起来主要有以下几个方面。

(1) 各校区之间实验教学信息不畅。包括实验中心管理人员之间、实验中心与参与实验的师生之间、指导教师与学生之间难以做到实验教学信息的及时准确反馈。

(2) 实验教学管理难以统一,实验教学质量不能做到有效监控。

(3) 实验教学资源(包括师资、设备、软件、教材等)共享困难。

(4) 实验教学数据的收集、统计与汇总异常困难。

(5) 各校区之间实验教学资源配置不均衡,难以实现仪器设备的动态管理[2-3]。

(6) 由于跨校区实验运作所带来的不便,造成师生在不同校区之间流动带来时间浪费、交通困难、安全等实际问题[4]。

1.2 建立集中式管理体系是多校区实验教学困境的解决之道

网络信息平台及相关信息技术的发展,为高校多校区办学中实验教学及其管理困境的化解提供了可能性,解决之道在于建立基于网络的集中式实验教学管理体系。

集中式实验教学管理体系,是一种基于先进的信息化、网络化技术的新型教学管理模式。通过改革实验教学管理体制,同时以信息化技术搭建实验教学管理平台,整合不同校区实验教学资源,可以提供实验教学的教务管理、设备管理及实验教学课程建设等方面的管理及信息共享[5]。

2 多校区实验教学集中式管理体系建设的目标

基于先进网络信息技术的集中式实验教学管理体系的核心在于集中式管理平台建设,其主要目标如下。

2.1 实验教学和实验室管理全流程的实时信息化

为实验课教学流程和管理流程提供一个统一的网络工作平台,实现全流程的实时信息化,即在完成

[基金项目] 本课题为北京市高等教育学会"十二五"高等教育科学研究规划课题"实验教学远程监控动态管理系统研究与应用"(BG125YB094)(项目负责人:牛爱芳)阶段性成果

[作者简介] 董焱(1964—),男,新疆哈密人,博士研究生(管理学博士),北京联合大学管理学院教授,副院长,研究方向为信息管理与信息系统、信息文化、实验教学。

实验课教学流程的同时，实时地在线生成实验课教学相关信息，将实验教学信息的生成、记录、存储和使用在网络工作平台上统一起来。

2.2 实验教学资源的高效共享

利用信息网络工作平台，实验教学中心的各项资源（包括师资、设备、软件、教材、课件、教学参考资料等）理论上可以实现全面共享。

2.3 实验教学参加者及时高效的互动

网络工作平台同时可承担网络交流平台的功能，供学生、教师、实验技术人员和管理者通过该平台进行及时地交流和反馈。

2.4 实验室管理对教学的高效服务

利用网络工作平台，实验技术人员可为开展实验教学的师生提供快捷的实验教学资源部署、远程咨询和技术维护等服务[6]。

3 多校区实验教学集中管理体系的构建模式

北京联合大学的经济管理类专业广泛分散在管理学院、商务学院、旅游学院、生物化学工程学院、应用科技学院等多个学院，学科专业众多，学生达6000人以上。2008年在管理学院、商务学院实验教学中心基础上成立的北京联合大学经贸实验教学中心成为市级实验教学示范中心，几年来，中心探索学院间实验教学工作多方面的合作，以及不同校区间实验教学资源整合之路，在学校实验教学管理体制改革方面起到了成功的试水作用。

经贸实验教学中心配合学校学科专业调整，针对经济管理类教育教学改革的需要，通过建立校院两级、总分结合的实验中心管理运行机制，组建跨学科、专业的实验教学团队，同时，采用虚拟化技术建立跨校区、开放共享的实验教学环境，管理和共享经济管理类专业教学软件，校企合作、自主研发了实时、动态的实验教学监测管理系统（含"计算机辅助排课综合管理系统"和"指纹自动识别上机综合管理系统"）。通过上述手段，构建了基于先进网络信息技术的、可支撑多校区经济管理实验教学的集中管理体系，为高校多校区环境下实验教学的实施及资源共享探索了一条切实可行的道路（见图1）。

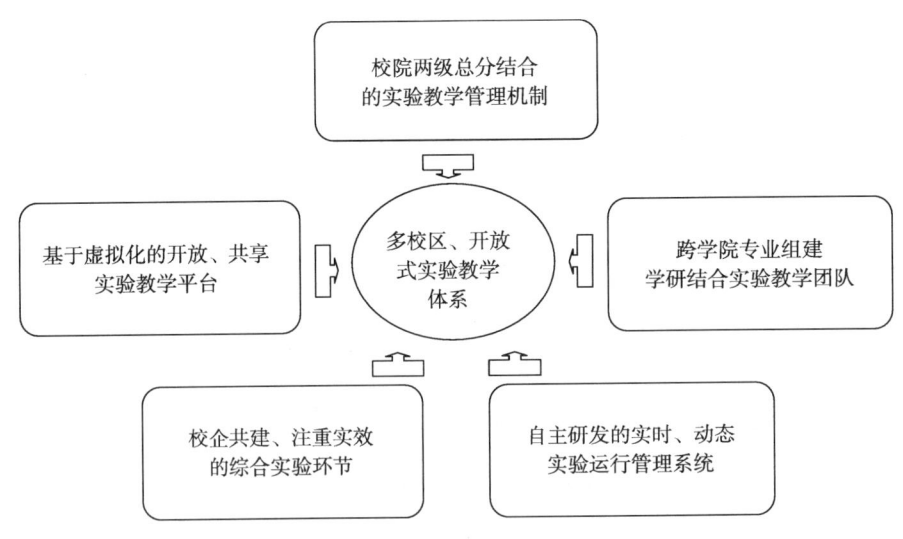

图1 多校区实验教学管理体系示例

3.1 理顺多校区实验教学管理体制

化解多校区实验教学管理难题，除技术解决方案外，首要问题是解决实验教学管理体制问题。只有理顺多校区高校的实验教学管理体制，才能有效地解决教学部门（院、系）与实验中心之间管理运行脱节问题，以及各校区之间在师资队伍、实验教学环境方面重复建设、资源不能共享等矛盾与冲突问题。

北京联合大学在经贸实验教学中心建设过程中，针对中心由位于商务学院的东校区中心和位于管理学院的北校区中心两个分中心组成的现实情况，建立起校院两级总分结合、有利于实验教学资源整合的管理体制（见图2）。具体来说，实验教学中心归校教务处领导（教务处实验教学科具体负责），中心主任负责中心整体规划和建设、项目申报、财政专项经费的统筹、中心形象设计与宣传、跨学院实验教学活动的组织协调；实验教学日常管理与运行由分中心主任分别负责；专业实验教学的实施、实验教师的安排由学院教务部门负责；同时鼓励两个分中心借助各自的优势，探索实验教学环境建设等方面的改革与创新。

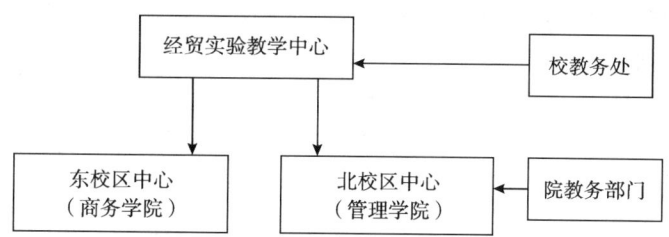

图2　校院两级实验教学管理体制示例

3.2　利用虚拟化技术构建多校区实验教学管理平台的基础环境

在现阶段，多校区实验教学集中管理平台应当建立在虚拟化技术基础环境之上。

虚拟化技术具有支持多种操作系统、安装快捷、集成度高、方便移植、有较强的容灾功能，实验教学中心可通过建立服务器池，建立桌面虚拟机环境，在同一系统上同时运行多台虚拟机、快速部署操作系统和应用软件等手段，构建全天候、灵活可靠的、多校区共享的虚拟实验教学环境[7]。利用虚拟化桌面技术等，还可以开发虚拟仿真性实验课程或实验环节，拓展专业实验教学的领域与实现手段[8-9]。

北京联合大学经贸实验教学中心与有关公司合作，进行了桌面虚拟化，开发虚拟机的电子教室功能等方面的虚拟管理系统试验。通过构建虚拟化实验教学环境，对中心整体网络环境和实验教学软、硬件资源进行部署整合，使校内各校区均可通过中心的虚拟网络教学平台获取和使用专业实验软件环境、进行开放性的实验教学活动和自主性学习，为集中式实验教学管理平台及未来的"实验教学云平台"打下基础（见图3）。

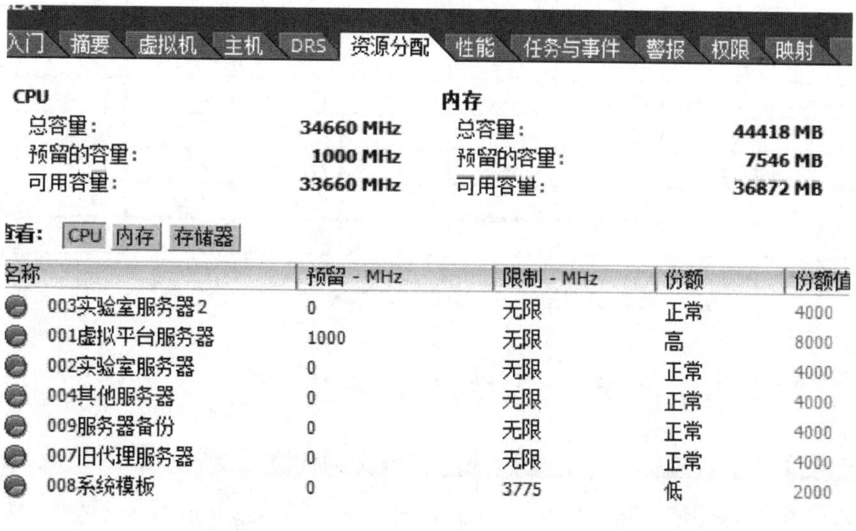

图3　基于虚拟化技术的实验教学基础环境

3.3　建立跨校区实验教学集中管理平台

利用虚拟化技术所构建的基础环境，可建立跨校区实验教学集中管理平台。该结构基于B/S结构，利用网络将本地或异地的不同实验用户与虚拟实验室连接起来，共享一个虚拟的实验空间，可支持用户进行远程实验和本地实验[10]。

该管理系统主要包括：（1）系统管理模块。包括基础数据、系统用户等相关数据的管理与维护。

(2) 实验课程及实验项目管理模块。实现对实验教学全过程各环节的动态管理。(3) 实验教学双向评价模块。实现课堂教师与学生之间的双向评价管理。(4) 仪器设备管理模块。对实验教学仪器设备使用、调配情况及故障报修的管理。(5) 资源共享管理模块。实验教学相关资料和实验课程内容建设的管理。(6) 师生互动资源交流平台模块。构建实验教学的师生互动交流的网上社区。(7) 汇总与报表模块。实现各类实验教学信息、设备使用信息的统计、汇总、上报及工作量核算等。(8) 实验教学成果管理模块。对实验教材、实验教学课件、科研论著及学生等获奖情况的统计、汇总与更新[10-11]。

实验教学中的一个突出的难点是实验教学效果的评价，原因在于学生的实验教学状态和过程的实时监控是一个难题[12]。主要体现在：学生的真实出勤情况难以准确记录与管理，授课教师的课堂管理和过程监控的难度非常大，对影响学生学习效果的许多"隐性"数据难于掌握，实验室管理人员的日常管理工作量非常繁杂而工作效率又不高等。

北京联合大学经贸实验教学中心通过校企合作研发"指纹识别自动上机综合管理系统"和"计算机辅助实验教学综合排课系统"，加强了对实验教学运行过程的有效监控，为实验教学效果和质量的提升提供了必要保证，并在全校7个校区试验推广，以实现在全校范围内对实验教学运行自动化、精细化、动态化和可视化管理（见图4）。

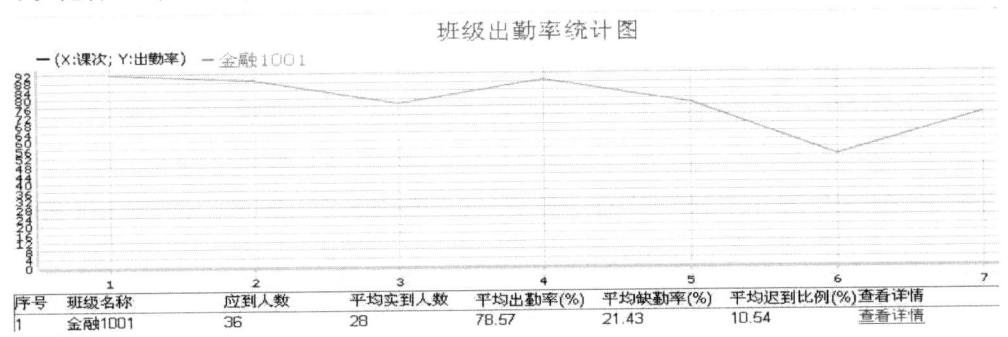

图4 指纹识别系统与计算机辅助排课系统实现动态监控

4 多校区实验教学集中管理实施中的问题及其克服

4.1 多校区实验教学集中管理体系存在信息沟通量巨大的问题

多校区实验教学集中管理体系建立以后，由于突破了单一校区实验教学运行管理模式，会使实验教学运行管理中的信息沟通量激增。必须由专人负责不同校区间实验教学与管理的协调工作，采用线上间接沟通和线下直接沟通相结合的方式解决此问题。

4.2 多校区实验教学集中管理平台对技术环境依赖性较强

虚拟化技术的实施要求服务器和大容量存储的性能更先进、更强大，实验教学动态监控系统不仅要求有相应的软件系统，而且需要有指纹读入装置和摄录设备等硬件的配合，大量的实时、多媒体形式的数据的存储、传输与处理对网络的性能也提出了较高的要求。这就要求各方面紧密跟踪信息技术和网络技术的最新进展，以使实验教学中心的环境建设具有先进性和适用性。

4.3 多校区实验教学管理平台与学校现有其他信息系统的协洽问题

如果实验教学管理平台不能与学校教务管理系统、学生管理系统、校园卡等连通和共享，会造成学生信息、教师信息、课程信息等相关数据输入比较烦琐。应当认真研究多校区实验教学管理平台与学校现有其他信息系统的协洽问题，规范数据交换格式，统一数据交换接口，以解决相关数据统一输入及在不同系统间共享的问题。

4.4 多校区实验教学资源综合利用的问题

在集中统一管理体系下，多校区的实验教学资源仍存在利用不足的可能性。实验教学中心应与各专业配合，加强实验教学改革，通过开发基于网络平台的仿真实验和虚拟实验，开展开放性的、可由学生自主选修的实验教学第二课堂，全面开展专业实验技能竞赛，将学生科技活动与兴趣小组引进实验室，开放周边的社会服务[13]，以提高各校区实验教学资源的综合效益。

5 结 语

高校多校区实验教学的运行管理从分散走向集中的问题，随着多校区办学成为普遍现象日益受到关注，网络等信息技术的快速发展，为建立集中式的实验教学管理体系提供了技术支持，针对多校区实验教学的管理问题人们提出了许多行之有效的方案。但由于实验教学改革不断深化，导致原有的问题尚待解决，新的问题又不断涌现。这就要求从事高校实验教学工作及管理的人员进行更为深入的探索与研究，并且要随时关注信息技术与网络技术的最新进展（如云技术、射频技术等），适时引入到实验教学管理体系的建构工作中，使多校区集中式实验教学管理体系得以高效、顺畅、安全地运转。

参考文献

[1] 谢佳, 张超. 多校区高校校区管理模式再探[J]. 宜春学院学报, 2009 (2)：183–184.

[2] 石义芳. 多校区模式下计算机实验教学综合信息平台的构建与研究[J]. 中国科教创新导刊, 2011 (26)：179–180.

[3] 廖君衡. 网络工具与多校区办学模式下的实验教学[J]. 新西部, 2009 (12)：147–148.

[4] 朱向运. 多校区办学模式下的实验教学管理[J]. 实验技术与管理, 2005, 22 (2)：100–101, 117.

[5] 余建波, 等. 高校实验教学信息化的建设与探索[J]. 实验室研究与探索, 2010, 29 (10)：149–153.

[6] 田曙坚, 王岩, 徐金荣. 实验教学中心信息化建设的认识与探索[J]. 实验室研究与探索, 2010, 29 (9)：92–94.

[7] 董焱. 基于虚拟化技术的实验教学中心环境构建[J]. 实验技术与管理, 2011, 28 (3)：299–302.

[8] 李潮锐. 虚拟仪器技术构建跨校区实验教学平台[J]. 实验技术与管理, 2007, 24 (1)：90–93.

[9] 陈萍, 周会超, 周虚. 构建虚拟仿真实验平台，探索创新人才培养模式[J]. 实验技术与管理, 2011, 28 (3)：277–280.

[10] 赵红, 李著成. 基于B/S的网络虚拟实验室系统构建与实现[J]. 实验技术与管理, 2011, 28 (9)：86–88.

[11] 同[2].

[12] 林先津. 机房实验教学管理系统学生状态监控的设计与实现[J]. 实验技术与管理, 2011, 28 (10)：96–99.

[13] 黄景荣, 唐治中, 计国菊. 多校区办学实验教学管理与效益的发挥[J]. 中国教育技术装备, 2007 (10)：112–114.

我国残疾人高等教育宏观结构研究

滕祥东　郝传萍　吕淑慧　朱　琳

1　我国残疾人高等教育发展与研究状态

残疾人高等教育包括特殊教育（如中、重度听力残疾人和视力残疾人在高等特殊教育学院就读）和普通教育（如肢体残疾人和轻度听力残疾人、视力残疾人在普通高校就读）两种方式。残疾人高等教育是我国高等教育的重要组成部分。自1985年山东滨州医学院首次招收残疾人大学生开始，我国残疾人高等教育发展已有26年的历史，共招收残疾人大学生近8万人。作为一项特殊的高等教育，目前中国残疾人高等教育得到了空前的发展。

与此相应的是，对残疾人高等教育的研究也经历了三个主要阶段：2000年以前，重点是对残疾人高等教育发展基本概况和实践进行简单的总结和梳理；2001—2005年是研究的第二阶段，开始了在理论层面对残疾人高等教育的发轫与发展、学科体系建立、人才培养体系、师资培训体系、区域均衡发展等多方面进行探讨；2006—2010年是研究的第三个阶段，在总结前20年中国残疾人高等教育经验的基础上，重点分析了中国残疾人特殊教育存在的各种问题，以国际残疾人特殊教育为研究视野，吸取发达国家特殊教育经验，结合中国国情，进行国内残疾人特教教育的改革，提出了未来中国残疾人高等教育发展趋势。近几年，中国残疾高等教育在理论研究层面上不断深化，广泛探讨了教育公平问题、法律保障体系、办学形式、不同层次人才培养模式、不同类型残疾人教育策略、管理体系、专业建设、支持系统、经费投入及就业等众多问题。

但是，在众多研究层面，中国残疾人高等教育过去多数是从具体问题的微观层面进行剖析，而从整体上对残疾人高等教育结构问题一直没有进行系统的研究。高等教育结构是高等教育系统内各要素的构成状态，分为宏观结构和微观结构。宏观结构指整个高等教育系统的构成，主要有层次结构、科类结构、形式结构、区域布局结构、管理体制结构等。本文在大量调研的基础上，以第一手调研材料，对我国残疾人高等教育的宏观结构问题进行分析。采取问卷调查和2009年残疾人事业年报数据分析相结合的方法，对我国现有专门招收残疾大学生、并以单考单招形式招生的16所高等院校进行调查，主要涉及残疾人高等教育的层次、体制、科类、形式、分布结构等内容。通过对残疾人高等教育宏观结构现状的分析与建议，期望能对优化我国残疾人高等教育的结构提供参考依据，寻求推动残疾人高等教育在新的历史阶段有效和规范发展的途径，促进残疾人高等教育科学发展。

2　我国残疾人高等教育结构的调查分析

2.1　层次结构

我国高等教育层次结构分为专科、本科和研究生教育三个层次。对目前我国残疾人高等教育层次结构调查结果显示：在调查的16所院校中，专科层次10所，占62.5%；本科层次4所，占25%；既有本科层次又有专科层次2所，占12.5%；残疾人高等教育以专科层次为主，没有研究生层次教育。表1。

[基金项目] 本文为全国教育科学"十二五"规划教育部重点课题"残疾人高等教育院校教师专业化特色研究"（课题编号：DFA110214）的研究成果，并得到北京市重点建设学科建设项目资助。

[作者简介] 滕祥东，北京联合大学特殊教育学院。

表1 我国残疾人高等教育层次结构

层次	研究生	本科	专科	本、专	合计
数量	0	4	10	2	16
%	0	25	62.50	12.50	100

中国残疾人事业发展年报数据也显示：2006—2009年特殊教育院校招收的、毕业于盲聋学校的本、专科层次的盲聋学生4300人，其中专科层次学生2834人，占66%。专科层次在高等教育层次结构中处于最下面的一层。从以上调查数据可看出：目前我国残疾人高等教育与普通高等教育层次还有较大差距。专科层次只是解决了部分残疾人上大学的问题，还不能满足残疾人接受更高层次高等教育的需要；并且从数量上也不能满足需求，2009年在盲聋学校就读的盲聋学生大约有10.5万人。应当提高残疾人高等教育办学层次，增加各层次招生人数，并适当发展研究生教育。

2.2. 体制结构

高等教育的体制结构是指宏观上高等学校的举办主体和行政管理的隶属关系。目前我国高等学校按行政隶属关系分为教育部直属、中央其他部委直属、省（直辖市）直属和省辖市所属，根据所属权和经费来源不同又分为公办、民办和公办民办二元制的高等院校。对我国残疾人高等教育体制结构的调查结果显示：在调查的16所院校中，13所为省（直辖市）所属，占81.25%，3所为省辖市所属学校，占18.75%，全部为公办学校。表2。

表2 我国残疾人高等教育体制结构

行政隶属关系	教育部直属	省（直辖市）直属	中央其他部委直属	省辖市所属	合计
数量	0	13	0	3	16
%	0	81.25	0	18.75	100

残疾人高等教育体制是由我国高等教育体制发展决定的，基本符合目前我国高等教育体制中"统一领导、分级管理"的特征。现阶段在社会主义市场经济体制下，我国高等教育体制结构正在向多元化方向发展，反映了高等教育管理体制与社会政治经济体制的协调发展。相比较，残疾人高等教育主要以省（直辖市）和省辖市管理为主，体制结构单一，与国家的政治经济体制发展缺乏一致性。残疾人高等教育体制是否能有效地发挥管理职能，是发展残疾人高等教育的关键。

2.3 科类结构

高等教育的科类结构是指高等教育发展中不同学科领域的构成状态，又称专业结构，是一种横向结构，它规定着所培养人才的专业类别和规格。我们国家本科专业分为哲学、经济学、法学、教育学、文学、历史学、理学、工学、农学、医学、管理学等11个学科门类；专科分为农林牧渔、交通运输、生化与药品、资源开发与测绘、材料与能源、土建、水利、制造、电子信息、环保气象与安全、轻纺食品、财经、医药卫生、旅游、公共事业、文化教育、艺术设计传媒、公安、法律等19个专业大类。

关于我国残疾人高等教育科类调查结果显示：在调查的16所院校中，本科设置的专业依次涉及文学、医学、工学、教育学等4个学科门类，专科设置的专业依次涉及艺术设计传媒、电子信息、医药卫生、公共事业、农林牧渔等5个专业大类；视障学生的专业设置主要是针灸推拿学和针灸推拿，听障学生的专业设置主要是艺术设计和装潢艺术设计，计算机科学与技术和计算机应用技术；目前残疾人高等教育设置的专业科类较少、单一，且都以目录内为主。

残疾人高等教育在设置专业时，更多地考虑的是残疾人的生理限制问题，尽量选择适合残疾人生理需要的专业，这与我们国家残疾人的支持与服务系统发展相对滞后有关。多学科、大专业、宽口径的设置应该能为残疾人高等教育提供多元化的专业选择，关键是相应的支持性服务要配套发展。

2.4 形式结构

高等教育的形式结构主要指普通高等教育、职业高等教育及成人高等教育等结构形式。调查结果显示：在调查的16所学校中，16所全部是全日制的学历教育并且为地方办的公立高等教育；4所为普通高等教育，10 所为高等职业技术教育，2 所既有普通高等教育又有高等职业技术教育；有 11 所高校开办了成人教育。目前残疾人高等教育的办学形式以全日制的学历教育和公立学校为主，主要是进行高等职业技术教育，多数高校开办了成人教育。

在二十多年的发展历程中，我国残疾人高等教育的办学形式在顺应国家主导形式的基础上，也形成了适合我国高等教育体制的办学特点。主要有：第一种是在全日制的公立学校中设立二级学院，或者在学校中建立系和专业，采取单考单招的形式，主要招收特教学校毕业的听障和视障学生；第二种是建立独立设置的专科院校，以招收残疾大学生为主；第三种是中等职业学校与有条件的高等院校合作开办残疾人大专班；第四种是残疾人参加自学考试和成人教育；第五种是残疾人进入普通高校进行随班就读。这些办学形式都是在发展过程中，适应国情，符合国家高等教育体制，满足残疾人接受高等教育的需求而形成的。一方面普通高校还不具备"无障碍"环境与条件，普通高考制度无法适应听障、视障和一些程度较重的肢体障碍学生的考试需要，特殊中等教育和基础教育水平与普通教育还有一定差距，因此残疾人高等教育在国家主导办学形式基础上实行单考单招，举办高等职业教育，开办成人教育，推动中等职业学校与高校联合办学等，以满足残疾人接受高等教育的数量上的需求。

2.5 区域布局结构

高等教育的区域布局结构是指高等学校的地区分布情况，即高等学校的数量、机构、类型、层次等方面在不同地区的分布比例。高等教育的区域布局结构既受各地经济文化发展水平、历史传统和文化环境的制约，也受国家政策的影响。

调查数据显示：调查的 16 所院校分布在不同的地区，其中华东和华中地区各有 4 所，占 25%；华南地区有 3 所，占 18.75%；华北地区有 2 所，占 12.50%；西南、西北和东北地区各有 1 所，占 6.25%。残疾人高等院校一半建在我国的中东部地区，并且是在北京、天津、上海、南京、广州等经济和文化较发达的城市。见表 3。

表 3 我国残疾人高等教育地区布局结构

地区	华北地区	东北地区	华东地区	华南地区	西北地区	华中地区	西南地区	合计
数量	2	1	4	3	1	4	1	16
%	12.50	6.25	25	18.75	6.25	25	6.25	100

高等教育是社会、经济和文化发展到一定程度的产物，残疾人高等教育更是社会文明和教育发展的标志。目前残疾人高等教育这种分布结构并不是某种设计的结果，而是在发展过程中形成的自然结果，这种分布基本与普通高等教育的发达地区、较发达地区、边远欠发达地区的梯层结构相似。发展残疾人高等教育不仅需要一定的物质条件和经济条件，更需要一定的社会文化条件和高等教育的基础。从办学效益讲，大城市经济发达、条件好、教育基础好，能够保证办学质量，便于发展残疾人高等教育；从社会人文角度讲，经济发达的城市，人们整体素质高、社会发展进程快，人文意识强，易于接受残疾人高等教育。中国有 8600 万残疾人，现有学校数量还远远不能满足残疾人接受高等教育的需要。中国地域辽阔、人口众多、地区差异较大，如何有计划地、合理地布局残疾人高等院校，需要在理论上和实践上进行深入的探讨。

3 对优化我国残疾人高等教育结构的建议

3.1 完善残疾人高等教育单考单招制度，提升层次结构

我国高等教育层次结构分为专科、本科和研究生教育三个层次。目前残疾人高等教育以专科层次为主，与普通高等教育的本、专层次结构基本对应，但没有研究生教育层次。建议残疾人高等教育的办学层次结构可基本保持本、专层次结构比例，适度增加本科生招生规模。同时研究残疾人高等教育研究生层次的单考单招制度，帮助残疾大学生实现接受研究生教育的梦想。

3.2 加强残疾人高等教育体制结构研究，明确教育管理运行机制的责任与归属

体制结构反映了高等教育行政主体、办学主体和经营主体之间的关系，并且受国家制度、经济体制、国家政体形式及民族文化传统的影响和制约。目前残疾人高等教育的管理体制与国家高等教育管理

体制是一致的，由国家统一领导，地方自主办学。教育部在基础教育二司设立特殊教育处负责义务教育阶段特殊教育工作，高校学生司本专科招生处指定专人负责残疾人高等教育考试招生录取事务。地方各级教育行政部门中则仅在基础教育处（科）中有一人兼管特殊教育。在这种不完善的管理体制下，残疾人高等教育在整体规划、政策导向、学科建设、办学资金和条件、师资队伍培养等多个方面，缺乏宏观统筹、协调、管理和指导。随着教育事业和残疾人事业的不断发展，残疾人教育已经突破义务教育向两头延伸，从学前教育、义务教育、高中教育、职业教育到高等教育、成人教育的残疾人教育体系已初步形成。残疾人高等教育管理体制需要尽快理顺，以便于残疾人高等教育规范、有序地发展。

3.3 改变残疾人高等教育专业设置单一的科类结构，实现残疾人高等教育多元化

高等教育的科类结构，一方面要与社会、经济、科学技术结构相适应，与国家的人才需求趋势相吻合，另一方面也要从高等教育自身的发展出发，建立宽窄适应、文理工协调发展的科类结构，满足人们接受高等教育的不同需求。进入高等学府的残疾人都是残疾人中的佼佼者和高智商群体，他们与健全的青年一样，渴望学习更多的知识与技能报效祖国，他们具有很大的潜能，如果专业设置只考虑他们的特殊性，将会极大限制他们潜能的发挥和自我价值的实现。不管在普通院校还是特殊教育院校学习，我们需要从"人"的角度去认识残疾人，从"权利"的高度去理解残疾人，从"社会"的视角去看待残疾人。在进行专业设置时，不单是要考虑其特殊性，还应从学校的公共设施、教学设施、生活问题等方面加强服务与支持系统的建设，为残疾人高等教育拓宽专业奠定基础，实现残疾人高等教育的多元化、多学科的专业设置。

3.4 优化残疾人高等教育形式结构，完善办学形式与实现多元化办学

我国残疾人高等教育办学形式在发展过程中，根据国家具体情况和实际条件，逐渐摸索和形成了能够初步满足残疾人接受高等教育需要的模式。但是随着社会的进步、经济的繁荣、高等教育的大众化趋势，残疾人高等教育必须在巩固现有办学形式的前提下，进一步完善各种办学形式，提高各级学校的教育质量，协调各种办学形式间的关系与功能，发挥现有办学形式的优势和作用，优化残疾高等教育形式结构，鼓励多元化办学，提高办学效益，促进残疾人高等教育在新的历史阶段向高水平发展。

3.5 平衡残疾人高等教育区域分布结构，兼顾西部残疾人高等教育的发展

根据调查，我国残疾人高等教育区域布局主要集中在中东部、南方沿海及发达的大城市地区，相对来说，西部及少数民族经济欠发达地区残疾人高等教育发展不足。为此，需要对残疾人高等教育进行合理的布局。院校主要分布在中东部，需要有计划和合理地布局。未来10年，残疾人高等教育的发展将会进入一个新的历史阶段，数量和质量上都会有一个较大的提高。对残疾人高等教育进行合理布局，需要从地域、经济、文化、人文意识、历史沿革、教育民主的高度等多角度、多维度综合进行计划和合理布局，保证残疾人高等教育的办学水平和教育质量。

参考文献

[1] 山东省滨州医学院"残疾人高等教育研究"课题组. 我国残疾人高等教育研究[J]. 教育研究, 2000 (1).
[2] 曲学利, 吕淑慧. 我国高等特殊教育的现状及发展研究[J]. 中国特殊教育, 2004 (6).
[3] 闫亚林. 高等教育层次和科类结构研究[D]. 上海: 华东师范大学博士论文, 2005.
[4] 朱宁波. 发展残疾人高等教育的目的追求[J]. 中国特殊教育, 2003 (5).
[5] 雷江华. 关于残疾学生在普通高等学校接受教育的思考[J]. 中国特殊教育, 2003 (5).
[6] 朴永馨. 残疾人高等教育的产生和发展[J]. 中国听力语言康复科学杂志, 2004 (4).
[7] 黄伟. 我国残疾人高等教育公平研究[J]. 中国特殊教育, 2011 (4).

基于云计算的电子商务安全问题研究

于 平 马桂真

云计算的内涵及特征

(一) 云计算的内涵

云计算是继个人计算机、互联网之后的第三次信息技术新浪潮,是新一代信息技术产业的重要组成部分,将引发信息产业商业模式的根本性改变。对于云计算的定义,业界都希望从自身的角度来定义。从电子商务的角度看,云计算就是在一个大规模的系统环境中,不同系统之间相互提供服务,软件都是以服务的方式运行,当所有这些系统相互协作,并在互联网上提供服务时,这些系统的总体就形成了云。

(二) 云计算的特征

1. 根据用户需要提供自助服务。用户能够在不和云服务提供商交互的情况下,根据需要自动获取所需计算资源或服务,比如服务时间和网络存储等。云服务提供商根据提供的资源或服务计费。

2. 使用宽带网络接入获取服务。云服务提供商通过网络提供云服务,支持各种标准接入手段,包括各种胖或瘦客户端平台(例如移动电话、笔记本电脑等),也包括其他传统的或基于云的服务,即云计算服务在网络中发生,在网络中传递。

3. 虚拟化。云提供商将计算资源都汇集到资源池中,使用多租户模式,按照用户需要,将不同的物理和虚拟资源动态地分配或再分配给用户使用。云计算支持用户在任意位置,使用各种终端从资源池获取应用服务,用户不需了解也不用担心资源池的具体位置。资源包括存储、处理能力、内存、网络带宽以及虚拟机等。虚拟的资源池是实现资源共享,提高计算效率的重要基础。

4. 快速弹性架构。用户可以随时根据自己的需要购买资源或服务,不必担心资源不够用或资源浪费,因为云可以快速、弹性地供应资源或服务,并且提供的资源或服务近乎无限;而云计算平台的建设者和运营商,也仅需在容量预警时,很简单地即可实现横向扩容,以应对增长的需求。

云计算对电子商务的影响

(一) 云计算使得企业电子商务安全性得到改善

随着云技术在企业中的应用,电子商务企业不必再担心由于各种电子商务安全问题而导致企业重要数据丢失或失窃。这是因为企业将数据存储在云端,云服务将会提供专业的、高效的、安全的数据存储。

(二) 云计算降低了电子商务企业的运营成本

应用云服务后,电子商务企业不必花费大量的精力、财力规划自己的数据中心,不必组建自己的IT管理团队,不必投入大量的费用购买软件,这些功能在云中能够更好地实现。云计算为电子商务企业提供了近乎无限的虚拟计算资源,提供了最优秀的管理团队,提供了不同程度不同类型的信息服务。

(三) 云计算为客户端带来更高的性能

随着云服务的应用,电子商务企业使用的所有的应用程序都是运行在云中而不是在台式机上,并且云中提供了近乎无限的存储容量,这样对客户端的硬件要求就很低,电子商务企业也不需投入大量资金

[作者简介] 于平,北京联合大学旅游学院旅游实践教学中心;马桂真,北京联合大学。

购买高性能的电脑。

（四）云计算能够促进企业之间的共享合作

在云计算中，所有的电子设备只要连接到互联网上，就可以对数据与应用进行操作。所以即使位于不同的地理位置，电子商务企业之间和企业内部通过云都可以轻松实现共享协作。有权限的人员可以利用基于云的项目管理，随时随地查看项目的文件、任务以及项目进展和更新情况。

基于云计算的电子商务安全问题的类别

（一）信息安全问题

电子商务中，订单信息、支付信息、商务往来的机密文件等需要在开放、共享的互联网络下进行，这就对电子商务企业平台的安全性、稳定性有了更高的要求。也就是对电子商务企业的数据中心硬件基础设施和信息的维护管理提出了更高的要求。对于电子商务企业来说，去选择实力强大的云计算服务，远比自己创建数据中心、自己管理维护，能够获得更高的安全保障。

（二）数据的存储安全

在传统的电子商务软件架构中，电子商务平台的任何正常或者非正常的中断，比如爆发计算机病毒、软件逻辑故障等，都可能丢失交易数据，造成巨大的经济损失。云中的数据存储采用的是分布式方式，具有高度冗余化的特点，这样就有利于保证云中的数据具有更高的可用性和可靠性，一旦数据出现了丢失或者错误，想要恢复时就会有众多的冗余原始数据供恢复。同样在云计算平台下软件的业务逻辑也可以被快速地重新组织，各种应用可随之高效恢复。

（三）用户终端安全问题

云计算技术对于用户终端的保护也提供了有力的支持。各杀毒软件厂商纷纷提出自己的云安全战略，但是他们关于云的含义各有不同，例如趋势科技是将后台庞大的服务器集群作为云，把病毒库特征码文件保存在互联网的云数据库中，云端的病毒库时时更新，用户不用更新数据库也根本感受不到服务器端的更新。后台的几万台云服务器具有强大的并行处理能力，在病毒和木马的威胁到达用户端之前对其拦截，将用户终端解放出来。

（四）信息保密问题

云环境中，用户对自己信息的保密性是完全可以放心的，因为在云的大规模分布式存储机制中，通常把完整的数据实体打散成一些"块"或者"碎片"，然后在不同的服务器上存储，甚至不同数据实体的内容可能存储在一个"块"中。因此，一个块可能是由一个很大的逻辑文件的一部分组成，也可能包含很多个很小的逻辑文件。所以用户若想获取云中的数据，必须获得大量的存储服务器的访问授权。因此一个非法用户获取云中数据是非常困难的。

（五）数据泄密问题

很多电子商务企业担心企业内部数据放到云中，会出现数据被盗或泄密问题。其实企业数据被盗有60%情况是由企业内部人员所为，而云计算中，大的信誉好的云服务商会设置一系列的安全管理条例，避免系统管理人员接触存储的企业数据，同时那些管理人员对企业的核心数据缺乏认知，造成的危害有限。

基于云计算的电子商务安全问题面临的风险

（一）云平台更容易遭受攻击

云计算最开始是在企业内部网络运行，并不对外开放，因此云计算在设计之初没有太多考虑安全性问题，从而导致云计算面临一系列安全问题。在云环境下，云暴露在公开的网络中，任何一个节点及它们的网络都可能受到攻击。另外在云环境中，用户、信息资源的高度集中，更容易成为黑客攻击的目标。

(二) 病毒日益猖獗

未来查毒软件将无法有效处理日益增多的恶意程序，来自互联网的主要威胁正在由电脑病毒转向恶意程序及木马，在这种情况下，采用特征库判别法显然已经过时。

(三) 安全和隐私保护问题

电子商务企业所有的敏感数据都掌握在云计算服务提供商手中，使得电子商务企业始终会担心信息的安全和个人隐私保护问题。目前云计算服务商一直宣称对于云中的数据，任何人都无法知道某条信息到底存放在哪里，信息是绝对安全的。但是其切实有效性还有待进一步验证。

(四) 系统升级问题

在云环境中，用户的服务系统更新和升级大多数是由用户在远程执行的，而不是采用传统的在本地按版本更新的方式，每一次升级都可能带来潜在的安全问题和对原有安全策略的挑战。

(五) 管理及法律风险

在云环境下，所有云上的信息处理、数据存储、安全维护等工作全都交给了云服务提供商，云服务提供商是否会妥善保管、处理、运用这些信息将会关系到企业的信息安全。因此，如何规范和监管云服务提供商的行为和服务，是一个亟待解决的问题。目前对于云中信息的处理缺乏有效的规范和立法，云环境提供商的信誉更多的依靠于用户的认同感，对云计算环境的规范和立法，是一个需要关注的问题。

(六) 未知的风险

未知的安全漏洞、软件版本、安全实践和代码更改等都可能给云计算带来安全威胁。

基于云计算的安全问题应对策略

(一) 云服务商的应对策略

对于云服务商，针对云计算环境下的电子商务信息安全防护要求，需要采用数据隔离、加密传输、访问控制、安全存储等一系列安全技术手段，为电子商务企业提供端对端的信息安全与隐私保护，从而保证用户信息的保密性、可用性和完整性。可以根据不同电子商务企业的具体需求，采用物理隔离、虚拟化和 Multi-tenancy 等方案来实现数据隔离。可以通过采用基于身份认证的权限控制方式，进行实时的用户身份监控、权限认证和证书检查来实现数据的访问控制。云计算系统应该提供数据的加密服务，对数据进行加密存储，防止数据被非法窥探或窃取。

(二) 电子商务企业的应对策略

对于电子商务企业，也要采取以下措施保证自身数据的安全。

1. 明智地选择云计算提供商。确保提供商在 IT 和安全服务方面都要有丰富的经验和很好的口碑。另外还有要明确当前自己企业所处的环境和所想达到的目标，小型电子商务企业希望通过使用云来提供文件共享类 IT 服务，大型企业则希望通过使用云来加强云备份，尽管有需求差异，但安全性、可用性和灵活性是不可缺少的。

2. 仔细阅读和咨询云服务提供商提供的隐私说明，确保云提供商有严格的数据管理标准条例，防止云计算提供者的超级用户有可能对企业的数据进行查看或修改，造成数据泄露。

3. 数据加密。电子商务企业在数据传输前对数据进行加密，在传输过程中即使被窃取，得到的也是乱码，能够保证数据的安全。加密的数据存储在云端，即使设施处于法律调查阶段，也会保证数据的安全性。

4. 监控数据。云监控通过和云计算平台的整合，针对网络、系统、应用等提供可用性、用户体验和安全性等方面的监控服务，保障云计算用户的业务稳定安全运行。当服务器端发生故障时，及时地给网站管理人员发送邮件和报警短信，第一时间了解网站状态，将故障修复时间降低到最小。同时也可以追踪用户访问网站的速度、协助用户判断故障等。电子商务企业使用监控系统，连续不断地监控云计算中的数据，可防止重要数据的丢失。

5. 数据备份。电子商务企业应该慎重考虑数据丢失的风险，定期进行数据的备份。在虚拟化的环境下，选择能支持基于磁盘的备份与恢复、能支持文件完整与增量备份的云服务，以便出现数据丢失时快速高效进行数据恢复。

结　　论

云计算强大的存储、运算功能以及理想的资源分配和共享模式为电子商务开辟了全新的发展领域，产生了全新的发展模式。电子商务企业选用云服务的最大障碍是云计算安全，但是随着云计算技术的飞速发展，各种新的云安全解决方案不断出现。各大云计算服务商也正着手制定各种相应的技术标准和管理流程，来防止用户数据的泄露，提高数据的安全性。同时，电子商务企业对电子商务的安全也不断提出新的具体的细化要求，促进云安全技术更进一步的发展。

参考文献

[1] 虚拟化与云计算小组．虚拟化与云计算［M］．北京：电子工业出版社，2009．
[2] 张恒喜，史争军．云时代电子商务安全研究［J］．现代商业，2011（14）．
[3] 周畅．基于云计算的电子商务探讨［J］．现代商贸工业，2011（16）．
[4] 陈龙，肖敏．云计算安全：挑战与策略［J］．数字通信，2010（3）．
[5] 云计算给点子商务带来的六大机遇［Z］．http：//www.zbintel.com/wz/11028696.htm．

大数据技术背景下的服务外包人才培养

于丽娟

一、服务外包产业发展

随着大数据、云计算、移动互联网、物联网等新技术的创新和应用，全球服务外包业已进入"3.0时代"。互联网数据中心（IDC）预测，到2017年，大数据技术和服务市场规模将达到324亿美元，年增长率将达27%。在3.0时代，服务外包的新业态将不断涌现，国家、城市、园区、企业等在技术模式、服务模式、运营模式、商业模式、供给模式、行业边界、服务内涵、竞争格局等方面展开了全方位竞争，这些都对服务外包企业提出了创新和转型升级的要求。

英国拉夫堡大学教授依兰·奥斯瑞认为，在"3.0时代"发包方不再仅仅要求降低成本，而是更关注一些增值服务，他们需要服务外包企业成为合作伙伴，需要服务外包企业从软件外包商向个性化解决方案提供商和集成综合服务提供商转型，并帮助他们更好地应对市场竞争。中国服务外包研究中心主任骞芳莉说，发包方更加重视利用外包实现自身业务流程的调整和转型，需要服务外包企业提供创新、有效的解决方案，为企业的转型提供咨询服务。发包方更加青睐利润分享协议、激励型协议、共享风险回报协议等新的定价模式。

IBM全球服务执行中心中国区总经理马塞尔·格瑞德曼认为，在"3.0时代"服务外包企业需要利用与客户相关的大数据，运用各种各样的应用软件对其进行分析和处理，研究出智能化、颠覆性的技术，为客户提供个性化的集成解决方案。由于大数据中的80%都是非结构化数据，本身并没有多大意义，因此企业必须具备挖掘和分析大数据的技术与能力，从数据中获得真正有价值的信息。

二、我国服务外包产业发展现状

近年来我国服务外包产业飞速增长，基本稳居世界第二大离岸服务外包承接国地位。据中国贸易报2014全球服务外包大会报道，2014年1~5月我国共签订服务外包合同65248份，合同金额400亿美元，同比增长43.5%；执行金额272.7亿美元，同比增长37.1%。

在这些数据背后，我国服务外包产业将面临着一系列挑战。从承接离岸服务外包的总额来看，与印度差距明显且有差距拉大的趋势；从服务外包成本优势来看，马来西亚、越南、柬埔寨、菲律宾等其他亚洲国家普遍具有成本优势，同样纷纷鼓励承接国际服务外包业务，这使得竞争日趋激烈。

再从我国的服务外包企业来看，统计数据显示，我国约有2.6万家服务外包企业，其中大部分是中小企业，普遍存在着创新和转型升级中投入不足的问题。依兰·奥斯瑞认为，中国服务外包企业虽然数量众多，但没有形成较大规模、有较强国际影响力的企业，没有像IBM那样能接到国际大单的大公司，没有企业带领国内同行共同创新和转型升级、克服企业规模偏小的不利因素。一些专家认为，我国服务外包企业需要从商务流程外包和信息技术外包向业务流程管理外包和知识流程外包转型，从被动外包商转为主动管理服务商。

中国服务外包研究中心调查结果显示，约有73%的企业认为人才缺乏是其发展过程中面临的主要问题，其中接近50%的受访企业认为难以招录到合适的中高端人才，行业平均人才缺口约为20%~30%。同时，我国服务外包产业人均产值不足3万美元。这些数据表明，我国服务外包产业最突出的问题是人才供给难以满足业务的快速发展，尤其是高层次人才的匮乏。骞芳莉表示，高层次人才供给明显跟不上产业发展需要，能够引领产业或者某个领域发展方向的领军型人才及具有国际视野、渠道和经验的国际化人才都非常缺乏，这是影响我国服务外包企业转型升级的主要原因。

[作者简介] 于丽娟，北京联合大学管理学院。

三、我国服务外包人才培养现状

服务外包产业具有人员流动率高，对人才的需求量大，以及批量招聘的特点，目前高等院校已成为我国服务外包人才培养的重要基地，很多高校通过改革教学体系培养服务外包人才，主要模式有以下两大类。

1. 改革人才培养教学体系和课程体系

根据服务外包人才的知识和能力需求特点，大多数高校对外包人才的培养是改革教学体系和课程体系。例如，北京联合大学在国家级和北京市级服务外包人才培养实验区的统筹下，系统构建了"一体两翼"的人才培养框架，构建了"三三分流"的课程体系实施方案。"一体两翼"是指以服务科学知识、服务意识、服务能力培养为主体，以信息技术运用能力培养为一翼，以服务外包业务领域工作能力培养为另一翼。"三三分流"是指大类培养与公共基础、分流培养与专业能力、综合应用与职业导向三个阶段，培养ITO、BPO和KPO三类服务外包人才。在具体实施时成立了服务外包实验班，改革课程体系，进行服务外包类课程建设和师资培养，与文思创新等服务外包企业广泛开展校企合作，共建校外实践基地。

对外经济贸易大学在信息管理与信息系统专业的课程体系中增加了服务外包相关课程，如金融业务管理、金融信息管理，其目标是培养金融行业服务外包人才。

2. 校企合作多种途径培养服务外包人才

在充分研究服务外包企业需求的基础上，结合学校办学实际，以多种校企合作模式培养服务外包人才，如共建服务外包学院或专业，为企业定向培养服务外包人才等。杭州师范大学挂牌成立杭州国际服务工程学院，与多家国内外知名企业如微软、IBM、思科、凯捷、东软等开展深度合作，建有"微软IT学院国际认证考试中心""IBM实验中心""思科网络实验室"等合作平台，与企业合作编写教材，覆盖金融、计算机、外语、实践实训等课程，在师资方面实现教师企业化，企业老师学校化。该校采用"2+1+1"的学程模式：前两年构筑公共和专业基础，以校内教师为主，企业专家为辅；第三年是专业课程和企业课程嵌入，企业专家授课为主，校内教师为辅，注重企业技能训练；第四年是能力提升训练，以企业实践为主，包括企业实习和毕业设计，采用专兼结合的双导师制，即校内教师与企业专家共同指导，实现人才培养与企业需求"无缝衔接"，实现为企业定向培养人才的目标。此模式充分发挥了高校学历教育优势和企业实务实践优势，是对学历教育和实训模式的综合和优化。

常熟理工学院国际服务工程学院实施学分制，嵌入的企业课程占有近23个学分，以企业需求为主构建教学内容，并在培养体系中引入了多家企业的课程，由学生自行选择。青岛理工大学建立和实践与教学体系紧密结合的大学生创新性实验，开展校内外学科竞赛及社会实践等系列活动。

四、大数据技术背景下的服务外包人才培养

高校对服务外包人才培养进行了有益的探索，为我国服务外包产业输送了大量人才。然而新兴技术不断涌现、大数据时代到来，服务外包产业提升需要更多高层次、具备新兴技术与大数据技术能力的服务外包人才。为此需要进一步改革现有的人才培养体系。

1. 服务外包人才的培养理念

服务外包人才与传统专业人才在知识、能力及素质的需求方面具有共同点。表现在他们都需要在知识、能力和素质三方面达到协调发展。面对当代社会知识量激增，知识陈旧率加快，获取知识的能力将比知识本身更重要，因此各类专业人才还必须具备创新精神和创新能力，具备可持续发展能力。因此，与传统专业人才培养相同，对服务外包人才的培养应树立以学生发展为中心的教育理念，并以学生成长和发展作为教育的核心价值取向。

2. 服务外包人才培养的专业领域

外包产业是现代高端服务业的重要组成部分，具有信息技术承载度高、附加值大、资源消耗低、环境污染少、吸纳就业（特别是大学生就业）能力强、国际化水平高等特点。目前，服务外包广泛应用于IT服务、人力资源管理、金融、会计、客户服务、研发、产品设计等众多领域，这在高校的专业人才培养方面具有普遍意义。调查显示，全球服务外包领域中扩张最快速的是IT服务、人力资源管理、媒体公关管理、客户服务、市场营销。随着服务外包产业发展和服务方式的创新，服务外包业务范围将不断扩

张，业务层次不断提高，服务的附加值也将明显增大。可见，服务外包人才既要具备某一专业领域的知识和能力，又要具备服务领域的知识和能力，同时又要面对当今科学技术高度分化又趋向综合性的要求，是一种跨专业领域的复合型人才。对服务外包人才培养应基于高校现有的专业如IT技术、人力资源管理、金融、会计等进行改革，在这些专业基础上，扩展服务外包领域相关的知识，以适应产业发展需要，使专业人才更适应服务型社会发展的需要。

3. 服务外包人才培养的课程体系

与传统专业人才相比，服务外包产业对人才的知识能力需求有明显不同。这类人才既需要具备所服务的专业领域的知识和技能，以胜任专业领域的工作任务，同时也需要具备服务外包领域的知识和技能。分析外包产业业务及职能，服务外包人才必须具备的服务领域的知识和能力包括：服务意识和服务能力；语言（国际语言）沟通与交流能力；服务项目管理能力。作为企业经营模式的创新，基于信息技术的服务外包业务将会得到不断发展，服务外包人才还需具备信息技术能力，特别是新兴技术，如云计算、3D打印技术、移动互联网、物联网等。大数据时代，发包业务很多都是基于大数据的分析与应用，这要求服务外包人才必须具有挖掘和分析大数据的技术与能力。

因此，基于某专业的服务外包人才培养应该扩展的知识或能力训练课程包括：服务外包知识类、人际沟通技巧类、语言交流类、信息技术类、数据挖掘与数据分析类等。当今世界科学技术的发展既高度分化，又趋向综合，各学科广泛交叉、相互渗透，很多重大问题都是涉及多学科的综合性课题，服务外包人才培养在课程体系上还应强调综合化，开设综合化课程和系列化课程，并应将跨学科的教学模式贯穿整个学习过程中。

4. 校企合作搭建实践教学平台

校企合作共建实践教学平台是提高人才培养质量的重要途径。这种实践平台可促使学生的理论知识与实践技能紧密结合，促进企业与学生的沟通和了解，缩短学生与用人企业需求的差距。校企合作的主要形式有：把企业部分真实的业务、开发环境移入学校；引入企业专家讲授企业实务知识和技术；企业专家与教师共同制订教学计划、编著教材；为服务外包企业制定订单式的课程体系，培养定制化的人才；将学生送到企业中参加工作实践，增进学生对企业文化和业务的理解，也为企业提供全方位选择人才的机会。

5. 其他创新与改革

考虑学生的个性化发展需要可采用学分制。学分制提供了一份富有弹性的指导性教学计划和一套灵活的管理制度，其出发点是使学生个性得到充分自由的全面发展，其归宿是培养更多的高质量人才。服务外包人才培养同样应积极推进学分制，给学生更多选择权，为学生全面发展提供一个广阔、自由选择的空间。

此外，还应建设具有丰富实践教学能力的教师队伍。调整教师考核机制，使教师有机会参加服务外包企业的实践，积累实践经验，提高他们的实践教学能力，尽可能地避免学校教学与企业实践的脱节。

参考文献

[1] 范丽敏. 中国服务外包业直面"3.0时代"[N]. 中国贸易报，2014.
[2] 鲍泓. 国家级服务外包人才培养模式创新实验区，中国高等院校服务外包人才培养课程体系建议书（2011）.
[3] 于丽娟，薛万欣，张士玉，等. BPO服务外包人才培养模式研究[J]. 科技管理研究，2011（9）.

档案部门参与非遗保护工作的优势与劣势分析

王巧玲 孙爱萍 陈文杰

自2003年联合国教科文组织通过《保护非物质文化遗产国际公约》以来，作为缔约国之一的中国便将"保护非物质文化遗产"（以下简称"非遗"）纳入了政府的职能范围，并在实践过程中逐步明确了文化行政部门在非遗保护领域的主管之责。然而"文化行政部门承担主管之责"并非意味着它是非遗保护工作的唯一主体。作为一项新兴的、涉及多方利益的、复杂的社会公共事务，非遗保护工作需要各相关主体的共同参与和协作努力。本文将以档案部门作为关注对象，着重分析其在参与非遗保护工作方面的优势和劣势，并就如何发挥优势、化解劣势提出相应的对策建议，以为更好地发挥档案部门在非遗保护领域中的作用提供参考借鉴。

1 档案部门参与非遗保护工作的优势

1.1 现代档案部门的使命定位与非遗保护根本目的基本一致

组织的使命定位，简单来说，即对组织的服务对象和服务功能的确定。现代档案部门的使命定位是与其传统的使命定位相对应的。新中国建立之初，档案部门的使命定位基本沿袭了古代的传统，即"党政机关存史、资政"。[1]然而，随着改革开放的深入和社会文明的进步，中国档案部门的性质已逐渐由政府机要单位转变为公共文化机构。与之相适应，档案部门的使命定位也逐渐转变为"为社会保留记忆、传承文化、提供信息"。

《中华人民共和国非物质遗产法（2011）》（以下简称《非遗法》）总则第四条规定，非遗保护工作要"有利于增强中华民族的文化认同，有利于维护国家统一和民族团结，有利于促进社会和谐和可持续发展"。[2]以此为据可以推断：从根本上说，非遗保护不是为了满足某一部分人当下的功利性需求，也不是要全面振兴所有的传统文化，以复活一个农耕时代的古老中国，其根本目的是为中国社会未来的可持续发展留存并提供精神财富。[3]由此可见，非遗保护的根本目的与现代档案部门的使命定位是基本一致的。

1.2 档案部门的业务环节与非遗保护工作的具体内容高度契合

根据《非遗法》的相关规定，非遗保护工作的具体内容主要包括：调查、认定、记录、建档、保存、传承、传播等七大类。具体来说，"调查"即确定某一地区或某种非物质文化的实际存在状况；"认定"即对某种具体的非物质文化的社会价值进行判断，以确定其是否应列为非物质文化遗产；"记录"即将非物质文化遗产所涉及的信息全面、真实地记录在适合的媒介载体上；"建档"即应用档案管理的原则和方法收集非遗档案，并对其进行科学整理使之有序化，以方便管理和利用；"保存"指使非遗档案得到长期、安全的保存；"传承"即让非遗所包含的核心知识、技术或技艺或生活方式被系统地继承；"传播"即让更多的人了解和关注非遗的相关信息。

一般来说，档案部门的具体业务主要由以下八个相互关联的环节构成：收集、鉴定、整理、保管、检索、编研、利用、统计。其中收集、鉴定、整理、保管、检索和统计是档案的基础工作，编研与利用是档案的开发利用工作。需要特别指出的是，口述历史档案的收集，通常也需要首先开展调查和记录

［基金项目］本文系国家社科基金面上项目"国家层面的私人档案信息资源体系建设研究"（项目批准号：12BTQ046）、北京联合大学社会科学类新起点计划项目（2013—2014年）"北京市档案部门参与非物质文化遗产保护工作的现状及对策研究"的阶段性成果。

［作者简介］王巧玲，孙爱萍，北京联合大学应用文理学院；陈文杰，北京市档案局。

工作。

对比非遗保护工作的具体内容和档案部门的业务环节，我们不难看出，口述档案的收集与非遗的调查与记录之间、一般档案的基础工作与非遗的建档与保存之间、档案的开发利用与非遗的传承与传播之间存在着高度契合关系，见表1。

表1 档案部门业务环节与非遗保护具体工作内容之间的对应契合关系

档案部门业务环节	口述历史档案的收集	一般档案的基础工作	档案的开发利用
非遗保护具体工作内容	非遗的调查、记录	非遗的建档、保存	非遗的传承、传播

1.3 非遗的档案化保护在中国具有十分重要的现实意义

所谓非遗的档案化保护，就是采用特定的手段将非遗以特定的方式记录在一定的载体上，从而形成物质化的档案，纳入到档案部门的管理范围，以档案系统的方式来保护它，以使其得以世代传承和传播。[4]

作为有着五千年悠久文明历史的国家，中国拥有数量惊人的非遗宝藏。据初步统计，全国各地现存的非遗项目达87万项之多；但与此同时，中国的非遗有很大一部分源自农耕时代甚至是原始氏族时代，其赖以生存的文化生态环境正在无可挽回地成为即将消失的历史。[5]

因此，在这样的背景下，对这些活态生存环境极其恶劣的非遗抢救性地实施档案化保护，从而使其所包含的有价值的信息得以流传后世，具有非常重要的现实意义。

1.4 档案部门是在非遗建档和保存方面最具有专业优势的机构

相对于其他各类组织或机构而言，档案部门应该说是在非遗建档和安全保存方面最具有专业优势的专门机构。档案部门不仅有成熟的收集档案材料并使之有序化的科学管理经验，有专门的适用于各种媒体介质档案安全存放的库房，还有成体系的相关管理机制和专职工作人员。因此，从理论上说，由档案部门指导非遗建档并接收非遗档案，是确保其得到永久妥善保存，方便社会公众查找利用的最佳选择。

1.5 很多档案部门已实际参与了非遗保护工作

实践中，已有很多档案部门实际参与了非遗保护工作，其中以云南省的情况最为突出。云南省境内少数民族众多，拥有丰富的非遗资源。少数民族档案是云南省档案部门的特色馆藏之一。根据笔者的调研，云南省档案部门还专门针对少数民族制定了分区分批实施调查、记录和建档的工作计划。目前云南省档案部门已经收集的少数民族档案有佤族土司的实物档案；傣族的贝叶经、折叠经和绵纸经；白族家谱档案；纳西族东巴文档案；拉祜族、基诺族、哈尼族的结绳、刻木记事和数豆计龄用的木、绳等。[6]虽然云南省档案部门所开展的工作没有直接以"非遗"为名头，但由于少数民族档案与非遗之间存在很强的渊源关系，云南省的档案部门实际参与了大量的非遗保护工作。

除了主动进行调查、记录和建档以外，将非遗档案接收进馆是近年来档案部门参与非遗保护工作最常见的一种方式。例如，截至2013年3月，广东清远市档案馆已先后接收了三批共47个非遗项目的档案资料，其中包括列入国家级非遗名录的瑶族耍歌堂，列入省级非遗名录的舞马鹿、舞被狮、凤舞、闹花灯、瑶族长鼓舞、小长鼓舞、英石假山盆景传统工艺、豆腐节等。[7]

2 档案部门参与非遗保护工作的劣势

2.1 主体身份未被明确写入相关法规性文件，导致档案部门参与非遗缺乏专项资金支持

根据笔者目前所收集到的资料，在2003年至今中国政府颁布的所有指导非遗保护工作开展的正式文件中，无论是国家层面的，还是地方层面的，都没有明确提到档案部门在非遗保护工作中的职责和地位。

以国家层面的情况为例，国家层面的法规性文件共有两部：《国务院办公厅关于加强我国非物质文化遗产保护工作的意见（2005）》（以下简称《意见》）和《非遗法》。其中，《意见》做出了建立非遗保护工作部际联席会议制度的决定，然而在联席会议的九个成员单位中并没有档案局。[8]在《非遗法》第四章第三十五条有关公共文化机构的非遗保护职责的相关规定中，所列举的公共文化机构只有图书

馆、文化馆、博物馆、科技馆，而没有档案馆。[9]

档案部门属于非生产性部门，其业务经费需要靠财政拨款支持。而在中国的体制背景下，主体身份没有被明确写入相关正式文件之中，就意味着档案部门参与非遗保护得不到政府的专项经费支持。根据笔者的实地调研，缺少经费支持正是档案部门目前在参与非遗保护工作中面临的最大困难之一。

2.2 对于非遗保护工作的意义被普遍误认为仅限于建档和保存，导致档案部门的作用很难获得关注和重视

尽管根据我们前面的理论分析，档案部门的业务工作与非遗保护工作的具体内容在诸多方面存在着高度契合关系，但从公众的认知情况来看，绝大部分的人都认为档案部门在非遗保护工作中能够发挥作用领域仅限于建档和保存，即使是在非遗档案管理的专业研究者中也不乏有人持这一观点。[10]

而与此同时，在政府主导的非遗保护工作中，"建档和保存"与"传承和传播"相比，前者在获得重视的倾向性方面存在明显的劣势。这是因为：第一，"建档和保存"工作相对比较隐性，且很难与"政绩"挂钩；而"传承和传播"工作则相对更显性，容易与经济发展、城市建设等通常的"政绩"指标相关联，更易获得外界的关注和支持。另外，中国的非遗保护工作还处在开展初期，很多非遗项目档案的累积数量和面临的安全风险还未在现实中形成对科学有序化管理与安全保存的迫切需求。

综上所述，由于公众的普遍误解，档案部门在非遗保护工作中的作用被人们主观缩小为仅与建档和保存有关，又由于"建档和保存"工作相对较难获得外界的关注和支持，且这类工作还未成为现实的迫切需求，档案部门在非遗保护工作中的作用在实践中往往容易被忽略，而这也对其参与非遗保护工作带来了很大的困扰。

2.3 改革还未深入开展，导致档案部门自身在全面参与非遗保护工作方面还欠缺足够的条件

无论是性质的转变，还是使命的重新定位，档案部门都还处在变革的过渡阶段。因此，在充分发挥档案部门的作用，参与除建档和保存以外的其他非遗保护工作上，尤其是在如何促进传播和传承上，档案部门自身在思想认识、组织设置、工作机制、管理经验以及相应场所的准备方面都还有所欠缺。这显然也是目前档案部门参与非遗保护工作亟待解决的问题。

3 发挥档案部门参与非遗保护工作优势、化解劣势的对策建议

就档案部门如何通过自身的努力发挥其参与非遗保护工作的优势、化解劣势，笔者有如下建议。

3.1 用现代档案部门使命定位的思想来统一内部工作人员的认识

要在档案部门内部掀起一场意识变革，促使内部工作人员认识到在新的历史时期档案部门作为公共文化机构，其使命定位必然要发生的转变，以及在上述背景下参与非遗保护工作对于推进档案部门实现上述转变、适应现代社会发展的需要，推进档案事业科学发展具有重要意义。同时要抓住目前中国政府正在酝酿修订《档案法》的机会，争取将相关的内容写入法律之中。

3.2 在档案部门内部设置专门负责推进参与非遗保护工作的组织机构

要针对非遗保护，在档案部门内部设置专门的组织机构，由其负责研究如何在工作体系设置上将参与非遗保护工作与档案部门的业务工作相关联，使参与非遗保护工作成为档案部门业务工作的有机组成部分，并积极推进档案部门参与非遗保护工作。

3.3 制定从最优势的地方入手，从优势扩展到化解劣势的非遗保护参与方案

在参与非遗保护工作的具体行动方案上，首先要以目前档案部门最具有专业组织优势的地方，同时也是最符合公众普遍认知的"建档和保存"入手，一方面建立与外界的联系，另一方面实现馆藏资源的优化；其次，在上述工作的基础上，改变工作模式，将被动接收转变为主动征集；同时建立界面良好的非遗档案数据库，实现对非遗档案资源的信息化管理；第三，在拥有一定馆藏的基础上，积极进行非遗档案馆藏资源开发，促进非遗的传承与传播；最后，全面参与非遗保护工作。

3.4 与其他政府部门、非营利组织、高校等相关单位建立战略合作伙伴关系

由于非遗保护工作需要大量的经费和人力，而根据前面的分析档案部门目前恰恰缺乏相应的支持；

又由于非遗保护工作本应是全社会的共同之责，同时中国目前在民众相关的意识觉醒和民间力量的兴起方面已为民间参与非遗保护工作准备了现实条件。例如，成立于2003年的北京文化遗产保护中心就是一个致力于文化遗产保护的民间机构。[11]因此，基于上述几个方面的考虑，笔者认为，档案部门在参与非遗保护工作的过程中，不仅要与其他相关政府部门建立合作关系，更要充分挖掘社会志愿资源，有计划、有目的地与相关的高校、研究机构、社会公益组织等民间力量建立战略合作伙伴关系，围绕非遗档案馆藏共同开发和开展调查记录、学术研究、特色教育、文化休闲等相关项目。

参考文献

[1] 王春晖. 我国公共档案馆职能现状分析与定位研究 [D]. 河南：郑州大学，2010：23－27.

[2] 中国非物质文化遗产网. http：//www. ihchina. cn/inc/faguiwenjian. jsp

[3] 曾平. 论我国非物质文化遗产保护的基本立场与核心理念——对《中华人民共和国非物质文化遗产法》的学理解读 [J]. 中华文化论坛，2011（3）：68－74.

[4] 吴品才，储蕾. 非物质文化遗产档案化保护的理论基础 [J]. 档案学通讯，2012（5）：75－77.

[5] 同 [3]。

[6] 云南档案信息网. http：//www. ynda. yn. gov. cn/ynda/2738188573441261568/

[7] 清远日报. 市群艺馆向市档案馆移交第三批市级非遗档案资料. 2013. 3. 28

[8][9] 中国非物质文化遗产网. http：//www. ihchina. cn/inc/faguiwenjian. jsp

[10] 陈祖芬. 非物质文化遗产档案管理主体研究——以妈祖信俗档案管理为例 [J]. 档案学通讯，2011，1990（1）16－19.

[11] 北京文化遗产保护中心官网. http：//www. bjchp. org/

Investigation and Study on the Present Situation of Enterprise Website Construction of Intellectual Property Agencies

Wang Xiaohong   Wu Jianping

1 INTRODUCTION

Intellectual property refers to creations of the mind: inventions, literary and artistic works, and symbols, names, images, and designs used in commerce. It has the characteristics of invisibility, dualism, validation and monopoly. With the continuous improvement of intellectual property protection, the role of intellectual property is emerging in the world economy and the development of science and technology. The intellectual property has become the strategic resource in national development and the core essential factor of international competitiveness. Electronic application refers to submitting application of intellectual property rights to the competent department of the national intellectual property in the form of electronic documents. In the patent law treaty and the detailed rules for the patent cooperation treaty drafted by the World Intellectual Property Organization (WIPO), the requirements of electronic application have been put forward and its legitimacy has been confirmed. The Japanese Patent Office is the first successful implementation of electronic application system. Since then, many countries have started to follow and consider the paperless patent literature as the development direction.

In China, although intellectual property system has just only 20 years of history, the speed of development is very fast. Take year 2012 as an example, it is reported that China ranks the first in the world in the number of patent application with 635,000 pieces, and the fourth in the international patent application with 19,926 pieces; China has reached 3.23 pieces per million population in terms of invention patent ownership; the number of trademark registered is 1,648,000 pieces and the cumulative effective registrations of trademark continue to rank the first in the world; the number of works registration is 688,000 pieces and the number of software copyright registration is 139,000 pieces and both break the record[1].

At present, the competition of intellectual property industry is very fierce, and the intellectual property agencies are usually small and medium - sized enterprises (SMEs). With the development of information technology and the increasing economic globalization, the intellectual property agencies want to promote publicity and provide information services, expand scope of business and international market, promote informatization construction and improve enterprise competitiveness through network. The role of website in the enterprise development has received more attention of SMEs. Under the e - commerce environment, how to establish a website and play its role fully will have the vital significance to realize the rapid development of intellectual property agency industry.

Now, the research perspectives on intellectual property could be summarized as follows:

One of the perspectives is based on the construction of network platform for intellectual property information. Xiaoqing Feng[2] pointed out that the construction of network platform for intellectual property information is an important part of enterprise information construction, and is also an important safeguard for the enterprise to

---

[Foundation Item] Philosophy and Social Science Plan Research Projects (11JGB040) from the Beijing Municipal Government.

[Author Introduction] Wang Xiaohong, Management College of Beijing Union University, E - mail: wxh8789@163.com; Wu Jianping, China Waterborne Transport Research Institute, E - mail: wujp@wti.ac.cn.

develop technological innovation activities and implement intellectual property strategy. Yu Jiang and Ye Chen[3] adopted the social network analysis which combined patent and trademark application data between 2000 – 2010 to analyze the network structure. Wei Huang, Ji Li and Wentao Wang[4] studied the network influence of provincial intellectual property office website of China by using link analysis.

The second perspective is based on the intellectual property culture. Fang Yao and Hua Liu[5] thought the practice of intellectual property culture in China mainly relies on the government. Hua Liu and Ying Zhou[6] structurally reflected current status of Chinese social public's IP protection awareness.

The third perspective is based on the information service system of intellectual property. Xiaofeng Yang[7] analyzed the current status of patent information services, problems and solutions based on a website sample survey method. Xiaoqing Feng[8] analyzed the present situation and problems of the service system construction of intellectual property in China.

Although there are quite a few researches on intellectual property, the researches involving the enterprises of intellectual property agency are comparatively few, especially website construction of intellectual property agencies. The agency work of intellectual property plays an important role in promoting the construction and development of the intellectual property system. It is necessary to analyze and study the present situation of website construction of intellectual property agencies, its problems and solutions.

This paper is organized as follows: first of all, it introduces the background of the research; secondly, it explains research content and object, data collection and analysis method; thirdly, it analyzes the survey results; fourthly, it provides some suggestions for enterprises to prompt and improve their website construction; last of the full text, it comes up with the foresight and future work.

II RESEARCH CONTENT AND METHOD

A. Research Content

E – commerce is becoming more and more popular in the world because of its convenience and absence of time and space limitations. Today, e – commerce has become a jot point of economy. Either the traditional manufacture or the new industry takes e – commerce as a new commercial mode of business operation, and invests to establish websites, so as to engage in commercial activities. Because of the improvement of enterprise operation environment and lower cost operation, e – commerce has been adopted by more and more SMEs to face market challenges and opportunities.

The enterprise website is an important window for external publicity through network, and an important platform to provide services. The website target audiences of intellectual property agencies usually have professional background, so the ability of website information and service is more targeted. Investigation on the present situation of website construction can provide better understanding of the network application of intellectual property agency industry. Some reasonable suggestions are put forward to solve the problems existing in the process of website construction and promotion, so enterprise websites can provide better service for the development of intellectual property agencies.

Based on literatures of website evaluation research and principles of measurability, integrity and feasibility, this paper carries out the research from the following aspects, as shown in Table I.

TABLE I
THE RESEARCH CONTENT

Aspects	Items
Website domain name and age	Domain name
	Domain name age

续表

Aspects	Items
Website information service	Website language
	Website column
	Website function
	Site map
	Three elements of page
	Traffic statistics
	Baidu snapshot date
Website influence	Website ranking
	Google PR
	Baidu inclusion
	Number of inverse link

Website domain name and age: website domain name and website domain name age.

Website information service: website language, website column, website function, sitemap, of three elements, website traffic statistics and Baidu snapshot date. The website functions mainly include data downloading, online consultation, message board, customer management, search function, business information, enterprise e-mail, online application and internal office, etc. The three elements of page include title, key words and description.

Website influence: website ranking, Google PR, Baidu inclusion and number of inverse link.

B. Research Object

Being the national cultural center with the most concentrated colleges, Beijing is the center of education, decision-making, high-level talents training, modern education thought and mode, international education exchange, scientific education research and education resource. In recent years, the intellectual property agency industry has developed continuously along with the market demand of Beijing. The development of intellectual property agencies in Beijing is faster than the other parts of China. Beijing has become the most intensive distribution area of national patent service organizations and professional talents. It is reported that the total of patent application in Beijing was 546,113 pieces which was the largest in China by the end of 2012[9], and the number of patent agents in Beijing accounts for about one third of the country's total. By the end of June 2013, there had been 255 patent agencies in Beijing which had registered on the website of State Intellectual Property Office of the People's Republic of China (http://www.cpo.cn.net/). Among them, 205 agencies (80.4%) have independent website domain names, and the rest have either established websites on the third-party platform or have yellow pages. Thus this paper selects the patent agencies in Beijing whose websites have independent domain names as research objects.

C. Data Collection Method

With the help of some research tools, the survey on the present situation of website construction of patent agencies in Beijing was made on December 12th - 16th in 2013. The work on data collection was done by six professionals, and three professionals in a group did a sample survey together in order to prevent deviation. Data collection is mainly divided into the following three steps.

Most of website domain names are obtained through the website of Beijing Intellectual Property Office (http://www.bjipo.gov.cn/) and others are found by Baidu search.

The information including website language, website column, website function, sitemap and traffic statistics, is collected by accessing websites directly. The information including title, key words and description of homepage is gathered by viewing source file of page. The entry is recorded as '1' if the website has the related content; otherwise it is recorded as '0'.

The information including website domain name age, website ranking, Baidu snapshot date, Google PR, Baidu inclusion and number of inverse link is gotten by the tools (http://tool.chinaz.com/).

D. Data Analysis Method

The statistical analysis software SPSS is used to analyze the survey results and some methods of statistical analysis are adopted, such as contingency analysis, variance analysis and T – test analysis.

Firstly, the overall situation of website construction is analyzed by calculating the proportion of each option that is the proportion of 1.

Secondly, the differentiation analysis of website construction is made. Enterprise websites are divided into four groups according to domain name age, that is, within 3 years (represented as a1), between 3 and 5 years (represented as a2), between 5 and 10 years (represented as a3) and more than 10 years (represented as a4). Then the contingency analysis between domain name age and information service is made; the variance analysis between domain name age and Google PR is completed; the T – test analysis between information service and Google PR is conducted.

III RESULTS AND ANALYSIS

A. Situation of Website Construction

- Website domain name and age

Domain name is the bond that links the enterprise and the Internet, and the sign of enterprises on the Internet. It plays an important role in identification of enterprise website. The domain name should not only be related to the industry, but also be in accordance with the marketing goal of enterprise. The survey indicates that there are 70 websites (34.1%) containing the IP (Intellectual Property) characters in the domain name.

Domain name age refers to the period from registration time to query time of domain name. It directly affects the credibility of domain name, and domain names of 10 years old have a big advantage[10]. The survey shows that the website domain name age of patent agencies in Beijing is comparatively long, with websites whose domain name age above 5 years accounting for about 70%. There are 52 websites (25.3%) whose domain name age is above 10 years, 92 websites (44.9%) whose domain name age is between 5 and 10 years, and 61 websites (29.8%) whose domain name age is less than 5 years. The website domain name age of Beijing Deheng Law Offices (http://www.dhl.com.cn/) has a history of nearly 17 years.

- Website information service

The statistical results of website information service are shown in Table II.

TABLE II
THE STATISTICAL RESULTS OF WEBSITE LANGUAGE, FUNCTION AND PAGE ELEMENTS

	Items	Number of agency	Percentage (%)
Website language	Chinese	202	98.5
	English	182	88.8
	Japanese	103	50.2
	Traditional Chinese	21	10.2
	German	4	2.0
	French	4	2.0
	Korean	44	21.5
	Russian	3	1.5

续表

Items		Number of agency	Percentage (%)
Website function	Data download	117	57.1
	Online consultation	48	23.4
	Message board	80	39.0
	Customer management	24	11.7
	Search function	65	31.7
	Business information	34	16.6
	Enterprise e-mail	17	8.3
	Online application	3	1.5
	Internal office	9	4.4
Page elements and other information	Title	195	95.1
	Key words	111	54.1
	Descriptions	102	49.8
	Traffic statistics	20	9.8
	Sitemap	26	12.7
	Independent title	93	45.4

Enterprise websites are usually operated in various languages to provide prosecution, litigation, transaction and consultation services relating to patent, trademark, copyright and other intellectual property related matters for customers from China and around the world. There are 182 websites (88.8%) with more than 2 languages, 113 websites (55.1%) with more than 3 languages, 51 websites (24.9%) with more than 4 languages, and 8 websites (3.9%) with more than 5 languages. It is shown that patent agencies in Beijing usually attach great importance to multi-language websites construction because they usually have foreign business and expect to develop international market through network. Yet without taking into full account of users' habits of different languages when agencies plan and construct their multi-language websites, the style and design of these websites are almost the same.

The enterprise websites of patent agencies in Beijing generally have the columns of about firm, company news, patent, trademark, copyright, regulation, professionals, links, download, contact us, etc. The column structure of website is simple. The column structure of enterprise website of Beijing Huicheng Zhilin Intellectual Property Agent Co., Ltd (http://www.zhilinlaw.com/) is shown in Fig. 1.

The statistical result of website functions, as shown in Table Ⅱ, demonstrates that enterprise websites of patent agencies in Beijing have only basic functions, such as data download, message board and search function. There are only 3 websites with online application platform; they are the website of Beijing Chofn Intellectual Property Agent Co., Ltd (http://www.chofn.com/), the website of Beijing Eastking Intellectual Property Right Agent Co., Ltd (http://www.eastking.net/) and the website of Beijing Drug IP Intellectual Property Agent Co., Ltd (http://www.drugip.com/). There are only 26 websites (12.7%) integrated with enterprise e-mail or internal office system. The patent

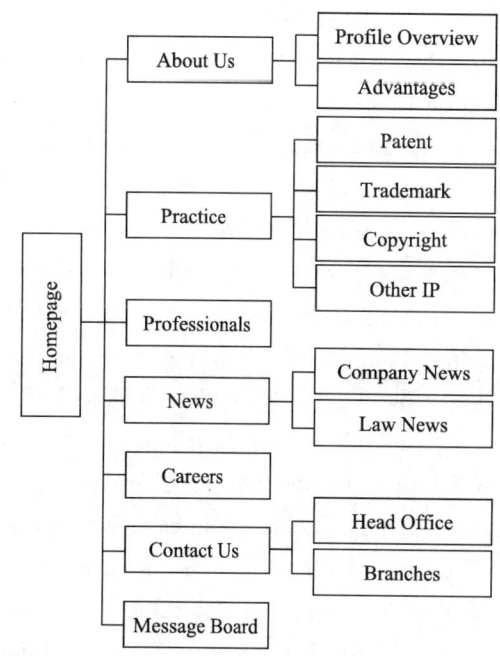

Fig. 1 The main website columns of Huicheng ZhilinIntellectual Property Agent Co., Ltd.

agencies in Beijing need to improve their website functions further.

Page title, usually displayed at the top of browser window, and whose role is to prompt page theme to search engine, is an important part of the search result. As shown in Table Ⅱ, most of website pages have set up page titles and there are only 45.4% of the websites whose each page is put up with the independent title, and most of the page titles are only the name or abbreviation name of enterprises. The survey indicates that enterprises do not conduct in-depth study on search engine and the page titles need to be improved, especially the title of each page.

Key words are used to specify page theme, and are the basis for search engine to judge page content. As shown in Table Ⅱ, there are only 54.1% of the websites whose homepage set up key words. This displays that about 46% of the websites are without key words, and the websites with key words also need further improvement in key word choice.

Description is used to illustrate the main content of website. It affects hits and it is also one part of the search result. As shown in Table Ⅱ, there are only 49.8% of the websites whose homepages have description information, while other 50.2% do not.

Website traffic is an important index to measure a website, and it can help enterprises to analyze the detailed data of visitors so as to increase website traffic[11]. The traffic statistics software can be installed to obtain the geographical location, source and numbers of visitors. As shown in Table Ⅱ, there are only 9.8% of the websites with traffic statistics software. This reflects that enterprises do not attach enough importance to traffic statistics and data analysis of visitors.

Sitemap is a navigation file generated according to structure, framework and content of website, and it is an indispensable factor of website optimization. Sitemap may facilitate spiders of search engine to grab pages and clearly understand website architecture, and it can increase numbers of important pages inclusion. As shown in Table Ⅱ, there are only 12.7% of the websites with sitemaps. This indicates that enterprises need to strengthen the awareness of submitting sitemap to search engine.

Baidu snapshot refers to a backup file of pure file generated when a page is included. Baidu snapshot date has become one of the criteria to evaluate the importance of website. Baidu snapshot is associated with update frequency of website. Usually websites update faster, and so does Baidu snapshot. The better snapshot date is always within 3 days. The survey indicates that there are 52 websites (25.4%) whose Baidu snapshot date is within 3 days; 40 websites (19.5%) whose Baidu snapshot date is from 3 to 30 days; 35 websites (17.1%) whose Baidu snapshot date is from 30 to 90 days; 78 websites (38%) whose Baidu snapshot date is above 90 days. These data show that the enterprises' less emphasis on website optimization has resulted in little unique content on their websites and the need to improve it.

- Website influence

Alexa[12] ranking can reflect the influence of website. One of the website optimization goals is to improve website ranking. The survey indicates the comparatively low website ranking of patent agencies. The website ranking of Beijing Chofn Intellectual Property Agent Co., Ltd. (http://www.chofn.com/) is the highest in patent agencies in Beijing, with its Alexa ranking 221,728.

Google PR (Page Rank) is a method for evaluating the importance of page and is used to represent page level. PR value is from 0 to 10; the higher the PR value is, the more important the page is. Usually the PR value above 7 illustrates that the website is very popular, and PR value of 4 means the website is good[13]. The survey shows that page level of patent agencies in Beijing is not high, with the PR value of 148 websites (72.2%) under 4; only 3 websites' PR value is 6, the highest figure. They are the website of Beijing Shengfeng Law Firm (http://www.lawyer8.com/), the website of Beijing Yingke Law Firm (http://www.yingkelawyer.com/) and the website of Beijing Zhongyin Law Firm (http://www.zhongyinlawyer.com/).

Baidu inclusion refers to the collected data of each page snapshot of a website, and it directly reflects the content and position of the website. The survey as shown in Table III indicates that Baidu inclusion quantity of patent agencies in Beijing is comparatively low and there are 89.8% websites whose Baidu inclusion quantity is under 1,000. The Baidu inclusion quantity of Bejing Deheng Law Offices (http://www.dhl.com.cn/) is up to 38,000 which is the highest in patent agencies in Beijing. The lower Baidu inclusion quantity reveals the slow updating of website information and the poor website navigation.

TABLE III
THE STATISTICAL RESULTS OF BAIDU INCLUSION AND NUMBER OF INVERSE LINK

Items		Number of agency	Percentage (%)
Baidu inclusion quantity	≤1000	184	89.8
	1000~5000	14	6.8
	5000~10000	2	1.0
	>10000	5	2.4
Number of inverse link	≤100	201	98.0
	>100	4	2.0

The number of inverse link is also an important part of the search result. External link pointing to the website of a patent agency is reverse link. The certain quantity and quality of reverse link are important to obtain good ranking, which can bring traffic and improve website ranking. The survey as shown in Table III demonstrates that numbers of inverse link of patent agencies in Beijing are very low and there are only 4 websites whose numbers of inverse link are above 100. They are the website of Beijing Shengfeng Law Firm (http://www.lawyer8.com/), the website of Beijing Yingke Law Firm (http://www.yingkelawyer.com/), the website of Beijing Dacheng Law Offices (http://www.dachengnet.com/) and the website of Beijing Chofn Intellectual Property Agent Co., Ltd (http://www.chofn.com/). The number of inverse link of Beijing Chofn Intellectual Property Agent Co., Ltd is 255, which is the highest in patent agencies in Beijing. This indicates that the construction of inverse link is ignored and the quality of inverse link is not very high.

B. Differentiation Analysis of Website Construction

- Website domain age and information service

The result of contingency analysis between domain name age and website information service is shown in Table IV. The result indicates that there is no significant difference between different domain name age and website function ($p > 0.05$), with the only exception of download function ($P < 0.05$). The reason may be that new websites are always willing to imitate mature well-known websites due to lack of experience. The websites whose domain name ages are more than 10 years old are more willing to provide download function for users because these websites usually have accumulated abundant network resources.

TABLE IV
THE RESULT OF CONTINGENCY ANALYSIS BETWEEN DOMAIN NAME AGE AND INFORMATION SERVICE

Items	Website domain name age				
	a1	a2	a3	a4	P (χ^2 Test)
Data download	47.2%	36.0%	59.8%	69.2%	0.025
Online consultation	11.1%	16.0%	30.4%	23.1%	0.096
Message board	27.8%	28.0%	43.5%	44.2%	0.208
Search function	22.2%	32.0%	27.2%	46.2%	0.061
Title	100%	96.0%	93.5%	94.2%	0.473
Independent title	36.1%	48.0%	50.0%	42.3%	0.511
Key words	69.4%	44.0%	51.1%	53.8%	0.189
Description	58.3%	36.0%	47.8%	53.8%	0.329

a1, a2, a3, a4 represent <3 years, 3~5 years, 5~10 years and >10 years respectively.

There is no significant difference between different domain name ages and three elements of page ($p > 0.05$). In general, the longer the website domain name age is; the more attention to content construction is paid. But the actual situation is not so, and the possible reason is that although patent agencies in Beijing set up page elements at the beginning of website construction, they do not pay attention to optimizing page elements and content due to lack of awareness of website promotion.

- Website domain name age and PR value

The result of homogeneity test of variance (F-test) between domain name age and PR value is shown in Table V, and the result of the least significant difference (LSD) between domain name age and PR value is shown in Table VI.

The results show that there is a significant difference between different domain name age groups and PR value ($P < 0.05$). Usually the older domain name age can bring more traffic and be very beneficial to improve website ranking in search engine.

TABLE V
THE RESULT OF VARIANCE ANALYSIS BETWEEN DOMAIN NAME AGE AND PR VALUE

	Items	SS	df	MS	F	P
PR	Inter-group	122.160	3	40.720	25.817	0.000
	Intra-group	317.030	201	1.577	-	-
	Total	439.190	204	-	-	-

TABLE VI
THE RESULT OF LSD ANALYSIS BETWEEN DOMAIN NAME AGE AND PR VALUE

(I) Website domain name age	(J) Website domain name age	MD (I-J)	STDEV	P
a1	a2	0.984*	0.327	0.003
a1	a3	1.705*	0.247	0.000
a1	a4	2.271*	0.272	0.000
a2	a3	0.721*	0.283	0.012
a2	a4	1.287*	0.306	0.000
a3	a4	0.566*	0.218	0.010

a1, a2, a3, a4 represent <3 years, 3~5 years, 5~10 years and >10 years respectively.

*. $\alpha = 0.05$.

- Website information service and PR value

Enterprise websites are divided into two groups according to Google PR value. As shown in Table VII, the result of T-test indicates that there is no significant difference in three elements of page in terms of different PR groups ($p > 0.05$). This result is consistent with the result of differentiation analysis between different domain name ages and three elements of page. But the actual situation is not so, and it is possible that enterprises do not pay attention to content optimization due to lack of consciousness of website promotion.

TABLE VII
THE RESULT OF T-TEST ANALYSIS BETWEEN PR VALUE AND INFORMATION SERVICE

Items	Google PR value		P (T-test)
	<4	≥4	
Data download	52.0%	70.2%	0.019
Online consultation	23.0%	24.6%	0.811

续表

Items	Google PR value		
	<4	≥4	P (T-test)
Message board	38.5%	40.4%	0.810
Search function	27.0%	43.9%	0.020
Title	95.3%	94.7%	0.687
Independent title	43.9%	49.1%	0.184
Key words	55.4%	50.9%	0.097
Description	50.0%	49.1%	0.265

For different PR groups, there are no significant differences between online consultation function and message board ($p > 0.05$), while there are significant differences between data download function and search function ($P < 0.05$). It is possible that websites with higher PR value are more willing to provide download and search function for users because they have rich network resources.

Through the investigation, the present situation of website construction of patent agencies in Beijing has been understood. The investigation shows that the domain name ages of enterprise websites are comparatively long; the website language is rich, but the website function is not very perfect; the Google PR value is relatively low, the website content updates slowly, the website navigation is not clear, and the quality of reverse link is not high. The difference analysis on website construction indicates that different domain name ages have a little effect on three elements of page and website function except download function, but there is a significant difference in Google PR value; the page three elements and the website functions have a little impact on Google PR value except download function and search function. In short, most of the websites of patent agencies in Beijing are information release websites with functions of data download, message board and internal search; the comprehensive quality of websites is not high; the website influence and radiation are comparatively small and the website usage is comparatively low.

IV DISCUSSION AND SUGGESTIONS

In view of the existing problems, some advice will be put forward through the reason analysis.

A. Consciousness of E-Commerce and Management

E-commerce can provide substantial benefits to SMEs through improved efficiency and raised business volume. It is very important that e-commerce can give a competitive advantage, and it can help strengthen market position and open up new business opportunities to improve profits.

The awareness of management and e-commerce of enterprises is relatively backward. Even today, some business decision-makers think that e-commerce means only sending business messages by e-mail, or just having a domain name registered on the Internet, or creating a website at World Wide Web. In fact, e-commerce is far more than that; it refers to a series of business activities in which inquiring, offering, ordering, marketing, advertising, paying and so on are handled or arranged through the Internet, intranet and extranet, etc. In addition, on the management side, there still exist some problems, such as unclear division of duties and labor, lack of person for network, and these problems will restrict the development of the enterprise.

The intellectual property agencies in Beijing should enhance the awareness of e-commerce. Enterprises also should apply a variety of ways to promote websites, not only the ways of the Internet, such as search engine optimization, reciprocal linking, but also the ways of traditional mass media, such as television and printing and advertising. The information management system of intellectual property agencies will be developed to realize the standardization of process management including patent application, fee payment, query of intellectual property review status and legal status.

B. Website Information Service

Based on the previous survey, it is shown that the majority of the websites of patent agencies in Beijing belong to information release websites, that is, the primary role of website is to publicize business philosophy, promote corporate culture and establish corporate image. Therefore, from the aspect of website information service, patent agencies in Beijing need to pay more attention to the following points:

- Paying attention to users' habits

With the acceleration of internationalization, a multi – language website has become an indispensable part of an enterprise. The website design style of different regions or countries varies greatly according to different users' habits. The page layout of Chinese websites is usually symmetrical and looks a bit complicated because of using more colors, pictures and animation. But those websites in European and American countries are usually concise because of using more text. So patent agencies in Beijing should pay considerable attention to users' habits of different areas and try to display pages in different styles and languages.

- Paying attention to information resource management

Now only a few enterprises use management system to manage information of patent, trademark, copyright and customers. Therefore, patent agencies in Beijing should speed up informatization construction of enterprises and use management system to manage enterprise customers and website content, and connect internal information with external information to enhance the working efficiency of enterprises through building network information platform, thus to achieve the maximization of efficiency and effectiveness.

Patent agencies in Beijing should reinforce the customer relation management, do market research on customer satisfaction, analyze the feed – back question in the BBS, e – mail and MSN, deal with the complaints of customers effectively, and improve communication with customers.

- Paying attention to page content quality

Page content is the most active factor in website and its role is to meet users'demands for information[14,15]. For any website, content quality is the core factor of website effect, and a website with high quality original content and rich information can usually get more traffic. With the rapid development of the Internet and the increasing number of users, the construction and maintenance of website content are also becoming more and more important. Patent agencies in Beijing should pay attention to the novelty and originality of website content, timely updating and regularly maintaining to avoid misleading users by out – of – date information, and attract more users to click and browse.

C. SEO Strategy

Search Engine Optimization (SEO) refers to using reasonable means to make the basic elements of website more suitable for search engine, more friendly to users, and more likely to be collected and prioritized by search engine[16]. SEO plays an important role in website promotion. Enterprise websites using SEO techniques can display their products and services to target customers and potential customers better, enhance enterprise popularity and improve enterprise influence, bring more customers for enterprise. The survey indicates that patent agencies in Beijing have not been fully aware of the necessity and importance of SEO to enterprise website, and have not yet implemented SEO strategy. Therefore, patent agencies in Beijing need to strengthen the awareness of SEO and implement SEO strategy actively in order to provide users with better information and services.

- Optimizing three elements of page

Each page can be set a unique and different title tag. The homepage title should follow the principle of "site name + key words", and the column title should follow the principle of "column name + site name". Setting different titles will help websites increase exposure rate. The homepage title can use patent agency name or website name, and other page titles can be associated with the content of each page. At the same time, attention should be paid to controlling the length of title, with no more than 30 Chinese characters.

Choose the right key words. Put important key words at the front of the title and pay attention to the numbers of key words in the title and their occurrence frequency in the article. Better choose no more than 5 key words and keep each key word in less than 8 Chinese characters.

The statements of description information should be smooth, with appropriate key words and no more than 80 Chinese characters. Different description information should be set up according to different pages of enterprise website. Description information may include the introduction of products and services, the company features and advantages, and contact information. It is better to use creative but not exaggerating statements to optimize description information and attract more possible users to access page.

- Optimizing website structure

Website structure tends to be flat structure which is beneficial for spiders of search engine to crawl and grab. Keep website directory as simple as possible with no more than 3 layers. Website column is a tree-like structure and website navigation should be clear. It is best to add text descriptions for pictures. To make link for each path will be conducive for spiders to find related pages quickly.

It is better to submit a sitemap actively to search engine. Search engine can use the sitemap to understand the internal structure of website clearly. If there is any change in the website, the sitemap will inform search engine immediately, which can improve the speed of page inclusion.

- Optimizing website link

Internal link refers to links between pages inside a website, and the reasonable website link can improve page inclusion and PR value. Internal link should try to use the text instead of image, flash and client script. It is very important to ensure that the internal link has unique URL, and each page has a link to homepage. In addition, according to Google rules, the number of internal links should be kept under 100.

The large number of external links can not only raise website ranking, but also bring more visitors to website indirectly. Establish exchange links to some related websites with higher PR value, but pay attention to the quality and quantity of exchange links and keep the number under 40. In addition, it is better to return partner's website irregularly to check the link to your website.

V CONCLUSION

The present situation of website construction of intellectual property agencies in Beijing is investigated from the aspects of website domain name and age, website information service and website influence. The main problems existing in the process of website construction and promotion are analyzed deeply. Then, some reasonable suggestions are put forward based on the investigation research. These research results can guide intellectual property agencies to establish their websites and play their role fully.

The investigation and study obtain the certain valuable conclusions, but there are still some limitations: the research objects are limited to patent agencies in Beijing and the research scope is small. The present situation of website construction of intellectual property agencies in other provinces and cities needs further research. All in above, we can believe under further research and practice concerning enterprise websites, the intellectual property agencies will have more achievements and contributions to the applications of e-commerce in the Internet.

ACKNOWLEDGMENT

This paper is supported by the Philosophy and Social Science Plan Research Projects: Research on the Networked Growth Performance of the Enterprises at the High-tech Industrial Park (11JGB040), from the Beijing Municipal Government.

We wish to thank professors Shiyv Zhang and Qiuyan Tao for the data analysis, and thank Jianhao Zhang for valuable discussions. We also want to thank my colleagues, Yilei Pei and Laiyv Liu, who helped and guided us to translate this paper into English.

REFERENCES

［1］ The Intellectual Property Development Research Center of the State Intellectual Property Office, "2012 The national intellectual property development report", May 2013.

［2］ Xiaoqing Feng, "Research on the construction of network platform for intellectual property information in China", *Journal of Hunan University (Social Sciences)*, Vol. 27, No. 3, pp. 137 – 142, May 2013.

［3］ Yv Jiang and Ye Chen, "A structure analysis of the global intellectual property rights network: based on patent data and trademark data", *Science & Technology Progress and Policy*, pp. 146 – 152, September 2013.

［4］ Wei Huang, Ji Li, and Wentao Wang, "Link – based analysis of the network influence of provincial intellectual property office website in China", *Information Science*, Vol. 30, No. 2, pp. 264 – 267, February 2012.

［5］ Fang Yao and Hua Liu, "The practice of intellectual property culture in China: status survey and policy suggestion", *Science & Technology Progress and Policy*, Vol. 30, No. 11, pp. 107 – 112, June 2013.

［6］ Hua Liu and Ying Zhou, "Survey of Chinese Public's IP protection awareness and pone recommendations", *China Soft Science*, pp. 103 – 111, October 2006.

［7］ Xiaofeng Yang, "Analysis on the current status of the domestic patent information", *Library Work and Study*, Vol. 205, No. 3, pp. 26 – 29, March 2013.

［8］ Xiaoqing Feng, "Study on the construction of service system of intellectual property to based on technical innovation and intellectual property strategy implement", *Science & Technology Progress and Policy*, Vol. 30, No. 2, pp. 112 – 114, February 2013.

［9］ The state intellectual property office, "The 2012 annual report of the state intellectual property office", http://www.sipo.gov.cn/ztzl/ywzt/zlwzn/2012qgzscqfzzkbg.pdf, May 2013.

［10］ Hui Zan, SEO actual combat password, Beijing: Electronic Industry Press, 2011.

［11］ Lingxia Chen, "Optimization of website search engine of provincial public libraries in China", *Library and Information Service*, Vol. 56, No. 21, pp. 88 – 91, November 2012.

［12］ Amazon, "Alexa the web information company", http://www.alexa.com, May 2008.

［13］ Xiaoli Yang, "Investigation and study on the SEO present situation of 20 domestic university library websites", *Library and Information Service*, Vol. 56, No. 13, pp. 105 – 108, July 2012.

［14］ Yasunori Shiono, Zhongli Kuang, Yoshitaka Nakagawa, Takaaki Goto, and Kensei Tsuchida, "Cooperative software development and usability evaluation: a web – based work management system for construction sites", *Journal of Software*, Vol. 5, No. 3, pp. 259 – 268, March 2010.

［15］ Zhongjun Li, "Research on the website key words seeding system based on SEO", *Journal of Computers*, Vol. 6, No. 1, pp. 75 – 82, January 2011.

［16］ Yongqi Ren and Yi Tang, "Research on search engine optimization based on user – centered", *Researches in Library Science*, No. 1, pp. 44 – 46, January 2009.

广州会展企业空间集聚特征与影响因素

方忠权

1 引 言

经过改革开放30多年的快速发展，会展业已经成为中国现代服务业的重要组成部分，是近年来最具活力的行业之一。特别是进入21世纪后，各级政府纷纷加大对会展业的投入，主要中心城市的会展企业数量显著增加，企业的空间分布呈明显的集聚态势。正是基于这种态势，北京、上海和广州提出要大力发展会展业集聚区，均希望通过打造集聚区来促进会展业的快速发展并提升区域会展业的竞争力。但从集聚发展与会展业竞争力的关系来看，中国会展业集聚程度偏低，企业规模偏小，集聚区综合配套与服务不够完善，业态较单一。因此，开展会展企业空间集聚研究，对于政府制定产业发展政策，引导和推进会展企业有效集聚，成功打造会展业集聚区，提升区域会展业的竞争力具有重要现实意义。

对于产业集聚现象，不同学科均给予了高度关注，并在不同的分析框架下进行论述，形成了具有代表性的马歇尔"三要素"学说、韦伯的"工业区位论"、克鲁格曼的"新经济地理思想"，以及波特的"集群学派"等许多理论[1-5]。长期以来，产业集聚研究主要集中在制造业领域。自20世纪70年代以后，全球呈现"工业型经济"向"服务型经济"转型的趋势，服务业得到迅速发展，在地理空间上的集聚趋势也进一步增强，因此，产业集聚的现有分析框架被越来越多地应用于服务业研究[6-9]。近年来，针对服务业内部各行业空间集聚的研究逐步增多。例如，杨永忠等研究了创意产业集聚区的形成路径与演化机理[10]；林彰平、闫小培对转型期广州市金融服务业空间格局变动过程及原因进行了研究，认为社会经济体制和金融管理体制转型、金融机构行为变化以及城市空间扩张分别是金融服务业空间格局变动的前提条件、微观基础和空间张力[11]；袁丰等引入空间点模式分析方法，探讨了1996—2006年苏州市区不同空间尺度上信息通信企业的时空集聚特征[12]；毕秀晶等运用GIS技术和社会网络分析方法探讨了上海大都市区软件产业的空间分布、演变特征及影响因素，发现上海软件产业空间分布的集聚化特征明显，但产业集聚中心位置发生了从中心城区向郊区的偏移[13]；王承云分析了日本研发产业的空间集聚与影响因素，利用统计数据考察了日本国内3302家R&D企业的空间分布和集聚现象，认为在日本研发产业的集聚和发展过程中，政策驱动和市场驱动起到了重要作用[14]；甄峰等以南京市为例，证实了汽车服务业集聚空间的出现以及不同行业类型的空间表现[15]。

作为现代服务业重要内容之一的会展业，从企业空间集聚角度进行的研究还极为少见。目前国外会展研究主要集中在会展的经济影响、会展地点的选择、会展旅游者的决策行为和会展目的地的营销等几方面[16-19]。中国会展业发展相对较晚，研究主要集中在会展业发展的问题与对策、会展对经济社会的影响、会展业竞争力评价和会展教育等方面[20-22]。基于"空间"视角的研究大致包括两个方面：一是关于会展产业集群的相关研究。Jin等实证研究了集群对展览目的地吸引力的影响，认为集群可以解释展览目的地吸引力的空间分布，并开发了相应的测量方法，测度了展览业中的集群效应[23]；Bathelt将会展看作"临时集群"，认为这样的"临时集群"是知识交流、网络建立以及创意产生的白热地带[24]；Wu等从系统动力学的视角考察不同因素如何对会展产业集群产生正或负的影响，表明会展产业集群的演化是来自内、外部系统的综合优势的结果，系统内部的供给因素和系统外部的市场需求是这种演化的关键[25]；张俐俐运用区位熵分析了广州会展产业集群的LQ系数，认为广州会展产业集群已经形成，

[基金项目] 教育部人文社科规划项目（10YJA79004）[Foundation: Humanities and Social Science Foundation of the Ministry of Education, No. 10YJA790047]。

[作者简介] 方忠权（1966—），男，湖北云梦人，博士，广州大学旅游学院教授，注册规划师，主要从事会展产业发展、旅游开发与规划研究。E-mail: fzq33@sina.com。

并有较高的集聚程度及一定的优势和特色[26];王永刚、郭旸通过聚类分析检验了中国会展业的集群化程度,并分析其"链群式结构"的演进趋势[27]。二是关于会展业空间布局的相关研究。叶洪涛论证了中国会展产业总体布局的基本发展战略,提出了优化会展业布局的措施[28];鞠航等基于不平衡发展理论和产业布局原理,论述了影响现代会展业布局的新因素,提出了会展业未来发展布局的创新模式[29];王云龙以北京、上海和广州为例,论述了会展经济的空间运动形式,认为会展业的空间结构变化主要表现为会展场馆的空间聚集与扩散,饭店、公司、资金、技术和专业人才等会展经济的生产要素依此聚散[30];朱海森分析了国际会展产业空间布局的特点,以德国和香港会展业布局的经验为例,分析了会展业布局的条件和要求[31]。

从国内外相关研究来看,虽然服务业空间集聚研究已经取得了比较丰富的成果,服务业内部不少行业也被独立出来单独进行研究,但将会展业从服务业中剥离出来全面系统地对其空间集聚问题进行的研究却明显不足。同时,现有的从空间视角对会展业进行的研究均比较宏观,大多注重总体布局与发展战略方面的研究,缺乏对城市尺度会展企业空间集聚的研究以及城市特定地段会展企业微观集聚案例的分析。本文运用广州市工商局提供的企业数据和问卷调查数据,采用 GIS 空间分析等方法从会展企业区位的角度全面分析广州会展企业空间分布、演变规律、集聚类型与影响因素。

2 数据来源与研究方法

2.1 数据来源

参照国家统计局制定的《国民经济行业分类》(GB/T4754—2002)对"会议与展览服务(L7491)"做出的界定,考虑会展业的现有统计情况及数据的可获取性,本文所研究的会展企业主要包括会展主办企业、会展场馆企业和会展服务企业三个会展业的主要组成部分,具体界定如下:会展主办企业是指会展活动的主办方或者专业的会展公司,一般以展览公司为中心,从事会展的策划开发、会展组织、会展宣传等;会展场馆企业是以场馆为中心的会展活动场地的出租和管理、场馆设施的更新与维护等的企业;会展服务企业是展览设计装饰、展台展位制作搭建、展具租用、展会广告宣传、展览贸易、展会信息咨询以及展品运输等企业。

基础数据主要来源于三个方面:①由广州市统计局数据中心和广州市工商管理局信息中心提供的会展企业名录,包括企业名称、地址、邮编、性质、成立年份、经营范围、营业收入、企业规模等特征数据,经过筛选,选定 1658 家会展企业进行分析;②实地调查获得数据。主要是对会展企业集中分布地段进行实地调查,获取必要的空间数据;③问卷调查获得数据。问卷调查由广东会展协会组织实施,在协会召开会议期间要求企业法人或总经理认真填写问卷并当场回收,因此调查结果真实反映了各因素对企业区位选择的影响。本次调查共发出问卷 302 份,均为有效问卷。

本文将每个企业看作空间上的一个点,利用地址信息并借助 Google Earth 对每个企业进行空间化处理,并与广州市电子地图匹配,再根据企业的成立时间,得到 1991 年、2002 年及 2011 年三个时间节点的广州市会展企业空间分布图。

2.2 研究方法

2.2.1 Ripley K 函数分析

Ripley K 函数是点格局分析的常用方法,本文运用 Ripley K 函数,将每个会展企业视为平面上的一个点,根据点坐标绘制点图,并以此为基础分析会展企业空间分布格局,即点格局。Ripley K 函数公式如下:

$$K(d) = A \sum_{i=1}^{n} \sum_{j=1}^{n} \frac{\delta_{ij}(d)}{n^2} \quad (1)$$

$$i, j = 1, 2, \cdots, n; \ i \neq j, \ d_{ij} \leq d, \ \delta_{ij}(d) = \begin{cases} 1 & (d_{ij} \leq d) \\ 0 & (d_{ij} > d) \end{cases}$$

$$L(d) = \sqrt{\frac{K(d)}{\pi}} - d \quad (2)$$

式中：A 为研究区域面积；n 为研究区域内会展企业个数；d 为距离尺度；d_{ij} 为企业 i 与企业 j 之间的距离。Besag 提出用 $L(d)$ 取代 $K(d)$，并对 $K(d)$ 做开方的线性变换，以保持方差稳定[32]。在随机分布的假设下，$L(d)$ 的期望值等于 0。$L(d)$ 与 d 的关系图可以用于检验依赖于尺度 d 的会展企业分布格局。$L(d)>0$ 表示会展企业有空间聚集分布的趋势；$L(d)<0$ 表示会展企业有空间均匀分布的趋势；$L(d)=0$ 表示企业呈随机的空间分布。$L(d)$ 的置信区间采用 Monte Carlo 方法求得。当企业分布格局为聚集分布时，可根据上述关系图得到聚集强度和聚集规模等信息。此时，偏离置信区间的最大值，即 $L(d)$ 的第一个峰值，可用来度量聚集强度，而 $L(d)$ 值第一个峰值所对应的 d 值表示空间聚集的特征空间尺度（characteristic spatial scale），可用来度量聚集规模。

2.2.2 核密度估计法

核密度估计是一种从数据样本本身出发研究数据分布特征的方法，适合于用可视化方法表示空间点模式，该方法通过考察规则区域中的点密度的空间变化来研究点的分布特征[33]，其结果可以用来平滑地识别并表示样本在研究区域内的集聚与分散情况[34]。本研究采用由 Silverman 提出的 KDF（kernel density function）密度分析法[35]，借助 ArcGIS9.2 实现对广州会展企业空间分布形态的分析。

3 空间集聚特征

3.1 广州会展业具有明显的空间集聚性，呈现由"单中心集聚"到"多中心集聚"的演变

为了探讨广州会展企业的空间分布与演变，根据广州会展业的发展历程，考虑到 1992 年以来新一轮改革开放大潮下广州会展业在探索展览专业化、促进服务功能现代化等方面的跨越式发展及 2003 年广州国际会展中心的投入使用给广州会展业带来的巨大影响，本文选择 1991 年、2002 年及 2011 年三个时间节点来考察广州会展企业空间集聚演变。首先采用核密度估计对会展企业空间分布进行分析（图1），总体来看，1991 年、2002 年和 2011 年广州会展企业在空间上均呈集聚分布。1991 年主要集中在流花地区，之后向天河地区扩散，到 2011 年已形成了流花、天河、东圃和琶洲 4 个明显的集聚区。

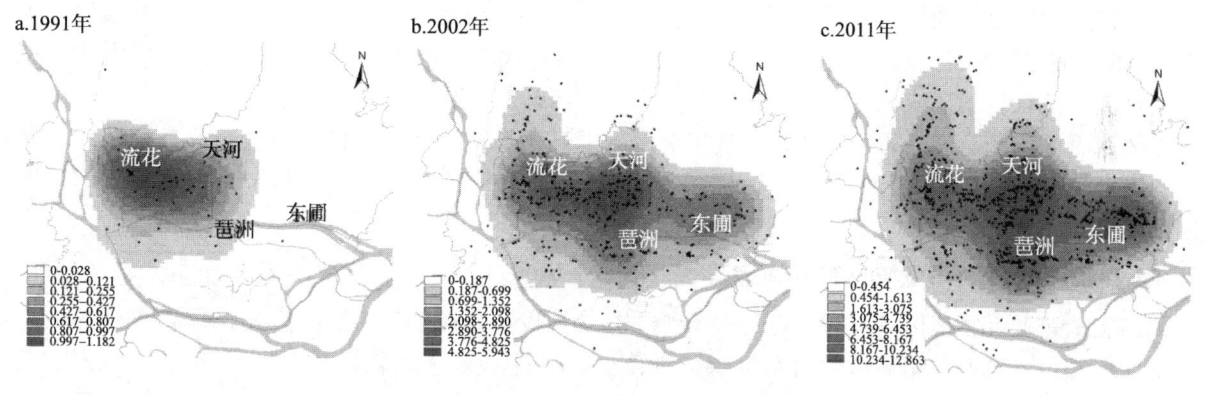

图1　广州会展企业空间分布密度图

为进一步分析集聚演变的过程，利用 ArcView 分别以流花展馆、天河体育中心、东圃广场和广州国际会展中心为圆心，以 500m 为单元进行缓冲区分析，结果表明：

1991 年前，广州会展企业主要分布在流花地区，形成了以流花展馆为中心、与周边宾馆酒店共同构成的会展集聚区。1991 年广州会展企业的 42.78% 分布在流花展馆周围 2.5km 半径范围内，8.31% 的企业分布在天河体育中心 2.5km 半径范围内，琶洲和东圃地区则没有分布。这一阶段形成了典型的"单中心集聚"的空间格局。

1992—2002 年，随着天河区作为广州新的 CBD 被开发与建设，吸引了大量会展企业向该区域集聚。2002 年，25.11% 的企业分布在天河体育中心周围 2.5km 半径范围内，较 1991 年的 8.31% 上升了 16.8%，流花地区则由 1991 年的 42.78% 降低到 17.42%，同时，东圃地区开始呈现集聚态势。这一阶段广州会展企业主要向东部扩散，呈现"双中心集聚"的空间格局。

2003—2011 年，由于政府的高度重视，广州会展业得到快速发展，会展企业数量显著增加，一些大型会展场馆的建设使会展企业的空间格局发生了很大变化，特别是广州国际会展中心的建设使会展企业开始

向广州南部扩展。2011年，流花、天河、东圃和琶洲地区会展企业所占比重分别为14.91%、25.82%、15.32%和9.87%。从空间分布密度图上可以看出，目前已经形成了以流花路展馆、天河体育中心、东圃广场和广州国际会展中心为中心的会展集聚区。这一阶段广州会展企业呈现"多中心集聚"的空间格局。

因此，广州会展企业空间格局呈现由"单中心集聚"到"双中心集聚"再到"多中心集聚"的演变规律。

3.2 集聚与扩散并存，并向城市新区发展

运用GIS空间分析功能，以500m×500m为空间单元从上述三个时间段进行分析，并以每个空间单元中的会展企业数量代表空间密度数值。计算表明，1991年有67家企业分布在27个单元格中，平均密度为2.48，标准差为1.27。这一阶段，会展企业的数量较少且分布的区域相对较小。从20世纪90年代初开始，会展业出现明显向东部天河一带扩散的趋势；到2002年，有715家企业分布在87个单元格中，平均密度为8.22，标准差为7.09。与1991年的数值相比，单元格面积、平均密度和标准差均有显著增加，单元格面积增加表明会展企业空间分布更广；平均密度增加表明每空间单元中企业分布的数量在增加，空间的集中分布趋势在增强；标准差的增大表明会展企业分布的空间差异在增大。2002年后，会展企业分布范围继续扩大，2011年1658家企业分布在113个单元格中，平均密度为14.67，标准差为15.39，表明扩散趋势和空间的集中分布程度继续增强，会展企业空间分布差异继续扩大。

从会展企业的扩散区域来看，主要是受城市空间向城市新区发展扩张的影响。20世纪70年代，由于广交会规模不断扩大，因而选择在流花路建设中国出口商品交易会展馆，当时的流花地区位于城市边缘，属于城市发展新区。此后，广州火车站、主要接待交易会来宾的东方宾馆新楼和流花宾馆，及其附近的电报电话大楼、邮政大楼、民航售票大楼等大型公共建筑相继建成，形成目前的发展格局。1979—1992年，由老城区向东是广州市最主要的城市空间扩展方向，天河区成为新的城市CBD。2000年，广州城市总体发展概念规划提出了促使城市由"单中心"向"多中心"转变的城市空间发展战略和"东进西联、南拓北优"的空间发展方针，明确了东、南是广州市中心城区发展的主要方向。因而，位于城市东部的东圃地区发展为新的CBD，而琶洲这一新区被规划定位为"以会展博览业为核心的城市副中心区"。与这种城市空间扩展相伴的是会展企业显著向东、南两个方向的扩散运动，主要表现为续流花集聚区之后天河集聚区的形成及近5年来琶洲和东圃集聚区的形成。

总体来看，广州会展企业空间格局呈现出高度的地理集聚特征和动态性，会展企业在空间的集聚程度并没有因为空间范围的扩展而降低，而是在扩散中集聚——在向城市新区扩散的同时，老区的集聚在不断加强。

3.3 各集聚区的强度和规模具有明显差异性

识别会展企业在哪些区域具有显著集聚特征，集聚强度、规模如何，能为政府选择在哪些区域并在多大范围内进行会展产业集聚区的打造提供科学依据。通过Crimestat软件对2011年流花、天河、东圃和琶洲4个区域的会展企业进行Ripley's K统计分析，其结果显示各区域企业的集聚程度均高于随机分布的最大值，显著性全部通过检验，表明在特定尺度范围内，4个区域的会展企业空间分布具有显著的集聚性，同时也验证了上述对会展企业空间集聚的判断。

进一步测算各集聚区的聚集强度和规模，结果表明不同地段的集聚存在明显差异（图2）。通过Ripley $L(d)$ 指数分析可知，流花、天河、东圃和琶洲4个区域的特征空间尺度分别为870m、1750m、900m和830m，相应的 $L(d)$ 峰值为308、380、450和360。数据表明，各区集聚规模和强度存在明显差异，集聚规模相当的区域集聚强度存在较大差异；集聚强度相差较小的区域集聚规模却相差较大。在4个区域中，天河区的集聚规模最大，基本是其他3个区的2倍，而其他3个区的集聚规模相差不大。从集聚强度来看，东圃区集聚强度最大，流花区最小。流花地区虽是最早的会展企业集聚区，但随着天河、东圃及琶洲地区会展企业的集聚发展，其集聚强度已明显落后于后者，集聚规模也不如天河及东圃，表明广州会展企业在迅速向新区扩散并集聚。

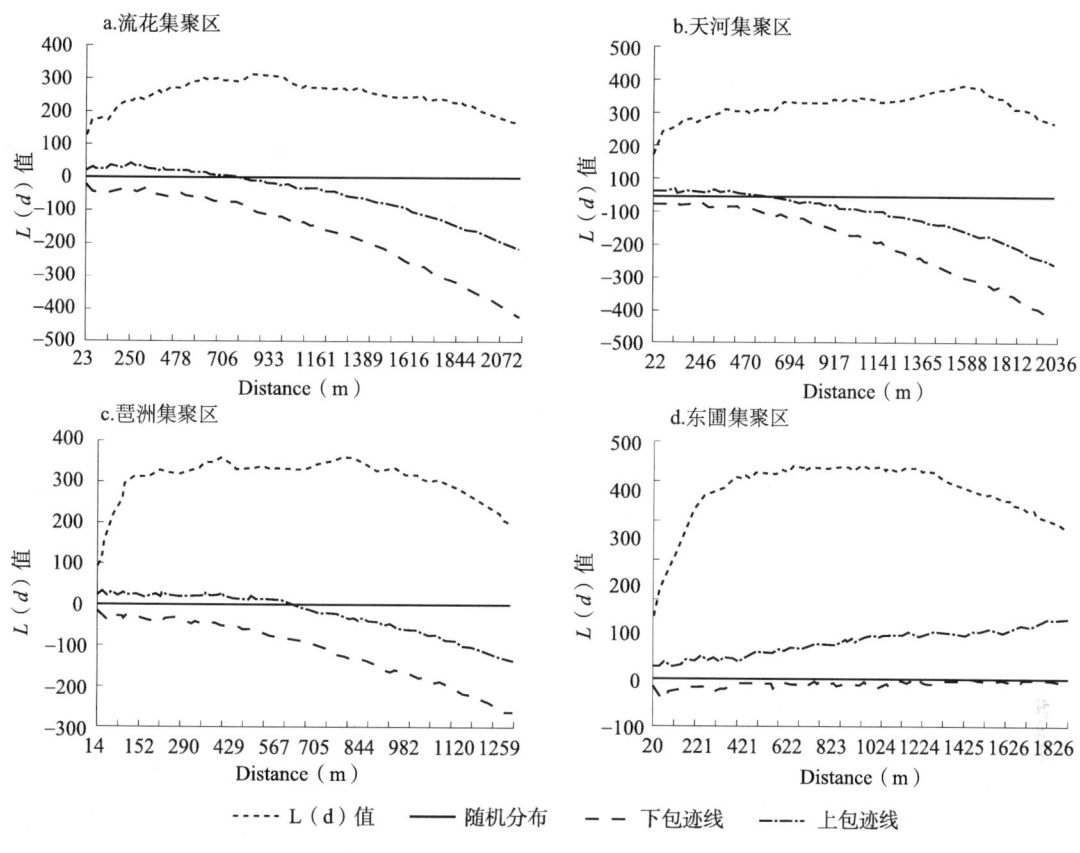

------- L（d）值 ——— 随机分布 — — 下包迹线 —·— 上包迹线

图2 各集聚区 Ripley $L(d)$ 指数分析

3.4 主要依托大型展馆及 CBD，形成了展馆依托型和 CBD 依托型两种类型

大型会展场馆往往成为会展企业集聚的中心，但是随着展馆区地价的快速增长及交通的显著改善带来的会展企业服务半径的扩大，使会展企业不必然在展馆周边集聚，而是选择与展馆有良好通达性和拥有良好商业环境的城市 CBD 作为企业区位。对会展企业集中的微观区位进行考察，发现广州会展企业集聚区大体可分为展馆依托型和 CBD 依托型两种主要类型。

展馆依托型集聚区：这类会展企业集聚区主要是依托大型展馆集聚会展企业及相关企业，由于是以一定数量的关键企业或大型设施作为核心，并在其周围有供应商和相关活动，它的结构类似于轮轴式集聚区。例如流花集聚区和琶洲集聚区均是这种类型。流花集聚区拥有流花展馆和广州锦汉展览中心两个主要的展馆，展览面积分别达 13 万 m^2 和 4 万 m^2。另外，一些酒店还拥有自己的展览场馆，如中国大酒店（展览面积 $3192m^2$）、东方宾馆（展览面积 $5672m^2$）等。在以流花展馆为中心的 5 分钟步行半径内，集中了众多展馆、会展企业，以及 30 多家三星级以上酒店和银行、商务楼宇、高档餐厅，形成了一个成熟的商务会展区域。琶洲集聚区拥有目前亚洲规模最大、设施最先进的国际会展中心（展览面积 33.8 万 m^2）以及广州保利世贸博览馆（展览面积 6.8 万 m^2）、广州国际采购中心（展览面积 4 万 m^2）、中洲国际展示中心（展览面积 3.6 万 m^2）等会展场馆，形成了以会展场馆的集聚为主体的功能特征，并吸引了五星级的香格里拉和威斯汀酒店、超甲级写字楼、大型广场及金融、信息咨询等相关行业。

这类区域由于大型场馆的存在，是展览活动发生的区域，是供应商、采购商和观众的集聚区。展馆依托型集聚区的企业规模一般较大，产业之间特别是上下游产业间联系密切，中小企业对核心企业的依赖性较大，虽然不一定和核心企业发生联系，但可以享受核心企业带来的外部经济。单个企业的垂直分离比较明显，例如一些展览公司拥有自己的展馆及展台搭建、宣传策划等展览服务公司。

CBD 依托型集聚区：这类会展企业集聚区主要是依托城市中央商务区的商务环境优势而集聚起来的，区内没有大型展览场馆，集中的是大量中小型会展企业，类似于马歇尔式的产业区。例如天河会展企业集聚区和东圃会展企业集聚区均是这种类型，2011 年，在天河和东圃集聚区 2.5 千米半径范围内（分别以天河体育中心和东圃广场为圆心）集聚的会展企业分别为 428 家和 254 家，两个区的集聚强度和规模均超过流花区和琶洲区。由于区内没有大型展馆,不是展览活动主要发生的区域,区内企业规模一般较小,多为展览设计装饰、展台展位制作搭建、展具租用、展会宣传广告、展览贸易、展会信息咨询以及展品运输等企业。企业之间联系不密切,单个企业垂直分离很弱。

总体来看,无论是考察空间分布形态还是 K 函数计算值,均表明广州会展企业具有显著集聚特征,并且集聚的强度和规模在不断增加,同时,在集聚过程中呈现从单中心集聚到多中心集聚的演变。从集聚的空间区位来看,主要在大型场馆周边和 CBD 区域集聚。不同时期广州会展企业空间集聚演变特征见表1。

表1 广州会展企业空间集聚演变

时间	企业数量（家）	集中分布地区（企业分布所占比重%）	空间分布形态	空间集聚模式	集聚强度和规模	集聚类型
1991 年	67	流花地区（42.78）	集中分布	单中心集聚	较低	展馆依托型
2002 年	715	流花地区（17.42）	集中与扩散并存	双中心集聚	显著增加	展馆依托型及 CBD 依托型
2011 年	1658	天河地区（25.11）	集中与扩散并存	多中心集聚	显著增加	展馆依托型及 CBD 依托型
		流花地区（14.91）				
		天河地区（25.82）				
		东圃地区（15.32）				
		琶洲地区（9.87）				

4 会展业空间集聚影响因素

影响企业区位选择的因素是复杂的,并且很多因素都难以量化,因此,调查问卷分析成为国际上惯用的一种研究服务业产业集聚的方法。Taylor 等对伦敦金融产业、Coffey 等对加拿大蒙特利尔的生产者服务业、Aguilera 对法国里昂商务服务业企业的空间集聚与区位选择的研究等,均采用了这一研究方法[36-38],该方法的优势是它可以反映出研究对象用现有的统计数据所无法反映的一些更为微观的经济学特征。另外,目前会展业的统计数据还不健全,因此本文采用问卷调查分析会展企业集聚的影响因素。

根据前人对企业空间集聚影响因素的研究成果及会展业的特征,本文设计了由 17 个项目组成的调查问卷。问卷的评价选项分为非常不重要、不重要、一般、重要、非常重要 5 级,从非常不重要到非常重要分别赋予 1~5 的数值,并对 302 家企业进行问卷调查,然后求出企业评价的平均值,结果见表2。

表2 广州会展企业集聚影响因素评价

类别	影响因素	得分
会展服务设施	大型展馆	4.13
	公共服务设施	3.97
整体商务环境	交通条件	4.08
	商业氛围	3.86
	办公楼品质	3.77
	区位知名度	3.49
	地价和房租	3.07
外部经济性	毗邻主要客户	3.61
	获得实时信息	3.52
	集聚效应	3.47
	获取其他企业的经营经验	3.41
	分享竞争者市场份额	3.35

续表

类别	影响因素	得分
人力资源	毗邻高校	3.43
	获取高素质劳动力	3.33
政府行为	城市规划	3.47
	政府优惠政策	3.12
	政府资金支持	2.97

总体来看，17个因素的平均得分为3.53，介于"一般"和"重要"之间，除"政府资金支持"外，其余16个因素的得分都大于3，表明这些因素对会展企业集聚的影响均在"一般"水平之上。如果将高于3.5分的因素作为集聚因素[39]，则影响会展企业集聚的因素有大型展馆、交通条件、公共服务设施、商业氛围、办公楼的品质、毗邻主要客户和获得实时信息7个因素，其中，得分高于4的大型展馆和交通条件是最主要的集聚因素。为综合分析各因素的影响，本文将17个因素分为会展服务设施、整体商务环境、外部经济性、政府行为和人力资源5个大类。

4.1 会展服务设施

会展服务设施包括大型展馆和相关公共服务设施两个因素。评价结果表明大型展馆位列影响因素的第一位，可见其对会展企业集聚的重要性。会展场馆是展览业发展的基础，被誉为会展经济发展的火车头，没有相当规模和配套设施齐全的会展场馆就难以催生具有影响力的品牌展会。由于会展业的快速发展，原有场馆不能满足需求而周边又没有足够的用地建设新的场馆，使地方政府不得不选择新的区位建设新场馆。大型场馆的建设将带来外部规模经济和范围经济，由此吸引大量会展企业向周边集聚并形成新的集聚区。因此，大型展馆的空间分布影响会展企业空间集聚的总体格局。流花集聚区是通过"广交会"围绕流花路展馆发展起来的，形成了初始的"单中心集聚"格局；20世纪90年代随着天河体育中心会展功能的发挥以及天河区作为新的城市CBD，会展业开始向东部扩散，在天河体育中心周边集聚；2003年广州国际会展中心投入使用，会展业开始向南部扩散，以琶洲为中心的周边区会展企业迅速集聚；2005年广州白云国际会议中心的投入使用又使会展业呈现向北部扩散的趋势，并最终形成了目前的"多中心集聚"的空间格局。

除大型展馆外，良好的公共服务设施也是会展企业选址考虑的重要因素，这些设施包括餐饮、住宿、仓储、信息咨询、邮局、快递、金融保险、通信等方面的设施，这些设施是会展企业从事经营活动的重要条件。

4.2 整体商务环境

良好的商务环境对服务业具有强大的吸引力，是形成服务业集聚区的重要因素[40]。CBD有最密集的信息和人口，商业活动最发达，容易获得各种高级劳动力，以及有良好的交通和通信设施，这不仅有利于生产者服务业的商务会面，也有利于信息的交流和机会的把握，因此许多高端生产者服务业聚集在CBD[41]。天河地区是广州从20世纪90年代初发展起来的CBD，东圃地区是最近几年发展起来的新的CBD。这些地区没有大型会展场馆，但具有良好的商业区位环境，除了交通便利能为琶洲地区的展会提供及时便捷的服务外，本地区商业发达、高档写字楼集中分布，为企业提供了良好的配套服务及办公场所，这种商业氛围对会展企业的选址均有很强的吸引力，使会展企业迅速集聚。

在整体商务环境的各因素中，"交通条件"的分值最高，达到4.08，表明交通对于会展企业选址的重要性。展会的举办会产生大量的人流和物流，便利的交通是最基本的保证。企业选址于交通条件较好的地区，可以降低运输费用，原材料、产品的输入输出也比较便利。另外，城市快速交通系统使会展场馆的服务半径和辐射力加大，使会展企业减少了对场馆的过分依赖，从而影响到会展企业的区位选择变化，会展企业有可能在没有大型展馆但商务环境良好的区域集聚，这就加大了展馆与会展业市场分离的倾向。天河区和东圃区之所以集聚大量的会展中小企业，与这两个地区到琶洲有便利的交通密切相关，天河区离琶洲乘地铁只需5站，东圃区距琶洲乘地铁只需2站，便利的交通使服务商在场馆外围一定的距离区域同样可以发挥自身的功能。另外，"地价和房租"的分值最低，只有3.07。针对这种情况，笔者对部分企业负责人进行了访谈，被访者普遍认为只要靠近主要展馆或者具有良好的商务环境，地价和房租即便高一些也可以接受。

4.3 外部经济性

外部经济性的平均分值为3.47，说明外部经济性对于会展企业集聚产生了比较重要的影响。Marshall认为，即使对于那些规模报酬不变或者规模报酬递减的行业，一个企业的生产成本也可能会由于本地区存在其他同行业企业而降低，这种溢出效应可能造成生产集中在个别地区[1]。许多生产者服务业的生产活动是非标准化的，需要频繁的信息联系，这种联系不仅包括客户和企业之间的密切联系，也包括不同行业的生产者服务企业由于相互依存的关系而产生的紧密联系。会展业由于涉及餐饮、住宿、物流运输、展台装修、物品租赁、贸易中介、金融保险、旅游、广告、通信等众多行业，因而尤其注重这种联系。这些"面对面"的交流能增强信任，有效地传递与分享企业的生产和管理知识，同时还能满足现代服务业企业即时投入和获得反馈信息的需要，节省大量的时间成本。因此，为了取得外部经济性，会展企业通常会聚集在通达性最好的城市中心区。

4.4 人力资源

人力资源特别是具有创新能力的人才是企业赢得竞争优势的根本保证，人力资源的丰裕程度是企业考虑的主要因素。由于目前的会展教育与企业需求之间存在一定的差距，高素质会展专业人才的缺乏成为制约会展经济发展的重要因素之一。从目前产业集聚影响因素的研究来看，人力资源在大尺度空间对企业集聚具有重要影响[7,42-43]，但在城市尺度空间上对企业区位选择的影响并不显著。从问卷调查结果看，"毗邻高校"和"获取高素质劳动力"的评价分值分别为3.43和3.33，位列17个因素的第11位和第14位。在对企业负责人的访谈中发现，对于"获取高素质劳动力"这一因素，他们认为只要在市区范围内，否则企业是否选择在集聚区驻扎对于获取高素质劳动力区别不大。这也说明同一因素在不同空间尺度对企业区位选择的影响程度是不同的[44]。

4.5 政府行为

政府主要通过城市规划、产业发展政策、金融手段、税收体制及其他优惠措施等一系列政策影响服务业集聚。对广州会展企业而言，政府行为的影响主要表现在城市规划对企业选址的影响。在目前会展业发展主要为政府主导的背景下，政府的发展规划首先决定了场馆的具体区位。其次，政府对规划打造的会展集聚区，必然会在相关配套设施的建设方面予以大力支持。例如，广州市提出要将琶洲地区培育成国际商务会展集聚中心；将流花地区打造成以流花展贸中心为核心的区域中小型专业会展集聚区，这些举措必然加速以场馆为依托的会展企业集聚区的形成。

2009年广州市政府出台了促进会展业发展的指导意见，并在展馆投资建设、运营方面均实施税收优惠政策，此外还设有会展专项资金。但就目前情况看，优惠力度太小，专项资金只是杯水车薪，而且仅有极少数几家企业能获得支持。大多数企业负责人认为，政府还没有对会展企业（特别是中小型会展企业）的发展形成有力支持，因此政府资金支持和优惠政策不作为重要考虑因素。

5 结论与讨论

中国产业空间集聚的研究还很不充分，现有研究主要是从区域尺度对整个制造业或服务业进行研究，基于城市尺度和企业层次的研究明显不足。本文运用企业层面数据和问卷调查数据，采用GIS空间分析等方法研究广州会展企业空间集聚特征与影响因素，研究结论对于会展产业政策的制定具有重要参考意义，同时也丰富了产业集聚，特别是会展产业集聚研究的空间尺度和实证研究成果。研究表明：

（1）广州会展企业具有明显的空间集聚性，并且集聚与扩散并存，在向城市新区扩散的同时，老区的集聚在不断加强。在这种集聚与扩散的时空过程中，形成了初始的"单中心集聚"空间格局及目前的"多中心集聚"空间格局。这种空间集聚特征与西方生产性服务业体现出的空间集聚性和由单中心到多中心的结构模式具有一致性，但与服务业内其他行业相比，却体现出了不同的空间变动特征。西方生产者服务业内部各行业空间分布的研究表明，一部分高端的生产者服务业，如银行、金融保险、法律咨询、房地产等仍高度集中在 CBD，而另一部分低端生产者服务业企业如技术服务、数据处理等行业则表现出较强的离心化趋势，呈现广域分散模式[45]。而会展企业在向新区扩散的同时，在 CBD 的集聚程度不仅没有减弱，反而不断加强。

（2）影响会展企业空间集聚的主要因素可以归纳为会展服务设施、整体商务环境、外部经济性、人力资源和政府行为 5 个方面。从所包含的具体因素来看，大型展馆和交通条件对会展企业集聚具有重要影响，而获取高素质的劳动力、政府的支持及地价和房租等因素的影响不明显，无论是问卷调查还是企业访谈均证实了这一结论。但从国内外对大都市生产者服务业的研究成果来看，交通的便利性、区位的形象和知名度、容易获得高素质的劳动力、办公楼的品质以及租金和物业成本等因素是企业在城市空间内部选址时首要的考虑因素[13-14,36-39,46]。这与会展企业集聚影响因素存在不同程度的差异，表明同一因素对不同类型企业的区位选择产生不同的影响。将本文的影响因素与国家、省等大区域尺度上会展业集聚的影响因素相比较，发现两者存在明显区别。在大区域尺度上，会展企业更多的考虑区域的经济发展水平、市场容量、经济对外开放度、基础设施等因素[28-31]，因此倾向于在大城市集聚。这种区别表明空间尺度对会展企业的区位选择产生影响，不同因素在不同尺度上影响企业区位选择的程度是不同的。另外，对会展企业不同集聚区规模和强度的研究表明，即便是在同一城市尺度空间内部，由于微观区位因子的差异，企业在城市内部的分布也不是同质的[47]。

（3）大型会展场馆往往成为会展企业集聚的中心，但是随着展馆区地价的快速增长及交通的显著改善带来的会展企业服务半径的扩大，使会展企业不必在展馆周边集聚，而是选择与展馆有良好通达性和拥有良好商业环境的城市 CBD 作为企业区位。因而形成了展馆依托型和 CBD 依托型两种主要集聚类型。同时，大量的企业选址在 CBD 集聚，也表明尽管交通和通信技术的发展缩短了交流距离和降低了交流成本，有利于企业的分散化，但对会展企业而言，面对面的交流依然重要。从问卷调查的结果看，接近主要客户、获得实时信息依然是重要的影响因素。

（4）目前，会展产业集群的概念已开始出现在一些学者的研究中或地方政府的政策中，但目前还未见有来自国内外的实证研究表明会展产业集群的存在，本文只是实证了会展企业空间集聚的存在及相应的集聚特征。特定产业的空间集聚是产业集群形成和发展的基础，但并非任何产业集聚都一定能发展为产业集群。产业集群的核心是企业间及企业与其他机构之间的联系以及互补性[48]。尽管中国会展企业在主要中心城市的特定地段的集聚态势日渐显著，但当前中国会展企业的空间集聚是否正在形成会展业集群？会展业集群化的程度如何？这是有待求证的问题。因此，一下步需要在两方面进行研究：第一，研究区域尺度（如珠三角、长三角等区域）会展企业空间集聚特征，并与城市尺度进行对比，揭示不同尺度空间会展企业的集聚机制；第二，在会展企业空间集聚研究的基础上，进一步考察企业间及企业与其他机构之间的联系以及互补性，即本地化的企业网络以及专业化分工协作等，对会展业集群予以识别。

致谢：本文的问卷调查是在 2012 年 6 月 28 日召开的广东会展协会理事扩大会议上进行的。整个调查由会展协会秘书长刘松萍教授组织实施，在此对刘教授及协会工作人员表示感谢！

参考文献

[1] Marshall A. Principles of Economics [M]. London: Macmillan, 1920.

[2] Weber A. Theory of the Location of Industries [M]. Chicago: The University of Chicago Press, 1965.

[3] Krugman P. Geography and Trade [M]. Boston: MIT Press, 1991.

[4] Fujita M, Krugman P, Venables A. The Spatial Economy: Cites, Regions, and International Trade [M]. Cambridge: MIT Press, 1999.

[5] Porter M E. The Competitive Advantage of Nations [M]. New York: The Free Press, 1990.

[6] Li Wenxiu, Tan Liwen. Two dimension evaluation model of services agglomeration and its experience study: The case of American service. China Industrial Economics, 2008 (4): 55-63. [李文秀, 谭力文. 服务业集聚的二维评价模型及实证研究——以美国服务业为例 [J]. 中国工业经济, 2008 (4): 55-63.]

[7] Chen Jianjun, Chen Guoliang, Huang Jie. Agglomeration on producer services and its affecting factors from the view of new economic geography: The empirical analyses based on the 222 cities in China. Management World, 2009 (4): 83-95. [陈

建军, 陈国亮, 黄洁. 新经济地理学视角下的生产性服务业集聚及其影响因素研究: 来自中国222个城市的经验证据 [J]. 管理世界, 2009 (4): 83-95.]

[8] Xue Dongqian, Shi Ning, Gong Xiaoxiao. Spatial features and agglomeration of producer services in Xi'an City, China. Scientia Geographica Sinica, 2011, 31 (10): 1195-1201. [薛东前, 石宁, 公晓晓. 西安市生产者服务业空间布局特征与集聚模式研究. 地理科学, 2011, 31 (10): 1195-1201.]

[9] Zhang Wang, Shen Yuming. The spatial characteristics of producer service agglomeration in Beijing-Tianjin-Hebei metropolitan region. Progress in Geography, 2012, 31 (6): 742-749. [张旺, 申玉铭. 京津冀都市圈生产性服务业空间集聚特征. 地理科学进展 [J], 2012, 31 (6): 742-749.]

[10] Yang Yongzhong, Huang Shuyi, Lin Minghua. Study on the formation path and evolution mechanism of the creative industrial zones. China Industrial Economics, 2011, (8): 128-138. [杨永忠, 黄舒怡, 林明华. 创意产业集聚区的形成路径与演化机理 [J]. 中国工业经济, 2011, (8): 128-138.]

[11] Lin Zhangping, Yan Xiaopei. Analysis on the change of the spatial pattern of financial service industry in Guangzhou during the transition period. Acta Geographica Sinica, 2006, 61 (8): 818-828. [林彰平, 闫小培. 转型期广州市金融服务业空间格局变动分析 [J]. 地理学报, 2006, 61 (8): 818-828.]

[12] Yuan Feng, Wei Yehua, Chen Wen. Spatial agglomeration and new firm formation in the information and communication technology industry in Suzhou. Acta Geographica Sinica, 2010, 65 (2): 153-163. [袁丰, 魏也华, 陈雯, 等. 苏州市区信息通讯企业空间集聚与新企业选址 [J]. 地理学报, 2010, 65 (2): 153-163.]

[13] Bi Xiujing, Wang Mingfeng, Li Jian. Agglomeration and suburbanization: A study on the spatial distribution of software industry and its evolution in metropolitan Shanghai. Acta Geographica Sinica, 2011, 66 (12): 1682-1694. [毕秀晶, 汪明峰, 李健. 上海大都市区软件产业空间集聚与郊区化 [J]. 地理学报, 2011, 66 (12): 1682-1694.]

[14] Wang Chengyun. Spatial agglomeration and influencing factors of Japanese R&D industry. Acta Geographica Sinica, 2010, 65 (4): 387-396. [王承云. 日本研发产业的空间集聚与影响因素分析 [J]. 地理学报, 2010, 65 (4): 387-396.]

[15] Zhen Feng, Yu Yang, Wang Xia et al. The spatial agglomeration characteristics of automotive service industry: A case study of Nanjing. Scientia Geographica Sinica, 2012, 32 (10): 1200-1208. [甄峰, 余洋, 汪侠, 等. 城市汽车服务业空间集聚特征研究: 以南京市为例 [J]. 地理科学, 2012, 32 (10): 1200-1208.]

[16] Kim S, Chon K, Chung K Y. Convention industry in South Korea: An economic impact analysis. Tourism Management, 2003, 24 (5): 533-541.

[17] Robin B, Deborah B, Paul R. An exploratory study of differences among meeting and exhibition planners in their destination selection criteria [J]. Journal of Convention & Event Tourism, 2008, 9 (4): 258-276.

[18] Siu N Y, Wan P Y K, Dong P. The impact of the servicescape on the desire to stay in convention and exhibition centers: The case of Macao [J]. International Journal of Hospitality Management, 2012, 31 (1): 236-246.

[19] Wang Y C, Fesenmaier D R. Identifying the success factors of web-based marketing strategy: An investigation of convention and visitors bureaus in the United States [J]. Journal of Travel Research, 2006, 44 (3): 239-249.

[20] Luo Qiuju, Pang Jiawen, Jin Wenmin. An empirical study on the economic impact of the events with input-output model: A case study of Canton Fair, China. Acta Geographica Sinica, 2011, 66 (4): 487-503. [罗秋菊, 庞嘉文, 靳文敏. 基于投入产出模型的大型活动对举办地的经济影响: 以广交会为例 [J]. 地理学报, 2011, 66 (4): 487-503.]

[21] Hu Ping. Study on evaluating and enhancing countermeasures of the MICE industry competitiveness: A case of Shanghai. Tourism Forum, 2009 (1): 114-119. [胡平. 基于钻石理论的会展业竞争力评价及其提升对策研究: 以上海为例 [J]. 旅游论坛, 2009 (1): 114-119.]

[22] Wu Shirong. A discussion of education model of operational talents in universities of China: A case study of practices in exhibition major. Modern University Education, 2009 (1): 104-112. [邬适融. 我国高校应用型人才培养模式的思考: 以会展专业为例 [J]. 现代大学教育, 2009 (1): 104-112.]

[23] Jin X, Weber K, Bauer T. Impact of clusters on exhibition destination attractiveness: Evidence from Mainland China [J]. Tourism Management, 2012, 33: 1429-1439.

[24] Bathelt H, Schuldt N. Between luminaries and meat grinders: International trade fairs as temporary clusters [J]. Regional Studies, 2008, 42 (6): 853-868.

[25] Wu X J, Sun M J. The system dynamics analysis on the evolvement of mechanism of convention and exhibition industry//Shen Gang, Huang Xiong. Advanced Research on Electronic Commerce, Web Application, and Communication [J]. Berlin: Springer Berlin Heidelberg, 2011: 167-172.

[26] Zhang Lili. Study of Guangzhou's convention and exhibition industry cluster based on LQ coefficient. International Economics and Trade Research, 2009, 25 (12): 67 - 71. [张俐俐. 基于 LQ 系数的广州会展产业集群 [J]. 国际经贸探索, 2009, 25 (12): 67 - 71.]

[27] Wang Yonggang, Guo Yang. Study on exhibition industry cluster evolution trend and development path in China. Inquiry into Economic Issues, 2011 (8): 48 - 53. [王永刚, 郭旸. 中国会展业集群化演进趋势及发展路径研究 [J]. 经济问题探索, 2011 (8): 48 - 53.]

[28] Ye Hongtao. Research on the distribution of convention and exhibition industry. Contemporary Economics, 2008 (8): 92 - 94. [叶洪涛. 我国会展产业布局分析 [J]. 当代经济, 2008 (8): 92 - 94.]

[29] Ju Hang, Tian Jinxin. Research on development distribution and innovation model of convention and exhibition industry. China Soft Science, 2006 (11): 131 - 136. [鞠航, 田金信. 城市会展产业的发展布局与创新模式研究 [J]. 中国软科学, 2006 (11): 131 - 136.]

[30] Wang Yunlong. On the mode of spatial movement of MICE economy: A case study of Beijing, Shanghai and Guangzhou. Human Geography, 2005, 20 (4): 26 - 29. [王云龙. 关于会展经济空间运动形式的分析: 以北京、上海与广州为例 [J]. 人文地理, 2005, 20 (4): 26 - 29.]

[31] Zhu Haisen. Study and inspiration on the spatial distribution of overseas MICE industry. Human Geography, 2004, 19 (5): 93 - 96. [朱海森. 海外会展业空间布局的研究及启示: 以德国、香港为例 [J]. 人文地理, 2004, 19 (5): 93 - 96.]

[32] Besag J E. Comments on Ripley's paper. Journal of the Royal Statistical Society, Series B, 1977, 39: 193 - 195.

[33] Wang Yuanfei, He Honglin. Methods of Spatial Data Analysis. Beijing: Science Press, 2007. [王远飞, 何洪林. 空间数据分析方法 [M]. 北京: 科学出版社, 2007.]

[34] Berke O. Exploratory disease mapping: Kriging the spatial risk function from regional count data [J]. International Journal of Health Geography, 2004, 3 (1): 18.

[35] Silverman B W. Density Estimation for Statistics and Data Analysis [M]. New York: Chapman and Hall, 1986.

[36] Taylor P J, Beaverstock J V, Cook G A S. Financial services clustering and its significance for London [M]. Corporation of London, 2003.

[37] Coffey W J, Drolet R, Polese M. The intrametropolitan location of high order services: Patterns, factors and mobility in Montreal [J]. Papers in Regional Science, 1996, 75 (3): 293 - 323.

[38] Aguilera A. Services relationship, market area and the intrametropolitan location of business services [J]. The Services Industries Journal, 2003, 23 (1): 43 - 58.

[39] Wang Jici, Song Xianghui, Li Guangyu. Agglomeration and dispersion of new and high technical industries in the Zhongguancun Area in Beijing. Acta Geographica Sinica, 1996, 51 (6): 481 - 488. [王缉慈, 宋向辉, 李光宇. 北京中关村高新技术企业的集聚与扩散 [J]. 地理学报, 1996, 51 (6): 481 - 488.]

[40] Illeris S. The Service Economy: A Geography Approach [M]. Chichester: John Wiley & Sons, 1996.

[41] Coffey W, Polèse M, Drolet R. Examining the thesis of CBD decline: Evidence from the Montreal metropolitan area [J]. Environment and Planning A, 1996, 28: 1795 - 1814.

[42] Monseny J J, López R M, Marsal E V. The mechanisms of agglomeration: Evidence from the effect of inter - industry relations on the location of new firms [J]. Journal of Urban Economics, 2011, 70: 61 - 74.

[43] Yu Pei, Sun Yongping. The impacts of agglomeration on MNE's location choice in China. Economic Research Journal, 2011, (1): 71 - 82. [余珮, 孙永平. 集聚效应对跨国公司在华区位选择的影响 [J]. 经济研究, 2011 (1): 71 - 82.]

[44] Rosenthal S S, Strange W C. The determinants of agglomeration [J]. Journal of Urban Economics, 2001, 50 (2): 191 - 229.

[45] Shearmur R, Alvergne C. Intrametropolitan patterns of high - order business service location: A comparative study of seventeen sectors in Lie - de - France [J]. Urban Studies, 2002, 39 (7): 1143 - 1163.

[46] Zhang Wenzhong. A study of metropolitan service industry location theory and substantiation. Geographical Research, 1999, 18 (3): 273 - 281. [张文忠. 大城市服务业区位理论及其实证研究 [J]. 地理研究, 1999, 18 (3): 273 - 281.]

[47] Wu F. Intrametropolitan FDI firm location in Guangzhou, China: A poisson and negative binomial analysis [J]. The Annals of Regional Science, 1999, 33: 535 - 555.

[48] Wei Houkai. Industrial Agglomeration and Cluster Strategy in China. Beijing: Economy Management Publishing House, 2008. [魏后凯. 中国产业集聚与集群发展战略 [M]. 北京: 经济管理出版社, 2008.]

旅游权内涵解析及其保险保障机制探讨

孔令学

1 旅游权概念界定与相关研究概述

旅游权作为一个新引入的法律概念，应明确其内涵，这需要借鉴相关国家和国际组织的定义，并结合已有研究成果和我国国情进行概念界定。

1.1 旅游权概念的引入

从我国政府工作报告多次提到的提高人民福祉，到《国民旅游休闲纲要（2013—2020）》提出满足人民群众日益增长的旅游休闲需求，都与保障公民旅游权直接相关。特别是第十二届全国人大常委会第二次会议通过的《中华人民共和国旅游法》（以下简称《旅游法》）在其总则部分第3条首次规定了公民旅游权，即"国家发展旅游事业，完善旅游公共服务，依法保护旅游者在旅游活动中的权利"。这是我国法律首次引入旅游权概念，并在《旅游法》相关条款中设计了比较完善的公民旅游权保障机制。有必要结合法定权利和旅游发展阐释公民旅游权的基本内涵，并在此基础上探讨我国公民旅游权的保障机制及其发展完善问题。

1.2 旅游权概念的国际借鉴

英美等发达国家由于社会经济发展水平较高，旅游保障机制比较健全，其公民旅游权主要涉及旅行自由等方面的权利，并通过司法判例的形式不断发展完善。如在1868年的克兰戴尔诉内华达州案例中，美国联邦最高法院首次确立了"迁徙权"。1948年12月10日，联合国大会第217A（Ⅲ）号决议通过并颁布的《世界人权宣言》第13条明确规定了旅游权，指出"（一）人人有权在各国境内自由迁徙和居住。（二）人人有权离开任何国家，包括其本国在内，并有权返回他的国家"。2010年欧盟强调旅游是最新的人权，并通过政府买单保障部分特需人群的旅游权。世界旅游组织《旅游权利法案与旅游者守则》指出，"每个人都有休息娱乐的权利，合理限定工时的权利，定期带薪休假的权利，在法律范围内不加限制地自由往来的权利，并已在全世界得到承认"。

1.3 旅游权相关研究概述

旅游权研究是个相对较新的领域，目前国内学界对旅游权的研究大致有两类：一类是从旅游伦理的视角研究旅游权利，如王德刚从本体论的角度出发，对"旅游权利"的本质、内涵、特点及实现途径进行了系统探讨，强调"旅游权利"实际包括闲暇权、娱乐权、带薪休假权和自由旅行权[1]。夏赞才、刘焱分析了旅游权利主张的哲学背景和典章依据，阐释了旅游权利价值和现实困境[2]。另一类是从法学的视角研究旅游权，如刘红婴从人权和权利义务的角度出发，对旅游权的含义、性质及其实现手段进行法理分析，提出其实现程序和行为规范[3]。郭志平认为，公民旅游权的主要内容包括旅游自由权、平等权、资源共享权和保障权，提出了公民旅游权的法律确认与保障措施建议[4]。概言之，作为专有的法律概念，有关公民旅游权的法律内涵及其保障机制的研究还有待深入，特别是从保险视角开展的研究尚属空白，本文拟作引玉之砖，以供方家批评。

1.4 我国公民旅游权概念界定

我国公民旅游权的界定既要契合我国的基本国情和旅游业发展现状，又要充分保障公民的旅游休闲权，满足人民群众日益增长的旅游休闲需求。基于此，我国公民旅游权可以有两种定义方式：一是性质

[作者简介] 孔令学（1969—），男，山东沂水人，博士，北京联合大学旅游学院副教授，主要研究方向为经济法、旅游标准化、金融制度，E-mail：lxkong@sohu.com。

界定，即公民旅游权是指公民在一定时期内离开惯常居住地进行休闲娱乐等非营利性活动的权利。二是综合定义，即公民旅游权是指公民自主自由旅行，进行休闲娱乐等非营利性活动，共享旅游资源，实现精神享受和自我发展的权利。后者更有利于旅游权保护机制研究，本文也在此概念基础上进行阐述。

2 旅游权内涵解析及其现实约束

旅游行为的复杂性和多样性决定了公民旅游权利的复杂性和多样性，公民旅游权内涵非常丰富，大致可分为两类七项权利。囿于基本国情和旅游业发展现状，我国公民旅游权的实现和保障机制还存在一定的现实约束，亟待改进和完善。

2.1 基础性公民旅游权

2.1.1 旅游保障视角下的旅游保障权

旅游虽然是旅游者的个人行为，但其背后却是国家和社会的综合制度保障，主要包括经济实力和社会结构支撑，基础设施与公共服务，闲暇时间和休闲文化保障等[5]，旅游保障权即体现为公民要求国家为其旅游休闲需求提供综合制度保障的权利。从旅游的视角看，经济实力直接体现为居民收入，居民收入和旅游消费之间是长期均衡关系，居民收入每增加1%，可以使旅游消费增加1.144%[6]。中产阶级收入稳定，旅游消费意愿和消费能力都比较强，构建以中产阶级为主体的纺锤形社会是旅游休闲发展的重要保障。基础设施是旅游休闲的物质载体，公共服务是满足公民旅游休闲需求的基本质量保障。闲暇时间是旅游休闲的重要时间保障，我国始于1995年的双休日制度，形成于1999年的"黄金周"长假制度，2008年调整后的国家法定节假日安排，以及同年施行的《职工带薪年休假条例》规定，形成了相对固定的闲暇时间安排。休闲文化通过影响旅游者的思想直接影响旅游决策和旅游过程，是旅游的内在支撑因素。

2.1.2 旅游过程视角下的旅游自由权

旅游是一种过程性行为，涉及旅游决策、准备、安排、出游、返程和再次旅游等多种具体行为，包括食、住、行、游、购、娱等多种消费行为。每个具体行为如何实施完全取决于旅游者的意愿，即旅游者具有完全的旅游自由权。从权利内容上看，旅游自由权是指旅游者不受其他因素影响，主要根据自己和家人的条件、兴趣和意愿自主地决定是否旅游、何时旅游、去何地旅游、以何种形式旅游、是否再次旅游等具体旅游事项。

2.1.3 旅游主体视角下的旅游平等权

旅游平等权是指公民所享有的旅游时不受歧视或其他不平等对待的权利，主要内涵有三：一是公民旅游时不分民族、种族、性别、年龄、宗教信仰、教育程度、职业和家庭收入，一律平等地享有旅游的权利；二是旅游服务者不得因旅游者的民族、种族、性别、年龄、宗教信仰、教育程度、职业和家庭收入差异，给予歧视或其他不平等待遇；三是国家对公民的旅游权实行平等保护，并对残障人士、老年人、青少年和妇女儿童等特殊人群实行特别保护。

2.2 消费性公民旅游权

2.2.1 旅游资源视角下的旅游资源共享权

根据《马尼拉世界旅游宣言》，各国的旅游资源同时由空间、设施、价值等组成，是最基本的旅游景观和历史、文化遗迹。旅游资源是人类遗产的重要组成部分，各国和整个国际社会都有义务采取必要的保护措施，并要保护和保障公民的旅游资源共享权。旅游资源共享权是指公民共同享有享用国家旅游资源的权利，特别是享有享用人类物质文化遗产和自然遗产的权利。旅游资源共享权主要体现在两个方面：一是国家及其授权的旅游资源管理者有义务在保护好旅游资源的同时尽可能地向全体公民及入境旅游者开放旅游；二是旅游资源是全人类的共有资源，应当允许旅游者低价甚至免费享用。

2.2.2 旅游发展视角下的旅游发展共享权

根据人类需求层次理论，旅游属于高层次需求，是提高公民自身综合素质、实现自我价值的重要途径。随着社会经济和旅游休闲的发展，公民有权利平等、持续地享受发展成果。旅游发展共享权主要包括两个方面：一是当代人的旅游发展共享权，二是当代人和后代人的旅游发展共享权。旅游发展共享权需要依靠国家和社会的力量予以保证，并通过旅游规划、旅游管理、生态环境保护等方面的制度和措施加以落实。

2.2.3 国际旅游视角下的出入境旅游权

公民出入境旅游权包括我国公民的出入境旅游权和外国公民到我国的入出境旅游权两个方面，出入境旅游者还依法享受前述平等待遇、资源共享等相关旅游权利。目前，我国公民自费出境旅游目的地国家或地区已超过140个，2012年共接待入境游客1.324亿人次，2011年实现国际旅游（外汇）收入484.64亿美元。2011年中国公民出境人数达到7025.00万人次，旅游业总收入2.25万亿元人民币[7]。近期，国家批准北京和上海对45个国家的外国人实行72小时过境免签政策，出入境旅游的内涵更加丰富。

2.2.4 消费视角下的公民旅游消费权

从消费的视角看，旅游是融合物质消费和精神消费的综合性消费行为，公民在旅游过程中应当享有作为消费者的相关权利，主要是《消费者权益保护法》所规定的消费者基本权利，包括以下八种权利[8]：一是安全权，即旅游者在接受旅游服务时享有人身、财产安全不受损害的权利。二是知情权，即旅游者享有知悉其接受的旅游服务的真实情况的权利。三是自主选择权，即旅游者享有自主选择旅游服务，自主选择旅游服务方式，自主选择提供服务的旅游经营者的权利。四是公平交易权，即旅游者在接受服务时，获得质量保障、价格合理、计量正确等公平交易条件，拒绝强制交易的权利。五是获得赔偿权，即旅游者因接受服务受到人身、财产损害的，享有依法获得赔偿的权利。六是获取知识权，即旅游者享有获得有关旅游消费和旅游消费者权益保护方面知识的权利。七是获得尊重权，即旅游者在接受旅游服务时，享有其人格尊严、民族风俗习惯得到尊重的权利。八是监督批评权，即旅游者享有对旅游服务以及保护旅游者权益工作进行监督的权利。

2.3 我国公民旅游权的现实约束

2.3.1 基础性公民旅游权的现实约束

在经济实力和居民收入方面，由于住房、养老、教育、医疗等支出巨大或保障不足，经济实力和消费预期仍在一定程度上制约着公民的旅游休闲消费。在社会结构方面，当前我国社会结构总体上还是传统的金字塔形，中等收入阶层占总人口的比例偏少[9]，不利于旅游业的全面发展。在基础设施方面，各类旅游基础设施数量和质量有待提高，而且还不同程度地存在侵占、挤占旅游休闲公共场所和公共资源的现象。在公共服务方面，旅游公共信息系统尚待完善，安全应急管理和应急救援管理能力还不能适应大规模出游需要。在闲暇时间方面，受带薪休假制度落实不到位、黄金周集中出游等因素影响，人均出游率和旅游质量仍待提高。在休闲文化方面，虽然《国民旅游休闲纲要》已经发布，但我国传统文化历来崇尚节俭，形成全民性的休闲文化还需假以时日。在旅游自由方面，现实中旅行社"倒卖"游客、导游人员强制消费等侵害公民旅游自由权的现象屡见不鲜，公民旅游自由权还有待进一步落实。在旅游平等方面，旅游服务企业及其从业人员直接或间接侵害旅游者平等权的现象仍时有发生，如旅行社对老年游客加收费用，旅游景区没有配套建设残障人士专用通道或设施，旅游饭店禁止某地人或某类人进入等。

2.3.2 消费性公民旅游权的现实约束

在资源共享方面，由于管理体制等方面的原因，部分旅游资源已成为某些地方和个人坐地生财的捷径，重开发轻保护、重收费轻服务的现象非常突出，无规划乱开发、高票价高收费等已成为阻碍旅游休闲发展的重要因素。在发展共享方面，由于地方保护和部门利益等方面的原因，存在着旅游资源过度开发和使用，有些甚至是破坏性开发和使用的现象，甚至形成少部分人受益大部分人受损，当代人受益后代人受损的恶性发展格局。在出入境旅游方面，现行旅游签证管理制度总体上还有待进一步完善，公民出入境旅游权也有待进一步扩大，特别是自助出入境旅游安排需要在制度上实现大的飞跃。在落实旅游者消费权利方面，虽然各级政府及其旅游、工商、质监等相关部门做了大量工作，也取得了不错的成效，但欺诈欺骗、强买强卖、侵犯人格尊严等侵害旅游者消费权的事件仍时有发生，有些甚至是行业性行为，亟待从制度和体制上进行改革、完善和加强。

3 公民基础性旅游权利保险保障机制探讨

虽然公民旅游权本质上属于私权利，但"行船跑马三分险"，基于旅游行业特点和我国公民旅游权的现实约束，仍需要借助国家公权力和相关制度安排全面、广泛地保护公民旅游权。本部分主要从基本保险制度，特别是体制机制方面，探讨我国公民基础性旅游权利的保险保障问题。

3.1 完善旅游和保险立法，加强公民旅游权的保险法律保障

《旅游法》在第56条规定了旅游经营者责任保险，即国家根据旅游活动的风险程度，对旅行社、住宿、旅游交通以及高空、高速、水上、潜水、探险等高风险旅游项目的经营者分类实施责任保险，但这尚不足以完全满足旅业业的风险保障要求。建议将来在《旅游法》修改时，要考虑在旅游经营和旅游服务合同、旅游安全、旅游监管、旅游者及其权利救济等相关内容中适当增加旅游保险的内容，特别是要细化规定，通过可操作性强的保险制度安排保护公民的旅游保障权、旅游自由权和旅游平等权。同时，在修订《保险法》时也要考虑旅游保险的特殊性及其适用问题，尤其注意要在强制责任保险、旅游资源保险、旅游安全保险等方面要和《旅游法》实现有机衔接。同时，在《旅游法》和《保险法》相关旅游保险规定的基础上，制定和完善相关行政法规、地方法规、行政规章和规范性文件，细化优化旅游保险管理规定和操作规范，形成上下位法相互衔接、各类旅游风险全面涵盖的公民旅游权保险保障法律法规体系。

3.2 完善社会保险制度，优化公民旅游保障权

目前，二元结构社会状态下，我国社会保险制度主要提供基本保障，对公民旅游权的保障作用并不是其主要目标，所以其制度设计上并没有特别考虑旅游权的保障问题。社会保险是公民旅游权最重要的经济保障手段之一，建议从以下几个方面着手改进、完善和优化：一是从根本上改变差别化的社会保险结构，改革城镇职工的社会保险制度，提高城镇职工社保水平，实现城镇职工和事业单位员工社会保险待遇统一化，并探索适合我国国情的公务员和农民社会保险制度。二是实行同工同保制度，如对实行劳务派遣用工人员实行与正职员工同样的社会保险待遇，提高2700万劳务派遣用工人员的经济收入和社会保障水平❶。三是构建三位一体的养老保险框架体系，实行社会养老保险为核心，企业补充养老保险和个人储蓄性商业养老保险为补充的综合性基本养老保险，保障退休人员的生活消费水平，保障其旅游休闲需求。四是对残疾人员、孕期妇女、高龄退休人员等特殊人员实行特别的社会保险保障制度，提高特需人员的社会保障水平和旅游休闲消费能力。五是优化基本医疗保险、工伤保险和失业保险制度，稳定居民收入和支出预期，提高其旅游休闲消费意愿和能力。

3.3 创新家庭和个人财产保险制度，保障公民经济实力

目前，我国大部分家庭对家庭财产保险和个人商业保险重视不够，投保险种主要集中在火灾险和盗抢险等财产损失险种上，投保比例和投保金额都明显偏低，需要改变保险理念，加大财产保险密度，增强家庭和个人财务风险防控能力，从而提高公民旅游休闲经济保障能力。一是创新财产保险产品，研发适合居民家庭和个人财务风险保障需求的保险产品，如健康保险、重大疾病保险等医疗保险等。二是完善投资型保险产品，优化财产保险结构，提高居民和家庭财产增值和稳定水平，扩大消费如优化分红保险制度、创新个税递延型保险等保险产品。三是支持部分保险公司实行专业化经营，专注于家财保险业务，扩大财产保险业务覆盖范围，提高保险服务质量和投保、理赔便利度。

3.4 加强旅游保险监督管理，提高旅游保险服务质量

保险公司和保险中介等保险机构作为市场经营主体，利润是其最基本的追求，要发挥保险的公民旅游权保障作用，除了完善前述相关制度安排外，还要建立有效的制度落实监管机制。从保险监管的视角看，目前应集中做好以下监管工作：一是制定相关的旅游保险监管行政规范，用法律法规引导保险机构及其从业人员依法合规经营。二是根据需要安排专门人员或专门机构负责旅游保险监管工作，或者协调旅游、保险、工商等相关部门建立旅游保险联合执法机构，优化旅游保险行政监管。三是赋予保险行业协会相应的旅游保险行业管理职责，并建立保险行业协会与旅游行业协会的合作机制，共同推进旅游保险工作。

---

❶ 一说为非官方统计数据6000万人。陈青松. 劳动合同法修正案草案首次审议，直指劳务派遣 [N]. 中国企业报，2012-07-02。

3.5 加强旅游保险宣传，提高旅游保险的认同度和接受率

我国旅游保险没有实行专门的行业准入资格管理，相关旅游保险的险种也多达上百种，但除了差强人意的旅行社强制责任险外，其他旅游保险业务开展情况远不能适应旅游业的发展需要，宣传不到位，保险意识薄弱是其中一个重要原因。笔者认为，可以从以下几方面加强旅游保险宣传，提高旅游保险的认同度和接受率：一是规定或要求旅行社、旅游景区等旅游企业在经营过程中做好旅游保险的宣传推广工作，如建立强制性的旅游风险告知制度，强制要求旅游企业向特定旅游者告知旅游风险，并向咨询或签约的旅游者介绍旅游安全和旅游保险知识。二是对导游等实行资格管理的部分旅游从业人员加强保险知识培训，并根据需要在旅游行业资格考试或考核时考查旅游保险知识。三是支持保险公司、保险代理公司和其他保险中介机构开展旅游保险业务，扩大旅游保险宣传。四是鼓励旅游管理部门、保险监管机构的官方网站、官方微博通过设立旅游保险专栏，建立与相关保险公司的网站链接等多种途径宣传旅游保险。五是探索外交部门和旅游部门在加强出入境旅游合作中的保险合作新形式，通过签证管理、领队管理等途径宣传旅游保险。六是旅游、保险等相关机构和企业要加强与各类新闻媒体的合作，通过现代传媒、出版物宣传旅游保险知识，提高旅游者对旅游保险的认同度。

4 公民消费性旅游权利保险保障机制探讨

旅游者的旅游消费主要是服务性消费，旅游服务质量直接影响旅游者的旅游休闲感受，从而影响旅游行业发展。良好的保险保障制度安排有助于保证和提高旅游服务质量，是实现公民旅游权，特别是公民消费性旅游权利，促进旅游行业持续健康发展的必要条件之一。

4.1 优化旅游资源财产保险制度，满足公民旅游资源共享需求

旅游吸引物等旅游资源是旅游企业生存和发展的根本要素，也是公民旅游权的重要载体，建议结合我国财产保险制度现状，从以下方面着手创新和优化我国旅游资源财产保险制度：一是实现商业保险与政策性保险相结合的旅游资源保险制度，扩大旅游资源的保险覆盖范围和保险保障水平。二是培育发展重点旅游资源保险专业中介机构，特别是文化遗产保险专业中介机构，实行中介机构代理承保、安全监管和代理理赔等专业管理，以专业保险提高旅游资源安全水平。三是完善火灾保险等传统企业财产保险制度，设计针对旅游资源的专项财产保险产品，提高旅游资源保险保障水平。四是探索创新地震、雷电等自然灾害等保险品种，研发文化遗产特种保险产品，实现和促进保险对旅游资源的特别保障。五是将重要旅游资源保险纳入再保险体系，集合保险行业力量，提高对旅游资源的保险保障能力。

4.2 完善旅游者安全保险制度，以安全保障促旅游发展

安全是公民旅游权的最重要基础，也是旅游者进行旅游选择的主要考量因素之一，交通意外保险等我国现有涉及旅游者安全的相关保险产品大都不是为旅游者单独设计的，而且也没有考虑到旅游的综合性和特殊性。建议引导和鼓励保险公司结合旅游特点，研发新的旅游保险产品，完善旅游保险制度，提高公民旅游自由保障水平。一是实行旅游综合保险保障，如开发旅游交通综合保险，对旅游者乘坐旅游汽车、火车、轮船和飞机等各类交通工具提供综合性的人身意外伤害保险，或者开发旅游综合意外伤害保险，对旅游者在旅游过程中的食、住、行、游、购、娱等消费行为提供综合性的保险保障。二是创新旅游保险产品品种，优化旅游保险产品体系，如实行综合保险和单项保险的保险责任可选性保险产品，以及开发针对度假旅游、自助旅游、自驾旅游、探险旅游和老年旅游等特种旅游的保险产品，研发和完善针对出境旅游的救援保险产品等，实现旅游保险对食、住、行、游、购、娱的全方位覆盖。三是创新旅游保险营销机制，优化旅游保险销售渠道，除了传统的旅行社代销、旅游景点代销、机票销售点代销和网上销售外，还可以开发营业网点销售、代理机构代销、银行代销、报纸销售、卡片销售和信函销售等新的销售形式，也可以借鉴山西等省经验，在全国推行旅行社责任险等旅游强制保险统保制度安排，提高旅游保险覆盖率。四是优化旅游保险销售模式，如借鉴香港旅游保险代理人制度经验，探索建立有中国特色的旅行社和导游人员代理销售旅游保险产品等新的旅游保险销售模式。五是灵活设计各类旅游保险产品生效（使用）范式，如试行一次销售全年适用，或者提前购买，电话、短信或网络通知启用等新型旅游保险产品生效范式。六是提高旅游保险保障水平，如提高保险金额，扩大保险赔偿范围，加快

保险赔付速度等，以旅游安全促进旅游行业发展。

4.3 完善旅游企业责任保险制度，提高对旅游者的保障水平

旅游者和旅游企业的权利义务是对等的，明确或扩大旅游企业的义务就是明确或扩大旅游者的权利，从保险的视角看，可以进一步完善旅游企业责任保险制度，保障公民的旅游权利。一是在原来的旅行社责任保险基础上，进一步扩大强制性责任保险的参保旅游企业范围，要尽快涵盖旅行社、旅游承运人、旅游景点、旅游娱乐场所、旅游饭店和旅游购物商店等经营主体。二是改革旅游企业责任保险制度，提高保险金额，优化理赔程序，实行旅游企业无责垫付制度等。三是改革旅行社质量保证金制度，试行质量保证金与旅行社责任保险的有机结合，如将部分质量保证金转为投保责任险，扩大责任险的承保范围和赔偿金额。四是引入保险中介服务机构，完善旅游保险服务，如由保险中介机构代理旅游企业责任保险，代理垫付。五是探索建立旅游保险与旅游遇险救援协作机制和协调机制，特别是要提高旅游意外伤害的救援救助和医疗救治保障水平，满足旅游者的多样化旅游需求，促进旅游新业态发展。

4.4 建立健全出入境旅游保险体系，保障公民出入境旅游权

出入境旅游风险相对较高，但目前其保险保障与境内旅游相比较弱，保险体系不够健全是重要原因。要适应我国公民出入境旅游快速发展的需要，建议从以下方面着手建立健全出入境旅游保险体系：一是制定扶持政策，鼓励和支持国内保险公司、保险代理公司等保险机构在境外设立分支机构，拓展旅游保险等相关业务。二是支持保险机构在我国公民出境旅游主要目的地国家或地区设立境外代理机构，重点做好公民出境旅游保险理赔等相关服务。三是加强旅游和保险监管合作，如借鉴英国外交部的"行前须知"运动安排，加强外交、旅游部门和保险机构间的合作，提高旅游者出入境旅游安全和保险意识，及时发现出入境旅游保险中存在的问题，并依法处罚。四是借鉴新加坡的"旅安"旅行保险计划，研究制订我国统一的出入境旅行保险计划，联合有救援能力的商业公司或医疗机构对出入境旅游实行全方位保险救援安排，至少要包括以下保障：全天候快速救援热线电话、紧急救援服务、足额救援费用、保险公司预付医疗救护费用、回国救治费用保障和行李遗失赔偿等。

说明：本文于 2013 年 3 月 28 日根据外审专家的意见进行了修改，并参照 2013 年 4 月 25 日第十二届全国人大常委会第二次会议通过的《旅游法》相关条款作了个别调整。

参考文献

[1] Wang Degang. Discussion about tourism rights again [J]. *Journal of Beijing International Studies University*, 2011 (7): 1–6. [王德刚. 再论旅游权利 [J]. 北京第二外国语学院学报, 2011 (7): 1–6.]

[2] Xia Zancai, Liu Yan. On tourism rights [J]. *Tourism Tribune*, 2010 (5): 14–19. [夏赞才, 刘焱. 论旅游权利 [J]. 旅游学刊, 2010 (5): 14–19.]

[3] Liu Hongying. On the elucidation for tourism right by legal theory [J]. *Tourism Tribune*, 2006 (9): 11–14. [刘红婴. 旅游权的法理释义 [J]. 旅游学刊, 2006 (9): 11–14.]

[4] Guo Zhiping. On legal recognition and safeguard of tourism right [J]. *Journal of Jimei University (Philosophy and Social Sciences Edition)*, 2011 (3): 109–114. [郭志平. 试论公民旅游权的法律确认与保障 [J]. 集美大学学报（哲学社会科学版）, 2011 (3): 109–114.]

[5] Kong Lingxue. Comparison and reference of Brazil, China's tourism market development [J]. *Journal of Latin American Studies*, 2012 (1): 64–67. [孔令学. 巴西、中国旅游市场发展比较与借鉴 [J]. 拉丁美洲研究, 2012 (1): 64–67.]

[6] Yao Lifen, Long Ruyin, LI Qingchen. Cointegration relationship analysis of tourism income and consumption in China [J]. *Geography and Geo-Information Science*, 2010 (6): 93–95. [姚丽芬, 龙如银, 李庆辰. 中国居民收入与旅游消费关系的协整分析 [J]. 地理与地理信息科学, 2010 (6): 93–95.]

[7] National Tourism Bureau. 2012 inbound tourism statistics, 2012 statistical bulletin of China tourism [EB/OL]. http://www.cnta.gov.cn/html/2012-10/2012-10-25-9-0-71726.html, 2012-10-25. [国家旅游局. 2012 年入境游统计. 2011 年中国旅游业统计公报 [EB/OL]. http://www.cnta.gov.cn/html/2012-10/2012-10-25-9-0-

71726. html，2012 – 10 – 25.］

［8］Li Xiuna，Kong Lingxue. *Tourism Laws and Regulations*［M］. Beijing：Beijing Yanshan Press，2012. 242 – 246.［李秀娜，孔令学. 旅游法律法规［M］. 北京：北京燕山出版社，2012.］

［9］Institute for Urban and Environmental Studies Chinese Academy of Social Sciences. *City Blue Book：China City Development Report No. 4：Focus on People's Livelihood*［M］. Beijing：Social Sciences Academic Press，2011.8.［中国社会科学院城市发展与环境研究所. 城市蓝皮书：中国城市发展报告 No.4——聚焦民生［M］. 北京：社会科学文献出版社，2011.8.］

会展旅游带动效应的统计研究
——以北京为例

石美玉　王春才

一、引　言

21世纪是服务经济的时代，在经济发展全球化、一体化的趋势下，会展业自从1851年诞生于欧洲以来，形成了以欧洲和美洲为龙头，以亚太地区为强大新生力量的全球化产业，被称为无烟产业、朝阳产业。会展旅游作为服务业的重要组成部分之一，以附加值高、产业关联性强等特点在创汇、扩大内需、增加就业等方面起着重要作用，尤其是通过关联效应和乘数效应带动了其他相关产业的极大发展。如今，会展旅游已逐步发展为新的经济增长点，它所发挥的作用越来越引起人们的关注，素有城市经济发展的"助推器"之称。

会展旅游是以会议、展览、节庆活动等为主要吸引物，吸引旅游者前往会展举办地参加会议、展览及相关活动，满足旅游者人际交流需求的一种综合性旅游产品，与会展业密不可分。就本文而言，涉及的会展业主要包含会议、展览、节事活动和奖励旅游，而会展旅游并不完全等同于会展业，会展旅游主要是因参加会议、展览、节事活动和奖励旅游等延伸出来的旅游活动，包含会议旅游、展览旅游（含会议附设展览旅游）、节事活动旅游和奖励旅游等。会展旅游既涉及前期的会展活动，又涉及延伸的相关活动，同时，还涉及交通、住宿、餐饮、娱乐等相关产业。因此，会展旅游统计涉及的范围非常广泛。

会展旅游对经济发展的带动作用可通过量化为数字比例关系来体现。然而，这一助推器的带动作用的量化统计在国内外仍未形成一个统一的标准和认识。目前，国际上通常将会展业的带动系数比例大致定为1∶5~1∶10。而我国按照国际传统将这种比例定为固定值1∶9，且一般认为会展旅游的带动系数也是如此，虽然可以简化会展旅游带动作用的测算，却不甚科学。因为国家地域的不同、会奖类别的不同、类别划分标准的不同等差异，会对相关产业产生不同的带动作用。因此，以1∶9的固定值来测算我国会展旅游的带动作用存在许多弊端，既没有与时俱进地与新的国际惯例接轨，也没有考虑到我国会展旅游的真实发展现状。李杰（2007）认为，当前由于对会展经济"1∶9产业带动效应"的过度渲染，使许多地方干部群众在思想认识上产生偏差。这个缺乏科学依据的"定数值"变成了各地盲目举办会展活动的依据，有的地区竟相把会展业确定为当地重点发展的行业，试图将本地的整体经济带动起来。

尽管目前对此相关问题有一些研究，但此前的研究大都偏重于宏观描述或一般性研究，缺乏全面系统及更具说服力的数据统计和定量分析。况且，到目前为止，国际上还没有真正建立起公认的会展旅游统计体系，这给研究会展旅游的带动效应也带来了一定的影响。本文选择北京会展旅游的带动效应为研究对象，采用较为全面的调研和统计，并结合投入产出核算方法，客观全面地探讨和反映北京会展旅游的带动效果，具有科学性、系统性和全面性。本文对会展旅游统计的核心产业采用直接统计法和相关系数推算法，直接向统计对象发放统计表，按统计指标要求填写一定期间内的会展旅游数据，然后收集汇总。再依据不同行业或部门与会展旅游关联程度的不同，运用调查问卷和投入产出的方法，对与会展旅游相关的产业或部门分别测算其带动系数，从而推算出北京会展旅游对北京国民经济的总体带动效应。

二、文献综述

由于会展业还是一个新兴产业，人们更多关注会展与旅游结合的开发模式、与经济发展挂钩等实际

[作者简介] 石美玉（1972—），女（朝鲜族），吉林延吉人，教授，经济学博士，研究领域为会展旅游、非物质文化遗产旅游、旅游购物与旅游商品开发。E-mail：lytmeiyu@buu.edu.cn；王春才（1963—），男，河南平顶山人，副教授，经济学博士，研究领域为会展经济、会展城市、会展旅游。E-mail：lytchuncai@buu.edu.cn。

问题,学术界对会展业的研究也多集中在企业的市场营销渠道方面和对城市经济的增长作用方面。按研究视角的不同,可划分为概念理论和作用两大方面。

1. 会展旅游的概念

对于会展旅游的概念,不同学者有着各自的见解,主要从四方面来界定:(1)从旅游产品的角度来看,何建英(2004)认为会展旅游是指以会议、展览为主要吸引物,吸引旅游者前往会展举办地参加会议、展览及相关活动,满足旅游者人际交流需求的一种综合性旅游产品。(2)从会展与旅游的关系角度看,王云龙(2003)认为会展旅游是指旅游属性结合会展活动特点衍生出来的行为,但不包括旅游业对会展的多元化经营业务。会展旅游业是综合会展业和旅游业两大产业优势形成的新型产业。(3)从会展旅游经济的角度来看,王保伦(2003)认为会展旅游是为会议和展览活动的举办提供展会场之外的、且与旅游业务相关的服务,并从中获取一定收益的经济活动。他认为,我们所提倡的会展旅游不是让旅游企业去举办各种会议和展览,而是让旅游企业发挥行业功能优势,为会展的举办提供相应的外围服务。(4)从旅游供求两个方面来定义,林越英(2002)认为从旅游需求来看,会展旅游是指特定群体到特定地方去参与各类会议、展览活动,并附带相关的参观、游览及考察内容的一种旅游活动形式;从旅游供给来看,会展旅游是特定机构或企业以组织参与各类会议、展览等相关活动为目的而推出的一种专项旅游产品。从这些概念中可以看出,会展与旅游之间具有天然融合的关系,会展旅游具有极强的带动作用。

2. 会展旅游的作用

会展业能够带来经济效益,不仅仅指会议和展览可促成商品或服务成交带来收益,如参展商的订单收益,以及由会展所带来的门票收入、广告收入等,还包括为其他行业,如餐饮、交通、酒店等带来的收益。郑建瑜(2000)认为,会展经济已成为新的经济增长点,会展业有助于提高城市的就业水平,并推动社会实现可持续发展。此外,会展旅游还是提高国际化城市地位的重要举措,能提升城市环境形象和政府形象,提高举办地文明程度,促进信息知识的交流与传播。

会展业能促进相关产业的快速发展。会展业之所以能成为城市经济的新亮点,关键在于它具有强大的产业带动效应。林越英(2002)认为,旅游业与会展业有机组合,具有明显的关联、带动及辐射作用。旅游业是会展的前提条件,会展业是构成会展旅游的核心基础,会展旅游能够带动以旅游业为主的交通、住宿、餐饮、商业、金融、房地产、文化艺术等第三产业的发展。一个成功会展活动的举办离不开四个相关单位,即组织单位、接待单位、场馆单位、参与单位。不同类型的会展会吸引不同行业、不同层次的参与单位,从而来带动各个行业的发展。

尽管如此,国内外对会展业和会展旅游带动作用的统计研究却十分薄弱,缺乏专门深入的研究。胡平(2006)认为,会展业作为前景广阔的朝阳产业,对相关产业有巨大的拉动作用。他通过以上海新国际博览中心作为案例,对会展业的经济效应做实证研究,得出以下结论:上海展览业的拉动效应为1:8.4,已接近发达国家水平;不同展览的经济带动作用各不相同,参观人数多的品牌国际展的经济拉动作用更大;展览会对展览搭建公司以及当地住宿餐饮影响巨大。余向平(2006)运用凯恩斯经济学乘数效应和萨缪尔森经济学乘数与加速效应相互作用原理,解释会展业的产业带动效应,从经济学角度更加证实了会展业对社会经济发展的重要作用。卡尔(2000)提出了城市旅游统计的规范,但并没有涉及会展领域。Kim(2003)等运用投入产出模型,从会展产业的产出、就业、收入、增加值等方面对韩国会展业的经济影响进行了分析,并比较了会展业与其他出口业的乘数效应、汇率收益和替代效应,认为会展业对韩国的经济影响更体现在国家层面上,而非某一特定地区。

综上所述,专家学者均对会展旅游的带动作用给予肯定和关注,但是带动作用的统计问题,即会展旅游在何种程度上带动相关产业发展却尚属空白。本文主要从支出和收入两个角度对会展旅游数据进行调研和收集,支出部分主要调研与会展旅游直接相关的单位所主办或承办的会议支出情况,收入部分主要调研与会展旅游有关联的相应行业企业的总收入中来自会展的收入比例。

三、会展旅游统计现状与存在的问题

目前,就会展旅游的相关统计而言,国际上在会展分类、相关界定、统计标准等方面仍"各自为政",尚未形成统一的划分标准。相对而言,在相关统计中,对展览、奖励旅游等相关项目有较为统一的统计标准,统计内容基本包括时间、规模、人数、收入等主要方面。但对会议方面的统计,特别是对国际会议的统计方面存在比较混乱的现象,没有一个较为认可的统一标准,这给与此相关的会议旅游统计及其相关带动效应的测算等都带来了一定的困难。

1. 国际会议界定

国际上有多个机构对国际会议进行认定和统计,如国际大会与会议协会(ICCA)、国际社团组织联盟(UIA)、国际会议专家联盟(MPI)、国际奖励旅游管理者协会(SITE)、联合国世界旅游组织(UNWTO)等(见表1)。但到目前为止,国际上并没有一个完全统一的国际会议统计标准。由于每个组织规定的统计标准都不尽不同,所以,会造成认定或统计上的明显偏差。如 ICCA 规定的国际会议标准至少有 50 个参会者,定期组织举行会议(不包括一次性会议)且必须在至少 3 个国家轮流举行;而 UIA 国际会议标准规定至少有 300 个参会者,国外参加者至少占总量的 40%,参加会议的国家至少有 5 个,最短会期为 3 天(见表1)。

表1 国际会议的不同界定

标准来源	参会人数	参会者来自国家数	国外参会者比重	会期	举办频率	会议地点
ICCA(国际大会与会议协会)	至少50人	—	—	—	定期举办	至少在3个国家轮流举行
UIA(国际社团组织联盟)	至少300人	至少5个国家	至少40%	3天以上	—	—
UNWTO(联合国世界旅游组织)	至少10人	—	—	4小时以上	—	在商业性场所举办
西班牙旅游研究院	至少50人	至少3个国家	至少40%	4小时以上	—	—
新加坡会议社团组织	至少300人	至少5个国家	至少40%	3天以上	—	—
TCEA(台湾国际会议展览协会)	至少100人	至少5个国家	40%或80人以上	—	—	—
日本国际观光局振兴会	至少20人	至少2个国家	—	—	—	—
中国国际会议推展社团组织	至少50人	至少2个国家	至少20%	—	—	—
中国有关文件规定(统计用)	—	至少3个国家(不含港、澳、台地区)	—	—	—	—

我国尚无国际会议的权威统计标准。目前,根据国家有关文件的规定,来自 3 个或 3 个以上国家或地区(不含港、澳、台地区)的代表参加,以交流为主要目的而举办的研讨会、报告会、交流会、论坛及国际组织的行政会议,可称为国际会议。但由于该标准太低,其统计数据与 ICCA 的统计结果相差甚远。

2. 会议统计标准

目前,国内外对会议的统计主要存在两个方面的问题,一是缺乏统一的权威统计标准,二是统计的内容和项目存在差异。同时,与会展相关的行业及部门的统计覆盖不充分,统计误差较大。因此,不同机构相同项目类别的统计数据之间可比性不强。

(1)国(境)外不同国家或地区对会议的统计

①美国统计。美国会议统计指标中包括:会议数量、会议巡回的区域数目、国际会议的首脑们、每个地区的会议数、每个国家的会议数、每个城市的会议数、参会人数、会议频率、会议持续时间、使用的会议场馆、会议主题、参会注册费用和花费等。

②ICCA 统计。ICCA 对会议的统计主要是按 ICCA 制定的国际会议标准进行统计(见表1),统计结果主要用来对举办国际会议的国家或城市进行分析和排序。尽管 ICCA 和 UIA 统计中有很多重合的节事活动,但从市场角度来看最重要的区别是,UIA 包括同一地点举办的节事活动,而 ICCA 的节事活动必须在至少三个国家间轮流举行。

③UIA 统计。UIA 对会议的统计主要是按照 UIA 制定的国际会议标准来统计,其中没有包括在 UIA 统计中的有:纯粹国内会议,以及只有的宗教、教育、政治、商业或运动属性的会议;严格限制参会者的会议;公司会议和奖励会议。

④UNWTO 统计。UNWTO 主要是负责处理各类旅游业相关事宜，并根据统计数据制作世界旅游排行榜，其中对会议的统计项目涉及较少，主要包括参会人数、支出费用、参会者特征等。其会议统计标准主要有：至少有 10 人以上的参加者；在商业性场所举办；最短会期为 4 小时。

⑤欧洲统计。欧洲国家会议统计数据主要由各大场馆提供，包括各场馆会议室类型、年举办会议次数、收入等，缺乏国家整体会议产业数据。

⑥韩国统计。韩国会议统计的一大特点是，对会议主承办方的国际会议申办情况进行了细致调查，如会议申办情况、所属国际机构、近期是否有申办意图、困难及建议等都做了深入细致的调查，为政府制定相关政策提供了重要信息。但韩国会议产业方面的数据量较小，且分类过于精细，不适合我国国情。

⑦澳门统计。澳门会议统计项目包含：会议数量、持续时间、参会人数、会议类型、会议主题、收入等。但会展行业调查涉及内容较少，并未作为重点行业而进行相关行业带动数据的测算。

（2）国内会议统计。

国内城市对会议的统计较为混乱，除了实施统计的城市数量较少外，在现有开展会议统计的城市中普遍存在统计标准不统一、统计项目不一致等问题，个别城市只是简单统计一下举办会议数量等。同时，更为严重的问题还表现在：第一，现有会议统计体系漏掉许多与会议直接或间接相关的一些数据，所统计出来的数据不能客观反映会议产业的发展实际；第二，部分城市目前还没有将会议与展览分开统计，而是统计会展的整体状况；第三，没有一个权威机构来直接负责制定会议统计标准和统计体系。比较而言，北京市统计局对会展业及会展旅游的统计项目较为全面，基本包含了会展及会展旅游的主要方面。

3. 存在的主要问题

可以看出，目前国内外对会议的统计存在的主要问题是：第一，缺乏统一的统计标准；第二，统计的内容和项目存在差异；第三，与会展相关的行业及部门的统计覆盖不充分，统计误差较大；第四，没有一个权威机构来直接负责制定会议统计标准和统计体系。

因此，就会议的统计标准和统计体系而言，目前国内外没有一个完整的标准和体系可以使用。相对而言，国外的某些标准和体系可以借鉴，如 UNWTO 的会议标准中对会议举办地的要求是必须在商业性场所举办，最短会期为 4 小时；ICCA 的会议标准中关于参会人数有至少 50 个参会者等规定。就北京目前关于会议的统计而言，其统计体系相对较为完整，但仍存在统计项目和统计覆盖面需要完善等问题。在统计效果分析方面，韩国的投入产出分析比较有借鉴意义。因此，我们主要借鉴以上的相关标准和做法来进行本文的分析和研究。

四、会展旅游带动效应的统计测算

1. 相关界定

鉴于会展旅游涉及范围广，目前国内外对会展旅游的统计标准和要求不统一，国内统计也存在多种统计标准，会展旅游对相关行业的带动作用难以测算等，本文采取两种方法予以解决，一是明确会展旅游统计的相关定义，二是尽可能选取较全面的与会展旅游相关的产业，并分别测算其相关系数，然后汇总。

首先，根据会议规模的大小，会议可分为小型会议（参会人数 50～100 人）、中型会议（参会人数 100～500 人）和大型会议（参会人数 500 人以上）。国际会议是指来自一定数量国家的参会者为解决互相关心的问题、协调彼此利益、相互交流信息等，在一定时间聚集在一定商业性场所而举行的交流活动，要求：与会者来自三个或三个以上国家，与会人数不低于 50 人，活动时间不少于 4 小时；国内会议是指一定数量的参会者为解决互相关心的问题、协调彼此利益、相互交流信息等，在一定时间聚集在一定商业性场所而举行的交流活动，要求：与会者来自三个以下国家，与会人数不少于 50 人，活动时间不少于 4 小时；国际展览会，就国际展览联盟（UFI）的国际展会标准而言，需至少连续举办 3 届，展出面积 20000 平方米以上，国外参展商至少达 20%，国外观众至少达 4%。这一标准高于我国目前的国际展会统计标准，对会议附设展而言这一国际展会标准显得很高。结合会议附设展的特点，本文将国际展览会标准界定为：连续举办 3 届，展出面积达 5000 平方米以上，国外参展商至少达 10%，国外观众至少达 3%；达不到国际展览会标准的其他展会都统计为国内展览会。

其次，会展旅游是利用参加各种会议、展览或大型活动而开展的特殊旅游活动，这种旅游的费用往往不需游客承担，具有奖励或激励特性。会展旅游直接收入包括场馆单位收入、举办单位收入、会展专业服务机构收入等三者之和。会展旅游间接收入为与会展配套及关联的行业和部门的收入之和。会展旅游的总收入为会展直接收入、会展间接收入和会展游客消费诱发收入之和。

2. 统计与测算方法

本文基于支出法和收入法进行问卷调查，收集数据。支出法、收入法和投入产出法相结合，能够较全面反映会展旅游的带动效应。其中，直接统计部分由于北京市统计局数据较为详细，可直接采用北京市统计局现有的统计结果；间接带动效应部分，由本文分析、测算得出会展旅游活动对相关产业部门的带动系数，通过带动系数，得出整体的带动效应。

3. 调研对象的选取

会展旅游的主办或承办单位重点选取了事业单位、企业、协会和会展承办公司。对主办或承办方，重点从支出角度分析其支出结构、支出涉及的主要产业或部门等。

会展旅游相关行业单位的选取，重点是从收入角度，了解其各自收入中来自会展旅游的收入所占的份额。会展旅游相关行业重点选取住宿、餐饮、搭建、交通、广告和翻译等。

五、会展旅游带动效应的调研与测算结果分析

1. 基于收入角度的调研与分析

基于收入角度的调研，部分具体调研结果如表2所示。

表2 收入法调研结果（部分调研样本）

序号	业务大类	总收入/万元	会展旅游收入占比/%	备注
1	策划、搭建	30000	42	
2		—	80	搭建业务来自会展旅游比例90%
3		80000	100	
4		130000	100	
5	展品生产	22000	90	
6	翻译		旺季30~40 淡季10	
7		—	50	
8		500	70	
9		180	20	
10	广告	—	20~30	
11	酒店	—	5~40	淡季5% 旺季40%
12	餐饮	300	10	
13	交通	—	5~50	淡季约5% 旺季约50%
14		—	80以上	
15	场馆	46600	100	

由调研的样本数据可以看出，会展旅游相关服务公司收入中，来自会展旅游的收入所占比重比较大。其中，策划、搭建公司来自会展旅游的收入能占到总收入的40%~100%；展品生产、销售类公司其会展旅游收入占到90%以上；翻译类公司的会展旅游收入随会展旅游活动的淡旺季而有所不同，基本能占到总收入的20%~40%，最高可占到总收入的70%；广告公司的会展旅游收入占总收入的20%~30%；酒店总收入中，来自与会展旅游有关的收入占5%~40%，这部分也与会议的淡旺季有关，其中，旺季达40%；餐饮企业其会展旅游相关收入能占总收入10%左右；而汽车租赁等会展旅游服务公司的会

展旅游相关收入也能占到40%～50%，旺季时甚至达到80%。

根据现有调研结果并结合2010年北京市相关行业统计数据，对五类行业（交通、住宿、餐饮、租赁、广告）初步测算，用其各自的平均占比乘以2010年统计出来的营业额，得出对这些相关行业的带动效应达735亿元。

2. 基于支出角度的调研与分析

从支出角度调研统计的主要结果如表3所示。

表3 会展旅游活动费用支出结构（部分调研样本） 单位：元

活动名称或性质	规模/人	场馆租赁费	设备租赁费	场馆施工和各种制作费	图书印刷费	广播电视费	汽车租赁费	文化体育娱乐费	餐饮费	住宿费	交通运输费	保险费	商务服务费	管理运营费	广告	其他	合计
培训会	总人数70	6000	500	450	2600	0	0	0	6430	0	400	0	0	0	0	4000	20380
企业年会	总人数110	16800	0	0	0	0	0	11000	88000	36850	0	0	0	0	0	0	152650
国际美食文化节		20000	0	25600	24500	0	0	10000	0	0	0	0	20000	0	100000	0	200100
国际组织年会		955000	784000	1340000	150000	175000		185000	1409410	73500	297000	500000	293907	281000	60000	305000	6808817
年会	总人数50，外国人20	35000		2000		2000	6000	80000	120000		5000						250000
专业委员会年会	总人数200	189200	56280		96650		8000	26000	52000	129430			4000				561560
协会会议	总人数120	8000		2460					23440	1500			1300			5000	41700
培训会	总人数83，外国人11	50000	10000		20000				44000	86400	8000			88000			306400
协会国际论坛	总人数150，外国人60	20000	8000		5000				60000	68000			40000			51000	252000
培训会	总人数230	10000	20000	20000	20000				10000	50000	5000						229000
学会会议	总人数530	1500000		330000			190000		30000	700000	360000		270000	1500000		220000	5100000
公司年会	总人数900	1300000	1600000	1510000		500000	760000	850000	1900000				600000			650000	9670000
年度庆典	总人数1200	320000		1150000	50000		300000	1000000	150000	800000	50000	30000	650000			700000	5200000
企业年会	总人数6000，外国人4000	600000		300000			70000		60000	30000			250000		90000		1400000
培训会	总人数58	160000							60000	120000						40000	380000
旅游节		11000	39280	3344977	144967		6000	4132045	116243	2400	89361.5	0	2426223	34362.5		325000	10671859

从支出法调研数据中可以看出，参加会议人数规模最大的为6000人，规模较少的则有50人参加，涵盖了典型的国际或国内年会、研讨会、培训会等会议性质，各支出项目与国民经济相关部门相对应，所占平均比例及诱发效果，如表4所示。

表4 支出法调研结果及对国民经济相关行业部门带动效果

序号	支出项目	对应国民经济部门	所占比例%	金额（亿元）	生产诱发乘数	生产诱发效果（亿元）
1	场馆租赁费	72 房地产业 34 租赁和商务服务业	17.97	38.24457	2.563	98.02083
2	设备租赁费	73 租赁业 18 电气机械及器材制造业 20 仪器仪表及文化办公用机械制造业	7.49	15.92835	11.89	189.388
3	场馆施工和各种制作费	48 建筑安装业	15.74	33.48759	8.249	276.2391
4	图书印刷费	23 印刷业和记录媒介的复制	1.47	3.1357	3.401	10.66452
5	广播电视费	60 电信和其他信息传输服务业	0.37	0.79775	8.603	6.863043
6	汽车租赁费	73 租赁业	2.95	6.283341	3.666	23.03473
7	文化体育娱乐费	90 文化艺术业，92 娱乐业	11.65	24.79775	3.123	77.44337
8	餐饮费	67 餐饮业 05 食品制造及烟草加工业	7.77	16.53781	7.259	120.0479
9	住宿费	66 住宿业	9.54	20.29436	3.509	71.21291
10	交通运输费	55 航空运输业 17 交通运输设备制造业	3.69	7.841973	7.383	57.89729
11	保险费	70 保险业	1.02	2.165872	2.528	5.475325
12	商务服务费	74 商务服务业	10.35	22.0342	7.628	168.0769
13	管理运营费	42 公共管理和社会组织	3.93	8.355472	3.363	28.09945
14	广告	74 商务服务业 36 综合技术服务业	0.49	1.048251	7.628	7.99606
15	其他	57 装卸搬运和其他运输服务业，58 仓储业，59 邮政业	5.57	11.84702	8.643	102.3938
	合　计		100.00	212.8	6.10	1242.853304

表中数据显示，活动费用的支出方向涉及15个类别，其中，场馆租赁费支出最大，占到总支出的17.79%；其次是场馆施工和各种制作费、文化体育娱乐费、商务服务费的支出，分别占到总支出的15.74%、11.65%和10.35%。再次是住宿费、餐饮费和设备租赁费，分别占到9.54%、7.77%和7.49%。此外，交通运输费和汽车租赁费分别占3.69%和2.95%，而管理运营费和其他业务支出分别占3.93%和5.57%。从目前对会展旅游样本的调研看，其支出涉及范围较广，因此，会展旅游对相关行业的带动作用将非常可观。

根据北京市统计局公布的相关数据，2011年北京共举办会议28.55万次，举办展览1380个，会展收入212.8亿元。结合北京市2010年投入产出表提供的数据和本次调研数据，计算出各产业部门的生产诱发乘数和各个支出项所代表的国民经济分类大类的系数，从而得到2011年利用会展旅游支出费用相关系数法求得的生产诱发经济效果为1242.85亿元。随着北京会展数量的逐年增加、会展规模的扩大、会展时间的延长、会展地点的多样化，北京会展旅游将会对其他产业产生更大的带动作用。

3. 会展游客旅游支出带动效应分析

根据北京市2010年投入产出表提供的数据，可计算出各产业部门（42×42部门）的生产诱发乘数，如表5所示。

表5 北京市2010年国民经济部门生产诱发系数表

序号	国民经济各部门	生产诱发乘数
1	造纸印刷及文教体育用品制造业	3.401
2	通用、专用设备制造业	3.977
3	交通运输设备制造业	4.320
4	通信设备、计算机及其他电子设备制造业	4.626
5	交通运输及仓储业	3.752
6	邮政业	2.721
7	信息传输、计算机服务和软件业	3.356
8	批发和零售业	2.773
9	住宿和餐饮业	3.509
10	租赁和商务服务业	3.666
11	文化、体育和娱乐业	3.123

根据《2011年北京国内旅游抽样调查分析报告》及北京市旅游发展委员会提供的相关资料得出：北京会展游客旅游消费支出总额为223.8亿元，详细情况如表6所示。

表6 北京市会展游客旅游总支出

旅游消费	支出额（亿元）
入境游客	52.4
国内来京游客	157.4
市民在京游	14
合计	223.8

以参加会展为来访目的的游客，其具体支出项目构成如表7所示。

表7 北京市会展游客旅游支出项目构成

来访目的 支出项目(%)	会展
购物费	23.3
餐饮费	17.4
住宿费	34.4
长途交通费	17.8
景点游览费	1.6
市内交通费	4.9
娱乐费	0.5
邮电通信费	0.1
其他费用	0

根据以上几个表格提供的数据信息，可以计算出北京市会展游客旅游支出项目对国民经济相应行业部门的带动效果，如表8所示。

表8 北京市会展游客旅游支出项目对国民经济相应行业部门的带动效果

支出项目	所占比重（%）	金额（亿元）	对应国民经济行业部门	生产诱发乘数	生产诱发效果（亿元）	所占比重（%）
住宿	34.4	76.9872	31 住宿和餐饮业	3.509	270.148	35.7
餐饮	17.4	38.9412	31 住宿和餐饮业	3.509	136.645	18.0

续表

支出项目	所占比重（%）	金额（亿元）	对应国民经济行业部门	生产诱发乘数	生产诱发效果（亿元）	所占比重（%）
交通（长途+市内）	17.8+4.9=22.7	50.8026	27 交通运输及仓储业	3.752	190.611	25.2
购物	23.3	52.1454	30 批发和零售业	2.773	144.599	19.1
景点游览、娱乐	1.6+0.5=2.1	4.6998	41 文化、体育和娱乐业	3.123	14.677	1.9
邮电通信	0.1	0.2238	28 邮政业 29 信息传输、计算机服务和软件业	2.721 3.356 3.039 （取均值）	0.680	0.1
合计	100	223.8		合计	757.36	100

由上表可以看出，2010年北京市会展游客旅游总支出为223.8亿元，为北京市的住宿业、餐饮业、交通业等相关行业带来的带动效应共计757.36亿元。其中，对住宿业的带动效应最大，达到270.148亿元，占到总带动效果的35.7%；其次是交通业，达到190.611亿元，占到总带动效果的25.2%；再次则是购物和餐饮业，各行业带动比例如图1所示。

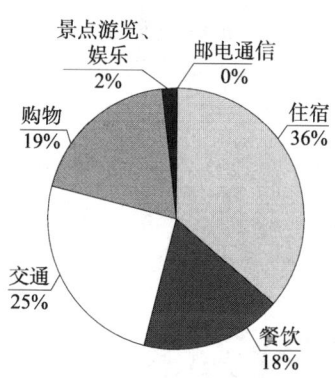

图1　北京市会展游客旅游支出带动效应构成

4. 会展旅游总带动效应分析

从以上各类核算数据可以看出，北京会展旅游的总带动效应非常显著。由于会展与旅游所具有的天然融合关系，使得会展活动与旅游活动密不可分，二者之间相互促进。同时，会展旅游又具有附加值高、产业关联性强等特点，会展旅游对交通、餐饮、住宿、购物、广告、通信、娱乐等相关产业有很强的带动作用。总体而言，会展旅游总收入等于会展旅游直接收入、间接收入和会展游客消费中非重复的消费诱发收入之和。根据北京市统计局相关统计和本调研相关计算，2011年北京会展旅游直接收入212.8亿元，通过测算间接带动收入达1242.85亿元，会展游客消费对相关行业的带动效应为757.36亿元。其中，会展旅游间接收入主要是根据会展主办方或承办方提供的支出法调研材料，通过投入产出法算出各项带动系数，再结合2011年北京市统计数据计算得到。会展游客消费收入是游客在参会之外而发生的消费，在原来的统计数据和大多数文献中，这一部分并没有在相应的直接和间接收入中体现。同时，在会展游客消费诱发收入中，有些项目已部分体现在会展旅游间接收入中，部分项目还没有体现在间接收入中，如购物等。本文在全面分析的基础上，尽可能全面地探讨并核算了北京会展旅游的带动效应。综合以上各项直接和间接带动测算结果，2011年北京市会展旅游的总带动效应为2008.35亿元人民币，综合带动系数达到8.44。这一数据显示，会展旅游对相关产业的带动效应非常显著。

结　论

会展旅游具有附加值高、产业关联性强等特点，对交通、餐饮、住宿、购物、广告、通信、娱乐等相关产业有很强的带动作用。但在现有的会展旅游相关统计中，存在许多影响统计结果的问题，并进而影响到对会展旅游带动效应的测算。本文在分析当前国内外会展旅游统计状况的基础上,结合北京会展旅游发展及相关统计现状,明确会展旅游统计范围,提出会展旅游总收入等于会展旅游直接收入、间接收入和会展游客消费中非重复的消费诱发收入之和,详细调研北京会展旅游数据,并运用支出法、收入法和投入产出法相结合的方法,较全面地测算了北京会展旅游对相关行业的带动效应,带动系数达8.44,进一步验证了会展旅游具有较强的带动效应。

参考文献

[1] Karl W. Wöber. Standardizing City Tourism Statistics [J]. Annals of Tourism Research, 2000, 27 (1): 51-68.
[2] Kim Samuel Seongseop, Chon Kaye, Chung Kyu Yoop. Convention Industry in South Korea: An Economic Impact Analysis [J]. Tourism Management, 2003, 24 (5): 533-541.
[3] 何建英. 论会展旅游的概念内涵 [J]. 哈尔滨商业大学学报(社会科学版), 2004 (3): 98-99.
[4] 胡平, 杨杰. 会展业经济拉动效应的实证研究——以上海新国际博览中心为例 [J]. 旅游学刊, 2006, 21 (11).
[5] 李杰. 对会展产业带动系数的理性分析 [J]. 经济纵横, 2007 (10).
[6] 林越英. 对我国会展旅游发展若干问题的初步探讨 [J]. 北京第二外国语学院学报, 2002 (6).
[7] 王保伦. 会展旅游发展模式之探讨 [J]. 旅游学刊, 2003, 18 (1).
[8] 王云龙. 会展活动与旅游活动的比较——兼论会展旅游概念的界定 [J]. 旅游学刊, 2003, 18 (5).
[9] 余向平. 会展业的产业带动效应及其经济学分析 [J]. 商业研究, 2006 (18).
[10] 郑建瑜. 上海会展业现状及发展趋势分析 [J]. 旅游学刊, 2000 (6).
[11] 钟汶利. 我国会展业的竞争优势分析 [D]. 镇江: 江苏大学, 2010.

旅游吸引力与城市休闲气质的探讨

宁泽群

一、问题的提出

城市旅游问题是旅游研究的一个重要内容。它对于旅游者的吸引力何在一直是研究者关注的中心问题。从传统的旅游资源与规划的角度来看,旅游的历史人文资源和自然资源是构成吸引旅游者前往旅游的资源基础。尽管一些研究者对城市旅游资源的理解略有不同,但基本都是在原有的旅游理论框架中讨论的。但是,从我国城市旅游的发展现状来看,存在着许多问题。这些问题不仅仅是城市旅游发展的市场问题,对于城市本身的发展也具有重要的理论和现实意义。

我们先从北京和上海两个城市的相关数据比较中来看一下这一问题的潜在意义。我们都知道,北京是世界闻名的历史古都,历史悠久,人文遗产古迹繁多,可以说,几乎在北京的任何一个角落里,都能够挖掘出一段历史故事。林语堂在《大城北京》一书中,曾经这样形容北京:"北京曾经是世界上最大的开放性都城之一。它吸引着来自世界各地的人们。巴黎和北京被人们公认为世界上两个最美的城市。"❶ 上海则是我国近代形成的最大商业城市,经贸交易十分活跃,特别是在20世纪30年代,商业繁华程度达到了鼎盛,曾经被誉为东方小巴黎。

从传统旅游发展的观点来看,北京的优势是毋庸置疑的❷。事实上,在改革开放后的相当一段时期里,北京也一直是中国旅游业发展的龙头。但是,21世纪以后,一些统计数据显示出了不同的现象(如表1所示)。

表1 北京与上海的国内旅游比较

年份	北京			上海			人均消费比较
	国内游客/万人次	国内旅游收入/亿元	人均消费/元	国内游客/万人次	国内旅游收入/亿元	人均消费/元	
2000	10186	683	670.53	7848.1	775	987.5	B<S
2001	11007	887.7	806.49	8254.5	806	976.44	B<S
2002	11500	930	808.7	8760	907	1035.39	B<S
2003	8700	706	811.49	7603.6	1079	1419.07	B<S
2004	11950	1145	951.16	8505.1	1216	1429.73	B<S
2005	12500	1300	1040	9011.9	1308	1451.41	B<S
2006	13200	1482.7	1123.26	9683.9	1419	1465.32	B<S
2007	14280	1753.6	1228.01	10210.2	1611	1577.83	B<S
2007	4354774	457962	1051.63	5200981	467297	898.48	B>S

资料来源:高峻主编:《中国城市旅游发展报告(2009版)》。人均消费作者根据数据计算。❸

从表1中,我们可以发现,尽管北京的国内旅游人数始终多于上海(2007年除外),但国内旅游的收入则是此起彼伏的,2000年、2003年、2004年、2005年、2007年上海均高于北京,而人均消费的比

[基金项目] 本研究受北京市哲学社会科学规划项目(11JGB041)资助。
[作者简介] 宁泽群(1954—),男,教授,北京联合大学现代休闲方式与旅游发展研究所所长,主要研究方向为休闲与旅游发展、旅游经济产业与政策,Email:ningzequn@163.com。

❶ 林语堂.大城北京,西安:陕西师范大学出版社,2008:5.
❷ 北京的全国重点文物保护单位有98处,而上海只有19处,且上海的多数是近现代的文物,而北京则是历史悠久的古迹。
❸ 高峻.中国城市旅游发展报告(2009版),北京:中国旅游出版社,2009,第34、36、54、56页。

较，上海始终大于北京。

我们再来看一下国际旅游的情况，如表2所示。

表2　北京与上海的国际旅游人数比较

年份	北京 海外游客（人次）	上海 海外游客（人次）	比较
2000	2820911	1814027	B > S
2001	2857872	2042636	B > S
2002	3103836	2725263	B > S
2003	1851245	2447089	B < S
2004	3154950	3854505	B < S
2005	3629142	4445428	B < S
2006	3902923	4646303	B < S
2007	4354774	5200981	B < S

资料来源：同表1。

表2的数据显示，2002年以前，北京的国际旅游人数大于上海，而2003年以后，上海的国际旅游人数则大于北京。

从表1和表2的数据比较中，我们发现了一个需要我们深入思考的问题：北京拥有如此众多的传统旅游资源（主要是历史人文资源）❶，为什么上海会在某些方面慢慢领先了呢？而上海能够吸引旅游者的又是什么呢？

二、什么构成城市旅游者的吸引力

对于城市旅游吸引力的探讨，国内外学者做过不少理论探索。如 Myriam Jansen Verbake（1986）提出了城市内部的旅游系统问题，认为这一系统是由城市旅游资源、旅游者、广告商与开发商构成。后来，Jansen Verbeke（1988）将城市旅游产品划分为两个层面：第一要素是历史性建筑、都市风光、博物馆、画廊、戏院、体育和其他各项活动；第二要素则是饭店、餐厅、商场、购物场所和其他服务。第一要素是旅游的核心产品，第二要素是旅游的非核心产品，而交通和旅游基础设施则是辅助因素。在Jansen Verbeke对城市旅游产品的划分中，多数都是物态的旅游吸引物，少数是非物态的活动，如都市风光、体育和其他各项活动等。不过，Jansen Verbeke的定义是从城市旅游的具体现象出发，一般性抽象不足，结果导致一些城市旅游现象与其定义产生矛盾。正如我们所知道的，作为免税自由港的香港被称为旅游购物的天堂，显然，香港作为旅游城市的重要标志，就是商场与购物，按照Jansen Verbeke的划分，它必然属于城市旅游的第一要素。

对旅游吸引的明确定义，是由Neil Leiper 1979年提出的，之后他在1990年加以修正。他将旅游吸引力定义为一个系统，这一系统由人的需要、有吸引力的地方，以及连接旅游地和旅游者的相关信息媒介三者构成，只有三者共存，才形成旅游吸引力系统。

国际学者对旅游吸引力的研究主要体现在区域吸引和吸引物的吸引两个方面。区域吸引的主要理论观点体现在游憩商务区（RBD, Recreational Business District）的概念上，它是由Stansfield & Rickert（1970）提出的。它主要指为季节性涌入城区的游客的需要，城区内集中布置饭店、娱乐业、新奇物和礼品商品的街区。后来，RBD被引申为旅游商业区（TBD, Tourism Business District）。❷ 而吸引物研究的主要观点主要体现在有形吸引物和无形吸引物的分析上，有形吸引物主要集中在对城市建筑及其设施研究，无形吸引物主要集中在城市的文化节事和会展活动方面。

我国学者对城市旅游的定义则相对宽泛，以至于很难把握。如宋家增（1996）将都市旅游定义为以都市风貌、风光、风物、风情为特色的旅游。然而，风貌、风光、风物、风情的内容具体体现为什么，

---

❶ 如果不考虑上海周边地区，单纯从上海本身来看，上海的旅游自然资源似乎也不如北京。
❷ 从RBD引申到TBD的过程，我们不难发现，RBD和TBD的对象群体是有所不同。

它们之间有什么区别和联系。这些都缺乏明确的内涵和界定，以至于将都市旅游引申是以商务旅游、会议旅游和国内外交流活动是其发展的重点上。并且，在概念上又细分为城市旅游和都市旅游。以城市的大小来区分城市旅游和都市旅游的区别❶。此外，我国学者对城市旅游（或都市旅游）的研究更多倾向于旅游城市的供给一方的研究，如旅游业与城市发展的关系（于英士1994，张广瑞1994）、市场宣传推广（白祖诚1994，李蕾蕾1995、1997、1999）、城市旅游的规划与管理（陈传康1996，尚文生等1998）。而基于 Neil Leiper 的城市旅游吸引力系统的分析，几乎没有。尽管我国学者接受了城市旅游（RBD, Recreational Business District）的概念，但他们更多将其理解为旅游商务区（TBD, Tourism Business District）。（关于两者的区别，我们将在后面进行分析。）国内研究者往往在概念不清晰的情况下，就延续既定的模糊内涵来做进一步的论证、分析和推广。

实际上，笔者认为在 Leiper 的旅游吸引力系统的理论中，"存在着人的需要"是吸引力系统理论的首要条件。在旅游市场中，旅游活动是由供求双方决定的。在旅游者拥有很大自由选择权的情况下，旅游者的需求起到更大的作用。我们知道，旅游需求是由旅游动机引发，它服从于旅游者旅游体验的需要，是旅游者休闲方式的一种表现形式。根据 S. E. Ios – Ahola（1991）的观点，旅游者的动机来自他对压抑的单调重复的日常生活和工作环境的逃避，并希望通过旅游来寻求心理的补偿。旅游者通过旅游这种"非惯常环境"来获得在日常生活中所没有的愉悦体验。❷ 由此，西方学者将这种现象定义为旅游的"推—拉"模式。"推"从旅游者的心理动机来看，主要体现为有逃避、自我发现、休息放松、名望、挑战、冒险等因素；"拉"则是指旅游目的地以独特的自然景观、历史悠久的名胜古迹、文化活动、体育运动等对旅游者的吸引。❸

但是，我们所要提出的问题是：在"推—拉"模式的不同种类中，旅游者在旅游活动中究竟需要体验什么？他们追求的形而上的心理补偿究竟是什么？

为了解决这一问题，我们认为，答案需要从旅游本身的定义去寻找。

旅游的定义，尽管学术界始终没有一个被一致认同的说法，但在我们所熟悉的旅游定义中，它还是可以分为三大类别：经济性的定义、技术性的定义、文化性的定义。经济性的定义实际上是对旅游产业群的定义，如 Soukhanov, Anne H 和 Ellis, Kaethe 主编的《韦斯伯斯特大学词典》中对旅游的定义是"以娱乐为目的的旅行，为旅游者提供旅程和服务的行业"❹。技术性的定义则主要从统计的层面来获取旅游现象的基本数据和发展规模。这一定义是由世界旅游组织和加拿大旅游局于1991年达成的共识。而加拿大规范旅游的技术性定义的最初动机恰恰是出于旅游对社会经济发展的重要性的计量需要。❺ 从前两种定义来看，它们基本上都基于旅游业的发展，而并非是旅游现象本身。相比之下，旅游的文化性定义更贴近旅游者所追求的目的。如法国学者让·梅特森认为，"旅游是一种休闲活动，它包括旅行或在离开定居地点较远的地方逗留。其目的是在于消遣、休息或为了丰富他的经历和文化教育。"❻

在梅特森的定义中，它反映了旅游者活动的三个关键要素：异地、休闲、获取心理补偿的体验。然而，我们需要进一步探究的是，旅游者为什么要前往异地，难道在本地就不能获得心理上的补偿了吗？S. E. Ios – Ahola 从心理需求的解释为我们提供了解锁的钥匙：旅游者是为了逃避压抑的日常生活和工作

---

❶ 事实上，国际上并没有城市旅游和都市旅游之分。尽管在英文中，城市的表达可以使用不同的词汇，如 city（城市、都市），town（城镇、城市中心区），abad（网络词汇中的城市），conurbation（有卫星城的大都市），metropolis（首府，重要中心城市），但是我国的城市旅游和都市旅游对应于英文似乎只有一个词，即 urban tourism。有的学者将 city break 看作城市旅游是不准确的。City break 是指一些旅馆针对周末短途出游者给出的优惠房价。即使引申到周末的短途出游行为，也不能作为城市旅游的完整现象来考察。此外，城市旅游应该根据其特性来界定，而不是根据城市的大小来界定。

❷ 张凌云将旅游的本质定义为"非惯常环境的体验和生活方式"，本文作者是基本赞同的。但本文作者认为，这一定义的不足在于旅游者在非惯常环境中并不是一种一般性的常规体验，它是有特定的限定意义，即应该是有异于旅游者居住地文化的异文化体验，这是休闲方式的一种类型。张凌云的观点可参见他的《旅游学研究的新框架：对非惯常环境下消费者行为和现象的研究》，旅游学刊，2008（10）。

❸ 作者一直没有寻找到"推—拉"模式理论的提出者，而这一观点引自古诗韵、保继刚的《城市旅游研究进展》，旅游学刊，1999（2）。

❹ Soukhanov, Anne H & Ellis, Kaethe (eds) 1984, Websters Ⅱ New Riverside University Dictionary, Houghton Mifflin, Boston.

❺ 加拿大第一任旅游部长 Tom McMillan 曾经因为受到内阁其他同僚针对旅游业和其发展数据的质疑，而开始对旅游统计数据质量重视，进而与世界旅游组织在1991年达成共识，并于1994年开发了附属于国民经济账户系统之外的旅游卫星账户（TSA, Tourism Satellite Account）。

❻ 谢彦君. 基础旅游学（第二版），北京：中国旅游出版社，2004：66。

环境。而导致这一逃避的根源在于社会经济高速发展中经济利益驱动所导致的生活与工作的压迫感和非自由状态。❶ 德国著名哲学家，法兰克福学派的代表人物赫伯特·马尔库塞在1964年发表的《单向度的人》就深刻地揭示了经济高速增长给人们带来的异化现象。❷ 他认为现代社会用经济的高速增长所带来的物质利益，压制了人们追寻自由的本性需求。在这种背景下，人们追求对日常生活的逃避就不是什么奇怪的事情了。

由于这一日常生活与工作的压迫感，使得人们无法在原来的生活与工作环境中释放压力和寻找自我，从而产生了逃避熟悉生活环境的心理需求。旅游者通过对异地文化（或者称为非居住地文化）的感知、体验和比较，来缓解原来生活状况所带来的心理落差，以达到自我心理的平衡和满足。旅游者的异地游历过程既体验了不同于自己惯常的生活形态，也通过非常规的生活消费行为释放自己的心理压力。如许多旅游者在旅游途中的消费行为都是依据享乐原则，而不是居家过日子的节俭原则而发生的。这种消费行为并不单单是物质的追求，而表现出一种自我释放的含义。❸

通过上面的分析，我们不难看出，旅游者前往异地的心理需求是为了体验异文化的不同，来达到心理上的补偿。而不同地域的文化差异就是旅游者产生前往体验的吸引力所在。不过，由于不同地域的文化差异是由当地的地理构造、气候条件等一系列自然因素影响下的人们的生活方式积淀的结果，所以其文化特色的表达方式是不同的，这种文化可能是食文化（如中国许多城市的特色饮食）、可能是购物文化（如香港等发达商业城市的商业购物）、可能是节庆文化（如世界一些著名的电影节、体育赛事，以及巴西和其他一些地方的狂欢节等）。

三、城市休闲气质：城市文化氛围的集中体现

一个城市是通过什么方式来感召旅游者前往的呢？❹ 显然是它的文化魅力，而这种魅力是通过它的休闲气质来渲染的。

文化是一个形而上的概念。像许多内涵丰富的概念一样，文化也是歧义多解的词汇。美国人类学家克罗伯（A. L. Kroeber）和克拉克洪（C. Kluckhohn）（1952）出版的《文化：关于概念和定义的探讨》一书中，列举出他们所能搜集到的1871年至1951年八十年间关于"文化"的161个定义。❺ 不过，尽管这一概念存在着不同的解释，但文化成为一门学科的独立研究对象则是在20世纪20年代英美出现了人类文化学之后，而这些文化人类学家在诠释文化含义时，都强调了文化是一个"整体"。如英国文化人类学奠基人爱德华·伯内特·泰勒（Edward Burnett Tylor, 1871）在《原始文化》一书中指出，文化是一个复杂的总体，包括知识、信仰、艺术、道德、法律、风俗以及人类在社会里所得到的一切能力与习惯。我国著名的社会学家沙莲香也认为，"所谓文化，就是人们在长期的社会生活中凝聚起来的生活方式之总体。首先，文化本身是一种生活方式，其中包括思考方式和行为方式"。"其实，文化是生活方式的总体。"❻

实际上，文化虽然是人们生活方式累积的结果，但它应该包含两个层面：感性层面和理性层面。❼ 感性层面体现在人们日常生活的方方面面，诸如吃、喝、拉、撒、睡等风俗习惯；理性层面则体现在意识结构的知识体系之中。在文化的历史延续中，感性层面的时间传递有两种方式：一种人们之间的言语

---

❶ 这就是为什么大众旅游现象出现在经济高速增长时期，而不是之前。我们通常只从消费者经济收入达到一定水平来解释大众旅游的兴起，而忽视了大众旅游出现的特定社会心理需求现象。本文因为不是在这里讨论这一问题，所以在这里不作深入的探讨。

❷ 卢瑾. 发达工业社会中人的异化——马尔库塞的单向度理论解读［J］. 理论观察，2008（1）。

❸ 与这种现象类似的是，在现代社会中一些女性为了表达对家庭日常生活压抑和对男权压迫的不满，而到商场肆意购物。这种行为同样是一种心理释放。

❹ 对于旅游者的吸引，旅行社一直使用"招徕"这一术语，但这个词是一个经营性词汇，它不能反映旅游的基本含义。我认为，旅游者之所以对一个城市感兴趣，是由于这个城市的魅力所在，因此，我使用了"感召"这个词来表达城市对旅游者的吸引。

❺ 转引自刘跃进：文化就是社会化——广义"文化"概念的逻辑批判，北方论丛，1999（3）。

❻ 同附注15。

❼ 我在这里对文化的分类与 H. H. Stern（1992：208）的文化分类不同。H. H. Stern 根据文化的结构和范畴的特点，将文化分为广义和狭义两种概念，广义的文化是从一个社会的总体是由物质、心理和制度三个方面构成来划分的。狭义的文化是指人们普遍的社会习惯，如衣食住行、风俗习惯、生活方式、行为规范等。而我的划分是从一个外来进入者对当地文化的认知发展过程来划分的。这种认知必然是一个从感性认识逐步上升到理性认识的过程。所以，进入者对异文化的认识是从感性层面逐步渗透到理性层面的。

和行为的互动感知和传递，这种传递会形成一个区域内特有的人们相互制约的社会心理和生活习俗，另一种则是以表演或口头记述的休闲娱乐方式来再现，这种再现可能是节事娱乐活动，也可能是文化娱乐的表演再现。理性层面的时间传递方式则是知识体系——物化的（如书籍等）和非物化的（如法律制度等）❶。由于感性层面的文化更容易被感知，所以，一个城市的文化氛围往往是由这个城市的感性层面文化积淀来营造的，即是由休闲娱乐方式和活动所营造出来的。这种由休闲娱乐方式和活动行为营造出来的氛围，被定义为这个城市的"休闲气质"。❷

一个城市具有的"休闲气质"应该由以下几点来进行判断。

首先，城市的"休闲气质"是从当地居民的生活方式中渗透出来的，因此，这种气质是依托当地居民的生活而显现出来的，离开了当地居民的生活，这种气质的荡然无存。一些城市将一些古老街区开发为专门招徕旅游者的观光街区，而剥离了当地居民的生活。这些区域内的城市休闲气质就会消散。

其次，城市的"休闲气质"就像人的气质一样，是天生遗传的。它体现了当地居民生活方式的一种历史的累积，即使时代发生了巨大的变化，但生活方式的改变需要较长的时间，它需要观念和社会群体心理的转变，因此，城市的"休闲气质"会具有一定的历史遗传，保持一定时期的稳定性。

最后，城市的"休闲气质"主要通过当地居民的休闲娱乐方式来集中体现出来。因为，如果我们需要了解当地居民的生活方式，需要较长时间的体验，而当地的休闲娱乐方式则是对当地生活方式的演示和再现，这些休闲娱乐方式往往能够以感性的方式，使得外来者很快能感知当地文化，从而被这种文化所吸引。

由此可见，一个城市的"休闲气质"并不单纯是一个地理空间的氛围，我们之所以不用"气氛""环境"等词来形容它，是因为它是一种活的生命体，它体现的是一个地区的人的群体的活动集合，这种集合既保留着该地区人们生活方式的历史累积延续下来印记，又会随着时代发展所引起的物质、心理和制度的变化而相应变化。它既有自己独有的特征，又会随着时代变化形成新的独有特征。

我们在前面指出，旅游的本质是旅游者从居住地到非居住地来体验当地居民生活文化方式的一种休闲行为。这种休闲行为包含着对不同于旅游者居住地的异文化的综合体验，它既可能是探源的（历史文化的），也可能是即时享受的（当代文化的）。这是因为旅游体验是综合而复杂的，因而，我国旅游学界通常将其简单概括为吃、住、行、游、购、娱六大要素。实际上，这种体验就是旅游者希望通过了解和感受旅游目的地当地居民的真实生活方式，以获得不同文化形态的差异的比较、沟通与理解，来达到自己在原来居住地所不能获取的心理补偿。正是由于城市的"休闲气质"是这个城市散发出来的文化特质，所以，显而易见的是，一个城市的"休闲气质"是吸引旅游者前往的重要因素，它的浓郁程度决定了旅游者被吸引的程度。

通过前面的分析，我们不难发现，城市的"休闲气质"与旅游吸引力之间存在着密切的关系。城市"休闲气质"不同于传统旅游资源吸引力的关键在于，它是这个城市文化的一种凝聚力，是这个城市文化的灵魂体现。它并不具体体现在某一点、某个景区、某个街区上，而是这个城市整体散发出来的魅力。❸ 就像某首歌曲中表达的那样：千万里我追寻着你，可是你却并不在意，你不像是在我梦里，在梦里你是我的唯一。

四、结论：问题的初步解答

现在，我们回到文章最初提出的问题上。为什么北京拥有如此众多的传统旅游资源的情况下，上海能够在某些方面慢慢领先于北京，吸引了更多的旅游者呢？

（1）传统旅游资源与城市休闲气质对旅游者的吸引是不同的。北京尽管拥有众多的传统旅游资源，

---

❶ 城市建筑介于两者之间，从感知的角度，建筑的造型、风格、色彩都成为吸引力外来者关注的城市休闲气质，但建筑的构造原理及其历史内涵则往往成为这个城市的理性层面的文化知识体系的一个重要组成部分。

❷ 气质通常是用来形容"人"的。它是指根据人的姿态、长相、穿着、性格、行为等元素结合起来，给别人的一种感觉。而根据心理学的解释，气质（temperament）是指表现人的心理活动的强度、速度、灵活性与指向性等方面的一种稳定的心理特征，它是人的天性。一般来说，形容场所的感觉是用气氛来形容，而对较大区域的感觉则用环境来表示。

❸ 实际上，作为城市休闲气质具体体现的休闲娱乐活动本身，就是一种强吸引力。在英文中，娱乐一词"entertainment"的拉丁文词根"tenare"的意思，就是"抓住你，触及你的灵魂"。转引自楼嘉军：《上海城市娱乐研究》，上海：文汇出版社，2008，第2页。

但是，这种传统旅游资源的形态更多的是以建筑遗产的形态展示给旅游者的，虽然，建筑文化是城市文化的一部分，但是建筑文化并不是城市"休闲气质"的主导方面，建筑文化只有承载了休闲娱乐的功能以后，才构成城市休闲气质的组成部分。城市休闲气质的主导方面应该是当地居民的休闲娱乐活动。上海的休闲娱乐活动相对于北京更为丰富，特别是上海的夜生活，不论是居民的参与程度，还是范围，都超过了北京。有资料显示，上海南京路超过100万的高峰客流是出现在夜市；上海商家全天的营业额，有一半是在夜市赚来的。上海这种夜生活的浓郁气氛，恰恰是城市休闲气质的一种体现，也是吸引旅游者前往的重要因素。

（2）城市休闲气质具有遗传性。它是当地居民生活方式（特别是休闲娱乐方式）的一种文化体现，随着历史时间的延续，这种文化体现会沉淀在当地居民的潜意识之中，内化成一种当地社会的民风民俗，它通过社会心理层面和集体无意识来左右当地居民的行为。我们都知道，上海在20世纪30年代是被称为东方的"冒险家的乐园"，中外五湖四海的人们聚集在上海，造就了中外文化混杂融合的独特娱乐氛围，如上海当时有中国最高的餐饮大楼——国际饭店，有最开放的娱乐场所——大世界，有最洋派的爵士乐队和赛马，有最时髦的化装舞会和选美大赛等，因而使得上海成为当时中国最繁华的城市。表3中的数据显示了20世纪30年代上海娱乐业在中国发展的龙头地位。

表3　20世纪30年代上海与国内六大城市娱乐场所的比较

城市	戏院	百分比	电影院	百分比	舞厅	百分比	游乐场	百分比
上海	81	63.78	44	36.36	28	65.12	9	39.13
香港	—	—	24	19.83	7	16.28	—	—
北平	17	13.39	10	8.26	—	—	1	4.35
天津	14	11.02	23	19.01	5	11.63	6	26.09
武汉	5	3.94	9	7.44	3	6.98	3	13.04
广州	10	7.87	11	9.09	—	—	4	17.39
总计	127	100	121	100	43	100	23	100

资料转引楼嘉军：《上海城市娱乐研究》，上海：文汇出版社，2008，第59页。

显然，上海这种娱乐文化积淀的遗传性多于北京。

（3）城市休闲气质的基本特征是休闲娱乐的平民化。尽管北京是当代中国的文化之都，各类文化娱乐产业都呈现一种蓬勃发展的趋势。但受政治中心的影响，北京的文化娱乐更多体现一种理性文化的特征，相反，上海的休闲娱乐活动更加随意，更加平民化。如上海的夜生活是老少咸宜的。上海的夜生活，不可无商店、酒吧、外滩。著名的摄影艺术家编号233认为，北京有魅力而不性感，而上海却处处散发着一种城市独特的性感。我们在前面强调指出，城市的休闲气质主要体现为一种感性文化，而不是一种理性文化。

（4）商业街区的繁荣是城市休闲气质的另一个重要体现。如Stansfield & Rickert提出的RBD（游憩商务区）概念，就体现为休闲娱乐与商业区域的有机结合。它对旅游者的吸引力要远远大于传统旅游资源。Myriam Jansen Verbeke（1991）认为发展休闲购物旅游是城市传统中心区、败落的旅游胜地，甚至郊区再生的驱动力。Shaw & Williams（1994）甚至指出，在许多城市，商店和饭店对于某类旅游者而言可能是最大的吸引物。❶ 楼嘉军在研究上海娱乐业发展时发现，上海在19世纪40年代开埠以后，在英租界、法租界和华界交接的洋泾浜两岸地区商业、住宿业、娱乐业的发展繁荣，甚至超过了传统人文景观和自然景观对上海市民的吸引力度。❷ 可见，商业的繁荣是城市休闲气质的重要组成部分，它对旅游者具有强烈的吸引力。上海的商业繁荣历来胜于北京。而20世纪90年代以后，上海经济社会的高速发展所带来的浓郁的商业繁荣气氛，更加增强了它对旅游者的吸引力。

通过上面的分析，我们可以发现，由城市居民生活方式所体现出来的文化感性层面所凝聚而成的城市休闲气质，是旅游吸引力的重要要素。因此，如何培养、营造和保持一个城市的休闲气质，对这个城

---

❶ 张蕾，赵中华，贾志宏. 国外城市旅游研究进展[J]. 旅游科学，2005（2）.
❷ 楼嘉军. 上海城市娱乐研究[M]. 上海：文汇出版社，2008：24-27.

市的旅游发展具有重要的意义。这也是本文探讨此问题的初衷所在。

参考文献

[1] 宋家增. 发展都市旅游之我见 [J]. 旅游学刊, 1996 (3): 23-25.
[2] 古诗韵, 保继刚. 城市旅游研究进展 [J]. 旅游学刊, 1999 (2): 15-20.
[3] 张侠. 都市旅游发展与政府职能研究 [D]. 武汉: 华中师范大学, 2009.
[4] 楼嘉军. 上海城市娱乐研究 [J]. 上海: 文汇出版社, 2008.
[5] 张凌云. 旅游学研究的新框架: 对非惯常环境下消费者行为和现象的研究 [J]. 旅游学刊, 2008 (10): 12-16.
[6] 谢彦君. 基础旅游学 [M]. 2版. 北京: 中国旅游出版社, 2004.
[7] 卢瑾. 发达工业社会中人的异化——马尔库塞的单向度理论解读 [J]. 理论观察, 2008 (1): 53-54.
[8] 刘跃进. 文化就是社会化——广义"文化"概念的逻辑批判 [J]. 北方论丛, 1999 (3): 46-54.
[9] 张蕾, 赵中华, 贾志宏. 国外城市旅游研究进展 [J]. 旅游科学, 2005 (2): 17-23.

开展人力资源开发研究 促进中青年教师队伍建设

曲学利 孔 军 方祖成

在高等教育人才培养质量要求不断提高，应用型大学建设对教师队伍执教水平的要求不断提高的双重背景下，努力开展教师队伍建设，特别是中青年教师队伍建设的研究和服务工作，提高人事工作的科研和服务水平，不仅是当前加强人事工作的一项迫切任务，而且是人事工作向人力资源开发的研究和服务转变的必然要求。

1 人力资源开发的研究和服务是当前人事工作的迫切任务

随着这些年北京联合大学的建设和应用型人才培养工作的深入，应用型的教师队伍建设已成为学校工作的重中之重。如何提高教师，特别是中青年教师适应应用型教育的理论知识和技能，学校应采取什么政策和措施来加强中青年教师队伍建设，如何培养中青年教师队伍中的领军人物，如何引进带头人，如何从高等院校政策和制度的层面将中青年教师的职业生涯发展需要和学校事业的发展需要结合起来，是学校在新时期的建设和发展对人事工作提出的新任务和新要求，要适应和服务于这种要求，就需要从传统的对人和对事的管理向人力资源开发（研究）和服务转变；把这些新任务和新要求变成人事工作新的发展机遇，把大力开展人力资源开发的研究、服务作为一件重要工作。[1]

人事工作，是涉及"人"和"事"的管理工作，是与学校每个教职员工的成长、成才，工作、学习和生活息息相关的。传统的人事管理就是告诉人们"如何把事情做对"，"如何把一件事情做好"，对人的评价是诊断性评价，即"哪些做对了，哪些做错了"。而从现代人力资源开发的研究、服务的角度说，人事工作是应该研究如何制定有利于教职员工个人职业生涯发展需要和学校事业发展需要的政策和制度，让人们知道"如何做对的事"，"哪些事情该做，哪些事情不该做"，是以"人的发展为主，寻找新的方式或者改变方式去发现和寻找人才"，对人的评价也是发展性评价，即"找出个人的优缺点有哪些，且指明如何发展"，并能够根据政策和制度为教职员工职业生涯发展提供更好的服务，帮助教职员工更好地成长[2-3]。

在这种理念指导下，研究和做好应用型大学的人事工作，能为学校提高人才培养质量提供良好的师资队伍条件，为学校的可持续发展奠定坚实的基础。对于这样一门很有研究价值的学问，应该下力气去做，并做好。

2 中青年教师队伍建设是学校进一步发展的关键性工作

2.1 中青年教师是学校教育教学的中坚力量

以北京联合大学为例，目前学校45岁（含45岁，下同）以下的中青年教师是1133人，占教师总人数的70.8%，占比较高；2011年，学校新晋升副高级专业技术人员62名，硕士、博士（共57人）和40岁以下人员（平均年龄38.8岁）已成为主体；新晋升正高级专业技术人员32名，硕士、博士（27人）和50岁以下人员（平均年龄45.9岁）已成为主体。因此，中青年教师理应成为学校人才队伍建设的重中之重，把他们培育好、发展好已经是学校进一步发展的关键性工作。

2.2 中青年教师对自身成长和专业化发展要求十分迫切

通过近年来校人事处在研究项目中对中青年教师的调查发现，绝大部分中青年教师对职业生涯成长和专业化发展的要求十分迫切。

[作者简介] 曲学利（1955—），男，北京人，北京联合大学人事处处长，研究员，研究方向为人力资源与高等教育管理。

首先，在对自我的评价中，绝大部分中青年教师都对自己的精神状态和工作状况给予了积极的肯定，达到了88.7%；在教学中，绝大部分中青年教师都对自己的积极努力和做法给予了肯定，认可率也达到了88%。

其次，71%的中青年教师更希望在专业技能方面有所提高，加快学到专业技能，使自己的专业执教能力得到提升；77%的中青年教师希望参加在职进修的内容是：提高教学科研水平、更新知识；而参加进修的主要原因为：提高教学科研水平、更新知识。可以看出，绝大部分中青年教师对自身教学科研水平的提高以及专业技能的学习具有很强的迫切性。调查中还发现，近两年，中青年教师在职参加国内外访问学者和攻读博士学位的人数在增加，这说明中青年教师在职业生涯成长和专业化发展中十分注重提高自身的学历和开拓自己的视野。

2.3 中青年教师中的校级领军人物数量太少

还是以北京联合大学为例，学校45岁以下正高级专业技术职务的教师共32名，应用文理学院7名，师范学院6名，商务学院、生物化学工程学院、自动化学院和校级直属科研单位各3名，特殊教育学院、校直属教学单位各2名，旅游学院和信息学院各1名；其他4所学院目前还没有45岁以下正高级专业技术职务的教师。32名45岁以下正高级专业技术职务的教师占全校正高级专业技术职务教师的24.3%，不到1/4；40岁以下比例更少，只占6.7%。

2012年上半年，学校人事处对全校45岁以下1000多名中青年教师进行了情况分析，经过对比目前他们在教学、科研和社会服务等方面的综合情况并进行了甄选，最后只有7名中青年教师在正高级职称、科研项目、获奖情况、教学等方面的条件基本符合"北京市长城学者培养计划"的入选条件；校人事处将建议学校进一步下大力气在政策和措施方面对7名中青年教师进行培育，争取在这7人中培育出进入"北京市长城学者培养计划"的候选人选。

目前学校重点建设学科和专业带头人共计29位，45岁以下的只有6位；专业负责人共计78名，45岁以下的只有26位，只占1/3；学校7门基础课程（群）中，主持公共基础课程群建设的负责人中没有45岁以下的中青年教师。

另外，45岁以下教师中，博士比例为21.4%；40岁以下的教师中，博士比例为20.6%。

总之，45岁以下的教师中，拥有正高级专业技术职务的少，学科、专业负责人少，特别是40岁以下的更少，学校中青年教师中校级的领军人物亟须加大培养的力度。

3 努力开展中青年教师培育、扶持的研究和服务工作

在"从现代人力资源开发、研究和服务角度搞好应用型大学人事工作"理念的指导下，根据学校中青年教师队伍在专业化成长中存在的问题和职业生涯发展上的迫切需求，学校相继开展了如下工作。

3.1 助推学校制定中青年教师队伍建设目标和各项计划

在学校"十二五"规划目标中明确提出：要培养100名左右具有创新意识，素质精良，有发展潜力的中青年骨干教师，采取各种有效措施，提升中青年骨干教师队伍的整体素质，特别是要切实提高青年教师的教学和科研能力；成立教师教学发展中心，借助校内外教学专家的帮助对中青年教师进行深度指导，形成全方位的师资培训体系，加强对中青年教师职业生涯规划和专业化发展的指导和服务水平。

为落实学校"十二五"规划上述目标，校人事处又助推学校制订了"人才强校四项计划"，其中包括针对学科（专业）带头人后备人选及教学、科研骨干教师的"人才提升计划"及针对优秀青年博士教师的"人才培育计划"和"团队扶持计划"。计划中明确提出：对现有各学科、各专业中的优秀中青年教师进行培养提升，鼓励和支持其出国进修、申报各类教学科研奖项，对获得国家奖励的，视奖励等级给予配套奖励；加强对优秀青年人才的培养和培育，通过加大经费投入、专项经费资助、配备优秀导师等措施，实现培育突出人才项目等目标。这些措施将有效地满足中青年教师的职业生涯发展和专业化发展的需求。为进一步加强中青年教师培育工作，在学校2012年人才工作会上，又提出了《关于加强中青年教师培养和资助工作的意见（征求意见稿）》，依托学科建设平台，通过向重点学科倾斜、建设团队和协同创新平台等措施，重点加大对45岁以下、具有博士学位、副高以下专业技术职务教师的培养与资助的力度。

3.2 制定管理办法,做好资助培养工作

为确保"人才强校四项计划"保质保量地实施,校人事处在征求各教学单位和相关职能部门意见和建议的基础上,制订和实施了具体的"人才提升计划"、"人才培育计划"和"团队扶持计划"等项目的人员遴选方案,以及各资助项目的实施和经费管理办法;在组织各教学单位积极申报的基础上,经过组织校内专家的评比遴选,2011年和2012年通过的"人才提升计划"和"人才培育计划"共资助了全校50多名中青年优秀教师、57名优秀的青年博士教师。

3.3 组织开展校级、市级各种科研项目

为了能够达到既把以上各项计划的实施当作经常性的工作抓紧抓好,又能够作为科研的项目,以科研探索的精神创新出成果的目的,还需要申报相关的科研、教研项目,如学校已成功申报的以"北京联合大学中青年教师队伍专业化建设"为内容的4项科研和教研项目。

有了各级教研和科研项目作为推动,师资队伍建设工作就有了一个科学研究的平台,在日常工作中,不但要思考如何按照各项政策及规章制度把工作做好、做规范,更重要的是要思考如何以科学研究的精神和态度,改革创新出中青年教师人才培养的新思路和新办法来。把人事部门的日常管理工作和中青年教师人力资源开发的研究结合起来,既促进了人事工作在管理、服务等方面的拓展,提高了工作的效率和满意度,又提升了人事干部工作的科学化研究和服务水平,促进了人事干部自身的职业生涯发展,稳定了人事干部队伍。

今后,做好研究和服务型的人事工作,促进中青年教师专业化发展,需要人事干部进一步帮助和协调各个学院和教学单位,针对中青年教师中已经遴选出的领军人物、带头人后备人选、骨干教师、青年优秀博士教师等各个层次的人员,制订详细可实施的培育计划,努力、认真地抓几年,真正培养出一大批能够为北京联合大学应用型大学建设做出贡献的优秀中青年骨干教师。人事工作要按照学校在人才工作会上提出的要求:为中青年人才施展才华搭好舞台,提供道具,让他们成为这个舞台上的中坚力量。

参考文献

[1] 曲学利,闫宏,李娟娟. 关注职业化发展,促进专业化成长——高校中青年教师职业现状的分析与思考[J]. 北京联合大学学报:自然科学版,2011,25(4):79-82.
[2] 夏侃,周静珍. 高校教师的团队激励研究[J]. 经济师,2006(11):117-118.
[3] 李志明. 高等学校激励理论的应用与激励机制的构建[J]. 兰州交通大学学报,2008,27(5):146-149.

农村老年人休闲生活方式研究

——以北京郊区农村调查为例

李 享

新时期，我国提出中国梦的奋斗目标，这不只是一个富裕梦，还是对幸福和有尊严生活的期许[1]。这自然也是 1.94 亿中国老年人[2]的渴望。因此，重视老年人的休闲生活，是维护其有尊严晚年的重要内容。

一、研究背景

（一）我国老年人口数量及老龄化速度惊人

截至 2012 年年底，中国 60 岁及以上老年人口数量已达到 1.94 亿人，老龄化水平达到 14.3%；预计到 2015 年，老年人口数量将达到 2.16 亿人，约占总人口数的 16.7%；中国老年人口数量到 2053 年将达到峰值，即 4.87 亿人，比 2010 年增长 7 倍，占总人口的 34.8%；届时，每 3 个人当中就会有 1 个 60 岁以上的老年人[2]。

从一些大城市来看，上述指标更高，比如北京市，截至 2011 年年底，60 岁及以上的户籍老年人口已达 247.9 万人，占全市户籍人口的 19.4%[3]。

（二）农村人口老龄化现象严重并呈加速发展趋势

城乡二元老龄化空间结构中，农村老龄化率为 18.3%，（城市老龄化率为 8.0%），全国有 62.8% 的老年人居住在农村[4]，以目前全国 60 岁及以上老年人口基数推算，即超过 1.2 亿人。2010 年底北京市 60 岁及以上农村老年人就已经超过 100 万人。

（三）农村老年人闲暇时间充裕与精神慰藉问题凸显

当温饱问题基本解决，闲暇时间充裕后，多数老年人又处于多数子女外出务工，常年与其分离的生活状况下，农村老年人留守现象更加突出，2012 年全国约有 5000 万农村留守老年人[2]。再加之农村老年人文化程度相对较低，文化活动设施和活动场所匮乏，继而使农村老年人闲暇时间的合理利用与精神慰藉问题更加凸显，甚至会导致相关的精神或躯体疾患，严重影响老年人的生活质量。

二、研究现状

（一）国外相关文献研究综述

尽管老年人可参加的休闲活动依然很多，但他们参加的活动数量和活动强度都在逐渐下降。老年化过程伴随的是老年活动项目的不断变化，但有一个趋势非常明显，随着年龄的增长，老年人更喜欢选择容易完成的活动，放弃有些要求的活动。而且，老年休闲活动对老年人保持活跃、促进身体健康、拥有好的精神状态都是有积极的作用的[5]。

休闲项目代表着活动的数量和种类，是我们日常生活方式的一个常规部分，当人们扩大了休闲项目时，他们对于由年龄增长所带来的身体功能的变化会适应的更好。国外 Ragheb 和 Griffith 研究者研究发现，扩大休闲活动的广度，比单纯地局限于频繁地参与某些特定的活动，对于老年人休闲生活的最优化更为重要。Guinn 对老年人进行调查发现，休闲活动的广度和生活满意度存在着积极的关系。Bevil 和

[作者简介] 李享，北京联合大学旅游学院教授，实证研究室负责人、硕士生导师，主要从事休闲/旅游市场及行为等方面的实证研究，E-mail：lytlixiang@buu.edu.cn。

Mattoon 研究发现休闲活动越广泛,生活满意度越高。对于那些生活满意度高的老年人来说,他们有许多休闲活动并经常参与[6]。

大量研究表明拥有更多休闲活动的老年人,或者说是休闲项目越丰富,他们的生活满意度就越高。可见,休闲活动对老年人们的休闲生活起着不可忽视的作用。在老龄化的社会,老年人只有参与到多项休闲活动当中,才能在晚年生活享受幸福和快乐[7]。

Sasidharan Vinod *et al.* 学者通过对老年人休闲生活的研究认为,老年人的健康和快乐与社会对他们参与休闲活动的支持度有很大的关系,他强调了休闲的社会支持,并且调查了自身社会资源如家庭成员、朋友和周围人等他们的休闲生活和快乐程度的影响。可见,老年人的休闲活动影响着自身的健康与快乐,因为老年人们可以通过休闲活动来放松身心,尽情地享受生活带来的美好。而且,现今社会给予了老年人们一些优惠政策的支持,这就使得老年人们的休闲生活变得更为丰富多彩[8]。

(二) 国内老年休闲研究现状

中国老龄科学研究中心最近完成的一项调查表明,中国农村现有 35.1% 的老人经常感到孤独。在农村,目前靠子女赡养的老人占总数的 86.1%,老人们除已养成勤劳的习惯外,经济上的困难迫使相当多的老人在晚年仍不得不从事生产劳动,其中,在农村 60~64 岁的老人中仍在劳动的占 62.7%;而 65 岁以上的老年人中,农村有 35% 的参与劳动[9]。有子女赡养的老人,其生活水平也不高,在南方和北方的不少农村,老人们一般只停留在吃饱穿暖的水平,精神方面的需求几乎没有涉及。可见,农村老年人的休闲生活还是比较缺乏的[10]。

总体来讲,国内关于老年人的休闲研究,其对象以城市老年人为主,忽视农村老年人;研究内容以局部调查及休闲生活为主,忽视老年视角的主观休闲价值观研究;研究意义以经济价值分析为主,忽视人类发展视角的社会效益综合研究[11]。

三、研究方法

(一) 方法选择缘由

休闲是文化的一部分,但也受到区域资源的多寡影响。因而,可以预期到不同区域(社会、文化)的休闲参与,其活动种类、形态、资源与参与类型会有差异。以美国和加拿大为代表的休闲研究,在北美已经发展了半个世纪以上。但是,因为东西方文化的差异,现存文献中的休闲活动量表在亚洲使用的时候,难以把握其有效性。鉴于目前欠缺适合的休闲活动量表。本研究希望能通过运用文化人类学所常用的自由列举(Free Listing)法,对我国农村老年人休闲生活方式类型、主观休闲价值观进行研究,并为进一步发展相应的休闲活动量表提供研究基础。

(二) 自由列举法的含义

自由列举法,即若已知集合(或类)的每一个元素,而且元素个数"相当有限",我们可以通过"列举"其所有元素的方法来表示它;如果集合(或类)的元素有"很多",甚至"无限多"以至于很难或无法将其所有元素一一列出,但其元素又具有很明显的"规律",我们可以用"…"略过规律性比较明显的大量元素。列举法的实质是给出了集合(或类)的外延,因此又称为外延法。如果在列举法中列出了集合(或类)的所有元素,此时称为完全列举法,否则就称为部分列举法。

自由列举法的特点,即非引导性,适合于休闲研究对象对休闲感受的主观性研究;其探索性的特点适合于休闲研究的探索性阶段。

四、研究过程

(一) 调查概况

本调查于 2012 年 3 月调查了北京市所有 9 个远郊区县,针对 60 岁及以上农村老年人,共随机获得有效样本 482 个。调查内容包括休闲方式,即"日常主要休闲方式/或闲暇时都做些什么/做什么事情会使你快乐";另一方面还调查了农村老年人的闲暇时间分配,具体包括起居时间、工作时间及闲暇时间分配状况。

(二)北京市农村老年人的休闲方式

调查表明,北京市农村老年人的休闲方式共分为三大类、40小类和122项。

1. "劳作类"包括:干农活占11%、做家务占10%、做针线活占2%、照顾老人占1%。
2. "简单(非技能)休闲方式类"包括:看电视占37%、散步占30%、聊天占21%、打牌占14%、打麻将占9%、待着占9%、唱歌跳舞占4%、健身运动占4%、旅游占3%、看书报占2%、串门占2%、养宠物占2%、睡觉占1%、骑车占1%。
3. "技能类"包括:刺绣占1%、玩电脑占1%、老年大学(占比不到1%)、玩乐器(占比不到1%)。

上述归纳表明,劳作类休闲方式占比较大,一方面体现了农村老年人的休闲意识缺失;另一方面体现了农村老年人的劳作习惯。多数农村老年人采取简单(非技能)类休闲方式,体现出农村老年人休闲生活方式的单一。从人数的集中程度来说,农村老年人的休闲方式大致相同,无非是看电视,散步,聊天;休闲场所也无非是在家里,在村庄里很是局限;而农村老年人很少采取技能类的休闲方式,或许在此方面存在地域性差别,有待进一步的调查研究。

(三)北京市农村老年人的时间分配

北京市的农村老年人从起居时间来看,他们的起床时间大都集中在5点到6点(见图1),睡觉时间大都集中在21点到22点(见图2)。

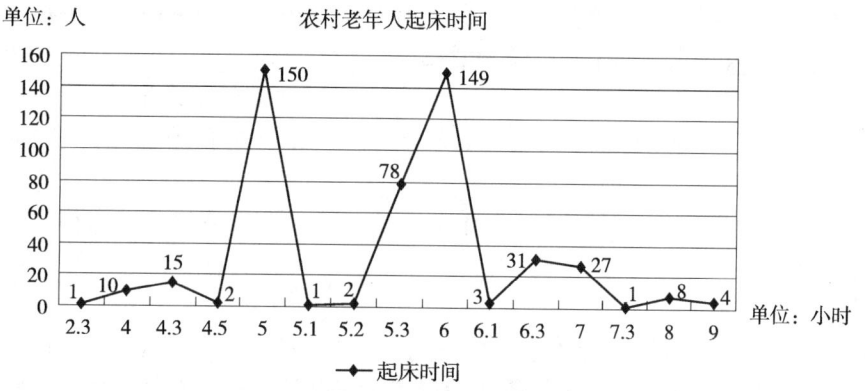

图1 北京市农村老年人样本群体的起床时间

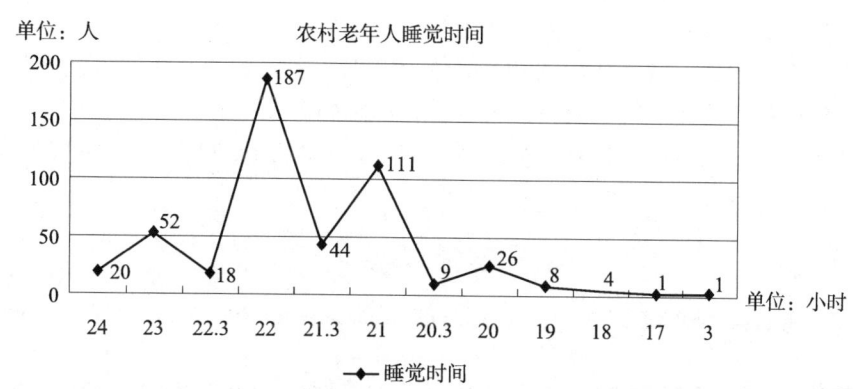

图2 北京市农村老年人样本群体的睡觉时间

北京市农村老年人样本群体的工作时间和闲暇时间如表1所示,从中可知农闲季节里,人均休闲时间为6.3小时/天,而在农忙季节里,这一指标则为3小时/天;农闲季节里,人均工作时间为2.5小时/天,而在农忙季节里,这一指标则为5.7小时/天;通常干家务活儿的时间人均为2.5小时/天,说明农闲季节里的工作时间基本为家务劳动时间。

表 1　北京市农村老年人样本群体的工作及闲暇时间

		农闲季节里通常的休闲时间（小时/天）	农忙季节里通常的休闲时间（小时/天）	农闲季节通常干农活儿或工作的时间/或不工作（小时/天）	农忙季节通常干农活儿或工作的时间/或不工作（小时/天）	通常干家务活儿时间（小时/天）
N	有效	662	662	662	662	662
	缺失	0	0	0	0	0
均值		6.299	3.076	2.542	5.668	2.549
中值		6.000	2.000	1.000	6.000	2.000
众数		4.0	0	0	0	2.0
标准差		4.5171	3.5263	3.3817	4.5966	2.5378
极小值		0	0	0	0	0
极大值		24.0	18.0	24.0	24.0	24.0

（四）北京市农村老年人的休闲满意度

针对休闲满意度问题，本研究还进行了部分非结构性访谈调查。调查表明农村老年人比较容易满足，调查的结果是多数老年人满意或比较满意现在的休闲生活方式，普遍感觉幸福。

这是一种简单、质朴、平实的幸福，正如林语堂所谓"幸福：一是睡在自家的床上。二是吃父母做的饭菜。三是听爱人给你说情话。四是跟孩子做游戏"。

这是一种充满人生及宗教哲理的真实的幸福，亦如那个诞生了（欲意取代 GDP 的）GNH（国民幸福指数）的伟大小国——不丹，他们认为"国民幸福大约是：顺利地出生、幸福地生活、安详地死去"。[12]

这亦充分体现了休闲满意度、满足感的主观特性，即"子非鱼，安知鱼之乐？"

五、研究结论

本研究表明性别和年龄都不是影响农村老年人选择不同休闲方式的因素，不同区域对休闲活动存在着相关性，不同区县的农村老年人选择的休闲活动有较小幅度的变化。农村老年人农忙季节的休闲时间少于农闲季节的休闲时间，因此，在农忙季节的休闲活动减少，农闲季节的休闲活动增加。不仅如此，干家务活的时间长短也影响着农村老年人参与休闲活动的多少。

总体来讲，农村老年人普遍缺乏现代意义上的休闲意识，多以各种劳作的方式来打发闲暇时间，休闲活动半径较小，休闲方式简单、传统，休闲要求低，休闲满意度高。

本研究存在调查的持续性、区域性差异与经济关联等方面的局限性问题，有待今后的进一步研究。

参考文献

[1] 吴忠民. 中国梦的新起点 [EB/OL]. http：//news. xinhuanet. com/2013lh/2013 - 03/17/c_ 115055390. htm，2013 - 03 - 17/2013 - 03 - 31.
[2] 中国老龄科学研究中心. 中国老龄事业发展报告（2013）[M]. 北京：社会科学文献出版社，2013.
[3] 北京市老龄工作委员会. 北京市 2011 年老年人口信息和老龄事业发展状况报告 [R]. 2011.
[4] 人民日报海外版. 中国老年人口过亿农村社会保障制度严重滞后 [EB/OL]. http：//bbs. xs163. net/read - htm - tid - 1908847 - page - 1. html，2011 - 05 - 19/2012 - 10 - 08.
[5] Sasidharan Vinod et al. Older adults'physical activity participation and perceptions of wellbeing：examining the role of social support for leisure [J]. Managing Leisure，2006（3）：164 - 185.
[6] 朱群英. 老年休闲行为研究及对休闲供给的启示——以杭州市为例 [J]. 浙江工商大学，2008，12.
[7] 丁志宏. 我国老年人休闲活动的特点分析及思考——以北京市为例 [J]. 兰州学刊，2010（9）.
[8] Gerard T. Kyle，Andrew J. Momen，et al. Commitment to public leisure service providers：a conceptual and psychometric analysis [J]. Journal of Leisure Research，2006（1）：78 - 103.

［9］彭世明. 中国人口老龄化发展趋势预测研究报告［R］. 2007.

［10］郝洪儒. 关注农村老人的精神生活［N］. 中国老年报, 2004（2）.

［11］黄璜."积极老龄化"理论视角下的老龄旅游产业发展战略［R］. 中国旅游学术年会2012.

［12］沈颢,（不丹）卡玛·尤拉. 国民幸福［M］. 北京：北京大学出版社, 2011.

刍议我国中小企业发展面临的困境与突破

张永敬

中小企业作为我国国民经济的重要组成部分，在扩大就业、推动经济增长等方面具有不可替代的作用。据统计，我国工商注册登记的中小企业占全部注册企业总数的99%；中小企业工业总产值、销售收入、实现利税分别占总量的60%、57%和40%；流通领域中小企业占全国零售网点的90%以上；中小企业大约提供了75%的城镇就业机会。因而，促进中小企业发展，意义重大，任务艰巨。❶

一、我国中小企业发展面临的挑战

当前，中小企业的生存困境时下又成为我国实业界和政府忧虑的一大问题，其主要体现在：

1. 创新能力不足

我国中小企业主要集中在传统产业，创新能力不强，部分行业产能过剩、布局雷同现象突出；服务业中小企业发展滞后，产业结构不合理；高耗能行业总产值占工业比重高。区域发展不均衡，中西部地区中小企业发展不足。由于中小企业普遍缺乏资金、技术、人才、信息，要实现产业结构优化，任务重，压力大。

2. 资源环境约束压力加大

我国中小企业多处于产业链底端，产品附加值低，消化成本能力弱。一些中小企业资源利用率低，环境污染重，安全隐患多。在当前国内土地、能源、环境等制约因素影响下，初级产品和大宗商品等原材料价格和劳动力成本面临上升压力，中小企业走"拼资源、拼价格、拼环境"的老路已难以为继。

3. 市场环境不容乐观

在国际贸易领域，针对外来产品的保护主义日益抬头，技术性贸易壁垒等贸易保护手段不断翻新、更趋隐蔽，贸易摩擦范围逐步从传统产业向高新技术产业蔓延，人民币升值压力加大，中小企业进入国际市场面临更大困难。可以预料的是今后围绕市场、资源、人才、技术、标准等的国际竞争将更加激烈。

4. 制约中小企业成长的体制机制因素依然存在

中小型金融机构发育不足，中小企业融资难问题依然突出；涉企收费偏多偏高，违规收费屡禁不止，中小企业负担依然较重；公共服务基础设施薄弱，服务质量有待提高；行业性垄断依然存在，部分行业准入条件偏高；创业门槛较高，企业设立前置审批复杂。不少中小企业技术和管理落后，产品趋同，国内市场同质化竞争和不公平竞争现象没有根本改变。

二、引导我国中小企业走出困境的对策建议

目前，解决中小企业所面临的困境问题，应对症下药，从以下几个方面入手予以支持与引导。

1. 实施相对稳健的货币政策和差别化的信贷扶持

高通货膨胀环境本身对于中小企业而言非常不利，从中长期看，中小企业发展需要一个平稳的物价环境。这主要是由于中小企业往往处于中下游产业，国有大型企业往往处于上游产业，上游产品价格上涨就会转嫁到下游产业，也就是说，在高通胀条件下中小企业与国有大型企业利润分配上的再调整，对于中小企业不利。在这方面，应在制定宏观政策时更多地考虑多种政策造成的叠加效应和中小企业的承受力。由于货币政策与物价指标存在一定的时滞性，考虑到经济增长、工业增速、企业效益等指标出现

[作者简介] 张永敬，北京联合大学。

❶ 苗圩. 加大工作力度 狠抓政策落实 促进中小企业发展取得新成效 [J]. 中国中小企业，2012（1）。

放缓迹象,未来货币政策可本着相机抉择的原则适当微调调控的力度和方式,在整体维持物价相对稳定的前提下,保证中小企业发展的合理经营规划和市场预期,切实引导实业走向繁荣。

同时,对于中小企业融资成本高、融资难等问题,应全面落实支持中小企业发展的金融政策,建立健全应急状态下的金融保障,完善中小企业金融服务差异化监管政策,重点加强和改善中小企业金融服务。积极引导银行业金融机构创新体制机制,创新金融产品、服务和贷款抵质押方式,积极发展中小金融机构,扩大对中小企业的贷款规模和比重。应当建立更多的国有或民营的中小银行,特别是专门为中小企业提供信贷服务的金融机构。这样能够促进金融领域的良性竞争,降低企业融资借贷的难度,中小银行与中小企业的合作更加相匹配,因为其与国有大银行相比具有低成本、高效率、专业性强的服务等优势。中小银行由于规模的原因导致其必然以为中小企业提供贷款为主要盈利模式,数量众多,广泛分布的中小银行十分适合后危机时代我国中小企业发展的需要。同时我国的银行业应当降低中小企业申请信用贷款的门槛,适当修改对其信用评定的标准,为中小企业融资设立专门的服务部门,增加效率、简化程序,使金融机构的信用管理机制更加完善和合理,让中小企业能够拥有一个良好的融资环境。金融部门应结合实际不断创新,以满足中小企业融资的需要,积极开展中小企业互助性信用担保和供应链融资,为其提供更加优质同时也能降低自身风险的全新的金融服务产品,消除银行和企业之间的信息不对称问题,从而拓宽融资渠道,实现银行与企业的双赢。

2. 加大财政扶持力度,扩大中小企业市场发展空间

2011年修订后出台的《中小企业划型标准》中首次提出了微型企业的类型,较为真实地反映出我国当前中小企业经济运行状况,特别是小型和微型企业经济基础相对薄弱、科研能力总体偏低,是财政政策的扶植重点,有利于实施更有针对性的优惠政策。在当前我国年财政收入增至10万亿元以上的背景下,财税部门应积极研究结构性减税政策,进一步减轻中小企业负担。可以说,2009年开始的由生产型增值税转为消费型增值税改革,起到了促进企业固定资产更新换代的作用,也显示了政府扶助企业的用心良苦。然而目前我国生产型中小企业中比重最大的是以加工、制造为主的劳动密集型产业,固定资产在资本中的比例并不高,因此消费型增值税对长三角、珠三角大量的纺织、服装制造等中小企业的惠及程度还有待提升。在针对中小企业的结构性减税方面,建议对劳动密集型的制造业和服务业中小企业降低税率或采用13%的低税率进行优惠;适当提高对中小企业职工福利费支出准予扣除的比例,以帮助中小企业有更大的空间改善员工福利,缓解用工难的现状;将我国年出口量大且劳动密集型的出口企业,如服装、玩具、鞋帽制造等中小企业等退税率提高到最大值17%,以降低其产品成本,缓解其因国际市场排斥和员工工资上涨导致的利润缩水。

国际金融危机条件下暴露出中小企业发展存在的深层次问题是长期国内需求不足的条件下,过度依靠外需和出口,且外部市场发生变化对于中小企业而言具有高度的风险。因此,扩大内需将是今后我国财税部门长期坚持的一项战略任务,也是中小企业扩大市场发展空间的必要条件。在当前实施的稳中求进的财政政策中,还应从单纯地鼓励人们增加开支与促进收入增长,转向调整居民收入结构,降低基尼指数,以利于真正拉动广大群众的一般消费需求,为中小企业发展提供更为广阔的市场空间。同时,要切实放宽市场准入,破除各种有形和无形的障碍,积极鼓励和引导中小企业以多种形式进入基础产业和基础设施、市政公用事业、社会服务等领域,拓展业务发展空间,促进社会就业。例如,为加大对中小企业参与政府采购的政策扶持力度,财政部、工业和信息化部出台了《政府采购促进中小企业发展暂行办法》,在综合考虑国际上对中小企业政策的接受程度和中国中小企业较多等因素的基础上,规定2012年起中小企业获得政府采购额的比例为30%,并把中小企业所获份额的60%预留给了小型和微型企业。对于类似的各项财税优惠政策,应充分发掘政策潜力确保执行到位。

3. 因地制宜,促进中小企业转型升级

我国的中小企业大多是劳动密集型企业,成本低是其最大的优势,然而近年来生产成本的上升,使得我国中小企业价格优势不再,最直接的表现在制造加工业开始大量向印度、越南、马来西亚等地转移。从表面上看,我国中小企业陷入困境是国内紧缩的信贷政策、生产成本上涨、用工荒、订单锐减等因素的集中爆发,但在实质上,更多的是经济体自身内在的原因,是经济运行过程中战略性结构性矛盾积累到一定程度的集中爆发,是多年来所累积的制度和政策的综合产物。将中小企业发展存在的问题放

大到整个经济发展中来看，实际上这正是一个经济体向中等收入阶段迈进时必然面临的问题。世界银行的研究报告指出，一个国家在从低收入阶段向中等收入阶段过渡时所采取的发展方式、战略以及政策措施，在进入中等收入阶段之后将不起作用。这就意味着必须要实现转型，即中央提出来的加快发展方式转变和经济结构战略性调整。因此，目前我国中小企业发展到了一个亟待转型的阶段。按照新近出台的《"十二五"中小企业成长规划》精神，我国中小企业转型措施应主要包括三大方面：一是引导中小企业进入现代农业、现代服务业、战略性新兴产业，支持中小企业在科技研发、工业设计、技术咨询、软件和信息服务、现代物流等生产性服务业领域以及家政、养老等生活性服务业领域的发展；鼓励中小企业进入服务外包、游戏动漫、文化创意、电子商务、总部经济等新兴领域，拓展发展空间。二是加强区域合作与交流，引导东部中小企业向中西部有序转移，加快中西部中小企业发展，促进区域协调发展。按照"布局合理、特色鲜明、用地集约、生态环保"的原则，积极推动以上下游企业分工协作、品牌企业为主导、专业市场为导向的产业集群建设。加强统筹规划，坚持市场导向，突出地区优势和特色，发展专业化产业集群。适应不同地区、不同行业的特点，探索多种类型的产业集群发展模式。加强产业集群环境建设，改善产业集聚条件。三是支持中小企业专业化发展，提高生产工艺、产品质量、服务水平、市场专业化水平，鼓励中小企业走差异化成长道路，赢得市场竞争优势。

4. 构建中小企业发展支撑服务平台

为了提高中小企业转型效率和市场竞争力，有必要进一步加快中小企业信息化服务体系建设，各级政府要积极组织实施中小企业信息化建设社会化服务体系。一是要推进网络基础设施的建设。要加快对现有信息网络的升级改造，加快信息传输平台、多媒体宽带网建设和完善。政府要加大资金投入，建设一个"宽带、高速、大容量、高水平"的信息主干网，逐步清除部门间、地区间的网络分割壁垒、资源垄断和体制性障碍。二是要注重中小企业数据库建设。建设一个面向中小企业技术创新、非营利性的数据资料库，专门向中小企业传播技术信息和技术知识，促进中小企业间的技术合作和企业网络的发展。要积极引进国内外有关的企业新产品数据库、新技术数据库等，为中小企业提供决策依据。三是要完善现有的中小企业信息网、技术创新信息网等网站的功能，为中小企业更好地提供信息采编、信息检索、信息咨询等网络服务。中小企业必须要以不断提高自身的创新能力、加强人力资本积累等为核心，积极推动自身实现转型。中小企业信息化服务体系的建设，有利于中小企业在转型过程中更有效地获取经济、技术、市场、人才等方面的信息，有利于中小企业以更少的成本、更方便的途径利用各种社会资源，加快转型步伐。

总之，帮助、引导中小企业走出困境，一方面固然要在尊重市场经济规律的同时，积极实施相应的金融和财税等扶持政策，另一方面也要认清中小企业困境成因的长期性和复杂性，这其中不仅涉及资金缺乏和市场萎缩问题，更涉及中小企业技术发展瓶颈和产业结构升级问题。对此，我们除了采取必要的调控政策和保障手段外，更应着眼于长远和大局，加强自主创新，积极推动中小企业转型升级和构建发展支撑服务平台，力争相关扶持政策的精、细、准，以求实效。

网络时代听力有障碍年轻群体娱乐休闲研究

陈文力

1 引　言

随着我国休闲产业的蓬勃发展，人们的娱乐休闲活动越来越丰富多彩[1]，但是听力有障碍的残疾人的娱乐休闲活动就逊色了许多。中华人民共和国国家统计局公布的《第二次全国残疾人抽样调查报告》显示，全国大约有2075万听力有障碍的残疾人，其中6~14岁儿童中，就有11万人。这样一个庞大的弱势群体的娱乐休闲需求长期得不到满足会直接影响他们的身心健康[2]。

本文所研究的听力有障碍的残疾人是指包括聋哑人在内的所有听力存在缺陷的弱势群体。听力有障碍的残疾人分为轻度、中度和重度听力障碍。轻度听力有障碍的人是指当有背景噪声时不能像正常人一样听清对方所说的话，这部分人群特征就是人们常说的"耳背"。他们一般不承认由于听力原因而引起相互交流所产生的困难，这个群体目前人数比较多。中度听力有障碍的人是指那些明显感到听力上有困难的群体，当对方说话比较慢时，他们一般也能够听懂对方所说的话。重度听力有障碍的人主要是指听力严重受损甚至一点都听不见的聋哑人，与这部分人群的交流主要是通过两个渠道：一是通过唇语进行交流，但要求聋人从小受过唇语训练；二是双方利用手语进行交流。听力有障碍的人由于交流和语言上的困难，他们缺乏做出回应的信心，在对问题的理解上与健全人也有很大的差异[3]。但这个弱势群体与健全人一样有娱乐休闲的需求，开展这方面的研究对这个弱势群体来说具有重要意义。

2　文献回顾

近年来，欧美等发达国家的专家学者开始关注残疾人的基本生活条件和娱乐休闲需求。对于残疾人的分类，国外专家倾向于分成两大类：一类是精神方面的残疾，另一类是身体方面的残疾。听力有障碍的残疾人属于身体方面的残疾人。瑞格利（Wrigley）对听力有障碍群体的定义是"听力有障碍的人是指那些在正常情况下，由于各种因素影响接收声音而听不到或很难听懂别人所说的话的人群"[4]。国外专家经过大量研究，发现了能够帮助这个弱势群体娱乐休闲的一些方法。其中，深度休闲理论[5]是富有成效的研究成果之一。斯特宾斯（Stebbins）对深度休闲的定义是"业余爱好者的一系列追求、沉溺于某种癖好者或自愿参与追寻有趣的活动者。例如，他们围绕着这个事业自己着手开始学习所需的特殊技能、知识和经验"[6]。斯特宾斯指出深度休闲与随意休闲的区别，随意休闲是指那些直接的、本质的休闲，一般与短期的娱乐活动有关，不需要或很少需要特殊训练就能进行的娱乐活动[7]。随意休闲包括几种类型，如玩耍、休闲、被动娱乐（如看电视）、主动娱乐（如玩游戏）、友好的会谈和感官刺激（如同学聚会）。而深度休闲包括三种类型：一是在艺术、科技、运动和娱乐表演等方面的业余爱好者[8]；二是沉溺于某种癖好者[9]；三是从事自愿和非营利活动的志愿者[10]。第一种类型需要艺术、科技、运动和娱乐表演的专家给予指导才能完成相应的娱乐休闲活动。第二种类型是指收藏家、手工艺者、游戏玩家、文人墨客等，他们同样也需要掌握专业知识和受过专门的训练。第三种类型是从事自愿和非营利活动的志愿者，例如组织免费健康咨询等活动，而提供咨询的志愿者是要具备一定专业知识的人才。因此，国外所指的深度休闲活动一般是需要专门的知识和技能，需要经过专门的训练才能完成。国外专家认为对残疾人提供深度休闲教育，使他们获得休闲技能后，再通过参加深度休闲活动来满足他们的娱乐休闲需求。目前，国内对这个弱势群体的研究主要集中在医学治疗和如何开展特殊教育方面，而对他们的娱乐休闲需求研究与国外相比差距较大。

［作者简介］陈文力（1954—），男，北京人，北京联合大学旅游学院副教授，研究方向为残疾人娱乐休闲研究、旅游信息化研究，E-mail: chen2007w@126.com。

3　研究内容与方法

为保证研究的可靠性，笔者选择中度和重度听力有障碍的年轻群体作为研究对象。一方面，这个群体在听力上有明显的障碍，不会不承认自己在这方面的缺陷；另一方面，他们是年轻的一代，受过特殊教育，容易理解要调查的内容。另外，鉴于聋哑人与健全人在思维方式上存在差异，笔者在与中学和大学在读的聋哑人通过QQ和举行座谈会等方式进行多次交流的基础上设计了调查问卷，然后使用德尔菲法请了8名在北京第四聋哑学校和北京联合大学特殊教育学院从事特殊教育工作的老师对调查问卷进行评价，根据老师们的意见修改了调查问卷。调查问卷内容包括受访者的基本情况、与外界沟通的方式、沟通障碍以及这种障碍影响心情的程度、所喜欢的娱乐活动、心情郁闷时排解的方式、喜欢上网的程度和每天上网所花费的时间以及上网的目的和上网聊天的对象等。

调查过程中，对北京第四聋哑学校的60名高二学生发放调查问卷，回收有效问卷59份。对北京联合大学特殊教育学院的40名大二学生发放调查问卷，回收有效问卷34份。北京第四聋哑学校的受访者中女性33人，占56%，男性26人，占44%；完全听不到声音的占56.7%，完全不能说话的占53.3%，不会唇语的占59.3%。北京联合大学特殊教育学院的受访者中女性17人，占50%，男性17人，占50%；完全听不到声音的占32.3%，完全不能说话的占12.9%，不会唇语的占21.9%。

被调查的高中生主要由重度听力有障碍的人组成，女性偏多。而被调查的大学生则由中度和重度听力有障碍的人组成，男女比例相同。本次调查样本的大部分人都与健全人交流有困难，具有明显的听力有障碍年轻群体的特征，符合本次调查样本的要求。

4　调研结果与分析

利用SPSS16.0统计分析软件对回收的93份有效问卷进行了统计分析，其结果分为以下三部分加以说明。

4.1　听力有障碍年轻群体的沟通障碍与沟通方式

在访谈中，笔者了解到聋哑人称健全人为听人，称自己为聋人。大多数聋人都非常愿意与听人进行交流，且在性别上无明显差异。但聋人在思考问题和表述问题上与听人之间存在较大的差异，究其原因是他们长期生活在无声的世界里，与听人的交流机会比较少，因此双方很容易产生交流上的障碍。通过调查得知，聋人不愿意与听人交流的只占5%，聋人与听人交流的主要障碍是听力障碍和语言理解或意思表达困难所带来的障碍，其次是聋人存在自卑感，没有勇气与听人交流。

听力有障碍的年轻群体在与同学和与父母交流时多采用面对面的交流，交流方式主要是通过唇语和手语。而他们与其他听人的交流多采用QQ和短信，这两种交流方式由于不需要声音的传递，对他们来说减少了交流上的障碍，而且简单易学。本次调查结果显示，通过网络手段进行交流的百分比很高，而且这种交流方式可以有效的避免听力障碍和自卑情绪。因此，笔者认为网络对听力有障碍的年轻群体与外界沟通具有较大的影响。

4.2　娱乐活动对听力有障碍的年轻群体的影响

娱乐休闲活动可以扩大听力有障碍年轻群体的交友范围，培养他们更多的情趣爱好，进而改变他们的生活态度和性格，使他们能够健康快乐地成长。娱乐活动对听力有障碍年轻群体影响的统计结果如表1所示。其中影响最大的是培养了多个兴趣，其次是改变了生活态度，而影响最小的是改变了职业意向。但是利用网络进行背对背的工作比起面对面的工作更适合这个弱势群体，笔者认为，应深入挖掘通过网络娱乐休闲方式来激发听力有障碍年轻群体对在网络上开展工作的兴趣，进而改变他们的职业意向，引导他们掌握从事网络工作所需的技能，为听力有障碍的年轻群体的就业探索一条新路。

表1 娱乐活动对听力有障碍的年轻群体的影响

娱乐活动对听力有障碍的年轻群体的影响 Recreational activities on the hearing handicapped young group	高中生 Senior high school students				大学生 College students			
	男 Male		女 Female		男 Male		女 Female	
	频数 Frequency	百分比(%)	频数 Frequency	百分比(%)	频数 Frequency	百分比(%)	频数 Frequency	百分比(%)
培养了多个兴趣 Cultivate a number of interest	15	57.7	22	64.7	7	41.2	10	58.8
改变了生活态度 Changed their attitude towards life	12	46.2	13	38.2	9	52.9	9	60.0
扩大了朋友圈 Expand the circle of friends	9	34.6	15	44.1	3	17.6	7	41.2
改变了性格 Changed personality	12	46.2	9	26.5	2	11.8	6	35.3
改变了职业意向 Changing the occupation intentions	6	23.1	8	23.5	2	11.8	4	23.5

听力有障碍的年轻群体在排解心情郁闷时，高中生首先选择的方式是上网，其次才选择散步和睡觉；而大学生首先选择的是睡觉，其次才是选择散步和上网。高中生用上网来排解心情郁闷的方式，表现出他们渴望与外界交流的愿望，希望能够通过外界的帮助来解除烦恼。而大学生更多地选择睡觉，反映了他们自我解脱的倾向，这也是大学生更加成熟的表现，但若不能自我排解的话，就会产生精神抑郁，进而造成严重的后果。这个群体在不开心时排解郁闷方式的统计结果如表2所示。其中，吃东西和购物经过卡方检验，高中学生男女之间和大学生男女之间均有显著差异，男生很少通过吃东西或购物来排解心情郁闷。排解郁闷方式中的聊天经过卡方检验，大学生男女之间有显著差异，男生很少通过聊天来排解心情郁闷。这些特征与听人的特征是相吻合的。

表2 听力有障碍的年轻群体在不开心时排解郁闷的方式

排解郁闷的方式 Depressed untangle way	高中生 Senior high school students				大学生 College students			
	男 Male		女 Female		男 Male		女 Female	
	频数 Frequency	百分比(%)	频数 Frequency	百分比(%)	频数 Frequency	百分比(%)	频数 Frequency	百分比(%)
上网 Surf the internet	11	42.3	14	41.2	4	23.5	6	37.5
睡觉 Sleep	10	38.5	13	38.2	9	52.9	9	52.9
散步 Take a walk	10	38.5	15	44.1	7	41.2	8	47.1
聊天 Chat	9	34.6	11	32.4	1	5.9	6	35.3
旅游 Tourism	4	15.4	4	11.8	3	17.6	4	23.5
乱扔东西 Throw things	5	19.2	4	11.8	3	17.6	1	5.9

续表

排解郁闷的方式 Depressed untangle way	高中生 Senior high school students				大学生 College students			
	男 Male		女 Female		男 Male		女 Female	
	频数 Frequency	百分比 （％）	频数 Frequency	百分比 （％）	频数 Frequency	百分比 （％）	频数 Frequency	百分比（％）
吃东西 Eat something	1	3.8	10	29.4	0	0	7	41.2
购物 Shopping	0	0	7	20.6	0	0	6	35.3

听力有障碍的年轻群体最喜欢的娱乐休闲活动是上网，所占比例高达70％以上，其中，大学的男生最高，百分比达到94.1％，无论高中生还是大学生，男生的上网兴趣都比女生高。除了上网，体育活动、看书、看电影、逛公园等也是高中受访者比较喜欢的娱乐休闲活动，他们与大学生的娱乐休闲需求的差异主要体现在大学生比高中生更加对旅游和逛街感兴趣，而不论大学生还是高中生都很少去泡吧，显然泡吧这种面对面交流的方式并不适合他们。从统计结果明显看出，这个群体的兴趣爱好是比较广泛的，但与听人的娱乐休闲需求还是有一定的差别，他们更喜欢那些不需要直接用语言交流的娱乐活动。听力有障碍的年轻群体平时最喜欢的娱乐活动的统计结果如表3所示。其中，打球、游泳、滑冰等体育活动经过卡方检验，大学生男女之间有显著差异，男生更喜欢体育活动。而逛街经过卡方检验，高中学生男女之间也有显著差异，女生更喜爱逛街。因此，从性别的差异上来看，男生偏爱体育活动、上网，而女生则更喜欢逛街和上网，这个结果与听人的性别差异基本一致。

表3 听力有障碍的年轻群体平时最喜欢的娱乐活动

娱乐活动 Recreational activities	高中生 Senior high school students				大学生 College students			
	男 Male		女 Female		男 Male		女 Female	
	频数 Frequency	百分比 （％）	频数 Frequency	百分比 （％）	频数 Frequency	百分比 （％）	频数 Frequency	百分比（％）
上网 Surf the internet	22	84.6	27	79.4	16	94.1	12	70.6
打球、游泳、滑冰等体育活动 Basketball, swimming, skating and other sports activities	21	80.8	21	61.8	14	82.4	8	47.1
看书 Read books	14	53.8	25	73.5	11	64.7	11	64.7
看电影 Watch movies	13	50.0	21	61.8	10	58.8	8	47.1
逛公园 The park	13	50.0	19	55.9	11	64.7	7	41.2
旅游 Tourism	11	42.3	15	44.1	11	64.7	9	52.9
购物 Shopping	7	26.9	20	58.8	9	52.9	9	52.9
书法 Calligraphy	3	11.5	3	8.8	2	11.8	4	23.5
泡吧 Go to the bar	2	7.7	2	5.9	3	17.6	2	11.8

根据以上统计分析，可以得出结论，通过网络方式的娱乐休闲活动对听力有障碍的年轻群体的影响是显著的。

4.3 网络对听力有障碍的年轻群体娱乐休闲的影响

根据本次统计结果，高中生拥有电脑的比例达85%，大学生拥有电脑的比例达73.5%；喜欢经常上网的高中学生比例达75%，大学生比例达73.5%，高中生与大学生没有明显差异。高中生和大学生的上网时间主要集中在每天2~4小时，高中生在家里和学校每天花费2~4小时上网的比例分别为38.3%和58.3%。大学生在家里和学校花费2~4小时上网的比例分别为29.5%和58.8%。而花费10小时以上的高中生和大学生在校期间都为0，在家期间也只占6.8%，沉溺于网络的学生基本没有。

高中生和大学生上网目的统计结果如表4所示，他们上网都偏重于QQ聊天、看电影和新闻、下载资料和看在线小说、打游戏。其中，打游戏经过卡方检验大学生和高中生男女之间均有显著差异，高中男生比女生高出31%，大学男生比女生高出53%，明显看出男生比女生更加迷恋网络游戏。从统计结果看，网上购物的比例无论是高中生还是大学生都比较低，而这种购物方式由于避开了面对面的交流，对聋哑人购物应该更加有利，因此从事特殊教育的学校应该开设网络购物方面的课程，引导他们改变传统的购物方式。另外，利用网络开展工作的学生较少，其中大学男生百分比最高，而调查样本中的高中女生没有在网上开展工作的经历。通过座谈了解到，大学生利用网络开展工作主要是网络广告设计，而高中生则是开网店卖商品。有过网络工作经历的学生都感到在网络上开展工作不仅能带来收入，而且也能带来满足感，使他们感到与听人的差距在缩小。

表4 听力有障碍年轻群体的上网目的

上网的目的 The purpose of Enternet	高中生 Senior high school students				大学生 College students			
	男 Male		女 Female		男 Male		女 Female	
	频数 Frequency	百分比 （%）	频数 Frequency	百分比 （%）	频数 Frequency	百分比 （%）	频数 Frequency	百分比（%）
QQ聊天 QQ chat	22	84.6	27	79.4	16	94.1	15	88.2
看电影 Watch movies	24	92.3	26	76.5	15	88.2	10	58.8
看新闻 Watch the news	16	61.5	20	58.8	14	82.4	11	64.7
下载资料 Download data	13	50.0	18	52.9	8	47.1	10	58.8
看在线小说 Read the online novel	8	30.8	19	55.9	7	41.2	7	41.2
打游戏 Play game	18	69.2	13	38.2	13	76.5	4	23.5
听音乐 Listen to the music	8	32.0	12	35.3	5	29.4	4	23.5
去开心网等社区网站 To happy net community website	2	7.7	14	41.2	11	64.7	4	23.5
网上购物 Online shopping	5	20.0	5	14.7	5	29.4	2	12.5

续表

上网的目的 The purpose of Enternet	高中生 Senior high school students				大学生 College students			
	男 Male		女 Female		男 Male		女 Female	
	频数 Frequency	百分比 (%)	频数 Frequency	百分比 (%)	频数 Frequency	百分比 (%)	频数 Frequency	百分比(%)
写博客 Blog	5	19.2	16	47.1	4	23.5	3	18.8
发表文章 Published articles	3	11.5	10	29.4	2	11.8	4	23.5
结交新朋友 Make new friends	2	7.7	8	23.5	4	23.5	3	17.6
工作 Work	2	7.7	0	0	5	29.4	4	23.5

上网聊天的对象，不论是高中生还是大学生，都是与同学、朋友上网聊天的比例最大，其次是与亲人。而与老师通过网络交流的比例并不高，其中女生与老师交流的百分比大于男生，经卡方检验与老师聊天的大学男女生之间具有显著差异，女生比男生高出41%，显示出女生与老师的沟通热情远高于男生。另外，与陌生人（听人）的网聊比例较少，而且大学生低于高中生，这表明听力有障碍的学生随着年龄的增长与听人的交流呈下降趋势，究其原因是由于他们与听人之间的交流障碍所造成的挫折感促使他们与听人进行交流的热情越来越低。

5 利用网络开展听力有障碍的年轻群体学习和娱乐活动的研究

随着互联网的普及，听力有障碍年轻群体的触网人数与年轻的健全人一样呈逐年增长的趋势。研究如何通过网络来满足这个群体的娱乐休闲需求和提供培训来掌握网络工作的技能，既可以提高他们的就业能力，又可以改善这个弱势群体的生活质量。

5.1 网络时代满足听力有障碍年轻群体的网络学习和网络娱乐需求的解决方案

互联网的普及为满足听力有障碍年轻群体的娱乐休闲需求提供了一条新的途径，这条途径不仅可以有效地避开聋人与听人的交流障碍，降低他们的自卑感，还可以培养他们在网上开展工作的兴趣，扩大他们的就业机会。除此之外，作为听人除了学校的学习外，还有许多社会上的各种学习班，为他们提供了更多的充电机会，而聋人继续学习的机会就非常少。探讨通过网络来解决这个问题是一个大胆的创新，但是到目前为止，网络上还没有专门为这个弱势群体开发的学习和娱乐软件。

依据深度休闲理论，对这个弱势群体培训网络技能，使他们能够利用网络来满足娱乐休闲需求。要想实现这个设想，关键在于开发出适合他们的网络软件（网络娱乐软件和网络学习软件）。开发软件的步骤是在网络娱乐和学习专家以及特教老师的配合下，指导学生提出网络娱乐和学习的需求。根据这些需求，由软件开发公司与网络娱乐和学习专家合作进行需求分析，并由软件开发公司进行软件开发。经系统测试合格后，由软件开发公司的培训师对特教老师进行培训，使他们掌握软件的操作技能，然后为学生讲授和组织学生在网上试用该软件，并征求学生的意见，根据学生的意见配合网络娱乐和学习专家向软件开发公司提出改进意见。软件开发公司修改软件后，再由学生试用，直到学生满意为止，最终作为这个弱势群体在网络上开展娱乐和学习的平台。在开发网络学习软件时，可以侧重开发有助于就业的教学辅助软件。例如，电脑美术、电脑广告设计、网络游戏的制作与维护、网站设计与维护、电子商务平台数据维护以及其他适合弱势群体在网上开展工作的学习软件。在开展弱势群体网络娱乐和学习活动时，关注那些对网络产生兴趣并渴望利用网络开展工作的聋人，在培训机构讲师和特教老师的配合下，完成对他们的技能培训。

技能培训的目的一方面是让这个群体掌握网络娱乐休闲的技能，以满足他们的娱乐休闲需求；另一方面通过培训网络工作的技能，来提高他们的就业能力。因此技能考核的权威性就显得尤为重要，技能证书的发放应由政府主导的技能鉴定部门来核发。取得证书的聋人可以通过为弱势群体提供职业介绍的机构来双向选择工作。网络时代满足听力有障碍的年轻群体网络学习和娱乐需求的解决方案如图1所示。

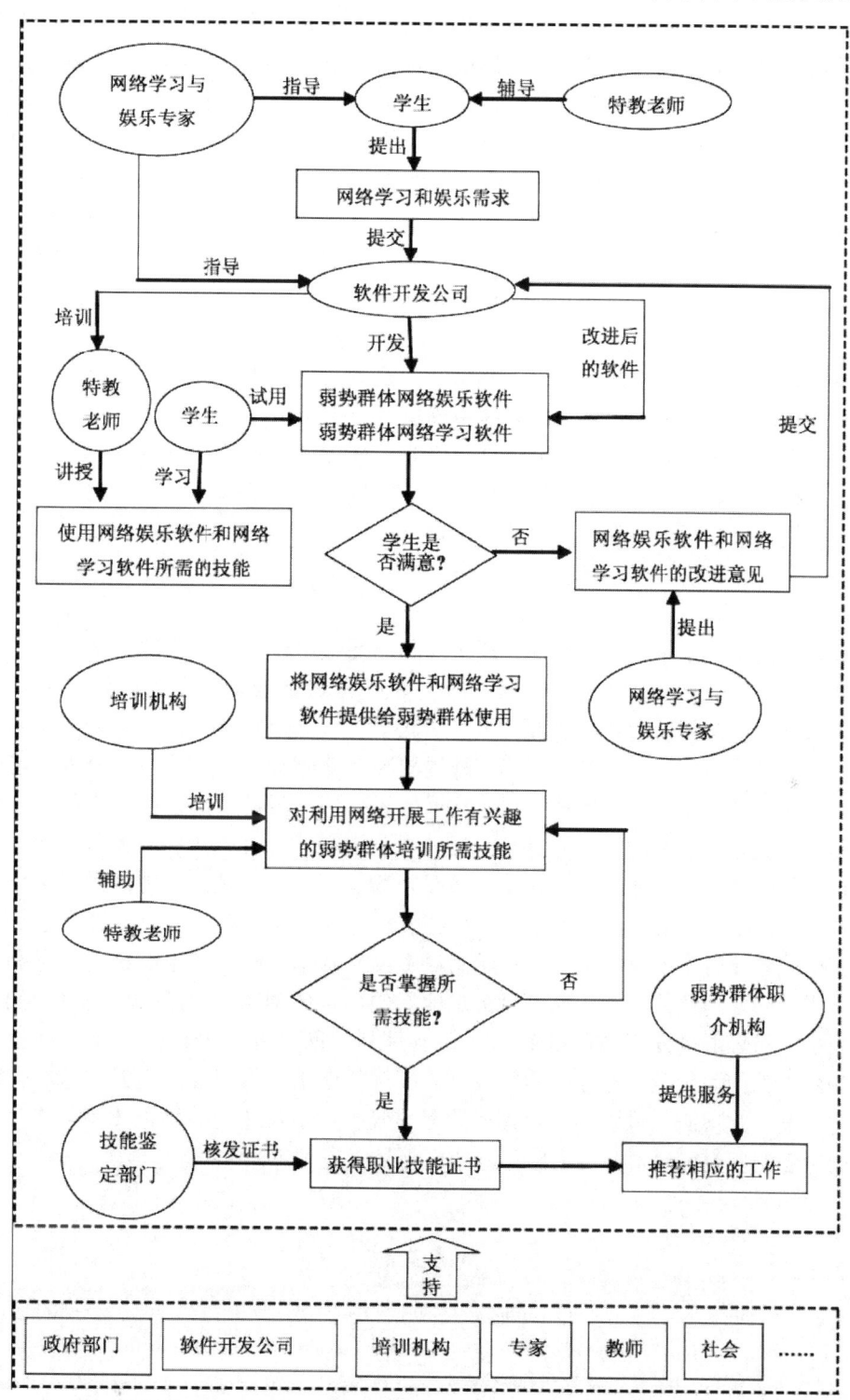

图1　网络时代满足听力有障碍的年轻群体网络学习和娱乐需求的解决方案

5.2 政府和社会的支持是实施解决方案的前提条件

开发针对这个弱势群体的网络娱乐和学习软件以及为他们提供技能培训和介绍工作是一个系统工程，涉及软件开发经、培训、硬件设备的费用支出，以及开设技能课程、职业鉴定、职业介绍等。要实现这个系统工程,需要政府的大力支持,软件开发公司、网络娱乐和学习专家、培训机构和从事特教教师们的积极参与以及社会的关注与捐赠。

首先是政府的大力支持。一方面,政府应加大宣传力度,引起社会的广泛关注,鼓励热心于这个弱势群体的专家学者从事这方面的研究,鼓励听人多学一些与聋人交流的方法,并作为志愿者多去聋哑人学校为这个弱势群体服务;另一方面,制定相关政策来鼓励企事业单位和个人积极为这个弱势群体提供相应的培训和适合他们的工作岗位。政府还应提供一定的经费来扶持适合这个弱势群体的网络娱乐和学习软件的开发。例如,投入一定的经费来研究这个弱势群体的网络娱乐和学习需求,开发满足这些需求的示范软件。除此之外,通过建立专门为弱势群体进行职业培训、就业指导和职业介绍的指导中心以及负责弱势群体职业技能鉴定的机构来推动解决方案的实施。

其次是网络娱乐和学习的专家与学校领导的热心支持。由于特教老师对网络娱乐和学习的规则以及所需技能了解有限,很难正确地引导学生提出适合他们的需求。需求的获取,可采用特教老师配合下的专家讲授、问卷调查、焦点访谈等方法。在学校开展网络娱乐和学习活动时,要增设学习这方面技能的课程,需要学校领导的支持才能实现。学校领导可以考虑与网络娱乐和学习专家签订协议,定期请这方面的专家来校参与教学和共同组织网络娱乐和网络学习活动。也可以通过宣传,引起网络娱乐和学习专家的关注,使专家能够自愿地为这个弱势群体免费提供专业指导。

最后是社会的广泛关注。对这个弱势群体开展网络娱乐和学习活动光靠政府的力量是不够的。由于政府的财力有限。在现有的条件下,还不能完全独立解决这个弱势群体的所有休闲需求。如果能够引起社会的广泛关注,捐赠一些善款,就能弥补政府在财力上的不足。

6 小 结

娱乐休闲活动对健全人来说是一种享受,通过这种享受,可以调节人们的心情,从而达到心情愉悦的目的。而听力有障碍的群体由于存在与健全人交流的困难,造成这个弱势群体与健全人的世界相隔绝,他们所能参与的娱乐休闲活动就会非常有限,长此下去,会影响到他们的身心健康。

为了满足这个弱势群体的娱乐休闲需求,国外提出深度休闲理论,并认为这个理论能够较好地帮助这个群体。深度休闲理论强调通过掌握技能后所开展的娱乐休闲活动对满足残疾人的娱乐休闲需求的作用。在我国加强对残疾人娱乐休闲需求的研究,提供适合这个弱势群体的公共文化服务,在残疾人学校设置更多的适合他们的技能培训课程以及开发网络娱乐和学习软件,是满足他们的娱乐休闲需求的一个设想。要想实现这个设想,需要政府、专家、从事特殊教育的工作者以及全社会的大力支持。

通过本次调研能明显看出,听力有障碍的学生对上网有浓厚兴趣,如果能正确引导和开发适合这个弱势群体的网络娱乐和学习软件,则不仅可以满足他们的娱乐休闲需求,还可以激发他们利用网络开展工作的兴趣,为这个弱势群体开辟新的就业途径。但是利用网络开展工作,需要掌握相应的技能,因此,探讨有哪些网络工作适合听力有障碍的年轻人,以及如何培养他们在网上开展这些工作的能力是值得进一步研究的课题。此项研究可以扩展到其他类型的残疾人,对他们的娱乐休闲和终身学习具有一定实际意义。希望笔者的研究能够对听力有障碍的年轻群体有所帮助。

参考文献

[1] Smith L J. Leisure recreation and tourism [J]. *Annals of Tourism Research*, 1991, 18 (1): 85-100.

[2] Chen Wenli, Jia Chunying, Liu Rui. The effects analysis of recreation and leisure activities to the hearing handicapped young groups [A]. //: Ma Huidi. *Proceedings of 2009 Chinese Leisure and Social Progress Academic Conference* [C]. Beijing: China Tourism Press, 2010. 147-159. [陈文力,贾春英,刘睿. 娱乐休闲活动对听力有障碍的年轻群体的影响及分析 [A]. //: 马惠娣. 2009 中国休闲与社会进步学术年会文集 [C]. 北京:中国旅游出版社,2010. 147-159.]

[3] Chen Wenli, Wu Ning. The discussion of entertainment treatment to Chinese young hearing handicapped [A]. //: Ning Zequn. *Proceedings of the Modern Way of Leisure and Tourism Development the International Symposium* [C]. Beijing: China Tourism Press, 2007. 396-411. [陈文力,吴宁. 对我国听力有障碍的年轻群体进行娱乐治疗的探讨 [A]. //: 宁泽群. 现代休闲方式与旅游发展国际学术研讨会论文集 [C]. 北京:中国旅游出版社,2007. 396-411.]

［4］ Wrigley O. *The Politics of Deafness* ［M］. Washington：Gallaudet University Press，1996. 25.

［5］ Lin Shanru. Serious leisure and information behavior research ［J］. *Library and Information Journal*，2007，3（1/2）：15 - 22. ［林珊如. 深度休闲与资讯行为研究［J］. 图书资讯学刊，2007，3（1/2）：15 - 22.］

［6］ Stebbins R A. Serious Leisure：A conceptual statement ［J］. *Pacific Sociological Review*，1982，25（2）：251 - 272.

［7］ Stebbins R A. Casual leisure：A conceptual statement ［J］. *Leisure Studies*，1997，16（1）：17 - 25.

［8］ Stebbins R A. *Amateurs，Professionals，and Serious Leisure* ［M］. Sherbrooke：McGill - Queen's University Press，1992. 3 - 15.

［9］ Olmsted A D. Hobbies and serious leisure ［J］. *World Leisure & Recreation*，1993，35（1）：26 - 32.

［10］ Stebbins R A. Volunteering：A serious leisure perspective ［J］. *Nonprofit and Voluntary Sector Quarterly*，1996，25（2）：211 - 224.

旅游服务外包的理论建构研究

范 蓓 田彩云

1 问题的提出

在信息技术革命、经济全球化以及市场竞争加剧的共同推动下，越来越多的企业或机构为突出竞争优势，降低运营成本，将有限的资源配置在核心领域中，而将其非核心业务以外包的方式交由其他专业供应商完成。发展服务外包已经成为新时期产业升级的重要方式。据工信部估计，2010年中国服务外包产业规模超2700亿元，同比增长35%。按过去5年（2006—2010）年均30%至50%的增速发展，预计到2015年末，中国服务外包产业规模将突破万亿元大关。而服务业的兴旺发达是社会转型，即由工业化后期向后工业化社会演进的重要标志。

服务外包业是基于服务业价值链的要素重组，是对现有旅游产业的流程再造，是从根本上解决目前我国旅游产业"散、小、弱、差"的战略选择。服务外包既有利于大中型旅游企业做大做强，又为小微型旅游企业拓展了生存空间，从而形成旅游业新的专业分工格局，是对现有旅游产业要素和价值链的解构和重构，是旅游业从传统服务业向现代服务业转型升级的一次革命性跃升。

在2010年9月举办的第一届"中国服务"发展论坛上，与会专家明确提出，旅游业是最有可能、最有条件成为"中国服务"战略的核心产业，未来"中国服务"可以从旅游业起步。旅游业作为一种高成长性的服务产业，具有较好的产业渗透和扩张能力，将"非核心"的业务通过外包的方式加以整合、重组和创新，是旅游业在新竞争环境下的一种新的战略发展机遇。因此，研究旅游服务外包不仅对于旅游产业的转型升级、保持旅游业可持续的健康发展具有重大的现实意义，而且对于在当下纷乱复杂的国际政治和经济环境中探索和构建具有我国社会主义市场经济特色的"中国服务"理论体系更具有深远的历史意义。

2 相关研究综述

服务外包的迅猛发展，激发国内外学者对服务外包的内涵、动因、理论基础、功能效应等方面展开研究。通过案例和实证研究，开展了物流、软件、金融、信息技术等典型行业和地区服务外包实践的分析。而旅游服务外包的研究，主要聚焦在三个方面：（1）旅游服务外包整体发展的描述（王琼英，2009；项园园，2007；Lamminmaki，2008），着重对旅游、会展及酒店等发展服务外包的可行性和必要性、外包管理及发展模式、路径等方面进行探讨；（2）旅游服务外包专项研究（杨海红，2009；陈攀，2010；杨文丽，2002；Chatzoglou，Sarigiannidis，2009），主要集中在对旅行社、饭店、旅游景区人力资源外包，旅行社差旅、专项旅游业务，饭店业财务管理等外包的现状、动机及绩效的分析；（3）旅游业发展服务外包的作用及对产业、区域发展的影响，这方面的研究成果主要有：张文建和华建平（2008）提出了商务会展服务外包是实现旅游产业发展方式转变的必由之路；梁峰（2010）研究了服务外包对我国传统旅游价值链的影响。总之，与旅游服务外包丰富多彩的实践相比，关于旅游服务外包的理论研究相对较为薄弱。目前的研究主要着眼于对现象的描述分析或对某项具体的、职能性的服务外包业务的研究，尚未形成一个完整、清晰的旅游服务外包的理论分析框架，对实践的研究以点展开，零散且存在研究空白。本文试图从理论上对旅游服务外包给予解释并对其实

[基金项目] 教育部课题《面向区域企业集群的服务外包人才产学研合作教育机制研究》（DIA100287）；国家级服务外包人才培养模式创新实验区课题《现代旅游业服务外包人才需求研究》（sk201023x）资助。

[作者简介] 范蓓（1961—），女，北京联合大学旅游学院副研究员，研究方向为服务经济、旅游人力资源开发与管理；田彩云（1972—），女，博士，北京联合大学旅游学院副教授，研究方向为旅游经济分析、现代旅游服务管理和休闲农业。

践进行体系化归纳和系统性梳理。

3 旅游服务外包的理论模型构建

3.1 旅游服务外包的概念范畴边界

"外包（outsourcing）"一词，最早出现在1990年哈默尔（Hamel）和普拉哈拉德（Praharad）发表的《企业的核心竞争力》一文中，指企业在内部资源有限的情况下，将生产链中一些非核心的业务发包给第三方企业完成的生产经营方式（郑建伟，曾松，2008）。如果外包的对象是制造业中的某个环节为制造外包，而以服务活动为对象则是服务外包。随着全球经济从"产品经济"到"服务经济"的转变，服务外包成为主要的外包方式，对其概念、分类进行清晰界定是深入开展理论研究的前提。

迄今为止，学术界和产业界对服务外包的概念尚未形成一致的观点。归纳起来可以分为三大类（袁欣，2010）：第一类是从性质的角度来界定，认为服务外包是指依据双方议定的标准，成本和条件的合约，将原来由企业内部完成的工作外包给外部专业服务提供商来完成的一种服务模式或经营方式；第二类是从类别范畴的角度来界定，认为服务外包是IT服务市场的一部分，信息技术外包（ITO）和业务流程外包（BPO），中国"服务外包"主要政府管理部门商务部也用这种方式来定义；第三类是将上述两类定义方式合并在一起的界定方式，认为服务外包是基于IT技术的业务流程外包，建立在IT技术和网络平台以上的任何可外包的作业经数据化之后转移出去的业务流程和办公作业，都属于服务外包。目前"服务外包"概念表述虽未一致，但普遍认可它是基于信息网络技术的企业非核心业务的服务业转移。

我们认为，旅游服务外包，是指企业将自身生产业务活动中非核心的旅游服务业务委托给第三方专业服务提供商来完成的经济活动。旅游服务外包的概念包括了如下内涵：

第一，服务外包存在于旅游相关产业企业之间，外包的"外"指企业之外，是企业之间的分工与合作，是以企业作为业务发包与承包活动的主体。

第二，企业服务活动中非核心的旅游服务业务和内容是外包的主要对象，企业在保持生产链条性质不发生实质性变化的情况下，把链条中的某个环节或区段的旅游服务业务，通过契约的方式转移给专业服务机构。这些服务活动通常是其非核心或不具有比较优势的项目，但并不一定是其不重要的项目。旅游企业缺乏技术优势的一些核心业务往往也采取外包形式，例如酒店把餐饮业务外包给外部餐饮管理公司。

第三，服务外包是企业充分利用企业外部资源完成内部分工的一种经营行为或经济活动，是企业选择纵向一体化和依靠市场机制实现交易行为从而完成经营活动之外的第三个选择。

依据发包方和承包方企业空间和国别分布关系差异，可以把外包划分为国内外包和国际外包两种类型（卢峰，2007）。如旅游服务外包的发包方与承包方同属特定国家的企业，则属于国内外包，称"在岸外包（onshore outsourcing）"；如发包方与承包方分属不同国家的企业，则属于国际外包，称"离岸外包（offshore outsourcing）"。如国内旅行社承接国际企业的商务旅游活动业务，便是国际旅游服务外包。

3.2 旅游服务外包的理论模型

通过对旅游服务外包的概念及内涵的界定与分析，我们构建了旅游服务外包的理论模型（见图1）。

理论模型包括"外包的主体"和"外包的内容"两个维度。旅游服务外包的主体是参与完成旅游服务外包的企业，包括发包方和接包方。旅游服务外包的内容是指服务外包企业（承接服务外包业务的企业）向客户提供的旅游外包业务，是发包方非核心的、不直接创造价值的后台支持业务，即相关性、支持性和边缘性业务。下面对旅游服务外包主体及其相关关系进行详细阐述。

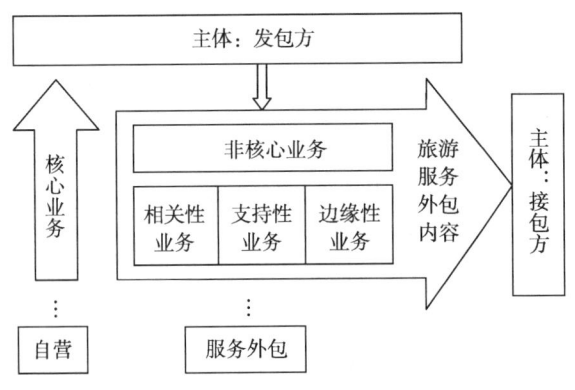

图1 旅游服务外包模型

3.2.1 旅游服务外包的主体及其关系

旅游服务外包的主体即发包方和接包方，分别是旅游服务业务的需求方和供给方，其关系如表1所示。

表1 旅游服务外包业务的主体和客体

主体（发包企业）	客体（接包企业）
非旅游企业	旅游企业
旅游企业	非旅游企业、旅游企业

旅游企业是指为旅游者旅游消费实现提供旅游服务，在旅游消费服务领域中进行独立经营核算的经济单位，包括有赖于旅游者的存在而生存的直接旅游企业，如旅行社，饭店、餐馆、旅游商店、交通公司、旅游景点、娱乐经营企业等；间接从旅游消费中获益的企业，如管理公司、旅行公司、服务公司、影视公司、出版单位、通信设施以及食品、卫生等生活服务部门；旅游组织，包括相关的政府机构、旅游院校、旅游科研机构等（宁泽群，2005）。旅游企业的旅游服务业务是指企业为实现旅游消费所包含的所有生产环节和活动，既包括旅游者能接触和感知的主要旅游服务，也包括为完成旅游消费活动所需要的一切后台运行支持和辅助功能性活动。非旅游企业涉及面非常广，是指除旅游企业以外的所有企业或机构。

旅游服务外包主体之间通常以协议或合同的方式进行合作以及约束相互行为，彼此以旅游服务业务作为合作基点，在合约期内完成外包任务：一是旅游企业以服务供应商的身份提供其他非旅游企业所需的旅游服务，二是旅游企业把自己的非核心业务外包给其他专业的非旅游企业或把部分旅游服务业务再分包给其他旅游企业完成。外包的类型既有单项服务外包，即将旅游业务的某一个环节外包；还有全部业务外包，即将旅游服务的整个环节全部外包。外包至少存在两个企业，存在双方合作与多方合作关系。发包可以是一级发包，也可以是多级发包。同一旅游企业可能在不同的业务项目中分别承担发包方和接包方的角色和职能。

对于发包方，要求企业对外包的旅游服务业务提出明确的项目需求，同时具有一定的项目管理水平、人力资源和沟通控制能力。对于接包方，要求企业具有一定的服务品质，具有成本、质量控制能力，交流能力和商业信誉，同时做到不外泄发包方信息，不侵犯发包方依法享有的商标、专利、著作权等知识产权权利。为保证项目实施成功，双方要就项目协商制订实施计划、对质量和进度进行严格控制并做好风险管理。服务质量保证是双方由一次性服务转变为存续长期、可信赖外包关系的基础。

3.2.2 旅游服务外包的内容

旅游服务外包的内容是指接包方为发包方提供的旅游外包业务。我们以旅游服务外包企业关系为基础，研究了目前不同旅游服务外包主体之间存在的主要外包内容及类别（见表2、表3）。

表 2　旅游服务外包业务的主要内容

发包方	接包方	服务外包业务及内容
非旅游企业	旅游企业	酒店、票务、租车预订：为企业商务活动提供酒店预订、票务预订和租车预订业务，这是比较低端的旅游服务外包内容（梁峰，2010）。目前承接此类业务的主要有：在线旅游企业，如携程、e龙和芒果网；专业商旅公司，如国航运通、中航嘉信、HRG中国等
		旅游信息咨询服务：为企业提供旅游前期准备、行程安排与管理、后期服务等消费分析方案或报告，包括旅游健康咨询、旅游安全、旅游线路设计、旅游活动安排、旅游花费管理等内容。这要求旅游企业具有高素质管理咨询人才、分析技术工具和方法。目前能承接此类业务的主要是具有专门咨询服务部门的大型商旅公司
		商旅管理业务：商旅管理公司等承接企业、有规模的社团组织和政府部门等运营主体的差旅管理业务。为客户提供差旅计划、活动策划等全方位的商旅打包服务，提供全程服务及管理活动，并有效执行差旅政策。目前主要是商务旅行公司、商务差旅管理公司、部分在线旅游企业开展此类外包业务
		商务旅游服务：根据各企业个性化需求，为企业组织公务性旅游活动（商务旅游、会议旅业游、奖励旅游、商务考察、培训旅游、疗养旅游、体育旅游等）提供交通、住宿、餐饮、导游、咨询、设计、管理等一条龙旅游服务，包括组织、策划、接待各种商务活动、安排对口商务考察和洽谈，量身定做旅游项目和行程。旅行社、旅行公司、会展公司等承接此类业务
		商务会展业务：为企业提供会展策划、会展管理、会展营销、展场及展台设计、会展现场服务、会展信息、会展财务管理等业务。主要是专门的会展公司、专业展览企业、会议中心、会展中心、酒店等承接此类业务
		节事节庆安排：为企业各种节假日、节日和事件活动（周年庆、促销活动、年会等）提供项目策划、项目服务及管理业务，包括庆典仪式、展览展示、演讲、文化娱乐、摄影摄像、大型文艺演出等表演活动。会议酒店、会议展览公司、度假村等旅游企业承接此类业务

表 3　旅游服务外包业务的主要内容

发包方	接包方	服务外包业务及内容
旅游企业	非旅游企业	办公业务：为旅游企业完成旅游供给活动提供的专业IT技术支持服务，包括企业网络接入、桌面管理到远程技术支持、定制数据库开发与管理、应用软件开发等服务内容
		人力资源：旅游企业将内部部分人力资源及其相关活动委托给专业、高效的外部服务商，包括员工的派遣，工作技术含量和员工素质要求不高，需求量大的基层岗位，如保洁、保安、工程维修、绿化等采用该种方式（陈攀，2010）；人力资源各项管理活动的外包，如雇用和招聘、工资和缴税、医疗及福利、培训与教育等。目前，旅行社、酒店和旅游景旅区人力资源外包普遍存在
		财务/会计：外包的主要业务包括程序化的一般旅游会计业务、会计报表监控、薪资管理、银行调解准备、资本与风险管理以及交易管理等方面
		客户交互服务：外包的主要业务包括呼叫中心、预订中心、联络中心、客户分析、客户支持服务、订单处理等
		知识流程服务：为旅游企业提供解决方案。包括提供分析咨询工具和相关报告，如旅游区规划、公园设计、旅游目的地策划、旅游企业运营管理及营销策划、旅游项目投资论证、客源地市场开发等
	旅游企业	细分的旅游服务：旅游企业将旅游服务环节中的部分业务外包给其他专业旅游公司，服务外包内容涉及旅游活动的各个方面，如旅行社、酒店、景区等将票务、营销、预订、差旅管理外包给在线旅游企业或商旅公司；酒店把运营管理交给专业的酒店管理集团；专业展览、会展公司将展会搭建、布景设计、礼仪服务等外包给其他专业开展此类业务的旅游企业；旅行社将导游服务、翻译服务外包给导游服务中心；旅游总社将目的地的接待活动委托地接社完成，旅游景区策划、目的地营销外包给旅游院校和旅游规划公司等

3.3　旅游服务外包的分类

结合上文从类别范畴对服务外包的概念梳理以及旅游服务外包业务的主要内容，我们将旅游服务外包分为三类：

（1）IT基础设施及应用服务外包，是指企业将旅游信息化建设、运营服务交给专业化企业完成。包括各类网上预订业务、涉及旅游企业IT基础运营的各类办公业务，应用软件系统开发与管理等。

（2）业务流程外包，是指企业将旅游流程或职能外包给供应商，并由供应商对这些流程进行重组，包括旅游企业提供的商旅管理、商务旅游、商务会展等专项业务以及旅游企业外包的非核心旅游业务，如人力资源、会计业务、客户支持等。

（3）知识服务外包，是指和旅游企业、旅游产品和市场开发相关的研究、策划、规划和咨询活动，包括旅游信息咨询服务、知识流程服务等。

4 旅游服务外包的特征

4.1 服务水平层次化

旅游服务外包的对象是旅游业务，其本质就是"服务"。服务对象需求的异质性和企业需要在有限资源基础上进行有效市场竞争决定了外包服务的层次性特征。根据发包方业务需求的知识及技术含量水平的差异，旅游服务外包的内容可分为三个层次。低端旅游服务外包，主要是指发包方需求的服务内容相对比较固定和程序化，从根本上讲，接包方不是每次都要做出大的调整和决策，而是建立某些制度、规则或政策就能完成。内容主要是酒店、票务、租车预订；员工的派遣；一般会计业务；工资和缴税；呼叫中心和预订中心等。中端旅游服务外包，主要是指根据特定发包方的特定需求提供的具有针对性的专项旅游服务，包括旅游信息服务、旅游企业所需的后台办公网络接入、桌面管理到远程技术支持、培训与教育、会计报表监控等。高端旅游服务外包，是指接受发包方特定委托的个性化、定制化的旅游服务（陈攀，2010），如为非旅游企业提供的旅游咨询、打包的商旅管理、商务旅游和商务会展业务，为旅游企业提供的定制数据库和应用软件开发、知识服务等。需要注意的是，这种划分方法具有相对性和动态性。

4.2 服务手段IT化

服务外包在技术手段上强调信息传输手段和交易平台的IT化，这已经成为共识（袁欣，2010），旅游服务外包也不例外。IT基础设施及应用服务外包，实际上是利用IT工具来为企业提供IT服务。每一项旅游业务流程、知识服务外包业务背后都离不开IT的支持，这种支持或是通过硬件系统平台完成的，抑或是通过软件辅助来完成的。例如人力资源外包业务，服务外包企业要利用自身内部的信息系统平台，根据旅游企业人力资源的雇佣和招聘、工资和缴税、医疗及福利、培训与教育等一系列具体职能，开发新的适合该企业的系统，从而使得企业人力资源的规划和管理在该系统下进行优化和整合，并实现与其他部门业务之间的交互性。旅游信息咨询、知识流程外包等无不是基于信息网络技术的，其服务性工作都是通过计算机操作完成，并采用现代通信手段进行交付。依托信息技术和现代管理理念对传统旅游服务进行改造，旅游服务外包的IT化特征将体现得越来越明显。

4.3 服务链条网状化

旅游产业群体的内涵广泛，几乎涉及国民经济消费领域的大多数产业。旅游直接影响的产业包括吃、住、行、游、购、娱等部门，间接影响的产业则包括金融、通信、环保、印刷等58个部门。另外，旅游活动从空间表现形式上来看是一种旅游客源地与旅游目的地之间的通道式流动。旅游所涉及产业的广泛性、丰富性以及旅游的跨区域性，决定了旅游服务外包的业务范围广泛且彼此关联。非旅游企业可以把其中一块或多块旅游业务发包给一个或多个旅游企业，第二个接包的旅游企业把部分业务再分包给一个或多个非旅游企业，以此衍生出以旅游服务业务作为连接点，多级相连，环环相扣的外包网络结构。由于不同的接包企业可能分布于不同地区，使得服务链条在组织结构和空间分布上形成纵向化网状式结构。特别是随着信息技术成果的商业性普及与推广，在传统的人与人的服务界面之外，还增加了人与技术的界面，即通过"人—技术—人"的界面来提供服务（李华，等，2009），从而改变了传统旅游服务生产与消费同时进行的特性。旅游业务可以在信息和电子商务技术条件下，形成"一对多"的外包企业关系，以信息技术为支持平台的服务链条网状模式将会成为现代旅游服务外包的主要特征。

5 旅游服务外包的理论解释

关于服务外包的理论解释，国内外许多学者从各个不同的角度进行了探讨，但各种理论的关注点不同。我们考虑了旅游行业的特质及发展现状，构建了一个旅游服务外包产生机制模型（见图2），从旅游服务外包发生的基础条件、主要驱动力和外在客观要求三方面探讨其产生的基础、动力机理以及维持和引导的经济力量。

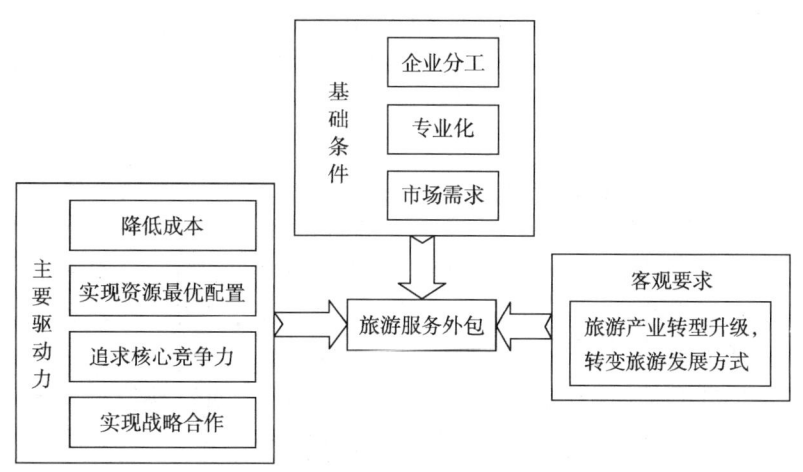

图2 旅游服务外包产生机制模型

5.1 企业分工、专业化和市场需求是旅游服务外包发生的基础条件

企业分工是企业在各个市场区域和生产过程的相对分散化；专业化则是生产要素在分散的市场区域和生产过程中各个生产片段上的相对集中，它是企业将主要精力放在最擅长的领域，在其核心能力所及的范围内的经营。分工的前提主要源自比较优势，而比较优势的发挥导致专业化程度的提高。旅游服务外包发生的根本原因就在于旅游业务具有形成分工和专业化的自然禀赋以及由此带来的经济性。根据"斯密定理"，分工和专业化受市场范围的限制。也就是说，市场的扩大使分工进一步发展后，专业化的生产者才能实际出现和存在❶。因此，旅游服务外包的出现和发展也是旅游市场需求的结果。

商务旅游、商务会展等旅游业务，对于非旅游企业来讲，无疑可以形成生产服务过程职能的专业化，将企业内部的职能独立出来，外包于专业的旅游企业是其理性的选择。随着现代企业市场拓展与商务活动的开展，必将促进旅游服务外包企业的大幅度增长，企业专业化方式随企业在产业间的扩展而广泛扩展。

旅游企业的生产过程是提供满足旅游消费的旅游资源、旅游设施和旅游服务的过程，涉及游览、餐饮、住宿、交通、娱乐等直接服务和租车、保险、咨询、教育等相关服务的提供。这些彼此关联的旅游业务由于不同的生产特性很容易形成分工和专业化。而且旅游生产链条长、各个环节活动范围广泛决定了分工和专业化程度相当高。当不同的旅游企业专业化某些业务后，便产生了"服务内部化"向"服务外部化"转变的社会分工，从而形成了不同职能细分的服务外包组织。开展服务外包，细分的不同旅游企业将会集中于某一产品领域的生产，专门化经营在提高企业管理水平的同时，也提高了服务品质，因此能够更好地满足旅游市场对服务项目与功能的专业化、多样化的需求，以分工为基础的服务外包市场就会得到进一步的发展。

5.2 降低成本、实现资源最优配置、追求核心竞争力和实现战略合作是旅游服务外包的主要驱动力

服务外包的驱动力是指企业服务外包所必需的推动力。其主要驱动力包括成本、资源优化配置、核心竞争力提升、寻求战略合作这四方面。各个动力之间并非彼此孤立，而是相互联系、渗透和转换，共同推进旅游服务外包的发展。

---

❶ 亚当·斯密. 国民财富的性质和原因的研究 [M]. 郭大力、王亚南译. 商务印书馆，1981：5-10。

第一，企业降低成本的推动力。服务外包作为企业的一种选择，会受到成本的约束。生产成本与交易成本构成了企业的全部成本。由于每个企业的资源禀赋不同，受到的"成本—效益"约束也不同。非旅游企业将生产过程中的非核心的旅游业务分包给具有比较优势的专门服务提供的旅游企业完成。规模较大的旅游企业接包商可能通过规模经济获得成本优势，并提供标准性能和质量稳定的服务。如非旅游企业将酒店、票务预订服务交由携程、e龙等旅游电子商务企业完成，这种外包合作除了可以获得相比自营业务的成本优势外，非旅游企业还可将节省下来的资源用于强化自我优势，提高技术水平上，使得企业的生产成本进一步降低，收益进一步增加。另外，由于服务外包是通过企业相互合作而非通过市场进行资源配置的方式，能避免交易中的盲目性，减少搜寻民航、铁路信息的成本，降低与目的地住宿、餐饮讨价还价的价格机制运行成本，有效降低了交易的费用。

第二，资源优化配置的推动力。外包的一个基本特征是，企业在保持最终产出或产出组合不变的前提下把某些投入性活动转移出去。企业利用外部的专业化资源完成非核心的环节，将有限的资源合理配置和优化，通过专注于具有核心能力的服务，把资源配置到绩效显著的生产环节。如西门子、通用、惠普等大型电子科技企业，人员规模大，商务活动频繁，因此选择将商旅管理外包给中航嘉信完成❶，由其提供定制的差旅服务、管理和控制，把自己的人力、物力、财力等资源则集中于主营业务电子产品的生产运营上，这样既降低了成本，又实现了资源的优化配置。

第三，核心竞争力提升推动力。根据核心竞争力理论，企业具有各种各样的能力，但那些能够给企业带来长期竞争优势和超额利润的能力才是企业的核心能力。核心能力是企业增强竞争力、获得竞争优势的关键。为了在激烈的市场竞争环境中获得竞争优势，企业把非核心的、次要的业务外包出去，利用有限资源专注于核心资源的开发，把精力投入到具有核心竞争力的研发与培育方面。如旅游景区专注于为游客提供参观游览、休闲度假等旅游服务与功能，而将内部人力资源及其相关活动外包给专业的外部服务商完成，强化自身核心能力，增强自身竞争优势。

第四，寻求战略合作推动力。企业选择外包传统认为是基于成本节约，而不是一种战略动机。基于成本动机的外包被称为战术的或传统的外包。然而，随着外包的发展，外包的原因开始由战术原因转向战略原因。当企业许多服务过程都需要采取分散、无组织的方式外包时，企业依赖过多的、多类型的供给者，这时是不能获得预期的成本节约的。企业便选择一家提供综合服务的供应商来完成，"战略合作伙伴"的外包关系就产生了。另外，对于传统认为并不适合的一些更加核心与高端的生产服务活动外包时，发包企业也选择这种方式。例如，酒店投资方（业主方）将酒店的经营管理和运作委托专业的酒店管理公司来完成，双方以切实的战略利益为结合点建立战略伙伴关系，发包方在获得相应需求的基础上，也获得了技能、技术、知识的转移。

5.3 旅游产业转型升级、转变旅游发展方式是旅游服务外包的客观要求

旅游产业转型升级、转变旅游发展方式，具体表现为旅游业由规模扩张向质量提升、由低端建设向高端拓展、由资源依赖向创新驱动、由粗放经营向集聚发展转变。势在必行的旅游产业转型升级，是旅游服务外包发展的一个良好契机。旅游服务外包由于其产生的产业融合效应、企业集群和结构重塑效应以及技术创新和溢出效应，而成为旅游产业转型升级的一个有效途径。

第一，产业融合效应。旅游服务外包的出现，使旅游企业和各类型的非旅游企业发生业务联系，推动旅游业与其他产业走向融合。同时，旅游服务外包使旅游服务的价值创造过程嵌入到其他产业的价值链当中，成为产业链上的增值点。如旅游企业为各类企业提供商务旅游、会议展览服务，提供旅游信息咨询及全程差旅管理等服务时，这些旅游业务融入到各类企业的整体运营当中，成为一个职能模块，被分包出来。企业需求的广度和深度提高了旅游供给的质量，组织、信息技术、知识和社会资本作为主要的生产要素推动着旅游产业不断发展，使旅游产出呈现信息技术承载度高、高附加价值的知识密集型特征，为旅游产业的转型升级提供动力。

第二，企业集群和结构重塑效应。企业是产业结构升级的组织载体和中心环节，实现产业结构升级最终体现为企业转型升级。实现旅游服务外包，有利于承担相同专项服务外包职能的旅游企业形成基于

---

❶ 资料来源：对中航嘉信商务旅行管理有限公司管理人员的调研访谈。

开拓共同市场的较稳定的专业化分工与协作关系的企业集群，这不仅促进了旅游企业间通过有序竞争进行技术创新、服务创新、管理创新或运用信息技术改造传统作业方式上的尝试与创新，而且企业之间专业化程度的提高可以使不同旅游企业日益专精于某一项业务，实现创新专业化，每个企业负担的创新投资成本也大大降低。企业的竞争和模仿，便会触发企业的产品结构与产业结构发生改变，向着合理化与高级化的方向移动。同时，旅游企业把非主营业务进行剥离，集中企业的经济资源于核心业务上。这不仅促进了企业内部资源的重新配置，而且深入到不同业务环节在企业内外对企业结构进行重组。降低了企业运行成本，提高了企业的运行效率。

第三，技术创新和溢出效应。技术进步是推动产业结构升级优化的主要力量。基于信息和网络技术的旅游服务外包可以加快旅游信息化的进程，并从旅游运行方式、市场渠道等方面加速旅游产业和市场结构的调整。携程、e龙等在线旅游企业在旅游信息查询、在线预订服务、旅游信息导航等方面发挥着越来越重要的作用。另外，承接服务外包特别是国际服务外包，可以促进旅游企业技术水平的提升。例如承接国际软件和通信服务行业商务会展服务外包业务，可以促使旅游企业不断进行技术研发和创新，并获得国际技术外溢效应，从而促进接包方产业技术水平的提升，进而促进产业结构的优化。而旅游企业在接受专业IT技术支持服务时，不断学习、效仿和追赶，可以加快技术创新的速度，提升旅游产品的层次和服务水平，实现企业更快成长，最终带动整个产业的升级。

6　研究展望

本文梳理了旅游服务外包实践和理论基础，初步构建了一个抽象层次上的理论框架。旅游服务外包的后续研究应致力于以下三个方面：（1）理论深化。深入探究并规范确定旅游服务外包的内涵和外延，研究服务外包和制造外包之间存在的异同之处，明确其理论基础和作用机制。随着实践的发展，旅游服务外包的性质、目的、模式也在发生深刻的变化，理论将会进一步发展和完善。（2）旅游服务外包的实证研究。旅游服务外包在实践中尽管已经存在并不断发展，但其所涉及的企业组织方式、外包的动因和风险、外包的模式和路径、外包的效应、外包所需的环境和人才建设、外包对地区和国家经济发展以至全球化层面的影响（如对外依存度、服务贸易壁垒和国际贸易等）及发展趋势等将是深入探讨的课题。（3）研究方法的探讨。旅游服务外包产生的总量及对微观企业和旅游产业的贡献等需要采集数据进行定量研究，从而逐步丰富和完善旅游服务外包的理论和实证研究。

参考文献

[1] Lamminmaki D. Accounting and the management of outsourcing: An empirical study in the hotel industry [J]. Management Accounting Research, 2008, 19 (2): 163-181.
[2] Chatzoglou P, Sarigiannidis L. Business outsourcing and organizational performance: the case of the Greek hotel industry [J]. International Journal of Services Technology and Management, 2009, 11 (2): 105-127.
[3] 陈攀. 旅游景区人力资源外包研究 [D]. 湘潭: 湘潭大学, 2010: 15-17.
[4] 卢峰. 当代服务外包的经济学观察: 产品内分工的视角 [J]. 世界经济, 2007 (8): 22-35.
[5] 梁峰. 服务外包对我国传统旅游价值链的影响及对策研究 [J]. 特区经济, 2010 (5): 159-160.
[6] 李华, 董明, 汪应洛. 基于信息技术的服务外包 [M]. 西安: 西安交通大学出版社, 2009.
[7] 宁泽群. 旅游经济、产业与政策 [M]. 北京: 中国旅游出版社, 2005.
[8] 王琼英. 会展业服务外包发展模式研究及前景展望 [J]. 浙江树人大学学报, 2009 (11): 39-44.
[9] 项园园. 试论新时期我国旅游业服务外包的发展 [J]. 消费导刊, 2007 (11): 49-51.
[10] 杨海红. 旅行社承接服务外包研究 [D]. 上海: 上海师范大学, 2009: 11-19.
[11] 杨文丽. 构建中国星级酒店竞争优势途径——业务外包 [J]. 旅游科学, 2002 (3): 5-10.
[12] 袁欣. 服务外包: 概念、本质、效应 [J]. 国际经贸探索, 2010 (9): 10-14.
[13] 郑建伟, 曾松. 国际外包理论与战略 [M]. 北京: 经济管理出版社, 2008.
[14] 张文建, 华建平. 商务会展服务外包: 实现旅游产业发展方式的转变 [J]. 社会科学, 2008 (7): 69-75.

Studies on the Issue of Trust in Tourism Group – buying

Li Zheng

I INTRODUCTION

In recent years, the development of the Internet in China is very fast. The number of Internet users increases rapidly. According to the 29th China Internet Development Statistics Report released by CNNIC (China Internet Network Information Center) in January 2012, Chinese netizens continued its growth and the number exceeded 500 million in 2011. Internet penetration rate reached 38.3%.[1] With the increasing number of Chinese Internet users, as well as the improvement of the online shopping environment, e – Business in China shows a good trend of development after the dotcom bubble in 2001. As a new e – Business model, group – buying is accepted gradually by the netizens.

By the end of 2011, group buyers passion kept consistent, the number of group buying user is up to 64.65 million. Annual growth rate of group buyer is as high as 244.8%.[1] Almost all of China's Internet giants have set foot in this area. As an effective tool for the Internet industry profitability and enhancement stickiness, the websites promote the development of the industry of group – buying. But it is undeniable that the amount of group buying websites had seen the declination since the second half of the year. There are many reasons. Among them, the trust insufficient in group – buying is an important one, it limited the rapid development in groupbuying market. Actually, the market still needs to cultivate continually.

This study is carried out for the issue of trust in tourism group – buying. By summing up the theories of trust in the tourism group – buying, trust factors affecting the behavior of consumers in their group – buying process are analyzed. Ways to build consumer trust in the tourism group – buying are studied. At last, ideas and proposals to solve the crisis of confidence in the process of China's tourism group – buying are put forward.

II THE BASIC CONCEPTS OF TOURISM GROUP – BUYING AND TRUST

A. Concept of tourism group – buying

The group – buying was first introduced in the 1990s, it refers to purchasing behavior of the products or services at below market prices for some certain groups order from the suppliers for large quantities.[2] Tourism group – buying means that its purchase targets are tourism products or services in particular.

As a new e – Business model, group – buying has several form, such as organizations of the consumer themselves, organized by professional group – buying websites, organized by the suppliers and etc. Through group – buying the consumers can enhance the bargaining power with the suppliers, access to goods at very low prices, so it caused great concern by consumers, suppliers and even the capital market. Groupbuying has become a new consumption patterns popularly among netizens. With the prosperity and development of Chinese e – Business market, group – buying has completed the transition from small merchandise to large ones. However, due to product attributes and profitability as well as the limitations of consumer attitudes, now the group – buying products are mainly limited to items that closely related to the daily lives of consumers, such as dining, hairdressing, entertainment and etc. Tourism group – buying is in the early stage of development right now, only few websites get involved in

---

[Author Introduction] Li Zheng, Business College of Beijing Union University. E – mail: li.zheng@buu.edu.cn.

this area, the related research is also not rich. With the evolution of travel patterns and maturing of e – Business, tourism group – buying will definitely become a huge business opportunities and potential markets in the world. Correspondingly, the consumer trust issues in tourism group – buying are becoming increasingly important.

B. The definition of trust in e – Business environment

The trust issues related to many fields such as sociology, psychology, economics, management, marketing and etc. Scholars with different background and different disciplines had different views, so they defined in different ways. This feature also extends to the academic term of e – Business environment.

In e – Business environment, the definition of trust can be summarized as two kinds. [3] The first one emphasized from the perspective of consumer trust in the bargaining relationship. Typical scholars include Roger C. Mayer, James H. Davis and F. David Schoorman. They believed that trust can be expressed as a dependent variable influenced by the independent variables including abilities to be trusted, benevolence, integrity and propensity to trust. [4] The trust is based on the expected subjective wishes, and it is also a relationship between the two sides of buyers and sellers. Another point of view focused on online trust in the trading environment. Corritore et al (2003) defined that online trust is a relationship between individual consumers with specific trading websites or providing information websites. [5]

Based on the above viewpoints, the author of this paper considers that the trust in e – Business environment can be defined as follows: Trust is the expectation for the specific behavior of the businesses throughout the consumers' full purchase process in the risk and uncertain environment of e – Business, and on this basis the confidence and the subjective will which the trust main body depends on the trust objects.

III THEORETICAL ANALYSIS ON TRUST IN TOURISM GROUPBUYING

About theoretical research on trust, the typical conceptual model should be the one built by Mayer (Mayer et al., 1995)[4] and the one put forward by McKnight (McKnight, et al., 2002)[6]. See Fig. 1 and Fig. 2.

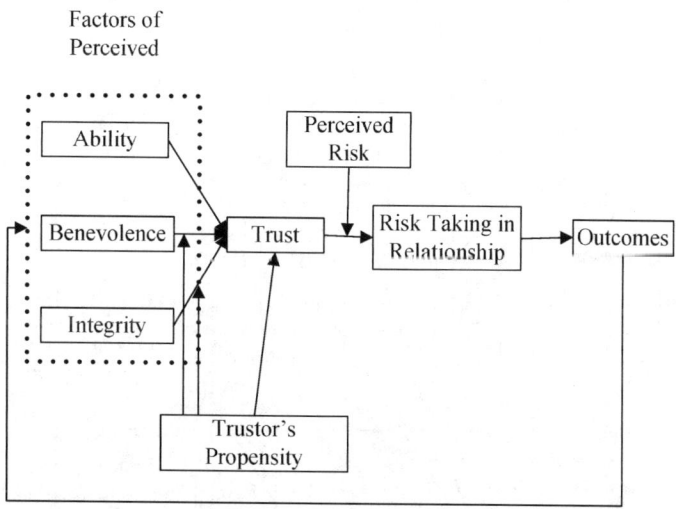

Fig. 1 Proposed Model of Trust[4]

It can be seen from Fig. 1 that trust was in fact exhibited the willingness of the trust main body to take risks, and the trust behavior is a risk – taking behavior. Ability, benevolence, integrity of trust object and trustor's propensity have become the main factors affecting trust. Suppose the trustors' trust level exceeds the perceived risk threshold, they will take some risks to implement those trust – related behaviors (Mayer et al., 1995).

In tourism group – buying, the purchase process is completed on the network, the product is usually not an actual freight, and consumers often need to go through a long period before their travel experiences, so they often worry about whether they can enjoy the travel services, what the qualities are, whether they will be cheated. In this process, consumers are disadvantageous and vulnerable. However, due to different status of merchants and consumers, they own asymmetric information, so it is difficult for consumers to monitor the suppliers effectively. In this regard, we believe that Mayer's trust conceptual model is equally applicable to tourism group – buying. It should be said that ability, benevolence and integrity are the main characteristics of trust objects in tourism group – buying. If the supplier has these three characteristics, then with the influence of trustor's propensity, it will make consumers to produce a certain degree of trust feelings, and lead to produce positive outcomes. Even though there may be some uncertainties or unpredictable results in this process, however, due to the foregoing reasons, consumers have established a trust relationship with the suppliers, they are willing to bear the risks that might existed in this relationship.

From Fig. 2, it can be seen more clearly that consumers' trust to the suppliers is composed by two parts: trusting intentions and trusting beliefs. They are influenced by two main factors (Trust Building Levers and Institutional/Structural Factors). Their results will act on consumers' behavioral intentions. Due to the special characteristics of tourism groupbuying, consumers' trust to the suppliers is mainly based on the perceived vendor reputation and the perceived site quality. This is the significant difference between tourism group – buying and other e – Business activities. For example, if we are not satisfied with the goods bought from the Internet, we can return or exchange. But for tourism group – buying, it is impossible. We obtain the real feelings only when we begin the journey, or even until the end of the tourism activities. On the other hand, the price of tourism group – buying is lower than the usual market price and the online price, so the profit margins of travel suppliers, service providers and other businesses in the supply chain will get smaller. The consumer would be worried about whether this will affect the quality of tourism products, and whether the suppliers will cancel many of the original services. Channels for the consumers to investigate or monitor the suppliers are few. At this time, a good reputation of the suppliers and service providers and high quality websites will become the most important factors affecting the consumers' trust.

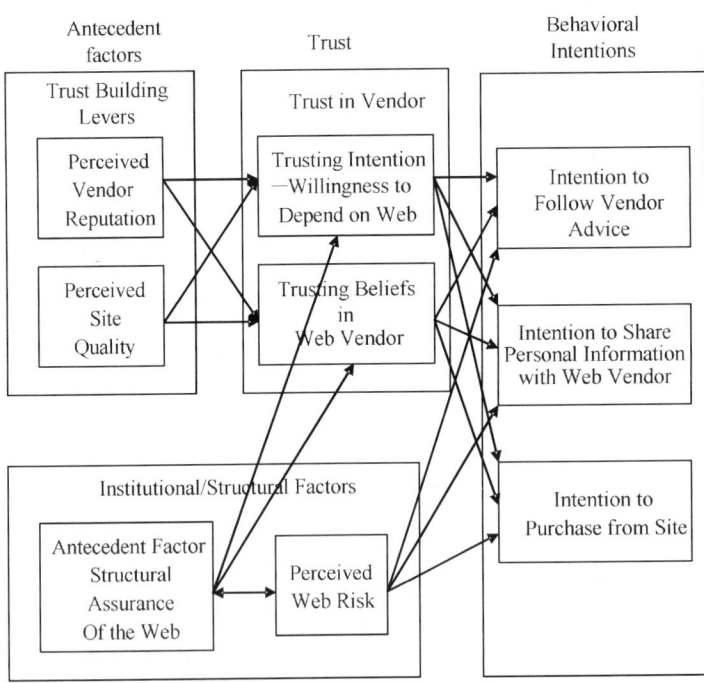

Fig. 2　TBM – Trust building model[6]

In addition, consumers' trust to the travel suppliers and service providers, as well as their perceived risk of online shopping will directly lead to their behavioral intentions, which includes intention to follow vendors advice, intention to share personal information with web vendors, intention to purchase from website.

IV WAYS TO BUILD CONSUMER TRUST IN TOURISM GROUPBUYING

Group – buying is a new development of the Internet in China in 2010, the number of group – buying websites increased rapidly. So it pushes the fast development of tourism groupbuying. But by 2011, its growth rate is gradually reduced due to various reasons. Among them, how to build consumer trust in the field is an important one. Here we studied from three aspects.

A. Consumer trust established before tourism group – buying

According to the latest statistical report of the China Internet Network Information Center, China's Internet groupbuying users reached 64.65 million by the end of 2011. The proportion reached 12.6%[1], in which mainly young netizens. The biggest characteristic of the young netizens is willing to try new things, but at the same time, their interest shifted rapidly. Therefore, those travel suppliers and service providers should pay special attention to the consumers' behavioral intentions, try their best to show appropriate elements so as to meet the needs of the tourism group – buying netizens, and prompt the netizens to establish their trust tendency and initial trust quickly.

In advertising and marketing fields, we had a very famous model called AIDA. AIDA stands for Attention, Interest, Desire and Action and attempts to explain the various stages through which a consumer passes before he or she makes a brand choice. Fig. 3 shows the model. It reflects the process of consumers from being drawn attention to produce action. This model was invented in 1898 by E. St. Elmo Lewis. We still use the AIDA model to understand consumer behavior today.

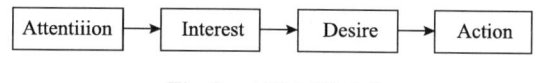

Fig. 3 AIDA Model

Later, in order to pay more attention to maintain the existing customers, Lewis and other scholars from marketing field optimized it to AIDAS. That is to add a key part of Satisfaction at the end of the model. So the model became:

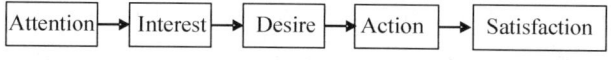

Fig. 4 AIDAS Model

This model reflects that the suppliers were not only care about the consumer consumption behavior, but also pay great attention about the feelings after the process. They hope the consumers were satisfied throughout the marketing process and got good experiences and good results, and thus caused their spending again in the future. At the same time, they want to produce a positive suggestion or impact on the consumers' friends and their family members, thus lead to more people's attention and more generation of consumer behavior.

However, only these models are not perfect. The author of this paper believes consumer trust is an important factor to make them taking action from Desire. This is the most critical part to avoid the loss of potential customers. In other words, it is also the most important step to convert click to purchase. For these reasons, the model can be further amended as Fig. 5.

Among the trust elements to tourism suppliers, brand is the core. In fact, the brand represents the credibility of the supplier. Good reputation will increase the attractiveness of the brand to tourism group – buying netizens, expand its influence and improve its profits. Conversely, if the supplier is fraudulent in the process of consumer consumption, its credibility will be affected, the brand will also be tarnished and the ultimate benefit of the company will be affected. The brand is a kind of accumulation, this accumulation often takes years. So, for tourism suppliers and service providers, if they want the tourism group – buying activities to be carried out smoothly and continually, they should always pay attention to maintaining the brand's reputation. At the same time, the suppliers should study consumers' behavioral characteristics, especially those young netizens, and then apply their research outcomes to the marketing process. In this way, the suppliers are able to make the consumers produce trust at the beginning of the business.

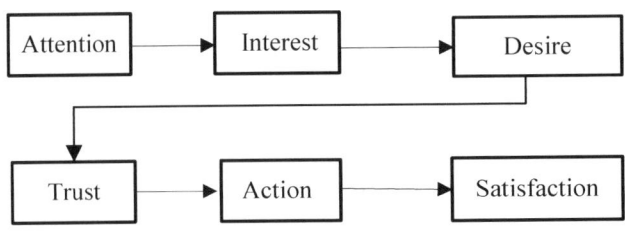

Fig. 5 AIDTAS Model

B. Consumer trust established in the process of tourism group – buying

This means the whole process of tourism consumption from registration, login, purchase, and experience until the end. In order to maintain consumer trust, the tourism suppliers and service providers should pay attention to establish a good security system which can guarantee the registration safety, the login safety, and online payment safety. Suppliers should pay particular attention to win more praise from the consumers by providing good products and services because of the reduction of profit margins, and make efforts to enhance consumer confidence by various means in this process. In this way, tourism vendors could attract more consumers, via small profits but quick turnover, they might have the maximization of profits.

C. Consumer trust established after tourism group – buying

Trust and distrust behavior exists only in asymmetric information environment full of risks and uncertainties. It is obvious that the uncertainties in the process of online transactions are much higher than the uncertainty of the traditional transaction. Online transactions for consumers may bring two risks: one is system dependent uncertainty; the other is transaction specific uncertainty. In order to help consumers to prevent the occurrence of these two risks, or in order to enhance consumers' confidence, reduce their fears and anxieties in the process of tourism group – buying, it is very important to establish consumer trust after their tourism group-buying.

In this field, the vendors have a lot of work to do. For example, they can make appropriate commitments that if the consumers' interests lose due to business reasons, the suppliers or the providers should bear the corresponding compensation. On the other hand, they should develop interaction platform such as forum, discussion board or community to let the consumers publish their opinions, views and comments, exchange and share their information and experiences, and promote the birth of new tourism group-buying products or organizations.

In addition, it is not required to provide appropriate logistics and distribution for products of tourism group – buying, the cost of this step could be saved. So the vendors should devote their contributes more on travel services and post – sale services so as to improve the quality of the services. For example, they should listen carefully to the feedback from consumers of tourism group – buying. If there does exist problems in the process of tourism group-buying, the vendor must compensate the consumers for the reasonable demands through a certain way. For those tourism group – buying customers who spend more than a certain limit, the vendors can upgrade them to be VIP customers, and provide them more preferential price. We even suggest that the vendors permit consumers to establish groups in accordance with their own wishes, and provide them better services and supports.

The purpose of all these should be done by vendors is to improve consumer trust. The merchants will get more opportunities and profits only when they are highly recognized.

V CONCLUSIONS

Group – buying is an emerging model of e – Business, tourism group – buying attracted more attention of many Internet users, especially young netizens due to the particularity of its products. Unlike B2C, C2C, B2B and other e – Business modes, the development trends of tourism group – buying tend to C2B or B2T (Business to Team). The consumers improve their bargaining abilities via organizations of group. This can meet young netizens' personalized demands greatly. However, consumer trust issues in tourism group – buying greatly affect the healthy development of this new industry. So, it is necessary to analyze the factors of trust affecting the behavior of tourism group – buying consumers, study the ways to build consumer trust so as to promote the sustained development of tourism group – buying.

Tourism group – buying based on the open network environment will weaken consumer trust basis because of its particularity. The presence of uncertainty or risk will also make it more difficult to build consumer confidence in the process of group – buying. In order to maintain the tourism group – buying activities being carried out smoothly and continuously, bring acquisition both for consumers and vendors, creating and maintaining trust between buyers and sellers will become the core factors of a successful e – Business form. For the suppliers, they should have the corresponding capacities, benevolences and integrities. For the commerce websites providing platforms for tourism group – buying, they should provide protection in technical capacity, system reliability, security of transactions, and create an easy and convenient environment for consumers to operate. In addition, in order to ensure the interests of both the consumers and the sellers, the effectiveness of a third – party certification will have a significant impact on consumers' trust.

REFERENCES

[1] China Internet Network Information Center. The 29th Statistical Report on Internet Development. [EB/OL]. http://www.cnnic.cn/en/index/index.htm.

[2] Jinying Li. Developments and Countermeasures of group – buying. Finance & Economy, 2007 (4): 22 – 23.

[3] Shuojia Guo. Research on Antecedents of Consumer Trust in B2C Electronic Commerce. Huazhong University of Science and Technology. 2006. 10.

[4] Mayer R C, Davis J H, Schoorman F D. An integration model of organizational trust. The Academy of Management Review, 1995, 20 (3): 709 – 734.

[5] Corritore C L, Kracher B, Wiedenbeck S. On – line trust: concepts, evolving themes, a model. Int. J. Human – Computer Studies, 2003, 58: 737 – 758.

[6] D. Harrison McKnight et al. The impact of initial consumer trust on intentions to transact with a web site: a trust building model. Journal of Strategic Information Systems 2002, 11: 297 – 323.

云数字档案馆安全运营管理机制研究

——以区域性档案局（馆）为承建方为例

徐 华 薛四新 刘宗渊

1 引 言

云数字档案馆即是基于云计算技术构建的数字档案馆系统，是面向档案形成机构（立档单位）、档案管理机构、档案利用者（包括机构和社会公众）等提供档案数字资源采集、整理、编目、管理、保存和利用服务的行业云。云数字档案馆的落地和推广，安全运营机制是保证。但是，不同的档案云建设主体，其运营机理不同，安全机制也不相同。基于我国的国情，本文以区域性档案行业主管机构即档案局（馆）作为档案云建设责任者为例，考虑云特点，研究其安全责任主体、安全组织体系、安全制度、安全岗位设置、安全角色职责和安全保障体系等，为后续的档案云实践提供借鉴。

2 云数字档案馆安全界定

"安全是一个系统保护信息和系统资源真实性、机密性、完整性的能力，是理解、管理、控制和缓解机构关键性资产所面临的风险。"[1]云数字档案馆架构包括 SaaS、PaaS 和 IaaS 三个服务层级，分别提供"软件即服务""平台即服务""硬件即服务"。完整意义上的云数字档案馆，可以给不同用户提供不同层级的服务。

区域性云数字档案馆是面向其直属和下属机构搭建的，从事档案资源采集、档案业务管理、档案信息长期保存、档案资源利用的信息系统，通常覆盖一定的区域范围。数字档案馆中最重要的关键性资产是海量的档案数字资源，它保存着时代的记忆，反映社会的历史，能快速敏捷地通过网络被利用，通过数据挖掘和知识管理，给人类提供行动决策的依据。因此云数字档案馆中要保护的是档案数字资源、档案管理系统以及软硬件基础设施的安全，最终目标是通过建立安全的软硬件基础设施运行环境和系统以保障档案数字资源的安全。档案数字资源安全性要素主要包括[2]：

（1）机密性：防止未授权泄露敏感信息，包括有意或无意的行为。

（2）完整性：包括内容完整性和数量完整性。内容完整性是指只有得到允许的人才能够修改数据，并且能够判别出数据是否已被篡改。数量完整性是指保存在数据中心的电子档案的数量不变，不会发生丢失等现象。

（3）可用性：得到授权的用户能够及时地、不受干扰地访问网络和档案数据，使用系统信息。

（4）可控性：可以控制授权范围内的信息流向以及行为方式。

（5）可审查性：对出现的安全问题可提供调查的依据和手段。

考虑档案数字资源对硬软件资源的依附性，云数字档案馆安全侧重在硬件安全、网络安全、虚拟化安全、应用安全、多租户安全、分布式系统安全、档案数据安全、用户安全、安全管理等方面。

3 云数字档案馆安全与传统 IT 安全的异同

云数字档案馆存在的安全威胁主要包括信息泄露，非授权访问、使用、篡改和破坏，系统漏洞，恶意内部用户、恶意外部攻击，抵赖行为，物理故障，网络病毒等。传统的安全技术包括密码技术、认

[基金项目] 文章系北京市科技计划课题"基于异构系统的电子档案凭证性保障核心技术开发与应用"（编号：Z111100075011001）的阶段性成果。

[作者简介] 徐华，北京联合大学应用文理学院；薛四新，清华大学档案馆；刘宗渊，北京市档案局。

证、授权和审计技术、监控技术、恶意代码检测与防范技术、防火墙技术、虚拟专网技术、入侵检测技术、网络脆弱性检测、安全接入技术、安全隔离与交换技术、垃圾邮件防范与处理技术、应急响应技术等，将仍然会继续应用在云数字档案馆本身的安全管理和安全保障领域[3]。

但是，考虑云数字档案馆的资源共享性，集中部署特点及其采用虚拟化技术、分布式技术、多租户技术的特点，其安全的特征主要呈现于：

（1）安全隐患大。云数字档案馆内部系统无边界、流动性大、IT资源、信息资源、用户数据、用户应用的高度集中，带来的安全隐患比传统IT模式大。

（2）保护力度巨变。采用虚拟技术，将一个物理机虚拟出无数虚拟机的方法，使物理机安全保护转向虚拟机的管理和控制。这种物理计算资源共享带来的虚拟机安全包括虚拟机监督程序的安全和虚拟机镜像安全。需要检测虚拟镜像中恶意软件、盗版软件。多租户环境下，一台物理机运行多台虚拟机同时为多用户服务，虚拟机的非完全独立性，恶意用户可攻击其他用户，避免与竞争对手共享物理机是防范旁通道攻击的理想方法。

（3）保密强度不同。数据拥有者与数据的物理存储地相分离，会带来用户隐私安全隐患。传统的解决方法是对数据预先加密。但如果用户对数据预加密，云计算中心就无法对密文做任何有意义的计算，无法为用户提供云存储以外的任何云计算服务。完全同态加密（云端在密文上的操作直接对应明文上的相应操作）提供了新的技术途径。另外支持检索的加密使高安全敏感度的用户可以有效地对存储在云端的加密数据进行管理。

（4）法律风险大。未来云数字档案馆的信息流动性大，信息服务或用户数据可能分布在不同地区甚至不同国家，在政府信息安全监管和管理等方面可能存在法律差异与纠纷；同时由于虚拟化等技术引起的用户间物理界限模糊而可能导致的司法取证问题也不容忽视。

（5）信任机制建立需待时日。云数字档案馆的承建方是行业性档案主管机构，面向所管辖的立档单位用户，宏观层面上公信力是足够的。但是不同的立档单位的文件在归档前需要安全隔离，自身档案的安全存放以及容灾备份，个人存档和其他不存在隶属关系的社会机构存档，信任机制建立有一个过程。需要有法律规范、服务水平协议（SLA）等社会手段和技术手段来提高其信任度。

（6）安全即服务（SecaaS）可提供更大范围的安全保障。云数字档案馆提供的SecaaS在反病毒、防火墙、安全监测和数据安全等领域具有传统IT安全保护不可比拟的优越性，实现了安全服务功能集中化和规模化。

因此，云数字档案馆安全的策略、管理、技术手段在沿用传统IT安全的基础上，需要有创新性的发展。

4 云数字档案馆的安全责任主体

从我国国情考虑，目前数字档案馆的建设基本是区域性档案行业主管机构〔档案局（馆）〕为主体承建方，建设中可以根据其综合能力（包括人力、物力、财力和持续运维能力）来组合使用云计算的任意两个或三个层级的服务模式。由于档案行业档案信息化人才不足、档案管理软件使用普及有待推进、档案数据安全有特殊要求，云数字档案馆的建设通常也是分层次进行，重点在SaaS层（面向立档单位和档案管理业务人员提供应用软件服务），IaaS和PaaS仅提供支撑该SaaS层运行所必需的硬软件和环境支持，暂不向档案用户提供该两层租用服务。

考虑档案局（馆）承担云数字档案馆的建设，因而档案局（馆）既是云服务提供商又是应用提供商，其身份可以认定为档案云服务集成商。安全责任主体见图1。

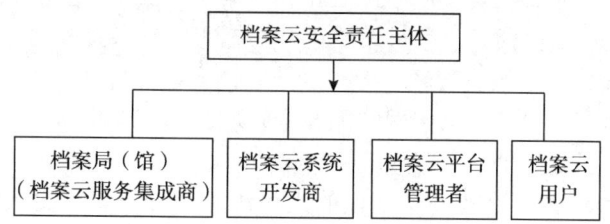

图1 档案云安全责任主体

（1）档案局（馆）：档案云建设的投资方、管理者、使用者、档案云服务集成商。负责制定适合本行业的安全战略、安全规划、法律遵从、合规性审计流程，完成风险评估、价值和成本分析，安全需求分析，用户规模和档案数字信息资源总量和存量分析，形成安全组织管理体系，明确人员分工和职责权限，制定安全规章制度，动态评估反馈，不断持续改进来确保云数字档案馆的安全运营。

（2）档案云系统开发商：档案云建设的具体实施者。在充分理解档案行业主管机构的安全战略和需求后，设计云安全架构，选择安全的软硬件资源以及安全核心技术，制定档案业务战略、业务支撑、运营支撑、管理支撑流程及具体步骤和操作，集成建设档案云平台。

（3）档案云平台管理者：可以是档案局（馆）内设人员，也可以委托第三方进行。完成对应档案云管理平台的业务支撑服务（BSS）、运维支撑服务（OSS）、管理支撑服务（MSS）。管理者可分为应用管理员、平台管理员、运维管理员，分别管理档案云业务、档案用户订阅和配置、个性化定制、SLA 管理、用户行为分析统计、软硬件资源监控、档案云安全运行等事务，及时处理安全漏洞和隐患，动态反映档案用户的健康运行状态。

（4）档案云用户：档案云的终端用户。有不同级别的档案馆、不同立档单位的档案室和档案检索利用者。终端用户的安全意识、主机安全、身份认证和访问控制的密码安全都直接影响到档案云的安全。

5　云数字档案馆安全组织框架设计

针对我国的档案行政管理体制，区域性的档案局（馆）是云数字档案馆的投资方和管理者。面对局（馆）合一、全员实施、在不改变当前局（馆）部门设置的情况，云数字档案馆的安全组织框架可以建设如图 2 所示。

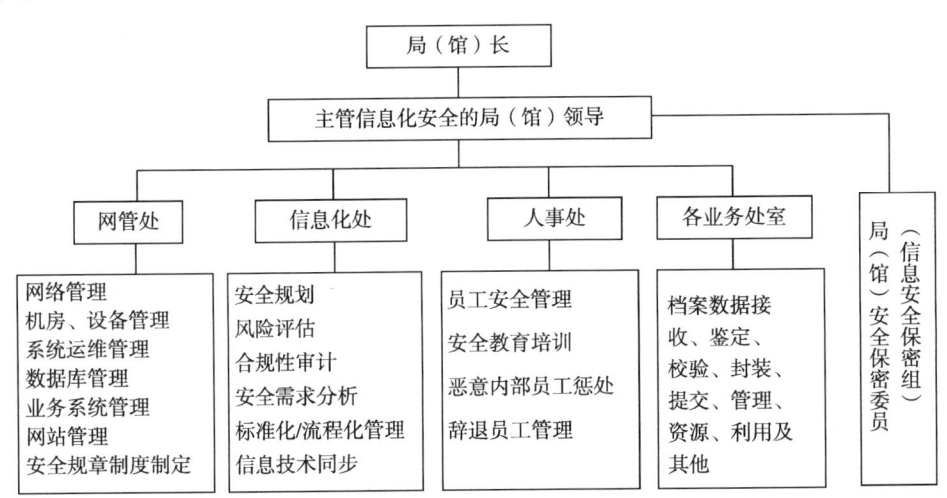

图 2　以档案局（馆）为承建方的云数字档案馆安全组织框架

本着"领导集中统一、机构设置协调、职责分工明确、联系渠道畅通"的原则，主管机要与信息安全的局（馆）领导是云数字档案馆安全的第一责任人，成立安全保密委员会，下设信息安全保密组，各处、室部门领导是该组成员，肩负安全职责。拆分上述安全责任主体的任务，下设安全岗，可由兼职人员承担。一旦出现云数字档案馆安全问题，信息安全保密组能迅速聚合，第一时间里反馈、协调、处理，恢复档案云的正常运行。

（1）信息化处安全职能：在安全保密委员会的领导下，负责牵头策划信息化安全战略、安全规划、法律遵从、合规性审计流程，完成风险评估、价值和成本分析，安全需求分析，用户规模和档案数字资源总量和存量分析等。动态评估反馈，不断持续改进，实施安全一票否决制。

（2）网管处安全职能：作为运维管理者，牵头云数字档案馆交付使用后的安全运行。包括网络、机房、设备、运维系统、数据库、业务系统、网站等安全管理，制定安全规章制度。是安全管理实施的执行部门。作为牵头方，也可以委托第三方完成。

（3）人事处安全职能：负责对涉及安全岗位的人员配备、辞退员工处理、恶意内部员工防范和惩处、安全教育培训等。

（4）各业务处室安全职能：按照云数字档案馆的业务管理流程，分别负责对应立档单位提交的档案数字资源安全接收、鉴定、校验、封装、提交。是档案数字资源在不同阶段的安全责任人。操作中要确保自身本机安全，密码管理，权限控制，识别档案在流转中不同阶段上下游部门人员的身份等。

（5）不同的档案云建设主体，可根据自己的建制情况，或在网管处或在信息化处统一或分别设置应用管理员和平台管理员，完成系统配置、用户管理、SLA 管理、容量管理、收费管理、统计分析等任务。

6 云数字档案馆安全运营制度设计

健全的规章制度和规范的操作流程是云数字档案馆安全运行的保证。区域性档案行业主管机构承建的档案云在提供服务时，要根据自身平台建设、机构建制以及人员情况制定相关标准规范。

（1）档案云安全体系结构设计规范：包括认证授权、访问控制、保密性、完整性、不可抵赖性、业务流程、技术规范、人和组织管理、安全体系结构文档、安全和隐私原则、法律和标准遵从等。

（2）档案云安全组织和程序章程：包括安全治理战略、安全组织机构、安全管理范围、安全职责权限等。

（3）档案云风险管理制度：包括风险分析、风险识别、风险评估、风险控制、评估文档等。

（4）档案云运维管理制度：包括管理目标、管理的参与对象、服务生命周期管理、服务动态伸缩、灵活的定价策略、信息安全管理、安全特征优先级、审计流程等。

（5）档案云数据安全管理：包括数据封装、数据传输、数据存储、数据隔离、数据隐私、数据残留处理等。

（6）档案云虚拟化管理制度：包括服务器虚拟化、软件虚拟化、网络虚拟化、存储虚拟化、文件虚拟化、虚拟机管理等策略和实施。

（7）档案云用户管理制度：包括用户身份认证、权限划分、密钥管理、安全行为控制、统计分析、许可证与计费等。

（8）档案用户服务水平（SLA）管理制度：包括不同用户享用的服务水平、技术水平。如系统响应时间、错误解决时间、虚拟机和存储空间使用数目、软件应用平台类型、服务时间、用户安全优先级等。

（9）档案云多租户安全管理制度：包括多租户数据存储模式、元数据开发模式、租户间安全隔离等。

（10）档案云安全应急响应制度：包括应急流程、安全优先级、阻断隔离、灾后恢复等。

（11）档案云安全管理培训制度：包括入职安全教育、安全知识考核、现场体验、预演、不同安全岗的定期教育等。

除上述基于档案云特点的制度规范外，传统的 IT 安全管理制度仍然有效，如：人员安全管理规范、机房及物理设备管理规范、操作安全管理规范、电子废弃物处置办法、计算机及相关设备管理办法、信息网络安全保密管理规定、计算机及移动存储设备安全保密管理规定、计算机房安全保密管理规定、电子邮箱使用安全保密管理规定等。

7 云数字档案馆安全角色分工

从云数字档案馆的安全责任主体分析看，档案云系统开发商在完成设计、开发、测试工作，交付给档案局（馆）运行使用后，承担的是后续硬件或软件基础维护工作，档案云的日常运营管理权在档案局（馆）。从目前情况看，数字档案馆与实体档案馆将在较长时间内共存，档案业务管理应该在档案局（馆），运营和维护可以部分委托第三方进行。因此在不改变建制的情况下，可以设置安全角色进行管理。

7.1 局（馆）安全保密委员会（下设信息安全保密组）

由主管保密工作的局领导、主管信息化工作的局领导以及各部门负责人组成。指导全局（馆）的安全工作，审查云数字档案馆安全策略以及有关的安全原则和规章制度，监督其实施，定期检查并评价档案云安全情况，分析解决安全问题，督促持续改进。

7.2 硬件（IaaS）安全岗（可分类设多人协同完成）

负责物理安全、网络安全和服务连续性。物理安全包括环境安全管理（制定温度、湿度、静电防尘等一系列安全要素的参数指标体系）、设备自身的安全管理（选型、安装、登记、使用和维修管理等）。机房管理，自动化监控。设置最小特权机制，限定仅授权人员才能管理客户应用程序和服务；网络安全包括网络边际设置防火墙、入侵检测和防护系统；服务连续性指24小时提供SLA协议范围内稳定服务。

7.3 平台（PaaS）安全岗（可分类设多人协同完成）

操作系统、支撑软件环境、应用软件、虚拟软件的安全维护。可设应用管理员、平台管理员，对软件资源监控安全管理。

7.4 应用（SaaS）安全岗（可设多人协同完成）

设应用管理员对档案管理应用软件的安全运营管理，各业务处室安全员负责自身提交数据的安全。

7.5 档案用户管理岗

鉴于目前建设的档案云主要侧重在SaaS服务，安全管理主要体现在用户认证与访问控制、权限管理、用户安全底线行为监控、SLA协议管理与监督、用户行为统计等。

8 云数字档案馆安全保障体系建设

云数字档案馆的技术安全应该是由预防、保护、检测、监控、应急处理而形成的闭环控制系统。在安全体系结构设计时，既要考虑云计算所要遵从的法律法规和标准，又要考虑认证授权、访问控制、保密性、完整性、不可抵赖性、安全管理等要素。因此其安全运营保障体系应包括防御系统、监控系统、容灾备份系统、应急响应系统和技术支撑系统，通过安全法规体系、安全组织体系、安全管理制度体系、安全人员培养和培训体系来保证。

防御内容包括入侵检测、多重防火墙、主动审计、虚拟专网、加密、访问控制等；监控内容包括负载均衡、网络流量分析、虚拟机资源使用、物理机运行状况、机房、病毒等；容灾备份内容有数据冗余设置、异地备份、热备和磁带机多重备份等措施；应急响应内容包括不同资产安全优先级处理、最优原则的危险隔离和阻断、快速响应机制、灾难恢复等；技术资源涉及云安全的核心技术使用。

云数字档案馆的安全运营涉及技术、管理、法规制度等内容。宏观层面上，要充分考虑云计算必须遵从的安全类法律法规和标准；中观层面要规划安全战略、安全组织体系、安全制度体系、安全管理体系、安全人员培训体系、安全运营流程设计等；微观层面要对安全岗位人员分工、职责权限、工作流程、沟通协调、安全教育内容制定、安全审查、安全评价以及持续改进制定可操作性的程序文件，才能确保云数字档案馆的运营安全。

参考文献

[1]（美）Eric Cole. 网络安全宝典（第2版）[M]. 曹继军译. 北京：清华大学出版社，2010.
[2] 同[1]。
[3] 李德毅主编. 云计算技术发展报告[M]. 北京：科学出版社，2012.
[4] 虚拟化与云计算小组. 云计算宝典技术与实践[M]. 北京：电子工业出版社，2011.
[5] 虚拟化与云计算小组. 云计算实践之道——战略蓝图与技术架构[M]. 北京：电子工业出版社，2011.

"金蝉"不再"脱壳"
——论营业转让中债权人的利益保护

郭娅丽

1 问题缘起：营业转让中债务人"金蝉脱壳"现象频发

营业转让的商事实践在我国早已存在，司法实践中亦有成案。特别是在国企改制过程中，通过营业转让逃废、悬空债务的行为大量出现。据统计，人民法院受理的各类经济纠纷案件中，因企业改制而引发的债务纠纷案件占此类案件的近70%，并有逐渐上升趋势。[1]具体表现为：（1）剥离优质资产设立新公司，不承担或少承担原企业的债务；（2）将企业的资产转移给其他主体，实行部分公司制改造，原企业仍然存在但无力清偿债务或宣告破产；（3）将财产全部转移给股东，股东将这些财产用于设立新公司、导致债权落空[2]；（4）将企业的资产转移给其他主体，注销该企业等，这些行为的实质就是使"金蝉脱壳"之计，侵害债权人的利益。最高法院对此作出了司法解释，但由于法官对其法理基础理解歧义，导致司法实践中类似案件审理结果差异较大而带来了诸多迷乱。根据任何人不得从违法行为中获利的法律公理性原则，认真审视相关司法解释，探寻"金蝉"不再"脱壳"的制度措施，从而遏止营业转让中严重损害债权人利益的行为，是本文的主旨所在。

2 本源探寻：营业转让中债权人利益保护的深层原因

2.1 现代经济组织中债权的优越地位是债权人利益保护的经济根源

法学家拉德布鲁赫在其著作《法学导论》中指出："社会生产关系完全以所有权为中心的中世纪的社会形式是静态的，今天资本主义法律形式已完全变为动态的，债权表现的权力欲及利息欲，在今天都是经济目的。债权已不是取得物权和物的利用的手段，它本身就是法律生活的目的。经济价值不是暂时静止地存在于物权，而是从一个债权向另一个债权不停地移动。"[3]的确，现代社会商品经济高度发达，经济形态由"相对静止"向"频繁交易"变化，社会经济组织的存在依靠各种各样的债权关系得以维持，交易链条上的任一环节断裂，均可能导致整个交易链条的断裂，立法对债权人的利益保护正缘于"债权在近代法中占优越地位"。

2.2 现代经济组织中债权人的弱势地位是债权人利益保护的制度根源

与债权的优越地位相对，债权人在营业转让中则处于弱势地位，这是因为：营业转让作为重大交易行为属股东大会决议事项，股东是公司"内部人"，可以透过股东大会这一会议体机构投票表决对营业转让同意与否。而公司债权人通常被认为是公司的"外部人"，当公司就营业转让形成决议时，一般无须债权人参与决策，或履行通知程序，或征得债权人同意，即使债权人不同意并不影响营业转让的效力，因此，通常说，债权人事实上被剥夺了参与营业转让的决策权；而债权人与股东不同的投资风险倾向进一步加剧了其不利地位，与公司通过契约安排次级债权的债权人、未来债权人（侵权债权人）母子公司中的子公司的债权人[4]等则承担着更大的风险。现代公司法理论充分关注到这一点，认为公司在追求股东利益最大化的同时，应该兼顾其他利害相关者的利益：债权人对公司的专用性投资有其正当性基础，该种利益诉求应得到满足。如果说保护股东利益是对交易效率的追求，那么保护债权人利益则是对交易安全的尊重和满足。可见，现代经济组织中债权人的弱势地位是债权人利益保护的制度根源。

[基金项目] 北京联合大学北京市级重点建设学科"经济法学"建设科研项目（LDJJF013）的阶段性成果。
[作者简介] 郭娅丽（1969—），女，北京联合大学商务学院副教授，法学博士，研究方向：商法、经济法。

3 法理追问：营业转让中债务承担规则的诸多迷乱

营业转让本质上是一种合同，对于前述严重侵害债权人利益的行为，依据当时的法律[1]，从理论上说，可以保护自己的债权免受侵害。但是：第一，《合同法》赋予债权人的撤销权难以真正得到贯彻实施。债权人在整个改制活动中属于外部人，改制企业是否应通知债权人，在改制的相关文件中并不明确；且债权人要证明价格不合理，由于企业的个体差异较大，对企业整体价值的衡量很难有合适的参照，聘请专业机构重新评估需要改制企业的配合，且成本高昂，事实上不具有可操作性。第二，《企业破产法》（试行）提供的解决方案无法实现。该法规定的撤销权只能由清算组向法院申请追回财产，债权人不能行使该项权利。正是基于上述背景下，最高人民法院推出了《关于审理与企业改制相关民事纠纷案件若干问题的规定》（以下简称《企业改制规定》）及一系列相关文件。然而，由于法官对这些文件中的具体规定理解歧义，不但未从根本上解决债权人保护问题，却引发了更多的争议，产生了如下质疑。

3.1 营业转让中的现时债权人——"债随物走"的意外礼物？

《企业改制规定》着眼于保护现时债权人的利益，第6、7条规定要求"新设公司在所接收的财产范围内与原企业承担连带民事责任"，权威人士将其归纳为"债务随财产变动原则"[5]。该原则属于企业法人财产原则派生出来的两个原则之一，归纳其核心意思如下：企业法人的财产是企业对外承担债务的一般担保，债务人的财产处分行为减少了自己的法人财产，降低了清偿能力，所以，接收财产的企业应该在接收财产范围内对原企业债务承担连带责任[6]。仔细分析该种债务承担规则，至少有以下几点质疑。

（1）对"债随物走"的法律性质认定不清

对该类资产转移的法律性质认定存在较大分歧，大致有三种观点：①"企业分立说"[7]；②"转投资说"[5]；③"合并分立说"[8]。

笔者认为，上述观点均有存疑之处，这是因为：

"企业分立说"不能成立。企业分立有不同的情形[9]，要经过严格的分立程序暂且不论，公司分立是在原有公司的基础上"一分为二"或"一分为多"，分立的结果是产生新的独立的企业法人组织[10]。而部分改制转让给既存公司的两种情形并不产生新的企业法人组织。至于先派生分立再与其他股东联合设立新公司的情形，显然不能简单归为企业分立。

"转投资说"不能成立。我国台湾学者武忆舟先生对转投资有一个经典定义："所谓'转投资'，应以章程有明文规定，照必须长期经营为目的之投资，并经认股手续缴纳股款者而言。其一时收买股票等理财目的之不包括在内。"[11]转投资是公司作为投资主体，以公司法人财产作为出资而成为另一公司的股东，从而形成母子公司、相互持股公司，形成稳固的企业集团的手段。转投资可以现金、实物、无形财产等单一财产作为出资形式，也可以集合体的营业作为出资形式，出资人获得股权。《企业改制规定》中的资产转移行为与转投资的后种出资方式的确相同，但性质迥异：转投资行为中，当营业整体转移给新的受让人时，转让人获得公司的股权，转让人和受让人之间成为股东与公司的产权联结关系；而《企业改制规定》中转让人将营业财产转让于受让人后，转让人和受让人之间不能有任何产权联结关系。故定性为转投资不能成立。

"合并分立说"也不能成立。该观点所称的"合并分立"说称为"分立合并"说也许更为恰当，因为该类资产转移是先从一公司中分离部分财产，然后移转至另一个或几个既存公司；或者两个或数个公司先将其部分财产分离出来，而以各个公司的其他部分财产共同设立一个或几个新公司的形态等，是分立在先，合并在后。但是，如果称为分立、合并，那么依照《公司法》规定要求履行分立程序、合并程序，无论存续分立，还是派生分立，应有新公司的产生，合并也应是不同独立主体的按照法律和合同规定的条件和程序组成一个公司的行为，而上述五类行为主要是资产转移的行为，具体说是部分或全部财产由一个主体转移至另一个主体的行为，不是主体之间的分立和合并行为。

综上，对于该类资产转移行为，实质是不同主体之间的买卖行为，但其标的具有特殊性，为具有有

---

[1] 参见《合同法》第74条和《企业破产法》（试行）第35条。

机性的统一整体，该项资产的转移不会带来企业组织结构的变化，一般伴随着债权债务关系的清理、劳动关系是否承继等问题，该资产转移行为的实质是营业转让。

(2)"债随物走"原则混淆了债的担保和债的保全制度

最高法院《企业改制规定》所确立的"债随物走"原则，要求新设公司以所接收的财产对原企业的债权人承担责任，混淆了债的担保和债的保全制度。学者敏锐地指出："债务随企业财产变动原则"扩充第三人为求偿对象范围，将对债权人的一般担保变为具有物权性质、对物可追索的优先受偿的特别担保[12]，"实际上创设了一种超级担保权益——既具有扩展债务人范围的人保性质，又具有追及变动财产的担保优先性"[13]，违背了债的担保和债的保全基本法理。具体来说：

①转让人将财产转移给受让人后，该财产成为受让人财产的组成部分，受让人以其全部财产对原企业的债权人提供的是一般担保，而非特别担保。而条文中所说的"以所接收的财产"承担责任，恰恰是对"向新设公司主张债权的债权人"提供了特别担保，享有优先于其他债权人的受偿权。但是，按照特别担保的原理，以及我国《担保法》和《物权法》的规定，特别担保必须履行担保物登记手续或占有担保物才能生效，或取得对抗第三人的效力。该条文并未指出须履行公示程序却取得了对抗其他债权人的效力，显然难以自圆其说。

②"债随物走"原则不能解决第6、7条所指出的逃废债务问题，该问题应由债的保全制度解决。《企业改制规定》第6条规定的"企业同时转移财产和债务"的情况解决的是优惠性清偿问题：因部分改制导致的移转到新设公司的债权人，与留在原来企业的无担保债权人之间的不公平受偿，其适用的前提是无力清偿债务；否则，就会出现实践中判断"合法投资"与"逃废债务"的困扰[12]。殊不知，病症并不在于"以企业实物出资是否构成剥离资产"，或者"原企业转移财产后是否取得相应股权"，而在于这种转移是否害及债权。对于部分财产的转让未获得相应对价或虽然获得对价，但因转让导致原企业无力清偿债务，害及债权实现，则债权人享有撤销权，可由破产管理人请求法院予以撤销来解决，追回财产复归于原债务人，由全体债权人按照法定顺序集体受偿，并非对最先主张债权的人优先清偿该种行为，这正是新《企业破产法》第32条的规定。《企业改制规定》第7条的适用范围为只转移资产不转移负债的情况，指债务人借改制之名、恶意逃债的违法行为，实质是欺诈行为。而对欺诈行为的认定，主观因素的衡量是首要考虑的问题，但该条并未涉及，我国《破产法》对于欺诈行为有规定，管理人可行使撤销权保护债权人的利益，但立法仅仅列举几种行为，未对欺诈的客观外在表现作出认定，且限于企业已经进入破产申请阶段，对于遏止逃废债务行为的作用实在有限。

③"债随物走"原则歪曲了连带责任的基本法理

最高人民法院《企业改制规定》所确立的"债随物走"原则，在第6条、7条要求新设公司与原企业承担连带责任，值得肯定。但是令人困惑的是，第24条、25条、26条却只要求受让方承担责任，可见关于连带责任的规定并未贯彻到底。并且，连带责任的承担规则是：新设公司与原企业任何一方应就债务负有全部清偿责任，至于各自应承担的份额，即新设公司（或原公司）对债权人承担全部清偿责任之后的追偿份额，只是连带责任人的内部责任而已。"新设公司所在接收财产范围内"与原公司承担连带责任，歪曲了连带责任的基本法理。况且，"新设公司所接收财产范围"如何认定也颇为棘手，如原企业转让资产后获得对新设公司的股权价值如何认定、资产和负债同时转移的场合负债能否从该转移价格中扣除等。倘若以转让的价格为依据，二者往往以较低的价格成交（这一点在我国现阶段评估体制和信用机制未很好建立起来之前很容易做到），则正好中了恶意串通的双方当事人的圈套。由此看来，"债随物走"原则并非现时债权人的意外礼物，而是在人格延续前提下完璧归赵的结果。

3.2 营业转让中的未来债权人——置之不理的权宜之策？

从我国目前立法来看，营业转让中债权人的保护主要关注的是现时债权人，未来债权人还未进入立法者的视野。当转让人在转让营业后，使用该转让人产品的消费者在若干年后可能受到侵害，该转让人在经营期间产生的环境污染可能在若干年后得以显现等，类似问题可能更多地涉及产品责任、环境侵权责任等问题，因此而产生的未来债权人如何得到法律救济，在我国《产品质量法》《消费者权益保护法》

以及有关环境保护的法律法规中尚未规定，在《中华人民共和国侵权责任法草案专家建议稿》❶，以及2008年12月《侵权责任法草案》审议稿❷中未提及，在2009年12月26日全国人大常委会第十二次会议通过的《侵权责任法》第五章"产品责任"（第41～47条）中并未规定。

4 他山之石：营业转让中债权人利益保护制度的梳理

4.1 制定法对营业转让中债权人的保护制度

4.1.1 债权人知情权的保护

基于债权人的利益保护，民法中规定债权让与时要求履行"通知"义务、债务承担时要求取得债务人的"同意"，而在商法中，公告是公司向众多特定的债权人和债务人发出意思表示最主要的法定方式。这是因为：首先，公告是转让人和受让人最有效率的选择。"公司是一系列契约的联结"，无数个债权债务关系维系公司的运营，尽管每个债权债务关系中债权人、债务人均为特定，但当公司（特别是股份公司）作出营业转让的决议时，有特定的商业时机，如果要求公司与之通过个别通知、逐一地与之达成一致意思表示，由于各个债权人债务人人数众多，各自所处的位置、具体的变动情况复杂，公司与债权人之间不像股东会议有定期会议和临时会议召开一样，一般并没有固定的时间商定债权债务的履行，无须定期向债权人债务人公布其经营决策等，所以需要耗费较长的时间，那样恐怕已经贻误最佳的时机。第二，营业转让对多数债权人债权的实现不会造成影响或影响甚微。如公司的债权人（债务人）人数众多，其中大多数债权人债权数额较小如公司债券持有人，而这部分债权人可能占据较大比例，公司营业转让对他们的债权利益实现影响不大。第三，债权人以异议或沉默作出意思表示以维护他们的利益是最经济的选择。公司营业转让时，从维护债权人利益考虑，通过公告程序，给予他们作出意思表示的权利，在规定期限内，只要提出异议，且异议成立，那么应对债权人提供担保；如果公告期满，未提出异议，或虽有异议但不成立，则可以合理推定，公司与债权人之间达成债权转让或与债务人之间达成债务移转的合意。

这方面法国的公示制度颇具特色，商事营业资产的出卖建立了两个层次的公示制度：一为地方性的公示制度，要求买受人在买卖合同签字之日起的15日内，在商事营业资产被经营的行政区或省内具有刊登法律公告的报刊上，公示商事营业资产买卖合同，目的在于对本地的第三人予以公告；二为全国性的公示制度，在第一种报刊公示进行之日起15日内在《民商事公告之官方公报》上进行。为了确保所有商事营业资产买卖均遵循公示原则，规定了公示的效力：当买受人履行公示义务后，出卖人的债权人即享有反对权（异议权）和竞价权；如买受人不履行公示义务，并不影响买卖合同的效力，但买受人不得将价款支付给出卖人；否则，买受人仍然要对出卖人的债权人承担支付价款的义务，通过对支付价款的限制来约束转让人和受让人，防止他们恶意串通，保护转让人的债权人[14]。

4.1.2 债权人撤销权的保护制度

对诈害债权人进行法律保护，各国立法中均有撤销权制度的规定，最有代表性的当属美国《统一欺诈性产权转让法》，主要内容有：第一，欺诈性产权转让的表现形式有两种：事实欺诈（纯粹欺诈）和推定欺诈。所谓事实欺诈，是指债务人有妨碍、延误、欺诈目前和将来债权人实际意图而从事的转让行为；所谓推定欺诈，是指从行为的客观特征及结果来分析，无须考虑行为人的主观意图，只要具有诈害债权人的事实，就推定为欺诈[15]。第二，为了增加司法操作上的可行性，法院总结出11个"欺诈标识"，从目的要素、时间要素、对价要素来审查是否为欺诈行为，并规定了例外情形。在此基础上，作为兜底要素，赋予法官自由裁量权，只要法官内心确信转让行为具有欺诈即可作出宣判，即使根据其他三个要素审查确定并非欺诈也不例外。第三，对受到欺诈性产权转让损害的债权人的救济方法，因到期债权和未到期债权而不同。当债权到期时，他可以针对任何购买者或从该购买交易中直接或间接得利的人向法院提出：（1）取消该项产权转让或废止义务，直至能使其债权得到清偿。（2）产权转让无效，对

---

❶ 参见杨立新：《中华人民共和国侵权责任法草案专家建议稿》第101～110条，第117～121条。资料来源：http://gxh.fyfz.cn/blog/gxh/index.aspx?blogid=278579. 2009年4月25日访问。

❷ 参见2008年12月22日《侵权责任法草案》审议稿第39～45条，第67～71条。资料来源：http://www.pei chang.cn/2860w.html. 2009年4月26日访问。

被转让财产实行强制执行❶。对未到期的债权，法院可以对被他起诉的人采取以下措施：（1）防止被告处分其财产。（2）派一个清算人去保管财产。（3）取消产权转让或废止义务。（4）视案件情形发展的要求作出任何命令❷。第（4）被认为是一个开放性的规定，赋予了法院最大限度的自由裁量权，能够及时采用恰当的方式来保全债权，是对债权人利益予以充分保护的有效措施。

4.1.3 根据外观主义法理保护债权人利益

外观主义法理，是指交易行为的效果以当事人行为的外观为标准，即公示于外表的事实，即使与真实的情况不符合，亦应确认外表事实所产生的法律效果，以维护交易安全。在商号转让引起营业转让的情形下，商号作为企业对外活动的标志，相对人基于对商号的信赖所作出的行为应得到法律的尊重和维护。如德国、韩国、日本等商法典均规定：营业受让人继续使用转让人的商号时，对于转让人因营业而产生的债务，受让人亦负清偿责任。即以继续使用商号为条件，受让人加入到转让人和对原营业上的债权人之间的债务关系中来，与转让人共同对原营业债权人负清偿责任。但是，恶意债权人应排除在外，立法亦持肯定态度，如《日本商法典》第 27 条有此规定。

4.1.4 连带责任制度保护债权人利益

"如果制度规定具有信息优势的人群同时必须对被监督对象的行为承担连带责任（风险），这部分人群也就获得了监督他人的激励和名义（权利）。就整个社会而言，这种基于信息优势的连带责任就是一种相对有效的制度安排。"[16] 营业转让中，双方当事人在缔结合同时会尽职调查对方的情况，是处于信息优势的一方；而转让人的债权人是处于信息弱势的一方，对于转让人和受让人之间进行的营业转让未必知悉，对作为担保债权的责任财产的变化难以真正把握其实情，对减少责任财产的真正的责任人不能准确确定。要求二者承担连带责任的制度设计加强了对债权的担保，使债权人债权实现具有双重保障，这种立法例在《日本商法典》《德国商法典》《俄罗斯民法典》《澳门商法典》中均有体现。

4.1.5 特殊债权人的自我保护机制

一般债权人之外，公司可能还存在两类特殊的债权人，他们可以依据其特殊方式参与公司内部经营，以更充分地维护自身权益：第一，金融债权人以股东身份参与公司治理。当公司主要依赖银行融资时，银行对公司就具有较强的控制力，债权人同时兼具股东身份，可以知悉公司经营状况，通过行使表决权及时维护自身权益，如德国的全能银行和日本的主银行制度。第二，债券持有人以参加公司债债权人会议参与公司治理。公司债债权人会议是债权人团体意思表达的非常设机构，营业转让属于重大交易行为，尽管各国立法并未明确将其列入债权人会议审议的范围，但根据该会议的职权范围当属其中。根据会议的表决程序可以形成决议，经过法院认可，发生法律效力，对全体公司债债权人有约束力。日本、法国、意大利等均规定了该制度。

4.2 判例法对营业转让中债权人的保护制度

制定法确立的上述规则侧重于对营业转让中现时债权人的保护，美国判例法上发展出来的继受人责任制度则为对未来债权人保护提供了新的思路。

（1）传统的继受人责任规则的产生及适用

继受人责任规则是 19 世纪后半期及 20 世纪早期出现的公司法的产物，起源于美国的判例法，是指当一个公司从另外一个公司购买大量财产时，原则上购买公司（受让人）并不需要承担出售公司的债务，即债务不承担规则。但严格遵循该规则有违公平、正义时，法官根据衡平法的精神，在四种例外情况下，受让人作为转让人的继受人或称为后继者，要求承担转让人的债务。四种例外情况包括：①明示或者默示的合同约定；②欺诈性转让；③实质合并原则；④实质存续原则[17]。

对于后两者，均有作为一项有机体的营业财产的转让行为，且受让方延续该项营业行为，这实际上就是我们所指的营业转让。对此美国法院均规定了严格的适用条件，实质合并的情形应该承担与合并同样的概括承担权利义务的后果，即对于转让方的债务（包括非欺诈性转让情形），受让方应该当然承继；实质存续由于交易的双方当事人是同一的控制人，具有关联关系，存在利益上的牵扯，交易并不是在完

---

❶ 参见《美国统一欺诈性转让法》第 9 条 1 项。
❷ 参见《美国统一欺诈性转让法》第 10 条。

全公开竞争的条件下进行,价格不公平的可能性较大,法院可据此推定交易不公平,是一种欺诈行为。作为推定原则,当然允许当事人通过反证加以推翻;否则,对转让公司解散注销情形下,转让人的债务应由受让人承担。可见,传统继受人责任规则的价值在于赋予法官自由裁量权,当受让人与转让人之间的非常规交易明显违反公平正义原则时,法官可据此作出判决,直达交易的实质,要求受让人对转让人的合同侵权人和未来侵权人承担责任,一定程度上对债权人提供了更充分的救济手段。

(2) 新继受人责任规则的产生及发展

传统继受人规则的适用条件非常严格,而精明的商人往往"上有政策,下有对策",对适用条件只要稍做改变就可避免适用,如实质合并原则的核心要素在于经营延续和股东存续,即交易对价为股份,如受让人以现金为对价,继受人与缺陷产品的风险产生没有任何关系时,传统继受人责任规则不能适用;实质存续原则的核心是实际控制人同一两个公司从事相同业务,但只要对业务稍做调整即可达到同样效果,由此导致对未来债权人的利益保护不周。而此时,美国法院面对实践中越来越多的生产商已经解散的产品责任案件,从法理上讲,法院可有两种选择❶:一是要求股东退回公司解散时分配得到的财产,但股东承担的是有限、不连带责任,债权人要充分受偿,必须起诉所有的股东,而作为产品责任的未来债权人中消费者居多,由于诉讼成本(包括寻找众多股东的成本)高昂必然放弃债权;二是改变清算规则为未来债权人预留部分财产,但预留多少、预留财产如何管理等都是难以妥善解决的问题。而且,根据1984年修改的《美国示范公司法》规定:合法债权在公司解散公告发布后5年内可提出,而产品造成的侵权损害往往发生在5年以后。美国法院迫于公共政策的压力,将目光转向受让了原产品制造商主要财产的继受人身上,要求继受人承担产品侵权责任,这就是新继受人责任规则。该原则是对继受人责任规则的合理借鉴和发展,法院在司法实践中还为其寻找了新的理论依据:产品存续原则和事业存续原则[18],从而给予未来侵权债权人以充分的法律救济。

产品存续原则和事业存续原则作为新继受人责任规则的主要内容,侧重于强调业务经营的延续,放弃了所有者的延续条件,从而扩大了适用范围。自从在产品责任中适用开始,出于公共政策的目标,美国一些法院在判例中进一步扩展了其适用范围,如劳工法中的"单一雇主"或"同一企业"标准、环境法中确定环境污染的承担主体等。从产品存续原则和事业存续原则的适用条件分析,是对实质合并和实质存续原则的继承和发展,其内核依然包含了营业转让的本质特征。因此,美国判例法发展出来的新继受人责任制度对营业转让中债权人的保护具有重要的借鉴意义,对于符合适用条件的情形,未来债权人可以要求受让人对转让人原先所制造和销售的相同产品中存在的缺陷承担严格的产品责任,更进一步,对于未来的环境侵权责任、侵害劳动者权益的责任亦可纳入适用范围,从而使营业转让中对债权人的保护制度更加完善。

5 解决之道:建立债权人利益保护的防范机制

5.1 完善债权人知情权的实现程序,建立债权保护的事前防范机制

(1) 建立商事公告制度,赋予债权人反对权(异议权)和竞价权,保护债权人的知情权

营业转让时,应分别根据不同的债权人设定不同的程序,根据公司债权人债权数额的大小不同,达到一定债权额的债权人应履行个别通知程序;对于其他债权人,则以公告方式通知。为了避免双方恶意串通损害债权人利益,公告程序必须对转让行为有一定的限制,这方面法国法为我们提供了可资借鉴的经验:当买受人履行公示义务后,出卖人的债权人即享有反对权(异议权)和竞价权。

(2) 建立债券持有人会议制度,保护公司债债权人的利益

发行债券是部分企业融资的重要方式,我国《证券法》第16条规定:符合条件的股份有限公司和有限责任公司可以发行债券。但我国证券法的性质体现为纵向调整有余而横向调整不足,如债券发行中侧重于发行的条件、程序的调整,对于公司债券发行人和持有人之间的关系调整不足,特别是对于债券

---

❶ 注:这两种选择在1984年修改的《美国模范公司法》中得到体现。第14.07节(d)(2):除非14.08节(d)小节(法院程序)另有规定,如公司资产已在清算中分配,则针对被解散公司的股东,范围为其按比例应承担的主张份额或者在清算中分配给其的公司资产,两者中较少者,但股东就本节规定的所有的主张承担的全部义务不得超过其被分配的公司资产总额。参见沈四宝编译:《最新美国标准公司法》,法律出版社2006年3月版,第206页。

持有人的利益保护不够。营业转让事关公司的存亡，应属于债权人会议审议的范围，根据会议的表决程序形成关于撤销公司营业转让、要求公司履行债务，以及公司不履行债务时的对策等决议，经过法院认可，发生法律效力，对全体公司债债权人有约束力。借鉴日本、法国、意大利等国规定，我国亦应建立债券持有人会议，营业转让中债券持有人可以通过这个会议体机制主动积极地维护自身权益。

（3）利用金融债权人的特有机制，完善金融债权人的自我保护

在我国，金融机构往往就是公司最大债权人，随着金融机构的股份制改造，金融机构成为独立的市场主体，独立享有权利和承担义务，首先应注意控制风险，包括缔约前对债务人的基本信息、对内对外的法律关系等进行尽职调查，对债务人的偿债能力进行风险评估，通过契约条款作出有利于债权实现的清偿的约定，如要求债务人提供担保，保证优先受偿；定型化契约中约定较高利率，约定公司如有资产收购等重大事情时，应事先取得债权人同意或书面通知，如债权人不同意或公司无法补提充足的担保品时，金融机构即得使加速清偿条款。在合同有效期间内银行以其特有的业务范围可以对企业的运营形成监督机制，此外可以通过对债务人参股而成为股东参与公司治理等。

5.2 夯实债务承担规则的法理基础，重构债权保护的事后救济机制

（1）重新阐释"债随物走"原则，保护现时债权人的利益

如前文所述，"债随物走"原则违反基本法理的弊病是显而易见的，有学者甚至认为该原则"是将营业转让中的债务承担过分简单化了"，"是无视私法的一般规则"。[19]笔者认为，最高法院关于《企业改制规定》的司法解释中对该原则的阐释的确存在前述的问题，但循着"债随物走"的思路，对该原则限制一些条件，进行重新阐释，却是一个简便易行、操作性较强的规则，对债权人的利益保护非常有利。这些限制条件包括：第一，明示或默示的约定。如果双方当事人以合同或其他方式约定受让人承担转让人的债务，这是契约自由原则的体现，只要不违反法律的规定，应予准许"债随物走"。第二，转让存在欺诈性。规定推定性欺诈，根据司法实践经验归纳"欺诈标识"，于此时可以"债随物走"。第三，依据外观主义原理，在营业转让附商号转让的情形下，商号构成债务承担的外观时，可以"债随物走"。第四，受让人继续转让人的事业，受让人与转让人之间存在持续关系，即使受让人未受让转让人的商号，但对外宣称是转让人的延续时，可以"债随物走"。后两者或者可称为"债随人走"，即构成了人格的延续，受让人应承担转让人所承担的责任。

（2）借鉴美国判例法的继受人责任规则，保护未来债权人的利益

美国判例法确立的继受人责任规则对于解决我国在企业改制中大量脱壳经营逃废债务问题有很高的借鉴价值。传统继受人责任规则中实质存续原则和新继受人责任规则认定的适用条件可以为我们所用：转让人和受让人的实际控制人同一，转让人在将优质资产转让后，成立一新公司，只不过改头换面而已；两个公司基本从事相同业务，新公司正是为了有效利用原公司的资产、商誉，保持了业务活动的延续性；转让公司解散消失，正是我们看到的新公司成立，原公司解散并不办理清算注销手续，董事、高级管理人员"人间蒸发"现象；两公司之间确实发生了资产转移，是以合法的形式掩盖非法的目的行为。"无论股权买卖，还是资产买卖，在一定程度上说，都是企业人格的一种延伸。这是继受人责任、企业债务的承受、资产买卖中劳动关系延续等制度的基本根据。"[20]根据实质胜于形式的实质公平原则，法官可以要求受让人来承担转让人的债务，避免"金蝉"一再脱壳的现象发生[21]。

对于未来的侵权债权人，借鉴美国《第三次侵权法重述：产品责任》第三章第12条规定：后手对前手通过商业方式销售的缺陷产品造成损害的责任——获得前手公司或者其他商业实体财产的后手应对前手通过商业方式销售或者以其他方式分销的缺陷产品造成的损害承担责任，如果这种获得：（a）附有使后手承担这种责任的协议要求；或者（b）是前手为了逃避的债务或者责任所进行的欺诈性财产转让行为；或者（c）构成了与前手的合并或者合营；或者结果是后手成为前手的延续[22]。在侵权责任法部分应确立受让人承担转让人债务的责任。但受让人承担的责任并非没有限制，有学者主张在破产公司进行资产收购时，为了避免未来侵权债权人不公平地获得一笔"横财"，可参照既存破产债权人的债权在破产财产分配中获得清偿的比例适用继受人责任规则[23]。

（3）规定转让人和受让人承担连带责任，使债权人债权实现具有双重保障

营业转让中转让人和受让人承担连带责任属于"共同行为"引起的连带责任，由于营业转让行为使

转让人对债权人的责任财产发生了变化，可能危及债权人债权的实现，法律设定二者承担连带责任，彼此具有互相监督的内在激励，可以最低的成本获得最大的效益，使债权人债权实现获得双重保障。唯应注意的是，受让人对转让人的债权人承担全部责任，在内部责任分担方面有最高额的限制，如我国香港地区《业务转让（保护债权人）条例》规定：营业受让人对原营业债务承担的债务数额，不得超过转让营业的价值总额。这是立法为了平衡债权人和受让人之间利益而作出的选择。

参考文献

[1] 钱卫清，李智慧. 企业改制操作与诉讼实务［M］. 北京：法律出版社，2003.1.

[2] 唐丽子. 国有企业重组改制中的债务转移法律问题研究［D］. 北京：对外经贸大学，2005：22-26；蔺莉，曹柯. 对公司脱壳经营的对策分析［DB/OL］. http：//www.law-lib.com/，2008年3月19日访问.

[3] ［德］拉德布鲁赫. 法学导论［M］. 米健，朱林译. 北京：中国大百科全书出版社，1997：78-79. 转引自［日］我妻荣. 债权在近代法中的优越地位［M］. 王书江，张雷译. 北京：中国大百科全书出版社，1999：6-7.

[4] 王勇. "从属公司债权人保护"的法律体系构建——试析关联企业中特殊债权人问题［J］. 河北法学，2004（8）：109-110.

[5] 彭冰. 债务随财产变动原则研究［A］. 北京大学法学院. 江流有声：北京大学法学院百年院庆文存之民商法学·经济法学卷［C］. 北京：法律出版社，2004：300-313，306-313.

[6] 刘敏. 企业改制案件审理中的疑难问题解析——解读《最高人民法院关于审理与企业改制相关民事纠纷案件若干问题的规定》［A］. 最高人民法院民事审判第二庭. 民商事审判指导［C］. 北京：人民法院出版社，2005：36.

[7] 李国光. 最高人民法院关于企业改制司法解释条文释义及案例解析［M］. 北京：人民法院出版社，2003：30.

[8] 吴伟央. 公司财产、负债及人员等同时转让的行为性质及债务承担——兼评"中国进出口银行诉广州万宝电器、万宝冰箱等公司借款纠纷案"［DB/OL］. http：//www.civillaw.com.cn/article/default.asp，上传时间：2007-11-02，访问时间：2008-11-20.

[9] 何秉群. 企业法人分立后原企业的债务由谁承担［J］. 河北法学，1995（2）：38-39.

[10] 冯果. 公司法［M］. 武汉：武汉大学出版社，2007：291.

[11] 武忆舟. 公司法论［M］. 台北：三民书局有限公司，1995：46.

[12] 王军. 评"企业债务随企业财产变动原则"——法释〔2003〕1号司法解释的一个理论误区［A］. 王卫国. 法大民商经济法评论·第三卷［C］. 北京：人民法院出版社，2007：97，99.

[13] 彭冰. "债随物走原则"的重购与发展——企业重大资产出售中的债权人保护［J］. 法律学，2004（6）：150.

[14] George Ripert et Rene Roblot, pp. 482-483. 转引自张民安. 商法总则制度研究［M］. 北京：法律出版社，2007：359.

[15] 汪华志. 公司欺诈性财产权转让行为及其法律控制［M］. 北京：中国检察出版社，2007：226；王海明. 美国《统一欺诈性转让法》一瞥及其借鉴［J］. 环球法律评论，2007（2）：76-80.

[16] 张维迎. 信息、激励与连带责任. 信息、信任与法律［M］. 北京：生活·读书·新知三联书店，2003：163-164.

[17] Philadelphia Elec. Co. v. Hercules, 762 F.2d 303 (3d Cir. 1985). 转引自彭冰. 美国法上的继受人责任［J］. 环球法律评论，2008（2）：67-68.

[18] 彭冰. 美国法上的继受人责任［J］. 环球法律评论，2008（2）：72；宋巨伟. 美国资产收购中的后继者责任规则研究——以保护潜在侵权债权人利益为研究视角［D］. 上海：华东政法大学，2008：25.

[19] 朱慈蕴. 营业规制在商法中的地位［J］. 清华法学，2008（4）.

[20] 许德风. 论企业买卖——以瑕疵与缔约行为为中心［D］. 北京：北京大学，2004. 摘要部分.

[23] 李鹭芸，马春久. 王新华："金蝉"一再脱壳［J］. 环球人物，2007（1）.

[22] 肖永平，等译. 侵权法重述：产品责任［M］. 北京：法律出版社，2006：293.

[23] rederick Tung +, Taking Future Claims Seriously: Future Claims and Successor Liability in Bankruptcy, Case Western Reserve Law Review, 1999. 转引自宋巨伟. 美国资产收购中的后继者责任规则研究——以保护潜在侵权债权人利益为研究视角［D］. 上海：华东政法大学，2008：29.

中小企业社会网络与其成长绩效的关系研究
——基于北京地区 200 家企业的调研

陶秋燕　汪昕宇　陈雄鹰

引　言

在竞争激烈、产品快速升级换代的环境下，企业已经难以完全依靠自身力量立足并取得发展，企业成长越来越依赖外部资源的获取，而资源获取渠道通常来自于由各种关系交织成的复杂、交叉重叠的社会网络。特别是在当前"开放式发展"的时代背景下，企业已经意识到通过契约关系、合作网络、社会关系与企业、大学、科研机构、政府和中介机构等联结形成的协同合作网络，将更有利于自身的生存与发展。对于占全国企业 95% 以上的中小企业来说，它们面临着整体实力不强、发展方式转变不快、融资渠道不畅等问题，而产生这些问题的根源是企业内生资源不足、成长能力弱，使得企业可获得和利用的资源十分有限。企业承受着巨大的生存压力，完全依靠自身力量获取和积累成长所需资源，培育生产、营销和研发等方面的竞争能力已不现实，企业亟须与其他各种组织建立多维联系，形成协同网络，以促进资源溢出与共享。

虽然越来越多的中小企业开始通过各种渠道来拓展自己的社会关系网络以获取自己所需的资源，但企业在社会网络建设方面还很不成熟，政府及其相关部门在帮助企业搭建社会关系网络平台方面也未能充分发挥支持作用，从而影响了中小企业的健康和可持续发展。因此，客观地评价企业社会网络状态及其对企业成长绩效的作用，将有利于发现中小企业在社会网络建设及其成长方面存在的问题，以便及时采取措施改进并完善自己的社会关系网络。

基于上述考虑，利用北京地区 200 家中小企业的调研数据，从企业社会网络建设中的网络规模、关系强度和关系质量 3 个方面对企业社会网络现状与企业成长绩效之间的关系进行分析，挖掘其中存在的问题，并提出相关建议以促进中小企业社会关系网络的建设和企业的健康可持续成长。

1　文献回顾与理论假设

1.1　文献回顾

企业成长理论研究起源于潘洛斯 1959 年出版的《企业成长理论》，但迄今为止企业成长理论还没有统一的分析框架。各种有关企业成长的观点散见于各种理论分析框架，包括斯密的分工理论、马歇尔的内部成长观点、SCP 范式、产业生命周期理论、交易成本经济学、资源基础理论、演化经济学和波特的五力模型等。后来随着实践中大量网络组织的涌现，网络化成长也开始成为企业成长理论研究的重点之一。因此，企业成长理论包括内生成长理论、外生成长理论以及网络化成长理论。

网络最初来自社会学家对社会交换的研究。埃默森[1]通过网络这一概念对松散的社会结构进行形式化，并把研究的重点从行动者的自身属性研究转移到行为者之间的关系研究，认为关系是行动者彼此交换资源的渠道，这种关系进一步形成了社会网络。20 世纪 70 年代以来，中小企业、高科技新兴产业、区域产业集群迅速发展，传统的经济增长模式与产业组织结构开始受到越来越大的挑战，各种企业网络化组织的涌现，企业网络开始成为促进企业成长的重要动力，网络化成长也随之成为企业成长理论的重要分支。

［基金项目］北京市哲学社会科学规划项目（11JGB040）。
［作者简介］陶秋燕（1965—），女，湖北省应城人，博士，北京联合大学教授，研究方向为中小企业管理；汪昕宇（1975—），女，山西忻州市人，博士，北京联合大学副教授，研究方向为人力资源和中小企业管理。

在交易成本理论范式下，Richardson认为企业间合作是介于市场与科层制之间稳定的中间型组织[2]。阿尔钦指出许多长期合同关系模糊了市场与企业之间的界限[3]。威廉姆森对原有的认为中间型组织不稳定的观点进行了修正，认为位于两极之间的中间型组织形式也可以长期、稳定地存在[4]。Powell把交易组织形式分为市场、网络与科层制，认为网络已经成为一种稳定的介于市场与科层制之间的第三种交易组织形式[5]。Ring和Van de Von从不确定性和对信任的依赖程度分析了网络在交易治理中的比较优势，认为在中等不确定程度下，网络可以依托中等程度的信任实现交易的有效治理[6]。

同样，资源基础理论也开始拓展自身的研究范式，认为企业不仅仅可以通过内部资源获得竞争优势，也可以通过企业间的关系和网络识别，获得和利用外部的互补性资源来获得竞争优势。Pfeffer和Salancik认为企业成长必然要通过各种关系与网络和外部其他组织进行资源交换，而有效地管理企业之间的关系与网络是企业实现成长的关键[7]。Gulati认为除了二元企业之间的关系，企业还嵌入在更大范围的网络中，这一网络对于企业识别、获得和利用外部资源具有重要影响[8]。Grant和Baden Fuller认为企业可以利用网络中其他企业所拥有的知识来实现多元化生产[9]。Dyer和Nobeoka认为企业网络可以实现企业间的知识生产、转移和重组，可以获得更加多元化的知识[10]。

国内对于企业成长机制以及企业网络化成长的研究起步较晚，研究主题与国外相似，主要包括以下几个方面：①企业成长因素与机制。已有研究对企业成长动力[11]、成长方式[12]、成长要素[13-14]和影响因素[15-16]等问题进行分析，邬爱其提出内部成长、并购成长和网络化成长等3种企业成长机制[17]。②企业成长能力与评价。众多学者从不同的要素角度定义并测量了企业成长能力。张玉利提出通过组织学习来培养知识管理能力[18]；林汉川构建了中小企业成长能力的评价指标体系[19]；李维安提出基于盈利能力和发展能力的企业成长性评价[20]；田晓明和张玉利等提出了动态能力的测量结构[21-22]。③企业网络化成长。邬爱其根据网络联接节点的差别将本地网络分为3个层次[23]；魏江的集群创新系统总体模型包括核心价值网络、可控支持网络和不可控支持网络3个层次的网络[24]；刘存福等人认为中小企业依靠社会网络可有效解决内生资源不足的问题[25]。众多学者探讨了集群企业的网络关系问题[26-27]，分析了中小企业网络及创新网络问题[28-29]，探讨了创业网络对企业绩效的影响等问题[30]。总之，对网络化成长的研究从关注企业社会网络结构开始，逐渐转向研究企业战略网络的结构、特征和关系。

国外的研究成果奠定了企业成长理论的基础概念与理论体系。国外企业网络研究涉及理论、实证和案例分析等多个方面，但多数侧重静态因素分析，在网络演化、成长路径演化等动态方面尚有空间，且对中国境内的企业关注较少。国内研究视角和方法多样，主要探讨在复杂多变的环境中企业的成长模式与成长能力等，缺少量化的模型研究和实证支撑，也较少探讨企业社会网络建设与成长绩效之间的关系，也就难以发现企业在社会网络建设中存在的问题。并且，已有研究对企业网络建设和网络化成长中政府政策支持方面的问题研究较少，而政府相关部门以及政策方面的支持对于企业社会网络建设和成长是十分重要的。

1.2 研究假设

分析企业社会网络特征与中小企业成长之间的关系需要确定衡量企业社会网络的维度。根据已有理论和实证研究，企业的社会网络特征可以从关系强度、关系质量和网络规模等维度来进行衡量，下面将从这几个维度来检验企业社会网络现状与企业成长绩效之间的关系，并先假设这几个维度与企业成长绩效之间存在正相关关系。

H_1：企业与合作伙伴联系越频繁，越有利于企业的成长（关系强度）。

H_2：企业与合作伙伴的关系越好，越有利于企业的成长（关系质量）。

H_3：企业建立的合作伙伴关系越多，越有利于企业的成长（网络规模）。

2 研究设计

2.1 变量的选择与测量

2.1.1 被解释变量的选择与测量

已有研究对直接用于衡量企业成长绩效指标的研究还不统一，多数采用销售额、市场份额、资产和社会知名度的变化等指标进行衡量。然而，企业成长不仅体现在经济效益方面，还应该包括企业规模和内部管理的变化。其中，企业规模的变化能够体现企业成长"量"的变化，而企业内部管理的变化则体现企业成长"质"的变化，企业规模的扩大和内部管理的改善都意味着企业的成长。

因此，从企业规模的变化、企业销售额的变化和企业内部管理的变化3个方面来衡量企业的成长绩效，且每个变量按照有所减少、基本没变化、一直平稳增加和一直快速增加进行1~4的赋值。

2.1.2 解释变量的选择与测量

企业社会网络是指企业与供应商、客户企业、同行、科研院校和政府部门等组织机构，在企业成长与发展过程中形成的关系集合，为了检验企业社会网络特征与企业成长绩效的关系，根据文献研究和实地调查访谈结果，分别选取体现网络质和量特征的3个变量。其中，在社会网络质的维度上选取关系强度和关系质量2个变量；在社会网络量的维度上选取网络规模1个变量，具体变量的测度方法见表1。

表1 解释变量及其测量方法

变量	问题	测量
关系强度	与主要合作伙伴交流的频率：最近半年以来，贵企业与以上部门每月联系（包括电话、传真、登门、办事等）的次数是多少？	(1) 0次；(2) 1~2次；(3) 3~5次；(4) 6~8次；(5) 9~10次；(6) 10次以上，分别赋值为1~6；直接赋值
关系质量	对主要伙伴合作的满意度：与伙伴合作，对企业成长和发展的帮助有多大？	(1) 极少；(2) 帮助较少；(3) 帮助程度一般；(4) 比较有帮助；(5) 非常有帮助，分别赋值为1~5；直接赋值
网络规模	主要合作伙伴的数量之和	过去1年中，企业主要接触和联系的机构有多少家？直接加总测算

2.1.3 数据的收集与样本统计

数据的收集分为三个阶段：第一阶段为企业访谈阶段，共访谈了15家科技型企业，为设计问卷提供依据；第二阶段为试调研阶段，共对北京中关村科技园区、中关村软件园、北京经济技术开发区等高端产业园区的50家企业进行了调研，根据调研结果对问卷进行了修订，并确定了最终的调查问卷；第三阶段为正式调查阶段，调查了中关村科技园、中关村软件园、北京经济技术开发区、中关村数字电视产业园、朝阳区产业园等高端产业园区的200家企业，具体样本分布见表2。

表2 研究样本

指标	类别	样本数	百分比/%
主导业务所属行业领域	电子与信息技术	103	51.5
	生物工程和新医药技术	18	9.0
	新材料及应用技术	5	2.5
	先进制造技术	51	25.5
	现代农业技术行业	3	1.5
	新能源与高效节能技术行业	6	3.0
	环境保护新技术行业	3	1.5
	其他	11	5.5
员工规模	300人以上	105	52.5
	101~300人	43	21.5
	11~100人	48	24.0
	10人及以下	4	2.0
样本来源区域	中关村科技园	46	23.0
	中关村软件园	40	20.0
	北京经济技术开发区	65	32.5
	中关村数字电视产业园	21	10.5
	其他	28	14.0

续表

指标	类别	样本数	百分比/%
企业类型	国有企业	20	10.0
	股份制	60	30.0
	外商独资	24	12.0
	中外合资	18	9.0
	民营企业	78	39.0

采用 SPSS 17.0 和 AMOS 17.0 统计分析软件作为数据分析工具。目前对 AMOS 涉及的结构方程模型所需要的样本容量要求看法不一,但通常认为样本容量至少在 100~120,以便使用极大似然法(ML)对结构模型进行估计,因此,上述有效样本 200 份,已达到样本分析要求。

2.1.4 研究方法与模型构建

根据上述讨论的企业网络特征的 3 个方面与企业成长绩效关系的假设,运用结构方程模型,构建如图 1 所示的概念模型。

3 实证分析

3.1 信度检验

信度检验是对量表的稳定性和一致性的研究。根据前文的讨论,关系强度、关系质量、网络规模,以及企业成长绩效都是由多指标项构成的,需要利用因素提取法来进行测度,所以需要对 4 个变量进行信度检测。采用克朗巴赫(Cronhach)α 系数法对这 4 个变量进行信度检测,结果见表 3。

表 3 关系强度、关系质量、网络规模和成长绩效的信度检验结果

项目内容(简写)	相关系数	相关系数	相关系数	相关系数
与政府部门的交往频率	0.515			
与科研院校的交往频率	0.772			
与供应商的交往频率	0.653			
与同行的交往频率	0.530			
与行业协会的交往频率	0.394			
与中介机构的交往频率	0.439			
与金融机构的交往频率	0.674			
与政府部门交往对企业的帮助程度		0.503		
与科研院校交往对企业的帮助程度		0.686		
与供应商交往对企业的帮助程度		0.529		
与同行交往对企业的帮助程度		0.471		
与行业协会交往对企业的帮助程度		0.325		
与中介机构交往对企业的帮助程度		0.344		
与金融机构交往对企业的帮助程度		0.563		
与政府部门交往的数量			0.674	
与科研院校交往的数量			0.825	
与供应商交往的数量			0.794	
与同行交往的数量			0.713	
与行业协会交往的数量			0.485	
与中介机构交往的数量			0.404	
与金融机构交往的数量			0.774	
企业人员规模的变化				0.591
企业销售额的变化				0.584
企业内部管理的变化				0.367
Cronhach α	0.691	0.738	0.801	0.693

从表3的信度检验结果可以看出 Item – to – total 相关系数均大于0.30，且 Cronbachα 系数均近似等于或大于0.70，这表明关系强度、关系质量、网络规模和企业成长绩效的信度检验符合统计要求。

3.2 效度检验

效度是指量表的指标能够真正衡量研究人员所要衡量的事物的真实程度，用于揭示结构变量和它的测量指标之间的关系。采用因子分析法对含有多项指标的变量进行效度检测。首先对关系强度、关系质量和网络规模进行样本充分性检验，即样本充分性的KMO测试系数检测和巴特莱特球体检验（Bartlett Test of Sphericity），判断其是否可以进行因子分析。在此基础上，采用主成分分析法提取因子，并按照极大方差法进行因子旋转，将特征值大于1作为因子提取标准。当指标项的因子荷载值均大于0.5时，而且累积解释方差的比例大于50%，说明该多指标项的变量符合结构效度的要求。关系强度、关系质量、网络规模和成长绩效的具体效度检测结果见表4。

表4 关系强度、关系质量、网络规模和成长绩效的效度检验结果

因子	KMO值	Bartlett卡方值	因子载荷（最小值）	累计方差解释率/%	Sig.
关系强度	0.722	107.996	0.526	57.442	0.000
关系质量	0.780	105.774	0.564	50.437	0.000
网络规模	0.796	257.926	0.591	54.508	0.000
成长绩效	0.601	122.198	0.648	62.207	0.000

从表4的效度分析结果可以看出，KMO值均大于0.70，Bartlett显著性概率均为0.000，因子负荷值均大于0.50，且累计方差解释率的比例均大于50%，表明关系强度、关系质量、网络规模和成长绩效的效度检测符合统计要求。

3.3 模型分析结果与检验

根据前文提出的社会网络对企业成长绩效的影响模型（见图1），利用结构方程模型分析软件 AMOS 17.0，采用验证性因子分析法对模型进行验证，得到了结构方程模型的检验结果（见表5）和模型拟合指数（见表6）。

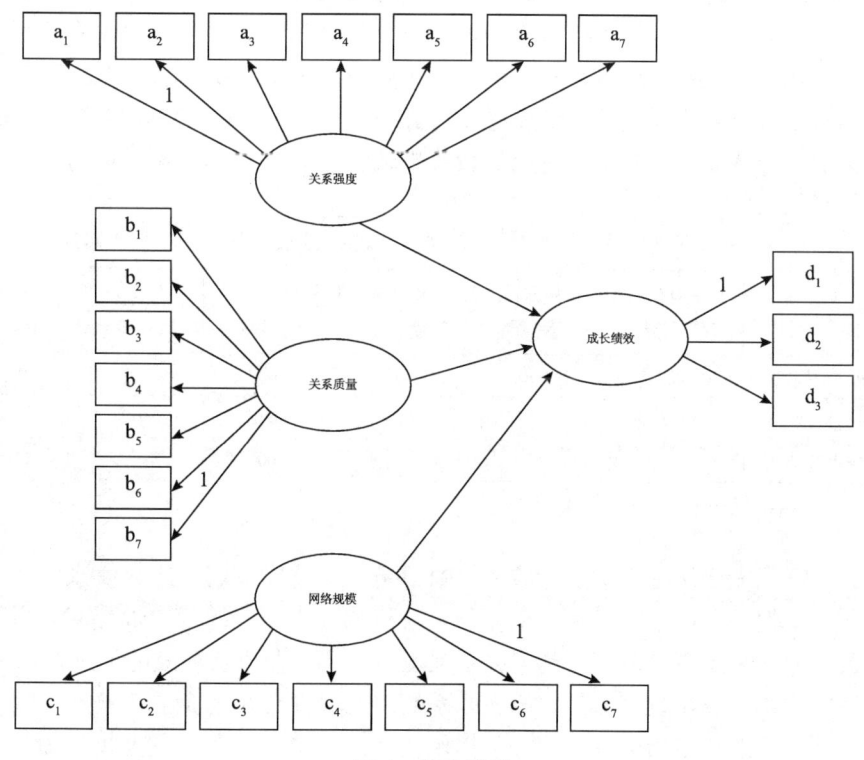

图1 概念模型

表5　社会网络特征对中小企业成长绩效的影响路径系数表

关系	标准化路径系数	C. R. 值	P	对应假设	检验结果
关系强度→成长绩效	0.128	2.984	*	H_1	通过
关系质量→成长绩效	0.149	2.177	*	H_2	通过
网络规模→成长绩效	0.366	3.255	***	H_3	通过

注：* 表示 $P<0.05$，*** 表示 $P<0.00$。

表6　社会网络特征对中小企业成长绩效影响的拟合指数表

拟合指数	χ^2/df	RMR	RMSEA	GFI	AGFI	CFI	NFI	IFI
统计值	2.427	0.070	0.071	0.821	0.814	0.940	0.913	0.924
判断标准	(2, 5)	<0.08	<0.08	>0.8	>0.8	>0.9	>0.9	>0.9

由表5和表6的结果来看，3个网络特征维度对中小企业成长绩效均有积极显著的影响。

3.4　结果的分析与讨论

从以上模型的拟合与检验结果可以看出，关系强度、关系质量和网络规模都与中小企业的成长绩效呈显著正相关。企业与合作伙伴之间的联系越频繁（关系强度）、与合作伙伴的协作对企业的帮助越大（关系质量）、与企业合作的机构数量越多，企业的成长绩效就越好。其中，网络规模对企业成长绩效的影响最大，其标准路径系数达到0.366，远高于另外2个解释变量，表示在当前企业成长环境状态下，网络规模相比关系强度和关系质量更能促进企业的成长。如前所述，关系质量和关系强度是用于反映企业社会网络关系"质"的指标，而网络规模是反映企业社会网络关系"量"的指标。模型检验结果反映出当前中小企业社会网络关系的建立更多的是依赖于"量"的累计，而在"质"的建设上还很欠缺。这样的结论一方面带给我们一些思考，为什么中小企业社会网络关系的"质"还较低？另一方面，我们还需要对关系强度、关系质量以及网络规模3个变量各自包含的指标项与企业成长绩效之间作出进一步的分析，以反映每个变量中各指标项所发挥的作用，并有利于我们揭示关系强度和关系质量对中小企业成长绩效影响不大（虽然影响是显著的）的原因。

3.4.1　关系强度变量中各指标项与中小企业成长绩效的关系

为了揭示关系强度变量中各指标项与中小企业成长绩效之间的关系，将表3中所列的7个表示关系强度的指标项与企业成长绩效指标进行相关分析。由于企业绩效变量中包含3个指标项，需要将3个指标项整合成一个指数来参与相关分析，为此，利用前面在检验企业成长变量效度时所做的因子分析结果，按照3个指标的因子载荷，计算出企业成长绩效指数，然后再计算各指标项与企业成长绩效指数之间的相关系数，结果见表7。

表7　关系强度变量中的7个指标项与中小企业成长绩效之间的相关系数

		与政府部门联系频率	与科研院校联系频率	与供应商联系频率	与同行联系频率	与协会联系频率	与中介联系频率	与金融机构联系频率
企业成长绩效指数	皮尔逊相关系数	0.263*	0.060	0.027	0.032	0.230**	0.076	0.060
	双侧检验	0.000	0.530	0.728	0.685	0.008	0.457	0.370
	样本量				200			

注：* 表示 $P<0.05$，** 表示 $P<0.01$。

由表7可知，关系强度变量的7个指标项中，中小企业与政府部门、协会联系的频率与企业成长绩效之间呈显著正相关，但关联度不高，并且企业与金融机构、中介、同行、供应商和科研院校联系的频率与企业成长绩效之间的关系不显著，限制了关系强度对中小企业成长绩效的促进作用。

分析结果表明，中小企业与政府部门、协会联系的密切程度在帮助企业了解相关政策信息和获取政府部门支持、获得协会资源与帮助等方面发挥了作用。然而，中小企业与其他机构的频繁联系并没有帮助企业获取更多的资金、技术和其他资源的支持，从而间接地反映出中小企业在与金融机构、科研院校以及中介方面的关系还很不理想。

3.4.2 关系质量变量中各指标项与中小企业成长绩效的关系

同理,将表3中所列的7个表示关系质量的指标项分别与企业成长绩效指数进行相关分析,计算出各指标项与中小企业成长绩效指数之间的相关系数,结果见表8。

表8 关系质量变量中的7个指标项与中小企业成长绩效之间的相关系数

		与政府部门联系效果	与科研院校联系效果	与供应商联系效果	与同行联系效果	与协会联系效果	与中介联系效果	与金融机构联系效果
企业成长绩效指数	皮尔逊相关系数	0.175*	0.092	0.069	0.156*	0.160	0.096	0.338**
	双侧检验	0.013	0.270	0.373	0.049	0.065	0.350	0.000
	样本量				200			

注:* 表示 $P<0.05$,** 表示 $P<0.01$。

由表8可知,关系质量变量的7个指标项中,中小企业与政府部门、同行和金融机构联系的效果与企业成长绩效之间呈显著正相关,但关联度不高,并且企业与其他机构的联系与企业成长绩效之间的关系不显著。

分析结果表明,中小企业与政府部门、同行以及金融机构的合作质量对于企业成长是非常重要的,来自政府部门、同行以及金融机构的合作与支持相比其他机构更有利于促进企业成长。然而,科研院校、供应商、协会、中介对中小企业成长的促进作用还很有限,这也反映出了这些机构在扶持中小企业成长方面的作用还没有得到充分发挥,有待进一步的开发和挖掘。

3.4.3 网络规模变量中各指标项与中小企业成长绩效的关系

同理,将表3中所列的7个表示网络规模的指标项分别与企业成长绩效指数进行相关分析,计算出各指标项与中小企业成长绩效指数之间的相关系数,结果见表9。

表9 网络规模变量中的7个指标项与中小企业成长绩效之间的相关系数

		与政府部门联系数量	与科研院校联系数量	与供应商联系数量	与同行联系数量	与协会联系数量	与中介联系数量	与金融机构联系数量
企业成长绩效指数	皮尔逊相关系数	0.063	0.253**	0.212**	0.182**	0.173*	0.210**	0.074
	双侧检验	0.379	0.000	0.003	0.010	0.014	0.003	0.295
	样本量				200			

注:* 表示 $P<0.05$,** 表示 $P<0.01$。

由表9可知,网络规模变量的7个指标项中,中小企业与科研院校、供应商、同行、协会以及中介等机构联系的数量与企业成长绩效之间呈显著正相关,关联度总体高于关系强度和关系质量。但企业与政府部门和金融机构联系的频率与企业成长绩效之间的关系不显著。

分析结果表明,中小企业通过大量建立与科研院校、供应商、同行、协会以及中介机构的联系对企业获取资源与支持有明显帮助。但这种方式并不适用于企业从政府部门与金融机构获得支持,企业与政府部门和金融机构的联系频率对企业成长没有明显影响。

4 结论与建议

4.1 结论

在文献研究的基础上,通过对北京高端产业园区内200家中小企业的调研数据进行实证分析,运用结构方程建模探讨了社会网络特征和中小企业成长绩效的关系,主要结论如下。

1)社会网络特征的不同维度对中小企业成长绩效的影响不同,且企业在社会网络"质"与"量"的建设方面不均衡。关系强度、关系质量和网络规模3个社会网络特征维度与中小企业成长绩效之间存在显著正相关关系。然而,不同社会网络维度对中小企业成长绩效的影响程度不同,其中,网络规模是反映中小企业社会网络"量"的维度,其对企业成长的影响最大,而反映社会网络"质"的关系强度和关系质量 2 个维度对企业成长的影响较小。这说明现阶段中小企业更多地通过与合作伙伴建立"量"的关系来建设自己的社会网络,在社会网络"质"的建设方面还很欠缺。

2)中小企业与政府部门和金融机构的联系对企业成长的作用相对较大,也比较显著,但两个机构发挥的作用主要取决于机构与企业之间的联系效果。企业与政府部门和金融机构的合作效果好,才能建立稳定的联系,并获得来自两类机构的支持。政府部门和金融机构是中小企业成长过程中最重要的两类机构。政府部门为企业发展提供政策支持和服务,金融机构为企业提供发展资金,没有这两类机构的支持,中小企业的发展举步维艰。然而,现实是这两类机构对中小企业的支持还远远不够,尤其是金融机构,其对中小企业的资金扶持有限一直都是制约中小企业发展的主要瓶颈。如何建立中小企业与政府部门和金融机构良好的合作关系,不仅是中小企业需要重点解决的问题,也是政府部门需要重点思考和改革的问题。

3)科研院所和中介机构在促进中小企业成长方面的作用没有得到充分发挥。科研院所和中介机构为中小企业提供技术支持、技术转移和技术孵化等帮助,尤其是在当前大力推行协同创新发展模式的形势下,中小企业加强与科研院所和中介机构的合作,有利于提升企业的创新能力,促进企业的创新发展。然而,分析结果显示,当前中小企业与科研院所和中介机构的联系主要通过增加与科研院所和中介机构的合作数量来实现相互联结,缺乏深入合作,这不利于企业长远、可持续的发展。

4.2 建议

1)从中小企业自身来说,要强化企业自主创新和协作体系建设,发挥企业的主体作用。

首先,建立以企业为核心、高校和科研单位为依托、产学研紧密合作的机制。企业需要从自身的相对优势出发,与高校和科研机构在重大项目的攻关、技术培训、管理咨询和相互兼职等领域进行全方位合作,发挥产学研各自的优势,开发共性技术、关键技术和前瞻性技术,构建互通有无、协助发展的良好环境。

其次,推动中小企业间的广泛合作,排除恶性竞争,建立企业间的协作。建立企业之间松散的、动态的、开放的虚拟创新组织,利用现代信息技术进行知识、技术和信息的交流和有效沟通;开展技术援助,向合作伙伴提出产品改进建议等。

最后,加强与政府部门的沟通与合作,推动政府部门与企业之间的协同创新。通过项目研发、项目共建等形式与政府部门建立良好的合作关系,在为政府服务的同时获得政府的支持。

2)从政府部门来说,应加强政策引导和保障体制建设,营造良好的宏观环境。

第一,积极加强政府的宏观引导和支持作用,充分发挥对社会中介的支持作用。政府部门应在宏观层面上厘清思路和理顺机制,对企业实施积极的引导与调控,为培育、扶持、保护和发展中小企业营造良好的宏观环境。

第二,政府有关部门应不断改进和完善各种政策措施,积极促进中小企业的发展,如通过倾斜政策、税收和信贷等优惠政策、技术扶持政策等引导和促进企业的快速成长,为中小企业的成长和发展提供支持。

第三,大力加强配套的交通、信息、通信、电力、教育、文化和科技等相关基础设施建设,并以环境创新和制度建设为着力点,吸引聚集创新型人才,营造有利于中小企业发展的文化环境和制度环境。

参考文献

[1] 吴波,贾生华. 区域产业集群演进中集群企业网络化成长机制与模式研究 [M]. 杭州:浙江大学出版社,2008.
[2] Richardson G B. The Organization of Industry [J]. Economic Journal, 1972 (82): 883-896.
[3] Alchian A, Demsetz H. Production, information costs and economic organization [J]. America Economic Review, 1972 (62): 777-795.
[4] Oliver E. Williamson. The Economic Institutions of Capitalism [M]. Canada Free Press, 1985.
[5] Powell W W. Neither Market Nor Hierarchy: Network Forms of Organization [J]. Research in Organizational Behavior, 1990 (12): 295-336.
[6] Ring P S, Van de Von. Developmental Processes of Cooperative Inter-organizational Relationships [J]. Academy of Manage-

ment Review, 1994, 19 (1): 118 – 190.
- [7] PfefferJ, Salancik G R. The External Control of Organization: A Resource Dependence Perspective [M]. New York: New York Harper and Row press, 1978.
- [8] Gulati R. Alliance and Networks [J]. Strategic Management Journal, 1998 (19): 293 – 317.
- [9] Grant R M, Baden – Fuller C. A Knowledge accessing Theory of Strategy Alliances [J]. Journal of Management Studies, 2004, 41 (1): 61 – 84.
- [10] Dyer J H K, Nobeoka. Creating and Managing a High Performance Knowledge Sharing Network: the Toyota Case [J]. Strategic Management Journal, 2000 (21): 345 – 367.
- [11] 杨杜. 企业成长论 [M]. 北京: 中国人民大学出版社, 1995.
- [12] 李华晶, 朱建武. 企业成长三维研究框架初探 [J]. 研究与发展管理, 2005 (4): 76 – 82.
- [13] 贾生华, 邬爱其, 张学华. 企业集群化成长障碍调查: 以浙江省为例 [J]. 经济理论与经济管理, 2003 (7): 69 – 74.
- [14] 雷家骕. 企业成长的本质、要素与途径 [N]. 中国高新技术产业导报, 2005 – 12 – 2 (007).
- [15] 雷家骕. 恰当认识企业成长的本质及其影响因素 [J]. 化工管理, 2009 (1): 87 – 90.
- [16] 吕一博, 苏敬勤, 傅宇. 中国中小企业成长的影响因素研究——基于中国东北地区中小企业的实证研究 [J]. 中国工业经济, 2008 (1): 14 – 23.
- [17] 邬爱其. 企业网络化成长——国外企业成长研究新领域 [J]. 外国经济与管理, 2005 (10): 10 – 17.
- [18] 张玉利, 徐海林. 中小企业成长中的复杂性管理及知识显性化问题研究 [J]. 外国经济与管理, 2002 (3): 18 – 23.
- [19] 林汉川, 叶红雨. 论我国高新技术中小企业成长的市场环境 [J]. 研究与发展管理, 2001 (10): 37 – 41.
- [20] 李维安, 张国萍. 经理层治理评价指数与相关绩效的实证研究——基于中国上市公司治理评价的研究 [J]. 经济研究, 2005 (11): 87 – 98.
- [21] 田晓明, 蒋勤峰, 王重鸣. 企业动态能力与企业创业绩效关系实证研究——以270家孵化企业为例分析 [J]. 科学学研究, 2008 (4): 812 – 819.
- [22] 胡望斌, 张玉利, 牛芳. 我国新企业创业导向、动态能力与企业成长关系实证研究 [J]. 中国软科学, 2009 (4): 107 – 118.
- [23] 邬爱其. 集群企业网络化成长机制研究——对浙江三个产业集群的实证研究 [D]. 杭州: 浙江大学, 2004: 43 – 68.
- [24] 魏江. 产业集群——创新系统与技术学习 [M]. 北京: 科学出版社, 2003.
- [25] 刘存福, 侯光明, 李存金. 中小民营企业集群的社会网络分析及发展趋势探讨 [J]. 科学学与科学技术管理, 2005 (7): 144 – 148.
- [26] 魏江, 勾丽. 基于动态网络关系组合的集群企业成长研究——以正泰集团为例 [J]. 经济地理, 2009 (5): 787 – 793.
- [27] 贾生华, 田家欣, 李生校. 全球网络、本地网络对集群企业技术能力的影响 [J]. 浙江大学学报: 人文社会科学版, 2008 (3): 126 – 135.
- [28] 池仁勇. 中小企业创新网络的理论与实践 [M]. 北京: 科学出版社, 2009.
- [29] 孟庆敏, 梅强. 开放式创新环境下科技服务业与制造企业的知识转移过程研究——以某校技术转移中心为例 [J]. 科技进步与对策, 2012 (23): 137 – 142.
- [30] 吴冰, 王重鸣, 唐宁玉, 等. 高科技产业创业网络、绩效与环境研究: 国家级软件园的分析 [J]. 南开管理评论, 2009, 12 (3): 10 – 15.

保险合同可争议制度研究

常 敏

1 引 言

保险合同可争议制度是指保险人因投保人未如实告知而争议保险合同有效性的制度，具体包括保险人争议保险合同有效性的事由、期间及法律效果等的制度组合。❶ 保险合同可争议制度本为私法自治的产物，首先体现为保险合同约定的可争议条款。所有的保险合同均是可以争议的，在保险业界，保险合同通常会约定超乎人们生活想象的争议保险合同有效性的条款。世界范围内的保险立法，基于对被保险人利益保护的关注，普遍介入保险合同当事人拟定可争议条款的过程，限制保险人争议保险合同有效性的空间遂成为常态，从而形成了保险法上特有的保险合同可争议规范。可争议规范的形成更多地反映并维系着社会公众对保险业的信心和期待利益。保险立法例上的可争议规范成为保险合同可争议制度的价值中枢。

我国《保险法》第 16 条为保险合同可争议规范的体系化规定。该条的基本内容可以归纳为：保险人仅得以投保人故意或重大过失未如实告知重要事实为由，解除保险合同；前述解除权，仅能于可争议期间内行使；但是，保险人在订立合同时已知有解除合同的事由，或者超过可争议期间的，不得解除保险合同。《保险法》第 16 条相比较我国 1995 年颁布的保险法，在制度设计上更多地关注了被保险人利益的保护，以多重限制进一步缩小了保险人争议保险合同有效性的空间，这种制度体系的完备而产生的变化，为我国保险法理论和司法实务提出了许多新的课题，值得深入研究。

2 保险合同的可争议条款：自治与强制

投保人未如实告知，保险人有解除保险合同的权利，自治空间十分广阔，这是由保险合同的特性决定的。保险合同为机会性法律行为，分散被保险人的危险为其目的和功能。但保险人所承担的保险责任，仅以保险人合理评估风险并选择承担的危险为限。投保人对保险标的危险情况的如实告知，对保险人评估风险有直接的影响，保险人决定承保以及确定保险费率，均以投保人告知的真实危险状况为基础。保险合同订立时还有信息不对称的特征，投保人对保险标的危险状况最为了解，投保人"逆选择"的心理会助长其隐瞒保险人评估风险可能不承保或提高保险费率的危险状况，增加了保险人承担责任的概率和风险成本。保险人为保护自身的利益，均会在保险合同中约定可争议条款，投保人未如实告知的，保险人有权解除保险合同或不承担保险责任。约定可争议条款，与其说是合同当事人基于诚实信用和私法自治的产物，不如说是保险人管控危险的必不可少的一种工具。因为保险业的特殊发展历程，保险合同的格式化为其基本形式，可争议条款的约定更难以真实地反应被保险人的意思。"每个人都知道，合同的订立并不是关于合同条款的负责任的谈判协商的结果。"❷ 这样，作为管控危险的工具被使用的可争议条款，过多地考量了保险人的利益而极少顾忌被保险人的利益，必首先受到保险制度的"诚实信用"原则以及保险费和危险负担的"对价平衡"原则❸的检视。

[作者简介] 常敏，北京联合大学应用文理学院法律系副教授。

❶ 一般而言，保险合同因为违反法律而无效、因为意思表示瑕疵不成立或者无效、因为保险人依照法律规定或者合同约定的事由而解除，或者因为违反先契约义务而撤销的，均属于保险合同可争议制度的范围。但本文仅讨论保险人因投保人未如实告知而争议保险合同有效性的制度。

❷ ［德］康拉德·茨威格特，海因·克茨：《合同法中的自由与强制》，孙宪忠译，载《民商法论丛》（第 9 卷），法律出版社 1998 年版，第 361 页。

❸ "诚实信用"和"对价平衡"的原则，被称之为保险合同可争议制度的法理基础。见江朝国：《保险法基础理论》，中国政法大学出版社 2002 年版，第 233 页。

在这个层面上，世界范围内的保险立法例对于保险合同的可争议条款，始终施加着持续的关注和影响。保险立法例对可争议条款的审视，不在于应否给予保险人解除合同的权利，而是要确保保险人争议保险合同有效性的空间的合理性。投保人在订立保险合同时未如实告知的，若其事实对保险人评估风险不产生影响，允许保险人解除保险合同，对于被保险人而言，过于苛刻，这不符合诚实信用与对价平衡的原则。保险人能以什么样的事由争议保险合同的有效性，单纯指望保险公司在合同中加以限定，也是不现实的。历史经验表明，不同法域的保险立法例，对于保险合同的可争议事由均有规定，以此限定保险人依照合同约定争议保险合同有效性的空间。保险立法例对于保险合同的可争议事由，从投保人告知义务的条件、❶ 投保人未如实告知的主观过错❷，以及投保人未如实告知的"重大性"❸ 等不同方面作出规范，形成了具有强行法性质的可争议规范。强行法的"目的就在于通过限制当事人权利和法律行为的类型，或者通过规制基于私法自治而形成的法律关系，从而缩减私法自治的空间。"❹

关于可争议条款的自治和强制，还有一个较为引人注目的现象。保险合同约定的可争议条款，因为保险市场自身发展的需要，曾经历了一场意义深远的"自我矫正"的运动。在人寿保险领域，合同的可争议成为人寿保险单的信用水平下降的重要原因之一，因为保险人可以随时对保险合同的有效性提出争议，被保险人（受益人）不能不怀疑其最终能否取得保险给付，在 19 世纪后愈加明显，严重制约了人寿保险市场的发展。为了提升社会公众对人寿保险的信赖，拓展保险市场的发展空间，英国的保险公司自 19 世纪中期自行在人寿保险单中使用"不可争议条款"。❺ 不可争议条款的产生，是人寿保险合同约定可争议条款的一项重大发展，并非源自于法律的强制。❻ 不可争议条款的产生具有两个积极的作用：其一，为被保险人高度信任保单所能带来的利益提供了保障，经过可争议期间，被保险人（受益人）所受保险保障是稳定而不可动摇的；其二，消弱了保险人随时争议合同有效性的强势地位，从而减少诉讼成本的开支。❼ 因为如此，美国的州保险立法才不失时机地跟进，于 20 世纪初期将之规定为寿险保单的必要条款，并强制要求人寿保险单约定符合法律规定的不可争议条款。第一个要求寿险合同订入不可争议条款的立法，为美国纽约州于 1906 年制定的阿姆斯特朗法；其后 10 年间，约有半数的州都通过了类似的立法。❽ 州法要求保险合同写入 2 年不可争议条款的，即使保险合同没有约定此类条款，在保险单签发 2 年后，保险人也不能对合同的有效性提出争议。❾

在我国，作为合同约定的可争议条款的意思自治始终受到尊重。但是，保险法并没有放任可争议条款的随意性，而是经历了一个逐步强制的过程。在 1995 年保险法颁布前，我国保险公司在合同中约定可争议条款，不论是财产保险还是人身保险，几乎没有约束。但问题一直存在，保险人基于投保人未如实告知解除合同的，法律是否应当或者如何对之加以约束？1995 年颁布的《保险法》第 16 条❿的内容虽简单，但迈出了我国保险法限制保险人解除合同的重要一步。因为学者过多地关注了该条有关"保险人

---

❶ 除海上保险外，投保人的告知义务依赖于保险人的询问；保险人未询问的，投保人不承担如实告知义务，此乃保险法上的询问告知主义。英美法系判例法，以及大陆法系的瑞士、法国、芬兰等国的保险合同法，均规定有询问告知主义。我国保险法和台湾地区保险法亦同。

❷ 例如，大陆法系保险立法例所称投保人的"故意"或者"重大过失"。英美法系判例法的主流立场认为，被保险人为"隐瞒"的，当其行为构成对保险人订立合同的"诈欺"或"恶意"时，保险人才能解除合同。

❸ 例如，未如实告知"足以影响保险人决定是否同意承保或者提高保险费率"的，则具有重大性。

❹ 齐晓琨：《论违法合同效力的实质问题》，载全国博士后管理委员会等主编《法治文明与公平正义》，中国社会科学出版社 2010 年版，第 310－311 页。

❺ 不可争议条款是人寿保险合同约定的一个条款，基本内容为：在合同成立后被保险人生存至合同约定的可争议期间（1 年或者 2 年）届满，保险人不得以被保险人订立合同时未如实告知为由而否认保险合同的有效性。

❻ 十分遗憾的是，身处 21 世纪的我国人寿保险业至今在寿险合同的可争议条款方面仍无作为。以前，我国的寿险合同仅仅拟订有保险合同可争议的内容，并无"不可争议"的内容。自 2009 年 10 月 1 日后，寿险合同开始写入"不可争议"的内容，但基本上是复制我国《保险法》第 16 条的规定。很显然，我国的寿险合同约定的"不可争议"之内容，是因为保险法的强制而写入的。

❼ WilliamF. Young, Incontestabale － AstoWhat?, 1964 *U. Ill.* L. F. 323 (1964).

❽ Ralph W. Hratt, The Incontestable Clause in Life Insurance Policies － A Statute of Limitations, but Not a Confession of Judge － ment, 7*U. NewarkL. Rev.* 130 (1941－1942).

❾ *BankersSec. LifeIns. v. Killingsworth*, 1955OK166, 284P. 2d734.

❿ 该条第 2 款规定："订立保险合同，保险人应当向投保人说明保险合同的条款内容，并可以就保险标的或者被保险人的有关情况提出询问，投保人应当如实告知。投保人故意隐瞒事实，不履行如实告知义务，或者因过失未履行如实告知义务，足以影响保险人决定是否同意承保或者提高保险费率的，保险人有权解除保险合同。"

有权解除保险合同"的描述，多将之理解为赋予保险人"法定解除权"的规定，❶ 保险人依照该条享有十分有利的解约权，❷ 对该条所具有的限制保险人解除权的强行法内容认识不足。但全面审视该条内容，不难发现，该条虽有赋予保险人解除保险合同的权利的表述，然其核心内容却是限制保险人行使保险合同的解除权：保险人解除合同以投保人的"故意"或"过失"为必要，更以未如实告知的事项限于"重要事实"❸ 为条件。前述条文不仅有限制保险人合同解除权的立法目的，而且有限制保险人合同解除权的客观功效。❹

当然，前述《保险法》第16条作为限制保险人解除权的规定，因为缺乏约束保险人解除权的期间限制，受到保险法理论和实务的不断抨击。尤其是，我国的人寿保险业，作为长期的险种，已经出现"在保险事故发生时，保险人借口投保人告知不实，不愿承担责任，故意为难，拒付保险金等"等乱象，危害被保险人应有的保障，也不利于我国人寿保险业的发展，呼吁立法增设合同不可争议的规范。❺ 人民法院在司法实务中，也迫切感受到保险法的前述条文因为缺乏可争议期间的规定，不能有效地平衡因为随时解除合同而形成的被保险人不受保护的利益失衡局面。综合各种因素的评估，2009年第2次修订保险法时增加规定了保险合同的"可争议期间"和"弃权"制度，并相应限缩了投保人未如实告知的主观过错类型以及可争议事由的范围，使得我国《保险法》第16条关于保险合同的可争议规范的面貌有了较为彻底的改观，更加清晰地展示了其作为强行法的特征。

强行法是当事人在订立合同时不得违反的法律规范。当保险合同约定的可争议条款与强行法不同，会发生什么样的后果？我国保险法对此没有规定。在我国私法理论和实务上，依照强行法对当事人的意思表示效力的影响程度的差异，将强行法区分为"管理性规范"与"效力性规范"，"违反效力性强制规定的，人民法院应当认定合同无效；违反管理性强制规定的，人民法院应当根据具体情形认定其效力。"❻ 依照上述逻辑，不论《保险法》第16条为效力性规范还是管理性规范，都会发生合同约定的可争议条款是否无效的问题。

不能不引起注意的是，我国民法对于效力性规范和管理性规范并没有提供区分标准，判断《保险法》第16条的规范性质就成为问题。已有学者对我国有关强行法区分为管理性规范和效力性规范并进而决定法律行为效力的学说提出质疑，批评其为法律实证主义的僵硬态度，因为这种区分过于关注法律规范的表面性质。❼ 当我们在审视保险合同约定的可争议条款的内容时，并不会当然涉及该条款"无效"的问题，基于当事人的意思自治而成立的可争议条款，仅仅因为不符合保险法上的可争议规范就断定其无效，缺乏说服力。同时我们注意到，保险法上的合同可争议规范的目的，在于限制保险人的解除权，而不在于排除保险人的解除权，合同约定的可争议条款违反保险法上的可争议规范，并不影响保险人合同解除权的存在。在这个意义上，以管理性规范或效力性规范限定《保险法》第16条的强行法性质，并进而决定合同约定的可争议条款的效力，无疑人为地增加了处理此等问题的复杂程度。意大利《民法典》第1932条规定，第1892条❽的规定"如果不是更有利于被保险人，则不得违反。违反上述规定的不利于被保险人的条款，将被相应的法律规定所替代"。❾ 同时考虑到，不可争议规范的基本目的在于限制保险人的解除权，保险人的解除权基础❿为合同约定的可争议条款，合同约定的可争议条款的效力应

---

❶ 邹海林. 保险法 [M]. 人民法院出版社，1998：149；温世扬. 保险法 [M]. 法律出版社，2004：168.
❷ 陈之楚. 不可抗辩条款在我国寿险合同中的应用 [J]. 现代财经（天津财经学院学报）. 2003（3）.
❸ 李玉泉. 保险法（第二版）[M]. 法律出版社，2003：58.
❹ 1995年《保险法》生效后，我国保险公司开始在合同中写入该法第16条规定的内容，对保险公司拟定可争议条款产生了实质性的影响。
❺ 徐晓棠. 保险呼唤不可抗辩条款 [J]. 华南金融研究，2001（2）.
❻ 最高人民法院《关于当前形势下审理民商事合同纠纷案件若干问题的指导意见》（2009年7月）。
❼ 齐晓琨. 论违法合同效力的实质问题 [M] //全国博士后管理委员会，等法治文明与公平正义.
❽ 意大利《民法典》第1892条是有关保险人解除保险合同的事由（投保人故意或重大过失为重要事实的未如实告知）以及可争议期间（保险人知其实事后3个月）的规定。
❾ 我国台湾地区"保险法"第54条、澳门《商法典》第964条有类似的规定。
❿ 保险人依照保险法的规定或者保险合同的约定，可以解除保险合同。保险合同可以约定保险人解除合同的任何事由，除非保险法另有规定。法律规定保险人解除合同的事由，充其量仅是数百年的保险实务中的合同约定保险人解除合同的个别事由。保险法规定保险人可以解除保险合同，实属多余。

当得到尊重。因此，保险合同约定的可争议条款，并不因违反保险法上的可争议规范而无效；保险合同约定的可争议条款违反保险法上的可争议规范，若其约定更有利于被保险人，则依照其约定；反之，则以保险法的相应规定取代合同条款约定的相应内容。

我国《保险法》第16条的规定为强行法，至少表明保险人在订立合同时不得以任何理由进行规避，例如保险合同中有关保险人行使解除权的条件、可争议期间、弃权等约定，不得违反其相应规定。同时也表明，强行法在限制保险人解除合同的权利时，势必为保护被保险人的利益而特别设计，均属于法律中的特别规定，依照我国《立法法》第84条❶的规定，不受"法律不溯及既往的原则"限制，《保险法》第16条应当无条件地适用于2009年10月1日前订立的保险合同。"保险合同成立于保险法施行前，保险法施行后，保险人以投保人未履行如实告知义务或者申报被保险人年龄不真实为由，主张解除合同的，适用保险法的规定。"❷

3 保险合同的可争议事由

保险立法例对可争议事由的基本价值判断为：投保人故意或过失为重要事实的未如实告知。保险合同的可争议事由，分为主观和客观两个方面。在主观上，投保人未如实告知的，是否应当以其存在主观上的过错为条件，保险立法例有不同的规定。在不同的法域，投保人未如实告知的主观过错，因为描述投保人行为的用语和法律环境的差异，存在很大的差异。在客观上，投保人未如实告知的事项，仅以重要事实为限，但保险立法例对于重要事实的取舍或判断基准，亦有不同。

3.1 投保人未如实告知的过错

在英美法上，通常用"隐瞒"和"不实陈述"来概括投保人未如实告知的行为。构成"隐瞒"的，投保人的主观心理状态一般为"故意"，但也包括"非故意"的未将有关事实告知保险人的情形，不论投保人是有意还是无意"隐瞒"，法院在实务上则是以投保人构成"诈欺"来定性"隐瞒"的。构成"不实陈述"的，通常并不考虑投保人是否有诈欺的意图。❸ 在英美保险法上，诈欺意味着行为人以不真实的信息对意思表示相对人的误导，至于行为人有无误导相对人的故意或过失，不属于应当考虑的因素；故英美保险法并不存在大陆法系用以描述投保人的主观过错的"故意"或者"过失"这样的制度体系，而是以投保人的未如实告知在事实上对保险人的误导作为判断依据的。

在大陆法系，行为人的过错构成其行为可归责性的要件，为自己责任原则的核心要素。投保人未如实告知重要事实的，保险人仅得以投保人主观上存在过错，争议保险合同的有效性。投保人未如实告知的过错，包括故意和过失两种基本形态。在德国法上，投保人未告知或者不实告知保险人重要事实无过失的，保险人不得解除保险合同。❹ 德国保险法以投保人未如实告知"无过失"排除保险人争议合同有效性的权利，相应地则以投保人的过错，作为保险人争议合同有效性的主观事由，包括投保人的故意和过失；至于投保人未如实告知的行为如何，在所不问。我国台湾地区"保险法"第64条以"故意"或者"过失"限定可争议保险合同的主观事由，但其区分投保人未如实告知的行为类型，分别以故意或者过失加以限定，有别于德国保险法的规定。对于隐匿和不实告知行为，以投保人的故意为必要；对于遗漏，则以投保人的过失为必要。❺ 在意大利、日本和韩国，投保人未如实告知有故意或者重大过失的，保险人才可以解除保险合同；因为投保人一般过失或者轻过失未如实告知的，保险人不得解除保险合同。❻

我国保险法有关投保人未如实告知的主观过错之规定，前后的立场有所不同。1995年保险法强调，投保人的故意或者过失在确定可争议事由时具有意义：就投保人的隐瞒行为而言，以投保人有故意为必

---

❶ 我国《立法法》第84条规定："法律、行政法规、地方性法规、自治条例和单行条例、规章不溯及既往，但为了更好地保护公民、法人和其他组织的权利和利益而作的特别规定除外。"
❷ 最高人民法院《关于适用〈中华人民共和国保险法〉若干问题的解释（一）》（法释［2009］12号）第4条。
❸ John F. Doobyn, *Insurance Law*, West Publishing Co. (1981), pp. 144–149.
❹ 参见德国《保险契约法》第16条第3款和第17条第2款。
❺ 参见汪信君、廖世昌：《保险法理论与实务》，元照出版公司2006年版，第48页。
❻ 参见意大利《民法典》第1892条、日本《商法》第644条、韩国《商法典》第651条。

要；投保人隐瞒以外的其他未如实告知的行为，则以投保人有过失为必要。❶ 如此规定，与我国台湾地区"保险法"第64条如出一辙。但是，2009年修订后的保险法，对于投保人的主观过错做了较为明显的调整，不论投保人未如实告知的行为方式如何，仅在投保人存在故意或者重大过失的情形下，保险人才能解除保险合同。❷ 这样规定更有利于保护被保险人的利益。我国《保险法》第16条有关投保人未如实告知的过错的规定，只承认投保人的故意或重大过失，与意大利、日本和韩国等保险立法例相同。如此规定至少表明，投保人未如实告知时没有过失，或者仅有一般过失或轻过失的，保险人不得解除合同。保险人行使合同解除权，对于投保人未如实告知是否存在故意或者重大过失，负有举证责任。

这里还应当注意一个问题。保险立法例对投保人的主观过错的限制性规定，并不妨碍保险合同约定具有特色的可争议条款。合同约定的可争议条款就投保人的主观心理状态所为表述，与保险法限定的投保人的主观心理状态不同的，应当以保险法的规定取代合同约定的相应内容，但合同约定的内容更有利于被保险人的，应从其约定。例如，保险合同若仅约定投保人故意未如实告知，保险人可以解除合同时，保险人则不得再以《保险法》第16条规定的"重大过失"作为解除合同的事由。

3.2 未如实告知的重大性

在订立保险合同时，投保人对保险人承担如实告知的义务。投保人不告知、虚伪告知或者告知不完整（遗漏）等，表明投保人对于应当告知的事实做出了不真实的陈述，本文将其统称为"未如实告知"。前已言之，保险立法例对于不同形式的未如实告知，作为可争议事由，对投保人提出了故意或者过失的主观心理状态的要求。但这并不充分，因为诚实信用和对价平衡的原则，对于投保人的未如实告知还提出了"重大性"的要求，符合重大性要求的未如实告知，才能作为争议保险合同有效性的事由。未如实告知的重大性，是指投保人对重要事实的陈述不真实。保险立法例几乎一致的立场是，投保人为重要事实的未如实告知，保险人可以解除保险合同。相对应而言，投保人未如实告知的，若其内容非为重要事实，保险人不得解除保险合同。何为重要事实？重要事实是指"估计危险的事实"，即影响保险人对于承保的危险进行评估或估计的事实。

保险立法例对于估计危险的事实所为规定，并没有实质性的差异。❸ 在英美保险法上，就海上保险而言，重要事实为"凡能影响谨慎的保险人确定保险费的事项，以及决定是否承保的事项"；❹ 就其他保险而言，投保人"隐瞒"的事实，限于重要事实，是指"那些影响特定的保险人决定据此签发保单或者据此以特定的保险费水平签发保单的事实"；❺ 但投保人"不实陈述"的事项，则应当具有"重要性"，即诱使谨慎的保险人订立保险合同的不实陈述，如果没有这个陈述，保险人将拒绝承保或者收取较高的保险费。❻ 不论描述"重要事实"的用语有何变化，英美保险法上的"不实陈述"的"重要性"只不过是重要事实的另一种表述方式，因为投保人"不实陈述"的事项，与保险人是否订立保险合同或者决定特定的保险费率相关。在大陆法系的保险立法例上，因为成文法的概念抽象性的要求，对重要事实也有类似的表述。一类立法例将重要事实与保险人订立合同或决定保险费率相关联，例如，德国法将重要事实表述为"对保险人订立契约或者决定契约内容产生影响的危险情况"，❼ 意大利法将之称为"保险人如果知道真相即不会同意给予同样条件的"的事实。❽ 我国《保险法》第16条第2款将重要事实限定为"足以影响保险人决定是否同意承保或者提高保险费率的"事实，与前述立法例在表述方式上相同。另

---

❶ 参见1995年《保险法》第17条第2款。
❷ 参见《保险法》第16条第2款。依照相同的机理，在发生保险事故后，保险人以投保人未如实告知而拒绝承担保险责任的，亦以投保人有故意或重大过失为必要，参见《保险法》第16条第4款和第5款。
❸ 但是，究竟应当以何人的认知作为判断重要事实的标准，在学理和司法实务上存在"主观说"和"客观说"的对立。主观说以订立保险合同的特定保险人或者被保险人对于危险重要性的认知，作为判断重要事实的标准，相应区分为保险人主观说和被保险人主观说。客观说则以谨慎的保险人或者合理预见的被保险人对于危险重要性的认知，作为判断重要事实的标准，相应区分为保险人客观说和被保险人客观说。参见汪信君、廖世昌：《保险法理论与实务》，元照出版公司2006年版，第35-40页。
❹ 参见英国1906年《海上保险法》第18条第2款。
❺ John F. Doobyn, *Insurance Law*, p.144.
❻ John F. Doobyn, *Insurance Law*, p.150.
❼ 参见德国《保险契约法》第16条第1款。
❽ 参见意大利《民法典》第1892条第1款。

一类立法例则将重要事实直接与保险人评估风险相关联,例如,我国澳门商法将重要事实表述为"能影响风险评估的一切情况",❶ 我国台湾地区"保险法"将之概括为"足以变更或减少保险人对于危险之估计者"。❷ 除上述以外,保险人在订立合同时询问的事项,在不同法域,都是被推定为"重要事实"的。例如,我国澳门《商法典》第 973 条第 2 款规定,"如保险人向投保人交付问卷以便投保人填写,则推定调查表所载情况对风险评估有影响。"

我国保险法对"重要事实"的表述,在法律修订过程中是有所变化的。有学者认为,2002 年《保险法》第 17 条将未如实告知区分为"故意隐瞒事实、不如实告知和因过失未履行如实告知义务两类。就前者而言,其构成要件是具有欺诈意图和行为虚伪,但对于蓄意的隐瞒并未要求具有重大性;而后者的构成要件则干脆少了'重大性'。……修订后的《保险法》在第 16 条中引入了'重大性'标准。这一规定在客观上减轻了投保人的告知义务,有助于在保险事故发生时,真正受到损害的被保险人能够及时获得救助。"❸ 如果对比 2002 年《保险法》第 17 条第 2 款和 2009 年修订后的《保险法》第 16 条第 2 款,并不能得出 2002 年《保险法》对于未如实告知没有"重大性"要求的结论,更无法得出对于未如实告知的"重大性"要求是我国 2009 年《保险法》新引入制度的结论。

我国 1995 年颁布的保险法及其后两次修订的保险法,虽然没有使用"重要事实"这一术语,但其制度构成均十分清晰地表达了"重要事实"在评价未如实告知的法律效果方面存在的必要性。2002 年《保险法》第 17 条第 2 款所称"故意隐瞒"的事实,仅限于第 16 条第 1 款项下保险人询问的事实,即推定的重要事实;该款后段所称"足以影响保险人决定是否同意承保或者提高保险费率的"事实,本身就是重要事实。❹ 在订立保险合同时,保险人询问投保人的事项,与保险人决定同意承保或者提高保险费率的事实,并非一一对应的关系,保险人询问的事项,并不一定会影响保险人决定是否同意承保或者提高保险费率,故推定的重要事实与重要事实的内涵与外延会有所不同。为了切实贯彻诚实信用和对价平衡的原则,更好地保护被保险人的利益,2009 年修订后的《保险法》第 16 条第 2 款将重要事实统称为"足以影响保险人决定是否同意承保或者提高保险费率"的事实。❺

当保险立法例采用"询问告知主义"立场时,重要事实首先表现为推定的重要事实,以保险人询问的事项为限。保险人的询问限定了投保人履行如实告知义务的范围。保险人在订立保险合同时所为询问,直接效果在于"激活"投保人履行如实告知义务,在签发保险单以前,保险人没有询问的,投保人以诚实信用推定保险人已知所有的必要情况,没有义务将其知道或者应当知道的重要情况告知保险人。❻ 在保险人询问的事项中,凡属估计危险的事实,均为重要事实;与之相对应,保险人未询问的事项,不论该事项是否为估计危险的事实,均被排除于重要事实之外。因此,重要事实是保险人询问的估计危险的事实。投保人在订立保险合同时,对于保险人询问以外的事项未如实告知,即使该事实在性质上构成估计危险的事实,保险人亦不得以投保人未如实告知为由,对保险合同的有效性提出争议。

4 保险合同的可争议期间

保险合同的可争议期间是保险合同可争议制度的构成要素,原本属于合同当事人意思自治的内容。因为保险法上的可争议规范的介入,保险人以格式条款滥用其争议保险合同的优势地位的空间(例如,不约定争议期间或者约定不合理的争议期间)受到了限制。保险法上的可争议规范规定的可争议期间,称之为"可争议法定期间"。保险合同约定的可争议期间依照具体险种的性质与目的,可以作出有利于被保险人的变通,但期间的起算和长短不得超过"可争议法定期间"。

---

❶ 参见我国澳门《商法典》第 973 条第 1 款。
❷ 参见我国台湾地区"保险法"第 64 条第 2 款。
❸ 胡晓珂:《保险法二次修订之理念与路径选择》,《法商研究》2009 年第 6 期。
❹ 参见李玉泉:《保险法》(第二版),法律出版社 2003 年版,第 58-59 页。
❺ 但是,我国《保险法》第 16 条对于不真实陈述的"重大性"的改革并不彻底,仍然有所疏漏。在发生保险事故后,保险人以投保人故意未如实告知而拒绝承担保险责任的,仍以推定的重要事实为必要,即投保人对于保险人询问的事项未如实告知的,仅考虑投保人未如实告知的故意,至于投保人未如实告知的事实是否影响保险人评估承保风险或者对保险事故的发生是否有影响,在所不问。参见《保险法》第 16 条第 4 款。
❻ John F. Doobyn, *Insurance Law*, p. 147.

4.1 保险立法例上的可争议期间

可争议法定期间在保险立法例上表现为两种形式：短期可争议期间和长期可争议期间。短期可争议期间以保险人已知投保人为重要事实的未如实告知为条件，长期可争议期间则以保险合同的成立为条件。

有的保险立法例仅规定有短期可争议期间。例如，意大利《民法典》第1892条规定，保险人自知道投保人故意或重大过失为不正确申明或不告知之日起3个月内，未对保险合同表示异议的，丧失异议权。我国澳门《商法典》第974条规定，保险人于知悉投保人故意不告知或不正确告知之日起1个月内不为撤销保险合同的意思表示，则丧失撤销保险合同的权利；第975条规定，若投保人非故意的不告知或不正确告知，保险人在知其事实后2个月内可以解除保险合同或提议投保人支付新保险费。有的保险立法例则同时规定有短期可争议期间和长期可争议期间。例如，1899年颁布的、后经多次修改的日本《商法》第644条规定：投保人因故意或重大过失为重要事实的未如实告知，保险人可以解除合同；但自保险人知其事实后1个月内不行使解除合同的权利的，其解除权消灭；自合同订立时起经过5年的，亦同。我国台湾地区"保险法"第64条第3款规定，保险人基于投保人违反"据实说明义务"而享有的"解除契约权"，"自保险人知有解除之原因后经过1个月不行使而消灭；或契约订立后经过2年，即有可以解除之原因，亦不得解除契约"。在英美法系，并不存在与大陆法系保险立法例规定的适用于所有保险合同的可争议法定期间相同或者类似的制度，短期可争议期间依照判例法上的"弃权"规则，由法官依照个案确定，成文法仅有适用于人身保险的长期可争议期间的规定；❶ 例如美国各州的保险法对于人身保险均规定有"自保险单签发之日起2年"的可争议期间。

我国《保险法》第16条第3款规定："前款规定的合同解除权，自保险人知道有解除事由之日起，超过三十日不行使而消灭。自合同成立之日起超过二年的，保险人不得解除合同；发生保险事故的，保险人应当承担赔偿或者给付保险金的责任。"从法律规范的形式和内容上看，我国保险法与大陆法系的许多保险立法例几近相同，不仅有短期可争议期间的规定，而且有长期可争议期间的规定，只是在期间计算的长短上有所不同。

4.2 可争议期间与除斥期间

我国保险法规定的可争议法定期间是否为除斥期间？目前，在我国保险法理论上，有将《保险法》第16条第3款规定的"可争议期间"定性为除斥期间的；❷ 有将之定性为除斥期间的，但却与英美法上的"不可争议条款"相联系，试图找寻"可争议期间"存在的制度性基础；❸ 也有将之直接等同于英美法上的"不可争议期间"的，只字不提除斥期间。❹

除斥期间为大陆法系民法上的一种"期间"制度。除斥期间是法律规定或者当事人意定的权利存续期间，经过该期间，权利人不行使权利的，其权利消灭。除斥期间在我国民法上适用于"形成权"，但它却是一个不变期间，当事人不得以其意思表示对该期间进行延长，该期间也不会发生中止或中断的现象。除斥期间的完成，将确定的发生权利消灭的效果。《保险法》第16条规定的可争议期间完成，保险人解除合同的权利将确定地归于消灭，此与我国民法关于除斥期间的制度相吻合。

从民法除斥期间的效果上看，权利人的权利因为期间经过而消灭，与英美法上的权利人因为"弃权"或"禁止反言"而失权的效果并无二致，但二者在权利消灭的基础上却有所不同。依照大陆法系民法，保险人的解除权因为除斥期间完成而消灭的，并不取决于保险人是否有放弃权利的明示或默示的意思，仅因期间的完成就发生权利消灭的效果；而依照英美法上的"弃权"或"禁止反言"规则，保险人因为可争议期间的完成，解除合同的权利消灭，其依据是保险人有放弃或者禁止反言的明示或者默示的意思，诸如将不可争议条款写入保险合同。在这个意义上，我国保险法规定的可争议期间，因为不依赖

---

❶ John F. Doobyn, *Insurance Law*, pp. 173–176.
❷ 参见邹海林：《保险法》，人民法院出版社1998年版，第150页；温世扬主编：《保险法》，法律出版社2003年版，第171页。
❸ 参见刘学生：《论不可抗辩规则——我国〈保险法〉第16条第3款之解析》，《保险法评论》（第3卷），法律出版社2010年12月版。
❹ 梁鹏. 保险法修改中的不可争条款 [M] //保险法评论（第2卷）. 法律出版社, 2009.

于"弃权"或"禁止反言"而独立发生效果，当为除斥期间，与英美法上本属"弃权"和"禁止反言"制度的"不可争议期间"相比较，性质不同。

这里需要强调的是，我国保险法理论将"可争议期间"定性为除斥期间，事实上还受到了居于强势地位的民法学有关除斥期间的理论的影响以及理解大陆法系民法体系化的期间制度的惯性思维的支配。❶ 同时，我国保险法规定的可争议期间，作为除斥期间，更是完善和推进我国民法上的除斥期间制度发展的历史必然。因为合同法已经构建了解除权消灭的除斥期间制度，❷ 这一制度体系是完整的，足以包容保险法有关限制保险人解除权的期间制度，《保险法》第 16 条在修订时增加规定的可争议法定期间，只不过是将合同法的除斥期间，以特别法的形式加以落实而已。总之，2009 年修订保险法时规定的短期和长期可争议法定期间，是我国民法上的除斥期间制度在保险法上的自然延伸，而非引入什么新规则。

4.3 可争议期间与普通法上的不可争议条款

在第二次修订保险法的过程中，因为过多地检讨了 1995 年保险法欠缺限制保险人解除权的可争议期间的规定，同时或多或少地注意到普通法国家的人寿保险单自行成长的"不可争议条款"所内含的 2 年不可争议期间，以致不少人将我国《保险法》第 16 条第 3 款规定的"可争议法定期间"与普通法上的不可争议条款相联系，❸ 甚至认为第 16 条第 3 款借鉴了普通法上的不可争议条款。❹

大陆法系民法的除斥期间，有着悠久的历史，其发展变化向来是自成体系的，我国亦然。保险立法例上以除斥期间呈现的可争议期间，自然应当遵循除斥期间的基本制度构造。普通法上并不存在大陆法系民法所概括的除斥期间制度，不可争议条款虽是一个相对年轻的制度，但在制度结构上与大陆法系民法上的除斥期间不同。不可争议条款仅是保险业自身为了消除社会公众对保险业的疑虑，在特定的历史条件下使用的一种合同条款，❺ 适用于人寿保险等保险合同，仅仅是普通法上特有的"弃权"和"禁止反言"制度的组成部分。❻ 除斥期间与不可争议条款无法相提并论，相互的影响也十分有限。有学者认为，"美国关于不可争议条款的立法影响了许多国家，世界许多国家的法律都规定了不可争议条款"，并列举了日本《商法》第 644 条、我国澳门《商法典》第 1041 条，以及我国台湾地区"保险法"第 64 条。❼ 不可争议条款产生于英国，但其成文法的发展则在美国，美国各州围绕不可争议条款的立法，是否影响了世界范围内的保险立法例（尤其是大陆法系的保险立法例），似乎没有事实能够证实。

我国《保险法》第 16 条规定的可争议期间，除了承继我国合同法关于除斥期间的制度结构外，更有短期和长期可争议期间的区分，并适用于所有的保险合同，更不专门针对人寿险保单。这些内容，均是普通法上的不可争议条款不具有甚至排斥的内容。不可争议条款有其特定的适用场景，其发展之初仅以人寿保险为限，许多健康和意外伤害保险也采用不可争议条款，但是团体人寿保险是不适用不可争议条款的。❽ 健康和意外伤害保险采用不可争议条款的，许多州的立法接受美国保险全国联合会（the National Association of Insurance Commissioners）1950 年制定的《统一个人意外伤害与健康保险单条款法》（the Uniform Individual Accident and Sickness Policy Provisions Law），适用保单签发之日的 3 年可争议期

---

❶ 在我国台湾地区，对于可争议期间，理论和实务均将之归类为"除斥期间"，少有人从除斥期间的制度体系之外审视其性质。参见刘宗荣：《保险法》，三民书局 1995 年版，第 128 页；梁宇贤：《保险法新论》，中国人民大学出版社 2001 年版，第 169 页。

❷ 我国《合同法》第 95 条规定："法律规定或者当事人约定解除权行使期限，期限届满当事人不行使的，该权利消灭。法律没有规定或者当事人没有约定解除权行使期限，经对方催告后在合理期限内不行使的，该权利消灭。"

❸ 刘学生：《论不可抗辩规则——我国〈保险法〉第 16 条第 3 款之解析》，《保险法评论》（第 3 卷）。

❹ 参见梁鹏：《借鉴而来的错误——新增订不可控辩条款存在的问题》，《中国保险报》2008 年 9 月 1 日。

❺ 参见文娟：《不可控辩条款之"不争期间"性质辨析》，《晋中学院学报》2009 年第 5 期，第 83 页。

❻ 英国伦敦无争议寿险公司于 1848 年在保单中声明放弃以任何理由作为争议保险合同有效性的权利。英国寿险公司这一创新观念在保险人中被评价为是"保险保证学说"的超技术应用，是保险人对社会公众的信用保证。随后，美国曼哈顿寿险公司于 1864 年率先在保险条款中引进了不可争议条款。不久后发生的美国南北战争，使美国经济萧条，导致大量保险人破产。在此政治、经济环境下，保险业者为向公众显示保险业经营的诚信品质和寿险产品的可信赖程度，在保险合同自由竞争过程中，各寿险公司纷纷选择采用不可争议条款。至 1870 年后，不可争议条款亦被美国寿险市场广泛采用，成为寿险保单的标准条款。参见陈之楚：《不可抗辩条款在我国寿险合同中的应用》，《现代财经》（天津财经学院学报）2003 年第 3 期。

❼ 参见梁鹏：《保险人抗辩权限制研究》，中国人民公安大学出版社 2008 年版，第 310 页。该书作者所引证的立法例，均为大陆法系的成文法，有其固有的规范形成路径和体系，在内容上完全不同于美国有关不可争议条款的州立法，仅有"可争议期间"的形式上的相似。这些立法例甚至都没有显示出一点借鉴美国有关不可争议条款的州立法的痕迹。

❽ Kenneth S. Abraham, *Insurance Law and Regulation*, the Foundation Press Inc. (1990), p. 332.

间，有些州将之缩短为 2 年。❶ 不同的州法院对于保险人不受不可争议条款约束的"例外"判例或立场，差别更是巨大。❷ 于此情形下，我国 2009 年修订保险法时又是借鉴美国哪个州的保险立法呢？事实上，我国《保险法》第 16 条根本就没有而且没有必要借鉴英美法上的不可争议条款，我国《保险法》第 16 条规定的内容，连美国有关不可争议条款的州立法的影子都见不到。将我国保险法规定的可争议期间，与普通法上的不可争议条款相联系，在立法上缺乏事实依据，在法律解释上陷入方法论错误。

以普通法上的不可争议条款，审视我国《保险法》第 16 条规定的可争议期间，会产生许多不应有的混乱。在保险法的第二次修订过程中，有学者怀揣我国保险法借鉴普通法上的不可争议条款的心理暗示，接受了《保险法》第 16 条借鉴普通法上的不可争议条款的假象。把两个结构体系不同的制度进行比较，肯定会出现"排异"现象。有人提出，我国《保险法》第 16 条规定的可争议期间，显系借鉴我国台湾地区"保险法"第 64 条第 3 款的规定，而第 64 条第 3 款又在借鉴其他国家的规定的过程中存在错误；该条规定适用于财产保险、可争议期间自合同成立时起算、以及没有任何例外的 2 年可争议期间，都是错误的借鉴。❸ 还有不少文章在讨论我国《保险法》第 16 条第 3 款时，声称第 16 条引进了"不可争议条款"，并以"不可争议条款"作为参照系，分析第 16 条第 3 款存在的不足以及应当采取的改进措施。❹ 我国《保险法》第 16 条第 3 款未借鉴普通法上的不可争议条款，以"不可争议条款"对我国保险法规定的可争议期间品头论足，实在是毫无意义。❺

4.4 可争议期间完成的效果

可争议期间制度的设立，目的在于排除保险人争议保险合同的有效性的机会，故可争议期间完成的，不论在普通法抑或大陆法上，保险人解除保险合同的权利归于消灭。但是，仍有两个被学界和实务界普遍关注的问题值得研究。

其一，保险事故发生在可争议期间，但被保险人嗣可争议期间完成后，始向保险人请求承担保险责任的，保险人可否以投保人故意或过失未如实告知重要事实为由，主张解除保险合同或拒绝承担保险责任？在美国，因为不可争议条款适用于人寿保险，而且条款的内容均含有可争议期间完成前被保险人"生存"这样一个基本条件，如果在可争议期间内，被保险人死亡的，不可争议条款的适用条件丧失，保险人争议保险合同的有效性，不受不可争议条款的约束。"如果在法定的 1 年或 2 年期间结束前死亡的，不可争议条款不产生效力，而且保险人在此后任何时间内，对基于保险单提起的诉讼均可进行抗辩。"❻ 我国《保险法》第 16 条对于保险事故发生在可争议期间的后果未作规定，但并不表明可争议期间完成后，保险人就不能以投保人未如实告知解除合同或拒绝承担保险责任。可争议期间作为除斥期间，不允许保险人在可争议期间完成后以投保人未如实告知为由解除合同或拒绝承担保险责任，目的在于保障被保险人预期的合理期待：基于保险合同承保的不确定危险的发生而享有的合同利益，在可争议期间完成后，不因投保人未如实告知而受任何影响。被保险人预期的合理期待的基础正是保险合同承保的不确定危险，在可争议期间完成前尚未发生。保险事故如果发生于可争议期间完成前，保险合同承保的危险已经发生，可争议期间保障被保险人预期的合理期待的基础丧失，仍然禁止保险人在可争议期间

---

❶ J. Ron Stegall, Jr., Legal Issues Arising in Connection With the "Time Limit on Certain Defenses" Provision, 46 *Tort & Ins. L. J.* 73 (2011).

❷ 例如，对于人寿保险的冒名诈欺，绝大多数州郡将之作为不可争议条款适用的例外，并有扩张适用的趋势。但是，加州最高法院则采取保守的立场，不承认冒名诈欺的适用例外，因为"不可争议条款要求保险人在签发保险单之前或者其后的 2 年期间内应当对诈欺进行调查"，而保险人只顾收取保费直至被保险人死亡都没有进行相应的调查。参见 Amex Life Assurance Co. v. Superior Court, 930 P. 2d1264 (Cal. 1997)。加州保险法也相应地对冒名诈欺的适用例外作出了限定，参见 Cal. Ins. Code § 10113.5。另外，在意外伤害和健康保险领域，不可争议条款的适用例外，情形更比人寿保险更为复杂。

❸ 参见梁鹏：《借鉴而来的错误—新增订不可控辩条款存在的问题》，《中国保险报》2008 年 9 月 1 日。

❹ 参见贺克玲：《评新〈保险法〉新增不可抗辩条款的修法价值与建议》，《金融发展研究》2009 年第 7 期；罗秀兰：《论保险法上的不可抗辩条款及其修订》，《法学杂志》2009 年第 12 期；任以顺、刘宝琳：《新〈保险法〉不可抗辩条款之立法不足与完善建议》，《上海保险》2010 年第 5 期；刘子操：《不可抗辩条款存在的缺陷与弥补措施》，《上海保险》2010 年第 7 期。

❺ 在这个问题上，我国保险法没有吸收和借鉴普通法上的不可争议条款，并不表明我国的人寿保险公司在开发设计寿险保单条款时不能借鉴美国法上的不可争议条款。保险合同的自治属性允许保险公司在可争议条款中引入美国人寿保险公司普遍使用的"不可争议条款"的内容，只要其引入符合我国《保险法》第 16 条的规定或者更有利于被保险人的利益。

❻ JohnF. Doobyn, *Insurance Law*, p.164.

完成后争议保险合同的有效性，缺少正当性。何况，因为保险事故发生于可争议期间完成前，被保险人已知或者应知投保人未如实告知将对其合理期待产生的影响，仍给予被保险人此时的合理期待与其预期的合理期待相同的保护，无异于被保险人因为保险事故的发生而提前享受了可争议期间完成的利益，不符合可争议期间的制度目的，更会诱发被保险人不当利用可争议期间完成以获得不合理给付的道德危险，违反诚实信用原则。因此，保险事故发生于可争议期间内，被保险人在其后任何时间向保险人索赔的，保险人均得以投保人未如实告知为由解除合同或拒绝承担保险责任。

其二，可争议期间完成后，保险人发现投保人在订立保险合同时有未如实告知以外的其他欺诈保险人的行为的，保险人是否可以对保险合同的有效性提出争议？在美国，因为不可争议条款给予人寿保险的被保险人（受益人）对保险合同约定的利益所产生的合理期待以更强的信心保障，除条款已经写明的投保人未交纳保险费外，经过2年可争议期间，人寿保险合同的有效性似乎不容置疑。在许多州，可争议期间完成，保险人不得以被保险人的"隐瞒"或"不实陈述"争议保险合同的有效性，也不得以被保险人违反条件或保证争议保险合同的有效性，[1]这必然引发相当多的案型涉及不可争议条款的适用问题。因为冒名诈欺而引发的争议，最为典型。冒名者以被保险人的名义接受体检并申请保险，被保险人没有签署寿险申请，只是被写在了保险单上，法院以保险人和被保险人欠缺意思表示一致保险合同不成立为由，判决保险人不受不可争议条款的约束。[2]在后来发生的一些案件中，有些法院对冒名诈欺的适用例外予以扩展，认为只要有冒名体检的情形，保险人就可解除保险合同。[3]更有法院认为，即使被保险人申请投保并签署了投保书，但被保险人阻截邮寄给其指明的医生的邮件、虚报健康信息并伪造医生签名的，保险人亦不受不可争议条款的约束。[4]总体而言，可争议期间完成后，保险人仍得以保险合同的不成立或者无效、合同约定的除外责任为由，对抗被保险人或者受益人的保险给付请求。然而在我国，因为《保险法》第16条规定的可争议期间被限定适用于投保人的未如实告知，故不会存在美国法上曾经发生的如此多的疑问。当投保人在订立保险合同时，有未如实告知以外的其他欺诈保险人的行为[5]的，例如雇佣冒名者从事体检或代订保险合同，因为并不涉及投保人的未如实告知，保险人仍可以独立的保险合同不成立或者无效为由，对抗被保险人的给付请求，这与保险法规定的可争议期间完成与否不发生关系。

5　保险合同的可争议与保险弃权

保险合同可争议制度与保险人的"弃权"之间有着紧密的联系。在普通法国家，弃权和禁止反言本身就是限制保险人争议保险合同有效性的强力措施。保险人通过使用复杂的保单语言以及设计苛刻的保险条款而获得了过度且不合理的争议保险合同有效性的便利，被保险人在保险人享受这些便利时受到了不公正的对待，其对保险合同约定的利益具有的合理期待受到威胁，普通法国家的法院则以弃权与禁止反言缩减保险人享有的过度且不合理的争议保险合同有效性的便利，以保护被保险人对合同利益的合理期待，维持和增强社会公众对保险业的信心。[6]弃权和禁止反言在普通法上是不同的，但在保险法上，法官总是以各自的观点利用弃权或禁止反言，在投保人未如实告知的场合，经常是不作严格区分的。[7]保险合同均为可争议的合同，在普通法国家，投保人未如实告知，除不可争议条款阻止保险人争议保险合同的有效性外，弃权和禁止反言在阻止保险人争议保险合同的有效性方面更是价值明显。在订立保险合同时，保险人已知投保人未如实告知，仍然签发保险单；或者在保险合同成立后，保险人已知投保人未如实告知，继续收取保险费的，均因为弃权而不得对保险合同的有效性提出争议。弃权和禁止反言在

---

[1] John F. Doobyn, *Insurance Law*, p. 164.

[2] *Maslin v. Columbian Nat'l Life Ins. Co.*, 3F. Supp. 368 (S. D. N. Y. 1932); *Ludwinska v. John Hancock Mut. Life Ins. Co.*, 317Pa. 577, 178A. 28 (1935); *Petaccio v. New York Life Ins. Co.*, 125Pa. Super. 15, 189A. 697 (Pa. 1937); *Obartuch v. Sec. Mut. LifeIns. Co.*, 114F. 2d873 (7thCir. 1940), *cert. den.*, 312 U. S. 696 (1941).

[3] *Blair v. Berkshire Life Ins. Co.*, 429F. 2d996, 999 (3d Cir. 1970); *Strawbridge v. New York Life Insurance Co.*, 504F. Supp. 824, 830 - 31 (D. N. J. 1980).

[4] *UnityMut. LifeIns. Co. v. Moses*, 621F. Supp. 13 (E. D. Pa.), *aff'd.*, 780F. 2d1015 (3dCir. 1985).

[5] 与此有相同或类似效果的情形，包括但不限于无保险利益、未交纳保险费、违反保证条款、违反危险增加的通知义务、合同约定的除外责任等影响保险合同的有效性或保险人拒绝承担保险责任的事由。

[6] JohnF. Doobyn, *Insurance Law*, pp. 172 - 173.

[7] Edwin W. Patterson, *Essentials of Insurance Law*, (1957), p. 494.

英美法上发挥着强行法的功能，对保险合同可争议制度的方方面面均有适用，而事实上，英美法上的"不可争议条款"及其相关的制度设计，更无法离开弃权和禁止反言这一制度基础。

但在大陆法国家，因为并不存在普通法基于判例法形成和发展的弃权与禁止反言制度体系，成文法也缺乏能够等同于普通法上的弃权与禁止反言的制度构造。在保险合同可争议制度方面，限制保险人的解除权主要是通过除斥期间等制度来实现的。保险人争议保险合同有效性的权利，在除斥期间经过后归于消灭。然而，保险人在订立保险合同时，已知投保人未如实告知、或者在合同成立后已知投保人未如实告知，而此时除斥期间尚未开始或者完成，对保险人争议保险合同的有效性之权利是否产生影响？大陆法系的保险立法例对此保持沉默的，不在少数。这种现象说明，利用除斥期间约束保险人解除保险合同的权利，作用是有限的，对于保护被保险人的合同利益是不充分的。当然，在除斥期间完成之前，保险人的合同解除权是否因保险人自己的行为而"丧失"，有必要在法律上作出特别规定。有保险立法例对此作出了规定。例如，日本《商法》第644条第1款规定，投保人因故意或者重大过失未如实告知重要事实，保险人可以解除保险合同；但是，保险人已知或者应知该事实的，不在此限。❶ 如此规定，可以在除斥期间不能完全阻止保险人解除合同的缝隙中，发挥限缩保险人解除合同的空间的作用，具有相当于普通法上的弃权的某些效果，但其制度基础并非保险人权利的放弃，制度结构也难说完整。保险人已知或者应知投保人未如实告知的事实，保险人不得解除保险合同，在解释论上则有"缔约过失相抵论"❷"投保人告知义务免除论"❸ 等见解。

投保人未如实告知，但保险人已知其事实的，保险人解除保险合同的权利是否会相应消灭？这个问题，在我国保险法的制度构造上，曾经是一个不小的问题。2009年修订前的保险法，对此没有任何规定。理论上，早就有人主张建立和完善我国保险法上的"弃权制度"来弥补成文法上的漏洞；❹ 学界也不断有人提起借鉴和吸收普通法上的弃权和禁止反言规则。在司法实务上，个案判决则探索性地运用了弃权与禁止反言规则，"保险合同作为最大诚信合同，对保险人的要求是'弃权与禁止反言'，弃权即保险合同一方当事人放弃他在保险合同中享有的相关权利；禁止反言指保险合同一方当事人既然已经放弃根据保险合同而享有的某种权利，将来则不允许反悔再向对方主张这种已放弃的权利。"❺ 因为学说的推动和司法实务的应用，修订后的保险法借鉴吸收了普通法上的弃权和禁止反言规则的经验，规定了具有我国特色的"保险弃权"的雏形。《保险法》第16条第6款规定："保险人在合同订立时已经知道投保人未如实告知的情况的，保险人不得解除合同；发生保险事故的，保险人应当承担赔偿或者给付保险金的责任。"我国保险法引入保险弃权制度，不影响我国私法所确立的除斥期间制度具有的功能，与除斥期间制度形成互补的关系；弃权制度在强制保险合同的可争议事项上，仅仅是辅助性的制度设计，在除斥期间制度无法限缩保险人解除合同的空间的缝隙中，发挥限制保险人解除权的作用。

投保人未如实告知的，保险人以某种方式（明示或者默示）使被保险人相信保险合同是不可争议的，则保险人不得再以投保人未如实告知为由解除保险合同。这是保险弃权制度的核心价值。《保险法》第16条第6款规定的弃权构成，在法条中所包括的要素是可以做如上的解释的。但要注意的是，第16条第6款项下的弃权制度，是我国保险法引入保险弃权制度过程中的雏形，功能并不完整，适用场景有限。保险人解除权的丧失，仅以保险人订立合同时"知道"或者"明知"投保人未如实告知的情形为限，既不包括保险人因为过失而未知（应当知道）投保人未如实告知的情形，也不包括保险人在保险合同订立后"知道"或者"明知"投保人未如实告知的情形。

---

❶ 该条所称保险人已知或者应知的事实，为投保人订立合同时，应当告知的重要事实。保险人已知或者应知的事实，限于估计危险的事实本身，而非投保人的未如实告知行为。我国台湾地区保险法对此未作类似于日本商法的规定，但理论和实务依照"保险法"第62条的解释认为，对保险人已知或者应知的事实，即使投保人未如实告知，保险人也不得解除合同。

❷ 投保人未如实告知的，犯有"缔结契约的过失"应受惩罚，然而保险人知道或者应知这些事实时，同样犯有"缔结契约之过失"，"两者相抵，故保险人解除契约之权应受剥夺，此乃依保险契约法理推论之结果。"江朝国：《保险法基础理论》，中国政法大学出版社2002年版，第232页。

❸ 保险人已知或者应知的事实，并不影响保险人评估风险，投保人对此免于承担如实告知义务，即使投保人未如实告知，保险人也不得解除合同。参见梁宇贤：《保险法新论》（修订新版），中国人民大学出版社2004年版，第112页。

❹ 参见邹海林：《责任保险论》，第152页下。

❺ 中华人民共和国海南省海口市中级人民法院民事判决书［（2005）海中法民三初字第2号］（海南宏业毛纺有限公司与香港民安保险有限公司海口分公司等财产保险合同纠纷案）。

我国保险法已有保险弃权限制保险人合同解除权的雏形，则其进一步的发展和完善将是可以期待的，完善后的弃权制度限缩保险人合同解除权的功能将更全面：(1) 保险人订立合同时，因为过失而未知投保人未如实告知的，保险人亦不得解除合同。因为保险人在订立保险合同前，对投保人告知的事实应当予以调查，保险人怠于调查而不知投保人未如实告知的，其向投保人签发保险单的行为足以使投保人相信，保险人已知投保人未如实告知的事实，且投保人未如实告知的事实并没有误导保险人订立合同或确定保险费率，则保险单的有效性不受争议，保险人已经放弃了争议保险合同有效性的权利。❶
(2) 在保险合同成立后，保险人知道投保人未如实告知的，仍然继续向投保人收取保险费或者通知投保人增收保险费，保险人不得以投保人未如实告知解除合同。对于估计危险的事实，投保人未如实告知的，保险人在保险合同成立后知道该事实，不论是保险人调查所知还是投保人通知保险人其未如实告知，保险人继续收取保险费，足以使投保人相信保险合同的有效性不受争议，保险人丧失解除合同的权利。❷

投保人未如实告知，保险人已知或者应知其事实而不得解除保险合同的，发生弃权的相对效力，即仅在保险人已知或者应知投保人未如实告知的事实上发生弃权的效果，保险人不得以同一事实主张解除合同或者拒绝承担保险责任。保险人因投保人未如实告知的其他事实所享有的争议保险合同的有效性的权利，不受影响。

6 小　　结

保险合同的可争议属于私法自治的范畴，因其事关诚实信用和对价平衡原则的贯彻，保险立法例对之进行了多方位的强制。在不同的法域，保险立法例强制保险合同约定的可争议条款的规范内容，基本目标都是一致的，即不断地限缩保险人争议保险合同有效性的空间。在这一过程中，可争议规范的强行法功能、法定的可争议事由、可争议期间，以及可利用的保险弃权制度，在限制保险人的合同解除权方面扮演着十分重要的角色。我国保险法经过 2009 年的修订，可争议规范的制度结构已经相对完善。尤其是，可争议期间的制度安排，保持了我国私法既有的除斥期间制度体系。再者，在除斥期间外，借鉴其他保险立法例的经验引入保险弃权制度，为更加全面地限缩保险人的合同解除权奠定了基础。

---

❶ 理由可以是"投保人告知义务免除论"，参见梁宇贤：《保险法新论》（修订新版），中国人民大学出版社 2004 年版，第 112 页。
❷ Raoul Colinvaux, *The Law of Insurance*, Sweet & Maxwell, (5th ed. 1984), p. 93.

建筑师事务所绩效考核管理体系设计

蔡 红　李树贤

中国建筑市场的快速发展,使其成为全球第三大市场,吸引着众多国外建筑企业包括建筑设计企业的竞相加入,使我国建筑师事务所面临着来自国内大型设计企业与国外设计企业的双重压力。建筑师事务所要想在竞争中获得生存与发展,就必须要提高自身的实力。建筑师事务所的核心竞争力来自那些拥有专业技术和专业知识的专业设计人员,如何激发他们的积极性,从而提高企业的创造力,是事务所内部管理的关键,因此需要有科学全面的绩效考核体系来激励设计人员。

1 建筑师事务所绩效管理的主要特点

1.1 我国建筑师事务所绩效管理的发展历程

我国建筑师事务所的绩效管理经历了4个阶段:赏罚调剂阶段、主观评价阶段、德能勤绩评价阶段、量化考核与目标考核阶段[1]。目前大多数建筑设计企业的绩效管理考核都处于上述4个阶段之内。如今国外很多企业在考核体系中采用了平衡计分卡(BSC)这一绩效管理工具,该工具使设计企业可以改变原来仅仅以财务指标为考核重心的方法,形成更为全面合理的绩效管理体系。

1.2 建筑师事务所员工的特点

建筑师事务所的特点是:员工人数为100人以下,部门设置少,设计人员比例大,其核心竞争力就是那些具有专业技术和专业知识的专业设计人员,即知识型员工。他们的主要特点为:

(1) 具有知识资本,即知识资源和知识创新能力。

(2) 自主性强。他们不希望依赖别人的指导和管理来完成工作,而更愿意依靠自我来完成目标。

(3) 有更高的追求。他们喜欢挑战,追求完美,赢得他人的肯定和尊重,实现自我价值是他们奋斗的目标。

(4) 工作富于创造性。知识型员工从事的不是简单重复的体力劳动,而是以知识创新为核心的工作。

(5) 忠诚度差。他们注重自身的发展,当企业不再满足其发展时便会希望跳槽,流动意愿强。

1.3 知识型员工绩效考核中存在的问题

知识型员工绩效考核中存在的主要问题有:

(1) 劳动过程难以监控。知识型员工主要从事脑力劳动,其工作没有预定的流程,且劳动时间随机,没有可供参考的标准,这样便很难对其进行监控与考核。

(2) 工作成果不易衡量。知识型员工的工作成果评价以完成的质量为重,而非以数量为主。因此,如何公正合理地定量化考核其工作质量,是知识型员工绩效考核的一个重要问题。另外,知识型员工工作的复杂性以及不确定性使得对于他们工作的失误很难进行界定,这样就无法对知识型员工的工作绩效进行准确地评价,也就无法对员工给予有效的激励。

(3) 考核阶段、考核指标及标准难以确定。知识型员工的工作知识含量高、挑战性大,工作成果在短期内难以体现,一般需要较长时间来完成,这使得知识型员工的阶段性考核及考核指标的设定成为一大难题。

2 建筑师事务所设计人员工作分析

对设计人员进行绩效考核,不仅要了解其工作特点,更要熟知他们的工作情况,这样才能便于考核

[作者简介] 蔡红(1967—),女,北京联合大学工程管理系主任,教授。主要研究方向为建设工程管理。

的操作。设计人员的工作流程如图1所示。经分析，设计人员的岗位职责如表1所示。

图1 设计人员工作流程

表1 设计人员岗位职责

职位	岗位职责	
	文案工作	绘图工作
施工图设计相关		
专业负责人	1. 按照工程主持人的详细性工作周期及时间节点控制制定本专业的详细性工作周期 2. 把控本专业的所有技术细节 3. 根据项目要求及工程主持人、经理要求在施工期间配合工地服务 4. 给下级设计师和设计助理派发设计任务单 5. 对设计人员进行绩效考核	1. 制作建筑设计总说明 2. 根据工程主持人确定的定位坐标及单体方案平立剖确定单体各层定位轴线 3. 绘制单体平面的柱、墙等结构性控制构建并确定洞口 4. 控制立面、剖面及详图
设计师	对设计人员进行绩效考核	根据专业负责人要求绘制项目相关施工图
设计助理	1. 根据项目经理、工程主持人的要求做项目相关会议的会议记录并整理会议纪要 2. 配合项目经理、工程主持人做文字录入工作 3. 对设计人员进行绩效考	1. 根据项目经理和专业负责人要求配合相关制图工作 2. 施工图整理、排版、布局、标注尺寸等图面工作
方案设计相关		
项目建筑师	1. 熟悉所设计元素的客户要求 2. 配合客户完善设计任务书 3. 确定方案的设计方向 4. 根据项目经理制定的整体框架性周期及进度制定方案阶段的设计进度 5. 确定方案设计成果及设计汇报的形式 6. 配合项目经理与客户沟通 7. 对施工图设计提出方案要求 8. 确定方案设计的相关人员 9. 协调组织专业工程师提供方案的专业支持、确定专业方案意向 10. 与项目经理共同组织方案阶段与项目有关的各种会议 11. 根据项目进度给主创建筑师及设计助理派发设计任务单 12. 根据项目要求派遣相关人员外出工作 13. 对设计人员进行绩效考核 14. 在方案结束后及时组织方案总结	1. 手绘草图（包括计算机手工相结合） 2. 组织方案成果文件
主创设计师	1. 根据项目进度及项目建筑师的要求给下级建筑师和设计助理派发设计任务单 2. 根据设计任务书、客户书面要求编制方案阶段的统一技术措施 3. 对设计师进行绩效考核 4. 积极了解新技术、新材料并对项目建筑师提出建议	1. 根据项目建筑师确定的设计方向进行深化设计 2. 根据项目建筑师要求组织方案成果的制作 3. 编写方案设计说明 4. 向施工图团队提交方案条件，其中总图控制定位要精确，每一单体应至少保证一个控制坐标点精确
建筑师	1. 对设计师进行绩效考核。 2. 根据主创建筑师的要求进行深化设计和项目制图 3. 熟练使用sketchup、photoshop并根据方案需要制作项目表现文件	
设计助理	1. 根据项目建筑师、主创设计师的要求做项目相关会议的会议记录并整理会议纪要 2. 配合项目建筑师、主创设计师做文字录入工作 3. 对主建筑师进行绩效考核	1. 根据项目建筑师和主创设计师的要求配合相关制图工作 2. 方案成果的整理、排版、布局、标注尺寸等图面工作 3. 熟练使用sketchup、photoshop并根据方案需要制作项目表现文件

3 建筑师事务所绩效考核体系设计

3.1 确定绩效考核指标体系

设计人员的绩效考核指标分为两个级别：

（1）一级指标：工作业绩、工作态度、工作能力。

（2）二级指标：设计人员的关键业绩指标，即 KPI 指标。设计人员的 KPI 指标包括：产值指标完成率、图纸合格率、出图及时率、顾客满意率、图纸使用效率、技术创新率、错误数量与错误程度等。其中，产值指标完成率为年度实收产值与年初计划产值之比；图纸合格率为年度合格项目总数与年度规定范围内项目总数之比；出图及时率为按期出图项目总数与出图项目总数之比；顾客满意率为顾客满意项目总数与当年已竣工项目总数之比；图纸使用效率为可用图纸张数与所用纸张总数之比；技术创新率为年度拥有技术创新的出图项目总数与年度出图项目总数之比；错误数量与错误程度则为审图时发现的错误总数及该错误所引发的后果严重程度。

在个体考核指标体系中，个人所属团队绩效评价情况应占一定比重。设计团队的平衡计分卡指标如表 2 所示。

表 2 设计团队的平衡计分卡指标

财务目标	产值指标完成率
	总资产报酬率
	成本费用利用率
	项目盈利率
客户角度	客户满意度
	市场占有率
	投标中标率
	客户保留率
内部流程	质量控制指标
	创新指标
	经营管理效率指标
学习与发展	员工满意度
	员工稳定性
	员工培训

设计人员全面绩效考核指标体系如图 2 所示。

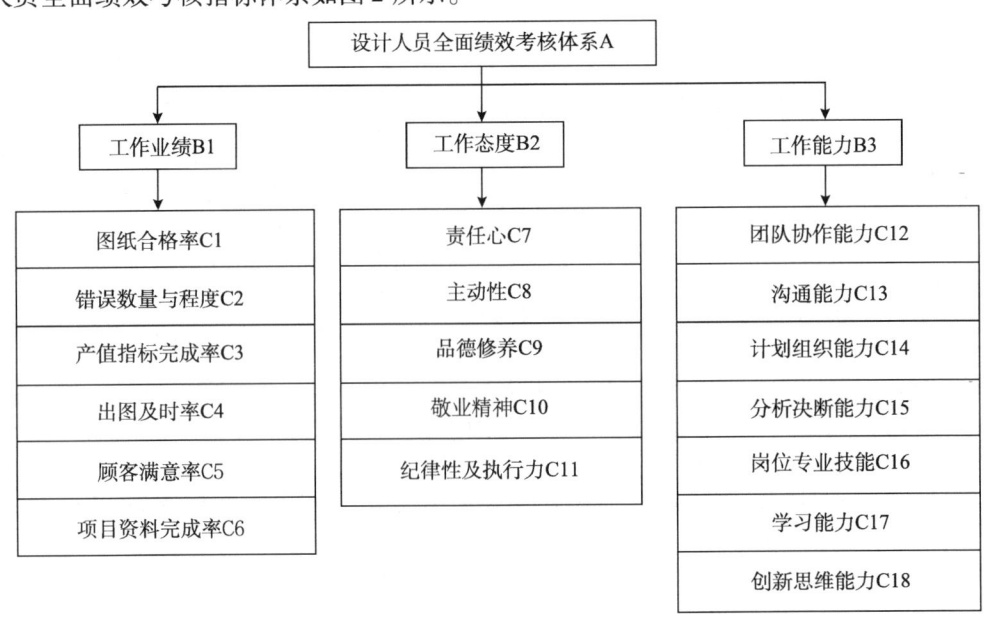

图 2 设计人员全面绩效考核指标体系

3.2 确定考核指标权重

权重确定方法采用层次分析法（AHP）。针对设计人员绩效考核指标体系中的工作业绩、工作态度、工作能力三项一级考核指标，经计算后，确定一级指标的权重，如表3所示。

表3 一级指标权重

一级绩效考核指标	权重
工作业绩 B1	60%
工作态度 B2	15%
工作能力 B3	25%

3.3 确定考核标准

（1）工作业绩考核标准。根据设计企业的战略目标，项目管理办公室与设计人员共同设定本企业的绩效计划，如表4所示，确定设计人员工作业绩考核标准[2]。

表4 项目绩效计划

	指标项	目标
工作业绩指标	图纸合格率	年度合格项目总数/年度规定范围内项目总数×100%　不低于 %
	产值指标完成率	年度实收产值/年初计划产值×100%　不低于 %
	出图及时率	未拖期出图项目总数/出图项目总数×100%　不低于 %
	顾客满意率	顾客满意项目总数/当年已竣工项目总数×100%　不低于 %
	项目资料完整率	实收资料数/应收资料数×100%　不低于 %

（2）工作态度及工作能力考核标准。通过收集企业中"优秀""良好""合格"和"不合格"的设计人员的行为资料，从这些资料中提炼出各工作态度及工作能力指标的考核等级标准。设计人员工作态度考核标准如表5所示，工作能力考核标准如表6所示。

表5 设计人员工作态度考核标准

态度指标名称	工作态度考核标准			
	优	良	合格	不合格
责任心	竭尽所能任劳任怨地完成任务	工作积极，出色完成份内工作	能自动自觉完成任务	敷衍无责任感，粗心大意；交付工作常需督导才完成
主动性	主动收集信息并加以分析，主动开辟出多种独特的方式和渠道，以及采取很多次的主动行为以完成工作	分析现成的信息，运用常规的方式和渠道，并开辟出其他方式和渠道，以及采取多次的主动行为以完成工作	有不止一次的主动行为，在别人的指导下能运用常规的方式完成工作	完成工作多数需要别人督促，工作经常拖沓
品德修养	具有较高的品德修养和理论水平，大公无私、言行足为楷模	能坚持政治理论学习、公而忘私、品行良好、言行得体、平易近人	品行正常，公私分明，尚能洁身自爱	涵养欠佳、言行随便。政治理论水平一般或较低
敬业精神	热爱本职工作，能够坚定不移地沿着既定目标前进，并能保持对目标的持续关注和全力投入的能力	对工作兴趣强烈，可以在没有外部要求的情况下为工作付出额外时间与精力	乐于追求更出色的工作结果，但没有职业满足感，尽自己的能力继续提高工作效率并完成任务	所完成的工作仅能满足客户的要求或忽视客户要求，改进工作方式有限，但仅仅能提供要求的服务和设计质量，并厌倦长期从事本工作
纪律性及执行力	认真执行公司规章制度和组织纪律，工作中坚持原则，服从组织决议	能执行公司规章制度和组织纪律，工作中比较坚持原则	能基本坚持原则。虽有未遵守纪律和原则的行为，但未对工作造成不良后果	对上级指示、规定执行不及时，有时对自身要求不够严格，违反公司纪律，甚至造成不良后果
对应分值	100	80	60	40

表6 设计人员工作能力考核标准

能力指标名称	工作能力考核标准			
	优	良	合格	不合格
团队协作能力	能经常不计个人得失，主动与他人进行协作	当别人找到他时，基本上能尽力帮别人解决问题	多数情况下能与同事互相帮助，保持和睦相处	很多时候不会主动协助他人；事不关己，高高挂起。对本职工作有不满情绪，经常牢骚满腹
沟通能力	善于与上下周围人群沟通，平衡各方关系，能自发与人合作	乐意与人沟通，协调关系，能顺利达成任务	尚能与人合作，达成工作要求	协调不善，致使工作较难开展；不与人合作，工作无法开展
计划组织能力	能依据工作目标，预见工作的要求与不利因素并做出切实可行的计划，能变通地执行计划，组织实施严密有条理，合理调配有关资源，善于总结提高	能依据工作目标，基本预见工作的要求与不利因素并做出切实可行的计划，能按计划执行工作，组织实施基本严密有条理，基本能合理调配有关资源，能够总结提高	尚能依据工作目标做出计划，能按计划执行，组织实施有条理，能调配有关资源	不能依据工作目标做出切实可行的计划，未能按计划执行，组织实施缺乏条理，缺乏合理调配资源的能力
分析决断能力	善于分析问题，把握问题的本质，能快速分析解决问题的办法，果断选择以解决问题	懂得分析问题，找寻问题的本质与解决办法，能快速选择以解决问题	基本能够分析问题以及解决问题的办法，基本能选择办法以解决问题	缺乏分析问题、解决问题的能力，遇到问题犹豫不决
设计岗位专业技能	具备扎实的设计专业知识，熟练掌握本学科设计工作的技术、技巧，经验丰富	熟悉与建筑设计相关学科的知识，掌握设计工作的技术技巧，经验较丰富	具备本学科设计专业知识，对相关知识有一定了解，基本掌握设计工作	有一定岗位专业知识，但不全面，相关知识了解不够，经验不够
学习能力	面对工作需要能快速更新自己的知识结构和概念，并能够通过培训向他人进行传授并指导他人开展工作	面对工作需要能吸收新的知识和概念，最终具备设计相关专业的最前沿知识并应用到工作中	面对工作需要能吸收新的知识和概念，部分具备设计相关专业的最前沿知识，并在指导下能够应用到相关工作中	面对工作需要能吸收部分新知识，也能具备设计相关专业的最前沿知识，但应用不到相关工作中；面对工作需要不吸收新知识，依然难于具备设计相关专业的前沿知识，在工作中，只能凭老本吃饭
创新思维能力	对工作不断提出创新的、突破性的改进提案和新思路，多数能够被采纳和实施	有时工作提出创新的、突破性的改进提案和新思路，多数能够被采纳和实施	能对工作提出创新的、突破性的解决方案，少数方案被采纳和实施	能对工作提出新思路，但多数不切合实际；缺乏创新能力，基本上不能提出突破性的设计方案和思路
对应分值	100	80	60	40

3.4 考核流程

（1）制定绩效考核计划与绩效考核标准。由项目管理办公室填写业绩绩效考核计划表与绩效考核标准表。项目管理办公室填写完上述表格后提交给总经理审核，审核合格则发布给所有参与绩效考核的员工进行查看。

（2）填写工作周报与个人项目总结表。每周末由设计人员填写工作周报中本周工作计划完成情况汇报，提交给各专业负责人审核，审核不合格的发回给设计人员修改，审核合格的则由专业负责人填写下周计划。下周计划填写完发给设计人员进行确认，设计人员不确认发回给各专业负责人协商修改，确认后提交给项目管理办公室，由项目管理办公室在次周周一进行汇总。

（3）绩效考核。1）月度考核：每月月底由项目管理办公室发起考核，所有参与绩效考核的人员进行评分工作，填写专业设计员工绩效考核表，评分完毕由项目管理办公室审核汇总，并填写月度考核总结表。2）项目业绩考核：每半年由项目管理办公室发起考核，所有被考核人填写项目业绩考核表，进行项目业绩自我评分，评分完提交给各专业负责人进行审核，审核合格后提交给项目管理办公室审核汇总。

3.5 考核结果的应用

（1）与工资挂钩。设计人员的工资＝基本工资＋绩效工资（绩效工资是以设计人员的项目提成额为基础）。绩效工资＝预付绩效工资＋剩余绩效工资＊绩效考核系数。

（2）职位等级调整。企业可根据年度绩效考核结果，对设计师的职位等级进行晋级、保留原级、降级。

（3）培训计划，包括绩效考核培训计划和员工培训计划。

（4）员工发展计划。绩效考核结果包括各指标的得分，以及其他员工对自己的意见汇总。将考核结果反馈给员工，使他们不仅有了改进工作的依据和目标，在企业战略目标的指导下，设计人员还将不断提高工作能力，开发自身潜能，不断改进和优化工作方式，最终实现个人职业目标和企业目标。

4 结 论

企业的发展需要企业有全面科学的绩效考核体系，建筑师事务所的绩效考核既要考虑中小企业的特征，还要结合知识型员工的特点及设计人员的岗位职责，深入了解企业的实际情况。

绩效考核指标的确定需要结合企业的发展目标、员工的工作分析，融合关键绩效指标法和平衡计分卡法，这样绩效考核才能更科学、合理、易操作。

绩效考核过程并不仅仅是绩效评分，还需要有绩效反馈与改进，需要与员工薪酬等挂钩，才能充分发挥绩效考核的激励作用。

参考文献

[1] 俞辉."平衡计分卡"在设计单位绩效考核中的应用探索［J］.优秀民营设计论坛，2006（4）：17-19.
[2] 张旭.SZ建筑设计院的绩效考评体系改进研究［D］.西安：西北大学，2007.
[3] 尹隆森，孙宗虎.目标分解与绩效考核设计实务［M］.北京：人民邮电出版社，2006：12-14.
[4] STEPHEN EMMITT. Design management for architects［M］. U.K：Blackwell Publishing，2007.
[5] 姜定维.KPI——关键绩效指引成功［M］.北京：北京大学出版社，2004：98-99.
[6] 胡勇军.绩效考评与管理［M］.北京：机械工业出版社，2007（1）：115.
[7] 吕思泓.济南舜华建设发展有限公司绩效考核体系分析与设计［D］.天津：天津大学，2008.
[8] 冯杰.建筑设计企业基于创新激励的绩效管理研究［J］.建筑经济，2008（9）：100-101.

发明专利

(19) 中华人民共和国国家知识产权局

(12) 发明专利

(10) 授权公告号 CN101502307B
(45) 授权公告日 2012.05.23

(21) 申请号 200910079478.7
(22) 申请日 2009.03.12
(73) 专利权人 北京联合大学生物化学工程学院
地址 100023 北京市朝阳区垡头西里三区18号
(72) 发明人 龚平　赵有玺　卢鑫鑫　周贺新
(74) 专利代理机构 北京科龙寰宇知识产权代理有限
责任公司　11139
代理人 孙皓晨　费碧华

审查员 王文庆

(51) Int. Cl.
A23L1/076 (2006.01)
A23L1/29 (2006.01)

(56) 对比文件
CN　1321442A，2001.11.14，权利要求1、4.
杨晓萍等. 油菜花粉破壁方法研究.《华中农业大学学报》. 2004，第23卷（第6期），671-672.

权利要求书1页　说明书5页　附图1页

(54) 发明名称
蜂花粉无糖活性速溶颗粒

(57) 摘要
本发明提供一种蜂花粉活性成分速溶颗粒的制备方法及产品，是采用复合酶酶解破壁方法进行蜂花粉破壁后与常用赋型剂制备成颗粒。植物复合水解酶酶解蜂花粉是现今最新的工艺方法，与其他方法相比较，该方法具有简单、条件温和、容易操作、反应过程耗时短、破壁率高等显著特点。蜂花粉经酶解后，其中的主要活性成分含量显著提高，所含致敏物质被酶解分解，从而既大幅度提高了产品的营养价值，又提高了花粉产品的食用安全性，提升了产品品质。

CN 101502307 B 权 利 要 求 书

1. 一种蜂花粉活性成分速溶颗粒的制备方法，主要包括以下步骤。

A. 配制柠檬酸缓冲溶液：将柠檬酸5.50~50.50g和柠檬酸钠14.70~60.00溶于150~200ml去离子水中，调整缓冲溶液的pH值至2.5~6.8，取60~120ml缓冲溶液倒入250ml的锥形瓶中；

B. 将所述缓冲溶液在灭菌锅中0.05~0.50Mpa，灭菌15~45min，取出冷却后备用；

C. 取植物复合水解酶80~400μL，将其加入到上述冷却的缓冲溶液中至溶解，再称取经干热灭菌的蜂花粉5~45g加入到该锥形瓶中，混和均匀；所述植物复合水解酶为纤维素酶1~5份，果胶酶1~5份，蛋白酶1~5份，均为重量份；

D. 摇床培养：在转速120~250rpm，反应温度30~45℃，提取时间2~10h，pH2.5~6.8的条件下，确保花粉酶解破壁充分；

E. 反应混合液经减压过滤得提取液，冷冻干燥得到浓缩液；

F. 将过滤后的不溶性固形物在40~120℃恒温烘箱烘干至恒重；

G. 制粒：将所述浓缩液、所述不溶性固形物与药物学常用无糖型赋型剂、溶剂混合后制成颗粒。

2. 根据权利要求1所述的制备方法，其特征在于所述植物复合水解酶为纤维素酶、果胶酶、蛋白酶的重量比为1:1:1的混合物。

3. 根据权利要求1所述的制备方法，其特征在于所述摇床培养的条件为反应温度45℃，提取时间6h，pH3.4。

4. 根据权利要求1所述的制备方法，其特征在于所述制粒包括以下步骤，分别称取如下重量份数的原料：所述浓缩液20~80份、可溶性淀粉20~50份、不溶性固形物10~90份、木糖醇2~10份、羧甲基纤维素2~10份和麦芽糊精10~50份混合均匀，加入30~100ml乙醇溶液和食用香精适量活成团状，于20目筛上搓成颗粒，散开，30~60℃烘干1~4h。

5. 根据权利要求4所述的制备方法，其特征在于所述制粒包括以下步骤。分别称取如下重量份数的原料：所述浓缩液50份、可溶性淀粉30份、不溶性固形物20份、木糖醇3份、羧甲基纤维素4份和麦芽糊精25份混合均匀，加入50ml乙醇溶液和占原料总重0.5%~1%的食用香精活成团状，于20目筛上搓成颗粒，散开，40℃烘干2小时。

6. 根据权利要求4或5所述的制备方法，其特征在于所述乙醇溶液为蒸馏水和无水乙醇按体积比1:4~4:1配制而成。

7. 一种蜂花粉活性成分速溶颗粒，其特征在于，它是根据权利要求1-6任一项所述的方法制备得到的。

8. 权利要求7所述的蜂花粉活性成分速溶颗粒作为食品添加剂或在制备医药保健品中的用途。

蜂花粉无糖活性速溶颗粒

技术领域

[0001] 本发明涉及一种蜂花粉无糖活性速溶颗粒及其制备方法，属于医药、保健食品领域。

背景技术

[0002] 自《本草纲目》以来，蜂花粉的全面复合型营养和神奇功效，一直受到国人追捧，在中国民间具有广泛的药用和食用群体。近年来，在部分功能性食品和药品不断出现安全事故的背景下，追求平衡健康、重视食疗食补以及回归天然的科学理念再度回归。近年来，蜂花粉其产品的开发利用研究在国内外已再次引起广泛地开展，已引起人们的重视。欧、美一些国家兴起花粉热，利用花粉食品，提高食品业营养价值。我国也利用花粉作食品添加剂和医药保健品，提高食品的营养价值和防病治病的功能。

[0003] 蜂花粉是蜜蜂从种子植物的花朵上采集花粉过程中形成的花粉团，含有人体所必需的蛋白质（SOD、多种氨基酸）、脂类、碳水化合物、多种维生素（维生素C、E、A、D、P、B_1、B_6）和微量元素（K、P、Fe、Cu、Mn、Mg、Ca、Zn等），以及对人体生理机能有特殊功效的黄酮类、核酸、天然植物激素、性激素和促性腺激素等多种生物活性物质，在国际上蜂花粉被称为"完全营养品"，它具有明显的增强人体免疫力、抗疲劳、延缓衰老、美容以及治疗前列腺疾病等作用。

[0004] 我国幅员辽阔，蜂花粉资源丰富，特别是近年来，我国油菜的栽种面积增加，因而油菜蜂花粉是高产价廉的蜂花粉。虽然油菜蜂花粉对人体有许许多多的益处，但其固有的腥涩气味以及一定的致敏性往往使部分消费者避而远之。

[0005] 根据花粉的结构可知，成熟的花粉壁分为明显的2层，即内壁和外壁。外壁较厚、硬而缺乏弹性，主要成分是纤维素，具有抗酸、抗生物分解的特性。外壁通常有萌发孔或沟缝，为外壁最薄弱的地方，花粉粒萌发时由此伸出花粉壁。其外壁结构中的孢粉素具有耐酸、耐碱、耐温、耐压，以及对胃酸和其他消化系统酶非常稳定的理化特性。不少研究表明，当花粉进入人体的消化道时，虽然可以通过表面的萌发孔释放一些营养成分，但为数极少。因此，为了提高花粉的开发利用价值，对其进行特殊的破壁处理就显得尤为重要。

[0006] 花粉破壁是指花粉的细胞受到不同程度的损伤，以便花粉内含营养物质的释放、吸收和利用。它是花粉加工中的一个关键技术。

[0007] 目前国内外报道的花粉破壁方法包括湿法破壁和干法破壁。主要湿法破壁方法有：温差破壁法、机械破壁法、有机溶剂破壁法、发酵酶解破壁法等；主要干法破壁主法有微波辐射破壁法和气流粉碎法。现有的破壁方法虽然各有其优点，但是缺点同样明显，或者处理周期长，对花粉的营养成分破坏较大；或者破壁过程中产生大量热量，导致花粉酶活的丧失；或者工艺复杂且成本昂贵，增加产品成本，在生产中不易推广使用。

发明内容

[0008] 为了解决上述问题，本发明的目的在于提供一种蜂花粉活性成分速溶颗粒的制备方法及产品，是采用复合酶酶解破壁方法进行蜂花粉破壁后与常用赋型剂制备成颗粒。植物复合水解酶酶解蜂花粉是现今最新的工艺方法。与其他方法相比较，该方法具有简单、条件温和、容易操作、反应过程耗时短、破壁率高等显著特点。蜂花粉经酶解后，其中的主要活性成分含量显著提高，所含致敏物质被酶解分解，不仅大幅度提高了产品的营养价值，同时又提高了花粉产品的食用安全性，提升了产品品质。

[0009] 为了达到所述目的，本发明提供一种蜂花粉活性成分速溶颗粒的制备方法，其主要包括以下步骤：

[0010] 1. 配制柠檬酸缓冲溶液：将柠檬酸5.50~50.50g和柠檬酸钠14.70~60.00g溶于150~200ml去离子水中，调整缓冲溶液的pH值为2.5~6.8，取60~120ml缓冲溶液倒入250ml的锥形瓶中；

[0011] 2. 将所述缓冲溶液在灭菌锅中0.05~0.50Mpa,灭菌15~45min,取出冷却后备用;

[0012] 3. 取植物复合水解酶80~400μl,将其加入到上述冷却的缓冲溶液中至溶解,再称取经干热灭菌的蜂花粉5~45g加入到该锥形瓶中,混和均匀;

[0013] 4. 摇床培养:在转速120~250rpm,反应温度30~45℃,提取时间2~10h,pH2.5~6.8的条件,确保花粉酶解破壁充分;

[0014] 5. 反应混合液经减压过滤得提取液,测量提取液总体积,并测其总黄酮、SOD酶活力,再取50ml冷冻干燥得到浓缩液,计算蜂花粉提取率。

[0015] 6. 将过滤后的不溶性固形物(其主要成分包括纤维素、半纤维素、花粉多糖、脂肪、蛋白质和矿物质)取样,在40~120℃恒温干燥箱烘干,至含水量2.5%~12.5%。

[0016] 7. 制粒:将上述浓缩液、不溶性固形物与药物学常用赋型剂(无糖型)、溶剂混合后制成颗粒。

[0017] 其中,所述植物复合水解酶选自纤维素酶、果胶酶、蛋白酶中的一种以上任意比例混合物,优选含纤维素酶:果胶酶:蛋白酶的重量比为1~5:1~5:1~5,更优选纤维素酶:果胶酶:蛋白酶的重量比为1:1:1。

[0018] 所述摇床培养的条件优选为反应温度45℃,提取时间6h,pH3.4。

[0019] 所述步骤7中的制粒例如可以采用药典所述的配方和方法。在本发明的较佳实施例中,采用如下方法。

[0020] 分别称取如下重量份数的原料:所述浓缩液20~80份、可溶性淀粉20~50份、不溶性固形物10~90份、木糖醇2~10份、羧甲基纤维素2~10份和麦芽糊精10~50份混合均匀,加入乙醇溶液30~100ml和食用香精适量活成团状,于20目筛上搓成颗粒,散开,30~60℃烘干1~4h。通风冷却,装袋。

[0021] 其中,优选的,是将所述浓缩液50份、可溶性淀粉30份、不溶性固形物20份、木糖醇3份、羧甲基纤维素4份和麦芽糊精25份混合均匀,加入50ml乙醇溶液和占原料总重0.5%~1%的食用香精活成团状,于20目筛上搓成颗粒,散开,40℃烘干2h。

[0022] 其中,所述乙醇溶液为蒸馏水和无水乙醇按体积比1:4~4:1配制而成,优选体积比1:1。

[0023] 经本发明方法制备得到的提取液总体积为200-280ml,蜂花粉提取率为25%~55%,不溶性固形物含水量为2.5%~12.5%。所制得的油菜蜂花粉颗粒按《中国药典》(2005版)颗粒剂进行理化质量检查。

[0024] 本发明得到的酶解蜂花粉颗粒破壁率高,活性成分含量大大提高,花粉黄酮含量平均提高了2.07倍,花粉SOD酶活力也有较高的保留。酶解花粉其感官指标亦有显著提升:颜色由酶解前因花源差异导致的花粉颗粒自然色差,改善为均一柔和淡黄色;口感由酶解前微涩味,改善为具有植物自然清新及低度甜味。花粉经酶解后,过敏原被水解破坏,提高了产品生物安全度。

附图说明

[0025] 图1为蜂花粉速溶颗粒剂展示图;

图1

[0026] 图2为蜂花粉速溶颗粒剂5min溶解图；

图2

[0027] 图3为蜂花粉速溶颗粒剂展示图。

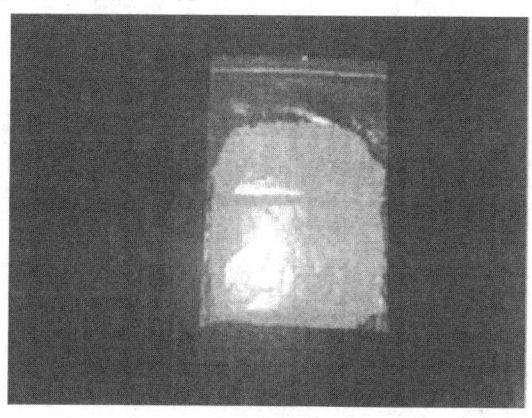

图3

具体实施方式

[0028] 下面结合实施例对本发明作进一步说明，应该理解的是，这些实施例仅用于例证的目的，决不限制本发明的保护范围。

[0029] [对照例1] 本例为空白对照组。

[0030] 配制柠檬酸缓冲溶液，将柠檬酸5.50~50.50g和柠檬酸钠14.70~60.00g溶于200ml去离子水中，调整缓冲溶液的pH值至2.5~6.8，取80ml缓冲液倒入250ml的锥形瓶中；将所述缓冲溶液在灭菌锅中0.1Mpa，灭菌20min，取出冷却后备用。

[0031] 将20g经干热灭菌的蜂花粉加入到上述缓冲液中，上摇床培养，在转速为120rpm，反应温度45℃，提取时间6h，pH3.4的条件下，充分破壁。反应混合液经减压抽滤后，测量得到的提取液体积为200ml，之后取50ml浓缩，液冷冻干燥，测得其总黄酮含量为247.249mg/100g，其SOD酶活力为203.160U/mL。

[0032] 将抽滤后的不溶性固形物取样，在40~120℃恒温烘箱烘干至恒重计算含水量为4.5%。

[0033] 将上述浓缩液50g、可溶性淀粉30g、不溶性固形物20g、木糖醇3g、羧甲基纤维素4g和麦芽糊精25g混合均匀，加入50ml乙醇溶液（蒸馏水和无水乙醇按体积比1:1配置而成）和食用香精（占原料总重的0.6%）活成团状，于20目筛上搓成颗粒，散开，40℃烘干2h即得本发明颗粒。

[0034] [实施例1]

[0035] 缓冲溶液的制备同对照例1。取80μl植物复合水解酶（纤维素酶:果胶酶:蛋白酶的重量比为1:1:1），和20g蜂花粉同时加入到缓冲液中，在转速为120rpm，反应温度45℃，提取时间6h，pH3.4

的条件下，充分破壁。反应混合液经减压抽滤后，测量得到的提取液体积为250ml，之后取50ml浓缩，冷冻干燥，测得其总黄酮含量为335.520mg/100g，其SOD酶活力为149.96U/mL。

[0036] 将抽滤后的不溶性固形物取样，在40~120℃恒温烘箱烘干至恒重计算含水量为5.0%。

[0037] 将上述浓缩液50g、可溶性淀粉30g、不溶性固形物20g、木糖醇3g、羧甲基纤维素4g和麦芽糊精25g混合均匀，加入50ml乙醇溶液（蒸馏水和无水乙醇按体积比1:1配置而成）和食用香精（占原料总重的0.6%）活成团状，于20目筛上搓成颗粒，散开，40℃烘干即得本发明颗粒。

[0038] ［实施例2］

[0039] 缓冲溶液的制备同对照例1。取80μl植物复合水解酶（纤维素酶:果胶酶:蛋白酶的重量比为2:1:1），和20g蜂花粉同时加入到缓冲液中，在转速为150rpm，反应温度45℃，提取时间6h，pH3.4的条件下，充分破壁。反应混合液经减压抽滤后，测量得到的提取液体积为280ml，之后取50ml浓缩，冷冻干燥，测得其总黄酮含量为352.603mg/100g，其SOD酶活力为203.15U/mL。

[0040] 将抽滤后的不溶性固形物取样，在60℃恒温烘箱烘干至恒重计算含水量为2.5%。

[0041] 将上述浓缩液20g、可溶性淀粉50g、不溶性固形物50g、木糖醇7g、羧甲基纤维素6g和麦芽糊精25g混合均匀，加入70ml乙醇溶液（蒸馏水和无水乙醇按体积比1:4配置而成）和食用香精（占原料总重的1%）活成团状，于20目筛上搓成颗粒，散开，40℃烘干即得本发明颗粒。

[0042] ［实施例3］

[0043] 缓冲溶液的制备同对照例1。取100μl植物复合水解酶（纤维素酶:果胶酶:蛋白酶的重量比为5:3:1），和40g蜂花粉同时加入到缓冲液中，在转速为150rpm，反应温度45℃，提取时间10h，pH6.8的条件下，充分破壁。反应混合液经减压抽滤后，测量得到的提取液体积为250ml，之后取50ml提取液冷冻干燥得到浓缩液，测得其总黄酮含量为389.063mg/100g，其SOD酶活力为214.14U/mL。

[0044] 将抽滤后的不溶性固形物取样，在100℃恒温烘箱烘干至恒重计算含水量为10.0%。

[0045] 将上述浓缩液80g、可溶性淀粉40g、不溶性固形物10g、木糖醇8g、羧甲基纤维素4g和麦芽糊精15g混合均匀，加入80ml乙醇溶液（蒸馏水和无水乙醇按体积比4:1配置而成）和食用香精（占原料总重的0.7%）活成团状，于20目筛上搓成颗粒，散开，60℃烘干2h即得本发明颗粒。

[0046] ［实施例4］

[0047] 缓冲溶液的制备同对照例1。取200μl植物复合水解酶（纤维素酶:果胶酶:蛋白酶的重量比为1:4:2），和30g蜂花粉同时加入到缓冲液中，在转速为150rpm，反应温度40℃，提取时间4h，pH3.4的条件下，充分破壁。反应混合液经减压抽滤后，测量得到的提取液体积为210ml，之后取50ml提取液冷冻干燥得到浓缩液，测得其总黄酮含量为439.063mg/100g，其SOD酶活力为256.61U/mL。

[0048] 将抽滤后的不溶性固形物取样，在80℃恒温烘箱烘干至恒重计算含水量为6.0%。

[0049] 将上述浓缩液20g、可溶性淀粉20g、不溶性固形物90g、木糖醇8g、羧甲基纤维素10g和麦芽糊精40g混合均匀，加入100ml乙醇溶液（蒸馏水和无水乙醇按体积比1:1配置而成）和食用香精（占原料总重的0.8%）活成团状，于20目筛上搓成颗粒，散开，40℃烘干4h即得本发明颗粒。

[0050] ［实施例5］

[0051] 缓冲溶液的制备同对照例1。取300μl植物复合水解酶（纤维素酶:果胶酶:蛋白酶的重量比为2:4:3），和10g蜂花粉同时加入到缓冲液中，在转速为150rpm，反应温度35℃，提取时间6h，pH4.5的条件下，充分破壁。反应混合液经减压抽滤后，测量得到的提取液体积为270ml，之后取50ml提取液冷冻干燥得到浓缩液，测得其总黄酮含量为472.190mg/100g，其SOD酶活力为267.30U/mL。

[0052] 将抽滤后的不溶性固形物取样，在120℃恒温烘箱烘干至恒重计算含水量为5.8%。

[0053] 将上述浓缩液50g、可溶性淀粉30g、不溶性固形物60g、木糖醇2g、羧甲基纤维素10g和麦芽糊精15g混合均匀，加入40ml乙醇溶液（蒸馏水和无水乙醇按体积比2:1配置而成）和食用香精（占原料总重的0.9%）活成团状，于20目筛上搓成颗粒，散开，20℃烘干3h即得本发明颗粒。

[0054] ［实施例6］

[0055] 缓冲溶液的制备同对照例1。取400μl植物复合水解酶（纤维素酶:果胶酶:蛋白酶的重量比为5:2:4），和20g蜂花粉同时加入到缓冲液中，在转速为120rpm，反应温度45℃，提取时间5h，pH3.4

的条件下，充分破壁。反应混合液经减压抽滤后，测量得到的提取液体积为240ml，之后取50ml提取液冷冻干燥得到浓缩液，测得其总黄酮含量为512.813mg/100g，其SOD酶活力为320.77U/mL。

[0056] 将抽滤后的不溶性固形物取样，在105℃恒温烘箱烘干至恒重计算含水量为11.2%。

[0057] 将上述浓缩液50g、可溶性淀粉40g、不溶性固形物10g、木糖醇3g、羧甲基纤维素10g和麦芽糊精25g混合均匀，加入50ml乙醇溶液（蒸馏水和无水乙醇按体积比1:3配置而成）和食用香精（占原料总重的0.5%）活成团状，于20目筛上搓成颗粒，散开，40℃烘干1h即得本发明颗粒。

[0058] 以上所述仅为本发明的较佳实施例，对本发明而言仅仅是说明性的，而非限制性的。本专业技术人员理解，在本发明权利要求所限定的精神和范围内可对其进行许多改变，修改，甚至等效，但都将落入本发明的保护范围内。

发明专利证书

证书号 第1308678号

发 明 名 称：电梯的防坠落机构及装有这种机构的电梯

发 明 人：张子义；杨志勤；谭蒲苗；朱家潮；蔺廿辉；张鹤；陶大伟

专 利 号：ZL 2011 1 0296880.8

专利申请日：2011年09月30日

专 利 权 人：北京联合大学

授权公告日：2013年11月13日

　　本发明经过本局依照中华人民共和国专利法进行审查，决定授予专利权，颁发本证书并在专利登记簿上予以登记。专利权自授权公告之日起生效。

　　本专利的专利权期限为二十年，自申请日起算。专利权人应当依照专利法及其实施细则规定缴纳年费。本专利的年费应当在每年09月30日前缴纳。未按照规定缴纳年费的，专利权自应当缴纳年费期满之日起终止。

　　专利证书记载专利权登记时的法律状况。专利权的转移、质押、无效、终止、恢复和专利权人的姓名或名称、国籍、地址变更等事项记载在专利登记簿上。

局长 田力普

关于"助眠卧室系统"的说明

1 成果简介

失眠困扰着很多人。目前对抗失眠常用的方法是采用医药或营养品,也有采用一些改善卧室环境的技术方案。例如,有一个专利申请公开了一种整体卧室设计,它是通过床上和床周围用品的布置设计,达到改善睡眠环境的目的,但这种改善仅限于视觉效果。另一个专利技术方案是通过控制卧室的温度和湿度来营造舒适的睡眠环境,这一方案也只是从温度和湿度两个方面来改善睡眠环境。

"助眠卧室系统"发明专利推出了一种全新卧室系统,它包括卧室内的床、室内灯具、空调、湿度调节器、控制器、从室内向室外排气的气泵、音频播放装置、视频播放装置、噪声发生器、电磁波发生器、利眠气体喷射器、呼吸遥测器、室内压力检测器,以及设置在室外的室内低压报警器。

"助眠卧室系统"发明专利克服了目前现有其他发明专利在技术上的局限性,从多方面同时解决睡眠的环境问题,不仅助人入睡,而且能够使人安眠,确保睡眠质量,为失眠者带来福音。

2 应用范围及其应用前景

采用本发明的助眠安系统,可以根据失眠患者的具体需求提供适合于该患者的睡眠环境,不仅助其入睡,而且能够使其安眠,还可以在患者小睡将醒时通过降低空气密度和/或喷入利眠气体而抑制其醒来,从而确保其睡眠质量。

目前其他发明的技术方案及其实施例中的各细节部分都很容易在市场上获得,而本发明的基本框架是对现有技术的结合。还需要指出的是,本发明的外延不仅包括了目前其他发明专利的各种特征及其技术方案,而且只要这些组合在本申请的权利要求书的范畴内,就还包括这些特征和技术方案的各种组合。

3 成果转让方式

本专利的发明人服从学校及学校科研处的领导与安排,相关事宜双方可以协商解决。

说 明 书

助眠卧室系统

1 技术领域

本发明是一种助人入睡并且能够安眠的助眠卧室系统。

2 研制背景

失眠困扰着很多人。目前对抗失眠常用的方法是采用医药或营养品，也有采用一些改善卧室环境的技术方案。申请号为200610126806.0的中国专利申请公开了一种整体卧室设计，它是通过床上和床周围用品的布置设计，达到改善睡眠环境的效果，但这种改善仅限于视觉效果。公开号为WO2008/056717的PCT申请提出的技术方案是通过控制卧室的温度和湿度来营造舒适的睡眠环境，这一专利也是从温度和湿度来改善睡眠环境。

3 发明内容

本发明的目的是为了克服现有专利技术的局限性，从多方面同时解决睡眠的环境问题，不仅助人入睡，而且能够使人安眠，确保睡眠质量，为失眠者带来福音。

本发明推出了一种全新的助眠卧室系统，它包括卧室及其室内的床、灯具、空调、湿度调节器、控制器、从室内向室外排气的气泵、音频播放装置、视频播放装置、噪声发生器、电磁波发生器、利眠气体喷射器、呼吸遥测器、室内压力检测器，以及设置在室外的室内低压报警器。卧室为气密和光密封的，具有良好的隔音效果，不仅与室外隔音，而且能够隔离气泵的工作噪声。呼吸遥测器与控制器联接，用于遥测睡眠者的呼吸，当检测到睡眠者呼吸深度增加时就会向控制器传送信号。控制器还与卧室内的空调、湿度调节器、灯具、气泵、利眠气体喷射器、噪声发生器和电磁波发生器连接，用于根据编程控制卧室内的空调、湿度调节器、灯具、噪音发生器和电磁波发生器中至少之一的运行，并根据来自呼吸遥测器的信号控制气泵和/或利眠气体喷射器的运行。室内压力检测器与室外报警器配合，当室内压力低于设定的阈值时，室外报警器就会发出报警信号。控制器中不仅储存有用于发现睡眠者渐醒的呼吸深度上限值，而且储存有一呼吸深度下限值，当呼吸遥测器检测到睡眠者的呼吸深度低于该下限时，控制影片播放装置和/或视频播放装置就会逐渐减弱音量和/或视频的亮度。控制器内还装有计时器并储存有睡眠者正常的一次睡眠时间值（其作用将在后文中予以阐述）。室内灯具优选能在控制器的控制下产生有利于失眠症患者睡眠的特定效果的灯光。

人们关于睡眠的传统认识是，环境越安静、光线越暗，越适合睡眠。然而最新的医学研究发现，这并不是对任何人都通用的"公理"。一些失眠症患者往往越是夜深人静越是不能入睡，相反，特定的噪声、特定波长的昏暗灯光，反而容易使这些失眠症患者的大脑皮层疲劳，抑制了神经元兴奋的传播，或者直接使这些神经元疲劳，有利于他们入睡，甚至其他特定的电磁波也有利于某些人的睡眠。室内的温度和湿度也应调节得有利于睡眠。另一个影响睡眠的因素是室内含氧量，一般来说，含氧量越高，人的大脑越清醒，就越不利于睡眠。所以，本发明的助眠卧室系统中的卧室是气密的，而且系统里装有排气泵，可以适当地降低卧室内的氧气含量，从而抑制大脑的清醒和兴奋，确保睡眠质量。特别是当呼吸遥测器检测到睡眠者呼吸加深，即睡眠者有可能醒来时，就会向控制器发出信号，而控制器接到这个信号后就会判断睡眠者是否已经睡够事先预定的睡眠时间。当睡眠者的睡眠时间尚未达到事先预定的时间时，气泵就会向室外排出空气，将室内的空气密度降低，从而使睡眠者由于缺少氧气而再次睡熟。控制器中设定一个室内压力安全预定值，当室内压力传感器检测到的室内气压低于该安全预定值时，控制器即停止气泵的工作。当呼吸遥测器检测到睡眠者呼吸加深并向控制器发出信号，而控制器接到这个信号后，就会判断睡眠者尚未睡够事先预定的睡眠时间，控制器即刻启动利眠气体喷射器进行喷射，但该喷射器内的利眠气体装入量不得超过该气体对人体的安全极限。当然，气泵和利眠气体喷射器也可以在睡眠开始时使用，应视失眠患者的具体情况而定。气泵和利眠气体喷射器可以同时启动，也可以分别启动。

利眠气体可以采用芬太尼，但必须慎重，应采用微量。系统中的利眠气体喷射器中只能装入对人体基本上没有危害的一次用量，避免喷入过量而对睡眠者造成伤害，并优选有利于睡眠效果的某些植物释放的气体。

可以根据患者的特定情况对控制器编程。例如，如果失眠症患者适合于在某种频率的噪音下睡眠，则可控制噪声发生器发出该频率的噪声。如果患者适合在特定的迷幻灯光下睡眠，则可控制室内灯具发出该特定的迷幻灯光。例如，灯具可以尽可能靠近天花板，并将其分布构成设置为有益于睡眠的图案，如星空、夏夜花草等，也可以构成一幅三维立体画，睡眠者读画时大脑容易产生疲劳，读出画中画后，又容易使人对环境产生模糊感觉，这些都有利于睡眠者入睡。

综上所述，采用本发明的助眠卧室系统，可以根据失眠患者的具体需求提供适合于该患者的睡眠环境，不仅助其入睡，还可以在患者小睡将醒时通过降低空气密度和/或喷入利眠气体而抑制其醒来，从而确保其睡眠质量。本发明的实施将为众多失眠患者带来福音，彻底改变其失眠不治的状况。

4　具体实施

下面描述一优选实施例。

本实施例中的卧室为一名患者使用，因此卧室面积可以为$10m^2$左右，房间带有一个边长约为0.5m的方形窗户，装有隔音玻璃和隔音且不透光窗帘。窗帘同样为方形，其各边应从窗户的相应边分别延伸出0.5m以上，以确保遮光和隔音效果。床南北向放置，床头朝北，床尾朝南。这是为了使人睡眠时顺磁场，有利于睡眠。视频播放装置设置在床头的前方，并带有投影仪，以便向侧墙壁上投影，方便睡眠者观看，该视频播放装置可以借助U盘播放。音频播放装置设置在床头上，带有一个小功率音箱。在床头的上方设置一个呼吸遥测器。例如，将一个二氧化碳瞬时检测器与一个控制器联接，二氧化碳瞬时检测器能够向控制器传送睡眠者呼吸的强弱信号，控制器中设有呼吸深度的一个阈值。控制器还与视频播放装置和音频播放装置联接，以实现对它们的控制，并且还与设置在墙上的气泵和同样设置在床头上方的利眠气体喷射器联接。气泵设置在穿过墙体的一个空洞中，在该空洞的内侧设有单向阀，使得气体只能排出，不能进入室内。所述单向阀的阀片和阀座都采用减震材料，气泵空洞设置在离床最远的位置，以将噪声减至最小。室内还装有一个室内压力传感器，其分别与控制器和设置在室外的报警器联接。控制器内设有室内压力的安全下限值，当室内空气压力低于该安全下限值时，控制装置停止气泵工作。这不仅是为了避免由于过分缺氧而对睡眠者的健康造成损害，而且也能避免因门内外压差过大，开门时伤及室内开门的人。由于报警器上设置了一个更低的室内气压下限值，当室内气压低于该下限值时，报警器开始报警。控制器或者气泵一旦出现故障，而没有及时停止气泵，室外的人得到报警信号就会及时打开卧室门，恢复室内正常的气压和空气量。

在本实施例中，在床头上方，在适合睡眠者观看的位置上设有一组灯具，该灯具为一暗橙色圆盘。采用这种设计是因为暗橙色易使睡眠者产生虚幻的想象，从而产生模糊意识，使人尽快进入梦乡。

在本实施例中，利眠气体采用合欢花排出的气体，该气体基本上对人体无副作用。

在本实施例中，视频播放装置中装有催眠师的催眠表演影视资料。

目前现有发明的技术方案及其实施例中的各细节部分都很容易获得，而本发明方案是将这些现有技术的基本框架结合在一起。但这种结合本身对于本领域技术人员来说绝非一件容易的事，相反，往往需要科研人员付出创造性的劳动。还需要指出的是，本发明的外延不仅包含了以上直接描述了的各种特征和由这些特征组成的技术方案，而且还包括了这些特征和技术方案的各种组合。

权 利 要 求 书

助眠卧室系统包括卧室及室内的床、灯具、空调、湿度调节器、控制器、用于从室内向室外排出空气的气泵、音频播放装置、视频播放装置、噪声发生器、电磁波发生器、利眠气体喷射器、呼吸遥测器、室内压力检测器,以及设置在室外的室内低压报警器。卧室为气密和光密封的,具有良好的隔音效果,不仅与室外隔音,而且隔离所述气泵的工作噪声。呼吸遥测器与控制器联接,用于遥测睡眠者的呼吸,当检测到呼吸深度增加时,立刻向控制器传送信号。控制器还与卧室内的空调、湿度调节器、灯具、气泵、利眠气体喷射器、噪声发生器和电磁波发生器联接,它根据已经编好的程序来控制卧室内的空调、湿度调节器、灯具、噪声发生器和电磁波发生器的运行,并根据来自呼吸遥测器的信号控制气泵和/或利眠气体喷射器运行。室内压力检测器与室外报警器配合,当室内压力低于设定的阈值时,室外报警器便发出警报。控制器中不仅设有用于发现睡眠者渐醒的呼吸深度上限值,而且还设有一呼吸深度下限值,当呼吸遥测器检测到睡眠者的呼吸深度低于该下限时,控制影片播放装置和/或视频播放装置就会逐渐减弱音量或视频的亮度。

摘　要

　　助眠卧室系统包括卧室及室内的床、灯具、空调、湿度调节器、控制器、气泵、音频播放装置、视频播放装置、噪声发生器、电磁波发生器、利眠气体喷射器、呼吸遥测器、室内压力检测器，以及设置在室外的室内低压报警器。卧室为气密和光密封的，具有良好的隔音效果，不仅与室外隔音，而且能够隔离气泵的工作噪声。呼吸遥测器与控制器连接，用于遥测睡眠者的呼吸，当检测到睡眠者呼吸深度增加时，就会向控制器传送信号。控制器还与卧室内的空调、湿度调节器、灯具、气泵、利眠气体喷射器、噪声发生器和电磁波发生器控制连接，并根据已经编好的程序来控制卧室内的空调、湿度调节器、灯具、噪音发生器和电磁波发生器的运行。

一种高精度电子微距测量装置简介

微距测量是大学物理实验和生产实践中经常遇到的测量技术。然而，在基础物理实验室中现有传统实验设备存在着精度低、读数困难、测量效率低等问题。为了解决此类问题，我们研究开发了高精度电子微距测量装置。

本设计是以51单片机为信息处理的核心，利用其内部定时计数模块测量旋转编码器的角位移，再通过角位移和实际位移的对应函数关系计算出实际移动的距离。显示部分利用1602液晶屏显示位移值。本测量装置可以很方便地安装在需要微距测量的多种实验仪器上，如牛顿环、杨氏模量测量仪、速度测量仪等。此装置的测量精度高达0.01mm，且在液晶屏上直接显示出测量数据，大大节省了测量时间。下图为该装置的实物图。

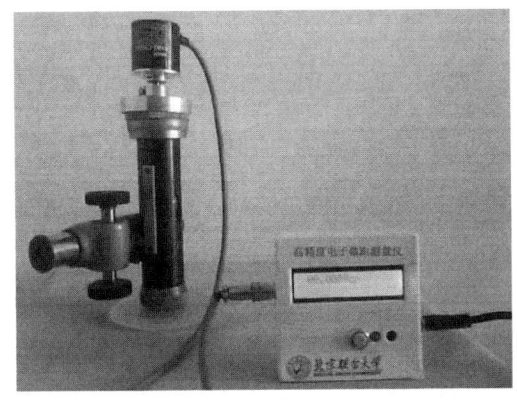

该装置的总体设计思路是：设计使微调旋钮和旋转编码器的转轴同步，当微调时旋转编码器同步旋转。旋转编码器的作用是通过光电转换将输出轴上的机械几何位移量转换成数字脉冲量，微处理器再对编码器输出的脉冲进行计算并判断其旋转方向。最后可以通过软件处理计算出绝对位移 Δd，并实时显示在液晶屏上。该装置的设计框图见下图。

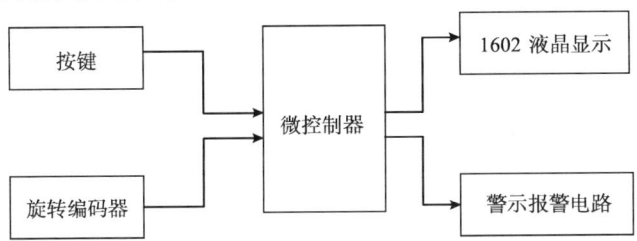

学术著作

汽车发动机构造、原理与维修

于增信

概 要

汽车工业作为国民经济的支柱产业得到了迅猛发展，中国已成为全球第一汽车消费和制造大国，且仍以较快的速度发展。与国际接轨、运作高效、功能健全的汽车服务业正蓬勃发展，业务内容涵盖了汽车检修、售后技术支持、汽车改装、汽车测试等汽车技术服务和汽车营销、汽车保险、汽车金融、汽车贸易、汽车文化、汽车救援、二手车评估、汽车回收、汽车租赁、汽车美容、服务代理，等等。且新的服务项目不断衍生，创造了约占整个汽车产业链70%的利润，已成为极具规模和吸引力的"黄金产业"，从业人员队伍迅速扩大。

现代汽车集各项高新技术于一体，是典型的机电一体化产品，汽车检修已成为经验判断、各总成拆装、调整、修复工艺与先进设备仪器的定量分析、诊断及排除故障相结合的综合技术，加之汽车服务业的快速发展和变革，我国汽车后市场急需大量高素质的人才。

作者根据汽车后市场对人才素质的要求、汽车技术与检修技术的发展和多年来的教学、科研经验，编著此书，期望为汽车服务产业人才培养及与汽车相关专业或领域人员的学习提供支持。

全书将汽车发动机构造、原理、拆装、检修、调整及必要的基础知识等融为一体，注重理论知识与实践技能相结合、构造和原理与检修和基本故障现象相结合、基本知识与先进技术及其发展趋势相结合，以揭示发动机结构因素、使用因素、技术状况、检修因素等与整机性能、基本故障现象的内在联系，建立构造、原理基本知识与新技术及检修、诊断等实际应用的关系，为学习者构筑持续发展的知识与技能平台。

全书强调概念清晰和知识的实用性、适用性和系统性，内容按循序渐进、理论实践相结合、继承与发展的原则组织安排，力求深入浅出、简明扼要、通俗易懂；集学习内容与学习指导于一体，每章都有明确的学习目标、本章小结、复习思考题和警示的注意事项，以便读者自主学习。

建筑智能化系统工程实训

苏 玮　阴振勇　杜明芳　杨晓玲

概　要

智能建筑是现代化建筑与高新信息技术完美结合的产物，是多学科、多技术系统的综合集成。智能建筑利用系统集成的方法，将计算机技术、通信技术、控制技术与建筑艺术有机结合，通过对设备的自动控制，对信息资源的管理和对使用者的信息服务以及与建筑的优化组合，可获得的投资合理、适合信息社会需要并具有安全、高效、舒适、便利等灵活特点的建筑物。因此，建筑智能电气与智能化专业是对建筑科学的有利支撑，同时，建筑业的需求又推动了智能建筑电气与智能化的发展。

近十多年来，随着信息技术迅速进入建筑领域，对建筑智能化技术人才提出了大量需求与更高要求。但是智能建筑专业人才培养的速度、特别是人才培养的质量还远远不能满足蓬勃发展的智能建筑市场对人才的需求，其目前实践教学的理念与相关软/硬件条件的严重滞后是主要原因之一。智能建筑相关专业实践教学环节的研究以至于实践教学质量管理体系的建立已成为一个亟待解决的问题。

本书以实际工程为背景，在对建筑智能化实践教学研究的基础上，开发出一种以就业为导向、符合专业培养目标要求的楼宇自动化工程训练方法。

全书共分七章：智能家居系统实训、基于LONWORKS技术实训、门禁与指纹识别技术实训、消防系统实训、组态王技术实训、综合布线系统实训和楼宇智能化系统集成实训等内容。

本书由北京联合大学苏玮教授主编。其中，第一章、第二章由苏玮编写，第三章、第七章由杜明芳编写，第四章、第五章由阴振勇编写，第六章由杨晓玲编写。全书由北京联合大学范同顺教授主审。

高寒地区矿山深部通风防尘技术研究

杨 鹏　吕文生

内容简介

本书将高寒地区气候的独特性及其矿井通风系统及井下空气环境等相互制约条件有机地结合起来，对高寒地区矿井的风流流动规律、增氧技术及可行性、通风系统评价指标和方法、通风系统优化、有毒有害气体扩散规律、粉尘治理、井下空气环境指标、井下空气环境参数实时监测系统等问题进行了深入系统的研究。本书可供矿业、安全等学科领域的研究生以及从事矿业安全管理和研究的工程技术人员参考。

概　要

随着社会物质文明的高度发展，人类对矿产资源的依赖性越来越强。这种大背景下，我国资源的需求压力不断加大，正在转向过去由于开采条件限制、尚未充分开发的西部高原寒冷地区迈进，但高原严酷和脆弱的自然生态环境对于人类的资源开发活动是一个天然障碍。研究高寒地区采矿相关的职业健康，优化高寒地区地下矿井通风系统，改善井下作业的空气环境，对实现安全高效、可持续的高原采矿，保障我国的矿产资源的稳定供应，具有十分重要的现实意义和深远的战略价值。

高寒地区的长期低温和缺氧环境，给矿山生产及生产管理带来许多不利影响。由于不同季节的差异巨大，为了确保井下工作面有足够的风量，以及避免过大的风速引起有害的扬尘对矿山职工身体健康带来危害，做好高寒地区井下巷道及作业面抑尘工作就显得尤为重要。

针对上述难题，国家科学技术部发起了本课题。作为"十一五"国家科技支撑项目和国家自然科学基金委员会资助课题，本课题研究对象为青海省锡铁山铅锌矿。研究主要反映了课题组在2007—2012年执行期间，对高寒矿山进行调研、分析、现场测试等一系列工作后，开展理论研究、实验研究等所取得的成果。研究了高海拔脆弱环境下绿色开采系统的基础理论，并进一步研究了高海拔矿山缺氧、低气压环境对矿山工作人员的影响，模拟高原的疲劳程度指标测试研究；研究了高原习服机理及影响因素，提出了有利于高原习服的各种方法；在低海拔矿山采矿规程、技术要求的基础上，研究针对高原缺氧、低气压环境，提出采用富氧室提高矿山生产人员工作能力和保障其健康安全的理论。本课题通过对高寒地区矿井风流流动规律、增氧技术及可行性、通风系统鉴定指标、评价方法、井下环境标准、通风系统优化、有毒有害气体扩散规律、粉尘治理、井下环境参数实时监测系统等问题进行深入系统的研究的基础将理论研究与实验研究相结合，对高寒矿井通风系统进行了评价并提出了井下环境的建议标准，应用国内外著名的通风仿真专业软件 Ventism 和 MVSS 等对该矿井的通风系统进行了优化研究，并应用 FLUENT 软件对矿井有毒有害气体的扩散规律进行了模拟研究。此外，还对高寒矿井的防尘措施进行了探讨，对粉尘的扩散规律和化学抑尘剂等进行了研究，提出了合理的粉尘治理方案。在理论研究成果的基础上，开发了具有自主知识产权的高原非煤矿山井下空气环境参数实时监测仪和高原非煤矿井采掘工作面增氧方法及装置，申请并获得了国家专利局的发明专利。

本研究将高寒地区气候的独特性与矿井通风系统及井下空气环境等相互制约的条件有机地结合起来，研究了通风除尘和供氧通风等技术在高寒气候下的适用性和可靠性，一定程度上丰富了世界高原采矿与矿井通风等理论方法和技术，为国内外采矿工作者和学习者提供了一种新的方法和思路。

建筑供配电与照明

范同顺　苏　玮

概　要

本书是建筑电气与智能化专业系列教材之一，已入选国家"十二五"普通高等教育本科规划教材；北京市2013年精品教材。本教材强调了供配电与照明技术并重、传统技术与高新技术融合、基本理论与工程实际有机结合等原则，力求满足相关专业人才培养目标的要求。

由于本书参照《供配电系统设计规范》GB50052、《建筑照明设计标准》GB 50034、《民用建筑电气设计规范》JGJ 16、《建筑物防雷设计规范》GB50057等现行国家工程建设标准的内容编写及其参考了大量工程资料，遵循供配电与照明技术并重、传统技术与高新技术融合、基本理论与工程实际有机结合等原则，所以教学内容完全贴近现代建筑电气和智能建筑工程实际，并结合实际工程设计图纸和工程案例讲解知识内容，使得学生可以学到与实际工程相吻合的建筑供配电与照明知识和工程技能，较好地掌握了实际变配电及电气照明工程的设计内容和方法。教学效果良好

本书由北京联合大学范同顺教授、苏玮教授主编。其中，第一章由苏玮、马东晓、卢春焕编写；第二章、第三章由施卫华、范同顺编写；第四章由范同顺、蒋蔚编写。

工业工程现场改善与应用

程 光

概 要

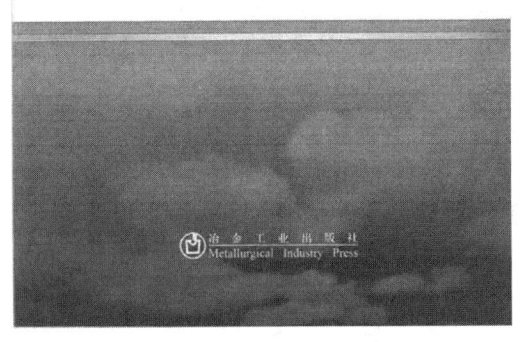

工业工程（Industrial Engineering, I.E）起源于20世纪初的美国，该学科是一个技术与管理相结合的学科，在西方先进国家影响极为广泛，有着复合型、应用型学科的特点，其内涵与外延随着时代的发展、科技的进步也在同步发展过程中。该学科的核心是通过对生产制造、产品及服务系统中涉及的人、物料、设备、方法、环境及信息等组成的综合系统的设计、改善达到系统的运行及使用效率最高、成本最低、质量保证和安全。

在生产现场进行改善的方法和技术既是工业工程最基础、最传统的应用领域，也是中国企业与国外先进企业差距较大的领域，无论是在制造业还是在服务业，这些技术方法和手段都可以得到广泛的应用。当前的中国，急需发展方式的转变，改变高污染、高能耗、低附加值的生产方式，在这转变过程中工业工程的理论和基本方法将起到重要作用，这已被西方先进国家的经济发展证实。

制造业是实现国家工业化、现代化的基础和原动力，是国家综合实力的支柱。一个国家只有有了强大的制造能力，才能成为真正的经济强国，我国目前已经成为了世界制造大国，但离成为制造强国的距离还很远，突出表现就是制造企业生产过程中的生产效率低下、资源消耗量大，生产过程对人和环境的影响没有作为重点考虑的因素。当前，我国工业化的进程正处在由低级向高级发展的中间阶段，要完全实现工业化、成为工业化的强国，根据发达国家走过的经验，还需要经过不懈地努力。

人类的生产制造发展过程实际上也是一个生产效率不断改善的过程，从原始的刀耕火种、手工生产发展到工业化大规模生产直到今天的特性化的敏捷制造、精益制造、可重构制造。在这一生产进步发展过程中，生产制造伴随着生产技术、生产效率的不断提高和改善。

工业工程现场改善及提高是指在不增加更多资源投入的前提下，使生产制造过程更流畅，单位时间产量提高，并达到绿色、节能的集约型生产制造过程。近年来，随着制造业企业竞争的加剧，特别是世界金融危机暴发后，制造业企业获取利润越来越难，因此，如何在车间生产现场降低成本、降低消耗、提高生产效率有着更重要的意义。现代化的制造企业应该具备高的灵活性、高效率的企业运行能力、集约型的生产方式等，为了更好地满足现代化企业的需求，近年来许多新的制造技术被提出并在生产现场得到广泛应用，如丰田生产系统（TPS）、精益制造（LP）、柔性制造系统（FMS）及近几年才提出的可重构制造系统（RMS）、约束理论（TOC）、同步流制造（SFM）。与此同时，许多关键技术和工具发展起来满足当前车间制造的需求，从材料资源规划（MRP）到准时化生产（JIT），从全面质量管理（TQM）到先进计划系统（APS），从优化生产技术（OPT）到MRPII等。所有这些先进的方法和技术必须以现场获得的数据为基础开展工作，因而现场改善并获得相关基础数据将更加重要。

服饰品设计

张嘉秋

概 要

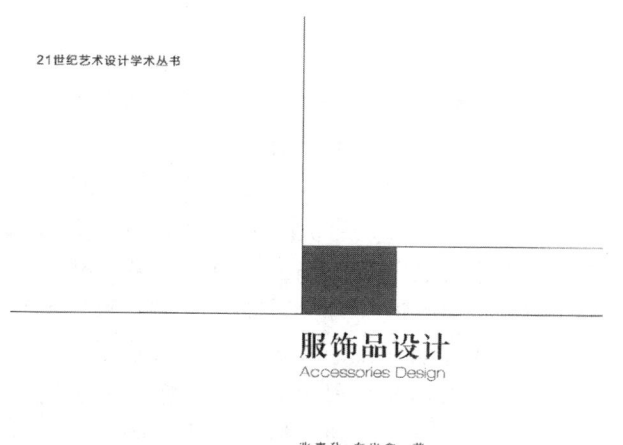

服饰艺术具有广泛的群众性，服饰品是服饰艺术整体的一个重要组成部分，它标志着一个人的风度气质和文化修养，是直接影响人们形象的重要因素。随着人们对服饰的整体需求的提高，服饰品逐渐地演变成为服装表现形式的一种延伸，已成为服装整体美不可或缺的一部分，同时其实用价值也使之成为了人们生活中的必需品，服饰品设计的重要性也就不言而喻了。

装饰是人类在社会实践中改变事物原貌使其不断增益、美化的活动，它不仅是人们对社会现实生活感性认知最生动的提炼与表现，而且是一种"有意味的形式"，成为人们寄托情思、宣泄情感、表达心境与意志的载体。人类服装是从身体装开始的，从严格意义上讲，服饰品是先于服装出现的，人类在其身体表面加些附属的东西使之美观、适宜，这种活动本身即为装饰的过程。服装装饰不仅体现在服装表面的配饰、纹样、图案和色彩等因素上，同时也体现着依据服装的功能应运而生的服饰品体系。服饰品以自身的形式特征及完整的社会功能而成为文化的符号，使人们的精神需求、审美需求以及生理需求不断地得到补偿和满足，其社会属性也不断得到认同与体现。

服装的发展过种就是服装装饰形式、装饰手段和装饰内容不断发展完善的过程。

本书由北京联合大学师范学院张嘉秋老师和车岩鑫老师撰写。作者结合多年教学经验，以图文并茂的形式概述了服饰品设计的发展历史、服饰品与服装的关系、服饰品的品牌与风格、服饰品整体搭配技巧等内容。本书内容丰富，由浅入深、循序渐进，为广大服装专业的师生、从事服装设计的人员，以及服装设计爱好者提供了一本既有理论依据，又可作为服饰图典的工具书。由于学识有限，加上时间仓促，书中不足在所难免，欢迎各位专家、读者——指出，以便再版时订正。

谢谢！

张嘉秋
北京联合大学师范学院
2012.7

《中国民族电影审美鉴赏》

茹秀华　赵　华

概　要

中国电影已经走过了百年风风雨雨，从第一部电影《定军山》到当下流行的电影《赵氏孤儿》《一九四二》《泰囧》等，国产片已经形成了强大的阵营，构成了世界电影的重要组成部分。中国电影艺术道路，有着独特的时代与历史文化语境，形成了自己的电影风格，显示了鲜明的民族性，深刻地反映了中国人民解放事业、社会主义建设，及对外改革开放艰难曲折的历程，承载了中国人民勤劳勇敢、真诚善良、热爱祖国、顽强拼搏、努力创新和积极进取的民族精神和民族个性，彰显了悠久的儒家精神和传统的人文道德情怀。为此，需要对中国民族电影的审美性及所表现出的深刻内涵进行充分的研究与挖掘，分析中国电影文化精神内涵和中国电影的民族艺术表现的喜闻乐见的大众化形式。

中国从延安文艺开始，一直对民族性与现代性（世界性）进行探讨。在特定的战争岁月，民族性必须凸显出重要的位置，同时，将民族性与政治性进行了成功的整合，中国的艺术作品成了民族抒情性的政治艺术作品。毛泽东在1938年《中国共产党在民族战争中的地位》中提出：要建立"新鲜活泼的、为中国老百姓所喜闻乐见的中国作风和中国气派"，因此民族性、时代性和世界性成为了中国电影发展的显著特色。

本书首先论述了中国电影的民族性与现代性的构成，分析了中国电影文本产生的文化语境。中国电影是从"五四运动"前后产生，经历了国内革命战争、抗日战争及解放战争，一直到社会主义建设各时期的政治风云及改革开放的时代洪流助推这样的文化语境逐步发展起来的。所以，中国民族电影与政治发展密切相关，大多数中国民族电影都包含着政治意义和政治目的，这是中国文化艺术的体制所决定的。电影的政治话语是中国电影永远的主潮。但是，由于政治本身的特殊性及中国发展道路的曲折性，导致了中国电影发展的起起落落，甚至在历史上被政治所颠覆、所批判，并与无数优秀的民族电影被扼杀。爱国主义是中华民族的优良传统，"位卑未敢忘忧国"，中国民族电影所表现的最大的主题就是爱国主义激情和英雄主义的献身精神。战争片构成了中国民族电影最主要的风景，从《八百壮士》《八女投江》《南征北战》《英雄儿女》到《台儿庄战役》《大决战》《建党伟业》等众多优秀电影，通过全景式的拍摄充分展示了中华民族保卫祖国领土完整，维护祖国尊严，保护中华儿女生命而为和平发展而进行的可歌可泣的斗争。

在中国电影的核心主题之中，歌颂新中国成立后社会主义农村建设，歌颂劳动与生产，表现改革开放后农村生产责任制及发家致富的经验，反映社会主义新农村新貌，及农村现代文明冲击下的新伦理道德建设等乡村电影，构成了中国民族电影的重要组成部分。随着当代中国社会的全面开放与外国影视文化思潮的影响，中国电影从20世纪80年代出现了最具有民族性内涵的"寻根文化"电影的探寻，一批文学作品被改编成电影，艺术家们从最古老的中华民族各个僻远的山寨、乡村及传说中寻找中国民族文化的品质特性，去开掘中华民族集体的顽强的民族生存意志与坚韧的民族毅力。中国电影的民族精神还包含了中国少数民族电影的重要业绩，少数民族电影浓郁的民族风情及各个民族为了祖国的建设，为了家乡的发展，以及为了本民族的利益而进行的民族解放斗争，民族经济建设及民族文化建构等，在电影中得到了充分的表现，清新、自然、古朴、率真、乐观、开朗、奔放、幽默、聪明是我国少数民族电影一贯的表现风格。从第六代导演开始，中国电影走向了多元主义，包括各种现代手法的运用，如意识流、象征主义、表现主义、新写实等，更多的是以"独立电影"或者"地下电影"的身份出现，全方位地表现了中国百姓当下的生存状态，这些电影丰富了中国民族电影的内容与表现手法，使中国电影更具有现代性和世界性。

　　本书是作者多年对中国民族电影思考与研究的结果，部分文章已经在相关电影或艺术刊物上发表。本书部分章节是与河北大学艺术学院潘先伟老师共同完成，同时，对百度电影相关词典及其他研究者的论文资料进行了参考，在此一并表示特别感谢！

英语口语比喻词语词典

张东昌

前 言

语言随着社会的发展而发展，而发展最快的是词汇。在社会各领域、阶层中新的词汇日益增多，日常口语交际中口语词尤为突出。随着我国国际化步伐的加快，人们对词汇的研究也不仅仅限于词汇本身，而且扩展到思维方式等的研究，人们不仅满足于对词汇字面意义的理解，而且寻求词汇所表达的真正意义以及其与思维方式的联系，以求达到更好的交流与融通。西方语用学在我国的引进，开拓了词汇研究的新领域，为解决上述问题提供了新的方法和路径。近年来，这方面比较突出的是对比喻词语的研究。我们在阅读英语书刊或同以英语为母语的人、尤其是同他（她）们中的年轻人交谈时，常常会遇到一些令人（特别是非母语学习者）费解的口语比喻词语表达法，而这些表达法又都有其固定的含义和搭配。例如，"be in high gear"原为汽车用语，意为"在最高速档"即"发动机全速运转"，在口语表达中用其比喻"全力进行"；"climb the wall"字面上是"爬墙头"的意思，而美国人却常用它表示"欣喜若狂"的意思。可见对这些表达法如果不能正确地理解和掌握，就难以学好地道的英语口语。英语日常口语词汇与典型的书面语言之间存在着很大差异。口语中包含着极为繁多的俚语、俗语、比喻词语等，而这些在其他词典中很难找到，如果翻阅资料，则如大海捞针，徒然费力，即使是综合性词典，虽然列入几条，然而挂一漏万，难以满足读者的要求，出于上述种种考虑，我们编纂了这本《英语口语比喻词语词典》。

许国璋先生在谈语言符号的任意性与理据时指出："文明社会时期创造的新词新语就不再是任意的了，而是立意的了，甚至即使是民间任意创造的词，也有语言文字学家赋予有理有据的形态了。因此，可以说，原始时期的语言符号是任意的，部落社会时期是约定俗成的，文明"社会时期是立意的。"英语也不例外。现代英语中出现的新词新语，一般来说都是立意的。然而，在语言发展的过程中，许多词语在形式上和意义上都发生了变化，原义可能逐渐消失，理据也变得模糊，难以理解。为此，本词典收录了近年来英国、美国、加拿大、澳大利亚等国最新出版的各种权威英语词典、口语参考书、小说、报刊、广播、电视中的大量口语词汇，特别是带有比喻性质的固定习语、惯用词、客套话及常用俗语、俚语等，共计千余条，以帮助了解讲英语国家的人民如何用这些比喻词语表达自己的生活起居、喜怒哀乐、文化社交以及爱与恨的情感，从中掌握地道的英语口语，提高口语水平和口语实践能力。本部词典主要供口译人员、导游、涉外工作者、英语师生及英语自学者使用。

《英语口语比喻词语词典》所选的比喻词语一般字面上难以领会，但又被普遍使用。这些词语涉及文化、历史和民俗等方面，充分反映了西方人的智慧、风趣和幽默，给人以丰富的想象和美的感受，无论在口语还是在书面语中均有不同程度的适应性和表力现，具有广泛的应用价值。本词典既收录了"文明用语"，亦收录了"粗脏话"等。编写粗脏话的目的在于帮助读者全面了解冒犯和侮辱人格的常见用语，从而能在与外国人实际交往中在偶发的特殊情况下，维护自己和祖国的尊严。书中所有词条均标有释义、示例两部分，以指导读者的实际使用。鉴于本部词典的对象是具有一定英语水平的人员，为了压缩篇幅，故略去了音标和词性。所有词、词条都按字母顺序编成条，供读者查阅。

蒋大平老师参加了本词典的编写工作；美国籍语言专家 Jim Nicols 和 John Alan Donohue，加拿大籍语言专家 James Flath，澳大利亚英语口语学专家 Kenneth Mark Kimmel 审阅了全稿英文部分；知识产权出版社对《英语口口语比喻词词典》的编纂工作给予了热情的帮助，在此，一并表示衷心感谢。

编纂这部《英语口语比喻词语词典》，尽管我们做了最大的努力，但仍会有许多不尽人意之处，竭诚欢迎广大同仁和读者指正。

编者
2012.2

汉英衔接文化性研究

张殿恩

概 要

本书是以汉英语料为基础,对汉英语衔接进行了对比研究。从语音、语法、语义和语用等方面对汉英语的衔接现象进行了对比研究,探讨了汉英语衔接的异同。这不仅有助于语言类型学的研究,而且还能为汉英语衔接性的翻译和教学提供重要的帮助。

本书主要包括以下三部分内容。第一部分导论,即本书第一章,主要说明了选题的意义、汉英衔接对比研究的概况、范围、界定、笔者的研究兴趣、主要内容、研究方法及各章节的主要内容。第一章强调了衔接是汉英语里非常重要的组成部分,在比较二者差异的基础上,从文化的取向探讨汉英语衔接的异同。第二部分,即本书第二章和第三章。第二章概述了汉英语衔接的研究概况,阐述了汉英语衔接的界定标准、基本特点及类别,综述了汉语英语衔接的研究情况。这部分是进行对比的基础和先决条件。第三章是本书研究的框架,也是本部分的重点,是汉英语衔接现象的多层次对比,包括语音层面的对比、语法层面的对比、语义层面的对比和语用层面的对比。第三部分,即本书第四章和结束语。第四章为语料的分析和讨论,包括语音、语法、语义和语用层面的分析与讨论。

本书研究采用的方法是语言对比。主要是双向对比,是以汉英语为出发点,考察两种语言的异同,探究了汉英语衔接现象,揭示了汉英语两种语言文化的差异。

现代流通企业知识资产评价研究简介

王 卓　王晓文

概 要

知识经济中的经济单位以知识型企业为主体，企业知识存量与结构是知识型企业竞争优势和未来收益的来源。现代流通产业是国民经济的先导产业，知识的物理测度是一项基础性微观研究，对于知识型流通企业的知识存量物理测度研究成果很少。本书着重从以下几个方面对现代流通企业知识资产如何进行评价展开研究。

首先从理论角度，分析论述知识、定义知识型企业，知识型流通企业，并在此基础上，结合国内外相关研究，将知识型企业知识看作一个系统，对其进行系统分析，将知识型企业的知识分为相互联系的外部关系知识、通用结构知识、专业结构知识、员工个人知识四个子系统。

其次，在 TRIZ 理论创新思想基础上，进行知识型企业的知识测度研究。阿奇舒勒将技术创新系统分解为用来描述技术系统特征的不同指标，在 TRIZ 理论应用于知识型企业的知识测评分析中，紧扣创新程度这一知识的核心价值。以不同载体形式的知识创新的不同等级程度作为测评的重点。依据 TRIZ 理论的技术等级划分，将其推广应用于知识创新的测评。

最后，对知识型流通企业的知识做实证分析与测评。根据知识系统的复杂性特点，选择网络层次分析法（ANP）。结合知识管理理论与企业管理实践建立了一套由 A、B、C、D 四层元素、元素群组成的指标体系，这一指标体系的元素层 D 层包括D1～D41 共计 41 个可行性指标。在对样本数据进行统计研究和理论分析的基础上，剖析知识型流通企业的特点。然后，对样本数据中的企业进行知识评价。确定不同决策对象的各元素的分值，采用 Saaty 0～9 等级方法确定相互联系不同元素之间、不同元素群之间的对比权重值。借助 SuperDecisions 多目标决策软件，得到最终的评价报告。ANP 报告中的数据为流通企业指出其知识结构的优势和存在问题所在；指导流通企业选择正确的知识管理策略。

金融创新与北京国际金融中心发展

——基于环境金融理论的研究

张 蓉

前 言

金融全球化发展使得资本流动和金融服务日益全球化，新兴市场国家的经济发展，对原有的国际金融中心格局产生了压力。国际金融中心的发展正在逐步分散，而不再集中在发达国家的某几个城市，国际金融中心之间的"替代"转移日趋激烈。因此，对于各国政府而言，如何通过金融机构的发展，以及政府各项优惠政策，推进本国或地区的中心城市发展成为国际金融中心，促进产业结构的调整，正成为政府推行金融全球化的目的之一。❶ 而随着低碳经济时代的来临，经济的发展呈现出了新的发展态势，关注绿色生态环境建设，转变经济增长模式，寻求可持续发展的经济增长，正在成为各国政府的共识。在此大背景下，国际金融中心的发展，必将受到直接的影响。如何在新的环境下，通过不断的金融创新，提高金融服务的效率和质量，建设绿色金融生态环境，从而增进金融中心的向心力和集聚力，是每个国际金融中心都将面临的机遇和挑战。

本研究是在理论和实证研究的基础上，从历史发展和现实存在的角度，对国际金融中心的发展问题，进行深入细致研究。主要是遵循国际金融中心形成和发展的路径依赖，从中发现金融中心发展的必然规律性，提出金融创新是国际金融中心发展的首要因素，而这其中外资银行（金融机构）、政府作用不容忽视，为北京的国际金融中心城市建设提供有益的思路和可借鉴的经验。

第一部分是理论部分的总结和归纳。金融发展理论、金融创新理论、环境金融理论、金融生态理论等与国际金融中心发展的互动性研究是本研究的重点。从理论上总结金融创新与环境金融（碳金融）的发展，碳金融发展与国际金融中心发展，可以为后续的实证研究提供基本的研究路径；第二部分是金融创新与国际金融中心的发展，即国外金融中心发展的研究借鉴。分别从传统和创新的角度进行论述，总结金融创新与金融中心发展的相互关系；第三部分是金融机构与国际金融中心发展、（源

---

❶ Rauch (1993) 提出，历史原因会影响工业城市的布局，其产生的重要不利因素会阻止企业从高成本、旧的所在地，向低成本、新的所在地转移。银行业也同样面临这个两难选择问题，众多银行集中在一个城市发展，会面临成本上升，竞争加剧等不利因素。但是，银行重新布局又很艰难，特别是大型的国际化银行尤甚。因此，政府政策更多是体现在如何吸引和鼓励更多的银行或金融机构流动到新的地区，支持其发展成为新的金融中心（Tschoegl, 2000）。[3]

于市场竞争的加剧）外资银行与国际金融中心发展的关系，以及作用发挥；第四部分国际金融中心发展中的政府作用；第五部分北京的发展之路（即是国际金融中心，又是世界城市的发展目标）。首先是国内发展的现状，如外资银行问题、世界城市发展中的环境金融理论问题、金融生态环境的建设、创新的动力、要素等，以及政府的统筹规划能力。其次是北京自身所要面临的问题。

投资项目金融价值评估

庞昊勇　秦　江　吕　强　王立军

概　要

一、主要内容

本书主要内容围绕"投资项目金融价值"的评估而展开，包括：投资项目金融评估的前提－市场调查与预测；投资项目金融评估的基础－项目可行性研究；投资项目金融评估的依据－资金的时间价值；投资项目金融评估的实质－项目投资决策；投资项目金融评估内容－技术评估、财务评估、宏观价值评估等。在上述内容中，贯彻了投资项目金融价值评估的原则、标准与程序，介绍了一系列的专门的金融价值评估的方法。

为了便于读者理解，本书通过两个现实的案例，系统地、有效地展示了"投资项目金融评估"的内容、过程、方法与结论，为读者深入理解和掌握"投资项目金融评估"的全部知识，提供了有力的帮助与参考。

最后，为了使"投资项目金融评估"更为规范，本书提供了投资项目金融价值评估报告（参考）规范。

二、主要特点

价值评估理论与实践经历了长期的发展，主要在"某项资产的价值评估""某个企业的价值评估"方面形成了较完整的方法与体系，但是，在"投资项目价值评估"方面、尤其是投资项目金融价值评估方面尚未形成完整的方法与体系，而且这方面的研究也很少，本书的创新之处也正在于此。本书开辟了从金融的视角论证投资项目价值的新路径，填补了价值评估理论与实践的空白。

本书从金融角度，提出了投资项目金融价值评估的原则、标准与程序，构建了专门的金融价值评估的系统方法，对于开展"投资项目金融价值评估，避免投资失误"有较大的推动与促进作用。

三、学术价值及应用价值

1. 学术价值

本书从金融的角度，提出了投资项目价值评估的独特观点；构建了"投资项目金融价值评估体系"；基本拟定了"投资项目金融价值评估的原则、标准、程序与规范"；形成了较完整的、独特的"投资项目金融价值评估方法"等。

2. 应用价值

在经济建设中，最大的失误就是投资项目决策的失误。为确保投资项目的正确性、可行性，必须开展投资项目金融价值的评估。投资项目的金融价值的评估与确定，恰恰是避免投资失误的最有效手段，是社会发展与经济建设所必需的，必须引起理论界、实业界的认识与高度重视。

  本书以案例的形式展示了已经实现的两个经过金融价值评估的投资项目，还有较多已经实现的案例没有在书中予以展示。截至目前为止，经过评估的投资项目运行良好，没有出现投资失误，基本实现了预期的金融价值。

庞昊勇
2014 年 9 月 5 日

北京零售业绿色经营发展研究

——基于理论与跨国零售实践

赵亚平

概　要

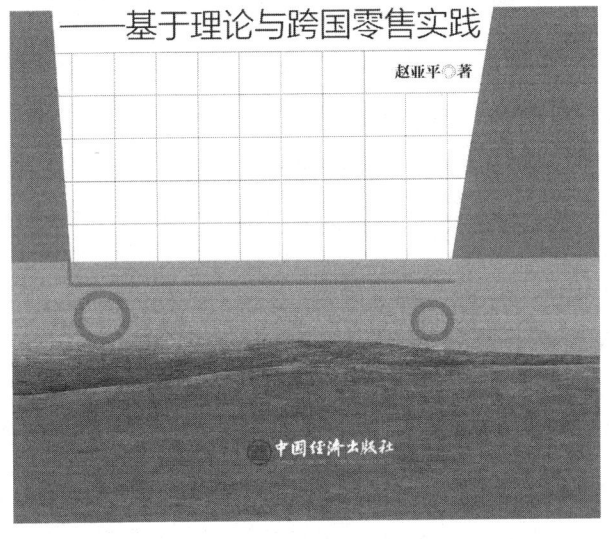

本书立足于推动北京零售业绿色经营发展进而促进北京"世界城市""国际商贸中心"的建设，结合规范研究与实证研究等方法，梳理零售绿色经营的理论基础、跨国零售在京绿色经营情况、北京零售业绿色经营情况，从宏观与微观两方面分析北京零售业绿色经营的优势与机遇、困难与障碍，并在借鉴跨国零售绿色经营经验的基础上，从政府、行业协会、零售企业三个层次提出进一步发展北京零售业绿色经营的对策。研究内容主要集中在3个关键问题（3W）：一是北京零售企业目前绿色经营的情况是怎样（What）？具体有哪些业态的零售商比较注重绿色经营？有代表性的零售商有哪些？绿色经营中存在的问题与障碍是什么？便于在发现问题、分析问题的基础上，提出推动零售绿色经营进一步发展的对策与措施。二是国际零售商进行着怎样的绿色经营活动（How）？包括它们在本国与东道国的绿色经营活动有什么不同？目前世界上著名的绿色零售商有哪些？它们的绿色经营进行到怎样的程度？从这些情况的梳理中，归纳出可供我们借鉴的经验。三是怎样才能推动北京零售企业绿色经营的发展（How）？包括政府采取怎样的措施能够推进零售商的绿色经营？行业协会应该开展哪些推动活动？零售商应该如何提高自身绿色经营的水平？即从应用的角度提炼出可供借鉴和操作的建议。

稀土催化材料在环境保护中的应用

赵 卓 彭 鹏 傅平丰

概 要

我国是世界上稀土资源最丰富的国家，其资源总量、工业储量、稀土产品都居世界领先地位，我国稀土的探明储量占世界稀土总量的80%以上。稀土元素特殊的电子结构决定了其功能独特，稀土金属活泼，几乎可与所有的元素发生作用形成化合物，从而具备独特的催化作用和性质，将其加入催化组分，会大大提高贵金属催化剂的抗毒性、高温稳定性和催化活性。研究发现，稀土代替部分贵金属制成的催化剂不仅成本低，而且能获得良好的能化效果，对于开拓稀土资源的综合利用，治理我国环境污染都有着至关重要的意义。

稀土元素因其特有的催化性能在多种催化材料中发挥着重要的作用。本书系统地讲述了稀土催化材料在环境保护领域中的应用。全书共分为8章，第1章稀土元素及其环境化学行为概述，介绍了稀土元素的概念、分类、资源分布及其环境化学行为；第2章稀土催化剂，阐述了稀土元素的性质及其在催化剂中的作用机理，以及稀土在催化中的应用；第3章稀土催化剂在光催化环境净化中的应用，论述了稀土修饰提高光催化剂的途径、机理及其在催化净化气相污染物、水体中有机污染物的应用；第4章稀土催化剂在汽车尾气净化中的应用，研究了汽车尾气排放状况及危害、稀土材料在汽车尾气净化催化剂中的应用；第5章稀土催化剂在工业废气净化中的应用，介绍了稀土氧化物在烟气脱硫过程的应用及稀土在工业废气和人居环境净化中的作用；第6章稀土催化剂在工业废水处理中的应用，探讨了稀土在工业废水处理中的强化催化机理及稀土催化剂处理各种工业废水；第7章稀土催化剂在催化燃烧中的应用，研究了催化燃烧的特点、应用，稀土在燃烧催化剂中的作用，以及稀土钙钛矿化合物在催化燃烧中的应用；第8章展望，提出了今后需要进一步在稀土催化材料研究方面开展的几项工作，以便更加合理地利用资源，保护环境。

本书由北京联合大学赵卓教授，中国人民解放军防化学院彭鹏博士，北京科技大学傅平丰博士共同完成。

《实用特殊教育研究方法概论》

刘全礼 邓 猛 熊 琪

概 要

改革开放以后,中国教育界出版了若干本教育研究的著作或教材。这些著作或教材有的专为研究生编写,有的专为教师编写,有的则是为教育系高年级本科生编写。它们或难或易,或艰涩或通俗,但往往具有一个共同的特征,就是过多的以域外的资料为素材,或者以域外的话语体系为参照系,使得本来应该根植于本土的一门学科,成为在中国表达的域外书。

同时,改革开放以后,我国的特殊教育专业有了很大的发展,特殊教育教师队伍得到快速的扩张,特殊教育的科研活动开始在各地有序地开展。但是,我们并没有一本以特殊教育视野为参照系的为特殊教育专业的学生和特殊教育教师使用的教育研究方法。这就是本书的写作初衷。

《实用特殊教育研究方法概论》由刘全礼设计了基本的结构和纲目,然后由作者分别撰写。第一、二、三、五章由刘全礼(北京联合大学特殊教育学院)完成,第四、六章由邓猛(北京师范大学教育学部教授)和熊琪(南京特殊教育职业技术学院,博士)完成。各章内容大致如下:

第一章主要介绍教育研究的基本内涵、教育研究的主要类别、步骤,以及一线教师和在校学生的研究特点。

第二章主要讲选题,从自由选题和限定选题两个角度,从选题的原则、方法、着眼点和文献研究—包括文献综述的基本方法等方面予以详细介绍。

第三章主要是介绍调查研究的方法,从实证的例证出发,介绍了调查研究的接本规范,接着详细介绍了问卷、访谈和观察研究的具体操作模式。

第四章主要介绍了质的研究,重点就特殊教育研究中如何更好地使用质的研究方法提供了相应的研究案例,便于读者把握。

第五章介绍实验研究,就实验研究中的主要要素、实验研究的基本步骤、基本的实验设计和实验结果的解释与表达进行了详略得当的介绍。

第六章主要介绍了如何表达研究的成果,包括详细介绍了文献的呈现、研究结果表达的规范格式和相应的案例。

[作者简介] 刘全礼,北京联合大学特殊教育学院;邓猛,北京师范大学教育学部教授;熊琪,南京特殊教育职业技术学院。

本书是我国第一本专门为特殊教育专业的学生和特殊教育教师撰写的如何开展特殊教育研究的指南性著作，针对性很强。

同时，本书从实用出发，在进行基本的论述后，提供了相当的研究实例，避免了过去许多教育研究类著作主要是照抄国外有关著作的纯纸上谈兵的做法。

再者，本书的内容基本上是作者们自己研究心得的一次表达，并非书本来书本去，其实例更是特殊教育工作者自己的研究成果，因此更具有非常强的本土特色。

教育基本问题专论

刘彦文

概　要

《教育基本问题专论》对教育的若干重点、热点问题进行了比较深入的专题性的探索思考,概要阐述了作者的一些基本认识。重点研究了教育本质问题、课程问题、道德教育、教师教育、个性化教育、因材施教与差异教育等六个专题。同时,附录部分还简要探讨了其他教育热点问题,包括终身教育、家庭教育、学前教育、教育先行和教育与消费等问题。本书力求既能丰富教育基本理论研究成果,启发研究者更进一步的深入研究和思考,又能对教育实践具有一定指导价值,推进教育改革和发展。本书不仅适用于广大从事教育研究和教育教学工作的教师和教育工作者,也适用于教育专业研究人员、学生。

学校食堂从业人员培训教材

闫喜霜　许荣华　姜　慧　张　琦

概　要

　　《学校食堂从业人员培训教材》是为各类学校食堂餐饮从业人员而编写的。全书共四篇：第一篇为基础篇，共五章，第一章为食品卫生基础知识，第二章为原料的卫生管理，第三章为烹调的卫生管理，第四章为服务的卫生管理，第五章为环境的卫生管理；第二篇职业道德，第一章为道德与职业道德概述，第二章学校食堂从业人员职业道德与职业守则，第三章：案例分析与反思；第三篇膳食营养，第一章人体需要的能量与营养素，第二章各类烹饪原料的营养，第三章平衡膳食与膳食指南，第四章营养配餐；第四篇法律法规，第一章《中华人民共和国劳动法》相关知识，第二章《中华人民共和国食品安全法》相关知识，第三章《餐饮业和集体用餐配送单位卫生规范》相关知识。

残疾儿童随班就读支持体系的研究与实践

王洙 许家成

概 要

该专著是基于国家一般课题《残疾儿童随班就读支持系统的研究与实践》在全国 200 个县作为项目单位的实践基础上出版的一部关于我国随班就读支持体系的系统研究。

本人对支持的概念及其支持系统进行了深入的研究,成为本人的重要的学术特点。本书反映了本人将支持的理念用于提升随班就读质量,有两点具体的贡献。

第一,提出了资源教室建设和运作,作为提升所办就读教学质量的重要专业支持体系,并逐步在北京和全国各地推广开来。

第二,对支持的理念进行了比较深入的研究。本人长期以来主张支持与支持体系。在对支持的研究的基础上,提出了支持性生活、支持性教育和支持就业的实践模式。

该专著出版与 2014 年国家 7 部委《特殊教育提升计划 2014—2016》的精神一致,对提升我国融合教育的质量,具有现实的理论价值和实践意义。

说明:本人原来申报的题目是《特殊儿童生涯发展与转衔教育》由于各种原因,未能在 2014 年 6 月出版。因此,将已经正式出版的本书作为本学期的代表性著作。特此说明。

许家成
2014 年 7 月 28 日

职业教育分级制研究

——职业教育分级框架与分级标准建构研究

李宇红

内容简介

本著作是基于北京市教委、北京市财政局关于《市场营销专业职业教育分级制度改革试验》项目研究；国家社会科学基金职业教育制度研究课题《我国现代职业教育体系研究》子课题（课题批准号 AJA110003）项目研究；北京高等教育学会《市场营销专业职业教育分级标准研究》（京高学会［2011］28 号）项目研究基础，历时3年，吸收 IT、互联网、医药、商业零售连锁等行业企业职业专家、培训专家、技师、工程师，还有以用友大学营销学院为代表的企业营销专家，同时还包括北京财贸职业学院、北京商业学校在内的中职、高职院校，共同组成研发项目团队，调研8大行业数20余家龙头企业近300个职业岗位，同时分析数百万字国内外职业教育研究资料，并于2011年9月开始进行市场营销专业职业教育分级试点实践。本著作将理论研究成果和实践试验结果进行整理出版，形成职业教育分级制度研究与实践系列研究著作，本专著是系列著作第一部。

本著作在第一版研究成果基础上进行了进一步理论研究和逻辑梳理。第一部分除了保持第一版中从国内外职业教育理论与实践的宏观视角对职业教育分级制度进行了解读，对市场营销职业教育分级个案研究项目进行了重点阐述以外，增加了职业教育及其体系、职业教育分级制度的研究，更清晰的明确了职业教育分级理念和框架是构建职业教育体系的核心和关键所在；第二部分提供从职业教育研究角度进行职业分析的方法，详细阐述如何通过职业分类、分级研究提供职业教育分级制度的客观依据以及如何进行职业标准研究为职业教育能力体系和教育标准建构奠定基础；相对于第一版本著作在第三部分除了详细论述市场营销专业构建职业教育分级标准的方法以及构成要素，增加了职业教育专业与职业教育标准的分析研究，对每个级别教育标准进行了描述和对比分析，在制定标准的依据、标准内涵、标准的科学性以及标准的特征等方面提供了详实的论证。

本著作是系列著作的第一部著作，重点解决分级框架和教育标准问题。第二部著作将着重于教学体系和课程原理的设计，包括职业课程设计理论、职业课程设计方法、市场营销职业课程开发、市场营销职业课程方案、教学组织与实施以及市场营销分级制人才培养质量监测与评价要素。

本著作成果分析了职业院校中专业与职业脱节、专业教育标准与行业企业标准脱节、所学内容与岗位工作内容脱节的问题，并从理念更新、方法创新、构建新体系等方面进行具体的方法论探索以及实践探索。

《职业教育教师教育研究》

李娟华

概 要

《职业教育教师教育研究》以对职业教育教师教育的历史考察作为起点,对职业教育教师教育研究的主要内容、职业教育教师教育研究的价值、职业教育教师教育的理论基础、我国职业教育教师教育的实施研究、发达国家职业教育教师培养与培训研究、我国职业教育教师教育保障体系研究,以及我国职业教育教师教育发展的对策与建议等问题分别进行了深入地探讨。

该书具有以下特点。第一,基础性。书中对职业教育教师教育的理论基础进行思考,分析职业教育教师教育与职业教育学、职业教育管理学、职业教育教师学、教师教育理论及政策科学与教育政策学等学科和理论的关系,这个研究具有一定的基础性。第二,系统性。该书对我国职业教育教师教育体系做了比较系统的分析,对我国职业教育教师教育的实施体系和保障体系进行研究,涉及我国职业教育教师教育的实施机构、我国职业教育教师教育的实施过程、我国职业教育教师教育管理体制、我国职业教育教师教育政策等问题,该研究框架具有一定的系统性。第三,一定的创新性。该书把职业教育教师教育作为一个整体,从职业教育教师教育理论基础、实施体系、保障体系、发展建议,及国外职业教育教师教育借鉴等方面多角度、较全面地对职业教育教师教育进行探讨,具有一定的创新性。

汉语盲文简写方案

钟经华

概　要

汉语盲文简写方案是应用型成果，具有较高的系统性、简明性，实用价值高。简写方案能够提高盲文的摸读和书写速度，能够区分同音词、提高准确性。本研究成果对汉语盲文简写国家标准的正式诞生有实质性的推动作用，为我国大陆1233万视力残疾人快捷地处理文字信息，共享信息时代的文明成果奠定了基础。

本简写方案能够减少盲文的方数、点数，加大盲文的信息密度，在盲人摸读和书写速度不变的情况下，简写方案可以间接地提高盲人的信息处理能力。对简写方案的需求是世界上各种语言盲文的共性，是有别于明眼文字的特殊性。本研究成果使得汉语盲文简写方案从无到有，实现了汉语盲文简写方案零的突破。

本简写方案包括15条简写规则，257个常用多音节定型简写词（含9个同音分化定型简写词），包括核心部分和扩展部分。

简写方案在"现代汉语通用平衡语料库"7千常用词范围内形成简写词1769个，其中新设计的简写词1055个。在2万常用词范围内形成简写词5033个，其中新设计的简写词2989个。通过对60万字中小学语文课文语料和200万字人民日报语料的检验，简写比例分别为33.51%、40.19%，省方比例分别为18.11%和21.72%（按百字185方计算）。本方案能够通过省方省点间接提高摸读和书写速度。

本方案还能够通过定型简写区分部分常用同音词，这是一个重大突破。现行盲文一般不标调（需要时才标调），存在因标调方式不统一造成的"一词多形"和同音词不标调造成的"一形多词"的现象。本方案有257个多音节词定型简写符号，每个符号只对应一个唯一确定的词，有明确的读音和词义。这些定型简写符号既表音又表义，因此，它们不存在"一词多形"和"一形多词"问题，不存在猜测读音和词义的问题。这些有固定读音和词义的定型简写符号在句子中就像固定的支点，能够缩小其他词的猜测范围，对于理解其他符号的读音和词义也有帮助作用。这对减少现行盲文的歧义是一个重要贡献。

本方案首创了同音同调词分化定型简写标志符号（23），将易混淆的需要区分的同音同调、同词性、有并列关系的词，使用标志符号进行区分。这样就使得分化定型词与其他同音词彻底不同形，从根本上解决了它们的混淆问题。

本研究提出了按盲文符号触觉可感性分类的概念和标准，将盲文符号分为：完善型、一般型、缺陷型、严重缺陷型四种。并对单方符号、两方组合符号的触觉可感性进行了具体的分析，这是对盲文基础研究的一项重要贡献。在不使用严重缺陷符号的前提下，发掘出了现行盲文充足的简写空间。简写方案不仅可以避开缺陷符号，还能够减少现行盲文中原有的严重缺陷型符号（qun）的出现频率，提高了汉语盲文的触觉品质。

本研究在提高简写效率和发挥简写符号的简写潜能两个方面都做了深入分析。一方面，通过词频统计分析简写规则覆盖到的词语使用频率；另一方面，采取根据有简写潜能的符号找常用词的逆向思维方式，充分发挥简写符号的潜能。由于需要在常用词与不同简写符号的简写潜能之间寻找平衡点，逆向思维可以减少交叉、混乱，从而取得简写效率和简写潜能的最大化。

本研究采取了定量与定性相结合的方法寻找适当的定型简写词，以定量方法为基础，再通过定性分析提高可靠性。

定量方法的应用主要表现为通过定型简写效率计算公式进行量化分析，为每个有简写潜能的符号找出5个候选，并给出候选词的词频等信息。定型简写是在简写规则的基础上进行的，简写规则覆盖的音节在定型简写时不再产生新的简写效率（每使用一次简写规则，减少1方）。简写效率还与简写词的原方数和定型简写符号的预期方数有关。定型简写效率计算公式如下所示：

定型简写效率 =（原方数 − 简写规则覆盖的音节数 − 定型简写符号的方数）× 使用频率

定性方法主要表现为由语言学家对通过定量分析选出的5个候选词进行语用分析，同时结合盲文专家（盲人）的实际经验，从中筛选出一个简写词；然后，再将专家给出的简写词到盲校师生中进行多次反复检验，最终确定合适的简写词。

本研究的突出特色是：①在继承基础上创新，简写方案兼容原方案，简写方案与原方案无任何符号冲突，学习过简写的人可以毫无困难地阅读原有的盲文出版物。②简明性与科学性兼顾，不仅提高了摸读和书写速度，还同时达到了区分同音词、提高科学性的目的。③简写效益与语音规律、摸读规律兼顾，在符合汉语语音规律、不增加触觉辨认困难的基础上，追求简写效益的最大化。④强化简写方案的规律性，尽量多地使用简写规则进行概括，降低盲人的记忆负担。⑤以大规模语料库为主，结合有针对性的动态语料，保障了本研究基础语料的平衡性和样本代表性，同时使用最新的语言分析处理技术解决了资料搜集与处理难度大的问题。⑥统一设计、分级选择、分级使用。先统一设计出简写规则和定型简写符号，将规律性强的简写规则，符合优选条件的多音节词的分化定型简写作为核心部分，经过审批后推广使用；其余作为扩展部分，供盲人自由选择使用。

本研究成果使得汉语盲文简写研究取得了突破性进展，以原始创新为主。定型简写、盲文符号触觉可感性分类的概念和标准、定型简写效率计算公式、简写设计原则、常用词优选条件等都是原始创新。

汉语现行盲文具有升级的潜力，简写是汉语盲文升级的必由之路。简写能够提高汉语盲文的科学性、简明性，能够提高盲文的摸读和书写速度，能够有效解决同音词的猜测问题。汉语盲文改革不应只着眼于基本方案的更迭，简写是汉语盲文改革的一个重要方面。

本课题研制出了比较符合汉语语言特点、现行盲文特点和盲文触觉规律的简写方案，使汉语盲文的科学性、简明性得到了较大提高，证明了汉语现行盲文具有通过简写提升品质的潜力。本研究成果对汉语盲文简写国家标准的正式诞生有实质性的推动作用。

简写是盲文研究的重要问题，涉及语言学、心理学、教育学等领域。本项目探讨了汉语语音及词汇的构成特点和使用规律、盲文符号的触觉可感性、简写的学习负担等问题。系统研究了常用词的盲文定型问题，深入研究了多音节同音词分化问题。本成果对汉语盲文的整体改革和发展有重要的参考价值，也为盲文数字化奠定了基础。

本研究成果使得汉语盲文第一次有了简写方案，它具有较高的系统性、简明性，实用价值高，是应用型成果。具有提高盲文的摸读和书写速度、区分同音词、提高准确性的实际意义。在目前盲文基本方案不通用的情况下，本研究成果不能直接在港澳台地区应用，港澳台地区仍然没有盲文简写方案。

对简写方案的需求是世界上各种语言盲文的共性。本研究成果具有与国际上盲文普遍简写的惯例接轨的重要意义，填补了我国汉语盲文简写方案的空白。

本研究成果受到了试验学校老师、盲生的好评，受到了学习过英语简写盲文的大学生的欢迎，也受到了盲文出版工作者的欢迎。盲文使用者和工作者普遍认为本研究成果已经比较成熟，有效提高了汉语现行盲文的简明性和准确性。

我国盲文研究的基础薄弱，黄乃先生逝世近 5 年来，除了本课题组发表的学术论文外，没有检索到其他正式发表的盲文研究学术论文。本课题研究使得我国盲文研究没有完全中断，并在一定程度上唤起了对盲文研究的重视。

《新时期职业院校创业教育理论与实践》

段素菊

概 要

　　21世纪是创业教育时代。这是因为，诸多实践业已表明，创业教育不仅能为学生实现顺利创业、社会经济发展提供帮助，更能为培养学生创业型人格、创新精神提供支持。《新时期职业院校创业教育理论与实践》从创业教育在职业教育发展中的现实问题出发，结合中外职业院校开展创业教育的历史与现实，从政治、经济、技术和社会等影响职业院校创业教育发展的外部因素进行研究分析，以解决社会发展的一些关键问题为诉求，来探讨我国职业院校创业教育的理论与实践，推动职业院校的转型与发展。《新时期职业院校创业教育理论与实践》立足于职业院校创业教育这一研究领域，试图通过理论分析与实践分析相结合的方式，更好地展现与分析创业教育在我国职业院校开展的实际情况。在事实分析的基础上，提出问题，并尝试提出解决途径，以支持创业教育在职业院校更好地开展。

"思想道德修养与法律基础"课教学设计

陈 勇 王 易 贾少英 王滨有

概 要

本成果是在2010年度教育部人文社会科学研究专项任务项目（高校思想政治理论课）科研项目初期研究成果的基础上，进一步深化研究的成果（项目批准号：10JDSZK044，批准经费5万元，2010年在北京联合大学科研处备案）。

2011年，教社科司函［2011］63号文件通知所有承担教育部人文社会科学研究专项任务项目的课题组，对初期研究成果进一步修改完善。2011年4月，我们在北京市科技协会召开了关于"进一步修改完善初期研究成果研讨会"。在研讨会上，北京市科技协会、北京理工大学、中国人民大学、北京化工大学、北京联合大学等院校的领导和相关专家教授夏强、张红峻、王易、张明德等，对初期研究成果的修改完善提出了很多宝贵意见。这次研讨会后，我们又召开了多次小型研讨会。在这些小型研讨会上，陈勇、王易等教授对初期研究成果的修改完善提出了很多建设性意见。经过一年多的努力，我们对初期研究成果进行了反复多次的修改和完善，从而使本成果有很多新的突破和创新。

2012年6月4日，教育部社会科学司关于2010年度教育部人文社会科学研究专项任务项目（高校思想政治理论课）结项情况的通知，公布了教育部人文社会科学研究专项任务项目的鉴定评审结果。该通知明确："我司组织专家对收到的48份2010年思想政治理论课专项任务项目和5份2009年延期结项项目结项材料进行了鉴定评审，评出优秀成果7项，合格成果46项。现对优秀成果予以表扬。"（见教社科司函［2012］119号）。本研究成果是上述7项被表扬的优秀成果之一，该成果被评为优秀成果结项，并在北京联合大学科研处备案。

大学生职业发展教育实证研究

葛海燕

内容简介

大学生职业发展教育是大学生职业生涯发展教育的简称，属于素质教育范畴。它是指在市场化背景下高校面向大学生开展的关于职业生涯规划、就业创业能力培养和择业咨询指导为一体的教育活动。我国关于大学生职业发展教育的理论研究和实践探索尚处于起步阶段。

《大学生职业发展教育实证研究》的作者以其所致力的大学生职业发展教育教学工作为背景积淀，从中萃取了一批其近年来开展的相关课题研究成果撰著成书，内容主要包括四部分：第一篇为大学生涯与职业规划，将职业生涯理论应用于大学生学习生活实际，为大学生的大学生涯设计和未来的职业发展规划提供一种参考。第二篇为大学生就业关系的实证分析，对北京地区15所不同层次高校入学生的高校属性、社会属性、学历属性和学生就业水平的相关性进行了切片分析。第三篇为北京地区高校大学生职业发展教育与毕业生就业能力对接的实证研究。第四篇为大学生就业指导课程体系建设的实践与思考。

心理学实验与生活

曾美英 晏 宁 毛荣建 李 伟

概 要

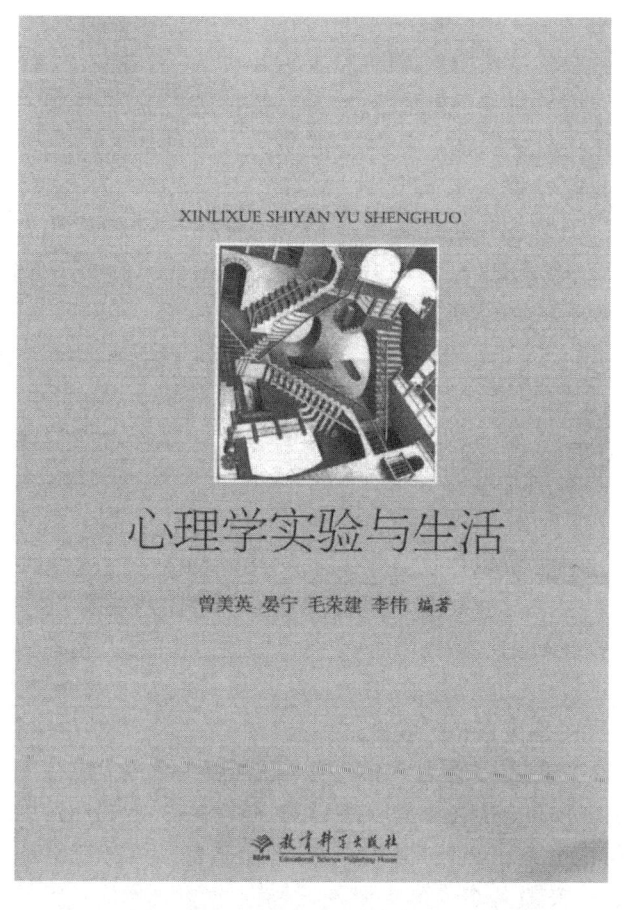

心理学是一门研究人类心理活动的科学，而人类的心理活动存在于日常的行为和活动当中。从这个意义上讲，心理学就是关于生活和社会的科学。实验是心理学的主导研究方法，是心理学科学性和严谨性的重要保障。心理学在追求科学实证的过程中，无数的学者力图超越经验，以实验的方法对人类的心理和行为进行分析，以实现心理学实验的最终目的：提示人类的心理现象，提高人类对自身生活的把握。

其实很多心理学实验并非我们如想象的那样完全在封闭的实验室里进行，而与我们的生活密切相关。心理学实验其实就是去芜存菁的生活，是浓缩的人生经验。心理学实验让我们在特定情境脉络中，清楚地看到喜爱、恐惧、顺从、怯懦等心理作用。我们常因为生活的急促忙乱，而忽略行为反应的其他意义。伟大的心理学实验则凸显这些被我们忽略的意义，让我们更能清楚地检视、了解自我。《心理学实验与生活》一书通过对59个经典心理学实验研究的介绍，并结合人们的日常生活和工作实际，对每一个实验结果的意义进行了阐释和说明，具有一定的学术价值和较强的独创性。

全书分为五个部分，分别为认知与学习、情绪与生活、行为与动机、自我与发展、社会与角色。该书在确保著作内容的科学性和严谨性的基础上，也从体例和语言上兼顾了作品的可读性，使读者在了解心理现象、认识心理效应、把握心理规律的同时，能结合生活的实际，了解每个行为背后所要表达的真实意义。

高校英语教师专业发展研究

谢职安

前 言

始于上世纪六十年代的教育改革使教师在教育教学中的作用变得愈发突出。目前,随着社会对教育重要性认识的深入,教师的专业发展受到国内外学者的广泛关注和研究。教师的专业发展是教师以个人成长为根本,以专业成熟为目标,以教师的知识、技能、信念、态度、情感等其他专业素质提高为内容,是一个终身的、个体专业发展的动态过程。

2007年教育部在《大学英语课程要求》中特别指出:教师素质是提高教学质量的关键,也是大学英语课程建设与发展的关键。作为高等学府的教育者,高校英语教师承担着大学英语教学、科学研究及社会服务三大使命。在如今英语教学环境复杂化、教学模式多元化的趋势下,大学英语教师如何提高自身的专业素质、实现自身的专业发展,这就需要广大英语教师及相关研究者积极探索、发现、归纳和总结,从实践上升到理论,再由理论来指导实践。

在此社会大背景下,本书的作者们非常有幸参加了为期两年的(2011年3至2013年1月)由北京外国语大学中国外语教育研究中心文秋芳教授主持的北京市高校英语教师跨校团队行动研究活动项目。在文教授带领下,通过团队的学习、交流与分享,以及教师个人的文献阅读、课堂录像、总结反思活动,我们的教学、科研、反思和合作等能力均得到了显著提高,成为教师专业发展研究的直接受益者。

在顺利完成文教授的项目后,我们的团队凝聚力增强,团队成员的科研意愿不减,对于教师专业发展的研究热情更是空前高涨。本书便是继文教授跨校团队项目后,我们北京联合大学团队的教师专业发展研究成果之一。

结合目前我国高校英语教师专业发展的研究趋势、文教授跨校教师合作团队中的研究重点、以及我们团队成员的研究兴趣点等因素,本书内容共分为如下四个章节:大学英语教师的专业发展现状及影响因素、包括行动研究在内的教师专业实践反思、教师认知及团队共同体发展、以及教师的信息素养。每一章节均有对目前相关领域学术界文献的综述,属于 library - based research,以期能够帮助读者了解高校英语教师发展的研究现状及研究概貌。

本书的撰写工作分工如下:谢职安负责全书选题、总体设计、审阅并校对稿件、全书质量把关,并撰写第一章和第二章的一部分,共计约5万字;何芳负责审阅并校对稿件,并撰写第三章和第四章的一部分,共计约5万字;王玮撰写第一章的一部分,共计约5万字;夏文红撰写第二章的一部分,共计约

5万字；马亚星撰写第三章的一部分，共计约5万字；叶秀娟撰写第四章的一部分，共计约5万字。

本书的撰写和出版得到了北京联合大学学术著作出版基金资助和北京市教委大学英语应用能力测试口试（TEP）专题项目的支持，在此一并表示衷心感谢！

在撰写过程中每位成员都付出了很大的努力，但由于笔者们的水平和能力有限，书中疏漏和不妥之处在所难免，敬请广大读者和专家学者对书中存在的问题给予批评指正。

谢职安
2014年春

第一作者简介：

谢职安：北京联合大学外语部教授，长期从事英语专业和大学英语教学，主要研究方向为社会语言学和二语习得。

喀斯特洞穴旅游开发与景观保护研究

王 静

概 要

  旅游业是快速发展的新兴产业，对拉动经济增长、促进居民消费、增加社会就业、促进文化交流、扩大国际交往等具有重要意义。党中央、国务院高度重视发展旅游业，已将旅游业发展纳入国家战略体系，《国务院关于加快发展旅游业的意见》（国发〔2009〕41号）明确提出要把旅游业培育成国民经济的战略性支柱产业和人民群众更加满意的现代服务业。力争到2020年我国旅游产业规模、质量、效益基本达到世界旅游强国水平。目前，已有27个省（自治区、直辖市）把旅游业作为支柱产业或第三产业的龙头加以发展，加快发展旅游业已成为我国转变增长方式、推动科学发展、构建和谐社会的战略性举措。旅游业的特点与政策机遇不仅为我国旅游资源开发带来机遇，同时也带来了挑战，如何对旅游资源进行科学地开发，如何深入地研究旅游资源保护，是促进旅游业可持续发展的基础。

  喀斯特洞穴（Karst cave）是自然赋予人类的遗产，也是一种独特的自然景观资源。洞穴景观是在漫长的地质年代里，在洞穴特定的环境条件下形成、积累、保存下来的，具有相当高的科学价值和旅游价值。此外，由于洞穴中常汇集摩崖石刻、碑刻、书法、壁画、古建筑等文化艺术人文景观，甚至因曾经是古人类居住栖息地而成为遗址宝地。因此，喀斯特洞穴景观是一种十分特殊的具有科学研究价值和观赏价值的不可再生的旅游资源，对其进行旅游开发和保护工作极为重要，本书主要讨论喀斯特洞穴的旅游开发与景观保护。

  本书主要分为九章，第一章、第二章和第三章是基础知识，主要是对旅游洞穴的定义、喀斯特洞穴的特点、喀斯特洞穴的环境和景观特点、类型等进行分析，第四章与第五章主要讨论喀斯特洞穴旅游开发理论与实证研究。在实证研究中，以河北承德兴隆溶洞为例，对溶洞中的景观进行评价，不仅从市场、客源等方面提出开发建议，还融入了对景区信息化建设的建议，以适应游客需求的新趋势。第六章至第九章主要讨论喀斯特景观保护的研究。旅游设施的建设和游客的涌入，洞穴水文地质条件和表层喀斯特特征的改变，往往导致洞穴环境的巨大变异，碳酸钙景观强烈风化，科学价值和观赏价值严重受挫，碳酸钙景观风化现象在旅游洞穴中屡见不鲜。多数研究认为，由旅游业发展引起的洞穴环境变化是主要原因，如不正确的新洞口开凿、洞穴不合理的灯光布置以及超出洞穴承载力的游客量等。本研究根据对白龙洞实地研究分析，认为由控制洞腔形态的岩体及其上覆土壤组成的土-岩系统通过影响洞穴风和新景观的形成条件对洞穴景观的风化也起着重要的作用。

  本研究结合已有的关于旅游洞穴景观恢复的研究方法和试验思路，在白龙洞景区建立野外试验场，模拟洞穴景观形成过程，运用水文地球化学试验的方法，论证改善表层喀斯特水文地质特征对促进洞穴碳酸钙景观沉淀的积极作用，进行景观复生试验。通过缜密选点和关键水文地球化学数据的确定，试验结果证明在喀斯特水进入洞穴后的滴落过程中，Ca^{2+}因沉积而在水溶液中的平均损失量远远超过雨水补给的长期滴水点和季节性滴水点的滴水，因此证明了当地喀斯特水代替大气降水不仅能够解决干燥洞穴中洞穴水来源不足的问题，而且能够通过补给表层喀斯特含水层对干旱洞穴景观的沉积起到促进作用，为恢复旅游洞穴中破损、干裂景观和保护旅游资源提供新的思路和方法。虽然过程中会引起洞穴空气中CO_2浓度增加，但是在较干燥的洞穴内一般通风条件较好，不会造成洞穴环境恶化。

  本研究依托旅游地学的基础知识与研究方法，对喀斯特洞穴的旅游开发和景观保护进行分析，既有以旅游发展为切入点、以经济效益为导向的开发措施，也有以地貌学和地质学为基础的景观保护措施，对喀斯特洞穴旅游发展具有较深刻的指导意义。

《旅游标准化导论》

张凌云　朱莉蓉

概　要

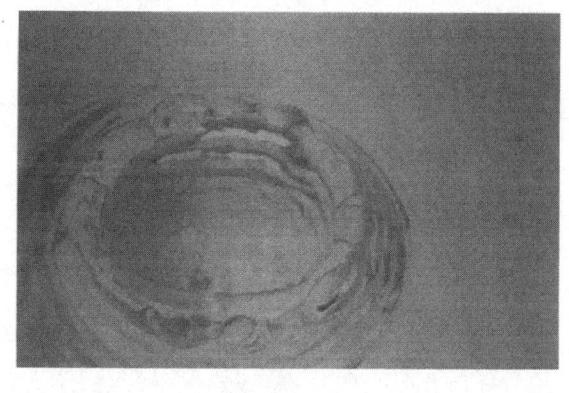

本书是国内第一本较为全面、系统地论述旅游标准化管理的专著。由旅游教育出版社，2014年3月出版，全书32.2万字。全书介绍了标准化工作的历史沿革、中外旅游标准化的发展现状和趋势、旅游标准概况、旅游标准编制、旅游标准化管理与创新等内容。该书对于从事旅游标准化研究、旅游标准编制和旅游标准化管理工作的人员有较大的参考价值。

附《旅游标准化导论》目录：

第一编　标准化基础知识

第一章　标准化概论　第一节　标准化基本概念；第二节　标准化发展简史；第三节　标准化原则与分类；第四节　标准化任务和作用

第二章　中国标准化管理运行体系　第一节　中国标准化法律法规；第二节　标准化管理体系及管理机构；第三节　标准化技术委员会—标准制定机构；第四节　标准化研究机构

第三章　国际标准化概述　第一节　国际和区域标准化组织；第二节　国际标准的制定程序和类型；第三节　国际标准的战略、政策与发展趋势；第四节　我国标准的国际化进程

第二编　中外旅游标准化概述

第四章　旅游的发展与旅游标准化　第一节我国旅游标准化的产生和发展；第二节旅游标准化的意义和作用；第三节我国旅游标准化历程和现状；第四节我国旅游标准化发展趋势及存在问题；第五节我国旅游标准化体系建设

第五章　国际旅游标准化　第一节　全球性组织；第二节　区域性组织；第三节　各国旅游标准化组织

第三编　旅游标准的结构

第六章　按照内容划分的结构　第一节　要素；第二节　条款

第七章　按照层次划分的结构　第一节　部分；第二节　章；第三节　条；第四节　段；第五节　列项；第六节　附录

第四编　旅游标准的编写

第八章　规范性要素的编写　第一节　标准名称；第二节　规范性技术要素的选择；第三节　要求；第四节　分类、标记和编码；第五节　术语和定义；第六节　符号、代号和缩略语；第七节　规范性引用文件；第八节　范围

第九章 资料性要素的编写 第一节 引言;第二节 前言;第三节 参考文献;第四节 索引;第五节 目次;第六节 封面

第十章 要素内容的表述 第一节条文的注、脚注和示例;第二节图;第三节表;第四节其他规则

第十一章 采用国际标准 第一节 采用国际标准的原则;第二节 采用国际标准的程度和方法;第三节 国家标准双编号方法和一致性程度标示方法;第四节 对国际标准相关内容的处理

第五编 旅游标准化管理概述

第十二章 旅游标准化管理概述 第一节旅游业制标的过程管理;第二节旅游标准的复审;第三节标准的实施;第四节标准实施的监督;第五节旅游标准的认证

第十三章 我国旅游标准化运行机制的提升与创新 第一节旅游业标准化的制定及修订体系;第二节旅游业标准化的分类实施;第三节 旅游标准化的宣传推广;第四节 旅游标准化的评估监督

主要参考文献

附录一:附表1.1 中华人民共和国行业标准类别一览表;附表1.2 省、自治区、直辖市行政区划代码表

附录二:附表2.1 推荐性国家标准项目建议书;附表2.2 北京市地方标准制定及修订项目申报书;附表2.3 意见汇总处理表;附件2.4 国家标准编制说明;附件2.5 国家标准函审结论;附件2.6 标准审查会会议纪要

附录三:《中华人民共和国标准化法》

附录四:《中华人民共和国标准化法实施条例》

张凌云

旅游公共服务：理论与实践

徐菊凤

概　　要

研究背景

本课题的研究背景主要来自以下三方面。

一、旅游市场需求结构变动凸显出我国旅游公共服务的缺失

中国经济的飞速发展，以及1999年开始实施"黄金周"制度，使我国国民旅游需求的总量、结构和方式在近十年发生了巨大变化。首先，国民人均年2.46人次的出游率，使得国民旅游需求成为市场核心需求，旅游服务供给的质量问题也就容易凸显为社会性"大问题"而非关涉及少数人的"小问题"。其次，旅游经验的丰富，助推大众旅游方式的改变和旅游品位的提高，旅游需求呈现常态化、散客化、休闲化、随机化趋势。北京、上海等重要旅游目的地所接待的散客量甚至高达80%~90%。这对我国传统的"入境游客+团队旅游"的旅游管理和服务模式提出了挑战，凸显出散客旅游所必须依赖的旅游公共服务供给明显不足，由此导致散客满意度偏低。同时，传统上狭窄的旅游行业管理路径难以覆盖旅游行业范围之外的其他公共要素。

二、各地旅游公共服务实践存在认知误区与失败教训

为了应对日益庞大的散客自由出行的需要，一些城市在最近十年开始探索建设了服务于散客的旅游公共服务设施。例如，北京曾在1990年尝试设立旅游咨询点；上海在1998年建立了旅游集散中心。然而，由于旅游公共服务体系建设问题涉及理念认知、项目建设、资金投入、效果监控、体制构建等诸多环节问题，且具有问题新、内容广、交叉性强、横向协调难度大等特征，因此，放眼全国，各地旅游公共服务体系建设总体上还处于起步探索阶段，许多地方政府和旅游管理部门对该类服务的需求、性质和规律还缺乏足够认知，在摸索建设的过程中暴露出思路、方法有失偏颇，机制、功能常失效的问题，一些地方的尝试显现明显的政绩工程痕迹。例如，全国有数十个城市仿效上海建设旅游集散中心，但大多数名不副实，鲜有成功；一些城市盲目追求公共服务的市场化，完全将承担公共服务和城市形象推介职责的公益机构交给以营利为目标的旅行社企业，导致公共服务功能难以发挥，等等。

三、学术界对旅游公共服务的研究零散而不足

有关公共服务领域的研究，理论学术界普遍聚焦于宏观的公共服务理论与实践，而对于旅游领域的公共服务问题鲜有人涉及。首次系统性探讨旅游公共服务问题的人来自国家旅游局官员，而学术界对于旅游公共服务问题的研究零散分布于若干细分领域，尤以旅游咨询中心和旅游集散中心方面的研究较多。总体上看，研究界对于我国旅游公共服务体系的个别问题研究较多，而系统性研究缺乏（2010年以后才出现），部分研究也不够契合实际，说服力不强。在国外，对旅游公共服务的研究，较多集中在旅游业中的犯罪、暴力和恐怖活动等问题上，仅有少数文献涉及旅游咨询中心服务和城市旅游发展中的公共交通问题，但没有直接以"旅游公共服务"为题的研究。相比学术研究，西方国家旅游公共服务的现实经验对于本课题的借鉴价值大于其理论研究。

研究方法

本研究采取了文献分析法、理论研究法，以及田野调查、访谈调研、问卷调研等实证研究方法。

首先，结合大量学术文献，在辨析旅游公共服务理论来源，以及各种旅游公共服务概念界定的基础上，提出了我们对于旅游公共服务及其体系的概念界定与认知，从理论上对旅游公共服务的内涵、外延、结构、类型进行了深入研究。其次，依据四个研究重点，有针对性地开展大量实证研究，深入国家与地方政府旅游管理部门和旅游公共服务机构与一线服务网点进行调研和体验。分别对国内7大城市和国外3个城市的旅游公共服务实践进行了考察调研。涉及30多家旅游管理机构和70多家旅游公共服务机构/网点。再次，展开问卷调研，了解旅游消费者对旅游公共服务的需求与认知。实施了三个层面的问卷调研：（1）国内游客对旅游公共服务的需求与认知；（2）国外游客对旅游公共服务的需求与认知；（3）游客对北京旅游资讯的需求与认知。最后，在翔实的理论研究和实证调研的基础上，对我国旅游公共服务领域的现状做出分析，并针对发现的理论和实践问题提出改进建议。

研究内容及结论

第一部分　旅游公共服务的理论研究。从理论上阐述了旅游公共服务的概念内涵、外延范畴与典型特征，辨析了其与公共产品和公共服务之间的理论关系，概括了旅游公共服务具有的三大类型与表现形式，并提出了旅游公共服务体系的整体结构框架。

首先，简要梳理了公共服务与公共产品之间在概念内涵与外延范围上的异同，从理论发展脉络梳理和学者争鸣中确认了二者的共性大于差异性。其次，对现有十多种关于旅游公共服务的概念界定进行了对比分析，分析了其优缺点，在此基础上，提出了我们对旅游公共服务的定义，认为旅游公共服务是为满足旅游者的普遍需要而由旅游等相关公共部门主导提供的具有公益性、共享性特点的产品和服务。再次，认为旅游公共服务的范畴包括了旅游基础设施、旅游市场推广、旅游权益保障三大分系统，其下还包括一般基础设施、旅游吸引物、旅游便捷交通、旅游市场培育、目的地形象推广、旅游市场秩序监管、游客权益保障、旅游者素质培育、旅游消费环境等十大子系统。政府部门，尤其是游客停留地的目的地地方政府，是旅游公共服务的主导供给者。最后，探究了旅游公共服务体系问题。认为旅游公共服务是在这样一个整体框架下产生并形成相互关系的：游客（尤其是散客）的普遍需求——希望借助当地公共设施实现自身便捷、自由、舒适的旅游活动的需求，是一般企业无能、不愿、甚至也没有责任提供的，只有政府有责任和义务弥补市场服务的不足，向到访的游客提供不以营利为主要目的的公益性服务。部分服务收费或委托企业经营，并不等同公共服务市场化。

第二部分　发达市场经济地区的旅游公共服务体系。着重介绍了市场经济发达地区几个著名国际旅游城市的旅游公共服务体系。重点论述了他们在旅游信息咨询服务、便捷旅游交通服务、游客权益维护服务、旅游安全保障服务等方面的具体措施与服务内容，并分析了其提供与保障旅游公共服务的体制和机制。

对著名旅游城市巴黎、东京和香港的旅游公共服务体系的研究表明，发达市场经济体制下的这些城市，在旅游公共服务方面都具有如下共同特征：著名景点普遍拥有发达而便捷的旅游公共交通服务体系，交通和旅游部门共同主导着多元化便捷"旅游+交通"准公共产品的供给，游客甚至可以享受到比普通居民更大的交通优惠；城市观光车和散客一日游产品实行特许经营方式；城市旅游咨询服务、免费资料、旅游咨询官方网站均由公共部门主导提供，经费从市场推广资金中列支。政府的旅游管理体制，以大部制作为行政设置方式，政府旅游部门合并在交通等其他公共部门之中，而具体旅游公共服务的提供——城市旅游推广、旅游信息服务、旅游统计分析等事宜，委托授权第三方公营机构（旅游局）提供服务。综上可以发现，为目的地提供旅游公共服务的，一是交通部门，二是旅游部门，还有一个是掌管旅游吸引物资源的其他公共部门。尽管不同城市的旅游局（第三方运营机构）的运营资金来源结构比例有所不同，但其公营（公益）机构的身份、使命和职能却高度一致。概言之，即使在市场化程度很高的地区，政府也在满足散客旅游需求方面充分发挥了弥补市场供给不足，为游客提供了便利、公益、均等的服务，维护了城市形象，保证了游客满意度。

第三部分　我国旅游公共服务的实证研究　从两个维度展开：其一，研究自助旅游市场对旅游公共服务的需求与评价；其二，对四大重点旅游公共服务的供给状况进行研究。研究对象以国内城市和旅游者为主，同时也适当介绍了国外情况和外国旅游者的需求。

市场需求问卷调研　对北京、上海和成都三地的国内外散客自助旅游者的问卷调查表明，一半左右的人会在出发前和到达目的地后查询旅游信息，超过2/3的旅游者曾因收集信息不充分/不准确而导致旅游行程不愉快。交通信息，尤其是通往景区的交通方式的信息，是游客最为需要的，而购物与娱乐信息则不太受重视。国内民众对于实体旅游咨询点（i小屋）和旅游信息触摸机的公益性功能还不够了解，但外国游客的认知度普遍高于国内游客。调研还表明，国内外散客一致认为，旅游安全、利益维护和通用基础设施这三个旅游公共服务要素的重要性最高；而城市内部的地铁、公交等公共交通，以及直通景区的交通条件被认为是最重要的。在旅游权益保障方面，消费者最看重的是在当地旅游不被骗和不挨宰。在安全保障方面，饮食安全和住宿安全最受关注，对预警提示和紧急救援服务的重视程度也较高，但对购买旅游保险的关注程度偏低。

旅游公共服务供给现状研究　我们选择了我国旅游服务体系中最为短缺、急需解决并且与旅游者需求最直接相关的四个领域作为研究重点，分别是旅游信息服务、目的地旅游便捷公共交通服务、旅游安全保障服务、旅游者利益维护服务。

在旅游公共信息服务方面，分析了国外旅游信息服务的发展历程和成功经验，以及国内若干城市旅游公共信息服务的实际供给状况。研究表明，向游客提供信息服务，维护和营造城市良好形象，是国外旅游局的主要职能之一。西方发达国家及地区普遍建立了面向散客的旅游公共信息服务体系，服务游客的旅游全程——游前、游中和游后。我国许多城市虽然也初步构建了旅游信息咨询中心和官方旅游网站，但普遍存在网点布局不合理、体制不顺畅、资金缺保障、功效不理想的现象。面向游客的官方旅游网站的功能，大多混合于旅游政务网站之中。在具体观察的五个城市——上海、杭州、南京、北京、成都中，杭州的服务信息体系最与国际接轨，运行机制和效果俱佳；上海、南京也保持了较好的效果，但仍有值得改进之处；北京、成都的效果不够理想。

目的地内的短程便捷旅游公共交通对于散客旅游具有十分重要的意义。国外旅游城市的公共交通和旅游专线，共同为散客旅游提供便利服务。旅游专线作为一种准公共产品，在政府主导或监管下运行，对于解决城市知名景点的一日游/半日游需求起到了"正规军"作用。我国城市的公共交通体系还不够发达，"城市观光车"这类旅游专线交通方式还刚刚起步，具有中国特色的旅游集散中心虽然在功能上类似国外旅游专线，但其准公共产品属性还没有获得广泛认可。部分地方构建的旅游集散中心，只交给某一旅行社经营，公益性、公正性无从体现。本研究分析了国内城市旅游集散中心的三种发展模式及其运行效果。指出以上海和杭州为代表的政府主导型模式体现出较鲜明的准公共产品性质，运行的社会和经济效果也比较好；以北京和成都为代表的政府引导型模式，具有一定的公共产品色彩，运行成败取决于具体运行机构的素质和能力；以深圳、武汉、昆明等其他城市为代表的市场主导型模式，完全由普通企业承担公共服务职能，违背了事物发展规律，最终没有成功。

在旅游安全保障服务方面，重点论述了安全保障对于游客出游和旅游目的地发展的重要性，分析了我国旅游安全保障体系的结构与类型。认为旅游安全保障体系包括旅游安全预警系统、旅游安全救援系统、旅游保险、旅游安全控制系统和旅游安全政策法规系统。这些子系统的运行目标，都是将不安全因素对旅游活动的干扰降至最低，从而最大限度地保证旅游者在旅游活动中应享有的权益。针对我国目前旅游安全保障体系存在的问题，本课题提出了旅游安全保障服务体系的改善对策。

在旅游消费者合法权益维护方面，以旅游者投诉及其处理为重点，论述了我国现有旅游投诉程序的制度建设和运行机制，认为行政机关在维护旅游者权益方面负有的公共管理职能主要体现在处罚违法经营行为和及时处理旅游消费权益纠纷两个方面。但是，旅游是一个综合性的消费活动，旅游活动会涉及多个行政机关的管理职能，相应的保障旅游者的合法权益必须协调各管理机关的职能才能完成。因此，我国以旅游局质监所和执法大队为主导的现有旅游者权益保护体制存在缺陷，尤其是散客权益不能得到有效的保障。课题介绍了杭州等地探索构建的综合性"目的地旅游质量监管机构"的做法，并提出了要抓住旅游法的立法契机，为旅游行政管理部门行使职能提供更多法律依据，同时，也期望行业协会和消费者团体能更多发挥维护旅游消费者权益的作用。

创新之处

本课题创新之处主要体现在以下四点。

（1）从理论和实践上对旅游公共服务问题进行了系统的、深入的研究，不像以往的研究那样分散、割裂；同时，有破有立，构建了较为严谨、完善的旅游公共服务理论体系。在理论分析之外，更有详尽的第一手调研资料和实证研究作为支撑，同时还有与国外情况的对比分析，保证了研究结论建立在翔实的理论和事实基础之上，所提出的观点及建议不空洞，具有针对性和可操作性。

（2）通过论析旅游业所蕴涵的公共服务要素和职能，鲜明地提出了旅游业属于"产业＋事业"的准公共服务领域，而不像以往我们所认为的那样是纯粹市场化经济领域。在此基础上，提出要转变政府旅游管理职能，以旅游者需求为核心作为工作的出发点和抓手。具体而言，要发生如下工作方式的转变：从服务团队旅游者转变为服务所有旅游者；从管理行业要素转变为管理游客需求；从"产业管理"转向"事业＋产业管理"。

（3）通过市场需求调研和国内外实践对比分析，论证了旅游信息服务和游客权益保护是政府旅游部门的重要职能。建议我国将这两项服务纳入政府旅游部门基本职能范畴，改变其现有的事业性机构从属地位。

（4）论证了目的地短程便捷旅游公共交通服务对于数量庞大的散客旅游和城市形象推广具有十分重要的意义，同时对于根治各地泛滥的"一日游"市场秩序也具有十分重要的作用，提出了新的便捷旅游交通建设思路。建议各地将便捷旅游交通纳入目的地综合公共服务范畴予以重视，同时，认为各地不宜一刀切地兴建名不副实的旅游集散中心，而应根据市场、资源条件适当兴建切实有效的具有准公共产品色彩的旅游专线。

应用价值

本课题的应用价值体现为以下几方面。

（1）可以为各地加强旅游公共服务建设提供充实的理论依据和清晰的规划发展思路，从而增强目的地竞争力和吸引力，提高游客满意度。

（2）能为各地旅游部门加强旅游信息服务，完善旅游公共信息服务体系提供指导。

（3）可以为各地构建便捷旅游交通服务体系提供指导，包括规划建设旅游集散中心（旅游专线）、开通城市观光巴士、建设通往著名景区的公共交通设施等。

（4）可以为各地诊断和治理"一日游"问题提供理论依据和解决思路。

（5）可以为重新认识旅游业的属性特征、重新定位旅游局的职能、完善旅游管理体制提供参考。